LANGENSCHEIDT
STANDARD DICTIONARIES

LANGENSCHEIDT'S
STANDARD DICTIONARY

OF THE ENGLISH AND SPANISH LANGUAGES

First Part

English≠Spanish

by

C. C. SMITH
G. A. DAVIES
H. B. HALL

LANGENSCHEIDT

BERLÍN · MUNICH · ZURICH

Contents
Materias

© 1966 Langenscheidt KG, Berlin und München
ISBN: 3-468-98052-3
Printed in Germany

Preface

We believe that this work will be a useful addition to the existing English-Spanish dictionaries, and that it will be found to serve a very wide range of purposes.

The dictionary is up-to-date in its treatment of neologisms, colloquial words, idioms and phrases, clichés and slang, and in its inclusion of large numbers of words drawn from sport, radio, television, the cinema, and other spheres which are the creation of our own times. Due attention has been paid to Americanisms in English. The writing of Spanish words has been governed by the *Nuevas Normas* issued by the Academy in 1952 and revised in 1959.

Notable features of the dictionary are: a phonetic transcription, in the alphabet of the International Phonetic Association, is given for every English headword; the stress of every word is indicated; syllabification dots show where each word should be divided at the end of a written line; in many cases, the "social class" of a word is indicated, and an attempt is made to render the word by another of equivalent class. The gender of every Spanish noun is given. Within each entry, the reader is offered many defining words to help his choice of an exact translation, and is given help with grammatical constructions.

We are indebted to a number of people, many of them past or present members of the University of Leeds, for expert advice generously given during many months of work. Sr Agustín de Irízar and Dr Manuel Bermejo Marcos have been untiring in their efforts to solve our problems. Much help has also come from Srta María Victoria Alvarez, Srta Paloma de Hita, Professor R. F. Brown, and Mr Peter Saword; also from Professor Keith Whinnom, and Col. Enrique Navasa of Madrid. To all of them our warmest thanks.

C.C.S.
G.A.D.
H.B.H.

Prólogo

Creemos que esta obra podrá ser considerada como una adición útil a los diccionarios inglés-español ya existentes, y que podrá resolver un buen número de problemas.

Nuestro diccionario está al día en su manera de tratar los neologismos, palabras coloquiales, giros y modismos, clichés y términos de argot, y contiene gran número de palabras que nos han sido suministradas por los deportes, la radio, la televisión, el cine, y otras formas de actividad que son creación de nuestra época. Hemos tenido en cuenta la gran importancia del inglés hablado en Estados Unidos. Respecto a la ortografía de las voces españolas, nos hemos atenido a las *Nuevas Normas* publicadas por la Real Academia de la Lengua en 1952 y corregidas en 1959.

Quien nos consulte apreciará las características siguientes: una pronunciación figurada, según el alfabeto de la Asociación Internacional de Fonética, acompaña a cada voz-guía inglesa; en todos los casos, se indica la acentuación de la palabra; hemos señalado la separación silábica por medio de puntos que indican dónde se debe dividir una palabra al final de un renglón escrito; en muchos casos, se ha señalado la "clase social" de una palabra, y se ha intentado traducirla con el equivalente castellano. Se precisa el género de cada sustantivo español. Dentro de cada artículo, el lector encontrará muchas palabras definidoras que le ayudarán a elegir la traducción exacta, y se le ayuda además con las construcciones gramaticales.

Hemos de poner de manifiesto la deuda que tenemos con varias personas — muchas de ellas miembros antiguos o actuales de la Universidad de Leeds — por los sagaces consejos que tan generosamente nos ofrecieron durante los largos meses de trabajo. Destaquemos a don Agustín de Irízar y al Dr don Manuel Bermejo Marcos, quienes se han mostrado en todo momento incansables en sus esfuerzos por resolver nuestros problemas. También hemos recibido una ayuda apreciable de las Srtas María Victoria Alvarez y Paloma de Hita, del Profesor R. F. Brown, de Mr Peter Saword, del Profesor Keith Whinnom, y del Coronel don Enrique Navasa, de Madrid. A todos ellos, nuestro más sincero agradecimiento.

C.C.S.
G.A.D.
H.B.H.

Directions for the use of the dictionary

Advertencias para facilitar la consulta del diccionario

1. Arrangement. A strict alphabetical order has been maintained throughout. The following forms will therefore be found in alphabetical order: the irregular forms of verbs, nouns, comparatives and superlatives; the inflected forms of the pronouns; and compounds.

Proper names and abbreviations are collected in special lists at the end of the dictionary.

2. Vocabulary. In many cases, the rarer words formed with -*ing*, -*er*, -*ness*, -*ist*, *un*-, *in*-, etc., are excluded, to avoid extending the size of the dictionary beyond all reasonable limits. The reader having some slight acquaintance with the processes of word-formation in the two languages will be able to look up the root word and form derived words from it.

Abstract nouns are often dealt with very briefly when they are adjacent to a root-word which has been fully dealt with. Thus the entry *fineness* fineza *f* etc. means: see the adjective *fine* and form other abstract nouns accordingly.

3. Separation of different senses. The various senses of each English word are made clear:

a) by symbols and abbreviated categories (see list on pp. 10—11);

b) by explanatory additions in italics, which may be a synonym (e.g. *face* [*grimace*] mueca *f*), or a complement (e.g. *face* faz *f of the earth*), or the object of a transi-

1. El orden alfabético queda rigurosamente establecido. Ocupan su lugar alfabético, por tanto: las formas irregulares de los verbos y sustantivos, del comparativo y del superlativo; las diferentes formas de los pronombres; y las palabras compuestas.

Los nombres propios y las abreviaturas van reunidos en listas especiales que se imprimen como apéndices.

2. Vocabulario. En muchos casos se excluyen las palabras derivadas menos corrientes, que se forman, p.ej., con -*ing*, -*er*, -*ness*, -*ist*, *un*-, *in*-, a fin de no extender más de lo razonable los límites del diccionario. El lector que tenga algún conocimiento de cómo se forman las palabras derivadas en los dos idiomas podrá buscar la palabra radical y formar sobre ella las derivadas que quiera.

Los sustantivos abstractos están tratados a menudo en forma somera cuando la palabra radical que les corresponde se ha tratado en forma extensa. Por tanto, el artículo *fineness* fineza *f* etc. quiere decir: véase el adjetivo *fine* para formar luego los sustantivos abstractos correspondientes.

3. Separación de las diversas acepciones. Las diversas acepciones de cada palabra inglesa se indican:

a) mediante signos y categorías abreviadas (véase la lista en las págs. 10—11);

b) mediante aclaraciones impresas en bastardilla, las cuales pueden ser un sinónimo (p.ej., *face* [*grimace*] mueca *f*), o complemento (p.ej., *face* faz *f of the earth*), u objeto

— 8 —

tive verb (e.g. *face danger* arrostrar), or the subject of an intransitive verb (e.g. *fall* [*wind*] amainar).

Sometimes, e.g. with many abstract nouns, these explanations are omitted, but can easily be supplied from the adjacent entry for the corresponding verb or root-word.

4. The different parts óf speech are indicated by numbers within each entry; the grammatical indication *adj.*, *su.*, etc., is omitted in all cases where the category is obvious.

5. The gender of every Spanish noun is indicated. Often in translating an English noun, two Spanish versions must be given, one for each gender: where the final o or e changes to *a* for the feminine, we write *passenger* pasajero (a *f*) *m*; where the *a* has to be added for the feminine, we write *teacher* profesor (-a *f*) *m*. In this second class, some endings carry an accent in the masculine which is not needed in the feminine, and this suppression is not indicated in the dictionary. The endings affected are: *-án*, *-ín*, *-ón* and *-és*, so that *idler* haragán (-a *f*) *m* means: haragán *m*, haragana *f*.

6. Syllabification dots. The centred dots within the English word show how it should be divided in writing, e.g. **ab·dom·i·nal.** If the syllabification dot coincides with the stress mark, the former is left out. The word may therefore also be divided at the point where the stress mark stands alone, e.g. **ab·ne'ga·tion.**

7. Phonetic transcription. The pronunciation of each headword and of many others is given in the alphabet of the International Phonetic Association (explanation on pp. 12—14). This is omitted only in the case of forms derived with one of the common suffixes (*-er*, *-ness*, etc.) and of compounds whose component parts are given independently elsewhere in the dictionary. In both cases, however, the stress of the word is always given.

de verbo transitivo (p.ej., *face danger* arrostrar), o sujeto de verbo intransitivo (p.ej., *fall* [*wind*] amainar).

Estas aclaraciones suelen omitirse en el caso de muchos sustantivos abstractos, etc., pero es fácil suplirlas refiriéndose al artículo del verbo o palabra radical correspondiente.

4. Las diferentes partes de la oración están indicadas dentro de cada artículo mediante números; las indicaciones gramaticales *adj.*, *su.*, etc., están suprimidas siempre cuando la categoría es obvia.

5. Se indica el género de cada sustantivo español. A veces, al traducir una palabra inglesa, hay que dar dos palabras españolas, una para cada género: cuando la o o la e final se cambia en *a* para formar el femenino, ponemos *passenger* pasajero (a *f*) *m*; cuando hay que añadir una *a* para la forma femenina, ponemos *teacher* profesor (-a *f*) *m*. En ciertas desinencias de esta segunda clase, el acento que lleva el género masculino se suprime en el femenino, supresión que no está indicada en el diccionario. Estas desinencias son: *-án*, *-ín*, *-ón*, *-és*, de manera que *idler* haragán (-a *f*) *m* quiere decir: haragán *m*, haragana *f*.

6. Puntos de silabeo. Los puntos centrales dentro de la palabra inglesa indican cómo se puede dividir la palabra escrita, p.ej., **ab·dom·i·nal.** Si el punto coincide con el acento, aquél queda suprimido. La palabra puede por tanto dividirse allí donde está el acento solo, p.ej., **ab·ne'ga·tion.**

7. La pronunciación figurada de cada palabra impresa en caracteres gruesos se da según el alfabeto de la Asociación Fonética Internacional (véase la explicación en las págs. 12—14). Esta pronunciación se omite en el caso de las palabras derivadas mediante uno de los sufijos corrientes (*-er*, *-ness*, etc.), y en el caso de las palabras compuestas cuyos elementos constan independientemente en otra parte del diccionario. En ambos casos, no obstante, se indica siempre dónde cae el acento.

8. Translation. In rare cases, accurate single-word translation is impossible or meaningless. Recognizing this obvious linguistic fact, we have in such cases either provided an explanation in italics in place of a translation, or have introduced the translation with the warning abbreviation *approx.* (= approximately).

When certain letters stand within brackets in a Spanish word, we indicate two forms that may be used indifferently or which are more or less synonymous, e.g. *village* puebl(ecit)o *m* means pueblo *m* and pueblecito *m*.

9. As appendices to the dictionary, the reader will find: a list of proper names, a list of abbreviations, a table of numerals, a note on the conjugation of the English verb, with a list of the parts of irregular verbs, and a table of weights, measures and coinage.

8. La traducción. En muy contados casos, la traducción exacta o resulta imposible o carece de sentido práctico. Ante este innegable hecho lingüístico, ponemos en dichos casos o una explicación en bastardilla, o, como advertencia al lector, la abreviatura *approx.* (= aproximadamente).

Cuando en una voz española ciertas letras están entre paréntesis, se trata de dos formas que se pueden usar indiferentemente o que son más o menos sinónimas, p.ej. *village* puebl(ecit)o *m* quiere decir pueblo *m* y pueblecito *m*.

9. Como apéndices, el diccionario tiene: una lista de nombres propios, una lista de abreviaturas, una lista de numerales, una nota sobre la conjugación del verbo inglés, con una lista de las partes de los verbos irregulares, y una tabla de pesos, medidas y moneda.

Key to the symbols and abbreviations
Explicación de los signos y abreviaturas

1. Symbols — Signos

~ ℃ ~ ℃ is the mark of repetition or tilde (swung dash). To save space, compound catchwords are frequently given with the aid of the tilde. The thick tilde (~) stands for the catchword at the beginning of the entry. The thin tilde (~) stands for: a) the preceding catchword, which itself may have been formed with the aid of a thick tilde; b) in the phonetic transcription, the entire pronunciation of the preceding catchword, or a part of it which remains unchanged. If the preceding catchword is given without phonetic transcription, the tilde refers to the last preceding phonetic transcription or indicates only a shifting stress.

~ ℃ ~ ℃ es la tilde o raya que indica repetición. Para reservar todo el espacio disponible a las voces-guía, las palabras compuestas se imprimen a menudo en forma abreviada mediante la tilde. La tilde gruesa (~) representa la voz-guía que encabeza el párrafo. La tilde delgada (~) representa: a) la voz-guía precedente, que puede ella misma estar formada mediante una tilde gruesa; b) en la pronunciación figurada, toda la pronunciación de la voz-guía precedente, o bien parte de ella que permanece intacta. Si la voz-guía se imprime sin pronunciación figurada, la tilde se refiere a la última pronunciación figurada, o bien indica solamente un cambio de acento.

When the initial letter changes from a capital to a small letter, or vice versa, the normal tilde mark is replaced by the sign ⚲ or ⚲ respectively.

El signo ⚲ ⚲ significa la repetición de la voz-guía con inicial cambiada (mayúscula en minúscula o viceversa).

Examples:

far ... ~-fetched
fore ... ~·gone: ~ *conclusion*
fair[1] [fɛə] ... **fair**[2] [~]
favour ['feivə] ... **favourable** ['~vərəbl]
foreign ... ⚲ *Office*

Ejemplos:

far ... ~-fetched
fore ... ~·gone: ~ *conclusion*
fair[1] [fɛə] ... **fair**[2] [~]
favour ['feivə] ... **favourable** ['~vərəbl]
foreign ... ⚲ *Office*

□ after an adjective or participle, means that from it an adverb may be formed regularly by adding -*ly*, or from adjectives ending in -*ic* by adding -*ally*, or by changing -*le* into -*ly* or -*y* into -*ily*; examples:

rich □ = *richly*
frantic □ = *frantically*
acceptable □ = *acceptably*
happy □ = *happily*

□ después de un adjetivo o participio significa que de él se puede formar regularmente el adverbio añadiendo -*ly*, o añadiendo -*ally* a los adjetivos que terminan en -*ic*, o cambiando -*le* en -*ly* e -*y* en -*ily*; ejemplos:

rich □ = *richly*
frantic □ = *frantically*
acceptable □ = *acceptably*
happy □ = *happily*.

F   familiar, colloquial, *familiar, coloquial.*

†   archaic, *arcaico.*

⚲   rare, little used, *raro, poco usado.*

⊞   scientific, learned, *científico, culto.*

⚘   botany, *botánica.*

⊕   technology, handicrafts, *tecnología, artes mecánicas.*

⚒   mining, *minería.*

⚔   military, *milicia.*

⚓   nautical, *náutica.*

♱   commerce, *comercio.*

🚂   railway, *ferrocarriles.*

✈   aviation, *aviación.*

✉   postal affairs, *correos.*

♪   music, *música.*

⚠   architecture, *arquitectura.*

⚡   electrical engineering, *electrotecnia.*

⚖   jurisprudence, *jurisprudencia.*

A⟋   mathematics, *matemáticas.*

✎   farming, *agricultura.*

⚗   chemistry, *química.*

⚕   medicine, *medicina.*

2. Abbreviations — Abreviaturas

a.	and, also, y, también.	mst	mostly, por la mayor parte.
abbr.	abbreviation, abreviatura.	opt.	optics, óptica.
acc.	accusative, acusativo.	orn.	ornithology, ornitología.
adj.	adjective, adjetivo.	o.s.	oneself, uno mismo, sí mismo.
adv.	adverb, adverbio.	p.	person, persona.
Am.	Americanism, americanismo.	paint.	painting, pintura.
anat.	anatomy, anatomía.	parl.	parliamentary, parlamenta-
approx.	approximately, aproximada-		rio.
	mente.	pharm.	pharmacy, farmacia.
ast.	astronomy, astronomía.	phls.	philosophy, filosofía.
attr.	attributive, atributivo.	phot.	photography, fotografía.
biol.	biology, biología.	phys.	physics, física.
b.s.	bad sense, mal sentido, peyo-	physiol.	physiology, fisiología.
	rativo.	pl.	plural, plural.
cj.	conjunction, conjunción.	poet.	poetry, poetic, poesía, poé-
co.	comic(al), cómico.		tico.
comp.	comparative, comparativo.	pol.	politics, política.
contp.	contemptuous, despectivo.	p.p.	past participle, participio del
dat.	dative, dativo.		pasado.
eccl.	ecclesiastical, eclesiástico.	pred.	predicative, predicativo.
e.g.	for example, por ejemplo.	pret.	preterit(e), pretérito.
esp.	especially, especialmente.	pron.	pronoun, pronombre.
etc.	et cetera, etcétera.	prov.	provincialism, provincia-
euph.	euphemism, eufemismo.		lismo.
f	feminine, femenino.	prp.	preposition, preposición.
fenc.	fencing, esgrima.	rhet.	rhetoric, retórica.
fig.	figurative, figurativo, figu-	S.Am.	Spanish Americanism, his-
	rado.		panoamericanismo.
f pl.	feminine plural, femenino al	Scot.	Scottish, escocés.
	plural.	sew.	sewing, costura.
freq.	frequently, frecuentemente.	sg.	singular, singular.
gen.	generally, generalmente.	sl.	slang, argot, germanía.
geog.	geography, geografía.	s.o.	someone, alguien.
geol.	geology, geología.	s.t.	something, algo.
ger.	gerund, gerundio.	su.	substantive, sustantivo.
gr.	grammar, grámatica.	subj.	subjunctive, subjuntivo.
hist.	history, historia.	sup.	superlative, superlativo.
hunt.	hunting, montería.	surv.	surveying, topografía, agri-
ichth.	ichthyology, ictiología.		mensura.
indic.	indicative, indicativo.	tel.	telegraphy, telegrafía.
inf.	infinitive, infinitivo.	teleph.	telephony, telefonía.
int.	interjection, interjección.	th.	thing, cosa.
Ir.	Irish, irlandés.	thea.	theatre, teatro.
iro.	ironical, irónico.	typ.	typography, tipografía.
irr.	irregular, irregular.	univ.	university, universidad.
lit.	literary, literario.	v.	vide (see), véase.
m	masculine, masculino.	v/aux.	auxiliary verb, verbo auxi-
metall.	metallurgy, metalurgia.		liar.
meteor.	meteorology, meteorología.	vet.	veterinary, veterinaria.
m f	masculine and feminine,	v/i.	intransitive verb, verbo in-
	masculino y femenino.		transitivo.
min.	mineralogy, mineralogía.	v/r.	reflexive verb, verbo reflexi-
mot.	motoring, automovilismo.		vo.
mount.	mountaineering, alpinismo.	v/t.	transitive verb, verbo tran-
m pl.	masculine plural, masculino		sitivo.
	al plural.	zo.	zoology, zoología.

Signos de la Asociación Fonética Internacional aplicados al inglés

Pronunciation key to the English language

A. Vocales y Diptongos

[ɑ:] sonido largo parecido al de *a* en *raro*: *far* [fɑ:], *father* ['fɑ:ðə].

[ʌ] *a* abierta, breve y oscura, que se pronuncia en la parte anterior de la boca sin redondear los labios: *butter* ['bʌtə], *come* [kʌm], *colour* ['kʌlə], *blood* [blʌd], *flourish* ['flʌriʃ], *two-pence* ['tʌpəns].

[æ] sonido breve, bastante abierto y distinto, algo parecido al de *a* en *parra*: *fat* [fæt], *ran* [ræn].

[ɛə] diptongo que se encuentra únicamente delante de la *r* muda. El primer y principal elemento se parece a la *e* de *perro*, pero es más abierto y breve; el segundo es una forma débil de la 'vocal neutra' (*v.* abajo): *bare* [bɛə], *pair* [pɛə], *there* [ðɛə].

[ai] sonido parecido al de *ai* en *estáis*, *baile*: *I* [ai], *lie* [lai], *dry* [drai].

[au] sonido parecido al de *au* en *causa*, *sauce*: *house* [haus], *now* [nau].

[ei] *e* medio abierta, pero más cerrada que la *e* de *hablé*; suena como si la siguiese una [i] débil, sobretodo en sílaba acentuada: *date* [deit], *play* [plei], *obey* [ə'bei].

[e] sonido breve, medio abierto, parecido al de *e* en *perro*: *bed* [bed], *less* [les].

[ə] 'vocal neutra', siempre átona; parecida a la *e* del artículo francés *le* y a la *a* final del catalán *casa*: *about* [ə'baut], *butter* ['bʌtə], *connect* [kə'nekt].

[i:] sonido largo, parecido al de *i* en *misa*, *vino*: *scene* [si:n], *sea* [si:], *feet* [fi:t], *ceiling* ['si:liŋ].

[i] sonido breve, abierto, parecido al de *i* en *filfa*, *esbirro*, pero más abierto: *big* [big], *city* ['siti].

[iə] diptongo cuyo primer y principal elemento es una *i* medio abierta, medio larga, seguida de una forma débil de la 'vocal neutra' [ə]: *here* [hiə], *hear* [hiə], *inferior* [in'fiəriə].

[ou] *o* larga, más bien cerrada, sin redondear los labios ni levantar la lengua; suena como si la siguiese una [u] débil: *note* [nout], *boat* [bout], *below* [bi'lou].

[ɔ:] vocal larga, bastante cerrada, entre *a* y *o*; le es algo parecida la *o* de *por*: *fall* [fɔ:l], *nought* [nɔ:t], *or* [ɔ:], *before* [bi'fɔ:].

[ɔ] sonido breve y abierto, parecido al de la *o* en *porra*, *corro*, pero más cerrado: *god* [gɔd], *not* [nɔt], *wash* [wɔʃ], *hobby* ['hɔbi].

[ɔi] diptongo cuyo primer elemento es una *o* abierta, seguido de una *i* abierta pero débil; parecido al sonido de *oy* en *doy*: *voice* [vɔis], *boy* [bɔi], *annoy* [ə'nɔi].

[ə:] forma larga de la 'vocal neutra' [ə], en sílaba acentuada; algo parecida al sonido de *eu* en la palabra francesa *leur*: *word* [wə:d], *girl* [gə:l], *learn* [lə:n], *murmur* ['mə:mə].

[u:] sonido largo, parecido al de *u*

en *cuna*, *duda*: *fool* [fu:l], *shoe* [ʃu:], *you* [ju:], *rule* [ru:l], *canoe* [kə'nu:].

[uə] diptongo cuyo primer elemento es una *u* medio larga, medio abierta, seguido de una forma débil de la 'vocal neutra' [ə]: *pure* [pjuə], *allure* [ə'ljuə].

[u] *u* pura pero muy rápida, más cerrada que la *u* de *burra*: *put* [put], *look* [luk], *careful* ['kɛəful].

B. Consonantes

[b] como la *b* de *cambiar*: *bay* [bei], *brave* [breiv].

[d] como la *d* de *andar*: *did* [did], *ladder* ['lædə].

[f] como la *f* de *filo*: *face* [feis], *baffle* ['bæfl].

[g] como la *g* de *golpe*: *go* [gou], *haggle* ['hægl].

[h] se pronuncia con aspiración fuerte, sin la aspereza gutural de la *j* en *Gijón*: *who* [hu:], *behead* [bi'hed].

[j] como la *y* de *cuyo*: *you* [ju:], *million* ['miljən].

[k] como la *c* de *casa*: *cat* [kæt], *kill* [kil].

[l] como la *l* de *loco*: *love* [lʌv], *goal* [goul].

[m] como la *m* de *madre*: *mouth* [mauθ], *come* [kʌm].

[n] como la *n* de *nada*: *not* [nɔt], *banner* ['bænə].

[p] como la *p* de *padre*: *pot* [pɔt], *top* [tɔp].

[r] la *r* escrita se pronuncia únicamente cuando está delante de vocal; en los demás casos es muda. Cuando se pronuncia, es un sonido muy débil, más bien semivocal, que no tiene nada de la vibración fuerte que caracteriza a la *r* española; se articula elevando la punta de la lengua hacia el paladar duro: *rose* [rouz], *pride* [praid], *there is* [ðɛər'iz].

[s] como la *s* de *casa*: *sit* [sit], *scent* [sent].

[t] como la *t* de *pata*: *take* [teik], *patter* ['pætə].

[v] inexistente en español; a diferencia de *b*, *v* en español, se pronuncia juntando la labio inferior con los dientes superiores: *vein* [vein], *velvet* ['velvit].

[w] como la *u* de *huevo*: *water* ['wɔ:tə], *will* [wil].

[z] como la *s* de *mismo*: *zeal* [zi:l], *hers* [hə:z].

[ʒ] inexistente en español; como la *j* de la palabra francesa *jour*: *measure* ['meʒə], *rouge* [ru:ʒ]. Aparece a menudo en el grupo [dʒ], que se pronuncia como el grupo *dj* de la palabra francesa *adjacent*: *edge* [edʒ], *gem* [dʒem].

[ʃ] inexistente en español; como *ch* en la palabra francesa *chose*: *shake* [ʃeik], *washing* ['wɔʃiŋ]. Aparece a menudo en el grupo [tʃ], que se pronuncia como la *ch* en *mucho*: *match* [mætʃ], *natural* ['nætʃrəl].

[θ] como la *z* de *zapato*: *thin* [θin], *path* [pɑ:θ].

[ð] forma sonorizada del anterior, algo como la *d* de *todo*: *there* [ðɛə], *breathe* [bri:ð].

[ŋ] como la *n* de *banco*: *singer* ['siŋə], *tinker* ['tiŋkə].

[x] sonido que en rigor no pertenece al inglés, pero que se encuentra en palabras escocesas, alemanas, etc. que se usan en inglés: como la *j* de *jamás*: *loch* [lɔx].

Nota: Importa que el lector se dé cuenta de la casi imposibilidad de explicar de modo satisfactorio los sonidos de una lengua en términos de otra. Lo que aquí se dice es a modo de aproximación y de ayuda general, sin que pretenda tener ningún rigor científico. Importa además reconocer que los sonidos que se explican aquí pueden variar mucho en cuanto se emplean juntamente con otros sonidos o en frases enteras.

— 14 —

La tilde [~], que aparece en la pronunciación figurada de ciertas palabras de origen francés, indica la nasalización de la vocal.

Los dos puntos [:] indican que la vocal anterior se pronuncia larga.

C. Acentuación

La acentuación de la palabra inglesa se indica colocando el acento ['] al principio de la sílaba acentuada, p.ej. *onion* ['ʌnjǝn]. Muchas palabras largas o compuestas tienen dos sílabas acentuadas (una quizá más ligeramente que la otra), lo cual se indica poniendo dos acentos: *falsification* ['fɔ:lsifi'keiʃn], *upstairs* ['ʌp'steǝz]. Uno de los acentos que lleva la palabra compuesta puede sin embargo suprimirse cuando la palabra tiene que someterse al ritmo de una frase entera, o cuando se emplea en función distinta (p.ej. como adjetivo o adverbio): *the upstairs rooms* [ði 'ʌpsteǝz 'rumz], *on going upstairs* [ɔn 'gouiŋ ʌp'steǝz].

Véanse también las *Advertencias*, núm. 7, y la *Explicación de los Signos*.

D. Sufijos sin pronunciación figurada

Para ahorrar espacio, las palabras derivadas mediante uno de los sufijos corrientes suelen escribirse en el diccionario sin pronunciación figurada propia. Su pronunciación puede comprobarse consultando el lector la pronunciación figurada de la voz-guía que encabeza el párrafo, añadiendo después la pronunciación del sufijo según esta lista:

-ability [-ǝbiliti]
-able [-ǝbl]
-age [-idʒ]
-al [-(ǝ)l]
-ally [-(ǝ)li]
-an [-(ǝ)n]
-ance [-(ǝ)ns]
-ancy [-ǝnsi]
-ant [-ǝnt]
-ar [-ǝ]
-ary [-(ǝ)ri]
-ation [-eiʃ(ǝ)n]
-cious [-ʃǝs]
-cy [-si]
-dom [-dǝm]
-ed [-d; -t; -id]*
-edness [-dnis; -tnis; -idnis]
-ee [-i:]
-en [-n]
-ence [-(ǝ)ns]

-ent [-(ǝ)nt]
-er [-ǝ]
-ery [-ǝri]
-ess [-is]
-fication [-fikeiʃ(ǝ)n]
-ial [-(ǝ)l]
-ian [-(jǝ)n]
-ible [-ǝbl]
-ic(s) [-ik(s)]
-ical [-ik(ǝ)l]
-ily [-ili]
-iness [-inis]
-ing [-iŋ]
-ish [-iʃ]
-ism [-iz(ǝ)m]
-ist [-ist]
-istic [-istik]
-ite [-ait]
-ity [-iti]
-ive [-iv]
-ization [-aizeiʃ(ǝ)n]

-ize [-aiz]
-izing [-aiziŋ]
-less [-lis]
-ly [-li]
-ment(s) [-mǝnt(s)]
-ness [-nis]
-oid [-ɔid]
-oidic [-ɔidik]
-or [-ǝ]
-ous [-ǝs]
-ry [-ri]
-ship [-ʃip]
-(s)sion [-ʃ(ǝ)n]
-sive [-siv]
-ties [-tiz]
-tion [-ʃ(ǝ)n]
-tious [-ʃǝs]
-trous [-trǝs]
-try [-tri]
-y [-i]

* [-d] tras vocales y consonantes sonoras; [-t] tras consonantes sordas; [-id] tras *d* y *t* finales.

The English Alphabet

a [ei], b [bi:], c [si:], d [di:], e [i:], f [ef], g [dʒi:], h [eitʃ], i [ai], j [dʒei], k [kei], l [el], m [em], n [en], o [ou], p [pi:], q [kju:], r [ɑ:], s [es], t [ti:], u [ju:], v [vi:], w ['dʌblju:], x [eks], y [wai], z [zed].

Normas
de ortografía en el inglés americano

Existen ciertas diferencias entre el inglés escrito en Gran Bretaña (British English, BE) y el inglés escrito en Estados Unidos (American English, AE). Son las principales:

1. **El guión** con que se escriben en BE muchas palabras compuestas se suprime a menudo en AE, p.ej. newsstand, soapbox, coed.

2. La **u** que se escribe en BE en las palabras que terminan en **-our** (p.ej. col*our*) se suprime en AE: col*or*, hum*or*, honorable.

3. Muchas palabras que en BE terminan en **-re** (p.ej. cent*re*) se escriben en AE **-er**, p.ej. cent*er*, fib*er*, theat*er* (pero no massacre).

4. En muchos casos las palabras que en BE tienen **ll** en posición media se escriben en AE con una **l**, p.ej. counci*l*or, quarre*l*ed, trave*l*ed. Sin embargo, hay palabras que en BE se escriben con una **l** que en AE se escriben con **ll**, p.ej. enro*ll*(s), fulfi*ll*(s), ski*ll*ful, insta*ll*ment.

5. En ciertos casos las palabras que en BE terminan en **-ence** se escriben en AE con **-ense**, p.ej. def*ense*, off*ense*.

6. Ciertas vocales finales, que no tienen valor en la pronunciación, se escriben en BE (p.ej. catalog*ue*) pero no en AE: catalog, dialog, prolog, program, envelop.

7. Se ha extendido más en AE que en BE la costumbre de escribir **e** en lugar de **ae** y **oe**, p.ej. an(a)emia, an(a)esthesia, subp(o)ena.

8. Algunas cononantes que en BE suelen escribirse dobles (p.ej. wa*gg*on) se escriben en AE sencillas, p.ej. wa*g*on, kidna*p*ed, worshi*p*ed.

9. En AE se suprime a veces la **u** del grupo **ou** que tiene BE, p.ej. mo(*u*)ld, smo(*u*)lder, y se escribe en AE pl*ow* en lugar del BE pl*ough*.

10. En AE suele suprimirse la **e** muda en las palabras como abridg(*e*)ment, acknowledg(*e*)ment.

11. Hay otras palabras que se escriben de distinto modo en BE y AE, p.ej. BE cheque = AE *check*, BE hallo, hullo = AE *hello*, BE cosy = AE *cozy*, BE moustache = AE *mustache*, BE gipsy = AE *gypsy*, BE sceptical = AE *skeptical*, BE grey = AE *gray*.

12. En AE se suelen escribir de distinto modo las siguientes palabras, pero sólo en tono familiar: BE although = AE *altho*, BE all right = AE *alright*, BE through = AE *thru*.

La pronunciación del inglés americano

Entre la pronunciación del inglés en Gran Bretaña (British English, BE) y la del inglés en Estados Unidos (American English, AE) existen múltiples diferencias que es imposible tratar aquí en forma adecuada. Señalamos únicamente las diferencias más notables:

1. **Intonación.** El AE se habla en un tono más monótono que el BE.

2. **Ritmo.** Las palabras que tienen dos sílabas o más después del acento principal ['] llevan en AE un acento secundario que no tienen en BE, p.ej. *dictionary* [AE ''dikʃəˈneri = BE 'dikʃənri], *secretary* [AE ''sekrəˈteri = BE 'sekrətri].

3. Muchas de las vocales breves acentuadas del BE se alargan en AE (*American drawl*), p.ej. *capital* [AE 'kæːpətəl = BE 'kæpitl].

4. Las consonantes sordas **p, t** del BE en posición intervocálica suelen sonorizarse bastante [b, d], p.ej. *property* [AE 'prabərti = BE 'prɔpəti], *united* [AE juˈnaidid = BE juˈnaitid].

5. La **r** escrita en posición final después de una vocal o entre vocal y consonante es normalmente muda en BE, pero se pronuncia claramente en AE, p.ej. *car* [AE kaːr = BE kaː], *care* [AE kɛr = BE kɛə], *border* [AE 'bɔːrdər = BE 'bɔːdə].

6. Una de las peculiaridades más notables del AE es la **nasalización** de las vocales antes y después de las consonantes nasales [m, n, ŋ].

7. La **o** [BE ɔ] suele pronunciarse en AE casi como una **a** oscura [AE a], p.ej. *dollar* [AE 'dalər = BE 'dɔlə], *college* [AE 'kalidʒ = BE 'kɔlidʒ], *lot* [AE lat = BE lɔt], *problem* [AE 'prabləm = BE 'prɔbləm].

8. El **a** [BE aː] se pronuncia en AE como [æ] o bien [æː] en palabras del tipo *pass* [AE pæ(ː)s = BE paːs], *answer* [AE 'æ(ː)nsər = BE 'aːnsə], *dance* [AE dæ(ː)ns = BE daːns], *laugh* [AE læ(ː)f = BE laːf].

9. La **u** [BE juː] en sílaba acentuada se pronuncia en AE como [uː], p.ej. *Tuesday* [AE 'tuːzdi = BE 'tjuːzdi], *student* [AE 'stuːdənt = BE 'stjuːdənt], pero no en *music* [AE, BE = 'mjuːzik], *fuel* [AE, BE = 'fjuːəl].

10. La sílaba final **-ile** (BE generalmente [-ail]) se pronuncia a menudo en AE como [-əl] o bien [-il], p.ej. *missile* [AE 'misəl, 'misil = BE 'misail], *textile* [AE 'tekstil = BE 'tekstail].

A

a [ei; ə] *article*: un, una; *10 miles an hour* 10 millas por hora; *2 shillings a pound* 2 chelines la libra.
A 1 ['ei 'wʌn] F de primera calidad; *F feel* ~ estar como un reloj.
a·back [ə'bæk] F atrás, hacia atrás; ⚓ en facha; F *taken* ~ desconcertado.
ab·a·cus ['æbəkəs], *pl.* **ab·a·ci** ['‿sai] ábaco *m* (*a.* △).
a·baft [ə'bɑ:ft] **1.** *adv.* a popa; **2.** *prp.* detrás de.
a·ban·don [ə'bændən] abandonar, desamparar; renunciar a, dejar; ~ o.s. to abandonarse a, entregarse a; **a'ban·doned** *adj.* abandonado, desamparado; **a'ban·don·ment** abandono *m*, desamparo *m*.
a·base [ə'beis] humillar, degradar; envilecer; **a'base·ment** humillación *f*, degradación *f*.
a·bash [ə'bæʃ] confundir, avergonzar; ~ed corrido, confundido; **a'bash·ment** confusión *f*, vergüenza *f*.
a·bate [ə'beit] *v/t.* disminuir, reducir; ⚖ suprimir, abolir; *price* rebajar; *enthusiasm etc.* moderar; *pride* abatir; *v/i.* menguar, disminuir; moderarse; (*price*) bajar; (*wind*) amainar; **a'bate·ment** disminución *f*; supresión *f*, abolición *f*; rebaja *f of price*; amaine *m*.
ab·a(t)·tis [ə'bætis] estacada *f*.
ab·at·toir ['æbətwɑ:] matadero *m*.
ab·ba·cy ['æbəsi] abadía *f*; **'ab·bess** abadesa *f*; **ab·bey** ['æbi] abadía *f*, convento *m*; **ab·bot** ['æbət] abad *m*.
ab·bre·vi·ate [ə'bri:vieit] abreviar; ⚖ simplificar; **ab·bre·vi'a·tion** abreviatura *f*.
ABC ['ei 'bi: 'si:] abecé *m*, abecedario *m*; rudimentos *m/pl.*
ab·di·cate ['æbdikeit] *v/t.* abdicar, renunciar; *he* ~s *his principles* abdica de sus principios; *v/i.* abdicar (*in favour of* en, en favor de); **ab·di'ca·tion** abdicación *f*, renuncia *f*.
ab·do·men ['æbdəmen; ⚕ æb-

'doumen] abdomen *m*, vientre *m*; **ab·dom·i·nal** [æb'dɔminl] abdominal.
ab·duct [æb'dʌkt] raptar; **ab'duc·tion** rapto *m*; ⚖, ⚕ abducción *f*.
a·bed [ə'bed] en cama.
ab·er·ra·tion [æbə'reiʃn] aberración *f* (*a. ast. a. opt.*).
a·bet [ə'bet] incitar, instigar; ⚖ (*mst aid and* ~) encubrir, ser cómplice; **a'bet·ment** incitación *f*, instigación *f*; ⚖ encubrimiento *m*, complicidad *f*; **a'bet·tor** instigador *m*; ⚖ cómplice *m/f*, encubridor *m*, fautor *m*.
a·bey·ance [ə'beiəns] suspensión *f*; ⚖ *in* ~ en suspenso, en desuso.
ab·hor [əb'hɔ:] aborrecer, abominar; **ab·hor·rence** [əb'hɔrns] aborrecimiento *m*, abominación *f*; *hold in* ~ detestar; **ab'hor·rent** ☐ repugnante, detestable (*to* a).
a·bide [ə'baid] [*irr.*] *v/i. lit.* morar, ~ *by* atenerse a; conformarse con, cumplir con; *v/t.* aguardar; conformarse con; *I cannot* ~ *him* no le puedo ver; **a'bid·ing** ☐ permanente, perdurable.
a·bil·i·ty [ə'biliti] habilidad *f*, capacidad *f*, talento *m*; aptitud *f*; *to the best of one's* ~ lo mejor que pueda (*or* sepa) uno; **a'bil·i·ties** *pl.* dotes *f/pl.* intelectuales.
ab·ject ['æbdʒekt] ☐ abyecto, vil, ruin; ~ *poverty* la mayor miseria; **ab'jec·tion**, **'ab·ject·ness** abyección *f*, bajeza *f*.
ab·jure [əb'dʒuə] renunciar (a), abjurar. [~ *case*).\
ab·la·tive ['æblətiv] ablativo *m* (*a.*)
a·blaze [ə'bleiz] ardiendo; *fig.* ardiente, ansioso.
a·ble ['eibl] ☐ hábil, capaz; *be* ~ poder; (*know how to*) saber; ~ *to pay* solvente; ~**-bod·ied** ['‿'bɔdid] sano, robusto; ⚓ ~ *seaman* marinero *m* de primera.
ab·lu·tion [ə'blu:ʃn] ablución *f*.
ab·ne·gate ['æbnigeit] abnegar, renunciar, rehusar; **ab·ne'ga·tion** abnegación *f*, renuncia *f*.

ab·nor·mal [æb'nɔ:ml] □ anormal; deforme; **ab·nor'mal·i·ty** anormalidad *f*; deformidad *f*.

a·board [ə'bɔ:d] ⚓ a bordo; *all ~!* ¡ señores viajeros, al tren! (*etc.*).

a·bode [ə'boud] **1.** *pret. a. p.p. of abide*; **2.** morada *f*, domicilio *m*; *take up one's ~* avecindarse, domiciliarse.

a·bol·ish [ə'bɔliʃ] abolir, anular, suprimir; **a'bol·ish·ment, ab·o·li·tion** [æbo'liʃn] abolición *f*, anulación *f*, supresión *f*; **ab·o'li·tion·ist** abolicionista *m/f*.

A-bomb ['eibɔm] = *atomic bomb* bomba *f* atómica.

a·bom·i·na·ble [ə'bɔminəbl] □ abominable, detestable; *taste etc.* pésimo; **a'bom·i·nate** [~neit] abominar; **a·bom·i'na·tion** abominación *f*; asco *m*.

ab·o·rig·i·nal [æbə'ridʒənl] **1.** □ aborigen, indígena; **2.** (*pl. mst* **ab·o'rig·i·nes** [~ini:z]) aborigen *m*.

a·bort [ə'bɔ:t] abortar (*a. fig.*); **a'bor·tion** aborto *m*; engendro *m*; *fig.* malogro *m*, fracaso *m*; **a'bor·tive** □ abortivo; ineficaz, sin resultado. [*in an.*)]

a·bound [ə'baund] abundar (*with,*)

a·bout [ə'baut] **1.** *prp.* (*nearly*) casi; *place* junto a; (*relating to*) de, acerca de; *~ 6 o'clock* a eso de las 6; *~ 6 days* unos 6 días; *~ the end* casi al final; *~ the fire* junto al fuego; *~ the house* por la casa; *he looked ~ him* miró a su alrededor; *he took her ~ the waist* la cogió por la cintura; *I have no money ~ me* no llevo dinero encima; *speak ~ the matter* hablar del asunto; *ask questions ~ s.t.* hacer preguntas acerca de algo; *what is it ~?* ¿de qué se trata?; *v. how, what;* **2.** *adv.:* *be ~* estar levantado; estar por aquí; *be ~ to do* estar para (*or* a punto de) hacer.

a·bove [ə'bʌv] **1.** *prp.* encima de, superior a; *~ 300* más de 300; *~ all* sobre todo; *not to be ~ doing s.t.* ser capaz de hacer algo; *fig. get ~ o.s.* engreírse; *fig. it is ~ me* no lo entiendo; **2.** *adv.* (por) encima; arriba; *v. over;* **3.** *adj.* susodicho; **a'bove-'board** sin rebozo; legítimo.

ab·ra·ca·dab·ra [æbrəkə'dæbrə] abracadabra *f*.

ab·rade [ə'breid] raer, raspar.

ab·ra·sion [ə'breiʒn] raedura *f*, rozadura *f*, raspadura *f*; abrasión *f*; **ab'ra·sive** ⊕ abrasivo *m*.

a·breast [ə'brest] de frente, de fondo; *fig. ~ of or with* al corriente de; al día de.

a·bridge [ə'bridʒ] abreviar; compendiar; privar; **a'bridg(e)·ment** abreviación *f*; compendio *m*; privación *f of rights.*

a·broad [ə'brɔ:d] fuera; en el extranjero; *go ~* ir al extranjero; *there is a rumour ~ that* corre el rumor de que; *it has got ~* se ha divulgado.

ab·ro·gate ['æbrougeit] revocar, abrogar; **ab·ro'ga·tion** abrogación *f*.

ab·rupt [ə'brʌpt] □ brusco, rudo; *event* precipitado; *terrain* escarpado; *style* cortado; **ab'rupt·ness** brusquedad *f*, rudeza *f*; precipitación *f*.

ab·scess ['æbsis] absceso *m*.

ab·scond [əb'skɔnd] huir de la justicia; F zafarse.

ab·sence ['æbsns] ausencia *f*; falta *f*; *~ of mind* distracción *f*, despiste *m* (F).

ab·sent 1. ['æbsnt] □ ausente; be *~* faltar; *fig.* = '~·mind·ed □ distraído; **2.** [æb'sent]: *~ o.s.* ausentarse (*from* de); **ab·sen·tee** [æbsn'ti:] absentista *m/f*; **ab·sen·tee·ism** absentismo *m*.

ab·sinth ['æbsinθ] ajenjo *m*.

ab·so·lute ['æbsəlu:t] □ absoluto (*a. gr.*); total; *denial* categórico, rotundo; *liar* redomado; *non·ense* puro; *~ly* absolutamente *etc.*; *~ly* ¡perfectamente!; **'ab·so·lute·ness** lo absoluto; **ab·so'lu·tion** absolución *f*; **'ab·so·lut·ism** absolutismo *m*.

ab·solve [əb'zɔlv] absolver (*from* de).

ab·sorb [əb'sɔ:b] absorber (*a. fig.*); *shock etc.* amortiguar; *~ed in* absorto en; **ab'sorb·ent** absorbente, hidrófilo.

ab·sorp·tion [əb'sɔ:pʃn] absorción *f* (*a. fig.*).

ab·stain [əb'stein] abstenerse (*from* de); *freq.* abstenerse de las bebidas alcohólicas; **ab'stain·er** *approx.* abstemio *m* (*freq. total ~*).

ab·ste·mi·ous [əb'sti:miəs] □ sobrio, abstemio.

ab·sten·tion [æb'stenʃn] abstención *f* (*parl.* de votar).

ab·sti·nence ['æbstinəns] abstinencia *f (from* de); **'ab·sti·nent** □ abstinente, abstemio.

ab·stract 1. ['æbstrækt] □ abstracto (*a. gr.*); recóndito; *in the* ~ en abstracto; **2.** [~] resumen *m*, extracto *m*; **3.** [æb'strækt] abstraer (*mentally*); *euph.* hurtar; ⚕ extraer; *book* compendiar; **ab'stract·ed** □ *fig.* distraído; **abstrac·tion** [æb'strækʃn] abstracción *f; euph.* hurto *m*; ⚕ extracto *m*; recogimiento *m* (del espíritu).

ab·struse [æb'stru:s] □ abstruso; **ab'struse·ness** lo abstruso; tenebrosidad *f*.

ab·surd [əb'sə:d] □ absurdo, irrazonable; ridículo; necio; **ab'surdi·ty** disparate *m*, absurdo *m*; tontería *f*, locura *f*.

a·bun·dance [ə'bʌndəns] abundancia *f*, copia *f*, caudal *m*; plenitud *f of heart etc.*; riqueza *f*; **a'bun·dant** □ abundante, copioso; *water* caudaloso; ~ *in* abundante en, rebosante de; **a'bun·dant·ly** copiosamente; ~ *clear* plenamente claro.

a·buse 1. [ə'bju:s] abuso *m*; (*insults*) denuestos *m/pl.*, improperios *m/pl.*; injurias *f/pl.*; **2.** [~z] abusar de; denostar; maltratar; **a'bu·sive** □ abusivo; insultante; *be* ~ soltar injurias.

a·but [ə'bʌt] *v/t. a. v/i.*: ~ *with*, ~ *on* confinar con, lindar con; *v/i.*: ~ *on*, ~ *against* apoyarse en (*penthouse etc.*); **a'but·ment** contrafuerte *m*, estribo *m*; **a'but·ter** propietario *m* colindante.

a·bysm [ə'bizm] *poet.* = *abyss;* **a'bys·mal** □ abismal; *fig.* profundo; **a·byss** [ə'bis] abismo *m*, sima *f*.

Ab·ys·sin·i·an [æbi'sinjən] abisinio *adj. a. su. m* (a *f*).

a·ca·cia [ə'keiʃə] acacia *f*.

ac·a·dem·ic [ækə'demik] □ académico; universitario; *argument etc.* bizantino, estéril; ~ *dress* vestidura*f* universitaria (*a. academicals pl.*); **ac·a'dem·i·cal** □ universitario.

a·cad·e·mi·cian [əkædə'miʃn] académico *m*; **a·cad·e·my** [ə'kædəmi] academia *f*. [(*a.* ⚘).\

a·can·thus [ə'kænθəs] acanto *m*\

ac·cede [æk'si:d]; ~ *to* consentir en, acceder a; *post* entrar en; *party* afiliarse a; *throne* subir a.

ac·cel·er·ate [æk'seləreit] acelerar; apresurar; **ac·cel·er'a·tion** aceleración *f*; **ac'cel·er·a·tor** *mot.* acelerador *m*.

ac·cent 1. ['æksnt] acento *m*; **2.** [æk'sent] acentuar; recalcar (*a. fig.*).

ac·cen·tu·ate [æk'sentjueit] = *accent* 2; **ac·cen·tu'a·tion** acentuación *f*.

ac·cept [ək'sept] aceptar (*a.* ~ *of, a.* ✝); *p.* admitir; **ac·cept·a'bil·i·ty** = *acceptableness*; **ac·cept·a·ble** [ək'septəbl] □ aceptable; grato; **ac'cept·a·ble·ness** aceptación *f*; aprobación *f*; **ac'cept·ance** aceptación *f* (*a.* ✝); acogida *f*; (*ideas*) acogida *f*, asenso *m*; **ac·cep·ta·tion** [æksep'teiʃn] acepción *f* (de una palabra); **ac'cept·ed** □ acepto; **ac'cept·er**, **ac'cept·or** aceptador *m*; ✝ aceptante *m*.

ac·cess ['ækses] acceso *m*, entrada *f* (*to* a); ⚕ acceso *m*, ataque *m*; *easy of* ~ abordable, tratable; accesible; **ac'ces·sa·ry** = *accessory* 2; **acces·si·bil·i·ty** [~i'biliti] accesibilidad *f*; **ac'ces·si·ble** [~əbl] □ accesible (*to* a); asequible; **ac'cession** acceso *m*, entrada *f*; accesión *f* (*treaty etc.*); entrada *f* en posesión *of estate etc.*; subida *f to throne*; (*property*) aumento *m*; ⚖ accesión *f*.

ac·ces·so·ry [æk'sesəri] **1.** □ accesorio; **2.** accesorio *m*; ⚖ cómplice *m/f*; **ac'ces·so·ries** [~riz] *pl.* accesorios *m/pl.*

ac·ci·dence ['æksidəns] *gr.* accidentes *m/pl.*

ac·ci·dent ['æksidənt] accidente *m*; ~ *insurance* seguro *m* contra accidentes; *by* ~ por casualidad; **ac·ciden·tal** [æksi'dentl] **1.** □ accidental, fortuito; ~ *death* muerte *f* accidental; **2.** ♪ accidente *m*.

ac·claim [ə'kleim] **1.** aclamar, ovacionar; **2.** aclamación *f*.

ac·cla·ma·tion [æklə'meiʃn] aclamación *f* (*freq.* ~*s pl.*); *by* ~ por aclamación.

ac·cli·mate [ə'klaimit] *esp. Am.* aclimatar.

ac·cli·ma·ti·za·tion [əklaimətai'zeiʃn] aclimatación *f*; **ac'cli·matize** aclimatar.

ac·cliv·i·ty [ə'kliviti] subida *f*.

ac·com·mo·date [ə'kɔmədeit] (*adapt*) acomodar, adaptar (*to* a);

ajustar; *differences* reconciliar, acomodar; proveer (*with* de); (*house*) alojar; **ac'com·mo·dat·ing** □ acomodadizo; **ac·com·mo'da·tion** acomodación *f*, adaptación *f*; acuerdo *m*, convenio *m*; transigencia *f*; alojamiento *m*; ✝ ~ *bill* pagaré *m* de favor; *seating* ~ plazas *f/pl.*, asientos *m/pl.*; *Am.* ~ *train* tren *m* ómnibus.

ac·com·pa·ni·ment [ə'kʌmpənimənt] acompañamiento *m* (*a.* ♪); accesorio *m*; **ac'com·pa·nist** acompañante (*a f*) *m*; **ac'com·pa·ny** acompañar (*by*, *with* de).

ac·com·plice [ə'kɔmplis] cómplice *m/f*, fautor *m*.

ac·com·plish [ə'kɔmpliʃ] acabar, completar; efectuar; *prophesy etc.* cumplir; **ac'com·plished** consumado, logrado; *fact* realizado; *p.* hábil; **ac'com·plish·ment** (*end*) conclusión *f*; logro *m*, éxito *m*; *mst pl.* talentos *m/pl.*, habilidades *f/pl.*

ac·cord [ə'kɔ:d] 1. acuerdo *m*, convenio *m*; armonía *f*; *of one's own* ~ espontáneamente, de su propio acuerdo; *with one* ~ de común acuerdo; 2. *v/i.* concordar (*with* con); *v/t.* conceder; **ac'cord·ance** conformidad *f*; *in* ~ *with* conforme a, de acuerdo con; **ac'cord·ant**: ~ *to*, ~ *with* conforme a; **ac'cording**: ~ *to* según; conforme a; ~ *as* según; **ac'cord·ing·ly** en conformidad: *and* ~ así pues, y por lo tanto.

ac·cor·di·on [ə'kɔ:diən] acordeón *m*.

ac·cost [ə'kɔst] abordar.

ac·cou·cheur [æku:'ʃə:], *f* **ac·cou'cheuse** [~z] comadrón (-a *f*) *m*.

ac·count [ə'kaunt] 1. narración *f*, relato *m*; cuenta *f* (*a.* ✝), cálculo *m*; estimación *f*, importancia *f*; *blocked* ~ cuenta *f* bloqueada; *current* ~ cuenta *f* corriente; *payment on* ~ pago *m* a cuenta; *by all* ~*s* por lo que dicen; *of no* ~ de poca importancia; *on his* ~ por él; *on his own* ~ por su propia cuenta; *on no* ~ de ninguna manera; *on* ~ *of* a causa de, por; *bring to* ~ pedir cuentas a; *give* (*or render*) *an* ~ *of* dar cuenta de; *give a good* ~ *of o.s.* dar buena cuenta de sí; *settle an* ~ liquidar una cuenta; *take into* ~*s, take* ~ *of* tener en cuenta; *turn to* ~ aprovechar, sacar provecho de; 2. *v/i.*: ~ *for* dar cuenta de, explicar; justificar; *l*

cannot ~ *for it* no me lo explico; *v/t.* considerar, tener por; **ac·count·a'bil·i·ty** responsabilidad *f*; **ac'count·a·ble** □ responsable; **ac'count·an·cy** contabilidad *f*; **ac'count·ant** contador *m*; contable *m*; **ac'count-book** libro *m* de cuentas; **ac'count·ing** contabilidad *f*.

ac·cou·tred [ə'ku:təd] equipado; **ac·cou·tre·ments** [ə'ku:təmənts] *pl.* arreos *m/pl.*; equipo *m*.

ac·cred·it [ə'kredit] acreditar (*a. diplomatic*); ~ *s.o. to a p.* acreditar a alguien cerca de una p.; ~ *s.t. to a p.* atribuir algo a una p.

ac·cre·tion [æ'kri:ʃn] aumento *m*; ⚜ acrecencia *f*, accesión *f*.

ac·crue [ə'kru:] aumentarse.

ac·cu·mu·late [ə'kju:mjuleit] acumular(se), amontonar(se); **ac·cu·mu'la·tion** acumulación *f*, aumento *m*; montón *m*; **ac·cu·mu·la·tive** [ə'kju:mjulətiv] □ acumulativo; **ac'cu·mu·la·tor** ⚡ acumulador *m*.

ac·cu·ra·cy ['ækjurəsi] exactitud *f*, precisión *f*; **ac·cu·rate** ['~rit] □ exacto, preciso; correcto.

ac·cursed [ə'kə:sid], **ac·curst** [ə'kə:st] maldito; *lit.* ~ *be* ¡ maldito sea!, ¡ mal haya!

ac·cu·sa·tion [ækju:'zeiʃn] acusación *f*; ⚜ denuncia *f*, delación *f*; **ac·cu·sa·tive** [ə'kju:zətiv] acusativo *m* (*a.* ~ *case*); **ac·cu·sa·to·ry** [ə'kju:zətəri] acusatorio; **ac·cuse** [ə'kju:z] acusar (*of* de); denunciar, delatar; *the* ~*d* ⚜ el acusado; **ac'cuser** acusador *m*.

ac·cus·tom [ə'kʌstəm] acostumbrar, avezar (*to* a); **ac'cus·tomed** acostumbrado; usual.

ace [eis] as *m* (*dice, cards, a. tennis; a. sl. fig.*); *Am.* F ~ *in the hole* triunfo *m* en reserva; *within an* ~ *of* a dos dedos de.

a·cer·bi·ty [ə'sə:biti] aspereza *f*.

ac·e·tate ['æsitit] acetato *m*; **a·ce·tic** [ə'si:tik] acético; **a·cet·i·fy** [ə'setifai] acetificar; **ac·e·tone** ['æsitoun] acetona *f*; **ac·e·tous** ['~təs] acetoso; agrio; **a·cet·y·lene** [ə'setili:n] acetileno *m*.

ache [eik] 1. doler; 2. dolor *m*; *full of* ~*s and pains* lleno de goteras.

a·chieve [ə'tʃi:v] lograr, conseguir; acabar; **a'chieve·ment** realización *f*, logro *m*; hazaña *f*, proeza *f*.

ach·ing ['eikiŋ] **1.** □ dolorido; **2.** dolor *m*. [romático.〉

ach·ro·mat·ic [ækrou'mætik] □ ac-〉

ac·id ['æsid] **1.** □ ácido, agrio; *v.* test; **2.** ácido *m*; **a·cid·i·fy** [ə'sidifai] acidificar; **a'cid·i·ty** acidez *f*; acedía *f of stomach*; **ac·i·do·sis** [æsi'dousis] acidosis *f*; **'ac·id-proof** a prueba de ácidos; **a·cid·u·late** [ə'sidjuleit] acidular; **a·cid·u·lous** [ə'sidjuləs] acídulo.

ac·knowl·edge [ək'nɔlidʒ] reconocer; *crime etc.* confesar; *favour etc.* agradecer; ✝ ~ *receipt* acusar recibo; **ac'knowl·edg(e)·ment** reconocimiento *m*; confesión *f*; agradecimiento *m*; ✝ acuse *m* de recibo.

ac·me ['ækmi] *lit. fig.* cima *f*, apogeo *m*, colmo *m*; ~ *of perfection* suma perfección *f*.

ac·o·nite ['ækənait] acónito *m*.

a·corn ['eikɔ:n] bellota *f*.

a·cous·tic, a·cous·ti·cal [ə'ku:stik(l)] □ acústico; **a'cous·tics** *mst pl.* acústica *f*.

ac·quaint [ə'kweint] enterar, avisar (*with, of* de); *be* ~*ed* conocerse; *be* ~*ed with* conocer; saber, estar al corriente de; *become* ~*ed with* (llegar a) conocer; ponerse al tanto de; **ac'quaint·ance** conocimiento *m* (*with* de); (*p.*) conocido *m*, conocido *m*.

ac·qui·esce [ækwi'es] asentir (*in* a), conformarse (*in* con); **ac·qui·es·cence** consentimiento *m*, aquiescencia *f* (*to* en); **ac·qui·es·cent** □ condescendiente; acomodadizo.

ac·quire [ə'kwaiə] adquirir, obtener; *language* aprender; ~ *a taste* for tomar gusto a; ~*d taste* gusto *m* adquirido; **ac'quire·ment** adquisición *f*; ~*s pl.* conocimientos *m/pl.*

ac·qui·si·tion [ækwi'ziʃn] adquisición *f*; ganancia *f*; **ac·quis·i·tive** [æ'kwizitiv] □ adquisitivo; codicioso; **ac'quis·i·tive·ness** codicia *f*.

ac·quit [ə'kwit] absolver (*a.* 🕮), exculpar (*of* de); ~ *o.s.* of duty etc. desempeñar, cumplir; ~ *o.s. well* (*ill*) hacerlo bien (mal); **ac'quit·tal** 🕮 absolución *f*; descargo *m of debt*; desempeño *m*; **ac'quit·tance** 🕮 quita *f*; descargo *m of debt*.

a·cre ['eikə] acre *m* (= 40,47 *áreas*); *God's* ~ camposanto *m*; **'acre·age** superficie *f* en acres; extensión *f* (de tierras).

ac·rid ['ækrid] acre; *fig.* áspero, desapacible.

ac·ri·mo·ni·ous [ækri'mounjəs] □ áspero, desabrido; **ac·ri·mo·ny** ['ækriməni] acrimonia *f*, aspereza *f*.

ac·ro·bat ['ækrəbæt] acróbata *m/f*; **ac·ro'bat·ic** □ acrobático; **ac·ro'bat·ics** acrobacia *f*; 🗡 vuelo *m* acrobático.

a·cross [ə'krɔs] **1.** *adv.* a través, de través; de una parte a otra, de un lado a otro; del otro lado; en cruz, transversalmente; **2.** *prp.* a(l) través de; del otro lado de.

act [ækt] **1.** *v/i.* actuar, obrar; funcionar, marchar; comportarse, conducirse; *thea.* trabajar; ~ *as* actuar de, hacer de ; ~ (*up*)*on* obrar con arreglo a; influir en; 🕮 atacar; ~ *for* representar; *Am.* F ~ *up* travesear; *v/t. thea.* representar; desempeñar (un papel); **2.** acto *m*, acción *f*, obra *f*; *parl.* decreto *m*, ley *f*; *thea.* acto *m*, jornada *f*; F *in the* ~ con las manos en la masa; ~*s pl. of the Apostles* Hechos *m/pl.* de los Apóstoles; **'act·a·ble** representable; **'act·ing 1.** *thea.* representación *f*; desempeño *m*; **2.** interino, suplente; ✝ ~ *partner* socio *m* interino.

ac·tion ['ækʃn] acción *f* (*a.* 🗡, *thea.*), acto *m*, hecho *m*; ⊕ mecanismo *m*; funcionamiento *m*, marcha *f*; (*horse*) marcha *f*; gesto *m*; 🕮 acción *f*, demanda *f*; *put into* ~ poner en marcha; *put out of* ~ inutilizar; parar; *take* ~ tomar medidas; **'ac·tion·a·ble** justiciable.

ac·tive ['æktiv] □ activo (*a. gr. a.* ✝); enérgico; vigoroso; *be on the* ~ *list* estar en activo; **ac'tiv·i·ty** actividad *f*; energía *f*; vigor *m*; *in full* ~ en plena actividad; *pl. esp.* ✝ negocios *m/pl.*; esfera *f* de actividad.

ac·tor ['æktə] actor *m*, cómico *m*; **ac·tress** ['æktris] actriz *f*.

ac·tu·al ['æktjuəl] □ verdadero, real, efectivo; actual; **ac·tu·al·i·ty** [æktju'æliti] realidad *f*; actualidad *f*; **ac·tu·al·ize** ['æktjuəlaiz] actualizar; realizar. [seguros.〉

ac·tu·ar·y ['æktjuəri] actuario *m* de〉

ac·tu·ate ['æktjueit] actuar; impeler; **ac·tu'a·tion** actuación *f*.

a·cu·men [ə'kju:men] perspicacia *f*; juicio *m* crítico.

a·cute [ə'kju:t] □ *all senses*: agudo; **a'cute·ness** agudeza *f*.

ad [æd] F = *advertisement* anuncio *m*; *classified* ~s *pl.* anuncios *m/pl.* por palabras.

ad·age ['ædidʒ] adagio *m*; refrán *m*.

ad·a·mant ['ædəmənt] *fig.* firme, intransigente; insensible (*to* a); **ad·a·man·tine** [~'mæntain] adamantino; *fig.* = *adamant*.

a·dapt [ə'dæpt] adaptar, acomodar, ajustar; *text* refundir; **a·dapt·a'bil·i·ty** adaptabilidad *f*; capacidad *f* para acomodarse; **a'dapt·a·ble** adaptable; **ad·ap'ta·tion** adaptación *f* (*to* a); refundición *f*; **a'dap·ter** *radio*: adaptador *m*.

add [æd] *v/t.* añadir, agregar (*to* a); Å sumar; *v/i.* ~ *to* aumentar; realzar; ~ *up to* subir a; *fig.* venir a ser, equivaler a.

ad·den·dum [ə'dendəm], *pl.* **ad·'den·da** [~ə] adición *f*, apéndice *m*.

ad·der ['ædə] víbora *f*.

ad·dict 1. [ə'dikt]: ~ *o.s.* entregarse (*to* a), enviciarse (*to* en, con); **2.** ['ædikt] adicto (a *f*) *m*; (*drugs*) toxicómano (a *f*) *m*; **ad'dict·ed**: ~ *to* aficionado a, adicto a; entregado a; **ad'dic·tion** (*drugs*) toxicomanía *f*.

ad·di·tion [ə'diʃn] añadidura *f*; adición *f*; Å suma *f*; *in* ~ además, a más; *in* ~ *to* además de; **ad'di·tion·al** adicional *f*, sentencia *f*.

ad·dle ['ædl] **1.** huero, *fig.* huero, atontado; confuso; **2.** enhuerar (*v/t. a. v/i.*).

ad·dress [ə'dres] **1.** *p.* dirigir la palabra a; *letter, protest etc.* dirigir (*to* a); ✝ consignar; ~ *o.s. to p.* dirigirse a; *th.* aplicarse a; **2.** (*house*) dirección *f*, señas *f/pl.*; sobrescrito *m*; ✝ consignación *f*; (*speech*) discurso *m*; (*skill*) destreza *f*; (*behaviour*) maneras *f/pl.*, modales *m/pl.*; *give an* ~ pronunciar un discurso; *pay one's* ~*es to a lady* hacer la corte a una señorita; **ad·dress·ee** [ædre·'si:] destinatario *m*; **ad'dress·o·graph** máquina *f* de direcciones.

ad·duce [ə'dju:s] aducir, alegar.

ad·ept ['ædept] **1.** diestro, experto (*at, in* en); **2.** perito *m*; *be an* ~ *at* ser maestro en (*or* de).

ad·e·qua·cy ['ædikwəsi] suficiencia *f*; adecuación *f*; **ad·e·quate** ['~kwit] ☐ suficiente; apropiado, adecuado.

ad·here [əd'hiə]: ~ *to* adherir a, pegarse a; *fig.* adherirse a, allegarse a; *promise* cumplir; *rule* observar; **ad·'her·ence**: ~ *to* adherencia *f* a, adhesión *f* a; (*rule*) observancia *f* de; **ad'her·ent 1.** adhesivo; **2.** partidario (a *f*) *m*.

ad·he·sion [əd'hi:ʒn] *mst* = *adherence*; ℱ adherencia *f*.

ad·he·sive [əd'hi:siv] ☐ adhesivo; ~ *plaster* esparadrapo *m*; ~ *tape* cinta *f* adhesiva.

a·dieu [ə'dju:] **1.** ¡adiós!; **2.** adiós *m*; *bid* ~ *to* despedirse de.

ad·i·pose ['ædipous] adiposo.

ad·it ['ædit] entrada *f*, acceso *m*; ✕ bocamina *f*.

ad·ja·cen·cy [ə'dʒeisənsi] adyacencia *f*, contigüidad *f*; **ad'ja·cent** ☐ adyacente, contiguo, inmediato (*to* a).

ad·jec·ti·val [ædʒek'taivl] ☐ adjetival, adjetivo (a); **ad·jec·tive** ['ædʒiktiv] adjetivo *m*.

ad·join [ə'dʒɔin] lindar con; **ad·'join·ing** colindante, lindero.

ad·journ [ə'dʒə:n] *v/t.* prorrogar, diferir; *session* clausurar, suspender; *v/i.*: ~ *to* trasladarse a; **ad'journ·ment** aplazamiento *m*; clausura *f*.

ad·judge [ə'dʒʌdʒ] decretar; condenar (*to* a); sentenciar, juzgar; *prize* adjudicar; ~ *s.o. guilty* declarar culpable a alguien; **ad'judge·ment** adjudicación *f*, sentencia *f*.

ad·ju·di·cate [ə'dʒu:dikeit] juzgar; declarar, pronunciar; **ad·ju·di'ca·tion** adjudicación *f*; juicio *m*, sentencia *f*.

ad·junct ['ædʒʌŋkt] auxiliar *m*, adjunto *m*; accesorio *m*.

ad·ju·ra·tion [ædʒuə'reiʃn] conjuro *m*, imprecación *f*; juramento *m*; **ad·jure** [ə'dʒuə] conjurar, imprecar; juramentar.

ad·just [ə'dʒʌst] ajustar; arreglar; *quarrel* conciliar; *apparatus etc.* ajustar, regular; ~ *o.s. to* adaptarse a; **ad'just·a·ble** ☐ ajustable, graduable, regulable; **ad'just·ment** ajuste *m*, regulación *f*; acuerdo *m*, convenio *m*; arreglo *m*.

ad·ju·tan·cy ['ædʒutənsi] ayudantía *f*; **'ad·ju·tant** ayudante *m*.

ad·lib [æd'lib] F **1.** a voluntad; a discreción; **2.** improvisar.

ad·min·is·ter [əd'ministə] *mst* administrar; *shock etc.* proporcionar; ~ *an oath* tomar juramento; **ad·min·is'tra·tion** administración *f*; gobierno *m*; dirección *f*; **ad-'min·is·tra·tive** [ˌ.trətiv] administrativo; **ad'min·is·tra·tor** [ˌ.treitə] administrador *m*; **ad'min·is·tra·trix** [ˌ.triks] administradora *f*.

ad·mi·ra·ble ['ædmərəbl] □ admirable; excelente.

ad·mi·ral ['ædmərəl] almirante *m*; **'ad·mi·ral·ty** almirantazgo *m*; ♀ Ministerio *m* de Marina; *First Lord of the* ~ *(British)* Ministro *m* de Marina.

ad·mi·ra·tion [ædmi'reiʃn] admiración *f*.

ad·mire [əd'maiə] admirar; **ad·'mi·rer** admirador (-a *f*) *m*.

ad·mis·si·bil·i·ty [ədmisə'biliti] admisibilidad *f*; **ad'mis·si·ble** □ admisible; **ad'mis·sion** admisión *f*, entrada *f* (*to* a); confesión *f* (*of* de); ~ *free* entrada *f* libre (*or* gratis).

ad·mit [əd'mit] *v/t.* admitir; aceptar; confesar, reconocer; *be* ~*ted to academy etc.* ingresar en; *v/i.*: ~ *of* admitir, dar lugar a; ~ *to* confesarse culpable de; **ad'mit·tance** entrada *f*, admisión *f*; ⚡ admitancia *f*; *No* ~ prohibida la entrada; **ad'mit·ted·ly** indudablemente; de acuerdo que..., es verdad que...

ad·mix·ture [əd'mikstʃe] mezcla *f*, adición *f*.

ad·mon·ish [əd'mɔniʃ] amonestar; reprender; aconsejar (*to inf.*); **ad·mo·ni·tion** [ædmə'niʃn] amonestación *f*; represión *f*; consejo *m*; advertencia *f*; **ad·mon·i·to·ry** [əd-'mɔnitəri] □ amonestador.

a·do [ə'du:] ruido *m*; aspaviento *m*; dificultad *f*; *without more* ~ sin más ni más; *much* ~ *about nothing* mucho ruido y pocas nueces.

a·do·be [ə'doubi] adobe *m*.

ad·o·les·cence [ædou'lesns] adolescencia *f*; **ad·o·les·cent** adolescente *adj. a. su. m/f*.

a·dopt [ə'dɔpt] adoptar; ~*ed son* hijo *m* adoptivo; **a'dop·tion** adopción *f*; *country of* ~ patria *f* adoptiva; **a'dop·tive** adoptivo; **a'dop·tive·ly** por adopción.

a·dor·a·ble [ə'dɔːrəbl] □ adorable; **ad·o·ra·tion** [ædɔː'reiʃn] adoración *f*; **a·dore** [ə'dɔː] adorar; **a'dor·er** adorador (-a *f*) *m*.

a·dorn [ə'dɔːn] adornar, engalanar, embellecer; **a'dorn·ment** adorno *m*.

ad·ren·al·in [əd'renəlin] adrenalina *f*.

a·drift [ə'drift] ♻ al garete, a la deriva (*a. fig.*); *turn* ~ abandonar a su suerte.

a·droit [ə'drɔit] □ diestro, hábil; mañoso; **a'droit·ness** destreza *f*, habilidad *f*; maña *f*.

ad·u·late ['ædjuleit] adular, lisonjear; **ad·u'la·tion** adulación *f*, lisonja *f*; **'ad·u·la·tor** adulador (-a *f*) *m*, lisonjero (a *f*) *m*; **'ad·u·la·to·ry** lisonjero.

a·dult ['ædʌlt] adulto *adj. a. su. m* (a *f*); ♀ *Education* enseñanza *f* de adultos.

a·dul·ter·ant [ə'dʌltərənt] adulterante *adj. a. su. m*; **a'dul·ter·ate** 1. [ˌreit] adulterar, falsificar; 2. [ˌrit] adulterado, falsificado; **a·dul·ter·a·tion** [ədʌltə'reiʃn] adulteración *f*, falsificación *f*; impureza *f*; **a'dul·ter·a·tor** adulterador (-a *f*) *m*; **a'dul·ter·er** adúltero *m*; **a'dul·ter·ess** adúltera *f*; **a'dul·ter·ous** □ adúltero; **a'dul·ter·y** adulterio *m*.

ad·um·brate ['ædʌmbreit] bosquejar; presagiar; **ad·um'bra·tion** bosquejo *m*; presagio *m*.

ad·vance [əd'vɑːns] 1. *v/i.* avanzar, adelantar(se); ascender *in rank*; *(price)* subir; *v/t.* avanzar, adelantar; *fig. cause etc.* fomentar, promover; *idea etc.* proponer; 2. ✕ *etc.* avance *m*; *fig.* progreso *m*, adelanto *m*; *(money)* anticipo *m*; ~*s pl.* requerimiento *m* amoroso; *in* ~ por adelantado, de antemano; *be in* ~ *of* adelantarse a; *thank in* ~ anticipar las gracias; 3. *adj.* adelantado, anticipado; ~ *guard* avanzada *f*; **ad'vanced** *adj. gen. a. pol.* avanzado; adelantado; *study* superior, alto; ~ *in years* entrado en años; **ad'vance·ment** progreso *m*; adelantamiento *m*; fomento *m*; ascenso *m*.

ad·van·tage [əd'vɑːntidʒ] ventaja *f* (*a. tennis*); beneficio *m*, provecho *m*; *take* ~ *of* aprovechar(se de), sacar ventaja de; *b.s.* embaucar, valerse de, abusar de; *have the* ~ *of s.o.* llevar ventaja a alguien; *show to* ~ lucir; **ad·van·ta·geous** [ædvən-'teidʒəs] □ ventajoso, provechoso.

ad·vent ['ædvənt] advenimiento *m*; *eccl.* ♀ Adviento *m*; **ad·ven·ti·tious** [ædven'tiʃəs] □ adventicio.

ad·ven·ture [əd'venҫ̌ə] 1. aventura

f; lance *m*; 2. aventurar(se); arriesgarse; **ad'ven·tu·rer** aventurero *m*; **ad'ven·tur·ess** aventurera *f*; **ad·'ven·tur·ous** □ aventurero, arrojado, emprendedor.

ad·verb ['ædvəːb] adverbio *m*; **ad·ver·bi·al** [əd'vəːbiəl] □ adverbial.

ad·ver·sar·y ['ædvəsəri] adversario (a *f*) *m*, contrario (a *f*) *m*; **ad·verse** ['‿vəːs] □ adverso, contrario; hostil; desfavorable; ‿ *balance* saldo *m* negativo; **ad·ver·si·ty** [əd'vəːsiti] adversidad *f*; infortunio *m*.

ad·vert¹ [əd'vəːt]: ‿ *to* referirse a, hacer referencia a.

ad·vert² ['ædvəːt] = *advertisement* anuncio *m*.

ad·ver·tise ['ædvətaiz] *v/t.* anunciar; publicar; ‿ *one's weakness* patentizar debilidad; *v/i.* poner un anuncio; ‿ *for* buscar por medio de anuncios; **ad·ver·tise·ment** [əd-'vəːtismənt] anuncio *m*; **ad·ver·tis·er** ['ædvətaizə] anunciante *m/f*; **'ad·ver·tis·ing** 1. publicidad *f*, propaganda *f*, anuncios *m/pl.*; 2. publicitario, de anuncios; ‿ *agen·cy* agencia *f* de publicidad.

ad·vice [əd'vais] consejo *m*; aviso *m*, informe *m*, noticia *f*; *take medical* ‿ consultar al médico; **ad'vice-boat** aviso *m*.

ad·vis·a·bil·i·ty [ədvaizə'biliti] conveniencia *f*; **ad·vis·a·ble** [əd-'vaizəbl] □ aconsejable, prudente, conveniente; **ad'vise** *v/t.* aconsejar (*to inf.*); avisar, informar (*a.* ✝); *v/i.*: ‿ *on* ser asesor en; **ad'vised** □ deliberado; *well* ‿ prudente; *you would be well* ‿ *to inf.* sería aconsejable que Vd. *subj.*; **ad'vis·ed·ly** [‿idli] deliberadamente, adrede; **ad'vis·er** consejero *m*, asesor *m*; **ad'vi·so·ry** [‿eri] consultivo.

ad·vo·ca·cy ['ædvəkəsi] ⚖ abogacía *f*; defensa *f*; intercesión *f*; **ad·vo·cate** 1. ['‿kit] ⚖ abogado *m*; defensor *m*; 2. ['‿keit] abogar por; propugnar, defender; proponer.

adze [ædz] azuela *f*.

ae·gis ['iːdʒis] égida *f*.

Ae·o·li·an [iː'oulian] eolio.

ae·on ['iːən] eternidad *f*; *phls.* eón *m*.

a·er·at·ed ['eiəreitid]: ‿ *water* (agua *f*) gaseosa *f*; **a·er·a·tion** aeración *f*.

a·e·ri·al ['eəriəl] 1. □ aéreo; ‿ *camera* aparato *m* de fotografía

aérea; ‿ *photograph* aerofoto *f*; ‿ *railway* funicular *m* aéreo; 2. antena *f*; ‿ *mast* torre *f* de antena.

a·er·ie ['eəri] *v.* eyrie.

a·er·o... ['eərou] aero...; **a·er·o·bat·ics** ['‿bætiks] *pl.* acrobacia *f* aérea; **a·er·o·drome** ['eərədroum] aeródromo *m*, campo *m* de aviación; **a·er·o·dy·nam·ic** ['‿dai'næmik] aerodinámico; **a·er·o·gram** ['‿græm] aerograma *m*, radiograma *m*; **a·er·o·lite** ['‿lait] aerolito *m*; **a·er·o·naut** ['‿nɔːt] aeronauta *m/f*; **a·er·o·nau·tic**, **a·er·o·nau·ti·cal** □ aeronáutico; **a·er·o·nau·tics** *sg. a. pl.* aeronáutica *f*; **'a·er·o·plane** avión *m*, aeroplano *m*; **a·er·o·stat** ['‿stæt] aerostato *m*; **a·er·o·stat·ic** aerostático.

aes·thete ['iːsθiːt] esteta *m/f*; **aes·thet·ic**, **aes·thet·i·cal** ['iːsθetik(l)] □ estético; **aes'thet·ics** *sg.* estética *f*.

a·far [ə'faː] (*mst* ‿ *off*) lejos, en (la) lontananza; *from* ‿ (des)de lejos.

af·fa·bil·i·ty [æfə'biliti] afabilidad *f*.

af·fa·ble ['æfəbl] □ afable.

af·fair [ə'fɛə] asunto *m*, negocio *m*; F cosa *f*; amorío *m*; ‿ *of honour* lance *m* de honor; ‿s *of state* asuntos *m/pl.* de estado.

af·fect [ə'fekt] afectar; conmover, enternecer, impresionar; tener que ver con; influir en; *he* ‿s *the free-thinker* se las echa de librepensador; **af·fec·ta·tion** [æfek'teiʃn] afectación *f*; amaneramiento *m*; cursilería *f*; melindre *m*, dengue *m*; **af·fect·ed** [ə'fektid] □ afectado; conmovido; amanerado; cursi; melindroso; **af'fect·ing** 1. □ conmovedor, tierno, patético; 2. *prp.* relativo a; **af'fec·tion** afecto *m*, cariño *m*, amor *m*; *esp.* ⚕ afección *f*; **af·'fec·tion·ate** ['‿kʃnit] □ cariñoso, afectuoso; **af'fec·tive** afectivo.

af·fi·ance [ə'faiəns] 1. palabra *f* de casamiento; 2. dar palabra de casamiento.

af·fi·da·vit [æfi'deivit] declaración *f* jurada.

af·fil·i·ate [ə'filieit] *v/t.* (a)filiar; ⚖ determinar la paternidad de; *v/i.* afiliarse (*with, to* a); ‿*d company* sociedad *f* filial, compañía *f* subsidiaria; **af·fil·i·a·tion** afiliación *f*.

af·fin·i·ty [ə'finiti] afinidad *f*; atracción *f*.

af·firm [ə'fə:m] afirmar, aseverar, declarar; **af·fir·ma·tion** [æfə:-'meiʃn] afirmación *f*, aseveración *f*, declaración *f*; **af·firm·a·tive** [ə'fə:-mətiv] **1.** □ afirmativo; **2.**: *answer in the ~* dar una respuesta afirmativa.

af·fix 1. ['æfiks] *gr.* afijo *m*; añadidura *f*; **2.** [ə'fiks] fijar; pegar, unir; añadir.

af·flict [ə'flikt] afligir, acongojar; *be ~ed with* sufrir de; **af·flic·tion** aflicción *f*, congoja *f*; miseria *f*.

af·flu·ence ['æfluəns] afluencia *f*; opulencia *f*; **'af·flu·ent 1.** □ opulento, acaudalado; **2.** afluente *m*.

af·flux ['æflʌks] aflujo *m*.

af·ford [ə'fɔ:d] dar, proporcionar, proveer; (*pay for*) costear; *I can ~ it* tengo con que comprarlo, puedo permitírmelo.

af·fray [ə'frei] refriega *f*, reyerta *f*.

af·for·est [æ'fɔrist] poblar de árboles, repoblar; **af·for·est'a·tion** repoblación *f* (forestal).

af·fran·chise [æ'fræntʃaiz] franquear, manumitir.

af·front [ə'frʌnt] **1.** afrentar, injuriar, ultrajar; (*verbally*) denostar; arrostrar; **2.** afrenta *f*, injuria *f*, ultraje *m*; denuesto *m*; *put an ~ upon, offer an ~ to* afrentar *etc.*

a·field [ə'fi:ld] en el campo, al campo; afuera; *far ~* muy lejos.

a·fire [ə'faiə] ardiendo; *be ~* arder.

a·flame [ə'fleim] en llamas.

a·float [ə'flout] a flote; en el mar; a nado; inundado; ✝ en circulación; *keep ~* mantener(se) a flote; *set ~* poner a flote; *esp.* ✝ sacar a flote.

a·foot [ə'fut] a pie; en pie; en marcha; *set ~* poner en marcha; *what is ~?* qué se está tramando?

a·fore [ə'fɔ:] ⚓ *v. before;* **'~·men·tioned,** '~·named, '~·said antedicho, susodicho, precitado; '~·thought premeditado; *malice ~* premeditación *f*.

a·fraid [ə'freid] temeroso, miedoso; *be ~* tener miedo (*of* de, a), temer; *be ~ to* tener miedo de *inf.*, temer *inf.*; *be ~ for* temer por; F *I'm ~ I have to go now* siento tener que irme ahora; F *I'm ~ he won't come* me temo que no venga.

a·fresh [ə'freʃ] de nuevo, otra vez.

Af·ri·can ['æfrikən] africano *adj. a.*

su. m (a *f*); **Af·ri·kaans** [⌐'kɑ:ns] africaans *m*; **Af·ri·kan·der** ['⌐kændə] africander *m*.

aft [ɑ:ft] a popa; en popa.

aft·er ['ɑ:ftə] **1.** *adv.* (*time*) después; (*place*) detrás; **2.** *prp.* (*time*) después de; (*place*) detrás de; *~ all* después de todo, con todo; *day ~ day* día tras día; *time ~ time* repetidas veces; *I'll go ~ him* voy detrás de él; *~ Velázquez* según Velázquez; ♀ *you!* ¡Pase Vd.!; *soon ~ having seen him* poco después de haberle visto; *~ hours* fuera de horas; **3.** *cj.* después (de) que; **4.** *adj.* posterior; ⚓ de popa; '~·birth secundinas *f/pl.*; '~·crop segunda cosecha *f*; '~·din·ner de sobremesa; '~·ef·fect efecto *m* resultante, consecuencia *f*; '~·glow celajes *m/pl.*; '~·life vida *f* futura; resto *m* de la vida; '~·math consecuencias *f/pl.*; repercusiones *f/pl.*; '~·noon tarde *f*; *good ~!* ¡buenas tardes!; '~·pains *pl.* dolores *m/pl.* de sobreparto; '~·taste dejo *m*, resabio *m*; '~·thought ocurrencia *f* tardía; '~·treat·ment tratamiento *m* postoperatorio; ~·wards ['⌐wədz] después, más tarde.

a·gain [ə'gein] otra vez, de nuevo, nuevamente; *~ and ~*, *time and ~* repetidas veces; *as much (many) ~* otro (os, as) tanto (os, as); *now and ~* de vez en cuando, una que otra vez; *never ~* nunca más; *do it ~* volver a hacerlo.

a·gainst [ə'geinst] contra; cerca de, al lado de; (*as*) ~ en contraste con; *~ his coming* para su venida; *over ~* enfrente de; *be ~* oponerse a; *he was ~ it* estaba en contra.

a·gape [ə'geip] boquiabierto.

ag·ate ['ægət] ágata *f*.

a·ga·ve [ə'geivi] agave *f*, pita *f*.

age [eidʒ] **1.** edad *f*; época *f*, siglo *m*; (*old*) ~ vejez *f*, senectud *f*; *at the ~ of* a la edad de; *in the ~ of Queen Anne* en la época de (*or* en tiempos de) la reina Ana; *of ~* mayor de edad; *come of ~* llegar a mayor edad; *over ~* demasiado viejo; *under ~* menor de edad; *what is your ~?* ¿qué edad tiene Vd.?, ¿cuántos años tiene Vd.?; F *wait for ~s* esperar una eternidad; **2.** envejecer(se); **a·ged** ['⌐id] viejo, anciano; [eidʒd]: *~ 20* de 20 años; **'age·less** que no tiene edad, inmemorial; eternamente joven; **'age-lim·it** edad *f* mínima *or* máxima; edad *f* de jubilación.

a·gen·cy ['eidʒənsi] agencia *f*; acción *f*; medio *m*, mediación *f*, instrumentalidad *f*.

a·gen·da [ə'dʒendə] orden *m* del día.

a·gent ['eidʒənt] agente *m*; apoderado *m*; representante *m*; *Am.* 🜃 jefe *m* de estación.

a·gent-pro·voc·a·teur [æʒũprɔvɔk-ətə:r] agente *m* provocador.

age-worn ['eidʒwɔ:n] caduco.

ag·glom·er·ate [ə'glɔməreit] aglomerar(se); **ag·glom·er'a·tion** aglomeración *f*.

ag·glu·ti·nate 1. [ə'glu:tineit] aglutinar(se); **2.** [‿nit] aglutinado; **ag·glu·ti·na·tion** [‿'neiʃn] aglutinación *f*; **ag·glu·ti·na·tive** [ə'glu:-tinətiv] aglutinante.

ag·gran·dize ['ægrəndaiz] engrandecer, agrandar; **ag·gran·dize·ment** [ə'grændizmənt] engrandecimiento *m*, agrandamiento *m*.

ag·gra·vate ['ægrəveit] agravar, exacerbar; F irritar, exasperar; **ag·gra'va·tion** agravación *f*, exacerbación *f*; circunstancia *f* agravante; F exasperación *f*.

ag·gre·gate 1. ['ægrigeit] *v/t.* agregar, unir; *v/i.* ascender a, sumar; **2.** ['‿git] ‿ agregado, unido, global; ‿ *value* valor *m* total (*or* global); **3.** [‿] agregado *m*, total *m*, conjunto *m*; *in the* ‿ en conjunto, en total; **ag·gre·ga·tion** [‿'geiʃn] agregación *f*.

ag·gres·sion [ə'greʃn] agresión *f*; **ag'gres·sive** [ə'gresiv] □ agresivo; *fig.* emprendedor; ‿ *war* guerra *f* agresiva; **ag'gres·sive·ness** acometividad *f*; **ag'gres·sor** agresor (-a *f*) *m*.

ag·grieved [ə'gri:vd] ofendido, desairado; agraviado.

a·ghast [ə'gɑ:st] espantado, horrorizado; pasmado (*at* de).

ag·ile ['ædʒail] □ ágil.

a·gil·i·ty [ə'dʒiliti] agilidad *f*.

a·ging ['eidʒiŋ] envejecimiento *m*.

ag·i·o ['ædʒou] agio *m*; **ag·i·o·tage** ['ædʒətidʒ] agio *m*, agiotaje *m*.

ag·i·tate ['ædʒiteit] *v/t.* agitar; perturbar, alborotar; *plans etc.* discutir (acaloradamente); *v/i.:* ‿ *for* hacer propaganda por; **ag·i'ta·tion**

agitación *f*; perturbación *f*; discusión *f*; *insidious* ‿ agitación *f* clandestina; **ag·i·ta·tor** agitador (-a *f*) *m*, instigador (-a *f*) *m*, alborotador (-a *f*) *m*.

a·glow [ə'glou] encendido, fulgurante.

ag·nate ['ægneit] agnado *adj. a. su. m* (a *f*).

a·go [ə'gou]: (*it is*) *a year* ‿ hace un año; *long* ‿ hace mucho tiempo, tiempo ha.

a·gog [ə'gɔg] ansioso, anhelante, ávido (*for* de); *set* ‿ excitar.

ag·o·nize ['ægənaiz] *v/t.* atormentar; *v/i.* retorcerse de dolor, sufrir intensamente; **'ag·o·niz·ing** ‿ desgarrador, angustioso.

ag·o·ny ['ægəni] angustia *f*, congoja *f*; (‿ *of death, mortal* ‿) agonía *f*; F ‿ *column* sección *f* de anuncios relativos a asuntos particulares (*parientes desaparecidos, etc.*).

a·grar·i·an [ə'greəriən] agrario *adj. a. su. m* (a *f*); **a'grar·i·an·ism** agrarismo *m*.

a·gree [ə'gri:] *v/i.* concordar (*esp. gr.*), estar de acuerdo (*with* con, *that* en que); ponerse de acuerdo; ‿ *on,* ‿ *to* convenir en, quedar en, acordar; *it does not* ‿ *with me* no me sienta (bien); *v/t.* be ‿*d* estar de acuerdo (*on* en, *that* en que); ‿*d* convenido, aprobado; ¿*d!* ¡Conforme!; **a'gree·a·ble** □ agradable, ameno; *p.* simpático; conforme (*to* con), dispuesto (*to* a); **a'gree·a·ble·ness** agrado *m*; amenidad *f*; **a'gree·ment** acuerdo *m*; convenio *m*; concordancia *f*; conformidad *f*; ‿ *to differ* desacuerdo *m* amistoso; *come to an* ‿ ponerse de acuerdo, concertarse.

ag·ri·cul·tur·al [ægri'kʌltʃurəl] agrícola; ‿ *adviser* agrónomo *m*; **ag·ri·cul·ture** ['‿tʃə] agricultura *f*; **ag·ri'cul·tur·(al·)ist** [‿tʃər(əl)ist] agricultor (-a *f*) *m*.

a·ground [ə'graund] varado, encallado; *run* ‿ varar, encallar.

a·gue ['eigju:] fiebre *f* intermitente; escalofrío *m*; **'a·gu·ish** palúdico; escalofriado.

ah [ɑ:] ¡ah!

a·ha [ɑ:'hɑ:] ¡ajá!

a·head [ə'hed] delante, al frente; ⚓ por la proa; adelante; *straight* ‿ todo seguido; *be* ‿ *of one's time* anticiparse a su época; get ~ of a p. adelantarse a una p.; go ~ ir adelante, continuar, avanzar; go ~! ¡adelante!; send ~ enviar por delante.

a·hoi, a·hoy [əˈhɔi] ¡ha!; ship ~! ¡Ah del barco!

aid [eid] **1.** ayudar, auxiliar, socorrer; **2.** ayuda f, auxilio m, socorro m; by (with) the ~ of con la ayuda de; al amparo de; in ~ of a beneficio de.

aide-de-camp [ˈeiddəˈkãːŋ] edecán m.

ai·grette [ˈeigret] airón m.

ai·guil·lette [eigwiˈlet] cordones m/pl.

ail [eil] v/i. estar enfermo; sufrir; v/t. afligir; inquietar; what ~s him? ¿qué tiene?

ail·e·ron [ˈeilərɔn] alerón m.

ail·ing [ˈeiliŋ] enfermizo, achacoso; enfermo; **'ail·ment** achaque m, dolencia f, enfermedad f.

aim [eim] **1.** v/i. apuntar (at a); fig. ~ at aspirar a, ambicionar; ~ to aspirar a, intentar; fig. ~ high picar muy alto; v/t. gun, remark etc. apuntar (at a); blow etc. asestar (at a); **2.** puntería f; fig. mira f, meta f, blanco m, designio m; take ~ apuntar; **'aim·less** □ sin objeto; desatinado; ~ly a la buena ventura, a la deriva.

ain't [eint] F = is not, are not etc.; has not, have not.

air[1] [ɛə] **1.** aire m; by ~ por avión; in the ~ fig. en el aire, indefinido; en proyecto; in the open ~ al aire libre, al raso; castles in the ~ castillos m/pl. en el aire; war in the ~ guerra f aérea; on the ~ en la radio; be on the ~ hablar por radio; emitir; clear the ~ airear la atmósfera; take the ~ tomar el fresco; walk on ~ estar bañado en agua de rosas; **2.** airear, orear, ventilar (a. fig.).

air[2] [~] aire m, aspecto m; ademán m; porte m; give o.s. ~s darse tono, envanecerse; with an ~ con aplomo; con garbo; ~s and graces refinamiento m afectado.

air[3] [~] ♪ aire m, tonada f.

air...: '~-base base f aérea; '~-bladder vejiga f natatoria; '~·borne ✈ en el aire, despegado; ✈ aerotransportado; germs etc. transmitido por el aire; '~-brake freno

m neumático; '~-cham·ber cámara f de aire; '~-con·di·tioned con aire acondicionado, refrigerado; '~-con·di·tion·er acondicionador m de aire; '~-cooled enfriado por aire; '~-craft avión m; ~ carrier porta(a)viones m; '~-cush·ion cojín m de aire, almohada f neumática; '~-ex·haust·er aspirador m; '~-field campo m de aviación; '~-force aviación f, fuerzas f/pl. aéreas; '~-gun escopeta f de aire comprimido; ~ host·ess azafata f, aeromoza f S.Am.

air·i·ness [ˈɛərinis] buena ventilación f; airosidad f; fig. ligereza f; alegría f.

air·ing [ˈɛəriŋ] ventilación f; oreo m; paseo m (para tomar el aire); take an ~ orearse, dar una vuelta.

air...: '~-jack·et chaqueta f salvavidas; ⊕ camisa f de aire; '~-less sin aire; sin viento; '~-lift puente m aéreo; '~-line línea f aérea; Am. línea f recta; '~-lin·er avión m de pasajeros, transaéreo m; '~-mail correo m aéreo; '~-man aviador m; '~-me'chan·ic mecánico m de aviación; '~-mind·ed interesado en aeronáutica; '2 Min·is·try Ministerio m del Aire; '~-pas·sen·ger pasajero m de avión; '~-pho·to (·graph) aerofoto f; '~-pi·lot piloto m; '~-plane Am. avión m; '~-pock·et bache m aéreo; '~-port aeropuerto m; '~-pres·sure presión f atmosférica; '~-pump bomba f de aire; '~-raid ataque m aéreo; ~ shelter refugio m antiaéreo; '~-screw hélice f de avión; '~-ship aeronave f; '~-sick mareado (en el aire); '~-speed velocidad f relativa al aire; ~ indicator velocímetro m aéreo; '~-tight hermético; '~-wom·an aviadora f; '~-wor·thy en condiciones de vuelo.

air·y [ˈɛəri] □ airoso; esp. room bien ventilado, ancho; fig. etéreo, ligero; (rude) impertinente; airily con desenvoltura; muy a la ligera.

aisle [ail] nave f lateral; thea. etc. pasillo m.

aitch [eitʃ] nombre de la h inglesa.

aitch·bone [ˈeitʃboun] rabad(ill)a f.

a·jar [əˈdʒɑː] entreabierto, entornado; fig. en desacuerdo.

a·kim·bo [əˈkimbou]: with arms ~ en jarras.

a·kin [ə'kin] consanguíneo (to de emparentado (to con); *fig.* análogo, semejante (to a).

al·a·bas·ter ['æləbɑ:stə] **1.** alabastro *m*; **2.** alabastrino.

a·lack [ə'læk] † *a.* ~-*a-day!* ¡ay!, ¡guay!

a·lac·ri·ty [ə'lækriti] alacridad *f*.

a·larm [ə'lɑ:m] **1.** alarma *f*; sobresalto *m*; ~ *and despondency* confusionismo *m* y desconcierto; *give the* ~, *raise an* ~, *sound the* ~ dar la alarma, tocar a rebato; **2.** alarmar, inquietar, asustar; **a'larm-bell** (campana *f* de) rebato *m*, timbre *m* de alarma; a'**larm-clock** (reloj *m*) despertador *m*; **a'larm-cord** 🔔 freno *m* de alarma; **a'larm·ist** **1.** alarmista *m/f*; **2.** alarmante.

a·lar·um [ə'leərəm] *mst* † *for alarm*; ⊕ timbre *m* del despertador.

a·las [ə'lɑ:s] ¡ay!

alb [ælb] *eccl.* alba *f*.

Al·ba·ni·an [æl'beinjən] albanés *adj. a. su. m* (-a *f*).

al·ba·tross ['ælbətrɔs] albatros *m*.

al·be·it [ɔ:l'bi:it] aunque, bien que.

al·bi·no [æl'bi:nou] albino (a *f*) *m*.

al·bum ['ælbəm] álbum *m*.

al·bu·men, al·bu·min ['ælbjumin] 🔬 albúmina *f*; 🔬 albumen *m*; **al'bu·mi·nous** albuminoso.

al·chem·ic, al·chem·i·cal [æl-'kemik(l)] □ alquímico; **al·che·mist** ['ælkimist] alquimista *m*; **'al·che·my** alquimia *f*.

al·co·hol ['ælkəhɔl] alcohol *m*; **al·co·hol·ic** alcohólico *adj. a. su. m* (a *f*), alcoholizado *adj. a. su. m* (a *f*); **'al·co·hol·ism** alcoholismo *m*; **'al·co·hol·ize** ['~laiz] alcoholizar.

al·cove ['ælkouv] nicho *m*, hueco *m*; gabinete *m of library*; cenador *m in garden*.

al·der ['ɔ:ldə] aliso *m*.

al·der·man ['ɔ:ldəmən] regidor *m*, concejal *m* (de cierta antigüedad); **al·der·man·ic** ['~mænik] de (un) concejal, edilicio; **al·der·man·ship** ['~mənʃip] regiduría *f*, concejalía *f*.

ale [eil] cerveza *f* (inglesa).

a·lee [ə'li:] a sotavento.

ale-house ['eilhaus] taberna *f*.

a·lem·bic [ə'lembik] alambique *m*.

a·lert [ə'lə:t] **1.** □ vigilante; vivo, listo; **2.** alerta *m*; *be on the* ~ estar alerta, estar sobre aviso; **a'lert·ness** vigilancia *f*; presteza *f*.

al·fal·fa [æl'fælfə] alfalfa *f*.

al·ga ['ælgə], *pl.* **al·gae** ['ældʒi:] alga *f*.

al·ge·bra ['ældʒibrə] álgebra *f*; **al·ge·bra·ic** [~'breiik] □ algebraico, algébrico.

a·li·as ['eiliæs] alias *adv. a. su. m*.

a·li·bi ['ælibai] coartada *f*; F excusa *f*, pretexto *m*.

al·ien ['eiliən] **1.** ajeno, extraño (to a); extranjero; **2.** extranjero (a *f*) *m*; **'al·ien·a·ble** enajenable, alienable; **al·ien·ate** ['~eit] enajenar, alienar; *be* ~*d from* enajenarse de; **al·ien·a·tion** enajenación *f*; alienación *f*; ~ *of mind* enajenación *f* mental; **'al·ien·ist** alienista *m/f*.

a·light¹ [ə'lait] ardiendo, encendido, iluminado.

a·light² [~] bajar, apearse; 🦋 aterrizar; ~ *on* posarse sobre; ~ *on one's feet* caer de pie.

a·lign [ə'lain] alinear; ~ *o.s. with* alinearse con; ponerse al lado de; **a'lign·ment** alineación *f*.

a·like [ə'laik] **1.** *adj.* semejante, parecido; *look* ~ parecerse; **2.** *adv.* igualmente, del mismo modo.

al·i·ment ['ælimənt] alimento *m*; **al·i·men·ta·ry** [~'mentəri] alimenticio; ~ *canal* tubo *m* digestivo; **al·i·men·ta·tion** alimentación *f*.

al·i·mo·ny ['æliməni] alimentos *m/pl.*

a·line(·ment) [ə'lain(mənt)] = *align (-ment)*.

al·i·quot ['ælikwɔt] (parte *f*) alícuota.

a·live [ə'laiv] vivo, viviente, con vida; *fig.* vivaz, activo; sensible (to a); *keep* ~ mantener(se) en vigor; F *look* ~ menearse; F *man* ~! ¡hombre!; *be* ~ *to* hacerse cargo de; apreciar; ~ *with* rebosante de, hormigueante de.

al·ka·li ['ælkəlai] álcali *m*; **al·ka·line** ['~lain] alcalino.

all [ɔ:l] **1.** *adj.* todo; ~ *day (long)* (durante) todo el día; ~ *kind(s) of books* toda clase de libros, libros de toda clase; *for* ~ *that* con todo, no obstante, así y todo; **2.** todo *m*; todos *m/pl.*, todas *f/pl.*; *my* ~ todo lo que tengo; ~ *of them* (ellos) todos; *at* ~ de cualquier manera; en lo más mínimo; siquiera un poco; *not at* ~ de ninguna manera;

no hay de qué; for ~ (that) I care igual me da; for ~ I know que yo sepa; quizá; **3.** *adv.* enteramente, del todo; *v. once*; ~ *the better* tanto mejor; ~ *but* casi, por poco; menos; *v. right, there.*

all-A·mer·i·can [ɔ:lǝ'merikǝn] que representa los EE.UU.; exclusivamente estadunidense.

al·lay [ǝ'lei] apaciguar, aquietar; *pain* aliviar, mitigar.

al·le·ga·tion [æle'geiʃn] aseveración *f*, alegación *f*, alegato *m*; **al·lege** [ǝ'ledʒ] declarar, sostener; *(as proof, excuse, etc.)* alegar; **al·leged** alegado; *(mst falsely)* supuesto, pretendido.

al·le·giance [ǝ'li:dʒns] fidelidad *f*, lealtad *f*; *(a. oath of ~)* homenaje *m*; *swear* ~ to rendir homenaje a.

al·le·gor·ic, **al·le·gor·i·cal** [æle-'gɔrik(l)] □ alegórico; **al·le·go·rize** [' æligǝraiz] alegorizar; **'al·le·go·ry** alegoría *f*.

al·le·lu·ia [æli'lu:jǝ] aleluya *f*.

al·ler·gy [ælǝdʒi] alergia *f*.

al·le·vi·ate [ǝ'li:vieit] aliviar; **al·le·vi·a·tion** alivio *m*.

al·ley [æli] callejuela *f*, callejón *m*; paseo *m in park*; **'al·ley·way** callejuela *f*, callejón *m*; pasadizo *m*.

al·li·ance [ǝ'laiǝns] alianza *f*; *form an* ~ formar una alianza.

al·li·ga·tor [' æligaitǝ] caimán *m*.

all-in [' ɔ:l'in] total, global; *charge* todo incluido; F rendido (de fatiga), agotado.

al·lit·er·ate [ǝ'litǝreit] usar aliteración; formar aliteración; **al·lit·er·'a·tion** aliteración *f*; **al'lit·er·a·tive** □ aliterado.

all-met·al [' ɔ:l'metl] enteramente metálico.

al·lo·cate [' ælǝkeit] asignar, señalar; repartir; **al·lo'ca·tion** asignación *f*; reparto *m*. [ción *f*.]

al·lo·cu·tion [ælou'kju:ʃn] alocu-]

al·lo·di·al [ǝ'loudiǝl] □ alodial.

al·lot [ǝ'lɔt] asignar, adjudicar; repartir; **al'lot·ment** asignación *f*; reparto *m*; lote *m*, porción *f*; parcela *f* (de tierra).

all-out [' ɔ:l'aut] **1.** *adj. supporter etc.* acérrimo; *effort etc.* total, máximo; **2.** *adv.* con todas las fuerzas; a máxima velocidad.

al·low [ǝ'lau] *(permit)* permitir, dejar *(to inf.)*; *(grant)* conceder, dar;

(admit) confesar; *discount* descontar; *he is ~ed to be* se reconoce que es; ~ *for* tomar en consideración, tener en cuenta; *it ~s of no excuse* no admite disculpa; **al'low·a·ble** □ permisible, admisible; **al'low·ance** *(grant)* concesión *f*; ración *f*, pensión *f*; *(discount)* descuento *m*, rebaja *f*; ⊕ tolerancia *f*; *make ~ for p.* disculpar; *th.* tener en cuenta.

al·loy [ǝ'lɔi] **1.** aleación *f*, liga *f*; *fig.* mezcla *f*; **2.** alear, ligar; *fig.* mezclar, adulterar.

all-round [' ɔ:l'raund] cabal; ✝ global; *player* competente en todos los aspectos del juego.

All Saints' Day ['ɔ:l'seintsdei] Día *m* de Todos los Santos *(1 noviembre).*

All Souls' Day [' ɔ:l'soulzdei] Día *m* de Difuntos *(2 noviembre).*

all-star [' ɔ:l'sta:] *sport, film, etc.:* compuesto de primeras figuras.

al·lude [ǝ'lu:d]: ~ *to* aludir a, hacer referencia a, mencionar.

al·lure [ǝ'ljuǝ] atraer, fascinar; **al'lure·ment** atractivo *m*, aliciente *m*; fascinación *f*; **al'lur·ing** □ atractivo, tentador.

al·lu·sion [ǝ'lu:ʒn] alusión *f*, referencia *f* (*to* a); **al'lu·sive** □ alusivo, referente (*to* a).

al·lu·vi·al [ǝ'lu:viǝl] □ aluvial; **al'lu·vi·on** [~ǝn], **al lu·vi·um** [~ǝm] aluvión *m*.

al·ly[1] **1.** [ǝ'lai] aliarse, unirse; *fig.* emparentarse (*to, with* con); *allied fig.* conexo, parecido; *allied to fig.* relacionado con; **2.** [' ælai] aliado *m*, confederado *m*; *The Allies* Los Aliados *m*|*pl.*

al·ly[2] [' æli] bolita *f*, canica *f*.

al·ma·nac [' ɔ:lmǝnæk] almanaque *m*.

al·might·i·ness [ɔ:l'maitinis] omnipotencia *f*; **al'might·y 1.** □ todopoderoso; F imponente, grandísimo; **2.** ♀ Todopoderoso *m*.

al·mond [' ɑ:mǝnd] almendra *f*; *(a. ~ tree)* almendro *m*.

al·mon·er [' ælmǝnǝ] limosnero *m*.

al·most [' ɔ:lmoust] casi.

alms [ɑ:mz] *sg. a. pl.* limosna *f*; **'~-house** hospicio *m*, asilo *m*.

al·oe [' ælou] áloe *m*, acíbar *m*.

a·loft [ǝ'lɔft] hacia arriba, en alto; ♼ en la arboladura.

a·lone [ǝ'loun] **1.** *adj.* solo; **2.** *adv.* solamente, sólo.

a·long [ə'lɔŋ] **1.** *adv.* a lo largo; adelante; *all* ~ desde el principio; ~ *with* junto con; **2.** *prp.* a lo largo de; por; al lado de; **a'long'side 1.** *adv.* ⚓ al costado, costado con costado; *bring* ~ costar; **2.** *prp. fig.* junto a, al lado de.

a·loof [ə'lu:f] reservado, huraño; *keep* ~ apartarse, alejarse (*from* de); *stand* ~ mantenerse apartado, mantenerse a distancia; **a'loof·ness** reserva *f*.

a·loud [ə'laud] en voz alta.

alp [ælp] *lit.* cumbre *f*; ⍰s *pl.* Alpes *m/pl.*; **al·pen·stock** ['ælpinstɔk] alpenstock *m*.

al·pha·bet ['ælfəbit] alfabeto *m*; **al·pha·bet·ic, al·pha·bet·i·cal** [~'be-tik(l)] ☐ alfabético.

Al·pine ['ælpain] alpino, alpestre; ⚜ ~ *sun* sol *m* de montaña; **'al·pin·ist** alpinista *m/f*.   [antes.⟩

al·read·y [ɔ:l'redi] ya; previamente,⟩

Al·sa·tian [æl'seiʃn] alsaciano *adj. a. su. m* (a *f*); ~ *dog* perro *m* lobo.

al·so ['ɔ:lsou] también, además; *racing:* ~ *ran* (caballo *m*) que no logró colocarse; F fracasado *m*.

al·tar ['ɔ:ltə] altar *m*; ara *f* (*lit.*); *high* ~ altar *m* mayor; '~**-piece** retablo *m*.

al·ter ['ɔ:ltə] cambiar(se), alterar, modificar; *Am.* F *animal* castrar; **'al·ter·a·ble** mudable; **al·ter'a·tion** alteración *f*, cambio *m* (*of, to* de); ⚕ ~s *pl.* reformas *f/pl.*

al·ter·cate ['ɔ:ltə:keit] altercar; **al·ter'ca·tion** altercado *m*.

al·ter·nate 1. ['ɔ:ltə:neit] alternar; *alternating current* corriente *f* alterna; **2.** [ɔ:l'tə:nit] ☐ alterno, alternativo; *on* ~ *days* cada dos días, un día sí y otro no; **3.** *Am.* suplente *m*, sustituto *m*; **al·ter·na·tion** [~'nei-ʃn] alternación *f*; **al'ter·na·tive** [~nətiv] **1.** ☐ alternativo; **2.** alternativa *f*; *I have no* ~ no puedo hacer otra cosa; no tengo elección; **al·ter·na·tor** ['~neitə] ⚡ alternador *m*.

al·though [ɔ:l'ðou] aunque; si bien.

al·tim·e·ter [æl'timitə] altímetro *m*.

al·ti·tude ['æltitju:d] altitud *f*; altura *f*, elevación *f*; *high* ~ *flight* vuelo *m* de altura.

al·to ['æltou] contralto *f*.

al·to·geth·er [ɔ:ltə'geðə] enteramente, del todo; en conjunto, en total.

al·tru·ism ['æltruizm] altruismo *m*; **'al·tru·ist** altruista *m/f*; **al·tru'is·tic** ☐ altruista, desinteresado.

al·um ['æləm] alumbre *m*; **a·lu·mi·na** [ə'lju:minə] alúmina *f*; **al·u·min(·i)·um** [ælju'minjəm, *Am.* ə'luminəm] aluminio *m*; **a·lu·mi·nous** [ə'lju:minəs] aluminoso.

a·lum·nus [ə'lʌmnəs] *m*, *pl.* **a·lum·ni** ['~nai]; **a·lum·na** ['~nə] *f*, *pl.* **a·lum·nae** ['~ni:] *mst Am.* graduado (a *f*) *m*.

al·ve·o·lar ['ælviələ] alveolar.

al·ways ['ɔ:lwəz] siempre; *as* ~ como (de) siempre.

am [æm; *in phrases freq.* əm] soy; estoy (*v. be*).

a·mal·gam [ə'mælgəm] amalgama *f*; **a'mal·gam·ate** [~meit] amalgamar(se); **a·mal·gam'a·tion** amalgamación *f*, unión *f* (*a.* ⚓).

a·man·u·en·sis [əmænju'ensis], *pl.* **a·manu'en·ses** [~si:z] secretario *m*, amanuense *m*.   [*m.*⟩

am·a·ranth ['æmərænθ] amaranto⟩

a·mass [ə'mæs] acumular, amontonar.

am·a·teur ['æmətə:] aficionado (a *f*) *m*; *b.s.* chapucero *m*, principiante *m/f*; **am·a'teur·ish** superficial, inexperto, chapucero.

am·a·tive ['æmətiv], **am·a·to·ry** ['~təri] amatorio, erótico.

a·maze [ə'meiz] asombrar, pasmar; **a'mazed** ☐ asombrado, pasmado (*at* de); *be* ~*d at* asombrarse de; **a'maze·ment** asombro *m*, aturdimiento *m*; pasmo *m*; **a'maz·ing** ☐ asombroso, pasmoso.

Am·a·zon ['æməzn] amazona *f*; *fig.* F marimacho *m*; **Am·a·zo·ni·an** [~'zounjən] amazónico.

am·bas·sa·dor [æm'bæsədə] embajador *m*; **am·bas·sa·do·ri·al** [~'dɔ:riəl] embajatorio; **am'bas·sa·dress** [~dris] embajadora *f*.

am·ber ['æmbə] **1.** ámbar *m*; **2.** ambarino, de ámbar; **am·ber·gris** ['~gri:s] ámbar *m* gris.

am·bi·dex·trous ['æmbi'dekstrəs] ☐ ambidextro.

am·bi·ent ['æmbiənt] ⚠ ambiente.

am·bi·gu·i·ty [æmbi'gjuiti] ambigüedad *f*, doble sentido *m*; **am'big·u·ous** ☐ ambiguo; equívoco, dudoso.

am·bi·tion [æm'biʃn] ambición *f* (*to, for* por), anhelo *m* (*to, for* de);

am·bi·tious ☐ ambicioso; *idea, plan* grandioso; *be ~ of (or for)* ambicionar.

am·ble ['æmbl] 1. (*horse etc.*) paso *m* de andadura; 2. amblar; *fig.* andar despacio; 'am·bler amblador *m*.

am·bro·si·a [æm'brouziə] ambrosía *f*; am·bro·si·al ☐ ambrosíaco; *fig.* celestial, delicioso.

am·bu·lance ['æmbjulɔns] (coche *m*) ambulancia *f*; *Am.* ~ box botiquín *m*; *Am.* F ~ chaser abogado *m* especializado en pleitos sobre accidentes; ~ man ambulanciero *m*; ~ station puesto *m* de socorro; 'am·bu·lant ambulante.

am·bu·la·to·ry ['æmbjulətəri] 1. ambulatorio, móvil; 2. paseo *m*; ⚠ galería *f*, deambulatorio *m*.

am·bus·cade [æmbəs'keid], am·bush ['æmbuʃ] 1. emboscada *f*; *lay (make) an ~* tender una celada *(for* a); *lie in ~* estar en acecho *(or* en celada); 2. acechar; tomar *(or* coger) por sorpresa.

a·mel·io·rate [ə'miːliəreit] mejorar(se); a·mel·io·ra·tion mejora *f*, mejoramiento *m*.

a·men ['ɑː'men] amén.

a·me·na·ble [ə'miːnəbl] sumiso, dócil; ☆ responsable; ~ *to argument* persuasible.

a·mend [ə'mend] enmendar (*a.* ☆ *a. parl.*); rectificar, reformar; a'mend·ment enmienda *f*; *Am.* enmienda *f* (de la Constitución de EE.UU.); a'mends [͜ dz] reparación *f*, recompensa *f*; *make ~ for* compensar, igualar; expiar.

a·men·i·ty [ə'miːniti] amenidad *f*; *amenities pl.* atractivos *m/pl.*, conveniencias *f/pl.*; comodidad *f*.

a·merce [ə'məːs] multar; a'merce·ment multa *f*.

A·mer·i·can [ə'merikən] 1. americano; ~ *cloth* hule *m*; ~ *leather* cuero *m* artificial; *Am.* ~ *Legion* organización *de* veteranos *de* las 2 *guerras mundiales*; 2. americano (a *f*) *m*; a'mer·i·can·ism americanismo *m*; a'mer·i·can·ize americanizar(se).

Am·er·in·di·an, Am·er·ind [æm-ə'rindjən, 'æmərind] amerindio *m*.

am·e·thyst ['æmiθist] amatista *f*.

a·mi·a·bil·i·ty [eimjə'biliti] afabilidad *f*, amabilidad *f*; 'a·mi·a·ble ☐ afable, amable; bonachón; simpático.

am·i·ca·ble ['æmikəbl] ☐ amigable, amistoso.

a·mid(st) [ə'mid(st)] entre, en medio de.

a·mid·ships [ə'midʃips] en medio del navío.

a·miss [ə'mis] mal, fuera de propósito; impropio; *take ~* llevar a mal; *it would not be ~ (for him)* no (le) estaría de más; *what is ~ with it?* ¿qué le pasa?

am·i·ty ['æmiti] concordia *f*, amistad *f*.

am·me·ter ['æmitə] amperímetro *m*.

am·mo·ni·a [ə'mounjə] amoníaco *m*; *liquid ~* amoníaco *m* líquido; am'mo·ni·ac [͜ æk], am·mo·ni·a·cal [æmou'naiəkl] amoníaco; *v. sal.*

am·mu·ni·tion [æmju'niʃn] 1. municiones *f/pl.*; *fig.* pertrechos *m/pl.*; 2. *attr.* de municiones.

am·nes·ty ['æmnesti] 1. amnistía *f*, indulto *m*; 2. indultar.

a·moe·ba [ə'miːbə] amiba *f*.

a·mong(st) [ə'mʌŋ(st)] entre, en medio de; *from ~* de entre.

a·mor·al [æ'mɔrəl] ☐ amoral.

am·o·rous ['æmərəs] ☐ amoroso; enamoradizo; *b.s.* mujeriego; 'am·o·rous·ness enamoramiento *m*.

a·mor·phous [ə'mɔːfəs] *min.* amorfo (*a. fig.*); *fig.* heterogéneo, abigarrado.

am·or·ti·za·tion [əmɔːti'zeiʃn] amortización *f*; am'or·tize [͜ taiz] amortizar.

a·mount [ə'maunt] 1.: ~ *to* valer, hacer, ascender a; *fig.* equivaler a, significar; 2. cantidad *f*, suma *f*, importe *m*; *to the ~ of* hasta la cantidad de.

a·mour [ə'muə] *mst iro.* amorío *m*; ~ *propre* amor *m* propio.

am·pere ['æmpɛə] amperio *m*.

am·phib·i·an [æm'fibiən] 1. anfibio *m*; 2. = am'phib·i·ous ☐ anfibio.

am·phi·the·a·tre ['æmfiθiətə] anfiteatro *m*.

am·ple ['æmpl] amplio; abundante; liberal; bastante; 'am·ple·ness amplitud *f*; abundancia *f*; suficiencia *f*.

am·pli·fi·ca·tion [æmplifi'keiʃn] amplificación *f* (*a. rhet. a. phys.*); am·pli·fi·er [' ͜ faiə] *radio*: amplificador *m*; 'am·pli·fy amplificar, ampliar; dilatar, extender; *radio*: ~*ing valve* lámpara *f* amplificadora;

am·pli·tude ['æ̩tjuːd] amplitud *f*; extensión *f*; *phys.* amplitud *f* (de oscilación).

am·poule ['æmpuːl] ampolla *f*.

am·pu·tate ['æmpjuteit] amputar; **am·pu'ta·tion** amputación *f*.

a·muck [ə'mʌk]: *run* ~ enloquecer, desbocarse (*a. fig.*), desmandarse.

am·u·let ['æmjulit] amuleto *m*.

a·muse [ə'mjuːz] divertir, entretener; distraer, solazar; **a'muse·ment** diversión *f*, entretenimiento *m*; pasatiempo *m*, recreo *m*; *for* ~ para divertirse; **a·mus·ing** □ divertido, entretenido; gracioso.

an [æn, ən] *article*: un, una.

an·a·bap·tist [ænə'bæptist] anabaptista *m/f*.

a·nach·ro·nism [ə'nækrənizm] anacronismo *m*.

a·n(a)e·mi·a [ə'niːmiə] anemia *f*; **a'n(a)e·mic** anémico.

an·(a)es·the·si·a [ænis'θiːziə] anestesia *f*; **an·(a)es·thet·ic** [ænis'θetik] □ anestésico *adj. a. su. m*; **an·(a)es·thet·ize** [ə'niːsθətaiz] anestesiar.

an·al·ge·si·a [ænəl'dʒiːziə] analgesia *f*.

an·a·log·ic, an·a·log·i·cal [ænə-'lɔdʒik(l)] □, **a·nal·o·gous** [ə'næləgəs] análogo; afín; **a'nal·o·gy** analogía *f*; afinidad *f*; *on the* ~ *of* por analogía con.

an·a·lyse ['ænəlaiz] analizar; **a·nal·y·sis** [ə'næləsis], *pl.* **a'nal·y·ses** [‿iːz] análisis *mst m*; **ana·lyst** ['ænəlist] analizador *m*; *public* ~ jefe *m* del laboratorio municipal; **an·a·lyt·ic, an·a·lyt·i·cal** [ænə'litik(l)] □ analítico.

an·ar·chic, an·ar·chi·cal [æ'nɑː-kik(l)] □ anárquico; **an·arch·ism** ['ænəkizm] anarquismo *m*; **an·arch·ist** anarquista *m/f*; **'an·arch·y** anarquía *f*; desorden *m*.

a·nath·e·ma [ə'næθimə] anatema *m*; **a'nath·e·ma·tize** anatematizar.

an·a·tom·i·cal [ænə'tɔmikl] □ anatómico; **a·nat·o·mist** [ə'nætəmist] anatomista *m/f*; **a'nat·o·mize** [‿aiz] anatomizar; *fig.* analizar minuciosamente; **a'nat·o·my** anatomía *f* (*a. fig.*).

an·ces·tor ['ænsistə] antepasado *m*, progenitor *m*; **an·ces·tral** [‿'ses-trəl] ancestral, hereditario; **an·ces·tress** ['ænsistris] antepasada *f*; **'an·**

ces·try ascendencia *f*, linaje *m*, abolengo *m*.

an·chor ['æŋkə] **1.** ⚓ *a. fig.* ancla *f*; *at* ~ al ancla, anclado; *cast (or drop)* ~ echar anclas; *weigh* ~ zarpar; **2.** *v/t.* anclar; sujetar; *v/i.* anclar, fondear; **'an·chor·age** ancladero *m*, fondeadero *m*.

an·cho·ret, an·cho·rite ['æŋkəret; '‿rait] anacoreta *m/f*.

an·cho·vy ['æntʃəvi] anchoa *f*.

an·cient ['einʃənt] **1.** □ antiguo; vetusto; **2.** *the* ~*s pl.* los antiguos *m/pl*.

an·cil·lar·y [æn'siləri] auxiliar; subordinado (*to* a).

and [ænd, ənd, F ən] y; (*before* i-, hi-) e; *thousands* ~ *thousands* miles y miles, millares; *try* ~ *inf.* tratar de *inf.*; *try* ~ *take it* cógelo si puedes; *after verbs of motion*: a (*e.g., go* ~ *see him* ir a verle).

An·dal·u·si·an [ændəl'uːziən] andaluz *adj. a. su. m.* (-a *f*).

an·ec·do·tal [ænek'doutl], **an·ec·dot·i·cal** [‿'dɔtikl] □ anecdótico; **an·ec·dote** ['ænikdout] anécdota *f*.

an·e·lec·tric [æni'lektrik] aneléctrico.

an·e·mom·e·ter [æni'mɔmitə] anemómetro *m*.

a·nem·o·ne [ə'neməni] ♀ anemone *f*; *zo.* anémona *f* (de mar).

an·er·oid ['ænərɔid] aneroide.

a·new [ə'njuː] de nuevo, otra vez.

an·gel ['eindʒl] ángel *m*; **an·gel·ic, an·gel·i·cal** [æn'dʒelik(l)] □ angélico.

an·ger ['æŋgə] **1.** cólera *f*, ira *f*, saña *f*; **2.** enojar, encolerizar, provocar.

an·gi·na [æn'dʒainə] angina *f*; ~ *pectoris* angina *f* de pecho.

an·gle ['æŋgl] **1.** ángulo *m*; *fig.* punto *m* de vista; **2.** pescar con caña (*for acc.*); ~ *for* F ir a la caza de; **'an·gler** pescador (-a *f*) *m* con caña.

An·gles ['æŋglz] *pl.* anglos *m/pl*.

An·gli·can ['æŋglikən] anglicano *adj. a. su. m* (a *f*); *Am. a.* inglés.

An·gli·cism ['æŋglisizm] anglicismo *m*.

an·gling ['æŋgliŋ] pesca *f* con caña.

An·glo-Sax·on ['æŋglou'sæksn] anglosajón *adj. a. su. m* (-a *f*).

an·gry ['æŋgri] □ colérico; enojado, enfadado; ⚕ inflamado; *get* ~ encolerizarse, montar en cólera (*with* *p.* con); *it makes me ~ me* enoja mucho.

an·guish ['æŋgwiʃ] angustia *f*, congoja *f*.

an·gu·lar ['æŋgjulə] ☐ angular; *fig.* torpe; *~ point* vértice *m*; **an·gu·lar·ity** [~'læriti] calidad *f* de lo angular; *fig.* torpeza *f*.

an·hy·drous [æn'haidrəs] anhidro.

an·i·line ['ænilain] anilina *f*.

an·i·mad·ver·sion [ænimæd'və:ʃn] censura *f*, animadversión *f*; **an·i·mad·vert** [~'və:t] censurar, reprochar ([up]on *acc.*); observar.

an·i·mal ['ænimǝl] 1. animal *m*; bestia *f*; 2. animal; *~ spirits pl.* vitalidad *f*; **an·i·mal·cule** [~'mælkju:l] animálculo *m*; **an·i·mal·ism** ['~mǝlizm] sensualidad *f*; **an·i·mal·i·ty** animalidad *f*.

an·i·mate 1. ['ænimeit] animar, alentar; 2. ['~mit] vivo; **'an·i·mat·ed** ☐ *fig.* vivo, vivaz, animado; **an·i·ma·tion** [æni'meiʃn] vivacidad *f*, animación *f*.

an·i·mos·i·ty [æni'mɔsiti], **an·i·mus** ['ænimǝs] animosidad *f*, rencor *m*, ojeriza *f*.

an·ise ['ænis] anís *m*; **an·i·seed** ['~si:d] 1. anís *m*; 2. *attr.* de anís.

an·kle ['æŋkl] tobillo *m*; *~ sock* escarpín *m*.

an·klet ['æŋklit] ajorca *f* para el pie.

an·nals ['ænlz] *pl.* anales *m/pl.*; *fig. a. lit.* fastos *m/pl.*

an·neal [ǝ'ni:l] reccer; templar (*a. fig.*).

an·nex 1. [ǝ'neks] añadir, adjuntar (to a); *esp. territory* anexar, apoderarse de; 2. ['æneks] apéndice *m*, aditamento *m*; **an·nex·a·tion** anexión *f*; **an·nexe** ['æneks] edificio *m* anexo, pabellón *m*.

an·ni·hi·late [ǝ'naiǝleit] aniquilar; **an·ni·hi·la·tion** aniquilamiento *m*.

an·ni·ver·sa·ry [æni'vǝ:sǝri] aniversario *m*.

an·no·tate ['ænouteit] anotar; comentar, glosar; **an·no·ta·tion** anotación *f*; comentario *m* (on, to sobre).

an·nounce [ǝ'nauns] anunciar, proclamar; **an'nounce·ment** anuncio *m*, aviso *m*, proclama *f*; **an'nounc·er** *radio:* locutor (-a *f*) *m*.

an·noy [ǝ'nɔi] molestar, fastidiar, jorobar (F); **an'noy·ance** molestia *f*, fastidio *m*; enojo *m*; **an'noyed**

enfadado, irritado, enojado; **an'noy·ing** ☐ molesto, fastidioso; *p.* importuno.

an·nu·al ['ænjuǝl] 1. ☐ anual; ♀ *~ ring* cerco *m*; 2. anuario *m*; ♀ planta *f* anual, anual *m*.

an·nu·i·tant [ǝ'njuitǝnt] rentista *m/f*, censualista *m/f*; **an'nu·i·ty** [~iti] renta *f* vitalicia (*a. ~ bond*), pensión *f* vitalicia.

an·nul [ǝ'nʌl] anular, cancelar; *laws* abrogar.

an·nu·lar ['ænjulǝ] ☐ anular.

an·nul·ment [ǝ'nʌlmǝnt] anulación *f*, cancelación *f*; abrogación *f*.

An·nun·ci·a·tion [ǝnʌnsi'eiʃn] Anunciación *f*.

an·ode ['ænoud] 1. ánodo *m*; 2. *attr.* de ánodo; *~ potential* potencial *m* anódico.

an·o·dyne ['ænoudain] anodino *adj. a. su. m.*

a·noint [ǝ'nɔint] *mst eccl.* untar, ungir; consagrar.

a·nom·a·lous [ǝ'nɔmǝlǝs] ☐ anómalo; **a'nom·a·ly** anomalía *f*.

a·non [ǝ'nɔn] 1. † luego, dentro de poco; *poet. ever and ~* de vez en cuando; 2. *abbr.* = anonymous.

an·o·nym·i·ty [ænǝ'nimiti] anónimo *m*; **a·non·y·mous** [ǝ'nɔnimǝs] ☐ anónimo.

an·oth·er [ǝ'nʌðǝ] otro; *just such ~* otro tal.

an·swer ['ɑ:nsǝ] 1. *v/t. p., question* contestar a, responder a, replicar a; *~ a letter* contestar (a) una carta; *~ the bell or the door* acudir a la puerta; *v/i.* responder, contestar, replicar; (*suffice*) servir, convenir; F *~ back* ser respondón; *~ for* responder de; *~ to description* corresponder a; *~ to the name of* atender por; 2. respuesta *f*, contestación *f* (to a); ⚕ solución *f*; ♫♫ réplica *f*; **'an·swer·a·ble** ☐ responsable (for de).

ant [ænt] hormiga *f*.

an't [ɑ:nt] F = are not, am not; *prov.* = is not.

an·tag·o·nism [æn'tægǝnizm] antagonismo *m*, rivalidad *f* (between entre); hostilidad *f* (to a); **an'tag·o·nist** antagonista *m/f*, adversario *m*; **an·tag·o·nis·tic** ☐ antagónico; contrario, opuesto (to a).

an·tag·o·nize [æn'tægǝnaiz] enemistarse con, contrariar.

ant·arc·tic [ænt'ɑːktik] antártico; ♀ *Circle* Círculo *m* Polar Antártico.

an·te ['ænti] *Am. poker:* 1. tanto *m*, apuesta *f*; 2. F (*mst ~ up*) *v/t. a. v/i.* poner un tanto, apostar; *v/i. fig.* contribuir.

an·te·ced·ence [ænti'siːdəns] precedencia *f*; *ast.* retrogradación *f*; **an·te'ced·ent** 1. □ precedente, antecedente (to a); 2. antecedente *m* (*a. gr.*); *his ~s pl.* sus antecedentes *m*/*pl.*

an·te·cham·ber ['æntitʃeimbə] antecámara *f*. [preceder.｜

an·te·date ['ænti'deit] antedatar;｜

an·te·di·lu·vi·an ['æntidi'luːviən] antediluviano.

an·te·lope ['æntiloup] antílope *m*.

an·ten·na [æn'tenə], *pl.* **an'ten·nae** [~niː] *all senses:* antena *f*.

an·te·ri·or [æn'tiəriə] anterior (to a).

an·te·room ['æntirum] antecámara *f*.

an·them ['ænθəm] motete *m*; *national ~* himno *m* nacional.

an·ther ['ænθə] antera *f*.

ant·hill ['ænthil] hormiguero *m*.

an·thol·o·gy [æn'θɔlədʒi] antología *f*.

an·thra·cite ['ænθrəsait] antracita *f*.

an·thrax ['ænθræks] ántrax *m*.

an·thro·poid ['ænθrəpɔid] antropoide; **an·thro·pol·o·gist** [~'pɔlədʒist] antropólogo *m*; **an·thro'pol·o·gy** antropología *f*; **an·thro·poph·a·gy** [ænθrou'pɔfədʒi] antropofagia *f*.

an·ti... ['ænti-] *in compounds* anti...

an·ti-air·craft ['ænti'ɛəkrɑːft]: *~ defence* defensa *f* antiaérea; *~ gun* cañón *m* antiaéreo.

an·ti·bi·ot·ic ['æntibai'ɔtik] antibiótico *m*.

an·tics ['æntiks] *pl.* bufonadas *f*/*pl.*, payasadas *f*/*pl.*; travesuras *f*/*pl.*

An·ti·christ ['æntikraist] Anticristo *m*.

an·tic·i·pate [æn'tisipeit] (*forestall*) anticipar, prevenir; (*foresee*) prever; (*expect*) esperar; (*look forward to*) prometerse; **an·tic·i'pa·tion** anticipación *f*, prevención *f*; previsión *f*; expectación *f*; esperanza *f*; *in ~* de antemano; *in ~ of* esperando; **an'tic·i·pa·to·ry** [~peitəri] que anticipa.

an·ti·cler·i·cal ['ænti'klerikl] anticlerical.

an·ti·cli·max ['ænti'klaimæks] *rhet.* anticlímax *m*; *fig.* decepción *f*.

an·ti·cor·ro·sive ['æntikə'rousiv] anticorrosivo.

an·ti·cy·clone ['ænti'saikloun] anticiclón *m*.

an·ti·daz·zle ['ænti'dæzl] *mot.* antideslumbrante.

an·ti·dote ['æntidout] antídoto *m* (*against, for, to* contra).

an·ti·fas·cist ['ænti'fæʃist, ~sist] antifascista *adj. a. su. m*/*f*.

an·ti·freeze ['ænti'friːz] *mot.* (solución *f*) anticongelante.

an·ti·fric·tion ['ænti'frikʃn] ⊕ antifriccional.

an·ti·ha·lo ['ænti'heilou] *phot.* antihalo *m*.

an·ti·knock ['ænti'nɔk] *mot.* antidetonante.

an·ti·mo·ny ['æntiməni] antimonio *m*.

an·tip·a·thy [æn'tipəθi] antipatía *f* (*between* entre); repugnancia *f* (*to* hacia).

an·tip·o·dal [æn'tipədl] □ antípoda; **an'tip·o·des** [~diːz] *pl.* antípodas *f*/*pl.*; **an·ti·pode** ['~poud] *fig. sg.* antípoda *m*.

An·ti·py·rin(e) [ænti'paiərin] antipirina *f*.

an·ti·quar·i·an [ænti'kwɛəriən] anticuario *adj. a. su. m*; **an·ti·quar·y** ['~kwəri] anticuario *m*, aficionado *m* de antigüedades; **an·ti·quat·ed** ['~kweitid] anticuado.

an·tique [æn'tiːk] 1. antíguo, viejo; 2. antigüedad *f*, antigualla *f*; **an·tiq·ui·ty** [~'tikwiti] antigüedad *f*; vetustez *f*.

an·ti·rust ['ænti'rʌst] antioxidante.

an·ti·sem·ite [ænti'siːmait] antisemita *m*/*f*; **an·ti·sem·it·ic** [~səm'itik] antisemítico; **an·ti·sem·i·tism** [~'semitizm] antisemitismo *m*.

an·ti·sep·tic [ænti'septik] antiséptico *adj. a. su. m*.

an·ti·skid ['ænti'skid] *mot.* antideslizante, antiderrapante.

an·tith·e·sis [æn'tiθisis], *pl.* **an·tith·e·ses** ['~siːz] antítesis *f*; **an·ti·thet·ic, an·ti·thet·i·cal** [~'θetik(l)] □ antitético.

ant·ler ['æntlə] cuerna *f*; *~s pl.* cornamenta *f*, cuernas *f*/*pl.*

an·to·nym ['æntənim] antónimo *m*.

a·nus ['einəs] ano *m*.

an·vil ['ænvil] yunque *m* (*a. fig.*).

anx·i·e·ty [æŋ'zaiəti] cuidado *m*; inquietud *f*, ansiedad *f* (*about* sobre); (*yearning*) ansia *f*, anhelo *m* (*for, to* de); ☜ ansiedad *f*.

anx·ious ['æŋkʃəs] □ inquieto, preocupado, ansioso; (*desirous*) deseoso (*for, to* de); *be* ~ *about* inquietarse por.

an·y ['eni] **1.** *pron.* alguno; cualquiera; (*negative sense*) ninguno; **2.** *adj.* algún; cualquier; (*negative sense*) ningún; *are there* ~ *nails?* ¿hay clavos?; ~ *book you like* cualquier libro; **3.** *adv. mst not translated:* ~ *more* más; '~**bod·y**, '~**one** alguien, alguno; *not* ~ nadie; '~**how** en todo caso, de todos modos; con todo; de cualquier modo; '~**thing** algo, cualquier cosa; ~ *but* (*that*) todo menos (eso); *not* ~ nada; '~**way** = *anyhow*; '~**where** en todas partes, en cualquier parte, dondequiera.

a·pace [ə'peis] aprisa.

a·part [ə'pɑːt] aparte, separadamente; aislado, separado; ~ *from* aparte de; *joking* ~ en serio; **a·part·heid** [ə'pɑːtait] separación *f* racial; **a'part·ment** habitación *f*, aposento *m*; *Am.* piso *m*; *Am.* ~ *hotel* hotel *m* de familias; *Am.* ~ *house* casa *f* de pisos; ~*s pl.* alojamiento *m*, casa *f*.

ap·a·thet·ic [æpə'θetik] □ apático; indiferente; '**ap·a·thy** apatía *f*; indiferencia *f* (*to* a).

ape [eip] **1.** mono *m* (*esp.* los antropomorfos); *fig.* mono (a *f*) *m* de imitación; remedador (-a *f*) *m*; **2.** imitar, remedar.

a·pe·ri·ent [ə'piəriənt] laxante *adj. a. su. m*; **a·pe·ri·tif** [ə'peritiv] aperitivo *m*.

ap·er·ture ['æpətjuə] abertura *f*; rendija *f*.

a·pex ['eipeks], *pl. freq.* **ap·i·ces** ['eipisiːz] ápice *m*; *fig.* cumbre *f*.

aph·o·rism ['æfərizm] aforismo *m*, apotegma *m*; **aph·o'ris·tic** □ aforístico.

aph·ro·dis·i·ac [æfrou'diziæk] afrodisíaco *adj. a. su. m*.

a·pi·a·ry ['eipiəri] colmenar *m*; **a·pi·cul·ture** ['ˌeipikʌltʃə] apicultura *f*.

a·piece [ə'piːs] cada uno; por persona.

ap·ish ['eipiʃ] simiesco; *fig.* necio, tonto.

A·poc·ry·pha [ə'pɔkrifə] *pl.* libros *m/pl.* apócrifos de la Biblia; **a'poc·ry·phal** apócrifo.

ap·o·gee ['æpoudʒiː] apogeo *m*.

a·pol·o·get·ic [əpɔlə'dʒetik] **1.** □ lleno de disculpas; **2.** *mst* ~*s pl. eccl.* apologética *f*; **a'pol·o·gist** apologista *m/f*; **a'pol·o·gize** [ˌ~dʒais] disculparse (*for* de; *to* con); pedir perdón; **a'pol·o·gy** disculpa *f*, excusa *f*; *lit.* apología *f*, defensa *f*; *an* ~ *for a house* una birria de casa; *make an* ~ disculparse.

ap·o·plec·tic, ap·o·plec·ti·cal [æpə'plektik(l)] □ apoplético; '**ap·o·plex·y** apoplejía *f*.

a·pos·ta·sy [ə'pɔstəsi] apostasía *f*; **a'pos·tate** [ˌ~stit] apóstata *m/f*; **a'pos·ta·tize** [ˌ~stətaiz] apostatar (*from* de).

a·pos·tle [ə'pɔsl] apóstol *m*; **ap·os·tol·ic, ap·os·tol·i·cal** [æpə'stɔlik(l)] □ apostólico.

a·pos·tro·phe [ə'pɔstrəfi] *gr.* apóstrofo *m*; *rhet.* apóstrofe *m or f*; **a'pos·tro·phize** apostrofar.

a·poth·e·car·y [ə'pɔθikəri] † boticario (a *f*) *m*.

a·poth·e·o·sis [əpɔθi'ousis] apoteosis *f* (*a. fig.*).

ap·pal [ə'pɔːl] espantar; infundir pasmo (*or* horror); **ap'pall·ing** □ espantoso; *taste etc.* pésimo.

ap·pa·ra·tus [æpə'reitəs] aparato *m*.

ap·par·el [ə'pærəl] *lit.* **1.** ataviar, vestir (*esp. p.p.*); **2.** atavío *m*, vestido *m*; (*a. wearing* ~) ropa *f*.

ap·par·ent [ə'pærənt] □ aparente; claro, manifiesto; *v. heir*; ~*ly* según parece, por lo visto; aparentemente; **ap·pa·ri·tion** [æpə'riʃn] aparición *f*; fantasma *m*.

ap·peal [ə'piːl] **1.** ⚖ apelar (*to* a; *against* de); suplicar (*to a p. for a th.* a una p. por algo); ~ *to* llamar la atención de *s.o.*; atraer, interesar *acc.*; recurrir a; *v. country*; **2.** ⚖ apelación *f*, recurso *m* de casación; súplica *f*, instancia *f*; llamamiento *m* (*to* a); atractivo *m*; *Court of* ⚖ Tribunal *m* de Apelación; *judge of* ~ juez *m* de alzadas; **ap'peal·ing** □ suplicante; atrayente.

ap·pear [ə'piə] parecer; aparecer (*mst suddenly*); *esp.* ⚖ comparecer; **ap'pear·ance** apariencia *f*, aspecto *m*; (*act*) aparición *f*; ⚖ comparecencia *f*; ~*s pl.* apariencias *f/pl.*; *keep up* (*or save*) ⁓s salvar las apariencias; *thea. make an* ⁓ salir; *put in an* ⁓ hacer acto de presencia; *to all* ⁓s aparentemente.

ap·pease [ə'piːz] apaciguar; *p.* desenojar; *hunger etc.* satisfacer, saciar; *passion* mitigar, aquietar; **ap-'pease·ment** pacificación *f.*

ap·pel·lant [ə'pelənt] apelante *adj. a. su. m/f;* **ap·pel·la·tion** [æpe-'leiʃn] nombre *m,* título *m.*

ap·pel·lee [æpe'liː] apelado (a *f*) *m.*

ap·pend [ə'pend] añadir; adjuntar; colgar; **ap'pend·age** añadidura *f;* accesorio *m,* apéndice *m;* **ap·pen-dec·to·my** [⁓'dektəmi] apendectomía *f;* **ap·pen·di·ci·tis** [⁓'saitis] apendicitis *f;* **ap'pen·dix** [⁓diks], *pl. a.* **ap'pen·di·ces** [⁓disiːz] apéndice *m* (*a.* ⁓).

ap·per·tain [æpə'tein]: ⁓ *to* pertenecer a; atañer a; relacionarse con; incumbir a.

ap·pe·tite ['æpitait] apetito *m,* apetencia *f* (*a. fig.*); *fig.* deseo *m,* anhelo *m* (*for* de); *eccl.* apetito *m* concupiscible.

ap·pe·tiz·er ['æpitaizə] apetite *m* (*a. fig.*); aperitivo *m;* **'ap·pe·tiz·ing** ☐ apetitoso.

ap·plaud [ə'plɔːd] *v/t.* aplaudir (*a. fig.*); *fig.* celebrar; *v/i.* aplaudir, dar palmadas.

ap·plause [ə'plɔːz] aplauso *m* (*a. fig.*); *fig.* aprobación *f,* elogio *m.*

ap·ple ['æpl] manzana *f;* (*a.* ⁓ *tree*) manzano *m; Adam's* ⁓ nuez *f* de la garganta; ⁓ *of discord* manzana *f* de la discordia; ⁓ *of one's eye* niñas *f/pl.* de los ojos; '⁓-**cart**: F *upset a p.'s* ⁓ dar al traste con los planes de una p.; '⁓-**jack** *Am.* aguardiente *m* de manzana; '⁓-**pie** pastel *m* (*or* empanada *f*) de manzanas; F *in* ⁓ *order* en perfecto orden; '⁓-**sauce** compota *f* de manzanas; *Am. sl.* coba *f,* jabón *m.*

ap·pli·ance [ə'plaiəns] instrumento *m,* herramienta *f;* dispositivo *m.*

ap·pli·ca·bil·i·ty [æplikə'biliti] aplicabilidad *f;* **'ap·pli·ca·ble** aplicable (*to* a); **'ap·pli·cant** suplicante *m/f;* aspirante *m/f,* pretendiente (a *f*) *m* (*for a post* a un puesto); **ap·pli·ca·tion** aplicación *f* (*to* a; *a.* = *industry*); solicitud *f* (*for* por), petición *f* (*for* de, por); *make an* ⁓ solicitar; dirigirse (*to* a).

ap·pli·qué [ə'pliːkei] (*a.* ⁓ *work*) encaje *m* de aplicación.

ap·ply [ə'plai] *v/t.* aplicar (*to* a); ⁓ *o.s. to* aplicarse a; *v/i.* ser aplicable; interesar; *cross out what does not* ⁓ táchese lo que no interese; ⁓ *to* referirse a; acudir a, dirigirse a; ⁓ *for* solicitar, pedir *acc.; applied mathematics* matemáticas *f/pl.* aplicadas.

ap·point [ə'pɔint] *date etc.* señalar, designar; *p.* nombrar; *house* amueblar; proveer; *well* ⁓*ed* bien amueblado; bien provisto (de muebles *etc.*); **ap'point·ment** señalamiento *m,* designación *f;* nombramiento *m to post;* (*post*) oficio *m;* cita *f with p.; make an* ⁓ citar(se); *by* ⁓ (*with royal arms etc.*) proveedores de; ⁓s *pl.* moblaje *m;* equipo *m.*

ap·por·tion [ə'pɔːʃn] prorratear; **ap'por·tion·ment** prorrateo *m.*

ap·po·site ['æpəzit] ☐ apropiado (*to* a); a propósito, oportuno; **'ap·po·site·ness** propiedad *f;* acierto *m;* oportunidad *f.*

ap·po·si·tion [æpə'ziʃn] juxtaposición *f; gr.* aposición *f;* (*seal*) impresión *f.*

ap·prais·al [ə'preizl] tasación *f,* valoración *f; fig.* aprecio *m;* **ap-'praise** [⁓eiz] tasar, valorar; *fig.* apreciar; **ap'praise·ment** = *appraisal;* **ap'prais·er** tasador *m.*

ap·pre·ci·a·ble [ə'priːʃəbl] ☐ apreciable, estimable; sensible, perceptible; **ap'pre·ci·ate** [⁓ʃieit] *v/t.* apreciar, estimar; percibir; *v/i.* aumentarse en valor; **ap·pre·ci-'a·tion** aprecio *m,* estimación *f;* percepción *f;* (*value*) aumento *m* en valor; **ap'pre·ci·a·tive** ☐, **ap-'pre·ci·a·to·ry** apreciativo; apreciador; agradecido; *be* ⁓ *of* agradecer *acc.*

ap·pre·hend [æpri'hend] aprehender, prender; *fig.* percibir, entender; temer, sospechar; **ap·pre'hen·sion** aprehensión *f,* prendimiento *m;* percepción *f,* comprensión *f;* temor *m,* recelo *m,* aprensión *f;* **ap·pre'hen·sive** ☐ aprensivo, miedoso (*of* de; *that* de que); tímido; perspicaz, comprensivo; *grow* ⁓ intimidarse.

ap·pren·tice [ə'prentis] **1.** aprendiz (-a *f*) *m; fig.* novicio (a *f*) *m;* **2.** poner de aprendiz; *be* ⁓*d to* estar de aprendiz con; **ap'prentice·ship** aprendizaje *m*, noviciado *m*.

ap·prise [ə'praiz] informar, avisar (of de).

ap·pro ['æprou] ✝ F: on ~ a prueba.

ap·proach [ə'proutʃ] **1.** *v/i.* acercarse, aproximarse (*a. fig.*; *freq.* to a); *v/t.* acercarse a, aproximarse a (*a. fig.*); *p.* abordar; *firm etc.* dirigirse a; **2.** acercamiento *m*; aproximación *f* (to a); acceso *m* (*a. fig.*); método *m*, camino *m*; camino *m* de entrada; ~es *pl.* ✗ aproches *m/pl.*; accesos *m/pl.*; **ap·'proach·able** abordable, accesible; **ap'proach·ing** próximo, cercano; que se acerca.

ap·pro·ba·tion [æprə'beiʃn] aprobación *f*; consentimiento *m*.

ap·pro·pri·ate 1. [ə'prouprieit] apropiar(se); *funds etc.* destinar (for a); **2.** [~priit] □ apropiado (to a), a propósito; apto, pertinente; **ap·pro·pri·a·tion** apropiación *f*; consignación *f*.

ap·prov·al [ə'pru:vəl] aprobación *f*; consentimiento *m*; visto *m* bueno; on ~ a prueba; **ap'prove** aprobar, sancionar, confirmar; ~ of aprobar, dar por bueno; **ap'proved** probado, acreditado; ~ school correccional *m*.

ap·prox·i·mate 1. [ə'prɔksimeit] aproximar(se) (to a); **2.** [~mit] □ aproximado, aproximativo; cercano, inmediato (to a); **ap·prox·i·ma·tion** [~'meiʃn] aproximación *f*; **ap'prox·i·ma·tive** [~ksimətiv] □ aproximativo.

ap·pur·te·nance [ə'pə:tinəns] (*freq.* ~s *pl.*) dependencia *f*; pertinencia *f*.

a·pri·cot ['eiprikɔt] albaricoque *m*.

A·pril ['eiprəl] abril *m*.

a·pron ['eiprən] delantal *m*; mandil *m of shoemaker, freemason etc.*; *thea.* visera *f*; **'~·string:** tied to the ~s of cosido a las faldas de.

ap·ro·pos [æprə'pou] **1.** *adj.* oportuno; **2.** *adv.* a propósito; **3.** *prp.* ~ of a propósito de; acerca de.

apse [æps] ábside *m*.

apt [æpt] □ apto; *remark etc.* a propósito; propenso (to a); listo (at en); **ap·ti·tude** ['~titju:d] aptitud *f*; **'apt·ness** acierto *m of remark etc.*

aq·ua·for·tis ['ækwə'fɔ:tis] agua-fuerte *f*.

aq·ua·ma·rine [ækwəmə'ri:n] agua-marina *f*; color *m* verde mar.

aq·ua·relle [ækwə'rel] acuarela *f*; **aq·ua'rel·list** acuarelista *m/f*.

a·quar·i·um [ə'kwɛəriəm] acuario *m*.

a·quat·ic [ə'kwaetik] **1.** acuático, acuátil; ~s *pl.*, ~ *sports pl.* deportes *m/pl.* acuáticos; **2.** animal *m* acuático; planta *f* acuática.

aq·ua·tint ['ækwətint] acuatinta *f*.

aq·ue·duct ['ækwidʌkt] acueducto *m*; **a·que·ous** ['eikwiəs] □ ácueo; acuoso.

aq·ui·line ['ækwilain] aguileño.

Ar·ab ['ærəb] árabe *adj. a. su. m/f*; ~ *quarter* morería *f*; F *street* ♀ golfillo *m*; chico *m* de la calle; **ar·a·besque** [~'besk] arabesco (*a. su. m*); *fig.* fantástico; **A·ra·bi·an** [ə'reibjən] árabe *adj. a. su. m/f*; *The ~ Nights* las Mil y una noches; **Ar·a·bic** ['ærəbik] árabe *adj. a. su. m*, arábigo *adj. a. su. m*; *gum* ♀ goma *f* arábiga.

ar·a·ble ['ærəbl] **1.** arable; **2.** (*or ~ land*) tierra *f* de labrantío.

a·rach·nid [ə'ræknid] arácnido *m*.

A·ra·gon·ese ['ærəgəni:z] aragonés *adj. a. su. m* (-a *f*).

ar·bi·ter ['ɑ:bitə] árbitro (a *f*) *m*; arbitrador (-a *f*) *m*; **ar·bi·trage** [ɑ:bi'trɑ:ʒ] ✝ arbitraje *m*; **ar'bit·ra·ment** *lit.* arbitramento *m*; **'ar·bi·trar·i·ness** arbitrariedad *f*; capricho *m*; **'ar·bi·trar·y** □ arbitrario; **ar·bi·trate** ['~treit] arbitrar; **ar·bi'tra·tion** arbitraje *m*; ⚖ arbitramento *m*; tercería *f*; *court of* ~ tribunal *m* de arbitraje; **'ar·bi·tra·tor** arbitrador *m*; ⚖ juez *m* árbitro.

ar·bor ['ɑ:bə] ⊕ eje *m*, árbol *m*; *Am.* ♀ *Day* fiesta *f* del árbol; **ar·bo·re·al** [ɑ:'bɔ:riəl], **ar'bo·re·ous** arbóreo; **ar·bo·res·cent** [ɑ:bə'resnt] □ arborescente; **ar·bo·ri·cul·ture** ['ɑ:bərikʌltʃə] arboricultura *f*.

ar·bour ['ɑ:bə] cenador *m*.

arc [ɑ:k] *all senses:* arco *m*; **ar·cade** [ɑ:'keid] arcada *f*; (*with shops*) pasaje *m*, soportales *m/pl.*

Ar·ca·dian [ɑ:'keidjən] arcadio *adj. a. su. m* (a *f*).

ar·ca·num [ɑ:'keinəm], *pl.* **ar·ca·na** [ɑ:'keinə] arcano *m*.

arch¹ [ɑ:tʃ] **1.** ⚠ *a. anat.* arco *m*;

bóveda *f*; ~ *of heaven* bóveda *f* celeste; **2.** △ abovedar; arquear.

arch² [ˌ] □ zumbón; chancero; travieso; astuto; *woman* coqueta.

arch³ [ˌ] principal; consumado.

ar·chae·ol·ogist [ɑːkiˈɔlədʒist] arqueólogo *m*; **ar·chae'ol·o·gy** arqueología *f*.

ar·cha·ic [ɑːˈkeiik] □ arcaico; **'ar·cha·ism** arcaísmo *m*.

arch·an·gel [ˈɑːkeindʒl] arcángel *m*.

arch·bish·op [ˈɑːtʃˈbiʃəp] arzobispo *m*; **arch'bish·op·ric** [ˌrik] arzobispado *m*.

arch·dea·con [ˈɑːtʃˈdiːkən] arcediano *m*.

arch·duch·ess [ˈɑːtʃˈdʌtʃis] archiduquesa *f*; **'arch'duch·y** archiducado *m*.

arch·duke [ˈɑːtʃˈdjuːk] archiduque *m*.

arch·er [ˈɑːtʃə] arquero *m*; **'arch·er·y** tiro *m* con arco.

ar·che·type [ˈɑːkitaip] arquetipo *m*.

arch-fiend [ˈɑːtʃˈfiːnd] Satanás *m*, el enemigo.

ar·chi·e·pis·co·pal [ɑːkiiˈpiskəpl] arzobispal.

ar·chi·pel·a·go [ɑːkiˈpeligou] archipiélago *m*.

ar·chi·tect [ˈɑːkitekt] arquitecto *m*; *fig.* artífice *m/f*; **ar·chi·tec·ton·ic** [ˌtɔnik] □ arquitectónico; **ar·chi·tec·ture** [ˌtʃə] arquitectura *f*.

ar·chives [ˈɑːkaivz] *pl.* archivo *m*; **'ar·chiv·ist** archivero (a *f*) *m*.

arch·ness [ˈɑːtʃnis] socarronería *f*, salero *m*; astucia *f*; (*woman's*) coquetería *f*.

arch·way [ˈɑːtʃwei] arcada *f*.

arc-lamp [ˈɑːklæmp] arco *m* voltaico.

arc·tic [ˈɑːktik] **1.** ártico; frígido; ♀ *Circle* Círculo *m* Polar Ártico; ♀ *Ocean* Océano *m* Boreal; **2.** zona *f* ártica.

ar·den·cy [ˈɑːdənsi] ardor *m*, celo *m*; vehemencia *f*; **'ar·dent** □ *mst fig.* ardiente, caluroso; fogoso; fervoroso, entusiasmado; ~ *spirits pl.* licores *m/pl.* espiritosos.

ar·dour [ˈɑːdə] ardor *m*; *fig.* fervor *m*, celo *m*; ahinco *m*.

ar·du·ous [ˈɑːdjuəs] □ arduo, penoso; riguroso.

are [ɑː] somos; estamos *etc.* (*v.* be).

a·re·a [ˈɛəriə] área *f*, extensión *f*; *geog.* región *f*, comarca *f*; △ *ap-*

prox. corral *m*, traspatio *m*; *danger* ~ zona *f* de peligro; *goal* ~ área *f* de meta; *prohibited* ~ zona *f* prohibida.

a·re·na [əˈriːnə] arena *f*, redondel *m*; *esp. bullfighting*: ruedo *m*; *fig.* lid *f*.

aren't [ɑːnt] = *are not*.

a·rête [æˈreit] *mount.* arista *f*.

ar·gent [ˈɑːdʒənt] argén *m*.

Ar·gen·tine [ˈɑːdʒəntain] argentino *adj. a. su. m* (a *f*); *the* ~ la Argentina.

ar·gil [ˈɑːdʒil] arcilla *f* figulina; **ar·gil·la·ceous** [ˌleiʃəs] arcilloso.

Ar·go·naut [ˈɑːgənɔːt] argonauta *m* (*a. zo.*).

ar·gu·a·ble [ˈɑːgjuəbl] discutible; **ar·gue** [ˌgjuː] *v/t.* argüir; sostener; ~ *into* persuadir a; ~ *out of* disuadir de; *v/i.* disputar, argumentar.

ar·gu·ment [ˈɑːgjumənt] argumento *m*; discusión *f*; disputa *f*; **ar·gu·men'ta·tion** raciocinación *f*, argumentación *f*; **ar·gu·men·ta·tive** [ˌˈmentətiv] □ argumentador.

a·ri·a [ˈɑːriə] aria *f*.

ar·id [ˈærid] árido, seco (*a. fig.*); **a'rid·i·ty** aridez *f*.

a·right [əˈrait] correctamente; acertadamente; a derechas; *set* ~ rectificar.

a·rise [əˈraiz] [*irr.*] *lit.* levantarse, alzarse; *fig.* surgir, aparecer; ~ *from* provenir de; **a'ris·en** *p.p. of* arise.

ar·is·toc·ra·cy [ærisˈtɔkrəsi] aristocracia *f* (*a. fig.*); **a·ris·to·crat** [ˈˌtəkræt] aristócrata *m/f*; **a·ris·to·'crat·ic, a·ris·to'crat·i·cal** □ aristocrático.

a·rith·me·tic [əˈriθmətik] aritmética *f*; **ar·ith·met·i·cal** [ˌˈmetikəl] □ aritmético; **a·rith·me·ti·cian** [ˌməˈtiʃn] aritmético *m*.

ark [ɑːk] arca *f*; ♀ *of the Covenant* arca *f* de la alianza; *Noah's* ♀ arca *f* de Noé.

arm¹ [ɑːm] brazo *m* (*a. of sea, chair*); ♀ rama *f*, gajo *m*; ~ *in* ~ de bracete; *infant in* ~s niño (a *f*) *m* de teta; *fig. with open* ~s con los brazos abiertos; *within* ~'s *reach* al alcance del brazo; *keep a p. at* ~'s *length* mantener a una p. a distancia; *take a p. in one's* ~ abrazar a una p.

arm² [ˌ] **1.** ✗ arma *f* (*mst in pl.*); *heraldry*: ~s *pl.* escudo *m*, blasón *m*; *infantry* ~ arma *f* de infantería; ~s *race* carrera *f* de armamentos; *under* ~s sobre las armas; *fig. be* *(all) up in* ~s poner el grito en el cielo; *rise up in* ~s alzarse en armas; *take up* ~s tomar las armas; **2.** ✗ armar(se); ⊕ armar.

ar·ma·da [ɑː'mɑːdə] armada *f; the* (*Invincible*) ♀ la (Armada) Invencible (*1588*).

ar·ma·ment ['ɑːməmənt] armamento *m;* **ar·ma·ture** ['ˌˈtjuə] armadura *f (a. ⚡, zo., ⚘); (dynamo)* inducido *m;* ~ *winder* bobinador *m.*

arm·chair ['ɑːmtʃeə] silla *f* de brazos; butaca *f;* sillón *m;* ~ *politician etc.* político *m etc.* de café.

...-armed [ɑːmd] de brazos...

Ar·me·ni·an [ɑː'miːnjən] armenio *adj. a. su. m (a.)*.

arm·ful ['ɑːmful] brazado *m.*

ar·mi·stice ['ɑːmistis] armisticio *m.*

arm·let ['ɑːmlit] brazal *m.*

ar·mo·ri·al [ɑː'mɔːriəl] heráldico.

ar·mo(u)r ['ɑːmə] **1.** ✗ armadura *f (a. suit of ~; a. zo. a. fig.);* blindaje *m;* escafandro *m;* **2.** blindar; ~*ed car* carro *m (or* coche *m)* blindado; **'~-clad, '~-plat·ed** blindado, acorazado; **'armour·er** armero *m;* **'ar·mo(u)r·y** armería *f; Am.* arsenal *m.*

arm·pit ['ɑːmpit] sobaco *m;* **'arm·rest** apoyo *m* para el brazo.

ar·my ['ɑːmi] ejército *m (a. fig.);* ~ *command,* ~ *staff* estado *m* mayor; **'~-corps** cuerpo *m* de ejército; **'~-list** lista *f* de oficiales del ejército.

ar·ni·ca ['ɑːnikə] árnica *f.*

a·ro·ma [ə'roumə] aroma *m,* fragancia *f;* **ar·o·mat·ic** [ærou'mætik] □ aromático, fragante.

a·rose [ə'rouz] *pret. of arise.*

a·round [ə'raund] **1.** *adv.* alrededor; a la redonda; por todos lados; F *be* ~ andar por allí; **2.** *prp.* alrededor de, en torno de; *Am. number* cerca de.

a·rouse [ə'rauz] despertar *(a. fig.); fig.* mover, excitar. [palma.)

ar·rack ['ærək] aguardiente *m* de)

ar·raign [ə'rein] ⚖ procesar; denunciar; reprender; **ar'raign·ment** ⚖ auto *m* de procesamiento; denuncia *f;* reprensión *f.*

ar·range [ə'reindʒ] *v/t.* arreglar, componer, ordenar; *time* fijar, citar; *dispute, agreement etc.* ajustar, componer; ♪ adaptar, refundir; *v/i.* hacer un arreglo (*with* con); convenir (*to* en); ~ *for* prevenir, disponer; **ar'range·ment** arreglo *m,* ordenación *f;* concierto *m,* convenio *m;* ajuste *m;* orden *m,* disposición *f;* ♪ adaptación *f,* refundición *f; come to an* ~ llegar a un acomodo, entenderse (*with* con); *make one's own* ~s obrar por su propia cuenta.

ar·rant ['ærənt] □ notorio, redomado, de siete suelas.

ar·ray [ə'rei] **1.** ✗ orden *m* de batalla; *fig.* aparato *m,* pompa *f; poet.* gala *f,* atavío *m;* **2.** ✗ formar las tropas; ataviar, componer.

ar·rear [ə'riə]: *mst* ~s *pl.* atrasos *m/pl.; in* ~s atrasado en pagos; **ar'rear·age** tardanza *f.*

ar·rest [ə'rest] **1.** arresto *m,* detención *f;* secuestro *m (of goods);* parada *f;* prórroga *f of judgment;* **2.** arrestar, detener; parar; prorrogar; *attention* llamar; **ar'rest·ing** impresionante.

ar·riv·al [ə'raivl] llegada *f;* persona *f or* cosa *f* que ha llegado; F *new* ~ recién nacido (a *f) m; fig.* advenimiento *m;* 🚂 ~ *platform* andén *m* de vacío; **ar'rive** llegar, arribar (*at* a).

ar·ro·gance ['ærəgəns] arrogancia *f,* soberbia *f;* **'ar·ro·gant** □ arrogante, soberbio; **ar·ro·gate** ['ærougeit] arrogar, usurpar (*mst to o.s.*); *qualities etc.* atribuirse, apropiarse.

ar·row ['ærou] flecha *f,* saeta *f;* **'~-head** punta *f* de flecha; **~·root** ['ærəruːt] arrurruz *m.*

arse [ɑːs] culo *m.*

ar·se·nal ['ɑːsinl] arsenal *m.*

ar·se·nic [ɑː'snik] arsénico *m;* **ar·sen·i·cal** arsénico.

ar·son ['ɑːsn] delito *m* de incendiar.

art¹ [ɑːt] arte *mst m in sg., f in pl.;* habilidad *f,* destreza *f; black* ~s *pl.* magia *f* negra; *fine* ~s *pl.* bellas artes *f/pl.; liberal* ~s *pl.* artes *f/pl.* liberales; ~s *and crafts pl.* artes *f/pl.* y oficios; *Bachelor of* ♀s (*abbr. B. A.*) Licenciado (a *f) m* en Filosofía y Letras; *Master of* ♀s (*abbr. M. A.*) Maestro (a *f) m* en Artes; *Faculty of* ♀s Facultad *f* de Filosofía y Letras.

art² [ˌ] † eres; estás (*v. be*).

ar·te·fact ['ɑːtifækt] artefacto *m.*

ar·te·ri·al [ɑː'tiəriəl] arterial; ~ *road* carretera *f* principal, autopista *f;* **ar·te·ri·o·scle·ro·sis** [ɑːtiəriousklɪə'rousis] arteriosclerosis *f;* **ar·ter·y** ['ɑːtəri] arteria *f (a. fig.).*

Ar·te·sian well [ɑːtiːzjən'wel] pozo *m* artesiano.

art·ful ['ɑːtful] □ artero, mañoso.
ar·thrit·ic [ɑː'θritik] artrítico; ar-
thri·tis [ɑː'θraitis] artritis f.
ar·ti·choke ['ɑːtitʃouk] alcachofa f;
Jerusalem ～ approx. girasol m.
ar·ti·cle ['ɑːtikl] 1. artículo m; ～s of
apprenticeship contrato m de aprendizaje; ～s of association escritura f
(or reglamento m) para una sociedad
anónima; 2. law, text articular;
acusar; apprentice etc. pactar, comprometer por escrito; ～d to agregado a, unido a.
ar·tic·u·late 1. [ɑː'tikjuleit] speech
articular; joints enlazar; 2. [～lit] □
(a. ar'ticu·lat·ed [～leitid]) articulado; distinto; capaz de hablar;
ar·tic·u'la·tion articulación f.
ar·ti·fice ['ɑːtifis] artificio m; destreza f, maña f; ar'tif·i·cer artífice
m/f; ar·ti·fi·cial [～'fiʃəl] □ artificial; postizo; afectado; ⚕ ～ person
persona f jurídica; ar·ti·fi·ci'al·i·ty
calidad f de lo artificial etc.
ar·til·ler·y [ɑː'tiləri] artillería f; ar-
'til·ler·y·man artillero m.
ar·ti·san [ɑːti'zæn] artesano (a f) m.
art·ist ['ɑːtist] artista m/f; ar·tiste
[ɑː'tiːst] artista m/f de teatro etc.;
ar·tis·tic, ar·tis·ti·cal [～'tistik(l)]
□ artístico; artificioso.
art·less ['ɑːtlis] □ natural, sencillo;
ingenuo; b.s. desmañado; 'art·less-
ness naturalidad f, sencillez f; candidez f.
art·y ['ɑːti] F ostentosamente artístico; p. cursi, repipi.
Ar·y·an ['ɛəriən] ario adj. a. su. m
(a f).
as [æz, əz] adv. a. cj. como; porque,
ya que; a medida que; tal como;
(temporal) cuando; (result) que, de
manera que; ～ ... ～ tan ... como; it
is ～ good ～ lost puede darse por perdido; v. far; ～ for, ～ to en cuanto a;
～ from date a partir de; ～ if, ～ though
como si subj.; ～ if to inf. como para
inf.; ～ it were por decirlo así; ～ per
según; v. such; ～ well también; ～
well ～ así como; tan bien como; ～
yet hasta ahora.
as·bes·tos [æz'bestɔs] asbesto m.
as·cend [ə'send] v/i. subir (a. ♪);
elevarse, encaramarse; (time) remontarse; v/t. river subir; mountain, throne subir a; as'cend·an·cy
ascendiente m, dominio m (over
sobre); as'cend·ant 1. ascendente;

predominante; 2. = ascendancy;
ast. ascendiente m; be in the ～ estar
predominante; estar en su cenit;
as'cend·en·cy, as'cend·ent = ascendancy, ascendant.
as·cen·sion [ə'senʃn] all senses: ascensión f; ♀ Day Día m de la Ascensión.
as·cent [ə'sent] ascenso m; subida f
of mountain etc.; (slope) cuesta f,
pendiente f; tramo m of stairs.
as·cer·tain [æsə'tein] averiguar; as-
cer'tain·a·ble □ averiguable; as-
cer'tain·ment averiguación f.
as·cet·ic [ə'setik] 1. □ ascético;
2. asceta m/f; as'cet·i·cism [～'tisi-
zm] ascetismo m.
as·crib·a·ble [əs'kraibəbl] atribuible; as'cribe atribuir; imputar,
achacar; as·crip·tion [əs'kripʃn]
atribución f.
a·sep·tic [ei'septik] aséptico.
a·sex·u·al [æ'seksjuəl] asexual.
ash¹ [æʃ] ♀
ash² [～](freq. pl. ash·es ['æʃiz]) ceniza f; ～es pl. cenizas f/pl. of dead;
♀ Wednesday Miércoles m de Ceniza.
a·shamed [ə'ʃeimd] □ avergonzado; be (or feel) ～ avergonzarse,
sonrojarse (at, of de; for por); be ～
of o.s. tener vergüenza de sí.
ash·can ['æʃkæn] Am. cubo m de la
basura.
ash·en¹ ['æʃn] ♀ de fresno.
ash·en² [～] ceniciento; face pálido.
ash·lar ['æʃlə] sillar m.
a·shore [ə'ʃɔː] a tierra; en tierra;
come ～, go ～ desembarcar; run ～, be
driven ～ encallar, varar.
ash...: '～-pan guardacenizas m; '～-
tray cenicero m.
ash·y ['æʃi] cenizoso.
A·sian ['eiʃn], A·si·at·ic [eiʃi'ætik]
asiático adj. a. su. m (a f).
a·side [ə'said] 1. aparte, a un lado;
Am. ～ from además de; 2. thea.
aparte m.
as·i·nine ['æsinain] asnal; fig. estúpido.
ask [ɑːsk] v/t. preguntar (a th. algo;
a p. a th. algo a una p.); pedir, rogar
(of, from a); ～ a p. for a th. pedir
algo a una p.; ～ that pedir que; invitar (to a); ～ (a p.) a question hacer
una pregunta (a una p.); v/i. ～
about, ～ after, ～ for preguntar por;
～ for pedir, reclamar; sl. he ～ed for

it se la buscó; *for the* ~*ing* sin más que pedirlo, con solo pedir; F *that's* ~*ing a lot* eso pone mucho.

a·skance [ə'skæns], **'a·skant** [ə-'skænt] al soslayo, al sesgo; *look* con recelo.

a·skew [ə'skju:] al soslayo, ladeado.

a·slant [ə'slɑ:nt] **1.** *adv.* oblicuamente; **2.** *prp.* a través de.

a·sleep [ə'sli:p] dormido, durmiendo; *fall* ~ dormirse.

asp[1] [æsp] *zo.* áspid *m.*

asp[2] [~] ⚮ *v.* aspen.

as·par·a·gus [əs'pærəgəs] espárrago *m.*

as·pect ['æspekt] aspecto *m*; apariencia *f*; *with southern* ~ con vistas al sur.

as·pen ['æspən] **1.** álamo *m* temblón; **2.** *wood* de álamo temblón; temblador.

as·per·gill, as·per·gil·lum ['æs-pədʒil, ~'dʒiləm] hisopo *m.*

as·per·i·ty [æs'periti] aspereza *f.*

as·per·sion [əs'pə:ʃən] difamación *f*, calumnia *f.*

as·phalt ['æsfælt] **1.** asfalto *m*; **2.** asfaltar.

as·pho·del ['æsʃədel] asfódel *m.*

as·phyx·i·a [æs'fiksiə] asfixia *f*; **as-'phyx·i·ate** asfixiar; **as·phyx·i·a·tion** asfixia *f.*

as·pic ['æspik] *manjar a base de gelatina, que contiene huevos, carne, etc.*

as·pir·ant [əs'paiərənt] aspirante *m/f (after, for, to* a*);* **as·pi·rate 1.** ['æspərit] aspirado; **2.** [~] aspirada *f*; **3.** ['~reit] aspirar; **as·pi·ra·tion** ✈ aspiración *f*; *fig.* anhelo *m (after, for* por*);* **as'pire** [əs'paiə] aspirar *(after, to* a*),* anhelar *(after, to* acc.*);* **as·pi·rin** ['æspərin] aspirina *f*; **as'pir·ing** [əs'paiəriŋ] ☐ ambicioso.

ass [æs] asno *m*, burro *m*; *fig.* burro *m*, mentecato *m*; *make an* ~ *of o.s.* ponerse en ridículo.

as·sail [ə'seil] acometer, arremeter contra; *fig.* asaltar; *fig.* inundar *(with* de*);* *task* acometer, emprender; **as'sail·ant, as'sail·ler** asaltador (-a *f*) *m*, agresor (-a *f*) *m*; atracador *m.*

as·sas·sin [ə'sæsin] asesino (a *f*) *m*; **as'sas·si·nate** [~neit] asesinar *(esp. por motivos políticos);* **as·sas·si·na·tion** asesinato *m.*

as·sault [ə'sɔ:lt] **1.** asalto *m (a. fig.;*

[up]*on* sobre); ⚔ carga *f*, ataque *m*; ⚖ violencia *f*; atraco *m*; **2.** asaltar; ⚔ cargar, atacar; ⚖ violentar; atracar.

as·say [ə'sei] **1.** ensaye *m*; **2.** *metals* ensayar; intentar, tratar (de); **as-'say·er** ensayador *m.*

as·sem·blage [ə'semblidʒ] asamblea *f*, reunión *f*; ⊕ montaje *m*; **as-'sem·ble** convocar; juntar(se), reunir(se); *troops* formar; ⊕ montar; **as'sem·bly** reunión *f*; asamblea *f (a.* ⚔), junta *f*; senado *m*; ⊕ montaje *m*, armadura *f*; ~ *line* cadena *f* de montaje; *Am. pol.* ~ *man* asambleísta *m en la asamblea legislativa;* ~ *room* sala *f* (de fiestas *etc.*); ~ *shop* taller *m* de montaje.

as·sent [ə'sent] **1.** asenso *m*, consentimiento *m*; aprobación *f*; **2.** consentir *(to* en), asentir *(to* a); ~ *to* aprobar *acc.*

as·sert [ə'sə:t] afirmar, declarar; hacer valer; **asser·tion** afirmación *f*, declaración *f*; **as'ser·tive** ☐ asertivo; *character* agresivo, presumido; **as'ser·tor** afirmador *m*, defensor *m.*

as·sess [ə'ses] gravar (con impuestos); *damage, tax etc.* fijar, determinar; valorar; apreciar; **as'sess·a·ble** ☐ ✝ gravable; **as'sess·ment** gravamen *m*; valoración *f*; aprecio *m*; **as'ses·sor** tasador *m*; asesor *m.*

as·set ['æset] posesión *f*; F ventaja *f*; **'as·sets** *pl.* ✝ activo *m*; *fig.* valores *m/pl.* positivos.

as·sev·er·ate [ə'sevəreit] aseverar, afirmar; **as·sev·er·a·tion** aseveración *f.*

as·si·du·i·ty [æsi'djuiti] asiduidad *f*, diligencia *f*; **as'sid·u·ous** ☐ asiduo, diligente, concienzudo.

as·sign [ə'sain] **1.** asignar, señalar; *goods* consignar, traspasar; achacar *(to* a *cause etc.*); **2.** ⚖ cesionario *m*, consignatorio *m*; **as'sign·a·ble** ☐ asignable; transferible; **as'sig·na·tion** [æsig'neiʃn] asignación *f*; ✝ consignación *f*, traspaso *m*; cita *f with p.*; **as·sign·ee** [æsi'ni:] = *assign* 2; *(bankruptcy)* síndico *m*; apoderado *m*; **as·sign·ment** [ə'sainmənt] asignación *f*; consignación *f*; *(task)* comisión *f*, encargo *m*; **as·sign·or** [æsi'nɔ:] ⚖ cesionista *m/f.*

as·sim·i·late [ə'simileit] asimilar(se) *(a. physiol. a. gr.),* asemejar(se) *(to,* *with* a); **as·sim·i·la·tion** asimilación *f*.

as·sist [ə'sist] ayudar, auxiliar; ∼ *at* asistir a; ∼ *in* tomar parte en; ∼ *in ger.* ayudar a *inf.*; **as'sist·ance** ayuda *f*, socorro *m*, auxilio *m*; **as'sist·ant 1.** auxiliar, ayudador; sub-; **2.** ayudante *m*, adjutor *m*; *v. shop.*

as·size [ə'saiz] tasa *f*; ∼*s pl.* sesión *f* de un tribunal de justicia.

as·so·ci·a·ble [ə'souʃiəbl] relacionable (*with* con); **as'so·ci·atę 1.** [∼ʃieit] asociar(se), juntar(se) (*with* a, con); ∼ *in* mancomunarse en; **2.** [∼ʃiit] asociado, coligado; con-; **3.** [∼ʃiit] asociado *m*, socio *m* (*a.* ✝), consocio *m*; miembro *m* correspondiente (de una academia;) compañero *m*, camarada *m/f*; **as·so·ci·a·tion** [∼si'eiʃn] asociación *f*; agrupación *f*, sociedad *f*; (*a. mutual* ∼) cooperativa *f*; ∼ *football* fútbol *m*.

as·so·nance ['æsənəns] asonancia *f*.

as·sort [ə'sɔːt] *v/t.* clasificar, compaginar; ✝ proveer de un surtido; *v/i.* convenir, concordar (*with* con); ∼ *well* (*ill*) (no) hacer juego (*with* con); **as'sort·ment** clasificación *f*; ✝ surtido *m*.

as·suage [ə'sweidʒ] apaciguar, mitigar; *appetite, passion etc.* saciar; **as·'suage·ment** mitigación *f*, alivio *m*.

as·sume [ə'sjuːm] *aspect* tomar; *authority etc.* apropiarse, agregarse; *burden* asumir; dar por sentado, suponer (*that* que); *assuming that* dado que; **as'sum·ing** □ presuntuoso, presumido; **as·sump·tion** [ə'sʌmpʃn] asunción *f*; suposición *f*; presunción *f*; *eccl.* ♀ Asunción *f*; *on the* ∼ *that* suponiendo que; **as'sump·tive** □ supuesto; arrogante.

as·sur·ance [ə'ʃuərəns] aseguramiento *m*; declaración *f*; garantía *f*; ✝ seguro *m*; confianza *f* en sí mismo; *b.s.* descoco *m*; **as'sure** asegurar (*a p. of a th.* a una p. de algo; *a.* ✝); declarar, afirmar, garantizar; **as'sured 1.** (*adv.* **as'sur·ed·ly** [∼ridli]) confiado; *b.s.* presumido; ∼*ly* ciertamente, de seguro; **2.** asegurado (*a f*) *m*; **as'sur·er** [∼rə] asegurado (*a f*) *m*; *a.* = **as'sur·or** [∼rə] asegurador *m*.

As·syr·i·an [ə'siriən] asirio.

as·ter ['æstə] aster *f*.

as·ter·isk ['æstərisk] asterisco *m*.

a·stern [ə'stəːn] a popa; *go* ∼ ciar.

asth·ma ['æsmə] asma *f*; **asth·mat·ic** [∼'mætik] **1.** *a.* **asth'mat·i·cal** □ asmático; **2.** asmático (*a f*) *m*.

as·tig·mat·ic [æstig'mætik] □ astigmático; **a'stig·ma·tism** [∼mə-tizm] astigmatismo *m*.

a·stir [əs'tə:] en movimiento; levantado (de la cama).

as·ton·ish [əs'tɔniʃ] asombrar, sorprender; pasmar; *be* ∼*ed* asombrarse, maravillarse (*at* de, con); **as'ton·ish·ing** □ asombroso, sorprendente; **as'ton·ish·ment** asombro *m*, sorpresa *f*; pasmo *m*.

as·tound [əs'taund] pasmar; aturdir.

as·tra·khan [æstrə'kæn] astracán *m*.

as·tral ['æstrəl] astral, sidéreo.

a·stray [ə'strei] extraviado, descarriado, despistado; *go* ∼ extraviarse, descarriarse (*a. fig.*); *lead* ∼ llevar por mal camino.

a·stride [ə'straid] **1.** *adv.* (*ride* montar) a horcajadas; **2.** *prp.* a caballo sobre, a horcajadas sobre.

as·trin·gent [əs'trindʒent] □ ♂ astringente; *fig. style* adusto, austero.

as·trol·o·ger [əs'trɔlədʒə] astrólogo *m*; **as·tro·log·i·cal** [æstrə'lɔdʒikl] □ astrológico, astrólogo; **as·trol·o·gy** [əs'trɔlədʒi] astrología *f*; **as·tron·o·mer** [əs'trɔnəmə] astrónomo *m*; **as·tro·nom·i·cal** [æstrə'nɔmikl] □ astronómico; *fig.* tremendo; **as·tron·o·my** [əs'trɔnəmi] astronomía *f*.

as·tute [əs'tjuːt] □ sagaz, perspicaz; astuto; **as'tute·ness** perspicacia *f*; astucia *f*.

a·sun·der [ə'sʌndə] separadamente; en dos; *lit. tear* ∼ hacer pedazos.

a·sy·lum [ə'sailəm] asilo *m*; amparo *m*; (*mental* ∼) manicomio *m*.

at [æt, *unstressed* ət] en; a; hacia; por; ∼ *Mérida* en Mérida; ∼ *school* en la escuela; ∼ *midday* a mediodía; ∼ *Christmas* en (*or* por) Navidades; ∼ *a low price* a un precio bajo; ∼ *Mary's* en casa de María; ∼ *that time* en aquella época; ∼ *the door* a la puerta; ∼ *table* a la mesa; ∼ *peace* en paz; ∼ *one blow* de un golpe; *be* ∼ *s.t.* estar ocupado con algo.

at·a·vism ['ætəvizm] atavismo *m*.

a·tax·y [ə'tæksi] ataxia *f*.

ate [et; eit] *pret. of* eat.

a·the·ism ['eiθiizm] ateísmo *m*; **'a-**

the·ist ateo (a *f*) *m*; **a·the'is·tic**, **a·the'is·ti·cal** □ ateísta, ateo.

ath·lete ['æθliːt] atleta *m/f*; ⚐ ~'s *foot* pie *m* de atleta; **ath·let·ic** [æθ'letik], **ath'let·i·cal** □ atlético; ~ *sports pl.* ejercicios *m/pl.* atléticos; **ath'let·ics** *pl.*, **ath'let·i·cism** [~tisizəm] atletismo *m*.

at-home [ət'houm] fiesta *f* (en una casa particular).

a·thwart [ə'θwɔːt] **1.** *prp.* a(l) través de; **2.** *adv.* de través, transversalmente.

a-tilt [ə'tilt] inclinado.

at·las ['ætləs] atlas *m*.

at·mos·phere ['ætməsfiə] atmósfera *f*; *fig.* ambiente *m*; **at·mos·pher·ic**, **at·mos·pher·i·cal** [~'ferik(l)] □ atmosférico; **at·mos·'pher·ics** *pl. radio:* mala atmósfera *f*, parásitos *m/pl.*

at·oll ['ætɔl] atolón *m*.

at·om ['ætəm] átomo *m* (*a. fig.*); **a·tom·ic** [ə'tɔmik] atómico; ~ *age* era *f* atómica; ~ *bomb* bomba *f* atómica; ~ *energy* energía *f* atómica; ~ *fission* fisión *f* nuclear; ~ *nucleus* núcleo *m* atómico; ~ *pile* pila *f* atómica; ~ *research* investigaciones *f/pl.* atómicas; **a'tom·ic·'pow·ered** impulsado por energía atómica; **at·om·ism** ['ætəmizm] atomismo *m*; **at·om'is·tic** □ atomístico; **'at·om·ize** reducir a átomos; *liquid* pulverizar; **'at·om·iz·er** pulverizador *m*.

a·ton·al [ei'tounəl] atonal; **a·ton'al·i·ty** atonalidad *f*.

a·tone [ə'toun] *v/t.* † conciliar; *v/i.:* ~ *for* expiar *acc.*; **a'tone·ment** expiación *f*; *Day of ♀* Día *m* de la Expiación.

a·ton·ic [æ'tɔnik] □ átono, atónico; **at·o·ny** ['ætəni] atonía *f*.

a·tro·cious [ə'trouʃəs] □ atroz; F malísimo, infame; **a·troc·i·ty** [ə'trɔsiti] atrocidad *f* (*a.* F).

at·ro·phy ['ætrəfi] **1.** atrofia *f*; **2.** atrofiar(se).

at·tach [ə'tætʃ] *v/t.* atar, pegar, prender (to a); † adjuntar; *importance, value etc.* dar, conceder (to a); ⚖ *p.* arrestar; *th.* incautarse; ~ *o.s.* to agregarse a; pegarse a; ~ *value* to conceder valor a, estimar; *fig. be* ~*ed to p. etc.* tener cariño a; *v/i.* ~ *to* corresponder a; **at'tach·a·ble** separable; *p.* casadero; ⚖ incautable;

at·ta·ché [ə'tæʃei] agregado *m*; ~ *case* cartera *f* (grande, para documentos); **at'tached** *male etc.* comprometido; agregado (to a); † adjunto (to a); **at'tach·ment** atadura *f*; ⊕ accesorio *m*; (*affection*) cariño *m* (to por, a), apego *m* (to a); (*loyalty*) adhesión *f*, lealtad *f*; ⚖ arresto *m*; incautación *f*.

at·tack [ə'tæk] **1.** acometer, embestir (*a. fig.*); atacar (*a.* ⚔ *a.* ⚕); **2.** ataque *m* (on contra, a, sobre; *a. fig.*); ⚔ ataque *m*, acceso *m*; **at'tack·a·ble** atacable; **at'tack·er** agresor (-a *f*) *m*.

at·tain [ə'tein] *v/t.* alcanzar, lograr, conseguir; *v/i.:* ~ *to* llegar a; **at'tain·a·ble** realizable; accesible; **at'tain·der** ⚖ muerte *f* civil; **at'tain·ment** logro *m*, obtención *f*; ~*s pl.* talentos *m/pl.*, conocimientos *m/pl.*

at·tar ['ætə] esencia *f* de rosas.

at·tem·per [ə'tempə] atemperar (*a. fig.*); modificar; calmar; acomodar (to a).

at·tempt [ə'tempt] **1.** ensayar, intentar (to *inf.*), tentar (to de); **2.** tentativa *f*, conato *m* (to de); atentado *m* (on *life* a, contra).

at·tend [ə'tend] *v/t.* acompañar; cortejar, servir; † aguardar; *course etc.* asistir a; ⚔ atender a, asistir; *well attended* (muy) concurrido; *v/i.* prestar atención (to a); asistir (*at* a); ~ *on* servir; *sick* atender a, asistir; ~ *to* work *etc.* atender a; **at'tend·ance** (*presence*) presencia *f* (*at* en), asistencia *f* (*at* a); (*gathering*) concurrencia *f*; ⚔ asistencia *f*; *obsequio m* (on de); *be in* ~ asistir; *dance* ~ *on* estar pendiente de los menores detalles de; **at'tend·ant 1.** concomitante ([up]on a); asistente (*at* a); **2.** criado (a *f*) *m*, sirviente (a *f*) *m*; mozo (a *f*) *m*; ordenanza *m*; *thea. etc.* acomodador (-a *f*) *m*.

at·ten·tion [ə'tenʃn] atención *f* (*a. fig.*); ~*!* ¡atención!; ✕ ~*!* ¡firmes!; *call* ~ *to* llamar la atención sobre; *give* (*or pay*) ~ prestar atención (to a); **at'ten·tive** □ atento (to a).

at·ten·u·ate [ə'tenjueit] atenuar (*a. fig.*); *attenuating circumstances pl.* circunstancias *f/pl.* atenuantes; **at'ten·u·at·ed** enflaquecido; **at·ten·u·a·tion** atenuación *f*.

at·test [ə'test] atestiguar; dar fe (to de); juramentar; **at·tes·ta·tion** [ætes'teiʃn] atestiguación *f*; atestación *f*; ʀʲ̣ autenticación *f*.

At·tic ['ætik] **1.** ático; **2.** ♀ desván *m*, sotabanco *m*; guardilla *f*.

at·tire [ə'taiə] *lit.* **1.** ataviar; adornar, componer; **2.** atavío *m*; adorno *m*.

at·ti·tude ['ætitju:d] actitud *f* (*a. fig.*; *to* a); ademán *m*; ✍ posición *f*; *strike an* ~ tomar una postura; ~ *of mind* actitud *f*, disposición *f* de ánimo; **at·ti·tu·di·nize** pavonearse; tomar posturas afectadas.

at·tor·ney [ə'tə:ni] † apoderado (a *f*) *m*; † ʀʲ̣ procurador *m*; *Am.* ʀʲ̣ *circuit* (*district*) ~ fiscal *m*; *letter* (or *warrant*) *of* ~ poder *m*, procuración *f*; *power of* ~ poder *m*; ♀ *General* fiscal *m* de la corona; *Am.* procurador *m* general; *by* ~ por poder.

at·tract [ə'trækt] atraer; *attention* llamar; **at·trac·tion** [~kʃən] atracción *f*; aliciente *m*; atractivo *m of p.esp.*; *thea.* programa *m*; **at·trac·tive** [~tiv] □ *mst fig.* atractivo, atrayente; agradable; **at·trac·tive·ness** atractivo *m*, hechizo *m*.

at·trib·ut·a·ble [ə'tribjutəbl] atribuible; **at·trib·ute 1.** [ə'tribju:t] atribuir, achacar; **2.** ['ætribju:t] atributo *m*; **at·tri·bu·tion** atribución *f*; **at·trib·u·tive** [ə'tribjutiv] □ atributivo.

at·tri·tion [ə'triʃn] roce *m*, desgaste *m*; *eccl.* atrición *f*; *war of* ~ guerra *f* de agotamiento; [armonizar con.]

at·tune [ə'tju:n] ♪ afinar; *fig.* ~ *to*]

au·burn ['ə:bən] castaño rojizo.

auc·tion ['ɔ:kʃn] **1.** almoneda *f*, subasta *f*; *sell by* (*Am.* at) ~, *put up for* ~ subastar, poner en pública subasta; *sale by* ~ subasta *f*; **2.** subastar (*freq.* ~ *off*); **auc·tion·eer** [~'niə] subastador *m*.

au·da·cious [ɔ:'deiʃəs] □ audaz, osado; *b.s.* descarado, fresco; **au·dac·i·ty** [ɔ:'dæsiti] audacia *f*, osadía *f*; *b.s.* descaro *m*.

au·di·bil·i·ty [ɔ:di'biliti] capacidad *f* de ser oído; **au·di·ble** ['ɔ:dəbl] □ audible; **'au·di·ble·ness** = *audibility*.

au·di·ence ['ɔ:djəns] auditorio *m*, público *m*; audiencia *f* (*with, of* con).

au·di·o·fre·quen·cy ['ɔ:diou'fri:kwənsi] *radio*: audiofrecuencia *f*.

au·di·on ['ɔ:diən] *radio*: audión *m*.

au·dit ['ɔ:dit] **1.** intervención *f*; **2.** intervenir; **au'di·tion** audición *f*; **'au·di·tor** interventor *m*; censor *m* de cuentas; **au·di·to·ri·um** [~'tɔ:riəm] sala *f*, anfiteatro *m*; **au·di·to·ry** ['~tɔri] auditivo.

au·ger ['ɔ:gə] barrena *f*.

aught [ɔ:t] algo; (*with negation*) nada; *for* ~ *I care* igual me da; *for* ~ *I know* que yo sepa.

aug·ment [ɔ:g'ment] aumentar(se), engrosar(se); **aug·men·ta·tion** aumento *m*, acrecentamiento *m*; **aug·'ment·a·tive** [~tətiv] □ aumentativo (*a. gr.*).

au·gur ['ɔ:gə] **1.** augur *m*; **2.** agorar, pronosticar; prometer (*well* bien, *ill* mal); **au·gu·ry** ['ɔ:gjuri] augurio *m*.

Au·gust ['ɔ:gəst] **1.** agosto *m*; **2.** ♀ [ɔ:'gʌst] □ augusto; **Au·gus·tan** [ɔ:'gʌstən] augustal; clásico.

auk [ɔ:k] alca *f*.

aunt [ɑ:nt] tía *f*; **aunt·ie, aunt·y** ['~ti] F tía *f*.

au·ra ['ɔ:rə] ambiente *m*; emanación *f*.

au·ral ['ɔ:rəl] auricular.

au·re·ole ['ɔ:rioul] *eccl.*, *ast.*, aureola *f*.

au·ri·cle ['ɔ:rikl] aurícula *f*; **au·ric·u·la** [ɔ:'rikjula] ♀ oreja *f* de oso; **au·ric·u·lar** □ auricular; ~ *witness* testigo *m* auricular.

au·rif·er·ous [ɔ:'rifərəs] aurífero.

au·rochs ['ɔ:rɔks] uro *m*.

au·ro·ra [ɔ:'rɔ:rə] aurora *f*; ~ *borealis* aurora *f* polar (or *boreal*); **au'ro·ral** matutino; *colour* rosáceo.

aus·cul·ta·tion [ɔ:skəl'teiʃn] auscultación *f*.

aus·pice [ɔ:spis] auspicio *m*; protección *f*; *under the* ~*s of* bajo los auspicios de; **aus·pi·cious** [~'piʃəs] □ propicio, favorable; de buen augurio.

aus·tere [ɔ:s'tiə] □ austero, severo; *style etc.* adusto; *taste* acerbo; **aus·ter·i·ty** [~'teriti] austeridad *f*, severidad *f*; adustez *f*.

aus·tral ['ɔ:strəl] austral.

Aus·tra·lian [ɔ:s'treiljən] australiano *adj.* *u.* *su.* *m* (a *f*).

Aus·tri·an ['ɔ:striən] austríaco *adj.* *a.* *su.* *m* (a *f*).

au·tarch·y ['ɔ:tɑ:ki] autarquía *f*.

au·then·tic [ɔ:'θentik] □ auténtico;

au·then·ti·cate [ˌkeit] autenticar; refrendar; au·then·ti·ca·tion autenticación *f*; refrendación *f*; au·then·tic·i·ty autenticidad *f*.

au·thor ['ɔ:θə] autor (-a *f*) *m*; au·thor·ess ['ɔ:θəris] *esp. lit.* autora *f*; au·thor·i·tar·i·an [ɔ:θɔri'tɛəriən] autoritario; au·thor·i·ta·tive [ˌtei-tiv] □ autorizado; perentorio; autoritario; au'thori·ty autoridad *f*; *the authorities* las autoridades; *on good* ~ de buena tinta; *under the* ~ *of* bajo la autoridad de; *in* ~ *over* al mando de; au·thor·i·za·tion [ɔ:θərai'zeiʃn] autorización *f*; 'au·thor·ize autorizar; 'au·thor·ship calidad *f or* profesión *f* de autor; paternidad *f* literaria *of work*.

au·to ['ɔ:tou] *Am.* automóvil *m*, coche *m*.

au·to... ['ɔ:to] auto...

au·to·bi·og·ra·pher [ɔ:toubai'ɔgrəfə] autobiógrafo (a *f*) *m*; 'au·to·bi·o·graph·ic, 'au·to·bi·o·graph·i·cal [ˌ'græfik(l)] □ autobiográfico; au·to·bi·og·ra·phy [ˌgrəfi] autobiografía *f*.

au·to·bus ['ɔ:toubʌs] autobús *m*.

au·to·cade ['ɔ:toukeid] *Am.* caravana *f* de automóviles.

au·toch·thon [ɔ:'tɔkθɔn] autóctono (a *f*) *m*; au'toch·tho·nous autóctono.

au·toc·ra·cy [ɔ:'tɔkrəsi] autocracia *f*; au·to·crat ['ɔ:təkræt] autócrata *m*/*f*; au·to'crat·ic, au·to'crat·i·cal □ autocrático; autoritario.

au·to·gi·ro ['ɔ:tou'dʒaiərou] autogiro *m*.

au·to·graph ['ɔ:təgrɑ:f] 1. autógrafo *adj. a. su. m*; 2. firmar; dedicar; au·to·graph·ic [ˌ'græfik] autográfico; au·tog·ra·phy [ɔ:'tɔgrəfi] ⊕ autografía *f*.

au·to·mat·ic [ɔ:tə'mætik] 1. □ automático; 2. pistola *f* automática; au·to·ma·tion automatización *f*; au·tom·a·ton [ɔ:'tɔmətən] *pl. mst* au'tom·a·ta [ˌtə] autómata *m* (*a. fig.*).

au·to·mo·bile ['ɔ:təmoubi:l] *esp. Am.* automóvil *m*, coche *m*.

au·ton·o·mous [ɔ:'tɔnəməs] □ autónomo; au'ton·o·my autonomía *f*.

au·top·sy ['ɔ:təpsi] autopsia *f*.

au·to·type ['ɔ:totaip] 1. autotipo *m*, facsímil *m*; 2. producir por la autotipia.

au·tumn ['ɔ:təm] otoño *m*; au·tum·nal [ɔ:'tʌmnəl] □ otoñal.

aux·il·ia·ry [ɔ:g'ziliəri] 1. auxiliar (*a. gr.*); subalterno; 2. aux·il·ia·ries [ˌiz] *pl.* tropas *f*/*pl.* auxiliares.

a·vail [ə'veil] 1. beneficiar, valer; ~ *o.s. of* valerse de, aprovechar; 2.: *of no* ~ inútil; *of what* ~ *is it?* ¿de qué sirve? (*to inf.*); a·vail·a·'bil·i·ty disponibilidad *f*; calidad *f* de asequible (*or* accesible); a'vail·a·ble □ disponible, asequible; *p.* accesible, tratable; *ticket* válido; *make* ~ disponer.

av·a·lanche ['ævəlɑ:ntʃ] alud *m*; *fig.* torrente *m*.

av·a·rice ['ævəris] avaricia *f*, mezquindad *f*; av·a'ri·cious □ avaro, avariento.

a·venge [ə'vendʒ] vengar, vindicar; ~ *o.s.* (*or be* ~d) vengarse ([up]on en); *avenging angel* ángel *m* vengador; a'veng·er vengador (-a *f*) *m*.

av·e·nue ['ævinju:] avenida *f*; *Am.* autopista *f*; *fig.* camino *m*, acceso *m*.

a·ver [ə'və:] afirmar, declarar.

av·er·age ['ævəridʒ] 1. promedio *m*, término *m* medio; ⚓ avería *f* (*general* gruesa; *particular* particular); *on* (*an or the*) ~ por regla general; 2. medio, de término medio; *a.b.s.* mediano, ordinario; 3. *v*/*t.* calcular el término medio de; prorratear; *v*/*i.* (*work etc.*) resultar por término medio, ser por regla general.

a·ver·ment [ə'və:mənt] declaración *f*; ⚖ comprobación *f*.

a·verse [ə'və:s]: ~ *from,* to opuesto a, adverso a; con antipatía hacia; *I am* ~ *to th.* siento repugnancia por; *I am* ~ *to ger.* tengo pocas ganas de *inf.*, me repugna *inf.*; a'verse·ness, a'ver·sion aversión *f* (*for, from,* to hacia), repugnancia *f* (*for from,* to por); *v. pet.*

a·vert [ə'və:t] apartar; *blow etc.* impedir, quitar.

a·vi·ar·y ['eiviəri] avería *f*, pajarera *f*.

a·vi·a·tion [eivi'eiʃn] aviación *f*; 'a·vi·a·tor aviador (-a *f*) *m*.

av·id ['ævid] □ ávido, ansioso (*of, for* de); a·vid·i·ty [ə'viditi] avidez *f*, ansia *f*.

av·o·ca·tion [ævou'keiʃn] vocación *f*; ocupación *f* accesoria; † distracción *f*.

a·vo·cet ['ævouset] avoceta *f.*

a·void [ə'vɔid] evitar (*doing* hacer); salvarse de; *duty etc.* eludir; 🏛 anular; **a'void·a·ble** evitable; eludible; **a'void·ance** evitación *f.*; 🏛 anulación *f.*; plaza *f* vacante.

av·oir·du·pois [ævədə'pɔiz] *sistema de pesos británico y estadounidense*; F gordura *f.*

a·vouch [ə'vautʃ] afirmar; garantizar; confesar.

a·vow [ə'vau] reconocer, confesar; **a'vow·al** reconocimiento *m*, confesión *f.*; **a'vow·edly** [⌣idli] sin rebozo, abiertamente.

av·unc·u·lar [ə'vʌŋkjuːlə] de un tío; como un tío.

a·wait [ə'weit] *lit. a. fig.* aguardar, esperar.

a·wake [ə'weik] 1. despierto; *fig.* despabilado, listo; *keep* ⌣ (*coffee etc.*) desvelar; *wide* ⌣ completamente despierto (*a. fig.*); *fig.* astuto; 2. [*irr.*] *v/t.* (*mst* **a'wak·en**) despertar; ⌣ *a p. to a th.* ponerle a uno al corriente de algo; *v/i.* despertar (se) (*a. fig.*); ⌣ *to* darse cuenta de.

a·ward [ə'wɔːd] 1. adjudicación *f.*; 🏛 sentencia *f*, fallo *m*; ⚔ *etc.* condecoración *f.*; (*prize*) premio *m* (*chief gordo*); 2. adjudicar; decretar; *prize etc.* conferir, conceder.

a·ware [ə'wɛə] consciente (*of* de); *be* ⌣ *of* estar enterado de; *become* ⌣ *of* enterarse de; darse cuenta de; **a'ware·ness** conciencia *f*, conocimiento *m.*

a·wash [ə'wɔʃ] a flor de agua; en el agua.

a·way [ə'wei] ausente; lejos; en otro lugar; (*with verbs, e.g. work* ⌣) con ahinco, sin cesar; *be* ⌣ estar fuera; ⌣ *with you!* ¡quita allá!; ¡lárgate!; *Am.* F ⌣ *back* hace mucho tiempo; ⌣ *team* equipo *m* de fuera; *play* ⌣ jugar fuera.

awe [ɔː] 1. temor *m* reverencial,

pasmo *m*; *stand in* ⌣ *of* reverenciar; **awe·some** ['⌣səm] □ pasmoso; aterrador; '⌣**-struck** pasmado.

aw·ful ['ɔːful] □ tremendo, pasmoso; impresionante; F malísimo, muy feo; ⌣*ly adv.* F excesivamente; terriblemente; **'aw·ful·ness** † veneración *f*; horror *m*; F enormidad *f.*

a·while [ə'wail] un rato; algún tiempo.

awk·ward ['ɔːkwəd] □ *p. etc.* desmañado, torpe, lerdo; *situation* embarazoso; violento; *problem* peliagudo, difícil, delicado; **'awk·ward·ness** desmaña *f*, torpeza *f*; delicadeza *f.*

awl [ɔːl] lezna *f*, subilla *f.*

awn [ɔːn] arista *f.*

awn·ing ['ɔːniŋ] toldo *m*; (*cart*) entalamadura *f*; (*window*) marquesina *f*; ⚓ toldilla *f.*

a·woke [ə'wouk] *pret. a. p.p. of awake* 2.

a·wry [ə'rai] de través, al sesgo; *fig.* equivocadamente; *go* ⌣, *turn* ⌣ salir mal, fracasar.

axe [æks] 1. hacha *f*; *fig.* (*costs etc.*) reducción *f*, cercenamiento *m*; *have an* ⌣ *to grind* actuar de una manera interesada; 2. *fig.* reducir, cercenar.

ax·i·om ['æksiəm] axioma *m*; **ax·i·o'mat·ic** □ axiomático.

ax·is ['æksis], *pl.* **ax·es** ['⌣siːz] eje *m* (*a.* ⚓ *a.* ⚕); *physiol.* axis *m.*

ax·le ['æksl] eje *m*, árbol *m*; ⌣ *box* caja *f* de eje; '⌣**-tree** eje *m* (de un carro).

ay(e) [ai] 1. *parl. a.* ⚓ sí; *for ever and* ⌣ siempre jamás; 2. sí *m*; *parl.* *the* ⌣*s have it* han ganado los que votaron por la moción.

a·za·lea [ə'zeiljə] azalea *f.*

az·i·muth ['æzimaθ] acimut *m*; **az·i·muth·al** [⌣'mjuːθl] □ acimu-⌐
a·zo·ic [ə'zouik] azoico. [tal.⌐

az·ure ['æʒə] azul *adj. a. su. m.*

B

baa [bɑ:] 1. balar; 2. balido *m*.
bab·ble ['bæbl] 1. barbullar, barbotear; *fig.* charlar, parlar; hablar indiscretamente; *(stream)* murmurar; 2. barboteo *m*; parloteo *m*; murmullo *m*; **'bab·bler** charlatán (-a *f*) *m*; **'bab·bling** *adj. talk* descosido.
babe [beib] *poet.* nene (a *f*) *m*, criatura *f*. [babel *m* or *f*.\
Ba·bel ['beibl] Babel *m or f*; ♀ *fig.*\
ba·boon [bə'bu:n] mandril *m*.
ba·by ['beibi] niño (a *f*) *m*; nene (a *f*) *m*, rorro (a *f*) *m*; *Am.* F *(woman)* rica *f*; *b.s.* aniñado (a *f*) *m*; ~ *of the family* benjamín *m*; *be left holding the* ~ cargar con la oveja muerta; ~ **grand** piano *m* de media cola; **'~·hood** [͵hud] infancia *f*; **'ba·by·ish** infantil.
Bab·y·lo·ni·an [bæbi'lounjən] babilonio *adj. a. su. m* (a *f*).
baby...: **'~·sit** F vigilar (*a los niños dormidos en ausencia de sus padres*); **'~·sit·ter** niñero (a *f*) *m*, cuidaniños *m*/*f S.Am.*; **'~·talk** habla *f* infantil.
bac·cha·nal ['bækənl] 1. = *bacchante*; 2. |bacanal; **'bac·cha·nals** *pl. or* **bac·cha·na·li·a** [͵'neiljə] *pl.* bacanales *f*/*pl.*; **bac·cha·na·li·an** bacanal; desenfrenado.
bac·chan·te [bə'kænti] bacante *f*; **bac'chan·tic** bacanal.
bac·cy ['bæki] F tabaco *m*.
bach·e·lor ['bætʃələ] soltero *m*; *old* ~ solterón *m*; *univ.* bachiller *m* (†), licenciado (a *f*) *m*; ~ *flat* piso *m* para soltero; ~ *girl* soltera *f* (que tiene sus propios recursos); **'~·hood** [͵hud] soltería *f*.
bac·il·la·ry [bə'siləri] bacilar; **ba·'cil·lus** [͵ləs], *pl.* **ba'cil·li** [͵lai] bacilo *m*.
back [bæk] 1. espalda *f*, dorso *m*; *(mountain)* lomo *m*; respaldo *m of chair*; dorso *m of cheque, hand etc.*; final *m of book*; *sport*: defensa *m*; *(at the)* ~ *of* tras, detrás de; *stage etc.* al fondo de; *behind one's* ~ a espaldas de uno (*a.fig.*); *on one's* ~ postrado, en cama; *(carrying s. t.)* a cuestas; *with one's* ~ *to the wall*

entre la espada y la pared; F *get (or put) a p.'s* ~ *up* enojar a una p.; *turn one's* ~ *on* volver la espalda a; 2. *adj.* trasero, posterior, de atrás; ~ *issue* número *m* atrasado; ~ *pay* sueldo *m* retrasado; 3. *adv.* (hacia) atrás; otra vez; de vuelta; ~ *and forth* de una parte a otra; ~ *in period* allá por; *some months* ~ hace unos meses; 4. *v/t.* apoyar (*a.* ~ *up*); *pol.* respaldar; *car* dar marcha atrás a; *horse* montar; *(bet)* apostar a; ♀ endosar; ~ *up* mover hacia atrás; ♣ ~ *water* ciar; *v/i.* retroceder, moverse hacia atrás; *(esp. horse)* cejar; F ~ *down* ceder; rajarse; F ~ *out* echarse atrás, desdecirse; ~ **al·ley** callejón *m* de atrás; **'~-'ben·cher** *diputado que no ocupa un escaño en la fila delantera*; **'~·bite** [*irr. bite*] cortar de vestir, murmurar; **'~·bone** espinazo *m*; *fig.* firmeza *f*; *fig.* to the ~ hasta la médula; **'~·chat** *sl.* réplica *f*; maldicencia *f*; **'~·cloth** telón *m* de fondo; ~ **'door** puerta *f* trasera; **'back·er** sostenedor (-a *f*) *m*; ♀ suscriptor (-a *f*) *m*, inversionista *m*/*f*.
back...: **'~·fire** 1. *mot.* petardeo *m*, falsa explosión *f*; 2. *mot.* petardear; *fig.* salir el tiro por la culata; **~·'gam·mon** chaquete *m*; **'~·ground** fondo *m*, último término *m*; *fig.* antecedentes *m*/*pl.*; educación *f*; ~ *music* música *f* de fondo; **'~·'hand** 1. *tennis etc.*: revés *m*; 2. = **'~·'hand·ed** dado con la vuelta de la mano; *fig.* falto de sinceridad, irónico; **'~-'hand·er** *tennis etc.*: revés *m*; **'back·ing** apoyo *m*; *esp.* ♀ reserva *f*.
back...: **'~·log** atrasos *m*/*pl.* (de pedidos pendientes); **'~-'num·ber** número *m* atrasado; *fig.* cero *m* a la izquierda; **'~-'ped·al** dar marcha atrás con los pedales, contrapedalear; **'~-'seat** asiento *m* de atrás; F *take a* ~ ceder su puesto, perder influencia; **'~·side** trasero *m*; nalgas *f*/*pl.*; **'~-slap·per** tipo *m* gua-

són, campechano *m*; '~-**slap·ping** espaldarazos *m/pl.*; *mutual* ~ bombo *m* mutuo; '~'**slide** [*irr.* (*slide*)] volver a las andadas, reincidir; '~'**slid·er** reincidente *m/f*; '~'**slid·ing** reincidencia *f*; '~'**stairs 1.** escalera *f* de servicio; **2.** F por enchufe; por intriga; clandestino; '~-**stitch 1.** pespunte *m*; **2.** pespuntar; '~-**stop** reja *f* (*or* red *f*) para detener la pelota; '~-**stroke** arrastre *m* de espaldas; ~ **talk** *Am.* F contestación *f* insolente; ~ **to back** dándose las espaldas; *Am.* F sucesivamente; '~-**track** *Am.* F volver pies atrás, retirarse.

back·ward ['bækwəd] **1.** *adj.* vuelto hacia atrás; (*country, pupil* atrasado; *p.* (*shy*) retraído, corto; **2.** *adv.* (*a.* '**back·wards**) (hacia) atrás; al revés; ~s *and forwards* de acá para allá; '**back·ward·ness** atraso *m*; cortedad *f*.

back...: '~-**wa·ter** brazo *m* de río estancado; remanso *m*; *fig.* lugar *m* (*or* condición *f*) atrasado(a); '~-**woods** *pl.* región *f* apartada (*compare* Las Batuecas *in Spain*); '~'**woods·man** patán *m*, hombre *m* de los *backwoods*.

ba·con ['beikən] tocino *m*; F *save one's* ~ salvar el pellejo; *sl.* bring home the ~ sacarse el gordo.

bac·te·ri·al [bæk'tiəriəl] □ bacteriano, bactérico; **bac·te·ri·o·log·i·cal** [bæktiəriə'lɔdʒikəl] □ bacteriológico; **bac·te·ri·ol·o·gist** [~'ɔl-ədʒist] bacteriólogo *m*; **bac'te·ri·um** [~iəm], *pl.* **bac'te·ri·a** [~iə] bacteria *f*.

bad [bæːd] □ malo; infeliz, desgraciado; (*rotten etc.*) dañado, podrido; (*harmful*) nocivo, dañoso; ⚕ indispuesto, enfermo; *coin* falso; *debt* incobrable; F *not* ~ bastante bueno (*or* bien); F *not too* ~ así así; *things are not so* ~ las cosas van bastante bien; ~ *blood* mala sangre *f*; *Am.* F *be in* ~ *with* tener enojada a una persona (*over a causa de*); *go* ~ (*food*) pasarse; *go to the* ~ caer en el mal; *look* ~ tener mala cara; F *he's a* ~ *one* [*freq.* ən] es un mal sujeto; *v. worse*; ~*ly adv.* mal; *he is* ~*ly off* le va muy mal de dinero; está malparado; *want* ~*ly* desear mucho; perderse por.

bade [beid] *pret. of* bid.

badge [bædʒ] insignia *f*, divisa *f*.

badg·er ['bædʒə] **1.** tejón *m*; **2.** molestar; fastidiar, acosar.

bad·i·nage [bædi'naːʒ] chanza *f*; guasa *f*.

bad lands ['bæd'lændz] *Am. tierras yermas en los estados de Nebraska y Dakota del Sur.*

bad·min·ton ['bædmintən] volante *m*.

bad·ness ['bædnis] maldad *f*; podredumbre *f*.

bad-tem·pered ['bæː'd'tempəd] de mal genio.

baf·fle ['bæfl] **1.** ⊕ (*a.* '~-*plate*) deflector *m*; *radio :* pantalla *f* acústica; **2.** frustrar, impedir; chasquear; desconcertar; *it* ~s *description* se escapa a la descripción.

bag [bæːg] **1.** maleta *f*; bolsa *f* (*a. zo.,* ⚕); (*hand-*) bolso *m*; (*big*) saco *m*; (*shoulder-*) zurrón *m*, mochila *f*; *hunt.* cacería *f* (de animales muertos de una vez); *diplomatic* ~ valija *f* diplomática; F ~s *pl.* pantalón *m*; *Am.* F *it's in the* ~ es cosa segura; *pack* ~ *and baggage* tomar el tole; F *there's* ~s *of room* hay sitio de sobra; **2.** [bæg] *v/t.* ensacar; *sl.* coger, asegurarse; *hunt.* cazar; *v/i.* (*garment etc.*) hacer bolsa.

bag·a·telle [bægə'tel] bagatela *f*.

bag·gage ['bægidʒ] *Am.* equipaje *m*; ✕ bagaje *m*; *contp.* mujercilla *f*; fulana *f*; ~ *car Am.* 🚃 vagón *m* de equipajes; '~-**check** *Am.* talón *m* de equipajes.

bag·gy ['bægi] holgado, que hace bolsa.

bag...: '~-**pipe** gaita *f*; '~-**snatch·er** ladrón *m* de bolsos, ratero (a *f*) *m*.

bail[1] [beil] ⚖ **1.** caución *f*, fianza *f*; ⚖ *admit to* ~ admitir a caución; *be* (*or* go, stand) ~ *for* salir fiador por; **2.** caucionar; ~ *out* poner en libertad bajo fianza.

bail[2] [~] ⚓ achicar.

bail[3] [~] *cricket:* travesaño *m* del rastrillo.

bail[4] [~] asa *f* *of kettle etc.*

bail·ee [bei'liː] ⚖ depositario *m*.

bail·iff ['beilif] ⚖ alguacil *m*, corchete *m*; mayordomo *m* *on estate.*

bail·ment ['beilmənt] ⚖ afianzamiento *m*; (*goods*) depósito *m*.

bail·or ['beilə] ⚖ depositador (-a *f*) *m*.

bairn [bɛən] *Scot.* niño (a *f*) *m*.

bait [beit] **1.** cebo *m*, carnada *f*; *fig.* aliciente *m*; (*deceitful*) señuelo *m*, añagaza *f*; *swallow the* ~ tragar el anzuelo; **2.** *trap etc.* poner cebo en; *dogs* azuzar; *horses on journey* dar pienso a; *fig.* acosar, atormentar.

bait·ing ['beitiŋ] acoso *m*.

baize [beiz] bayeta *f*; *green* ~ tapete *m* verde.

bake [beik] **1.** cocer al horno; *bricks etc.* cocer; endurecer; **2.** *Am.* banquete *m* al aire libre; '~**house** panadería *f*, tahona *f*.

ba·ke·lite ['beikəlait] baquelita *f*.

bak·er ['beikə] panadero *m*; **bak·er·y** panadería *f*; '**bak·ing** hornada *f*; cocción *f*; F *it's* ~ (*hot*) hace un calor sofocante; '**bak·ing-pow·der** polvos *m/pl.* de levadura, polvo *m* de hornear.

bak·sheesh ['bækʃiːʃ] propina *f*.

bal·a·lai·ka [bælə'laikə] balalaika *f*.

bal·ance ['bæləns] **1.** (*scales*) balanza *f*; equilibrio *m* (a. *fig.*); ✝ balance *m*; ✝ saldo *m* *of account etc.*; (*watch*) volante *m*; *esp. Am.* F resto *m*; ~ *in hand* ✝ alcance *m*; sobrante *m*; ~ *of payments* balance *m* de pagos; ~ *of power* equilibrio *m* político; ~ *of trade* balance *m* de comercio; *fig. in the* ~ en la balanza; *v. strike*; **2.** *v/t.* equilibrar; contrapesar (*with con*); ✝ saldar, finiquitar; *v/i.* equilibrarse, balancearse; menvarse; ~ *up* finiquitar; '~-**sheet** ✝ balance *m*, avanzo *m*.

bal·co·ny ['bælkəni] balcón *m*, mirador *m*; *thea.* anfiteatro *m*.

bald [bɔːld] ☐ calvo; *countryside* pelado; *fig.* sin adornos, franco, escueto, desnudo.

bal·da·chin ['bɔːldəkin] baldaquín *m*.

bal·der·dash ['bɔːldədæʃ] galimatías *m*; disparate *m*.

bald...: '~-**head**, '~-**pate** calvo *m*; '~-'**head·ed** calvo; F *go* ~ *into* meterse de ligero en; '**bald·ness** calvicie *f*; *fig.* desnudez *f*.

bal·dric ['bɔːldrik] tahalí *m*.

bale[1] [beil] ✝ **1.** fardo *m*, bala *f*; **2.** embalar.

bale[2] [~] ⚓ achicar; ✈ ~ *out* lanzarse en paracaídas.

bale·ful ['beilful] ☐ funesto; (*look*) triste.

balk [bɔːk] **1.** ⚷ lomo *m* (entre surcos); *fig.* obstáculo *m*, estorbo *m*; (*timber*) viga *f*; (*billiards*) cabaña *f*; **2.** *v/t.* frustrar, impedir; perder, evitar; *v/i.* (*horse*) plantarse (*a. fig.*; *at* al ver), repropriarse.

Bal·kan ['bɔːlkən] balcánico.

ball[1] [bɔːl] **1.** bola *f*; globo *m*, esfera *f*; (*tennis etc.*) pelota *f*; (*football*) balón *m*; (*cannon*) bala *f*; (*wool*) ovillo *m*; *Am. baseball*: tiro *m* falso; F *keep the* ~ *rolling* mantener en marcha (*esp.* la conversación); *Am.* F *play* ~ cooperar (*with con*); **2.** convertir en bolas; *sl.* ~ *up* echarlo todo a rodar.

ball[2] [~] baile *m*; *dress* ~ baile *m* de etiqueta.

bal·lad ['bæləd] romance *m*; ♪ balada *f*.

ball-and-sock·et ['bɔːlən'sɔkit]: ~ *joint* articulación *f* esférica.

bal·last ['bæləst] **1.** ⚓ lastre *m* (a. *fig.*); 🚂 balasto *m*; **2.** ⚓ lastrar; 🚂 balastar.

ball...: '~-'**bear·ing** cojinete *m* a bolas; '~-**boy** mozo *m* que recoge las pelotas; '~-**car·tridge** cápsula *f* con bala.

bal·let ['bælei] ballet *m*, baile *m*.

bal·lis·tics [bə'listiks] *mst sg.* balística *f*.

bal·loon [bə'luːn] **1.** 🎈 *a.* ✈ globo *m*; *mot.* ~ *tyre* llanta *f* balón; **2.** subir en un globo; ~ (*out*) hincharse como un globo; ** bal'loon-fab·ric** tela *f* de globo; **bal'loon·ist** ascensionista *m/f*.

bal·lot ['bælət] **1.** balota *f*, papeleta *f* (para votar); sufragio *m*; votación *f*; **2.** balotar, votar; ~ *for* determinar por balota; '~-**box** urna *f* electoral.

ball-point-pen ['bɔːlpɔint'pen] bolígrafo *m*. [baile.]

ball·room ['bɔːlrum] salón *m* de baile)

bal·ly·hoo [bæli'huː] **1.** F alharaca *f*; bombo *m*; propaganda *f* sensacional; **2.** *Am.* F dar bombo a.

balm [bɑːm] bálsamo *m* (a. *fig.*).

balm·y ['bɑːmi] ☐ balsámico, fragante; *sl.* chiflado.

ba·lo·ney [bə'louni] *sl.* sandez *f*, tontería *f*.

bal·sam ['bɔːlsəm] bálsamo *m*; **bal·sam·ic** [~'sæmik] ☐ balsámico.

bal·us·ter ['bæləstə] balaustre *m*.

bal·us·trade [bæləs'treid] balaustrada *f*, barandilla *f*.

bam·boo [bæm'buː] bambú *m*.

bam·boo·zle [bæm'buːzl] F embaucar, capotear.

ban [bæn] **1.** bando *m*, edicto *m*; bando *m* de destierro; excomunión *f*; prohibición *f* (*on* de); **2.** prohibir; proscribir; excomulgar; ~ *a p. from a th.* prohibir a una p. (el uso de) algo.

ba·nan·a [bə'nɑːnə] plátano *m*; banana *f* S.Am.; *radio*: ~ *plug* clavija *f* con hembrilla.

band [bænd] **1.** banda *f* (*a. radio*), faja *f*; (*edge of garment*) cenefa *f*; (*hat-*) cintillo *m*; (*group*) cuadrilla *f*, gavilla *f*; ♪ banda *f*, música *f*; **2.** orlar; rayar *with stripes*; (*group*) apandillar(se), acuadrillarse; ~ *together* asociarse.

band·age ['bændidʒ] **1.** vendaje *m*, venda *f*; *first aid* ~ vendaje *m* provisional; **2.** vendar. [de hierbas.)

ban·dan·na [bæn'dɑːnə] pañuelo *m*)

band·box ['bændbɔks] caja *f* de cartón; *as if he came out of a* ~ aseadísimo, acicalado.

ban·dit ['bændit] bandido *m*; **'ban·dit·ry** bandolerismo *m*, bandidaje *m*.   [tor de banda.)

band·mas·ter ['bændmɑːstə] direc-)

ban·do·leer [bændə'liə] bandolera *f*.

bands·man ['bændzmən] músico *m* de banda; **'band·stand** quiosco *m* de música; **'band·wag·on** *esp. Am.* F *pol. a. fig.* partido *m* político que triunfa; *get* (*climb*) *on the* ~ adherirse al partido que gana.

ban·dy ['bændi] **1.** hockey *m* (sobre hielo) (*a.* '~*-ball*); **2.** *ball* pelotear, pasar de uno a otro; *words etc.* cambiar, trocar; *a. fig.* ~ *about* divulgar, esparcir; **'~-leg·ged** estevado.

bane [bein] azote *m*; ruina *f*; *it's the* ~ *of my life!* ¡causará mi perdición!; **bane·ful** ['beinful] □ funesto; nocivo.

bang [bæŋ] **1.** ¡pum!; **2.** F precisamente (~ *across etc.*); *sl.* ~ *on* acertado; **3.** detonación *f*; estallido *m*; golpe *m on head etc.*; contusión *f*; *Am.* (*hair*) flequillo *m*; **4.** golpear, cerrar *etc.* con estrépito; *Am.* cortar en flequillo; *sl. price* rebajar.

ban·gle ['bæŋgl] ajorca *f*.

bang-up ['bæŋ'ʌp] *Am. sl.* de primera.

ban·ish ['bæniʃ] desterrar (*a. fig.*); **'ban·ish·ment** destierro *m*.

ban·is·ter ['bænistə] balaustre *m*; **ban·is·ters** ['~z] *pl.* barandilla *f*.

ban·jo ['bændʒou] banjo *m*.

bank [bæŋk] **1.** ribera *f*, orilla *f*, margen *f*; banda *f*, montón *m of clouds*; banco *m of sand*; (*hill*) loma *f*; batería *f of lamps*; hilera *f of oars*; ♦ banco *m*; (*in games*) banca *f*; (*piggy-*) ~ hucha *f*, alcancía *f*; ~ *of deposit* banco *m* de depósito; ~ *of issue* banco *m* de emisión; **2.** *v/t. fire* cubrir (*a.* ~ *up*); *water* represar, estancar; *pile* amontonar (*a.* ~ *up*); ✈ ladear; *v/i.* dedicarse a negocios de banca; depositar dinero (*with* en); ✈ ladearse; F ~ *on* contar con; **'bank·a·ble** recibidero (en un banco); **'bank-ac·count** cuenta *f* de banco; **'bank-bill** obligación *f* de banco; *Am.* = *banknote*; **'bank-book** libreta *f* (de depósitos); **'bank·er** banquero *m* (*a. in games*); **'bank-hol·i·day** día *m* feriado en que están cerrados los bancos; **'bank·ing 1.** rampas *f/pl.*, terraplén *m*; ♦ banca *f*; ✈ ladearse *m*; **2.** ♦ bancario; **'bank·ing-house** casa *f* de banca; **'bank-note** billete *m* de banco; **'bank-rate** tipo *m* de interés (*or* descuento) bancario; **bank·rupt** ['~rʌpt] **1.** quebrado *m*, fallido *m*; ~'s *estate* activo *m* de la quiebra; **2.** quebrado, insolvente; *fig.* ~ *in* (*or* ~ *of*) falto de; *go* ~ hacer bancarrota, quebrar; **3.** hacer quebrar, arruinar; **bank·rupt·cy** ['~rəptsi] bancarrota *f*, quiebra *f*; *declaration of* ~ declaración *f* de quiebra.

ban·ner ['bænə] **1.** bandera *f*, estandarte *m*; ~ *headlines pl.* titulares *m/pl.* sensacionales; **2.** *adj. Am.* primero en dignidad.

banns [bænz] *pl.* amonestaciones *f/pl.* (de matrimonio); *call the* ~ amonestar, correr las amonestaciones.

ban·quet ['bæŋkwit] **1.** banquete *m*; **2.** banquetear (*v/i. a. v/t.*); ~*ing hall* comedor *m* de gala.

ban·shee [bæn'ʃiː] *Scot., Ir.* hada *f* que anuncia una muerte.

ban·tam ['bæntəm] gallinilla *f* (de) Bantam; *fig.* persona *f* de pequeña talla y amiga de pelear; **'~-weight** peso *m* gallo.

ban·ter ['bæntə] **1.** zumba *f*, chanza *f*; **2.** chancear(se con); burlar(se de); '**ban·ter·er** zumbón (-a *f*) *m*.

bap·tism ['bæptizm] bautismo *m* (*a. fig.*); (*act*) bautizo *m*; **bap·tismal** [bæp'tizməl] bautismal.

bap·tist ['bæptist] bautista *m*; (*sect*) baptista *m*/*f*; '**bap·tis·ter·y** bautisterio *m*; **bap·tize** [ˌ'taiz] bautizar (*a. fig.*).

bar [bɑ:] **1.** barra *f* (*a.* ₤₤ *a.* heraldry); vara *f*, varilla *f*; (*securing*) tranca *f*; (*window*) reja *f*; (*tavern*) bar *m*; (*counter*) mostrador *m*; (*river*) barra *f*; ♪ compás *m*; *fig.* impedimento *m* (to para); *fig.* tribunal *m* of public opinion etc.; parallel ⌐s *pl.* (barras) paralelas *f*/*pl.*; ₤₤ be called to the ⌐ recibirse de abogado; ₤₤ prisoner at the ⌐ acusado *m*; ₤₤ stand at the ⌐ comparecer ante el tribunal (*a. fig.*); **2.** *door* atrancar; barrear; impedir, obstruir; prohibir; (*a.* ⌐ out) excluir.

barb [bɑ:b] lengüeta *f* of arrow etc.; *zo.* púa *f*; **barbed** armado de lengüetas (*or* púas); *fig.* incisivo, mordaz; ⌐ wire ⚔ alambre *m* de púas (de espino *for fences*).

bar·bar·i·an [bɑ:'bɛəriən] bárbaro *adj. a. su. m* (a *f*) (*a. fig.*); **bar·bar·ic** [ˌ'bærik] ▢ barbárico; de ruda magnificencia; **bar·ba·rism** ['ˌbərizm] barbarismo *m* of language etc.; barbarie *f*; **bar·bar·i·ty** [ˌ'bæriti] barbaridad *f*; **bar·ba·rize** ['ˌbəraiz] barbarizar; '**bar·ba·rous** ▢ bárbaro.

bar·be·cue ['bɑ:bikju:] barbacoa *f* S.Am.; *fiesta al aire libre en la que se come carne asada.*

bar·bel ['bɑ:bl] barbo *m*.

bar·ber ['bɑ:bə] barbero *m*, peluquero *m*; ⌐'s (*shop*) peluquería *f*.

bard [bɑ:d] bardo *m*.

bare [bɛə] **1.** ▢ desnudo; *head* descubierto; *landscape* pelado, raso; *clothes etc.* raído; *style* escueto; *room* con pocos muebles; desprovisto (*of* de); mero; *v. lay*, **2.** desnudar, descubrir; '⌐**-back** montado en pelo; *adv.* en pelo, sin montura; '**bare·faced** ▢ descarado, fresco; '**bare·fac·ed·ness** descaro *m*, desfachatez *f*; '**bare-'foot·ed** descalzo; '**bare-'head·ed** descubierto; '**bare-'leg·ged** en pernetas; '**bare-**

ly apenas, solamente; '**bare·ness** desnudez *f* (*a. fig.*); desabrigo *m*.

bar·gain ['bɑ:gin] **1.** pacto *m*, convenio *m*; (*cheap th.*) ganga *f*; negocio *m* ventajoso (para el comprador); ⌐ counter baratillo *m*; ⌐ price precio *m* irrisorio; F it's a ⌐! ¡hecho!; into the ⌐ de añadidura; por más señas; make (*or* strike) a ⌐ cerrar un trato; make the best of a bad ⌐ poner a mal tiempo buena cara; **2.** negociar; F regatear (*freq.* away); ⌐ for (*freq. with negative*) contar con.

barge [bɑ:dʒ] **1.** gabarra *f*, barcaza *f*; (*esp. ceremonial*) falúa *f*; **2.** F (*a.* ⌐ about) moverse pesadamente, dar tumbos; F ⌐ in entrar sin pedir permiso; irrumpir; F ⌐ into entrometerse en, inmiscuirse en; **bar'gee**, '**barge·man** gabarrero *m*.

bar·i·ron ['bɑ:aiən] hierro *m* en barras.

bar·i·tone ['bæritoun] barítono *m*.

bar·i·um ['bɛəriəm] bario *m*.

bark[1] **1.** corteza *f*; ⊕ casca *f* for tanning; **2.** descortezar; *skin* raer.

bark[2] [ˌ] **1.** ladrar (*a. fig.*: at a); ⌐ up the wrong tree tomar el rábano por las hojas; **2.** ladrido *m*; *sl.* tos *f*.

bark[3] [ˌ] ♫ = barque; *poet.* barca *f*.

bar·keep·er ['bɑ:ki:pə] tabernero *m*.

bar·ley ['bɑ:li] cebada *f*.

barm [bɑ:m] levadura *f* (de cerveza).

bar·maid ['bɑ:meid] moza *f* de taberna.

bar·man ['bɑ:mən] *v. bartender.*

barm·y ['bɑ:mi] espumoso; *sl.* chiflado.

barn [bɑ:n] granero *m*, troje *f*; *esp. Am.* establo *m*, cuadra *f*.

bar·na·cle[1] ['bɑ:nəkl] *orn.* bernicla *f*; *zo.* percebe *m*.

bar·na·cle[2] [ˌ] *vet.* acial *m*; F ⌐s gafas *f*/*pl.*

barn·storm ['bɑ:nstɔ:m] *Am. pol.* ir por el campo pronunciando discursos políticos.

ba·rom·e·ter [bə'rɔmitə] barómetro *m*; **bar·o·met·ric, bar·o·met·ri·cal** [bærə'metrik(l)] ▢ barométrico.

bar·on ['bærən] barón *m*; *fig.* potentado *m*; ⌐ of beef solomillo *m* doble (de carne de vaca); '**bar·on·age** nobleza *f*; '**bar·on·ess** baronesa *f*;

bar·on·et ['ːit] baronet *m*; **bar·on·et·cy** ['ːsi] título *m* de baronet; **ba·ro·ni·al** [bə'rouniəl] baronial; **bar·o·ny** ['bærəni] baronía *f*.

ba·roque [bə'rɔk] barroco *adj. a. su. m.* [barca *f*.

barque [bɑ:k] bricbarca *f*; *poet.*

bar·rack ['bærək] 1. (*mst* ːs *pl.*) cuartel *m*; F *approx.* caserón *m*; 2. F mofarse de; 'ː-square', 'ːyard plaza *f* de armas.

bar·rage ['bærɑ:ʒ] (*water*) presa *f*; ✗ barrera *f* de fuego; ː balloon globo *m* de barrera; *creeping* ː barrera *f* de fuego móvil.

bar·rel ['bærl] 1. tonel *m*, cuba *f*; (*gun, pen*) cañón *m*; (*capstan, watch*) cilindro *m*; ⊕ tambor *m*; 2. embarrilar, entonelar; '**bar·rel·or·gan** ♪ organillo *m*.

bar·ren ['bærən] □ estéril; árido; *fig.* infructuoso; '**bar·ren·ness** esterilidad *f*; aridez *f*.

bar·ri·cade [bæri'keid] 1. barricada *f*; 2. barrear, cerrar con barricadas.

bar·ri·er ['bæriə] barrera *f* (*a. fig.*); ✝ fielato *m*.

bar·ring ['bɑ:riŋ] F excepto, salvo.

bar·ris·ter ['bæristə] (*a.* ː-at-law) *British:* abogado *que tiene derecho a alegar en los tribunales superiores*; *Am.* F abogado *m*.

bar·row[1] ['bærou] carretilla *f*; carreta *f*; 'ː-boy carretonero *m* que vende fruta y legumbres en la calle.

bar·row[2] [ˏ] *hist.* túmulo *m*.

bar·tend·er ['bɑ:tendə] tabernero *m*, barman *m*.

bar·ter ['bɑ:tə] 1. permutación *f*, trueque *m* (de bienes); 2. trocar, permutar (*for por, con*); *b.s.* (*mst* ː away*) derrochar, malvender.

ba·salt ['bæsɔ:lt] basalto *m*; **ba·sal·tic** [bə'sɔ:ltik] basáltico.

base[1] [beis] □ bajo, humilde; vil, ruin; infame; *metals* bajo de ley.

base[2] [ˏ] 1. base *f*; △ basa *f*; 2. basar, fundar ([up]on en; *a. fig.*); ✗ aterrizar; ː o.s. on apoyarse en; *be* ːd [up]on estribar en, basarse en.

base...: 'ː-ball béisbol *m*; 'ː-less infundado; 'ː-line *surv.* línea *f* de base; *tennis:* línea *f* de saque; '**base·ment** sótano *m*.

base·ness ['beisnis] bajeza *f*, vileza *f* *etc.* (*v. base*[1]).

bash·ful ['bæʃful] □ tímido, encogido; vergonzoso.

bas·ic ['beisik] □ fundamental; ♏ básico; ♀ English (= *British, American, Scientific, International, Commercial English*) inglés *m* básico; ː slag escoria *f* básica.

ba·sil·i·ca [bə'zilikə] basílica *f*.

bas·i·lisk ['bæzilisk] basilisco *m*.

ba·sin ['beisn] (*small*) escudilla *f*, cuenca *f*; (*wash-*) jofaina *f*; (*river*) cuenca *f*; (*port*) dársena *f*; (*fountain*) taza *f*.

ba·sis ['beisis], *pl.* **ba·ses** ['ːi:z] base *f*, fundamento *m*; *on the* ː *of a* base de.

bask [bɑ:sk] asolearse, tomar el sol.

bas·ket ['bɑ:skit] cesta *f*; (*big*) cesto *m*; (*with two handles*) canasta *f*; 'ː-ball baloncesto *m*; ː din·ner, ː sup·per *Am. approx.* comida *f* campestre; '**bas·ket·ful** cestada *f*; '**bas·ket·work** cestería *f*.

Basque [bɑ:sk] 1. vasco *adj. a. su. m* (*a f*); 2. (*language*) vascuence *m*.

bas-re·lief [beisri'li:f] bajorrelieve *m*.

bass[1] [beis] ♪ bajo *m*. [*m*.]

bass[2] [bæs] corteza *f* de tilo; *Am.* ː wood tilo *m* americano.

bas·si·net [bæsi'net] cuna *f* hecha de mimbres.

bas·so ['bæsou]: ː profundo bajo *m* profundo.

bas·soon [bə'su:n] bajón *m*.

bas·tard ['bæstəd] □ bastardo *adj. a. su. m* (*a f*); '**bas·tar·dy** bastardía *f*.

baste[1] [beist] *sew.* hilvanar.

baste[2] [ˏ] *joint* pringar; F dar de palos.

bas·tion ['bæstiən] baluarte *m* (*a. fig.*).

bat[1] [bæt] *zo.* murciélago *m*; *blind as a* ː más ciego que un topo.

bat[2] [ˏ] 1. *sport:* maza *f*; *off one's own* ː sin ayuda; de suyo; *Am.* F *right off the* ː de repente, sin deliberación; 2. golpear (con un palo *etc.*); *Am.* F *come* (*or go*) *to* ː *for* ayudar.

bat[3] [ˏ] *Am.* guiñar; *without* ːting *an eyelid* sin emoción, sin pestañear.

batch [bætʃ] *cooking:* hornada *f*; colección *f*, grupo *m*; (*set*) tanda *f*; lío *m of papers.*

bate [beit] disminuir; *price* rebajar; *with* ːd *breath* con aliento suspenso.

Bath[1] [bɑ:θ]: ː *brick* piedra *f* para limpiar cuchillos; ♀-*chair* silla *f* de ruedas.

bath² [~] **1.** (pl. **baths** [bɑː̃z]) baño m; piscina f for swimming; fig. blood ~ carnicería f; take a ~ tomar un baño; **2.** v/t. bañar; v/i. tomar un baño.

bathe [beið] **1.** bañar(se); **2.** baño m (en el mar etc.); go for a ~ ir a bañarse.

bath·ing ['beiθiŋ] **1.** baño m; **2.** attr. de baño; '~-**cap** gorro m de baño; '~-**cos'tume** (a. '~-**suit**) traje m de baño; '~-**hut** caseta f; '~-**trunks** pl. taparrabo m; '~-**wrap** albornoz m.

ba·thos ['beiθɔs] paso m de lo sublime a lo ridículo (or trivial).

bath…: '~-**robe** Am. albornoz m; '~-**room** cuarto m de baño; ~ fixtures pl. aparatos m/pl. sanitarios; '~-**salts** pl. sales f/pl. de baño; '~-**tow·el** toalla f de baño; '~-**tub** bañadera f.

ba·tiste [bæ'tiːst] batista f.

bat·man ['bætmən] ordenanza m.

ba·ton ['bætən] ✗ bastón m; ♪ batuta f.

ba·tra·chi·an [bə'treikjən] batracio adj. a. su. m.

bat·tal·ion [bə'tæljən] batallón m.

bat·ten ['bætn] **1.** alfarjía f, lata f, listón m; **2.** listonar; asegurar con listones (✈ a. ~ down); esp. fig. ~ on cebarse en.

bat·ter ['bætə] **1.** pasta f, batido m; sport: bateador m; **2.** apalear; magullar; ✗ cañonear; fig. criticar severamente; ~ down, ~ in door etc. derribar; '**bat·ter·ed** apaleado, fig. ajado; '**bat·ter·ing** paliza f; castigo m; ~ ram ariete m; '**bat·ter·y** ✗, ♪, baseball: batería f; ♪ pila f, acumulador m; ⚡ violencia f (esp. assault and ~); '**bat·ter·y-charg·er** cargador m de acumulador.

bat·tle ['bætl] **1.** batalla f; combate m; ~ royal pelotera f; do ~ librar batalla; **2.** batallar (against contra; with con); luchar (for por); '~-**axe** hacha f de combate; fig. old ~ mujer f severa.

bat·tle·dore ['bætldɔː] raqueta f (en el juego de volante).

bat·tle…: '~-**dress** traje m de campaña; '~-**field** campo m de batalla; '~-**ments** ['bætlmənts] pl. almenas f/pl.; '~-**ship** acorazado m.

bat·tue [bæ'tuː] hunt. batida f.

bau·ble ['bɔːbl] chuchería f.

baulk [bɔːk] v. balk.

baux·ite ['bɔːksait] bauxita f.

Ba·var·i·an [bə'veəriən] bávaro adj. a. su. m (a f).

baw·bee [bɔː'biː] Scot. = halfpenny.

bawd [bɔːd] alcahueta f; '**bawd·y** ☐ obsceno, impúdico; ~ house lupanar m.

bawl [bɔːl] v/i. vocear, desgañitarse (freq. ~ out); ~ at s.o. reñir a una p. en voz alta; v/t. Am. sl. ~ out reñir, regañar.

bay¹ [bei] horse (caballo m) bayo approx.

bay² [~] ⚓ bahía f, abra f; (large) golfo m; ~ salt sal f morena.

bay³ [~] ⚠ crujía f; 🚢 nave f.

bay⁴ [~] 🌿 laurel m.

bay⁵ [~] **1.** ladrar, aullar; **2.** ladrido m, aullido m; at ~ acosado, acorralado; keep at ~ mantener a raya.

bay·o·net ['beiənit] **1.** bayoneta f; **2.** herir (or matar) con la bayoneta.

bay-win·dow ['bei'windou] ventana f saledizo, mirador m; sl. barriga f.

ba·zaar [bə'zaː] bazar m.

be [biː; bi] [irr.]: a) ser; estar; encontrarse; haber; existir; he is a doctor es médico; (location) he is in Madrid está en Madrid; (temporary state) he is ill está (or se encuentra) enfermo; there is, there are hay; so be it (or be it so) así sea; be that as it may sea como fuere; b) auxiliary verb with present participle: I am working trabajo, estoy trabajando; he is coming tomorrow viene mañana; c) auxiliary verb with inf.: I am to go to Spain he de ir a España; d) auxiliary verb with p.p.: ser, estar, quedar; passive (action): he was followed by the police fue seguido por la policía; passive (state): the door is closed la puerta está (or queda) cerrada; e) idioms: mother to ~ futura madre f; my wife to ~ mi futura (esposa); f) for phrases with prp., v. the prp.

beach [biːtʃ] **1.** playa f; **2.** v/t. ⚓ varar; '~-**comb·er** raquero m; '~-**head** ✗ cabeza f de playa.

bea·con ['biːkn] **1.** almenara f, alcandora f; faro m; (hill) hacho m; fig. amonestación f, guía f; **2.** iluminar, guiar.

bead [biːd] **1.** cuenta f, abalorio m; gota f; (gun) mira f globular; ~s pl. sarta f de cuentas; rosario m; tell one's ⁓s rezar el rosario; 2. v/t. adornar con abalorios; v/i. burbujear; 'bead·ing abalorio m; ⚕ astrágalo m, contero m.

bea·dle ['biːdl] bedel m; eccl. pertiguero m.

bead·y ['biːdi] adornado con abalorios; burbujeante; esp. eyes que tienen apariencia de gotas.

beak [biːk] pico m; nariz f (corva esp.); ⚖ rostro m; sl. magistrado m; 'beaked picudo.

beak·er ['biːkə] taza f grande; 🜍 probeta f con pico.

beam [biːm] 1. ⚔ viga f; ⚓ bao m; ⚓ (width) manga f; (plough) timón m; ✢ etc. a. fig. rayo m; (balance) astil m; ⊕ balancín m; on her ⁓ends ⚓ a punto de volcar; F fig. on one's ⁓ ends sin blanca; Am. F on the ⁓ siguiendo el buen camino; 2. brillar; fig. sonreír alegremente.

bean [biːn] ♣ haba f; judía f; Am. sl. cabeza f; F full of ⁓s rebosando de vitalidad; F I haven't a ⁓ no tengo un cuarto; '⁓-feast, bean·o ['biːnou] sl. fiesta f, juerga f; (meal)comilona f.

bear¹ [beə] 1. oso m; fig. hombre m ceñudo; ✝ bajista m/f; ✝ ⁓ market mercado m bajista; 2. ✝ jugar a la baja; ✝ hacer bajar el valor.

bear² [⁓] [irr.] v/t. llevar; (endure) soportar, aguantar; arms, date, inscription, name llevar; interest devengar; love etc. sentir, tener; weight cargar, sostener; child parir; inspection etc. tolerar, sufrir; fruit etc. rendir, producir; costs etc. pagar, costear; ⁓ away llevarse; ganarse; ⁓ down postrar; ⁓ o.s. comportarse; ⁓ out confirmar, apoyar; v/i. dirigirse (a); ⚓ the ship ⁓s north el barco lleva dirección norte; ⚓ ⁓ down upon correr sobre; caer sobre; ⁓ (up)on atañer a; F ⁓ up cobrar ánimo; ⁓ with tener paciencia con; bring to ⁓ pressure etc. ejercer ([up] on sobre); '⁓·a·ble □ llevadero.

beard [biəd] 1. barba f; ♣ arista f; 2. hacer cara a; retar; 'beard·ed barbudo; ♣ aristado; 'beard·less imberbe, lampiño.

bear·er ['beərə] portador (-a f) m (a. ✝); ♣ árbol m fructífero; poseedor (-a f) m of office.

bear·ing ['beəriŋ] aguante m; sustentamiento m; p.'s porte m, modales m/pl.; heraldry: blasón m; as-

pecto m of th.; relación f (on con); ⚓ marcación f; ⊕ cojinete m, apoyo m; take one's ⁓s ⚓ marcarse; fig. orientarse; lose one's ⁓s desorientarse.

beast [biːst] bestia f; fig. hombre m brutal; fig. persona f molesta; F th. cosa f mala (or molesta); ⁓ of burden bestia f de carga; F a ⁓ of a th. molesto, pesado; 'beast·li·ness bestialidad f; 'beast·ly bestial; F molesto, desagradable.

beat [biːt] 1. [irr.] v/t. batir, golpear, pegar; (defeat) vencer; record batir, superar; F sobrepasar, aventajar; F p. confundir; path abrir; hunt. ojear; drum tocar; carpet apalear; ♪ time llevar; v. retreat; sl. ⁓ it! ¡lárgate!; Am. F to ⁓ the band hasta más no poder; Am. F ⁓ one's way hacer un viaje sin pagar; ⁓ down abatir; ✝ price rebajar; ⁓ off rechazar; ⁓ up egg batir; sl. p. aporrear; v/i. batir; (heart) latir; ⚓ ⁓ about barloventear; F ⁓ about the bush andarse por las ramas, ir por rodeos; 2. golpe m; (heart⁓) latido m; (rhythm) marca f; ♪ compás m; (police) ronda f; off (outside) my ⁓ fuera de mi competencia; 3. F deslumbrado, perplejo; engañado; dead ⁓ sl. rendido; 'beat·en p.p. of beat 1; track trillado; 'beat·er hunt. ojeador m.

be·at·i·fi·ca·tion [biːætifiˈkeiʃn] beatificación f; be·at·i·fy beatificar; be·at·i·tude [⁓tjuːd] beatitud f; the ⁓s pl. las Bienaventuranzas.

beau [bou] galán m; b. s. petimetre m; ⁓ ideal lo bello ideal.

beau·ti·ful ['bjuːtəful] □ hermoso, bello; ⁓ly F maravillosamente, muy bien.

beau·ti·fy ['bjuːtifai] embellecer.

beau·ty ['bjuːti] belleza f, hermosura f; (woman) beldad f; F it's a ⁓ es bárbaro; sleeping ♀ la Bella Durmiente (del bosque); ⁓ contest concurso m de belleza; ⁓ parlour salón m de belleza; ⁓ spot (face) lunar m postizo; (place) sitio m pintoresco.

bea·ver ['biːvə] zo. castor m; (helmet) babera f; (hat) sombrero m de copa.

be·bop ['biːbɔp] variación sobre el jazz tradicional.

be·calm [biˈkɑːm] sosegar; ⚓ be ⁓ed encalmarse.

be·came [biˈkeim] pret. of become.

be·cause [bi'kɔz] porque; ~ of a causa de.

beck [bek] seña *f*; *at the* ~ *and call of* a disposición de.

beck·on ['bekn] hacer seña (*to* a); llamar con señas; *fig.* atraer.

be·come [bi'kʌm] [*irr.* (come)] *v/i.* ser, hacerse (*of* de); *what will* ~ *of me? ¿* qué será de mí?; *v/t. mst with su.* hacerse; *mst with adj.* ponerse; llegar a ser; convertirse en; (*action*) convenir a; (*clothes esp.*) sentar a, favorecer; **be'com·ing** □ decoroso; *clothes* que sienta bien.

bed [bed] **1.** cama *f*; (*a. animals*) lecho *m*; (*river-*) cauce *m*; ✗ macizo *m*, arriate *m*; ⊕ base *f*, apoyo *m*; *geol.* capa *f*, yacimiento *m*; ~ *and board* comida *f* y casa; ~ *jacket* mañanica *f*; *be brought to* ~ *of* parir; F *get up on the wrong side of the* ~ levantarse por los pies de la cama; *go to* ~ acostarse; *make the* ~ hacer la cama; *stay in* ~ guardar cama; *take to* (*one's*) ~ encamarse; **2.** acostar; ⊕ engastar, embutir; ✗ ~ (*out*) plantar en un macizo.

be·daub [bi'dɔ:b] embadurnar.

be·dazzle [bi'dæzl] deslumbrar.

bed·clothes ['bedklouðz] *pl.* ropa *f* de cama.

bed·ding ['bediŋ] ropa *f* de cama; colchón *m*; (*animals*) lecho *m*.

be·deck [bi'dek] acicalar, engalanar.

be·dev·il [bi'devl] endiablar (*a. fig.*); hechizar; **be'dev·il·ment** hechizo *m*; confusión *f*.

be·dew [bi'dju:] *poet.* rociar.

bed·fel·low ['bedfelou] compañero *m* de cama.

be·dim [bi'dim] oscurecer.

bed·lam ['bedləm] manicomio *m*; *fig.* belén *m*.

bed·lin·en ['bedlinin] ropa *f* de cama; las sábanas.

Bed·ou·in ['beduin] beduino *adj. a. su. m* (*a f*).

bed·pan ['bedpæn] silleta *f*.

be·drag·gle [bi'drægl] ensuciar; *clothes etc.* manchar.

bed...: '~-**rid**(·**den**) postrado en cama; '~-'**rock** *geol.* lecho *m* de roca; *fig.* fundamento *m*; '~-**room** dormitorio *m*, alcoba *f*; '~-**side:** *at the* ~ *of* a la cabecera de; *good* ~ *manner* mano *f* izquierda, diplomacia *f*; ~ *table* mesa *f* de noche; '~-'**sit·ting-room** (F '~-'**sit·ter**) salón

m con cama; '~-**sore** úlcera *f* de decúbito; '~-**spread** colcha *f*, sobrecama *m*; '~-**stead** cuja *f*; '~-**straw** cuajaleche *m*, amor *m* de hortelano; '~-**tick** cutí *m*; '~-**time** hora *f* de acostarse.

bee [bi:] abeja *f*; *Am. fig.* reunión *f*; F *have a* ~ *in one's bonnet* tener una idea fija.

beech [bi:tʃ] haya *f*; '~-**nut** hayuco *m*.

beef [bi:f] **1.** carne *f* de vaca; F fuerza *f* muscular; **2.** *Am.* F quejarse; '~-**eat·er** alabardero *m* de la Torre de Londres; ~**steak** ['bi:f'steik] biftec *m*, bistec *m*; '~-'**tea** caldo *m* concentrado de carne; '**beef·y** fornido; carnoso.

bee...: '~-**hive** colmena *f*; '~-**keep·er** colmenero *m*; '~-**keep·ing** apicultura *f*; '~-'**line** línea *f* recta *gen. in make a* ~ *for* ir en línea recta hacia.

been [bi:n, bin] *p.p. of be.*

beer [biə] cerveza *f*; *small* ~ cerveza floja; F bagatela *f*; '**beer·y** F de cerveza; alcohólico.

bees·wax ['bi:zwæks] cera *f* (de abejas).

beet [bi:t] remolacha *f*; *v. sugar* ~.

bee·tle[1] [bi:tl] ⊕ **1.** pisón *m*; **2.** apisonar.

beet·le[2] [~] *zo.* **1.** escarabajo *m*; **2.** *sl.* ~ *off* largarse, volver la cara.

bee·tle[3] [~] **1.** (sobre)saliente; ceñudo; **2.** sobresalir.

beet·root ['bi:tru:t] raíz *f* de remolacha.

beet·sug·ar ['bi:tʃugə] azúcar *m* de remolacha.

be·fall [bi'fɔ:l] [*irr.* (fall)] *v/t.* acontecer a, acaecer a; *v/i.* acontecer; **be'fall·en** *p.p. of befall.*

be·fit [bi'fit] cuadrar a, convenir a; **be·fit·ting** □ propio, conveniente.

be·fog [bi'fɔg] aneblar; *fig.* ofuscar.

be·fore [bi'fɔ:] **1.** *adv.* (*place*) (a)delante; *go* ~ ir adelante; ~ *and be-hind* por delante y por detrás; (*time*) antes; anteriormente; **2.** *cj.* antes (de) que; **3.** *prp.* (*place*) delante de; *judge etc.* ante; (*time*) antes de; *be* (*or go*) ~ *a p.* ir delante de una p., ir primero; **be'fore·hand** de antemano; *be* ~ *with* anticipar.

be·foul [bi'faul] ensuciar, emporcar.

be·friend [bi'frend] ofrecer amistad a; patrocinar.

beg [beg] *v/t.* suplicar, rogar (*of* a);

(*as beggar*) mendigar; *v. pardon, question*; *v/i.* mendigar, pordiosear; rogar (*for a th. acc.*; *of a p.* a); *fig.* go ~ging ofrecerse algo sin presentarse aceptador ninguno; ✝ *I* ~ *to inform you*... tengo el gusto de informarle...

be·gan [bi'gæn] *pret. of begin.*

be·get [bi'get] [*irr.* (get)] engendrar (*a. fig.*); **be'get·ter** engendrador *m.*

beg·gar ['begə] **1.** mendigo (a *f*) *m*, pordiosero (a *f*) *m*; F *contp.* tío *m*; **2.** empobrecer; *fig.* excederse de; *it* ~s *description* supera a toda descripción; '**beg·gar·li·ness** mendicidad *f*; '**beg·gar·ly** indigente; mezquino; '**beg·gar·y** mendicidad *f*; miseria *f*; *reduce to* ~ reducir a la miseria.

be·gin [bi'gin] [*irr.*] comenzar, empezar (*to* a); iniciar; ~ *by* comenzar por; ~ *on s.t.* emprender algo; ~ *with* comenzar con, principiar con; *to* ~ *with* para empezar; en primer lugar; ~ning *from date* a partir de; **be'gin·ner** principiante *m/f*; **be'gin·ning** comienzo *m*, principio *m*; *from* ~ *to end* del principio al fin, de cabo a rabo (F).

be·gone [bi'gɔn] ✝ ¡fuera!; ¡aléjate!

be·go·ni·a [bi'gounjə] begonia *f.*

be·got [bi'gɔt] *pret. a. p.p. of beget*; **be·got·ten** [bi'gɔtn] *p.p. of beget*; *the only* ♀ *Son* El Unigénito.

be·grime [bi'graim] embadurnar, embarrar; tiznar *with soot etc.*

be·grudge [bi'grʌdʒ] dar de mala gana; (*envy*) envidiar.

be·guile [bi'gail] engañar, seducir; *fig.* entretener; ~ *into* inducir (por engaño) en *acc.*, a *inf.*

be·gun [bi'gʌn] *p.p. of begin.*

be·half [bi'hɑ:f]: *on* ~ *of* a favor de, en nombre de; por.

be·have [bi'heiv] (com)portarse; ⊕ *etc.* funcionar, actuar; ~ *o.s.* portarse bien; **be'hav·io(u)r** [~jə] conducta *f*, comportamiento *m*; ⊕ *etc.* funcionamiento *m*; **be'hav·io(u)r·ism** behaviorismo *m.*

be·head [bi'hed] descabezar; decapitar.

be·held [bi'held] *pret. a. p.p. of behold.*

be·hest [bi'hest] orden *f.*

be·hind [bi'haind] **1.** *adv.* (por) detrás; (hacia) atrás; *be* ~ (*late*) retrasarse; F *be a bit* ~ estar un poco

atrasadillo; **2.** *prp.* detrás de; **be'hind·hand** con retraso, retrasado.

be·hold [bi'hould] [*irr.* (hold)] *lit.* **1.** contemplar; advertir, columbrar; **2.** ¡he aquí!; ¡mira(d)!; **be'hold·en** obligado; **be'hold·er** observador (-a *f*) *m.*

be·hove [bi'houv]: *it* ~s *a p. to inf.* incumbe a una p. *inf.*

beige [beiʒ] **1.** beige *m*; **2.** color de beige, amarillento.

be·ing ['bi:iŋ] ser *m*; existencia *f*; *in* ~ existente; *come into* ~ producirse; nacer.

be·jew·elled [bi'dʒu:əld] enjoyado.

be·la·bo(u)r [bi'leibə] apalear; *fig.* zurrar.

be·lat·ed [bi'leitid] □ demorado, tardío.

be·lay [bi'lei] **1.** [*irr.*] ⚓ amarrar a una cabilla *or* hierro; **2.** *mount.* atadura *f.*

belch [beltʃ] **1.** eructar, regoldar; *fig.* echar, arrojar; **2.** eructación *f*, regüeldo *m.*

bel·dam ['beldəm] *fig.* bruja *f.*

be·lea·guer [bi'li:gə] sitiar.

bel·fry ['belfri] campanario *m.*

Bel·gian ['beldʒən] belga *adj. a. su. m/f.*

be·lie [bi'lai] desmentir.

be·lief [bi'li:f] creencia *f*, crédito *m*; fe *f* (*in* en; *that* de que); (*opinion*) parecer *m*; *past all* ~ increíble; *to the best of my* ~ según mi leal saber y entender.

be·liev·a·ble [bi'li:vəbl] creíble.

be·lieve [bi'li:v] creer (*in* en); ~ *in story etc.* dar crédito a; F (*not*) ~ *in e.g. drink* (no) aprobar; *don't you* ~ *it!* ¡no lo crea(s)!; **be'liev·er** creyente *m/f*; F partidario (a *f*) *m* (*in* de).

be·lit·tle [bi'litl] *fig.* deprimir, despreciar.

bell [bel] campana *f*; (*hand-*) campanilla *f* (*a.* ♀); (*electric*) timbre *m*; (*animal's*) cencerro *m*; cascabel *m*; ♪ pabellón *m of trumpet etc.*; *fig. that rings a* ~ eso me suena.

bell·boy ['belbɔi] botones *m.*

belle [bel] beldad *f*, guapetona *f.*

belles-let·tres ['bel'letr] bellas letras *f/pl.*

bell...: '~**flow·er** campanilla *f*; '~**found·er** ⊕ campanero *m*; '~**glass** campana *f* de cristal; '~**hop** *Am sl.* botones *m.*

bel·li·cose ['belikous] belicoso; **bel·li·cos·i·ty** [‿'kɔsiti] belicosidad *f*.
bel·lied ['belid] panzudo; convexo, combado.
bel·lig·er·ent [bi'lidʒərənt] ☐ beligerante *adj. a. su. m/f*; **bel·lig·er·en·cy** beligerancia *f*.
bel·low ['belou] **1.** bramar; (*p*.) gritar, dar voces; **2** bramido *m*.
bel·lows ['belouz] *pl.* (*a pair of* un) fuelle *m* (*a. phot.*); (*forge*) barquín *m*.
bell...: '‿-rope cuerda *f* de campana; '‿-shaped acampanado.
bel·ly ['beli] **1.** vientre *f*; barriga *f* (*a. of vessel*); **2.** combarse; (*sail*) hacer bolso; **'bel·ly·ful** [‿ful] *sl.* panzada *f*; F have had a ‿ estar harto ya (of de).
be·long [bi'lɔŋ] pertenecer (*to* a); corresponder (*to* a); **be'long·ings** [‿iŋz] *pl.* bártulos *m/pl.*; F cosas *f/pl.*
be·lov·ed [bi'lʌvid] querido *adj. a. su. m* (a *f*).
be·low [bi'lou] **1.** *adv.* abajo, debajo; here ‿ en este mundo; **2.** *prp.* debajo de; *fig.* inferior a.
belt [belt] **1.** cinturón *m* (*a.* ⚔), cinto *m*; (*corset*) faja *f*; ⊕ correa *f*, cinta *f*; *fig.* zona *f*; *fig. below the* ‿ sucio, suciamente; *fig. tighten one's* ‿ ceñirse; **2.** *sl.* golpear con correa.
bel·ve·dere ['belvidiə] belvedere *m* (en forma de torre).
be·moan [bi'moun] lamentar.
be·muse [bi'mju:z] aturdir.
bench [ben(t)ʃ] banco *m* (*a.* ⊕); ⚖ tribunal *m*; ⚖ judicatura *f*; be on the ‿ ser juez (*or* magistrado); *v. treasury*; **'bench·er** *approx.* decano *m* de los colegios de abogados.
bend [bend] **1.** curva *f*; recodo *m*, curva *f in road*; ⚓ gaza *f*; F the ‿s *pl.* enfermedad *f* de los cajones de aire comprimido; F go round the ‿ volverse loco; **2.** [*irr.*] combar(se), encorvar(se); *body etc.* inclinar(se); *efforts etc.* dirigir (*to* a); *sail* envergar.
beneath [bi'ni:θ] = below; *fig.* ‿ me indigno de mí; *she married* ‿ her se casó con hombre de clase inferior.
Ben·e·dic·tine [beni'diktain] benedictino *adj. a. su. m* (a. *liqueur* [‿ti:n]).
ben·e·dic·tion [beni'dikʃn] bendición *f*.

ben·e·fac·tion [beni'fækʃn] beneficencia *f*; (*gift*) beneficio *m*; **'ben·e·fac·tor** bienhechor *m*; **'ben·e·fac·tress** bienhechora *f*.
ben·e·fice ['benifis] beneficio *m*; **be·nef·i·cence** [bi'nefisns] beneficencia *f*; **be'nef·i·cent** ☐ benéfico.
ben·e·fi·cial [beni'fiʃl] ☐ beneficioso; ⚖ que goza el usufructo de una propiedad; **ben·e'fi·ci·ar·y** beneficiario (a *f*) *m*; *eccl.* beneficiado *m*.
ben·e·fit ['benifit] **1.** beneficio *m* (*a. thea.*); (*insurance*) lucro *m*; for the ‿ of a beneficio de; **2.** beneficiar, aprovechar; sacar provecho (*by*, *from* de).
be·nev·o·lence [bi'nevələns] benevolencia *f*; **be'nev·o·lent** ☐ benévolo; *society* caritativo.
Ben·gal [beŋ'gɔ:l] bengalí; **Ben·'gal·i** [‿li] bengalí *adj. a. su. m/f*.
be·night·ed [bi'naitid] sorprendido por la noche; *fig.* ignorante.
be·nign [bi'nain] ☐ benigno (*a.* ⚕); **be·nig·nant** [bi'nignənt] ☐ saludable; benigno; **be'nig·ni·ty** benignidad *f*.
bent [bent] **1.** *pret. a. p.p. of* bend[2]; ‿ *on* resuelto a, empeñado en; **2.** inclinación *f*, propensión *f* (*for* a).
be·numb [bi'nʌm] entorpecer, entumecer.
ben·zene ['benzi:n] benceno *m*.
ben·zine ['benzi:n] bencina *f*.
be·queath [bi'kwi:ð] legar (*a. fig.*).
be·quest [bi'kwest] legado *m* (*a. th.*), manda *f*.
be·reave [bi'ri:v] [*irr.*] despojar; *esp.* the ‿d los afligidos; **be'reave·ment** *mst* aflicción *f*, duelo *m*.
be·reft [bi'reft] *pret. a. p.p. of* bereave; be ‿ of ser (*a.* estar) privado de.
be·ret ['berei] boina *f*.
ber·ry ['beri] baya *f*.
berth [bə:θ] **1.** ⚓ fondeadero *m*, amarradero *m for ship*; ⚓ F (*cabin*) camarote *m*; ⚓, 🚢 (*bunk*) litera *f*; F *fig.* puesto *m*; *give a wide* ‿ to esquivar, evitar; **2.** anclar, atracar.
ber·yl ['beril] berilo *m*.
be·seech [bi'si:tʃ] suplicar (*for acc.*); **be'seech·ing** ☐ suplicante.
be·set [bi'set] [*irr.* (set)] acosar (*a. fig.*), perseguir; *road* obstruir; ‿ting sin pecado *m* dominante.

be·side [bi'said] **1.** adv. v. ~s; **2.** prp. cerca de, junto a; en comparación con; ~ o.s. fuera de sí (with con); **be'sides** [~dz] **1.** adv. además, también; **2.** prp. además de; excepto.

be·siege [bi'si:dʒ] asediar (a. fig.), sitiar; **be'sieg·er** asediador m, sitiador m.

be·smear [bi'smiə] embarrar, embadurnar.

be·smirch [bi'smə:tʃ] ensuciar, manchar (a. fig.).

be·som ['bi:zm] escoba f.

be·sot·ted [bi'sɔtid] embrutecido.

be·sought [bi'sɔ:t] pret. a. p.p. of beseech.

be·spat·ter [bi'spætə] salpicar; fig. llenar (with de).

be·speak [bi'spi:k] [irr. (speak)] encargar; apalabrar; indicar; poet. hablar con.

be·spec·ta·cled [bi'spektəkld] con gafas.

be·spoke [be'spouk] pret. a. p.p. of bespeak; ~ tailor sastre m que confecciona a medida; ~ work trabajo m hecho a la medida; **be'spo·ken** p.p. of bespeak.

be·sprin·kle [bi'spriŋkl] salpicar (a. fig.), rociar.

best [best] **1.** adj. sup. mejor; óptimo; ~ girl novia f; ~ man padrino m de boda; v. seller; **2.** adv. sup. mejor; at ~ a lo más; I had ~ go más vale que yo vaya; **3.** su. lo mejor; v. Sunday; do one's ~ hacer como mejor pueda uno; for the ~ con la mejor intención; be for the ~ conducir al bien; F get the ~ of it vencer; make the ~ of salir lo mejor posible de; make the ~ of a bad job sobreponerse.

bes·tial ['bestjəl] □ bestial, brutal; **bes·ti·al·i·ty** [besti'æliti] bestialidad f, brutalidad f.

be·stir [bi'stə:]: ~ o.s. menearse (fig.).

be·stow [bi'stou] conferir, otorgar ([up]on a); **be'stow·al** otorgamiento m, donación f.

be·strew [bi'stru:] [irr.] esparcir; desparramar.

be·strid·den [bi'stridn] p.p. of bestride.

be·stride [bi'straid] [irr.] montar a horcajadas; cruzar de un tranco.

be·strode [bi'stroud] pret. of bestride.

bet [bet] **1.** apuesta f; (sum) postura f; **2.** apostar (on a); F you ~ (your life)! ¡ya lo creo!; I ~ you a shilling that te apuesto un chelín a que; I ~ you can a que puedes.

be·take [bi'teik] [irr. (take)]: ~ o.s. to darse a, aplicarse a; ir a, acudir a.

be·think [bi'θiŋk] [irr. (think)]: ~ o.s. of recapacitar acc.; considerar, recordar acc.; ~ o.s. to inf. ocurrírsele a uno inf.

be·thought pret. a. p.p. of bethink.

be·tide [bi'taid]: woe ~ the man who ...! ¡ay del que ...!

be·times [bi'taimz] temprano; en sazón.

be·to·ken [bi'toukn] presagiar; anunciar, indicar.

be·took [bi'tuk] pret. of betake.

be·tray [bi'trei] traicionar; delatar (a. fig.); fig. revelar, dejar ver; **be·'tray·al** traición f; fig. revelación f; ~ of trust abuso m de confianza; **be'tray·er** traicionero (a f) m, traidor (-a f) m.

be·troth [bi'trouð] prometer en matrimonio; be (or become) ~ed desposarse; **be'troth·al** desposorio m.

bet·ter¹ ['betə] **1.** adj. comp. mejor; he is ~ está mejor; get ~ mejorarse; v. half; **2.** adv. comp. mejor; ~ off más acomodado; so much the ~ tanto mejor; I had ~ go más vale que yo vaya; think ~ of it mudar de parecer; **3.** su. superior m; my ~s pl. mis superiores; get the ~ of llevar la ventaja a; **4.** v/t. mejorar; ~ o.s. mejorar su posición; v/i. progresar, mejorar(se).

bet·ter² [~] apostador (-a f) m.

bet·ter·ment mejoramiento m.

bet·ting ['betiŋ] apostar m; juego m.

be·tween [bi'twi:n] (poet. or prov. a. **be·twixt** [bi'twikst]) **1.** adv. (freq. in ~) en medio, entremedias; betwixt and ~ entre lo uno y lo otro, ni fu ni fa (F); **2.** prp. entre; ~ ourselves entre nosotros; **be'tween-decks** entrecubiertas f/pl.

bev·el ['bevl] **1.** biselado; **2.** ⊕ (instrument) cartabón m, escuadra f falsa; △ baivel m; ⊕ bisel m (a. ~ edge); **3.** v/t. ⊕ biselar; v/i. inclinarse; '~-**wheel** rueda f cónica.

bev·er·age ['bevəridʒ] bebida f.

bev·y ['bevi] (birds) bandada f; (ladies) grupo m.

be·wail [bi'weil] lamentar.

be·ware [bi'wɛə] precaverse (of de);
~! ¡atención!

be·wil·der [bi'wildə] aturdir, aturrullar; desconcertar; **be'wil·der·
ment** aturdimiento *m*; perplejidad *f*.

be·witch [bi'witʃ] hechizar (*a. fig.*),
embrujar; **be'witch·ment** hechizo
m (*a. fig.*); encanto *m*.

be·yond [bi'jɔnd] **1.** *adv.* más allá
(*a. fig.*), más lejos; F *it's* ~! ¡es el
colmo!; **2.** *prp.* más allá de; además
de; fuera de; superior a; ~ *the seas*
allende los mares; *get* ~ *a p.* hacérsele imposible a una p.; *it is* ~ *me*
está fuera de mi alcance; **3.** más
allá *m*.

bi... [bai] bi...

bi·as ['baiəs] **1.** sesgo *m*, diagonal *f*;
fig. pasión *f*, predisposición *f*, prejuicio *m*; *cut on the* ~ cortar al
sesgo; **2.** sesgar; *fig.* influir en,
torcer; *be* ~*sed* tener prejuicio, ser
partidista.

bib [bib] babador *m*, babero *m*.

Bi·ble ['baibl] Biblia *f*.

bib·li·cal ['biblikəl] □ bíblico.

bib·li·og·ra·pher [bibli'ɔgrəfə] bibliógrafo *m*; **bib·li·o·graph·ic,
bib·li·o·graph·i·cal** [ˌou'græfik(l)]
□ bibliográfico; **bib·li·og·ra·phy**
[ˌ'ɔgrəfi] bibliografía *f*; **bib·li·o·
ma·ni·a** [ˌou'meinjə] bibliomanía *f*;
bib·li·o'ma·ni·ac [ˌniæk] bibliómano *m*; **bib·li·o·phile** ['ˌoufail]
bibliófilo *m*.

bib·u·lous ['bibjuləs] □ *p.* bebedor,
borrachín; hidrófilo.

bi·car·bon·ate of so·da [bai'kɑː-
bənitəv'soudə] bicarbonato *m* sódico.

bi·ceps ['baiseps] bíceps *m*.

bick·er ['bikə] (*quarrel*) altercar,
pararse en quisquillas; (*stream*)
murmurar; **'bick·er·ing** riña *f*.

bi·cy·cle ['baisikl] **1.** bicicleta *f*;
2. andar en bicicleta; **'bi·cy·clist**
ciclista *m/f*.

bid [bid] **1.** [*irr.*] *lit.* mandar; ordenar; *cards*: pujar, marcar; licitar
at auction; *adieu etc.* decir, dar;
~ *fair to inf.* prometer *inf.*, dar in-
dicios de *inf.*; ~ *up* pujar; **2.** (*auction
etc.*) oferta *f*, postura *f*; (*cards*)
marca *f*; tentativa *f* (*to* de, *para*);
cards: no ~ paso; **'bid·den** *p.p. of
bid*; **'bid·der** licitador *m*, postor *m*;
highest ~ mejor postor *m*; **'bid·ding**

orden *f*; (*auction*) licitación *f*, postura *f*; *cards*: (*open the* abrir la,
close the cerrar la) declaración *f*.

bide [baid] † aguardar; ~ *one's time*
esperar la hora propicia.

bi·en·ni·al [bai'enjəl] ♧ (planta *f*)
bienal, bianual *m*.

bier [biə] féretro *m*, andas *f/pl.*

biff [bif] *sl.* bofetada *f*.

bi·fur·cate ['baifəːkeit] **1.** bifurcarse; **2.** bifurcado; **bi·fur'ca·tion**
bifurcación *f*.

big [big] grande (*a. fig.*); abultado,
voluminoso; (*mst* ~ *with child*)
encinta; F engreído; *fig.* importante; *sl. talk* ~ echar bravatas.

big·a·mist ['bigəmist] bígamo (*a f*)
m; **big·a·mous** [ˌməs] □ bígamo;
'big·a·my bigamia *f*.

bight [bait] gaza *f*; (*bay*) caleta *f*.

big·ness ['bignis] grandeza *f*; (*gran*)
tamaño *m*.

big·ot ['bigət] fanático (a *f*) *m*,
intolerante *m/f*; **'big·ot·ed** fanático,
intolerante; **'big·ot·ry** fanatismo *m*,
intolerancia *f*.

big·wig ['bigwig] F pájaro *m* de
cuenta, espadón *m*.

bike [baik] F bici *f*.

bi·lat·er·al [bai'lætərl] □ bilateral.

bil·ber·ry ['bilbəri] arándano *m*.

bile [bail] bilis *f*; *fig.* displicencia *f*.

bilge [bildʒ] ⚓ pantoque *m*; ⚓
(*a.* ~*water*) agua *f* de pantoque;
(*barrel*) barriga *f*; *sl.* disparates
m/pl.

bi·lin·gual [bai'liŋwəl] bilingüe.

bil·ious ['biljəs] □ bilioso (*a. fig.*).

bilk [bilk] estafar, defraudar.

bill¹ [bil] **1.** *zo.* pico *m*; uña *f of anchor*;
🪝 podadera *f* (*a.* ~*hook*); *geog.*
promontorio *m*; **2.** *esp. fig.* ~ *and
coo* acariciarse, besuquearse.

bill² [ˌ] **1.** ✝ cuenta *f*, factura *f*; *parl.*
proyecto *m* de ley; ✝ *Am.* billete *m*;
✝ letra *f* de cambio (*a.* ~ *of exchange*); (*notice*) cartel *m*; anuncio *m*;
thea. programa *m*; ⚖ alegato *m*; pedimento *m*; ~ *of fare* minuta *f*; ⚓ ~
of health patente *m* de sanidad;
~ *of lading* conocimiento *m* de embarque; ~ *of rights* declaración *f*
de derechos; ley *f* fundamental;
⚖ ~ *of sale* escritura *f* de venta;
2. *thea. etc.* anunciar.

bill·board ['bilbɔːd] *Am.* cartelera *f*,
tablón *m* de anuncios.

bil·let ['bilit] **1.** ✗ (lugar *m* de)

alojamiento *m*; **2.** leño *m*; *metall.* lingote *m*; **3.** ✗ alojar (*on* en casa de). **bil·let-doux** [bilei'du:] carta *f* amorosa.

bill·fold ['bilfould] *Am.* billetera *f*.
bill-hook ['bilhuk] podadera *f*.
bil·liard ['biljəd] de billar; '**~-cue** taco *m*; '**bil·liards** *pl.* billar *m*.
bil·lion ['biljən] *British* billón *m*; *Am.* mil millones.
bil·low ['bilou] **1.** oleada *f*; *poet.* ~s *pl.* piélago *m*; **2.** ondular, ondear; '**bil·low·y** ondoso.
bill-stick·er ['bilstikə] cartelero *m*.
bil·ly ['bili] (*a.* '**~-can**) lata *f* para calentar agua al aire libre; *Am.* cachiporra *f*; '**~-goat** macho *m* cabrío.

bin [bin] hucha *f*, arcón *m*; (*bread-*) nasa *f*.
bi·na·ry ['bainəri] binario.
bind [baind] [*irr.*] **1.** *v/t.* liar, atar (*to* a); ceñir (*with* con, de); *wound* vendar; *book* encuadernar; *cloth* ribetear; *corn* agavillar; ✗ estreñir; *fig.* obligar; ⚖ ~ *over* obligar legalmente (*to* a); ~ *a p.* apprentice poner en aprendizaje a una p.; *v/i.* atiesarse, aglutinarse, adherirse; **2.** *sl.* lata *f*; '**bind·er** atador (-a *f*) *m*; ✗ faja *f*; (*book-*) encuadernador *m*; ✗ atadora *f* agavilladora *f*; '**bind·ing 1.** obligatorio; *food* que estriñe; **2.** ligadura *f*; (*book-*) encuadernación *f*; *sew.* ribete *m*; '**bind·weed** enredadera *f*.
binge [bindʒ] *sl.* borrachera *f*; *go on a* ~ ir de juerga.
bin·na·cle ['binəkl] bitácora *f*.
bin·oc·u·lar [bai'nɔkjulə] binocular; **bin·oc·u·lars** [bi'nɔkjuləz] *pl.* gemelos *m/pl.*
bi·no·mi·al [bai'noumiəl] binomio.
bi·o·chem·i·cal [baiou'kemikl] bioquímico; '**bi·o'chem·ist** bioquímico *m*; '**bi·o'chem·is·try** bioquímica *f*.
bi·og·ra·pher [bai'ɔgrəfə] biógrafo (a *f*) *m*; **bi·o·graph·ic, bi·o·graph·i·cal** [ˌbaiou'græfik(l)] ☐ biográfico; **bi·og·ra·phy** [ˌˈɔgrəfi] biografía *f*.
bi·o·log·ic, bi·o·log·i·cal [baiə-'lɔdʒik(l)] ☐ biológico; **bi·ol·o·gist** [ˌˈɔlədʒist] biólogo *m*; **bi'ol·o·gy** biología *f*.
bi·par·ti·san [bai'pɑ:tizn] de dos partidos políticos.

bi·par·tite [bai'pɑ:tait] bipartido.
bi·ped ['baiped] 🚶 bípedo *adj. a. su. m.*
bi·plane ['baiplein] biplano *m*.
birch [bə:tʃ] **1.** ♣ abedul *m*; vara *f* de abedul, férula *f*; **2.** varear.
bird [bə:d] ave *f*, pájaro *m*; *sl.* sujeto *m*, tío *m*; F *be a night* ~ correrla; ~ *in the hand* pájaro *m* en mano; ~s *of a feather* gente *f* de una calaña; ~ *of passage* ave *f* de paso (*a. fig.*); *kill two* ~s *with one stone* matar dos pájaros de una pedrada; '**~-fan·ci·er** pajarero *m*; '**~-lime** liga *f*; '**~-seed** alpiste *m*; '**bird's-eye view** vista *f* de pájaro; '**bird's nest 1.** nido *m* de pájaro; **2.** buscar nidos.
birth [bə:θ] nacimiento *m* (*a. fig.*); ✂ parto *m*; linaje *m*; *fig.* origen *m*, comienzo *m*; *by* ~ de nacimiento; *give* ~ *to* parir, dar a luz; ~ *control* control *m* de natalidad; '**~-day** cumpleaños *m*; '**~-place** lugar *m* de nacimiento; '**~-rate** natalidad *f*; '**~-right** derechos *m/pl.* de nacimiento; primogenitura *f*.
bis·cuit ['biskit] **1.** galleta *f*; bizcocho *m* (*a. pottery*); **2.** bayo, pardusco.
bi·sect [bai'sekt] bisecar; **bi'sec·tion** bisección *f*.
bish·op ['biʃəp] obispo *m*; (*chess*) alfil *m*; '**bish·op·ric** obispado *m*.
bis·muth ['bizməθ] bismuto *m*.
bi·son ['baisn] bisonte *m*.
bis·sex·tile [bi'sekstail] bisiesto *adj. a. su. m.*
bit [bit] **1.** trozo *m*, porción *f*; (*horse's*) freno *m*; ⊕ barrena *f*; ~ *by* ~ poco a poco; *a good* ~ bastante; F (*p.*) *a* ~ *of a* hasta cierto punto; *not a* (*or one*) ~ ni pizca; *do one's* ~ hacer su contribución; *take the* ~ *in one's teeth* rebelarse; **2.** *pret. of* bite.
bitch [bitʃ] **1.** perra *f*; zorra *f*, loba *f*; (*woman*) zorra *f*, mujer *f* de mal genio; **2.** *sl.* chapucear.
bite [bait] **1.** mordedura *f*, dentellada *f*; bocado *m to eat*; (*snack*) refrigerio *m*; picadura *f of insect etc.*; *fig.* mordacidad *f*; *take a* ~ F comer algo; **2.** morder; (*fish, insect*) picar; ⊕ asir; (*acid*) corroer; (*sword*) herir; *sl. what's biting you?* ¿qué mosca te ha picado?; ~ *at* querer morder; '**bit·er**

mordedor (-a *f*) *m*; *the* ~ *bit* el
cazado cazador; '**bit·ing** □ penetrante; *fig.* mordaz. [la basura.)
bits-pail ['bitspeil] *Am.* cubo *m* de)
bit·ten ['bitn] *p.p. of bite* 2; *be* ~
fig. ser engañado; F ~ *with* con-
tagiado de.
bit·ter ['bitə] 1. □ amargo (*a. fig.*);
fight etc. encarnizado; *cold* cortante,
penetrante; 2. cerveza *f* clara.
bit·tern ['bitə:n] avetoro *m* común.
bit·ter·ness ['bitənis] amargura *f*,
amargor *m*; encarnizamiento *m of
fight etc.*
bit·ters ['bitəz] *pl.* bíter *m*.
bit·ter·sweet ['bitə:swi:t] agridulce.
bitts [bits] bitas *f/pl.*
bi·tu·men ['bitjumin] betún *m*;
bi·tu·mi·nous [~'tju:minəs] bituminoso.
biv·ouac ['bivuæk] 1. vivaque *m*
(al raso); 2. vivaquear.
biz [biz] F *v.* business.
bi·zarre [bi'za:] raro, grotesco.
blab [blæb] F 1. (*a.* **blab·ber**) chismoso (a *f*) *m*; 2. chismear; parlar;
divulgar; soplar (*sl.*).
black [blæk] 1. □ negro (*a. fig.*);
fig. aciago; *look* ceñudo; *look* ~ *at*
mirar con ceño; ~ *and blue* amoratado, acardenalado; ♀ *Death* peste *f*
negra; *in* ~ *and. white* en blanco
y negro; *por escrito; v. eye, market*;
2. ennegrecer; *shoes* limpiar; 3. negro (a *f*) *m* (*a. race*); color negro *m*;
(*mourning*) luto *m*.
black...: ~**·a·moor** ['~əmuə] negro
(a *f*) *m*; '~·**ball** dar bola negra a;
'~·**ber·ry** zarzamora *f*; '~·**bird**
mirlo *m*; '~·**board** pizarra *f*;
'~·**coat·ed** en chaqueta negra; ~
worker oficinista *m/f*; '**black·en** *v/t.*
ennegrecer; *fig.* denigrar; *v/i.* enne-
grecerse (*a. fig.*).
black...: ~**·guard** ['blæga:d] 1. pícaro *m*, bribón *m*, canalla *m*;
2. (*mst* '~·**guard·ly**) pillo, vil;
3. injuriar, vilipendiar; ~**head**
['blækhed] ♂ comedón *m*; '**black·
ing** betún *m*; '**black·ish** negruzco.
black...: '~·**jack** 1. cantimplora *f* (de
cuero); cachiporra *f* (con puño flexible); 2. aporrear; '~·**lead** 1. grafito *m*; lápiz *m*; 2. ennegrecer con
plombagina; '~·**leg** esquirol *m in
strike*; tramposo *m*; '~·'**let·ter** *typ.*
letra *f* gótica; '~·**list** lista *f* negra;
'~·**mail** 1. chantaje *m*; 2. amenazar

con chantaje; '~·**mail·er** chantajista *m/f*; '**black·ness** negrura *f*.
black...: '~·**out** 1. apagón *m*; ♂ amnesia *f* (*or* ceguera *f*) temporal;
2. *v/t.* apagar; *v/i.* padecer un
ataque de amnesia (*or* ceguera)
temporal; '~·**smith** herrero *m*;
'~·**thorn** endrino *m*; '**black·y** F
negro (a *f*) *m*.
blad·der ['blædə] vejiga *f*.
blade [bleid] hoja *f of knife etc.*;
(*cutting edge*) filo *m*; paleta *f* of
propeller; hoja *f of grass*; pala *f*
of oar, axe, hoe; (*p.*) buen mozo *m*;
♂ cuchilla *f*.
blam·a·ble ['bleiməbl] □ culpable;
'**blam·a·ble·ness** culpabilidad *f*.
blame [bleim] 1. culpa *f*; *bear the* ~
cargar con la culpa; *put* (*or lay*)
the ~ *on* echar la culpa a (*for* de);
2. culpar; *be to* ~ *for* tener la culpa
de.
blame·ful ['bleimful] censurable;
'**blame·less** □ inculpable, intachable; '**blame·less·ness** inculpa-
bilidad *f*; '**blame·wor·thi·ness**
culpabilidad *f*; '**blame·wor·thy**
censurable.
blanch [bla:ntʃ] *cooking*: blanquear;
blanquecer; (*p.*) palidecer.
blanc·mange [blə'mɔnʒ] *approx.*
crema *f* (de vainilla *etc.*).
bland [blænd] □ suave, blando;
'**blan·dish** engatusar, halagar;
'**blan·dish·ment** (*mst* ~*s pl.*) halago *m*, lisonja *f*.
blank [blæŋk] 1. □ *paper etc.* en blanco; vacío; *fig.* desconcertado; *look*
sin expresión; *verse* blanco, suelto;
~ *cartridge* cartucho *m* sin bala;
fire ~ usar municiones de fogueo;
2. (*space etc.*) blanco *m*; (*coin*) cospel
m; *fig.* falta *f* de sensaciones *etc.*;
billete *m* de lotería no premiado;
fig. draw (*a*) ~ no encontrar nada.
blan·ket ['blæŋkit] 1. manta *f*; cobija *f S.Am.*; *fig.* manto *m*; *fig.*
wet ~ aguafiestas *m/f*; 2. cubrir con
manta; ♧ quitar el viento a; *fig.*
suprimir; (*p.*) mantear; 3. comprensivo, general.
blank·ness ['blæŋknis] vacío *m*;
falta *f* de expresión.
blare [bleə] 1. (*trumpet*) sonar;
sonar muy fuerte; ~ (*out*) vociferar;
2. trompetazo *m*; estrépito *m*.
blar·ney ['bla:ni] 1. zalamerías *f/pl.*,
coba *f*; 2. halagar, dar coba.

bla·sé ['blɑːzei] hastiado; empalagado.

blas·pheme [blæs'fiːm] blasfemar (*against* contra); **blas'phem·er** blasfemador (-a *f*) *m*; **blas·phe·mous** ['blæsfiməs] ☐ blasfemo; **'blas·phe·my** blasfemia *f*.

blast [blɑːst] 1. ráfaga *f*; soplo *m of bellows*; trompetazo *m from trumpet*; carga *f* de pólvora; (*explosion*) sacudida *f*; presión *f*; ♀ tizón *m*, añublo *m*; *v. full-*; 2. volar, barrenar; ♀ añublar, marchitar; *fig.* arruinar; ⁓ (*it*)! ¡maldito sea!; **'⁓-fur·nace** ⊕ alto horno *m*; **'blast·ing** 1. de volar; 2. voladura *f*.

bla·tan·cy ['bleitənsi] vocinglería *f*; descaro *m*; **'bla·tant** ☐ vocinglero; descarado.

blath·er ['blæðə] 1. charla *f*; disparates *m/pl.*; 2. charlatanear.

blaze [bleiz] 1. llamarada *f*; hoguera *f*; F incendio *m*; *fig.* ardor *m*; *fig.* resplandor *m*; señal *f* (*hecha en los árboles para que sirva de guía*); (*on horse, cow*) estrella *f*; go to ⁓s! ¡en tu padre!; 2. *v/i.* arder, encenderse en llamas; *fig.* enardecerse; F ⁓ *away* ✗ seguir tirando; trabajar con ahinco; *v/t. trail* abrir; publicar, proclamar (*mst* ⁓ *abroad*); **'blaz·er** chaqueta *f* ligera.

bla·zon ['bleizn] 1. blasón *m* (*a. fig.*); 2. blasonar; proclamar; **'bla·zon·ry** blasón *m*; boato *m*.

bleach [bliːtʃ] 1. blanquear(se); 2. ♑ lejía *f*; **'bleach·er** blanqueador (-a *f*) *m*; lejía *f*, blanquimiento *m*; *Am.* ⁓s *pl.* gradas *f/pl.* al aire libre; **'bleach·ing** blanqueo *m*; **'bleaching-pow·der** polvos *m/pl.* de blanqueo; cloruro *m* de cal.

bleak [bliːk] ☐ desierto, solitario; (*bare*) pelado; *weather* frío, crudo; *fig. prospect* nada prometedor; *welcome* inhospitalario; **'bleak·ness** lo desierto, frío *m etc.*

blear [bliə] 1. (*a.* **blear·y** ☐) legañoso; turbio, indistinto; 2. enturbiar.

bleat [bliːt] 1. balido *m*; 2. balar.

bleb [bleb] ampolla *f*.

bled [bled] *pret. a. p.p. of bleed.*

bleed [bliːd] (*irr.*) 1. *v/i.* sangrar; ⁓ *to death* morir de desangramiento; 2. *v/t.* sangrar, desangrar; ⁓ (*white*) desangrar; **'bleed·ing** 1. ⚕ sangría *f*; 2. *sl.* maldito.

blem·ish ['blemiʃ] 1. mancha *f*, tacha *f* (*a. fig.*); 2. manchar, tachar (*a. fig.*).

blench [blentʃ] cejar, recular.

blend [blend] 1. mezclar(se), combinar(se); (*colours*) casar; 2. mezcla *f*, combinación *f*.

blende [blend] blenda *f*.

bless [bles] bendecir; favorecer (*with* con); F ⁓ *me!*, ⁓ *my soul!* ¡válgame Dios!; **bless·ed** ☐ *p.p. of bless*; bendito, bienaventurado; agraciado (*with* con); F santo; *well I'm* ⁓! ¡caramba!; **'bless·ed·ness** bienaventuranza *f*, santidad *f*; **'bless·ing** bendición *f* (*a. fig.*); beneficio *m*.

blest [blest] *poet. v. blessed.*

bleth·er ['bleðə] = *blather.*

blew [bluː] *pret. of blow*² *a. blow*³.

blight [blait] 1. ♀ añublo *m*; ♀ tizón *m*, roya *f*; *fig.* plaga *f*, infortunio *m*; 2. ♀ atizonar; arruinar; **'blight·er** *sl.* tío *m*; bribón *m*.

Blight·y ['blaiti] ✗ *sl.* Inglaterra *f*.

blind [blaind] 1. ☐ ciego (*a.* ⚠ *a. fig.*; *with* de, *to* a); oculto; ⁓ *in one eye* tuerto; *fig.* ⁓ *alley* callejón *m* sin salida; ⁓*ly fig.* a ciegas; 2. venda *f*; (*window*) celosía *f*, persiana *f*; *fig.* pretexto *m*; *Am. sl.* pantalla *f*; 3. cegar; deslumbrar.

blind...: **'⁓-fold** 1. con los ojos vendados; *fig.* sin reflexión; 2. vendar los ojos a; **'⁓-man's-buff** gallina *f* ciega; **'blind·ness** ceguedad *f*; **'blind-worm** lución *m*.

blink [bliŋk] 1. parpadeo *m*; (*gleam*) destello *m*; *Am. sl.* on the ⁓ incapacitado, desconcertado; 2. *v/t.* guiñar, cerrar momentáneamente; no hacer caso de; *v/i.* parpadear; (*light*) oscilar; **'blink·ers** *pl.* anteojera *f* (de caballo); **'blink·ing** F maldito.

bliss [blis] bienaventuranza *f*; arrobamiento *m*; **'bliss·ful** ☐ bienaventurado; deleitoso; **'bliss·ful·ness** embeleso *m*, éxtasis *m*.

blis·ter ['blistə] 1. ampolla *f*, vejiga *f*; 2. ampollar(se); ⁓*ing fig.* arrollador; *heat* abrasador.

blithe [blaið] ☐, ⁓**some** ['⁓səm] ☐ *mst poet.* alegre, jovial.

blith·er·ing ['bliðəriŋ] *sl.* charlatán; *fig.* consumado.

blitz [blits] 1. guerra *f* relámpago; *esp.* bombardeo *m* aéreo (alemán); 2. ✗ bombardear.

bliz·zard ['blizəd] ventisca *f.*

bloat [blout] hinchar(se), abotagarse; ˜ed abotagado; *fig.* hinchado (*with* de); **'bloat·er** arenque *m* ahumado.

blob [blɔb] gota *f*; burbuja *f.*

bloc [blɔk] bloque *m*; en ˜ en bloque.

block [blɔk] **1.** *stone, a. pol. a. mot.* bloque *m*; zoquete *m of wood*; (*butcher's, executioner's*) tajo *m*; (*pulley*) polea *f*, aparejo *m*; ⚠ manzana *f*, cuadra *f S.Am.*; 🚂 bloqueo *m*; *fig.* obstáculo *m*; *fig.* g upo m; F ˜*-buster* bomba *f* revientamanzanas; ˜ *letter* mayúscula *f*; **2.** obstruir, cerrar; ♱ bloquear; ˜ *in*, ˜ *out* esbozar; ˜ *up* tapar, cegar.

block·ade [blɔ'keid] **1.** bloqueo *m*; *v. run*; **2.** bloquear; **'˜-run·ner** forzador *m* de bloqueo.

block...: **'˜-head** zoquete *m*, zopenco (a *f*) *m*; **'˜-house** blocao *m*; **'˜-sys·tem** sistema *m* de bloqueo.

bloke [blouk] F tío *m*, sujeto *m.*

blonde [blɔnd] **1.** rubio; blondo; **2.** F rubia *f*; (*a.* ˜ *lace*) blonda *f.*

blood [blʌd] sangre *f*; linaje *m*, parentesco *m*; *b. s.* ira *f*, cólera *f*; (*p.*) currutaco *m*, galán *m*; *in cold* ˜ a sangre fría; ˜ *royal* estirpe *f* regia; *his* ˜ *ran cold* se le heló la sangre; *v. bad*; **'˜-guilt·y** culpable de homicidio; **'˜-heat** calor *m* de la sangre; **'˜-horse** caballo *m* de pura raza; **'˜-hound** sabueso *m* (*a. fig.*); **'blood·less** ▢ exangüe; pálido; *fig.* pacífico, incruento.

blood...: **'˜-let·ting** sangría *f*; **'˜-poi·son·ing** envenenamiento *m* de la sangre; **'˜-pres·sure** tensión *f* arterial; (*high*) hipertensión *f*; **'˜-shed** efusión *f* de sangre; matanza *f*; **'˜-shot** *eye* inyectado (de sangre); **'˜-thirst·y** ▢ sanguinario; **'˜-ves·sel** vaso *m* sanguíneo; **'blood·y** ▢ sangriento; *sl.* puñetero; *sl. as adv.* muy.

bloom¹ [blu:m] **1.** flor *f*; florecimiento *m*, floración *f*; vello *m on fruit*; *fig.* lozanía *f*; **2.** florecer; *fig.* lozanear.

bloom² [˜] *metall.* changote *m.*

bloom·er ['blu:mə] F gazapatón *m*; F ˜s *pl.* bragas *f*/*pl.*

bloom·ing ['blu:miŋ] ▢ floreciente (*a. fig.*); F condenado.

blos·som ['blɔsəm] **1.** flor *f*; flores

f/*pl.*; *in* ˜ en flor; **2.** florecer; *fig.* ˜ *into* convertirse en.

blot [blɔt] **1.** borrón *m* (*a. fig.*); **2.** manchar; borrar; (*mst* ˜ *out*) *light, view* oscurecer; *writing* borrar, tachar; *fig.* destruir; secar *with blotting-paper.*

blotch [blɔtʃ] mancha *f*; erupción *f on skin.*

blot·ter [blɔtə] papel *m* secante; borrador *m.*

blot·ting-pa·per ['blɔtiŋpeipə] papel *m* secante.

blot·to ['blɔtou] *sl.* borracho.

blouse [blauz] blusa *f.*

blow¹ [blou] golpe *m*; bofetada *f with hand*; choque *m*; *at one* ˜ de un golpe; *come to* ˜s venir a las manos; *that was a* ˜! ¡fue un golpe duro!

blow² [˜] [*irr.*] *poet.* florecer.

blow³ [˜] [*irr.*] **1.** *v/i.* soplar (*a. whale*); (*puff*) jadear, resoplar; (*hooter etc.*) sonar; *sl.* irse; *sl.* ˜ *in* entrar de sopetón; ˜ *on s. t.* enfriar soplando; ˜ *open* abrirse (por el viento); ˜ *over* pasar; ser olvidado; ˜ *up* estallar; *sl.* reventar (de ira); *v/t.* soplar; ♪ sonar, tocar; *fuse* quemar; *nose* sonar; (*fly*) depositar larvas en; *sl. money* despilfarrar; F ˜ *me!*, *I'm* ˜ *ed!* ¡no me digas!; ¡ahí va!; ˜ *a kiss* echar un beso; ˜ *out* apagar; ˜ *up* volar, hacer saltar; *balloon etc.* inflar; **2.** soplo *m*, soplido *m*; F *go for a* ˜ dar una vuelta; **'blow·er** soplador (-a *f*) *m*; ⊕ aventador *m*; *sl.* teléfono *m.*

blow...: **'˜-fly** moscarda *f*; **'˜-hole** *zo.* espiráculo *m*; respiradero *m*; **'˜-off** ⊕ escape *m*; **'˜-out** *mot.* pinchazo *m*; ⚡ quemadura *f*; *sl.* banquetazo *m*; **'˜-pipe** ⊕ soplete *m*; cerbatana *f of native*; **'blow·y** ventoso.

blowz·y ['blauzi] desaliñado; *face* coloradote.

blub·ber ['blʌbə] **1.** grasa *f* de ballena; (*weeping*) llanto *m*; **2.** lloriquear; llorar hasta hincharse los carrillos; **3.** (*lips*) befo *m.*

bludg·eon ['blʌdʒn] **1.** cachiporra *f*; **2.** aporrear; *fig.* obligar a porrazos (*into ger. a inf.*).

blue [blu:] **1.** azul; *bruise etc.* lívido, amoratado; F abatido, melancólico; **2.** azul *m*; ⚕ añil *m*; *pol.* conservador (-a *f*) *m*; **3.** azular; *washing* dar azulete a, añilar; F *money* despilfarrar.

blue...: '~-'**blood·ed** linajudo; '~-**book** *libro de informes oficiales*; *Am.* *registro de empleados del gobierno*; '~-**bottle** moscarda *f*; ♣ aciano *m* mayor; '~-'**dev·ils** *pl.* F melancolía *f*; '~-**jack·et** marinero *m* (de buque de guerra); ~ **laws** *pl. Am.* leyes *f/pl.* rigoristas severas; '**blue·ness** azul *m*; '**blue·print** cianotipo *m*, ferroprusiato *m*; *fig.* programa *m*, bosquejo *m*, anteproyecto *m*; **blues** *pl.* morriña *f*, murrias *f/pl.*; ♪ *música de jazz melancólica*; '**blue-stock·ing** literata *f*; marisabidilla *f*.

bluff [blʌf] **1.** □ escarpado; *p.* brusco, francote; **2.** risco *m*, promontorio *m* escarpado; amenaza *f* que no se puede realizar, bluf *m*; fanfarronada *f*; *call s.o.'s* ~ cogerle la palabra a uno; **3.** engañar, embaucar.

blu·ish ['bluːiʃ] azulado, azulino.

blun·der ['blʌndə] **1.** patochada *f*, coladura *f*, patinazo *m*; **2.** hacer una patochada *etc.*; desatinar (*a.* ~ *along*); F ~ *out* descolgarse con; '**blun·der·er** desatinado (*a f*) *m*.

blunt [blʌnt] **1.** □ embotado (*a. fig.*), despuntado; *fig.* obtuso, torpe; *manner* francote; **2.** embotar, despuntar; '**blunt·ness** embotamiento *m*; *fig.* brusquedad *f*, franqueza *f*.

blur [bləː] **1.** borrón *m*; contorno *m* borroso; **2.** manchar, borrar; empañar (*a. fig.*); ~*red esp. phot.* desfigurado, desdibujado.

blurb [bləːb] *sl.* anuncio *m* efusivo (*esp. de editor*).

blurt [bləːt] (*a.* ~ *out*) descolgarse con.

blush [blʌʃ] **1.** rubor *m*, sonrojo *m*; color *m* de rosa; *at first* ~ a primera vista; **2.** sonrojarse, ruborizarse (*at de*); ponerse colorado; ~ *to inf.* avergonzarse de *inf.*; '**blush·ing** ruboroso.

blus·ter ['blʌstə] **1.** borrasca *f* ruidosa; *fig.* jactancia *f*, fanfarronada *f*; **2.** *v/i.* (*wind etc.*) bramar; fanfarronear; *v/t.* ~ *forth*, ~ *out* decir ruidosamente; ~ *it out* defenderse echando bravatas; '**blus·ter·er** fanfarrón *m*; hombre *m* colérico.

bo·a ['bouə] boa *f* (*a. fur*).

boar [bɔː] verraco *m*; *wild* ~ jabalí *m*.

board [bɔːd] **1.** tabla *f*, tablero *m*; (*notice-*) tablón *m*; cartón *m for bind-ing*; ♣ bordo *m*; ✝ *etc.* junta *f*, consejo *m* de administración; *thea.* the ~s *pl.* las tablas; (*full*) ~ *and lodging* pensión *f* completa, comida *f* y casa; ♣ *on* ~ a bordo; *go by the* ~ ser abandonado; *tread the* ~s ser actor (*or* actriz); **2.** *v/t.* entablar (*a.* ~ *up*); ♣ abordar; ♣ embarcarse en; 🚌 *etc.* subir a; *p.* dar pensión completa a; *v/i.* (*a.* ~ *with*) hospedarse (con); '**board·er** huésped (-*a f*) *m*, cliente *m/f* habitual *or* fijo; *school:* interno (*a f*) *m*.

board·ing ['bɔːdiŋ] entablado *m*; ♣ abordaje *m*; '~-**house** pensión *f*, casa *f* de huéspedes; '~-**school** internado *m*.

board-room ['bɔːdrum] sala *f* de juntas.

boast [boust] **1.** jactancia *f*; baladronada *f*; *make* ~ *of* hacer gala de; **2.** jactarse (*about, of* de); ~ *about*, ~ *of* hacer alarde de; *fig. th.* enorgullecerse de, cacarear; '**boast·er** fanfarrón (-*a f*) *m*, plantista *m*; '**boast·ful** □ jactancioso.

boat [bout] **1.** barca *f*, bote *m*; (*large*) barco *m*; *be in the same* ~ correr los mismos peligros; *burn one's* ~s *pl.* quemar las naves; **2.** ir en bote; '**boating** canotaje *m*; '**boat-race** regata *f*; '**boat·swain** ['bousn] contramaestre *m*.

bob [bɔb] **1.** (*jerk*) sacudida *f*, meneo *m*; (*hair*) borla *f*; pelo *m* cortado corto; *sl.* chelín *m*; (*plumb-line*) plomo *m*; **2.** *v/t.* menear, sacudir; *hair* cortar corto; *v/i.* menearse; (*a.* ~ *up and down*) fluctuar.

bob·bin ['bɔbin] carrete *m* (*a.* ♀); bobina *f* (*a.* ♀); *sew.* canilla *f*.

bob·ble ['bɔbl] *Am.* F coladura *f*.

bob·by ['bɔbi] *sl.* polizonte *m*; '~-**socks** *pl.* escarpines *m/pl.*; '~-**soxer** *Am. sl.* chica *f* tobillera.

bob·sled ['bɔbsled], **bob·sleigh** ['bɔbslei] trineo *m* de balancín, bobsleigh *m*.

bob·tail ['bɔbteil] rabo *m* mocho; *v. rag-tag*.

bode [boud]: ~ *well* (*ill*) ser buena (mala) señal.

bod·ice ['bɔdis] corpiño *m*, almilla *f*; (*dress*) cuerpo *m*.

bod·i·less ['bɔdilis] incorpóreo.

bod·i·ly ['bɔdili] **1.** *adj.* corpóreo, corporal; **2.** *adv.* corporalmente; en conjunto; *lift etc.* en peso.

bod·kin ['bɔdkin] aguja *f* de jareta; (*hair*) espadilla *f*.

bod·y ['bɔdi] **1.** cuerpo *m*; persona *f*; (*dead*) cadáver *m*; ⊕ armazón *f*; *mot.* carrocería *f*, caja *f*; *in a* ∼ en bloque, todos juntos; ✕ *main* ∼ grueso *m*; **2.** ∼ *forth* dar cuerpo (*or* forma) a; encarnar; '∼-**guard** guardia *m* de corps; guardaespaldas *m*.

Boer [buə] bóer *adj. a. su. m/f*.

bog [bɔg] **1.** pantano *m*, ciénaga *f*; **2.**: *get* ∼*ged down* enfangarse; *fig.* empantanarse, atrancarse.

bog·gle ['bɔgl] sobresaltarse; cejar (*a. fig.*); ∼ *at* vacilar (*or* titubear) ante.

bog·gy ['bɔgi] pantanoso.

bo·gie ['bougi] 🚋 bogie *m*; *a.=bogy*.

bo·gus ['bougəs] falso, superchero.

bo·gy ['bougi] duende *m*, trasgo *m*; *the* ∼ *man* el coco; *fig.* espantajo *m*.

Bo·he·mi·an [bou'hi:mjən] bohemo *adj. a. su. m* (a *f*); *fig.* bohemio *adj. a. su. m* (a *f*).

boil[1] [bɔil] 🜊 divieso *m*, furúnculo *m*.

boil[2] [∼] **1.** hervir (*a. fig.*); *cooking*: cocer, salcochar; ∼ *down* reducir por cocción; ∼ *over* (*liquid*) irse; **2.**: *come to the* ∼ comenzar a hervir; '**boil·er** caldera *f* (*a.* ⊕); ∼-*room* sala *f* de calderas; ∼-*suit* mono *m*; '**boil·ing** hervor *m*; cocción *f*; ∼ *point* punto *m* de ebullición.

bois·ter·ous ['bɔistərəs] □ *wind etc.* borrascoso, proceloso; *p.* alborotador, bullicioso; *voices* vocinglero; '**bois·ter·ous·ness** tumulto *m*, bullicio *m*; vocinglería *f* of *voices*.

bold [bould] □ atrevido, osado; *b.s.* desenvuelto, descocado; (*steep*) escarpado; *fig.* claro, vigoroso; *typ.* negrita; *make* (*so*) ∼ (*as*) to atreverse a; '**bold·ness** osadía *f*; *b.s.* desenvoltura *f*, descoco *m*; *fig.* claridad *f*, vigor *m*.

bole [boul] tronco *m*.

boll [boul] cápsula *f*.

bol·lard ['bɔləd] bolardo *m*.

bo·lo·ney [bə'louni] = *baloney*.

Bol·she·vism ['bɔlʃəvizm] bolchevismo *m*; '**Bol·she·vist** bolchevista *adj. a. su. m/f*.

bol·ster ['boulstə] **1.** (*pillow*) travesero *m*; ⊕ plancha *f* de garnitura, cojín *m*; **2.** (*mst* ∼ *up*) sostener, reforzar; *fig.* alentar.

bolt [boult] **1.** (*door*) cerrojo *m*, pestillo *m*; ✕ saeta *f*; (*thunder*-) rayo *m*;

⊕ perno *m*; salida *f* (*or* fuga *f*) repentina (*for* para alcanzar); ∼ *upright* erguido; *fig.* ∼ *from the blue* acontecimiento *m* inesperado, *b.s.* rayo *m*; **2.** *v/t. door* acerrojar; ⊕ sujetar con perno, empernar; F *food* engullir; *v/i.* fugarse, escaparse (*esp. horse*); ∼ *out* salir de golpe; *Am. pol.* disidir; '**bolt·er** tamiz *m*; *Am. pol.* disidente *m*.

bolt·hole ['boulthoul] *fig.* refugio *m*; escapatoria *f*.

bomb [bɔm] **1.** bomba *f*; (*hand*) granada *f*; *v. atomic, incendiary etc.*; *fig. fall like a* ∼(*shell*) caer como una bomba; **2.** bombardear; ∼*ed out* desalojado (por causa de bombardeo).

bom·bard [bɔm'bɑ:d] bombardear; *fig.* llenar (*with* de); **bom'bard·ment** bombardeo *m*.

bom·bast ['bɔmbæst] ampulosidad *f*, rimbombancia *f*; **bom'bas·tic**, **bom'bas·ti·cal** □ ampuloso, rimbombante.

bomb·er ['bɔmə] bombardero *m*.

bomb·proof ['bɔmpru:f] a prueba de bombas.

bo·nan·za [bou'nænzə] F **1.** *fig.* filón *m*; **2.** lucrativo.

bon·bon ['bɔnbɔn] bombón *m*, confite *m*.

bond [bɔnd] **1.** lazo *m*, vínculo *m* (*a. fig.*); † obligación *f*; † bono *m*; † fianza *f* (de aduana); 🜨 aparejo *m*; † *in* ∼ en depósito; **2.** † obligar por fianza; † depositar mercancías en la Aduana; ∼*ed warehouse* almacén *m* de depósito; '**bond·age** esclavitud *f* (*a. fig.*), cautiverio *m*; '**bond**(s)-**man** siervo *m*; '**bond**(s)·**wom·an** sierva *f*.

bone [boun] **1.** hueso *m*; (*fish*-) espina *f*; ∼*s pl. a.* esqueleto *m*; huesos *m/pl. of the dead*; ∼ *of contention* manzana *f* de la discordia; *feel in one's* ∼*s* saber a buen seguro, estar totalmente seguro de; F *have a* ∼ *to pick with* tener que habérselas con; F *make no* ∼*s about* no andarse con rodeos en; **2.** *meat, fish* deshuesar; *Am.* F (*a.* ∼ *up*) quemarse las cejas, empollar; '**bone-meal** harina *f* de huesos; '**bon·er** *Am. sl.* patochada *f*; '**bone-set·ter** ensalmador *m*.

bon·fire ['bɔnfaiə] hoguera *f*.

bon·net ['bɔnit] **1.** (*woman's*) gorra

f, papalina *f*; (*child's*) capillo *m*; gorra *f* escocesa: *mot.* capó *m*; ⊕ sombrerete *m*; ♩ boneta *f*; **2.** cubrir (la cabeza).

bon·ny ['bɔni] *esp. Scot.* bonito, lindo; robusto.

bo·nus ['bounəs] adehala *f*; ✝ prima *f*. [huesoso.)

bon·y ['bouni] huesudo; ✿ *etc.*)

boo [bu:] **1.** *speaker etc.* silbar; **2.**: *not to say* ⁓ no decir chus ni mus.

boob [bu:b] *Am.* bobo *m*.

boo·by [bu:bi] bobo *m*, mentecato *m*; *orn.* bubia *f*; ⁓ *prize* premio *m* de consolación; '⁓-trap trampa *f* explosiva; zancadilla *f*.

boog·ie-woog·ie ['bugi'wugi] bugui-bugui *m*.

boo·hoo [bu'hu:] lloriquear.

book [buk] **1.** libro *m*; libreta *f for notes etc.*; libro *m* talonario *of cheques, tickets*; *bring s. o. to* ⁓ pedirle cuentas a una p.; ✝ *close the* ⁓s cerrar el borrador; *be in a p.'s good* (*bad*) ⁓s estar bien (mal) con una p.; **2.** ✝ asentar, anotar; *artist* escriturar; *room* reservar; *ticket* sacar; F (*police*) reseñar; ⁓ *through to* sacar un billete hasta; '⁓-bind·er encuadernador *m*; '⁓-case armario *m* para libros, estante *m*; '⁓-end sujetador *m* de libros; '**book·ie** F = **book-maker**; ' **book·ing-clerk** taquillero (a *f*) *m*; '**book·ing-of·fice** taquilla *f*; despacho *m* de billetes; '**book·ish** □ *learning* libresco; *p.* estudioso; *p.* ⁓ enteradillo; '**book-keep·er** tenedor *m* de libros; '**book-keep·ing** teneduría *f* de libros; '**book·let** folleto *m*, opúsculo *m*.

book...: '⁓-mak·er corredor *m* profesional de apuestas; '⁓-mark señal *f* de libros; '⁓-plate ex libris *m*; '⁓-rest atril *m*; '⁓-sell·er librero *m*; '⁓-worm polilla *f*; *fig.* ratón *m* de biblioteca.

boom[1] [bu:m] ♩ (*jib*) botalón *m*; botavara *f*.

boom[2] [⁓] ✝ **1.** auge *m*, prosperidad *f* repentina; **2.** ascender (los negocios), estar en bonanza.

boom[3] [⁓] **1.** estampido *m*; **2.** hacer estampido; estallar; (*voice*) resonar, retumbar.

boom·er·ang ['bu:məræŋ] bumerang *m*; *fig.* lo contraproducente.

boon[1] [bu:n] merced *f*, gracia *f*; (*gift*) dádiva *f*; favor *m*.

boon[2] [⁓] generoso, liberal; ⁓ *companion* amigo *m* íntimo, camarada *m*.

boor [buə] patán *m* (*a. fig.*); tosco *m*, palurdo *m*.

boor·ish ['buəriʃ] □ patán, tosco, palurdo.

boost ['bu:st] **1.** empujar; ✠ elevar; *fig.* promover, fomentar; ayudar; **2.**: *give a* ⁓ *to* dar bombo a; '**boost·er** reforzador *m*.

boot[1] [bu:t] † **1.**: *to* ⁓ también; **2.** aprovechar.

boot[2] [⁓] **1.** bota *f*; *mot.* maleta *f*; F *the* ⁓ *is on the other foot* los papeles están trastrocados; **2.** patear; *sl.* ⁓ *out* poner en la calle; '⁓-black *Am.* limpiabotas *m*; '**boot·ed** calzado con botas; **boot·ee** [bu:'ti:] (*woman's*) botina *f*, borceguí *m*; (*child's*) bota *f* de lana, borceguí *m*.

booth [bu:ð] caseta *f*; (*market*) puesto *m*; *teleph.* cabina *f*.

boot...: '⁓-lace cordón *m*; '⁓-leg·ger *Am.* contrabandista *m* en licores.

boots [bu:ts] *sg.* limpiabotas *m*, botones *m*.

boot-tree ['bu:ttri:] horma *f*.

boo·ty ['bu:ti] botín *m*, presa *f*.

booze [bu:z] F **1.** emborracharse; borrachear; **2.** bebida *f* (alcohólica); borrachera *f*; '**booz·y** F borracho.

bop [bɔp] *especie de jazz.*

bo·rax ['bɔ:ræks] bórax *m*.

bor·der ['bɔ:də] **1.** borde *m*, margen *m*, orilla *f*; (*frontier*) frontera *f*; ✿ arriate *m*; *sew.* orla *f*, orilla *f*; (*embroidered etc.*) cenefa *f*; **2.**: ⁓ *on* rayar en, frisar en; ⁓ *upon* lindar con, confinar con; **3.** fronterizo; '⁓-land región *f* (*or* zona *f*) fronteriza; '⁓-line *case etc.* dudoso, incierto.

bore[1] [bɔ:] **1.** ⊕ taladro *m*, barreno *m*; ✗ calibre *m*, alma *f*; *geol.* sonda *f*; *fig.* (*p.*) pelmazo *m*, pesado (a *f*) *m*, machaca *m*/*f*; (*th.*) molestia *f*, lata *f*; **2.** ⊕ taladrar, perforar; *fig.* aburrir; fastidiar, dar la lata a; *be* ⁓d *to death* aburrirse como una almeja.

bore[2] [⁓] *ola grande causada en los estuarios por la marea.*

bore[3] [⁓] *pret. of* bear[2].

bo·re·al ['bɔ:riəl] boreal, septentrional.

bore·dom ['bɔ:dəm] aburrimiento *m*, fastidio *m*.

bor·er ['bɔ:rə] ⊕ barrena *f*, taladro

m; zo. barrenillo *m, cualquier insecto que roe.*

bo·ric ac·id ['bɔːrik'æsid] ácido *m* bórico; **bo·ron** ['ˌrɔn] boro *m.*

bor·ing ['bɔːriŋ] ☐ aburrido, pesado.

born [bɔːn] **1.** *p.p. of* bear²; be ~ nacer; *I was* ~ nací; **2.** *adj.* actor nato; *liar* innato; *in all my* ~ *days* en mi vida.

borne [bɔːn] *p.p. of* bear² llevar *etc.*

bor·ough ['bʌrə] villa *f;* (*municipal*) ~ municipio *m,* municipalidad *f;* *parliamentary* ~ pueblo *m* con derecho de representación en el Parlamento.

bor·row ['bɔrou] pedir prestado (*of, from* a); *idea etc.* apropiarse; '**bor·row·er** prestatario (a *f*) *m,* comodatario *m;* el (la) que pide (*or* toma) prestado; '**bor·row·ing** acto *m* de pedir (*or* tomar) prestado; empréstito *m;* (*word*) préstamo *m.*

Bor·stal train·ing ['bɔːstl'treiniŋ] educación *f* correccional.

bos·cage ['bɔskidʒ] espesura *f,* matorral *m.*

bosh [bɔʃ] F palabrería *f,* necedades *f/pl.,* música *f* celestial.

bos·om ['buzəm] seno *m* (*a. fig.*), pecho *m;* (*garment*) pechera *f;* superficie *f of lake;* ~ *friend* amigo (a *f*) *m* íntimo (a).

boss¹ [bɔs] ⊕ clavo *m,* tachón *m;* protuberancia *f;* ⚠ crucería *f.*

boss² [ˌ] F **1.** jefe (a *f*) *m,* patrón (-a *f*) *m; esp. Am. pol.* cacique *m;* **2.** regentar, dirigir; mandar, dominar.

boss·y ['bɔsi] ☐ F mandón; tiránico.

bo·tan·ic, bo·tan·i·cal [bə'tænik(l)] ☐ botánico; **bot·a·nist** ['bɔtənist] botanista *m/f,* botánico *m/f;* **bot·a·nize** ['ˌnaiz] herborizar; '**bot·a·ny** botánica *f.*

botch [bɔtʃ] **1.** chapucería *f,* chafallo *m;* **2.** chapucear, chafallar; '**botch·er** chapucero (a *f*) *m.*

both [bouθ] ambos, los dos; ~ ... *and* tanto ... como; ~ *of them* ambos, los dos.

both·er ['bɔðə] F **1.** molestia *f,* lata *f;* pejiguera *f;* **2.** molestar; ~ *to* marse la molestia de; ~ (*it*)! ¡porras!; *he's always* ~*ing* me me está majando continuamente; **both·er·'a·tion** F ¡porras!

bot·tle ['bɔtl] **1.** botella *f;* frasco *m;*

(*water-*) cantimplora *f;* (*baby's*) biberón *m;* (*scent-*) pomo *m;* F *hit the* ~ emborracharse; **2.** embotellar (*a.* ~ *up; esp. fig.*); ~ *up emotion* contener; '**~-neck** cuello *m* (de una botella); *fig.* embotellamiento *m.*

bot·tom 1. fondo *m* (*a. fig.*); lecho *m,* cauce *m of river;* asiento *m of chair, bottle;* ⚓ (*ship's*) quilla *f,* casco *m;* F trasero *m; fig.* base *f,* fundamento *m; at the* ~ en el fondo; en el otro extremo; *fig. at* ~ en el fondo; *get to the* ~ *of a matter* profundizar (*or* fondear) un asunto; topar con la explicación de una cosa; *fig. be at the* ~ *of* ser causa (*or* motivo) de; **2.** ínfimo, más bajo; último; *Am.* ~ *dollar* último dólar *m;* **3.** poner fondo (*or* asiento) a; '**bot·tom·less** sin fondo; insondable; '**bot·tom·ry** préstamo *m* sobre

bough [bau] rama *f.* [casco y quilla.]

bought [bɔːt] *pret. a. p.p. of* buy.

bou·gie ['buːʒiː] candelilla *f.*

boul·der ['bouldə] canto *m* rodado.

bounce [bauns] **1.** (re)bote *m;* F fanfarronería *f;* **2.** (re)botar; F fanfarronear; ~ *in* (*out*) entrar (salir) sin ceremonia; ~ *a p. out of a th.* disuadir a una p. de algo a fuerza de amenazas; '**boun·cer** F embuste *m,* filfa *f; Am. sl.: el que echa a los alborotadores de un café etc.;* '**bounc·ing** fuerte, recio; frescachón.

bound¹ [baund] **1.** *pret. a. p.p. of* bind; **2.** *adj.* atado; *fig.* obligado; *fig.* ~ *to* seguro de *inf.;* ~ *up with* estrechamente relacionado con.

bound² [ˌ]: ~ *for* con rumbo a, con destino a.

bound³ [ˌ] **1.** límite *m,* linde *m a. f; in* ~*s* a raya; (*out of* ~*s* fuera de los límites; *fig. fix* (*the*) ~*s* fijar los jalones; **2.** limitar, deslindar.

bound⁴ [ˌ] **1.** salto *m,* brinco *m; v. leap;* **2.** saltar, brincar.

bound·ary ['baundəri] límite *m,* linde *m a. f;* lindero *m;* ~ *stone* hito *m,* mojón *m.*

bound·less ['baundlis] ☐ ilimitado.

boun·te·ous ['bauntiəs] ☐, **boun·ti·ful** ['ˌtiful] ☐ liberal, generoso; dadivoso.

boun·ty ['baunti] munificencia *f;* ⚔ *etc.* gratificación *f,* enganche *m;* (*esp. royal*) merced *f,* gracia *f;* ⊕ prima *f,* subvención *f.*

bou·quet [bu'kei] ♀ ramillete *m*; ramo *m*; (*wine*) aroma *m*, nariz *f*.

bour·geois¹ ['buəʒwɑ:] burgués *adj. a. su. m* (-a *f*).

bour·geois² [bə:'dʒɔis] *typ*. tipo *m* de 9 puntos.

bour·geoi·sie [buəʒwa:'zi:] burguesía *f*.

bout [baut] turno *m*; ⚔ ataque *m*; ✗ encuentro *m*; *fenc*. asalto *m*.

bo·vine ['bouvain] bovino; *fig*. lerdo.

bow¹ [bau] **1.** reverencia *f*, inclinación *f*; *make one's* ~ presentarse, debutar; **2.** *v/i*. hacer una reverencia *f* (*to* a); *fig*. ~ *to* someterse a; ~ *beneath* agobiarse con (*or* de; *a. fig*.); *v/t*. inclinar; *fig*. agobiar, oprimir (*mst* ~ *down*).

bow² [~] ⚓ proa *f*.

bow³ [bou] **1.** arco *m* (*a*. ♪); (*tie, knot*) lazo *m*; **2.** ♪ hacer pasos del arco. [gar.\

bowd·ler·ize ['baudləraiz] expur-\

bow·el ['bauəl] intestino *m*; ~s *pl*. entrañas *f/pl*. (*a. fig*.).

bow·er ['bauə] cenador *m*, glorieta *f*; *poet*. enramada *f*; *poet*. morada *f*; ⚓ (*a*. ~ *anchor*) ancla *f* de proa.

bow·ie·knife ['boui'naif] cuchillo *m* de monte.

bowl¹ [boul] (*large*) (al)jofaina *f*, palangana *f*; (*small*) escudilla *f*, tazón *m*; *fig*. copa *f* of *wine*); hornillo *m* of *pipe*; pala *f* of *spoon*; *geog*. cuenca *f*.

bowl² [~] **1.** bola *f*, bocha *f*; ~s *sg. a. pl*. juego *m* de las bochas; **2.** *v/t*. rodar; *sport*: arrojar; *fig*. ~ *over* desconcertar; *v/i*. rodar; *sport*: jugar a las bochas; arrojar la pelota; ~ *along* rodar, ir de prisa.

bow·leg·ged ['bou'legid] estevado, con las piernas en arco.

bowl·er ['boulə] *el que arroja la pelota*; (*hat*) hongo *m*.

bow...: ~·**line** ['boulin] ⚓ bolina *f*; '~·**man** arquero *m*, flechero *m*; '~·**sprit** bauprés *m*; '~·**string** cuerda *f* de arco; '~·'**tie** (corbata *f* de) lazo *m*; '~·'**win·dow** ventana *f* salediza.

bow-wow ['bau'wau] ¡guau!

box¹ [bɔks] **1.** ♀ boj *m*; caja *f* (*a*. ♪); (*large*) cajón *m*; cofre *m*, arca *f*; (*jewel-*) estuche *m*; ⊕ caja *f*, cojinete *m*; (*coach*) pescante *m*; *thea*. palco *m*; **2.** encajonar (*a. fig*.; *esp*. ~ *up*); *compass* cuartear.

box² [~] **1.** boxear; ~ *a. p.'s ear* dar un cachete a una p.; **2.**: ~ *on the ear* cachete *m*, puñetazo *m*; '~·'**calf** boxcalf *m*, piel *f* de becerro; '**box·er** boxeador *m*; *zo*. boxer *m*.

box·ing ['bɔksiŋ] boxeo *m*; '2-*Day* = *fiesta de San Esteban* (*26 diciembre*).

box...: '~·**num·ber** apartado *m*; '~·**of·fice 1.** taquilla *f*; **2.** *adj*. seguro de éxito popular; *be good* ~ ser taquillero; '~·**room** trastero *m*.

boy [bɔi] **1.** niño *m*; muchacho *m*, chico *m*; (*son*) hijo *m*; (*servant*) criado *m*, botones *m*; **2.** *adj*. joven; *v. scout*.

boy·cott ['bɔikət] **1.** boicotear; **2.** boicoteo *m*.

boy·hood ['bɔihud] muchachez *f*, puericia *f*; juventud *f*.

boy·ish ['bɔiiʃ] □ amuchachado; juvenil.

bra [brɑ] F = *brassière*.

brace [breis] **1.** ⊕ abrazadera *f*; refuerzo *m*, laña *f*; △ tirante *m*, riostra *f*; (*carriage*) sopanda *f*; *typ*. corchete *m*; ⚓ braza *f*; (*pair*) par *m*; ~s *pl*. tirantes *m/pl*.; ~ *and bit* berbiquí *m* y barrena; **2.** asegurar, reforzar; ⚓ bracear; *fig*., *esp*. ~ *o.s.* vigorizar(se); prepararse.

brace·let ['breislit] pulsera *f*, brazalete *m*.

brac·ing ['breisiŋ] que da vigor (*or* tono); tónico.

brack·en ['brækn] helecho *m*.

brack·et ['brækit] **1.** △ ménsula *f*, repisa *f*; (*gas*) mechero *m*; (*light*) brazo *m*; *typ*. corchete *m*; **2.** poner entre corchetes; *fig*. asociar, agrupar.

brack·ish ['brækiʃ] salobre.

bract [brækt] bráctea *f*.

brag [bræg] **1.** fanfarronada *f*; **2.** fanfarronear; ~ *of*, ~ *about* jactarse de.

brag·gart ['brægət] fanfarrón *m*, matasiete *m*.

Brah·man ['brɑ:mən], *mst* **Brah·min** ['~min] **1.** bracmán (-a *f*) *m*; **2.** bracmánico.

braid [breid] **1.** (*hair*) trenza *f*; trencilla *f*; ✗ galón *m*; **2.** trenzar; galonear.

braille [breil] alfabeto *m* de los ciegos.

brain [brein] **1.** cerebro *m*, sesos *m/pl*.; *fig*. (*mst* ~s *pl*.) intelecto *m*, cabeza *f*; *have s.t. on the* ~ ser obsesionado por algo, no poder quitar algo de la cabeza; F *pick a p.'s ~s* sacarle a uno el jugo; *rack one's ~s* devanarse los sesos; **2.** *sl.* romper la crisma a.

brain...: '~**-fag** fatiga *f* cerebral; '~-'**fe·ver** meningitis *f* cerebroespinal; '~·**less** □ tonto, insensato; '~-**pan** cráneo *m*, tapa *f* de los sesos; '~-**storm** frenesí *m*; **brain(s) trust** consultorio *m* intelectual.

brain...: '~-**wave** F idea *f* luminosa; '~-**work** trabajo *m* intelectual; '**brain·y** □: *be ~* ser sesudo, ser una hacha.

braise [breiz] guisar; estofar.

brake¹ [breik] ♣ helecho *m*; soto *m*.

brake² [~] **1.** ⊕ freno *m* (*a. fig.*); (*flax*) agramadera *f*; *mot.* rubia *f*; *~ pedal* pedal *m* de freno; *~ shoe* zapata *f*; **2.** ⊕ frenar; *flax* agramar; '**brake(s)·man** 🚂 guardafrenos *m*.

bram·ble ['bræmbl] zarza *f*; '**bram·bly** zarzoso.

bran [bræn] salvado *m*.

branch [brɑ:ntʃ] **1.** ♣ rama *f*; *fig.* ramo *m*, dependencia *f*; sección *f*; brazo *m of river*; ♀ sucursal *f*; **2.** (*a. ~ out*) ramificarse; ♣ echar ramas; extenderse; (*a. ~ off*) bifurcarse; separarse (*from* de); '**branch·ing** ≠ derivación *f*; '**branch-line** ramal *m*; línea *f* local; '**branch-'of·fice** sucursal *f*; '**branch·y** ramoso.

brand [brænd] **1.** tizón *m*; ↗ *etc.* hierro *m* de marcar; *esp. poet.* tea *f*; *poet.* espada *f*; ♀ marca *f*, sello *m*; **2.** marcar (con hierro candente); *fig.* tiznar (*acc.* de).

bran·dish ['brændiʃ] blandir.

brand-new ['brænd'nju:] enteramente nuevo, flamante.

bran·dy ['brændi] coñac *m*; '~-**ball** bombón *m* relleno de coñac.

brash [braeʃ] insolente, respondón; descarado; inculto; tosco.

brass [brɑ:s] latón *m*; F pasta *f*; plancha *f* conmemorativa (de latón); *fig.* descaro *m*; ♪ *the ~* el cobre; *~ band* charanga *f*, banda *f*; ☒ F *~ hat* espadón *m*; *Am.* F *~ knuckles* boxeador *m*; *sl. ~ tacks pl.* lo esencial; *get down to ~ tacks* ir al grano; '~-**found·er** latonero *m*.

brassière ['bræsiəɹ] sostén *m*.

bras·sy ['brɑ:si] de latón; *sound* áspero; *fig.* descarado; presuntuoso, presumido.

brat [bræt] F mocoso *m*, braguillas *m*.

bra·va·do [brə'vɑ:dou] bravata *f*, baladronada *f*.

brave [breiv] **1.** □ valiente, animoso; *lit.* magnífico, vistoso; **2.** desafiar, arrostrar; '**brav·er·y** valor *m*, valentía *f*.

bra·vo ['brɑː'vou] (*pl. ~[e]s*) **1.** asesino *m* pagado; **2.** ¡bravo!

brawl [brɔ:l] **1.** pendencia *f*; alboroto *m*; *poet.* murmullo *m*; **2.** alborotar, armar pendencia; '**braw·ler** pendenciero (a *f*) *m*.

brawn [brɔ:n] músculo *m*; *fig.* fuerza *f* muscular; (*meat*) carne *f* en gelatina; '**braw·ni·ness** fortaleza *f*; '**brawn·y** fuerte, vigoroso.

bray¹ [brei] **1.** rebuzno *m*; (*trumpet*) sonido *m* bronco; tintirintín *m*; (*laugh*) carcajada *f*; **2.** rebuznar; (*trumpet*) sonar con estrépito; (*laugh*) soltar una carcajada.

bray² [~] triturar.

braze [breiz] soldar.

bra·zen ['breizn] □ de latón; *fig.* descarado; '**bra·zen·ness** descaro *m*, desfachatez *f*.

bra·zier ['breiziə] brasero *m*; (*p.*) latonero *m*.

Bra·zil·ian [brə'ziljən] brasileño *adj. a. su. m* (a *f*).

Bra·zil-nut [brə'zil'nʌt] castaña *f* de Pará.

breach [bri:tʃ] **1.** rompimiento *m* (*a. fig.*), rotura *f*; violación *f*, infracción *f of rule*; ☒ brecha *f*; *~ of contract* infracción *f* de contrato; *~ of faith* abuso *m* de confianza, infidencia *f*; *~ of the peace* perturbación *f* del orden público; **2.** romper; ☒ abrir brecha en.

bread [bred] pan *m* (*a. fig.*); *earn one's ~ and butter* ganarse el pan; *know which side one's ~ is buttered* saber a qué carta quedarse; '~-**crumb** migaja *f* (de pan).

breadth [bredθ] anchura *f*; ⚓ (*beam*) manga *f*; *fig.* amplitud *f*; tolerancia *f*.

bread-win·ner ['bredwinə] el (la) que se gana la vida; productor (-a *f*) *m*.

break [breik] **1.** ruptura *f*; abertura *f*, grieta *f*; pausa *f*, intervalo *m*; interrupción *f*; (*rest*) descanso *m*; (*holiday*) asueto *m*; (*voice*) gallo *m*; (*carriage*) break *m*; partida *f at* *billiards*; ✝ (*price*) baja *f*; ~ *of day* alba *f*, amanecer *m*; *without a* ~ sin parar; F *give a p. a* ~ abrirle a uno la puerta; **2.** [*irr.*] *v/t.* romper, quebrantar (*a. fig.*); ≠ interrumpir; *bank* quebrar; *horse* domar, amansar; *impact* amortiguar, suavizar; *news* comunicar; *p.* arruinar; *record* batir, superar; ✄ abrir (*freq. fig.*: ~ *new ground* emprender algo nuevo); ~ *down* derribar; destruir; ~ *in* forzar, romper; ~ *in pieces* hacer pedazos; ~ *up* desmenuzar; *camp* levantar; *estate* parcelar; *organization* disolver; *ship* desguazar; *v/i.* romperse, quebrantarse; (*bank*) hacer bancarrota; (*boil*) reventar; (*day*) apuntar; (*health*) desfallecerse; (*voice*) mudar; ~ *away* desprenderse; separarse; ~ *down* perder la salud, decaer; prorrumpir en lágrimas; *mot.*, ⊕ tener averías; ~ *into a run* echar a correr; ~ *out* (*war*) estallar; ✄ declararse; ~ *up* hacerse pedazos; disolverse; (*meeting*) levantarse; (*school*) cerrarse; *v. a. broken*; **'break·a·ble** quebradizo, frágil; **'break·age** rotura *f*; ✝ indemnización *f* (por cosas quebradas); **'break·a·way** *sport*: escapada *f*; **'break·down** ✄ colapso *m*; ✄ (*nervous*) crisis *f* nerviosa; interrupción *f*, cesión *f*; *mot.* avería *f*; **'break·er** ⚓ cachón *m*.

break...: ~**fast** ['brekfəst] **1.** desayuno *m*; **2.** desayunar(se); ~**neck** ['breiknek] precipitado; arriesgado; *at* ~ *speed* a mata caballo; **'~-through** ✄ ruptura *f*; **'~-'up** desmoronamiento *m*; desintegración *f*; disolución *f*; *school*: clausura *f*; **'~·wa·ter** rompeolas *m*.

bream [briːm] brema *f*; *sea* ~ besugo *m*.

breast [brest] **1.** pecho *m* (*a. fig.*); seno *m*; *fig.* corazón *m*; pechuga *f* *of bird*; *make a clean* ~ *of* confesar con franqueza; **2.** arrostrar, hacer cara a.

breast...: **'~·bone** esternón *m*; **'~-pin** alfiler *m* de pecho; **'~·plate** peto *m*; **'~-stroke** brazada *f* de pecho; **'~·work** ✄ parapeto *m*.

breath [breθ] aliento *m*, respiración *f*; (*animals*) hálito *m* (*a. poet.* = *breeze*); (*pause*) respiro *m*, pausa *f*; *out of* ~ sin aliento; *short of* ~ corto de resuello; *under one's* ~ en

voz baja; *waste one's* ~ *on* gastar saliva en; **breathe** [briːð] *v/i.* respirar (*a. fig.*); (*heavily*) resollar; aspirar (*a.* ~ *in*); *v/t.* inspirar, respirar; exhalar; *fig.* sugerir; *v. last, word;* **'breath·er** respiro *m*.

breath·ing ['briːðiŋ] respiración *f*; **'~-space**, **'~-time** descanso *m*, respiro *m*.

breath·less ['breθlis] □ falto de aliento; **'breath·less·ness** falta *f* de aliento.

breath-tak·ing ['breθteikiŋ] □ *speed* vertiginoso; pasmoso.

bred [bred] *pret. a. p.p. of breed.*

breech [briːtʃ] ⊕ recámara *f*; **breech·es** ['∟iz] *pl.* calzones *m/pl.*; F *wear the* ~ llevar los calzones; **'breech-load·er** arma *f* de retrocarga.

breed [briːd] **1.** casta *f*, progenie *f*; raza *f*; *Am.* mestizo (a *f*) *m esp. White-Indian*; **2.** [*irr.*] *v/t.* criar, engendrar; *fig.* ocasionar, producir; educar; *v/i.* reproducirse; **'breed·er** criador (-a *f*) *m*; ~ *reactor* reactor-generador *m*; **'breed·ing** cría *f*; crianza *f* (*a. fig.*).

breeze[1] [briːz] **1.** brisa *f*; F bronca *f*; **2.** F: ~ *in* entrar sin preocupación.

breeze[2] [∟] *zo.* tábano *m*.

breez·y ['briːzi] □ ventilado; (*windy*) ventoso; *p.* animado, jovial.

breth·ren ['breðrin] hermanos *m/pl.*

breve [briːv] cuadrada *f*, breve *m*.

bre·vet ['brevit] graduación *f* honoraria.

bre·vi·a·ry ['briːviəri] breviario *m*.

brev·i·ty brevedad *f*.

brew [bruː] **1.** *v/t.* hacer, preparar; *fig.* urdir; *v/i.* prepararse; (*storm*) amenazar; **2.** poción *f*, brebaje *m*; mezcla *f*; **'brew·er** cervecero *m*; **'brew·er·y** fábrica *f* de cerveza.

bri·ar ['braiə] = *brier[1]* a. *brier[2]*.

brib·a·ble ['braibəbl] sobornable; **bribe** [braib] **1.** soborno *m*, cohecho *m*; **2.** sobornar, cohechar; **'brib·er** sobornador (-a *f*) *m*, cohechador (-a *f*) *m*; **'brib·er·y** soborno *m*, cohecho *m*.

brick [brik] **1.** ladrillo *m*; F *a regular* ~ un buen sujeto; *sl. drop a* ~ hacer una plancha; **2.** (*mst* ~ *up*) cerrar (con ladrillos); **'~·bat** trozo *m* de ladrillo; **'~·kiln** horno *m* de ladrillos; **'~·lay·er** ladrillador *m*; **'~·works** tejar *m*, ladrillar *m*.

brid·al ['braidl] 1. □ nupcial; 2. *mst poet.* boda *f*.

bride [braid] novia *f*, desposada *f*; '~·**groom** novio *m*, desposado *m*; '**brides·maid** madrina *f* de boda, prónuba *f*.

bridge[1] [bridʒ] 1. puente *m* (*a.* ♪); (*nose*) caballete *m*; (*billiards*) violín *m*; 2. tender un puente sobre; *fig.* ~ the gap llenar el vacío.

bridge[2] [~] *cards*: bridge *m*.

bridge·head ['bridʒhed] cabeza *f* de puente.

bri·dle ['braidl] 1. brida *f*, freno *m*; 2. *v/t.* enfrenar; *fig.* refrenar, reprimir; *v/i.* levantar la cabeza; *fig.* picarse (*at* por); *fig.* erguirse; '~·**path** camino *m* de herradura.

bri·doon [bri'duːn] bridón *m*.

brief [briːf] 1. □ breve, conciso; (*fleeting*) fugaz, pasajero; 2. epítome *m*, resumen *m*; (*papal*) breve *m*; ⚡ escrito *m*, memorial *m*; hold a ~ for abogar por (*a. fig.*); '~·**bag**, '~·**case** cartera *f*; '**brief·ness** brevedad *f*.

bri·er[1] ['braiə] ⚜ escaramujo *m*; zarza *f*.

bri·er[2] [~] pipa *f* (*esp.* aquélla hecha de madera de brezo; *a.* ~ *pipe*).

brig [brig] bergantín *m*.

bri·gade [bri'geid] brigada *f*; **brig·a·dier** [brigə'diə] brigadier *m*.

brig·and ['brigənd] bandido *m*, bandolero *m*; '**brig·and·age** bandolerismo *m*; latrocinio *m*.

bright [brait] □ claro, luminoso, brillante; *surface* lustroso, pulido; *colour* subido; *fig.* (*cheerful*) vivo, alegre; (*clever*) listo, talentoso; '**bright·en** *v/t.* pulir, abrillantar; *fig.* mejorar, avivar, animar; *v/i.* (*freq.* ~ *up*) avivarse, animarse; mejorar; '**bright·ness** claridad *f*, brillantez *f*; resplandor *m*; lustre *m*; lo subido *of colour*; *fig.* viveza *f*; talento *m*, viveza *f* de ingenio.

brill [bril] rodaballo *m*.

bril·lian·cy ['briljənsi] brillantez *f*, brillo *m*; '**bril·liant 1.** □ brillante, refulgente; *fig.* excelente, sobresaliente; (*showy*) vistoso; 2. brillante *m*.

brim [brim] 1. borde *m*, orilla *f*; ala *f* of hat; 2. (*a.* ~ over) rebosar (with de; *a. fig.*); '~·**ful**, '~·'**full** lleno hasta el borde; rebosante (with de); '~·**less** hat sin ala.

brim·stone ['brimstən] azufre *m*.

brin·dle(d) ['brindl(d)] manchado, mosqueado.

brine [brain] salmuera *f*; *poet.* piélago *m*.

bring [briŋ] [*irr.*] llevar; traer; conducir; ⚡ charge exponer; ⚡ suit entablar, armar; ~ about ocasionar, originar; ~ along llevar consigo; ~ away llevarse; ~ back devolver; *p.*, *th.* volver con; ~ down price rebajar; ⚔ derribar; *thea.* ~ down the house hacer que se venga abajo el teatro; ~ forth dar a luz, parir; *fig.* producir; ~ forward presentar; *date* adelantar; ✝ llevar a otra cuenta; ~ s.t. home to s.o. hacer que alguien se dé cuenta de algo; ~ in presentar; *fashion etc.* introducir; *income etc.* producir, rendir; *p.* hacer entrar; *verdict* dar; ~ off ⚡ exculpar; *success* conseguir; ~ on causar, inducir; ~ out th. sacar, hacer salir; *book* sacar a luz, publicar; *p.* hacer más afable, ayudar a adquirir confianza; ~ round (*win over*) ganar, convertir; ⚡ hacer volver en sí; ~ a p. to do s.t. inducir a alguien a hacer algo; ~ o.s. to inf. resignarse a inf., cobrar suficiente ánimo para inf.; ⚓ ~ to ponerse en facha; ~ together reunir; *enemies* reconciliar; ~ under sojuzgar, someter; ~ up p. criar, educar; *subject* sacar a colación; (*stop*) parar; F vomitar, arrojar.

brink [briŋk] borde *m*, orilla *f*; *fig.* on the ~ of a punto de.

brin·y ['braini] salado, salobre.

bri·quette [bri'ket] briqueta *f*.

brisk [brisk] 1. □ enérgico, vigoroso; despejado; animado, activo; *gait etc.* gallardo, airoso; 2. (*mst* ~ *up*) avivar, animar.

bris·ket ['briskit] pecho *m* de un animal, *esp. carne cortada del pecho para asar*.

brisk·ness ['brisknis] energía *f*; despejo *m*; *etc.*

bris·tle ['brisl] 1. cerda *f*; 2. erizarse; *fig.* (*freq.* ~ *up*) montar en cólera; *fig.* estar erizado (with de); '**bris·tled**, '**bris·tly** cerdoso; erizado.

Bri·tan·nic [bri'tænik] británico.

Brit·ish ['britiʃ] británico; inglés; the ~ *pl.* los ingleses; '**Brit·ish·er** *Am.* natural *m/f* de Gran Bretaña.

Brit·on ['britən] britano (a *f*) *m*; inglés (-a *f*) *m*.

brit·tle ['britl] quebradizo, frágil; 'brit·tle·ness fragilidad *f*, friabilidad *f*.

broach [broutʃ] **1.** asador *m*; (*spire*) aguja *f*; ⊕ broca *f*; **2.** *cask* espitar; *fig.* mencionar por primera vez; (*start using*) decentar.

broad [brɔːd] □ ancho, amplio; extenso, vasto; *outline etc.* claro, explícito; (*coarse*) grosero; *story* verde; *mind*, *view* liberal, tolerante; *accent* marcado, cerrado; ~ in outlook de amplias miras e ideas; ~ly en general; '~-axe ⊕ hacha *f* de carpintero; '~-cast **1.** ✗ sembrado al vuelo; *fig.* diseminado, divulgado; **2.** [*irr.* (*cast*)] *v/t.* ✗ sembrar al vuelo; *fig.* diseminar, divulgar; *radio*: emitir, radiar; *v/i.* hablar etc. por la radio; ~ing radiodifusión *f*; ~ing station emisora *f*; **3.** *radio*: emisión *f*, programa *m*; '~-cloth paño *m* fino; 'broad·en ensanchar(se); *fig.* ampliar(se); 'broad-'mind·ed liberal, tolerante; de miras amplias; 'broad·ness anchura *f*; *esp. fig.* amplitud *f*; liberalismo *m*, tolerancia *f*.

broad...: '~-sheet hoja *f* suelta impresa; '~-side ⚓ costado *m*, andanada *f*; *a.* = broadsheet; '~-sword espadón *m*.

bro·cade [brə'keid] brocado *m*; **bro'cad·ed** espolinado.

broc·co·li ['brɔkəli] brécol *m*.

bro·chure ['brɔʃjuə] folleto *m*.

brock [brɔk] tejón *m*.

brogue [broug] (*shoe*) abarca *f*; acento *m* irlandés.

broil [brɔil] **1.** pendencia *f*, camorra *f*; **2.** asar sobre ascuas (*or* a la parrilla); tostar (al sol); ~ing tórrido; 'broil·er pollo *m* para asar.

broke [brouk] *pret. of* break; *sl.* sin blanca.

bro·ken ['broukən] *p.p. of* break; *adj.* *ground* accidentado, desigual; *health* estropeado, deshecho; *language* chapurreado; *voice* cascado; (*despairing*) desesperado; '~-'heart·ed traspasado de dolor; 'bro·ken·ly con la voz cascada; acongojado; 'bro·ken-'wind·ed *vet.* corto de resuello.

bro·ker ['broukə] ✝ corredor *m*; ✝ agente *m* de negocios; prendero *m*; 'bro·ker·age, 'bro·king corretaje *m*.

bro·mide ['broumaid] bromuro *m*; F perogrullada *f*; **bro·mine** ['~miːn] bromo *m*.

bron·chi·al ['brɔŋkiəl] bronquial; **bron·chi·tis** [brɔŋ'kaitis] bronquitis *f*.

bron·co ['brɔŋkou] *Am.* potro *m* cerril; '~-bust·er *sl.* domador *m* de caballos, picador *m*.

bronze [brɔnz] **1.** bronce *m* (*a. fig.*); **2.** *attr.* de bronce; **3.** *v/t.* broncear; F (*beat*) zurrar; *v/i.* (*tan*) broncearse.

brooch [broutʃ] broche *m*.

brood [bruːd] **1.** camada *f*, cría *f*; *fig.* progenie *f*; ~ mare yegua *f* de cría; **2.** empollar; *fig.* ~ on, ~ over rumiar *acc.*; meditar *acc.* melancólicamente; 'brood·y clueca; *fig.* melancólico.

brook[1] [bruk] arroyo *m*.

brook[2] [~] *lit.* (*mst negative*) sufrir, aguantar.

brook·let ['bruklit] arroyuelo *m*.

broom [bruːm] escoba *f*; ♀ hiniesta *f*, retama *f*; '~-stick ['brumstik] palo *m* de escoba.

broth [brɔθ] caldo *m*.

broth·el ['brɔθl] burdel *m*, lupanar *m*.

broth·er ['brʌðə] hermano *m* (*a. fig.*); ~-hood ['~hud] fraternidad *f*; (*a. guild*) hermandad *f*; '~-in-law cuñado *m*; 'broth·er·ly fraternal.

brougham ['bruːəm] brougham *m*.

brought [brɔːt] *pret. a. p.p. of* bring.

brow [brau] ceja *f*; (*forehead*) frente *f*; cumbre *f of hill*; knit one's ~ fruncir las cejas; '~-beat [*irr.* (*beat*)] intimidar (con palabras); (*dominate*) imponerse a.

brown [braun] **1.** pardo, castaño, moreno; *bread* moreno; *paper* de embalar, de estraza; *shoes* de color; ~ sugar azúcar *f* terciada; **2.** color *m* pardo *etc.*; **3.** (*skin etc.*) broncear (se); poner(se) moreno; *cooking:* dorar(se); *sl.* be ~ed off estar harto (with de); 'brown·ie duende *m* moreno; *miembro joven de la Asociación de Girl Guides*; 'brown·ish que tira a moreno; 'brown·stone *Am. piedra arenisca de color pardo rojizo.*

browse [brauz] **1.** pimpollos *m/pl.*; **2.** herbajar; ramonear, rozar (on *acc.*); *fig.* leer por gusto.

Bru·in ['bruːin] oso *m*.

bruise [bruːz] **1.** contusión *f*, cardenal *m*, magulladura *f*; **2.** magullar; (*batter*) majar, machacar; **'bruis·er** *sl.* boxeador *m*.

Brum·ma·gem ['brʌmədʒəm] falso, postizo.

bru·nette [bruːˈnet] morena, trigueña *adj. a. su. f.*

brunt [brʌnt] ✗ embate *m*, acometida *f*; *fig.* bear the ~ of aguantar lo más recio de.

brush [brʌʃ] **1.** cepillo *m*; (*large*) escoba *f*, *pint.* pincel *m*, brocha *f*; (*fox*) rabo *m*; ⚡ escobilla *f*; ✗ escaramuza *f*; *Am.* = ~wood, backwoods; ~-stroke pincelada *f*; *give a p. a* ~ cepillar a una p.; *have a* ~ *with a p.* desavenirse con una p.; **2.** *v/t.* (a)cepillar; rozar *in passing*; ~ *aside* echar a un lado; ~ *away*, ~ *off* quitar con cepillo (*or* con la mano); ~ *down* (a)cepillar, limpiar, almo'nazar; ~ *up* acicalar; *fig.* repasar, refrescar; *v/i.*: ~ *against* rozar; ~ *by*, ~ *past* pasar rozando (*or* muy cerca); **'~·wood** matorral *m*, breñal *m*.

brusque [brusk] □ brusco, rudo.

Brus·sels ['brʌslz]: ~ *sprouts pl.* col *f* de Bruselas.

bru·tal ['bruːtl] □ brutal; feroz; **bru·tal·i·ty** [bruːˈtæliti] brutalidad *f*; ferocidad *f*; **bru·tal·ize** ['bruːtəlaiz] embrutecer; **brute** [bruːt] **1.** brutal; (*stupid etc.*) bruto; **2.** bruto *m*, bestia *f* (*a. fig.*); monstruo *m*; **'brut·ish** □ = brute 1; **'brut·ish·ness** brutalidad *f*.

bub·ble ['bʌbl] **1.** burbuja *f*, ampolla *f*; *fig.* bagatela *f*; (*fraud*) engañifa *f*; ~ *and squeak* carne fría frita con legumbres; **2.** burbujear, borbotar; ~ *over fig.* rebosar (*with* de).

buc·ca·neer [bʌkəˈniə] **1.** bucanero *m*; **2.** piratear.

buck [bʌk] **1.** *zo.* gamo *m*; (*goat*) macho *m* cabrío; (*rabbit*) conejo *m* macho; (*p.*) petimetre *m*; *Am. sl.* dólar *m*; *Am.* F *pass the* ~ echar la carga a otro; **2.** *v/i.* corcovear; F ~ *up* animarse, cobrar ánimo; F ~ *up!* ¡apúrate!; *v/t. Am.* F hacer frente a; *Am.* F embestir, arrojarse sobre; F ~ *up* animar.

buck·et ['bʌkit] cubo *m*, balde *m*; ⊕ paleta *f*; F *a drop in the* ~ una nonada; *sl. kick the* ~ estirar la pata; **'~·ful** contenido *m* de un cubo; F *rain* ~s llover a chuzos; **'~·shop** bolsín *m*.

buck·le ['bʌkl] **1.** hebilla *f*; **2.** *v/t.* hebillar; *v/i.* doblarse, encorvarse; ~ *down to* (*prp.*) dedicarse con empeño a; ~ *to* (*adv.*) emprender algo con ahínco; **'buck·ler** escudo *m*, rodela *f*.

buck·ram ['bʌkrəm] bucarán *m*.

buck...: '**~·shot** balines *m/pl.*; perdigón *m* zorrero; '**~·skin** cuero *m* de ante; '**~·wheat** alforfón *m*.

bud [bʌd] **1.** pimpollo *m*, brote *m*; *Am.* chica *f* que se presenta en la sociedad; *in* ~ en brote; *fig. nip in the* ~ cortar de raíz; **2.** *v/t.* ⚡ injertar de escudete; *v/i.* brotar, echar pimpollos; ~ding *lawyer etc.* abogado *m etc.* en ciernes.

bud·dy ['bʌdi] *Am.* F camarada *m*, compinche *m*.

budge [bʌdʒ] mover(se); *he did not dare to* ~ no osaba bullirse.

budg·et ['bʌdʒit] **1.** presupuesto *m*; *attr.* presupuestario; **2.** *v/i.*: ~ *for* presupuestar; **'budg·et·ar·y** presupuestario.

buff [bʌf] **1.** piel *f* de ante; *in* (*one's*) ~ en cueros; **2.** color de ante.

buf·fa·lo ['bʌfəlou], *pl.* **buf·fa·loes** ['~z] búfalo *m*.

buff·er ['bʌfə] 🚆 tope *m*; amortiguador *m*; F mastuerzo *m*; ~ *state* estado *m* tapón.

buf·fet[1] ['bʌfit] **1.** bofetada *f*; golpe *m*; **2.** abofetear; golpear; ~ing golpear *m* (*e.g. of sea*).

buf·fet[2] ['bufei] 🍴 fonda *f*, cantina *f*; (*sideboard*) aparador *m*; (*meal*) ambigú *m*.

buf·foon [bʌˈfuːn] bufón *m*; **buf·foon·er·y** bufonada *f*.

bug [bʌg] chinche *f*; *esp. Am.* bicho *m*, insecto *m*; *sl.* microbio *m*; *Am. sl.* estorbo *m*, traba *f*; F *big* ~ señorón *m*; ~·a·boo ['~əbuː], **bug·bear** espantajo *m* (*a. fig.*); coco *m*; **'bug·gy** lleno de chinches; **2.** calesa *f*.

bu·gle[1] ['bjuːgl] ♪ corneta *f*.

bu·gle[2] ['~] abalorio *m*.

bu·gler ['bjuːglə] corneta *m*.

buhl [buːl] taracea *f*.

build [bild] **1.** [*irr.*] construir, fabricar; *fig.* edificar (*on sobre*); fundar, establecer, componer; ⊕ ~ *in* empotrar; ~ *up* componer *from parts*;

armar; *fortalecer*; *fig.* crear: **2.** estructura *f*; *anat.* talle *m*; '**build·er** arquitecto *m*; constructor *m*; maestro *m* de obras; '**build·ing** edificio *m*; construcción *f*; *attr.* de construcción; relativo a edificios; ~ *contractor* contratista *m*; ~ *site* solar *m*; ~ *society* cooperativa *f* de construcciones; '**build-'up** composición *f*; *fig.* propaganda *f* previa.

built [bilt] *pret. a. p.p. of* build 1; '**built-'in** ⚘ empotrado; ⊕ incorporado, montado; ≉ interior; '**built-'up** urbanizado.

bulb [bʌlb] ♱ bulbo *m*; ≉ bombilla *f*; ampolleta *f of thermometer*; '**bulb·ous** bulboso.

Bul·gar·i·an [bʌl'gɛəriən] búlgaro *adj. a. su. m* (a *f*).

bulge [bʌldʒ] **1.** bombeo *m*, comba *f*, pandeo *m*; **2.** bombearse, combarse, pandearse; *bulging eyes* ojos *m/pl.* saltones.

bulk [bʌlk] bulto *m*, volumen *m*; grueso *m*; *fig.* la mayor parte; ⚓ carga *f*; *in ~ a granel*; ~ *goods pl.* mercancías *f/pl.* sueltas; '**~head** ⚓ mamparo *m*; '**bulk·i·ness** volumen *m*, bulto *m*; '**bulk·y** abultado, voluminoso.

bull¹ [bul] **1.** *zo.* toro *m*; ♱ *sl.* alcista *m*; *Am. sl.* detective *m*, policía *m*; *take the ~ by the horns* irse a la cabeza del toro; *attr.* macho; **2.** ♱ *sl.* jugar al alza; *sl.* chapucear.

bull² [⌣] *eccl.* bula *f*.

bull³ [⌣] disparate *m*.

bull·dog ['buldɔg] dogo *m*; *univ.* F bedel *m*.

bull·doze ['buldouz] F intimidar; *opposition* arrollar; '**bull·doz·er** empujadora *f* niveladora, motoniveladora *f*.

bul·let ['bulit] bala *f* (de fusil).

bul·le·tin ['bulitin] boletín *m*; anuncio *m*; *v. news-~*; *Am.* ~ *board* tablón *m* de anuncios.

bull...: '**~fight** corrida *f* de toros; '**~finch** camachuelo *m*; '**~frog** rana *f* toro.

bul·lion ['buljən] oro *m* (*or* plata *f*) en barras (*or* lingotes); (*fringe*) entorchado *m*.

bull·ock ['bulək] buey *m*.

bull·pen ['bul'pen] toril *m*; *Am.* F prevención *f* de policía.

bull's-eye ['bulzai] centro *m* del blanco; ⚓ cristal *m* de patente,

portilla *f*; *tipo de dulce*; ~ *pane* vidrio *m* abombado.

bul·ly¹ ['buli] **1.** matón *m*, valentón *m*; **2.** *Am.* F de primera; *a. int.* ¡bravo!; **3.** intimidar; tiranizar; ~ *s.o. into* forzar a uno con amenazas a que *subj.*

bul·ly² [⌣] carne *f* de vaca conservada en latas (*a.* ~ *beef*).

bul·rush ['bulrʌʃ] junco *m*; espadaña *f*.

bul·wark ['bulwək] baluarte *m* (*a. fig.*); ⚓ macarrón *m*.

bum¹ [bʌm] F culo *m*.

bum² [⌣] *Am.* F **1.** (*p.*) holgazán *m*, vagabundo *m*; (*spree*) jarana *f*, juerga *f*; **2.** holgazanear, vagabundear (*a. go on the* ~); *sl.* beber a pote; *sl.* mendigar; **3.** *sl.* inferior, chapucero; *feel* ~ sentirse muy malo.

bum·ble-bee ['bʌmblbi:] abejorro *m*.

bum·boat ['bʌmbout] bote *m* vivandero.

bump [bʌmp] **1.** topetón *m*; batacazo *m in falling*; sacudida *f*; (*lump etc.*) chichón *m*, hinchazón *f*; protuberancia *f*; comba *f on surface*; **2.** chocar contra, topetar (*a.~against*); ~ *along* botar, dar sacudidas; F ~ *into p.* topar; *Am. sl.* ~ *off* asesinar, despenar; **bump·er** ['bʌmpə] tope *m*; ≉ *a. mot.* parachoques *m*; copa *f* llena; *attr.* muy grande, abundante.

bump·kin ['bʌmpkin] patán *m*.

bump·tious ['bʌmpʃəs] □ F engreído, presuntuoso.

bump·y ['bʌmpi] abollado; *land* desigual; *air* agitado; *road* lleno de baches.

bun [bʌn] bollo *m*; (*hair*) moño *m*.

bunch [bʌntʃ] **1.** manojo *m*, atado *m*; ramo *m of flowers*; racimo *m of grapes*; F grupo *m*; F montón *m*; **2.** agrupar, juntar; '**bunch·y** racimoso.

bun·combe ['bʌŋkəm] *v.* bunk.

bun·dle ['bʌndl] **1.** lío *m*, bulto *m*; legajo *m of papers*; haz *f of sticks*; **2.** *v/t.* arropar, envolver (*mst* ~ *up*); F ~ *off* despachar sin ceremonia; *v/i.* escaparse, irse.

bung [bʌŋ] **1.** bitoque *m*; **2.** tapar (con bitoque); cerrar; F ~ *ed up mst* hinchado; cerrado.

bun·ga·low ['bʌŋgəlou] bungalow *m*, casa *f* de campo.

bung-hole ['bʌŋhoul] piquera *f.*

bun·gle ['bʌŋgl] **J.** chapucería *f*; 2. chapucear; **'bun·gler** chapucero (a *f*) *m*; **'bun·gling 1.** □ chapucero; 2. chapucería *f.*

bun·ion ['bʌnjən] hinchazón *f* en el pie, juanete *m.*

bunk[1] [bʌŋk] *sl.* palabrería *f*, música *f* celestial; *do a* ~ huir, volver la cara.

bunk[2] [~] camastro *m*, tarima *f* para dormir; F cama *f.*

bunk·er ['bʌŋkə] **1.** (*coal-*) carbonera *f*; ⚓ pañol *m* del carbón; *golf:* hoya *f* de arena, arenal *m*; 2. ⚓ proveer de carbón; F *get* ~*ed* empantanarse.

bun·kum [b'ʌŋkəm] *v.* **bunk.**

bun·ny ['bʌni] conejo *m.*

bun·ting[1] ['bʌntiŋ] *orn.* escribano *m*; *corn* ~ triguero *m.*

bun·ting[2] [~] ⊕ estameña *f*; ⚓ *etc.* banderas *f/pl.*, empavesado *m.*

buoy [bɔi] **1.** boya *f*; 2. aboyar; ~ *up* mantener a flote; *fig.* alentar.

buoy·an·cy ['bɔiənsi] fluctuación *f*, facultad *f* de flotar; ⚓ fuerza *f* ascensional; **'buoy·ant** □ boyante; *fig.* alegre, animado; ✝ al alza.

bur [bə:] ♀ erizo *m*; *fig.* persona *f* muy pegadiza.

Bur·ber·ry ['bə:bəri] gabardina *f.*

bur·den[1] ['bə:dn] **1.** carga *f* (*a. fig.*), gravamen *m*; ⚓ arqueo *m*; ⚓ peso *m* de la carga; 2. cargar (*a. fig.*; *with* de); **'bur·den·some** oneroso, gravoso.

bur·den[2] [~] ♪ estribillo *m*; *fig.* tema *m* principal.

bur·dock ['bə:dɔk] bardana *f.*

bu·reau [bjuə'rou], *pl. a.* **bu·reaux** ['~z] escritorio *m*; oficina *f*, agencia *f*; *Am.* ramo *m*, departamento *m*; **bu·reauc·ra·cy** [~'rɔkrəsi] burocracia *f*; **bu·reau·crat** ['bjuərou·kræt] burócrata *m/f*; **bu·reau·'crat·ic** □ burocrático.

bur·geon ['bə:dʒən] *lit.* **1.** retoño *m*; 2. retoñar.

bur·gess ['bə:dʒis] vecino (a *f*) *m* de una villa; *hist.* diputado *m.*

burgh ['bʌrə] *Scot.* villa *f.*

bur·glar ['bə:glə] escalador *m*; **bur·gla·ry** ['~əri] allanamiento *m* de morada; **bur·gle** ['bə:gl] *house* allanar, escalar.

bur·gun·dy ['bə:gəndi] vino *m* de Borgoña.

bur·i·al ['beriəl] entierro *m*; **'~-ground** cementerio *m.*

bu·rin ['bjuərin] buril *m.*

burl [bə:l] mota *f* en el paño.

bur·lap ['bə:ləp] harpillera *f.*

bur·lesque [bə:'lesk] **1.** burlesco, festivo; 2. parodia *f*; 3. parodiar.

bur·ly ['bə:li] membrudo, fornido.

Bur·mese [bə:'mi:z] birmano *adj. a. su. m* (*a. pl.*).

burn [bə:n] **1.** quemadura *f*; *Scot.* arroyo *m*; 2. [*irr.*] *v/t.* quemar; (*sun*) abrasar; ⊕ *fuel* funcionar con; *house etc.* (*a.* ~ *down*) incendiar; ⚡ ~ *out* fundir, quemar; ~ *up* consumir (*a. fig.*; *with* con, en); *v/i.* quemar (se); arder; incendiarse (*a.* ~ *down*); ~ *out* apagarse; ⚡ fundirse, quemarse; ~ *up* consumirse; arder mejor; *fig.* ~ *with* arder en (*or* de); *the light is* ~*ing* la luz está encendida; **'burn·er** mechero *m*; (*gas etc.*) quemador *m*, fuego *m*; **'burn·ing** □ ardiente (*a. fig.*); ~ *question* cuestión *f* palpitante.

bur·nish ['bə:niʃ] bruñir; **'bur·nish·er** bruñidor *m.*

burnt [bə:nt] *pret. a. p.p. of* **burn** 2; ~ *almond* almendra *f* dulce tostada; ~ *offering* holocausto *m.*

burr [bə:] **1.** sonido *m* fuerte de la erre; 2. pronunciar la erre con sonido fuerte.

bur·row ['bʌrou] **1.** madriguera *f*; (*rabbit's*) conejera *f*; 2. socavar; (*a.* ~ *through*) horadar.

bur·sa·ry ['bə:səri] beca *f*; tesorería *f* de un colegio.

burst [bə:st] **1.** reventón *m*; estallido *m*; (*leak*) fuga *f*; ✕ ráfaga *f* of *fire*; *fig.* arranque *m*, ímpetu *m*; 2. [*irr.*] *v/i.* reventar(se); estallar (*a. fig.*); ~ *into room* irrumpir en; *tears* prorrumpir en, deshacerse en; *threats etc.* desatarse en; ~ *out laughing* echarse a reír; ~ *with laughing* reventar de risa; *v/t.* reventar; romper.

bur·then ['bə:ðn] ⚓ arqueo *m.*

bur·y ['beri] enterrar, sepultar; *fig.* ocultar; *be buried in thought* estar absorto en meditación.

bus [bʌs] F autobús *m*; *sl. miss the* ~ perder la ocasión.

bus·by ['bʌzbi'] gorra *f* de húsar.

bush [buʃ] arbusto *m*; matorral *m*; ⊕ forro *m* de metal; **bush·el** ['buʃl] *medida de áridos* (= 36,36 *litros*; *Am.* = *35,24 litros*); **'bush-rang·er** *Australia*: bandido *m*; **bush·y** ['buʃi] *p.* peludo; *ground* matoso.

busi·ness ['biznis] negocio *m*, comercio *m*; (*firm*) empresa *f*; negocios *m/pl.*; (*calling*) empleo *m*, ocupación *f*; (*matter*) asunto *m*, cuestión *f*; *big* ~ comercio *m* en gran escala; *on* ~ de negocios; ~ *connections pl.* relaciones *f/pl.* comerciales; ~ *deal* trato *m* comercial; ~ *hours pl.* horas *f/pl.* de oficina; ~ *house* casa *f* de comercio; ~ *quarter* barrio *m* comercial; ~ *trip* viaje *m* de negocios; *do* ~ *with* comerciar con; *have no* ~ *to inf.* no tener derecho a *inf.*; *make it one's* ~ *to inf.* proponerse *inf.*; *F mean* ~ actuar (*or* hablar) en serio; *mind one's own* ~ no meterse donde no le llaman; *send a p. about his* ~ mandarle a uno a paseo; **'~-like** metódico, eficaz; negocioso; **'~-man** hombre *m* de negocios.

bus·kin ['bʌskin] borceguí *m*; *thea.* coturno *m*.

bus·man ['bʌsmən] conductor *m* de autobús; ~'s *holiday* día *m* de fiesta que pasa uno haciendo lo mismo que los otros días.

bust¹ [bʌst] busto *m*; pecho *m* de mujer.

bust² [~] *F* **1.** reventón *m*; † fracaso *m*; *go* ~ quebrar; **2.** romper(se), estropear(se).

bus·tard ['bʌstəd] avutarda *f*.

bus·tle ['bʌsl] **1.** bullicio *m*, animación *f*; (*esp. crowd*) bulla *f*; (*dress*) polisón *m*; **2.** *v/i.* menearse, apresurarse; (*a.* ~ *about*) bullir; *v/t.* impeler (a trabajar *etc.*); **'bus·tler** bullebulle *m/f*; **'bus·tling** ☐ hacendoso; *crowd* bullicioso.

bust-up ['bʌst'ʌp] *F* † quiebra *f*; (*quarrel*) riña *f*; (*row*) una *f* de Dios es Cristo.

bus·y ['bizi] **1.** ☐ ocupado (*at, with* en); activo; *b.s.* entrometido; bullicioso; *place* muy concurrido, de mucha actividad; *keep* ~ (*v/t.*) ocupar, (*v/i.*) estar ocupado; **2.** (*mst ~ o.s.*) ocupar(se) (*about, at, in, with* en, de, con); **'~-body** buscavidas *m/f*, entrometido (*a f*) *m*.

but [bʌt] **1.** *cj.* pero, mas (*lit.*); (*after negative*) sino; sino que; que no *subj.* (*e.g., not so busy* ~ *he can come*

no tan ocupado que no pueda venir); *he never walks* ~ *he falls* nunca anda sin caer; **2.** *prp.* excepto; solamente; *I cannot* ~ *inf.* no puedo menos de *inf.*; *v. last*; ~ *for* a no ser por; **3.** *adv.* solamente; *v. all*; *nothing* ~ nada más que; ~ *little* muy poco; **4.** *su.* pero *m*, objeción *f*.

butch·er ['butʃə] **1.** carnicero *m* (*a. fig.*); asesino *m*; **2.** *cattle* matar; dar muerte a; **'butch·er·y** carnicería *f* (*a. fig.*); (*place*) matadero *m*.

but·ler ['bʌtlə] despensero *m*; mayordomo *m*.

butt¹ [bʌt] **1.** cabo *m*, extremo *m*; mocho *m*; culata *f* *of gun*; colilla *f* *of cigarette*; ⊕ cabeza *f* de biela; (*target*) blanco *m*; *fig.* hazmerreír *m*; cabezada *f* *with head*; ~s *pl.* sitio *m* para tirar al blanco; **2.** dar cabezadas (*v/t.* contra); *F* ~ *in* interrumpir; *b. s.* entrometerse.

butt² [~] tonel *m*.

butte [bjuːt] *Am.* cerro *m*, monte *m* aislado.

but·ter ['bʌtə] **1.** mantequilla *f*; *F* ~ *would not melt in his mouth* es un mátalas callando, es una mosquita muerta; **2.** untar con mantequilla; *F* (*a.* ~ *up*) lisonjear; **'~-cup** ranúnculo *m*; **'~-fin·gered** desmañado en coger (la pelota *etc.*); **'~-fly** mariposa *f* (*a. fig.*); **'~-milk** leche *f* de manteca; **'but·ter·y** despensa *f*.

but·tock ['bʌtək] nalga *f* (*mst pl.*).

but·ton ['bʌtn] **1.** botón *m* (*a.* ♀); **2.** abotonar (*a.* ~ *up*); **'~-hole** **1.** ojal *m*; **2.** *sew.* abrir ojales en; *fig.* obligar a escuchar; **'~-hook** abotonador *m*.

but·tress ['bʌtris] **1.** contrafuerte *m* (*a. geog.*); *fig.* sostén *m*, apoyo *m*; *flying* ~ arbotante *m*; **2.** apoyar, reforzar (*a. fig.*).

bux·om ['bʌksəm] rolliza; frescachona.

buy [bai] [*irr.*] *v/t.* comprar (*from* a); *fig.* (*a.* ~ *off*) comprar, sobornar; ~ *out partner* comprar la parte de; ~ *up* † acaparar; *v/i. mst* ~ *and sell* traficar, comerciar; **'buy·er** comprador (-a *f*) *m*; **'buy·ing** compra *f*.

buzz [bʌz] **1.** zumbido *m*; *Am.* ~ *saw* sierra *f* circular; **2.** *v/i.* zumbar; ~ *about* cazclear; *sl.* ~ *off* largarse;

Am. teleph. colgar; *v/t. Am.* llamar por teléfono.

buz·zard [ˈbʌzəd] ratonero *m* común, águila *f* ratonera.

buzz·er [ˈbʌzə] *⚡* zumbador *m*.

by [bai] **1.** *prp.* por; *norm* según, de acuerdo con; *(in respect of)* de; *(time)* ~ *day* de día; ~ *3 o'clock* para las 3; ~ *now* ya, ahora; ~ *then* para entonces; antes de eso; *day* ~ *day* día por día; *(place)* ~ *me* cerca de mí, a mi lado; *north* ~ *east* norte por este; *side* ~ *side* lado a lado; *(manner)* ~ *easy stages* en cortas etapas; ~ *leaps and bounds* a pasos agigantados; ~ *lamplight* a la luz de una lámpara; ~ *land* por tierra; ~ *the dozen fig.* a docenas; ~ *twos* en pares; **⨯** *(multiplication)* por; ~ *far,* ~ *half* con mucho; ~ *o.s.* solo; ~ *the* ~ a propósito; ~ *the way* de paso; a propósito; **2.** *adv.* cerca; a un lado; aparte; ~ *and* ~ luego, pronto; ~ *and large* de un modo

general; *close* ~ cerca; **3.** *adj.* secundario, incidente.

bye-bye [ˈbaiˈbai] F ¡adiosito!; *(lulling children)* ¡ro ro!

by...: ˈ~-eˈlec·tion elección *f* complementaria; ˈ~·gone **1.** pasado; **2.** ~*s pl.*: *let* ~ *be* ~ olvidemos lo pasado; ˈ~-law estatuto *m*, reglamento *m*; ˈ~-name apodo *m*; ˈ~·pass **1.** desviación *f*; ⊕ tubo *m* de paso; **2.** desviar; evitar *(a. fig.)*; ˈ~-path trocha *f*; ˈ~-play *thea.* acción *f* aparte; escena *f* muda; ˈ~-prod·uct subproducto *m*; ⚗ derivado *m*; ˈ~-road camino *m* apartado; ˈ~-stand·er espectador (-a *f*) *m*, circunstante *m/f*; ˈ~-street callejuela *f*; ˈ~-way camino *m* apartado; camino *m* vecinal; ˈ~-word objeto *m* de burla *(or* aprobio); refrán *m*; *be a* ~ *for* ser notorio por.

By·zan·tine [biˈzæntain] bizantino *adj. a. su. m* (a *f*).

C

cab [kæb] taxi *m*; † cabriolé *m*; 🚂 casilla *f*.
ca·bal [kə'bæl] cábala *f*.
cab·a·ret ['kæbərei] cabaret *m*.
cab·bage ['kæbidʒ] col *f*; repollo *m*.
cab·ba·lis·tic,   cab·ba·lis·ti·cal [kæbə'listik(l)] □ cabalístico.
cab·by ['kæbi] F taxista *m*.
cab·in ['kæbin] cabaña *f*; ⚓ camarote *m*; *lorry,* ✈ cabina *f*; '**~-boy** mozo *m* de cámara; grumete *m*.
cab·i·net ['kæbinit] vitrina *f*; armario *m*; (*radio-*) caja *f*; *pol.* gabinete *m*, consejo *m* de ministros; *medicine* ~ botiquín *m*; '**~-mak·er** ebanista *m*.
ca·ble ['keibl] **1.** ⚓, *tel.* cable *m* (*a.* F); **2.** cablegrafiar; '**~-gram** cablegrama *m*; '**~-stitch** punto *m* en cruz.
cab·man ['kæbmən] taxista *m*; † cochero *m*.
ca·boo·dle [kə'bu:dl] *sl.*: *the whole* ~ lo todo.
ca·boose [kə'bu:s] cocina *f* en la cubierta de un buque.
cab·ri·o·let [kæbriou'lei] cabriolé *m*.
cab-stand ['kæbstænd] parada *f* de taxis.
ca'can·ny [kɔ:'kæni] trabajar con deliberada lentitud.
ca·ca·o [kə'kɑ:ou] cacao *m*.
cache [kæʃ] escondite *m*; ~ *of arms* alijo *m* de armas.
ca·chet ['kæʃei] sello *m*; *fig.* marca *f* de distinción.
cack·le ['kækl] **1.** cacareo *m*; risa *f* aguda; *sl.* cháchara *f*; **2.** cacarear; *sl.* chacharear; '**cack·ler** cacareador (-a *f*) *m*; *fig.* parlanchín (-a *f*) *m*.
ca·coph·o·ny [kæ'kɔfəni] cacofonía *f*.
cac·tus ['kæktəs] cacto *m*.
cad [kæd] F sinvergüenza *m*, pillo *m*.
ca·dav·er·ous [kə'dævərəs] □ cadavérico.
cad·die ['kædi] *golf: muchacho que lleva los instrumentos de juego.*
cad·dish ['kædiʃ] mal educado; de un malcriado.
cad·dy ['kædi] cajita *f* para té.

ca·dence ['keidəns] cadencia *f*; compás *m*.
ca·det [kə'det] cadete *m*; hijo *m* menor.
cadge [kædʒ] *v/t.* obtener mendigando; *v/i.* gorronear, vivir de gorra; '**cadg·er** gorrón (-a *f*) *m*.
ca·du·cous [kə'dju:kəs] caduco.
cae·cum ['si:kəm] intestino *m* ciego.
Cae·sar·i·an [si:'zɛəriən] cesario (*a.* ♂); cesariano.
cae·su·ra [si'zjuərə] cesura *f*.
ca·fé ['kæfei] café *m*; restaurante *m*.
caf·e·te·ri·a [kæfi'tiəriə] cafetería *f*.
caf·fe·ine ['kæfii:n] cafeína *f*.
cage [keidʒ] **1.** jaula *f* (*a.* ⚒); **2.** enjaular.
cage·y ['keidʒi] □ F astuto, taimado; cauteloso, reservado.
cairn [kɛən] montón *m* de piedras (como señal o mojón).
cais·son ['keisn] ⚒ cajón *m*; ⊕ cajón *m* hidráulico; ⚓ cajón *m* de suspensión.
ca·jole [kə'dʒoul] halagar, camelar; ~ *s.o. into s.t.* conseguir por medio de halagos que una p. haga algo; **ca'jol·er** lisonjero (-a *f*) *m*, zalamero (-a *f*) *m*; **ca'jol·er·y** engatusamiento *m*, zalamería *f*.
cake [keik] **1.** pastelillo *m*, bollo *m*; bizcocho *m*; (*soap*) pastilla *f*; *sl. take the* ~ ganar el premio; ser el colmo; **2.** apelmazarse; endurecerse.
cal·a·bash ['kæləbæʃ] calabaza *f*.
cal·a·mine ['kæləmain] calamina *f*.
ca·lam·i·tous [kə'læmitəs] □ calamitoso; **ca'lam·i·ty** calamidad *f*.
ca·lash [kə'læʃ] calesa *f*.
cal·car·e·ous [kæl'kɛəriəs] calcáreo.
cal·ci·fi·ca·tion [kælsifi'keiʃn] calcificación *f*; **cal·ci·fy** ['~fai] calcificar(se); **cal·ci·na·tion** [kælsi'neiʃn] calcinación *f*; **cal·cine** ['kælsain] calcinar(se); '**cal·cite** calcita *f*; **cal·ci·um** ['~siəm] calcio *m*.
cal·cu·la·ble ['kælkjuləbl] calculable; **cal·cu·late** ['~leit] *v/t.* calcular; ~*d to inf.* aprestado para *inf.*; *v/i.* calcular, conjeturar; ~ *on* contar

con; *calculating machine* máquina *f* de calcular; sumadora *f*; **cal·cu·la·tion** cálculo *m*, calculación *f*.

cal·en·dar ['kælində] **1.** calendario *m*; lista *f*; ~ *month* mes *m* del año; **2.** poner en la lista.

cal·en·der [~] ⊕ **1.** calandria *f*; **2.** calandrar.

calf [kɑ:f], *pl.* **calves** [kɑ:vz] ternero *m*; *fig.* F bobo *m*; (*or* '~**-leath·er**) piel *f* de becerro; *anat.* pantorrilla *f*; *zo.* (*seal etc.*) cría *f*; *in* ~, *with* ~ preñada; F ~ *love* amartelamiento*m*; *kill the fatted* ~ celebrar una fiesta de bienvenida; '~**-skin** piel *f* de becerro.

cal·i·brate ['kælibreit] calibrar; **cal·i·bre** ['~bə] calibre *m*; *fig.* capacidad *f*, aptitud *f*.

cal·i·co ['kælikou] calicó *m*.

Cal·i·for·nian ['kæli'fɔ:njən] californio *adj. a. su. m* (a *f*).

ca·liph ['kælif] califa *m*; **cal·iph·ate** ['~eit] califato *m*.

calk [kɔ:k] **1.** poner ramplones; **2.** ramplón *m* (*a.* **calk·in** ['kælkin]).

call [kɔ:l] **1.** llamada *f*; grito *m*; visita *f* (*pay hacer*); ⚖ citación *f*; ⚒ toque *m*, llamada *f*; (*bird's, bird-catcher's*) reclamo *m*; *hunt.* chilla *f*; ✝ demanda *f*; *fig.* (~ *to*) obligación *f* (a, de), necesidad *f* (de); *thea.* llamamiento *m*; demanda *f* (*for* por); ~ *girl* prostituta *f*, mujer *f* de lujo; ✝ ~ *money* dinero *m* a la vista; *radio:* ~ *sign* indicativo *m*; *port of* ~ puerto *m* de escala; *on* ~ disponible; ✝ *a* solicitud; *within* ~ al alcance de la voz; **2.** *v/t.* llamar; *meeting* convocar; invitar; calificar de; considerar, juzgar; *roll* pasar; llamar por teléfono; *cards:* (*bid*) marcar; *poker:* exigir la exposición de una mano; *attention* llamar (*to* sobre, a); *v. name, question; be* ~ *ed* llamarse; *v. bar;* ~ *back* hacer volver; *teleph.* volver a llamar; ~ *down* pedir al cielo; *Am.* F regañar; ~ *forth* sacar; *protest* originar, motivar; ~ *in p.* hacer entrar; *police* llamar; pedir la ayuda de; *thing issued* retirar; ~ *off* cancelar, abandonar; ~ *together* convocar; ~ *up memory* evocar; *teleph.* llamar; ⚒ llamar (al servicio militar); *v/i.* llamar (*a. teleph.*), dar voces; venir; hacer una visita; ~ *at house etc.* pasar por; ⚓ *port* hacer escala en; ~ *for* ir (*or* venir) por; exigir; pe-

dir; ~ *on* acudir a (*for* en busca de); visitar; invitar (*to* a); ~ *out* dar voces; '**call-box** cabina *f* telefónica; '**call-boy** *thea.* traspunte *m*; '**call·er** llamador (-a *f*) *m*; visita *f*.

cal·li·graph·ic [kæli'græfik] □ caligráfico; **cal·lig·ra·phy** [kə'ligrəfi] caligrafía *f*.

call·ing ['kɔ:liŋ] vocación *f*, profesión *f*; acción *f* de llamar *etc.*; *Am.* ~ *card* tarjeta *f* de visita.

cal·li·pers ['kælipəz] *pl.* calibrador *m*.

cal·lis·then·ics [kælis'θəniks] *mst sg.* calistenia *f*.

call-of·fice ['kɔ:lɔfis] *Am.* teléfono*m* público.

cal·los·i·ty [kæ'lɔsiti] callosidad *f*; '**cal·lous** □ calloso; *fig.* duro, insensible.

cal·low ['kælou] inexperto, sin plumas.

call-up [kɔ:l'ʌp] movilización *f*; servicio *m* militar; llamamiento *m*.

calm [kɑ:m] **1.** □ *weather* calmoso, bonancible; *p. etc.* tranquilo, sosegado; **2.** calma *f*; tranquilidad *f*, sosiego *m*; *v. dead;* **3.** (*a.* ~ *down*) calmar(se); tranquilizar(se), sosegar(se); ~ *down!* ¡tente quieto!; '**calm·ness** calma *f*; tranquilidad *f*.

ca·lor·ic [kə'lɔrik] calórico; *conductor of* ~ conductor *m* del calor; **cal·o·rie** ['kæləri] caloría *f*; **cal·o·rif·ic** [kælə'rifik] calorífico.

ca·lum·ni·ate [kə'lʌmnieit] calumniar; **ca·lum·ni·a·tion** calumnia *f*; **ca·lum·ni·a·tor** calumniador (-a *f*) *m*; **ca·lum·ni·ous** □ calumnioso, difamador; **cal·um·ny** ['kæləmni] calumnia *f*.

Cal·va·ry ['kælvəri] Calvario *m*; ♀ calvario *m*.

calve [kɑ:v] parir (*la vaca*); **calves** [kɑ:vz] *v. calf.*

Cal·vin·ism ['kælvinizm] calvinismo *m*.

ca·lyx ['keiliks], *pl.* **cal·y·ces** ['~lisi:z] ♀ cáliz *m*.

cam [kæm] leva *f*.

cam·ber ['kæmbə] ⊕ **1.** combadura *f*; **2.** combarse, arquearse.

cam·bric ['keimbrik] batista *f*.

came [keim] *pret. of* **come.**

cam·el ['kæml] *zo. a.* ♣ camello *m*.

ca·mel·li·a [kə'mi:ljə] camelia *f*.

cam·e·o ['kæmiou] camafeo *m*.

cam·er·a ['kæmərə] máquina *f*

(fotográfica); cámara f (de televisión); in ~ en secreto.

cami-knick·ers ['kæmi'nikəz] pl. combinación f con bragas en una sola pieza.

cam·o·mile ['kæməmail] camomila f: ~ tea manzanilla f.

cam·ou·flage ['kæmuflɑ:ʒ] 1. camuflaje m; 2. camuflar.

camp [kæmp] 1. campamento m; ~-bed catre m de tijera; ~-chair, ~-stool silla f plegadiza; 2. acampar; F alojarse temporalmente; ~ing site camping m.

cam·paign [kæm'pein] 1. campaña f; election ~ campaña f electoral; 2. hacer campaña (for a favor de); **cam'paign·er** veterano m (a. fig., esp. old ~); fig. paladín m.

cam·phor ['kæmfə] alcanfor m; **cam·phor·at·ed** ['~reitid] alcanforado.

cam·pus ['kæmpəs] Am. recinto m (de la Universidad).   [levas.

cam·shaft ['kæmʃɑ:ft] árbol m de**|**

can¹ [kæn] [irr.] puedo; sé; etc.

can² [~] 1. lata f, bote m; vaso m (de lata); 2. enlatar, conservar; Am. sl. poner en la calle; sl. carry the ~ pagar el pato; ~ning industry industria f conservera.

Ca·na·di·an [kə'neidjən] canadiense adj. a. su. m/f.

ca·nal [kə'næl] canal m (a. ⚡); **ca·nal·i·za·tion** [kænəlai'zeiʃn] canalización f; **'ca·nal·ize** canalizar.

ca·nard [kæ'nɑ:d] noticia f falsa.

ca·nar·y [kə'neəri] canario m.

ca·nas·ta [kə'næstə] cards: canasta f.

can·cel ['kænsl] v/t. cancelar (a. fig.); stamp: matar; v/i. ⊬ ~ out destruirse; **can·cel·la·tion** [kænse-'leiʃn] cancelación f, supresión f.

can·cer ['kænsə] ⚡ cáncer m; ♋ ast. Cáncer m; **'can·cer·ous** canceroso.

can·did ['kændid] ☐ franco; ~ly francamente.

can·di·date ['kændidit] candidato m (for para); opositor (-a f) m; **can·di·da·ture** ['~ʃə] candidatura f.

can·died ['kændid] azucarado.

can·dle ['kændl] candela f, bujía f; vela f; eccl. cirio m; ~ power bujía f; **Can·dle·mas** ['~məs] candelaria f; **can·dle·stick** candelero m; (low) palmatoria f.

can·dour ['kændə] candor m; franqueza f.

can·dy ['kændi] 1. azúcar m cande; Am. bombón m, dulce m; Am. ~ floss caramelo m americano; 2. v/t. azucarar; v/i. cristalizarse.

cane [kein] 1. ♀ caña f; ♀ caña f de azúcar; (stick) bastón m; school: palmeta f; ~ chair silla f de mimbre; 2. school: castigar con palmeta.

ca·nine ['keinain] 1. canino; 2. canino m, colmillo m (a. ~ tooth).

can·is·ter ['kænistə] bote m, lata f.

can·ker ['kæŋkə] 1. ⚡ úlcera f en la boca; ♀ cancro m; fig. corrupción f, peste f; 2. ulcerarse; corromperse; **'can·kered** fig. emponzoñado, corrompido; **'can·ker·ous** ulceroso.

canned [kænd] envasado; en lata; sl. ~ music música f en discos.

can·ner·y ['kænəri] fábrica f de conservas alimenticias.

can·ni·bal ['kænibl] 1. caníbal m; 2. antropófago.

can·non ['kænən] 1. ⚔ cañón m; artillería f; billiards: carambola f; 2. hacer carambola; rebotar (against, off contra); **can·non·ade** [~'neid] cañoneo m.

can·not ['kænɔt] no puedo; no sé; etc.

can·ny ['kæni] ☐ Scot. astuto; frugal, económico.

ca·noe [kə'nu:] 1. canoa f; 2. pasear en canoa.

can·on ['kænən] canon m; (p.) canónigo m; typ. gran canon m; ~ law derecho m canónico; **'can·on·ess** canonesa f; **can·on·i·cal** canónico; **can·on·i·za·tion** [~nai'zeiʃn] canonización f; **'can·on·ize** canonizar; **'can·on·ry** canonjía f.

can·o·py ['kænəpi] 1. dosel m; 🜂 baldaquín m; cielo m of bed; 2. endoselar.

cant¹ [kænt] 1. inclinación f, sesgo m; vaivén m; (crystal etc.) bisel m, chaflán m; 2. inclinar, sesgar; ladear (se); ~ over volcar.

cant² [~] 1. lenguaje m insincero, gazmoñería f; (jargon) jerga f, germanía f; 2. hablar insinceramente; hablar en jerga.

can't [kɑ:nt] = cannot.

can·ta·loup ['kæntəlu:p] cantalupo m, melón m.

can·tan·ker·ous [kən'tæŋkərəs] ☐ F arisco, intratable; quejumbroso; quisquilloso.

can·teen [kæn'ti:n] cantina *f*; (*bottle*) cantimplora *f*; juego *m* of cutlery.

can·ter ['kæntə] 1. medio galope *m*; 2. andar a medio galope.

can·thar·i·des [kæn'θæridi:z] *pl.* polvo *m* de cantárida.

can·ti·cle ['kæntikl] cántico *m*; ♫s *pl.* Cantar *m* de los Cantares.

can·ti·le·ver ['kæntili:və] viga *f* voladiza.

can·to ['kæntou] canto *m*.

can·ton 1. ['kæntɔn] cantón *m* (*a. heraldry*); 2. [kən'tu:n] ✗ acantonar; '**can·ton·ment** acantonamiento *m*.

can·vas ['kænvəs] cañamazo *m*, lona *f*; *paint.* lienzo *m*; under ~ en tiendas.

can·vass [~] 1. solicitación *f* (*esp.* de votos); sondeo *m*; *Am.* escrutinio *m*, pesquisa *f*; 2. *v/t.* escudriñar; *votes* solicitar; *opinion* sondear; *v/i.* solicitar; '**can·vass·er** solicitador (-a *f*) *m*.

caou·tchouc ['kautʃuk] caucho *m*.

cap [kæp] 1. gorra *f*; (*with peak*) gorra *f* de visera; (*cover*) tapa *f*, tapón *m*; caballete *m* of chimney; ⊕ casquete *m*; ⚓ tamborete *m*; cápsula *f* of gun, bottle; ~ and bells gorro *m* con campanillas; ~ and gown toga *f* y bonete; ~ in hand con el sombrero en la mano; the ~ fits viene de perilla; *polar* ~ casquete *m* polar; *put on one's thinking* ~ meditarlo bien; F *set one's* ~ *at a p.* proponerse conquistar a una p. como novio; 2. *head* cubrir con gorra; *hill* coronar; *vessel* poner tapa a; *work* poner remate a; *to* ~ *it all* para colmo de desgracias.

ca·pa·bil·i·ty [keipə'biliti] capacidad *f*, habilidad *f*; '**ca·pa·ble** □ capaz (of de), hábil.

ca·pa·cious [kə'peiʃəs] □ espacioso, capaz; *dress* holgado; **ca·pac·i·tate** [~'pæsiteit] habilitar, autorizar; **ca'pac·i·ty** 1. capacidad *f*; *mot.* cilindrada *f*; *in my* ~ *as* en mi calidad de; 2. *attr.* máximo; *thea.* lleno.

cap-à-pie [kæpə'pi:] de pies a cabeza.

ca·par·i·son [kə'pærisn] *lit.* 1. caparazón *m*; equipo *m*; 2. engualdrapar; *fig.* vestir soberbiamente.

cape¹ [keip] *geog.* cabo *m*, promontorio *m*.

cape² [~] capa *f*, esclavina *f*.

ca·per¹ ['keipə] ♀ alcaparra *f*.

ca·per² [~] 1. cabriola *f*; *fig.* travesura *f*; F lío *m*, embrollo *m*; *cut* ~*s* = 2. cabriolar.

ca·pi·as ['keipiæs]: *writ of* ~ orden *f* de arresto.

cap·il·lar·i·ty [kæpi'læriti] capilaridad *f*; **cap·il·lar·y** [kə'piləri] 1. capilar; 2. tubo *m* (*or* vaso *m*) capilar.

cap·i·tal ['kæpitl] 1. □ capital; ✝ de capital; F excelente, magnífico; 2. ✝ capital *m*; (*town*) capital *f*; △ capitel *m*; *typ.* (*or* ~ *letter*) mayúscula *f*; *fig.* make ~ out of aprovechar; '**cap·i·tal·ism** capitalismo *m*; '**cap·i·tal·ist** capitalista *m/f*; **cap·i·tal·is·tic** capitalista; **cap·i·tal·i·zation** [kəpitəlai'zeiʃn] capitalización *f*; **cap·i·tal·ize** capitalizar; *typ.* escribir (*or* imprimir) con mayúscula; ~ *on* aprovecharse de.

cap·i·ta·tion [kæpi'teiʃn] capitación *f*.

ca·pit·u·late [kə'pitjuleit] capitular; **ca·pit·u·la·tion** capitulación *f*.

ca·pon ['keipən] capón *m*.

ca·price [kə'pri:s] capricho *m*; **ca·pri·cious** [kə'priʃəs] □ caprichoso, caprichudo; **ca'pri·cious·ness** veleidad *f*, inconstancia *f*.

Cap·ri·corn ['kæprikɔ:n] Capricornio *m*.

cap·ri·ole ['kæprioul] corveta *f*.

cap·size [kæp'saiz] *v/i.* volcar, zozobrar; *v/t.* tumbar, volcar.

cap·stan ['kæpstən] cabrestante *m*.

cap·su·lar ['kæpsjulə] capsular; **cap·sule** ['kæpsju:l] ♀ *a.* ☣ cápsula *f*.

cap·tain ['kæptin] capitán *m* (*a. sport*); ~ *of industry* gran industrial *m*; **cap·tain·cy**, **cap·tain·ship** ['kæptinsi, '~inʃip] capitanía *f*.

cap·tion ['kæpʃn] 1. encabezamiento *m*; pie *m*; *film*: subtítulo *m*; 2. *Am.* intitular.

cap·tious ['kæpʃəs] □ criticón, reparador; quisquilloso; falso.

cap·ti·vate ['kæptiveit] *fig.* cautivar, fascinar; **cap·ti·va·tion** fascinación *f*; '**cap·tive** cautivo *adj. a. su. m* (a *f*); ~ *balloon* globo *m* cautivo; **cap·tiv·i·ty** [~'tiviti] cautiverio *m*.

cap·tor ['kæptə] apresador (-a *f*) *m*; **cap·ture** ['~tʃə] 1. apresamiento *m*; captura *f*; toma *f* of city etc.; (*p.*) prisionero (a *f*) *m*; presa *f*; 2.

apresar, capturar; *city etc.* tomar; *fig.* captar.

Cap·u·chin [ˈkæpjuʃin] capuchino *m.*

car [kɑ:] coche *m,* carro *m S.Am.*; (*tram-*) tranvía *m;* 🚂 vagón *m,* coche *m.*

car·a·bi·neer [kærəbiˈniə] carabinero *m.*

car·a·cole [ˈkærəkoul] **1.** caracol *m* (*horse*); **2.** caracolear.

ca·rafe [kəˈrɑ:f] garrafa *f.*

car·a·mel [ˈkærəmel] caramelo *m.*

car·at [ˈkærət] quilate *m.*

car·a·van [kærəˈvæn] caravana *f;* carricoche *m; mot.* remolque *m;* **car·a'van·se·rai** [ˌserai] caravasar *m.*

car·a·way [ˈkærəwei] alcaravea *f.*

car·bide [ˈkɑ:baid] carburo *m.*

car·bine [ˈkɑ:bain] carabina *f.*

car·bo·hy·drate [ˈkɑ:bouˈhaidreit] 🜨 hidrato *m* de carbono *m;* ⚗ carbohidrato *m,* fécula *f.*

car·bol·ic ac·id [kɑ:ˈbɔlikˈæsid] ácido *m* carbólico.

car·bon [ˈkɑ:bən] carbono *m; ⚡* carbón *m;* (*a. ~ paper*) papel *m* carbón; *~ copy* copia *f* al carbón; **car·bo·na·ceous** [ˌˈneiʃəs] carbonoso *m;* **car·bon·ate** [ˈˌbənit] carbonato *m;* **car·bon·ic** [ˌˈbɔnik] carbónico; *~ acid* ácido *m* carbónico; **car·bon·i·za·tion** [ˌbənaiˈzeiʃn] carbonización *f;* **ˈcar·bon·ize** carbonizar(se).

car·boy [ˈkɑ:bɔi] bombona *f.*

car·bun·cle [ˈkɑ:bʌŋkl] *min.* carbunclo *m; ⚗* carbunco *m;* F grano *m.*

car·bu·ret [ˈkɑ:bjuret] carburar; **ˈcar·bu·ret·ter** *mst* **ˈcar·bu·ret·tor** carburador *m.*

car·case, *mst* **car·cass** [ˈkɑ:kəs] cadáver *m* (de un animal); res *f* muerta; (*frame*) armazón *f.*

card[1] [kɑ:d] ⊕ **1.** carda *f;* **2.** *wool* cardar.

card[2] [ˌ] (*playing-*) carta *f;* ♣ *etc.* tarjeta *f,* postal *f;* (*index-*) ficha *f;* F (*tipo m*) salado *m; ~ catalogue* catálogo *m* de fichas, fichero *m; ~ game* juego *m* de naipes; *game of ~s* partida *f* de cartas; *like a house of ~s* como un castillo de naipes; F *on the ~s* probable; *have a ~ up one's sleeve* tener ayuda en reserva; *put one's ~s on the table* poner las cartas boca arriba; *speak by the ~* hablar con conocimiento de causa.

card·board [ˈkɑ:dbɔ:d] cartón *m; ~ box* caja *f* de cartón.

car·di·ac [ˈkɑ:diæk] cardíaco.

car·di·gan [ˈkɑ:digən] rebeca *f,* jersey *m.*

car·di·nal [ˈkɑ:dinl] **1.** □ cardinal; **2.** cardenal *m* (*a. orn.*); **car·di·nal·ate** [ˈˌeit] cardenalato *m.*

card...: **ˈ~-in·dex** fichero *m;* ˈ**~-sharp·er** fullero *m.*

care [kɛə] **1.** cuidado *m,* solicitud *f;* esmero *m,* atención *f;* cargo *m,* custodia *f; ~ of* (*abbr. c/o*) ... a manos de; *en casa de; take ~* tener cuidado; *take ~ of* cuidar de; F atender a; *with ~!* ¡atención!; ¡cuidado!; **2.** tener cuidado; *~ about* preocuparse de (*or* por); *~ for* cuidar; (*love*) querer, amar; desear; *I don't ~ for that* no me gusta eso; *~ to* tener ganas de; *would you ~ to say?* ¿quiere Vd. decirme?; F *I don't ~* (*twopence etc.*)! ¡no se me da un bledo! (*for de*); *well ~d for* bien cuidado. [inclinar.|

ca·reen [kəˈri:n] ⚓ carenar; volcar,|

ca·reer [kəˈriə] **1.** carrera *f; Am. ~ diplomat* diplomático *m* de carrera; **2.** correr a carrera tendida; **ca·reer·ist** [kəˈriərist] ambicioso (a *f*) *m.*

care·free [ˈkɛəfri:] despreocupado.

care·ful [ˈkɛəful] □ cuidadoso; esmerado; cauteloso; *appearance* acicalado; *be ~ to inf.* poner diligencia en *inf.; be ~ to say that* decir muy particularmente que; **ˈcare·ful·ness** cuidado *m;* esmero *m;* cautela *f.*

care·less [ˈkɛəlis] □ descuidado; desatento, desaplicado; alegre, sin cuidado; **ˈcare·less·ness** descuido *m;* negligencia *f;* indiferencia *f;* desaliño *m of appearance.*

ca·ress [kəˈres] **1.** caricia *f;* **2.** acariciar (*a. fig.*).

care·tak·er [ˈkɛəteikə] custodio *m,* conserje *m;* guardesa *f.*

care·worn [ˈkɛəwɔ:n] agobiado de inquietudes.

car·fare [ˈkɑ:fɛə] *Am.* pasaje *m.*

car·go [ˈkɑ:gou] carga *f,* cargamento *m; mixed* (*or general*) *~ carga f* mixta.

car·i·ca·ture [ˈkærikəˈtjuə] **1.** caricatura *f;* (*newspaper*) dibujo *m;* **2.** caricaturizar; **car·i·ca·tur·ist** [kærikəˈtjuərist] caricaturista *m/f,* dibujante *m/f.*

car·i·es ['kɛərii:z] caries *f*; **'car·i·ous** cariado.

car·mine ['ka:main] **1.** carmín *m*; **2.** carmíneo.

car·nage ['ka:nidʒ] carnicería *f*, mortandad *f*; **'car·nal** ☐ carnal; **car·nal·i·ty** [ˌ'næliti] carnalidad *f*; **car·na·tion** [ˌ'neiʃn] **1.** clavel *m*; **2.** encarnado.

car·ni·val ['ka:nivl] carnaval *m*, fiesta *f*, feria *f*.

car·ni·vore ['ka:nivɔ:] carnívoro *m*; **car·niv·o·rous** [ˌ'nivərəs] carnívoro.

car·ol ['kærl] **1.** villancico *m*; **2.** cantar villancicos. [rótida *f.*]

ca·rot·id [kə'rɔtid] (*a.* ~ *artery*) ca-ʃ

ca·rouse [kə'rauz] **1.** *a.* **ca'rous·al** jarana *f*, parranda *f*; **2.** jaranear, andar de parranda.

carp[1] [ka:p] *ichth.* carpa *f*.

carp[2] [ˌ] criticar, censurar; ~ *at* quejarse de.

car·park ['ka:pa:k] aparcamiento *m*.

car·pen·ter ['ka:pintə] **1.** carpintero *m*; **2.** carpintear; **'car·pen·try** carpintería *f*.

car·pet ['ka:pit] **1.** alfombra *f*, tapete *m*; *Am.* F *be on the* ~ estar sobre el tapete; F ser reprobado; **2.** alfombrar; *fig.* cubrir, revestir; F reprobar; **'~-bag·ger** aventurero *m* político; **'car·pet·ing** alfombrado *m*.

car·pet...: **'~-knight** soldado *m* de gabinete; **'~-slip·pers** *pl.* zapatillas *f*/*pl.*; **'~-sweep·er** barredera *f* de alfombras; (*machine*) aspirador *m* (de polvo).

car·riage ['kæridʒ] carruaje *m*; 🚃 vagón *m*; ⚔ cureña *f*; ✝ porte *m*; ⊕ carro *m*; (*bearing*) andares *m*/*pl.*, modo *m* de andar; ~ *free* franco de porte; ~ *paid* porte pagado.

car·riage...: **'~-and-'pair** coche *m* de dos caballos; **'~-door** portezuela *f*; **'~-drive** calzada *f*; **'~-road**, **'~-way** carretera *f*; calzada *f*.

car·ri·er ['kæriə] porteador *m*; trajinante *m*; empresa *f* de transportes; ⚓ porta(a)viones *m*; ✈ portador (-a *f*) *m*; *radio*: onda *f* portadora; **pi·geon** paloma *f* mensajera.

car·ri·on ['kæriən] carroña *f*; inmundicia *f*; ~ *crow* corneja *f* negra.

car·rot ['kærət] zanahoria *f*; **'car·rot·y** F pelirrojo.

car·ry ['kæri] **1.** *v/t.* llevar, traer; transportar; llevar encima *on p.*;

goods acarrear; *burden* sostener; *prize, election* ganar, lograr; ⚔ *fortress* conquistar, tomar; *proposition* hacer aceptar; ✝ *stock* tener en existencia; (*extend*) extender, llevar más lejos; ♪ llevar; *fig.* comprender, implicar; *v. day, effect, weight*; ~ *o.s.* andar (con garbo *etc.*); ~ *along* llevar consigo; ~ *away* llevarse; *fig.* encantar, arrebatar; ~ *everything before one* arrollarlo todo; ✝ ~ *forward* pasar; ~ *off* llevarse; (*kill*) matar; ~ *s.t. off* well salir airoso; ~ *on* continuar; *esp.* ✝ dirigir; promover; ~ *out* (*or through*) *plan* realizar, llevar a cabo; *repairs* hacer; ~ *over* guardar para más tarde; ✝ ~ *pasar*; ~ *through p.* sostener hasta el fin; *v/i.* (*reach*) alcanzar; ~ *on* continuar; F (*complain*) quejarse sin motivo; (*misbehave*) travesar; insistir, machacar (*about* en); ~ *on!* ¡adelante!; ¡siga!; F ~ *on* with tener un amorío con; ~*ing capacity* capacidad *f* de carga; **2.** ⚔ alcance *m*; **'~-cot** cuna *f* portátil, cochecito *m*.

cart [ka:t] **1.** carro *m*, carreta *f*; ~ *horse* caballo *m* de tiro; *hand* ~ carretilla *f*, carretón *m*; *fig.* put the ~ *before the horse* trastrocar las cosas; *sl.* *in the* ~ en un atolladero; **2.** carretear; F llevar (*esp.* con dificultad); **'cart·age** carretaje *m*; ✝ acarreo *m*.

car·tel ['ka:tel] ✝ *a.* ⚔ cartel *m*.

cart·er ['ka:tə] carretero *m*, trajinante *m*.

car·ti·lage ['ka:tilidʒ] cartílago *m*; **car·ti·lag·i·nous** [ˌ'lædʒinəs] cartilaginoso.

cart·load ['ka:tloud] carretada *f* (*a. fig.*).

car·tog·ra·pher [ka:'tɔgrəfə] cartógrafo *m*; **car'tog·ra·phy** cartografía *f*.

car·ton ['ka:tən] caja *f* de cartón, envase *m*.

car·toon [ka:'tu:n] **1.** *paint.* cartón *m*; caricatura *f*, dibujo *m*; *film*: dibujo *m* animado; **2.** caricaturizar.

car·touche [ka:'tu:ʃ] △ cartela *f*.

car·tridge ['ka:tridʒ] cartucho *m*.

cart-wheel ['ka:twi:l] rueda *f* de carro; *fig.* salto *m* mortal de lado; *Am. sl.* dólar *m*.

cart·wright ['ka:trait] carretero *m*.

carve [ka:v] *meat* trinchar; *stone etc.* esculpir, tallar (*in* en); *fig.* ~

one's *way through* hacerse un camino por; **'carv·er** trinchador (-a *f*) *m*; tallista *m/f*; escultor (-a *f*) *m*; ~s *pl.* cuchillo *m* y trinchante.

carv·ing ['kɑ:viŋ] acción *f* de trinchar; ⚓ *etc.* escultura *f*; obra *f* de talla.

cas·cade [kæs'keid] cascada *f*.

case¹ [keis] **1.** caja *f* (*a. typ.*); estuche *m*; funda *f*; (*window etc.*) marco *m*, bastidor *m*; (*cartridge- etc.*) cápsula *f*; (*glass*) vitrina *f*; *typ.* lower ~ caja *f* baja; upper ~ caja *f* alta; **2.** encajonar; enfundar.

case² [~] caso *m* (*a. ⚑ a. gr.*); 🜨 causa *f*, pleito *m*; F persona *f* divertida; *argumento m* convincente; *a* ~ *for* una razón por; *have a strong* ~ tener un argumento fuerte; *as the* ~ *may be* según el caso; *in* ~ en caso que; por si acaso; *in* ~ *of* en caso de; *in any* ~ en todo caso; *in such a* ~ en tal caso.

case·hard·en ['keishɑ:dn] ⊕ cementar; *fig.* ~ed insensible.

ca·se·in ['keisii:n] caseína *f*.

case-knife ['keisnaif] cuchillo *m* con vaina.

case·mate ['keismeit] casamata *f*.

case·ment ['keismənt] ventana *f* a bisagra; marco *m* (de una ventana); *poet.* ventana *f*.

cash [kæʃ] **1.** dinero *m* contante; pago *m* al contado; ~ *down, for* ~ al contado; *in* ~ en metálico; *be out of* ~ estar sin blanca; ~ *payment* pago *m* al contado; ~ *on delivery* pagar contra recepción; ~ *register* caja *f* registradora; **2.** *cheque* cobrar, hacer efectivo; F ~ *in on* sacar provecho de; '~-book libro *m* de caja; '~-box caja *f*; **cash·ier** [kæ'ʃiə] **1.** cajero (a *f*) *m*; **2.** destituir; degradar.

cash·mere [kæʃ'miə] casimir *m*.

cas·ing ['keisiŋ] cubierta *f*, envoltura *f*; cerco *m of window*; ⊕ tubería *f* de revestimiento.

ca·si·no [kə'si:nou] casino *m*.

cask [kɑ:sk] tonel *m*, barril *m*.

cas·ket ['kɑskit] cajita *f*, cofrecito *m*; *Am.* ataúd *m*.

cas·sa·tion [kæ'seiʃn] casación *f*.

cas·se·role ['kæsəroul] cacerola *f*.

cas·si·a ['kæsiə] casia *f*; canela *f* de la China.

cas·sock ['kæsək] sotana *f*.

cas·so·war·y ['kæsəweəri] casuario *m*.

cast [kɑ:st] **1.** echada *f*; lance *m of net*; molde *m*, forma *f*; *fig.* apariencia *f*, estampa *f*; *thea.* reparto *m*, personal *m*; ⊕ pieza *f* fundida; ♱ balance *m*; (*eye*) mirada *f* bizca; (*colour*) tinte *m*; **2.** [*irr.*] *v/t.* echar, lanzar; desechar; *eyes* volver; *shadow* proyectar; ⊕ fundir; *thea. parts* repartir; *lots* echar; *sum* (*a.* ~ *up*) calcular, sumar; ~ *iron* hierro *m* colado; ~ *steel* acero *m* colado; ~ (*a th.*) *in a p.'s teeth* echar a uno en la cara; ~ *away* desechar, abandonar; ♱ *be* ~ *away* ser un náufrago; ~ *down* derribar; *fig.* desanimar; *eyes* bajar; ~ *forth* despedir; ~ *loose* soltar; ~ *off* abandonar; ~ *on* (*knitting*) empezar con; ~ *out* arrojar; despedir; *v/i.* (*fishing*) lanzar, arrojar; ⊕ fundir; ~ *about for* buscar; ♱ ~ *off* desamarrar.

cas·ta·net [kæstə'net] castañuela *f*.

cast·a·way ['kɑ:stəwei] ♱ náufrago (a *f*) *m*; réprobo (a *f*) *m*.

caste [kɑ:st] casta *f*; *lose* ~ desprestigiarse.

cas·tel·lan ['kæstələn] castellano *m*, alcaide *m*; **cas·tel·lat·ed** ['kæsteleitid] almenado; encastillado.

cas·ter ['kɑ:stə] = *castor²*.

cas·ti·gate ['kæstigeit] castigar; **cas·ti·ga·tion** castigo *m*.

cast·ing ['kɑ:stiŋ] **1.** *vote* decisivo; **2.** ⊕ pieza *f* fundida.

cast-i·ron ['kɑ:st'aiən] hecho de hierro fundido; *fig.* fuerte, duro.

cas·tle ['kɑ:sl] **1.** castillo *m*; *chess:* torre *f*, roque *m*; ~ *in Spain* castillo *m* en el aire; **2.** *chess:* enrocar.

cas·tor¹ ['kɑ:stə] *pharm.* castóreo *m*; *sl.* sombrero *m*; ~ *oil* aceite *m* de ricino.

cas·tor² [~] ruedecilla *f* de mueble; vinagrera *f*; ~s *pl.* angarillas *f/pl.*; ~ *sugar* azúcar *m* extrafino.

cas·trate [kæs'treit] castrar; **cas·'tra·tion** castración *f*.

cas·u·al ['kæʒjuəl] **1.** □ casual; descuidado, indiferente; ~ *labourer* obrero *m* casual; **2.** *persona que recibe caridad de vez en cuando*; **'cas·u·al·ty** accidente *m*; ✗ baja *f*; víctima *f*.

cas·u·ist ['kæzjuist] casuista *m/f*; *b.s.* sofista *m/f*; **'cas·u·ist·ry** casuística *f*; razonamiento *m* falaz.

cat [kæt] gato *m*; azote *m* con

nueve ramales; ~-*burglar* balconero *m*; *bell the* ~ ponerle cascabel al gato; F *let the* ~ *out of the bag* revelar el secreto, cantar.

cat·a·clysm [ˈkætəklizm] cataclismo *m*. [ba *f*.]

cat·a·comb [ˈkætəkoum] catacum-

cat·a·logue, *Am. a.* **cat·a·log** [ˈkætələɔg] **1.** catálogo *m*; fichero *m*; **2.** catalogar.

cat·a·lyst [ˈkætəlist] catalizador *m*.

cat·a·pult [ˈkætəpʌlt] catapulta *f*; honda *f*.

cat·a·ract [ˈkætərækt]ʹ catarata *f* (*a.* 🜨).

ca·tarrh [kəˈtɑː] catarro *m*; **ca·tarrh·al** [kəˈtɑːrəl] catarral.

ca·tas·tro·phe [kəˈtæstrəfi] catástrofe *f*; **cat·a·stroph·ic** [kætəˈstrɔfik] □ catastrófico.

cat·call [ˈkætkɔːl] **1.** rechifla *f*, silba *f*; **2.** rechiflar, silbar.

catch [kætʃ] **1.** cogida *f*; presa *f*, botín *m*; pesca *f of fish*; (*lock*) pestillo *m*, aldabilla *f*; ♪ canon *m* de carácter cómico; (*deceit*) trampa *f*; **2.** [*irr.*] *v/t.* coger, atrapar; agarrar, asir; *fig.* comprender; llegar a oír; *fig.* sorprender; *breath* suspender; F ~ *it* merecerse un regaño; ~ *in the act* coger con las manos en la masa; *v. cold, fire, hold etc.*; F ~ *out p.* cazar, sorprender; coger en una falta; ~ *up p.* alcanzar; *th.* asir; **3.** *v/i.* enredarse, engancharse; ⊕ engranar; (*fire*) encenderse; 🜨 *be* ~*ing* ser contagioso; ~ *at* tratar de asir (*or* coger); ~ *on* prender en; F coger el tino; caer en la cuenta; ~ *up fig.* ponerse al día; ~ *up with* alcanzar, emparejar con; ʹ~*all Am.* armario *m etc.* destinado a contener toda clase de objeto; ʹ**catch·er** *Am. sport:* receptor *m*, parador *m*; ʹ**catch·ing** 🜨 contagioso; atrayente; ♪ pegajoso; ʹ**catch·ment ba·sin** cuenca *f*.

catch...: ʹ~*pen·ny* ♱ de pacotilla; ʹ~*phrase* tópico *m*; ʹ~*pole* alguacil *m*, corchete *m*; ʹ~*word typ.* reclamo *m*; *thea.* pie *m*; ʹ**catch·y** F pegajoso.

cat·e·chism [ˈkætikizm] catecismo *m*; (*method*) catequismo *m*; **cat·e·chize** [ˈ~kaiz] catequizar; **cat·e·chu·men** [ˌ~ˈkjuːmən] catecúmeno (a *f*) *m*.

cat·e·gor·i·cal [kætiˈgɔrikl] □ categórico; **cat·e·go·ry** [ˈ~gəri] categoría *f*.

cat·e·nar·y [kəˈtiːnəri] 🜨 catenaria *f*.

ca·ter [ˈkeitə]: ~ *for* abastecer, proveer; *fig.* proveer a; ʹ**ca·ter·er** abastecedor *m*; proveedor *m*; ʹ**ca·ter·ing** abastecimiento *m*.

ca·ter·pil·lar [ˈkætəpilə] oruga *f*.

cat·er·waul [ˈkætəwɔːl] marramizar; chillar.

cat·gut [ˈkætgʌt] cuerda *f* de tripa.

ca·thar·sis [kəˈθɑːsis] catarsis *f*.

ca·the·dral [kəˈθiːdrl] catedral *f*.

Cath·er·ine wheel [ˈkæθərin ˈwiːl] △ rosetón *m*; (*firework*) rueda *f* de fuegos artificiales.

cath·ode [ˈkæθoud] cátodo *m*; ~ *ray* tube tubo *m* de rayos catódicos.

cath·o·lic [ˈkæθəlik] **1.** □ *eccl.* católico; liberal, de amplias miras; **2.** católico (a *f*) *m*; **ca·thol·i·cism** catolicismo *m*.

cat·kin [ˈkætkin] amento *m*.

cat's-paw [ˈkætspɔː] *fig.* instrumento *m*.

cat·ti·ness [ˈkætinis] malicia *f*.

cat·tle [ˈkætl] ganado *m* (vacuno); ʹ~*breed·ing* cría *f* de ganado; ʹ~*rus·tler Am.* ladrón *m* de ganado; ʹ~*show* exposición *f* de ganado.

Cau·ca·sian [kɔːˈkeiziən] caucasiano *adj. a. su. m* (a *f*).

cau·cus [ˈkɔːkəs] camarilla *f* política.

cau·dal [ˈkɔːdl] *zo.* caudal.

cau·dle [ˈkɔːdl] bebida *f* caliente.

caught [kɔːt] *pret. a. p.p. of catch* 2 *a.* 3.

caul·dron [ˈkɔːldrən] calderón *m*.

cau·li·flow·er [ˈkɔliflauə] coliflor *f*.

caulk [kɔːk] calafatear; ʹ**caulk·er** calafate *m*.

caus·al [ˈkɔːzl] □ causal; **cau·sal·i·ty** [ˌ~ˈzæliti] causalidad *f*; ʹ**caus·a·tive** causativo; **cause 1.** causa *f* (*a.* ⚖); *make common* ~ *with* hacer causa común con; **2.** causar; ʹ**cause·less** □ sin causa.

cause·way [ˈkɔːzwei] calzada *f*; (*sea*) arrecife *m*.

caus·tic [ˈkɔːstik] **1.** cáustico *m*; **2.** □ cáustico (*a. fig.*).

cau·ter·i·za·tion [kɔːtəraiˈzeiʃn] cauterización *f*; ʹ**cau·ter·ize** cauterizar; ʹ**cau·ter·y** cauterio *m*.

cau·tion [ˈkɔːʃn] **1.** cautela *f*; (*warn-*

ing) amonestación *f*; F persona *f* extraordinaria; ~ *money* caución *f*; **2.** advertir, amonestar *(against contra)*; **'cau·tion·ar·y** amonestador.

cau·tious ['kɔːʃəs] □ cauteloso, precavido; **'cau·tious·ness** cautela *f*, circunspección *f*.

cav·al·cade [kævl'keid] cabalgata *f*.

cav·a·lier [kævə'liə] **1.** caballero *m*; galán *m*; **2.** altivo, desdeñoso.

cav·al·ry ['kævlri] caballería *f*.

cave [keiv] **1.** cueva *f*; **2.** ~ *in*: *v/i.* hundirse, derrumbarse; *v/t.* F quebrar.

ca·ve·at ['keiviæt] advertencia *f*; *t*ᵼ advertencia *f* de suspensión.

cave-man ['keivmən] troglodita *m*; hombre *m* de las cavernas.

cav·ern ['kævən] caverna *f*, antro *m*; **'cav·ern·ous** cavernoso.

cav·i·ar(e) ['kæviɑː, kævi'ɑː] caviar *m*.

cav·il ['kævil] **1.** crítica *f*, reparo *m*; **2.** sutilizar, criticquizar; ~ *at, about* poner peros a; **'cav·il·ler** criticón (-a *f*) *m*.

cav·i·ty ['kæviti] cavidad *f*.

ca·vort [kə'vɔːt] cabriolar.

caw [kɔː] **1.** graznar; **2.** graznido *m*.

cay·enne [kei'en] *(a.* ['keien] *pepper)* pimentón *m*.

cay·man ['keimən] caimán *m*.

cay·use ['kai'juːs] *Am.* F jaca *f* india.

cease [siːs] *v/i.* cesar *(from* de); ~ *from* dejar de; *v/t.* suspender, cesar; '~·'fire cese *m* de hostilidades; **'cease·less** □ incesante.

ce·dar ['siːdə] cedro *m*.

cede [siːd] ceder.

ceil·ing ['siːliŋ] techo *m*, cielo *m* raso; ⚓ techo *m*; *fig.* punto *m* más alto; ~ *price* precio *m* tope.

cel·an·dine ['seləndain] celidonia *f*.

cel·e·brant ['selibrənt] *eccl.* celebrante *m*; **'cel·e·brate** celebrar *(a. eccl.)*; **'cel·e·brat·ed** célebre, famoso *(for* por); **cel·e·'bra·tion** celebración *f*; *(party)* reunión *f*; *in* ~ *of* en conmemoración de; **'cel·e·bra·tor** parrandista *m/f*.

ce·leb·ri·ty [si'lebriti] celebridad *f* *(a. p.)*.

ce·ler·i·ty [si'leriti] celeridad *f*.

cel·er·y ['seləri] apio *m*.

ce·les·tial [si'lestjəl] celestial *(a. fig.)*.

cel·i·ba·cy ['selibəsi] celibato *m*; **cel·i·bate** ['~bit] célibe *adj. a. su. m/f*.

cell [sel] *(prison)* celda *f*; *biol.* célula *f*; *pol.* célula *f* (de comunistas); ⚡ elemento *m*; *(bees)* celdilla *f*.

cel·lar ['selə] **1.** sótano *m*; *(wine-)* bodega *f*; **2.** embodegar; **'cel·lar·age** almacenaje *m* en una bodega.

cel·list ['tʃelist] violoncelista *m/f*; **cel·lo** ['tʃelou] violoncelo *m*.

cel·lo·phane ['seləfein] *(papel m)* celofán *m*.

cel·lu·lar ['seljulə] celular; **cel·lule** ['~juːl] célula *f*; **cel·lu·loid** ['~juloid] celuloide *m*; **cel·lu·lose** ['~lous] celulosa *f*.

Celt [kelt] celta *m/f*; **'Celt·ic** céltico.

ce·ment [si'ment] **1.** cemento *m*; **2.** cementar; *fig.* consolidar; **ce·ment·a·tion** [siːmen'teiʃn] cementación *f*.

cem·e·ter·y ['semitri] cementerio *m*.

cen·o·taph ['senətɑːf] cenotafio *m*.

cense [sens] incensar; **'cen·ser** incensario *m*.

cen·sor ['sensə] **1.** censor *m*; **2.** censurar; **cen·so·ri·ous** [sen'sɔːriəs] □ hipercrítico, criticón; **cen·sor·ship** ['~səʃip] censura *f*.

cen·sur·a·ble ['senʃərəbl] □ censurable; **cen·sure** ['senʃə] **1.** censura *f*; **2.** censurar.

cen·sus ['sensəs] censo *m*.

cent [sent] centavo *m* *(Am. = ¹/₁₀₀ dólar)*; *per* ~ por ciento.

cen·taur ['sentɔː] centauro *m*.

cen·tau·ry ['sentɔːri] centaura *f*.

cen·te·nar·i·an [senti'nɛəriən] centenario *adj. a. su. m* *(a f)*; **cen·te·nar·y** [sen'tiːnəri] centenario *m*.

cen·ten·ni·al [sen'tenjəl] centenario *adj. a. su. m*.

cen·tes·i·mal [sen'tesiml] □ centesimal.

cen·ti... ['senti]: '~·grade centígrado; '~·gramme centígramo *m*; '~·me·tre centímetro *m*; '~·pede ['~piːd] ciempiés *m*.

cen·tral ['sentrəl] □ central; ~ *heating* calefacción *f* central; **cen·tral·i·za·tion** [~lai'zeiʃn] centralización *f*; **'cen·tral·ize** centralizar.

cen·tre, *Am.* **cen·ter** ['sentə] **1.** centro *m*; ~ *forward* delantero *m* centro; ~ *half* medio centro *m*; **2.** central; **3.** centrar; concentrarse *(on, about* en); ⊕ ~ *punch* punzón *m* de marcar.

cen·tric, cen·tri·cal ['sentrik(l)] □ céntrico; **cen·trif·u·gal** [sen'trifjug|] □ centrífugo; **cen'trip·e·tal** [~pitl] □ centrípeto.

cen·tu·ple ['sentjupl] 1. céntuplo; 2. centuplicar.

cen·tu·ry ['sentʃuri] siglo m.

ce·ram·ic [si'ræmik] cerámico; **ce·ram·ics** pl. cerámica f.

ce·re·al ['siəriəl] cereal adj. a. su. m.

cer·e·bral ['seribrəl] cerebral.

cere·cloth ['siəklɔθ] † mortaja f.

cer·e·mo·ni·al [seri'mounjəl] □ ceremonial adj. a. su. m; **cer·e'mo·ni·ous** □ ceremonioso; **cer·e·mo·ny** ['seriməni] ceremonia f; Master of Ceremonies maestro m de ceremonias; stand on ~ hacer ceremonias.

cer·tain ['sə:tn] □ cierto; know for ~ saber a buen seguro; make ~ asegurarse (de), cerciorarse (de); ~ly ciertamente; sin falta; **'cer·tain·ty** certeza f.

cer·tif·i·cate 1. [sə'tifikit] certificado m, título m; ~ of baptism (death, marriage) partida f de bautismo (defunción, casamiento); 2. [sə'tifikeit] certificar; ~d con título; **'cer·ti·fi·ca·tion** certificación f; **cer·ti·fy** ['~fai] certificar; garantizar; **cer·ti·tude** ['~tju:d] certeza f.

cer·vi·cal ['sə:vikl] cervical.

ces·sa·tion [se'seiʃn] cesación f; ~ of hostilities suspensión f de hostili-|
ces·sion ['seʃn] cesión f. [dades.|
cess·pool ['sespu:l] pozo m negro.

ce·ta·cean [si'teiʃjən] cetáceo adj. a. su. m.

chafe [tʃeif] 1. v/t. rozar, raer; calentar (frotando); fig. irritar, enfadar; 2. v/i. desgastarse (against contra); fig. irritarse, enfadarse; chafing dish escalfador m.

chaff [tʃɑ:f] 1. barcia f, aechaduras f/pl.; b.s. broza f, desecho m; (banter) zumba f, chanza f; 2. p. zumbarse de, dar chasco a.

chaf·fer ['tʃæfə] regatear.

chaf·finch ['tʃæfintʃ] pinzón m vulgar.

cha·grin ['ʃægrin] 1. desazón f, disgusto m; 2. desazonar, apesadumbrar.

chain [tʃein] 1. cadena f; phys. ~ reaction reacción f en cadena; ~ store tienda f de una cadena; 2. encadenar; **'~-smo·ker** fumador (-a f) m de un pitillo tras otro.

chair [tʃɛə] 1. silla f; cátedra f (a. professorial ~); presidencia f of meeting; take the ~ presidir; 2. p. in authority asentar; llevar en una silla; meeting presidir; '~·man, '~·woman presidente m; '~·man·ship presidencia f.

chaise [ʃeiz] calesa f, landó m; ~longue meridiana f.

chal·ice ['tʃælis] eccl. cáliz m.

chalk [tʃɔ:k] 1. geol. creta f; tiza f for drawing; French ~ jaboncillo m de sastre; esteatita f; F by a long ~ de mucho; 2. marcar con tiza; fig. apuntar (mst ~ up); **'chalk·y** cretoso.

chal·lenge ['tʃælindʒ] 1. desafío m (a. fig.), reto m; ✗ quién vive m; ⚖ recusación f; 2. desafiar (a. fig.), retar; ✗ dar el quién vive a; ⚖ recusar; disputar; dudar; **'chal·leng·er** desafiador (-a f) m; retador (-a f) m.

cha·lyb·e·ate [kə'libiit] ferruginoso.

cham·ber ['tʃeimbə] cámara f; recámara f of gun; lit. aposento m; ~ music música f de cámara; ~s pl. despacho m de un abogado (or juez); **cham·ber·lain** ['~lin] chambelán m, gentilhombre m de cámara; **'cham·ber·maid** camarera f, criada f (de un hotel); **'cham·ber·pot** orinal m.

cha·me·le·on [kə'mi:ljən] camaleón m.

cham·fer ['tʃæmfə] 1. chaflán m; 2. chaflanar.

cham·ois ['ʃæmwɑ:] zo. a. ⊕ gamuza f.

champ[1] [tʃæmp] morder; mordiscar.

champ[2] [~] Am. sl. campeón m.

cham·pagne [ʃæm'pein] champaña m.

cham·pi·on ['tʃæmpjən] 1. campeón m (a. fig.); paladín m (of a cause etc.); 2. defender; abogar por; **'cham·pi·on·ship** campeonato m.

chance [tʃɑ:ns] 1. ocasión f, oportunidad f; posibilidad f, probabilidad f; suerte f; riesgo m; by ~ por casualidad; look out for the main ~ estar a la caza de su propio provecho; stand a ~ tener una probabilidad (of de); take a (or one's) ~ aventurarse; take no ~s obrar con cautela; 2. casual; for-

tuito; **3.** *v/i.* acontecer, suceder; *~ upon* tropezar con; *v/t.* F arriesgar.
chan·cel [ˈtʃɑːnsəl] coro *m* y presbiterio *m*; ˈ**chan·cel·ler·y** cancillería *f*; ˈ**chan·cel·lor** canciller *m*; *v. exchequer*; ˈ**chan·cel·lor·ship** cancillería *f*.
chan·cer·y [ˈtʃɑːnsəri] ⚖ chancillería *f*; cancillería *f*.
chanc·y [ˈtʃɑːnsi] F arriesgado.
chan·de·lier [ʃændiˈliə] araña *f* (de luces).
chan·dler [ˈtʃɑːndlə] (*p.*) velero *m*; abacero *m*.
change [tʃeindʒ] **1.** cambio *m*; transformación *f*; muda *f of clothing*; (*a. small ~*) moneda *f* suelta; (*money returned*) vuelta *f*; *~ of heart* cambio *m* de sentimiento; *~ of life* menopausia *f*; *thea. ~ of scene* mutación *f*; *for a ~* por cambiar; **2.** *v/t.* cambiar; transformar; (*replace*) reemplazar; *clothes, opinion* cambiar de; *colour* demudarse; *~ places* trocarse (*with* con); *~ the subject* volver la hoja; *v/i.* cambiar, mudar; 🚂 transbordar, hacer transbordo; **change·aˈbil·i·ty** alterabilidad *f*; mutabilidad *f*; ˈ**change·a·ble** □ cambiable; inconstante, inestable; ˈ**change·less** inmutable; ˈ**change·ling** niño (a *f*) *m* cambiado por otro; ˈ**change-ˈo·ver** cambio *m*; ˈ**chang·ing-room** vestuario *m*.
chan·nel [ˈtʃænl] **1.** canal *m* (*a. radio*); brazo *m of river*; (*irrigation-*) cacera *f*; *fig.* vía *f*; *through the official ~s* pasando por los trámites oficiales; **2.** acanalar; *fig.* encauzar.
chant [tʃɑːnt] **1.** canto *m* llano; (*talking*) sonsonete *m*; **2.** cantar (el canto llano); *fig.* (*mst ~ away*) discantar, cantar la misma cantilena; ˈ**chan·try** capilla *f* (dotada para decir misas).
cha·os [ˈkeiɔs] caos *m*; **chaˈot·ic** □ caótico.
chap[1] [tʃæp] **1.** grieta *f*, hendedura *f*; **2.** agrietar(se).
chap[2] [~] mandíbula *f*, quijada *f*.
chap[3] [~] F tipo *m*, pájaro *m*; ˈ**~-book** librete *m* (de cuentos *etc.*).
chap·el [ˈtʃæpl] capilla *f*; templo *m* (de algunas sectas protestantes); *typ.* personal *m* de una imprenta.
chap·er·on [ˈʃæpəroun] **1.** acompañanta *f* de señorita, carabina *f*; **2.** acompañar (a una señorita), ir de carabina.
chap·lain [ˈtʃæplin] capellán *m*; ˈ**chap·lain·cy** capellanía *f*.
chap·let [ˈtʃæplit] guirnalda *f*, corona *f* de flores; *eccl.* rosario *m*.
chap·py [ˈtʃæpi] *sl.* tipo *m*.
chap·ter [ˈtʃæptə] capítulo *m*; *eccl. mst* cabildo *m*.
char[1] [tʃɑː] *ichth.* umbra *f*.
char[2] [~] carbonizar; chamuscar.
char-a-banc [ˈʃærəbæŋ] autocar *m*.
char·ac·ter [ˈkæriktə] carácter *m*; *thea.* personaje *m*; F tipo *m*, sujeto *m*; *in ~* conforme al tipo; **char·ac·terˈis·tic 1.** □ característico; propio (*of* de); **2.** característica *f*; distintivo *m*; **char·ac·ter·i·za·tion** [~raiˈzeiʃn] caracterización *f*; representación *f*; **char·ac·ter·ize** caracterizar.
cha·rade [ʃəˈrɑːd] charada *f*.
char·coal [ˈtʃɑːkoul] carbón *m* vegetal; carboncillo *m for drawing*; ˈ**~-burn·er** carbonero *m*.
charge [tʃɑːdʒ] **1.** carga *f of gun* (*a.* ⚡); *fig.* cargo *m*; ⚔ carga *f*; *eccl.*, ⚖ exhortación *f*, exhorto *m*; ⚖ acusación *f*; (*price*) precio *m*; *heraldry*: blasón *m*; *~s pl.* coste *m*; honorarios *m/pl.*; *in ~ of p.* a cargo de; *th.* encargado de; *free of ~* gratis; *give a p. in ~* entregar a la policía; *take ~ of* hacerse cargo de; **2.** *v/t.* cargar (*a.* ⚔, ⚡); *price* cobrar; ordenar, mandar (*to inf.*); *p.* cargar (*with* con, de); *~ s.t. to* (*the account of*) cargarle algo a uno en cuenta; *v/i.* cobrar (*freq.* mucho); ˈ**charge·a·ble** □ cobradero; ⚖ acusable (*with* de).
char·gé d'af·faires [ˈʃɑːʒei dæˈfɛə] encargado *m* de negocios.
charg·er [ˈtʃɑːdʒə] *poet.* caballo *m* de guerra, corcel *m*; ⚡ cargador *m*.
char·i·ot [ˈtʃæriət] carro *m* romano, carro *m* de guerra; **char·i·ot·eer** [~ˈtiə] (*classical*) auriga *m*.
char·i·ta·ble [ˈtʃæritəbl] □ caritativo; benéfico; *~ society* institución *f* benéfica.
char·i·ty [ˈtʃæriti] caridad *f*; *out of ~* por caridad; ˈ**~-ˈschool** colegio *m* para pobres.
char·la·tan [ˈʃɑːlətən] charlatán *m*, curandero *m*; ˈ**char·la·tan·ry** charlatanismo *m*.
char·lotte [ˈʃɑːlət] *cooking*: carlota *f*.

charm [tʃɑːm] **1.** hechizo *m*, encanto *m*; amuleto *m*; *fig.* encanto *m*; **~s** *pl.* hechizos *m/pl. of woman*; **2.** hechizar, encantar (*a. fig.*); **~ away** hacer desaparecer como por magia; llevarse misteriosamente; **'charm·er** encantador *m*; *fig.* hombre *m* de mucho encanto; **'charm·ing** □ encantador.

char·nel-house ['tʃɑːnlhaus] osario *m*.

chart [tʃɑːt] **1.** ♆ carta *f* de marear; tabla *f*, cuadro *m*; **2.** poner en una carta de marear; **~ a course** trazar un derrotero.

char·ter ['tʃɑːtə] **1.** carta *f*; carta *f* de privilegio, encartación *f*; **2.** estatuir; *ship* fletar; *bus etc.* alquilar; **'~-par·ty** carta *f* partida.

char·wom·an ['tʃɑːwumən] criada *f* por horas, asistenta *f*.

char·y ['tʃɛəri] □ avaro (*of* de); cuidadoso, cauteloso; *be* **~** *of ger.* esquivar, evitar *inf.*

chase[1] [tʃeis] **1.** caza *f*; persecución *f*; *give* **~** dar caza; **2.** perseguir; **~** *after* ir en pos de; *fig.* ir tras; **~ away** ahuyentar.

chase[2] [~] grabar; *jewel* engastar.

chase[3] [~] *typ.* rama *f*.

chas·er ['tʃeisə] ✈ avión *m* de caza; ♆ cazasubmarinos *m*.

chasm ['kæzm] grieta *f*; sima *f*; *fig.* abismo *m*.

chas·sis ['ʃæsi] chasis *m*, armazón *f*.

chaste [tʃeist] □ casto; *fig.* castizo, sin adorno.

chas·ten ['tʃeisn] castigar; *style* acendrar, apurar (*mst p.p.*); templar; **~ed** *p.* escarmentado.

chas·tise [tʃæs'taiz] *lit.* castigar; **chas·tise·ment** ['~tizmənt] castigo *m*.

chas·ti·ty ['tʃæstiti] castidad *f*; sencillez *f of style*.

chas·u·ble ['tʃæzjubl] casulla *f*.

chat [tʃæt] **1.** charla *f*, palique *m*; **2.** charlar.

chat·tels ['tʃætlz] *pl.* (*mst goods and* **~**) bienes *m/pl.* muebles.

chat·ter ['tʃætə] **1.** (*p.*) chacharrear; (*birds*) chirriar; (*teeth*) castañetear; **2.** cháchara *f*; chirrido *m*; castañeteo *m*; **'~-box** F parlanchín (-a *f*) *m*, tarabilla *f*.

chat·ty ['tʃæti] □ hablantín; *letter* lleno de noticias.

chauf·feur ['ʃoufə] chófer *m*.

Chau·tau·qua [ʃə'tɔːkwə] *Am.* reunión *f* cultural.

chau·vin·ism ['ʃouvinizm] chauvinismo *m*; **'chau·vin·ist** chauvinista *m/f*; **chau·vin·is·tic** □ chauvinista.

chaw [tʃɔː] F mascar; *Am. sl.* **~ up** hacer polvo.

cheap [tʃiːp] □ barato; (*selling cheap*) *fig.* de mal gusto, chabacano; F *feel* **~** sentirse avergonzado; *hold* **~** despreciar; F *on the* **~** barato; **'cheap·en** abaratar; *fig.* desprestigiar; **~** *o.s.* aplebeyarse; **'cheap-jack** buhonero *m*; **'cheap-skate** *Am. sl.* tacaño (a *f*) *m*.

cheat [tʃiːt] **1.** trampa *f*, fraude *m*; (*p.*) tramposo (a *f*) *m*, petardista *m/f*; **2.** trampear, petardear; defraudar; estafar ([*out*] *of acc.*); **'cheat·ing** trampa *f*, engaño *m*.

check [tʃek] **1.** parada *f* (súbita); rechazo *m*, repulsa *f* (*a.* ♟); impedimento *m* (*on* para), estorbo *m* (*on* a); control *m*, inspección *f* (*on* de); (*luggage-*) talón *m*; billete *m* de reclamo; ficha *f in games*; ⊕ tope *m*; (*square*) cuadro *m*; (*cloth*) paño *m* a cuadros; *chess*: (*in* en) jaque *m*; *Am.* cheque *m*; *Am.* cuenta *f*; F *hand in one's* **~s** estirar la pata; *hold in* **~** contener, refrenar; **2.** parar; rechazar, repulsar; impedir, estorbar; controlar, inspeccionar; *document* compulsar; *facts* comprobar; *Am. baggage* facturar; *chess*: dar jaque a; *Am.* **~** *in* inscribir el nombre (en el registro de un hotel); **~** *up* comprobar, verificar (*on acc.*); **'check·ers** *pl. Am.* juego *m* de damas; **'check·ing** control *m*, verificación *f*; **'check(·ing)-room** *Am.* guardarropa *f*; **'check-'mate 1.** mate *m*; **2.** dar mate a; **'check-'up** verificación *f*; ⚕ reconocimiento *m* general.

cheek [tʃiːk] mejilla *f*, carrillo *m*; F descaro *m*, frescura *f*; ⊕ quijada *f*; *v. jowl*; **'cheek·y** F descarado.

cheep [tʃiːp] piar.

cheer [tʃiə] **1.** humor *m* (*esp. of good* **~** de buen ánimo); comida *f* (*esp. make good* **~** banquetear); aplauso *m*; *three* **~s** ¡viva! (*for acc.*); **2.** *v/t.* alegrar, consolar (*a.* **~** *up*); aplaudir; animar con aplausos (*a.* **~** *on*); *v/i.* alegrarse, animarse (*a.* ~ *up*); ~ *up!* ¡ánimo!; '**cheer·ful** □ alegre; '**cheer·ful·ness**, '**cheer·i·ness** alegría *f*; complacencia *f*; **cheer·i·o** [ˌ~ri'ou] F ¡adiós!; ¡hasta la vista!; '**cheer·less** □ triste, melancólico; '**cheer·y** □ animado; jovial; *atmosphere etc.* acogedor.

cheese [tʃiːz] queso *m*; *cream* ~ requesón *m*; '~-**cloth** estopilla *f*; '~-**par·ing** 1. *fig.*, *mst* ~*s pl.* bagatelas *f/pl.*, frioleras *f/pl.*; 2. tacaño, roñoso.

chees·y ['tʃiːzi] caseoso; *sl.* elegante, de moda; *Am. sl.* tosco, sin valor.

chef [ʃef] jefe *m* de cocina.

chei·ro·man·cy ['kaiərəmænsi] quiromancia *f*.

chem·i·cal ['kemikl] 1. □ químico; 2. sustancia *f* química.

che·mise [ʃi'miːz] camisa *f* de mujer.

chem·ist ['kemist] ⚗ químico (*a f*) *m*; (*pharmaceutical* ~) boticario *m*, farmacéutico *m*; ~'s (*shop*) farmacia *f*; '**chem·is·try** química *f*.

cheque [tʃek] cheque *m*; *not negotiable* (*or crossed*) ~ cheque *m* cruzado; '~-**book** talonario *m* de cheques.

chequer ['tʃekə] 1. *mst* ~*s pl.* patrón *m* en forma de cuadros; 2. marcar con cuadros; '**cheq·uered** cuadrado; *fig.* variado.

cher·ish ['tʃeriʃ] estimar, apreciar; *hopes etc.* acariciar, abrigar.

che·root [ʃə'ruːt] tipo de puro.

cher·ry ['tʃeri] 1. cereza *f*; (*a.* ~ *tree*) cerezo *m*: 2. *attr.* rojo cereza (*a.* '~-**red**).

cher·ub ['tʃerəb] querubín *m*; **che·ru·bic** [ˌ'ruːbik] querúbico.

cher·vil ['tʃəːvil] perifollo *m*.

chess [tʃes] ajedrez *m*; '~-**board** tablero *m* (de ajedrez); '~-**man** trebejo *m*, pieza *f*.

chest [tʃest] arca *f*, cofre *m*; *anat.* pecho *m*; (*money-*) caja *f*; ~ *of drawers* cómoda *f*; ~ *trouble* catarro *m* crónico del pecho; *get a th. off one's* ~ desahogarse; '**chest·y** *sl.* engreído.

chest·nut ['tʃesnʌt] 1. castaña *f*; (*a.* ~ *tree*) castaño *f*; F chiste *m* ya conocido; 2. castaño, marrón.

chev·a·lier [ʃevə'liə] caballero *m*.

chev·i·ot ['tʃeviət] cheviot *m*.

chev·ron ['ʃevrən] ⚔ galón *m*; *heraldry:* cheurón *m*.

chev·y ['tʃivi] 1. caza *f*; 2. cazar;

F acosar; F ~ *s.o. into ger.* empujar a una p. a *inf.*

chew [tʃuː] 1. mascar, masticar; ~ *the cud* rumiar (*a. fig.*; *a.* ~ *s.t. over*); *Am. sl.* ~ *the rag* dar la lengua; 2. mascadura *f*; '**chew·ing-gum** chicle *m*.

chi·cane [ʃi'kein] 1. embuste *m*; 2. embustar; **chi'can·er·y** embuste *m*, trapaza *f*.

chick ['tʃik] pollito *m*; F crío (*a f*) *m*; **chick·en** ['tʃikin] pollo *m*, gallina *f*; F *she is no* ~ ya no es una pollita.

chick·en...: '~-**farm·er** avicultor *m*; '~-**feed** *sl.* pan *m* comido; *sl.* breva *f*; '~-**pox** varicela *f*; '**chick-pea** garbanzo *m*.

chic·o·ry ['tʃikəri] chicoria *f*.

chide [tʃaid] [*irr.*] *lit.* reprobar.

chief [tʃiːf] 1. □ principal; primero; ~ *clerk* oficial *m* mayor; 2. jefe *m*; ...-*in* ~ ... en jefe; ~ *of staff* jefe *m* de estado mayor; **chief·tain** ['~tən] jefe *m*, cacique *m*.

chil·blain ['tʃilblein] sabañón *m*.

child [tʃaild] niño (*a f*) *m*; hijo (*a f*) *m*; *attr.* muy joven; ~'s *play fig.* cosa *f* de coser y cantar; *from a* ~ desde niño; *with* ~ encinta; '~-**bed** parturición *f*; '~-**birth** parto *m*; '**child·hood** niñez *f*, infancia *f*; '**child·ish** □ pueril; *b.s.* aniñado; '**child·ish·ness** puerilidad *f*; niñería *f*; '**child·less** sin hijos; '**child·like** *fig.* propio de un niño; **children** ['tʃildrən] *pl. of* child.

Chil·e·an ['tʃiliən] chileno *adj. a. su. m* (*a f*).

chill [tʃil] 1. *lit.* frío; *manner* desapacible; 2. frío *m*; escalofrío *m* (*a.* ⚕); *take the* ~ *off liquid* entibiar; *room* calentar ligeramente; 2. *v/t.* enfriar (*a. metal*); *fig.* desalentar; ~*ed meat* carne *f* congelada; *v/i.* enfriarse; *esp.* ⚕ calofriarse; '**chill·i·ness**, '**chill·ness** frialdad *f* (*a. fig.*); '**chill·y** frío (*a. fig.*); *p.* friolero; *feeling* escalofriado.

chime [tʃaim] 1. campaneo *m*; (*peal*) repique *m*; carillón *m*; *fig.* conformidad *f*, acuerdo *m*; 2. repicar, sonar; *fig.* estar en armonía; F ~ *in with* soltar, saltar.

chi·me·ra [kai'miərə] quimera *f*; **chi·mer·i·cal** [ˌ'merik(l)] □ quimérico.

chim·ney ['tʃimni] chimenea

(*exterior*); tubo *m* de lámpara; *mount.* olla *f*, cañón *m*; '~-**piece** marco *m* de chimenea; '~-**pot** tubo *m* de chimenea; '~-**sweep**(·**er**) limpiachimeneas *m*.

chim·pan·zee [tʃimpən'zi:] chimpancé *m*.

chin[1] [tʃin] 1. barba *f*, barbilla *f*; *double* ~ papada *f*; F *keep one's* ~ *up* no desanimarse; *Am.* F *take it on the* ~ mantenerse firme.

chin[2] [~] *sl.* parlotear.

chi·na ['tʃainə] porcelana *f*; ♀-**man** chino *m*.

chine [tʃain] espinazo *m*; (*meat*) lomo *m*.

Chi·nese ['tʃai'ni:z] 1. chino *adj. a. su. m* (a *f*); 2. (*language*) chino *m*.

chink[1] [tʃiŋk] grieta *f*, hendedura *f*; resquicio *m* (*a. fig.*).

chink[2] [~] 1. sonido *m* metálico; tintineo *m*; 2. sonar, tintinear.

Chink[3] [~] *sl.* chino (a *f*) *m*.

chintz [tʃints] zaraza *f*.

chip [tʃip] 1. astilla *f*, brizna *f*; lasca *f of stone*; (*defect*) saltadura *f*, desportilladura *f*; patata *f* frita; *poker:* ficha *f*; ~ *off the old block* de tal palo tal astilla; F *have a* ~ *on one's shoulder* ser un resentido; 2. desportillar(se), astillar(se); F ~ *in* interrumpir (una conversación) (*with* diciendo); **chip·munk** ['tʃipmʌŋk] ardilla *f* listada; '**chip·py** *sl.* seco, poco interesante.

chi·rop·o·dist [ki'rɔpədist] quiropodista *m/f*; **chi'rop·o·dy** quiropodia *f*.

chirp [tʃə:p] 1. gorjear, pipiar; (*cricket*) chirriar; F hablar alegremente; 2. gorjeo *m*; chirrido *m*; '**chirp·y** F alegre.

chis·el ['tʃizl] 1. formón *m*, escoplo *m for wood*; cincel *m for stone*; 2. escoplear; cincelar; *sl.* timar; '**chis·el·er** F gorrón *m*.

chit[1] [tʃit] chiquillo (a *f*) *m*; ~ *of a girl* mujercilla *f*.

chit[2] [~] esquela *f*, nota *f*.

chit-chat ['tʃittʃæt] palique *m*; chismería *f*.

chiv·al·rous ['ʃivlrəs] □ caballeroso; '**chiv·al·ry** caballería *f*; (*spirit*) caballerosidad *f*.

chive [tʃaiv] cebollino *m*.

chiv·y ['tʃivi] F = *chevy*.

chlo·ral ['klɔ:rl] cloral *m*; **chlo·ride** ['~aid] cloruro *m*; ~ *of lime* cloruro *m* de cal; **chlo·rine** ['~i:n] cloro *m*; **chlo·ro·form** ['~əfɔ:m] 1. cloroformo *m*; 2. cloroformizar.

chock [tʃɔk] 1. cuña *f*; combo *m of barrel*; ♣ calzo *m*; 2. acuñar; afianzar con combos (*or* calzos); '~-**a**-'**block** apretado; atestado (*with* de); '~-'**full** de bote en bote.

choc·o·late ['tʃɔkəlit] chocolate *m*.

choice [tʃɔis] 1. elección *f*; preferencia *f*; ♥ *wide* ~ gran surtido *m*; *have no* ~ no tener alternativa; *make* (*or take*) *one's* ~ elegir, seleccionar; 2. selecto, escogido.

choir ['kwaiə] coro *m*.

choke [tʃouk] 1. *v/t.* estrangular; sofocar (*a. fig.*); tapar, atascar (*a.* ~ *up*); *fig.* ~ *back* retener; F ~ *off p.* parar; reprobar; *v/i.* sofocarse, ahogarse (*a. fig.*); atascarse, obstruirse; 2. ⊕ cierre *m*, obturador *m*; *mot.* estrangulador *m*; *mot.* aire *m*; ~ *coil* bobina *f* de reacción; '~-**bore** calibre *m* estrangulado; '~-**damp** mofeta *f*; '**chok·er** F cuello *m* alto.

chol·er·a ['kɔlərə] cólera *m*; '**chol·er·ic** colérico, irascible.

choose [tʃu:z] [*irr.*] escoger; elegir; seleccionar; ~ *between* optar entre; ~ *to inf.* optar por *inf.*; '**choos·y** F melindroso, quisquilloso.

chop[1] [tʃɔp] 1. golpe *m* cortante; tajada *f*; (*meat*) chuleta *f*; *sl.* ~*s pl.* boca *f*; labios *m/pl.*; ~ *and changes* altibajos *m/pl.*; cambios *m/pl.*; 2. *v/t.* cortar, tajar; tronchar (*freq.* ~ *off*); desmenuzar (*freq.* ~ *up*); *meat* picar; *v/i.* cambiar súbitamente; (*wind*) virar; ~ *and change* variar; cambiar de parecer.

chop[2] [~] ♥ sello *m*; F *first* ~ de primera calidad.

chop-house restaurán *m* barato; '**chop·per** hacha *f*; (*butcher's*) cuchilla *f*; '**chop·ping-block** tajo *m*; '**chop·py** *sea* agitado, picado; '**chop·stick** palillo *m* para comer (*de los chinos*).

cho·ral ['kɔ:rl] □ coral; **cho·ral(e)** [kɔ'rɑ:l] coral *m*.

chord [kɔ:d] acorde *m*; (*string*, ♪, ₳ *a. poet.*) cuerda *f*; *fig. strike the right* ~ juzgar bien el ambiente (de una reunión *esp.*).

chore [tʃɔ:] tarea *f* de ocasión; (*household*) ~*s pl.* quehaceres *m/pl.* domésticos.

chor·is·ter ['kɔristə] corista *m/f*.

cho·rus ['kɔ:rəs] **1.** coro *m*; **2.** hablar (*or* cantar) en coro.

chose [tʃouz] *pret.*, '**cho·sen** *p.p. of* choose.

chough [tʃʌf] chova *f*.

chow [tʃau] chao *m*; *Am. sl.* comida *f*.

chrism ['krizm] crisma *f*.

chris·ten ['krisn] bautizar; **Chris·ten·dom** ['∼dəm] cristiandad *f*; '**chris·ten·ing** bautismo *m*, bautizo *m*.

Chris·tian ['kristjən] □ cristiano *adj. a. su. m* (a *f*); ∼ *name* nombre *m* de pila; **Chris·ti·an·i·ty** [∼ti·'æniti] cristianismo *m*; **Chris·tian·ize** ['∼tjənaiz] cristianizar.

Christ·mas ['krisməs] Navidad(es) *f(pl.*); ∼ *Day* Día *m* de Navidad; ∼ *Eve* Noche *f* Buena; '∼**-box** aguinaldo *m*.

chro·mat·ic [krə'mætik] □ cromático; **chro'mat·ics** *pl. or sg.* cromática *f*.

chrome [kroum] (*a.* ∼ *yellow*) amarillo *m* de cromo; **chro·mi·um** ['∼jəm] cromo *m*; '**chro·mi·um-plat·ed** cromado; **chro·mo'lith·o·graph** cromolitografía *f*.

chron·ic ['krɔnik] □ crónico; F terrible, muy serio; '**chron·i·cle 1.** crónica *f*; **2.** anotar; narrar; '**chron·i·cler** cronista *m/f*.

chron·o·log·i·cal [krɔnə'lɔdʒikl] □ cronológico; ∼*ly* en orden cronológico; **chronol·o·gy** [krə'nɔlədʒi] cronología *f*.

chro·nom·e·ter [krə'nɔmitə] cronómetro *m*.

chrys·a·lis ['krisəlis] crisálida *f*.

chrys·an·the·mum [kri'sænθəməm] crisántemo *m*.

chub [tʃʌb] cacho *m*; '**chub·by** rechoncho; *face* mofletudo.

chuck¹ [tʃʌk] **1.** (*hen*) cloqueo *m*; *my* ∼! ¡amor mío!; **2.** cloquear.

chuck² [∼] **1.** F arrojar; ∼ *out* echar; ∼ *it!* ¡basta ya!; ∼ *under the chin* dar la mamola a; **2.** mamola *f*.

chuck³ [∼] ⊕ manguito *m*.

chuck·le ['tʃʌkl] **1.** reír entre dientes, soltar una risa sofocada; **2.** risa *f* sofocada.

chum [tʃʌm] **1.** F compinche *m*, compañero *m*; *be great* ∼*s* ser amigos íntimos; **2.** compartir un cuarto; F ∼ *up* entablar amistad.

chump [tʃʌmp] F zoquete *m*; (*meat*) lomo *m*; *sl.* melón *m*, calabaza *f*;

sl. (*p.*) majadero *m*; *sl. off one's* ∼ chiflado.

chunk [tʃʌŋk] F pedazo *m* grueso; *Am.* persona *f* rechoncha; '**chunk·y** *Am.* F corto y grueso; rechoncho.

church [tʃə:tʃ] **1.** iglesia *f*; ♀ *of England* Iglesia *f* Anglicana; **2.:** *be* ∼*ed* ser purificada *después de un parto*; '∼**-go·er** devoto (a *f*) *m*; '**church·ing** purificación *f de una mujer*; '**church'ward·en** capiller *m*; '**church·y** F beato; '**church'yard** cementerio *m*, camposanto *m*.

churl [tʃə:l] patán *m* (*a. fig.*), palurdo *m*; '**churl·ish** □ palurdo, tosco; (*niggardly*) mezquino.

churn [tʃə:n] **1.** mantequera *f*; **2.** batir en una mantequera; hacer (mantequilla); revolver, agitar (*a.* ∼ *up*).

chute [ʃu:t] salto *m* de agua; canalón *m in house*; tolva *f in mill*; tobogán *m ∙in swimming-pool*.

chut·ney ['tʃʌtni] salsa *f* picante.

chyle [kail] quilo *m*.

chyme [kaim] quimo *m*.

ci·ca·da [si'kɑ:də] cigarra *f*.

ci·ca·trice ['sikətris] ⚕ cicatriz *f*; **cic·a·tri·za·tion** [∼trai'zeiʃn] cicatrización *f*; '**cic·a·trize** cicatrizar (se).

ci·ce·ro·ne [tʃitʃə'rouni] *lit.* cicerone *m*.

ci·der ['saidə] sidra *f*.

ci·gar [si'gɑ:] (cigarro) puro *m*; **ci·gar-case** cigarrera *f*.

cig·a·rette [sigə'ret] cigarrillo *m*; pitillo *m*; '∼**-case** petaca *f*, pitillera *f*; '∼**-hold·er** boquilla *f*; '∼**-light·er** mechero *m*.

cil·i·ar·y ['siliəri] ciliar.

cinch [sintʃ] *Am. sl.* breva *f*.

cinc·ture ['siŋktʃə] *lit.* cinturón *m*.

cin·der ['sində] carbonilla *f*; ∼*s pl.* cenizas *f/pl.*.

cin·e·cam·er·a ['sinikæmərə] cámara *f* cinematográfica.

cin·e·ma ['sinimə] cine *m*; **cin·e·mat·o·graph** [∼'mætəgrɑ:f] **1.** cinematógrafo *m*; **2.** cinematografiar; **cin·e·mat·o·graph·ic** [∼'græfik] □ cinematográfico.

cin·er·ar·y ['sinərəri] cinerario.

cin·na·bar ['sinəbɑ:] cinabrio *m*.

cin·na·mon ['sinəmən] canela *f*.

ci·pher ['saifə] **1.** cifra *f*; cero *m*; (*p.*) cero *m* a la izquierda; *in* ∼ en cifra; **2.** cifrar; calcular.

cir·cle ['sə:kl] **1.** círculo *m* (*a. fig.*); *thea.* anfiteatro *m*; **2.** circundar, cercar; (*go round*) dar vueltas (a); girar; **cir·clet** ['⌐klit] venda *f*, faja *f* (para la cabeza).

cir·cuit ['sə:kit] circuito *m* (*a. ♪*); ⚡ *approx.* distrito *m*; *sport*: pista *f*; *v. short* ~; *∮* ~*breaker* cortacircuitos *m*; **cir·cu·i·tous** [sə'kjuitəs] □ tortuoso.

cir·cu·lar ['sə:kjulə] **1.** □ circular; *↑* ~ *note* carta *f* de crédito; ~ *saw* sierra *f* circular; **2.** circular *f* (*a.* ~ *letter*).

cir·cu·late ['sə:kjuleit] circular; **'cir·cu·lat·ing**: ~ *library* biblioteca *f* circulante; ~ *medium* moneda *f* corriente; **cir·cu'la·tion** circulación *f* (*a.* ↑).

cir·cum ['sə:kəm] circum, circun...; **cir·cum·cise** ['⌐saiz] circuncidar; **cir·cum·ci·sion** [⌐'siʒn] circuncisión *f*; **cir·cum·fer·ence** [sə'kʌmfərəns] circunferencia *f*; **cir·cum·flex** ['sə:kəmfleks] circunflejo *m*; **cir·cum·ja·cent** [⌐'dʒeisnt] circunjacente; **cir·cum·lo·cu·tion** [⌐lə'kju:ʃn] circunlocución *f*; circunloquio *m*; **cir·cum·loc·u·to·ry** [⌐'lɔkjutəri] perifrástico; **cir·cum·nav·i·gate** [⌐'nævigeit] circunnavegar; **cir·cum·nav·i·ga·tion** circunnavegación *f*; **cir·cum·scribe** ['⌐skraib] circunscribir (*a. fig.*); **cir·cum·scrip·tion** [⌐'skripʃn] circunscripción *f*; **cir·cum·spect** □ ['⌐spekt] circunspecto; **cir·cum·spec·tion** [⌐'spekʃn] circunspección *f*; **cir·cum·stance** ['⌐stəns] circunstancia *f*; *be in easy* ~*s* estar acomodado; *in* (*or under*) *the* ~*s* en las circunstancias; *under no* ~*s* de ninguna manera; **cir·cum·stan·tial** [⌐'stænʃl] □ circunstancial; ⚡ ~ *evidence* prueba *f* indiciaria; **cir·cum'stan·ti·ate** relatar con las circunstancias; **cir·cum·vent** [⌐'vent] embaucar; burlar.

cir·cus ['sə:kəs] circo *m*; (*in town*) plaza *f* redonda.

cir·rus ['sirəs], *pl.* **cir·ri** ['⌐ai] cirro *m*.

cis·co ['siskou] *Am.* arenque *m* de lago.

cis·tern ['sistən] arca *f*, depósito *m*; (*rainwater*) aljibe *m*; *hot-water* ~ termo *m*.

cit·a·del ['sitədl] ciudadela *f*.

ci·ta·tion [sai'teiʃn] citación *f* (*a.* ⚡); ⚔ mención *f*; **cite** [sait] citar; ⚔ mencionar.

cit·i·zen ['sitizn] ciudadano (a *f*) *m*; *Am.* ⚔ paisano *m*; **cit·i·zen·ship** ['⌐ʃip] ciudadanía *f*.

cit·ric ac·id ['sitrik'æsid] ácido *m* cítrico; **cit·ron** ['sitrən] (*tree*) cidro *m*; (*fruit*) cidra *f*; **cit·rus** ['⌐rəs] **1.** auranciáceo; **2.** cidro *m* (*el género Citrus*).

cit·y ['siti] **1.** ciudad *f*; *London*: *the* ♀ *el centro comercial de Londres*; **2.** ciudadano; ~ *council* ayuntamiento *m*; ~ *editor* redactor *m* encargado de las noticias financieras; *Am.* redactor encargado de las noticias locales; ~ *hall* palacio *m* municipal; *Am.* ~ *manager* administrador *m* municipal.

civ·ic ['sivik] cívico; ~ *centre* casa *f* consistorial; conjunto *m* de edificios municipales; ~*s sg.* ciencia *f* de los derechos *etc.* del ciudadano.

civ·il ['sivl] □ civil; ~ *defence* defensa *f* pasiva; ~ *servant* funcionario (a *f*) *m* del Estado; ♀ *service* burocracia *f* oficial; **ci·vil·ian** [si'viljən] paisano (a *f*) *m*; ~ *clothes pl.* traje *m* de paisano; **ci·vil·i·ty** civilidad *f*; **civ·i·li·za·tion** [⌐lai'zeiʃn] civilización *f*; **'civ·i·lize** civilizar.

clack [klæk] **1.** chasquido *m*; (*p.*) tarabilla *f*; ~ *valve* chapaleta *f*; **2.** hacer chasquido; sonar; (*chatter*) charlar.

clad [klæd] *lit. pret. a. p.p. of clothe.*

claim [kleim] **1.** demanda *f* (*a.* ⚡); petición *f*; pretensión *f* (*to a*); ⚔ pertinencia *f*; *lay* ~ *to* reclamar; **2.** demandar; reclamar; pretender (*to inf.*); afirmar; *attention* merecer; **'claim·a·ble** que se puede reclamar; **'claim·ant** demandante *m/f* (*a.* ⚡); pretendiente (a *f*) *m to throne.*

clair·voy·ance [klɛə'vɔiəns] clarividencia *f*; **clair'voy·ant(e)** visionario (a *f*) *m*; clarividente *m*.

clam [klæm] almeja *f*.

cla·mant ['klɛimənt] *lit.* estrepitoso.

clam·ber ['klæmbə] gatear, trepar; subir gateando (*up* a).

clam·mi·ness ['klæminis] frío *m* húmedo; **'clam·my** □ frío y húmedo.

clam·or·ous ['klæmərəs] □ clamoroso; **'clam·our 1.** clamor *m*, clamoreo *m*; **2.** clamorear, clamar (*for por*).

clamp [klæmp] **1.** abrazadera *f*; (*screw*) tornillo *m* de banco; (*potato-*) montón *m*; **2.** afianzar con abrazadera; *fig.* ~ *down on* apretar los tornillos a; suprimir.

clan [klæn] clan *m* (*a. fig.*).

clan·des·tine [klæn'destin] □ clandestino.

clang [klæŋ] **1.** sonido *m* metálico fuerte, clamoreo *m*; ~! ¡tolón!; **2.** (re)sonar; **'clang·er** F: *drop a* ~ hacer una plancha; meter la pata; **clang·or·ous** ['klæŋgərəs] estrepitoso; **'clang·o(u)r** estruendo *m*.

clank [klæŋk] **1.** sonido *m* metálico seco, rechino *m*; **2.** rechinar.

clan·nish ['klæniʃ] exclusivista; unido.

clap [klæp] **1.** palmoteo *m*, aplauso *m*; (*thunder*) trueno *m*; golpe *m* seco; *sl.* gonorrea *f*; **2.** dar palmadas, aplaudir; dar un golpe a (*on en*); ~ *eyes on* clavar la vista en; *Am.* F ~ *up* poner en la cárcel; = *place 2*, *put* 1; **'~board** *Am.* chilla *f*; **'clap·per** badajo *m*; **'clap·trap 1.** faramalla *f*; farfolla *f*; **2.** faramallón.

claque [klæk] claque *f*, t:fus *m*.

clar·et ['klærət] clarete *m*; *sl.* sangre *f*.

clar·i·fi·ca·tion [klærifi'keiʃn] aclaración *f*; **clar·i·fy** ['~fai] clarificar, aclarar.

clar·i·net [klæri'net] clarinete *m*.

clar·i·ty ['klæriti] claridad *f*.

clash [klæʃ] **1.** choque *m*; fragor *m*; **2.** chocar (*a. fig.*; *with* con); (*colours*) desentonar (*with* con).

clasp [kla:sp] **1.** broche *m*, corchete *m*; (*book-*) broche *m*, manecilla *f*; (*shoe-*) hebilla *f*; agarro *m of hand etc.*; (*handshake*) apretón *m*; **2.** abrochar; abrazar; agarrar; *hand* apretar; **'~-'knife** navaja *f*.

class [kla:s] **1.** clase *f*; *good* ~ de buena calidad; F *that's* ~ (*for you!*) ¡su padre!; **2.** clasificar; ~ *with* comparar con; **'~-'con·scious** celoso de las distinciones sociales.

clas·sic ['klæsik] clásico *adj. a. su.m*; *the* ~*s pl.* las obras clásicas (*esp.* griegas y latinas); las humanidades; **'clas·si·cal** □ clásico.

clas·si·fi·ca·tion [klæsifi'keiʃn] clasificación *f*; **clas·si·fy** ['~fai] clasificar.

class...: '~**room** aula *f*, clase *f*; '~-**'strug·gle** lucha *f* de clases; **'class·y** F elegante, de primera, muy pera.

clat·ter [klætə] **1.** martilleo *m*; repiqueteo *m*; estruendo *m*; trápala *f of hooves*; choque *m of plates*; rumor *m of conversation*; **2.** martillear; (*esp. metal*) guachapear; chocar; mover con estruendo confuso.

clause [klɔ:z] cláusula *f* (*a. gr.*).

claus·tral ['klɔ:strəl] claustral.

clav·i·cle ['klævikl] clavícula *f*.

claw [klɔ:] **1.** garra *f*; garfa *f esp. of bird of prey*; (*lobster's etc.*) pinza *f*; ⊕ garfio *m*, gancho *m*; **2.** arañar; agarrar; (*tear*) desgarrar.

clay [klei] arcilla *f*; ~ *pigeon* pichón *m* de barro; **clay·ey** ['kleii] arcilloso; **'clay-pit** barrera *f*.

clean [kli:n] **1.** *adj.* □ limpio (*a.fig.*); neto, distinto; *surface etc.* despejado, desembarazado; *limb etc.* bien formado; *fig.* diestro; *sl.* come ~ cantar; **2.** *adv.* enteramente; **3.** limpiar; ~ *out* limpiar vaciando; *sl.* be ~ed *out* quedar limpio; ~ *up* arreglar; *sl.* sacar de ganancia; **4.** *su.* limpia *f*; **'clean·ing** limpia *f*, limpiadura *f*; *attr.* de limpiar; ~ *woman* asistenta *f*; **clean·li·ness** ['klenlinis] limpieza *f*; esmero *m*; **clean·ly 1.** *adv.* ['kli:nli] limpiamente; en limpio; **2.** *adj.* ['klenli] esmerado; limpio; **clean·ness** ['kli:nnis] limpieza *f*; **cleanse** [klenz] *lit.* limpiar, purificar (*of* de); **clean-up** ['kli:n'ʌp] limpiadura *f*; *sl.* ganancia *f*.

clear [kliə] **1.** □ claro; *sky* despejado; libre (*of* de); completo, total; ~ sin deudas (*a. in the* ~); *as* ~ *as day* más claro que el sol; *get* ~ *of* deshacerse de, desembarazarse de; *place* salir de; **2.** *v/t.* aclarar, clarificar (*a.* ~ *up*); *table* despejar; (*a.* ~ *away*) levantar; *site* desmontar; quitar (*a.* ~ *away*, *off*); limpiar (*of* de); (*jump*) saltar por encima de; ⟂ absolver; probar la inocencia de; *ball* despejar; ♰ *cheque* hacer efectivo; ♰ *debt* liquidar (*a.* ~ *off*); ~ *a ship for action* alistar un buque para el combate; *v.* *throat*; *v/i.* abonanzar (*a.* ~ *up*); (*sky*) despejarse; F ~ *off* irse, escabullirse (*a.* ~ *out*); **'clear·ance** espacio *m* libre; acreditación *f of personnel*; ♰ negociación *f*; ⚓, ♰ despacho *m*; ⊕ espacio *m* muerto; *sport*: despeje *m*:

~ sale venta f de liquidación; **'clear-cut** claro, bien definido; **'clearing** claro m in wood; ✝ compensación f; ~ house cámara f de compensación; v. clear 1.

cleav·age ['kli:vidʒ] hendedura f; fig. división f; Am. sl. escote m.

cleave¹ [kli:v] [irr.] hender (a. fig.).

cleave² [~] fig. adherirse (to a); ~ together ser inseparables.

cleav·er ['kli:və] cuchilla f de carnicero.

clef [klef] clave f.

cleft [kleft] 1. grieta f, hendedura f; 2. pret. a. p.p. of cleave 1.

clem·en·cy ['klemənsi] clemencia f (a. meteor.); **'clem·ent** ☐ clemente.

clench [klentʃ] apretar, cerrar; = clinch.

cler·gy ['klə:dʒi] clero m, clerecía f; **'~·man** clérigo m, sacerdote m (esp. de la Iglesia Anglicana); pastor m.

cler·i·cal ['klerikl] ☐ clerical; oficinista, b.s. oficinesco; ~ error error m de pluma; ~ work trabajo m de oficina.

clerk [klɑ:k] oficinista m/f; Am. dependiente (a f) m; ₤ escribano m; eccl. clérigo m; v. town.

clev·er ['klevə] ☐ inteligente; hábil; listo; b.s. habilidoso; **'clev·er·ness** inteligencia f; habilidad f.

clew [klu:] ovillo m; v. clue.

cli·ché ['kli:ʃei] cliché m, frase f hecha.

click [klik] 1. golpecito m seco; piñoneo m of gun; chasquido m of tongue; taconeo m of heels; 2. piñonear; chasquear; sl. enamorarse, hacerse novios.

cli·ent ['klaiənt] cliente m/f; **cli·en·tèle** [kli:ã:n'tel] clientela f.

cliff [klif] risco m; (sea-) acantilado m.

cli·mate ['klaimit] clima m; fig. ambiente m; **cli·mat·ic** [klai'mætik] ☐ climático.

cli·max ['klaimæks] rhet. clímax m; colmo m; cima f de intensidad, punto m álgido.

climb [klaim] [irr.] 1. trepar, escalar; subir (a); F fig. ~ down cejar; desdecirse; 2. subida f; **'climb·er** mst alpinista m/f; fig. buscavidas m, tiralevitas m; ♀ enredadera f, trepadora f; **'climb·ing** mst alpinismo m; **'climb·ing-i·ron** garfio m.

clinch [klintʃ] 1. agarro m; ⊕ re-mache m; boxing: clincha f; 2. agarrar; remachar; luchar cuerpo a cuerpo; fig. argument remachar; v. clench; **'clinch·er** ⊕ remachador m; fig. argumento m decisivo.

cling [kliŋ] [irr.] adherirse (to a), pegarse (to a) (a. fig.); ~ to p. abrazarse a, quedar abrazado a; **'clinging** suspendido; p. pegajoso; dress muy ajustado.

clin·ic ['klinik] 1. clínica f; 2. = **'clin·i·cal** ☐ clínico; ~ thermometer termómetro m clínico.

clink [kliŋk] 1. tintín m; choque m of glasses; sl. trena f; 2. tintinear; chocar; **'clink·er** escoria f de hulla; ladrillo m muy duro.

clip¹ [klip] 1. esquileo m of wool; F golpe m; 2. trasquilar, esquilar; recortar; coin cercenar; ticket picar; words apocopar; F chapurrear; F (hit) golpear.

clip² [~] grapa f; (paper-) sujetapapeles m; sujetador m of pen; (brooch) alfiler m de pecho, clip m.

clip·per ['klipə] (a pair of ~s una) cizalla f; ✂ tijeras f/pl. podadoras; ⚓, ✈ clíper m; **'clip·pings** pl. recortes m/pl.; trasquilones m/pl. of wool; retales m/pl. of cloth.

clique [kli:k] pandilla f; peña f.

cloak [klouk] 1. capa f (a. fig.), capote m; ~ and dagger de capa y espada; 2. encapotar; fig. encubrir, disimular; **'~·room** guardarropa f; euph. aseos m/pl.; ⛟ consigna f.

clock [klɔk] 1. reloj m; sport: cronómetro m; against the ~ contra el reloj; 2.: ~ in fichar; **'~·wise** en la dirección de las agujas del reloj; **'~·work** aparato m de relojería; like ~ como un reloj.

clod [klɔd] tierra f, terrón m; (p.) palurdo m (a. **'~·hop·per**).

clog [klɔg] 1. zueco m; fig. traba f; estorbo m; 2. atascar(se) (a. fig.); (hamper) estorbar.

clois·ter ['klɔistə] 1. claustro m; 2. enclaustrar (a. fig.).

close 1. a) [klouz] fin m; conclusión f; at the ~ of day a la caída de la tarde; b) [klous] recinto m, cercado m; 2. [klouz] v/t. cerrar (a. ✝); hole tapar (a. ~ up); treaty concluir; ~d shop fig. coto m cerrado; ~ down cerrar definitivamente; closing date fecha f tope; ✝ closing price último precio m; v/i. cerrar(se); terminar; ~ in acercarse rodeando; ~ *in on* rodear; ~ *up* ponerse más cerca; (*wound*) cicatrizarse; **3.** [klous] □ cercano, próximo; *friendship etc.* estrecho, íntimo; *weave etc.* compacto, tupido; *argument* minucioso; *atmosphere* sofocante, mal ventilado; *imitation* arrimado; *score* igual, casi empatado; *translation* fiel; F (*mean*) avaro, mezquino; ~ *by*, ~ to cerca de; *v. quarter*, *season*, *shave*; ~*ly printed* de impresión compacta; '~-'**fist·ed** tacaño; '~-'**fit·ting** ajustado; '**close-ness** proximidad *f*; intimidad *f*; pesantez *f*, mala ventilación *f*; fidelidad *f to original.*

clos·et ['klɔzit] **1.** retrete *m*, gabinete *m*; (*cupboard*) armario *m*; *v. water-* **2.**: *be* ~*ed with* estar encerrado con.

close-up ['klousʌp] vista *f* de cerca.

clo·sure ['klouʒə] **1.** cierre *m*; clausura *f*; fin *m*, término *m*; *parl. apply the* ~ terminar el debate; **2.** *debate* terminar.

clot [klɔt] **1.** grumo *m*; cuajarón *m of blood etc.*; *sl.* papanatas *m*; **2.** cuajarse, coagularse.

cloth [klɔθ], *pl.* **cloths** [klɔθs, klɔːðz] tela *f*, paño *m*; (*table-*) mantel *m*; *fig.* clero *m*; *lay the* ~ poner la mesa; ~ *binding* encuadernación *f* en tela.

clothe [klouð] [*irr.*] vestir; *p.* trajear; *fig.* revestir; investir (*with de*).

clothes [klouðz] ropa *f*, vestidos *m/pl.*; '~-**bas·ket** cesto *m* de la colada; '~-**line** cordel *m* para tender la ropa; '~-**peg**, *Am.* '~-**pin** pinza *f*; '~-**press** guardarropa *f*, armario *m*.

cloth·ier ['klouðiə] fabricante *m* de ropa; (*shop*) pañero *m*.

cloth·ing ['klouðiŋ] ropa *f*, vestidos *m/pl.*; ropaje *m*; *attr.* textil.

cloud [klaud] **1.** nube *f* (*a. fig.*); *phys.* ~ *chamber* cámara *f* de niebla; *storm* ~ nubarrón *m*; *be under a* ~ estar desacreditado; estar mohíno; *fig. in the* ~*s th.* quimérico, ilusorio; *p.* distraído, despistado; **2.** anublar (*a. fig.*); ~ (*over*) anublarse; '~-**burst** chaparrón *m*; '**cloud·less** sin nubes, despejado; '**cloud·y** □ anublado, nuboso; *liquid* turbio; sombrío.

clout [klaut] **1.** F dar de bofetadas; **2.** F bofetada *f*; † trapo *m*.

clove¹ [klouv] clavo *m*; (*tree*) clavero *m*.

clove² [~] *pret. of cleave*¹; '**clo·ven** *p.p. of cleave*¹; *adj.*: ~ *hoof* pata *f* hendida.

clo·ver ['klouvə] trébol *m*; F *be in* ~ vivir holgadamente, darse buena vida.

clown [klaun] **1.** payaso *m in circus*; palurdo *m*; **2.** bufonearse; '**clown·ish** □ bufonesco.

cloy [klɔi] empalagar(se), hartar(se).

club [klʌb] **1.** porra *f*, cachiporra *f*; (*golf-*) palo *m*; (*society*) club *m*; casino *m*; *cards*: ~*s pl.* tréboles *m/pl.*, (*Spanish*) bastos *m/pl.*; **2.** *v/t.* aporrear; *v/i.*: ~ *together* unirse para el mismo fin; pagar cada uno su escote; '~-**house** *golf*: chalet *m*; '~-**man** casinista *m*.

cluck [klʌk] cloquear.

clue [kluː] indicio *m*; pista *f*.

clump [klʌmp] **1.** grupo *m* de árboles, arboleda *f*; masa *f* informe; **2.** andar pesadamente (*a.* ~ *along*).

clum·si·ness ['klʌmzinis] desmaña *f*, torpeza *f*; '**clum·sy** □ desmañado, torpe; (*badly done*) chapucero.

clung [klʌŋ] *pret. a. p.p. of cling.*

clus·ter ['klʌstə] **1.** grupo *m*; ♀ racimo *m*; **2.** agruparse; ♀ arracimarse; (*people*) apiñarse; ~ *around* reunirse en torno de.

clutch [klʌtʃ] **1.** agarro *m*; *mot.* (*pedal m de*) embrague *m*; nidada *f of eggs*; *in his* ~*es* en sus garras; **2.** agarrarse (*at a*); empuñar.

clut·ter ['klʌtə] **1.** desorden *m*, confusión *f*; (*with noise*) barahúnda *f*; **2.** poner en confusión; *be* ~*ed up with* estar atestado de.

coach [koutʃ] **1.** coche *m*; diligencia *f*; 🚃 coche *m*, vagón *m*; *mot.* autocar *m*, pullman *m*; *sport:* entrenador *m*; **2.** *team etc.* entrenar; *student* enseñar, preparar; '~-**build·er** carrocero *m*; '~-**house** cochera *f*; '~-**man** cochero *m*. [tor *m.*]

co·ad·ju·tor [kou'ædʒutə] coadju-]

co·ag·u·late [kou'ægjuleit] coagular;

co·ag·u·la·tion coagulación *f*.

coal [koul] **1.** carbón *m*; hulla *f*; (*freq.* ~*s pl.*) ascua *f*, brasa *f*; ~ *industry* industria *f* hullera; *haul over the* ~*s* echar un rapapolvo a; *v. Newcastle*; **2.** ⚓ tomar carbón; ~*ing station* estación *f* carbonera.

co·a·lesce [kouə'les] unirse; combinarse; *pol. etc.* incorporarse; **co·a'les·cence** unión *f*; combinación *f*.

coal·field ['koulfi:ld] yacimiento *m* de carbón; cuenca *f* minera.

co·a·li·tion [kouə'liʃn] *pol.* coalición *f*; unión *f*, combinación *f*.

coal...: '~·**pit** mina *f* de carbón; '~·**scut·tle** cubo *m* para carbón; '~·**tar** alquitrán *m* mineral.

coarse [kɔːs] □ basto, tosco; *fig.* grosero, rudo; '**coarse·ness** tosquedad *f*; grosería *f*, *etc.*

coast [koust] 1. costa *f*; litoral *m*; the ~ is clear no hay moros en la costa; 2. costear; *mot.* ir en punto muerto; ~ along avanzar sin esfuerzo; '**coast·al** costanero; '**coast·er** ♣ barco *m* costero; *Am.* trineo *m*; *Am.* ~ brake freno *m* de contrapedal; '**coast·guard** guardacostas *m*; '**coast·ing** navegación *f* costera; ~ trade cabotaje *m*.

coat [kout] 1. chaqueta *f*, americana *f*; (*overcoat*) abrigo *m*; (*layer*) capa *f*; mano *f* of paint; (*animal's*) pelo *m*; ~ of arms escudo *m* de armas; ~ of mail cota *f* de malla; *fig.* turn one's ~ cambiar de casaca; cut the ~ according to the cloth adaptarse a las circunstancias; 2. cubrir, revestir (*with* con, de); dar una mano de pintura a; '~·**hang·er** colgador *m*; '**coat·ing** capa *f*, baño *m*; tela *f* para chaquetas *etc.*; '**coat·stand** percha *f*.

coax [kouks] engatusar; conseguir por medio de halagos (*into ger.* que *subj.*); ~ a p. out of doing s.t. disuadir a una p. de hacer algo; '**coax·ing** □ lenguaje *m* almibarado; coba *f*; halagos *m/pl.*

cob [kɔb] jaca *f* fuerte; cisne *m* macho; (*loaf*) pan *m* redondo; (*maize*) mazorca *f*.

co·balt ['kɔ'bɔːlt] cobalto *m*; ~ blue azul *m* de cobalto.

cob·ble [kɔbl] 1. guija *f* (*a.* '~·**stone**); ~s *pl.* enguijarrado *m*; 2. enguijarrar; *shoes* remendar; *b.s.* chafallar; '**cob·bler** zapatero *m*, remendón *m*; bebida *f* helada; *Am.* pastel *m* de frutas.

cob·nut ['kɔbnʌt] avellana *f* grande.

cob·web ['kɔbweb] telaraña *f* (*a. fig.*).

co·caine [kə'kein] cocaína *f*.

coc·cyx ['kɔksiks] cóccix *m*.

coch·i·neal ['kɔtʃini:l] cochinilla *f*.

cock [kɔk] 1. gallo *m*; macho *m* de ave; ⊕ grifo *m*, espita *f*; martillo *m* of gun; vuelta *f* of hat; ~ of the walk gallito *m* del lugar; 2. *gun* amartillar; enderezar, volver hacia arriba; ladear on side; ~ed hat sombrero *m* de tres picos (*or* de candil); ~ one's eye at s.o. mirar con intención a una p.

cock·ade [kɔ'keid] escarapela *f*.

cock-and-bull sto·ry ['kɔkənd'bulstɔːri] cuento *m*, camelo *m*.

cock·a·too [kɔkə'tu:] cacatúa *f*.

cock·a·trice ['kɔkətrais] basilisco *m*.

cock·chaf·er ['kɔktʃeifə] abejorro *m*.

cock·crow ['kɔkkrou] canto *m* del gallo; aurora *f*; at ~ al amanecer.

cock·er ['kɔkə] cocker *m*.

cock...: '~-**eyed** ['kɔkaid] bizco; *sl.* ladeado; *sl. fig.* incomprensible, estúpido; '~-**fight**(·**ing**) pelea *f* de gallos.

cock·le[1] ['kɔkl] ♀ cizaña *f*.

cock·le[2] [~] 1. *zo.* berberecho *m*; the ~s of the heart lo más íntimo del corazón; 2. arrugar(se) (*a.* ~ up).

cock·ney ['kɔkni] *habitante de Londres*; *dialecto de ciertos barrios de Londres*.

cock·pit ['kɔkpit] cancha *f*, reñidero *m* de gallos; ✈ cabina *f*, carlinga *f*; *fig.* sitio *m* de muchos combates.

cock·roach ['kɔkroutʃ] cucaracha *f*.

cocks·comb ['kɔkskoum] cresta *f* de gallo; '**cock·sure** F demasiado seguro; presuntuoso; '**cock·tail** combinación *f*; ~ party cóctel *m*; '**cock·y** □ F engreído, hinchado.

co·co ['koukou] cocotero *m*.

co·coa ['koukou] cacao *m*; (*drink*) chocolate *m*.

co·co·nut ['koukənʌt] coco *m*.

co·coon [kə'ku:n] capullo *m*.

cod [kɔd] bacalao *m*.

cod·dle ['kɔdl] mimar; *egg* cocer en agua caliente sin hervir.

code [koud] 1. código *m* (✍ *a. fig.*); cifra *f*; *tel.* alfabeto *m* Morse; in ~ en cifra; 2. cifrar.

co·de·ine ['koudi:n] codeína *f*.

cod·fish ['kɔdfiʃ] bacalao *m*.

codg·er ['kɔdʒə] F (*freq. old* ~) tipo *m*, sujeto *m*.

cod·i·cil ['kɔdisil] codicilo *m*; **cod·i·fi·ca·tion** codificación *f*; **cod·i·fy** ['~fai] codificar.

cod·ling ['kɔdliŋ] ♀ manzana *f* de forma cónica.

cod·liv·er oil ['kɔdlivər'ɔil] aceite *m* de hígado de bacalao.

co-ed ['kou'ed] F **1.** coeducacional; **2.** alumna *f* de un colegio coeducacional.

co-ed-u-ca-tion [kouedju'keiʃn] coeducación *f*.

co-ef-fi-cient [koui'fiʃnt] coeficiente *adj. a. su. m.*

co-erce [kou'ɔːs] obligar, apremiar (*into ger.* a *inf.*); coercer; **co'er-ci-ble** coercible; **co'er-cion** [ʌʃn] compulsión *f*; coerción *f*; *under* ~ por fuerza mayor; **co'er-cive** □ coercitivo.

co-e-val [kou'iːvəl] □ coetáneo; contemporáneo.

co-ex-ist ['kouig'zist] coexistir (*with* con); **co'ex'ist-ence** coexistencia *f*, convivencia *f*; **'co-ex'ist-ent** coexistente.

cof-fee ['kɔfi] café *m*; '~-'**bean** grano *m* de café; '~-**grounds** heces *f/pl.* del café; '~-**pot** cafetera *f*; '~-**set** juego *m* de café.

coff-er ['kɔfə] cofre *m*, arca *f*; ⚠ artesón *m*; ~**s** *pl. fig.* fondos *m/pl.*; '~-**dam** ataguía *f*.

cof-fin ['kɔfin] **1.** ataúd *m*; **2.** *fig.* encerrar.

cog [kɔg] diente *m*; rueda *f* dentada.

co-gen-cy ['koudʒənsi] fuerza *f*; '**co-gent** □ convincente; lógico.

cogged [kɔgd] dentado; engranado.

cog-i-tate ['kɔdʒiteit] *v/i.* meditar, reflexionar; *v/t.* recapacitar; **cog-i-'ta-tion** meditación *f*, reflexión *f*.

co-gnac ['kounjæk] coñac *m*.

cog-nate ['kɔgneit] cognado *adj. a. su. m* (a *f*); afín.

cog-ni-tion [kɔg'niʃn] cognición *f*.

cog-ni-za-ble ['kɔgnizəbl] cognoscible; ⚖️ justiciable; '**cog-ni-zance** conocimiento *m*; ⚖️ competencia *f*; *take* ~ *of* reparar en; '**cog-ni-zant** instruido, noticioso (*of* de).

cog-no-men [kɔg'noumen] apodo *m*; apellido *m*. [tada.)

cog-wheel ['kɔgwiːl] rueda *f* den-)

co-hab-it [kou'hæbit] cohabitar; **co-hab-i'ta-tion** cohabitación *f*.

co-heir ['kou'ɛə] coheredero *m*; **co-heir-ess** ['kou'ɛəris] coheredera *f*.

co-here [kou'hiə] adherirse, pegarse (*ideas etc.*) enlazarse; **co-'her-en-cy** coherencia *f*; **co'her-ent** □ coherente; **co-her-er** [kou-'hiərə] *radio:* cohesor *m*.

co-he-sion [kou'hiːʒn] cohesión *f* (*a. fig.*); **co'he-sive** □ cohesivo.

coif-feur [kwɑː'fəː] peluquero *m*; **coif-fure** [ʌ'fjuə] peinado *m*.

coign of van-tage [kɔinəv'vɑːntidʒ] atalaya *f*; posición *f* ventajosa.

coil [kɔil] **1.** rollo *m*; ⚓ aduja *f of rope*; ⚡ carrete *m*; 🐍 serpentín *m*; † desorden *m*, barahunda *f*; ~ *spring* resorte *m* espiral; **2.** arrollar(se), enrollar(se); serpentear; ⚓ *rope* adujar.

coin [kɔin] **1.** moneda *f*; F *pay back in one's own* ~ pagar en la misma moneda; **2.** acuñar; *fig.* forjar; *word etc.* inventar, idear; '**coin-age** acuñación *f*; amonedación *f*; sistema *m* monetario; *fig.* invención *f*.

co-in-cide [kouin'said] coincidir (*with* con); **co-in-ci-dence** [kou'insidəns] coincidencia *f*; **co-in-ci'dent-al** □ coincidente; fortuito.

coin-er [kɔinə] monedero *m* (*esp.* falso).

coke [kouk] **1.** coque *m*; *Am.* F Coca-Cola *f*; **2.** convertir en coque.

col-an-der ['kʌləndə] escurridor *m*.

cold [kould] **1.** □ frío (*a. fig.*); ~ *meat* carne *f* fiambre; *be* ~ (*p.*) tener frío; (*weather*) hacer frío; (*th.*) estar frío; F *have* ~ *feet* encogérsele a uno el ombligo; **2.** frío *m*; 🇸 resfriado *m*; *catch* ~ resfriarse; F *leave out in the* ~ dejar al margen; '~-'**blood-ed** *zo.* de sangre fría; *fig.* insensible; (*cruel*) desalmado; '**cold-ness** frialdad *f*; indiferencia *f*.

cold...: '~-'**shoul-der** tratar con frialdad; '~-'**stor-age** almacenaje *m* frigorífico.

cole-slaw ['koulslɔː] ensalada de coles.

col-ic ['kɔlik] cólico *m*.

col-lab-o-rate [kə'læbəreit] colaborar; **col-lab-o-'ra-tion** colaboración *f*; **col'lab-o-ra-tor** colaborador (-a *f*) *m*; ✂ colaboracionista *m*.

col-lapse [kə'læps] **1.** 🇸 sufrir colapso; F desmayarse; ⚠ *etc.* hundirse; *fig.* fracasar; **2.** 🇸 colapso *m*; hundimiento *m*; fracaso *m*; **col-'laps-i-ble** plegable.

col-lar ['kɔlə] **1.** cuello *m*; (*animals a.* ⊕) collar *m*; F *slip the* ~ escaparse; **2.** prender por el cuello; *sl.* coger, prender; '~-**bone** clavícula *f*.

col-late [kɔ'leit] colacionar (*a. eccl.*); *text* cotejar.

col-lat-er-al [kɔ'lætərəl] □ colateral; ~ *security* garantía *f* subsidiaria.

col·la·tion [kɔ'leiʃn] colación *f* (*a. eccl.*); cotejo *m of text.*

col·league ['kɔli:g] colega *m.*

col·lect 1. ['kɔlekt] *eccl.* colecta *f*; **2.** [kə'lekt] *v/t.* acumular; reunir; *antiques etc.* coleccionar; *fares* cobrar; *taxes* colectar, recaudar; ~ *o.s.* recobrarse; ~ one's wits reconcentrarse; *v/i.* acumularse; reunirse; coleccionar; **col'lect·ed** ☐ *fig.* sosegado; **col'lec·tion** colección *f*; montón *m*; recaudación *f of taxes*; **col'lec·tive** ☐ colectivo (*a. gr.*); ~ *bargaining* trato *m* colectivo; ~ *farm* granja *f* colectiva; **col'lec·tive·ly** colectivamente; **col'lec·tiv·ism** colectivismo *m*; **col'lec·tor** coleccionador *m*; (*tax-*) recaudador *m*; ⚡ colector *m.* [chacha *f*.\

col·leen ['kɔli:n, kɔ'li:n] *Ir.* mu-/

col·lege ['kɔlidʒ] colegio *m*; colegio *m* de universidad; **col·le·gi·an** [kə'li:dʒiən] colegial *m*; **col'le·gi·ate** [~dʒiit] colegial; colegiado.

col·lide [kə'laid] chocar (*with* con; *a. fig.*); *fig.* entrar en conflicto.

col·lie ['kɔli] perro *m* pastor.

col·lier ['kɔliə] minero *m* de carbón; ⚓ barco *m* minero; **col'lier·y** ['kɔljəri] mina *f* de carbón.

col·li·sion [kə'liʒn] colisión *f*, choque *m* (*a. fig.*).

col·lo·ca·tion [kɔlə'keiʃn] colocación *f*; disposición *f.*

col·lo·di·on [kə'loudiən] colodión *m.*

col·lo·qui·al [kə'loukwiəl] ☐ popular, familiar; **col'lo·qui·al·ism** popularismo *m.*

col·lo·quy ['kɔləkwi] coloquio *m.*

col·lude [kɔ'lju:d] coludir; **col·lu·sion** [kɔ'lu:ʒn] colusión *f.*

co·lon ['koulən] *typ.* dos puntos; *anat.* colon *m.*

colo·nel [kə:nl] coronel *m*; **'colo·nel·cy** coronelía *f.*

co·lo·ni·al [kə'lounjəl] **1.** colonial; **2.** colono *m*; **col·o·nist** ['kɔlənist] colonizador *m*; colono *m*; **col·o·ni·za·tion** [kɔlənai'zeiʃn] colonización *f*; **'col·o·nize** colonizar.

col·on·nade [kɔlə'neid] △ columnata *f*; soportales *m/pl.*

col·o·ny ['kɔləni] colonia *f.*

col·o·phon ['kɔlɔfən] colofón *m.*

col·o·pho·ny [kɔ'lɔfəni] colofonía *f.*

co·los·sal [kə'lɔsl] ☐ colosal.

col·our, *Am.* **col·or** ['kʌlə] **1.** color *m* (*a. fig.*); ✕ ~s *pl.* bandera *f*; F

be off ~ estar indispuesto; change ~ mudar de color, demudarse; ~ *film* película *f* en colores; *call to the* ~s llamar al servicio militar; *show one's* ~s dejar ver uno su verdadero carácter; *fig. with flying* ~s con lucimiento; **2.** *v/t.* colorear (*a. fig.*), colorar; *v/i.* sonrojarse (*a.* ~ *up*); '~-**bar** barrera *f* racial; '~-**blind** daltoniano; '~-**blind·ness** daltonismo *m*; **'colo(u)red** *p.* de color; coloreado (*a. fig.*); **col·o(u)r·ful** ['~ful] ☐ lleno de color; vivo, animado; **'col·o(u)r·ing** colorido *m*; colorante *m* (*a.* ~ *matter*); (*complexion*) color *m*; **'col·o(u)r·ist** colorista *m/f*; **'colo(u)r·less** ☐ sin color, incoloro; *fig.* soso.

colt [koult] potro *m*; *fig.* mozuelo *m*; **'colts·foot** ♀ uña *f* de caballo.

col·um·bine ['kɔləmbain] aguileña*f.*

col·umn ['kɔləm] columna *f*; **co·lum·nar** [kə'lʌmnə] de columna; **col·um·nist** ['kɔləmnist] periodista *m*, columnista *m.*

col·za ['kɔlzə] colza *f.*

co·ma ['koumə] **1.** ⚕ coma *m*; **2.** ♀ manojito *m* (de hebras sedosas); *ast.* cabellera *f.*

comb [koum] **1.** peine *m*; almohaza *f for horse*; (*cock's*) cresta *f*; ⊕ carda *f*; *v.* curry-~; *v.* honey-~; **2.** peinar; *wool* cardar; *fig.* registrar (*or* explorar) con minuciosidad.

com·bat ['kɔmbət] **1.** combate *m* (*a. fig.*); ~ *duty* servicio *m* de frente; **2.** combatir(se); **'com·bat·ant** combatiente *m*; **'com·bat·ive** ☐ peleador.

comb·er ['koumə] ⊕ cardador *m*; ⚓ ola *f* encrestada.

com·bin·a·ble [kəm'bainəbl] combinable; **com·bi·na·tion** [kɔmbi'neiʃn] combinación *f* (*a. garment, mst* ~s *pl.*); ~ *lock* cerradura *f* de combinación; **com·bine 1.** [kəm'bain] combinar(se); **2.** ['kɔmbain] ✦ monopolio *m*; ⚡ (*a.* ~ *harvester*) cosechadora *f.*

comb·ings ['koumiŋz] *pl.* peinaduras *f/pl.*

com·bus·ti·ble [kəm'bʌstəbl] **1.** combustible; *fig.* ardiente; **2.** combustible *m*; **com·bus·tion** [kəm'bʌstʃən] combustión *f.*

come [kʌm] [*irr.*] venir; ir; ~! ¡ven!, ¡venga!; oh, ~! ¡pero mire!; *how* ~? F ¿cómo eso?; *that's what*

~s *of hesitating* eso lo trae el va- cilar; *coming!* ¡voy!; ~ *about* pasar; suceder (*that* que); realizarse; ~ *across* p. topar a; *th.* encontrar, dar con; ~ *along* venir, ir; ~ *along!* ¡ vamos!; ~ *at* alcanzar; (*attack*) arrojarse sobre; ~ *away* retirarse, marcharse; salir de casa *etc.*; ~ *back* volver; ~ *before* anteponerse a; llegar antes; ~ *by* conseguir; ~ *down* bajar; *fig.* desplomarse; ~ *down on* caer sobre; F regañar; ~ *down with* ✗ enfermar de; ~ *for* venir por; ~ *forward* presentarse, acudir; ~ *in* entrar; *fig.* ponerse en uso, ponerse de moda; empezar; llegar *in race*; ~ *in!* ¡adelante!; ~ *in useful* servir, ser útil; ~ *into estate* heredar; *v. own*; ~ *off* (*part*) soltarse; despren- derse; *fig.* (*event*) verificarse, cele- brarse; (*succeed*) tener éxito, verse logrado; ~ *off it!* F ¡ déjate de ton- terías!; ~ *off well* salir airoso; ~ *on* (*grow*) crecer; (*improve*) mejorar, hacer progresos; (*prosper*) medrar; ~ *on!* ¡vamos!, ¡despabílate!; (*en-couragement*) ¡ánimo!; ~ (*up*)*on* en- contrarse con; descubrir; ~ *out* salir; salir a luz; (*as new*) estrenarse, de- butar; (*news*) revelarse, traslucirse; (*workers*) declararse en huelga; ~ *out with* decir, revelar; ~ *over: what's* ~ *over you?* ¿qué te pasa?; ~ *over queer* F tener vahídos; ~ *round* ✗ volver en sí; (*visit*) ir a ver; (*agree*) convenir, asentir; dejarse persua- dir; ~ *to* a) *adv.* ✗ volver en sí; ⚓ parar, fachear; b) *prp.* heredar; *sum* subir a; ~ *to mind* ocurrirse; ~ *up* subir; aparecer; acercarse (*to* a); mencionarse *in conversation; univ.* matricularse; ~ *up to* estar a la altura de; ~ *up with th.* proponer; '~-back F rehabilitación f; res- puesta f aguda.

co·me·di·an [kə'miːdiən] cómico m; autor m de comedias; **co·me·di- enne** [ˌ.i'en] cómica f.

come-down ['kʌmdaun] F desazón f, humillación f; desgracia f.

com·e·dy ['kɔmidi] comedia f; (*mu- sical*) zarzuela f; (*behaviour*) co- micidad f.

come·li·ness ['kʌmlinis] gracia f, donaire m; '**come·ly** gentil, apuesto.

come-on ['kʌmɔn] *Am. sl.* añagaza f; desafío m; (*p.*) bobo m.

com·er ['kʌmə] *Am.* F persona f

que promete; *all* ~s *pl.* todos los contendientes.

co·mes·ti·bles [kə'mestiblz] *pl.* co- mestibles m/*pl.*

com·et ['kɔmit] cometa m.

com·fort ['kʌmfət] **1.** consuelo m, alivio m; (*physical*) confort m, co- modidad f; bienestar m; ~ *loving* comodón; **2.** consolar, aliviar; ✗ ayudar; '**com·fort·a·ble** ☐ cómo- do, confortable; *living* desahogado, holgado; '**com·fort·er** consolador (-a f) m; (*scarf*) bufanda f de lana; (*baby's*) chupete m; *Am.* colcha f, cobertor m; '**com·fort·ing** ☐ con- solador; '**com·fort·less** ☐ descon- solado; desolado, triste; *room* sin comodidad.

com·frey ['kʌmfri] consuelda f.

com·fy ['kʌmfi] ☐ F = *comfortable.*

com·ic ['kɔmik] **1.** ☐ (*mst* '**com·i- cal** ☐) cómico; divertido, entre- tenido; **2.** (*p.*) cómico m; revista f cómica (*infantil*), tebeo m.

com·ing ['kʌmiŋ] **1.** que viene, venidero; **2.** venida f, llegada f; ~ *and going* trajín m, ajetreo m.

com·i·ty ['kɔmiti] cortesía f.

com·ma ['kɔmə] coma f.

com·mand [kə'mɑːnd] **1.** orden f, mandato m; mando m, dominio m; ✗ comando m; ✗, ⚓ comandancia f; dominio m *of language*; *be at the* ~ *of* estar a la disposición de; *be in* ~ estar al mando; **2.** mandar, ordenar (*to* a); *respect* merecer, imponer; ✗, ⚓ comandar; **com- man·dant** [kɔmən'dænt] coman- dante m; **com·man·deer** [ˌ.'diə] ✗ *men* reclutar por fuerza; *stores etc.* expropiar; F apoderarse de; **com·mand·er** [kə'mɑːndə] ✗ co- mandante m; ⚓ capitán m de fra- gata; comendador m *of Order*; **com'mand·er-in-'chief** genera- lísimo m; **com'mand·ing** coman- dante; *fig.* imponente, dominante; *appearance* señorial; **com'mand- ment** mandamiento m.

com·mem·o·rate [kə'meməreit] conmemorar; **com·mem·o'ra·tion** conmemoración f (*in* ~ *of* en ... de); **com'mem·o·ra·tive** ☐ conmemo- rativo.

com·mence [kə'mens] comenzar, empezar (*ger. or to inf.* a *inf.*); **com'mence·ment** comienzo m, principio m.

com·mend [kə'mend] encomendar (to a); recomendar, alabar; **com'mend·a·ble** □ loable, recomendable; **com·men·da·tion** [kɔmen'deiʃn] alabanza *f*, encomio *m*; recomendación *f*; **com'mend·a·to·ry** [‿ətəri] laudatorio; comendatorio.

com·men·su·ra·ble [kə'menʃərəbl] □ conmensurable; **com'men·su·rate** □ proporcionado; ~ with conforme a.

com·ment ['kɔment] **1.** comento *m*; comentario *m* (on sobre); observación *f* (on sobre); (*conversational*) dicho *m*; **2.** comentar (on *acc.*); observar (*that* que); **'com·men·tar·y** comentario *m*; **'com·men·ta·tor** comentador *m*, comentarista *m*; *radio*: locutor *m*.

com·merce ['kɔmə:s] comercio *m*; *Chamber of* ♀ Cámara *f* de Comercio; **com·mer·cial** [kə'mə:ʃl] **1.** □ comercial; ~ *traveller* viajante *m*, agente *m* viajero *S.Am.*; **2.** *radio*: anuncio *m*, programa *m* publicitario; **com'mer·cial·ism** mercantilismo *m*; **com'mer·cial·ize** comercializar.

com·mis·er·ate [kə'mizəreit] compadecer; ~ *with* condolerse de; **com·mis·er·a·tion** [‿'reiʃn] conmiseración *f*.

com·mis·sar·i·at [kɔmi'sɛəriət] comisariato *m*, comisaría *f*; **com·mis·sar·y** ['‿səri] comisario *m* (a. ✕).

com·mis·sion [kə'miʃn] **1.** comisión *f* (a. ✝); ✕ nombramiento *m*; ⚖ perpetración *f* of *crime*; ✝ ~ *merchant* comisionista *m*; **2.** comisionar; ✕ nombrar; *ship* poner en servicio activo; **com·mis·sion·aire** [‿ə'nɛə] portero *m*, conserje *m*; **com'mis·sion·er** comisionado *m*; *Am.* miembro *m* de la junta municipal; ~ *for oaths* notario *m* público.

com·mit [kə'mit] cometer; *business* confiar; *parl. bill* someter (a una comisión); (*o.s.*) comprometer(se); ⚖ *p.* encarcelar, internar; ~ *to memory* aprender de memoria; ~ *to writing* poner por escrito; **com'mit·ment** obligación *f*; compromiso *m*; ⚖ auto *m* de prisión; *parl.* traslado *m* a una comisión; **com'mit·tal** ⚖ auto *m* de prisión;

entierro *m* of *body*; **com'mit·tee** comité *m*, comisión *f*.

com·mode [kə'moud] cómoda *f*; (*a. night* ~) sillico *m*; **com'mo·di·ous** □ cómodo, espacioso, holgado; **com·mod·i·ty** [kə'mɔditi] mercancía *f*; cosa *f* útil.

com·mo·dore ['kɔmədɔ:] comodoro *m*.

com·mon ['kɔmən] **1.** □ común; F ordinario; ♀ *Council* ayuntamiento *m*; ~ *law* derecho *m* consuetudinario; ~ *room* salón *m* (*de un colegio etc.*); ~ *sense* sentido *m* común; *attr.* cuerdo, racional; ~ *weal* bien *m* público; *in* ~ en común; *fig. in* ~ *with* de común con; **2.** campo *m* común, ejido *m*; **com·mon·al·ty** ['‿nlti] generalidad *f* de personas; **'com·mon·er** plebeyo *m*; *univ.* estudiante *m* que no tiene beca del colegio; **'com·mon·ness** F ordinariez *f*; **'com·mon·place 1.** perogrullada *f*; lugar *m* común; **2.** común, trivial; **com·mons** ['‿z] *pl.* estado *m* llano; (*food*) víveres *m/pl.*; *short* ~ ración *f* escasa; (*mst House of*) ♀ (Cámara *f* de) los Comunes; **'com·mon·wealth** nación *f*; república *f*; ♀ Mancomunidad *f*.

com·mo·tion [kə'mouʃn] conmoción *f*, tumulto *m*.

com·mu·nal ['kɔmjunl] □ comunal; **com·mune 1.** [kə'mju:n] *eccl.* comulgar; comunicar (*with* con); **2.** ['kɔmju:n] *pol.* comuna *f*.

com·mu·ni·ca·bil·i·ty [kəmju:nikə'biliti] comunicabilidad *f*; **com'mu·ni·ca·ble** □ comunicable; **com'mu·ni·cant** *eccl.* comulgante *m/f*; **com'mu·ni·cate** [‿keit] comunicar (*with* con); *eccl.* comulgar; (*buildings*) mandarse (*with* con); **com·mu·ni·ca·tion** comunicación *f*; *be in* ~ *with* estar en contacto con; **com'mu·ni·ca·tive** □ comunicativo. [nión *f.*\
com·mun·ion [kə'mju:njən] comu-∫
com·mu·ni·qué [kəm'ju:nikei] comunicado *m*, parte *m*.

com·mu·nism ['kɔmju:nizm] comunismo *m*; **'com·mu·nist 1.** comunista *m/f*; **2.** = **com·mu'nis·tic** □ comunista.

com·mu·ni·ty [kəm'ju:niti] comunidad *f*; sociedad *f*; (*local*) vecindario *m*; ~ *centre* centro *m* social; ~ *spirit* civismo *m*.

com·mut·a·ble [kəm'juːtəbl] conmutable; **com·mu·ta·tion** [kɔmjuː-'teiʃn] conmutación *f*; abono *m*; *Am.* ~ ticket billete *m* de abono; **com·mu·ta·tive** [kə'mjuːtɔtiv] conmutativo; **com·mu·ta·tor** ['kɔmjuːteitə] ≠ colector *m*; **com·mute** [kə'mjuːt] *v/t.* conmutar (*for*, to por, *into* en); *v/i. Am.* ser abonado al ferrocarril; viajar con billete de abono (*esp.* al trabajo); **com'mut·er** abonado *m* al ferrocarril.

com·pact 1. ['kɔmpækt] pacto *m*, convenio *m*; (*make-up*) estuche *m* de afeites; **2.** [kəm'pækt] compacto; conciso, breve; **3.** [~] condensar, hacer compacto; **com'pact·ness** densidad *f*; concisión *f*.

com·pan·ion [kəm'pænjən] compañero (*a f*) *m*; compañía *f*; ⚓ lumbrera *f*; ~ *in arms* compañero *m* de armas; **com'pan·ion·a·ble** □ sociable, simpático; **com'pan·ion·ship** compañerismo *m*.

com·pa·ny ['kʌmpəni] compañía *f* (*a.* ✗ *a. thea.*); ✝ sociedad *f*, empresa *f*; F (*p.*) visita *f*; *bad* ~ amistades *f/pl.* sospechosas; F *good* ~ compañero *m* simpático (*or* entretenido); *keep s.o.* ~ acompañar a, estar con; ir juntos; *part* ~ separarse, tomar rumbos distintos; *fig.* desunirse.

com·pa·ra·ble ['kɔmpərəbl] □ comparable; **com·par·a·tive** [kəm-'pærətiv] **1.** *gr.* comparativo *m*; **2.** □ comparado; *gr.* comparativo.

com·pare [kəm'pɛə] **1.** *beyond* ~, *without* ~, *past* ~ sin comparación; **2.** *v/t.* comparar (*with*, to con); *as* ~*d with* comparado con; *v/i.* compararse (*with* con); **com·par·i·son** [~'pærisn] comparación *f*; *in* ~ *with* en comparación con.

com·part·ment [kəm'pɑːtmənt] compartimiento *m*; 🚋 departamento *m*.

com·pass ['kʌmpəs] **1.** ⚓ brújula *f*; ♪ extensión *f*, límites *m/pl.* (de la voz *etc.*); confín *m*, circuito *m*; *fig.* alcance *m*; (*a pair of* un) ~*es pl.* compás *m*; **2.** rodear, ceñir; (*contrive*) conseguir; *fig.* alcanzar, abarcar.

com·pas·sion [kəm'pæʃn] compasión *f*, piedad *f*; *have* ~ *on* tener piedad de; *move to* ~ mover a compasión; **com'pas·sion·ate** [~-

ʃənit] □ compasivo; *on* ~ *grounds* por compasión.

com·pat·i·bil·i·ty [kəmpætə'biliti] compatibilidad *f*; **com'pat·i·ble** □ compatible.

com·pa·tri·ot [kəm'pætriət] compatriota *m/f.*

com·pel [kəm'pel] *p.* compeler (*to* a); *respect* imponer.

com·pen·di·ous [kəm'pendiəs] □ compendioso.

com·pen·di·um [kəm'pendiəm] compendio *m.*

com·pen·sate ['kɔmpenseit] *v/t.* compensar (*with* con); indemnizar (*for* de); *v/i.*: ~ *for* compensar; **com·pen'sa·tion** compensación *f*; indemnización *f*; ⊕ retribución *f*, recompensa *f*; **'com·pen·sa·tive**, **'com·pen·sa·to·ry** compensador, compensatorio.

com·pete [kəm'piːt] competir, hacer competencia (*for* para; *with* con).

com·pe·tence, **com·pe·ten·cy** ['kɔmpitəns(i)] competencia *f* (*a.* ⚖); capacidad *f*; aptitud *f*; **'com·pe·tent** □ competente (*a.* ⚖); capaz, hábil.

com·pe·ti·tion [kɔmpi'tiʃn] competencia *f*; concurso *m*; (*Civil Service etc.*) oposiciones *f/pl.*; *in* ~ *with* en competencia con; **com·pet·i·tive** [kəm'petitiv] □ competidor; *price* competitivo; *post* de (*or* por) concurso (*or* oposición); **com'pet·i·tor** competidor (-a *f*) *m*; opositor (-a *f*) *m* for post.

com·pi·la·tion [kɔmpi'leiʃn] compilación *f*; **com·pile** [kəm'pail] compilar.

com·pla·cence, **com·pla·cen·cy** [kəm'pleisns(i)] complacencia *f*; *b.s.* satisfacción *f* de sí mismo; **com'pla·cent** □ satisfecho (con poca razón) (*about* de).

com·plain [kəm'plein] quejarse (*about*, *of* de; *that* de que); ⚖ demandar; **com'plain·ant** ⚖ demandante *m/f*; **com'plaint** queja *f*; ⚖ querella *f*, demanda *f*; ⚕ enfermedad *f*, mal *m*; *lodge a* ~ hacer una reclamación.

com·plai·sance [kəm'pleizns] complacencia *f*; deferencia *f*; **com'plai·sant** □ complaciente, amable; *husband* consentido.

com·ple·ment ['kɔmplimənt] **1.** complemento *m* (*a. gr.*, Ⓐ); ⚓ personal *m*; **2.** complementar; **com·ple'men·tal, com·ple'men·ta·ry** complementario.

com·plete [kəm'pli:t] **1.** ☐ completo, entero; consumado; **2.** completar, llevar a cabo; *form* llenar; **com'ple·tion** cumplimiento *m*, terminación *f*.

com·plex ['kɔmpleks] **1.** ☐ complejo; complicado; **2.** ♂ complejo *m*; F idea *f* fija, prejuicio *m* irracional; **com·plex·ion** [kəm'plekʃn] tez *f*, color *m* de la cara; aspecto *m*, carácter *m*; **com'plex·i·ty** complejidad *f*.

com·pli·ance [kəm'plaiəns] sumisión *f* (with a), condescendencia *f* (with a); *in* ~ *with* accediendo a; de acuerdo con; **com'pli·ant** ☐ condescendiente; sumiso.

com·pli·cate ['kɔmplikeit] complicar; embrollar; **com·pli'ca·tion** complicación *f*.

com·plic·i·ty [kəm'plisiti] complicidad *f*.

com·pli·ment 1. ['kɔmplimənt] cumplimiento *m*, cumplido *m*; piropo *m* *to woman*; *send* ~s enviar saludos; **2.** ['~ment] cumplimentar; felicitar (on sobre); **com·pli'men·ta·ry** lisonjero; *ticket etc.* de regalo, de cortesía.

com·ply [kəm'plai] conformarse (with con); obedecer (with a); ~ *with* obrar de acuerdo con.

com·po·nent [kəm'pounənt] componente *adj. a. su. m* (a. ~ *part*).

com·port [kəm'pɔ:t] convenir (with a); ~ *o.s.* comportarse.

com·pose [kəm'pouz] componer (a. ♪ *a. typ.*); **com'posed,** *adv.* **com·pos·ed·ly** [kəm'pouzidli] *spirit* sosegado; compuesto (of de); *be* ~ *of* componerse de, estar compuesto de; **com'pos·er** ♪ compositor *m*; autor *m*; **com'pos·ing** composición *f*; *typ.* ~ *stick* componedor *m*; **com·pos·ite** ['kɔmpəzit] **1.** compuesto; **2.** compuesto *m*; ♀ ~s *pl.* compuestas *f/pl.*; **com·pos·i·tion** [kɔmpə'ziʃn] composición *f*; ✝ arreglo *m*, ajuste *m*; **com·pos·i·tor** [kəm'pɔzitə] cajista *m*; **com·post** ['kɔmpɔst] ♪ abono *m*; **com·po·sure** [kəm'pouʒə] compostura *f*, serenidad *f*.

com·pote ['kɔm'pout] compota *f*; conserva *f* (de fruta).

com·pound¹ 1. ['kɔmpaund] compuesto; ~ *fracture* fractura *f* complicada; ~ *interest* interés *m* complicada; **2.**[~] compuesto *m* (*a.* 🜚); *gr.* (*a.* ~ *word*) vocablo *m* compuesto; **3.** [kəm'paund] *v/t.* componer; *v/i.*: ~ *with* capitular con.

com·pound² ['kɔmpaund] comprender; encerrar; incluir.

com·pre·hen·si·ble [kɔmpri'hensəbl] ☐ comprensible; **com·pre·'hen·sion** comprensión *f*; **com·pre'hen·sive** ☐ comprensivo; **com·pre'hen·sive·ness** extensión *f*, alcance *m*.

com·press 1. [kəm'pres] comprimir; **2.** ['kɔmpres] compresa *f*; **com·pres·si·bil·i·ty** [kəmpresi'biliti] compresibilidad *f*; **com·pres·sion** [~'preʃn] compresión *f*; ~ *ratio* índice *m* de compresión; **com'pres·sor** compresor *m*.

com·prise [kəm'praiz] comprender; constar de; *range* abarcar.

com·pro·mise ['kɔmprəmaiz] **1.** compromiso *m*, componenda *f*; **2.** *v/t. affair* arreglar; *p.* comprometer; *v/i.* comprometer(se); *b.s.* transigir.

com·pul·sion [kəm'pʌlʃn] compulsión *f*; **com'pul·so·ry** [~səri] ☐ obligatorio; compulsivo.

com·punc·tion [kəm'pʌŋkʃn] compunción *f*.

com·put·a·ble [kəm'pju:təbl] calculable; **com·pu·ta·tion** [kɔmpju:'teiʃn] cómputo *m*, cálculo *m*; **com·pute** [kəm'pju:t] computar, calcular; **com'put·er** calculadora *f*.

com·rade ['kɔmreid] camarada *m*; ~ *in arms* compañero *m* de armas.

con¹ [kɔn] estudiar, repasar; aprender de memoria.

con² [~] *ship* gobernar.

con³ [~] *abbr.* = *contra* contra; *pro and* ~ en pro y en contra; *the pros and* ~s el pro y el contra.

con⁴ [~] *Am. sl.* **1.** (*a.* ~ *man*) timador *m*; **2.** timar.

con·cat·e·nate [kɔn'kætineit] concatenar; **con·cat·e'na·tion** concatenación *f*.

con·cave ['kɔn'keiv] ☐ cóncavo; **con·cav·i·ty** [~'kæviti] concavidad *f*.

con·ceal [kən'si:l] ocultar (*from* a, de); ⚖ encubrir; **con'ceal·ment** disimulación *f* *of feelings etc.*; encubrimiento *m*; *place of* ~ escondrijo *m*.

con·cede [kən'si:d] conceder.

con·ceit [kən'si:t] presunción *f*, engreimiento *m*, ínfulas *f/pl.*; *lit.* concepto *m*; **con'ceit·ed** □ engreído, afectado; *style* conceptuoso; **con'ceit·ed·ness** engreimiento *m*.

con·ceiv·a·ble [kən'si:vəbl] □ concebible; **con'ceive** *v/i.* concebir; *v/t.* imaginar, formar concepto de; *child* concebir; *plan* idear.

con·cen·trate 1. ['kɔnsentreit] concentrar(se); ~ *on* concentrar la atención en; concentrarse (*on ger.* a *inf.*); *fig.* hope *etc.* cifrar (*on* en); **2.** ['⸗trit] *esp.* ⚗ sustancia *f* concentrada; **con·cen'tra·tion** concentración *f* (*a.* ⚗); ~ *camp* campo *m* de concentración; **con'cen·tric** □ concéntrico.

con·cep·tion [kən'sepʃn] concepción *f*; idea *f*, concepto *m*.

con·cern [kən'sə:n] **1.** asunto *m*, negocio *m*; interés *m*, preocupación *f* (*for*, *with* por); inquietud *f* (*for* por); ✝ empresa *f*; F *esp.* the *whole* ~ el asunto entero; *of* ~ de importancia; *that's your* ~! ¡allá tú!; **2.** concernir, atañer; preocupar, inquietar; ~ *o.s. with* ocuparse de, interesarse por; *be* ~*ed in* estar interesado en; estar metido en; *be* ~*ed* estar preocupado (*with* por; *that* porque); *be* ~*ed to inf.* (me *etc.*) interesa *inf.*; *as far as he is* ~*ed* en cuanto le toca a él; *as* ~*s* respecto de; **con'cerned** □ interesado (*in* en); ocupado; inquietado (*at*, *about*, *for* por); *those* ~ los interesados; **con'cern·ing** *prp.* concerniente a; respecto de.

con·cert 1. ['kɔnsət] concierto *m* (*a.* ♪); *in* ~ de concierto; **2.** [kən'sə:t] concertar; **con·cer·ti·na** [kɔnsə-'ti:nə] concertina *f*.

con·ces·sion [kən'seʃn] concesión *f*; privilegio *m*; **con·ces·sion·aire** [kənseʃə'nɛə] concesionario *m*.

con·ces·sive [kən'sesiv] □ concesivo (*a.* ~ *gr.*).

conch [kɔŋk] caracola *f*.

con·cil·i·ate [kən'silieit] conciliar; (*win over*) ganar, granjear; **con·cil·i'a·tion** conciliación *f*; **con'cil·i·a·tor** conciliador *m*; **con'cil·i·a·to·ry** [⸗ətəri] conciliador, conciliatorio.

con·cise [kən'sais] □ conciso; **con'cise·ness** concisión *f* (*a.* **con'ci·sion**).

con·clave ['kɔnkleiv] cónclave *m*; asamblea *f*.

con·clude [kən'klu:d] concluir, terminar; sacar una consecuencia; *agreement* llegar a; *business* finalizar, dar por terminado; *to be* ~*d* continuará; **con'clud·ing** final.

con·clu·sion [kən'klu:ʒn] conclusión *f*; *in* ~ en conclusión; *try* ~*s with* participar en una contienda con; **con'clu·sive** □ conclusivo; (*decisive*) decisivo.

con·coct [kən'kɔkt] mezclar, confeccionar; *fig.* tramar, urdir; **con'coc·tion** confección *f*; *fig.* maquinación *f*, trama *f*.

con·com·i·tance, con·com·i·tan·cy [kən'kɔmitəns(i)] concomitancia *f*; **con'com·i·tant** concomitante *adj. a. su. m.*

con·cord 1. ['kɔŋkɔ:d] concordia *f*; *gr.*, ♪ concordancia *f*; **2.** [kən'kɔ:d] concordar (*with* con); **con'cord·ance** concordancia *f* (*a. eccl.*); **con'cord·ant** □ concordante; **con'cor·dat** [⸗dæt] concordato *m*.

con·course ['kɔŋkɔ:s] confluencia *f* *of rivers*; concurso *m*, reunión *f of people*; *Am.* 🚉 gran salón *m*.

con·crete 1. ['kɔnkri:t] □ concreto; ⊕ de hormigón; **2.** [~] ⊕ hormigón *m*; ~ *mixer* hormigonera *f*; **3.** [kən-'kri:t] cuajarse; solidificarse; **con·cre·tion** [kən'kri:ʃn] concreción *f*.

con·cu·bi·nage [kɔn'kju:binidʒ] concubinato *m*; **con·cu·bine** ['kɔŋkjubain] concubina *f*, barragana *f*.

con·cu·pis·cence [kən'kju:pisns] concupiscencia *f*; **con'cu·pis·cent** concupiscente.

con·cur [kən'kə:] concurrir; convenir (*with* con; *in* en); **con·cur·rence** [~'kʌrəns] concurrencia *f*; unión *f*; (*agreement*) acuerdo *m*; (*assent*) asenso *m*; *in* ~ *with* de acuerdo con; **con'cur·rent** □ concurrente.

con·cus·sion [kən'kʌʃn] sacudimiento *m*; 🇫 conmoción *f* cerebral.

con·demn [kən'dem] condenar (*to* a); censurar; ~*ed cell* celda *f* de los condenados a muerte; **con'dem·na·ble** condenable; **con·dem·na·tion** [kɔndem'neiʃn] condenación *f*; ⚖ condena *f*; censura *f*; **con·dem-**

na·to·ry [kən'demnətəri] condenador.

con·den·sa·ble [kən'densəbl] condensable; **con·den·sa·tion** [kɔnden'seiʃn] condensación *f*; (*a.* ⏦) compendio *m of material*; **con·dense** [kən'dens] condensar; *material* abreviar; **con'dens·er** ⊕, ⚡ condensador *m*.

con·de·scend [kɔndi'send] condescender (*to* en); dignarse (*to inf.*); **con·de'scend·ing** □ condescendiente; que trata (*or* se comporta) con aire protector (*or* de superioridad); **con·de'scen·sion** dignación *f*, condescendencia *f*.

con·di·ment ['kɔndimənt] condimento *m*.

con·di·tion [kən'diʃn] **1.** condición *f*; ⁓*s pl.* condiciones *f*/*pl.*, circunstancias *f*/*pl.*; *on* ⁓ *that* a condición (de) que; **2.** condicionar. acondicionar; determinar; **con·di'tion·al** □ condicional (*a. gr.*); ⁓ *upon* a condición de (que); **con'di·tion·al·ly** [⁓əli] con reservas; **con'di·tioned** (a)condicionado; determinado.

con·dole [kən'doul] condolerse (*with* de); **con'do·lence** pésame *m*, condolencia *f*; *express one's* ⁓*s* dar el pésame. [condominio *m*.\
con·do·min·i·um [kɔndə'miniəm]/ **con·do·na·tion** [kɔndou'neiʃn] condonación *f*; **con·done** [kən'doun] condonar.

con·duce [kən'dju:s] conducir (*to* a); **con'du·cive** conducente, contribuyente (*to* a).

con·duct 1. ['kɔndəkt] conducta *f*; **2.** [kən'dʌkt] conducir; llevar; *orchestra* dirigir; ♪ (*v.*/*i.*) llevar la batuta; ⁓ *o.s.* comportarse; **con·duct·i·bil·i·ty** [kəndʌkti'biliti] conductibilidad *f*; **con'duct·i·ble** [⁓təbl] conductivo; **con'duct·ing** ♪ dirección *f*; dirigir *m*; **con'duc·tion** conducción *f*; **con'duc·tive** □ conductivo; conductor; **con·duc·tiv·i·ty** [kɔndʌk'tiviti] conductibilidad *f*; **con·duc·tor** [kən'dʌktə] conductor *m* (*a. phys.*); ♪ director *m*; (*bus-*) cobrador *m*; *Am.* 🚃 revisor *m*; (*lightning-*) pararrayos *m*; **con'duc·tress** cobradora *f*.

con·duit ['kɔndjuit] conducto *m*, canal *m*.

cone [koun] cono *m* (*a.* ⚘); (*ice-cream* ⁓) barquillo *m*.

co·ney ['kouni] conejo *m*.

con·fab ['kɔnfæb] F **1.** = **con·fab·u·late** [kən'fæbjuleit] confabular; **2.** = **con·fab·u·la·tion** confabulación *f*; plática *f*.

con·fec·tion [kən'fekʃn] confección *f*, hechura *f*; (*sweetmeat*) confite *m*; **con'fec·tion·er** confitero *m*; pastelero *m*; **con'fec·tion·er·y** confites *m*/*pl.*; pasteles *m*/*pl.*; (*shop*) confitería *f*; pastelería *f*.

con·fed·er·a·cy [kən'fedərəsi] confederación *f*; ⚖ complot *m*; **con·'fed·er·ate 1.** [⁓rit] confederado; **2.** [⁓] confederado *m*; cómplice *m*; **3.** [⁓reit] confederarse; **con·fed·er·a·tion** confederación *f*.

con·fer [kən'fə:] *v*/*t.* conferir (*on* a); *v*/*i.* conferir (*with* con; *about*, *upon* acerca de, sobre); **con·fer·ence** ['kɔnfərəns] conferencia *f*; (*assembly*) congreso *m*.

con·fess [kən'fes] confesar (*to p.* a); ⁓ *to th.* reconocer, admitir; ⁓ *to God* confesarse a Dios; **con'fess·ed·ly** [⁓idli] según se admite; francamente; **con·fes·sion** [⁓'feʃn] confesión *f* (*a. eccl.*); *eccl.* (*a.* ⁓ *of faith*) credo *m*; ⁓ *box* confesonario *m*; **con'fes·sion·al 1.** confesional; **2.** confesonario *m*; **con'fes·sor** (*priest*) confesor *m*; (*sinner*) confesante *m*/*f*, penitente *m*/*f*.

con·fi·dant [kɔnfi'dænt] confidente *m*; **con·fi'dante** [⁓] confidenta *f*.

con·fide [kən'faid] *v*/*i.*: ⁓ *in* confiar en, fiarse de; ⁓ *to* hacer confidencias a; *v*/*t. th.* confiar (*to* a, en); **con·fi·dence** ['kɔnfidəns] confianza *f* (*in* en); confidencia *f*, secreto *m*; *in* ⁓ en confianza; *gain* ⁓ adquirir confianza; *Am.* ⁓ *man* timador *m*; **'con·fi·dent** □ seguro (*of* de; *that* de que); lleno de confianza; *b.s.* confiado; **con·fi'den·tial** □ confidencial; ⁓*ly* en confianza.

con·fig·u·ra·tion [kənfigju'reiʃn] configuración *f*.

con·fine 1. ['kɔnfain] *mst* ⁓*s pl.* confines *m*/*pl.* (*a. fig.*); **2.** [kən'fain] confinar (*s.o. to* en); encerrar; limitar; *be* ⁓*d to bed* tener que guardar cama; *be* ⁓*d* (*woman*) estar de parto; **con'fine·ment** confinamiento *m*; encierro *m*; encarcelamiento *m in prison*; ⚕ parto *m*, sobreparto *m*.

con·firm [kən'fə:m] confirmar (*a. eccl.*); ratificar, revalidar; **con·fir-**

ma·tion [kɔnfə'meiʃn] confirmación *f* (*a. eccl.*); **con·firm·a·tive** [kən'fə:mətiv], **con'firm·a·to·ry** [‿təri] confirmatorio; **con'firmed** confirmado (*a. eccl.*); (*by habit*) inveterado.

con·fis·cate ['kɔnfiskeit] confiscar; **con·fis'ca·tion** confiscación *f*; **con'fis·ca·to·ry** que confisca.

con·fla·gra·tion [kɔnflə'greiʃn] conflagración *f*.

con·flict 1. ['kɔnflikt] conflicto *m* (*a. fig.*); **2.** [kən'flikt]: ~ *with* estar en pugna con.

con·flu·ence ['kɔnfluəns] confluencia *f* (*a. ♣*); **con·flu·ent** ['‿fluənt] confluente *adj. a. su. m.*

con·form [kən'fɔ:m] *v/t.* conformar (*to* con); *v/i.*: ~ *to* conformarse con, allanarse a; **con'form·a·ble** □ conforme (*to* con); **con·for·ma·tion** [kɔnfɔ:'meiʃn] conformación *f*; **con·form·ist** [kən'fɔ:mist] conformista *m/f*; *fig.* que se allana a todo; **con'form·i·ty** conformidad *f*; *in* ~ *with* conforme a.

con·found [kən'faund] confundir; vencer; F ~ *it!* ¡demonio!; **con'found·ed** □ F condenado.

con·fra·ter·ni·ty [kɔnfrə'tə:niti] cofradía *f*; *fig.* confraternidad *f*.

con·front [kən'frʌnt] afrontar, carear; *s.o.* confrontar (*with* con); hacer cara a; *manuscripts* cotejar; *be* ~*ed with* encararse con; salírsele a uno; **con·fron·ta·tion** [kɔnfrʌn'teiʃn] confrontación *f*; cotejo *m*.

con·fuse [kən'fju:z] confundir (*s.t. with* con); ~ *the issue* oscurecer las cosas; **con'fused** □ confuso; perturbado, aturrullado; **con'fu·sion** confusión *f*; (*mental*) aturdimiento *m*; desorden *m*.

con·fut·a·ble [kən'fju:təbl] confutable; **con·fu·ta·tion** [kɔnfju:'teiʃn] confutación *f*; **con·fute** [kən'fju:t] confutar.

con·geal [kən'dʒi:l] congelar(se); (*blood*) coagular(se). [lación *f*.\

con·ge·la·tion [kɔndʒi'leiʃn] conge-/

con·gen·ial [kən'dʒi:niəl] □ congenial; *atmosphere etc.* agradable; **con·ge·ni·al·i·ty** [‿'æliti] simpatía *f*, afinidad *f*. [génito.\

con·gen·i·tal [kən'dʒenitl] □ con-/

con·ge·ri·es [kən'dʒiəri:z] 🄌 congerie *f*.

con·ger·['kɔngə] (*a.* ~ *eel*) congrio *m*.

con·gest [kən'dʒest] congestionar (se) (*a. ♣*); (*people*) apiñarse; ~*ed area* barrio *m* superpoblado; **con·'ges·tion** congestión *f*; ~ *of traffic* aglomeración *f* del tráfico.

con·glom·er·ate 1. [kɔn'glɔmərit] conglomerado *adj. a. su. m*; **2.** [‿reit] conglomerar(se); **con·glom·er·a·tion** conglomeración *f*.

con·grat·u·late [kən'grætjuleit] felicitar ([*up*]*on* por); **con·grat·u·la·tion** felicitación *f*, parabién *m*; ~*s!* ¡enhorabuena!; **con'grat·u·la·to·ry** congratulatorio.

con·gre·gate ['kɔŋgrigeit] congregar(se); **con·gre'ga·tion** *eccl.* congregación *f*; auditorio *m*; los fieles (de una iglesia); **con·gre'ga·tion·al** congregacionalista.

con·gress ['kɔŋgres] congreso *m*; ♀ Congreso *m* (*de Estados Unidos*); ~*man Am.* congresista *m*; **con·gres·sion·al** [‿'greʃnl] congresional.

con·gru·ence, con·gru·en·cy ['kɔŋgruəns(i)] = *congruity*; **con·gru·ent** = *congruous*; cia *f*; **con·gru·ent** = *congruous*; **con'gru·i·ty** congruencia *f*, conformidad *f*; **con·gru·ous** □ congruo (*with* con); conforme (*with* a a); **con·gru·ent** (*to* respecto a).

con·ic, con·i·cal ['kɔnik(l)] □ cónico; ~ *section* sección *f* cónica. **co·ni·fer** ['kounifə] conífera *f*; **co·'nif·er·ous** conífero.

con·jec·tur·al [kən'dʒektʃərəl] □ conjetural; **con'jec·ture 1.** conjetura *f*; **2.** conjeturar (*from* de, por).

con·join [kən'dʒɔin] juntar(se), unir (se); **con'joint** conjunto; **con·'joint·ly** de mancomún.

con·ju·gal ['kɔndʒugl] □ conjugal; **con·ju·gate** ['‿geit] **1.** *v/t.* conjugar; *v/i. biol.* reproducirse; **2.** ['‿git] 🄌 conjugado; **con·ju·ga·tion** ['‿geiʃn] conjugación *f* (*a. biol.*).

con·junct [kən'dʒʌŋkt] □ conjunto; **con'junc·tion** conjunción *f*; **con·junc·ti·va** [kɔndʒʌŋk'taivə] conjuntiva *f*; **con·junc·tive** [kən'dʒʌŋktiv] conjuntivo; ~ *mood* modo *m* conjuntivo; **con·junc·ti·vi·tis** [‿'vaitis] conjuntivitis *f*; **con'junc·ture** [‿tʃə] coyuntura *f*.

con·ju·ra·tion [kɔndʒuə'reiʃn] conjuro *m*; **con·jure 1.** [kən'dʒuə] *v/t.*

conjurar, pedir con instancia;
2. ['kʌndʒə] v/t. conjurar, exorcizar
(a. ~ away); ~ up hacer aparecer;
fig. evocar; v/i. escamotear; practicar las artes mágicas; 'con·jur·er,
'con·jur·or mágico m; escamoteador m, prestidigitador m; 'con·jur·ing-trick escamoteo m.

conk [kɔŋk] F 1. narigón m; 2.: mst
~ out ⊕ parar, tener averías; ⚙
perder el conocimiento.

con·nect [kə'nekt] conectar(se),
conexionar(se); asociar(se), enlazar
(se); 🚂 empalmar (with con);
teleph. poner en comunicación
(with con); con'nect·ed □ conexo;
asociado; enlazado (with con); well
~ de buena familia; be ~ with estar
asociado con; † ser un empleado de;
con'nect·ing que une, que conecta; ~ rod biela f; con'nec·tion v.
connexion; con'nec·tive □ conectivo; anat. ~ tissue tejido m conjuntivo.

con·nex·ion [kə'nekʃn] conexión f
(a. 🛠); fig. relación f; (family ~) parentesco m; unión f, enlace m;
🚂 correspondencia f (with con),
empalme m; ⊕ acoplamiento m; in
~ with a propósito de; in this ~ con
respecto a esto.

conn·ing-tow·er ['kɔniŋtauə] torreta f.

con·niv·ance [kə'naivəns] connivencia f; confabulación f (at, in
para); con'nive hacer la vista gorda
(at a); ~ with confabularse con.

con·nois·seur [kɔni'sə:] conocedor
(-a f) m; catador m of wine.

con·no·ta·tion [kɔnou'teiʃn] connotación f; con'note connotar.

con·nu·bi·al [kə'nju:biəl] □ conjugal, connubial.

con·quer ['kɔŋkə] conquistar (a.
fig.), vencer; 'con·quer·or conquistador (-a f) m; vencedor (-a f)
m.

con·quest ['kɔŋkwest] conquista f.

con·san·guin·e·ous [kɔnsæŋ'gwiniəs] consanguíneo; con·san'guin·i·ty consanguinidad f.

con·science ['kɔnʃns] conciencia f;
F in all ~ en realidad de verdad; ~
money dinero m que se paga para
descargar la conciencia; 'con·science·less desalmado; '~-strick·en contrito, arrepentido.

con·sci·en·tious [kɔnʃi'enʃəs] □

concienzudo; ~ objector pacifista m
que se niega a tomar las armas;
con·sci'en·tious·ness escrupulosidad f; industria f.

con·scious ['kɔnʃəs] □ consciente;
intencional; be ~ hacerse cargo,
tener conocimiento (of de; that de
que); ⚙ tener conocimiento; 'con·scious·ness conciencia f; ⚙ conocimiento m; phls. consciencia f; lose
(regain) ~ perder (recobrar) el
conocimiento.

con·script [kən'skript] reclutar;
con·script ['kɔnskript] recluta m,
quinto m; con·scrip·tion reclutamiento m; (llamada f al) servicio m
militar obligatorio.

con·se·crate ['kɔnsikreit] consagrar
(a. fig.); con·se'cra·tion consagración f.

con·sec·u·tive [kən'sekjutiv] consecutivo (a. gr.), sucesivo; con'sec·u·tive·ly sucesivamente.

con·sen·sus [kən'sensəs] consenso m.

con·sent [kən'sent] 1. consentimiento m (to en); by common ~ según la opinión unánime; 2. consentir (to en).

con·se·quence ['kɔnsikwəns] consecuencia f; of ~ de consecuencia; in ~
por consiguiente; in ~ of de resultas
de; take the ~s aceptar las consecuencias; 'con·se·quent 1. consiguiente; phls. consecuente; be ~ on
ser consecuencia de; 2. gr. consiguiente m; phls., 🜨 consecuente m;
con·se·quen·tial [~'kwenʃl] □ consiguiente; (proud) altivo; ~ on en
consecuencia de; con·se·quent·ly
['~kwentli] por consiguiente.

con·ser·va·tion [kɔnsə'veiʃn] conservación f; con·serv·a·tism [kən-
'sə:vətizm] conservatismo m; con·serv·a·tive [kən'sə:vətiv] □ conservativo; pol.
conservador (a. su. m); moderado,
cauteloso; con'ser·va·toire [~·
twa:] conservatorio m; con'ser·va·tor·y
[~tri] invernadero m; con'serve
1. conserva f, compota f; 2. conservar.

con·sid·er [kən'sidə] considerar;
con'sid·er·a·ble □ considerable;
con'sid·er·ate [~rit] □ considerado; con·sid·er·a·tion [~'reiʃn]
consideración f; † remuneración f;
in ~ of en consideración a; take
into ~ tomar en cuenta; without due

~ sin reflexión; **con'sid·er·ing 1.** *prp.* en consideración a; **2.** F *adv.* teniendo en cuenta las circunstancias.

con·sign [kən'sain] consignar (*a.* ✝); confiar, entregar; **con·sig·na·tion** [kɔnsai'neiʃn] consignación *f*; **con·sign·ment** [kən'sainmənt] consignación *f* (*a.* ✝); ✝ envío *m*, remesa *f*; **con·sign·ee** [kɔnsai'ni:] consignatorio *m*; **con·sign·er, con·sign·or** [kən'sainə] consignador *m*.

con·sist [kən'sist] consistir (*in, of* en); constar (*of* de); **con·sist·ence, con·sist·en·cy** consistencia *f*; consecuencia *f of actions*; **con·sist·ent** □ consistente; consonante (*with* con); *conduct* consecuente; ~ly sin excepción, continuamente; **con·'sis·to·ry** consistorio *m*.

con·sol·a·ble [kən'soulǝbl] consolable; **con·so·la·tion** [kɔnsǝ'leiʃn] consolación *f*, consuelo *m*.

con·sole 1. [kən'soul] consolar; **2.** ['kɔnsoul] △ consola *f*.

con·sol·i·date [kən'sɔlideit] consolidar (*a.* ✝); **con·sol·i·da·tion** consolidación *f*. [*m/pl.*]

con·sols [kən'sɔlz] *pl.* consolidados]

con·so·nance ['kɔnsǝnǝns] consonancia *f*; **'con·so·nant 1.** □ consonante (*a.* ♪); ~ *with* compatible con, conforme a; **2.** *gr.* consonante *f*; ~ *shift* alteración *f* de consonantes.

con·sort 1. ['kɔnsɔ:t] consorte *m/f*; ♣ buque *m* que acompaña a otro; *prince* ~ príncipe *m* consorte; **2.** [kən'sɔ:t] ~ *with* asociarse con; (*agree*) concordar con.

con·spic·u·ous [kən'spikjuǝs] □ visible, evidente; que llama la atención; *fig.* notable; *be* ~ *by one's absence* brillar por su ausencia.

con·spir·a·cy [kən'spirǝsi] conspiración *f*, complot *m*; **con·spir·a·tor** [~tǝ] conspirador (-a *f*) *m*; **con·spire** [~'spaiǝ] *v/t.* urdir, maquinar; *v/i.* conspirar (*to* a).

con·sta·ble ['kʌnstǝbl] policía *m* (*a. police* ~); *hist.* condestable *m*; **con·stab·u·lar·y** [kən'stæbjulǝri] guardia *f* civil, policía *f*.

con·stan·cy ['kɔnstǝnsi] constancia *f*; fidelidad *f*; **'con·stant 1.** □ constante; incesante; (*persistent*) porfiado; **2.** ⅄ constante *f*.

con·stel·la·tion [kɔnstǝ'leiʃn] constelación *f* (*a. fig.*).

con·ster·na·tion [kɔnstǝ'neiʃn] consternación *f*.

con·sti·pate ['kɔnstipeit] estreñir; **con·sti·pa·tion** estreñimiento *m*.

con·stit·u·en·cy [kən'stitjuǝnsi] distrito *m* electoral; **con·stit·u·ent 1.** constitutivo; *pol.* constituyente; ~ *assembly* cortes *f/pl.* constituyentes; **2.** constitutivo *m*, componente *m*; ⅄⅄ poderdante *m*; *pol.* elector *m*.

con·sti·tute ['kɔnstitju:t] constituir (*a p. judge* a una p. juez); **con·sti·'tu·tion** constitución *f*; **con·sti·'tu·tion·al 1.** □ constitucional; **2.** F paseo *m*; **con·sti·'tu·tion·al·ist** constitucional *m*; **con·sti·tu·tive** □ constitutivo, constituidor.

con·strain [kən'strein] constreñir, obligar (*to* a); imponer; detener, encerrar *in prison*; *pol.* ~ed (*embarrassed*) desconcertado; *smile* forzado; **con·'straint** coacción *f*, constreñimiento *m*; encierro *m*; *fig.* desconcierto *m*.

con·strict [kən'strikt] apretar; (*shrink*) encoger; **con·'stric·tion** constricción *f*; **con·'stric·tor** *anat.* constrictor *m*.

con·struct [kən'strʌkt] construir (*a. gr.*); **con·'struc·tion** construcción *f*; interpretación *f*, explicación *f*; *under* ~ en construcción; **con·'struc·tive** constructivo; *denial etc.* implícito; **con·'struc·tor** constructor *m*. [interpretar.]

con·strue [kən'stru:] *gr.* construir;]

con·sue·tu·di·nar·y [kɔnswi'tju:dinǝri] consuetudinario.

con·sul ['kɔnsl] cónsul *m*; **con·su·lar** ['kɔnsjulǝ] consular; **con·su·late** ['~lit] consulado *m*; **con·sul·ship** ['kɔnslʃip] consulado *m*.

con·sult [kən'sʌlt] consultar (*with* con); ~*ing attr.* consultor; ⅍ ~*ing room* consultorio *m*; **con·'sult·ant** consultor *m*; ⅍ especialista *m*; **con·sul·ta·tion** [kɔnsǝl'teiʃn] consulta *f* (*a.* ⅍), consultación *f*; **con·sult·a·tive** [kən'sʌltǝtiv] consultivo.

con·sum·a·ble [kən'sju:mǝbl] consumible; **con·'sume** consumir (*a. fig.*); **con·'sum·er** consumidor *m*; ~ *goods pl.* artículos *m/pl.* de consumo.

con·sum·mate 1. [kən'sʌmit] □ consumado, cabal; **2.** ['kɔnsʌmeit] consumar; **con·sum·ma·tion** [~'meiʃn] consumación *f*, perfección *f*.

con·sump·tion [kən'sʌmpʃn] consunción *f*; consumo *m of goods*; 🟋 tisis *f*; **con'sump·tive** ☐ consuntivo; 🟋 tísico *adj. a. su. m* (a *f*).

con·tact ['kɔntækt] **1.** contacto *m* (*a. fig.*, *🌣*); ~ lenses microlentillas *f/pl. get in* ~ *with* = **2.** [kən'tækt] F ponerse en contacto con.

con·ta·gion [kən'teidʒn] contagio *m* (*a. fig.*); **con'ta·gious** ☐ contagioso (*a. fig.*).

con·tain [kən'tein] contener (*a. 🗡*); *space* abarcar; ~ *o.s.* contenerse; *be* ~*ed in* caber en; *ser (exactamente) divisible por*; **con'tain·er** continente *m*; 🕆 *etc.* envase *m*, caja *f*; **con'tain·ment** 🗡 contención *f*.

con·tam·i·nate [kən'tæmineit] contaminar (*a. fig.*); *be* ~*ed by* contaminarse con (*or de*); **con·tam·i·na·tion** contaminación *f*; refundición *f*, fusión *f of text*.

con·tem·plate ['kɔntempleit] contemplar; proponerse (*doing* hacer); **con'tem·pla·tion** contemplación *f*; mira *f*, intención *f*; '**con·tem·pla·tive** ☐ contemplativo.

con·tem·po·ra·ne·ous [kəntempə'reinjəs] ☐ contemporáneo; **con·'tem·po·rar·y** contemporáneo *adj. a. su. m* (a *f*); coetáneo *adj. a. su. m* (a *f*).

con·tempt [kən'tempt] desprecio *m*, desdén *m*; 🜨 ~ *of court* contumacia *f*, rebeldía *f*; *hold in* ~ despreciar; **con'tempt·i·ble** ☐ despreciable; **con'temp·tu·ous** [~juəs] ☐ despreciativo, despectivo; desdeñoso (*of* para, hacia).

con·tend [kən'tend] *v/i.* contender (*with ... over* con ... sobre); luchar (*for* por); (*argument*) sostener; *v/t.* afirmar, sostener.

con·tent [kən'tent] **1.** contento (*with* de, con); *parl.* ~! ¡sí!; *not* ~! ¡no!; *be* ~ *to* quedar contento de; **2.** contentar; ~ *o.s.* contentarse (*with* con); **3.** contento *m*; *to one's heart's* ~ a gusto, hasta más no poder; **4.** ['kɔntent] contenido *m* (*freq.* ~*s pl.*); (*capacity*) cabida *f*; (*esp.* ⚗) componente *m*; **con'tent·ed** ☐ contento, satisfecho; **con'tent·ed·ness** contento *m*, satisfacción *f*.

con·ten·tion [kən'tenʃn] contienda *f*, disputa *f*; argumento *m*, aseveración *f* (*that* de que); **con'ten·tious** ☐ contencioso; (*quarrelsome*) pendenciero.

con·tent·ment [kən'tentmənt] contento *m*, satisfacción *f*.

con·ter·mi·nous [kɔn'təːminəs] contérmino, limítrofe.

con·test 1. ['kɔntest] debate *m*, disputa *f*; (*fight*) contienda *f*, lid *f* (*a. fig.*); (*competition*) concurso *m*; **2.** [kən'test] disputar, impugnar; tomar parte en un concurso; *election* ser candidato en; **con'test·ant** contendiente *m/f*; contrincante *m*; rival *m/f*.

con·text ['kɔntekst] contexto *m* (*a. fig.*); **con·tex·tu·al** [kən'tekstjuel] ☐ relativo al contexto; **con'tex·ture** [~tʃə] contextura *f*.

con·ti·gu·i·ty [kɔnti'gjuiti] contigüidad *f*; **con·tig·u·ous** ☐ [kən'tigjuəs] contiguo (*to* a).

con·ti·nence ['kɔntinəns] continencia *f*; **'con·ti·nent 1.** ☐ continente; **2.** continente *m*; *the* ♀ la Europa continental; **con·ti·nen·tal** [~'nentl] ☐ continental; ~ *climate* clima *m* continental.

con·tin·gen·cy [kən'tindʒənsi] contingencia *f*; **con'tin·gent 1.** ☐ contingente, eventual; dependiente (*on* de); **2.** contingente *m*.

con·tin·u·al [kən'tinjuəl] ☐ continuo, incesante; **con'tin·u·ance** continuación *f*; (*stay*) permanencia *f*; **con·tin·u·a·tion** continuación *f*; 🕆 prórroga *f*; **con'tin·ue** *v/t.* continuar; mantener; 🜨 aplazar; *to be* ~*d* continuará; *v/i.* continuar(se); ~ *doing* continuar haciendo; **con·ti·nu·i·ty** [kɔnti'njuːiti] continuidad *f*; *film*: escenario *m*; **con·tin·u·ous** [kən'tinjuəs] ☐ continuo (*a. 🌣*); ~ *showing* sesión *f* continua; **con·tin·u·um** [kən'tinjuəm] continuo *m*.

con·tort [kən'tɔːt] retorcer, deformar; **con'tor·tion** contorsión *f*; **con'tor·tion·ist** contorsionista *m/f*.

con·tour ['kɔntuə] contorno *m*; ~ *line* curva *f* de nivel.

con·tra ['kɔntrə] (en) contra.

con·tra·band ['kɔntrəbænd] (*attr.* de) contrabando *m*.

con·tract 1. [kən'trækt] *v/t.* contraer; *friendship* entablar; *v/i.* contraerse; comprometerse por contrato (*to* a); ~ *for* contratar; ~*ing party* contratante *m*; **2.** ['kɔntrækt] contrato *m*; 🕆 contrata *f*; *by* ~ por contrata; ~

work destajo *m*; **con·tract·ed** [kən-'trӕktid] contraído; encogido; **con·tract·i·bil·i·ty** calidad *f* de contractable; **con·tract·i·ble** contractable; **con·trac·tile** [ˌtail] contráctil; **con·trac·tion** contracción *f*; **con·trac·tor** contratista *m*/*f*; contratante *m*; *anat.* esfínter *m*; **con·trac·tu·al** [ˌtjuel] contractual.

con·tra·dict [kɔntrə'dikt] contradecir; **con·tra·dic·tion** contradicción *f*; **con·tra·dic·to·ry** □ contradictorio; *p.* contradictor.

con·tra·dis·tinc·tion [kɔntrədis-'tiŋkʃn] distinción *f* por oposición; *in* ~ *to* a diferencia de.

con·trap·tion [kən'trӕpʃn] dispositivo *m*, artificio *m*; *contp.* armatoste *m*.

con·tra·ri·e·ty [kɔntrə'raiəti] contrariedad *f*; **con·tra·ri·ly** ['ˌtrərili] con espíritu de contradicción; tercamente; **'con·tra·ri·ness** contrariedad *f*; (*obstinacy*) terquedad *f*; **con·tra·ri·wise** ['ˌwaiz] en contrario; F tercamente; **'con·tra·ry 1.** contrario; F [kən'treəri] obstinado, terco; que lleva la contra; *adv.* en contrario; ~ *to* contrario a; **2.** contrario *m*; *on the* ~ al contrario; *to the* ~ en contrario.

con·trast 1. ['kɔntrɑːst] contraste *m*; *in* ~ por contraste; *in* ~ *to* en contraposición a; **2.** [kən'trɑːst] *v/t.* poner en contraste; *v/i.* contrastar (*with* con).

con·tra·vene [kɔntrə'viːn] contravenir a; *statement* contradecir, resistir a; **con·tra·ven·tion** [ˌ'venʃn] contravención *f*; ‡‡ infracción *f*.

con·trib·ute [kən'tribjuːt] contribuir (*towards* a, para; *to ger.* a *inf.*); ~ *to paper* colaborar en; **con·tri·bu·tion** [kɔntri'bjuːʃn] contribución *f*; artículo *m*, escrito *m to paper*; **con·trib·u·tor** [kən'tribjuːtə] contribuidor (-a *f*) *m*, contribuyente *m*; colaborador (-a *f*) *m to paper*; **con·trib·u·to·ry** contribuidor (*to* a).

con·trite ['kɔntrait] □ contrito; **con·tri·tion** [kən'triʃn] contrición *f*.

con·triv·ance [kən'traivəns] invención *f*; (*apparatus*) artificio *m*; plan *m*; **con·trive** *v/t.* inventar; urdir, tramar; *v/i.*: ~ *to* ingeniarse a, lograr; ~ *well* componérselas (*in* para).

con·trol [kən'troul] **1.** mando *m*, gobierno *m*; inspección *f*, intervención *f* (*esp.* ✝); control *m*; ⊕ regulador *m*; ⨆ norma *f* de comprobación; dirección *f*; *attr.* de mando, de control; ~*s pl. esp.* ✈ aparatos *m*/*pl.* de mando; *remote* ~ comando *m* a distancia, telecontrol *m*; ✈ ~ *column* palanca *f* de mando; ~ *knob radio*: botón *m*, regulador *m*; ✈ ~ *panel* tablero *m* de instrumentos; *be in* ~ tener el mando, mandar; *get out of* ~ perder control; *get under* ~ conseguir dominar; **2.** mandar, gobernar; controlar, comprobar; ⊕ regular; *price* controlar; ~ *o.s.* dominarse; **con'trol·ler** inspector *m*; ✝ interventor *m*; director *m*; ⊕ regulador *m*; **con'trol·ling** predominante, decisivo; ✝ ~ *interest* interés *m* predominante.

con·tro·ver·sial [kɔntrə'vəːʃl] □ controvertible; contencioso; **'con·tro·ver·sy** controversia *f*; **'con·tro·vert** controvertir.

con·tu·ma·cious [kɔntju'meiʃəs] □ contumaz (*a.* ‡‡); **con·tu·ma·cy** ['kɔntjuməsi] contumacia *f*.

con·tu·me·li·ous [kɔntju'miːliəs] □ contumelioso; **con·tu·me·ly** ['kɔntjumli] contumelia *f*.

con·tuse [kən'tjuːz] contundir; **con·tu·sion** contusión *f*.

co·nun·drum [kə'nʌndrəm] acertijo *m*, adivinanza *f*.

con·va·lesce [kɔnvə'les] convalecer; **con·va·les·cence** convalecencia *f*; **con·va·les·cent** convaleciente *adj. a. su. m*/*f*; ~ *home* clínica *f* de reposo. [ción *f*.]

con·vec·tion [kən'vekʃn] convec-]

con·vene [kən'viːn] *v/i.* juntarse, reunirse; *v/t. meeting* convocar.

con·ven·ience [kən'viːnjəns] conveniencia *f*; comodidad *f*; (*time*) oportunidad *f*; *at your earliest* ~ cuando le sea conveniente; *public* ~ aseos *m*/*pl.*; *marriage of* ~ matrimonio *m* de conveniencia; **con'ven·ient** □ conveniente; cómodo; *time* oportuno; apto; *spot* alcanzadizo, céntrico.

con·vent ['kɔnvənt] convento *m* (de religiosas); **con·ven·ti·cle** [kən-'ventikl] conventículo *m*; **con'ven·tion** convención *f*; (*meeting*) asamblea *f*; **con'ven·tion·al** □ convencional; **con'ven·tion·al·ism**

convencionalismo *m*; formalismo *m*; **con·ven·tion·al·i·ty** [ˌ'næliti] formalismo *m*; apego *m* a las convenciones; **con'ven·tu·al** [ˌtjuəl] □ conventual.

con·verge [kən'vɔ:dʒ] convergir (*on* en); **con'ver·gence, con'ver·gen·cy** convergencia *f*; **con'ver·gent, con'verg·ing** convergente.

con·ver·sant [kən'vɔ:sənt] versado (*with* en); *become* ~ *with* familiarizarse con; **con·ver·sa·tion** [ˌ'seiʃn] conversación *f*, plática *f*; **con·ver·'sa·tion·al** □ de conversación; *p.* hablador, expansivo; **con·verse 1.** ['kɔnvɔ:s] □ contrario, inverso; **2.** [ˌ] plática *f*; ♀ inversa *f*; **3.** [kən'vɔ:s] conversar (*with* con); **con'ver·sion** conversión *f* (*to* a; *into* en); ♥ cambio *m*, conversión *f*; ✝, ⊕ reorganización *f*; ⚖ apropiación *f* ilícita.

con·vert 1. ['kɔnvɔ:t] converso (*a f*) *m*, convertido (*a f*) *m*; **2.** [kən'vɔ:t] convertir (*to* a); ⚖ apropiarse ilícitamente (*to one's own use* para uso propio); **con'vert·er** ⊕, ⚡ convertidor *m*; **con·vert·i·bil·i·ty** [ˌˌbiliti] convertibilidad *f*; **con'vert·i·ble** □ convertible; *mot.* transformable; descapotable.

con·vex ['kɔn'veks] □ convexo; **con'vex·i·ty** convexidad *f*.

con·vey [kən'vei] transportar, llevar; *current* transmitir; *news* comunicar; dar a entender (*to* a); ⚖ traspasar; **con'vey·ance** transporte *m*; vehículo *m*; (*a.* ⚡) transmisión *f*; comunicación *f*; ⚖ (escritura *f* de) traspaso *m*; *public* ~ vehículo *m* de transporte público; **con'vey·anc·er** escribano *m* que prepara escrituras de traspaso; **con'vey·or** (*or* ~ *belt*) correa *f* transportadora.

con·vict 1. ['kɔnvikt] presidiario *m*; **2.** [kən'vikt] condenar; declarar culpable (*of* de); **con·vic·tion** [kən'vikʃn] convencimiento *m*; ⚖ condena *f*; ~*s pl.* convicciones *f/pl.*, opiniones *f/pl.*

con·vince [kən'vins] convencer (*of* de); **con'vinc·ing** □ convincente.

con·viv·i·al [kən'viviəl] □ festivo, jovial; **con·viv·i·al·i·ty** [ˌvi'æliti] jovialidad *f*, sociabilidad *f*.

con·vo·ca·tion [kɔnvə'keiʃn] convocación *f*; (*meeting*) asamblea *f*.

con·voke [kən'vouk] convocar.

con·vo·lu·tion [kɔnvə'lu:ʃn] circunvolución *f* (*a.* ♫), repliegue *m*.

con·vol·vu·lus [kən'vɔlvjuləs] convólvulo *m*.

con·voy ['kɔnvɔi] **1.** convoy *m*; **2.** convoyar.

con·vulse [kən'vʌls] agitar(se); *nerves* convulsionar; *be* ~*d with laughter* desternillarse de risa; **con'vul·sion** convulsión *f* (*a. fig.*); ~*s pl.* (*of laughter*) paroxismo *m* de risa; **con'vul·sive** □ *cough etc.* convulsivo; convulso.

coo [ku:] arrullar.

cook [kuk] **1.** cocinero (*a f*) *m*; **2.** cocinar; cocer, guisar; *meal* preparar; F *accounts* falsificar; *sl.* ~ *up* maquinar, tramar; **'cook·er** hervidor *m*; (*gas-, etc.*) cocina *f*; ♀ fruta *f* para cocer; **'cook·er·y** arte *m* de cocina; ~ *book* libro *m* de cocina; **'cook·ie** *Am.* pastelito *m* dulce; **'cook·ing** cocina *f*; *attr.* de cocina(r); ~ *soda* bicarbonato *m* sódico; ~ *stove* cocina *f* económica.

cool [ku:l] **1.** □ fresco; tibio (*a. fig.*); *fig.* indiferente, frío; sereno, tranquilo; *b.s.* descarado, audaz; F sin exageración; *a* ~ *thousand* mil libras contantes y sonantes; **2.** fresco *m*; **3.** refrescar(se); (*a.* ~ *down*) moderarse; ~ *down!* ¡cálmate!; ~ *off fig.* enfriarse; **'cool·er** refrigerador *m*; *sl.* trena *f*; **'cool-'head·ed** sereno, sosegado.

coo·lie ['ku:li] culí *m*.

cool·ing ['ku:liŋ] refrigeración *f*; *attr.* refrigerante; *drink* refrescante; ~ *tower* torre *f* de refrigeración; **'cool·ness** frescura *f*; tibieza *f* (*a. fig.*), *etc.*

coomb [ku:m] hondonada *f*.

coon [ku:n] *Am.* F marrullero *m*; *contp.* negro *m*; *zo.* mapache *m*.

coop [ku:p] **1.** gallinero *m*, caponera *f*; **2.:** ~ *up* encerrar, enjaular.

co-op [kou'ɔp] F = *co-operative* (*store*).

coop·er ['ku:pə] barrilero *m*, tonelero *m*; **'coop·er·age** tonelería *f*.

co-op·er·ate [kou'ɔpəreit] cooperar; **co-op·er'a·tion** cooperación *f*; **co-'op·er·a·tive** [ˌpərətiv] **1.** cooperativo; *p.* socorrido; **2.** cooperativa *f*; ~ *store* tienda *f* cooperativa; **co-'op·er·a·tor** [ˌreitə] cooperario *m*, cooperador (-a *f*) *m*.

co-opt [kou'ɔpt] *nombrar (a una p. a un comité) por votación extraordinaria.*

co-or-di-nate 1. [kou'ɔːdinit] ☐ coordenado; *(equal)* igual; *gr.* coordinante; **2.** [⌣] ♣ coordenada *f*; **3.** [⌣neit] coordinar; **co-or-di-na-tion** coordinación *f*.

coot [kuːt] *zo.* focha *f* común; F bobo (a *f*) *m*; **coot-ie** ['⌣i] *sl.* piojo *m*.

cop [kɔp] *sl.* **1.** coger, prender; *you'll ⌣ it!* ¡las vas a pagar!; **2.** polizonte *m*, esbirro *m*; *be a fair ⌣* caerse con todo el equipo.

co-part-ner ['kou'pɑːtnə] consocio *m*; copartícipe *m/f*; **'co-part-ner-ship** coparticipación *f*; asociación *f*.

cope¹ [koup] **1.** *eccl.* capa *f* pluvial; ♣ albardilla *f*; **2.** ♣ poner albardilla a; abovedar.

cope² [⌣] *⌣ with* poder con, vencer.

co-pi-lot ['kou'pailət] copiloto *m*.

cop-ing ['koupiŋ] ♣ albardilla *f*; *⌣ stone* coronamiento *m*.

co-pi-ous ['koupjəs] ☐ copioso; **'co-pi-ous-ness** abundancia *f*, copia *f*.

cop-per¹ ['kɔpə] **1.** cobre *m*; *(utensil)* caldero *m*; *(money)* calderilla *f*; **2.** cubrir con cobre; **3.** de cobre, cobreño; *(colour)* cobrizo; **'⌣plate** plancha *f* de cobre; lámina *f*, estampa *f*; *attr.* bello, bien formado; **'cop-per-y** cobreño; *(colour)* cobrizo.

cop-per² [⌣] *sl.* polizonte *m*, esbirro *m*. [*m*.]

cop-pice ['kɔpis], **copse** [kɔps] soto⌣

cop-u-late ['kɔpjuleit] tener ayuntamiento; **cop-u'la-tion** ayuntamiento *m* carnal, cóito *m*; **cop-u-la-tive** ['⌣lətiv] copulativo.

cop-y ['kɔpi] **1.** copia *f*; ejemplar *m of book*; número *m of journal*; *typ.* material *m*, original *m*; *v. fair, rough*; **2.** copiar; imitar; *(counterfeit)* contrahacer; **'⌣book** cuaderno *m*; **'⌣cat** F imitador (-a *f*) *m*; **'⌣hold** posesión *f* por enfiteusis; **'copy-ing-ink** tinta *f* de copiar; **'copy-ist** copista *m/f*; **'copy-right** derecho *m* de propiedad literaria, copyright *m*; **'copy-writ-er** escritor *m* de anuncios.

co-quet [kou'ket] coquetear; **co-quet-ry** ['⌣kitri] coquetería *f*; **co-quette** [⌣'ket] coqueta *f*; **co-'quet-tish** ☐ coquetón, coqueta.

cor-al ['kɔrəl] coral *m*; *attr.* coralino; **cor-al-line** ['⌣lain] *zo.* coralina *f*.

cor-bel ['kɔːbl] ménsula *f*, repisa *f*.

cord [kɔːd] **1.** cuerda *f*; *anat.* cordón *m*; *(cloth)* pana *f*; **2.** acordonar; **'cord-age** ♣ cordaje *m*; cordería *f*; **'cord-ed** acordonado.

cor-dial ['kɔːdiəl] ☐ cordial *adj. a. su. m*; **cor-dial-i-ty** [⌣di'æliti] cordialidad *f*.

cord-mak-er ['kɔːdmeikə] cordelero *m*.

cor-don ['kɔːdən] **1.** cordón *m*; *sanitary ⌣* cordón *m* sanitario; **2.** *⌣ off* aislar con un cordón.

cor-do-van ['kɔːdəvən] cordobán *m*.

cor-du-roy ['kɔːdərɔi] pana *f*; *Am. ⌣ road* camino *m* de troncos.

core [kɔː] **1.** corazón *m*, centro *m*; *fig.* quid *m*, esencia *f*; ♣ foco *m*; alma *f of cable*; núcleo *m of electromagnet*.

co-re-li-gion-ist ['kouri'lidʒənist] correligionario (a *f*) *m*.

Co-rin-thi-an [kə'rinθiən] corintio *adj. a. su. m* (a *f*).

cork [kɔːk] **1.** corcho *m*; tapón *m* (de corcho); **2.** tapar con corcho (*a. ⌣ up*); **'cork-age** sobrecarga que se cobra en un restaurante sobre una botella de vino; **'cork-er** *sl.* argumento *m* irrefutable; *(lie)* camelo *m*; **'cork-ing** F excelente, bárbaro.

cork...: **'⌣jack-et** salvavidas *m* de corcho; **'⌣screw 1.** sacacorchos *m*; **2.** en caracol, en espiral; **3.** zaguear, moverse en espiral; **'⌣tipped** *cigarette* emboquillado; **'⌣tree** alcornoque *m*; **'cork-y** corchoso; F alegre, vivaracho.

cor-mo-rant ['kɔːmərənt] cormorán *m* grande; *fig.* persona *f* rapaz.

corn¹ [kɔːn] **1.** trigo *m*; *Am.* (a. *Indian ⌣*) maíz *m*; *Am. sl.* broma *f* gastada; *Am. ⌣ bread* pan *m* de maíz; **2.** acecinar; *⌣ed beef* carne *f* de vaca conservada en lata.

corn² [⌣] ♣ callo *m*.

corn...: **'⌣cob** *Am.* mazorca *f* de maíz; **'⌣crake** guión *m* de codornices.

cor-ne-a ['kɔːniə] córnea *f*.

cor-nel ['kɔːnl] cornejo *m*.

cor-nel-ian [kɔː'niːljən] cornalina *f*.

cor-ne-ous ['kɔːniəs] córneo.

cor-ner ['kɔːnə] **1.** ángulo *m*; esquina *f* (*esp. street-⌣*); *(inside)* rincón *m* (a. *fig.*); *fig.* apuro *m*, aprieto *m*;

sport: córner *m*; ✝ acaparamiento *m*; *fig.* turn the ~ ir saliendo del apuro, darse la vuelta a la tortilla; *out of the* ~ *of one's eye* con el rabillo del ojo; *cut* ~s atajar; ~ *flag* banderín *m*; ~ *room* habitación *f* de esquina; **2.** arrinconar (*a. fig.*); ✝ acaparar.

cor·ner...: '~-cup·board rinconera *f*; **'~-stone** piedra *f* angular (*a. fig.*); **'~-ways** diagonalmente.

cor·net ['kɔːnit] ♪ corneta *f*; cucurucho *m of paper etc.*; (*ice-cream*) barquillo *m*.

corn...: '~-ex·change bolsa *f* de granos; **'~-flour** harina *f* de maíz; **'~-flow·er** aciano *m*.

cor·nice ['kɔːnis] cornisa *f* (*a. mount.*).

Cor·nish ['kɔːniʃ] córnico *adj. a. su. m*.

corn...: '~-juice *Am.* chicha *f*; **'~-meal** harina *f* de maíz; **'~-pop·py** amapola *f*.

cor·nu·co·pi·a [kɔːnjuˈkoupjə] cornucopia *f*.

corn·y ['kɔːni] de trigo; *Am.* de maíz; ✱ calloso; *sl.* ♪ muy sentimental; *sl. joke etc.* pesado, viejo.

co·rol·la [kəˈrɔlə] corola *f*; **cor'ol·la·ry** corolario *m*; consecuencia *f* natural.

co·ro·na [kəˈrounə], *pl.* **co'ro·nae** [~niː] corona *f*; ⚠ cornisa *f*, coronamiento *m*; **co'ro·nal** coronal, coronario; **'co·ro·na·ry** ✱ coronario; ~ *thrombosis* trombosis *f* coronaria; **cor·o·na·tion** [kɔrəˈneiʃn] coronación *f*; **cor·o·ner** ['kɔrənə] juez *m* de primera instancia e instrucción; **cor·o·net** ['~nit] corona *f* (de conde *or* marqués); diadema *f*.

cor·po·ral ['kɔːpərəl] **1.** □ corporal; **2.** ✗ cabo *m*; *eccl.* corporal *m*; **cor·po·rate** ['~rit] □ corporativo; incorporado; **cor·po·ra·tion** [~ˈreiʃn] corporación *f*; F panza *f*, tripa *f*; ✝ sociedad *f* anónima; **cor·po·ra·tive** ['~rətiv] corporativo; **cor·po·re·al** [~ˈpɔːriəl] □ corpóreo; ▨ material, tangible.

corps [kɔː], *pl.* **corps** [kɔːz] cuerpo *m*; ~ *de ballet* cuerpo *m* de baile.

corpse [kɔːps] cadáver *m*.

cor·pu·lence, **cor·pu·len·cy** ['kɔːpjuləns(i)] corpulencia *f*; **'cor·pu·lent** corpulento.

cor·pus ['kɔːpəs], *pl.* **cor·po·ra** ['~pərə] cuerpo *m* (de leyes, escritos *etc.*); ♀ *Christi* Corpus *m*; ~ *delicti* cuerpo *m* de delito; **cor·pus·cle** ['kɔːpʌsl] corpúsculo *m*; (*blood*) glóbulo *m*.

cor·ral [kɔˈrɑːl] *esp. Am.* **1.** corral *m*; **2.** acorralar, encerrar.

cor·rect [kəˈrekt] **1.** □ exacto, justo; *behaviour* correcto, cumplido; *be* ~ *freq.* tener razón, acertar; **2.** corregir; *exam* puntuar, calificar; **cor'rec·tion** corrección *f*; calificación *f of exam paper*; I *speak under* ~ puede que esté equivocado; **cor'rec·tive** correctivo *adj. a. su. m*; **cor'rect·ness** corrección *f*, urbanidad *f*; exactitud *f*, fidelidad *f*; **cor'rec·tor** corrector *m*.

cor·re·late ['kɔrileit] **1.** correlacionar; **2.** correlativo *m*; **cor·re·la·tion** correlación *f*; **cor·rel·a·tive** [~ˈrelətiv] □ correlativo *adj. a. su. m*.

cor·re·spond [kɔrisˈpɔnd] corresponder (*to* a); corresponderse, cartearse (*with p.* con); **cor·re·spond·ence** correspondencia *f*; (*collected letters*) epistolario *m*; **cor·re·spond·ent 1.** □ correspondiente; **2.** correspondiente *m*; (*newspaper-*) corresponsal *m*; el (la) que escribe cartas.   [rredor *m*.\

cor·ri·dor ['kɔridɔː] pasillo *m*, co-\

cor·rob·o·rant [kəˈrɔbərənt] corroborante *adj. a. su. m*; **cor'rob·o·rate** [~reit] corroborar; **cor·rob·o·'ra·tion** corroboración *f*; **cor'rob·o·ra·tive** [~rətiv] corroborativo.

cor·rode [kəˈroud] corroer (*a. fig.*); **cor'ro·dent** corrosivo *adj. a. su. m*; **cor'ro·sion** corrosión *f*; **cor'ro·sive** □ corrosivo *adj. a. su. m*.

cor·ru·gate ['kɔrugeit] arrugar(se); ⊕ acanalar; ~d *iron* hierro *m* ondulado; ~d *paper* papel *m* ondulado.

cor·rupt [kəˈrʌpt] **1.** □ corrompido; *manners* estragado; *text* viciado, depravado; **2.** *v/t.* corromper; estragar; *v/i.* corromperse; (*rot*) podrirse; **cor'rupt·er** corruptor (-a *f*) *m*; **cor·rupt·i·bil·i·ty** [~əˈbiliti] corruptibilidad *f*; **cor'rupt·i·ble** □ corruptible; **cor'rup·tion** corrupción *f* (*a. fig.*); **cor'rup·tive** □ corruptivo.

cor·sage [kɔːˈsɑːʒ] corpiño *m*, jubón *m*; ✿ ramillete *m* para la cintura.

cor·sair ['kɔːsɛə] corsario *m*.
cors(e)·let ['kɔːslit] sostén-faja *f*.
cor·set ['kɔːsit] corsé *m*.
cor·ti·cal ['kɔːtikl] cortical.
cor·us·cate ['kɔrəskeit] coruscar;
  cor·us·ca·tion brillo *m*, relampagueo *m*.
cor·vette [kɔː'vet] corbeta *f*.
cor·vine ['kɔːvain] corvino.
cor·y·phae·us [kɔri'fiːəs], *pl*. **cor·y-**
  phae·i [\'fiːai] corifeo *m*; **co·ry-**
  phée [\'fei] prima bailarina *f*.
cosh [kɔʃ] *sl*. **1.** cachiporra *f*; **2.** dar
  de golpes con una cachiporra.
co·sig·na·to·ry ['kou'signətəri] co-
  signatorio *adj. a. su. m* (a *f*).
co·sine ['kousain] coseno *m*.
co·si·ness ['kouzinis] comodidad *f*;
  calor *m* acogedor *of room etc*.
cos·met·ic [kɔz'metik] **1.** cosmético;
  2. cosmético *m*, afeite *m*.
cos·mic, cos·mi·cal ['kɔzmik(l)] □
  cósmico; ~ *rays* rayos *m/pl*. cósmicos.
cos·mo·gra·pher [kɔz'mɔgrəfə] cosmógrafo *m*; **cos'mo·gra·phy** cosmografía *f*.
cos·mo·pol·i·tan [kɔzmə'pɔlitən]
  cosmopolita *adj. a. su. m/f*.
Cos·sack ['kɔsæk] cosaco *adj. a. su.*
  m (a *f*).
cos·set ['kɔsit] **1.** cordero *m* domesticado; **2.** mimar, acariciar.
cost [kɔst] **1.** precio *m*; coste *m*, costa
  f; ✝ *at* ~ a costa; *to my* ~ por mi
  daño; ~ *of living* costo *m* de la vida;
  ~*s pl*. 🏛 costas *f/pl*.; *at all* ~*s* a todo
  trance; **2.** [*irr.*] costar; ~ *what it*
  may cueste lo que cueste.
cos·ter ['kɔstə] = '~**mon·ger**
  vendedor *m* ambulante (de frutas,
  pescado *etc*.).
cost·ing ['kɔstiŋ] cálculo *m* de coste.
cos·tive ['kɔstiv] □ estreñido.
cost·li·ness ['kɔstlinis] carestía *f*;
  (*luxury*) fausto *m*; **'cost·ly** costoso,
  suntuoso.
cost-price ['kɔstprais] (*adv*. al) precio *m* de coste.
cos·tume ['kɔstjuːm] **1.** traje *m*;
  (*fancy-dress*) disfraz *m*; **2.** trajear;
  cos'tum·i·er [\~miə] sastre *m* de
  teatro.
co·sy ['kouzi] **1.** □ cómodo; *clothes*
  abrigado; *room* acogedor; *life* holgado; **2.** cubierta *f* para tetera.
cot [kɔt] catre *m*; camita *f* de niño,
  cuna *f*; ⚓ coy *m*.

co·te·rie ['koutəri] grupo *m*; camarilla *f*.
cot·tage ['kɔtidʒ] casita *f*; chalet *m*;
  (*labourer's etc*.) barraca *f*, choza *f*,
  cabaña *f*; *Am.* ~ *cheese* requesón
  m; **'cot·tag·er** habitante *m/f* de
  una choza; *Am*. veraneante *m/f*.
cot·ter ['kɔtə] chaveta *f*.
cot·ton ['kɔtn] **1.** algodón *m*; (*plant*)
  algodonero *m*; ~ *wool* algodón *m*
  (hidrófilo), ouata *f*; **2.** F convenir,
  congeniar; *sl*. ~ *on to* entender; F
  ~ *up* hacer buenas migas; **'~-grass**
  algodonosa *f*; **'cot·ton·y** algodonoso.   [*m*.\
co·tyl·e·don [kɔti'liːdən] cotiledón}
couch [kautʃ] **1.** sofá *m*, canapé *m*,
  meridiana *f*; *poet*. lecho *m*; **2.** acos-
  tar(se) (*now only p.p.*); *thoughts*
  expresar, formular; (*crouch*) agacharse; (*lie in wait*) emboscarse;
  '~-grass hierba *f* rastrera.
cough [kɔf] **1.** tos *f*; **2.** toser; ~ *down*
  speaker hacer callar (tosiendo); ~
  up expectorar; *sl*. descolgarse con;
  sl. sacar, producir; (*money*) desdinerarse.
could [kud] *pret. of* can.
couldn't ['kudnt] = *could not*.
cou·lee ['kuːli] *Am*. cañada *f*, quebrada *f*.
coul·ter ['koultə] reja *f* (del arado).
coun·cil ['kaunsl] junta *f*, consejo *m*;
  eccl. concilio *m*; (*town-*) concejo *m*,
  ayuntamiento *m*; **coun·ci(l)·lor**
  ['\~ilə] concejal *m*.
coun·sel ['kaunsəl] **1.** consejo *m*;
  deliberación *f*, consulta *f*; 🏛 abogado *m*; ~ *for the defence* defensor
  m; ~ *for the prosecution* fiscal *m*;
  keep one's own ~ guardar silencio;
  take ~ *with* consultar; **2.** aconsejar;
  coun·se(l)·lor ['\~lə] consejero (a *f*)
  m; *Ir*. abogado *m* (a. '~**-at-'law**).
count[1] [kaunt] **1.** cuenta *f*, cálculo
  m; suma *f*, total *m*; 🏛 cargo *m*;
  boxing: cuenta *f*; *lose* ~ perder la
  cuenta; **2.** *v/t*. contar; ~ *out* no
  incluir, no tener en cuenta; *boxing*:
  declarar vencido; *v/i*. contar; valer
  (*a*. ~ *for*); *that doesn't* ~ eso no vale;
  ~ *on* contar con; ~ *on one's fingers*
  contar por los dedos.
count[2] [\~] conde *m*.
coun·te·nance ['kauntinəns] **1.** semblante *m*, figura *f*; *be out of* ~ estar
  desconcertado; *keep one's* ~ mantenerse tranquilo; abstenerse de

reír; *lose* ~ perturbarse; *put out of*
~ desconcertar; **2.** dar aprobación
a; *(encourage)* apoyar.

count·er[1] ['kauntə] *(shop- etc.)*
mostrador *m*, contador *m*; *(check)*
ficha *f*, chapa *f*; *(horse's)* pecho *m*;
⚓ bovedilla *f*; *fenc.* contra *f*;
Geiger ~ contador *m* Geiger; *sl.*
under the ~ por la trastienda.

count·er[2] [~] **1.** en contra; ~ *to*
contrario a, opuesto a; *run* ~ *to*
oponerse a, ser contrario a; **2.** oponerse a; contradecir; contrarrestar;
blow parar; ~ *with* contestar con.

coun·ter·act [kauntə'rækt] contrarrestar; neutralizar; **coun·ter'ac·**
tion contrarresto *m*, neutralización *f*.

coun·ter·at·tack [ˈkauntərətæk]
1. contraataque *m*; **2.** contra-
atacar.

coun·ter·at·trac·tion [ˈkauntərə-
ˈtrækʃn] atracción *f* rival.

coun·ter·bal·ance 1. [ˈkauntəbæl-
əns] contrapeso *m*, contrabalanza *f*;
2. [~ˈbæləns] contrapesar, contra-
balancear.

coun·ter·blast [ˈkauntəblɑːst] *fig.*
respuesta *f* vigorosa *(to a)*; declaración *f* vigorosa.

coun·ter·charge [ˈkauntətʃɑːdʒ] recriminación *f*.

coun·ter·check [ˈkauntətʃek] oposición *f*, estorbo *m*; † segunda comprobación *f*.

coun·ter·clock·wise [ˈkauntəˈklɔk-
waiz] en sentido contrario al de las
agujas del reloj.

coun·ter·cur·rent [ˈkauntəˈkʌrənt]
contracorriente *f*.

coun·ter·es·pi·o·nage [ˈkauntər-
ˈespiənɑːʒ] contraespionaje *m*.

coun·ter·feit [ˈkauntəfiːt] **1.** falsificado, falseado, contrahecho; **2.** falsificación *f*, contrahechura *f*;
3. falsificar, falsear, contrahacer;
'**coun·ter·feit·er** falsificador (-a *f*)
m, falseador (-a *f*) *m*.

coun·ter·foil [ˈkauntəfɔil] talón *m*.

coun·ter·fort [ˈkauntəfɔːt] contrafuerte *m*.

coun·ter·mand 1. [ˈkauntəmɑːnd]
contramandato *m*, contraorden *f*;
2. [~ˈmɑːnd] contramandar, revocar.

coun·ter·march [ˈkauntəmɑːtʃ]
1. contramarcha *f*; **2.** contramar-
char.

coun·ter·mark [ˈkauntəmɑːk] **1.**
contramarca *f*; **2.** contramarcar.

coun·ter·move [ˈkauntəmuːv] con-
trajugada *f*.

coun·ter·or·der [ˈkauntərɔːdə] contraorden *f*.

coun·ter·pane [ˈkauntəpein] colcha
f, cobertor *m*.

coun·ter·part [ˈkauntəpɑːt] copia *f*,
imagen *f*; *(complement)* contra-
parte *f*, complemento *m*.

coun·ter·point [ˈkauntəpoint] con-
trapunto *m*.

coun·ter·poise [ˈkauntəpoiz] **1.** contrapeso *m*; **2.** contrapesar.

coun·ter·shaft [ˈkauntəʃɑːft] eje *m*
intermedio.

coun·ter·sign [ˈkauntəsain] **1.** con-
traseña *f* (*a.* ⚔); † *etc.* contramarca *f*; **2.** refrendar.

coun·ter·sink [kauntəˈsiŋk] avellanar.

coun·ter·stroke [ˈkauntəstrouk]
contragolpe *m*.

coun·ter·ten·or [ˈkauntəˈtenə] con-
tralto *m*. [contrapeso *m*.|

coun·ter·weight [ˈkauntəweit]|

count·ess [ˈkauntis] condesa *f*.

count·ing·house [ˈkauntiŋhaus]
escritorio *m*, despacho *m*; oficina *f*.

count·less [ˈkauntlis] sin cuento.

coun·tri·fied [ˈkʌntrifaid] rústico,
campesino; *contp.* palurdo.

coun·try [ˈkʌntri] **1.** país *m*; patria *f*;
(not town) campo *m*; *parl. appeal*
(or go) to the ~ celebrar elecciones
generales; ⚔ *live off the* ~ vivir
sobre el país; **2.** *attr.* de campo,
rural; ~ *club esp. Am.* club *m*
campestre; ~ *estate* finca *f*; ~ *folk*
gente *f* del campo; ~ *house* quinta *f*,
casa *f* de campo; ~ *life* vida *f* del
campo; ~ *seat* finca *f*, casa *f* solariega; '~·**man** campesino *m*; *fellow*
~ compatriota *m*; '~·**side** campo *m*;
(open ~*)* campiña *f*; '~·**wom·an**
campesina *f*.

coun·ty [ˈkaunti] condado *m*; *attr.*
aristocrático; ~ **seat** *Am.* = ~ **town**
cabeza *f* de partido.

coup [kuː] golpe *m*; ~ *d'état* golpe *m*
de estado; ~ *de grâce* golpe *m* de
gracia.

cou·ple [ˈkʌpl] **1.** par *m*; *(people)*
pareja *f*; F dos más o menos;
married ~ matrimonio *m*; **2.** juntar,
unir; *animals* aparear; ⊕ acoplar,
enganchar; F casar; '**cou·pler**

radio: acoplador *m*; **'cou·plet** pareado *m*; par *m* de versos.

cou·pling ['kʌpliŋ] ⊕ acoplamiento *m*; 🚂 enganche *m*.

cou·pon ['ku:pɔn] cupón *m*; (*football-*) boleto *m*.

cour·age ['kʌridʒ] valor *m*, valentía *f*; ~! ¡ánimo!; *pluck up* ~ hacer de tripas corazón; **cou·ra·geous** [kə-'reidʒəs] □ valiente.

cour·i·er ['kuriə] estafeta *f*, correo *m* diplomático; agente *m* de turismo.

course [kɔ:s] 1. curso *m*; ✕ trayectoria *f*; *fig.* proceder *m*, camino *m*; ⚓ rumbo *m*; plato *m of meal*; transcurso *m*, paso *m of time*; hilada *f of bricks*; corriente *f of water*; (*golf-*) campo *m*; (*race-*) pista *f*; *in due* ~ a su tiempo; andando el tiempo; *in the* ~ *of* durante; *of* ~ por supuesto, desde luego; *give* ~ *to* dar curso a; 2. *v/t*. dar caza a, perseguir; *v/i*. correr (*freq.* ~ *along*).

court [kɔ:t] 1. corte *f*; ⚖ tribunal *m*; *sport*: pista *f*; ⚔ patio *m*; (*house*) palacete *m*, mansión *f* suntuosa; *Am. General* ♀ Asamblea *f* Legislativa; *in open* ~ en pleno tribunal; *pay one's* ~ *to* hacer la corte a; 2. cortejar, galantear; hacer la corte a; *favour etc.* solicitar, buscar; **'~-card** carta *f* de figura; **'~-day** día *m* hábil; **cour·te·ous** ['kə:tiəs] □ cortés; **cour·te·san**, *a.* **cour·te-zan** [kɔ:ti'zæn] cortesana *f*, hetera *f*; **cour·te·sy** ['kə:tisi] cortesía *f*, gentileza *f*; **court-house** ['kɔ:t-'haus] palacio *m* de justicia; **cour·ti·er** ['~jə] cortesano *m*; **'court·ly** urbano, elegante; *b.s.* obsequioso, halagüeño; ~ *love* amor *m* cortés.

court...: **'~·'mar·tial** 1. consejo *m* de guerra; 2. someter a consejo de guerra; **'~·'plas·ter** esparadrapo *m*; **'~·ship** cortejo *m*; noviazgo *m*; **'~·yard** patio *m*, atrio *m*.

cous·in ['kʌzn] primo (a *f*) *m*; *first* ~, ~ *german* primo (a *f*) *m* carnal; *country* ~ pariente *m* pueblerino.

cove[1] [kouv] 1. ⚓ cala *f*, ensenada *f*; escondrijo *m*; ⚔ bovedilla *f*; 2. abovedar.

cove[2] [~] *sl.* tío *m*, tipo *m*.

cov·e·nant ['kʌvinənt] 1. pacto *m*, convenio *m*; *Bible*: ♀ Alianza *f*; 2. pactar, convenir.

cov·er ['kʌvə] 1. (*lid*) tapa *f*, cubierta *f*; (*cutlery*) cubierto *m*; colcha *f on bed*; forro *m*, cubierta *f of book*; portada *f of magazine*; (*insurance*) cobertura *f*; *mot.* (*a. outer* ~) cubierta *f*; *fig. b.s.* disimulación *f*, pretexto *m*; ~ *charge* precio *m* del cubierto; *break* ~ salir a campo raso; *take* ~ abrigarse (*from de*); esconderse; *under* ~ clandestinamente; *under* ~ *of* so pretexto de; *under separate* ~ por separado; 2. cubrir (*a. fig.*); revestir; tapar *with lid etc.*; (*hide*) ocultar; *fig.* disimular; *fig.* incluir; *distance* recorrer; ✕ apuntar a, dominar; *retreat* cubrir; (*stallion*) cubrir; ~ *in* llenar; ~ *over* cubrir, revestir (*with de, con*); ~ *up* tapar, correr el velo sobre; *fig.* ocultar; disimular; **~ed wire** alambre *m* forrado; **'cov·er·ing** cubierta *f*, envoltura *f*; ~ *letter* carta *f* adjunta; **cov·er·let** ['~lit] cubrecama *m*, colcha *f*.

cov·ert ['kʌvət] 1. □ cubierto, secreto, disimulado; 2. *zo.* guarida *f*; abrigo *m*; ♣ soto *m*.

cov·et ['kʌvit] codiciar; **'cov·et·ous** □ codicioso (*of de*); avaro; **'cov·et·ous·ness** codicia *f*; avaricia *f*.

cov·ey ['kʌvi] nidada *f* de perdices; *fig.* grupo *m*, peña *f*.

cow[1] [kau] vaca *f*; hembra *f* del elefante *etc.*

cow[2] [~] intimidar, acobardar.

cow·ard ['kauəd] □ cobarde *adj. a. su. m*; **'cow·ard·ice**, **'cow·ard·li·ness** cobardía *f*; **'cow·ard·ly** cobarde.

cow·boy ['kaubɔi] vaquero *m*; gaucho *m S.Am.*; **'cow·catch·er** *Am.* 🚂 rastrillo *m* delantero, quitapiedras *m*. [causa de miedo).]

cow·er ['kauə] agacharse (*esp.* por)

cow·herd ['kauhə:d] pastor *m* de ganado; **'cow·hide** cuero *m*; (*whip*) zurriago *m*.

cowl [[kaul] capucha *f*; (*habit*) cogulla *f*; (*chimney-*) sombrerete *m*.

cow...: **'~·pox** vacuna *f*; **'~·punch·er** *Am.* F vaquero *m*; **'~·shed** establo *m*; **'~·slip** primavera *f*.

cox [kɔks] F 1. = *coxswain*; 2. *v/i*. servir de timonel; *v/t*. gobernar.

cox·comb ['kɔkskoum] farolero *m*, mequetrefe *m*.

cox·swain ['kɔkswein, 'kɔksn] timonel *m*.

coy [kɔi] □ reservado, tímido, recatado; **'coy·ness** recato *m*, timidez *f*.

coz·en ['kʌzn] *lit.* defraudar, engañar.

co·zy ['kouzi] = *cosy*.

crab[1] [kræb] cangrejo *m*, centolla *f*; *ast.* ♋ Cáncer *m*; ⊕ torno *m*; grúa *f*; *catch a ~* faltar con el remo.

crab[2] [~] ♣ (*freq.* '*~-ap·ple*) manzana *f* silvestre; (*tree*) manzano *m* silvestre; F persona *f* desabrida; **crab·bed** □ avinagrado, amargado; (*disagreeable*) desabrido, desapacible; *writing* indescifrable, mal formado.

crab-louse ['kræblaus] ladilla *f*.

crack [kræk] **1.** grieta *f*, hendedura *f*; (*sound*) crujido *m*; chasquido *m* (*a. of whip*), estallido *m*; F instante *m*; *sl.* chiste *m*, cuchufleta *f*; *attr.* F de primera; F *shot* certero; *at* (*the*) *~ of dawn* al romper el alba; **2.** *v/t.* agrietar, hender; hacer chasquear; *safe, bottle* abrir; *joke* decir, contar; *nut* cascar; *sl. ~ up* elogiar; *v/i.* agrietarse, henderse; chasquear; (*window*) rajarse; (*voice*) cascarse; F *~ down on* castigar severamente; F *~ up* fracasar; (⚔ *etc.*) desbaratarse; ⚗ perder la salud; '*~-brained* chiflado, loco; **'cracked** agrietado; *window* rajado; F chiflado; **'crack·er** triquitraque *m*, petardo *m*; (*biscuit*) cracker *m*; *Am.* blanco *m* de baja clase; **'crack·er·jack** *Am.* F la monda, el *non plus ultra*; **'crack-jaw** trabalenguas *m*; **'crack·le 1.** crujir, crepitar; **2.** crujido *m*, crepitación *f*; **'crack·ling** chicharrón *m*; = *crackle* **2**: **crack·nel** ['~nl] *approx.* galleta *f* ligera; turrón *m*; **'crack-up** F fracaso *m*; ⚗ colapso *m*; ✈ aterrizaje *m* violento.

cra·dle ['kreidl] **1.** cuna *f* (*a.* ⚓ *a. fig.*); ⚒ artesa *f* oscilante; ⚠ plataforma *f* colgante; *~ song* canción *f* de cuna; **2.** poner en la cuna; *fig.* criar.

craft [krɑːft] oficio *m*, empleo *m*; (*skill*) destreza *f*; *b.s.* maña *f*, astucia *f*; ⚓ embarcación *f*, barco *m*; **craft·i·ness** astucia *f*, socarronería *f*; **'crafts·man** artesano *m*, artífice *m*; **'crafts·man·ship** artesanía *f*, artificio *m*; **'craft·y** □ astuto, socarrón.

crag [kræg] peñasco *m*, risco *m*, despeñadero *m*; **'crag·gy** peñascoso, escarpado, arriscado.

crake [kreik] polluela *f*.

cram [kræm] embutir, rellenar; *hen* cebar; F empollar; F *~ o.s.* (*with food*) hartarse; '*~-full* atestado, repleto (*of* de); '**cram·mer** F empollón (*-a f*) *m*.

cramp [kræmp] **1.** ⊕ grapa *f*; ⊕ abrazadera *f*; ⚕ calambre *m*; **2.** engrapar, lañar; *~ (one's style)* cortarle las alas a uno; '**cramped** estrecho, apretado; ⚕ entumecido; '**cramp-iron** grapa *f*, laña *f*.

cran·ber·ry ['krænbəri] arándano *m* agrio.

crane [krein] **1.** *orn.* grulla *f* (común); ⊕ grúa *f*; **2.** levantar (*or* mover) con grúa; *neck* estirar; **crane-fly** ['~flai] típula *f*; **'crane's-bill** geranio *m*, pico *m* de cigüeña.

cra·ni·um ['kreiniəm] cráneo *m*.

crank [kræŋk] **1.** ⊕ manivela *f*, manubrio *m*; F persona *f* rara, maniático *m*; extravagante *m*; concepto raro *m*; **2.** *mot.* hacer arrancar con la manivela (*a. ~ up*); '*~-case* cárter *m* del cigüeñal; '**crank·i·ness** F chifladura *f*, desequilibrio *m*; '**crank·shaft** eje *m* del cigüeñal; '**crank·y** chiflado, extravagante.

cran·nied ['krænid] grietado, grietoso; '**cran·ny** grieta *f*, hendedura *f*.

crape [kreip] crespón *m*.

craps [kræps] *Am.* juego *m* de los dados.

crap·u·lence ['kræpjuləns] crápula *f*; '**crap·u·lent** crapuloso.

crash [kræʃ] **1.** (*noise*) estrépito *m*, estallido *m*; *mot.*, 🚗 *etc.* accidente *m*, choque *m*, encontronazo *m*; *fig.* fracaso *m*; ✈ quiebra *f*; *~ helmet* casco *m* protector; *~ landing* aterrizaje *m* violento; **2.** romperse con estrépito; *mot.*, 🚗 tener un accidente; ✈ estrellarse; ✈ quebrar; *~ a party sl.* colarse, entrar de gorra; *~ into* chocar con, estrellarse contra.

crass [kræs] tupido, espeso; *fig.* craso.

crate [kreit] caja *f*, cajón *m* (de embalaje); jaula *f* (de listones).

cra·ter ['kreitə] cráter *m*.

cra·vat [krə'væt] corbata *f*.

crave [kreiv] implorar, solicitar; ansiar, anhelar (*for, after acc.*).

cra·ven ['kreivn] cobarde *adj. a. su. m.*

crav·ing ['kreiviŋ] ansia *f*; regosto *m*, deseo *m* vehemente (*for* de).

craw·fish ['krɔ:fiʃ] **1.** ástaco *m*; **2.** *Am.* F desdecirse, rajarse.

crawl [krɔ:l] **1.** arrastramiento *m*; (*on all fours*) gateamiento *m*; *swimming*: crol *m*, crawl *m*; corral *m* (para peces); **2.** arrastrarse; gatear, ir a gatas; F (*a.* ~ *along*) ir a paso de tortuga; F *fig.* ~ *with* estar cuajado (*or* plagado) de; pulular de.

cray·fish ['kreifiʃ] ástaco *m*.

cray·on ['kreiɔn] **1.** creyón *m*, tizna *f*; **2.** dibujar con creyón.

craze [kreiz] **1.** manía *f* (*for* por), locura *f*; (*fashion*) moda *f*; be the ~ estar de moda; **2.** estriar; **'cra·zed** enloquecido, alocado; **'cra·zi·ness** locura*f*; chifladura *f*; **'cra·zy** □ loco (*for, about* por); chiflado; *idea* disparatado; △ en mosaico; △ *building etc.* desvencijado; *drive* ~ volver loco; *quite* ~, *Am. sl.* ~ *as a bedbug* loco rematado; ~ *quilt* centón *m*.

creak [kri:k] **1.** crujido *m*, chirrido *m*; rechinamiento *m*; **2.** crujir, chirriar; rechinar; **'creak·y** □ rechinador.

cream [kri:m] **1.** crema *f*; nata *f*; *fig.* flor *f* y nata (*of* de); *cold* ~ crema *f*; ~ *of tartar* crémor *m* (tártaro); **2.** formar nata; *milk* desnatar; *butter* batir; *fig.* quitar lo mejor de; **3.** color de crema; **'cream·er·y** mantequería *f*; lechería *f*; **'cream·y** □ cremoso.

crease [kri:s] **1.** pliegue *m*, arruga *f*; (*fold*) doblez *m*; (*trousers*) raya *f*; ~ *resisting* inarrugable; **2.** arrugar (se), plegar(se).

cre·ate [kri'eit] crear; originar, ocasionar; *sl.* hacer alharacas; **cre'a·tion** creación *f*; **cre'a·tive** creador; fecundo; **cre'a·tor** creador *m*; **crea·ture** ['kri:tʃə] criatura *f*; (*p.*) hechura *f*; *Am.* bicho *m*; ~ *comforts pl.* las cosas que confortan el *cuerpo.*

crèche [kreʃ] guardería *f* infantil.

cre·dence ['kri:dəns] fe *f*, creencia *f*; *give* ~ *to* dar fe a; **cre·den·tials** [kri'denʃlz] *pl.* credenciales *f/pl.*

cred·i·bil·i·ty [kredi'biliti] credibili-

dad *f*; **cred·i·ble** ['kredəbl] □ creíble.

cred·it ['kredit] **1.** crédito *m* (*a.* ✝); *on* ~ a crédito; *give* ~ *to* creer; ✝ abrir crédito a; *do a p.* ~ honrar; *take* ~ *for* atribuirse el crédito de; **2.** *attr.* ✝ crediticio; **3.** creer; ✝ acreditar; ~ *a p. with* atribuir a una p. el mérito de; **'cred·it·a·ble** □ estimable, honorable; **'cred·i·tor** acreedor (-a *f*) *m*.

cre·du·li·ty [kri'dju:liti] credulidad *f*; **cred·u·lous** □ crédulo.

creed [kri:d] credo *m*.

creek [kri:k] cala *f*, ensenada *f*; *Am.* río *m*, riachuelo *m*.

creel [kri:l] cesta *f* (para pescado); jaula *f* de mimbre (para la langosta).

creep [kri:p] **1.** [*irr.*] arrastrarse; gatear; moverse despacio y con cautela; (*flesh*) sentir hormigueo; ~ *up on s.o.* acercarse a uno sin que se dé cuenta; **2.** arrastramiento *m*; *sl.* be a ~ reptar; ~*s pl.* hormigueo *m*; *give the* ~*s* horripilar; **'creep·er** (planta *f*) enredadera *f*; **'creep·y** hormigueante; horripilante.

cre·mate [kri'meit] incinerar; **cre·ma·tion** incineración *f* (de cadáveres); **crem·a·to·ri·um** [kremə'tɔ:riəm], *Am.* **cre·ma·to·ry** ['~təri] horno *m* crematorio.

cren·el·(l)at·ed ['krenileitid] almenado.

Cre·ole ['kri:oul] criollo *adj. a. su. m* (a *f*).

cre·o·sote ['kriəsout] creosota *f*.

crep·i·tate ['krepiteit] crepitar; **crep·i'ta·tion** crepitación *f*.

crept [krept] *pret. a. p.p. of* creep 1.

cre·pus·cu·lar [kri'pʌskjulə] crepuscular.

cres·cent ['kresnt] **1.** creciente *f*; **2.** cuarto *m* creciente (*or* menguante); *heraldry*: creciente *m*; (*street*) calle *f* en forma de cuarto creciente.

cress [kres] mastuerzo *m*.

cres·set ['kresit] tedero *m*.

crest [krest] cresta *f*; **'crest·ed** crestado; ~ *lark* cogujada *f*; **'crest·fall·en** alicaído, abatido.

cre·ta·ceous [kri'teiʃəs] cretáceo.

cre·tin ['kretin] cretino *m*.

cret·onne [kre'tɔn] cretona *f*.

cre·vasse [kri'væs] grieta *f* en un helero; *Am.* brecha *f* en un dique.

crev·ice ['krevis] grieta *f*.

crew[1] [kru:] ♠ tripulación *f*; equipo *m*; (*gang*) banda *f*, pandilla *f*.

crew[2] [ ] *pret. of* crow 2.

crib [krib] **1.** pesebre *m*; cama *f* pequeña para niños; F *school*: chuleta *f*; F plagio *m*; *Am.* hucha *f* para maíz; *sl.* crack *a* ~ robar una casa; **2.** F plagiar; F usar una chuleta; **'crib·bage** *juego de naipes*.

crick [krik] tortícolis *m* (*esp.* ~ *in the neck*); calambre *m*.

crick·et[1] ['krikit] *zo.* grillo *m*.

crick·et[2] [ ] **1.** cricquet *m*; F juego *m* limpio; **2.** jugar al cricquet; **'crick·et·er** cricquetero *m*.

cri·er ['kraiə] pregonero *m*.

crime [kraim] crimen *m*.

crim·i·nal ['kriminl] criminal *adj. a. su. m/f*; **crim·i·nal·i·ty** [~'næliti] criminalidad *f*.

crimp[1] [krimp] ✂, ♠ reclutar por fuerza.

crimp[2] [ ] **1.** rizar, encrespar; ~*ing iron* encrespador *m*; **2.** rizo *m*; *sl. put a* ~ *in* estorbar.

crim·son ['krimzn] **1.** carmesí *adj. a. su. m*; **2.** enrojecer(se).

cringe [krindʒ] **1.** agacharse, encogerse; *fig.* reptar; **2.** servilismo *m*.

crin·kle ['kriŋkl] **1.** arruga *f*; *sl.* parné *m*; **2.** arrugar(se); (*hair*) rizar (se); **'crink·ly** arrugado; rizado.

crin·o·line ['krinəli:n] crinolina *f*.

crip·ple ['kripl] **1.** lisiado (*a f*) *m*, mutilado *m* (*a f*), tullido (*a f*) *m*; **2.** lisiar, mutilar; *ship* desarbolar; *fig.* perjudicar, estropear.

cri·sis ['kraisis], *pl.* **cri·ses** ['~si:z] crisis *f*.

crisp [krisp] **1.** □ crespo, rizado; frágil pero duro; tostado; *style* cortado; *air* fresco, refrescante; *su.* ~*s pl.* patatas *f/pl.* inglesas; **2.** encrespar, rizar; tostar *in oven*.

criss-cross ['kriskrɔs] **1.** cruz *f*; líneas *f/pl.* cruzadas; **2.** *adv.* en cruz; **3.** trazar líneas cruzadas (sobre); entrecruzarse; F ~ (*my heart*)! ¡palabra de honor!

cri·te·ri·on [krai'tiəriən], *pl.* **cri·te·ri·a** [~ə] criterio *m*.

crit·ic ['kritik] crítico *m*; *b.s.* criticón (-*a f*) *m*; **'crit·i·cal** □ crítico; (*hyper-*) criticón; *be* ~ *of* criticar; **crit·i·cism** ['~sizm], **cri·ti·que** [kri'ti:k] crítica *f*; **crit·i·cize** ['~saiz] criticar.

croak [krouk] **1.** (*crow*) graznar;

(*frog*) croar; (*p.*) gruñir; *sl.* estirar la pata; **2.** graznido *m*; canto *m of frog*; **'croak·er** gruñidor *m*.

Cro·at ['krouət], **Cro·a·tian** [krou-'eiʃn] croata *adj. a. su. m/f*.

cro·chet ['krouʃei] **1.** croché *m*; **2.** hacer croché.

crock [krɔk] vasija *f* de barro; F (*p.*) carcamal *m*; (*car*) cacharro *m*; **'crock·er·y** loza *f*; vajilla *f*, los platos.

croc·o·dile ['krɔkədail] cocodrilo *m*; ~ *tears* lágrimas *f/pl.* de cocodrilo.

cro·cus ['kroukəs] azafrán *m*.

croft·er ['krɔftə] arrendatario *m* de una finca pequeña.

crom·lech ['krɔmlek] crómlech *m*.

crone [kroun] vieja *f* arrugada.

cro·ny ['krouni] F compinche *m*.

crook [kruk] **1.** (*shepherd's*) cayado *m*; ⊕ gancho *m*; (*bend*) curva *f*; F criminal *m*, fullero *m*; *v. hook*; **2.** encorvar(se); **crook·ed** ['~kid] □ encorvado, curvo; *fig.* torcido, avieso; F *go* ~ torcerse.

croon [kru:n] canturrear; **'croon·er** vocalista *m/f* (*sentimental*).

crop [krɔp] **1.** cosecha *f* (*a. fig.*); *orn.* buche *m*; (*hair*) cabellera *f*, corte *m* de pelo; (*whip*) látigo *m* mocho; **2.** *v/t.* cortar; desorejar; *top* desmochar; trasquilar (*a. fig.*); *grass* pacer; *v/i.* ~ *up geol.* aflorar; F manifestarse inesperadamente; salir; **'crop·per** ♀ que da cosecha; *sl.* caída *f* severa; F *come a* ~ caer; fracasar.

cro·quet ['kroukei] juego *m* de croquet.

cro·sier ['krouʒə] báculo *m* del obispo.

cross [krɔs] **1.** cruz *f*; *biol.* cruzamiento *m*; (*burden*) cruz *f*; *on the* ~ diagonalmente; *make the sign of the* ♀ hacer la señal de la cruz; **2.** □ transversal; opuesto (*to a*); F malhumorado; F arisco, de mal genio; *get* ~ enfadarse, ponerse furioso; *at* ~ *purposes* sin comprenderse uno a otro; **3.** *v/t.* atravesar, cruzar; *p.* contrariar; *breed* cruzar; ~ *o.s.* santiguarse; ~ *out* tachar; ~ *one's mind* ocurrírsele a uno; *teleph.* the wires are ~ed hay un cruce en las líneas; *v/i.* cruzar (*a. letters*); ~ *over* atravesar de un lado a otro; **'~-bar** travesaño *m*; **'~-beam** viga *f* transversal; **'~-**

bench *parl. escaños de los indepen-
dientes;* '**~-bow** ballesta *f;* '**~-breed**
1. híbrido; 2. cruzar; '**~-'coun·try**
a campo traviesa; ~ *race* cross *m;*
'**~-cur·rent** contracorriente *f;*
'**~-cut** *saw* sierra *f* de trazar;
'**~-ex·am·i'na·tion** 🕭 repre-
gunta *f;* interrogatorio *m* severo;
~-ex·am·ine ['krɔsig'zæmin] 🕭
repreguntar; interrogar; '**~-eyed**
bizco; '**~-grained** de contrafibra;
fig. áspero, ♦esquivo; *be* ~ ser de
mala uva; '**cross·ing** 🕭 travesía *f;*
(roads) cruce *m; (ford)* vado *m.*
cross...: '**~-'legged** con las piernas
cruzadas; en cuclillas; '**~·ly** con
enfado; resentido; '**~-patch** F
malhumorado (a *f*) *m;* '**~-road**
camino *m* que cruza; *(a. ~s pl.)*
cruce *m,* encrucijada *f;* '**~-sec·tion**
sección *f* transversal; *fig.* sección
f representativa; '**~·wise** al través;
en cruz; '**~·word** *(a. ~ puzzle)*
crucigrama *m.*
crotch [krɔtʃ] bifurcación *f; anat.*
horcajadura *f;* **crotch·et** ['~it] ♩
negra *f;* capricho *m;* '**crotch·et·y**
F caprichoso; *(disagreeable)* desabrido.
crouch [krautʃ] agacharse, encogerse.
croup¹ [kruːp] *(horse's)* grupa *f.*
croup² [~] 🐾 crup *m.*
crou·pi·er ['kruːpiə] coime *m.*
crow [krou] 1. corneja *f; as the* ~
flies en derechura; *Am.* F *eat* ~ cantar la palinodia; *Am.* F *have a* ~ to
pick with tener que habérselas con;
2. *[irr.]* cantar (el gallo); *fig.* alardear, exultar; '**~·bar** palanca *f.*
crowd [kraud] 1. multitud *f,* muchedumbre *f;* gentío *m; contp.* vulgo *m;*
sport: espectadores *m/pl.; follow
the* ~ irse tras el hilo de la
gente; *fig. pass in a* ~ no descollar; 2. *v/t.* amontonar, atestar;
people apiñar *(a. ~ together);* ~ *on
sail* hacer fuerza de vela; ~ed atestado *(with* de); concurrido; *be* ~ed
out (place) estar de bote en bote; (*p.*)
ser excluido; *v/i.* agolparse, arremolinarse *(a. ~ together, ~ around).*
crow·foot ['kroufut] ranúnculo *m.*
crown [kraun] 1. corona *f;* cruz *f of
anchor;* copa *f of hat;* cima *f of hill;*
⚠ coronamiento *m;* 2. coronar;
completar, terminar; *(reward)* premiar; *sl.* golpear en la cabeza.

crow's-nest ['krouznest] 🕭 torre *f*
de vigía.
cru·cial ['kruːʃiəl]☐ decisivo, crítico;
shape cruciforme; **cru·ci·ble** ['kruː-
sibl] crisol *m (a. fig.);* **cru·ci·fix**
['~fiks] crucifijo *m,* cruz *f;* **cru·ci-
fix·ion** [~'fikʃn] crucifixión *f;* '**cru-
ci·form** cruciforme; **cru·ci·fy** ['~-
fai] crucificar; *fig.* mortificar.
crude [kruːd] ☐ *(raw)* crudo; *fig.*
tosco, grosero; *b.s. work* chapucero;
⚠ *etc.* sin labrar; '**crude·ness,**
cru·di·ty ['~iti] tosquedad *f;*
grosería *f,* rudeza *f.*
cru·el ['kruəl] ☐ cruel *(a. fig.);*
'**cruel·ty** crueldad *f.*
cru·et ['kruːit] vinagrera *f;* '**~-stand**
angarillas *f/pl.*
cruise [kruːz] 1. viaje *m* por mar,
crucero *m;* excursión *f;* 2. cruzar;
cruising speed velocidad *f* de crucero; *mot.* velocidad *f* económica;
'**cruis·er** 🕭 crucero *m;* '**~-weight**
peso *m* medio fuerte.
crul·ler ['krʌlə] *Am.* buñuelo *m.*
crumb [krʌm] 1. migaja *f (a. fig.);*
miga *f of loaf;* 2. desmigar; cubrir
con migajas; **crum·ble** ['~bl] *v/t.*
desmigar; *v/i.* desmoronarse *(a.
fig.; a. ~ away);* '**crum·bling,**
'**crum·bly** desmenuzable, desmoronadizo; **crumb·y** ['krʌmi] lleno
de migajas.
crum·my ['krʌmi] *Am. sl.* sucio;
joke gastado; *bar etc.* de baja categoría.
crum·pet ['krʌmpit] bollo *m* blando
tostado.
crum·ple ['krʌmpl] arrugar(se),
plegar(se); *(dress)* ajar(se); *fig. (a.
~ up)* ceder, desplomarse.
crunch [krʌntʃ] ronzar; *(ground)*
crujir.
cru·sade [kruː'seid] 1. cruzada *f (a.
fig.);* 2. participar en una cruzada;
~ *for* hacer campaña en pro de *(or
por);* **cru'sad·er** cruzado *m.*
crush [krʌʃ] 1. aplastar; *grapes etc.*
prensar, estrujar; *stones etc.* moler;
dress ajar; *fig.* abrumar, anonadar;
~*ing fig.* aplastante; 2. presión *f*
violenta, aplastamiento *m; (crowd)*
agolpamiento *m,* bullaje *m; sl. have
a* ~ *on* perder la chaveta por;
'**crus·her** molino *m* (de piedra *esp.*).
crust [krʌst] 1. corteza *f;* (🐾 *a. wine)*
costra *f;* 🐾 escara *f; (old bread)*
mendrugo *m;* 2. encostrarse;

'crust·y ☐ costroso; *fig.* áspero, desabrido.
crutch [krʌtʃ] muleta *f* (*a. fig.*).
crux [krʌks] enigma *m*; lo esencial.
cry [krai] 1. grito *m*; lloro *m*, lamento *m*; (*seller's*) pregón *m*; be a far ~ estar lejos, ser mucho camino; *have a* (*good*) ~ llorar (a mares); *in full* ~ acosando de cerca; 2. gritar; llorar; *wares* pregonar; ~ *down* rebajar, desacreditar; ~ *for* clamar por; ~ *for joy* llorar de alegría; ~ *off* retirarse, rajarse; *s.t.* renunciar (a), romper; ~ *out* gritar, publicar en voz alta; ~ *out* (*against*) protestar (contra); ~ *up* encarecer; '~-ba·by llorón (-a *f*) *m*; 'cry·ing *fig.* atroz, enorme.
crypt [kript] cripta *f*; 'cryp·tic ☐ oculto, misterioso.
crys·tal ['kristl] 1. cristal *m*; *as clear as* ~ tan claro como el agua; 2. = crys·tal·line ['~təlain] cristalino; crys·tal·li·za·tion cristalización *f*; 'crys·tal·lize cristalizarse; ~*d fruit* fruta *f* escarchada.
cub [kʌb] cachorro *m*; *fig.* rapaz *m*.
cub·by·hole ['kʌbihoul] chiribitil *m*.
cube [kju:b] 1. cubo *m*; ~ *root* raíz *f* cúbica; 2. cubicar; 'cu·bic, 'cu·bi·cal ☐ cúbico.
cu·bi·cle ['kjubikl] cubículo *m*.
cu·bism ['kju:bizm] cubismo *m*; 'cu·bist cubista *m*.
cuck·old ['kʌkəld] 1. cornudo *m*; 2. encornudar, poner los cuernos a.
cuck·oo ['kuku:] 1. cuc(lill)o *m*; 2. *sl.* chiflado.
cu·cum·ber ['kju:kʌmbə] cohombro *m*, pepino *m*; *cool as a* ~ fresco como una lechuga; *fig.* sosegado.
cud [kʌd] bolo *m* alimenticio; *v.chew.*
cud·dle ['kʌdl] 1. abrazo *m*, caricia *f*; 2. acariciar, abrazar; ~ *up* arrimarse (*to* a).
cudg·el ['kʌdʒl] 1. porra *f*; *take up the* ~*s for* ir a la defensa de; 2. aporrear, apalear; ~ *one's brains* devanarse los sesos.
cue [kju:] *billiards*: taco *m*; *thea.* pie *m*, apunte *m*; (*hair*) coleta *f*; *take one's* ~ *from* seguir el ejemplo de.
cuff[1] [kʌf] 1. bofetada *f*; 2. abofetear, dar de bofetadas.
cuff[2] [~] (*shirt-, etc.*) puño *m*; (*hand-*)~*s pl.* esposas *f/pl.*; '~-links *pl.* gemelos *m/pl.*
cui·rass [kwi'ræs] coraza *f*.

cui·sine [kwi'zi:n] cocina *f*.
cu·li·nar·y ['kʌlinəri] culinario.
cull [kʌl] *lit.* entresacar, espigar.
culm [kʌlm] cisco *m*.
cul·mi·nate ['kʌlmineit] culminar (*a. ast.*); ~ *in* terminar en; cul·mi·na·tion culminación *f*; *fig.* colmo *m*, apogeo *m*.
cul·pa·bil·i·ty [kʌlpə'biliti] culpabilidad *f*; cul·pa·ble ☐ culpable.
cul·prit ['kʌlprit] culpado (a *f*) *m*; reo *m*; F bribón *m*.
cult [kʌlt] culto *m*.
cul·ti·va·ble ['kʌltivəbl] cultivable.
cul·ti·vate ['kʌltiveit] cultivar (*a. fig.*); *fig.* ~*d* culto, refinado; cul·ti·va·tion cultivo *m*; 'cul·ti·va·tor cultivador *m*; ⊕ cultivadora *f*.
cul·tur·al ['kʌltʃərəl] ☐ cultural.
cul·ture ['kʌltʃə] cultura *f*; cultivo *m* (*a.* 🜨); 'cul·tured culto; '~-me·di·um medio *m* de cultivo.
cul·vert ['kʌlvət] alcantarilla *f*.
cum·ber ['kʌmbə] estorbar; molestar; ~some ['~səm], cum·brous ['~brəs] ☐ molesto, pesado.
cu·mu·la·tive ['kju:mjulətiv] ☐ cumulativo; cu·mu·lus ['~ləs], *pl.* cu·mu·li ['~lai] cúmulo *m*.
cu·ne·i·form ['kju:niifɔ:m] cuneiforme.
cun·ning ['kʌniŋ] 1. ☐ astuto, taimado; *Am.* precioso, mono; 2. astucia *f*; sagacidad *f*.
cup [kʌp] 1. taza *f*; *eccl. a.* 🜚 cáliz *m*; (*fig. a. prize*) copa *f*; *in one's* ~*s* bebido; 2. ahuecar; poner en forma de taza (*or* bocina); ~·board ['kʌbəd] armario *m*; aparador *m*; ~ *love* amor *m* interesado; '~-shaped en forma de taza.
cu·pid·i·ty [kju:'piditi] codicia *f*.
cu·po·la ['kju:pələ] cúpula *f*.
cup·ping-glass ['kʌpiŋglɑ:s] ventosa *f*.
cu·pre·ous ['kju:priəs] cúprico; cobrizo.
cur [kə:] perro *m* de mala raza; (*p.*) canalla *m*.
cur·a·bil·i·ty [kjuərə'biliti] curabilidad *f*; 'cur·a·ble curable.
cu·ra·cy ['kjuərəsi] vicaría *f*; cu·rate ['~rit] vicario *m*, cura *m*; cu·ra·tor [~'reitə] conservador *m*.
curb [kə:b] 1. barbada *f* (de la brida); (*pavement*) encintado *m*; (*well*) brocal *m*; *fig.* impedimento *m*, estorbo *m* (on para); 2. proveer de barbada

(*or* encintado); *fig.* refrenar, reprimir; '~-'**mar·ket** *Am.* ✝ bolsín *m*.

curd [kəːd] cuajada *f*; **cur·dle** ['~dl] cuajar(se); ~ *the blood* horripilar.

cure [kjuə] 1. cura *f*; *fig.* curato *m*; 2. curar; '~-all panacea *f*.

cur·few ['kəːfjuː] queda *f*.

cu·ri·o ['kjuəriou] curiosidad *f*; **cu·ri'os·i·ty** [~'ɔsiti] curiosidad *f*; '**cu·ri·ous** ☐ curioso.

curl [kəːl] 1. rizo *m*, bucle *m of hair*; espiral *f of smoke*; ondulación *f*; 2. rizar(se), encrespar(se); ondular (se); *lips* fruncir; (*waves*) encresparse; ~ *up* arrollarse; (*p*.) acurrucarse; *Am.* F abatirse.

curl·ing ['kəːliŋ] *sport*: curling *m* (*juego sobre un campo de hielo*); '~-i·ron, '~-tongs *pl.* encrespador *m*; '**curl·y** crespo, encrespado, rizado.

cur·mudg·eon [kəː'mʌdʒn] erizo *m*, mezquino *m*, cicatero *m*.

cur·rant ['kʌrənt] (*dried*) pasa *f* de Corinto; (*fresh*) grosella *f*; ~ (*bush*) grosellero *m*.

cur·ren·cy ['kʌrənsi] moneda *f* (en circulación); *fig.* uso *m* corriente; *fig.* extensión *f*, propagación *f*; '**cur·rent** 1. ☐ corriente; *be* ~ correr, ser de actualidad; ~ *events* actualidades *f/pl.*; ~ly actualmente; 2. corriente *f* (*a.* ⚡).

cur·ric·u·lum [kə'rikjuləm], *pl.* **cur'ric·u·la** [~lə] programa *m* de estudios.

cur·ri·er ['kʌriə] curtidor *m*.

cur·ry¹ ['kʌri] 1. cari *m*, curry *m*; 2. preparar con cari; '~-pow·der polvo *m* (de especias) para preparar el cari.

cur·ry² [~] *leather* curtir; *horse* almohazar; ~ *favour* buscar favores; '~-comb almohaza *f*.

curse [kəːs] 1. maldición *f*; blasfemia *f*; (*oath*) palabrota *f*; 2. *v/t.* maldecir; echar pestes de; *be* ~*d with* padecer de; tener que aguantar; *v/i.* blasfemar; (*a.* ~ *and swear*) soltar palabrotas.

cur·sive ['kəːsiv] cursivo.

cur·so·ry ['kəːsəri] ☐ precipitado, apresurado; *glance* rápido.

curt [kəːt] ☐ brusco, áspero, conciso; '**curt·ness** brusquedad *f*.

cur·tail [kəː'teil] cercenar (*a. fig.*), reducir; privar (*of* de); **cur'tail·ment** cercenamiento *m*, reducción *f*; privación *f*.

cur·tain ['kəːtn] 1. cortina *f* (*a.* ✕); (*heavy*) cortinón *m*; *thea.* telón *m*; *pol.* iron ~ telón *m* de acero; 2. proveer de cortina; separar con cortina (*a.* ~ *off*); '~-rais·er pieza *f* preliminar; '~-ring anilla *f*; '~-rod barra *f* de cortina.

curt·s(e)y ['kəːtsi] 1. reverencia *f*; *drop a* ~ = 2. hacer una reverencia (*to* a).

cur·va·ture ['kəːvətʃə] curvatura *f*.

curve [kəːv] 1. curva *f*; 2. encorvar (se); voltear en curva *through air*.

cush·ion ['kuʃn] 1. cojín *m*, almohadón *m*; *billiards*: baranda *f*; *fig.* ✝ colchón *m*; 2. amortiguar; proteger con cojines; ⊕ acojinar.

cush·y ['kuʃi] *sl.* fácil, agradable; holgado.

cusp [kʌsp] cúspide *f*.

cuss [kʌs] *Am.* F 1. blasfemia *f*, ajo *m*; *sl.* tipo *m*, tío *m*; 2. blasfemar, soltar un ajo; '**cuss·ed** ['kʌsid] maldito; '**cuss·ed·ness** terquedad *f* (*esp. pure* ~).

cus·tard ['kʌstəd] natillas *f/pl.*; flan *m*.

cus·to·di·an [kʌs'toudiən] custodio *m*; **cus·to·dy** ['kʌstədi] custodia *f*; *in* ~ en prisión; *take into* ~ arrestar.

cus·tom ['kʌstəm] costumbre *f*; ✝ clientela *f*, parroquia *f*; ~*s pl.* aduana *f*; *derechos m/pl.* de aduana; ~*s house* aduana *f*; ~*s post* puesto *m* aduanero; **cus·tom·ar·y** ['~əri] ☐ acostumbrado, de costumbre; '**cus·tom·er** cliente *m*; F tío *m*; '**cus·tom-made** *Am.* hecho a la medida.

cut [kʌt] 1. corte *m*; (*blow*) golpe *m* cortante, tajo *m*; tajada *f of meat*; (*deletion*) corte *m*; ✝ reducción *f*; ✂ herida *f*, incisión *f*; corte *m*, hechura *f of dress*; (*proportion*) parte *f*; (*insult*) desaire *m*, zaherimiento *m*; ✄ apagón *m*; *sl.* tajada *f*; *short* ~ atajo *m*; 2. [*irr.*] *v/t.* cortar; *corn* segar; *esp. hole* practicar, hacer; *stone etc.* tallar; (*divide*) partir, dividir; ✝ *losses* abandonar; *class* fumarse; *p.* desairar, zaherir; fingir no ver; F *caper etc.* ejecutar, presentar; *tooth* salirle a uno (un diente); ~ *across* cortar al través; atravesar; *fig.* ir en contra de; ~ *away* separar (cortando); *back* acortar, recortar; ~ *down* cortar, derribar; *costs* aminorar; *price* rebajar; ~ *off* cortar (*a.* ⚡); *leg* amputar; ~ *open* abrir (cortando); ~

out (re)cortar; *hole etc.* practicar, hacer; *stone* tallar, labrar; *fig.* suprimir; *be* ~ *out for* tener talento especial para; *have one's work* ~ *out* tener trabajo de sobra (*to inf.* para poder *inf.*); F ~ *it out!* ¡déjese de eso!; *v. short*; ~ *up* desmenuzar; *meat* picar; F *fig.* criticar severamente; F *be* ~ *up* acongojarse, afligirse (*about* por); *v/i.* cortar; ~ *in* interrumpir, interponerse; **3.** cortado; ⊕ labrado; ~ *glass* cristal *m* tallado; ~ *and dried* preparado (*or* convenido) de antemano; ~ *off* aislado, incomunicado.

cu·ta·ne·ous [kju'teiniəs] cutáneo.

cut·a·way ['kʌtəwei] (*a.* ~ *coat*) chaqué *m*.

cute [kju:t] □ F mono; astuto.

cu·ti·cle ['kju:tikl] *anat.,* ♀ cutícula *f*.

cut·lass ['kʌtləs] chafarote *m*.

cut·ler ['kʌtlə] cuchillero *m*; **'cut·ler·y** cuchillería *f*; cubertería *f*.

cut·let ['kʌtlit] chuleta *f*.

cut...: '~-**off** *Am.* atajo *m*; '~-'**out** diseño *m* para recortar; *⚡* portafusible *m*; ⊕ válvula *f* de escape; '~-**purse** carterista *m*; ratero *m*; **'cut·ter** cortador (-a *f*) *m*; ⊕ cortadora *f*; ⚓ cúter *m*; ⚓ escampavía *f*; **'cut-throat 1.** asesino *m*; **2.** sanguinario, cruel; *competition* intenso, implacable; **'cut·ting 1.** □ cortante; *fig.* mordaz; ~ *edge* filo *m*; **2.** corte *m*, cortadura *f*; (*paper*) recorte *m*; 🚞 *etc.* trinchera *f*, desmonte *m*; 🚞 zanja *f* ferroviaria.

cut·tle ['kʌtl] jibia *f* (*mst* '~-**fish**).

cy·a·nide ['saiənaid] cianuro *m*; ~ *of potassium* cianuro *m* de potasio.

cyc·la·men ['sikləmən] ciclamino *m*, pamporcino *m*.

cy·cle ['saikl] **1.** ciclo *m* (*a.* ♪ *etc.*); F bicicleta *f*; **2.** montar (*or* ir) en bicicleta; **cy·clic, cy·cli·cal** ['saiklik(l)] □ cíclico; **'cy·cling** ciclismo *m*; **'cy·clist** ciclista *m/f*.

cy·clo·pae·di·a [saiklə'pi:diə] enciclopedia *f*.

cy·clone ['saikloun] ciclón *m*; borrasca *f*.

cy·clo·tron ['saiklətrɔn] ciclotrón *m*.

cyg·net ['signit] pollo *m* de cisne.

cyl·in·der ['silində] cilindro *m*; ⊕ ~ *block* bloque *m* de cilindros; *mot.* ~ *capacity* cilindrada *f*; *hot-water* ~ termo *m*; **cy'lin·dric, cy'lin·dri·cal** □ cilíndrico.

cym·bal ['simbl] címbalo *m*.

cyn·ic ['sinik] **1.** (*a.* **'cyn·i·cal** □) cínico; **2.** cínico *m*; **cyn·i·cism** ['~sizm] cinismo *m*.

cy·no·sure ['sinəzjuə] *fig.* (*esp.* ~ *of every eye*) miradero *m*.

cy·press ['saipris] ciprés *m*.

cyst [sist] quiste *m*; **'cyst·ic** *anat.* cístico; *⚕* quístico; **cys·ti·tis** [sis'taitis] cistitis *f*.

Czar [zɑ:] zar *m*; **Czar·i·na** [zɑ:'ri:nə] zarina *f*.

Czech [tʃek] **1.** checo *adj. a. su. m* (a *f*); **2.** (*language*) checo *m*.

Czech·o·Slo·vak ['tʃekou'slouvæk] checoslovaco *adj. a. su. m* (a *f*).

D

'd F = had; would.

dab [dæb] **1.** golpe *m* ligero; soba *f*; untadura *f of liquid*; brochazo *m of paint*; pizca *f*, porción *f* pequeña; *ichth.* lenguado *m*; *be a ~ hand at* ser perito en; **2.** golpear (*or* tocar) ligeramente; sobar; untar; *~ on paint* embadurnar de.

dab·ble ['dæbl] salpicar, mojar; *feet etc.* chapotear; *~ in* interesarse en, ser aficionado a; *b.s.* meterse en, mangonear en; ✝ especular en, jugar a; '**dab·bler** aficionado(a *f*) *m*.

dace [deis] albur *m*.

dad [dæd], **dad·dy** ['~i] F papá *m*, papaíto *m*. [típula *f*.]

dad·dy-long-legs ['dædi'lɔŋlegz] F)

da·do ['deidou] friso *m* (de pared).

daf·fo·dil ['dæfədil] dafodelo *m*; narciso *m*.

dag·ger ['dægə] daga *f*, puñal *m*; *be at ~s drawn* ser enemigos; *look ~s at* apuñalar con la mirada.

da·go ['deigou] *sl. contp.* = *español*, *portugués*, *italiano*.

dahl·ia ['deiljə] dalia *f*.

dai·ly ['deili] diario *adj. a. su. m*; F asistenta *f*.

dain·ti·ness ['deintinis] delicadeza *f*, melindre *m*; primor *m*, esmero *m*; '**dain·ty 1.** □ delicado, regalado; de buen gusto, precioso; *b.s.* quisquilloso, remilgado; **2.** golosina *f*.

dair·y ['dɛəri] ✝ lechería *f*; (*farm*) quesería *f*, vaquería *f*; '**~maid** lechera *f*; '**~man** lechero *m*.

da·is ['deiis] estrado *m*.

dai·sy ['deizi] margarita *f*, maya *f*; *sl.* primor *m*.

dale [deil] valle *m*.

dal·li·ance ['dæliəns] frivolidad *f*; coquetería *f*; '**dal·ly** coquetear (*with* con); (*sport*) juguetear; (*delay*) tardar; (*idle*) holgar.

dam¹ [dæm] madre *f* (de un animal).

dam² [~] **1.** presa *f*; embalse *m*; **2.** represar (*a. fig.*); *~ up* cerrar, tapar.

dam·age ['dæmidʒ] **1.** daño *m*, perjuicio *m*; ⊕ *etc.* avería *f*; ⚖ *~s pl.* daños *m/pl.* y perjuicios; **2.** dañar,

perjudicar; averiar; *mot. etc.* causar daño a; *mot. etc. be ~ed* sufrir daño; '**dam·age·a·ble** ⚖ susceptible de indemnización.

dam·a·scene ['dæməsi:n] ataujía *f*.

dam·ask ['dæməsk] **1.** damasco *m*; ⊕ ataujía *f*; damasquinado *m*; *attr.* de damasco; ⊕ de ataujía; **2.** *cloth* adamascar; ⊕ damasquinar.

dame [deim] dama *f*; *sl.* tía *f*.

damn [dæm] **1.** condenar (*a. eccl.*), censurar; maldecir; *~ it!* ¡maldito sea!; **2.** terno *m*, palabrota *f*; *sl. I don't care a ~* maldito lo que me importa; *sl. not worth a ~* de poca monta; '**dam·na·ble** □ destestable; **dam'na·tion** condenación *f*; *~!* ¡cáspita!; **damned** *eccl.* condenado; F maldito, condenado; *adv.* extremadamente; **damn·ing** ['dæmiŋ] damnificador.

damp [dæmp] **1.** húmedo; mojado; **2.** humedad *f*; *fig.* abatimiento *m*, desaliento *m*; **3.** (*a.* '**damp·en** humedecer, mojar; (*dull*) amortiguar, amortecer; *fig.* desalentar; (*a. ~ down*) cubrir; '**damp·er** registro *m*; ♪ sordina *f*; tiro *m* (de chimenea); '**damp·ish** algo húmedo; '**damp-proof** a prueba de humedad.

dam·sel ['dæmzl] ✝, *lit.* damisela *f*.

dam·son ['dæmzn] ciruela *f* damascena.

dance [dɑːns] **1.** baile *m*, danza *f*; *formal ~* baile de etiqueta; **2.** bailar, danzar (*a. fig.*); '**~floor** pista *f* de baile; '**danc·er** bailador (-a *f*) *m*; danzante (a *f*) *m*; (*professional*) bailarín (-a *f*) *m*.

danc·ing ['dɑːnsiŋ] baile *m*; *attr.* de baile; '**~girl** bailarina *f*, corista *f*; '**~part·ner** pareja *f* de baile.

dan·de·li·on [dændi'laiən] diente *m* de león.

dan·der ['dændə] *sl.* cólera *f*, mal genio *m*; *get a p.'s ~ up* enojar a una p.

dan·dle ['dændl] *child* hacer saltar sobre las rodillas.

dan·driff ['dændrif], **dan·druff** ['dændrəf] caspa *f*.

dan·dy ['dændi] **1.** currutaco *m*; *sl.* cosa *f* excelente; **2.** *sl.* de primera; **'dan·dy·ism** dandismo *m*.

Dane [dein] danés (-a *f*) *m*; *Great* ♀ mastín *m* danés.

dan·ger ['deindʒə] peligro *m*; *out of ~* fuera de peligro; **'~-list:** *be on the ~* estar de cuidado; **'~-mon·ey** prima *f* de riesgos; **'dan·ger·ous** ☐ peligroso; **'dan·ger-sig·nal** señal *f* de peligro.

dan·gle ['dæŋgl] colgar(se) en el aire; bambolearse; *~ after* ir tras de.

Dan·ish ['deiniʃ] danés *adj. a. su. m.*

dank [dæŋk] húmedo, liento.

dap·per ['dæpə] ☐ apuesto, gallardo.

dap·ple ['dæpl] motear, salpicar de manchas; **'dap·pled** moteado, salpicado de manchas; *horse* rodado; **'dap·ple-'grey** caballo *m* rucio rodado.

dare [dɛə] *v/i.* osar (*to inf.*), atreverse (*to* a); *I ~ say* quizá; concedo (*that* que); *v/t. s.o.* desafiar; *gaze* resistir; **'~-dev·il** temerario (a *f*) *m*; **'dar·ing** ☐ **1.** atrevido, osado; **2.** atrevimiento *m*, osadía *f*.

dark [dɑːk] **1.** ☐ oscuro; *complexion* moreno, trigueño; enigmático, secreto; ignorante; (*evil*) malvado, alevoso; ♀ *Ages* edades *f/pl.* bárbaras; *~ horse fig.* ganador *m* inesperado; candidato *m* poco conocido; *~ room* cuarto *m* oscuro; *get ~* hacerse de noche; *keep ~* mantener secreto, reservar; **2.** oscuridad *f*, tinieblas *f/pl.*; *in the ~* a oscuras (*a. fig.*); *keep s.o. in the ~* no revelar a una p. cierta noticia; **'dark·en** oscurecer(se); *fig.* entristecer; *fig.* confundir, turbar; *never ~ a p.'s door* nunca ir a ver a una p.; **'dark·ish** algo oscuro; **'dark·ness** oscuridad *f*; *fig.* maldad *f*; *fig.* ignorancia *f*; **'dark·y** F negro (a *f*) *m*.

dar·ling ['dɑːliŋ] **1.** querido (a *f*) *m*; *my ~!* ¡amor mío!; **2.** querido, predilecto.

darn¹ [dɑːn] F = *damn*.

darn² [~] **1.** zurcido *m*, zurcidura *f*; **2.** zurcir.

darn·ing ['dɑːniŋ] acción *f* de zurcir; zurcidura *f*; cosas *f/pl.* por zurcir; **'~-nee·dle** aguja *f* de zurcir.

dart [dɑːt] **1.** ⚔ dardo *m*, venablo *m*; (*game*) rehilete *m*; movimiento *m* rápido; *~board* blanco *m*; **2.** lanzarse, precipitarse; moverse rápidamente.

Dar·win·ism ['dɑːwinizm] Darvinismo *m*.

dash [dæʃ] **1.** choque *m*; rociada *f* *of water etc.*; pequeña cantidad *f*; raya *f with pen*; *typ.* guión *m*; *fig.* arrojo *m*, brío *m*; carrera *f* corta (*for* hasta *etc.*); *cut a ~* lucir; **2.** *v/t.* romper, estrellar (*against* contra); rociar, salpicar; despedazar (*mst ~ to pieces*); *hope* frustrar; *~ (it)!* ¡porras!; *~ against* estampar contra; *~ off letter* escribir de prisa; *v/i.* estrellarse; (*waves*) romperse; correr; F *~ away*, *~ off* marcharse; F *~ in (out)* entrar (salir) como un rayo; F *~ up* acercarse (rápidamente); **'~-board** tablero *m* de instrumentos, panel *m*; **'dash·ing** ☐ brioso, arrojado; apuesto, guapo.

das·tard ['dæstəd] alevoso; **'das·tard·ly** cobarde, alevoso, vil.

da·ta ['deitə] *pl.* datos *m/pl.*

date¹ [deit] ♀ dátil *m*; (*tree*) datilera *f* (*a. ~ palm*).

date² [~] **1.** fecha *f*; F cita *f*; † plazo *m*; *Am.* F novio (a *f*) *m*; *what is the ~?* ¿a cuántos estamos?; F *make a ~* citar (*with* a); *out of ~* anticuado; (*up*) *to ~* hasta la fecha; *up to ~* al día; moderno; **2.** fechar; *Am.* F citar; *~ back to* remontarse a; *~ from* datar de; *~d* fechado; *fig.* anticuado; **'~-less** sin fecha; *fig.* inmemorial; **'~-line** línea *f* de cambio de fecha.

da·tive ['deitiv] dativo *m* (*a. ~ case*).

da·tum ['deitəm] dato *m*.

daub [dɔːb] **1.** embadurnar; *paint.* pintorrear; **2.** embadurnamiento *m*; *paint.* pintarrajo *m*; **'daub·(st)er** pintamonas *m*.

daugh·ter ['dɔːtə] hija *f*; **'~-in-law** ['dɔːtərinlɔː] nuera *f*; **'daugh·ter·ly** filial, como una hija.

daunt [dɔːnt] acobardar, desalentar; **'~-less** ☐ intrépido, impávido.

dav·it ['dævit] pescante *m*.

da·vy¹ ['deivi] ⚒ (*mst ~ lamp*) lámpara *f* de seguridad.

da·vy² [~]: *take one's ~* jurar, prestar juramento.

daw·dle ['dɔːdl] F *v/i.* holgazanear; andar muy despacio; *v/t. ~ away* malgastar; **'daw·dler** F holgazán (-a *f*) *m*; *fig.* dormilón (-a *f*) *m*.

dawn [dɔːn] **1.** amanecer *m*, alba *f*; *esp. fig.* aurora *f*; *from* ～ *to dusk* de sol a sol; *get up with the* ～ madrugar; **2.** amanecer, apuntar el día; *fig.* ～ *on s.o.* caer uno en la cuenta.

day [dei] día *m*; *eccl.* fiesta *f*; *fig.* palma *f*, victoria *f*; ～ *after* ～, ～ *in*, ～ *out* día tras día; *the* ～ *after* el día siguiente; *the* ～ *before* el día anterior; la víspera de *event etc.*; *by* ～ de día; *by the* ～ a jornal; *good* ～! ¡buenos días!; *to this* ～ hasta el día de hoy; *call it a* ～ dejar de trabajar *etc.*; *carry the* ～ ganar la victoria; *v. off etc.*; '～·book diario *m*; '～·break amanecer *m*; '～·dream ensueño *m*; '～·la·bo(u)r·er jornalero *m*; '～·light luz *f* del día; *in broad* ～ en pleno día; *fig. see* ～ comprender; ver el final de un trabajo; '～·nurse·ry guardería *f* para niños; '～·star *poet.* sol *m*; lucero *m* del alba; '～·time día *m*; '～-to-'day diario, cotidiano.

daze [deiz] **1.** aturdir, ofuscar; deslumbrar; **2.** aturdimiento *m*; *in a* ～ aturdido.

daz·zle ['dæzl] **1.** deslumbrar (*a. fig.*), ofuscar; **2.** deslumbramiento *m*.

dea·con ['diːkn] diácono *m*; **dea·con·ess** ['diːkənis] diaconisa *f*; '**dea·con·ry** diaconía *f*.

dead [ded] **1.** muerto; difunto; insensible (*to* a); *leaf* marchito, seco; *hands etc.* entumecido; *colour* apagado; *sound* sordo; ∮ sin corriente; (*obsolete*) anticuado, obsoleto; ～ *calm* calma *f* chicha; ～ *centre* punto *m* muerto; *v. heat*; ～ *letter fig.* letra *f* muerta; *v. level*; ～ *load* carga *f* fija; *v. loss*; ～ *march* marcha *f* fúnebre; ～ *stop* parada *f* en seco; ～ *water* agua *f* tranquila; ～ *weight* peso *m* muerto; *fig.* carga *f* onerosa; ～ *wood* leña *f* seca; *fig.* material *m* inútil; **2.** *adv.* completamente, absolutamente; ～ *drunk* borracho como un tronco; ～ *set* empeñado (*on* en); ～ *tired* hecho polvo, muerto de cansancio; **3.:** *the* ～ *pl.* los muertos; *fig.* lo más profundo; *in the* ～ *of night* en las altas horas; *in the* ～ *of winter* en lo más recio del invierno; '～-'beat **1.** hecho polvo, agotado; **2.** *Am. sl.* gorrón (-a *f*) *m*; holgazán (-a *f*) *m*; '**dead-·en** amortiguar, amortecer; '**dead-**

'**end** callejón *m* sin salida (*a. fig.*); *Am.* ～ *kids* chicos *m*/*pl.* de las calles; '**dead·line** fecha *f* tope, línea *f* tope; '**dead·lock** *fig.* punto *m* muerto; '**dead·ly 1.** mortal; fatal (*a. fig.*); *fig.* abrumador; **2.** *adv.* sumamente; '**dead·ness** inercia *f*; pérdida *f* de vida; falta *f* de vida.

dead...: '～·net·tle ortiga *f* muerta; '～·pan *sl.* (semblante *m*) sin expresión.

deaf [def] sordo (*to* a); ～ *as a post* sordo como una tapia; '**deaf·en** ensordecer; (*noise*) asordar; '**deaf·mute** sordomudo (a *f*) *m*.

deal[1] [diːl] tabla *f* de pino (*or* de abeto).

deal[2] [～] **1.** negocio *m*, negociación *f*; ✝ trato *m*, transacción *f*; *Am.* convenio *m*, acuerdo *m*; *cards*: reparto *m*, mano *f*; (*turn*) turno *m*; porción *f*; *a good* ～ bastante; *a great* ～ mucho; *it's a* ～! ¡trato hecho!; *give a square* ～ tratar con justicia a; *make a great* ～ *of p.* estimar mucho a; *th.* dar importancia a; **2.** [*irr.*] *v*/*t. blow* asestar, dar; (*esp.* ～ *out*) repartir; *cards* dar; *v*/*i.* negociar, comerciar (*in* en); *cards*: ser mano; ～ *with p.* tratar a (*or* con); *subject* tratar de; '**deal·er** ✝ comerciante *m* (*in* en); *cards*: mano *f*; *sharp* ～ taimado *m*; '**deal·ing** (*mst* ～*s pl.*) comercio *m*, trato *m*; relaciones *f*/*pl.*

dealt [delt] *pret. a. p.p. of deal*[2].

dean [diːn] *eccl.* deán *m*; *univ. etc.* decano *m*; '**dean·er·y** deanato *m*; (*residence*) decanato *m*.

dear [diə] **1.** □ *p. etc.* querido; *purchase* caro, costoso; *shop etc.* carero; *fig. pay* ～*ly for* pagar caro *acc.*; **2.** querido (a *f*) *m*; persona *f* simpática; *my* ～! ¡querido (a) mío (a)!, ¡hombre!; **3.** F *oh* ～!, ～ *me!* ¡Dios mío!; ¡caramba!; '**dear·ness** cariño *m*; ✝ carestía *f*; **dearth** [dɔːθ] carestía *f*, escasez *f*; **dear·y** ['diəri] F queridito (a *f*) *m*.

death [deθ] muerte *f*; fallecimiento *m*, defunción *f*; *be at* ～*'s door* estar a la muerte; *do* (*put*) *to* ～ dar la muerte a; ～ *penalty* pena *f* de muerte; *tired to* ～ rendido, fatigado; *fig.* harto (*of* de); *to the* ～ a muerte; '～·bed lecho *m* de muerte; '～·blow golpe *m* mortal; '～·less inmortal; '**death·ly** mortal; *fig.* profundo;

'**death-rate** mortalidad *f*; '**death-roll** número *m* de muertos; '**death's-head** calavera *f*; '**death-war·rant** sentencia *f* de muerte.

dé·bâ·cle [dei'baːkl] derrota *f*, caída *f*; fracaso *m*.

de·bar [di'baː] excluir (*from* de); prohibir.

de·base [di'beis] degradar, envilecer; *coinage* adulterar; **de'base-ment** envilecimiento *m*.

de·bat·a·ble [di'beitəbl] □ discutible, contestable; dudoso; **de'bate** 1. debate *m*, discusión *f*; 2. discutir, debatir (*with* con); disputar (*on* de, sobre; *with* con); (*think*) deliberar; **de'bat·er** polemista *m*/*f*; controversista *m*/*f*; *parl. etc.* discutidor (-a *f*) *m*, orador (-a *f*) *m*.

de·bauch [di'bɔːtʃ] 1. libertinaje *m*; 2. corromper; viciar; **deb·au'chee** libertino (a *f*) *m*; **de'bauch·er·y** libertinaje *m*.

de·ben·ture [di'bentʃə] vale *m*, obligación *f*.

de·bil·i·tate [di'biliteit] debilitar; **de'bil·i·ty** debilidad *f*.

deb·it ['debit] 1. debe *m* (*a. ~ side*); (*entry*) cargo *m*; 2. cargar.

de·bouch [di'bautʃ] desembocar.

de·bris ['debriː] escombros *m*/*pl.*, desechos *m*/*pl*.

debt [det] deuda *f*; *deeply in ~* lleno de deudas; *be in ~* tener deudas; *be £5 in ~* deber 5 libras (*to* a); *be in a p.'s ~ fig.* estar agradecido a una p.; *run into ~* contraer deudas, endeudarse; '**debt·or** deudor (-a *f*) *m*.

de·bunk [diː'bʌŋk] F *p.* desenmascarar; desacreditar.

dé·but ['deibuː] estreno *m*, debut *m*; *make one's ~ thea.* estrenarse, debutar; (*in society*) ponerse de largo, presentarse en la sociedad; **dé·bu·tante** [debjutãːnt] muchacha *f* que se presenta en la sociedad.

dec·ade ['dekeid] década *f*; decenio *m*, década *of years*.

de·ca·dence ['dekədəns] decadencia *f*; '**de·ca·dent** decadente.

de·camp [di'kaemp] largarse, marcharse; ✕ decampar, levantar el campo.

de·cant [di'kaent] decantar; **de'cant·er** garrafa *f*.

de·cap·i·tate [di'kæpiteit] degollar; **de·cap·i'ta·tion** degollación *f*.

de·car·bon·ize [di'kaːbənaiz] descarburar, quitar la carbonilla a.

de·cay [di'kei] 1. decadencia *f*, decaimiento *m*; caries *f* *of teeth*; podredumbre *f*; 2. decaer; *esp.* ⚗ *a. fig.* desmoronarse; cariarse; pudrirse.

de·cease [di'siːs] *esp.* ⚖ 1. fallecimiento *m*; 2. fallecer; *the ~d* el (la) difunto (a).

de·ceit [di'siːt] engaño *m*; fraude *m*; **de'ceit·ful** □ engañoso; (*lying*) mentiroso; **de'ceit·ful·ness** duplicidad *f*, bellaquería *f*.

de·ceive [di'siːv] engañar; defraudar; *be ~d freq.* equivocarse; **de'ceiv·er** engañador (-a *f*) *m*, impostor (-a *f*) *m*.

de·cel·er·ate [diː'seləreit] moderarse la marcha.

De·cem·ber [di'sembə] diciembre *m*.

de·cen·cy ['diːsnsi] decencia *f*; '**de·cen·cies** *pl.*: *the ~* las buenas costumbres *f*/*pl.*; (*comforts*) comodidades *f*/*pl*.

de·cen·ni·al [di'senjəl] decenal; **de'cen·ni·um** [~jəm] decenio *m*.

de·cent ['diːsnt] □ decente; F *he's a ~ sort* es (una) buena persona; F *h₂ was ~ to me* estuvo amable conmigo.

de·cen·tral·i·za·tion [diːsentrəlai'zeiʃn] descentralización *f*; **de'cen·tral·ize** descentralizar.

de·cep·tion [di'sepʃn] engaño *m*, fraude *m*, decepción *f*; **de'cep·tive** □ engañoso; ilusorio.

de·cide [di'said] decidir (*to inf. or -se a inf.*); *in favour of* a favor de; [*up*]*on* por); *attitude* determinar; **de'cid·ed** □ decidido, resuelto; indudable; *~ly* indudablemente.

de·cid·u·ous [di'sidjuəs] □ deciduo.

dec·i·mal ['desiml] decimal *adj. a. su. m*; *~ point* punto *m* decimal, coma *f*; **dec·i·mate** ['~meit] diezmar (*a. fig.*); **dec·i'ma·tion** decimación *f*.

de·ci·pher [di'saifə] descifrar (*a. fig.*); **de'ci·pher·a·ble** [~rəbl] descifrable; **de'ci·pher·ment** desciframiento *m*.

de·ci·sion [di'siʒn] decisión *f*; ⚖ resolución *f*, fallo *m*; (*resoluteness*) firmeza *f*; *make* (*or take*) *a ~* tomar una decisión; **de·ci·sive** [di'saisiv] □ decisivo; (*conclusive*) terminante.

deck [dek] 1. ⚓ cubierta *f*; (*omnibus*) planta *f*; *Am. cards*: baraja *f*; 2. *lit.* ataviar, engalanar; '~'**chair** hamaca *f*, tumbona *f*; ...'**deck·er**: *e.g. two-~* de dos plantas.

de·claim [di'kleim] declamar; ~ *against* protestar contra.

dec·la·ma·tion [deklə'meiʃn] declamación *f*; **de·clam·a·to·ry** [di-'klæmətəri] declamatorio.

de·clar·a·ble [di'kleərəbl] declarable; **dec·la·ra·tion** [deklə'reiʃn] declaración *f* (*a.* ⚖); **de'clar·a·to·ry** [~tɔri] declaratorio; **de·clare** [di'kleə] declarar; afirmar; ~ *o.s.* pronunciarse (*in favour of* en favor de); *F well, I ~!* ¡vaya, vaya!; *nothing to ~* nada de pago; **de-'clared** □ manifiesto.

de·clen·sion [di'klenʃn] declinación *f* (*a. gr.*).

de·clin·a·ble [di'klainəbl] declinable; **dec·li·na·tion** [dekli'neiʃn] declinación *f* (*ast. a.* ⚓); *Am.* denegación *f*; **de·cline** [di'klain] 1. *v/t.* rehusar, no aceptar; *gr.* declinar; *v/i.* declinar (*a. fig.*); negarse (*to* a); 2. declinación *f* (*a. fig.*); ♪ *etc.* bajón *m*; ocaso *m of sun*; baja *f of prices*; F tisis *f*; *be on the ~* ir disminuyendo.

de·cliv·i·ty [di'kliviti] declive *m*.

de·clutch ['di:'klʌtʃ] desembragar.

de·code ['di:'koud] descifrar.

dé·colle·té·e [dei'kɔltei] escotado.

de·com·pose [di:kəm'pouz] descomponer(se); **de·com·po·si·tion** [di:kɔmpə'ziʃn] descomposición *f*.

de·con·tam·i·nate [di:kən'tæmineit] descontaminar; **de·con·tam·i'na·tion** descontaminación *f*; ~ *squad* cuadrilla *f* de descontaminación.

de·con·trol ['di:kən'troul] 1. supresión *f* del control; 2. suprimir el control (de).

dec·o·rate ['dekəreit] decorar, adornar; *room* empapelar, pintar; ✕ condecorar; **dec·o'ra·tion** adorno *m*, ornato *m*; ✕ condecoración *f*; *Am.* ♀ *Day* (*30 mayo*) *dia para decorar las tumbas de los soldados muertos en batalla*; **dec·o·ra·tive** ['dekərətiv] □ decorativo; bonito; **dec·o·ra·tor** ['~reitə] adornista *m/f*; (*piʌtor m*) decorador *m*.

dec·o·rous ['dekərəs] □ decoroso; **de·co·rum** [di'kɔ:rəm] decoro *m*.

de·coy [di'kɔi] 1. señuelo *m* (*a. fig.*);

(*a.* **de'coy-duck**) reclamo *m*; trampa *f*; 2. atraer con señuelo.

de·crease 1. ['di:kri:s] disminución *f*; 2. [di:'kri:s] disminuir(se).

de·cree [di'kri:] 1. decreto *m*; 2. decretar.

de·crep·it [di'krepit] decrépito; **de'crep·i·tude** [~tju:d] decrepitud *f*.

de·cry [di'krai] desacreditar; rebajar.

dec·u·ple ['dekjupl] 1. décuplo *adj. a. su. m*; 2. decuplicar.

ded·i·cate ['dedikeit] dedicar; **ded·i'ca·tion** dedicación *f*; dedicatoria *f in book*; **'ded·i·ca·to·ry** dedicatorio.

de·duce [di'dju:s] deducir; **de'duc·i·ble** deducible.

de·duct [di'dʌkt] restar; **de'duc·tion** deducción *f*; ✝ descuento *m*; **de'duc·tive** □ deductivo.

deed [di:d] 1. hecho *m*, acto *m*, hazaña *f*; ⚖ escritura *f*, documento *m*; 2. *Am.* traspasar por escritura.

deem [di:m] juzgar, considerar; (*believe*) creer.

deep [di:p] 1. □ hondo, profundo; ♪ grave, bajo; *colour* oscuro; subido; *p.* insondable, astuto; ~ *in debt* lleno de deudas; ~ *in thought* absorto en la meditación; *fig.* ~ *in s.t.* muy metido en; *F go off the ~ end* montar en cólera; 2. *poet.* piélago *m*; '~'**breath·ing** gimnasia *f* respiratoria; '~'**chest·ed** ancho de pecho; '**deep·en** profundizar(se); *voice* ahuecar; *colour* hacer(se) más oscuro (*or* subido); *sorrow* intensificar(se); **deep-'root·ed** profundamente arraigado; **deep-'seat·ed** con profundas raíces.

deer [diə] ciervo *m*; '~-**stalk·er** cazador *m* de venado; '~-**stalk·ing** caza *f* de venado.

de·face [di'feis] desfigurar, deformar; **de'face·ment** desfiguración *f*, deformación *f*.

de·fal·cate ['di:fælkeit] desfalcar; **de·fal'ca·tion** desfalco *m*; '**de·fal·ca·tor** defraudador (*-a f*) *m*.

def·a·ma·tion [defə'meiʃn] difamación *f*; **de·fam·a·to·ry** [di'fæmətəri] difamatorio; **de·fame** [di-'feim] difamar; mancillar; **de'fam·er** difamador (*-a f*) *m*.

de·fault [di'fɔ:lt] 1. omisión *f*, descuido *m*; falta *f*, incumplimiento *m*; ⚖ rebeldía *f*; *in ~ of* por falta de;

make ～ no comparecer; faltar; **2.** faltar; ⚖ caer en rebeldía; ponerse en mora; ✝ demorar los pagos; **de'fault·er** ⚖ rebelde *m*; ✝ persona *f* que demora los pagos; ⚒ delincuente *m*.

de·feat [di'fi:t] **1.** derrota *f*; **2.** vencer (*a. fig.*); derrotar; *fig. e.g.* hopes frustrar; **de'feat·ism** derrotismo *m*; **de'feat·ist** derrotista *m/f*.

de·fect [di'fekt] defecto *m*; **de'fec·tion** defección *f*, deserción *f*; **de·'fec·tive** □ defectuoso; defectivo (*a. gr.*); *child etc.* anormal; falto (*in* de).

de·fence, Am. de·fense [di'fens] defensa *f* (*a. sport*); **de'fence·less** indefenso.

de·fend [di'fend] defender (*from* de); **de'fen·dant** (*civil*) demandado (a *f*) *m*; (*criminal*) acusado (a *f*) *m*, reo *m*; **de'fend·er** defensor *m*.

de·fen·si·ble [di'fensəbl] defendible; **de'fen·sive 1.** □ defensivo; **2.** defensiva *f*; *be on the* ～ estar a la defensiva.

de·fer[1] [di'fə:] diferir, aplazar; ～red *payment* pago *m* a plazos; ～red *annuity* cuota *f* de pensión.

de·fer[2] [～] deferir (*to* a); **defer·ence** ['defərəns] deferencia *f*; *in* ～ *to, out of* ～ *to* obedeciendo a, teniendo respeto a; **def·er·en·tial** [～'renʃl] □ deferente.

de·fer·ment [di'fə:mənt] aplazamiento *m*; prórroga *f* (*a.* ⚒).

de·fi·ance [di'faiəns] desafío *m*; oposición *f* terca; *bid* ～ *to* desafiar; *in* ～ *of* a despecho de, con infracción de; **de'fi·ant** □ desafiador; provocador.

de·fi·cien·cy [di'fiʃənsi] deficiencia *f*, carencia *f*; ～ *disease* mal *m* carencial; **de'fi·cient** insuficiente; incompleto; deficiente; *be* ～ *in* carecer de.

def·i·cit ['defisit] déficit *m*.

de·fi·er [di'faiə] desafiador (-a *f*) *m*.

de·file[1] [di'fail] **1.** desfiladero *m*; **2.** ⚒ desfilar.

de·file[2] [～] manchar, ensuciar (*a. fig.*); profanar, contaminar; **de·file·ment** profanación *f*, contaminación *f*.

de·fin·a·ble [di'fainəbl] definible; **de'fine** definir, delimitar, determinar; **def·i·nite** ['definit] □ definido (*a. gr.*); *statement etc.* categó-

rico; distinto, preciso; *quite* ～ indudable; **def·i·ni·tion** definición *f*; claridad *f*; *by* ～ por definición; **de·'fin·i·tive** □ definitivo; categórico; ～*ly* en definitiva.

de·flate [di'fleit] desinflar; ✝ deflacionar; **de'fla·tion** desinflación *f*; ✝ deflación *f*; **de'fla·tion·a·ry** deflacionista.

de·flect [di'flekt] desviar (*a. fig.*; *from* de); **de'flec·tion**, *mst* de**flex·ion** [di'flekʃən] desviación *f*.

de·flow·er [di:'flauə] desflorar; *fig.* despojar.

de·form [di'fɔ:m] deformar; ～ed deforme, mutilado; **de·for'ma·tion** deformación *f*; **de'form·i·ty** deformidad *f*.

de·fraud [di'frɔ:d] defraudar (*of* de).

de·fray [di'frei] *costs* sufragar, costear.

de·freez·er [di:'fri:zə] anticongelante *m*.

de·frost·er [di:'frɔstə] desescarchador *m*.

deft [deft] □ diestro (*at* en); *touch* ligero.

de·funct [di'fʌŋkt] **1.** difunto; *fig.* muerto, inexistente; **2.** *the* ～ el (la) difunto (a).

de·fy [di'fai] desafiar (*a. fig.*); oponerse a.

de·gen·er·a·cy [di'dʒenərəsi] depravación *f*; **de'gen·er·ate 1.** [～rit] □ degenerado *adj. a. su. m* (a *f*); **2.** [～reit] degenerar (*into* en); **de·gen·er·a·tion** [～'reiʃn] degeneración *f*; **de'gen·er·a·tive** degenerativo.

deg·ra·da·tion [degrə'deiʃn] degradación *f*, envilecimiento *m*; **de·grade** [di'greid] degradar, envilecer; ～ *o.s. freq.* aplebeyarse.

de·gree [di'gri:] grado *m* (Å *etc.*); *univ.* título *m*, licenciatura *f*; ✝ grada *f*; rango *m*, condición *f* social; *by* ～*s* poco a poco; *in no* ～ de ninguna manera; *in some* ～ hasta cierto punto; en cierto modo; *to the highest* ～ en sumo grado; *to a* ～ un tanto; *take a* ～ recibir un título; graduarse, licenciarse (*in* en).

de·hy·drat·ed [di:'haidreitid] deshidratado; **de·hy·dra·tion** deshidratación *f*.

de·ice ['di:'ais] ✈ deshelar.

de·i·fi·ca·tion [di:ifi'keiʃn] deificación *f*; **de·i·fy** ['di:ifai] deificar.

deign [dein]: ~ to dignarse *inf.*

de·ism ['di:izm] deísmo *m*; **'de·ist** deista *m/f*; **de'is·tic, de'is·ti·cal** □ deísta.

de·i·ty ['di:iti] deidad *f*; the ♀ Dios.

de·ject [di'dʒekt] abatir, desanimar; **de'ject·ed** □ abatido; **de'ject·ed·ness, de'jec·tion** abatimiento *m*.

de·lay [di'lei] **1.** tardanza *f*, retraso *m*; dilación *f*; **2.** *v/i.* tardar (*in* en); *v/t.* diferir, dilatar; ~*ed action attr.* de acción retardada.

de·le ['di:li:] *typ.* **1.** dele *m*; **2.** borrar, quitar.

de·lec·ta·ble [di'lektəbl] □ *co. or lit.* deleitable; **de·lec·ta·tion** [di:lek'teiʃn] delectación *f*.

del·e·ga·cy ['deligəsi] delegación *f*; **del·e·gate 1.** ['~geit] delegar (*to* a); *p.* diputar; **2.** ['~git] delegado (a *f*) *m*; diputado (a *f*) *m*; **del·e·ga·tion** [~'geiʃn] delegación *f* (*a. body*); diputación *f*.

de·lete [di:'li:t] tachar, suprimir, borrar; **del·e·te·ri·ous** [deli'tiəriəs] □ deletéreo; **de·le·tion** [di:'li:ʃn] supresión *f*.

delf(t) [delf(t)] porcelana *f* de Delft.

de·lib·er·ate 1. [di'libəreit] *v/t. s.t.* meditar; *v/i.* deliberar (*on* sobre); **2.** [~rit] □ premeditado, reflexionado; (*cautious*) cauto, circunspecto; *movement etc.* lento, espacioso; ~*ly freq.* de propósito, con premeditación; **de'lib·er·ate·ness** premeditación *f*; **de·lib·er·a·tion** [~'reiʃn] deliberación *f*; premeditación *f*; **de'lib·er·a·tive** [~reitiv] □ deliberativo.

del·i·ca·cy ['delikəsi] delicadeza *f*; (*titbit*) golosina *f*; **del·i·cate** ['~kit] □ delicado; *food* exquisito; *action* considerado; **del·i·ca·tes·sen** [deli-kə'tesn] tienda *f* que se especializa en manjares exquisitos.

de·li·cious [di'liʃəs] □ delicioso, exquisito.

de·light [di'lait] **1.** deleite *m*, delicia *f*; *a* ~ *to the eye* un gozo para la retina; *take* ~ *in* deleitarse en *inf.*, con *su.*; **2.** deleitarse (*in* en, con); *be* ~*ed to* tener mucho gusto en; **de'light·ful** [~ful] □ delicioso, precioso; **de'light·ful·ness** encanto *m*, delicia *f*.

de·lim·it [di:'limit], **de'lim·i·tate** [~teit] delimitar; **de·lim·i'ta·tion** delimitación *f*.

de·lin·e·ate [di'linieit] delinear; bosquejar (*a. fig.*); **de·lin·e·a·tion** delineación *f*; bosquejo *m*; **de'lin·e·a·tor** delineador (-a *f*) *m*; ⊕ delineante *m*.

de·lin·quen·cy [di'liŋkwənsi] ♂ɫ delincuencia *f*; (*guilt*) culpa *f*; (*omission*) descuido *m*; **de'lin·quent** delincuente *adj. a. su. m/f*; culpable *adj. a. su. m/f*.

de·lir·i·ous [di'liriəs] □ delirante; **de'lir·i·ous·ness** delirio *m*; **de'lir·i·um** [~əm] delirio *m*; ~ *tremens* [~ 'tri:menz] delirium *m* tremens.

de·liv·er [di'livə] librar (*from* de); (*a.* ~ *up*, ~ *over*) entregar; ✂ distribuir, repartir; *speech* pronunciar; *blow* asestar; ♂ *woman* partear; *message* comunicar; *ball* lanzar; *be* ~*ed of* parir *acc.*; **de'liv·er·ance** liberación *f*, rescate *m*; **de'liv·er·y** liberación *f*, salvación *f*; ✂ repartido *m*; ♂ parto *m*, alumbramiento *m*; entrega *f of goods, writ*; modo *m* de expresarse; *attr.* de entrega; de reparto; **de'liv·er·y 'serv·ice** servicio *m* a domicilio.

dell [del] vallecito *m*.

de·louse [di:'laus] despiojar, espulgar.

del·ta ['deltə] delta *f*; *geog.* delta *m*.

de·lude [di'lu:d] engañar, deludir (*into* para que); *easily* ~*d* iluso.

del·uge ['delju:dʒ] **1.** diluvio *m*; **2.** inundar (*with* de).

de·lu·sion [di'lu:ʒn] engaño *m*; ilusión *f*, alucinación *f*; **de'lu·sive** [~siv] □, **de'lu·so·ry** [~səri] delusorio, ilusorio; decepcionante.

de luxe [di'lʌks] de lujo.

delve [delv] cavar (*into* en; *a. fig.*).

dem·a·gog·ic, dem·a·gog·i·cal [demə'gɔgik(l)] □ demagógico; **dem·a·gogue** ['~gɔg] demagogo *m*; **'dem·a·gog·y** demagogia *f*.

de·mand [di'mɑ:nd] **1.** demanda *f* (*a.* ✝, ♂ɫ); exigencia *f*; *on* ~ a solicitud; *be in* ~ tener demanda; *fig.* ser solicitado; ~ *note* apremio *m* de pago; **2.** demandar; exigir (*of* a), solicitar perentoriamente (*of* de); **de'mand·ing** exigente.

de·mar·cate ['di:mɑ:keit] demarcar; **de·mar'ca·tion** (*line of* línea *f* de) demarcación *f*.

de·mean[1] [di'mi:n] (*mst* ~ *o.s.*) degradar(se).

de·mean[2] [~]: ~ *o.s.* comportarse;

de·'mean·o(u)r [ˌ‿ə] porte *m*, conducta *f*.

de·ment·ed [di'mentid] ☐ demente.

de·mer·it [di:'merit] demérito *m*.

de·mesne [di'mein] heredad *f*, hacienda *f*; tierras *f/pl.* solariegas (*freq.* ‿ *land*).

dem·i... ['demi] medio, semi...

dem·i·john ['demidʒɔn] damajuana *f*.

de·mil·i·ta·ri·za·tion [di:militərai-'zeiʃn] desmilitarización *f*; de'mil·i·ta·rize desmilitarizar.

de·mise [di'maiz] **1.** ꜯ transferencia *f*; traspaso *m of title or estate*; fallecimiento *m of p.*; **2.** transferir, traspasar.

de·mob [di:'mɔb] F = demobilize; de·mo·bi·li·za·tion ['di:moubilai-'zeiʃn] desmovilización *f*; de'mo·bi·lize desmovilizar.

de·moc·ra·cy [di'mɔkrəsi] democracia *f*; dem·o·crat ['deməkræt] demócrata *m/f*; dem·o'crat·ic, dem·o'crat·i·cal ☐ democrático; de·moc·ra·tize [di'mɔkrətaiz] democratizar.

de·mol·ish [di'mɔliʃ] demoler, derribar; *argument etc.* destruir; F zamparse; dem·o·li·tion [demə-'liʃn] demolición *f*, derribo *m*.

de·mon ['di:mən] demonio *m*; de·mo·ni·ac [di:'mouniæk] **1.** (*a.* de·mo·ni·a·cal [di:mə'naiəkl] ☐) demoníaco; **2.** energúmeno (a *f*) *m*; de·mon·ic [di:'mɔnik] demoníaco.

de·mon·stra·ble ['demənstrəbl] ☐ demostrable; dem·on·strate ['‿streit] demostrar; *pol.* hacer una manifestación; dem·on'stra·tion demostración *f*; *pol.* manifestación *f*; de·mon·stra·tive [di'mɔnstrə-tiv] **1.** ☐ demostrativo (*a. gr.*); *p.* exagerado, exaltado; **2.** demostrativo *m*; dem·on·stra·tor ['demənstreitə] demostrador (-a *f*) *m*; *univ.* ayudante *m*, mozo *m* de laboratorio; *pol.* manifestante *m*.

de·mor·al·i·za·tion [dimɔrəlai-'zeiʃn] desmoralización *f*; de'mor·al·ize desmoralizar; de'mor·al·iz·ing desmoralizador.

de·mote [di:'mout] degradar; de·'mo·tion degradación *f*.

de·mur [di'mə:] **1.** reparo *m*, pega *f*; **2.** poner pegas, objetar.

de·mure [di'mjuə] ☐ grave, solemne; (*modest*) recatado; *b. s.* gaz-

moño; de'mure·ness gazmoñería *f*; recato *m*.

de·mur·rage [di'mʌridʒ] estadía *f*; de'mur·rer objeción *f*; ꜯ excepción *f*.

de·my [di'mai] papel *m* marquilla.

den [den] (*animal's, robber's*) madriguera *f*; F (*room*) cuchitril *m*; F cuarto *m* de estudio; *opium* ‿ fumadero *m* de opio.

de·na·tion·al·ize [di:'næʃnəlaiz] desnacionalizar.

de·ni·a·ble [di'naiəbl] negable; de·'ni·al negación *f*; (*refusal*) denegación *f*; (*a. self-*‿) abnegación *f*; de'ni·er negador (-a *f*) *m*.

den·i·grate ['di:nigreit] denigrar.

den·im ['denim] (*freq.* ‿*s pl.*) dril *m* de algodón.

den·i·zen ['denizn] habitante *m/f*; extranjero (a *f*) *m* naturalizado (a).

de·nom·i·nate [di'nɔmineit] denominar; de·nom·i'na·tion denominación *f*; categoría *f*; *eccl.* secta *f*, confesión *f*; valor *m of coin etc.*; de·nom·i'na·tion·al *mst eccl.* sectario; de·nom·i·na·tive [‿nətiv] denominativo (*a. gr.*); de'nom·i·na·tor [‿neitə] denominador *m*; *common* ‿ denominador *m* común.

de·no·ta·tion [di:nou'teiʃn] denotación *f*; designación *f*; significación *f*; de'note denotar; señalar, designar; significar.

de·nounce [di'nauns] denunciar; censurar, reprender; de'nounce·ment denuncia *f*; censura *f*, reprensión *f*.

dense [dens] ☐ denso, compacto; *undergrowth etc.* tupido; F duro de mollera; 'dense·ness *mst* estupidez *f*; 'den·si·ty densidad *f* (*a. phys.*).

dent [dent] **1.** abolladura *f*; mella *f in edge*; **2.** abollar(se); mellar.

den·tal ['dentl] **1.** dental; odontológico; ‿ *science* odontología *f*; **2.** ꝺ dental *f*; den·tate ['‿teit] dentado; den·ti·frice ['‿tifris] dentífrico *m*; 'den·tist dentista *m*, odontólogo *m*; 'den·tist·ry odontología *f*; den·ture ['‿tʃə] dentadura *f*; (*esp.* ‿*s pl.*) dentadura *f* postiza.

de·nu·da·tion [di:nju'deiʃn] denudación *f*; despojo *m*; de'nude denudar; despojar (*of* de).

de·nun·ci·a·tion [dinʌnsi'eiʃn] denuncia *f* (*a.* ꜯ), denunciación *f*;

de·nun·ci·a·tor denunciador (-a *f*) *m*; 🜊 denunciante *m*/*f*.

de·ny [di'nai] negar; *request etc.* denegar; *report* desmentir; ~ o.s. abnegarse; ~ o.s. *th.* negarse, no permitirse.

de·o·dor·ize [di:'oudəraiz] desodorizar; **de'o·dor·ant** desodorante *m*.

de·part [di'pɑ:t] *v/i.* partir, marcharse; (*train etc.*) salir, tener su salida; ~ *from truth etc.* apartarse de, desviarse de; *the* ~*ed* el (la) difunto (a); *v/t.*: ~ *this life* partir de esta vida; **de'part·ment** departamento *m*; sección *f,* ramo *m*; *Am.* ministerio *m*; ~ *store* almacenes *m*/*pl.*; **de·part'men·tal** □ departamental; **de'par·ture** [~tʃə] partida *f*, salida *f*; *fig.* desviación *f*; *attr.* 🚗 *etc.* de salida; *new* ~ un curso (*or* rumbo) nuevo.

de·pend [di'pend] 🜊 pender, colgar; ~ (*up*)*on* depender de; *p. etc.* contar con, confiar en; F *it* ~*s* eso depende; **de'pend·a·ble** □ *p.* formal, confiable; seguro; **de'pend·ant** familiar *m*/*f* dependiente; **de'pend·ence** dependencia *f* (*on* de); confianza *f* (*on* en); apoyo *m* (*on* sobre); **de'pend·en·cy** *mst* posesión *f*, colonia *f*; **de'pend·ent** **1.** □ dependiente (*on* de); pendiente (*on* de); *gr.* subordinado; **2.** *v. dependant.*

de·pict [di'pikt] representar, describir; *paint.* pintar, dibujar.

de·pil·a·to·ry [de'pilətəri] depilatorio *adj. a. su. m.*

de·plete [di'pli:t] agotar; *stock etc.* mermar; 🜍 depauperar; **de'ple·tion** agotamiento *m*; 🜍 depauperación *f*.

de·plor·a·ble [di'plɔ:rəbl] □ deplorable; **de·plore** [di'plɔ:] deplorar.

de·ploy [di'plɔi] ✗ desplegar; *fig.* organizar; **de'ploy·ment** despliegue *m*.

de·po·nent [di'pounənt] **1.** *gr.* deponente; **2.** 🜊 deponente *m*.

de·pop·u·late [di:'pɔpjuleit] despoblar; **'de·pop·u'la·tion** despoblación *f*.

de·port [di'pɔ:t] deportar; ~ o.s. comportarse; **de·por'ta·tion** deportacion *f*; **de·port·ee** [di:pɔ:'ti:] deportado (a *f*) *m*; **de'port·ment** porte *m*, continente *m*; conducta *f*.

de·pose [di'pouz] deponer (*a.* 🜊).

de·pos·it [di'pɔzit] **1.** depósito *m* (*a.* ♰); *geol.* yacimiento *m*; ✝ señal *f*; (*house etc.*) desembolso *m* inicial; 🜍 poso *m*; **2.** depositar (*with* en); ✝ dar para señal; 🜍 sedimentar; **de'pos·i·ta·ry** (*p.*) depositario (a *f*) *m*; **dep·o·si·tion** [depə'ziʃn] deposición *f* (*a.* 🜊); *eccl., paint.* descendimiento *m* (de Cristo); **de·pos·i·tor** [di'pɔzitə] depositador (-a *f*) *m*; ✝ cuentacorrentista *m*/*f*, imponente *m*; **de'pos·i·to·ry** depositaría *f*, almacén *m*; *fig.* filón *m*.

de·pot ['depou] depósito *m*, almacén *m*; *Am.* 🚂 estación *f*.

dep·ra·va·tion [deprə'veiʃn] depravación *f*, perversión *f*; **de·prave** [di'preiv] depravar; **de'praved** depravado; **de·prav·i·ty** [di'prævviti] depravación *f*, estragamiento *m*.

'dep·re·cate ['deprikeit] desaprobar, lamentar; **dep·re·ca·tory** ['~təri] de desaprobación.

de·pre·ci·ate [di'pri:ʃieit] depreciar(se); desestimar, despreciar; **de·pre·ci·a·tion** depreciación *f*; **de'pre·ci·a·to·ry** [~təri] despectivo.

dep·re·da·tion [depri'deiʃn] depredación *f*; ~*s pl.* estragos *m*/*pl.*; **'dep·re·da·tor** depredador *m*.

de·press [di'pres] deprimir (*a. fig.*); (*dispirit*) desalentar, desanimar; *price* hacer bajar; ~*ed area* zona *f* deprimida, abatido; **de'press·ing** □ deprimente; triste; **de·pres·sion** [di'preʃn] depresión *f* (*a.* ✈, ♰); ✝ flojedad *f*; crisis *f* económica; *meteor.* depresión *f*, borrasca *f*; *geog.* hondonada *f*.

dep·ri·va·tion [depri'veiʃn] privación *f*; *a great* ~ una gran pérdida; **de·prive** [di'praiv] privar (*of* de).

depth [depθ] profundidad *f* (*a. fig.*); fondo *m* of building; ~ *charge* carga *f* de profundidad; *in the* ~ *of* en lo más recio de, en pleno ...; *be out of one's* ~ cubrirle a uno (el agua); *fig. get out of one's* ~ meterse en honduras; *the* ~ *s pl.* ♰ el abismo, el piélago.

dep·u·ta·tion [depju'teiʃn] diputación *f*; **de·pute** [di'pju:t] diputar; **dep·u·tize** ['depjutaiz] *Am.* diputar; ~ *for s.o.* sustituir a; **'dep·u·ty** **1.** diputado *m* (*a. pol.*); sustituto *m*, suplente *m*; **2.** *attr.* teniente, suplente.

de·rail [di'reil] (hacer) descarrilar; **de'rail·ment** descarrilamiento *m*.

de·range [di'reindʒ] desarreglar, descomponer; *p.* volver loco; **de-'range·ment** desarreglo *m*, descompostura *f*; ♣ trastorno *m* mental. [impuestos sobre.]

de·rate [di:'reit] *property* reducir los]

Der·by ['dɑːbi] *sport*: derby *m*; **'der·by** *Am.* (*hat*) hongo *m*.

der·e·lict ['derilikt] 1. abandonado; *Am.* negligente; 2. *esp.* ⚓ derrelicto *m*; *Am.* pelafustán (-a *f*) *m*; **der·e·lic·tion** [deri'likʃn] abandono *m*; ~ *of duty* negligencia *f* (de sus deberes).

de·ride [di'raid] ridiculizar, mofarse de.

de·ri·sion [di'riʒn] mofa *f*, befa *f*; **de·ri·sive** [di'raisiv] □ mofador; **de'ri·so·ry** [~səri] mofador; *quantity etc.* irrisorio, ridículo.

de·riv·a·ble [di'raivəbl] derivable; deducible; **der·i·va·tion** [deri-'veiʃn] derivación *f*; **de·riv·a·tive** [di'rivətiv] 1. □ derivativo, derivado (*a. gr.*); 2. derivativo *m* (*a. gr.*, ♣); **de·rive** [di'raiv] derivar(se) (*from* de); *profit* sacar (*from* de); *be* ~*d from* provenir de.

der·ma·tol·o·gist [dəːmə'tɔlədʒist] dermatólogo *m*; **der·ma'tol·o·gy** dermatología *f*.

der·o·gate ['derəgeit] detraer (*from* de); *b.s.* desmerecerse; **der·o'ga·tion** menosprecio *m*; **de·rog·a·to·ry** [di'rɔgətəri] □ despreciativo, despectivo.

der·rick ['derik] grúa *f*; (*oil-*) torre *f* de perforación, derrick *m*.

des·cant [dis'kænt] *fig.* discantar (*upon* sobre).

de·scend [di'send] descender, bajar (*from* de); ~ (*up*)*on* caer sobre; *fig.* ~ *to* rebajarse a; ~ (*or be* ~*ed*) *from* descender de; **de'scend·ant** descendiente *m/f*.

de·scent [di'sent] descendimiento *m* (*a. eccl.*); (*fall*) descenso *m* (*a. fig.*); (*origin*) descendencia *f* (*from* de); ♣♣ herencia *f*; *geog.* declive *m*; *esp.* ⚓ invasión *f*.

de·scrib·a·ble [dis'kraibəbl] descriptible; **de'scribe** describir (*a. A*); ~ *as* calificar de.

de·scrip·tion [dis'kripʃn] descripción *f*; clase *f*. género *m*; **de'scrip·tive** □ descriptivo; *style* pintoresco.

de·scry [dis'krai] divisar, columbrar.

des·e·crate ['desikreit] profanar; **des·e'cra·tion** profanación *f*.

des·ert¹ 1. ['dezət] a) desierto; inhabitado; b) desierto *m*, yermo *m*; 2. [di'zəːt] *v/t.* ✗ desertar; abandonar, desamparar; *v/i.* ✗, ♣♣ desertar (*from* de; *to* a); ♣♣ abandonar el domicilio conyugal.

de·sert² [di'zəːt] (*a.* ~*s pl.*) merecimiento *m*, mérito *m*; *get one's* ~*s* llevar su merecido.

de·sert·er [di'zəːtə] desertor *m*; **de'ser·tion** deserción *f*, abandono *m*.

de·serve [di'zəːv] merecer (*of* de, para con); *he got what he* ~*d* llevó su merecido; **de'serv·ed·ly** [~vidli] merecidamente; **de'serv·ing** □ merecedor (*of* de); digno (*of* de).

des·ha·bille ['dezæbiːl] desabillé *m*.

des·ic·cate ['desikeit] desecar; **des·ic'ca·tion** desecación *f*.

de·sid·er·a·tum [di'sidə'reitəm] desiderátum *m*.

de·sign [di'zain] 1. ⊕ *etc.* diseño *m*, traza *f*; (*pattern*) dibujo *m*; (*sketch*) bosquejo *m*; (*purpose*) designio *m*, intención *f*; *by* ~ intencionalmente; ⚠ *modern* ~ estilo *m* moderno, moderno diseño *m*; *F have* ~*s on* tener sus proyectos sobre; 2. diseñar, trazar; dibujar; (*purpose*) idear, proyectar; *be* ~*ed to* estar proyectado para; *well* (*badly*) ~*ed house* bien (mal) distribuido.

des·ig·nate 1. ['dezigneit] designar; nombrar; (*point to*) señalar; 2. ['~nit] designado, nombrado; **des·ig'na·tion** nombramiento *m*; (*title etc.*) denominación *f*.

de·sign·ed·ly [di'zainidli] adrede; **de'sign·er** dibujante *m*; diseñador *m*; **de'sign·ing** intrigante.

de·sir·a·ble [di'zaiərəbl] □ deseable, apetecible; **de·sire** [di'zaiə] 1. deseo *m* (*for*, *to* de); 2. desear (*to inf.*; *a p. to* que una p. *subj.*); **de·sir·ous** [di'zaiərəs] □ deseoso (*of* de; *to inf.* de *inf.*; *that* de que *subj.*).

de·sist [di'zist] desistir (*from* de).

desk [desk] pupitre *m*; (*a. writing* ~) escritorio *m*; mesa *f*.

des·o·late 1. ['desəleit] asolar; *p.* entristecer; 2. ['~lit] □ desierto, solitario; despoblado; (*in ruins*)

arruinado; (*forlorn*) lúgubre, triste;
des·o'la·tion soledad *f*; desolación
f; (*act*) arrasamiento *m*.
de·spair [dis'peə] **1.** desesperación *f*;
2. desesperar (*of* de); **de·spair·ing**
[dis'peəriŋ] □ desesperado.
des·patch = *dispatch*.
des·per·a·do [despə'rɑ:dou] bandido *m*; forajido *m*.
des·per·ate ['despərit] □ desesperado; *situation etc.* grave; *fight*
encarnizado; (*bold*) temerario; **des·
per·a·tion** [despə'reiʃn] desesperación *f*; *in* ~ desesperado.
des·pi·ca·ble ['despikəbl] □ despreciable; vil, ruin.
de·spise [dis'paiz] despreciar; desdeñar. [de.\
de·spite [dis'pait] *prp.* a despecho/
de·spoil [dis'pɔil] despojar (*of* de);
de'spoil·ment despojo *m*.
de·spond [dis'pɔnd] desalentarse,
desanimarse; desesperar (*of* de);
de'spond·en·cy [‿dənsi] desánimo
m; desesperanza *f*; **de'spond·ent**
□ abatido, alicaído; *be* ~ andar de
capa caída.
des·pot ['despɔt] déspota *m*; **des·
'pot·ic** □ despótico; **des·pot·ism**
['‿pətizm] despotismo *m*.
des·sert [di'zə:t] postre *m*; ~*-spoon*
cuchara *f* de postre.
des·ti·na·tion [desti'neiʃn] destino
m (*a.* 🚂), paradero *m*; **des·tine**
['‿tin] destinar (*to, for* a, para);
be ~*d to* estar destinado a; **'des·
ti·ny** destino *m*, hado *m*.
des·ti·tute ['destitju:t] indigente;
desprovisto (*of* de); **des·ti'tu·tion**
indigencia *f*.
de·stroy [dis'trɔi] destruir (*a.*
fig.); matar; (*annihilate*) aniquilar;
de'stroy·er destructor *m* (*a.* ⚓).
de·struct·i·bil·i·ty [distrʌkti'biliti]
destructibilidad *f*; **de'struct·i·ble**
[‿əbl] destructible; **de'struc·tion**
destrucción *f* (*a. fig.*); ⚔ *etc.* estragos *m/pl.*; **de'struc·tive** □ destructivo (*a. fig.*); *child* revoltoso;
nocivo (*of* a); **de'struc·tive·ness**
espíritu *m* de destrucción; **de·
'struc·tor** incinerador *m* (de basuras).
des·ue·tude [di'sju:itju:d] desuso *m*.
des·ul·to·ri·ness ['desəltərinis] calidad *f* de inconexo (*or* deshilvanado);
'des·ul·to·ry □ inconexo, deshilvanado; intermitente.

de·tach [di'tætʃ] separar, desprender; ✕ destacar; **de'tach·a·ble**
separable, desmontable; suelto;
de'tached separado, desprendido;
fig. imparcial, objetivo; ~ *house*
hotel *m*; *become* ~ desprenderse,
separarse; **de'tach·ment** separación *f*, desprendimiento *m*; *fig.*
objetividad *f* (*of mind* de ánimo);
✕ destacamento *m*.
de·tail 1. ['di:teil] detalle *m*, pormenor *m*; ✕ destacamento *m*; *in* ~
en detalle; *go into* ~ menudear;
2. [di'teil] detallar; ✕ destacar;
'de·tailed *account etc.* detallado,
detenido.
de·tain [di'tein] detener (*a.* ⚖);
(*delay*) retener; **de·tain·ee** [‿ni:]
detenido *m*; **de'tain·er** ⚖ detención *f*.
de·tect [di'tekt] descubrir, percibir;
de'tect·a·ble perceptible; **de'tec·
tion** descubrimiento *m*; **de'tec·
tive** detective *m*; *attr.* policíaco,
de detective; **de'tec·tor** descubridor *m*; *radio a.* ⚡: detector *m*.
dé·tente [dei'tɑ̃:nt] *pol.* détente *f*.
de·ten·tion [di'tenʃn] detención *f*,
arresto *m*; *unlawful* ~ detención *f*
ilegal.
de·ter [di'tə:] disuadir (*from* de);
impedir (*from que subj.*).
de·ter·gent [di'tə:dʒənt] detergente
adj. a. su. m.
de·te·ri·o·rate [di'tiəriəreit] *v/t.*
deteriorar; *v/i.* empeorarse; **de·te·
ri·o'ra·tion** deterioro *m*, empeoramiento *m*.
de·ter·ment [di'tə:mənt] disuasión
f.
de·ter·mi·na·ble [di'tə:minəbl] □
determinable; **de'ter·mi·nant** determinante *adj. a. su. m*; **de'ter·
mi·nate** [‿nit] □ determinado; definitivo, distinto; **de·ter·mi'na·
tion** determinación *f*; (*resolve*)
empeño *m*; **de'ter·mi·na·tive**
[‿neitiv] determinativo (*a. gr.*);
de'ter·mine [‿min] determinar (*to*
inf.); determinarse (*to* a); ocasionar,
dar motivo a; ~ *on* optar por; resolverse a; **de'ter·mined** □ resuelto;
(*stubborn*) porfiado.
de·ter·rent [di'terənt] **1.** disuasivo;
2. lo que disuade; impedimento *m*;
(*threat*) amenaza *f*.
de·test [di'test] detestar; **de'test·
a·ble** □ detestable; **de·tes·ta·tion**

[di:tes'teiʃn] detestación f; persona f detestada; hold in ~ execrar.
de·throne [di'θroun] destronar; **de'throne·ment** destronamiento m.

det·o·nate ['detouneit] (hacer) detonar; **'det·o·nat·ing-cap** cápsula f fulminante; **det·o'na·tion** detonación f; **det·o·na·tor** ['~tə] detonador m, cápsula f fulminante.

de·tour [di'tuə], **dé·tour** ['deituə] desvío m, rodeo m.

de·tract [di'trækt]: ~ from quitar atractivo a; rebajar, quitar mérito a; **de'trac·tive** detractor; **de'trac·tor** calumniador (-a f) m.

de·train [di:'trein] ⚒ (hacer) bajar del tren.

det·ri·ment ['detrimənt] perjuicio m, detrimento m; to the ~ of en perjuicio de; **det·ri·men·tal** [detri'mentl] □ perjudicial (to a, para).

de·tri·tus [di'traitəs] detrito m.

deuce [dju:s] 1. dice: dos m; tennis: a dos; 2. F diantre m, demonio m; what the ~ ...? ¿qué demonios ...?

de·val·u·a·tion [di:vælju'eiʃn] desvalorización f; **de'val·ue** desvalorizar.

dev·as·tate ['devəsteit] devastar; **'dev·as·tat·ing** □ fig. arrollador; **dev·as'ta·tion** devastación f.

de·vel·op [di'veləp] v/t. desarrollar (a. Å), desenvolver; phot. revelar; land urbanizar; ⚒ etc. explotar; v/i. desarrollarse; F (esp. be ~ing) ir, progresar; **de'vel·op·er** phot. revelador m; **de'vel·op·ing** phot. revelado m; **de'vel·op·ment** desarrollo m, desenvolvimiento m; phot. revelado m; (a. urban ~) urbanización f; ⚒ explotación f; fig. (esp. new ~) acontecimiento m nuevo, novedad f; ~ area zona f con tendencia a paro laboral severo.

de·vi·ate ['di:vieit] desviar(se) (from de); **de·vi'a·tion** desviación f (a. compass).

de·vice [di'vais] ⊕ dispositivo m, aparato m; fig. recurso m, ardid m; emblema m; (motto) lema m; nuclear ~ ingenio m nuclear; leave to one's own ~s dejar a uno que haga lo que le dé la gana.

dev·il ['devl] 1. diablo m (a. fig.); F arrojo m, ardor m; ⚖ abogado m principiante; typ. mozo m recadero; plato m picante; the ~! ¡diablos!;

poor ~! ¡pobre diablo!; F like the ~ como el diablo; F talk of the ~! ¡hablando (del ruin) de Roma, por la puerta asoma!; F there'll be the ~ to pay nos sentarán las costuras; F raise the ~ armarla; 2. preparar con mucho picante; Am. vejar; ⚖ ~ for trabajar de abogado para (un principal); **'dev·il·ish** □ diabólico; adv. F extremadamente; **'dev·il-may-'care** F despreocupado; temerario; **'dev·il·ment** maldad f; (mischief) diablura f; **'dev·il·ry** diablura f.

de·vi·ous ['di:viəs] □ apartado, aislado; path tortuoso.

de·vise [di'vaiz] 1. ⚖ legado m; 2. idear, proyectar; hacer proyectos; ⚖ legar; **de·vis·er** [di'vaizə] autor m, inventor m; **de·vi·sor** [devi'zɔ:] ⚖ testador m.

de·vi·tal·ize [di:'vaitəlaiz] debilitar.

de·void [di'vɔid] desprovisto (of de).

dev·o·lu·tion [di:və'lu:ʃn] ⚖ traspaso m; biol. degeneración f; parl. delegación f (de poderes); **de·volve** [di'vɔlv] v/t.: ~ upon transmitir a; transferir a; v/i.: ~ upon, ~ to incumbir a, corresponder a.

de·vote [di'vout] dedicar; ~ o.s. to dedicarse a; **de'vot·ed** □ devoto; dedicado (to a); (letter) your ~ servant suyo afmo.; **dev·o·tee** [devou'ti:] devoto (a f) m; **de·vo·tion** [di'vouʃn] devoción f (to a); (studies etc.) dedicación f (to a); ~s pl. oraciones f/pl.; rezo m; **de'vo·tion·al** □ piadoso, devoto.

de·vour [di'vauə] devorar (a. fig.); F food zamparse; ~ed with consumido de (or por); **de'vour·ing** devorador (a. fig.).

de·vout [di'vaut] □ devoto, piadoso; (earnest) cordial; **de'vout·ness** piedad f.

dew [dju:] 1. rocío m; 2. rociar; **'~-drop** gota f de rocío; **'~-lap** papada f; **'dew-pond** charca f formada por el rocío; **'dew·y** rociado; eyes húmedos; fig. ~ eyed ingenuo.

dex·ter·i·ty [deks'teriti] destreza f; **dex·ter·ous** ['~tərəs] □ diestro (at, in en).

di·a·be·tes [daiə'bi:ti:z] diabetes f; **di·a'be·tic** diabético adj. a. su. m (a f). ['bɔlik(l)] □ diabólico.\
di·a·bol·ic, di·a·bol·i·cal [daiə-/

di·a·dem ['daiədem] diadema *f.*

di·ag·nose ['daiəgnouz] diagnosticar; **di·ag'no·sis** [‿sis], *pl.* **di·ag·'no·ses** [‿si:z] diagnosis *f.*

di·ag·o·nal [dai'ægənl] **1.** ☐ diagonal *adj. a. su. f* (⚓ *a. cloth*).

di·a·gram ['daiəgræm] diagrama *m*, esquema *m*; **di·a·gram·mat·ic** [daiəgrə'mætik] ☐ esquemático.

di·al ['daiəl] **1.** esfera *f*, cuadrante *m*; *teleph.* disco *m*; *radio*: dial *m*; **2.** *teleph.* marcar; ‿*ling* tone tono *m* (de marcar).

di·a·lect ['daiəlekt] dialecto *m*; **di·a'lec·tic, di·a'lec·ti·cal** ☐ dialéctico; **di·a'lec·tics** dialéctica *f.*

di·a·logue, *Am. a.* **di·a·log** ['daiələg] diálogo *m.*

di·am·e·ter [dai'æmitə] diámetro *m*; **di·a·met·ri·cal** [daiə'metrikl] ☐ diametral; ‿*ly opposed* diametralmente opuesto (*to* a).

di·a·mond ['daiəmənd] diamante *m*; (*shape*) losange *m*; *cards*: ‿*s pl.* diamantes *m/pl.*, (*Spanish*) oros *m/pl.*; ‿ *cut* ‿ tal para cual; ‿ *jubilee* sexagésimo aniversario *m*; ‿ *wedding* bodas *f/pl.* de diamante; '‿-'**cut·ter** diamantista *m.*

di·a·pa·son [daiə'peisn] diapasón *m*; (*voice*) extensión *f.*

di·a·per ['daiəpə] **1.** labor *f* con motivos en forma de diamantes; *Am.* pañal *m*; **2.** adornar con motivos en forma de diamantes.

di·aph·a·nous [dai'æfənəs] ☐ diáfano.

di·a·phragm ['daiəfræm] diafragma *m* (*a. teleph.*).

di·ar·rhoe·a [daiə'riə] diarrea *f.*

di·a·rist ['daiərist] diarista *m/f*; **'di·ary** diario *m.* [mia *f.*\

di·a·ther·my ['daiəθə:mi] diater-\

di·a·ton·ic [daiə'tɔnic] diatónico.

di·a·tribe ['daiətraib] diatriba *f.*

dib·ble ['dibl] ⚒ **1.** plantador *m*; **2.** *plants* (*freq.* ‿ *in*) plantar con plantador.

dibs [dibz] *sl.* parné *m.*

dice [dais] [*pl. of* die²] **1.** dados *m/pl.*; (*shape*) cubitos *m/pl.*, cuadritos *m/pl.*; *load the* ‿ cargar los dados; **2.** jugar a los dados; *vegetables* cortar en cuadritos; '‿-**box** cubilete *m.*

dick [dik] *Am. sl.* detective *m*; *take one's* ‿ jurar.

dick·ens ['dikinz] F diantre *m*; *the* ‿ *of a* ... un tremendo ...

dick·er ['dikə] *Am.* regatear.

dick·(e)y ['diki] F (*a.* ‿-*bird*) pájaro *m*; pechera *f* postiza *to wear*; *mot.* asiento *m* del conductor; asiento *m* trasero (descubierto).

dic·ta·phone ['diktəfoun] dictáfono *m.*

dic·tate 1. ['dikteit] mandato *m*; **2.** [dik'teit] dictar; mandar, disponer (*a. fig.*); **dic'ta·tion** dictado *m*; = *dictate*; *take* ‿ escribir al dictado; **dic'ta·tor** dictador *m*; **dic·ta·to·ri·al** [diktə'tɔ:riəl] ☐ dictatorio; *manner etc.* dictatorial, mandón; **dic'ta·tor·ship** [dik'teitəʃip] dictadura *f.*

dic·tion ['dikʃn] dicción *f*, lenguaje *m*; **dic·tion·ar·y** ['dikʃənri] diccionario *m.*

dic·tum ['diktəm], *pl.* **dic·ta** ['‿tə] aforismo *m*; ⚖ *etc.* dictamen *m.*

did [did] *pret. of* do.

di·dac·tic [di'dæktik] ☐ didáctico.

did·dle ['didl] *sl.* estafar; engañar.

didn't ['didnt] = *did not*.

die¹ [dai] [*ger. dying*] morir (*of, from* de); ‿ *away* acabarse gradualmente; desaparecer; ‿ *down* (*fire*) extinguirse, morir; sosegarse (*a. fig.*); ‿ *off* morir, extinguirse; ‿ *out* extinguirse, desaparecer; F ‿ *hard* rendirse de mala gana; F *never say* ‿! ¡ánimo!; *be dying to* morirse por; *be dying for* (*s.t.*) apetecer mucho, morir por (una cosa).

die² [‿] [*pl. dice*] dado *m*; (*pl. dies* [daiz]) ⊕ troquel *m*; matriz *f*, molde *m*; *as straight as a* ‿ más derecho que una vela; *the* ‿ *is cast* la suerte está echada.

die...: '‿-'**cast·ing** ⊕ pieza *f* fundida a troquel; '‿-**hard** intransigente (*a. su. m*); acérrimo, empedernido.

di·e·lec·tric [daii'lektrik] dieléctrico *adj. a. su. m.*

Die·sel en·gine ['di:zl'endʒin] motor *m* Diesel.

die-sink·er ['daisiŋkə] grabador *m* de troqueles.

die-stock ['daistɔk] terraja *f.*

di·et ['daiət] **1.** régimen *m*, dieta *f*; *pol. etc.* dieta *f*; **2.** *v/t.* poner a dieta; *v/i.* estar a dieta (*a. be on a* ‿); '**di·e·tar·y** dietético; **di·e·ti·cian** [daiə'tiʃn] dietético *m.*

dif·fer ['difə] diferenciar, discordar (*with, from* de); diferenciarse (*from* de); **dif·fer·ence** ['difrəns] diferencia *f* (*a.* ⚥); *it makes no ~ lo mismo da*; *split the ~* partir la diferencia; **'dif·fer·ent** □ diferente, distinto (*from* de); **dif·fer·'en·tial** [~ʃl] **1.** diferencial; *~ calculus* cálculo *m* diferencial; **2.** diferencial *f* (⚥ *a. mot.*); **dif·fer·'en·ti·ate** [~ʃieit] *v/t.* distinguir (*between* entre); *v/i.* diferenciarse (*a.* ♀ *etc.*).

dif·fi·cult ['difikəlt] □ difícil; **'dif·fi·cul·ty** dificultad *f*; aprieto *m*; *difficulties pl.* ✝ *etc.* aprietos *m/pl.*, apuros *m/pl.*; *make difficulties* poner reparos (*for s.o.* a).

dif·fi·dence ['difidəns] cortedad *f*, timidez *f*; **'dif·fi·dent** □ tímido, apocado.

dif·fuse 1. [di'fju:z] difundir(se) (*a. fig.*); **2.** [~s] □ difuso (*a. fig.*); **dif'fused** [~zd] *light etc.* difuso; **dif·'fu·sion** [~zən] difusión *f*; **dif·'fu·sive** [~siv] □ difusivo; *speech* difuso.

dig [dig] **1.** [*irr.*] cavar, excavar; F empellar, empujar; ⚔ *~ in* atrincherarse; F *~ into* engolfarse en; *~ up* desenterrar; **2.** empujón *m*; F *fig.* indirecta *f*, zumba *f*; F excavación *f*.

di·gest 1. [di'dʒest] digerir (*a. fig.*); compendiar, resumir; **2.** ['daidʒest] resumen *m*; ⚖ digesto *m*; **di·gest·i·bil·i·ty** [~ə'biliti] digestibilidad *f*; **di'gest·i·ble** digerible; **di'ges·tion** digestión *f*; **di'ges·tive** digestivo.

dig·ger ['digə] cavador *m*; **dig·gings** ['~iŋz] *pl.* F alojamiento *m*, pensión *f*; *Am.* excavaciones *f/pl.*

dig·it ['didʒit] ⚓ dígito *m*; **'dig·it·al** digital.

dig·ni·fied ['dignifaid] grave, solemne; **dig·ni·fy** ['~fai] dignificar.

dig·ni·tar·y ['dignitəri] dignatario *m*; **'dig·ni·ty** dignidad *f*; *beneath one's ~* impropio; *stand (up)on one's ~* indignarse, ponerse en su lugar.

di·gress [dai'gres] hacer una digresión, apartarse del tema; **di·'gres·sion** [~ʃn] digresión *f*.

digs [digz] *pl.* F alojamiento *m*, pensión *f*.

dike [daik] **1.** dique *m* (*a. fig. a. geol.*); **2.** contener con un dique.

di·lap·i·date [di'læpideit] *furniture etc.* desmantelar(se); *house* des-

moronar(se); **di·lap·i·dat·ed** desmoronado; **di·lap·i·da·tion** dilapidación *f of fortune*; desmoronamiento *m*; desmantelamiento *m*.

di·lat·a·bil·i·ty [daileitə'biliti] dilatabilidad *f*; **di'lat·a·ble** dilatable; **dil·a'ta·tion** dilatación *f*; **di'late** dilatar(se) (*upon* sobre); **di'la·tion** dilatación *f*; **dil·a·to·ri·ness** ['dilətərinis] tardanza *f*; **'dil·a·to·ry** □ dilativo; tardón (F).

di·lem·ma [di'lemə] dilema *m* (*a. phls.*), perplejidad *f*, apuro *m*; *be in a ~* estar en un dilema.

dil·et·tan·te, *pl.* **dil·et·tan·ti** [dili'tænti, *pl.* ~'tænti:] diletante *m/f*; aficionado (*a. f*) *m*.

dil·i·gence ['dilidʒəns] diligencia *f*; **'dil·i·gent** □ diligente, trabajador.

dil·ly-dal·ly ['dilidæli] F vacilar; (*loiter*) holgazanear, perder el tiempo.

di·lute [dai'lju:t] **1.** diluir (*a. fig.*); **2.** diluido; **di'lu·tion** dilución *f*.

di·lu·vi·al [dai'lu:viəl] *geol.* diluvial; *hist.* diluviano.

dim [dim] **1.** □ *light* débil, mortecino; *fig.* confuso, indistinto; F atontado (*a. ~-witted*); F *take a ~ view of th.* reprobar; **2.** amortiguar; *mot.* poner a media luz; *fig.* ofuscar, oscurecer; (*glass*) empañarse.

dime [daim] *Am.* moneda de diez centavos (*de un dólar*); *~ novel* novela *f* sensacional. [sión *f.*\

di·men·sion [di'menʃn] dimen-\

di·min·ish [di'miniʃ] disminuir(se);

dim·i·nu·tion [dimi'nju:ʃn] disminución *f*; **di'min·u·tive** [~jutiv] **1.** □ *gr.* diminutivo; (*small*) diminuto, menudo; **2.** *gr.* diminutivo *m*.

dim·ple ['dimpl] **1.** hoyuelo *m*; **2.** formar(se) hoyuelos; (*water*) rizar(se); **'dim·pled** que tiene hoyuelos.

din [din] **1.** estruendo *m* continuo; barahunda *f* (*e.g. of market*); **2.** atolondrar con reiteraciones.

dine [dain] *v/i.* cenar; *~ out* cenar fuera; *v/t.* dar de cenar a; **'din·er** convidado *m*; comensal *m*; *Am.* 🚃 coche-comedor *m*.

ding [diŋ] repicar; F repetir insistentemente; **~-dong** ['~dɔŋ] repique *m*; tintín *m*; *~!* ¡tolón!; *attr. battle* encarnizado.

din·gey, din·ghy ['diŋgi] bote *m*; 🛟 *rubber ~* bote *m* salvavidas.

din·gle ['diŋgl] cañada *f* pequeña.
din·gy ['dindʒi] □ deslustrado, desmejorado; sórdido; *colour* sombrío, tétrico.
din·ing... ['dainiŋ...]: '~**-car** coche-comedor *m*; '~**-hall** comedor *m*; '~**-room** comedor *m*; ~ *suite* comedor *m*; ~ *table* mesa *f* de comer.
dink·ey ['diŋki] *Am.* locomotora *f* de maniobras.
dink·y ['diŋki] F mono; pequeñito.
din·ner ['dinə] cena *f*; comida *f at midday*; banquete *m*; '~**-jack·et** smoking *m*; '~**-pail** *Am.* fiambrera *f*; '~**-par·ty** banquete *m*; '~**-ser·vice** vajilla *f*; '~**-suit** smoking *m*.
dint [dint] **1.** † golpe *m*; *by ~ of* a fuerza de; **2.** abollar.
di·o·ce·san [dai'ɔsisn] diocesano *adj. a. su. m.*; **di·o·cese** ['daiəsis] diócesi(s) *f*.
di·op·tric [dai'ɔptrik] **1.** dióptrico; **2.** ~*s pl.* dióptrica *f*.
di·o·ra·ma [daiə'rɑ:mə] diorama *m*.
dip [dip] **1.** *v/t.* bañar, sumergir (*a.* ⊕); *flag* bajar, saludar con; *pen* mojar; *cloth* teñir; meter, mojar (*into* en); *mot.* poner a media luz; *v/i.* sumergirse; inclinarse hacia abajo, ladearse; (*disappear*) desaparecer, bajar; *geol.* buzar; F ~ *into* meterse en; *book* hojear; **2.** baño *m* (*a. liquid*), inmersión *f*; inclinación *f*, ladeo *m*; depresión *f in road, horizon*; F baño *m* de mar; (*candle*) vela *f* de sebo; *geol.* buzamiento *m*.
diph·the·ri·a [dif'θiəriə] difteria *f*.
diph·thong ['difθɔŋ] diptongo *m*.
di·plo·ma [di'ploumə] diploma *m*; **di·plo·ma·cy** diplomacia *f*; **dip·lo·mat** ['dipləmæt] diplomático *m*; **dip·lo·mat·ic, dip·lo·mat·i·cal** □ diplomático; **dip·lo·mat·ics** *sg.* diplomática *f*; **di·plo·ma·tist** [di'ploumətist] diplomático *m* (*a. fig.*).
dip·per ['dipə] cazo *m*; *orn.* mirlo *m* acuático; *ast. the* ♀ el Carro; '**dip·py** *sl.* loco.
dip·so·ma·ni·a [dipsou'meiniə] dipsomanía *f*; **dip·so·ma·ni·ac** [~niæk] dipsomaníaco (a *f*) *m*.
dire ['daiə] horrendo, calamitoso; extremado.
di·rect [di'rekt] **1.** □ directo (*a. gr.*); sincero, abierto; ~ *current* corriente *f* continua; ✕ ~ *hit* impacto *m* directo; ~ *speech* oración *f* directa; **2.** *adv.* derecho, en derechura; =

~*ly*; **3.** dirigir (*to, towards, at* a, hacia); mandar, ordenar (*to inf.*); **di'rec·tion** dirección *f*; (*order*) orden *f*, instrucción *f*; ~*s for use* modo *m* de empleo; *in the ~ of* en la dirección de; **di'rec·tion·al** *radio*: direccional; ~ *aerial* antena *f* orientable; **di'rec·tion-find·er** radiogoniómetro *m*; **di'rec·tion-find·ing** radiogoniometría *f*; **di'rec·tive** [~tiv] **1.** directivo; **2.** directorio *m*; **di'rect·ly 1.** *adv.* en el acto, en seguida; precisamente; **2.** *cj.* en cuanto; **di'rect·ness** derechura *f*; franqueza *f*.
di·rec·tor [di'rektə] director *m* (*a. film*); † *board of ~s* junta *f*, consejo *m* de administración; **di'rec·to·rate** [~rit] † dirección *f*; directorio *m*; **di'rec·tor·ship** cargo *m* de director; **di'rec·to·ry** directorio *m*; *teleph.* guía *f* telefónica.
dire·ful ['daiəful] □ calamitoso.
dirge [də:dʒ] endecha *f*.
dir·i·gi·ble ['diridʒəbl] dirigible *adj. a. su. m.*
dirk [də:k] puñal *m*.
dirt [də:t] mugre *f*, suciedad *f*; (*mud*) lodo *m*; (*filth, a. fig.*) porquería *f*; obscenidad *f*; F *fling* ~ *at* calumniar; '~**-cheap** F tirado; '~**-track** *sport:* pista *f* de ceniza; '**dirt·y 1.** □ sucio (*a. fig.*); (*stained*) manchado; indecente, obsceno; *v. trick*; **2.** ensuciar; manchar.
dis·a·bil·i·ty [disə'biliti] inhabilidad *f*, impedimento *m*.
dis·a·ble [dis'eibl] inhabilitar, incapacitar (*for, from* para); **dis·a·bled** incapacitado; impedido; mutilado; **dis'a·ble·ment** inhabilitación *f*.
dis·a·buse [disə'bju:z] desengañar (*of* de).
dis·ac·cord [disə'kɔ:d] **1.** desacuerdo *m*; **2.** discordar.
dis·ad·van·tage [disəd'vɑ:ntidʒ] desventaja *f*; *taken at a ~* colocado en una situación violenta; **dis·ad·van·ta·geous** [disædvɑ:n'teidʒəs] □ desventajoso.
dis·af·fect·ed [disə'fektid] desafecto (*towards* hacia); **dis·af'fec·tion** malquerencia *f*; *esp. pol.* descontento *m*.
dis·a·gree [disə'gri:] desavenirse (*with* con); discrepar (*with* de); no estar de acuerdo (*on* sobre); (*quarrel*) altercar; ~ *with* (*food*) sentar

mal a; **dis·a'gree·a·ble** □ desagradable; *p.* displicente, de mal genio; desabrido(*to* con); **dis·a'gree·ment** desacuerdo *m*; discrepancia *f*; disconformidad *f* (*with* con); (*quarrel*) altercado *m*.

dis·al·low ['disə'lau] desaprobar, rechazar; *goal* anular.

dis·ap·pear [disə'piə] desaparecer; **dis·ap'pear·ance** [ˌˈpiərəns] desaparición *f*.

dis·ap·point [disə'pɔint] decepcionar; desilusionar; *hopes* frustrar; **dis·ap'point·ing** □ decepcionante; **dis·ap'point·ment** decepción *f*, desilusión *f*; chasco *m*; ~ *in love* amor *m* fracasado.

dis·ap·pro·ba·tion [disæprou'beiʃn] desaprobación *f*.

dis·ap·prov·al [disə'pru:vl] desaprobación *f*; **dis·ap'prove** desaprobar (*of th. acc.*); ~ *of p.* tener poca simpatía a.

dis·arm [dis'ɑ:m] desarmar; **dis'ar·ma·ment** desarme *m*.

dis·ar·range ['disə'reindʒ] desarreglar, descomponer; **dis·ar'range·ment** desarreglo *m*.

dis·ar·ray [disə'rei] desorden *m*, descompostura *f*.

dis·as·ter [di'zɑ:stə] desastre *m*; **dis'as·trous** □ desastroso, catastrófico.

dis·a·vow ['disə'vau] desconocer; repudiar, renunciar; **dis·a'vow·al** desconocimiento *m*; repudio *m*, renuncia *f*.

dis·band [dis'bænd] *v/t. troops* licenciar; *organization* disolver; *v/i.* desbandarse; **dis'band·ment** licenciamiento *m*.

dis·bar [dis'bɑː] ⚖ excluir del foro.

dis·be·lief ['disbi'li:f] incredulidad *f* (*a. eccl.*); **dis·be·lieve** ['disbi'li:v] descreer (*a. eccl.*); **'dis·be'liev·er** incrédulo (*a f*) *m*; *esp. eccl.* descreído (*a f*) *m*.

dis·bur·den [dis'bə:dn] descargar; ~ *o.s. of* descargarse de.

dis·burse [dis'bə:s] desembolsar; **dis'burse·ment** desembolso *m*.

disc [disk] = *disk*.

dis·card 1. [dis'kɑ:d] (*a. cards*) descartar, echar a un lado; **2.** ['diskɑ:d] descarte *m*.

dis·cern [di'sə:n] discernir, percibir; **dis'cern·i·ble** [ˌəbl] □ perceptible; **dis'cern·ing** □ discernidor,

perspicaz; **dis'cern·ment** discernimiento *m*, perspicacia *f*.

dis·charge [dis'tʃɑ:dʒ] **1.** *v/t.* descargar; *duty* desempeñar; *worker* despedir; *patient* dar de alta; *troops* licenciar; *abscess* sajar; *v/i.* (*river,* ⚡) descargar; *⚡* supurar; **2.** descarga *f*; descargo *m of debt*; desempeño *m*; despedida *f*, desacomodo *m*; ⚔ licenciamiento *m*; *⚡* supuración *f*; **dis'charg·er** ⚡ excitador *m*.

dis·ci·ple [di'saipl] discípulo (a *f*) *m*; **dis'ci·ple·ship** discipulado *m*.

dis·ci·plin·a·ble ['disiplinəbl] disciplinable; castigable; **dis·ci·pli·nar·i·an** [ˌˈnɛəriən] ordenancista *m/f*; **dis·ci'pli·na·ry** [ˌəri] disciplinario; **dis·ci·pline** ['ˌplin] **1.** disciplina *f*; (*punishment*) castigo *m*; **2.** disciplinar; castigar.

dis·claim [dis'kleim] desconocer, negar; ⚖ renunciar; **dis'claim·er** negación *f*; renuncia *f*.

dis·close [dis'klouz] revelar; divulgar, propalar; **dis'clo·sure** [ˌ3ə] revelación *f*; divulgación *f*.

dis·col·o·(u)r·a·tion [diskʌlə'reiʃn] descoloramiento *m*; **dis'col·o·(u)r** descolorar(se).

dis·com·fit [dis'kʌmfit] † derrotar; desconcertar; frustrar; **dis'com·fi·ture** [ˌtʃə] desconcierto *m*; frustración *f*.

dis·com·fort [dis'kʌmfət] **1.** incomodidad *f*; **2.** inquietar.

dis·com·pose [diskəm'pouz] inquietar, desasosegar; (*ruffle*) descomponer; **dis·com'po·sure** [ˌ3ə] inquietud *f*; desconcierto *m*; descompostura *f*.

dis·con·cert [diskən'sə:t] desconcertar; **dis·con'cert·ing** □ desconcertante.

dis·con·nect ['diskə'nekt] ⚡, ⊕ desconectar; desacoplar; **'dis·con·'nect·ed** □ desconectado; *speech* inconexo; **'dis·con'nec·tion** desunión *f*; incoherencia *f*.

dis·con·so·late [dis'kɔnsəlit] □ desconsolado (*a. fig.*).

dis·con·tent ['diskən'tent] **1.** descontento *m*; **2.** descontentar; **'dis·con'tent·ed** □ descontento; **dis·con'tent·ment** descontento *m*.

dis·con·tin·u·ance ['diskən'tinjuəns] (*a.* **dis·con·tin·u'a·tion**) descontinuación *f*; **'dis·con'tin·ue** [ˌnju:] descontinuar; cesar de; *pa-*

per anular el abono de; **'dis·con·'tin·u·ous** ☐ discontinuo (*a.* ⅋).

dis·cord ['diskɔ:d], **dis'cord·ance** discordia *f*; ♪ disonancia *f*; *fig.* sow ~ sembrar cizaña; **dis'cord·ant** ☐ discorde (*a. fig.*); *fig.* disonante.

dis·count 1. ['diskaunt] descuento *m*, rebaja *f*; *at a* ~ al descuento; *fig.* be *at a* ~ no valorarse en su justo precio; **2.** [dis'kaunt] descontar (*a. fig.*); desestimar; *report* considerar exagerado; **dis'count·a·ble** descontable.

dis·coun·te·nance desaprobar; **dis·'coun·te·nanced** desconcertado; (*abashed*) corrido.

dis·cour·age [dis'kʌridʒ] desalentar, desanimar; disuadir (*from* de); desaprobar; **dis'cour·age·ment** desaliento *m*; disuasión *f*; desaprobación *f*.

dis·course 1. ['diskɔ:s] discurso *m*; *hold* ~ *with* platicar con; **2.** [dis-'kɔ:s] discurrir (*about, upon* sobre).

dis·cour·te·ous [dis'kə:tiəs] ☐ descortés; **dis'cour·te·sy** [~tisi] descortesía *f*.

dis·cov·er [dis'kʌvə] descubrir; revelar; manifestar; **dis'cov·er·er** descubridor *m*; **dis'cov·er·y** descubrimiento *m*; revelación *f*; manifestación *f*.

dis·cred·it [dis'kredit] **1.** descrédito *m*; (*doubt*) duda *f*, desconfianza *f*; **2.** desacreditar; (*disbelieve*) descreer; **dis'cred·it·a·ble** ☐ ignominioso, deshonroso.

dis·creet [dis'kri:t] ☐ discreto.

dis·crep·an·cy [dis'krepənsi] discrepancia *f*. [continuo.)

dis·crete [dis'kri:t] ⋔ discreto; dis-)

dis·cre·tion [dis'kreʃn] discreción *f*; *at one's* ~ a discreción; *years* (*or age*) *of* ~ edad *f* de discernimiento; **dis'cre·tion·al** ☐, **dis'cre·tion·ar·y** discrecional.

dis·crim·i·nate [dis'krimineit] distinguir (*between* entre); ~ *against* hacer distinción en perjuicio de; **dis'crim·i·nat·ing** ☐ discernidor, perspicaz; de buen gusto, fino; ♰ *duty* diferencial; parcial; **dis·crim·i·na·tion** discernimiento *m*, discreción *f*; *b.s.* tratamiento *m* parcial (*against* de); *racial* ~ discriminación *f* racial; **dis'crim·i·na·tive** [~neitiv] ☐, **dis'crim·i·na·to·ry** ☐ discernidor; *b.s.* parcial.

dis·cur·sive [dis'kə:siv] ☐ divagador, difuso; *phls.* que raciocina.

dis·cus ['diskəs] *sport*: disco *m*.

dis·cuss [dis'kʌs] hablar de, tratar de; *theme etc.* versar sobre; (*argue*) discutir; **dis'cus·sion** discusión *f*; tratamiento *m*, exposición *f of theme*.

dis·dain [dis'dein] **1.** desdén *m*; **2.** desdeñar; **dis'dain·ful** [~ful] ☐ desdeñoso.

dis·ease [di'zi:z] enfermedad *f*; **dis·'eased** enfermo; morboso; *fig.* depravado.

dis·em·bark ['disim'bɑ:k] desembarcar; **dis·em·bar·ka·tion** [disembɑ:'keiʃn] desembarco *m*.

dis·em·bar·rass ['disim'bærəs] desembarazar, despejar (*of* de); *fig.* librar de turbación.

dis·em·bod·y [disim'bɔdi] *soul* separar del cuerpo; ✗ licenciar.

dis·em·bow·el [disim'bauəl] desentrañar.

dis·en·chant ['disin'tʃɑ:nt] desencantar (*a. fig.*).

dis·en·cum·ber ['disin'kʌmbə] descombrar; desembarazar (*of* de).

dis·en·gage ['disin'geidʒ] ⊕ soltar, desenganchar; *p.*, ♰ *etc.* despeñar(se); ✗ retirar(se); **'dis·en·'gaged** *esp.* libre, desocupado; **'dis·en'gage·ment** *mot.* desembrague *m*; ⊕ desunión *f*; ♰ *etc.* desempeño *m*; ✗ retirada *f*; *pol.* neutralización *f*.

dis·en·tan·gle ['disin'tæŋgl] librar (*from* de); desenredar; *fig.* ~ *o. s. from* desenredarse de; **'dis·en'tan·gle·ment** desenredo *m*.

dis·es·tab·lish ['disis'tæbliʃ] *eccl.* separar del Estado; **'dis·es'tab·lish·ment** *eccl.* separación *f* del Estado.

dis·fa·vo(u)r ['dis'feivə] **1.** disfavor *m*; desaprobación *f*; *fall into* ~ caer en la desgracia; **2.** desfavorecer; *action* desaprobar.

dis·fig·ure [dis'figə] desfigurar; **dis'fig·ure·ment** desfiguración *f*.

dis·fran·chise ['dis'fræntʃaiz] privar de derechos de ciudadano; **dis·fran·chise·ment** [dis'fræntʃizmənt] privación *f* de derechos de ciudadano.

dis·gorge [dis'gɔ:dʒ] *v/t.* vomitar, arrojar; *fig. e.g. booty* devolver; *v/i.* (*river*) desembocar.

dis·grace [dis'greis] **1.** desgracia *f*, disfavor *m*; ignominia *f*; escándalo *m*; *fall into* ~ caer en la desgracia; **2.** deshonrar, desacreditar; ~ *o.s.* deshonrarse, desacreditarse; **dis·'grace·ful** [~ful] □ ignominioso, vergonzoso; ~! ¡qué vergüenza!.

dis·grun·tled [dis'grʌntld] descontento ⟨at de⟩; ⟨moody⟩ veleidoso.

dis·guise [dis'gaiz] **1.** disfrazar ⟨as de; a. fig.⟩; voice cambiar, disfrazar; **2.** disfraz *m*; it's a blessing in ~ no hay mal que por bien no venga.

dis·gust [dis'gʌst] **1.** repugnancia *f*, aversión *f* ⟨at hacia⟩; fill with ~ dar asco; **2.** repugnar, dar asco a; be ~ed with sentir repugnancia hacia; **dis·'gust·ing** □ repugnante, asqueroso; ofensivo.

dish [diʃ] **1.** plato *m*, fuente *f*; cooking: plato *m*, manjar *m*; wash the ~es fregar los platos; **2.** servir en un plato; sl. vencer, burlar; F ~ up servir.

dis·ha·bille [disæ'bi:l] desabillé *m*.

dis·har·mo·ny [dis'hɑ:məni] disonancia *f*.

dish-cloth ['diʃklɔθ] paño *m* de cocina; approx. estropajo *m*.

dis·heart·en [dis'hɑ:tn] desalentar; abatir.

di·shev·el(l)ed [di'ʃevld] hair despeinado, desgreñado; desaliñado.

dis·hon·est [dis'ɔnist] □ fraudulento; no honrado; **dis·hon·est·y** [~'ɔnisti] fraude *m*; falta *f* de honradez.

dis·hon·o(u)r [dis'ɔnə] **1.** deshonra *f*, deshonor *m*; **2.** deshonrar, afrentar; cheque etc. negarse a aceptar (or pagar); **dis·'hon·o(u)r·a·ble** □ deshonroso.

dish...: '~-pan Am. jofaina *f* para fregar los platos; '~-rag Am. = dish-cloth; '~-wash·er friegaplatos *m*; ⊕ lavadora *f* de platos; '~-wa·ter lavazas *f/pl.*

dis·il·lu·sion [disi'lu:ʒn] **1.** desilusión *f*; **2.** desilusionar; **dis·il·lu·sion·ment** desilusión *f*.

dis·in·cli·na·tion [disinkli'neiʃn] aversión *f*, antipatía *f* ⟨for, to hacia⟩; **dis·in·cline** ['~'klain] s.o. hacer (a uno) poco dispuesto ⟨to a⟩; '**dis·in·'clined** poco dispuesto ⟨to a⟩.

dis·in·fect [disin'fekt] desinfectar; '**dis·in·'fect·ant** desinfectante *m*; **dis·in·'fec·tion** desinfección *f*.

dis·in·fla·tion ['disin'fleiʃn] desinflación *f*.

dis·in·gen·u·ous ['disin'dʒenjuəs] □ doble, insincero.

dis·in·her·it ['disin'herit] desheredar; **dis·in·'her·it·ance** desheredación *f*.

dis·in·te·grate [dis'intigreit] desagregar(se), disgregar(se); **dis·in·te·'gra·tion** desagregación *f*, disgregación *f*.

dis·in·ter ['disin'tə:] desenterrar.

dis·in·ter·est·ed [dis'intristid] □ desinteresado; **dis·'in·ter·est·ed·ness** desinterés *m*.

dis·join [dis'dʒɔin] desunir; **dis·'joint** [~t] dislocar; fig. desordenar; **dis·'joint·ed** desarticulado; speech inconexo.

dis·junc·tion [dis'dʒʌŋkʃn] disyunción *f*; **dis·'junc·tive** □ disyuntivo ⟨a. gr.⟩.

disk [disk] disco *m*; mot. ~ clutch embrague *m* de disco; ✗ ~ harrow grada *f* de discos.

dis·like [dis'laik] **1.** p.: I ~ him le tengo aversión, me es antipático; th.: I ~ that eso no me gusta; I ~ walking no me gusta ir a pie; **2.** aversión *f*, antipatía *f* ⟨for, of hacia, a⟩; take a ~ to coger antipatía a; ~d malquisto; poco grato, impopular.

dis·lo·cate ['disləkeit] dislocar; traffic interceptar; fig. embrollar; **dis·lo·'ca·tion** dislocación *f* ⟨a. geol.⟩; ⟨traffic⟩ interceptación *f*; fig. embrollo *m*.

dis·lodge [dis'lɔdʒ] desalojar ⟨a. ✗⟩; quitar de su sitio, hacer caer.

dis·loy·al [dis'lɔiəl] □ desleal; '**dis·'loy·al·ty** deslealtad *f*.

dis·mal ['dizml] □ fig. sombrío, tenebroso, tétrico; ⟨sad⟩ triste, lúgubre; F pésimo.

dis·man·tle [dis'mæntl] desmontar, desarmar; house desmantelar; ⚓ desaparejar; ✗ desguarnecer; **dis·'man·tling** desmonte *m*; desmantelamiento *m*.

dis·mast [dis'mɑ:st] desarbolar.

dis·may [dis'mei] **1.** consternación *f*, conturbación *f*; ⟨discouragement⟩ desánimo *m*; **2.** consternar, turbar ⟨a. fill with ~⟩; desanimar.

dis·mem·ber [dis'membə] desmembrar; **dis·'mem·ber·ment** desmembración *f*.

dis·miss [dis'mis] *v/t.* despedir, destituir; ✗ licenciar; ⚖ rechazar; dar permiso a *p.* para irse; *possibility etc.* descartar, echar a un lado; ~ *(from one's mind)* poner en olvido; *be* ~*ed the service* ser separado del servicio; *v/i.* ✗ romper filas; **dis'miss·al** despedida *f*, destitución *f*; ✗ licenciamiento *m*; ⚖ rechazamiento *m*; permiso *m* para irse.

dis·mount [dis'maunt] desmontar (se).

dis·o·be·di·ence [disə'biːdjəns] desobediencia *f*; **dis·o'be·di·ent** ☐ desobediente; **'dis·o'bey** desobedecer.

dis·o·blige ['disə'blaidʒ] ser poco servicial a *(una p.)*; **'dis·o'blig·ing** ☐ poco servicial.

dis·or·der [dis'ɔːdə] 1. desorden *m*; ✚ trastorno *m*; *(indisposition)* destemplanza *f*; tumulto *m*, motín *m*; *mental* ~ trastorno *m* mental; 2. desordenar, desarreglar; **dis'or·dered** ☐ desordenado; *stomach* alterado; **dis'or·der·ly** desordenado; *(riotous)* alborotador; *conduct* escandaloso ~ *house euph.* burdel *m*.

dis·or·gan·i·za·tion [disɔːgənai-'zeiʃn] desorganización *f*; falta *f* de organización; **dis'or·gan·ize** desorganizar.

dis·own [dis'oun] repudiar, desconocer; renegar de.

dis·par·age [dis'pæridʒ] desacreditar; *(with words)* menospreciar, hablar mal de; **dis'par·age·ment** descrédito *m*; menosprecio *m*, detracción *f*; **dis'par·ag·ing** ☐ despreciativo; ~*ly* en términos despreciativos, con desdén.

dis·pa·rate ['dispərit] ☐ dispar, distinto; **dis·par·i·ty** [dis'pæriti] disparidad *f*.

dis·pas·sion·ate [dis'pæʃnit] ☐ desapasionado, imparcial.

dis·patch [dis'pætʃ] 1. despachar; *goods* consignar, enviar; *(death-blow)* rematar; *meal* despabilar; 2. despacho *m*; consignación *f*; *(speed)* prontitud *f*; **dis'patch-rid·er** correo *m*. [*esp. fig.* desvanecer.|

dis·pel [dis'pel] disipar, dispersar;|

dis·pen·sa·ble [dis'pensəbl] dispensable; prescindible; **dis'pen·sa·ry** dispensario *m*; **dis·pen·sa·tion** [dispen'seiʃn] dispensación *f*; *eccl. etc.* dispensa *f*; designio *m* divino.

dis·pense [dis'pens] *v/t.* dispensar; ⚖ administrar; *pharm.* preparar; ~ *from* eximir de; *v/i.*: ~ *with* deshacerse de; prescindir de; *oath etc.* eximir de; **dis'pens·er** dispensador *m*; *pharm.* farmacéutico *m*.

dis·perse [dis'pɔːs] dispersar(se); **dis'per·sal**, **dis'per·sion** dispersión *f (a. of Jews)*; *opt.* descomposición *f*; **dis'per·sive** ☐ dispersivo.

dis·pir·it [dis'pirit] desalentar; **dis'pir·it·ed** ☐ desalentado; abatido.

dis·place [dis'pleis] sacar de su sitio; destituir; *(replace)* suplir, reemplazar; *phys.* desplazar; ~*d person (abbr.* D. P.) desplazado (a *f*) *m*; **dis'place·ment** desplazamiento *m*; cambio *m* de situación, destitución *f*; remplazo *m (by* con).

dis·play [dis'plei] 1. despliegue *m of quality*; exhibición *f*; pompa *f*, aparato *m*; ostentación *f (esp. b.s.)*; ~ *cabinet* vitrina *f*; ~ *window* escaparate *m*; 2. desplegar; exhibir; ostentar; *quality* revelar.

dis·please [dis'pliːz] desagradar, desplacer; *(annoy)* enojar, enfadar; **dis'pleased** ☐ disgustado *(at, with* de, con); enfadado, indignado; **dis'pleas·ing** ☐ desagradable, ingrato; **dis'pleas·ure** [~'pleʒə] desagrado *m*; disgusto *m (at* por, a causa de); enojo *m*, indignación *f*; *incur s.o.'s* ~ incurrir en el enojo de una *p.*

dis·port [dis'pɔːt]: ~ *o.s.* divertirse *(esp.* alborozadamente), juguetear.

dis·pos·a·ble [dis'pouzəbl] disponible; **dis'pos·al** disposición *f*; arreglo *m*, ajuste *m of a matter*; ✚ *etc.* consignación *f*, donación *f*; *(sale)* venta *f*; *at one's* ~ a su disposición; **dis'pose** *v/t.* disponer, arreglar; inducir, mover *(to* a); determinar, decidir; *v/i.* ~ *of* disponer de; *(rid)* deshacerse de, quitarse de; *rights* enajenar; *problem etc.* solucionar; *food* comer; *property* vender; **dis'posed** dispuesto *(to* a); *well* ~ bien dispuesto *(towards* hacia); **dis·po·si·tion** [~pə-'siʃn] disposición *f*, orden *m*; *(character)* índole *f*, natural *m*; decreto *m*; ⚖ *(will)* legado *m*; propensión *f (to* a); plan *m*; ✗ *make* ~*s* hacer preparativos.

dis·pos·sess [dispə'zes] desposeer, privar *(of* de); *tenant* desahuciar;

dis·pos·ses·sion [ˌ'seʃn] desposeimiento *m*; desahucio *m*.

dis·pro·por·tion ['disprə'pɔːʃn] desproporción *f*; **dis·pro'por·tion·ate** [ˌit] □ desproporcionado; (*large*) desmesurado, indebido.

dis·prove ['dis'pruːv] confutar, refutar.

dis·pu·ta·ble [dis'pjuːtəbl] disputable; **dis'pu·tant** disputador *m*; **dis·pu·ta·tion** [ˌ'teiʃn] disputa *f*; **dis·pu'ta·tious** □ disputador; **dis'pute 1.** disputa *f*, contienda *f*; beyond (*or* without) ~ sin disputa; in ~ disputado; **2.** *v/t.* disputar; *v/i.* disputar, discutir (*about*, over sobre).

dis·qual·i·fi·ca·tion [diskwɔlifi'keiʃn] inhabilitación *f*, impedimento *m*; *sport*: descalificación *f*; **dis'qual·i·fy** [ˌfai] inhabilitar, incapacitar (*for* para); *sport*: descalificar.

dis·qui·et [dis'kwaiət] **1.** inquietud *f*, desasosiego *m*; **2.** inquietar; **dis'qui·et·ing** inquietante; **disqui·e·tude** [ˌ'kwaiitjuːd] inquietud *f*.

dis·qui·si·tion [diskwi'ziʃn] disertación *f*, disquisición *f*.

dis·re·gard ['disri'gɑːd] **1.** indiferencia *f* (*for* a); (*neglect*) descuido *m*; with complete ~ for sin atender en lo más mínimo a; **2.** desatender, descuidar; (*ignore*) no hacer caso de.

dis·re·pair ['disri'pɛə] mal estado *m*; fall into ~ desmoronarse (*esp. building*).

dis·rep·u·ta·ble [dis'repjutəbl] □ de mala fama, mal reputado; *house* de mal vivir; **dis·re·pute** ['ˌri'pjuːt] mala fama *f*, descrédito *m*; bring into ~ desacreditar.

dis·re·spect ['disris'pekt] desacato *m*, falta *f* de respeto; **dis·re·spect·ful**['ˌ'pektful] □ irrespetuoso, desacatador.

dis·robe ['dis'roub] desnudar(se) (*of* de; *a. fig.*).

dis·rupt [dis'rʌpt] romper; *fig.* desbaratar, desorganizar; **dis'rup·tion** rompimiento *m*; desordenamiento *m*, confusión *f*; desbaratamiento *m*, desorganización *f*.

dis·sat·is·fac·tion ['dissætis'fækʃn] descontento *m*; desagrado *m*; **'dissat·is'fac·to·ry** [ˌtəri] □ poco satisfactorio; **'dis'sat·is·fy** [ˌfai] desagradar, descontentar.

dis·sect [di'sekt] disecar; *fig.* hacer

la disección de; **dis·sec·tion** [di'sekʃn] disección *f*; análisis *m* minucioso.

dis·sem·ble [di'sembl] *v/t.* disimular, encubrir; *v/i.* disimular, ser hipócrita; **dis'sem·bler** disimulador (-a *f*) *m*.

dis·sem·i·nate [di'semineit] diseminar, difundir; **dis·sem·i'na·tion** difusión *f*.

dis·sen·sion [di'senʃn] disensión *f*, discordia *f*; *eccl.* disidencia *f*.

dis·sent [di'sent] **1.** disentir (*from* de); *eccl.* disidir; **2.** disentimiento *m*; *eccl.* disidencia *f*; **dis'sent·er** *mst eccl.* disidente *m*; **dis·sen·tient** [di'senʃiənt] **1.** disidente, desconforme; **2.** disidente *m*.

dis·ser·ta·tion [disə'teiʃn] disertación *f* (*on* sobre).

dis·serv·ice ['dis'səːvis] deservicio *m* (*to* a); render a ~ to perjudicar.

dis·sev·er [dis'sevə] partir, separar.

dis·si·dence ['disidəns] disidencia *f*; **'dis·si·dent** disidente *adj. a. su. m*.

dis·sim·i·lar ['di'similə] □ disimilar (*a. gr.*), desemejante (*to* de); **dis·sim·i·lar·i·ty** ['ˌ'læriti] desemejanza *f*.

dis·sim·u·late [di'simjuleit] = *dissemble*; **dis·sim·u'la·tion** disimulación *f*.

dis·si·pate ['disipeit] *v/t.* disipar; *money* despilfarrar; *v/i.* disiparse; (*p.*) entregarse a los vicios; **'dis·sipat·ed** disoluto; **dis·si'pa·tion** disipación *f* (*a. fig.*); libertinaje *m*.

dis·so·ci·ate [di'souʃieit] disociar; ~ o.s. from hacerse insolidario de; **dis·so·ci'a·tion** disociación *f*.

dis·sol·u·bil·i·ty [disɔlju'biliti] disolubilidad *f*; **dis·sol·u·ble** [di'sɔljubl] disoluble.

dis·so·lute ['disəluːt] □ disoluto; **dis·so'lu·tion** disolución *f*.

dis·solv·a·ble [di'zɔlvəbl] disoluble; **dis'solve** *v/t.* disolver (*a. fig.*); *v/i.* disolverse; *fig.* desvanecerse; ~ into tears deshacerse en lágrimas; **dis'solv·ent** disolvente *adj. a. su. m*.

dis·so·nance ['disənəns] disonancia *f* (*a. fig.*); **'dis·so·nant** disonante (*a. fig.*).

dis·suade [di'sweid] disuadir (*from* de); **dis·sua·sion** [di'sweiʒən] disuasión *f*; **dis·sua·sive** [di'sweisiv] □ disuasivo.

dis·taff ['dista:f] rueca *f*; *fig. on the* ~ *side* por parte de madre.

dis·tance ['distəns] **1.** distancia *f* (*a. fig.*); lejanía *f*, lontananza *f*; *fig.* reserva *f*, recato *m*; *paint.* término *m*; *at a* ~ a distancia; *in the* ~ a lo lejos, en lontananza; *from a* ~ de lejos; *fig. keep at a* ~ no tratar con familiaridad; *keep one's* ~ mantenerse a distancia; *striking* ~ alcance *m*; **2.** distanciar; *sport:* dejar atrás (*a. fig.*); **'dis·tant** □ distante; lejano; (*slight*) leve, ligero; *fig.* indiferente, frío; *relation* lejano; *be* ~ *with s.o.* tratar con frialdad.

dis·taste ['dis'teist] aversión *f*, repugnancia *f* (*for, towards* hacia, por); **dis'taste·ful** [~ful] □ desagradable, poco grato (*to* a); (*annoying*) enfadoso.

dis·tem·per¹ [dis'tempə] **1.** pintura *f* al temple; **2.** pintar al temple.

dis·tem·per² [~] *vet.* moquillo *m*; *pol.* desorden *m*, destemplanza *f*.

dis·tend [dis'tend] dilatar(se), distender(se), hinchar(se); **dis'ten·sion** distensión *f*, dilatación *f*.

dis·tich ['distik] dístico *m*.

dis·til(l) [dis'til] destilar (*a.* ⚗); **dis·til·late** ['~eit] ⚗ destilar; **dis·til·la·tion** [~'leiʃən] destilación *f*; **dis'till·er** destilador *m*; **dis'till·er·y** destilería *f*.

dis·tinct [dis'tiŋkt] □ distinto; claro, inequívoco;! positivo; *as* ~ *from* a diferencia de; **dis'tinc·tion** distinción *f*; individualidad *f* of style; sobresaliente *m* in exam; *draw a* ~ *between* hacer una distinción entre; *have the* ~ *of ger.* haberse distinguido por *inf.*; **dis'tinc·tive** □ distintivo, característico; **dis'tinct·ness** claridad *f*.

dis·tin·guish [dis'tiŋgwiʃ] distinguir (*between* entre); ~ *o.s.* distinguirse; *be* ~*ed from* distinguirse de; **dis'tin·guish·a·ble** distinguible; **dis'tin·guished** distinguido; conocible (*by* por).

dis·tort [dis'tɔ:t] torcer (*a. fig.*), deformar; **dis'tor·tion** torcimiento *m*, deformación *f*; *radio etc.*: distorsión *f*.

dis·tract [dis'trækt] distraer; (*confuse*) aturdir, confundir; (*madden*) volver loco; **dis'tract·ed** □ aturdido; enloquecido; **dis'tract·ing** □ que distrae (la atención);

dis·trac·tion distracción *f*; diversión *f*; aturdimiento *m*, perplejidad *f*; locura *f*; *drive s.o. to* ~ volver loco.

dis·train [dis'trein]: ~ *upon* secuestrar, embargar; **dis'traint** secuestro *m*, embargo *m*.

dis·traught [dis'trɔ:t] demente; (*agitated*) muy turbado.

dis·tress [dis'tres] **1.** pena *f*, angustia *f*; (*straits*) apuro *m*, miseria *f*; (*danger*) peligro *m*; = *distraint*; ✈ agotamiento *m*; ~ *rocket* cohete *m* de señales; ~ *signal* señal *f* de peligro; **2.** apenar, afligir; agotar; **dis'tressed** *freq.* preocupado (*for* por); **dis'tress·ing** □ penoso, que da pena.

dis·trib·ute [dis'tribju:t] distribuir, repartir (*among* entre); **dis·tri'bu·tion** distribución *f*, repartimiento *m*; **dis'trib·u·tive** □ distributivo (*a. gr.*); **dis'trib·u·tor** distribuidor (-a *f*) *m*; ⊕, ⚡ distribuidor *m*; ⬆ distribuidora *f* (*a. films*).

dis·trict ['distrikt] comarca *f*, región *f*; *pol.* distrito *m*; ⚖ jurisdicción *f*.

dis·trust [dis'trʌst] **1.** desconfianza *f*, recelo *m*; **2.** desconfiar de, recelar; **dis'trust·ful** [~ful] □ desconfiado; (*suspicious*) receloso.

dis·turb [dis'tə:b] *p.* molestar, estorbar; inquietar, perturbar; *order* alborotar; *balance of mind* trastornar; **dis'turb·ance** alboroto *m*, disturbio *m*; (*disquiet*) desasosiego *m*; trastorno *m* of mind.

dis·un·ion ['dis'ju:njən] desunión *f*; **dis·u·nite** ['disju'nait] desunir(se) (*a. fig.*).

dis·use ['dis'ju:s] desuso *m*: *fall into* ~ caer en desuso; **dis'used** [~zd] *mst building* abandonado.

di·syl·lab·ic ['disi'læbik] □ disílabo; **di·syl·la·ble** [di'siləbl] disílabo *m*.

ditch [ditʃ] **1.** zanja *f*; (*road*) cuneta *f*; ✕ foso *m*; *to the last* ~ hasta quemar el último cartucho; **2.** *v/i.* abrir zanjas; *v/t. sl.* zafarse de; ✈ *sl.* ~ *a plane* amarar, tomar agua; **'ditch·er** cavador *m* de zanjas.

dith·er ['diðə] F **1.** estremecimiento *m*; nerviosismo *m*; *be all of a* ~, *be in a* ~ = **2.** estar muy nervioso, estar a(l) quite y pon; (*hesitate*) vacilar.

dit·to ['ditou] ídem, ídem.

dit·ty ['diti] cancioneta *f*.

di·ur·nal [dai'ə:nl] □ diurno, diario.

di·va·ga·tion [daivə'geiʃn] divagación f.

di·van [di'væn] diván m; ~ bed cama f turca.

dive [daiv] **1.** sumergirse; *swimming*: zambullirse *into water*, bucear *under water*; ✕ picar; F ~ *into pocket* meter la mano en; *building* entrar de prisa en; *matter* engolfarse en; **2.** *swimming*: salto m de trampolín, zambullida f; ✕ picado m; F (*esp. low*) ~ tasca f; '**div·er** buzo m; *orn.* colimbo m.

di·verge [dai'vəːdʒ] divergir; (*road*) bifurcarse; **di'ver·gence, di'ver·gen·cy** divergencia f; discrepancia f; **di'ver·gent** □ divergente; discrepante.

di·verse [dai'vəːs] □ diverso; variado; **di·ver·si·fi·ca·tion** diversificación f; **di'ver·si·fy** [~fai] diversificar; **di'ver·sion** [~ʃn] diversión f (*a.* ✕); (*traffic-*) desviación f; **di'ver·si·ty** diversidad f.

di·vert [dai'vəːt] divertir; *traffic* desviar.

di·vest [dai'vest] desnudar; *fig.* despojar (*of* de); ~ *o.s. of fig.* renunciar a.

di·vide [di'vaid] **1.** *v/t.* partir, dividir (*freq.* ~ *up*; *into* en); ♫ dividir (*by* por); *fig.* dividir, sembrar la discordia entre; ~ *out* repartir; *v/i.* dividirse (*into* en); **2.** *geog.* divisoria f; **div·i·dend** ['dividend] †, ♫ dividendo m; **di'vid·ing** [di'vaidiŋ] divisorio; ~ *line* línea f divisoria.

div·i·na·tion [divi'neiʃn] adivinación f; **di·vine** [di'vain] **1.** □ divino (*a. fig.*); *v. service*; **2.** sacerdote m; teólogo m; **3.** adivinar (*a. fig.*); **di'vin·er** adivinador m; (*water*) zahorí m.

div·ing ['daiviŋ] salto m de trampolín, el bucear *etc.*; '~**-bell** campana f de bucear; '~**-suit** escafandra f.

di·vin·ing-rod [di'vainiŋrɔd] varilla f de zahorí; **di·vin·i·ty** [di'viniti] divinidad f; teología f.

di·vis·i·bil·i·ty [divizi'biliti] divisibilidad f; **di'vis·i·ble** [~zəbl] divisible; **di'vi·sion** [~ʒn] división f (*a.* ♫, ✕); sección f; *fig.* discordia f; división f; *parl.* votación f; **di'vi·sion·al** ✕ divisional; **di'vi·sor** [~zə] divisor m.

di·vorce [di'vɔːs] **1.** disolución f del matrimonio; divorcio m; *fig.* sepa-

ración f, divergencia f; *get a* ~ divorciarse; **2.** divorciar; *fig.* separar; **di·vor'cee** [~sei] divorciado (a f)m.

di·vulge [dai'vʌldʒ] divulgar; revelar.

dix·ie ['diksi] ✕ *sl.* olla f de campaña; ♀ *el Sur de Estados Unidos.*

diz·zi·ness ['dizinis] vértigo m; '**diz·zy 1.** □ vertiginoso; aturdido, confuso; *height* que produce vértigo; F alegre; *sl.* estupendo; *be* ~ tener vértigos; ♂ tener vahidos; **2.** (*a. make* ~) causar vértigos, marear.

do [duː] [*irr.*] (*v. a. done*) **1.** *v/t.* hacer; obrar; ejecutar; terminar; *thea.* desempeñar, representar; *cooking*: asar, cocer; *distance* recorrer; *duty* cumplir con; *hair* peinar; *homage* rendir, tributar; *problem* resolver; *room* limpiar; *sl.* visitar de turista; *sl.* estafar, timar (*a.* ~ *down*); *v. best, death, time etc.*; F ~ *o.s. well* regalarse; ~ (*over*) *again* repetir; *sl.* ~ *in* apalear; asesinar; ~ *out* decorar; F ~ *out of* hacer perder; ~ *up laces etc.* liar, atar; *parcel* empaquetar; *room* renovar el papel *etc.* de; **2.** *v/i.* actuar, proceder; convenir, ser suficiente; estar, encontrarse; *that will* ~ basta ya; eso sirve; *that won't* ~ no sirve; no vale; *how do you* ~? encantado, mucho gusto; ¿cómo está Vd.?; ~ *badly* ir perdiendo, sufrir reveses; salir mal; ~ *well* tener éxito; salir bien *in exam*; ~ *away with* quitar, suprimir; ~ *for p.* ser cocinera (*or* asistenta) de; F acabar con; ~ *with* conformarse con; *I could* ~ *with me* apetece; necesito; *have nothing to* ~ *with* no tener nada que ver con; ~ *without* pasarse sin, prescindir de; **3.** *v/aux.* a) *question*: ~ *you know him?* ¿le conoce Vd.?; b) *negation with not*: *I* ~ *not know him* no le conozco; c) *emphasis*: *I* ~ *feel better* ciertamente me encuentro mejor; ~ *come and see me* le ruego que venga a verme; *I* ~ *tell the truth* yo sí que digo la verdad; d) *to avoid repetition of a verb*: ~ *you like London?—I* ~ ¿le gusta Londres?—Sí; *you write better than I* ~ Vd. escribe mejor que yo; *I take a bath every day—so* ~ *I* me baño todos los días—yo también; e) *inversion after adv.*: *seldom does she come here* (ella) rara vez viene por aquí; **4.** *su.* F (*swindle*) estafa *f*; (*party*) reunión *f*, guateque *m*; *make* ~ *with* conformarse con; hacer lo posible con.

doc [dɔk] F = *doctor*.

doc·ile ['dousail] dócil *f*; **do·cil·i·ty** [dou'siliti] docilidad *f*.

dock[1] [dɔk] recortar; *tree* desmochar; *pay* reducir, rebajar.

dock[2] [~] ♣ acedera *f*, romaza *f*.

dock[3] [~] **1.** ♣ (*with gates*) dique *m*; dársena *f*; *esp. Am.* muelle *m*; ⚓ barra *f*; ~s *pl.* puerto *m*; *dry* ~ dique *m* seco; *floating* ~ dique *m* flotante; **2.** (hacer) entrar en dique; atracar al muelle; **'dock·er** trabajador *m* portuario, cargador *m*.

dock·et ['dɔkit] rótulo *m*, marbete *m*; etiqueta *f*; ⚖ orden *m* del día; *pay* ~ *approx.* sobre *m* de paga.

dock·yard ['dɔkjɑːd] arsenal *m*.

doc·tor ['dɔktə] **1.** doctor *m* (*a.* ⚕); ⚕ médico *m*; **2.** F medicinar; reparar; F castrar; adulterar, falsificar; **doc·tor·ate** ['~rit] doctorado *m*.

doc·tri·naire [dɔktri'nɛə] doctrinario *adj. a. su. m*; **doc·tri·nal** [~'trainl] □ doctrinal; **doc·trine** ['~trin] doctrina *f*.

doc·u·ment 1. ['dɔkjumənt] documento *m*; **2.** ['~mənt] documentar; **doc·u·men·tal, doc·u·men·ta·ry** □ documental; ~ (*film*) documental *m*; **doc·u·men'ta·tion** documentación *f*.

dod·der ['dɔdə] **1.** ♣ cúscuta *f*; **2.** temblar; (*totter*) tambalear; **'dod·der·ing** chocho.

dodge [dɔdʒ] **1.** regate *m* (*a. fig.*); (*trick*) truco *m*; ⊕ ingenio *m*, artificio *m*; **2.** *v/t.* evadir (moviéndose bruscamente); (*elude*) dar esquinazo a; *v/i.* F *fig.* escurrir el bulto; ~ *around* andar a saltos; ~ *round the corner* volver la esquina; **dodg·ems** ['dɔdʒəms] coches *m/pl.* de choque; **'dodg·er** *fig.* remolón (-a *f*) *m*; fullero (a *f*) *m*; *Am.* anuncio *m* de mano; *Am.* pan *m* de maíz.

doe [dou] gama *f*; hembra *f* del conejo (*or* de la liebre).

do·er ['du:ə] hacedor *m*.

does [dʌz] hace *etc.* (*v. do*).

doe·skin ['douskin] piel *f* de ante.

dog [dɔg] **1.** perro *m*; *hunt.* sabueso *m*; (*male of fox*) zorro *m*; (*wolf*) lobo *m*; F tío *m*; F *b.s.* tunante *m*; ⊕ grapa *f*; (*a. fire* ~) morillo *m*; F *go to the* ~*s* arruinarse; entregarse al vicio; *Am.* F *put on the* ~ darse ínfulas; *gay* ~ calavera *m*; *gay old* ~ viejo *m* verde; *every* ~ *has his day* todo llega en este mundo; **2.** seguir de cerca, perseguir; '~**-cart** coche *m* de dos ruedas, dócar *m*; '~**-days** *pl.* canícula *f*.

doge [doudʒ] dux *m*.

dog-fight ['dɔgfait] *mst fig.* escaramuza *f*, refriega *f*; ✈ combate *m* aéreo.

dog·ged ['dɔgid] □ tenaz, terco; **'dog·ged·ness** tenacidad *f*.

dog·ger·el ['dɔgərəl] versos *m/pl.* ramplones.

dog·go ['dɔgou] F: *lie* ~ no moverse; **'dog·gy 1.** perrito *m*; **2.** canino; *Am.* aparatoso, emperejilado; **'dog-'Lat·in** latín *m* macarrónico.

dog·ma ['dɔgmə] dogma *m*; **dog·mat·ic, dog·mat·i·cal** [dɔg'mæ-tik(l)] □ dogmático (*a. fig.*); arrogante, autoritario; **dog'mat·ics** *pl. or sg.* dogmática *f*; **dog·ma·tism** ['~mətizm] dogmatismo *m*; **'dog·ma·tist** dogmatizador *m*; **dog·ma·tize** ['~taiz] dogmatizar.

dog...: '~**-rose** rosal *m* silvestre, escaramujo *m*; '~**-('s)-eared** *book* sobado, muy usado; '~**-'tired** rendido, cansadísimo; '~**-track** canódromo *m*.

doi·ly ['dɔili] pañito *m* (de adorno).

do·ing ['du:iŋ] **1.** *present participle of do*; *nothing* ~! de ninguna manera; **2.**: *esp.* ~*s pl.* actos *m/pl.*, hechos *m/pl.*; conducta *f*; *sl.* ⊕ *etc.* chismes *m/pl.*; *great* ~*s* gran actividad *f*, tremolina *f*.

dol·drums ['dɔldrəmz] *pl.* ⚓ zona *f* de las calmas; *fig. be in the* ~ tener murria; (*th.*) languidecer.

dole [doul] **1.** limosna *f*; subsidio *m* de paro; F *be on the* ~ estar parado; **2.** repartir, distribuir (*mst* ~ *out*).

dole·ful ['doulful] □ triste, lúgubre; **'dole·ful·ness** tristeza *f*, melancolía *f*.

doll [dɔl] **1.** muñeca *f*; *Am. sl.* mozuela *f*; **2.** F engalanarse, emperejilarse (*a.* ~ *up*).

dol·lar ['dɔlə] dólar *m*.

dol·lop ['dɔləp] F grumo *m*; porción *f*.

doll·y ['dɔli] F muñequita *f*.

dol·o·mite ['dɔləmait] dolomita *f*.

dol·o·rous ['dɔlərəs] † lastimoso, apenado; triste.

dol·phin ['dɔlfin] delfín *m.*

dolt [doult] bobalicón *m*, mastuerzo *m*; **'dolt·ish** ☐ bobalicón, atontado.

do·main [də'mein] dominio *m*; *fig.* campo *m.*

dome [doum] cimborrio *m*; cúpula *f.*

do·mes·tic [də'mestik] **1.** ☐ doméstico; casero; *pol. strife* intestino; ~ *science college* escuela *f* de hogar; academia *f* gastronómica; **2.** doméstico *m*; **do'mes·ti·cate** [‿keit] domesticar; ~*d p.* hogareño; **do·mes·ti'ca·tion** domesticación *f*; **do·mes·tic·i·ty** [doumes'tisiti] domesticidad *f.*

dom·i·cile ['dɔmisail] **1.** *esp.* ⚖ domicilio *m*; **2.** domiciliar(se); **dom·i·cil·i·ar·y** [dɔmi'siljəri] domiciliario.

dom·i·nance ['dɔminəns] dominación *f*; **'dom·i·nant** dominante *adj. a. su. f* (♪); **dom·i·nate** ['‿neit] dominar; **dom·i'na·tion** dominación *f*; **dom·i·neer** [dɔmi'niə] dominar, tiranizar (*over acc.*); **dom·i·'neer·ing** ☐ dominante, dominador.

Do·min·i·can [də'minikən] **1.** dominicano; **2.** dominico *m.*

do·min·ion [də'minjən] dominio *m*; *the* 2s *pl.* los dominios británicos.

dom·i·no ['dɔminou] (*carnival*) dominó *m*; ficha *f* del dominó; **dom·i·noes** ['‿z] *pl.* (juego *m* de) dominó *m.*

don[1] [dɔn] *univ.* (*Oxford a. Cambridge*) preceptor *m*, catedrático *m*, *fellow* (*véase*) de un colegio.

don[2] [‿] ponerse.

do·nate [dou'neit] donar; **do'na·tion** donación *f.*

done [dʌn] **1.** *p.p. of do*; *freq.* ser hecho, estar hecho (*a. cooking*); *have* ~ haber terminado; *have* ~ *with th.* haber terminado con; *p. freq.* no tener nada que ver con; *ger.* haber terminado de *inf.*, haber dejado de *inf.*; *it's not* ~ *to inf.* no es elegante *inf.*; *well* ~! ¡bien!; **2.** *adj.* terminado; F (*a.* ~ *in*, ~ *up*) rendido, hecho cisco; F ~ *for* fuera de combate; ⚓ desahuciado; **3.** *int.* ¡terminado!; ✝ ¡trato hecho!.

don·jon ['dɔndʒən] torre *f* del homenaje.

don·key ['dɔŋki] burro *m*; ~ *engine* pequeña máquina *f* de vapor.

do·nor ['dounə] donador *m*; -donante *m/f*; *blood* ~ donante *m/f* de sangre.

don't [dount] **1.** = do not; **2.** F prohibición *f.*

doom [du:m] **1.** *mst b.s.* destino *m*, hado *m*; perdición *f*, muerte *f*; juicio *m* final; **2.** predestinar (a la muerte, a la perdición); condenar (a muerte); **dooms·day** ['du:mzdei] día *m* del juicio final.

door [dɔ:] puerta *f* (*a. fig.*); (*street-*) portal *m*; portezuela *f of vehicle*; *front* ~, *main* ~ puerta *f* principal; *side* ~ puerta *f* accesoria; *behind closed* ~s a puertas cerradas; *next* ~ en la casa de al lado; *next* ~ *to* al lado de; *fig.* que raya en; *out of* ~s al aire libre, afuera; *lay the blame at s.o.'s* ~ echarle a uno la culpa (*for* de); *show to the* ~ acompañar a la puerta; *show s.o. the* ~ enseñar la puerta a; **'~·han·dle** tirador *m* (*or* resbalón *m*) de puerta; picaporte *m*; **'~·keep·er**, **'~·man** portero *m*; **'~·nail**: *dead as a* ~ más muerto que mi abuela; **'~·post** jamba *f* (de una puerta); **'~·way** portal *m*, puerta *f*; *stand in the* ~ estar a la puerta.

dope [doup] **1.** grasa *f* lubricante; barniz *m* (*a.* ✈); *sl.* narcótico *m*; *sl.* informe *m*; *sl.* (*p.*) bobo *m*; **2.** *sl.* dar (*or* poner) un narcótico a; *Am. sl.* pronosticar; **'dope·y** *sl.* bobalicón.

dor·mant ['dɔ:mənt] *mst fig.* durmiente, inactivo; latente.

dor·mer(-win·dow) ['dɔ:mə('windou)] buhardilla *f.*

dor·mi·to·ry ['dɔ:mitəri] dormitorio *m*; ⚔ compañía *f.*

dor·mouse ['dɔ:maus] (*pl.* **dor·mice** ['dɔ:mais]) lirón *m.*

dor·sal ['dɔ:sl] ☐ dorsal.

dose [dous] **1.** dosis *f*; **2.** administrar una dosis a (*a.* ~ *a p. with*); *wine* adulterar. [dormir.]

doss-house ['dɔshaus] *sl.* casa *f* de]

dos·si·er ['dɔsiei] expediente *m*; (*police etc.*) ficha *f.*

dot [dɔt] **1.** punto *m*; F *on the* ~ en punto; **2.** poner punto a; puntear, salpicar de puntos; *fig.* esparcir, desparramar (*a.* ~ *about*); *sl.* ~ *s.o. one* dar de bofetadas a; ~*ted with* salpicado de.

dot·age ['doutidʒ] chochez *f*; *be in one's* ~ chochear; **do·tard** ['‿əd] viejo (a *f*) *m* chocho (a); **dote**

[dout] chochear; ~ (*up*)*on* estar loco por (*or* con); **'dot·ing** ☐ chocho (*a. fig.*); (*doltish*) lelo.

dot·ty ['dɔti] *sl.* chiflado.

dou·ble ['dʌbl] **1.** doble (*a.* ✿); dos veces; doblado; *fig.* doble, falso; ~ *meaning* doble sentido *m*; **2.** doble *m* (*a. p.*); ~*s pl.* tennis: juego *m* de dobles; *at the* ~ a paso ligero; **3.** *v/t.* doblar (*a. bridge*); *p.* ser el doble de; ~*d up* doblado; agachado; *be* ~*d up with laughter* desternillarse de risa; *v/i.* doblarse; (*a.* ~ *up*) agacharse; F ~ *up* compartir dos la misma habitación; (*a.* ~ *back*) virar; **'~·bar·relled** de dos cañones; *fig.* ambiguo; **'~·bass** contrabajo *m*; **'~·bed** cama *f* de matrimonio; **'~·breast·ed** *jacket* cruzado, de dos filas; **'~·cross** *sl.* hacer una mala faena a; **'~·deal·er** artero *m*; traidorzuelo *m*; **'~·deal·ing** doblez *f*; **'~·edged** de dos filos; **'~·en·try** † partida *f* doble; **'~·fea·ture** *esp. Am.* de dos películas de largo metraje; **'dou·ble·'quick** ✗ a paso ligero (*or* redoblado); F lo más pronto posible.

dou·blet ['dʌblit] † jubón *m*; (*pair*) pareja *f*; etimología *f* doble.

doubt [daut] **1.** *v/i.* dudar (*whether* que *subj.*); tener dudas; *v/t.* dudar; *I* ~ *it* lo dudo; **2.** duda *f*; *beyond* ~ sin duda; *in* ~ dudoso; *no* ~ sin duda; *without* ~ indudablemente; *call in* ~ poner en duda; **'doubt·er** escéptico (a *f*) *m*; **doubt·ful** ['~ful] ☐ dudoso (*a. character*); **'doubt·less** *adv.* sin duda, indudablemente.

douche [du:ʃ] **1.** ducha *f*; ✗ jeringa *f*, maqueta *f*. **2.** duchar(se).

dough [dou] masa *f*, pasta *f*; *sl.* pasta *f*, guita *f*; **'~·boy** *Am.* F soldado *m* de infantería; **'~·nut** buñuelo *m*; **'dough·y** pastoso; que sabe a pasta, crudo.

dour ['duə] severo, austero; (*obstinate*) terco.

douse [daus] moja*r*, calar *with water*; *v.* dowse.

dove [dʌv] paloma *f*; **'~·cot(e)** palomar *m*; **'~·tail** ⊕ **1.** cola *f* de milano; **2.** ensamblar a cola de milano; *fig.* corresponder, ajustarse.

dow·a·ger ['dauədʒə] viuda *f* de un titulado (*or* hidalgo); señora *f* anciana.

dow·dy ['daudi] ☐ *p.*, *dress* poco

elegante, poco atractivo; *dress* fuera de moda.

dow·el ['dauəl] clavija *f*.

dow·er ['dauə] viudedad *f*.

down¹ [daun] vello *m*; plumón *m* *of bird, mattress*.

down² [~] *geog.* (*esp.* ~*s pl.*) terreno ondulado y pelado sobre roca de creta; = dune.

down³ [~] **1.** *adv.* abajo; hacia abajo, para abajo; (*to ground*) en tierra; (*south*) hacia el sur; ~ *below* allá abajo; ~ *from* desde; ~ *to* hasta; *be* ~ (*price*) haber bajado; F estar abatido; (*battery etc.*) estar agotado; *sport*: quedarse atrás, perder; F *be* ~ *on p.* tener una inquina a; tratar severamente; *be* ~ *and out* estar arruinado, estar en las últimas; **2.** *prp.* abajo de; ~ *river* río abajo; ~ *the street* calle abajo; **3.** *int.* ¡abajo!; ~ *with* ...! ¡muera ...!; **4.** *adj.* train etc. descendente; **5.** F echar a tierra; *food* tragar; ~ *tools* declararse en huelga; **6.** *su. v. up* 5; **7.** *Down-Easter* etc. *Am.* habitante de la Nueva Inglaterra, *esp. de Maine*; **'~·cast** alicaído, abatido; **'~·fall** caída *f*, ruina *f*; **'~·grade** F *be on the* ~ ir cuesta abajo (*fig.*); **'~·heart·ed** abatido, desanimado; **'~·hill 1.** *adj.* en declive; **2.** *adv.* cuesta abajo (*a. fig.*); **'~·pour** chaparrón *m*; aguacero *m*; **'~·right 1.** *lie* etc. categórico, absoluto; patente, evidente; *p.* franco, abierto; **2.** *adv.* absolutamente, completamente; **'~·stairs 1.** abajo; en el piso de abajo; **2.** piso *m* inferior; **'~·stream** aguas abajo, río abajo; **'~·stroke** (*pen*) palote *m*, pierna *f*; ⊕ carrera *f* descendente; **'~·town** *esp. Am.* en el centro de la ciudad; **'~·trod·den** pisoteado (*a. fig.*); oprimido; **'~·ward 1.** descendente; **2.** (*a.* **'~·wards**) hacia abajo.

down·y ['dauni] velloso; plumoso; *sl.* despabilado, taimado.

dow·ry ['dauəri] dote *f*.

dowse [dauz] *light* apagar; **'dows·er** zahorí *m*; **'dows·ing-rod** varilla *f* de zahorí.

do·yen ['dwaiən] decano *m*.

doze [douz] **1.** dormitar (*a.* ~ *away*); ~ *off* quedarse medio dormido; **2.** sueño *m* ligero; *have a* ~ echar una siestecita.

doz·en ['dʌzn] docena *f*; *baker's* ~ docena *f* de fraile; *talk 19 to the* ~ hablar más que 7.

drab [dræb] **1.** gris amarillento; *fig.* monótono; **2.** ramera *f*.

drachm [dræm], **drach·ma** ['dræk-mə] dracma *f* (*a. pharm.*).

draft [drɑːft] **1.** = *draught*; † giro *m*, letra *f* de cambio; ✕ quinta *f*; (*sketch*) bosquejo *m*; borrador *m*, versión *f* of *article etc.*; *attr. horse etc.* de tiro; **2.** *article* redactar; *plan* bosquejar; *Am.* ✕ quintar; ✕ destacar; **draft·ee** [drɑːfˈtiː] *Am.* ✕ quinto *m*; **'drafts·man** = *draughtsman*.

drag [dræg] **1.** rastra *f* (*a.* ⚓); ↙ grada *f*; narria *f* *for wood etc.*; ⚓ (*a.* ~ *net*) red *f* barredera; ⚓ resistencia *f* al avance; *fig.* estorbo *m*, demora *f*; F cuesta *f* dura; *Am. sl.* influencia *f*; **2.** *v/t.* arrastrar; ⚓ rastrear; = *dredge*[1] 2; ~ *along* arrastrar consigo (*or* tras sí); ~ *out* hacer demasiado largo (*or* lento); *v/i.* arrastrarse (*along the ground* por el suelo); ⚓ rastrear (*for* en busca de); † decaer; (*time*) pesar.

drag·on ['drægən] dragón *m*; F *fig.* fiera *f*; F (*duenna*) carabina *f*; **'~·fly** libélula *f*, caballito *m* del diablo.

dra·goon [drəˈguːn] **1.** ✕ dragón *m*; **2.** tiranizar; ~ *into ger.* obligar por intimidación a *inf.*

drain [drein] **1.** (*outlet*) desaguadero *m*; alcantarilla *f*, boca *f* de alcantarilla *in street*; *fig.* desaguadero *m* (*on* de); ~ *pipe* tubo *m* de desagüe (*a. fig.*); **2.** *v/t.* desaguar; ↙ avenar; 🌿 *wound* drenar; *glass* apurar; *lake* desangrar (*a.* ~ *off*); *vessel* escurrir; *v/i.* desaguar (*into* en); **'drain·age** desagüe *m*, avenamiento *m*; (*system*) alcantarillado *m*; ~ *basin* cuenca *f* de un río; ↙ ~ *channel* zanja *f*; **'drain·ing-board** escurridero *m*.

drake [dreik] pato *m* macho.

dram [dræm] dracma *f*; cantidad *f* pequeña *of brandy etc.*

dra·ma ['drɑːmə] drama *m* (*a. fig.*); **dra·mat·ic** [drəˈmætik] □ dramático (*a. fig.*); **dram·a·tist** ['dræmətist] dramaturgo *m*; **'dram·a·tize** dramatizar.

drank [dræŋk] *pret. of* drink.

drape [dreip] colgar, adornar con colgaduras; vestir (con telas de muchos pliegues; *in* de); **'drap·er** pañero *m*, lencero *m*; **'dra·per·y** colgaduras *f/pl.*, ropaje *m*; pañería *f* (*a.* ~ *shop*); (*haberdashery*) mercería *f*.

dras·tic ['dræstik] □ drástico.

draught [drɑːft] tiro *m* (*a. chimney*); corriente *f* de aire; (*drink*) trago *m*; ⚓ calado *m* *of ship*; ⚓ (*net*) rastreo *m*; *attr. horse* de tiro; *beer* de barril, al grifo; ~*s pl.* juego *m* de damas; *v. draft*; *at a* ~ de un trago; **'~-board** tablero *m* (del juego de damas); **'~-horse** caballo *m* de tiro; **'draughts·man** dibujante *m*; (*professional*) delineante *m*; **'draughts·man·ship** arte *m* del dibujante (*or* delineante); **'draught-y** airoso; *house* ventilado, aireado, lleno de corrientes de aire.

draw [drɔː] **1.** [*irr.*] *v/t.* arrastrar, tirar de (*a.* ~ *along*); (*take out*) sacar; (*lengthen*) alargar; atraer; *bow* tender; *breath* aspirar; *cheque* girar, librar; *curtain* correr; *drawing* dibujar; *fowl* destripar; *line* trazar, tirar; *lots* echar; *money, prize* sacar; *salary* cobrar; *sword, water* sacar; ⚓ *water* calar; ~ *aside p.* apartar; ~ *back* retirar; *curtain* descorrer; ~ *forth* hacer salir, producir; ~ *off* sacar, extraer; *liquid* trasegar; ~ *on p.* engatusar; *glove* ponerse; ~ *out* sacar; *p.* hacer hablar; *b.s.* sonsacar; ~ *up* redactar; *chair* acercar; ✕ ordenar para el combate; ~ *o.s. up* enderezarse, ponerse en su lugar; ~ (*up*)*on* † girar a cargo de; *fig.* inspirarse en; *v/i.* (*chimney*) tirar; *sport:* empatar; atraer; (*artist*) dibujar; moverse (*aside* a un lado *etc.*); ~ *back* retroceder, cejar (*a. fig.*); ~ *near* acercarse (*to* a); ~ *up* pararse (*sharp* en seco); ~ *to a close* estar para terminar; **2.** *sport:* empate *m*; *chess:* tablas *f/pl.*; *lottery:* sorteo *m*; F función *f* taquillera (*or* de mucho éxito); **'~·back** inconveniente *m* (*to* en); † (*excise*) reembolso *m*; **'~·bridge** puente *m* levadizo; **draw'ee** † librado *m*, girado *m*; **'draw·er 1.** ['drɔːə] dibujante *m*; † girador *m*, librador *m*; **2.** ['drɔː] cajón *m*; ~*s pl.* calzoncillos *m/pl.*; bragas *f/pl.* de mujer.

draw·ing ['drɔːiŋ] dibujo *m*; ~ *instruments pl.* instrumentos *m/pl.* de dibujar; '~-ac'count cuenta *f* corriente; '~-board tablero *m* de dibujo; '~-pen tiralíneas *m*; '~-pin chincheta *f*; '~-room salón *m*; recepción *f*; *Am.* 🔲 departamento *m* reservado; *attr.* de buen gusto.

drawl [drɔːl] 1. *v/t. words* arrastrar; *v/i.* hablar lentamente arrastrando las palabras; 2. habla *f* lenta y pesada.

drawn [drɔːn] 1. *p.p. of draw* 1; 2. *adj. game* empatado; *face* ojeroso, cansado; *sew.* ~ *work* calado *m*.

dray [drei] carro *m* (*esp.* para barriles de cerveza).

dread [dred] 1. pavor *m*, temor *m*; *fill with* ~ infundir pavor a; 2. temer; *I* ~ *to think of it* me horroriza pensar en ello; 3. espantoso; **dread·ful** ['~ful] 1. □ terrible, espantoso; F desagradable; F malísimo; 2.: *penny* ~ folletín *m* horrendo; **dread·nought** ['~nɔːt] acorazado *m*, dreadnought *m*.

dream [driːm] 1. sueño *m* (*a. fig.*); (*a. day-*) ensueño *m*; 2. [*irr.*] soñar (*of* con); ~ *away* (*e.g. the day*) pasar (el día) soñando; **'dream·er** soñador (-a *f*) *m*; *fig.* fantaseador (-a *f*) *m*; **'dream-like** de ensueño; **dreamt** *pret. a. p.p. of dream* 2; **'dream·y** □ *p.* distraído, muy en las nubes; entre sueños, nebuloso.

drear·i·ness ['driərinis] tristeza *f*; monotonía *f*; **'drear·y** □ triste, melancólico; monótono.

dredge[1] [dredʒ] ⚓ 1. draga *f*, rastra *f*; 2. dragar; rastrear; ~ *up* pescar (*a. fig.*); **'dredg·er**[1] ⚓ draga *f*; **'dredg·ing** obras *f/pl.* de dragado.

dredge[2] [~] espolvorear; **'dredg·er**[2] azucarero *m*, especiero *m*.

dregs [dregz] *pl.* heces *f/pl.* (*a. fig.*).

drench [drentʃ] 1. *vet.* poción *f*; (*shower*) chaparrón *m*; 2. mojar, empapar; F *be* ~*ed* calarse, estar calado; **'drench·er** F chaparrón *m*; **'drench·ing** torrencial.

dress [dres] 1. vestido *m*, ropa *f*; (*a. fig.*) atavío *m*; (*woman's*) vestido *m*; ~ *ball* baile *m* de etiqueta; *thea.* ~ *rehearsal* ensayo *m* general; *full* ~ traje *m* de etiqueta; *v. fancy*; 2. *v/t.* vestir (*a. fig.*; *in black* de negro); (*a.* ~ *up*) ataviar, adornar (*in* con, de); *hair* peinar; *horse*, *skins* peinar, almohazar; *stone* labrar; *window* poner; *wound* curar,

vendar; 🖋 abonar; ✂ alinear; F ~ *down* dar un rapapolvo a; *v/i.* (*a. get* ~*ed*) vestirse; ~ (*well*) vestir(se) (bien); ~ *up* acicalarse; vestirse de etiqueta; '~-'cir·cle *thea.* anfiteatro *m*; '~-'coat frac *m*; '~-de'sign·er modisto *m*; **'dress·er** aparador *m* con estantes; *Am.* cómoda *f* con espejo.

dress·ing ['dresiŋ] (*act*) el vestir(se); 🖋 vendaje *m*; (*food*) salsa *f*, condimento *m*; 🖋 abono *m*; '~-case neceser *m*; '~-'down F rapapolvo *m*; '~-gown bata *f*; '~-room vestidor *m*; *thea.* camarín *m*, camerino *m*; '~-sta·tion puesto *m* de socorro; '~-ta·ble tocador *m*.

dress...: '~-mak·er costurera *f*, modista *f*; '~-mak·ing costura *f*; '~-pa·rade ✂ parada *f*; '~-'shirt camisa *f* de pechera dura; '~-'suit traje *m* de etiqueta; **'dress·y** F acicalado; elegante.

drew [druː] *pret. of draw* 1.

drib·ble ['dribl] gotear, caer gota a gota; (*mouth*) babear; *football*: driblar.

drib·let ['driblit] adarme *m*; *in* ~*s* por adarmes.

dried [draid] secado; *fruit* paso; *vegetables* seco.

drift [drift] 1. (impulso *m* de una) corriente *f*; ⚓ deriva *f*; *fig.* sentido *m*, tendencia *f*; *fig.* giro *m*; *b.s.* (*esp. pol.*) inacción *f*; (*snow- etc.*) montón *m*; *geol.* terrenos *m/pl.* de acarreo; ✕ galería *f* horizontal que sigue el filón; ~ *from the land* despoblación *f* del campo; 2. *v/t.* impeler, llevar; amontonar; *v/i.* ir a la deriva (*a.* ~ *along*); *fig.* vivir sin rumbo; '~-ice hielo *m* a la deriva; '~-wood madera *f* de deriva.

drill [dril] 1. ⊕ taladro *m*; (*pneumatic*) ~ perforadora *f*, martillo *m* picador; 🖋 hilera *f*; 🖋 (*machine*) sembradora *f*; ✕ instrucción *f*; *fig.* disciplina *f*; *sl.* rutina *f*; 2. *v/t.* ⊕ taladrar; 🖋 sembrar con sembradora; ✕ enseñar instrucción a; *v/i.* perforar (*for oil* en busca de); ✕ hacer instrucción; **'drill·ing** perforación *f for oil etc.*

drink [driŋk] 1. bebida *f*; beber *m* (*en exceso*); (*swig*) trinquis *m*, trago *m*; *have a* ~ tomar unas copas, tomar algo; *take a* ~ echar un trago; 2. beber (*a. fig.*); ~ *a p.'s health* brindar por alguien; ~ *down* beber de una vez; *esp. fig.* ~ *in* beber; ~ *out of* beber de; ~ *up* tragar, apurar; **'drink·a·ble** bebible, potable.

drink·ing...: **'~-bout** juerga *f* de borrachera; **'~-foun·tain** fuente *f*; **'~-song** canción *f* de taberna; **'~-wa·ter** agua *f* potable.

drip [drip] **1.** goteo *m*; △ alero *m*; *sl.* bobalicón (-a *f*) *m*; tontaina *m*/*f*; **2.** gotear, caer gota a gota; F ~*ping wet* calado.

drip·ping ['dripiŋ] pringue *m*.

drive [draiv] **1.** *mot.* paseo *m* (en coche); calzada *f up to house*; *sport*: golpe *m* fuerte (*tennis*: a ras de la red); *fig.* vigor *m*, energía *f*; campaña *f* vigorosa (*to para*); ⊕ mecanismo *m* de transmisión; † venta *f* de liquidación; *hunt.*, ⚔ batida *f*; **2.** [*irr.*] *v/t.* impeler, empujar; mover, actuar (*a. fig.*); ⊕ impulsar; *mot. etc.* conducir, guiar; *p.* llevar en coche; *fig. p.* forzar (*to* a); *sport*: golpear con gran fuerza; *p. crazy etc.* volver; ~ *away* (*or off*) ahuyentar; ~ *back* obligar a retroceder; ~ *in* (*or home*) hincar, remachar; ~ *a good bargain* hacer un buen trato; *v/i.* conducir; ~ *at th. fig.* insinuar, querer decir; *Am.* ~ *away* trabajar mucho; *mot.* ~ *on* seguir adelante; *the rain was driving down* llovía a chuzos.

drive-in ['draiv'in] *Am.* motocine *m*.

driv·el ['drivl] **1.** babear; ~ *away fortune* malgastar; **2.** música *f* celestial, monserga *f*.

driv·en ['drivn] *p.p. of* drive 2.

driv·er ['draivə] conductor *m*; 👷 maquinista *m*; ⊕ rueda *f* motriz; persona *f* despótica.

driv·ing ['draiviŋ] **1.** conducción *f*; **2.** *adj. freq.* motriz; *rain* torrencial, recio; *attr.* ~ *instructor* instructor *m* de conducción; ~ *licence* permiso *m* (*or carnet m*) de conducir; ~ *mirror* retrovisor *m*; ~ *school* escuela *f* automovilista; **'~-belt** correa *f* de transmisión.

driz·zle ['drizl] **1.** llovizna *f*; **2.** lloviznar.

droll [droul] (*adv.* drolly) gracioso, festivo; (*odd*) raro; **'droll·er·y** chuscada *f*.

drom·e·dar·y ['drʌmədəri] dromedario *m*.

drone [droun] **1.** *zo.* zángano *m* (*a. fig.*); (*noise*) zumbido *m*; **2.** zumbar; hablar monótonamente (*a.* ~ *on*).

drool [dru:l] **1.** babear; **2.** *Am.* F bobería *f*.

droop [dru:p] *v/t.* inclinar, dejar caer; *v/i.* inclinarse; pender, colgar; *fig.* decaer; *fig.* (*lose heart*) desalentarse; **'droop·ing** □ caído, inclinado; lánguido.

drop [drɔp] **1.** gota *f* (*a.* 🍬); (*fall*) baja *f*, caída *f* repentina; (*slope*) cuesta *f*, declive *m*, pendiente *f*; *mount.* precipicio *m*; lanzamiento *m by parachute*; *thea.* (*a.* ~ *curtain*) telón *m* de boca; ~ *by* ~ gota a gota; ~ *light* lámpara *f* colgante; *Am.* F *get* (*have*) *the* ~ *on coger* (llevar) la delantera a; F *take a* ~ beber; F *have taken a* ~ *too much* llevar una copa de más; **2.** *v/t.* dejar caer; inclinar; *hunt.* derribar; abandonar; omitir, suprimir; *claim* renunciar a; *consonant* comerse; *curtsy* hacer; *money* perder; *passenger, subject* dejar; *voice* bajar; ~ *that!* ¡deja eso!; *v. anchor*; ~ *a hint* soltar una indirecta; ~ *in the post* echar al buzón; *v/i.* caer; bajar (*a.* ~ *down*); (*crouch*) agacharse; *fig.* cesar, terminar; (*drip*) gotear; ~ *behind* quedarse atrás; ~ *dead* caer muerto; ~ *in* (*or by, over*) visitar de paso; ~ *off esp.* quedarse dormido; ~ *out* darse de baja, retirarse; ~ *out of sight* desaparecer; **'drop·let** gotita *f*; **'drop·ping** goteo *m*; ~*s pl.* excremento *m* (de los animales); **'drop-scene** telón *m* de boca.

drop·si·cal ['drɔpsikl] □ hidrópico; **'drop·sy** hidropesía *f*.

dross [drɔs] escoria *f* (*a. fig.*).

drought [draut] sequía *f*; **'drought·y** árido, seco.

drove [drouv] **1.** manada *f*, piara *f*; *fig.* muchedumbre *f*; **2.** *pret. of* drive 2; **'dro·ver** ganadero *m*; boyero *m*, pastor *m*.

drown [draun] *v/t.* anegar (*a. fig.*; *in* en); *sound* apagar; *v/i.* (*or be* ~*ed*) ahogarse; perecer ahogado, anegarse.

drowse [drauz] adormecer(se); **'drow·si·ness** somnolencia *f*, modorra *f*; **'drow·sy** □ soñoliento; *be* ~ tener sueño.

drub [drʌb] apalear; tundir; *fig.*

vencer, derrotar; **'drub·bing** paliza *f* (*a. fig.*); *fig.* derrota *f*.

drudge [drʌdʒ] **1.** esclavo *m* del trabajo (*or* de la cocina), azacán (-a *f*) *m*; **2.** azacanarse, afanarse; **'drudg·er·y** perrera *f*, trabajo *m* penoso.

drug [drʌg] **1.** droga *f* (*a. b.s.*), medicamento *m*; (*esp. to sleep*) narcótico *m*; ✝ ~ on the market artículo *m* invendible; *Am.* ~ store farmacia *f*, droguería *f*; **2.** administrar narcóticos a, narcotizar; aletargar; **drug·gist** ['drʌgist] farmacéutico *m*; ~s (*shop*) farmacia *f*.

dru·id ['druːid] druida *m*.

drum [drʌm] **1.** tambor *m* (*a.* ⊕); (*big*) timbal *m*; (*ear-*) tímpano *m*; (*oil- etc.*) bidón *m*; **2.** *v/i.* ♪ tocar el tambor; tamborilear *with fingers*; *v/t.* ~ into *s.o.* meterle a uno en la cabeza; ✕ ~ out expulsar; **'~·head** piel *f* (*or* parche *m* de tambor); ~ court martial consejo *m* de guerra sumarísimo (*or* al frente del enemigo); **'drum·mer** tambor *m*; **'drum·stick** palillo *m*, maza *f*.

drunk [drʌŋk] **1.** *p.p. of* drink 2; **2.** borracho (*a. fig.*); get ~ emborracharse; **drunk·ard** ['~əd] borracho (a *f*) *m*; **'drunk·en** borracho, dado a la bebida; **'drunk-en·ness** embriaguez *f*.

dry [drai] **1.** □ seco; *climate etc.* árido; *fig.* aburrido, sin interés; *appearance* (*of p.*) enjuto; *humour* approx. raro, peculiar; *Am.* F prohibicionista; F (*thirsty*) sediento; *bread freq.* sin mantequilla; *Am.* F ~ goods *pl.* lencería *f*; **2.** secar(se) (*a.* ~ up); *sl.* ~ up callarse, dejar de hablar.

dry-clean ['drai'kliːn] limpiar en seco; **'dry-'clean·ing** limpieza *f* en seco.

dry·ness ['drainis] sequedad *f*; (*climate*) aridez *f*.

dry...: **'~-'nurse** ama *f* seca, niñera *f*; **'~-'rot** ♠ putrefacción *f* fungoide; *fig.* corrupción *f* interna; **'~-'shod** a pie enjuto.

du·al ['djuːəl] *gr.* dual; doble; ~ control doble mando *m*; **'du·al·ism** dualismo *m*.

dub [dʌb] *film* doblar; *knight* armar caballero; apodar *with name*; **'dub·bing** *film*: doblaje *m*.

du·bi·ous ['djuːbiəs] □ dudoso; be ~

dudar, tener dudas (*of, about, over* sobre, de); **'du·bi·ous·ness** duda *f*, incertidumbre *f*.

du·cal ['djuːkl] ducal.

duc·at ['dʌkət] ducado *m* (*dinero*).

duch·ess ['dʌtʃis] duquesa *f*.

duch·y ['dʌtʃi] ducado *m* (*título*).

duck¹ [dʌk] *orn.* pato *m*; ánade *m*; F ~! ¡querida!

duck² [~] **1.** zambullida *f in water*; agachada *f to escape*; **2.** chapuzar(se) *in water*; agachar(se) *to escape*; *Am.* F ~ out esfumarse.

duck³ [~] (*cloth*) dril *m*, brin *m*; ~s *pl.* pantalón *m* de dril.

duck·ling ['dʌkliŋ] patito *m*, anadón *m*.

duck·y ['dʌki] F **1.** ¡querida!; **2.** mono, majo.

duct [dʌkt] conducto *m* (*a.* ✿).

duc·tile ['dʌktail] □ dúctil (*a. fig.*).

duc·til·i·ty [~'tiliti] ductilidad *f*.

dud [dʌd] **1.** ✕ granada *f etc.* fallida; *fig.* fallo *m*; (*fake*) filfa *f*; **2.** fallido, huero; falso.

dude [djuːd] petimetre *m*, cursi *m*; *Am.* ~ ranch rancho *m* para turistas.

dudg·eon ['dʌdʒn]: in high ~ muy enojado.

due [djuː] **1.** *adj.* debido; ✝ pagadero; conveniente, oportuno; 🕰 *etc.* (que) debe llegar; ~ to por causa de; debido a; be ~ to *p.* deberse a; *th.* ser ocasionado por; be ~ to *inf.* deber *inf.*; (*time*) estar para *inf.*; *fall* ~ vencer; **2.** *adv.* ♁ derecho, en derechura; precisamente; **3.** *su.* (*right*) derecho *m*; (*desert*) merecimiento *m*; (*debt*) deuda *f*; ~s *pl.* ✝ derechos *m/pl.*; *b.s.* get one's ~ llevar su merecido.

du·el ['djuːəl] **1.** duelo *m*; **2.** batirse en duelo; **'du·el·list** duelista *m*.

du·et(to) [djuˈet(ou)] dúo *m*.

duff·el ['dʌfl] paño *m* de lana basta; ~ coat comando *m*.

duff·er ['dʌfə] tonto *m*, zoquete *m*.

dug [dʌg] **1.** *pret. a. p.p. of* dig; **2.** *zo.* ubre *f*, pezón *m*; **'~-out** ✕ refugio *m* subterráneo; *Am.* cobertizo *m* bajo.

duke [djuːk] duque *m*; **'duke·dom** ducado *m*.

dull [dʌl] **1.** (*adv.* dully) lerdo, estúpido; insensible; (*tedious etc.*) insulso, aburrido; *colour* apagado; *day* gris; *edge* embotado; *pain, sound* sordo; *surface* deslustrado, mate; ✝ inactivo, flojo; **2.** embotar (*a. fig.*); deslustrar; *enthusiasm* enfriar; *p.* entorpecer; '**dull·ness** estupidez *f*; insensibilidad *f* etc. (*v. dull*).

du·ly ['dju:li] *v. due*; debidamente; a su (debido) tiempo.

dumb [dʌm] ☐ mudo; F estúpido, lerdo; *deaf and* ~ sordomudo; *v. show*; *strike* ~ dejar sin habla, pasmar; '~**bell** pesa *f*; *Am. sl.* estúpido *m*; ~**'found** dejar sin habla, pasmar; '**dumb·ness** mudez *f*; F estupidez *f*; '**dumb-'wait·er** estante *m* giratorio; *Am.* montaplatos *m*.

dum·my ['dʌmi] **1.** (*tailor's*) maniquí *m*; ✝ envase *m* vacío; (*baby's*) chupete *m*; *bridge:* (be hacer de) muerto *m*; ✝ (*p.*) testaferro *m*; **2.** falso, postizo.

dump [dʌmp] **1.** descargar de golpe; (*rid*) deshacerse de; *rubbish* vaciar; ✝ *goods* inundar el mercado con; F ~ *down meter*; **2.** basurero *m*, escorial *m*; ✗ depósito *m*; *sl. contp.* pueblucho *m*, poblachón *m*; F (be [*down*] *in the* tener) ~*s pl.* murria *f*; '**dump·ing** ✝ dumping *m*; '**dump·ing-ground** basurero *m*; '**dump·ling** *bola de masa hervida* (*or cocida*); '**dump·y** regordete, culibajo.

dun[1] [dʌn] pardo, castaño oscuro.

dun[2] [~] **1.** acreedor *m* importuno; **2.** molestar, dar la lata a.

dunce [dʌns] zopenco (a *f*) *m*; **dun·der·head** ['dʌndəhed] zoquete *m*.

dune [dju:n] duna *f*.

dung [dʌŋ] **1.** estiércol *m*; **2.** estercolar.

dun·geon ['dʌndʒn] mazmorra *f*, calabozo *m*.

dung·hill ['dʌŋhil] estercolero *m*.

duo ['dju:ou] dúo *m*.

du·o·dec·i·mal [dju:ou'desiml] duodecimal; **du·o'dec·i·mo** [~mou] duodécimo, dozavo; *typ. in* ~ en dozavo.

dupe [dju:p] **1.** primo *m*, inocentón *m*; **2.** embaucar; (*swindle*) timar.

du·plex ['dju:pleks] dúplice, doble; *Am.* ~ *house* casa *f* para dos familias.

du·pli·cate 1. ['dju:plikit] a) (*in* por) duplicado; b) duplicado *m*; **2.** [~keit] duplicar; **du·pli·ca·tion** [~'keiʃn] duplicación *f*; '**du·pli·ca·tor** duplicador *m*, multicopista *m*;

du·plic·i·ty [dju:'plisiti] duplicidad *f*, doblez *f*.

du·ra·bil·i·ty [djuərə'biliti] durabilidad *f*, duración *f*; '**du·ra·ble** ☐ durable, duradero; ~ *goods pl.* artículos *m/pl.* duraderos; **du·ra·tion** [~'reiʃn] duración *f*.

du·ress [djuə'res] (*under* por) coacción *f*.

du·ring ['djuəriŋ] durante.

durst [də:st] ✝ *pret. of* dare.

dusk [dʌsk] crepúsculo *m*, anochecer *m*; *poet.* oscuridad *f*; '**dusk·i·ness** oscuridad *f*; color *m* sombrío; '**dusk·y** ☐ oscuro, sombrío; *complexion* moreno.

dust [dʌst] **1.** polvo *m*; (*refuse*) basura *f*; *fig.* cenizas *f/pl.*; *sl.* pasta *f*; *bite the* ~ morder el polvo; *raise a* ~ armarla; *throw* ~ *in one's eyes* engañar; **2.** quitar el polvo, despolvorear; *cooking:* espolvorear; '~**bin** cubo *m* de la basura; '~**-bowl** *Am.* estepa *f*, terreno *m* estéril a causa de la erosión; '~**-cart** camión *m* de la basura; '~**-cov·er** guardapolvo *m*; sobrecubierta *f of book*; '**dust·er** plumero *m*, (*rag*) gamuza *f*, trapo *m*; (*blackboard-*) borrador *m*; *Am.* guardapolvo *m*; '**dust·i·ness** calidad *f* de polvoroso (*or* empolvado); '**dust·ing** *sl.* paliza *f*; '**dust-'jack·et** sobrecubierta *f*; '**dust·man** basurero *m*; '**dust·pan** cogedor *m*; '**dust-'up** F riña *f*, pelea *f*; '**dust·y** polvoriento, empolvado; *sl. not so* ~ bastante bien (*or* bueno).

Dutch [dʌtʃ] holandés *adj. a. su. m*; *Am. in* ~ en desgracia; F *double* ~ galimatías *m*, chino *m*; '**Dutch·man** holandés *m*; '**Dutch·wom·an** holandesa *f*.

du·ti·a·ble ['dju:tiəbl] sujeto a derechos de aduana; **du·ti·ful** ['~ful] ☐ obediente, respetuoso; (*obliging*) servicial.

du·ty ['dju:ti] deber *m*, obligación *f* (*to a*, para con); (*esp. duties pl.*) tarea *f*, faena *f*; ~ derechos *m/pl.* de aduana; *off* ~ libre; ✗ franco de servicio; *on* ~ de servicio; de guardia; *in* ~ *bound* obligado (*to a*); *do* ~ *for* servir en lugar de; *take up one's duties* entrar en funciones; '~**'free** ✝ libre de derechos de aduana; '~**ser·geant** (*police*) sargento *m* de servicio.

dwarf [dwɔːf] **1.** enano *m*; **2.** enano; diminuto; **3.** achicar; *fig.* empequeñecer; '**dwarf·ish** □ enano, diminuto.

dwell [dwel] [*irr.*] morar, habitar; ~ (*up*)*on* explayarse en; hacer hincapié en; '**dwell·ing** morada *f*, vivienda *f*; **dwell·ing-house** casa *f*, domicilio *m*; **dwelt** [dwelt] *pret. a. p.p. of* **dwell.**

dwin·dle ['dwindl] disminuirse, menguar (*a.* ~ *away*); quedar reducido (*into* a); '**dwin·dling** disminución *f*, mengua *f* (*a.* ~ *away*).

dye [dai] **1.** tinte *m*; matiz *m*, color *m*; *fig. of deepest* ~ de lo más vil; **2.** teñir (*s.t. black* de negro); *v. wool*; '**dy·er** tintorero *m*; '**dye-stuff**

tinte *m*, materia *f* colorante; '**dye-works** tintorería *f*.

dy·ing ['daiiŋ] **1.** moribundo; agonizante; *moments* final; **2.** *ger. of* **die**[1].

dy·nam·ic [dai'næmik] **1.** □ (*a.* **dy-'nam·i·cal** □) dinámico (*a. fig.*); **2.** *fig.* dinámica *f*; **dy'nam·ics** *sg.* dinámica *f*; **dy·na·mite** ['dainəmait] **1.** dinamita *f*; **2.** volar con dinamita; **dy·na·mo** ['dainəmou] dínamo *f*.

dy·nas·tic [di'næstik] □ dinástico; **dy·nas·ty** ['dinəsti] dinastía *f*.

dys·en·ter·y ['disntri] disentería *f*.

dys·pep·sia [dis'pepsiə] dispepsia *f*; **dys'pep·tic** □ dispéptico; melancólico.

E

each [i:tʃ] **1.** *adj.* cada; todo; **2.** *pron.* cada uno; ~ *other* uno(s) a otro(s), el uno al otro; mutuamente; **3.** *adv.* por persona.

ea·ger ['i:gə] □ ansioso; anhelante; impaciente; vehemente; *be* ~ *for* anhelar; *be* ~ *to* tener vivo deseo de; **'ea·ger·ness** ansia *f*; anhelo *m etc.*

ea·gle ['i:gl] águila *f*; *eye* (de) lince.

ear¹ [iə] ♀ espiga *f*.

ear² [~] oreja *f*; (*sense*) oído *m*; ♪ *by* ~ de oído; *be all* ~*s* ser todo oídos; *give* ~ *to* prestar oído a; *have a good* ~ tener buen oído; *turn a deaf* ~ hacerse el sordo; ~**ache** ['iəreik] dolor *m* de oídos; **'~-drum** tímpano *m*. [dəm] condado *m.*)

earl [ə:l] conde *m*; **earl·dom** ['~-]

ear·ly ['ə:li] **1.** *adj.* temprano (*a.* ♀); primero, primitivo; precoz; *reply* pronto; *at an* ~ *date* en fecha próxima; ~ *bird* madrugador (-a *f*) *m*; ~ *life* juventud *f*; **2.** *adv.* temprano; con tiempo; *arrive 5 minutes* ~ llegar con 5 minutos de anticipación; *book* ~ reservar con mucha anticipación; ~ *last century* a principios del siglo pasado; ~ *in the morning* muy de mañana.

ear·mark ['iəma:k] *fig.* reservar, poner aparte (*for* para); destinar (*for* a).

earn [ə:n] ganar(se); adquirir, obtener; *praise etc.* merecer(se), granjearse; ♀ (*bonds*) *interest* devengar.

ear·nest¹ ['ə:nist] prenda *f*, señal *f*; (*a.* '~-mon·ey) arras *f/pl.*

ear·nest² [~] □ serio; formal; *desire* ardiente; *in* (*good*) ~ (muy) de veras, en serio; **'ear·nest·ness** seriedad *f*; formalidad *f*.

earn·ings ['ə:niŋz] *pl.* sueldo *m*; ingresos *m/pl.*; ganancias *f/pl.*

ear...: '~**phones** *pl.* auriculares *m/pl.*; '~**piece** *teleph.* auricular *m*; '~**ring** (*long*) pendiente *m* (*round*) arete *m*; '~**shot**: *within* ~ al alcance del oído; '~**split·ting** *shout* desaforado; *noise* que rompe el tímpano.

earth [ə:θ] **1.** tierra *f* (*a.* ⚡); *zo.* madriguera *f*; F *cost the* ~ costar un

potosí; *down-to-*~ práctico; *get back to* ~ volver a la realidad; *run to* ~ encontrar (tras larga búsqueda); **2.** ⚡ conectar a tierra; ✗ ~ *up* acollar; **'earth·en** de tierra; *pot* de barro; **'earth·en·ware** loza *f* de barro; cacharros *m/pl.*; **'earth·ly** terrenal, mundano; F *he hasn't an* ~ no tiene posibilidad alguna; *be of no* ~ *use* no servir para nada en absoluto; **'earth·quake** terremoto *m*; **'earth·work** terraplén *m*; **'earth·worm** lombriz *f*; **'earth·y** terroso; *fig.* telúrico; (*coarse*) grosero.

ear...: '~**trum·pet** trompetilla *f* (acústica); '~**wig** tijereta *f*.

ease [i:z] **1.** facilidad *f*; soltura *f*; comodidad *f of living etc.*; alivio *m from pain*; naturalidad *f of manner*; *at* ~ cómodo; *a sus anchas*; *ill at* ~ incómodo; ✗ *stand at* ~! en su lugar ¡descanso!; *life of* ~ vida *f* desahogada; *take one's* ~ descansar; *with* ~ fácilmente, con facilidad; **2.** *v/t.* aliviar, mitigar; (*soften*) suavizar; *weight* aligerar; *pressure* aflojar; *mind* tranquilizar; *v/i.* (*wind*) amainar; (*rain*) moderarse; ~ *off*, ~ *up* suavizarse, aligerarse.

ea·sel ['i:zl] caballete *m*.

ease·ment ['i:zmənt] ⚖ servidumbre *f*.

eas·i·ness ['i:zinis] facilidad *f*; soltura *f*.

east [i:st] **1.** este *m*, oriente *m*; **2.** *adj.* del este, oriental; **3.** *adv.* al este, hacia el este.

East·er ['i:stə] pascua *f florida* (*or* de Resurrección); (*period*) semana *f* santa; *attr. ... de* pascua; ~ *Day*, ~ *Sunday* Domingo *m* de Resurrección.

east·er·ly ['i:stəli] *direction* hacia el este; *wind* del este; **east·ern** ['~tən] oriental; **'east·ern·er** habitante *m/f* del este; **east·ern·most** ['istənmoust] (el) más oriental; **east·ward(s)** ['i:stwəd(z)] hacia el este.

eas·y ['i:zi] **1.** □ fácil; *conditions* cómodo, holgado; *manner* natural, afable; *pace* lento, pausado; *virtue* laxo; *p.* de moralidad laxa; ♀ *money*

abundante; F p. fácil de engañar; v.
street, term; ~ to get on with muy
afable; ~ to run de fácil manejo; 2.
adv. F fácilmente; take it ~ descansar; b.s. haraganear; ir despacio;
take it ~! ¡cálmese!; '~-'chair butaca f, sillón m; '~-going acomodadizo; (careless) descuidado; (lazy)
holgazán.

eat [i:t] 1. [irr.] comer; meal tomar;
consumir with envy etc.; sl. what's
~ing you? ¿qué mosca te ha picado?; ~ away, ~ into corroer; fig.
carcomer; fig. mermar; ~ up comerse; devorar; 2. sl. ~s pl. comida
f (muy sabrosa); 'eat·a·ble comestible; eat·a·bles ['~z] pl. comestibles m/pl.; 'eat·en p.p. of eat 1;
'eat·er: be a big ~ tener siempre
buen apetito; ser comilón; 'eat·ing el
comer; 'eat·ing-house bodegón m.

eau de Co·logne ['oudəkə'loun]
(agua f de) Colonia f.

eaves [i:vz] pl. alero m; 'eaves·drop
escuchar a las puertas; fisgonear;
'eaves·drop·per escuchador m escondido, fisgón m.

ebb [eb] 1. menguante m, reflujo m;
~ tide marea f menguante; at a low
~ decaído; 2. bajar; fig. decaer, disminuir.

eb·on·ite ['ebənait] ebonita f; 'eb-
on·y (attr. de) ébano m.

e·bul·li·ent [i'bʌljənt] fig. exaltado,
entusiasta; **eb·ul·li·tion** [ebə'liʃn]
fig. arranque m.

ec·cen·tric [ik'sentrik] 1. □ excéntrico; 2. ⊕ excéntrica f; (p.) excéntrico m; **ec·cen·tric·i·ty** [eksen-
'trisiti] excentricidad f (a. fig.).

ec·cle·si·as·tic [ikli:zi'æstik], adj.
mst **ec·cle·si·as·ti·cal** □ eclesiástico adj. a. su. m.

ech·e·lon ['eʃəlɔn] 1. escalón m;
2. escalonar.

ech·o ['ekou] 1. eco m; 2. v/t. repetir; opinion hacerse eco de; v/i. resonar; ~sound·er ['~saundə] sonda
f acústica.   [llo m.)

é·clat ['eiklɑ:] éxito m brillante; bri-)

ec·lec·tic [ek'lektik] □ ecléctico adj.
a. su. m; **ec'lec·ti·cism** [~tisizm]
eclecticismo m.

e·clipse [i'klips] 1. eclipse m (a. fig.);
2. eclipsar (a. fig.); **e'clip·tic** eclíptica f.

ec·logue ['eklɔg] égloga f.

e·co·nom·ic [i:kə'nɔmik], **e·co-**

'nom·i·cal □ económico; frugal;
rent justo; **e·co'nom·ics** pl. economía f política; **e·con·o·mist** [i'kɔ-
nəmist] economista m/f; **e'con·o-
mize** [~maiz] economizar (on en);
e'con·o·my economía f; frugalidad f.

ec·sta·sy ['ekstəsi] éxtasis m; go
into ecstasies extasiarse (over ante);
ec·stat·ic [eks'tætik] □ extático.

ec·ze·ma ['eksimə] eczema m.

ed·dy ['edi] 1. remolino m; 2. arremolinarse.

edge [edʒ] 1. (cutting) filo m, corte
m; (border) margen m, borde m,
orilla f; canto m of table etc.; (end)
extremidad f; on ~ de canto; fig.
nervioso; F have the ~ on llevar ventaja a; put an ~ on afilar; set a p.'s
teeth on ~ dar dentera a una p.;
2. v/t. afilar; orlar; sew. ribetear;
v/i. ~ along avanzar de lado; ~ in
abrirse paso (poco a poco); ~ up to
acercarse con cautela a.

edge...: '~-tool herramienta f de
filo; '~ways, '~wise de canto, de
lado; not to let a p. get a word in ~
no dejar meter baza a nadie.

edg·ing ['edʒiŋ] orla f, ribete m.

edg·y ['edʒi] F nervioso.

ed·i·ble ['edibl] comestible.

e·dict ['i:dikt] edicto m.

ed·i·fi·ca·tion [edifi'keiʃn] edificación f; **ed·i·fice** ['~fis] edificio m
(imponente); **ed·i·fy** ['~fai] edificar; 'ed·i·fy·ing □ edificante.

ed·it ['edit] script preparar (or corregir) para la imprenta; paper dirigir, redactar; book editar; ~ed by
(en) edición de; **e·di·tion** [i'diʃn]
edición f; typ. tirada f; **ed·i·tor**
['editə] director m, redactor m of
paper; editor m of book; **ed·i·to·ri·
al** [~'tɔ:riəl] artículo m de fondo; ~
staff redacción f; **ed·i·tor·ship** ['~-
təʃip] dirección f.

ed·u·cate ['edjukeit] educar; instruir; ~d culto; **ed·u·ca·tion** educación f; instrucción f; cultura f;
elementary ~ primera enseñanza f;
secondary ~ segunda enseñanza f;
Ministry of ♀ Ministerio m de Educación (Nacional); **ed·u·ca·tion·al**
□ educacional; docente; film etc.
instructivo; **ed·u·ca·tive** educativo; **ed·u·ca·tion(·al)·ist** [~ʃn(əl)-
ist] educacionista m/f; **ed·u·ca·tor**
educador (-a f) m.

e·duce [i'dju:s] educir, sacar.
e·duc·tion [i'dʌkʃn] educción f; ⊕ evacuación f; **e'duc·tion-pipe** tubo m de emisión.
eel [i:l] anguila f.
e'en [i:n] = even.
e'er [εə] = ever.
ee·rie, **ee·ry** ['iəri] ☐ misterioso; horripilante; inquietante.
ef·face [i'feis] borrar; ~ o.s. retirarse modestamente, lograr pasar inadvertido.
ef·fect [i'fekt] 1. efecto m; resultado m; impresión f; fuerza f; ~s pl. efectos m/pl.; for ~ sólo por impresionar; in ~ en efecto, en realidad; law vigente; of no ~ inútil; to this ~ con este propósito; carry into ~ poner en ejecución; feel the ~ of estar resentido de; give ~ to poner en efecto; put into ~ poner en vigor; take ~ (law) ponerse en vigor; (remedy) surtir efecto; 2. efectuar, llevar a cabo; **ef'fec·tive 1.** ☐ eficaz; potente, impresionante; efectivo; ⚒, ⚓ útil para todos servicios; ⚒ become ~ entrar en vigor; ⊕ ~ capacity capacidad f útil; ⊕ ~ power potencia f real; 2. ⚒ ~s pl. efectivos m/pl.; **ef'fec·tu·al** [~juəl] eficaz; **ef'fec·tu·ate** [~jueit] efectuar.
ef·fem·i·na·cy [i'feminəsi] afeminación f; **ef'fem·i·nate** [~nit] ☐ afeminado.
ef·fer·vesce [efə'ves] estar (or entrar) en efervescencia; bullir; **ef·fer'ves·cence** efervescencia f; **ef·fer'ves·cent** efervescente (a. fig.).
ef·fete [e'fi:t] gastado; decadente.
ef·fi·ca·cious [efi'keiʃəs] ☐ eficaz; **ef·fi·ca·cy** ['~kəsi] eficacia f.
ef·fi·cien·cy [e'fiʃnsi] eficiencia f; eficacia f; capacidad f; ⊕ rendimiento m; **ef'fi·cient** [~ʃnt] ☐ eficiente; eficaz; capaz; ⊕ de buen rendimiento.
ef·fi·gy ['efidʒi] efigie f.
ef·flo·resce [eflɔ:'res] ♀ florecer; ⌂ eflorecerse; **ef·flo'res·cence** eflorescencia f (a. ⌂); **ef·flo'res·cent** eflorescente (a. ⌂).
ef·flu·ent ['efluənt] (corriente f) efluente; **ef·flu·vi·um**, pl. **ef'flu·vi·a** [e'flu:viəm, ~viə] efluvio m, emanación f; tufo m.
ef·fort ['efət] esfuerzo m (to por); F tentativa f; resultado m; spare no ~

to no regatear medio para; **'ef·fort·less** ☐ fácil, nada penoso.
ef·fron·ter·y [e'frʌntəri] descaro m, impudencia f.
ef·fu·sion [i'fju:ʒn] efusión f; **ef'fu·sive** [~siv] ☐ efusivo.
eft [eft] tritón m.
egg¹ [eg]: ~ on incitar (to a), impulsar (to a).
egg² [~] huevo m; sl. tío m; sl. bad ~ calavera m, sinvergüenza m; as sure as ~s sin duda alguna; **'~-cup** huevera f; **'~-flip** yema f mejida; **'~-head** Am. intelectual m; **'~-shell** cáscara f de huevo.
eg·lan·tine ['egləntain] eglantina f.
e·go ['egou] el yo; **'e·go·ism** egoísmo m; **'e·go·ist** egoísta m/f; **e·go·'is·tic, e·go'is·ti·cal** ☐ egoísta; **e·go·tism** ['egoutizm] egotismo m; **'e·go·ist** egotista m/f; **e·go'tis·tic, e·go'tis·ti·cal** ☐ egotista.
e·gre·gious [i'gri:dʒəs] ☐ enorme, chocante.
e·gress ['i:gres] salida f.
E·gyp·tian [i'dʒipʃn] egipcio adj. a. su. m (a f).
eh [ei] ¿cómo?; ¿qué?; ¿no?
ei·der ['aidə] (a. '~-'duck) eider m; **'~-down** edredón m.
eight [eit] ocho (a. su. m); sl. have one over the ~ llevar una copa de más; **eight·een** ['ei'ti:n] dieciocho; **'eight'eenth** [~θ] décimoctavo; **eighth** [~θ] octavo (a. su. m); **eight·i·eth** ['~iiθ] octogésimo; **'eight·y** ochenta.
ei·ther ['aiðə, 'i:ðə] 1. adj. cualquier ... de los dos; 2. pron. uno u otro, cualquiera de los dos; 3. cj. ~ ... or o ... o; 4. adv. tampoco.
e·jac·u·late [i'dʒækjuleit] exclamar, proferir (de repente); **e·jac·u'la·tion** exclamación f.
e·ject [i'dʒekt] expulsar, echar, arrojar; tenant desahuciar; **e'jec·tion** expulsión f; desahucio m from house; **e'jec·tor** ⊕ eyector m, expulsor m; ⚒ ~ seat asiento m expulsor.
eke [i:k] : ~ out hacer llegar; suplir las deficiencias de (with con); livelihood ganar a duras penas.
el [el] Am. F = elevated (railroad) ferrocarril m elevado.
e·lab·o·rate 1. [i'læbərit] ☐ complicado; primoroso; detallado; rebuscado; **2.** [~reit] v/t. elaborar; v/i. ex-

plicarse (~ on explicar) con muchos detalles; ~ on ampliar; **e·lab·o·ra·tion** [~'reiʃn] elaboración f; complicación f etc.

e·lapse [i'læps] pasar, transcurrir.

e·las·tic [i'læstik] □ elástico adj. a. su. m; ~ band gomita f; **e·las·tic·i·ty** [~'tisiti] elasticidad f.

e·late [i'leit] regocijar, exaltar; be ~d alegrarse (at, with de); **e'la·tion** regocijo m, viva alegría f, júbilo m.

el·bow ['elbou] **1.** codo m (a. ⊕); (bend) recodo m; at one's ~ a la mano; muy cerca; out at ~s raído; bend the ~ empinar el codo; **2.** empujar con el codo; ~ one's way (through) abrirse paso codeando; '~-grease F codo m; esfuerzo m, aplicación f; '~-room espacio m suficiente; libertad f de acción.

eld·er¹ ['eldə] **1.** mayor; **2.** mayor m/f; eccl. anciano m; ~s pl. jefes m/pl. (de tribu); my ~s pl. mis mayores.

el·der² [~] ♣ saúco m.

eld·er·ly ['eldəli] mayor, de edad.

eld·est ['eldist] (el) mayor.

e·lect [i'lekt] **1.** elegir, escoger; ~ to optar por inf.; decidir inf.; **2.** elegido; eccl. electo; the ~ los elegidos; president ~ presidente m electo; **e'lec·tion** elección f; **e·lec·tion·eer·ing** campaña f electoral; b.s. maniobras f/pl. electorales; **e'lec·tive 1.** □ electivo; 2. Am. asignatura f electiva; **e'lec·tor** elector (-a f) m; **e'lec·tor·al** electoral; Am. ~ college colegio m electoral; ~ roll lista f electoral; **e'lec·tor·ate** [~rit] electorado m.

e·lec·tric [i'lektrik] □ eléctrico; fig. cargado de emoción; muy tenso, candente; ~ blanket calienta-camas m; ~ blue azul (m) eléctrico; ~ chair silla f eléctrica; **e'lec·tri·cal** □ eléctrico; ~ engineer ingeniero m electricista; ~ engineering electrotecnia f; **e·lec·tri·cian** [~'triʃn] electricista m; **e·lec'tric·i·ty** [~siti] electricidad f; ~ supply suministro m eléctrico; **e·lec·tri·fi·ca·tion** electrificación f; **e'lec·tri·fy** [~fai] electrificar; electrizar (a. fig.).

e·lec·tro [i'lektrou] electro...; **e'lec·tro·cute** [~trəkju:t] electrocutar; **e·lec·tro·cu·tion** electrocución f; **e'lec·trode** [~troud] electrodo m; **e'lec·tro·dy·nam·ics** sg. electro-

dinámica f; **e·lec·trol·y·sis** [~'trolisis] electrólisis f; **e'lec·tro·mag·net** electroimán m; **e'lec·tro·met·al·lur·gy** electrometalurgia f; **e'lec·tro·mo·tor** electromotor m.

e·lec·tron [i'lektrɔn] electrón m; attr. = **e·lec'tron·ic** □ electrónico; ~ brain cerebro m electrónico; **e·lec'tron·ics** sg. electrónica f.

e·lec·tro·plate [i'lektroupleit] **1.** galvanizar; **2.** artículo m galvanizado; **e·lec·tro·type** [i'lektroutaip] electrotipo m. [m.\

e·lec·tu·ar·y [i'lektjuəri] electuario\

el·e·gance ['eligəns] elegancia f; '**el·e·gant** □ elegante.

el·e·gi·ac [eli'dʒaiək] elegíaco.

el·e·gy ['elidʒi] elegía f.

el·e·ment ['elimənt] all senses: elemento m; ~s pl. elementos m/pl., nociones f/pl.; be in one's ~ estar en su elemento; **el·e'men·tal** □ elemental; **el·e'men·ta·ry** □ elemental; ~ school escuela f primaria.

el·e·phant ['elifənt] elefante m; white ~ maula f; **el·e·phan·tine** [~'fæntain] elefantino; fig. mastodóntico.

el·e·vate ['eliveit] elevar; p. exaltar; ascender in rank; '**el·e·vat·ed** elevado (a. fig.); Am. F (a. ~ railroad) ferrocarril m elevado; **el·e'va·tion** all senses: elevación f; '**el·e·va·tor** Am. ascensor m; (goods) montacargas m; Am. ✔ elevador m de granos; ✈ timón m de profundidad.

e·lev·en [i'levn] once (a. su. m); **e'lev·enth** [~θ] undécimo, onceno.

elf [elf] duende m; (dwarf) enano m.

e·lic·it [i'lisit] (son)sacar, lograr obtener.

e·lide [i'laid] elidir.

el·i·gi·bil·i·ty [elidʒə'biliti] elegibilidad f; '**el·i·gi·ble** □ elegible; aceptable, adecuado; bachelor de partido.

e·lim·i·nate [i'limineit] eliminar; solution etc. descartar; suprimir; **e·lim·i'na·tion** eliminación f etc.

e·li·sion [i'liʒn] elisióг f.

é·lite [ei'li:t] élite f; lo selecto, flor f y nata.

e·lix·ir [i'liksə] elixir m.

E·liz·a·be·than [ilizə'bi:θn] isabelino.

elk [elk] alce m.

ell [el] † approx. ana f (= 45 pulgadas).

el·lipse [i'lips] elipse *f*; **el'lip·sis** [~-sis], *pl.* **el'lip·ses** [~si:z] elipsis *f*; **el'lip·tic, el'lip·ti·cal** [~tik(l)] □ elíptico.

elm [elm] olmo *m*.

el·o·cu·tion [elə'kju:ʃn] elocución *f*; (arte *m* de la) declamación *f*; **el·o·'cu·tion·ist** profesor (-a *f*) *m* de elocución.

e·lon·gate ['i:lɔŋgeit] alargar, extender; **e·lon'ga·tion** alargamiento *m*, extensión *f*; *ast.* elongación *f*.

e·lope [i'loup] fugarse (con un amante); **e'lope·ment** fuga *f*.

el·o·quence ['eləkwəns] elocuencia *f*; **'el·o·quent** □ elocuente.

else [els] **1.** *adj.* otro; *all* ~ todo lo demás; *anyone* ~ (cualquier) otro; *nobody* ~ ningún otro; *nothing* ~ nada más; *how* ~? ¿de qué otra manera?; *what* ~? ¿qué más?; **2.** *adv.* (ade)más; F de otro modo; *or* ~ o bien, si no; **'else'where** en (*or* a) otra parte.

e·lu·ci·date [i'lu:sideit] aclarar, dilucidar, elucidar; **e·lu·ci'da·tion** aclaración *f*, elucidación *f*.

e·lude [i'lu:d] *blow etc.* eludir, esquivar, evitar; *grasp* escapar de; *it* ~s me se me escapa; **e'lu·sive** [i'lu:siv] □ fugaz; evasivo; *p.* difícil de encontrar; **e'lu·sive·ness** lo fugaz *etc.*

elves [elvz] *pl. of* elf.

em [em] *typ.* eme *f*.

e·ma·ci·at·ed [i'meiʃieitid] demacrado, extenuado; **e·ma·ci·a·tion** [imeisi'eiʃn] demacración *f*.

em·a·nate ['eməneit] emanar; **em·a'na·tion** emanación *f* (*a. phys.*).

e·man·ci·pate [i'mænsipeit] emancipar; **e·man·ci'pa·tion** emancipación *f*; **e'man·ci·pa·tor** emancipador *m*, libertador *m*.

e·mas·cu·late [i'mæskjuleit] *fig.* mutilar, debilitar; estropear; ~d *style* empobrecido; **e·mas·cu'la·tion** *fig.* mutilación *f*.

em·balm [im'bɑ:m] embalsamar; **em'balm·ment** embalsamamiento *m*.

em·bank·ment [im'bæŋkmənt] terraplén *m*; dique *m*.

em·bar·go [em'bɑ:gou] **1.** embargo *m*; prohibición *f* (*on* de), suspensión *f*; **2.** embargar.

em·bark [im'bɑ:k] *v/t.* embarcar; *v/i.* embarcarse (*for* con rumbo a);

~ (*up*)*on* emprender; **em·bar·ka·tion** [emba:'keiʃn] embarco *m of people*; embarque *m of goods*.

em·bar·rass [im'bærəs] desconcertar, turbar, azorar; molestar; poner en un aprieto; *be* ~ed azorarse, estar azorado; **em'bar·rass·ing** □ embarazoso, desconcertador; vergonzoso; molesto; *moment, situation* violento; **em'bar·rass·ment** desconcierto *m*, (per)turbación *f*, azoramiento *m*; apuro *m*; estorbo *m*.

em·bas·sy ['embəsi] embajada *f*.

em·bat·tled [im'bætld] en orden de batalla; *city* sitiado; △ almenado.

em·bed [im'bed] empotrar, clavar, hincar (*in* en).

em·bel·lish [im'beliʃ] embellecer; adornar, guarnecer; **em'bel·lish·ment** embellecimiento *m*; adorno *m*.

em·ber-days ['embədeiz] *pl.* témporas *f/pl.* [ascua *f*.]

em·bers ['embəz] *pl.* rescoldo *m*,]

em·bez·zle [im'bezl] malversar, defalcar; **em'bez·zle·ment** malversación *f*, desfalco *m*; **em'bez·zler** malversador *m*.

em·bit·ter [im'bitə] amargar; *relations* envenenar.

em·blem ['embləm] emblema *m*; **em·blem·at·ic, em·blem·at·i·cal** [embli'mætik(l)] □ emblemático.

em·bod·i·ment [im'bɔdimənt] encarnación *f*, personificación *f*; **em·'bod·y** encarnar, personificar; (*include*) incorporar.

em·bold·en [im'bouldn] envalentonar.

em·bo·lism ['embəlizm] embolia *f*.

em·boss [im'bɔs] realzar, labrar de realce; estampar en relieve.

em·brace [im'breis] **1.** abrazar(se); (*include*) abarcar; *offer* aceptar; **2.** abrazo *m*.

em·bra·sure [im'breiʒə] △ alféizar *m*; ⚔ tronera *f*, cañonera *f*.

em·bro·ca·tion [embrou'keiʃn] embrocación *f*.

em·broi·der [im'brɔidə] bordar, recamar; *fig.* adornar con detalles ficticios; **em'broi·der·y** bordado *m*.

em·broil [im'brɔil] embrollar, enredar; ~ *with* indisponer con; **em·'broil·ment** embrollo *m*, enredo *m*.

em·bry·o ['embriou] **1.** embrión *m*; *in* ~ en embrión; **2.** = **em·bry·on·ic** [~'ɔnik] □ embrionario.

e·mend [i:'mend] enmendar; **e-men'da·tion** enmienda *f*.

em·er·ald ['emərəld] **1.** esmeralda *f*; **2.** esmeraldino.

e·merge [i'mə:dʒ] salir, surgir, emerger; aparecer; resultar (de una investigación) (*that* que); **e'mer·gence** salida *f*, aparición *f*; **e'mer·gen·cy** necesidad *f* urgente, aprieto *m*, situación *f* imprevista; ∼ *brake* freno *m* de auxilio; ∼ *exit* salida *f* de urgencia; ∼ *landing* aterrizaje *m* forzoso; ∼ *measure* medida *f* de urgencia.

em·er·y ['eməri] esmeril *m*; '∼**-cloth** tela *f* de esmeril.

e·met·ic [i'metik] emético *adj. a. su. m*.

em·i·grant ['emigrənt] emigrante *adj. a. su. m/f*; **em·i·grate** ['∼greit] emigrar; **em·i'gra·tion** emigración *f*.

em·i·nence ['eminəns] eminencia *f* (*a. title*); '**em·i·nent** □ eminente.

em·is·sar·y ['emisəri] emisario *m*; **e·mis·sion** [i'miʃn] emisión *f*.

e·mit [i'mit] emitir; *smoke etc.* arrojar, despedir; *cry* dar; *sound* producir.

e·mol·u·ment [i'mɔljumənt] emolumento *m*.

e·mo·tion [i'mouʃn] emoción *f*; **e'mo·tion·al** □ emocional; *moment* de mucha emoción; *p.* exaltado; demasiado sensible; **e'mo·tive** □ emotivo.

em·pan·el [im'pænl] *jury* elegir, inscribir.

em·per·or ['empərə] emperador *m*.

em·pha·sis ['emfəsis], *pl.* **em·pha·ses** ['∼si:z] énfasis *m*; **em·pha·size** ['∼saiz] acentuar (*a. fig.*); *fig.* subrayar, recalcar; **em·phat·ic** [im-'fætik] □ enfático; enérgico; *be* ∼ *that* insistir en que.

em·pire ['empaiə] imperio *m*.

em·pir·ic [em'pirik] empírico *adj.* (*mst* **em'pir·i·cal** □) *a. su. m*; **em-'pir·i·cism** empirismo *m*; **em'pir·i·cist** empírico *m*.

em·place·ment [im'pleismənt] sitio *m*, colocación *f*; ✗ emplazamiento *m*.

em·ploy [im'plɔi] **1.** emplear; servirse de; **2.** empleo *m*; servicio *m*; ocupación *f*; *in the* ∼ *of* empleado por; **em·ploy·ee** [emplɔi'i:] empleado (a *f*) *m*, dependiente (a *f*) *m*;

em·ploy·er [im'plɔiə] patrón *m*; **em'ploy·ment** empleo *m*; ocupación *f*; servicio *m*; *full* ∼ pleno empleo *m*; *level of* ∼ nivel *m* de trabajo; ∼ *agency* agencia *f* de colocaciones; ♀ *Exchange* bolsa *f* de trabajo.

em·po·ri·um [em'pɔ:riəm] emporio *m*.

em·pow·er [im'pauə] autorizar (*to* a); habilitar (*to* para que); facultar (*to* para).

em·press ['empris] emperatriz *f*.

emp·ti·ness ['emptinis] vacío *m*; vaciedad *f*, vacuidad *f*; **emp·ty** ['empti] **1.** vacío; (*fruitless*) vano, inútil; *house, place* desocupado; *post* vacante; *vehicle* sin carga; F hambriento; **2.** *v/t.* vaciar; *contents* descargar, verter; *place* desocupar, dejar vacío; *v/i.* vaciarse; (*drain away*) desaguar; (*place*) ir quedando vacío (*or* desocupado); ∼ *into* (*river*) desembocar en; **3.** botella *f* etc. vacía; **empties** *pl.* envases *m/pl.*; '∼-'hand·ed con las manos vacías, manivacío.

e·mu ['i:mju:] emú *m*.

em·u·late ['emjuleit] emular; **em-u'la·tion** emulación *f*; '**em·u·lous** □ émulo; emulador (*of* de).

e·mul·sion [i'mʌlʃn] emulsión *f*.

en·a·ble [i'neibl] permitir (*to inf.*); habilitar (*to* para que); poner en condiciones (*to* para).

en·act [i'nækt] decretar; *law* dar, promulgar; *thea.* representar, realizar; **en'act·ment** ley *f*, estatuto *m*; promulgación *f of law*.

en·am·el [i'næml] **1.** esmalte *m*; **2.** esmaltar, pintar al esmalte.

en·am·o(u)r [i'næmə] enamorar; *be* ∼*ed of p.* estar enamorado de; *th.* tener gran afición a.

en·camp [in'kæmp] acampar(se); **en'camp·ment** campamento *m*.

en·case [in'keis] encaj(on)ar; encerrar.

en·cash·ment [in'kæʃmənt] cobro *m*.

en·chain [in'tʃein] encadenar.

en·chant [in'tʃɑ:nt] encantar (*a. fig.*); **en'chant·er** hechicero *m*; **en'chant·ing** □ encantador; **en-'chant·ress** hechicera *f*.

en·cir·cle [in'sə:kl] cercar; rodear, circunvalar; *waist* ceñir; ✗, *pol.* envolver; **en'cir·cle·ment** ✗, *pol.* envolvimiento *m*.

en·clave ['enkleiv] enclave *m.*

en·close [in'klouz] cercar, encerrar; (*include*) incluir; remitir adjunto, adjuntar *with letter*; **en'clo·sure** [~ʒə] (*place*) cercado *m*, recinto *m*; (*act*) encerramiento *m*; cosa *f etc.* inclusa *in letter.*

en·co·mi·ast [en'koumiæst] encomiasta *m/f*; **en'co·mi·um** [~miəm] encomio *m.*

en·com·pass [in'kʌmpəs] abarcar; (*surround*) rodear; (*bring about*) lograr.

en·core [ɔŋ'kɔ:] 1. ¡bis!; 2. pedir la repetición de *a th.*, a *a p.*; 3. repetición *f*, bis *m.*

en·coun·ter [in'kauntə] 1. *all senses:* encuentro *m*; 2. encontrar(se con), tropezar con.

en·cour·age [in'kʌridʒ] animar, alentar (to a); *industry* fomentar, reforzar; *growth* estimular; fortalecer *in a belief*; **en'cour·age·ment** estimulo *m*, incentivo *m*; aliento *m*; fomento *m*; *give* ~ *to* infundir ánimo(s) a; **en'cour·a·ging** □ alentador, esperanzador; favorable.

en·croach [in'kroutʃ] pasar los límites (on de); invadir (on *acc.*); *fig.* usurpar (on *acc.*); **en'croach·ment** invasión *f*; intrusión *f*; *fig.* usurpación *f.*

en·crust [in'krʌst] incrustar(se).

en·cum·ber [in'kʌmbə] estorbar; gravar, cargar *with debts etc.*; *place* llenar; **en'cum·brance** estorbo *m*, impedimento *m*; gravamen *m*, carga *f*; *without* ~ sin familia.

en·cy·clo·pae·di·a [ensaiklou'pi:diə] enciclopedia *f*; **en·cy·clo'pae·dic** enciclopédico.

end [end] 1. fin *m*, final *m*; extremo *m*, cabo *m*; remate *m*; límite *m*; *sport*: lado *m*; desenlace *m of play*; (*object*) fin *m*, objeto *m*; *at the* ~ *of* al cabo de; *century etc.* a fines de; *in the* ~ al fin y al cabo; *on* ~ de punta, de canto; *3 days on* ~ 3 días seguidos; *for days on* ~ durante una infinidad de días; *no* ~ *of* un sinfín de, la mar de; *to the* ~ *that* a fin de que; *to this* ~ con este propósito; *be at an* ~ estar terminado; *come to an* ~ terminarse; *keep one's* ~ *up* no cejar, defenderse bien; *make an* ~ *of* acabar con; *make both* ~s *meet* hacer llegar el dinero; *put an* ~ *to* poner fin a; *stand on* ~ poner(se) de punta; 2. final; 3. *v/t.*

acabar, terminar; *v/i.* terminar (*in* en; *with* con; *by present participle*); acabar; (*route*) morir; ~ *up* acabar; ir a parar (*at* en).

en·dan·ger [in'deindʒə] poner en peligro, comprometer.

en·dear [in'diə] hacer querer; ~ *o.s. to* hacerse querer de; **en'dear·ing** □ atractivo, simpatiquísimo; **en'dear·ment** palabra *f* cariñosa, ternura *f*, caricia *f.*

en·deav·o(u)r [in'devə] 1. esfuerzo *m*, empeño *m*; tentativa *f*; 2. esforzarse (to por), procurar (to *inf.*).

en·dem·ic [en'demik] 1. *a.* **en'dem·i·cal** □ endémico; 2. endemia *f.*

end·ing ['endiŋ] fin *m*, conclusión *f*; desenlace *m of book etc.*; *gr.* desinencia *f.*

en·dive ['endiv] escarola *f*, endibia *f.*

end·less ['endlis] □ inacabable, interminable; ⊕ sin fin.

en·dorse [in'dɔ:s] endosar; *fig.* aprobar, confirmar; *licence* poner nota de inhabilitación en; **en'dor·see** [endɔ:'si:] endosatario *m*; **en·dorse·ment** [in'dɔ:smənt] endoso *m*; *fig.* aprobación *f*, confirmación *f*; nota *f* de inhabilitación *in licence*; **en'dors·er** endosante *m/f.*

en·dow [in'dau] dotar (*a. fig.*) (*with* con, *fig.* de); fundar; **en'dow·ment** dotación *f*; fundación *f*; *fig.* dote *f*, prenda *f.*

en·due [in'dju:] dotar (*with* de).

en·dur·a·ble [in'djuərəbl] tolerable, soportable; **en'dur·ance** resistencia *f*, paciencia *f*; aguante *m*; *past* ~ inaguantable; ~ *race* carrera *f* de resistencia; **en·dure** [in'djuə] *v/t.* aguantar, soportar, tolerar; resistir; *v/i.* (per)durar; sufrir sin rendirse.

end·way(s) ['endwei(z)], **end·wise** ['~waiz] de punta; de pie; de lado.

en·e·ma ['enimə] enema *f.*

en·e·my ['enimi] enemigo *adj. a. su. m* (*a f*) (*of* de).

en·er·get·ic [enə'dʒetik] □ enérgico; **'en·er·gize** activar; excitar (*a. ƒ*); **'en·er·gy** energía *f.*

en·er·vate ['enə:veit] enervar; **'en·er·vat·ing** enervador, deprimente; **en·er'va·tion** enervación *f.*

en·fee·ble [in'fi:bl] debilitar; **en·'fee·ble·ment** debilitación *f.*

en·fi·lade [enfi'leid] 1. enfilar; 2. enfilada *f.*

en·fold [in'fould] envolver, abrazar; estrechar (entre los brazos).

en·force [in'fɔːs] *law* hacer cumplir, poner en vigor; *demand* insistir en; imponer (*upon* a); **en'force·ment** ejecución *f of law*; imposición *f*.

en·fran·chise [in'fræntʃaiz] conceder el derecho de votar a; (*free*) emancipar; **en'fran·chise·ment** [‿tʃizmənt] concesión *f* del derecho de votar; emancipación *f*.

en·gage [in'geidʒ] *v/t.* (*contract*) apalabrar; *taxi etc.* alquilar; *servant* ajustar, tomar a su servicio; *attention* atraer, ocupar; *p.* entretener *in conversation;* ⊕ (*a.* ‿ *with*) engranar con; ⊕ *coupling* acoplar; ✕ *enemy* trabar batalla con; *be* ‿*d* estar prometido (*to* para casarse con); *teleph.* estar comunicando; *be* ‿*d in* estar ocupado en, dedicarse a; *get* ‿*d* prometerse; *v/i.* (*promise*) comprometerse (*to* a); ⊕ engranar (*in*, *with* con); ‿ *in* ocuparse en, dedicarse a; **en'gage·ment** (*contract*) contrato *m*, ajuste *m*; (*appointment*) compromiso *m*, cita *f*; (*to marry*) palabra *f* de casamiento; (*period of* ‿) noviazgo *m*; ✕ combate *m*, acción *f*.

en·gag·ing [in'geidʒiŋ] □ simpático, atractivo, agraciado.

en·gen·der [in'dʒendə] engendrar (*a.* †), dar lugar a, suscitar.

en·gine ['endʒin] motor *m*; 🚂 máquina *f*, locomotora *f*; **'en·gined** de ... motores; **'en·gine-driv·er** maquinista *m*.

en·gi·neer [endʒi'niə] **1.** ingeniero *m* (*a.* ✕, ⚓); mecánico *m*; *Am.* 🚂 maquinista *m*; **2.** F lograr, agenciar, gestionar; **en·gi'neer·ing** (*attr.* de) ingeniería *f*.

en·gine-room ['endʒinrum] sala *f* de máquinas.

Eng·lish ['iŋgliʃ] inglés *adj. a. su. m*; *the* ‿ los ingleses; **'Eng·lish·man** inglés *m*; **'Eng·lish·wom·an** inglesa *f*.

en·gorge [in'gɔːdʒ] atracar(se).

en·grain [in'grein] *v.* ingrain.

en·grave [in'greiv] grabar (*a. fig.*); burilar; **en'grav·er** grabador *m*; **en'grav·ing** grabado *m*.

en·gross [in'grous] absorber; ☧ redactar en forma legal; poner en limpio; **en'gross·ment** absorción *f*; copia *f* caligráfica.

en·gulf [in'gʌlf] sumergir, hundir, tragar(se).

en·hance [in'hɑːns] realzar; *price* aumentar; **en'hance·ment** realce *m*.

e·nig·ma [i'nigmə] enigma *m*; **e·nig·mat·ic, e·nig·mat·i·cal** [e-nig'mætik(l)] □ enigmático.

en·join [in'dʒɔin] mandar, ordenar (*to inf.*); imponer (*on* a); *Am.* ☧ prohibir (*from inf.*).

en·joy [in'dʒɔi] *health, possessions* gozar de, disfrutar de; *advantages* poseer; *meal* comer con gusto; *hə* ‿*s swimming* le gusta nadar; *b.s.* ‿ *ger.* gozarse en *inf.*; ‿ *o.s.* divertirse mucho, pasarlo bien; *did you* ‿ *the play?* ¿le gustó la comedia?; **en-'joy·a·ble** □ deleitable, agradable; divertido; **en'joy·ment** placer *m*; goce *m*; gusto *m*; disfrute *m of in-heritance etc.*

en·lace [in'leis] en(tre)lazar; ceñir.

en·large [in'lɑːdʒ] *v/t.* agrandar, ensanchar; aumentar; ampliar (*a. phot.*); *v/i.*: ‿ *upon* tratar con más extensión; exagerar; **en'large·ment** ensanche *m*; extensión *f*; aumento *m*; ampliación *f* (*a. phot.*); **en'larg·er** *phot.* ampliadora *f*.

en·light·en [in'laitn] ilustrar, iluminar; instruir (*in* en); *can you* ‿ *me?* ¿puede Vd. ayudarme? (*about* en el asunto de); **en'light·en·ment** ilustración *f*.

en·list [in'list] ✕ alistar(se); *support* conseguir; ✕ ‿*ed man* soldado *m* raso.

en·liv·en [in'laivn] vivificar, avivar, animar.

en·mesh [in'meʃ] coger en la red; ⊕ engranar.

en·mi·ty ['enmiti] enemistad *f*.

en·no·ble [i'noubl] ennoblecer.

e·nor·mi·ty [i'nɔːmiti] *fig.* enormidad *f*; **e'nor·mous** □ enorme.

e·nough [i'nʌf] bastante; suficiente; *be kind* ‿ *to* tener la amabilidad de; *more than* ‿ más que suficiente (*to* para); *I've had* ‿ *of him* estoy harto de él; *I had* ‿ *to do to get home* me costó trabajo llegar a casa; *v. sure*; *that's* ‿! ¡basta!

en·quire [in'kwaiə] = inquire.

en·rage [in'reidʒ] enfurecer, hacer rabiar.

en·rich [in'ritʃ] enriquecer; *soil fer-*

tilizar; **en·rich·ment** enriquecimiento *m*; fertilización *f*.

en·rol(l) [in'roul] alistar(se) (*a.* ✗); inscribir(se), matricular(se); **en·'rol(l)·ment** alistamiento *m*; inscripción *f*.

en·sconce [in'skɔns]: ~ *o.s.* instalarse cómodamente, acomodarse.

en·semble [ã:'sã:mbl] (*dress*) conjunto *m*; F traje *m*; ♪ agrupación *f*.

en·shrine [in'ʃrain] *fig.* encerrar.

en·sign ['ensain] bandera *f*; *Am.* alférez *m*.

en·slave [in'sleiv] esclavizar; **en·'slave·ment** esclavitud *f*; (*act*) avasallamiento *m*.

en·snare [in'snɛə] entrampar.

en·sue [in'sju:] seguirse, resultar; sobrevenir.

en·sure [in'ʃuə] asegurar.   '

en·tab·la·ture [en'tæblətʃə] cornisamento *m*.

en·tail [in'teil] 1. vínculo *m*, vinculación *f*; 2. ocasionar, causar; suponer; ♁ vincular.

en·tan·gle [in'tæŋgl] enmarañar, enredar; **en·'tan·gle·ment** embrollo *m*, enredo *m* (*amoroso etc.*); *barbed wire* ~ alambrada *f*.

en·ter ['entə] *v/t.* entrar en; penetrar en; *society* ingresar en, matricularse en; *member* matricular; asentar, registrar *in records*; *protest* formular; ✝ *order* asentar, anotar; *child* inscribir como futuro alumno (*for de*); ~ *a p.'s head* ocurrírsele a uno; ~ *up* ✝ *ledger* hacer, llevar; *diary* poner al día; *v/i.* entrar; *thea.* entrar en escena; *sport:* participar (*for en*), presentarse (*for a*); ~ *into* participar en; *agreement* firmar; *conversation* entablar; *plans* formar parte de; *relations* establecer; ~ *into the spirit of* dejarse emocionar por; empaparse en; ~ (*up*)*on career* emprender; *office* tomar posesión de; *term* empezar.

en·ter·ic [en'terik] entérico; **en·ter·i·tis** [ˌtə'raitis] enteritis *f*.

en·ter·prise ['entəpraiz] empresa *f*; (*spirit*) iniciativa *f*; *private* ~ iniciativa *f* privada; **'en·ter·pris·ing** ☐ emprendedor.

en·ter·tain [entə'tein] (*amuse*) entretener, divertir; *guest* recibir; festejar, agasajar; *idea, hope* abrigar; considerar; *they* ~ *a great deal* reciben mucho en casa; **en·ter·**

'tain·er actor *m*, músico *m* (*etc.*); **en·ter'tain·ing** ☐ entretenido, divertido; **en·ter'tain·ment** entretenimiento *m*, diversión *f*; espectáculo *m*; función *f*; ~ *tax* impuesto *m* sobre los espectáculos.

en·thral(l) [in'θrɔ:l] *fig.* encantar, embelesar; cautivar.

en·throne [in'θroun] entronizar; **en'throne·ment** entronización *f*.

en·thuse [in'θju:z] F: ~ *over* entusiasmarse mucho por.

en·thu·si·asm [in'θju:ziæzm] entusiasmo *m* (*for* por); **en'thu·si·ast** [ˌæst] entusiasta *m/f*; **en·thu·si·'as·tic** ☐ entusiasta; entusiástico; lleno de entusiasmo (*about, over* por).

en·tice [in'tais] tentar, atraer (con maña); seducir; **en'tice·ment** tentación *f*; seducción *f*.

en·tire [in'taiə] entero; completo; **en'tire·ly** enteramente; **en'tire·ty**: *in its* ~ enteramente, completamente; en su totalidad.

en·ti·tle [in'taitl] *book* intitular; ~ *to* dar derecho a (*acc., inf.*); *be* ~*d to* tener derecho a.

en·ti·ty ['entiti] entidad *f*, ente *m*.

en·tomb [in'tu:m] sepultar.

en·to·mol·o·gy [entə'mɔlədʒi] entomología *f*.

en·tour·age [ɔntu'rɑ:ʒ] séquito *m*.

en·trails ['entreilz] *pl.* entrañas *f/pl.*

en·trance[1] ['entrəns] entrada *f*; ingreso *m*; *thea.* entrada *f* en escena; ~ *examination* examen *m* de ingreso; ~ *fee* cuota *f*.

en·trance[2] [in'trɑ:ns] encantar, embelesar, hechizar; extasiar.

en·trant ['entrənt] principiante *m/f*; *sport:* participante *m/f*.

en·treat [in'tri:t] rogar, suplicar (insistentemente) (*to inf.*); **en·'treat·y** ruego *m*, súplica *f* (insistente).

en·trench [in'trentʃ] ✗ atrincherar(se); *fig.* ~ *o.s.* establecerse firmemente; **en'trench·ment** trinchera *f*, atrincheramiento *m*.

en·trust [in'trʌst] confiar (*to a*; *a p. with a th.* algo a alguien).

en·try ['entri] entrada *f*; ingreso *m*; (*street*) bocacalle *f*; ♁ toma *f* de posesión (*on* de); *sport:* (*total*) participación *f*; (*p.*) participante *m/f*; artículo *m in dictionary*; apunte *m in diary*; ✝

partida *f*; *no* ~ prohibido el paso; dirección prohibida; ~ *permit* permiso *m* de entrada; *book-keeping by double (single)* ~ contabilidad *f* por partida doble (simple).

en·twine [in'twain] entretejer; entrelazar.

e·nu·mer·ate [i'nju:məreit] enumerar; e·nu·mer'a·tion enumeración *f*.

e·nun·ci·ate [i'nʌnsieit] enunciar; pronunciar; e·nun·ci'a·tion enunciación *f*; pronunciación *f*.

en·vel·op [in'veləp] envolver (*in* en); ✂ ~*ing movement* movimiento *m* envolvente; en·ve·lope ['enviloup], *Am. a.* en·vel·op [in'veləp] sobre *m*; ✂ envoltura *f*; en·vel·op·ment [in'veləpmənt] envolvimiento *m*.

en·ven·om [in'venəm] envenenar (*a. fig.*).

en·vi·a·ble ['enviəbl] □ envidiable; 'en·vi·ous □ envidioso; *be* ~ *of* tener envidia de.

en·vi·ron·ment [in'vaiərənmənt] medio *m* ambiente; en·vi·rons ['environz] *pl.* alrededores *m/pl.*, inmediaciones *f/pl.*

en·vis·age [in'vizidʒ] prever; concebir, representarse; contemplar.

en·voy ['envɔi] enviado *m*.

en·vy ['envi] 1. envidia *f*; 2. envidiar (*a p. a th.* algo a alguien); *p.* tener envidia a.

e·paul·ette [epɔ:l'et] charretera *f*.

e·pergne [i'pɔ:n] centro *m* de mesa.

e·phem·er·al [i'fi:mərəl] efímero.

ep·ic ['epik] 1. □ épico; 2. épica *f*, epopeya *f*.

ep·i·cure ['epikjuə] gastrónomo *m*; ep·i·cu·re·an [~'riən] epicúreo *adj. a. su. m* (*a. fig.*).

ep·i·dem·ic [epi'demik] 1. □ epidémico; 2. epidemia *f*.

ep·i·der·mis [epi'də:mis] epidermis *f*.

ep·i·gram ['epigræm] epigrama *m*; ep·i·gram·mat·ic, ep·i·gram·mat·i·cal [~grə'mætik(l)] □ epigramático.

ep·i·lep·sy ['epilepsi] epilepsia *f*; ep·i'lep·tic epiléptico *adj. a. su. m* (*a f*).

ep·i·logue ['epiləg] epílogo *m*.

E·piph·a·ny [i'pifəni] Epifanía *f*.

e·pis·co·pa·cy [i'piskəpəsi] episcopado *m*; e'pis·co·pal episcopal; e'pis·co·pate [~pit] episcopado *m*.

ep·i·sode ['episoud] episodio *m*; ep·i·sod·ic, ep·i·sod·i·cal [~'sɔd-ik(l)] □ episódico.

e·pis·tle [i'pisl] epístola *f*; e'pis·to·lar·y [~tələri] epistolar.

ep·i·taph ['epitɑ:f] epitafio *m*.

ep·i·thet ['epiθet] epíteto *m*.

e·pit·o·me [i'pitəmi] epítome *m*, compendio *m*; *fig.* representación *f* en miniatura, resumen *m*; e'pit·o·mize epitomar, compendiar; *fig.* representar en miniatura.

ep·och ['i:pɔk] época *f*; '~-mak·ing que hace época.

Ep·som salts ['epsəm'sɔ:lts] *pl.* sal *f* de la Higuera.

e·qua·bil·i·ty [ekwə'biliti] uniformidad *f*; tranquilidad *f*, ecuanimidad *f*; 'eq·ua·ble □ *climate etc.* igual, uniforme; *temperament* tranquilo, ecuánime.

e·qual ['i:kwl] 1. □ igual (*to* a); *fig.* ~ *to task* con fuerzas para; *occasion* al nivel de; 2. igual *m/f*; 3. ser igual a; e·qual·i·ty [i'kwɔliti] igualdad *f*; e·qual·i·za·tion [i:kwəl-ai'zeiʃn] igualación *f*; 'e·qual·ize *v/t.* igualar; *v/i. sport:* lograr el empate. [nimidad *f*.\

e·qua·nim·i·ty [i:kwə'nimiti] ecua-/

e·quate [i'kweit] igualar, considerar equivalente (*to, with* a); e'qua·tion ecuación *f*; e'qua·tor ecuador *m*; e·qua·to·ri·al [ekwə'tɔ:riəl] □ ecuatorial.

eq·uer·ry [e'kweri] caballerizo *m* (del rey).

e·ques·tri·an [i'kwestriən] 1. ecuestre; 2. jinete ⟨a *f*⟩ *m*.

e·qui·dis·tant ['i:kwi'distənt] □ equidistante.

e·qui·lat·er·al ['i:kwi'lætərəl] □ equilátero.

e·quil·i·brist [i:'kwilibrist] equilibrista *m/f*; e·qui'lib·ri·um [~əm] equilibrio *m*.

e·quine ['i:kwain] 🐎 equino; caballar, hípico.

e·qui·noc·tial [i:kwi'nɔkʃl] equinoccial; e·qui·nox ['~nɔks] equinoccio *m*.

e·quip [i'kwip] equipar; ⊕ ~*ped with* dotado de; *be well* ~*ped to inf.* estar bien dotado para *inf.*; e·quip·ment [i'kwipmənt] equipo *m*; material *m*; avíos *m/pl.*; equipaje *m*; pertrechos *m/pl.*; (*mental*) aptitud *f*.

e·qui·poise ['ekwipɔiz] **1.** equilibrio *m*; contrapeso *m*; **2.** equilibrar; contrapesar.

eq·ui·ta·ble ['ekwitəbl] □ equitativo; **'eq·ui·ty** equidad *f* (*a.* ɪ̌ɪ̌); † *equities pl.* acciones *f/pl.* de dividendo no fijo.

e·quiv·a·lence [i'kwivələns] equivalencia *f*; **e'quiv·a·lent** equivalente *adj. a. su. m* (to a).

e·quiv·o·cal [i'kwivəkl] □ equívoco, ambiguo; **e'quiv·o·cate** [‿keit] soslayar el problema, usar equívocos (para no contestar directamente); **e·quiv·o'ca·tion** equívoco *m*.

e·ra ['iərə] era *f*, época *f*. [*m*.]

e·rad·i·cate [i'rædikeit] desarraigar, extirpar; **e·rad·i'ca·tion** desarraigo *m*, extirpación *f*.

e·rase [i'reiz] borrar (*a. fig.*); **e'ras·er** goma *f* de borrar; **e'ra·sure** [‿ʒə] borradura *f*.

ere [ɛə] † **1.** *cj.* antes (de) que; **2.** *prp.* antes de; ~ *long* dentro de poco.

e·rect [i'rekt] **1.** □ erguido, derecho; *hair etc.* erizado; **2.** erigir, construir, levantar; ⊕ montar; *principles* formular; constituir (into en); **e'rec·tion** construcción *f*, estructura *f*; (*act*) erección *f*; ⊕ montaje *m*; **e'rect·ness** lo erguido *etc.*; **e'rec·tor** constructor *m*.

erg [ə:g] ergio *m*.

er·got ['ə:gət] cornezuelo *m*.

er·mine ['ə:min] armiño *m*.

e·rode [i'roud] *soil* erosionar(se), causar erosión en; *metal etc.* corroer, desgastar(se).

e·ro·sion [i'rouʒn] erosión *f*; desgaste *m*; **e'ro·sive** [‿siv] erosivo.

e·rot·ic [i'rɔtik] □ erótico; erotómano; (*obscene*) sicalíptico; **e'rot·i·cism** [‿sizm] erotomanía *f*; sicalipsis *f*.

err [ə:] errar, equivocarse; (*sin*) pecar; ~ *on the side of* pecar por exceso de.

er·rand ['erənd] recado *m*, mandado *m*; *run* ~*s* ir a los mandados; '~*-boy* mandadero *m*, recadero *m*.

er·rant ['erənt] errante; *knight* andante; (*erring*) equivocado.

er·rat·ic [i'rætik] □ irregular, inconstante; *performance, record etc.* desigual; *behaviour* excéntrico; *geol.*, ⚒ errático; **er·ra·tum** [i'rɑ:təm], *pl.* **er'ra·ta** [‿ə] errata *f*.

er·ro·ne·ous [i'rounjəs] □ erróneo.

er·ror ['erə] error *m*, yerro *m*; equivocación *f*; *in* ~ por equivocación.

e·ruc·ta·tion [i:rʌk'teiʃn] ⚕ eructo *m*.

er·u·dite ['erudait] □ erudito; **er·u·di·tion** [‿'diʃn] erudición *f*.

e·rupt [i'rʌpt] (*volcano*) entrar en erupción; ⚒ hacer erupción; *fig.* irrumpir (*into* en); (*anger*) estallar; **e'rup·tion** erupción *f* (*a.* ⚒); explosión *f of anger etc.*; **e'rup·tive** eruptivo.

er·y·sip·e·las [eri'sipiləs] erisipela *f*.

es·ca·la·tor ['eskəleitə] escalera *f* móvil (*or* rodante).

es·ca·pade [eskə'peid] travesura *f*, aventura *f*; **es·cape** [is'keip] **1.** *v/t.* evitar, eludir; *death* escapar a; *vigilance* burlar; (*forget*) olvidársele (a uno); (*meaning*) *p.* escaparse a; ~ *notice* pasar inadvertido; *a cry* ~*d him* no pudo contener un grito; *v/i.* escapar(se); evadirse; (*gas etc.*) fugarse; ~ *from p.* escaparse a; *prison* escaparse de; **2.** escape *m*, fuga *f*; fuga *f of gas etc.*; *fig.* escapatoria *f* (*from duties etc.*); *have a narrow* ~ escaparse por un pelo; **es'cape·ment** ⊕ escape *m*; **es'cap·ism** escapismo *m*.

es·carp [is'kɑ:p] **1.** (*a.* **es'carp·ment**) escarpa *f*; **2.** escarpar.

es·cheat [is'tʃi:t] **1.** reversión *f* de bienes mostrencos; **2.** *v/t.* confiscar; transferir (al estado *etc.*); *v/i.* revertir (al estado *etc.*).

es·chew [is'tʃu:] evitar; renunciar a.

es·cort 1. ['eskɔ:t] ⚔ escolta *f*; acompañante *m/f*; **2.** [is'kɔ:t] escoltar; acompañar.

es·cri·toire [eskri'twa:] escritorio *m*.

es·cutch·eon [is'kʌtʃn] escudo *m* de armas; *fig.* honor *m*.

Es·ki·mo ['eskimou] esquimal *m/f*.

e·so·ter·ic [esou'terik] □ esotérico.

es·pe·cial [is'peʃl] □ especial; particular; **es'pe·cial·ly** especialmente; sobre todo; máxime.

es·pi·o·nage [espiə'nɑ:ʒ] espionaje *m*. [(*mst* marítimo).]

es·plan·ade [esplə'neid] paseo *m*]

es·pous·al [is'pauzl] *fig.* adhesión *f* (*of* a); **es'pouse** [‿z] casarse con; *fig.* adherirse a, abrazar.

es·py [is'pai] divisar.

es·quire [is'kwaiə] *on envelopes:* Sr. don; *v.* squire.

es·say 1. [e'sei] intentar (*to inf.*); (*test*) ensayar; **2.** ['esei] ensayo *m*; **'es·say·ist** ensayista *m/f*.

es·sence ['esns] esencia *f*; **es·sen·tial** [i'senʃl] **1.** □ esencial; indispensable, imprescindible; ~ *oil* aceite *m* esencial; **2.** esencial *m*.

es·tab·lish [is'tæbliʃ] establecer; fundar; *facts* verificar; ~ *that* comprobar que; ⍦*ed Church* iglesia *f* del Estado; **es'tab·lish·ment** establecimiento *m*; fundación *f*; ✗ efectivos *m/pl.*, fuerzas *f/pl.*; *the* ⍦ centro del poder efectivo en Inglaterra; † *etc.* personal *m*.

es·tate [is'teit] (*land etc.*) finca *f*, hacienda *f*, heredad *f*; ⚖ (*property*) bienes *m/pl.* (relictos); herencia *f*; *pol.* estado *m*; ~ *agent* corredor *m* de fincas; ~ *car* rubia *f*; ~ *duty* impuesto *m* sobre los bienes relictos; *real* ~ bienes *m/pl.* raíces; *third* ~ estado *m* llano; F *fourth* ~ la prensa.

es·teem [is'ti:m] **1.** estima *f*; consideración *f*, aprecio *m*; **2.** estimar, apreciar; *I should* ~ *it a favour if* agradecería que.

Es·tho·ni·an [es'tounjən] **1.** estonio *adj. a. su. m* (*a f*); **2.** (*language*) estonio *m*.

es·ti·ma·ble ['estiməbl] estimable.

es·ti·mate 1. ['estimeit] estimar; apreciar; calcular (*that* que); computar, tasar (*at* en); hacer un presupuesto (*for* de); **2.** ['~mit] estimación *f*; tasa *f*; cálculo *m*; presupuesto *m for work*; **es·ti'ma·tion** estimación *f*; *in my* ~ según mis cálculos; en mi opinión.

es·trange [is'treindʒ] enajenar, apartar; *become* ~*d* malquistarse; **es'trange·ment** enajenamiento *m*, extrañamiento *m*; desavenencia *m*.

es·tu·ar·y ['estjuəri] estuario *m*, ría *f*.

et·cet·er·a [it'setrə] etcétera; ~*s pl.* adiciones *f/pl.*, adornos *m/pl.*

etch [etʃ] grabar al agua fuerte; **'etch·ing** aguafuerte *f*.

e·ter·nal [i'tə:nl] □ eterno; (*a. b.s.*) sempiterno; **e'ter·nal·ize** [~nəlaiz] eternizar; **e'ter·ni·ty** eternidad *f*; **e·ter·nize** [i'tə:naiz] eternizar.

e·ther ['i:θə] éter *m*; **e·the·re·al** etéreo (*a. fig.*); **'e·ther·ize** eterizar.

eth·i·cal ['eθikl] □ ético; honrado; **'eth·ics** *mst sg.* ética *f*; moralidad *f*.

E·thi·o·pi·an [i:θi'oupiən] etíope *adj. a. su. m/f*.

eth·nog·ra·phy [eθ'nɔgrəfi] etnografía *f*; **eth'nol·o·gy** [~'lədʒi] etnología *f*.

et·i·quette [eti'ket] etiqueta *f*; honor *m* profesional.

E·ton crop ['i:tn'krɔp] corte *m* a lo garçón.

et·y·mo·log·i·cal [etimə'lɔdʒikl] □ etimológico; **et·y·mol·o·gy** [~'mɔlədʒi] etimología *f*.

eu·cha·rist ['ju:kərist] Eucaristía *f*.

eu·gen·ics [ju:'dʒeniks] *sg.* eugenismo *m*.

eu·lo·gist ['ju:lədʒist] elogiador *m*; **eu·lo·gize** ['~dʒaiz] elogiar, encomiar; **eu·lo·gy** ['~dʒi] elogio *m*, encomio *m*.

eu·nuch ['ju:nək] eunuco *m*.

eu·phe·mism ['ju:fimizm] eufemismo *m*; **eu·phe'mis·tic, eu·phe'mis·ti·cal** □ eufemístico.

eu·phon·ic [ju:'fɔnik] □, **eu·phon·i·ous** ['~iəs] □ eufónico; **eu·pho·ny** ['ju:fəni] eufonía *f*.

eu·re·ka [juə'ri:kə] ¡eureka!

Eu·ro·pe·an [juərə'pi:ən] europeo *adj. a. su. m* (*a f*).

Eu·ro·vi·sion [juərə'viʒn] Eurovisión *f* (*sistema europeo de televisión*). [nasia *f*.⧵

eu·tha·na·si·a [ju:θə'neiziə] eutа-⧸

e·vac·u·ate [i'vækjueit] evacuar; desocupar; **e·vac·u'a·tion** evacuación *f*; **e·vac·u'ee** evacuado (*a f*) *m*.

e·vade [i'veid] evadir, eludir; *v. issue*.

e·val·u·ate [i'væljueit] evaluar; **e·val·u'a·tion** evaluación *f*.

ev·a·nesce [i:və'nes] desvanecerse; **ev·a'nes·cence** desvanecimiento *m*; **ev·a'nes·cent** □ evanescente.

e·van·gel·ic, e·van·gel·i·cal [i:væn'dʒelik(l)] □ evangélico; **e·van·ge·list** [i'vændʒilist] evangelizador *m*; *the* ⍦ Evangelista *m*; **e'van·ge·lize** evangelizar.

e·vap·o·rate [i'væpəreit] evaporar (se) (*a. fig.*); ⍦ *milk* leche *f* evaporada; **e·vap·o'ra·tion** evaporación *f*.

e·va·sion [i'veiʒn] evasiva *f*, evasión *f*; **e'va·sive** [~siv] □ evasivo; *be* ~ contestar con evasivas.

eve [i:v] víspera *f*; *on the* ~ *of* la víspera de, en vísperas de.

e·ven[1] ['i:vn] **1.** *adj.* □ llano, liso; igual; *temperature etc.* constante, invariable; *treatment* imparcial; *temper* sereno, apacible; *par;* *be* ~ estar en paz (*with* con); *get* ~ desquitarse (*with* con); *that makes us* ~ (*game*) eso iguala el tanteo; **2.** *adv.* aun, hasta; incluso; tan siquiera; ~ *as* precisamente cuando, en el mismo momento en que; ~ *if,* ~ *though* aunque, aun cuando; ~ *so* aun así; *not* ~ ni (...) siquiera; F *break* ~ salir sin ganar ni perder; **3.** *v/t.* igualar, allanar; ~ *out ps.* hacer iguales; *th.* repartir con justicia; ~ *up score etc.* igualar, nivelar; *v/i.:* ~ *up* pagar, ajustar cuentas (*with* con).

e·ven[2] [~] *poet.* anochecer *m.*

e·ven...: '~'**hand·ed** imparcial; '~·**tem·pered** apacible, ecuánime.

eve·ning ['i:vniŋ] tarde *f;* anochecer *m;* noche *f; good* ~! ¡buenas tardes!; *musical* ~ velada *f* musical; *attr. star etc.* vespertino; *paper* de la tarde; ~ *dress* traje *m* de etiqueta.

e·ven·ness ['i:vənnis] igualdad *f;* lisura *f;* uniformidad *f;* imparcialidad *f;* serenidad *f.*

e·ven·song ['i:vənsɔŋ] vísperas *f/pl.*

e·vent [i'vent] suceso *m,* acontecimiento *m;* caso *m;* consecuencia *f; sport:* prueba *f,* carrera *f etc.;* ~*s pl.* (*programme*) programa *m; at all* ~*s, in any* ~ en todo caso; *in the* ~ *of* en caso de; **e'vent·ful** [~ful] □ *life* azaroso, accidentado; memorable; *match etc.* lleno de emoción, lleno de incidentes.

e·ven·tu·al [i'ventjuəl] □ final; consiguiente; eventual; ~*ly* finalmente, con el tiempo; al fin y al cabo; **e·ven·tu·al·i·ty** [~'æliti] eventualidad *f.*

ev·er ['evə] siempre; alguna vez; (*negative sense*) jamás, nunca; ~ *after,* ~ *since* desde entonces; (*cj.*) después (de) que; F ~ *so* (— *adj.*) muy; F ~ *so* (*much*) (*adv.*) muchísimo; F ~ *so many things* la mar de cosas; *as* ~ como siempre; (*in letter*) tu amigo, un abrazo; *as soon as* ~ *I can* lo más pronto que pueda; *for* ~ para siempre; *for* ~ *and* ~ por siempre jamás; *hardly* ~ casi nunca; *better than* ~ mejor que nunca; F *the best* ~ el mejor que se ha visto nunca; F *did you* ~? ¿se vió jamás tal cosa?;

did you ~ *meet him?* ¿llegó Vd. a conocerle?; '~·**green** (planta *f*) de hoja perenne; ~'**last·ing** □ sempiterno, perpetuo, perdurable; *b.s.* aburrido; '~·**more** eternamente; *for* ~ por siempre jamás.

ev·er·y ['evri] cada, todo; todos (los *etc.*); ~ *bit as good* de ningún modo inferior (*as* a); ~ *bit a man* todo un hombre; ~ *now and then* de vez en cuando; ~ *one* cada uno; ~ *one of them* todos ellos; ~ *other day* un día sí y otro no, cada dos días; ~ *ten years* cada diez años; *her* ~ *look* todas sus miradas; '~·**bod·y** todos, todo el mundo; '~·**day** diario; rutinario; acostumbrado, corriente; '~·**thing** todo; *he paid for* ~ lo pagó todo; *time is* ~ el tiempo lo es todo; '~·**where** en (por, a) todas partes; ~ *you go* (por) dondequiera que vayas.

e·vict [i'vikt] desahuciar; **e'vic·tion** desahucio *m.*

ev·i·dence ['evidəns] **1.** ⚖ prueba *f,* declaración *f,* testimonio *m,* deposición *f;* (*sign*) prueba *f,* indicio *m;* evidencia *f; in* ~ manifiesto, visible; *give* ~ deponer, prestar declaración, dar testimonio; **2.** evidenciar; *be* ~*d by* estar probado por; '**ev·i·dent** □ evidente, claro; manifiesto; *be* ~ *in* manifestarse en; *be* ~ *from* resultar de; deducirse de, quedar bien claro de; **ev·i·den·tial** [~'denʃl] □ indicador, probatorio.

e·vil ['i:vl] **1.** □ *p.* malo, malvado, perverso; *th.* pernicioso; *the* ~ *eye* aojo *m,* mal *m* de ojo; **2.** mal *m,* maldad *f;* '~'**doer** malhechor *m.*

e·vince [i'vins] dar señales de, mostrar; indicar.

e·vis·cer·ate [i'visəreit] destripar.

ev·o·ca·tion [evou'keiʃn] evocación *f;* **e·voc·a·tive** [i'vɔkətiv] □ evocador, sugestivo.

e·voke [i'vouk] evocar.

ev·o·lu·tion [i:və'lu:ʃn] evolución *f* (*a. biol. a.* ✕); desarrollo *m;* ✗ extracción *f* de raíces; **ev·o·lu·tion·a·ry** evolutivo.

e·volve [i'vɔlv] *v/t.* evolucionar, desarrollar; *heat etc.* desprender; *v/i.* evolucionar, desarrollarse.

ewe [ju:] oveja *f.*

ew·er ['ju:ə] aguamanil *m.*

ex [eks] **1.** *prp. dividend* sin participación en; *works* en; ~ *officio* de oficio; **2.** antiguo; ... que fue; ex...; ~-*minister* ex ministro *m.*

ex·ac·er·bate [eks'æsəbeit] exacerbar.

ex·act [ig'zækt] **1.** □ exacto; puntual; **2.** exigir (*from* a); *obedience etc.* imponer (*from* a); **ex'act·ing** exigente; *conditions* severo; **ex'ac·tion** exacción *f* (*a. b.s.*); **ex'act·i·tude** [‿titju:d] exactitud *f*; **ex'act·ly** exactamente; (*time*) en punto; (*as answer*) exacto; *how many were there,* ~? ¿cuántos había, en concreto?; **ex'act·ness** exactitud *f.*

ex·ag·ger·ate [ig'zædʒəreit] exagerar; **ex·ag·ger'a·tion** exageración *f.*

ex·alt [ig'zɔ:lt] exaltar; elevar; ensalzar; **ex·al·ta·tion** exaltación *f*; elevación *f*; **ex·alt·ed** [ig'zɔ:ltid] exaltado, elevado.

ex·am [ig'zæm] F examen *m.*

ex·am·i·na·tion [igzæmi'neiʃn] examen *m*; ⚕ reconocimiento *m*; ⚖ interrogación *f*; investigación *f* (*into* de); registro *m of baggage*; **ex'am·ine** [‿min] examinar; ⚖ interrogar; (*closely*) escudriñar; *baggage* registrar; ~ *into* indagar, investigar; **ex·am·i'nee** examinando (a *f*) *m*; **ex'am·in·er** examinador *m*; inspector *m.*

ex·am·ple [ig'zɑ:mpl] ejemplo *m*; ejemplar *m*; ⚖ problema *m*; *for* ~ por ejemplo; *make an* ~ *of* castigar de modo ejemplar; *set an* ~ dar ejemplo.

ex·as·per·ate [ig'sɑ:spəreit] exasperar, irritar, sacar de quicio; **ex·as·per'a·tion** exasperación *f.*

ex·ca·vate ['ekskəveit] excavar; **ex·ca'va·tion** excavación *f*; **'ex·ca·va·tor** (*p.*) excavador *m*; ⊕ excavadora *f.*

ex·ceed [ik'si:d] exceder (de); *limit* rebasar; *speed limit* sobrepasar; *expectations* superar; ~ *o.s.* excederse; **ex'ceed·ing** extraordinario; † = **ex'ceed·ing·ly** sumamente, sobremanera.

ex·cel [ik'sel] *v/t.* aventajar, superar; *v/i.* sobresalir (*in* en); **ex·cel·lence** ['eksələns] excelencia *f*; **'Ex·cel·len·cy** Excelencia *f*; **'ex·cel·lent** □ excelente.

ex·cept [ik'sept] **1.** exceptuar, excluir; **2.** *cj.* † ~ (*that*) a menos que; **3.** *prp.* excepto, salvo, fuera de; ~ *for* excepto; dejando aparte, sin

contar; **ex'cept·ing** *prp.* excepto, a excepción de; **ex'cep·tion** excepción *f*; *with the* ~ *of* a excepción de; *take* ~ ofenderse (*to* por); **ex'cep·tion·a·ble** recusable; **ex'cep·tion·al** □ excepcional.

ex·cerpt 1. [ek'sə:pt] citar; sacar; **2.** ['eksə:pt] cita *f*, extracto *m*; separata *f from journal.*

ex·cess [ik'ses] exceso *m* (*a. fig.*); *fig.* desmán *m*, desafuero *m*; † excedente *m*; *attr.* excedente, sobrante; *in* ~ *of* superior a; *carry to* ~ llevar al exceso; ~ *fare* suplemento *m*; ~ *luggage* exceso *m* de peso; ~ *profits tax* impuesto *m* sobre ganancias excesivas; **ex'ces·sive** □ excesivo; sobrado.

ex·change [iks'tʃeindʒ] **1.** cambiar (*for* por); *prisoners, stamps etc.* canjear; *shots* cambiar; *courtesies* hacerse; **2.** cambio *m*; canje *m*; (*cultural etc.*) intercambio *m*; *teleph.* central *f* telefónica; † (*Stock* ♀) Bolsa *f*; (*corn etc.*) lonja *f*; *in* ~ *for* a cambio de; *bill of* ~ letra *f* de cambio; ~ *control* control *m* de divisas; (*rate of*) ~ (tipo *m* de) cambio *m*; **ex'change·a·ble** cambiable, canjeable.

ex·cheq·uer [iks'tʃekə] erario *m*, hacienda *f*, tesoro *m* (público); *Chancellor of the* ♀ Canciller *m* del Tesoro (= *Ministro de Hacienda*); ~ *bills* bonos *m/pl.* del Tesoro.

ex·cise¹ [ek'saiz] (recaudación *f* de) impuestos *m/pl.* interiores.

ex·cise² [‿] eliminar, quitar; cortar; **ex·ci·sion** [ek'siʒn] excisión *f*; corte *m.*

ex·cit·a·bil·i·ty [iksaitə'biliti] excitabilidad *f*; exaltación *f*; **ex'cit·a·ble** □ excitable; exaltado; nervioso; **ex·ci·ta·tion** [eksi'teiʃn] excitación *f*; **ex·cite** [ik'sait] emocionar; entusiasmar; (*stimulate*) excitar, estimular; (*rouse*) provocar; *get* ~*d* emocionarse; alborotarse; entusiasmarse (*about, over* por); **ex'cite·ment** emoción *f*; entusiasmo *m*; excitación *f*; **ex'cit·ing** □ emocionante; conmovedor; apasionante; excitante.

ex·claim [iks'kleim] *v/t.* decir con vehemencia; *v/i.* exclamar; ~ *against* acusar vivamente.

ex·cla·ma·tion [eksklə'meiʃn] exclamación *f*; ~ *mark* punto *m* de

admiración; **ex·clam·a·to·ry** [ˌ~ 'klæmətəri] □ exclamatorio.
ex·clude [iks'kluːd] excluir; exceptuar.
ex·clu·sion [iks'kluːʒn] exclusión f; to the ~ of con exclusión de; **ex·'clu·sive** [ˌsiv] □ exclusivo; privativo; policy etc. exclusivista; (sole) único; club etc. selecto; ~ of fuera de, sin contar.
ex·cog·i·tate [eks'kɔdʒiteit] excogitar.
ex·com·mu·ni·cate [ekskə'mjuːnikeit] excomulgar; **ex·com·mu·ni·'ca·tion** excomunión f.
ex·co·ri·ate [eks'kɔːrieit] excoriar; fig. azotar.
ex·cre·ment ['ekskrimənt] excremento m; **ex·cre·men·tal** [ˌ~'mentl] excremental; **ex·cre·men·ti·tious** [ˌ~'tiʃəs] excrementicio.
ex·cres·cence [iks'kresns] excrecencia f; **ex·'cres·cent** excrecente.
ex·crete [eks'kriːt] excretar; **ex·'cre·tion** excreción f; **ex·'cre·tive** excrementicio; **ex·'cre·to·ry** excretorio.
ex·cru·ci·at·ing [iks'kruːʃieitiŋ] □ agudísimo, atroz.
ex·cul·pate ['ekskʌlpeit] exculpar; **ex·cul·'pa·tion** exculpación f.
ex·cur·sion [iks'kəːʃn] excursión f; ~ train tren m botijo, tren m de recreo.
ex·cus·a·ble [iks'kjuːzəbl] □ perdonable, disculpable; **ex·'cuse 1.** [iks·'kjuːz] disculpar, perdonar (a p. a th. algo a alguien); excusar; dispensar (from de); ~ me! ¡dispense Vd.!; **2.** [iks'kjuːs] excusa f; disculpa f; pretexto m.
ex·e·at ['eksiæt] permiso m (para estar ausente).
ex·e·cra·ble ['eksikrəbl] □ execrable; **ex·e·crate** ['ˌkreit] execrar; **ex·e·'cra·tion** execración f; abominación f.
ex·e·cu·tant [ig'zekjutənt] ♪ ejecutante m/f; **ex·e·cute** ['eksikjuːt] ejecutar (a. ♪); llevar a cabo, cumplir; ⚖ man ejecutar, ajusticiar; document otorgar; legalizar; **ex·e·'cu·tion** ejecución f (a. ♪ a. ⚖); ⚖ otorgamiento m; legalización f; **ex·e·'cu·tion·er** verdugo m; **ex·ec·u·tive** [ig'zekjutiv] **1.** □ ejecutivo; **2.** ♰ gerente m, director m; pol. poder m ejecutivo; autoridad f

suprema; Am. ejecutivo m; **ex·'ec·u·tor** [ˌtə] albacea m, ejecutor m testamentario.
ex·em·plar [ig'zemplə] modelo m, patrón m; **ex·'em·pla·ri·ness** ejemplaridad f; **ex·'em·pla·ry** ejemplar.
ex·em·pli·fi·ca·tion [igzemplifi'keiʃn] ejemplificación f; ⚖ copia f notarial; **ex·'em·pli·fy** [ˌfai] ejemplificar; ⚖ hacer copia notarial de.
ex·empt [ig'zempt] **1.** exento (from de); **2.** exentar, eximir (from de); dispensar, exceptuar; **ex·'emp·tion** exención f.
ex·e·quies ['eksikwiz] pl. funerales m/pl.
ex·er·cise ['eksəsaiz] **1.** all senses: ejercicio m; take ~ hacer ejercicios; **2.** v/t. power, profession ejercer; care poner (in en); right valerse de; (train) ejercitar (in en); mind, p. preocupar; dog llevar de paseo; horse entrenar; v/i. ejercitarse; hacer ejercicios.
ex·ert [ig'zəːt] ejercer; ~ o.s. esforzarse; afanarse; trabajar etc. demasiado; **ex·'er·tion** esfuerzo m; afán m; trabajo m etc. excesivo.
ex·es ['eksiz] sl. = expenses gastos m/pl.
ex·e·unt ['eksiʌnt] éxeunt.
ex·fo·li·ate [eks'foulieit] exfoliar(se).
ex·ha·la·tion [ekshə'leiʃn] exhalación f; espiración f of air; **ex·hale** [ˌ'heil] air espirar; exhalar.
ex·haust [ig'zɔːst] **1.** agotar (a. fig.); fig. apurar; debilitar; (tire) cansar; be ~ed (tired) estar rendido; **2.** ⊕ (tubo m de) escape m; gases m/pl. de escape; attr. de escape; ~ pipe tubo m de escape; ~ valve válvula f de escape; **ex·'haust·i·ble** agotable; **ex·'haust·ing** □ duro, que agota; **ex·'haus·tion** agotamiento m (a. fig.); fig. postración f; **ex·'haus·tive** □ exhaustivo, comprensivo.
ex·hib·it [ig'zibit] **1.** signs etc. mostrar, manifestar, exhibir; exhibit exponer; film etc. presentar; **2.** objeto m expuesto; pieza f de museo; ⚖ documento m; on ~ expuesto; **ex·hi·bi·tion** [eksi'biʃn] paint. etc. exposición f; exhibición f; demostración f; univ. beca f; make an ~ of o.s. ponerse en ridículo; on ~ expuesto; **ex·hi·bi·tion·er** becario m; **ex·hi·bi·tion·ist** exhibicionista m/f; **ex·hib·i·tor** [ig'zibitə] expositor m.

ex·hil·a·rate [ig'ziləreit] alegrar, regocijar; excitar; levantar el ánimo de; **ex'hil·a·rat·ing** ☐ que regocija *etc.*; tónico, vigorizante; **ex·hil·a'ra·tion** alegría *f*, regocijo *m*; excitación *f*.

ex·hort [ig'zɔːt] exhortar (*to* a); **ex·hor·ta·tion** [egzɔː'teiʃn] exhortación *f*; **ex'hor·ta·to·ry** [‿təri] exhortatorio.

ex·hu·ma·tion [ekshju:'meiʃn] exhumación *f*; **ex'hume** exhumar; desenterrar (*a. fig.*).

ex·i·gence, **ex·i·gen·cy** ['eksidʒəns(i)] exigencia *f*, necesidad *f* (urgente); caso *m* de urgencia; **'ex·i·gent** exigente; urgente.

ex·ile ['eksail] 1. destierro *m*, exilio *m*; (*p.*) desterrado (a *f*) *m*, exilado (a *f*) *m*; 2. desterrar, exil(i)ar.

ex·ist [ig'zist] existir; **ex'ist·ence** existencia *f*; vida *f*; *be in ~* existir; *in ~* = **ex'istent** existente; actual; **ex·ist'en·tial·ism** existencialismo *m*.

ex·it ['eksit] 1. salida *f*; *thea.* mutis *m*; ~ *permit* permiso *m* de salida; 2. *thea.* hacer mutis; ~ *Macbeth* váse Macbeth.

ex·o·dus ['eksədəs] éxodo *m*.

ex·on·er·ate [ig'zɔnəreit] exculpar, disculpar (*from blame* de); exonerar (*from duty* de); **ex·on·er'a·tion** exculpación *f*; exoneración *f*.

ex·or·bi·tance [ig'zɔːbitəns] exorbitancia *f*; **ex'or·bi·tant** ☐ exorbitante, excesivo.

ex·or·cism ['eksɔːsizm] exorcismo *m*; **'ex·or·cist** exorcista *m/f*; **ex·or·cize** ['‿saiz] exorcizar, conjurar.

ex·ot·ic [eg'zɔtik] 1. ☐ exótico; 2. ♀ planta *f* exótica.

ex·pand [iks'pænd] *v/t.* extender; ensanchar; dilatar; *market etc.* expansionar; ℟ *equation* desarrollar; *v/i.* extenderse; dilatarse; (*p.*) hacerse más expansivo; **ex·panse** [‿'pæns] extensión *f*; envergadura *f of wings*; **ex'pan·si·ble** expansible; **ex'pan·sion** expansión *f*; dilatación *f*; ensanche *m of town etc.*; ♰ desarrollo *m*; **ex'pan·sive** ☐ expansivo (*a. fig.*); **ex'pan·sive·ness** afabilidad *f*.

ex·pa·ti·ate [eks'peiʃieit] espaciarse; extenderse (*on en* alabanzas *etc.* de).

ex·pa·tri·ate [eks'pætrieit] 1. desterrar; ~ *o.s.* expatriarse; 2. expa-

triado (a *f*) *m*; **ex·pa·tri'a·tion** expatriación *f*.

ex·pect [iks'pekt] esperar (*of* de; *that* que *subj.*); contar con; prometerse; *baby* esperar; (*foresee*) prever; F suponer; F *be ~ing* estar encinta; F *I ~ he'll be there* supongo que estará allí; *just what I ~ed* ya me lo figuraba; **ex'pect·an·cy** (*state*) expectación *f*; expectativa *f* (*of* de); **ex'pect·ant** ☐ expectante; ~ *mother* mujer *f* encinta; **ex·pec'ta·tion** expectación *f*; expectativa *f*; ~*s pl.* esperanza *f* de heredar *in will*; *beyond ~* mejor de lo que se esperaba; *in ~ of* esperando; ~ *of life* expectativa *f* de vida, índice *m* vital.

ex·pec·to·rate [eks'pektəreit] expectorar; **ex·pec·to'ra·tion** expectoración *f*.

ex·pe·di·ence, **ex·pe·di·en·cy** [iks'piːdiəns(i)] conveniencia *f*; oportunidad *f*; **ex'pe·di·ent** 1. ☐ conveniente; oportuno; ventajoso; 2. expediente *m*, recurso *m*; **ex·pe·dite** ['ekspidait] *progress* facilitar; *business* despachar; (*speed up*) acelerar; **ex·pe·di·tion** [‿'diʃn] expedición *f*; **ex·pe'di·tion·ar·y** expedicionario; **ex·pe'di·tious** ☐ expeditivo, pronto.

ex·pel [iks'pel] expeler, despedir; arrojar; *p.* expulsar.

ex·pend [iks'pend] expender, gastar (*on en*; *in doing* haciendo); *time* pasar; *resources* consumir, agotar; **ex'pend·a·ble** prescindible; **ex'pend·i·ture** [‿itʃə] gasto (s) *m(pl.)*; desembolso *m*; **ex·pense** [‿'pens] gasto *m*; costa *f*; expensas *f/pl.*; *at my ~* corriendo yo con los gastos; *at the ~ of fig.* a expensas de; *at great ~* gastándose muchísimo dinero; ~ *account* cuenta *f* de gastos; *go to ~* meterse en gastos; **ex'pen·sive** ☐ caro, costoso; *shop etc.* carero.

ex·pe·ri·ence [iks'piəriəns] 1. experiencia *f*; 2. experimentar; *loss, fate* sufrir; *difficulty* tener; **ex'pe·ri·enced** experimentado; perito; versado (*in* en).

ex·per·i·ment 1. [iks'perimənt] experimento *m*; prueba *f*; 2. [‿ment] hacer experimentos, experimentar (*on en, with con*); **ex·per·i·men·tal** [eksperi'mentl] ☐ experimental.

ex·pert ['ekspəːt] 1. ☐ experto, perito (*at, in* en); hábil; ℟ *witness* pericial; **2.** e*x*perto *m*, perito *m* (*at*, *in* en); **ex·pert·i·se** [ekspə:'ti:z], 'expert·ness pericia *f*; habilidad *f*.

ex·pi·ate ['ekspieit] expiar; **ex·pi'a·tion** expiación *f*; **ex·pi·a·to·ry** ['~təri] expiatorio.

ex·pi·ra·tion [ekspaiə'reiʃn] vencimiento *m*, expiración *f of term*; espiración *f of air*; **ex'pire** *v/i.* (*die*) expirar; (*term*) vencer, expirar, cumplirse; (*ticket*) caducar; *v/t. air* expeler, espirar; **ex'pi·ry** = *expiration*.

ex·plain [iks'plein] explicar; *mystery* aclarar; *plan* exponer; *conduct* explicar, justificar; ~ *o.s.* explicarse; hablar más claro; justificar su conducta; ~ *away* justificar hábilmente, dar razones convincentes de; *difficulty* salvar hábilmente; **ex'plaina·ble** explicable.

ex·pla·na·tion [eksplə'neiʃn] explicación *f*; aclaración *f*, *etc.*; **ex·plana·to·ry** [iks'plænətəri] explicativo.

ex·ple·tive [eks'pli:tiv] voz *f* expletiva, reniego *m*; (*oath*) palabrota *f*.

ex·pli·ca·ble ['eksplikəbl] explicable.

ex·plic·it [iks'plisit] □ explícito.

ex·plode [iks'ploud] *v/t.* volar, hacer saltar; *theory* refutar, desmentir; *v/i.* estallar, hacer explosión; reventar *with anger etc.*

ex·ploit 1. [iks'plɔit] explotar; **2.** ['eksplɔit] hazaña *f*, proeza *f*; **ex·ploi'ta·tion** explotación *f*.

ex·plo·ra·tion [eksplɔ:'reiʃn] exploración *f*; **ex'plor·a·to·ry** [~rətəri] preparatorio, de sondaje; **ex·plore** [iks'plɔ:] explorar; *fig.* examinar, sondar; **ex'plor·er** explorador *m*.

ex·plo·sion [iks'plouʒn] explosión *f* (*a. fig.*); **ex'plo·sive** [~siv] □ explosivo *adj. a. su. m* (*a. fig.*).

ex·po·nent [eks'pounənt] exponente *m/f*; partidario (a *f*) *m*; intérprete *m/f*; ℞ exponente *m*.

ex·port 1. [eks'pɔ:t] exportar; **2.** ['ekspɔ:t] exportación *f* (*a.* ~s *pl.*); ~ *trade* comercio *m* de exportación; **ex'port·a·ble** exportable; **ex·por'ta·tion** exportación *f*; **ex·port·er** exportador *m*.

ex·pose [iks'pouz] exponer (*a. phot.*); *plot etc.* desenmascarar; ~ *o.s. to* exponerse a; *be* ~*d* quedar al descubierto; **ex'posed** *adj. position* expuesto, desabrigado, al descubierto; *flank* desguarnecido; **ex·po·si·tion** [ekspə'ziʃn] exposición *f*.

ex·pos·tu·late [iks'pɔstjuleit] protestar; ~ *with* reconvenir a; tratar de convencer a; **ex·pos·tu'la·tion** protesta *f*; reconvención *f*; esfuerzo *m* por convencer(le *etc.*).

ex·po·sure [iks'pouʒe] exposición *f* (*a. phot.*); desenmascaramiento *m of plot etc.*; *die from* ~ morir de frío; ~ *meter* fotómetro *m*, exposímetro *m*; ~ *time* tiempo *m* de exposición.

ex·pound [iks'paund] exponer, explicar; comentar.

ex·press [iks'pres] **1.** □ expreso; explícito, categórico; *letter* urgente; *Am.* ~ *company* compañía *f* de expreso; ~ *train* rápido *m*; **2.** rápido *m* (*a.* ~ *train*); **3.** *adv.* por carta (*etc.*) urgente; **4.** expresar; *juice* exprimir; ~ *o.s.* expresarse; **ex'pres·sion** *all senses*: expresión *f*; **ex'pres·sive** □ expresivo; **ex'press·ly** expresamente, categóricamente; adrede.

ex·pro·pri·ate [eks'prouprieit] expropiar; **ex·pro·pri'a·tion** expropiación *f*.

ex·pul·sion [iks'pʌlʃn] expulsión *f*.

ex·punge [eks'pʌndʒ] borrar, tachar.

ex·pur·gate ['ekspə:geit] expurgar; **ex·pur'ga·tion** expurgación *f*; **ex·'pur·ga·to·ry** [~gətəri] expurgatorio.

ex·qui·site ['ekskwizit] **1.** □ exquisito, primoroso; *pain* agudísimo; **2.** petimetre *m*.

ex·serv·ice·man ['eks'sə:vismən] excombatiente *m*.

ex·tant [eks'tænt] existente.

ex·tem·po·rar·y [iks'tempərəri], **ex·tem·po·re** [eks'tempəri] **1.** *adj.* improvisado; **2.** *adv.* de improviso, sin preparación; *speak* ~ = **ex·tem·po·rize** [iks'tempəraiz] improvisar.

ex·tend [iks'tend] extender(se); *building etc.* ensanchar, ampliar; *hand* tender; *term etc.* prolongar (se); *thanks, welcome* dar, ofrecer; *athlete* exigir el máximo esfuerzo a; ~ *over*, ~ *to* (*include*) abarcar.

ex·ten·si·ble [iks'tensibl] extensible; **ex'ten·sion** extensión *f*; ⚠ *etc.* ensanche *m*, ampliación *f*; prolongación *f of term etc.*; ✝ prórroga *f*; *teleph.* línea *f* derivada; ⚡ ~ *cord* cordón *m* de extensión; **ex'ten·sive** □ extenso; vasto, dilatado; *use etc.*

abundante, general; *travel* ~*ly* viajar por muchos países *etc.*

ex·tent [iks'tent] extensión *f*; alcance *m*; amplitud *f*; *to the* ~ *of* hasta el punto de; *to the full* ~ en toda su extensión; *to a certain* ~, *to some* ~ hasta cierto punto; *to a great* ~ en gran parte; *to such an* ~ *that* hasta tal punto que; *to that* ~ hasta ahí.

ex·ten·u·ate [eks'tenjueit] atenuar, disminuir, mitigar; *extenuating circumstances pl.* circunstancias *f/pl.* atenuantes; **ex·ten·u·a·tion** atenuación *f*, mitigación *f*.

ex·te·ri·or [eks'tiəriə] exterior *adj. a. su. m.*

ex·ter·mi·nate [eks'tə:mineit] exterminar; **ex·ter·mi·na·tion** exterminio *m*.

ex·ter·nal [eks'tə:nl] **1.** □ externo; exterior; ~ *trade* comercio *m* exterior; **2.** ~*s pl.* exterioridad *f*, aspecto *m* exterior.

ex·tinct [iks'tiŋkt] *volcano etc.* extinto, apagado; *animal* extinto, extinguido; **ex·tinc·tion** extinción *f*.

ex·tin·guish [iks'tiŋgwiʃ] extinguir; apagar; *right etc.* suprimir; **ex·tin·guish·er** extintor *m*.

ex·tir·pate [ˈekstə:peit] extirpar; **ex·tir·pa·tion** extirpación *f*.

ex·tol [iks'tɔl] ensalzar, celebrar.

ex·tort [iks'tɔ:t] obtener (*or* sacar) por fuerza; **ex·tor·tion** *all senses:* exacción *f*; **ex·tor·tion·ate** [~ʃnit] □ exorbitante, excesivo; *p., means* injusto; **ex·tor·tion·er** desollador *m*; concusionario *m*.

ex·tra [ˈekstrə] **1.** *adj.* extra (...); de más, de sobra; *charge etc.* extraordinario, suplementario; *part* de repuesto; adicional; ~ *charge* suplemento *m*, recargo *m*; ~ *pay* pay sobresueldo *m*; *sport:* ~ *time* prórroga *f*; **2.** *adv.* especialmente, extraordinariamente; *with verbs:* más; de sobra; **3.** *su.* extra *m on bill*; exceso *m*; cosa *f* adicional; *Am.* (pieza *f* de) repuesto *m*; *thea.* comparsa *m/f*; ~*s pl.* comparsería *f*.

ex·tract 1. [ˈekstrækt] cita *f*, trozo *m*; *pharm.* extracto *m*; **2.** [iks'trækt] extraer (*a.* ⩎); sacar; **ex·trac·tion** extracción *f*.

ex·tra·dit·a·ble [ekstrə'daitəbl] sujeto a la extradición; **ex·tra·dite** extradicionar, obtener la extradi-

ción de; **ex·tra·di·tion** [~'diʃn] extradición *f*.

extra...: '~·ju·di·cial extrajudicial; '~·mu·ral de extramuros; fuera del recinto de la escuela (*or* universidad *etc.*); *course* para externos.

ex·tra·ne·ous [eks'treinjəs] extraño; ajeno (*to* a).

ex·traor·di·nar·y [iks'trɔ:dnri] □ extraordinario.

ex·trav·a·gance [iks'trævigəns] prodigalidad *f*, despilfarro *m*; gasto *m* (*or* lujo *m*) excesivo; extravagancia *f*; **ex·trav·a·gant** □ *p.* pródigo, despilfarrado(r); *price* exorbitante; *praise* excesivo; *living* muy lujoso; *ideas etc.* extravagante, estrafalario; **ex·trav·a·gan·za** [ekstrævə'gænzə] obra *f* extravagante y fantástica.

ex·treme [iks'tri:m] **1.** □ extremo; *case freq.* excepcional; ~*ly* extremadamente, sumamente; **2.** extremo *m*; extremidad *f*; *in the* ~ en sumo grado; *go to* ~*s* propasarse; pasar de lo razonable; tomar medidas extremas; **ex·trem·ist** extremista *m/f*; **ex·trem·i·ty** [~'tremiti] extremidad *f*; medida *f* extrema; rigor *m*; **ex·trem·i·ties** [~z] *pl.* extremidades *f/pl. of body*; medidas *f/pl.* extremas; *be driven to* ~ estar muy apurado.

ex·tri·cate [ˈekstrikeit] librar, extraer, sacar (*from* de); **ex·tri·ca·tion** libramiento *m*, extricación *f*.

ex·trin·sic [eks'trinsik] □ extrínseco.

ex·tro·vert [ˈekstrouvə:t] extrovertido *m*.

ex·trude [eks'tru:d] empujar hacia fuera; sacar.

ex·u·ber·ance [ig'zju:bərəns] exuberancia *f*; euforia *f*; **ex·u·ber·ant** □ exuberante; eufórico.

ex·u·da·tion [eksju:'deiʃn] exudación *f*; **ex·ude** [ig'zju:d] *v/i.* exudar; rezumarse; *v/t.* dejar escapar, destilar, rezumar.

ex·ult [ig'zʌlt] exultar; regocijarse (*at, in* por; *to find* al encontrar); triunfar (*over* sobre); **ex·ult·ant** □ regocijado, ufano, triunfante; **ex·ul·ta·tion** [egzʌl'teiʃn] exultación *f*.

eye [ai] **1.** *mst* ojo *m*; *sew.* corcheta *f*; ⚘ yema *f*; ⚘ *black* ~ ojo *m* amoratado; *in the* ~*s of* a los ojos de; *with an* ~ *to ger.* con la intención de *inf.*; pensando en *acc.*; *be all* ~*s* ser todo ojos; F *be up to one's* ~s tener trabajo hasta encima de la cabeza; *catch the* ~ llamar la atención; *catch s.o.'s* ~ atraer la atención de uno; *cry one's* ~s *out* llorar a mares; F *give the glad* ~ *to* echar los ojazos a; *have an* ~ *for* tener gusto por; saber apreciar *acc.*; *have an* ~ *to* vigilar; tener en cuenta; F *have one's* ~ *on* tener los ojos en; vigilar; (*desire*) echar el ojo a; F *it's all my* ~! ¡es puro cuento!; *keep an* ~ *on* vigilar; echar una mirada a; *make* ~s *at* hacer guiños a; *open s.o.'s* ~s *to* hacer que uno se dé cuenta de; (*not to*) *see* ~ *to* ~ (*with*) (no) estar completamente de acuerdo (con); *set* ~s *on a p.* ponerle los ojos encima a uno; *shut one's* ~s *to* hacer la vista gorda a; *not to shut one's* ~s *to* tener en cuenta; *turn a blind* ~

fingir no ver (*on acc.*), hacer la vista gorda (*to* a); **2.** ojear; mirar (detenidamente *etc.*); '~·**ball** globo *m* del ojo; '~·**brow** ceja *f*; '~-**catch·er** cosa *f etc.* que llama la atención; ...**eyed** [aid] de ... ojos, de ojos ...

eye...: '~-**glass** anteojo *m*; lente *m*; monóculo *m*; '~·**lash** pestaña *f*; '**eye·let** ojete *m.*

eye...: '~·**lid** párpado *m*; '~-**o·pen·er** revelación *f*, sorpresa *f* grande; acontecimiento *m* asombroso; '~-**piece** *opt.* ocular *m*; '~·**sight** (alcance *m* de la) vista *f*; '~·**sore** monstruosidad *f*, cosa *f* que ofende la vista; '~-**tooth** colmillo *m*; '~-**wash** *sl.* tonterías *f/pl.*; protestación *f* insincera; alabanza *f* insincera; '~-'**wit·ness** testigo *m* presencial.

ey·rie, ey·ry ['aiəri, 'ɛəri] aguilera *f.*

F

fa·ble ['feibl] fábula *f*.

fab·ric ['fæbrik] tejido *m*, tela *f*; △ fábrica *f*; **fab·ri·cate** ['⁓keit] fabricar (*a. fig.*); *fig.* inventar, falsificar; **fab·ri·ca·tion** fabricación *f*; *fig.* mentira *f*, falsificación *f*.

fab·u·lous ['fæbjuləs] □ fabuloso.

fa·çade [fə'sɑːd] fachada *f*; *fig.* apariencia *f*, barniz *m*.

face [feis] **1.** cara *f*; semblante *m*, rostro *m*; superficie *f*; faz *f of the earth*; (*grimace*) mueca *f*; (*effrontery*) desfachatez *f*; (*prestige*) prestigio *m*, apariencias *f/pl.*; esfera *f of watch*; ⚒ cara *f* de trabajo; ⁓ *downwards* boca abajo; ⁓ *to* ⁓ cara a cara; *in* (*the*) ⁓ *of* ante; luchando contra; a pesar de; *on the* ⁓ *of it* a primera vista; *lose* ⁓ desprestigiarse; F *make* (*or pull*) ⁓*s* hacer carantoñas (*at a*), hacer muecas (*at a*); *save* (*one's*) ⁓ salvar las apariencias; *say s.t. to one's* ⁓ decir a!go por (*or* en) la cara de uno; *set one's* ⁓ *against* mostrarse contrario a; F *show one's* ⁓ dejarse ver; ⁓ *value* ♰ valor *m* nominal; *fig.* valor *m* aparente, significado *m* literal; **2.** *v/t. danger* arrostrar, hacer cara a; *p., enemy* encararse con; *problem* afrontar; *facts* reconocer, aceptar; (*building*) mirar hacia, estar enfrente de; ⊕ revestir; (*a*)forrar; ⊕ (*a.* ⁓ *off*) alisar; *be* ⁓*d with* presentársele a uno; ⁓ *it out* mantenerse firme; insistir descaradamente en ello; *v/i.* : ⁓ *about* dar media vuelta; ⁓ *on* to dar a, dar sobre; ⁓ *up* to dar cara a; ⁓ *up to it* reconocerlo; '⁓-lift cirugía *f* estética; '⁓-pow·der polvos *m/pl.*; 'fac·er percance *m*; problema *m* desconcertante.

fac·et ['fæsit] faceta *f* (*a. fig.*); 'fac·et·ed labrado en facetas.

fa·ce·tious [fə'siːʃəs] □ gracioso, chistoso (*freq.* en momento inoportuno); guasón.

face-work·er ['feiswəːkə] ⚒ picador *m*.

fa·cial ['feiʃl] **1.** □ facial; **2.** *Am.* masaje *m* facial.

fac·ile ['fæsail] fácil, vivo; *b.s.* ligero, superficial; **fa·cil·i·tate** [fə'siliteit] facilitar; **fa·cil·i·ta·tion** facilitación *f*; **fa·cil·i·ty** facilidad *f*.

fac·ing ['feisiŋ] ⊕ revestimiento *m*; *sew.*: ⁓*s pl.* vueltas *f/pl.*

fac·sim·i·le [fæk'simili] facsímil *adj. a. su. m*.

fact [fækt] hecho *m*; realidad *f*; ⁓*s pl.* 🄓 datos *m/pl.*; *the* ⁓ *is that* ello es que; *the* ⁓ *of the matter is* en verdad; *in* (*point of*) ⁓ en realidad; '⁓-find·ing ... de investigación, de indagación; [sión *f*.]

fac·tion ['fækʃn] facción *f*; disen-⌐

fac·tious ['fækʃəs] □ faccioso; 'fac·tious·ness disensión *f*, espíritu *m* de partido.

fac·ti·tious [fæk'tiʃəs] □ facticio.

fac·tor ['fæktə] factor *m* (Å *a. fig.*); *fig.* elemento *m*, hecho *m*; ♰ agente *m*; 'fac·to·ry fábrica *f*, factoría *f*.

fac·to·tum [fæk'toutəm] factótum *m*.

fac·tu·al ['fæktjuəl] □ objetivo; que consta de hechos (*or* datos).

fac·ul·ty ['fækəlti] *all senses:* facultad *f*.

fad [fæd] F manía *f*, capricho *m*; novedad *f*; 'fad·dy caprichoso; aficionado a novedades; descontentadizo.

fade [feid] desteñir(se), descolorar (se); (*flower*) marchitar(se); ⁓ *away*, ⁓ *out* desdibujarse; desvanecerse (*a. radio*); apagarse; ⁓ *in*, ⁓ *up* (hacer) aparecer gradualmente; *film:* ⁓ *to* fundir a; 'fade·less que no se descolora; 'fad·ing *radio:* desvanecimiento *m*

fae·ces ['fiːsiːz] *pl.* excrementos *m/pl.*

fag [fæg] F **1.** faena *f*, trabajo *m* penoso; *school:* alumno *m* joven que trabaja para otro mayor; *sl.* pitillo *m*; **2.** *v/i.* hacer faenas rudas; *v/t.* fatigar, cansar; *be* ⁓*ged out* estar rendido; '⁓-'end F cabo *m*, desperdicios *m/pl.*; *sl.* colilla *f*.

fag·ot, fag·got ['fægət] haz *m* (*or* gavilla *f*) de leña; astillas *f/pl.*

Fahr·en·heit ['færənhait]: ⁓ *ther-*

mometer termómetro *m* de Fahrenheit.

fail [feil] 1. *v/i.* fracasar; frustrarse, malograrse; no surtir efecto; *(supply)* acabarse; *(voice)* desfallecer; ser suspendido *in exam*; ✝ quebrar, hacer bancarrota; ~ *to* dejar de; no lograr; *he* ~*ed to appear* no se presentó, 🔬 no compareció; *often not translated: I* ~ *to see how* no veo cómo; ~ *in duty etc.* faltar a; *v/t.* faltar a; *p.* faltar a sus obligaciones a; *pupil* suspender; *exam* salir mal en, no aprobar; *(strength etc.)* abandonar; *words* ~ *me* no encuentro palabras (para expresarme)〈 2. F *univ.* suspenso *m*; *without* ~ sin falta; **'fail·ing** 1. falta *f*, defecto *m*, flaqueza *f*; 2. *prp.* a falta de; **fail·ure** ['feiljə] fracaso *m*; malogro *m*; falta *f*, omisión *f*; *(p.)* fracasado (a *f*) *m*; ⚡ corte *m*; suspenso *m in exam*; ✝ quiebra *f*, bancarrota *f*; *the* ~ *to* el dejar de, la omisión de.

fain [fein] ✝ 1. *adj.* dispuesto; 2. *adv.* de buena gana.

faint [feint] 1. □ débil; *sound etc.* indistinto, casi imperceptible; *resemblance* ligero; *line etc.* tenue; *I haven't the* ~*est (idea)* no tengo la más remota idea; 🔬 *feel* ~ sentir vahidos; 2. desmayarse, desfallecer *(with* de*)*; 3. desmayo *m*, desfallecimiento *m*; ~**-heart·ed** ['~'ha:tid] □ medroso, pusilánime; **'faint·ness** debilidad *f*; tenuidad *f*; 🔬 desfallecimiento *m*.

fair[1] [fɛə] 1. □ *(beautiful)* hermoso, bello; *hair* rubio; *skin* blanco; *(just)* justo, equitativo; *hearing* imparcial; *name* honrado; *prospects* favorable; *sky* sereno, despejado; *weather* bueno; *chance, warning* razonable; *(middling)* regular, mediano; *the* ~ *(sex)* el bello sexo; *it's not* ~*!* ¡no hay derecho!; ~ *copy* copia *f* en limpio; *make a* ~ *copy of* poner en limpio; ~ *game* caza *f* legal; *fig.* objeto *m* legítimo; *by* ~ *means* por medios rectos; ~ *play* juego *m* limpio; 2. *adv.* directamente; exactamente; justamente; *play* ~ jugar limpio; *speak a p.* ~ hablar a una p. cortésmente.

fair[2] [~] feria *f*; *(fun-)* parque *m* de atracciones; verbena *f*; '~**-ground** real *m*.

fair·ly ['fɛəli] *v. fair*[1]; bastante; medianamente; completamente;

'fair·ness justicia *f*, imparcialidad *f*; blancura *f of skin*; *in all* ~ para ser justo; **'fair·'spo·ken** bien hablado; **'fair·way** ⚓ canalizo *m*; **'fair-weath·er friend** amigo *m* en la prosperidad.

fair·y ['fɛəri] 1. hada *f*; 2. feérico, mágico; de hada(s); ~ *light* farolillo *m*; **'Fair·y·land** tierra *f* de las hadas; **'fair·y·tale** cuento *m* de hadas; fantástico, de ensueño.

faith [feiθ] fe *f*; confianza *f (in* en*)*; *in good* ~ de buena fe; *break* ~ faltar a la palabra *(with* dada a*)*; *keep* ~ cumplir su palabra *(with* dada a*)*; **faith·ful** ['~ful] □ fiel, leal; puntual; *the* ~ *pl.* los fieles; *yours* ~*ly* atentamente le saluda; **'faith·ful·ness** fidelidad *f*, lealtad *f*; **'faith-heal·ing** curación *f* por fe; **'faith·less** □ infiel, desleal; falso; **'faith·less·ness** infidelidad *f*, deslealtad *f*.

fake [feik] F 1. falsificación *f*, impostura *f*; filfa *f*; *(p.)* impostor *m*, farsante *m (Am. a.* **'fak·er**); 2. falso, fingido, falsificado; 3. *(a.* ~ *up)* contrahacer, falsificar, fingir.

fal·con ['fɔ:lkən] halcón *m*; **'fal·con·er** halconero *m*, cetrero *m*; **'fal·con·ry** halconería *f*, cetrería *f*.

fall [fɔ:l] 1. caída *f*; ✝ baja *f*; *esp. Am.* otoño *m*; declive *m*, desnivel *m in ground*; *(water-)* salto *m* de agua, cascada *f*, catarata *f (a.* ~*s pl.)*; *the* ♀ la Caída; *ride for a* ~ ir a acabar mal; 2. *[irr.]* caer(se); disminuir; *(level, price)* bajar; ⚔ caer, rendirse; *(wind)* amainar; sucumbir *(to* ante*)*; *his face fell* se inmutó; *the anniversary* ~*s on a Tuesday* el aniversario cae en martes; ~ *asleep* dormirse; ~ *away* enflaquecer; apostatar; ~ *back* retroceder; ⚔ replegarse *(on sobre)*; ~ *back (up)on* recurrir a; ~ *behind* quedarse atrás; *v. stool*; ~ *down* caerse; F fracasar; ~ *due* vencer; ~ *flat* caer de bruces, caer de boca; *(suggestion)* caer en el vacío; ~ *for p.* enamorarse de; *trick* dejarse engañar por; ~ *in (roof)* desplomarse; ⚔ alinearse; ~ *in love* enamorarse *(with* de*)*; ~ *in with p.* encontrarse con; *idea* convenir en; ~ *into error etc.* incurrir en; *category* estar incluido en; *conversation* entablar; *habit* adquirir; *three parts etc.* dividirse en; ~ *off* desprenderse; caerse; *(quantity)* disminuir; *(qua!-*

ity) empeorar; ~ *on* ✕ *etc.* caer sobre, echarse sobre; ~ *out* reñir (*with* con), pelearse (*with* con), indisponerse (*with* con); resultar (*that* que); ✕ romper filas; *v. short*; ~ *through* fracasar, quedar en nada; ~ *to* empezar a comer; (*duty*) competer a, corresponder a; ~ *to ger.* empezar a *inf.*

fal·la·cious [fə'leiʃəs] □ erróneo, delusorio, ilusorio; *b.s.* sofístico.

fal·la·cy ['fæləsi] error *m*; sofisma *m*.

fall·en ['fɔːlən] *p.p. of* fall 2.

fall guy ['fɔːl'gai] *Am. sl.* pato *m*, cabeza *f* de turco.

fal·li·bil·i·ty [fæli'biliti] falibilidad *f*; **fal·li·ble** ['fæləbl] □ falible.

fall·ing ['fɔːliŋ]: '~-'**off** disminución *f*; empeoramiento *m*; '~-'**sick·ness** mal *m* caduco; '~-**star** estrella *f* fugaz.

fal·low ['fælou] **1.** barbechado; *lie* ~ estar en barbecho; **2.** barbecho *m*; **3.** barbechar; '~-**deer** gamo *m*.

false [fɔːls] □ falso; *p.* desleal, pérfido; *teeth etc.* postizo; *be* ~ *to, play* ~ traicionar; ~ *bottom* doble fondo *m*; ~ *imprisonment* detención *f* ilegal; **false·hood** ['~hud] mentira *f*; falsedad *f*; **'false·ness** falsedad *f*; perfidia *f*.

fal·set·to [fɔːl'setou] falsete *m*.

fal·si·fi·ca·tion ['fɔːlsifi'keiʃn] falsificación *f*; **fal·si·fy** ['~fai] falsificar; **fal·si·ty** ['~ti] falsedad *f*.

fal·ter ['fɔːltə] *v/i.* vacilar, titubear; (*voice*) desfallecer, empañarse; *v/t.* decir titubeando.

fame [feim] fama *f*; **famed** famoso (*for* por), afamado.

fa·mil·iar [fə'miljə] **1.** □ familiar (*to* a) (*a. b.s.*); conocido; íntimo; *be* ~ *with* estar familiarizado con, ser conocedor de; **2.** familiar *m* (*a. eccl.*; *a.* ~ *spirit*); **fa·mil·i·ar·i·ty** [~li'æriti] familiaridad *f* (*a. b.s*); conocimiento *m*; intimidad *f*; **fa·mil·iar·i·za·tion** [~ljərai'zeiʃn] familiarización *f*; **fa·mil·iar·ize** [~'miljəraiz] familiarizar (*o.s. with* -se con).

fam·i·ly ['fæmili] **1.** familia *f*; **2.** familiar; casero; *business* de familia; *butcher etc.* doméstico; *in the* ~ *way* en estado de buena esperanza, encinta; ~ *allowance* subsidio *m* familiar; ~ *income* entradas *f/pl.* familiares; ~ *man* padre *m* de familia;

hombre *m* casero; ~ *tree* árbol *m* genealógico.

fam·ine ['fæmin] hambre *f*; carestía *f of goods.*

fam·ished ['fæmiʃt] famélico, hambriento.

fa·mous ['feiməs] □ famoso, célebre (*for* por); F ~*ly* a las mil maravillas.

fan¹ [fæn] **1.** abanico *m*; ventilador *m*; ✗ aventador *m*; (*machine*) aventadora *f*; **2.** abanicar; ventilar; ✗ aventar; *fire* avivar, soplar; *fig.* excitar, atizar.

fan² [~] F aficionado (a *f*) *m*, entusiasta *m/f*; admirador (-a *f*) *m*.

fa·nat·ic, fa·nat·i·cal [fə'nætik(l)] □ fanático *adj. a. su. m* (a *f*); **fa·nat·i·cism** fanatismo *m*.

fan·ci·er ['fænsiə] criador *m* aficionado.

fan·ci·ful ['fænsiful] □ caprichoso; fantástico; imaginario.

fan·cy ['fænsi] **1.** fantasía *f*; imaginación *f*; capricho *m*, antojo *m*; afición *f*, gusto *m*; quimera *f*, suposición *f* arbitraria; *take a* ~ *to* aficionarse a; *p.* prendarse de; *take* (*or tickle*) *one's* ~ atraer, cautivar; **2.** de fantasía; de lujo, de adorno; *ideas etc.* extravagante; *price* exorbitante; ~ *dress* disfraz *m*; ~ *dress ball* baile *m* de trajes; ~-*free* libre de amores; ~ *goods pl.* géneros *m/pl.* de fantasía; **3.** imaginar(se), figurarse; antojarse; aficionarse a, encapricharse por; ~ *meeting you!* ¡qué casualidad encontrarle a Vd.!; *just* ~! ¡imagínate!; '~-**work** *sew.* labores *f/pl.*

fan·fare ['fænfeə] *approx.* toque *m* de trompeta, fanfarria *f*.

fan·light ['fænlait] abanico *m*.

fang [fæŋ] colmillo *m*; ⊕ diente *m*.

fan·mail ['fænmeil] F cartas *f/pl.* escritas por admiradores.

fan·ta·sia [fæn'teiziə] ♩ fantasía *f*; **fan·tas·tic** [~'tæstik] □ fantástico; **fan·ta·sy** ['~təsi] fantasía *f*.

far [fɑː] **1.** *adj.* lejano, distante; más lejano; **2.** *adv.* lejos, a lo lejos (*a.* ~ *away, off*); *how* ~ *is it* (*to*)? ~ ¿ cuánto hay de aquí (a)?; ~ *and away* con mucho; ~ *and near,* ~ *and wide* por todas partes; ~ *better* mucho mejor; ~ *the best* con mucho el mejor; ~ *from ger.* lejos de *inf.*; ~ *from it!* ¡nada de eso!; ~ *be it from me to inf.* no permita Dios que *subj.*; *by* ~ con mucho; *as* ~ *as* hasta; *as*

~ *as* I *know* que yo sepa; *in so* ~ *as* en tanto que; *so* ~ hasta aquí; (*time*) hasta ahora; *go* ~ *to* contribuir mucho a; *go so* ~ *as to inf.* llegar a *inf.*; ~**·a·way** ['fɑːrəwei] remoto; *look* preocupado, distraído.

farce [fɑːs] farsa *f*; *fig.* tontería *f*, absurdo *m*; **far·ci·cal** ['ˌikl] □ ridículo, absurdo.

fare [fɛə] **1.** precio *m* (del billete); billete *m*; ⚓ pasaje *m*; (*p.*) pasajero (a *f*) *m*; (*food*) comida *f*; **2.** pasarlo, irle a uno (bien *etc.*); suceder; '~-**'well 1.** ¡adiós! **2.** adiós *m*, despedida *f*; *bid* ~ despedirse (*to* de); **3.** ... de despedida.

far... [fɑː]: '~-**'fetched** inverosímil, poco probable; forzado, traído por los cabellos; '~-**'flung** extenso.

far·i·na·ceous [færi'neiʃəs] farináceo.

farm [fɑːm] **1.** granja *f*; cortijo *m*; estancia *f* *S. Am.*; (*oyster- etc.*) criadero *m*; = ~*house*; **2.** *v/t.* cultivar, labrar; ~ *out* arrendar, dar en arriendo; *v/i.* cultivar la tierra; ser agricultor; *he* ~*s in* Kent tiene tierras en Kent; '**farm·er** granjero *m*, agricultor *m*; labrador *m*; estanciero *m S.Am.*; '**farm·hand** labriego *m*; peón *m S.Am.*; '**farm·house** alquería *f*, cortijo *m*; '**farm·ing 1.** agricultura *f*; labranza *f*, cultivo *m*; **2.** agrícola; *land* labrantío, de labor; **farm·stead** ['ˌsted] alquería *f* (y sus dependencias); '**farm·yard** corral *m*.

far-off ['fɑːr'ɔf] lejano, remoto.

far·ra·go [fə'reigou] fárrago *m*.

far-reach·ing ['fɑːr'riːtʃiŋ] trascendental; de mucho alcance.

far·ri·er ['færiə] herrador *m*; *vet.* albéitar *m*.

far·row ['færou] **1.** lechigada *f*; **2.** parir (*la cerda*).

far-sight·ed ['fɑː'saitid] □ clarividente; previsor; **far-'sight·ed·ness** clarividencia *f*; previsión *f*.

far·ther ['fɑːðə], **far·thest** ['ˌðist] *comp. a. sup. of* far.

far·thing ['fɑːðiŋ] cuarto *m* de penique; *fig.* ardite *m*.

fas·ci·nate ['fæsineit] fascinar, encantar; **fas·ci·nat·ing** □ fascinador, encantador; **fas·ci·na·tion** fascinación *f*, encanto *m*.

Fas·cism ['fæʃizm] fascismo *m*; '**Fas·cist** fascista *adj. a. su. m/f*.

fash·ion ['fæʃn] **1.** moda *f*; estilo *m*; uso *m*, manera *f*; buen tono *m*; *in* ~ de moda; *out of* ~ pasado de moda; *in the Spanish* ~ a la (manera) española; *set the* ~ imponer la moda (*for* de); **2.** formar; labrar; forjar; adaptar; modelar; '**fash·ion·a·ble** □ de moda; de buen tono, elegante; *be* ~ estar de moda; '**fash·ion-de'sign·er** modisto *m*; '**fash·ion-mod·el** modelo *m/f*; '**fash·ion-pa'rade**, '~-'**show** desfile *m* de modelos; '**fash·ion-'plate** figurín *m* de moda.

fast[1] [fɑːst] **1.** *adj.* rápido, veloz; ligero; (*firm*) fijo, firme; *colour* sólido, inalterable; *friend* leal; *living* disoluto; F *make* ~ muy coqueta; *fresca*; *make* ~ sujetar, amarrar; F *pull a* ~ *one* jugar una mala pasada (*on* a); **2.** *adv.* rápidamente; de prisa; ~ *asleep* profundamente dormido; *be* ~ (*clock*) adelantar; *hold* ~ mantenerse firme.

fast[2] [ˌ] **1.** ayuno *m*; **2.** ayunar; '~-**day** día *m* de ayuno.

fas·ten ['fɑːsn] *v/t.* asegurar, fijar; atar; sujetar, pegar; *door* cerrar; *dress* abrochar; ~ *on blame etc.* achacar a; *v/i.* ~ (*up*)*on* agarrarse de; *fig.* fijarse en; '**fas·ten·er**, '**fas·ten·ing** (*lock*) cerrojo *m*; cierre *m*; broche *m*, corchete *m on dress*; (*paper-*) grapa *f*.

fas·tid·i·ous [fæs'tidiəs] □ quisquilloso, delicado; exigente; descontentadizo.

fast·ness ['fɑːstnis] ✕ plaza *f* fuerte; lo más intrincado *of mountain etc.*

fat [fæt] **1.** gordo, grueso; *land* fértil; *living, profits* pingüe; *meat* poco magro; F *iro. a* ~ *lot* muy poco; *get* ~ engordar; **2.** grasa *f*; *the* ~ *of the land* lo mejor y más rico de la tierra; *now the* ~ *is in the fire* aquí se va a armar la gorda.

fa·tal ['feitl] □ fatal, funesto (*to* para); **fa·tal·ism** ['ˌəlizm] fatalismo *m*; '**fa·tal·ist** fatalista *m/f*; **fa·tal·i·ty** [fə'tæliti] fatalidad *f*; (*p.*) muerto *m*, muerte *f*.

fate [feit] hado *m*; suerte *f*, destino *m*; *the* ♀*s pl.* las Parcas; **fat·ed** ['ˌid] fatal; ~ *to* predestinado a; **fate·ful** ['ˌful] □ fatal, funesto, fatídico.

fat·head ['fæthed] F idiota *m/f*.

fa·ther ['fɑːðə] **1.** padre *m*; ♀ *Christmas* Papá Noel *m*; **2.** engendrar; prohijar; servir de padre a; ~ *on* atribuir a, achacar a; **fa·ther·hood**

['⌣hud] paternidad *f*; **'fa·ther-in-law** suegro *m*; **'fa·ther·land** patria *f*; **'fa·ther·less** huérfano de padre; **'fa·ther·ly** paternal.

fath·om ['fæðəm] 1. braza *f*; 2. ♓ sond(e)ar (*a. fig.*); *fig.* penetrar; profundizar; entender; **'fath·om·less** insondable (*a. fig.*).

fa·tigue [fə'ti:g] 1. fatiga *f* (*a.* ⊕), cansancio *m*; ✄ faena *f*; 2. fatigar, cansar; **fa'tigue-par·ty** destacamento *m* de trabajo.

fat·ness ['fætnis] gordura *f*; fertilidad *f*; **'fat·ten** engordar (*a. v/i.*); **'fat·ty** 1. graso; ~ *degeneration* degeneración *f* grasosa; 2. F gordi(n)flón *m*.

fa·tu·i·ty [fə'tjuiti] fatuidad *f*, simpleza *f*; **fat·u·ous** ['fætjuəs] □ fatuo, simple.

fau·cet ['fɔ:sit] *esp. Am.* grifo *m*.

faugh [fɔ:] ¡bah!

fault [fɔ:lt] 1. falta *f* (*a. sport*); culpa *f*; imperfección *f* *in manufacture etc.*; ⊕, ✗ avería *f*, desperfecto *m*, defecto *m*; *geol.* falla *f*; *at* ~ culpable; *to a* ~ excesivamente, sumamente; *it's your* ~ Vd. tiene la culpa; *find* ~ criticar, censurar (*with acc.*); 2. tachar, encontrar defectos en; **'~·find·er** criticón (-a *f*) *m*; **'~·find·ing** 1. criticón, reparón; 2. manía *f* de criticar; **'fault·less** □ impecable, intachable; **'fault·y** □ defectuoso, imperfecto.

faun [fɔ:n] fauno *m*.

fau·na ['fɔ:nə] fauna *f*.

fa·vo(u)r ['feivə] 1. favor *m*; (*approval*) aprobación *f*; (*support*) amparo *m*; privanza *f at court*; (*token*) prenda *f*; ✝ grata *f*, atenta *f*; ~*s pl.* favores *m/pl. of woman*; *in* ~ of a favor de; *be in* ~ of *p.* estar por; *th.* aprobar, ser partidario de; *ger.* estar por *inf.*, apoyar la idea de *inf.*; *be in* ~ tener mucha aceptación; *be in* ~ *with* tener el apoyo de; gozar de favor cerca de; *do a* ~ hacer un favor; *find* ~ *with s. o.* caerle en gracia a uno; 2. favorecer; apoyar; **fa·vo(u)r·a·ble** ['~vərəbl] □ favorable; **fa·vo(u)red** ['~vəd] favorecido; *well* ~ bien parecido; **fa·vo(u)r·ite** ['~vərit] 1. favorito, predilecto; 2. favorito (a *f*) *m* (*a. sport*); **'fa·vo(u)r·it·ism** favoritismo *m*. [de cervato.﹚

fawn¹ [fɔ:n] *zo.* cervato *m*; color *m*﹚

fawn² [⌣] adular, lisonjear (*on acc.*); (*animal*) acariciar (*on acc.*); **'fawn·ing** servil, lisonjero.

faze [feiz] *Am.* F inquietar, molestar.

fe·al·ty ['fi:əlti] † homenaje *m*, fidelidad *f*.

fear [fiə] 1. miedo *m* (*of a, de*), temor *m*; aprensión *f*; *for* ~ of temiendo, por miedo de; *for* ~ *that* por miedo de que; *go in* ~ *of one's life* temer por su vida; *F no* ~! ¡ni hablar!; 2. *v/t.* temer; *v/i.* tener miedo (*to inf. de inf.*); ~ *for* temer por; **fear·ful** ['~ful] □ *p.* temeroso (*of de*), tímido, aprensivo; *th.* pavoroso, horrendo; **'fear·less** □ intrépido, audaz; ~ *of* sin temor a; **'fear·less·ness** intrepidez *f*.

fea·si·ble ['fi:zəbl] factible, posible; *make* ~ posibilitar.

feast [fi:st] 1. banquete *m*, festín *m*; (*day*) fiesta *f*; 2. *v/t.* festejar; agasajar; banquetear; ~ *one's eyes* recrear la vista (*on mirando*); *v/i.* banquetear; ~ *on* regalarse con.

feat [fi:t] hazaña *f*, proeza *f*.

feath·er ['feðə] 1. pluma *f*; ⊕ lengüeta *f*; ⊕ cuña *f*; *in fine etc.* ~ de buen humor; *show the white* ~ volver las espaldas, mostrarse cobarde; *that is a* ~ *in his cap* es un triunfo para él; 2. emplumar; ~ *one's nest* ponerse las botas, hacer su agosto; **'~·bed** plumón *m*; **'~·brained** cascabelero; **'feath·ered** plumado; alado; **'feath·er·edge** filván *m*; **'feath·er-stitch** punto *m* de espina; **'feath·er-weight** peso *m* pluma; **'feath·er·y** ligero como pluma.

fea·ture ['fi:tʃə] 1. rasgo *m*; característica *f*; facción *f of face*; (*film*) atracción *f* principal; artículo *m* *in paper*; ~*s pl.* facciones *f/pl.*; 2. delinear; representar; *film* ofrecer; destacar; *actor* presentar; **'fea·ture·less** sin rasgos distintivos, monótono. [*adj. a. su. m.*﹚

feb·ri·fuge ['febrifju:dʒ] febrífugo﹚

fe·brile ['fi:brail] febril.

Feb·ru·ar·y ['februəri] febrero *m*.

feck·less ['feklis] □ irreflexivo, descuidado; *Am.* débil.

fec·u·lent ['fekjulənt] feculento.

fe·cund ['fi:kʌnd] fecundo; **fe·cun·date** ['fi:kʌndeit] fecundar; **fe·cun·'da·tion** fecundación *f*; **fe·cun·di·ty** [fi'kʌnditi] fecundidad *f*.

fed [fed] *pret. a. p.p. of* feed 2; be ~ up estar harto (*with* de).

fed·er·al ['fedərəl] □ federal; '**fed·er·al·ism** federalismo *m*; '**fed·er·al·ist** federalista *m/f*; '**fed·er·al·ize** confederar(se); **fed·er·ate** ['~reit] confederar(se); **fed·er·a·tion** federación *f*; **fed·er·a·tive** ['~reitiv] federativo.

fee [fi:] derechos *m/pl.*; honorarios *m/pl.*; (*entrance*) cuota *f*; (*tip*) gratificación *f*; *school*: ~s *pl.* cuota *f* de enseñanza; ~ *simple* herencia *f* libre de condición.

fee·ble ['fi:bl] □ débil; flojo; irresoluto; '~-'**mind·ed** imbécil; '**fee·ble·ness** debilidad *f*; flojedad *f*.

feed [fi:d] **1.** comida *f*; ✗ pienso *m*, pasto *m*; F cuchipanda *f*, comilona *f*; ⊕ (*tubo m*), dispositivo *m* de) alimentación *f*; **2.** [*irr.*] *v/t.* dar de comer a; nutrir; alimentar (*a.* ⊕); *fire* cebar; *v. fed*; ~ *up animals* cebar, engordar; *v. fed*; *v/i.* comer; alimentarse (on de); ✗ pacer; '~-**back** *radio:* realimentación *f*; '**feed·er** ⊕ alimentador *m*; *geog.* afluente *m*; (*baby's*) babero *m*; '**feed·er line** 🔗 ramal *m* tributario; '**feed·ing** alimentación *f*; ⊕ *attr.* de alimentación; '**feed·ing-bot·tle** biberón *m*; '**feed·ing-stuffs** ✗ piensos *m/pl.*

feel [fi:l] **1.** [*irr.*] *v/t.* sentir; experimentar, percibir; (*touch*) palpar, tocar; *pulse* tomar; reconocer; ~ *that* creer que, parecerle a uno que; *v/i.* sentirse; ~ *bad*, ~ *ill* sentirse mal; ~ *cold* (*p.*) tener frío; (*th.*) estar frío; ~ *for* condolerse de; ~ *like doing* tener ganas de hacer; ~ *rough etc.* ser áspero *etc.* al tacto; ~ *up to* creerse capaz de; *I don't* ~ *quite myself* no me encuentro muy bien de salud; **2.** tacto *m*; sensación *f*; '**feel·er** *zo.* antena *f*; *zo.* tentáculo *m*; *pol. etc.* sondeo *m*; tentativa *f*; '**feel·ing 1.** □ sensible; compasivo; ~ly con honda emoción; **2.** tacto *m*; sensación *f*; sentimiento *m*; sensibilidad *f*; (*opinion*) parecer *m*; (*foreboding*) presentimiento *m*; *with* ~ con emoción; (*angrily*) con pasión; *hurt one's* ~s herir los sentimientos de uno.

feet [fi:t] *pl. of* foot pies *m/pl.*

feign [fein] fingir; ~ *mad(ness)* fingirse loco; ~ *sleep* fingirse dormido; ~ *to do* fingir hacer; '**feigned** fingido.

feint [feint] **1.** artificio *m*, engaño *m*; (*fencing*) finta *f*; **2.** hacer una finta.

fe·lic·i·tate [fi'lisiteit] felicitar; **fe·lic·i·ta·tion** felicitación *f*; **fe'lic·i·tous** □ feliz, oportuno; **fe'lic·i·ty** felicidad *f*; ocurrencia *f* oportuna.

fe·line ['fi:lain] felino.

fell[1] [fel] **1.** *pret. of* fall 2; **2.** *tree* talar; derribar; *cattle* acogotar.

fell[2] [~] *poet.* cruel; feroz; destructivo.

fell[3] [~] *geog.* montaña *f*; (*moor*) páramo *m*, brezal *m*.

fel·low ['felou] compañero *m*; prójimo *m*; (*equal*) igual *m/f*; (*other half*) pareja *f*; *univ. approx.* miembro *m* de la junta de gobierno de un colegio; *univ.* becario *m*; socio *m*, miembro *m of society*; F tipo *m*, sujeto *m*, individuo *m*; *nice* ~ buen chico *m*; *poor* ~ (!) pobrecito *m*; *young* ~ chico *m*; *now listen, young* ~ oiga Vd., joven; *a* ~ *can't do this all day* uno no puede hacer esto todo el día; '~-'**be·ing** prójimo *m*; '~-'**cit·i·zen** conciudadano *m*; '~-'**coun·try·man** compatriota *m*; '~-'**crea·ture** prójimo *m*; '~-'**feel·ing** simpatía *f*, afinidad *f*; '~-'**mem·ber** consocio *m*; ~**ship** ['~ʃip] compañerismo *m*; compañía *f*; hermandad *f*; *univ.* (*office*) dignidad *f* del *fellow*; *univ.* (*grant*) beca *f*; '~-'**trav·el·ler** compañero *m* de viaje (*a. fig.*); *pol.* filocomunista *m/f*.

fel·on ['felən] criminal *m*, delincuente *m/f* de mayor cuantía; **fe·lo·ni·ous** [fi'lounjəs] □ criminal; delincuente; **fel·o·ny** ['feləni] crimen *m*, delito *m* de mayor cuantía.

felt[1] [felt] *pret. a. p.p. of* feel 1.

felt[2] [~] **1.** fieltro *m* (*a.* ~ *hat*); **2.** cubrir con fieltro.

fe·male ['fi:meil] hembra *adj. a. su. f* (*a.* ⊕); femenino.

fem·i·nine ['feminin] femenino; *contp.* afeminado; **fem·i·nin·i·ty** feminidad *f*; '**fem·i·nism** feminismo *m*; '**fem·i·nist** feminista *m/f*.

fen [fen] pantano *m*.

fence [fens] **1.** cerca *f*, valla *f*, cercado *m*; *sl.* receptor *m* de cosas robadas; *sit on the* ~ ver los toros desde la barrera; (*estar a*) ver venir; **2.** *v/t.* cercar; proteger, defender (*from* de); ~ *in* encerrar con cerca; ~ *off* separar con cerca; *v/i. fig.* defenderse con evasivas; *sport*: esgrimir; **'fen·cer** esgrimidor (-a *f*) *m*; **fenc·ing** ['fensiŋ] esgrima *f; attr.* de esgrima; ~ *post* poste *m* de cerca.

fend [fend]: ~ *for o.s.* defenderse (a sí mismo), apañárselas por su cuenta; ~ *off* parar; desviar; **'fend·er** guardafuego *m; Am. mot.* parachoques *m*; guardafango *m; Am.* 🚂 trompa *f;* ⚓ defensa *f.*

fen·nel ['fenl] hinojo *m.*

fen·ny ['feni] pantanoso.

fer·ment 1. ['fəːmənt] fermento *m*; fermentación *f; fig.* agitación *f*; **2.** [fəˈment] (hacer) fermentar; **fer·men·ta·tion** [fəːmenˈteiʃn] fermentación *f;* **fer'ment·a·tive** [~tə-tiv] fermentativo.

fern [fəːn] helecho *m.*

fe·ro·cious [fəˈrouʃəs] □ feroz; **fe·roc·i·ty** [fəˈrɔsiti] ferocidad *f.*

fer·ret ['ferit] **1.** hurón *m* (*a. fig.*); **2.** cazar con hurones; ~ *about* buscar revolviéndolo todo; ~ *out* husmear; *secret* lograr saber.

fer·ric ['ferik] férrico; **fer·ro·concrete** ['ferouˈkɔŋkriːt] ferrohormigón *m;* **fer·rous** ['ferəs] ferroso.

fer·rule ['feruːl] regatón *m;* ⊕ virola *f.*

fer·ry ['feri] **1.** pasaje *m*; balsadero *m;* (*boat*) balsa *f*, barca *f* (de pasaje); **2.** pasar ... a través del río *etc.*; **'~·boat** balsa *f*, barca *f;* **'fer·ry·man** balsero *m.*

fer·tile ['fəːtail] fértil (*of, in* en; *a. fig.*), fecundo; **fer·til·i·ty** [fəːˈtil-iti] fertilidad *f*, fecundidad *f;* **'fer·ti·lize** fertilizar, fecundar; 🖉 abonar; **'fer·ti·liz·er** fertilizante *m,* abono *m.*

fer·ule ['feruːl] férula *f.*

fer·ven·cy ['fəːvənsi] *fig.* fervor *m;* **'fer·vent** □, **fer·vid** ['fəːvid] □ fervoroso, ardiente.

fer·vo·(u)r ['fəːvə] fervor *m,* ardor *m.*

fes·tal ['festl] □ festivo.

fes·ter ['festə] ulcerarse, enconarse (*a. fig.*).

fes·ti·val ['festəvl] **1.** fiesta *f;* ♪ festival *m;* **2.** festivo; **fes·tive** ['~iv] □ festivo; regocijado; *the ~ season mst* Navidades *f/pl.;* **fes'tiv·i·ty** fiesta *f;* festividad *f;* regocijo *m.*

fes·toon [fesˈtuːn] **1.** *sew.* festón *m;* **2.** *sew.* festonear; *fig.* engalanar, adornar.

fetch [fetʃ] *v/t.* traer; ir por, ir a buscar; hacer venir; *blow* dar; *price* venderse por (*or* a); *sigh* proferir; F atraer; ~ *up* vomitar; *v/i.* ~ *up* al llegar por fin a, ir a parar a; ~ *and carry* trajinar; ser un esclavo del trabajo; **'fetch·ing** □ F atractivo.

fête [feit] **1.** fiesta *f;* **2.** festejar.

fet·id ['fetid] □ fétido.

fet·ish ['fetiʃ] fetiche *m.*

fet·lock ['fetlɔk] espolón *m;* (*hair*) cernejas *f/pl.*

fet·ter ['fetə] **1.** grillete *m;* ~*s pl.* grillos *m/pl.* (*a. fig.*); **2.** encadenar; trabar (*a. fig.*); *fig.* estorbar.

fet·tle ['fetl] estado *m,* condición *f; in fine* ~ de buen humor; en buenas condiciones.

feud [fjuːd] enemistad *f* heredada (entre dos familias *etc.*); vendetta *f,* odio *m* de sangre; **feu·dal** ['~dl] □ feudal; **feu·dal·ism** ['~əlizm] feudalismo *m;* **feu·dal·i·ty** ['~ˈdæliti] feudalidad *f;* (*holding*) feudo *m;* **feu·da·to·ry** ['~dətəri] feudatorio *adj. a. su. m.*

fe·ver ['fiːvə] fiebre *f;* calentura *f;* **fe·vered** ['fiːvəd] *mst fig.* febril; **'fe·ver·ish** □ febril (*a. fig.*), calenturiento.

few [fjuː] pocos; (alg)unos; *a* ~ unos cuantos; *not a* ~ no pocos; F *a good* ~ un buen número (de); ~ *and far between* muy raros; *the* ~ la minoría.

fi·an·cé(e *f***)** [fiˈɑ̃nsei] *approx.* novio (a *f*) *m,* prometido (a *f*) *m.*

fi·as·co [fiˈæskou] fiasco *m.*

fi·at ['faiæt] fíat *m,* autorización *f; Am.* ~ *money* billetes *m/pl.* sin respaldo.

fib [fib] F **1.** mentirilla *f,* bola *f;* **2.** decir mentirillas; **'fib·ber** F mentirosillo (a *f*) *m.*

fi·bre ['faibə] fibra *f; fig.* carácter *m;* **fi·brin** ['~brin] fibrina *f;* **'fi·brous** □ fibroso.

fib·u·la ['fibjulə] *anat.* peroné *m.*

fick·le ['fikl] inconstante, mudable, veleidoso; **'fick·le·ness** inconstancia *f,* veleidad *f.*

fic·tion ['fikʃn] ficción *f;* novelas *f/pl.,* género *m* novelístico; **'fic·tion·al** □ novelesco.

fic·ti·tious [fikˈtiʃəs] □ ficticio.

fid·dle ['fidl] **1.** ♪ violín *m*; F trampa *f*; *be fit as a* ~ andar como un reloj; *play second* ~ desempeñar un papel secundario; **2.** ♪ tocar el violín; *sl.* agenciarse; ~ *away* desperdiciar; ~ *with* jugar con, manosear; **fid·dle-de-dee** ['~di'di:] ¡tonterías!; **'fid·dler** violinista *m/f*; **'fid·dle·sticks** ¡qué disparate!; **'fid·dling** trivial, insignificante; molesto.

fi·del·i·ty [fi'deliti] fidelidad *f*.

fidg·et ['fidʒit] F **1.** (*p.*) persona *f* inquieta; ~*s pl.* agitación *f* nerviosa; *have the* ~*s* no poder estar quieto; **2.** agitarse nerviosamente; ~ *with* manosear, jugar con; **'fidg·et·y** F nervioso, azogado; *be* ~ tener azogue.

fi·du·ci·ar·y [fi'dju:ʃiəri] fiduciario *adj. a. su. m.*

fief [fi:f] feudo *m*.

field [fi:ld] **1.** campo *m* (*a.* ⚔, ⚒, *sport*); prado *m*, pradera *f*; esfera *f* *of activities*; competidores *m/pl. in race*; *take the* ~ salir a palestra; **2.** *ball* parar, recoger; *team* presentar; **'~-day** ⚔ día *m* de maniobras; *fig.* día *m* de gran éxito; **'field·er** el que recoge la pelota.

field...: **'~·fare** zorzal *m* real; **'~-glass·es** *pl.* gemelos *m/pl.* (de campo); **'~-gun** cañón *m* de campaña; **'~-kit·chen** cocina *f* de campaña; **'~-mar·shal** *approx.* mariscal *m* de campo; capitán *m* general del ejército; **'~-'of·fi·cer** jefe *m*; **'~-sports** *pl.* caza *f*; **'~-work** trabajo *m* en el propio campo.

fiend [fi:nd] demonio *m*, diablo *m*; desalmado *m*; fanático *m* (*for* de); **'fiend·ish** □ diabólico.

fierce [fiəs] □ feroz, fiero; furioso; *heat* intenso; *supporter etc.* acérrimo; **'fierce·ness** ferocidad *f*; violencia *f*; intensidad *f*.

fi·er·y ['faiəri] □ ardiente; caliente; *fig.* vehemente; *horse* fogoso; *speech* apasionado.

fife [faif] pífano *m*.

fif·teen ['fif'ti:n] quince (*a. su. m*); **'fif'teenth** [~θ] decimoquinto; **fifth** [fifθ] **1.** □ quinto; **2.** quinto *m*; quinta parte *f*; ♪ quinta *f*; **fif·ti·eth** ['~tiiθ] quincuagésimo; **'fif·ty** cincuenta; **'fif·ty-'fif·ty:** *go* ~ ir a medias, pagar a escote.

fig [fig] (*green*) higo *m*; (*early*) breva *f*; ~*-leaf fig.* hoja *f* de parra;

~*-tree* higuera *f*; *I don't care a* ~ *for him* no se me da un higo.

fight [fait] **1.** pelea *f*, combate *m*; lucha *f* (*for* por); combatividad *f*, brío *m*; *Am.* riña *f*; *put up a good* ~ dar buena cuenta de sí; *show* ~ enseñar los dientes; **2.** [*irr.*] *v/t.* combatir; batirse con; luchar con(tra); *battle* dar; *bull* lidiar; ~ *it out* decidirlo luchando; ~ *off* rechazar; *v/i.* batirse, pelear; luchar (*against* con, contra; *for* por); ~ *back* resistir; ~*ing chance* posibilidad *f* de éxito; ~*ing fit* en excelente salud; **'fight·er** combatiente *m/f*; luchador (-a *f*) *m*; ✈ caza *m*; ~*-bomber* cazabombardero *m*; **'fight·ing** combate *m*; lucha *f*; pendencia *f*; *attr.* guerrero; *cock* de pelea.

fig·ment ['figmənt] ficción *f*, invención *f*. [figurante (a *f*) *m.*\
fig·u·rant(e) ['figjurənt;(~'rænti)]|
fig·ur·a·tive ['figərətiv] □ *sense* figurado; figurativo.

fig·ure ['figə] **1.** figura *f*; tipo *m* *of body*; (*sketch etc.*) dibujo *m*, figura *f*; A figura *f*; (*number*) cifra *f*; número *m*; † precio *m*; (~ *of speech*) figura *f*, tropo *m*; *fig.* exageración *f*; *be good at* ~*s* ser fuerte en matemáticas; *cut a* ~ hacer papel; **2.** *v/t.* figurar; representar; *Am.* imaginar; *Am.* calcular (*a.* ~ *up*); ~ *out* calcular; resolver; descifrar; *v/i.* figurar (*as* como, *among* entre); *Am.* figurarse; *Am.* ~ *on* contar con; incluir; proyectar; esperar; ~ *out at* venir a ser; **'~-head** ⚓ mascarón *m* (de proa); *fig.* figurante (a *f*) *m*; **'~-skat·ing** patinaje *m* de figuras.

fig·u·rine ['figjuri:n] figurina *f*.

fil·a·ment ['filəmənt] *all senses*: filamento *m*.

fil·bert ['filbə:t] avellana *f*.

filch [filtʃ] sisar, ratear.

file¹ [fail] **1.** carpeta *f*; fichero *m*; archivo *m*; legajo *m*; (*row*) fila *f*, hilera *f*; *the* ~*s pl.* los archivos; **2.** *v/t.* archivar (*a.* ~ *away*); clasificar; registrar; *v/i.* ~ *by*, ~ *past* desfilar; ~ *out* salir en fila; *filing-cabinet* archivador *m*; *filing-clerk* archivero *m*.

file² [~] ⊕ **1.** lima *f*; **2.** limar; **'~-cut·ter** picador *m* de limas.

fil·i·al ['filjəl] □ filial; **fil·i·a·tion** [fili'eiʃn] filiación *f*.

fil·i·bus·ter ['filibʌstə] **1.** filibustero *m*; *Am. parl.* (*p.*) obstruccionista *m*; (*act*) maniobra *f* obstruccionista; **2.** *Am. parl.* usar de maniobras obstruccionistas.

fil·i·gree ['filigri:] filigrana *f*.

fil·ings ['filiŋz] *pl.* limaduras *f/pl.*

fill [fil] **1.** llenar(se) (*with* de); rellenar(se); *post* ocupar; *vacancy* cubrir; *sails* hinchar(se); *space* llenar (*or* ocupar) completamente; *tooth* empastar; *tyre* inflar; ~ *in form* llenar; *hole* terraplenar; llenar; *details* añadir; *outline etc.* completar; ~ *out Am. form* llenar; (*p.*) engordar; *fig.* completar; ~ *up* llenar; colmar; **2.** hartazgo *m*; pipa *f* *of tobacco*; *eat one's* ~ hartarse; *have one's* ~ darse un hartazgo (*of* de).

fill·er ['filə] cargador *m of pen*.

fil·let ['filit] **1.** *all senses*: filete *m*; **2.** *fish* quitar la raspa de, cortar en filetes.

fill·ing ['filiŋ] relleno *m*; ⊕ empaquetadura *f*; empaste *m of tooth*; *mot.* ~ *station* estación *f* de servicio.

fil·lip ['filip] capirotazo *m with finger*; *fig.* estímulo *m*. [vivaz.\

fil·ly ['fili] potra *f*; *fig.* muchacha *f*∫

film [film] **1.** película *f*; capa *f of dust*; *fig.* velo *m*; *phot. a. thea.* película *f*, film *m*; ~ *strip* tira *f* de película; **2.** filmar; hacer una película de; rodar; ~ *over* empañarse, cubrirse con película; '~**star** estrella *f* (*or* astro *m*) de cine; '**film·y** □ transparente, diáfano.

fil·ter ['filtə] **1.** filtro *m*; **2.** filtrar(se); ~ *in*, ~ *through* infiltrarse; *fig.* introducirse; '~**pa·per** papel *m* de filtro.

filth [filθ] inmundicia *f*; suciedad *f*, mugre *f*; '**filth·y** □ inmundo (*a. fig.*); sucio, mugriento.

fil·trate ['filtreit] filtrar(se); **fil'tra·tion** filtración *f*.

fin [fin] *all senses*: aleta *f*.

fi·nal ['fainl] **1.** □ final, último; decisivo, definitivo, terminante; ~*ly* finalmente, por último; **2.** *sport*: final *f*; *univ.* ~*s pl.* examen *m* final; **fi·nale** [fi'nɑ:li] ♪ final *m*; **fi·nal·ist** ['fainəlist] finalista *m/f*; **fi·nal·i·ty** [~'næliti] finalidad *f*; decisión *f*.

fi·nance [fi'næns] **1.** finanzas *f/pl.*; fondos *m/pl.*; asuntos *m/pl.* financieros; **2.** financiar; **fi'nan·cial** [~ʃl] □ financiero; bancario; monetario; **fi'nan·cier** [~siə] financiero *m*.

finch [fintʃ] *v. chaf*~ *etc.*

find [faind] **1.** [*irr.*] encontrar, hallar; dar con; descubrir; ⚖ declarar, fallar; (*supply*) proveer; lograr obtener, lograr reunir; ~ *o.s. fig.* descubrir su verdadera vocación; *all found* todo incluido; ~ *out* averiguar; (llegar a) saber; F conocer el juego de, calar; ~ *out about* informarse sobre; **2.** hallazgo *m*; '**find·er** el (la) que halla; *phot.* visor *m*; '**find·ing** descubrimiento *m*; ~*s pl.* ⚖ fallo *m*; recomendaciones *f/pl. of report*.

fine[1] [fain] **1.** □ fino; bello, hermoso; escogido, primoroso; refinado; *p.* admirable; magnífico; *iro.* bueno, lindo; *be* ~ (*weather*) hacer buen tiempo; *that's* ~! ¡estupendo!; *have a* ~ *time* divertirse mucho; F *you're a* ~ *one!* ¡qué tío!; ~ *arts pl.* bellas artes *f/pl.*; **2.** *adv.* F muy bien; *cut it* ~ dejarse muy poco tiempo; *feel* ~ estar de primera; **3.** *meteor.* buen tiempo *m*.

fine[2] [~] ⚖ **1.** multa *f*; *in* ~ en resumen; **2.** multar.

fine-drawn ['fain'drɔ:n] fino, sutil.

fine·ness ['fainnis] fineza *f etc.* (*v. fine*[1]); ley *f of metals*. [*m/pl.*\

fin·er·y ['fainəri] galas *f/pl.*, adornos∫

fi·nesse [fi'nes] discriminación *f* sutil; artificio *m*, sutileza *f*; tino *m*; *cards*: impase *m*.

fin·ger ['fiŋgə] **1.** dedo *m*; *little* ~ dedo *m* meñique; *middle* ~ dedo *m* del corazón; *ring* ~ dedo *m* anular; *have a* ~ *in the pie* meter su cucharada; *put one's* ~ *on* señalar acertadamente; *slip through one's* ~*s* escaparse de entre los dedos de uno; *twist s.o. round one's little* ~ hacer con uno lo que le da la gana; **2.** manosear; ♪ pulsar; ♪ teclear (*v/i.*); '~**board** teclado *m*; '**fin·gered** con ... dedos; '**fin·ger·ing** ♪ digitación *f*.

fin·ger...: '~**nail** uña *f*; '~**post** poste *m* indicador; '~**print** **1.** huella *f* dactilar; **2.** tomar las huellas dactilares a; '~**stall** dedil *m*; '~**tip** punta *f* del dedo; *have at one's* ~*s* saber al dedillo.

fin·i·cal ['finikl] □, '**fin·ick·ing**, '**fin·ick·y** melindroso, superferolítico.

fin·ish ['finiʃ] **1.** *v/t.* acabar (*a.* ⊕, *a.* ~ *up*); terminar; concluir; consumar; ~ off completar; rematar; acabar con; F p. despachar; ~ed goods pl. productos m/pl. acabados; ~ing touch última mano f, aderezo m definitivo; v/i. acabar (by por; ger. de inf.); ~ up ger. terminar ger.; ~ up at ir a parar a; 2. fin m, final m; conclusión f; remate m; sport: poste m de llegada; ⊕ acabado m; 'fin·ish·er acabador m; ⊕ máquina f acabadora.

fi·nite ['fainait] □ finito (a. gr.).

Finn [fin] finlandés (-a f) m; Finn·ish ['~iʃ] finlandés adj. a. su. m.

fir [fəː] abeto m; Scotch ~ pino m; '~-cone piña f (de abeto).

fire ['faiə] 1. fuego m; (damaging) incendio m; (warming) fuego m, lumbre f; fig. ardor m; viveza f; be on ~ estar ardiendo; catch ~ encenderse; open ~ abrir fuego; play with ~ fig. jugar con fuego; set on ~, set ~ to pegar fuego a; take ~ encenderse; 2. v/t. encender, incendiar, quemar; pottery etc. cocer; gun, shot disparar; F p. despedir; fig. excitar, enardecer; ~ off descargar; v/i. encenderse; ✗ hacer fuego; mot. dar explosiones; ~ at, ~ (up)-on hacer fuego sobre, tirar a; F ~ away! ¡adelante!; Am. ~ up enfurecerse (at con); 3. ¡fuego!; '~-a·larm alarma f de incendios; '~-arm arma f de fuego; '~-ball bola f de fuego; '~-box caja f de fuego; '~-brand fig. partidario m violento; '~-brick ladrillo m refractario; '~-bri·gade cuerpo m de bomberos; '~-bug Am. F incendiario m; '~-cur·tain thea. telón m a prueba de incendios; '~-damp ✗ grisú m; '~-de·part·ment Am. servicio m de bomberos; '~-dog morillo m; '~-en·gine bomba f de incendios; '~-es·cape escalera f de incendios; '~-ex·tin·guish·er extintor m; '~-fly luciérnaga f; '~-guard alambrera f; guardafuego m; '~-in·sur·ance seguro m de incendios; '~-i·rons pl. útiles m/pl. de chimenea; '~-light·er approx. astillas f/pl. para encender el fuego, tea f; '~-man bombero m; 👫 fogonero m; '~-place chimenea f; hogar m; '~-plug boca f de agua; '~-proof incombustible, a prueba de fuego; '~-side 1. hogar m; 2. familiar, hogareño, doméstico; '~-sta·tion

parque m de bomberos; '~-wood leña f; '~-works fuegos m/pl. artificiales; fig. explosión f de cólera etc.

fir·ing ['faiəriŋ] (fuel) combustible m; (act) incendio m; cocción f of pottery etc.; mot. encendido m; ✗ disparo m; tiroteo m; ~ squad pelotón m de ejecución.

fir·kin ['fəːkin] approx. cuñete m (= 45,5 litros).

firm [fəːm] 1. □ firme; 2. firma f, casa f de comercio, empresa f.

fir·ma·ment ['fəːməmənt] firmamento m.

firm·ness ['fəːmnis] firmeza f.

first [fəːst] 1. adj. primero; original, primitivo; 2. adv. primero; en primer lugar; ~ of all, ~ and foremost ante todo; at ~ al principio; 3. primero (a f) m; ✝ ~s pl. artículos m/pl. de primera calidad; ✝ ~ of exchange primera f de cambio; from the ~ desde el principio; from ~ to last desde el principio hasta el fin, de todo en todo; be the ~ to inf. ser el primero en inf.; go ~ entrar etc. el primero; 👫 viajar en primera; '~-'aid primera curación f, primeros auxilios m/pl.; ~ kit botiquín m; ~ post puesto m de socorro; '~-born primogénito (a f) m; '~-class de primera (clase); ~ e'di·tion edición f príncipe; '~-fruits pl. primicias f/pl.; '~-hand de primera mano; 'first·ly en primer lugar; first night estreno m; first pa·pers Am. solicitud f preliminar de carta de naturaleza; 'first-rate excelente, de primera.

firth [fəːθ] ría f, estuario m.

fis·cal ['fiskl] fiscal; monetario.

fish [fiʃ] 1. pez m; (as food) pescado m; F tipo m, tío m; have other ~ to fry tener cosas más importantes que hacer; 2. v/t. pescar; river pescar en; F ~ out sacar; v/i. pescar; ~ for tratar de pescar; F compliment etc. andar a la pesca de; '~-bone raspa f, espina f (de pez); '~-bowl pecera f.

fish·er·man ['fiʃəmən] pescador m; 'fish·er·y pesquería f, pesquera f.

fish-hook ['fiʃhuk] anzuelo m.

fish·ing ['fiʃiŋ] pesca f; '~-boat barca f pesquera; '~-grounds pl. pesquera f; '~-rod caña f (de pescar); '~-tack·le aparejo *m* de pescar.

fish...: '~-mon·ger pescadero *m*; ~'s = '~-shop pescadería *f*; '~-plate 🔧 eclisa *f*; '~-wife pescadera *f*; 'fish·y *eye* vidrioso; F sospechoso; it's ~ me huele a camelo.

fis·sion ['fiʃn] *phys.* fisión *f*; *biol.* escisión *f*; 'fis·sion·a·ble fisionable; **fis·sure** ['fiʃə] 1. grieta *f*, hendedura *f*; 2. agrietar(se), hender(se).

fist [fist] puño *m*; F escritura *f*; ~*ful* puñado *m*; fist·i·cuffs ['~ikʌfs] *pl.* puñetazos *m/pl.*

fis·tu·la ['fistjulə] fístula *f*.

fit[1] [fit] 1. ☐ apto, a propósito; adecuado, conveniente, apropiado; listo (*for* para); hábil (*for a post* para); digno (*for a king* de); 🦴 sano, bien de salud; ~ *to eat* bueno de comer; *the wine is not ~ to drink* el vino no se puede beber; *see ~* juzgar conveniente (*to inf.*); *survival of the ~test* supervivencia *f* de los mejor dotados; 2. *v/t.* ajustar, acomodar (*to* a); encajar (*a.* ⊕); adaptar (*for* para); *clothes* probar (*a.* ~ *on*); *p.* (*clothes*) sentar a, venir bien a; *description* cuadrar con; *facts* estar de acuerdo con; ⊕ ~ *in*(*to*) encajar en; ~ *out*, ~ *up* equipar (*with* con); ⚓ armar; *v/i.* ajustarse; (*clothes*) entallar; encajar *in place*; (*facts*) estar de acuerdo; ~ *in* caber; ⊕ encaiarse en; F *fig.* acomodarse; ~ *in with* cuadrar con, concordar con; (*p.*) llevarse bien con; *the dress fits well* el vestido le sienta bien, el vestido entalla bien; 3. ajuste *m*, corte *m*; ⊕ encaje *m*; it's *a good* ~ le sienta bien.

fit[2] [~] acceso *m*, ataque *m*; arranque *m* *of anger*; *by* ~*s and starts* a saltos, a rachas.

fit·ful ['fitful] ☐ espasmódico, caprichoso; 'fit·ment mueble *m*; 'fit·ness aptitud *f*, conveniencia *f*; 🦴 (buena) salud *f*; 'fit·ter ⊕ mecánico *m* ajustador; 'fit·ting 1. ☐ conveniente, apropiado; *it is not ~ that* no está bien que *subj.*; 2. prueba *f of dress*; ajuste *m*; (*size*) medida *f*; ~*s pl.* guarniciones *f/pl.*; (*metal*) herrajes *m/pl.*; muebles *m/pl.*

five [faiv] cinco (*a. su. m*); ~*s sg.* juego *m* de pelota (*estilo inglés*); ~ *year plan* plan *m* quinquenal.

fix [fiks] 1. fijar (*a. phot.*), asegurar;

attention fijar (*on* en); *bayonet* calar; *blame* colgar (*on* a); *date* fijar, señalar (*a.* ~ *on*); *eyes* clavar (*on* en); *price* determinar, decidir; (*establish*) precisar; *sl.* pagar en la misma moneda; *Am.* F = ~ *up* arreglar; componer; decidir, organizar; F ~ (*up*)*on* escoger, elegir; F ~ *up with* arreglarlo con; *p.* proveer de; 2. F aprieto *m*; fix'a·tion fijación *f*; **fix·a·tive** ['~ətiv] fijativo *adj. a. su. m*; fixed ['~t] (*adv.* fix·ed·ly ['~idli]) *all senses*: fijo; 'fix·er *phot.* fijador *m*; 'fix·ing fijación *f etc.*; *Am.* F ~*s pl.* accesorios *m/pl.*, guarniciones *f/pl.*; 'fix·i·ty fijeza *f*; = fix·ture ['~tʃə] cosa *f* fija; instalación *f* fija; *sport*: (fecha *f* de un) partido *m*; *fig.* (*p.*) ostra *f*; *lighting* ~*s pl.* guarniciones *f/pl.* de alumbrado.

fizz [fiz] 1. sisear; 2. siseo *m*; F gaseosa *f*; 'fiz·zle 1. sisear débilmente; F ~ *out* (*candle*) apagarse; *fig.* no dar resultado, fracasar; 2. siseo *m* débil; F fracaso *m*; 'fiz·zy gaseoso.

flab·ber·gast ['flæbəgɑ:st] pasmar, aturdir.

flab·by ['flæbi] ☐ flojo; blanducho; *fig.* débil.

flac·cid ['flæksid] ☐ fláccido.

flag[1] [flæg] 1. bandera *f*, pabellón *m*; (*small*) banderín *m*; ~ *of truce*, *white* ~ bandera *f* de parlamento; 2. hacer señales con bandera (a).

flag[2] [~] 🔺 1. losa *f*; 2. enlosar.

flag[3] [~] ♣ lirio *m*.

flag[4] [~] flaquear, decaer; (*conversation etc.*) languidecer; (*enthusiasm etc.*) aflojar, enfriarse.

flag·day ['flægdei] día *m* de la banderita; *Am. Flag Day* fiesta *f* de la bandera (*14 junio*).

flag·el·late ['flædʒeleit] flagelar; **flag·el·la·tion** flagelación *f*.

flag·on ['flægən] *approx.* jarro *m*; ✝ botella *f* de unos 2 litros.

fla·grant ['fleigrənt] ☐ notorio, escandaloso.

flag...: '~-pole, '~-staff asta *f* de bandera; '~-ship capitana *f*; '~-stone losa *f*.

flail [fleil] 1. 🌾 mayal *m*; 2. *v/t. fig.* golpear, azotar; *v/i.*: ~ *about* debatirse.

flair [fleə] instinto *m*, aptitud *f* especial (*for* para).

flake [fleik] 1. escama *f*; hojuela *f*;

copo m of snow; **2.** v/t. separar en escamas; v/i. desprenderse en escamas; **'flak·y** escamoso; desmenuzable.

flam·beau ['flæmbou] antorcha f.

flam·boy·ant [flæm'bɔiənt] □ extravagante; flameante (a. △).

flame [fleim] **1.** llama f; fuego m; co. novio (a f) m; **2.** llamear; brillar; fig. estallar, encenderse (a. ~ up); ~ up inflamarse; '~**·throw·er** lanzallamas m.

flange [flænd3] pestaña f, reborde m.

flank [flæŋk] **1.** costado m; ijada f of animal; ✕ flanco m; **2.** flanquear; be ~ed by tener a su lado; (p.) ir escoltado por.

flan·nel ['flænl] franela f; (face-) paño m; ~s pl. pantalones m/pl. de franela; ropa f interior de lana.

flap [flæp] **1.** fald(ill)a f on dress; cartera f of pocket; hoja f plegadiza f of table; solapa f of envelope; aletazo m of wing; sl. lío m; estado m nervioso; **2.** v/t. batir; sacudir; agitar; v/i. aletear; sl. ponerse nervioso.

flare [flɛə] **1.** v/i. resplandecer, llamear, destellar; ~ up encenderse; fig. (p.) encolerizarse; estallar; v/t. skirt nesgar; **2.** llamarada f, destello m; (signal) cohete m de señales; (skirt) nesga f; '~**-up** llamarada f; fig. arranque m of anger; manifestación f súbita, estallido m of trouble.

flash [flæʃ] **1.** relámpago m of lightning (a. fig.); destello m, ráfaga f of light; fogonazo m of gun; rayo m of hope etc.; (moment) instante m; phot. = ~light; esp. Am. flash m, noticia f de última hora, mensaje m urgente; in a ~ en un instante; ~ of wit rasgo m de ingenio; ~ in the pan esfuerzo m abortado, éxito m único; **2.** v/i. relampaguear; destellar; ~ past pasar como un rayo; v/t. light despedir; look dirigir rápidamente; message transmitir rápidamente; F hacer ostentación de (a. ~ about); '~**·back** film: escena f retrospectiva; '~**·bulb** bombilla f fusible (or de flash); '~**·light** phot. flash m, magnesio m; (torch) linterna f eléctrica; '~**·point** punto m de inflamación; '**flash·y** □ llamativo; de relumbrón; p. charro, chulo.

flask [flɑːsk] frasco m; redoma f; 🜍 matraz m.

flat [flæt] **1.** □ llano; (smooth) liso; (even) igual; horizontal; (stretched out) tendido; denial terminante; drink muerto; feeling de abatimiento; p. alicaído; taste insípido; tone monótono; tyre desinflado; voice desafinado; ♪ bemol; ↑ flojo; ~ roof azotea f; sport: 400 metres ~ 400 metros lisos; v. fall 2; **2.** adv.: sing ~ desafinar; turn down ~ rechazar de plano; F go ~ out ir a máxima velocidad; **3.** piso m; palma f of hand; plano m of sword; ♪ bemol m; ⚓ banco m; pantano m; mot. sl. pinchazo m; '~**-foot** Am. sl. polizonte m; '~**-foot·ed** que tiene los pies planos; F fig. pedestre, desmañado; indiscreto; Am.F inflexible; '~**-'i·ron** plancha f; '**flat·ness** llanura f; fig. insipidez f; '**flat·ten** allanar; aplanar(se); aplastar; ✕ ~ out enderezarse.

flat·ter ['flætə] adular, lisonjear; (clothes, picture) favorecer; '**flat·ter·er** adulador (-a f) m; '**flat·ter·ing** □ lisonjero; halagüeño; '**flat·ter·y** adulación f, lisonja f.

flat·u·lence, flat·u·len·cy ['flætjuləns(i)] flatulencia f; fig. hinchazón f; '**flat·u·lent** □ flatulento; fig. hinchado.

flaunt [flɔːnt] v/t. ostentar, lucir; v/i. pavonearse.

fla·vo(u)r ['fleivə] **1.** sabor m; gusto m; condimento m (a. ~ing); **2.** sazonar, condimentar; fig. dar un sabor característico a; '**fla·vo(u)red** con sabor a...; '**fla·vo(u)r·less** insípido, soso.

flaw [flɔː] tacha f; imperfección f; desperfecto m; defecto m (a. 🜛 a. ⊕); (crack) grieta f; '**flaw·less** □ intachable, perfecto.

flax [flæks] lino m; '**fla·xen** de lino; hair muy rubio.

flay [flei] desollar; fig. azotar; (criticize) flagelar.

flea [fliː] pulga f; '~**-bite** picadura f de pulga; fig. pérdida f (or gasto m) insignificante.

fleck [flek] **1.** mancha f, punto m; **2.** puntear, salpicar (with de).

flec·tion ['flekʃn] flexión f.

fled [fled] pret. a. p.p. of flee.

fledge [fled3] emplumar; ~d plumado; fully ~d fig. hecho y derecho;

fledg(e)·ling ['ˌliŋ] volantón *m*, pajarito *m*.
flee [fli:] [*irr.*] huir (*from* de).
fleece [fli:s] **1.** vellón *m*; lana *f*; *Golden* ♀ vellocino *m* de oro; **2.** esquilar; F pelar, mondar; '**fleec·y** lanudo; *cloud* aborregado.
fleet [fli:t] **1.** □ *poet.* veloz, ligero; **2.** flota *f*; armada *f*; escuadra *f of cars*; ♀ *Street* la prensa (*londinense*); '**fleet·ing** □ fugaz, efímero, pasajero.
Flem·ish ['flemiʃ] flamenco *adi. a. su. m.*
flesh [fleʃ] carne *f* (*a. fig.*); *in the* ~ en persona; *put on* ~ echar carnes; *of* ~ *and blood* de carne y hueso; '**flesh·ly** carnal, sensual; '**flesh-wound** herida *f* superficial; '**flesh·y** (*fat*) gordo; ♀ *etc.* carnoso.
flew [flu:] *pret. of fly* 2.
flex [fleks] **1.** doblar(se); **2.** ⚡ hilo *m*, cordón *m* (de la luz); **flex·i·bil·i·ty** [ˌˈbiliti] flexibilidad *f* (*a. fig.*); '**flex·i·ble** □ flexible (*a. fig.*); **flex·ion** ['flekʃn] flexión *f* (*a. gr.*); **flex·or** ['ˌksə] (músculo *m*) flexor *m*; **flex·ure** ['flekʃə] flexión *f*; corvadura *f*.
flick [flik] **1.** dar un capirotazo a; rozar levemente; *whip* chasquear; ~ *away* quitar *etc.* rápidamente; **2.** capirotazo *m of finger*; chasquido *m of whip*; golpe *m* rápido y ligero; *sl.* película *f*; *sl.* ~*s pl.* cine *m*.
flick·er ['flikə] **1.** (*light*) parpadear; brillar con luz mortecina; (*flame*) vacilar; (*movement*) oscilar, vibrar; *fig.* fluctuar; **2.** parpadeo *m*; luz *f* mortecina; *without a* ~ of sin la menor señal de.
flight [flait] ⚔ vuelo *m*; (*distance*) recorrido *m*; (*unit*) escuadrilla *f*; ⚔ trayectoria *f of bullet etc.*; (*flock of birds*) bandada *f*; (*escape*) huida *f*, fuga *f*; escalera *f*, tramo *m of steps*; ~ *of fancy* sueño *m*, ilusión *f*; *put to* ~ ahuyentar; *take* ~ alzar el vuelo; *take to* ~ ponerse en fuga; '**flight·y** □ coqueta, frívolo, veleidoso.
fli·er ['flaiə] *v. flyer.*
flim·sy ['flimzi] **1.** □ débil, endeble; *fig.* baladí, frívolo; *cloth* muy delgado; **2.** papel *m* muy delgado.
flinch [flintʃ] acobardarse, retroceder (*from* ante); desistir de miedo (*from* de); *without* ~*ing* sin vacilar.
fling [fliŋ] **1.** baile *m* escocés; *have a* ~

at intentar; *have one's* ~ correrla; **2.** [*irr.*] *v/i.* arrojarse; ~ *out* salir muy enfadado; *v/t.* arrojar; tirar (*a.* ~ *away*); echar (*a.* ~ *out*); ~ *o.s.* arrojarse; ~ *down* echar al suelo; ~ *open* abrir de golpe.
flint [flint] pedernal *m*; piedra *f of lighter*; '**flint·y** *fig.* empedernido.
flip [flip] **1.** capirotazo *m*; ⚔ *sl.* vuelo *m*; **2.** *coin etc.* echar de un capirotazo; mover de un tirón.
flip·pan·cy ['flipənsi] ligereza *f*, frivolidad *f*; '**flip·pant** □ ligero, frívolo.
flip·per ['flipə] aleta *f* (*a. sl.*).
flirt [flə:t] **1.** coqueta *f*; mariposón *m*; **2.** coquetear (*with con*), flirtear, mariposear; *fig.* ~ *with idea* acariciar con poca seriedad; *death* jugar con; **flir'ta·tion** coqueteo *m*; flirteo *m*.
flit [flit] revolotear; volar con vuelo cortado; pasar rápidamente *before eyes etc.*; F mudarse a la chita callando.
flitch [flitʃ] hoja *f* de tocino.
fliv·ver ['flivə] F coche *m* barato.
float [flout] **1.** boya *f*, corcho *m*; balsa *f*; carroza *f in procession*; **2.** *v/t.* poner a flote; ⚓ emitir; *company* lanzar; *v/i.* flotar; (*bather*) hacer la plancha; '**float·a·ble** flotable; **float'a·tion** flotación *f*; '**float·ing** *mst* flotante; *voter* indeciso.
flock¹ [flɔk] **1.** rebaño *m*; bandada *f of birds*; *eccl.* grey *f*; gentío *m of people*; **2.** congregarse, reunirse; *come* ~*ing* venir en masa.
flock² [ˌ] (*wool*) borra *f*.
floe [flou] témpano *m* de hielo.
flog [flɔg] azotar; F ~ *a dead horse* machacar en hierro frío; '**flog·ging** paliza *f*, zurra *f*.
flood [flʌd] **1.** inundación *f*; diluvio *m*; avenida *f in river*; *fig.* torrente *m*, plétora *f*; (*a.* ~ *tide*) pleamar *f*; *the* ♀ el Diluvio; *in* ~ crecido; **2.** *v/t.* inundar (*with* de; *a. fig.*), anegar; *v/i.* desbordar; ~ *in etc.* entrar a raudales; '~-gate compuerta *f*; esclusa *f*; '~-light **1.** foco *m*; **2.** iluminar con foco(s).
floor [flɔ:] **1.** suelo *m*; (*storey*) piso *m*; fondo *m of sea*; *parl.* hemiciclo *m*; *first* ~ primer piso *m*, piso *m* principal; *Am.* = *ground* ~ piso *m* bajo, planta *f* baja; *have the* ~, *hold the* ~ tener la palabra; *take the* ~ salir a bailar; *fig.* salir a

palestra; ~ show atracciones f/pl.
(en la pista de baile); **2.** solar,
entarimar; p. derribar; fig. dejar
sin réplica posible, confundir; '~-
cloth bayeta f; **'floor·ing** entarimado m, piso m, suelo m; **'floor-
walk·er** Am. superintendente m/f
de división.

flop [flɔp] **1.** dejarse caer pesadamente; sl. fracasar; thea. venirse al
foso; **2.** thea. caída f; sl. fracaso m;
Am. sl. ~-house posada f de baja
categoría; **'flop·py** flojo, colgante.

flo·ra ['flɔ:rə] flora f.

flo·ral ['flɔ:rəl] floral; de flores.

flo·res·cence [flɔ:'resns] florescencia f.

flor·id ['flɔrid] □ florido; face encarnado, subido de color.

flor·in ['flɔrin] florín m (Brit. =
2 chelines).

flo·rist ['flɔrist] florista m/f; ~'s floristería f.

floss [flɔs] seda f floja (a. ~ silk);
'floss·y Am. sl. vistoso, cursi.

flo·ta·tion [flou'teiʃn] flotación f; ✝
lanzamiento m.

flo·til·la [flə'tilə] flotilla f.

flot·sam ['flɔtsəm] pecios m/pl., restos m/pl. flotantes.

flounce[1] [flauns] **1.** volante m;
2. guarnecer con volantes.

flounce[2] [⌐]: ~ out salir airado,
alejarse indignado.

floun·der[1] ['flaundə] ichth. platija f.

floun·der[2] [⌐] revolcarse, forcejear
(a. ~ about).

flour ['flauə] harina f.

flour·ish ['flʌriʃ] **1.** rúbrica f, rasgo
m in writing; ♪ floreo m; ♪ toque m
de trompeta; ademán m of hand;
with a ~ triunfalmente; **2.** v/i. florecer; prosperar; crecer rápidamente;
v/t. weapon blandir; stick menear;
fig. hacer alarde de, mostrar
orgullosamente; **'flour·ish·ing** □
floreciente; (healthy) como un reloj.

flout [flaut] mofarse de, burlarse de.

flow [flou] **1.** corriente f; flujo m;
(amount) caudal m; curso m; torrente m of words etc.; **2.** fluir;
correr; (tide) subir; (hair) ondear;
(blood) derramarse; fig. abundar
(with en); ~ away deslizarse; ~ from
fig. proceder de; ~ into (river)
desembocar en.

flow·er ['flauə] **1.** flor f; fig. flor f
(y nata); in ~ en flor; **2.** florecer;

'~-**bed** cuadro m, macizo m; '~-**pot**
tiesto m, maceta f; **'flow·er·y** florido (a. fig.).

flown [floun] p.p. of fly 2.

flu [flu:] F = influenza gripe f.

fluc·tu·ate ['flʌktjueit] fluctuar;
fluc·tu'a·tion fluctuación f.

flue [flu:] humero m, (cañon m de)
chimenea f.

flu·en·cy ['fluənsi] fluidez f, facilidad f; dominio m (in language de);
'flu·ent □ flúido, fácil; corriente;
be ~ in German, speak German ~ly
dominar el alemán.

fluff [flʌf] pelusa f, tamo m, lanilla f;
F bit of ~ falda f, tia f; **'fluff·y** velloso; que tiene mucha pelusa.

flu·id ['flu:id] flúido adj. a. su. m (a.
⚥); líquido m; **flu'id·i·ty** fluidez f.

fluke [flu:k] zo. trematodo m; ichth.
platija f; ⚓ uña f; F chiripa f.

flum·mox ['flʌməks] F confundir,
desconcertar.

flung [flʌŋ] pret. a. p.p. of fling 2.

flunk [flʌŋk] Am. F v/t. p. reprobar,
dar calabazas a; exam perder; v/i.
salir mal.

flunk·(e)y ['flʌŋki] lacayo m (a. fig.).

flu·o·res·cence [fluə'resns] fluorescencia f; **flu·o'res·cent** fluorescente.

flur·ry ['flʌri] **1.** agitación f; conmoción f; nevisca f, ráfaga f of snow;
2. agitar, hacer nervioso.

flush [flʌʃ] **1.** ⊕ nivelado; igual,
parejo; F adinerado; **2.** rubor m,
sonrojo m; abundancia f; fig. vigor
m, plenitud f; cards: flux m; **3.** v/t.
limpiar con chorro de agua (a. ~
out); game levantar; v/i. ruborizarse, sonrojarse.

flus·ter ['flʌstə] **1.** confusión f, aturdimiento m; **2.** confundir, aturdir.

flute [flu:t] **1.** ♪ flauta f; ⚔ estría f;
2. estriar, acanalar.

flut·ter ['flʌtə] **1.** revoloteo m of
wings; palpitación f of heart; fig.
agitación f; emoción f; sl. apuesta f;
2. v/t. agitar, menear; v/i. (bird etc.)
revolotear; (heart) palpitar; (flag)
ondear; agitarse.

flux [flʌks] fig. flujo m; ⚒ fundente
m; (state) continua mudanza f.

fly [flai] **1.** mosca f; (trouser-) bragueta f; thea. flies pl. bambalinas
f/pl.; die like flies morir como chinches; **2.** [irr.] v/i. volar; (rush) precipitarse; (escape) evadirse, huir; l

must ~ tengo que darme prisa; *the flag is* ~*ing* la bandera está izada; *send* ~*ing* echar a rodar; *v. let*; ~ *at* lanzarse sobre; ~ *away* irse volando; ~ *in the face of* estar abiertamente opuesto a; desafiar; ~ *into a passion* montar en cólera; ~ *off (part)* desprenderse; *(bird)* alejarse volando; ~ *open* abrirse de repente; *v/t.* hacer volar; 🗲 dirigir; transportar en avión; *ocean etc.* atravesar (en avión); *distance* recorrer (en avión); *flag* llevar, tener izado; *danger* huir (de); *country* abandonar; *let* ~ descargar, proferir (*at* contra); **3.** F despabilado, avispado.

fly-blown ['flaibloun] lleno de cresas; *fig.* contaminado.

fly·er ['flaiə] aviador *m*; tren *m etc.* rápido; *Am. sl.* empresa *f* arriesgada.

fly·ing ['flaiiŋ] **1.** vuelo *m*; aviación *f*; **2.** *attr.* de vuelo; de aviación; *adj.* volante, volador; rápido, veloz; *visit* muy breve; ~ *boat* hidroavión *m*; ~ *bomb* bomba *f* volante; ~ *field* campo *m* de aviación; ~ *fish* pez *m* volador; ~ *machine* avión *m*; ~ *saucer* platillo *m* volante; ~ *start* salida *f* lanzada; *get off to a* ~ *start* comenzar muy felizmente.

fly…: '~**leaf** hoja *f* de guarda; '~**weight** peso *m* mosca; '~**wheel** volante *m* (*de motor*).

foal [foul] **1.** potro (*a f*) *m*; **2.** parir (*la yegua*).

foam [foum] **1.** espuma *f*; ~ *rubber* espuma *f* de látex (*or* de caucho); **2.** espumar; echar espuma; ~ *at the mouth* espumajear; '**foam·y** espum(aj)oso.

fob[1] [fɔb] faltriquera *f* del reloj.

fob[2] [~]: ~ *off* apartar de un propósito con excusas; ~ *off with* persuadir a aceptar de modo fraudulento.

fo·cal ['foukl] focal; *phot.* ~ *distance* distancia *f* focal; *phot.* ~ *plane* plano *m* focal; ~ *point* punto *m* focal.

fo·cus ['foukəs] **1.** foco *m* (*a. fig.*); *in* ~ enfocado; *out of* ~ desenfocado; **2.** enfocar; *attention* fijar, concentrar (*on* en).

fod·der ['fɔdə] forraje *m*.

foe [fou] *lit.* enemigo *m*.

foe·tus ['fiːtəs] feto *m*.

fog [fɔg] **1.** niebla *f* (*a. fig.*); *fig.* confusión *f*; *phot.* velo *m*; **2.** *fig.* oscurecer; *issue* entenebrecer; *phot.* ve-

lar(se); '~**-bound** inmovilizado por la niebla.

fo·g(e)y ['fougi]: *old* ~ viejo *m* de ideas anticuadas.

fog·gy ['fɔgi] brumoso, nebuloso (*a. fig.*); *phot.* velado; *it is* ~ hay niebla; *I haven't the foggiest idea* no tengo la más remota idea; '**fog·horn** sirena *f* (de niebla).

foi·ble ['fɔibl] flaco *m*.

foil[1] [fɔil] hojuela *f* (de metal); *fig.* contraste *m*.

foil[2] [~] **1.** frustrar; *attempt* desbaratar; **2.** *fenc.* florete *m*.

foist [fɔist]: ~ *on* encajar a, lograr con engaño que … acepte; imputar a.

fold[1] [fould] 🐑 **1.** redil *m*, apriscom; *eccl.* rebaño *m*; **2.** apriscar.

fold[2] [~] **1.** doblez *m*, pliegue *m* (*a. geol.*); arruga *f*; **2.** plegar(se), doblar(se); envolver (*in* en); *wings* recoger; ~ *one's arms* cruzar los brazos; ~ *in one's arms* abrazar tiernamente; ~ *down* doblar hacia abajo; ~ *up* doblar(se); F 🕆 quebrar; entrar en liquidación, liquidarse; '**fold·er** carpeta *f*; *(brochure)* folleto *m*.

fold·ing ['fouldiŋ] plegadizo; plegable; '~**-bed** catre *m* de tijera; '~**-chair** silla *f* de tijera; '~**-door(s** *pl.*) puerta *f* plegadiza.

fo·li·age ['fouliidʒ] follaje *m*; **fo·li·a·tion** foliación *f*.

fo·li·o ['fouliou] folio *m*; libro *m* en folio.

folk [fouk] *pl.* gente *f*; nación *f*; raza *f*; tribu *f*; F (*a.* ~*s pl.*) familia *f*; *the old* ~ los viejos; F *hullo* ~*!* ¡hola, amigos!

folk·lore ['fouklɔː] folklore *m*; '**folk·song** canción *f* popular (*or* tradicional).

fol·low ['fɔlou] *v/t.* seguir; seguir la pista a; *news* interesarse en; *profession* ejercer; *p.* comprender; *argument* seguir el hilo de; ~ *through*, ~ *up* llevar hasta el fin; proseguir; *v. suit*; *v/i.* seguirse; resultar; *as* ~*s* como sigue; *it* ~*s that* síguese que; ~ *on from* ser la consecuencia lógica de; '**fol·low·er** partidario (*a f*) *m*; secuaz *m*; imitador (*-a f*) *m*; discípulo *m*; '**fol·low·ing 1.** partidarios *m/pl.*; secuaces *m/pl.*; séquito *m*; **2.** siguiente; *the* ~ lo siguiente; ~ *wind* viento *m* en popa; '**fol·low-**

'**up** *letter* recordativo; subsiguiente; de continuación.

fol·ly ['fɔli] locura *f*, desatino *m*.

fo·ment [fou'ment] fomentar (*a.* ⚙); provocar; nutrir; **fo·men'ta·tion** fomento *m* (*a.* ⚙); ⚙ fomentación *f*.

fond [fɔnd] □ cariñoso, afectuoso; *be* ~ *of* ser aficionado a, ser amigo de; *p.* tener mucho cariño a.

fon·dle ['fɔndl] acariciar.

fond·ness ['fɔndnis] cariño *m*; afición *f* (*for* a).

font [fɔnt] pila *f*.

food [fu:d] comida *f*; alimento *m*, alimentación *f*; provisiones *f/pl.*; (*dish*) manjar *m*; (*material*) comestible *m*; *fig.* alimento *m*, pábulo *m*; *give* ~ *for thought* dar materia en que pensar; '~**poi·son·ing** botulismo *m*; '~**stuffs** *pl.* comestibles *m/pl.*, artículos *m/pl.* alimenticios; '~**val·ue** valor *m* alimenticio.

fool [fu:l] **1.** tonto (*a f*) *m*, necio (*a f*) *m*; (*jester*) bufón *m*; *make a* ~ *of* poner en ridículo; *play the* ~ hacer el tonto; *all* ~*'s day* (*1 abril*) día *m* de inocentes (*28 diciembre*); ~*'s errand* empresa *f* descabellada; misión *f* inútil; ~*'s paradise* bienestar *m* ilusorio; **2.** *Am.* F tonto; **3.** *v/t.* engañar, embaucar; confundir; F ~ *away* malgastar; *v/i.* chancear; tontear; (*a.* ~ *about*) juguetear (*with* con), divertirse (*with* con); F *no* ~*ing* en serio; *Am.* F ~ *around* malgastar el tiempo neciamente; *Am.* F ~ *with* manosear neciamente.

fool·er·y ['fu:ləri] bufonada *f*; tontería *f*; '**fool·hard·y** □ temerario; '**fool·ish** □ tonto, necio; *remark etc.* disparatado; indiscreto; ridículo; '**fool·ish·ness** tontería *f*, necedad *f*; estupidez *f*; ridiculez *f*; '**fool·proof** ⊕ a prueba de impericia; F infalible; '**fools·cap** *approx.* papel *m* tamaño folio.

foot [fut] **1.** (*pl.* feet) pie *m*; pata *f* of *animal etc.*; ✗ infantería *f*; *on* ~ a pie; *fig.* en marcha; *fall on one's feet fig.* caer de pie; *keep one's feet* mantenerse en pie; *put one's* ~ *down* adoptar una actitud firme; F *mot.* acelerar; F *put one's* ~ *in it* meter la pata; *set on* ~ promover, iniciar; **2.** ~ *the bill* pagar la cuenta; *fig.* pagar el pato; ~ *it* ir andando; '~**and·'mouth** (**dis·ease**) fiebre *f* aftosa; '~**ball** fútbol *m*;

(*ball*) balón *m*; ~ *player* futbolista *m*; ~ *pool* quinielas *f/pl.*; '~**board** estribo *m*; '~**brake** pedal *m* del freno; freno *m* de pie; '~**bridge** puente *m* para peatones; '**foot·ed** de ... pies; '**foot·fall** pisada *f*, paso *m*; '**foot·hills** *pl.* colinas *f/pl.* al pie de una sierra; estribaciones *f/pl.*; '**foot·hold** (asidero *m* para el) pie *m*, pie *m* firme.

foot·ing ['futiŋ] pie *m*; posición *f* estable(cida); condición *f*; *on an equal* ~ en un mismo pie de igualdad (*with* con); *on a war* ~ en pie de guerra; *gain a* ~ lograr establecerse.

foo·tle ['fu:tl] F hacer el tonto; ~ *away* disipar neciamente; '**foot·ling** baladí, insignificante.

foot...: '~**lights** *pl.* candilejas *f/pl.*; '~**loose** libre; andariego; '~**man** lacayo *m*; '~**note** nota *f*; apostilla *f*; '~**pad** salteador *m* de caminos; '~**path** senda *f*, sendero *m*; '~**plate** plataforma *f* del maquinista; '~**print** huella *f*; '~**rest** apoyapié *m*; '~**rule** regla *f* de un pie; '~**sore** con los pies cansados; '~**step** paso *m*; '~**stool** escabel *m*; '~**wear** calzado *m*; '~**work** *sport*: juego *m* de piernas.

fop [fɔp] petimetre *m*, currutaco *m*; '**fop·per·y** afectación *f*; '**fop·pish** □ currutaco, afectado.

for [fɔː, fə, fo, f] **1.** *prp.* para; por; a causa de; en honor de; en lugar de; ~ *all his wealth* a pesar de su riqueza; ~ *all that* con todo; ~ *3 days* (*past*) (durante) 3 días; (*present a. future*) por 3 días; *as* ~ en cuanto a; *as* ~ *me* por mi parte; *but* ~ a no ser por; F *I'm* ~ *London* yo voy a Londres; F *I'm all* ~ *it* lo apruebo sin reserva; *it is* ~ *you to decide* le toca a Vd. decidir; F *now we're* ~ *it* ahora nos va a tocar la gorda; *oh* ~ ... *!* ¡quién tuviera ...!; ~ *time* ~ *dinner* hora *f* de comer; *there is nothing* ~ *it but to* no queda más remedio que *inf.*; *if it were not* ~ *him* si no fuera por él; *were it not* ~ *that* si no fuera por eso; **2.** *cj.* pues, ya que.

for·age ['fɔridʒ] **1.** forraje *m*; **2.** forrajear; dar forraje a; *fig.* buscar (*for acc.*).

for·ay ['fɔrei] correría *f*, incursión *f*.

for·bade [fə'beid] *pret. of* forbid.

for·bear [fɔː'bɛə] [*irr.*] abstenerse (*from* de); contenerse; **for'bear-**

ance paciencia *f*, dominio *m* sobre sí mismo.

for·bears ['fɔːbɛəz] *pl.* antepasados *m/pl.*

for·bid [fə'bid] [*irr.*] prohibir (*to inf.*; *a p. a th.* algo a alguien); God ~! ¡no lo permita Dios!; **for'bid·den** *p.p. of forbid;* **for'bid·ding** □ formidable; repugnante.

for·bore, **for·borne** [fɔː'bɔː(n)] *pret. a. p.p. of forbear.*

force [fɔːs] **1.** fuerza *f*; personal *m*; ✕ cuerpo *m*; ✕ ~s *pl.* fuerzas *f/pl.* (armadas); F the ~ la policía; by ~ a la fuerza; by ~ of a fuerza de; in ~ en gran número; in ~ (*law*) vigente, en vigor; be in ~ (*price etc.*) regir, imperar; v. join; **2.** *mst* forzar (*to a inf.*; *upon a p.* a uno a aceptar); obligar; violentar; ⚡ hacer madurar temprano; ~d to me veo obligado a; ~ back hacer retroceder; ~ down (hacer) tragar por fuerza; ✈ obligar a aterrizar; ~ in introducir por fuerza; ~ o.s. *inf.* hacer un esfuerzo por *inf.*; ~ open forzar; ~ a smile sonreír forzadamente; **'forced** (*adv.* forc·ed·ly ['~idli]) *mst* forzado; smile que no le sale a uno; **force·ful** ['~ful] □ vigoroso, poderoso; **'force·meat** relleno *m* (de carne picada).

for·ceps ['fɔːseps] fórceps *m*; tenacillas *f/pl.*; **force-pump** ['fɔːspʌmp] bomba *f* impulsora.

for·cible ['fɔːsəbl] □ vigoroso, poderoso, enérgico; concluyente; *entry* a viva fuerza.

forc·ing-house ['fɔːsiŋhaus] invernadero *m*.

ford [fɔːd] **1.** vado *m*; **2.** vadear; **'ford·a·ble** vadeable.

fore [fɔː] **1.** *adv.*: to the ~ en la delantera; destacado; come to the ~ empezar a destacar; ⚓ ~ and aft de (*etc.*) popa a proa; **2.** *adj.* anterior, delantero; ⚓ de proa; '~·arm antebrazo *m*; ~'bode presagiar, pronosticar; ~'bod·ing presagio *m*, presentimiento *m*; '~·cast **1.** pronóstico *m*; **2.** [*irr.* (cast)] pronosticar, prever; '~·cas·tle ['fouksl] castillo *m* de proa; ~'close excluir; ⚖ extinguir el derecho de redimir; '~·fa·thers *pl.* antepasados *m/pl.*; '~·fin·ger dedo *m* índice; '~·foot pata *f* delantera; '~·front vanguardia *f*; sitio *m* de actividad más in-

tensa; ~'go [*irr.* (go)] renunciar, privarse de; ~'go·ing anterior, precedente; ~'gone: ~ conclusion conclusión *f* (*or* resultado *m*) inevitable; ~'ground primer plano *m* (*or* término *m*); '~·hand directo *m*; ~·head ['fɔrid] frente *f*.

for·eign ['fɔrin] extranjero; *trade etc.* exterior; extraño, ajeno (to a); ~ exchange divisas *f/pl.*; ♀ Office Ministerio *m* de Asuntos Exteriores; ~ trade comercio *m* exterior; **'for·eign·er** extranjero (a *f*) *m*.

fore...: '~'know·ledge presciencia *f*; '~·land cabo *m*, promontorio *m*; '~·leg pata *f* delantera; '~·lock copete *m*; take time by the ~ tomar la ocasión por los cabellos; '~·man capataz *m*; maestro *m* de obras; ⚖ presidente *m* del jurado; '~·mast trinquete *m*; '~·most delantero; primero; principal; '~·noon mañana *f*.

fo·ren·sic [fə'rensik] forense.

fore...: '~'run·ner precursor (-a *f*) *m*; ~·sail ['~seil, ⚓ '~sl] trinquete *m*; ~'see [*irr.* (see)] prever; ~'see·a·ble □ previsible; ~'shad·ow prefigurar, prever, anunciar; '~·shore playa *f* (entre los límites de pleamar y bajamar); ~'short·en escorzar; '~·sight previsión *f*; '~·skin prepucio *m*.

for·est ['fɔrist] bosque *m*; *attr.* forestal, del bosque.

fore·stall [fɔː'stɔːl] *th.* prevenir; *p.* anticipar (e impedir).

for·est·er ['fɔristə] silvicultor *m*; ingeniero *m* forestal (*or* de montes); (*keeper*) guardabosques *m*; **'for·est·ry** silvicultura *f*.

fore...: '~·taste anticipo *m*; ~'tell [*irr.* (tell)] predecir, pronosticar; presagiar; ~'thought providencia *f*, prevención *f*; *b.s.* premeditación *f*; '~·top cofa *f* de trinquete; ~'warn prevenir; be ~ed precaverse; '~·word prefacio *m*.

for·gath·er [fɔː'gæðə] reunirse.

for·gave [fə'geiv] *pret. of forgive.*

forge¹ [fɔːdʒ] **1.** (*fire*) fragua *f*; (*blacksmith's*) herrería *f*; (*factory*) fundición *f*; **2.** *metal* forjar, fraguar;

money etc. falsificar, contrahacer; **'forg·er** falsificador *m;* **'for·ger·y** falsificación *f.*

forge² [⌣]: ⌣ *ahead* avanzar constantemente; adelantarse muchísimo a todos.

for·get [fə'get] [irr.] *v/t.* olvidar(se de) *(to inf.)*; ⌣ *o.s.* propasarse; F ⌣ *it!* ¡no se preocupe!; *v/i.* olvidarse; *I forgot freq.* se me olvidó; **for'get·ful** [⌣ful] □ olvidadizo; descuidado; **for'get·ful·ness** olvido *m;* descuido *m;* **for'get-me-not** nomeolvides *f.*

for·give [fə'giv] [irr.] perdonar *(acc. acc.;* a *p. [for]* a *th.* algo a alguien); **for'giv·en** *p.p. of* forgive; **for-'give·ness** perdón *m;* misericordia *f;* **for'giv·ing** □ perdonador; magnánimo. [privarse de.⟩

for·go [fɔ:'gou] [irr. (go)] renunciar, ⟩

for·got [fə'gɔt], **for'got·ten** [⌣n] *pret. a. p.p. of* forget.

fork [fɔ:k] 1. tenedor *m;* ⚡ horca *f;* horquilla *f (a.* ⊕); bifurcación *f in road;* horcajo *m in river;* horcadura *f in tree;* *anat.* horcajadura *f,* entrepierna *f;* 2. *v/i. (road)* bifurcarse; *v/t.* cultivar (cavar, hacinar *etc.)* con horquilla *f;* F ⌣ *out* desembolsar de mala gana; F ⌣ *over* entregar; **'forked** ahorquillado; *road* bifurcado; *lightning* en zigzag.

for·lorn [fə'lɔ:n] abandonado, desamparado; *appearance* triste, de abandono; ⌣ *hope* empresa *f* desesperada; cosa *f* sumamente dudosa.

form [fɔ:m] 1. forma *f;* figura *f;* *(condition)* estado *m;* *(formality)* formalidad *f; (seat)* banco *m; school:* clase *f; (document)* hoja *f,* formulario *m; be in (good)* ⌣ *sport:* estar en forma; *(witty)* estar de vena; *be bad* ⌣ ser de mal gusto; *for* ⌣'*s sake* por pura fórmula; 2. formar(se); *habit* adquirir; ⚡ alinearse, formar *(a.* ⌣ *up).*

for·mal ['fɔ:ml] □ formal; *manner etc.* ceremonioso; *visit* de cumplido; *dress etc.* de etiqueta; **'for·mal·ist** formalista *m/f.;* **for·mal·i·ty** [fɔ:-'mæliti] formalidad *f;* etiqueta *f; without formalities* prescindiendo de los trámites de costumbre; **for·mal·ize** ['fɔ:məlaiz] formalizar.

for·mat ['fɔ:mæt] formato *m.*

for·ma·tion [fɔ:'meiʃn] *all senses:* formación *f;* **form·a·tive** ['fɔ:mə-tiv] formativo.

for·mer ['fɔ:mə] antiguo; anterior; primero, precedente; ex...; *the* ⌣ ése *etc.,* aquél *etc.;* **'for·mer·ly** antes, antiguamente. [fórmico.⟩

for·mic ['fɔ:mik]: ⌣ *acid* ácido *m*⟩ **for·mi·da·ble** ['fɔ:midəbl] □ formidable.

form·less ['fɔ:mlis] □ informe.

for·mu·la ['fɔ:mjulə], *pl. mst* **for·mu·lae** ['⌣li:] fórmula *f;* **for·mu·lar·y** ['⌣ləri] formulario *adj. a. su. m;* **for·mu·late** ['⌣leit] formular; **for·mu·la·tion** formulación *f.*

for·ni·cate ['fɔ:nikeit] fornicar; **for·ni·ca·tion** [⌣'keiʃn] fornicación *f.*

for·sake [fə'seik] [irr.] abandonar, dejar; desamparar; *opinion* renegar de; **for'sak·en** *p.p. of* forsake.

for·sook [fə'suk] *pret. of* forsake.

for·sooth [fə'su:θ] *iro.* en verdad.

for·swear [fɔ:'swɛə] [irr. *(swear)]* abjurar; ⌣ *o.s.* perjurarse; **for-'sworn** perjuro.

fort [fɔ:t] fuerte *m,* fortín *m.*

forte [⌣] *fig.* fuerte *m.*

forth [fɔ:θ] (a)delante; (a)fuera; *v. so; from this day* ⌣ de hoy en adelante; **⌣'com·ing** venidero, próximo; *book etc.* de próxima aparición; *p.* abierto, afable; *be* ⌣ *freq. th.* ser disponible; **'⌣'right** directo; franco; terminante; **'⌣'with** en el acto, sin dilación.

for·ti·eth ['fɔ:tiiθ] cuadragésimo.

for·ti·fi·ca·tion [fɔ:tifi'keiʃn] fortificación *f;* **for·ti·fy** ['⌣fai] ⚔ fortificar; *wine* encabezar; *opinion* corroborar; *p.* animar; *p.* confirmar *(in belief* en); **for·ti·tude** ['⌣tju:d] fortaleza *f,* valor *m,* resistencia *f.*

fort·night ['fɔ:tnait] quince días *m/pl.,* quincena *f; this day* ⌣ de hoy en quince (días); **'fort·night·ly** (que sale *etc.)* cada quince días; quincenal(mente). [fuerte.⟩

for·tress ['fɔ:tris] fortaleza *f,* plaza *f*⟩ **for·tu·i·tous** [fɔ:'tju:itəs] □ fortuito, casual; **for'tu·i·ty** casualidad *f.*

for·tu·nate ['fɔ:tʃnit] □ afortunado; feliz; ⌣*ly* afortunadamente.

for·tune ['fɔ:tʃn] fortuna *f;* suerte *f; cost a* ⌣ valer un dineral; *tell one's* ⌣ decirle a uno la buenaventura; **'⌣-hunt·er** aventurero *m;* **'⌣-tel·ler** adivina *f.*

for·ty ['fɔːti] cuarenta. [nal m.]
fo·rum ['fɔːrəm] foro m; fig. tribu-
for·ward ['fɔːwəd] 1. adj. delantero;
adelantado; precoz; ⚓ de proa;
F descarado, impertinente; ☂ ~
delivery entrega f en fecha futura;
~ line línea f delantera; 2. adv.
(hacia) adelante; ⚓ hacia la proa;
~ march! de frente ¡mar!;
3. sport: delantero m; 4. project fomentar, promover, favorecer; ☙
hacer seguir; expedir; enviar; ~ing
agent agente m expedidor.
for·ward·ness ['fɔːwədnis] precocidad f; F descaro m, impertinencia f.
for·wards ['fɔːwədz] = forward 2.
for·went [fɔːˈwent] pret. of forgo.
fosse [fɔs] ✕ foso m; anat. fosa f.
fos·sil ['fɔsl] fósil adj. a. su. m (a.
fig.); **'fos·sil·ized** fosilizado.
fos·ter ['fɔstə] 1. fomentar, favorecer; criar; 2.: ~ brother hermano m
de leche; ~ mother madre f adoptiva; (nurse) ama f de leche.
fought [fɔːt] pret. a. p.p. of fight 2.
foul [faul] 1. □ sucio, puerco; asqueroso; air viciado; blow, play
sucio, feo; breath fétido; deed vil;
weather feo, muy malo; fall ~ of
indisponerse con, ponerse a malas
con; 2. falta f, juego m sucio;
3. ensuciar; chocar contra; enredarse
en; obstruir; sport: cometer una
falta contra; ~-mouthed ['~ˈmauðd]
malhablado, deslenguado; '~-
'smell·ing hediondo.
found[1] [faund] pret. a. p.p. of find 1.
found[2] [~] fundar, establecer; basar.
found[3] [~] ⊕ fundir.
foun·da·tion [faunˈdeiʃn] fundación
f; fig. fundamento m, base f; ~s pl.
▲ cimientos m/pl.; **foun'da·tion-
school** escuela f dotada; **foun'da·
tion-stone** primera piedra f.
found·er ['faundə] 1. fundador (-a
f) m; 2. ⊕ fundidor m; 3. ⚓ irse a
pique, hundirse (a. fig.). [sito.]
found·ling ['faundliŋ] niño m expó-
found·ress ['faundris] fundadora f.
found·ry ['faundri] fundición f.
fount poet. [faunt] fuente f; typ.
[fɔnt] fundición f.
foun·tain ['fauntin] fuente f (a.fig.);
surtidor m; '~-'head fig. fuente f,
origen m; '~-'pen (pluma f) estilográfica f; plumafuente f S.Am.
four [fɔː] cuatro (a. su. m); on all ~s a
gatas; fig. en completa armonía

(with con); '~-'en·gined cuatrimotor; '~-'flush·er Am. sl. impostor m, embustero m; '~-fold
1. adj. cuádruple; 2. adv. cuatro
veces; '~-'foot·ed cuadrúpedo;
'four-'square fig. firme; franco,
sincero; 'four-'stroke de cuatro
tiempos; **four·teen** ['~ˈtiːn] catorce; **four·teenth** ['~ˈtiːnθ] decimo-
cuarto; **fourth** [fɔːθ] 1. cuarto;
2. cuarto m; cuarta parte f; ♪
cuarta f; 'fourth·ly en cuarto lugar; 'four-wheel 'drive tracción f
a las cuatro ruedas.
fowl [faul] ave f (de corral); gallina f;
pollo m; ~ pest peste f aviar; 'fowl-
er cazador m de aves.
fowl·ing ['fauliŋ] caza f de aves; '~-
piece escopeta f.
fox [fɔks] 1. zorra f; (dog-) zorro m
(a. fig.); 2. F engañar, confundir;
foxed ['~t] manchado.
fox...: '~-glove dedalera f; '~-hole
✕ hoyo m de protección; '~-hound
perro m raposero; '~-hunt cacería f
de zorras; '~-trot fox m; 'fox·y fig.
taimado, astuto.
foy·er ['fɔiei] vestíbulo m, hall m.
fra·cas ['fræːkaː] gresca f, riña f.
frac·tion ['frækʃn] ঀ fracción f,
quebrado m; fig. parte f muy pequeña; 'frac·tion·al □ fraccionario.
frac·tious ['frækʃəs] □ reacio, rebelón, arisco.
frac·ture ['fræktʃə] 1. fractura f;
2. fracturar(se), quebrar(se).
frag·ile ['frædʒail] frágil; quebradizo; delicado; **fra·gil·i·ty** [frə-
ˈdʒiliti] fragilidad f.
frag·ment ['frægmənt] fragmento
m; 'frag·men·tar·y □ fragmentario. ['fra·grant □ fragante.]
fra·grance ['freigrəns] fragancia f;
frail [freil] □ frágil; fig. débil, endeble; 'frail·ty fig. debilidad f, flaqueza f.
frame [freim] 1. estructura f; esqueleto m; marco m of picture; sew.,
⊕ bastidor m; armadura f of spectacles; ⊕ armazón m; p.'s forma f,
figura f; ⚓ cuaderna f; ~ of mind
estado m de ánimo; 2. formar; inventar; construir; picture poner un
marco a; fig. servir de marco a;
question formular, expresar; esp.
Am. sl. incriminar por medio de una
estratagema; arreglar bajo cuerda;
'frame-up esp. Am. F estratagema f

para incriminar a alguien; complot m; **'frame·work** ⊕ armazón f, esqueleto m, armadura f; fig. sistema m, organización f.

franc [fræŋk] franco m.

fran·chise ['fræntʃaiz] derecho m de votar, sufragio m.

Fran·cis·can [fræn'siskən] franciscano adj. a. su. m.

Frank¹ [fræŋk] franco m.

frank² [~] □ franco.

frank³ [~] ✂ franquear.

frank·in·cense ['fræŋkinsens] incienso m.

frank·ness ['fræŋknis] franqueza f.

fran·tic ['fræntik] □ frenético, furioso; F desquiciado with worry.

fra·ter·nal [frə'tɔ:nl] □ fraternal, fraterno; **fra'ter·ni·ty** fraternidad f, hermandad f; Am. univ. club m de estudiantes; **frat·er·ni·za·tion** [frætənai'zeiʃn] fraternización f; **'frat·er·nize** fraternizar.

frat·ri·cide ['freitrisaid] fratricidio m; (p.) fratricida m.

fraud [frɔ:d] fraude m; (p.) impostor m, farsante m; **fraud·u·lence** ['~juləns] fraudulencia f; **'fraud·u·lent** □ fraudulento. [lleno de.｜

fraught [frɔ:t]: ~ with cargado de,｜

fray¹ [frei] v/i. deshilacharse; ~ed raído; v/t. desgastar. [riña f.｜

fray² [~] combate m; refriega f,｜

fraz·zle ['fræzl] F 1.: in a ~ rendido de cansancio; beat to a ~ cascar; 2. desgastar; rendir de cansancio.

freak [fri:k] 1. capricho m of imagination; (p.) fenómeno m; (a. ~ of nature) monstruo m, monstruosidad f; curiosidad f; 2. = **'freak·ish** □ caprichoso; inesperado, imprevisto. [pecoso.｜

freck·le ['frekl] peca f; **'freck·led**｜

free [fri:] 1. □ mst libre (from, of de); franco; exento (from de); inmune (from contra); p. liberal; (not fixed) suelto; (untied) desatado; (for nothing) gratuito; be ~ to inf. poder libremente inf.; be ~ with dar abundantemente; no regatear; be ~ with money ser manirroto; make ~ with usar como si fuera cosa propia; set ~ libertar; ~ and easy despreocupado, poco ceremonioso; ~ of charge gratis; ✝ ~ on board franco a bordo; ~ fight, F ~ for all sarracina f, riña f general; ~ trade libre cambio m; ~ wheel rueda f libre;

2. librar (from de), libertar; eximir, exentar (from, of de); place etc. desembarazar, despejar; knot etc. soltar, desenredar; **'~·boot·er** filibustero m; **'free·dom** libertad f; exención f, inmunidad f; ~ of a city ciudadanía f de honor; ~ of speech libertad f de la palabra.

free...: **'~·hand** hecho a pulso; **'~·hold** feudo m franco; **'~·hold·er** poseedor m de feudo franco; **'~·kick** golpe m franco; **'~·lance** (periodista m etc.) independiente; **'~·man** hombre m libre; ciudadano m de honor of city; **'~·ma·son** francmasón m; **'~·ma·son·ry** francmasonería f; fig. compañerismo m; **'~·'think·er** librepensador (-a f) m; **'~·'think·ing** librepensamiento m; **'~·'will** (libre) albedrío m; of one's own ~ por voluntad propia.

freeze [fri:z] 1. [irr.] helar(se); congelar(se) (a. fig., ✝ etc.); ~ to death morir de frío; F ~ out competitor deshacerse de (quitándole la clientela); 2. helada f; congelación f of wages etc.; **'freez·ing** □ glacial (a. fig.), helado; F it's ~ cold hace terriblemente frío; ~ mixture mezcla f refrigerante; ~ point punto m de congelación.

freight [freit] 1. flete m, carga f; Am. attr. de mercancías; 2. fletar, cargar; **'freight·age** flete m; **'freight-car** Am. vagón m de mercancías; **'freight·er** buque m de carga.

French [frentʃ] francés adj. a. su. m; ~ bean judía f; take ~ leave despedirse a la francesa; ~ window puerta f ventana; **'~·man** francés m; **'~·wom·an** francesa f.

fren·zied ['frenzid] □ frenético; **'fren·zy** frenesí m, delirio m.

fre·quen·cy ['fri:kwənsi] frecuencia f (a. ✔); **fre·quent** 1. ['~kwənt] □ frecuente; 2. [~'kwent] frecuentar; **fre'quent·er** frecuentador (-a f) m.

fres·co ['freskou], pl. **fres·co(e)s** ['~z] fresco m.

fresh [freʃ] □ fresco; nuevo, reciente; air puro; face de buen color; water dulce; wind recio; p. nuevo, novicio; F fresco, descarado; in the ~ air al aire libre; **'fresh·en** refrescar(se); **'fresh·er** F = **'fresh·man** estudiante m de primer año; **'fresh·ness** frescura f; novedad f;

'**fresh·wa·ter** de agua dulce; *Am.* bisoño.

fret[1] [fret] ⊕ **1.** calado *m*; **2.** adornar con calados.

fret[2] [⌣] **1.** *v/t.* raer, rozar, corroer; *p.* irritar, molestar; *v/i.* inquietarse, apurarse, impacientarse (*at* por); **2.** estado *m* inquieto.

fret[3] [⌣] ♪ traste *m*.

fret·ful ['fretful] □ displicente, descontentadizo, impaciente.

fret-saw ['fretsɔ:] sierra *f* de calados.

fret·work ['fretwə:k] calado *m*.

fri·a·ble ['fraiəbl] friable.

fri·ar ['fraiə] fraile *m*; fray *in titles*; '**fri·ar·y** convento *m* de frailes.

fric·as·see [frikə'si:] fricasé *m*.

fric·tion ['frikʃn] rozamiento *m* (*a. fig.*), fricción *f*; *fig.* desavenencia *f*; *attr.* = '**fric·tion·al** de rozamiento, de fricción. [Viernes *m* Santo.↓

Fri·day ['fraidi] viernes *m*; Good ♀↓

fridge [fridʒ] F = *refrigerator* nevera *f*, refrigerador *m*.

friend [frend] amigo (*a f*) *m*; ♀ cuáquero (*a f*) *m*; ~! ¡gente de paz!; be ~s with ser amigo de; make ~s with trabar amistad con; '**friend·less** sin amigos; '**friend·li·ness** cordialidad *f*, amigabilidad *f*; '**friend·ly** amistoso; cordial, amigable; *place etc.* acogedor; *v. society*; '**friend·ship** amistad *f*.

frieze [fri:z] friso *m*.

frig·ate ['frigit] fragata *f*.

fright [frait] susto *m*, sobresalto *m*; terror *m*; (*p.*) espantajo *m*; '**fright·en** asustar, espantar, sobresaltar; ~ *away*, ~ *off* ahuyentar, espantar; be ~*ed of* tener miedo a; **fright·ful** ['⌣ful] □ espantoso, horrible, horroroso (*a. fig.*); F tremendo; '**fright·ful·ness** horror *m*; ⚔ terrorismo *m*.

frig·id ['fridʒid] □ frío; frígido; **fri·gid·i·ty** [fri'dʒid] frialdad *f*; frigidez *f*.

frill [fril] lechuga *f*, volante *m*; ~s *pl. fig.* afectación *f*, adornos *m/pl.*

fringe [frindʒ] **1.** franja *f*; borde *m*; orla *f*; flequillo *m of hair*; **2.** orlar (*with* de) (*a. fig.*).

frip·per·y ['fripəri] perifollos *m/pl.*; cursilería *f*.

frisk [frisk] *v/i.* retozar, cabriolar, juguetear; *v/t. sl.* palpar, registrar, cachear; '**frisk·y** □ retozón, juguetón; *horse* fogoso.

frit·ter ['fritə] **1.** fruta *f* de sartén,

buñuelo *m*; **2.:** ~ *away* desperdiciar, disipar.

fri·vol·i·ty [fri'vɔliti] frivolidad *f*; **friv·o·lous** ['frivələs] □ frívolo; trivial.

frizz [friz] pelo *m* de rizos muy apretados; **friz·zle** ['⌣l] freír, asar; '**friz·zled**, '**friz·zly** muy ensortijado.

fro [frou]: *to and* ~ de un lado a otro, de aquí para allá.

frock [frɔk] vestido *m*; '~-**coat** levita *f*.

frog [frɔg] rana *f*; ~ *in the throat* carraspera *f*; '~-**man** hombre-rana *m*.

frol·ic ['frɔlik] **1.** juego *m* alegre; travesura *f*; **2.** retozar, juguetear; **frol·ic·some** ['⌣səm] □ retozón, juguetón; (*mischievous*) travieso.

from [frɔm, frəm] de; desde; *message* de parte de; *date* a partir de; *price* desde … en adelante; ~ *above* desde encima; ~ *among* de entre; ~ *afar* desde lejos; ~ *memory* de memoria; ~ *what he says* según lo que dice; *judging* ~ juzgando por; *take s.t.* ~ *s.o.* quitar algo a alguien.

frond [frɔnd] fronda *f*.

front [frʌnt] **1.** frente *m* (*a.* ⚔, *meteor., pol.*); parte *f* delantera (*or* anterior); fachada *f of house*; principio *m of book*; pechera *f of shirt*; *fig.* apariencia *f* falsa; *in* ~ delante (*of* de); *come to the* ~ empezar a destacar; *put on a bold* ~ hacer de tripas corazón; **2.** delantero, anterior; primero; *door* puerta *f* principal; ⚔ ~ *line* primera línea *f*; ~ *wheel drive* tracción *f* a las ruedas delanteras; **3.:** ~ *on* (*to*) dar a; '**front·age** fachada *f*; terreno *m* delante de una casa; '**fron·tal** frontal; ⚔ de frente; **fron·tier** ['⌣jə] **1.** frontera *f*; **2.** fronterizo; **fron·tis·piece** ['⌣ispi:s] ⚓ fachada *f*; ⚠ frontispicio *m*; *typ.* portada *f*; '**front-page** de primera página; *fig.* muy importante.

frost [frɔst] **1.** helada *f*; escarcha *f* (*a. hoar* ~, *white* ~); *sl.* fracaso *m*; **2.** cubrir de escarcha; *plant* quemar; ~*ed glass* vidrio *m* deslustrado; '~-**bite** congelación *f*; '**frost-bit·ten** congelado, helado; '**frost·y** □ helado; escarchado; *fig.* glacial.

froth [frɔθ] **1.** espuma *f*; *fig.* bachillerías *f/pl.*; **2.** espumar; ~ *at the* *mouth* espumajear; **'froth·y** ☐ espumoso; *fig.* frívolo.

frown [fraun] **1.** ceño *m*; entrecejo *m*; **2.** fruncir el entrecejo; ~ *at* mirar con ceño; ~ *on* desaprobar.

frow·sy, frow·zy ['frauzi] desaliñado; maloliente.

froze [frouz] *pret. of* freeze 1; **'froz·en** *p.p. of* freeze 1 *a. adj.*; ~ *foods* alimentos *m/pl.* congelados.

fruc·ti·fy ['frʌktifai] *v/t.* fecundar; *v/i.* fructificar.

fru·gal ['fru:gəl] ☐ frugal; **fru·gal·i·ty** [fru'gæliti] frugalidad *f.*

fruit [fru:t] **1.** fruto *m* (*a. fig.*); fruta *f*; ~ *salts* sal *f* de fruta; ~ *tree* árbol *m* frutal; **2.** dar fruto, frutar; **'fruit·er·er** frutero *m*; ~*'s* frutería *f*; **fruit·ful** ['~ful] ☐ fructífero; *fig.* fructuoso, provechoso; **fru·i·tion** [fru'iʃn] cumplimiento *m*; fruición *f*; *come to* ~ verse logrado; **'fruit·less** ☐ infructuoso; **'fruit·y** con sabor de fruta; F verde.

frump [frʌmp] espantajo *m*, mujer *f* descuidada en el vestir; **'frump·ish** desaliñada.

frus·trate [frʌs'treit] frustrar; *plot* desbaratar; **frus·tra·tion** frustración *f*; desazón *f*.

fry [frai] **1.** fritada *f*; **2.** *ichth.* pececillos *m/pl.*; F *small* ~ gente *f* menuda; **3.** freír(se); *fried fish* pescado *m* frito; **'fry·ing-pan** sartén *f*.

fuch·sia ['fju:ʃə] fucsia *f*. [dido.\ **fud·dled** ['fʌdld] borracho; atur-J

fudge [fʌdʒ] **1.** hacer de modo chapucero; **2.** *dulce de leche, azúcar, etc.*

fu·el ['fjuəl] **1.** combustible *m*; carburante *m*; *fig.* pábulo *m*; **2.** aprovisionar(se) de combustible.

fug [fʌg] aire *m* viciado (*or* confinado, cargado).

fu·gi·tive ['fju:dʒitiv] **1.** fugitivo; fugaz; de interés pasajero; **2.** fugitivo (a *f*) *m*, evadido *m*.

fugue [fju:g] fuga *f*.

ful·crum ['fʌlkrəm] fulcro *m*.

ful·fil [ful'fil] cumplir; realizar; *condition etc.* llenar; *orders* ejecutar; **ful·'fil·ment** cumplimiento *m*; realización *f*; ejecución *f*.

full¹ [ful] **1.** (*adv. fully*) *mst* lleno; *fig.* pleno; (*complete*) cabal, íntegro; *account* extenso; *bus* completo; *dress* (*formal*) de etiqueta; *meal* abundante; *member* de número; *session* plen(ari)o; *skirt* amplio; F ~ *up bus* completo; harto *with food*; *beat by a* ~ *minute* aventajar en un minuto largo; *a* ~ *hour* una hora entera; ~ *moon* luna *f* llena, plenilunio *m*; ~ *powers* plenos poderes *m/pl.*; *at* ~ *speed* a máxima velocidad, a toda máquina; ~ *stop* punto *m*; *fig.* parada *f* completa; *in* ~ *view* totalmente visible; **2.** *adv.* de lleno; ~ *well* muy bien, sobradamente; **3.**: *in* ~ sin abreviar, por extenso; *pay in* ~ pagar la deuda entera; *to the* ~ completamente, al máximo.

full² [~] ⊕ abatanar.

full...: **'~-'blast** a máxima velocidad (*or* capacidad); en plena actividad; **'~-'blood·ed** vigoroso; de raza; **'~-'blown** hecho y derecho, desarrollado; ♀ abierto; **'~-'bod·ied** fuerte; *wine* generoso; **'~-'dress** de etiqueta, de gala.

full·er ['fulə] ⊕ batanero *m*; ~*'s earth* tierra *f* de batán.

full...: **'~-(y)-'fash·ioned** de costura francesa; **'~-(y)-'fledged** *fig.* hecho y derecho; **'~-grown** crecido; **'~-'length** de cuerpo entero; ~ *film* (cinta *f* de) largo metraje *m*.

ful(l)·ness ['fulnis] plenitud *f*; *in the* ~ *of time* a su debido tiempo.

full-time ['fultaim] (*adj.* que trabaja) jornada *f* completa, jornada *f* de costumbre; *adj.* en plena dedicación.

ful·mi·nate ['fʌlmineit] **1.** *v/t.* fulminar; *fulminating powder* pólvora *f* fulminante; *v/i.* ~ *against* tronar contra; **2.** 🜍 fulminato *m*; **ful·mi·'na·tion** fulminación *f*.

ful·some ['fulsəm] ☐ exagerado; repugnante; servil.

fum·ble ['fʌmbl] *v/t.* manosear, revolver *etc.* torpemente; *ball* dejar caer; ~ *one's way* ir a tientas; *v/i.* ~ *for* buscar con las manos; ~ *with* tocar (*or* manejar *etc.*) torpemente; tratar torpemente de abrir *etc.*

fume [fju:m] **1.**: ~*s pl.* humo *m*, gas *m*, vapor *m*; **2.** humear; (*p.*) enfadarse; echar pestes (*at th.* contra, *p.* de).

fu·mi·gate ['fju:migeit] fumigar; **fu·mi·'ga·tion** fumigación *f*.

fun [fʌn] diversión *f*; alegría *f*; *be* (*good, great*) ~ ser (muy) divertido;

for ~, in ~ en broma; *have ~* divertirse; *make ~ of* burlarse de, hacer chacota de.

func·tion ['fʌŋkʃn] **1.** función *f*; acto *m*, ceremonia *f*; cargo *m*; **2.** funcionar; '**func·tion·al** □ funcional; '**func·tion·ar·y** funcionario *m*.

fund [fʌnd] **1.** fondo *m* (*a. fig.*); *~s pl.* fondos *m/pl.*; *be in ~s* estar en fondos; **2.** *debt* consolidar.

fun·da·men·tal [fʌndə'mentl] □ fundamental; **fun·da'men·tals** [~z] *pl.* fundamentos *m/pl.*

fu·ner·al ['fjuːnərəl] **1.** entierro *m*, funerales *m/pl.*; *~ director* director *m* de funeraria; **2.** funeral, fúnebre; **fu·ne·re·al** [~'niəriəl] □ fúnebre, funéreo. [atracciones.\

fun·fair ['fʌnfɛə] parque *m* de\ **fun·gous** ['fʌŋgəs] fungoso; **fun·gus** ['fʌŋgəs], *pl.* **fun·gi** ['~gai] hongo *m*. [(*m*) funicular.\

fu·nic·u·lar [fju'nikjulə] (ferrocarril)\

funk [fʌŋk] F **1.** canguelo *m*, jindama *f*; (*p.*) gallina *m/f*, mandria *m/f*; *in a ~* aterrado; **2.** retraerse por miedo de; '**funk·y** F cobarde, miedoso. [chimenea *f.*\

fun·nel ['fʌnl] embudo *m*; ♆, 🚂\

fun·ny ['fʌni] □ cómico, gracioso, divertido; chistoso; (*strange*) raro, curioso; *the ~ thing about it is* (*that*) lo gracioso del caso es (que); *find it ~ that*, *strike s.o. as ~ that* hacerle a uno mucha gracia que; '**~bone** F hueso *m* de la alegría.

fur [fɜː] **1.** piel *f*; pelo *m*; saburra *f on tongue*; sarro *m in kettle etc.*; **2.** de piel(es); *~ coat* abrigo *m* de pieles; **3.** guarnecer *etc.* con pieles; depositar sarro en.

fur·bish ['fɜːbiʃ] pulir; *~ up* renovar, restaurar. [nético; violento.\

fu·ri·ous ['fjuəriəs] □ furioso; fre-\

furl [fɜːl] ♆ aferrar; arrollar.

fur·long ['fɜːlɔŋ] estadio *m*.

fur·lough ['fɜːlou] **1.** licencia *f*; **2.** dar licencia a.

fur·nace [ˈfɜːnis] horno *m*; lugar *m* de mucho calor.

fur·nish ['fɜːniʃ] suministrar, proporcionar (*with acc.*); equipar (*with con*); *proof* aducir; *room* amueblar (*with de*); '**fur·nish·ings** *pl.*, **fur·ni·ture** ['fɜːnitʃə] muebles *m/pl.*, mueblaje *m*, mobiliario *m*; *piece of ~* mueble *m*.

fur·ri·er ['fʌriə] peletero *m*.

fur·row ['fʌrou] **1.** surco *m*; **2.** surcar.

fur·ry ['fɜːri] peludo.

fur·ther ['fɜːðə] **1.** *adj.* más lejano; nuevo, adicional; *till ~ orders* hasta nueva orden; **2.** *adv.* más lejos, más allá (*a. ~ on*); además; **3.** promover, fomentar; adelantar; '**fur·ther·ance** promoción *f*, fomento *m*; adelantamiento *m*; '**fur·ther·more** además; '**fur·ther·most** más lejano.

fur·thest ['fɜːðist] **1.** *adj.* más lejano; extremo; **2.** *adv.* (lo) más lejos.

fur·tive ['fɜːtiv] □ furtivo.

fu·ry ['fjuəri] furor *m*, furia *f*; frenesí *m*; *like ~* a toda furia.

furze [fɜːz] aulaga *f*, tojo *m*.

fuse [fjuːz] **1.** fundir(se) (*a. ⚡*); fusionar(se); *the lights ~d* se fundieron los plomos; **2.** ⚡ plomo *m*, fusible *m*; ✗ espoleta *f*, mecha *f*; *~ box* caja *f* de fusibles.

fu·se·lage ['fjuːzilɑːʒ] fuselaje *m*.

fu·si·ble ['fjuːzəbl] fusible, fundible.

fu·sil·ier [fjuːzi'liə] fusilero *m*.

fu·sil·lade [fjuːzi'leid] descarga *f* cerrada; *fig.* torrente *m*.

fu·sion ['fjuːʒn] fusión *f* (*a. fig.*), fundición *f*.

fuss [fʌs] **1.** (*noisy*) bulla *f*, alharaca *f*; (*excessive display*) aspaviento *m*, hazañería *f*; (*trouble*) lío *m*; (*formalities*) ceremonia *f*; *kick up a ~, make a great ~* dar cuatro voces, hacer una algarada; *armar un lío; make a ~ of* hacer mimos a; *there's no need to make such a ~* no es para tanto; **2.** agitarse, inquietarse (por pequeñeces); '**fuss·y** □ F exigente; remilgado.

fus·tian ['fʌstiən] fustán *m*, pana *f*.

fust·y ['fʌsti] □ mohoso, rancio; que huele a cerrado.

fu·tile ['fjuːtail] □ inútil, vano, infructuoso; frívolo; **fu·til·i·ty** [fjuˈtiliti] inutilidad *f*, lo inútil; frivolidad *f*.

fu·ture ['fjuːtʃə] **1.** futuro; **2.** porvenir *m*, futuro *m*; ♣ *~s pl.* futuros *m/pl.*; *in* (*the*) *~* en el futuro, en lo sucesivo; *in the near ~* en fecha próxima; '**fu·tur·ism** futurismo *m*; **fu·tu·ri·ty** [fjuˈtjuəriti] estado *m* futuro.

fuzz [fʌz] tamo *m*, pelusa *f*; '**fuzz·y** □ borroso; *hair* muy ensortijado.

G

gab [gæb] F locuacidad *f*; cháchara *f*; *have the gift of the ~* tener mucha labia, ser un pico de oro.
gab·ar·dine [ˈgæbədiːn] gabardina*f*.
gab·ble [ˈgæbl] **1.** algarabía *f*; cotorreo *m*; **2.** *v/t.* farfullar, decir atropelladamente; *v/i.* farfullar; cotorrear.
gab·er·dine [ˈgæbədiːn] gabardina*f*.
ga·ble [ˈgeibl] aguilón *m*; '*~-end* hastial *m*.
gad [gæd] (*mst ~ about*) andar de aquí para allá; corretear; viajar mucho; '**gad·a·bout** F corretero (*a f*) *m*, persona *f* andariega.
gad·fly [ˈgædflai] tábano *m*.
gadg·et [ˈgædʒit] F artilugio *m*, chisme *m*.
Gael·ic [ˈgeilik] gaélico *adj. a. su. m.*
gaff [gæf] arpón *m*, garfio *m*; ♣ cangrejo *m*; *sl.* teatrucho *m*; *sl. blow the ~* descubrir el pastel, levantar la liebre.
gaffe [gæf] F plancha *f*.
gaf·fer [ˈgæfə] vejete *m*; tío *m*; (*foreman*) capataz *m*; (*boss*) jefe *m*.
gag [gæg] **1.** mordaza *f* (*a. fig.*); *thea.* morcilla *f*; *parl.* clausura *f*; F chiste *m*; *sl.* timo *m*; **2.** amordazar (*a. fig.*); *thea.* meter morcillas; F chunguear.
gai·e·ty [ˈgeiəti] alegría *f*, regocijo *m*; diversión *f* alegre.
gai·ly [ˈgeili] alegremente.
gain [gein] **1.** ganancia *f*; aumento *m*; provecho *m*; ✗ amplificación *f*; **2.** *v/t.* ganar; conseguir; (*clock*) adelantarse; *v/i.* crecer, medrar; ganar terreno; *~ on* ir alcanzando; '**gain·er:** *be the ~* salir ganando; **gain·ful** [ˈ~ful] ☐ ganancioso; *~ employment* trabajo *m* remunerado; **gain·ings** [ˈ~iŋz] *pl.* ganancias *f/pl.*
gain·say [geinˈsei] *lit.* contradecir, negar.
gait [geit] paso *m*, andar *m*.
gai·ter [ˈgeitə] polaina *f*.
gal [gæl] *Am. sl.* chica *f*.
ga·la [ˈgɑːlə] fiesta *f*; *~ dress* vestido *m* de gala.

gal·ax·y [ˈgæləksi] *ast.* galaxia *f*; *fig.* constelación *f*, pléyade *f*.
gale [geil] ventarrón *m*; (*esp. southerly*) vendaval *m*; *poet.* brisa *f*.
gall[1] [gɔːl] bilis *f*, hiel *f* (*a. fig.*); vejiga *f* de la bilis; *fig.* rencor *m*; *Am. sl.* descaro *m*.
gall[2] [~] ♀ agalla *f*.
gall[3] [~] **1.** *vet.* matadura *f*; **2.** lastimar rozando; *fig.* irritar, mortificar.
gal·lant [ˈgælənt] **1.** ☐ (*brave*) gallardo, valiente; lucido; **2.** [*mst* gəˈlænt] ☐ galante; **3.** [~] galán *m*; '**gal·lant·ry** gallardía *f*, valor *m*, bizarría *f*; galantería *f*, galanteo *m*.
gal·leon [ˈgæljən] galeón *m*.
gal·ler·y [ˈgæləri] galería *f* (*a.* ✗, *thea.*); *art ~* museo *m* de arte; *play to the ~* actuar para la galería.
gal·ley [ˈgæli] ♣ *a. typ.* galera *f*; ♣ cocina *f*, fogón *m*; '*~-proof* galerada *f*; '*~-slave* galeote *m*.
Gal·lic [ˈgælik] galo; **Gal·li·can** [ˈ~kən] galicano.
gal·li·vant [gæliˈvænt] F callejear; andar de visitas; viajar mucho; pindonguear.
gal·lon [ˈgælən] galón *m* (= *4,546 litros, Am. 3,785 litros*).
gal·lop [ˈgæləp] **1.** galope *m*; galopada *f*; *at full ~* a galope tendido, a uña de caballo; **2.** galopar; '**gal·lop·ing** ✗ galopante.
gal·lows [ˈgælouz] *sg.* horca *f*; '*~-bird* carne *f* de horca.
ga·lore [gəˈlɔː] a porrilla, en abundancia.
ga·losh [gəˈlɔʃ] chanclo *m*.
gal·van·ic [gælˈvænik] ☐ galvánico; **gal·va·nism** [ˈgælvənizm] galvanismo *m*; '**gal·va·nize** galvanizar; **gal·va·no·plas·tic** [gælvənouˈplæstik] galvanoplástico [táctica *f*.)
gam·bit [ˈgæmbit] gambito *m*; *fig.*)
gam·ble [ˈgæmbl] **1.** jugar; **2.** jugada *f*; empresa *f* arriesgada; '**gambler** jugador (-a *f*) *m*, tahúr *m*.
gam·bling [ˈgæmbliŋ] juego *m*; '*~-den*, '*~-house* garito *m*, casa *f* de juego.
gam·bol [ˈgæmbl] **1.** brinco *m*; re-

tozo *m*; **2.** brincar, retozar, juguetear.
game [geim] **1.** juego *m* (*a.* F); partida *f*; (*match*) partido *m*; deporte *m*; *bridge*: manga *f*; *hunt.* caza *f*; **big ~** caza *f* mayor; **~ of chance** juego *m* de azar; F **the ~ is up** ya se acabó; *play* **the ~** *fig.* jugar limpio; **2.** F animoso, valiente; *leg* cojo; **be ~ for anything** atreverse a todo; **3.** jugar (por dinero); **'~-bag** morral *m*; **'~-cock** gallo *m* de pelea; **'~-keep·er** guardabosques *m*; **'~-licence** licencia *f* de caza; **game·ster** ['~stə] jugador (-a *f*) *m*, tahur *m*; **'gam·ing** juego *m*.
gam·ma ['gæmə] gama *f*; **'~-rays** *pl.* rayos *m/pl.* gama.
gam·mer ['gæmə] abuelita *f*, vieja *f*.
gam·mon ['gæmən] **1.** a) jamón *m*; b) curar (jamón); **2.** a) lance *m* del juego del chaquete; engaño *m*; b) ganar doble partida al chaquete; engañar.
gamp [gæmp] F paraguas *m*.
gam·ut ['gæmət] gama *f*.
gam·y ['geimi] manido, salvajino.
gan·der ['gændə] ganso *m* (macho).
gang [gæŋ] **1.** cuadrilla *f*; pandilla *f*; brigada *f* *of workers*; juego *m* *of tools*; **2.** *Scot.* ir; **~ up** conspirar, obrar de concierto (*against*, *on* contra); **3.** ⊕ múltiple; **gang·er** ['gæŋə] capataz *m*; **'gang·plank** ⚓ plancha *f*.
gan·grene ['gæŋgriːn] gangrena *f*.
gang·ster ['gæŋstə] pistolero *m*, atracador *m*; gángster *m*, pandillero *m*.
gang·way ['gæŋwei] paso *m*, pasadizo *m*, pasillo *m*; ⚓ plancha *f*, pasadera *f*; ⚓ (*opening*) portalón *m*; ⚓ pasamano *m*; **~!** ¡abran paso!
gan·try ['gæntri] caballete *m*.
gaol [dʒeil] cárcel *f*.
gap [gæp] portillo *m*, abertura *f*; brecha *f*, boquete *m*; quebrada *f* *in mountains*; vacío *m*, hueco *m*, claro *m*, laguna *f*.
gape [geip] **1.** bostezo *m*; abertura *f*, hendedura *f*; **2.** bostezar; embobarse, estar boquiabierto; **~ at** mirar boquiabierto, embobarse de (*or* con, en).
ga·rage ['gærɑːʒ; 'gæridʒ] **1.** garaje *m*; **2.** dejar en garaje.
garb [gɑːb] **1.** traje *m*, vestido *m*; ropaje *m* (*a. fig.*); **2.** vestir.

gar·bage ['gɑːbidʒ] basura *f*, bazofia *f*, desperdicios *m/pl.*; **~ can** *Am.* cubo *m* de basuras.
gar·ble ['gɑːbl] mutilar; falsear (por selección).
gar·den ['gɑːdn] **1.** jardín *m*; (*fruit a. vegetables*) huerto *m*; **2.** cultivar un huerto (*or* jardín); trabajar en el huerto (*or* jardín); **'gar·den·er** jardinero (a *f*) *m*; hortelano (a *f*) *m*; **'gar·den·ing** jardinería *f*; horticultura *f*.
gar·gle ['gɑːgl] **1.** gargarizar, hacer gárgaras *f/pl.*; **2.** gargarismo *m*.
gar·goyle ['gɑːgɔil] gárgola *f*.
gar·ish ['gɛəriʃ] ☐ chillón, llamativo.
gar·land ['gɑːlənd] **1.** guirnalda *f*; **2.** enguirnaldar.
gar·lic ['gɑːlik] ajo *m*.
gar·ment ['gɑːmənt] prenda *f* (de vestir).
gar·ner ['gɑːnə] almacenar.
gar·net ['gɑːnit] granate *m*.
gar·nish ['gɑːniʃ] adornar, guarnecer; aderezar (*a. cooking*); **'gar·nish·ing** adorno *m*.
gar·ni·ture ['gɑːnitʃə] adorno *m*, guarnición *f*. [m.\]
gar·ret ['gærit] guardilla *f*, desván|
gar·ri·son ['gærisn] **1.** guarnición *f*; **2.** guarnecer, guarnicionar; poner en guarnición.
gar·ru·li·ty [gæ'ruːliti] garrulidad *f*; **gar·ru·lous** ['gæruləs] ☐ gárrulo.
gar·ter ['gɑːtə] liga *f*; **~-belt** *Am.* portaligas *m*; *Order of the* ♀ orden *f* de la Jarretera.
gas [gæs] **1.** *pl.* **gas·es** ['~iz] gas *m*; F parloteo *m*; *Am.* **= gasoline**; *mot.* **step on the ~** acelerar la marcha; **2.** asfixiar con gas; F parlotear; **'~-bag** ✈ cámara *f* de gas; F charlatán (-a *f*) *m*; **'~-brack·et** brazo *m* de lámpara de gas; **'~-burn·er** mechero *m* de gas; **'~-'cook·er** cocina *f* de (*or* a) gas; **gas·e·ous** ['geiziəs] gaseoso; **'gas-fire** estufa *f* de gas; **'gas-fit·ter** gasista *m*; **'gas-fit·tings** *pl.* instalación *f* del gas; guarniciones *f/pl.* del gas.
gash [gæʃ] **1.** cuchillada *f*, chirlo *m*; raja *f*, hendedura *f*; **2.** acuchillar, herir.
gas·ket ['gæskit] ⚓ tomador *m*; ⊕ empaquetadura *f*.
gas...: **'~-light** luz *f* de gas, alumbrado *m* de gas; **'~-main(s)** cañería

f (maestra) de gas; '~-**man·tle** manguito *m* incandescente; '~-**mask** careta *f* antigás; '~-**me·ter** contador *m* de gas; **gas·o·line** ['gæsəli:n] *Am. mot.* gasolina *f*; **gas·o·me·ter** [gæ'sɔmitə] gasómetro *m*; '**gas-ov·en** cocina *f* de (*or* a) gas.

gasp [gɑːsp] 1. (*esp. last* ~) boqueada *f*; grito *m* entrecortado; 2. boquear; ~ *for breath* jadear; *fig.* ~ *for* anhelar.

gas-proof ['gæs'pruːf] a prueba de gas; '**gas-range** cocina *f* de (*or* a) gas; '**gas-ring** hornilla *m* de gas; '**gas-stove** cocina *f* de (*or* a) gas; '**gas-sy** gaseoso; *fig.* hinchado.

gas·tric ['gæstrik] gástrico; **gas·tri·tis** [gæs'traitis] gastritis *f*.

gas·tron·o·mist [gæs'trɔnəmist] gastrónomo (a *f*) *m*; **gas'tron·o·my** gastronomía *f*.

gas-works ['gæswəːks] fábrica *f* de gas.

gat [gæt] *Am. sl.* arma *f* de fuego, revólver *m*.

gate [geit] puerta *f*; verja *f of iron*; portal *m of town*; (*wicket*) portillo *m*; (*level crossing*) barrera *f*; *sport:* entrada *f*; '~-**crash·er** *sl.* intruso (a *f*) *m*; '~-**leg**(·**ged**)**ta·ble** mesa *f* de alas abatibles; '~-**mon·ey** *sport:* ingresos *m/pl.* de entrada; '~-**way** portal *m*; entrada *f*.

gath·er ['gæðə] 1. *v/t.* recoger; reunir; acumular; *wood, flowers* coger; *crops* cosechar; *sew.* fruncir; *fig.* colegir, inferir, sacar la consecuencia (*that* que); *I* ~ *from A. that* ... según lo que me ha dicho A. ...; ~ *dust* empolvarse; ~ *speed* ir cada vez más rápidamente; ~ *strength* cobrar fuerzas; ~ *in* recoger; *money* recaudar; ~ *together* reunir, juntar; ~ *up* recoger; *v/i.* reunirse, juntarse, congregarse (*a.* ~ *together*); acumularse; condensarse; (*clouds*) amontonarse; ✟ formar pus; 2. (*mst* ~*s pl.*) frunce *m*; '**gath·er·ing** reunión *f*, asamblea *f*; muchedumbre *f*; acumulación *f*; recolección *f*; ✟ absceso *m*.

gaud·y ['gɔːdi] □ chillón, llamativo, vistoso.

gauge [geidʒ] 1. (norma *f* de) medida *f*; calibre *m*; indicador *m*; manómetro *m*; ⊕ calibrador *m*; *carpentry:* gramil *m*; ⛓ entrevía *f*,

ancho *m*; 2. medir; calibrar; aforar; *fig.* estimar.

Gaul [gɔːl] galo (a *f*) *m*.

gaunt [gɔːnt] □ flaco, desvaído, macilento; sombrío.

gaunt·let ['gɔːntlit] guantelete *m*; guante *m*; *run the* ~ correr baquetas; *take up the* ~ recoger el guante; *throw down the* ~ arrojar el guante.

gauze [gɔːz] gasa *f*; '**gauz·y** diáfano.

gave [geiv] *pret. of give.*

gav·el ['gævl] martillo *m de los presidentes y subastadores.*

gawk [gɔːk] F 1. zote *m*, bobo *m*; 2. papar moscas; '**gawk·y** torpe, desgarbado.

gay [gei] □ alegre, festivo; *appearance* brillante, vistoso; *b.s.* ligero de cascos.

gaze [geiz] 1. mirada *f* fija; contemplación *f*; 2. *a.* ~ *at*, ~ *on* mirar con fijeza, contemplar.

ga·zelle [gə'zel] gacela *f*.

ga·zette [gə'zet] 1. gaceta *f*; 2. publicar en la gaceta oficial; **gaz·et·teer** [gæzi'tiə] diccionario *m* geográfico.

gear [giə] 1. aparejo *m*, pertrechos *m/pl.*, herramientas *f/pl.*; F cosas *f/pl.*, chismes *m/pl.*; (*attire*) atavío *m*; (*harness*) arreos *m/pl.*, arneses *m/pl.*; ⊕ aparato *m*, mecanismo *m*; ⊕ engranaje *m*, rueda dentada *f*; *mot.* marcha *f* (*low, bottom* primera, *second* segunda, *top* tercera *or* cuarta), velocidad *f*; *in* ~ en juego; *put into* ~ engranar; *throw out of* ~ desengranar; *fig.* desconcertar; 2. aparejar; ⊕ engranar; ~ *up* multiplicar; ~ *down* desmultiplicar; ~ (*in*)*to* engranar con; '~-**box**, '~-**case** caja *f* de velocidades (*or* de engranajes); '**gear·ing** engranaje *m*; '**gear-le·ver**, '**gear-shift** *Am.* (palanca *f* de) cambio *m* de marchas.

gee [dʒiː] *esp.* ~ *up*! ¡arre!; *Am.* ¡caramba!

geese [giːs] *pl. of goose.*

gee·zer ['giːzə] *sl.* vejancón *m*, tío *m*.

gel·a·tin(**e**) ['dʒelətin] gelatina *f*; **ge·lat·i·nize** [dʒi'lætinaiz] gelatinizar(se); **ge·lat·i·nous** gelatinoso.

geld [geld] [*irr.*] castrar; '**geld·ing** caballo *m* castrado.

gel·id ['dʒelid] gélido, helado.

gel·ig·nite ['dʒelignait] gelatina *f* explosiva.

gem [dʒem] **1.** gema *f*, piedra *f* preciosa; *fig.* joya *f*, preciosidad *f*.

gen [dʒen] *sl.* información *f*.

gen·der ['dʒendə] género *m*.

gene [dʒi:n] *biol.* gen *m*.

gen·e·a·log·i·cal [dʒi:niə'lɔdʒikl] □ genealógico; **gen·e·al·o·gy** [dʒi:n-i'ælədʒi] genealogía *f*.

gen·er·a ['dʒenərə] *v. genus*.

gen·er·al ['dʒenərəl] **1.** □ general; *become ~* generalizarse; *in ~, as a ~ rule* en general, por lo general, por regla general; *~ election* elecciones *f/pl.* generales; **2.** ⚔ general *m*; F (= *~ servant*) criada *f* para todo; **gen·er·al·i·ty** [~'ræliti] generalidad *f*; **gen·er·al·i·za·tion** [~rəl-ai'zeiʃn] generalización *f*; **'gen·er·al·ize** generalizar; **'gen·er·al·ly** generalmente, en general, por lo común; **'gen·er·al·ship** generalato *m*; estrategia *f*; dirección *f*, don *m* de mando.

gen·er·ate ['dʒenəreit] engendrar (*a.* ⚕), generar (*a.* ⚡); *generating station* central *f* (generadora); **gen·er·a·tion** generación *f*; **'gen·er·a·tive** generativo; **'gen·er·a·tor** generador *m* (*a.* ⚡, ⊕).

ge·ner·ic [dʒi'nerik] genérico.

gen·er·os·i·ty [dʒenə'rɔsiti] generosidad *f*; **'gen·er·ous** □ generoso; dadivoso; amplio, abundante.

gen·e·sis ['dʒenisis] génesis *f*; *Bible:* ♀ Génesis *m*.

ge·net·ic [dʒi'netik] □ genético, genésico; **ge'net·ics** genética *f*.

gen·ial ['dʒi:njəl] □ afable, complaciente, cordial; suave; **ge·ni·al·i·ty** [~ni'æliti] afabilidad *f*, cordialidad *f*.

gen·i·tals ['dʒenitlz] *pl.* órganos *m/pl.* genitales.

gen·i·tive ['dʒenitiv] genitivo *m* (*a. ~ case*).

gen·ius ['dʒi:njəs] *pl.* **gen·i·i** ['~niai] (*deidad, espíritu tutelar*), *pl.* **gen·i·uses** ['~njəsiz] (*facultad, persona*) genio *m*.

gen·o·cide ['dʒenəsaid] genocidio *m*.

Gen·o·ese [dʒenou'i:z] genovés *adj. a. su. m* (-a *f*).

gent [dʒent] F = *gentleman*.

gen·teel [dʒen'ti:l] □ *mst iro.* fino, cortés, elegante, de buen tono; afectado, cursi; **gen'teel·ism** locución *f* afectada (*or* cursi).

gen·tian ['dʒenʃiən] genciana *f*.

gen·tile ['dʒentail] no judío *adj. a. su. m* (a *f*); (*pagan*) gentil *adj. a. su. m/f*.

gen·til·i·ty [dʒen'tiliti] *mst iro.* fineza *f*, buen tono *m*; cursilería *f*; † nobleza *f*.

gen·tle ['dʒentl] □ suave, dulce; benigno; sosegado; *esp. animals* manso, dócil; moderado; ligero; lento, pausado; bien nacido; † caballeroso; **'~·folk(s)** gente *f* bien nacida; **'~·man** caballero *m*, señor *m*; (*at court*) gentilhombre *m*; *he is no ~* es un mal caballero; **~'s** *agreement* acuerdo *m* verbal; **'~·man·ly** caballeroso; **'gen·tle·ness** suavidad *f*, dulzura *f*; mansedumbre *f*; **'gen·tle·wom·an** dama *f*, señora *f*; **'gen·tly** suavemente; poco a poco, despacio; ~! ¡paso!

gen·try ['dʒentri] gente *f* bien nacida; alta burguesía *f*; pequeña aristocracia *f*; *contp.* gentuza *f*.

gen·u·flec·tion, gen·u·flex·ion [dʒenju'flekʃn] genuflexión *f*.

gen·u·ine ['dʒenjuin] □ auténtico, legítimo, genuino; sincero; **'gen·u·ine·ness** autenticidad *f*, legitimidad *f*; sinceridad *f*.

ge·nus ['dʒi:nəs], *pl.* **gen·er·a** ['dʒenərə] género *m*.

ge·od·e·sy [dʒi'ɔdisi] geodesia *f*.

ge·og·ra·pher [dʒi'ɔgrəfə] geógrafo *m*; **ge·o·graph·i·cal** [~ə'græfikl] □ geográfico; **ge·og·ra·phy** [~'ɔgrəfi] geografía *f*.

ge·o·log·ic, ge·o·log·i·cal [dʒiə-'lɔdʒik(l)] □ geológico; **ge·ol·o·gist** [dʒi'ɔlədʒist] geólogo *m*.

ge·o·met·ric, ge·o·met·ri·cal [dʒiə-'metrik(l)] □ geométrico; **ge·om·e·try** [~'ɔmitri] geometría *f*.

ge·o·phys·ics [dʒiou'fiziks] geofísica *f*.

ge·o·pol·i·tics [dʒiou'pɔlitiks] geopolítica *f*.

ge·ra·ni·um [dʒi'reinjəm] geranio *m*. [tría *f*.╲]

ger·i·a·trics [dʒeri'ætriks] geria-

germ [dʒə:m] *biol., fig. a.* ⚕ germen *m*; ⚕ microbio *m*.

Ger·man¹ ['dʒə:mən] **1.** alemán *adj. a. su. m* (-a *f*); ⚕ *~ measles* rubéola *f*; ⊕ *~ silver* plata *f* alemana; *~ text typ.* letra *f* gótica; **2.** (*language*) alemán *m*.

ger·man² [~]: *brother etc. ~* hermano *m etc.* carnal; **ger·mane**

[dʒə:'mein] relacionado (*to* con); pertinente (*to* a); oportuno.

Ger·man·ic [dʒə:'mænik] germánico.

germ-car·ri·er ['dʒə:mkæriə] portador *m* de gérmenes.

ger·mi·cide ['dʒə:misaid] germicida *m*.

ger·mi·nal ['dʒə:minl] germinal; **ger·mi·nate** ['ˌneit] (hacer) germinar; **ger·mi'na·tion** germinación *f*.

germ-proof ['dʒə:mpru:f] a prueba de gérmenes.

ger·ry·man·der ['dʒerimændə] *pol.* falsificar elecciones.

ger·und ['dʒərənd] gerundio *m*.

ges·ta·tion [dʒes'teiʃn] gestación *f*.

ges·tic·u·late [dʒes'tikjuleit] accionar, gesticular, manotear; **ges·tic·u'la·tion** gesticulación *f*, manoteo *m*.

ges·ture ['dʒestʃə] **1.** gesto *m*, ademán *m*; demostración *f*; (*small token*) muestra *f*, detalle *m*; *empty* ~ pura formalidad *f*; *noble* ~ rasgo *m*; **2.** hacer ademanes.

get [get] [*irr.*] **1.** *v/t.* obtener, adquirir; lograr, conseguir; coger; (*grasp*) asir, agarrar *S.Am.*; recibir; *wage etc.* cobrar; ganar; tomar, prender; (*hit*) dar en; captar; comprender; alcanzar; cazar; hallar; (*fetch*) buscar, traer; sacar; (dis)poner; procrear; *have got* tener; *have got to inf.* tener que *inf.*; ~ *it sl.* ser castigado; F (*do you*) ~ *it?* ¿ comprendes?; F ~ *it bad* sufrir mucho; *I'll* ~ *him one day!* *sl.* ¡algún día me lo cargaré!; ~ *a p. to do s.t.* lograr que una p. haga algo; F ~ *religion* darse a la religión; ~ *s.t.* done hacer (*or* mandar) hacer una cosa; *that's what* ~*s me!* *sl.* ¡eso es lo que me irrita!; F ~ *across* hacer entender; ~ *away* quitar (de en medio); separar; conseguir que (una p.) se escape; ~ *back* recobrar.) ~ *down* bajar; descolgar; tragar; apuntar; F (*state of mind*) abatir; ~ *in* hacer entrar; *harvest* recoger; *word* decir; *blow* dar; ~ *off clothes etc.* quitar(se); *stain* sacar; despachar; (*punishment*) librar; aprender; ~ *on clothes etc.* ponerse; ~ *out* sacar; publicar; *problem* resolver; ~ *over* hacer pasar por encima de; F hacer entender; terminar; *let's* ~ *it over!*

¡vamos a concluir de una vez!; ~ *through* conseguir pasar (por); ~ *up* levantar; (hacer) subir; organizar; presentar; (*dress*) ataviar; (*disguise*) disfrazar; **2.** *v/i.* hacerse, llegar a ser, ponerse, volverse, quedar(se); ir; *sl.* largarse; venir; llegar; ~ *going* ponerse en marcha; empezar; ~ *going!* ¡menearse!; ~ *home* llegar a casa; *fig.* dar en el blanco; ~ *a p.p. or adj. is often translated by passive, v/i. or v/r. corresponding to p.p. or adj.:* ~ *beaten* ser vencido; ~ *dark* oscurecer; ~ *old* envejecer(se); ~ *angry* enfadarse; ~ *married* casarse; ~ *about* ir a muchos sitios; (*after sickness etc.*) estar levantado y moverse; (*report*) divulgarse; ~ *abroad* salir (al extranjero); (*report*) divulgarse; ~ *across* lograr cruzar; F *thea.* surtir efecto, tener éxito; F indisponerse con; ~ *ahead* (*of*) adelantar (se a); ~ *along* seguir andando; (*depart*) marcharse; (*manage*) ir tirando; *how are you* ~*ting along?* ¿cómo te va?; ~ *along with* avenirse con; ~ *along with you!* ¡no digas bobadas! ~ *along without* pasarse sin; ~ *around* viajar mucho; (*report*) divulgarse; ~ *around to s.t.* llegar a una cosa (con el tiempo); ~ *at* alcanzar, llegar a; atacar; descubrir, averiguar; querer decir; F apuntar a; F sobornar; (*spoil*) estropear; ~ *away* escapar(se); conseguir marcharse; alejarse; ~ *away with fig.* hacer impunemente; ~ *back* volver; retroceder; ~ *behind* penetrar; quedarse atrás; ~ *by* lograr pasar; eludir; F arreglárselas; ~ *down* bajar; ~ *down to* emprender; *problem* abordar; ~ *down to work* ponerse a trabajar; ~ *in* (lograr) entrar (en); llegar, volver a casa; *pol.* ser elegido; ~ *in with* congraciarse con; hacerse amigo de; ~ *into* (lograr) entrar (en); *vehicle* subir a; *difficulties etc.* meterse en; *clothes* ponerse; ~ *off* apearse (de); bajar (de); marcharse; *punishment* librarse de; escaparse; ✈ despegar; ~ *off!* ¡suelta!; ¡fuera!; ~ *off with sl.* enamorar; ~ *on* subir a; ponerse encima de; (*make progress*) adelantar; (*continue*) seguir; (*prosper*) medrar, tener éxito; *it's* ~*ting on for 8* falta poco para las 8; ~ *on with a p.* congeniar con; llevarse (bien) con; ~

out salir; escaparse; (*news*) hacerse público; ~ *out of vehicle* bajar de; *responsibility etc.* librarse de; evadir; ~ *over* atravesar; *obstacle* vencer, superar; *illness etc.* reponerse de, salir de; *fright* sobreponerse a; ~ *round* dar la vuelta a; *difficulty* soslayar; *p.* persuadir; ~ *through* (conseguir) pasar por; *time* pasar; *money* gastar; llegar al final de; terminar; penetrar; *exam* aprobar; ~ *through to* comunicar con; ~ *to* llegar a; empezar a; aprender a; ~ *together* reunirse; ~ *up* levantarse; ponerse de pie; subir; (*wind*) empezar a soplar recio; (*fire*) avivarse; **get-at-a-ble** [get'ætəbl] accesible; **get-a-way** ['getəwei] *sport:* salida *f*; escapatoria *f*; *make one's* ~ escaparse; **'get-up** (*dress*) atavío *m*; presentación *f*.

gew-gaw ['gju:gɔ:] fruslería *f*, chuchería *f*.

gey-ser ['gaizə] géiser *m*; ['gi:zə] calentador *m*.

ghastly ['gɑ:stli] horrible; pálido; cadavérico; F malo, desagradable, aburrido.

gher-kin ['gə:kin] pepinillo *m*.

ghet-to ['getou] judería *f*.

ghost [goust] fantasma *m*, aparecido *m*, espectro *m*; alma *f*, espíritu *m*; sombra *f*; *Holy* ♀ Espíritu *m* Santo; ~ (*-writer*) escritor *m* fantasma; *give up the* ~ entregar el alma; perder la esperanza; *not the* ~ *of a chance* ni la más remota posibilidad; **'ghostly** espectral; espiritual; **'ghostwrite** componer escritos por otra persona.

ghoul [gu:l] demonio *m* necrófago; persona *f* de gustos inhumanos; **'ghoul-ish** espantosamente cruel y malsano.

gi-ant ['dʒaiənt] **1.** gigante *m*; **2.** gigantesco; **'gi-ant-ess** giganta *f*.

gib-ber ['dʒibə] farfullar; hablar de una manera ininteligible; decir disparates; **'gib-ber-ish** galimatías *m*, guirigay *m*.

gib-bet ['dʒibit] **1.** horca *f*; **2.** ahorcar; *fig.* exponer a la vergüenza.

gibe [dʒaib] **1.** mofarse (*at* de); **2.** mofa *f*, escarnio *m*, pulla *f*.

gib-lets ['dʒiblits] *pl.* menudillos *m/pl.*

gid-di-ness ['gidinis] vértigo *m*; mareo *m*; atolondramiento *m*; fri-

volidad *f*; **'gid-dy** □ vertiginoso; mareado; atolondrado; ligero de cascos.

gift [gift] **1.** regalo *m*, dádiva *f*; (*esp. spiritual*) don *m*; (*personal quality*) dote *f*, talento *m*, prenda *f*; *eccl.* ofrenda *f*; ⚥ donación *f*; *sl.* ganga *f*; *deed of* ~ escritura *f* de donación; *I wouldn't have it as a* ~ no lo quiero ni regalado; *don't look a* ~ *horse in the mouth* a caballo regalado no le mires el diente; **2.** dotar; **'gift-ed** talentoso.

gig [gig] calesín *m*; ⚓ canoa *f*.

gi-gan-tic [dʒai'gæntik] □ gigantesco.

gig-gle ['gigl] (reír con) risilla *f* sofocada (*or* tonta).

gild [gild] **1.** = *guild*; **2.** [*irr.*] (sobre)dorar; **'gild-er** dorador (-a *f*) *m*; **'gild-ing** doradura *f*.

gill¹ [dʒil] cuarta parte *f* de una pinta (*approx.* 1/8 *litro*).

gill² [gil] *ichth.* agalla *f*; ♀ laminilla *f*; *fig.* papad(ill)a *f*.

gil-lie ['gili] ayudante *m* (*or* criado *m*) escocés.

gilt [gilt] **1.** *pret. a. p.p. of gild*; **2.** dorado *m*; *fig.* atractivo *m*; **'~-edged** con los cantos dorados; *fig.* de toda confianza, de primer orden; ~ *security* papel *m* del Estado.

gim-crack ['dʒimkræk] **1.** fruslería *f*; **2.** de baratillo; mal hecho.

gim-let ['gimlit] barrena *f* de mano.

gim-mick ['gimik] *sl.* treta *f*, artilugio *m*; *thea.* truco *m* característico; ✝ truco *m* publicitario.

gin¹ [dʒin] (*drink*) ginebra *f*.

gin² [~] **1.** trampa *f*; ⊕ desmotadera *f* de algodón; **2.** coger con trampa; ⊕ desmotar.

gin-ger ['dʒindʒə] **1.** jengibre *m*; F brío *m*, viveza *f*; **2.** rojo; **3.** F (*mst* ~ *up*) animar, estimular; **'~-'ale,** **'~-'beer,** **'~-'pop** cerveza *f* de jengibre; gaseosa *f*; **'~-bread** pan *m* de jengibre; **'~-group** F grupo *m* de activistas; **'gin-ger-ly 1.** *adj.* cuidadoso, delicado; **2.** *adv.* con tiento, con pies de plomo; **'gin-ger-snap** galleta *f* de jengibre. [(*a f*).\]

gip-sy ['dʒipsi] gitano *adj. a. su. m*\

gi-raffe [dʒi'rɑ:f] jirafa *f*.

gird [gə:d] [*irr.*] ceñir; rodear; ~ *o.s. for the fray* aprestarse a la lucha.

gird·er ['gəːdə] viga f.

gird·le ['gəːdl] 1. cinto m; (belt a. fig.) cinturón m; (corset) faja f; 2. ceñir; cercar.

girl [gəːl] (mst young) niña f; muchacha f, chica f; (young woman) joven f; (servant) criada f; '~friend amiguita f; novia f; **girl·hood** ['~hud] niñez f; mocedad f; **'girl·ish** □ de niña; juvenil; afeminado; **'girl·ish·ness** aire m (or modales m/pl.) de niña.

girt [gəːt] pret. a. p.p. of gird.

girth [gəːθ] 1. (horse's) cincha f; cintura f; corpulencia f; circunferencia f; 2. (a. ~ up) cinchar.

gist [dʒist] esencia f, quid m, meollo m.

give [giv] 1. [irr.] v/t. dar; proporcionar; ofrecer; (as present) regalar; (pass on) transmitir; disease contagiar con; punishment imponer, condenar a, castigar con; aid prestar; (produce) dar por resultado, arrojar, producir; (cause) ocasionar; (hand over) entregar; (grant) otorgar, conceder; time, energy dedicar, consagrar; sacrificar; (impart) comunicar; lecture explicar; thea. representar; speech pronunciar; F ~ it to a p. regañar a una p.; pegar a una p.; ~ us a song! ¡cántanos algo!; ~ away regalar; (get rid of) deshacerse de; (sell cheaply) malvender; (disclose) revelar; (betray) traicionar; ~ away the bride ser padrino de boda; ~ back devolver; ~ forth publicar, divulgar; emitir, despedir; ~ in entregar; ~ off emitir, despedir, echar; ~ out distribuir, repartir; anunciar; divulgar; afirmar; emitir, despedir; ~ over entregar; transferir; F cesar (de); dejar (de); ~ up entregar; ceder; cesar (de), dejar (de); renunciar (a); ⚔ desahuciar; (for lost) dar por perdido; ~ o.s. up to entregarse a; dedicarse a; 2. [irr.] v/i. dar; ceder; (weaken) flaquear; (break) romperse; (cloth etc.) dar de sí; ~ in ceder; consentir; darse por vencido; ~ out agotarse; fallar; F ~ over cesar; ~ up rendirse, darse por vencido; perder la esperanza; 3. elasticidad f; **give-and-take** ['givən'teik] toma y daca m; concesiones f/pl. mutuas; **give-a·way** ['givə'wei] revelación f indiscreta; ~ price precio m obsequio; **'giv·en**

p.p. of give; ~ that dado que; ~ to dado a, adicto a; **'giv·er** dador (-a f) m, donador (-a f) m.

giz·zard ['gizəd] molleja f; it sticks in my ~ no lo puedo tragar.

gla·ci·al ['gleisiəl] □ glacial; **gla·ci·a·tion** glaciación f; **gla·cier** ['glæsjə] ventisquero m, glaciar m; **gla·cis** ['glæsis] glacis m.

glad [glæd] □ contento, satisfecho; alegre, gozoso; be ~ alegrarse (of, to de); tener mucho gusto (to en); ~ly con mucho gusto; alegremente; **glad·den** ['~dn] alegrar, regocijar.

glade [gleid] claro m (en un bosque), calvero m.

glad·i·a·tor ['glædieitə] gladiador m; **glad·i·o·lus** [glædi'ouləs], pl. **glad·i·o·li** [~'oulai] estoque m, gladíolo m.

glad·ness ['glædnis] alegría f, gozo m; contento m; **glad·some** ['~səm] poet. alegre.

glad·stone ['glædstən] (a. ~ bag) maletín m.

glam·or·ous ['glæmərəs] □ encantador, hechicero; **glam·our** ['~mə] encanto m, hechizo m; ~ girl glamour f, chica f picante.

glance [glɑːns] 1. (look) ojeada f, vistazo m; (light) destello m; golpe m oblicuo; resbalón m, rebote m of projectile; at a ~ de un vistazo; at first ~ a primera vista; 2. destellar; (a. ~ off) rebotar de soslayo; ~ at ojear, echar un vistazo a; book (a. ~ over, ~ through) hojear; examinar de paso.

gland [glænd] anat., ⚘ glándula f; ⊕ prensaestopas m; **glan·dered** ['~əd] amormado; **glan·ders** ['~əz] sg. muermo m; **glan·du·lar** ['~julə] glandular.

glare [gleə] 1. luz f deslumbradora; deslumbramiento m; mirada f feroz; 2. relumbrar, deslumbrar; mirar ferozmente, echar fuego por los ojos; **glar·ing** ['~riŋ] □ deslumbrador; colour chillón; de mirada feroz; fig. manifiesto, craso.

glass [glɑːs] 1. vidrio m, cristal m; (drinking) vaso m; (wine) copa f; (beer) caña f; (spyglass) catalejo m; barómetro m; (mirror) espejo m; ~es pl. gafas f/pl., anteojos m/pl., lentes m/pl.; (binoculars) gemelos m/pl.; 2. de vidrio, de cristal; ~ case escaparate m, vitrina f; ~ door puerta f vidriera (or de cristales); '~-

blow·er soplador *m* de vidrio; '~-
cut·ter cortavidrio *m*; **glass·ful**
['~ful] vaso *m*; '**glass·house**
invernadero *m*; *sl.* ✗ cárcel *f*
militar; '**glass·i·ness** lo espejado,
vidriosidad *f*.

glass…: '~·**pa·per** (papel *m* de) lija*f*;
'~·**ware** cristalería *f*; '~·**works** *pl.*
⊕ vidriería *f*, cristalería *f*; '**glass·y**
□ vítreo; *water* espejado; *eyes* vidrioso.

glaze [gleiz] **1.** vidriado *m*, barniz *m*;
2. vidriar; poner vidrios a; ~*d paper*
papel *m* satinado; **gla·zier** ['~iə]
vidriero *m*; '**glaz·ing** vidriado *m*;
vidrios *m*/*pl.*

gleam [gli:m] **1.** rayo *m*, destello *m*;
a. fig. vislumbre *f*; brillo *m*; **2.** brillar, destellar.

glean [gli:n] espigar (*a. fig.*); '**glean·
er** espigador (-a *f*) *m*; **glean·ings**
['~iŋz] *pl.* moraga *f*; *fig.* fragmentos
m/*pl.* recogidos.

glebe [gli:b] *eccl.* terreno *m* beneficial; *poet.* suelo *m*.

glee [gli:] regocijo *m*, júbilo *m*; ♪
canción *f* para voces solas; ~ *club*
orfeón *m*; **glee·ful** ['~ful] □ alegre,
regocijado.

glen [glen] cañada *f*.

glen·gar·ry [glen'gæri] gorra *f* escocesa.

glib [glib] □ de mucha labia; *explanation* fácil; '**glib·ness** labia *f*; facilidad *f*.

glide [glaid] **1.** deslizamiento *m*; ✗
planeo *m*; **2.** deslizarse; ✗ planear;
~ *away*, *off* escurrirse; '**glid·er**
planeador *m*; (*light*) velero *m*; ~
pilot piloto *m* de planeador; '**glid·
ing** vuelo *m* a vela.

glim·mer [glimə] **1.** luz *f* trémula;
a. fig. vislumbre *f*; **2.** brillar con
luz tenue y vacilante.

glimpse [glimps] **1.** vistazo *m*, vislumbre *f*; *catch a* ~ *of* vislumbrar;
2. vislumbrar, entrever; ver por un
momento.

glint [glint] **1.** destello *m*, reflejo *m*,
centelleo *m*; **2.** destellar, centellear.

glis·ten ['glisn] relucir, brillar,
centellear.

glit·ter ['glitə] **1.** resplandecer, ruti-
lar; *all that* ~*s is not gold* no es oro
todo lo que reluce; **2.** resplandor *m*;
brillo *m*; '**glit·ter·ing** resplandeciente, brillante, reluciente.

gloam·ing ['gloumiŋ] crepúsculo *m*.

gloat [glout] (*mst* ~ *over*) deleitarse
(en); relamerse.

glob·al ['gloubl] mundial, global;
globe [gloub] globo *m*; esfera *f*;
geog. bola *f* del mundo; '**globe-
trot·ter** trotamundos *m*; **glo·bose**
['~ous], **glob·u·lar** ['glɔbjulə] □
globoso; **glo·bos·i·ty** [glou'bɔsiti]
globosidad *f*; **glob·ule** ['glɔbju:l]
glóbulo *m*.

gloom [glu:m], '**gloom·i·ness** tenebrosidad *f*, lobreguez *f*, oscuridad
f; melancolía *f*, abatimiento *m*,
pesimismo *m*; '**gloom·y** □ tenebroso, lóbrego; abatido, melancólico, pesimista.

glo·ri·fi·ca·tion [glɔ:rifi'keiʃn] glorificación *f*; **glo·ri·fy** ['~fai] glorificar; '**glo·ri·ous** □ glorioso; F
magnífico, estupendo.

glo·ry ['glɔ:ri] **1.** gloria *f*; *be in
one's* ~ estar en sus glorias; **2.** (*rejoice*) gloriarse (*in* en); (*boast*) gloriarse (*in* de).

gloss[1] [glɔs] **1.** glosa *f*; **2.** glosar.

gloss[2] [~] **1.** lustre *m*, brillo *m*; *put
a* ~ *on* sacar brillo a; ~ *paint* pintura *f* esmalte; **2.** pulir, lustrar;
~ *over* paliar, colorear.

glos·sa·ry ['glɔsəri] glosario *m*.

gloss·i·ness ['glɔsinis] lustre *m*,
brillantez *f*; '**gloss·y** □ lustroso,
pulido; *paper*, *cloth* satinado.

glot·tis ['glɔtis] glotis *f*.

glove [glʌv] guante *m*; **gloved** [~d]
enguantado; '**glov·er** guantero
(a *f*) *m*.

glow [glou] **1.** incandescencia *f*;
brillo *m*; calor *m*; luz *f* (difusa);
arrebol *m* *of sky*; color *m* vivo;
sensación *f* de bienestar; ardor *m*;
2. estar candente; brillar; estar encendido; arder.   [ceño.]
glow·er ['glauə]: ~ *at* mirar con)
glow·ing ['glouiŋ] candente; encendido; ardiente; *fig.* entusiasta.

glow-worm ['glouwə:m] luciérnaga *f*.

glu·cose ['glu:kous] glucosa *f*.

glue [glu:] **1.** cola *f*; **2.** encolar,
pegar; '~-**pot** cazo *m* (de cola);
'**glue·y** pegajoso; encolado.

glum [glʌm] □ taciturno, sombrío,
malhumorado.

glut [glʌt] **1.** hartazgo *m*; supera-
bundancia *f*; *be a* ~ *on the market*
abarrotar el mercado; abarrotarse
S.Am.; **2.** hartar; *market* inundar.

glu·ti·nous [ˈgluːtinəs] ☐ glutinoso.
glut·ton [ˈglʌtn] glotón (-a *f*) *m*;
zo. glotón *m*; *be a ~ for* ser insaciable de; **'glut·ton·ous** ☐ glotón; **'glut·ton·y** glotonería *f*.
glyc·er·in(e) [ˈglisərin] glicerina *f*.
G-man [ˈdʒiːmæn] *Am.* F agente *m* secreto federal.
gnarled [nɑːld] nudoso, rugoso; (*weather-beaten*) curtido.
gnash [næʃ] rechinar (los dientes).
gnat [næt] mosquito *m*; jején *m* S.Am.
gnaw [nɔː] roer; **'gnaw·ing 1.** roedura *f*; **2.** roedor.
gnome [noum] gnomo *m*; **gnom·ic** [ˈnoumik] gnómico.
gnu [nuː] ñu *m*.
go [gou] **1.** [*irr.*] (*v. a. going, gone*) ir; viajar, caminar; (*no direction indicated*) andar; (*depart*) irse, marcharse; desaparecer; eliminarse; (*give way*) ceder, romperse, hundirse; ⊕ funcionar, trabajar, marchar; seguir; hacer (gestos *or* movimientos); (*be current*) correr; (*be habitually*) andar; (*turn out*) resultar, salir; (*become*) hacerse, ponerse, volverse; (*food*) pasarse; (*milk*) cortarse; (*be sold*) venderse; (*time*) pasar; (*reach*) alcanzar, llegar; (*fit*) ajustarse, caber; (*belong*) (*deber*) colocarse; *as far as it ~es* dentro de sus límites; *as they etc. ~* considerando lo que corre; F *here ~es!* ¡vamos a ver!; F *how ~es it?* ¿qué tal?; *the story ~es* se dice; *there ~es the bell* allí suena el timbre; *who ~es there?* ¿quién vive?; *~ and* (*or* to) *see* ir a ver; *v. bad*; *~ blind* quedarse ciego; *~ hungry* pasar hambre; *~ hunting* ir de caza; *sl. ~ it* ir a toda velocidad; obrar enérgicamente; correrla; *sl. ~ it alone* obrar sin ayuda; *~ one better* quedar por encima (*than* de); *~ about* andar (de un sitio para otro); circular; ocuparse en; emprender; hacer las gestiones para; ⚓ virar; *~ abroad* ir al extranjero; salir; *~ against* ir en contra de; oponerse a; chocar con; *~ ahead* ir adelante, continuar, avanzar; *~ ahead!* ¡adelante!; *~ along* ir por; marcharse; seguir andando; *~ at* lanzarse sobre; acometer; *~ away* irse, marcharse; desaparecer; *~ back* volver, regresar; retroceder; *~* *back on* desdecirse de; faltar a; *~ before* ir a la cabeza de; anteceder; comparecer ante; *~ behind* ir detrás de; *~ behind a p.'s back* obrar a espaldas de uno; *~ between* interponerse; mediar (entre); *~ beyond* ir más allá (de); exceder; *~ by* pasar (por); atenerse a; juzgar por; regirse por; *~ by the name of* conocerse por el nombre de; *~ down* bajar; (*sun*) ponerse; (*ship*) hundirse; sucumbir (*before* ante); F aceptarse, tragarse; pasar a la historia; *~ for* ir por; F atacar; F *that ~es for me too* yo contigo; *~ in* entrar (en); (*fit*) caber (en); *~ in for* dedicarse a; tomar parte en; *exam* tomar, presentarse para; comprar; *~ into* entrar en; caber en; investigar; *~ in with* asociarse con; *~ off* irse, marcharse; (*gun*) dispararse; (*explosion*) estallar; deteriorarse; *~ on* seguir (adelante); durar; pasar; F machacar; F echar pestes; *thea.* salir a escena; F *~ on!* ¡anda!; F *how are you ~ing on?* ¿qué tal?, ¿cómo te va?; F *~ on at* reñir; *~ on to inf.* pasar luego a *inf.*; *~ on to say* decir a continuación; *~ on with* continuar, proseguir; *~ out* salir; (*light*) apagarse; F pasar de moda; *~ over* recorrer, atravesar; examinar, repasar; (*to another party, etc.*) pasarse a; *~ round* dar la vuelta a; circular; (*revolve*) girar; (*suffice*) alcanzar para todos; *~ round to* hacer una visita a; *~ through* pasar por; atravesar; penetrar; sufrir; experimentar; (*spend*) (mal)gastar; examinar; *~ through with* llevar a cabo; *~ to* (*bequest*) pasar a; servir para, ayudar a; destinarse a; *~ under* (*ship*) hundirse; arruinarse; fracasar; *name* pasar por; *~ up* subir (a); (*explode*) estallar; *~ with* acompañar; (*agree*) estar de acuerdo con; hacer juego con; ir bien con; *~ without* pasarse sin; **2.** F (*occurrence*) suceso *m*; (*fix*) lío *m*; energía *f*; turno *m*; F *be on the ~* trajinar; F *have a ~* probar suerte; tentar; *in one ~* de una vez, de un tirón; F *is it a ~?* ¿hace?; F *it's a ~!* ¡trato hecho!; F *it's all the ~* hace furor; *sl. it's no ~* es inútil; no puede ser; F *it's your ~* te toca a ti; *make a ~ of* tener éxito en.

goad [goud] **1.** aguijada *f*; (*a. fig.*) aguijón *m*; **2.** aguijonear; *fig.* irritar, incitar; ~ *into* provocar a; ~ *into fury* irritar hasta la furia.

go·a·head ['gouǝhed] **1.** emprendedor; **2.** permiso *m* (*or* señal *f*) para seguir adelante.

goal [goul] meta *f*; *sport*: portería *f*, meta *f*; (*score*) gol *m*, tanto *m*; '~·keep·er portero *m*, guardameta *m*; '~·post poste *m* de la portería, larguero *m*.

goat [gout] cabra *f*, macho *m* cabrío; *sl. get a p.'s* ~ irritar a una p.; **goat·ee** perilla *f*; **goat·herd** ['~hǝ:d] cabrero *m*; '**goat·ish** cabruno; lascivo.

gob [gɔb] salivazo *m*; *sl.* boca *f*; *Am.* F marino *m*; **gob·bet** ['~it] bocado *m*; pedazo *m*.

gob·ble ['gɔbl] **1.** engullir; (*turkey*) gluglutear; **2.** gluglú *m* of *turkey*; **gob·ble·dy·gook** ['gɔbldiguk] *Am. sl.* jerga *f* burocrática.

go·be·tween ['goubitwi:n] medianero (a *f*) *m*, tercero (a *f*) *m*; *b.s.* alcahuete (a *f*) *m*.

gob·let ['gɔblit] copa *f*.

gob·lin ['gɔblin] duende *m*, trasgo *m*.

go-by ['goubai]: F *give the* ~ *to* desairar; pasar por alto de; evitar.

go-cart ['gouka:t] cochecito *m* de niño; andaderas *f/pl.*

god [gɔd] dios *m*; ♀ Dios *m*; ~s *thea.* F paraíso *m*, gallinero *m*; *please* ♀ plegue a Dios; ♀ *willing* Dios mediante; '**god·child** ahijado (a *f*) *m*; '**god·daugh·ter** ahijada *f*; '**god·dess** diosa *f*; '**god·fa·ther** padrino *m*; '**god-fear·ing** timorato; '**god-for·sak·en** dejado de la mano de Dios; abandonado; desierto; '**god·head** divinidad *f*; '**god·less** descreído; '**god·like** (de aspecto) divino; '**god·li·ness** piedad *f*, santidad *f*; '**god·ly** piadoso; '**god·moth·er** madrina *f*; *fairy* ~ hada madrina *f*; '**god·par·ents** *pl.* padrinos *m/pl.*; '**god·send** divina merced *f*; cosa *f* llovida del cielo; '**god-'speed** bienandanza *f*; adiós *m*; *bid* (*or wish*) ~ desear un feliz viaje (*or* buena suerte).

go·er ['gouǝ] corredor (-a *f*) *m*.

go-get·ter ['gou'getǝ] *sl.* persona *f* emprendedora, buscavidas *m/f*.

gog·gle ['gɔgl] **1.** salirse a una p.

los ojos de la cabeza; **2.** ~s *pl.* anteojos *m/pl.*; *sl.* gafas *f/pl.*

go·ing ['gouiŋ] **1.** yendo, que va; en marcha, funcionando; F en venta; F disponible; F existente; *be* ~ *to inf.* ir a *inf.*; *it's* ~ *on for 5 o'clock* son casi las 5; *keep* ~ seguir; no cejar; *set* ~ poner en marcha; ~ *concern* empresa *f* en pleno funcionamiento (*or* que marcha bien); ~, ~, *gone!* ¡a la una, a las dos, a las tres!; **2.** ida *f*; partida *f*, salida *f*; marcha *f*, velocidad *f*; estado *m* del camino (*sport*: de la pista); *good* ~! ¡bien hecho!; '**go·ings-'on** *pl.* F actividades *f/pl.* (dudosas); jarana *f*.

goi·tre ['gɔitǝ] bocio *m*; **goi·trous** ['gɔitrǝs] que tiene bocio.

gold [gould] **1.** oro *m*; **2.** de oro, áureo; *Am. sl.* ~ *brick* estafa *f*; ~ *leaf* oro *m* batido; ~ *plate* vajilla *f* de oro; ~ *standard* patrón *m* oro; '~·crest reyezuelo *m* sencillo; '~·dig·ger *sl.* aventurera *f*; '**gold·en** áureo, de oro; dorado; *fig.* excelente, próspero, feliz; ~ *jubilee* quincuagésimo aniversario *m*; ~ *mean* justo medio *m*; ~ *wedding* bodas *f/pl.* de oro; '**gold·finch** jilguero *m*; '**gold·fish** pez *m* de colores; ~ *bowl* pecera *f*; '**gold-mine** mina *f* de oro; *fig.* río *m* de oro, potosí *m*; '**gold·smith** orfebre *m*.

golf [gɔlf] golf *m*; ~ *club* (*stick*) palo *m* de golf; club *m* de golf; '**golf·er** jugador (-a *f*) *m* de golf; '**golf·links** terreno *m* (*or* campo *m*) de golf.

gol·li·wog(g) ['gɔliwɔg] negrito *m*.

go·losh [gǝ'lɔʃ] chanclo *m*.

gon·do·la ['gɔndǝlǝ] ⚓ góndola *f*; 🚃 barquilla *f*.

gone [gɔn] (*p.p. of go*) ido; pasado; desaparecido; arruinado; (*lost*) perdido; (*used up*) agotado; muerto; F chiflado; *be* ~!, *get you* ~! ¡vete!; F *far* ~ muy adelantado; cerca de la muerte; muy borracho; *sl.* ~ *on* loco por; enamorado de; ~ (*with child*) encinta; *it has* ~ *4 o'clock* ya dieron las 4; '**gon·er** *sl.* persona *f* (dada por) muerta.

gong [gɔŋ] gong(o) *m*, batintín *m*.

good [gud] **1.** bueno; F ~ *and adj. or adv.* bien, muy; ~ *at* hábil en; *be* ~ *for* ser bueno para; servir para; F tener fuerzas para; F ser capaz de (hacer *or* pagar *or* dar); *that's a* ~ *one!* ¡ésa sí que es buena!; **2.** bien *m*; provecho *m*, utilidad *f*; ~*s pl.* bienes *m/pl.*; ✝ géneros *m/pl.*, mercancías *f/pl.*; *do* ~ hacer bien; sentar bien; *for* ~ *(and all)* (de una vez) para siempre; *for the* ~ *of* en bien de, para el bien de; *it is no* ~ es inútil, no sirve (para nada); *he is up to no* ~ está urdiendo algo malo; *the* ~ lo bueno; los buenos; *what is the* ~ *of?* ¿para qué sirve?; *to the* ~ en el haber, de sobra; ~*s station* estación *f* de mercancías; ~*s train* (tren *m* de) mercancías *m*; **~-bye 1.** [gud'bai] adiós *m*; **2.** ['gud'bai] ¡adiós!; '~-**for-liv-ing 1.** inútil; **2.** haragán (-a *f*) *m*; '**good·li·ness** hermosura *f*; excelencia *f*; '**good-look·ing** bien parecido; '**good·ly** hermoso; considerable; '**good-'na·tured** bondadoso; bonachón; '**good·ness** bondad *f*; *(food)* sustancia *f*, lo mejor; ~*!* ¡válgame Dios!; *for* ~*' sake!* ¡por Dios!; '**good'will** buena voluntad *f* *(towards hacia)*; buena gana *f*; ✝ clientela *f*, buen nombre *m*; ~ *mission* misión *f* de buena voluntad.

good·y¹ ['gudi] golosina *f*.

good·y² [~] *(a.* ~-~) beato *adj. a. su. m* (a *f*); santito *adj. a. su. m* (a *f*).

goo·ey ['gu:i] *sl.* pegajoso, empalagoso.

goof [gu:f] *sl.* bobo (a *f*) *m*; '**goof·y** *sl.* bobo.

goon [gu:n] *Am. sl.* zoquete *m*; gángster *m*, gorila *m*.

goose [gu:s], *pl.* **geese** [gi:s] ganso (a *f*) *m*, oca *f*, ánsar *m*; *fig.* tonto (a *f*) *m*; plancha *f* de sastre; *cook a p.'s* ~ pararle los pies a una p., acabar con una p.

goose·ber·ry ['guzbəri] uva espina *f*; F *play* ~ hacer de carabina.

goose...: '~-**flesh**, '~-**pim·ples** carne *f* de gallina; '~-**step** paso *m* de ganso.

gore¹ [gɔ:] sangre *f* (derramada).

gore² [~] **1.** *sew.* nesga *f*; **2.** cornear, acornar; *sew.* nesgar.

gorge [gɔ:dʒ] **1.** garganta *f*, barranco *m*; *(meal)* atracón *m*; *my* ~ *rises at me* da asco; **2.** *v/t.* engullir; *v/i.* atracarse.

gor·geous ['gɔ:dʒəs] □ magnífico, brillante, vistoso; F maravilloso,

hermoso; '**gor·geous·ness** magnificencia *f*, vistosidad *f*.

gor·mand·ize ['gɔ:məndaiz] glotonear.

gorse [gɔ:s] tojo *m*, aulaga *f*.

gor·y ['gɔ:ri] □ ensangrentado; sangriento.

gosh [gɔʃ] *sl.* ¡caray!

gos·hawk ['gɔshɔ:k] azor *m*.

gos·ling ['gɔzliŋ] ansarino *m*.

gos·pel ['gɔspl] evangelio *m*.

gos·sa·mer ['gɔsəmə] (hilos *m/pl.* de) telaraña *f* (volantes); ✝ gasa *f* sutil.

gos·sip ['gɔsip] **1.** hablador (-a *f*) *m*; *b.s.* chismoso (a *f*) *m*, murmurador (-a *f*) *m*; ✝ comadre *f*; *(conversation)* charla *f*; comadreo *m*, murmuración *f*, chismes *m/pl.*, habladurías *f/pl.*; *piece of* ~ chisme *m*, hablilla *f*; ~ *column* gacetilla *f*; **2.** charlar; *b.s.* chismear; '**gos·sip·y** chismoso, hablador.

got [gɔt], ✎ *or Am.* **got·ten** ['~tn] *pret. a. p.p. of get.*

Goth [gɔθ] *hist.* godo (a *f*) *m*; *fig.* bárbaro (a *f*) *m*; '**Goth·ic** gótico *(a. su. m)*; godo.

gouge [gaudʒ] **1.** ⊕ gubia *f*; **2.** *(mst* ~ *out)* excavar con gubia, acanalar; *Am. sl.* estafar; ~ *a p.'s eyes out* sacarle los ojos a una p.

gourd [guəd] calabaza *f*.

gour·mand ['guəmənd] glotón *m*.

gour·met ['guəmei] gastrónomo *m*.

gout [gaut] ✻ gota *f*; '**gout·y** □ gotoso.

gov·ern ['gʌvən] *v/t.* gobernar, regir *(a. fig., gr.)*; dominar; *v/i.* gobernar; ~*ing body* junta *f* directiva; ~*ing principle* principio *m* rector; '**gov·ern·a·ble** □ gobernable, dócil; '**gov·ern·ess** institutriz *f*; '**gov·ern·ment** gobierno *m*; *(a. gr.)* régimen *m*; *attr.* = **gov·ern·men·tal** [~'mentl] gubernativo, gubernamental, del gobierno; '**gov·er·nor** gobernador *m*; director *m*; alcaide *m of prison*; F jefe *m*; F *(father)* progenitor *m*, viejo *m S.Am.*; ⊕ regulador *m*.

gown [gaun] **1.** *(dress)* vestido *m*; *univ.* toga *f*; traje *m* talar; **2.** vestir (con toga).

grab [græb] **1.** arrebatar; agarrar, coger; *fig.* apropiarse; ~ *at* tratar de agarrar; **2.** arrebatiña *f*; agarro *m*; F robo *m*; ⊕ gancho *m* arrancador; ⊕ cubeta *f* draga, cuchara *f* de dos mandíbulas; '**grab·ber** avaro (a *f*) *m*; ladrón (-a *f*) *m*.

grace [greis] 1. (*favour, attractiveness, a. eccl.*) gracia *f*; elegancia *f*; armonía *f*, decoro *m*; (*at table*) bendición *f* de la mesa; (*deferment*) respiro *m*, demora *f*; ♀s Gracias *f*/*pl.*; ~ note nota *f* de adorno; *act of* ~ gracia *f*; *with* (*a*) *good* (*bad*) ~ de buen (mal) talante; *good* ~s favor *m*; *get into a p.'s good* ~s congraciarse con una p.; *period of* ~ plazo *m*; *Your* ♀ Vuestra Ilustrísima; *eccl.* Monseñor, su Reverendísima; 2. adornar, embellecer; favorecer; honrar; **grace·ful** ['~ful] □ agraciado, gracioso; elegante; '**grace·ful·ness** gracia *f*, graciosidad *f*; elegancia *f*; '**grace·less** □ réprobo; desgraciado, sin gracia.

gra·cious ['greiʃəs] □ clemente, benigno, graciable; gracioso; *good* (*ness*) ~! ¡Dios mío!; '**gra·cious·ness** clemencia *f*; afabilidad *f*.

gra·da·tion [grə'deiʃn] graduación *f*; gradación *f*; paso *m* (gradual).

grade [greid] 1. grado *m*; (*quality*) clase *f*, calidad *f*; (*mark*) nota *f*; (*slope*) pendiente *f*; *make the* ~ vencer los obstáculos, tener éxito; *Am.* 🚃 ~ *crossing* paso *m* a nivel; *Am.* ~ *school* escuela *f* primaria; 2. graduar, clasificar; *cattle* cruzar; 🚃 *etc.* nivelar, explanar.

gra·di·ent ['greidiənt] declive *m*, pendiente *f*.

grad·u·al ['grædjuəl] □ gradual; **grad·u·ate** 1. ['~eit] graduar(se); 2. ['~it] graduado *adj. a. su. m* (a *f*); **grad·u·a·tion** [~'eiʃn] graduación *f*.

graft¹ [graːft] 1. ✒, 🌿 injerto *m*; 2. ✒, 🌿 injertar (*in, upon* en).

graft² [~] 1. corrupción *f*, soborno *m*, chanchullos *m*/*pl.*; *sl.* hard ~ trabajo *m* muy duro; '**graft·er** *Am.* F chanchullero *m*.

Grail [greil] grial *m*.

grain [grein] 1. grano *m*; cereales *m*/*pl.*; fibra *f*, hebra *f* *of wood*; vena *f*, veta *f* *of stone*; flor *f* *of leather*; granilla *f* *of cloth*; (*particle*) pizca *f*; *against the* ~ *fig.* a contrapelo; *it goes against the* ~ *with me* se me hace cuesta arriba; *dyed in the* ~ teñido en rama; *with a* ~ *of salt* con un grano de sal; *saw with the* ~ ase-

rrar a hebra; 2. vetear; '**grain·ing** veteado *m*.

gram·mar ['græmə] gramática *f*; ~ *school* instituto *m* (de segunda enseñanza); (*private*) colegio *m*; *Am.* escuela *f* intermedia; **gram·mar·i·an** [grə'meəriən] gramático *m*; **gram·mat·i·cal** [grə'mætikl] □ gramático, gramatical.

gram(me) [græm] gramo *m*.

gram·o·phone ['græməfoun] gramófono *m*, gramola *f*; fonógrafo *S.Am.*; ~ *pick-up* pick-up *m*; ~ *record* disco *m* (de gramófono).

gram·pus ['græmpəs] orca *f*.

gran·a·ry ['grænəri] granero *m*.

grand [grænd] 1. □ magnífico, imponente, grandioso; espléndido; *p.* distinguido, soberbio; *style* elevado, sublime; noble; magno; gran(de); estupendo; ♀ *Duke* gran duque *m*; 2. ♪ (*a.* ~ *piano*) piano *m* de cola; *Am. sl.* mil dólares *m*/*pl.*; '**gran·dad** ['grændæd] F abuelito *m*; **gran·dam(e)** ['~dæm] abuela *f*; anciana *f*; '**grand·child** nieto (a *f*) *m*; '**grand·daugh·ter** nieta *f*; **gran·dee** [græn'diː] grande *m* (de España); **gran·deur** ['grændʒə] magnificencia *f*, grandiosidad *f*; grandeza *f*; sublimidad *f*; '**grand·fa·ther** abuelo *m*; ~('*s*) *clock* reloj *m* de caja (*or* de pie).

gran·dil·o·quence [græn'diləkwəns] grandilocuencia *f*; **gran·dil·o·quent** □ grandílocuo.

gran·di·ose ['grændious] □ grandioso; *b.s.* exagerado, hinchado.

grand·ma ['grænmɑ] F abuelita *f*.

grand·moth·er ['grænmʌðə] abuela *f*; '**grand·ness** = grandeur.

grand·pa ['grænpɑ] F abuelito *m*.

grand...: '~-**par·ents** *pl.* abuelos *m*/*pl.*; ~**sire** ['~saiə] † abuelo *m*; antepasado *m*; '~-**son** nieto *m*; '~-**stand** tribuna *f*.

grange [greindʒ] granja *f*; casa *f* de campo; *Am.* asociación *f* agrícola.

gran·ite ['grænit] granito *m*; **gra·nit·ic** [græ'nitik] granítico.

gran·ny ['græni] F nana *f*, abuelita *f*; viejecita *f*.

grant [graːnt] 1. concesión *f*; otorgamiento *m*; donación *f*; (*subsidy*) subvención *f*; (*for study*) beca *f*, pensión *f*; 👥 cesión *f*; 2. conceder; otorgar, 👥 ceder; donar; asentir a; *take for* ~*ed* dar por supuesto, descontar; ~ed *that* dado que; ~*ing this* (*to*) *be so* dado que asi sea; *God* ~! ¡ojalá!, ¡Dios lo quiera!; **gran'tee** ⚖ cesionario (a *f*) *m*; **grant-in-aid** ['grɑːntin'eid] subvención *f*, pensión *f*; **grant-or** [~'tɔː] ⚖ cesionista *m*/*f*.

gran-u-lar ['grænjulə] granular; **gran-u-late** ['~leit] granular(se); **gran-u-la-tion** granulación *f*; **gran-ule** ['~juːl] gránulo *m*.

grape [greip] uva *f*; *unfermented* ~ *juice* mosto *m*; *sour* ~*s*! ¡están verdes!; '~**fruit** toronja *f*, pomelo *m*; '~**shot** metralla *f*; '~**sug-ar** glucosa *f*; '~**vine** vid *f*, parra *f*; *sl.* sistema de comunicación clandestina, rumores *m*/*pl.*

graph [grɑːf] gráfico *m*; ~ *paper* papel *m* cuadriculado; '**graph-ic** □ gráfico; ~*arts* artes *f*/*pl.* gráficas; **graph-ite** ['~fait] grafito *m*; **graph-ol-o-gy** [~'fɔlədʒi] grafología *f*.

grap-nel ['græpnəl] ⚓ rezón *m*, arpeo *m*; ✕ áncora *f*.

grap-ple ['græpl] 1. ⚓ arpeo *m*, rezón *m*; asimiento *m*; *wrestling:* presa *f*; ⊕ garfio *m*; 2. *v/t.* ⚓ aferrar; agarrar, asir; *v/i.*: ~ *with* ⚓ aferrar con; luchar (a brazo partido) con; *fig.* esforzarse por resolver; '**grap-pling-iron** arpeo *m*, garfio *m*.

grasp [grɑːsp] 1. agarro *m*, asimiento *m*; (*handclasp*) apretón *m*; (*power*) poder *m*; (*range*) alcance *m*, comprensión *f*; *have a good* ~ *of* saber a fondo; *within the* ~ *of* al alcance de; 2. *v/t.* agarrar, asir, empuñar; *hand* estrechar; apoderarse de; *fig.* comprender; *v/i.*: ~ *at* hacer por asir; '**grasp-ing** □ codicioso, tacaño.

grass [grɑːs] 1. hierba *f*; (*sward*) césped *m*; (*grazing*) pasto *m*; *go to* ~ ir al pasto; *fig.* descansar; *put out to* ~ echar al pasto; 2. cubrir de hierba; apacentar; '~**hop-per** saltamontes *m*; '~**land** pradera *f*; '~**plot** césped *m*; '~**roots** *Am.* básico; rústico, provinciano; popular; '~**wid-ow(-er)** F mujer *f* cuyo marido (hombre *m* cuya mujer) está ausente; '**grass-y** herboso; herbáceo.

grate[1] [greit] parrilla *f*; reja *f*; (*fireplace*) hogar *m*.

grate[2] [~] *v/t. food* rallar; *teeth* hacer

rechinar; *v/i.* rechinar; ~ (*up*)*on fig.* irritar; ~ *on the ear* herir el oído.

grate-ful ['greitful] □ agradecido, reconocido; *th.* grato, agradable; *be* ~ *for* agradecer.

grat-er ['greitə] rallador *m*.

grat-i-fi-ca-tion [grætifi'keiʃn] satisfacción *f*; placer *m*; **grat-i-fy** ['~fai] satisfacer; complacer; '**grat-i-fy-ing** satisfactorio; grato.

grat-ing ['greitiŋ] 1. □ rechinador, áspero; irritante; 2. reja *f*, verja *f*; rechinamiento *m*.

gra-tis ['greitis] 1. *adv.* gratis; 2. *adj.* gratuito.

grat-i-tude ['grætitjuːd] agradecimiento *m*, reconocimiento *m*, gratitud *f*.

gra-tu-i-tous [grə'tjuːitəs] □ gratuito; **gra-tu-i-ty** gratificación *f*.

gra-va-men [grə'veimen] ⚖ querella *f*; lo más grave (de una acusación).

grave[1] [greiv] grave (*a. gr.*); solemne; serio.

grave[2] [~] 1. fosa *f*, sepultura *f*; (*esp. monument*) tumba *f*, sepulcro *m*; 2. [*irr.*] grabar, esculpir; '~**dig-ger** sepulturero *m*, enterrador *m*.

grav-el ['grævl] 1. grava *f*, recebo *m*; ✚ litiasis *f*, arenillas *f*/*pl.*; 2. engravar, recebar; desconcertar; '**grav-el-ly** arenisco, cascajoso.

grav-en ['greivən] *p.p. of* grave; ~ *image* ídolo *m*.

grave...: '~**stone** lápida *f* sepulcral; '~**yard** cementerio *m*, campo *m* santo.

grav-ing dock ['greiviŋ'dɔk] dique *m* de carena.

grav-i-tate ['græviteit] gravitar; *fig.* dejarse atraer [*to*(*wards*) por]; **grav-i-ta-tion** gravitación *f*; **grav-i-ta-tion-al** gravitatorio, gravitacional.

grav-i-ty ['græviti] gravedad *f*; seriedad *f*, solemnidad *f*; *centre of* ~ centro *m* de gravedad; *specific* ~ peso *m* específico.

gra-vy ['greivi] salsa *f*; jugo *m* (de la carne); *Am. sl.* ganga *f*; '~**boat** salsera *f*.

gray [grei] = grey.

graze [greiz] 1. *v/t. grass* pacer; *cattle etc.* apacentar, pastar; *v/i.* pacer; 2. a) *v/t.* rozar; raspar; b) *su.* roce *m*, abrasión *f*, desolladura *f*.

gra·zier ['greiziə] ganadero *m*.

grease 1. [gri:z] engrasar; *v. palm²*; **2.** [gri:s] grasa *f*; (*dirt*) mugre *f*; '~-**box**, '~-**cup** vaso *m* de engrase, caja *f* de sebo; '~-**gun** *mot.* engrasador *m* de compresión; '~-**paint** maquillaje *m*; '~-**proof** impermeable a la grasa; *paper* apergaminado; **greas·er** ['gri:zə] engrasador *m*; *Am. sl. contp.* hispanoamericano *m*; '**greas·ing** *mot.*, ⊕ engrase *m*.

greas·y ['gri:zi] □ grasiento, pringoso; *surface* resbaladizo; *p.* adulón.

great [greit] **1.** gran(de); enorme, vasto; importante; *lit.* magno; principal; mucho; *time* largo; F excelente, estupendo; F ~ *at* fuerte en; ~ *on* aficionado a; **2.** the ~ los grandes; '~-**aunt** tía abuela *f*; '~-**coat** sobretodo *m*; '~-'**grand·child** bisnieto (a *f*) *m*; '~-'**grand·fa·ther** bisabuelo *m*; '~-'**grand·moth·er** bisabuela *f*; '~-'~-'**grand·fa·ther** tatarabuelo *m*; '~-'~-'**grand·son** tataranieto *m*; '~-'**heart·ed** magnánimo, valiente; '**great·ly** grandemente, mucho, muy; '**great·ness** grandeza *f*. [pullín *m*.]

grebe [gri:b] somormujo *m*, zam-

Gre·cian ['gri:ʃn] griego.

greed [gri:d], '**greed·i·ness** codicia *f*, avaricia *f*; voracidad *f*, gula *f*; '**greed·y** □ codicioso, avaro; (*for food*) goloso, voraz.

Greek [gri:k] **1.** griego *adj. a. su. m* (a *f*); **2.** (*language*) griego *m*; *that is ~ to me* no entiendo palabra.

green [gri:n] **1.** verde; fresco; *complexion* pálido; (*raw*) crudo; F (*inexperienced*) novato; F (*credulous*) crédulo, bobo; *grow ~, look ~* verdear; **2.** verde *m*; prado *m*; césped *m*; ~*s pl.* verduras *f/pl.*; *bright ~* verdegay *adi. a. su. m*; *dark ~* verdinegro; '~-**back** *Am.* billete *m* de banco; '~(-'**baize**) **table** tapete *m* verde; '**green·er·y** verde *m*, verdura *f*.

green···: '~-**finch** verderón *m* común; '~-**fly** pulgón *m*; '~-'**gage** claudia *f*; '~-**gro·cer** verdulero (a *f*) *m*; '~-**gro·cer·y** verdulería *f*; '~-**horn** bisoño *m*; bobo *m*; '~-**house** invernáculo *m*; '**green·ish** verdoso.

Green·land·er ['gri:nləndə] groenlandés (-a *f*) *m*.

green light F señal *f* para seguir adelante, autorización *f*; '**green·ness** verdor *m*; F inexperiencia *f*, credulidad *f*.

green···: '~-**stuff** verduras *f/pl.*; '~-**sward** césped *m*.

greet [gri:t] saludar; recibir; *senses* presentarse a; (*welcome*) dar la bienvenida a; '**greet·ing** saludo *m*, salutación *f*; (*welcome*) bienvenida *f*; ~*s* (*in letters*) recuerdos *m/pl.*, expresiones *f/pl.*

gre·gar·i·ous [gre'geəriəs] □ gregario; sociable.

grem·lin ['gremlin] ✕ *sl.* duendecillo *m*.

gre·nade [gri'neid] ✕ granada *f*; **gren·a·dier** [grenə'diə] granadero *m*.

grew [gru:] *pret. of* grow.

grey [grei] **1.** □ gris (*a. fig.*); *horse* rucio; *weather* pardo; ♀ *Friar* franciscano *m*; ~ *hair(s)* canas *f/pl.*; ~ *matter anat.* materia *f* gris, seso *m*; **2.** (*colour*) gris *m*; (*horse*) (caballo) rucio *m*; **3.** volver(se) gris; (*hair*) encanecer; '~-'**haired**, '~-'**head·ed** canoso; '**grey·hound** galgo *m*, lebrel *m*; '**grey·ish** grisáceo; *hair* entrecano.

grid [grid] reja *f*; parrilla *f*; ⚡ red *f*; *radio:* rejilla *f*; *mot. sl.* armatoste *m*, rácano *m*; '**grid·i·ron** parrilla *f*; reja *f*; *Am.* campo *m* de fútbol; 🔲 emparrillado *m*.

grief [gri:f] dolor *m*, pesar *m*, aflicción *f*; *come to ~* malograrse; sobrevenirle *a una p.* una desgracia.

griev·ance ['gri:vəns] agravio *m*; motivo *m* de queja; **grieve** [gri:v] afligir(se), acongojar(se) (*at, over* de, por); ~ *for* llorar; '**griev·ous** □ doloroso, penoso; opresivo; lamentable, grave; '**griev·ous·ness** gravedad *f*, opresión *f*; dolor *m*.

grill [gril] **1.** parrilla *f*; (*meat*) asado *m* a la parrilla; **2.** asar a la parrilla; *sl.* atormentar, interrogar; '~-**room** parrilla *f*.

grille [gril] rejilla *f*; (*window*) reja *f*; (*screen*) verja *f*.

grim [grim] □ severo; ceñudo; feroz; inflexible; horroroso; F muy aburrido, desagradable; ~ *facts* hechos *m/pl.* inexorables.

gri·mace [gri'meis] **1.** mueca *f*, gesto *m*, visaje *m*; **2.** hacer muecas (*or* visajes).

gri·mal·kin [gri'mælkin] gato *m*; gata *f* vieja.

grime [graim] 1. mugre *f*; tizne *mst m*; 2. enmugrecer; 'grim·y □ mugriento, sucio.

grin [grin] 1. sonrisa *f* (abierta *or* burlona *or* feroz); (*grimace*) mueca *f*; 2. sonreír (mostrando los dientes *or* irónicamente *or* ferozmente); ~ *and bear it* poner al mal tiempo buena cara.

grind [graind] 1. [*irr.*] *v/t.* moler; pulverizar; (*sharpen*) amolar, afilar; *teeth etc.* hacer rechinar; *dentistry*: desgastar; (*oppress*) oprimir; ~ *down* desgastar; pulverizar; F oprimir, agobiar; ~ *out* (re)producir mecánicamente (*or* laboriosamente); *v/i.* moler(se); trabajar (*or* estudiar) laboriosamente; F quemarse las cejas; 2. molienda *f*; F trabajo *m* de negros; F rutina *f*; 'grind·er amolador *m*, afilador *m*; (*coffee etc.*) molin(ill)o *m*; (*stone, tooth*) muela *f*; 'grind·ing 1. pulverización *f*; amoladura *f*; molienda *f*; (*teeth*) rechinamiento *m*; *dentistry*: desgaste *m*; 2. opresivo, agobiante; 'grind·stone muela *f*, piedra *f* de amolar; *keep one's nose to the* ~ batir el yunque.

grip [grip] 1. asir, agarrar; (*squeeze*) apretar; *wheel* agarrarse (a); *fig.* absorber la atención (a); 2. asimiento *m*, agarro *m*; (*handle*) agarradero *m*, empuñadura *f*; (*clutches*) garras *f/pl.*; (*handshake*) apretón *m*; *fig.* dominio *m*, comprensión *f*; (*bag*) maletín *m* (con cremallera); *come to* ~*s with* luchar (a brazo partido) con; F *lose one's* ~ estar desbordado.

gripe [graip] 1. *esp.* ~*s pl.* retortijón *m* de tripas; 2. dar cólico a; *Am. sl.* quejarse.

grip·sack ['gripsæk] *Am.* maletín *m*.

gris·ly ['grizli] horripilante, espantoso; F desagradable.

grist [grist] molienda *f*; *all is* ~ *that comes to his mill* saca partido de todo.

gris·tle ['grisl] ternilla *f*, cartílago *m*; 'gris·tly ternilloso, cartilaginoso.

grit [grit] 1. arena *f*, cascajo *m*; *geol.* arenisca *f*; F valor *m*, firmeza *f*; ~*s* cereales *m/pl.* a medio moler; 2. (hacer) rechinar; 'grit·ty arenisco.

griz·zle ['grizl] F gimotear; 'griz-

zled = *grizzly* 1; 'griz·zly 1. gris, grisáceo; canoso; 2. oso *m* gris.

groan [groun] 1. gemido *m*, quejido *m*; 2. gemir, quejarse; (*with weight*) crujir.

groats [grouts] *pl.* avena *f* a medio moler.

gro·cer ['grousə] tendero (a *f*) *m* (de ultramarinos), abacero (a *f*) *m*; abarrotero (a *f*) *m S. Am.*; **gro·cer·ies** ['~riz] *pl.* comestibles *m/pl.*, ultramarinos *m/pl.*; abarrotes *m/pl. S.Am.*; 'gro·cer's (shop), 'gro·cery store tienda *f* de ultramarinos (*or* de comestibles), abacería *f*, colmado *m*; tienda *f* de abarrotes *S.Am.*

grog [grɔg] grog *m*; 'grog·gy F vacilante, inseguro; turulato; débil; † calamocano; *boxing*: grogui.

groin [grɔin] *anat.* ingle *f*; △ arista *f* de encuentro.

groom [grum] 1. mozo *m* de caballos; *palace*: gentilhombre *m*; lacayo *m*; = *bridegroom*; 2. *horse* almohazar, cuidar; *p.* acicalar; *fig.* preparar (para un puesto *or* para la vida pública); *well-*~*ed* acicalado; elegante.

groove [gru:v] 1. ranura *f*, estría *f*, acanaladura *f*; *gramophone record*: surco *m*; *fig.* rutina *f*; 2. estriar, acanalar.

grope [group] andar a tientas; ~ *one's way* tentar el camino; ~ *for* buscar (a tientas).

gross [grous] 1. □ *size*: grueso, espeso; enorme; total; † bruto; *character* grosero; *error etc.* craso; 2. gruesa *f*; *by the* ~ en gruesas; *in* (*the*) ~ en grueso; al por mayor; 'gross·ness gordura *f*, grosería *f*; enormidad *f*.

gro·tesque [grou'tesk] □ grotesco.

grot·to ['grɔtou] gruta *f*.

grouch [grautʃ] *Am.* F 1. mal humor *m*; 2. estar de mal humor, refunfuñar; 'grouch·y F malhumorado, refunfuñador.

ground[1] [graund] *pret. a. p.p. of grind*; ~ *glass* vidrio *m* deslustrado.

ground[2] [~] 1. suelo *m*; (*earth a.* ⚡) tierra *f*; terreno *m* (*a. fig.*); *sport*: campo *m*; ⚓ fondo *m*; (*reason*) causa *f*, motivo *m*; (*basis*) fundamento *m*; *paint.* primera capa *f*, fondo *m*; ~*s pl.* terreno *m*, jardines *m/pl.*; *fig.* fundamento *m*, motivo *m*; (*sediment*) poso *m*; F *down to the* ~ completa-

mente, como un guante; *on the* ~
sobre el terreno; *on the* ~(s) *of* con
motivo de, en virtud de; *on the*
~(s) *that* porque, por *inf.*; pretex-
tando que; *fall to the* ~ venirse al
suelo (*a. fig.*); *give* ~ ceder terreno;
hold (*or stand*) *one's* ~ mantenerse
firme; 2. ⚓ (hacer) varar; poner
en tierra; ⚡ conectar con tierra;
establecer; basar; enseñar los rudimentos (*in de*); ✈ *be* ~*ed* no poder
despegar; *well* ~*ed* bien fundado;
versado (*in* en).

ground...: '~-**'floor** piso *m* bajo,
planta *f* baja; '~-**less** ☐ infundado;
'~-**nut** cacahuete *m*; '~-**'plan**
planta *f*; '~-**'rent** *approx.* canon *m*.
ground·sel ['graunsl] ♣ hierba *f*
cana.

ground...: '~-**staff** ✈ personal *m* de
tierra; '~-**'swell** mar *m* de fondo;
'~-**wire** ⚡ toma *f* de tierra; '~-**work**
fundamento *m*, cimiento *m*.

group [gru:p] 1. grupo *m*, agrupación
f; 2. agrupar(se); 3. colectivo.

grouse[1] [graus] *orn. black* ~ gallo *m*
lira; *red* ~ lagópodo *m* escocés.

grouse[2] [~] F 1. (motivo *m* de)
queja *f*; 2. quejarse, refunfuñar.

grove [grouv] soto *m*, arboleda *f*,
boscaje *m*.

grov·el ['grɔvl] arrastrarse; envile-
cerse; **'grov·el·(l)er** persona *f* servil; **'grov·el·(l)ing** 1. rastrero, servil; 2. servilismo *m*.

grow [grou] [*irr.*] *v/i.* crecer; culti-
varse; (*become*) hacerse, ponerse,
volverse; ~ *a. adj. is often translated by v/i. or v/r. corresponding to
adj.:* ~ *angry* enfadarse; ~ *cold* enfriarse; ~ *dark* oscurecer(se); ~ *fat*
engordar; ~ *old* envejecer(se); ~
into hacerse, llegar a ser; F ~ *on a p.*
gustar cada vez más a una p.; (*habit*)
arraigar en una p.; ~ *out of* resultar
de; *clothes* hacérsele pequeña a una
p. la ropa; *habit* perder (con el
tiempo); ~ *to inf.* llegar a *inf.*; ~ *up*
hacerse hombre (*or* mujer) (*custom*) imponerse; **'grow·er** cultivador (-a *f*) *m*.

growl [graul] 1. gruñido *m*; rezongo *m*; 2. gruñir, regañar; rezongar; decir rezongando.

growl·er ['graulə] gruñón (-a *f*) *m*;
Am. sl. jarro *m* para cerveza.

grown [groun] 1. *p.p of grow*;
2. *adj.* crecido, adulto, maduro; ~

over with cubierto de; '~-**'up** 1. *adj.*
adulto; 2. *su.* persona *f* mayor;
growth [grouθ] crecimiento *m*;
desarrollo *m*; aumento *m*; cobertura *f*, vegetación *f*; ✱ tumor *m*;
3 days' ~ *on the chin* barba *f* de
3 días.

grub [grʌb] 1. larva *f*, gusano *m*;
contp. puerco (a *f*) *m*; *sl.* alimento
m, comida *f*; 2. *v/t.* desmalezar; (*a.*
~ *out*, ~ *up*) arrancar, desenterrar;
v/i. cavar; afanarse (*a.* ~ *away*);
emplearse en oficios bajos; ~ *for* buscar (cavando *or* laboriosamente);
'grub·by sucio, mugriento; **'grub-
stake** *Am.* anticipo *m* (*dado a un
explorador minero*) *a cambio de una
participación en los beneficios.*

grudge [grʌdʒ] 1. (motivo *m* de)
rencor *m*, inquina *f*, resentimiento
m; *bear* (*or have*) *a* ~ *against* guardar rencor a; 2. escatimar, dar de
mala gana; envidiar; ~ *no pains* no
perdonar esfuerzos; **grudg·ing·ly**
['~iŋli] de mala gana.

gru·el ['gruəl] *approx.* gachas *f/pl.*;
'gru·el·(l)ing 1. castigo *m*; 2. riguroso, penoso.

grue·some ['gru:səm] ☐ pavoroso,
horripilante.

gruff [grʌf] ☐ *voice* (b)ronco; *manner* brusco, malhumorado.

grum·ble ['grʌmbl] 1. queja *f*,
regaño *m*; ruido *m* sordo; 2. quejarse (*at* de); murmurar; refunfuñar; (*thunder*) retumbar (a lo
lejos); **'grum·bler** murmurador
(-a *f*) *m*, gruñón (-a *f*) *m*.

grump·y ['grʌmpi] ☐ F malhumorado, gruñón.

grunt [grʌnt] 1. gruñido *m*; 2. gruñir.

guar·an·tee [gærən'ti:] 1. garantía *f*;
persona *f* de quien se saca fiador;
garante *m/f*, fiador (-a *f*) *m*; 2. garantizar; F asegurar; **guar·an·tor**
[~'tɔ:] garante *m/f*; **'guar·an·ty**
garantía *f*.

guard [gɑ:d] 1. (*in general, p., act,
a. of sword*) guarda *f*; (*fencing*, ✗
duty, regiment) guardia *f*; (*soldier*)
guardia *m*; (*sentry*) centinela *m*;
(*safeguard*) resguardo *m*; ⚒ jefe *m*
de tren; ~*'s van* furgón *m*; *off* (*one's*)
~ desprevenido; *on* ~ en guardia;
✗ de guardia; alerta; *change* ~ relevar la guardia; *mount* ~ montar la
guardia; 2. *v/t.* guardar, proteger,

defender (*against, from* de); vigilar;
escoltar; *v/i.* ~ *against* guardarse de;
'guard·ed ☐ guardado; cauteloso,
reservado, circunspecto; **'guard·i-
an** guardián (-a *f*) *m*; protector (-a
f) *m*; ₷ tutor (-a *f*) *m*; ~ *angel*
ángel *m* custodio (*or* de la guarda);
'guard·i·an·ship ₷ tutela *f*; protección *f*; **guards·man** ['gɑ:dz-
mən] ⚔ guardia *m*.

Gua·te·ma·lan [gwɑti'mɑ:lən] guatemalteco *adj. a. su. m* (a *f*).

gua·va ['gwɑ:və] guayaba *f*.

gudg·eon ['gʌdʒən] *ichth.* gobio *m*;
fig. bobo (a *f*) *m*; ⊕ gorrón *m*; ⊕
cuello *m* de eje; **'~-pin** perno *m* de
émbolo.

gue(r)·ril·la [gə'rilə] guerrilla *f*;
guerrillero (a *f*) *m*; ~ *war(fare*)
guerra *f* de guerrillas.

guess [ges] **1.** adivinación *f*, conjetura *f*, suposición *f*; **2.** adivinar,
conjeturar, suponer; *esp. Am.* creer;
~ *at* conjeturar, estimar aproximadamente; **'guess·work** conjetu-
ra(s) *f(pl.).*

guest [gest] huésped (-a *f*) *m*; (*at
meal*) convidado (a *f*) *m*; **'guest-
house** casa *f* de huéspedes.

guf·faw [gʌ'fɔ:] **1.** risotada *f*;
2. reírse a carcajadas.

guid·ance ['gaidəns] gobierno *m*,
conducta *f*, dirección *f*; consejo *m*.

guide [gaid] **1.** (*p.*) guía *m/f*; (*book*,
⊕, *fig. etc.*) guía *f; attr.* de guía;
Girl ♀ exploradora *f*; **2.** guiar; orientar; gobernar; ~*d missile* proyectil *m*
(tele)dirigido; **'~-book** guía *f* (del
viajero); **'~-post** poste *m* indicador.

guild [gild] gremio *m*; cofradía *f*;
'Guild'hall casa *f* de ayuntamiento
(*esp. London*).

guile [gail] astucia *f*, maña *f*, malicia *f*, engaño *m*; **guile·ful** ['~ful] ☐
astuto, mañoso; **'guile·less** ☐ cándido, inocente, sincero.

guil·le·mot ['gilimɔt] arao *m* común.

guil·lo·tine [gilə'ti:n] **1.** guillotina *f*
(*a.* ⊕); **2.** guillotinar.

guilt [gilt] culpa(bilidad) *f* (*a.*
'guilt·i·ness); **'guilt·less** ☐ libre
de culpa, inocente (*of* de); **'guilt·y**
☐ culpable; *plead* ~ confesarse culpable.

guin·ea ['gini] guinea *f* (= *21 chelines*); **'~-fowl** gallina *f* de Guinea;
'~-pig cobayo *m*.

guise [gaiz] apariencia *f*; traje *m*;
manera *f*; pretexto *m*; *in the* ~ *of*
disfrazado de; *under the* ~ *of* so capa
de.

gui·tar [gi'tɑ:] guitarra *f*; **guit·ar-
ist** guitarrista *m/f.*

gulch [gʌltʃ] *Am.* barranco *m.*

gulf [gʌlf] golfo *m*; abismo *m* (*a.
fig.*); vorágine *f.*

gull¹ [gʌl] *orn.* gaviota *f.*

gull² [~] **1.** primo *m*, bobo *m*; **2.** engañar; inducir con engaños (*into* a).

gul·let ['gʌlit] esófago *m*; garganta *f.*

gul·li·bil·i·ty [gʌli'biliti] credulidad
f, tragaderas *f/pl.*; **gul·li·ble** ['~əbl]
crédulo, simplón.

gul·ly ['gʌli] barranco *m*, hondonada
f; canal *m*; (*a.* '**~-hole**) (*gutter*)
arroyo *m*, alcantarilla *f.*

gulp [gʌlp] **1.** trago *m*, sorbo *m*;
2. *v/t.* (*a.* ~ *down*) tragar, engullir;
emotion ahogar; *v/i.* ahogarse momentáneamente.

gum¹ [gʌm] *anat.* encía *f.*

gum² [~] **1.** goma *f*; (*chewing-*) chicle
m; (*adhesive*) cola *f*; ~*s pl. Am.*
chanclos *m/pl.* de goma; **2.** engomar, pegar con goma; F (*esp.* ~ *up*)
atascar; **'~-boots** botas *f/pl.* de goma; **'~-tree** gomero *m*, eucalipto
m; F *up a* ~ en un aprieto; **'gummy** gomoso.

gum·boil ['gʌmbɔil] flemón *m.*

gump [gʌmp] F majadero *m.*

gump·tion ['gʌmpʃn] F sentido *m*
común; *Am.* energía *f.*

gun [gʌn] **1.** arma *f* de fuego; cañón
m; (*sporting*) escopeta *f*; (*rifle*) fusil
m; *Am.* F revólver *m*, pistola *f*; (*shot*)
cañonazo *m*; F *big* (*or great*) ~
pájaro *m* gordo; *stick to one's* ~*s*
seguir en sus trece; *a 21-*~ *salute*
una salva de 21 cañonazos; **2.** *Am.* F
andar a caza (*for* de); **'~-boat** cañonero *m*; **'~-car·riage** cureña *f*; **'~-
cot·ton** algodón *m* pólvora; **'~-fire**
cañoneo *m*; **'~-li·cence** licencia *f* de
armas; **'~-man** gángster *m*, pistolero *m*; **'~-met·al** bronce *m* de cañón; **'gun·ner** ⚔, ⚓, ⚔ artillero *m.*
gun...: **'~-pow·der** pólvora *f*; **'~-
run·ning** contrabando *m* de ar-
mas; **'~-shot** cañonazo *m*, escopetazo *m*, tiro *m* de fusil; *within* ~ a
tiro de fusil; **'~-smith** escopetero *m*,
armero *m*; **'~-stock** caja *f* (de fusil);
'~-tur·ret torre(ta) *f*; **gun·wale**
['gʌnəl] borda *f*, regala *f.*

gur·gle ['gəːgl] **1.** (*liquid*) gluglú *m*, gorgoteo *m*; (*baby*) gorjeo *m*; **2.** gorgotear, hacer gluglú; (*baby*) gorjear(se).

gush [gʌʃ] **1.** chorro *m*, borbotón *m*; *fig.* efusión *f*; **2.** chorrear, borbotar; manar a borbotones (*from de*); *fig.* hacer extremos; **'gush·er** pozo *m* de petróleo; *fig.* persona *f* efusiva; **'gush·ing** □ *fig.* efusivo.

gus·set ['gʌsit] escudete *m*.

gust [gʌst] ráfaga *f*, racha *f*; *fig.* acceso *m*, arrebato *m*, explosión *f*.

gus·to ['gʌstou] gusto *m*; entusiasmo *m*.

gus·ty ['gʌsti] borrascoso.

gut [gʌt] **1.** intestino *m*, tripa *f*; cuerda *f* de tripa; ⚓ estrecho *m*; *Am. sl.* descaro *m*; ~s *sl.* agallas *f/pl.*; F sustancia *f*; **2.** destripar; saquear (*or* destruir) lo interior de.

gut·ta·per·cha ['gʌtə'pəːtʃə] gutapercha *f*.

gut·ter ['gʌtə] **1.** *street*: arroyo *m*; *roadside*: cuneta *f*; *roof*: canal *m*, gotera *f*; *fig.* barrios *m/pl.* bajos; **2.** *v/t.* acanalar; *v/i.* gotear; (*candle*) correrse; ~ **press** prensa *f* sensacional(ista); '~**-snipe** golfillo *m*.

gut·tur·al ['gʌtərəl] □ (sonido *m*) gutural.

guy[1] [gai] **1.** muñeco *m*, mamarracho *m*; espantajo *m*; *Am.* F tío *m*, tipo *m*; **2.** ridiculizar.

guy[2] [~] (*a.* ~ *rope*) viento *m*; retenida *f*.

guz·zle ['gʌzl] tragar, engullir; beber con exceso.

gym [dʒim] = *gymnasium*.

gym·kha·na [dʒim'kɑːnə] fiesta *f* deportiva.

gym·na·si·um [dʒim'neizjəm] gimnasio *m*; **gym·nast** ['dʒimnæst] gimnasta *m/f*; **gym'nas·tic 1.** □ gimnástico; **2.** ~s *pl.* gimnasia *f*.

gyn·ae·col·o·gist [gaini'kɔlədʒist] ginecólogo *m*; **gyn·ae'col·o·gy** ginecología *f*.

gyp [dʒip] *sl.* **1.** estafa *f*; estafador *m*; **2.** estafar.

gyp·se·ous ['dʒipsiəs] yesoso.

gyp·sum ['dʒipsəm] yeso *m*.

gy·rate [dʒaiə'reit] girar; **gy'ra·tion** giro *m*, vuelta *f*; **gy·ra·to·ry** ['dʒaiərətəri] giratorio.

gy·ro·com·pass ['dʒaiərə'kʌmpəs] brújula *f* giroscópica, girocompás *m*; **gy·ro·scope** ['gaiərəskoup] giroscopio *m*; **gy·ro·scop·ic** [~'kɔpik] giroscópico.

gyve [dʒaiv] *poet.* **1.** ~s *pl.* grillos *m/pl.*; **2.** engrillar.

H

h [eitʃ]: *drop one's h's* hablar con poca corrección.

ha [haː] ¡ah!

ha·be·as cor·pus ['heibiæs 'kɔːpəs] hábeas corpus *m*.

hab·er·dash·er ['hæbədæʃə] mercero (a *f*) *m*; *Am.* camisero (a *f*) *m*; ∼'s (*shop*) mercería *f*; *Am.* camisería *f*; **'hab·er·dash·er·y** mercería *f*.

hab·it ['hæbit] costumbre *f*; hábito *m* (*a. dress*); *v. riding-*∼; *be in the* ∼ *of ger.* acostumbrar *inf.*, soler *inf.*; **'hab·it·a·ble** habitable, vividero; **hab·i·tat** ['∼tæt] habitat *m*, habitación *f*; **hab·i·'ta·tion** habitación *f*; **'hab·it·'form·ing** que conduce al hábito morboso.

ha·bit·u·al [hə'bitjuəl] □ habitual, acostumbrado; **ha'bit·u·ate** [∼eit] habituar, acostumbrar (*to* a); **ha·'bit·u·é** [∼ei] habituado (a *f*) *m*, asiduo (a *f*) *m*.

hack¹ [hæk] 1. ⊕ piqueta *f*; corte *m*, hachazo *m*; mella *f*; puntapié *m* (en la espinilla); 2. cortar, acuchillar; picar; mellar; dar un puntapié (en la espinilla); ∼*ing cough* tos *f* seca.

hack² [∼] 1. caballo *m* de alquiler; rocín *m*; (*a.* ∼*-writer*) escritorzuelo (a *f*) *m*, plumífero (a *f*) *m*; 2. de alquiler; mercenario; *fig.* trillado, gastado, sin originalidad.

hack·le ['hækl] ⊕ rastrillo *m*; *orn.* plumas *f/pl.* del pescuezo.

hack·ney ['hækni] = *hack²* 1, 2; ∼ *carriage* coche *m* de alquiler; **'hack·neyed** *v. hack² 2 fig.*

hack·saw ['hæksɔː] sierra *f* de arco para metales.

had [hæd, həd] *pret. a. p.p. of* have.

had·dock ['hædək] eglefino *m*.

Had·es ['heidiːz] F infierno *m*.

haem·or·rhage ['hemɔridʒ] hemorragia *f*; **haem·or·rhoids** ['∼rɔidz] *pl.* hemorroides *f/pl.*

haft [haːft] mango *m*, puño *m*.

hag [hæg] (*mst fig.*) bruja *f*; F callo *m*.   [trasojado, trasnochado.⟩

hag·gard ['hægəd] □ macilento;⟩

hag·gish ['hægiʃ] □ de bruja.

hag·gle ['hægl] (*a.* ∼ *over*) regatear; **'hag·gling** 1. regateo *m*; 2. regatón.

hag·rid·den ['hægridn] atormentado (por una pesadilla); F dominado por una mujer.

hail¹ [heil] 1. granizo *m*, pedrisco *m*; *fig.* granizada *f*; 2. granizar (*a. fig.*).

hail² [∼] 1. *v/t.* llamar; saludar; aclamar; *v/i.*: ∼ *from* proceder de, ser natural de; 2. llamada *f*, grito *m*; saludo *m*; ∼! ¡salud!, ¡salve!; *within* ∼ al habla.

hail·stone ['heilstoun] piedra *f* de granizo; **'hail·storm** granizada *f*.

hair [hɛə] pelo *m*; cabello *m*; (*head of*) ∼ cabellera *f*; (*down*) vello *m*; *sl. keep your* ∼ *on!* ¡serénate!; F *let one's* ∼ *down* echar una cana al aire; *tear one's* ∼ mesarse los cabellos; F *not to turn a* ∼ no inmutarse; ∼'s *breadth* (ancho *m* de un) pelo *m*; *escape by a* ∼'s *breadth* escapar por un pelo; '∼·**brush** cepillo *m* para el cabello; '∼·**cut** corte *m* de pelo; *get a* ∼ hacerse cortar el pelo; '∼·**do** F peinado *m*; '∼·**dress·er** peluquero (a *f*) *m*; ∼'s (*shop*) peluquería *f*; '∼·**dry·er** secador *m* para el pelo.

hair...: '∼·**less** sin pelo; pelón, calvo; '∼·**net** redecilla *f*; '∼·**pin** horquilla *f*; ∼ *bend* viraje *m* en horquilla; '∼·**rais·ing** horripilante, espeluznante; '∼·**split·ting** 1. quisquilla *f*, argucia *f*; 2. quisquilloso; **'hair·y** peludo, velloso.

hake [heik] merluza *f*.

hal·cy·on ['hælsiən] 1. alción *m*; 2. apacible, feliz.

hale [heil] sano, robusto; ∼ *and hearty* sano y fuerte.

half [haːf] 1. *su.* mitad *f*; *school:* trimestre *m*; ⚼ parte *f*; ∼ *and* ∼ mitad y mitad; F *better* ∼ cara mitad *f*; *by* ∼ con mucho; ∼ *halves* a medias; *go halves with* ir a medias con; *in* ∼ en dos mitades; 2. *adj.* medio, semi...; ∼ *a crown,* ∼*-crown* media corona *f*; *a pound and a* ∼; *one and a* ∼ *pounds* libra *f* y media;

two and a ~ hours, two hours and a ~
dos horas *f/pl.* y media; **3.** *adv.*
medio, a medias, mitad, semi...;
casi; *~ asleep* medio dormido, semi-
dormido, dormido a medias; *~
dressed* a medio vestir; F *not ~*
mucho; F *not ~!* ¡ya lo creo!; F
not ~ bad bastante bueno; **~-back**
['ˌʌˈbæk] medio *m*;~-**baked** ['ˌʌˈbeikt]
fig. poco maduro, incompleto;
'**~-bind·ing** media pasta *f*;
'**~-bound** encuadernado en media
pasta; '**~-bred** mestizo; '**~-breed**
mestizo (a *f*) *m*; '**~-broth·er** medio
hermano *m*; '**~-caste** mestizo *adj.
a. su. m* (a *f*); '**~-full** a medio
llenar, mediado; '**~-heart·ed** □ sin
ánimo, indiferente; *effort* débil;
'**~-hol·i·day** medio día *m* festivo;
'**~-length** de medio cuerpo;
'**~-mast:** (*at*) *~* a media asta;
'**~-meas·ure** medida *f* poco eficaz;
'**~-moon** media luna *f*; '**~-mourn-
ing** medio luto *m*; '**~-pay** media
paga *f*; **~-pen·ny** ['heipni] **1.** medio
penique *m*; **2.** de medio penique;
'**~-price** a mitad de precio;
~-seas-o·ver ['haːfsiːzˈouvə] F calamocano; '**~-time** *sport*: descanso *m*; '**~-tone** fotograbado *m*
a media tinta; '**~-truth** verdad *f*
a medias; '**~-way 1.** *adv.* a medio
camino; **2.** *adj.* intermedio; *~ between* equidistante de; *~ house*
venta *f* situada a mitad del camino;
fig. punto *m* intermedio, término *m*
medio; '**~-wit·ted** imbécil; '**~-
'year·ly** semestral.
hal·i·but ['hælibət] halibut *m*.
hall [hɔːl] vestíbulo *m*; sala *f*; recibimiento *m*; casa *f* señorial; =
guild~, music~, *town ~*; *univ.*: residencia *f*; comedor *m*; paraninfo *m*.
hal·le·lu·jah [hæliˈluːjə] aleluya *f*.
hall·mark ['hɔːlmaːk] **1.** marca *f* del
contraste; *fig.* sello *m*; **2.** contrastar;
fig. sellar.
hal·lo [həˈlou] *v.* hullo.
hal·loo [həˈluː] **1.** ¡hola!; *hunt.*
¡sus!; **2.** grita *f*; llamada *f*; **3.** llamar; *hunt.* azuzar.
hal·low ['hælou] santificar; **Hall-
low-e'en** ['ˌʌiːn] víspera *f* de Todos
los Santos.
hall-stand ['hɔːlˈstænd] perchero *m*.
hal·lu·ci·na·tion [həluːsiˈneiʃn] alucinación *f*.
ha·lo ['heilou] halo *m*; *fig.* aureola *f*.

halt [hɔːlt] **1.** alto *m*, parada *f*; 🚋
apeadero *m*; interrupción *f*; *call a ~*
mandar hacer alto; *call a ~ to*
atajar; *come to a ~* pararse; inte-
rrumpirse; **2.** hacer alto; parar(se);
(*hesitate*) vacilar; † (*be lame*) cojear;
(*stammer*) tartamudear; **3.** cojo;
4. *~!* ¡alto!
hal·ter ['hɔːltə] cabestro *m*, ronzal
m; (*noose*) dogal *m*.
halt·ing ['hɔːltiŋ] □ vacilante, titubeante.
halve [haːv] **1.** partir por mitad;
2. halves [ˌʌz] *pl. of* half.
hal·yard ['hæljəd] driza *f*.
ham [hæm] jamón *m*, pernil *m*; *sl.*
~ (*actor*) comicastro *m*, maleta *m*;
sl. radio: radioaficionado *m*.
ham·burg·er ['hæmbəːgə] hamburguesa *f*.
ham·let ['hæmlit] aldehuela *f*, caserío *m*.
ham·mer ['hæmə] **1.** martillo *m*;
♪ macillo *m*; percusor *m of firearm*;
F *~ and tongs* violentamente, a más
no poder; *come under the ~* subas-
tarse; **2.** martillar; batir; (*a. ~ in*)
clavar (con martillo); *Stock Exchange:* declarar insolvente; *~
(away) at* trabajar asiduamente en;
insistir con ahinco en; *~ out* extender bajo el martillo; *fig.* elaborar
(trabajosamente).
ham·mock ['hæmək] hamaca *f*; ⚓
coy *m*.
ham·per ['hæmpə] **1.** cesto *m*, canasta *f*, excusabaraja *f*; **2.** estorbar,
embarazar, impedir.
ham·ster ['hæmstə] hámster *m*.
ham·string ['hæmstriŋ] **1.** tendón *m*
de la corva; **2.** desjarretar; *fig.* incapacitar.
hand [hænd] **1.** mano *f*; (*worker*)
operario (a *f*) *m*, obrero (a *f*) *m*,
peón *m*; (*measure*) palmo *m*; manecilla *f of clock*; aguja *f of instrument*;
(*writing*) escritura *f*; (*signature*)
firma *f*; aplausos *m/pl.*; *fig.* habilidad *f*; *fig.* influencia *f*; *all ~s* ⚓
toda la tripulación; *fig.* todos *m/pl.*;
at ~ a mano; *at first ~* de primera
mano, directamente; *at the ~s of*
de manos de; *be an old ~* ser perro
viejo; *be a good ~ at* tener buena
mano para; *~ in glove* uña y carne;
bear a ~ arrimar el hombro; *by ~*
a mano; *change ~s* cambiar de
dueño; *live from ~ to* mouth vivir

de la mano a la boca; *get one's* ~ *in* hacerse la mano; *have a* ~ *in* tomar parte en, tener mano en; *have a free* ~ tener carta blanca; *keep one's* ~ *in* conservar la práctica (*at de,* en); *in* ~ entre manos; *money* contante; dominado; *put in* ~ empezar; *take in* ~ hacerse cargo de; disciplinar; entrenar; *lay* ~*s on* echar mano a; conseguir; *eccl.* imponer las manos a; *lend a* ~ arrimar el hombro; ~*s off!* ¡fuera las manos!; *keep one's* ~*s off* no tocar; *on* ~ a la mano; entre manos; disponible; *on one's* ~*s* a su cargo; *on all* ~*s* por todas partes; *on the one* ~ por una parte; *on the other* ~ por otra parte; *out of* ~ en seguida; desmandado; ~ *over fist* rápidamente; *take a* ~ tomar parte, intervenir (*at, in* en); *to* (*one's*) ~ a mano; ~ *to* ~ cuerpo a cuerpo; *come to* ~ venir a mano; (*letter*) llegar a las manos; *put one's* ~ *to* emprender; firmar; *turn one's* ~ *to* dedicarse a; *he can turn his* ~ *to anything* vale tanto para un barrido como para un fregado; ~*s up!* ¡arriba las manos!; *v. high;* **2.** dar; entregar; alargar; ~ *down* bajar; *p.* ayudar a bajar; transmitir; ⚖ dictaminar; ~ *in* entregar; *p.* ayudar a entrar; ~ *out* distribuir; *p.* ayudar a salir; ~ *over* entregar; ~ *round* repartir; (hacer) pasar de uno a otro; '~**bag** bolso *m*, bolsa *f*; '~**ball** balonmano *m*; '~**bar·row** carretilla *f*; carretón *m* de mano; '~**bell** campanilla *f*; '~**bill** hoja *f* volante; '~**book** manual *m*; (*guide*) guía *f*; '~**brake** freno *m* de mano; '~**cuff 1.** ~*s pl.* esposas *f/pl.*; **2.** poner las esposas a; '**hand·ed** de ... mano(s); de mano(s) ...; para ... personas; **hand·ful** ['~ful] puñado *m*, manojo *m*; *F be a* ~ tener el diablo en el cuerpo.

hand·i·cap ['hændikæp] **1.** desventaja *f*, obstáculo *m*; handicap *m* (*a. sport*); **2.** perjudicar, dificultar; handicapar.

hand·i·craft ['hændikrɑ:ft] artesanía *f*; destreza *f* manual; '**hand·i·ness** destreza *f*; conveniencia *f*; '**hand·i·work** obra *f* (hecha a mano); hechura *f*.

hand·ker·chief ['hæŋkətʃif] pañuelo *m*.

han·dle ['hændl] **1.** mango *m*, puño *m*; asidero *m*; (*lever*) palanca *f*; asa *f of basket, jug etc.*; tirador *m of door, drawer etc.*; (*winding*) manubrio *m*; *fig.* F título *m*; *fig.* pretexto *m*; *sl. fly off the* ~ salirse de sus casillas; **2.** tocar, manosear; manejar, manipular; gobernar; (*deal in*) comerciar en; '~**bar** manillar *m*.

han·dling ['hændliŋ] manejo *m*; gobierno *m*; tratamiento *m*; manoseo *m*.

hand...: '~'**made** hecho a mano; ~ *paper* papel *m* de tina; '~**maid** (**en**) † *or fig.* criada *f*, sirvienta *f*; '~**-me-downs** *Am.* F *pl.* ropa *f* hecha; traje *m* de segunda mano; '~**-out** *Am.* F limosna *f*; F distribución *f*; F nota *f* de prensa; '~'**picked** escogido a mano; '~**rail** pasamano *m*, barandal *m*; '~**shake** apretón *m* de manos.

hand·some ['hænsəm] □ hermoso, guapo; buen mozo; *treatment etc.* generoso; *fortune etc.* considerable.

hand...: '~'**spring** voltereta *f* sobre las manos; '~**work** trabajo *m* a mano; obra *f* hecha a mano; '~**writ·ing** escritura *f*, letra *f*; '**hand·y** □ a mano; conveniente, práctico, manuable; útil; *p.* diestro, hábil; ~ *man* factótum *m*; *come in* ~ venir bien.

hang [hæŋ] **1.** [*irr.*] *v/t.* colgar; suspender; *wallpaper* pegar; *head* inclinar; (*execute*) ahorcar; (*drape*) poner colgaduras en; *I'll be* ~*ed if I will* que me cuelguen si lo hago; ~ *it* (*all*)! ¡por Dios!; ~ *fire* estar en suspenso; ~ *out* tender; ~ *up* colgar; interrumpir; suspender; *v/i.* colgar, pender; estar suspendido; (*be executed*) ser ahorcado; (*garments*) caer; ~ *in the balance* estar pendiente de un hilo; ~ *about* frecuentar, rondar; (*idle*) haraganear; ~ *back* resistirse a pasar adelante; vacilar; ~ *on* colgar de; agarrarse (*to* a); persistir; depender de; estar pendiente de; F esperar; ~ *out* asomarse (*of* por); *sl.* vivir; ~ *over* cernerse sobre; ~ *together* mantenerse unidos; ser consistente; **2.** caída *f of garment*; F modo *m* de manejar; F sentido *m*; *get the* ~ *of* (lograr) entender; *I don't care a* ~ no me importa un ardite.

hang·ar ['hæŋə] hangar *m.*

hang·dog ['hæŋdɔg] avergonzado; rastrero.

hang·er ['hæŋə] percha *f*, colgadero *m*; ~**on** ['~r'ɔn] *contp. fig.* parásito *m*, pegote *m.*

hang·ing ['hæŋiŋ] 1. colgante; digno de la horca; ~ *committee paint.* junta *f* de una exposición; 2. ahorcadura *f*; ~**s** *pl.* colgaduras *f/pl.*

hang·man ['hæŋmən] verdugo *m.*

hang·out ['hæŋ'aut] *sl.* guarida *f*, nidal *m.*

hang·o·ver ['hæŋouvə] F resto *m*; *sl.* resaca *f after drinking.*

hank [hæŋk] madeja *f.*

han·ker ['hæŋkə]: ~ *after* ambicionar, añorar; ~ *for* anhelar; **'han·ker·ing** anhelo *m*, ambición *m*; antojo *m*; añoranza *f.*

hank·y-pank·y ['hæŋki'pæŋki] F truco *m*, superchería *f.*

han·som ['hænsəm] cab *m.*

hap [hæp] † casualidad *f*; suerte *f*; **'hap'haz·ard** 1. casualidad *f*; 2. fortuito, casual; **'hap'haz·ard·ly** a troche y moche; **'hap·less** ☐ desgraciado.

ha'p'orth ['heipəθ] F = *halfpenny worth* valor *m* de medio penique.

hap·pen ['hæpən] pasar, suceder, ocurrir, acontecer, acaecer; *he* ~*ed to be at home* se hallaba en casa por casualidad; *as it* ~*s, it* ~*s that* da la casualidad que; *whatever* ~*s suceda lo que suceda*, venga lo que viniere; *Am.* F ~ *in(to)* entrar por casualidad; ~ *(up)on* tropezar con; acertar con; **'hap·pen·ing** suceso *m*, acontecimiento *m.*

hap·pi·ly ['hæpili] felizmente, afortunadamente.

hap·pi·ness ['hæpinis] felicidad *f*, dicha *f.*

hap·py ['hæpi] ☐ feliz, dichoso; *sl.* entre dos luces; *be* ~ *to* alegrarse de, tener gusto en; *be* ~ *about* estar contento de; *v. medium*; **'~-go-luck·y** despreocupado, imprevisor.

ha·rangue [hə'ræŋ] 1. arenga *f*; 2. arengar.

har·ass ['hærəs] acosar, hostigar; preocupar; agobiar; ⚔ picar.

har·bin·ger ['hɑ:bindʒə] 1. precursor *m*, heraldo *m*; 2. anunciar.

har·bo·(u)r ['hɑ:bə] 1. puerto *m*; 2. abrigar (*a. fig.*); encubrir;

'~-'**dues** derechos *m/pl.* de puerto; '~-'**mas·ter** capitán *m* de puerto.

hard [hɑ:d] 1. *adj.* duro, endurecido; sólido, firme; difícil, arduo, penoso; fuerte, recio, severo, inflexible; *water* crudo; *climate* áspero; *blow* rudo; *it is* ~ *to know* es difícil saber; *he is* ~ *to beat* es malo de vencer, es difícil de vencer; ~ *to deal with* intratable; *be* ~ *(up)on p.* estar muy duro con; *clothing etc.* gastar, echar a perder; ~ *and fast* inflexible; ~ *cash* dinero *m* contante; ~ *court* pista *f* dura; ~ *currency* moneda *f* dura; ~ *drinker* bebedor (-a *f*) *m* empedernido (a); ~ *facts* hechos *m/pl.* innegables; ~ *liquor* licor *m* espiritoso; ~ *of hearing* duro de oído; 2. *adv.* duro, duramente; de firme; difícilmente; con ahinco; *look* fijamente; ~ *by* muy cerca; F ~ *up* apurado; *be* ~ *put to it* encontrar difícil; *estar en un aprieto*; *go* ~ *with a p.* irle mal a una p.; *ride* ~ cabalgar fuerte; 3. F = *hard labour* trabajos *m/pl.* forzados; '~-'**bit·ten** terco; '~-'**boiled** *egg* duro; F endurecido; '**hard·en** endurecer(se) (*a.* ✝); solidificar(se).

hard…: '~-'**head·ed** astuto, práctico, poco sentimental; '~-'**heart·ed** ☐ duro de corazón, sin entrañas; **har·di·hood** ['~ihud] temeridad *f*; '**har·di·ness** vigor *m*, robustez *f*; audacia *f*; '**hard·ly** duramente; difícilmente; mal; (*scarcely*) apenas, casi no; ~ *ever* casi nunca; '**hard·ness** dureza *f*; dificultad *f*; fuerza *f*; rigor *m.*

hard…: '~-**pan** *Am.* subsuelo *m* (arcilloso y) duro; *fig.* base *f* sólida; '~-**shell** de caparazón duro; *Am. fig.* intransigente; '**hard·ship** penas *f/pl.*, penalidad *f*; infortunio *m*; apuro *m*, privación *f*; '**hard·ware** ferretería *f*, quincalla *f*; ~ *shop* quincallería *f*, ferretería *f*; '**hard·wear·ing** resistente, duradero; '**hard-'work·ing** trabajador, hacendoso; '**har·dy** ☐ robusto; audaz; ⚘ resistente.

hare [hɛə] liebre *f*; '~-**bell** campanilla *f* azul; '~-**brained** ligero de cascos; '~-**lip** *anat.* labio *m* leporino.

ha·rem ['hɛərem] harén *m.*

har·i·cot ['hærikou] (*a.* ~ *bean*)

judía *f* blanca, alubia *f*; ~ *mutton* guisado *m* de carnero.

hark [hɑːk] (*a.* ~ *at*, ~ *to*) escuchar; ~ *back hunt.* volver sobre la pista; *fig.* ~ *back to matter* volver a; *earlier occasion* recordar.

har·lot ['hɑːlət] ramera *f*; '**har·lot·ry** prostitución *f*.

harm [hɑːm] **1.** daño *m*; mal *m*; perjuicio *m*; *out of* ~'*s way a (or en)* salvo; *there's no* ~ *no* hay ningún mal (*in en*); **2.** hacer mal (a), hacer daño (a); dañar; perjudicar; **harm·ful** ['~ful] □ dañino, dañoso, perjudicial, nocivo; '**harm·less** □ inocuo, inofensivo.

har·mon·ic [hɑːˈmɔnik] **1.** □ armónico; **2.** armónica *f*; **har·mon·i·ca** [~ikə] armónica *f*; **har·mo·ni·ous** [hɑːˈmounjəs] armonioso; **har·mo·ni·um** [hɑːˈmounjəm] armonio *m*; **har·mo·nize** [ˈhɑːmənaiz] armonizar; '**har·mo·ny** armonía *f*.

har·ness 1. guarniciones *f*/*pl.*, arreos *m*/*pl.*; † ⚔ arnés *m*; *die in* ~ morir con las botas puestas; *get back in* ~ volver a la rutina; **2.** enjaezar, poner guarniciones a; *fig.* hacer trabajar, utilizar; '~**mak·er** guarnicionero *m*.

harp [hɑːp] **1.** arpa *f*; **2.** tañer el arpa; ~ *on* repetir constantemente; *stop* ~*ing on it!* ¡no machaques!; '**harp·ist** arpista *m*/*f*.

har·poon [hɑːˈpuːn] **1.** arpón *m*; **2.** arpon(e)ar.

har·py ['hɑːpi] arpía *f*.

har·ri·dan ['hæridən] bruja *f*.

har·ri·er ['hæriə] acosador *m*, asolador *m*; *sport*: corredor *m* a través del campo; *hunt.* perro *m* lebrel; *orn.* aguilucho *m*.

har·row ['hærou] **1.** ✍ grada *f*; **2.** ✍ gradar; *fig.* atormentar, horrorizar; '**har·row·ing** horrendo, conmovedor. [mentar, inquietar.]

har·ry ['hæri] acosar; asolar; ator-

harsh [hɑːʃ] □ áspero; *colour* chillón; duro, severo, cruel; '**harsh·ness** aspereza *f*; rigor *m*; dureza *f*.

hart [hɑːt] ciervo *m*.

har·um-scar·um ['hɛərəmˈskɛərəm] F tarambana *adj. a. su. m*/*f*.

har·vest ['hɑːvist] **1.** cosecha *f*, recolección *f*; (*reaping*) siega *f*; *vendimia f of grape*; ~ *festival*, ~ *thanksgiving* fiesta *f* de la cosecha; **2.** cosechar (*a. fig.*); recoger; '**har-**

vest·er segador (-a *f*) *m*; (*machine*) cosechadora *f*.

has [hæz, həz] ha; tiene (*v. have*); '~**-been** F persona *f* (*or* cosa *f*) que ya no sirve; vieja gloria *f*.

hash [hæʃ] picadillo *m*; F embrollo *m*; lío *m*; F *make a* ~ *of* estropear; F *settle a p.'s* ~ acabar con una p.

hasp [hɑːsp] portacandado *m*, aldaba *f* de candado; manecilla *f*.

has·sock ['hæsək] *eccl.* cojín *m*.

hast [hæst] † has; tienes (*v. have*).

haste [heist] prisa *f*, apresuramiento *m*, precipitación *f*; *make* ~ darse prisa (*to para, en*), apresurarse (*to a*); *more* ~ *less speed, make* ~ *slowly* vísteme despacio que estoy de prisa; **has·ten** ['heisn] *v*/*t.* apresurar, abreviar, acelerar; *v*/*i.* apresurarse (*to a*), darse prisa (*to para, en*); **hast·i·ness** ['heistinis] apresuramiento *m*, precipitación *f*; impaciencia *f*; '**hast·y** □ apresurado, precipitado; impaciente; inconsiderado.

hat [hæt] sombrero *m*; *sl.* *my* ~! ¡vaya!; *keep it under your* ~ de esto no digas ni pío; *take off one's* ~ descubrirse; *take off one's* ~ *to fig.* quitarse el sombrero y hacer reverencia a; *talk through one's* ~ decir disparates; '~**-box** sombrerera *f*.

hatch[1] [hætʃ] **1.** *orn.* nidada *f*, pollada *f*; (*door*) media puerta *f*, postigo *m*; (*trap*) trampa *f*; compuerta *f*; ⚓ escotilla *f*; **2.** *v*/*t.* empollar, sacar del cascarón; *fig.* tramar, idear; *v*/*i.* salir del huevo; empollarse; *fig.* madurarse.

hatch[2] [~] plumear.

hatch·et ['hætʃit] destral *m*, machado *m*, hacha *f*; *bury the* ~ echar pelillos a la mar; '~**-face** cara *f* de cuchillo.

hatch·way ['hætʃwei] ⚓ escotilla *f*.

hate [heit] **1.** odio *m* (*for* a), aborrecimiento *m* (*for* de); **2.** odiar, aborrecer; **hate·ful** ['~ful] □ odioso, aborrecible; '**hat·er** aborrecedor (-a *f*) *m*; **ha·tred** ['heitrid] = hate 1.

hat·ter ['hætə] sombrerero *m*; *mad as a* ~ más loco que una cabra.

haugh·ti·ness ['hɔːtinis] altanería *f*, altivez *f*; '**haugh·ty** □ altanero, altivo.

haul [hɔːl] **1.** tirón *m*; (*journey*) recorrido *m*, trayecto *m*; redada *f* of

fish (*a. fig.*); *fig.* botín *m*, ganancia *f*;
2. tirar (de); arrastrar; acarrear,
transportar; ⚓ (*a.* ~ *at*, ~ *on*)
halar; ⚓ ~ *down* arriar; ⚓ ~ (*the
wind*) virar para ceñir el viento;
'haul·age acarreo *m*, transporte *m*;
arrastre *m*, gastos *m/pl.* de acarreo;
tracción *f*; ~ *contractor* contratista
m de transportes.   [pierna *f.*)
haunch [hɔ:ntʃ] anca *f*; (*meat*))
haunt [hɔ:nt] **1.** nidal *m*, querencia *f*,
lugar *m* frecuentado (*of* por);
(*animals'*) guarida *f*; **2.** frecuentar,
rondar; *fig.* perseguir; (*ghosts*) aparecer en, andar por; ~*ed house*
casa *f* de fantasmas; **'haunt·ing**
persistente, obsesionante.
Ha·van·a [hə'vænə] (*or* ~ *cigar*)
habano *m*.
have [hæv, həv] **1.** [*irr.*] *v/t.* tener;
poseer; gozar de; contener; ob-
tener; *food, drink, lessons* tomar;
(*cause*) hacer; sentir; pasar; decir;
coger; vencer; dejar perplejo; engañar; tolerar, permitir; *child* tener,
dar a luz; ~ *just p.p.* acabar de *inf.*;
~ *to do* tener que hacer; ~ *to do
with* tener que ver con; *I* ~ *my hair
cut* me hago cortar el pelo; *he
had a suit made* mandó hacer un
traje; *he had his leg broken se* (le)
rompió una pierna; *I would* ~ *you
know* sepa Vd.; *as Plato has it*
según Platón; *he will* ~ *it that*
sostiene que; *I had (just) as well ...*
lo mismo da que yo ...; *I had better
go* más vale que yo vaya; *I had
rather go* preferiría ir; *it is not to
be had* no se puede conseguir; no
se vende; F *I* ~ *been had* me han
engañado; *sl.* he has had it se acabó
para él; ya perdió la oportunidad;
we can't ~ *that* no se puede consentir (eso); *let a p.* ~ *it* facilitárselo
a una p.; F dar una paliza a una p.;
F decirle cuatro verdades a una p.;
~ *about one* llevar consigo; ~ *at
him!* ¡dale!; F ~ *it in for* tener
tirria a; ~ *on* F *p.* tomar el pelo a;
th. llevar puesto; ~ *it out* resolverlo
discutiendo (*or* peleando); F ~ *a
p. up* llevar a una p. ante los tribunales. **2.** *v/aux.* haber; **3.** *mst
the* ~*s* los ricos *m/pl.*
ha·ven ['heivn] puerto *m*; abrigo *m*,
refugio *m*.
have-not ['hævnɔt]: *mst the* ~*s pl.*
los desposeídos *m/pl.*

haven't ['hævnt] = *have not.*
hav·er·sack ['hævəsæk] morral *m*,
mochila *f*.
hav·oc ['hævək] estrago *m*, destrucción *f*, ruina *f*; *make* ~ *of, play* ~
with (*or among*) hacer estragos en
(*or* entre).
haw[1] [hɔ:] ♠ baya *f* del espino.
haw[2] [~] **1.** *mst hum and* ~ vacilar
(al hablar); **2.** tosecilla *f* (falsa).
hawk[1] [hɔ:k] **1.** *orn.* halcón *m*; *v.
sparrow*; **2.** cazar con halcones;
'hawk·ing halconería *f*, cetrería *f*.
hawk[2] [~] carraspear.
hawk[3] [~] vender por las calles;
pregonar (*a. fig.*); **hawk·er** ['hɔ:kə]
vendedor (-a *f*) *m* ambulante.
haw·ser ['hɔ:zə] guindaleza *f*, cable
m, calabrote *m*.
haw·thorn ['hɔ:θɔ:n] espino *m*.
hay [hei] **1.** heno *m*; ~ *fever* fiebre *f*
del heno; *sl. hit the* ~ acostarse;
make ~ *of* confundir, desbaratar;
make ~ *while the sun shines* hacer
su agosto; **2.** segar el heno; '~·**cock**
montón *m* de heno; '~·**loft** henil *m*;
'~·**rick**, '~·**stack** almiar *m*; '~·**seed**
simiente *f* de heno; *Am. sl.* patán *m*;
'~·**wire** *sl.* en desorden; loco.
haz·ard ['hæzəd] **1.** azar *m*; riesgo
m, peligro *m*; *run a* ~ correr riesgo;
2. arriesgar; *remark etc.* aventurar;
'haz·ard·ous ☐ peligroso, arriesgado.
haze[1] [heiz] calina *f*; *fig.* confusión *f*,
vaguedad *f*.
haze[2] [~] vejar; *Am.* dar novatada a.
ha·zel ['heizl] **1.** avellano *m*; **2.** avellanado; '~·**nut** avellana *f*.
ha·zy ['heizi] calinoso; *fig.* confuso,
vago.
H-bomb ['eitʃbɔm] = *hydrogen
bomb* bomba *f* de hidrógeno.
he [hi:] **1.** él; ~ *who* el que, quien;
2. macho *m*, varón *m*.
head [hed] **1.** cabeza *f*; *lit. or iro.*
testa *f*; cabecera *f of bed*; espuma *f
of beer*; punta *f of arrow*; altura *f*
de caída *of water*; culata *f of
cylinder*; ⚓ proa *f*; *geog.* punta *f*;
♠ cabezuela *f*; (*p.*) jefe *m*, director
(-a *f*) *m*; (*title*) encabezamiento *m*;
sección *f*; *fig.* crisis *f*; *he is* (*or
stands*) ~ *and shoulders above the
rest* sobresale de cabeza y hombros;
fig. no le llegan a la suela del
zapato; *crowned* ~ testa *f* coronada;
~ *first* de cabeza; ~ *of hair* cabellera

f; ~s or tails cara o cruz; *I can't make* ~ *or tail of it* no le veo ni pies ni cabeza; *from* ~ *to foot* de pies a cabeza; ~ *over heels* patas arriba; *fig.* completamente, perdidamente; *off one's* ~ delirante, fuera de sí, loco; *(up)on one's (own)* ~ a su responsabilidad; *out of one's own* ~ de su cosecha; *over one's* ~ fuera de su alcance; por encima de uno; *bring to a* ~ ✝ ultimar; provocar; *come to a* ~ madurar, llegar a la crisis; ♨ supurar; *get it into one's* ~ *that* metérsele a uno en la cabeza que; *give him his* ~ darle rienda suelta; *it goes to his* ~ se le sube a la cabeza; *keep one's* ~ ser dueño de sí mismo; *lose one's* ~ perder los estribos; *talk one's* ~ *off* hablar por los codos; *he took it into his* ~ *to* se le ocurrió *inf.*; **2.** principal, primero; delantero, de frente; ⚓ de proa; superior; **3.** *v/t.* encabezar, estar a la cabeza de; acaudillar; dirigir; poner cabeza a; *football* cabecear; ~*ed for* con rumbo a; ~ *off* interceptar; desviar; distraer; atajar; *v/i.* dirigirse (*for, towards* hacia); *Am.* (*stream*) nacer; ~*ing for* ⚓ con rumbo a; **'head·ache** dolor *m* de cabeza; *fig.* quebradero *m* de cabeza; **'head-dress** toca *f*, tocado *m*; **'head·ed** con (*or* de) cabeza ...; **'head·er** ⚓ tizón *m*; F caída *f* de cabeza, salto *m* de cabeza; *football*: cabezazo *m*; **'head-gear** tocado *m*; sombrero *m*, gorro *m*; cabezada *f of horse*; **'head·i·ness** impetuosidad *f*, fogosidad *f*; terquedad *f*; fuerza *f* embriagadora; **'head·ing** encabezamiento *m*, título *m*; **'head·land** promontorio *m*; **'head·less** sin cabeza; descabezado; *fig.* sin jefe.

head...: **'~·light** ⚙ farol *m*; *mot.* faro *m*; **'~·line** titular *m*, cabecera *f*; F *he hits the* ~s se habla mucho de él en los periódicos; **'~·long 1.** *adj.* de cabeza, precipitado; **2.** *adv.* de cabeza, precipitadamente; **'~·man** jefe *m*, cacique *m*; (*foreman*) capataz *m*; **'~·mas·ter** director *m* (de colegio *etc.*); **'~·mis·tress** directora *f* (de colegio *etc.*); **'~·on** de frente; ~ *collision* choque *m* de frente; **'~·phones** *pl.* auriculares *m/pl.*; **'~·piece** casco *m*; F cabeza *f*; ♪

auriculares *m/pl.*; *typ.* cabecera *f*; **'~·quar·ters** *pl.* ⚔ cuartel *m* general; sede *f*; jefatura *f*; oficina *f* central; **'head·ship** dirección *f*, jefatura *f*; **'heads·man** verdugo *m*.

head...: **'~·stone** lápida *f* mortuoria; **'~·strong** voluntarioso, impetuoso, cabezudo; **'~·wat·ers** *pl.* cabecera *f* (de un río); **'~·way** *make* ~ adelantar, hacer progresos; **'~·wind** viento *m* contrario; **'head·y** □ impetuoso, fogoso; terco; *wine* cabezudo, embriagador.

heal [hi:l] curar, sanar (*of* de); *cut etc.* cicatrizar(se); *fig.* remediar; ~ *up* cicatrizarse; **'heal·ing 1.** □ curativo, sanativo; cicatrizal; **2.** cura(ción) *f*; cicatrización *f*.

health [helθ] salud *f*; (*public*) sanidad *f*; *be in good* (*bad*) ~ estar bien (mal) de salud; *drink* (*to*) *the* ~ *of* beber a la salud de; **health·ful** ['~·ful] □ sano; saludable, higiénico; **'health·i·ness** buena salud *f*; salubridad *f*; **'health-re·sort** balneario *m*; **'health·y** □ sano, saludable; *place etc.* salubre.

heap [hi:p] **1.** montón *m* (*a. fig.*); pila *f*, hacina *f*; F *we have* ~s *of time* nos sobra tiempo; F *struck all of a* ~ anonadado; **2.** amontonar, hacinar, apilar (*a.* ~ *up*); ~ *favours upon* colmar de favores; **3.** *adv.* F ~s mucho.

hear [hiə] [*irr.*] oír, sentir; escuchar; ~ *about*, ~ *of* oír hablar de, enterarse de; *I won't* ~ *of it* no lo permito; ¡ni hablar!; ~ *from* recibir carta de, tener noticias de; ~ *that* oír decir que; ~! ~! ¡muy bien!; **heard** [hə:d] *pret. a. p.p. of* hear; **hear·er** ['hiərə] oyente *m/f*; **'hear·ing** (*sense*) oído *m*; audiencia *f*; ♨ vista *f*; *in our* ~ en nuestra presencia; *within* ~ al alcance del oído; ~ *aid* aparato *m* del oído; **heark·en** ['ha:·kən] *mst* ~ *to* escuchar; hacer caso de; **hear·say** ['hiəsei] rumor *m*, voz *f* común; *by* ~ de oídas.

hearse [hə:s] coche *m* (*or* carro *m*) fúnebre.

heart [ha:t] corazón *m* (*a. fig.*); cogollo *m of lettuce*; (*soul*) alma *f*; prenda *f* (*a. dear* ~; *v. sweet*~); *cards*: ~s *pl.* corazones *m/pl.*, (*Spanish*) copas *f/pl.*; ~ *and soul* con toda el alma; *after my own* ~ de los que me gustan, enteramente a mi gusto; *at* ~ en el fondo; *be sick at* ~ tener la muerte en el alma; *have at* ～ tener presente; *by* ～ de memoria; *have one's* ～ *in one's mouth* tener el alma en un hilo; *from the* ～ de todo corazón; *have the* ～ *to* tener corazón para; *in good* ～ *p.* lleno de confianza, ilusionado; *soil* en buen estado; *in his* ～ *of* ～*s* en lo más recóndito de su corazón; *lose* ～ descorazonarse; *set one's* ～ *on* tener la esperanza puesta en; poner el corazón en; *take* ～ cobrar ánimo; *take to* ～ tomar a pecho(s); *wear one's* ～ *on one's sleeve* llevar el corazón en la mano; *with all my* ～ con toda mi alma; '～**ache** angustia *f*, pesar *m*; '～**at'tack** ataque *m* cardíaco; '～**beat** latido *m* del corazón; '～**break** congoja *f*, angustia *f*; '～**break·ing** □ angustioso, desgarrador; '～**bro·ken** con el corazón partido, acongojado, afligido; '～**burn** ✗ acedía *f*; '～**burn·ing** descontento *m*, envidia *f*, rencor *m*; '～**com·plaint** afección *f* cardíaca; '**heart·ed** de corazón...; '**heart·en** alentar, animar; '**heart·felt** cordial, sincero, hondo.

hearth [hɑ:θ] hogar *m* (*a. fig.*), chimenea *f*.

heart·i·ness ['hɑ:tinis] cordialidad *f*, sinceridad *f*; vigor *m*; campechanía *f*; '**heart·less** □ despiadado, empedernido; '**heart·rend·ing** angustioso, desgarrador, que parte el corazón.

heart...: '～**s·ease** ♀ trinitaria *f*; '～**strings** *pl. fig.* fibras *f*/*pl.* del corazón; '**heart·y 1.** □ cordial, sincero, vigoroso, robusto; campechano; *be a* ～ *eater* tener buen diente; **2.** ✿ compañero *m*; *univ.* deportista *m.*

heat [hi:t] **1.** calor *m* (*a. fig.*); ardor *m*; calefacción *f*; *zo.* celo *m*; *sport*: eliminatoria *f*; *dead* ～ empate *m*; *in* ～ en celo; **2.** calentar(se) (*a.* ～ *up*); acalorar(se) (*a. fig.*); '**heat·ed** □ acalorado; '**heat·er** calentador *m.*

heath [hi:θ] brezal *m*; ♀ brezo *m*; *native* ～ patria *f* chica.

hea·then [hi:ðən] gentil *adj. a. su. m*/*f*, pagano *adj. a. su. m* (a *f*); F bárbaro *adj. a. su. m* (a *f*); '**hea·then·ish** □ pagano; bárbaro; '**hea·then·ism** gentilidad *f*, paganismo.

heath·er ['heðə] brezo *m.* [*m.*]

heat·ing ['hi:tiŋ] **1.** calefacción *f*, caldeo *m*; **2.** de calefacción, de caldeo; calentador.

heat...: '～'**proof** termorresistente, a prueba de calor; '～**-stroke** ✗ insolación *f*; '～**-val·ue** poder *m* calorífico; '～**-wave** ola *f* de calor.

heave [hi:v] **1.** esfuerzo *m* (para levantar); echada *f*; henchidura *f*; náusea *f*; jadeo *m*; **2.** *v/t.* levantar; cargar; lanzar; tirar; ♪ jalar; *sigh* exhalar; *v/i.* levantarse con esfuerzo; subir y bajar; palpitar; ♪ basquear; ♪ (*at capstan*) virar; ♪ *in(to) sight* aparecer; ♪ ～ *to* ponerse al pairo; *it makes me* ～ me da asco.

heav·en ['hevn] (*a.* ～*s pl.*) cielo *m*; (*good*) ♀*s!* ¡Dios mío!; '**heav·en·ly** celestial (*a. fig.*); *ast.* celeste; **heav·en·ward(s)** ['～wəd(z)] hacia el cielo.

heav·i·ness ['hevinis] peso *m*; pesadez *f* (*a. fig.*); letargo *m*, modorra *f*; torpeza *f*; opresión *f*; abundancia *f*; fuerza *f.*

heav·y ['hevi] □ pesado; *atmosphere* opresivo; *burden fig.* oneroso; *cloth, line, sea* grueso; ✗ *current*, ✗ *fire* intenso; *emphasis, expense, meal, rain* fuerte; *feeling* aletargado; *heart* triste; *liquid* espeso; *loss* considerable; *movement* lento, torpe; *population, traffic* denso; *responsibility* grave; *sky* encapotado; *soil* arcilloso; *surface* difícil; *task* duro, penoso; *yield* abundante; *be a* ～ *drinker* (*eater, smoker*) beber (comer, fumar) mucho; '～**-weight** *boxing*: peso *m* pesado; *fig.* persona *f* de peso.

He·bra·ic [hi'breiik] □ hebraico.

He·brew ['hi:bru:] hebreo *adj. a. su. m* (a *f*).

hec·a·tomb ['hekətoum] hecatombe *f.*

heck·le ['hekl] interrumpir (a un orador).

hec·tare ['hektɛə] hectárea *f.*

hec·tic ['hektik] □ F agitado, febril; ✗ héc(t)ico.

hec·tor ['hektə] *v/t.* intimidar con bravatas; *v/i.* echar bravatas.

hedge [hedʒ] **1.** seto *m* (vivo); cerca *f*; **2.** *v/t.* cercar con seto; ～ *about*, ～ *in* rodear, encerrar; poner obstáculos a; ～ *off* separar (por un seto); ～ *a bet* hacer apuestas compensatorias; *v/i.* eludir la respuesta, contestar con evasivas; vacilar; '～**hog** erizo *m*; *Am.* puerco *m* espín; '～**-hop** ✈ *sl.* volar a ras de tierra; '～**row** seto *m* vivo; '~-'spar·row acentor *m* común.

he·don·ism ['hi:dənizm] hedonismo *m*.

heed [hi:d] **1.** atención *f*, cuidado *m*; *give* ~ *to* poner atención en; *take no* ~ *of* no hacer caso de; **2.** atender (a), hacer caso (de); **heed·ful** ['~ful] □ atento (*of* a); cuidadoso; **'heed·less** □ desatento, descuidado; distraído.

hee-haw ['hi:'hɔ:] **1.** rebuzno *m*; *fig.* risotada *f*; **2.** rebuznar; reírse a carcajadas.

heel¹ [hi:l] **1.** *anat.* calcañar *m*; *anat. a. fig.* talón *m*; tacón *m of shoe*; parte *f* inferior; parte *f* trasera; restos *m/pl.*; *sl. mst Am.* sinvergüenza *m*; *be at* (*or on*) *a p.'s* ~*s* pisarle los talones a una p.; *cool one's* ~*s* hacer antesala; *down at* ~ desaliñado, mal vestido; *take to one's* ~*s* poner pies en polvorosa; **2.** *shoe* poner tacón a; *football* talonar; '~-'click·ing taconazo *m*; **'heeled** *Am.* F provisto de dinero; **'heel·er** *Am. sl.* muñidor *m*.

heel² [~] ⚓ escorar; ~ *over* zozobrar.

heel-tap ['hi:ltæp] ⊕ tapa *f* (del tacón); escurridura *f*.

heft [heft] *v. haft*; **1.** *Am.* F mayor parte *f*; **2.** *Am.* F sopesar; **'heft·y** F pesado; fuerte, fornido. [nía *f*.]

he·gem·o·ny [hi'gemɔni] hegemonía]

he-goat ['hi:gout] macho *m* cabrío.

heif·er ['hefə] novilla *f*, vaquilla *f*.

heigh [hei] ¡oye!, ¡eh!

heigh-ho ['hei'hou] ¡ay!

height [hait] altura *f*; elevación *f*; altitud *f*; (*top*) cima *f*; *p.'s* estatura *f*; (*hill*) cerro *m*; crisis *f*; *the* ~ *of madness* el colmo de la locura; **'height·en** elevar; hacer más alto; aumentar; (*enhance*) realzar; intensificar, avivar.

hei·nous ['heinəs] □ atroz, nefando.

heir [ɛə] heredero *m*; *be* ~ *to* heredar; ~ *apparent*, ~ *at law* heredero *m* forzoso; **'heir·dom** herencia *f*; **'heir·ess** heredera *f*; F soltera *f* adinerada; **'heir·less** sin heredero; **heir·loom** ['~lu:m] reliquia *f* de familia.

held [held] *pret. a. p.p. of hold* 2.

hel·i·cal ['helikl] espiral.

hel·i·cop·ter ['helikɔptə] helicóptero *m*.

he·li·o·graph ['hi:liougra:f] heliógrafo *m*; **he·li·o·gra·vure** ['hi:liougrə'vjuə] heliograbado *m*; **he·li·o·trope** ['heljətroup] heliotropo *m*.

he·li·um ['hi:liəm] helio *m*.

hell [hel] infierno *m*; (*a. gambling-*~) garito *m*; *sl. like* ~! ¡ni hablar!; F *oh* ~! ¡demonio!; *go to* ~! ¡vete al diablo!; F *what the* ~....? ¿qué demonios...?; F *a* ~ *of a noise* un ruido de todos los demonios; F *raise* ~ armar la de Dios es Cristo; *go* ~ *for leather* ir como el demonio, ir disparado.

hel·le·bore ['helibɔ:] eléboro *m*.

Hel·lene ['heli:n] heleno (a *f*) *m*.

hell·ish ['heliʃ] □ infernal, diabólico.

hel·lo ['hʌ'lou; he'lou] v. hullo.

helm [helm] (caña *f or* rueda *f* del) timón *m*.

hel·met ['helmit] casco *m*; † yelmo *m*.

helms·man ['helmzmən] timonel *m*.

help [help] **1.** ayuda *f*, auxilio *m*; socorro *m*; remedio *m*; (*p.*) criada *f*; (*servants*) servidumbre *f*; ~! ¡socorro!; F *lady* ~ asistenta *f*; *mother's* ~ niñera *f*; criada *f*; *by the* ~ *of* con la ayuda de; *call for* ~ pedir socorro; *there's no* ~ *for it* no hay (más) remedio; **2.** *v/t.* ayudar (*to* a); auxiliar; socorrer; *pain* aliviar; remediar; facilitar; (*at table*) servir; ~ *a p. to a th.* servirle algo a una p.; ~ *o.s.* servirse; valerse por sí mismo; *I could not* ~ *laughing* no pude menos de reír; (*not*) *if I can* ~ *it* si puedo evitarlo; *it can't be* ~*ed* no hay (más) remedio; ~ *a p. on with* (*dress*) ayudar a una p. a ponerse; ~ *out* ayudar (a salir *or* a bajar); *v/i.* ayudar (*a.* ~ *out*); **'help·er** ayudador (-a *f*) *m*; ayudante *m*; asistente (a *f*) *m*; colaborador (-a *f*) *m*; **help·ful** ['~ful] □ útil, provechoso; *p.* servicial, comprensivo; **'help·ing** ración *f*, porción *f*; plato *m*; **'help·less** □ impotente; incapaz; desamparado; **'help·less·ness** impotencia *f*; incapacidad *f*; desamparo *m*; **'help·mate**, **'help·meet** buen(a) compañero (a *f*) *m*; esposo (a *f*) *m*.

hel·ter-skel·ter ['heltə'skeltə] atropelladamente.

helve [helv] mango *m*, astil *m*.

hem¹ [hem] **1.** dobladillo *m*, bastilla *f*; (*edge*) orilla *f*; **2.** dobladillar, bastillar; ~ *in* encerrar, cercar.

hem² [~] **1.** destoserse; **2.** ¡ejem!

he-man ['hi:mæn] *sl.* machote *m*.

hem·i·sphere ['hemisfiə] hemisferio *m*.

hem·i·stich ['hemistik] hemistiquio *m*.

hem·lock ['hemlɔk] cicuta *f*.

he·mo... *v.* haemo...

hemp [hemp] cáñamo *m*; **'hemp·en** cañameño.

hem·stitch ['hemstitʃ] **1.** vainica *f*; **2.** hacer vainica (en).

hen [hen] gallina *f*; (*female bird*) hembra *f*; ~'s egg huevo *m* de gallina.

hen·bane ['henbein] beleño *m*.

hence [hens] (*a. from* ~) (*place*) de aquí, desde aquí; fuera de aquí; (*time*) desde ahora; (*therefore*) por lo tanto, por eso; ~! ¡fuera (de aquí)!; *a year* ~ de aquí a un año; **'~·forth**, **'~·for·ward** de aquí en adelante.

hench·man ['hentʃmən] secuaz *m*; muñidor *m*; guardaespaldas *m*; † paje *m*.

hen·dec·a·syl·lab·ic [hen'dekəsi-'læbik] endecasílabo.

hen·house ['henhaus] gallinero *m*.

hen·na ['henə] alheña *f*.

hen...: **'~·par·ty** F tertulia *f* de mujeres; **'~·pecked** dominado por su mujer.

hep [hep]: *Am. sl.* enterado; **'~·cat** *Am. sl.* conocedor (-a *f*) *m* del jazz.

he·pat·ic [hi'pætik] hepático.

hep·ta·gon ['heptəgən] heptágono *m*.

her [hɔ:, hə] **1.** *possessive* su(s); **2.** *pron. acc.* la; *dat.* le; (*after prp.*) ella.

her·ald ['herəld] **1.** heraldo *m*; *fig.* anunciador *m*, precursor *m*; **2.** anunciar, proclamar; ser precursor de; **he·ral·dic** [he'rældik] □ heráldico; **her·ald·ry** ['herəldri] heráldica *f*.

herb [hɔ:b] hierba *f*; **her·ba·ceous** [~'beiʃəs] herbáceo; **'herb·age** herbaje *m*; ɹ̣̇ derecho *m* de pastoreo; **'herb·al** herbario *adj. a. su. m*; **'her·bal·ist** herbolario (a *f*) *m*; **her·bar·i·um** [~'bɛəriəm] herbario *m*; **her·biv·o·rous** [~'bivərəs] herbívoro.

Her·cu·le·an [hɔ:kju'li:ən] hercúleo.

herd [hɔ:d] **1.** manada *f*, hato *m*, rebaño *m*; piara *f of swine*; *fig.* muchedumbre *f*; *the common* ~ el vulgo; ~ *instinct* instinto *m* gregario; **2.** *v/t.* guardar; reunir (*or* llevar) en manada; *v/i.* (*a.* ~ *together*) reunirse en manada; ir juntos; **'herds·man** manadero *m*, pastor *m*; vaquero *m*.

here [hiə] aquí; acá; ~! ¡presente!; ~ *and there* aquí y allá; ~ *below* aquí abajo; ~'*s to...!* ¡vaya por...!; ¡a la salud de...!; ~ *it is* aquí lo tiene Vd.; *come* ~! ¡ven acá!; *that's neither* ~ *nor there* eso no viene al caso.

here·a·bout(s) ['hiərəbaut(s)] por aquí (cerca); **here·aft·er** [hiər-'ɑ:ftə] **1.** de aquí en adelante; en lo futuro; en la vida futura; **2.** lo futuro; vida *f* futura; **'here'by** por este medio; por la presente.

her·ed·it·a·ment [heri'ditəmənt] bienes *m/pl.* heredables; **he·red·i·tar·y** [hi'reditəri] hereditario; **he·'red·i·ty** herencia *f*.

here·in ['hiər'in] aquí dentro; en esto; **here·in'aft·er** más abajo, más adelante; **here·in·be'fore** en lo precedente; **here·of** [hiər'ɔv] de esto.

her·e·sy ['herəsi] herejía *f*.

her·e·tic ['herətik] **1.** (*mst* **he·ret·i·cal** □ [hi'retikl]) herético; **2.** hereje *m/f*.

here·to·fore ['hiətu'fɔ:] hasta ahora; antes; **here·up·on** ['hiərə'pɔn] en esto; en seguida; **'here'with** con esto; adjunto.

her·it·a·ble ['heritəbl] heredable; **'her·it·age** herencia *f*.

her·maph·ro·dite [hɔ:'mæfrədait] hermafrodita *adj. a. su. m*.

her·met·ic [hɔ:'metik] □ hermético.

her·mit ['hɔ:mit] ermitaño *m*; **'her·mit·age** ermita *f*.

her·ni·a ['hɔ:njə] hernia *f*; **'her·ni·al** herniario.

he·ro ['hiərou], *pl.* **he·roes** ['~z] héroe *m*; **he·ro·ic** [hi'rouik] □ heroico; **her·o·ine** ['herouin] heroína *f*; **'her·o·ism** heroísmo *m*.

her·o·in ['herouin] *pharm.* heroína *f*.

her·on ['herən] garza *f* real.

her·ring ['heriŋ] arenque *m*; **'her·ring-bone** ⊕ espinapez *m*; ~ *pattern* muestra *f* espiga; ~ *stitch* punto *m* de escapulario.

hers [hɔ:z] (el) suyo, (la) suya *etc*.

her·self [hɔ:'self] (*subject*) ella misma; *acc., dat.* se; (*after prp.*) sí (misma).

hes·i·tance, hes·i·tan·cy ['hezitəns(i)] vacilación *f*; **hes·i·tant** ['ˌ~-tənt] ☐ vacilante, irresoluto; **hes·i-tate** ['ˌ~teit] vacilar (*about, over, to* en); *speech*: titubear; **hes·i'ta·tion** vacilación *f*, irresolución *f*; titubeo *m*.

hes·sian ['hesiən] tejido *m* basto de cáñamo y yute.

het [het]: F *get* ~ *up* aturrullarse, acalorarse (*about, over* por).

het·er·o·dox ['hetərədɔks] heterodoxo; '**het·er·o·dox·y** heterodoxia *f*; **het·er·o·dyne** ['ˌ~dain] heterodino *adj. a. su. m*; **het·er·o·ge·ne·i·ty** [ˌ~roudʒi'niːiti] heterogeneidad *f*; **het·er·o·ge·ne·ous** ['ˌ~rou'dʒiːniəs] heterogéneo.

hew [hjuː] [*irr.*] cortar, tajar; hachear; labrar; picar; ~ *down* talar; ~ *out* excavar; tallar; *fig.* hacerse; **hewn** [hjuːn] *p.p. of hew*.

hex·a·gon ['heksəgən] hexágono *m*; **hex·ag·o·nal** [hek'sægənl] ☐ hexagonal; **hex·am·e·ter** [hek'sæmitə] hexámetro *m*.

hey [hei] ¡eh!, ¡oye!

hey·day ['heidei] auge *m*, apogeo *m*; buenos tiempos *m/pl.*; flor *f* de edad.

hi [hai] ¡oye!, ¡eh!, ¡hala!

hi·a·tus [hai'eitəs] laguna *f*; interrupción *f*; *gr.*, ✿ hiato *m*.

hi·ber·nate ['haibəːneit] *biol.* hibernar; invernar; **hi·ber'na·tion** hibernación *f*; invernada *f*.

hic·cup, *a.* **hic·cough** ['hikʌp] **1.** hipo *m*; **2.** *v/t.* decir con hipos; *v/i.* hipar.

hick [hik] *Am. sl.* palurdo *m*; *attr.* de aldea. [cano.\]

hick·o·ry ['hikəri] nogal *m* ameri-\]
hid [hid] *pret. a.* **hid·den** ['hidn] *p.p. of hide².*

hide¹ [haid] piel *f*, pellejo *m*; (*esp. tanned*) cuero *m*.

hide² [ˌ~] [*irr.*] **1.** *v/t.* esconder (*from* de), ocultar (*from a, de*); (en)cubrir; disimular; *v/i.* esconderse, ocultarse (*from* de); **2.** *hunt.* trepa *f*; '**hide-and-'seek** escondite *m*; *play* (*at*) ~ jugar al escondite.

hide·bound ['haidbaund] *fig.* rígido; conservador; aferrado a la tradición.

hid·e·ous ['hidiəs] ☐ horrible; feo; monstruoso.

hide-out ['haidaut] F escondrijo *m*, guarida *f*.

hid·ing¹ ['haidiŋ] F paliza *f*, tunda *f*.

hid·ing² [ˌ~] ocultación *f*; *in* ~ escondido; *go into* ~ ocultarse, refugiarse; '**~-place** escondrijo *m*.

hie [hai] *poet.* (*ger. hying*) ir de prisa.

hi·er·arch·y ['haiərɑːki] jerarquía *f*.

hi·er·o·glyph ['haiərəglif] jeroglífico *m*; **hi·er·o'glyph·ic** ☐ jeroglífico *adj. a. su. m*.

hi-fi ['hai'fai] = *high fidelity* (de) alta fidelidad *f*.

hig·gle ['higl] regatear.

hig·gle·dy-pig·gle·dy ['higldi-'pigldi] F *contp.* **1.** *adj.* revuelto; **2.** *adv.* confusamente.

high [hai] **1.** *adj.* ☐ (*v. a.* ~*ly*) alto; *altar, mass, street* mayor; *colour, price* subido; *game* manido; *manner* altanero; *meat* pasado; *number, speed* grande; *polish* brillante; *priest* sumo; *quality* superior; *3 feet* ~ 3 pies de alto; ~ *and dry* en seco; F ~ *and mighty* encopetado; ~*est bid* mejor postura *f*; *with a* ~ *hand* arbitrariamente, despóticamente; ~ *antiquity* antigüedad *f* remota; ♀ *Church* Alta Iglesia *f*; ✕ ~ *command* alto mando *m*; ♀ *Court* tribunal *m* supremo; ~ *diving* saltos *m/pl.* de palanca; ✄ ~ *frequency* alta frecuencia *f*; ~ *life* alta sociedad *f*; ~ *living* vida *f* regalada; *v. spirit. tea, tension, etc.*; ~ *treason* alta traición *f*; *v. water*; ~ *wind* ventarrón *m*; ~ *words* palabras *f/pl.* airadas; **2.** *meteor.* (zona *f* de) alta presión *f*; ♀ = *High Street*; ♀ *Am.* = *High School*; *on* ~ en las alturas, en el cielo; **3.** *adv.* altamente; (en) alto; fuertemente; a gran precio; lujosamente; ~ *and low* por todas partes; *aim* ~ *fig.* picar muy alto; *fly* ~ ✈ volar por alto; *fig.* picar muy alto; '**~-'backed** de respaldo alto; '**~-ball** *Am.* highball *m*; '**~-born** linajudo; '**~-brow** F intelectual *adj. a. su. m/f.*; '**~-class** de marca, de clase superior; '**~-'col·oured** de colores vivos; *fig.* exagerado; '**~-fa'lu·tin(g)** **1.** pomposidad *f*, presunción *f*; **2.** pomposo, presuntuoso; '**~-flown** hinchado, altisonante; '**~-grade** de calidad superior; '**~-'hand·ed** arbitrario, despótico; '**~-'hat** *Am. sl.* **1.** esnob *m/f*; **2.** encopetado; **3.** tratar con desdén; '**~-'heeled** *shoes* de tacones altos; '**~-jump** salto *m* de altura; '**~-land·er** montañés (-a *f*) *m* (de Escocia); '**lands** tierras f/pl. altas, montañas f/pl.; '~·light toque m de luz; fig. momento m culminante; 'high·ly altamente; mucho, muy; sumamente; muy favorablemente; speak ~ of decir mil bienes de; think ~ of tener en mucho; ~ bred animals de buena raza; ~ paid muy bien pagado; ~ seasoned picante; ~ strung muy excitable, neurasténico; 'high·'mind·ed magnánimo, de nobles pensamientos; 'high·ness altura f; ≈ Alteza f.

high...: '~·pow·ered de gran potencia; '~·'pres·sure de alta presión; fig. enérgico, urgente; '~·'road carretera f, camino m real (a. fig.); '~·'sound·ing altisonante; '~·speed de alta velocidad; '~·'spir·it·ed animoso; horse fogoso; '~·test fuel supercarburante m; '~·'toned F de alto copete; de buen tono; de tono elevado; '~·way = ~·road; ~ code código m de circulación; '~·way·man salteador m de caminos.

hi(gh)·jack·er ['haidʒækə] Am. F atracador m.

hike [haik] F 1. caminata f, excursión f a pie; 2. dar una caminata, ir de excursión; 'hik·er F excursionista m/f.

hi·lar·i·ous [hi'lɛəriəs] □ hilarante.

hi·lar·i·ty [hi'læriti] hilaridad f.

hill [hil] colina f, cerro m, otero m, collado m; (slope) cuesta f; ~·bil·ly ['~bili] Am. F rústico m montañés; '~·climb·ing mot. subida f de cuestas; ~ (con)test prueba f de subida de cuestas; 'hill·i·ness montuosidad f; hill·ock ['~ɔk] altillo m, montículo m, altozano m; 'hill·side ladera f; 'hill·y accidentado, montuoso; road de fuertes pendientes.

hilt [hilt] puño m, empuñadura f; up to the ~ hasta las cachas.

him [him] acc. lo, le; dat. le; (after prp.) él.

him·self [him'self] (subject) él mismo; acc., dat. se; (after prp.) sí (mismo); by ~ solo, por sí (solo); he said to ~ dijo para sí.

hind¹ [haind] cierva f.

hind² [~] trasero, posterior; ~ leg pata f trasera; ~ quarters cuarto m trasero; hin·der ['hində] v/t. estorbar, dificultar; ~ from impedir inf. (or que subj.); hind·most ['haindmoust] posterior, último.

hin·drance ['hindrəns] obstáculo m, estorbo m, impedimento m (to para).

Hin·du, a. Hin·doo ['hin'du:] hindú adj. a. su. m/f.

Hin·du·sta·ni [hindu'stæni] 1. indostánico; indostanés adj. a. su. m (-a f); 2. (language) indostaní m, indostánico m.

hinge [hindʒ] 1. gozne m, pernio m, bisagra f; a. zo. charnela f; fig. eje m; off the ~ desquiciado; 2. v/t. engoznar, embisagrar; v/i.: ~ (up)on girar sobre; fig. depender de.

hin·ny ['hini] burdégano m.

hint [hint] 1. indirecta f; indicación f; consejo m; take the ~ darse por aludido; darse cuenta de la indirecta; aprovechar la indicación; 2. echar indirectas; (a. ~ at) insinuar.

hin·ter·land ['hintəlænd] traspaís m.

hip¹ [hip] anat. cadera f; ~ and thigh sin piedad.

hip² [~] ♀ escaramujo m.

hip³ [~]: int. ~! ~! hurra(h)! ¡hurra!, ¡viva! [asiento.]

hip-bath ['hipbɑ:θ] baño m de]

hip-bone ['hipboun] cía f.

hipped¹ [hipt] △ a cuatro aguas.

hipped² [~] melancólico; Am. sl. obsesionado.

hip·po ['hipou] F = hip·po·pot·a·mus [hipə'pɔtəməs], pl. a. hip·po·'pot·a·mi [~mai] hipopótamo m.

hire ['haiə] 1. alquiler m, arriendo m; salario m, jornal m of p.; for (or on) ~ de alquiler; 2. alquilar, arrendar (a. ~ out); tomar en arriendo; p. contratar; hire·ling ['~liŋ] contp. alquiladizo adj. a. su. m (a f), mercenario adj. a. su. m (a f); 'hire·'pur·chase compra f a plazos.

hir·sute ['hə:sju:t] hirsuto.

his [hiz] 1. su(s); 2. pron. (el) suyo, (la) suya etc.

hiss [his] 1. siseo m, silbido m; 2. silbar, sisear (a. ~ off).

hist [s:t] ¡chitón!, ¡silencio!

his·tol·o·gy [his'tɔlədʒi] histología f.

his·to·ri·an [his'tɔ:riən] historiador (-a f) m; his·tor·ic, his·tor·i·cal [~'tɔrik(l)] □ histórico; his·to·ri·og·ra·pher [~tɔ:ri'ɔgrəfə] historiógrafo m; his·to·ry ['~təri] historia f.

his·tri·on·ic [histri'ɔnik] □ histriónico, teatral.

hit [hit] 1. golpe m (bien dado); tiro m certero; acierto m; fig., thea., ♪

éxito *m*, sensación *f*; ✗ impacto *m*; sátira *f*; **make a ~ with** caer en gracia a; **2.** golpear, pegar; (*collide with*) chocar con(tra), dar con; *target* dar en, acertar; (*wound*) herir; (*damage*) hacer daño a; afectar; *Am.* F llegar a; **~ a p. a blow** asestarle un golpe a una p.; **~ at** dirigir (un) golpe(s) a; *fig.* satirizar, apuntar a; **~ off** remedar; *resemblance* coger; **~ it off with** hacer buenas migas con; **~ or miss** a la buena ventura; **~ out** atacar; repartir golpes; **~ (up)on** dar con; tropezar con; **l ~ on the idea** se me ocurrió la idea; **~ and run** atacar y retirarse; **he ~ his head against a tree** dio con la cabeza contra un árbol; **~ the nail on the head** dar en el clavo; **it ~s you in the eye** salta a la vista; **'~-and-'run driv·er** *mot.* conductor *m* que atropella y huye.

hitch [hitʃ] **1.** tirón *m*; ⚓ cote *m*, vuelta *f* de cabo; obstáculo *m*, dificultad *f*; *without a ~* a pedir de boca; **2.** mover de un tirón; amarrar; enganchar; atar; **~ up** *trousers* alzar; **'~-hike** hacer autostop.

hith·er ['hiðə] *mst lit.* acá, hacia acá; **~ and thither** acá y acullá; **hith·er·to** ['~'tu:] hasta ahora.

hive [haiv] **1.** *a. fig.* colmena *f*; **~s** *# urticaria *f*; **2.** enjambrar; acopiar (miel); *fig.* vivir aglomerados.

ho [hou] ¡eh!; ¡alto!; ¡hola!

hoar [hɔː] † cano; vetusto.

hoard [hɔːd] **1.** tesoro *m* (escondido); provisión *f*; acumulamiento *m*; **2.** (*a. ~ up*) atesorar; acumular (en secreto).

hoard·ing[1] ['hɔːdiŋ] atesoramiento *m*; acumulación *f*; acaparamiento *m*.

hoard·ing[2] [~] valla *f* de construcción; (*for posters*) cartelera *f*.

hoar·frost ['hɔːfrɔst] escarcha *f*.

hoar·i·ness ['hɔːrinis] canicie *f*; vetustez *f*.

hoarse [hɔːs] □ ronco, enronquecido; **'hoarse·ness** ronquedad *f*; # ronquera *f*.

hoar·y ['hɔːri] cano; vetusto.

hoax [houks] **1.** mistificación *f*; burla *f*; engaño *m*; **2.** mistificar; burlar; engañar.   [chimenea.]

hob[1] [hɔb] repisa *f* interior de la]

hob[2] [~] = *hobgoblin*; *Am.* F **play ~ with** trastornar.

hob·ble ['hɔbl] **1.** cojera *f*; maniota *f*; **2.** *v/i.* cojear; *v/t.* manear.

hob·ble·de·hoy ['hɔbldi'hɔi] mozalbete *m* desgarbado.

hob·by ['hɔbi] pasatiempo *m*, afición *f*; tema *f*, manía *f*; *orn.* alcotán *m*; '**~-horse** caballito *m* (de niños); caballo *m* mecedor; *fig.* tema *f*, caballo *m* de batalla.

hob·gob·lin ['hɔbgɔblin] duende *m*, trasgo *m*.

hob·nail ['hɔbneil] clavo *m* de botas.

hob·nob ['hɔbnɔb] F codearse (*with* con).

ho·bo ['houbou] *Am.* vagabundo *m*.

hock[1] [hɔk] **1.** *zo.* corvejón *m*; **2.** desjarretar.

hock[2] [~] vino *m* (blanco) del Rin.

hock[3] [~] *sl.* **1.** empeño *m*; **2.** empeñar; '**~-shop** casa *f* de empeños.

hock·ey ['hɔki] hockey *m*.

ho·cus-po·cus ['houkəs'poukəs] abracadabra *m*, mistificación *f*; engaño *m*; pasapasa *m*.

hod [hɔd] cuezo *m* (para llevar mortero y ladrillos).

hoe [hou] **1.** azada *f*, azadón *m*; sacho *m*; **2.** azadonar; sachar.

hog [hɔg] **1.** cerdo *m*, puerco *m* (*a. fig.*); F **go the whole ~** llegar hasta el extremo; liarse la manta a la cabeza; **2.** *sl.* acaparar; tragarse lo mejor de; *credit etc.* atribuirse todo; **hog·gish** ['~iʃ] □ puerco; glotón; **hogs·head** ['~zhed] pipa *f*, bocoy *m*; *medida de capacidad* (= 52,5 *o* 54 *galones ingleses*); '**hog·skin** piel *f* de cerdo; '**hog·wash** bazofia *f*.

hoi(c)k [hɔik] ✈ (hacer) encabritarse.

hoist [hɔist] **1.** montacargas *m*; elevador *m* *S.Am.*; cabria *f*; alzamiento *m*; **2.** alzar; *flag* enarbolar; ⚓ izar.

hoi·ty-toi·ty ['hɔiti'tɔiti] **1.** petulante, presuntuoso, picajoso; **2.** ¡cáspita!; ¡tate!.

ho·kum ['houkəm] *Am. sl.* efectismo *m*; cursilería *f*; tonterías *f/pl.*

hold [hould] **1.** agarro *m*; asimiento *m*; *wrestling*: presa *f*; *fig.* dominio *m*, influencia *f*; *fig.* arraigo *m*; (*place to grip*) asidero *m*, asa *f*; ⚓ bodega *f*; ♪ calderón *m*; *catch* (*or get, lay, take*) **~ of** agarrar, coger; apoderarse de; *have a ~ on* (*or over*) dominar; *keep ~ of* seguir agarrado a; **2.** *v/t.* tener; retener, guardar; detener; (*in place*) sujetar; agarrar, coger; contener, tener cabida para; mantener; sostener (*a. ♪*); juzgar;

post ocupar; *meeting* celebrar; *this box won't ~ them all* en esta caja no caben todos; ~ *back* retener; detener; refrenar; ~ *down* sujetar; oprimir; F ~ *down a job* mantenerse en un puesto; estar a la altura de un cargo; ~ *in* refrenar; ~ *off* mantener a distancia; ~ *on* sujetar; ~ *out* extender, ofrecer; *over* aplazar, diferir; ~ *up* (*support*) apoyar, sostener; (*raise*) levantar; (*stop*) detener; parar; suspender; interrumpir; (*rob*) saltear; (*gangsters*) atracar; **3.** [*irr.*] *v/i.* mantenerse firme, resistir, aguantar; (de)tenerse; ser valedero; (*weather*) continuar; (*stick*) pegarse; ~ *back* refrenarse; vacilar; ~ *forth* perorar (*about, on* sobre); ~ *good* (*or true*) ser valedero; ~*hard!* ¡tente!, ¡para!; ~ *off* mantenerse a distancia, esperar; ~ *on* agarrarse bien; aguantar; persisitir; ~ *on!* ¡espera!; ~ *out* resistir; durar; ~ *out for s.t.* no cejar hasta que se conceda algo; insistir en algo; ~ *to* atenerse a; afirmarse en; ~ *up* mantenerse en pie; (*weather*) seguir bueno; ~ *with* estar de acuerdo con; aprobar; '**hold-all** funda *f*, neceser *m*; '**hold-er** (*p.*) tenedor (-a *f*) *m*; (*tenant*) arrendatario (a *f*) *m*; (*office-, title-*) titular *m/f*; (*handle*) asidero *m*; receptáculo *m*; ⊕ soporte *m*; (*pad*) agarrador *m*; (*in compounds*) porta ...; '**hold-fast** grapa *f*; '**hold-ing** posesión *f*; tenencia *f*; propiedad *f*; ✝ ~*s* valores *m/pl.* en cartera; ✝ ~ *company* sociedad *f* de control; compañía *f* tenedora; '**hold-o-ver** *Am.* resto *m*, sobras *f/pl.*; consecuencias *f/pl.*; '**hold-up** F detención *f*; interrupción *f*; (*gangsters*) atraco *m*.

hole [houl] **1.** agujero *m*; cavidad *f*; (*a. golf*) hoyo *m*; bache *m* in *road*; rotura *f* in *clothes*; boquete *m* in *wall*; guarida *f* of *animals*; *fig.* cuchitril *m*; F *in a ~* en un aprieto; F *pick ~s* in encontrar defectos en; **2.** agujerear; *ball* meter en el hoyo; '**hole-and-'cor-ner** furtivo.

hole-y ['houli] F agujereado.

hol-i-day ['hɔlədi] **1.** día *m* de fiesta, día *m* festivo; asueto *m*; ~(*s pl.*) vacaciones *f/pl.*; ~*s with pay* vacaciones *f/pl.* retribuidas; ~ *camp* colonia *f* veraniega; **2.** veranear;

pasar las vacaciones; '~-**mak·er** veraneante *m/f*; turista *m/f*.

ho·li·ness ['houlinis] santidad *f*.

hol·ler ['hɔlə] F gritar; llamar a gritos.

hol·low ['hɔlou] **1.** □ hueco, ahuecado; *eyes* hundido; *fig.* vacío, falso; *voice* sepulcral, cavernoso; **2.** F *adv.* *beat (all)* ~ cascar, vencer completamente; **3.** hueco *m*; (con)cavidad *f*; depresión *f*; hondón *m* in *terrain*; **4.** (*a.* ~ *out*) ahuecar, excavar, vaciar; '~-'**ground** vaciado; '**hol·low·ness** concavidad *f*; oquedad *f* (*a. fig.*); falsedad *f*.

hol·ly ['hɔli] acebo *m*.

hol·ly·hock ['hɔlihɔk] malva *f* loca, malvarrosa *f*.

holm-oak ['houm'ouk] encina *f*.

hol·o·caust ['hɔləkɔːst] holocausto *m*; *fig.* destrucción *f* ocasionada por un incendio.

hol·ster ['houlstə] pistolera *f*.

ho·ly ['houli] santo; sagrado; ♀ *of Holies* sanctasanctórum *m*; ♀ *Thursday* jueves *m* santo; ~ *water* agua *f* bendita; ♀ *Week* semana *f* santa.

hom·age ['hɔmidʒ] homenaje *m*; *do (or pay, render)* ~ rendir homenaje (*to* a).

home [houm] **1.** hogar *m*; domicilio *m*, casa *f*; patria *f* (chica); (*institution*) asilo *m*; (*habitat*) habitación *f*; *sport:* meta *f*; *children's games:* la madre; *at* ~ en casa; *fig.* a gusto; **2.** *adj.* casero, doméstico; de casa; nativo; nacional; *a few ~ truths* cuatro verdades; ~ *life* vida *f* de familia; ♀ *Office* Ministerio *m* del Interior; (*Spain*) Ministerio *m* de la Gobernación; ~ *rule* autonomía *f*; ♀ *Secretary* Ministro *m* del Interior; (*Spain*) Ministro *m* de la Gobernación; ~ *straight racing:* recta *f* de la llegada; ~ *team* equipo *m* de casa; **3.** *adv.* a casa; en casa; a fondo; *be* ~ estar de vuelta; *bring s.t.* ~ *to s.o.* hacer que alguien se dé cuenta de algo; *come* ~ volver a casa; *it came* ~ *to me* me llegó al alma; me di cuenta de ello; *hit (or strike)* ~ herir en lo vivo; dar en el blanco; ⊕ meter a fondo; **4.** volver a casa; buscar la querencia; ✕ ~ *on the target* buscar al blanco; '~-'**baked** hecho en casa; '~-'**brewed** fermentado en casa; ~ *e·co'nom·ics Am.* economía *f* doméstica; '~-'**grown**

de cosecha propia; del país; '**home·less** sin casa ni hogar; '**home·li·ness** sencillez *f*; domesticidad *f*; comodidad *f*; *Am.* fealdad *f*; '**home·ly** sencillo, llano; casero; familiar; *Am.* feo.

home...: '~·**made** casero, de fabricación casera; '~·**sick** nostálgico; *be* ~ tener morriña; '~·**sick·ness** morriña *f*, nostalgia *f*; '~·**spun 1.** hilado (*or* tejido) en casa; casero; *fig.* llano; **2.** tela *f* de fabricación casera; '~·**stead** hacienda *f*, granja *f*; heredad *f*; casa *f*, caserío *m*; '~·**ward**(s) hacia casa; hacia la patria; ⚓ ~ *bound* con rumbo al puerto de origen; '~·**work** deberes *m/pl.*

hom·i·cide ['hɔmisaid] homicidio *m*; (*p.*) homicida *m/f*.

hom·i·ly ['hɔmili] homilía *f*.

hom·ing ['houmiŋ] vuelta *f* (al palomar); ~ *pigeon* paloma *f* mensajera; ~ *rocket* cohete *m* autodirigido buscador del blanco.

ho·moe·o·path ['houmjəpæθ] homeópata *m*; **ho·moe·o'path·ic** [~'opəθist] homeópata *m*; **ho·moe·'op·a·thy** homeopatía *f*.

ho·mo·ge·ne·i·ty [hɔmoudʒe'ni:iti] homogeneidad *f*; **ho·mo·ge·ne·ous** [~'dʒi:niəs] □ homogéneo; **ho·mol·o·gous** [hɔ'mɔləgəs] homólogo; **ho'mol·o·gy** [~dʒi] homología *f*; **hom·o·nym** ['hɔmənim] homónimo *m*; **ho·mo·sex·u·al** ['houmou'seksjuəl] homosexual.

hone [houn] **1.** piedra *f* de afilar; **2.** afilar.

hon·est ['ɔnist] □ honrado, recto, probo; (*chaste, decent, reasonable*) honesto; sincero, genuino; '**hon·es·ty** honradez *f*, rectitud *f* *etc.*

hon·ey ['hʌni] miel *f*; *Am.* (*my*) ~! ¡vida mía!; '~·**bee** abeja *f* (obrera); '**hon·ey·comb** panal *m*; '**hon·ey·combed** apanalado; acribillado; **hon·eyed** ['hʌnid] meloso, melifluo; '**hon·ey·moon 1.** luna *f* de miel, viaje *m* de novios; **2.** pasar la luna de miel; '**hon·ey·pot** mielera *f*; **hon·ey·suck·le** ['~sʌkl] madreselva *f*.

honk [hɔŋk] **1.** graznido *m* of *goose*; bocinazo *m* of *horn*; **2.** graznar; bocinar.

honk·y-tonk ['hɔŋkitɔŋk] *Am. sl.*

taberna *f* (*or* cabaret *m*) de mala fama.

hon·o·rar·i·um [ɔnə'rɛəriəm] honorario *m* (*mst pl.*); **hon·or·ar·y** ['ɔnərəri] honorario; no remunerado.

hon·o·(u)r ['ɔnə] **1.** honor *m*; (*esp. good name*) honra *f*; condecoración *f*; ~s *pl.* honores *m/pl.*; *last* ~s honras *f/pl.* (fúnebres); *point of* ~ punto *m* de honor; *word of* ~ palabra *f* de honor; *Your* ♀ vuestra merced; 🔯 Su Señoría; *in* ~ *of* en honor de; (*up*)*on my* ~ a fe mía; *do the* ~s *of the house* hacer los honores de la casa; **2.** honrar (*a.* ✝); *signature etc.* hacer honor a.

hon·o·(u)r·a·ble ['ɔnərəbl] □ honorable; honrado; (*conferring honour*) honroso; *Right* ♀ Ilustrísimo; ~ *mention* mención *f* honorífica; '**hon·o·(u)r·a·ble·ness** honorabilidad *f*, honradez *f*.

hooch [hu:tʃ] *Am. sl.* licor *m*.

hood [hud] capucha *f*, capilla *f*; (*univ., penitent's, hawk's*) capirote *m*; *mot.* capota *f*; *Am. mot.* capó *m*; *Am. sl.* criminal *m*; '**hood·ed** encapuchado; encapirotado.

hood·lum ['hu:dləm] *Am.* F matón *m*, gori!a *m*.

hoo·doo ['hu:du:] aojo *m*; mala suerte *f*; *put the* ~ *on* aojar.

hood·wink ['hudwiŋk] vendar los ojos a; engañar.

hoo·ey ['hu:i] *sl.* tonterías *f/pl.*, música *f* celestial.

hoof [hu:f] **1.** casco *m*, pezuña *f*; **2.** F ~ *it* marcharse; ir a pie; **hoofed** [hu:ft] ungulado.

hook [huk] **1.** gancho *m* (*a. boxing*); garfio *m*; (*fishing*) anzuelo *m*; (*door etc.*) aldabilla *f*; (*hanger*) colgadero *m*; ~s *and eyes* corchetes *m/pl.*; *by* ~ *or by crook* por fas o por nefas; ~, *line and sinker* totalmente; **2.** *v/t.* enganchar (*a. fishing*); pescar (*a. fig.*); encorvar; *sl.* hurtar; *sl.* ~ *it* largarse; ~ *up* enganchar; abrochar; *v/i.* engancharse; encorvarse; **hooked** [~t] ganchudo; '**hook-up** combinación *f*; conexión *f*; ⚡ acoplamiento *m*; *radio*: estaciones *f/pl.* conjugadas; '**hook·y:** *play* ~ hacer novillos.

hoo·li·gan ['hu:ligən] gamberro *m*, rufián *m*, camorrista *m*; '**hoo·li·gan·ism** gamberrismo *m*.

hoop [hu:p] **1.** aro *m*; ~ *skirt* miriñaque *m*; **2.** enarcar; **'hoop·er** tonelero *m*.

hoo·poe ['hu:pu:] abubilla *f*.

hoot [hu:t] **1.** ululato *m of owl*; bocinazo *m of horn*; ⚓, ⊕ toque *m* de sirena; (*laugh*) risotada *f*; grito *m*; **2.** *v/i.* ulular; gritar; *mot.* tocar la bocina; ⚓, ⊕ tocar la sirena; *v/t.* manifestar a gritos; dar grita a; silbar, abuchear (*a.* ~ *at*, ~ *off*, ~ *out*); **'hoot·er** sirena *f*; *mot.* bocina *f*.

hop¹ [hɔp] ♀ lúpulo *m* (*a.* ~s *pl.*).

hop² [~] **1.** salt(it)o *m*, brinco *m*; 🦋 vuelo *m*, etapa *f*; F baile *m*; ~, *skip and jump* triple salto *m*; **2.** *v/i.* brincar, saltar; danzar; F ~ *off* marcharse; bajar de; F ~ *on* subir a; *v/t.* atravesar (de un salto); F ~ *it* escabullirse; largarse.

hope [houp] **1.** esperanza *f*; **2.** esperar (*for acc.*, *to inf.*); ~ *in* confiar en; ~ *against* ~ esperar desesperando; **'hope·ful** ['~ful] □ esperanzado; optimista; esperanzador, que da esperanzas, prometedor; *be* ~ *that* esperar que; **'hope·less** □ desesperanzado; desesperado; imposible; ✠ desahuciado.

hop·per ['hɔpə] ⊕ tolva *f*; 🚃 vagón *m* tolva *m*; **hop·ping** ['hɔpiŋ]: F *he is* ~ *mad* está que bota.

hop·scotch ['hɔpskɔtʃ] infernáculo *m*.

horde [hɔ:d] horda *f*.

ho·ri·zon [hə'raizn] horizonte *m*; **hor·i·zon·tal** [hɔri'zɔntl] □ horizontal.

hor·mone ['hɔ:moun] hormona *f*.

horn [hɔ:n] **1.** cuerno *m*; asta *f of stag, bull*; ♪ trompa *f*; *mot.* bocina *f*, claxon *m*; ~ *of plenty* cuerno *m* de la abundancia; *on the* ~s *of a dilemma* entre la espada y la pared; **2.** *sl.* ~ *in* entrometerse; **horned** ['~id, *in compounds* hɔ:nd] cornudo; de cuernos ...

hor·net ['hɔ:nit] avispón *m*; *stir up a* ~s' *nest* armar cisco.

horn·less ['hɔ:nlis] sin cuernos; mocho; **'horn·pipe** ♪ cornamusa *f*; baile *m* vivaz (de marineros); **'horn-rimmed 'spec·ta·cles** anteojos *m/pl.* de concha; **horn·swoggle** ['~swɔgl] *Am. sl.* **1.** timo *m*; pamplinas *f/pl.*; **2.** timar; **'horn·y** □ córneo; *hands* calloso.

hor·o·scope ['hɔrəskoup] horóscopo *m*; *cast a* ~ sacar un horóscopo.

hor·ri·ble ['hɔrəbl] □ horrible, horroroso; **hor·rid** ['hɔrid] □ horroroso, horrible; F muy antipático; **hor·rif·ic** [hɔ'rifik] horrendo, horrífico; **hor·ri·fy** ['~fai] horrorizar; **hor·ror** ['hɔrə] horror *m* (*of a*); *the* ~s espasmo *m* de horror; espanto *m*. [ses *m/pl.*\

hors d'œuvres [ɔ:'də:vr] entreme-\

horse [hɔ:s] **1.** *zo.*, *gymnastics*: caballo *m*; ⚔ caballería *f*; ⊕ caballete *m*; ~ *of a different colour* harina *f* de otro costal; *eat like a* ~ comer como una vaca; *get on one's high* ~ darse aires de suficiencia; F *hold your* ~s! ¡para!, ¡despacito!; *take* ~ montar a caballo; ~ *artillery* artillería *f* montada; **2.** montar; proveer de caballos; **'~·back**: *on* ~ a caballo; **'~-box** vagón *m* para caballerías; **'~-break·er** domador *m* de caballos; **'~-chest·nut** castaña *f* de Indias; (*a.* ~ *tree*) castaño *m* de Indias; **'~-col·lar** collera *f*; **'~-deal·er** chalán *m*; ♀ **Guards** *pl.* guardias *f/pl.* montadas; **'~-hair** crin *f*; **'~-laugh** F risotada *f*; **'~-man** jinete *m*, caballista *m*; **'~-man·ship** equitación *f*, manejo *m* (del caballo); ~ **op·er·a** *Am. sl.* película *f* que se desarrolla en el oeste de EE.UU.; **'~-play** payasadas *f/pl.*, travesuras *f/pl.*, pelea *f* amistosa; **'~-pow·er** caballo *m* (de fuerza); **'~-race** carrera *f* de caballos; **'~-rad·ish** rábano *m* picante; **'~-sense** sentido *m* común; **'~-shoe** herradura *f*; **'~-show** concurso *m* hípico; **'~-whip** látigo *m*; **'~-wom·an** amazona *f*.

hors·y ['hɔ:si] caballuno; aficionado a caballos; carrerista.

hor·ti·cul·tur·al [hɔ:ti'kʌltʃərəl] hortícola; **'hor·ti·cul·ture** horticultura *f*; **hor·ti'cul·tur·ist** horticultor (-a *f*) *m*.

hose [houz] **1.** † calzas *f/pl.*; ✝ medias *f/pl.*, calcetines *m/pl.*; (*a.* **'~-pipe**) mang(uer)a *f*; **2.** regar (*or* limpiar) con manga.

ho·sier ['houʒə] calcetero (a *f*) *m*; **'ho·sier·y** calcetería *f*; géneros *m/pl.* de punto.

hos·pice ['hɔspis] hospicio *m*.

hos·pi·ta·ble ['hɔspitəbl] □ hospitalario.

hos·pi·tal ['hɔspitl] hospital *m*; **hos·pi·tal·i·ty** [ˌ~'tæliti] hospitalidad *f*; **hos·pi·tal·ize** ['ˌ~təlaiz] hospitalizar; **'hos·pi·tal·'ship** buque hospital *m*; **'hos·pi·tal-train** tren hospital *m*.

host[1] [houst] huésped *m* (*a. zo.*, ♀); anfitrión *m at meal*; hospedero *m of inn*.

host[2] [~] ✠ hueste *f*, ejército *m*; muchedumbre *f*; sinnúmero *m*; *Lord of* ~s Señor *m* de los ejércitos.

host[3] [~] *eccl.* hostia *f*.

hos·tage ['hɔstidʒ] rehén *m*.

hos·tel ['hɔstəl] albergue *m*; residencia *f* (de estudiantes).

host·ess ['houstis] huéspeda *f* (*v. host*[1]); ✈ azafata *f*.

hos·tile ['hɔstail] hostil; **hos·til·i·ty** [hɔs'tiliti] hostilidad *f*; *start hostilities* romper las hostilidades.

hos·tler ['ɔslə] = *ostler.*

hot [hɔt] caliente; *climate* cálido; *day* caluroso, de calor; *sun* ardiente, abrasador; *taste* picante; ⊕ en caliente; *fig. dispute* acalorado; *supporter* vehemente, acérrimo; *p.* enérgico; apasionado; lujurioso; F *situation* difícil, de mucho peligro; *sl.* robado; *Am. sl.* radiactivo; *be* ~ (*p.*) tener calor; (*weather*) hacer calor; (*th.*) estar caliente; F ~ *air* palabrería *f*; F ~ *dog* perro *m* caliente; *go like* ~ *cakes* venderse como pan bendito; *sl.* ~ *stuff* caliente; de rechupete; experto; **'hot-bed** almajara *f*; *fig.* semillero *m*, foco *m*.

hotch·potch ['hɔtʃpɔtʃ] olla *f* podrida; mezcolanza *f*, baturrillo *m*.

ho·tel [hou'tel] hotel *m*.

hot...: '~**foot** a toda prisa; '~**head** persona *f* exaltada (*or* impetuosa); '~**house** invernáculo *m*; '~**plate** calienta-platos *m*; hornillo *m* eléctrico; '~**pot** estofado *m*; '~**press** prensar en caliente; ~ *rod Am. sl.* bólido *m*; '~-'**wa·ter:** ~ *bottle*, ~ *bag* bolsa *f* de agua caliente.

hound [haund] **1.** perro *m* (de caza); podenco *m*; sabueso *m* de Artois; *fig.* canalla *m*; **2.** acosar, perseguir; ~ *on* incitar (*to* a).

hour ['auə] hora *f*; *fig.* momento *m*; *after* ~s fuera de horas; *by the* ~ por horas; *the small* ~s las altas horas; '~-**glass** reloj *m* de arena;

'~-**hand** horario *m*; '**hour·ly** (de) cada hora; por hora.

house 1. [haus], *pl.* **hous·es** ['hauziz] casa *f* (*a.* ✝); *thea.* sala *f*, público *m*, entrada *f*; edificio *m*; *parl.* cámara *f*; *univ.* colegio *m*; ~ *and home* hogar *m*; F *it's on the* ~ está pagado (por el dueño); *keep* ~ llevar la casa; tener casa propia; *attr.* de (la) casa, domiciliario, doméstico; **2.** [hauz] *v/t.* alojar; domiciliar; almacenar; meter (en); ⊕ encajar; ⚓ estibar; *v/i.* vivir, alojarse; ~-**a·gent** ['haus~] corredor *m* de casas; '~**boat** habitación *f* flotante; '~-**break·er** ladrón *m* con escala; demoledor *m* de casas; '~-**coat** bata *f*; '~-**fly** mosca *f* doméstica; '~**hold** casa *f*; familia *f*; menaje *m*; *attr.* casero, doméstico; *royal* ~ corte *f*; ~ *troops* guardia *f* real; *be a* ~ *word* andar en lenguas; '~**hold·er** cabeza *f* de familia; amo (a *f*) *m* de casa; inquilino (a *f*) *m*; '~-**keep·er** ama *f* de casa (*or* de llaves); '~**keep·ing 1.** gobierno *m* de la casa; quehaceres *m/pl.* domésticos; **2.** doméstico; '~**maid** criada *f*; '~-**paint·er** pintor *m* de brocha gorda; '~-**phy'si·cian** médico *m* residente; '~-**room** alojamiento *m*; cabida *f* (de una casa); *give* ~ *to* alojar, tener en casa; '~-**to-'house** de casa en casa; a domicilio; '~**top** tejado *m*; *shout from the* ~s pregonar a los cuatro vientos; '~-**train·ed** bien enseñado, limpio; '~-**warm·ing** (*a.* ~ *party*) fiesta *f* de estreno de una casa; ~**wife** ['~waif] ama *f* de casa; madre *f* de familia; mujer *f* casada; ['hʌzif] estuche *m* de costura; ~**wife·ly** ['~waifli] de ama de casa; hacendoso.

hous·ing ['hauziŋ] alojamiento *m*; (provisión *f* de) vivienda *f*; casas *f/pl.*; (*storage*) almacenaje *m*; ⊕ encaje *m*; ⊕ cárter *m*, caja *f*; ~ *estate* bloque *m* de casas protegidas; ~ *shortage* crisis *f* de vivienda.

hove [houv] *pret. a. p.p. of heave 2.*

hov·el ['hɔvl] casucha *f*, cuchitril *m*, tugurio *m*.

hov·er ['hɔvə] cernerse; revolotear; planear; estar suspendido; flotar (en el aire); rondar; vacilar; ✈ ~(*ing*) *plane* helicóptero *m*.

how [hau] cómo; *price*: a cómo; *before adj. or adv.* qué, cuán; ~ *large it is!* ¡qué grande es!, ¡cuán grande es!; ~ *large is it?* ¿cómo es de grande?, ¿de qué tamaño es?; *he does not know* ~ *large it is* no sabe lo grande que es, no sabe cuán grande es; ~ *are you?* ¿cómo está Vd.?; ¿qué tal? (F); ~ *about ...?* ¿qué tal si ...?; ¿qué te parece ...?; ¿qué tal anda ...?; *v. else, far;* ~ *long* cuánto tiempo; ~ *many* cuántos; ~ *much* cuánto; ~ *often* cuántas veces; ~ *old is he?* ¿cuántos años tiene?, ¿qué edad tiene?; ~**d'ye-do** [¹ʌdiˈduː] F lío *m*, berenjenal *m*; ~**ev-er 1.** *adv.* comoquiera que; por más que; *(with adj. or adv.)* por (muy) ... que; ~ *clever he is* por (muy) hábil que sea; ~ *hot it is* por mucho calor que haga; ~ *much* por mucho que; **2.** *conj.* sin embargo, no obstante, con todo.

how-itz-er [ˈhauitsə] obús *m*.

howl [haul] **1.** aullido *m*; alarido *m*; chillido *m*; ♫ silbido *m*; **2.** aullar; dar alaridos; F reír a carcajadas; ~ *down* abuchear; **'howl-er** F plancha *f*, falta *f* garrafal; **'howl-ing 1.** aullador; F formidable, clamoroso; **2.** aullido(s) *m(pl.)*.

hoy[1] [hɔi] ¡eh!, ¡hola!   [caza *f*.]

hoy[2] [~] ♣ buque *m* costero; bar-]

hub [hʌb] cubo *m*; *fig.* eje *m*, centro *m*; **'~-cap** tapacubos *m*.

hub-bub [ˈhʌbʌb] baraúnda *f*, batahola *f*; alboroto *m*.

hub(·by) [ˈhʌb(i)] F marido *m*.

huck-ster [ˈhʌkstə] **1.** buhonero *m*; mercachifle *m*; **2.** (re)vender; regatear.

hud-dle [ˈhʌdl] **1.** pelotón *m*, montón *m*; grupo *m* apretado; *sl.* *go into a* ~ ir aparte para conferenciar; **2.** *v/t.* amontonar; confundir; hacer precipitadamente; *v/i.* amontonarse, apretarse (*a.* ~ *together, up*); acurrucarse (*a.* ~ *up*).   [tono *m.*]

hue[1] [hjuː] color *m*, tinte *m*; matiz *m*;]

hue[2] [~]: ~ *and cry* alarma *f*; protesta *f* clamorosa.

huff [hʌf] mal humor *m*, pique *m*; rabieta *f*; *in a* ~ ofendido; **'huff·y** □ malhumorado, ofendido; enojadizo.

hug [hʌg] **1.** abrazo *m*; **2.** abrazar; apretujar; *coast etc.* no apartarse de; *fig.* afirmarse en; *fig.* acariciar; ~ *o.s.* congratularse (*on* de, por).

huge [hjuːdʒ] □ enorme, inmenso, descomunal; **'huge·ness** inmensidad *f*.

hug·ger-mug·ger [ˈhʌgəmʌgə] F **1.** confusión *f*, desorden *m*; **2.** confuso; desordenado; **3.** *adv.* desordenadamente.   [*adj. a. su. m* (a *f*).]

Hu-gue-not [ˈhjuːgənɔt] hugonote]

hulk [hʌlk] ♣ casco *m* (arrumbado); pontón *m*, carraca *f*; *fig.* armatoste *m*; **'hulk·ing** grande y pesado.

hull [hʌl] **1.** ♣ casco *m*; ♣ vaina *f*, cáscara *f*; **2.** mondar; desvainar; ♣ dar en el casco de.

hul·la·ba·loo [hʌləbəˈluː] baraúnda *f*, batahola *f*; vocería *f*.

hul·lo [ˈhʌˈlou] ¡hola!; *teleph.* ¡oiga!; *(answering teleph.)* ¡diga!

hum [hʌm] **1.** zumbido *m*; tararareo *m*; murmullo *m*; **2.** zumbar; *tune* tararear; *v. haw;* F *make things* ~ avivarlo; desplegar gran actividad.

hu·man [ˈhjuːmən] □ humano *adj. a. su. m*; **hu·mane** [hjuːˈmein] □ humano; compasivo; **hu·man·ism** [ˈhjuːmənizm] humanismo *m*; **'hu·man·ist** humanista *m/f*; **hu·man·i·tar·i·an** [hjuːmæniˈteəriən] humanitario *adj. a. su. m* (a *f*); **hu·man·i·ty** humanidad *f*; *humanities pl.* humanidades *f/pl.*; **hu·man·i·za·tion** [hjuːmənaiˈzeiʃn] humanización *f*; **'hu·man·ize** humanizar.

hum·ble [ˈhʌmbl] **1.** □ humilde; *my* ~ *self, your* ~ *servant* un servidor; *eat* ~ *pie* humillarse y pedir perdón; **2.** humillar.

hum·ble-bee [ˈhʌmblbiː] abejorro *m*.   [dad *f.*]

hum·ble-ness [ˈhʌmblnis] humil-]

hum·bug [ˈhʌmbʌg] **1.** bola *f*, farsa *f*; embaucamiento *m*; disparate *m*; (*p.*) farsante *m/f*, charlatán (-a *f*) *m*, embaucador (-a *f*) *m*; (*sweet*) caramelo *m* de menta; **2.** embaucar.

hum·ding·er [hʌmˈdiŋə] *Am. sl.* (*p.*) machote *m*; cosa *f* estupenda.

hum·drum [ˈhʌmdrʌm] monótono; rutinario; aburrido.

hu·mid [ˈhjuːmid] húmedo; **hu·mid·i·ty** humedad *f*.

hu·mil·i·ate [hjuːˈmilieit] humillar; **hu·mil·i·a·tion** humillación *f*.

hu·mil·i·ty [hjuːˈmiliti] humildad *f*.

hum·ming-bird [ˈhʌmiŋbəːd] colibrí *m*; **hum·ming-top** [ˈhʌmiŋtɔp] trompa *f*.

hum·mock ['hʌmək] morón *m*, montecillo *m*.

hu·mor·ist ['ĥju:mərist] humorista *m/f*; persona *f* chistosa.

hu·mor·ous ['hju:mərəs] □ festivo, chistoso, humorístico.

hu·mo(u)r ['hju:mə] **1.** humor *m*; humorismo *m*; capricho *m*; (*situation*) comicidad *f*; *in a good (bad)* ~ de buen (mal) humor; *be in the* ~ *for* estar (de humor) para; *out of* ~ de mal humor; **2.** seguir el humor a; complacer; mimar; **'hu·mo(u)r·less** sin (sentido de) humor.

hump [hʌmp] **1.** joroba *f*, corcova *f*, giba *f*; montecillo *m*; 🐫 lomo *m* para maniobras de gravedad); *fig.* mal humor *m*, abatimiento *m*; *give a p. the* ~ jorobar; **2.** corcovar(se); *fig.* jorobar; F llevar al hombro; **'hump·back**, **'hump·backed** *v.* hunchback.

humph [mm] ¡bah!, ¡qué va!

hump·ty-dump·ty ['hʌmpti'dʌmpti] F persona *f* rechoncha.

hump·y ['hʌmpi] desigual; giboso.

hu·mus ['hju:məs] humus *m*.

hunch [hʌntʃ] **1.** *v.* hump; tajada *f*, pedazo *m* grande; F idea *f*, corazonada *f*, sospecha *f*; **2.** encorvar (*a.* ~ *up*); **'hunch·back** corcova *f*, joroba *f*; (*p.*) corcovado (*a f*) *m*, jorobado (*a f*) *m*; **'hunch·backed** corcovado, jorobado.

hun·dred ['hʌndrəd] **1.** cien(to); **2.** ciento *m*; centenar *m*; centena *f*; *in (by)* ~s a centenares; **'hun·dred·fold 1.** *adj.* céntuplo; **2.** *adv.* cien veces; **hun·dredth** ['~θ] centésimo (*a. su. m*); **'hun·dred·weight** (= 50,8 Kg.) *approx.* quintal *m*.

hung [hʌŋ] *pret. a. p.p. of* hang 1.

Hun·gar·i·an [hʌŋ'gɛəriən] **1.** húngaro *adj. a. su. m* (*a f*); **2.** (*language*) húngaro *m*.

hun·ger ['hʌŋgə] **1.** hambre *f* (*a. fig.*) (for de); ~ *strike* huelga *f* de hambre; **2.** hambrear; tener hambre (*after, for* de).

hun·gry ['hʌŋgri] □ hambriento; *land* pobre, estéril; *be* ~ tener hambre, tener ganas (*for* de).

hunk [hʌŋk] F buen pedazo *m*, rebanada *f* gruesa.

hunk·y(-do·ry) ['hʌŋki('dɔ:ri)] *Am. sl.* magnífico, de órdago.

hunt [hʌnt] **1.** (partida *f* de) caza *f*, cacería *f*; montería *f*; *on the* ~ *for*

a caza de; **2.** *v/t.* cazar; perseguir; buscar; *hounds etc.* emplear en la caza; *country* recorrer de caza; ~ *out*, ~ *up* rebuscar; *v/i.* cazar, buscar (*a.* ~ *for*); *go* ~*ing* ir de caza; **'hunt·er** cazador *m*; caballo *m* de caza; (*watch*) saboneta *f*; **'hunt·ing 1.** caza *f*; montería *f*; **2.** cazador; de caza; **'hunt·ing-box** pabellón *m* de caza; **'hunt·ing-ground** cazadero *m*; **'hunt·ress** cazadora *f*; **'hunts·man** montero *m*, cazador *m*.

hur·dle ['hɜ:dl] valla *f* (*a. sport*); **'hur·dler** corredor (-a *f*) *m* en las carreras de vallas; **'hur·dle-race** carrera *f* de vallas. [nillo *m*.⟩
hur·dy-gur·dy ['hɜ:digə:di] orga-⟩

hurl [hɜ:l] **1.** lanzamiento *m*; **2.** lanzar, arrojar.

hurl·y-burl·y ['hɜ:libə:li] batahola *f*, tumulto *m*. [¡viva …!⟩
hur·ra(h) [hu'rɑ:] ¡hurra!; ~ *for* …⟩

hur·ri·cane ['hʌrikən] huracán *m*.

hur·ried ['hʌrid] □ apresurado; hecho de (*or* a) prisa.

hur·ry ['hʌri] **1.** prisa *f*; *in a* ~ de prisa; *be in a* ~ (*to*) tener prisa (por); *is there any* ~? ¿corre prisa?; *F I shan't come back here in a* ~ aquí no pongo los pies nunca más; **2.** *v/t.* apresurar, dar prisa a, acelerar (*a.* ~ *on*, ~ *up*); ~ *away*, ~ *off* hacer marchar de prisa; *v/i.* apresurarse (*to* a), darse prisa (*a.* ~ *up*) (*to* para, en); ~ *away*, ~ *off* marcharse de prisa; ~ *over* pasar rápidamente por; concluir a prisa; hacer con precipitación; **'~·scur·ry 1.** atropello *m*, precipitación *f*; **2.** precipitadamente, atropelladamente.

hurt [hɜ:t] **1.** daño *m*, mal *m*; dolor *m*; herida *f*; **2.** [*irr.*] *v/t.* lastimar, dañar; herir; perjudicar; hacer mal a; doler; ofender; *get* ~ lastimarse; *v/i.* doler; hacer mal; F sufrir daño; **hurt·ful** ['~ful] □ dañoso, perjudicial.

hur·tle ['hɜ:tl] arrojarse con violencia; volar; caer con violencia.

hus·band ['hʌzbənd] **1.** marido *m*, esposo *m*; **2.** economizar; manejar con economía; **'hus·band·man** labrador *m*, granjero *m*, agricultor *m*; **'hus·band·ry** labranza *f*, agricultura *f*; granjería *f*; economía *f*; (buen) gobierno *m*.

hush [hʌʃ] **1.** silencio *m*; quietud *f*;

2. v/t. acallar; apaciguar; ~ up
echar tierra a; v/i. callar(se);
3. ¡chito!, ¡chitón!; '~-'~ F muy
secreto; '~-mon·ey F precio m del
silencio (de una p.).

husk [hʌsk] **1.** cascabillo m; cáscara
f (a. fig.); vaina f; **2.** descascarar;
desvainar; '**husk·i·ness** ronquedad f; '**husk·y¹** □ ronco; ♀ casca-
rudo; F fornido.

hus·ky² ['hʌski] esquimal adj. a. su.
m/f; perro m esquimal, husky m.

hus·sar [hu'zɑː] húsar m.

hus·sy ['hʌsi] mujerzuela f; sinver-
gonzona f.   [f/pl.]

hus·tings ['hʌstiŋz] pl. elecciones]

hus·tle ['hʌsl] **1.** prisa f; actividad f
(febril); empuje m; ~ and bustle
actividad f bulliciosa; **2.** v/t. empujar; atropellar; apresurar, dar prisa
a; v/i. apresurarse; F menearse;
'**hus·tler** F persona f de empuje;
trafagón m.

hut [hʌt] cabaña f; barraca f (a. ⚔);
casucha f; casilla f; cobertizo m.

hutch [hʌtʃ] conejera f for rabbit;
jaula f; arca f; cabaña f.

hut·ment ['hʌtmənt], **hut·ted camp**
['hʌtid kæmp] campamento m de
barracas.

huz·za [hu'zɑː] † ¡viva!, ¡vítor!

hy·a·cinth ['haiəsinθ] jacinto m.

hy·ae·na [hai'iːnə] hiena f.

hy·brid ['haibrid] híbrido adj. a.
su. m (a f); '**hy·brid·ism** hibri-
dismo m; '**hy·brid·ize** hibridar.

hy·dra ['haidrə] hidra f.

hy·dran·gea [hai'dreindʒə] hortensia f.

hy·drant ['haidrənt] boca f de riego.

hy·drate ['haidreit] **1.** hidrato m;
2. hidratar(se).

hy·drau·lic [hai'drɔːlik] **1.** □ hidráulico; **2.** ~s hidráulica f.

hy·dro... ['haidrou...] hidr(o)...;
'~'car·bon hidrocarburo m; '~'chlo-
ric ac·id ácido m clorhídrico;
'~-dy'nam·ics hidrodinámica f;
'~-e'lec·tric hidroeléctrico; ~ generating station central f hidro-
eléctrica; **hy·dro·gen** ['haidridʒən]
hidrógeno m; ~ bomb bomba f de
hidrógeno; **hy·dro·gen·at·ed** [hai-
'drɔdʒineitid], **hy'drog·e·nous** hi-
drogenado; **hy'drog·ra·phy** [~grə-
fi] hidrografía f; **hy·dro·path·ic**
['haidrou'pæθik] **1.** hidropático; **2.**
(a. ~ establishment) establecimiento

m hidropático; **hy·drop·a·thy** [hai-
'drɔpəθi] hidropatía f.

hy·dro...: '~'pho·bi·a hidrofobia f;
'~·plane hidroplano m; '~'stat·ic
1. hidrostático; **2.** ~s hidrostática f.

hy·drox·ide [hai'drɔksaid] hidró-]
hy·e·na [hai'iːnə] hiena f. [xido m.]

hy·giene ['haidʒiːn] higiene f; **hy-**
'**gi·en·ic 1.** □ higiénico; **2.** ~s
higiene f.   [metro m.]

hy·grom·e·ter [hai'grɔmitə] higró-]

Hy·men ['haimen] himeneo m; ⚥
anat. himen m; **hy·me·ne·al**
[~'niːəl] nupcial.

hymn [him] **1.** himno m; **2.** v/t.
ensalzar con himnos; v/i. cantar
himnos; **hym·nal** ['~nəl], '**hymnbook** himnario m.

hy·per·bo·la [hai'pəːbələ] Ⱥ hipérbola f; **hy·per·bo·le** [~li] rhet.
hipérbole f; **hy·per·bol·ic** [~'bɔlik],
hy·per·bol·i·cal □ hiperbólico;
hy·per·crit·i·cal ['~'kritikl] □ hipercrítico; **hy'per·tro·phy** [~trəfi]
hipertrofia f.

hy·phen ['haifən] guión m; **hy-
phen·ate** [~eit] unir (or separar or
escribir) con guión; ~d American
norteamericano (a f) m de nacimiento extranjero.

hyp·no·sis [hip'nousis] hipnosis f.
hyp·not·ic [hip'nɔtik] □ hipnótico
adj. a. su. m (a f); **hyp·no·tism**
['~nətizm] hipnotismo m; '**hyp·no-
tist** hipnotista m/f; **hyp·no·tize**
['~taiz] hipnotizar.

hy·po ['haipou] hiposulfito m sódico.

hy·po·chon·dri·a [haipou'kɔndriə]
hipocondría f; **hy·po·chon·dri·ac**
[~driæk] hipocondríaco adj. a. su. m
(a f); **hy·poc·ri·sy** [hi'pɔkrəsi]
hipocresía f; **hyp·o·crite** ['hipəkrit]
hipócrita m/f; **hyp·o·crit·i·cal** □
hipócrita; **hy·po·der·mic** [haipə-
'dəːmik] hipodérmico; **hy·pot·e·
nuse** [hai'pɔtinjuːz] hipotenusa f;
hy'poth·e·cate [~θikeit] hipotecar;
hy'poth·e·sis [~θisis], pl. **hy-
'poth·e·ses** [~θisiːz] hipótesis f;
hy·po·thet·ic, hy·po·thet·i·cal [~
pə'θetik(l)] □ hipotético.

hys·sop ['hisəp] ♀, eccl. hisopo m.

hys·te·ri·a [his'tiəriə] ♂ histerismo
m; excitación f loca; **hys·ter·ic,**
mst **hys·ter·i·cal** [his'terik(l)] □
histérico; **hys·ter·ics** paroxismo m
histérico; go into ~ ponerse histérico.

I

I [ai] yo.

i·am·bic [ai'æmbik] yámbico; **'i·amb, i'am·bus** [ˌbəs] yambo *m*.

I·be·ri·an [ai'biəriən] **1.** ibero (a *f*) *m*; **2.** ibérico.

i·bex ['aibeks] rebeco *m*.

ice [ais] **1.** hielo *m*; (*to eat*) helado *m*; *break the* ~ romper el hielo; F *cut no* ~ no pinchar ni cortar; **2.** *v/t.* helar; (*with sugar*) alcorzar, garapiñar; *v/i.* helarse (*a.* ~ *up*); '~-age período *m* glacial; '~-axe piolet *m*; **ice·berg** ['ˌbəːg] témpano *m*, iceberg *m*.

ice...: '~-bound helado; preso entre los hielos; '~-box *Am.*, '~-chest nevera *f*; '~-break·er ♨ rompehielos *m*; '~-cream helado *m*, mantecado *m*; '~-floe témpano *m*; '~-'hock·ey hockey *m* sobre hielo.

Ice·land·er ['aisləndə] islandés (-a *f*) *m*; **Ice·land·ic** [ais'lændik] islandés *adj. a. su. m.*

ich·thy·ol·o·gy [ikθi'ɔlədʒi] ictiología *f*.

i·ci·cle ['aisikl] carámbano *m*.

i·ci·ness ['aisinis] frialdad *f* (de hielo).

ic·ing ['aisiŋ] formación *f* de hielo; alcorza *f*, capa *f* de azúcar *on cake*.

i·con ['aikɔn] icono *m*; **i·con·o·clast** ['ai'kɔnəklæst] iconoclasta *m/f*.

i·cy ['aisi] □ helado, glacial (*a. fig.*); gélido (*mst lit.*).

i·de·a [ai'diə] idea *f*, concepto *m*; *bright* ~ ocurrencia *f*, idea *f* luminosa; *form* (*or get*) *an* ~ *of* hacerse una idea de; F *the very* ~! ¡ni hablar!; **i'de·al 1.** □ ideal; perfecto; **2.** ideal *m*; **i'de·al·ism** idealismo *m*; **i'de·al·ist** idealista *m/f*; **i·de·al·is·tic** □ idealista; **i'de·al·ize** [ˌaiz] idealizar.

i·den·ti·cal [ai'dentikl] □ idéntico; **i'den·ti·cal·ness** identidad *f*; **i·den·ti·fi·ca·tion** identificación *f*; ~ *mark* señal *f* (*or* marca *f*) de identificación *f*; *v. a. identity*; **i'den·ti·fy** [ˌfai] identificar; **i'den·ti·ty** identidad *f*; ~ *card* cédula *f* personal, carnet *m*; ~ *disc* placa *f* (*or* chapa *f*) de identidad.

id·e·o·log·i·cal [aidiə'lɔdʒikl] □ ideológico; **id·e·ol·o·gy** [ˌ'ɔlədʒi] ideología *f*.

id·i·o·cy ['idiəsi] idiotez *f*, imbecilidad *f*.

id·i·om ['idiəm] modismo *m*, idiotismo *m*; lenguaje *m*; idioma *m*; estilo *m*; **id·i·o·mat·ic** [idiə'mætik] □ idiomático.

id·i·o·syn·cra·sy [idiə'siŋkrəsi] idiosincrasia *f*.

id·i·ot ['idiət] idiota *m/f*, tonto (a *f*) *m*, imbécil *m/f*; **id·i·ot·ic** [idi'ɔtik] □ idiota, necio, imbécil.

i·dle ['aidl] **1.** □ ocioso; desocupado; ⊕ parado; inactivo; *p. contp.* holgazán, perezoso; vano, inútil; *talk* vacío, frívolo; ~ *hours* ratos *m/pl.* perdidos, horas *f/pl.* de ocio; ~ *question* pregunta *f* ociosa; ⊕ *run* ~ marchar en vacío; **2.** *v/t.* (*mst* ~ *away*) gastar ociosamente; perder; *v/i.* haraganear; vagar; ⊕ marchar en vacío; **'i·dle·ness** ociosidad *f*; desocupación *f*; holgazanería *f*; pereza *f*; frivolidad *f*; **'i·dler** ocioso (a *f*) *m*, haragán (-a *f*) *m*, zángano *m*.

i·dol ['aidl] ídolo *m*; **i·dol·a·ter** [ai'dɔlətə] idólatra *m*; **i'dol·a·tress** idólatra *f*; **i'dol·a·trous** □ idólatra; idolátrico; **i'dol·a·try** idolatría *f*; **i·dol·ize** ['aidəlaiz] idolatrar.

i·dyll ['aidil] idilio *m*; **i'dyl·lic** □ idílico.

if [if] **1.** si; ~ *only...!* ¡ojalá (que)...!; ~ *so* si es así; **2.** hipótesis *f*; duda *f*; ~*s and buts* peros *m/pl.*, dudas *f/pl.*; **'if·fy** *Am.* F dudoso.

ig·loo ['iglu] iglú *m*.

ig·ne·ous ['igniəs] ígneo.

ig·nite [ig'nait] encender(se); **ig·ni·tion** [ˌ'niʃn] ignición *f*; *mot.* encendido *m*; ~ *key* llave *f* de contacto.

ig·no·ble [ig'noubl] □ innoble.

ig·no·min·i·ous [ignə'miniəs] □ ignominioso; **'ig·no·min·y** ignominia *f*.

ig·no·ra·mus [ignə'reiməs] ignorante *m/f*; **ig·no·rance** ['ignərəns] ignorancia *f*; **'ig·no·rant** ignorante;

F inculto; *be ~ of* ignorar, desconocer; **ig·nore** [ig'nɔː] desatender, no hacer caso de (*a p.*).

i·lex ['aileks] encina *f*.

ilk [ilk] (mismo) nombre *m*; F especie *f*, jaez *m*.

ill [il] **1.** *su.* mal *m*; desgracia *f*; daño *m*; **2.** *adj.* malo; enfermo; *fall (or take) ~* caer (*or* ponerse) enfermo; **3.** *adv.* mal; *v. ease; take it ~* tomarlo a mal.

I'll [ail] = *I will, I shall*.

ill-ad·vised ['iləd'vaizd] malaconsejado.

il·la·tive [i'leitiv] ilativo.

ill...: '**~-'bred** malcriado; '**~-dis-'posed** malintencionado; maldispuesto (*to[wards]* a, hacia).

il·le·gal [i'liːgəl] □ ilegal; **il·le·gal·i·ty** [ili'gæliti] ilegalidad *f*.

il·leg·i·ble [i'ledʒəbl] □ ilegible.

il·le·git·i·ma·cy [ili'dʒitiməsi] ilegitimidad *f*; **il·le'git·i·mate** [~mit] □ ilegítimo.

ill...: '**~-'fat·ed** aciago; malhadado; malogrado; '**~-'fa·vo(u)red** feo, mal parecido; '**~-'feel·ing** hostilidad *f*, rencor *m*; '**~-'got·ten** mal adquirido; '**~-'hu·mo(u)red** malhumorado.

il·lib·er·al [i'libərəl] □ iliberal; **il·lib·er·al·i·ty** [ilibə'ræliti] ilibe-\

il·lic·it [i'lisit] □ ilícito. [ralidad *f*.\

il·lim·it·a·ble [i'limitəbl] ilimitable.

il·lit·er·a·cy [i'litərəsi] analfabetismo *m*; **il·lit·er·ate** ['~rit] □ analfabeto *adj. a. su. m* (*a f*); iletrado.

ill...: '**~-'judged** imprudente; '**~-'man·nered** grosero, mal educado; '**~-'na·tured** malicioso; malhumorado.

ill·ness ['ilnis] enfermedad *f*, mal *m*.

il·log·i·cal [i'lɔdʒikl] □ ilógico.

ill...: **~-o·mened** ['il'oumend] de mal agüero; '**~-'starred** malhadado; '**~-'tem·pered** de mal genio; malhumorado; '**~-'timed** intempestivo; '**~-'treat** maltratar.

il·lu·mi·nant [i'ljuːminənt] (tipo *m* de) alumbrado *m*; **il'lu·mi·nate** [~neit] iluminar, alumbrar (*a. fig.*); **~d** *sign* letrero *m* luminoso; **il'lu·mi·nat·ing** instructivo, aclaratorio; **ǂ** de alumbrado; **il·lu·mi'na·tion** iluminación *f*; alumbrado *m*; **il'lu·mi·na·tive** [~neitiv] iluminativo; **il'lu·mi·na·tor** iluminador (*-a f*) *m*; **il'lu·mine** [~min] = *illuminate*.

ill-use ['il'juːz] maltratar.

il·lu·sion [i'luːʒn] ilusión *f*; **il'lu·sive** [~siv] □, **il'lu·so·ry** [~səri] □ ilusorio.

il·lus·trate ['iləstreit] ilustrar; **il·lus'tra·tion** ilustración *f*; '**il·lus·tra·tive** □ ilustrativo; *be ~ of* ejemplificar; '**il·lus·tra·tor** ilustrador (*-a f*) *m*.

il·lus·tri·ous [i'lʌstriəs] □ ilustre.

ill-will ['il'wil] mala voluntad *f*; rencor *m*, odio *m*.

I'm [aim] = *I am*.

im·age ['imidʒ] **1.** imagen *f*; *be the very* (F *spitting*) *~ of* ser el vivo retrato de; **2.** representar; retratar; imaginar; reflejar; '**im·age·ry** imaginería *f*.

im·ag·i·na·ble [i'mædʒinəbl] imaginable; **im'ag·i·nar·y** imaginario; **im·ag·i·na·tion** [~'neiʃən] imaginación *f*; **im'ag·i·na·tive** [~nətiv] □ imaginativo; **im'ag·i·na·tive·ness** imaginativa *f*; **im'ag·ine** [~dʒin] imaginar(se), figurarse; *just ~!* ¡imagínese *f*.

im·be·cile ['imbisiːl] □ imbécil *adj. a. su. m/f*; **im·be·cil·i·ty** [~'siliti] imbecilidad *f*.

im·bibe [im'baib] (em)beber; *fig.* embeberse de (*or* en).

im·bro·glio [im'brouliou] embrollo *m*, lío *m*.

im·bue [im'bjuː] *fig.* imbuir (*with* de, en); empapar; teñir.

im·i·ta·ble ['imitəbl] imitable; **im·i·tate** [~teit] imitar; *b.s.* remedar; **im·i'ta·tion** imitación *f*; *b.s.* remedo *m*; *attr.* imitado, artificial; *~ jewels* joyas *f/pl.* de imitación; '**im·i·ta·tive** □ imitativo; imitador; '**im·i·ta·tor** imitador (*-a f*) *m*.

im·mac·u·late [i'mækjulit] □ sin mancha, limpísimo; inmaculado; correcto; ♀ *Conception* Inmaculada (*or* Purísima) Concepción *f*.

im·ma·nent ['imənənt] inmanente.

im·ma·te·ri·al [imə'tiəriəl] □ inmaterial; sin importancia; indiferente.

im·ma·ture [imə'tjuə] inmaturo; verde; **im·ma'tu·ri·ty** inmadurez *f*, inexperiencia *f*.

im·meas·ur·a·ble [i'meʒərəbl] □ inmensurable, inmenso.

im·me·di·ate [i'miːdjət] inmediato; **im'me·di·ate·ly 1.** *adv.* inmediatamente, luego, en seguida; **2.** *cj.* así que, luego que.

im·me·mo·ri·al [imi'mɔːriəl] □ in-memorial, inmemorable.

im·mense [i'mens] □ inmenso, enorme, vasto; *sl.* estupendo; **im-'men·si·ty** inmensidad *f*.

im·merse [i'mɔːs] sum(erg)ir; ~ o.s. *in fig.* sumergirse en; ~ed *in fig.* absorto en; **im'mer·sion** inmersión *f*, sumersión *f*; ~ heater calentador *m* de inmersión.

im·mi·grant ['imigrənt] inmigrante *adj. a. su. m/f*; **im·mi·grate** ['~greit] inmigrar; **im·mi'gra·tion** inmigración *f*.

im·mi·nence ['iminəns] inminencia *f*; **'im·mi·nent** □ inminente.

im·mo·bile [i'moubail] inmóvil, inmoble; **im·mo·bil·i·ty** [imou'biliti] inmovilidad *f*; **im·mo·bi·lize** [i'moubilaiz] inmovilizar.

im·mod·er·ate [i'mɔdərit] □ inmoderado; **im'mod·er·ate·ness** inmoderación *f*.

im·mod·est [i'mɔdist] □ inmodesto, impúdico; **im'mod·es·ty** inmodestia *f*, impudicia *f*.

im·mo·late ['imouleit] inmolar; **im-mo'la·tion** inmolación *f*.

im·mor·al [i'mɔrəl] □ inmoral; **im-mo·ral·i·ty** [imə'ræliti] inmoralidad *f*.

im·mor·tal [i'mɔːtl] □ inmortal *adj. a. su. m/f*; **im·mor·tal·i·ty** [~-'tæliti] inmortalidad *f*; **im'mor·tal·ize** [~təlaiz] inmortalizar.

im·mov·a·ble [i'muːvəbl] **1.** □ inmoble, inmóvil; inalterable; **2.** ~s *pl.* bienes *m/pl.* inmuebles.

im·mune [i'mjuːn] inmune (*from, to* contra); exento (*from* de); **im-'mu·ni·ty** inmunidad *f*; exención *f*; **'im·mu·nize** [~aiz] inmunizar.

im·mure [i'mjuə] emparedar.

im·mu·ta·bil·i·ty [imjuːtə'biliti] inmutabilidad *f*; **im'mu·ta·ble** □ inmutable.

imp [imp] trasgo *m*, duende *m*, diablillo *m* (*a. fig.*).

im·pact ['impækt] impacto *m* (*a. fig.*), choque *m*; *fig.* efecto *m*.

im·pair [im'pɛə] perjudicar, menoscabar, deteriorar, debilitar.

im·pale [im'peil] empalar, espetar.

im·pal·pa·ble [im'pælpəbl] □ impalpable; *fig.* intangible.

im·pan·(n)el [im'pænl] = *empanel*.

im·part [im'pɑːt] comunicar, hacer saber; impartir.

im·par·tial [im'pɑːʃl] □ imparcial; **im·par·ti·al·i·ty** ['~ʃi'æliti] imparcialidad *f*.

im·pass·a·ble [im'pɑːsəbl] □ intransitable, impracticable.

im·passe [æm'pɑːs] callejón *m* sin salida (*a. fig.*).

im·pas·sioned [im'pæʃnd] apasionado, ardiente.

im·pas·sive [im'pæsiv] □ impasible; **im'pas·sive·ness** impasibilidad *f*.

im·pa·tience [im'peiʃns] impaciencia *f*; **im'pa·tient** □ impaciente (*at, with* con, de, por); intolerante (*of* con, para); *be(come)* (*or get, grow*) ~ impacientarse (*at, with* ante, con; *to* por); *make* ~ impacientar.

im·peach [im'piːtʃ] acusar (de alta traición); procesar; censurar; tachar; **im'peach·a·ble** censurable; susceptible de ser procesado; **im-'peach·ment** procesamiento *m* (por alta traición); acusación *f*.

im·pec·ca·bil·i·ty [impekə'biliti] impecabilidad *f*; **im'pec·ca·ble** □ impecable, intachable.

im·pe·cu·ni·ous [impi'kjuːniəs] inope, indigente.

im·pede [im'piːd] dificultar, estorbar; impedir.

im·ped·i·ment [im'pedimənt] impedimento *m* (*a. ⚖*); estorbo *m* (*to* para); *speech:* defecto *m* del habla; **im·ped·i·men·ta** [~'mentə] *pl.* equipaje *m*; ✗ impedimenta *f*.

im·pel [im'pel] impeler, impulsar (*to* a).

im·pend [im'pend] pender; ser inminente; amenazar; **im'pend·ing** inminente; pendiente.

im·pen·e·tra·bil·i·ty [impenitrə'biliti] impenetrabilidad *f*; **im'pen·e·tra·ble** □ impenetrable (*by, to* a).

im·pen·i·tence [im'penitəns] impenitencia *f*; **im'pen·i·tent** □ impenitente, incorregible.

im·per·a·tive [im'perətiv] **1.** □ imperativo; imperioso; indispensable; *gr.* ~ *mood* = **2.** *gr.* (modo) imperativo *m*.

im·per·cep·ti·ble [impə'septəbl] □ imperceptible.

im·per·fect [im'pɔːfikt] □ imperfecto (*a. gr.*); deficiente, defectuoso; **im·per·fec·tion** [~pə'fekʃn] imperfección *f*; desperfecto *m*.

im·pe·ri·al [im'piəriəl] **1.** □ impe-

rial; imperatorio; **2.** (*beard*) perilla *f*;
im·pe·ri·al·ism imperialismo *m*;
im·pe·ri·al·ist imperialista *m/f*;
im·pe·ri·al·is·tic imperialista.

im·per·il [im'peril] poner en peligro, arriesgar.

im·pe·ri·ous [im'piəriəs] ☐ imperioso, arrogante; apremiante.

im·per·ish·a·ble [im'periʃəbl] imperecedero.

im·per·ma·nent [im'pə:mənənt] no permanente, fugaz.

im·per·me·a·ble [im'pə:miəbl] impermeable.

im·per·son·al [im'pə:snl] ☐ impersonal; **im·per·son·al·i·ty** [‿sə-'næliti] impersonalidad *f*.

im·per·son·ate [im'pə:səneit] hacerse pasar por; hacer el papel de; *thea.* imitar; **im·per·son·a·tion** representación *f*; *thea.* imitación *f*; **im'per·son·a·tor** representador (-a *f*) *m*; *thea.* imitador (-a *f*) *m*.

im·per·ti·nence [im'pə:tinəns] impertinencia *f*; insolencia *f*; **im'per·ti·nent** ☐ impertinente; insolente.

im·per·turb·a·bil·i·ty ['impətə:bə-'biliti] imperturbabilidad *f*; **im·per'turb·a·ble** ☐ imperturbable.

im·per·vi·ous [im'pə:viəs] ☐ impermeable, impenetrable (*to* a); *fig.* insensible (*to* a).

im·pet·u·os·i·ty [impetju'ɔsiti] impetuosidad *f*; irreflexión *f*; **im'pet·u·ous** ☐ impetuoso; irreflexivo; **im·pe·tus** ['‿pitəs] ímpetu *m*; impulso *m* (*a. fig.*).

im·pi·e·ty [im'paiəti] impiedad *f*.

im·pinge [im'pindʒ] incidir ([*up*]*on* en); chocar ([*up*]*on* con); tocar ([*up*]*on* en); **im'pinge·ment** choque *m*; infracción *f*.

im·pi·ous ['impiəs] ☐ impío.

imp·ish [impiʃ] ☐ endiablado; travieso; juguetón.

im·pla·ca·bil·i·ty [implækə'biliti] implacabilidad *f*; **im'pla·ca·ble** ☐ implacable.

im·plant [im'plɑ:nt] implantar; inculcar.

im·plau·si·ble [im'plɔ:zəbl] inverosímil.

im·ple·ment 1. ['implimənt] utensilio *m*, herramienta *f*, instrumento *m*; ‿s *pl.* 𝄡 apero *m*; **2.** ['‿ment] poner por obra; llevar a cabo; cumplir; **im·ple·men·ta·tion** [‿'teiʃn] cumplimiento *m*, ejecución *f*.

im·pli·cate ['implikeit] implicar; comprometer; enredar; **im·pli·ca·tion** inferencia *f*; insinuación *f*; complicidad *f*; ‿s *pl.* trascendencia *f*, consecuencias *f/pl.*

im·plic·it [im'plisit] ☐ implícito; *faith etc.* absoluto, incondicional, ciego.

im·plied [im'plaid] implícito; *be* ‿ sobre(e)ntenderse.

im·plore [im'plɔ:] implorar; **im'plor·ing** [‿riŋ] ☐ suplicante.

im·ply [im'plai] implicar; (pre)suponer; dar a entender; insinuar.

im·po·lite [impə'lait] ☐ descortés, mal educado.

im·pol·i·tic [im'pɔlitik] ☐ impolítico.

im·pon·der·a·ble [im'pɔndərəbl] **1.** imponderable; **2.** ‿s *pl.* elementos *m/pl.* imponderables.

im·port 1. ['impɔ:t] ✝ importación *f*; mercancía *f* importada; importancia *f*; significado *m*; ‿ *duty* derechos *m/pl.* de entrada; **2.** [im'pɔ:t] importar (*a.* ✝); significar; **im'por·tance** importancia *f*; **im'por·tant** ☐ importante; de categoría; **im·por·ta·tion** [‿'teiʃn] importación *f*; **im'port·er** importador (-a *f*) *m*.

im·por·tu·nate [im'pɔ:tjunit] ☐ importuno, insistente; **im·por·tune** [‿'pɔ:tju:n] importunar; insistir en una pretensión; **im·por·tu·ni·ty** importunidad *f*; insistencia *f*.

im·pose [im'pouz] imponer; cargar; hacer aceptar; ‿ *upon* embaucar; abusar de; molestar; **im'pos·ing** ☐ imponente, impresionante, impetuoso; **im·po·si·tion** [‿pə'ziʃn] imposición *f*; carga *f*; abuso *m*; *school*: ejercicio *m* de castigo.

im·pos·si·bil·i·ty [impɔsə'biliti] imposibilidad *f*; **im'pos·si·ble** ☐ imposible.

im·post ['impoust] impuesto *m*; **im·pos·tor** [im'pɔstə] impostor (-a *f*) *m*, embaucador (-a *f*) *m*; **im'pos·ture** [‿tʃə] impostura *f*, fraude *m*.

im·po·tence ['impətəns] impotencia *f*; **'im·po·tent** impotente.

im·pound [im'paund] acorralar; encerrar; 𝓉𝓉 embargar, confiscar.

im·pov·er·ish [im'pɔvəriʃ] empobrecer; **im'pov·er·ish·ment** empobrecimiento *m*.

im·prac·ti·ca·bil·i·ty [impræktikə-

'biliti] impracticabilidad *f;* **im·prac·ti·ca·ble** □ impracticable; intratable; **im'prac·ti·cal** *v. unpractical.*

im·pre·cate ['imprikeit] imprecar; **im·pre'ca·tion** imprecación *f;* **im·pre·ca·to·ry** ['⌣keitəri] imprecatorio.

im·preg·na·bil·i·ty[impregnə'biliti] inexpugnabilidad *f;* **im'preg·na·ble** □ inexpugnable; **im·preg·nate** ['⌣neit] impregnar; empreñar; *biol.* fecundar; imbuir; **im·preg·'na·tion** impregnación *f;* fecundación *f.*

im·press 1. ['impres] impresión *f;* huella *f; fig.* sello *m;* **2.** [im'pres] imprimir; estampar; *(of emotions)* impresionar, imponer; grabar, inculcar *(s.t. on the mind* algo en el ánimo); *goods* confiscar, apoderarse de; ⚔ reclutar (a la fuerza); **im'press·i·ble** impresionable; **im'pres·sion** [⌣ʃn] impresión *f (a. fig.);* huella *f; fig.* efecto *m; make an ⌣* hacer efecto; *make an ⌣ on* impresionar; *be under the ⌣ that* tener la impresión de que; **im'pres·sion·a·ble** impresionable; **im'pres·sion·ist** impresionista *m/f;* **im'pres·sive** □ impresionante; imponente.

im·print 1. [im'print] imprimir; estampar; *fig.* grabar; **2.** ['imprint] impresión *f;* huella *f; typ.* pie *m* de imprenta.

im·pris·on [im'prizn] encarcelar, aprisionar; **im'pris·on·ment** encarcelamiento *m;* prisión *f.*

im·prob·a·bil·i·ty [imprɔbə'biliti] improbabilidad *f,* inverosimilitud *f;* **im'prob·a·ble** □ improbable, inverosímil.

im·promp·tu [im'prɔmtju:] **1.** *su.* improvisación *f;* **2.** *adj.* improvisado; espontáneo; **3.** *adv.* de improviso.

im·prop·er [im'prɔpə] □ impropio; incorrecto; indecoroso; *⌣ fraction* fracción *f* impropia; **im·pro·pri·e·ty** [imprə'praiəti] inconveniencia *f;* indecencia *f;* indecoro *m;* impropiedad *f of language.*

im·prov·a·ble [im'pru:vəbl] mejorable.

im·prove [im'pru:v] *v/t.* mejorar; perfeccionar; ✍ abonar; enmendar; reformar; *opportunity* aprove-

char; *yield etc.* aumentar; *v/i.* mejorar(se), medrar; perfeccionarse; aumentar(se); hacer progresos *in studies etc.; ⌣ upon* mejorar, perfeccionar; aventajar; **im·'prove·ment** mejora *f;* ✍ mejoría *f;* perfeccionamiento *m;* ✍ abono *m;* enmienda *f;* reforma *f;* aprovechamiento *m;* aumento *m;* progreso *m.*

im·prov·i·dence [im'prɔvidəns] imprevisión *f;* **im'prov·i·dent** □ impróvido, desprevenido.

im·prov·ing [im'pru:viŋ] edificante, instructivo.

im·pro·vi·sa·tion [imprəvai'zeiʃn] improvisación *f;* **im·pro·vise** ['⌣vaiz] improvisar.

im·pru·dence [im'pru:dəns] imprudencia *f;* **im'pru·dent** □ imprudente, malaconsejado.

im·pu·dence ['impjudəns] impudencia *f,* descaro *m,* insolencia *f,* desvergüenza *f;* '**im·pu·dent** □ impudente, descarado, insolente, desvergonzado.

im·pugn [im'pju:n] impugnar; poner en tela de juicio.

im·pulse ['impʌls] impulso *m,* impulsión *f;* ímpetu *m;* arranque *m,* arrebato *m;* **im'pul·sion** impulsión *f;* **im'pul·sive** □ impulsivo; irreflexivo; **im'pul·sive·ness** irreflexión *f,* carácter *m* impulsivo.

im·pu·ni·ty [im'pju:niti] impunidad *f; with ⌣* impunemente.

im·pure [im'pjuə] □ impuro; adulterado; deshonesto; **im'pu·ri·ty** [⌣riti] impureza *f.*

im·put·a·ble [im'pju:təbl] imputable; **im·pu·ta·tion** [⌣'teiʃn] imputación *f;* **im·pute** [⌣'pju:t] imputar (to a).

in [in] **1.** *prp.* en; dentro de; *⌣ Spain* en España; *⌣ 1960* en (el año) 1960; *⌣ the box* en (or dentro de) la caja; *⌣ a week* dentro de una semana, de aquí a 8 días; *the biggest ⌣ Spain* el más grande de España; *all the soldiers ⌣ the army* todos los soldados del ejército; *⌣ this way* de esta manera; *dressed ⌣ white* vestido de blanco; *furnished ⌣ walnut* amueblado de nogal; *better ⌣ health* mejor de salud; *⌣ the morning* por la mañana; *at 7 ⌣ the morning* a las 7 de la mañana; *⌣ the daytime* de día, durante el día; *⌣ writing* por escrito; *⌣*

my opinion a mi parecer; ~ *(good) time (early)* a tiempo, con tiempo; *(eventually)* andando el tiempo, con el tiempo; ~ *the Spanish fashion* a la (manera) española; ~ *the rear* a retaguardia; ~ *the reign of* bajo el reinado de; *one* ~ *four* uno sobre cuatro; *day* ~, *day out* día tras día; F *there's nothing* ~ *it* van muy iguales; no da ningún resultado; no tiene importancia; *it is not* ~ *him to* no es capaz de; *he has it* ~ *him to* tiene capacidad (*or* predisposición) para; ~ *that* en que, por cuanto; ~ *saying this* al decir esto; **2.** *adv.* (a)dentro; *be* ~ estar en casa (*or* en su oficina *etc.*); *haber llegado; parl.* estar en el poder; F estar en sazón; F estar de moda; *is John* ~? ¿está Juan?; F *be* ~ *for* estar expuesto a; *exam* presentarse a; *post* ser candidato a, solicitar; *competition* concurrir a; F *you're* ~ *for it now* la vas a pagar; F *you don't know what you're* ~ *for* no sabes lo que te pescas; F *be* ~ *on (it)* estar en el secreto, estar al tanto de; F *be (well)* ~ *with* estar muy metido con; estar asociado con; ~ *here* aquí dentro; ~ *there* allí dentro; **3.** *su.* ~*s and outs pl.* recovecos *m/pl.*; pormenores *m/pl.*

in·a·bil·i·ty [inə'biliti] incapacidad *f*; impotencia *f*; imposibilidad *f*.

in·ac·ces·si·bil·i·ty ['inæksesə'biliti] inaccesibilidad *f*; **in·ac'ces·si·ble** □ inaccesible; inasequible.

in·ac·cu·ra·cy [in'ækjurəsi] inexactitud *f*; incorrección *f*; **in'ac·cu·rate** [~rit] □ inexacto; incorrecto.

in·ac·tion [in'ækʃn] inacción *f*.

in·ac·tive [in'æktiv] □ inactivo; **in·ac'tiv·i·ty** inactividad *f*.

in·ad·e·qua·cy [in'ædikwəsi] insuficiencia *f*; **in'ad·e·quate** [~kwit] □ insuficiente, inadecuado.

in·ad·mis·si·bil·i·ty ['inədmisə'biliti] no admisibilidad *f*; **in·ad'mis·si·ble** □ inadmisible.

in·ad·vert·ence, in·ad·vert·en·cy [inəd'və:təns(i)] inadvertencia *f*; **in·ad'vert·ent** □ inadvertido; accidental; ~*ly a.* sin querer.

in·ad·vis·a·ble [inəd'vaizəbl] □ imprudente, no aconsejable.

in·al·ien·a·ble [in'eiliənəbl] □ inalienable.

in·am·o·ra·ta [inæmə'rɑ:tə] amada *f*.

in·ane [i'nein] □ necio, fatuo, inane.

in·an·i·mate [in'ænimit] □ inanimado.

in·a·ni·tion [inə'niʃn] inanición *f*.

in·an·i·ty [i'næniti] fatuidad *f*, sandez *f*; inanidad *f*.

in·ap·pli·ca·bil·i·ty ['inæplikə'biliti] no aplicabilidad *f*; **in'ap·pli·ca·ble** inaplicable.

in·ap·po·site [in'æpəzit] □ impertinente, inaplicable.

in·ap·pre·hen·si·ble [inæpri'hensəbl] □ inaprensible.

in·ap·pro·pri·ate [inə'proupriit] □ impropio, inoportuno, inadecuado.

in·ar·tic·u·late [inɑ:'tikjulit] □ *p.* incapaz de expresarse; inarticulado; **in·ar'tic·u·late·ness** (*p.'s*) incapacidad *f* para expresarse; falta *f* de articulación.

in·ar·tis·tic [inɑ:'tistik] □ antiestético; *p.* falto de talento artístico.

in·as·much [inəz'mʌtʃ]: ~ *as* ya que; en cuanto.

in·at·ten·tion [inə'tenʃn] desatención *f*; **in·at'ten·tive** □ desatento; distraído; descuidado.

in·au·di·ble [in'ɔ:dəbl] □ inaudible, imperceptible.

in·au·gu·ral [i'nɔ:gjurəl] inaugural; **in'au·gu·rate** [~reit] inaugurar; **in·au·gu'ra·tion** inauguración *f*; ♀ *day Am. día de la instalación del presidente.*

in·aus·pi·cious [inɔ:s'piʃəs] □ poco propicio, desfavorable; ominoso.

in·board ['inbɔ:d] ♣ **1.** *adj.* interior; **2.** *adv.* hacia dentro (del casco).

in·born ['in'bɔ:n] innato.

in·bred ['in'bred] innato; engendrado por endogamia.

in·breed·ing ['inbri:diŋ] endogamia *f*.

in·cal·cul·a·ble [in'kælkjuləbl] □ incalculable.

in·can·des·cence [inkæn'desns] incandescencia *f*; **in·can'des·cent** incandescente.

in·can·ta·tion [inkæn'teiʃn] conjuro *m*; ensalmo *m*.

in·ca·pa·bil·i·ty [inkeipə'biliti] incapacidad *f*, inhabilidad *f*; **in'ca·pa·ble** □ incapaz; inhábil; imposibilitado; **in·ca·pac·i·tate** [inkə'pæsiteit] incapacitar (*for, from* para); imposibilitar; **in·ca'pac·i·ty** incapacidad *f*; insuficiencia *f*.

in·car·cer·ate [in'kɑ:səreit] encarcelar; in·car·cer'a·tion encarcelamiento *m*.

in·car·nate 1. [in'kɑ:nit] encarnado; 2. ['inkɑ:neit] encarnar; in·car'na·tion encarnación *f*.

in·case [in'keis] *v*. encase.

in·cau·tious [in'kɔ:ʃəs] ☐ incauto, imprudente.

in·cen·di·ar·y [in'sendjəri] incendiario *adj. a. su. m* (a *f*); ~ bomb bomba *f* incendiaria.

in·cense¹ ['insens] 1. incienso *m* (*a. fig.*); 2. incensar.

in·cense² [in'sens] encolerizar, indignar.

in·cen·tive [in'sentiv] incentivo *adj. a. su. m*.

in·cep·tion [in'sepʃn] principio *m*, comienzo *m*; inauguración *f*; in·'cep·tive incipiente; *gr.* incoativo.

in·cer·ti·tude [in'sə:titju:d] incertidumbre *f*.

in·ces·sant [in'sesnt] ☐ incesante.

in·cest ['insest] incesto *m*; in·ces·tu·ous [in'sestjuəs] ☐ incestuoso.

inch [intʃ] 1. pulgada *f* (= *2,54 cm.*); *fig.* pizca *f*; ~es *pl. a.* estatura *f*; ~ by ~, by ~es palmo a palmo; every ~ a man nada menos que todo un hombre; *within an* ~ of a dos dedos de; 2.: ~ forward etc. avanzar etc. palmo a palmo.

in·cho·ate [in'koueit] incipiente, rudimentario; in·cho·a·tive ['inkoueitiv] incoativo.

in·ci·dence ['insidəns] incidencia *f*; frecuencia *f*; extensión *f*; *angle of* ~ ángulo *m* de incidencia; 'in·ci·dent 1. incidente *m*; episodio *m*; ocurrencia *f*; suceso *m*; 2. incidente; propio (*to* de); in·ci·den·tal [~'dentl] 1. cosa *f* accesoria (*or* sin importancia); 2. ☐ incidental, incidente; accesorio; casual; ~ly *a.* a propósito.

in·cin·er·ate [in'sinəreit] incinerar; in·cin·er'a·tion incineración *f*; in·'cin·er·a·tor incinerador *m*.

in·cip·i·ent [in'sipiənt] incipiente.

in·cise [in'saiz] cortar; grabar; tallar; in·ci·sion [~'siʒn] incisión *f*; in·ci·sive [~'saisiv] ☐ incisivo; *fig.* tajante; in·ci·sor [~zə] incisivo *m*.

in·cite [in'seit] incitar, mover (*to* a); in·'cite·ment incitación *f*; incitamento *m*.

in·ci·vil·i·ty [insi'viliti] descortesía *f*, incivilidad *f*.

in·clem·en·cy [in'klemənsi] inclemencia *f*; intemperie *f of weather*; in·'clem·ent inclemente, riguroso; *weather* destemplado.

in·cli·na·tion [inkli'neiʃn] inclinación *f*; declive *m*; tendencia *f*; afición *f* (*for* a); gana(s) *f(pl.)* (*to, for* de); in·cline [~'klain] 1. *v/t.* inclinar (*a. fig.*), ladear; ~ed plane plano *m* inclinado; *fig.* be ~ed to inclinarse a; *v/i.* inclinarse (*to* a); ladearse; estar inclinado, estar ladeado; 2. *su.* [mst '~klain] declive *m*, pendiente *f*.

in·close [in'klouz] *v*. enclose.

in·clude [in'klu:d] incluir; adjuntar; comprender; be ~d *in* figurar en; *everything* ~d todo comprendido; *including* incluso, inclusive; *not including* no comprendido.

in·clu·sion [in'klu:ʒn] inclusión *f*; in·'clu·sive 1. ☐ *adj.* inclusivo; completo; be ~ of incluir; ~ terms todo incluido; 2. *adv.* inclusive; *Sunday to Saturday* ~ del domingo al sábado inclusive.

in·cog [in'kɔg] F, in·cog·ni·to [~ni·tou] 1. incógnito *m*; 2. de incógnito.

in·co·her·ence, in·co·her·en·cy [inkou'hiərəns(i)] incoherencia *f*; in·co'her·ent ☐ incoherente; sin pies ni cabeza.   [☐ incombustible.]

in·com·bus·ti·ble [inkəm'bʌstəbl]|

in·come ['inkəm] ingreso(s) *m(pl.)*; renta *f*; entrada *f*; *annual* ~ ingresos *m/pl.* anuales; *family* ~ entradas *f/pl.* familiares; in·com·er ['inkʌmə] recién llegado (a *f*) *m*; forastero (a *f*) *m*; sucesor (-a *f*) *m*; in·come-tax ['inkəmtæks] impuesto *m* sobre la renta.

in·com·ing ['inkʌmiŋ] 1. entrada *f*; ~s *pl.* ingresos *m/pl.*; 2. entrante; *tide* ascendente.

in·com·men·su·ra·ble [inkə'menʃərəbl] ☐ inconmensurable; in·com'men·su·rate [~rit] inconmensurable, desproporcionado.

in·com·mode [inkə'moud] incomodar, molestar; in·com'mo·di·ous [~iəs] ☐ incómodo.

in·com·mu·ni·ca·bil·i·ty ['inkəmju:nikə'biliti] incomunicabilidad *f*; in·com'mu·ni·ca·ble ☐ incomunicable; in·com·mu·ni·ca·do [inkəmjuni'kɑ:dou] incomunicado.

in·com·pa·ra·ble [in'kɔmpərəbl] ☐ incomparable.

in·com·pat·i·bil·i·ty ['inkəmpætə-'biliti] incompatibilidad *f*; **in·com·'pat·i·ble** ☐ incompatible.

in·com·pe·tence, in·com·pe·ten·cy [in'kɔmpitəns(i)] incompetencia *f*; incapacidad *f*; inhabilidad *f*; **in·'com·pe·tent** ☐ incompetente; inhábil; incapaz.

in·com·plete [inkəm'pli:t] ☐ incompleto; defectuoso; inconcluso.

in·com·pre·hen·si·bil·i·ty [inkəm-prihensə'biliti] incomprensibilidad *f*; **in·com·pre'hen·sible** ☐ incomprensible.

in·com·press·i·ble [inkəm'presəbl] incompresible.

in·con·ceiv·a·ble [inkən'si:vəbl] ☐ inconcebible.

in·con·clu·sive [inkən'klu:siv] ☐ inconcluyente; poco convincente; indeterminado; **in·con·clu·sive·ness** lo inconcluyente; indeterminación *f*.

in·con·gru·i·ty [inkɔŋ'gruiti] incongruencia *f*; **in'con·gru·ous** ☐ incongruo.

in·con·se·quence [in'kɔnsikwəns] inconsecuencia *f*; **in'con·se·quent** ☐ inconsecuente; **in·con·se·quen·tial** [ʌ'kwenʃl] ☐ inconsecuente; sin trascendencia.

in·con·sid·er·a·ble [inkən'sidərəbl] ☐ insignificante; pequeño; **in·con·'sid·er·ate** [ʌrit] ☐ desconsiderado.

in·con·sist·en·cy [inkən'sistənsi] inconsistencia *f*, inconsecuencia *f*; **in·con'sist·ent** ☐ inconsistente, inconsecuente. [inconsolable.)

in·con·sol·a·ble [inkən'soulabl] ☐)

in·con·spic·u·ous [inkən'spikjuəs] ☐ que no llama la atención; poco aparente; modesto.

in·con·stan·cy [in'kɔnstənsi] inconstancia *f*, veleidad *f*; **in'con·stant** ☐ inconstante, veleidoso.

in·con·test·a·ble [inkən'testəbl] incontestable.

in·con·ti·nence [in'kɔntinəns] incontinencia *f* (*a.* 🦠); **in'con·ti·nent** ☐ incontinente; ʌly *a.* en seguida.

in·con·tro·vert·i·ble ['inkɔntrə-'və:təbl] ☐ incontrovertible.

in·con·ven·ience [inkən'vi:njəns] **1.** incomodidad *f*, inconveniencia *f*, molestia *f*; inoportunidad *f*; **2.** incomodar, molestar; **in·con'ven·ient** ☐ incómodo, inconveniente, molesto; inoportuno.

in·con·vert·i·bil·i·ty ['inkənvə:tə-'biliti] inconvertibilidad *f*; **in·con·'vert·i·ble** ☐ inconvertible.

in·cor·po·rate 1. [in'kɔ:pəreit] incorporar (*in*[to], *with* a, con, en); incluir; comprender; ⚖ constituir(se) en corporación (*or* sociedad anónima); **2.** [in'kɔ:pərit] incorpóreo; asociado, incorporado; **in'cor·po·rat·ed** [ʌreitid] ✝ *Am.* sociedad *f* anónima (*abbr.* S.A.); **in·cor·po·'ra·tion** incorporación *f*; constitución *f* en sociedad anónima.

in·cor·po·re·al [inkɔ:'pɔ:riəl] incorpóreo, incorporal.

in·cor·rect [inkə'rekt] ☐ incorrecto; inexacto; erróneo.

in·cor·ri·gi·bil·i·ty [inkɔridʒə'biliti] incorregibilidad *f*; **in'cor·ri·gi·ble** ☐ incorregible, empecatado.

in·cor·rupt·i·ble [inkə'rʌptəbl] ☐ incorruptible.

in·crease 1. [in'kri:s] *v/t.* aumentar; acrecentar; multiplicar; *v/i.* aumentarse; crecer; multiplicarse; *increasing* creciente; *increasingly* cada vez más; **2.** [inkri:s] aumento *m*, incremento *m*; crecimiento *m*; ganancia *f*; alza *f in price*; *be on the* ʌ ir en aumento.

in·cred·i·bil·i·ty [inkredi'biliti] incredibilidad *f*; **in'cred·i·ble** ☐ increíble.

in·cre·du·li·ty [inkri'dju:liti] incredulidad *f*; **in'cred·u·lous** [in-'kredjuləs] ☐ incrédulo.

in·cre·ment ['inkrimənt] incremento *m*; añadidura *f*; (*a.* ʌ *value*) plusvalía *f*.

in·crim·i·nate [in'krimineit] acriminar, incriminar; **in'crim·i·na·to·ry** [ʌəri] acriminador, incriminador.

in·crust [in'krʌst] incrustar(se); **in·crus'ta·tion** incrustación *f*; costra *f*.

in·cu·bate ['inkjubeit] empollar, incubar; **in·cu'ba·tion** incubación *f*; **'in·cu·ba·tor** incubadora *f*; **in·cu·bus** ['ʌbəs] íncubo *m*.

in·cul·cate ['inkʌlkeit] inculcar (*in* en); **in·cul'ca·tion** inculcación *f*.

in·cul·pate ['inkʌlpeit] inculpar; **in·cul'pa·tion** inculpación *f*; **in·'cul·pa·to·ry** [ʌpətəri] inculpador.

in·cum·ben·cy [in'kʌmbənsi] *eccl.* (duración *f* de un) beneficio *m* eclesiástico; **in'cum·bent 1.** *eccl.*

beneficiado *m*; **2.** incumbente, obligatorio; *be ~ upon* incumbir a.

in·cu·nab·u·la [inkju'næbjulə] *pl. typ.* incunables *m/pl.*

in·cur [in'kə:] incurrir en; *debt* contraer.

in·cur·a·bil·i·ty [inkjuərə'biliti] incurabilidad *f*; **in'cur·a·ble** □ incurable.

in·cu·ri·ous [in'kjuəriəs] □ poco curioso.

in·cur·sion [in'kə:ʃn] incursión *f*, invasión *f*; *fig.* penetración *f*.

in·debt·ed [in'detid] adeudado; reconocido; obligado; *be ~ to* estar en deuda con; **in'debt·ed·ness** deuda *f*; obligación *f*.

in·de·cen·cy [in'di:snsi] indecencia *f*; **in'de·cent** □ indecente; *~ assault approx.* tentativa *f* de violación.

in·de·ci·pher·a·ble [indi'saifərəbl] indescifrable.

in·de·ci·sion [indi'siʒn] indecisión *f*; irresolución *f*; **in·de·ci·sive** [~'saisiv] □ indeciso; inconcluyente; dudoso.

in·de·clin·a·ble [indi'klainəbl] indeclinable.

in·dec·o·rous [in'dekərəs] □ indecoroso; **in'dec·o·rous·ness** = **in·de·co·rum** [indi'kɔ:rəm] indecoro *m*.

in·deed [in'di:d] verdaderamente, de veras; por cierto; en efecto (*a.* yes, ~); *~?* ¿de veras?; yes, ~! ¡sí, por cierto!

in·de·fat·i·ga·ble [indi'fætigəbl] □ infatigable, incansable.

in·de·fen·si·ble [indi'fensəbl] □ indefendible.

in·de·fin·a·ble [indi'fainəbl] indefinible.

in·def·i·nite [in'definit] □ indefinido; incierto; vago.

in·del·i·ble [in'delibl] □ indeleble; *~ pencil* lápiz tinta *m*.

in·del·i·ca·cy [in'delikəsi] falta *f* de delicadeza; grosería *f*; **in'del·i·cate** [~kit] □ poco delicado, indecoroso, grosero.

in·dem·ni·fi·ca·tion [indemnifi-'keiʃn] indemnización *f*, resarcimiento *m*; **in'dem·ni·fy** [~fai] indemnizar, resarcir (*a p. for, from, against* a una p. de); **in'dem·ni·ty** (*compensation*) indemnización *f*; indemnidad *f*.

in·dent 1. ['indent] mella *f*; muesca *f*; ✝ pedido *m*; ⚔ requisición *f*; = *indenture*; **2.** [in'dent] mellar; (en)dentar; *typ.* sangrar; ⚏ redactar (por duplicado) un contrato (de aprendizaje); *~ upon a p. for s.t.* pedir algo a una p.; **in·den'ta·tion** mella *f*; muesca *f*; *typ.* sangría *f* = **in'den·tion**; **in'den·ture** [~tʃə] **1.** escritura *f*; contrato *m* (de aprendizaje); **2.** contratar (como aprendiz).

in·de·pend·ence [indi'pendəns] independencia *f*; **in·de'pend·ent** □ independiente *adj. a. su. m/f*; *of ~ means* acomodado.

in·de·scrib·a·ble [indis'kraibəbl] □ indescriptible; *b.s.* incalificable.

in·de·struct·i·ble [indis'trʌktəbl] □ indestructible.

in·de·ter·mi·na·ble [indi'tə:minəbl] □ indeterminable; **in·de'ter·mi·nate** [~nit] □ indeterminado; vago.

in·dex ['indeks] **1.** (*pl. a.* **in·di·ces** ['indisi:z]) (*finger, of book*) índice *m*; ♈ exponente *m*; ⚲ *eccl.* índice *m* expurgatorio; **2.** *book* poner índice a; *entry* poner en un índice.

In·di·a ['indjə]: *~ paper* papel *m* de China, papel *m* biblia; *~ rubber* goma *f* de borrar; caucho *m*.

In·di·an ['indjən] **1.** indio (a *f*) *m*; (*Red*) *~* piel roja *m/f*; **2.** indio; *~ club* maza *f* (de gimnasia); *~ corn* maíz *m*; *~ file* fila *f* india; *Am.* F *~ giver* dador *m* interesado (*or* de toma y daca); *~ ink* tinta *f* china; *~ summer* veranillo *m* de San Martín.

in·di·cate ['indikeit] indicar, señalar; **in'di·ca·tion** indicio *m*, señal *f*; indicación *f*; **in·dic·a·tive** [in'dikətiv] indicativo *adj. a. su. m*; *be ~ of* indicar; **in·di·ca·tor** ['~keitə] indicador *m* (*a.* ⊕, ⚒).

in·di·ces ['indisi:z] *pl. of index.*

in·dict [in'dait] acusar (ante el juez) (*for, on a charge of* de); encausar; **in'dict·a·ble** denunciable, procesable; **in'dict·ment** acusación *f*; ⚏ sumaria *f*.

in·dif·fer·ence [in'difrəns] indiferencia *f*; desapego *m*; falta *f* de importancia; **in·dif·fer·ent** □ indiferente; desinteresado; imparcial; *quality* mediano, ordinario.

in·di·gence ['indidʒəns] indigencia *f*.

in·dig·e·nous [in'didʒinəs] indígena (to de).

in·di·gent ['indidʒənt] indigente.

in·di·gest·i·ble [indi'dʒestəbl] □ indigestible, indigesto; **in·di'ges·tion** indigestión f, empacho m.

in·dig·nant [in'dignənt] □ indignado (at a p. con[tra]; at a th. de, por); **in·dig'na·tion** indignación f; ~ meeting mitin m de protesta; **in·'dig·ni·ty** [~niti] indignidad f, afrenta f.

in·di·go ['indigou] añil adj. a. su. m.

in·di·rect [indi'rekt] □ indirecto.

in·dis·cern·i·ble [indi'sə:nəbl] imperceptible.

in·dis·ci·pline [in'disiplin] indisciplina f.

in·dis·creet [indis'kri:t] □ indiscreto; **in·dis·cre·tion** [~'kreʃn] indiscreción f.

in·dis·crim·i·nate [indis'kriminit] □ promiscuo, sin distinción; falto de discernimiento; **'in·dis·crim·i·'na·tion** falta f de discernimiento; indistinción f.

in·dis·pen·sa·ble [indis'pensəbl] □ indispensable, imprescindible.

in·dis·pose [indis'pouz] indisponer (for para); **in·dis'posed** ☞ indispuesto; mal dispuesto; **in·dis·po·si·tion** [indispə'ziʃn] indisposición f (to para).

in·dis·pu·ta·ble ['indis'pju:təbl] □ indisputable, incontestable.

in·dis·so·lu·bil·i·ty ['indisɔlju'biliti] indisolubilidad f; **in·dis·so·lu·ble** [~'sɔljubl] □ indisoluble.

in·dis·tinct [indis'tiŋkt] □ indistinto; **in·dis'tinct·ness** indistinción f, vaguedad f; falta f de claridad.

in·dis·tin·guish·a·ble [indis'tiŋgwiʃəbl] indistinguible.

in·dite [in'dait] componer; redactar; poner por escrito.

in·di·vid·u·al [indi'vidjuəl] **1.** individuo m; mst contp. sujeto m; **2.** □ individual; personal; particular; **in·di'vid·u·al·ist** individualista m/f; **in·di·vid·u·al·i·ty** [~'æliti] individualidad f; **in·di'vid·u·al·ize** [~əlaiz] individuar.

in·di·vis·i·bil·i·ty ['indivizi'biliti] indivisibilidad f; **in·di'vis·i·ble** □ indivisible.

In·do... ['indou] indo...; '~-Eu·ro·'pe·an indoeuropeo adj. a. su. m;

In·do·ne·sian [indou'ni:zjən] indonesio adj. a. su. m (a f).

in·doc·tri·nate [in'dɔktrineit] adoctrinar (with en).

in·do·lence ['indələns] indolencia f; pereza f; **'in·do·lent** □ indolente (a. ☞); perezoso.

in·dom·i·ta·ble [in'dɔmitəbl] □ indómito, indomable.

in·door ['indɔ:] interior; de casa; de puertas adentro; sport: en sala; ~ aerial antena f de interior; ~ games diversiones f/pl. de salón; ~ plant planta f de salón; ~ swimming-bath piscina f cubierta; **in·doors** ['in'dɔ:z] en casa; (a)dentro; bajo techado.

in·dorse etc. [in'dɔ:s] = endorse etc.

in·du·bi·ta·ble [in'dju:bitəbl] □ indudable.

in·duce [in'dju:s] inducir (a. ✍) (to a); producir; ocasionar; sleep provocar; ~d current corriente f inducida; **in'duce·ment** incentivo m; aliciente m; estímulo m.

in·duct [in'dʌkt] eccl. instalar; **in·'duct·ance** inductancia f; **in'duc·tion** phls., ✍ inducción f; eccl. instalación f; ~ coil carrete m de inducción; **in'duc·tive** □ inductivo.

in·dulge [in'dʌldʒ] v/t. desires gratificar, dar rienda suelta a; p. consentir, mimar; dar gusto a; v/i.: ~ in darse a, entregarse a; darse el lujo de, permitirse; **in'dul·gence** indulgencia f (a. eccl.); mimo m; gratificación f; abandono m (in a); desenfreno m; **in'dul·gent** □ indulgente.

in·dus·tri·al [in'dʌstriəl] industrial; ~ court tribunal m industrial; **in·'dus·tri·al·ism** industrialismo m; **in'dus·tri·al·ist** industrial(ista) m; **in'dus·tri·al·ize** [~aiz] industrializar; **in'dus·tri·ous** □ industrioso, aplicado; **in'dus·tri·ous·ness** industria f, aplicación f, laboriosidad f.

in·dus·try ['indəstri] industria f; laboriosidad f, diligencia f; heavy ~ industria f pesada.

in·e·bri·ate 1. [i'ni:brieit] embriagar, emborrachar; **2.** [i'ni:briit] borracho adj. a. su. m (a f); **in·e·bri·'a·tion, in·e·bri·e·ty** [ini:'braiəti] embriaguez f.

in·ed·i·ble [in'edibl] incomible.
in·ed·it·ed [in'editid] inédito.
in·ef·fa·ble [in'efəbl] □ inefable.
in·ef·face·a·ble [ini'feisəbl] □ imborrable.
in·ef·fec·tive [ini'fektiv], **in·ef'fec·tu·al** [ˌtjuəl] □ ineficaz; vano; *p.* incapaz.
in·ef·fi·ca·cious [inefi'keiʃəs] □ ineficaz; **in'ef·fi·ca·cy** [ˌkəsi] ineficacia *f.*
in·ef·fi·cien·cy [ini'fiʃənsi] ineficiencia *f;* **in·ef'fi·cient** □ ineficiente, ineficaz.
in·e·las·tic [ini'læstik] inelástico.
in·el·e·gance [in'eligəns] inelegancia *f;* **in'el·e·gant** □ inelegante.
in·el·i·gi·bil·i·ty [inelidʒə'biliti] no elegibilidad *f;* **in'el·i·gi·ble** □ inelegible.
in·ept [i'nept] □ inepto; **in'ept·i·tude** [ˌitju:d], **in'ept·ness** inepcia *f,* ineptitud *f.* [dad *f.*]
in·e·qual·i·ty [ini'kwɔliti] desigualdad *f.*
in·eq·ui·ta·ble [in'ekwitəbl] injusto; **in'eq·ui·ty** injusticia *f.*
in·e·rad·i·ca·ble [ini'rædikəbl] □ no extirpable.
in·ert [i'nə:t] □ inerte; **in·er·tia** [i'nə:ʃiə], **in'ert·ness** inercia *f.*
in·es·cap·a·ble [inis'keipəbl] ineludible.
in·es·sen·tial ['ini'senʃl] 1. cosa *f* sin importancia; 2. no esencial.
in·es·ti·ma·ble [in'estiməbl] inestimable.
in·ev·i·ta·bil·i·ty [in'evitə'biliti] inevitabilidad *f,* necesidad *f;* **in'ev·i·ta·ble** □ inevitable, ineludible; **in·'ev·i·ta·ble·ness** = *inevitability.*
in·ex·act [inig'zækt] inexacto; **in·ex'act·i·tude** [ˌitju:d], **in·ex'act·ness** inexactitud *f.*
in·ex·cus·a·ble [iniks'kju:zəbl] □ inexcusable, imperdonable.
in·ex·haust·i·bil·i·ty ['inigzɔːstə'biliti] lo inagotable; **in·ex'haust·i·ble** □ inagotable, inexhausto.
in·ex·o·ra·bil·i·ty [ineksərə'biliti] inexorabilidad *f;* **in'ex·o·ra·ble** □ inexorable.
in·ex·pe·di·en·cy [iniks'pi:diənsi] inoportunidad *f,* inconveniencia *f,* imprudencia *f;* **in·ex'pe·di·ent** inoportuno, inconveniente, imprudente.
in·ex·pen·sive [iniks'pensiv] □ barato, económico.

in·ex·pe·ri·ence [iniks'piəriəns] inexperiencia *f,* falta *f* de experiencia; **in·ex'pe·ri·enced** inexperto, novel.
in·ex·pert [ineks'pə:t] □ imperito, inexperto, inhábil.
in·ex·pli·ca·ble [in'eksplikəbl] □ inexplicable.
in·ex·press·i·ble [iniks'presəbl] □ inexpresable, indecible.
in·ex·pres·sive [iniks'presiv] □ inexpresivo.
in·ex·tin·guish·a·ble [iniks'tiŋgwiʃəbl] □ inextinguible.
in·ex·tri·ca·ble [in'ekstrikəbl] □ inextricable.
in·fal·li·bil·i·ty [infælə'biliti] infalibilidad *f;* **in'fal·li·ble** □ infalible.
in·fa·mous ['infəməs] □ infame; ⅌⅛ infamante; **in·fa·my** ['ˌmi] infamia *f.*
in·fan·cy ['infənsi] infancia *f (a. fig.);* ⅌⅛ menor edad *f; from* ~ desde niño; **in·fant** ['ˌfənt] 1. criatura *f,* infante *m;* niño (a *f) m;* ⅌⅛ menor *m/f;* ~ *school* escuela *f* de párvulos; 2. infantil.
in·fan·ta [in'fæntə] infanta *f;* **in·'fan·te** [ˌti] infante *m.*
in·fan·ti·cide [in'fæntisaid] infanticidio *m; (p.)* infanticida *m/f;* **in·fan·tile** ['infəntail] infantil; pueril; aniñado; ~ *paralysis* parálisis *f* infantil.
in·fan·try ['infəntri] infantería *f;* **'in·fan·try·man** infante *m,* soldado *m* de infantería.
in·fat·u·ate [in'fætjueit] apasionar, amartelar; *be* ~*d with* apasionarse de *(or* por); F estar chiflado por; **in·fat·u·a·tion** apasionamiento *m;* F chifladura *f.*
in·fect [in'fekt] infectar; inficionar *(a. fig.);* contagiar *(a. fig.); fig.* influenciar; **in'fec·tion** infección *f;* contagio *m (a. fig.);* **in'fec·tious** □ infeccioso; contagioso *(a. fig.);* **in'fec·tive** infectivo.
in·fe·lic·i·tous [infi'lisitəs] □ infeliz; desacertado; *style* impropio; **in·fe·'lic·i·ty** infelicidad *f;* desacierto *m;* impropiedad *f.*
in·fer [in'fə:] inferir; deducir, colegir; F conjeturar; **in'fer·a·ble** deducible, ilativo; **in·fer·ence** ['infərəns] inferencia *f;* **in·fer·en·tial** [ˌ'renʃl] □ ilativo; **in·fer·en·tial·ly** [ˌ'renʃəli] por inferencia.
in·fe·ri·or [in'fiəriə] inferior *adj. a.*

su. *m/f*; **in·fe·ri·or·i·ty** [ˌri'ɔriti] inferioridad *f*; ~ *complex* complejo *m* de inferioridad.

in·fer·nal [in'fɔːnl] □ infernal; ~ *machine* máquina *f* infernal; **in·fer·no** [in'fɔːnou] infierno *m*.

in·fer·tile [in'fɔːtail] infecundo, estéril, infértil; **in·fer·til·i·ty** [ˌ'tiliti] infecundidad *f etc.*

in·fest [in'fest] infestar; *be* ~*ed with* estar plagado de; **in·fes·ta·tion** infestación *f*.

in·fi·del ['infidəl] infiel *adj. a. su. m/f*; pagano *adj. a. su. m* (a *f*); descreído *adj. a. su. m* (a *f*); **in·fi·del·i·ty** [ˌ'deliti] infidelidad *f* (*to* para [con]); perfidia *f*.

in·fight(·ing) ['infait(iŋ)] *boxing*: cuerpo a cuerpo *m*.

in·fil·trate ['infiltreit] infiltrar(se en); **in·fil'tra·tion** infiltración *f*.

in·fi·nite ['infinit] □ infinito; **in·fin·i·tes·i·mal** [ˌ'tesiml] infinitesimal (*a. Ⱥ*); **in'fin·i·tive** infinitivo *m* (*a.* ~ *mood*); **in'fin·i·tude** [ˌtjuːd] infinitud *f*, infinidad *f*; **in'fin·i·ty** infinidad *f*; sinfín *m*; Ⱥ infinito *m*.

in·firm [in'fɔːm] enfermizo, achacoso; débil; inestable; ~ *of purpose* irresoluto; **in'fir·ma·ry** enfermería *f*; hospital *m*; **in'fir·mi·ty** achaque *m*; enfermedad *f*; debilidad *f*; (*moral*) flaqueza *f*; inestabilidad *f*. [(en la mente).\
in·fix [in'fiks] encajar; clavar; fijar /
in·flame [in'fleim] inflamar (*a. fig. a.* Ⱥ); *be* ~*d with* inflamarse de (*or* en).

in·flam·ma·bil·i·ty [inflæmə'biliti] inflamabilidad *f*; **in'flam·ma·ble** □ inflamable; **in·flam·ma·tion** [inflə'meiʃn] inflamación *f* (*a.* Ⱥ); **in·flam·ma·to·ry** [in'flæmətəri] Ⱥ inflamatorio; inflamador; *speech* incendiario.

in·flate [in'fleit] hinchar (*a. fig.*); inflar; **in'fla·tion** inflación *f* (*a.* ✝); **in'fla·tion·ar·y** inflacionista; **in·'flat·or** bomba *f* (para inflar).

in·flect [in'flekt] torcer, encorvar; *voice* modular; *gr.* declinar, conjugar; ~*ed gr.* flexional; **in'flec·tion** = *inflexion*.

in·flex·i·bil·i·ty [infleksə'biliti] inflexibilidad *f*; **in'flex·i·ble** □ inflexible; **in'flex·ion** [ˌʃn] inflexión *f*.

in·flict [in'flikt] inferir, infligir (*on* a); *damage* causar; F ~ *o.s. on a p.* molestar a una p. acompañándole; **in'flic·tion** imposición *f*; castigo *m*; sufrimiento *m*.

in·flo·res·cence [inflə'resns] inflorescencia *f*. [**2.** afluir.\
in·flow ['inflou] **1.** afluencia *f*; /
in·flu·ence ['influəns] **1.** influencia *f*, influjo *m* ([*up*]*on* sobre); valimiento *m* (*with* cerca de); ascendiente *m* (*over* sobre); F *have* ~ tener buenas aldabas; **2.** influir en, influenciar; **in·flu·en·tial** [ˌ'enʃl] □ influ(y)ente; *p.* prestigioso.

in·flu·en·za [influ'enzə] gripe *f*, trancazo *m*.

in·flux ['inflʌks] afluencia *f*.

in·form [in'fɔːm] *v/t.* informar (*of* de, *about* sobre); avisar, comunicar; enterar; (*well*) ~*ed* entendido; *be* (*well*) ~*ed about* estar enterado de, estar al corriente de; *keep a p.* ~*ed about* tener una p. al corriente de; *v/i.*: ~ *against* delatar; **in'for·mal** □ de confianza, sin ceremonia; familiar; sencillo; (*unofficial*) extraoficial; (*irregular*) informal; **in·for·mal·i·ty** [ˌ'mæliti] falta *f* de ceremonia; familiaridad *f*; sencillez *f*; informalidad *f*; **in'form·ant** informante *m/f*; informador (-a *f*) *m*; = *informer*; **in·for·ma·tion** [infə'meiʃən] información *f* (*a. piece of* ~); informe(s) *m(pl.)*; noticia(s) *f(pl.)*; dato(s) *m(pl.)*; conocimientos *m/pl.*; Ⱥ denunciación *f*, delación *f*; ~ *bureau* oficina *f* de información; *gather* ~ tomar informes, informarse (*about* sobre); **in·form·a·tive** [in'fɔːmətiv] informativo; **in'form·er** Ⱥ denunciante *m/f*, delator (-a *f*) *m*; F soplón *m*.

in·frac·tion [in'frækʃn] infracción *f*.

in·fra·red ['infrə'red] infrarrojo.

in·fre·quen·cy [in'friːkwənsi] infrecuencia *f*; **in'fre·quent** □ poco frecuente, infrecuente.

in·fringe [in'frindʒ] infringir, violar (*a.* ~ *upon*); **in'fringe·ment** infracción *f*, transgresión *f*.

in·fu·ri·ate [in'fjuərieit] enfurecer, poner furioso.

in·fuse [in'fjuːz] *all senses*: infundir (*into* a, en); **in'fu·sion** [ˌʒn] infusión *f*; **in·fu·so·ri·a** [infjuː'sɔːriə] *pl.* infusorios *m/pl.*

in·gen·ious [in'dʒi:njəs] ☐ ingenioso, inventivo, hábil; listo; **in·ge·nu·i·ty** [indʒi'njuiti] ingenio *m*, ingeniosidad *f*; inventiva *f*; maña *f*; **in·gen·u·ous** [in'dʒenjuəs] ☐ ingenuo; **in'gen·u·ous·ness** ingenuidad *f*.

in·gest [in'dʒest] ingerir; **in'ges·tion** ingestión *f*.

in·gle-nook [ingl'nuk] rincón *m* de la chimenea.

in·glo·ri·ous [in'glɔ:riəs] ☐ ignominioso; desconocido, sin fama.

in·go·ing ['ingouiŋ] **1.** entrada *f* (*a.* ⚓); **2.** entrante.

in·got ['iŋgət] lingote *m*; ~ *steel* acero *m* en lingotes.

in·grain ['in'grein] teñido en rama; *fig.* (*a.* '**in'grained** [~d]) arraigado, inveterado; innato.

in·gra·ti·ate [in'greiʃieit]: ~ *o.s.* congraciarse, insinuarse (*with* con); **in'gra·ti·a·ting** ☐ insinuante; congraciador; **in·grat·i·tude** [~'grætitju:d] ingratitud *f*, desagradecimiento *m*.

in·gre·di·ent [in'gri:diənt] ingrediente *m*, componente *m*.

in·gress ['ingres] ingreso *m*; acceso *m*.

in·grow·ing ['ingrouiŋ] que crece hacia dentro; ~ *nail* uñero *m*.

in·gui·nal ['iŋgwinəl] inguinal.

in·hab·it [in'hæbit] habitar; **in'hab·it·a·ble** habitable; **in'hab·it·an·cy** 🏛 habitación *f*; **in'hab·it·ant** habitante *m*/*f*.

in·hal·ant [in'heilənt] inhalante *m*; **in·ha·la·tion** [inhə'leiʃn] ✹ inhalación *f*; **in·hale** [~'heil] inspirar; ✹ inhalar; ✹ **hal·er** ✹ inhalador *m*.

in·har·mo·ni·ous [inha:'mounjəs] inarmónico; *fig.* discorde, poco armonioso.

in·here [in'hiə] ser inherente (*in* a); residir (*in* en); **in'her·ence, in·'her·en·cy** [~rəns(i)] inherencia *f*; **in'her·ent** ☐ inherente (*in* a).

in·her·it [in'herit] heredar; **in'her·it·a·ble** ☐ heredable; heredero; **in'her·it·ance** herencia *f*; patrimonio *m*; **in'her·i·tor** heredero *m*; **in'her·i·tress, in'her·i·trix** [~triks] heredera *f*.

in·hib·it [in'hibit] inhibir; *eccl.* prohibir; impedir (*from inf.*); **in·hi·bi·tion** [~'biʃn] inhibición *f*; **in·'hib·i·to·ry** [~təri] inhibitorio.

in·hos·pi·ta·ble [in'hɔspitəbl] ☐ inhospitalario, inhóspito; **in·hos·pi·tal·i·ty** ['~'tæliti] inhospitalidad *f*.

in·hu·man [in'hju:mən] ☐ inhumano; **in·hu·man·i·ty** [~'mæniti] inhumanidad *f*.

in·hu·ma·tion [inhju:'meiʃn] inhumación *f*.

in·hume [in'hju:m] inhumar.

in·im·i·cal [i'nimikəl] enemigo (*to* de); contrario (*to* a).

in·im·i·ta·ble [i'nimitəbl] ☐ inimitable.

in·i·tial [i'niʃl] **1.** ☐ inicial *adj. a. su. f*; **2.** marcar (*or* firmar) con iniciales; **in·i·ti·ate 1.** [i'niʃiit] iniciado *adj. a. su. m* (a *f*); **2.** [i'niʃieit] iniciar (*into* en); **in·i·ti·a·tion** iniciación *f*; **in'i·ti·a·tive** [~ʃiətiv] **1.** iniciativa *f*; *on one's own* ~ por su propia iniciativa; *take the* ~ tomar la iniciativa; **2.** iniciativo; **in'i·ti·a·tor** [~ʃieitə] iniciador (-a *f*) *m*; **in'i·ti·a·to·ry** [~ʃiətəri] iniciativo; de iniciación.

in·ject [in'dʒekt] inyectar (*into* en); *fig.* introducir, injertar; **in'jec·tion** inyección *f*.

in·ju·di·cious [indʒu'diʃəs] ☐ imprudente, indiscreto.

in·junc·tion [in'dʒʌŋkʃn] mandato *m*, precepto *m*; 🏛 entredicho *m*.

in·jure ['indʒə] *body* lastimar, herir, ✹ lesionar, (*esp. permanently*) lisiar; (*damage*) dañar, perjudicar, averiar; *feelings, reputation* injuriar, ofender; **in·ju·ri·ous** [in'dʒuəriəs] ☐ dañoso, perjudicial; nocivo; injurioso; **in·ju·ry** ['indʒəri] herida *f*, lesión *f*; perjuicio *m*, daño *m*; injuria *f*.

in·jus·tice [in'dʒʌstis] injusticia *f*.

ink [iŋk] **1.** tinta *f*; **2.** entintar (*a.* ~ *in*); '~**-e·ras·er** goma *f* para tinta.

ink·ling ['iŋkliŋ] atisbo *m*; sospecha *f*; indicio *m*; idea *f*.

ink…: '~**-pad** almohadilla *f* (*or* tampón *m*) de entintar; '~**-pot** tintero *m*; '~**-stand** escribanía *f*; '~**-well** tintero *m*; '**ink·y** manchado de tinta; (negro) como la tinta.

in·laid ['inleid] *pret. a. p.p. of inlay*; ~ *floor* entarimado *m*; ~ *work* taracea *f*.

in·land ['inlǝnd] **1.** interior *m* (del país); **2.** (del) interior; ♀ *Revenue* delegación *f* de contribuciones; **3.** [in'lænd] *adv.* tierra adentro; **in·land·er** ['inlǝndǝ] habitante *m/f* del interior.

in·lay ['in'lei] **1.** [*irr.* (*lay*)] taracear, embutir, incrustar; **2.** taracea *f*, embutido *m*.

in·let ['inlet] entrante *m*, ensenada *f*, cala *f*; ⊕ admisión *f*; ~ *valve* válvula *f* de admisión.

in·mate ['inmeit] residente *m/f*; inquilino (-a *f*) *m*; preso (a *f*) *m*.

in·most ['inmoust] (más) interior; más íntimo, más recóndito.

inn [in] posada *f*, mesón *m*; (*poor, wayside*) venta *f*; (*bigger*) fonda *f*; ♀s *pl.* of *Court* Colegio *m* de abogados (*London*).

in·nate ['i'neit] □ innato.

in·ner ['inǝ] interior, interno; secreto, oculto; *mot. etc.* ~ *tube* cámara *f*; **'in·ner·most** = *inmost*.

in·nings ['ininz] *sport*: turno *m*, entrada *f*; *fig.* oportunidad *f*.

inn·keep·er ['inki:pǝ] posadero (a *f*) *m*, mesonero (a *f*) *m*; ventero (a *f*) *m*; fondista *m/f*.

in·no·cence ['inǝsns] inocencia *f*; **in·no·cent** ['~snt] □ inocente *adj. a. su. m/f* (*of* de).

in·noc·u·ous [i'nɔkjuǝs] □ inocuo.

in·no·vate ['inouveit] innovar; **in·no'va·tion** innovación *f*; **'in·no·va·tor** [~tǝ] innovador (-a *f*) *m*.

in·nu·en·do [inju'endou] indirecta *f*, insinuación *f*, pulla *f*.

in·nu·mer·a·ble [i'nju:mǝrǝbl] □ innumerable.

in·ob·serv·ance [inǝb'zǝ:vǝns] inobservancia *f*.

in·oc·u·late [i'nɔkjuleit] inocular; **in·oc·u'la·tion** inoculación *f*.

in·o·dor·ous [in'oudǝrǝs] inodoro.

in·of·fen·sive [inǝ'fensiv] □ inofensivo; **in·of'fen·sive·ness** inocuidad *f*.

in·op·er·a·tive [in'ɔpǝrǝtiv] inoperante.

in·op·por·tune [in'ɔpǝtju:n] □ inoportuno; ~*ly* a deshora.

in·or·di·nate [in'ɔ:dinit] □ desmesurado, excesivo; inordenado.

in·or·gan·ic [inɔ:'gænik] inorgánico.

in·pa·tient ['inpeiʃǝnt] paciente *m/f* interno (a).

in·put ['input] ⊕, ⚡ (potencia *f* de)

entrada *f*; ✝ dinero *m* invertido (*or* gastado).

in·quest ['inkwest] diligencias *f/pl.* previas; encuesta *f*.

in·quire [in'kwaiǝ] preguntar (*about, after, for* por; *of* a); pedir informes (*about* sobre); ~ *into* inquirir, averiguar, indagar; **in'quir·er** preguntador (-a *f*) *m*, interrogante *m/f*; investigador (-a *f*) *m*; inquiridor (-a *f*) *m*; **in'quir·ing** □ curioso, investigador; **in'quir·y** pregunta *f*; encuesta *f*; (*esp.* 🔖) pesquisa *f*; investigación *f*; petición *f* de informes; *make inquiries* pedir informes (*of* a; *about, on* sobre); **in'quir·y·'of·fice** oficina *f* de informaciones.

in·qui·si·tion [inkwi'ziʃn] inquisición *f*; ♀ Inquisición *f*, Santo Oficio *m*; **in'quis·i·tive** □ *b.s.* curioso, preguntón; especulativo; **in'quis·i·tive·ness** curiosidad *f*; **in'quis·i·tor** inquisidor *m*; **in·quis·i·to·ri·al** [~'tɔ:riǝl] □ inquisitorial.

in·road ['inroud] incursión *f*; *fig.* invasión *f*, usurpación *f* (*into, on* de).

in·rush ['inrʌʃ] afluencia *f*; irrupción *f*.   [salubre.\
in·sa·lu·bri·ous [insǝ'lu:briǝs] in-\
in·sane [in'sein] □ insano, loco, demente; (*senseless*) insensato; **in·san·i·tar·y** [~'sænitǝri] □ insalubre, antihigiénico; **in'san·i·ty** insania *f*, locura *f*, demencia *f*.

in·sa·ti·a·bil·i·ty [inseiʃiǝ'biliti] insaciabilidad *f*; **in'sa·ti·a·ble, in·'sa·ti·ate** [~ʃiǝt] insaciable.

in·scribe [in'skraib] inscribir (*a. fig.*, ✝, ⚖); *book* dedicar.

in·scrip·tion [in'skripʃn] inscripción *f*; dedicatoria *f* in *book*.

in·scru·ta·bil·i·ty [inskru:tǝ'biliti] inescrutabilidad *f*; **in'scru·ta·ble** □ inescrutable, insondable.

in·sect ['insekt] insecto *m*; **in'sec·ti·cide** [~isaid] insecticida *adj. a. su. m*; **in·sec·tiv·o·rous** [~'tivǝrǝs] insectívoro.

in·se·cure [insi'kjuǝ] □ inseguro; **in·se'cu·ri·ty** [~riti] inseguridad *f*.

in·sem·i·na·tion [insemi'neiʃn] inseminación *f*, fecundación *f*; *artificial* ~ fecundación *f* artificial.

in·sen·sate [in'senseit] insensato; (*unfeeling*) insensible; **in·sen·si·**

bil·i·ty [‿sə'biliti] insensibilidad *f*; desmayo *m*; inconsciencia *f*; impasibilidad *f*; **in'sen·si·ble** ☐ insensible (*of*, *to* a); inconsciente (*of* de); impasible; imperceptible; **in·'sen·si·tive** insensible (*to* a).

in·sep·a·ra·bil·i·ty [insepərə'biliti] inseparabilidad *f*; **in'sep·a·ra·ble** ☐ inseparable.

in·sert 1. [in'səːt] insertar, inserir; introducir; **2.** ['insəːt] inserción *f*; hoja *f* insertada; **in'ser·tion** inserción *f*; *sew.* entredós *m*.

in·set ['inset] inserción *f*; intercalación *f*, encaje *m*; *typ.* medallón *m*, mapa *m* (*or* grabado *m*) en la esquina de la página.

in·shore ['in'ʃɔː] **1.** *adj.* cercano a la orilla; **2.** *adv.* cerca de la orilla; hacia la orilla.

in·side ['in'said] **1.** interior *m*; parte *f* de dentro; F entrañas *f/pl.*; *on the* ‿ por dentro; ‿ *out* al revés; *turn* ‿ *out* volver(se) al revés; **2.** *adj.* interior; interno; F secreto, confidencial; *sport:* ‿ *left* interior *m* izquierdo; ‿ *right* interior *m* derecho; **3.** *adv.* (a)dentro, hacia dentro; por dentro; **4.** *prp.* dentro de; **'in'sid·er** miembro *m*; iniciado (a *f*) *m*; persona *f* enterada (*or* privilegiada).

in·sid·i·ous [in'sidiəs] ☐ insidioso.

in·sight ['insait] penetración *f* (psicológica); perspicacia *f*; intuición *f*; *get an* ‿ *into* formarse una idea de.

in·sig·ni·a [in'signiə] *pl.* insignias *f/pl.*

in·sig·nif·i·cance, *a.* **in·sig·nif·i·can·cy** [insig'nifikəns(i)] insignificancia *f*; **in·sig'nif·i·cant** ☐ insignificante.

in·sin·cere [insin'siə] ☐ poco sincero, falso; **in·sin'cer·i·ty** [‿'seriti] falta *f* de sinceridad, falsedad *f*.

in·sin·u·ate [in'sinjueit] insinuar; ‿ *o.s. into* insinuarse en; introducirse en; **in'sin·u·at·ing** ☐ insinuador; **in·sin·u·a·tion** insinuación *f*; indirecta *f*, pulla *f*.

in·sip·id [in'sipid] ☐ insípido, soso, insulso; **in·si'pid·i·ty** insipidez *f*, sosería *f*, insulsez *f*.

in·sist [in'sist] insistir ([*up*]*on* en, sobre; *on ger.* en *inf.*; *that* en que); empeñarse (en); porfiar; **in'sist·ence** insistencia *f*, empeño *m*, porfía *f*; **in'sist·ent** ☐ insistente, porfiado; urgente.

in·so·bri·e·ty [insou'braiəti] intemperancia *f*; embriaguez *f*. [ción *f*.\
in·so·la·tion [insou'leiʃn] ⚕ insola-|
in·sole ['insoul] plantilla *f*.

in·so·lence ['insələns] insolencia *f*, descaro *m*; **'in·so·lent** ☐ insolente, descarado.

in·sol·u·bil·i·ty [insɔlju'biliti] insolubilidad *f*; **in'sol·u·ble** [‿jubl] ☐ insoluble; *problem* indescifrable.

in·sol·ven·cy [in'sɔlvənsi] insolvencia *f*; **in'sol·vent** insolvente.

in·som·ni·a [in'sɔmniə] insomnio *m*.

in·so·much [insou'mʌtʃ]: ‿ *as* ya que; ‿ *that* hasta tal punto que.

in·spect [in'spekt] inspeccionar; examinar; registrar; ✗ pasar revista a; **in'spec·tion** inspección *f*; examen *m*; registro *m*; ✗ revista *f*; ‿ *pit* foso *m* de reconocimiento; **in·'spec·tor** inspector *m*; interventor *m*; 🚂 revisor *m*; **in'spec·tor·ate** [‿tərit] inspectorado *m*.

in·spi·ra·tion [inspə'reiʃn] inspiración *f*; *find* ‿ *in* inspirarse en; **in·spire** [‿'spaiə] inspirar; mover (*to* a); ‿ *s.t. in a p. or a p. with s.t.* inspirar algo a (*or* en) una p.; **in·spir·it** [‿'spirit] alentar, animar.

in·sta·bil·i·ty [instə'biliti] in(e)stabilidad *f*; inconstancia *f*, volubilidad *f*.

in·stall [in'stɔːl] instalar; **in·stal·la·tion** [instə'leiʃn] instalación *f*.

in·stal(l)·ment [in'stɔːlmənt] entrega *f*; ✝ plazo *m*; *payment by* (*or in*) ‿*s* pago *m* a plazos.

in·stance ['instəns] **1.** ejemplo *m*, caso *m*; vez *f*, ocasión *f*; petición *f*; (*urgent request a.* ⚖) instancia *f*; *at the* ‿ *of* a instancia de; *for* ‿ por ejemplo; *in the first* ‿ en primer lugar; **2.** poner por caso, citar (como ejemplo).

in·stant ['instənt] **1.** instante *m*, momento *m*; *in an* ‿, *on the* ‿, *this* ‿ al instante, en seguida; **2.** *cj.*: the ‿ luego que, en cuanto; **3.** ☐ inmediato, urgente; corriente; *the 10 th* ‿ (*mst inst.*) el 10 del (mes) corriente; **in·stan·ta·ne·ous** [‿'teinjəs] ☐ instantáneo; **in·stan·ter** [in'stæntə], **in·stant·ly** ['instəntli] inmediatamente, al instante.

in state [in'steit] instalar.

in·stead [ins'ted] en cambio; en lugar de ello (*or* él, ella, *etc.*); ‿ *of* en lugar de, en vez de.

in·step ['instep] empeine *m*.
in·sti·gate ['instigeit] instigar; **in-sti'ga·tion** instigación *f*; *at the ~ of* a instigación de; **'in·sti·ga·tor** instigador (-a *f*) *m*.
in·stil(l) [in'stil] instilar; infundir, inculcar (*in*[to] para); **in·stil·la·tion** [insti'leifn] instilación *f*; inculcación *f*.
in·stinct 1. ['instiŋkt] instinto *m*; **2.** [in'stiŋkt]: *~ with* animado de, lleno de; **in'stinc·tive** □ instintivo.
in·sti·tute ['institju:t] **1.** instituto *m*; asociación *f* (profesional); $\chi^{\cdot}_{b}$ *~s pl.* instituta *f*; **2.** instituir; *proceedings etc.* iniciar, entablar; *p.* nombrar ([*in*]to para); instalar ([*in*]to en); **in·sti'tu·tion** institución *f*; fundación *f*, establecimiento *m*; iniciación *f*; instituto *m*; asilo *m*; costumbre *f*; F cosa *f* (*or* persona *f*) muy conocida; **in·sti·tu·tion·al·ize** [~əlaiz] reglamentar.
in·struct [in'strʌkt] instruir (*about*, *in* de, en, sobre); mandar (*to* a); **in-'struc·tion** instrucción *f*; *~s pl.* instrucciones *f*/*pl.*; orden *f*; *~s for use* modo *m* de empleo; *on the ~s of* por orden de; **in'struc·tion·al** educacional; **in-'struc·tive** □ instructivo; **in-'struc·tor** instructor *m*; *Am. univ.* profesor *m* (auxiliar); **in'struc·tress** instructora *f*.
in·stru·ment ['instrumənt] *all senses*: instrumento *m*; *~s pl.* ♩, ♬ instrumental *m*; *mot.*, ✈ *~ board*, *~ panel* tablero *m* de instrumentos; *fly on ~s* volar por instrumentos; **in-stru·men·tal** [~'mentl] instrumental; *be ~ in* contribuir (materialmente) a, intervenir en, ayudar a; **in·stru'men·tal·ist** instrumentista *m*/*f*; **in·stru·men·tal·i·ty** [~'tæliti] intervención *f*, mediación *f*, agencia *f*; **in·stru·men'ta·tion** instrumentación *f*.
in·sub·or·di·nate [insə'bɔ:dnit] insubordinado;' **in·sub·or·di'na·tion** insubordinación *f*.
in·suf·fer·a·ble [in'sʌfərəbl] □ insufrible, inaguantable.
in·suf·fi·cien·cy [insə'fifənsi] insuficiencia *f*; **in·suf'fi·cient** □ insuficiente.
in·su·lar ['insjulə] insular, isleño; *fig.* de miras estrechas; **in·su·lar·i·ty** [~'læriti] insularidad *f*; *fig.*

estrechez *f* de miras; **in·su·late** ['~leit] aislar; **'in·su·lat·ing** aislador; *~ tape* cinta *f* aisladora; **in·su'la·tion** aislamiento *m*; **'in·su·la·tor** aislador *m*, aislante *m*.
in·su·lin ['insjulin] insulina *f*.
in·sult 1. ['insʌlt] insulto *m*, ultraje *m*, injuria *f*; **2.** [in'sʌlt] insultar, ultrajar, injuriar; **in'sult·ing** □ insultante, injurioso.
in·su·per·a·bil·i·ty [insju:pərə'biliti] lo insuperable; **in'su·per·a·ble** □ insuperable.
in·sup·port·a·ble [insə'pɔ:təbl] □ insoportable.
in·sur·ance [in'fuərəns] aseguramiento *m*; ✝ seguro *m*; *~ company* compañía *f* de seguros; *~ policy* póliza *f*; *~ premium* prima *f*, premio *m*; **in'sur·ant** asegurado (a *f*) *m*; **in·sure** [in'fuə] asegurar; **in'sured** asegurado (a *f*) *m*; **in'sur·er** asegurador (-a *f*) *m*.
in·sur·gent [in'sə:dʒənt] insurgente *adj. a. su. m*/*f*, insurrecto *adj. a. su. m* (a *f*).
in·sur·mount·a·ble [insə'mauntəbl] insuperable.
in·sur·rec·tion [insə'rekfn] insurrección *f*, levantamiento *m*; **in-sur'rec·tion·al**, **in·sur'rec·tion·ary** insurreccional; **in·sur'rec·tion·ist** [~fnist] insurrecto (a *f*) *m*, sedicioso (a *f*) *m*.   [ileso.\
in·tact [in'tækt] intacto, íntegro,]
in·take ['inteik] ⊕ admisión *f*, toma *f*, entrada *f*; cantidad *f* admitida; número *m* admitido.
in·tan·gi·bil·i·ty [intændʒə'biliti] intangibilidad *f*; **in'tan·gi·ble** [~dʒəbl] □ intangible.
in·te·ger ['intidʒə] (número *m*) entero *m*; **in·te·gral** ['~grəl] **1.** □ (*whole*) íntegro; (*component*) integrante; $\mathcal{A}$ integral; **2.** $\mathcal{A}$ integral *f*; **in·te·grant** ['~grent] integrante; **in·te·grate** ['~greit] integrar (*a.* $\mathcal{A}$); combinar en un todo (*with* con); **in·te'gra·tion** integración *f*; **in·teg·ri·ty** [~'tegriti] integridad *f*, probidad *f*.
in·teg·u·ment [in'tegjumənt] integumento *m*.
in·tel·lect ['intilekt] intelecto *m*, entendimiento *m*; **in·tel'lec·tu·al** [~tjuəl] □ intelectual *adj. a. su. m*/*f*; **in·tel·lec·tu·al·i·ty** ['~æliti] intelectualidad *f*.

in·tel·li·gence [in'telidʒəns] inteligencia *f*; información *f*, noticias *f/pl.*; ~ *quotient* cociente *m* intelectual; ~ *service* ⚔ servicio *m* de información; ~ *test* prueba *f* (*or* test *m*) de inteligencia; **in·tel·li·genc·er** *mst* † noticiero *m*; espía *m*; gaceta *f*.

in·tel·li·gent [in'telidʒənt] ☐ inteligente; **in·tel·li·gent·si·a** [~'dʒent-siə] intelectualidad *f*; **in·tel·li·gi·bil·i·ty** [~dʒə'biliti] inteligibilidad *f*; **in·tel·li·gi·ble** ☐ inteligible.

in·tem·per·ance [in'tempərəns] intemperancia *f*; inmoderación *f*; exceso *m* en la bebida; **in·tem·per·ate** [~rit] ☐ intemperante; inmoderado; descomedido; dado a la bebida.

in·tend [in'tend] pensar, proponerse; (*mean*) querer decir (*by* con); destinar (*for* a, para); ~ *to do* pensar hacer; **in·tend·ant** intendente *m*; **in·tend·ed 1.** pensado; deseado; F prometido; *be* ~ *to* tener por fin; **2.** F prometido (a *f*) *m*, novio (a *f*) *m*.

in·tense [in'tens] ☐ intenso; fuerte; extremado; *p.* apasionado; **in·tense·ness** intensidad *f*; fuerza *f*; apasionamiento *m* of *p.*

in·ten·si·fi·ca·tion [intensifi'keiʃn] intensificación *f*; **in·ten·si·fy** [~fai] intens(ific)ar(se); reforzar (*a. phot.*); **in·ten·si·ty** = *intenseness*; **in·ten·sive** ☐ = *intense*; intensivo.

in·tent [in'tent] **1.** ☐ absorto (*on* en); resuelto (*on* a); **2.** intento *m*, propósito *m*; *to all* ~*s and purposes* prácticamente, en realidad; *with* ~ *to* con el propósito de; **in·ten·tion** intención *f*; intento *m*, propósito *m*; significado *m*; **in·ten·tion·al** [~ʃnl] ☐ intencional; ~*ly* adrede, de propósito; **in·ten·tioned** intencionado; **in·tent·ness** atención *f*; ahinco *m*.

in·ter [in'tə:] enterrar, sepultar.

in·ter... ['intə] inter...; entre.

in·ter·act [intər'ækt] obrar recíprocamente; **in·ter·ac·tion** interacción *f*; efecto *m* recíproco.

in·ter·breed ['intə'bri:d] [*irr.*(*breed*)] cruzar(se).

in·ter·ca·late [in'tə:kəleit] intercalar; **in·ter·ca·la·tion** intercalación *f*.

in·ter·cede [intə'si:d] interceder, mediar (*with* con, *for* por).

in·ter·cept [intə'sept] interceptar;

detener; ⚔ cortar; **in·ter·cep·tion** interceptación *f*; **in·ter·cep·tor** interceptador *m* (*a.* ⚔).

in·ter·ces·sion [intə'seʃn] intercesión *f*.

in·ter·change 1. [intə'tʃeindʒ] (inter)cambiar(se), trocar(se); alternar(se); **2.** ['~'tʃeindʒ] intercambio *m*; canje *m* of *prisoners*, *publications*; alternación *f*; **in·ter·change·a·ble** intercambiable.

in·ter·com [intə'kɔm] F sistema *m* de intercomunicación.

in·ter·com·mu·ni·cate [intəkə-'mju:nikeit] comunicarse; **in·ter·com·mu·ni·ca·tion** intercomunicación *f*; comercio *m*; **in·ter·com·mun·ion** [~jən] intercomunión *f*.

in·ter·con·nect ['intəkə'nekt] interconectar.

in·ter·con·ti·nen·tal ['intəkɔnti-'nentl] intercontinental.

in·ter·course ['intəkɔ:s] (*social*) trato *m*; comercio *m*; intercambio *m*; (*sexual*) coito *m*, trato *m* sexual.

in·ter·de·nom·i·na·tion·al [intədi-nɔmi'neiʃnl] interconfesional.

in·ter·de·pend·ent [intədi'pendənt] interdependiente.

in·ter·dict 1. [intə'dikt] entredecir, interdecir; **2.** ['intədikt] entredicho *m*, interdicto *m*; **in·ter·dic·tion** interdicción *f*.

in·ter·est ['intrist] **1.** interés *m* (*a.* †); † rédito *m*; participación *f*; influencia *f* (*with* sobre); ~*s pl.* intereses *m/pl.*; personas *f/pl.* interesadas; *bear* ~ devengar intereses; *be of* ~ *to* interesar; *in the* ~ *of* en interés de; *put out at* ~ poner a interés; *repay with* ~ *fig.* devolver con creces; *take an* ~ interesarse (*in th.* en, *p.* por); **2.** interesar (*in* en); *be* ~*ed in*, ~ *o.s. in* interesarse por (*or* en); **in·ter·est·ed** ☐ interesado; ~ *party* interesado (a *f*) *m*; **in·ter·est·ing** ☐ interesante.

in·ter·fere [intə'fiə] (entro)meterse, mezclarse, intervenir (*in* en); ~ *with* estorbar; dificultar; meterse con; F tocar, manosear; *phys.* interferir; **in·ter·fer·ence** entrometimiento *m*; intervención *f*; estorbo *m*; *phys.*, ⚡ interferencia *f*; **in·ter·fer·ing** entrometido.

in·ter·fuse [intə'fju:z] mezclar(se).

in·ter·im ['intərim] **1.** intervalo *m*, intermedio *m*, ínterin *m*; *in the* ~

entretanto, en el ínterin, interina-
mente; **2.** interino; provisional.
in·te·ri·or [in'tiəriə] **1.** interior *m*;
2. interior, interno; ~ *decoration* decoración *f* de interiores.
in·ter·ject [intə'dʒekt] interponer;
interrumpir (con); **in·ter'jec·tion**
gr. interjección *f*; exclamación *f*.
in·ter·lace [intə'leis] entrelazar(se),
entretejer(se).
in·ter·lard [intə'lɑːd] *fig.* insertar,
interpolar; ~ *with* salpicar de.
in·ter·leave [intə'liːv] interfoliar.
in·ter·line [intə'lain] interlinear;
sew. entretelar; **in·ter·lin·e·ar** [in-
tə'liniə] interlineal; **in·ter·lin·e·a·
tion** ['~lini'eiʃn] interlineación *f*;
in·ter·lin·ing ['~lainiŋ] *sew.* entre-
tela *f*.
in·ter·link [intə'liŋk] eslabonar.
in·ter·lock [intə'lɔk] enclavar(se);
engranar; en(tre)lazar(se); ~*ing
device* sistema *m* de cierre (*or* de
enclavamiento); ~ *stitch* punto *m* indesmallable.
in·ter·lo·cu·tion [intəlou'kjuːʃn] in-
terlocución *f*; **in·ter·loc·u·tor** [~-
'lɔkjutə] interlocutor (-a *f*) *m*;
in·ter'loc·u·to·ry 🏛 interlocuto-
rio; dialogístico.
in·ter·lope [intə'loup] ser intruso;
entrometerse; ✝ traficar sin autorización; **'in·ter'lop·er** intruso (a *f*)
m; ✝ intérlope *m*.
in·ter·lude ['intəluːd] ♪ interludio
m; *thea.* intermedio *m*; intervalo *m*;
descanso *m*.
in·ter·mar·riage [intə'mæridʒ] matrimonio *m* entre parientes; matrimonio *m* entre personas de distintas
razas; **'in·ter'mar·ry** casarse(personas emparentadas *or* de distintas
razas).
in·ter·me·di·ar·y [intə'miːdiəri] intermediario *adj. a. su. m* (a *f*); **in·
ter·me·di·ate** [~'miːdiət] ☐ (inter)-
medio; intermediario; ~ *stop* escala *f*.
in·ter·ment [in'təːmənt] entierro *m*.
in·ter·mez·zo [intə'medzou] ♪ intermezzo *m*; *thea.* intermedio *m*.
in·ter·mi·na·ble [in'təːminəbl] ☐
interminable, inacabable.
in·ter·min·gle [intə'miŋgl] entre-
mezclar(se), entreverar(se).
in·ter·mis·sion [intə'miʃn] interrupción *f*; intervalo *m*, pausa *f*;
thea. entreacto *m*; 📺 intermisión *f*.

in·ter·mit·tent [intə'mitənt] ☐ intermitente (*a.* ⚙ʸ); ~*ly* a intervalos.
in·ter·mix [intə'miks] entremez-
clar(se).
in·tern [in'təːn] recluir, internar.
in·tern(e) ['intəːn] ⚙ practicante *m*
de hospital.
in·ter·nal [in'təːnl] ☐ interno, interior; ~-com'bus·tion en·gine motor *m* de explosión, motor *m* de
combustión interna.
in·ter·na·tion·al [intə'næʃnl] **1.** ☐
internacional; ~ *law* derecho *m* internacional (*or* de gentes); **2.** ⚲ *pol.*
Internacional *f*; *sport*: partido *m*
internacional; jugador (-a *f*) *m* internacional; **in·ter'na·tion·al·ism**
internacionalismo *m*; **in·ter'na·
tion·al·ize** [~əlaiz] internacionali-
zar.
in·ter·ne·cine war [intə'niːsain'wɔː]
guerra *f* de aniquilación mutua.
in·tern·ee [intəː'niː] internado (a *f*)
m; **in'tern·ment** internamiento *m*;
~ *camp* campo *m* de internamiento.
in·ter·pel·late [in'təːpeleit] interpe-
lar; **in·ter·pel'la·tion** interpela-
ción *f*.
in·ter·pen·e·trate [intə'penitreit]
compenetrarse.
in·ter·plan·e·tar·y [intə'plænitəri]
interplanetario.
in·ter·play ['intə'plei] interacción *f*.
in·ter·po·late [in'təː'pouleit] interpolar; **in·ter·po'la·tion** interpola-
ción *f*.
in·ter·pose [intə'pouz] interponer
(se); **in·ter·po·si·tion** [intəːpə-
'ziʃn] interposición *f*.
in·ter·pret [in'təːprit] interpretar;
in·ter·pre'ta·tion interpretación *f*;
in'ter·pre·ta·tive interpretativo;
in'ter·pret·er intérprete *m/f*.
in·ter·reg·num ['intə'regnəm] inte-
rregno *m*.
in·ter·ro·gate [in'terəgeit] interrogar, examinar; **in·ter·ro'ga·tion**
interrogación *f*, examen *m*; *note* (*or
mark or point*) *of* ~ (punto *m* de) interrogación *f*; **in·ter·rog·a·tive** [~-
tə'rɔgətiv] ☐ interrogativo *adj. a.
su. m*; **in·ter'rog·a·to·ry** [~təri]
1. interrogatorio *m*; **2.** interrogativo.
in·ter·rupt [intə'rʌpt] interrumpir;
(entre)cortar; **in·ter'rupt·ed·ly** in-
terrumpidamente; **in·ter'rupt·er**
interruptor (-a *f*) *m*; **in·ter'rup·
tion** interrupción *f*.

in·ter·sect [intə'sekt] *v/t.* cortar; *v/i.* intersecarse; **in·ter'sec·tion** intersección *f;* cruce *m.*

in·ter·space ['intə'speis] 1. espacio *m* intermedio, intervalo *m;* 2. espaciar.

in·ter·sperse [intə'spə:s] esparcir, entremezclar; salpicar *(with* de).

in·ter·state ['intə'steit] *Am.* interestatal.

in·ter·stel·lar ['intə'stelə] interestelar.

in·ter·stice [in'tə:stis] intersticio *m;* **in·ter·sti·tial** [intə'stiʃl] □ intersticial.

in·ter·twine [intə'twain] entrelazar (se), entretejer(se); trenzar.

in·ter·val ['intəvəl] intervalo *m (a.* ♪); *thea.* entreacto *m;* descanso *m (a. sport);* pausa *f; at ~s* de vez en cuando, a intervalos.

in·ter·vene [intə'vi:n] intervenir, interponerse, mediar; **in·ter·ven·tion** [~'venʃn] intervención *f.*

in·ter·view ['intəvju:] 1. entrevista *f;* *(press etc.)* interviú *f; have an ~ with =* 2. entrevistarse con, interviuvar; **'in·ter·view·er** interviuvador (-a *f) m;* interrogador (-a *f) m.*

in·ter·weave [intə'wi:v] [*irr.(weave)*] entretejer *(a. fig.).*

in·tes·ta·cy [in'testəsi] falta *f* de testamento; **in'tes·tate** [~tit] intestado.

in·tes·ti·nal [in'testinl] intestinal; **in'tes·tine** [~tin] intestino *adj. a. su. m; large ~* intestino *m* grueso; *small ~* intestino *m* delgado.

in·ti·ma·cy ['intiməsi] intimidad *f;* F trato *m* sexual; **in·ti·mate** 1. ['~meit] intimar; dar a entender; 2. ['~mit] a) □ íntimo; estrecho; *knowledge* profundo, detallado; *become ~* intimarse *(with* con); b) amigo (a *f) m* de confianza; **in·ti·ma·tion** [~'meiʃn] intimación *f;* insinuación *f,* indirecta *f;* indicio *m.*

in·tim·i·date [in'timideit] intimidar, amedrentar, acobardar; **in·tim·i·'da·tion** intimidación *f;* **in·tim·i·'da·tor·y** [~'deitəri] amenazador.

in·to ['intu, *before consonant* 'intə] en; a; dentro de; hacia el interior de; *~ the garden* al jardín; *fall ~ the sea* caer al *(or* en el) mar; *put it ~ the box* meterlo dentro de la caja.

in·tol·er·a·ble [in'tɔlərəbl] □ intolerable, inaguantable; **in'tol·er·ance**

intolerancia *f;* **in'tol·er·ant** □ intolerante *(of* con, para).

in·to·na·tion [intou'neiʃn] entonación *f;* **in·to·nate** ['~neit], **in·tone** [in'toun] entonar; *eccl.* salmodiar.

in·tox·i·cant [in'tɔksikənt] 1. embriagador; 2. bebida *f* alcohólica; **in'tox·i·cate** [~keit] embriagar *(a. fig.);* 🕱 intoxicar; **in·tox·i·'ca·tion** embriaguez *f (a. fig.);* 🕱 intoxicación *f.*

in·trac·ta·bil·i·ty [intræktə'biliti] intratabilidad *f;* **in'trac·ta·ble** □ *p.* intratable, insumiso; *materials* difícil de trabajar; *problem* insoluble.

in·tra·mu·ral ['intrə'mjuərəl] interior, situado intramuros.

in·tran·si·gent [in'trænsidʒənt] intransigente.

in·tran·si·tive [in'trɑ:nsitiv] □ intransitivo *adj. a. su. m.*

in·tra·state [intrə'steit] *Am.* de dentro de un estado. [venoso.]

in·tra·ve·nous ['intrə'vi:nəs] intra-ʃ

in·trench [in'trentʃ] *v.* entrench.

in·trep·id [in'trepid] □ intrépido; **in·tre·pid·i·ty** [intri'piditi] intrepidez *f.*

in·tri·ca·cy ['intrikəsi] intrincación *f;* **in·tri·cate** ['~kit] □ intrincado.

in·trigue [in'tri:g] 1. intriga *f;* amorío *m* secreto, lío *m; thea.* enredo *m;* 2. intrigar; tener un lío; **in'tri·guer** intrigante *m/f.*

in·trin·sic [in'trinsik] □ intrínseco.

in·tro·duce [intrə'dju:s] introducir; meter, insertar; *p. to a p., parl. bill* presentar; dar a conocer; *book* prologar; *subject into conversation* sacar a colación; **in·tro·duc·tion** [~'dʌkʃn] introducción *f;* inserción *f;* presentación *f of p.;* prólogo *m to book; letter of ~* carta *f* de recomendación; **in·tro·duc·to·ry** [~təri] introductor; preliminar.

in·tro·it ['introit] introito *m.*

in·tro·spec·tion [introu'spekʃn] introspección *f;* **in·tro·spec·tive** □ introspectivo.

in·tro·ver·sion [introu'və:ʃn] introversión *f;* **in·tro·vert** [~'və:t] introvertido *adj. a. su. m (a f).*

in·trude [in'tru:d] *v/t.* introducir (sin derecho), meter, encajar *(in* en); imponer *(upon* a); *v/i.* (entro)meterse, encajarse *(upon* en); pegarse; estorbar; **in'trud·er** intruso (a *f) m.*

in·tru·sion [in'tru:ʒn] intrusión *f*; **in·tru·sive** [in'tru:siv] □ intruso.

in·trust [in'trʌst] *v. entrust.*

in·tu·i·tion [intju'iʃn] intuición *f*; **in·tu·i·tive** [ˌ'tjuitiv] □ intuitivo.

in·un·date ['inʌndeit] inundar; **in·un'da·tion** inundación *f.*

in·ure [i'njuə] acostumbrar, endurecer (*to* a).

in·vade [in'veid] invadir (*a. fig.*); **in'vad·er** invasor (-a *f*) *m*; **in'vad·ing** invasor.

in·val·id 1. [in'vælid] inválido, nulo; **2.** ['invəli(:)d] ⚔, ⚓ inválido *adj. a. su. m* (a *f*); enfermo *adj. a. su. m* (a *f*); ~ *carriage* cochecillo *m* de inválido; ~ *chair* sillón *m* para inválidos; **3.** [invə'li:d] incapacitar; ⚔, ⚓ (*a.* ~ *out*) licenciar por invalidez; **in·val·i·date** [in'vælideit] invalidar; **in·val·i'da·tion** invalidación *f*; **in·va·lid·i·ty** [invə'liditi] invalidez *f.*

in·val·u·a·ble [in'væljuəbl] □ inestimable, inapreciable.

in·var·i·a·ble [in'vɛəriəbl] □ invariable.

in·va·sion [in'veiʒn] invasión *f* (*a. fig.*, ⚔).

in·vec·tive [in'vektiv] invectiva *f*; improperio *m.*

in·veigh [in'vei]: ~ *against* vituperar, invectivar.

in·vei·gle [in'vi:gl] engatusar (*into* para que); inducir (engañosamente) (*into* a); **in'vei·gle·ment** engatusamiento *m*, persuasión *f.*

in·vent [in'vent] inventar; idear; fingir; **in'ven·tion** invención *f*, invento *m*; (*faculty*) inventiva *f*; ficción *f*; **in'ven·tive** □ inventivo; **in'ven·tive·ness** inventiva *f*; **in·ven·tor** inventor (-a *f*) *m*; **in·ven·to·ry** ['invəntri] **1.** inventario *m*; existencias *f/pl.*; **2.** inventariar.

in·verse ['in'və:s] □ inverso; **in·ver·sion** [in'və:ʃn] inversión *f.*

in·vert 1. [in'və:t] invertir; trastrocar; volver al revés; ~*ed commas pl.* comillas *f/pl.*; **2.** ['invə:t] invertido (a *f*) *m.*

in·ver·te·brate [in'və:tibrit] invertebrado *adj. a. su. m.*

in·vest [in'vest] *v/t.* ✝ invertir, colocar; ~ *with honour* investir de (*or* con); *garment, quality* revestir de (*or* con); ⚔ sitiar, cercar; *v/i.:* ~ *in* poner (*or* invertir) dinero en; F comprar.

in·ves·ti·gate [in'vestigeit] investigar; averiguar; examinar; **in·ves·ti'ga·tion** investigación *f*; averiguación *f*; pesquisa *f*; **in'ves·ti·ga·tor** [ˌgeitə] investigador (-a *f*) *m.*

in·ves·ti·ture [in'vestitʃə] investidura *f*; **in'vest·ment** ✝ inversión *f*, colocación *f* (de fondos); ⚔ sitio *m*, cerco *m*; investidura *f*; ✝ ~*s pl.* valores *m/pl.* en cartera, fondos *m/pl.* invertidos; ~ *trust* compañía *f* inversionista; **in'vest·or** inversionista *m/f*; accionista *m/f*, inversor (-a *f*) *m.*

in·vet·er·a·cy [in'vetərəsi] lo inveterado; **in'vet·er·ate** [ˌrit] □ inveterado; *p.* habitual; *b.s.* empedernido.

in·vid·i·ous [in'vidiəs] □ aborrecible, odioso; parcial, injusto.

in·vig·i·late [in'vidʒileit] vigilar (durante los exámenes).

in·vig·or·ate [in'vigəreit] vigorizar, tonificar; **in'vig·or·a·ting** vigorizador; **in·vig·or'a·tion** tonificación *f.*

in·vin·ci·bil·i·ty [invinsi'biliti] invencibilidad *f*; **in'vin·ci·ble** □ invencible.

in·vi·o·la·bil·i·ty [invaiələ'biliti] inviolabilidad *f*; **in'vi·o·la·ble** □ inviolable; **in'vi·o·late** [ˌlit] inviolado.

in·vis·i·bil·i·ty [invizə'biliti] invisibilidad *f*; **in'vis·i·ble** □ invisible; ~ *ink* tinta *f* simpática.

in·vi·ta·tion [invi'teiʃn] invitación *f*, convite *m*; **in·vite** [in'vait] invitar (*to* a); (*esp. to food, drink*) convidar (*to* a); **in'vi·ting** □ atrayente; incitante; provocativo; *food* apetitoso.

in·vo·ca·tion [invou'keiʃn] invocación *f*; evocación *f* of *spirits.*

in·voice ['invɔis] **1.** factura *f*; **2.** facturar.

in·voke [in'vouk] invocar; *spirits* evocar.

in·vol·un·tar·y [in'vɔləntəri] □ involuntario.

in·vo·lute ['invəlu:t] intrincado; vuelto hacia dentro; enrollado en espiral; **in·vo'lu·tion** intrincación *f*; *biol.*, ⚘ involución *f*; ⚕ elevación *f* a potencias.

in·volve [in'vɔlv] envolver; (*entangle*) enredar, enmarañar; complicar; (*entail*) traer consigo, acarrear; implicar; comprometer; *get* ~*d in* meterse en, embrollarse en; **in'volve·ment** envolvimiento *m*;

enredo *m*; complicación *f*; compromiso *m*; apuro *m*, dificultad *f*.

in·vul·ner·a·bil·i·ty [invʌlnərə'biliti] invulnerabilidad *f*; **in'vul·ner·a·ble** □ invulnerable.

in·ward ['inwəd] **1.** *adj.* interior, interno; **2.** *adv.* (*mst* **in·wards** ['ˌz]) hacia dentro, para dentro, interiormente; **3.** *su.* F ˌs ['inədz] *pl.* entrañas *f/pl.*; interiores *m/pl.*; **'in·ward·ly** interiormente; (hacia) dentro; para sí; **'in·ward·ness** esencia *f*; espiritualidad *f*.

in·wrought ['in'rɔːt] entretejido; incrustado, embutido (*with* con; *in*, *on* en).

i·od·ic [ai'ɔdik] yódico; **i·o·dide** ['aiədaid] yoduro *m*; **i·o·dine** ['ˌdiːn] yodo *m*.

i·o·do·form [ai'ɔdəfɔːm] yodoformo *m*.

i·on ['aiən] ion *m*.

I·o·ni·an [ai'ounjən] jonio *adj. a. su. m* (a *f*), jónico *adj. a. su. m* (a *f*).

I·on·ic[1] [ai'ɔnik] jónico.

i·on·ic[2] [ˌ] *phys.* iónico; **i·on·ize** ['aiənaiz] ionizar.

i·o·ta [ai'outə] (*letter*) iota *f*; *fig.* jota *f*, ápice *m*, pizca *f*.

ip·e·cac·u·an·ha [ipikækju'ænə] ipecacuana *f*.

I·ra·ni·an [i'reinjən] iranio *adj. a. su. m* (a *f*), iranés *adj. a. su. m* (-a *f*).

I·ra·qi [i'rɑːki] irakí *adj. a. su. m/f*.

i·ras·ci·bil·i·ty [iræsi'biliti] irascibilidad *f*, iracundia *f*; **i'ras·ci·ble** [ˌsibl] □ irascible, iracundo.

i·rate [ai'reit] airado, colérico.

ire ['aiə] *poet.* ira *f*, cólera *f*.

ir·i·des·cence [iri'desns] iridescencia *f*, irisación *f*; **ir·i'des·cent** iridescente, irisado; tornasolado.

i·ris ['aiəris] *opt.* iris *m*; ♀ lirio *m*; *phot.* ˌ *diaphragm* diafragma *m* iris.

I·rish ['aiəriʃ] irlandés *adj. a. su. m*; *the* ˌ *pl.* los irlandeses; **'I·rish·ism** idiotismo *m* irlandés; **'I·rish·man** irlandés *m*; **'I·rish·wom·an** irlandesa *f*.

irk [əːk] fastidiar, molestar.

irk·some ['əːksəm] □ fastidioso, molesto, cargante, pesado; **'irk·some·ness** fastidio *m*, molestia *f*, tedio *m*.

i·ron ['aiən] **1.** hierro *m* (*a. fig.*, *tool*, *weapon*, *golf*); (*a. flat-* ˌ) plancha *f*; ˌs *pl.* hierros *m/pl.*, grillos *m/pl.*; *put in* ˌs aherrojar; *strike while the* ˌ

is hot a hierro candente batir de repente; **2.** de hierro; férreo (*a. fig.*); ˌ *curtain* telón *m* de acero; ˌ *lung* pulmón *m* de hierro; ˌ *ore* mineral *m* de hierro; ˌ *ration* ración *f* de reserva; **3.** *clothes* planchar; aherrojar; herrar; ˌ *out* allanar; **'ˌbound** zunchado con hierro; *fig.* férreo, inflexible; *coast* escabroso; **'ˌ·clad** acorazado *adj. a. su. m*; **'i·ron-found·ry** fundición *f* de hierro.

i·ron·ic, **i·ron·i·cal** [ai'rɔnik(l)] □ irónico.

i·ron·ing ['aiəniŋ] **1.** planchado *m*; **2.** de planchar; **'ˌ·board** tabla *f* de planchar.

i·ron...: 'ˌ·mas·ter fabricante *m* de hierro; '\~·mon·ger ferretero *m*, quincallero *m*; ˌ*s* (*shop*) ferretería *f*, quincallería *f*; '\~·mon·ger·y quincalla *f*, ferretería *f*; 'ˌ·mould mancha *f* de orín; '♀·sides *pl. hist.* caballería *f* de Cromwell; 'ˌ·stone mineral *m* de hierro; 'ˌ·work herraje *m*; obra *f* de hierro; '\~·works herrería *f*; fábrica *f* de hierro.

i·ro·ny ['aiərəni] ironía *f*.

ir·ra·di·ance, **ir·ra·di·an·cy** [i'reidiəns(i)] luminosidad *f*; irradiación *f*; **ir'ra·di·ant** luminoso, radiante.

ir·ra·di·ate [i'reidieit] *v/t. phys.*, 🜊 irradiar; iluminar(se de); *fig.* derramar; *v/i.* brillar; **ir·ra·di'a·tion** irradiación *f*.

ir·ra·tion·al [i'ræʃnl] □ irracional (*a.* 🜊); **ir·ra·tion·al·i·ty** [ˌʃə'næliti] irracionalidad *f*.

ir·re·claim·a·ble [iri'kleiməbl] □ irrecuperable; irredimible, incorregible; inservible.

ir·rec·on·cil·a·ble [i'rekənsailəbl] □ irreconciliable, intransigente.

ir·re·cov·er·a·ble [iri'kʌvərəbl] irrecuperable; incobrable.

ir·re·deem·a·ble [iri'diːməbl] irredimible; ♱ perpetuo, no reembolsable, no amortizable.

ir·re·duc·i·ble [iri'djuːsəbl] irreducible.

ir·ref·u·ta·ble [i'refjutəbl] □ irrefutable.

ir·reg·u·lar [i'regjulə] **1.** □ irregular; **2.** ✗ guerrillero *m*; **ir·reg·u·lar·i·ty** [ˌ'læriti] irregularidad *f*.

ir·rel·e·vance, **ir·rel·e·van·cy** [i'relivəns(i)] inconexión *f*; impertinencia *f*; inaplicabilidad *f*; **ir·rel·e·vant** □ fuera de propósito; impertinente; inaplicable; *be* ~ no hacer al caso.

ir·re·li·gion [iri'lidʒn] irreligión *f*; **ir·re·li·gious** [~dʒəs] □ irreligioso.

ir·re·me·di·a·ble [iri'mi:diəbl] □ irremediable.

ir·re·mis·si·ble [iri'misəbl] □ irremisible.

ir·re·mov·a·ble [iri'mu:vəbl] □ inamovible.

ir·rep·a·ra·ble [i'repərəbl] □ irreparable.

ir·re·place·a·ble [iri'pleisəbl] insustituible, irreemplazable.

ir·re·press·i·ble [iri'presəbl] indomable; incorregible, incontrolable.

ir·re·proach·a·ble [iri'prout∫əbl] □ irreprochable.

ir·re·sist·i·bil·i·ty ['irizistə'biliti] lo irresistible; invencibilidad *f*; **ir·re·'sist·i·ble** □ irresistible.

ir·res·o·lute [i'rezəlu:t] □ irresoluto, irresuelto, indeciso; **ir'res·o·lute·ness**, **ir·res·o'lu·tion** irresolución *f*, indecisión *f*.

ir·re·spec·tive [iris'pektiv] □: ~ *of* aparte de, prescindiendo de, sin consideración a.

ir·re·spon·si·bil·i·ty ['irispɔnsə'biliti] irresponsabilidad *f*; **ir·re'spon·si·ble** □ irresponsable.

ir·re·triev·a·ble [iri'tri:vəbl] irrecuperable, irreparable.

ir·rev·er·ence [i'revərəns] irreverencia *f*; **ir'rev·er·ent** □ irreverente.

ir·re·vers·i·ble [iri'və:səbl] irreversible; irrevocable.

ir·rev·o·ca·bil·i·ty [irevəkə'biliti] irrevocabilidad *f*; **ir'rev·o·ca·ble** □ irrevocable.

ir·ri·gate ['irigeit] regar; irrigar (*a.* 🖋); **ir·ri'ga·tion** riego *m*; irrigación *f*; ~ *channel* acequia *f*, canal *m* de riego.

ir·ri·ta·bil·i·ty [iritə'biliti] irritabilidad *f*; **ir·ri·ta·ble** □ irritable; irascible; nervioso; **'ir·ri·tant** irritante *adj. a. su. m*; **ir·ri·tate** ['~teit] irritar; exasperar; azuzar; molestar; **'ir·ri·tat·ing** □ irritador, irritante; enojoso; molesto; **ir·ri'ta·tion** irritación *f*.

ir·rup·tion [i'rʌp∫n] irrupción *f*.

is [iz] es; está (*v. be*).

i·sin·glass ['aiziŋglɑ:s] cola *f* de pescado.

Is·lam ['izlɑ:m] islam *m*; **Is·lam·ic** [iz'læmik] islámico.

is·land ['ailənd] **1.** isla *f*; refugio *m* *in road*; **2.** isleño; **'is·land·er** isleño (a *f*) *m*.

isle [ail] *mst poet.* isla *f*; **is·let** ['ailit] isleta *f*; islote *m*.

ism [izm] F *mst contp.* ismo *m*; teoría *f*; sistema *m*.

isn't ['iznt] = *is not*.

i·so... ['aisou] iso...; **'~·bar** [~bɑ:] isobara *f*.

i·so·late ['aisəleit] aislar; apartar; **i·so'la·tion** aislamiento *m*, apartamiento *m*; ~ *hospital* hospital *m* de aislamiento (*or* de contagiosos); **i·so'la·tion·ism** aislacionismo *m*; **i·so'la·tion·ist** aislacionista *adj. a. su. m*, aislamentista *adj. a. su. m*.

i·sos·ce·les [ai'sɔsəli:z] isósceles.

i·so·therm ['aisouθə:m] isoterma *f*.

i·so·tope ['aisoutoup] isótopo *m*.

Is·rael·i [iz'reili] israelí *adj. a. su. m/f*.

Is·ra·el·ite ['izriəlait] israelita *adj. a. su. m/f*.

is·sue ['isju:, 'i∫u:] **1.** salida *f*; distribución *f*; ✠ emisión *f* of *coins*, *shares*, *stamps*; *publishing*: edición *f*, impresión *f*, tirada *f*; (*copy*) número *m*, entrega *f*; (*question*) cuestión *f*, problema *m*, punto *m* en disputa; (*outcome*) resultado *m*, consecuencia *f*, éxito *m*; (*offspring*) sucesión *f*, prole *f*; 🖋 flujo *m*; *at* ~ en disputa, en cuestión; *without* ~ sin sucesión; *side* ~ cuestión *f* secundaria; *evade the* ~ esquivar la pregunta; *face the* ~ afrontar la situación; *force the* ~ forzar una decisión; *join* (*or take*) ~ *with* oponer; llevar la contraria a; no estar de acuerdo con; disputar con; **2.** *v/t.* distribuir; expedir; ✠ emitir; poner en circulación; publicar; *decree* promulgar; *v/i.* salir; brotar; provenir; emanar; fluir; ~ *in* dar por resultado; **3.** 🔩 reglamentario; **'is·sue·less** sin sucesión.

isth·mus ['isməs] istmo *m*.

it [it] **1.** (*subject, but gen. omitted*) él, ella, ello; *acc.* lo, la; *dat.* le; *after prp.* él, ella, ello; ~ *is I* (*or* F ~'s *me*) soy yo; ~ *is raining* llueve; ~ *is said that* se dice que; ~ *is true that* es verdad que; ~ *is 2 o'clock* son las 2; F *how goes* (*or is*) ⌒? ¿qué tal?; *that's* ⌒ eso es; ya está; está bien; F *this is* ⌒ ya llegó la hora; **2.** F aquél *m*; atracción *f* sexual; lo necesario; (= *Italian*) vermut *m* italiano; **3.** F *pred.*: *you're* ⌒ *children's games*: tú te quedas; *he thinks he's* ⌒ se da mucho tono.

I·tal·ian [i'tæljən] **1.** italiano *adj. a. su. m* (a *f*); **2.** (*language*) italiano *m*.

i·tal·ic [i'tælik] **1.** (*a.* ⌒) itálico; **2.** *typ. mst* ⌒s (letra *f*) bastardilla *f*; *in* ⌒s en bastardilla; **i·tal·i·cize** [i'tælisaiz] poner en (letra) bastardilla; subrayar.

itch [itʃ] **1.** ⚕ sarna *f*; picazón *f*; comezón *f*, prurito *m* (*a. fig.* for por, to de); **2.** picar; sentir comezón; *my arm* ⌒es me pica el brazo; ⌒ *to* sentir comezón (*or* prurito) de, rabiar por; '**itch·ing** prurito *m*, comezón *f* (*a. fig.*); *have an* ⌒ *palm* ser codicioso; '⌒-'**pow·der** polvos *m*/*pl.* de 'pica-pica'; '**itch·y** picante; sarnoso.

i·tem ['aitem] **1.** ítem *m*, artículo *m*; ☩ partida *f*; número *m in pro-gramme*; (*newspaper*) noticia *f*, suelto *m*; detalle *m*; **2.** *adv.* ítem; **i·tem·ize** ['aitəmaiz] detallar, especificar.

it·er·ate ['itəreit] iterar; **it·er'a·tion** iteración *f*; **it·er·a·tive** ['itərətiv] ⫶ iterativo.

i·tin·er·ant [i'tinərənt] ambulante, errante; **i·tin·er·ar·y** [ai'tinərəri] **1.** itinerario *m*; ruta *f*; guía *f*; **2.** itinerario; **i·tin·er·ate** [i'tinəreit] viajar; seguir un itinerario.

its [its] **1.** su(s); **2.** *pron.* (el) suyo, (la) suya *etc.*

it's [its] = *it is*, *it has*.

it·self [it'self] (*subject*) él mismo, ella misma, ello mismo; *acc.*, *dat.* se; (*after prp.*) sí (mismo [a]).

I've [aiv] = *I have*.

i·vo·ry ['aivəri] **1.** marfil *m*; *sl. ivories pl.* teclas *f*/*pl.* de piano; bolas *f*/*pl.* de billar; dientes *m*/*pl.*; **2.** de marfil; *poet.* ebúrneo.

i·vy ['aivi] hiedra *f*.

J

jab [dʒæb] **1.** (*poke*) hurgonazo *m*; (*prick*) pinchazo *m*, piquete *m*; (*with elbow*) codazo *m*; *boxing*: golpe *m* rápido (dado sin extender el brazo); **2.** hurgonear; pinchar; clavar; dar un codazo a; golpear.

jab·ber ['dʒæbə] **1.** (*a. ~ing*) jerigonza *f*; farfulla *f*, chapurreo *m*; **2.** farfullar, chapurrear; parlotear.

jack [dʒæk] **1.** ⊕, *mot.* gato *m*; ⚡ enchufe *m* hembra; (*p.*) hombre *m*, mozo *m*; ⚓ marinero *m*; *cards*: sota *f*; *bowls*: boliche *m*; *zo.* macho *m*; *ichth.* lucio *m* (joven); ⚓ bandera *f* de proa; torno *m* de asador; sacabotas *m* (*a. boot ~*); **2.**: *~ up* alzar con el gato; *esp. Am. price* subir, aumentar.

jack·al ['dʒækɔ:l] *zo.* chacal *m*; *fig.* paniaguado *m*.

jack·a·napes ['dʒækəneips] mequetrefe *m*; 'jack·ass burro *m* (*a. fig.*); 'jack·boots botas *f/pl.* fuertes; 'jack·daw grajilla *f*.

jack·et ['dʒækit] chaqueta *f*, americana *f*; saco *m S.Am.*; cubierta *f*; envoltura *f*; ⊕ camisa *f*, chaqueta *f*; (*book-*) sobrecubierta *f*, camisa *f*; *potatoes in their ~s* patatas *f/pl.* enteras (*or* con su piel).

jack...: '~-in-of·fice mandarín *m*; funcionario *m* engreído e impertinente; '~-in-the-box caja *f* sorpresa; '~-knife navaja *f*; ~ *dive* salto *m* de la carpa; '~-of-'all-trades factótum *m*; hombre *m* de muchos oficios (*and master of none* y maestro de ninguno); '~-of-'all-work factótum *m*; '~o'-lan·tern fuego *m* fatuo; '~-plane garlopa *f*; '~-pot *cards*: bote *m*; premio *m* gordo; *mst Am.* F hit the ~ tener mucha suerte; dar en el blanco.

Jac·o·be·an [dʒækə'bi:ən] de la época de Jacobo I; **Jac·o·bin** ['dʒækəbin] jacobino *adj. a. su. m* (a *f*); **Jac·o·bite** ['~bait] jacobita *adj. a. su. m/f*.

jade¹ [dʒeid] **1.** rocín *m*; *contp.* mujerzuela *f*, picarona *f*; mozuela *f*; **2.** cansar, rendir; saciar.

jade² [~] *min.* jade *m*.

jag [dʒæg] **1.** diente *m*; púa *f*; mella *f*; (*tear*) siete *m*; *sl.* turca *f*, juerga *f*; **2.** dentar; mellar; rasgar; **jag·ged** ['~id], 'jag·gy dentado, desigual, mellado; áspero; rasgado (en sietes); *sl.* borracho.

ja·gu·ar ['dʒægjuə] jaguar *m*.

jail [dʒeil] **1.** cárcel *f*; **2.** encarcelar; '~-bird presidiario *m*; malhechor *m*. **jail·er** ['dʒeilə] carcelero *m*.

ja·lop·(p)y [dʒə'lɔpi] *esp. Am.* F *mot.*, ⚡ cacharro *m*, armatoste *m*.

jam¹ [dʒæm] **1.** *approx.* mermelada *f*, confitura *f*, compota *f*; F *and ~ on it* y un jamón con chorreras; **2.** hacer mermelada de.

jam² [~] **1.** apiñadura *f*; (*stoppage*) atasc(amient)o *m*; agolpamiento *m of people*; *sl.* aprieto *m*, lío *m*; *traffic ~* aglomeración *f* de tráfico, ensalada *f*; F ~ *session* concierto *m* improvisado de jazz; **2.** apiñar(se); apretar(se); atascar(se); *radio*: interferir; ~ *on brakes* echar (*or* poner) con violencia; *hat* encasquetar(se).

Ja·mai·ca [dʒə'meikə] (~ *rum*) ron *m* de Jamaica; **Ja·mai·can** [~kən] jamaicano *adj. a. su. m* (a *f*).

jamb [dʒæm] jamba *f*.

jam·bo·ree [dʒæmbə'ri:] F franchela *f*, juerga *f*; congreso *m* de (niños) exploradores.

jam·jar ['dʒæmdʒɑ:] pote *m* para mermelada.

jan·gle ['dʒæŋgl] **1.** sonido *m* discordante, cencerreo *m*; **2.** cencerrear, (hacer) sonar de manera discordante; 'jan·gling discordante, estridente, desapacible. [serje *m*.]

jan·i·tor ['dʒænitə] portero *m*, con-] **Jan·u·ar·y** ['dʒænjuəri] enero *m*.

Jap [dʒæp] F japonés *adj. a. su. m* (-a *f*).

ja·pan [dʒə'pæn] **1.** laca *f* negra; charol *m*; obra *f* laqueada japonesa; **2.** barnizar con laca japonesa; charolar.

Jap·a·nese [dʒæpə'ni:z] **1.** japonés *adj. a. su. m* (-a *f*); the ~ *pl.* los japoneses; **2.** (*language*) japonés *m*.

jar¹ [dʒɑ:] tarro *m*; pote *m*; (*with handles*) jarra *f*; (*narrow-necked*) botija *f*; (*large*) tinaja *f*; Leyden ~ botella *f* de Leiden.

jar² [~] **1.** choque *m*, sacudida *f*; ruido *m* desapacible; sorpresa *f* desagradable; discordia *f*; **2.** chocar; sacudir; (hacer) vibrar; (*colours*) chillar; chirriar; ser discorde; ~ (*up*)on irritar, poner(le a una p.) los nervios en punta.

jar³ [~] F: on the ~ = ajar.

jar·gon ['dʒɑ:gən] jerigonza *f*; (*specialist*) jerga *f*; (*gibberish*) guirigay *m*.

jas·min(e) ['dʒæsmin] jazmín *m*.

jas·per ['dʒæspə] jaspe *m*.

jaun·dice ['dʒɔ:ndis] 🗡 ictericia *f*; **'jaun·diced** 🗡 ictérico; cetrino; *fig.* avinagrado, envidioso.

jaunt [dʒɔ:nt] **1.** caminata *f*, excursión *f*, paseo *m*; **2.** hacer una caminata, ir de excursión; **'jaun·ti·ness** viveza *f*, garbo *m*, soltura *f*; **'jaun·ty** □ garboso, airoso, ligero; vivaracho; de buen humor.

Jav·a·nese [dʒɑːvəˈniːz] javanés *adj. a. su. m* (-a *f*).

jave·lin ['dʒævlin] jabalina *f*; *throwing the* ~ lanzamiento *m* de jabalina.

jaw [dʒɔ:] **1.** quijada *f*, mandíbula *f*, maxilar *m*; *sl.* cháchara *f*, chismes *m/pl.*, charla *f*; ⊕ mordaza *f*, mandíbula *f*; ~s *pl.* boca *f*, garganta *f*; *fig.* garras *f/pl.*, fauces *f/pl.*; I hold your ~! ¡cállate la boca!; **2.** F *v/i.* chismear, charlar; *v/t.* regañar; '~-bone maxilar *m*, quijada *f*, mandíbula *f*; '~-break·er F trabalenguas *m*, palabra *f* kilométrica, terminacho *m* impronunciable.

jay [dʒei] *orn.* arrendajo *m*; F necio (a *f*) *m*; '~-walk·er peatón *m* imprudente.

jazz [dʒæz] **1.** jazz *m*; **2.** de jazz; **3.** *v/t.* sincopar; *v/i.* tocar (*or* bailar) el jazz; '~-'band orquesta *f* de jazz, jazz-band *m*; **'jazz·y** F sincopado; de colores chillones.

jeal·ous ['dʒeləs] □ celoso, envidioso; cuidadoso, vigilante; be ~ of a p. tener celos de una p.; **'jeal·ous·y** celos *m/pl.*; envidia *f*; (*care*) celo *m*.

jeans [dʒi:nz] *pl.* F pantalones *m/pl.* de pirata.

jeep [dʒi:p] jeep *m*.

jeer [dʒiə] **1.** mofa *f*, befa *f*, escarnio *m*; (*shout*) grito *m* de sarcasmo (*or* protesta *etc.*); **2.** mofarse (*at* de), befar; **'jeer·er** mofador (-a *f*) *m*; **'jeer·ing** □ mofador.

je·june [dʒi'dʒu:n] seco, árido; aburrido, insípido.

jel·ly ['dʒeli] **1.** jalea *f*, gelatina *f*; **2.** convertir(se) en jalea; '~-fish medusa *f*.

jem·my ['dʒemi] palanqueta *f*.

jeop·ard·ize ['dʒepədaiz] arriesgar, comprometer; **'jeop·ard·y** riesgo *m*, peligro *m*.

jer·e·mi·ad [dʒeri'maiæd] jeremiada *f*.

jerk [dʒə:k] **1.** tirón *m*, sacudida *f*, arranque *m*; espasmo *m* muscular; by (*or* in) ~s a sacudidas; *sl.* put a ~ in it menearse; F *physical* ~s ejercicios *m/pl.* físicos; **2.** *v/t.* sacudir; mover a tirones; arrojar; *Am. meat* atasajar; I ~ed it away from him se lo quité de una sacudida; *v/i.* sacudirse; avanzar a tirones.

jer·kin ['dʒə:kin] justillo *m*.

jerk·wa·ter ['dʒə:kwɔ:tə] *Am.* F de poca monta.

jerk·y ['dʒə:ki] □ espasmódico, desigual; que se mueve a tirones.

jer·ry ['dʒeri] F orinal *m*; F ♀ (soldado) alemán *m*.

jer·ry-build·ing ['dʒeribildiŋ] construcción *f* (barata y) defectuosa; **'jer·ry-built** mal construido, de pacotilla.

jer·sey ['dʒə:zi] jersey *m*.

jes·sa·mine ['dʒesəmin] jazmín *m*.

jest [dʒest] **1.** chanza *f*, broma *f*; (*esp. verbal*) chiste *m*; cosa *f* de risa; in ~ de guasa, en broma; **2.** bromear, chancear(se); **'jest·er** bufón *m*.

Jes·u·it ['dʒezjuit] jesuita *adj. a. su. m*; **Jes·u·it·ic, Jes·u·it·i·cal** □ jesuítico.

jet¹ [dʒet] *min.* azabache *m*.

jet² [~] **1.** chorro *m*, surtidor *m*; (*burner*) mechero *m*; ⊕, 🛩 *attr.* a reacción, a chorro; ~ engine reactor *m*, motor *m* a chorro; ~ plane avión *m* a reacción; ~ propulsion propulsión *f* por reacción (*or* a chorro); **2.** *v/t.* echar en chorro; *v/i.* chorrear.

jet-black ['dʒet'blæk] azabachado.

jet…: '~-'pow·ered, '~-pro'pelled a reacción.

jet·sam ['dʒetsəm] ⚓ echazón *f*; *fig.* persona *f* rechazada o maltratada por la sociedad.

jet·ti·son ['dʒetisn] 1. ⚓ echazón *f*; 2. ⚓ echar al mar; *fig.* desechar, librarse de.

jet·ty ['dʒeti] malecón *m*; muelle *m*; embarcadero *m*.

Jew [dʒuː] judío (a *f*) *m*; ~'s harp birimbao *m*.

jew·el ['dʒuːəl] 1 joya *f*; alhaja *f* (*a. fig.*); piedra *f* preciosa; rubí *m* *of watch*; 2. enjoyar; '~-'case joyero *m*; 'jew·el·led *watch* con rubíes; 'jew·el·(l)er joyero *m*; ~'s (*shop*) joyería *f*; 'jew·el·ry, 'jew·el·ler·y joyas *f*/*pl.*; ✝ joyería *f*.

Jew·ess ['dʒuːis] judía *f*; 'Jew·ish judío; Jew·ry ['dʒuəri] judería *f*, los judíos *m*/*pl.*

jib [dʒib] 1. ⚓ foque *m*; ⊕ aguilón *m*; *fig. the cut of his* ~ su pergeño *m*; 2. (*horse*) plantarse; resistirse, negarse (*at* a); 'jib-'boom botalón *m* de foque. [*gibe*.⏐

jibe [dʒaib] *Am.* F concordar; *v.*⏐

jif·fy ['dʒifi] F instante *m*; *in a* ~ en un santiamén.

jig [dʒig] 1. jiga *f*; ⊕ plantilla *f* (de guía); 2. bailar (la jiga); mover(se) a saltitos.

jig·ger ['dʒigə] *sl.* chisme *m*, dispositivo *m*.

jig·gered ['dʒigəd] F rendido; *I'm* ~ *if* ... que me cuelguen si ...

jig-saw ['dʒigsɔː] sierra *f* de vaivén; ~ *puzzle* rompecabezas *m*.

jilt [dʒilt] dar calabazas a, dejar plantado.

jim-jams ['dʒimdʒæmz] *sl.* delirium *m* tremens; *it gives me the* ~ me horripila.

jim·my ['dʒimi] *Am.* palanqueta *f*.

jin·gle ['dʒiŋgl] 1. (re)tintín *m*, cascabeleo *m*; rima *f* infantil; 2. *v/t.* hacer sonar; *v/i.* cascabelear, tintinear.

jin·go ['dʒiŋgou] patriotero (a *f*) *m*, jingoísta *m*/*f*; F *by* ~! ¡caramba!; 'jin·go·ism jingoísmo *m*, patriotería *f*.

jinks [dʒiŋks]: *high* ~*s pl.* jolgorio *m*; regocijo *m*.

jinx [~] *Am. sl.* cenizo *m*, pájaro *m* de mal agüero, duendecillo *m*.

jit·ney ['dʒitni] *Am. sl. moneda de 5 centavos*; coche *m* de pasaje.

jit·ter ['dʒitə] *sl.* 1. temblar, estre-

mecerse; bailar; 2. ~*s pl.* inquietud *f*, nerviosidad *f*; ~·bug ['~bʌg] *sl.* (aficionado [a *f*] *m* a) bailar el jazz; 'jit·ter·y *sl.* agitado, nervioso, inquieto.

jiu-jit·su [dʒuː'dʒitsuː] jiu-jitsu *m*.

jive [dʒaiv] *sl.* (modo *m* de) bailar el jazz.

job [dʒɔb] 1. tarea *f*, quehacer *m*; labor *m*; trabajo *m*; (*post*) empleo *m*, puesto *m*; (*piece-work, contract*) destajo *m*; F asunto *m*; F cosa *f* difícil, faena *f*; *sl.* crimen *m*, robo *m*; *by the* ~ a destajo; *it's a good* ~ (*that*) menos mal (que); *make a* (*good*) ~ *of it* hacerlo bien; *be on the* ~ estar trabajando; *sl.* estar al pie; *be out of a* ~ estar sin trabajo; *a bad* ~ mala situación *f*, caso *m* desahuciado; *odd* ~ tarea *f* suelta; *odd* ~ *man* hombre *m* que hace de todo; ~ *lot* ✝ lote *m* suelto de mercancías, saldo *m*; ~ *work typ.* remiendo *m*; 2. alquilar; ceder por contrato; ✝ comprar y vender como corredor; ✝ especular; trabajar a destajo.

job·ber ['dʒɔbə] destajista *m*/*f*; ✝ agiotista *m*; ✝ corredor *m*; ✝ intermediario *m*; *b.s.* chanchullero *m*; 'job·ber·y chanchullos *m*/*pl.*; ✝ agiotaje *m*; *piece of* ~ chanchullo *m*; 'job·bing 1. ✝ agiotaje *m*; ✝ comercio *m* de intermediario; trabajo *m* a destajo; 2. que trabaja a destajo.

jock·ey ['dʒɔki] 1. jockey *m*; 2. *v/t.* embaucar (*into* para que); *v/i.* maniobrar (*for* para obtener).

jo·cose [dʒə'kous] □, **joc·u·lar** ['dʒɔkjulə] □ jocoso.

joc·und ['dʒɔkənd] jocundo.

jog [dʒɔg] 1. empujoncito *m*, codazo *m*, sacudimiento *m* (ligero); trote *m* corto, paso *m* lento; *fig.* estímulo *m*; 2. *v/t.* empujar (*or* sacudir) levemente; *fig.* estimular; *memory* refrescar; *v/i.* (*mst* ~ *along*, ~ *on*) andar a trote corto, avanzar despacio.

jog·gle ['dʒɔgl] 1. traqueo *m*, sacudimiento *m*; ⊕ ensambladura *f* dentada; 2. traquear, sacudir.

jog-trot ['dʒɔg'trɔt] trote *m* corto; *fig.* rutina *f*.

john·ny ['dʒɔni] F tipo *m*, chico *m*; currutaco *m*; *Am.* ~ *cake* pan *m* de maíz.

join [dʒɔin] 1. juntura *f*, costura *f*; 2. *v/t.* unir, juntar; ⊕ ensamblar, acoplar; *lines* empalmar; reunirse con, unirse a; *society* ingresar en, hacerse socio de; ✂ alistarse en; ~ *battle* trabar batalla; ~ *company* (*with*) reunirse (con); asociarse (con); F ~ *forces* juntar meriendas; ~ *hands* darse las manos; ~ *one's regiment* (*ship*) incorporarse a su regimiento (barco); ~ *a p. in* acompañar a una p. en; *v/i.* juntarse, unirse; (*lines*) empalmar; ~ *in* tomar parte (en), participar (en); ~ *up* alistarse; ~ (*up*) *with* asociarse con, acompañar.

join·er ['dʒɔinə] carpintero *m* (de blanco); ensamblador *m*; *Am.* F persona *f* que se hace miembro de muchas asociaciones; **'join·er·y** carpintería *f*.

joint [dʒɔint] **1.** junt(ur)a *f*; *anat.* articulación *f*, coyuntura *f*; ⚘ nudo *m*; ⚙ empalme *m*; ⊕ ensambladura *f*; (*hinge*) bisagra *f*; cuarto *m of meat*; *sl.* garito *m*; *sl.* fonducho *m*; *out of* ~ descoyuntado; *fig.* fuera de quicio; *put out of* ~ descoyuntar; *put a p.'s nose out of* ~ suplantar a una p.; **2.** □ (en) común; mutuo; colectivo; conjunto; combinado; (*in compounds*) co...; ~ *account* cuenta *f* indistinta; ~ *communiqué* comunicado *m* conjunto; ~ *heir* coheredero (a *f*) *m*; ~ *responsibility* responsabilidad *f* solidaria; ~ *stock* fondo *m* social; **3.** juntar, unir; ⊕ ensamblar; articular; **'joint·ed** articulado; ⚘ nudoso; **'joint-stock 'com·pa·ny** sociedad *f* anónima.

joist [dʒɔist] vig(uet)a *f*.

joke [dʒouk] **1.** broma *f*, chanza *f*; (*esp. verbal*) chiste *m*; (*laughing matter*) cosa *f* de reír; (*p.*) hazmerreír *m*; *play a* ~ (*on*) gastar una broma (a); *tell a* ~ contar un chiste; **2.** bromear, chancear(se); decir chistes; hablar en broma; F chunguear; **'jok·er** bromista *m/f*; guasón (-a *f*) *m*; *cards*: comodín *m*; *Am.* escapatoria *f*, cláusula *f* que permite evadir un contrato.

jol·li·fi·ca·tion [dʒɔlifi'keiʃn] regocijo *m*, alborozo *m*; festividades *f/pl.*; **'jol·li·ty** alegría *f*, regocijo *m*; diversión *f*.

jol·ly ['dʒɔli] **1.** □ alegre, regocijado; jovial; divertido; F achispado; F agradable, estupendo; **2.** *adv.* F muy; ~ *well* de lo lindo; *you've* ~

well got to no tienes más remedio que; **3.** F (*a.* ~ *along*) engatusar, seguir el humor a.

jol·ly-boat ['dʒɔlibout] esquife *m*.

jolt [dʒoult] **1.** sacudida *f*; choque *m*; (*a.* ~*ing*) traque(te)o *m*; **2.** sacudir; traque(te)ar; **'jolt·y** desigual; que traquetea.

jon·quil ['dʒɔŋkwil] junquillo *m*.

josh [dʒɔʃ] *Am. sl.* **1.** broma *f*; **2.** burlarse de, tomar el pelo a.

jos·ser ['dʒɔsə] *sl.* tipo *m*, tío *m*.

jos·tle ['dʒɔsl] **1.** empujón *m*, empellón *m*, codazo *m*; **2.** empujar, dar empellones; codear.

jot [dʒɔt] **1.** jota *f*, pizca *f*; *I don't care a* ~ (*about*) no se me da un bledo (de); **2.**: ~ *down* apuntar; **'jot·ter** taco *m* para notas; **'jot·ting** apunte *m*.

jour·nal ['dʒə:nl] (✝ libro *m*) diario *m* (⚓ de navegación); (*newspaper*) periódico *m*; (*review*) revista *f*; ⊕ gorrón *m*, mangueta *f*; '~-'**bear·ing**, '~-'**box** ⊕ cojinete *m*; ⚙ caja *f* de grasas; **jour·nal·ese** ['dʒə:nə'li:z] lenguaje *m* periodístico; **'jour·nal·ism** periodismo *m*; **'jour·nal·ist** periodista *m/f*; **jour·nal·is·tic** □ periodístico.

jour·ney ['dʒə:ni] **1.** viaje *m*; **2.** viajar; '~-**man** oficial *m*.

joust [dʒaust] **1.** justa *f*, torneo *m*; **2.** justar.

jo·vi·al ['dʒouviəl] □ jovial; **jo·vi·al·i·ty** [~'æliti] jovialidad *f*.

jowl [dʒaul] quijada *f*; carrillo *m*; papada *f of cattle*; *cheek by* ~ lado a lado.

joy [dʒɔi] alegría *f*, júbilo *m*, regocijo *m*; deleite *m*; *a* ~ *to the eye* un gozo para la retina; **joy·ful** ['~ful] □ alegre, regocijado; **'joy·ful·ness** alegría *f*; **'joy·less** □ sin alegría, triste; deprimente; **'joy·ous** □ alegre; **'joy-ride** F excursión *f* (desautorizada) en coche *etc.*; **'joy-stick** ⚹ *sl.* palanca *f* de gobierno.

ju·bi·lant ['dʒu:bilənt] □ jubiloso; triunfante; **ju·bi·la·tion** júbilo *m*; **ju·bi·lee** ['~li:] *hist., eccl.* jubileo *m*; quincuagésimo aniversario *m*; (*rejoicing*) júbilo *m*.

Ju·da·ism ['dʒu:deiizm] judaísmo *m*.

judge [dʒʌdʒ] **1.** juez *m*; *fig.* conocedor (-a *f*) *m*; *sport*: árbitro *m*; *be no* ~ *of* no entender de; **2.** juzgar; considerar; opinar; *judging by* a juzgar por; ~ by appearances juzgar sobre apariencias; '~-'ad·vo·cate ✕ auditor m de guerra.

judg(e)·ment ['dʒʌdʒmənt] juicio m; ⚖ sentencia f, fallo m; entendimiento m, discernimiento m; opinión f; in my ~ a mi parecer; pronounce ~ pronunciar sentencia (on en, sobre); sit in ~ on juzgar; to the best of my ~ según mi leal saber y entender; ♀ Day día m del juicio (final); ~ seat tribunal m.

ju·di·ca·ture ['dʒuːdikətʃə] judicatura f.

ju·di·cial [dʒuːˈdiʃl] □ judicial; juicioso; ~ murder asesinato m legal.

ju·di·cious [dʒuːˈdiʃəs] □ juicioso, sensato.

jug [dʒʌg] 1. jarro m; pote m; sl. chirona f; 2. sl. encarcelar; ~ged hare liebre f en estofado.

Jug·ger·naut ['dʒʌɡənɔːt] fig. monstruo m destructor de los hombres.

jug·gins ['dʒʌɡinz] F bobo m, inocentón m.

jug·gle ['dʒʌɡl] 1. juego m de manos; b.s. engaño m; 2. v/t. escamotear; b.s. falsear; ~ a p. out of s.t. quitar algo a una p. por maña; v/i. hacer juegos malabares (or de manos); b.s. hacer trampas; ~ with fig. arreglar de otro modo; b. s. falsear; '**jug·gler** malabarista m/f, jugador (-a f) m de manos; b.s. tramposo (a f) m; † juglar m; '**jug·gler·y** juegos m/pl. malabares (or de manos); b.s. trampas f/pl.; fraude m.

Ju·go·slav ['juːɡouˈslɑːv] yugo(e)slavo adj. a. su. m (a f).

jug·u·lar ['dʒʌɡjulə] yugular; ~ vein vena f yugular.

juice [dʒuːs] (esp. fruit-) zumo m; jugo m; mot. sl. gasolina f; ⚡ sl. corriente f; **juic·i·ness** ['~inis] jugosidad f; '**juic·y** □ zumoso, jugoso, F picante, sabroso. [pastilla f.\

ju·jube ['dʒuːdʒuːb] ♣ azufaifa f;\

ju·jut·su [dʒuːˈdʒutsuː] jiu-jitsu m.

juke-box ['dʒuːkbɔks] tocadiscos m (tragaperras).

ju·lep ['dʒuːlep] julepe m.

Ju·ly [dʒuːˈlai] julio m.

jum·ble ['dʒʌmbl] 1. revoltijo m; confusión f; mezcolanza f; 2. mezclar, emburujar; confundir; '~-sale venta f de objetos usados.

jum·bly ['dʒʌmbli] revuelto, emburujado.

jum·bo ['dʒʌmbou] F elefante m; Am. attr. enorme.

jump [dʒʌmp] 1. salto m, brinco m; Am. F get (have) the ~ on llevar la ventaja a; give a ~ dar un salto; 2. v/t. saltar; horse hacer saltar; F ~ the gun madrugar; F ~ the queue salirse de su turno; ~ the rails descarrilar; ~ ship desertar del buque; v/i. saltar; brincar; dar saltos; bailar; ✕ lanzarse; fig. ~ at lanzarse sobre, apresurarse a aprovechar; ~ down bajar de un salto; ~ on (board) saltar a; F regañar, poner verde; ~ over saltar (por); ~ to conclusions juzgar al (buen) tuntún; '**jump·er** saltador (-a f) m; (dress) suéter m, jersey m; blusa f; ✕ barrena f de percusión; ⚡ hilo m de cierre; '**jump·ing-board** trampolín m; '**jump·ing-'off ground** fig. trampolín m; ✕ base f avanzada; '**jump·y** saltón; fig. asustadizo, nervioso.

junc·tion ['dʒʌŋkʃn] juntura f, unión f; conexión f; confluencia f of rivers; 🚂 (estación f de) empalme m; ⚡ ~ box caja f de empalmes; **junc·ture** ['~tʃə] coyuntura f; (critical) trance m; 🔩 jun-\
June [dʒuːn] junio m. [tura f.\

jun·gle ['dʒʌŋgl] jungla f; selva f; fig. maraña f.

jun·ior ['dʒuːnjə] 1. menor, más joven; más nuevo; subalterno; juvenil; Paul Jones, ~ Paul Jones, hijo; Am. ~ high school escuela f de bachillerato elemental; ~ partner socio m menos antiguo; 2. menor m/f; joven m/f; hijo m; alumno (a f) m de 8 a 11 años; Am. univ. estudiante m/f de penúltimo año; he is my ~ by 3 years, he is 3 years my ~ es 3 años más joven que yo, le llevo 3 años.

ju·ni·per ['dʒuːnipə] enebro m.

junk[1] [dʒʌŋk] ♣ junco m.

junk[2] [~] F trastos m/pl. viejos; (iron) chatarra f; (cheap goods) baratijas f/pl.; fig. disparates m/pl.; ⚓ (salt meat) carnaje m; ~ shop tienda f de trastos viejos; ~ yard parque m de desechos.

jun·ket ['dʒʌŋkit] 1. dulce m de leche cuajada; (a. ~ing) franca·chela f, festividades f/pl.; Am. jira f; 2. festejar; banquetear; Am. ir de jira.

jun·ta ['dʒʌntə] junta *f*; camarilla *f*; **jun·to** ['ʌtou] camarilla *f*.

ju·rid·i·cal [dʒuə'ridikl] □ jurídico.

ju·ris·dic·tion [dʒuəris'dikʃn] jurisdicción *f*; **ju·ris·pru·dence** ['ʌpru:dəns] jurisprudencia *f*.

ju·rist ['dʒuərist] jurista *m*.

ju·ror ['dʒuərə] (miembro *m* de un) jurado *m*.

ju·ry ['dʒuəri] jurado *m*; **'ju·ry-box** tribuna *f* del jurado; **'ju·ry·man** (miembro *m* de un) jurado *m*.

ju·ry-mast ['dʒuərimɑ:st] bandola *f*.

just [dʒʌst] **1.** *adj.* □ justo; recto; exacto; **2.** *adv.* justamente, exactamente, ni más ni menos; precisamente, sólo, no más; apenas; recientemente, recién; en el (*or* este) mismo instante; F absolutamente, completamente; *I have* (*had*) ~ *finished it* acabo (acababa) de acabarlo; ~ *appointed* recién nombrado; ~ *received* acabado de recibir; *he was* ~ *going* estaba a punto de marchar; ~ *imagine!* ¡imagínese!!; ~ *let me see!* ¡pues a ver!; *it's* ~ *perfect!* ¡es absolutamente perfecto!; ~ *as* en el momento en que; (tal) como; ~ *as you wish* como Vd. quiera; ~ *by* muy cerca (de); *v. now*.

jus·tice ['dʒʌstis] justicia *f*; juez *m*; ♀ *of the Peace approx.* juez *m* de paz; *Lord Chief* ♀ Justicia *m* Mayor; *court of* ~ tribunal *m* de justicia; *do* ~ *to p.* hacer justicia a, tratar debidamente; *meal* hacer los debidos honores a; *do oneself* ~ quedar bien.

jus·ti·fi·a·ble ['dʒʌstifaiəbl] justificable; **'jus·ti·fi·a·bly** con razón, con justicia.

jus·ti·fi·ca·tion [dʒʌstifi'keiʃn] justificación *f*.

jus·ti·fy ['dʒʌstifai] justificar (*a. typ.*); dar motivo para; ~ *o.s.* sincerarse; acreditarse; *be justified in* tener motivo para.

just·ly ['dʒʌstli] justamente, con justicia; con derecho; debidamente; exactamente.

just·ness ['dʒʌstnis] justicia *f*; rectitud *f*; exactitud *f*.

jut [dʒʌt] **1.** saliente *m*, saledizo *m*; **2.** (*a.* ~ *out*) sobresalir, resaltar.

Jute¹ [dʒu:t] juto (*a f*) *m*.

jute² [ʌ] yute *m*.

ju·ve·nile ['dʒu:vənail] **1.** joven *m/f*; niño (*a f*) *m*; **2.** juvenil; de (*or* para) niños (*or* menores); ♀ *Court* tribunal *m* juvenil; ~ *delinquency* delincuencia *f* de menores; ~ *delinquent* delincuente *m/f* juvenil; ~ *lead thea.* galán *m* joven.

jux·ta·pose [dʒʌkstə'pouz] yuxtaponer; **jux·ta·po·si·tion** [ʌpə'ziʃn] yuxtaposición *f*.

K

Kaf·(f)ir ['kæfə] cafre *adj. a. su.*
m/f.
kale [keil] col *f* (rizada); *Am. sl.*
guita *f.*
ka·lei·do·scope [kə'laidəskoup] ca·
l(e)idoscopio *m*; *fig.* escena *f* ani·
mada y variadísima.
kan·ga·roo [kæŋgə'ru:] canguro *m.*
ka·o·lin ['keiəlin] caolín *m.*
kedge [kedʒ] anclote *m.*
keel [ki:l] **1.** ⚓, *orn.,* ♕ quilla *f*;
on an even ~ ⚓ en iguales calados;
en equilibrio (*a. fig.*); *fig.* derecho,
estable; **2.**: ~ *over* ⚓ dar de quilla;
volcar(se); F caerse patas arriba;
'**keeled** *zo.,* ♕ carinado; **keel·haul**
['~hɔ:l] castigar pasando por debajo
de la quilla.
keen [ki:n] □ agudo; *edge* afilado;
wind penetrante; sutil; perspicaz;
mordaz; *price* bajo; *emotion* vivo,
ardiente, sentido; *appetite* bueno;
p. entusiasta, celoso; ansioso; F be
~ *on th.* ser muy aficionado a; *p.*
estar prendado de; *I'm not very* ~
on him no es santo de mi devoción;
be ~ *to inf.* ansiar *inf.*, tener vivo
deseo de *inf.*; **~·edged** ['~edʒd]
cortante, afilado; '**keen·ness** agu·
deza *f*; perspicacia *f*; viveza *f*;
entusiasmo *m*; afición *f*; ansia *f.*
keep [ki:p] **1.** mantenimiento *m*;
subsistencia *f*; comida *f*; *hist.* to·
rreón *m*, torre *f* del homenaje; F *for*
~*s* para siempre, para guardar; *earn*
one's ~ estar (*or* trabajar) por la co·
mida; producir (*or* trabajar) ba·
stante; **2.** [*irr.*] *v/t.* guardar; tener
guardado; (re)tener; reservar; (*not*
give back) quedarse con; preser·
var; conservar; mantener; defen·
der; cuidar, custodiar; (*delay a p.*)
detener, entretener; *promise* cum·
plir; *house, accounts* llevar; *position*
mantenerse (firme) en; *hotel, shop*
dirigir; *law* observar; ~ *a p. waiting*
hacer esperar a una p.; ~ *away*
mantener a distancia; no dejar
acercarse; ~ *back* retener; ocultar;
no dejar avanzar; reprimir; ~ *by*
guardar (para un apuro); ~ *down*

no dejar subir; sujetar; opri·
mir; dominar; limitar; *price* mante·
ner bajo; ~ *a p. from ger.* no dejar
inf. a una p.; ~ *s.t. from a p.* ocultar
algo a una p.; ~ *in p.* no dejar salir,
tener encerrado; *feelings* contener;
fire mantener encendido; ~ *off* tener
a raya; cerrar el paso a; no dejar
penetrar; ~ *on* no quitarse; tener
puesto (*or* encendido *etc.*); ~ *out*
excluir; no dejar entrar (*or* pene·
trar); ~ *s.t. to o.s.* guardar algo en
secreto; ~ *together* mantener unido;
~ *under* sujetar; tener oprimido; ~
up mantener, conservar; sostener;
p. hacer trasnochar; ~ *it up* no cejar;
3. [*irr.*] *v/i.* quedar(se); permane·
cer; seguir, continuar; mantenerse;
conservarse; estar(se); ~ *doing* se·
guir haciendo, continuar haciendo;
how are you ~*ing*? ¿cómo estás? ~
still! ¡estáte quieto!; ~ *well* con·
servarse bien; ~ *at* no cejar en;
insistir en; F ~ *at it* machacar; ~
away mantenerse alejado (*from place*
de); no dejarse ver; abstenerse
(*from th.* de); no meterse (*from p.*
con); ~ *back* hacerse a un lado; ~
clear of mantenerse libre de; no
meterse con; ~ *from* guardarse de,
abstenerse de; F ~ *in with* cultivar,
mantener buenas relaciones con;
~ *off* mantenerse a distancia; *grass*
no pisar; no tocar; *if the rain*
~*s off* si no llueve; ~ *on* continuar
(*with* con); seguir (*doing* haciendo);
~ *out!* ¡prohibida la entrada!; ~ *out*
of place no entrar en; *affair* no
meterse en; *trouble* evitar; ~ *to*
direction llevar; limitarse a; cum·
plir con; ~ *to one's bed* guardar
(la) cama; ~ *together* mantenerse
unidos; ~ *up* continuar; no reza·
garse; ~ *up with* ir al paso de; emu·
lar; proseguir; ~ *with* seguir acom·
pañando.
keep·er ['ki:pə] guarda *m*; custodio
m; (*park- etc.*) guardián (-a *f*) *m*;
(*owner*) dueño (a *f*) *m*; (*a. game*~)
guardabosques *m*; archivero *m*;
'**keep·ing** custodia *f*; guarda *f*;

protección *f*; mantenimiento *m*; conservación *f*; observación *f*; celebración *f*; *in* ~ *with* de acuerdo con, en armonía con; *out of* ~ *with* en desacuerdo con; **keep·sake** ['∼seik] recuerdo *m*.

keg [keg] cuñete *m*, barrilete *m*.

ken [ken] **1.** alcance *m* de la vista; comprensión *f*, conocimiento *m*; **2.** † *or prov.* saber, (re)conocer.

ken·nel ['kenl] **1.** perrera *f*; jauría *f of hounds*; *fig.* cuchitril *m*; **2.** tener (*or* encerrar *or* estar) en perrera.

kept [kept] *pret. a. p.p. of* keep 2.

kerb(·stone) ['kə:b(stoun)] encintado *m*.

ker·chief ['kə:tʃif] pañuelo *m*, pañoleta *f*.

ker·nel ['kə:nl] almendra *f*, núcleo *m*; grano *m*; *fig.* meollo *m*.

ker·o·sene ['kerəsi:n] keroseno *m*.

kes·trel ['kestrəl] cernícalo *m* vulgar.

ketch [ketʃ] queche *m*.

ketch·up ['ketʃəp] salsa *f* de tomate *etc.*

ket·tle ['ketl] *approx.* olla *f* en forma de cafetera, tetera *f*; pava *f S.Am.*; *here's a (pretty)* ~ *of fish!* ¡vaya un lío!; '**∼·drum** timbal *m*.

key [ki:] **1.** llave *f* (*a.* ⊕); tecla *f of piano, typewriter*; *tel.* manipulador *m*; ⊕ chaveta *f*, cuña *f*; *fig.*, ♪ clave *f*; ♪ tonalidad *f*, tono *m*; *in* ~ *a* tono, templado; *off* ~ desafinado, desafinadamente; ~ *industry* industria *f* clave; ~ *man* hombre *m* indispensable; **2.** ⊕ enchavetar, acuñar; ♪ afinar; '**∼·board** teclado *m*; '**∼·hole** ojo *m* (de la cerradura); '**∼·note** (nota *f*) tónica *f*; *fig.* idea *f* fundamental; '**∼·ring** llavero *m*; '**∼·stone** ⚠ clave *f*; *fig.* piedra *f* angular.

khak·i ['kɑːki] (de) caqui *m*.

kib·itz·er ['kibitsə] *Am.* F entrometido (a *f*) *m*; mirón (-a *f*) *m*.

ki·bosh ['kaibɔʃ] *sl.*: *put the* ~ *on* acabar con, desbaratar.

kick [kik] **1.** puntapié *m*; patada *f*; coz *f of animal*; culatazo *m of firearm*; *fig.* (fuerza *f* de) reacción *f*; *sl.* fuerza *f of drink*; *Am.* F queja *f*, protesta *f*; F *I get a* ~ *out of me* emociona, encuentro placer en; F *it's got a* ~ *to it* esto está que rabia; patea *S.Am.*; **2.** *v/t.* dar un puntapié a; dar de coces a; *goal* mar-

car; ~ *downstairs* echar escalera abajo; ~ *one's heels* esperar con impaciencia; ~ *out* echar (a puntapiés); ~ *up the dust* levantar una polvareda; ~ *up a row* meter bulla; armar camorra; *v/i.* dar coces; cocear (*a. fig.*); dar culatazo(s); *football*: chutar; ~ *against the pricks* dar coces contra el aguijón; '**kick·er** caballo *m* coceador; *Am.* F reparón (-a *f*) *m*, persona *f* quejumbrosa; '**kick·ing** coces *f/pl.*, pataleo *m*; '**kick·'off** *football*: saque *m* inicial.

kid [kid] **1.** (*meat* carne *f* de) cabrito *m*, chivo *m*; (*leather*) cabritilla *f*; F crío *m*, niño (a *f*) *m*, chico (a *f*) *m*, chaval (-a *f*) *m*; *sl.* broma *f*; F *the* ~*s* la chiquillería *f*; ~ *gloves* guantes *m/pl.* de cabritilla; F trato *m* muy blando; **2.** *sl.* embromar, tomar el pelo a; *I was only* ~*ding* lo decía en broma; '**kid·dy** F niño (a *f*) *m*.

kid·nap ['kidnæp] secuestrar; '**kid·nap·(p)er** secuestrador (-a *f*) *m*, ladrón *m* de niños.

kid·ney ['kidni] riñón *m*; *fig.* especie *f*, índole *f*; ~ *bean* judía *f*, habichuela *f*.

kill [kil] **1.** matar (*a. fig.*); destruir, eliminar; *feeling* apagar; *parl. bill* ahogar; F hacer morir de risa; F hacer una impresión irresistible; ~ *off* exterminar; ~ *time* matar (*or* engañar) el tiempo; **2.** matanza *f*; golpe *m* (*or* ataque *m*) final; '**kill·er** matador (-a *f*) *m*; asesino *m*; '**kill·ing 1.** matanza *f*; *Am.* F éxito *m* financiero; **2.** ☐ matador; destructivo; abrumador; F cómico; F irresistible; '**kill·joy** aguafiestas *m/f*.

kiln [kiln, ⊕ kil] horno *m*; '**∼·dry** secar al horno.

kil·o·cy·cle ['kilousaikl] kilociclo *m*; **kil·o·gram(me)** ['∼græm] kilo (gramo) *m*; **kil·o·me·ter, kil·o·metre** ['kiləmi:tə] kilómetro *m*; **kil·o·watt** ['kiləwɔt] kilovatio *m*; '**kil·o·watt-'hours** kilovatios-hora *m/pl.*

kilt [kilt] **1.** tonelete *m* (*de los montañeses de Escocia*); **2.** plegar; arremangar.

kin [kin] familia *f*, parientes *m/pl.*, parentela *f*; *fig.* especie *f*; *next of* ~ pariente(s) *m(pl.)* más próximo(s).

kind [kaind] **1.** clase *f*, género *m*, especie *f*, suerte *f*; *a ~ of* uno a modo de; F *~ of* casi, más o menos, vagamente; *pay in ~* pagar en especie (*fig.* en la misma moneda); *of a ~* de una misma clase; *b.s.* inferior; *of all ~s* toda clase de..., ...de todas clases; *nothing of the ~!* ¡nada de eso!; **2.** □ bondadoso, bueno; benigno; amable; *v. regard*; *be ~ to* ser amable con, ser bueno para (con); *be so ~ as* to tener la bondad de.

kind·er·gar·ten [ˈkindəgɑːtn] jardín *m* de (la) infancia.

kind-heart·ed [ˈkaindˈhɑːtid] de buen corazón, bondadoso.

kin·dle [ˈkindl] encender(se) (*a. fig.*).

kind·li·ness [ˈkaindlinis] bondad *f*, benignidad *f*, benevolencia *f*.

kin·dling [ˈkindliŋ] (*act*) encendimiento *m*; (*wood*) leña *f* menuda.

kind·ly [ˈkaindli] **1.** *adj.* bondadoso, benévolo; *climate* benigno; **2.** *adv.* bondadosamente; benignamente; *~ wait a moment* haga el favor de esperar un momento; *take ~ to* aceptar de buen grado; sufrir; *he'd take it ~ if you...* le estaría agradecido si...

kind·ness [ˈkaindnis] bondad *f*; benevolencia *f*; amabilidad *f*; favor *m*.

kin·dred [ˈkindrid] **1.** (*kinship*) parentesco *m*; afinidad *f*; (*ps.*) parentela *f*, familia *f*, parientes *m/pl.*; **2.** allegado; afín.

kin·e·mat·o·graph [kainiˈmætəgrɑːf] cinematógrafo *m*.

ki·net·ic [kaiˈnetik] cinético *f*; **ki·net·ics** cinética *f*.

king [kiŋ] rey *m* (*a. fig., chess, cards*); *draughts*: dama *f*; *~'s English* inglés *m* correcto; † *~'s evil* escrófula *f*; **'king·cup** botón *m* de oro; **'king·dom** reino *m*; **'king·fish·er** martín *m* pescador; **'king·ly** real, regio; digno de un rey; **king·pin** perno *m* real, perno *m* pinzote; pivote *m*; *fig.* persona *f* principal, elemento *m* fundamental; **'king·post** pendolón *m*; **'king·ship** dignidad *f* real; monarquía *f*; **'king-size** F de tamaño extra.

kink [kiŋk] **1.** coca *f*, enroscadura *f*; *fig.* chifladura *f*, peculiaridad *f*;

2. formar cocas; **'kink·y** enroscado, ensortijado.

kin...: *~s·folk* [ˈkinzfouk] parentela *f*, familia *f*, parientes *m/pl.*; **'~·ship** parentesco *m*, afinidad *f*; **'~s·man** pariente *m*; **'~·wom·an** parienta *f*.

ki·osk [ˈkiːɔsk] quiosco *m*; *teleph.* cabina *f*.

kip [kip] *sl.* **1.** sueño *m*; **2.**: *~ down* echarse.

kip·per [ˈkipə] **1.** arenque *m* ahumado; *sl.* tío *m*; *sl.* mujerzuela *f*; **2.** curar al humo.

kirk [kəːk] *Scot.* iglesia *f*.

kiss [kis] **1.** beso *m*; ósculo *m* (*lit.*); *fig.* roce *m*; **2.** besar(se); **'~-proof** indeleble.

kit [kit] avíos *m/pl.*; ✂ equipo *m*; (*travel*) equipaje *m*; (*tools*) herramental *m*; (*first aid*) botequín *m*; cubo *m*; **'~-bag** ✂ saco *m*; saco *m* de viaje.

kitch·en [ˈkitʃin] cocina *f*; *~ sink* fregadero *m*; *~ utensils* batería *f* de cocina; **kitch·en·ette** [~ˈnet] cocina *f* pequeña.

kitch·en...: '~-'gar·den huerto *m*; '~-maid fregona *f*; '~-range cocina *f* económica.

kite [kait] *orn.* milano *m* real; cometa *f*; ✈ giro *m* ficticio; *sl.* fly *a ~* sondar la opinión; intentar un timo; *~ balloon* globo *m* cometa.

kith [kiθ]: *~ and kin* parientes *m/pl.* (y amigos *m/pl.*).

kit·ten [ˈkitn] gatito (*a f*) *m*; '**kit·ten·ish** juguetón; coquetón.

kit·ty [ˈkiti] F minino *m*; *cards etc.*: puesta *f*, bote *m*.

klax·on [ˈklæksn] claxon *m*.

klep·to·ma·ni·a [kleptouˈmeiniə] cleptomanía *f*; **klep·to·ma·ni·ac** [~niæk] cleptómano (*a f*) *m*.

knack [næk] tino *m*; maña *f*, destreza *f*; hábito *m*; truco *m*.

knack·er [ˈnækə] matarife *m* de caballos; contratista *m* de derribos.

knag [næg] nudo *m*.

knap·sack [ˈnæpsæk] mochila *f*, barjuleta *f*.

knave [neiv] bellaco *m*, bribón *m*; *cards*: sota *f*; **knav·er·y** [~əri] bellaquería *f*, bribonería *f*.

knav·ish [ˈneiviʃ] □ bellaco, bribón, ruin.

knead [niːd] amasar, sobar; '**kneading** amasijo *m*, soba *f*.

knee [ni:] **1.** rodilla *f*; ⊕ ángulo *m*, cod(ill)o *m*; *on bended* ⸜, *on one's* ⸜s de rodillas; *fall on one's* ⸜s caer de rodillas; *go down on one's* ⸜s *to* implorar de rodillas; *bring a p. to his* ⸜s vencer a una p., humillar a una p.; **2.** dar un rodillazo a; *trousers* formar rodilleras en; '⸜-**breech·es** calzón *m* corto; '⸜-**cap** rótula *f*, choquezuela *f*; '⸜-**deep** metido hasta las rodillas; '⸜-**joint** articulación *f* de la rodilla; **kneel** [ni:l] [*irr.*] (*a.* ⸜ *down*) arrodillarse, hincar la rodilla (*to* ante); estar de rodillas.

knell [nel] doble *m*, toque *m* de difuntos; *fig.* mal agüero *m*.

knelt [nelt] *pret. a. p.p. of kneel.*

knew [nju:] *pret. of know.*

knick·er·bock·ers ['nikəbɔkəz] *pl.* pantalones *m/pl.* cortos; '**knick·ers** *pl.* F bragas *f/pl.*, pantalones *m/pl.* de señora; = *knickerbockers.*

knick-knack ['niknæk] chuchería *f*, baratija *f*; chisme *m*.

knife [naif] **1.** [*pl.* knives] cuchillo *m*; navaja *f*; ⊕ cuchilla *f*; *to the* ⸜ a muerte; *have one's* ⸜ *into* tener inquina a; **2.** acuchillar; apuñalar; '⸜-**box** portacubiertos *m*; '⸜-**edge** filo *m* (de cuchillo); '⸜-**grind·er** amolador *m*.

knight [nait] **1.** caballero *m*; *chess:* caballo *m*; **2.** armar caballero; **knight-er·rant** ['nait'erənt] caballero *m* andante; '**knight-'er·rant·ry** caballería *f* andante; **knight·hood** ['⸜hud] caballería *f*; título *m* de caballero; '**knight·ly** caballeroso, caballeresco.

knit [nit] [*irr.*] *v/t.* hacer (a punto de aguja); *brows* fruncir; (*a.* ⸜ *together*) enlazar, unir; *v/i.* hacer calceta (*or* media *or* punto); (*bone*) soldarse; (*a.* ⸜ *together*) enlazarse, unirse; '**knit·ting** labor *f* de punto; '**knit·ting-ma·chine** máquina *f* de hacer punto *etc.*; '**knit·ting-nee·dle** aguja *f* de hacer calceta; '**knit·wear** géneros *m/pl.* de punto.

knives [naivz] *pl. of knife.*

knob [nɔb] protuberancia *f*, bulto *m*; botón *m*, perilla *f*; tirador *m* of door, drawer; puño *m* of stick; (*fragment*) terrón *m*; '**knobbed**, '**knob·bly**, '**knob·by** nudoso; '**knob-stick** bastón *m* (nudoso); *sl.* esquirol *m*.

knock [nɔk] **1.** golpe *m*; porrazo *m*; aldabonazo *m*, llamada *f* *on door*;

⊕ golpeo *m*; **2.** *v/t.* golpear; chocar contra; *Am. sl.* criticar, calumniar; hacer competencia (injusta) a; ⸜ *about* pegar; maltratar; ⸜ *down* derribar; echar por tierra; *price* rebajar; *auction:* adjudicar, rematar (*to* a, *for* en); ⊕ desmontar; *mot.* atropellar; ⸜ *in* hacer entrar a golpes; *nail* clavar; ⸜ *off* quitar (de un golpe); hacer caer; F *work* terminar, suspender; ✝ rebajar; F ejecutar prontamente; *sl.* apropiarse, robar; ⸜ *out mst boxing:* poner fuera de combate, noquear; eliminar; suprimir; ⸜ *over* volcar; ⸜ *together* construir (*or* armar) de prisa; ⸜ *up* despertar; F agotar, reventar; *building* construir a la ligera; *v/i.* llamar a la puerta; ⊕ golpear, martillear; F ⸜ *about* vagabundear, ver mucho mundo; *he's* ⸜*ing about* estará por ahí; ⸜ *against* chocar contra; ⸜ *into* topar con; F ⸜ *off* acabar (el trabajo), terminar; ⸜ *up tennis:* pelotear; ⸜ *up against* chocar contra; tropezar con; ⸜-**a·bout** ['⸜əbaut] **1.** farsa *f* bulliciosa; **2.** bullicioso, turbulento; *clothes* para todos los días; '⸜-**down** que derriba; abrumador; ⸜ *price* precio *m* obsequio; '**knock·er** aldaba *f*; *Am. sl.* criticón (-a *f*) *m*; '**knock·er-'up** despertador (-a *f*) *m*; '**knock-kneed** patizambo; *fig.* débil, irresoluto; '**knock-'out** *boxing:* (*a.* ⸜ *blow*) knockout *m*, noqueada *f*; *sport:* eliminación *f* progresiva; *sl.* moza *f* (*or* cosa *f*) estupenda.

knoll [noul] otero *m*, montículo *m*.

knot [nɔt] **1.** nudo *m* (*a. fig.,* ⚓, ✿); (*bow*) lazo *m*; corrillo *m* of people; *tied up in* ⸜s confuso, enmarañado; perplejo; **2.** *v/t.* anudar, atar; *v/i.* hacer nudos; enmarañarse; '**knot·ty** nudoso; *fig.* difícil, complicado, espinoso.

knout [naut] knut *m*.

know [nou] **1.** [*irr.*] saber; (*be acquainted with*) conocer; (*recognize*) reconocer; ⸜ *best* saber lo que más conviene; ⸜ *French* saber francés; ⸜ *how to inf.* saber *inf.*; ⸜ *of* saber de; tener conocimiento de; *come (or get) to* ⸜ *p.* llegar a conocer; *th.* enterarse de; **2.:** F *be in the* ⸜ estar enterado (*about* de);

know·a·ble ['nouəbl] conocible; **'know-all** sabelotodo *m/f*; **'know-how** F habilidad *f*, destreza *f*; experiencia *f*; **'know·ing** □ inteligente; sabio; entendido; *b.s.* astuto; malicioso; ~ *full well that* a sabiendas de que; ~*ly* a sabiendas; **knowledge** ['nɔlidʒ] conocimiento(s) *m(pl.)*; saber *m*; *to my* ~ según mi leal saber y entender; que yo sepa; por lo que yo sé; *without my* ~ sin saberlo yo; **'know·ledge·able** □ enterado, conocedor; **known** [noun]

p.p. of know; make ~ publicar, comunicar.

knuck·le ['nʌkl] **1.** nudillo *m*; jarrete *m of meat*; **2.:** ~ *down to inf.* ponerse a *inf.* con ahinco; ~ *under* someterse; **'~-dust·er** puño *m* de hierro.

Ko·ran [kɔ'rɑːn] Alcorán *m*, Corán *m*.

kow·tow ['kau'tau] saludar humildemente; humillarse (*to ante*).

ku·dos ['kjuːdɔs] F renombre *m*, prestigio *m*.

L

lab [læb] F = *laboratory.*

la·bel ['leibl] **1.** rótulo *m*, marbete *m*, etiqueta *f*; tejuelo *m of book*; *fig.* calificación *f*, apodo *m*; **2.** rotular, poner etiqueta a; *fig.* calificar (*as* de); apodar.

la·bi·al ['leibiəl] labial *adj. a. su. f.*

lab·or·a·to·ry [lə'bɔrətəri] laboratorio *m*; ~ *assistant* ayudante (a *f*) *m* (*or* mozo *m*) de laboratorio.

la·bo·ri·ous [lə'bɔːriəs] □ laborioso.

la·bo(u)r ['leibə] **1.** trabajo *m*; labor *f*; faena *f*; esfuerzo *m*; pena *f*; (*a.* ~ *force*) mano *f* de obra; clase *f* obrera; (dolores *m/pl.* del) parto *m*; *Ministry of* ♀ Ministerio *m* de Trabajo; *hard* ~ trabajos *m/pl.* forzados; *be in* ~ estar de parto; **2.** *attr.* de trabajo; laboral; obrero; *pol.* ♀ laborista; ~ *camp* campamento *m* de trabajo; ~ *dispute* conflicto *m* laboral; ♀ *Exchange* bolsa *f* de trabajo; ♀(*Party*) Partido *m* Laborista; ~ *turnover* rotación *f* de la mano de obra; *mst Am.* ~ *union* sindicato *m* (de trabajadores de la misma rama) industrial; **3.** *v/t.* desarrollar con nimiedad; insistir en; *v/i.* trabajar (*at* en); afanarse (*to* por); moverse penosamente; ~ *under* sufrir; ~ *under a delusion* estar equivocado; **'la·bo(u)red** penoso, dificultoso; fatigoso; *style* premioso; **'la·bo(u)r·er** trabajador *m*; obrero *m*; (*day-*) jornalero *m*; (*unskilled*) peón *m*; bracero *m*; (*farm-*) labriego *m*; **'la·bo(u)r·ing** trabajador, obrero; **la·bo(u)r·ite** ['~rait] laborista *m/f*; **'la·bour-'sav·ing** que ahorra trabajo.

la·bur·num [lə'bəːnəm] laburno *m*, codeso *m*.

lab·y·rinth ['læbərinθ] laberinto *m*; **lab·y·rin·thine** [~'rinθain] laberíntico.

lac [læk] laca *f*.

lace [leis] **1.** cordón *m of shoes etc.*; encaje *m*; (*trimming*) puntilla *f*; **2.** atar; enlazar(se); *sew.* guarnecer con encajes; F (*a.* ~ *into*) dar una paliza a; *drink* echar licor a.

lac·er·ate ['læsəreit] lacerar; *feelings* herir; **lac·er·a·tion** laceración *f*.

lach·ry·mal ['lækriml] lagrimal; **lach·ry·ma·to·ry** ['~mətəri] lacrimatorio, lagrimal; ~ *gas* gas *m* lacrimógeno; **lach·ry·mose** ['~mous] lacrimoso.

lack [læk] **1.** carencia *f*; falta *f*; necesidad *f*; ausencia *f*; *for* (*or through*) ~ *of* por falta de; **2.** *v/t.* carecer de; necesitar; *he* ~*s money* le (hace) falta dinero; *v/i.*: *be* ~*ing* faltar; *he is* ~*ing in* le falta.

lack·a·dai·si·cal [lækə'deizikl] □ lánguido; indiferente; distraído.

lack·ey ['læki] lacayo *m*; *fig.* secuaz *m* servil.

lack·lus·ter, lack·lus·tre ['læklʌstə] deslustrado, inexpresivo, apagado.

la·con·ic [lə'kɔnik] □ lacónico.

lac·quer ['lækə] **1.** (*a.* ~ *work*) laca *f*, maque *m*; **2.** laquear. maquear.

lac·ta·tion [læk'teiʃn] lactancia *f*.

lac·te·al ['læktiəl] lácteo; *anat.* quilífero.

lac·tic ['læktik] láctico.

lac·tose ['læktouz] lactosa *f*.

la·cu·na [lə'kjuːnə] laguna *f*.

lad [læd] muchacho *m*, mozalbete *m*, zagal *m*, rapaz *m*; F *a bit of a* ~ un chico poco formal.

lad·der [lædə] **1.** escala *f* (*a.* ⚓); escalera *f* de mano; *fig.* escalón *m*; carrera *f in stocking*; **2.** *stocking*: hacer(se) una carrera; **'~-proof** *stocking* indesmallable.

lade [leid] [*irr.*] cargar; *v. ladle* 2; **'lad·en** cargado; **lad·ing** ['leidiŋ] cargamento *m*, flete *m*.

la·dle ['leidl] **1.** cucharón *m*, cazo *m*; **2.** sacar (*or* servir) con cucharón (*a.* ~ *out*).

la·dy ['leidi] señora *f*; (*noble*) dama *f*; *young* ~ señorita *f*; *ladies and gentlemen!* ¡(señoras y) señores!; ♀ *Chapel* Capilla *f* de la Virgen; ♀ *Day* día *m* de la Anunciación (*25 marzo*); F ~ *doctor* médica *f*; ~ *of the house* señora *f* de la casa; ~*'s maid* doncella *f*; ~*'s* (*or ladies'*) *man*

Perico *m* entre ellas; '~-bird mariquita *f*, vaca *f* de San Antón; '~-in-'wait·ing dama *f* (de honor); '~-kill·er F tenorio *m*; '~·like delicado; bien educado; elegante, distinguido; *contp.* afeminado; '~-love amada *f*, querida *f*; '~·ship: her ~, Your ♀ Su Señoría.

lag[1] [læg] **1.** retraso *m*, retardo *m*; **2.** (*a.* ~ *behind*) rezagarse; retrasarse.

lag[2] [~] ⊕ revestir, forrar; *boiler* calorifugar.

lag[3] [~] *sl.* **1.** presidiario *m*; **2.** encarcelar.

la·ger (**beer**) ['lɑːgə (biə)] cerveza *f* tipo Pilsen.

lag·gard ['lægəd] rezagado (a *f*) *m*; holgazán (-a *f*) *m*; persona *f* irresoluta.

la·goon [lə'guːn] laguna *f*.

la·i·cize ['leiəsaiz] laicizar.

laid [leid] *pret. a. p.p. of* lay[4] 2; *be* ~ *up* tener que guardar cama (*with* a causa de); ~ *paper* papel *m* vergé (*or* vergueteado).

lain [lein] *p.p. of* lie[2] 2.

lair [lɛə] cubil *m*, guarida *f*.

laird [lɛəd] *Scot.* señor *m*, propietario *m*.

la·i·ty ['leiiti] legos *m/pl.*, laicado *m*.

lake[1] [leik] lago *m*.

lake[2] [~] (*colour*) laca *f*.

lake-dwel·ling ['leikdweliŋ] habitación *f* lacustre.

lam [læm] *sl.* pegar, tundir (*a.* ~ *into*).

la·ma ['lɑːmə] lama *m*.

lamb [læm] **1.** cordero (a *f*) *m* (*a. fig.*); (*older*) borrego (a *f*) *m*; (*meat*) carne *f* de cordero; **2.** parir (*la oveja*).

lam·baste [læm'beist] F dar una paliza a; poner como un trapo.

lam·bent ['læmbənt] *flame* vacilante; centelleante.

lamb...: '~·like (manso) como un cordero; '~·skin corderina *f*, piel *f* de cordero; '~s·wool añinos *m/pl.*

lame [leim] **1.** □ cojo; lisiado; *excuse* débil, poco convincente; *metre* defectuoso; ~ *duck* persona *f* incapacitada (*or* ✝ insolvente); *Am.* político *m* derrotado; **2.** lisiar, encojar; incapacitar; '**lame·ness** cojera *f*; incapacidad *f*; *fig.* debilidad *f*.

la·ment [lə'ment] **1.** lamento *m*, queja *f*; *poet. etc* elegía *f*; **2.** lamen-

tar(se de), llorar (*a.* ~ *for*, *over*); **lam·en·ta·ble** ['læməntəbl] □ lamentable, deplorable; lastimero; **lam·en'ta·tion** lamentación *f*.

lam·i·na ['læminə], *pl.* **lam·i·nae** ['~niː] lámina *f*; '**lam·i·nar** laminar; **lam·i·nate** ['~neit] laminar; dividir en láminas; *wood* contraplacar; **lam·i·nate** ['~nit], **lam·i·nat·ed** ['~neitid] laminado.

lamp [læmp] lámpara *f*; linterna *f*; (*street*) farol *m*, farola *f*; *mot.* faro *m*; (*bulb*) bombilla *f*; *fig.* antorcha *f*; '~-**black** negro *m* de humo; '~-'**brack·et** brazo *m* (de lámpara); '~-**chim·ney**, '~-**glass** tubo *m* (de lámpara); '~-**hold·er** portalámpara(s) *m*; '~-**light** luz *f* de (la) lámpara; '~-**light·er** farolero *m*.

lam·poon [læm'puːn] **1.** pasquín *m*; **2.** pasquinar.

lamp-post ['læmppoust] poste *m* de farol.

lam·prey ['læmpri] lamprea *f*.

lamp-shade ['læmpʃeid] pantalla *f*.

lance [lɑːns] **1.** lanza *f*; **2.** (a)lancear; ✞ abrir con lanceta; '~-'**cor·po·ral** soldado *m* (de) primera; **lan·ce·o·late** ['lænsiəlit] lanceolado; **lanc·er** ['lɑːnsə] lancero *m*; ~s (*dance*) lanceros *m/pl.*

lan·cet ['lɑːnsit] lanceta *f*; ~ *arch* ojiva *f* aguda; ~ *win·dow* ventana *f* ojival.

land [lænd] **1.** *all senses:* tierra *f*; (*soil*) suelo *m*; (*nation*) país *m*; (*a. tract of* ~) terreno *m*; *by* ~ por tierra; *dry* ~ tierra *f* firme; *native* ~ patria *f*; *promised* ~ tierra *f* de promisión; ~ *forces* fuerzas *f/pl.* terrestres; ~ *reform* reforma *f* agraria; *see how the* ~ *lies* tantear (*or* reconocer) el terreno; **2.** *v/t. passengers* desembarcar; *goods* descargar; ✞ poner en tierra; F conseguir, ganar; *blow* asestar; *boxing:* conectar; *v/i.* desembarcar; ✞ aterrizar; ✞ (*on sea*) amerizar, amarar; llegar; F caer; (*a.* ~ *up*) ir a parar; '~-**a·gent** corredor *m* de fincas rurales; administrador *m*; '**land·ed** hacendado; que consiste en tierras; ~ *gentry* pequeña aristocracia *f* rural; ~ *property* bienes *m/pl.* raíces.

land...: '~·**fall** ⚓ aterrada *f*; '~-**hold·er** terrateniente *m/f*.

land·ing ['lændiŋ] aterraje *m*; desembarco *m of passengers*; desembarque *m of cargo*; ⚓ aterrizaje *m*; (*stairs*) descanso *m*, rellano *m*; ~ *craft* barcaza *f* de desembarco; ~ *gear* tren *m* de aterrizaje; ~ *ground* campo *m* de aterrizaje; ~ *run* recorrido *m* de aterrizaje; '~-**net** salabardo *m*; '~-**stage** (des)embarcadero *m*.

land...: '~-**la·dy** dueña *f*; patrona *f*, huéspeda *f of boarding-house*; '~-**locked** cercado de tierra; '~-**lord** propietario *m*, dueño *m of property*; patrón *m of boarding-house*; posadero *m*, mesonero *m of inn*; '~-**lub·ber** ⚓ *contp.* hombre *m* de tierra; '~-**mark** ⚓ marca *f* (de reconocimiento); mojón *m*; punto *m* destacado; *fig.* monumento *m*, acontecimiento *m* que hace época; '~-**own·er** terrateniente *m/f*, propietario (a *f*) *m*; ~-**scape** ['læn-skeip] paisaje *m*; ~ *gardener* arquitecto *m* de jardines; ~ *painter* paisajista *m/f*; '~-**slide** corrimiento *m* de tierras (*a.* '~-**slip**); *pol.* victoria *f* electoral arrolladora; ~-**tax** contribución *f* territorial; ~-**ward** ['~wəd] hacia tierra.

lane [lein] (*country*) camino *m* (vecinal), vereda *f*; (*town*) callejón *m*; *sport*: calle *f*; *mot.* senda *f*; ⚓ ruta *f* de navegación.

lang·syne ['læŋ'sain] *Scot.* (tiempo *m* de) antaño.

lan·guage ['læŋgwidʒ] lenguaje *m* (*faculty of speech, particular mode of speech, style*); lengua *f*, idioma *m of nation*; *bad* ~ palabrotas *f/pl.*; *use bad* ~ ser mal hablado; *strong* ~ palabras *f/pl.* mayores.

lan·guid ['læŋgwid] □ lánguido; '**lan·guid·ness** languidez *f*.

lan·guish ['læŋgwiʃ] languidecer; afectar languidez; mostrarse sentimental; consumirse (*for* por); pudrise *in prison*; '**lan·guish·ing** □ lánguido; sentimental.

lan·guor ['læŋgə] languidez *f*; '**lan·guor·ous** □ lánguido; enervante.

lank [læŋk] □ alto y flaco; *hair* lacio; '**lank·y** □ larguirucho.

lan·tern ['læntən] linterna *f* (*a.* ⚠); *fanal m of lighthouse*; ⚓ faro(l) *m*; *dark* ~ linterna *f* sorda; *magic* ~ linterna *f* mágica; ~ *lecture* conferencia *f* con proyecciones; '~-**jawed** chupado de cara; '~-**slide** diapositiva *f*.

lan·yard ['lænjəd] acollador *m*.

lap¹ [læp] **1.** regazo *m*; falda *f*; *fig.* seno *m*; *sport*: vuelta *f*; (*stage*) etapa *f*; ⊕ traslapo *m*; **2.** envolver (*in* en); traslapar(se) (*a.* ~ *over*); juntar a traslapo; *sport*: aventajar en una vuelta entera; ~ *about* (*with*) cercar (de).

lap² [~] **1.** lametada *f*; chapaleteo *m of waves*; **2.** lamer; (*waves*) chapalear; ~ *up* beber con la lengua; (*a. fig.*) tragar.

lap-dog ['læpdɔg] perro *m* faldero.

la·pel [lə'pel] solapa *f*.

lap·i·dar·y ['læpidəri] lapidario *adj. a. su. m.*

Lap·land·er ['læplændə], **Lapp** [læp] lapón (-a *f*) *m*.

lap·pet ['læpit] pliegue *m*.

lapse [læps] **1.** (*moral, of time*) lapso *m*; desliz *m*; recaída *f* (*into* en); (*mistake*) equivocación *f*; ⚖ caducidad *f*, prescripción *f*; **2.** (*time*) transcurrir; pasar; caer (*in* la culpa *or* en el error); recaer (*into* en); ⚖ caducar, prescribir.

lap·wing ['læpwiŋ] avefría *f*.

lar·board ['la:bəd] (de) babor.

lar·ce·ny ['la:sni] latrocinio *m*; *petty* ~ robo *m* de menor cuantía.

larch [la:tʃ] alerce *m*.

lard [la:d] **1.** manteca *f* (de cerdo), lardo *m*; **2.** lard(e)ar, mechar; *fig.* adornar (*with* con), salpicar (*with* de); '**lard·er** despensa *f*; '**lard·y** mantecoso.

large [la:dʒ] grande; *as* ~ *as life* de tamaño natural; *en* persona; *at* ~ en libertad, suelto; en general; extensamente; por todas partes; *on the* ~ *side* algo grande; '**large·ly** grandemente; en gran parte; '**large·ness** grandeza *f*; gran tamaño *m*; vastedad *f*; '**large·scale** en gran(de) escala; '**large·sized** de gran tamaño. [dádiva *f* espléndida.]

lar·gess(e) ['la:dʒes] largueza *f*;)

lar·i·at ['læriət] lazo *m*.

lark¹ [la:k] *orn.* alondra *f* común.

lark² [~] **1.** juerga *f*; travesura *f*; broma *f*; **2.** (*a.* ~ *about*) hacer travesuras; andar de jarana.

lark·spur ['la:kspə:] espuela *f* de caballero.

lar·va ['la:və], *pl.* **lar·vae** ['~vi:] larva *f*; **lar·val** ['~vl] larval.

lar·yng·i·tis [lærin'dʒaitis] laringitis *f*.

lar·ynx ['læriŋks] laringe *f*.
las·civ·ious [ləˈsiviəs] □ lascivo.
lash [læʃ] **1.** tralla *f*; azote *m*; (*whip*) látigo *m*; (*stroke*) latigazo *m* (*a. fig.*); coletazo *m of tail*; *anat.* pestaña *f*; **2.** azotar, fustigar (*a. fig.*); provocar (*into hasta*); *tail* agitar; chocar con; (*bind*) atar, ⚓ trincar; ∼ *out* tirar coces; dar golpes furiosos; estallar; '**lash·ing** azotamiento *m*; atadura *f*; ⚓ trinca *f*; ∼s *sl.* montones *m*/*pl.*, derroche *m*.
lass [læs] chica *f*, muchacha *f*; zagala *f*; moza *f*; **las·sie** [ˈ∼i] muchachita *f*.
las·si·tude ['laesitju:d] lasitud *f*.
las·so [læˈsu:] **1.** lazo *m*; **2.** lazar.
last¹ [lɑ:st] **1.** *adj.* último; postrero; final; extremo; *week etc.* pasado; *the* ∼ *to* el último en; *at the* ∼ *moment* a última hora; *before* ∼ antepasado; ∼ *but one* penúltimo; **2.** último (*a f*) *m*; última cosa *f*; fin *m*; *my* ∼ mi última carta; *at* ∼ por fin; *at long* ∼ al fin y al cabo; *to the* ∼ hasta el fin; *breathe one's* ∼ exhalar el último suspiro; *see the* ∼ *of* no volver a ver; **3.** *adv.* por último; por última vez; finalmente; ∼ *but not least* el último pero no el peor; *arrive* ∼ llegar el último.
last² [∼] (per)durar; continuar; permanecer; resistir; subsistir, sostenerse, conservarse (*a.* ∼ *out*).
last³ [∼] horma *f* (del calzado); *stick to your* ∼! ¡zapatero, a tus zapatos!
last·ing ['lɑ:stiŋ] □ duradero, perdurable; constante; *colour* sólido.
last·ly ['lɑ:stli] por último, finalmente.
latch [lætʃ] picaporte *m*; pestillo *m* de golpe; aldabilla *f*; *on the* ∼ cerrado con picaporte; '∼-**key** llavín *m*.
late [leit] **1.** *adj.* tardío; *hour* avanzado; reciente, de hace poco; (*dead*) fallecido, difunto; (*former*) antiguo, ex...; *a* ∼ *twelfth-century text* un texto de fines del siglo doce; *it is* ∼ es tarde; *he is* ∼ llega tarde; *I was* ∼ *in ger.* tardé en *inf.*; *be 2 minutes* ∼ 🕐 *etc.* llegar con 2 minutos de retraso; *get* (*or grow*) ∼ hacerse tarde; *keep* ∼ *hours* acostarse a las altas horas de la noche; *of* ∼ *years* en estos últimos años; **2.** *adv.* tarde; ∼ *in the afternoon* a última

hora de la tarde; ∼ *in life* a una edad avanzada; ∼ *in the year* hacia fines del año; *as* ∼ *as* todavía en; hasta; *at the* ∼*st* a más tardar; ∼*r on* más tarde; *of* ∼ últimamente, recientemente; '∼-**com·er** recién llegado (*a f*) *m*; rezagado (*a f*) *m*; '**late·ly** hace poco; últimamente, recientemente.
la·ten·cy ['leitənsi] estado *m* latente.
late·ness ['leitnis] retraso *m*; lo avanzado *of the hour*; lo tarde; lo reciente.
la·tent ['leitənt] □ latente.
lat·er·al ['lætərəl] □ lateral.
lath [lɑ:θ] listón *m*.
lathe [leið] torno *m*.
lath·er ['lɑ:ðə] **1.** jabonadura(s) *f*(*pl.*), espuma *f* (de jabón); **2.** *v/t.* (en)jabonar; *sl.* zurrar; *v/i.* hacer espuma.
Lat·in ['lætin] **1.** latino *adj. a. su. m* (*a f*); **2.** (*language*) latín *m*; '∼-**A'mer·i·can** latinoamericano *adj. a. su. m* (*a f*); '**Lat·in·ism** latinismo *m*.
lat·i·tude ['lætitju:d] latitud *f*; *fig.* libertad *f*; **lat·i'tu·di·nal** latitudinal; **lat·i·tu·di·nar·i·an** [ˈ∼ˈnɛəriən] latitudinario *adj. a. su. m* (*a f*).
la·trine [ləˈtri:n] letrina *f*.
lat·ter ['lætə] más reciente; posterior; último; segundo *of* 2; *the* ∼ éste *etc.*; ∼ *end* muerte *f*; *the* ∼ *end* (*or part*) *of* fines de; '∼-**day** moderno, reciente; '**lat·ter·ly** recientemente, últimamente.
lat·tice ['lætis] **1.** enrejado *m* (*a.* '∼-**work**); celosía *f*; **2.** enrejar.
Lat·vi·an ['lætviən] letón *adj. a. su. m* (-a *f*).
laud [lɔ:d] *mst lit.* **1.** alabanza *f*; ∼s *eccl.* laudes *f*/*pl.*; **2.** alabar, loar, elogiar; **laud·a'bil·i·ty** laudabilidad *f*; '**laud·a·ble** □ laudable, loable; **laud·a·to·ry** ['∼ətəri] □ laudatorio.
laugh [lɑ:f] **1.** risa *f*; (*loud*) carcajada *f*, risotada *f*; *have the* ∼ *of* quedar por encima de; **2.** reír(se); ∼ *at* reírse de, burlarse de; ∼ *off* tomar a risa; ∼ *out* (*loud*) reírse a carcajadas; '**laugh·a·ble** □ risible, irrisorio; divertido; '**laugh·ing** **1.** risa *f*; **2.** risueño, reidor; ∼ *matter* cosa *f* de risa; '**laugh·ing-stock** hazmerreír *m*; '**laugh·ter** risa(s) *f* (*pl.*).

launch [lɔ:ntʃ] **1.** botadura *f*; (*boat*) lancha *f*; **2.** *v/t. ship* botar, echar al agua; (*throw, publicize, set up*) lanzar; dar principio a; poner en operación; ✝ emitir; *v/i.*: ~ *forth*, ~ *out* lanzarse, salir; ~ (*out*) *into* lanzarse a; engolfarse en; emprender; *speech* desatarse en; **'launch·ing** botadura *f*; lanzamiento *m*; iniciación *f*; ✝ emisión *f*; **launch·ing-site** rampa *f* de lanzamiento.

laun·der ['lɔ:ndə] *v/t.* lavar (y planchar); *v/i.* resistir el lavado.

laun·dress ['lɔ:ndris] lavandera *f*; **'laun·dry** lavadero *m*; lavandería *f* *S.Am.*; (*clothes*) ropa *f* lavada (*or* por lavar).

lau·re·ate ['lɔ:riit] (poeta *m*) laureado.

lau·rel ['lɔrl] laurel *m*; *win* ~*s* cargarse de laureles, laurearse.

la·va ['lɑ:və] lava *f*.

lav·a·to·ry ['lævətəri] wáter *m*, excusado *m*, inodoro *m*, retrete *m*; (*washplace*) lavabo *m*; *public* ~ evacuatorio *m* (público).

lave [leiv] *mst poet.* lavar, bañar.

lav·en·der ['lævində] espliego *m*, lavanda *f*.

lav·ish ['læviʃ] **1.** ☐ pródigo (*of* de, *in* en); profuso; **2.** prodigar; ~ *s.t. upon a p.* colmar a una p. de algo; **'lav·ish·ness** prodigalidad *f*; profusión *f*.

law [lɔ:] ley *f*; (*study, body of*) derecho *m*; jurisprudencia *f*; *sport*: regla *f*; ~ *and order* orden *m* público; *by* ~ según la ley; *in* ~ según derecho; ...*-in-*~ político; *go to* ~ poner pleito, recurrir a la ley; *have the* ~ *of* (*or on*) llevar a los tribunales; *lay down the* ~ hablar autoritariamente; *practise* ~ ejercer (la profesión) de abogado; *take the* ~ *into one's own hands* tomarse la justicia por su mano; **'~-a·bid·ing** observante de la ley; morigerado; **'~-break·er** infractor (-a *f*) *m* de la ley; **'~-court** tribunal *m* de justicia; **'law·ful** ☐ lícito, legítimo, legal; **'law·giv·er** legislador (-a *f*) *m*; **'law·less** ☐ ilegal; desaforado, desordenado; sin leyes.

lawn[1] [lɔ:n] linón *m*.

lawn[2] [~] césped *m*; **'~-mow·er** cortacésped *m*; **'~-'ten·nis** lawn-tennis *m*, tenis *m*.

law·suit ['lɔ:sju:t] pleito *m*, litigio *m*,

proceso *m*; **law·yer** ['~jə] abogado *m*; jurisconsulto *m*.

lax [læks] (*morally*) laxo; indisciplinado; negligente; vago; **lax·a·tive** [~ətiv] laxante *adj. a. su. m*; **'lax·i·ty**, **'lax·ness** laxitud *f*; relajamiento *m*; negligencia *f*.

lay[1] [lei] *pret. of* lie[2] 2.

lay[2] [~] *lit.* trova *f*, romance *m*; caución *f*.

lay[3] [~] laico, lego, seglar; profano.

lay[4] [~] **1.** disposición *f*, situación *f*; *sl.* negocio *m*; **2.** [*irr.*] *v/t.* poner, colocar, dejar; (*ex*)tender; acostar; derribar; acabar con; ✗ apuntar; *bet* hacer; *blame, foundations* echar; *claim* presentar; *dust* matar; *eggs, table* poner; *fears* aquietar; *fire* preparar; *ghost* conjurar; *money* apostar; *plans* formar; 🚂 *track* tender; ~ *aside*, ~ *away* echar a un lado, arrinconar; ahorrar; ~ *bare* poner al descubierto; ~ *before* presentar a; exponer ante; ~ *by* poner a un lado; guardar; ahorrar; ~ *down arms* deponer; *burden* posar; *life* dar; *principle* asentar; *ship* colocar la quilla de; guardar; afirmar (*that* que); ~ *in* (*stocks of*) proveerse de; almacenar; ~ *low* derribar; poner fuera de combate; ~ *off* poner a un lado; *workers* despedir (temporalmente); ~ *on* colocar sobre; aplicar; imponer; *blows* descargar; *water etc.* instalar; F ~ *it on* (*thick*) (*beat*) zurrar; (*exaggerate*) recargar las tintas; (*flatter*) adular; ~ *open* abrir; poner al descubierto; exponer (*a. fig.*); ~ *out* (*ex*)tender; F derribar, poner fuera de combate; disponer; trazar; ✝ invertir; gastar; ~ *o.s. out* hacer un gran esfuerzo (*to por*); molestarse (*for* por); ~ *up* almacenar, guardar, ahorrar; 🛏 obligar a guardar cama; ⚓ amarrar; *mot.* encerrar; *v/i.* (*hens*) poner; apostar (*a.* ~ *a wager*) (*that* a que); ~ *about one* dar palos de ciego; *sl.* ~ *into* atacar, dar una paliza a; ~ *off sl.* dejar en paz, quitarse de encima; *sl.* dejar; ⚓ virar de bordo; F ~ *on* descargar golpes; **'~-by** *mot.* apartadero *m*.

lay·er 1. ['leiə] capa *f*; lecho *m*; *geol.* estrato *m*; (gallina *f*) ponedora *f*; ✓ acodo *m*; **2.** ['leə] acodar.

lay·ette [lei'et] canastilla *f*, ajuar *m* (de niño).

lay-fig·ure ['lei'figǝ] maniquí m.

lay·ing ['leiiŋ] colocación f; tendido m of cable; postura f of eggs; ~ on of hands imposición f de manos.

lay·man ['leimǝn] seglar m, lego m; profano m.

lay...: '~-off paro m involuntario; '~-out trazado m; disposición f; equipo m.

laze [leiz] holgazanear; '**laz·i·ness** pereza f, indolencia f, holgazanería f; '**la·zy** □ perezoso, indolente, holgazán; '**la·zy-bones** gandul (-a f) m.

lea [li:] poet. prado m.

lead[1] [led] 1. plomo m; ⚓ sonda f, escandallo m; typ. regleta f; mina f in pencil; ~s pl. chapas f/pl. de plomo; ~ pencil lápiz m; ~ poisoning plumbismo m; 2. emplomar; typ. regletear; ~ed lights cristales m/pl. emplomados.

lead[2] [li:d] 1. delantera f, cabeza f (a. sport); iniciativa f; dirección f, mando m; ejemplo m; guía f; indicación f; sport: liderato m; cards: mano f; thea. papel m principal; traílla f for dog; ⚡ conductor m, avance m; cards: it's my ~ yo soy mano; be in the ~ ir en cabeza; take the ~ tomar la delantera (or la cabeza or el mando); 2. v/t. conducir; guiar; encabezar; dirigir; mandar; life llevar; mover (to inf. a inf.); card salir con; ~ astray llevar por mal camino; ~ on fig. incitar (to a); seducir; v/i. llevar la delantera; tener el mando; conducir (to a); cards: ser mano; ~ off empezar; sport: abrir el juego; ~ up to conducir a; preparar (el terreno para).

lead·en ['ledn] plúmbeo, de plomo; colour plomizo; fig. pesado; fig. triste.

lead·er ['li:dǝ] jefe (a f) m, líder m, caudillo m; guía m/f; conductor (-a f) m; cuadrillero m of gang; cabecilla m of rebels; director m of band; primer violín m of orchestra; artículo m de fondo in newspaper; '**lead·er·ship** jefatura f, liderato m; mando m, dirección f; iniciativa f; (powers of) ~ dotes f/pl. de mando; '**lead·er-'wri·ter** editorialista m.

lead·ing ['li:diŋ] 1. dirección f; 2. principal, capital; director; primero; ~ article artículo m de fondo;

~ lady dama f, primera actriz f; ~ man primer galán m; ~ question ✝ pregunta f capciosa; '~-strings pl. andadores m/pl.

leaf [li:f] 1. (pl. leaves) hoja f; shake like a ~ temblar como un azogado; take a ~ from a p.'s book seguir el ejemplo de una p.; turn over a new ~ reformarse; 2. mst Am. ~ through hojear; '~-bud yema f; '**leaf·less** deshojado, sin hojas; '**leaf·let** ['~lit] hoja f volante, folleto m; '**leaf-mould** abono m verde; '**leaf·y** frondoso.

league [li:g] 1. (measure) legua f; pol., sport: liga f; ♀ of Nations Sociedad f de las Naciones; in ~ coligado; F de manga; in ~ with de acicate con; 2. (co)ligar(se).

leak [li:k] 1. ⚓ vía f de agua; gotera f in roof; (aperture) agujero m, rendija f; salida f, escape m, fuga f of gas, liquid; 2. ⚓ hacer agua; salirse; gotear(se); ~ out rezumarse (a. fig.); fig. filtrarse; '**leak·age** escape m; derrame m; filtración f; fig. divulgación f no autorizada, noticia f oficiosa; '**leak·y** ⚓ que hace agua; roof llovedizo; que se rezuma; agujereado.

lean[1] [li:n] flaco; meat magro; year etc. de carestía.

lean[2] [~] 1. [irr.] ladear(se), inclinar(se); ~ against arrimar(se) a; ~ back reclinarse, echar el cuerpo atrás; ~ out asomarse a; ~ to inclinarse a (or hacia); ~ (up)on apoyarse en; 2. (a. fig. lean·ing) inclinación f.

lean·ness ['li:nnis] flaqueza f; magrez f; fig. carestía f.

leant [lent] pret. a. p.p. of lean[2] 1.

lean-to ['li:n'tu:] colgadizo m.

leap [li:p] 1. salto m, brinco m; by ~s and bounds a pasos agigantados; ~ in the dark salto m en el vacío; 2. saltar (a. ~ over); dar un salto (a. fig.); '~-frog 1. fil derecho m, pídola f; 2. jugar a la pídola; saltar; **leapt** [lept] pret. a. p.p. of leap 2; '**leap-year** año m bisiesto.

learn [lǝ:n] [irr.] aprender (to a); instruirse (about en); enterarse de a fact; I ~ed the news yesterday supe la noticia ayer; live and ~ vivir para ver; **learn·ed** ['~id] □ docto, sabio; erudito; profession liberal; '**learn·er** principiante m/f, aprendiz (-a f) m; estudioso (a f) m; 'learn·ing el aprender; estudio m; erudición f, saber m; learnt [lə:nt] pret. a. p.p. of learn.

lease [li:s] 1. (contrato m de) arrendamiento m; let out on ~ dar en arriendo; take on a new ~ of life recobrar su vigor; renovarse; 2. arrendar; dar (or tomar) en arriendo; ~·hold ['~hould] 1. arrendamiento m; bienes raíces m/pl. arrendados; 2. arrendado; '~·hold·er arrendatario (a f) m.

leash [li:ʃ] 1. traílla f; 2. atraillar.

least [li:st] 1. adj. menor; más pequeño; mínimo; 2. adv. menos; 3. su. lo menos, menor m/f; the ~ of the apostles el menor de los apóstoles; at ~ a lo menos, al menos, por lo menos; at the (very) ~ lo menos; not in the ~ de ninguna manera; nada; to say the ~ para no decir más.

leath·er ['leðə] 1. cuero m; piel f; F pellejo m; (wash-) gamuza f; 2. de cuero; 3. F zurrar; leath·er·ette [~'ret] cuero m artificial; leath·ern ['leðən] de cuero; 'leath·er·y correoso; skin curtido.

leave [li:v] 1. permiso m; ✕ (a. ~ of absence) licencia f; (a. ~-taking) despedida f; by your ~ con permiso de Vd.; on ~ de licencia; take (one's) ~ despedirse (of de); 2. [irr.] v/t. dejar; abandonar; salir de; marcharse de; legar in will; entregar; ceder; F ~ it at that dejar así las cosas; darse por satisfecho; ~ it to me yo me encargaré de eso; it ~s much to be desired deja mucho que desear; 3 from 5 ~s 2 de 5 a 3 van 2, 5 menos 3 son 2; ~ alone p. dejar en paz; no meterse con; th. no tocar, no manosear; ~ it alone! ¡déjalo! ~ behind dejar atrás; olvidar; ~ off clothes no ponerse, quitarse; habit renunciar a; ~ out omitir; v/i. irse, marcharse; salir (for para); ~ off ger. cesar de inf., dejar de inf.

leav·en ['levn] 1. levadura f; fig. influencia f, estímulo m, mezcla f; 2. (a)leudar; fig. entremezclar; penetrar e influenciar.

leaves [li:vz] pl. of leaf.

leav·ings ['li:viŋz] pl. sobras f/pl.

Leb·a·nese ['lebəni:z] libanés adj. a. su. m (-a f).

lech·er·ous ['letʃərəs] ☐ lascivo; 'lech·er·y lascivia f.

lec·tern ['lektən] atril m.

lec·ture ['lektʃə] 1. conferencia f; univ. mst lección f, clase f; fig. sermoneo m; read a p. a ~ sermonear a una p.; 2. dar una conferencia, dar conferencias (or lecciones) (on sobre); fig. sermonear; 'lec·tur·er conferenciante m/f; conferencista m/f S.Am.; univ. approx. profesor m adjunto; 'lec·ture-room sala f de conferencias; univ. aula f, sala f de clase; 'lec·ture·ship approx. cargo m de profesor adjunto.

led [led] pret. a p.p. of lead² 2.

ledge [ledʒ] repisa f, (re)borde m; (shelf) anaquel m; retallo m along wall; antepecho m of window.

ledg·er ['ledʒə] † libro m mayor; ⊕ travesaño m de andamio.

lee [li:] ♣ (attr. de) sotavento m; (shelter) socaire m.

leech [li:tʃ] sanguijuela f (a. fig.); † médico m.

leek [li:k] puerro m.

leer [liə] 1. mirada f (de reojo) con una sonrisa impúdica (or maligna); 2. mirar (de reojo) con una sonrisa impúdica (or maligna) (at acc.).

lees [li:z] pl. heces f/pl., poso m.

lee·ward ['li:wəd] (attr. de, adv. a) sotavento m.

lee·way ['li:wei] ♣ deriva f; fig. atraso m, pérdida f de tiempo; Am. F sobra f de tiempo, libertad f; ♣ make ~ derivar, abatir; fig. make up ~ salir del atraso.

left¹ [left] pret. a. p.p. of leave 2; be ~ quedar(se); be ~ over sobrar.

left² [~] 1. su. izquierda f; pol. izquierda(s) f(pl.); on (or to) the ~ a la izquierda; 2. adj. izquierdo; pol. izquierdista; siniestro (lit.); 3. adv. a (or hacia) la izquierda; '~·hand: ~ drive mot. conducción f a la izquierda; ~ side izquierda f; '~·'hand·ed ☐ zurdo; fig. p. torpe, desmañado; compliment ambiguo, insincero; marriage de la mano izquierda; ⊕ a izquierdas; 'left·ist izquierdista adj. a. su. m/f.

left...: '~·'lug·gage of·fice consigna f; '~·'o·vers pl. sobras f/pl.; '~·'wing pol. izquierdista.

leg [leg] pierna f; pata f of animals, furniture; (support) pie m; pernil m of pork, trousers; caña f of stocking;

(*stage*) etapa *f*, recorrido *m*; F *give a p. a ~ up* ayudar a una p. a subir; F *be on one's last ~s* estar en las últimas; *pull a p.'s ~* tomar el pelo a una p. [cia *f.*]

leg·a·cy ['legǝsi] legado *m*, heren-

le·gal ['li:gǝl] ▢ legal; lícito; jurídico; *v. proceeding*; ~ *adviser* jurisconsulto *m*, abogado *m*; ~ *costs* litisexpensas *f/pl.*; ~ *entity* persona *f* jurídica; **le·gal·i·ty** [li'gæliti] legalidad *f*; **le·gal·i·za·tion** [li:gǝlai-'zeiʃn] legalización *f*; **'le·gal·ize** legalizar.

leg·ate ['legit] legado *m*.

leg·a·tee [legǝ'ti:] legatario (a *f*) *m*.

le·ga·tion [li'geiʃn] legación *f*.

leg·end ['ledʒǝnd] leyenda *f*; **'leg·end·ar·y** legendario.

leg·er·de·main ['ledʒǝdǝ'mein] juego *m* de manos; trapacería *f*.

legged [legd, 'legid] de ... piernas; **leg·gings** ['~z] *pl.* polainas *f/pl.*; **'leg·gy** zanquilargo.

leg·i·bil·i·ty [ledʒi'biliti] legibilidad *f*; **leg·i·ble** ['ledʒǝbl] ▢ legible.

le·gion ['li:dʒǝn] legión *f* (*a. fig.*); **'le·gion·ar·y** legionario *adj. a. su. m.*

leg·is·late ['ledʒisleit] legislar; **leg·is·la·tion** legislación *f*; **'leg·is·la·tive** ▢ legislativo; **'leg·is·la·tor** legislador (-a *f*) *m*; **leg·is·la·ture** ['~tʃǝ] legislatura *f*.

le·git·i·ma·cy [li'dʒitimǝsi] legitimidad *f*; **le'git·i·mate** 1. [~mit] ▢ legítimo; admisible; 2. [~meit] legitimar (*a.* **le'git·i·mize**); **le'git·i·ma·tion** legitimación *f*.

leg·ume ['legju:m] legumbre *f*; **le·gu·mi·nous** leguminoso.

lei·sure ['leʒǝ] 1. ocio *m*, tiempo *m* libre, desocupación *f*; *be at ~* estar desocupado; *at your ~* en sus ratos libres, cuando tenga tiempo; 2. de ocio, desocupado, de pasatiempo; **'lei·sured** desocupado; *class* acomodado; **'lei·sure·ly** 1. *adj.* pausado, lento; 2. *adv.* pausadamente, despacio, con calma.

lem·on ['lemǝn] 1. limón *m*; (*a. ~ tree*) limonero *m*; 2. *attr.* de limón; (*colour*) limonado; **lem·on·ade** [~-'neid] limonada *f*, gaseosa *f* de limón; **'lem·on·'squash** limonada *f* (natural); zumo *m* de limón; **'lem·on·'squeez·er** exprimelimones *m*.

lend [lend] [*irr.*] prestar; *fig.* dar, añadir; ~ *o.s.* to prestarse a; ~*ing*

library biblioteca *f* circulante; **'lend·er** prestador (-a *f*) *m*.

length [leŋθ] largo(r) *m*, longitud *f*; ⚓ eslora *f*; *racing*: cuerpo *m*; duración *f* *of time*; corte *m* *of cloth*; tramo *m* *of track, road etc.*; *at ~* por fin; *at (great) ~* detenidamente, por extenso; *v. full-~*; *go to any ~* no pararse en barras; hacer todo lo posible (to para); *go to great ~s in* extremarse en; *go to the ~ of* llegar al extremo de; **'length·en** alargar (se), prolongar(se); **'length·ways**, **'length·wise** longitudinal(mente); a lo largo.

le·ni·ent ['li:niǝnt] ▢ indulgente, clemente, poco severo; **le·ni·ence**, **le·ni·en·cy** ['~niǝns(i)], **len·i·ty** ['leniti] lenidad *f*; **'len·i·tive** lenitivo *adj. a. su. m.*

lens [lenz] *opt., phot.* lente *f*; *anat.* cristalino *m*; ~ *system* sistema *m* de lentes.

lent¹ [lent] *pret. a. p.p. of lend.*

Lent² [~] cuaresma *f*.

Lent·en ['lentǝn] cuaresmal.

len·til ['lentil] lenteja *f*.

le·o·nine ['li:ǝnain] leonino.

leop·ard ['lepǝd] leopardo *m*.

lep·er ['lepǝ] leproso (a *f*) *m*.

lep·ro·sy ['leprǝsi] lepra *f*; **'lep·rous** leproso. [majestad *f.*]

lese-maj·es·ty ['li:z'mædʒisti] lesa

le·sion ['li:ʒǝn] lesión *f*.

less [les] 1. *adj.* (*size, degree*) menor, inferior; (*quantity*) menos; 2. *adv., prp.* menos; ~ *and* ~ cada vez menos; (*at*) ~ *than* (en) menos que; ~ *than 4* menos de 4; ~ *than you say* menos de lo que dices; *grow* ~ menguar, disminuir(se); *no* ~ (*than*) nada menos (que); *no* ~ *a p. than* no otro que.

...less [lis] sin...

les·see [le'si:] arrendatario (a *f*) *m*.

less·en ['lesn] *v/t.* disminuir, (a)-minorar, reducir; *v/i.* disminuir(se), reducirse, menguar.

less·er ['lesǝ] menor, más pequeño; inferior.

les·son ['lesn] lección *f*; *fig.* escarmiento *m*; ~*s pl.* clases *f/pl.*; *learn one's* ~ *fig.* escarmentar(se); *teach* (or *give*) *a* ~ *dar clase*; dar una lección (*a. fig.*).

les·sor [le'sɔ:] arrendador (-a *f*) *m*.

lest [lest] de miedo que, para que no, no sea que.

let[1] [let] [*irr.*] *v/t.* dejar, permitir (*he let me go* me dejó ir, me permitió ir); *property* alquilar, arrendar; ~ *inf.* = *imperative*: ~ *him come!* ¡que venga!; ~'*s go!* ¡vamos! ~ *alone* no tocar; dejar en paz; sin mencionar, ni mucho menos; F ~ *well alone* por es meneallo; dejar las cosas como están; F ~ *be* dejar en paz; ~ *by* dejar pasar; ~ *down* (dejar) bajar; *tyre* deshinchar; *fig. p.* dejar plantado, faltar a, desilusionar; ~ *a p. down gently* castigar a una p. con poca severidad; ~ *o.s. down by* descolgarse con; ~ *fly* disparar (*at* contra); soltar (palabras duras) (*at* contra); ~ *go* soltar; *property* vender; (*miss, pass*) dejar pasar; F ~ *o.s. go* desfogarse; dejar de cuidarse *in appearance*; F ~ *a p. in for* meter a una p. en; ~ *in*(*to*) dejar entrar (en); *visitor* hacer pasar; ~ *a p. into a secret* revelar un secreto a una p.; ~ *a p. know* hacer saber a una p., avisar a una p.; ~ *loose* soltar; ~ *off gun* disparar; *p.* perdonar, dejar libre; ~ *out* dejar salir; poner en libertad; acompañar a la puerta; soltar; divulgar; (*for hire*) alquilar; *fire* dejar apagarse; *garment* ensanchar; ~ *through* dejar pasar (por); *v/i.* alquilarse (*at, for* en); F ~ *on* dejar saber; revelar el secreto; F ~ *up* moderarse (*on* en); trabajar menos, cesar.

let[2] [~]: *without* ~ *or hindrance* sin estorbo ni obstáculo.

le·thal ['li:θl] □ mortífero; *esp. poison* letal.

le·thar·gic, le·thar·gi·cal [le'θɑ:-dʒik(l)] □ letárgico; **leth·ar·gy** ['leθədʒi] letargo *m* (*a. fig.*).

let·ter ['letə] **1.** carta *f*; letra *f* *of alphabet, typ. a. fig.*; ~*s pl.* (*learning etc.*) letras *f/pl.*; ~ *of credit* carta *f* de crédito; *by* ~ por escrito, por carta; *man of* ~*s* literato *m*; *small* ~ minúscula *f*; *to the* ~ a(l pie de) la letra; **2.** rotular; estampar con letras; '~**-bal·ance** pesacartas *m*; '~**-box** buzón *m*; '~**-case** cartera *f*; '**let·tered** *p.* letrado; rotulado, marcado con letras; '**let·ter-file** carpeta *f*, archivo *m*; '**let·ter-ing** inscripción *f*, letras *f/pl.*

let·ter...: '~**-press** texto *m* impreso; '~**-press** prensa *f* de copiar cartas.

let·ting ['letiŋ] arrendamiento *m*.

let·tuce ['letis] lechuga *f*.

let-up ['letʌp] F calma *f*, tregua *f*, descanso *m*.

leu·k(a)e·mia [lju'ki:miə] leucemia *f*.

Le·vant·ine [li'væntain] levantino *adj. a. su. m* (*a f*).

lev·ee[1] ['levi] besamanos *m*, recepción *f*.

lev·ee[2] [~] *Am.* ribero *m*, dique *m*.

lev·el ['levl] **1.** (*flat place*) llano *m*; llanura *f*; (*instrument, altitude, degree*) nivel *m*; *dead* ~ superficie *f* completamente llana; *fig.* uniformidad *f*, monotonía *f*; *on a* ~ *with* al nivel de (*a. fig.*); a ras de, a flor de; *fig.* parangonable con; *sl. on the* ~ honrado; sin engaño, en serio; **2.** *v/t.* nivelar (*a. surv.*); igualar; allanar; derribar; *site* desmontar; *blow* asestar; *weapon* apuntar; *fig.* dirigir; ~ *with the ground* arrasar; ~ *down* rebajar (al mismo nivel); igualar; ~ *up* levantar (al mismo nivel); igualar; *v/i.*: ~ *at*, ~ *against* apuntar a; ~ *off* nivelarse; ✘ enderezarse; (*prices*) estabilizarse; **3.** raso, llano, plano; a nivel; nivelado; igual; *fig.* juicioso, ecuánime; *dead* ~ completamente a nivel; *my* ~ *best* todo lo que puedo; ~ *crossing* paso *m* a nivel; **4.** *adv.* a nivel; ras con ras; '~-'**head·ed** sensato, juicioso; '**lev·el·(l)ing 1.** nivelación *f etc.*; **2.** nivelador.

le·ver ['li:və] **1.** palanca *f* (*a. fig.*); **2.** apalancar; '**le·ver·age** apalancamiento *m*; *fig.* influencia *f*, ventaja *f*.

lev·er·et ['levərit] lebrato *m*.

le·vi·a·than [li'vaiəθən] leviatán *m*; *fig.* buque *m* enorme.

lev·i·tate ['leviteit] elevar(se) (por medios espiritistas).

Le·vite ['li:vait] levita *m*.

lev·i·ty ['leviti] frivolidad *f*, levedad *f*.

lev·y ['levi] **1.** exacción *f* (de tributos); impuesto *m*; ✘ leva *f*, reclutamiento *m*; **2.** *tax* exigir, recaudar; ✘ reclutar.

lewd [lu:d] □ lascivo, impúdico; '**lewd·ness** lascivia *f*, impudicia *f*.

lex·i·cal ['leksikl] □ léxico.

lex·i·cog·ra·pher [leksi'kɔgrəfə] lexicógrafo *m*; **lex·i·co·graph·i·cal** [~kou'græfikl] □ lexicográfico; **lex·i·cog·ra·phy** [~'kɔgrəfi] lexicografía *f*; **lex·i·con** ['leksikən] léxico *m*.

li·a·bil·i·ty [laiə'biliti] obligación *f*,

compromiso *m*; responsabilidad *f*; riesgo *m*, exposición *f*; tendencia *f*; F desventaja; **†** *liabilities pl.* pasivo *m*, deudas *f/pl.*

li·a·ble ['laiəbl] responsable (*for* de); obligado; expuesto, sujeto, propenso (*to* a); ⁓ *to duty* sujeto a derechos.

li·ai·son [li'eizɔ:ŋ] enlace *m* (*a.* ✗); (*affair*) lío *m*, relaciones *f/pl.* amorosas; ⁓ *officer* (oficial *m* de) enlace *m*.

li·ar ['laiə] embustero (*a f*) *m*, mentiroso (*a f*) *m*.

li·ba·tion [lai'beiʃn] libación *f*.

li·bel ['laibl] **1.** (*written*) libelo *m* (*on* contra); difamación *f*, calumnia *f* (*on* de); **2.** difamar, calumniar; '**li·bel·(l)ous** ☐ difamatorio, calumnioso.

lib·er·al ['libərəl] **1.** ☐ liberal (*a. pol.*); generoso; tolerante; abundante; **2.** liberal *m/f*; '**lib·er·al·ism** liberalismo *m*; **lib·er·al·i·ty** [⁓'ræliti] liberalidad *f*.

lib·er·ate ['libəreit] libertar, librar (*from* de); '**lib·er·a·tion** liberación *f*; '**lib·er·a·tor** libertador (-a *f*) *m*.

lib·er·tin·age ['libətinidʒ] libertinaje *m*; **lib·er·tine** ['libətain] libertino.

lib·er·ty ['libəti] libertad *f*; ♣ licencia *f*; *take liberties* permitirse (*or* tomar) libertades; *be at* ⁓ estar en libertad; *be at* ⁓ *to do* tener permiso para (*or* derecho de) hacer; *set at* ⁓ poner en libertad. [noso.)

li·bid·i·nous [li'bidinəs] ☐ libidi-)

li·brar·i·an [lai'breəriən] bibliotecario (*a f*) *m*; **li·brar·y** ['laibrəri] biblioteca *f*; (*esp. private*) librería *f*.

li·bret·tist [li'bretist] libretista *m/f*.

li·bret·to [li'bretou] libreto *m*.

Lib·y·an ['libiən] **1.** libio (*a f*) *m*; **2.** *p.* libio; líbico.

lice [lais] *pl. of louse*.

li·cence ['laisəns] licencia *f*; permiso *m*; autorización *f*; título *m*; cédula *f*; (*excess*) desenfreno *m*.

li·cense [⁓] **1.** *v. licence*; **2.** licenciar; autorizar; dar licencia (*or* cédula *or* privilegio) a; **li·cen·see** [⁓'si:] concesionario (*a f*) *m*; persona *f* que obtiene licencia.

li·cen·ti·ate [lai'senʃiit] licenciado (*a f*) *m*.

li·cen·tious [lai'senʃəs] ☐ licencioso, disoluto.

li·chen ['laiken] liquen *m*.

lich·gate ['litʃgeit] puerta *f* de cementerio.

lick [lik] **1.** lamedura *f*; lamida *f* *S.Am.*; lengüetada *f*; F velocidad *f*; **2.** lamer; F vencer; F zurrar; ⁓ *the dust* morder el polvo; F ⁓ *into shape* dar forma a; adiestrar; habilitar; ⁓ *one's lips* relamerse; '**lick·ing** lamedura *f*; F zurra *f*; '**lick·spit·tle** lameculos *m*.

lic·o·rice ['likəris] regaliz *m*.

lid [lid] tapa(dera) *f*; cobertera *f* of pan etc.; *anat.* párpado *m*; *sl.* (*hat*) techo *m*; F *that's put the* ⁓ *on it* eso es ⌐el colmo; se acabó.

lie¹ [lai] **1.** mentira *f*; *give the* ⁓ *to* dar el mentís a; desmentir; *tell a* ⁓ = **2.** mentir.

lie² [⁓] **1.** disposición *f*; ⁓ *of the land* configuración *f* del terreno; *fig.* estado *m* de las cosas; **2.** [*irr.*] echarse, acostarse; estar echado, estar tumbado; descansar; estar (situado), hallarse; (*stretch*) extenderse; yacer, estar enterrado *in grave*; † dormir; ⚖ ser admisible; *about* estar esparcido(s); F holgazanear; ⁓ *back* recostarse; ⁓ *down* echarse, acostarse, tenderse; F ⁓ *down under it, take it lying down* tragarlo, soportarlo sin chistar; ⁓ *in* (*prp.*) consistir en; depender de; (*adv.*) estar de parto; ⁓ *in wait for* acechar; F ⁓ *low* agacharse, no chistar; ⁓ *over* aplazarse, quedar en suspenso; ⚓ ⁓ *to* estar (*or* ponerse) a la capa; ⁓ *under* estar bajo (el peso de); estar sometido (*or* expuesto) a; ⁓ *up* descansar; guardar cama; ⚓ estar amarrado; ⁓ *with* † dormir con; *fig.* corresponder a; *it* ⁓*s with you* la responsabilidad recae sobre Vd.

lie·a·bed ['laiəbed] dormilón (-a *f*) *m*.

lief [li:f] de buena gana; '**lief·er:** *I would* ⁓ *inf.* preferiría *inf.*

liege [li:dʒ] *hist.* **1.** feudatario; **2.** (*a.* '⁓-**man** ['⁓mæn]) vasallo *m*; (*a.* ⁓ *lord*) señor *m* feudal.

li·en ['li:ən] derecho *m* de retención.

lieu [lju:]: *in* ⁓ *of* en lugar de.

lieu·ten·ant [lef'tenənt, ⚓ *a. Am.* lu:'tenənt] lugarteniente *m*; ✗ teniente *m*; ⚓ teniente *m* de navío; ✗ *second* ⁓ alférez *m*; ⚓ *sub-*⁓ alférez *m* de navío; '⁓-**colo·nel** teniente coronel *m*; '⁓-**com'mand·er**

capitán m de corbeta f; '~-'**gen·er-al** teniente general m.

life [laif] (pl. lives) vida f; (modo m de) vivir m; ser m, existencia f; vivacidad f, animación f; (period of validity) vigencia f; be the ~ and soul of the party ser el alma de la fiesta; for ~ de por vida; for one's ~, for dear ~ para salvarse la vida; a más no poder; F for the ~ of me así me maten; from ~ del natural; never in my ~ en mi vida; F not on your ~! ¡ni hablar!; en absoluto; see ~ ver mundo; take one's ~ in one's hands jugarse la vida; this is the ~! ¡cómo la mamamos!, ¡esto es jauja!; to the ~ al vivo; ~ sentence condena f a perpetuidad; '~-**an·nu·i·ty** vitalicio m; '~-**as·sur·ance** seguro m sobre la vida; '~-**belt** (cinturón m) salvavidas m; '~-**blood** sangre f vital; fig. alma f, nervio m, sustento m; '~-**boat** lancha f de socorro; (ship's) bote m salvavidas, bote m de salvamento; '~-**buoy** guindola f; '~-**guard** ✕ guardia m de corps; '~-**in·ter·est** usufructo m (vitalicio) (in de); '~-**'jack·et** chaleco m salvavidas; '~-**less** □ sin vida, muerto; exánime; fig. desanimado; flojo; deslucido; '~-**less·ness** falta f de vida; inercia f; desánimo m etc.; '~-**like** natural; from ~ del natural; '~-**line** cuerda f salvavidas; '~-**long** de toda la vida; '~-**pre·serv·er** cachiporra f; '~-**'sav·ing** (de) salvamento m; '~-**'size** de tamaño natural; '~-**time** (transcurso m de la) vida f.

lift [lift] 1. alzamiento m; esfuerzo m para levantar, empuje m para arriba; ayuda f (para levantar); (passenger) ascensor m, elevador m S.Am.; (cargo) montacargas m; F viaje m en coche ajeno; ✕ sustentación f; ⊕ altura f de elevación; ⊕ carrera f de valve; fig. estímulo m; give a p. a ~ ayudar a una p.; llevar a una p. gratis en coche. 2. v/t. levantar, alzar, elevar (a. ~ up); transportar (en avión); restrictions suprimir; hat quitarse; sl. ratear, robar; F plagiar; v/i. levantarse; (clouds etc.) disiparse; '~-**at·tend·ant** ascensorista m/f; '**lift·ing** 1. levantamiento m; 2. ascensional, levantador.

lig·a·ment ['ligəmənt] ligamento m.

lig·a·ture ['ligətʃuə] 1. ligadura f (a. ♪, ♫); typ. ligado m; 2. ligar.

light[1] [lait] 1. luz f (a. fig. a. window); lumbre f; fuego m for cigarette etc.; ⊕ faro m; fig. aspecto m, punto m de vista; ~s pl. luces f/pl., conocimientos m/pl.; according to his ~s según Dios le da a entender; against the ~ al trasluz; at first ~ al rayar el día; in the ~ of a la luz de (a. fig.); bring (come) to ~ sacar (salir) a luz, descubrir(se); cast (or shed or throw) ~ on aclarar; F give a ~ to dar fuego a; put a ~ to encender; see the ~ ver la luz; caer en la cuenta; convertirse; ~ bulb bombilla f; ~ wave onda f luminosa; 2. claro; hair rubio; skin blanco; 3. [irr.] v/t. (ignite) encender; alumbrar, iluminar (a. ~ up); v/i. (mst ~ up) encenderse; alumbrarse, iluminarse; brillar; Am. sl. ~ into atacar; Am. sl. ~ out largarse.

light[2] [~] 1. adj. □ a. adv. ligero (a. fig.); (slight) leve; (bearable) llevadero; (unencumbered) desembarazado; (fickle, wanton) liviano; (cheerful) alegre; reading ameno, de puro entretenimiento; ⊕ en lastre; ⚓ vacío; ~ opera opereta f, zarzuela f; make ~ of no dar importancia a; 2.: ~ (up)on dar con, tropezar con; (bird) posarse en.

light·en[1] ['laitn] iluminar(se); clarear; relampaguear.

light·en[2] [~] load etc. aligerar(se); heart alegrar(se).

light·er[1] ['laitə] encendedor m; (petrol-) mechero m.

light·er[2] [~] ⊕ gabarra f, barcaza f.

light...: '~-**'fin·gered** largo de uñas; '~-**fit·ting** guarnición f (or artefacto m) del alumbrado; '~-**'head·ed** mareado; ligero de cascos; ✣ delirante; '~-**'heart·ed** □ alegre (de corazón); poco serio; '~-**house** faro m; '~-(**house**)-**keep·er** torrero m.

light·ing ['laitiŋ] alumbrado m; iluminación f; encendido m; ~ engineering luminotecnia f; ✦ ~ point tomacorriente m para lámpara; ~-up time hora f de encender los faros.

light·ly ['laitli] adv. ligeramente; levemente; frivolamente; sin pensarlo bien; '**light·ness** ligereza f; levedad f; agilidad f; claridad f, luminosidad f.

light·ning ['laitniŋ] relámpago m, rayo m (a. ~-flash); relampagueo m;

attr. relámpago, relampagueante; '~-con·duc·tor, '~-rod pararrayos *m.*

lights [laits] *pl.* bofes *m/pl.*, livianos *m/pl.*

light·ship ['laitʃip] buque *m* faro.

light-weight ['laitweit] persona *f* de poco peso (*a. fig.*); *boxing*: peso *m* ligero.

light-year ['lait'jə:] año *m* luz.

lig·ne·ous ['ligniəs] leñoso; **lig·nite** ['lignait] lignito *m*; **lig·num vi·tae** ['lignəm 'vaiti:] palo *m* santo; (*tree*) guayacán *m*.

like [laik] **1.** *adj.* parecido (a), semejante (a); igual; propio de, característico a; como; ~..., ~.... tal..., tal...; ~ *father*, ~ *son* tal palo, tal astilla; *in* ~ *cases* en casos parecidos; *he has a house* ~ *mine* tiene una casa semejante a la mía; *eyes* ~ *stars* ojos como estrellas; *be* ~ parecerse a; *that's just* ~ *him* eso es muy de él; † *he is* ~ *to die* es probable que muera; *feel* ~ *ger.* tener ganas de *inf.*; *something* ~ algo así como; *that's more* ~ *it!* eso (sí que) se llama hablar; eso sí que es mejor; *what is he* ~? ¿cómo es?; **2.** *adv. or prp.* como; del mismo modo (que); igual (que); tal como; ~ *a hero* como un héroe; *nothing* ~ ni con mucho; **3.** *conj.* F como, del mismo modo que; F ~ *we used to* (*do*) como hacíamos; **4.** *su.* semejante *m/f*, semejanza *f*; ~*s pl.* simpatías *f/pl.*, gustos *m/pl.*; *and the* ~, F *and such* ~ y otros por el estilo; F *the* ~(*s*) *of him* otro(s) como él; **5.** *vb.* gustar; querer; estar aficionado a; *I* ~ *bananas* me gustan los plátanos; *I don't* ~ *bull-fighting* no estoy aficionado a los toros; *how do you* ~ *Madrid?* ¿qué te parece Madrid?; *as you* ~ como quieras, como gustes; *I should* ~ *time* desearía tiempo; *I should* ~ *to know* quisiera saber; *would you* ~ *to go to Madrid?* ¿te gustaría ir a Madrid?

lik(e)·a·ble ['laikəbl] simpático.

like·li·hood['laiklihud] probabilidad *f*; '**like·ly 1.** *adj.* probable; verosímil; prometedor; *he is* ~ *to die* es probable que muera; *not* ~! ¡ni hablar!; **2.** *adv.* probablemente.

like...: '~-'**mind·ed** animado por los mismos sentimientos; '**lik·en** com-

parar (*to con*), asemejar (*to a*); '**like·ness** parecido *m*, semejanza *f*; imagen *f*; (*portrait*) retrato *m*; *family* ~ aire *m* de familia; '**like·wise** asimismo, igualmente; además; lo mismo.

lik·ing ['laikiŋ] gusto *m* (*for* por); afición *f* (*for* a); simpatía *f* (*for p.* hacia), cariño *m* (*for p.* a); *take a* ~ *to* tomar gusto a, cobrar afición a; *p.* tomar cariño a; *to one's* ~ del gusto de uno.

li·lac ['lailək] (de color de) lila *f*.

lilt [lilt] (canción *f* alegre con) ritmo *m* marcado.

lil·y ['lili] lirio *m*; azucena *f*; ~ *of the valley* muguete *m*, lirio *m* de los valles.

limb[1] [lim] miembro *m* *of body*; rama *f* *of tree*; F muchacho (*a f*) *m* travieso(a); F *be out on a* ~ estar en un atolladero.

limb[2] [~] *ast.*, ✿ limbo *m*.

lim·ber[1] ['limbə] **1.** ágil, flexible; **2.** hacer flexible; ~ *up* agilitarse.

lim·ber[2] [~] **1.** ✕ armón *m* (de artillería); **2.** (*a.* ~ *up*) colocar el armón.

lim·bo ['limbou] limbo *m*.

lime[1] [laim] **1.** cal *f*; (*a. bird-*~) liga *f*; **2.** encalar; untar con liga.

lime[2] [~] ✿ (*a.* ~ *tree*) tilo *m*.

lime[3] [~] ✿ lima *f*; (*tree*) limero *m*; '~-**juice** jugo *m* de lima.

lime...: '~-**kiln** horno *m* de cal; '~-**light** luz *f* de calcio; *thea.* luz *f* del proyector; *be in the* ~ estar a la vista del público; '~-**stone** (piedra *f*) caliza *f*.

lim·er·ick ['limərik] *especie de* quintilla *f* jocosa.

lim·it ['limit] **1.** límite *m*, confín *m*; *know no* ~*s* ser infinito; F *that's the* ~! ¡es el colmo!, ¡no faltaba más!; *to the* ~ hasta no más; **2.** limitar (*to* a), restringir; **lim·i·ta·tion** limitación *f*, restricción *f*; ⚖ prescripción *f*; '**lim·it·ed** limitado, restringido; ~ (*liability*) *company* sociedad *f* anónima, sociedad *f* (de responsabilidad) limitada; *Am.* 🚂 ~ (*express train*) tren *m* de composición limitada; '**lim·it·less** ☐ ilimitado.

limn [lim] † pintar, ornar.

lim·ou·sine ['limuzi:n] limousine *f*, limusina *f*.

limp[1] [limp] **1.** cojera *f*; **2.** cojear.

limp² [～] ☐ flojo, lacio; flexible.
lim·pet ['limpit] lapa *f; fig.* persona *f* tenaz.
lim·pid ['limpid] ☐ límpido, cristalino, transparente; **lim'pid·i·ty**, **'lim·pid·ness** limpidez *f*, claridad *f*.
lim·y ['laimi] calizo; pegajoso.
linch·pin ['lintʃpin] pezonera *f*.
lin·den ['lindən] tilo *m (a. ～ tree).*
line¹ [lain] **1.** línea *f*; cuerda *f*; ♱ cordel *m; fishing:* sedal *m*; ♱ ramo *m*, género *m*; ⚓ vía *f; typ.* renglón *m; poet.* verso *m;* (*row*) hilera *f;* (*wrinkle*) arruga *f;* F especialidad *f;* F profesión *f;* F plan *m*, norma *f*; ～*s* pl. principios *m/pl.*, normas *f/pl.;* plan *m; thea.* papel *m;* ✕ líneas *f/pl.;* ♱ formas *f/pl.;* ～ *of battle* línea *f* de batalla; *ship of the* ～ navío *m* de línea; F *hard* ～*s* mala suerte *f; draw the* ～ no pasar más allá (*at* de); *drop a* ～ poner unas letras (*to* a); *teleph.* hold the ～! ¡un moment(it)o!, ¡no cuelgue Vd.!; *in* ～ *with* conforme a, de acuerdo con; *that is not in my* ～ eso no es de mi especialidad; *fall into* ～ *with* conformarse con; *on the* ～*s of* conforme a, a tenor de; *sl. shoot a* ～ darse bombo; *take a ... line* adoptar una actitud ...; **2.** *v/t.* rayar; linear; *face etc.* arrugar; alinear (*a. ～ up*); ～ *the streets* ocupar las aceras; *v/i.*: ～ *up* alinearse; ponerse en fila; hacer cola; formar(se).
line² [～] *clothes* forrar; ⊕ revestir; *brakes* guarnecer; F ～ *one's pockets* ponerse las botas.
lin·e·age ['liniidʒ] linaje *m*; **lin·e·al** ['liniəl] ☐ lineal; en línea recta; **lin·e·a·ment** ['～iəmənt] lineamento *m*; **lin·e·ar** ['～iə] lineal; de longitud.
lin·en ['linin] **1.** lino *m*, hilo *m;* (*a piece of un*) lienzo *m;* (*sheets, underclothes etc.*) ropa *f* blanca; *dirty* ～ ropa *f* sucia; **2.** de lino; '～**-clos·et**, '～**-cup·board** armario *m* para ropa blanca; '～**-drap·er** lencero (a *f*) *m;* ～'*s* (*shop*) lencería *f*.
lin·er ['lainə] ♱ vapor *m* de línea, transatlántico *m*; **lines·man** ['lainzmən] *sport:* juez *m* de línea; ⚓ guardavía *m;* ⚡ celador *m;* '**line-'up** alineación *f*, formación *f*.

ling¹ [liŋ] *ichth. approx.* abadejo *m* largo.
ling² [～] ♣ *approx.* brezo *m*.
lin·ger ['liŋgə] (*a. ～ on*) tardar (en marcharse [*or* morirse]); quedarse; persistir; ～ *over* hacer (*or* comer) despacio; dilatarse en; reflexionar; '**lin·ger·ing** ☐ prolongado, dilatado, lento, persistente.
lin·ge·rie ['lɛ̃:nʒəri:] ropa *f* blanca (*or interior*) de mujer, lencería *f*.
lin·go ['liŋgou] F lengua *f*, jerga *f*, galimatías *m*.
lin·guist ['liŋgwist] poligloto (a *f*) *m;* **lin'guis·tic** ☐ lingüístico; **lin·'guis·tics** lingüística *f*.
lin·i·ment ['linimənt] linimento *m*.
lin·ing ['lainiŋ] forro *m of clothes;* ⊕ revestimiento *m;* guarnición *f of brakes.*
link¹ [liŋk] **1.** eslabón *m; fig.* enlace *m;* ⊕ varilla *f*, corredera *f;* **2.** eslabonar(se), enlazarse (*a. ～ up*).
link² [～] *hist.* hacha *f* de viento.
link·age ['liŋkidʒ] enlace *m*, eslabonamiento *m;* ⊕ varillaje *m*.
links [liŋks] *pl.* campo *m (or terreno m)* de golf.
lin·net ['linit] pardillo *m* común.
li·no ['lainou] F, **li·no·le·um** [li-'nouljəm] linóleo *m*.
lin·o·type ['lainoutaip] linotipia *f*.
lin·seed ['linsi:d] linaza *f;* ～ *oil* aceite *m* de linaza.
lint [lint] hilas *f/pl.*
lin·tel ['lintl] dintel *m*.
li·on ['laiən] león *m (a. astr. a. fig.); fig.* celebridad *f;* ～*'s share* parte *f* del león; *put one's head in the* ～*'s mouth* meterse en la boca del lobo; **'li·on·ess** leona *f;* **'li·on·ize** tratar como a una celebridad.
lip [lip] labio *m (a. fig.,* ✿*);* pico *m of jug;* borde *m of cup; sl.* insolencia *f; hang on a p.'s* ～*s* estar pendiente de las palabras de una p.; *keep a stiff upper* ～ no inmutarse; '～**-serv·ice** jarabe *m* de pico; '～**-stick** rojo *m* de labios, lápiz *m* labial.
liq·ue·fac·tion [likwi'fækʃn] licuefacción *f;* **liq·ue·fi·a·ble** ['～faiəbl] liquidable; **liq·ue·fy** ['～fai] liqui-
li·queur [li'kjuə] licor *m.* [dar(se).⎬
liq·uid ['likwid] **1.** líquido *m; gr.* líquida *f;* **2.** ☐ líquido; *fig.* límpido; ♱ realizable; ♱ ～ *assets* activo *m* líquido.

liq·ui·date ['likwideit] *all senses*: liquidar(se); **liq·ui·da·tion** liquidación *f*; **'liq·ui·da·tor** liquidador (-a *f*) *m*.

liq·uor ['likə] licor *m*; bebida *f* alcohólica; *in* ~ borracho.

liq·uo·rice ['likəris] regaliz *m*.

lisp [lisp] **1.** ceceo *m*; balbuceo *m as of child*; **2.** cecear; balbucear.

lis·som(e) ['lisəm] ágil, flexible.

list[1] [list] **1.** lista *f*, relación *f*; (*registration*) matrícula *f*; escalafón *m of officials*; orillo *m*, tira *f of cloth*; **2.** poner en una lista; hacer una lista de; inscribir; *it is not* ~*ed* no consta (en la lista).

list[2] [⌣] ⚓ **1.** escora *f*; **2.** escorar.

list[3] [⌣] † escuchar.

lis·ten ['lisn] escuchar, oír (*to acc.*); prestar atención, dar oídos, atender (*to a*); ~ *in* (*to*) *radio*: escuchar la radio; escuchar por radio; estar a la escucha (de); (*eavesdrop*) escuchar a hurtadillas; **'lis·ten·er** oyente *m/f*; *radio*: (*a.* **'lis·ten·er-'in**) radioescucha *m/f*, radioyente *m/f*.

lis·ten·ing ['lisniŋ] escucha *f*; *attr.* de escucha; **'~-post** puesto *m* de escucha. [tico, indiferente.\

list·less ['listlis] □ lánguido, apá-\

lists [lists] *pl. hist.* liza *f*.

lit [lit] *pret. a. p.p. of light*[1] *3*; ~ *up sl.* achispado.

lit·a·ny ['litəni] letanía *f*.

lit·er·a·cy ['litərəsi] capacidad *f* de leer y escribir.

lit·er·al ['litərəl] □ literal.

lit·er·ar·y ['litərəri] □ literario; **lit·er·ate** ['litərit] que sabe leer y escribir; **lit·e·ra·ti** [litə'rɑ:ti] *pl.* literatos *m/pl.*; **lit·e·ra·ture** ['litəritʃə] literatura *f*; F impresos *m/pl.*, folletos *m/pl*.

lithe(·some) ['laið(səm)] ágil, esbelto, flexible.

lith·o·graph ['liθəgrɑ:f] **1.** litografía *f*; **2.** litografiar; **li·thog·ra·pher** [li'θɔgrəfə] litógrafo *m*; **lith·o·graph·ic** [liθə'græfik] litográfico; **li·thog·ra·phy** [li'θɔgrəfi] litografía *f*.

Lith·u·a·ni·an [liθju'einjən] lituano *adj. a. su. m* (a *f*).

lit·i·gant ['litigənt] litigante *adj. a. su. m/f*; **lit·i·gate** ['~geit] litigar; **lit·i·ga·tion** litigio *m*, litigación *f*; **li·ti·gious** [li'tidʒəs] □ litigioso.

lit·mus ['litməs] tornasol *m*.

li·tre ['li:tə] litro *m*.

lit·ter ['litə] **1.** litera *f*; ⚕ camilla *f*; lecho *m*, cama *f* de paja *for animals*; camada *f of young animals*; (cosas *f/pl*. esparcidas en) desorden *m*, revoltillo *m*; (*rubbish*) desperdicios *m/pl*., basura *f*; **2.** poner en desorden; esparcir (cosas por); dar cama de paja; (*give birth*) parir.

lit·tle ['litl] **1.** *adj.* pequeño; chico; menudo; poco; escaso; (*mean*) mezquino; ~ *money* poco dinero; *no* ~ *money* mucho dinero; *a* ~ *money* un poco de dinero; *a* ~ *house* una casa pequeña, una casita; *the* ~ *ones* los pequeños, los chiquillos, la gente menuda; *his* ~ *ways* sus cos(it)as; ~ *people* hadas *f/pl*.; **2.** *adv.* poco; *a* ~ *better* un poco mejor, algo mejor; ~ *does he know that* no tiene la menor idea de que; *not a* ~ *surprised* muy sorprendido; **3.** *su.* poco; *he knows* ~ sabe poco; ~ *he knows!* ¡maldito lo que él sabe!; *a* ~ un poco; ~ *by* ~ poco a poco; *for a* ~ (por *or* durante) un rato; *in* ~ en pequeño; *make* ~ *of* sacar poco en claro de; *not a* ~ mucho; **'lit·tle·ness** pequeñez *f*; poquedad *f*; mezquindad *f*.

lit·to·ral ['litərəl] litoral *adj. a. su. m*.

li·tur·gi·cal [li'tə:dʒikl] litúrgico.

lit·ur·gy ['litədʒi] liturgia *f*.

liv·a·ble ['livəbl] *life* llevadero *f* habitable; F (*mst* **'~-with**) *p.* tratable.

live 1. [liv] *v/i.* vivir (*by, off, on* de); *long* ~*!* ¡viva(n)!; ~ *high* (*or well*) darse buena vida; ~ *in* vivir en, habitar; estar interno; ~ *on* seguir viviendo; ~ *together* convivir; ~ *to see* (vivir bastante para) ver; presenciar; ~ *up to promise* cumplir; *standard* vivir (*or* ser) en conformidad con; ~ *up to one's income* gastarse toda la renta; ~ *within one's means* vivir con arreglo a los ingresos; *v/t. life* llevar; *experience* vivir; ~ *down* lograr borrar; ~ *out* vivir hasta el fin de; *life* pasar el resto de; **2.** [laiv] vivo; ardiente, encendido; *issue etc.* de actualidad; ⚡ con corriente; ✗ cargado; ~ *coal* ascua *f*; ~ *weight* peso *m* en vivo; *sl.* ~ *wire* polvorilla *m/f*; **'live·a·ble** *v. livable*; **live·li·hood** ['laivlihud] vida *f*, sustento *m*; **live·li·ness**

['‿linis] viveza *f*, vivacidad *f*; animación *f*; **live·long** ['livlɔŋ] *lit.* duradero; *all the* ~ *day* todo el santo día; **live·ly** ['laivli] vivo, vivaz; animado, bullicioso; alegre. **liv·er¹** ['livə]: *fast* ~ calavera *m*; *good* ~ goloso *m*.

liv·er² [‿] hígado *m*.

liv·er·y ['livəri] librea *f*; *poet.* vestiduras *f/pl.*; pensión *f* (*or* alquiler *m*) de caballos; ~ *company* gremio *m de la Ciudad de Londres*; ~ *stable* caballeriza *f* (*or* cochera *f*) de alquiler.

lives [laivz] *pl. of* life¹; **'live·stock** ganado *m*, ganadería *f*.

liv·id ['livid] lívido; F furioso.

liv·ing ['liviŋ] **1.** vivo, viviente; vital; ~ *conditions* condiciones *f/pl.* de vida; *in* ~ *memory* de que hay memoria; *que se recuerde*; ~ *wage* jornal *m* suficiente para 'vivir'; **2.** vida *f*; sustento *m*; modo *m* de vivir; *eccl.* beneficio *m*; *the* ~ los vivientes; *earn* (*or* make) *a* ~ ganarse la vida; **'~-room** sala *f* de estar, living *m*.

liz·ard ['lizəd] lagarto *m*.

lla·ma ['lɑːmə] llama *f*.

lo [lou] *mst* ~ *and behold!* ¡he aquí!, ¡mirad!

loach [loutʃ] locha *f*.

load [loud] **1.** carga *f* (*a. fig.*, ⊕, ♂); peso *m*; F ~*s pl.* gran cantidad *f*, montones *m/pl.*; ~ *test* prueba *f* de (*or* en) carga; **2.** *v/t.* cargar (*with* con, de); (*oppress*) agobiar (*with* con, de); (*favour*) colmar (*with* de); ~*ed question* intencionado; *dice* cargados; *v/i.* (*a.* ~ *up*) cargar(se); tomar carga; **'load·er** cargador *m*; **'load·ing 1.** cargamento *m*, carga *f*; **2.** de carga; cargador; **'load-line** línea *f* de (flotación con) carga; **'load·stone** piedra *f* imán.

loaf¹ [louf] (*pl. loaves*) pan *m*; (*large*) hogaza *f*; pilón *m of sugar*.

loaf² [‿] F haraganear, gandulear.

loaf·er ['loufə] haragán (-a *f*) *m*, gandul (-a *f*) *m*; (*street-*) azotacalles *m/f*.

loam [loum] marga *f*; **'loam·y** margoso.

loan [loun] **1.** préstamo *m*; (*public*) empréstito *m*; *on* ~ prestado; *ask for the* ~ *of* pedir prestado *acc.*; **2.** *mst Am.* prestar.

loath [louθ] poco dispuesto (*to* a); *be* ~ *for a p. to* no querer que una p. *subj.*; *nothing* ~ de buena gana; **loathe** [louð] abominar, detestar, aborrecer; *I* ~ *cheese* me da asco el queso; **loath·ing** ['‿ðiŋ] asco *m*, detestación *f*, repugnancia *f*; **loathsome** ['‿ðsəm] asqueroso, repugnante, nauseabundo.

loaves [louvz] *pl. of* loaf¹.

lob [lɔb] *tennis:* **1.** voleo *m* alto; **2.** volear por alto.

lob·by ['lɔbi] **1.** vestíbulo *m*; pasillo *m*; antecámara *f*; *Am. parl.* camarilla *f* de cabilderos; **2.** *parl.* cabildear; **'lob·by·ist** *parl.* cabildero *m*.

lobe [loub] *anat.*, ♀ lóbulo *m*.

lob·ster ['lɔbstə] langosta *f*; bogavante *m*.

lo·cal ['loukəl] **1.** □ local; vecinal; *he's a* ~ *man* es de aquí; *teleph.* ~ *call* llamada *f* local; ~ *colour* color *m* local; ~ *government* administración *f* local; **2.** 🚃 (*a.* ~ *train*) tren *m* ómnibus (*or* suburbano); F *the* ~ la taberna *f*; F ~*s pl.* vecindario *m*; **lo·cale** [lou'kɑːl] lugar *m*; escenario *m* (de acontecimientos); **lo·cal·i·ty** [‿'kæliti] localidad *f*; situación *f*; **lo·cal·ize** ['‿kəlaiz] localizar.

lo·cate [lou'keit] situar; colocar; localizar, hallar; *be* ~*d* estar situado, hallarse; **lo·ca·tion** localidad *f*; situación *f*; colocación *f*; ubicación *f*; localización *f*; *film:* rodaje *m* fuera del estudio.

loch [lɔx] *Scot.* lago *m*; ría *f*.

lock¹ [lɔk] **1.** cerradura *f*; traba *f*; retén *m*; (*wrestling a.* ⚔) llave *f*; esclusa *f on canal etc.*; F ~, *stock and barrel* por completo; *under* ~ *and key* bajo llave; **2.** *v/t.* cerrar con llave; encerrar; ⊕ trabar, enclavar; ~ *in* encerrar; ~ *out* cerrar la puerta a; ~ *up* encerrar; encarcelar; *capital* inmovilizar; *v/i.* cerrarse con llave; ⊕ trabarse; ~ *up* echar la llave.

lock² [‿] mechón *m*; guedeja *f*; bucle *m*; ~*s pl.* cabellos *m/pl.*

lock·er ['lɔkə] armario *m* (particular); cajón *m* cerrado con llave; **lock·et** ['‿it] medallón *m*, guardapelo *m*.

lock...: '~-'**gate** puerta *f* de esclusa; '~-**jaw** trismo *m*; '~-**keep·er** esclusero *m*; '~·nut contratuerca *f*; '~·'out cierre *m*, paro *m* voluntario de patronos; '~·smith cerrajero *m*; '~·stitch punto *m* de cadeneta; '~·up 1. cierre *m*; cárcel *f*; 2. con cerradura; ~ *garage* jaula *f*.

lo·co ['loukou] *Am. sl.* loco.

lo·co·mo·tion [loukə'mouʃn] locomoción *f*; lo·co·mo·tive ['~·tiv] 1. locomotora *f*; 2. locomotor.

lo·cum (te·nens) ['loukəm ('tenənz)] interino (a *f*) *m*.

lo·cust ['loukəst] langosta *f* (a. *fig.*); ♉ (a. ~ *tree*) acacia *f* falsa, algarrobo *m*.

lo·cu·tion [lou'kju:ʃn] locución *f*.

lode [loud] filón *m*; '~·star estrella *f* polar; *fig.* norte *m*; '~·stone piedra *f* imán.

lodge [lɔdʒ] 1. casita *f*; casa *f* de campo; casa *f* de guarda; (*porter's*) portería *f*; (*masonic*) logia *f*; 2. *v/t.* alojar, hospedar; colocar, depositar; introducir; *complaint* formular; *v/i.* alojarse; hospedarse; ir a parar; fijarse; 'lodg(e)·ment alojamiento *m*; depósito *m*; ✗ posición *f* ganada; 'lodg·er huésped (-a *f*) *m*; 'lodg·ing alojamiento *m*, hospedaje *m*; (a. ~s *pl.*) habitación *f*, aposento *m*; (*without board*) cobijo *m*; 'lodg·ing-house casa *f* de huéspedes.

loft [lɔft] desván *m*; pajar *m* *for straw*; *eccl.* galería *f*; 'loft·i·ness ['~inis] altura *f*; eminencia *f*; nobleza *f*; altanería *f*; 'loft·y □ alto, elevado; eminente; noble; sublime; altanero.

log [lɔg] 1. leño *m*, tronco *m*, troza *f*; ♣ corredera *f*; = ~-*book*; *v. sleep*; 2. cortar (y transportar) leños; apuntar, registrar.

log·a·rithm ['lɔgəriθm] logaritmo *m*.

log...: '~-book ♣ cuaderno *m* de bitácora, diario *m* de navegación; ✈ libro *m* de vuelo(s); ⊕ cuaderno *m* de trabajo; '~-cab·in cabaña *f* de madera; log·ger·head ['lɔgəhed]: *be at* ~s estar de pique; 'log·ging explotación *f* forestal; transporte *m* de leños.

log·ic ['lɔdʒik] lógica *f*; 'log·i·cal □ lógico; lo·gi·cian [lɔ'dʒiʃən] lógico (a *f*) *m*; lo·gis·tic [lɔ'dʒistik] logístico; ~s logística *f*.

log·roll·ing ['lɔgrouliŋ] F toma y daca *m*; sistema *m* de bombos

mutuos; *Am. pol.* trueque *m* de favores políticos.

loin [lɔin] ijada *f*; lomo *m* (a. *of meat*); *gird up one's* ~s *fig.* apercibirse para la lucha; '~·cloth taparrabo *m*.

loi·ter ['lɔitə] holgazanear, perder el tiempo; rezagarse; vagar; 'loi·ter·er holgazán (-a *f*) *m*; vago (a *f*) *m*; rezagado (a *f*) *m*.

loll [lɔl] repantigarse (a. ~ *about*); apoyarse con indolencia (*against*, *on* en); (*tongue*) colgar hacia fuera.

lol·li·pop ['lɔlipɔp] F gilda *f*.

lol·lop ['lɔləp] F correr (*or* moverse) torpemente, arrastrar los pies.

lol·ly ['lɔli] *sl.* parné *m*.

lol·ly-ice ['lɔli'ais] F polo *m*.

Lom·bard ['lɔmbəd] lombardo *adj. a. su. m* (a *f*).

Lon·don ['lʌndən] *adj.* londinense; 'Lon·don·er londinense *m/f*.

lone [loun] solo, solitario; soltero; aislado; 'lone·li·ness soledad *f*; 'lone·ly, lone·some ['~səm] solitario, solo; aislado, remoto.

long[1] [lɔŋ] 1. *adj.* largo; extenso; prolongado; F alto; *it is 4 feet* ~ tiene 4 pies de largo; *be* ~ *in ger.* tardar en *inf.*; ✝ *at* ~ *date* a largo plazo; *in the* ~ *run* a la larga; ~ *wave radio:* (de) onda *f* larga; *it is a* ~ *way (away, off)* está muy lejos, dista mucho; 2. *su.* largo (*or* mucho) tiempo *m*; *the* ~ *and the short of it is (that)* en resumidas cuentas; *before* ~ en breve, dentro de poco; *for* ~ largo (*or* mucho) tiempo; *take* ~ *to inf.* tardar en *inf.*; 3. *adv.* largo (*or* mucho) tiempo; largo rato; largamente; ~ *before* mucho antes; *as* ~ *as* mientras; con tal que *subj.*; *as* ~ *ago as 1950* ya en 1950; F *so* ~! ¡hasta luego!; *so* ~ *as* con tal que; ~*er* más tiempo; *how much* ~*er?* ¿cuánto tiempo más?; *no* ~*er* ya no; no más.

long[2] [~] anhelar (*for acc., to inf.*), suspirar (*for,* to por).

long...: '~·boat lancha *f*; '~·bow arco *m*; '~·'dat·ed a largo plazo; '~·'dis·tance a (larga *or* gran) distancia; *sport:* de fondo; *teleph.* ~ *call* conferencia *f* interurbana; ~ *flight* vuelo *m* a distancia; lon·gev·i·ty [lɔn'dʒeviti] longevidad *f*; 'long·hand escritura *f* normal (*or* sin abreviaturas).

long·ing ['lɔniŋ] **1.** anhelo *m*, añoranza *f*, ansia *f* (*for* de); **2.** □ anhelante.

long·ish ['lɔniʃ] algo (*or* bastante) largo.

lon·gi·tude ['lɔndʒitju:d] longitud *f*; **lon·gi·tu·di·nal** [~inl] □ longitudinal.

long...: '~-'**jump** salto *m* de longitud; '~-'**leg·ged** zancudo; '~-'**lived** de larga vida, duradero; '~-'**play·ing** de larga duración; '~-'**range** ✕ de gran alcance; ✈ de gran autonomía; '~-**shore·man** estibador *m*, obrero *m* portuario; '~-'**sight·ed** présbita; *fig.* previsor, sagaz; '~-'**stand·ing** existente desde hace mucho tiempo; '~-'**suf·fer·ing** sufrido; '~-'**term** a largo plazo; '~-**ways** longitudinalmente, a lo largo; '~-'**wind·ed** □ prolijo.

loo [lu:] *sl.* retrete *m*.

look [luk] **1.** mirada *f*, vistazo *m*; (*a.* ~s *pl.*) aspecto *m*, apariencia *f*; aire *m*; *good* ~s *pl.* buen parecer *m*; *by the* ~ *of things* por lo visto; F *get* (*or have*) *a* ~ *in* poder participar; tener posibilidad de ganar; *have* (*or take*) *a* ~ *at* echar un vistazo a; *have a* ~ *for* buscar; *I like the* ~ *of him* me hace buena impresión; **2.** *v/i.* mirar; parecer; tener aire (de); buscar; considerar; ~ *before you leap* antes que te cases, mira lo que haces; ~ *here!* ¡oye!; ~ *like* parecerse a; *it* ~s *like rain* parece que va a llover; ~ *well* (*p.*) tener buena cara; *it* ~s *well on you* te sienta bien; ~ *about* mirar alrededor; ~ *about for* andar buscando; ~ *about one* mirar a su alrededor; *fig.* considerar las cosas con calma; ~ *after* ocuparse de, cuidar de; ~ *at* mirar; ~ *away* desviar los ojos; ~ *back* mirar hacia atrás; *fig.* volverse atrás; ~ *back on* recordar, evocar; ~ *down on* dominar; *fig.* mirar por encima del hombro, despreciar; ~ *for* buscar; esperar; ~ *forward to* anticipar con placer, esperar con ilusión; F ~ *in* hacer una visita breve (*on* a), pasar por la casa *etc.* (*on* de); mirar la televisión; ~ *into* investigar, examinar; ~ *on* mirar, estar de mirón; ~ *on to* caer a, dar a; ~ *out!* ¡cuidado!, ¡ojo!; ~ *out for* buscar; estar a la expectativa de; tener cuidado con; ~ *out of window* mirar por;

~ *out on* dar a, caer a; ~ *round* volver la cabeza; = ~ *about*; ~ *through window* mirar por; *book* hojear; (*search*) rebuscar entre, registrar; ~ *to* ocuparse de, mirar por; *p.* contar con, acudir a; tener puestas las esperanzas en; ~ *to a p. to inf.* esperar que una p. *subj.*; ~ *up* levantar los ojos; F mejorar; ~ (*up*)*on fig.* considerar, estimar; ~ *up to* respetar, admirar; **3.** *v/t.* *emotion* expresar con la mirada; *age* representar; ~ *a p. in the face* mirar a una p. cara a cara (*a. fig.*); ~ *out* buscar; escoger; ~ *over* examinar; recorrer; ~ *up* buscar, averiguar, consultar; F visitar; ~ *a p. up and down* mirar a una p. de arriba abajo.

look·er-on ['lukər'ɔn] espectador (-a *f*) *m*, mirón (-a *f*) *m*.

look·ing-glass ['lukiŋglɑ:s] espejo *m*.

look-out ['luk'aut] (*p.*) vigía *m*, atalaya *m*; (*tower*) atalaya *f*; observación *f*, vigilancia *f*; perspectiva *f*; *be on the* ~ (*for*) estar a la mira (de); F *a poor* ~ *for* mala perspectiva para; F *that's his* ~ ¡eso a él!, ¡allá él!

loom[1] [lu:m] telar *m*.

loom[2] [~] surgir, asomar(se), aparecer (*a.* ~ *up*); vislumbrarse; *fig.* amenazar; ~ *large* abultar; *fig.* ser (*or parecer*) de gran importancia.

loon [lu:n] *Scot.* patán *m*; granuja *m*; tipo *m*.

loon·y ['lu:ni] *sl.* loco *adj. a. su. m* (a *f*).

loop [lu:p] **1.** gaza *f*, lazo *m*; (*fastening*) presilla *f*; (*bend*) curva *f*, vuelta *f*, recodo *m*; ✈ circuito *m* cerrado; *radio*: ~ *aerial* antena *f* de cuadro; **2.** *v/t.* hacer gaza con; asegurar con gaza (*or* presilla); enlazar; ✈ ~ *the* ~ hacer (*or* rizar) el rizo; *v/i.* formar lazo(s); serpentear; '~-**hole** ✕ aspillera *f*, tronera *f*; *fig.* escapatoria *f*, evasiva *f*; '~-**line** ⚐ vía *f* apartadero, vía *f* de circunvalación; ✈ circuito *m* en bucle.

loose [lu:s] **1.** □ (*free; separate*) suelto, desatado; (*not tight*) flojo, movedizo; (*unpacked*) sin envase; *dress* holgado; *wheel, pulley etc.* loco; *connexion* desconectado; poco exacto; aproximado; negligente; *thinking* ilógico, incoherente; *morals* relajado; *woman* fácil; ✻ suelto de vientre; ~ *change* suelto *m*; ~ *end* cabo *m* suelto; *be at a* ~ *end* estar desocupado; *become* (*or get, work*) ~ aflojarse, desatarse; *break* ~ desatarse; escaparse; *fig.* desencadenarse; *cast* (*or let, set, turn*) ~ soltar; **2.** soltar; desatar; aflojar; (*a.* ~ *off*) disparar; ~ *one's hold on* soltar; **3.**: F *be on the* ~ estar en libertad; estar de juerga; '**~-leaf**: ~ *book* cuaderno *m* de hojas sueltas (*or* movibles); **loos·en** ['luːsn] desatar(se), aflojar(se), soltar(se); ~ *up muscles* desentumecer; '**loose·ness** soltura *f*; flojedad *f*; holgura *f*; relajación *f*; ✻ diarrea *f*.

loot [luːt] **1.** botín *m*; F ganancias *f*/*pl.*; **2.** saquear, pillar; '**loot·er** saqueador (-a *f*) *m*.

lop [lɔp] *tree* (des)mochar; cercenar; ~ *away, off* cortar.

lope [loup] ir a medio galope, correr a paso largo.

lop...: '**~-eared** de orejas caídas; '**~-'sid·ed** desproporcionado; ladeado; desequilibrado (*a. fig.*).

lo·qua·cious [lou'kweiʃəs] ☐ locuaz; **lo·quac·i·ty** [lou'kwæsiti] locuacidad *f*.

lord [lɔːd] **1.** señor *m*; (*title*) lord *m*; *the* ♀ *the* el Señor; *my* ~ señor; Su Señoría; ♀'*s Prayer* padrenuestro *m*; ♀'*s Supper* (última) Cena *f*; *parl. the* (*House of*) ♀*s* (la Cámara de) los Lores. **2.**: ~ *it* hacer el señor; mandar despóticamente; ~ *it over* señorear, dominar; '**lord·li·ness** señorío *m*; altivez *f*; suntuosidad *f*; '**lord·ly** señoril; altivo; imperioso; esplénдido; '**lord·ship** (*title*) señoría *f*; (*rule*) señorío *m*.

lore [lɔː] saber *m* (popular), ciencia *f*.

lor·gnette ['lɔːnjet] impertinentes *m*/*pl*.

lor·ry ['lɔri] (auto)camión *m*.

lose [luːz] [*irr.*] *v*/*t*. perder; hacer perder; *that lost us the war* eso nos hizo perder la guerra; ~ *o.s.* perderse, errar el camino; *fig.* ensimismarse; *fig.* confundirse; *v*/*i*. perder; ser vencido; (*clock*) atrasar; '**los·er** perdidoso (a *f*) *m*, perdedor (-a *f*) *m*; F *come off the* ~ salir perdiendo; '**los·ing** perdidoso; *team* vencido.

loss [lɔs] pérdida *f*; F *be a dead* ~ ser inútil; ser una nulidad; *be a total* ~ considerarse totalmente perdido; *at*

a ~ ✝ con pérdida; *be at a* ~ estar perplejo, no saber qué hacer; *be at a* ~ *for* no encontrar; *be at a* ~ *to inf.* no saber cómo *inf*.

lost [lɔst] *pret. a p.p. of* **lose**; ~ *in* abismado en, absorto en; *be* ~ *on a p.* no aprovechar a una p.; *pasar* inadvertido por una p.; ~ *to* insensible a; inaccesible a; '**~-'prop·er·ty of·fice** oficina *f* de objetos perdidos.

lot [lɔt] ✝ lote *m*; porción *f*; (*fate*) suerte *f*; solar *m for building*; F gran cantidad *f*; F (*p.*) sujeto *m*, tipo *m*; F *a* ~ *of*, ~*s of* mucho, la mar de; F *a* ~ *of people* mucha gente; F *a bad* ~ un mal sujeto; *draw* ~*s* echar suertes; *fall to a p.'s* ~ caerle a una p. en suerte; incumbirle a una p.; F *the* ~ todo; *throw in one's* ~ *with* unirse a la suerte de.

lo·tion ['louʃn] loción *f*.

lot·ter·y ['lɔtəri] lotería *f*.

lo·tus ['loutəs] loto *m*.

loud [laud] ☐ alto; fuerte, recio; ruidoso, estrepitoso; *colour* chillón; (*in bad taste*) charro, cursi; '**loud·ness** (gran) ruido *m*; sonoridad *f*; fuerza *f*; *fig.* mal gusto *m*; '**loud·'speak·er** altavoz *m*, altoparlante *m*.

lounge [laundʒ] **1.** salón *m*; sala *f* (de estar); sofá *m*; ~ *suit* traje *m* de calle; **2.** arrellanarse, repantigarse; pasearse perezosamente; haraganear; ~ *about* tirarse a la bartola; '**loung·er** haragán (-a *f*) *m*; azotacalles *m*/*f*.

lour ['lauə] *v. lower²*.

louse [laus] (*pl. lice*) piojo *m*; **lous·y** ['lauzi] piojoso; *sl.* asqueroso, vil, malísimo.

lout [laut] patán *m*; gamberro *m*; '**lout·ish** grosero, zafio.

lov·a·ble ['lʌvəbl] ☐ amable.

love [lʌv] **1.** amor *m* (*of, for, towards* de, a); querer *m*; cariño *m*; (*p.*) amado (a *f*) *m*, querido (a *f*) *m*; F monada *f*, preciosidad *f*; *tennis*: cero *m*; *attr.* de amor, amoroso; *for* ~ por amor; F gratis; *for the* ~ *of* por el amor de; *give* (*or send*) *one's* ~ *to* (*in letters*) mandar cariñosos saludos a; *in* ~ *with* enamorado de; *fall in* ~ enamorarse (*with* de); *make* ~ *to* hacer el amor a; cortejar; F *not for* ~ *nor money* por nada del mundo; **2.** amar, querer; tener cariño a; ser muy aficionado a; *I should* ~ *to inf.* me gustaría mucho *inf.*; '**~-af·fair** amores *m*/*pl.*; amorío(s) *m*(*pl.*) (F);

'~-**bird** periquito *m*; *fig.* palomito *m*; '~-**child** hijo (a *f*) *m* del amor; '**love·less** sin amor; '**love-let·ter** carta *f* de amor; '**love·li·ness** belleza *f*, hermosura *f*; encanto *m*; exquisitez *f*; **love·lorn** ['~lɔ:n] suspirando de amor, abandonado de su amante; '**love·ly** bello, hermoso; encantador; exquisito; precioso; *Am.* simpático; '**love-mak·ing** galanteo *m*; trato *m* sexual; '**love-match** matrimonio *m* por amor; '**lov·er** amante *m/f*; aficionado (a *f*) *m* (of a), amigo (a *f*) *m* (of de); ~*s pl.* amantes *m/pl.*, novios *m/pl.*; '**love·sick** enfermo de amor, amartelado. [amante; cariñoso.)

lov·ing ['lʌviŋ] □ amoroso,)

low[1] [lou] **1.** bajo; *bow* profundo; *blow* sucio; *dress* escotado; *price* módico; *stocks* escaso; *diet* deficiente; ♪ grave; *spirits* abatido; *health* débil, gravemente enfermo; *rank* humilde; *manners* grosero; *character* vil, rastrero; *joke* verde; *opinion* malo; ~ *comedy* farsa *f*; ~ *trick* partida *f* serrana; F *be* ~ *on* estar escaso de; **2.** *meteor.* área *f* de baja presión; F punto *m* bajo; *mot.* primera marcha *f*; **3.** *adv.* bajo; bajamente; en voz baja.

low[2] [~] **1.** mugir; **2.** mugido *m*.

low...: '~-**born** de humilde cuna; '~-**brow** F (persona *f*) nada intelectual; '~-'**down 1.** bajo, vil; **2.** ['~] *sl.* verdad *f*, informes *m/pl.* confidenciales; pormenores *m/pl.*

low·er[1] ['louə] **1.** más bajo *etc.* (*v. low*); inferior; bajo; ~ *classes* clase *f* baja; **2.** bajar; disminuir; *price* rebajar; ♣ arriar; 🎖 debilitar; abatir; humillar; ~ *one's guard* aflojar la guardia.

low·er[2] ['lauə] **1.** fruncir el entrecejo, mirar con ceño; (*sky*) encapotarse; '**low·er·ing** ceñudo; encapotado; amenazador.

low·land ['loulənd] tierra *f* baja; '**low·li·ness** humildad *f*; '**low·ly** humilde; '**low-'necked** escotado; '**low·ness** bajeza *f etc.*; '**low-'pres·sure** de baja presión; '**low-'ten·sion** de baja tensión.

loy·al ['lɔiəl] □ leal, fiel; '**loy·al·ist** legitimista *adj. a. su. m/f*, gubernamental *adj. a. su. m/f*; *Spain:* republicano *adj. a. su. m* (a *f*); '**loy·al·ty** lealtad *f*, fidelidad *f*.

loz·enge ['lɔzindʒ] pastilla *f*; ⚭ *a. heraldry:* losange *m*.

lub·ber ['lʌbə] ♣ marinero *m* de agua dulce; bobalicón *m*; '**lub·ber·ly** torpe, tosco.

lu·bri·cant ['lu:brikənt] lubri(fi)cante *adj. a. su. m*; **lu·bri·cate** ['~keit] lubri(fi)car, engrasar; **lu·bri·'ca·tion** lubri(fi)cación *f*, engrase *m*; '**lu·bri·ca·tor** lubri(fi)cador *m*; **lu·bric·i·ty** [lju:'brisiti] lubricidad *f*.

lu·cerne [lu:'sə:n] alfalfa *f*.

lu·cid ['lusid] □ lúcido; **lu·cid·i·ty** lucidez *f*.

luck [lʌk] suerte *f*, ventura *f*; fortuna *f*; azar *m*; *good* ~ (buena) suerte *f*; *bad* ~, *hard* ~, *ill* ~ mala suerte *f*; *be in* ~ estar de suerte; F *be down on one's* ~, *be out of* ~ estar de malas; *no such* ~! ¡ojalá!; *try one's* ~ probar fortuna; *with any* ~ a lo mejor; '**luck·i·ly** afortunadamente, por fortuna; '**luck·less** desafortunado, desdichado; '**luck·y** □ afortunado; de buen agüero; *be* ~ tener (buena) suerte; tener buena sombra; ~ *hit*, ~ *break* racha *f* de suerte, chiripa *f*; ~ *bag*, ~ *dip approx.* tómbola *f*.

lu·cra·tive ['lu:krətiv] □ lucrativo, provechoso; **lu·cre** ['lu:kə] † lucro *m*; *filthy* ~ el vil metal.

lu·cu·bra·tion [lu:kju'breiʃn] lucubración *f*.

lu·di·crous ['lu:dikrəs] □ absurdo, ridículo.

luff [lʌf] **1.** orza *f*; **2.** orzar.

lug [lʌg] **1.** oreja *f*; ⊕ orejeta *f*; agarradera *f*; (*movement*) (es)tirón *m*; **2.** arrastrar; tirar de; F ~ *about* llevar consigo (con dificultad); *fig.* ~ *in* traer a colación.

lug·gage ['lʌgidʒ] equipaje *m*; '~-**boot** maleta *f*; '~-**car·ri·er**, '~-**grid** portaequipajes *m*; '~-**rack** rejilla *f*; '~-**van** furgón *m* de equipajes.

lug·ger ['lʌgə] lugre *m*.

lu·gu·bri·ous [lu:'gju:briəs] □ lúgubre.

luke·warm ['lu:kwɔ:m] tibio (*a. fig.*), templado; *fig.* indiferente.

lull [lʌl] **1.** recalmón *m*, intervalo *m* de calma; *fig.* tregua *f*, respiro *m*; **2.** arrullar; adormecer; *fig.* tranquilizar; (*storm*) amainar.

lull·a·by ['lʌləbai] nana *f*, canción *f* de cuna.

lum·ba·go [lʌm'beigou] lumbago *m*.

lum·ber ['lʌmbə] **1.** trastos *m/pl.* viejos; maderos *m/pl.*, maderas *f/pl.*

(de sierra); **2.** moverse pesadamente (*or* con ruido sordo); cortar árboles; **'lum·ber·ing** pesado; **'lum·ber·jack, 'lum·ber·man** hachero *m*, maderero *m*, leñador *m*; **'lum·ber·room** trastera *f*.

lu·mi·nar·y ['lu:minəri] lumbrera *f*; **'lu·mi·nous** □ luminoso.

lump [lʌmp] **1.** terrón *m* (*a. of sugar*); masa *f*; borujo *m*; (*swelling*) bulto *m*, hinchazón *f*; protuberancia *f*; (*pellet*) pella *f*; (*p.*) zoquete *m*; nudo *m in throat*; ∼ *sugar* azúcar *m* en terrón; ∼ *sum* suma *f* global; **2.** *v/t.* amontonar; aborujar; F aguantar, tragar; ∼ *together* agrupar, mezclar; *v/i.* aborujarse; **'lump·ing** F grueso, pesado; **'lump·ish** torpe, pesado; **'lump·y** □ aterronado; borujoso; *sea* agitado, picado.

lu·na·cy ['lu:nəsi] locura *f*.

lu·nar ['lu:nə] lunar.

lu·na·tic ['lu:nətik] loco *adj. a. su. m* (*a f*), demente *adj. a. su. m/f*; ∼ *asylum* manicomio *m*; F ∼ *fringe* elementos *m/pl.* fanáticos (y estrafalarios).

lunch [lʌntʃ] **1.** almuerzo *m*, comida *f* (*a. more formally* **'lunch·eon** ['˵ən]); lonche *m S.Am.*; (*snack*) bocadillo *m*, merienda *f*; **2.** almorzar, comer; tomar un bocadillo, merendar.

lung [lʌŋ] pulmón *m*.

lunge [lʌndʒ] **1.** *fenc.* estocada *f*; arremetida *f*; **2.** dar una estocada; arremeter (*at* contra).

lu·pin(e) ['lu:pin] altramuz *m*.

lurch[1] [ləːtʃ] **1.** sacudida *f*, tumbo *m*; tambaleo *m* repentino; **2.** dar sacudidas, dar un tumbo, tambalearse.

lurch[2] [˵]: *leave in the* ∼ dejar plantado.

lure [ljuə] **1.** cebo *m*; señuelo *m* (*a. fig.*); aliciente *m*, seducción *f*; **2.** atraer (con señuelo); tentar; seducir.

lu·rid ['ljuərid] □ *colour of skin etc.* lívido, cárdeno; *dress etc.* chillón; *account* sensacional; *detail* espeluznante.

lurk [ləːk] ocultarse; estar en acecho; moverse furtivamente.

lus·cious ['lʌʃəs] □ delicioso, rico, exquisito, suculento; *b.s.* empalagoso.

lush [lʌʃ] jugoso, lozano.

lust [lʌst] **1.** lujuria *f*, lascivia *f*; (*greed*) codicia *f*; **2.** lujuriar; ∼ *after* codiciar; **'lust·ful** □ lujurioso, lascivo.

lus·tre ['lʌstə] lustre *m*, brillo *m*; **'lus·tre·less** sin brillo, deslustrado.

lus·trous ['lʌstrəs] □ lustroso.

lust·y ['lʌsti] □ vigoroso, fornido, robusto; lozano.

lute [lu:t] ♪ laúd *m*.

Lu·ther·an ['lu:θərən] luterano *adj. a. su. m* (*a f*); **'Lu·ther·an·ism** luteranismo *m*.

lux·u·ri·ance [lʌgˈzjuəriəns] lozanía *f*, exuberancia *f*; **lux·u·ri·ant** □ lozano, exuberante; **lux·u·ri·ate** [˵rieit] crecer con exuberancia; deleitarse (*in* con), entregarse al lujo (*in* de); **lux·u·ri·ous** [˵riəs] □ lujoso; **lux·u·ry** ['lʌkʃəri] lujo *m*; *attr.* de lujo.

ly·ce·um [lai'siəm] liceo *m*.

ly·ing ['laiiŋ] **1.** *ger. of lie*[1] *a. lie*[2]; **2.** *adj.* mentiroso; **'˵'in** parto *m*; ∼ *hospital* casa *f* de maternidad.

lymph [limf] linfa *f* (*a. poet.*); **lym·phat·ic** [˵'fætik] □ (*vaso m*) linfático.

lynch [lintʃ] linchar; **'˵-law** ley *f* de Lynch.

lynx [liŋks] lince *m*; *be* ∼*-eyed* tener ojos de lince.

lyre [laiə] lira *f*.

lyr·ic ['lirik] **1.** lírico; **2.** poesía *f* lírica; letra *f* (de una canción); **'lyr·i·cal** □ lírico; F elocuente, entusiasmado.

M

ma [mɑ:] F mamá *f*.

ma'am [mæm, F məm, m] = *madam*.

ma·ca·bre [mə'kɑːbr] macabro.

mac·ad·am [mə'kædəm] macadán *m*; **mac'ad·am·ize** macadamizar.

mac·a·ro·ni [mækə'rouni] macarrones *m/pl*.

mac·a·roon [mækə'ruːn] macarrón *m* (de almendras), mostachón *m*.

mace [meis] maza *f*; (*spice*) macis *f*; '~-**bear·er** macero *m*.

mac·er·ate ['mæsəreit] macerar(se); **mac·er'a·tion** maceración *f*.

mach·i·na·tion [mæki'neiʃn] maquinación *f*; **mach·i·na·tor** ['~tə] maquinador (-a *f*) *m*; **ma·chine** [mə'ʃiːn] **1.** máquina *f* (*a. fig.*); aparato *m*; *mot.* coche *m*; (*cycle*) bicicleta *f*; ✈ avión *m*; *pol.* organización *f*, camarilla *f*; *attr.* mecánico, a máquina; ~ *fitter* montador *m*; **2.** elaborar (*or* cabar, coser) a máquina; **ma'chine-gun 1.** ametralladora *f*; **2.** ametrallar; **ma'chine-made** hecho a máquina; **ma'chin·er·y** maquinaria *f*; mecanismo *m* (*a. fig.*); **ma'chine·shop** taller *m* de máquinas; **ma'chine-tool** máquina herramienta *f*; **ma'chin·ist** operario (a *f*) *m* de máquina, mecánico *m*.

mack·er·el ['mækrəl] caballa *f*; '~-**sky** cielo *m* aborregado.

mack·in·tosh ['mækintɔʃ] impermeable *m*.

mac·ro... ['mækrou] macro...

mad [mæːd] □ loco, demente; F furioso; *dog* rabioso; *idea* insensato; F *be* ~ *about* (*on, for*) estar loco por, ser muy aficionado a; F *be* ~ *about* (*or at*) estar furioso con (*or* contra, por); *drive* ~ enloquecer, volver loco; F *get* ~ encolerizarse; *go* ~ volverse loco, enloquecer; F *like* ~ como un loco.

mad·am ['mædəm] señora *f*; F niña *f* precoz, niña *f* repipi.

mad·cap ['mædkæp] **1.** locuelo (a *f*) *m*, tarambana *m/f*; **2.** atolondrado; **mad·den** ['mædn] enloquecer; en-

furecer; *it's* ~*ing* es para volverse loco.

made [meid] *pret. a. p.p. of make* 1.

made-up ['meid'ʌp] hecho; compuesto; *story* ficticio; *face* pintado, maquillado; *dress* confeccionado.

mad·house ['mædhaus] manicomio *m*; casa *f* de locos (*a. fig.*); '**mad·man** loco *m*; '**mad·ness** locura *f*, demencia *f*; rabia *f*; furia *f*.

mad·ri·gal ['mædrigəl] madrigal *m*.

mael·strom ['meilstroum] remolino *m*, vórtice *m*.

mag·a·zine [mægə'ziːn] revista *f*; ✗ almacén *m*; ✗ polvorín *m for powder*; ⚓ santabárbara *f*.

ma·gen·ta [mə'dʒentə] magenta *f*.

mag·got ['mægət] cresa *f*, gusano *m*; '**mag·got·y** agusanado.

mag·ic ['mædʒik] **1.** magia *f*; *as if by* ~ (como) por ensalmo; **2.** mágico; *v. lantern*; ~ *wand* varilla *f* de virtudes; '**mag·i·cal** □ mágico; **ma·gi·cian** [mə'dʒiʃn] mágico *m*, mago *m*; (*conjuror*) prestidigitador *m*.

mag·is·te·ri·al [mædʒis'tiəriəl] □ magistral; **mag·is·tra·cy** ['~trəsi] magistratura *f*; **mag·is·trate** ['~trit] magistrado *m*; juez *m* (municipal).

mag·na·nim·i·ty [mægnə'nimiti] magnanimidad *f*; **mag·nan·i·mous** [~'næniməs] magnánimo.

mag·nate ['mægneit] magnate *m*.

mag·ne·sia [mæg'niːʃə] magnesia *f*; **mag·ne·sium** [~ziəm] magnesio *m*.

mag·net ['mægnit] imán *m*; **mag·net·ic** [~'netik] □ magnético; **mag·net·ism** ['~nitizm] magnetismo *m*; **mag·net·i·za·tion** [~tai'zeiʃn] magnetización *f*, iman(t)ación *f*; '**mag·net·ize** magnetizar, iman(t)ar; **mag·ne·to** [mæg'niːtou] magneto *f*.

mag·nif·i·ca·tion [mæghifi'keiʃn] *opt.* (*high* gran, *low* pequeño) aumento *m*, (*high* alto, *low* bajo) enfoque *m*; *fig.* exageración *f*.

mag·nif·i·cence [mæg'nifisns] magnificencia *f*; **mag'nif·i·cent** magnífico; **mag·ni·fy** ['~fai] *opt.* aumentar, magnificar; agrandar; *fig.* exagerar; ~*ing glass* lupa *f*, lente *f* de aumento; **mag·ni·tude** [ˈ~tjuːd] magnitud *f*; *star of the first* ~ estrella *f* de primera magnitud.

mag·no·li·a [mægˈnouljə] magnolia *f*.

mag·pie [ˈmægpai] urraca *f*, marica *f*.

ma·hog·a·ny [məˈhɔgəni] caoba *f*.

Ma·hom·et·an [məˈhɔmitən] mahometano *adj. a. su. m* (a *f*).

maid [meid] criada *f*, camarera *f*; *mst lit.* doncella *f*, virgen *f*; muchacha *f*; soltera *f*; ~ *of honour* dama *f* de honor; *old* ~ solterona *f*.

maid·en [ˈmeidn] **1.** *mst lit.* doncella *f*, virgen *f*; muchacha *f*; soltera *f*; **2.** virginal, intacto; (de) soltera; *speech* primero; *voyage* inaugural; ~ *name* apellido *m* de soltera; ˈ~**hair** ♀ culantrillo *m*, cabellos *m/pl.* de Venus; ˈ~**head** doncellez *f*; himen *m*; ˈ~**hood** doncellez *f*; ˈ**maid·en·ly** virginal; recatado, modesto.

maid-of-all-work [ˈmeidəvˈɔːlwəːk] criada *f* para todo; ˈ**maid·serv·ant** criada *f*, sirvienta *f*.

mail[1] [meil] ✗ (cota *f* de) malla *f*.

mail[2] [~] **1.** ✍ correo *m*; correspondencia *f*; mala *f*; **2.** echar al correo, despachar; enviar (por correo).

mail...: ˈ~**-bag** valija *f*, mala *f*; ˈ~**-boat** vapor *m* correo; ˈ~**-box** *Am.* buzón *m*; ˈ~**-car·ri·er** *Am.* cartero *m*; ˈ~**-coach** diligencia *f*, coche *m* correo; ˈ~**-or·der firm**, *Am.* ˈ~**-order house** casa *f* de ventas por correo; ˈ~**-train** (tren *m*) correo *m*.

maim [meim] tullir; mutilar; estropear.

main [mein] **1.** principal; maestro; mayor; *by* ~ *force* por fuerza mayor; ✗ ~ *plane* ala *f*; *the* ~ *thing* lo más importante, lo esencial; **2.** cañería *f* (maestra); *poet.* océano *m*; ~*s pl.* ⚡ red *f* (eléctrica); *in the* ~ en general, en su mayoría; ˈ~**land** tierra *f* firme, continente *m*; ˈ**main·ly** principalmente, mayormente.

main...: ~**mast** [ˈ~mɑːst, ⚓ ˈ~məst] palo *m* mayor; ~**sail** [ˈ~seil, ⚓ ˈ~sl] vela *f* mayor; ~**spring** muelle *m* real; *fig.* causa *f* (*or* motivo *m*) principal, origen *m*; ˈ~**stay** ⚓ estay *m* mayor; *fig.* sostén *m* principal; ℀-**Street** calle *f* mayor.

main·tain [meinˈtein] mantener, sostener; ⊕ entretener.

main·te·nance [ˈmeintinəns] mantenimiento *m*; sustento *m*; (gastos *m/pl.* de) conservación *f*; ⊕ entretenimiento *m*.

main·top [ˈmeintɔp] ⚓ cofa *f* mayor.

maize [meiz] maíz *m*.

ma·jes·tic [məˈdʒestik] ☐ majestuoso; **maj·es·ty** [ˈmædʒisti] majestad *f*; *His* ♀ Su Majestad *f*; *Your* ♀ (Vuestra) Majestad.

ma·jor [ˈmeidʒə] **1.** mayor (*a.* ♪); principal; importante; **2.** mayor *m/f* de edad; ✗ comandante *m*; *phls.* mayor *f*; *Am. univ.* especialidad *f*; **3.** *Am. univ.* especializarse (*in* en); ˈ~**-do·mo** [ˈ~doumou] mayordomo *m*; ˈ~**-gen·er·al** general *m* de división; **ma·jor·i·ty** [məˈdʒɔriti] mayoría *f*, mayor número *m*; ✗ comandancia *f*; mayor edad *f*.

make [meik] **1.** [*irr.*] *v/t.* hacer; crear; formar; construir; practicar, ejecutar, efectuar; constituir; causar, ocasionar; componer; producir; terminar, acabar; creer; deducir, inferir; calcular; (*acquire*) ganar, obtener, granjear, adquirir; (*act as*) servir de, portarse como; (*agree on*) convenir en; (*compel*) forzar, obligar, compeler (*inf. a inf.*); (*equal*) ser (igual a); (*induce*) inclinar, inducir (*inf. a inf.*); (*manufacture*) fabricar, confeccionar, elaborar; (*prepare*) aderezar, preparar, disponer, arreglar; (*reach*) alcanzar, llegar a (*a.* ⚓); ⚡ *circuit* cerrar; *mistake* cometer; *speech* pronunciar; ~ *a. adj. is often translated by v/t. corresponding to adj.:* ~ *rich* enriquecer; F ~ *a p.* hacerle la fortuna a una p., ser causa del éxito de una p.; *I made him write the letter* le hice escribir la carta; *that* ~*s 50* con éste van cincuenta; *I made one of the group* yo era (uno) del grupo; ~ *believe* fingir(-se); ~ *good damage* reparar; *loss* compensar, indemnizar; completar, suplir; probar; *promise* cumplir; *accusation* hacer bueno; F salir bien, tener éxito; F ~ *it* (*arrive*) llegar; (*succeed*) tener éxito; conseguir lo deseado; ~ *or break*, ~ *or mar* hacer la fortuna o ser la ruina de; ~ *into* convertir en, transformar en; ~ *of* sacar de, pensar de, inferir de; ~ *out document* extender; (*perceive*) distinguir, vislumbrar; *writing* descifrar; (*un-*

derstand) entender; justificar; dar la impresión de; sugerir; declarar; ~ *over* ceder, traspasar, transferir; ~ *up* hacer; preparar; fabricar; inventar; componer, formar; *collection* reunir; *total* completar; *typ.* compaginar; *clothes* confeccionar; *face* pintar, maquillar; *fire* echar carbón *etc.* a; *loss* subsanar; (re)compensar, indemnizar; *parcel* empaquetar; *time* recuperar; ~ *it up* hacer las paces; 2. [*irr.*] *v/i.*: ~ *as if to*, ~ *as though to inf.* hacer como si quisiese *inf.*, fingir que va a *inf.*, aparentar *inf.*; ~ *after* (per)seguir; ~ *away with* llevarse, hurtar; suprimir; destruir; *p.* matar; ~ *away with o.s.* suicidarse; ~ *for place* dirigirse a, encaminarse a; *result* contribuir a, conducir a; (*attack*) abalanzarse sobre; ~ *off* largarse, escaparse; ~ *off with* alzarse con, llevarse; escaparse con; *mst Am.* F ~ *out* arreglárselas, salir bien; *how did you* ~ *out?* ¿cómo te fue?; ~ *to inf.* ir a, hacer ademán de *inf.*; ~ *towards* dirigirse a; ~ *up* pintarse, maquillarse; *thea.* caracterizarse; ~ *up for* compensar; suplir; *lost time* recobrar; ~ *up to* (procurar) congraciarse con; halagar; adular; galantear; 3. hechura *f*; confección *f*; corte *m of clothes*; manufactura *f*, fabricación *f*; (*brand*) marca *f*; modelo *m*; *sl.* be on the ~ echar el agua a su molino; *our own* ~ de fabricación propia; '~-be·lieve 1. ficción *f*, simulación *f*; 2. simulado, falso, fingido; 'mak·er hacedor (-a *f*) *m*, creador (-a *f*) *m*; fabricante *m*; artífice *m/f*; constructor (-a *f*) *m*; confeccionador (-a *f*) *m*; ♀ Hacedor *m*.

make...: '~-shift 1. improvisación *f*; expediente *m*; arreglo *m* provisional; 2. improvisado, provisional; '~-up composición *f*; carácter *m*, modo *m* de ser; hechura *f*, confección *f of clothes*; maquillaje *m*, cosmético(s) *m(pl.) for face*; *thea.* caracterización *f*; *typ.* imposición *f*; ~ *man films*: maquillador *m*; '~-weight contrapeso *m*; *fig.* tapa(a)gujeros *m*.

mak·ing ['meikiŋ] creación *f*; formación *f*; fabricación *f*, confección *f*; hechura *f*; elementos *m/pl.* necesarios; *have the* ~*s of* (*p.*) tener talento para ser; *it was the* ~ *of him* fue la causa de su éxito.

mal·a·chite ['mæləkait] malaquita *f*.
mal·ad·just·ment ['mælə'dʒʌstmənt] mal ajuste *m*; inadaptación *f*.
mal·ad·min·is·tra·tion ['mælədminis'treiʃn] mala administración *f*.
mal·a·droit [mælə'drɔit] torpe.
mal·a·dy ['mælədi] mal *m*, enfermedad *f*.
mal·aise [mæ'leiz] malestar *m*.
ma·lar·i·a [mə'lɛəriə] paludismo *m*, malaria *f*; ma·lar·i·al palúdico.
Ma·lay [mə'lei] 1. malayo (a *f*) *m*; (*language*) malayo *m*; 2. malayo (*a.* Ma·lay·an).
mal·con·tent ['mælkəntent] malcontento *adj.* *a.* *su.* *m* (a *f*).
male [meil] 1. macho; masculino; ~ *child* hijo *m* varón; ~ *nurse* enfermero *m*; ~ *screw* tornillo *m* (macho); 2. macho *m*; varón *m*.
mal·e·dic·tion [mæli'dikʃn] maldición *f*. [hechor (-a *f*) *m*.
mal·e·fac·tor ['mælifæktə] mal-
ma·lev·o·lence [mə'levələns] malevolencia *f*; ma'lev·o·lent □ malévolo.
mal·for·ma·tion ['mælfɔ:'meiʃn] malformación *f*, deformidad *f*.
mal·ice ['mælis] malicia *f*, mala voluntad *f*; ♣ intención *f* delictuosa; *bear* ~ guardar rencor.
ma·li·cious [mə'liʃəs] □ malicioso, maligno; rencoroso.
ma·lign [mə'lain] 1. □ maligno; 2. calumniar, difamar; ma·lig·nan·cy [mə'lignənsi] malignidad *f*; ma'lig·nant maligno; ma'lig·ni·ty malignidad *f*.
ma·lin·ger [mə'liŋgə] fingirse enfermo; ma'lin·ger·er enfermo (a *f*) *m* fingido (a).
mal·lard ['mæləd] pato *m* real, ánade *m* real.
mal·le·a·bil·i·ty [mæliə'biliti] maleabilidad *f* (*a. fig.*); 'mal·le·a·ble maleable (*a. fig.*).
mal·let ['mælit] mazo *m*, mallo *m*.
mal·low ['mælou] malva *f*.
mal·nu·tri·tion ['mælnju:'triʃn] desnutrición *f*.
mal·o·dor·ous ['mæ'loudərəs] □ maloliente.
mal·prac·tice ['mæl'præktis] procedimientos *m/pl.* ilegales; abuso *m* de autoridad.
malt [mɔ:lt] 1. malta *f*; ~ *liquor* cerveza *f*; 2. preparar la malta; ~*ed milk* harina *f* lacteada.

Mal·tese ['mɔːl'tiːz] maltés *adj. a. su. m* (-a *f*); ~ *cross* cruz *f* de Malta.
mal·treat [mæl'triːt] maltratar; **mal'treat·ment** maltrat(amient)o *m.*
malt·ster ['mɔːltstə] preparador *m* de malta.
mal·ver·sa·tion [mælvə'seiʃn] malversación *f.*
ma·ma, mam·ma [məˈmɑː] mamá *f.*
mam·mal ['mæməl] mamífero *m*; **mam·ma·li·an** [məˈmeiliən] mamífero *adj. a. su. m.*
mam·moth ['mæməθ] 1. mamut *m*; 2. gigantesco.
mam·my ['mæmi] F mamaíta *f*; *Am.* nodriza *f* negra.
man [mæn, *in compounds* ... mən] 1. (*pl.* men) hombre *m*; varón *m*; el género humano; (*servant*) criado *m*; (*workman*) obrero *m*; ✗ soldado *m*; pieza *f in chess, etc.*; *a* ~ *needs friends* uno necesita amigos; ~ *about town* señorito *m*; F ~ *alive!* ¡hombre!; ~ *and boy* desde pequeño; ~ *and wife* marido *m* y mujer *f*; ~ *in the street* hombre *m* medio, hombre *m* de la calle; ~ *of the world* hombre *m* de mundo; *no* ~ nadie; *to a* ~ por unanimidad, como un solo hombre; *todos sin excepción*; 2. ⚓ tripular; ✗ guarnecer; proveer de gente (armada); *guns* servir.
man·a·cle ['mænəkl] 1. manilla *f*; ~*s pl.* esposas *f/pl.*; 2. poner esposas a.
man·age ['mænidʒ] *v/t.* manejar; manipular; llevar; conseguir (hacer); guiar; regir; administrar; *business* dirigir; *house* gobernar; F comer; *can you* ~ 2 *more?* ¿puedes llevar 2 más?; *can you* ~ 10 *o'clock?* ¿puedes venir a las 10?; *v/i.* arreglárselas, componérselas; ir tirando; ~ *to inf.* lograr *inf.*, arreglárselas para *inf.*, ingeniarse para *inf.*; ~ *without* pasarse sin; **'man·age·a·ble** ☐ manejable; dócil; **'man·age·ment** dirección *f*, gerencia *f*; administración *f*; *thea.* empresa *f*; manejo *m*; gobierno *m*; conducta *f*; **'man·ag·er** director *m*, gerente *m*; administrador (-a *f*) *m*; jefe *m*; *thea.* empresario *m*; *she is a good* ~ es buena administradora, es muy económica; **'man·ag·er·ess** directora *f*; jefa *f*;

administradora *f*; **man·a·ge·ri·al** [ˌmænəˈdʒiəriəl] ☐ directivo; administrativo.
man·ag·ing ['mænidʒiŋ] directivo; *b.s.* mandón; ~ *director* director *m* gerente.
man-at-arms ['mænət'ɑːmz] hombre *m* de armas.
man·da·rin ['mændərin] mandarín *m*; ♀ (*a.* 'man·da·rine) mandarina *f.*
man·da·tar·y ['mændətəri] mandatario *m*; **man·date** ['ˌdeit] 1. mandato *m*; 2. asignar por mandato; ~*d territory* país *m* bajo mandato; **man·da·to·ry** ['ˌdətəri] 1. obligatorio; conferido por mandato; 2. mandatario *m.*
man-day ['mæn'dei] día-hombre *m.*
man·di·ble ['mændibl] mandíbula *f.*
man·do·lin(e) ['mændəlin] mandolina *f.*
man·drake ['mændreik] mandrágora *f.*
man·drel ['mændril] ⊕ mandril *m.*
man·drill [ˌ] *zo.* mandril *m.*
mane [mein] crin(es) *f(pl.)*; melena *f of lion.*
man-eat·ing ['mæniːtiŋ] antropófago; caníbal.
ma·neu·ver [məˈnuːvə] *v.* manoeuvre.
man·ful ['mænful] ☐ valiente, resuelto.
man·ga·nese [ˌmæŋgəˈniːz] manganeso *m*; ~ *steel* acero *m* al manganeso.
mange [meindʒ] *vet.* roña *f*, sarna *f.*
man·ger ['meindʒə] pesebre *m*; *dog in the* ~ perro *m* del hortelano.
man·gle¹ ['mæŋgl] 1. exprimidor *m* de la ropa; rodillo *m*; 2. pasar por el exprimidor.
man·gle² [ˌ] lacerar, destrozar; mutilar (*a. fig.*); magullar; *fig.* estropear.
man·gy ['meindʒi] sarnoso, roñoso.
man...: '~·han·dle ⊕ mover a brazo; (*roughly*) maltratar; '~·hole registro *m*, pozo *m* de visita; agujero *m* de hombre *in boiler*; '~·hood virilidad *f*; naturaleza *f* humana; hombres *m/pl.*; '~-'hour hora-hombre *f*; '~·hunt persecución *f* de un criminal.
ma·ni·a ['meiniə] manía *f*; **ma·ni·ac** ['ˌiæk] 1. maníaco (a *f*) *m*; 2. (*a.* **ma·ni·a·cal** [məˈnaiəkl] ☐) maníaco.

man·i·cure ['mænikjuə] 1. manicura f; 2. hacer manicura a; '~-case, '~-set estuche m de manicura.

man·i·cur·ist ['mænikjuərist] manicuro (a f) m.

man·i·fest ['mænifest] 1. □ manifiesto; make ~ poner de manifiesto; 2. ♧ manifiesto m; 3. manifestar; hacer patente, revelar; **man·i·fes·'ta·tion** manifestación f; **man·i·fes·to** [~'festou] manifiesto m.

man·i·fold ['mænifould] 1. □ múltiple; multiforme; numeroso; 2. sacar muchas copias de.

man·i·kin ['mænikin] maniquí m; enano m.

ma·nip·u·late [mə'nipjuleit] manipular, manejar; **ma·nip·u·la·tion** manipulación f, manejo m; **ma·'nip·u·la·tive** de manipulación; **ma·'nip·u·la·tor** manipulador (-a f) m.

man·kind [mæn'kaind] humanidad f, raza f humana; ['~] sexo m masculino; '**man·li·ness** virilidad f, masculinidad f; hombr(ad)ía f; '**man·ly** varonil; masculino; valiente.

man·na ['mænə] maná m.

man·ne·quin ['mænikin] maniquí m/f, modelo f; ~ parade desfile m de modelos.

man·ner ['mænə] manera f, modo m; ademán m, aire m of p.; clase f; ~s pl. modales m/pl., maneras f/pl., crianza f, educación f; costumbres f/pl.; he has no ~s tiene malos modales, no tiene crianza, es un mal criado; after (or in) the ~ of a la manera de; all ~ of toda clase de; by no ~ of means de ningún modo; in a ~ (of speaking) en cierto modo; como si dijéramos; in this ~ de este modo, de esta forma; to the ~ born avezado desde la cuna; '**man·nered** style amanerado; de modales...; '**man·ner·ism** amaneramiento m of style; hábito m; idiosincrasia f; '**man·ner·ly** cortés, bien criado.

man·nish ['mæni] hombruno.

ma·noeu·vra·ble, Am. a. **ma·neu·ver·a·ble** [mə'nu:vrəbl] maniobrable; **ma·'noeu·vre**, Am. a. **ma·'neu·ver** [~və] 1. maniobra f; 2. v/t. hacer maniobrar, manipular; lograr con maniobras; v/i. maniobrar.

man-of-war ['mænəv'wɔ:] buque m de guerra. [metro m.]

ma·nom·e·ter [mə'nɔmitə] manó-/

man·or ['mænə] solar m, finca f solariega, señorío m; (a. '~-house) casa f señorial, casa f solariega; **ma·no·ri·al** [mə'nɔ:riəl] señorial; solariego.

man-pow·er ['mænpauə] mano f de obra; potencial m humano.

manse [mæns] Scot. casa f del párroco.

man-serv·ant ['mænsə:vənt] criado m.

man·sion ['mænʃn] palacio m, hotel m, casa f grande; casa f solariega.

man·slaugh·ter ['mænslɔ:tə] homicidio m (sin premeditación).

man·tel ['mæntl] manto m (de chimenea); '~-piece, '~-shelf repisa f de chimenea.

man·til·la [mæn'tilə] mantilla f.

man·tle ['mæntl] 1. manto m (a. fig., zo.): (incandescent ~) manguito m incandescente; 2. v/t. cubrir; ocultar; v/i. extenderse; (cheeks) ponerse encendido.

man·trap ['mæntræp] cepo m.

man·u·al ['mænjuəl] 1. □ manual; 2. manual m; ♪ teclado m de órgano.

man·u·fac·to·ry [mænju'fæktəri] fábrica f.

man·u·fac·ture [mænju'fæktʃə] 1. fabricación f; (product) manufactura f; 2. fabricar (a. fig.); manufacturar, elaborar; **man·u'fac·tur·er** fabricante m, industrial m, manufacturero m; **man·u'fac·tur·ing** 1. manufacturero, fabril; 2. fabricación f.

ma·nure [mə'njuə] 1. estiércol m, abono m; 2. estercolar, abonar.

man·u·script ['mænjuskript] manuscrito adj. a. su. m.

Manx [mæŋks] 1. de la Isla de Man; 2. lengua f de la Isla de Man; the ~ los habitantes de la Isla de Man.

man·y ['meni] 1. muchos (a. ~ a, ~ a one); ~ a time muchas veces; ~ people mucha gente f; as ~ as tantos como; as ~ as 50 hasta 50; how ~ cuántos; so ~ tantos; too ~ demasiados; one too ~ uno de más; 2. gran número m; muchos (as f/pl.) m/pl.; a good ~ un buen número (de); a great ~ muchísimos; the ~ la mayoría, las masas; '~-'col·oured multicolor; '~-'sid·ed multilátero; fig. polifacético; complejo.

map [mæp] 1. mapa m, carta f geográfica; F off the ~ remoto, aislado;

2. trazar el mapa (*or* plano) de; *fig.* planear, proyectar (*a.* ~ *out*).

ma·ple ['meipl] arce *m*.

map-mak·ing['mæp'meikiŋ], **map·ping** ['mæpiŋ] cartografía *f*.

mar [mɑ:] estropear; desfigurar; echar a perder; *enjoyment* aguar.

Mar·a·thon ['mærəθən] (*or* ~ *race*) carrera *f* de Maratón.

ma·raud [mə'rɔ:d] merodear; **ma·'raud·er** merodeador (-a *f*) *m*.

mar·ble ['mɑ:bl] **1.** mármol *m*; canica *f in game*; **2.** marmóreo (*a. fig.*); de mármol; **3.** crispir; jaspear.

March[1] [mɑ:tʃ] marzo *m*; *mad as a ~ hare* loco como una cabra.

march[2] [~] **1.** marcha *f* (*a.* ♪, *fig.*); *steal a ~ on a p.* ganarle por la mano a una p.; ✕ ~ *past* desfile *m*; **2.** *v/i.* marchar; caminar con resolución; ✕ *quick* ~! de frente ¡mar!; ~ *on* seguir marchando; ~ *past* desfilar (ante); *v/t. p. etc.* hacer marchar; llevar; *distance* llevar andado, recorrer marchando.

march[3] [~] *hist.* marca *f*, frontera *f* (*mst* ~es *pl.*).

march·ing ['mɑ:tʃiŋ] de marcha; en marcha; *get one's* ~ *orders* F ser despedido.   [quesa *f*.\

mar·chion·ess ['mɑ:ʃənis] mar-\

mar·co·ni·gram [mɑ:'kounigræm] radiograma *m*.

mare [mɛə] yegua *f*; ~'*s nest* parto *m* de los montes, hallazgo *m* ilusorio.

mar·ga·rine [mɑ:dʒə'ri:n] margarina *f*.

mar·gin ['mɑ:dʒin] margen *mst m* (*a. typ.*, ✝ ~ *of profit*); reserva *f*; sobrante *m*; ~ *of error* margen *m* de error; ~ *of safety* margen *m* de seguridad; *in the* ~ al margen; **'mar·gin·al** □ marginal; ~ *note* acotación *f*.   [celular.\

Ma·ri·a [mə'raiə]: F *Black* ~ coche *m*\

mar·i·gold ['mærigould] caléndula *f*, maravilla *f*.   [guana *f*.\

mar·i·jua·na [mæri'wɑ:nə] mari-\

ma·rine [mə'ri:n] **1.** marino, marítimo; **2.** marina *f*; soldado *m* de marina; ~s *pl.* infantería *f* de marina; *tell that to the* ~s! ¡a otro perro con ese hueso!; **mar·i·ner** ['mærinə] marinero *m*, marino *m*.

mar·i·o·nette [mæriə'net] marioneta *f*, títere *m*.

mar·i·tal ['mæritl] □ marital; matrimonial; ~ *status* estado *m* civil.

mar·i·time ['mæritaim] marítimo.

mar·jo·ram ['mɑ:dʒərəm] mejorana *f*; orégano *m*.

mark[1] [mɑ:k] (*coin*) marco *m*.

mark[2] [~] **1.** señal *f*; (*distinguishing*, *trade-*) marca *f*; impresión *f*; (*trace*) huella *f*; (*stain*) mancha *f*; (*sign*) indicio *m*; (*target*) blanco *m*; (*label*) marbete *m*; *exam*: calificación *f*, nota *f*; distinción *f*, categoría *f*; (*level*) nivel *m*; *sport*: raya *f*; *hit the* ~ dar en el blanco, acertar; *make one's* ~ firmar con una cruz; *fig.* señalarse, distinguirse; *of* ~ célebre, distinguido; *up to the* ~ satisfactorio; a la altura de las circunstancias; *wide of the* ~ alejado de la verdad; errado; **2.** *v/t.* señalar; marcar; (*stain*) manchar; notar; apuntar; distinguir; *exam*: dar nota a, calificar; (*label*) rotular; indicar (el precio de); ~ *down* ✝ rebajar (el precio de); apuntar; *fig.* señalar, escoger; ~ *off* señalar; separar; definir; jalonar; ~ *out* trazar; marcar; definir; jalonar; (*select*) escoger; *v. time*; **marked** [mɑ:kt] marcado; señalado; notable; ~ *man* hombre *m* que ha llamado la atención; futura víctima *f*; **mark·ed·ly** ['mɑ:kidli] marcadamente; notablemente; **'mark·er** marcador *m* (*a. billiards*); ficha *f*; registro *m* *in book*.

mar·ket ['mɑ:kit] **1.** mercado *m*; (*a.* ~ *place*) plaza *f* (del mercado); ✝ bolsa *f*; *fig.* tráfico *m*; venta *f*; *be in the* ~ *for* estar dispuesto a comprar; *black* ~ estraperlo *m*, mercado *m* negro; bolsa *f* negra *S.Am.*; ~ *garden* huerto *m*; (*large*) huerta *f*; ~ *gardener* hortelano *m*; ~ *price* precio *m* corriente (*or* de mercado); ~ *research* análisis *m* de mercados; *on the* ~ de venta; en la bolsa; *play the* ~ jugar a la bolsa; *ready* ~ fácil salida *f*; **2.** vender, poner a la venta; llevar al mercado; **'mar·ket·a·ble** □ vendible, comerciable; **mar·ket·eer** [~'tiə]: *black* ~ estraperlista *m/f*; **'mar·ket·ing** venta *f*, comercialización *f*.

mark·ing ['mɑ:kiŋ] señal *f*; marca *f*; pinta *f* *on animals*; coloración *f*; '~**ink** tinta *f* de marcar.

marks·man ['mɑ:ksmən] tirador (-a *f*) *m*; **'marks·man·ship** buena puntería *f*.

marl [mɑ:l] marga *f*.

mar·ma·lade ['mɑːməleid] mermelada f (de naranjas amargas).

mar·mo·re·al [mɑːˈmɔːriəl] □ *poet.* marmóreo.

mar·mo·set ['mɑːməzet] tití m.

mar·mot ['mɑːmət] marmota f.

ma·roon¹ [məˈruːn] **1.** (*colour*) marrón m; (*firework*) petardo m; **2.** marrón.

ma·roon² [⁓] abandonar (en una isla desierta).

mar·quee [mɑːˈkiː] entoldado m.

mar·quess, *mst* **mar·quis** ['mɑːkwis] marqués m. , [ría f.] **mar·que·try** ['mɑːkitri] marquete-

mar·riage ['mæridʒ] matrimonio m; (*wedding*) boda(s) f (pl.), casamiento m; *fig.* unión f; by ⁓ político; civil ⁓ matrimonio m civil; ⁓ licence licencia f para casarse; ⁓ lines partida f de matrimonio; ⁓ portion dote f; related by ⁓ emparentado; '**marriage·a·ble** casadero, núbil.

mar·ried ['mærid] p. casado; *state etc.* conyugal; get ⁓ casarse (*to* con).

mar·row ['mærou] médula f (*or* medula f), tuétano m; meollo m (*a. fig.*); to the ⁓ hasta los tuétanos; ⚥ (*vegetable*) ⁓ calabacín m; '⁓·bone hueso m con tuétano; ⁓s pl. co. rodillas f/pl.

mar·ry ['mæri] v/t. (*give or join in marriage*) casar (*to* con); (*take in marriage*) casar(se) con; *fig.* unir; v/i. casarse; ⁓ again casarse en segundas nupcias; ⁓ into family emparentar con.

marsh [mɑːʃ] pantano m, marjal m; marisma f; ciénaga f; ⁓ fever paludismo m; ⁓ gas gas m de los pantanos.

mar·shal ['mɑːʃəl] **1.** mariscal m; maestro m de ceremonias; *Am.* oficial m de justicia; jefe m de policía; **2.** ordenar; conducir con ceremonia; dirigir; '**mar·shal·ling·'yard** 🚆 playa f de clasificación; '**marshmal·low** ♣ malvavisco m; bombón m de merengue blando; '**marsh'mari·gold** calta f (palustre); '**marsh·y** pantanoso.

mar·su·pi·al [mɑːˈsjuːpiəl] marsupial adj. a. su. m.

mart [mɑːt] emporio m; (*auctionroom*) martillo m; *poet.* plaza f del mercado.

mar·ten ['mɑːtin] marta f; garduña f.

mar·tial ['mɑːʃəl] □ marcial; castrense; ⁓ law ley f marcial; under ⁓ law en estado de sitio.

mar·tin¹ ['mɑːtin] orn. avión m.

Mar·tin² [⁓]: *St.* ⁓'s summer veranillo m de San Martín.

mar·ti·net [mɑːtiˈnet] ordenancista m/f.

Mar·tin·mas ['mɑːtinməs] día m de San Martín (*11 noviembre*).

mar·tyr ['mɑːtə] **1.** mártir m/f; **2.** martirizar; '**mar·tyr·dom** martirio m; '**mar·tyr·ize** martirizar.

mar·vel ['mɑːvəl] **1.** maravilla f; prodigio m; **2.** maravillarse (*at* con, de).

mar·vel·(l)ous ['mɑːviləs] □ maravilloso.

Marx·ism ['mɑːksizm] marxismo m.

mar·zi·pan [mɑːziˈpæn] mazapán m.

mas·ca·ra [mæsˈkɑːrə] tinte m para las pestañas.

mas·cot ['mæskət] mascota f.

mas·cu·line ['mæskjulin] **1.** masculino; varonil; (*mst of woman*) hombruno; **2.** *gr.* masculino m.

mash [mæʃ] **1.** mezcla f; amasijo m; baturrillo m; *brewing*: malta f remojada; ⚘ afrecho m remojado; puré m (de patatas); **2.** majar, machacar; mezclar; amasar; despachurrar; ⁓ed potatoes puré m de patatas (papas *S.Am.*).

mask [mɑːsk] **1.** máscara f (*a. fig.*); careta f, antifaz m; (*p.*) máscara m/f; v. masque; (*death*) ⁓ mascarilla f; **2.** enmascarar; ocultar; ⁓ed ball baile m de máscaras.

mas·och·ism ['mæzəkizm] masoquismo m.

ma·son ['meisn] ⚠ cantero m, albañil m; (*free-*) (franc)masón m; **ma·son·ic** [məˈsɔnik] masónico; '**ma·son·ry** cantería f, albañilería f; sillería f; (franc)masonería f.

masque [mɑːsk] mascarada f; mojiganga f; **mas·quer·ade** [mæskəˈreid] **1.** mascarada f; (baile m de) máscaras f/pl.; *fig.* farsa f; **2.** enmascararse, ir disfrazado (*as* de); *fig.* hacer el papel (*as* de).

mass¹ [mæs] *eccl.* misa f; High ⁓ misa f mayor; Low ⁓ misa f rezada.

mass² [⁓] **1.** masa f (*a. phys.*); bulto m (informe); macizo m *of mountains*; montón m, gran cantidad f; muchedumbre f; the ⁓es pl.

las masas; the (great) ~ of la mayoría de; in the ~ en conjunto; ~ meeting mitin m popular; ~ production producción f en serie; ~ unemployment desempleo m en masa; 2. juntar(se) en masa, reunir(se); concentrar(se).

mas·sa·cre ['mæsəkə] 1. matanza f; carnicería f; 2. hacer una carnicería de, masacrar.

mas·sage ['mæsa:ʒ] 1. masaje m; 2. dar masaje a.

mas·seur [mæ'sə:] masajista m; **mas'seuse** [~z] masajista f.

mas·sive ['mæsiv] macizo, sólido; abultado; '**mas·sive·ness** macicez f, solidez f; gran bulto m.

mast¹ [mɑ:st] ♣ mástil m, palo m, árbol m; radio: torre f.

mast² [~] beech: hayuco m; oak: bellota f. [... palos.\

mast·ed ['mɑ:stid] ♣ arbolado; de\

mas·ter ['mɑ:stə] 1. señor m; amo m of house etc.; (owner) dueño m; (graduate, expert, teacher a. fig.) maestro m; profesor m in secondary school; director m of college; ♣ capitán m; patrón m of small craft; (young) señorito m; maestre m of military order; v. art, ceremony; old ~ pintura f de uno de los grandes maestros; be ~ of dominar; poseer; be ~ of the situation ser dueño del baile; I am the ~ here aquí mando yo; be one's own ~ ser independiente; trabajar por su propia cuenta; 2. maestro; fig. magistral, superior, principal; 3. dominar (a. fig.); llegar a ser maestro en; vencer; '**mas·ter-'build·er** arquitecto m; maestro m de obras; constructor m; **mas·ter·ful** ['~ful] □ imperioso, dominante; '**mas·ter-key** llave f maestra; '**mas·ter·ly** magistral; maestro; perfecto.

mas·ter...: '~piece obra f maestra; '~stroke golpe m maestro; '**mas·ter·y** maestría f; dominio m; autoridad f.

mast·head ['mɑ:sthed] ♣ tope m.

mas·tic ['mæstik] mástique m; ♀, pharm. almáciga f.

mas·ti·cate ['mæstikeit] mas(ti)car; **mas·ti'ca·tion** masticación f; **mas·ti·ca·to·ry** ['~təri] masticatorio.

mas·tiff ['mæstif] mastín m; perro m alano.

mast·oid ['mæstɔid] mastoides adj. a. su. f.

mat¹ [mæt] 1. estera f; esterilla f; (round) ruedo m; felpudo m at door; salvamanteles m for table; (lace etc.) tapetito m; greña f of hair; 2. esterar; enmarañar(se), entretejerse.

mat² [~] mate.

match¹ [mætʃ] cerilla f, fósforo m, mixto m; cerillo m S.Am.; (fuse) mecha f.

match² [~] 1. igual m/f; compañero (a f) m; pareja f; matrimonio m; sport: partido m; concurso m; be a ~ for poder con; (colour etc.) hacer juego con; good ~ buena pareja f; buen partido m in marriage; meet one's ~ hallar la horma de su zapato; 2. v/t. (pair) emparejar; parear; igualar; competir con; colour etc. hacer juego con; ~ a p. against another hacer que una p. compita con otro; v/i. hacer juego, casar; ~ing, to ~ acompañado; a juego con; a tono (con).

match-box ['mætʃbɔks] cajita f de cerillas, fosforera f.

match·less ['mætʃlis] sin par, incomparable; '**match-mak·er** casamentero (a f) m.

match·wood ['mætʃwud] madera f para fósforos; astillas f/pl.

mate¹ [meit] chess: 1. mate m; 2. dar jaque mate (a).

mate² [~] 1. compañero m, camarada m; (married) cónyuge m/f, consorte m/f; ♣ primer oficial m, segundo m, piloto m; (assistant) ayudante m, peón m; zo. macho m, hembra f; 2. casar(se); zo. parear (se), acoplar(se); mating season época f de celo.

ma·te·ri·al [mə'tiəriəl] 1. □ material; importante, esencial; considerable; 2. (ingredient, equipment a. fig.) material m; (substance) materia f; fig. datos m/pl.; (cloth) tejido m, tela f; ~s pl. material(es) m(pl.); raw ~s materias f/pl. primas; writing ~s efectos m/pl. de escritorio; **ma·te·ri·al·ism** materialismo m; **ma·te·ri·al·ist** materialista adj. a. su. m/f; **ma·te·ri·al·is·tic** □ materialista; **ma·te·ri·al·i·za·tion** [~riəlai'zeiʃn] materialización f; realización f; **ma·te·ri·al·ize** materializar(se); realizarse.

ma·ter·nal [mə'tə:nl] □ materno; affection etc. maternal; **ma·ter·ni·ty** [~niti] maternidad f; ~ benefit subsidio m de natalidad; ~ hospital casa f de maternidad.

math·e·mat·i·cal [mæθi'mætikl] □ matemático; **math·e·ma·ti·cian** [‚məˈtiʃn] matemático m; **math·e·mat·ics** [‚ˈmætiks] mst sg. matemáticas) f(pl.).   [tarde.)

mat·i·née ['mætinei] función f de)

mat·ins ['mætinz] pl. maitines m/pl.

ma·tri·arch ['meitriɑːk] matriarca f; **ma·tri·cide** ['‚said] matricidio m; (p.) matricida m/f.

ma·tric·u·late [mə'trikjuleit] matricular(se); **ma·tric·u·la·tion** matriculación f.

mat·ri·mo·ni·al [mætri'mounjəl] □ matrimonial; conyugal; **mat·ri·mo·ny** ['mætriməni] matrimonio m; vida f conyugal.

ma·trix ['meitriks] matriz f.

ma·tron ['meitrən] matrona f; hospital: enfermera f jefa; school: ama f de llaves; **'ma·tron·ly** matronal; respetable; maduro y algo corpulento.

mat·ter ['mætə] 1. materia f (a. 🜨); material m; tema m; asunto m, cuestión f; motivo m; cosa f; printed ~ impresos m/pl.; a ~ of cosa de; obra de; a ~ of course por rutina; be a ~ of course ser de cajón; ~ of fact hecho m positivo; as a ~ of fact en realidad; el caso es que; ~ of form pura formalidad f; in the ~ of en materia de; ~ in hand asunto m de que se trata; no ~ no importa; no ~ how de cualquier modo; no ~ who quienquiera; to make ~s worse para colmo de desgracias; for that ~ en cuanto a eso; what ~? ¿qué importa?; what's the ~? ¿qué hay?; what's the ~ with smoking? ¿qué inconveniente hay en fumar?; what's the ~ with you? ¿qué te pasa?, ¿qué tienes?; 2. importar; it does not ~ no importa, es igual; what does it ~? ¿qué importa?; '~-of-'fact prosaico; práctico, positivista; flemático.

mat·ting ['mætiŋ] estera f.

mat·tock ['mætək] azadón m.

mat·tress ['mætris] colchón m.

ma·ture [mə'tjuə] 1. □ maduro (a. fig.); 🜊 vencido, pagadero; 2. madurar; 🜊 vencer; **ma'tu·ri·ty** madurez f; 🜊 vencimiento m.

ma·tu·ti·nal [mætjuˈtainl] □ matutino.

maud·lin ['mɔːdlin] sensiblero; llorón.

maul [mɔːl] magullar; maltratar (a. fig.); F manosear.

maun·der ['mɔːndə] hablar (or errar) como atontado; chochear.

Maun·dy Thurs·day ['mɔːndiˈθəːzdi] Jueves m Santo.

mau·so·le·um [mɔːsəˈliːəm] mausoleo m.

mauve [mouv] (de) color m de malva.

mav·er·ick ['mævərik] Am. res f sin marcar; pol. disidente m.

maw [mɔː] estómago m; ruminant: cuajar m; bird: molleja f; F buche m; fig. abismo m.

mawk·ish ['mɔːkiʃ] □ insulso; empalagoso, dulzarrón; sensiblero; **'mawk·ish·ness** sensiblería f etc.

max·il·lar·y [mækˈsiləri] maxilar.

max·im ['mæksim] máxima f; **max·i·mum** ['‚əm] 1. máximo; 2. máximo m, máximum m.

May[1] [mei] 1. mayo m; ~ Queen maya f; ♀ 🜊 flor f del espino blanco); 2. go ~ing ir a la fiesta de mayo.

may[2] [‚] [irr.] poder; ser posible; tener permiso para; I ~ come puede (ser) que yo venga; yes, I ~ sí, es posible; if I ~ si me lo permites; ~ I come in? ¿se puede (pasar)?; it ~ be that puede ser que, tal vez, quizás; it ~ snow puede (ser) que nieve, es posible que nieve; ~ you be lucky! ¡que tengas suerte!

may·be ['meibiː] quizá(s), tal vez, acaso.

May-day ['meidei] (fiesta f del) primero m de mayo.

may·on·naise [meiəˈneiz] mayonesa f.

may·or [mɛə] alcalde m; **'may·or·al** de alcalde; **'may·or·al·ty** alcaldía f; **'may·or·ess** alcaldesa f.

may·pole ['meipoul] mayo m.

maze [meiz] laberinto m; fig. enredo m, perplejidad f; **'ma·zy** □ laberíntico; perplejo.

me [miː, mi] me; (after prp.) mí; with ~ conmigo.

mead [miːd] 1. aguamiel f, hidrom(i)el m; 2. poet. = meadow.

mead·ow ['medou] prado m; (big) pradera f; henar m for hay; **'~·sweet** reina f de los prados.

mea·ger, mea·gre ['miːgə] □ escaso, exiguo, pobre; magro, flaco;

'mea·ger·ness, 'mea·gre·ness escasez *f etc.*

meal¹ [mi:l] comida *f.*

meal² [⌣] harina *f* (a medio moler).

meal-time ['mi:ltaim] hora *f* de comer.

meal·y ['mi:li] harinoso; pálido; '**~-mouthed** mojigato; excesivamente circunspecto.

mean¹ [mi:n] □ humilde, pobre; inferior; vil, bajo; sórdido; mezquino, tacaño; *Am.* F malo, desconsiderado.

mean² [⌣] 1. medio; *in the ~ time* = *~time;* 2. medio *m;* promedio *m,* término *m* medio; ℞ media *f;* ~s *sg. or pl.* medio(s) *m(pl.);* manera *f;* ~s *pl.* recursos *m/pl.,* medios *m/pl.,* dinero *m; by all ~s* por todos los medios; F por cierto, con mucho gusto, no faltaba más; *by any ~s* de cualquier modo que sea; *not by any ~s* = *by no ~s* de ningún modo; *by fair ~s or foul* por las buenas o por las malas; *by ~s of* por medio de, mediante; *by this ~s* por este medio, de este modo; *~s to an end* medio *m* para conseguir un fin.

mean³ [⌣] [*irr.*] querer decir (*by* con); significar (*to* para); destinar (*for* para); decir en serio; *~ to inf.* pensar *inf.,* proponerse *inf.;* he didn't *~ to do it* lo hizo sin querer; *~ well (ill)* tener buenas (malas) intenciones.

me·an·der [mi'ændə] 1. meandro *m,* serpenteo *m;* 2. serpentear; errar.

mean·ing ['mi:niŋ] 1. □ significativo; 2. significado *m,* sentido *m; what's the ~ of ...?* ¿qué significa ...?; '**mean·ing·less** sin sentido; insignificante; insensato.

mean·ness ['mi:nnis] humildad *f etc.* (*v.* **mean¹**).

meant [ment] *pret. a. p.p. of* **mean³.**

mean·time ['mi:ntaim], **mean·while** ['mi:nwail] entretanto, mientras tanto.

mea·sles ['mi:zlz] sarampión *m;* '**mea·sly** F pobre, despreciable.

meas·ur·a·ble ['meʒərəbl] □ mensurable; apreciable.

meas·ure ['meʒə] 1. medida *f* (*a. fig.*); (*rule*) regla *f;* ♩ compás *m; parl.* (proyecto *m* de) ley *f; dry ~* medida *f* para áridos; *~ of capacity* medida *f* de capacidad; *beyond ~* hasta no más; excesivamente; *for*

good ~ por añadidura; *in a ~, in some ~* hasta cierto punto; *in (a) great ~* en gran manera; *made to ~* hecho a medida; *take a p.'s ~ fig.* tomarle las medidas a una p.; 2. medir (*a. ~ off, ~ out*); *p. for height* tallar; *p. for clothes* tomar las medidas a; *~ one's length* medir el suelo; *~ up to* estar a la altura de; *~d* moderado; acompasado; deliberado; '**mea·sure·less** □ inmensurable, inmenso; '**meas·ure·ment** medida *f;* medición *f.*

meas·ur·ing ['meʒəriŋ] 1. medición *f;* 2. de medir.

meat [mi:t] carne *f;* † comida *f;* † alimento *m; fig.* meollo *m,* sustancia *f; cold ~* fiambre *m; ~ ball* albóndiga *f; ~ fly* mosca *f* de la carne; *~ pie* pastel *m* de carne, empanada *f;* '**~-safe** fresquera *f;* '**meat·y** carnoso; *fig.* sustancioso.

me·chan·ic [mi'kænik] mecánico *m;* **me'chan·i·cal** □ mecánico; maquinal (*a. fig.*); *~ engineering* ingeniería *f* mecánica; **me·chan·ics** [mi'kæniks] *mst sg.* mecánica *f;* mecanismo *m,* técnica *f.*

mech·a·nism ['mekənizm] mecanismo *m; phls.* mecanicismo *m;* **mech·a·nize** ['~naiz] mecanizar.

med·al ['medl] medalla *f;* **me·dal·lion** [mi'dæljən] medallón *m;* **med·al·(l)ist** ['medlist] medallista *m;* persona *f* condecorada con una medalla.

med·dle ['medl] entrometerse (*in* en); meterse (*with* con); '**med·dler** entrometido (a *f*) *m;* **med·dle·some** ['~səm] □ entrometido; '**med·dle·some·ness** entrometimiento *m.*

me·di·ae·val = **medieval.**

me·di·al ['mi:diəl] □ medial; '**me·di·an** mediano.

me·di·ate 1. □ ['mi:diit] mediato; 2. ['mi:dieit] mediar (*between* entre, *for* por, *in* en); **me·di'a·tion** mediación *f;* '**me·di·a·tor** mediador (-a *f*) *m.*

med·i·cal ['medikəl] médico; de medicina; medicinal; *~ board* tribunal *m* médico; *~ certificate* certificado *m* médico; *~ corps* cuerpo *m* de sanidad; *~ jurisprudence* medicina *f* legal; *~ man* médico *m; ~ practitioner* médico (a *f*) *m; ~ officer* jefe *m* de sanidad municipal; ✂ oficial *m* médico; ~ *student* estudiante *m/f* de medicina; **me·'dic·a·ment** medicamento *m*.

med·i·cate ['medikeit] medicar; impregnar; **med·i·ca·tion** medicación *f*.

me·dic·i·nal [me'disinl] □ medicinal; **med·i·cine** ['medsin] medicina *f*; medicamento *m*; ~ *chest* botiquín *m*; ~ *man* curandero *m*; hechizador *m*; *take one's* ~ pagar las consecuencias.

me·di·e·val [medi'i:vəl] □ medieval; **me·di·e·val·ism** medievalismo *m*; **me·di·e·val·ist** medievalista *m/f*.

me·di·o·cre [mi:di'oukə] mediano, mediocre; **me·di·oc·ri·ty** [~'ɔkriti] mediocridad *f*, medianía *f* (*a. p.*).

med·i·tate ['mediteit] meditar (*on acc.*); reflexionar (*on en, sobre*); **med·i·ta·tion** meditación *f*, reflexión *f*; **'med·i·ta·tive** □ meditabundo, meditador.

me·di·um ['mi:diəm] **1.** *pl. a.* **me·dia** ['~diə] medio *m*; (*p.*) médium *m*; *happy* ~ justo medio *m*; *through the* ~ *of* por medio de; **2.** mediano, intermedio, regular; '**~-sized** de tamaño median(an)o.

med·lar ['medlə] níspola *f*; (*a.* ~ *tree*) níspero *m*.

med·ley ['medli] mezcla *f*, mezcolanza *f*; miscelánea *f*; ♪ popurrí *m*.

me·dul·la [mi'dʌlə] médula *f*.

meed [mi:d] *poet.* galardón *m* (merecido).

meek [mi:k] □ manso, dócil, humilde; '**meek·ness** mansedumbre *f* etc.

meer·schaum ['miəʃəm] (pipa *f* de) espuma *f* de mar.

meet[1] [mi:t] *lit.*, † conveniente.

meet[2] [~] **1.** [*irr.*] *v/t.* encontrar(se con); (*come across*) tropezar con; (*on arrival*) ir a recibir, esperar; (*become acquainted with*) conocer; (*fight*) batirse con; *sport*: enfrentarse con; (*connect with* 🚢 *etc.*) empalmar con; (*suffer*) tener que aguantar; (*answer*) responder a; (*fall in with*) conformarse a; *request, need* satisfacer; *bill* pagar; *obligations* cumplir; *expense* hacer frente a; *go to* ~ ir al encuentro de; ~ *a p. half-way fig.* partir la diferencia, hacer concesiones a una p.; *v. please*; *v/i.* encontrarse; reunirse;

conocerse; verse; (*fight*) batirse; (*join*) confluir; ~ *with* encontrarse con; reunirse con; *loss etc.* sufrir; *accident* tener; *till we* ~ *again* hasta más ver, hasta la vista; **2.** concurso *m* de cazadores (*or* deportistas).

meet·ing ['mi:tiŋ] reunión *f*; sesión *f*; (*public*) mitin *m*; encuentro *m*; (*by appointment*) cita *f*; confluencia *f of rivers*; *sport*: concurso *m*; '**~-place** lugar *m* de reunión (*or* de cita).

meg·a·cy·cle ['megəsaikl] megaciclo *m*; **meg·a·lo·ma·ni·a** [~'lou'meinjə] megalomanía *f*; **meg·a·phone** ['~foun] megáfono *m*; **meg·a·ton** ['~tʌn] megatón *m*.

mel·an·chol·ic [melən'kɔlik] melancólico; **mel·an·chol·y** ['~kɔli] **1.** melancolía *f*; **2.** melancólico.

mê·lée ['melei] pelea *f* confusa, refriega *f*.

mel·lif·lu·ent [me'lifluənt], *mst* **mel·lif·lu·ous** melifluo.

mel·low ['melou] **1.** □ maduro, sazonado; *fig.* blando, suave, meloso; melodioso; *wine* añejo; *sl.* entre dos luces; **2.** madurar(se); suavizar(se); '**mel·low·ness** madurez *f etc.*

me·lo·di·ous [mi'loudjəs] □ melodioso; **me·lo·di·ous·ness** melodía *f*; '**mel·o·dra·ma** melodrama *m*; **mel·o·dra'mat·ic** melodramático; '**mel·o·dy** melodía *f*.

mel·on ['melən] melón *m*.

melt [melt] (*snow*) derretir(se); (*metal*) fundir(se); disolver(se); *fig.* ablandar(se); ~ *away* disolverse, desvanecerse; ~ *down* fundir; ~ *into tears* deshacerse en lágrimas.

melt·ing ['meltiŋ] **1.** fusión *f*; derretimiento *m*; **2.** □ fundente; *fig.* tierno, dulce; '**~-point** punto *m* de fusión; '**~-pot** crisol *m* (*a. fig.*).

mem·ber ['membə] miembro *m* (*a. parl.*); socio (*a f*) *m*, individuo *m of society*; *parl.* diputado *m* (*Spanish*: a Cortes); '**mem·ber·ship** calidad *f* de miembro (*or* socio); asociación *f*; (número *m* de) miembros *m/pl. or* socios *m/pl.*; ~ *fee* cuota *f* (de socio).

mem·brane ['membrein] membrana *f*. [*m.*]

me·men·to [me'mentou] recuerdo]

mem·oir ['memwɑ:] memoria *f*; biografía *f*; ~*s pl.* memorias *f/pl.*

mem·o·ra·ble ['meməʳəbl] ☐ memorable.

mem·o·ran·dum [memə'rændəm] apunte m, memoria f; pol. memorándum m, memorando m.

me·mo·ri·al [mi'mɔ:riəl] 1. conmemorativo; 2. monumento m (conmemorativo); (document) memorial m; **me'mo·ri·al·ist** (professional) memorialista m/f, suplicante m/f; **'me'mo·rial·ize** conmemorar; dirigir un memorial a.

mem·o·rize ['meməraiz] aprender de memoria.

mem·o·ry ['meməri] memoria f; recuerdo m; from ~ de memoria; in ~ of en memoria de.

men [men] pl. of man.

men·ace ['menəs] 1. amenaza f; F sujeto m peligroso (or fastidioso); 2. amenazar.

me·nag·er·ie [mi'nædʒəri] casa f (or colección f) de fieras.

mend [mend] 1. v/t. remendar; componer, reparar; mejorar; reformar; (darn) zurcir; ~ one's ways enmendarse; v/i. mejorar(se); 2. remiendo m; (darn) zurcido m; be on the ~ ir mejorando.

men·da·cious [men'deiʃəs] ☐ mendaz; **men·dac·i·ty** [~'dæsiti] mendacidad f.

men·di·can·cy ['mendikənsi] mendicidad f; **'men·di·cant** mendicante adj. a. su. m/f; **men'dic·i·ty** [~siti] mendicidad f.

mend·ing ['mendiŋ] compostura f; reparación f; (darning) zurcidura f; (clothes) ropa f de repaso.

men·folk ['menfouk] F hombres m/pl.

me·ni·al ['mi:niəl] mst contp. 1. bajo; servil; doméstico; 2. criado (a f) m; lacayo m.

men·in·gi·tis [menin'dʒaitis] me- **men·stru·al** ['menstruəl] menstrual; **men·stru·a·tion** menstruación f.

men·su·ra·tion [mensju'reiʃn] mensura(ción) f.

men·tal ['mentl] ☐ mental; ~ arithmetic cálculo m mental; ~ derangement trastorno m mental; ~ home, ~ hospital manicomio m; ~ reservation reserva f mental; ~ly ill alienado; **men·tal·i·ty** [~'tæliti] mentalidad f.

men·thol ['menθɔl] mentol m.

men·tion ['menʃən] 1. mención f; alusión f; 2. mencionar, mentar;

(in passing) aludir a; don't ~ it! ¡no hay de qué!, ¡de nada!; not to ~ sin contar; además de.

men·tor ['mentɔ:] mentor m.

men·u ['menju:] lista f (de platos), minuta f, menú m.

mer·can·tile ['mə:kəntail] mercantil, comercial; ~ marine marina f mercante.

mer·ce·nar·y ['mə:sinəri] ☐ mercenario (⚔ a. su. m); interesado.

mer·cer ['mə:sə] mercero m; sedero m; **'mer·cer·y** mercería f; sedería f.

mer·cer·ize ['mə:səraiz] mercerizar.

mer·chan·dise ['mə:tʃəndaiz] mercancía(s) f(pl.), géneros m/pl.

mer·chant ['mə:tʃənt] 1. comerciante m/f, negociante m; F sujeto m; 2. mercantil; ⚓ mercante; **'mer·chant·a·ble** comerciable; **'mer·chant·man** buque m mercante.

mer·ci·ful ['mə:siful] ☐ misericordioso, piadoso; clemente.

mer·ci·less ['mə:silis] ☐ despiadado, inhumano.

mer·cu·ri·al [mə:kjuəriəl] mercurial; (lively) vivo; (changeable) veleidoso.

mer·cu·ry ['mə:kjuri] mercurio m.

mer·cy ['mə:si] misericordia f, compasión f; clemencia f; favor m; merced f; be at the ~ of estar a la merced de; it is a ~ that gracias a Dios que; ~ killing eutanasia f.

mere[1] [miə] ☐ mero; simple; solo, no más que; ~(st) nonsense puro disparate m; a ~ nothing una friolera; ~ words palabras f/pl. al aire; ~ly meramente; sólo, nada más que.

mere[2] [~] lago m.

mer·e·tri·cious [meri'triʃəs] ☐ de oropel, postizo.

merge [mə:dʒ] v/t. unir; mezclar; ♦ fusionar, enchufar; v/i. fundirse, ♦ fusionarse; ~ into ir convirtiéndose en; perderse en; **'merg·er** fusión f.

me·rid·i·an [mə'ridiən] 1. geog., ast. meridiano m; mediodía m; 2. meridiano; **me'rid·i·o·nal** ☐ meridional.

me·ringue [mə'ræŋ] merengue m.

mer·it ['merit] 1. mérito m, merecimiento m; ~s ⚖ méritos m/pl.; circunstancias f/pl. (de cada caso); 2. merecer, ser digno de; **mer·i·to·ri·ous** [~'tɔ:riəs] ☐ meritorio.

mer·maid ['mə:meid] sirena *f*; **mer·man** ['ˌmən] tritón *m*.

mer·ri·ment ['merimənt] alegría *f*, regocijo *m*, alborozo *m*; hilaridad *f*.

mer·ry □ alegre, regocijado, alborozado; *sl.* calamocano; *make ~* divertirse, regocijarse; *~ Christmas!* ¡felices pascuas!; '*~-go-round* tiovivo *m*, caballitos *m/pl.*; '*~-mak-ing* festividades *f/pl.*; alborozo *m*.

mes·en·ter·y ['mesəntəri] mesenterio *m*.

mesh [meʃ] **1.** malla *f*; ⊕ engran(aj)e *m*; *fig.* (*freq. ~es*) red *f*, trampa *f*; ⊕ *be in ~* estar engranado; **2.** *v/t. fig.* enredar; *v/i.* engranar (*with con*).

mes·mer·ism ['mezmərizm] mesmerismo *m*; '**mes·mer·ize** hipnotizar.

mes·on ['mi:zən] *phys.* mesón *m*.

mess¹ [mes] **1.** revoltijo *m*, lío *m*, confusión *f*; asco *m*, suciedad *f*; *be in a ~* estar revuelto; (*p.*) estar en un aprieto; *make a ~ of =* **2.** *v/t.* (*a. ~ up*) echar a perder; desordenar; ensuciar; *v/i.*: F *~ about* perder el tiempo (*in tonterías*); trabajar con desgana; *~ about with* manosear; divertirse con; *stop ~ing about!* ¡déjate de tonterías!.

mess² [~] **1.** † plato *m* de comida; ✕, ⚓ rancho *m*; **2.** comer (juntos); arrancharse.

mes·sage ['mesidʒ] recado *m*, mensaje *m*; *mst tel.* parte *m*; *leave a ~* dejar un recado.

mes·sen·ger ['mesindʒə] mensajero (a *f*) *m*; mandadero (a *f*) *m*, recadero (a *f*) *m*; *~ boy* botones *m*.

Mes·sieurs, *mst* **Messrs** ['mesəz] s(eño)res *m/pl.*

mess·mate ['meismeit] compañero *m* de rancho, comensal *m*; '**mess-tin** ✕ plato *m* de campaña.

mes·suage ['meswidʒ] ⚖ finca *f*.

met [met] *pret. a. p.p. of* **meet²** 1.

met·a·bol·ic [metə'bɔlik] metabólico; **me'tab·o·lism** metabolismo *m*.

met·al ['metl] **1.** metal *m*; *road:* grava *f*; *fig.* temple *m*; *fig.* ánimo *m*, brío *m*; *~s pl.* 🚆 rieles *m/pl.*; *~ polish* lustre *m* para metales; **2.** metálico; **3.** *v/t. road* engravar; **me'tal·lic** [mi'tælik] □ metálico; **met·al·lif·er·ous** [metə'lifərəs] metalífero; **met·al·lur·gic, met·al-** **lur·gi·cal** [ˌlə:dʒik(l)] metalúrgico; '**met·al·lur·gy** metalurgia *f*; '**met·al·work** metalistería *f*.

met·a·mor·phose [metə'mɔ:fouz] metamorfosear; **met·a'mor·pho·sis** [ˌfəsis], *pl.* **met·a'mor·pho·ses** [ˌfəsi:z] metamorfosis *f*.

met·a·phor ['metəfə] metáfora *f*; **met·a·phor·ic, mst met·a·phor·i·cal** [ˌ'fɔrik(l)] □ metafórico.

met·a·phys·i·cal [metə'fizikl] □ metafísico; **met·a'phys·ics** *mst sg.* metafísica *f*.

mete [mi:t] (*mst ~ out*) repartir, distribuir; F *punishment* dar, imponer.

me·te·or ['mi:tjə] meteorito *m*; *fig.* meteoro *m*; **me·te·or·ic** [mi:ti'ɔrik] meteórico; **me·te·or·ite** ['mi:tjərait] bólido *m*; **me·te·or·o·log·i·cal** [mi:tjərə'lɔdʒikl] □ meteorológico; **me·te·or·ol·o·gist** [ˌ'rɔlədʒist] meteorologista *m/f*; **me·te·or'ol·o·gy** meteorología *f*.

me·ter ['mi:tə] **1.** contador *m*; medidor *m S.Am.*; *v.* metre; **2.** medir (con contador).

meth·ane ['meθein] metano *m*.

me·thinks [mi'θiŋks] (*pret. methought*) † *or co.* me parece.

meth·od ['meθəd] método *m*, procedimiento *m*, sistema *m*; orden *m*; razón *f*; **me·thod·ic, mst me·thod·i·cal** [mi'θɔdik(l)] □ metódico; ordenado; **Meth·od·ism** ['meθədizm] metodismo *m*; '**Meth·od·ist** metodista *m/f*; '**meth·od·ize** metodizar; **meth·od·ol·o·gy** [ˌ'dɔlədʒi] metodología *f*.

meth·yl ['meθil] metilo *m*; *~ alcohol* alcohol *m* metílico; **meth·yl·at·ed spir·it** ['meθileitid 'spirit] alcohol *m* metilado (*or* desnaturalizado).

me·tic·u·lous [mi'tikjuləs] □ meticuloso; minucioso.

me·tre ['mi:tə] *all senses:* metro *m*.

met·ric ['metrik] métrico; *~ system* sistema *m* métrico; '**met·ri·cal** □ métrico; '**met·rics** *pl. a. sg.* métrica *f*.

me·trop·o·lis [mi'trɔpəlis] metrópoli *f*; **me·tro·pol·i·tan** [metrə-'pɔlitən] **1.** metropolitano; ♀ *Railway* metro(politano) *m*; **2.** *eccl.* metropolitano *m*.

met·tle ['metl] ánimo *m*, brío *m*; temple *m*; *be on one's ~* estar dispuesto a hacer grandes esfuerzos; *put a p. on his ~* picar a una p. en

el amor propio; **met·tle·some** ['͟səm] brioso, fogoso, animoso.
mew[1] [mju:] *orn.* gaviota *f*.
mew[2] [͟] **1.** maullido *m of cat*; **2.** maullar.
mewl [mju:l] maullar; lloriquear.
mews [mju:z] caballeriza *f*.
Mex·i·can ['meksikən] mejicano (*in Mexico* mexicano) *adj. a. su. m* (a *f*).
mez·za·nine ['mezəni:n] entresuelo *m*.
mi·aow [mi'au] **1.** miau *m*; **2.** maullar.
mi·as·ma [mai'æzmə], *pl. a.* **mi·'as·ma·ta** [͟tə] miasma *m*; **mi·'as·mal** □ miasmático.
mi·ca ['maikə] mica *f*.
mice [mais] *pl. of* mouse.
Mich·ael·mas ['miklməs] fiesta *f* de San Miguel (*29 septiembre*).
mi·cro... ['maikrou] micro...
mi·cro·bus ['maikroubʌs] microbus *m*; **mi·cro·cosm** ['͟kozm] microcosmo *m*; **'mi·cro·film** microfilm *m*; **'mi·cro·groove** microsurco.
mi·crom·e·ter [mai'krɔmitə] micrómetro *m*; **mi·cro·phone** ['maikrəfoun] micrófono *m*; **mi·cro·scope** ['͟skoup] microscopio *m*; **mi·cro·scop·ic, mi·cro·scop·i·cal** [͟s'kɔpik(l)] □ microscópico.
mid [mid] medio; *poet.* = amid; **~-'air:** *in* ~ en medio del aire; **'~-course:** *in* ~ a media carrera; **'~-day 1.** mediodía *m*; **2.** de(l) mediodía.
mid·den ['midn] muladar *m*.
mid·dle ['midl] **1.** centro *m*, medio *m*, mitad *f*; (*waist*) cintura *f*; *in the* ~ *of* en medio de; en pleno; *in the* ~ *of the afternoon* a media tarde; *towards* (*or in*) *the* ~ *of June* a mediados de junio; **2.** medio, intermedio; de en medio; central; mediano; ~ *age* mediana edad *f*; ♀ *Ages* Edad *f* Media; ~ *class*(*es pl.*) clase *f* media; ~ *distance* segundo término *m*; **'~-'aged** de mediana edad, de edad madura; **'~-'class** de la clase media; **'~-man** intermediario *m*; corredor *m*; **'~-most** más céntrico; **'~-sized** de tamaño mediano; *p.* de estatura mediana; **'~-weight** *boxing:* peso *m* medio.
mid·dling ['midliŋ] **1.** *adj.* mediano, regular; mediocre; **2.** *adv.* así, así; medianamente.

mid·dy ['midi] = *midshipman*.
midge [midʒ] mosca *f* pequeña; enano (a *f*) *m*; **midg·et** · ['͟it] **1.** enano (a *f*) *m*; **2.** (en) miniatura.
mid·land ['midlənd] **1.** del interior, del centro (de un país); **2.** *the* ♀s *pl. región central de Inglaterra*; **'mid·night** (de) medianoche *f*; *burn the* ~ *oil* quemarse las cejas; **mid·riff** ['͟rif] diafragma *m*; **'mid·ship·man** guardia marina *m*; *in medio del navío*; **midst** [midst] **1.** *in the* ~ *of* entre, en medio de; *in our* ~ entre nosotros; **2.** *prp. poet.* = *amidst*; **'mid·stream:** *in* ~ en medio de la corriente; **'mid·sum·mer** pleno verano *m*; solsticio *m* de verano; ♀ *Day* fiesta *f* de San Juan (*24 junio*); **'mid·way 1.** (situado) a mitad del camino; **2.** mitad *f* del camino; *Am.* avenida *f* central; **'mid·wife** comadrona *f*, partera *f*; **mid·wife·ry** ['midwifri] partería *f*; **'mid·win·ter** pleno invierno *m*; solsticio *m* de invierno.
mien [mi:n] *lit.* semblante *m*; porte *m*, aire *m*.
might [mait] **1.** fuerza *f*, poder(ío) *m*; *with* ~ *and main* con todas sus *etc.* fuerzas, a más no poder; **2.** *pret. of* may[2]; podría *etc.*; ser posible; ojalá; *for many phrases, v.* may; *they* ~ *arrive today* es posible que lleguen hoy; **might·i·ness** ['͟inis] fuerza *f*; poder(ío) *m*; grandeza*f*; **'might·y 1.** □ fuerte, potente; F enorme; **2.** *adv.* F muy.
mi·gnon·ette [minjə'nət] reseda *f*.
mi·graine ['mi:grein] jaqueca *f*, migraña *f*. **[2.** (*bird*) ave *f* de paso.)
mi·grant ['maigrənt] **1.** migratorio; **mi·grate** [mai'greit] emigrar; **mi·'gra·tion** migración *f*; **mi·gra·to·ry** ['͟grətəri] migratorio.
mike [maik] *sl.* micrófono *m*.
milch [miltʃ]: ~ *cow* vaca *f* lechera.
mild [maild] □ suave; manso; blando; apacible; dulce; *weather* templado; ♣ benigno; (*slight*) ligero; *to put it* ~*ly* para no decir más.
mil·dew ['mildju:] **1.** moho *m*; añublo *m on wheat*; mildeu *m on vine*; **2.** enmohecer(se).
mild·ness ['maildnis] suavidad *f etc.*
mile [mail] milla *f* (= *1609,34 m.*).
mil(e)·age ['mailidʒ] número *m* de millas; distancia*f* en millas; *approx.* kilometraje *m*.

mile·stone ['mailstoun] piedra *f* miliar(ia); mojón *m*; *fig.* be *a* ~ hacer época.

mi·lieu ['mi:ljə:] medio *m*, ambiente *m*.

mil·i·tan·cy ['militənsi] belicosidad *f*; **'mil·i·tant** □ militante; belicoso; agresivo; **mil·i·ta·rism** ['~rizəm] militarismo *m*; **'mil·i·tar·ize** militarizar; **'mil·i·tar·y 1.** □ militar; de guerra; **2.** the ~ los militares; **mil·i·tate** ['~teit] militar (*against* contra; *in favour of* a favor de); **mi·li·tia** [mi'liʃə] milicia *f*; **mi'li·tia·man** [~mən] miliciano *m*.

milk [milk] **1.** leche *f*; ~ *diet* régimen *m* lácteo; ~ *of human kindness* compasión *f*; ~ *of magnesia* leche *f* de magnesia; ~ *tooth* diente *m* de leche; *powdered (whole)* ~ leche *f* en polvo (no desnatada); **2.** *v/t.* ordeñar; *fig.* chupar; *v/i.* dar leche; **'milk·'and·'wa·ter** débil, flojo; **'milk·er** ordeñador (-a *f*) *m*; vaca *f etc.* lechera; **'milk·float** carro *m* de la leche; **'milk·ing** ordeño *m*; **'milk·ing·ma'chine** ordeñadora *f* (mecánica).

milk...: '~·maid lechera *f*; **'~·man** lechero *m*; **'~·'shake** batido *m* de leche; **'~·sop** marica *m*; **'milk·y** lechoso; ♀ *Way* Vía *f* Láctea.

mill[1] [mil] **1.** molino *m*; molinillo *m for coffee etc.*; (*factory*) fábrica *f*, taller *m*; *spinning*: hilandería *f*; *weaving*: tejeduría *f*; F pugilato *m*; F *go through the* ~ pasar por muchas cosas en la vida; aprender por experiencia; entrenarse rigurosamente; *put a p. through the* ~ pasar por la piedra; **2.** *v/t.* moler; ⊕ fresar; *coin* acordonar; *cloth* abatanar; *chocolate* batir; ~ed *edge* cordoncillo *m*; *v/i.*: ~ *around* circular en masa, moverse con impaciencia.

mill[2] [~] *Am.* milésimo *m* de dólar.

mil·len·ni·al [mi'leniəl] milenario; **mil·le·nar·y** ['~əri] milenario *adj. a. su. m*; **mil'len·ni·um** [~iəm] milenario *m*, milenio *m*.

mil·le·pede ['milipi:d] miriápodo *m*.

mill·er ['milə] molinero *m*.

mil·les·i·mal [mi'lesiməl] milésimo.

mil·let ['milit] mijo *m*.

mill-hand ['milhænd] obrero (a *f*) *m*, operario (a *f*) *m*. [*m/pl.*]

mil·li·ard ['miljɑ:d] mil millones}

mil·li·gram(me) ['miligræm] miligramo *m*.

mil·li·litre ['milili:tə] mililitro *m*.

mil·li·me·tre ['milimi:tə] milímetro *m*.

mil·li·ner ['milinə] sombrerera *f*, modista *f* (de sombreros); **'mil·li·ner·y** sombrerería *f*; sombreros *m/pl.* de señora.

mill·ing ['miliŋ] molienda *f*; cordoncillo *m of coin*; ⊕ ~ *cutter* fresa *f*; ~ *machine* fresadora *f*.

mil·lion ['miljən] millón *m*; *three* ~ *men* tres millones de hombres; **mil·lion·aire** [~'nɛə] millonario (a *f*) *m*; **mil·lionth** ['miljənθ] millonésimo *adj. a. su. m*.

mill...: '~·pond represa *f* de molino, cubo *m*; **'~·race** caz *m*; **'~·stone** piedra *f* de molino, muela *f*.

mil·om·e·ter [mai'lɔmitə] *approx.* cuentakilómetros *m*.

milt[1] [milt] *ichth.* lecha *f*.

milt[2] [~] *anat.* bazo *m*.

mime [maim] **1.** mimo *m*; pantomima *f*, mímica *f*; **2.** *v/t.* remedar, hacer en pantomima; *v/i.* hacer de mimo. [meógrafo *m.*]

mim·e·o·graph ['mimiəgra:f] mi-}

mim·ic ['mimik] **1.** mímico; fingido; **2.** remedador (-a *f*) *m*; **3.** remedar; imitar; **'mim·ic·ry** mímica *f*, remedo *m*; *zo.* mimetismo *m*.

min·a·ret ['minəret] alminar *m*.

min·a·to·ry ['minətəri] amenazador.

mince [mins] **1.** *v/t.* picar; desmenuzar; *not to* ~ *matters*, *not to* ~ *one's words* no tener pelos en la lengua; *v/i.* andar con pasos menuditos; hablar remilgadamente; **2.** carne *f* picada (*a.* ~d *meat*); **'~·meat** conserva *f* de fruta picada y especias; *make* ~ *of* hacer pedazos; **'~·'pie** pastel *m* de mincemeat; **'minc·er** molinillo *m*, máquina *f* de picar carne, picadora *f*.

minc·ing ['minsiŋ] remilgado, afectado; **'~·ma·chine** = *mincer*.

mind [maind] **1.** mente *f*; (*intellect*) inteligencia *f*, entendimiento *m*; (*not matter*) espíritu *m*; ánimo *m*; juicio *m*; (*opinion*) parecer *m*; inclinación *f*; gusto *m*; memoria *f*; ~*'s eye* imaginación *f*; *change one's* ~ cambiar de opinión, mudar de parecer; *give one's* ~ *to* aplicarse a; *give a p. a piece of one's* ~ decirle cuatro verdades a una p.; *I have (half) a* ~ *to go*, *I have a good* ~ *to go* estoy por ir; tengo ganas de ir; por poco me marcho; *know one's own* ~ saber lo que uno quiere; *bear (or keep) in* ~ tener presente, tener en cuenta; *have in* ~ pensar en; tener pensado; *put a p. in*~*of* recordarle a una p.; *be in one's right* ~ estar en sus cabales; *make up one's* ~ resolverse, decidirse (*to* a); determinar (*to inf.*); tomar partido; *of one* ~ unánimes; *have s.t. on one's* ~ estar preocupado; *out of* ~ olvidado; *time out of* ~ tiempo *m* inmemorial; *out of one's* ~ fuera de juicio, (como) loco; *set one's* ~ *on* desear con vehemencia; estar resuelto a; *it slipped my* ~ se me escapó de la memoria; *speak one's* ~ decir su parecer, hablar con franqueza; *with one* ~ unánimemente; **2.** *v/t.* (*heed*) fijarse en, hacer caso de; (*bear in* ~) tener en cuenta; cuidar; (*beware of*) tener cuidado de; (*remember*) acordarse de; obedecer; (*worry*) preocuparse de; (*be put out by*) sentir molestia por; tener inconveniente en; *do you* ~ *the noise?* ¿le molesta el ruido?; *do you* ~ *lending it to me?* ¿no te importa prestármelo?; *would you* ~ *taking off your hat?* ¿quiere hacer el favor de quitarse el sombrero?; *v. business*; *v/i.* tener cuidado; sentir molestia; tener inconveniente; ~! ¡cuidado!; *never*~! ¡no haga-Vd. caso!; ¡no importa!; ¡no se preocupe!; ¿qué más da?; '**mind·ed** inclinado, dispuesto; de pensamientos...; '**mind·ful** □ atento (*of* a), cuidadoso (*of* de); '**mind·less** □ estúpido; negligente (*of* de).

mine¹ [main] (el) mío, (la) mía *etc.*

mine² [~] **1.** mina *f* (*a.* ♣, ✕, *fig.*); **2.** *v/t.* extraer; minar (*mst* ✕); ✕, ♣ sembrar minas en; *v/i.* dedicarse a la minería; extraer minerales; ✕ minar; '~**field** campo *m* de minas; '~**lay·er** buque *m* minador; '**min·er** minero *m*.

min·er·al ['minərəl] mineral *adj. a. su. m*; ~ *water* agua *f* mineral; gaseosa *f* (*a.* F ~s); '**min·er·al·ize** mineralizar; **min·er·al·o·gist** [~'rælədʒist] mineralogista *m/f*; **min·er·al·o·gy** mineralogía *f*.

mine·sweep·er ['mainswi:pə] barreminas *m*, dragaminas *m*.

min·gle ['miŋgl] mezclar(se), confundir(se) (*in*, *with* con); asociarse (*with* con).

min·gy ['mindʒi] F cicatero, tacaño.

min·i·a·ture ['minjətʃə] **1.** miniatura *f*; modelo *m* pequeño; **2.** (en) miniatura; diminuto.

min·im ['minim] ♪ blanca *f*; *pharm.* mínima *f*; *eccl.* mínimo *m*; '**min·i·mal** [~l] mínimo; '**min·i·mize** minimizar, reducir al mínimo; atenuar; empequeñecer; menospreciar; **min·i·mum** ['~məm] **1.** mínimo *m*, mínimum *m*; **2.** mínimo.

min·ing ['mainiŋ] **1.** minería *f*; extracción *f*; **2.** minero; ~ *engineer* ingeniero *m* de minas.

min·ion ['minjən] favorito (a *f*) *m*; paniaguado *m*; satélite *m*; *typ.* miñona *f*.

min·is·ter ['ministə] **1.** ministro *m*; **2.** ministrar; atender (*to* a); **min·is·te·ri·al** [~'tiəriəl] □ *pol.* ministerial; de ministro.

min·is·trant ['ministrənt] **1.** ministrador; **2.** *eccl.* oficiante *m*; **min·is·tra·tion** ayuda *f*; servicio *m*; *eccl.* ministerio *m*; '**min·is·try** ministerio *m*; *eccl.* sacerdocio *m*.

mink [miŋk] (piel *f* de) visón *m*.

min·now ['minou] pececillo *m* de agua dulce.

mi·nor ['mainə] **1.** menor (*a.* ♪); menor de edad; secundario; subalterno; *detail* sin importancia; ~ *key* tono *m* menor; ~ *third* tercera *f* menor; **2.** menor *m/f* de edad; *phls.* menor *f*; *Am. univ.* asignatura *f* secundaria; **mi·nor·i·ty** [mai'nɔriti] minoría *f*; (*age*) minoridad *f*; ~ *government* gobierno *m* minoritario.

min·ster ['minstə] iglesia *f* de un monasterio; catedral *f*.

min·strel ['minstrəl] juglar *m*, trovador *m*; cantor *m*; cómico *m* (disfrazado de negro); **min·strel·sy** ['~si] canto *m*; *hist.* arte *m* del trovador (*or* juglar); *hist.* gaya ciencia *f*.

mint¹ [mint] ♀ hierbabuena *f*, menta *f*; (*sweet*) pastilla *f* de menta.

mint² [~] **1.** casa *f* de moneda; *a* ~ *of money* un dineral; **2.** sin usar; **3.** acuñar; *fig.* inventar; '**mint·age** acuñación *f*; moneda *f* acuñada.

min·u·et [minju'et] minué *m*, minuete *m*.

mi·nus ['mainəs] **1.** *prp.* menos; F sin; **2.** *adj.* negativo; **3.** (signo) menos *m*.

mi·nute [mai'nju:t] □ diminuto, menudo; minucioso.

min·ute ['minit] **1.** minuto *m*; *fig.* instante *m*, momento *m*; *(note)* nota *f*, minuta *f*; ~s *pl.* acta(s) *f(pl.)*; **2.** levantar acta de; minutar; ~book libro *m* de actas; 'min·ute·hand minutero *m*.

mi·nu·ti·a [mai'nju:ʃiə], *mst pl.* mi·'nu·ti·ae [~ʃii:] detalle(s) *m(pl.)* minucioso(s).

minx [miŋks] picaruela *f*, moza *f* descarada.

mir·a·cle ['mirəkl] milagro *m*; **mi·rac·u·lous** [mi'rækjuləs] □ milagroso.

mi·rage ['mira:ʒ] espejismo *m*.

mire ['maiə] fango *m*, lodo *m*.

mirk [mə:k] = *murk*.

mir·ror ['mirə] **1.** espejo *m* (*a. fig.*); *mot.* retrovisor *m*; **2.** reflejar.

mirth [mə:θ] regocijo *m*, alegría *f*; hilaridad *f*, risa *f*; **mirth·ful** ['~ful] □ alegre; reidor; '**mirth·less** □ triste, sin alegría.

mir·y ['maiəri] lodoso, fangoso; ~ *place* lodazal *m*.

mis... [mis] mal...

mis·ad·ven·ture ['misəd'ventʃə] desgracia *f*, accidente *m*.

mis·al·li·ance [misə'laiəns] casamiento *m* desigual.

mis·an·thrope ['mizənθroup] misántropo *m*; **mis·an·throp·ic, mis·an·throp·i·cal** [~'θrɔpik(l)] □ misantrópico; **mis·an·thro·pist** [mi'zænθrəpist] misántropo *m*; **mis·'an·thro·py** misantropía *f*.

mis·ap·pli·ca·tion ['misæpli'keiʃn] aplicación *f* errada; abuso *m*; **mis·ap·ply** ['~ə'plai] aplicar mal; abusar de.

mis·ap·pre·hend ['misæpri'hend] entender mal; '**mis·ap·pre·hen·sion** equivocación *f*; concepto *m* erróneo; *be under a* ~ estar equivocado.

mis·ap·pro·pri·ate ['misə'prouprieit] malversar; '**mis·ap·pro·pri·a·tion** malversación *f*.

mis·be·got(·ten) ['misbi'gɔt(n)] bastardo, ilegítimo.

mis·be·have ['misbi'heiv] portarse mal; *(child)* ser malo; '**mis·be·hav·io(u)r** [~jə] mala conducta *f*, mal comportamiento *m*.

mis·be·lief ['misbi'li:f] error *m*; creencia *f* heterodoxa; '**mis·be·'liev·er** heterodoxo (a *f*) *m*.

mis·cal·cu·late ['mis'kælkjuleit]

calcular mal; '**mis·cal·cu·la·tion** cálculo *m* errado; desacierto *m*.

mis·car·riage [mis'kæridʒ] malparto *m*, aborto *m*; malogro *m*, fracaso *m*; & extravío *m*; ~ *of justice* error *m* judicial; **mis'car·ry** malparir, abortar; salir mal, malograrse; & extraviarse.

mis·ce·ge·na·tion [misidʒi'neiʃn] entrecruzamiento *m* de razas.

mis·cel·la·ne·ous [misi'leinjəs] misceláneo. [nea *f*.\
mis·cel·la·ny [mi'seləni] miscelá-)

mis·chance [mis'tʃa:ns] mala suerte *f*; infortunio *m*; accidente *m*.

mis·chief ['mistʃif] daño *m*; mal *m*; malicia *f*; travesura *f*, diablura *f* *esp. of child*; F (*p.*) diablillo *m*; '~maker enredador (-a *f*) *m*, chismoso (a *f*) *m*; alborotador (-a *f*) *m*.

mis·chie·vous ['mistʃivəs] dañoso, perjudicial; malo; malicioso; *child* travieso.

mis·con·ceive ['miskən'si:v] entender mal, formar un concepto erróneo de; **mis·con·cep·tion** ['~'sepʃn] concepto *m* erróneo, equivocación *f*.

mis·con·duct 1. ['mis'kɔndəkt] mala conducta *f*; adulterio *m*; **2.** ['~kən'dʌkt] dirigir mal; ~ *o.s.* portarse mal.

mis·con·struc·tion ['miskən'strʌkʃn] mala interpretación *f*; **mis·con·strue** ['~'stru:] interpretar mal.

mis·count ['mis'kaunt] **1.** contar mal; **2.** cuenta *f* errónea.

mis·cre·ant ['miskriənt] malandrín *adj. a. su. m* (-a *f*), bellaco *adj. a. su. m* (a *f*).

mis·deal ['mis'di:l] [*irr.* (*deal*)] dar mal (las cartas).

mis·deed ['mis'di:d] malhecho *m*, delito *m*.

mis·de·mean·o(u)r ['misdi'mi:nə] mala conducta *f*; ⚖ delito *m* de menor cuantía.

mis·di·rect ['misdi'rekt] dirigir mal; extraviar; '**mis·di·'rec·tion** mala dirección *f*; instrucciones *f/pl.* erradas.

mi·ser ['maizə] avaro (a *f*) *m*.

mis·er·a·ble ['mizərəbl] □ triste; miserable; lastimoso; despreciable; F indispuesto.

mi·ser·ly ['maizəli] avariento, tacaño.

mis·er·y ['mizəri] sufrimiento *m*; aflicción *f*; infelicidad *f*; miseria *f*.

mis·fire ['mis'faiə] 1. falla *f* de tiro (*mot.* de encendido); 2. fallar.

mis·fit ['misfit] cosa *f* mal ajustada; traje *m* que no cae bien; (*p.*) inadaptado (a *f*) *m*.

mis·for·tune [mis'fɔ:tʃn] desgracia *f*, infortunio *m*, desventura *f*.

mis·giv·ing [mis'giviŋ] recelo *m*, duda *f*; presentimiento *m*.

mis·gov·ern ['mis'gʌvən] gobernar mal, desgobernar; **'mis'gov·ern·ment** desgobierno *m*; mala administración *f*. [aconsejar mal.\

mis·guide ['mis'gaid] dirigir mal;/

mis·han·dle ['mis'hændl] manejar mal; maltratar.

mis·hap ['mishæp] contratiempo *m*, accidente *m*; desgracia *f*.

mis·in·form ['misin'fɔ:m] informar mal, dar informes erróneos a; **'mis·in·for'ma·tion** informes *m/pl.* erróneos (*or* falsos).

mis·in·ter·pret ['misin'tə:prit] interpretar mal; **'mis·in·ter·pre'ta·tion** mala interpretación *f*.

mis·judge ['mis'dʒʌdʒ] juzgar mal; **'mis'judg(e)·ment** juicio *m* equivocado (*or* injusto).

mis·lay [mis'lei] [*irr.* (*lay*)] extraviar, perder.

mis·lead [mis'li:d] [*irr.* (*lead*)] extraviar; despistar; engañar; **mis'lead·ing** engañoso.

mis·man·age ['mis'mænidʒ] administrar mal, manejar mal; **'mis'man·age·ment** mala administración *f*, desgobierno *m*; mal manejo *m*.

mis·no·mer ['mis'noumə] nombre *m* equivocado (*or* inapropiado).

mi·sog·a·mist [mi'sɔgəmist] misógamo (a *f*) *m*.

mi·sog·y·nist [mai'sɔdʒinist] misógino *m*; **mi'sog·y·ny** misoginia *f*.

mis·place ['mis'pleis] colocar mal; poner fuera de su lugar; extraviar; *~d affection etc.* equivocado, inmerecido; **'mis'place·ment** colocación *f* fuera de lugar; extravío *m*.

mis·print ['mis'print] 1. errata *f*, error *m* de imprenta; 2. imprimir mal.

mis·pro·nounce ['misprə'nauns] pronunciar mal; **mis·pro·nun·ci·a·tion** ['~prənʌnsi'eiʃn] mala pronunciación *f*.

mis·quo·ta·tion ['miskwou'teiʃn] cita *f* falsa (*or* equivocada); **'mis'quote** citar mal.

mis·read ['mis'ri:d] [*irr.* (*read*)] leer mal; interpretar mal.

mis·rep·re·sent ['misrepri'zent] desfigurar, falsificar; describir engañosamente; **'mis·rep·re·sen'ta·tion** falsificación *f*, tergiversación *f*; descripción *f* falsa.

mis·rule ['mis'ru:l] 1. desgobierno *m*; desorden *m*; 2. desgobernar.

miss[1] [mis] señorita *f*; muchacha *f*; F niña *f* precoz.

miss[2] [~] 1. tiro *m* errado; (*mistake*) desacierto *m*; (*failure*) malogro *m*, fracaso *m*; 2. *v/t.* aim, target, vocation errar; chance, train etc. perder; solution no acertar; *th. sought* no encontrar; (*regret absence of*) echar de menos; meaning no entender; omitir (*a. ~ out*); (*overlook*) pasar por alto; *~ one's footing* perder el pie; the shot just *~ed* me por poco la bala me mató; I *~ed your lecture* perdí su conferencia, no pude asistir a su conferencia; I *~ed what you said* se me escapó lo que dijo Vd.; *v/i.* errar el blanco; fallar, salir mal; *mot.* ratear.

mis·sal ['misəl] misal *m*.

mis·shap·en ['mis'ʃeipən] deforme.

mis·sile ['misail] proyectil *m*; arma *f* arrojadiza.

miss·ing ['misiŋ] ausente; perdido; ✗ desaparecido; *be ~* faltar.

mis·sion ['miʃn] misión *f*; **'mis·sion·ar·y** misionero *adj. a. su. m* (a *f*).

mis·sis ['misiz] F: the *~* la parienta.

mis·sive ['misiv] misiva *f*.

mis·spell ['mis'spel] [*irr.* (*spell*)] deletrear (*or* escribir) mal; **'mis'spell·ing** error *m* de ortografía.

mis·spend ['mis'spend] [*irr.* (*spend*)] malgastar, desperdiciar, perder.

mis·state ['mis'steit] relatar mal; **'mis'state·ment** relación *f* inexacta (*or* falsa).

mis·sus ['misəz] = missis.

miss·y ['misi] F señorita *f*, hija *f* mía.

mist [mist] 1. niebla *f*; (*low*) neblina *f*; bruma *f* at sea; (*slight*) calina *f*; Scotch *~* llovizna *f*; 2. an(i)eblar(se); empañar(se).

mis·tak·a·ble [mis'teikəbl] confundible, equívoco; **mis·take** [~'teik] 1. [*irr.* (*take*)] *v/t.* entender mal;

confundir, equivocar(se en); ~ A for
B equivocar A con B; be ~n enga-
ñarse; equivocarse (for con); v/i. ↖
equivocarse; **2.** equivocación f;
error m; falta f in exercise; by ~ por
equivocación; sin querer; and no ~!
¡sin duda alguna!, ¡ya lo creo!;
make a ~ equivocarse; **mis'tak·en**
□ equivocado; erróneo, incorrecto;
~ identity identificación f errónea.
mis·ter ['mistə] señor m (abbr. **Mr**).
mis·time ['mis'taim] hacer (or decir) a deshora; cronometrar mal.
mis·tle thrush [misl θrʌʃ] zorzal m
charlo.
mis·tle·toe ['misltou] muérdago m.
mis·trans·late ['mistræns'leit] traducir mal; **'mis·trans'la·tion** mala
traducción f.
mis·tress ['mistris] ama f de casa;
dueña f; maestra f (de escuela),
profesora f; amante f, querida f;
señora f (abbr. **Mrs** ['misiz]).
mis·trust ['mis'trʌst] **1.** desconfiar
de; dudar de; **2.** desconfianza f, recelo m; **'mis'trust·ful** [~ful] □
desconfiado, receloso.
mist·y ['misti] □ nebuloso, brumoso; fig. vaporoso, vago; glass empañado.
mis·un·der·stand ['misʌndə'stænd]
[irr. (stand)] entender mal, comprender mal; **'mis·un·der'standing** equivocación f, concepto m
erróneo; desavenencia f; malentendido m.
mis·use 1. ['mis'ju:z] emplear mal;
abusar de; maltratar; **2.** ['~'ju:s]
mal uso m, abuso m; maltratamiento m.
mite¹ [meit] zo. ácaro m (doméstico).
mite² [~] (coin) ardite m; (contribution) óbolo m; pizca f; niño (a f) m
muy pequeño (a).
mit·i·gate ['mitigeit] mitigar; **mit-
i'ga·tion** mitigación f.
mi·tre, mi·ter ['maitə] **1.** mitra f;
⊕ inglete m; ~ joint ensambladura f
de inglete; **2.** ⊕ ingletear.
mit·t(en) ['mit(n)] mitón m, guante
m con solo el pulgar separado; Am.
sl. mano f; sl. get (give) the ~ recibir
(dar) calabazas.
mix [miks] mezclar, mixturar; flour,
plaster etc. amasar; drinks preparar;
salad aderezar; combinar; confundir; ~ed mixto; mezclado; (assorted)

variado, surtido; ~ up confundir; be
(or get) ~ed up in (or with) mezclarse
en, mojar en; v/i. mezclarse; (p.)
asociarse; (get on well) llevarse bien;
~ in (or with) high society frecuentar
la alta sociedad; **'mix·er** mezclador
m (a. radio); F persona f sociable;
be a good ~ tener don de gentes;
mix·ture ['~tʃə] mezcla f, mixtura f; **'mix-'up** confusión f; F lío
m, enredo m.
miz·en, miz·zen ['mizn] (palo m de)
mesana f.
miz·zle ['mizl] F zafarse; F llovizar.
mne·mon·ic [ni'mɔnik] **1.** (m)ne-
motécnico; **2. mne'mon·ics** (m)ne-
motécnica f.
moan [moun] **1.** gemido m, quejido
m; **2.** gemir; F quejarse.
moat [mout] **1.** foso m; **2.** fosar.
mob [mɔb] **1.** gentío m, muchedumbre f; b.s. chusma f, turba f, populacho m; sl. pandilla f; **2.** atropellar;
atacar en masa; festejar tumultuo-
samente.
mob-cap ['mɔbkæp] cofia f.
mo·bile ['moubail] móvil, movible;
mo·bil·i·ty [mou'biliti] movilidad
f; **mo·bi·li·za·tion** [moubilai'zeiʃn]
movilización f; **'mo·bi·lize** movilizar.
mob-law ['mɔblɔ:] ley f de Lynch.
moc·ca·sin ['mɔkəsin] mocasín m.
mock [mɔk] **1.** burla f; make a ~ of
poner en ridículo; **2.** fingido, simulado; burlesco; **3.** v/t. burlarse de,
mofarse de; (mimic) remedar; frustrar; decepcionar; v/i. mofarse (at
de); **'mock·er** mofador (-a f) m;
'mock·er·y mofa f, burla f; hazmerreír m; parodia f, mal remedo
m; make a ~ of hacer ridículo;
'mock-he'ro·ic heroicocómico;
'mock·ing 1. burlas f/pl.; **2.** □ burlón; **'mock·ing-bird** sinsonte m;
'mock-'or·ange jeringuilla f;
'mock-up maqueta f, modelo m en
escala natural.
mod·al ['moudl] □ modal; **mo-
dal·i·ty** [mou'dæliti] modalidad f.
mode [moud] modo m (a. phls., ♪);
manera f; (fashion) moda f.
mod·el ['mɔdl] **1.** modelo m (a. fig.);
△ maqueta f; (fashion) ~ modelo
m/f; attr. modelo; ~ aeroplane aero-
modelo m; ~ town ciudad f modelo;
2. v/t. modelar (on sobre); planear
(after, on según); v/i. servir de

modelo; **mod·el·(l)er** ['mɔdlə] modelador (-a f) m; '**mod·el·ling** modelado m.

mod·er·ate 1. ['mɔdərit] □ moderado (*pol. a. su. m*); regular, mediocre; *price* módico; **2.** ['ˌreit] moderar(se), templar(se); (*wind*) amainar; **mod·er·a·tion** [ˌ'reiʃn] moderación f; *in* ~ con moderación; '**mod·er·a·tor** moderador (-a f) m; árbitro m; *eccl. presidente de la asamblea de la Iglesia Escocesa.*

mod·ern ['mɔdən] **1.** moderno; **2.**: *the* ~*s pl.* los modernos; '**mod·ern·ism** modernismo m; **mo·der·ni·ty** [mɔ'də:niti] modernidad f; '**mod·ern·ize** modernizar(se).

mod·est ['mɔdist] □ modesto; moderado; púdico; '**mod·es·ty** modestia f; moderación f; pudor m.

mod·i·cum ['mɔdikəm] cantidad f módica, poco m.

mod·i·fi·a·ble ['mɔdifaiəbl] modificable; **mod·i·fi·ca·tion** [ˌfi'keiʃn] modificación f; **mod·i·fy** ['ˌfai] modificar(se). [gante.]

mod·ish ['moudiʃ] de moda, ele-)

mod·u·late ['mɔdjuleit] modular; **mod·u·la·tion** modulación f; *radio: frequency* ~ modulación f de frecuencia; '**mod·u·la·tor** modulador m.

Mo·gul [mou'gʌl]: *the Great* ~ el Gran Mogol; ♀ magnate m.

mo·hair ['mouhɛə] moer m.

Mo·ham·med·an [mou'hæmidən] mahometano *adj. a. su. m* (a f).

moi·e·ty ['mɔiəti] mitad f; parte f.

moist [mɔist] húmedo; mojado; **mois·ten** ['mɔisn] humedecer(se); mojar(se); '**moist·ness, mois·ture** ['ˌtʃə] humedad f.

moke [mouk] *sl.* burro m.

mo·lar ['moulə] molar m, muela f.

mo·las·ses [mə'læsiz] melaza(s) f(*pl.*).

mold [mould] *v.* mould.

mole [moul] *zo.* topo m; (*spot*) lunar m; ♻ malecón m, muelle m; ♓ mola f.

mo·lec·u·lar [mou'lekjulə] molecular; **mol·e·cule** ['mɔlikju:l] molécula f.

mole·hill ['moulhil] topera f; *make a mountain out of a* ~ hacer de una pulga un elefante; '**mole·skin** piel f de topo.

mo·lest [mou'lest] importunar; faltar

al respeto a; molestar; **mo·les·ta·tion** [moules'teiʃn] importunidad f; vejación f; molestia f.

moll [mɔl] *sl.* amiga f, ramera f.

mol·li·fy ['mɔlifai] apaciguar, mitigar.

mol·lusc ['mɔləsk] molusco m.

mol·ly·cod·dle ['mɔlikɔdl] **1.** niño m mimado; alfeñique m, marica m; **2.** mimar.

mol·ten ['moultən] fundido; derretido; *lava etc.* líquido.

mo·ment ['moumənt] momento m; instante m; importancia f; *at any* ~ de un momento a otro; *at* (*or for*) *the* ~ de momento, por ahora; *at this* ~ en este momento; *in a* ~ en un momento; '**mo·men·tar·y** □ momentáneo; **mo·men·tous** [ˌ'mentəs] □ grave, trascendental, de suma importancia; **mo·men·tum** [ˌtəm] *phys.* momento m; ímpetu m; *gather* ~ cobrar velocidad.

mon·ad ['mɔnæd] mónada f.

mon·arch ['mɔnək] monarca m; **mo·nar·chic, mo·nar·chi·cal** [mɔ'nɑ:kik(l)] □ monárquico; **mon·arch·ism** ['mɔnəkizm] monarquismo m; **mon·arch·y** ['ˌki] monarquía f.

mon·as·ter·y ['mɔnəstri] monasterio m; **mo·nas·tic, mo·nas·ti·cal** [mə'næstik(l)] □ monástico.

Mon·day ['mʌndi] lunes m.

mon·e·tar·y ['mʌnitəri] monetario; pecuniario; ~ *reform* reforma f monetaria.

mon·ey ['mʌni] dinero m; plata f *esp. S.Am.*; (*coin*) moneda f; *keep in* ~ proveer de dinero; *make* ~ ganar dinero; (*business*) dar dinero; *throw good* ~ *after bad* echar la soga tras el caldero; *v. paper; ready* ~ dinero *m* contante; '~**box** hucha f; '~**chang·er** cambista *m*/f; **mon·eyed** ['mʌnid] adinerado.

mon·ey...: '~**grub·ber** avaro (a f) m; '~**lend·er** prestamista *m*/f; '~**mar·ket** mercado *m* monetario; '~**or·der** *approx.* giro *m* postal; '~'**s-worth**: *get one's* ~ *out of* sacar el valor de.

mon·ger ['mʌŋgə] traficante *m*/f en...; tratante *m* en...; *fig.* propalador (-a f) m de...

Mon·gol ['mɔŋgɔl], **Mon·go·lian** [ˌ'gouljən] **1.** mogol *adj. a. su. m* (-a f); **2.** (*language*) mogol m.

mon·grel ['mʌŋgrəl] **1.** perro *m* mestizo, perro *m* callejero; mestizo (a *f*) *m*; **2.** mestizo.

mon·i·tor ['mɔnitə] **1.** *school*: monitor *m*; *radio*: radiorreceptor *m* de contrastación; *radio*: (p.) escucha *m*/*f*; **2.** vigilar; regular; contrastar; radiocaptar.

monk [mʌŋk] monje *m*.

mon·key ['mʌŋki] **1.** mono (a *f*) *m*, mico (a *f*) *m*; *fig.* diablillo *m*; ⊕ maza *f*; *sl.* 500 libras *f*/*pl.* esterlinas; F *get one's ∼ up* hinchársele a uno las narices; F *make a ∼ out of* tomar el pelo a; F *∼ business* trampería *f*, malas mañas *f*/*pl.*; F *∼ tricks* travesuras *f*/*pl.*, diabluras *f*/*pl.*; **2.** F hacer payasadas; *∼ (about) with* manosear; meterse con; '*∼-nut* cacahuete *m*; '*∼-puz·zle* araucaria *f*; '*∼-wrench* ⊕ llave *f* inglesa.

monk·ish ['mʌŋkiʃ] *mst contp.* frailuno, de monje.

mo·no... ['mɔnou] mono...; **mon·o·chrome** ['mɔnəkroum] monocromo *adj. a. su. m*; **mon·o·cle** ['mɔnɔkl] monóculo *m*; **mo'noc·u·lar** [∼kjulə] monóculo *m*; **mo'nog·a·my** [∼gəmi] monogamia *f*; **mon·o·gram** ['mɔnəgræm] monograma *m*; **mon·o·graph** ['∼grɑːf] monografía *f*; **mon·o·lith** ['mɔnəliθ] monolito *m*; **mon·o·logue** ['mɔnələg] monólogo *m*; **mon·o·ma·ni·a** ['mɔnou'meiniə] monomanía *f*; **mon·o·plane** ['mɔnəplein] monoplano *m*; **mo·nop·o·list** [mə'nɔpəlist] monopolista *m*/*f*; acaparador (-a *f*) *m*; **mo'nop·o·lize** [∼laiz] monopolizar; acaparar (*a. fig.*); **mo'nop·o·ly** monopolio *m*; **mon·o·syl·lab·ic** ['mɔnəsi'læbik] □ *word* monosílabo; monosilábico; **mon·o·syl·la·ble** ['∼læbl] monosílabo *m*; **mon·o·the·ism** ['mɔnouθi:izm] monoteísmo *m*; **mon·o·tone** ['mɔnətoun] monotonía *f*; **mo·not·o·nous** [mə'nɔtənəs] □ monótono; **mo'not·o·ny** [∼təni] monotonía *f*; **Mon·o·type** ['mɔnətaip] monotipia *f*.

mon·soon [mɔn'suːn] monzón *m or f*.

mon·ster ['mɔnstə] monstruo *m*; *attr.* enorme, monstruoso. [día *f*.]

mon·strance ['mɔnstrəns] custo-

mon·stros·i·ty [mɔns'trɔsiti] monstruosidad *f*; '**mon·strous** □ monstruoso.

mon·tage [mɔn'tɑːʒ] montaje *m*.

month [mʌnθ] mes *m*; *100 pesetas a ∼ 100 pesetas mensuales*; F *in a ∼ of Sundays* en mucho tiempo; '**month·ly 1.** mensual(mente); **2.** revista *f* mensual.

mon·u·ment ['mɔnjumənt] monumento *m*; **mon·u·men·tal** [∼'mentl] □ monumental; notable; *iro.* garrafal.

moo [muː] **1.** mugido *m*; **2.** mugir, hacer mu.

mooch [muːtʃ]: F *∼ about* vagar, haraganear; *∼ along* andar arrastrando los pies.

mood[1] [muːd] *gr.* modo *m*.

mood[2] [∼] humor *m*; capricho *m*; *be in a good (bad) ∼* estar de buen (mal) humor; *be in the ∼* estar de vena (*for para*).

mood·i·ness ['muːdinis] mal humor *m*; melancolía *f*; carácter *m* caprichoso.

mood·y ['muːdi] □ de mal humor; melancólico; caprichoso.

moon [muːn] **1.** luna *f*; *poet.* mes *m*; *v. full, new*; F *once in a blue ∼* de Pascuas a Ramos; **2.** mirar a las musarañas, andar distraído (*mst ∼ about*); '**∼beam** rayo *m* de luna; '**moon·light 1.** luz *f* de la luna; F *∼ flit* mudanza *f* a la chita callando; **2.** = '**moon·lit** iluminado por la luna; *night* de luna.

moon...: '**∼shine** *Am.* F pamplinas *f*/*pl.*, música *f* celestial; F licor *m* destilado ilegalmente; '**∼shin·er** *Am.* F fabricante *m* de licor ilegal; '**∼stone** adularia *f*; '**∼struck** lunático; aturdido.

Moor[1] [muə] moro (a *f*) *m*.

moor[2] [∼] páramo *m*, brezal *m*.

moor[3] [∼] ⚓ *v/t.* amarrar; *v/i.* echar las amarras.

moor·hen ['muəhen] polla *f* de agua.

moor·ings ['muəriŋz] *pl.* ⚓ amarras *f*/*pl.*; (*place*) amarradero *m*.

Moor·ish ['muəriʃ] moro; ⚔ *etc.* árabe.

moor·land ['muələnd] = *moor*[2].

moose [muːs] alce *m* de América (*a.* '**∼·deer**).

moot [muːt] **1.** *hist.* asamblea *f* de ciudadanos; **2.**: *∼ point, ∼ question* punto *m* discutible; **3.** proponer para la discusión.

mop [mɔp] **1.** fregasuelos *m*; mata *f*, greña *f* *of hair*; **2.** fregar; limpiar;

secar; ~ *up* secar; limpiar (*a.* ✂ *fig.*); *sl.* beber(se); *sl.* acabar con, liquidar.

mope [moup] **1.** estar abatido (*or* aburrido); andar alicaído; **2.** melancólico (a *f*) *m*; ~s *pl.* melancolía *f*; **'mop·ing** ☐, **'mop·ish** ☐ abatido, melancólico.

mo·quette [mə'ket] moqueta *f*.

mo·raine [mɔ'rein] *geol.* morena *f*.

mor·al ['mɔrəl] **1.** ☐ moral, ético; virtuoso; honesto; ~ *victory* victoria *f* moral; **2.** moraleja *f*; ~s *pl.* moral *f*; moralidad *f*; costumbres *f/pl.*; **mo·rale** [mɔ'rɑːl] moral *f*; **mo·ral·ist** ['mɔrəlist] moralista *m/f*; moralizador (-a *f*) *m*; **mo·ral·i·ty** [mə'ræliti] moralidad *f etc.*; **mor·al·ize** ['mɔrəlaiz] moralizar.

mo·rass [mə'ræs] cenagal *m*, pantano *m* (*a. fig.*).

mor·a·to·ri·um [mɔrə'tɔːriəm] moratoria *f*.

mor·bid ['mɔːbid] ☐ mórbido, morboso; *mind* malsano, enfermizo; **mor'bid·i·ty**, **'mor·bid·ness** morbosidad *f*; lo malsano.

mor·dant ['mɔːdənt] **1.** mordaz; **2.** mordiente *m*.

more [mɔː] *adj.*, *adv.*, *su.* más; ~ *and* ~ ⌐ada vez más; ~ *or less* (poco) más o menos; *v.* than; *no* (*or not any*) ~ ya no, no más; *once* ~ otra vez, una vez más; *so much* (*or all*) *the* ~ tanto más; *the* ~ *the merrier* cuanto(s) más, mejor; *the* ~ ... *the* ~ ... cuanto más ... (tanto) más ...

more·o·ver [mɔː'rouvə] además (de eso), por otra parte.

mor·ga·nat·ic [mɔːgə'nætik] ☐ morganático.

morgue [mɔːg] depósito *m* de cadáveres.

mor·i·bund ['mɔribʌnd] moribundo.

Mor·mon ['mɔːmən] **1.** mormón (-a *f*) *m*; **2.** mormónico.

morn [mɔːn] *poet.* mañana *f*, alborada *f*.

morn·ing ['mɔːniŋ] **1.** mañana *f*; *good* ~! ¡buenos días!; *in the* ~ por la mañana; *at 6 o'clock in the* ~ a las 6 de la mañana; *to-morrow* ~ mañana por la mañana; **2.** matutino, matinal, de (la) mañana; ~ *coat* chaqué *m*; ~ *sickness* achaques *m/pl.* mañaneros; ~ *star* lucero *m* del alba.

Mo·roc·can [mə'rɔkən] marroquí *adj. a. su. m/f*, marrueco *adj. a. su. m* (a *f*).

mo·roc·co [mə'rɔkou] (*or* ~ *leather*) marroquí *m*, tafilete *m*.

mo·ron ['mɔːrɔn] imbécil *m/f*.

mo·rose [mə'rous] ☐ malhumorado, sombrío.

mor·phi·a ['mɔːfjə], **mor·phine** ['mɔːfiːn] morfina *f*.

mor·phol·o·gy [mɔː'fɔlədʒi] morfología *f*.

mor·row ['mɔrou] *mst poet.* día *m* siguiente; mañana *m*; *on the* ~ al día siguiente.

Morse [mɔːs] (*a.* ~ *code*) (alfabeto) Morse *m*.

mor·sel ['mɔːsəl] pedazo *m*; bocado *m*.

mor·tal ['mɔːtl] ☐ mortal *adj. a. su. m/f*; **mor·tal·i·ty** [mɔː'tæliti] mortalidad *f*.

mor·tar ['mɔːtə] mortero *m* (*a.* ✂).

mort·gage ['mɔːgidʒ] **1.** hipoteca *f*; **2.** hipotecar; **mort·ga·gee** [~gə'dʒiː] acreedor (-a *f*) *m* hipotecario (a); **mort·ga·gor** [~gə'dʒɔː] deudor (-a *f*) *m* hipotecario (a).

mor·tice ['mɔːtis] = *mortise*.

mor·ti·cian [mɔː'tiʃn] *Am.* director *m* de pompas fúnebres.

mor·ti·fi·ca·tion [mɔːtifi'keiʃn] mortificación *f*; humillación *f*.

mor·ti·fy ['mɔːtifai] *v/t.* mortificar; humillar; *v/i.* ✿ gangrenarse.

mor·tise ['mɔːtis] **1.** muesca *f*, mortaja *f*; **2.** hacer muescas en.

mor·tu·ar·y ['mɔːtjuəri] **1.** depósito *m* de cadáveres; **2.** mortuorio.

mo·sa·ic¹ [mə'zeiik] mosaico *m*.

Mo·sa·ic² [~] mosaico.

Mos·lem ['mɔzlem] musulmán *adj. a. su. m* (-a *f*).

mosque [mɔsk] mezquita *f*.

mos·qui·to [məs'kiːtou], *pl.* **mos·qui·toes** [~z] mosquito *m*; ~ *net* mosquitero *m*.

moss [mɔs] musgo *m*; *geog.* pantano *m*; **'moss·y** musgoso.

most [moust] **1.** *adj.* ☐ más; la mayor parte de; los más, la mayoría de; casi todos; ~ *people* la mayoría de la gente; *v.* part; **2.** *adv.* más; muy, sumamente; de lo más; ~ *of all* sobre todo; *a* ~ *interesting book* un libro interesantísimo, un libro de lo más interesante; **3.** *su.* la mayor parte; el mayor número, los más; *at* (*the*) ~ a lo más, a lo sumo, cuando más; *make the* ~ *of* sacar el mejor partido de; exagerar.

...most [moust, məst] *sup.* más...

most·ly ['moustli] por la mayor parte; principalmente; en general.

mote [mout] mota *f*; átomo *m*.

mo·tel [mou'tel] *Am.* motel *m*.

mo·tet [mou'tet] motete *m*.

moth [mɔθ] mariposa *f* (nocturna); polilla *f in clothes etc.*; '~·**ball** bola *f* de naftalina; '~·**eat·en** apolillado.

moth·er ['mʌðə] 1. madre *f*; *attr.* madre, maternal, materno; ♀ *Church* la santa madre iglesia; iglesia *f* metropolitana; ~ *country* (madre) patria *f*; ~ *love* amor *m* maternal; ~ *tongue* lengua *f* materna; ~ *wit* sentido *m* común; ingenio *m*; 2. servir de madre a; mimar; *animal* ahijar; **moth·er·hood** ['~hud] maternidad *f*; madres *f*/*pl.*; '**moth·er-in-law** suegra *f*; '**moth·er·land** (madre) patria *f*; '**moth·er·less** huérfano de madre, sin madre; '**moth·er·ly** maternal.

moth·er...: '~·**of-'pearl** 1. nácar *m*; 2. nacarado; '~·**ship** buque *m* nodriza.

mo·tif [mou'ti:f] ♪, *art*: motivo *m*; tema *m*; *sew.* adorno *m*.

mo·tion ['mouʃn] 1. movimiento *m*; ⊕ marcha *f*, operación *f*; ⊕ mecanismo *m*; *parl.* moción *f*; ademán *m*; señal *f*; ✠ movimiento *m* del vientre, deyección *f*; *bring forward* (*or propose*) *a* ~ presentar una moción; *carry a* ~ (hacer) adoptar una moción; (*set*) *in* ~ (poner) en marcha; 2. *v/t.* indicar a *una p.* con la mano *etc.* (*to inf.* que *subj.*); *v/i.* hacer señas; '**mo·tion·less** inmóvil; '**mo·tion-pic·ture** *Am.* 1. película *f*; 2. cinematográfico.

mo·ti·vate ['moutiveit] motivar; **mo·ti·va·tion** motivación *f*.

mo·tive ['moutiv] 1. motivo *m*; 2. motor, motivo; ~ *power* fuerza *f* motriz; '**mo·tive·less** sin motivo.

mot·ley ['mɔtli] 1. abigarrado; vario; 2. botarga *f*.

mo·tor ['moutə] 1. motor *m*; = ~-*car*; 2. motor; ~ *ambulance* ambulancia *f*; ~ *mechanic* mecánico *m* (de automóviles); ~ *ship*, ~ *vessel* motonave *f*; 3. ir (*or* viajar) en automóvil; '~·**bike** F moto *f*; '~·**boat** gasolinera *f*, motora *f*,

motorbote *m*; '~·'**bus** autobús *m*; '~·**cade** ['~keid] *Am.* caravana *f* de automóviles; '~·**car** auto(móvil) *m*, coche *m*; carro *m S.Am.*; '~·**coach** autocar *m*; '~·'**cy·cle** moto(cicleta) *f*; '~·**cy·cling** motorismo *m*; '~·**cy·clist** motociclista *m*/*f*, motorista *m*/*f*; **mo·tor·ing** ['moutəriŋ] automovilismo *m*; ~ *school* escuela *f* automovilista; '**mo·tor·ist** automovilista *m*/*f*; **mo·tor·i·za·tion** [~rai'zeiʃn] motorización *f*; '**mo·tor·ize** motorizar; '**mo·tor-launch** lancha *f* (*or* canoa *f*) automóvil.

mo·tor...: '~·'**lor·ry** camión *m*; '~·**man** 🚋 conductor *m* (de locomotora eléctrica); '~·**road** autopista *f*; '~·'**scoot·er** vespa *f*; '~·'**spir·it** bencina *f*, gasolina *f*.

mot·tled ['mɔtld] jaspeado, abigarrado.

mot·to ['mɔtou], *pl.* **mot·toes** ['~z] lema *m*; *heraldry*: divisa *f*.

mo(u)ld¹ [mould] mantillo *m*; (*fungus*) moho *m*; (*iron* ~) mancha *f* de orín.

mo(u)ld² [~] 1. molde *m*; cosa *f* moldeada; *fig.* carácter *m*; 2. moldear; vaciar; amoldar (*a. fig.*) ([*up*]*on a*).

mo(u)ld·er¹ ['mouldə] moldeador (-a *f*) *m*.

mo(u)ld·er² [~] (*a.* ~ *away*) desmoronarse; convertirse en polvo; decaer.

mo(u)ld·i·ness ['mouldinis] moho *m*, enmohecimiento *m*.

mo(u)ld·ing ['mouldiŋ] amoldamiento *m*; vaciado *m*; 🏛 moldura *f*.

mo(u)ld·y ['mouldi] mohoso, enmohecido; *fig.* rancio, anticuado.

moult [moult] 1. muda *f*; 2. mudar (la pluma).

mound [maund] montón *m*; montículo *m*; terraplén *m*.

mount [maunt] 1. *poet. a. geog.* monte *m*; *horse etc.*: montura *f*, cabalgadura *f*; engaste *m of jewel*; base *f*; soporte *m*; fondo *m*; 2. *v/t.* montar (*a.* ⊕); (*climb*) subir; (*get on to*) subir a (*or* en); poner a caballo; proveer de caballos; *jewel* engastar; *v. guard*; *v/i.* subir a caballo; montar(se); aumentar (*a.* ~ *up*).

moun·tain ['mauntin] 1. montaña *f*; (*pile*) montón *m*; ~ *chain* cordillera *f*; ~ *range* sierra *f*; ~ *side* falda *f* (*or* ladera *f*) de una montaña; **2.** montañés, de montaña; **moun·tain·eer** [͵i'niə] **1.** montañés (-a *f*) *m*; montañero (a *f*) *m*, alpinista *m*/*f*; **2.** dedicarse al montañismo; **moun·tain'eer·ing 1.** montañismo *m*; alpinismo *m*; **2.** montañero; **'moun·tain·ous** montañoso; *fig.* enorme.

moun·te·bank ['mauntibæŋk] saltabanco *m*, saltimbanqui *m*, charlatán *m*.

mount·ing ['mauntiŋ] montadura *f*; ⊕ montaje *m*; engaste *m* ͵of jewel; soporte *m*; base *f*.

mourn [mɔ:n] *v*/*t*. llorar (la muerte de); lamentar; llevar luto por; *v*/*i*. lamentarse; estar de luto; **'mourn·er** doliente *m*/*f*; (*hired*) plañidera *f*; **mourn·ful** ['͵ful] □ triste, lúgubre, lastimero; **'mourn·ful·ness** tristeza *f*, melancolía *f*.

mourn·ing ['mɔ:niŋ] **1.** luto *m*, duelo *m*; lamentación *f*; be in ͵ estar de luto; be in ͵ for llevar luto por; *deep* ͵ luto *m* riguroso; *half* ͵ medio luto *m*; **2.** de luto.

mouse 1. [maus] (*pl.* mice) ratón *m*; **2.** [mauz] cazar ratones; **mous·er** ['mauzə] gato *m* cazador de ratones; **'mouse-trap** ratonera *f*.

mous·tache [məs'ta:ʃ] bigote(s) *m*(*pl.*), mostacho *m*.

mous·y ['mausi] *p.* silencioso, tímido; *colour* pardusco.

mouth [mauθ] *pl.* **mouths** [mauðz] **1.** boca *f* (*a. fig.*); (des)embocadura *f* of river; boquilla *f* of wind-instrument; down in the ͵ deprimido, alicaído; keep one's ͵ shut tener la boca cerrada, guardar un secreto; not to open one's ͵ no decir esta boca es mía; **2.** [mauð] *v*/*t*. pronunciar (con rimbombancia), proferir; *v*/*i*. hablar exagerando los movimientos de la boca; **mouthed** [mauðd] de boca ...; **mouth·ful** ['͵ful] bocado *m*.

mouth...: '͵-or·gan armónica *f* (de boca); '͵-piece boquilla *f*; *teleph.* micrófono *m*; *fig.* portavoz *m*; '͵-wash enjuague *m*.

mov(e)·a·ble ['mu:vəbl] **1.** movible; **2.** ͵s *pl.* bienes *m*/*pl.* muebles.

move [mu:v] **1.** *v*/*t*. mover; poner en marcha; trasladar *from one place to another*; *house* mudar de; (*disturb*) remover, sacudir; menear; *bowels*

exonerar; *emotion:* conmover, enternecer; *parl.* proponer; ͵ *a p. to inf.* mover (*or* impeler) a una p. a *inf.*; ͵ *away* alejar; apartar; quitar; ͵ *on* hacer circular; adelantar; ͵ *up* ascender; subir; *v*/*i.* moverse; trasladarse; caminar; ponerse en marcha; menearse; mudar de casa; *games:* hacer una jugada; (*traffic*) circular; (*bowels*) exonerarse; ͵ *about* ir y venir; moverse; ͵ *away* apartarse; marcharse; ͵ *forward* avanzar; ͵ *in* instalarse (en); *society* frecuentar, alternar con; ͵ *off* alejarse; ͵ *on* avanzar; seguir (andando); circular; ͵ *out* salir; abandonar la casa; ͵ *up* ascender, subir; **2.** movimiento *m*; paso *m*; acción *f*; maniobra *f*; *game:* jugada *f*; mudanza *f of house*; on the ͵ en movimiento; de viaje; F get *a* ͵ *on* menearse, darse prisa; F get *a* ͵ *on!* ¡anda, espabílate!; *have first* ͵ *games:* salir; make *a* ͵ dar un paso; hacer una jugada; ponerse en marcha; whose ͵ is it? ¿a quién le toca (jugar)?; **'move·ment** movimiento *m* (*a. fig.*); ⊕ mecanismo *m*; juego *m*; ♪ tiempo *m*; ☆ defecación *f*; ✝ actividad *f*; circulación *f of traffic;* **'mov·er** movedor (-a *f*) *m*; móvil *m*; (*proposer*) autor (-a *f*) *m*; prime ͵ ⊕ máquina *f* motriz; *phls.* primer motor *m*; *fig.* promotor (-a *f*) *m*.

mov·ie ['mu:vi] *Am.* F película *f*; ͵s *pl.* cine *m*.

mov·ing ['mu:viŋ] □ motor; movedor; movedizo; *fig.* conmovedor; ͵ *picture* = *motion picture;* ͵ *spirit* alma *f*.

mow [mou] [*irr.*] segar (*a.* ͵ *down*); **'mow·er** segador (-a *f*) *m*; = *mowing-machine;* **'mow·ing 1.** siega *f*; **2.** segador; **'mow·ing-ma·chine** segadora *f* mecánica; cortacésped *m for lawn;* **mown** *p.p. of* mow.

Moz·ar·ab [mouz'ærəb] mozárabe *m*/*f*; **Moz'ar·ab·ic** mozárabe.

much [mʌtʃ] *adj.* mucho; *adv.* mucho; (*before p.p.*) muy; (*almost*) casi, más o menos; (*by far*) con mucho; *su.* mucho; as ͵, so ͵ tanto; as ͵ again, as ͵ more otro tanto más; as ͵ as tanto como; how ͵ cuánto; however ͵ por mucho que; make ͵ of dar mucha importancia a;

p. agasajar; ~ *as I should like* por
más que yo quisiera; *not ~ of a ...
... de poca cuantía*; pobre, malo;
not so ~ as ni siquiera; *think ~ of*
estimar en mucho; *not to think
~ of* tener en poco; *I thought as ~*
ya me lo figuraba; *too ~* demasiado;
'much·ness: F *much of a ~* lo mismo poco más o menos.

mu·ci·lage ['mju:silidʒ] mucílago
m; **mu·ci·lag·i·nous** [ˌ~'lædʒinəs]
mucilaginoso.

muck [mʌk] **1.** ✗ estiércol *m*; suciedad *f*; F porquería *f* (*a. fig.*);
2. estercolar; F ~ *about* perder el
tiempo; F ~ *about with* manosear;
F ~ *up* ensuciar; estropear; **muck-
rake** ['~ɹeik] escarbar vidas ajenas;
'muck·rak·er escarbador (-a *f*) *m*
de vidas ajenas; **'muck-up** F lío *m*,
fracaso *m*; **'muck·y** F puerco, sucio,
asqueroso.

mu·cous ['mju:kəs] mucoso; ~
membrane mucosa *f*.

mu·cus [~] moco *m*, mucosidad *f*.

mud [mʌd] lodo *m*, barro *m*; fango
m (*a. fig.*); *sling ~ at* F vilipendiar;
stick in ~ atollarse; **'~-'bath**
lodos *m/pl.*

mud·dle ['mʌdl] **1.** embrollo *m*,
confusión *f*; F lío *m*; *get into a ~*
embrollarse; *make a ~* armar un
lío; **2.** *v/t.* embrollar, confundir (*a.
~ up*); *p.* aturdir; *v/i.* obrar confusamente (*or* sin ton ni son); ~
through salir del paso sin saber
cómo; **'~-head·ed** atontado, estúpido; confuso.

muddy ['mʌdi] **1.** □ lodoso, fangoso; *liquid* turbio; **2.** enlodar;
enturbiar; manchar (*a. fig.*).

mud...: **'~-'flats** *pl.* marisma *f*;
'~guard guardabarros *m*; **'~-lark**
F galopín *m*.

muff[1] [mʌf] *sport:* dejar escapar
(la pelota); perder (la ocasión).

muff[2] [~] manguito *m*.

muf·fin ['mʌfin] *approx.* mollete *m*.

muf·fle ['mʌfl] **1.** ⊕ mufla *f*;
2. embozar(se), tapar(se) (*a. ~ up*);
envolver; amortiguar (el ruido de);
drum enfundar; **'muf·fler** bufanda *f*; ♩ sordina *f*; ⊕ silenciador *m*.

muf·ti ['mʌfti] traje de paisano;
in ~ vestido de paisano.

mug [mʌg] **1.** taza *f* (alta sin platillo); barro *m*, jarra *f* of *beer*; *sl.*
(*face*) hocico *m*, jeta *f*; *sl.* (*p.*)

primo *m*, maleta *m* (*a.* **mug·gins**
['mʌginz]); **2.** *sl.* (*a. ~ up*) empollar.

mug·gy ['mʌgi] húmedo y sofocante.

mug·wump ['mʌgwʌmp] *Am. pol.*
(republicano *m*) independiente.

mu·lat·to [mju'lætou] mulato *adj.
a. su. m* (a *f*).

mul·ber·ry ['mʌlbəri] mora *f*; (*a. ~
tree*) morera *f*, moral *m*; *attr.
.(colour)* morado.

mulch [mʌlʃ] ✗ (cubrir con) estiércol *m*, paja *f* y hojas *f/pl.*

mulct [mʌlkt] **1.** ✎ multa *f*;
2. multar (*a p.* [*in*] a una *p.* en);
~ *of* quitar.

mule [mju:l] mulo (a *f*) *m*; (*slipper*)
babucha *f*; *fig.* sujeto *m* terco; ⊕
máquina *f* de hilar intermitente, sel-
factina *f*; **mu·le·teer** [ˌ~i'tiə] mu-
l(at)ero *m*, arriero *m*; **'mule-track**
camino *m* de herradura.   [nado.)

mul·ish ['mju:liʃ] □ terco, obsti-)

mull[1] [mʌl] calentar con especias.

mull[2] [~] chapucear, estropear; ~
over reflexionar sobre.

mul·let ['mʌlit] (*red*) salmonete *m*;
(*grey*) mújol *m*.

mul·li·gan ['mʌligən] *Am. sl.* puchero *m*; **mul·li·ga·taw·ny** [mʌli-
gə'tɔ:ni] sopa *f* muy condimentada.

mul·lion ['mʌljən] **1.** △ parteluz *m*;
2. dividir con parteluz.

mul·ti·col·o(u)red   ['mʌltikʌləd]
multicolor; **mul·ti·far·i·ous** [ˌ~-
'fɛəriəs] □ múltiple, vario; **mul·ti-
form** ['~fɔ:m] multiforme; **mul·ti-
lat·er·al** [ˌ~'lætərəl] □ multilátero;
mul·ti·mil·lion·aire ['~miljə'nɛə]
multimillonario (a *f*) *m*; **mul·ti·ple**
['mʌltipl] **1.** múltiple; múltiplo; ~
firm casa *f* con muchas sucursales; ~
stores cadena *f* de almacenes;
2. múltiplo *m*; *lowest common ~*
mínimo común múltiplo *m*; **mul·
ti·pli·cand** [ˌ~'kænd] multiplicando
m; **mul·ti·pli·ca·tion** multiplicación *f*; ~ *table* tabla *f* de multiplicar; **mul·ti·plic·i·ty** [ˌ~'plisiti] mul-
tiplicidad *f*; **mul·ti·pli·er** ['~plaiə]
multiplicador *m*; **mul·ti·ply** ['~plai]
multiplicar(se);   **mul·ti·tude**
['~tju:d] multitud *f*, muchedumbre
f; **mul·ti·tu·di·nous** [ˌ~dinəs] □
multitudinario; muy numeroso.

mum[1] [mʌm] **1.** callado; *keep ~*
callarse; **2.** ~*('s the word)!* ¡chito!,
¡chitón!

mum² [~] F mamá *f.*

mum·ble ['mʌmbl] mascullar, musitar.

mum·bo jum·bo ['mʌmbou 'dʒʌmbou] F fetiche *m*; conjuro *m*; mistificación *f*.

mum·mer ['mʌmə] máscara *m*/*f*; *contp.* comicastro *m*; '**mum·mer·y** momería *f*, mojiganga *f*; *fig.* ceremonia *f* vana.

mum·mi·fi·ca·tion [mʌmifi'keiʃn] momificación *f*; **mum·mi·fy** ['~fai] momificar(se).

mum·my¹ ['mʌmi] momia *f.*

mum·my² [~] F mamáita *f.*

mumps [mʌmps] *sg.* papera *f*, parótidas *f*/*pl.*

munch [mʌntʃ] ronzar.

mun·dane ['mʌndein] □ mundano.

mu·nic·i·pal [mju:'nisipl] □ municipal; **mu·nic·i·pal·i·ty** [~'pæliti] municipio *m*; **mu·nic·i·pal·ize** [~əlaiz] municipalizar.

mu·nif·i·cence [mju:'nifisns] munificencia *f*; **mu·nif·i·cent** □ munífico.

mu·ni·ments ['mju:nimənts] documentos *m*/*pl.* (probatorios), archivos *m*/*pl.*   [ciones *f*/*pl.*]

mu·ni·tions ['mju:niʃnz] *pl.* muni-]

mu·ral ['mjuərəl] 1. mural; 2. pintura *f* mural.

mur·der ['mə:də] 1. asesinato *m*; homicidio *m*; 2. asesinar; *fig.* arruinar, estropear; *play* degollar; '**mur·der·er** asesino *m*; '**mur·der·ess** asesina *f*; '**mur·der·ous** □ asesino, homicida; sanguinario; intolerable.

murk [mə:k] oscuridad *f*, lobreguez *f*; **murk·y** ['mə:ki] □ oscuro, lóbrego; tenebroso (*a. fig.*).

mur·mur ['mə:mə] 1. murmullo *m*, murmurio *m* (*a. fig.*); 2. murmurar (*a. fig.*) (*a.* ~ *against*, ~ *at*).

mur·rain ['mʌrin] morriña *f.*

mus·ca·dine ['mʌskədin], **mus·cat** ['~kət], **mus·ca·tel** [~'tel] moscatel *adj. a. su. m*

mus·cle ['mʌsl] 1. músculo *m*; *fig.* fuerza *f* muscular; 2.: *sl.* ~ *in* entrar (*or* establecerse) por fuerza (en un negocio ilegal); **mus·cu·lar** ['mʌskjulə] (*of muscle*) muscular; (*having muscles*) musculoso; fornido.

Muse¹ [mju:z] musa *f.*

muse² [~] meditar, reflexionar, rumiar; estar distraído; ~ (*up*)*on* contemplar.

mu·se·um [mju:'ziəm] museo *m.*

mush¹ [mʌʃ] gacha(s) *f*(*pl.*); *fig.* disparates *m*/*pl.*; *fig.* sensiblería *f.*

mush² [~] *Am.* (hacer un) viaje *m* con trineo tirado por perros.

mush·room ['mʌʃrum] 1. seta *f*, hongo *m*; champiñón *m*; *attr.* que aparece de la noche a la mañana; 2. aparecer de la noche a la mañana; crecer rápidamente.

mush·y ['mʌʃi] pulposo, mollar; *fig.* sensiblero.

mu·sic ['mju:zik] música *f*; F *face the* ~ pagar el pato; *set to* ~ poner música a, musicar; '**mu·si·cal** □ músico, musical; *be very* ~ tener mucho talento para la música; ~ *box* caja *f* de música; ~ *comedy* zarzuela *f*; ~ *instrument* instrumento *m* músico.

mu·sic-hall ['mju:zikhɔ:l] teatro *m* de variedades.   [*m.*]

mu·si·cian [mju:'ziʃn] músico (a *f*)]

mu·sic...: ~-*pa·per* papel *m* de música; '~-*stand* atril *m.*

musk [mʌsk] (olor *m* de) almizcle *m*; ♀ almizcleña *f.*

mus·ket ['mʌskit] mosquete *m*; **mus·ket·eer** [~'tiə] mosquetero *m*; '**mus·ket·ry** mosquetes *m*/*pl.*; (*troops*) mosquetería *f*; fuego *m* de fusilería; tiro *m* de fusil.

musk·y ['mʌski] almizcleño, almizclado.

Mus·lim ['mʌzlim] *v.* Moslem.

mus·lin ['mʌzlin] muselina *f.*

mus·quash ['mʌskwɔʃ] (piel de *f*) rata *f* almizclera.

muss [mʌs] *Am.* F 1. desaliño *m*, confusión *f*; 2. desarreglar, poner en confusión.

mus·sel ['mʌsl] mejillón *m.*

Mus·sul·man ['mʌslmən] musulmán *adj. a. su. m* (-a *f*).

must¹ [mʌst, məst] deber; tener que; haber de; *probability*: deber (de); *I* ~ *do it now* tengo que hacerlo ahora; *I* ~ *keep my word* debo cumplir lo prometido; *he* ~ *be there by now* ya debe (de) estar allí, ya estará allí; *there* ~ *be an explanation* ha de haber una explicación; *it* ~ *be about 2* serán las 2; *he* ~ *have gone* habrá ido.

must² [~] moho *m.*

must³ [~] mosto *m of wine.*

mus·tache [məs'tæʃ] *Am. v.* moustache.

mus·tard ['mʌstəd] mostaza *f*; **'mus·tard-pot** mostacera *f*.

mus·ter ['mʌstə] **1.** asamblea *f* (*a.* ✕); ✕ revista *f*; lista *f*, matrícula *f*; ⚓ rol *m*; *pass* ~ pasar revista; ser aceptable; **2.** *v/t.* llamar a asamblea; juntar para pasar revista; *fig.* (*a.* ~ *up*) cobrar, juntar; *v/i.* juntarse.

mus·ti·ness ['mʌstinis] moho *m*; ranciedad *f*; olor *m* a humedad; **'mus·ty** mohoso; rancio; que huele a humedad.

mu·ta·bil·i·ty [mjuːtə'biliti] mutabilidad *f*; **'mu·ta·ble** □ mudable; **mu'ta·tion** mutación *f*.

mute [mjuːt] **1.** □ mudo; silencioso; **2.** mudo (*a f*) *m*; ♪ sordina *f*; *gr.* (letra *f*) muda *f*; **3.** poner sordina a; apagar.

mu·ti·late ['mjuːtileit] mutilar; **mu·ti'la·tion** mutilación *f*.

mu·ti·neer [mjuːti'niə] amotinado(r) *m*; **'mu·ti·nous** □ amotinado; turbulento, rebelde; **'mu·ti·ny 1.** motín *m*, sublevación *f*; **2.** amotinarse, sublevarse.

mutt [mʌt] *sl.* bobo *m*.

mut·ter ['mʌtə] **1.** murmullo *m*, rumor *m*; **2.** *v/t.* murmurar, mascullar; *v/i.* murmurar.

mut·ton ['mʌtn] carne *f* de carnero; *leg of* ~ pierna *f* de carnero; **'~-'chop** chuleta *f* de carnero.

mu·tu·al ['mjuːtjuəl] □ mutuo; F común; ~ *aid* socorros *m/pl.* mutuos; ~ *consent* común acuerdo *m*; ~ *insurance* seguro *m* mutuo; **mu·tu·al·i·ty** [~'æliti] mutualidad *f*.

muz·zle ['mʌzl] **1.** hocico *m*; bozal *m for dog*; boca *f of gun*; **2.** abozalar; (*gag*) amordazar; **'~-load·er** arma *f* que se carga por la boca.

muz·zy ['mʌzi] □ confuso, aton-) **my** [mai, *a.* mi] mi(s). [tado.)

my·ope ['maioup] miope *m/f*; **my·op·ic** [~'ɔpik] □ miope *adj. a. su. m/f*; **my·o·pi·a** [~'oupiə], **my·o·py** ['~oupi] miopia *f*.

myr·i·ad ['miriəd] **1.** miríada *f*; **2.** miríada de, sin cuento.

myr·mi·don ['məːmidən] *contp.* secuaz *m* fiel, satélite *m*; esbirro *m*.

myrrh [məː] mirra *f*.

myr·tle ['məːtl] arrayán *m*, mirto *m*.

my·self [mai'self] (*subject*) yo mismo, yo misma; *acc., dat.* me; (*after prp.*) mí (mismo, misma).

mys·te·ri·ous [mis'tiəriəs] □ misterioso.

mys·ter·y ['mistəri] misterio *m*; arcano *m*; *thea.* auto *m*, misterio *m*; † oficio *m*, mester *m*; (*a.* ~ *novel*) novela *f* policíaca.

mys·tic ['mistik] **1.** (*a.* **'mys·ti·cal**) □ místico; **2.** místico (*a f*) *m*; **mys·ti·cism** ['~sizm] misticismo *m*, mística *f*; **mys·ti·fi·ca·tion** [~fi'keiʃn] mistificación *f*; *b.s.* superchería *f*; perplejidad *f*; misterio *m*; **mys·ti·fy** ['~fai] mistificar; dejar perplejo; ofuscar.

myth [miθ] mito *m*; **myth·ic**, **myth·i·cal** ['~ik(l)] □ mítico; fabuloso.

myth·o·log·ic, **myth·o·log·i·cal** [miθə'lɔdʒik(l)] □ mitológico; **my·thol·o·gy** [~'θɔlədʒi] mitología *f*.

myx·o·ma·to·sis [miksəmə'tousis] mixomatosis *f*.

N

nab [næb] coger, atrapar, prender.
na·bob ['neibɔb] nabab *m*.
na·celle [nə'sel] ⚓ barquilla *f*.
na·cre ['neikə] nácar *m*; **na·cre·ous** ['⌣kriəs] nacarino, nacarado.
na·dir ['neidiə] *ast.* nadir *m*; *fig.* punto *m* más bajo.
nag[1] [næg] jaca *f*; *contp.* rocín *m*.
nag[2] [⌣] regañar, importunar (*a.* ⌣ *at*); machacar; *fig.* hostigar, remorder.
Nai·ad ['naiæd] náyade *f*.
nail [nail] 1. *anat.* uña *f*; ⊕ clavo *m*; *on the* ⌣ en el acto; *pay on the* ⌣ pagar a toca teja; *bite one's* ⌣s comerse las uñas; 2. clavar (*a. fig.*), enclavar; clavetear; F coger; ⌣ *down* sujetar con clavos; ⌣ *a p. down* comprometer a una p. (*to a*); poner a una p. entre la espada y la pared; ⌣ *up* cerrar con clavos; ⌣ (*to the counter*) demostrar la falsedad de, poner término a; '⌣-**brush** cepillo *m* para las uñas; '⌣-**file** lima *f* para las uñas; '⌣-**scis·sors** *pl.* tijeras *f/pl.* para las uñas.
na·ive [nai'i:v], **na·ive** [neiv] □ ingenuo, cándido, sencillo; **na·ive·té** [nai'i:vtei], **na·ive·ty** ['neivti] ingenuidad *f etc.*
na·ked ['neikid] desnudo (*a. fig.*), en cueros; *with the* ⌣ *eye* a simple vista; '**na·ked·ness** desnudez *f*.
nam·by-pam·by ['næmbi'pæmbi] 1. soso, ñoño; melindroso; 2. ñoño (*a f*) *m*, mirliflor *m/f*, melindroso (*a f*) *m*; insulseces *f/pl.*
name [neim] 1. nombre *m* (*a. fig.*); (*surname*) apellido *m*; reputación *f*; *b.s.* apodo *m*; título *m of book etc.*; linaje *m*; *by* ⌣, *in* ⌣ de nombre; *by the* ⌣ *of* llamado, nombrado; bajo el nombre de; *call a p.* ⌣s poner motes a, injuriar; *in the* ⌣ *of* en nombre de, de parte de; *make a* ⌣ *for o.s.* darse a conocer; *my* ⌣ *is* me llamo; *what is your* ⌣? ¿cómo se llama?; 2. nombrar; designar; (*mention*) mentar; *date, price etc.* fijar, señalar; bautizar *with Christian name*; apellidar *with surname*;

⌣*d p.* llamado; '**name·less** □ anónimo, sin nombre; *vice* nefando; '**name·ly** a saber (*abbr. viz.*); '**name-plate** placa *f* rotulada, letrero *m* con nombre; '**name·sake** tocayo (a *f*) *m*, homónimo (a *f*) *m*.
nan·ny ['næni] F niñera *f*; '⌣-**goat** F cabra *f*.
nap[1] [næp] *cloth:* lanilla *f*, flojel *m*.
nap[2] [⌣] 1. sueño *m* ligero, dormirela *m*; (*afternoon*) siesta *f*; *take a* ⌣ descabezar el sueño; dormir la siesta; 2. dormitar; *catch* ⌣*ping* coger desprevenido.
nap[3] [⌣] *juego de naipes*; F *go* ⌣ jugarse el todo.
na·palm ['neipɑ:m] jalea *f* de gasolina. 　　　　[⌣ *of the neck*).\
nape [neip] cogote *m*, nuca *f* (*mst*/
naph·tha ['næfθə] nafta *f*; **naph·tha·lene** ['⌣li:n] naftaleno *m*, naftalina *f*.
nap·kin ['næpkin] servilleta *f* (*a. table-*⌣); pañal *m* (*a. baby's* ⌣); '⌣-**ring** servilletero *m*.
nap·py ['næpi] F pañal *m*.
nar·cis·sus [nɑ:'sisəs] narciso *m*.
nar·co·sis [nɑ:'kousis] narcosis *f*, narcotismo *m*; **nar·cot·ic** [⌣'kɔtik] narcótico *adj. a. su. m*; **nar·co·tize** ['nɑ:kətaiz] narcotizar.
nard [nɑ:d] nardo *m*.
nark [nɑ:k] *sl.* soplón *m*.
nar·rate [næ'reit] narrar, referir, relatar; **nar·ra·tion** narración *f*, relato *m*; **nar·ra·tive** ['⌣rətiv] 1. □ narrativo; 2. narrativa *f*, narración *f*; **nar·ra·tor** [⌣'reitə] narrador (-a *f*) *m*.
nar·row ['nærou] 1. □ estrecho (*a. fig.*); *passage etc.* angosto; reducido; *p.* de miras estrechas; *p.* tacaño; ⌣ *circumstances* estrechez *f*; 2. ⌣s *pl.* ⚓ estrecho *m*; desfiladero *m*; 3. estrechar(se), (en)angostar (se); reducir(se); encoger(se); '⌣-**gauge** 🚃 de vía estrecha; '⌣-'**mind·ed** □ intolerante; de miras estrechas; '**nar·row·ness** estrechez *f*, angostura *f*; intolerancia *f*.

nar·whal ['nɑ:wəl] narval *m*.

na·sal ['neizl] ☐ nasal *adj: a. su. f*; speak ~ly ganguear; **na·sal·i·ty** [~'zæliti] nasalidad *f*; **na·sal·ize** ['~zəlaiz] nasalizar.

nas·cent ['næsnt] naciente.

nas·ti·ness ['nɑ:stinis] suciedad *f* etc.

na·stur·tium [nə'stə:ʃəm] capuchina *f*.

nas·ty ['nɑ:sti] ☐ sucio, asqueroso; feo, repugnante; indecente; horrible; malévolo; F peligroso; F difícil.

na·tal ['neitl] natal; **na·tal·i·ty** [nə'tæliti] natalidad *f*.

na·tion ['neiʃn] nación *f*.

na·tion·al ['næʃnl] ☐ nacional *adj. a. su. m/f*; ~ debt deuda *f* pública; ♀ Socialism nacionalsocialismo *m*; **'na·tion·al·ism** nacionalismo *m*; **'na·tion·al·ist** nacionalista *adj. a. su. m/f*; **na·tion·al·i·ty** [næʃə'næliti] nacionalidad *f*; **na·tion·al·ize** ['næʃnəlaiz] nacionalizar.

na·tion-wide ['neiʃnwaid] por (*or* de) toda la nación.

na·tive ['neitiv] 1. ☐ nativo (*a.* ✕); natural; indígena, originario (*to* de); ~ tongue lengua *f* materna; F go ~ vivir como los indígenas; 2. natural *m/f*; indígena *m/f*; nacional *m/f*; I am a ~ of soy natural de, nací en.

na·tiv·i·ty [nə'tiviti] natividad *f*; (Christmas) Navidad *f*; art: nacimiento *m*; ~ play auto *m* del nacimiento.

nat·ty ['næti] ☐ F fino, elegante; apuesto; majo.

nat·u·ral ['nætʃrəl] 1. ☐ natural (*a.* ♩); nativo; innato; *p.* sencillo, llano; normal; child ilegítimo; ~ history historia *f* natural; ~ sciences *pl.* ciencias *f/pl.* naturales; 2. (*p.*) idiota *m/f*; ♩ nota *f* natural; ♩ becuadro *m*; Am. F cosa *f* de éxito certero; **'nat·u·ral·ism** naturalismo *m*; **'nat·u·ral·ist** naturalista *m/f*; **'nat·u·ral·ist·ic** ☐ naturalista; **nat·u·ral·i·za·tion** [~lai-'zeiʃn] naturalización *f*; ~ papers carta *f* de naturaleza; **'nat·u·ral·ize** naturalizar; **nat·u·ral·ly** naturalmente; F desde luego, claro; **'nat·u·ral·ness** naturalidad *f*.

na·ture ['neitʃə] naturaleza *f*; *p.'s* natural *m*, temperamento *m*; (kind) género *m*, clase *f*; from ~ del natu-

ral; in the ~ of algo como; good ~ buen natural *m*; afabilidad *f*; **'na·tured** de carácter..., de condición...

naught [nɔ:t] nada; cero *m*; bring to ~ frustrar; destruir; come to ~ malograrse; reducirse a nada; set at ~ despreciar; contravenir; **naugh·ti·ness** ['~tinis] travesura *f* etc.; **'naugh·ty** travieso, pícaro; desobediente; story verde; don't be ~! (to child) ¡no seas malo!

nau·se·a ['nɔ:siə] náusea *f*, asco *m*; **nau·se·ate** ['~sieit] dar asco (a); **'nau·se·at·ing**, **'nau·seous** ☐ nauseabundo; asqueroso.

nau·ti·cal ['nɔ:tikl] ☐ náutico, marítimo; ~ mile milla *f* marina.

na·val ['neivəl] naval, de marina; ~ base base *f* naval; ~ (dock)yard arsenal *m*; ~ officer oficial *m* de marina.

nave [neiv] ⌂ nave *f* (principal).

na·vel ['neivəl] ombligo *m*.

nav·i·ga·ble ['nævigəbl] river etc. navegable; ship etc. gobernable, dirigible; **nav·i·gate** ['~geit] navegar; ship marear; **nav·i·ga·tion** navegación *f*, náutica *f*; mareaje *m*; **'nav·i·ga·tor** navegador *m*, navegante *m*.

nav·vy ['nævi] peón *m* (caminero), bracero *m*.

na·vy ['neivi] marina *f* de guerra; armada *f*; ~ blue azul *m* marino (*or* de mar).

nay [nei] 1. † or prov. no; lit. más aun, mejor dicho; 2. negativa *f*.

Naz·a·rene [næzə'ri:n] nazareno *adj. a. su. m* (a *f*).

Na·zi ['nɑ:tsi] nazi *adj. su. m/f*; **Nazism** nazismo *m*.

neap [ni:p] marea *f* muerta (*a.* ~ tide).

Ne·a·pol·i·tan [niə'pɔlitən] napolitano *adj. a. su. m* (a *f*).

near [niə] 1. *adj.* cercano, próximo; inmediato, vecino; relationship estrecho, íntimo; translation etc. aproximativo; ~ side mot. lado *m* izquierdo (Am. derecho); it was a ~ thing escapé etc. por un pelo; 2. *adv.* cerca; ~ at hand a la mano, cerca; come (*or* draw) ~ acercarse (to a); 3. *prp.* (*a.* ~ to) cerca de; próximo a, junto a; hacia; casi; 4. acercarse a, aproximarse a; **near·by** ['~bai] 1. *adj.* próximo, cercano; 2. *adv.* cerca; **'near·ly** casi; de cerca; aproximadamente; not ~ ni con mucho; *I ⁓lost it* por poco lo perdí; *we very ⁓ bought it* en poco estuvo que lo comprásemos; **'near·ness** proximidad *f*, cercanía *f*; intimidad *f*; **'near·'sight·ed** miope, corto de vista.

neat [ni:t] □ pulcro, esmerado, aseado; primoroso; *(shapely)* bien hecho, bien proporcionado; *(skilful)* diestro; *drink* puro, sin mezcla; **'neat·ness** pulcritud *f* etc.

neb [neb] *Scot.* pico *m*; nariz *f*; punta *f*.

neb·u·la ['nebjulə] nebulosa *f*; **'neb·u·lar** *ast.* nebuloso; **'neb·u·lous** □ nebuloso.

nec·es·sar·y ['nesisəri] **1.** □ necesario, preciso, indispensable; **2.** cosa *f* necesaria, requisito *m* indispensable; lo necesario (*a. necessaries pl.*); **ne·ces·si·tate** [ni'sesiteit] necesitar, exigir; **ne'ces·si·tous** necesitado, indigente; **ne'ces·si·ty** necesidad *f*; requisito *m* indispensable; indigencia *f*; *of ⁓* de (*or* por) necesidad; *in case of ⁓* si fuese necesario; en caso de urgencia; *be under the ⁓ of ger.* verse obligado a *inf.*

neck [nek] **1.** cuello *m*; pescuezo *m* of *animal*; gollete *m of bottle*; mástil *m of violin etc.*; *geog.* istmo *m*; *sew.* escote *m* (*a. '⁓·line*); *⁓ and ⁓* (a las) parejas; *⁓ and crop* enteramente; de cabeza; *sl. get it in the ⁓* recibir una peluca, pagarla(s), cargársela; **2.** *sl.* acariciarse, besuquearse; **neck·er·chief** ['nekətʃif] pañoleta *f*, pañuelo *m* de cuello; **neck·lace** ['⁓lis], **neck·let** ['⁓lit] collar *m*; **'neck·tie** corbata *f*.

ne·crol·o·gy [ne'krɔlədʒi] necrología *f*; **nec·ro·man·cy** ['nekroumænsi] necromancía *f*, nigroman-cía *f*.

nec·tar ['nektə] néctar *m*.

née [nei] nacida (*f*); *Rosa Bell, ⁓ Martin* Rosa Martin de Bell.

need [ni:d] **1.** necesidad *f* (*for, of* de); requisito *m*; urgencia *f*; carencia *f*, falta *f* (*for, of* de); *bodily ⁓s pl.* menesteres *m/pl.*; *if ⁓ be* si fuera necesario; *in ⁓* necesitado; *be (or stand) in ⁓ of, have ⁓ of* necesitar; *in case of ⁓* en caso de necesidad (*or* urgencia); **2.** *v/t.* necesitar; requerir, exigir; carecer de; deber *inf.*; tener que *inf.*; *I ⁓ it* me hace falta, me falta, lo necesito; *I ⁓ to do it* tengo que hacerlo, debo hacerlo; *he ⁓s*

watching hay que vigilarle; *a visa is ⁓ed* se exige visado; *it ⁓ not be done* no es preciso hacerlo; *v/i.* estar necesitado; **need·ful** ['⁓ful] **1.** □ necesario; **2.** F lo necesario, *en quibus m*; **'need·i·ness** necesidad *f*, estrechez *f*.

nee·dle ['ni:dl] **1.** aguja *f*; **2.** *mst Am.* F aguijar; fastidiar; *drink* añadir alcohol a; **'⁓·case** alfiletero *m*.

need·less ['ni:dlis] innecesario, superfluo, inútil; *⁓ to say* excusado es decir, huelga decir; claro está.

nee·dle...: **'⁓·wom·an** costurera *f*; *be a good ⁓* coser bien; **'⁓·work** costura *f*; labor *f* (de aguja); bordado *m*.

needs [ni:dz] necesariamente, forzosamente; **'need·y** □ necesitado, indigente.

ne'er [neə] *poet.* nunca; **'⁓·do·well** holgazán *m*, perdulario *m*.

ne·far·i·ous [ni'feəriəs] □ nefario, malo, atroz.

ne·gate [ni'geit] negar; anular, invalidar; **ne'ga·tion** negación *f*, negativa *f*; anulación *f*; **neg·a·tive** ['negətiv] **1.** □ negativo; **2.** negativa *f*; *phot.* negativo *m*; *gr.* negación *f*; *⁊* electricidad *f* negativa; *⁊* polo *m* negativo; **3.** negar; desaprobar; poner veto a; anular.

neg·lect [ni'glekt] **1.** negligencia *f*, descuido *m*; abandono *m*; inobservancia *f*; *(self-)* dejadez *f*; *fall into ⁓* caer en desuso; **2.** descuidar, desatender; abandonar; *duty etc.* faltar a; *(ignore)* no hacer caso de; *⁓ to inf.* dejar de *inf.*, olvidarse de *inf.*; **neg·'lect·ful** [⁓ful] □ negligente, descuidado; *be ⁓ of* descuidar.

neg·li·gée ['negli:ʒei] salto *m* de cama; bata *f*.

neg·li·gence ['neglidʒəns] negligencia *f*, descuido *m*; **'neg·li·gent** □ negligente, descuidado.

neg·li·gi·ble ['neglidʒəbl] insignificante; despreciable.

ne·go·ti·a·bil·i·ty [nigouʃiə'biliti] negociabilidad *f*; **ne'go·ti·a·ble** □ negociable; *road etc.* transitable; **ne'go·ti·ate** [⁓eit] *v/t.* negociar; gestionar, agenciar; pasar por; *obstacle* salvar; *bend* tomar; *v/i.* negociar; *enter into ⁓ with* entrar en tratos con; **ne'go·ti·a·tion** negociación *f*; gestión *f*; **ne'go·ti·a·tor** negociador (-a *f*) *m*.

ne·gress ['ni:gris] negra *f*; **ne·gro** ['ni:grou], *pl.* **ne·groes** ['‿z] negro *adj. a. su. m*; **ne·groid** ['ni:grɔid] negroide.

neigh [nei] **1.** relincho *m*; **2.** relinchar.

neigh·bo(u)r ['neibə] **1.** vecino (a *f*) *m*; prójimo (a *f*) *m*; **2.** (*a.* ‿ *upon*) colindar con, estar contiguo a; **'neigh·bo(u)r·hood** vecindad *f*, vecindario *m*; alrededores *m/pl.*; *in the* ‿ *of* cerca de; **'neigh·bo(u)r·ing** vecino, colindante, cercano; de al lado; **'neigh·bo(u)r·ly** (de) buen vecino; amistoso.

nei·ther ['naiðə, 'ni:ðə] **1.** ninguno (de los dos), ni uno ni (el) otro; **2.** *adv.* ni; ‿ ... *nor* ni ... ni; **3.** *conj.* ni; tampoco; ni ... tampoco.

nem·e·sis ['nemisis] *fig.* justicia *f*, justo castigo *m*.

ne·ol·o·gism [ni'ɔlɔdʒizm] neologismo *m*.

ne·on ['ni:ɔn] neón *m*, neo *m*.

ne·o·phyte ['ni:oufait] neófito (a *f*) *m*.

neph·ew ['nevju:] sobrino *m*.

nep·o·tism ['nepɔtizm] nepotismo *m*.

Ne·re·id ['niəriid] ɲereida *f*.

nerve [nə:v] **1.** nervio *m* (*a. fig.*); (*courage*) valor *m*, ánimo *m*; *sl.* descaro *m*, tupé *m*; F ‿s *pl.* nerviosidad *f*; *get on a p.'s* ‿s crisparle los nervios a una p.; ‿ *centre* centro *m* nervioso; *fig.* punto *m* neurálgico; **2.** esforzar, animar; **'‿-'cell** neurona *f*; célula *f* nerviosa; **'nerve-'rack·ing** horripilante, irritante.

nerv·ous ['nə:vəs] □ nerv(i)oso; tímido; ‿ *breakdown* crisis *f* nerviosa; ‿ *exhaustion* neurastenia *f*; ‿ *system* sistema *m* nervioso; **'nerv·ous·ness** nerviosidad *f*, nerviosismo *m*; timidez *f*.

nerv·y ['nə:vi] F nervioso; *Am. sl.* descaroso.

nest [nest] **1.** nido *m* (*a. fig.*); nidada *f of eggs or young birds*; nidal *m of hen*; juego *m of drawers etc.*; **2.** anidar; buscar nidos; **'nest-egg** nidal *m*; *fig.* ahorros *m/pl.*, buena hucha *f*; **nes·tle** ['nesl] abrigar(se); anidar(se); arrimar(se) (*up to* a); apretar(se) (*up to* contra); **nest·ling** ['nesliŋ] pajarito *m* en el nido.

net¹ [net] **1.** red *f* (*a. fig.*); (*fabric*) tul *m*; redecilla *f for hair etc.*;

2. coger (con red); enredar; cubrir con red.

net² [‿] ✝ **1.** neto, líquido; ‿ *income* renta *f* neta; ‿ *price* precio *m* neto; ‿ *weight* peso *m* neto; **2.** ganar (*or* producir) en neto.

neth·er ['neðə] inferior, más bajo; ‿ *regions* infierno *m*; **'‿-·most** (el *etc.*) más bajo.

net·ting ['netiŋ] red(es) *f(pl.)*; obra *f* de malla.

net·tle ['netl] **1.** ortiga *f*; **2.** irritar, provocar; **'‿-rash** urticaria *f*.

net·work ['netwə:k] red *f* (*a. fig.*); malla *f*.

neu·ral·gia [njuə'rældʒə] neuralgia *f*; **neu·ras·the·ni·a** [njuərəs-'θi:niə] neurastenia *f*; **neu·rasthen·ic** [‿'θenik] neurasténico; **neu·ri·tis** [njuə'raitis] neuritis *f*; **neu·rol·o·gist** [‿'rɔlədʒist] neurólogo *m*; **neu·rol·o·gy** [‿'rɔlədʒi] neurología *f*; **neu·ro·path** [‿rou-'pæθ] neurópata *m/f*; **neu·ro·path·ic** [‿rou'pæθik] neuropático; **neu·ro·sis** [‿'rousis] neurosis *f*; **neu·rot·ic** [‿'rɔtik] □ neurótico *adj. a. su. m* (a *f*).

neu·ter ['nju:tə] neutro.

neu·tral ['nju:trəl] **1.** □ neutral, ⚥, ♂, ♑, zo. neutro; **2.** neutral *m/f*; *mot. in* ‿ en punto muerto; **neu·tral·i·ty** [nju:'træliti] neutralidad *f*; **neu·tral·i·za·tion** [nju:trəlai'zeiʃn] neutralización *f*; **'neu·tral·ize** neutralizar.

neu·tron ['nju:trɔn] neutrón *m*.

nev·er ['nevə] nunca, jamás; de ningún modo; ni siquiera; ‿ *again* nunca más; ‿ *fear!* ¡no hay cuidado!; ‿ *a word* ni una palabra; **'never'more** nunca más; **never·the·less** [‿ðə'les] sin embargo, no obstante, con todo.

new [nju:] **1.** *adj.* nuevo; (*fresh*) fresco; *bread* tierno; *p.* inexperto; F *what's* ‿? ¿qué hay de nuevo?; ‿ *moon* novilunio *m*; ♀ *Testament* Nuevo Testamento *m*; ♀ *Year* Año *m* Nuevo; ♀ *Year's Day* día *m* de Año Nuevo; ♀ *Yorker* neoyorquino (a *f*) *m*; ♀ *Zealander* neozelandés (-a *f*) *m*; **2.** *adv.* recién; **'new-'born** recién nacido; **'new-'com·er** recién llegado (a *f*) *m*; **new·fan·gled** ['‿-fæŋgld] *contp.* recién inventado, moderno; **'newish** bastante nuevo; **'new-laid** *egg* recién puesto, fresco; **'new·ly** nuevamente, recién; ~ *wed* recién casado; **'new·ness** novedad *f*; inexperiencia *f*.

news *mst sg.* noticia(s) *f* (*pl.*); nueva (s) *f* (*pl.*), novedad *f*; *radio:* noticiario *m*; *it was* ~ *to me* me cogió de nuevas; *what's the* ~? ¿qué hay de nuevo? *he is in the* ~ se oye hablar mucho de él; **'~·a·gen·cy** agencia *f* de información; **'~·a·gent** vendedor (-a *f*) *m* de periódicos; **'~-'bul-le·tin** (boletín *m* de) noticias *f/pl.*, noticiario *m*; **'~·pa·per** periódico *m*, diario *m*; *attr.* periodístico; **'~-pa·per·man** periodista *m*; **'~-print** papel *m* prensa; **'~-reel** noticiario *m*, actualidades *f/pl.*; **'~-room** gabinete *m* de lectura; **'~-stand** quiosco *m* de periódicos; **news·y** ['nju:zi] F lleno de noticias; *p.* noticioso.

newt [nju:t] tritón *m*.

next [nekst] **1.** *adj.* próximo, siguiente; *year etc.* que viene; inmediato; *house etc.* de al lado, vecino; otro; *it's the* ~ *but one* es el segundo después de éste; ~ *day* día *m* siguiente; *v. door;* *on the* ~ *page* a la vuelta, a la página siguiente; ~ *time* la próxima vez; ~ *week* la semana que viene; **2.** *adv.* luego, inmediatamente, después; la próxima vez; ~ *best thing* lo mejor después de eso; ~ *to* junto a, al lado de; primero después de; casi; ~ *to nothing* casi nada; *v. what*.

nib [nib] pico *m*; plumilla *f*, plumín *m* of fountain-pen.

nib·ble ['nibl] (*a.* ~ *at*) mordiscar; (*fish*) picar; *grass* rozar; *fig.* criticar; *fig.* tantear, considerar.

nibs [nibz]: *sl. his* ~ su señoría.

nice [nais] □ ameno, agradable; bonito (*a. iro.*); bueno; *p.* simpático, amable; primoroso; fino, delicado; escrupuloso; exacto; meticuloso; F ~ *and adj.* muy; bastante; *often rendered by diminutive* -ito; ~ *and early* tempranito; *it's* ~ *and warm* hace un calor agradable; F *not* ~feo; ~ *point* punto *m* delicado; **'~-look-ing** F mono, guapo; **'nice·ness** amenidad *f*; lo simpático, simpatía *f etc.*; **nice·ty** ['~iti] exactitud *f*; sutileza *f*; refinamiento *m*; *niceties pl.* detalles *m/pl.*; *to a* ~ con la mayor precisión.

niche [nitʃ] nicho *m*; *fig.* colocación *f* conveniente.

nick [nik] **1.** mella *f*; muesca *f*; *in the* (*very*) ~ *of time* de perilla, en el momento preciso (*or* crítico); **2.** mellar, hacer muescas en; *sl.* robar, ratear.

nick·el ['nikl] **1.** níquel *m* (*a. Am. moneda de 5 centavos*); **2.** niquelar (*a.* '~-**plate**).

nick·name ['nikneim] **1.** apodo *m*, sobrenombre *m*, mote *m*; **2.** apodar, motejar.

nic·o·tine ['nikəti:n] nicotina *f*.

niece [ni:s] sobrina *f*.

niff [nif] *sl.* olor *m*.

nif·ty □ ['nifti] *sl.* elegante, pera; excelente, de primera; hábil.

nig·gard ['nigəd] tacaño *adj. a. su. m* (*a f*); **'nig·gard·ly** tacaño, avariento, mezquino.

nig·ger ['nigə] F *contp.* negro (*a f*) *m*; ~ *in the woodpile* gato *m* encerrado; *work like a* ~ trabajar como un negro.

nig·gle ['nigl] inquietarse por pequeñeces; **'nig·gling** nimio, minucioso; mezquino; insignificante.

nigh [nai] † *or prov.* cerca (de); casi.

night [nait] noche *f*; *attr.* nocturno; *at* ~, *by* ~, *in the* ~ de noche, por la noche; *good* ~! ¡buenas noches!; *last* ~ anoche; F *make a* ~ *of it* estar de juerga hasta muy entrada la noche; *the* ~ *before last* anteanoche; **'~·cap** gorro *m*; F resopón *m*; **'~-club** cabaret *m*; **'~-dress** camisón *m* (de noche); **'~-fall** anochecer *m*; *at* ~ al anochecer; **'~-fight·er** ✠ caza *m* nocturno; **'~-gown** *v.* night-dress; **night·in·gale** ['~ingeil] ruiseñor *m*; **'night-light** mariposa *f*; **'night·ly** de noche, (de) todas las noches.

night...: **'~·mare** pesadilla *f* (*a. fig.*); **'~-school** escuela *f* nocturna; **'~-shade** dulcamara *f*, hierba *f* mora; *deadly* ~ belladona *f*; **'~'watch-man** sereno *m*, vigilante *m* de noche.

ni·hil·ism ['naiiilizm] nihilismo *m*; **'ni·hil·ist** nihilista *m/f*.

nil [nil] nada *f*, cero *m*.

nim·ble ['nimbl] □ ágil, activo, ligero; listo.

nim·bus ['nimbəs] nimbo *m*.

nin·com·poop ['ninkəmpu:p] F bobo (a *f*) *m*, simplón (-a *f*) *m*, papirote *m*.

nine [nain] nueve (*a. su. m*); F *be dressed up to the* ~*s* estar hecho un

brazo de mar; '**∿·pins** *pl.* (juego *m* de) bolos *m*/*pl.*; **nine·teen** ['∿'ti:n] diecinueve; '**nine'teenth** [∿θ] decimonoveno, decimonono; **nine·tieth** ['∿tiiθ] nonagésimo; '**nine·ty** noventa.   [tecato (a *f*) *m*.\
nin·ny ['nini] F bobo (a *f*) *m*, men-∫
ninth [nainθ] noveno, nono.
nip[1] [nip] **1.** pellizco *m*, mordisco *m*; viento *m* frío; helada *f*; **2.** pellizcar, mordiscar; helar; (*wind*) picar; *sl.* coger, ratear.
nip[2] [∿] trago *m*, sorb(it)o *m*.
nip[3] [∿] F correr; ∿ *in* colarse; ∿ *off* pirarse.
nip·per ['nipə] *sl.* chiquillo *m*.
nip·ple ['nipl] pezón *m*; tetilla *f of male or bottle*; ⊕ boquilla *f* roscada, manguito *m* de unión; (*lubricating*) engrasador *m*.
nip·py ['nipi] ágil, listo.
nit [nit] liendre *f*.
ni·trate ['naitreit] nitrato *m*.
ni·tre, ni·ter ['naitə] nitro *m*.
ni·tric ac·id ['naitrik'æsid] ácido *m* nítrico.
ni·tro·gen ['naitridʒən] nitrógeno *m*; **ni·trog·e·nous** [∿'trɔdʒinəs] nitrogenado.
ni·trous ['naitrəs] nitroso.
nix [niks] *sl.* nada.
no [nou] **1.** *adv.* no; **2.** *adj.* ninguno; ∿ *man's land* tierra *f* de nadie; ∿ *one* nadie, ninguno; *with* ∿ sin; **3.** *su.* no *m*; voto *m* negativo.
nob[1] [nɔb] *sl.* cabeza *f*.
nob[2] [∿] *sl.* pez *m* gordo; elegante *m*, majo *m*.
nob·ble ['nɔbl] *sl. p.* sobornar; *th.* birlar, ratear; *horse* narcotizar, estropear.
no·bil·i·ty [nou'biliti] nobleza *f*; hidalguía *f esp. of conduct*.
no·ble ['noubl] **1.** □ noble; hidalgo, caballeroso; sublime; **2.** (*a.* '∿·**man**) noble *m*; hidalgo *m*; '**no·ble·ness** nobleza *f*; hidalguía *f*; '**no·ble·wom·an** dama *f* noble, hidalga *f*.
no·bod·y ['noubədi] **1.** nadie, ninguno; *a* ∿ un (don) nadie, un cualquiera.
noc·tur·nal [nɔk'tə:nl] nocturno.
nod [nɔd] **1.** menear la cabeza de arriba abajo; (*doze*) dar cabezadas, cabecear; indicar con la cabeza; decir que sí con la cabeza; ∿*ding acquaintance* conocimiento *m* superficial; **2.** cabezada *f*; inclinación *f*

de la cabeza; señal *f* hecha con la cabeza.
nod·dle ['nɔdl] F cabeza *f*, mollera *f*.
node [noud] ♗, *ast.*, *phys.* nodo *m*; ♧ nudo *m*.
nod·u·lar ['nɔdjulə] nodular.
nod·ule ['nɔdju:l] nódulo *m*.
nog·gin ['nɔgin] vaso *m* pequeño; *medida de licor* (= *1,42 decilitros*).
no·how ['nouhau] F de ninguna manera.
noise [nɔiz] **1.** ruido *m*; clamor *m*; estrépito *m*; F *big* ∿ pez *m* gordo; **2.**: ∿ *abroad* divulgar, publicar.
noise·less ['∿lis] □ silencioso, sin ruido.   [trépito *m*; lo ruidoso.\
nois·i·ness ['nɔizinis] ruido *m*, es-∫
noi·some ['nɔisəm] apestoso; asqueroso; malsano, nocivo.
nois·y ['nɔizi] □ ruidoso, estrépitoso, clamoroso.
no·mad ['nɔməd] nómada *adj. a. su. m*/*f*; **no·mad·ic** [nou'mædik] □ nómada.
nom-de-plume ['nɔmdə'plum] seudónimo *m*.   [nomenclatura *f*.\
no·men·cla·ture [nou'menklətʃə]∫
nom·i·nal ['nɔminl] □ nominal; ∿ *value* valor *m* nominal; **nom·i·nate** ['∿neit] nombrar, proponer como candidato (*for* a); **nom·i·na·tion** nombramiento *m*, nominación *f*; propuesta *f*; **nom·i·na·tive** ['∿nətiv] nominativo *adj. a. su. m*; **nom·i·nee** [∿'ni:] candidato *m* nombrado (*or* propuesto).   [in..., falta *f* de.\
non [nɔn] *in compounds*: no, des...,∫
non-age ['nounidʒ] minoridad *f*.
non-a·ge·nar·i·an [nounədʒi'nɛəriən] nonagenario (a *f*) *m*, noventón (-a *f*) *m*.
non-ag·gres·sion ['nɔnə'greʃn]: no agresión *f*; ∿ *pact* pacto *m* de no agresión.
non-al·co·hol·ic ['nɔnælkə'hɔlik] no alcohólico.
non-ap·pear·ance ['nɔnə'piərəns] ausencia *f*; ♗♗ no comparecencia *f*.
non-at·tend·ance ['nɔnə'tendəns] falta *f* de asistencia, ausencia *f*.
nonce [nɔns]: *for the* ∿ por esta vez, por el momento.
non-cha·lance ['nɔnʃələns] indiferencia *f*; aplomo *m*; descuido *m*; '**non-cha·lant** □ indiferente; descuidado.
non-com·bat·ant ['nɔn'kɔmbətənt] no combatiente *adj. a. su. m*/*f*.

non·com·mis·sioned ['nɔnkə'miʃ-ənd]: ~ officer ✗ sargento m or cabo m; ~ officers pl. approx. clases f/pl. (de tropa).

non·com·mit·al ['nɔnkə'mitl] que no compromete; ambiguo, evasivo.

non·com·pli·ance ['nɔnkəm'plai-əns] falta f de cumplimiento, desobediencia f (with de).

non·con·duc·tor ['nɔnkən'dʌktə] ⚡ aislador m.

non·con·form·ist ['nɔnkən'fɔ:mist] disidente adj. a. su. m/f; eccl. no conformista adj. a. su. m/f; 'non·con'form·i·ty disidencia f; no conformismo m.

non·de·script ['nɔndiskript] indefinido, inclasificable; b.s. mediocre.

none [nʌn] 1. pron. (p.) nadie; (p., th.) ninguno; (th.) nada; ~ of that nada de eso; ~ of them ninguno de ellos; 2. adv. no; de ninguna manera, nada; ~ the less sin embargo.

non·en·ti·ty [nɔ'nentiti] nulidad f, cero m a la izquierda. [esencial.↓

non·es·sen·tial ['nɔni'senʃəl] no↑

non·fer·rous ['nɔn'ferəs] no ferroso.

non·fic·tion ['nɔn'fikʃn] literatura f no novelesca.

non·in·ter·ven·tion ['nɔnintə-'venʃn] no intervención f.

non·lad·der·ing ['nɔn'lædəriŋ] indesmallable.

non·pa·reil [nɔnpə'rel] (persona f or cosa f) sin par; typ. nomparell m.

non·par·ty ['nɔn'pɑːti] pol. independiente. [confundir.↓

non·plus ['nɔn'plʌs] dejar perplejo,↑

non·prof·it (-mak·ing) ['nɔn'prɔf-it (meikiŋ)]: ~ institution institución f no lucrativa.

non·res·i·dent ['nɔn'rezidənt] transeúnte adj. a. su. m/f.

non·sense ['nɔnsəns] disparate m, desatino m, tontería f; ~! ¡tonterías!; **non·sen·si·cal** [˰'sensikəl] □ disparatado, tonto, desatinado.

non·shrink ['nɔn'ʃriŋk] inencogible.

non·skid ['nɔn'skid] antideslizante, antirresbaladizo.

non·smok·er ['nɔn'smoukə] no fumador m.

non·stop ['nɔn'stɔp] 1. adj. 🚂 directo; ✗ sin escalas; continuo; 2. adv. sin parar.

non·un·ion [nɔn'juːnjən] no sindicalizado.

noo·dle ['nuːdl] F bobo (a f) m; F cabeza f; cooking: tallarín m; ~ soup sopa f de pastas.

nook [nuk] rincón m, escondrijo m.

noon [nuːn] 1. mediodía m (a. '~day, '~tide); fig. apogeo m; at ~ a(l) mediodía; 2. de mediodía, meridional.

noose [nuːs] 1. lazo m (corredizo); (hangman's) dogal m; 2. coger con↓

nope [noup] Am. F no. [lazo.↑

nor [nɔː] ni, no, tampoco; neither... ~ ... ni ... ni ...; ~ I ni yo tampoco; ~ was this all y esto no fue todo.

Nor·dic ['nɔːdik] nórdico.

norm [nɔːm] norma f; modelo m; pauta f; 'nor·mal □ 1. normal (a. Ⓐ); regular, corriente; ~ school escuela f normal; 2. estado m normal, nivel m normal; 'nor·mal·ize normalizar.

Nor·man ['nɔːmən] normando adj. a. su. m (a f).

north [nɔːθ] 1. norte m; 2. adj. del norte, septentrional; 3. adv. al norte, hacia el norte; '~·east noreste adj. (a. '~·'east·er·ly, '~·'east·ern) a. su. m; **north·er·ly** ['˰ðəli] direction hacia el norte; wind del norte; **north·ern** ['˰ən] (del) norte, norteño, septentrional; 'north·ern·er habitante m/f del norte; 'north·ern·most (el) más norte; 'north·ward(s) hacia el norte.

north...: '~·'west noroeste adj. (a. '~·'west·er·ly, '~·'west·ern) a. su. m.

Nor·we·gian [nɔː'wiːdʒən] 1. noruego adj. a. su. m (a f); 2. (language) noruego m.

nose [nouz] 1. nariz f; narices f/pl. (F); hocico m of animals; (sense of smell) olfato m; ✗ morro m; ⚓ proa f; blow one's ~ sonarse (las narices); follow one's ~ ir todo seguido; dejarse llevar por el instinto; have a good ~ for tener buen olfato para; look down one's ~ at mirar por encima del hombro; pay through the ~ dejarse desollar; turn up one's ~ at desdeñar; under the (very) ~ of en las barbas de; 2. v/t. husmear, olfatear (a. ~ out); restregar la nariz contra; ~ one's way avanzar con cautela; v/i.: ~ about curiosear; '~·bag morral m, cebadera f; **nosed** de nariz...

nose...: '~·dive ✗ picado m verti-

cal; (*involuntary*) caída *f* de morro;
'~·gay ramillete *m*.

nos·(e)y ['nouzi] F curioso; ♀ *Parker*
fisgón (-a *f*) *m*.

nos·tal·gi·a [nɔs'tældʒiə] nostalgia *f*,
añoranza *f*; **nos'tal·gic** [‿dʒik] □
nostálgico.   [nariz *f*.]

nos·tril ['nɔstril] (ventana *f* de la)|

nos·trum ['nɔstrəm] remedio *m*
secreto, panacea *f*.

not [nɔt] no; ~ *I* yo no; ~ *to say*
por no decir; ~ *thinking that* sin
pensar que; *I think* ~ creo que no,
no lo creo; *why* ~? ¿cómo no?

no·ta·bil·i·ty [noutə'biliti] notabilidad *f*; **no·ta·ble** ['noutəbl] **1.** □
notable, señalado; **2.** notabilidad *f*;
~*s pl*. notables *m/pl*.

no·tar·i·al [nou'tɛəriəl] □ notarial;
no·ta·ry ['noutəri] notario *m* (*a.*
~ *public*).

no·ta·tion [nou'teiʃn] notación *f*.

notch [nɔtʃ] **1.** muesca *f*, mella *f*;
Am. desfiladero *m*; **2.** mellar, cortar
muescas en; *fig*. señalar.

note [nout] **1.** nota *f* (*a. ♩*); apunte
m; marca *f*, señal *f*; (*letter*) esquela
f, recado *m*; (*bank-*) billete *m*; ✝ vale
m; *of* ~ notable; *make a* ~ *of*
apuntar; *take* ~ *of* poner atención a;
take ~*s* tomar notas, sacar apuntes;
2. notar, observar, advertir; anotar,
apuntar (*a.* ~ *down*); '~·book cuaderno *m*, libro *m* de apuntes, libreta *f*; '~·case cartera *f*; 'not·ed
conocido, célebre (*for* por); 'note-
pa·per papel *m* para cartas; 'note-
wor·thy notable, digno de notarse.

noth·ing ['nʌθiŋ] **1.** nada *f*; ♬ cero *m*;
friolera *f*, nadería *f* (*a. mere* ~);
sweet ~*s pl*. ternezas *f/pl.*; ~ *else*
nada más; ~ *much*, ~ *to speak of*
poca cosa; *for* ~ (*free*) gratis, de balde; (*in vain*) en vano, en balde; *come
to* ~ fracasar, reducirse a nada; *make*
~ *of* no sacar nada de, no entender;
no aprovecharse de; no dar importancia a; *think* ~ *of* tener en poco;
tener por fácil; no hacer caso de;
2. *adv*. de ninguna manera, en
nada; ~ *daunted* sin arredrarse; ~
less no menos; ni con mucho;
'noth·ing·ness nada *f*, inexistencia
f.

no·tice ['noutis] **1.** aviso *m*; (*poster
etc*.) letrero *m*, anuncio *m*, cartel *m*;
(*review*) reseña *f*, crítica *f*; (*reference*) nota *f*, mención *f*; observa-

ción *f*, atención *f*; *at short* ~
a corto plazo, con poco tiempo de
aviso; *give* ~ *that* avisar que; *give
a p. a week's* ~ despedir con una
semana de plazo; avisar con una
semana de anticipación; *take* ~ *of*
observar, hacer caso de; *until
further* ~ hasta nuevo aviso;
2. notar, observar; hacer caso de;
reparar, advertir, fijarse en; *book*
reseñar; 'no·tice·a·ble □ evidente,
perceptible; notable; 'no·tice-
board tablón *m* de anuncios.

no·ti·fi·a·ble ['noutifaiəbl] de declaración obligatoria; **no·ti·fi·ca-
tion** [‿fi'keiʃn] notificación *f*.

no·ti·fy ['noutifai] notificar, comunicar, intimar, avisar.

no·tion ['nouʃn] noción *f*, idea *f*;
capricho *m*; inclinación *f*; *Am*. ~*s
pl*. mercería *f*; artículos *m/pl*. de
fantasía; 'no·tion·al □ nocional;
especulativo.

no·to·ri·e·ty [noutə'raiəti] mala fama *f*; escándalo *m*; notoriedad *f*;
no·to·ri·ous [nou'tɔːriəs] □ de
mala fama; notorio; célebre (*for*
por).

not·with·stand·ing [nɔtwiθ'stænd-
iŋ] **1.** *prp*. a pesar de; **2.** *adv*. no
obstante; **3.** *conj.* (*a.* ~ *that*) a pesar
de que.

nou·gat ['nuːgɑː] *approx*. turrón *m*.

nought [nɔːt] ♬ cero *m*; nada.

noun [naun] nombre *m*, sustantivo
m.

nour·ish ['nʌriʃ] nutrir, alimentar,
sustentar; *fig*. fomentar, abrigar;
'nour·ish·ing nutritivo, alimenticio; 'nour·ish·ment nutrimento
m, alimento *m*; nutrición *f*.

nov·el ['nɔvl] **1.** nuevo, original, insólito; **2.** novela *f*; **nov·el·ette**
[nɔvə'let] novela *f* corta; **nov·el-
'et·tish** novelero; 'nov·el·ist novelista *m/f*; **nov·el·ty** ['nɔvlti] novedad *f*; innovación *f*; ✝ baratija *f*.

No·vem·ber [nou'vembə] noviembre *m*.

nov·ice ['nɔvis] novicio (a *f*) *m*
(*a. eccl*.); principiante *m/f*.

no·vi·ci·ate, no·vi·ti·ate [nou'viʃiit]
noviciado *m*.

now [nau] **1.** ahora; ya; *before* ~
antes, ya; *from* ~ *on(ward)* de aquí
en adelante; *just* ~ ahora mismo;
hace poco; ~ *and again*, ~ *and then*
de vez en cuando, una que otra

vez; ~ ... ~ ... ora ... ora ..., ya ...
ya ...; **2.** *cj.* ahora bien, pues; ~
(*that*) ya que; **3.** actualidad *f.*
now·a·days ['nauədeiz] hoy en día,
actualmente. [manera.\
no·way(s)['nouwei(z)] F de ninguna\
no·where ['nouwɛə] en (*or* a)
ninguna parte; ~ *else* en ninguna
otra parte.
no·wise ['nouwaiz] de ninguna manera. [so; pestífero.\
nox·ious ['nɔkʃəs] ☐ nocivo, daño-/
noz·zle ['nɔzl] ⊕ tobera *f*, inyector
m; boquerel *m*, lanza *f* of hose.
nu·cle·ar ['nju:kliə] nuclear; ~ *fission* fisión *f* nuclear, escisión *f*
nuclear; ~ *physics* física *f* nuclear;
nu·cle·us ['⌣kliəs] núcleo *m.*
nude [nju:d] desnudo *adj. a. su. m.*
nudge [nʌdʒ] **1.** codazo *m* (ligero); **2.** dar una codazo a.
nud·ism ['nju:dizm] desnudismo *m*;
'**nud·ist** desnudista *m/f*; '**nu·di·ty**
desnudez *f.*
nu·ga·to·ry ['nju:gətəri] fútil, ineficaz, insignificante.
nug·get ['nʌgit] pepita *f* (de oro).
nui·sance ['nju:sns] molestia *f*,
fastidio *m*; plaga *f*; lata *f* (F); (*p.*)
moscón *m*; *what a* ~! ¡qué lata!,
¡qué fastidio!; *be a* ~, *make a* ~ *of
o.s.* dar la lata.
null [nʌl] nulo, inválido (*a.* ~ *and
void*); **null·li·fy** ['⌣lifai] anular, invalidar; '**nul·li·ty** nulidad *f* (*a. p.*).
numb [nʌm] **1.** ☐ entumecido; insensible; **2.** entumecer; entorpecer.
num·ber ['nʌmbə] **1.** número *m*;
(*figure*) cifra *f*; ~*s pl. poet.* versos
m/pl.; *a* ~ *of* una porción de, varios; *v.* back-~; *sl. look after* ~
one cuidar de sí mismo; **2.** numerar; contar; poner número a; (*total*)
ascender a; *be* ~*ed among* figurar
entre, hallarse entre; *his days are*
~*ed* tiene los días contados; '**num-
ber·less** innumerable, sin número;
'**num·ber·plate** *mot.* placa *f* de
matrícula.
numb·ness ['nʌmnis] entumecimiento *m*; insensibilidad *f.*
nu·mer·al ['nju:mərəl] **1.** numeral;
2. número *m*, cifra *f*, guarismo *m*;
nu·mer·a·tion numeración *f*; '**nu-
mer·a·tor** numerador *m.*
nu·mer·i·cal [nju'merikl] ☐ numérico. [roso; muchos.\
nu·mer·ous ['nju:mərəs] ☐ nume-/

nu·mis·mat·ic [nju:miz'mætik] ☐
numismático; **nu·mis'mat·ics** *mst
sg.* numismática *f*; **nu·mis·ma·tist**
[nju'mizmətist] numismático *m.*
num·skull ['nʌmskʌl] F zote *m*,
majadero *m.*
nun [nʌn] monja *f*, religiosa *f.*
nun·ci·o ['nʌnʃiou] nuncio *m* (apostólico). [monjas.\
nun·ner·y ['nʌnəri] convento *m* de/
nup·tial ['nʌpʃəl] **1.** nupcial; **2.** ~*s*
['⌣lz] *pl.* nupcias *f/pl.*
nurse [nə:s] **1.** enfermera *f*; nodriza *f*, ama *f* de leche (*a.* wet-~);
(*children's*) niñera *f*; **2.** *v/t. sick*
cuidar; *child* criar, amamantar;
mecer *in arms*; (*caress*) acariciar;
fig. fomentar; ~ *a cold* tratar de cu-
rarse de un resfriado; *v/i.* ser enfermera; '~**maid** niñera *f.*
nurs·er·y ['nə:sri] cuarto *m* de los
niños; 🖉 criadero *m*, semillero *m*;
🖉, *fig.* plantel *m*; ~ *school* jardín *m*
de la infancia; '~**man** horticultor
m; encargado *m* de un semillero;
'~**rhyme** canción *f* infantil.
nurs·ing ['nə:siŋ] lactancia *f*; crianza *f*; asistencia *f*; profesión *f* de
enfermera; ~ *home* clínica *f.*
nur·ture ['nə:tʃə] **1.** nutrición *f*;
crianza *f*, educación *f*; **2.** nutrir,
alimentar; criar, educar.
nut [nʌt] nuez *f*; ⊕ tuerca *f*; *sl.*
cabeza *f*; *sl.* pisaverde *m*; *Am. sl.*
tonto *m*; *sl. be* ~*s on* estar loco por;
sl. drive ~*s* volver loco; *a hard* ~
to crack hueso *f* duro de roer.
nu·ta·tion [nju:'teiʃn] nutación *f.*
nut·crack·er ['nʌtkrækə], *mst* (*a pair
of* un) ~*s pl.* cascanueces *m*; **nut·meg**
['⌣meg] nuez *f* moscada.
nu·tri·ent ['nju:triənt] **1.** nutritivo;
2. nutrimento *m*; '**nu·tri·ment**
nutrimento *m.*
nu·tri·tion [nju:'triʃn] nutrición *f*,
alimentación *f*; **nu'tri·tion·al value** valor *m* nutritivo; **nu'tri·tious,
nu·tri·tive** ['⌣tiv] ☐ nutritivo, alimenticio.
nut·shell ['nʌtʃel] cáscara *f* de nuez;
in a ~ en resumidas cuentas; **nut·ty**
['nʌti] de nuez; que sabe a nueces;
sl. loco (*on* por).
nuz·zle ['nʌzl] *v/t.* hocicar; acariciar
con el hocico; *v/i.* arrimarse cómodamente (*in to, up to* a).
ny·lon ['nailən] nylón *m.*
nymph [nimf] ninfa *f.*

O

o [ou] ¡oh!, ¡ay!; ~ *that* ...! ¡ojalá (que) ...!

oaf [ouf] zoquete *m*, bobalicón *m*, patán *m*; **'oaf·ish** lerdo, zafio.

oak [ouk] **1.** roble *m*; **2.** de roble; **'~-ap·ple**, **'~-gall** agalla *f* (de roble); **'oak·en** ⚹ de roble.

oa·kum ['oukəm] estopa *f* (de calafatear).

oar [ɔː] remo *m*; (*p.*) remero (a *f*) *m*; *fig. put one's* ~ *in* meter baza; *fig. rest on one's* ~*s* descansar; dormir en los laureles; **oars·man** ['ɔːzmən] remero *m*. [oasis *m.*\

o·a·sis [ou'eisis], *pl.* **o'a·ses** [~si:z]\

oast [oust] secadero *m* para lúpulo.

oat [out] avena *f* (*mst* ~*s pl.*); *rolled* ~*s* copos *m/pl.* de avena; **'~·cake** torta *f* de avena; **'oat·en** de avena.

oath [ouθ], *pl.* **oaths** [ouðz] juramento *m*, jura *f*; *b.s.* blasfemia *f*, reniego *m*; *administer an* ~ *to* tomar juramento a; *on* ~ bajo juramento; *put a p. on* ~ hacer prestar juramento a una p.; *take an (or the)* ~ prestar juramento (*on* sobre).

oat·meal ['outmiːl] harina *f* de avena.

ob·du·ra·cy ['ɔbdjurəsi] obstinación *f*, terquedad *f*; **ob·du·rate** ['~rit] □ obstinado, terco; empedernido.

o·be·di·ence [ə'biːdjəns] obediencia *f*; *in* ~ *to* conforme a; **o'be·di·ent** □ obediente.

o·bei·sance [ou'beisns] reverencia *f*, acato *m*; homenaje *m*; *do (or make, pay)* ~ *to* acatar, tributar homenaje a.

ob·e·lisk ['ɔbilisk] obelisco *m*.

o·bese [ou'biːs] obeso; **o'bese·ness**, **o'bes·i·ty** obesidad *f*.

o·bey [ə'bei] obedecer; *instructions* cumplir, observar; obrar de acuerdo con.

ob·fus·cate ['ɔbfʌskeit] ofuscar.

o·bit·u·ar·y [ə'bitjuəri] **1.** necrología *f*; *eccl.* obituario *m*; **2.** necrológico; ~ *notice* necrología *f*.

ob·ject 1. ['ɔbdʒikt] objeto *m*; (*thing*) cosa *f*, artículo *m*; *contp.* mama-

rracho *m*, facha *f*; *gr.* complemento *m*; *cost no* ~ no importa (el) precio; **2.** [əb'dʒekt] *v/t.* objetar; *v/i.* poner reparos, hacer objeciones, oponerse (*to* a); sentir disgusto (*to* por); *if you don't* ~ si no tiene Vd. inconveniente; **'~-glass** ['ɔbdʒiktglɑːs] objetivo *m*.

ob·jec·tion [əb'dʒekʃn] objeción *f*, reparo *m*; dificultad *f*, inconveniente *m*; *raise* ~*s to* poner reparos a; *there is no* ~ no hay inconveniente; **ob'jec·tion·a·ble** □ molesto, desagradable; ofensivo; censurable.

ob·jec·tive [əb'dʒektiv] □ objetivo *adj. a. su. m*; **ob·jec'tiv·i·ty** objetividad *f*.

ob·ject...: **'~-lens** objetivo *m*; **'~-les·son** lección *f* práctica, ejemplo *m*; **ob·jec·tor** [əb'dʒektə] objetante *m/f*; *v. conscientious*.

ob·jur·gate ['ɔbdʒəːgeit] increpar, reprender.

ob·late ['ɔbleit] □ *eccl.* oblato; ⚹ achatado por los polos.

ob·la·tion [ou'bleiʃn] oblación *f*; (*gift*) oblata *f*.

ob·li·ga·tion [ɔbli'geiʃn] obligación *f*; deber *m*; compromiso *m*; *eccl. of* ~ de precepto; *be under (an)* ~ *to a p.* deber favores a una p.; *be under* ~ *to inf.* correr obligación a *inf.*; *without* ~ sin compromiso; **ob·lig·a·to·ry** ['~gətəri] obligatorio.

o·blige [ə'blaidʒ] obligar, forzar (*to* a); complacer, hacer un favor a; *much* ~*d* muy agradecido (*for* por); *much* ~*d!* ¡se agradece!; *I should be much* ~*d if* ... agradecería que ...; ~ *with* hacer el favor de; **o·blig·ing** □ atento, servicial, complaciente.

ob·lique [ə'bliːk] □ oblicuo; indirecto, evasivo; **ob'lique·ness**, **ob'liq·ui·ty** [~kwiti] oblicuidad *f*; desviación *f*; aberración *f*.

ob·lit·er·ate [ə'blitəreit] borrar; destruir, aniquilar; ⚸ obliterar; **ob·lit·er'a·tion** borradura *f*; des-

trucción *f*; aniquilación *f*; 🪦 oblite-
ración *f*.

ob·liv·i·on [ə'bliviən] olvido *m*;
ob'liv·i·ous □ olvidado, inconsciente (*of*, *to* de).

ob·long ['ɔblɔŋ] **1.** oblongo, rectangular, cuadrilongo; **2.** rectángulo *m*,
cuadrilongo *m*.

ob·lo·quy ['ɔblɔkwi] difamación *f*,
calumnia *f*; deshonra *f*.

ob·nox·ious [əb'nɔkʃəs] □ detestable, ofensivo, odioso.

o·boe ['oubou] oboe *m*.

ob·scene [ɔb'si:n] □ obsceno, indecente; **ob'scen·i·ty** [⹁iti] obscenidad *f*.

ob·scu·ran·tism [ɔbskjuə'ræntizm]
oscurantismo *m*; **ob·scure** [əb-
'skjuə] **1.** □ oscuro (*a. fig.*); **2.**
oscurecer; eclipsar; esconder;
ob'scu·ri·ty oscuridad *f* (*a. fig.*).

ob·se·quies ['ɔbsikwiz] *pl.* exequias *f/pl.*

ob·se·qui·ous [əb'si:kwiəs] □ servil;
obsequioso; **ob'se·qui·ous·ness**
servilismo *m*; obsequiosidad *f*.

ob·serv·a·ble [əb'zə:vəbl] □ ob-
servable; **ob'serv·ance** observancia *f*; práctica *f*, costumbre *f*;
ob'serv·ant □ observador; atento;
perspicaz; vigilante; **ob·ser·va·**
tion [ɔbzə:'veiʃn] observación *f*;
experiencia *f*; *under* ~ vigilado;
🚃 *car* vagón-mirador *m*; **ob·serv·**
a·to·ry [əb'zə:vətri] observatorio *m*;
ob'serve observar; decir; *festival,*
silence guardar; *p.* vigilar; **ob'serv·**
er observador (*-a f*) *m*.

ob·sess [əb'ses] obsesionar, causar
obsesión a; **ob·ses·sion** [əb'seʃn]
obsesión *f*.

ob·so·les·cence [ɔbsə'lesns] caída *f*
en desuso; **ob·so·les·cent** que cae
en desuso.

ob·so·lete ['ɔbsəli:t] anticuado, desusado; *biol.* rudimentario.

ob·sta·cle ['ɔbstəkl] obstáculo *m*;
impedimento *m*; inconveniente *m*;
~ *race* carrera *f* de obstáculos.

ob·ste·tri·cian [ɔbste'triʃn] obstétrico *m*; **ob'stet·rics** [⹁riks] obstetricia *f*.

ob·sti·na·cy ['ɔbstinəsi] obstinación
f etc.; **ob·sti·nate** ['⹁nit] □ obstinado, terco, porfiado; pertinaz.

ob·strep·er·ous [əb'strepərəs] □
turbulento, desmandado.

ob·struct [əb'strʌkt] *v/t.* obstruir;

action estorbar; *pipe etc.* atorar; *v/i.*
estorbar; **ob'struc·tion** obstrucción
f (*a. parl.*); estorbo *m*; **ob'struc·**
tion·ist obstruccionista *m/f*; **ob·**
'struc·tive □ obstructivo; estor-
bador.

ob·tain [əb'tein] *v/t.* obtener; adquirir; lograr, conseguir; *v/i.* existir, prevalecer; **ob'tain·a·ble** asequible; *be* ~ 🛉 estar de venta.

ob·trude [əb'tru:d] *v/t. opinions*
imponer (*on* a), introducir a la
fuerza; *v/i.* entrometerse; **ob'tru·**
sion imposición *f*; entrometimiento *m*; **ob'tru·sive** [⹁siv] □
entrometido, intruso; importuno.

ob·tuse [əb'tju:s] □ ⹁ obtuso (*a.* ⦞,
fig.); *p.* estúpido, duro de mollera;
ob'tuse·ness embotadura *f*; *fig.*
estupidez *f*.

ob·verse ['ɔbvə:s] (*adj.* del) anverso
m.

ob·vi·ate ['ɔbvieit] obviar, evitar,
eliminar.

ob·vi·ous ['ɔbviəs] □ evidente, obvio, patente; poco sutil, transparente.

oc·ca·sion [ə'keiʒən] **1.** ocasión *f*;
vez *f*; coyuntura *f*, sazón *f*; motivo *m*; *on* ~ de vez en cuando; *on*
the ~ *of* con motivo de; *rise to the* ~
estar a la altura de las circunstancias; **2.** ocasionar; **oc'ca·sion·al** □
poco frecuente; uno que otro; ~
table mesilla *f*; ~*ly* de vez en
cuando.

oc·ci·dent ['ɔksidənt] *lit.* occidente
m; **oc·ci·den·tal** [⹁'dentl] □ occidental.

oc·cult [ɔ'kʌlt] □ oculto, secreto;
misterioso; sobrenatural; **oc·cult·**
ism ['ɔkəltizm] ocultismo *m*; **'oc·**
cult·ist ocultista *m/f*.

oc·cu·pan·cy ['ɔkjupənsi] ocupan-
cia *f*, tenencia *f*; **'oc·cu·pant** ocupante *m/f*; (*tenant*) inquilino (*a f*)
m; **oc·cu·pa·tion** ocupación *f* (*a.*
⚔); tenencia *f*, inquilinato *m*; **oc·**
cu'pa·tion·al de oficio, profesional;
~ *disease* enfermedad *f* profesional;
~ *risks* iro. gajes *m/pl.* del oficio;
~ *therapy* terapia *f* laboral; **oc·cu·**
pi·er ['⹁paiə] inquilino (*a f*) *m*;
oc·cu·py ['⹁pai] ocupar; *house* habitar; *time* emplear, pasar; ~ *o.s.*
(*or be occupied*) *in or with* ocuparse
de *or* en *or* con.

oc·cur [ə'kə:] (*happen*) ocurrir, suceder, acontecer; (*be found*) encontrarse; *it ~ed to me* (*to inf.*) se me ocurrió (*inf.*); **oc·cur·rence** [ə'kʌrəns] acontecimiento *m*, ocurrencia *f*; caso *m*, aparición *f*; *be of frequent ~* suceder a menudo.

o·cean ['ouʃn] océano *m*; *fig. ~s of* la mar de; **o·ce·an·ic** [ouʃi'ænik] oceánico.

o·chre ['oukə] ocre *m*.

o'clock [ə'klɔk] = *of the clock*; *it is 1 ~* es la una; *it is 5 ~* son las cinco; *at 2 ~* a las dos.

oc·ta·gon ['ɔktəgən] octágono *m*; **oc·tag·o·nal** [ɔk'tægənl] octagonal.

oc·tane ['ɔktein] octano *m*; *high ~ petrol* gasolina *f* de alto octanaje.

oc·tave ['ɔktiv] octava *f*; **oc·ta·vo** [~'teivou] (libro *m*) en octavo.

Oc·to·ber [ɔk'toubə] octubre *m*.

oc·to·ge·nar·i·an ['ɔktoudʒi'nɛəriən] octogenario *adj. a. su. m* (a *f*).

oc·to·pus ['ɔktəpəs] pulpo *m*.

oc·u·lar ['ɔkjulə] □ ocular *adj. a. su. m*; **'oc·u·list** oculista *m/f*.

odd [ɔd] *number* impar; desigual; (*isolated*) suelto, desparejado; (*extra*) sobrante; (*queer*) raro, extraño, estrambótico; (*occasional*) tal cual; *20 ~* veinte y pico, veinte y tantos; *~ moments* momentos *m/pl.* de ocio; *at ~ times* de vez en cuando; *be ~ man out* diferenciarse de los demás; estar excluido; ser de más; **'odd·i·ty** rareza *f*, exentricidad *f*; ente *m* singular; cosa *f* rara; **'odd·ment** retal *m*; artículo *m* suelto; sobra *f*; **odds** [ɔdz] *mst pl.* (*advantage*) ventaja *f*. superioridad *f*; (*chances*) probabilidades *f/pl.*; *betting*: puntos *m/pl.* de ventaja; *~ and ends* retazos *m/pl.*; chismes *m/pl.*; materiales *m/pl.* sobrantes; *the ~ are* lo más probable es que; *against ~* contra una fuerza superior; *be at ~* estar reñido, estar de punta (*with* con); *give ~* dar ventaja; *it makes no ~* lo mismo da; *set at ~* enemistar; F *what's the ~?* ¿qué importa?

ode [oud] oda *f*.

o·di·ous ['oudjəs] □ odioso, detestable, infame; **o·di·um** ['oudiəm] oprobio *m*; odiosidad *f*; odio *m*.

o·don·to·lo·gy [ɔdɔn'tɔlədʒi] odontología *f*.

o·dor·if·er·ous [oudə'rifərəs] □

odorífero; **'o·dor·ous** oloroso, oliente.

o·do(u)r ['oudə] olor *m*; fragancia *f*; *fig.* sospecha *f*; *fig.* estimación *f*; *be in bad ~* tener mala fama; *be in bad ~ with* llevarse mal con; **'o·do(u)r·less** inodoro.

oec·u·men·i·cal [i:kju:'menikl] □ ecuménico.

oe·de·ma [i:'di:mə] edema *m*.

o'er [ɔuə] = *over*.

oe·soph·a·gus [i:'sɔfəgəs] esófago *m*.

of [ɔv, *unstressed* əv, v] de; *I was robbed ~ my money* me robaron el dinero; *how kind ~ you to inf.* qué amable ha sido Vd. en *inf.*; *a friend ~ mine* un amigo mío; *it smells ~ roses* huele a rosas; *love ~ country* amor *m* a la patria; *~ a morning* † *or* F por la mañana; *I dream ~ you* sueño contigo; *I think ~ you* pienso en ti.

off [ɔf] **1.** *adv.* lejos, a distancia; fuera; *mst in combination with vb.*: *be ~*, *go ~* marcharse *etc.*; *3 miles ~* a 3 millas (de distancia); *the exam is 3 days ~* faltan 3 días para el examen; *far ~*, (*a long*) *way ~* muy lejos; *~ and on* ya bien, ya mal; de vez en cuando, a intervalos; *hands ~!* ¡fuera las manos!; *have one's shoes ~* estar descalzo; *be badly ~* andar mal de dinero; *be well ~* estar acomodado; *there is nothing ~* † no hay descuento; **2.** *prp.* lejos de; fuera de; separado de; de, desde; ⚓ a la altura de, frente a; al lado de; *work* libre de; *he has a button ~ his coat* a su chaqueta le falta un botón; *a street ~ the square* una calle que sale de la plaza; **3.** *adj.* separado; terminado; quitado; ⚡ desconectado; ⊕ parado; *water etc.* cortado; *brake* desapretado; *light* apagado; *tap* cerrado; *food* un poco pasado; *time* libre, sin trabajo; *side* derecho, de la derecha; F *~ day* día *m* malo, día *m* nulo; *day ~* día *m* libre; *~ season* estación *f* muerta; **4.** *su.* paro *m* (*a. ~ position*); **5.** *int.* ¡fuera (de aquí)! (*a. ~ with you!*).

of·fal ['ɔfəl] despojos *m/pl.*; asadura *f*, menudencias *f/pl.*

off-du·ty hours ['ɔ:fdju:ti 'auəz] horas *f/pl.* libres (de servicio).

of·fence [ə'fens] ofensa *f*; ⚖ violación *f* de la ley, delito *m*; ⚔ ofensiva *f*; give ~ ofender; no ~ (*meant*) sin ofender a Vd.; take ~ ofenderse, resentirse (*at* de, por).

of·fend [ə'fend] ofender; be ~ed tomarlo a mal; ~ against pecar contra; violar; **of'fend·er** delincuente *m/f*; culpable *m/f*; ofensor (-a *f*) *m*; first ~ delincuente *m/f* sin antecedente penal.

of·fense [ə'fens] = *offence*.

of·fen·sive [ə'fensiv] **1.** □ ofensivo, injurioso; repugnante; agresivo; **2.** ofensiva *f*; take the ~ tomar la ofensiva.

of·fer ['ɔfə] **1.** oferta *f* (*a.* ✝), ofrecimiento *m*; ✝ on ~ en oferta; **2.** ofrecer (*a.* ~ up); *prospect etc.* deparar, brindar; *resistance* oponer, intentar; ~ to *inf.* ofrecerse a *inf.*; **'of·fer·ing** ofrecimiento *m*; *eccl.* ofrenda *f*; tributo *m*.

of·fer·to·ry ['ɔfətəri] ofertorio *m*; ofrenda *f*; ~ box cep(ill)o *m*.

off-hand ['ɔːf'hænd] **1.** *adj.* informal, brusco; despreocupado; improvisado; **2.** *adv.* de improviso, sin pensarlo.

of·fice ['ɔfis] oficina *f*; (*room*) despacho *m*, escritorio *m*; (*lawyer's*) bufete *m*; (*function*) oficio *m* (*a. eccl.*); (*post*) cargo *m*; good ~s buenos oficios *m/pl.*; be in ~ estar en el poder, estar en funciones; ~ worker oficinista *m/f*.

of·fi·cer ['ɔfisə] **1.** oficial *m* (*a.* ⚔); funcionario *m*; dignatario *m*; (*agente m de*) policía *m*; **2.** mandar; proveer de oficiales; be well ~ed tener buena oficialidad.

of·fi·cial [ə'fiʃl] **1.** □ oficial; formal; autorizado; ✱ oficinal; **2.** oficial *m* (*público*), funcionario *m*; **of'fi·cial·dom** círculos *m/pl.* oficiales; *contp.* burocracia *f*.

of·fi·ci·ate [ə'fiʃieit] oficiar (*as* de).

of·fic·i·nal [ɔfi'sainl, ɔ'fisinl] oficinal.

of·fi·cious [ə'fiʃəs] oficioso, entrometido.

off·ing ['ɔfin] *mst* in the ~ cerca (⚓ de la costa), en perspectiva.

off...: '~print separata *f*, tirada *f* aparte; '~set **1.** compensación *f*; ⚠ retallo *m*; *typ.* offset *m*; ⚙ acodo *m*; ⊕ recodo *m*; **2.** compensar; '~shoot vástago *m*; *fig.* ramal *m*; '~side *sport*: fuera de juego, offside; '~spring vástago *m*; prole *f*,

descendencia *f*; *fig.* resultado *m*; '~stage (de) entre bastidores.

of·ten ['ɔfn, 'ɔftən], †, *poet. or in composition* oft [ɔft] a menudo, muchas veces, con frecuencia; as ~ as siempre que, tantas veces como; how ~ cuántas veces; not ~ pocas veces. [['oudʒaiv) ojiva *f.*)

o·gi·val [ou'dʒaivəl] ojival; **o·give**/

o·gle ['ougl] echar miradas amorosas (*or* incitantes) (a).

o·gre ['ougə] ogro *m*.

oh [ou] ¡oh!, ¡ay!

oil [ɔil] **1.** *mst* aceite *m*; *geol. etc.* petróleo *m*; *paint., eccl.* óleo *m*; paint in ~s pintar al óleo; strike ~ *fig.* enriquecerse de súbito; ~ lamp velón *m*, quinqué *m*; candil *m*; **2.** lubri(fi)car, engrasar; aceitar; *sl.* be well ~ed ir a la vela; '~can aceitera *f*; '~cloth hule *m*; F linóleo *m*; '~field campo *m* petrolífero; '~gauge manómetro *m* de aceite; '~paint·ing pintura *f* al óleo; '~skin hule *m*; ~s *pl.* ⚓ chubasquero *m*; '~stove *cooking*: cocina *f* de petróleo; *heating*: estufa *f* de petróleo; '~tank·er ⚓ (buque) petrolero *m*; '~well pozo *m* de petróleo; **'oil·y** □ aceitoso, oleaginoso; *p.* zalamero, excesivamente obsequioso.

oint·ment ['ɔintmənt] ungüento *m*.

O. K., o·kay ['ou'kei] **1.** ¡está bien!; **2.** aprobar; **3.** aprobado; en buen orden; satisfactorio; **4.** visto *m* bueno.

old [ould] viejo; anciano (*p. only*); (*long-standing, former*) antiguo; *wine* añejo; grow ~ envejecer(se); how ~ is he? ¿cuántos años tiene?, ¿qué edad tiene?; he is 6 years ~ tiene 6 años (de edad); of ~ antiguamente, de antiguo; ~ age vejez *f*, senectud *f*; ~ age pension subsidio *m* de vejez; ~ boy antiguo alumno *m*; F viejo *m*; F amigo *m* mío; *Am.* ♀ Glory bandera de los EE.UU.; my ~ man F el pariente; ♀ Testament Antiguo Testamento *m*; my ~ woman F la parienta; '**old·en** † *or poet.* antiguo; '**old-'fash·ioned** anticuado, pasado de moda; '**old·ish** que va para viejo, algo viejo; '**old-'maid·ish** de solterona; remilgado; **old·ster** ['~stə] *Am.* F viejo *m*.

o·le·ag·i·nous [ouli'ædʒinəs] oleaginoso.

o·le·o·graph ['ouliougrɑːf] oleografía *f*.

ol·fac·to·ry [ɔl'fæktəri] olfativo, olfatorio.

ol·i·garch·y ['ɔligɑːki] oligarquía *f*.

ol·ive ['ɔliv] **1.** aceituna *f*, oliva *f*; (*a*. ~ tree) olivo *m*; ~ oil aceite *m* (de oliva); **2.** aceitunado; '~-grove olivar *m*.

O·lym·pi·ad [ou'limpiæd] olimpíada *f*.

O·lym·pi·an [ou'limpiən] olímpico; **O'lym·pic Games** *pl.* Juegos *m/pl.* Olímpicos.

om·e·let, om·e·lette ['ɔmlit] tortilla *f*.

o·men ['oumen] agüero *m*, presagio *m*.

om·i·nous ['ɔminəs] □ ominoso.

o·mis·sion [ou'miʃn] omisión *f*; sin of ~ pecado *m* por omisión.

o·mit [ou'mit] omitir/olvidar; suprimir; ~ to *inf.* dejar de *inf.*

om·ni·bus ['ɔmnibəs] **1.** autobús *m*; **2.** general, para todo.

om·nip·o·tence [ɔm'nipɔtəns] omnipotencia *f*; **om'nip·o·tent** □ omnipotente.

om·ni·pres·ence [ˈɔmni'prezəns] omnipresencia *f*; **'om·ni'pres·ent** □ omnipresente.

om·nis·cience [ɔm'nisiəns] omnisciencia *f*; **om'nis·cient** □ omnisciente, omniscio.

om·niv·o·rous [ɔm'nivərəs] omnívoro.

on [ɔn] **1.** *prp.* en, sobre, encima de; (*concerning*) sobre, (acerca de); ~ arriving al llegar; ~ Sunday el domingo; ~ Sundays los domingos; ~ the third of May el tres de mayo; ~ and after a partir de; ~ his arrival a su llegada; ~ holiday de vacaciones; ~ my responsibility bajo mi responsabilidad; ~ the next page a la página siguiente; ~ this model según este modelo; get ~ a train subir a un tren; F have you any change ~ you? ¿tienes cambio encima?; F this is ~ me esto corre por mi cuenta; (*drinks*) invito yo; march ~ London marchar hacia Londres; turn one's back ~ a p. volver la espalda a una p.; **2.** *adv.* (hacia) adelante; encima; *vb.* seguir *ger.*: read ~ seguir leyendo; farther ~ más allá, más adelante; later

~ más tarde; ~ and ~ sin cesar; *v. so*; **3.** *adj. clothes* puesto; *light* encendido; ↯ conectado; ⊕ (puesto) en marcha; *brake* apretado; *tap* abierto; *side* izquierdo; ✝ *the deal is* ~ se ha cerrado el trato; *the race is* ~ ha comenzado la carrera; F *that's not* ~! ¡eso no se hace!, ¡no hay derecho!; *what's* ~? *thea.* ¿qué representan?; **4.** *su.* marcha *f* (*a.* ~ position).

once [wʌns] **1.** *adv.* una vez; (*formerly*) antes, antiguamente; at ~ en seguida, inmediatamente; (*in one go*) de una vez; all at ~ (*suddenly*) de repente; (*in one go*) de una vez; (*all together*) todos juntos; (*just*) for ~ una vez siquiera; ~ (and) for all una vez para siempre; ~ in a while de tarde en tarde, de vez en cuando; ~ more otra vez; ~ upon a time there was érase que se era, había una vez; **2.** *su.* (una) vez *f*; this ~ esta vez; **3.** *cj.* una vez que.

once-o·ver ['wʌnsouvə] *sl.* vistazo *m*, examen *m* (rápido).

one [wʌn] **1.** un(o); solo, único; un tal; igual; his ~ care su único cuidado; it is all ~ (to me) (me) es igual (or indiferente); ~ day un día; ~ Jones un tal Jones; ~ or two unos pocos; **2.** uno (a *f*) *m*; alguno (a *f*) *m*; (*hour*) la una; (*indefinite*) se, uno; *v.* any, every, no; *the black book and the grey* ~ el libro negro y el gris; *the little* ~s los pequeños, los chiquillos, la gente menuda; ~ and all todos; ~ another se, uno(s) a otro(s); ~ by ~ uno a uno; ~ does not know no se sabe, uno no sabe; ~ must work hay que trabajar; ~'s su, el ... de uno; *the* ~ *that* (or who) el (la) que; *that* ~ ése (a *f*) *m*, aquél (-la *f*) *m*; *this* ~ éste (a *f*) *m*; '~-eyed tuerto; '~-'hand·ed manco; '~-'horse F insignificante, de poca monta; 'one·ness unidad *f*; 'one-'piece enterizo, de una pieza.

on·er·ous ['ɔnərəs] □ oneroso.

one...: ~'self (*subject*) uno mismo, una misma; (*acc., dat.*) se; (*after prp.*) sí (mismo), sí (misma); by ~ solo; por sí mismo; '~-'sid·ed □ unilateral; desequilibrado; parcial; *contest* desigual; '~-time antiguo; '~-way: ~ *street* calle *f* de dirección única; ~ *traffic* dirección *f* obligatoria.

on·ion ['ʌnjən] cebolla f.

on·look·er ['ɔnlukə] mirón (-a f) m, espectador (-a f) m.

on·ly ['ounli] **1.** adj. solo, único; **2.** adv. (tan) sólo, solamente; únicamente; no más que; nada más; he ~ wanted... quería... nada más; if ~....! ojalá...!; ~ just hace un momento; apenas; the ~ thing lo único m; **3.** cj. ~ (that) sólo que, pero.

on·o·mat·o·poe·ia [ɔnəmætə'pi:ə] onomatopeya f.

on·rush ['ɔnrʌʃ] arremetida f; torrente m; ímpetu m.

on·set ['ɔnset] ataque m; acceso m, comienzo m (a. 🐾).

on·slaught ['ɔnslɔ:t] embestida f furiosa.

o·nus ['ounəs] (no pl.) carga f, responsabilidad f.

on·ward ['ɔnwəd] **1.** adj. progresivo; hacia adelante; **2.** adv. (hacia) adelante (a. **on·wards** ['~z]).

on·yx ['ɔniks] ónice m.

oo·dles ['u:dlz] F: ~ of la mar de, montones de.

ooze [u:z] **1.** lama f, cieno m; **2.** rezumarse (a. ~ out), exudar.

o·pac·i·ty [ou'pæsiti] opacidad f.

o·pal ['oupəl] ópalo m; **o·pal·es·cent** ['~'lesnt] opalescente.

o·paque [ou'peik] ☐ opaco.

o·pen ['oupən] **1.** ☐ abierto; (uncovered) descubierto, destapado; (unfolded) desplegado, extendido; event etc. público; libre; p. franco; mind receptivo, sin prejuicios; race muy igual; sea alto; ~ to expuesto a; accesible a; ~ to conviction dispuesto a dejarse convencer; ~ question f pendiente(or sin resolver); ~ secret secreto m a voces; keep ~ house ser muy hospitalario, invitar a casa todo el mundo; leave ~ fig. dejar sin resolver; **2.:** in the ~ al aire libre; en el campo; al descubierto; bring into the ~ hacer público; **3.** v/t. abrir; (uncover) descubrir, destapar; desplegar, extender (a. ~ out); parcel deshacer; exhibition etc. inaugurar; dar principio a; ~ up abrir; explorar; (disencumber) franquear; v/i. abrir(se) (a. ~ out); comenzar; extenderse; (play) estrenarse; ~ into comunicar con; (street etc.) desembocar en; ~ on (tc) dar a, mirar a; ~ up franquearse, descubrir el pecho; 🐾 romper el fuego;

'~·**cast** 🐾 a (or de) cielo abierto; '~·**hand·ed** ☐ liberal, dadivoso; '**o·pen·ing 1.** abertura f; brecha f in wall; claro m in woods; thea., school, chess: apertura f; ✝ salida f; oportunidad f; (job) vacante f; **2.** de apertura; inaugural; remark etc. primero; '**o·pen·mind·ed**☐receptivo; imparcial; '**o·pen·mouthed** boquiabierto; **o·pen·ness** ['oupnnis] espaciosidad f; abertura f; fig. franqueza f.

op·er·a ['ɔpərə] ópera f; '~·**glass(·es** pl.) gemelos m/pl. de teatro; '~·**hat** clac m; '~·**house** teatro m de la ópera; '~·**sing·er** cantante m/f de la ópera, operista m/f.

op·er·ate ['ɔpəreit] v/t. hacer funcionar; actuar; impulsar; manejar, dirigir; v/i. funcionar; ✝, 🐾,🐾 operar; ~ on producir efecto en; 🐾 operar (for de); **op·er·at·ic** [~'rætik] operístico; **op·er·at·ing** ['ɔpəreitiŋ] operante; ~ expenses pl. gastos m/pl. de explotación; ~ table mesa f de operaciones; v. theatre; **op·er·a·tion** operación f (a. 🐾, ✝, 🐾); funcionamiento m; explotación f; manejo m; procedimiento m; in ~ 🚂 en vigor; ⊕ en funcionamiento; come into ~ entrar en vigor; put into ~ poner por obra; **op·er·a·tion·al** 🐾 de operaciones;🐾 en condiciones de servicio; ⊕ capaz de funcionar; **op·er·a·tive 1.** ['~reitiv] ☐ operativo; 🚂 en vigor; 🐾 operatorio; **2.** ['~rə·tiv] operario (a f) m; **op·er·a·tor** ['~reitə] ⊕ maquinista m/f; 🐾, film: operador (-a f) m; ✝ agente m, corredor m de bolsa; teleph. telefonista m/f.

op·er·et·ta [ɔpə'retə] opereta f; Spain: zarzuela f.

oph·thal·mi·a [ɔf'θælmiə] oftalmía f; **oph'thal·mic** oftálmico; **oph·thal·mol·o·gist** [~'mɔlədʒist] oftalmólogo m.

o·pi·ate ['oupiit] **1.** opiata f, narcótico m; **2.** opiato.

o·pine [ou'pain] opinar; **o·pin·ion** [ə'pinjən] opinión f, parecer m, juicio m, concepto m; public ~ opinión f pública; be of (the) ~ opinar, ser de la opinión (that que); have a high ~ of o.s. pagarse de sí mismo; in my ~ a mi parecer; **o'pin·ion·at·ed** [~eitid] porfiado, pertinaz; dogmático.

o·pi·um ['oupjəm] opio *m*.

o·pos·sum [ə'pɔsəm] zarigüeya *f*.

op·po·nent [ə'pounənt] adversario (a *f*) *m*, contrincante *m*, contrario (a *f*) *m*.

op·por·tune ['ɔpɔtju:n] □ oportuno, tempestivo; **'op·por·tun·ism** oportunismo *m*; **'op·por·tun·ist** oportunista *m/f*; **op·por'tu·ni·ty** oportunidad *f*, ocasión *f* (of ger., to inf. de inf.).

op·pose [ə'pouz] oponerse a; resistir, combatir; (set against) oponer; **op'posed** opuesto; *be ~ to* oponerse a; **op'pos·ing** opuesto, contrario; **op·po·site** ['ɔpəzit] **1.** □ opuesto, contrario; de enfrente; F *~ number* persona *f* que ocupa un puesto correspondiente, colega *m*; *the house ~* la casa de enfrente; **2.** *prp*. (a. *~ to*) enfrente de, frente a; **3.** *adv*. enfrente; **4.** *su*. lo contrario, lo opuesto; **op·po'si·tion** oposición *f*; resistencia *f*; ✝ competencia *f*.

op·press [ə'pres] oprimir; agobiar; **op·pres·sion** [ə'preʃn] opresión *f*; agobio *m*; **op·pres·sive** [~siv] □ opresivo; agobiador; *weather* sofocante; **op·pres·sor** [ə'presə] opresor (-a *f*) *m*.

op·pro·bri·ous [ə'proubriəs] □ oprobioso; **op'pro·bri·um** [~briəm] oprobio *m*.

opt [ɔpt] optar (for por).

op·tic ['ɔptik], **'op·ti·cal** □ óptico; **op·ti·cian** [ɔp'tiʃn] óptico *m*; **'op·tics** *sg*. óptica *f*.

op·ti·mism ['ɔptimizm] optimismo *m*; **'op·ti·mist** optimista *m/f*; **op·ti'mis·tic** □ optimista; **op·ti·mum** ['~məm] (lo) óptimo.

op·tion ['ɔpʃn] opción *f* (on a); **'op·tion·al** □ opcional, discrecional, facultativo.

op·u·lence ['ɔpjuləns] opulencia *f*; **'op·u·lent** □ opulento.

or [ɔː] o; (before o-, ho-) u; *after negative* ni; *either ... ~ ... o ... o ...*; *~ else* o bien, si no.

or·a·cle ['ɔrəkl] oráculo *m*; F *work the ~* dirigirlo todo entre bastidores; **o·rac·u·lar** [ɔ'rækjulə] de oráculo; *fig*. sentencioso; misterioso.

o·ral ['ɔːrəl] oral; *anat*. bucal.

or·ange ['ɔrindʒ] **1.** naranja *f*; (a. *~ tree*) naranjo *m*; *~ blossom* azahar *m*; **2.** (a)naranjado; **or·ange·ade** ['~'eid] naranjada *f*.

o·rate [ɔː'reit] *co*. perorar; **o'ra·tion** oración *f*, discurso *m*; **or·a·tor** ['ɔrətə] orador (-a *f*) *m*; **or·a·tor·i·cal** [ɔrə'tɔrikl] oratorio; **or·a·to·ri·o** [~'tɔːriou] ♪ oratorio *m*; **or·a·to·ry** ['ɔrətəri] oratoria *f*; *eccl*. oratorio *m*.

orb [ɔːb] orbe *m*, globo *m*; **or·bit 1.** órbita *f* (a. *fig*.); *go into ~* entrar en órbita; **2.** girar (alrededor de); **'or·bit·al** orbital.

or·chard ['ɔːtʃəd] huerto *m*, huerta *f* (de árboles frutales); (*esp. apple ~*) pomar *m*.

or·ches·tra ['ɔːkistrə] orquesta *f*; *thea. ~ stall* butaca *f* de platea; **or·ches·tral** [ɔː'kestrl] orquestal; **or·ches·trate** ['ɔːkistreit] orquestar.

or·chid ['ɔːkid], **or·chis** ['ɔːkis] orquídea *f*.

or·dain [ɔː'dein] ordenar (a. *eccl*.); decretar; disponer.

or·deal [ɔː'di:l] prueba *f* rigurosa, experiencia *f* penosa; *hist*. ordalías *f/pl*.

or·der ['ɔːdə] **1.** (method, class, disposition, peace) orden *m*; (command, society) orden *f*; ✝ pedido *m* for goods; ✝ libranza *f* for money; *~ of the day* ✗ orden *f* del día; *fig*. moda *f*, lo que es de rigor; *in ~* en regla, reglamentario; *~en orden*; ⊕ en funcionamiento; *in ~ that* para que; *in ~ to* para; *of the ~ of* del orden de; *on the ~s of* por orden de; *out of ~* desarreglado, descompuesto; ⊕ que no funciona; *parl*. fuera de orden; *till further ~s* hasta nueva orden; *to ~* por encargo especial; ✝ a la orden; *call to ~* llamar al orden; *it is on ~* está pedido; *keep ~* mantener el orden; *put in ~* poner en orden, arreglar; *take (holy) ~s* ordenarse; **2.** ordenar; mandar; (arrange) disponer; *goods* encargar, pedir; *~ a suit* mandar hacer un traje; *I ~ed them to go* les mandé ir, mandé que fuesen; *~ about, ~ around* mandar (para acá y para allá), ser muy mandón con; *~ out* mandar salir; **'~-book** ✝ libro *m* de pedidos; **'or·der·ly 1.** ordenado; metódico; regular; tranquilo; obediente; ✗ *~ officer* oficial *m* del día; ✗ *~ room* oficina *f*; **2.** ✗ ordenanza *m*; ✗ enfermero *m*.

or·di·nal ['ɔːdinl] ordinal *adj. a. su. m*.

or·di·nance ['ɔːdinəns] ordenanza *f*, decreto *m*.

or·di·nar·y ['ɔːdnri] 1. ☐ común, corriente, normal; òrdinario (*a. b.s.*); ~ *seaman* simple marin(er)o *m*; ~ *share* ♆ acción *f* ordinaria; 2.: *out of the* ~ fuera de lo común, extraordinario.

or·di·nate ['ɔːdnit] ordenada *f*.

or·di·na·tion [ɔːdi'neiʃn] ordenación *f*.

ord·nance ['ɔdnəns] artillería *f*; pertrechos *m*/*pl*. de guerra (*a.* ~ *stores*); ♀ *Corps* Cuerpo *m* de Armamento y Material; ♀ *Survey map approx.* mapa *m* del estado mayor.

or·dure ['ɔːdjuə] excremento *m*, inmundicia *f*.

or·e [ɔː] mineral *m*, mena *f*.

or·gan ['ɔːgən] *all senses*: órgano *m*; '~-grind·er organillero (a *f*) *m*; or·gan·ic [ɔː'gænik] ☐ orgánico; or·gan·ism ['ɔːgənizm] organismo *m*; 'or·gan·ist organista *m*/*f*; or·gan·i·za·tion [~nai'zeiʃn] organización *f*, organismo *m*; 'or·gan·ize organizar(se); *sl.* agenciar; 'or·gan·iz·er organizador (-a *f*) *m*.

or·gy ['ɔːdʒi] orgía *f*.

o·ri·el ['ɔːriəl] mirador *m*.

o·ri·ent ['ɔːriənt] 1. ♀ Oriente *m*; oriente *m of pearl*; 2. ['~ent] orientar; o·ri·en·tal [~'entl] ☐ oriental *adj. a. su. m*/*f*; o·ri·en·tate ['ɔrienteit] orientar(se); o·ri·en·ta·tion orientación *f*.

or·i·fice ['ɔrifis] orificio *m*.

or·i·gin ['ɔridʒin] origen *m*.

o·rig·i·nal [ə'ridʒənl] 1. ☐ original; primitivo, primordial; ~ *sin* pecado *m* original; 2. original *m* (*a. p.*); prototipo *m*; o·rig·i·nal·i·ty [~'næliti] originalidad *f*.

o·rig·i·nate [ə'ridʒineit] originar(se); ~ *from*, ~ *in a th.* traer su origen de; ~ *with a p.* ser obra de; o'rig·i·na·tor creador (-a *f*) *m*, inventor (-a *f*) *m*, autor (-a *f*) *m*.

o·ri·ole ['ɔːrioul] oropéndola *f*.

or·mo·lu ['ɔːməluː] oro *m* molido; bronce *m* dorado.

or·na·ment 1. ['ɔːnəmənt] adorno *m*, ornato *m*; ornamento *m* (*a. fig.*); ~s *pl. eccl.* ornamentos *m*/*pl.*; 2. ['~ment] adornar, ornamentar; or·na·'men·tal ☐ ornamental, decorativo.

or·nate [ɔː'neit] ☐ muy ornado; *language* florido.

or·ni·tho·log·i·cal [ɔːniθə'lɔdʒikl]

☐ ornitológico; or·ni·thol·o·gist [~'θɔlədʒist] ornitólogo *m*; or·ni·'thol·o·gy ornitología *f*.

or·phan ['ɔːfən] huérfano *adj. m* (*a f*) (*adj. a. ~ed*); or·phan·age ['~idʒ] orfanato *m*.

or·tho·dox ['ɔːθədɔks] ortodoxo; 'or·tho·dox·y ortodoxia *f*.

or·tho·graph·ic, or·tho·graph·i·cal [ɔːθə'græfik(l)] ☐ ortográfico; or·thog·ra·phy [ɔː'θɔgrəfi] ortografía *f*.

or·tho·pae·dic [ɔːθou'piːdik] ortopédico; or·tho'pae·dics *sg.* ortopedia *f*; or·tho'pae·dist ortopedista *m*/*f*.

os·cil·late ['ɔsileit] oscilar; os·cil'la·tion oscilación *f*; 'os·cil·la·tor oscilador *m*; os·cil·la·to·ry ['~təri] oscilatorio.

os·cu·late ['ɔskjuleit] *mst co.* besar (se).

o·sier ['ouʒə] mimbre *m or f*; (*bush*) mimbrera *f*.

os·prey ['ɔspri] águila *f* pescadora.

os·se·ous ['ɔsiəs] óseo; os·si·fi·ca·tion [ɔsifi'keiʃn] osificación *f*; os·si·fy ['~fai] osificar(se); os·su·ar·y ['ɔsjuəri] osario *m*.

os·ten·si·ble [ɔs'tensəbl] ☐ supuesto, pretendido, aparente.

os·ten·ta·tion [ɔsten'teiʃn] ostentación *f*; aparato *m*, boato *m*; os·ten·'ta·tious ☐ ostentoso, aparatoso; *p.* ostentativo.

os·te·ol·o·gy [ɔsti'ɔlədʒi] osteología *f*.

ost·ler ['ɔslə] mozo *m* de cuadra.

os·tra·cism ['ɔstrəsizm] ostracismo *m*; os·tra·cize ['~saiz] condenar al ostracismo, excluir de la sociedad.

os·trich ['ɔstritʃ] avestruz *m*.

oth·er ['ʌðə] 1. otro (*than que*); *the* ~ *day* el otro día; *some* ~ *day* otro día; *the* ~ (*one*) el otro; *this house and the* ~ (*one*) esta casa y la otra; *the* ~s los otros, los demás; *v. each*; *somebody or* ~ alguien; 2. *adv.*: ~ *than* de otra manera que; otra cosa que; '~·wise de otra manera, otramente; *si no*; (*in other respects*) por lo demás.

o·ti·ose ['ouʃious] ☐ ocioso, superfluo.

ot·ter ['ɔtə] nutria *f*.

Ot·to·man ['ɔtəmən] otomano *adj. a. su. m* (*a f*); ♀ otomana *f*.

ought [ɔːt] 1. = *aught* algo; 2. *v*/*aux*. *mst* deber; *I* ~ *to do it* debo (debiera *or* debería) hacerlo; *I ~ to have done it* debiera haberlo hecho; *he ~ to have arrived* debe de haber llegado; *you ~ to have seen it* era de ver; *one ~ to drink water* conviene beber agua.

ounce [auns] onza *f* (= *28,35 gr.*) (*a. zo.*); *fig.* pizca *f*.

our ['auə] nuestro(s), nuestra(s); **ours** ['auəz] (el) nuestro, (la) nuestra *etc.*; **our'selves** (*subject*) nosotros mismos, nosotras mismas; (*acc., dat.*) nos; (*after prp.*) nosotros (mismos), nosotras (mismas).

oust [aust] desposeer; expulsar, desalojar; desahuciar.

out [aut] **1.** *adv.* afuera, fuera, hacia fuera; *a. in combination with vb.*: *come ~, go ~* salir; *run ~* salir corriendo; *be ~* haber salido; estar fuera (de casa); estar fuera de moda; (*book*) haberse publicado; (*fire*) estar apagado; (*secret*) haber salido a luz; (*striker*) estar en huelga; *sport*: estar fuera de juego; *Mr Jones ~* no está el señor Jones; *be ~ for* buscar; ambicionar; *be ~ to inf.* esforzarse por *inf.*; proponerse *inf.*; *be ~ and about* estar levantado y salir; *have a day ~* tener un día libre; pasar el día fuera de casa; **2.** *prp. ~ of* fuera de; de; entre; de entre; por; sin; *a chapter ~ of a novel* un capítulo de una novela; *read ~ of a novel* leer en una novela; *~ of petrol* sin gasolina; *~ of spite* por despecho; *6 ~ of 7* de cada 7, 6; **3.** *int. ~ with him!* ¡fuera con él!; F *~ with it!* ¡desembucha!; ¡habla sin rodeos!

out...: [~] '~-and-'~ perfecto, rematado; *b.s.* redomado; ~'**bid** [*irr.* (*bid*)] licitar más que; sobrepujar; '~**board** (*~ motor* motor *m*) fuera de borda; '~**break** erupción *f*; estallido *m*; rompimiento *m of war*; brote *m of disease*; '~**build·ing** dependencia *f*, edificio *m* accesorio; cobertizo *m*; '~**burst** explosión *f*, arranque *m*, acceso *m*; '~**cast** paria *m/f*, proscrito (a *f*) *m*; ~'**class** ser muy superior a, aventajar con mucho; '~**come** resultado *m*, consecuencia *f*; '~**crop** *geol.* afloramiento *m*; '~**cry** grito *m*, clamoreo *m*; protesta *f* (ruidosa); ~'**dat·ed** fuera de moda, anticuado; ~'**dis·tance** dejar atrás; ~'**do** [*irr.* (*do*)] exceder, sobrepujar; *he was not to be outdone* no se quedó en menos; '~**door** *adj.* al aire libre;

externo; '~'**doors 1.** *adv.* fuera de casa, al aire libre; **2.** *su.* aire *m* libre, campo *m* raso.

out·er ['autə] exterior, externo; ~ *cover* cubierta *f of tyre*; ~ *space* espacio *m* exterior; '~**most** (el) más exterior; extremo.

out...: '~**fall** desembocadura *f*; '~**fit** equipo *m*; (*suit*) traje *m*; (*tools*) juego *m* de herramientas; F ✕ cuerpo *m*; F organización *f*; '~**fit·ter** camisero (a *f*) *m*; ~'**flank** ✕ flanquear; *fig.* burlar; '~**flow** efusión *f*, derrame *m*, desagüe *m*; '~**go·ing 1.** saliente; **2.** (*mst ~s pl.*) gastos *m/pl.*; ~'**grow** [*irr.* (*grow*)] crecer más que; hacerse demasiado grande (*or viejo*) para; *I have ~n my shoes* se me quedan chicos los zapatos; '~**growth** excrecencia *f*; *fig.* consecuencia *f*; '~**house** ~*building*.

out·ing ['autiŋ] excursión *f*, paseo *m*, jira *f*.

out...: ~'**land·ish** estrafalario; ~'**last** durar más que; sobrevivir a; '~**law 1.** proscrito *m*, forajido *m*; **2.** proscribir; declarar fuera de la ley; '~**law·ry** proscripción *f*; bandolerismo *m*; '~**lay** desembolso *m*; '~**let** salida *f* (*a. fig.*, ✝); ⚡ toma *f* de corriente; '~**line 1.** contorno *m*, perfil *m*; trazado *m*; bosquejo *m* (*a. fig.*); *in ~ fig.* a grandes rasgos; **2.** perfilar, trazar; bosquejar (*a. fig.*); *policy* prefigurar; *be ~d against* destacarse contra; ~'**live** sobrevivir a; durar más que; '~**look** perspectiva(s) *f(pl.)* (*a. fig.*); punto *m* de vista; actitud *f*; '~**ly·ing** remoto; exterior; de las afueras; ~**ma'noeu·vre** superar en la táctica; vencer por su mejor táctica; ~'**mod·ed** anticuado, fuera de moda; ~'**num·ber** exceder en número; '~**of-'doors** = *outdoors*; '~**pace** dejar atrás; '~**pa·tient** paciente *m/f* externo (a) (del hospital); '~**post** avanzada *f*, puesto *m* avanzado; '~**pour·ing** chorro *m*; efusión *f* (*a. fig.*); '~**put** producción *f*; ⊕ rendimiento *m*; ⚡ potencia *f* de salida; ~ *valve* válvula *f* de salida.

out·rage ['autreidʒ] **1.** atrocidad *f*; ultraje *m*, atropello *m*; violación *f* (*on* de); **2.** ultrajar; violentar; violar; **out'ra·geous** □ atroz; ultrajoso; violento; F monstruoso, inaudito.

out...: '~**rid·er** escolta *m* a caballo;

motociclista *m* de escolta; '~·**rig**-**ger** ♣ botalón *m*; ♣ (bote *m* con) portarremos *m* exterior; ♣ balancín *m*; ~**right 1.** ['autrait] *adj.* comple-to, cabal, franco; **2.** [aut'rait] *adv.* de una vez, de un golpe; enteramente, de plano; sin rodeos; ~**ri·val** sobre-pujar, exceder; ~**run** [*irr.* (run)] co-rrer más que; *fig.* exceder; pasar los límites de; '~·**set** principio *m*, co-mienzo *m*; ~'**shine** [*irr.* (shine)] bri-llar más que; *fig.* eclipsar, superar en brillantez; '~·**side 1.** exterior *m*; superficie *f*; apariencia *f*; *at the* ~ a lo sumo, cuando más; *on the* ~ por fuera; **2.** *adj.* exterior, externo; superficial; ajeno; extremo; *sport:* ~ *right* (*left*) extremo *m* derecho (izquierdo); **3.** *adv.* (a)fuera; ~ *of* = **4.** *prp.* fuera de; para; '~·**sid**-**er** forastero (a *f*) *m*; intruso (a *f*) *m*; desplazado (a *f*) *m*; *racing:* caba-llo *m* que no figura entre los favori-tos; '~·**size** de tamaño extraordina-rio; '~·**skirts** *pl.* afueras *f/pl.*, alre-dedores *m/pl.*, cercanías *f/pl.*; ~-'**smart** F ser más listo que; enga-ñar; ~'**spok·en** □ franco, abierto; *be* ~ no tener pelos en la lengua; '~-'**spread** extendido, desplegado; ~-'**stand·ing** destacado, descollante; sobresaliente; ✝ pendiente, sin pa-gar; ~'**stay** quedarse más tiempo que; ~'**stretched** extendido; ~-'**strip** dejar atrás, aventajar; ~'**vote** vencer en las elecciones; *proposal* rechazar por votación.

out·ward ['autwəd] **1.** □ exterior, externo; aparente; ~ *journey* (viaje *m* de) ida *f*; **2.** *adv.* (*mst* **out·wards** ['~z]) exteriormente, hacia fuera.

out...: ~'**wear** [*irr.* (wear)] durar más que; gastar; ~'**weigh** pesar más que; valer más que; ~'**wit** ser más listo que; burlar; '~-'**worn** gas-tado; anticuado.

o·val ['ouvl] **1.** oval(ado); **2.** óvalo *m*.

o·va·ry ['ouvəri] ovario *m*.

o·va·tion [ou'veiʃn] ovación *f*.

ov·en ['ʌvn] horno *m*, cocina *f*.

o·ver ['ouvə] **1.** *adv.* (por) encima; al otro lado; de un lado a otro; al revés; patas arriba; otra vez; de aña-didura; *all* ~ por todas partes; *he is all* ~ *mud* está cubierto de lodo; *all* ~ *again* de nuevo; ~ *against* enfrente de; en contraste con; ~ *and* ~ *again* repetidas veces; ~ *here* acá; por

aquí; ~ *there* allá; *10 times* ~ 10 ve-ces (seguidas); **2.** *prp.* sobre, (por) encima de; al otro lado de; por, a través de; más allá de; *number* más de; (*concerning*) acerca de; por causa de; superior a; *all* ~ *Europe* por toda Europa; *be* ~ *30* tener más de 30 años; ~ *and above* además de, en ex-ceso de; ~ *the way* enfrente, al otro lado; **3.** adicional, excesivo; aca-bado, concluido; *it's all* ~ se acabó.

o·ver...: '~'**act** exagerar (el papel); '~·**all 1.** global; de conjunto; **2.** guardapolvo *m*; ~s *pl.* mono *m*; ~'**awe** intimidar; ~'**bal·ance** (hacer) perder el equilibrio; ~'**bear·ing** □ despótico, dominante; ~'**blown** marchito, pasado; '~·**board** ♣ al mar, al agua; *man* ~*!* ¡hombre al agua!; *throw* ~ echar por la borda; F deshacerse de, aban-donar; ~'**bur·den** sobrecargar; oprimir, agobiar; ~'**cast** *sky* enca-potado; '~·**charge** sobrecargar; ✝ cobrar un precio excesivo (a); '~·**coat** abrigo *m*, sobretodo *m*, gabán *m*; ~'**come** [*irr.* (come)] vencer; superar; (*sleep etc.*) rendir; '~·'**con**-**fi·dent** □ demasiado confiado (*of* en); '~·**con'sump·tion** ✝ super-consumo *m*; ~'**crowd** apiñar, ates-tar; congestionar; ~'**crowd·ing** so-brepoblación *f*, congestionamiento *m*; ~'**do** [*irr.* (do)] exagerar; llevar a exceso, excederse en; *food* recocer, requemar; ~ *it* F trabajar demasiado, fatigarse; ~'**done** [ouvə'dʌn] exa-gerado; ['ouvə'dʌn] *food* muy he-cho, requemado, pasado; '~·**draft** ✝ giro *m* en descubierto, saldo *m* deu-dor; '~·'**draw** [*irr.* (draw)] ✝ girar en descubierto; '~·'**dress** vestirse con exceso; '~·'**drive** *mot.* super-directa *f*; '~·**due** atrasado; ✝ ven-cido y no pagado; ~'**eat** [*irr.* (eat)] comer con exceso, atracarse; ~-em'**ploy·ment** superempleo *m*; '~-'**es·ti·mate** estimar en valor exce-sivo; tener un concepto exagerado de; '~·**ex'pose** *phot.* sobreexponer; '~·**ex'po·sure** *phot.* sobreexposi-ción *f*; '~·**feed** [*irr.* (feed)] sobre-alimentar; ~'**flow 1.** [ouvə'flou] [*irr.* (flow)] desbordar(se); rebosar (*a. fig.*) (*with* de); *the river* ~*ed its banks* se desbordó el río; **2.** ['ouvə-flou] desbordamiento *m*; derrame *m*; (*pipe*) rebosadero *m*, vertedor *m*, cañería f de desagüe; '~·**grown** entapizado, revestido, cubierto (*with* de); demasiado grande (para su edad); ~**hang 1.** ['~'hæŋ] [*irr.* (*hang*)] sobresalir (por encima de); estar pendiente (sobre); *fig.* amenazar; **2.** ['~hæŋ] proyección f; alero m of *roof*; ~'**haul 1.** revisar; rehabilitar, componer; (*catch up*) alcanzar; **2.** repaso m, revisión f; ~**head 1.** [ouvə'hed] *adv.* por lo alto, por encima de la cabeza; **2.** ['ouvəhed] *adj.* de arriba, aéreo; ✝ general; ~ *cable* ⚡ línea f aérea; ~ *railway* ferrocarril m elevado; **3.** ✝ ~s *pl.* gastos m/pl. generales; ~'**hear** [*irr.* (*hear*)] oír (por casualidad); acertar a oír; *conversation* sorprender; '~'**heat** recalentar; '~·**in'dulge** mimar demasiado; ~ *in* tomar con exceso; ~'**joyed:** *be* ~ no caber de contento (*at* con); '~·**land** por tierra, (por vía) terrestre; ~'**lap 1.** traslapar(se);*fig.* coincidir en parte; **2.** solapo m, traslapo m; *fig.* coincidencia f (parcial); ~'**lay 1.** [ouvə'lei] [*irr.* (*lay*)] cubrir (*with* con); dar una capa a; **2.** ['ouvəlei] capa f; cubierta f; '~'**leaf** a la vuelta; ~'**load 1.** ['ouvə'loud] sobrecargar; **2.** ['ouvəloud] sobrecarga f; ~'**look** (*p.*) dominar con la vista; (*building*) dar a, caer a; vigilar; (*leave out*) pasar por alto, no hacer caso de; (*tolerate*) disimular; (*forgive*) perdonar; (*wink at*) hacer la vista gorda a; ~'**lord** señor m; jefe m supremo; '~'**much** demasiado; '~'**night** de la noche a la mañana; *stay* ~ pernoctar (*at* en); '~·**plus** sobrante m; ~'**pow·er** vencer; subyugar; dominar; *senses* embargar; '~·**pro'duc·tion** superproducción f; '~'**rate** exagerar el valor de; ~'**reach:** *mst* ~ *o.s.* excederse; pasarse de listo; ~'**ride** [*irr.* (*ride*)] no hacer caso de; anular; poner a un lado; ~'**rid·ing** predominante, decisivo; ~'**rule** anular; ⚖ denegar; ~'**run** [*irr.* (*run*)] invadir; infestar; *time etc.* exceder; '~'**sea·s 1.** *adj.* de ultramar; **2.** *adv.* allende el mar, en ultramar; '~'**see** [*irr.* (*see*)] superentender, fiscalizar; '~·**se·er** superintendente m/f; sobrestante m; (*foreman*) capataz m; ~'**shad·ow** (en)sombrear; *fig.* eclipsar; '~·**shoe** chanclo m; '~'**shoot** [*irr.* (*shoot*)] tirar más allá de; 🦌 sobrepasar; ~ *the mark* pasar de la raya, excederse;

'~·**sight** descuido m, inadvertencia f; equivocación f; (*supervision*) vigilancia f; '~·**sim·pli·fi'ca·tion** supersimplificación f; '~'**sleep** [*irr.* (*sleep*)] dormir demasiado; *I overslept* durmiendo se me pasó la hora; '~·**spill** desparramamiento m de población; '~'**state** exagerar; '~'**step** exceder; ~ *the mark* propasarse; '~·**stock:** *be* ~ed with tener surtido excesivo de; '~'**strain 1.** fatigar excesivamente; **2.** fatiga f excesiva; tensión f excesiva; '~'**strung** sobreexcitado, nervioso; *piano* cruzado; '~·**sub'scribe** contribuir más de lo pedido; '~·**sup'ply** proveer en exceso.

o·vert ['ouvə:t] □ abierto, manifiesto.

over...: ~'**take** [*irr.* (*take*)] alcanzar; pasar, adelantar(se) a; *fig.* coger, sorprender; '~'**tax** oprimir con tributos; *fig.* agobiar; exigir demasiado a; ~ *o.s.* fatigarse demasiado; ~·**throw 1.** [ouvə'θrou] [*irr.* (*throw*)] echar abajo; volcar; derrocar, derribar (*a. fig.*); **2.** ['ouvəθrou] derrocamiento m, derribo m; '~·**time** horas f/pl. extraordinarias; '~·**tone** ♪ armónico m; *fig.* sugestión f, resonancia f; '~'**top** descollar sobre.

overture ['ouvətjuə] ♪ obertura f; *fig.* proposición f; sondeo m.

o·ver...: ~'**turn** [ouvə'tə:n] *v/t.* volcar, trastornar; *v/i.* volcar; ⚓ zozobrar; ~·**ween·ing** arrogante, presuntuoso; '~·**weight 1.** sobrepeso m, peso m de añadidura; **2.** excesivamente pesado; *be* ~ pesar demasiado; ~'**whelm** abrumar; anonadar; inundar; ~ *with favours* colmar de favores; ~'**whelm·ing** □ arrollador, aplastante, abrumador; '~'**work 1.** trabajo m excesivo; **2.** [*irr.* (*work*)] (hacer) trabajar demasiado; '~'**wrought** agotado por el trabajo; sobreexcitado.

o·vi·form ['ouvifɔ:m] oviforme; **o·vip·a·rous** [ou'vipərəs] ovíparo; **o·void** ['ouvɔid] ovoide *adj. a. su. m.*

owe [ou] *v/t.* deber; estar agradecido por; ~ *a p. a grudge* guardar rencor a una p.; *v/i.* tener deudas; estar en deuda (*for* por).

ow·ing ['ouiŋ] sin pagar; debido; ~ *to* debido a, por causa de; *be* ~ *to* deberse a.

owl [aul] (*barn-*) lechuza f común;

(*little*) mochuelo *m* común; (*long-eared*) búho *m* chico; (*tawny*) cárabo *m*; **owl·et** ['aulit] lechuza *f etc.* pequeña; **'owl·ish** ☐ de búho; parecido a un búho; estúpido.

own [oun] **1.** propio; particular; *my ~ self* yo (*after prp.* mí) mismo; yo por mi parte; **2.** *my ~* (lo) mío; *come into one's ~* entrar en posesión de lo suyo; *tener el éxito merecido; get one's ~ back* tomar su revancha; *hold one's ~* no cejar, mantenerse firme; *on one's ~* por su propia cuenta; a solas; *a house of one's ~* una casa propia; **3.** poseer; ser dueño de; (*acknowledge*) reconocer; (*admit*) confesar (*a.* F *~ up* [*to*]).

own·er ['ounə] amo (*a f*) *m*, dueño (*a f*) *m*, poseedor (-*a f*) *m*, propie-

tario (*a f*) *m*; **'own·er·ship** posesión *f*, propiedad *f*.

ox [ɔks], *pl.* **ox·en** ['ɔksən] buey *m*.

ox·al·ic ac·id [ɔk'sælik 'æsid] ácido *m* oxálico.

ox·ide ['ɔksaid] óxido *m*; **ox·i·dize** ['ɔksidaiz] oxidar(se).

Ox·o·ni·an [ɔk'sounjən] oxoniense *adj. a. su. m/f.*

ox·y·a·cet·y·lene ['ɔksiə'setiliːn]: *~ burner* soplete *m* oxiacetilénico.

ox·y·gen ['ɔksidʒən] oxígeno *m*; **ox·y·gen·ate** [ɔk'sidʒineit] oxigenar.

ox·y·hy·dro·gen ['ɔksi'haidridʒən] gas *m* oxhídrico.

oys·ter ['ɔistə] ostra *f*; **'~-bed** ostral *m*; **'~-'catch·er** *orn.* ostrero *m*.

o·zone ['ouzoun] ozono *m*.

P

P [pi:]: *mind one's Ps and Qs* cuidarse de no meter la pata, andar con cuidado con lo que dice uno.
pa [pɑ:] F papá *m*.
pace [peis] **1.** paso *m*; marcha *f*; velocidad *f*; *keep* ~ *with* llevar el mismo paso con; *fig.* correr parejas con; *put through one's* ~*s* poner a uno a prueba; demostrar las cualidades de uno; *set the* ~ establecer el paso; **2.** *v/t. distance* medir a pasos (*a.* ~ *out*); *room* pasearse por; *competitor* marcar el paso para; *v/i.*: ~ *up and down* pasearse de un lado a otro; **'pace-mak-er** el que marca el paso, el que abre carrera.
pach·y·derm ['pækidə:m] paquidermo *m*.
pa·cif·ic [pə'sifik] □ pacífico; **pac-i-fi-ca-tion** [pæsifi'keiʃn] pacificación *f*; **'pac-i-fism** pacifismo *m*; **'pac-i-fist** pacifista *m/f*; **pac-i-fy** ['pæsifai] pacificar; apaciguar, calmar.
pack [pæk] **1.** (*bundle*) lío *m*, fardo *m*; (*animal's*) carga *f*; (*rucksack*) mochila *f* (*a.* ✕); paquete *m*; *Am.* cajetilla *f of cigarettes*; jauría *f of hounds*; manada *f of wolves*; baraja *f of cards*; montón *m of lies*; ~ *animal* bestia *f* de carga; **2.** *v/t. case etc.* hacer; embaular *in trunk*, encajonar *in box*; (*a.* ~ *up*) empacar, empaquetar; (*wrap*) envasar; *place, container* atestar, llenar (*with* de); apretar *tightly*; meter apretadamente (*a.* ~ *in*); *court* llenar de partidarios; *the hall was* ~*ed* la sala estuvo de bote en bote; *be* ~*ed with* estar lleno de; *send* ~*ing* despedir con cajas destempladas; F ~ *it in*, ~ *it up* dejarlo; ~ *off* despachar; *v/i.* hacer las maletas; ~ *up* hacer el equipaje; F terminar; liar el petate; **'pack-age 1.** paquete *m*; bulto *m*; **2.** empaquetar; envasar; **'pack-er** embalador (-a *f*) *m*; **pack-et** ['ɾt] paquete *m*; cajetilla *f of cigarettes etc.*; (*a.* '~*-boat*) paquebote *m*; **'pack-horse** caballo *m* de carga; **'pack-ing** (*act*) embalaje *m*, envase *m*;

(*material, outer*) envase *m*; (*inner*) relleno *m*, empaquetadura *f*; ~ *case* cajón *m* de embalaje.
pact [pækt] **1.** pacto *m*; **2.** pactar.
pad¹ [pæd] (*a.* ~ *about etc.*) andar, pisar (sin hacer ruido *etc.*).
pad² [ɾ] **1.** almohadilla *f*, cojinete *m*; (*ink-*) tampón *m*, almohadilla *f* para entintar; bloc *m of paper*; **2.** rellenar, forrear; *shoulders* bombear; *book etc.* hinchar con mucha paja (*a.* ~ *out*); **'pad-ding** relleno *m*; paja *f in book etc.*
pad·dle ['pædl] **1.** canalete *m*, zagual *m*; **2.** *v/i.* remar con canalete; mojarse los pies, chapotear *in sea*; *v/t.* impulsar con canalete; '~*-steam-er* vapor *m* de ruedas; '~*-wheel* rueda *f* de paletas.
pad·dock ['pædək] *approx.* potrero *m*; *racing*: corral *m*.
pad·dy¹ ['pædi] (*rice*) arroz *m*.
pad·dy² [ɾ] F rabieta *f*.
pad·lock ['pædlɔk] **1.** candado *m*; **2.** cerrar con candado.
pae·di·a·tri·cian [pi:diə'triʃn] pediatra *m/f*.
pa·gan ['peigən] pagano *adj. a. su. m* (a *f*); **'pa·gan·ism** paganismo *m*.
page¹ [peidʒ] **1.** (*boy*) paje *m*; **2.** (*in hotel*) buscar llamando, hacer llamar por el botones *etc.*
page² [ɾ] **1.** página *f*; *typ.* plana *f of newspaper etc.*; **2.** paginar.
pag·eant ['pædʒənt] espectáculo *m* brillante; desfile *m*; representación *f* de un episodio histórico *etc.* en una serie de cuadros; **'pag·eant·ry** pompa *f*, boato *m*; lo espectacular.
pag·i·nate ['pædʒineit] paginar; **pag·i'na·tion** paginación *f*.
pa·go·da [pə'goudə] pagoda *f*.
paid [peid] *pret. a. p.p. of pay* 2; asalariado; *put* ~ *to* acabar con; ~ *up share* liberado.
pail [peil] cubo *m*, balde *m*.
pail·lasse [pæl'jæs] jergón *m*.
pain [pein] **1.** dolor *m*; ✗ ~*s pl.* (*labour*) dolores *m/pl.* del parto; ~*s fig.* trabajo *m*; *on* ~ *of* so pena de; *be in* ~ estar con dolor; *get for*

one's ⁓s lograr después de tantos trabajos; *I have a* ⁓ *in my side* me duele el costado; *take* ⁓s esmerarse (*over en*); *take* ⁓s *to inf.* poner especial cuidado en *inf.*; **2.** doler; dar lástima; **pain·ed** *expression* de disgusto; *voice* dolorido; **pain·ful** ['⁓ful] □ doloroso; *penoso; decision* muy difícil; *duty* nada grato; **'pain·less** □ indoloro, sin dolor; **'pains·tak·ing** □ *p., th.* esmerado; cuidadoso; laborioso.

paint [peint] **1.** pintura *f*; colorete *m for face*; *v. wet*; **2.** pintar (*red de* rojo); *face* pintarse; ⁓ *out* tachar con una mano de pintura; **'⁓-brush** (*small*) pincel *m*; (*large*) brocha *f*.

paint·er¹ ['peintə] pintor (-a *f*) *m*; (*house*-) pintor *m* de brocha gorda.

paint·er² ['peintə] ⚓ amarra *f*.

paint·ing ['peintiŋ] pintura *f*; cuadro *m*; **'paint-roll·er** rodillo *m* pintor.

pair [pɛə] **1.** par *m*; pareja *f of people*; *a* ⁓ *of scissors* unas tijeras; **2.** aparear(se) (*a. zo., a.* ⁓ *off*).

pa·ja·mas [pə'dʒɑːməz] *pl. Am.* pijama *m*.

pal [pæl] F **1.** compañero (a *f*) *m*; amigo (a *f*) *m*; **2.:** ⁓ *up* hacerse amigos; ⁓ *up with* hacerse amigo de.

pal·ace ['pælis] palacio *m*.

palaeo- *v.* *paleo*-.

pal·at·a·ble ['pælətəbl] □ sabroso, apetitoso; F comible; *fig.* aceptable.

pal·a·tal ['pælətl] palatal *adj. a. su. f*; **'pal·a·tal·ize** palatalizar(se).

pal·ate ['pælit] paladar *m* (*a. fig.*).

pa·la·tial [pə'leiʃəl] □ suntuoso.

pal·a·tine ['pælətain] palatino.

pa·lav·er [pə'lɑːvə] (*discussion*) conferencia *f*, parlamento *m*; F lío *m*; trámites *m/pl. etc.* largos y molestos; (*words*) palabrería *f*.

pale¹ [peil] **1.** □ pálido; *colour* claro; *grow* ⁓ = **2.** palidecer; descolorarse; *fig.* dejar de tener importancia (*before ante*).

pale² [⁓] = *paling*; *beyond the* ⁓ excluido de la buena sociedad, indeseable.

pale·ness ['peilnis] palidez *f*.

pa·le·og·ra·phy [peili'ɔgrəfi] paleografía *f*.

pa·le·on·tol·o·gy [pæliɔn'tɔlədʒi] paleontología *f*.

Pal·es·tin·i·an [pæles'tiniən] palestino *adj. a. su. m* (a *f*).

pal·ette ['pælit] paleta *f*; ⁓ *knife* espátula *f*.

pal·frey ['pɔːlfri] palafrén *m*.

pal·ing ['peiliŋ] estaca *f*; (*fence*) estacada *f*.

pal·i·sade [pæli'seid] estacada *f*.

pall¹ [pɔːl] paño *m* mortuorio; *eccl.* palio *m*; capa *f of smoke*.

pall² [⁓] perder su sabor (*on para*), dejar de gustar (*on a*), empalagar (*on a*).

pal·let¹ ['pælit] (*bed*) jergón *m*.

pal·let² [⁓] ⊕ uña *f*.

pal·liasse [pæl'jæs] jergón *m*.

pal·li·ate ['pælieit] paliar; **pal·li·a·tive** ['pæliətiv] paliativo *adj. a. su. m*.

pal·lid ['pælid] □ pálido; **'pal·lid·ness, pal·lor** ['pælə] palidez *f*.

palm¹ [pɑːm] ♀ palma *f* (*a. fig.*), palmera *f*; ♀ *Sunday* Domingo *m* de Ramos.

palm² [⁓] **1.** palma *f of hand*; *grease s.o.'s* ⁓ untar la mano a alguien; **2.** *card etc.* escamotear; ⁓ *off* encajar (*on a*); **palm·is·try** ['⁓istri] quiromancia *f*; **'palm-oil** aceite *m* de palma; **'palm-tree** palmera *f*; **'palm·y** próspero, floreciente.

pal·pa·ble ['pælpəbl] □ palpable (*a. fig.*).

pal·pi·tate ['pælpiteit] palpitar; **pal·pi'ta·tion** palpitación *f*.

pal·sy ['pɔːlzi] perlesía *f*.

pal·try ['pɔːltri] □ insignificante, mezquino, baladí.

pam·pas ['pæmpəs] pampas *f/pl.*

pam·per ['pæmpə] mimar, consentir, regalar.

pam·phlet ['pæmflit] octavilla *f*; folleto *m*, panfleto *m*; **pam·phlet·eer** [⁓'tiə] folletista *m/f*.

pan¹ [pæn] **1.** cazuela *f*; cacerola *f*; (*frying*-) sartén *f*; perol *m*; **2.** *v/t. gold* separar en la gamella; F *play* dar un palo a; *cinema:* panoramicar; *v/i.:* ⁓ *out* tener éxito; resultar (de modo satisfactorio *etc.*).

pan²... [⁓] pan...

pan·a·ce·a [pænə'siə] panacea *f*.

pan·ache [pən'æʃ] penacho *m*.

pan·cake ['pænkeik] hojuela *f*, tortita *f*; ⁓ *landing* aterrizaje *m* a vientre.

pan·de·mo·ni·um [pændi'mounjəm] ruido *m* de todos los diablos, pandemonio *m*.

pan·der ['pændə] 1. alcahuetear; ~ to ser indulgente a; desvivirse por complacer a; procurar sin escrúpulo satisfacer a; 2. alcahuete *m*.

pane [pein] cristal *m*, (hoja *f* de) vidrio *m*.

pan·e·gyr·ic [pæni'dʒirik] panegírico *m*.

pan·el ['pænl] panel *m*; (*door-*) entrepaño *m*; (*ceiling-*) artesón *m*; (*wall-*) panel *m*; *sew.* paño *m*; *paint.* tabla *f*; tablero *m of instruments*; (*list*) lista *f*; tribunal *m of experts etc.*; '**pan·el·led** artesonado; con paneles; de tableros; '**pan·el·ling** entrepaños *m/pl. of door*; artesonado *m of ceiling*; paneles *m/pl. of wall*.

pang [pæŋ] punzada *f*, dolor *m* (agudo); ~ *of conscience* remordimiento *m*.

pan·han·dle ['pænhændl] *Am.* F pedir limosna; '**pan·han·dler** *Am.* F mendigo *m*.

pan·ic ['pænik] 1. pánico *m*; 2. (terror *m*) pánico *m*; 3. llenarse (sin motivo) de terror; aterrarse, ser preso de un terror pánico; '~**strick·en** lleno de terror, muerto de miedo; '**pan·ick·y** F asustadizo.

pan·nier ['pæniə] cuévano *m*; serón *m*; ~ *bags pl.* (*motor-cycle*) carteras *f/pl.*

pan·o·ply ['pænəpli] panoplia *f*; *fig.* esplendor *m*.

pan·o·ra·ma [pænə'ra:mə] panorama *m*; **pan·o·ram·ic** [~'ræmik] ☐ panorámico.

pan·sy ['pænsi] ♀ pensamiento *m*; F maricón *m*.

pant [pænt] jadear; resollar; ~ *after*, ~ *for* anhelar, suspirar por.

pan·tech·ni·con [pæn'teknikən] camión *m* de mudanzas.

pan·the·ism ['pænθiizm] panteísmo *m*; **pan·the'is·tic** ☐ panteísta; **pan·the·on** ['pænθiən] panteón *m*.

pan·ther ['pænθə] pantera *f*.

pant·ies ['pæntiz] *pl.* F (*a pair of* unas) bragas *f/pl.*

pan·to·mime ['pæntəmaim] pantomima *f*; (*British*) zarzuela en época de Navidades, a base de cuentos de hadas etc.

pan·try ['pæntri] despensa *f*.

pants [pænts] *pl.* F calzoncillos *m/pl.*; *Am.* pantalones *m/pl.*

pap [pæp] papilla *f*, gachas *f/pl.*

pa·pa [pə'pɑ:] papá *m*.

pa·pa·cy ['peipəsi] papado *m*, pontificado *m*.

pa·pal ['peipəl] ☐ papal, pontifical.

pa·per ['peipə] 1. papel *m*; (*news-*) periódico *m*; (*learned*) comunicación *f*, ponencia *f*; (*written*) artículo *m*; ~*s pl.* (*identity etc.*) documentación *f*; *brown* ~ papel de embalar, papel *m* de estraza; *on* ~ sobre el papel; 2. *attr.* ... de papel; ~ *money* papel *m* moneda; 3. *wall* empapelar; '~**bag** saco *m* de papel; '~**chase** rallye-paper *m*; '~**clip** sujetapapeles *m*; clip *m*; '~**fast·en·er** grapa *f*; '~**hang·er** empapelador *m*; '~**knife** cortapapeles *m*; '~**mill** fábrica *f* de papel; '~**weight** pisapapeles *m*; **pa·per·y** ['~ri] parecido al papel; delgado como el papel.

pa·pier mâché ['pæpjei'mɑ:ʃei] (*attr.* de) cartón *m* piedra.

pa·pist ['peipist] papista *m/f*; **pa·pis·try** ['peipistri] papismo *m*.

pa·py·rus [pə'paiərəs] papiro *m*.

par [pɑ:] 1. par *f*; *above* ~ a premio; *below* ~ ✝ a descuento; ✗ indispuesto; *fig.* inferior a la calidad normal; *golf: 5 under* ~ 5 bajo par; *be on a* ~ correr parejas (*with con*); 2. *value* nominal; *standard* normal.

par·a·ble ['pærəbl] parábola *f*.

pa·rab·o·la [pə'ræbələ] parábola *f*; **par·a·bol·ic**, **par·a·bol·i·cal** [pærə'bɔlik(l)] ☐ parabólico.

par·a·chute ['pærəʃuːt] 1. paracaídas *m*; 2. lanzar(se) en paracaídas; '**par·a·chut·ist** paracaidista *m*.

pa·rade [pə'reid] 1. ✗ desfile *m*, parada *f*; (*road*) paseo *m*; *fig.* alarde *m*, ostentación *f*; *make a* ~ *of* hacer alarde de; ~ *ground* plaza *f* de armas; 2. *v/t.* ✗ formar; *streets* desfilar por; *th.* pasear (*through the streets* por las calles); (*show off*) hacer gala *or* alarde) de, lucir; *v/i.* desfilar; formar en parada.

par·a·digm ['pærədaim] paradigma *m*.

par·a·dise ['pærədais] paraíso *m*.

par·a·dox ['pærədɔks] paradoja *f*; *fig.* persona *f etc.* enigmática; **par·a'dox·i·cal** ☐ paradójico.

par·af·fin ['pærəfin] petróleo *m*, keroseno *m*; ~ *wax* parafina *f*.

par·a·gon ['pærəgən] dechado *m*.

par·a·graph ['pærəgrɑːf] párrafo *m*;

typ. suelto *m*; *new* ~ (punto y) aparte.

Pa·ra·guay·an ['pærə'gwaijən] paraguayq *adj. a. su. m* (a *f*).

par·a·keet ['pærəki:t] perico *m*, periquito *m*.

par·al·lel ['pærələl] **1.** paralelo; ≠ en paralelo; *run* ~ *to* ir en línea paralela a; **2.** (línea *f*) paralela *f*; *geog.*, *fig.* paralelo *m*; ≠ *in* ~ en paralelo; *without* ~ nunca visto; *have no* ~ no tener par; **3.**: *be* ~*led by* ir parejo con, correr parejas con; tener su paralelo en; '**par·al·lel·ism** paralelismo *m*; **par·al'lel·o·gram** [~ə-græm] paralelogramo *m*.

par·a·lyse ['pærəlaiz] paralizar (*a. fig.*); **pa·ral·y·sis** [pə'rælisis] parálisis *f*; **par·a·lyt·ic** [pærə'litik] ☐ paralítico *adj. a. su. m* (a *f*).

par·a·mount ['pærəmaunt] supremo; *importance* capital.

par·a·mour ['pærəmuə] *lit. or co.* querido (a *f*) *m*.

par·a·no·ia [pærə'nɔijə] paranoia *f*.

par·a·pet ['pærəpit] parapeto *m*.

par·a·pher·na·li·a [pærəfə'neiljə] F avíos *m*/*pl.*, chismes *m*/*pl.*; molestias *f*/*pl.*, trámites *m*/*pl.* engorrosos.

par·a·phrase ['pærəfreiz] **1.** paráfrasis *f*; **2.** parafrasear.

par·a·site ['pærəsait] parásito *f* (*a. fig.*); **par·a·sit·ic, par·a·sit·i·cal** [~'sitik(l)] ☐ parasítico, parasitario; parásito (*on de*).

par·a·sol [pærə'sɔl] sombrilla *f*, quitasol *m*. [caidista *m*.|

par·a·troop·er ['pærətru:pə] para-|

par·a·ty·phoid ['pærə'taifɔid] (fiebre *f*) paratifoidea *f*.

par·boil ['pɑ:bɔil] sancochar.

par·cel ['pɑ:sl] **1.** paquete *m*; lío *m*; parcela *f of land*; **2.** (*a.* ~ *out*) *land* parcelar; repartir; ~ *up* empaquetar, embalar; **par·cel post** (servicio *m* de) paquetes *m*/*pl.* postales.

parch [pɑ:tʃ] (re)secar, (re)quemar; *plants* agostar; *be* ~*ed* (*with thirst*) morirse de sed.

parch·ment ['pɑ:tʃmənt] pergamino *m*.

par·don ['pɑ:dn] **1.** perdón *m*; ✝✝ indulto *m*; *I beg your* ~ le pido perdón, perdone; *I beg your* ~? ¿cómo?; **2.** perdonar, dispensar; ✝✝ indultar; ~ *me* dispense Vd.; perdone Vd.; '**par·don·a·ble** ☐ perdonable.

pare [pɛə] *stick etc.* adelgazar; *fruit etc.* mondar; *nails* cortar; *fig.* reducir, ir reduciendo (*a.* ~ *away*, ~ *down*).

par·ent ['pɛərənt] **1.** padre *m*, madre *f*; ~*s pl.* padres *m*/*pl.*; **2.** madre; '**par·ent·age** nacimiento *m*; linaje *m*; **pa·ren·tal** [pə'rentl] de padre y madre, de los padres.

pa·ren·the·sis [pə'renθisis], *pl.* **pa'ren·the·ses** [~si:z] paréntesis *m*; **par·en·thet·ic, par·en·thet·i·cal** [pærən'θetik(l)] ☐ entre paréntesis; explicativo.

par·ent·hood ['pɛərənthud] paternidad *f or* maternidad *f*; el ser padre(s), el tener hijos.

pa·ri·ah ['pæriə] paria *m*/*f*.

pa·ri·e·tal [pə'raiitl] parietal.

par·ish ['pæriʃ] **1.** parroquia *f* (*a.* ~ *church*); **2.** *attr.* parroquial; ~ *priest* párroco *m*; ~ *register* registro *m* parroquial; **pa·rish·ion·er** [pə'riʃənə] feligrés (-a *f*) *m*.

Pa·ri·sian [pə'rizjən] parisiense *adj. a. su. m*/*f*, parisino *adj. a. su. m* (a *f*). [dad *f*.|

par·i·ty ['pæriti] paridad *f*, igual-|

park [pɑ:k] **1.** parque *m*; jardines *m*/*pl.*; *mot.* parque *m* de automóviles; **2.** *v*/*t.* estacionar; aparcar; F poner, dejar; *v*/*i.* estacionarse; aparcar; '**park·ing** estacionamiento *m*; aparcamiento *m*; *no* ~ prohibido estacionarse; ~ *attendant* celador *m*; ~ *lights pl.* luces *f*/*pl.* de estacionamiento; ~ *meter* reloj *m* de estacionamiento.

par·lance ['pɑ:ləns] lenguaje *m*.

par·ley ['pɑ:li] **1.** parlamento *m*; **2.** parlamentar.

par·lia·ment ['pɑ:ləmənt] parlamento *m*; (*Spanish*) Cortes *f*/*pl.*; *Houses of* ♀ Cámara *f* de los Lores y la de los Comunes; *member of* ~ diputado *m*, miembro *m* del parlamento; **par·lia·men·tar·i·an** [~men'teəriən] parlamentario *adj. a. su. m* (a *f*); **par·lia·men·ta·ry** [~'mentəri] parlamentario.

par·lo(u)r ['pɑ:lə] salón *m*, saloncito *m*; *eccl.* locutorio *m*; ~ *game* juego *m* de salón; '~-**maid** camarera *f*.

par·lous ['pɑ:ləs] peligroso; *state* lamentable.

pa·ro·chi·al [pə'roukjəl] ☐ parroquial; *fig.* de miras estrechas, mezquino.

par·o·dist [ˈpærədist] parodista *m/f*; **ˈpar·o·dy 1.** parodia *f*; **2.** parodiar.

pa·role [pəˈroul] **1.** palabra *f* (de honor); libertad *f* bajo palabra; **on ~** bajo palabra; **put on ~ = 2.** dejar libre bajo palabra.

par·ox·ysm [ˈpærəksizm] paroxismo *m*.

par·quet [ˈpɑːkei] parquet *m*, entarimado *m* (de hojas quebradas); **ˈpar·quet·ry** (obra *f* de) entarimado *m*.

par·ri·cide [ˈpærisaid] parricidio *m*; (*p.*) parricida *m/f*.

par·rot [ˈpærət] loro *m*, papagayo *m*; **~ fashion** mecánicamente.

par·ry [ˈpæri] *fenc.* parar, quitar; *fig.* esquivar, desviar (hábilmente).

parse [pɑːz] *gr.* analizar.

Par·see [pɑːˈsiː] parsi *m/f*.

par·si·mo·ni·ous [pɑːsiˈmounjəs] □ parsimonioso; **par·si·mo·ny** [ˈpɑːsiməni] parsimonia *f*.

pars·ley [ˈpɑːsli] perejil *m*.

pars·nip [ˈpɑːsnip] chirivía *f*.

par·son [ˈpɑːsn] clérigo *m*, cura *m*; párroco *m*; **ˈpar·son·age** casa *f* del cura.

part [pɑːt] **1.** parte *f*; porción *f*; ⊕ pieza *f*; *thea. a. fig.* papel *m*; ♩ parte *f*; (*place*) lugar *m*, comarca *f*; (*duty*) deber *m*; **~s** *pl.* † prendas *f/pl.*; (*region*) región *f*; **three ~s** tres cuartos; casi; **travel in foreign ~s** viajar por el extranjero; **~ of speech** parte *f* de la oración; **~ and parcel** parte *f* esencial; **man of ~s** hombre *m* de mucho talento; **for my (own) ~** por mi parte; **for the most ~** por la mayor parte; **in ~** en parte; **in good ~** en buena parte; **in these ~s** por aquí; en estos contornos; **on my ~** por mi parte; **do one's ~** cumplir con su obligación; **it is not my ~ to** no me toca a mí *inf.*; **look the ~** vestir el cargo; **take ~ in** tomar parte en; **2.** *adv.* (en) parte; **3.** *adj.* parcial; co...; con; **~ author** coautor (-a *f*) *m*; **4.** *v/t.* separar; dividir; partir; *v. company*; **~ one's hair** hacerse la raya; *v/i.* separarse; (*come apart*) desprenderse; romperse; **~ from** despedirse de; **~ with** deshacerse de; ceder, entregar; *money* pagar, dar.

par·take [pɑːˈteik] [*irr.* (*take*)]: **~ of food etc.** comer *etc.*, aceptar; *quality* tener algo de.

par·terre [pɑːˈtɛə] *Am. thea.* anfiteatro *m* debajo de la galería.

part-ex·change [ˈpɑːtiksˈtʃeindʒ]: **in ~** como parte del pago.

par·tial [ˈpɑːʃl] □ parcial; **~ to** aficionado a; **par·ti·al·i·ty** [pɑːʃiˈæliti] (*bias*) parcialidad *f*; **~ for, ~ to** afición *f* a.

par·tic·i·pant [pɑːˈtisipənt] *mst* partícipe *m/f*; combatiente *m/f* **in fight**; **par·tic·i·pate** [~peit] participar, tomar parte (*in* en); **par·tic·i·pa·tion** participación *f*; **par·ti·ci·ple** [ˈpɑːtsipl] participio *m*; **past ~** participio *m* de pasado; **present ~** participio *m* de presente.

par·ti·cle [ˈpɑːtikl] partícula *f*; pizca *f*.

par·ti·col·oured [ˈpɑːtikʌləd] abigarrado.

par·tic·u·lar [pəˈtikjulə] **1.** □ particular; (*detailed*) detallado, minucioso; (*scrupulous*) escrupuloso; (*fastidious*) exigente, quisquilloso (*about*, [*as to*] *what* en cuanto a, en asuntos de); **be very ~ about** cuidar mucho de; **that ~ person** esa persona (y no otra); **2.** particularidad *f*; detalle *m*; **~s** *pl.* detalles *m/pl.*; informe *m* pormenorizado; **in ~** en particular; **par·tic·u·lar·i·ty** [~ˈlæriti] particularidad *f*; **par·tic·u·lar·ize** *v/t.* particularizar; *v/i.* dar todos los detalles.

part·ing [ˈpɑːtiŋ] **1.** separación *f*; despedida *f*; raya *f* **in hair**; **~ of the ways** *fig.* momento *m* de separación; **2.** ... de despedida.

par·ti·san [pɑːtiˈzæn] **1.** partidario (a *f*) *m*; ⚔ partisano *m*, guerrillero *m*; **2.** partidista; **~ spirit** partidismo *m*.

par·ti·tion [pɑːˈtiʃn] **1.** partición *f*, división *f*; **~** (*wall*) tabique *m*; **2.** (*share*) repartir; *country, room* dividir; **~ off** tabicar, separar con tabique.

par·ti·tive [ˈpɑːtitiv] □ partitivo.

part·ly [ˈpɑːtli] en parte; en cierto modo.

part·ner [ˈpɑːtnə] **1.** † socio (a *f*) *m*; compañero (a *f*) *m* (*a. cards*); pareja *f* **in dance, tennis etc.**; (*married*) cónyuge *m/f*; **2.** acompañar; **be ~ed by** ir acompañado de; **ˈpart·ner·ship** † sociedad *f*; asociación *f*; vida *f* etc. en común; **enter into ~** asociarse (*with* con).

part...: '~-own·er condueño (a *f*) *m*; '~-pay·ment: in ~ como parte del pago.

par·tridge ['pɑ:tridʒ] perdiz *f*.

part-time ['pɑ:t'taim] **1.** *adj.* en dedicación parcial, que trabaja por horas; **2.** *adv.*: work ~ trabajar por horas.

par·ty ['pɑ:ti] **1.** *pol.* partido *m*; grupo *m*; ✗ pelotón *m*; *hunt. etc.* partida *f*; (*gathering*) reunión *f*; (*informal*) tertulia *f*; (*merry*) fiesta *f*, guateque *m*; ⚓ parte *f*; interesado (a *f*) *m*; F individuo *m*; be ~ to estar interesado en; ser cómplice en; *I will not be a* ~ *to* no quiero tener nada que ver con; *v. third*; **2.** *attr. pol.* de partido; *dress* de gala; ~ *leader* jefe *m* de partido; ~ *line teleph.* línea *f* de dos o más abonados; *pol.* línea *f* de partido; ~ *politics b.s.* politiqueo *m*, partidismo *m*; *Am.* ~ *ticket* candidatura *f* apoyada por un partido; ~ *wall* pared *f* medianera.

par·ve·nu ['pɑ:vənju:] arribista *m/f*.

pas·chal ['pɑ:skəl] pascual.

pa·sha ['pæʃə] pachá *m*, bajá *m*.

pass [pɑ:s] **1.** *geog.* puerto *m*, paso *m*, desfiladero *m*; ✗ *etc.* pase *m* (*a. fenc., sport*); salvoconducto *m*; *thea.* entrada *f* de favor; *univ. etc.* nota *f* de aprobado; *fig.* condición *f*; coyuntura *f*; *make a* ~ *at* requebrar de amores, echar un piropo a; **2.** *v/i.* pasar; *univ. etc.* aprobar, ser aprobado; *come to* ~ suceder, acontecer; *let* ~ dejar pasar, no hacer caso de; ~ *away* fallecer; ~ *by* (*adv.*) pasar de largo; (*prp.*) pasar delante de, pasar cerca de; ~ *for* pasar por; ~ *off* pasar; ~ *on* fallecer; pasar; ~ *out* salir; F desmayarse, caer redondo; ~ *through* pasar por; *v/t.* pasar; pasar por delante de; (*overtake*) pasar, dejar atrás; *p.* cruzarse con *on street etc.*; *bill, candidate, exam, proposal* aprobar; *opinion* expresar; *sentence* pronunciar, dictar; ~ (*me*) *the salt, please* ¿me hace el favor de pasar la sal?; ~ *by* no hacer caso de, pasar por alto; ~ *off coin etc.* pasar; *offence* disimular; ~ *o.s. off as* hacerse pasar por; ~ *on* pasar, transmitir; dar, decir; ~ *over* pasar por alto; postergar *for promotion*; ~ *round* pasar de uno a otro; F ~ *up* renunciar a, rechazar; '**pass·a·ble** ☐ (*tolerable*) pasadero, pasable; *pass etc.* pasadero, transitable.

pas·sage ['pæsidʒ] paso *m*; ⚓, ♪ pasaje *m*; △ pasillo *m*, galería *f*; (*alley*) callejón *m*; (*underground*) pasadizo *m*; trozo *m of book*; *parl.* (*process*) trámites *m/pl.*, (*final*) aprobación *f of bill*; *bird of* ~ ave *f* de paso (*a. fig.*); ~ *of arms* combate *m*; ~ *of time* paso *m* del tiempo; *in the* ~ *of time* andando el tiempo; '~-mon·ey pasaje *m*; '~-way = *passage* △ *etc.*

pass-book ['pɑ:sbuk] libreta *f* de banco.

pass·é ['pæsei] pasado (de moda).

pas·sen·ger ['pæsindʒə] pasajero (a *f*) *m*, viajero (a *f*) *m*; ~ *train* tren *m* de pasajeros.

passe-par·tout ['pæspɑ:'tu:] paspartú *m*.

pass·er-by, *pl.* **pass·ers-by** ['pɑ:sə(z)'bai] transeúnte *m/f*.

pass·ing ['pɑ:siŋ] **1.** paso *m*; (*death*) fallecimiento *m*; *in* ~ de pasada, de paso; **2.** pasajero; ~ *fancy* capricho *m*; **3.** *adv.* † muy; '~-bell toque *m* de difuntos.

pas·sion ['pæʃən] pasión *f*; (*arranque m de*) cólera *f*; *have a* ~ *for* tener pasión por; **pas·sion·ate** ['~ʃənit] ☐ apasionado; (*angry*) colérico; *believer, desire* vehemente, ardiente; '**pas·sion-flow·er** pasionaria *f*; '**pas·sion-play** drama *m* de la Pasión.

pas·sive ['pæsiv] **1.** ☐ pasivo; inactivo, inerte; **2.** voz *f* pasiva; '**pas·sive·ness**, **pas·siv·i·ty** [~'siviti] pasividad *f*; inercia *f*.

pass-key ['pɑ:ski:] llave *f* maestra.

Pass·o·ver ['pɑ:souvə] Pascua *f* de los hebreos.

pass·port ['pɑ:spɔ:t] pasaporte *m*.

pass·word ['pɑ:swə:d] santo *m* y seña.

past [pɑ:st] **1.** *adj.* pasado (*a. gr.*); *all that is now* ~ todo eso se acabó ya; *for some time* ~ de algún tiempo a esta parte; ~ *master fig.* maestro *m*, consumado (*adj.*) (*at, in* en); **2.** *adv.* por delante; *rush* ~ pasar precipitadamente; **3.** *prp. place* (*beyond*) más allá de; (*in front of*) por delante de; *number* más de; *time etc.* después de; *half* ~ 2 las 2 y media; *it's* ~ *12* dieron las 12 ya;

F *I wouldn't put it* ~ *him* le creo capaz de eso; ~ *belief* increíble; ~ *comprehension* incomprensible; ~ *all doubt* fuera de toda duda; ~ *hope* sin esperanza; **4.** *su.* pasado *m* (*a. gr.*); antecedentes *m/pl.*; *woman with a* ~ mujer *f* que tiene historia.

paste [peist] **1.** pasta *f*; engrudo *m for sticking*; diamante *m* de imitación, bisutería *f*; **2.** engrudar; pegar (con engrudo); *sl.* pegar; *sport: sl.* cascar; '~**board** (*attr.* de) cartón *m*.

pas·tel ['pæstəl] pastel *m*; pintura *f* al pastel; ~ *shade* tono *m* pastel.

pas·tern ['pæstə:n] cuartilla *f* (del caballo).

pas·teur·ize ['pæstəraiz] pasteurizar.

pas·tille [pæs'ti:l] pastilla *f*.

pas·time ['pɑ:staim] pasatiempo *m*.

pas·tor ['pɑ:stə] pastor *m*; '**pas·to·ral** *lit.* pastoril; *economy etc.* pastoral; *eccl.* pastoral (*a. su. f*).

pas·try ['peistri] (*dough*) pasta *f*; (*collectively*) pastas *f/pl.*, pasteles *m/pl.*; (*art*) pastelería *f*; *flaky* (*or puff*-) ~ hojaldre *m*; '~**cook** pastelero (a *f*) *m*; repostero (a *f*) *m*.

pas·tur·age ['pɑ:stjurid3] = *pasture* 1.

pas·ture ['pɑ:stʃə] **1.** (*herbage, land*) pasto *m*, pastura *f*; (*land*) dehesa *f*; **2.** *v/t.* animals apacentar, pastorear; *herbage* comer; *v/i.* pastar, pacer.

past·y 1. ['peisti] *material* pastoso; *colour* pálido; **2.** ['pæsti] pastel *m* (de carne), empanada *f*.

pat [pæt] **1.** palmadita *f*; (*affectionate*) caricia *f*; palmada *f on shoulder*; pastelillo *m of butter*; **2.** dar una palmadita a; *shoulder* dar una palmada en; *dog etc.* acariciar (con la mano); pasar la mano por; ~ *on the back fig.* felicitar; **3.** *adj.* oportuno; apto; **4.** *adv.* *have* (*off*) ~ saber al dedillo.

patch [pætʃ] **1.** remiendo *m in dress*; parche *m on tyre, wound*; lunar *m postizo on face*; (*stain etc.*) mancha *f*; (*small area*) pequeña extensión *f*; ✍ terreno *m*, cuadro *m*; F *it's not a* ~ *on* no se puede de ningún modo comparar con; **2.** remendar; ~ *up quarrel* componer; remendar (*or* componer) de modo provisional; ~**work** ['pætʃwə:k] labor *f* de retazos; ~ *quilt* centón *m*; '**patch·y** desigual, poco uniforme.

pate [peit] mollera *f*.

pat·en ['pætən] patena *f*.

pat·ent ['peitnt, *Am.* 'pætnt] **1.** ☐ patente, palmario; ✝ de patente, patente, patentado; *letters* ~ *pl.* tente *m* de privilegio; ~ *leather* charol *m*; ~ *medicine* específico *m*; **2.** patente *f*, privilegio *m* de invención; ~ *agent* agente *m* de patentes; ~ *office* oficina *f* de patentes; **3.** patentar; **pat·ent·ee** [peitən'ti:] poseedor *m* de patentes.

pa·ter·nal [pə'tə:nl] ☐ *quality* paternal; *relation* paterno; **pa·ter·ni·ty** paternidad *f*.

path [pɑ:θ], *pl.* **paths** [pɑ:ðz] senda *f*, sendero *m*; *fig.* camino *m*, trayectoria *f*; curso *m*; rastro *m*; marcha *f of storm*.

pa·thet·ic [pə'θetik] ☐ patético, conmovedor.

path·o·log·i·cal [pæθə'lɔd3ikl] ☐ patológico; **pa·thol·o·gist** [pə'θɔlə-d3ist] patólogo *m*; **pa·thol·o·gy** patología *f*.

pa·thos ['peiθɔs] patetismo *m*, lo patético.

path·way ['pɑ:θwei] = *path*.

pa·tience ['peiʃns] paciencia *f*; *cards*: solitario *m*; *be out of* ~ *with* no poder más sufrir, no tener simpatía alguna a; '**pa·tient 1.** ☐ paciente, sufrido; **2.** paciente *m/f*, enfermo (a *f*) *m*.

pa·ti·o ['pɑ:tiou] *Am.* patio *m*.

pa·tri·arch ['peitriɑ:k] patriarca *m*; **pa·tri·ar·chal** ☐ patriarcal.

pa·tri·cian [pə'triʃn] patricio *adj. a. su. m* (a *f*).

pat·ri·mo·ny ['pætriməni] patrimonio *m*.

pa·tri·ot ['pætriət] patriota *m/f*; **pa·tri·ot·ic** [~'ɔtik] ☐ patriótico; **pa·tri·ot·ism** ['~ətizm] patriotismo *m*.

pa·trol [pə'troul] **1.** ✕ *etc.* patrulla *f*; ronda *f*; *Am.* ~ *wagon* camión *m* de policía; **2.** patrullar (*v/t.* por); *fig.* rondar, pasearse (por); ~**man** [pə'troulmæn] *Am.* guardia *m* municipal.

pa·tron ['peitrən] ✝ parroquiano (a *f*) *m*; *lit.* mecenas *m*; *eccl.* patrono (a *f*) *m* (*a.* ~ *saint*); patrocinador (-a *f*) *m of enterprise*; **pa·tron·age** ['pætrənid3] *lit.* mecenazgo *m*; *eccl.* patronato *m*; patrocinio *m of enterprise; under the* ~ *of* bajo los auspicios de; **pa·tron·ize** ['pætrənaiz] *shop* ser parroquiano de; *enterprise* patrocinar; *b.s.* tratar con aire protector; **'pa·tron·iz·ing** □ *tone etc.* protector.

pat·ten ['pætn] zueco *m*, chanclo *m*.

pat·ter ['pætə] **1.** (*a.* ~ *about*) andar con pasos ligeros; (*rain*) tamborilear; **2.** pasos *m/pl.* ligeros *of feet*; tamborileo *m of rain etc.*; golpeteo *m*; ✝ jerga *f* (publicitaria *etc.*); (*rapid speech*) parloteo *m*.

pat·tern ['pætən] **1.** (*design*) diseño *m*, dibujo *m*; modelo *m*; patrón *m for dress etc.*; **2.** modelar (on sobre); **'~-mak·er** ⊕ carpintero *m* modelista.

pat·ty ['pæti] empanada *f*.

pau·ci·ty ['pɔːsiti] escasez *f*, insuficiencia *f*.

paunch [pɔːntʃ] panza *f*; **'paunch·y** panzudo.

pau·per ['pɔːpə] pobre *m/f*, indigente *m/f*; **'pau·per·ism** pauperismo *m*; **'pau·per·ize** empobrecer.

pause [pɔːz] **1.** pausa *f*; *give* ~ *to* hacer vacilar, dar que pensar a; **2.** hacer una pausa, detenerse (brevemente); reflexionar.

pave [peiv] pavimentar, enlosar; ~ *the way* preparar el terreno (for a); **'pave·ment** acera *f*; pavimento *m*.

pa·vil·ion [pə'viljən] pabellón *m*; *sport*: caseta *f*, vestuario *m*.

pav·ing-stone ['peiviŋstoun] losa *f*.

paw [pɔː] **1.** pata *f*; (*cat's etc.*) garra *f*; (*lion's*) zarpa *f*; **2.** (*lion etc.*) dar zarpazos a; F manosear; *p.* sobar; ~ *the ground* piafar.

pawn[1] [pɔːn] *chess*: peón *m*; *fig.* instrumento *m*.

pawn[2] [~] **1.**: *in* ~ en prenda; **2.** empeñar, dejar en prenda; **'~-bro·ker** prestamista *m*, prendero *m*; **'~-bro·ker's**, **'~-shop** casa *f* de empeños, prendería *f*; monte *m* de piedad; **'~-tick·et** papeleta *f* de empeño.

pay [pei] **1.** paga *f*; sueldo *m*; *in the* ~ *of* asalariado de, al servicio de; *on half* ~ a medio sueldo; **2.** [*irr.*] *v/t.* pagar; *account* liquidar; (*be profitable*) ser provechoso a, rendir (bien, *etc.*); *attention* prestar; *respects* ofrecer; *visit* hacer; ~ *back* devolver; reembolsar; *fig.* pagar en la misma moneda; ~ *down* pagar al contado; pagar como desembolso inicial; ~ *off* pagar, liquidar; amortizar; *scores* ajustar; *workmen* pagar y despedir;

~ *out* desembolsar; *rope* ir dando; *p.* pagar en la misma moneda; ~ *up* pagar (de mala gana); *v/i.* pagar (*for acc.*); (*be profitable*) rendir, ser provechoso; *it doesn't* ~ *to* vale más no *inf.*; **'pay·a·ble** pagadero; **'pay·day** día *m* de paga; **pay dirt** *Am.* grava *f* provechosa; **pay·ee** [~'iː] portador (-a *f*) *m*; tenedor (-a *f*) *m*; **'pay·er** pagador (-a *f*) *m*; **'pay·ing** provechoso; que rinde bien; ~ *guest* pensionista *m/f*; **'pay-load** carga *f* útil; **'pay·mas·ter** oficial *m* pagador; **'pay·ment** pago *m* (*a. fig.*); *in* ~ *for* en pago de; *on* ~ *of* pagando; *monthly* ~ mensualidad *f*.

pay...: **'~-off** F colmo *m*; resultado *m*; momento *m* decisivo; **'~-pack·et** sobre *m* de paga; **'~-roll** nómina *f*; **'~-sta·tion** *Am.* teléfono *m* público.

pea [piː] guisante *m*; *be as like as 2* ~*s* parecerse como dos gotas de agua.

peace [piːs] paz *f*; *at* ~ en paz; *the (King's)* ~ orden *m* público; ~ *loving nation* nación *f* amante de la paz; *hold one's* ~ guardar silencio; *keep the* ~ mantener la paz; *make* ~ hacer las paces (*with* con); **'peace·a·ble** □ pacífico; sosegado; **peace·ful** ['~ful] □ tranquilo; **'peace·mak·er** pacificador (-a *f*) *m*; árbitro *m*.

peach[1] [piːtʃ] ⚘ melocotón *m*; (*a.* ~ *tree*) melocotonero *m*; *sl.* monada *f*; *sl.* (*girl*) botón *m*, real moza *f*.

peach[2] [~] *sl.* soplar (on contra).

pea·cock ['piːkɔk] pavo *m* real, pavón *m*.

peak [piːk] pico *m*; cima *f*; cumbre *f* (*a. fig.*); visera *f of cap*; ~ *hours pl.* horas *f/pl.* punta; ~ *load* carga *f* máxima; ~ *season* época *f* más popular del año; ~ *traffic* movimiento *m* máximo; **peaked** [piːkt] *cap* con visera; **'peak·y** pálido, enfermizo.

peal [piːl] **1.** repique(teo) *m*; (*set*) juego *m* de campanas; ~ *of laughter* carcajada *f*; ~ *of thunder* trueno *m*; **2.** *v/i. a. v/t.* repicar, tocar a vuelo.

pea·nut ['piːnʌt] cacahuete *m*; ~ *butter* manteca *f* de cacahuete.

pear [pɛə] pera *f*; (*a.* ~ *tree*) peral *m*; ~ *shaped* de forma de pera.

pearl [pɜːl] perla *f* (*a. fig.*); ~ *barley* cebada *f* perlada; *attr.* = **'pearl·y** de perla(s); color de perla; perlino; nacarado.

peas·ant ['pezənt] campesino (a *f*) *m*, labrador (-a *f*) *m*; **'peas·ant·ry**

campesinos *m/pl.*, gente *f* del campo.

pea-shoot·er ['pi:ʃu:tə] cerbatana *f*.

pea-soup ['pi:'su:p] puré *m* de guisantes; **pea-'soup·er** F niebla *f* muy densa, puré *m* de guisantes.

peat [pi:t] turba *f*; '~-**bog** turbera *f*; '**peat·y** turboso.

peb·ble ['pebl] guija *f*, guijarro *m*; '**peb·bly** guij(arr)oso.

pec·ca·dil·lo [pekə'dilou] falta *f* leve.

peck[1] [pek] *medida de áridos* (= 9,087 *litros*); *a* ~ *of trouble* la mar de disgustos.

peck[2] [~] **1.** picotazo *m*; F beso *m* poco cariñoso; **2.** picotear; ~ *at food* comer melindrosamente; '**peck·er**: F *keep your* ~ *up!* ¡ánimo!; '**peck·ish**: F *be* ~ andarle a uno el gusanillo.

pec·to·ral ['pektərəl] pectoral *adj. a. su. m*.

pec·u·la·tion [pekjuleiʃn] peculado *m*.

pe·cul·iar [pi'kju:ljə] ☐ peculiar; singular; ~ *to* propio de, privativo de; **pe·cu·li·ar·i·ty** [~li'æriti] peculiaridad *f*; singularidad *f*; rasgo *m* característico.

pe·cu·ni·ar·y [pi'kju:njəri] pecuniario.

ped·a·gog·ic, ped·a·gog·i·cal [pedə'gɔdʒik(l)] ☐ pedagógico; '**ped·a·gogue** [~gɔg] pedagogo *m* (*a. b.s.*); **ped·a·go·gy** ['~gi] pedagogía *f*.

ped·al ['pedl] **1.** pedal *m*; **2.** *v/i.* pedalear; *v/t.* impulsar pedaleando.

ped·ant ['pedənt] pedante *m*; **pe·dan·tic** [pi'dæntik] ☐ *p.* pedante; *manner* pedantesco; **ped·ant·ry** ['pedəntri] pedantería *f*.

ped·dle ['pedl] andar vendiendo (de puerta en puerta); '**ped·dler** *Am.* = *pedlar*.

ped·es·tal ['pedistl] pedestal *m*; **pe·des·tri·an** [pi'destriən] **1.** de (*or para*) peatones; pedestre (*a. fig.*); **2.** peatón *m*; paseante *m/f*.

ped·i·cure ['pedikjuə] quiropedia *f*.

ped·i·gree ['pedigri:] **1.** genealogía *f*, linaje *m*; árbol *m* genealógico; **2.** de raza.

ped·i·ment ['pedimənt] frontón *m*.

ped·lar ['pedlə] vendedor *m* ambulante, buhonero *m*.

pe·dom·e·ter [pi'dɔmitə] podómetro *m*.

peek [pi:k] **1.** mirada *f* furtiva; *take a* ~ (*at*) = **2.** mirar furtivamente.

peel [pi:l] **1.** piel *f*; (*removed*) pieles *f/pl.*, monda *f*, peladura(s) *f(pl.)*; **2.** *v/t.* pelar, mondar; *paper etc.* quitar (una capa de); ~ *off dress* quitarse; *v/i.* 🐟 pelarse; ~ *off* desconcharse; F (*p.*) desnudarse; '**peel·ings** *pl.* monda *f*, peladuras *f/pl.*

peep[1] [pi:p] **1.** pío *m*; **2.** piar.

peep[2] [~] **1.** mirada *f* (rápida, furtiva, por una rendija *etc.*); **2.** (*a.* ~ *at*) mirar (rápidamente, furtivamente, por una rendija *etc.*); atisbar; (*a.* ~ *out*) asomar; empezar a dejarse ver; '**peep·er** *sl.* ojo *m*; '**peep-hole** mirilla *f in door*, atisbadero *m*; '**peep-show** mundonuevo *m*; F vistas *f/pl.* sicalípticas.

peer[1] [piə] (*a.* ~ *at*) mirar de cerca; mirar con ojos de miope; ~ *into* mirar (de cerca) lo que hay dentro de.

peer[2] [~] (*noble*) par *m*; (*equal*) igual *m*; '**peer·age** nobleza *f*, paría *f*; '**peer·ess** paresa *f*; '**peer·less** sin par, incomparable.

peeved [pi:vd] F negro, irritado; **pee·vish** ['pi:viʃ] ☐ malhumorado, displicente, cojijoso; '**pee·vish·ness** mal humor *m*, displicencia *f*.

pee·wit ['pi:wit] avefría *f*.

peg [peg] **1.** clavija *f*, claveta *f*; (*tent-etc.*) estaca *f*; (*clothes-*) pinza *f*; colgadero *m for coats*; *fig.* pretexto *m*; *take s.o. down a* ~ bajarle los humos a uno; **2.** enclavijar; (*a.* ~ *down*) estaquillar; (*a.* ~ *out*) *area* señalar con estacas; *clothes* tender (con pinzas); *prices* fijar, estabilizar; F ~ *away* machacar; persistir, afanarse (*at* en); *sl.* ~ *out* estirar la pata; '~-**top** peonza *f*.

peign·oir ['peinwɑ:] bata *f*; peinador *m*.

pe·jo·ra·tive ['pi:dʒərətiv] ☐ peyorativo.

pel·i·can ['pelikən] pelícano *m*.

pel·let ['pelit] bolita *f*; bodoque *m*; 🐟 perdigón *m*.

pell-mell ['pel'mel] *adv.* en tropel, atropelladamente; precipitadamente.   [talino.)

pel·lu·cid [pe'lju:sid] diáfano, cris-)

pe·lo·ta [pe'loutə] pelota *f* (vasca).

pelt[1] [pelt] (*skin*) pellejo *m*.

pelt[2] [~] **1.** *v/t.* tirar, arrojar; apedrear *with stones*; *they ~d him with tomatoes* le tiraron tomates; *v/i.*

llover a cántaros (*a. ~ with rain*); F ir a máxima velocidad; **2.** F (*at*) *full ~* a máxima velocidad, a todo correr.

pel·vis ['pelvis] pelvis *f*.

pen[1] [pen] **1.** pluma *f*; (*fountain-*) estilográfica *f*; **2.** escribir; redactar.

pen[2] [~] ✎ **1.** corral *m*, redil *m*; **2.** [*irr.*] encerrar, acorralar.

pe·nal ['pi:nl] penal; *~ code* código *m* penal; *~ servitude* trabajos *m/pl.* forzados; **pe·nal·ize** ['~əlaiz] penar; (*accidentally, unfairly*) perjudicar; *sport*: castigar; **pen·al·ty** ['penlti] pena *f*; multa *f*; castigo *m*; *sport*: pénalty *m*; *~ area* área *f* de castigo; *~ kick* golpe *m* de castigo, pénalty *m*.

pen·ance ['penəns] penitencia *f*.

pence [pens] *pl. of penny*.

pen·chant ['pɑ:ŋʃɑ:ŋ] predilección *f* (*for por*), afición *f* (*for a*).

pen·cil ['pensl] **1.** lápiz *m*; rayo *m of light*; **2.** escribir con lápiz; **'pen·cil-sharp·en·er** sacapuntas *m*.

pend·ant ['pendənt] **1.** pendiente *f*; **2.** pendiente *m*, medallón *m*.

pend·ing ['pendiŋ] **1.** *adj.* pendiente; **2.** *prp.* durante; hasta.

pen·du·lous ['pendjuləs] colgante; **pen·du·lum** ['~ləm] péndulo *m*.

pen·e·trate ['penitreit] penetrar; **'pen·e·trat·ing** □ penetrante (*a. fig.*); **pen·e'tra·tion** penetración *f*; **'pen·e·tra·tive** □ penetrante.

pen·guin ['peŋgwin] pingüino *m*.

pen·hold·er ['penhouldə] portaplumas *m*.

pen·i·cil·lin [peni'silin] penicilina *f*.

pen·in·su·la [pi'ninsjulə] península *f*; **pen'in·su·lar** peninsular.

pe·nis ['pi:nis] pene *m*.

pen·i·tence ['penitəns] penitencia *f*, arrepentimiento *m*; **'pen·i·tent** □ penitente *adj. a. su. m/f*; compungido, arrepentido; **pen·i·ten·tial** [~'tenʃl] penitencial; **pen·i·ten·tia·ry** [~'tenʃəri] *Am.* cárcel *f*, presidio *m*.

pen·knife ['pennaif] navaja *f*.

pen·man·ship ['penmənʃip] caligrafía *f*.

pen-name ['penneim] seudónimo *m*.

pen·nant ['penənt] ⚓ gallardete *m*; banderola *f*.

pen·ni·less ['penilis] sin dinero.

pen·non ['penən] pendón *m*.

pen·ny ['peni] penique *m*; *Am.* centavo *m*; *cost a pretty ~* costar un

dineral; **'~-a-'lin·er** escritorzuelo *m*; **'~-'dread·ful** revista *f* juvenil de bajísima calidad; **'~-in-the-'slot ma·chine** tragaperras *m*; **'~·weight** *peso* (= *1,555 gr.*); **'~·worth** ['penəθ] valor *m* de un penique; *fig.* pizca *f*.

pen·sion ['penʃn] **1.** pensión *f*; jubilación *f*; ✗ retiro *m*; **2.** pensionar; jubilar (*a. ~ off*); **'pen·sion·er** pensionado (a *f*) *m*, pensionista *m/f*; ✗ inválido *m*.

pen·sive ['pensiv] □ pensativo; melarcólico; preocupado.

pent [pent] *pret. a. p.p. of pen*[2]; *~ up* reprimido.

pen·ta·gon ['pentəgən] pentágono *m*; **pen·tag·o·nal** [~'tægənl] pentagonal.

pen·tath·lon [pen'tæθlɔn] péntatlo *m*.

Pen·te·cost ['pentikɔst] Pentecostés *f*; **pen·te'cos·tal** de Pentecostés.

pent·house ['penthaus] colgadizo *m*; *Am.* casa *f* de azotea.

pen·ul·ti·mate [pin'ʌltimit] penúltimo.

pe·num·bra [pi'nʌmbrə] penumbra *f*.

pe·nu·ri·ous [pi'njuəriəs] □ miserable, pobrísimo; **pen·u·ry** ['penjuri] miseria *f*, pobreza *f*.

pen-wip·er ['penwaipə] limpiaplumas *m*.

pe·o·ny ['piəni] peonía *f*.

peo·ple ['pi:pl] **1.** (*nation*) pueblo *m*, nación *f*; (*lower orders*) pueblo *m*, plebe *f*; (*in general*) gente *f*; personas *f/pl.*; *my etc. ~* mi *etc.* familia; *the ~ of London* los londinenses, los habitantes de Londres; *English ~* los ingleses; *the English ~* el pueblo inglés; *old ~* los viejos; *some ~* algunos; *there are some ~ who say* hay quien dice que; *~ say that* se dice que; *I like the ~ here* aquí la gente es muy simpática; **2.** poblar.

pep [pep] *sl.* **1.** ánimo *m*, vigor *m*; **2.**: *~ up* animar, estimular.

pep·per ['pepə] **1.** pimienta *f*; (*plant*) pimiento *m*; **2.** sazonar con pimienta; *fig.* salpicar; acribillar *with shot*; **'~-box**, **'~-pot** pimentero *m*; **'~·corn** grano *m* de pimienta; **'~·mint** (pastilla *f etc.* de) menta *f*; **'pep·per·y** picante; *fig.* enojadizo, de malas pulgas.

pep·tic ['peptik] péptico.

per [pə:] por; *~ annum* al año; *~ cent*

por ciento; *increase by 50* ~ *cent* aumentar en un 50 por ciento; ~ *capita*, ~ *person* por persona; cada uno; ~ *se* de por sí; *as* ~ según; F *as* ~ *usual* lo de siempre.

per·am·bu·late [pə'ræmbjuleit] *v/t.* recorrer (para inspeccionar); *v/i.* pasearse, deambular; **per·am·bu-'la·tion** visita *f* de inspección; paseo *m*; viaje *m*; **per·am·bu·la·tor** ['præmbjuleitə] cochecito *m* de niño.

per·ceive [pə'si:v] percibir; ver; notar; comprender.

per·cent·age [pə'sentidʒ] porcentaje *m*; proporción *f*; *sl.* tajada *f*; *attr.* porcentual.

per·cep·ti·ble [pə'septəbl] ☐ perceptible; **per'cep·tion** percepción *f*; comprensión *f*; perspicacia *f*; **per'cep·tive** ☐ perspicaz, penetrante.

perch[1] [pə:tʃ] *ichth.* perca *f*.

perch[2] [~] **1.** *medida de longitud* (5,029 m.); (*bird's*) percha *f*; posición *f* elevada; *fig.* posición *f* al parecer segura; **2.** *v/i.* posar(se); encaramarse; colocarse *etc.* en una posición elevada; *v/t.* colocar (en una posición elevada).

per·chance [pə'tʃɑ:ns] quizá, por ventura.

per·cip·i·ent [pə'sipiənt] perspicaz, penetrante.

per·co·late ['pə:kəleit] filtrar(se), infiltrar(se); **'per·co·la·tor** *approx.* cafetera *f* filtradora.

per·cus·sion [pə:'kʌʃn] (♪ *attr.* de) percusión *f*; ~ *cap* cápsula *f* fulminante.

per·di·tion [pə:'diʃn] perdición *f*; infierno *m*.

per·e·gri·na·tion [perigri'neiʃn] peregrinación *f*; ~*s pl. co.* vagabundeo *m*.

per·emp·to·ry [pə'remtəri] ☐ perentorio; *p.* imperioso, autoritario.

per·en·ni·al [pə'renjəl] ☐ perenne *adj. a. su. m* (*a.* ♣).

per·fect 1. ['pə:fikt] ☐ perfecto (*a. gr.*); **2.** [~] (*a.* ~ *tense*) perfecto *m*; **3.** [pə'fekt] perfeccionar; **per'fect·i·bil·i·ty** [~i'biliti] perfectibilidad *f*; **per'fect·i·ble** [~təbl] perfectible; **per'fec·tion** perfección *f*; *to* ~ a la perfección; **per'fec·tion·ist** persona *f* que lo quiere todo perfecto; detallista *m/f*.

per·fid·i·ous [pə'fidiəs] ☐ pérfido;

per'fid·i·ous·ness, **per·fi·dy** ['pə:-fidi] perfidia *f*.

per·fo·rate ['pə:fəreit] perforar, horadar; ~*d stamp* dentado; **per·fo-'ra·tion** perforación *f*; trepado *m of stamp.*

per·force [pə'fɔ:s] forzosamente.

per·form [pə'fɔ:m] *v/t. task etc.* realizar, cumplir, hacer; *functions* desempeñar; ♪ *etc.* ejecutar; *play* representar, poner; *v/i.* ♪ tocar; *thea.* representar, actuar; tener un papel; ⊕ funcionar; **per'form·ance** ejecución *f* (*a.* ♪); desempeño *m*; *thea.* representación *f*; función *f*; actuación *f* (brillante *etc.*); ⊕ funcionamiento *m*; rendimiento *m*; comportamiento *m*; performance *m in race etc.*; **per'form·er** artista *m/f*; actor *m*, actriz *f*; ♪ ejecutante *m/f*; *etc.*; **per'form·ing** *animal* amaestrado.

per·fume 1. ['pə:fju:m] perfume *m*; **2.** [pə'fju:m] perfumar; **per'fum·er** perfumista *m/f*; **per'fum·er·y** (*factory*) perfumería *f*; perfumes *m/pl.*

per·func·to·ry [pə'fʌŋktəri] ☐ superficial, hecho *etc.* a la ligera.

per·haps [pə'hæps, præps] tal vez, quizá(s); puede que.

per·il ['peril] peligro *m*, riesgo *m*; **'per·il·ous** ☐ peligroso, arriesgado; *come* ~*ly close to* acercarse de modo peligroso a; *fig.* rayar en.

per·i·me·ter [pe'rimitə] perímetro *m*.

pe·ri·od ['piəriəd] período *m* (*a. gr.*), época *f*; término *m*; *typ.* punto *m*; *school*: clase *f*, hora *f*; ✾ ~*s pl.* reglas *f pl.*; ~ *furniture* muebles *m/pl.* de época; **pe·ri·od·ic** [~'ɔdik] periódico; **pe·ri·od·i·cal 1.** ☐ periódico; **2.** periódico *m*, publicación *f* periódica.

per·i·pa·tet·ic [peripə'tetik] ☐ ambulante, sin residencia fija; *phls.* peripatético.

pe·riph·er·y [pe'rifəri] periferia *f*.

pe·riph·ra·sis [pə'rifrəsis], *pl.* **pe-'riph·ra·ses** [~si:z] perífrasis *f*; **per·i·phras·tic** [peri'fræstik] ☐ perifrástico.

per·i·scope ['periskoup] periscopio *m*.

per·ish ['periʃ] *v/i.* perecer; (*material*) deteriorarse; ~ *the thought!* ¡ni por pensamiento!; *v/t.* deteriorar, echar a perder; F *be* ~*ed with cold* estar aterido; **'per·ish·a·ble 1.** perecedero; *food etc.* corruptible, que no se conserva bien; **2.** ⁓s *pl.* mercancias *f/pl.* corruptibles; **'per·ish·er** *sl.* tio *m*; *(little ⁓)* tunante *m*; **'per·ish·ing** *sl.*: *it's ⁓ cold* hace un frío helador.

per·i·style ['peristail] peristilo *m.*

per·i·to·ni·tis [peritə'naitis] peritonitis *f.*

per·i·win·kle ['periwiŋkl] ♀ *(vinca)*-pervinca *f; zo.* litorina *f.*

per·jure ['pə:dʒə]: ⁓ *o.s.* perjurar (se); **'per·jured** *p.* perjuro; *evidence* falso; **'per·jur·er** perjuro *m*; **'per·ju·ry** perjurio *m; commit ⁓* jurar en falso; dar falso testimonio.

perk [pə:k] F: ⁓ *up* reanimarse, sentirse mejor.

perks [pə:ks] *pl.* F = *perquisites.*

perk·y ['pə:ki] F de excelente humor; despabilado.

perm [pə:m] F **1.** permanente *f;* **2.**: *have one's hair ⁓ed* hacerse una permanente.

per·ma·nence ['pə:mənəns], **'per·ma·nen·cy** permanencia *f;* **'per·ma·nent** ☐ permanente; fijo; duradero; ⁓ *wave* ondulación *f* permanente; ⁓ *way* vía *f.*

per·man·gan·ate [pə:'mæŋgəneit] permanganato *m.*

per·me·a·bil·i·ty [pə:miə'biliti] permeabilidad *f;* **'per·me·a·ble** ☐ permeable; **per·me·ate** ['⁓mieit] penetrar; saturar; impregnar.

per·mis·si·ble [pə'misəbl] ☐ permisible; **per·mis·sion** [⁓'miʃn] permiso *m;* **per·mis·sive** [⁓'misiv] permisivo.

per·mit 1. [pə'mit] permitir *(to inf.,* que *subj.);* ⁓ *of* permitir, dar lugar a; *weather ⁓ting* si lo permite el tiempo; **2.** ['pə:mit] permiso *m;* licencia *f;* ✝ permiso *m* de importación *etc.*

per·mu·ta·tion [pə:mju:'teiʃn] permutación *f.*

per·ni·cious [pə'niʃəs] ☐ pernicioso, funesto.

per·nick·et·y [pə'nikiti] F quisquilloso, remirado.

per·o·ra·tion [perə'reiʃn] peroración *f.*

per·ox·ide [pə'rɔksaid] peróxido *m;* F ⁓ *blonde* rubia *f* de bote.

per·pen·dic·u·lar [pə:pən'dikjulə] ☐ perpendicular *adj. a. su. f.*

per·pe·trate ['pə:pitreit] perpetrar;

per·pe'tra·tion perpetración *f;* **'per·pe·tra·tor** perpetrador *(-a f)* *m.*

per·pet·u·al [pə'petjuəl] ☐ perpetuo; ⁓ *motion* movimiento *m* perpetuo; **per'pet·u·ate** [⁓eit] perpetuar; **per·pet·u'a·tion** perpetuación *f;* **per·pe·tu·i·ty** [pə:pi'tjuiti] perpetuidad *f; in ⁓* para siempre.

per·plex [pə'pleks] confundir, dejar perplejo; **per'plexed** ☐ perplejo; **per'plex·ing** ☐ confuso, que causa perplejidad; **per'plex·i·ty** perplejidad *f.*

per·qui·site ['pə:kwizit] gaje *m;* ⁓s *pl.* gajes *m/pl.; salary and ⁓s* un sueldo y lo que cae.

per·se·cute ['pə:sikju:t] perseguir, acosar; **per·se'cu·tion** persecución *f;* ⁓ *mania* mania *f* persecutoria; **per·se·cu·tor** ['⁓tə] perseguidor *m.*

per·se·ver·ance [pə:si'viərəns] perseverancia *f;* **per·se·vere** [⁓'viə] perseverar, persistir *(in* en); **per·se'ver·ing** ☐ perseverante.

Per·sian ['pə:ʃn] persa *adj. a. su. m/f.*

per·sist [pə'sist] persistir; porfiar, empeñarse *(in* en); **per·sist·ence**, **per·sist·en·cy** [pə'sistəns(i)] persistencia *f;* porfia *f;* pertinacia *f of disease etc.;* **per'sist·ent** ☐ persistente, porfiado; *disease etc.* pertinaz.

per·son ['pə:sn] persona *f; in ⁓* en persona; *in the ⁓ of* en la persona de; **'per·son·a·ble** bien parecido; **'per·son·age** personaje *m;* **'per·son·al 1.** ☐ personal; *(private)* privado; de uso personal; *cleanliness etc.* corporal; *interview etc.* en persona; ⁓ *property* bienes *m/pl.* muebles; *become ⁓* (pasar a) hacer critica personal; *make a ⁓ appearance* aparecer en persona; **2.** *Am.* F nota *f* de sociedad; **per·son·al·i·ty** [⁓sə'næliti] personalidad *f;* **per·son·al·ty** ['⁓snlti] bienes *m/pl.* muebles; **per·son·ate** ['⁓səneit] hacerse pasar por; *thea. etc.* hacer el papel de; **per·son·i·fi·ca·tion** [⁓sɔnifi'keiʃn] personificación *f;* **per·son·i·fy** [⁓'sɔnifai] personificar; **per·son·nel** [⁓sə'nel] personal *m;* ⁓ *management* relaciones *f/pl.* personales; ⁓ *manager* jefe *m* del personal.   [perspectiva *f.*\

per·spec·tive [pə'spektiv] *(in* en)\

per·spi·ca·cious [pə:spi'keiʃəs] □ perspicaz; **per·spi·cac·i·ty** [ˌ‿'kæsiti] perspicacia *f*.

per·spi·ra·tion [pə:spə'reiʃn] transpiración *f*, sudor *m*; **per·spire** [pəs'paiə] transpirar, sudar; **per·spir·ing** sud(or)oso.

per·suade [pə'sweid] persuadir, inducir (*to* a); convencer (*of* de, *that* de que).

per·sua·sion [pə'sweiʒən] persuasiva *f*; (*act*) persuasión *f*; (*creed*) creencia *f*, secta *f*.

per·sua·sive [pə'sweisiv] □ persuasivo.   [dón; fresco.|

pert [pə:t] □ impertinente, respon-|

per·tain [pə:'tein]: ~ *to* (*concern*) referirse a, tener que ver con; (*belong to*) pertenecer con.

per·ti·na·cious [pə:ti'neiʃəs] □ pertinaz; **per·ti·nac·i·ty** [ˌ‿'næsiti] pertinacia *f*.

per·ti·nence, **per·ti·nen·cy** ['pə:tinəns(i)] pertinencia *f*; **'per·ti·nent** □ pertinente, oportuno.

pert·ness ['pə:tnis] impertinencia *f*, frescura *f*.

per·turb [pə'tə:b] perturbar, inquietar; **per·tur·ba·tion** [pə:tə:-'beiʃn] perturbación *f*.

pe·rus·al [pə'ru:zl] lectura *f* (cuidadosa); **pe·ruse** [pə'ru:z] leer (con atención), examinar.

Pe·ru·vi·an [pə'ru:viən] peruano *adj. a. su. m* (a *f*); ~ *bark* quina *f*.

per·vade [pə:'veid] extenderse por, difundirse por; impregnar, ocupar; **per'va·sive** [ˌ‿siv] penetrante; que lo impregna (*or* ocupa) todo.

per·verse [pə'və:s] □ perverso; avieso; contumaz; **per'verse·ness** = *perversity*; **per'ver·sion** perversión *f* (a. ✺); **per'ver·si·ty** perversidad *f*; contumacia *f*.

per·vert **1.** [pə'və:t] pervertir; *taste etc.* estragar; *talent* emplear mal; **2.** ['pə:və:t] ✺ pervertido (a *f*) *m*; (*apostate*) apóstata *m/f*.

per·vi·ous ['pə:viəs] permeable (*to* a).

pes·ky ['peski] *esp. Am.* molesto.

pes·si·mism ['pesimizm] pesimismo *m*; **'pes·si·mist** pesimista *m/f*; **pes·si·mis·tic** □ pesimista.

pest [pest] *zo.* plaga *f*; insecto *m etc.* nocivo; *fig.* (*p.*) machaca *f*; (*th.*) molestia *f*; **'pes·ter** molestar, acosar (con preguntas *etc.*), importunar.

pes·tif·er·ous [pes'tifərəs] pestífero; **pes·ti·lence** ['pestiləns] pestilencia *f*; **'pes·ti·lent** pestilente; *fig.* engorroso; **pes·ti·len·tial** [ˌ‿'lenʃl] pestilencial.

pes·tle ['pesl] mano *f* de almirez.

pet¹ [pet]: *be in a* ~ estar de mal humor, estar enojado.

pet² [ˌ‿] **1.** animal *m* doméstico (*or* de casa); (*p.*) favorito (a *f*) *m*, persona *f* muy mimada; F yes, *my* ~ sí, rico; F *he's rather a* ~ es simpatiquísimo; **2.** *animal* doméstico, de casa, domesticado; (*favourite*) favorito; ~ *aversion* bestia *f* negra, pesadilla *f*; (*p.*) hincha *m/f*; ~ *name* nombre *m* cariñoso; diminutivo *m*; **3.** *v/t.* acariciar; (*spoil*) mimar; *v/i.* F besuquearse, sobarse.

pet·al ['petl] pétalo *m*.

pe·ter ['pi:tə]: ~ *out* (*supply*) agotarse; ir disminuyendo; parar en nada; (*plan etc.*) no dar resultado.

pe·ti·tion [pi'tiʃn] **1.** petición *f*, memoria *f*, instancia *f*; **2.** suplicar, rogar (*for acc.*; *to inf.* que *subj.*); dirigir una instancia a; **pe'ti·tion·er** suplicante *m/f*.

pet·rel ['petrəl] petrel *m*, paíño *m*.

pet·ri·fac·tion [petri'fækʃn] petrificación *f*.

pet·ri·fy ['petrifai] petrificar(se) (*a. fig.*).

pet·rol ['petrəl] gasolina *f*; bencina *f for lighter*; ~ *engine* motor *m* de gasolina; ~ *pump* surtidor *m* de gasolina; ~ *station* estación *f* de gasolina; ~ *tank* depósito *m* (de gasolina).

pe·tro·le·um [pi'trouljəm] petróleo *m*; ~ *jelly* vaselina *f*, jalea *f* de petróleo.

pe·trol·o·gy [pe'trɔlədʒi] petrología *f*.

pet·ti·coat ['petikout] enagua(s) *f(pl.)*; (*slip*) combinación *f*; (*stiff*) falda *f* can-can; *attr. ...* de mujer(es).

pet·ti·fog·ging ['petifɔgiŋ] insignificante; hecho *etc.* para entenebrecer (un asunto).

pet·ti·ness ['petinis] insignificancia *f etc.*

pet·tish ['petiʃ] □ malhumorado (de modo pueril).

pet·ty ['peti] □ insignificante, pequeño; despreciable; *p.* intolerante; que se para en menudencias; rencoroso; reparón; ~ *cash* gastos *m/pl.* menores; *v. larceny;* ~ *officer* suboficial *m* de marina; ~ *sessions pl. tribunal presidido por juez de paz.*

pet·u·lance ['petjuləns] mal humor *m;* **pet·u·lant** ['‿lənt] □ malhumorado, enojadizo.

pew [pju:] banco *m* de iglesia; F asiento *m;* F *take a* ~*!* ¡siéntate!

pew·ter ['pju:tə] *(attr.* de) peltre *m.*

pha·lanx ['fælæŋks] falange *f.*

phan·tasm ['fæntæzm] fantasma *m;* **phan·tas·ma·go·ri·a** [‿mə'gɔ:riə] fantasmagoría *f.*

phan·tom ['fæntəm] **1.** fantasma *m;* **2.** fantasmal.

phar·i·sa·ic, phar·i·sa·i·cal [færiseiik(l)] □ farisaico.

Phar·i·see ['færisi:] fariseo *m.*

phar·ma·ceu·ti·cal [fɑ:mə'sju:tikl] farmacéutico; **phar·ma·cist** ['fɑ:-məsist] farmacéutico *m;* **phar·ma·col·o·gy** [‿'kɔlədʒi] farmacología *f;* '**phar·ma·cy** farmacia *f.*

phar·inx ['færiŋks] faringe *f.*

phase [feiz] fase *f,* etapa *f.*

pheas·ant ['feznt] faisán *m.*

phe·nom·e·nal [fi'nɔminl] □ fenomenal; **phe'nom·e·non** [‿nən], *pl.* **phe'nom·e·na** [‿nə] fenómeno *m.*

phew [fju:] ¡puf!; ¡caramba!

phi·al ['faiəl] frasco *m* (pequeño), redoma *f.*

phi·lan·der [fi'lændə] flirtear, mariposear; **phi'lan·der·er** tenorio *m.*

phil·an·throp·ic [filən'θrɔpik] □ filantrópico; **phi·lan·thro·pist** [fi-'lænθrəpist] filántropo (*a f*) *m;* **phi'lan·thro·py** filantropía *f.*

phi·lat·e·list [fi'lætəlist] filatelista *m/f;* **phi'lat·e·ly** filatelia *f.*

phi·lip·pic [fi'lipik] filípica *f.*

Phi·lip·pine ['filipain] filipino *adj. a. su. m* (a *f*).

Phi·lis·tine ['filistain] filisteo (a *f*) *m.*

phil·o·log·i·cal [filə'lɔdʒikl] □ filológico; **phi·lol·o·gist** [fi'lɔlədʒist] filólogo *m;* **phi'lol·o·gy** filología *f.*

phi·los·o·pher [fi'lɔsəfə] filósofo *m;* ~*'s stone* piedra *f* filosofal; **phil·o·soph·ic, phil·o·soph·i·cal** [filə-'sɔfik(l)] □ filosófico; **phi·los·o·phize** [fi'lɔsəfaiz] filosofar; **phi'los·o·phy** filosofía *f;* ~ *of life* filosofía *f* de la vida.

phil·tre, phil·ter ['filtə] filtro *m.*

phle·bi·tis [fli'baitis] flebitis *f.*

phlegm [flem] flema *f* (*a. fig.*);

phleg·mat·ic [fleg'mætik] □ flemático.

Phoe·ni·cian [fi'niʃn] fenicio *adj. a. su. m* (a *f*).

phoe·nix ['fi:niks] fénix *m.*

phone [foun] F = *telephone.*

pho·net·ic [fou'netik] □ fonético; **pho·ne·ti·cian** [founi'tiʃn] fonetista *m/f;* **pho·net·ics** [fou'netiks] fonética *f.*

pho·no·graph ['founəgrɑ:f] fonógrafo *m.*

pho·nol·o·gy [fou'nɔlədʒi] fonología *f.*

pho·n(e)y ['founi] *sl.* **1.** farsante *m/f;* persona *f* insincera; **2.** falso, postizo; sospechoso; insincero.

phos·phate ['fɔsfeit] fosfato *m.*

phos·pho·resce [fɔsfə'res] fosforecer; **phos·pho'res·cent** fosforescente; **phos·phor·ic** [‿'fɔrik] fosfórico; **phos·pho·rous** ['‿fərəs] fosforoso; **phos·pho·rus** ['‿] fósforo *m.*

pho·to ['foutou] F foto *f;* '~**e'lec·tric 'cell** célula *f* fotoeléctrica; ~**en·grav·ing** [‿in'greiviŋ] fotograbado *m;* '~**'fin·ish** (resultado *m* comprobado por) fotocontrol *m; fig.* final *m* muy reñido; '~**flash** flash *m,* magnesio *m;* **pho·to·gen·ic** [‿'dʒenik] fotogénico (*a.* F).

pho·to·graph ['foutəgrɑ:f] **1.** fotografía *f* (*foto*); **2.** fotografiar; **pho·tog·ra·pher** [fə'tɔgrəfə] fotógrafo (a *f*) *m;* **pho·to·graph·ic** [foutə-'græfik] □ fotográfico; **pho·tog·ra·phy** [fə'tɔgrəfi] fotografía *f* (*arte*).

pho·to·gra·vure [foutəgrə'vjuə] fotograbado *m,* huecograbado *m;* **pho·tom·e·ter** [fou'tɔmitə] fotómetro *m;* **pho·to·stat** ['foutoustæt] **1.** fotóstato *m;* **2.** fotostatar; **pho·to·'syn·the·sis** [fou'tɔmitə] fotosíntesis *f;* '**pho·to·te'leg·ra·phy** fototelegrafía *f;* **pho·to·type** ['‿taip] fototipo *m.*

phrase [freiz] **1.** frase *f* (*a.* ♪); expresión *f,* locución *f;* **2.** expresar; **phra·se·ol·o·gy** [‿i'ɔlədʒi] fraseología *f.*

phre·net·ic [fri'netik] □ frenético.

phre·nol·o·gy [fri'nɔlədʒi] frenología *f.*

phthis·i·cal ['θaisikl] tísico; **phthi·sis** ['‿sis] tisis *f.*

phut [fʌt] *sl.: go* ~ romperse, estropearse; *fig.* fracasar.

phys·ic ['fizik] † medicina *f;* ~*s sg.*

física *f*; **'phys·i·cal** ☐ físico; ~ *condition* estado *m* físico; ~ *culture* cultura *f* física; **phy·si·cian** [fi'ziʃn] médico *m*; **phys·i·cist** ['~sist] físico *m*.

phys·i·og·no·my [fizi'ɔnəmi] fisonomía *f*; **phys·i·og·ra·phy** [~'ɔg-rəfi] fisiografía *f*; **phys·i·ol·o·gy** [~'ɔlədʒi] fisiología *f*.

phy·sique [fi'zi:k] físico *m*.

pi·an·ist ['pjænist, 'piənist] pianista *m/f*.

pi·a·no[1] ['pja:nou] *adv.* piano, suavemente.

pi·an·o[2] ['pjænou, 'pja:nou, pi'a:n-ou], *a.* **pi·an·o·for·te** [pjænou'fɔ:ti] piano(forte) *m*.

pi·az·za [pi'ædʒə] *Am.* pórtico *m*, galería *f*.

pic·a·yune [pikə'ju:n] *Am.* **1.** persona *f* insignificante; bagatela *f*; **2.** de poca monta.

pic·ca·nin·ny ['pikənini] negrito (a *f*) *m*.

pick [pik] **1.** (~*axe*) (zapa)pico *m*, piqueta *f*; (*choice*) derecho *m* de elección; (*best*) lo más escogido, flor *f* y nata; F *it's your* ~ a ti te toca elegir; **2.** *v/t.* escoger (con cuidado); *bone* roer; *flower* coger; *fruit* recoger; *lock* forzar, abrir con ganzúa; *nose* hurgarse; *team* seleccionar; *teeth* mondarse; ~ *one's way* andar con mucho tiento; *v.* bone, crow, pocket; ~ *off paint etc.* separar, arrancar; (*shoot*) matar de un tiro; matar con tiros sucesivos; ~ *out* escoger; *colour etc.* hacer resaltar; (*identify*) conocer, identificar; (*discern*) lograr ver; ~ *over* ir revolviendo y examinando; ~ *up* recoger *from floor etc.*; (*recover*) recobrar; (*casually*) saber (*or* encontrar *etc.*) por casualidad; (*learn*) lograr aprender; *radio:* captar; *v/i.* ~ *and choose* (hacer melindres al) escoger; *Am.* F ~ *at*, F ~ *on* perseguir, criticar; ~ *up* ∦ reponerse; ~**-a·back** ['~əbæk] sobre los hombros; **'~·axe** v. pick 1; **picked** [pikt] escogido; **'pick·er** recogedor *m*.

pick·et ['pikit] **1.** estaca *f*; ✗ piquete *m*; (guardia *f* de) vigilante(s) *m*(*pl.*) huelgista(s); **2.** *v/t. factory* cercar con un cordón de huelguistas; *v/i.* estar de guardia (los vigilantes huelguistas).

pick·ing ['pikiŋ] recolección *f* of

fruit etc.; ~*s pl.* sobras *f/pl.*; (*profits*) ganancias *f/pl.*; lo robado *from theft.*

pick·le ['pikl] **1.** (*as condiment*) encurtido *m* (*a.* ~*s pl.*); (*fish, olives*) escabeche *m*; (*meat*) adobo *m*; (*salted*) salmuera *f*; F apuro *m*; lío *m*; F (*p.*) pillo *m*; **2.** escabechar; adobar; conservar; ~*d sl.* ajumado.

pick...: '~**-me-up** F reconstituyente *m*; ∦ tónico *m*; '~**·pock·et** ratero *m*, carterista *m*; '~**-up** pick-up *m*; ~ *arm* palanca *f*.

pic·nic ['piknik] **1.** jira *f*, excursión *f* campestre, picnic *m*; *sl.* cosa *f* fácil; *go for a* ~ = **2.** ir de jira, merendar *etc.* en el campo.

pic·to·ri·al [pik'tɔ:riəl] ☐ pictórico; *magazine* gráfico, ilustrado.

pic·ture ['piktʃə] **1.** cuadro *m*, pintura *f*; (*portrait*) retrato *m*; (*photo*) fotografía *f*; lámina *f in book*; *television:* cuadro *m*; (*spoken etc.*) descripción *f*; (*mental*) imagen *f*; visión *f* de conjunto; F *the* ~*s* el cine; *a* ~ *of health* la salud personificada; *the other side of the* ~ el reverso de la medalla; F *put a p. in the* ~ poner a una p. al corriente de una cosa; **2.** *attr. paper* ilustrado; *hat* de alas anchas; **3.** pintar; describir; ~ (*to o.s.*) imaginarse, representarse; '~**-frame** marco *m*; '~**-gal·ler·y** museo *m* de pintura; '~**-go·er** aficionado (a *f*) *m* al cine; '~**-pal·ace** cine *m*; '~**-'post·card** postal *f* ilustrada.

pic·tur·esque [piktʃə'resk] ☐ pintoresco.

pidg·in ['pidʒin] (*chino* = *business*): ~ *English* lengua franca (inglés-chino) comercial del Lejano Oriente.

pie [pai] (*sweet*) pastel *m*; (*meat- etc.*) empanada *f*; *v.* finger.

pie·bald ['paibɔ:ld] pío, de varios colores; abigarrado.

piece [pi:s] **1.** (*fragment*) pedazo *m*, fragmento *m*; trozo *m*; ♪, *thea.*, ✗, ⊕, *coin, chess etc.*: pieza *f*; *chess etc. a.* ficha *f*; F (*girl*) pizpireta *f*; *by the* ~ por pieza; *in* ~*s* hecho pedazos, roto; desmontado; *of a* ~ *with* de la misma clase que; *conforme a; two-shilling* ~ moneda *f* de 2 chelines; ~ *of advice* consejo *m*; ~ *of furniture* mueble *m*; ~ *of ground* terreno *m*; solar *m*; ~ *of news* noticia *f*; *break*

to (or in) ⌄s hacer pedazos; go to ⌄s
fig. sufrir un ataque de nervios; perder la salud; (*team*) desalentarse por
completo; *take to* ⌄s desmontar;
2. (*a.* ⌄ *together*) juntar (las piezas
de); *fig.* atar cabos (e ir comprendiendo); '⌄**meal** *adv.* a trozos; sin
sistema fijo; '⌄**work** trabajo *m* a
destajo.

pied [paid] *animal* pío, de varios
colores; *bird* manchado.

pier [piə] △ estribo *m*, pila *f of
bridge*; pilar *m*, columna *f*; ⚓
muelle *m*, malecón *m*, embarca-
dero *m*.

pierce [piəs] penetrar; taladrar, horadar, perforar; agujerear; pinchár;
atravesar; **pierc·ing** ['piəsiŋ] □
penetrante, agudo.

pi·e·ty ['paiəti] piedad *f*, devoción *f*.

pif·fle ['pifl] F disparates *m/pl.*,
tonterías *f/pl.*; **pif·fling** F de poca
monta, insignificante.

pig [pig] cerdo *m*, puerco *m*, cochino
m; F (*p.*) marrano *m*; *metall.* lingote *m*; *buy a* ⌄ *in a poke* cerrar un
trato a ciegas; F *make a* ⌄ *of o.s.*
comer demasiado; darse un atracón
(*over* de).

pi·geon ['pidʒin] paloma *f*; '⌄**hole**
1. casilla *f*; **2.** encasillar; clasificar;
archivar (*fig.* en la memoria); (*shelve*)
dar carpetazo a.

pig·ger·y ['pigəri] pocilga *f*.

pig·head·ed ['pig'hedid] □ terco,
cabezudo.

pig·i·ron ['pigaiən] hierro *m* en lingotes.

pig·ment ['pigmənt] pigmento *m*.

pig·my pigmeo *adj. a. su. m.*

pig...: '⌄**skin** piel *f* de cerdo; ⌄**sty**
['⌄stai] pocilga *f*, cochiquera *f* (*a.
fig.*); '⌄**tail** trenza *f*, coleta *f*.

pike [paik] ✕ pica *f*; *ichth.* lucio *m*;
'**pik·er** *Am. sl.* cicatero *m*; cobarde
m; '**pike-staff:** *as plain as a* ⌄
claro como la luz del día.

pil·chard ['piltʃəd] sardina *f* arenque.

pile[1] [pail] **1.** montón *m*, pila *f*;
mole *f of buildings*; F fortuna *f*;
phys. (*atomic* ⌄) pila *f*; **2.** (*a.* ⌄ *up*)
amontonar(se), apilar(se), acumu-
lar(se); F ⌄ *in(to)* entrar todos (en);
⌄ *on* ir aumentando; ⌄ *it on* exagerar.

pile[2] [⌄] △ pilote *m*.

pile[3] [⌄] pelo *m of carpet*; pelillo *m
of cloth*.

pile-driv·er ['paildraivə] martinete
m.

piles [pailz] *pl.* ✱ almorranas *f/pl.*

pil·fer ['pilfə] ratear; '**pil·fer·ing**
ratería *f*.

pil·grim ['pilgrim] peregrino (*a f*)
m, romero (*a f*) *m*; '**pil·grim·age**
peregrinación *f*, romería *f*; *make a* ⌄
ir en romería.

pill [pil] píldora *f*; *sl.* pelota *f*.

pil·lage ['pilidʒ] **1.** pillaje *m*; **2.** pillar.

pil·lar ['pilə] pilar *m*, columna *f*;
fig. sostén *m*; *chase from* ⌄ *to post*
no dejar a sol ni a sombra; '⌄**box**
buzón *m*.

pill·box ['pilbɔks] fortín *m*.

pil·lion ['piljən]: ⌄ *seat* asiento *m*
de atrás; *ride* ⌄ ir en el asiento de
atrás.

pil·lo·ry ['piləri] **1.** picota *f*; **2.** *fig.*
poner en ridículo, satirizar.

pil·low ['pilou] **1.** almohada *f*;
2. apoyar sobre una almohada;
servir de almohada a; '⌄**case**,
'⌄**slip** funda *f* de almohada.

pi·lot ['pailət] **1.** ✈ piloto *m*; ⚓
práctico *m*; ⌄ *light mot.*, ✕ luz *f*
de situación; mechero *m* encendedor *on stove*; ⌄ *plant* planta *f*
piloto, fábrica *f* experimental;
2. pilotar; *fig.* guiar; conducir.

pi·men·to [pi'mentou] pimienta *f*.

pimp [pimp] **1.** alcahuete *m*; **2.** alcahuetear.

pim·ple ['pimpl] grano *m*; '**pim·ply**
granujoso.

pin [pin] **1.** alfiler *m*; ⊕ perno *m*;
(*wooden*) clavija *f*; ⌄s *pl. sl.* piernas
f/pl.; *like a new* ⌄ como una plata;
for 2 ⌄s por menos de nada; ⌄s *and
needles* F hormiguillo *m*; **2.** prender
con alfiler(es); sujetar (con perno
etc.); ⌄ *down fig.* inmovilizar; *p.*
obligar a que concrete; ⌄ *s.t. on s.o.
fig.* acusar (falsamente) a uno de
algo; ⌄ *up* fijar (con alfileres).

pin·a·fore ['pinəfɔ:] delantal *m* (de
niña).

pin·cers ['pinsəz] *pl.* (*a pair of* ⌄)
unas) tenazas *f/pl.*, pinzas *f/pl.*

pinch [pintʃ] **1.** pellizco *m with
fingers; cooking:* pizca *f*; pulgarada *f
of snuff; at a* ⌄ si es realmente necesario, en caso de apuro; *feel the* ⌄
pasar apuros; **2.** *v/t.* pellizcar *with
fingers; finger* cogerse *in door etc.;*
(*shoe*) apretar; *sl.* (*steal*) birlar, guin-

dar; (*arrest*) prender; *v*/*i*. (*shoe*) apretar; *fig*. economizar; privarse de lo necesario; **pinched** [~t] aterido, chupado (*with cold* de).

pinch·beck ['pintʃbek] (*attr*. de) similor *m*.

pinch-hit ['pintʃhit] *Am*. batear de emergente.

pin·cush·ion ['pinkuʃin] acerico *m*.

pine[1] [pain] ♀ pino *m*.

pine[2] [~] languidecer, consumirse (*a*. ~ *away*); ~ *for* penar por, anhelar.

pine...: '~·**ap·ple** ananás *m*, piña *f*; '~-**cone** piña *f*; '~-**need·le** aguja *f* de pino; '~-**wood** pinar *m*.

ping [piŋ] **1.** sonido *m* metálico; **2.** hacer un sonido metálico (como una bala).

ping-pong ['piŋpɔŋ] ping-pong *m*.

pin·ion ['pinjən] **1.** ⊕ piñón *m*; *poet*. ala *f*; **2.** *bird* cortar las alas a; *p*. atar los brazos de.

pink[1] [piŋk] **1.** ♀ clavel *m*, clavellina *f*; F *in the* ~ en perfecta salud; *in the* ~ *of* en perfecto estado de; **2.** rosado; color de rosa (*a*. *su*. *m*); *pol*. rojillo.

pink[2] [~] *sew*. ondear, picar.

pink[3] [~] *mot*. picar (por auto-encendido).

pin-mon·ey ['pinmʌni] alfileres *m*/*pl*.

pin·nace ['pinis] pinaza *f*.

pin·na·cle ['pinəkl] ♙ pináculo *m*, chapitel *m*; cumbre *f* (*a*. *fig*.).

pin...: '~-**point** *fig*. indicar con toda precisión; '~-**prick** alfilerazo *m*; *fig*. molestia *f* pequeña; '~-**stripe** (pantalón *m*) a rayas; '~-**ta·ble** billar *m* romano (*or* automático).

pint [paint] pinta *f* (= *0,568*, *Am*. *0,473 litros*).

pin-up ['pinʌp] F foto *f* de muchacha guapa, pin-up *f*; *fig*. mujer *f* ideal.

pi·o·neer [paiə'niə] **1.** explorador *m* *in country*; ✂ zapador *m*; (*early settler*) colonizador *m*; iniciador *m*, promotor *m of scheme*; *be a* ~ *in the study of* ser de los primeros en estudiar *acc*.; **2.** *v*/*i*. explorar; *v*/*t*. *settlement etc*. preparar el terreno para; *scheme*, *study* iniciar, promover.

pi·ous ['paiəs] □ piadoso, devoto.

pip[1] [pip] *vet*. pepita *f*; *sl*. *it gives me the* ~ me fastidia terriblemente.

pip[2] [~] ♀ pepita *f*; punto *m on card*; estrella *f on uniform*.

pip[3] [~] F (*defeat*) vencer; *exam* no aprobar; (*wound*) herir (con bala *etc*.).

pipe [paip] **1.** tubo *m*, caño *m*, cañería *f*; conducto *m*; cañón *m of organ*; ♪ caramillo *m*; pipa *f for tobacco*; ♪ ~*s* *pl*. gaita *f*; ~ *dream* esperanza *f* imposible; ~ *tobacco* tabaco *m* de pipa; **2.** *v*/*t*. conducir en cañerías *etc*.; decir en voz atiplada; *v*/*i*. tocar el caramillo; *sl*. ~ *down* callarse; F ~ *up* comenzar a hablar (inesperadamente); '~-**clay** **1.** albero *m*; **2.** blanquear con albero; '~-**line** (*oil*) oleoducto *m*; cañería *f*; '**pip·er** flautista *m*/*f*; (*bag*-) gaitero *m*; *pay the* ~ cargar con los gastos.

pip·ing ['paipiŋ] **1.** cañería(s) *f*(*pl*.); *sew*. ribete *m*; **2.**: ~ *hot* bien caliente.

pip·it ['pipit] bisbita *f*.

pip·pin ['pipin] camuesa *f*.

pi·quan·cy ['pi:kənsi] picante *m*; **pi·quant** ['pi:kənt] □ picante.

pique [pi:k] **1.** pique *m*, resentimiento *m*; *be in a* ~ estar resentido; **2.** picar, herir; ~ *o.s. upon* enorgullecerse de.

pi·ra·cy ['paiərəsi] piratería *f*; **pirate** ['~rit] **1.** pirata *m*; ~ *radio* emisora *f* ilegal; **2.** pillar, robar; publicar fraudulentamente; ~*d edition* edición *f* furtiva; **pi·rat·i·cal** [pai'rætikl] □ pirático.

pi·rou·ette [piru'et] **1.** pirueta *f*; **2.** piruetear.

piss [pis] **1.** orina *f*; **2.** mear.

pis·til ['pistil] pistilo *m*.

pis·tol ['pistl] pistola *f*; revólver *m*.

pis·ton ['pistən] émbolo *m*, pistón *m*; '~-**ring** aro *m* (*or* segmento *m*) de pistón; '~-**rod** vástago *m* de émbolo; '~-**stroke** carrera *f* del émbolo.

pit [pit] **1.** hoyo *m*, hoya *f*, foso *m*; ✗ mina *f* (de carbón); (*quarry*) cantera *f*; *thea*. parte *f* posterior del patio; boca *f of stomach*; *fig*. abismo *m*; (*danger*) escollo *m*; **2.** marcar (con hoyas) (*match*) oponer (*against* a).

pit-(a-)pat ['pit(ə)'pæt]: *go* ~ latir rápidamente, hacer tictac.

pitch[1] [pitʃ] **1.** pez *f*, brea *f*; ~ *dark* negro como boca de lobo; **2.** embrear.

pitch[2] [~] **1.** (*throw*) lanzamiento *m*, echada *f*; ♙ cabezada *f*; ♪ tono *m*;

(slope) grado *m* de inclinación; pendiente *f of roof*; *sport*: terreno *m*, campo *m*; *(salesman's)* puesto *m*; *fig.* punto *m*, grado *m*, extremo *m*; **2.** *v/t.* arrojar, echar; lanzar; *tent* armar; ♪ graduar el tono de; *note* entonar, dar; F *tale* contar; ~ed *battle* batalla *f* campal; *v/i.* caerse *(into* en); ♣ cabecear; ~ *forward* caer de cabeza; F ~ *in* ponerse a trabajar con afán; comenzar a comer; F ~ *into* arremeter contra, atacar vigorosamente; F ~ *on* elegir.

pitch·er[1] ['pitʃə] cántaro *m*, jarro *m*.

pitch·er[2] [~] *Am.* botador *m*.

pitch·fork ['pitʃfɔ:k] **1.** horca *f*, tornadera *f*, bielda *f*; **2.**: *fig.* ~ *s.o. into* s.t. imponer inesperadamente a alguien una tarea.

pitch-pine ['pitʃpain] pino *m* de tea.

pit·e·ous ['pitiəs] □ lastimero, lastimoso.

pit·fall ['pitfɔ:l] *fig.* escollo *m*, trampa *f*.

pith [piθ] ♀ médula *f* (*a. fig.*); *fig.* meollo *m*, jugo *m*; *(strength)* vigor *m*.

pit-head ['pithed] bocamina *f*.

pith·y ['piθi] □ *fig.* sucinto, expresivo, lacónico.

pit·i·a·ble ['pitiəbl] □ enternecedor, digno de compasión.

pit·i·ful ['pitiful] □ lastimero, lastimoso; *(contemptible)* despreciable, lamentable.

pit·i·less ['pitilis] □ despiadado, implacable.

pit·tance ['pitəns] miseria *f*, renta *f* miserable; recursos *m/pl.* insuficientes.

pi·tu·i·tar·y [pi'tju:itəri] **1.** pituitario; **2.** (*a.* ~ *gland*) glándula *f* pituitaria.

pit·y ['piti] **1.** piedad *f*, compasión *f*; lástima *f*; *for* ~*'s sake!* ¡por piedad!; *it is a* ~ *(that)* es lástima (que *subj.*); *more's the* ~ desgraciadamente; *take* ~ *on* tener piedad de, apiadarse de; *what a* ~*!* ¡qué lástima!; **2.** tener piedad de, compadecer(se de).

piv·ot ['pivət] **1.** pivote *m*, gorrón *m*; *fig.* punto *m* central; **2.** *v/t.* montar sobre un pivote; *v/i.* girar (*on* sobre); *fig.* ~ *on* depender de; '**piv·o·tal** central, fundamental.

pix·ie ['piksi] duende *m*.

pix·i·lat·ed ['piksəleitid] *Am. sl.* chiflado; aturrullado.

pla·card ['plækɑ:d] **1.** cartel *m*, pancarta *f*; **2.** *wall* llenar de carteles.

pla·cate [plə'keit] aplacar.

place [pleis] **1.** sitio *m*, lugar *m*; *(enclosed)* local *m*; *(post)* puesto *m*, empleo *m*; *(rank)* lugar *m*, puesto *m*; *(seat)* plaza *f*; *cubierto m at table*; Å *to the third* ~ en milésimas; ~ *of worship* templo *m*, edificio *m* de culto; F *at my* ~ en mi casa; *in* ~ en su sitio; oportuno; *in his* ~ en su lugar; *in* ~ *of* en lugar de; *in the first* ~ en primer lugar; *out of* ~ fuera de (su) lugar; fuera de serie; fuera de propósito; *give* ~ *to* ceder el paso a; *it is not his* ~ *to* no le cumple a él *inf.*; *put s.o. in his* ~ bajarle los humos a uno; *know one's* ~ ser respetuoso; *take* ~ tener lugar; verificarse; **2.** colocar, poner; fijar; colocar *in post etc.*; *(recall)* acordarse bien de; *(identify)* identificar; *sport*: be ~d colocarse; '~-**kick** puntapié *m* colocado; '~-**name** topónimo *m*.

plac·id ['plæsid] □ plácido; **pla-'cid·i·ty** placidez *f*.

pla·gi·a·rism ['pleidʒiərizm] plagio *m*; '**pla·gi·a·rist** plagiario (a *f*) *m*; '**pla·gi·a·rize** plagiar.

plague [pleig] **1.** peste *f*, plaga *f*; **2.** plagar, infestar; *fig.* atormentar, molestar, acosar.

pla·guy ['pleigi] F engorroso.

plaice [pleis] platija *f*.

plaid [plæd] plaid *m*, manta *f* escocesa.

plain [plein] **1.** □ sencillo, llano; sin adornos; *(unmixed)* natural, puro; *face* sin atractivo, ordinario; *in* ~ *clothes* en traje de calle, de paisano; *in* ~ *English* hablando sin rodeos; *be* ~ *with* hablar claro a; *it is* ~ *that* es evidente que; ~ *knitting* punto *m* de media; ~ *truth* verdad *f* lisa y llana; **2.** *adv.* claro, claramente; **3.** llano *m*, llanura *f*; '~-**clothes man** agente *m* de policía que lleva traje de calle; '**plain·ness** llaneza *f*, franqueza *f*; falta *f* de atractivo *of face etc.*

plains·man ['pleinzmən] llanero *m*.

plain·song ['pleinsɔŋ] canto *m* llano.

plain·tiff ['pleintif] demandante *m/f*; '**plain·tive** □ dolorido, plañidero.

plait [plæt] **1.** trenza *f*; **2.** trenzar.

plan [plæn] **1.** proyecto *m*, plan *m*; ⚠ plano *m*; esquema *m*; programa *m*; *v.* five; **2.** *v/t.* planear, planificar; proyectar; idear; ~ned economy economía *f* dirigida; ~ning board comisión*f* planificadora; *v/i.* hacer proyectos (for para); ~ to proponerse *inf.*, pensar *inf.*

plane[1] [plein] **1.** plano; **2.** ⚔ plano *m*; *fig.* nivel *m*, esfera *f*; ✈ avión *m*; ala *f*; ⊕ cepillo *m* (de carpintero); **3.** ⊕ acepillar; desbastar (*a.* ~ down).

plane[2] [~] ♧ plátano *m* (*a.* ~ tree).

plan·et ['plænit] planeta *m*.

plane·ta·ble ['pleinteibl] plancheta *f*.

plan·e·tar·i·um [plæni'tɛəriəm] planetario *m*; **plan·e·tar·y** ['~təri] planetario.

pla·nim·e·try [plæ'nimitri] planimetría *f*.

plan·ish ['plæniʃ] aplanar.

plank [plæŋk] **1.** tablón *m*, tabla *f* (gruesa); ~s *pl.* tablaje *m*; *mst Am. parl.* artículo *m* (de un programa político); **2.** entablar, entarimar; F ~ down tirar, colocar firmemente; **'plank·ing** tablaje *m*; ⚓ maderamen *m* de cubierta.

plan·ning ['plæniŋ] planificación *f*.

plant [plɑːnt] **1.** ♧ planta *f* (*a.* ⊕); ⊕ instalación *f*, maquinaria *f*; ⚡ grupo *m* electrógeno; (*factory*) fábrica *f*; *sl.* estratagema *f* para incriminar a una p.; **2.** plantar; (*sow*) sembrar; sentar, colocar; *blow* plantar; *sl.* ~ a th. on a p. ocultar algo para incriminar a una p.

plan·tain ['plæntin] llantén *m*.

plan·ta·tion [plæn'teiʃn] plantación *f of tea, sugar etc.*; vega *f S.Am. of tobacco*; arboleda *f of trees*; **plant·er** ['plɑːntə] plantador *m*; colono *m*.

plaque [plɑːk] placa *f*.

plas·m(a) ['plæzm(ə)] plasma *m*.

plas·ter ['plɑːstə] **1.** yeso *m*; ⚠ argamasa *f*; (*layer*) enlucido *m*; ✚ emplasto *m*; (*adhesive*) esparadrapo *m*; ~cast vaciado *m*; ✚ tablilla *f* de yeso; ~ of Paris yeso *m* mate; **2.** enyesar, enlucir; ✚ emplastar; *fig.* cubrir, llenar (*with* de); *posters* pegar; *sl.* ~ed ajumado; **'plas·ter·er** enlucidor *m*, yesero *m*.

plas·tic ['plæstik] **1.** plástico; ~ sur-

gery cirugía *f* estética (*or* plástica); **2.** plástico *m*; **plas·ti·cine** ['~tisiːn] plasticina *f*; **plas·tic·i·ty** [~'tisiti] plasticidad *f*.

plate [pleit] **1.** plato *m*; (*plaque*) placa *f*; ⊕ lámina *f*, chapa *f*, plancha *f*; (*silver*) vajilla *f* de plata; *typ.* lámina *f*; *phot.* placa *f*; (*a. dental* ~) (placa *f* de la) dentadura *f* postiza; *racing:* premio *m*; F *hand s.o. s.t. on a* ~ servirle algo a alguien en bandeja; F *have a lot on one's* ~ estar muy ocupado; **2.** planchear, chapear; niquelar *etc.*

pla·teau ['plætou] meseta *f*.

plate·ful ['pleitful] plato *m*.

plate...: '~-glass vidrio *m* cilindrado; '~-hold·er *phot.* portaplacas *m*; '~-lay·er peón *m* (ferroviario).

plat·form ['plætfɔːm] plataforma *f*; tablado *m*; tribuna *f at meeting*; ⚑ andén *m*; *esp. Am. pol.* programa *m* electoral.

plat·ing ['pleitiŋ] enchapado *m*; capa *f* metálica.

plat·i·num ['plætinəm] platino *m*; ~ blonde rubia *f* platino.

plat·i·tude ['plætitjuːd] lugar *m* común, perogrullada *f*, platitud *f*; **plat·i·tu·di·nous** □ lleno de lugares comunes *etc.*

pla·toon [plə'tuːn] pelotón *m*.

plat·ter ['plætə] fuente *f*.

plau·dits ['plɔːdits] aplausos *m/pl.*

plau·si·ble ['plɔːzəbl] □ especioso, aparente; *p.* bien hablado pero nada confiable.

play [plei] **1.** juego *m* (*a.* ⊕), recreo *m*; *thea.* obra *f* dramática, pieza *f*; *fair* (*foul*) ~ juego *m* limpio (sucio); ~ *on words* juego *m* de palabras; *sport: in* ~ en juego; *out of* ~ fuera de juego; *come into* ~ entrar en juego; *go to the* ~ ir al teatro; *make great* ~ *with* recalcar, insistir en; **2.** *v/i.* jugar (*at* a); divertirse; ♪ tocar; *thea.* representar; (*fountain*) correr; (*light*) reverberar; ~ *fast and loose with* portarse de modo irresponsable con; ~ *for time* tratar de ganar tiempo; ~ (*up*)*on* valerse de; ~ *up to* hacer la pelotilla a; *v/t. card* jugar; *game, cards etc.* jugar a; *opponent* jugar con(tra); *player* incluir *in team*; ♪ tocar; *thea. play* representar, poner; *part* hacer; *fig.* desempeñar; *character* hacer el papel de; *trick* hacer (on a); *fish* dejar que se canse; *hose* dirigir; ~ *back* repetir (lo grabado); *v. ball*; ~ *off* A *against* B oponer A a B; *be* ~*ed out* estar agotado (*a. fig.*); F ~ *up* burlarse de (la autoridad de); '~**bill** cartel *m*; '~**boy** señorito *m* amante de los placeres; '**play·er** jugador (-a *f*) *m*; *thea.* actor *m*, actriz *f*; ♩ músico (a *f*) *m*; '**play·fel·low** compañero *m* de juego; **play·ful** ['~ful] □ juguetón; *remark* dicho en broma.

play...: '~**go·er** aficionado (a *f*) *m* al teatro; '~**ground** patio *m* de recreo; '~**house** teatro *m*; *Am.* casita *f* de muñecas.

play·ing...: '~**card** carta *f*; '~**field** campo *m* de deportes.

play...: '~**mate** compañero (a *f*) *m* de juego; '~**off** (partido *m* de) desempate *m*; '~**pen** parque *m* (de niño), corral *m*; '~**thing** juguete *m* (*a. fig.*); '~**time** hora *f* de recreo; '~**wright** dramaturgo *m*.

plea [pliː] pretexto *m*, disculpa *f*; ⚖ (alegato *m* de) defensa *f*; contestación *f* a la demanda; (*request*) petición *f* (*for* a favor de); *put in a* ~ *for p.* hablar por; *th.* pedir.

plead [pliːd] *v/i.* suplicar (*with acc.*), rogar (*with s.o. for* a uno que conceda); ⚖ abogar; '**plead·er** ⚖ abogado *m*; '**plead·ing** (*a.* ~*s pl.*) súplicas *f*/*pl.*; ⚖ alegatos *m*/*pl.*

pleas·ant ['pleznt] □ agradable; *surprise etc.* grato; *manner, style* ameno; *p.* simpático; '**pleas·ant·ry** chiste *m*, dicho *m* gracioso.

please [pliːz] *v/i.* gustar; dar satisfacción; ~ *tell me* haga Vd. el favor de decirme, dígame por favor; *as you* ~ como Vd. quiera; *if you* ~! iro. ¡fíjese!; *v/t.* gustar, dar gusto a, caer en gracia a; ~ *o.s.* hacer únicamente lo que uno quiere; ~ *yourself!* como Vd. quiera; *be* ~*d* estar contento; *be* ~*d to* complacerse en; *we are* ~*d to inform you* nos es grato informarle; *I am* ~*d to meet you* tengo mucho gusto en conocerle; *be* ~*d with* estar satisfecho de; '**pleased** alegre; contento; **pleas·ing** ['pliːziŋ] □ agradable, grato.

pleas·ur·a·ble ['pleʒərəbl] □ agradable, deleitoso.

pleas·ure ['pleʒə] placer *m*; gusto *m*; deleite *m*; (*will*) voluntad *f*; *it is a* ~ es un placer; *with (great)* ~ con (mucho) gusto; ~ *trip* viaje *m* de recreo; *take* ~ *in* deleitarse en *su., inf.*; *b.s.* gozarse en *inf.*

pleat [pliːt] 1. pliegue *m*; 2. plegar, plisar. [*a. su. m* (a *f*).|

ple·be·ian [pliˈbiːən] plebeyo *adj.*]

pleb·i·scite ['plebisit] plebiscito *m*.

plebs [plebz] plebe *f*.

pledge [pledʒ] 1. (*security*) prenda *f* (*a. fig.*); (*promise*) promesa *f*; (*toast*) brindis *m*; *as a* ~ *of* en señal de; F *sign the* ~ jurar abstenerse del alcohol; 2. (*pawn*) empeñar; (*promise*) prometer; (*toast*) brindar por.

ple·na·ry ['pliːnəri] plenario.

plen·i·po·ten·ti·ar·y [plenipəˈtenʃəri] plenipotenciario *adj. a. su. m.*

plen·i·tude ['plenitjuːd] plenitud *f*.

plen·te·ous ['plentiəs] □, **plen·ti·ful** ['plentiful] □ copioso, abundante.

plen·ty ['plenti] 1. abundancia *f*; *in* ~ en abundancia; *we have* ~ *of* tenenos bastante..., tenemos una cantidad suficiente de; 2. F: *know* ~ saber (lo) bastante; ~ *of people do* hay muchos que lo hacen; 3. *Am.* F completamente.

ple·o·nasm ['pliːənæzm] pleonasmo *m*.

pleth·o·ra ['pleθərə] plétora *f*; **ple·thor·ic** [pleˈθɔrik] □ pletórico.

pleu·ri·sy ['pluərisi] pleuresía *f*.

pli·a·ble ['plaiəbl] □, **pli·ant** ['plaiənt] □ flexible, plegable; *fig.* dócil, manejable.

pli·ers ['plaiəz] *pl.* (*a pair of* ~ unos) alicates *m*/*pl.*

plight[1] [plait] empeñar.

plight[2] [~] apuro *m*, aprieto *m*; condición *f* (inquietante), situación *f* (difícil).

plim·solls ['plimsəlz] zapatillas *f*/*pl.* de goma.

plinth [plinθ] plinto *m*.

plod [plɔd] (*a.* ~ *on,* ~ *one's way*) avanzar (*or* caminar) laboriosamente; trabajar laboriosamente (*away at* en); '**plod·der** estudiante *m*/*f etc.* más aplicado que brillante; '**plod·ding** □ perseverante, laborioso. [(oír un paf.|

plop [plɔp] 1. ¡paf!; 2. caer dejando]

plot[1] [plɔt] ⚹ parcela *f*, terreno *m*; (*building-*) solar *m*; cuadro *m* (de hortalizas *etc.*).

plot[2] [~] 1. complot *m*, conspiración

f; *thea. etc.* argumento *m*, trama *f*, intriga *f*; **2.** *v/t. course etc.* trazar; *downfall etc.* tramar, maquinar; *v/i.* conspirar, intrigar (to para); '**plot·ter** conspirador (-a *f*) *m*, conjurado (a *f*) *m*.

plough [plau] **1.** arado *m*; **2.** *v/t.* arar; *fig.* surcar; *univ. sl.* dar calabazas a, escabechar; †~ *back* reinvertir; ~ *up* arrancar con el arado; *v/i.* arar; *fig.* ~ *through snow etc.* abrirse con dificultad paso por; *book* leer con dificultad; '**plough·ing** arada *f*; '**plough·man** arador *m*; '**plough·share** reja *f* del arado.

plov·er ['plʌvə] chorlito *m*.

plow [plau] *Am.* = **plough**.

pluck [plʌk] **1.** valor *m*, ánimo *m*; **2.** *v/t.* coger; arrancar; *bird* desplumar; *guitar* puntear; *v. courage*; *v/i.*: ~ *at* tirar de, dar un tirón a; '**pluck·y** ['plʌki] □ valiente, animoso.

plug [plʌg] **1.** tapón *m*, taco *m*; tampón *m* (*a.* ⚕); *mot.* bujía *f*; ⚡ enchufe *m*; ⚡ (*wall*-) toma *f*; (*fire*-) boca *f* de agua; *sl.* anuncio *m* (*or* publicidad *f*) incidental; **2.** *v/t.* tapar, obturar; *tooth* empastar; *sl.* (*strike*) pegar; *sl.* (*shoot*) pegar un tiro a; *radio etc. sl.* dar publicidad incidental a; machacar en; ⚡ ~ *in* enchufar; *v/i. sl.* (*a.* ~ *away*) trabajar con ahinco (at en), seguir trabajando a pesar de todo; '~-**in** enchufable; '**plug·'ug·ly** *Am. sl.* bullanguero *m*.

plum [plʌm] ciruela *f*; (*a.* ~ *tree*) ciruelo *m*; F lo mejor; (*post*) pingüe destino *m*.

plum·age ['plu:midʒ] plumaje *m*.

plumb [plʌm] **1.** plomada *f*; **2.** *adj.* vertical, a plomo; **3.** *adv.* verticalmente, a plomo; F completamente; **4.** *fig.* sond(e)ar; **plum·ba·go** [~-'beigou] plombagina *f*; **plumb·er** ['~mə] fontanero *m*; **plum·bic** ['~mbik] plúmbico *m*; **plumb·ing** ['~miŋ] (*craft*) fontanería *f*; (*piping*) instalación *f* de cañerías; '**plumb·line** cuerda *f* de plomada.

plume [plu:m] pluma *f*; penacho *m on helmet, of smoke*.

plum·met ['plʌmit] **1.** plomada *f*; **2.** caer a plomo.

plump[1] [plʌmp] **1.** rechoncho, rollizo; *fowl etc.* gordo; **2.** engordar (*v/i. a. v/t.*); hinchar(se).

plump[2] [~] **1.** dejar(se) caer pesadamente; ~ *for* optar por; **2.** *adv.* de lleno.

plump·ness ['plʌmpnis] gordura *f*.

plum-pud·ding ['plʌm'pudiŋ] *pudín inglés* (*de Navidad*).

plun·der ['plʌndə] **1.** botín *m*, pillaje *m*; **2.** saquear, pillar; '**plun·der·er** saqueador *m*.

plunge [plʌndʒ] **1.** zambullida *f*; salto *m*; **2.** zambullir(se); sumergir (se); *fig.* arrojar(se); precipitar(se); hundir(se) *into grief etc.*; *dagger* hundir; (*horse*) corcovear; ⚓ cabecear; **plung·er** ['plʌndʒə] émbolo *m*.

plu·per·fect ['plu:'pə:fikt] pluscuamperfecto *m*.

plu·ral ['pluərəl] plural *adj. a. su. m*; **plu·ral·i·ty** [~'ræliti] pluralidad *f*.

plus [plʌs] **1.** *prp.* más, y; **2.** *adj.* ⚡ positivo; adicional; F y algo más, y pico; ~**fours** ['~'fɔ:z] *pl.* pantalones *m/pl.* holgados de media pierna.

plush [plʌʃ] **1.** felpa *f*; **2.** F lujoso, de buen tono.

plu·toc·ra·cy [plu:'tɔkrəsi] plutocracia *f*; **plu·to·crat** ['~təkræt] plutócrata *m/f*.

plu·to·ni·um [plu:'touniəm] plutonio *m*.

plu·vi·om·e·ter [plu:vi'ɔmitə] pluviómetro *m*.

ply [plai] **1.:** *three* ~ de tres capas; *wool* de tres cordones; **2.** *v/t. tool* manejar, menear (vigorosamente); *trade* ejercer; *p.* acosar, importunar *with questions*; ofrecer repetidas veces; *v/i.*: ~ *between* hacer el servicio entre; '~**wood** madera *f* contrachapeada, panel *m*.

pneu·mat·ic [nju'mætik] □ neumático; ~ *drill* perforadora *f*, martillo *m* picador; ~ *tyre* neumático *m*.

pneu·mo·ni·a [nju'mounjə] pulmonía *f*.

poach[1] [poutʃ] *v/t. a. v/i.* cazar (*or* pescar) en vedado; *fig.* cazar en finca ajena.

poach[2] [~] *egg* escalfar.

poach·er ['poutʃə] cazador *m* furtivo; '**poach·ing** caza *f* furtiva.

pock·et ['pɔkit] **1.** bolsillo *m*; *fig.* bolsa *f* (*a.* ✕, *geol.*), cavidad *f*; ✈ bolsa *f* de aire; *be in* ~ salir ganando; *be out of* ~ salir perdiendo; *pick s.o.'s* ~ robar la cartera *etc.* a alguien; **2.** embolsar; *b.s.* apropiarse; **3.** *attr.*

... de bolsillo; '~·**book** cartera *f*, portamonedas *m*; '~·**knife** cortaplumas *m*; '~·**mon·ey** dinero *m* para pequeños gastos personales; '~·**size** de bolsillo.

pock·marked ['pɔkmɑ:kt] picado de viruelas; *fig.* marcado de hoyos.

pod [pɔd] vaina *f*.

podg·y ['pɔdʒi] F gordinflón.

po·di·um ['poudiəm] ⚠ podio *m*.

po·em ['pouim] poesía *f*, poema *m*.

po·et ['pouit] poeta *m*; **po·et·as·ter** [~'tæstə] poetastro *m*; '**po·et·ess** poetisa *f*; **po·et·ic**, **po·et·i·cal** [pou-'etik(l)] □ poético; ~ *justice* justicia *f* poética; **po·et·ics** *pl.* poética *f*; '**po·et·ry** poesía *f*; *attr.* de poesía.

pog·rom ['pɔgrəm] pogrom(o) *m*, persecución *f* (antisemítica).

poign·an·cy ['pɔinənsi] patetismo *m*; intensidad *f*; '**poign·ant** □ conmovedor, patético; intenso, agudo.

point [pɔint] **1.** punto *m* (*a. sport, typ.*, ⚓; = *place, time*); (*sharp*) punta *f*; puntilla *f* of *pen*; *geog.* punta *f*, cabo *m*; cuarta *f* of *compass*; (*objective*) propósito *m*, finalidad *f*; gracia *f*, lo esencial of *joke*; rasgo *m* of *character*; ⚡ enchufe *m*, toma *f*; 🔍 ~s *pl.* agujas *f*/*pl.*; *the* ~ *is that* lo importante es que; *there is no* ~ *in ger.* no vale la pena *inf.*; ~ *of order* cuestión *f* de procedimiento; ~ *of view* punto *m* de vista; *in* ~ *of* en cuanto a; *in* ~ *of fact* en realidad; *off the* ~ fuera de propósito; *on* ~*s boxing*: por puntos; *up to a* ~ hasta cierto punto; *be beside the* ~ no venir al caso; *be on the* ~ *of* estar a punto de; *carry one's* ~ salirse con la suya; *come to the* ~ ir al grano, dejarse de historias; *keep to the* ~ no salir del tema; *make a* ~ *of ger.* insistir en *inf.*, no dejar de *inf.*; *make the* ~ *that* hacer ver que; *see the* ~ caer en la cuenta; *I do not see the* ~ *of ger.* no creo que sea necesario *inf.*; *speak to the* ~ hablar al caso; *stretch a* ~ hacer una excepción; **2.** *v/t.* (*sharpen*) afilar, aguzar; *pencil* sacar punta a; *gun etc.* apuntar (*at* a); ~ *a finger at* señalar con el dedo; ~ *out* indicar, señalar; advertir (*that* que); *v/i.*: *it* ~*s west* está orientado hacia el oeste; ~ *at* señalar (con el dedo); ~ *to* señalar; indicar (*a. fig.*); '~·'**blank** (*adj.* hecho *etc.*) a quemarropa (*a. fig.*); '~·**du·ty** control *m* de la circulación;

'**point·ed** □ puntiagudo; *remark* inequívoco; lleno de intención; '**point·er** indicador *m on gauge*; *fig.* indicación *f* (*to* de); (*dog*) perro *m* de muestra; '**point·less** □ inútil; '**point-to-'point** *carrera de caballos a través del campo.*

poise [pɔiz] **1.** equilibrio *m*; aplomo *m*; confianza *f* en sí mismo; **2.** *v/t.* equilibrar; balancear; *be* ~*d* estar suspendido; cernerse; *be* ~*d to inf.* estar ya en condiciones de *inf.*

poi·son ['pɔizn] **1.** veneno *m* (*a. fig.*); **2.** *attr.* venenoso; ~ *gas* gas *m* asfixiante; **3.** envenenar (*a. fig.*); '**poi·son·er** envenenador (-a *f*) *m*; '**poi·son·ing** envenenamiento *m*; '**poi·son·ous** □ venenoso; F pésimo.

poke [pouk] **1.** empuje *m*, empujón *m*; codazo *m*; hurgonazo *m* of *fire*; **2.** *v/t.* empujar; *hole* hacer a empujones; *fire* hurgar, atizar; introducir (*into* en); ~ *fun at* burlarse de; ~ *one's nose into* meterse en; *v/i.*: ~ *about*, ~ *around* andar buscando (vagamente).

pok·er[1] ['poukə] *approx.* atizador *m*, badila *f*.

po·ker[2] [~] *cards*: póker *m*, póquer *m*; ~ *face* cara *f* impasible.

pok·y ['pouki] *room* muy pequeño, mezquino.

po·lar ['poulə] polar; ~ *bear* oso *m* blanco; **po·lar·i·ty** [pou'lærəti]polaridad *f*; **po·lar·i·za·tion** [poulərai-'zeiʃn] polarización *f*; '**po·lar·ize** polarizar.

Pole[1] [poul] polaco (a *f*) *m*.

pole[2] [~] *geog.*, ⚡ *etc.* polo *m*.

pole[3] [~] *medida de longitud* (= *5,029 m.*); *palo m*, vara *f* larga; (*flag-*) asta *f*; (*tent-*) mástil *m*; (*telegraph-*) poste *m*; (*vaulting- etc.*) pértiga *f*; *sl. up the* ~ en un aprieto; chiflado; '~·**ax(e)** desnucar; '~·**cat** turón *m*; *Am.* mofeta *f*.

po·lem·ic [pɔ'lemik] **1.** (*a.* **po·lem·i·cal** □) polémico; **2.** (*a.* **po·lem·ics** *pl.*) polémica *f*.

pole·star ['poulstɑ:] estrella *f* polar; *fig.* norte *m*.

pole·vault ['poulvɔ:lt] salto *m* con pértiga.

po·lice [pə'li:s] **1.** policía *f*; ~ *court* tribunal *m* de policía; ~ *force* (cuerpo *m* de) policía *f*; ~ *state* estado-policía *m*; **2.** *frontier* vigilar, patrullar; *area* mantener servicio de policía en; '**~·man** guardia m, policíam; agente m de policía; '**~·sta·tion** comisaría f; '**~·wom·an** policía m femenino.

pol·i·cy ['pɔlisi] política f; programa m político; normas f/pl. de conducta of *newspaper etc.*; (*insurance*) póliza f; ~ *holder* tenedor (-a f) m de póliza.

po·li·o(**·my·e·li·tis**) ['pouliou(maiə-'laitis)] polio(mielitis) f.

Pol·ish¹ ['pouliʃ] polaco *adj. a. su. m*.

pol·ish² ['pɔliʃ] **1.** (*shine*) lustre m, brillo m, bruñido m; (*act*) pulimento m; (*shoe-*) betún m; (*floor-*) cera f de lustrar; *fig.* finura f; perfección f; **2.** *floor etc.* encerar, sacar brillo a; *pans etc.* abrillantar; *shoes* limpiar; *silver etc.* pulir; ⊕ pulimentar; *fig.* (a. ~ *up*) pulir, limar; F *~ off* acabar con; '**pol·ished** *fig.* fino, elegante, acabado; '**pol·ish·er** (*p.*) pulidor (-a f) m; (*machine*) enceradora f; '**pol·ish·ing 1.** el pulir *etc.*; **2.** *attr.* de lustrar *etc.*; ~ *machine* enceradora f.

po·lite [pə'lait] □ cortés, atento, fino; *society* bueno, culto; **po'lite·ness** cortesía f *etc.*

pol·i·tic ['pɔlitik] □ prudente, aconsejable; *body* ~ el estado; **po·lit·i·cal** [pə'litikl] □ político; **pol·i·ti·cian** [pɔli'tiʃn] político m; *b.s.* politiquero m; **pol·i·tics** ['pɔlitiks] política f; *v. party*; **pol·i·ty** ['pɔliti] gobierno m; estado m.

pol·ka ['pɔlkə] polca f; *Am.* diseño m de puntos.

poll [poul] **1.** (*election*) votación f, elección f; (*total votes*) votos m/pl.; (*public opinion* ~) organismo m de sondaje; (*inquiry*) encuesta f, sondeo m; *go to the* ~(s) ir a votar; *take a* ~ hacer una encuesta; **2.** *v/t. votes* recibir; *cattle* descornar; *v/i.* recibir (muchos, *10.000 etc.*) votos.

pol·lard ['pɔləd] **1.** árbol m desmochado; **2.** desmochar; **3.** desmochado.

pol·len ['pɔlin] polen m; **pol·lin·ate** ['pɔlineit] fecundar (con polen).

poll·ing ['pouliŋ] votación f; '**~·booth** caseta f de votar; '**~·day** día m de elecciones; '**~·sta·tion** urnas f/pl. electorales.

poll-tax ['poultæks] capitación f.

pol·lute [pə'lu:t] *water etc.* contami-

nar, ensuciar; *fig.* corromper; **pol·lu·tion** contaminación f; corrupción f.

po·lo ['poulou] polo m.

pol·troon [pɔl'tru:n] cobarde m/f.

po·lyg·a·mist [pə'ligəmist] polígamo (a f) m; **po·lyg·a·my** [pə'ligəmi] poligamia f; **pol·y·glot** ['pɔliglɔt] políglotо *adj. a. su. m* (a f); **pol·y·gon** ['~gən] polígono m; **po·lyg·o·nal** [pə'ligənl] poligonal; **pol·y·phon·ic** [~'fɔnik] □ polifónico; **pol·yp** ['~ip], **pol·y·pus** ['~pəs] pólipo m; **pol·y·syl·lab·ic** ['pɔli'sil'læbik] □ polisílabo; **pol·y·syl·la·ble** ['~siləbl] polisílabo m; **pol·y·tech·nic** [~'teknik] escuela f de formación profesional; **pol·y·the·ism** ['~θiizm] politeísmo m; **po·ly·thene** ['~θi:n] politene m.

po·made [pə'mɑ:d], **po·ma·tum** [pə'meitəm] pomada f.

pome·gran·ate ['pɔmigrænit] granada f.

pom·mel ['pʌml] **1.** pomo m; **2.** apuñear, dar de puñetazos.

pomp [pɔmp] pompa f; **pom·pos·i·ty** [pɔm'pɔsiti] pomposidad f *etc.*; '**pomp·ous** □ pomposo; *language* hinchado.

pond [pɔnd] charca f; (*artificial*) estanque m; (*fish-*) vivero m.

pon·der ['pɔndə] *v/t. a. v/i.* ponderar, considerar con especial cuidado; meditar (*on, over acc.*); '**pon·der·ous** □ pesado; laborioso.

pone [poun] *Am.* pan m de maíz.

pon·iard ['pɔnjəd] *lit.* puñal m.

pon·tiff ['pɔntif] pontífice m; **pon·tif·i·cal** □ pontificio, pontifical; **pon·tif·i·cate 1.** [~kit] pontificado m; **2.** [~keit] pontificar.

pon·toon [pɔn'tu:n] pontón m; *cards:* veintiuna f; ~ *bridge* puente m de pontones.

po·ny ['pouni] jaca f, caballito m, poney m; *Am.* F chuleta f.

pooch [pu:tʃ] *Am. sl.* perro m.

poo·dle ['pu:dl] perro m de lanas.

pooh [pu:] ¡bah!, ¡qué va!

pooh-pooh [pu:'pu:] rechazar con desdén; negar importancia a.

pool [pu:l] **1.** charca f; (*artificial*) estanque m; (*swimming-*) piscina f; pozo m, remanso m *in river*; charco m *of spilt liquid*; *billiards:* trucos m/pl.; *cards etc.:* polla f; (*football-*) quinielas f/pl.; *fig.* mancomunidad *f*, fusión *f* de intereses; ✝ fondo *m* común; 2. *resources* juntar, mancomunar.

poop [puːp] popa *f*.

poor [pue] □ pobre; *quality* malo, bajo; *spirit* mezquino; *the* ~ los pobres; *be in* ~ *health* tener mala salud; '~-**box** cepo *m* para los pobres; '~-**house** asilo *m* de los pobres; '~-**law** *ley acerca de los menesterosos*; '**poor·ly** 1. *adj.* enfermo; 2. *adv.* pobremente; mal.

pop[1] [pɔp] 1. ligera detonación *f*; taponazo *m of cork*; ruido *m* seco *of fastener etc.*; F gaseosa *f*; 2. *v/t*. F poner (rápidamente); *sl.* empeñar; F ~ *the question* declararse; *v/i.* estallar (con ligera detonación); reventar; F ~ *in* entrar de sopetón, dar un vistazo; F ~ *out* salir un momento; F ~ *up* aparecer inesperadamente; 3. ¡pum!

pop[2] [~] F (*abbr. of popular*): ~ *concert* concierto *m* popular.

pop[3] [~] *mst Am.* F papá *m*.

pop·corn ['pɔpkɔːn] *esp. Am.* rosetas *f/pl.*, palomitas *f/pl.*

pope [poup] papa *m*; **pop·er·y** ['~əri] papismo *m*.

pop-eyed ['pɔpaid] de ojos saltones.

pop·gun ['pɔpɡʌn] taco *m*, fusil *m* de juguete.

pop·ish ['poupiʃ] papista, católico.

pop·lar ['pɔplə] (*white*) álamo *m*; (*black*) chopo *m*.

pop·lin ['pɔplin] popelín *m*, popelina *f*.

pop·py ['pɔpi] amapola *f*, adormidera *f*; '~-**cock** F ¡tonterías! (*a. su. f/pl.*).

pop·sy ['pɔpsi] *sl.* chica *f*.

pop·u·lace ['pɔpjuləs] pueblo *m*; *contp.* populacho *m*.

pop·u·lar ['pɔpjulə] □ popular; **pop·u·lar·i·ty** [~'læriti] popularidad *f*; **pop·u·lar·ize** ['~ləraiz] popularizar, vulgarizar.

pop·u·late ['pɔpjuleit] poblar; **pop·u·la·tion** población *f*; habitantes *m/pl.*

pop·u·lous ['pɔpjuləs] □ populoso.

por·ce·lain ['pɔːslin] porcelana *f*.

porch [pɔːtʃ] pórtico *m*; entrada *f*.

por·cu·pine ['pɔːkjupain] puerco *m*\

pore[1] [pɔː] poro *m*. [espín.\

pore[2] [~]: ~ *over* estar absorto en el estudio de; estudiar larga y detenidamente.

pork [pɔːk] carne *f* de cerdo (*or* puerco); '**pork·er** cerdo *m*, cochino *m*; '**pork·y** F gordo.

por·no·graph·ic [pɔːnə'ɡræfik] pornográfico; **por·no·gra·phy** [pɔː'nɔɡrəfi] pornografía *f*.

po·ros·i·ty [pɔː'rɔsiti], **po·rous·ness** ['pɔːrəsnis] porosidad *f*; **po·rous** ['pɔːrəs] □ poroso.

por·phy·ry ['pɔːfiri] pórfido *m*.

por·poise ['pɔːpəs] marsopa *f*.

por·ridge ['pɔridʒ] *approx.* gachas *f/pl.* de avena.

port[1] [pɔːt] ⚓ (*harbour*) puerto *m*.

port[2] [~] ⚓ (~*hole*) portilla *f*; ✝ tronera *f*; ⊕ lumbrera *f*.

port[3] [~] ⚓ 1. (*a.* ~ *side*) babor *m*; 2. *helm* poner a babor.

port[4] [~] vino *m* de Oporto.

port·a·ble ['pɔːtəbl] portátil.

por·tage ['pɔːtidʒ] porteo *m*.

por·tal ['pɔːtl] puerta *f* (grande e imponente).

port·cul·lis [pɔːt'kʌlis] rastrillo *m*.

por·tend [pɔː'tend] pronosticar; presagiar, augurar.

por·tent ['pɔːtent] presagio *m*, augurio *m*; **por·ten·tous** □ portentoso.

por·ter ['pɔːtə] portero *m*, conserje *m*; ☵ mozo *m* (de estación); (*beer*) cerveza *f* negra; ~'s *lodge* conserjería *f*; **por·ter·age** ['~ridʒ] porte *m*; '**por·ter·house**: *Am.* ~ *steak* biftec *m* de filete.

port·fo·li·o [pɔːt'fouljou] cartera *f* (*a. pol.*), carpeta *f*; *without* ~ sin cartera.

port·hole ['pɔːthoul] portilla *f*.

por·ti·co ['pɔːtikou] pórtico *m*.

por·tion ['pɔːʃn] 1. porción *f*, parte *f*; (*dowry*) dote *f*; (*helping*) ración *f*; 2. (*a.* ~ *out*) repartir, dividir.

port·li·ness ['pɔːtlinis] corpulencia *f*; '**port·ly** corpulento; grave.

port·man·teau [pɔːt'mæntou] baúl *m* de viaje; ~ *word* palabra *f* híbrida.

por·trait ['pɔːtrit] retrato *m*; ~ *painter* = '**por·trait·ist** retratista *m/f*; **por·trai·ture** ['~tʃə] arte *m* de retratar; retrato *m*.

por·tray [pɔː'trei] retratar; *fig.* describir; **por·tray·al** *fig.* descripción *f* (gráfica), representación *f*.

Por·tu·guese [pɔːtju'ɡiːz] 1. portugués *adj. a. su. m* (-a *f*); 2. (*language*) portugués *m*.

pose [pouz] 1. postura *f of body*; *fig.* afectación *f*, pose *f*; 2. *v/t. problem* plantear; *question* hacer, formular; v/i. (*model*) posar; darse tono (*affectedly*); ~ *as* hacerse pasar por, echárselas de; **'pos·er** pregunta *f* (*or* problema *m*) difícil.

posh [pɔʃ] F elegante, de lujo, lujoso; de mucho rumbo; cursi.

po·si·tion [pə'ziʃn] 1. posición *f*, situación *f*; categoría *f*; (*post*) puesto *m*, colocación *f*; (*opinion*) opinión *f*; *be in a* ~ *to* estar en condiciones de *inf.*; 2. colocar, disponer.

pos·i·tive ['pɔzətiv] 1. □ positivo (*a.* ⚡, ⚸, *phot.*); (*affirmative*) afirmativo; (*emphatic*) enfático, categórico; *be* ~ *that* estar seguro de que; F *it's a* ~ *nuisance* es realmente una molestia; ~*ly* realmente, absolutamente; 2. *phot.* positiva *f*; **'pos·i·tiv·ism** positivismo *m*.

pos·se ['pɔsi] *Am.* fuerza civil armada bajo el mando del *Sheriff* etc.; *fig.* grupo *m*, pelotón *m*.

pos·sess [pə'zes] poseer (*a. be* ~*ed of*); ~ *o.s.* of tomar posesión de, apoderarse de; *be* ~*ed by idea* estar dominado por; *what can have* ~*ed you?* ¿cómo lo has podido hacer?; **pos·sessed** [~t] poseído, poseso; **pos·ses·sion** [pə'zeʃn] posesión *f*; ~*s pl.* bienes *m/pl.*; *in the* ~ *of* en poder de; *take* ~ *of* tomar posesión de; **pos·ses·sive** [pə'zesiv] 1. □ *gr.* posesivo; *love etc.* dominante, tiránico; 2. posesivo *m*; **pos·ses·sor** poseedor (-a *f*) *m*.

pos·si·bil·i·ty [pɔsə'biliti] posibilidad *f*; **'pos·si·ble** □ posible; *as frequent(ly) as* ~ lo más frecuente(mente) posible; *as soon as* ~ cuanto antes; *do as much as* ~ *to* hacer lo posible para; *bring as much as* ~ traer todo lo que puede uno; **'pos·si·bly** posiblemente; tal vez; *if I* ~ *can* a serme posible; *he cannot* ~ *go* le es absolutamente im-

post[1] [poust] poste *m*. [posible ir.]

post[2] [~] 1. (*job*) puesto *m*; destino *m*; cargo *m*; ✗ etc. puesto *m*; ✍ correo *m*; (*casa f de*) correos; (*collection*) recogida *f*; (*delivery*) entrega *f*; *by* ~ por correo; *by return of* ~ a vuelta de correo; *go to the* ~ ir a correos, ir al buzón; 2. *poster etc.* fijar, pegar; ✍ echar al correo; mandar por correo, despachar; ✗ etc. situar, apostar; mandar (*to a*); *keep a p.* ~*ed* tener a una p. al corriente.

post·age ['poustidʒ] franqueo *m*, porte *m*; ~ *due* a pagar; ~ *stamp* sello *m* (de correo), estampilla *f* *S.Am.*

post·al ['poustəl] □ postal, de correos; *Am.* ~ (*card*) postal *f*; ~ *order approx.* giro *m* postal.

post…: **'~·box** buzón *m*; **'~·card** (tarjeta *f*) postal *f*; **'~·date** poner fecha adelantada a.

poste res·tante ['poust'resta:nt] lista *f* de correos.

post·er ['poustə] cartel *m*.

pos·te·ri·or [pɔs'tiəriə] 1. posterior; 2. F *co.* asentaderas *f/pl.*

pos·ter·i·ty [pɔs'teriti] posteridad *f*.

pos·tern ['poustə:n] postigo *m*.

post·free ['poust'fri:] porte pagado, franco de porte.

post·grad·u·ate ['poust'grædjuit] postgraduado *adj. a. su. m* (a *f*); ~ *course* curso *m* para postgraduados.

post·haste ['poust'heist] a toda prisa, con toda urgencia.

post·hu·mous ['pɔstjuməs] □ póstumo.

pos·til·(l)ion [pəs'tiljən] postillón *m*.

post…: **'~·man** cartero *m*; **'~·mark** 1. matasellos *m*; 2. matar (el sello de); **'~·mas·ter** administrador *m* de correos; ♀ *General* director *m* general de correos.

post·me·rid·i·an ['poustmə'ridiən] postmeridiano; **post·mor·tem** ['~·'mɔ:təm] autopsia *f*.

post…: **'~·of·fice** (casa *f* de) correos; ~ *general* administración *f* de correos; ~ *box* apartado *m* (de correos); ~ *savings bank* caja *f* postal de ahorros; **'~·paid** porte pagado, franco de porte.

post·pone [poust'poun] aplazar; **post'pone·ment** aplazamiento *m*.

post·pran·di·al [poust'prændiəl] *co.* de sobremesa; *walk etc.* que se da después de comer.

post·script ['pousskript] posdata *f*.

pos·tu·late 1. ['pɔstjulit] postulado *m*; 2. ['~leit] postular; **pos·tu·la·tion** postulación *f*.

pos·ture ['pɔstʃə] 1. postura *f*, actitud *f*; 2. adoptar una actitud (afectada).

post·war ['poust'wɔ:] de (la) pos(t)guerra.

po·sy ['pouzi] ramillete *m* de flores.

pot [pɔt] 1. (*cooking*) olla *f*, puchero *m*, marmita *f*; (*preserving*) tarro *m*, pote *m*; (*flower-*) tiesto *m*; (*chamber-*)

orinal *m*; F copa *f*; F ～*s pl.* montones
m|*pl.*; F big ～ pez *m* gordo; F go to ～
echarse a perder, arruinarse; **2.** *v*|*t.*
food conservar (en botes *etc.*); *plant*
poner en tiesto; ✗ F matar (a tiros);
v|*i.* F disparar (*at* contra).

pot·ash ['pɔtæʃ] potasa *f.*

po·tas·si·um [pə'tæsiəm] potasio *m.*

po·ta·tions [pou'teiʃnz] *pl.* libacio-
nes *f*|*pl.*

po·ta·to [pə'teitou], *pl.* **po·ta·toes**
[～z] patata *f*, papa *f S.Am.*

pot...: '～**-bel·lied** barrigón; '～**-boil·
er** obra *f* mediocre compuesta para
ganar dinero.

po·ten·cy ['poutənsi] potencia *f*;
'**po·tent** □ potente; poderoso, eficaz; *drink etc.* fuerte; **po·ten·tate**
['～teit] potentado *m*; **po·ten·tial**
[pə'tenʃl] potencial *adj. a. su. m*;
po·ten·ti·al·i·ty [～ʃi'æliti] potencialidad *f.*

poth·er ['pɔðə] alharaca *f*, aspaviento *m*; lío *m.*

pot-hole ['pɔthoul] bache *m in road*;
geol. marmita *f* de gigante; '～**-hol·
ing** espeleología *f.*

po·tion ['pouʃn] poción *f*, pócima *f.*

pot-luck ['pɔt'lʌk]: take ～ comer
(*fig.* tomar) lo que haya.

pot-shot ['pɔtʃɔt] tiro *m* a corta distancia; tiro *m* al azar.

pot·ter[1] ['pɔtə] ocuparse en fruslerías; ～ round the house hacer bagatelas en casa.

pot·ter[2] [～] alfarero *m*; ～'s clay arcilla *f* de alfarería; ～'s wheel torno *m*
de alfarero; '**pot·ter·y** (*works, art*)
alfarería *f*; (*pots*) cacharros *m*|*pl.*;
(*archaeological etc.*) cerámicas *f*|*pl.*

pot·ty ['pɔti] *sl.* (*small*) insignificante, miserable; (*mad*) chiflado.

pouch [pautʃ] bolsa *f*; *hunt. etc.* morral *m*, zurrón *m*; (*tobacco-*) petaca *f*;
✗ cartuchera *f.*

poul·ter·er ['poultərə] pollero *m.*

poul·tice ['poultis] **1.** cataplasma *f*,
emplasto *m*; **2.** poner una cataplasma a, emplastar.

poul·try ['poultri] aves *f*|*pl.* de
corral; ～ farm granja *f* avícola; ～
house gallinero *m*; ～ keeper avicultor *m.*

pounce [pauns] **1.** salto *m*; ataque *m*
súbito; **2.** atacar súbitamente; ～ on
saltar sobre (*a. fig.*), precipitarse
sobre, caer sobre.

pound[1] [paund] libra *f* (= *453,6*

gr.); ～ (*sterling*) libra *f* (esterlina)
(*abbr.* £ = *20 shillings*).

pound[2] [～] corral *m* de concejo.

pound[3] [～] *v*|*t.* machacar, martillar,
aporrear; dar de puñetazos *with
fists*; (*grind*) moler; ✗ bombardear;
v|*i.* dar golpes (*at* en); *door etc.*
aporrear (en); (*run*) correr *etc.*
pesadamente.

pound·age ['paundidʒ] impuesto *m*
exigido por cada libra.

pound·er ['paundə] de ... libras.

pour [pɔ:] *v*|*t.* (*a.* ～ out) echar, ver-
ter, derramar (*a. fig.*); *smoke* arro-
jar; ～ away, ～ out vaciar; *v*|*i.* correr,
fluir (abundantemente); (*rain*) diluviar; ～ in (*out*) entrar (salir) a
raudales, entrar (salir) a montones.

pout [paut] **1.** puchero *m*, mala
cara *f*; **2.** *v*|*t.*: ～ one's lips = *v*|*i.*
hacer pucheros, poner mala cara.

pov·er·ty ['pɔvəti] pobreza *f*, miseria *f*; escasez *f*; ～ stricken extremadamente pobre.

pow·der ['paudə] **1.** polvo *m*; (*face-*)
polvos *m*|*pl.*; (*gun-*) pólvora *f*;
2. (*reduce to* ～) pulverizar(se); (*dust
with* ～) polvorear; *face, o.s.* empolvarse, ponerse polvos; ～ed milk
leche *f* en polvo; '～**-com·pact** polvera *f*; '～**-puff** borla *f* para empolvarse; '**pow·der·y** *substance* en
polvo; pulverizado; *surface* polvoriento; empolvado.

pow·er ['pauə] poder *m* (*a.* ∰);
poderío *m*; autoridad *f*; *pol.*, ⚖
potencia *f*; ⊕ potencia *f*, energía *f*;
⚡ fuerza *f*; (*gift*) facultad *f* (*of* de);
(*drive*) empuje *m*, energía *f*; the ～s
that be las autoridades (actuales);
be in ～ estar en el poder; do all in
one's ～ hacer lo posible (*to* por);
'～**-cut** corte *m* de corriente, apagón
m; '～**-drill** taladradora *f* de fuerza;
pow·er·ful ['～ful] □ poderoso; ⊕
potente; *build* fuerte; *emotion etc.*
intenso; *argument* convincente;
'**pow·er-house** central *f* eléctrica;
⊕ fábrica *f* de fuerza motriz;
'**pow·er·less** □ impotente; sin
fuerzas (*to* para); sin autoridad (*to*
para).

pow·er...: '～**-line** ⚡ línea *f* de
fuerza; '～**-load·er** ✗ rompedora-
cargadora *f*; '～**-plant** grupo *m* electrógeno; '～**-sta·tion** central *f* eléctrica; '～**-tool** herramienta *f* mecánica.

pow·wow ['pau'wau] *fig.* conferencia *f*.

pox [pɔks] F sífilis *f*.

prac·ti·ca·ble ['præktikəbl] □ practicable, hacedero; **'prac·ti·cal** □ práctico; ~ *joke* trastada *f*, broma *f* pesada; **prac·ti·cal·i·ty** [⌣'kæliti] espíritu *m* práctico; **prac·ti·cal·ly** ['⌣kli] prácticamente; casi, punto menos que.

prac·tice ['præktis] **1.** práctica *f*; costumbre *f*; ejercicio *m*; ⚖ clientela *f*; *in* ~ (*not theory*) en la práctica; *be out of* ~ haber perdido la costumbre; *sport:* estar desentrenado; *make a* ~ *of ger.* acostumbrar *inf.*; *put into* ~ poner por obra; ~ *makes perfect* la práctica hace maestro; **2.** *Am.* = *practise*.

prac·tise [⌣] *v/t.* practicar; '*profession etc.* ejercitar, ejercer; *piano etc.* hacer prácticas de; *sport:* hacer ejercicios de, entrenarse en; ~ *ger.* ensayarse a *inf.*; *v/i.* ensayarse, hacer ensayos (*on* en); (*professionally*) ejercer (*as* de); ⚖ practicar la medicina; **'prac·tised** *eye etc.* experto; **'prac·tis·ing** practicante.

prac·ti·tion·er [præk'tiʃnə] facultativo *m*, práctico *m*; *general* ~ médico *m* general.

prag·mat·ic [præg'mætik] □ pragmático.

prai·rie ['preəri] pradera *f*, pampa *f* S.Am.

praise [preiz] **1.** alabanza(s) *f(pl.)*, elogio(s) *m(pl.)*; **2.** alabar, elogiar; **'~·wor·thy** □ loable, digno de alabanza.

pram [præm] F cochecito *m* de niño.

prance [prɑːns] cabriolar, encabritarse.

prank [præŋk] travesura *f*; broma *f*.

prate [preit] parlotear, charlar.

prat·tle ['prætl] **1.** parloteo *m*; (*child's*) balbuceo *m*; **2.** parlotear; (*child*) balbucear.

prawn [prɔːn] gamba *f*; (*large*) langostino *m*.

pray [prei] *v/i.* (*say one's prayers*) rezar; orar (*for* por, *to* a); *v/t.* rogar, pedir, suplicar (*for acc.*); ~ *tell* me haga el favor de decirme.

pray·er ['preə] oración *f*, rezo *m*; (*entreaty*) súplica *f*, ruego *m*; *Book of Common* ♀ *liturgia de la Iglesia Anglicana*; *say one's* ~*s* rezar; '~·**book** devocionario *m*, misal *m*.

pre... [priː, pri] pre...; ante...

preach [priːtʃ] predicar (*a.* F, *b.s.*); *advantages etc.* celebrar; **'preach·er** predicador *m*; **'preach·ing** predicación *f*; *b.s.* sermoneo *m*.

pre·am·ble [priː'æmbl] preámbulo *m*.

pre·ar·range [priːə'reindʒ] arreglar (*or* fijar) de antemano.

preb·end ['prebənd] prebenda *f*; **'pre·ben·dar·y** prebendado *m*.

pre·car·i·ous [pri'kɛəriəs] □ precario.

pre·cau·tion [pri'kɔːʃn] precaución *f*; **pre'cau·tion·ar·y** de precaución, preventivo.

pre·cede [priː'siːd] preceder; **pre'ced·ence**, **pre'ced·en·cy** [⌣dəns(i)] precedencia *f*; *take* ~ *over* primar sobre; **prec·e·dent** ['presidənt] precedente *m*; **pre'ced·ing** precedente.

pre·cen·tor [priː'sentə] chantre *m*.

pre·cept ['priːsept] precepto *m*; **pre·cep·tor** [pri'septə] preceptor *m*.

pre·cinct ['priːsiŋkt] recinto *m*; *Am.* distrito *m* electoral; barrio *m*; ~*s pl.* contornos *m/pl.*; *within the* ~*s of* dentro de los límites de.

pre·ci·os·i·ty [presi'ɔsiti] preciosismo *m*.

pre·cious ['preʃəs] **1.** □ precioso; *p.* amado, querido; *style* afectado, rebuscado; **2.** *adv.* F muy.

prec·i·pice ['presipis] precipicio *m*, despeñadero *m*; **pre·cip·i·tance**, **pre·cip·i·tan·cy** [pri'sipitəns(i)] precipitación *f*; **pre'cip·i·tate 1.** [⌣teit] precipitar (*a.* ♣); **2.** [⌣] ♣ precipitado *m*; **3.** [⌣tit] precipitado; **pre·cip·i·ta·tion** [⌣'teiʃn] precipitación *f*; **pre'cip·i·tous** □ escarpado, cortado a pico.

pré·cis ['preisiː] resumen *m*.

pre·cise [pri'sais] □ preciso, exacto; (*too* ~) afectado; *p.* escrupuloso, meticuloso; ~*ly!* perfectamente, eso es; **pre'cise·ness**, **pre·ci·sion** [pri'siʒn] (*attr.* de) precisión *f*, exactitud *f*.

pre·clude [pri'kluːd] excluir, imposibilitar.

pre·co·cious [pri'kouʃəs] □ precoz; **pre'co·cious·ness**, **pre·coc·i·ty** [pri'kɔsiti] precocidad *f*.

pre·con·ceived ['priːkən'siːvd] preconcebido.

pre·con·cep·tion ['priːkən'sepʃn] preconcepción f.

pre·cool ['priː'kuːl] preenfriar.

pre·cur·sor [priː'kəːsə] precursor (-a f) m.

pred·a·to·ry ['predətəri] rapaz, de rapiña; depredador.

pre·de·cease ['priːdiˈsiːs] morir antes que.

pre·de·ces·sor ['priːdisesə] predecesor (-a f) m, antecesor (-a f) m.

pre·des·ti·na·tion [priːdestiˈneiʃn] predestinación f; **pre·des·tine** [priː'destin] predestinar.

pre·de·ter·mine ['priːdi'təːmin] predeterminar.

pre·dic·a·ment [pri'dikəmənt] apuro m, situación f difícil; phls. predicamento m.

pred·i·cate ['predikit] gr. predicado m.

pre·dict [pri'dikt] pronosticar, predecir; **pre·dic·tion** [ˌ'dikʃn] pronóstico m, predicción f.

pre·di·lec·tion [priːdiˈlekʃn] predilección f.

pre·dis·pose ['priːdis'pouz] predisponer; **pre·dis·po·si·tion** ['ˌdispə-'ziʃn] predisposición f.

pre·dom·i·nance [pri'dɔminəns] predominio m; **pre·dom·i·nant** □ predominante; ˌly por la mayor parte, en su mayoría; **pre·dom·i·nate** [ˌneit] predominar.

pre·em·i·nence [priː'eminəns] preeminencia f; **pre·'em·i·nent** □ preeminente.   [empción f.⎫

pre·emp·tion [priː'empʃn] pre-⎭

preen [priːn] feathers arreglarse (con el pico); fig. ˌ o.s. pavonearse, atildarse.

pre·ex·ist ['priːigˈzist] preexistir; **'pre·ex'ist·ence** preexistencia f; **'pre·ex'ist·ent** preexistente.

pre·fab ['priːfæb] F casa f prefabricada; **'pre'fab·ri·cate** [ˌrikeit] prefabricar; ˌd prefabricado.

pref·ace ['prefis] 1. prólogo m, prefacio m; 2. book etc. prologar; fig. decir etc. a modo de prólogo a; introducir; be ˌd by tener ... a modo de prólogo.

pref·a·to·ry ['prefətəri] preliminar, a modo de prólogo.

pre·fect ['priːfekt] prefecto m; school: monitor m.

pre·fer [pri'fəː] preferir (to inf.; A to B A a B); p. ascender, pro-

mover to post; charge etc. hacer, presentar; **pref·er·a·ble** ['prefər-əbl] □ preferible; **'pref·er·a·bly** preferentemente, más bien; **'pref·er·ence** preferencia f; ˌ shares pl. acciones f/pl. preferentes; **pref·er·en·tial** [ˌ'renʃl] □ preferente; **pre·fer·ment** [pri'fəːmənt] promoción f, ascenso m.

pre·fix 1. ['priːfiks] prefijo m; 2. [priːˈfiks] prefijar.

preg·nan·cy ['pregnənsi] embarazo m; **'preg·nant** □ embarazada, encinta, en estado; fig. preñado, lleno (with de).

pre·heat ['priː'hiːt] precalentar.

pre·hen·sile [pri'hensail] prensil.

pre·his·tor·ic ['priːhis'tɔrik] prehistórico.

pre·ig·ni·tion ['priːigˈniʃn] preignición f.

pre·judge ['priːˈdʒʌdʒ] prejuzgar.

prej·u·dice ['predʒudis] 1. prejuicio m; parcialidad f; without ˌ to sin perjuicio de; 2. chances etc. perjudicar; prevenir, predisponer (against contra); ˌd parcial, interesado; lleno de prejuicios.

prej·u·di·cial [predʒu'diʃl] □ perjudicial.

prel·ate ['prelit] prelado m.

pre·lim·i·nar·y [pri'liminəri] preliminar adj. a. su. m; **pre'lim·i·na·ries** [ˌz] pl. preliminares m/pl., preparativos m/pl.

prel·ude ['preljuːd] 1. preludio m (a. ♪); 2. preludiar (a. ♪).

pre·mar·i·tal [pri'mæritl] premarital.

pre·ma·ture [premə'tjuə] prematuro; ˌ baldness calvicie f precoz.

pre·med·i·tate [priː'mediteit] premeditar; **pre·med·i'ta·tion** premeditación f.

pre·mi·er ['premjə] 1. primero, principal; 2. primer ministro m; **pre·mi·ère** ['premiəə] estreno m; **'pre·mi·er·ship** cargo m del primer ministro.

prem·ise ['premis] premisa f; ˌs pl. local m, casa f, tienda f etc.; on the ˌs en el local, in situ.

pre·mi·um ['priːmjəm] ✝ premio m; (insurance) prima f; be at a ˌ ✝ estar sobre la par; fig. estar en gran demanda; put a ˌ on estimular, fomentar; premiar (de modo injusto).

pre·mo·ni·tion [priːməˈniʃn] presentimiento *m*, premonición *f*; **pre·mon·i·to·ry** [priˈmɔnitəri] □ premonitorio.

pre·na·tal [ˈpriːˈneitl] prenatal.

pre·oc·cu·pa·tion [priːɔkjuˈpeiʃn] preocupación *f*; **pre·oc·cu·pied** [ˌɔkjupaid] preocupado; **pre·oc·cu·py** [ˌpai] preocupar.

pre·or·dain [ˈpriːɔːˈdein] predestinar.

prep [prep] F = *preparation*, *preparatory*.

pre·pack·aged [priˈpaekidʒd] precintado.

prep·a·ra·tion [prepəˈreiʃn] preparación *f*; ~*s pl.* preparativos *m*/*pl.*; **pre·par·a·to·ry** [ˌtəri] 1. preparatorio, preliminar; ~ *school* escuela privada para los muchachos de 8 a 12 años (*que pasan después a una public school*); 2. *adv.*: ~ *to* con miras a, antes de.

pre·pare [priˈpeə] preparar(se), disponer(se), prevenir(se); ~ *to* disponerse a; *be* ~*d* estar listo; *be* ~*d to* estar dispuesto a; *be* ~*d for anything* estar dispuesto a aguantarlo todo; *no dejarse sorprender*; **pre·par·ed·ness** preparación *f* (*militar etc.*).

pre·pay [ˈpriːˈpei] [*irr.* (*pay*)] pagar por adelantado; **ˈpreˈpay·ment** pago *m* adelantado.

pre·pon·der·ance [priˈpɔndərəns] preponderancia *f*; **preˈpon·der·ant** □ preponderante; **preˈpon·der·ate** [ˌreit] preponderar.

prep·o·si·tion [prepəˈziʃn] preposición *f*; **prep·o·si·tion·al** □ preposicional.

pre·pos·sess·ing [priːpəˈzesiŋ] □ agradable, atractivo.

pre·pos·ter·ous [priˈpɔstərəs] □ absurdo, ridículo.

pre·puce [ˈpriːpjuːs] prepucio *m*.

pre·req·ui·site [ˈpriːˈrekwizit] requisito *m* previo.

pre·rog·a·tive [priˈrɔgətiv] prerrogativa *f*.

pres·age [ˈpresidʒ] 1. presagio *m*; 2. **pre·sage** [ˌ, *a.* priˈseidʒ] presagiar.

pres·by·ter [ˈprezbitə] presbítero *m*; **Pres·by·te·ri·an** [ˌˈtiəriən] presbiteriano *adj. a. su. m* (a *f*); **pres·by·ter·y** [ˈˌtəri] presbiterio *m*.

pre·sci·ence [ˈpreʃiəns] presciencia *f*; **ˈpre·sci·ent** presciente.

pre·scribe [prisˈkraib] prescribir, ordenar; ✗ recetar.

pre·scrip·tion [prisˈkripʃn] prescripción *f*; ✗ receta *f*; **preˈscrip·tive** □ legal; sancionado por la costumbre.

pre·seal·ed [priˈsiːld] precintado.

pres·ence [ˈprezns] presencia *f*; asistencia *f* (*at* a); ~ *of mind* presencia *f* de ánimo; *in the* ~ *of* ante, en presencia de.

pres·ent¹ [ˈpreznt] 1. □ presente, actual; ~*!* ¡presente!; *those* ~ los presentes; ~ *company excepted* mejorando lo presente, con perdón de los presentes; *be* ~ asistir (*at* a); 2. presente *m*; actualidad *f*; *gr.* tiempo *m* presente; *at* ~ actualmente; *al presente*; *for the* ~ por ahora.

pre·sent² [priˈzent] presentar, ofrecer, dar; *case* exponer; ~ *o.s.* presentarse; ~ *arms!* ¡presenten armas!; ~ *with* obsequiar con; *occasion* deparar.

pres·ent³ [ˈpreznt] regalo *m*, presente *m*; *make a* ~ *of* regalar; *fig.* dar medio regalado.

pre·sent·a·ble [priˈzentəbl] presentable.

pres·en·ta·tion [prezənˈteiʃn] presentación *f*; (*present*) obsequio *m*; ~ *copy* ejemplar *m* con dedicatoria del autor.

pres·ent-day [ˈprezntdei] actual.

pre·sen·ti·ment [priˈzentimənt] presentimiento *m*, corazonada *f*; *have a* ~ *that* presentir que.

pres·ent·ly [ˈprezntli] luego, dentro de poco.

pres·er·va·tion [prezəˈveiʃn] conservación *f*; preservación *f*; *in good* ~ bien conservado; **pre·serv·a·tive** [priˈzɔːvətiv] preservativo *adj. a. su. m.*

pre·serve [priˈzɔːv] 1. conservar; preservar (*from* contra); guardar (*from* de); 2. conserva *f*; confitura *f*, compota *f*; *hunt.* vedado *m*; **preˈserved** *food* en conserva; **preˈserv·er** preservador *m*.

pre·side [priˈzaid] presidir (*at*, *over acc.*).

pres·i·den·cy [ˈprezidənsi] presidencia *f*; **ˈpres·i·dent** presidente *m*; *Am.* ✝ director *m*; *Am. univ.* rector *m*; **pres·i·den·tial** [ˌˈdenʃl] presidencial.

press [pres] **1.** ⊕ *etc.* prensa *f*; imprenta *f*; (*pressure*) presión *f*; urgencia *f* *of affairs*; apiñamiento *m* *of people*; *be in* ~ estar en prensa; *go to* ~ entrar en prensa; *have a bad* ~ tener mala prensa; **2.** *v/t.* ⊕ *etc.* prensar; apretar; *button etc.* pulsar, presionar, empujar; *clothes* planchar; *fig.* abrumar, acosar; apremiar; *claim* insistir en; ~ *s.t.* (*up*)*on s.o.* insistir en que uno acepte algo; ~ *s.o. to do s.t.* instar a uno a hacer algo; *be* ~*ed for time* tener poco tiempo; ~ *the point* insistir (*that* en que); ~ *into service* utilizar; *v/i.* urgir, apremiar; (*people*) apiñarse; *time* ~*es* el tiempo apremia; ~ *for* hacer propaganda a favor de; reclamar, pedir con urgencia; ~ *forward*, ~ *on* seguir adelante (a pesar de todo); **3.** *attr.* de prensa; de presión; '~-**a·gen·cy** agencia *f* de información; ~ **agent** agente *m* de publicidad; '~-**box** tribuna *f* de la prensa; '~-'**con·fer·ence** conferencia *f* de prensa; '~-**cut·ting** recorte *m* de periódico; '**press·ing** □ urgente, apremiante, acuciante; '**press·man** periodista *m*; '**press·mark** signatura *f*.

pres·sure ['preʃə] presión *f* (*a.* ⊕, *meteor.*); *fig.* urgencia *f*, apremio *m*; ⚕ tension *f* (nerviosa); impulso *m*, influencia *f*; '~-**cook·er** olla *f* a presión; '~-**gauge** manómetro *m*; '~-**group** grupo *m* de presión; '**pres·sur·ized cabin** cabina *f* a presión (*or* altimática). [*m.*\]

press-view ['presvju:] pre-estreno *m*
pres·ti·dig·i·ta·tion ['prestididʒi-'teiʃn] prestidigitación *f*.
pres·tige [pres'ti:ʒ] prestigio *m*.
pre·stressed con·crete ['pri:strest kɔnkri:t] hormigón *m* pretensado.
pre·sum·a·bly [pri'zju:məbli] *adv.* según cabe presumir; ~ *it was he* supongó que era él; **pre'sume** presumir, suponer; ~ *to atreverse a;* ~ (*up*)*on* abusar de.
pre·sump·tion [pri'zʌmpʃn] presunción *f*; pretensión *f*; *the* ~ *is that* puede presumirse que; **pre'sump·tive** *heir* presunto; **pre'sump·tu·ous** [~tjuəs] □ presuntuoso, presumido.
pre·sup·pose [pri:sə'pouz] presuponer; **pre·sup·po·si·tion** [pri:sʌpə-'ziʃn] presuposición *f*.

pre·tence, *Am.* **pre·tense** [pri'tens] (*claim*) pretensión *f*; (*display*) ostentación *f*; (*pretext*) pretexto *m*; fingimiento *m*; *false* ~*s pl.* fraude *m*.
pre·tend [pri'tend] (*feign*) fingir, aparentar; (*claim*) pretender (*to acc.*); ~ *to quality* afirmar tener; ~ *to be asleep* fingir dormir, fingirse dormido; ~ *to be ill* fingirse enfermo; ~ *to be su.* fingirse *su.*, hacerse el (la) *su.*; **pre'tend·ed** □ pretendido; **pre'tend·er** pretendiente *m/f*.
pre·ten·sion [pri'tenʃn] pretensión *f*; *have* ~*s to culture* tener pretensiones de cultura.
pre·ten·tious [pri'tenʃəs] □ pretencioso, presuntuoso; (*ostentatious*) aparatoso, ambicioso; cursi.
pret·er·it(e) ['pretərit] pretérito *m*.
pre·ter·nat·u·ral [pri:tə'nætʃrəl] □ preternatural.
pre·text ['pri:tekst] pretexto *m*; *under* ~ *of* so pretexto de.
pret·ti·fy ['pritifai] embellecer adornar (de modo ridículo).
pret·ti·ness ['pritinis] lindeza *f*.
pret·ty ['priti] **1.** □ bonito, guapo, lindo; precioso, mono; *sum etc.* considerable; *iro.* bueno; **2.** *adv.* bastante, algo; ~ *difficult* bastante difícil; ~ *much the same* más o menos lo mismo; ~ *near ruined* casi arruinado; *be sitting* ~ estar en posición muy ventajosa.
pre·vail [pri'veil] prevalecer, imponerse; (*conditions*) reinar, imperar; ~ *upon* persuadir, inducir (*to* a); *be* ~*ed upon to* dejarse persuadir a *inf.*; **pre'vail·ing** reinante, imperante; predominante; general.
prev·a·lence ['prevələns] uso *m* corriente, costumbre *f*; frecuencia *f*; predominio *m*; '**prev·a·lent** □ corriente; extendido; frecuente; predominante.
pre·var·i·cate [pri'værikeit] buscar evasivas, tergiversar.
pre·vent [pri'vent] impedir ([*from*] *ger. inf.*), evitar, estorbar; **pre'vent·a·ble** evitable; **pre'vent·a·tive** [~tətiv] *v. preventive;* **pre'ven·tion** prevención *f*; el impedir; **pre·ven·tive** **1.** □ preventivo, impeditivo; ~ *medicine* medicina *f* preventiva; **2.** preservativo *m*.
pre·view ['pri:vju:] pre-estreno *m*; *fig.* vista *f* anticipada.

pre·vi·ous ['pri:viəs] □ previo, anterior; F prematuro; ~ *to* antes de; ~*ly* previamente, con anticipación; antes.

pre-war ['pri:'wɔ:] de (la) preguerra.

prey [prei] **1.** presa *f*, víctima *f*; *bird of* ~ ave *f* de rapiña; *be a* ~ *to* ser víctima de; **2.**: ~ (*up*)*on* atacar, alimentarse de, pillar; *mind etc.* agobiar, remorder, preocupar.

price [prais] **1.** precio *m*; *at any* ~ a toda costa; *not at any* ~ de ningún modo; ~ *control* control *m* de precios; ~ *list* lista *f* de precios; **2.** tasar, fijar el precio de; '**price-less** inapreciable; F divertidísimo, absurdo.

prick [prik] **1.** pinchazo *m*, punzada *f*; alfilerazo *m* *with pin*; **2.** *v/t.* pinchar, punzar; agujerear; marcar con agujerillos; *conscience* remorder; ✗ ~ *out* plantar; ~ *up one's ears* aguzar las orejas; *v/i.*: ~ *up* prestar atención; **prick·le** ['~l] espina *f*, pincho *m*, púa *f*; '**prick-ly** espinoso; lleno de púas; *p.* malhumorado; ✗ ~ *heat* salpullido *m* causado por exceso de calor; ~ *pear* chumbera *f*.

pride [praid] **1.** orgullo *m*; *b.s.* soberbia *f*, arrogancia *f*; *take* ~ *of place* venir primero, ocupar el primer puesto; *take* (*a*) ~ *in* = **2.**: ~ *o.s. on* enorgullecerse de, preciarse de.

priest [pri:st] sacerdote *m*; cura *m*; '**priest·ess** sacerdotisa *f*; '**priest-hood** ['~hud] (*function*) sacerdocio *m*; (*priests collectively*) clero *m*; '**priest·ly** sacerdotal.

prig [prig] presumido (*a f*) *m*; pedante *m/f*; mojigato *m*; '**prig-gish** □ presumido; pedante; mojigato.

prim [prim] □ (*a.* ~ *and proper*) remilgado; etiquetero, estirado.

pri·ma·cy ['praiməsi] primacía *f*; **pri·ma don·na** ['pri:mə dɔnə] primadonna *f*, diva *f*; **pri·ma·ri·ly** ['~rili] ante todo; '**pri·ma·ry 1.** □ primario; **2.** *Am. parl. elección preliminar para nombrar candidatos*; **pri·mate** ['~mit] *eccl.* primado *m*; *zo.* primate *m*.

prime [praim] **1.** primero; principal; fundamental; *quality* selecto, de primera clase; ✗ primo; ~ *minister* primer ministro *m*; ~

number número *m* primo; **2.** flor *f*, lo mejor; ~ *of life* la flor de la vida; **3.** *gun, pump* cebar; *surface etc.* preparar; *fig.* informar de antemano, instruir clandestinamente; (*with drink*) hacer beber, emborrachar.

prim·er ['praimə] cartilla *f*; libro *m* de texto elemental.

pri·me·val [prai'mi:vəl] primitivo, prístino.

prim·ing ['praimiŋ] preparación *f*; primera capa *f of paint*; *attr.* de cebar.

prim·i·tive ['primitiv] □ primitivo; rudimentario, sencillo; F sucio, sórdido. ؛

pri·mo·gen·i·ture [praimou'dʒenitʃə] primogenitura *f*.

pri·mor·di·al [prai'mɔ:diəl] □ primordial.

prim·rose ['primrouz] primavera *f*; ~ *path* caminito *m* de rosas.

prince [prins] príncipe *m*; '**prince-ly** principesco, magnífico; **prin-cess** [prin'ses; *before name* 'prinsis] princesa *f*.

prin·ci·pal ['prinsəpəl] **1.** □ principal; *gr.* ~ *parts pl.* partes *f/pl.* principales; **2.** principal *m* (*a.* ✝, ₰); director (*-a f*) *m of college etc.*; **prin·ci·pal·i·ty** [prinsi'pæliti] principado *m*.

prin·ci·ple ['prinsəpl] principio *m*; *in* ~ en principio; *on* ~ por principio.

print [print] **1.** (*mark*) marca *f*, impresión *f*; *typ.* tipo *m*; (*picture*) estampa *f*, grabado *m*; *phot.* impresión *f*, positiva *f*; (*cloth, dress*) estampado *m*; *in* ~ impreso; disponible; *in* (*cold*) ~ en letras de molde; *out of* ~ agotado; **2.** *dress* estampado; **3.** (hacer) imprimir (*a. phot.*); (*write*) escribir en caracteres de imprenta; '**print·ed** impreso; *dress etc.* estampado; *v. matter*; '**print·er** impresor *m*; ~'*s devil* aprendiz *m* de imprenta; ~'*s ink* tinta *f* de imprenta.

print·ing ['printiŋ] impresión *f*; tipografía *f*; (*quantity*) tirada *f*; *attr.* ... de imprenta; '~-**frame** prensa *f* de copiar; '~-**ink** tinta *f* de imprenta; '~-**of·fice** imprenta *f*; '~-**press** prensa *f* de imprenta.

pri·or ['praiə] **1.** anterior; previo; **2.** *adv.*: ~ *to* antes de; hasta; **3.** *eccl.* prior *m*; '**pri·or·ess** priora *f*;

pri·or·i·ty [ˌ'ɔriti] prioridad *f*, precedencia *f*; **pri·o·ry** ['ˌ'əri] priorato *m*.

prise [praiz]: ~ *open* abrir por fuerza; abrir con una palanca; ~ *up* levantar con una palanca.

prism ['prizm] prisma *m*; ~ *binoculars* prismáticos *m/pl.*; **pris·mat·ic** [priz'mætik] □ prismático.

pris·on ['prizn] cárcel *f*, prisión *f*; *put in* ~ encarcelar; ~ *camp* campamento *m* para prisioneros; **'pris·on·er** ⚒ preso (a *f*) *m*; ✗ prisionero *m*; *take* ~ hacer prisionero.

pris·sy ['prisi] *Am.* F remilgado, melindroso.

pris·tine ['pristain] prístino.

pri·va·cy ['praivəsi] secreto *m*, reserva *f*, retiro *m*; aislamiento *m*; intimidad *f*.

pri·vate ['praivit] **1.** □ privado; particular; secreto, reservado; *report etc.* confidencial; *conversation etc.* íntimo; *view* particular, personal; ~*!* prohibida la entrada; ~ *enterprise* iniciativa *f* privada; *in* ~ *life* en la intimidad; *parl.* ~ *member* miembro *m* (*que no lo es del gobierno*); ~ *secretary* secretario *m* particular; ~ *view* inauguración *f* privada; **2.** ✗ (*or* ~ *soldier*) soldado *m* raso; ~*s pl.*, ~ *parts pl.* partes *f/pl.* pudendas; *in* ~ en privado, en secreto.

pri·va·teer [praivi'tiə] corsario *m*.

pri·va·tion [prai'veiʃn] estrechez *f*, miseria *f*.

pri·va·tive ['privətiv] privativo.

priv·et ['privit] ligustro *m*.

priv·i·lege ['privilidʒ] **1.** privilegio *m*, prerrogativa *f*; **2.** privilegiar; *be* ~*d to* tener el privilegio de; **'priv·i·leged** privilegiado.

priv·y ['privi] **1.** □: *be* ~ *to* estar enterado secretamente de; ♀ *Council* consejo *m* privado; ~ *parts pl.* partes *f/pl.* pudendas; ~ *purse* gastos *m/pl.* personales del monarca; ♀ *Seal* sello *m* pequeño; **2.** retrete *m*.

prize¹ [praiz] **1.** premio *m*; ⚓ *etc.* presa *f*; **2.** premiado; digno de premio; de primera clase; ~ *money* premio *m*; ⚓ parte *f* de presa; **3.** apreciar, estimar.

prize² [ˌ] = *prise*.

prize…: **'~-fight·er** boxeador *m* profesional; **'~-giv·ing** distribu-

ción *f* de premios; **'~-win·ner** premiado (a *f*) *m*.

pro¹ [prou] en pro de; *v. con.*

pro² [ˌ] F profesional *m/f*.

prob·a·bil·i·ty [prɔbə'biliti] probabilidad *f*; *in all* ~ según toda probabilidad; **'prob·a·ble** □ probable; **'prob·a·bly** probablemente; *he* ~ *forgot* lo habrá olvidado.

pro·bate ['proubit] verificación *f* oficial de los testamentos.

pro·ba·tion [prə'beiʃn] probación *f*; ⚒ *approx.* libertad *f* condicional; *on* ~ a prueba; ⚒ bajo libertad condicional; ~ *officer oficial que vigila las personas que están en régimen de libertad condicional*; **pro·'ba·tion·ar·y** de prueba; ⚒ ~ *period* período *m* de libertad condicional; **pro'ba·tion·er** ⚒ persona *f* en régimen de libertad condicional; *eccl.* novicio (a *f*) *m*; ✚ aprendiza *f* de enfermera.

probe [proub] **1.** ✚ sonda *f*; (*rocket*) cohete *m*, proyectil *m*; *fig.* F investigación *f* (*into* de), encuesta *f*; **2.** ✚ sondar, tentar; *fig.* indagar, investigar.

prob·i·ty ['proubiti] probidad *f*.

prob·lem ['prɔbləm] problema *m*; *attr.* F difícil; **prob·lem·at·ic**, **prob·lem·at·i·cal** [ˌbli'mætik(l)] problemático, dudoso. [F nariz *f*.]

pro·bos·cis [prə'bɔsis] próboscide *f*.

pro·ce·dur·al [prə'siːdʒərəl] procesal; **pro'ce·dure** [ˌdʒə] procedimiento *m*, proceder *m*; trámites *m/pl.*

pro·ceed [prə'siːd] proceder; (*continue*) seguir, continuar; obrar; ~ *against* proceder contra, procesar; ~ *from* proceder de, provenir de; salir de; ~ *on one's way* seguir su camino; ~ *to election* proceder a; *place* ir a, trasladarse a; ~ *to say etc.* decir *etc.* a continuación; (*unexpectedly*) ~ *to inf.* ponerse a *inf.*; ~ *with* proseguir; **pro'ceed·ing** procedimiento *m*; ~*s pl.* actos *m/pl.*; transacciones *f/pl.*; (*published*) actas *f/pl.*; ⚒ *take* ~ proceder, proceder *m*, procedimiento *m*; *take* (*legal*) ~*s* entablar demanda, instruir causa; *take* ~*s against* proceder contra; **pro·ceeds** ['prou-siːdz] *pl.* ganancia *f*, producto *m*; ingresos *m/pl.*

proc·ess ['prouses] **1.** procedimiento *m*, proceso *m*; *in* ~ *of construction* bajo construcción, en (vía de) construcción; in the ~ of time andando el tiempo; **2.** ⊕ preparar, tratar (into para hacer); **'pro·cess·ing** tratamiento m; **pro·ces·sion** [prǝ'seʃn] desfile m; eccl. procesión f; funeral ~ cortejo m fúnebre.

pro·claim [prǝ'kleim] proclamar; ~ o.s. king proclamarse rey.

proc·la·ma·tion [prɔklǝ'meiʃn] proclamación f.

pro·cliv·i·ty [prǝ'kliviti] propensión f, inclinación f.

pro·cras·ti·nate [prǝ'kræstineit] hablar etc. paro aplazar una decisión, no decidirse; **pro·cras·ti·na·tion** falta f de decisión, dilación f, discusión f etc. dilatoria.

pro·cre·ate ['proukrieit] procrear; **pro·cre·a·tion** procreación f; **'pro·cre·a·tive** procreador.

proc·tor ['prɔktǝ] ⚓ procurador m; univ. oficial que cuida de la disciplina.

pro·cur·a·ble [prǝ'kjuǝrǝbl] asequible.

proc·u·ra·tor ['prɔkjureitǝ] procurador m.

pro·cure [prǝ'kjuǝ] v/t. obtener (a p. a th. algo para alguien), conseguir; lograr; gestionar; girl obtener para la prostitución; v/i. alcahuetear; **pro'cure·ment** obtención f; **pro'cur·er** alcahuete m; **pro'cur·ess** alcahueta f.

prod [prɔd] **1.** empuje m; codazo m with elbow; **2.** empujar; codear with elbow; fig. pinchar.

prod·i·gal ['prɔdigǝl] □ pródigo (of de); the ~ son el hijo pródigo; **prod·i·gal·i·ty** [~'gæliti] prodigalidad f.

pro·di·gious [prǝ'didʒǝs] □ prodigioso; enorme, ingente; **prod·i·gy** ['prɔdidʒi] prodigio m; (a. child ~, infant ~) niño m prodigio.

pro·duce 1. ['prɔdjuːs] producto(s) m(pl.) (esp. agrícolas); **2.** [prǝ'djuːs] producir; line prolongar; (show) presentar, mostrar; sacar; (cause) causar, ocasionar, motivar; thea. (stage) presentar; actors dirigir; **pro'duc·er** productor (-a f) m; thea. director m de escena.

prod·uct ['prɔdǝkt] producto m; **pro·duc·tion** [prǝ'dʌkʃn] producción f; producto m; thea. (re)presentación f; **pro'duc·tive** □ pro-

ductivo; ~ of que produce...; abundante en, prolífico en; error etc. con tendencia a causar...; **pro·duc·tiv·i·ty** [prɔdʌk'tiviti] productividad f.

prof [prɔf] F profesor m.

prof·a·na·tion [prɔfǝ'neiʃn] profanación f; **pro·fane** [prǝ'fein] **1.** □ profano; impío; language etc. fuerte, indecente; **2.** profanar; **pro·fan·i·ty** [prǝ'fæniti] blasfemia f, impiedad f; F lenguaje m indecente, palabrotas f/pl.

pro·fess [prǝ'fes] profesar; declarar, confesar; regret etc. manifestar; ~ o.s. unable to inf. declararse incapaz de inf.; ~ to be su. pretender ser su.; **pro'fessed** □ declarado; b.s. supuesto; eccl. profeso; **pro'fess·ed·ly** [~idli] declaradamente; b.s. supuestamente.

pro·fes·sion [prǝ'feʃn] profesión f; **pro'fes·sion·al** □ profesional (a. su. m/f), de profesión; **pro'fes·sion·al·ism** [~ǝlizm] sport: profesionalismo m.

pro·fes·sor [prǝ'fesǝ] profesor (-a f) m (universitario [a]), catedrático (a f) m; **pro'fes·sor·ship** cáte-\
prof·fer ['prɔfǝ] ofrecer; [dra f.\
pro·fi·cien·cy [prǝ'fiʃǝnsi] pericia f, habilidad f; **pro'fi·cient** □ perito, hábil (at, in en).

pro·file ['proufail] perfil m.

prof·it ['prɔfit] **1.** ganancia f (✝, a. ~s pl.); fig. provecho m, beneficio m; utilidad f; ~ and loss ganancias f/pl. y pérdidas; **2.** v/t. servir a, aprovechar a; v/i.: ~ by, ~ from aprovechar, sacar partido de; he does not seem to have ~ed no parece haber sacado provecho de ello; **'prof·it·a·ble** □ provechoso; **prof·it·eer** [~'tiǝ] **1.** acaparador m, el que hace ganancias excesivas; **2.** hacer ganancias excesivas; **prof·it·eer·ing** (negocios m/pl. que dan) ganancias f/pl. excesivas; **'prof·it·less** □ inútil; **prof·it·shar·ing** ['~ʃɛǝriŋ] participación f en los beneficios by workers, reparto m de los beneficios by company.

prof·li·ga·cy ['prɔfligǝsi] libertinaje m; **prof·li·gate** ['~git] □ libertino adj. a. su. m.

pro·found [prǝ'faund] □ profundo; **pro·fun·di·ty** [~'fʌnditi] profundidad f.

pro·fuse [prə'fju:s] □ profuso, abundante; pródigo; **pro'fuse·ness**, **pro·fu·sion** [‿'fju:ʒn] profusión *f*.

pro·gen·i·tor [prou'dʒenitə] progenitor *m*; **prog·e·ny** ['prɔdʒini] progenie *f*, prole *f*.

prog·no·sis [prɔg'nousis], *pl.* **prog·'no·ses** [‿si:z] pronóstico *m*.

prog·nos·tic [prɔg'nɔstik] **1.** pronóstico *m*; **2.** pronosticador, pronóstico; **prog'nos·ti·cate** [‿keit] pronosticar; **prog·nos·ti'ca·tion** pronosticación *f*, pronóstico *m*.

pro·gram *Am.*, **pro·gramme** ['prougræm] programa *m*.

prog·ress 1. ['prougres] progreso(s) *m(pl.)*; marcha *f*; *in* ‿ en vía de realizarse *etc.*; *make* ‿ = **2. pro·gress** [prə'gres] progresar, hacer progresos; **pro'gres·sion** [‿ʃn] progresión *f* (*a.* ♃); **pro'gres·sive** □ progresivo; *pol.* progresista (*a. su. m/f*).

pro·hib·it [prə'hibit] prohibir; **pro·hi·bi·tion** [proui'biʃn] prohibición *f*; **pro·hi'bi·tion·ist** *Am.* prohibicionista *m/f*; **pro·hib·i·tive** [prə'hibitiv] □ prohibitivo; *price* exorbitante.

proj·ect ['prɔdʒekt] proyecto *m*.

pro·ject [prə'dʒekt] *v/t.* proyectar; *v/i.* (sobre)salir; resaltar; **pro·jec·tile** [prə'dʒektail] proyectil *m*; **pro·'ject·ing** saliente; **pro'jec·tion** proyección *f*; (*overhang etc.*) saliente *m*, resalto *m*; **pro'jec·tor** *film*: proyector *m*.

pro·le·tar·i·an [proule'teəriən] proletario *adj. a. su. m* (*a f*); **pro·le·'tar·i·at(e)** [‿riət] proletariado *m*.

pro·lif·ic [prə'lifik] □ prolífico (*of* en).

pro·lix ['prouliks] prolijo; **pro'lix·i·ty** prolijidad *f*.

pro·logue, *Am. a.* **pro·log** ['proulɔg] prólogo *m* (*a. fig.*).

pro·long [prə'lɔŋ] prolongar, alargar; **pro·lon·ga·tion** [proulɔŋ-'geiʃn] prolongación *f*.

prom·e·nade [prɔmi'na:d] **1.** paseo *m*; (*seaside*) paseo *m* marítimo; ‿ *deck* cubierta *f* de paseo; **2.** pasear (se).

prom·i·nence ['prɔminəns] prominencia *f*; *fig.* eminencia *f*; **'prom·i·nent** □ saliente, prominente; *eyes* saltones; *fig.* eminente, conspicuo.

prom·is·cu·i·ty [prɔmis'kju:iti] pro-

miscuidad *f*; **prom·mis·cu·ous** [prə-'miskjuəs] □ promiscuo.

prom·ise ['prɔmis] **1.** promesa *f*; *have* ‿, *be of (great)* ‿ prometer (mucho); **2.** prometer (*to inf.*); asegurar; (*augur*) augurar, pronosticar; *I* ‿ *you* se lo aseguro; *v. land*; **'prom·is·ing** □ que promete; **'prom·is·so·ry note** pagaré *m*.

prom·on·to·ry ['prɔməntri] promontorio *m*.

pro·mote [prə'mout] promover, fomentar; ascender *in rank*; *discussion etc.* estimular, facilitar; *parl. bill* presentar; *campaign* apoyar; ✝ *business* gestionar; *company* fundar, financiar; **pro'mot·er** promotor *m*; ✝ fundador *m*; *boxing:* empresario *m*, promotor *m*; **pro'mo·tion** promoción *f*, fomento *m*; ascenso *m in rank*.

prompt [prɔmpt] **1.** □ pronto, puntual; **2.** *adv.* puntualmente; *5 o'clock* ‿ las 5 en punto; **3.** mover, incitar, estimular (*to* a); *thought etc.* inspirar, sugerir; *thea.* apuntar; **4.** ✝ plazo *m*; ✝ *thea.* apuntador *m*; '‿-box concha *f*; **'prompt·er** apuntador *m*; **promp·ti·tude** ['‿itju:d], **'prompt·ness** prontitud *f*, puntualidad *f*.

pro·mul·gate ['prɔməlgeit] promulgar; **pro·mul·ga·tion** promulgación *f*.

prone [proun] postrado (boca abajo); *fig.* ‿ *to* propenso a; **'prone·ness** *fig.* propensión *f* (*to* a).

prong [prɔŋ] punta *f*, púa *f*; **pronged** [‿d] de ... puntas.

pro·nom·i·nal [prə'nɔminl] □ pronominal.

pro·noun ['prounaun] pronombre *m*.

pro·nounce [prə'nauns] *v/t.* pronunciar (*a. ♃*); (*with adj.*) declarar, juzgar; *v/i.:* ‿ *on* expresar una opinión sobre, juzgar *acc.*; **pro·'nounced** marcado, fuerte; decidido; **pro'nounce·ment** declaración *f*; decisión *f*; opinión *f*.

pron·to ['prɔntou] *Am.* F pronto.

pro·nun·ci·a·tion [prənʌnsi'eiʃn] pronunciación *f*.

proof [pru:f] **1.** prueba *f* (*a. typ.*); graduación *f* normal *of alcohol*; *in* ‿ *of* en prueba de, en comprobación de; *be* ‿ *against* ser (*or* estar) a prueba de; **2.** *drink* de graduación normal; ~ *against* a prueba de; *bullet*-~ a prueba de balas; **3.** impermeabilizar; '~-**read·er** corrector *m* (de pruebas); '~-**sheets** pruebas *f/pl.*; '~-**spir·it** licor *m* de prueba.

prop [prɔp] **1.** △ puntal *m*; sostén *m* (*a. fig.*); ✗ entibo *m*; ✗ rodrigón *m*; **2.** (*a. ~ up*) apuntalar; apoyar, sostener (*a. fig.*).

prop·a·gan·da ['prɔpə'gændə] propaganda *f*; **prop·a'gan·dist** propagandista *m/f*; **prop·a·gate** ['prɔpəgeit] propagar; **prop·a'ga·tion** propagación *f*.

pro·pel [prə'pel] ⊕ impeler, impulsar; empujar; **pro'pel·lent** propulsor *m*; **pro'pel·ler** hélice *f*; **pro·'pel·ling pen·cil** lapicero *m*.

pro·pen·si·ty [prə'pensiti] propensión *f* (*to* a).

prop·er ['prɔpə] □ propio (*to* de); conveniente, apropiado; (*decent*) decente, decoroso; (*prim and ~*) relamido, etiquetero; F (*fully formed*) hecho y derecho; consumado; *row etc.* de todos los diablos; *what is ~* lo que está bien; *architecture ~* la arquitectura propiamente dicha; *in the ~ sense of the word* en el sentido estricto de la palabra; *~ name* nombre *m* propio; '**prop·er·ly**: *do s.t. ~* hacer algo bien (*or* como hace falta); (*correctly*) correctamente, debidamente; *behave ~* portarse correctamente, portarse decorosamente; *it puzzled him ~* le confundió completamente; '**prop·er·ty** (*estate, quality*) propiedad *f*; hacienda *f*; bienes *m/pl.*; *man of ~* hacendado *m*; *thea. properties pl.* accesorios *m/pl.*; '**prop·er·ty-tax** impuesto *m* sobre la propiedad.

proph·e·cy ['prɔfisi] profecía *f*; **proph·e·sy** ['~sai] profetizar; *fig.* augurar, prever.

proph·et ['prɔfit] profeta *m*; **prophet·ic, proph·et·i·cal** [prə'fetik(l)] □ profético.

pro·phy·lac·tic [prɔfi'læktik] □ profiláctico *adj. a. su. m.*

pro·pin·qui·ty [prə'piŋkwiti] propincuidad *f*; (*kinship*) consanguinidad *f*.

pro·pi·ti·ate [prə'piʃieit] propiciar; conciliar; **pro·pi·ti·a·tion** propiciación *f*; **pro'pi·ti·a·to·ry** [~ʃiətəri] propiciatorio, conciliatorio.

pro·pi·tious [prə'piʃəs] □ propicio.

pro·por·tion [prə'pɔ:ʃn] **1.** proporción *f*; *in ~ as* a medida que; *in ~ to* en proporción con, a medida de; *out of ~* desproporcionado; *be out of ~* no guardar proporción (*to, with* con); **2.**: *well etc. ~ed* bien *etc.* proporcionado; **pro'por·tion·al** □ proporcional; *~ representation* representación *f* proporcional; **pro·'por·tion·ate** [~it] □ proporcionado.

pro·pos·al [prə'pouzəl] propuesta *f*, proposición *f*; oferta *f*; (*a. ~ of marriage*) oferta *f* de matrimonio, declaración *f*; **pro'pose** *v/t.* proponer; ofrecer; *v/i.* proponer; (*marriage*) pedir la mano, declararse (*to* a); *~ to inf.* proponerse *inf.*, pensar *inf.*; **pro'pos·er** *parl. etc.* proponente *m*; **pro·po·si·tion** [prɔpə-'ziʃn] proposición *f*; oferta *f*; F empresa *f*, cosa *f*, problema *m*.

pro·pound [prə'paund] proponer.

pro·pri·e·tar·y [prə'praiətəri] propietario; *article* patentado; **pro·'pri·e·tor** propietario *m*; dueño *m*; **pro'pri·e·tress** propietaria *f*; dueña *f*; **pro'pri·e·ty** corrección *f*; conveniencia *f*; decoro *m*; *proprieties pl.* decoro *m*, convenciones *f/pl.*

pro·pul·sion [prə'pʌlʃn] propulsión *f*.

pro·rate [prou'reit] *Am.* **1.** prorrata *f*; **2.** prorratear.

pro·ro·ga·tion [prourə'geiʃn] prórroga *f*, prorrogación *f*; **pro·rogue** [prə'roug] prorrogar.

pro·sa·ic [prou'zeiik] □ prosaico.

pro·scribe [prəs'kraib] proscribir.

pro·scrip·tion [prəs'kripʃn] proscripción *f*.

prose [prouz] **1.** prosa *f*; **2.** *attr.* de (*or* en) prosa.

pros·e·cute ['prɔsikju:t] 𝓐 procesar, enjuiciar; proseguir, continuar; **pros·e'cu·tion** 𝓐 (*case*) proceso *m*, causa *f*; 𝓐 (*side*) parte *f* actora; prosecución *f*; **pros·e·cu·tor** acusador *m*; (*a. public ~*) fiscal *m*.

pros·e·lyte ['prɔsilait] prosélito (a *f*) *m*; **pros·e·lyt·ism** ['~litizm] proselitismo *m*; '**pros·e·lyt·ize** *v/i.* ganar prosélitos.

pros·o·dy ['prɔsədi] métrica *f*, prosodia *f*.

pros·pect 1. ['prɔspekt] perspectiva *f*; (*view*) vista *f*; (*expectation*) expectativa *f*, esperanza *f*; (*chance*) probabilidad *f* (de éxito *etc.*); *have in ~* esperar, anticipar; *hold out a ~ of* dar esperanzas de; **2.** [prəs'pekt] *v/t.* explorar; *v/i.*: *~ for* buscar; **pro'spec·ting** ✕ prospección *f*; **pro'spec·tive** □ anticipado, esperado; futuro; **pros'pec·tor** ✕ prospector *m*; **pro'spec·tus** [\~təs] prospecto *m*.

pros·per ['prɔspə] *v/i.* prosperar, medrar; *v/t.* favorecer, fomentar; **pros·per·i·ty** [prɔs'periti] prosperidad *f*; **pros·per·ous** ['\~pərəs] □ próspero.

pros·ti·tute ['prɔstitjuːt] **1.** prostituta *f*; **2.** prostituir; **pros·ti'tu·tion** prostitución *f*.

pros·trate 1. ['prɔstreit] postrado (*a. fig.*); *fig.* abatido (*with* por); **2.** postrar (*a. fig.*); *fig.* abatir; *~ o.s.* postrarse; **pros'tra·tion** postración *f* (*a. fig.*); *fig.* abatimiento *m*.

pros·y ['prouzi] prosaico, aburrido.

pro·tag·o·nist [prou'tægənist] protagonista *m/f*.

pro·tect [prə'tekt] proteger (*from* de, contra); **pro'tec·tion** protección *f*; **pro'tec·tion·ist** proteccionista *adj. a. su. m/f*; **pro'tec·tive** □ protector; *~ custody* custodia *f* preventiva; *~ duty* impuesto *m* proteccionista; **pro'tec·tor** protector *m*; **pro'tec·tor·ate** [\~tərit] protectorado *m*.

pro·té·gé(e) ['prɔteiʒei] protegido (a *f*) *m*, ahijado (a *f*) *m*.

pro·te·in ['proutiːn] proteína *f*.

pro·test 1. ['proutest] protesta *f*; queja *f*; *under ~* haciendo objeciones; **2.** [prə'test] protestar (*against* de, *that* de que); quejarse; *innocence, loyalty etc.* declarar (enérgicamente).

Prot·es·tant ['prɔtistənt] protestante *adj. a. su. m/f*; **'Prot·es·tant·ism** protestantismo *m*.

prot·es·ta·tion [proutes'teiʃn] protesta *f*.

pro·to·col ['proutəkɔl] protocolo *m*.

pro·ton ['proutɔn] protón *m*.

pro·to·plasm ['proutəplæzm] protoplasma *m*.

pro·to·type ['proutətaip] prototipo *m*.

pro·tract [prə'trækt] prolongar; **pro'tract·ed** □ largo, prolongado; **pro'trac·tion** prolongación *f*; **pro'trac·tor** transportador *m*.

pro·trude [prə'truːd] *v/t.* sacar fuera; *v/i.* (sobre)salir, salir fuera; **pro'trud·ing** saliente; *eyes, teeth* saltones.

pro·tu·ber·ance [prə'tjuːbərəns] protuberancia *f*, saliente *m*; **pro'tu·ber·ant** □ protuberante, saliente, prominente.

proud [praud] □ orgulloso; *b.s.* soberbio, engreído; (*imposing*) espléndido, imponente; *be ~ of* enorgullecerse de; ufanarse de; *be ~ to* tener el honor de; F *do o.s. ~* darse buena vida; F *do a p. ~* agasajar a una p., hacer fiestas a una p.

prove [pruːv] *v/t.* (com)probar; demostrar; *will* verificar; *v/i.* resultar (*that* que; *true* verdadero); *~ otherwise* salir de otro modo; *~ to be* resultar (ser), salir.

prov·e·nance ['prɔvinəns] (*punto m* de) origen *m*.

prov·en·der ['prɔvində] forraje *m*; *co.* comida *f*.

prov·erb ['prɔvəb] refrán *m*, proverbio *m*; **pro·ver·bi·al** [prə'vəː-biəl] □ proverbial.

pro·vide [prə'vaid] *v/t.* suministrar, surtir; proporcionar; proveer, abastecer (*with* de); *v/i.*: *~ against* precaverse de; *~ for* prevenir; prever; *dependents* asegurar el porvenir de; *~ that* disponer que, estipular que; **pro'vid·ed** (**that**) con tal que.

prov·i·dence ['prɔvidəns] providencia *f*; previsión *f*; ♀ (*Divina*) Providencia; **'prov·i·dent** □ providente, previsor; *~ society* sociedad *f* de socorro mutuo; **prov·i·den·tial** [\~'denʃl] □ providencial.

pro·vid·er [prə'vaidə] proveedor (-a *f*) *m*.

prov·ince ['prɔvins] provincia *f*; *fig.* competencia *f*, jurisdicción *f*.

pro·vin·cial [prə'vinʃl] **1.** provincial; de provincia; *contp.* provinciano; **2.** provinciano (a *f*) *m*; **pro'vin·cial·ism** provincialismo *m*.

pro·vi·sion [prə'viʒn] **1.** provisión *f*; (*condition*) disposición *f*, estipulación *f*; *~s pl.* provisiones *f/pl.*, víveres *m/pl.*; *make ~ for* prevenir; *dependents* asegurar el porvenir de; **2.** aprovisionar, abastecer; **pro'vi·sion·al** □ provisional, interino.

pro·vi·so [prə'vaizou] estipulación *f*; salvedad *f*.

prov·o·ca·tion [prɔvə'keiʃn] provocación *f*; **pro·voc·a·tive** [prə'vɔkə-tiv] □ provocativo.

pro·voke [prə'vouk] provocar (*to* a), incitar (*to* a); causar, motivar; (*anger*) irritar, indignar; **pro'vok·ing** □ provocativo; irritante, enojoso.

prov·ost ['prɔvəst] preboste *m*; *univ.* rector *m*; *Scot. approx.* alcalde *m*; *eccl.* prepósito *m*; ✕ [prə'vou] ~ *marshal* capitán preboste *m*.

prow [prau] proa *f*.

prow·ess ['prauis] valor *m*; habilidad *f*, destreza *f*.

prowl [praul] 1. ronda *f* en busca de presa *etc.*; *be on the* ~ = 2. rondar (en busca de presa *etc.*); vagar (*v/t.* por); ~ **car** *Am.* coche *m* de policía.

prox·im·i·ty [prɔk'simiti] proximidad *f*; inmediaciones *f/pl.*; **prox·i·mo** ['~mou] ✝ del mes próximo.

prox·y ['prɔksi] (*power*) prɔcuración *f*, poder *m*; (*p.*) apoderado (a *f*) *m*; *by* ~ por poder(es).

prude [pru:d] remilgada *f*, gazmoña *f*.

pru·dence ['pru:dəns] prudencia *f*; **'pru·dent** □ prudente.

prud·er·y ['pru:dəri] remilgo *m*, gazmoñería *f*; **'prud·ish** □ remilgado, gazmoño.

prune[1] [pru:n] ciruela *f* pasa.

prune[2] [~] podar; escamondar (*a. fig.*); **'prun·ing** poda *f*; ~ *shears pl.* podadera *f*.

pru·ri·ence, pru·ri·en·cy ['pruəri-əns(i)] salacidad *f*, lascivia *f*; **'pru·ri·ent** □ salaz, lascivo.

Prus·sian ['prʌʃn] prusiano *adj. a. su. m* (a *f*); ~ *blue* azul *m* de Prusia.

prus·sic ac·id ['prʌsik'æsid] ácido *m* prúsico.

pry[1] [prai] fisgar, fisgonear; curiosear; entrometerse (*into* en); **'pry·ing** □ fisgón, entrometido; curioso.

pry[2] [~] = *prise*.

psalm [sɑ:m] salmo *m*; **'psalm·ist** salmista *m*; **psal·mo·dy** ['sælmədi] salmodia *f*.

psal·ter ['sɔ:ltə] salterio *m*.

pseu·do... ['psju:dou] seudo...; falso, fingido; **pseu·do·nym** ['~dənim] seudónimo *m*; **pseu·don·y·mous** ['~'dɔniməs] □ seudónimo.

pshaw [pʃɔ:] ¡bah!

psych- psic-, psiqu-; *the Academy recommends the spelling* sic-, siqu-.

psy·che ['saiki] psique *f*.

psy·chi·a·trist [sai'kaiətrist] psiquiatra *m/f*; **psy'chi·a·try** psiquiatría *f*.

psy·chic, psy·chi·cal ['saikik(l)] □ psíquico.

psy·cho·a·nal·y·sis [saikouə'næləsis] psicoanálisis *m*; **psy·cho·an·a·lyst** [~'ænəlist] psicoanalista *m/f*.

psy·cho·log·i·cal [saikə'lɔdʒikl] □ psicológico; **psy·chol·o·gist** [sai-'kɔlədʒist] psicólogo *m*; **psy'chol·o·gy** psicología *f*.

psy·cho·sis [sai'kousis] psicosis *f*.

ptar·mi·gan ['tɑ:migən] perdiz *f* blanca (*or* nival).

pto·maine ['toumein] ptomaína *f*; ~ *poisoning* envenenamiento *m* ptomaínico.

pub [pʌb] F taberna *f*, tasca *f*; '~-**crawl** *sl.* 1. chateo *m* (de tasca en tasca); *go on a* ~ = 2. ir de chateo, copear, alternar.

pu·ber·ty ['pju:bəti] pubertad *f*.

pu·bes·cence [pju'besns] pubescencia *f*; **pu'bes·cent** pubescente.

pub·lic ['pʌblik] 1. □ público; ~ *address system* sistema *m* amplificador (de discursos públicos); ~ *enemy* enemigo *m* público; ~ *house* taberna *f*; *Am.* posada *f*; ~ *library* biblioteca *f* pública; ~ *spirit* civismo *m*; *v. school, utility etc.*; 2. público *m*; *in* ~ en público; **pub·li·can** ['~kən] tabernero *m*; **pub·li'ca·tion** publicación *f*; **pub·li·cist** ['~sist] publicista *m*; **pub'lic·i·ty** [~siti] publicidad *f*; ~ *agent* agente *m* de publicidad; **pub·li·cize** ['~saiz] publicar, dar publicidad a, anunciar; **'pub·lic-'spir·it·ed** □ *action* de buen ciudadano; *p.* lleno de civismo.

pub·lish ['pʌbliʃ] publicar; **'pub·lish·er** editor *m*; **'pub·lish·ing** publicación *f* de libros; ~ *house* casa *f* editorial. [rojizo.|

puce [pju:s] (de) color purpúreo|

puck [pʌk] duende *m*.

puck·er ['pʌkə] 1. *sew.* frunce *m*, fruncido *m*; (*accidental*) buche *m*; 2. (*a.* ~ *up*) *v/t. sew., brow* fruncir; *v/i.* arrugarse, formar buches.

pud·ding ['pudiŋ] pudín *m*.

pud·dle ['pʌdl] 1. charco *m*; 2. ⊕ pudelar; **'pud·dler** ⊕ pudelador *m*; **'pud·dling-fur·nace** horno *m* de pudelar.

pu·er·ile ['pjuərail] pueril; **pu·er·il·i·ty** [~'riliti] puerilidad *f*.

puff [pʌf] **1.** resoplido *m*, resuello *m*; soplo *m of air*, racha *f of wind*; bocanada *f*, humareda *f of smoke*; *cookery*: pastelillo *m* de crema; (*advert etc.*) bombo *m*; **2.** *v/t.* soplar; ~ *out smoke etc.* echar, arrojar; ~ *up* hinchar, inflar; *v/i.* soplar; (*a.* ~ *and blow*) jadear, acezar, resollar; ~ *at* chupar; ~ *out* (*train*) salir echando humo; **puffed** *eye* hinchado; *be* ~ (*out of breath*) estar sin aliento, acezar; *be* ~ *up with pride* engreírse; **'puff·er** F locomotora *f*.

puf·fin ['pʌfin] frailecillo *m*.

puff-pas·try ['pʌf'peistri] hojaldre *m*; **puf·fy** hinchado.

pug(-dog) ['pʌg(dɔg)] doguillo *m*.

pu·gil·ism ['pju:dʒilizm] pugilato *m*; **'pu·gil·ist** púgil *m*.

pug·na·cious [pʌg'neiʃəs] □ pugnaz; **pug·nac·i·ty** [~'næsiti] pugnacidad *f*.

pug-nosed ['pʌgnouzd] chato, braco.

puke [pju:k] vomitar.

puk·ka ['pʌkə] F genuino; elegante, lujoso.

pull [pul] **1.** tirón *m*; estirón *m*; chupada *f at pipe*; cuerda *f of bell*; *typ.* primeras pruebas *f/pl.*; F (*drink*) trago *m*; F (*influence*) buenas aldabas *f/pl.*; F *it's a long* ~ es mucho camino; **2.** *v/t.* tirar de; (*drag*) arrastrar; *muscle* torcerse, dislocarse; *face(s)* hacer; ~ *about* manosear, estropear; ~ *along* arrastrar; ~ *back* tirar hacia atrás; ~ *down house* derribar, demoler; *grade, price etc.* rebajar; ~ *in rope* cobrar; *suspect* detener; ~ *off* arrancar; quitar de un tirón; F ~ *it off* lograrlo, llevarlo a cabo, vencer (inesperadamente); ~ *out* sacar; arrancar; (*stretch*) estirar; ~ *through* sacar de una enfermedad *etc.*; ~ *to pieces* deshacer, hacer pedazos; *fig. argument* deshacer; *p.* criticar severamente; ~ *o.s. together* sobreponerse, recobrar la calma; ~ *up root etc.* arrancar; *car* parar; *v/i.* tirar, dar un tirón; ~ *at pipe* chupar; *rope etc.* tirar de; ~ *in* 🚉 llegar al andén; *mot.* parar junto a la acera; ~ *on* tirar de; ~ *out* 🚉 salir de la estación; ⚓ retirarse; ~ *through* 🏥 recobrar la salud; salir de un apuro; ~ *up* pararse, detenerse; mejorar su posición.

pul·let ['pulit] poll(it)a *f*.

pul·ley ['puli] polea *f*.

Pull·man car ['pulmən'kɑ:] coche *m* Pullman.

pull·o·ver ['pulouvə] jersey *m*.

pul·mo·nar·y ['pʌlmənəri] pulmonar.

pulp [pʌlp] **1.** pulpa *f*; pasta *f* (*a. wood-*~); **2.** hacer pulpa.

pul·pit ['pulpit] púlpito *m*.

pulp·y ['pʌlpi] pulposo.

pul·sate [pʌl'seit] pulsar, latir, vibrar; **pul·sa·tion** pulsación *f*, latido *m*.

pulse [pʌls] **1.** pulso *m*; *feel one's* ~ tomar el pulso a; **2.** pulsar, latir.

pul·ver·i·za·tion [pʌlvərai'zeiʃn] pulverización *f*; **'pul·ver·ize** pulverizar(se); F cascar.

pum·ice ['pʌmis] (*a.* '~*-stone*) piedra *f* pómez.

pum·mel ['pʌml] *v. pommel*.

pump[1] [pʌmp] **1.** bomba *f*; **2.** sacar (*or* elevar *etc.*) con bomba; *arm* mover rápidamente de arriba para abajo; F *p.* sonsacar; ~ *dry* secar con bomba(s); ~ *up tyre* inflar.

pump[2] [~] (*shoe*) zapatilla *f*.

pump·kin ['pʌmpkin] calabaza *f*.

pun [pʌn] **1.** juego *m* de palabras (*on* sobre); **2.** jugar del vocablo (*a.* ~ *on*).

punch[1] [pʌntʃ] **1.** ⊕ punzón *m*; **2.** punzar, taladrar; *ticket* picar.

punch[2] [~] **1.** (*blow*) puñetazo *m*; F empuje *m*, vigor *m*; *pull one's* ~*es* no emplear toda su fuerza; **2.** dar un puñetazo a, pegar con los puños; golpear; *Am. cattle* guiar; acorralar; cuidar.

punch[3] [~] (*drink*) ponche *m*.

punch-ball ['pʌntʃbɔ:l] saco *m* de arena, punching *m*.

punc·til·i·o [pʌŋk'tiliou] puntillo *m*, etiqueta *f*; **punc·til·i·ous** [~'tiliəs] □ puntilloso, etiquetero.

punc·tu·al ['pʌŋktjuəl] □ puntual; **punc·tu·al·i·ty** [~'æliti] puntualidad *f*.

punc·tu·ate ['pʌŋktjueit] puntuar (*a. fig.*); **punc·tu·a·tion** puntuación *f*.

punc·ture ['pʌŋktʃə] **1.** *mot. etc.* pinchazo *m*; puntura *f*, punzada *f of skin*; ⚕ punción *f*; *have a* ~ tener un neumático pinchado; **2.** pinchar; perforar, punzar.

pun·dit ['pʌndit] *contp.* erudito *m*; experto *m*.

pun·gen·cy ['pʌndʒənsi] picante *m*; lo acre; mordacidad *f*; **'pun·gent** ☐ picante; *smell* acre; *remark etc.* mordaz, áspero.

pun·ish ['pʌniʃ] castigar; F maltratar; *(tax)* exigir esfuerzos sobrehumanos a; **'pun·ish·a·ble** ☐ punible, castigable; **'pun·ish·ment** castigo *m*; F tratamiento *m* severo.

pu·ni·tive ['pjuːnitiv] punitivo.

punk [pʌŋk] *Am.* 1. basura *f*, fruslerías *f/pl.*; 2. *sl.* malo, baladí.

pun·ster ['pʌnstə] persona *f* aficionada a los juegos de palabras.

punt[1] [pʌnt] ⚓ 1. batea *f*; 2. *v/i.* ir en batea; *v/t.* impeler con botador.

punt[2] [ˏ] jugar, hacer apuestas; **'punt·er** jugador *m*.

pu·ny ['pjuːni] encanijado; insignificante; *effort etc.* débil.

pup [pʌp] 1. cachorro (a *f*) *m*; 2. parir *(la perra)*.

pu·pil ['pjuːpl] alumno (a *f*) *m*; *anat.* pupila *f*.

pup·pet ['pʌpit] títere *m*; *(p.)* marioneta *f*; ~ *régime* régimen *m* marioneta; **'~-show** (función *f* de) títeres *m/pl.*

pup·py ['pʌpi] cachorro (a *f*) *m*; perrito (a *f*) *m*.

pur·blind ['pɜːblaind] cegato; *fig.* falto de comprensión.

pur·chase ['pɜːtʃəs] 1. compra *f*; *fig.* agarre *m* firme; ⊕ apalancamiento *m*; ~ *tax* impuesto *m* de venta; *get a ~ on rock etc.* tener donde agarrarse; *make ~s* hacer compras; 2. comprar, adquirir; *purchasing power* poder *m* adquisitivo; **'pur·chas·er** comprador (-a *f*) *m*.

pure [pjuə] ☐ puro; **'~-bred** de pura sangre; **'pure·ness** pureza *f*.

pur·ga·tion [pɜːˈgeiʃn] purgación *f*; **pur·ga·tive** ['ˏgətiv] purgativo; purgante (*a. su. m*); **'pur·ga·to·ry** purgatorio *m*.

purge [pɜːdʒ] 1. ⚕ purga *f*, purgante *m*; *pol.* purga *f*, depuración *f*; 2. purgar; purificar, depurar; *pol. party* purgar, depurar; *member* liquidar.

pu·ri·fi·ca·tion [pjuərifiˈkeiʃn] purificación *f*, depuración *f*; **pu·ri·fi·er** ['ˏfaiə] *(water-)* depurador *m*; **pu·ri·fy** ['ˏfai] purificar, depurar; *metall.* acrisolar; **'pu·rist** purista *m/f*, casticista *m/f*.

pu·ri·tan ['pjuəritən] puritano *adj.*

a. su. m (a *f*); **pu·ri·tan·i·cal** [ˏˈtænikl] ☐ puritano; **pu·ri·tan·ism** ['ˏtənizm] puritanismo *m*.

pu·ri·ty ['pjuəriti] pureza *f*.

purl [pɜːl] 1. punto *m* de media invertido; 2. hacer un punto de media invertido.

purl·er ['pɜːlə] F: *come a ~* caer pesadamente, caer de cabeza.

pur·lieu ['pɜːljuː] *fig.* competencia *f*; *~s pl.* alrededores *m/pl.*, inmediaciones *f/pl.*

pur·loin [pɜːˈlɔin] hurtar, robar.

pur·ple ['pɜːpl] 1. purpúreo, morado; ~ *patch* trozo *m* de estilo hinchado, pasaje *m* demasiado sentimental *etc.*; 2. púrpura *f*; 3. purpurar.

pur·port 1. ['pɜːpət] significado *m*, tenor *m*; intención *f*; 2. [pəˈpɔːt] significar, dar a entender (*that* que); ~ *to inf.* pretender *inf.*

pur·pose ['pɜːpəs] 1. propósito *m*, intención *f*; resolución *f*; *novel with a ~* novela *f* de tesis; *strength of ~* resolución *f*; *for the ~ of ger.* con el fin de *inf.*; *on ~* adrede, de propósito; *to good ~* con buenos resultados; *to no ~* inútilmente, en vano; *serve one's ~* servir para el caso; 2. proponerse; proyectar; **pur·pose·ful** ['ˏful] ☐ determinado, resuelto; **'pur·pose·less** ☐ sin propósito fijo, sin fin determinado; **'pur·pose·ly** *adv.* adrede, de propósito.

purr [pɜː] 1. *(cat, motor)* ronronear; *fig.* decir suavemente; 2. ronroneo *m*.

purse [pɜːs] 1. bolsa *f*; *Am.* bolso *m*; *(prize)* premio *m*; 2. *lips* fruncir; **'purs·er** contador *m* de navío; **'purse-strings:** *hold the ~* tener las llaves de la caja.

pur·su·ance [pəˈsjuːəns]: *in ~ of* con arreglo a, cumpliendo; **pur'su·ant:** ~ *to* de acuerdo con.

pur·sue [pəˈsjuː] *(hunt)* seguir (la pista de), cazar; *(a. fig.)* perseguir; acosar; *pleasures etc.* dedicarse a; *plan* proceder de acuerdo con; *profession* ejercer; *study, inquiry* proseguir; **pur'su·er** perseguidor (-a *f*) *m*; **pur'suit** [ˏˈsjuːt] caza *f*, busca *f*; persecución *f*; *(occupation)* ocupación *f*; *(pastime)* pasatiempo *m*; *in ~ of* en pos de; ~ *plane* avión *m* de caza. [lento.|

pu·ru·lent ['pjuərulənt] ☐ puru-|

pur·vey [pə:'vei] suministrar, abastecer, proveer; **pur'vey·ance** suministro *m*, abastecimiento *m*; **pur'vey·or** abastecedor (-a *f*) *m*, proveedor (-a *f*) *m*.
pur·view ['pə:vju:] alcance *m*, esfera *f*.
pus [pʌs] pus *m*.
push [puʃ] **1.** empuje *m*, empujón *m*; ✕ ofensiva *f*, avance *m*; F *at a* ~ si es absolutamente necesario; *sl. get the* ~ ser despedido; *sl. give a p. the* ~ despedir a una p.; **2.** *v/t.* empujar; *enterprise* promover, fomentar; *claim* proseguir; F *product* hacer una campaña publicitaria a favor de; *p.* incitar, obligar (*to a*); F (*prod*) pinchar; ~ *one's way* abrirse paso empujando; F *be* ~*ed for* tener muy poco ... disponible; andar muy escaso de; ~ *away* apartar con la mano; empujar; ~ *back* echar atrás; ~ *in* introducir a la fuerza; ~ *off* ⚓ desatracar; ~ *out* empujar hacia fuera; expulsar; ~ *through measure* hacer aceptar a la fuerza; *v/i.* empujar, dar un empujón; hacer esfuerzos; ~ *off* ⚓ desatracarse, apartarse de la orilla; F largarse, marcharse; ~ *on* seguir adelante, continuar (a pesar de todo); avanzar; '~**bike** F bici(cleta) *f*; '~**but·ton** (*attr.* que tiene) pulsador *m*, botón *m* de llamada *etc.*; ~ *control* mando *m* por botón; **push·ful** ['~ful] □, **push·ing** □ emprendedor, vigoroso; *b.s.* agresivo; '**push·ful·ness** empuje *m*; '**push·o·ver** F cosa *f* muy fácil; persona *f* muy fácil de (con)vencer *etc.*; breva *f*.
pu·sil·la·nim·i·ty [pju:silə'nimiti] pusilanimidad *f*; **pu·sil·lan·i·mous** [~'læniməs] □ pusilánime.
puss(·y) ['pus(i)] minino *m*, micho *m*; F moza *f*; *sl.* cara *f*; '**puss·y·foot** *Am.* F moverse a paso de gato, andar a tientas; no declararse.
pus·tule ['pʌstju:l] pústula *f*.
put [put] [*irr.*] **1.** *v/t.* poner; colocar; (*insert*) meter; *weight* lanzar, arrojar; *question* hacer; *motion* proponer, someter a votación; (*expound*) exponer, presentar; expresar, redactar *in words*; (*translate*) traducir (*into a*); (*estimate*) computar, estimar; *tasar* (*at en*); *for many phrases, see the corresponding su.*; ~ *it about that* dar a entender que; ~ *across meaning* comunicar, hacer entender;

idea, product hacer aceptar; F ~ *it across* (*deceive*) engañar, embaucar; (*defeat*) cascar; ~ *aside* (*reject*) rechazar; (*save*) poner aparte, ahorrar; ~ *away* (*keep*) guardar; (*save*) ahorrar; volver a poner en su lugar; F *food* zampar; (*imprison*) encarcelar; *lunatic* meter en un manicomio; ~ *back th.* devolver a su lugar; *clock, process* retardar, atrasar; *function etc.* aplazar; ~ *by* poner aparte; *money* ahorrar; ~ *down revolt* suprimir; *burden* poner en el suelo; soltar; apuntar *in writing*; ⸆ sentar (*to en la cuenta de*); *I could not* ~ *the book down* me era imposible dejar el libro de la mano; ~ *down as* juzgar; ~ (*it*) *down to* atribuir(lo) a, achacar(lo) a; ~ *forth book etc.* publicar; *bud etc.* producir, echar; *effort* emplear; ~ *forward* presentar, proponer; *function, date* adelantar; ~ *o.s. forward* ofrecerse (con poca modestia), llamar sobre sí la atención; ~ *in* meter, insertar, introducir; *claim* presentar; *remark* interponer; *time* dedicar; ~ *off* (*postpone*) aplazar, dejar para después; *p.* quitar las ganas de, hacer perder el sabor de (*fig. el deseo de*); *scent* desviar de, apartar de; (*dissuade*) disuadir; (*evade*) dar largas a, apartar de su propósito (con evasivas); ~ *on clothes* ponerse; *shoes* calzarse; F ~ *it on* exagerar; emocionarse demasiado; darse tono; ✗ engordar; ~ *out hand etc.* extender; *head etc.* asomar, sacar; *tongue* sacar; *shoot* echar; *bone* dislocar; *book* publicar; *fire, light* apagar; (*expel*) poner en la calle; (*inconvenience*) molestar, incomodar; (*disconcert*) desconcertar; ~ *over idea, product* hacer aceptar; *meaning* comunicar; ~ *o.s. over* impresionar con su personalidad; ~ *right watch* poner en hora; *difficulty* resolver, arreglar; *mistake* corregir; ~ *through task* llevar a cabo; *proposal* hacer aceptar; *teleph.* poner (*to con*); ~ *it to p.* decirlo a; sugerirlo a; proponerlo a; *be hard* ~ *to it to* tener mucha dificultad en *inf.*; ~ *together* añadir; juntar; ⊕ montar; ~ *up building* construir; *sword* envainar; *umbrella* abrir; *price* aumentar; *prize* ofrecer; *money* poner, contribuir; *game* levantar; *candidate* nombrar; apoyar; *guest* hospedar; *p.* ~

up to incitar a; **2.** *v/i.*: ~ *about* ⚓ cambiar de rumbo; ~ *in* ⚓ entrar a puerto; ~ *in at* ⚓ hacer escala en; ~ *in for post* presentarse a, solicitar; ~ *off*, ~ *out* ⚓ hacerse a la mar; ~ *up at* hospedarse en; ~ *up for* ser candidato a; ~ *up with* aguantar, resignarse a; ~ *upon* molestar, incomodar.

pu·ta·tive ['pju:tətiv] putativo.

pu·tre·fac·tion [pju:tri'fækʃħ] putrefacción *f*.

pu·tre·fy ['pju:trifai] pudrirse.

pu·tres·cence [pju:'tresns] pudrición *f*; **pu'tres·cent** putrescente.

pu·trid ['pju:trid] □ podrido, putrefacto; F malísimo, pésimo.

putt [pʌt] **1.** golpe *m* corto; **2.** golpear con poca fuerza.

put·ty ['pʌti] **1.** masilla *f*; **2.** enmasillar.

put-up job ['putʌp'dʒɔb] *sl.* cosa *f* proyectada y preparada de antemano; asunto *m* fraudulento.

puz·zle ['pʌzl] **1.** problema *m*, enigma *m*; (*game*) rompecabezas *m*, acertijo *m*; **2.** *v/t.* intrigar, confundir, dejar perplejo; ~ *out* descifrar, resolver; *v/i.*: ~ *over* tratar de resolver, devanarse los sesos para descifrar; **'puz·zled** intrigado; perplejo; **'puz·zler** engima *m*, problema *m* difícil; **'puz·zling** enigmático, misterioso.

pyg·my ['pigmi] pigmeo *adj. a. su. m.*

py·ja·mas [pə'dʒɑ:məz] *pl.* pijama *m*.

py·lon ['pailən] pilón *m*; ⚡ torre *f* de conducción eléctrica.

py·or·rh(o)e·a [paiə'riə] piorrea *f*.

pyr·a·mid ['pirəmid] pirámide *f*; **py·ram·i·dal** [pi'ræmidl] piramidal.

pyre ['paiə] pira *f*; *fig.* hoguera *f*.

py·ret·ic [pai'retik] pirético.

py·ri·tes [pai'raiti:z] pirita *f*.

py·ro... ['paiərou] piro...; **py·ro·'tech·nics** *pl.* pirotecnia *f*.

py·thon ['paiθən] pitón *m*.

pyx [piks] *eccl.* píxide *f*.

Q

quack[1] [kwæk] *approx.* **1.** graznido *m*; **2.** graznar.

quack[2] [~] **1.** charlatán *m*, curandero *m*; **2.** falso; *remedy* de curandero; **quack·er·y** ['~əri] charlatanismo *m*.

quad [kwɔd] = *quadrangle, quadrat, quadruplet(s)*.

quad·ran·gle ['kwɔdræŋgl] cuadrángulo *m*; △ patio *m*.

quad·rant ['kwɔdrənt] cuadrante *m*.

quad·rat ['kwɔdræt] cuadrado *m*, cuadratín *m*; **quad·rat·ic** [kwɔ-'drætik] de segundo grado; **quad·ra·ture** ['kwɔdrətʃə] cuadratura *f*.

quad·ri·lat·er·al [kwɔdri'lætərəl] cuadrilátero *adj. a. su. m*.

quad·ri·par·tite [kwɔdri'pɑːtait] cuadripartido.

quad·ru·ped ['kwɔdruped] **1.** cuadrúpedo *m*; **2.** (*a.* **quad·ru·pe·dal** [kwɔ'druːpidl] cuadrúpedo; **quad·ru·ple 1.** ['kwɔdrupl] cuádruple; **2.** [~] cuádruplo *m*; **3.** [~'rupl] cuadruplicar(se); **quad·ru·plets** [kwɔd'ruːplits] *pl.* cuatrillizos (as *f/pl.*) *m/pl.*; **quad·ru·pli·cate 1.** [kwɔ'druːplikit] (*in* por) cuadruplicado; **2.** [~keit] cuadruplicar.

quaff [kwɑːf] † beber; ~ *off* beberse *acc.*, apurar.

quag·mire ['kwægmaiə] tremedal *m*, cenegal *m*.

quail[1] [kweil] *orn.* codorniz *f*.

quail[2] [~] acobardarse, descorazonarse.

quaint [kweint] □ curioso, original; pintoresco; típico; **'quaint·ness** singularidad *f*; lo pintoresco; tipismo *m*.

quake [kweik] temblar, trepidar, estremecerse (*with, for* de).

Quak·er ['kweikə] cuáquero *m*; **'Quak·er·ism** cuaquerismo *m*.

qual·i·fi·ca·tion [kwɔlifi'keiʃn] calificación *f*; requisito *m*; modificación *f*, restricción *f*; *have the* ~*s* llenar los requisitos; *without* ~ sin reserva; **qual·i·fied** ['~faid] *p.* c(u)alificado, habilitado, capacitado, competente; modificado, limitado;

qual·i·fy ['~fai] *v/t.* calificar (*a. gr.*); habilitar; modificar, limitar; *drink*' aguar; *v/i.* habilitarse, capacitarse; llenar los requisitos; *qualifying examination* examen *m* eliminatorio; **qual·i·ta·tive** ['~teitiv] □ cualitativo; **'qual·i·ty** (*type, character*) calidad *f*, categoría *f*, clase *f*; (*characteristic*) cualidad *f*, virtud *f*; *the* ~ la aristocracia; *of low* ~ de baja calidad; *he has many good qualities* tiene muchas buenas cualidades.

qualm [kwɔːm, kwɑːm] 🏥 bascas *f/pl.*, náusea *f*; duda *f*, escrúpulo *m of conscience*; inquietud *f*; **'qualm·ish** □ bascoso.

quan·da·ry ['kwɔndəri] incertidumbre *f*, perplejidad *f*, dilema *m*; *be in a* ~ estar en un dilema.

quan·ti·ta·tive ['kwɔntiteitiv] □ cuantitativo; **'quan·ti·ty** cantidad *f*; *unknown* ~ incógnita *f* (*a. fig.*); ~ *surveyor* aparejador *m*.

quan·tum ['kwɔntəm] cantidad *f*; *phys.* cuanto *m*; ~ *theory* teoría *f* cuántica (*or* de los cuanta).

quar·an·tine ['kwɔrənti:n] **1.** cuarentena *f*; *place in* ~ = **2.** poner en cuarentena.

quar·rel ['kwɔrəl] **1.** riña *f*, disputa *f*; (*violent*) reyerta *f*, pendencia *f*; *pick a* ~ buscar camorra; **2.** reñir, disputar; pelear; **quar·rel·some** ['~səm] □ pendenciero.

quar·ry[1] ['kwɔri] **1.** cantera *f*; *fig.* mina *f*; **2.** sacar, extraer (*a. fig.*).

quar·ry[2] [~] *hunt.* presa *f*.

quar·ry·man ['kwɔrimən] cantero *m*.

quart [kwɔːt] *cuarto de galón* (= *1,136 litros*); *fenc.* [kɑːt] cuarta *f*.

quar·ter ['kwɔːtə] **1.** cuarto *m*, cuarta parte *f*; *heraldry:* cuartel *m*; (*3 months*) trimestre *m*; cuarto *m of moon*; barrio *m of town*; *fig.* procedencia *f*; *Am.* moneda de 25 *centavos*; (*weight*) (= *28 libras* = *12,7 Kg.*) *approx.* arroba *f*, ~*s pl.* vivienda *f*; ✗ cuartel *m*, alojamiento *m*; ~ *of an hour* cuarto *m* de hora; *from all* ~s de todas partes; *in this* ~ por aquí; *at close* ~s de cerca; ✗ casi cuerpo a cuerpo; ✗ *give no* ~ no dar cuartel; *have free* ~s tener alojamiento gratis; **2.** cuartear; *meat* descuartizar; *heraldry:* cuartelar; ✗ acuartelar; *be* ~ed (*up*) *on* estar alojado en casa de; '~-**day** día *m* en que se paga un trimestre; '~-**deck** alcázar *m*; '**quar·ter·ly 1.** trimestral; **2.** publicación *f* trimestral; **3.** cada tres meses, por trimestres; '**quar·ter·mas·ter** *approx.* furriel *m*, comisario *m*; **quar·tern** ['~ən] cuarta *f*; (*a.* ~ *loaf*) pan *m* de 4 libras.

quar·tet(te) [kwɔ:'tet] cuarteto *m*.

quar·to ['kwɔ:tou] en cuarto; (*paper*) tamaño holandesa.

quartz [kwɔ:ts] cuarzo *m*.

quash [kwɔʃ] anular, invalidar.

qua·si ['kweisai] cuasi ...

qua·ter·na·ry [kwə'tə:nəri] cuaternario (*a. geol.*).

quat·rain ['kwɔtrein] estrofa *f* de 4 versos.

qua·ver ['kweivə] **1.** temblor *m*; ♪ trémolo *m*; (*note*) corchea *f*; **2.** temblar, vibrar; ♪ gorjear, trinar; '**qua·ver·ing** □, '**qua·ver·y** trémulo. [dero *m*.\

quay [ki:] muelle *m*, desembarca-\

quea·si·ness ['kwi:zinis] bascas *f*/*pl.*; propensión *f* a la náusea; '**quea·sy** □ bascoso; delicado; *conscience* escrupuloso; *I feel* ~ me siento mal.

queen [kwi:n] **1.** reina *f* (*a. chess*); *cards:* dama *f*, (*Spanish*) caballo *m*; ~ *bee* abeja *f* reina; ~ *mother* reina *f* madre; **2.** *pawn* coronar; ~ *it* pavonearse; '**queen·like**, '**queen·ly** regio, de reina.

queer [kwiə] **1.** □ raro, extraño; misterioso; excéntrico, extravagante; F ♂ enfermo; F maricón (*a. su. m*); F ♂ *feel* ~ sentirse indispuesto; **2.**: *sl.* ~ *the pitch* crear dificultades a, chafar la guitarra a.

quell [kwel] reprimir, domar; calmar.

quench [kwentʃ] *thirst etc.* apagar; extinguir, ahogar; ⊕ templar; '**quench·er** F trago *m*; '**quench·less** □ inapagable.

quern [kwə:n] molinillo *m* de mano.

quer·u·lous ['kwerуləs] □ quejumbroso, quejicoso.

que·ry ['kwiəri] **1.** (*abbr.* **qu.**) pregunta *f*; duda *f*; punto *m* de interrogación [?]; **2.** preguntar; expresar dudas acerca de, dudar de; no estar conforme con.

quest [kwest] **1.** busca *f*, búsqueda *f*; pesquisa *f*; *in* ~ *of* en busca de; **2.** buscar (*for acc.*).

ques·tion ['kwestʃn] **1.** pregunta *f*; (*affair*) asunto *m*, cuestión *f*; problema *m*; ~ *mark* punto *m* de interrogación; *beyond all* ~ fuera de (toda) duda; *in* ~ en cuestión; *beg the* ~ ser una petición de principio; *call in* ~ poner en duda; *come into* ~ empezar a discutirse; *it is a* ~ *of* se trata de; *the* ~ *is* el caso es; *that is the* ~ ahí está el problema; *that is out of the* ~ es totalmente imposible; *there is no* ~ *of* no se trata de; **2.** interrogar, hacer preguntas a; examinar; (*doubt*) poner en duda; desconfiar de; '**ques·tion·a·ble** □ cuestionable, dudoso; **ques·tion·naire** [kestiə'nɛə, kwestʃə'nɛə] cuestionario *m*; '**ques·tion·er** interrogador (-a *f*) *m*.

queue [kju:] **1.** cola *f*; **2.** hacer cola (*a.* ~ *up*).

quib·ble ['kwibl] **1.** evasión *f*, sofistería *f*; retruécano *m*; **2.** sutilizar; jugar del vocablo; buscar evasivas; '**quib·bler** sofista *m*/*f*.

quick [kwik] **1.** rápido, veloz; pronto; vivo; ágil; *ear* fino; *eye*, *wit* agudo; **2.** carne *f* viva; *the* ~ los vivos; *cut to the* ~ herir en lo vivo; **3.** *v.* ~*ly*; ~ *march!* de frente ¡mar!; '~-**change ac·tor** transformista *m*; '**quick·en** acelerar(se), apresurar; vivificar; '**quick·fir·ing** de tiro rápido; **quick·ie** ['~i] F pregunta *f* relámpago; '**quick·lime** cal *f* viva; '**quick·ly** pronto; de prisa, rápidamente; '**quick·ness** presteza *f*, celeridad *f*; prontitud *f*; viveza *f*, penetración *f* *of mind*.

quick...: '~-**sand** arena *f* movediza; '~-**set** ✓ plantón *m* (*esp.* espino *m*); seto *m* vivo (*a.* ~ *hedge*); '~-'**sight·ed** de vista aguda; '~-**sil·ver** azogue *m*, mercurio *m*; '~-'**tem·pered** de genio vivo; '~-'**wit·ted** agudo, perspicaz.

quid[1] [kwid] mascada *f* (de tabaco).

quid[2] [~] *sl.* libra esterlina.

quid·di·ty ['kwiditi] *phls.* esencia *f*; sutileza *f*.

quid pro quo ['kwid prou 'kwou] compensación *f*; recompensa *f*.

qui·es·cence [kwai'esns] quietud *f*, tranquilidad *f*; **qui·es·cent** □ quieto, inactivo; latente.

qui·et ['kwaiət] **1.** □ (*silent*) silencioso, callado; (*motionless, not excited*) quieto, tranquilo; reposado; *colour* no llamativo; *market* encalmado; *celebration etc.* sin ceremonias, más bien privado; *all* ~ sin novedad; *be* ~, *keep* ~ (*p.*) callarse; **2.** silencio *m*; tranquilidad *f*, reposo *m*; F *on the* ~ a la sordina; **3.** calmar(se); **4.** ~! ¡silencio!; '**qui·et·en** calmar(se), tranquilizar(se); F callarse (*a.* ~ *down*); '**qui·et·ism** quietismo *m*; '**qui·et·ist** quietista *m/f*; '**qui·et·ness**, **qui·e·tude** ['~tju:d] tranquilidad *f*, quietud *f*; silencio *m*. [gracia; muerte *f*.\
qui·e·tus [kwai'i:təs] golpe *m* de\
quill [kwil] **1.** pluma *f*; cañón *m* (de pluma); (*spine*) púa *f*; (*bobbin*) canilla *f*; **2.** plegar; '**quill-pen** pluma *f* de ave (para escribir).

quilt [kwilt] **1.** colcha *f*; **2.** acolchar; estofar; pespunt(e)ar; '**quilt·ing** colchadura *f*; (*art*) piqué *m*.

quince [kwins] membrillo *m*.

qui·nine [kwi'ni:n, *Am.* 'kwainain] quinina *f*.

quin·quen·ni·al [kwiŋ'kwenjəl] □ quinquenal.

quin·quen·ni·um [kwiŋ'kweniəm] quinquenio *m*. [*f/pl.*) *m/pl.*\
quins [kwinz] F quintillizos (as\
quin·sy ['kwinzi] angina *f*.

quint·es·sence [kwin'tesns] quinta esencia *f*.

quin·tet(te) [kwin'tet] quinteto *m*.

quin·tu·ple ['kwintjupl] **1.** quíntuplo; **2.** quintuplicar(se); **quin·tu·plets** ['~plits] *pl.* quintillizos (as *f/pl.*) *m/pl.*

quip [kwip] agudeza *f*, pulla *f*, chiste *m*.

quire ['kwaiə] mano *f* de papel.

quirk [kwə:k] (*oddity*) capricho *m*, peculiaridad *f*; (*quip*) agudeza *f*; (*flourish*) rasgo *m*; ⚠ avivador *m*.

quit [kwit] **1.** *v/t.* dejar, abandonar; salir de; desocupar; *Am.* ~ *ger.* dejar de *inf.*, desistir de *inf.*; *v/i.* retirarse, despedirse; rajarse; cejar; **2.** libre (*of* de); absuelto.

quite [kwait] totalmente, completamente; (*rather*) bastante; ~ *a hero* todo un héroe; ~ (*so*)! efectivamente, perfectamente; ~ *that*! ¡lo menos eso!, ¡ya lo creo!; F ~ *the go*, ~ *the thing* muy de moda.

quits [kwits] en paz (*with* con); *cry* ~ hacer las paces.

quit·ter ['kwitə] F *approx.* faltón *m*, inconstante *m*; catacaldos *m*.

quiv·er[1] ['kwivə] **1.** temblar, estremecerse; **2.** temblor *m*.

quiv·er[2] ['kwivə] carcaj *m*, aljaba *f*.

quix·ot·ic [kwik'sɔtik] □ quijotesco.

quiz [kwiz] **1.** encuesta *f*; acertijo *m*; *radio:* concurso *m* radiofónico; **2.** interrogar; mirar con curiosidad; '**quiz·zi·cal** □ burlón.

quod [kwɔd] *sl.* chirona *f*.

quoin [kɔin] ⚠ esquina *f*; piedra *f* angular; *typ.* cuña *f*.

quoit [kɔit] tejo *m*; ~*s pl.* juego *m* de tejos (*or* aros).

quon·dam ['kwɔndæm] antiguo.

quo·rum ['kwɔːrəm] quórum *m*.

quo·ta ['kwoutə] cuota *f*; contingente *m*, cupo *m*.

quo·ta·tion [kwou'teiʃn] cita *f*, citación *f*; ✝ cotización *f*; **quo'ta·tion-marks** *pl.* comillas *f/pl.*

quote [kwout] citar; ✝ cotizar (*at* en).

quoth [kwouθ]: ✝ ~ *I* dije (yo).

quo·tient ['kwouʃənt] cociente *m*.

R

rab·bet ['ræbit] **1.** rebajo *m*; ensambladura *f*; ~ *plane* guillame *m*; **2.** embarbillar, ensamblar a rebajo.

rab·bi ['ræbai] rabino *m*; (*before name*) rabí *m*.

rab·bit ['ræbit] conejo *m*; *Welsh* ~ pan *m* con queso tostado; *Am.* ~ *fever* tularemia *f*.

rab·ble ['ræbl] canalla *f*, chusma *f*; '~**-rous·er** agitador *m*.

rab·id ['ræbid] □ rabioso (*a. fig.*); *fig.* fanático.

ra·bies ['reibi:z] rabia *f*.

race¹ [reis] raza *f* (*a. biol.*); estirpe *f*, casta *f*; *human* ~ género *m* humano.

race² [~] **1.** carrera *f*; regata *f* *on water*; (*current*) corriente *f* fuerte; (*mill-*) caz *m*, saetín *m*; ~*s pl.* carreras *f/pl.*; **2.** *v/i.* competir; ir a máxima velocidad; ⊕ girar a velocidad excesiva, embalarse; *v/t.* hacer correr; competir con; '~**course** hipódromo *m*, cancha *f* *S.Am.*

race-ha·tred ['reis'heitrid] odio *m* racial. [carrera.]

race-horse ['reishɔ:s] caballo *m* de

race-meet·ing ['reis'mi:tiŋ] concurso *m* hípico, reunión *f*.

rac·er ['reisə] caballo *m* (*or coche m etc.*) de carrera.

race-track ['reistræk] pista *f*, cancha *f* *S.Am.*; *mot.* autódromo *m*.

ra·cial ['reifl] □ racial; **ra·cial·ism** ['~fəlism] racismo *m*.

rac·i·ness ['reisinis] sal *f*, vivacidad *f*, picante *m*.

rac·ing ['reisiŋ] carreras *f/pl.*; *attr.* de carrera(s); ~ *car* coche *m* de carreras; ~ *cyclist* corredor *m* ciclista; ~ *motorist* corredor *m* automovilista.

rack¹ [ræk] **1.** estante *m*, anaquel *m*; (*torture*) potro *m*; ⊕ cremallera *f*; (*hat- etc.*) percha *f*, cuelgacapas *m*; **2.** atormentar; *v.* brain.

rack² [~]: *go to* ~ *and ruin* arruinarse.

rack³ [~] *wine* trasegar, embotellar (*a.* ~ *off*).

rack·et¹ ['ræket], **racquet** [~] raqueta *f*; ~*s pl.* especie de *tenis jugado contra frontón*.

rack·et² [~] **1.** alboroto *m*, baraúnda *f*, jaleo *m*, estrépito *m*; *F* estafa *f*, chantaje *m*, trapacería *f*; **2.** jaranear; hacer ruido; **rack·et·eer** [~'tiə] *esp. Am.* *F* estafador *m*, chantajista *m*, trapacista *m*; **rack·et·eer·ing** *esp. Am.* *F* chantaje *m* sistematizado.

rack-rent ['rækrent] alquiler *m* exorbitante.

ra(c)·coon [rə'ku:n] mapache *m*.

rac·y ['reisi] □ fuerte; picante; castizo; *style* salado, vivaz.

ra·dar ['reidɑ:] radar *m*.

rad·dle ['rædl] **1.** almagre *m*; **2.** almagrar.

ra·di·al ['reidiəl] □ radial; ~ *engine* motor *m* radial.

ra·di·ance, ra·di·an·cy ['reidiəns(i)] brillantez *f*, resplandor *m*; '**ra·di·ant** □ radiante (*a. fig.*); brillante.

ra·di·ate 1. ['reidieit] (ir)radiar; *happiness etc.* difundir; **2.** ['~it] radiado; **ra·di·a·tion** (ir)radiación *f*; **ra·di·a·tor** ['~eitə] radiador *m*.

rad·i·cal ['rædikəl] □ *all senses:* radical *adj. a. su. m*; '**rad·i·cal·ism** radicalismo *m*.

ra·di·o ['reidiou] **1.** radio *f* (*a.* ~ *set*); radio(tele)fonía *f*; rayos *m/pl.* X (*or* Roentgen); *on* (*or over*) the ~ por radio; ~ *drama*, ~ *play* comedia *f* radiofónica; ~ *engineering* técnica *f* radiofónica; ~ *fan* radioexperimentador *m*; ~ *station* emisora *f*; ~ *studio* estudio *m* (de emisión); **2.** radiar, transmitir por radio; '~**ac·tive** radiactivo; '~**ac·tiv·i·ty** radiactividad *f*; **ra·di·o·gram** ['~græm] (*message*) radiograma *m*; (*set*) radiogramola *f*, radiofonógrafo *m* *S. Am.*; **ra·di·o·graph** ['~grɑ:f] **1.** radiografía *f*; **2.** radiografiar; **ra·di·og·ra·phy** [reidi'ɔgrəfi] radiografía *f*; **ra·di·ol·o·gy** [reidi'ɔlədʒi] radiología *f*; **ra·di·os·co·py** [~'ɔskəpi] radioscopia *f*; '**ra·di·o·tel·e·gram** radiograma *m*; **ra·di·o·tel·e·scope** radiotelescopio *m*; '**ra·di·o·ther·a·py** radioterapia *f*.

rad·ish ['rædif] rábano *m*.

ra·di·um ['reidiəm] radio *m*.

ra·di·us ['reidiəs], *pl.* **ra·di·i** ['ˌai] *all senses*: radio *m*; *within a ~ of* en un radio de.

raff·ish ['ræfiʃ] disipado, de vida airada.

raf·fle ['ræfl] **1.** rifar, sortear; **2.** rifa *f*.

raft [rɑːft] **1.** balsa *f*, almadía *f*; **2.** transportar en balsa; **'raft·er** ⚠ cab(r)io *m*; (*a.* **'rafts·man**) almadiero *m*.

rag[1] [ræg] trapo *m*, andrajo *m*, harapo *m*; F (*newspaper*) periodicucho *m*; *in ~s* harapiento, andrajoso; F *feel like a ~* estar hecho cisco; *put on one's glad ~s* endomingarse.

rag[2] [ˌ] *sl.* **1.** *v/t.* embromar, dar guerra a; *v/i.* guasearse, bromear, fisgar; **2.** guasa *f*, broma *f* pesada; broma *f* estudiantil; función *f* estudiantil benéfica.

rag·a·muf·fin ['rægəmʌfin] granuja *m*, galopín *m*.

rag-bag ['rægbæg] talego *m* de recortes; *fig.* mezcolanza *f*, cajón *m* de sastre.

rage [reidʒ] **1.** rabia *f*, furor *m*; manía *f*, afán *m* (*for* de); *it's all the ~* es la moda, es la última; **2.** rabiar; (*storm etc.*) bramar.

rag·ged ['rægid] □ harapiento, andrajoso; *edge* desigual, mellado; ♪ poco suave.

rag·ing ['reidʒiŋ] rabioso, furibundo.

rag·man ['rægmən] trapero *m*.

ra·gout ['ræguː] guisado *m*.

rag...: **'~·tag** F chusma *f* (*freq. ~ and bobtail*); **'~·time** ♪ tiempo *m* sincopado.

raid [reid] **1.** correría *f*, incursión *f*; ✈ ataque *m*, bombardeo *m*; **2.** invadir; atacar; ✈ bombardear.

rail[1] [reil] **1.** baranda *f*, barandilla *f*, pasamanos *m*; 🚂 riel *m*, carril *m*; *by ~* por ferrocarril; ✝ *~s pl.* acciones *f/pl.* de sociedades ferroviarias; *get (or go or run) off the ~s* descarrilar; *fig.* extraviarse; **2.** (*a. ~ in, ~ off*) poner cerca (*or* barandilla) a; 🚂 transportar por ferrocarril.

rail[2] [ˌ]: *~ at, ~ against* protestar amargamente contra.

rail[3] [ˌ] *orn.* rascón *m*.

rail·ing ['reiliŋ] (*a. ~s pl.*) verja *f*, barandilla *f*.

rail·lery ['reiləri] burla *f*, mofa *f*.

rail·road **1.** ['reilroud] *Am.* = **rail·way** ['reilwei] ferrocarril *m*; **2.** *attr.* ... ferroviario; **3.** *Am.* llevar a cabo muy precipitadamente; *sl.* encarcelar falsamente.

rail·way·man ['reilweimən] ferroviario *m*.

rai·ment ['reimənt] *lit.* vestimenta *f*.

rain [rein] **1.** lluvia *f* (*a. fig.*); **2.** llover (*a. fig.*); *~ cats and dogs* llover a cántaros; *'~·bow* arco iris *m*; *'~·coat* impermeable *m*; *'~·drop* gota *f* de agua; *'~·fall* precipitación *f*; (*cantidad f de*) lluvia *f*; *~·gauge* ['ˌgeidʒ] pluviómetro *m*; **'rain·i·ness** lo lluvioso; **'rain·proof** impermeable; **'rain·wa·ter** agua *f* llovediza; **'rain·y** □ lluvioso; *~ day* día *m* de lluvia.

raise [reiz] levantar, alzar, elevar, subir, erguir; ⚡ elevar (a una potencia); ascender *in rank*; *sunken vessel* sacar a flote; *army* reclutar; *building* erigir; *claim* formular; *crop* cultivar; *dead* resucitar; *doubts, hopes* suscitar, excitar; *flag* izar, enarbolar; *livestock* criar; *money* reunir; *objection* poner, hacer; *question* plantear, suscitar; *siege, voice* levantar; *v. Cain*; *~ a loan* reunir fondos; *~ one's hat* descubrirse; **raised** en relieve.

ra·ja(h) ['rɑːdʒə] rajá *m*.

rake[1] [reik] **1.** (*garden-*) rastrillo *m*; (*farm-*) rastro *m*; (*fire-*) hurgón *m*; **2.** *v/t.* rastrillar; *fire* hurgar; *~ together* (*off*) reunir (quitar) con el rastrillo; *~ up the past etc.* remover; *sacar a relucir*; ✕, ⚓ barrer; *v/i.* rastrear; *'~·off sl.* tajada *f*.

rake[2] [ˌ] ⚓ **1.** inclinación *f*; **2.** inclinar.

rake[3] [ˌ] libertino *m*, calavera *m*.

rak·ish ['reikiʃ] **1.** ⚓ de palos inclinados; veloz, ligero; gallardo (*a. fig.*); *at a ~ angle hat* echado al lado, a lo chulo; **2.** □ *p.* libertino.

ral·ly[1] ['ræli] **1.** *mst pol.* reunión *f*, manifestación *f*; ✈, ✝ recuperación *f*; ✕ repliegue *m*; *mot.* rallye *m*; *tennis*: peloteo *m*; **2.** *v/i.* reunirse; ✈, ✝ recuperarse; ✕ replegarse, rehacerse; *v/t.* reanimar.

ral·ly[2] [ˌ] ridiculizar, embromar, burlarse de.

ram [ræm] **1.** *zo.* carnero *m*; *ast.* Aries *m*; ✕ ariete *m*; ⚓ espolón *m*; ⊕ pisón *m*; **2.** dar contra; ⚓ atacar con espolón; apisonar; (*fill*) rellenar (*with* de); ~ *s.t.* into introducir algo por fuerza (*or* apretadamente) en.

ram·ble ['ræmbl] **1.** paseo *m* por el campo, excursión *f* a pie; **2.** salir de (*or* hacer una) excursión a pie; divagar *in speech*; **'ram·bler** excursionista *m*/*f*; ~ *rose* rosal *m* trepador; **'ram·bling 1.** □ errante; ❦ trepador; *speech* divagador; *house* laberíntico, construido sobre un plano poco lógico; **2.** excursionismo *m*.

ram·i·fi·ca·tion [ræmifi'keiʃn] ramificación *f*; **ram·i·fy** ['~fai] ramificarse.

ram·mer ['ræmə] ⊕ pisón *m*.

ramp¹ [ræmp] *sl.* estafa *f*; usura *f*.

ramp² [~] rampa *f*; descendedero *m*; **'ram·page** *co.* **1.** *v*/*i.* = **2.**: *be on the* ~ desbocarse, desenfrenarse; **'ramp·an·cy** exuberancia *f*; desenfreno *m*; **'ramp·ant** □ prevaleciente; exuberante; desenfrenado; *heraldry*: rampante; *be* ~ cundir.

ram·part ['ræmpɑ:t] muralla *f*; terraplén *m*.

ram·rod ['ræmrɔd] baqueta *f*, atacador *m*.

ram·shack·le ['ræmʃækl] desvencijado, destartalado, ruinoso.

ran [ræn] *pret. of* run 1.

ranch [rɑ:ntʃ] *Am.* hacienda *f*, rancho *m S.Am.*; **'ranch·er** *Am.* ganadero *m*.

ran·cid ['rænsid] □ rancio; **ran·'cid·i·ty, 'ran·cid·ness** rancidez *f*, ranciedad *f*.

ran·cor·ous ['ræŋkərəs] □ rencoroso.

ran·co(u)r ['ræŋkə] rencor *m*.

ran·dom ['rændəm] **1.**: *at* ~ al azar; **2.** fortuito, casual, impensado; aleatorio; ~ *distribution* distribución *f* aleatoria; ~ *sample* muestra *f* seleccionada al azar; ~ *shot* tiro *m* sin puntería.

rang [ræŋ] *pret. of* ring² 2.

range [reindʒ] **1.** alcance *m*; extensión *f*; serie *f*; ♂ gama *f* (de frecuencias); ✝ surtido *m*; gama *f of colours*; escala *f of prices, speeds*; amplitud *f of variation*; extensión *f of voice*; (*cattle-*) dehesa *f*; (*mountain-*) sierra *f*, cordillera *f*; (*stove*) fogón *m*; ✗ alcance *m* (de tiro); ✗ campo *m* de tiro; ⚓, ✗ autono-

mía *f*, radio *m* de acción; *take the* ~ averiguar la distancia; *within* ~ al alcance (*a. fig.*); **2.** *v*/*t.* ordenar; clasificar; colocar; *country* recorrer; *v*/*i.* extenderse; variar; alinearse; **'~find·er** telémetro *m*; **'rang·er** guardabosques *m*.

rank¹ [ræŋk] **1.** (*row*) fila *f* (*a.* ✗), hilera *f*; (*status*) grado *m*, graduación *f*, rango *m*; dignidad *f*, categoría *f*; ✗ *the* ~*s*, *the* ~ *and file* soldados *m*/*pl.* rasos; *fig.* masa *f*; *join the* ~*s* alistarse; *rise from the* ~*s* ascender desde soldado raso; **2.** *v*/*t.* clasificar, ordenar; *v*/*i.* clasificarse; figurar; ~ *above* ser superior a; ~ *among* estar al nivel de; ~ *as* equivaler a; figurar como; ~ *with* equipararse con.

rank² [~] □ *growth* lozano, exuberante; *smell etc.* maloliente, rancio; *fig. b.s.* redomado.

ran·kle ['ræŋkl] *v*/*i.* roer, afligir (*with acc.*).

rank·ness ['ræŋknis] exuberancia *f of growth*; fetidez *f of smell*.

ran·sack ['rænsæk] saquear; registrar (de arriba abajo).

ran·som ['rænsəm] **1.** rescate *m*; *eccl.* redención *f*; **2.** rescatar; redimir.

rant [rænt] **1.** lenguaje *m* campanudo (*or* declamatorio); **2.** despotricar, delirar, hablar con violencia; hablar en un estilo hinchado; **'rant·er** fanfarrón *m*; declamador *m*.

ra·nun·cu·lus [rə'nʌŋkjuləs] ranúnculo *m*.

rap [ræp] **1.** golpecito *m*; *not to care a* ~ no importarle un bledo a uno; *sl. take the* ~ pagar la multa; **2.** golpear; ~ *a p.'s knuckles fig.* reprender severamente a una p.; ~ *out order* espetar.

ra·pa·cious [rə'peiʃəs] □ rapaz; **ra·pac·i·ty** [rə'pæsiti] rapacidad *f*.

rape¹ [reip] **1.** violación *f*, estupro *m*; **2.** violar, forzar, estuprar.

rape² [~] ❦ colza *f*; **'~-oil** aceite *m* de colza; **'~·seed** nabina *f*.

rap·id ['ræpid] **1.** □ rápido, veloz; **2.** ~*s pl.* rápidos *m*/*pl.*, recial *m*, rabión *m*; **ra·pid·i·ty** [rə'piditi] rapidez *f*.

ra·pi·er ['reipiə] estoque *m*.

rap·ine ['ræpain] *lit.* rapiña *f*.

rap·proche·ment [ræ'prɔʃmɑ̃:ŋ] *pol.* acercamiento *m*.

rapt [ræpt] arrebatado, transportado; ~ *attention* atención *f* fija.

rap·ture ['ræptʃə] rapto *m*, éxtasis *m*, arrobamiento *m*; *in* ~s extasiado; *go into* ~s extasiarse; '**rap·tur·ous** □ extático.

rare [rɛə] □ raro, poco común; peregrino; *phys.* ralo; *esp. Am. meat* poco hecho; ~*ly* rara vez.

rare·bit ['rɛəbit] *v. rabbit.*

rar·e·fac·tion [rɛəri'fækʃn] rarefacción *f*; **rar·e·fy** ['~fai] enrarecer; '**rare·ness**, '**rar·i·ty** rareza *f*.

ras·cal ['rɑːskəl] pillo *m*, pícaro *m*; **ras·cal·i·ty** ['~kæliti] picardía *f*; **ras·cal·ly** ['~kəli] pícaro, truhanesco.

rash[1] [ræʃ] □ temerario; precipitado.

rash[2] [~] 🞳 erupción *f* (cutánea).

rash·er ['ræʃə] magra *f*, lonja *f*.

rash·ness ['ræʃnis] temeridad *f*; precipitación *f*.

rasp [rɑːsp] 1. escofina *f*; 2. escofinar, raspar; decir en voz áspera.

rasp·ber·ry ['rɑːzbəri] frambuesa *f*.

rasp·er ['rɑːspə] raspador *m*.

rasp·ing ['rɑːspiŋ] 1. □ *voice* áspero; 2. ~s *pl.* raspaduras *f*/*pl.*

rat [ræt] 1. rata *f*; *sl.* canalla *m*; *pol.* desertor *m*; *sl.* ~s! ¡narices!; *smell a* ~ oler el poste; 2. cazar ratas; *pol. a.* F desertar, ser esquirol; *sl.* ~ *on* chivatear contra, soplar contra.

rat·a·ble ['reitəbl] □ sujeto a contribución (municipal *etc.*); tasable.

ratch [rætʃ], **ratch·et** ['rætʃit] trinquete *m*; '~-**wheel** rueda *f* de trinquete.

rate[1] [reit] 1. proporción *f*; relación *f*; tanto *m* (por ciento); (*speed*) velocidad *f*, paso *m*; (*price*) tasa *f*, precio *m*; (*hotel*) tarifa *f*; *mst* ~s *pl.* contribución *f* (municipal *etc.*); *at a cheap* ~ a un precio reducido; *at the* ~ *of* a razón de; *at any* ~ de todas formas; *at that* ~ de ese modo; ~ *of exchange* cambio *m*; ~ *of interest* tipo *m* de interés; ~ *of taxation* nivel *m* de impuestos; 2. tasar (*at* en), valorar; clasificar; imponer contribución (municipal) a; ~ *s.o. highly* tener muy buen concepto de alguien.

rate[2] [~] regañar, reñir.

rate-pay·er ['reitpeiə] contribuyente *m*/*f*.

rath·er ['rɑːðə] (*more*) mejor, primero, más bien; (*somewhat*) algo, bastante; F ~! ['rɑː'ðə] ¡ya lo creo!; *or* ~ mejor dicho; *I had (or would)* ~ preferiría *inf.*; me gustaría más *inf.*; *I* ~ *expected it* ya lo preveía.

rat·i·fi·ca·tion [rætifi'keiʃn] ratificación *f*; **rat·i·fy** ['~fai] ratificar.

rat·ing[1] ['reitiŋ] clasificación *f*; contribución *f*; ⚓ (*ship*) clase *f*; ⚓ marinero *m*.

rat·ing[2] [~] represión *f*.

ra·tio ['reiʃiou] relación *f*, razón *f*, proporción *f*.

ra·tion ['ræʃn] 1. ración *f*; ✗ ~s *pl.* suministro *m*; ~ *book (or* ~ *card)* cartilla *f* de racionamiento; *off the* ~ no racionado; 2. racionar.

ra·tion·al ['ræʃnl] □ racional, razonable; **ra·tion·al·ism** ['~nəlizm] racionalismo *m*; '**ra·tion·al·ist** racionalista *m*/*f*; **ra·tion·al·i·ty** [~'næliti] racionalidad *f*; **ra·tion·al·i·za·tion** ['~nəlai'zeiʃn] racionalización *f*; '**ra·tion·al·ize** hacer racional, organizar racionalmente; buscar pretexto racional a.

ra·tion·ing ['ræʃniŋ] racionamiento *m*. [ing sabotaje *m*.]

rat·ten ['rætn] sabotear; '**rat·ten-**

rat·tle ['rætl] 1. golpeteo *m*; traqueteo *m*; crujido *m*; sonsonete *m*; (*instrument*) matraca *f*, carraca *f*; (*child's*) sonajero *m*; *death* ~ estertor *m*; 2. *v/i.* sonar, crujir, castañetear; F ~ *on* parlotear; *v/t.* agitar, sacudir; F desconcertar; ~ *off* enumerar rápidamente; '~-**brained**, '~-**pat·ed** ligero de cascos; '**rat·tler** *Am.* F = '**rat·tle·snake** serpiente *f* de cascabel; '**rat·tle-trap 1.** desvencijado; 2. armatoste *m*.

rat·tling ['rætliŋ] ruidoso; F *at a* ~ *pace* a gran velocidad; F *adv.* ~ *good* realmente estupendo.

rat·ty ['ræti] *sl.* amostazado.

rau·cous ['rɔːkəs] □ estridente, ronco.

rav·age ['rævidʒ] 1. estrago *m*, destrozo *m*; 2. destrozar, asolar; pillar.

rave [reiv] delirar, desvariar; F ~ *about* pirrarse por, entusiasmarse por; ~ *at* insultar frenéticamente de palabra.

rav·en ['reivn] cuervo *m*.

rav·en·ous ['rævnəs] □ famélico, voraz, hambriento; *be* ~*ly hungry* tener una hambre canina; '**rav·en·ous·ness** voracidad *f*.

ra·vine [rəˈviːn] barranco *m.*,

rav·ings [ˈreiviŋz] *pl.* delirio *m*, desvarío *m*.

rav·ish [ˈræviʃ] encantar, embelesar; *lit.* robar, violar; **ˈravˈishˈer** raptor *m*; **ˈravˈishˈing** □ encantador, embelesador; **ˈravˈishˈment** éxtasis *m*; rapto *m*.

raw [rɔː] **1.** □ *food, weather* crudo; *spirit* puro; *substance* en bruto, sin refinar, crudo; *(inexperienced)* novato; F ~ *deal* tratamiento *m* injusto; *v. material*; ~ *recruit* soldado *m* bisoño; **2.** carne *f* viva; F *it gets me on the* ~ me hiere en lo más vivo; **ˈ~-boned** huesudo; **ˈrawˈness** crudeza *f*; inexperiencia *f*.

ray[1] [rei] **1.** rayo *m*; ♀ bráctea *f*; ✶ ~ *treatment* tratamiento *m* con rayos; **2.** emitir rayos.

ray[2] [ʌ] *ichth.* raya *f*.

ray·on [ˈreiɔn] rayón *m*.

raze [reiz] arrasar, asolar (*a.* ~ *to the ground*).

ra·zor [ˈreizə] *(open)* navaja *f*; *(safety-)* maquinilla *f* de afeitar; ✶ máquina *f* de afeitar, rasurador *m*; **ˈ~-blade** hoja *f* (*or* cuchilla *f*) de afeitar; **ˈ~-strop** suavizador *m*.

razz [ræz] *Am. sl.* echar un rapapolvo a; ridiculizar.

raz·zle(-dazˈzle) [ˈræzl(dæzl)] *sl.* borrachera *f*; *go on the* ~ andar de parranda.

re [riː] respecto a, con referencia a.

re... [ʌ] re...

reach [riːtʃ] **1.** alcance *m*; extensión *f*, distancia *f*; capacidad *f*; *(river)* extensión *f* entre dos recodos; *beyond* ~, *out of* ~ fuera de alcance; *within* (*easy*) ~ al alcance de; **2.** *v/i.* extenderse; *with hand* (*freq.* ~ *out*) alargar (*or* tender) la mano (*for* para tomar); *it won't* ~ no llega; *v/t.* alcanzar; llegar a; lograr; *hand* alargar; *age* cumplir.

reach-me-down [ˈriːtʃmiˈdaun] traje *m etc.* que se compra ya confeccionado.

re·act [riˈækt] reaccionar (*against* contra; *to* a, ante; *upon* sobre).

re·acˈtion [riˈækʃn] reacción *f*; **reˈacˈtionˈarˈy** *esp. pol.* reaccionario *adj. a. su. m* (*a f*).

re·acˈtive [riˈæktiv] reactivo; **reˈacˈtor** *phys.* reactor *m*.

read 1. [riːd] *(irr.)* *v/t.* leer; interpretar, descifrar; *typ.* corregir;

univ. estudiar, cursar; *thermometer etc.* consultar; ~ *out* anunciar; ~ *over* repasar; *v/i.* leer; *(notice etc.)* rezar, decir; *(thermometer etc.)* indicar, marcar; ~ *aloud* leer en alta voz; ~ *between the lines* *fig.* leer entre líneas; **2.** [red] *pret. a. p.p. of* **1**; *adj. well* ~ leído, instruido.

read·a·ble [ˈriːdəbl] □ legible; digno de leerse, entretenido.

read·er [ˈriːdə] lector (-a *f*) *m*; *typ.* corrector *m*; *(book)* libro *m* de lectura; *univ.* profesor que ocupa el *segundo rango, después del catedrático*; **ˈreadˈerˈship** número *m* total de lectores (de un periódico); *univ.* puesto del *reader*.

read·i·ly [ˈredili] *adv.* de buena gana; fácilmente; **ˈreadˈiˈness** prontitud *f*; alacridad *f*; buena disposición *f*; *in* ~ preparado, listo; ~ *of mind* (*or wit*) viveza *f*.

read·ing [ˈriːdiŋ] lectura *f* (*a. parl*); interpretación *f*; *(MS)* lección *f*; *(thermometer etc.)* indicación *f*, lectura *f*; *attr.* ... de lectura; ~ *room* sala *f* de lectura.

re·ad·just [ˈriːəˈdʒʌst] reajustar; *pol. etc.* reorientar; **ˈreˈadˈjustˈment** reajuste *m*; reorientación *f*.

re·ad·mit [ˈriːədˈmit] readmitir.

read·y [ˈredi] **1.** □ listo, preparado (*for* para; *to* para *inf.*); pronto; (*inclined*) dispuesto (*to* a); ✶ contante, efectivo; *answer* fácil; *wit* agudo, vivo; ~ *reckoner* libro *m* de cálculos hechos; ~ *for action* dispuesto para el combate; *fig.* lanza en ristre; ~ *for use*, ~ *to use* listo para usar; ~ *to serve* preparado; *get* (*or make*) ~ preparar(se), disponer (se); **2.:** *at the* ~ ✕ listo para tirar; apercibido; en ristre; **ˈ~-made**, **ˈ~-to-ˈwear** ya hecho, confeccionado.

re·af·firm [ˈriːəˈfəːm] reafirmar, reiterar.

re·af·for·es·ta·tion [ˈriːəfɔristˈeiʃn] repoblación *f* forestal.

re·a·gent [riˈeidʒənt] reactivo *m*.

re·al [riəl] □ real; verdadero; auténtico; genuino; legítimo; *v. estate*; **ˈreˈalˈism** realismo *m*; **reˈalˈisˈtic** □ realista; **reˈalˈiˈty** [riˈæliti] realidad *f*; **reˈalˈizˈaˈble** [ˈriəlaizəbl] □ realizable; **reˈalˈiˈzaˈtion** comprensión *f*; realización *f of plan, a.* ✶; verificación *f*; **ˈreˈalˈize** darse cuenta de; reconocer; ✶ realizar;

plan etc. realizar, llevar a cabo; **'real·ly** en realidad; verdaderamente, realmente; ~? ¿de veras?

realm [relm] reino *m*; *Peer of the* ~ miembro de la Cámara de los Lores.

re·al·tor ['rialtə] *Am.* corredor *m* de bienes raíces (*or* de fincas); **'real·ty** ɪ̃z̃ bienes *m|pl.* raíces.

ream[1] [ri:m] (*paper*) resma *f*; F montón *m*.

ream[2] [~] ⊕ escariar; **'ream·er** escariador *m*.

re·an·i·mate [ri'ænimeit] reanimar.

reap [ri:p] segar; cosechar (*a. fig.*); **'reap·er** segador (-a *f*) *m*; (*machine*) segadora *f*; **'reap·ing** siega *f*; **'reap·ing-hook** hoz *f*.

re·ap·pear ['ri:ə'piə] reaparecer; **'re·ap'pear·ance** reaparición *f*.

re·ap·point ['ri:ə'pɔint] volver a nombrar.

rear[1] [riə] *v/t.* criar; (*build*) erigir, alzar; *v/i.* encabritarse, ponerse de manos.

rear[2] [~] **1.** parte *f* posterior (*or* trasera); cola *f*; ✕ última fila *f*; ✕ retaguardia *f*; *bring up the* ~ cerrar la marcha; *at the* ~ *of*, *in* (*the*) ~ *of* detrás de; ✕ *in the* ~ a retaguardia; **2.** trasero, posterior; de cola; ~ *wheel drive* mando *m* de las ruedas traseras; **'~-'ad·mi·ral** contraalmirante *m*; **'~-guard** retaguardia *f*; **'~-lamp** luz *f* piloto (*or* trasera).

re·arm ['ri:'ɑ:m] rearmar(se); **'re·'ar·ma·ment** [~məmənt] rearme *m*.

rear·most ['riəmoust] trasero, último.

re·ar·range ['ri:ə'reindʒ] ordenar de nuevo; ♪ volver a adaptar.

rear·ward ['riəwəd] **1.** *adj.* trasero, de atrás; **2.** *adv.* (*a.* **'rear·wards** [~z]) hacia atrás.

rea·son ['ri:zn] **1.** razón *f*; motivo *m*, causa *f*; sensatez *f*, moderación *f*; *by* ~ *of* a causa de; en virtud de; *for this* ~ por esta razón; *within* ~ dentro de lo razonable; *listen to* ~ meterse en razón; *it stands to* ~ (*that*) es evidente (que), es lógico (que); **2.** *v/i.* razonar, discurrir; *v/t.* razonar; resolver pensando (*a.* ~ *out*); ~ *a p. into* (*out of*) *a th.* lograr con razones que una p. acepte (abandone) algo; ~*ed* razonado; **'rea·son·a·ble** □ razonable; justo, equi-

tativo; *p.* sensato; **'rea·son·ing** razonamiento *m*; argumento *m*.

re·as·sem·ble ['ri:ə'sembl] volver a reunir(se); ⊕ montar de nuevo.

re·as·sert ['ri:ə'sə:t] reiterar, reafirmar.

re·as·sur·ance ['ri:ə'ʃuərəns] noticia *f* (*or* promesa *f etc.*) tranquilizadora; **re·as·sure** ['~'ʃuə] tranquilizar; alentar; **re·as'sur·ing** □ tranquilizador.

re·bate[1] ['ri:beit] **1.** rebaja *f*, descuento *m*; **2.** rebajar, descontar.

re·bate[2] [~, 'ræbit] ⊕ *v. rabbet.*

reb·el 1. ['rebl] rebelde *m|f*; **2.** [~] rebelde (*mst* **re·bel·lious** [ri'beljəs]); **3.** [ri'bel] rebelarse, sublevarse; **re'bel·lion** [~jən] rebelión *f*, sublevación *f*.

re·birth ['ri:bə:θ] renacimiento *m*.

re·bore ['ri:bɔ:] **1.** ⊕ rectificar; **2.** rectificado *m*.

re·bound [ri'baund] **1.** rebotar; **2.** rebote *m*; *on the* ~ de rebote, de rechazo.

re·buff [ri'bʌf] **1.** repulsa *f*, desaire *m*; **2.** rechazar, desairar.

re·build ['ri:'bild] [*irr.* (*build*)] reedificar, reconstruir.

re·buke [ri'bju:k] **1.** reprensión *f*, reprimenda *f*; **2.** reprender, censurar.

re·bus ['ri:bəs] jeroglífico *m*.

re·but [ri'bʌt] rebatir, refutar; **re'but·tal** refutación *f*.

re·cal·ci·trant [ri'kælsitrənt] recalcitrante, refractorio.

re·call [ri'kɔ:l] **1.** revocación *f*; retirada *f of ambassador, capital*; llamada *f* (para que vuelva una p.); *thea.* llamada *f* a escena; *beyond* ~, *past* ~ irrevocable; **2.** revocar; *ambassador, capital* retirar; llamar; hacer volver; recordar, traer a la memoria.

re·cant [ri'kænt] retractar(se); **re·can·ta·tion** [ri:kæn'teiʃn] retractación *f*.

re·ca·pit·u·late [ri:kə'pitjuleit] recapitular; **'re·ca·pit·u'la·tion** recapitulación *f*.

re·cap·ture ['ri:'kæptʃə] **1.** represa *f*, recobro *m*; **2.** represar, recobrar; volver a prender; *memory* hacer revivir.

re·cast ['ri:'kɑ:st] [*irr.* (*cast*)] ⊕ refundir (*a. fig.*).

re·cede [ri'si:d] retroceder, retirarse, alejarse; (*price*) bajar.

re·ceipt [ri'si:t] **1.** recibo *m*; cobranza *f*; ✝ ~s *pl.* ingresos *m/pl.*; **2.** dar recibo (por).

re·ceiv·a·ble [ri'si:vəbl] admisible; recibidero; ✝ por cobrar; **re'ceive** recibir, admitir; *guest etc.* acoger; *money* cobrar; *tennis etc.*: ser restador; **re'ceived** admitido, aprobado; **re'ceiv·er** recibidor (-a *f*) *m*; destinatario (a *f*) *m*; *radio:* receptor *m*; *teleph.* auricular *m*; *phys.*, 🜖 recipiente *m*; 🜨 *(official ~) approx.* síndico *m*; **re'ceiv·ing** recepción *f* (*a. radio*); ~ set radiorreceptor *m*.

re·cen·sion [ri'senʃn] recensión *f*.

re·cent ['ri:snt] □ reciente, nuevo.

re·cep·ta·cle [ri'septəkl] receptáculo *m* (*a.* 🜬).

re·cep·tion [ri'sepʃn] recepción *f* (*a. radio*); recibimiento *m*; acogida *f*; *(royal)* besamanos *m*; **re'cep·tion·ist** recibidor (-a *f*) *m*; **re'cep·tion·room** sala *f* de recibo.

re·cep·tive [ri'septiv] □ receptivo; **re·cep'tiv·i·ty** receptividad *f*.

re·cess [ri'ses] vacaciones *f/pl.*, intermisión *f*; *esp. parl.* suspensión *f*; intermedio *m between sittings*; 🜨 rebajo *m*; △ hueco *m*, nicho *m*; ~es *pl. fig.* entrañas *f/pl.*; lo más recóndito.

re·ces·sion [ri'seʃn] retirada *f*, retroceso *m* (*a.* ✝); ✝ recesión *f*; **re'ces·sion·al** himno *m* (de fin de oficio).

re·cher·ché [rə'ʃɛəʃei] rebuscado.

re·ci·pe ['resipi] receta *f*.

re·cip·i·ent [ri'sipiənt] recibidor (-a *f*) *m*, recipiente *m/f*.

re·cip·ro·cal [ri'siprəkəl] **1.** □ recíproco, mutuo; **2.** A recíproca *f*, inverso *m*; **re'cip·ro·cate** [~keit] *v/i.* 🜨 oscilar, alternar; usar de reciprocidad, corresponder; *v/t.* intercambiar; corresponder a; devolver; **re·cip·ro'ca·tion** reciprocación *f*; **rec·i·proc·i·ty** [resi'prɔsiti] reciprocidad *f*.

re·cit·al [ri'saitl] relación *f*, narración *f*; ♪ recital *m*; 🜨 parte *f* expositiva (de un documento); **rec·i·ta·tion** [resi'teiʃn] recitación *f*; recitado *m*; **rec·i·ta·tive** [~tə'ti:v] ♪ recitativo *adj. a. su. m*; recitado *m*; **re·cite** [ri'sait] recitar; declamar; narrar, referir; **re'cit·er** recitador (-a *f*) *m*.

reck·less ['reklis] □ temerario; imprudente; inconsiderado; **'reck-**less·ness** temeridad *f*; imprudencia *f*.

reck·on ['rekn] *v/t.* contar, calcular; estimar; considerar (*as como; that* que); ~ *up* calcular, computar; *v/i.* calcular; F estimar, creer; ~ (*up*)*on* contar con; ~ *with* tener en cuenta; **'reck·on·er** calculador *m*; *v. ready* ~; **'reck·on·ing** cuenta *f*; cálculo *m*; *be out in one's* ~ equivocarse en el cálculo; *day of* ~ día *m* de ajuste de cuentas.

re·claim [ri'kleim] reclamar; amansar, reformar; *land* recuperar, hacer utilizable; (*from sea*) ganar; ⊕ utilizar, regenerar; **re'claim·a·ble** reclamable; utilizable.

rec·la·ma·tion [reklə'meiʃn] reclamación *f*; recuperación *f*, utilización *f*; *land* ~ rescate *m* de terrenos.

re·cline [ri'klain] reclinar(se), recostar(se); ~ *upon fig.* contar con, fiarse de; **re'clin·ing chair** sillón *m* reclinable, poltrona *f*.

re·cluse [ri'klu:s] recluso, solitario *adj. a. su. m* (a *f*).

rec·og·ni·tion [rekəg'niʃn] reconocimiento *m*; **rec·og·niz·a·ble** ['~naizəbl] □ reconocible; **rec·og·ni·zance** [ri'kɔgnizəns] 🜨 reconocimiento *m*; obligación *f* contraída; **rec·og·nize** ['rekəgnaiz] reconocer; admitir, confesar.

re·coil [ri'kɔil] **1.** recular, retroceder (de espanto); ✕ retroceder, rebufar; ~ *on* recaer sobre; **2.** reculada *f*, retroceso *m* (*a.* ✕); ✕ rebufo *m*.

rec·ol·lect [rekə'lekt] recordar, acordarse de; **rec·ol·lec·tion** [rekə-'lekʃn] recuerdo *m*.

re·com·mence ['ri:kə'mens] recomenzar.

rec·om·mend [rekə'mend] recomendar, encarecer; **rec·om'mend·a·ble** recomendable; **rec·om·men·'da·tion** recomendación *f*; **rec·om'mend·a·to·ry** [~ətəri] recomendatorio.

rec·om·pense ['rekəmpens] **1.** recompensa *f*, compensación *f*; **2.** recompensar (*for acc.*).

re·com·pose ['ri:kəm'pouz] recomponer.

rec·on·cil·a·ble ['rekənsailəbl] reconciliable; **'rec·on·cile** (re)conciliar; ~ *o.s. to* resignarse a, acomodarse con; **'rec·on·cil·er** reconciliador (-a *f*) *m*; **rec·on·cil·i·a·tion** [ˈ‿siliˈeiʃn] reconciliación *f*.

rec·on·dite [riˈkɔndait] □ recóndito.

re·con·di·tion [ˈriːkənˈdiʃn] reacondicionar.

re·con·nais·sance [riˈkɔnisəns] reconocimiento *m*.

rec·on·noi·ter, rec·on·noi·tre [rekəˈnɔitə] reconocer.

re·con·quer [ˈriːˈkɔŋkə] reconquistar; **'re·con·quest** [‿kwest] reconquista *f*.

re·con·sid·er [ˈriːkənˈsidə] repensar, reconsiderar; **'re·con·sid·er·'a·tion** reconsideración *f*.

re·con·sti·tute [ˈriːˈkɔnstitjuːt] reconstituir; **'re·con·sti'tu·tion** reconstitución *f*.

re·con·struct [ˈriːkənsˈtrʌkt] reconstruir; reedificar; **'re·con'struc·tion** reconstrucción *f*.

re·con·ver·sion [ˈriːkənˈvəːʃn] reconversión *f*, reorganización *f*; **'re·con'vert** reconvertir, reorganizar.

re·cord 1. [ˈrekɔːd] registro *m*; partida *f*; documento *m*; relación *f*; (*p.'s history*) historial *m*, curriculum vitae *m*, carrera *f*, antecedentes *m*/*pl*.; reputación *f*; ⚖ acta *f*; *sport*: record *m*, marca *f*; ♩ disco *m*; ‿s *pl*. archivos *m*/*pl*.; *esp. Am.* off the ‿ no oficial, confidencial(mente); *place* on ‿ dejar constancia de; *it is on* ‿ *that* consta que; *beat* (*or break*) *the* ‿ batir la marca; *set up* (*or establish*) *a* ‿ establecer un record; ‿ *card* ficha *f*; ‿ *library* discoteca *f*; ☸ Office Archivo *m* Nacional; **2.** [‿] *attr*. sin precedentes, máximo; ‿ *time* tiempo *m* record; **3.** [riˈkɔːd] registrar; hacer constar, consignar; inscribir; archivar; indicar; *voice etc.* registrar, grabar; **re'cord·er** registrador *m*, archivero *m*; ⚖ *approx*. juez *m* municipal; ♩ caramillo *m*; ⊕ indicador *m*; **re'cord·ing** grabación *f*; **'re·cord-'play·er** tocadiscos *m*.

re·count¹ [riˈkaunt] (re)contar, referir.

re·count² [ˈriːˈkaunt] *parl*. segundo escrutinio *m*.

re·coup [riˈkuːp] recobrar; indemnizarse por.

re·course [riˈkɔːs] recurso *m*; *have* ‿ *to* recurrir a.

re·cov·er¹ [riˈkʌvə] *v*/*t*. recobrar, recuperar; *money* reembolsarse;

recaudar; *v*/*i*. ✠ restablecerse (*a*. ✝), reponerse; ⚖ ganar (‿ *in a suit* un pleito).

re·cov·er² [ˈriːˈkʌvə] recubrir.

re·cov·er·a·ble [riˈkʌvərəbl] recuperable; **re'cov·er·y** recobro *m*, recuperación *f*; ✠ restablecimiento *m*, mejoría *f*; recaudación *f* of *money*.

rec·re·ate [ˈrekrieit] recrear(se), divertir(se); **rec·re'a·tion** recreación *f*; *school*: recreo *m*; ‿ *ground* campo *m* de deportes; **'rec·re·a·tive** recreativo.

re·crim·i·nate [riˈkrimineit] recriminar; **re·crim·i'na·tion** recriminación *f*.

re·cru·desce [riːkruˈdes] recrudecer; **re·cru'des·cence** recrudescencia *f*.

re·cruit [riˈkruːt] **1.** recluta *m*; *fig*. novicio *m*; **2.** reclutar, alistar; ✠ *etc*. restablecer(se), rehacer(se); **re'cruit·ing, re'cruit·ment** reclutamiento *m*.

rec·tan·gle [ˈrektæŋgl] rectángulo *m*; **rec'tan·gu·lar** [‿gjulə] □ rectangular.

rec·ti·fi·a·ble [ˈrektifaiəbl] rectificable; **rec·ti·fi·ca·tion** [‿fiˈkeiʃn] rectificación *f*; **rec·ti·fi·er** [ˈ‿faiə] *mst* rectificador *m*; ⊕ (*crankshafts etc*.) rectificadora *f*; **rec·ti·fy** [ˈ‿fai] *all senses*: rectificar; **rec·ti·lin·e·al** [rektiˈlinjəl], **rec·ti·lin·e·ar** [‿njə] □ rectilíneo; **rec·ti·tude** [ˈ‿tjuːd] rectitud *f*, probidad *f*.

rec·tor [ˈrektə] *Scot. univ*. rector *m*; *eccl*. párroco *m*; **rec·tor·ate** [ˈ‿rit], **'rec·tor·ship** rectorado *m*; **'rec·to·ry** rectoría *f*; casa *f* del cura.

rec·tum [ˈrektəm] recto *m*.

re·cum·bent [riˈkʌmbənt] □ reclinado, recostado; *statue* yacente.

re·cu·per·ate [riˈkjuːpəreit] *v*/*t*. recuperar; *v*/*i*. ✠ restablecerse; **re·cu·per'a·tion** recuperación *f*; ✠ restablecimiento *m*; **re'cu·per·a·tive** [‿rətiv] recuperativo.

re·cur [riˈkəː] repetirse, producirse de nuevo, volver a ocurrir; (*idea*) volver a la mente; ‿ *ring decimal* decimal *f* (*or* fracción *f*) periódica pura; **re·cur·rence** [riˈkʌrəns] repetición *f*, reaparición *f*; **re'cur·rent** □ repetido; recurrente (*a. anat.*, ✠); ♉ periódico.

re·curve [riːˈkəːv] recorvar(se).

rec·u·sant ['rekjuzənt] recusante *adj. a. su. m/f.*

red [red] **1.** rojo (*a. pol.*); colorado; encarnado; *wine* tinto; *face* encendido *with anger*, ruboroso *with shame*; *sl. paint the town* ~ echar una cana al aire; ♀ *Cross* Cruz *f* Roja; ~ *currant* grosella *f* roja; ~ *deer* ciervo *m* común; ~ *heat* calor *m* rojo; ~ *herring fig.* pista *f* falsa, ardid *m* para apartar la atención del asunto principal; ~ *lead* minio *m*; ~ *tape* papeleo *m*, formalidades *f/pl.*, burocracia *f*; **2.** (color *m*) rojo *m*; (*pol.*) rojo *m*; *see* ~ sulfurarse, encolerizarse; F *be in the* ~ estar adeudado, estar en el libro de los morosos.

red·act [ri'dækt] redactar; **re'dac·tion** redacción *f*.

red·breast ['redbrest] (*freq. robin* ~) petirrojo *m*; **'red·cap** *Am.* mozo *m* de estación; ✕ *sl.* policía *m* militar; **red·den** ['redn] *v/t.* enrojecer, teñir de rojo; *v/i.* enrojecer(se) *with anger*; ponerse colorado, ruborizarse *with shame*; **'red·dish** rojizo; **red·dle** ['⌐⌐] almagre *m*, almazarrón *m*.

re·dec·o·rate ['ri:'dekəreit] *room* renovar; **'re·dec·o'ra·tion** renovación *f*.

re·deem [ri'di:m] redimir; *promise* cumplir; *pledge etc.* rescatar, desempeñar; ✝ amortizar; ~*ing virtue* virtud *f* compensadora; **re'deem·a·ble** redimible; ✝ amortizable; **Re'deem·er** Redentor *m*.

re·de·liv·er ['ri:di'livə] volver a entregar.

re·demp·tion [ri'dempʃn] redención *f*; rescate *m*; desempeño *m*; ✝ amortización *f*; *beyond* ~, *past* ~ sin esperanza, que no tiene remedio; **re'demp·tive** redentor.

re·de·ploy·ment ['ri:di'plɔiment] reorganización *f*.

red...: '~·haired, **'~·head·ed** pelirrojo; **'~·hand·ed** con las manos en la masa, en flagrante; **'~·hot** candente; *fig.* vehemente, acérrimo; *news* de última hora.

re·di·rect ['ri:di'rekt] *letter* reexpedir.

re·dis·cov·er ['ri:dis'kʌvə] volver a descubrir.

re·dis·trib·ute ['ri:dis'tribju:t] distribuir de nuevo.

red-let·ter day ['redletə'dei] día *m* festivo; *fig.* día *m* señalado.

red-light dis·trict ['redlait'distrikt] barrio *m* de los lupanares, barrio *m* chino.

red·ness ['rednis] rojez *f*, lo rojo.

re·do ['ri:'du:] [*irr.* (do)] rehacer.

red·o·lence ['redələns] fragancia *f*, perfume *m*; **'red·o·lent** perfumado (*of* como); *fig. be* ~ *of* recordar, hacer pensar en.

re·dou·ble [ri'dʌbl] redoblar (*a. bridge*); intensificar.

re·doubt [ri'daut] reducto *m*; **re'doubt·a·ble** temible, formidable.

re·dound [ri'daund]: ~ *to* redundar en (*or* en beneficio de).

re·draft ['ri:'dra:ft] **1.** nuevo borrador *m*; ✝ (letra *f* de) resaca *f*; **2.** *or* **re·draw** ['ri:'drɔ:] [*irr.* (draw)] volver a dibujar (*or* redactar).

re·dress [ri'dres] **1.** reparación *f*, compensación *f*, resarcimiento *m*; derecho *m* a satisfacción; **2.** reparar, resarcir; enmendar; equilibrar.

red...: '~·skin piel roja *m/f*; **'~·start** colirrojo *m* real.

re·duce [ri'dju:s] *v/t.* reducir (*to* a, hasta; *a.* ♈, ♎); disminuir; abreviar; *price* rebajar; degradar *in rank*; *fort etc.* reducir, tomar; ~ *to writing* poner por escrito; *v/i.* ✄ adelgazar; **re'duc·i·ble** reducible; **re'duc·tion** [ri'dʌkʃn] reducción *f*; di(s)minución *f*; abreviación *f*; rebaja *f* *of price*; reducción *f*, toma *f* *of fort etc.*

re·dun·dance, **re·dun·dan·cy** [ri'dʌndəns(i)] redundancia *f*; **re'dun·dant** □ redundante; *be* ~ estar de más.

re·du·pli·cate [ri'dju:plikeit] reduplicar; **re·du·pli·ca·tion** reduplicación *f*.

re·dye ['ri:'dai] reteñir.

re·ech·o [ri:'ekou] repercutirse, resonar.

reed [ri:d] ♉ carrizo *m*, junco *m*, caña *f*; ♪ lengüeta *f*; ♪ (*pipe*) caramillo *m*.

re·ed·it ['ri:'edit] reeditar.

re·ed·u·ca·tion ['ri:edju'keiʃn] reeducación *f*. [alto y delgado.)

reed·y ['ri:di] *place* cañoso; *voice*]

reef[1] [ri:f] escollo *m*, arrecife *m*.

reef[2] [~] ⚓ **1.** rizo *m*; **2.** arrizar.

reef·er[1] ['ri:fə] chaquetón *m*.

reef·er[2] [~] *sl.* pitillo *m* de mariguana.

reek [ri:k] **1.** vaho *m*; hedor *m*; **2.** vahear, humear; heder, oler (*of* a).

reel [ri:l] **1.** carrete *m*, tambor *m*; (*fishing*) carrete(l) *m*; *sew.* broca *f*, devanadera *f*; ♪ *baile escocés*; *phot.*, *film*: rollo *m*, cinta *f*, película *f*; F off the ~ seguido(s); **2.** *v/t.* devanar; ~ off enumerar rápidamente, ensartar; *v/i.* tambalear(se); (*enemy*) cejar.

re·e·lect ['ri:i'lekt] reelegir.

re·el·i·gi·ble ['ri:'elidʒəbl] reelegible.

re·en·act ['ri:i'nækt] 🏛 volver a promulgar; *thea.* volver a representar.

re·en·gage ['ri:in'geidʒ] contratar de nuevo. [(se).]

re·en·list ['ri:in'list] reenganchar)

re·en·ter ['ri:'entə] reingresar en, reentrar en; **re·en·trant** [ri:'entrənt] entrante.

re·es·tab·lish ['ri:is'tæbliʃ] restablecer; **'re·es'tab·lish·ment** restablecimiento *m*.

reeve [ri:v] ⚓ *v/i.* laborear; *v/t.* pasar (por un ojal *etc.*).

re·ex·change ['ri:iks'tʃeindʒ] ✝ (letra *f* de) resaca *f*, recambio *m*.

re·fec·tion [ri'fekʃn] refacción *f*; **re'fec·to·ry** [⌐təri] refectorio *m*.

re·fer [ri'fə:] *v/t.* remitir (*a th. to a p.* algo a una p., *a p. to a th.* una p. a algo); *v/i.*: ~ *to* referirse a, hacer referencia (*or* alusión) a; **ref'er·a·ble** ~ *to* referible a, asignable a; **ref·er·ee** [refə'ri:] **1.** *all senses:* árbitro *m*; **2.** arbitrar; **ref·er·ence** ['refrəns] referencia *f*; alusión *f*; recomendación *f*; (*a.* ~ *mark*) llamada *f*; *with* (*or in*) ~ *to* en cuanto a, respecto a (*or* de); *make* ~ *to* referirse a, hacer alusión a; *terms of* ~ puntos *m/pl.* de consulta; *work of* ~, ~ *book* libro *m* de consulta; ~ *library* biblioteca *f* de consulta; ~ *number* número *m* de referencia; ~ *point* punto *m* de referencia.

ref·er·en·dum [refə'rendəm] referéndum *m*.

re·fill ['ri:'fil] **1.** repuesto *m*, recambio *m*; mina *f* *for pencil*; **2.** rellenar.

re·fine [ri'fain] *v/t.* refinar (*a.* ⊕); purificar; ⊕ acrisolar, acendrar (*a. fig.*); *v/i.*: ~ (*up*)*on* sutilizar *acc.*; mejorar *acc.*; **re'fined** fino, refinado; *b.s.* redicho; **re'fine·ment** refinamiento *m*; esmero *m*, urbanidad *f*; ⊕ refinación *f*; **re'fin·er** refinador *m*; **re'fin·er·y** refinería *f*.

re·fit ['ri:'fit] **1.** reparar(se) (*a.* ⚓), componer(se); **2.** (*a.* **re'fit·ment**) reparación *f*, compostura *f*.

re·flect [ri'flekt] *v/t.* reflejar; *v/i.* (*think*) reflexionar; *that* ~*s well* (*ill*) *upon him* eso le revela bajo una luz (poco) favorable; **re'flec·tion** reflejo *m*, reflexión *f*; (*thinking*) reflexión *f*, consideración *f*, meditación *f*; (*censure*) reproche *m* (*on* a); *cast* ~*s on* reprochar *acc.*; **re'flec·tive** □ reflexivo; **re'flec·tor** reflector *m*; *mot.* rear ~ (placa *f* de) captafaros *m*.

re·flex ['ri:fleks] reflejo *adj. a. su. m*; ~ *action physiol.* (acto *m*) reflejo *m*; **re'flex·ive** [ri'fleksiv] □ reflexivo.

re·float ['ri:'flout] sacar a flote.

re·flux ['ri:flʌks] reflujo *m*.

re·for·est·a·tion ['ri:fɔris'teiʃn] repoblación *f* forestal.

re·form [ri'fɔ:m] **1.** reforma(ción) *f*; **2.** reformar(se), enmendar(se); reconstituir (*mst* **re-form** ['ri:-'fɔ:m]); **ref·or·ma·tion** [refə-'meiʃn] reformación *f*; *eccl.* ♀ Reforma *f*; **re·form·a·to·ry** [ri'fɔ:-mətəri] reformatorio *adj. a. su. m* (*mst* de *jóvenes*); **re'formed** reformado; **re'form·er** reformador (-a *f*) *m*.

re·found ['ri:'faund] refundir.

re·fract [ri'frækt] refractar; ~*ing telescope* telescopio *m* de refracción; **re'frac·tion** refracción *f*; **re'frac·tive** refractivo; **re'frac·tor** refractor *m*; **re'frac·to·ri·ness** lo refractario (*a.* 🜍), obstinación *f*; **re'frac·to·ry** refractario (*a.* 🜍), obstinado.

re·frain[1] [ri'frein] abstenerse (*from* de).

re·frain[2] [~] estribillo *m*.

re·fresh [ri'freʃ] refrescar; **re'fresh·er** F refresco *m*; ~ *course* curso *m* de repaso; **re'fresh·ing** ⌐ refrescante; **re'fresh·ment** refresco *m*; ~*s pl.* refrescos *m/pl.*; ~ *room* cantina *f*.

re·frig·er·ant [ri'fridʒərənt] refrigerante *adj. a. su. m*; **re'frig·er·ate** [⌐reit] refrigerar; **re'frig·er·at·ing** refrigerativo; refrigerante; **re'frig·er·a·tion** refrigeración *f*; **re'frig·er·a·tor** nevera *f*, refrigerador *m*; 🜍 refrigerante *m*; ~ *lorry* camión *m* frigorífico.

re·fu·el [ri:'fjuəl] reabastecer(se) de

combustible, rellenar (de combustible).

ref·uge ['refjuːdʒ] refugio *m*, asilo *m*; *fig.* recurso *m*, amparo *m*; *mount.* albergue *m*; *take* ~ guarecerse; *take* ~ *in* acogerse a; **ref·u·gee** [ˌ·'dʒiː] refugiado (a *f*) *m*; ~ *camp* campo *m* de refugiados.

re·ful·gence [ri'fʌldʒəns] refulgencia *f*; **re'ful·gent** □ refulgente.

re·fund 1. [riː'fʌnd] devolver, reintegrar; **2.** ['riːfʌnd] devolución *f*.

re·fur·bish ['riː'fəːbiʃ] restaurar, repulir. [nuevo.]

re·fur·nish ['riː'fəːniʃ] amueblar de]

re·fus·al [ri'fjuːzl] negativa *f*; denegación *f*; rechazamiento *m*; ✝ opción *f* (exclusiva).

re·fuse 1. [ri'fjuːz] *v/t.* rehusar, (de)negar, rechazar; no querer aceptar; ~ *o.s.* *s.t.* privarse de algo; *v/i.* (*horse*) rehusar, plantarse; ~ *to inf.* negarse a *inf.*, rehusar *inf.*; *he* ~*d* se negó a hacerlo; **2. re'fuse** ['refjuːs] desechado; **3.** [ˌ·] basura *f*; desperdicios *m/pl.*; sobras *f/pl.*; ~ *lorry* camión *m* de la basura.

ref·u·ta·ble ['refjutəbl] □ refutable; **ref·u'ta·tion** refutación *f*; **re·fute** [ri'fjuːt] refutar, rebatir.

re·gain [ri'gein] (re)cobrar.

re·gal ['riːgəl] □ regio; real.

re·gale [ri'geil] regalar(se) (*on* con); agasajar, festejar.

re·ga·li·a [ri'geiliə] *pl.* insignias *f/pl.* (reales).

re·gard [ri'gɑːd] **1.** consideración *f*, respeto *m*; estimación *f*; (*gaze*) mirada *f*; ~*s pl.* recuerdos *m/pl.*; *having* ~ *to* considerando; *in* (*or with*) ~ *to* con respecto a, en cuanto a; *out of* ~ *for* por respeto a; *with kind* ~*s* con muchos recuerdos; **2.** considerar (*as* como); observar; respetar; mirar; tocar a; *as* ~*s* por lo que se refiere a; **re'gard·ful** □ atento (*of* a); **re'gard·ing** en cuanto a; relativo a; **re'gard·less 1.:** ~ *of* indiferente a; sin hacer caso de; sin miramientos de; **2.** *adv.* F pese a quien pese, a pesar de todo.

re·gat·ta [ri'gætə] regata *f*.

re·gen·cy ['riːdʒənsi] regencia *f*.

re·gen·er·ate 1. [ri'dʒenəreit] regenerar; **2.** [ˌ·rit] regenerado; **re·gen·er'a·tion** regeneración *f*; **re'gen·er·a·tive** [ˌ·rətiv] *radio:* regenerador.

re·gent ['riːdʒənt] regente *adj. a. su. m/f.*

reg·i·cide ['redʒisaid] regicidio *m*; (*p.*) regicida *m/f.*

ré·gime [rei'ʒiːm], **reg·i·men** ['redʒimen] régimen *m*.

reg·i·ment 1. ['redʒimənt] regimiento *m*; **2.** ['ˌ·ment] *fig.* organizar muy estrictamente, reglamentar; **reg·i'men·tal** de(l) regimiento; **reg·i'men·tals** [ˌ·tlz] *pl.* ✕ uniforme *m*; **reg·i·men'ta·tion** organización *f* estricta.

re·gion ['riːdʒən] región *f*, comarca *f*; zona *f*; *in the* ~ *of fig.* alrededor de; **'re·gion·al** □ regional.

reg·is·ter ['redʒistə] **1.** registro *m* (*a.* ♪); lista *f*, padrón *m* *of members*; *univ.*, ♟ matrícula *f*; ⊕ indicador *m*, registrador *m*; (*parish*) ~ registro *m* parroquial; ~ *office* *approx.* juzgado *m* (municipal); ♟ ~ *ton* tonelada *f* de registro (= *2,832m³*); **2.** *v/t.* registrar; inscribir, matricular; ⊕ indicar *emotion* manifestar; *letter* certificar; *luggage* facturar; *v/i.* inscribirse, matricular; *typ.* corresponder, estar en registro; *fig.* producir impresión; **'reg·is·tered** *letter* certificado; ~ *design* diseño *m* registrado; ~ *trade mark* marca *f* registrada.

reg·is·trar [redʒis'trɑː] registrador *m*, archivero *m*; **reg·is'tra·tion** [ˌ·'treiʃn] registro *m*, inscripción *f*, matrícula *f*; ~ *fee* derechos *m/pl.* de matrícula; ~ *number* *mot.* matrícula *f*; **'reg·is·try** registro *m*, archivo *m*; ~ *office* *approx.* juzgado *m* (municipal), registro *m* civil; *servants'* ~ agencia *f* de colocaciones.

re·gress ['riːgres] retroceso *m*; **re·gres·sion** [ri'greʃn] regresión *f*; **re·gres·sive** [ri'gresiv] □ regresivo.

re·gret [ri'gret] **1.** sentimiento *m*, pesar *m*; remordimiento *m*; *to my* ~ a mi pesar; ~*s pl.* excusas *f/pl.*; **2.** sentir, lamentar; arrepentirse de; **re'gret·ful** [ˌ·ful] □ pesaroso; arrepentido; ~*ly* con pesar, sentidamente; **re'gret·ta·ble** □ lamentable, deplorable.

reg·u·lar ['regjulə] **1.** □ regular (*a. eccl.*); normal; uniforme; ordenado; *attender etc.* asiduo; *reader* habitual; F cabal, verdadero; ✕ regular, de línea; **2.** *eccl.* regular *m*;

✗ soldado *m* de línea; F parroquiano *m*, asiduo *m*; **reg·u·lar·i·ty** [‿'læriti] regularidad *f*; orden *m*; '**reg·u·lar·ize** regularizar.

reg·u·late ['regjuleit] regular (*a.* ⊕), arreglar, ajustar; '**reg·u·lat·ing** ⊕ regulador; **reg·u·la·tion 1.** regulación *f*; regla *f*, reglamento *m*; **2.** reglamentario; '**reg·u·la·tor** regulador *m* (*a.* ⊕).

re·gur·gi·tate [ri:'gə:dʒiteit] *v/t.* vomitar (sin esfuerzo); *v/i.* regurgitar.

re·ha·bil·i·tate [ri:ə'biliteit] rehabilitar; '**re·ha·bil·i·ta·tion** rehabilitación *f*.

re·hash ['ri:'hæʃ] *fig.* **1.** refundir, rehacer; **2.** refundición *f*.

re·hears·al [ri'hə:sl] enumeración *f*, repetición *f*; *thea.*, ♪ ensayo *m*; **re·hearse** [ri'hə:s] enumerar, repetir; *thea.*, ♪ ensayar.

reign [rein] **1.** reinado *m*; *fig.* (pre)dominio *m*; **2.** reinar; *fig.* imperar, prevalecer; *‿ing* reinante.

re·im·burse ['ri:im'bə:s] reembolsar; '**re·im'burse·ment** reembolso *m*.

rein [rein] **1.** rienda *f*; *give ‿ to* dar rienda suelta a; **2.** *v/t.*: ‿ *in*, ‿ *back* refrenar; *v/i.*: ‿ *in* detenerse.

rein·deer ['reindiə] reno *m*.

re·in·force ['ri:in'fɔ:s] reforzar (*a. fig.*); *‿d concrete* hormigón *m* armado; '**re·in'force·ments** *pl.* refuerzos *m/pl.*

re·in·state ['ri:in'steit] reinstalar; rehabilitar; '**re·in'state·ment** reinstalación *f*.

re·in·sur·ance ['ri:in'ʃuərəns] reaseguro *m*; **re·in·sure** ['‿'ʃuə] reasegurar.

re·in·vest ['ri:in'vest] reinvertir.

re·is·sue ['ri:'isju:] **1.** *book* reimprimir; *patent etc.* reexpedir; *film* reestrenar; **2.** reimpresión *f* etc.

re·it·er·ate ['ri:'itəreit] reiterar; **re·it·er'a·tion** reiteración *f*.

re·ject [ri'dʒekt] *offer etc.* rechazar; *application* denegar; *plan etc.* desechar; *solution* descartar; **re'jec·tion** rechazamiento *m*; denegación *f*, desestimación *f*; **re'jec·tor cir·cuit** *radio*: circuito *m* de repulsor.

re·joice [ri'dʒɔis] alegrar(se), regocijar(se) (*at, by* de); **re'joic·ing 1.** □ regocijado; **2.** (*freq. ‿s pl.*) regocijo *m*, júbilo *m*, alegría *f*.

re·join 1. ['ri:'dʒɔin] reunirse con, volver a juntarse con; reincorporarse a; **2.** [ri'dʒɔin] replicar; **re'join·der** réplica *f*.

re·ju·ve·nate [ri'dʒu:vineit] rejuvenecer; **re·ju·ve·nes·cence** [‿'nesns] rejuvenecimiento *m*.

re·kin·dle ['ri:'kindl] reencender.

re·lapse [ri'læps] **1.** ⚕ recaída *f*, recidiva *f*; reincidencia *f* *into crime etc.*; **2.** ⚕ recaer; reincidir *into crime etc.*; *eccl.* relapso *m into sin, heresy.*

re·late [ri'leit] *v/t.* relatar, contar; relacionar (*to, with* con); *v/i.*: ‿ *to* relacionarse con; **re'lat·ed** *subject* afín, conexo; *he is ‿ to me* es pariente mío.

re·la·tion [ri'leiʃn] (*narration*) relato *m*, relación *f*; (*‿ship*) conexión *f*, relación *f* (*to, with* con); (*kin*) pariente *m/f*; *‿s pl.* (*kin*) parientes *m/pl.*; (*good etc.*) relaciones *f/pl.*; *in ‿ to* respecto de; *public ‿s office* departamento *m* de relaciones públicas; **re'la·tion·ship** conexión *f*, afinidad *f* (*to, with* con); (*kinship*) parentesco *m*.

rel·a·tive ['relətiv] **1.** □ relativo (*to* a); **2.** *gr.* relativo *m*; (*kin*) pariente *m/f*; **rel·a'tiv·i·ty** relatividad *f*.

re·lax [ri'læks] *v/t.* relajar, aflojar; mitigar, suavizar; *v/i.* esparcirse, expansionarse, descansar; relajarse, mitigarse; F *‿!* ¡cálmate!; **re·lax·a·tion** esparcimiento *m*, recreo *m*, descanso *m*; relajación *f*, aflojamiento *m*.

re·lay¹ [ri'lei] **1.** parada *f*, posta *f* *of horses etc.*; *tanda f of workmen*; relevo *m*; ⚡ relai(s) *m*; ‿ *race* (carrera *f* de) relevos *m/pl.*; **2.** *radio*: retransmitir.

re·lay² ['ri:'lei] volver a colocar.

re·lease [ri'li:s] **1.** liberación *f*; excarcelación *f from prison*; descargo *m from obligation*; *film*: estreno *m* general; ⚖ cesión *f*; ⊕, *phot.* disparador *m*; **2.** soltar, libertar; descargar, absolver *from obligation*; *pressure etc.* aflojar; *brake* soltar; *film* estrenar; ⚖ ceder.

rel·e·gate ['religeit] relegar; **rel·e'ga·tion** relegación *f*.

re·lent [ri'lent] ablandarse, ceder; **re'lent·less** □ implacable, despiadado.

rel·e·vance, rel·e·van·cy ['relivəns(i)] pertinencia *f*; **'rel·e·vant** □ pertinente.

re·li·a·bil·ity [rilaiə'biliti] confiabilidad *f*; formalidad *f*; seguridad *f*; **re'li·a·ble** □ confiable; seguro; de fiar, de confianza; *p.* formal, de mucha formalidad; *news* fehaciente.

re·li·ance [ri'laiəns] confianza *f* (*on* en); dependencia *f* (*on* de).

re·li·ant [ri'laiənt] confiado; dependiente.

rel·ic ['relik] reliquia *f* (*a. eccl.*), vestigio *m*; **rel·ict** ['relikt] viuda *f*.

re·lief [ri'li:f] alivio *m*; desahogo *m*; consuelo *m*; aligeramiento *m*; relevación *f*; (*a. poor* ～) socorro *m*, auxilio *m*; ⚔ (*troops*) relevo *m*; ⚔ descerco *m*, socorro *m* of *town*; ⚖ relieve *m*; ⚖ satisfacción *f*, remedio *m*; *throw into* ～ hacer resaltar; F *that's a* ～! ¡menos mal!; ～ *map* mapa *m* en relieve; ～ *train* tren *m* suplementario; ～ *work* trabajos *m*/*pl.* de socorro; ～ *works* obras *f*/*pl.* públicas (para aliviar el desempleo).

re·lieve [ri'li:v] aliviar; (*reassure*) tranquilizar; *burden* aligerar; *poor* socorrer; *headache etc.* quitar, suprimir; ⚔ *men* relevar; ⚔ *town* socorrer, descercar; destituir (*of post* de); relevar, exonerar (*of duty* de); ～ *nature* hacer del cuerpo; ～ *one's feelings* desahogarse.

re·lie·vo [ri'li:vou] relieve *m*.

re·li·gion [ri'lidʒən] religión *f*.

re·li·gious [ri'lidʒəs] □ religioso; ～*ly fig.* puntualmente; **re'li·gious·ness** religiosidad *f*.

re·lin·quish [ri'liŋkwiʃ] abandonar, renunciar (a); **re'lin·quish·ment** abandono *m*, renuncia *f*.

rel·i·quar·y ['relikwəri] relicario *m*.

rel·ish ['reliʃ] **1.** sabor *m*, gusto *m*; apetito *m*, apetencia *f*; (*sauce*) salsa *f*; **2.** saborear; gustar de; tener buen apetito para.

re·luc·tance [ri'lʌktəns] desgana *f*, renuencia *f*, aversión *f*; *with* ～ a desgana; **re'luc·tant** □ maldispuesto; poco dispuesto (*to* a); ～*ly* a regañadientes, de mala gana.

re·ly [ri'lai]: ～ (*up*)*on* confiar en, fiarse de; contar con.

re·main [ri'mein] **1.** quedar(se), permanecer; (*be left over*) sobrar; ～ *the same*, ～ *unchanged* seguir

siendo lo mismo; **2.** ～*s pl.* restos *m*/*pl.*; sobras *f*/*pl.*; *mortal* ～ restos *m*/*pl.* mortales; **re'main·der 1.** resto *m*; 𝔸 residuo *m*, resta *f*; (*books*) restos *m*/*pl.* de edición; **2.** *books* saldar.

re·make ['ri:'meik] rehacer.

re·mand [ri'mɑ:nd] **1.** reencarcelar; **2.**: *be on* ～ estar detenido.

re·mark [ri'mɑ:k] **1.** observación *f*; **2.** *v/t.* observar, notar; *v/i.* hacer una observación ([*up*]*on* sobre); **re'mark·a·ble** □ notable; raro.

re·mar·ry ['ri:'mæri] volver a casarse.

re·me·di·a·ble [ri'mi:diəbl] □ remediable; **re·me·di·al** [ri'mi:diəl] □ remediador.

rem·e·dy ['remidi] **1.** remedio *m*; **2.** remediar.

re·mem·ber [ri'membə] acordarse de, recordar; (*mst in commands*) tener presente; ～ *me to him!* ¡déle Vd. recuerdos míos!; **re'mem·brance** recuerdo *m*, memoria *f*; recordación *f*; *in* ～ *of* que conmemora; ～*s pl.* recuerdos *m*/*pl.*

re·mind [ri'maind] recordar (*a p. of a th.* algo a una p.); ～ *o.s. that* recordarse que; **re'mind·er** recordatorio *m*, advertencia *f*.

rem·i·nisce [remi'nis] contar los recuerdos; **rem·i·nis·cence** [remi'nisns] reminiscencia *f*; **rem·i·nis·cent** □ evocador; recordativo; *be* ～ *of* recordar *acc.*

re·miss [ri'mis] □ negligente, descuidado; **re'mis·si·ble** [‿əbl] remisible; **re·mis·sion** [‿'miʃn] remisión *f*; **re'miss·ness** negligencia *f*, descuido *m*.

re·mit [ri'mit] *all senses:* remitir; **re'mit·tance** remesa *f*; **re·mit'tee** consignatorio (a *f*) *m*; **re'mit·tent** (fiebre *f*) remitente; **re'mit·ter** remitente *m*/*f*.

rem·nant ['remnənt] resto *m*, residuo *m*; ✝ retazo *m* of *cloth*.

re·mod·el ['ri:'mɔdl] modelar de nuevo; refundir.

re·mon·strance [ri'mɔnstrəns] protesta *f*, reconvención *f*; **re'mon·strant** protestante *adj. a. su. m*/*f*; **re'mon·strate** [‿streit] reconvenir (*with* a); protestar (*against* contra); poner reparos (*on* a).

re·morse [ri'mɔːs] remordimiento *m*; **re'morse·ful** [‿ful] □ arrepentido; re'morse·less □ implacable, despiadado.

re·mote [ri'mout] □ remoto; v. *control*; re'mote·ness apartamiento m, alejamiento m.

re·mount [ri:'maunt] 1. v/t. remontar (a. ✕); v/i. volver a subir; 2. remonta f (a. ✕).

re·mov·a·ble [ri'mu:vəbl] separable; amovible; re'mov·al [~vəl] removimiento m, remoción f; mudanza f *of furniture*; destitución f, deposición f *from office*; ⊕ separación f *of part*; eliminación f *of obstacle, waste*; ✗ extirpación f; re·move [~'mu:v] 1. v/t. quitar, remover; trasladar (to a); *furniture* mudar; destituir *from office*; borrar *from list*; ⊕ *part* separar, retirar; *obstacle, waste* eliminar; ✗ extirpar; v/i. mudarse, trasladarse; 2. grado m; re'mov·er agente m de mudanzas.

re·mu·ner·ate [ri'mju:nəreit] remunerar; re·mu·ner·a·tion remuneración f; re'mu·ner·a·tive [~rətiv] □ remunerador.

Ren·ais·sance [ri'neisəns] Renacimiento m.

re·nal ['ri:nl] renal.

re·name ['ri:'neim] dar nuevo nombre a.

re·nas·cence [ri'næsns] renacimiento m.

rend [rend] [*irr.*] *lit.* rasgar, hender.

ren·der ['rendə] hacer, volver; *service, honour, thanks* dar; *fat* derretir; (*translate*) traducir; ♪ interpretar, ejecutar; ✝ *account* pasar; ⊕ rendir, producir; 'ren·der·ing interpretación f; traducción f *etc.*

ren·dez·vous ['rɔndivu:] (lugar m de una) cita f.

ren·di·tion [ren'diʃn] ♪ ejecución f.

ren·e·gade ['renigeid] renegado *adj. a. su. m* (a f).

re·new [ri'nju:] renovar; reanudar; re'new·a·ble renovable; re'new·al [~əl] renovación f; reanudación f.

ren·net ['renit] cuajo m.

re·nounce [ri'nauns] renunciar (*un derecho, a una cosa*).

ren·o·vate ['renouveit] renovar; ren·o'va·tion renovación f.

re·nown [ri'naun] *lit.* renombre m, nombradía f; re'nowned *lit.* renombrado, ínclito.

rent¹ [rent] 1. *pret. a. p.p. of rend*; 2. rasgón m; *fig.* cisma m.

rent² [~] 1. alquiler m; arriendo m; 2. alquilar; arrendar; 'rent·a·ble arrendable; 'rent·al alquiler m, arriendo m; 'rent-'free exento de alquiler.

re·nun·ci·a·tion [rinʌnsi'eiʃn] renuncia(ción) f.

re·o·pen ['ri:'oupn] reabrir(se); 're·'o·pen·ing reapertura f.

re·or·ga·ni·za·tion ['ri:ɔ:gənai'zeiʃn] reorganización f; 're'or·gan·ize reorganizar.

rep [rep] ✝ reps m.

re·paint ['ri:'peint] repintar.

re·pair¹ [ri'pɛə] 1. reparación f; compostura f; (*esp. shoes*) remiendo m; ~s *pl.* reparaciones f/pl.; in (*good*) ~ en buen estado; ~ *shop* taller m de reparaciones; 2. reparar; componer; *shoes etc.* remendar.

re·pair² [~]: ~ to ir a, encaminarse a.

rep·a·ra·ble ['repərəbl] reparable; rep·a'ra·tion reparación f; satisfacción f; ~s *pol.* indemnizaciones f/pl.; *make* ~s dar satisfacción.

rep·ar·tee [repɑ:'ti:] réplicas f/pl. agudas.

re·pass ['ri:'pɑ:s] repasar.

re·past [ri'pɑ:st] comida f.

re·pa·tri·ate 1. [ri:'pætrieit] repatriar; 2. [ri:'pætriit] repatriado m; 're·pa·tri·a·tion repatriación f.

re·pay [ri:'pei] [*irr.* (*pay*)] pagar, devolver; reembolsar; *p.* resarcir, compensar; re'pay·a·ble reembolsable; re'pay·ment reembolso m; devolución f.

re·peal [ri'pi:l] 1. revocación f, abrogación f; 2. revocar, abrogar.

re·peat [ri'pi:t] 1. v/t. repetir; *thanks etc.* reiterar; (*aloud*) recitar; ✝ ~ *an order (for)* repetir el pedido (de); v/i. repetirse; (*rifle, clock, taste*) repetir; 2. ♪ repetición f; *radio* (a. ~ *broadcast*): retransmisión f; ✝ (*freq.* ~ *order*) pedido m de repetición; re'peat·ed □ repetido; re'peat·er reloj m (rifle m *etc.*) de repetición.

re·pel [ri'pel] rechazar, repeler; *fig.* repugnar; re'pel·lent repugnante.

re·pent [ri'pent] arrepentirse (*of* de). re·pent·ance [ri'pentəns] arrepentimiento m; re'pent·ant □ arrepentido.

re·peo·ple ['ri:'pi:pl] repoblar.

re·per·cus·sion [ri:pə:'kʌʃn] repercusión f (a. *fig.*); *fig.* resonancia f.

rep·er·toire ['repətwɑː], **rep·er·to·ry** ['repətəri] repertorio *m* (*a. fig.*).

rep·e·ti·tion [repi'tiʃn] repetición *f*; ✝ ~ *order* pedido *m* de repetición; **re'pet·i·tive** ☐ reiterativo.

re·pine [ri'pain] quejarse (*at* de), afligirse.

re·place [ri:'pleis] reemplazar, sustituir (*with*, *by* por); reponer, colocar nuevamente; **re'place·ment** (*th.*) repuesto *m*; (*p.*) sustituto *m*; (*act*) reposición *f*; reemplazo *m*.

re·plant ['ri:'plɑːnt] replantar.

re·plen·ish [ri'pleniʃ] rellenar, reaprovisionar; **re'plen·ish·ment** rellenado *m*, reaprovisionamiento *m*.

re·plete [ri'pliːt] repleto (*with* de); **re'ple·tion** repleción *f*; hartazgo *m of food*.

rep·li·ca ['replikə] *paint. etc.* copia *f*, reproducción *f* (exacta); *fig.* segunda edición *f*.

re·ply [ri'plai] 1. responder, contestar; ~ *to a letter* contestar (a) una carta; 2. respuesta *f*, contestación *f*; ~ *postcard* tarjeta *f* de porte pagado.

re·port [ri'pɔːt] 1. (*official*) informe *m*; parte *m*; relato *m*; (*newspaper*) información *f*, reportaje *m*, crónica *f*; *school*: papeleta *f*, nota *f*; estampido *m of gun*; *annual* ~ memoria *f* anual; 2. *v/t.* relatar; *event etc.* informar acerca de; *crime* denunciar; ~ *that* comunicar que, informar que; *v/i.* hacer un informe (*on* acerca de); presentarse (*at* en); **re'port·er** reportero *m*.

re·pose [ri'pouz] 1. reposo *m*; 2. descansar, reposar; ~ *trust etc. in* poner confianza *etc.* en; **re·pos·i·to·ry** [ri'pozitəri] guardamuebles *m*; repositorio *m*; (*p.*) depositario *m*.   [recobrar *acc.*\

re·pos·sess ['riːpə'zes]: ~ *o.s. of*]

rep·re·hend [repri'hend] reprender; **rep·re'hen·si·ble** ☐ reprensible; **rep·re'hen·sion** reprensión *f*.

rep·re·sent [repri'zent] representar; ⚖ ser apoderado de; ✝ ser agente (*or* representante) de; **rep·re·sen·'ta·tion** representación *f*; **rep·re·'sent·a·tive** [~tətiv] 1. ☐ representativo; 2. representante *m/f*; ⚖ apoderado *m*; *House of* ~*s Am.* Cámara *f* de Representantes.

re·press [ri'pres] reprimir; **re·pres·sion** [ri'preʃn] represión *f*; **re·'pres·sive** ☐ represivo.

re·prieve [ri'priːv] 1. respiro *m*; ⚖ indulto *m*, suspensión *f* (*esp.* de la pena de muerte); 2. indultar, suspender la pena de muerte de.

rep·ri·mand ['reprimɑːnd] 1. reprimenda *f*; 2. reprender, reconvenir.

re·print ['riː'print] 1. reimprimir; 2. reimpresión *f*.

re·pris·al [ri'praizl] represalia *f*; *take* ~*s* tomar represalias.

re·proach [ri'proutʃ] 1. reproche *m*; oprobio *m*; baldón *m*; 2. reprochar (*s.o. for*, *with a th.* algo a alguien); **re'proach·ful** [~ful] ☐ acusador, reprensor.

rep·ro·bate ['reproubeit] réprobo *adj. a. su. m* (*a f*); **rep·ro'ba·tion** reprobación *f*.

re·pro·duce [riːprə'djuːs] reproducir(se); **re·pro·duc·tion** [~'dʌkʃn] reproducción *f*; **re·pro'duc·tive** ☐ reproductor; *organ etc.* de la generación.

re·proof [ri'pruːf] reproche *m*, reprensión *f*.

re·prov·al [ri'pruːvl] reprobación *f*; **re·prove** [~'pruːv] reprobar, reprender (*s.o. for s.t.* algo a alguien).

rep·tile ['reptail] reptil *adj. a. su. m*.

re·pub·lic [ri'pʌblik] república *f*; **re'pub·li·can** republicano *adj. a. su. m* (*a f*); **re'pub·li·can·ism** republicanismo *m*.

re·pub·li·ca·tion ['riːpʌbli'keiʃn] reedición *f*.

re·pub·lish ['riː'pʌbliʃ] reeditar.

re·pu·di·ate [ri'pjuːdieit] *charge etc.* desechar, negar, rechazar; *obligation etc.* desconocer, rechazar; *wife* repudiar; **repu·di·a·tion** desconocimiento *m*; repudiación *f* *etc.*.

re·pug·nance [ri'pʌgnəns] repugnancia *f*; **re'pug·nant** ☐ repugnante.

re·pulse [ri'pʌls] 1. repulsión *f*, repulsa *f*, rechazo *m*; 2. rechazar, repulsar; **re'pul·sion** repulsión *f*, repugnancia *f*; **re'pul·sive** ☐ repulsivo, repelente.

re·pur·chase [riː'pəːtʃəs] readquirir.

rep·u·ta·ble ['repjutəbl] ☐ *firm* acreditado; *p.* honroso, estimable; **rep·u·ta·tion** [~'teiʃn] reputación *f*, fama *f*; **re·pute** [ri'pjuːt] 1. reputación *f*; *by* ~ según la opinión común; *of* ~ acreditado; 2. reputar; *be* ~*d to be or as* ser tenido por, tener

fama de; **re'put·ed** supuesto; **re·'put·ed·ly** según la opinión común.
re·quest [ri'kwest] **1.** petición *f*, instancia *f*, solicitud *f*; ✝ demanda *f*; *at the* ~ *of* a petición (*or* instancia) de; *by* ~ a petición; *on* ~ a solicitud; ~ *programme* programa *m* a petición de radioyentes; ~ *stop* parada *f* discrecional; **2.** pedir; solicitar; suplicar.
re·qui·em ['rekwiem] réquiem *m*.
re·quire [ri'kwaiə] necesitar; exigir; requerir (*of* a; *a p. to do* que una p. haga); **re'quire·ment** requerimiento *m*; requisito *m*; necesidad *f*.
req·ui·site ['rekwizit] **1.** preciso, indispensable; **2.** requisito *m*; *toilet* ~s *pl.* artículos *m/pl.* de limpieza; **req·ui·si·tion 1.** requisición *f* (*a.* ⚔); pedido *m*; requerimiento *m*; **2.** ⚔ requisar; exigir.
re·quit·al [ri'kwaitl] compensación *f*; desquite *m*.
re·quite [ri'kwait] (re)compensar; desquitarse; corresponder a.
re-read ['ri:'ri:d] [*irr.* (*read*)] releer.
re·re·dos ['riədɔs] retablo *m*.
re·sale ['ri:'seil] reventa *f*.
re·scind [ri'sind] rescindir.
re·scis·sion [ri'siʒn] rescisión *f*.
re·script ['ri:skript] rescri(p)to *m*.
res·cue ['reskju:] **1.** salvamento *m*; liberación *f*; rescate *m*; **2.** salvar; librar, libertar; rescatar; **'res·cu·er** salvador (-a *f*) *m*.
re·search [ri'sə:tʃ] investigación *f* (*in, into* de); ~ *establishment* instituto *m* de investigaciones; ~ *worker* = **re'search·er** investigador (-a *f*) *m*.
re·seat ['ri:'si:t] *valves* reasentar.
re·sell ['ri:'sel] [*irr.* (*sell*)] revender.
re·sem·blance [ri'zembləns] semejanza *f*, parecido *m* (*to* a); **re'sem·ble** [~bl] asemejarse a, parecerse a.
re·sent [ri'zent] resentirse de (*or* por); tomar a mal; **re'sent·ful** [~ful] □ resentido, ofendido (*at, of* por); **re'sent·ment** resentimiento *m*.
res·er·va·tion [rezə'veiʃn] (*act*) reserva *f*; reservación *f*; (*mental*) reserva *f*; salvedad *f*; (*in argument*) distingo *m*; plaza *f* reservada *on train etc.*; *Am.* reserva *f* (de indios *etc.*)
re·serve [ri'zə:v] **1.** reserva *f* (*a.* ⚔, ✝); *sport:* suplente *m/f*; *in* ~ de reserva; ~ *price* precio *m* mínimo; **2.** reservar; ~ *one's strength* reser-

varse; **re'served** □ reservado, callado; sigiloso; ~ *seat* plaza *f* reservada.
re·serv·ist [ri'zə:vist] reservista *m*.
res·er·voir [rezəvwɑ:] embalse *m*, pantano *m of water*; depósito *m*; *fig.* fondo *m*.
re·set ['ri:set] ⊕ reajustar; *jewel* reengastar; *typ.* recomponer.
re·set·tle ['ri:'setl] *p.* restablecer; *land* colonizar; **'re·set·tle·ment** restablecimiento *m*; colonización *f*.
re·shuf·fle ['ri:'ʃʌfl] **1.** *government* reconstruir; **2.** reconstrucción *f*.
re·side [ri'zaid] residir (*fig. in* en); **.res·i·dence** ['rezidəns] residencia *f*; ~ *permit* visado *m* de permanencia; **'res·i·dent 1.** residente; **2.** residente *m/f*, vecino (a *f*) *m*; **res·i·den·tial** [~'denʃl] residencial.
re·sid·u·al [ri'zidjuəl] residual; **re·'sid·u·ar·y** restante; residual; ⚖ ~ *legatee* legatario (a *f*) *m* universal; **res·i·due** ['rezidju:] residuo *m*; resto *m*; ✝ *etc.* superávit *m*; **re·sid·u·um** [ri'zidjuəm] *esp.* 🜍, ⚗ residuo *m*.
re·sign [ri'zain] *v/t.* dimitir, renunciar, resignar; ~ *o.s.* resignarse (*to* a), conformarse (*to* con); *v/i.* dimitir (*from* de); **res·ig·na·tion** [rezig'neiʃn] dimisión *f* (*from* de), renuncia *f*; resignación *f*; conformidad *f* (*to* con); **re·signed** [ri'zaind] □ resignado.
re·sil·i·ence [ri'ziliəns] resistencia *f*; elasticidad *f*; *fig.* resistencia *f*, poder *m* de recuperación; **re'sil·i·ent** elástico; resistente (*a. fig.*).
res·in ['rezin] **1.** resina *f*; **2.** tratar con resina; **'res·in·ous** resinoso.
re·sist [ri'zist] resistir (a); oponerse a; **re'sist·ance** resistencia *f* (*a. phys.*, ⚡); **re'sist·ant** resistente; **re'sis·tor** ⚡ resistor *m*.
re·sole ['ri:'soul] (sobre)solar.
res·o·lute ['rezəlu:t] □ resuelto; **'res·o·lute·ness** resolución *f*.
res·o·lu·tion [rezə'lu:ʃn] resolución *f*; *parl. etc.* acuerdo *m*; *pass a* ~ tomar un acuerdo; *good* ~s buenos propósitos *m/pl.*
re·solv·a·ble [ri'zɔlvəbl] soluble.
re·solve [ri'zɔlv] **1.** *v/t. all senses:* resolver (*into* en); *v/i.* resolverse (*into* en; *to* a); *parl. etc.* acordar (*to do* hacer); ~ (*up*)*on ger.* acordar *inf.*; **2.** resolución *f*; **re'solved** resuelto.

res·o·nance ['rezənəns] resonancia *f*; **'res·o·nant** ☐ resonante.

re·sorp·tion [ri'sɔːpʃn] resorción *f*.

re·sort [ri'zɔːt] **1.** recurso *m*; punto *m* de reunión; *health* ~ balneario *m*; *seaside* ~ punto *m* marítimo de veraneo, playa *f*; *summer* ~ punto *m* de veraneo; *in the last* ~, *as a last* ~ en último caso; **2.**: ~ *to* recurrir a, acudir a; *place* frecuentar.

re·sound [ri'zaund] resonar, retumbar; **re'sound·ing** ☐ sonoro; *fig.* clamoroso, resonante.

re·source [ri'sɔːs] recurso *m*, expediente *m*; inventiva *f*; ~s *pl.* recursos *m/pl.*; **re'source·ful** [~ful] ☐ inventivo, ingenioso; **re'source·ful·ness** inventiva *f*, iniciativa *f*.

re·spect [ris'pekt] **1.** (*esteem*) respeto *m*, consideración *f* (*for* por); (*aspect, relation*) respecto *m*; ~s *pl.* recuerdos *m/pl.*, saludos *m/pl.*; *in* ~ *of* respecto a (*or* de); *in this* ~ por lo que se refiere a esto; *out of* ~ *for* por consideración a; *with* ~ *to* con respecto a; *pay one's* ~s *to* cumplimentar a; **2.** respetar; estimar; *law etc.* atenerse a; **re·spect·a'bil·i·ty** respetabilidad *f*; **re·spect·a·ble** ☐ respetable; apreciable; **re'spect·ful** [~ful] ☐ respetuoso; *Yours* ~*ly* le saluda atentamente; **re'spect·ful·ness** acatamiento *m*; **re'spect·ing** con respecto a, en cuanto a; **re'spec·tive** ☐ respectivo; **re'spec·tive·ly** respectivamente.

res·pi·ra·tion [respə'reiʃn] respiración *f*.

res·pi·ra·tor ['respəreitə] máscara *f* (*or* careta *f*) antigás; **re·spir·a·to·ry** [ris'paiərətəri] respiratorio *m*.

re·spire [ris'paiə] respirar.

res·pite ['respait] **1.** respiro *m*, respiradero *m*; ♫ prórroga *f*; *without* ~ sin tregua, sin respirar; **2.** aplazar, prorrogar; *p.* suspender la ejecución de.

re·splend·ence, re·splend·en·cy [ris'plendəns(i)] resplandor *m*; **re'splend·ent** ☐ resplandeciente.

re·spond [ris'pɔnd] responder; ~ *to treatment etc.* reaccionar a, ser sensible a; **re'spond·ent** ♫ demandado *adj. a. su. m* (a *f*).

re·sponse [ris'pɔns] respuesta *f*; *fig.* reacción *f* (*to* a); *eccl.* responsorio *m*.

re·spon·si·bil·i·ty [rispɔnsə'biliti]

responsabilidad *f* (*for* de); **re'spon·si·ble** responsable (*for* de); *post* de confianza; **re'spon·sive** ☐: ~ *to* sensible a.

rest[1] [rest] **1.** descanso *m*, reposo *m*; *fig.* paz *f*; (*support*) apoyo *m*; ♪ silencio *m*, pausa *f*; *at* ~ reposado; *fig.* en paz; *take a* ~ descansar un rato; **2.** *v/i.* descansar; holgar; posar(se) (*on* en); apoyarse (*on* en); (*matter*) quedar; *fig.* ~ (*up*)*on* descansar sobre; estribar en; *fig.* ~ *with* depender de; residir en; ~ *assured that* tener la seguridad de que; *v/t.* descansar; apoyar (*on* en).

rest[2] [~] resto *m*; ♱ reserva *f*; *the* ~ lo demás, los demás *etc.*; *for the* ~ por lo demás.

re·state·ment ['riːsteitmənt] nueva exposición *f*.

res·tau·rant ['restərɔːŋ] restaurante *m*, restorán *m*; ~ *car* coche *m* restaurante, coche-comedor *m*.

rest-cure ['restkjuə] cura *f* de reposo.

rest·ful ['restful] ☐ descansado, sosegado; tranquilizador.

res·ting-place ['restiŋpleis] *fig.* última morada *f* (*a. last* ~).

res·ti·tu·tion [resti'tjuːʃn] restitución *f*; *make* ~ indemnizar.

res·tive ['restiv] ☐ intranquilo, inquieto; *horse etc.* rebelón; **'res·tive·ness** intranquilidad *f*.

rest·less ['restlis] ☐ inquieto; desasosegado; (*sleepless*) insomne; turbulento; **'rest·less·ness** inquietud *f*; desasosiego *m*; insomnio *m*; turbulencia *f*.

re·stock ['riː'stɔk] reaprovisionar; repoblar.

res·to·ra·tion [restə'reiʃn] restauración *f*; devolución *f*; **re·stor·a·tive** [ris'tɔrətiv] reconstituyente *adj. a. su. m.*

re·store [ris'tɔː] restaurar; devolver; ~ *a p. to liberty* (*health*) devolver la libertad (la salud) a una p.; **re'stor·er** restaurador (-a *f*) *m*; *hair* ~ loción *f* capilar, restaurador *m* del cabello.

re·strain [ris'train] contener, refrenar, reprimir, tener a raya; ~ *s.o. from ger.* impedir que alguien *subj.*; **re'strained** templado, cohibido; refrenado; **re'straint** moderación *f*, comedimiento *m*; restricción *f*.

re·strict [ris'trikt] restringir, limitar; *be* ~*ed to* (*quality*) ser privativo de; **re·stric·tion** restricción f, limitación f; **re·stric·tive** □ restrictivo; ~ *practices pl.* normas f/pl. restrictivas.

re·sult [ri'zʌlt] **1.** resultado m; *as a* ~ por consiguiente; *as a* ~ *of* de resultas de; **2.** resultar (*from* de); ~ *in* terminar en, parar en; **re'sult·ant** resultante *adj. a. su. f* (⊕).

ré·su·mé ['rezju·mei] resumen m.

re·sume [ri'zju:m] reasumir; *journey etc.* reanudar; *seat* volver a tomar; **re·sump·tion** [ri'zʌmpʃn] reasunción f; reanudación f.

re·sur·gence [ri'sə:dʒəns] resurgimiento m; **re'sur·gent** que está en trance de renacer.

res·ur·rect [rezə'rekt] resucitar; **res·ur'rec·tion** resurrección f.

re·sus·ci·tate [ri'sʌsiteit] resucitar (*v/t. a. v/i.*); **re·sus·ci'ta·tion** resucitación f.

re·tail 1. ['ri:teil] venta f al por menor; *by* ~ al por menor; ~ *price* precio m al por menor (*or* al detalle); **2.** [~] *adj., adv.* al (por) menor; **3.** [ri:'teil] *v/t.* vender al (por) menor (*or* al detalle); *gossip* repetir; *v/i.* venderse al (por) menor (*at* a); **re'tail·er** detallista m/f, comerciante m/f al por menor.

re·tain [ri'tein] retener; conservar; quedarse con; *lawyer* ajustar; *player* contratar; **re'tain·er** *hist.* adherente m, secuaz m; criado m; ⚖ (*a. retaining fee*) ajuste m, anticipo m.

re·take ['ri:'teik] [irr. (*take*)] volver a tomar.

re·tal·i·ate [ri'tælieit] desquitarse; tomar represalias; vengarse (*on* en); **re·tal·i'a·tion** desquite m; represalias f/pl.; venganza f; **re'tal·i·a·to·ry** [~əri] vengativo.

re·tard [ri'tɑ:d] retardar, retrasar.

retch [ri:tʃ] (esforzarse por) vomitar.

re·tell ['ri:'tel] [irr. (*tell*)] recontar.

re·ten·tion [ri'tenʃn] retención f (*a.* 🖋), conservación f; **re'ten·tive** □ retentivo.

re·think ['ri:'θiŋk] [irr. (*think*)] repensar.

ret·i·cence ['retisəns] reserva f; **'ret·i·cent** □ reservado.

re·tic·u·late [ri'tikjulit], **re'tic·u·lat·ed** [~leitid] reticular; **ret·i·cule** ['retikju:l] ridículo m; (*a.* **re·ti·cle** ['retikl]) *opt.* retículo m.

ret·i·na ['retinə] retina f.

ret·i·nue ['retinju:] séquito m, comitiva f.

re·tire [ri'taiə] *v/i.* retirarse (*a.* ✗); recogerse *to bed etc.*; jubilarse *from post,* retirarse *from army*; *v/t.* jubilar; **re'tired** jubilado, ✗ retirado; **re'tire·ment** retiro m; ✗ retirada f; jubilación f *from post;* ~ *pay* ✗ retiro m; ~ *pension* jubilación f, pensión f de retiro; **re'tir·ing** □ retraído, reservado; *member* saliente.

re·tort [ri'tɔ:t] **1.** réplica f; 🝪 retorta f; **2.** replicar (*a. v/i.*); *insult etc.* devolver; *argument* redargüir.

re·touch ['ri:'tʌtʃ] retocar (*a. phot.*).

re·trace [ri'treis] volver a trazar; repasar; ~ *one's steps* desandar lo andado, volver sobre sus pasos.

re·tract [ri'trækt] retractar(se); retraer(se); ⊕ replegar; **re'tract·a·ble** retractable; ✗ replegable; **re·trac'ta·tion, re'trac·tion** retracción f, retractación f.

re·treat [ri'tri:t] **1.** retiro m (*a. eccl.*); retraimiento m; ✗ retirada f; **2.** ✗ retirarse, batirse en retirada (*a. beat a* ~); retroceder.

re·trench [ri'trentʃ] *v/t.* cercenar; *v/i.* economizar; **re'trench·ment** cercenadura f; economías f/pl.

re·tri·al ['ri:'traiəl] revisión f.

ret·ri·bu·tion [retri'bju:ʃn] justo castigo m; desquite m.

re·triev·a·ble [ri'tri:vəbl] reparable; recuperable.

re·trieve [ri'tri:v] (re)cobrar; *fortunes* reparar; *loss* resarcirse de; *hunt.* cobrar; **re'triev·er** perro m cobrador.

ret·ro... ['retrou] retro...; **re'tro·ac·tive** □ retroactivo; **ret'ro·cede** retroceder; **ret·ro'ces·sion** retroceso m; **ret·ro·gra'da·tion** *ast.* retrogradación f; **'ret·ro·grade 1.** retrógrado; **2.** *ast.* retrogradar.

ret·ro·gres·sion [retrou'greʃn] *ast.* retrogradación f; **re'tro·spect** ['~spekt] retrospección f; *in* ~ retrospectivamente; **ret'ro·spec·tion** retrospección f, consideración f de lo pasado; **ret'ro·spec·tive** □ retrospectivo; ⚖ retroactivo.

re·try ['ri:'trai] ⚖ rever.

re·turn [ri'tə:n] **1.** vuelta f, regreso m; devolución f *of book etc.*; 🕊 etc. reaparición f; (*reply*) respuesta f; recompensa f *for kindness*; (*report*) informe m, relación f; *parl.* elección *f*; resultado *m* (del escrutinio); △ marco *m*; vuelta *f*; ✝ (*freq.* ~s *pl.*) ganancia *f*, rédito *m on capital etc.*; ingresos *m/pl.*; ~s *pl.* (*official*) estadística *f*; (*tax* ~) declaración *f* (de renta); *many happy* ~s *of the day!* ¡que tú cumplas muy felices!; *in* ~ en cambio, en recompensa (*for* de); *by* ~ (*of post*) a vuelta de correo; ~ *match* (partido *m* de) desquite *m*, revancha *f*; ~ *ticket* (F ~) billete *m* de ida y vuelta; **2.** *v/i.* volver, regresar; (*reply*) responder; (*reappear*) reaparecer; ✝ revertir; ~ *to theme, habit* volver a; *v/t.* devolver; ✝ producir, rendir; *parl.* elegir; *ball* restar; *kindness etc.* corresponder a; *suit of cards* devolver; *thanks* dar; *verdict* dictar; *visit* pagar; **re'turn-a·ble** restituible; 🏛 devolutivo; ~ *empties* envases *m/pl.* a devolver; **re'turn·ing-of·fi·cer** *approx.* escudriñador *m.*

re·un·ion ['riːjuːnjən] reunión *f*; **re-u·nite** ['riːjuː'naɪt] reunir(se); reconciliar(se).

rev [rev] *mot.* F **1.** revolución *f*; **2.** (*a.* ~ *up*) girar (el motor); acelerar.
re·val·or·i·za·tion [riːvælərai'zeiʃn], **re·val·u·a·tion** [~vælju'eiʃn] revalor(iz)ación *f*; **re'val·or·ize** [~ʹɔːraiz], **re·val·ue** [~'vælju:] revalorizar.
re·veal [ri'viːl] revelar; **re'veal·ing** □ revelador.
re·veil·le [ri'væli] (toque *m* de) diana *f.*
rev·el ['revl] **1.** (*freq.* ~s *pl.*) jarana *f*, juerga *f*, fiesta *f* bulliciosa; **2.** jaranear; ir de parranda; ~ *in* deleitarse en.
rev·e·la·tion [revi'leiʃn] revelación *f.*
rev·el·(l)er ['revlə] jaranero *m*, juerguista *m/f*; **'rev·el·ry** jolgorio *m*, jarana *f*, diversión *f* tumultuosa.
re·venge [ri'vendʒ] **1.** venganza *f*; **2.** vengar(se); ~ *o.s.* (*or be* ~*d*) *on* vengarse en; **re'venge·ful** [~ful] □ vengativo; **re'venge·ful·ness** sed *f* de venganza; **re'veng·er** vengador (-a *f*) *m.*
rev·e·nue ['revinjuː] rentas *f/pl.* públicas; (*a.* ~s *pl.*) ingresos *m/pl.*; rédito *m*, renta *f*; ~ *cutter* guardacostas *m*; ~ *officer* aduanero *m*; ~ *stamp* sello *m* fiscal.
re·ver·ber·ate [ri'vəːbəreit] retumbar; (*light*) reverberar; **re·ver·ber-**
a·tion el retumbar; reverberación *f*; **re'ver·ber·a·tor** reverberador *m*; **re'ver·ber·a·to·ry fur·nace** horno *m* de reverbero.
re·vere [ri'viə] reverenciar, venerar; **rev·er·ence** ['revərəns] **1.** reverencia *f*; *Your* ♀ (su) Reverencia; **2.** reverenciar; **'rev·er·end 1.** reverendo; **2.** sacerdote *m*, pastor *m.*
rev·er·ent ['revərənt] □ reverente; **rev·er·en·tial** [~'renʃl] □ reverencial.
rev·er·ie ['revəri] ensueño *m.*
re·ver·sal [ri'vəːsəl] inversión *f*; cambio *m* completo *f of policy etc.*; 🏛 revocación *f*; **re·verse** [~'vəːs] **1.** (lo ~) lo contrario; *fig.* revés *m*, contratiempo *m*; reverso *m of coin*; revés *m of cloth*; ⊕ marcha *f* atrás; *quite the* ~ todo lo contrario; **2.** inverso, invertido; contrario; *mot.* ~ *gear* cambio *m* de marcha atrás; **3.** *v/t.* invertir; *opinion* cambiar completamente de; trastrocar; volver al revés; 🏛 revocar; ⊕ poner en marcha atrás; *v/i.* dar la marcha atrás; **re'vers·i·ble** *coat etc.* reversible; **re'vers·ing** ⊕ ... de marcha atrás.
re·ver·sion [ri'vəːʃn] reversión *f* (*a.* 🏛 *a. biol.*); *fortune in* ~ bienes *m/pl.* reversibles; **re'ver·sion·ar·y** reversible.
re·vert [ri'vəːt] volver(se) (*to* a); revertir (*a.* 🏛); *biol.* saltar atrás.
rev·er·y = *reverie.*
re·vet·ment [ri'vetmənt] ⊕ revestimiento *m.*
re·view [ri'vjuː] **1.** revista *f* (⚓, ✕, *magazine*); repaso *m*; 🏛 revisión *f*; reseña *f of book*; **2.** rever (*a.* 🏛); repasar; ⚓, ✕ pasar revista a, revistar; *book* reseñar; **re'view·er** crítico *m.*
re·vile [ri'vail] ultrajar, injuriar.
re·vise [ri'vaiz] **1.** revisar; *lesson* repasar; *book* corregir, refundir; **2.** *typ.* segunda prueba *f*; **re'vis·er** revisor (-a *f*) *m*; *typ.* corrector *m.*
re·vi·sion [ri'viʒn] revisión *f*; repaso *m*; corrección *f*, refundición *f of book*; *typ.* corrección *f.*
re·vis·it [ri'viːzit] volver a visitar.
re·vi·so·ry [ri'vaizəri] revisor.
re·vi·tal·ize ['riː'vaitəlaiz] revivificar.
re·viv·al [ri'vaivl] reanimación *f*; renacimiento *m*; *thea.* reposición *f*;

eccl. despertamiento *m* religioso; **re·vive** [ʌ'vaiv] *v/t.* reanimar; restablecer; *fire* avivar; *hopes* despertar; *play* reponer; *v/i.* reanimarse; volver en si; renacer; restablecerse; **re·viv·i·fy** [ʌ'vivifai] revivificar.

rev·o·ca·ble ['revəkəbl] ☐ revocable; **rev·o·ca·tion** [ʌ'keiʃn] revocación *f*.

re·voke [ri'vouk] *v/t.* revocar; *v/i. cards:* renunciar.

re·volt [ri'voult] **1.** rebelión *f*, sublevación *f*; **2.** *v/i.* rebelarse, sublevarse; *v/t. fig.* dar (*or* causar) asco a; repugnar; **re'volt·ing** ☐ asqueroso, repugnante.

rev·o·lu·tion [revə'lu:ʃn] revolución *f* (*a.* ⊕, *pol.*); vuelta *f*, rotación *f*; **rev·o'lu·tion·ary** revolucionario *adj. a. su. m* (a *f*); **rev·o·'lu·tion·ize** revolucionar.

re·volve [ri'vɔlv] *v/i.* girar, dar vueltas; *ast.* revolverse; *fig.* depender (*round de*); *v/t.* (hacer) girar; *fig.* ponderar; **re'volv·er** revólver *m*; **re'volv·ing** giratorio; rotativo.

re·vue [ri'vju:] *thea.* revista *f*.

re·vul·sion [ri'vʌlʃn] ⚕ revulsión *f*; asco *m*; reacción *f*, cambio *m* repentino; **re'vul·sive** ☐ ⚕ revulsivo.

re·ward [ri'wɔːd] **1.** recompensa *f*, premio *m*, galardón *m*; £5 ʌ 5 libras de hallazgo; **2.** recompensar, premiar; **re'ward·ing** ☐ remunerador.

re·word ['riː'wəːd] formular en otras palabras.

re·write ['riː'rait] [*irr.* (*write*)] refundir; escribir de nuevo.

rhap·so·dize ['ræpsədaiz] *fig.*: ʌ *over* entusiasmarse por, extasiarse ante; **'rhap·so·dy** rapsodia *f*; *fig.* transporte *m* (de admiración *etc.*).

rhe·o·stat ['riːoustæt] reóstato *m*.

rhet·o·ric ['retərik] retórica *f*; **rhe·tor·i·cal** [ri'tɔrikl] ☐ retórico; **rhet·o·ri·cian** [retə'riʃn] retórico *m*.

rheu·mat·ic [ruː'mætik] ☐ reumático; ʌs F *pl.* = **rheu·ma·tism** ['ruːmətizm] reumatismo *m*.

rhi·no[1] ['rainou] *sl.* parné *m*.

rhi·no[2] [ʌ] = **rhi·noc·er·os** [rai-'nɔsərəs] rinoceronte *m*.

rhomb, rhom·bus ['rɔm(bəs)] rombo *m*.

rhu·barb ['ruːbɑːb] ruibarbo *m*.

rhyme [raim] **1.** rima *f*; poesía *f*; *without* ʌ *or reason* sin ton ni son; **2.** rimar; **'rhym·er, rhyme·ster** ['ʌstə] rimador (-a *f*) *m*.

rhythm [riðm] ritmo *m*; **'rhyth·mic, 'rhyth·mi·cal** ☐ rítmico.

rib [rib] **1.** *anat.*, ⚓ costilla *f*; ⚘ nervio *m*; △ nervadura *f*; **2.** F tomar el pelo a.

rib·ald ['ribəld] obsceno; irreverente y regocijado; **'rib·ald·ry** obscenidad *f*; irreverencia *f* regocijada.

rib·and ['ribənd] = *ribbon*.

ribbed [ribd] nervudo; rayado.

rib·bon ['ribən] cinta *f* (*a. type-writer* ʌ); ✂ galón *m*; ʌs *pl. fig.* trizas *f/pl.*; F ʌs *pl.* riendas *f/pl.*; ʌ *development* desarrollo *m* en línea.

rice [rais] arroz *m*; ʌ *field* arrozal *m*; ʌ *paper* papel *m* de paja de arroz.

rich [ritʃ] ☐ rico; (*lavish*) suntuoso; exquisito; *colour* vivo; *food* rico, sabroso; *profits* pingüe; *soil* fértil; *style* opulento, copioso; *b.s.* empalagoso; *voice* sonoro; *wine* generoso; F muy divertido; *be* ʌ *in* abundar de (*or* en); ʌ *milk* leche *f* sin desnatar; **rich·es** ['ʌiz] *pl.* riqueza *f*; **'rich·ness** riqueza *f*; fertilidad *f* of *soil etc.*

rick[1] [rik] 𝒗 **1.** *approx.* montón *m* de paja (*or* heno *etc.*), almiar *m*; **2.** recoger en montones.

rick[2] [ʌ] *v.* wrick.

rick·ets ['rikits] ⚕ raquitismo *m*, raquitis *f*; **'rick·et·y** ⚕ raquítico; *fig.* desvencijado, destartalado.

ri·co·chet ['rikəʃei] rebotar.

rid [rid] [*irr.*] librar, desembarazar (*of de*); *be* ʌ *of* estar libre de; *get* ʌ *of* deshacerse de; **'rid·dance** libramiento *m*; *good* ʌ! ¡enhoramala!, ¡vete con viento fresco!

rid·den ['ridn] *p.p. of ride* 2; ʌ *by horse* montado por.

rid·dle[1] ['ridl] acertijo *m*, adivinanza *f*; (*p. etc.*) enigma *m*.

rid·dle[2] [ʌ] **1.** criba *f* (gruesa); (*potato* ʌ) escogedor *m*; **2.** cribar; acribillar *with shot.*

ride [raid] **1.** cabalgata *f*; paseo *m*, viaje *m* (a caballo, en coche *etc.*); camino *m* de herradura; *sl. take s.o. for a* ʌ decepcionar a alguien; *Am. sl.* pasear a alguien; **2.** *v/i.* montar, cabalgar; ir, viajar, pasear (se) (en coche *etc.*); flotar; ʌ *at* *anchor* estar fondeado; ~ *for a fall* presumir demasiado; *v/t. horse etc.* montar; *bicycle* ir en; *a distance* recorrer (a caballo *etc.*); *waves* hender, surcar; ~ *down* revolcar, atropellar; ~ *out storm* capear, hacer frente a; '**rid·er** jinete (a *f*) *m*, caballero *m*; (*cyclist*) ciclista *m/f*; (*clause*) aditamento *m*; ⊕ pilón *m*.

ridge [ridʒ] cadena *f*, sierra *f of hills*; cresta *f of hill*; △ caballete *m* (*a.* ✒); ✒ caballón *m*.

rid·i·cule ['ridikjuːl] **1.** irrisión *f*, burlas *f/pl.*; **2.** ridiculizar, poner en ridículo; **ri'dic·u·lous** [~juləs] □ ridículo.

rid·ing ['raidiŋ] **1.** equitación *f*; **2.** ... de montar; '**~-hab·it** traje *m* de montar; '**~-school** picadero *m*, escuela *f* de equitación.

rife [raif] corriente, frecuente; general; endémico; ~ *with* lleno de; *be* ~ cundir.

riff-raff ['rifræf] chusma *f*, bahorrina *f*.

ri·fle[1] ['raifl] robar; saquear.

ri·fle[2] [~] **1.** rifle *m*, fusil *m*; ~*s pl.* rifleros *m/pl.*; **2.** ⊕ rayar; '~·**man** riflero *m*.

ri·fling ['raifliŋ] ⊕ rayado *m*.

rift [rift] hendedura *f*, rendija *f*; *fig.* grieta *f*, desavenencia *f*.

rig[1] [rig] *sl. election* falsificar; ~ *the market* manipular la lonja.

rig[2] [~] **1.** ⚓ aparejo *m*; F atuendo *m*; **2.** ⚓ aparejar, enjarciar; F ~ *out* ataviar; F ~ *up* improvisar; '**rig·ger** ⚓ aparejador *m*; ✂ mecánico *m*; '**rig·ging** jarcia *f*; aparejo *m*; cordaje *m*.

right [rait] **1.** □ *side* derecho; (*correct*) correcto, exacto; (*true*) verdadero; (*just*) justo, equitativo; (*proper*) indicado, debido; (*in mind*) cuerdo; *conditions* favorable; *th. sought* que hace falta, que se busca; *be* ~ (*p.*) tener razón; *be* ~ *to inf.* hacer bien in *inf.*; *that's* ~ eso es; *put* (*or set*) ~ arreglar, ajustar; *all* ~! ¡bueno!; ¡conforme!; ¡está bien!; (*answering call*) ¡voy!; *be all* ~ estar bien (de salud); *it will be all* ~ todo se arreglará; *are we on the* ~ *road?* ¿vamos por buen camino?; **2.** *adv.* derechamente; directamente; bien; completamente; exactamente; correctamente; a la derecha; † muy; ~ *away* en seguida; ~ *here* aquí

mismo; F ~ *now* ahorita; **3.** derecho *m* (*to a su.*, *inf.*); justicia *f*; título *m*; privilegio *m* (*of ger.* de *inf.*); (*side*) derecha *f* (*a. pol.*); *boxing:* derechazo *m*; ~*s pl.* propiedad *f of story etc.*; ~ *of way* derecho *m* de paso; *mot.* prioridad *f*; *by* ~(*s*) en justicia, según derecho; *by* ~ *of* por razón de; *in his own* ~ por derecho propio; *on* (*or to*) *the* ~ a la derecha; *be in the* ~ tener razón; *set* (*or put*) *to* ~*s* arreglar, ajustar; **4.** enderezar (*a.* ⚓); corregir, rectificar; ~·**an·gle** ['~'æŋgl] △ ángulo *m* recto; ~*d* rectangular; **right·eous** ['~ʃəs] □ justo, honrado, probo; '**right·eous·ness** honradez *f*, probidad *f*; **right·ful** ['~ful] □ justo; legítimo; '**right-'hand**: ~ *drive mot.* conducción *f* a la derecha; ~ *side* derecha *f*; '**right-'hand·ed** que usa (*or* ⊕ para) la mano derecha; '**right·ist** derechista *adj. a. su. m/f*; '**right-'mind·ed** honrado; '**right·ness** derechura *f*; justicia *f*; '**right-wing** *pol.* derechista.

rig·id ['ridʒid] □ rígido; **ri'gid·i·ty** rigidez *f*.

rig·ma·role ['rigməroul] galimatías *m*, relación *f* disparatada.

rig·or ['raigɔː] ✆ escalofríos *m/pl.*; ~ *mor·tis* ['mɔːtis] rigidez *f* cadavérica; **rig·or·ous** ['rigərəs] □ riguroso.

rig·o(u)r ['rigə] rigor *m*, severidad *f*.

rile [rail] F sulfurar, irritar, reventar.

rill [ril] *poet.* riachuelo *m*.

rim [rim] borde *m*, canto *m*; llanta *f of wheel.*

rime[1] [raim] *poet.* rima *f*.

rime[2] [~] (*frost*) escarcha *f*.

rind [raind] corteza *f*; cáscara *f*; piel *f*.

ring[1] [riŋ] **1.** (*finger-*) anillo *m*; círculo *m*; (*iron*) argolla *f*; (*boxing-*) cuadrilátero *m*; (*bull-*) redondel *m*, plaza *f*; corro *m of people*; ✝ confabulación *f*, pandilla *f*; (*on large scale*) cartel *m*; **2.** cercar, rodear (*by, with* de).

ring[2] [~] **1.** campanilleo *m*; toque *m* (de timbre); llamada *f at door*; *teleph.* telefonazo *m*; **2.** *v/i.* sonar; resonar (*with* con); (*bell*) repicar; campanillear; llamar *at door*; (*ears*) zumbar; ~ *off teleph.* colgar; *v/t. small bell* tocar; *large bell* tañer;

(hacer) sonar; *teleph.* llamar (por teléfono) (*a.* ~ up); **'ring·er** campanero *m*; **'ring·ing 1.** □ resonante; **2.** repique *m of bells*; zumbido *m in ears*; **'ring·lead·er** cabecilla *m*; **ring·let** ['~lit] rizo *m*; **'ring·worm** tiña *f*.

rink [riŋk] pista *f*.

rinse [rins] **1.** aclarar; enjuagar (*a.* ~ out); **2.** = **'rins·ing** aclaración *f*; enjuague *m*.

ri·ot ['raiət] **1.** tumulto *m*, alboroto *m*, motín *m*; orgía *f* (*a. fig.*); run ~ desenfrenarse; F *it was a* ~ eso fue de miedo; **2.** amotinarse, alborotarse; **'ri·ot·er** manifestante *m/f*; amotinado(r) *m*; **'ri·ot·ous** □ alborotado; *life* desenfrenado; *party* bullicioso; F ~ly funny tremendamente divertido.

rip[1] [rip] **1.** rasgón *m*, rasgadura *f*; **2.** rasgar(se); ~ off arrebatar; ~ up desgarrar, romper.

rip[2] [~] calavera *m*.

rip·cord ['ripkɔːd] 🪂 cabo *m* de desgarre.

ripe [raip] □ maduro; **'rip·en** madurar; **'ripe·ness** madurez *f*.

ri·poste [ri'poust] *fenc.* estocada *f*; *fig.* respuesta *f* aguda, réplica *f*.

rip·ping ['ripiŋ] □ *sl.* bárbaro, de aúpa.

rip·ple ['ripl] **1.** rizo *m*; ondulación *f*; (*sound*) murmullo *m*; **2.** rizar(se), encrespar(se); (*sound*) murmurar.

rise [raiz] **1.** subida *f*, alza *f*, elevación *f of prices etc.*; ascenso *m in rank*; crecida *f of river*; nacimiento *m of spring*; (*hill*) cuesta *f*, elevación *f*; *fig.* origen *m*; give ~ to dar origen a, motivar, ocasionar; **2.** [*irr.*] subir; alzarse; levantarse; ponerse en pie; ascender *in rank*; (*sun*) salir; (*river*) nacer, brotar; (*swell*) hincharse; (*revolt*) sublevarse; (*cake*) leudarse; *parl.* suspenderse (la sesión); ~ to ser capaz de; *occasion* estar a la altura de, corresponder dignamente a; (*mountain*) elevarse a, alcanzar; **ris·en** ['rizn] *p.p. of* rise; **'ris·er**: *early* ~ madrugador (-a *f*) *m*.

ris·i·bil·i·ty [rizi'biliti] risibilidad *f*; **'ris·i·ble** □ risible.

ris·ing ['raiziŋ] **1.** (*revolt*) sublevación *f*; levantamiento *m*; salida *f of sun*; *parl.* término *m* (de sesión); **2.** naciente, ascendiente; *sun* saliente; *ground* que sube; *generation* nuevo.

risk [risk] **1.** riesgo *m*; peligro *m*; *at the* ~ of con peligro de, arriesgando; run a (or the) ~ of ger. correr riesgo de *inf.*; **2.** arriesgar, exponer(se a); ~ ger. arriesgarse a *inf.*; **'risk·y** □ arriesgado, aventurado.

ris·sole ['risoul] *approx.* croqueta *f*, albóndiga *f*.

rite [rait] rito *m*; *last* (or *funeral*) ~s *pl.* exequias *f/pl.*; **rit·u·al** ['ritjuəl] □ ritual *adj. a. su. m.*

ri·val ['raivl] **1.** rival *m/f*, competidor (-a *f*) *m*; **2.** rival, competidor (*a.* 🌲); **3.** rivalizar con, competir con; **'ri·val·ry** rivalidad *f*, competencia *f*.

riv·er ['rivə] río *m*; *down* ~ río abajo; *up* ~ río arriba; *attr.* fluvial; **'~-side** ribera *f*, orilla *f*; *attr.* ribereño.

riv·et ['rivit] **1.** roblón *m*, remache *m*; **2.** ⊕ remachar; *fig.* clavar (*on*, *to* en).

riv·u·let ['rivjulit] riachuelo *m*.

roach [routʃ] *ichth.* escarcho *m*; *Am.* cucaracha *f*.

road [roud] camino *m* (*to de*; *a. fig.*); carretera *f*; (*in town*) calle *f*; *by* ~ por carretera; ⚓ ~s *pl.* rada *f* (*a.* '~-stead); *hold the* ~ agarrarse al camino; **'~-hog** conductor *m* poco considerado, asesino *m* de carretera; **'~-house** albergue *m* de carretera; **'~-mend·er** peón *m* caminero; **'~-race** carrera *f* sobre carretera; **'~-sense** *mot.* instinto *m* del buen conductor; **'~-side** borde *m* del camino; **road·ster** ['~stə] coche *m* (or bicicleta *f etc.*) de turismo; **'road-'us·er** usuario *m* de la vía pública; **'road·way** calzada *f*.

roam [roum] *v/i.* vagar; callejear *in town*; *v/t.* vagar por; recorrer; **'roam·er** vag(abund)o *m*.

roan [roun] (*caballo m*) ruano; ⊕ badana *f*.

roar [rɔː] **1.** rugir; bramar; (*with laughter*) reírse a carcajadas; **2.** rugido *m*; bramido *m*; **roar·ing** ['~riŋ] **1.** *v.* roar 2; **2.** □ rugiente; 🌲 *etc.* floreciente; F de aúpa.

roast [roust] **1.** asar; *coffee* tostar; **2.** asado; *coffee* tostado; ~ *beef* rosbif *m*; **3.** carne *f* asada, asado *m*; *rule the* ~ mandar.

rob [rɔb] robar (s.o. of s.t. algo a alguien); saltear on highway); **'rob·ber** ladrón m; salteador m (de caminos); **'rob·ber·y** robo m.

robe [roub] **1.** túnica f, manto m; 🕆 toga f; vestido m talar; ~s pl. traje m de ceremonia; gentlemen of the ~ la curia; **2.** vestir(se).

rob·in ['rɔbin] petirrojo m.

ro·bot ['roubɔt] autómata m, robot m.

ro·bust [rə'bʌst] ☐ robusto; recio; vigoroso; **ro'bust·ness** robustez f.

rock¹ [rɔk] roca f; peña f; 🕆 escollo m; sl. diamante m; the ♀ el Peñón (de Gibraltar); get down to ~ bottom llegar a lo más bajo; ~ crystal cristal m de roca; ~ salt sal f gema.

rock² [~] mecer(se), balancear(se); (violently) sacudir(se).

rock-bot·tom ['rɔk'bɔtəm] F price más bajo, mínimo.

rock·er ['rɔkə] (eje m de) balancín m.

rock·er·y ['rɔkəri] jardincito m rocoso, cuadro m alpino.

rock·et¹ ['rɔkit] cohete m; sl. peluca f; ~ propulsion propulsión f a cohete.

rock·et² [~] ♀ oruga f.

rock...: '~·fall deslizamiento m de montaña; '~-gar·den = rockery.

rock·ing... ['rɔkiŋ]: '~-chair mecedora f; '~-horse caballo m de balancín.

rock·y ['rɔki] rocoso, peñascoso; sl. inestable.

ro·co·co [rə'koukou] rococó adj. a. su. m.

rod [rɔd] medida de longitud (= 5,029 m.); var(ill)a f; barra f; vástago m; (fishing-) caña f; Am. sl. quitapenas m.

rode [roud] pret. of ride 2.

ro·dent ['roudənt] roedor m.

ro·de·o [rou'deiou] Am. rodeo m.

rod·o·mon·tade [rɔdə'mɔnteid] fanfarronada f.

roe¹ [rou] hueva f (a. hard ~); soft ~ lecha f.

roe² [~] zo. corzo (a f) m; '~-buck corzo m.

ro·ga·tion [rou'geiʃn] eccl. rogación f.

rogue [roug] pícaro m, pillo m; canalla m; ~s' gallery fichero m de delin-

cuentes; **'ro·guer·y** picardía f; **'ro·guish** ☐ pícaro, picaruelo; travieso.

roist·er ['rɔistə] jaranear; **'roist·er·er** jaranero m.

role [roul] thea. papel m (a. fig.); play (or take) a ~ hacer un papel.

roll [roul] **1.** rollo m; ⊕ rodillo m; (bread-) panecillo m; bollo m; (list) lista f; retumbo m of thunder; redoble m of drum; (gait) bamboleo m; 🕆 balance(o) m; Am. fajo m of notes; **2.** v/t. hacer rodar; soil allanar; cigarette liar; eyes poner en blanco; tongue vibrar; ~ up arrollar, enrollar; sleeves arremangar; ~ed gold oro m laminado; v/i. rodar; revolcarse on ground; (land) ondular; (thunder) retumbar; (gait) bambolearse; 🕆 balancearse; F be ~ing in nadar en; ~ up (car etc.) llegar; F (p.) aparecer, presentarse; '~-call (acto m de pasar) lista f; **'roll·er** ♪, ⊕ rodillo m; 🕆 ola f larga; (mst ~ bandage) venda f enrollada; Am. ~ coaster montaña f rusa; ~ skates patines m/pl. de ruedas; ~ towel toalla f de rodillo; **'roll-film** película f en rollo.

rol·lick ['rɔlik] juguetear; **'rol·lick·ing** alegre, jovial.

roll·ing ['rouliŋ] **1.** rodante; rodadero; ground ondulado; **2.** rodadura f; 🕆 balanceo m; ~ mill tren m de laminación; ~ pin rodillo m; '~-stock material m rodante.

roll-top desk ['roultɔp'desk] buró m, escritorio m de tapa rodadera.

ro·ly-po·ly ['rouli'pouli] pudín en forma de rollo.

Ro·man ['roumən] romano adj. a. su. m (a f); typ. (mst ♀) tipo m romano.

ro·mance [rə'mæns] **1.** novela f; ficción f; lo pintoresco of history etc.; F amoríos m/pl., amores m/pl.; (language) romance m; **2.** soñar; exagerar; **3.** románico, romance.

Ro·man·esque [roumə'nesk], **Ro·man·ic** [rou'mænik] románico.

ro·man·tic [rə'mæntik] **1.** ☐ romántico; affair novelesco; p. sentimental; place pintoresco, encantado; **2.** romántico m; **ro'man·ti·cism** romanticismo m.

Rom·ish ['roumiʃ] mst contp. (cató lico) romano.

romp [rɔmp] **1.** retozo m, trisca **2.** retozar, juguetear, triscar home ganar fácilmente; **'romp·ers** pelele *m*, mono *m*.

rood [ru:d] cruz *f*, crucifijo *m*.

roof [ru:f] **1.** tejado *m*, techo *m*; (*flat*) azotea *f*; ~ *of the mouth* paladar *m*; **2.** (*freq.* ~ *in*, *over*) techar; **'roof·ing 1.** techumbre *f*; **2.** ... para techos.

rook¹ [ruk] **1.** *orn.* graja *f*; **2.** trampear, estafar.

rook² [~] *chess:* torre *f*, roque *m*.

rook·er·y ['rukəri] nidada *f* de grajas.

rook·ie ['ruki] ⚔ *sl.* bisoño *m*.

room [rum, ru:m] cuarto *m*, habitación *f*; pieza *f*; (*large*) aposento *m*; (*space*) sitio *m*, espacio *m*; cabida *f*; ~*s pl.* alojamiento *m*; *make* ~ hacer lugar; *there is no* ~ *for* no cabe(n); **...roomed** [ru:md] de ... piezas; **'room·er** *Am.* subinquilino (a *f*) *m*; huésped *m/f*; **'room·ing-house** *Am.* casa *f* donde se alquilan cuartos; **'room-mate** compañero (a *f*) *m* de cuarto; **'room·y** □ espacioso, holgado.

roor·back ['ru:bæk] *Am.* libelo *m* político.

roost [ru:st] **1.** percha *f*; gallinero *m*; *rule the* ~ mandar; **2.** (*bird*) descansar (en una percha); *fig.* pasar la noche; **'roost·er** gallo *m*.

root [ru:t] **1.** *all senses:* raíz *f*; *take* (*or strike*) ~ echar raíces, arraigar; ~ *idea* idea *f* fundamental; ~ *and branch* del todo; **2.** *v/t.:* ~ *out,* ~ *up* arrancar, desarraigar, desenterrar, extirpar; F buscar; F hacer salir; *v/i.* ♣ arraigar(se); (*pig*) hozar, hocicar; *Am. sl.* ~ *for* hacer propaganda por; gritar por el éxito de; ~ **'root·er** *Am. sl.* entusiasta *m*, partidario *m* (for de).

rope [roup] **1.** cuerda *f*; soga *f*; (*esp.* ♣) maroma *f*, cable *m*; collar *m of pearls*; *mount. on the* ~ atado(s); *know the* ~*s* saber cuántas son cinco; **2.** atar, amarrar con cuerda(s) *etc.*; ~ *off* cercar con cuerdas; F ~ *a p. in* entruchar a una p., persuadir a una p. a que tome parte (*for s.t.* en algo); **'~-lad·der** escala *f* de cuerda; **'~-mak·er** cordelero *m*.

rop·y ['roupi] *liquid* viscoso.

ro·sa·ry ['rouzəri] *eccl.* rosario *m*; ♣ jardín *m* de rosales.

rose¹ [rouz] ♣ rosa *f*; (*colour*) color *m* de rosa; roseta *f of can*; ⚠ rosetón *m* (*a.* ~ *window*).

rose² [~] *pret. of rise* 2.

ro·se·ate ['rouziit] róseo, rosado.

rose·bud ['rouzbʌd] capullo *m* de rosa.

rose·mar·y ['rouzməri] romero *m*.

ro·sette [rou'zet] escarapela *f*; ⚠ rosetón *m*.

ros·in ['rɔzin] **1.** colofonia *f*; **2.** frotar con colofonia.

ros·ter ['rɔstə] lista *f*.

ros·trum ['rɔstrəm] tribuna *f*; ♪ atril *m*.

ros·y ['rouzi] □ (son)rosado; *prospect* prometedor.

rot [rɔt] **1.** putrefacción *f*, podredumbre *f*; *sl.* tonterías *f/pl.*; **2.** pudrir(se), corromper(se).

ro·ta ['routə] lista *f* (de tandas *etc.*).

ro·ta·ry ['routəri] rotativo, rotatorio; ~ *press* prensa *f* rotativa; **ro·tate** [rou'teit] (hacer) girar; alternar(se); **ro·ta'tion** rotación *f* (*a.* ✎); alternación *f*; *in* ~ por turno; **ro·ta·to·ry** [~'tətəri] *v. rotary*.

rote [rout]: *by* ~ de coro, maquinalmente.

ro·tor ['routə] rotor *m*.

rot·ten ['rɔtn] □ podrido, corrompido; *food* putrefacto; *wood* carcomido; *sl.* vil, ruin; *sl. feel* ~ estar muy malo; **'rot·ten·ness** podredumbre *f*, putrefacción *f*.

rot·ter ['rɔtə] *sl.* canalla *m*, sinvergüenza *m*.

ro·tund [rou'tʌnd] □ rotundo; *figure* corpulento; **ro'tun·da** [~də] ⚠ rotonda *f*; **ro'tun·di·ty** rotundidad *f*.

rou·ble ['ru:bl] rublo *m*.

rouge [ru:ʒ] **1.** colorete *m*, arrebol *m*; **2.** ponerse colorete, arrebolarse.

rough [rʌf] **1.** □ áspero; tosco; *estimate* aproximado; *ground* quebrado; *manners* grosero; *material* crudo, bruto; *play* duro; *sea* bravo; *treatment* brutal; *weather* tempestuoso; *work* chapucero; de preparación; ~ *and ready* tosco (pero eficaz); F *cut up* ~ sulfurarse; ~ *copy*, ~ *draft* borrador *m*; **2.** terreno *m* áspero, superficie *f* áspera; F *matón m*; *in the* ~ en bruto; *take the* ~ *with the smooth* aceptar la vida como es, tomarse las cosas filosóficamente; **3.** F ~ *it* pasar apuros, vivir sin comodidades; ~ *out* bosquejar, trazar de modo provisional; **'rough·age** alimento *m* poco digerible; **'rough·cast** mezcla *f* gruesa; **'rough·en** poner(se) áspero (*or* tosco).

rough...: ~**hewn** [ˈˌˈhjuːn] desbastado; **'~·house** *sl.* trapatiesta *f*, trifulca *f*; **'~·neck** *Am. sl.* canalla *m*; matón *m*; **'rough·ness** aspereza *f*, tosquedad *f etc.*; **'rough-rid·er** domador *m* de caballos; **'rough-shod:** *ride* ~ *over* tratar sin miramientos, imponerse a.

rou·lette [ruːˈlet] ruleta *f*.

Rou·ma·nian *v.* Rumanian.

round [raund] **1.** □ redondo (*a. number, sum*); *denial etc.* rotundo, categórico; ~ *table* mesa *f* redonda; ~ *trip* viaje *m* de ida y vuelta; **2.** *adv.* alrededor; (*freq.* ~ *about*) a la redonda; *all* ~ por todos lados; *all the year* ~ durante todo el año; 2 *feet* ~ 2 pies en redondo; **3.** *prp.* alrededor de; cerca de, cosa de; ~ *about 5 o'clock* a eso de las 5; ~ *the corner* a la vuelta de esquina; ~ *the town* por la ciudad; **4.** esfera *f*; círculo *m*; (*daily*) rutina *f*; (*tradesman's etc.*) recorrido *m*; (*slice*) rodaja *f*; (*drinks*) ronda *f*; *sport:* (*stage*) vuelta *f*; (*lap*) circuito *m*; *boxing:* asalto *m*; ✗ salva *f*; ✗ tiro *m*, cartucho *m*; **5.** redondear (~ *off*, ~ *out*); *corner etc.* doblar; ~ *up* acorralar, rodear *S.Am.*

round·a·bout [ˈraundəbaut] **1.** indirecto; ambagioso; **2.** tiovivo *m*; (*traffic-*) glorieta *f*; **'round·head** *hist.* cabeza *f* pelada; **'round·ly** *adv.* rotundamente; **'round·ness** redondez *f*; **'round-'shoul·dered** cargado de espaldas; **rounds·man** [ˈ~zmən] proveedor *m* casero; repartidor *m*; **'round-ta·ble con·fer·ence** reunión *f* de mesa redonda; **'round-'up** rodeo *m*.

rouse [rauz] despertar(se); *emotion* excitar; provocar *to fury etc.*; *game* levantar; **'rous·ing** conmovedor, emocionado.

roust·a·bout [ˈraustəˈbaut] *Am.* peón *m* (*esp.* portuario).

rout¹ [raut] **1.** derrota *f* completa, fuga *f* desordenada; *put to* ~ = **2.** derrotar (completamente).

rout² [~] *v.* root².

route [ruːt, ✗ raut] ruta *f*, itinerario *m*, camino *m*; **'~·march** marcha *f* (de entrenamiento).

rou·tine [ruːˈtiːn] **1.** rutina *f*; **2.** rutinario.

rove [rouv] vagar, errar (*the country*

por el campo); **'rov·er** vagabundo (a *f*) *m*; **'rov·ing** errante; ambulante; *disposition* andariego.

row¹ [rou] fila *f* (*a. thea. etc.*), hilera *f*; *in a* ~ seguidos.

row² [~] ♱ **1.** *v/i.* remar; *v/t.* conducir remando; **2.** paseo *m* en bote.

row³ [rau] F **1.** (*noise*) ruido *m*, jaleo *m*, tremolina *f*, estrépito *m*; (*quarrel*) bronca *f*, pelea *f*, camorra *f*; lío *m*, escándalo *m*; follón *m*; **2.** pelearse (con); reñir.

row·an [ˈrauən, ˈrouən] serbal *m*.

row-boat [ˈroubout] bote *m* (de remos).

row·dy [ˈraudi] quimerista *adj. a. su. m.*

row·er [ˈrouə] remero (a *f*) *m*; **'row·ing** remo *m*; ~ *boat* bote *m* (de remos).

row·lock [ˈrɔlək] escalamera *f*.

roy·al [ˈrɔiəl] □ real; regio; **'roy·al·ism** sentimiento *m* monárquico, monarquismo *m*; **'roy·al·ist** monárquico (a *f*) *m*; **'roy·al·ty** realeza *f*; personajes *m/pl.* reales; derechos *m/pl.* de autor.

rub [rʌb] **1.** frotamiento *m*; roce *m*, rozadura *f*; *there's the* ~ ahí está el busilis; **2.** *v/t.* frotar; (*hard*) (r)estregar; limpiar frotando; ~ *down horse* almohazar; ~ *in* hacer penetrar frotando; ~ *it in* F reiterar (una cosa desagradable); ~ *off* quitar frotando; ~ *out* borrar; *sl.* asesinar; ~ *up* pulir; ~ *the wrong way* frotar a contrapelo; *v.* shoulder; *v/i.:* ~ *against*, ~ *on* rozar *acc.*; ~ *along* F ir tirando.

rub-a-dub [ˈrʌbədʌb] rataplán *m*.

rub·ber [ˈrʌbə] caucho *m*, goma *f*; (*eraser*) goma *f* de borrar; ⊕ paño *m etc.* de pulir; *bridge:* juego *m* (primero *etc.*); *Am.* ~*s pl.* chanclos *m/pl.*; *attr.* de caucho, de goma; ~ *band* gom(it)a *f*; *Am. sl.* ~ *check* cheque *m* no cobradero; ~ *solution* disolución *f* de goma; **'~·neck** *Am. sl.* **1.** mirón (-a *f*) *m*; **2.** curiosear; **'~·'stamp 1.** estampilla *f* (*or* sello *m*) de goma; **2.** F aprobar maquinalmente.

rub·bish [ˈrʌbiʃ] basura *f*; desperdicios *m/pl.*; desecho(s) *m(pl.)*; *fig.* disparates *m/pl.*, tonterías *f/pl.*; ~ *dump* vertedero *m*; **'rub·bish·y** de bajísima calidad.

rub·ble ['rʌbl] cascote *m*, escombros *m/pl.*; (*filling*) cascajo *m*.
rube [ru:b] *Am. sl.* campesino *m*.
ru·bi·cund ['ru:bikənd] rubicundo.
ru·bric ['ru:brik] rúbrica *f* (*a. eccl.*); **ru·bri·cate** ['ˌkeit] rubricar.
ru·by ['ru:bi] 1. rubí *m*; 2. de color de rubí.
ruck [rʌk] *racing*: the ~ el grueso del pelotón; *fig.* vulgo *m*.
ruck(·le) ['rʌk(l)] (*mst* ~ *up*) arrugar (se).
ruck·sack ['ruksæk] mochila *f*.
ruc·tion ['rʌkʃn] F disturbio *m*, jaleo *m*; disgusto *m*.
rud·der ['rʌdə] timón *m* (*a.* ✈), gobernalle *m*.
rud·dle ['rʌdl] 1. almagre *m*; 2. marcar con almagre; **'rud·dy** rubicundo; rojizo; *sl.* condenado.
rude [ru:d] □ grosero, descortés; ofensivo, (*rough*) inculto, rudo, tosco; **'rude·ness** grosería *f*; rudeza *f*.
ru·di·ment ['ru:dimənt] *biol.* rudimento *m*; ~s *pl. fig.* rudimentos *m/pl.*; **ru·di·men·ta·ry** [ˌˈmentəri] *biol.* rudimental; *fig.* rudimentario.
rue¹ [ru:] ♀ ruda *f*.
rue² [ˈ] arrepentirse de, lamentar.
rue·ful ['ru:ful] □ triste; arrepentido; lamentable; **'rue·ful·ness** tristeza *f*.
ruff¹ [rʌf] gorguera *f*.
ruff² [ˈ] *cards*: 1. fallada *f*; 2. fallar.
ruf·fi·an ['rʌfjən] rufián *m*; canalla *m*; **'ruf·fi·an·ly** brutal.
ruf·fle ['rʌfl] 1. *sew.* volante *m*; 2. descomponer; perturbar; *water etc.* agitar, rizar; *sew.* fruncir.
rug [rʌg] alfombr(ill)a *f*; tapete *m*; manta *f* (de viaje).
rug·by ['rʌgbi] rugby *m*.
rug·ged ['rʌgid] □ *country* áspero, escabroso; *character* robusto; *b.s.* rudo, tosco; **'rug·ged·ness** escabrosidad *f etc.*
ru·in ['ru:in] 1. ruina *f*; arruinamiento *m*; perdición *f*; ~s *pl.* ruinas *f/pl.*; lay in ~s asolar; 2. arruinar; perder; estropear; estragar; **ru·in·'a·tion** F arruinamiento *m*; **'ru·in·ous** □ ruinoso.
rule [ru:l] 1. regla *f* (*a. eccl.*); reglamento *m*; norma *f*; mando *m*; dominio *m*; ⚖ fallo *m*, decisión *f*; (*a. standing* ~) estatuto *m*; ⊕ metro *m*

(plegable *etc.*); *as a* ~ por regla general; ~ *of the road* reglamento *m* del tráfico; ⚖ ~ *of three* regla *f* de tres; ~ *of thumb* regla *f* empírica; *be the* ~ ser de regla; *make it a* ~ *to* hacerse una regla de; 2. *v/t.* mandar, gobernar (*a.* ~ *over*); regir; *line* trazar, tirar; *paper* rayar, reglar; ~ *that* decretar que; ~ *out* excluir; *be* ~*d by* guiarse por; *v/i.* gobernar; reinar; prevalecer; ✝ (*price*) regir; **'rul·er** gobernante *m/f*; (*for lines*) regla *f*; **'rul·ing** 1. *esp.* ⚖ fallo *m*; 2. ✝ *price* que rige; imperante.
rum¹ [rʌm] ron *n*; *Am.* aguardiente *m*.
rum² [ˈ] *sl.* extraño, misterioso.
Ru·ma·nian [ru:ˈmeinjən] 1. rumano *adj. a. su. m* (a *f*); 2. (*language*) rumano *m*.
rum·ble¹ ['rʌmbl] 1. retumbo *m*; ruido *m* sordo; *Am.* ~ *seat* asiento *m* trasero (descubierto); 2. retumbar; F (*stomach*) sonar.
rum·ble² [ˈ] *sl.* calar.
ru·mi·nant ['ru:minənt] rumiante *adj. a. su. m*; **'ru·mi·nate** [ˌneit] rumiar (*a. fig.*); **ru·mi·na·tion** rumia(ción *f*) *f*.
rum·mage ['rʌmidʒ] 1. buscar (*in* en) revolviéndolo todo; registrar; 2. *attr.* ~ *sale* venta *f* de prendas usadas.
rum·my¹ ['rʌmi] *sl.* extraño, misterioso.
rum·my² [ˈ] *cards*: rummy *m*.
ru·mo(u)r ['ru:mə] 1. rumor *m*; 2. rumorear; *it is* ~*ed* (*that*) se rumorea (que).
rump [rʌmp] *anat.* trasero *m*, ancas *f/pl.*; *cooking*: cuarto *m* trasero.
rum·ple ['rʌmpl] ajar, chafar.
rump·steak ['rʌmp'steik] biftec *m*.
rum·pus ['rʌmpəs] F tumulto *m*, batahola *f*, revuelo *m*.
rum-run·ner ['rʌmrʌnə] *Am.* contrabandista *m* de bebidas alcohólicas.
run [rʌn] 1. [*irr.*] *v/i.* correr; apresurarse; (*continue*) seguir; (*reach*) extenderse; (*liquid*) correr, fluir; (*transport*) circular, ir; competir *in race*; (*melt*) derretirse; (*colour*) desteñirse; *thea.* mantenerse en la cartelera; ⊕ funcionar, marchar, andar; 🖋 supurar; *parl.* ser candidato; ~ *across a p.* topar a una p.; ~ *away* huir; escaparse; (*horse*) dispararse;

~ *away with* arrebatar; fugarse con; *race* ganar fácilmente; ~ *down* (*watch*) acabarse la cuerda; ~ *dry* secarse; ~ *for parl.* ser candidato para; ~ *high* (*river*) estar crecido; (*feelings*) encenderse; ~ *in* entrar corriendo; ~ *in the family* venir de familia; ~ *into* extenderse a; (*meet*) topar a; (*crash*) chocar con; ~ *on* continuar; F parlotear; ~ *out* salir corriendo; (*stock*) agotarse, acabarse; (*term*) expirar; ~ *over* desbordar, rebosar; *v. short*; ~ *through money* derrochar, consumir; *book* hojear; ~ *to* extenderse a; F costear; ~ *up* acudir corriendo; ~ (*up*)*on* (*thoughts*) concentrarse en; ~ *up against* tropezar con, chocar con; ~ *with* abundar en; nadar en; ~ *with sweat* chorrear de sudor; **2.** [*irr.*] *v/t.* correr; *blockade* forzar, burlar; *business* dirigir, organizar; *candidate* proponer, apoyar; *city* gobernar; *contraband* pasar; *distance, race* correr; *errand* hacer; *line* trazar; *machine* manejar; *temperature* tener; *vehicle* poseer; ~ *down* (*car*) atropellar; (*police*) acorralar, cazar; *reputation* desacreditar, desprestigiar, denigrar; ~ *be ~ down* estar debilitado; ~ *hard* acosar, hacer pasar apuros; ~ *in* ⊕, *mot.* rodar, ablandar; F *criminal* meter en la cárcel; ~ *into* hacer chocar con; ~ *off liquid* vaciar; *typ.* tirar, imprimir; ~ *over text* repasar; (*search*) registrar a la ligera; *p.* atropellar; ~ *one's eye over* examinar *acc.*; ~ *one's hand over* pasar la mano por, recorrer con la mano; ~ *a p. through* traspasar, espetar; ~ *up flag* izar; *debts* incurrir en; *house* construir (rápidamente); **3.** carrera *f* (*a. sport*); corrida *f*; *mot.* paseo *m* en coche; trayecto *m*, recorrido *m of vehicle*; ♪ glisado *m*, fermata *f*; ♫ (*a. day's* ~) singladura *f*; *thea.* serie *f* de representaciones; ⚡ terreno *m* de pasto; ♰ demanda *f* (*on de*); ♰ tendencia *f of market*; ♰ asedio *m* (*on a bank* de un banco); curso *m*, desarrollo *m of play etc.*; (*progress*) marcha *f*, progreso *m*; *the common* ~ el común (de las gentes); *in the long* ~ a la larga; *on the* ~ en fuga desordenada; (*prisoner*) fugado; *have the* ~ *of* tener libre uso de.

run·a·bout ['rʌnəbaut] *mot.* coche *m* pequeño.

run·a·way ['rʌnəwei] **1.** fugitivo *m*; caballo *m* desbocado; **2.** *victory* fácil; *marriage* clandestino.

rune [ruːn] runa *f*.

rung[1] [rʌŋ] *p.p. of ring*[2].

rung[2] [~] escalón *m* (*a. fig.*).

run·ic ['ruːnik] rúnico.

run·let ['rʌnlit], **run·nel** ['rʌnl] arroyuelo *m*.

run·ner ['rʌnə] corredor (-a *f*) *m*; caballo *m*; ⚔ ordenanza *m*, mensajero *m*; *patín m of sledge*; tapete *m of table*; ♣ serpa *f*; ~**-up** ['~ər'ʌp] subcampeón *m*.

run·ning ['rʌniŋ] **1.** *water* corriente; *knot* corredizo; *writing* cursivo; *commentary* continuo; ✹ supurante; *two days* ~ dos días seguidos; ~ *start* salida *f* lanzada; **2.** carrera *f*; ⊕ marcha *f*, funcionamiento *m of machine*; administración *f*, dirección *f of business*; *be in the* ~ tener posibilidades de ganar; '~**-board** *mot.* estribo *m*; '~-'**in** *mot.* (*adv. en*) rodaje *m*.

runt [rʌnt] redrojo *m*, enano *m* (*a. fig.*).

run·way ['rʌnwei] ✈ pista *f* de aterrizaje; *hunt.* pista *f*.

ru·pee [ruː'piː] rupia *f*.

rup·ture ['rʌptʃə] **1.** ✹ hernia *f*, quebradura *f*; *fig.* ruptura *f*; **2.** ✹ quebrarse (*a.* ~ *o.s.*).

ru·ral ['ruərəl] ☐ rural.

rush[1] [rʌʃ] ♣ junco *m*.

rush[2] [~] **1.** ímpetu *m*; ataque *m* (*a.* ✕), acometida *f*; torrente *m of words etc.*; (*haste*) prisa *f*, precipitación *f*; agolpamiento *m of people*; (*disorderly*) desbandada *f* general; ♰ demanda *f* extraordinaria (*for, on* de); ♰ ~ *order* pedido *m* urgente; ~ *hours* horas *f/pl.* de máximo tránsito; **2.** *v/i.* precipitarse, lanzarse; venir *etc.* de prisa; ~ *at* arremeter contra; ~ *in* entrar precipitadamente; ~ *into print* publicar una obra sin reflexionar; *v/t. work* despachar (*or* ejecutar) de prisa; ✕ asaltar; *sl.* hacer pagar; *parl.* ~ *through* aprobar de prisa.

rush·y ['rʌʃi] juncoso.

rusk [rʌsk] galleta *f* dura.

rus·set ['rʌsit] (*color m*) bermejo, rojizo.

Rus·sia leath·er ['rʌʃə'leðə] piel *f* de Rusia; '**Rus·sian 1.** ruso *adj. a. su. m* (*a f*); **2.** (*language*) ruso *m*.

rust [rʌst] **1.** orín *m*, herrumbre *f*; ⚘ roya *f*; **2.** aherrumbrar(se), oxidar(se), tomarse de orín.

rus·tic ['rʌstik] **1.** □ rústico, palurdo; **2.** rústico *m*, palurdo *m*; **rus·ti·cate** ['ˌkeit] *v/t. univ.* suspender temporalmente; *v/i.* rusticar; **rus·ti'ca·tion** rusticación *f*; *univ.* suspensión *f* temporal; **rus·tic·i·ty** [ˌ-'tisiti] rusticidad *f*.

rus·tle ['rʌsl] **1.** (hacer) susurrar; (hacer) crujir; *Am.* F hurtar; **2.** (*a.* **'rus·tling**) crujido *m of paper*; susurro *m of wind*.

rust...: '**ˌ·less** inoxidable; '**ˌ·proof**, '**ˌ·re·sist·ant** a prueba de herrumbre; '**rust·y** mohoso, enmohecido, herrumbroso, oxidado; *fig.* torpe.

rut¹ [rʌt] *zo.* **1.** celo *m*; **2.** caer (*or* estar) en celo.

rut² [ˌ] rodera *f*, rodada *f*, carril *m*; bache *m*; *fig.* rutina *f*; *be in a ˌ fig.* ir encarrilado.

ruth·less ['ruːθlis] □ despiadado; implacable; '**ruth·less·ness** implacabilidad *f*.

rut·ted ['rʌtid] *road* lleno de baches.

rut·ting ['rʌtiŋ] *zo.* en celo; *ˌ season* época *f* de celo.

rut·ty ['rʌti] = *rutted*.

rye [rai] centeno *m*.

S

sab·bath ['sæbǝθ] (*Christian*) domingo *m*; (*Jewish*) sábado *m*.
sab·bat·ic, sab·bat·i·cal [sǝ'bæt-ik(l)] □ sabático.
sa·ble ['seibl] 1. *zo.* cebellina *f*; *heraldry*: sable *m*; 2. negro.
sab·o·tage ['sæbǝtɑ:ʒ] 1. sabotaje*m*; 2. sabotear; **sab·o·teur** [sæbǝ'tǝ:] saboteador *m*.
sa·bre ['seibǝ] 1. sable *m*; 2. herir a sablazos.
sac·cha·rin ['sækǝrin] sacarina *f*; **sac·cha·rine** ['‿rain] sacarino; *fig.* azucarado.
sac·er·do·tal [sæsǝ'doutl] □ sacerdotal.
sack[1] [sæk] 1. saco *m*, costal *m*; (*a. ‿ coat*) saco*m*, americana *f*; F *give the ‿* despedir; F *get the ‿* ser despedido; 2. ensacar; F despedir.
sack[2] [‿] 1. saqueo *m*; *put to ‿* = 2. saquear.
sack·cloth ['sækklǝθ], **'sack·ing** (h)arpillera *f*; **sack·ful** ['‿ful] saco *m* (lleno).
sac·ra·ment ['sækrǝmǝnt] sacramento *m*; **sac·ra·men·tal** [‿'mentl] sacramental.
sa·cred ['seikrid] □ sagrado; **'sa·cred·ness** santidad *f*.
sac·ri·fice ['sækrifais] 1. sacrificio*m*; víctima *f*; † *at a ‿* con pérdida; 2. sacrificar; † malvender.
sac·ri·fi·cial [sækri'fiʃl] de sacrificio.
sac·ri·lege ['sækrilidʒ] sacrilegio *m*; **sac·ri·le·gious** [‿'lidʒǝs] sacrílego.
sa·crist, sac·ris·tan ['sækrist(ǝn)] sacristán *m*.
sac·ris·ty ['sækristi] sacristía *f*.
sad [sæd] □ triste; lamentable; *grow ‿* entristecerse.
sad·den ['sædn] entristecer.
sad·dle ['sædl] 1. silla *f*; (*cycle*-)sillín *m*; (*hill*) collado *m*; 2. ensillar (*a. ‿ up*); *fig. ‿ with* echar a cuestas a; *‿ o.s. with cargar con*; **'‿·backed** ensillado; **'‿·bag** alforja *f*; **'‿·cloth** sudadero *m*; **'sad·dler** talabartero *m*, guarnicionero *m*; **'sad·dler·y** talabartería *f*.

sad·ism ['sædizm] sadismo *m*; **sad·is·tic** □ sádico.
sad·ness ['sædnis] tristeza *f*.
sa·fa·ri [sǝ'fɑ:ri] safari *f*.
safe [seif] 1. □ seguro; intacto, ileso; *p.* digno de confianza; *‿ from* a salvo de, al abrigo de; *‿ and sound* sano y salvo; *to be on the ‿ side* para mayor seguridad; 2. caja *f* de caudales; *‿ deposit* cámara *f* acorazada; *‿ keeping* custodia *f*; lugar *m* seguro; *be in ‿ keeping* (*p.*) estar en buenas manos; **'‿·blow·er** ladrón*m* de cajas de caudales; *‿* **con·duct** salvoconducto *m*; **'‿·guard** 1. salvaguardia *f*; protección *f*; 2. salvaguardar; **safe·ly** con toda seguridad; *arrive etc.* sin accidente, sin novedad; **'safe·ness** seguridad *f*.
safe·ty ['seifti] 1. seguridad *f*; 2. *attr.* de seguridad; **'‿·belt** ✠ cinturón*m* de seguridad; *‿* **cur·tain** *thea.* telón *m* de seguridad; **'‿·pin** imperdible *m*; *‿* **ra·zor** maquinilla *f* de afeitar; **'‿·valve** válvula *f* de seguridad.
saf·fron ['sæfrǝn] 1. azafrán *m*; 2. azafranado.
sag [sæg] 1. combarse, hundirse; ✙ bajar; *fig.* aflojarse; 2. comba *f*.
sa·ga ['sɑ:gǝ] saga *f*.
sa·ga·cious [sǝ'geiʃǝs] □ sagaz.
sa·gac·i·ty [sǝ'gæsiti] sagacidad *f*.
sage[1] [seidʒ] □ sabio *adj. a. su. m* (*a f*).
sage[2] [‿] ♀ salvia *f*.
sa·go ['seigou] sagú *m*.
said [sed] *pret. a. p.p.* of *say*; *esp.* ⚖ *the ‿ articles* dichos artículos, los cuales artículos.
sail [seil] 1. vela *f*; paseo *m* en barco (de vela); aspa *f* of *mill*; *in full ‿* a todo trapo; *set ‿* hacerse a la vela; 2. *v/i.* navegar; darse a la vela; flotar; *‿ into sl.* atacar; *v/t. boat* gobernar; *sea* navegar; **'‿·cloth** lona *f*; **'sail·ing** *be plain ‿* ser cosa de coser y cantar; *‿ orders pl.* últimas instrucciones *f/pl.*; **'sail·ing-ship** velero *m*; **'sail·or** marinero *m*, marino *m*; *be a bad ‿* marearse fácil-

mente; **'sail·plane** velero *m*, planeador *m*.

sain·foin ['seinfɔin] pipirigallo *m*.

saint [seint] santo (a *f*) *m*; (*before
most m names*) San ...; **'saint·ed**
santo; que en santa gloria esté;
'saint·li·ness santidad *f*; **'saint·ly**
santo.

sake [seik]: *for the* ~ *of* por, por
motivo de, en atención a; *for my* ~
por mí; *for God's* ~ por el amor de
Dios.

sal [sæl]: ~ *ammoniac* sal *f* amoníaca;
~ *volatile* sal *f* volátil.

sa·la·cious [sə'leiʃəs] □ salaz.

sal·ad ['sæləd] ensalada *f*; ~ *bowl*
ensaladera *f*; ~ *dressing* mayonesa *f*,
aliño *m*.

sal·a·man·der ['sæləmændə] salamandra *f*.

sa·la·mi [sə'lɑ·mi] salami *m*.

sal·a·ried ['sælərid] *post* retribuido;
~ *employees* empleados *m*/*pl*. (de
oficina); **'sal·a·ry** sueldo *m*; **'sal·a·-
ry-earn·er** persona *f* que gana un
sueldo.

sale [seil] venta *f*; (*clearance* ~)
saldo *m*, liquidación *f*; (*a. public* ~)
(pública) subasta *f*; *for* ~, *on* ~ de
venta, en venta; se vende; **'sale·a·-
ble** vendible; **'sale-room** sala *f*
de subastas.

sales... [seilz]: **'~·man** dependiente
m, vendedor *m*; viajante *m*; **'~·man·-
ship** arte *m* de vender; **'~·wom·an**
dependienta *f*, vendedora *f*.

sa·li·ent ['seiliənt] □ (*fig.* sobre)-
saliente *adj. a. su. m*.

sa·line 1. ['seilain] salino; 2. [sə'lain]
saladar *m*; **sa·lin·i·ty** [sə'liniti] salinidad *f*.

sa·li·va [sə'laivə] saliva *f*; **sal·i·-
var·y** ['sælivəri] salival; **sal·i'va·-
tion** salivación *f*.

sal·low¹ ['sælou] ♣ sauce *m*.

sal·low² [~] cetrino, amarillento;
'sal·low·ness amarillez *f*.

sal·ly ['sæli] 1. ✕ salida *f* (*a. fig.*);
2. hacer una salida; ~ *forth* salir
resueltamente.

salm·on ['sæmən] (color *m*) salmón
m.

sa·loon [sə'lu·n] salón *m*; ⚓ cámara
f; *Am.* bar *m*, taberna *f*; *mot.*
limousine *f*, limusina *f*; **sa'loon-
car** 🚗 coche-salón *m*.

salt [sɔ·lt] 1. sal *f*; ~*s pl.* sales *f*/*pl.*
medicinales; *old* ~ lobo *m* de mar;

~ *of the earth* sal *f* de la tierra;
2. salado; salobre; 3. salar; ~ *away*
ocultar para uso futuro.

salt...: **'~-cel·lar** salero *m*; **'salt-
ness** salinidad *f*; **salt·pe·tre** ['~'pi·-
tə] salitre *m*; **'salt-works** salinas
f/*pl.*; **'salt·y** salado.

sa·lu·bri·ous [sə'lu·briəs] □ salubre; **sa·lu·bri·ty** [sə'lu·briti],
sal·u·tar·i·ness ['sæljutərinis] salubridad *f*; **sal·u·tar·y** ['sæljutəri]
□ saludable.

sal·u·ta·tion [sælju'teiʃn] salutación *f*; **sa·lu·ta·to·ry** [səl'ju·tətəri]
de salutación; **sa·lute** [sə'lu·t]
1. saludo *m*; *co.* beso *m*; salva *f of
guns*; 2. saludar.

sal·vage ['sælvidʒ] 1. salvamento *m*;
objetos *m*/*pl.* salvados; 2. salvar.

sal·va·tion [sæl'veiʃn] salvación *f*;
♀ Army Ejército *m* de Salvación;
sal'va·tion·ist miembro *m* del
Ejército de Salvación.

salve¹ [sælv] salvar.

salve² [sɑ·v] 1. *mst fig.* ungüento *m*;
2. curar (con ungüento); *fig.* tranquilizar.

sal·ver ['sælvə] bandeja *f*.

sal·vo¹ ['sælvou] salvedad *f*, reserva *f*.

sal·vo² [~] ✕ salva *f*.

Sa·mar·i·tan [sə'mæritn] samaritano *adj. a. su. m* (a *f*); *good* ~
buen samaritano *m*.

same [seim] mismo; igual, idéntico;
all the ~ a pesar de todo; *it is all
the* ~ *to me* me es igual, lo mismo
me da; *the* ~ ... *as* el mismo ... que;
the ~ *to you* igualmente; **'sameness** igualdad *f*; identidad *f*; monotonía *f*.

samp [sæmp] *Am.* maíz *m* molido
grueso.

sam·ple ['sɑ·mpl] 1. *esp.* ♣ muestra *f*; 2. probar; *wine etc.* catar;
⚕ muestrear; **'sam·pler** (*p.*) catador *m*; *sew.* dechado *m*; **'sam·pling**
⚕ muestreo *m*.

san·a·tive ['sænətiv], **san·a·to·ry**
['~təri] sanativo; **san·a·to·ri·um**
[~'tɔ·riəm] sanatorio *m*.

sanc·ti·fi·ca·tion [sæŋktifi'keiʃn]
santificación *f*; **sanc·ti·fy** ['~fai]
santificar; **sanc·ti·mo·ni·ous** [~-
'mounjəs] □ mojigato, santurrón;
sanc·tion ['sæŋkʃn] 1. sanción *f*;
2. sancionar, autorizar; **sanc·ti·ty**
['~titi] santidad *f*; inviolabilidad *f*;

~ of the mails secreto m de correspondencia; **sanc·tu·ar·y** ['ˌtjuəri] santuario m; (high altar) sagrario m; fig. refugio m; seek ~ acogerse a sagrado; **sanc·tum** ['ˌtəm] lugar m sagrado; fig. despacho m particular.

sand [sænd] **1.** arena f; ~s pl. arenal m, playa f (arenosa); Am. sl. resolución f; **2.** enarenar.

san·dal¹ ['sændl] sandalia f.

san·dal² [ˌ], '~·wood sándalo m.

sand...: '~·bag saco m terrero; '~·bank banco m de arena; '~·blast ⊕ chorro m de arena; '~·glass reloj m de arena; '~·pa·per **1.** papel m de lija; **2.** lijar; '~·pit arenal m; '~·stone piedra f arenisca.

sand·wich ['sænwidʒ, '~witʃ] **1.** sándwich m; bocadillo m; **2.** poner (entre dos cosas or capas); apretujar; intercalar.

sand·y ['sændi] arenoso; hair rojo.

sane [sein] □ cuerdo, sensato.

San·for·ize ['sænfəraiz] Am. sanforizar.

sang [sæŋ] pret. of sing.

san·gui·nary ['sæŋgwinəri] □ sanguinario; sangriento; **san·guine** ['ˌgwin] optimista; **san·guin·e·ous** [ˌniəs] sanguíneo.

san·i·tar·y ['ˌtəri] □ sanitario; ~ inspector inspector m de sanidad; ~ towel compresa f higiénica, paño m higiénico.

san·i·ta·tion [sæni'teiʃn] sanidad f; instalación f sanitaria, servicios m/pl.; saneamiento m in house; 'san·i·ty cordura f, sensatez f.

sank [sæŋk] pret. of sink 1.

San·skrit ['sænskrit] sánscrito adj. a. su. m.

sap¹ [sæp] ⚓ savia f; jugo m; fig. vitalidad f; sl. simplón m.

sap² [ˌ] **1.** ⚔ zapa f; **2.** ⚔ zapar; socavar; strength minar.

sa·pi·ence ['seipiəns] mst iro. sapiencia f; '**sa·pi·ent** □ mst iro. sapiente.

sap·ling ['sæpliŋ] pimpollo m, árbol m nuevo; fig. jovenzuelo m.

sap·o·na·ceous [sæpou'neiʃəs] 🝆 or co. saponáceo.

sap·per ['sæpə] zapador m.

sap·phire ['sæfaiə] zafiro m.

sap·py ['sæpi] jugoso; fig. enérgico; sl. tonto.

Sar·a·cen ['særəsn] sarraceno m.

sar·casm ['sɑːkæzm] sarcasmo m;

sar·cas·tic, sar·cas·ti·cal □ sarcástico.

sar·coph·a·gus, pl. **sar·coph·a·gi** [sɑːˈkɔfəgəs, ˌdʒai] sarcófago m.

sar·dine [sɑːˈdiːn] sardina f.

Sar·din·i·an [sɑːˈdinjən] sardo adj. a. su. m (a f).

sar·don·ic [sɑːˈdɔnik] □ burlón, irónico; sardónico S.Am.

sar·to·ri·al [sɑːˈtɔːriəl] □ de sastrería; relativo al vestido.

sash¹ [sæʃ] marco m (corredizo) de ventana.

sash² [ˌ] faja f; ⚔ fajín m.

sash-win·dow ['sæʃ'windou] ventana f de guillotina.

sat [sæt] pret. a. p.p. of sit.

sa·tan·ic [sə'tænik] □ satánico.

satch·el ['sætʃl] cabás m; cartapacio m.

sate [seit] v. satiate.

sa·teen [sæ'tiːn] satén m.

sat·el·lite ['sætəlait] satélite adj. a. su. m.

sa·ti·ate ['seiʃieit] saciar, hartar; **sa·ti·a·tion, sa·ti·e·ty** [sə'taiəti] saciedad f, hartura f.

sat·in ['sætin] raso m.

sat·ire ['sætaiə] sátira f; **sa·tir·ic, sa·tir·i·cal** [sə'tirik(l)] □ satírico; **sat·i·rist** ['sætərist] escritor m satírico; '**sat·i·rize** satirizar.

sat·is·fac·tion [sætis'fækʃn] satisfacción f; **sat·is·fac·to·ry** [ˌtəri] □ satisfactorio.

sat·is·fied ['sætisfaid] satisfecho; be ~ that estar convencido de que; **sat·is·fy** ['ˌfai] satisfacer.

sat·u·rate ['sætʃəreit] saturar; empapar; **sat·u·ra·tion** saturación f.

Sat·ur·day ['sætədi] sábado m.

sat·ur·nine ['sætənain] saturnino.

sat·yr ['sætə] sátiro m.

sauce [sɔːs] salsa f; (sweet) crema f; F impertinencia f, frescura f; '~·boat salsera f; '~·pan cacerola f, cazo m; '**sauc·er** platillo m.

sau·ci·ness ['sɔːsinis] F impertinencia f, descaro m, desfachatez f; **sau·cy** ['sɔːsi] F impertinente, descarado; fresco; coqueta.

saun·ter ['sɔːntə] **1.** paseo m lento y tranquilo; **2.** pasearse despacio y tranquilamente; deambular.

sau·ri·an ['sɔːriən] saurio m.

sau·sage ['sɔsidʒ] embutido m, salchicha f, chorizo m.

sav·age ['sævidʒ] **1.** □ salvaje;

attack feroz; F rabioso; **2.** salvaje *m/f;* **3.** *(animal)* embestir; **'sav·age·ness, 'sav·age·ry** salvajismo *m;* salvajería *f;* ferocidad *f.*

sa·van·na(h) [sə'vænə] sabana *f.*

save [seiv] **1.** *v/t.* salvar *(from* de); *time, money* ahorrar; *trouble* evitar; *(keep)* guardar; *v/i.* ahorrar, economizar; **2.** *lit. prp. a. cj.* salvo, excepto; ~ *for* excepto, si no fuera por; ~ *that* excepto que.

sav·e·loy ['sæviloi] salchichón *m* seco y sazonado.

sav·ing ['seiviŋ] **1.:** ~ *clause* cláusula *f* que contiene una salvedad; ~ *grace* único mérito *m;* **2.** economía *f;* ~s *pl.* ahorros *m/pl.;* '~s**bank** caja *f* de ahorros.

sav·io(u)r ['seivjə] salvador (-a *f) m;* ♀ Salvador *m.*

sa·voir faire ['sævwa:'fɛə] desparpajo *m,* destreza *f,* aptitud *f* práctica.

sa·vo(u)r ['seivə] **1.** sabor *m,* gust(ill)o *m;* **2.** *v/i.* saber *(of* a), oler *(of* a) *(a. fig.);* *v/t.* saborear; **sa·vo(u)r·i·ness** ['~rinis] sabor *m;* **'sa·vo(u)r·less** insípido; **'sa·vo(u)r·y 1.** sabroso; salado; **2.** entremés *m* salado.

sa·vo(u)r·y ['seivəri] ♀ tomillo *m* salsero.

sa·voy [sə'vɔi] col *f* de Saboya.

sav·vy ['sævi] *sl.* **1.** comprender; **2.** comprensión *f.*

saw¹ [sɔ:] *pret. of* see.

saw² [~] refrán *m,* dicho *m.*

saw³ [~] ⊕ **1.** sierra *f;* **2.** (a)serrar; '~·**dust** serrín *m;* '~·**fish** pez *m* sierra; '~·**horse** burro *m;* '~·**mill** aserradero *m;* **sawn** [sɔ:n] *p.p. of* saw³ **2;** **saw·yer** ['~jə] aserrador *m.*

Sax·on ['sæksn] sajón *adj. a su. m* (-a *f).*

sax·o·phone ['sæksəfoun] saxofón *m.*

say [sei] **1.** [*irr.*] decir; afirmar; *(text)* rezar; ~ *grace* bendecir la mesa; ~ *mass* decir misa; *that is to* ~ es decir; *to* ~ *nothing of* eso sin tomar en cuenta; *do you* ~ *(so)?* ¿de veras?; *you don't* ~ *(so)!* ¡parece mentira!; *I should* ~ *so!* ¡ya lo creo!; ~ *to o.s.* decir para sí; *it is said* se dice; *I* ~*!, Am.* ~! ¡oiga!; ¡vaya!; **2.** voz *f,* (uso *m* de la) palabra *f;* *let him have his* ~ que hable él; *have a (or some)* ~ *in a th.* tener voz y voto; *have no* ~ *in a th.*

no tener voz en capítulo; **'say·ing** dicho *m,* refrán *m; as the* ~ *goes* como dice el refrán; *it goes without* ~ eso cae de su peso.

scab [skæb] costra *f;* *vet.* roña *f;* F esquirol *m.*

scab·bard ['skæbəd] vaina *f.*

scab·by ['skæbi] costroso.

sca·bi·es ['skeibii:z] sarna *f.*

sca·bi·ous ['skeibiəs] escabiosa *f.*

sca·brous ['skeibrəs] escabroso.

scaf·fold ['skæfəld] cadalso *m;* = **'scaf·fold·ing** andamiaje *m,* andamio *m.*

scald [skɔ:ld] **1.** escaldadura *f;* **2.** escaldar; *(mst* ~ *out)* limpiar con agua caliente; *milk* calentar.

scale¹ [skeil] **1.** *(fish-)* escama *f;* **2.** *v/t.* escamar; descostrar; ⊕ raspar; *teeth* quitar el sarro a; *v/i.* descamarse *(freq.* ~ *off).*

scale² [~] **1.** platillo *m* de balanza; *(a pair of* una) ~s *pl.* balanza *f; ast.* Balanza *f; turn the* ~s decidir; **2.** pesar.

scale³ [~] **1.** escala *f (a.* ♪); *to* ~ según escala; *on a large* ~ en gran-(de) escala; **2.** *mountain* escalar, trepar a; ~ *down* reducir según escala.

scal·lop ['skɔləp] **1.** *zo.* venera *f;* *sew.* festón *m;* **2.** *sew.* festonear.

scalp [skælp] **1.** cuero *m* cabelludo; cabellera *f;* **2.** escalpar.

scal·pel ['skælpəl] escalpelo *m.*

scal·y ['skeili] escamoso.

scamp [skæmp] **1.** tunante *m/f,* bribón (-a *f) m; (child)* diablillo *m;* **2.** chapucear, frangollar; **'scamp·er 1.** *(a.* ~ *away,* ~ *off)* escabullirse, escaparse precipitadamente; **2.** huida *f etc.* precipitada.

scan [skæn] *v/t.* escudriñar, examinar; explorar *(a. television);* *verse* escandir; *v/i.* estar bien medido.

scan·dal ['skændl] escándalo *m;* ⚖ difamación *f; what a* ~!, *it's a* ~! ¡qué vergüenza !; **'scan·dal·ize** escandalizar; **'scan·dal·mon·ger** chismoso (a *f) m;* difamador (-a *f) m;* **'scan·dal·ous** ☐ escandaloso.

Scan·di·na·vi·an [skændi'neivjən] escandinavo *adj. a. su. m* (a *f).*

scan·ner ['skænə] *(radar)* antena *f* direccional giratoria; *(television)* dispositivo *m* explorador.

scan·sion ['skænʃn] escansión *f.*

scant [skænt] *lit. v.* scanty.

scant·i·ness ['skæntinis] escasez *f*, insuficiencia *f*.

scant·ling ['skæntliŋ] escantillón *m*; cuartón *m*; mínimo *m*.

scant·y ['skænti] □ escaso, corto; insuficiente.

scape·goat ['skeipgout] cabeza *f* de turco.

scape·grace ['skeipgreis] bribón (-a *f*) *m*; pillo (a *f*) *m*.

scap·u·lar ['skæpjulə] **1.** *anat.* escapular; **2.** *eccl.* escapulario *m*.

scar[1] [ska:] **1.** 𝔰 cicatriz *f*, señal *f* (*a. fig.*); **2.** *v/t.* señalar; *v/i.* cicatrizarse.

scar[2] [ʌ] paraje *m* rocoso; despeñadero *m*.

scar·ab ['skærəb] escarabajo *m*.

scarce [skeəs] escaso; raro; F *make* o.s. ~ escabullirse, esfumarse; **'scarce·ly** apenas; con dificultad; ~ *anybody* casi nadie; ~ *ever* casi nunca; **'scar·ci·ty** escasez *f*; rareza *f*; carestía *f*.

scare [skeə] **1.** espantar, asustar; ~ *away* ahuyentar; ~d sobresaltado; **2.** susto *m*, sobresalto *m*; '~·**crow** espantapájaros *m*; *fig.* espanto *m*; '~·**head** *Am.* títulares *m/pl.* grandes y sensacionales; '~·**mon·ger** alarmista *m/f*.

scarf[1] [ska:f] bufanda *f*; (*head*-)pañuelo *m*; '~·**skin** epidermis *f*.

scarf[2] [ʌ] **1.** ⊕ ensambladura *f* francesa; **2.** unir con ensambladura francesa.

scar·i·fi·ca·tion [skeərifi'keiʃn] 𝔰 escarificación *f*; *fig.* crítica *f* mordaz; **scar·i·fy** ['~fai] 𝔰, 𝒜 escarificar; *fig.* criticar severamente.

scar·la·ti·na [ska:lə'ti:nə] escarlatina *f*.

scar·let ['ska:lit] **1.** escarlata *f*, grana *f*; **2.** de color escarlata, de grana; ~ *fever* escarlatina *f*; ♀ ~ *runner* judía *f* de España.

scarp [ska:p] escarpa *f*, declive *m*.

scarred [ska:d] señalado de cicatrices.

scarves [ska:vz] *pl. of scarf*.

scar·y ['skeəri] F asustadizo.

scath·ing ['skeiðiŋ] □ acerbo, mordaz.

scat·ter ['skætə] **1.** esparcir, desparramar(se); ⚒ dispersar(se); ~d disperso; **2.** 𝒜 dispersión *f*; '~·**brain** F cabeza *m/f* de chorlito.

scav·enge ['skævindʒ] limpiar (las calles), recoger la basura; **'scav·en·ger** basurero *m*; *zo.* animal *m etc.* que se alimenta de carroña.

sce·nar·i·o [si'na:riou] guión *m*; **sce'nar·ist** guionista *m/f*.

scene [si:n] escena *f* (*a. thea.*); vista *f*, perspectiva *f*; paisaje *m*; teatro *m of events*; escenario *m of crime*; F escándalo *m*, jaleo *m*; *behind the* ~*s* entre bastidores; '~·**paint·er** escenógrafo *m*; **scen·er·y** ['~əri] paisaje *m*; *thea.* decoración(es) *f(pl.)*; decorado *m*; '**scene-shift·er** tramoyista *m*.

sce·nic ['si:nik] □ pintoresco; escénico; ~ *railway* montaña *f* rusa.

scent [sent] **1.** perfume *m*, olor *m*; (*sense*) olfato *m*; *hunt.* rastro *m*, pista *f*; **2.** perfumar; *danger etc.* sospechar, percibir; (*freq.* ~ *out*) olfatear, husmear; **'scent·ed** perfumado; **'scent·less** inodoro.

scep·tic ['skeptik] escéptico (a *f*) *m*; **'scep·ti·cal** □ escéptico; **scep·ti·cism** ['~sizm] escepticismo *m*.

scep·tre ['septə] cetro *m*.

sched·ule ['ʃedju:l, *Am.* 'skedju:l] **1.** lista *f*; *esp.* 𝔱𝔞 inventario *m*, apéndice *m*; programa *m*; cuestionario *m*; *esp. Am.* horario *m*; calendario *m* (de operaciones proyectadas); *on* ~ puntual; **2.** catalogar; fijar la hora de; proyectar; ~d *for demolition* se prevé su demolición.

scheme [ski:m] **1.** esquema *m*; plan *m*, proyecto *m*; (*plot*) ardid *m*, intriga *f*; **2.** *v/t.* proyectar; *b.s.* tramar; *v/i. b.s.* intrigar; **'schem·er** intrigante *m/f*.

schism ['sizm] cisma *m*; **schis·mat·ic** [siz'mætik] **1.** (*a.* **schis·'mat·i·cal** □) cismático; **2.** cismático *m*.

schist [ʃist] esquisto *m*.

schiz·o·phre·ni·a [skitsə'fri:njə] esquizofrenia *f*; **schiz·o·'phre·nic** □ esquizofrénico.

schol·ar ['skɔlə] (*pupil*) colegial (-a *f*) *m*, escolar *m/f*; (*learned p.*) erudito (a *f*) *m*; *univ.* becario (a *f*) *m*; **'schol·ar·ly** *adj.* erudito; **'schol·ar·ship** erudición *f*; *univ.* beca *f*.

scho·las·tic [skə'læstik] □ escolástico *adj. a. su. m*.

school[1] [sku:l] *v. shoal*[1].

school[2] [ʌ] **1.** escuela *f* (*a.* ~ *of thought*); colegio *m*; *public* ~ *England: approx.* internado *m* privado

(con dote); *Am. a. Scot.* escuela *f* pública; *v. driving, grammar etc.*; high ~ *Am. a. Scot.* instituto *m*; *primary* ~ escuela *f* primaria; *secondary* ~ escuela *f* secundaria; **2.** instruir, enseñar; disciplinar; '~**boy** colegial *m*, escolar *m*; '~**fel·low,** '~**mate** compañero (a *f*) *m* de clase; '~**girl** colegiala *f*, escolar *f*; '**school- ing** instrucción *f*, enseñanza *f*.
school...: '~**man** escolástico *m*; '~**mas·ter** (*grammar school*) profesor *m* (de instituto); (*others*) maestro *m*; '~**mis·tress** (*grammar school*) profesora *f*; (*others*) maestra *f*; '~**room** (sala *f* de) clase *f*; '~**teach·er** maestro (a *f*) *m*.
schoon·er ['sku:nə] ♒ goleta *f*; *Am.* vaso *m* grande para cerveza.
sci·at·i·ca [sai'ætikə] ciática *f*.
sci·ence ['saiəns] ciencia *f*.
sci·en·tif·ic [saiən'tifik] ☐ científico.
scin·til·late ['sintileit] centellear, chispear; *fig.* brillar; '**scin·til·lat- ing** ☐ *fig.* brillante.
sci·on ['saiən] vástago *m* (a. *fig.*).
scis·sion ['siʒn] escisión *f*; **scis·sors** ['sizəz] *pl.* (*a pair of* unas) tijeras *f/pl.*
scle·ro·sis [skliə'rousis] esclerosis *f*.
scoff [skɔf] **1.** mofa *f*, befa *f*; **2.** mofarse, burlarse (*at* de); *sl.* engullir; '**scoff·er** mofador (-a *f*) *m*, burlón (-a *f*) *m*.
scold [skould] **1.** regañona *f*; **2.** regañar, reprender; '**scold·ing** reprensión *f*, regaño *m*.
scol·lop ['skɔləp] *v.* scallop.
sconce¹ [skɔns] candelabro *m* de pared.
sconce² [~] ✗ fortín *m*.
scon(e) [skɔn, skoun] *torta escocesa.*
scoop [sku:p] **1.** pal(et)a *f*; (*water-*) achicador *m*; cuchara *f* (de draga); ✗ espátula *f*; *sl.* ganancia *f*; *sl.* primera publicación *f* de una noticia; **2.** (*mst* ~ *out*) sacar con pal(et)a; *water* achicar; *hole* excavar; *sl.* adelantarse a (un rival) publicando una noticia.
scoot·er ['sku:tə] (*child's*) patinet(te) *f*; (*adult's*) vespa *f*.
scope [skoup] alcance *m*; extensión *f*; envergadura *f*; oportunidad *f*; esfera *f* de acción; *have free* ~ tener carta blanca; *there is* ~ *for* hay campo para.

scorch [skɔːtʃ] *v/t.* chamuscar; (*sun, wind*) abrasar; ~*ed earth* tierra *f* quemada; *v/i.* F *mot.* ir volando; '**scorch·er** F día *m* de mucho calor.
score [skɔː] **1.** (*cut*) muesca *f*, entalladura *f*; (*line*) raya *f*; ♪ partitura *f*; (*20*) veintena *f*; *sport:* tanteo *m*; *four* ~ ochenta; *by the* ~ a granel; *on the* ~ *of* con motivo de; *on that* ~ a ese respecto; *pay off old* ~*s* ajustar cuentas viejas; *what's the* ~? ¿cómo estamos?; *keep* (*the*) ~ tantear; **2.** *v/t.* rayar; hacer cortes en; ♪ instrumentar; *sport: goal* marcar; *points* ganar; *total* apuntar (a. ~ *up*); *Am.* F criticar severamente; *v/i.* marcar (un tanto), ganar (puntos); (*keep total*) tantear; F ~ *off a p.* triunfar a expensas de alguien; *that doesn't* ~ eso no puntúa; '**score·board** tanteador *m*; '**scor·er** (*player*) marcador *m*; (*recorder*) tanteador *m*.
sco·ri·a, *pl.* **sco·ri·ae** ['skɔːriə, '~rii:] escoria *f*.
scorn [skɔːn] **1.** desprecio *m*, desdén *m*; **2.** despreciar, desdeñar; ~ *to* no dignarse *inf.*, desdeñarse de *inf.*; '**scorn·ful** ['~ful] ☐ desdeñoso.
scor·pi·on ['skɔːpjən] alacrán *m*.
Scot [skɔt] escocés (-a *f*) *m*.
Scotch¹ [skɔtʃ] **1.** escocés *m*; *the* ~ los escoceses; **2.** F *whisk(e)y m* escocés.
scotch² [~] **1.** calce *m*, cuña *f*; **2.** *wheel* calzar, engalgar; *rumour* desmentir; *plan etc.* frustrar.
scot-free ['skɔt'fri:] impune.
Scots [skɔts] escocés; '**Scots·man** escocés *m*; '**Scots·wom·an** escocesa *f*.
Scot·tish ['skɔtiʃ] escocés.
scoun·drel ['skaundrl] canalla *m*, bribón *m*.
scour¹ ['skauə] *dish* fregar, estregar; *channel* limpiar; ✗ purgar.
scour² [~] *v/i.:* ~ *about* buscar por todas partes (*for acc.*); *v/t. country* recorrer, explorar (*for* buscando).
scourge [skəːdʒ] *lit.* **1.** azote *m* (a. *fig.*); **2.** azotar, hostigar.
scout¹ [skaut] **1.** explorador *m*, escucha *m*; F busca *f*, reconocimiento *m*; *univ.* fámulo *m*, criado *m*; *Boy* ♀ (niño *m*) explorador *m*; **2.** explorar; reconocer; F ~ *for* buscar.
scout² [~] desmentir; rechazar con desdén.
scow [skau] gabarra *f*.

scowl [skaul] **1.** ceño *m*, sobrecejo *m*; **2.** fruncir el ceño; mirar con ceño (*a.* ~ *at*).

scrab·ble ['skræbl] garrapatear.

scrag [skræg] **1.** pescuezo *m*; **2.** torcer el pescuezo a; *sl.* aporrear; **scrag·gi·ness** ['~inis] flaqueza *f*; **'scrag·gy** □ enjuto, flaco.

scram [skræm] *esp. Am. sl.* **1.** largarse, dar un zarpazo; **2.** *int.* ¡lárgate!

scram·ble ['skræmbl] **1.:** ~ *up* trepar a, subir gateando a; ~ *for* disputarse a gritos, andar a la rebatiña por; ~*d eggs* huevos *m/pl.* revueltos; **2.** subida *f* (*up* a); arrebatiña *f*, pelea *f* (*for* por).

scrap [skræp] **1.** pedazo *m*, fragmento *m*; *sl.* riña *f*, bronca *f*; ~*s pl.* sobras *f/pl.*; desperdicios *m/pl.*; *not a* ~ ni pizca; *contp.* ~ *of paper* papel *m* mojado; **2.** *v/t.* desechar; ⚓ reducir a chatarra; *v/i. sl.* reñir; '~**book** álbum *m* de recortes.

scrape [skreip] **1.** raspadura *f*; F aprieto *m*, lío *m*; **2.** *v/t.* raspar, raer; ♪ *co.* rascar; (*a.* ~ *against*) rozar; ~ *off* quitar raspando; ~ *together*, ~ *up* arañar; ~ *acquaintance with* lograr conocer; *v/i.*; F ~ *along* ir tirando; F ~ *through exam* aprobar justo; '**scrap·er** (*tool*) raspador *m*, rascador *m*; limpiabarros *m for shoes*; '**scrap·ing(s)** raspadura(s) *f(pl.)*; ~*s fig.* hez *f*.

scrap...: '~**heap** montón *m* de desechos; '~**i·ron** chatarra *f*, hierro *m* viejo; '**scrap·py** □ fragmentario, inconexo.

scratch [skrætʃ] **1.** rasguño *m*, arañazo *m*; raya *f on stone etc.*; *sport:* línea *f* de partida; *be* (*or come*) *up to* ~ estar en buena condición; (*p.*) estar al nivel de las circunstancias; *start from* ~ empezar sin nada, empezar desde el principio; **2.** *competitor* sin ventaja; *team etc.* improvisado, reunido de prisa; **3.** *v/t.* rasguñar; rascar; *stone* rayar; *earth* escarbar; *sport etc.*: borrar, retirar; ~ *out* borrar, raspar; *v/i.* rasguñar; rascarse; (*pen*) raspear; (*chicken*) escarbar; *sport:* retirarse; '**scratch·y** *pen* que raspea; *tone* áspero.

scrawl [skrɔːl] **1.** garrapatear; **2.** garrapatos *m/pl.*

scraw·ny ['skrɔːni] F descarnado.

scream [skriːm] **1.** chillido *m*, grito *m*; F *he's a* ~ es un chistoso; **2.** chillar, gritar (*a.* ~ *out*); *abuse etc.* vociferar.

scree [skriː] *ladera de montaña cubierta de piedras movedizas.*

screech [skriːtʃ] *v.* scream; '~**owl** lechuza *f* común.

screed [skriːd] escrito *m* largo y aburrido.

screen [skriːn] **1.** (*cinema etc.*) pantalla *f*; (*folding*) biombo *m*; (*sieve*) tamiz *m*; ✂ cortina *f*; *phot.* retícula *f*; *the* ~ la pantalla; ~ *advertising* publicidad *f* cinematográfica; *phot. focussing* ~ placa *f* esmerilada; **2.** (*hide*) ocultar; (*protect*) proteger, abrigar; (*sift*) tamizar; *film* proyectar; *suspects* investigar.

screw [skruː] **1.** tornillo *m*; (*thread*) rosca *f*; ⚓, ✈ hélice *f*; *sl.* sueldo *m*; F *he has a* ~ *loose* le falta un tornillo; F *put the* ~(*s*) *on* apretar los tornillos a; **2.** atornillar; ~ *down* fijar con tornillos; ~ *up* atornillar; *paper, face* arrugar; ~ *up one's courage* cobrar ánimo; '~**ball** *Am. sl.* estrafalario, excéntrico *adj. a. su. m*; '~**driv·er** destornillador *m*; '~**jack** gato *m* de tornillo; '~**pro·pel·ler** hélice *f*; '**screw·y** *Am. sl.* chiflado.

scrib·ble ['skribl] **1.** garrapatos *m/pl.*; **2.** garrapatear; ~ *over* emborronar; '**scrib·bler** autorzuelo *m*.

scribe [skraib] † *or co.* escriba *m*; amanuense *m/f*; *contp.* escritorzuelo *m*.

scrim·mage ['skrimidʒ] arrebatiña *f*, pelea *f*.

scrimp [skrimp] **1.** escatimar; **2.** (*a.* '**scrimp·y**) escatimoso.

scrip [skrip] vale *m*, abonaré *m*.

script [skript] escritura *f*, letra *f* (*cursiva*); manuscrito *m*; *film:* guión *m*; ~ *writer* guionista *m/f*.

Scrip·tur·al ['skriptʃərəl] escrituario; bíblico; **Scrip·ture** ['~tʃə] Sagrada Escritura *f*; (*lesson*) Historia *f* Sagrada.

scrof·u·la ['skrɔfjulə] escrófula *f*; '**scrof·u·lous** □ escrofuloso.

scroll [skroul] rollo *m* de pergamino *etc.*; △ voluta *f*.

scro·tum ['skroutəm] escroto *m*.

scrounge [skraundʒ] *sl.* **1.:** *be on the* ~ = **2.** *v/i.* ir de gorra, gorronear, sablear; *v/t.* sacar por medio de gorronería.

scrub¹ [skrʌb] ⚜ maleza *f*, matas *f*/*pl*., monte *m* bajo.

scrub² [‿] 1. fregar, (r)estregar; 2. fregado *m* (*a.* '**scrub·bing**); *Am.* jugador *m* no adiestrado.

scrub·bing-brush ['skrʌbiŋbrʌʃ] bruza *f*, estregadera *f*.

scrub·by ['skrʌbi] achaparrado, enano.

scruff of the neck ['skrʌfəvðə'nek] pescuezo *m*; '**scruf·fy** F sucio, desaliñado, piojoso.

scrum, scrum·mage ['skrʌm(idʒ)] arrebatiña *f*; *rugby*: melée *f*.

scrump·tious ['skrʌmpʃəs] *sl.* de rechupete.

scrunch [skrʌntʃ] ronzar.

scru·ple ['skru:pl] 1. escrúpulo *m* (*a. pharm.* = *20 granos* = *1,296 gramos*); *make no* ‿ to no vacilar en; 2. escrupulizar, vacilar (*to* en); **scru·pu·lous** ['‿juləs] ☐ escrupuloso (*about* en cuanto a); '**scru·pu·lous·ness** escrupulosidad *f*.

scru·ti·neer [skru:ti'niə] escudriñador *m*; '**scru·ti·nize** escudriñar; examinar; *votes* escrutar; '**scru·ti·ny** escrutinio *m*; examen *m*.

scud [skʌd] correr (llevado por el viento); deslizarse rápidamente.

scuf·fle ['skʌfl] 1. refriega *f*, riña *f*; 2. pelear(se).

scull [skʌl] 1. remo *m* ligero; espadilla *f*; 2. remar (con remo ligero); cinglar.

scul·ler·y ['skʌləri] trascocina *f*, fregadero *m*, office *m*.

sculp·tor ['skʌlptə] escultor *m*.

sculp·tur·al ['skʌlptʃərəl] ☐ escultural; **sculp·ture** ['skʌlptʃə] 1. escultura *f*; 2. esculpir; '**sculp·tur·ing** escultura *f*.

scum [skʌm] espuma *f*; *metall.* escoria *f*; verdín *m on pond*; *fig.* heces *f*/*pl*.

scup·per ['skʌpə] imbornal *m*.

scurf [skə:f] caspa *f*; '**scurf·y** caspposo.

scur·ril·i·ty [skʌ'riliti] grosería *f*, procacidad *f*; '**scur·ril·ous** ☐ grosero, procaz; difamatorio.

scur·ry ['skʌri] 1. escabullirse; 2. carrera *f* precipitada.

scur·vy¹ ['skə:vi] 🇽 escorbuto *m*.

scur·vy² [‿] ☐ vil, despreciable.

scut [skʌt] rabito *m*.

scutch·eon ['skʌtʃn] *v.* escutcheon.

scut·tle¹ ['skʌtl] (*coal-*) cubo *m*.

scut·tle² [‿] ⚓ 1. escotilla *f*; 2. barrenar, dar barreno a.

scut·tle³ [‿] 1. fuga *f* (*or* retirada *f*) precipitada; 2. escabullirse, echar a correr.

scythe [saið] 1. guadaña *f*; 2. guadañar.

sea [si:] mar *m or f*; océano *m*; (*waves*) marejada *f*; *at* ‿ en el mar; *fig.* (*all*) *at* ‿ despistado, perplejo; *by* ‿ por mar; *go to* ‿ hacerse marinero; *put to* ‿ hacerse a la mar; *sl. half* ‿s *over* ajumado; '**‿board** litoral *m*; '**‿dog** lobo *m* de mar; '**‿far·ing** marinero; ‿ *food Am.* (*a.* ‿s *pl.*) mariscos *m*/*pl.*; '**‿go·ing** de alta mar; '**‿green** verdemar; '**‿gull** gaviota *f*; '**‿horse** caballito *m* de mar.

seal¹ [si:l] *zo.* foca *f*.

seal² [‿] 1. sello *m*; *great* ‿ sello *m* real; 2. sellar; cerrar; lacrar *with wax*; *fig.* decidir, confirmar; ‿ *off* obturar; ‿ *up* cerrar; ⊕ precintar; ‿ (*with lead*) emplomar.

sea-legs ['si:legz] pie *m* marino; *get one's* ‿ acostumbrarse a la vida de a bordo.

sea-lev·el ['si:levl] nivel *m* del mar.

seal·ing ['si:liŋ] caza *f* de la foca.

seal·ing-wax ['si:liŋwæks] lacre *m*.

sea-lion ['si:laiən] león *m* marino.

seal·skin ['si:lskin] piel *f* de foca.

seam [si:m] 1. *sew.* costura *f*; ⊕ juntura *f*; *geol.* filón *m*, veta *f*; *burst at the* ‿s descoserse; 2. coser.

sea·man ['si:mən] marinero *m*; '**sea·man·ship** marina *f*, náutica *f*.

seam·less ['si:mlis] sin costura, inconsútil.

seam·stress ['semstris] costurera *f*.

seam·y ['si:mi]: ‿ *side fig.* el revés de la medalla.

sé·ance ['seiɑ̃:ns] sesión *f* de espiritismo.

sea...: '**‿-piece** marina *f*; '**‿plane** hidroavión *m*; '**‿port** puerto *m* de mar.

sear [siə] chamuscar; (*wind*) abrasar; *fig.* marchitar; 🇽 cauterizar; ‿*ing pain* dolor *m* punzante.

search [sə:tʃ] 1. busca *f*, buscada *f*, búsqueda *f* (*for* de); registro *m of house etc.*; 🇽 pesquisa *f*; *in* ‿ *of* en busca de; 2. buscar (*a.* ‿ *for*); *place* explorar, registrar; *conscience* examinar; 🇽 tentar; ‿ *out* descubrir buscando; ‿ *into* investigar; F ‿ *me!*

¡qué sé yo!; **'search·er** buscador (-a *f*) *m*; **'search·ing** ☐ *look* penetrante; *question* agudo; **'searchlight** reflector *m*; **'search-warrant** mandamiento *m* judicial.

sea...: **~·scape** ['si:skeip] marina *f*; **'~·ser·pent** serpiente *f* de mar; **'~·shore** playa *f*; orilla *f* del mar; **'~·sick** mareado; *be* ~ marearse; **'~·sick·ness** mareo *m*; **'~·side** playa *f* (a. ~ *place*, ~ *resort*); orilla *f* del mar; *go to the* ~ ir a una playa (a veranear).

sea·son ['si:zn] **1.** estación *f of year*; (*indefinite*) época *f*; *social, sport*: temporada *f*; (*opportune time*) sazón *f*; *at this* ~ en esta época (del año); *in* (*good or due*) ~ a su tiempo; (*fruit*) en sazón; *out of* ~ fuera de sazón; *at the height of the* ~ en plena temporada; *with the compliments of the* ~ deseándole felices Pascuas *etc.*; *close* ~ veda *f*; **2.** sazonar, condimentar; *wood* curar; *fig.* templar; *fig.* acostumbrar (to a); **'sea·son·a·ble** ☐ propio de la estación; oportuno; **sea·son·al** ['si:znl] ☐ estacional; según la estación; **'sea·son·ing** condimento *m*; aderezo *m*; **'sea·son-'tick·et** abono *m* (de temporada); ~ *holder* abonado *m*.

seat [si:t] **1.** asiento *m*, silla *f*; *thea.* localidad *f*; *parl.* escaño *m*; 🏇 *etc.* plaza *f*; residencia *f*; sede *f of government*; fondillos *m/pl. of trousers*; ~ *of war* teatro *m* de guerra; *v. country*; *take a back* ~ dejar de figurar, quedar humillado; **2.** (a)sentar; establecer, fijar; *chair* poner asiento a; (*hall*) tener asientos para; *valve* ajustar; ~ *o.s.* sentarse; *be* ~*ed* estar sentado; **'seat·er** *mot.*, 🏇 *de ...* plaza(s); **'seat·ing** **ca'pac·i·ty** número *m* de asientos.

sea-ur·chin ['si:'ə:tʃin] erizo *m* de mar; **'sea-'wall** dique *m* (marítimo); **sea·ward** ['~wəd] **1.** *adj.* del lado del mar; **2.** *adv.* (a. **seawards** ['~z]) hacia el mar.

sea...: **'~·weed** alga *f* (marina); **'~·wor·thy** marinero, en condiciones de hacerse a la mar.

se·cant ['si:kənt] secante *adj. a. su. f.*

sec·a·teurs [sekə'tə:z] (*a pair of* una) podadera *f*.

se·cede [si'si:d] separarse; **se'ced·er** separatista *m*.

se·ces·sion [si'seʃn] secesión *f*; **se·'ces·sion·ist** secesionista *m*.

se·clu·ded [si'klu:did] retirado, apartado; **se'clu·sion** [~ʒn] recogimiento *m*, retiro *m*.

sec·ond ['sekənd] **1.** ☐ segundo; *be* ~ *to none* no irle en zaga a nadie; *on* ~ *thoughts* después de pensarlo bien; *v. fiddle*; ~ *sight* doble vista *f*; **2.** segundo *m*; *duel*: padrino *m*; *boxing*: segundante *m*; *♪* segunda *f*; ✝ ~*s pl.* artículos *m/pl.* de segunda calidad; **3.** apoyar, secundar; *p.* [si'kənd] trasladar temporalmente; **'sec·ond·ar·y** ☐ secundario (*a. school*); **'sec·ond-'best 1.** expediente *m*, sustituto *m*; **2.** (el) mejor después del primero; F *come off* ~ quedarse en segundo lugar; **'sec·ond·er** el (la) que secunda una moción; **'sec·ond-'hand 1.** de segunda mano, de lance; ~ *bookseller* librero *m* de viejo; ~ *bookshop* librería *f* de viejo; **2.** segundero *m of watch*; **'sec·ond·ly** en segundo lugar; **'sec·ond-'rate** de segunda categoría; de calidad inferior.

se·cre·cy ['si:krisi] secreto *m*; discreción *f*; **se·cret** ['~krit] **1.** ☐ secreto; oculto; clandestino; **2.** secreto *m*; *in* ~ en secreto; *be in the* ~ estar en el secreto.

sec·re·tar·i·al [sekri'tɛəriəl] de secretario; ~ *course* curso *m* de secretaria; **sec·re·tar·i·at(e)** ['~ət] secretaría *f*.

sec·re·tar·y ['sekrətri] secretario (a *f*) *m*; ♀ *of State* Ministro *m*; *Am.* Ministro *m* de Asuntos Exteriores; **'sec·re·tar·y·ship** secretaría *f*.

se·crete [si'kri:t] esconder; *physiol.* secretar; **se'cre·tion** *physiol.* secreción *f*; **se'cre·tive** ☐ callado, reservado; sigiloso; *be* ~ *about* hacer secreto de.

sect [sekt] secta *f*; **sec·tar·i·an** [~'tɛəriən] sectario *adj. a. su. m* (a *f*).

sec·tion ['sekʃn] *mst* sección *f*; región *f of country*; barrio *m of city*; tramo *m of road etc.*; sector *m of opinion*; **'sec·tion·al** ☐ seccional; ⊕ fabricado en secciones; regional, local; **'sec·tion-mark** párrafo *m*.

sec·tor ['sektə] sector *m*.

sec·u·lar ['sekjulə] ☐ secular; seglar; **sec·u·lar·i'za·tion** secularización *f*; **'sec·u·lar·ize** secularizar.

se·cure [si'kjuə] **1.** □ seguro; firme, fijo; a salvo; ~ *against*, ~ *from* asegurado contra; **2.** asegurar (*against*, *from* contra); (*obtain*) conseguir, obtener.

se·cu·ri·ty [si'kjuəriti] seguridad *f*; protección *f*; ✝ fianza *f on loan*, prenda *f*; (*p.*) fiador *m*; *stand* ~ *for* salir fiador de; *fig.* salir por; **se'cu·ri·ties** *pl.* valores *m/pl.*, obligaciones *f/pl.*

se·dan [si'dæn] silla *f* de manos (*a.* ~ *chair*); *mot.* sedan *m*.

se·date [si'deit] □ sosegado, sentado, grave; **se'date·ness** compostura *f*, gravedad *f*.

sed·a·tive ['sedətiv] sedante *adj. a. su. m*; calmante *adj. a. su. m*.

sed·en·tar·y ['sedntəri] □ sedentario.

sedge [sedʒ] juncia *f*.

sed·i·ment ['sedimənt] sedimento *m* (*a. geol.*); poso *m*; **sed·i·men·ta·ry** [~'mentəri] sedimentario (*a. geol.*).

se·di·tion [si'diʃn] sedición *f*.

se·di·tious [si'diʃəs] □ sedicioso.

se·duce [si'djuːs] seducir; **se'duc·er** seductor *m*; **se·duc·tion** [~'dʌkʃn] seducción *f*; **se'duc·tive** □ seductor.

sed·u·lous ['sedjuləs] □ diligente, asiduo.

see¹ [siː] [*irr.*] *v/i. a. v/t.* ver; observar; percibir; *fig.* comprender; (*visit*) visitar; (*receive*) recibir; (*vide*) véase; *I* ~ lo veo; ¡ya comprendo!; ~ *for yourself* véalo Vd.; *let's* ~ a ver; *let me* ~ vamos a ver; ~ *about a th.* atender a; encargarse de; ~ *off* despedir(se de); ~ *out* acompañar a la puerta; ~ *through a p.* calarle a uno; ~ *a p. through* ayudarle a uno hasta el fin; ~ *a th. through* llevar algo a cabo; ~ *to* atender a; ~ (*to it*) *that* hacer que, cuidar de que; ~ *home* acompañar a casa.

see² [~] sede *f; Holy* ♀ Santa Sede *f*.

seed [siːd] **1.** semilla *f*, simiente *f*; *fig.* germen *m*; ~ *potato* patata *f* de siembra; *go (or run) to* ~ granar, dar en grana; *fig.* echarse a perder; **2.** *v/t.* land sembrar; *sport*: seleccionar; *v/i.* dejar caer semillas; '~·bed (or '~-plot) semillero *m*; **seed·i·ness** ['~inis] F achaque *m*; **'seed·ling** planta *f* de semillero; **seeds·man** ['~zmən] vendedor *m* de semillas; **'seed·y** F ✿ canijo, ojeroso; ✿

achacoso; *appearance* raído; *place* asqueroso.

see·ing ['siːiŋ] **1.** vista *f*, visión *f*; *worth* ~ que vale la pena de verse; **2.** *cj.* ~ *that* visto que.

seek [siːk] [*irr.*] (*a.* ~ *after*, ~ *for*) buscar; *post* pretender, solicitar; *honour* ambicionar; (*search*) recorrer buscando; ~ *to* intentar, tratar de; **'seek·er** buscador (-a *f*) *m*.

seem [siːm] parecer; **'seem·ing 1.** □ aparente; **2.** apariencia *f*; **'seem·li·ness** decoro *m*; **'seem·ly** decoroso, decente, correcto.

seen [siːn] *p.p. of* see¹.

seep [siːp] rezumarse, filtrar(se); **'seep·age** filtración *f*.

seer ['siːə] vidente *m/f*, profeta *m*.

see·saw ['siːˈsɔː] **1.** columpio *m*; *fig.* vaivén *m*; **2.** columpiarse.

seethe [siːð] hervir.

seg·ment ['segmənt] segmento *m*.

seg·re·gate ['segrigeit] segregar; **seg·re'ga·tion** segregación *f*.

seine [sein] jábega *f*.

seis·mo·graph ['saizməɡrɑːf] sismógrafo *m*.

seize [siːz] *v/t.* agarrar, asir, coger; apoderarse de; ✝✝ *p.* prender; *property* embargar; secuestrar; *opportunity* aprovechar; *v/i.* ⊕ (*a.* ~ *up*) (*valve, piston*) agarrotarse; (*motor*) calarse; ~ (*up*)*on fig.* fijarse en; **sei·zure** ['~ʒə] asimiento *m*; captura *f*; ✝✝ prendimiento *m*; embargo *m*; ✿ ataque *m*.

sel·dom ['seldəm] rara vez, raramente.

se·lect [si'lekt] **1.** escoger, elegir; *sport*: seleccionar; **2.** selecto, escogido; **se'lec·tion** selección *f* (*a.* ♀, *zo.*); elección *f*; ♪ selecciones *f/pl.*; ✝ surtido *m*; **se'lec·tive** □ selectivo (*a. radio*); **se·lec·tiv·i·ty** [~'tiviti] *radio*: selectividad *f*; **se'lect·man** *Am.* concejal *m*; **se'lec·tor** *radio*: selector *m*; *sport*: seleccionador *m*.

self [self] **1.** *pron.* se *etc.*; (*after prps.*) sí mismo *etc.*; ✝ *or* F = myself *etc.*; **2.** *adj. esp.* ♀ unico'or; **3.** *su.* (*pl.* **selves** [selvz]) uno mismo *m*; *the* ~ el yo; (*all*) *by one's* ~ (*unaided*) sin ayuda de nadie; (*alone*) completamente a solas; ~-a'base·ment rebajamiento *m* de sí mismo; ~-'act·ing automático; '~-ad'ver·tise·ment autobombo *m*; '~-as'surance confianza *f* en sí mismo; '~-'cen·tred, *Am.* '~-'cen·tered egocéntrico; '~-'com·mand dominio *m* sobre sí mismo; '~-con'ceit presunción *f*, arrogancia *f*; '~-'con·fi·dence confianza *f* en sí mismo; '~-'con·scious ☐ cohibido, tímido; ~-con'tained ['ˌkən'teind] independiente; reservado; *flat* completo en sí mismo; '~-con'trol autodominio *m*, dominio *m* sobre sí mismo; '~-de'fence (*in* en) defensa *f* propia; '~-de'ni·al abnegación *f*; '~-de·ter·mi'na·tion autodeterminación *f*; '~-'ed·u·cat·ed autodidacto; '-ef·'fac·ing modesto, humilde; '~-es·'teem amor *m* propio; '~-'evi·dent patente, palmario; '~-'gov·ern·ment autogobierno *m*, autonomía *f*; '~-'fill·ing de relleno automático; '~-'in·ter·est egoísmo *m*; 'self·ish ☐ egoísta; 'self·ish·ness egoísmo *m*.

self...: '~-'made man hijo *m* de sus propias obras; '~-'por·trait autorretrato *m*; '~-pos'sessed sereno, dueño de sí mismo; '~-pre·ser·'va·tion propia conservación *f*; '~-pro'pelled autopropulsado; automotriz (*f only*); '~-re'li·ance confianza *f* en sí mismo; '~-re'li·ant confiado en sí mismo; '~-re'spect amor *m* propio, dignidad *f*; '~-'right·eous ☐ santurrón; '~-same *lit.* mismísimo, mismo; '~-'sat·is·fied pagado de sí mismo; '~-'seek·ing egoísta; '~-'serv·ice res·tau·rant autoservicio *m*; '~-'start·er *mot.* arranque *m* automático; '~-'styled supuesto, sediciente; '~-suf'fi·cien·cy independencia *f*; confianza *f* en sí mismo; '~-'willed terco, obstinado.

sell [sel] [*irr.*] 1. *v/t.* vender (*a. fig.*); *Am.* F *idea* hacer aceptar; ✝ ~ off liquidar; ~ out saldar; *be sold out* estar agotado; *sl. be sold on* estar cautivado por; *v/i.* venderse, estar de venta; *Am.* F ser aceptable; ~ out, ~ up venderlo todo, realizar; 2. F decepción *f*, estafa *f*; 'sell·er vendedor (-a *f*) *m*; ✝ *good* ~ artículo *m* que se vende bien; *best* ~ éxito *m* de librería; 'sell·ing-price precio *m* de venta.

selt·zer ['seltsə] (*or* ~ *water*) agua *f* (de) Seltz.

sel·vage, sel·vedge ['selvidʒ] borde *m*, orillo *m*.

se·man·tics [si'mæntiks] semántica *f*.

sem·a·phore ['seməfɔ:] 1. semáforo *m*; 2. comunicar por semáforo.

sem·blance ['sembləns] apariencia *f*; simulacro *m*.

se·mes·ter [sə'mestə] semestre *m*.

sem·i... ['semi] semi...; medio...; '~-breve semibreve *f*; '~-'cir·cle semicírculo *m*; '~'co·lon punto *m* y coma; '~-de'tached semiseparado; '~-'fi·nal semifinal *f*.

sem·i·nal ['si:minl] seminal.

sem·i·nar ['seminɑ:], sem·i·nar·y ['~ɔri] seminario *m*.

sem·i-of·fi·cial ['semiə'fiʃl] ☐ semioficial.   [corchea *f*.]

sem·i·qua·ver ['semikweivə] semi-

Sem·ite ['si:mait] semita *m/f*; Se·mit·ic [si'mitik] semítico.

sem·i·tone ['semitoun] semitono *m*.

sem·i·vow·el ['semi'vauəl] semivocal *f*.

sem·o·li·na [semə'li:nə] sémola *f*.

sem·pi·ter·nal [sempi'tə:nl] ☐ *lit.* sempiterno.

semp·stress ['sempstris] costurera *f*.

sen·ate ['senit] senado *m*; *univ.* *approx.* claustro *m*.

sen·a·tor ['senətə] senador *m*; sen·a·to·ri·al [ˌ'tɔ:riəl] ☐ senatorial.

send [send] [*irr.*] enviar, mandar, despachar; remitir; expedir; *ball* lanzar; *telegram* poner; (*with adj.*) hacer, volver; *v.* pack 2, word 1; ~ *away* despedir; despachar; ~ *back* devolver; ~ *down univ.* expulsar; ~ *for* enviar por; ~ *in p.* hacer entrar; ~ *name etc.* presentar; ~ *off p.* despedir; expedir; ~ *on* hacer seguir, dar curso a; ~ *out smoke etc.* arrojar, despedir; *signal* emitir; *invitations* mandar; distribuir; 'send·er remitente *m/f*; ⚡ transmisor *m*; 'send-'off despedida *f*; principio *m*.

se·nile ['si:nail] senil, caduco; se·nil·i·ty [si'niliti] vejez *f*; ⚕ debilidad *f* senil.

sen·ior ['si:njə] 1. mayor (de edad); más antiguo *in post* (to que); (*after names*) padre; ✝ ~ *partner* socio *m* más antiguo; 2. mayor *m/f*; decano *m in group*; *univ.* alumno *m* del último año; *he is my* ~ *by a year* tiene un año más que yo; sen·ior·i·ty [si:ni'ɔriti] antigüedad *f*; prioridad *f*.

sen·sa·tion [sen'seiʃn] sensación *f*; sen·sa·tion·al ☐ sensacional; sen·'sa·tion·al·ism sensacionalismo *m*.

sense [sens] **1.** sentido *m*; sensación *f*; juicio *m*; opinión *f* *of meeting*; **common** (*or* **good**) ~ sentido *m* común; **be out of one's** ~s haber perdido el juicio; **bring one to his** ~s hacerle volver en sí; **make** ~ tener sentido; *talk* ~ hablar con juicio; *in* *a* ~ en cierto sentido; *in the full* ~ *of the word* en toda la extensión de la palabra; **2.** sentir, percibir.

sense·less ['senslis] ☐ sin sentido; (*mad*) insensato; **'sense·less·ness** insensatez *f*.

sen·si·bil·i·ty [sensi'biliti] sensibilidad *f* (*to* a).

sen·si·ble ['sensəbl] ☐ (*reasonable*) sensato, cuerdo; (*feeling*) sensible; **be** ~ **of** estar consciente de, darse cuenta de; **'sen·si·ble·ness** sensatez *f*.

sen·si·tive ['sensitiv] ☐ sensitivo; sensible (*to* a); impresionable; (*touchy*) susceptible; *phot.* sensibilizado; **'sen·si·tive·ness**, **sen·si·tiv·i·ty** [~'tiviti] sensibilidad *f* (*to* a); susceptibilidad *f*.

sen·si·tize ['sensitaiz] sensibilizar.

sen·so·ri·al [sen'sɔːriəl], **sen·so·ry** ['~səri] sensorio.

sen·su·al ['sensjuəl] ☐ sensual; **'sen·su·al·ism** sensualismo *m*; **'sen·su·al·ist** sensualista *m/f*; **sen·su·al·i·ty** [~'æliti] sensualidad *f*.

sen·su·ous ['sensjuəs] ☐ sensual.

sent [sent] *pret.* *a.* *p.p. of* **send**.

sen·tence ['sentəns] **1.** ᴢᵗᶻ sentencia *f*, condena *f*; fallo *m*; *gr.* frase *f*; oración *f*; *serve one's* ~ cumplir su condena; **2.** sentenciar, condenar (*to* a).

sen·ten·tious [sen'tenʃəs] ☐ sentencioso; **sen'ten·tious·ness** estilo *m* sentencioso.

sen·tient ['senʃnt] sensitivo, que siente.

sen·ti·ment ['sentimənt] sentimiento *m*; *v.* ~**ality**; **sen·ti·men·tal** [~'mentl] ☐ sentimental; *b.s.* sensiblero; ~ *value* valor *m* sentimental; **sen·ti·men·tal·i·ty** [~'tæliti] sentimentalismo *m*; sensiblería *f*.

sen·ti·nel ['sentinl], **sen·try** ['sentri] centinela *m*.

sen·try...: '~**-box** garita *f* de centinela; '~**-go** turno *m* de centinela.

se·pal ['siːpəl] sépalo *m*.

sep·a·ra·ble ['sepərəbl] ☐ separable; **sep·a·rate 1.** ['seprit] ☐ separado; distinto; suelto; **2.** ['~əreit] separar(se) (*from* de); desprender(se); apartar(se); **sep·a'ra·tion** separación *f*; **sep·a·ra·tist** ['~ərətist] separatista *m/f*; **sep·a·ra·tor** ['~əreitə] *all senses:* separador *m*.

se·pi·a ['siːpjə] *ichth.* jibia *f*; *paint.* sepia *f*.

se·poy ['siːpɔi] cipayo *m*.

sep·sis ['sepsis] sepsis *f*.

Sep·tem·ber [sep'tembə] se(p)tiembre *m*.

sep·tic ['septik] séptico.

sep·tu·a·ge·nar·i·an ['septjuedʒi'neəriən] septuagenario *adj.* *a.* *su.* *m* (*a f*).

se·pul·chral [si'pʌlkrəl] sepulcral (*a. fig.*); **sep·ul·chre** ['sepəlkə] *lit.* **1.** sepulcro *m*; **2.** sepultar en sepulcro; **sep·ul·ture** ['sepəltʃə] *lit.* sepultura *f*.

se·quel ['siːkwəl] continuación *f* *of story*; resultado *m* (*to act* de); *in the* ~ como consecuencia.

se·quence ['siːkwəns] (orden *m* de) sucesión *f*; serie *f*; *film:* secuencia *f*; *gr.* ~ *of tenses* sucesión *f* de tiempos; **'se·quent** consecutivo.

se·ques·ter [si'kwestə] secuestrar; ~ *o.s.* apartarse (*from* de); ~*ed spot* aislado, retirado.

se·ques·trate [si'kwestreit] ᴢᵗᶻ secuestrar; **se·ques·tra·tion** [siː-kwes'treiʃn] secuestro *m*; **'se·ques·tra·tor** secuestrador *m*.

se·quin ['siːkwin] lentejuela *f*.

se·quoi·a [si'kwɔiə] secoya *f*.

se·ragl·io [se'rɑːliou] seralio *m*.

ser·aph ['serəf], *pl.* *a.* **ser·a·phim** ['~fim] serafín *m*; **se·raph·ic** [se'ræfik] ☐ seráfico.

Serb, Ser·bi·an [səːb, '~jən] servio *adj.* *a.* *su.* *m* (*a f*).

sere [siə] seco, marchito.

ser·e·nade [seri'neid] **1.** serenata *f*; **2.** dar serenata a.

se·rene [si'riːn] ☐ sereno; *Your 2 Highness* Su Serenidad; **se·ren·i·ty** [si'reniti] serenidad *f*.

serf [səːf] siervo (*a f*) *m* (de la gleba); **'serf·dom** servidumbre *f* (de la gleba).

serge [səːdʒ] estameña *f*.

ser·geant ['sɑːdʒnt] sargento *m*; '~**-ma·jor** *approx.* sargento *m* mayor, brigada *m*.

se·ri·al ['siəriəl] **1.** ☐ consecutivo; en serie; *number* de serie; *story* por entregas; **2.** serial *m*, novela *f* por entregas.

se·ries ['siəri:z] *sg. a. pl. all senses:* serie *f*; ⚡ connect or join in ~ conectar en serie; '~-wound arrollado en serie.

se·ri·ous ['siəriəs] □ serio; *news, condition* grave; *be* ~ (*p.*) tomar las cosas en serio; 'se·ri·ous·ness seriedad *f*; gravedad *f*.

ser·jeant ['sɑ:dʒnt] *hist.* notario *m* de categoría (*a.* ~ *at law*).

ser·mon ['sə:mən] sermón *m* (*a. iro.*); 'ser·mon·ize sermonizar.

se·rol·o·gy [siə'rɔlədʒi] serología *f*.

ser·pent ['sə:pənt] serpiente *f*, sierpe *f*; **ser·pen·tine** ['~ain] **1.** serpentino; **2.** *min.* serpentina *f*.

ser·rate ['serit], **ser·rat·ed** [se'reitid] serrado; **ser'ra·tion** endentadura *f*.

ser·ried ['serid] apretado, apiñado.

se·rum ['siərəm] suero *m*.

serv·ant ['sə:vənt] criado (a *f*) *m*; sirviente (a *f*) *m*; servidor (-a *f*) *m*; ~s *pl.* servidumbre *f*; ~s' hall comedor *m* de servicio; *v. civil.*

serve 1. [sə:v] *v/t. p.* servir (a); estar al servicio de; *food* servir (*a.* ~ *out,* ~ *up*); abastecer; ser útil a; *tennis:* sacar; 🏛 *writ* entregar (*on a p.* a una p.); *it* ~s *him right* bien merecido lo tiene; *v. sentence*; *v/i.* servir (*a.* ✗) (*as, for* de); ~ *at table* servir a la mesa; **2.** *tennis:* saque *m*; 'serv·er *tennis:* saque *m/f*; pala *f for fish etc.*; *eccl.* acólito *m*.

serv·ice ['sə:vis] **1.** servicio *m*; vajilla *f*, juego *m*, servicio *m of crockery*; *tennis:* saque *m*; ⚓ forro *m* de cable; 🏛 entrega *f*; (*a. divine* ~) oficio *m* divino; misa *f*; *at your* ~ servidor de Vd.; *be at a p.'s* ~ estar a la disposición de alguien; *be of* ~ servir, ayudar; ✗ *see* ~ prestar servicio; ✗ *active* ~ servicio *m* activo; *be on active* ~ estar de activo; *after-sales* ~ servicio *m* de atención; ✗ *the* ~s *pl.* las fuerzas armadas; *v. civil.* **2.** ⊕ atender, mantener, reparar; 'serv·ice·a·ble □ servible; útil; duradero.

serv·ice...: '~-line *tennis:* línea *f* de saque; '~-man militar *m*; ~ *sta·tion* estación *f* de servicio; '~-tree serbal *m*.

ser·vi·ette [se:vi'et] servilleta *f*; ~ *ring* servilletero *m*.

ser·vile ['sə:vail] □ servil; **ser·vil·i·ty** [.~'viliti] servilismo *m*.

ser·vi·tude ['sə:vitju:d] servidumbre *f*; *v. penal.*

ses·a·me ['sesəmi] ♀ *a. fig.* sésamo *m*; *open* ~! ¡sésamo ábrete!

ses·qui·pe·da·li·an ['seskwipi'deiljən] sesquipedal (*a. fig.*).

ses·sion ['seʃn] sesión *f*; *univ.* curso *m*; *v. petty*; F reunión *f*; F entrevista *f*; 'ses·sion·al de una sesión.

set [set] **1.** [*irr.*] *v/t.* poner, colocar; situar; establecer; arreglar, preparar; *alarm-clock* regular; 🦴 *bone* reducir; *dog* azuzar (*at, on* a que embista a); *example* dar; *hair* fijar, marcar; *jewel* engastar, montar; *price* fijar; *problem* poner; *sail* desplegar; *saw* triscar; *task* imponer, asignar; *teeth* apretar; *time* fijar; *trap* armar; *watch* poner en hora; *v. fashion, fire, foot, heart, liberty, music, sail, store*; ~ *going* poner en marcha; ~ *a p. laughing* hacer reír a una p.; ~ *against* indisponer con; ~ *o.s. against* oponerse resueltamente a; ~ *apart* separar, segregar; ~ *aside* poner aparte; reservar; *petition* desatender; 🏛 anular; ~ *at ease, at rest* tranquilizar; ~ *back* detener; entorpecer; poner obstáculos a; ~ *down* poner por escrito; depositar; *passenger* dejar (apearse); ~ *forth* exponer; ~ *off* (*explode*) hacer estallar; (*contrast*) hacer resaltar, poner de relieve (*against* contra); ~ *out* exponer; sacar y disponer; ~ *up* fundar; *house, shop* poner; establecer, instalar; *p.* erigir (*as* en); *cry* levantar; ⊕ armar, montar; ~ *up* (*in type*) componer; *be well* ~ *up for* estar bien provisto de; ~ *upon* acometer; *be* ~ *upon* estar resuelto a; **2.** *v/i.* (*sun*) ponerse; (*jelly, mortar*) cuajarse; (*gum etc.*) endurecerse; *hunt.* estar de muestra (*dog*); ~ *about* ger. ponerse a *inf.*; ~ *about th.* emprender; *p.* F aporrear; atacar; ~ *forth* salir, partir; ponerse en camino; ~ *in* comenzar, declararse; (*night*) cerrar; ~ *off* partir; ~ *on* atacar; ~ *out* partir, ponerse en camino; ~ *out to inf.* ponerse a *inf.*; tener la intención de *inf.*; ~ *to* aplicarse (con vigor), empezar; ~ *up* as erigirse en, constituirse en, dárselas de; **3.** *adj. purpose* resuelto, determinado; inflexible *in* *belief*; (*rigid*) rígido; (*usual*) reglamentario; *price etc.* fijo, firme; *barometer* estable; ~ (*up*)*on* empeñado en; ~ *with* adornado de; ~ *phrase* frase *f* hecha; *paint. etc.* ~ *piece* grupo *m*; ~ *speech* discurso *m* preparado de antemano; **4.** *su.* juego *m*; serie *f*; servicio *m* (de mesa); tendencia *f of mind*; pandilla *f*, clase *f of people*; caída *f of dress*; *thea.* decorado *m*, decoración *f*; (*radio-*) (aparato *m* de) radio *f*; ⊕ tren *m of gears*; *tennis:* set *m*; ✐ planta *f* de transplantar; *smart* ⁓ mundo *m* elegante.

set·back ['setbæk] contratiempo *m*, revés *m*; △ retraqueo *m*; '**set-'off** adorno *m*; contraste *m*; ✝ *etc.* compensación *f*; '**set-square** cartabón *m*.

set·tee [se'ti:] canapé *m*, sofá *m*.

set·ter ['setə] el que pone *etc.* (*v.* set 1); *hunt.* perro *m* de muestra.

set·ting ['setiŋ] puesta *f of sun*; engaste *m*, montadura *f of jewels*; ⊕ ajuste *m*; alrededores *m/pl. of place*; *fig.* marco *m*; ♪ versión *f*, arreglo *m*; *thea.* escena *f*, escenario *m*; '~-**lotion** *hair:* fijador *m*; '~-**up** establecimiento *m*; ⊕ ajuste *m*; composición *f of type.*

set·tle ['setl] **1.** banco *m* (largo); **2.** *v/t.* colocar; fijar; establecer; arreglar; calmar, sosegar; *account* ajustar, liquidar (*a.* ~ *up*); *fig.* saldar cuentas con (*a.* ~ *with*); *date* fijar; *deal* firmar; *income* asignar (*on* a); *land* colonizar, poblar; F *p.* vencer, confundir; *people* establecer; *quarrel* componer; *question* decidir, resolver; *v/i.* (*freq.* ~ *down*) asentarse (*liquid, building*); (*a.* ~ *o.s.*) sentarse, reposarse; (*bird etc.*) posar(se); (*p.*) instalarse, establecerse *in house, in town*; (*a.* ~ *down*) ⚓ hundirse lentamente; (*weather*) serenarse; *fig.* normalizarse; ~ *down to work* ponerse a trabajar; ~ *on* fijar; escoger; ~ *up* ajustar cuentas (*with* con).

set·tle·ment ['setlmənt] establecimiento *m*; ✝ ajuste *m*, pago *m*, liquidación *f of account*; ⚖ asignación *f* (*on* a); (*agreement*) convenio *m*; colonización *f of land*; (*village*) colonia *f*, caserío *m*, núcleo *m* rural.

set·tler ['setlə] colono (a *f*) *m*; colonizador *m*.

set·tling ['setliŋ] arreglo *m of dispute*; ✝ ajuste *m*; *v.* settle 2.

set...: '~-'**to** F disputa *f*; pelea *f*; '~-'**up** F tinglado *m*, sistema *m*, organización *f*; *Am. sl.* invitación *f* a beber.

sev·en ['sevn] siete (*a. su. m*); **sev·en·teen** ['~'ti:n] diecisiete; **sev·en·'teenth** [~θ] decimoséptimo; **sev·enth** ['~θ] □ séptimo (*a. su. m*); **sev·en·ti·eth** ['~tiiθ] septuagésimo; '**sev·en·ty** setenta.

sev·er ['sevə] separar, cortar; *relations* romper.

sev·er·al ['sevrəl] □ diversos, varios; respectivos; distintos; ⚖ *joint and* ~ solidario; '**sev·er·al·ly** respectivamente; separadamente.

sev·er·ance ['sevərəns] separación *f*; ruptura *f of relations.*

se·vere [si'viə] □ severo; *weather, winter, critic* riguroso; *storm* violento; *loss, wound* grave; *pain* intenso; *style* adusto; **se·ver·i·ty** [~'veriti] severidad *f*; rigor *m etc.*

Se·vil·lian [se'viljən] sevillano *adj. a. su. m* (a *f*).

sew [sou] [*irr.*] coser; ~ *up* zurcir.

sew·age ['sju:idʒ] aguas *f/pl.* residuales; ~ *farm* estación *f* depuradora.

sew·er ['sjuə] albañal *m*, alcantarilla *f*; '**sew·er·age** alcantarillado *m*.

sew·ing ['souiŋ] **1.** (labor *m* de) costura *f*; **2.** ... de coser; '~-**ma·chine** máquina *f* de coser.

sewn [soun] *p.p. of* sew.

sex [seks] **1.** sexo *m*; *attr.* sexual; ~ *appeal* atracción *f* sexual, gancho *m*; **2.** *chicks etc.* sexar.

sex·a·ge·nar·i·an [seksədʒi'nεəriən] sexagenario *adj. a. su. m* (a *f*); **sex·en·ni·al** □ [sek'senjəl] sexenal; **sex·tant** ['sekstənt] sextante *m*.

sex·ton ['sekstən] sacristán *m*; sepulturero *m*.

sex·tu·ple ['sekstjupl] séxtuplo.

sex·u·al ['seksjuəl] □ sexual; ~ *desire* instinto *m* sexual; *v. intercourse*; **sex·u·al·i·ty** [~'æliti] sexualidad *f*.

sh [ʃ]: ~! ¡chitón!, ¡chis!

shab·bi·ness ['ʃæbinis] lo raído *etc.*; '**shab·by** □ *p.* pobremente vestido; *dress* raído, gastado; *place* en mal estado; *treatment* ruin, vil.

shack [ʃæk] *esp. Am.* chabola *f*, choza *f*.

shack·le ['ʃækl] **1.** grillete *m*, grillos *m*/*pl*. (*a. fig.*); *fig.* (*mst ~s pl.*) trabas *f*/*pl*.; ⊕, ⚓ eslabón *m*; **2.** encadenar; trabar; *fig.* poner trabas a.

shade [ʃeid] **1.** sombra *f*; matiz *m* of *colour*, *meaning*, *opinion*; tonalidad *f* of *colour*; (*fraction*) poquito *m*; (*lamp*-) pantalla *f*; (*eye*-) visera *f*; *in the ~ of* a la sombra de; F *put in the ~* oscurecer; **2.** dar sombra a; (*protect*) resguardar; *paint.* sombrear; *~ away*, *~ off* cambiar poco a poco (*into* hasta hacerse), transformarse gradualmente (*into* en).

shad·i·ness ['ʃeidinis] lo umbroso *etc*. (*v. shady*); **'shad·ing** sombreado *m for eyes*; degradación *f of colours*.

shad·ow ['ʃædou] **1.** *all senses*: sombra *f*; *the ~s* las tinieblas; *~ boxing* boxeo *m* (*fig.* disputa *f*) con un adversario imaginario; **2.** sombrear; (*follow*) seguir y vigilar; (*mst ~ forth*) anunciar; indicar vagamente; **'shad·ow·y** umbroso, sombroso; *fig.* vago, indefinido.

shad·y ['ʃeidi] sombreado, umbroso; F turbio, sospechoso; F *on the ~ side of 40* más allá de 40 (años).

shaft [ʃɑ:ft] (*arrow*) flecha *f*, dardo *m*; (*handle*) mango *m*; vara *f* of *carriage*; agudeza *f* of *wit*; rayo *m* of *light*; ⊕ eje *m*; árbol *m*; ⚒ pozo *m*.

shag [ʃæg] 🕆 felpa *f*; tabaco *m* picado.

shag·gy ['ʃægi] velludo, peludo; *sl.* *~ dog story* chiste *m* goma.

sha·green [ʃə'gri:n] chagrén *m*, zapa *f*.

Shah [ʃɑ:] cha(h) *m*.

shake [ʃeik] **1.** [*irr.*] *v/t.* sacudir (*a. ~ off*); agitar; *head* mover, menear; *building* hacer retemblar; (*perturb*) perturbar; F sorprender; *hand* estrechar; *~ (on it)! ¡*chócala!; *~ hands* estrecharse la mano; *~ down* bajar sacudiendo; *~ off fig.* zafarse de, dar esquinazo a; librarse de; *~ up* remover, agitar; *fig.* descomponer; F reorganizar; *v/i.* agitarse; (*earth*) (re)temblar (*at*, *with* de); bambolear; ♪ trinar; *~ with laughter* desternillarse de risa; **2.** sacudida *f*, sacudimiento *m*; meneo *m*, movimiento *m* of *head*; vibración *f* of *vehicle*; ♪ trino *m*; F instante *m*; F batido *m* (de leche *etc*.); F *no great ~s* poco extraordinario; *in a brace of ~s* en un periquete; '~·'down cama *f* improvisada; *Am. sl.* exacción *f* de dinero; *Am.* ⚓ viaje *m* de pruebas; **'shak·en** *p.p. of shake* 1; **'shak·er** (*cocktail*-) coctelera *f*.

shake-up ['ʃeik'ʌp] F conmoción *f*; reorganización *f*.

shak·i·ness ['ʃeikinis] falta *f* de solidez; **'shak·y** □ tembloroso; *fig.* poco sólido; débil, debilitado.

shale [ʃeil] esquisto *m*; *~ oil* aceite *m* esquistoso. [*futuro etc.*]

shall [ʃæl] [*irr.*] *v/aux.* que forma el]

shal·lot [ʃə'lɔt] chalote *m*.

shal·low ['ʃælou] **1.** poco profundo; *fig.* somero, superficial; *p.* frívolo; **2.** *~s pl.* bajío *m*; **3.** hacer(se) menos profundo; **'shal·low·ness** poca profundidad *f*; *fig.* superficialidad *f*.

sham [ʃæm] **1.** falso, fingido, postizo; *~ fight* simulacro *m* de combate; **2.** impostura *f*, engaño *m*; (*p.*) impostor *m*, farsante *m*; **3.** *v/i. a. v/t.* fingir(se), simular.

sham·ble ['ʃæmbl] andar arrastrando los pies.

sham·bles ['ʃæmblz] *pl. or sg.* (lugar *m* de gran) matanza *f*; ruina *f*, escombrera *f*.

shame [ʃeim] **1.** vergüenza *f*; oprobio *m*, deshonra *f*; (*for*) *~!*, *~ on you!* ¡qué vergüenza!; *what a ~!* ¡qué lástima!; *put to ~* avergonzar; *fig.* superar con mucho; **2.** avergonzar.

shame-faced ['ʃeimfeist] □ vergonzoso, avergonzado; **'shame-faced·ness** vergüenza *f*.

shame·ful ['ʃeimful] □ vergonzoso; ignominioso; **'shame·ful·ness** ignominia *f*.

shame·less ['ʃeimlis] □ descarado, desvergonzado; **'shame·less·ness** descaro *m*, desvergüenza *f*.

sham·my ['ʃæmi] gamuza *f*.

sham·poo [ʃæm'pu:] **1.** lavar la cabeza (*v/t. a*); **2.** champú *m*.

sham·rock ['ʃæmrɔk] trébol *m* (*emblema nacional irlandés*).

shang·hai [ʃæŋ'hai] ⚓ *sl.* embarcar emborrachando.

shank [ʃæŋk] zanca *f of bird*; caña *f of leg*; ♀ tallo *m*; ⊕ mango *m*; *ride ♀s mare or pony* ir en coche de San Fernando.

shan't [ʃɑ:nt] = *shall not*.

shan·ty ['ʃænti] choza *f*, cabaña *f*; ♪ saloma *f*.

shape [ʃeip] **1.** forma *f*; figura *f*; contorno *m*; configuración *f*; take ~ tomar forma; irse perfilando; *in bad* ~ ✗ muy enfermo; arruinado; **2.** formar(se); modelar; tallar; *fig. course etc.* determinar; dirigir; **shaped** de ... forma; en forma de...; 'shape·less ▭ informe; 'shape·liness buen talle *m*; elegancia *f*; 'shape·ly bien formado, bien tallado; (bien) proporcionado, elegante; de buen talle.

share [ʃɛə] **1.** parte *f*, porción *f*; participación *f*; interés *m*; cuota *f*, contribución *f*; ✝ acción *f*; *have a* ~ *in* participar en; *go* ~*s* ir a escote; ~ *and* ~ *alike* por partes iguales; **2.** *v/t.* (com)partir, dividir; *fig.* poseer en común; ~ *out* repartir; *v/i.*: ~ *in* tener parte en, participar en (*fig.* de); '~·crop·per aparcero *m*; '~·hold·er accionista *m/f*; '~·out reparto *m*.

shark [ʃɑːk] *ichth.* tiburón *m*; F estafador *m*; F caimán *m*; *Am. sl.* perito *m*, as *m*.

sharp [ʃɑːp] **1.** ▭ agudo; puntiagudo; *bend* fuerte; *edge* afilado; *feature* bien marcado; *hearing* fino; *mind* listo, vivo; *outline* definido; *pace* rápido; *pain* agudo; *photo* nítido; *sight, wind* penetrante; *taste* acerbo, acre; *temper* áspero; *tongue* mordaz; *turn* (*tight*) cerrado, (*unexpected*) repentino; ♪ sostenido; F astuto, mañoso; avispado; **2.** *adv.* ♪ desafinadamente; F *4 o'clock* ~ las 4 en punto; *he turned* ~ *left* torció repentinamente a la izquierda; F *look* ~! ¡pronto!; *if you don't look* ~ si no te meneas; **3.** ♪ sostenido *m*; F estafador *m*; 'sharp·en afilar, aguzar (*a. fig.*); *pencil* sacar punta a; *feeling* agudizar; 'sharp·en·er afilador *m*, máquina *f* de afilar; 'sharp·er estafador *m*; *cards*: fullero *m*; 'sharp·ness agudeza *f etc.* (*v. sharp*).

sharp...: '~·shoot·er tirador *m* certero; '~·'sight·ed de vista penetrante; '~·'wit·ted perspicaz.

shat·ter ['ʃætə] romper(se), hacer (se) pedazos, estrellar(se); *health* quebrantar; *nerves* destrozar; *hopes* destruir.

shave [ʃeiv] **1.** [*irr.*] afeitar(se); ⊕ (a)cepillar; (*skim*) pasar rozando; **2.** afeitada *f*, afeitado *m*; *have a* ~

afeitarse; *have a close* ~ escaparse por un pelo; *a close* ~, *a narrow* ~ cosa *f* de milagro; 'shav·er: F *young* ~ rapaz *m*.

Sha·vi·an ['ʃeivijən] shaviano.

shav·ing ['ʃeiviŋ] **1.** afeitada *f*; el afeitarse; ~*s pl.* virutas *f/pl.*, acepilladuras *f/pl.*; **2.** *attr.* de afeitar; '~·brush brocha *f* (de afeitar).

shawl [ʃɔːl] chal *m*.

she [ʃiː] **1.** ella; **2.** hembra *f*.

she-... hembra *f of animals*.

sheaf [ʃiːf] (*pl.* sheaves) ✗ gavilla *f*; haz *m*; fajo *m of papers*.

shear [ʃiə] **1.** [*irr.*] esquilar; trasquilar; ~ *off* cortar; ~ *through* hender, cortar; **2.** (*a pair of* unas) ~*s pl.* tijeras *f/pl.* (de jardín); ⊕ cizalla *f*; 'shear·ing esquileo *m*; ~*s pl.* lana *f* esquilada.

sheath [ʃiːθ] vaina *f* (*a.* ♀); estuche *m*, funda *f*; cubierta *f*; **sheathe** [ʃiːð] envainar; enfundar; ⊕ revestir; 'sheath·ing ⊕ revestimiento *m*, forro *m*.

sheaves [ʃiːvz] *pl. of* sheaf.

she-bang [ʃə'bæŋ] *Am. sl.* taberna *f*; equipo *m*; *the whole* ~ todo el negocio.

shed[1] [ʃed] [*irr.*] *tears, light* verter; *blood* derramar; *skin etc.* mudar; *clothes, leaves* despojarse de; ~ *light on fig.* arrojar luz sobre.

shed[2] [~] cobertizo *m*; (*industrial*) nave *f*.

sheen [ʃiːn] lustre *m*, brillo *m*; 'sheen·y lustroso.

sheep [ʃiːp] oveja *f*; carnero *m*; *pl.* ganado *m* lanar; '~·cot *v.* ~·fold; '~·dog perro *m* pastor; '~·fold redil *m*, aprisco *m*; 'sheep·ish ▭ corrido; tímido; 'sheep·ish·ness timidez *f*.

sheep...: '~·man *Am.* dueño *m* de ganado lanar; '~·run *v.* ~·walk; '~·skin zamarra *f*, badana *f*; '~·walk pasto *m* (*or* dehesa *f*) de ovejas.

sheer[1] [ʃiə] **1.** *adj.* completo, cabal; puro; consumado; (*steep*) escarpado; *cloth* diáfano; fino; **2.** *adv.* directamente, completamente.

sheer[2] [~] **1.** ♣ desviarse; ~ *off fig.* desviarse, largarse; **2.** ♣ desviación *f*; ♣ arrufadura *f*.

sheet [ʃiːt] (*bed-*) sábana *f*; hoja *f of paper, tin*; lámina *f of metal, glass*; (*news-*) periódico *m*; exten-

sión *f of water etc.*; ⚓ escota *f*;
~ *copper etc.* cobre *m etc.* en láminas; '**~-an·chor** ⚓ ancla *f* de la
esperanza; *fig.* áncora *f* de salvación; '**sheet·ing** tela *f* para sábanas;
'**sheet-light·ning** relámpago *m* difuso.

sheik(h) [ʃeik] jeque *m.*

she·kel [ʃekl] siclo *m*; *sl.* ~s *pl.* parné
m.

shelf [ʃelf] (*pl.* **shelves**) estante *m*,
anaquel *m*; ⚓ banco *m* de arena,
bajío *m*; *on the* ~ arrinconado, olvidado; (*girl*) *be on the* ~ quedarse
para vestir santos.

shell [ʃel] 1. cáscara *f of egg, nut,*
building; concha *f*, caparazón *m*,
carapacho *m of mollusc, tortoise etc.*;
vaina *f of pea*; ⊕ armazón *f*; cubierta *f*; ✗ granada *f*, proyectil *m*,
bomba *f*; 2. des(en)vainar, descascarar; ✗ bombardear; *sl.* ~ *out*
money desembolsar; (*v/i.*) desdina-
rarse.

shel·lac [ʃeˈlæk] (goma *f*) laca *f.*

shelled [ʃeld] dotado de cáscara ...;
(*without*) sin cáscara *etc.*

shell...: '**~-fire** cañoneo *m*; '**~-fish**
mariscos *m/pl.*; *zo.* crustáceo *m*;
'**~-proof** a prueba de granadas;
'**~-shock** neurosis *f* de guerra.

shel·ter [ʃeltə] 1. abrigo *m*, asilo *m*,
refugio *m*; (*mountain-*) albergue *m*;
fig. resguardo *m*; *take* ~ = 2. *v/i.*
abrigarse, refugiarse, guarecerse;
v/t. abrigar; guarecer; proteger.

shelve¹ [ʃelv] *fig.* arrinconar; dar
carpetazo a; aplazar indefinida-
mente.

shelve² [~] *geog.* estar en declive.

shelves [ʃelvz] *pl. of* **shelf** estante *m*
etc.; (*a.* **shelv·ing**) estantería *f.*

she·nan·i·gans [ʃiˈnænigənz] F em-
bustes *m/pl.*

shep·herd [ʃepəd] 1. pastor *m*;
2. guiar. dirigir; '**shep·herd·ess**
pastora *f.*

sher·bet [ˈʃəːbət] sorbete *m.*

sher·iff [ˈʃerif] sheriff *m* (*oficial de*
justicia inglés o norteamericano).

sher·ry [ˈʃeri] jerez *m.*

shew [ʃou] ✎ = *show* mostrar *etc.*

shib·bo·leth [ˈʃibələθ] santo *m* y
seña; *fig.* dogma *m* hoy desacreditado; convencionalismo *m.*

shield [ʃiːld] 1. escudo *m* (*a. fig.*);
⊕ blindaje *m*; 2. escudar (*a. fig.*),
proteger, resguardar (*from* de).

shift [ʃift] 1. cambio *m*; movimiento
m, cambio *m* de sitio; tanda *f*,
turno *m at work*; astucia *f*; recurso
m, expediente *m*; *make* ~ ingeniarse
(*to* por), arreglárselas (*to* para);
make ~ *with* ayudarse con; *make* ~
without pasarse sin; 2. *v/t.* cambiar
(de sitio); mover; *v/i.* cambiar (de
sitio, de puesto); moverse; (*move*
house) mudar; (*wind*) cambiar; F
ir a gran velocidad; ~ *for o.s.* ayudarse (a sí mismo); '**shift·ing** mudable; ~ *sands pl.* arenas *f/pl.* movedizas; '**shift·less** ☐ agalbanado,
indolente, inútil; '**shift·y** ☐ taimado, furtivo.

shil·ling [ˈʃiliŋ] chelín *m*; *the King's*
~ *approx.* enganche *m*; *cut off with*
a ~ desheredar.

shil·ly-shal·ly [ˈʃiliʃæli] vacilar.

shim·mer [ˈʃimə] 1. reflejo *m* (*or*
resplandor *m*) trémulo; 2. rielar.

shim·my¹ [ˈʃimi] *Am. sl.* shimmy *m*
(*baile*).

shim·my² [~] F camisa *f.*

shin [ʃin] 1. (*or* '**~-bone**) espinilla *f*;
2.: ~ *up* trepar a.

shin·dy [ˈʃindi] F cisco *m*, alboroto
m; *kick up a* ~ armar camorra.

shine [ʃain] 1. lustre *m*, brillo *m*;
buen tiempo *m*; F *take the* ~ *out of*
eclipsar; *Am. sl.* *take a* ~ *to* tomar
simpatía por; 2. [*irr.*] *v/i.* brillar
(*a. fig.*), lucir (*a. fig.*); *v/t. shoes*
limpiar; sacar brillo a.

shin·gle¹ [ˈʃiŋgl] 1. ripia *f*; (*hair*)
corte *m* a lo garçón; 2. cubrir con
ripias; *hair* cortar a lo garçón.

shin·gle² [~] guijo *m*; guijarral *m*;
playa *f* guijarrosa.

shin·gles [ˈʃiŋglz] ✚ *pl.* herpes *m*
or *f/pl.*

shin·gly [ˈʃiŋgli] guijarroso.

shin·ing [ˈʃainiŋ], **shin·y** [ˈʃaini] ☐
brillante, lustroso.

ship [ʃip] 1. buque *m*, navío *m*,
barco *m*; ~'*s company* tripulación *f*;
merchant ~ mercante *m*; 2. *v/t.*
embarcar; ✝ transportar; enviar,
expedir; *mast* izar; *oars* desarmar;
v/i. embarcarse; '**~-board**: *on* ~
a bordo; '**~-build·er** constructor *m*
de buques, ingeniero *m* naval;
'**~-build·ing** construcción *f* de
buques; '**~-ca·nal** canal *m* de navegación; '**~-chan·dler** abastecedor
m de buques; '**ship·ment** embarque *m*; envío *m*, remesa *f*;

'**ship·own·er** naviero *m*; '**ship·per** exportador *m*; remitente *m*; '**ship·ping** buques *m/pl.*, flota *f*, marina *f*; navegación *f*; embarque *m of goods*; ⁓ *agent* agente *m* marítimo; ⁓ *company* compañía *f* naviera.

ship...: '⁓-**shape** en buen orden; '⁓-**wreck 1.** naufragio *m*; **2.** naufragar (*a. be* ⁓ed); '⁓-**wrecked** náufrago; '⁓-**wright** carpintero *m* de navío; = ⁓builder; '⁓-**yard** astillero *m*, varadero *m*.

shire ['ʃaiə, *in compounds* ... ʃiə] condado *m*; ⁓ *horse* caballo *m* de tiro (inglés).

shirk [ʃəːk] *v/t.* eludir, esquivar, desentenderse de; *v/i.* faltar al deber, gandulear; '**shirk·er** gandul *m*.

shirt [ʃəːt] camisa *f*; *sl.* keep one's ⁓ on quedarse sereno; '⁓-**front** pechera *f*; '**shirt·ing** † tela *f* para camisas; '**shirt-sleeve 1.:** *in* ⁓s en mangas de camisa; **2.** F sencillo, directo; '**shirt·y** *sl.* furioso, negro.

shiv·er¹ ['ʃivə] estrellar(se), hacer (se) añicos.

shiv·er² [⁓] **1.** (*fear*) temblor *m*; (*cold*) tiritón *m*; F *the* ⁓s *pl.* dentera *f*, grima *f*; *it gives me the* ⁓s me da miedo; **2.** estremecerse; temblar *with fear*; tiritar *with cold*; '**shiv·er·y** estremecido; (*cold*) friolento.

shoal¹ [ʃoul] **1.** banco *m*, cardumen *m*; *fig.* muchedumbre *f*; **2.** reunirse en gran número.

shoal² [⁓] **1.** bajío *m*, banco *m* de arena; **2.** disminuir en profundidad.

shock¹ [ʃɔk] ⚜ tresnal *m*.

shock² [⁓] **1.** choque *m* (*a.* ⚡); sacudida *f*; temblor *m* de tierra; sobresalto *m*; conmoción *f* desagradable; ✇ shock *m*; ✕ ⁓ *troops pl.* tropas *f/pl.* de asalto; **2.** *fig.* chocar; sobresaltar; escandalizar; *be* ⁓ed asombrarse (*at* de).

shock³ [⁓] greña *f of hair*.

shock-ab·sorb·er ['ʃɔkəbsɔːbə] *mot.* amortiguador *m*.

shock·er ['ʃɔkə] *sl.* novelucha *f*.

shock·ing ['ʃɔkiŋ] □ chocante; escandaloso; *taste* pésimo.

shod [ʃɔd] *pret. a. p.p. of* shoe 2.

shod·dy ['ʃɔdi] **1.** paño *m* burdo de lana; lana *f* regenerada; **2.** de pacotilla, de pésima calidad; *Am.* ⁓ *aristocracy* ricachos *m/pl.* ostentosos y vulgares.

shoe [ʃuː] **1.** zapato *m*; (*horse-*) herradura *f*; (*brake-*) zapata *f*; *I wouldn't be in his* ⁓s no quisiera estar en su pellejo; **2.** [irr.] calzar; *horse* herrar; '⁓-**black** limpiabotas *m*; '⁓-**black·ing** betún *m*; '⁓-**horn** calzador *m*; '⁓-**lace** cordón *m*; '⁓-**mak·er** zapatero *m*; '⁓-**shop** zapatería *f*; '⁓-**string** *Am.* cordón *m*; F *on a* ⁓ con muy poco dinero.

shone [ʃɔn] *pret. a. p.p. of* shine 2.

shoo [ʃuː] **1.** *birds* oxear; ahuyentar; **2.** ¡zape!, ¡ox!

shook [ʃuk] *pret. of* shake 1.

shoot [ʃuːt] **1.** ⚘ renuevo *m*, vástago *m*; cacería *f*; tiro *m* (al blanco); conducto *m* inclinado; **2.** [irr.] *v/t.* disparar; tirar; herir (*or* matar) con arma de fuego; (*execute*) fusilar; *bolt* correr; *bridge* pasar debajo de; *film* rodar; *rapids* salvar; *rubbish* verter; *sun* tomar la altura de; ⁓ *down* derribar; ⁓ *up sl.* destrozar a tiros; *v/i.* tirar (*at* a); *football:* chutar; ⚘ brotar; (*pain*) punzar; ⁓ *ahead* adelantarse mucho (*of* a); ⁓ *by*, ⁓ *past* pasar como un meteoro; ⁓ *forth* brotar; ⁓ *off*, ⁓ *out* salir disparado, precipitarse; ⁓ *up* crecer rápidamente, espigar; (*price*) elevarse rápidamente.

shoot·ing ['ʃuːtiŋ] **1.** tiros *m/pl.*; tiroteo *m*, cañoneo *m*; caza *f* con escopeta; rodaje *m of film*; *go* ⁓ ir a la caza; **2.** *pain* punzante; '⁓-**box** pabellón *m* de caza; '⁓-**brake** rubia *f*; '⁓-**gal·ler·y** galería *f* de tiro (al blanco); '⁓-'**star** estrella *f* fugaz.

shop [ʃɔp] **1.** tienda *f*; (*large*) almacén *m*; ⊕ taller *m*; F *talk* ⁓ hablar del propio trabajo; **2.** ir de compras (*mst go* ⁓ping); '⁓-**as'sist·ant** dependiente (a *f*) *m*; '⁓-**keep·er** tendero (a *f*) *m*; '⁓-**lift·er** mechera *f*; '**shop·per** comprador (-a *f*) *m*; '**shop·ping** compras *f/pl.*; ⁓ *centre* zona *f* de tiendas.

shop...: '⁓-**soiled** deteriorado; '⁓-**stew·ard** representante *m* de los obreros en la sección de una fábrica; '⁓-**walk·er** vigilante (a *f*) *m*; '⁓-**win·dow** escaparate *m*, vidriera *f S.Am.*

shore¹ [ʃɔː] playa *f*, orilla *f*, ribera *f*; *on* ⁓ en tierra.

shore² [⁓] **1.** puntal *m*; **2.** apuntalar; *fig.* apoyar.

shorn [ʃɔ:n] *p.p. of* shear 1 esquilar *etc.*; ~ *of* despojado de.

short [ʃɔ:t] **1.** corto, breve; *p.* bajo; (*brusque*) brusco, seco; *memory* flaco; *pastry* quebrad(iz)o; ~ *wave radio:* onda *f* corta; *by a* ~ *head* por una cabeza escasa; *5* ~ *5* de menos, faltan 5; *for* ~ para abreviar; *in* ~ en breve; ~ *for* forma abreviada de; ~ *of* falto de, escaso de; *nothing* ~ *of* nada menos que; ~ *of lying* fuera de mentir; *cut* ~ acortar, abreviar; interrumpir; *fall* ~ *of* no alcanzar, no llegar a; no corresponder a; *run* ~ acabarse; *run* ~ *of* acabársele a uno; *stop* ~ parar de repente; *stop* ~ *of* detenerse antes de llegar a; *work* ~ *time* trabajar en jornadas reducidas; **2.** *film:* corto metraje *m*; ⚡ cortocircuito *m*; F ~s *pl.* pantalones *m/pl.* cortos; **3.** *v.* ~-*circuit;* 'short·age escasez *f*, falta *f*, carestía *f*; † déficit *m.*

short...: '~·bread, '~·cake torta *f* seca y quebradiza; '~-'cir·cuit **1.** cortocircuito *m*; **2.** poner(se) en cortocircuito; ~'com·ing defecto *m*; ~ *cut* atajo *m*; '~-'dat·ed † a corto plazo; 'short·en acortar(se), reducir(se); 'short·en·ing acortamiento *m.*

short...: '~-'fall déficit *m*; '~-hand taquigrafía *f*; ~ *writer* taquígrafo (a *f*) *m*; ~ *typist* taquimeca(nógrafa) *f*; '~-'hand·ed falto de mano de obra; '~-'lived efímero; 'short·ly *adv.* en breve, dentro de poco; próximamente; 'short·ness pequeñez *f.*

short...: '~-'sight·ed miope, corto de vista; *fig.* falto de previsión; '~-'tem·pered enojadizo; '~-term a plazo corto; '~-'wave *radio:* ... de onda corta; '~-'wind·ed corto de resuello.   [**2.** *silk* tornasolado.⎮

shot[1] [ʃɔt] **1.** *pret. a. p.p. of* shoot 2;⎮

shot[2] [⌐] tiro *m*, disparo *m*; balazo *m*; (*a. small* ~) perdigones *m/pl.*; (*p.*) tirador (-a *f*) *m*; *sport:* tiro *m at goal*; (*stroke*) golpe *m*; (*weight*) pesa *f*; F tentativa *f*, conjetura *f*; *phot.* fotografía *f*; *film:* fotograma *m*; 💉 inyección *f*; dosis *f*; *sl.* trago *m of rum etc.*; *have a* ~ probar suerte; *have a* ~ *at fig.* hacer una tentativa de; F *not by a long* ~ ni con mucho; F *like a* ~ acto seguido; como una bala; F

big ~ pez *m* gordo; '~·gun escopeta *f*; F ~ *marriage* casamiento *m* a la fuerza.

should [ʃud] **1.** *v/aux. que forma el condicional etc.:* I ~ *do it if I could* lo haría si pudiese; **2.** deber: *he* ~ *be here soon* debe llegar dentro de poco; *he* ~ *know that* debiera saberlo; *he* ~ *have gone last week* debiera haber ido la semana pasada.

shoul·der ['ʃouldə] **1.** hombro *m*; espaldas *f/pl.*; lomo *m of hill etc.*; *give a p. the cold* ~ volver la espalda a una p.; *put one's* ~ *to the wheel* arrimar el hombro; *rub* ~s *with* codearse con; ~ *to* ~ hombro a hombro; **2.** llevar al hombro; *fig.* cargar con; empujar con el hombro; ✗ ~ *arms!* ¡armas al hombro!; '~-blade omóplato *m*; '~-knot dragona *f*; '~-strap tirante *m*, hombrera *f.*

shout [ʃaut] **1.** grito *m*; voz *f*; **2.** gritar; dar voces; ~ *down p.* protestar hasta hacer callar; *play* hundir a gritos.

shove [ʃʌv] **1.** empujón *m*; **2.** *v/i.* dar empujones; ~ *off* ⚓ alejarse; *sl.* marcharse; *v/t.* empujar.

shov·el [ʃʌvl] **1.** pala *f*; cogedor *m*; **2.** traspalar; '~-board juego *m* de tejo.

show [ʃou] **1.** [*irr.*] *v/t.* mostrar, enseñar; (*prove*) probar, demostrar; señalar; manifestar; *film* poner, proyectar; *goods, pictures* exhibir; *loss* dejar; ~ *in* hacer pasar; ~ *off* hacer gala de; ~ *out* acompañar a la puerta; ~ *up* hacer subir; F desenmascarar; *v/i.* mostrarse, (a)parecer; (*film*) representarse; ~ *off* lucirse; fachendear; F ~ *up* acudir, presentarse; **2.** (*display*) exhibición *f*; exposición *f*; (*outward*) apariencia *f*; (*pomp*) boato *m*; manifestación *f*, demostración *f of feeling*; *thea.* función *f*, espectáculo *m*; 🎪 feria *f*; *sl.* cosa *f*, empresa *f*; ~ *of hands* votación *f* por manos levantadas; *dumb* ~ pantomima *f*; *on* ~ expuesto; F *give the* ~ *away* tirar de la manta; (*involuntary*) clarearse; *make a* ~ *of* hacer gala de; fingir; *sl. run the* ~ ser el todo; mandar; '~-case vitrina *f* (de exposición); '~-down F momento *m* decisivo, revelación *f* decisiva.

show·er ['ʃauə] **1.** chaparrón *m*, chubasco *m*; aguacero *m*; *fig.* rociada *f*, lluvia *f*; (~-*bath*) ducha *f*; **2.** llover; derramar; *fig.* ~ *with* colmar de; ~-**bath** ['~bɑ:θ] ducha *f*; '**show·er·y** lluvioso.

show·i·ness ['ʃouinis] boato *m*; aparatosidad *f*; '**show·ing** (*poor etc.*) actuación *f* (defectuosa *etc.*); '**show·man** empresario *m*; *fig.* hombre *m* ostentoso; '**show·man·ship** teatralidad *f*; **shown** [ʃoun] *p.p. of show* 1; '**show·room** salón *m* de demostraciones; '**show-win·dow** *Am.* escaparate *m*; '**show·y** □ vistoso, llamativo; aparatoso; *p.* ostentoso.

shrank [ʃræŋk] *pret. of shrink*.

shrap·nel ['ʃræpnl] metralla *f*.

shred [ʃred] **1.** triza *f*, jirón *m*; fragmento *m*; *fig.* pizca *f*; **2.** [*irr.*] hacer trizas; desmenuzar.

shrew [ʃru:] *zo.* musaraña *f* (*a.* '~-*mouse*); *fig.* arpía *f*, mujer *f* regañona, fierecilla *f*.

shrewd [ʃru:d] □ astuto, sagaz; '**shrewd·ness** astucia *f*, sagacidad *f*.

shrew·ish ['ʃru:iʃ] □ regañón.

shriek [ʃri:k] **1.** alarido *m*, chillido *m*; **2.** chillar (*a. fig.*).

shrill [ʃril] **1.** □ chillón (*a. fig.*), agudo y penetrante; **2.** chillar.

shrimp [ʃrimp] *zo.* camarón *m*; *fig.* enano *m*.

shrine [ʃrain] relicario *m*; capilla *f*, sepulcro *m* (de santo).

shrink [ʃriŋk] [*irr.*] *v/i.* encogerse, contraer(se); mermar; (*a.* ~ *back*) acobardarse, retirarse (*from, at* ante); ~ *from ger.* no atreverse a *inf.*; *v/t.* encoger, contraer; ⊕ ~ *on* montar en caliente; '**shrink·age** encogimiento *m*, contracción *f*.

shriv·el ['ʃrivl] (*a.* ~ *up*) marchitar(se), arrugar(se); avellanarse.

shroud [ʃraud] **1.** sudario *m*, mortaja *f*; *fig.* velo *m*; **2.** amortajar; *fig.* velar.

shrouds [ʃraudz] ⚓ obenques *m/pl.*

Shrove·tide ['ʃrouvtaid] carnestolendas *f/pl.*; **Shrove Tues·day** martes *m* de carnaval.

shrub [ʃrʌb] arbusto *m*; **shrub·ber·y** ['~əri] plantío *m* de arbustos.

shrug [ʃrʌg] **1.** encogerse de hombros; **2.** encogimiento *m* (de hombros).

shrunk [ʃrʌŋk] *pret. a. p.p. of*

shrink; '**shrunk·en** *adj.* encogido; *fig.* mermado.

shud·der ['ʃʌdə] **1.** estremecerse; **2.** estremecimiento *m*.

shuf·fle ['ʃʌfl] **1.** *v/t.* mezclar, revolver; *cards* barajar; ~ *off* deshacerse de; **2.** *v/i.* arrastrar los pies; andar (bailar *etc.*) arrastrando los pies; **3.** *cards:* (*act*) barajadura *f*; (*turn*) turno *m* de barajar.

shun [ʃʌn] esquivar, evitar; retraerse de.

shunt [ʃʌnt] **1.** ⚡ derivación *f*, shunt *m*; *Am.* 🚂 aguja *f*, cambio *m* de vía; **2.** ⚡ poner en derivación; 🚂 maniobrar; apartar; '**shunt·er** 🚂 guardagujas *m*, obrero *m* del servicio de maniobras; '**shunt·ing** 🚂 maniobras *f/pl.*; ~ *engine* locomotora *f* de maniobras.

shut [ʃʌt] [*irr.*] *v/t.* cerrar; ~ *down factory* cerrar; *machine* parar; ~ *in* encerrar; cercar, rodear; ~ *off water etc.* cortar; aislar (*from de*); ~ *out* excluir; negar la entrada a; ~ *up* (en)cerrar; *opening* obturar; F *p.* hacer callar, reducir al silencio; *v/i.* cerrarse (*a.* ~ *down etc.*); F ~ *up* callarse; F ~ *up!* ¡cállate!; '~-**down** cierre *m*; ~**out** *Am. sport:* victoria *f* en que el contrario no gana un tanto; '**shut·ter** contraventana *f*; *phot.* obturador *m*.

shut·tle ['ʃʌtl] **1.** lanzadera *f*; ~ *service* tren *m etc.* que hace viajes cortos entre dos puntos; **2.** hacer viajes cortos entre dos puntos; '~-**cock** volante *m*.

shy¹ [ʃai] **1.** □ tímido; recatado; huraño; vergonzoso; *be* (F *fight*) ~ *of* (tratar de) evitar; *sl. I'm £10* ~ me faltan 10 libras; **2.** espantarse, respingar (*at* al ver).

shy² [~] F **1.** lanzar, arrojar; **2.** echada *f*; *have a* ~ probar; *have a* ~ *at* hacer una tentativa de.

shy·ness ['ʃainis] timidez *f*; recato *m*; vergüenza *f*.

shy·ster ['ʃaistə] *sl., esp. Am.* abogado *m* trampista.

Si·a·mese [saiə'mi:z] siamés *adj. a. su. m* (-a *f*).

Si·be·ri·an [sai'biəriən] siberiano *adj. a. su. m* (a *f*).

sib·i·lant ['sibilənt] □ sibilante *adj. a. su. f*.

sib·yl ['sibil] sibila *f*.

sib·yl·line [si'bilain] sibilino.

Si·cil·ian [si'siljən] siciliano *adj. a. su. m* (a *f*).

sick [sik] enfermo; mareado; *be ~* estar enfermo; sentirse mareado; vomitar; *be ~ of* estar harto de; *get ~ of* coger asco a, hacérsele pesado; *go (Am. take) ~* caer enfermo; ausentarse debido a enfermedad; '**~·bay** enfermería *f*; '**~·bed** lecho *m* de enfermo; '**sick·en** *v/i.* enfermar; *~ at* sentir náuseas ante; *~ for* añorar; ♣ mostrar síntomas de; *v/t.* dar asco a; '**sick·en·ing** □ asqueroso, nausea-; **sick·le** ['sikl] hoz *f.* [bundo.] **sick-leave** ['sikli:v] permiso *m* de convalecencia; '**sick·li·ness** achaque *m*; palidez *f*; '**sick·ly** *p.* enfermizo, achacoso; pálido; *smell* nauseabundo; *taste* débil; *taste* empalagoso; '**sick·ness** enfermedad *f*, mal *m*; náusea *f*; '**sick-pay** subsidio *m* de enfermedad.

side [said] 1. lado *m*; costado *m* of *body, ship*; cara *f* of *solid, record*; falda *f*, ladera *f* of *hill*; orilla *f* of *lake*; (*party*) partido *m*; *sport:* equipo *m*; *fig.* aspecto *m*; F tono *m*, postín *m*; *~ by ~* lado a lado; *by the ~ of* al lado de; *on all ~s* por todas partes; *on the ~* F incidentalmente, de paso; *sl.* bajo cuerda; *take ~s* tomar partido; 2. lateral; secundario; indirecto; 3.: *~ with* declararse por; '**~·arms** armas *f/pl.* de cinto; '**~·board** aparador *m*; **~·car** sidecar *m*; '**sid·ed** de ... lados.

side...: '**~·face** (de) perfil *m*; '**~·light** luz *f* de costado; *fig.* detalle *m* (*or* información *f*) incidental; '**~·line** ⊕ apartadero *m*; *sport:* línea *f* lateral; *fig.* empleo *m* (*or* negocio *m*) suplementario; '**~·long** oblicuo; lateral; *glance* de soslayo. **si·de·re·al** [sai'diəriəl] sidéreo.

side...: '**~·sad·dle** 1. silla *f* de mujer; 2. *adv.* a mujeriegas, a la inglesa; '**~·show** caseta *f* (de feria); '**~·slip** ✈, *mot.* deslizamiento *m* lateral; '**~·step** 1. esquivada *f* lateral; 2. *fig.* evitar, esquivar; '**~·stroke** natación *f* de costado; '**~·track** 1. ⊕ apartadero *m*, vía *f* muerta; 2. *fig.* desviar, apartar; '**~·walk** *Am.* acera *f*; **side·ward** ['~wəd] *adj.* oblicuo; *adv.* (*a.* **side·wards** ['~z], '**side·ways**, '**side·wise**) de lado, hacia un lado.

si·dle ['saidl]: *~ up to* acercarse cautelosamente (*or* servilmente) a.

siege [si:dʒ] cerco *m*, sitio *m*; *lay ~ to* asediar (*a. fig.*).

sieve [siv] 1. cedazo *m*, tamiz *m*; (*kitchen*) coladera *f*; 2. = sift. **sift** [sift] tamizar, cerner; *fig.* examinar.

sigh [sai] 1. suspiro *m*; 2. suspirar (*after, for* por).

sight [sait] 1. vista *f* (*a.* ⚓); visión *f*; escena *f*; espectáculo *m*; cosa *f* digna de verse; ✕ puntería *f*; F espantajo *m*; *~s pl.* cosas *f/pl.* de interés turístico; monumentos *m/pl.*; ✕ miras *f/pl.*; *at ~, on ~, at first ~* a primera vista; ⚓ a la vista; *by ~* de vista; (*with*)*in ~ of* a la vista de; *out of ~* invisible; *catch ~ of* alcanzar a ver; *lose ~ of* perder de vista (*a. fig.*); 2. avistar, divisar; *gun* apuntar; '**~·see·ing** excursionismo *m*, turismo *m*; '**~·se·er** excursionista *m/f*, turista *m/f*; '**~·read·ing**, '**~·sing·ing** ejecución *f* a la primera lectura.

sign [sain] 1. señal *f*; indicio *m*; ♐, ♪ *etc.* signo *m*; (*trace*) huella *f*, vestigio *m*; (*notice*) letrero *m*; (*shop-*) rótulo *m*; *~s pl.* señas *f/pl.*; *in ~ of* en señal de; *show ~s of* dar muestras de; 2. *v/t.* firmar; *~ away* ceder; *~ on, ~ up* contratar; *~ed and sealed* firmado y lacrado; *v/i.* firmar; *~ off* terminar; *~ on* fichar (*for* por).

sig·nal ['signl] 1. señal *f*; *teleph.* *engaged ~, Am. busy ~* señal *f* de ocupado; *~s pl.* ✕ (cuerpo *m* de) transmisiones *f/pl.*; 2. □ señalado, notable; 3. señalar; hacer señales (*to* a); comunicar por señales (*that* que); '**~·box** garita *f* de señales; **sig·nal·ize** ['~nəlaiz] distinguir, marcar; '**sig·nal·man** ⊕ guardavía *m*; ✕ soldado *m* de transmisiones.

sig·na·to·ry ['signətəri] firmante *adj. a. su. m* (a *f*), signatorio *adj. a. su. m* (a *f*); **sig·na·ture** ['signitʃə] firma *f*; *typ.*, ♪ signatura *f*; ⚓ marca *f*; *~ tune* sintonía *f*.

sign·board ['sainbɔ:d] letrero *m*, muestra *f*; '**sign·er** firmante *m/f*. **sig·net** ['signit] sello *m*; '**~·ring** sortija *f* de sello.

sig·nif·i·cance, **sig·nif·i·can·cy** [sig'nifikəns(i)] significación *f*, significado *m*; **sig·nif·i·cant** □

significante, significativo; **sig·ni·fi'ca·tion** significación *f*; **sig'nif·i·ca·tive** [ˌkətiv] significativo.

sig·ni·fy ['signifai] significar; *it does not* ~ no importa.

sign...: '~-**paint·er** rotulista *m*; '~-**post** 1. poste *m* indicador; señal *f*; 2. señalizar.

si·lence ['sailəns] 1. silencio *m*; ~! ¡silencio!; 2. acallar (*a. fig.*), imponer silencio a; **'si·lenc·er** mot. silenciador *m*.

si·lent ['sailənt] □ silencioso; callado; *be* ~, remain ~ callarse; ~ *film* película *f* muda; *Am.* † ~ *partner* socio *m* comanditario.

sil·hou·ette [silu'et] 1. silueta *f*; 2.: *be* ~d *against* destacarse sobre (*or* contra).

sil·i·ca ['silikə] sílice *f*; **sil·i·cate** ['silikit] silicato *m*; **si·li·ceous** [si'lifəs] silíceo.

silk [silk] 1. seda *f*; 2. *attr.* de seda; ~ *hat* sombrero *m* de copa; **'silk·en** de seda; sedoso; **'silk·i·ness** lo sedoso; **'silk-'stock·ing** *Am.* 1. aristócrata *m/f*; 2. aristocrático; **'silk·worm** gusano *m* de seda; **'silk·y** □ sedoso.

sill [sil] (*window-*) alféizar *m*; ante-pecho *m*; (*door-*) umbral *m*.

sil·li·ness ['silinis] necedad *f*, ton-tería *f*; **sil·ly** ['sili] □ tonto, necio. bobo; ~ *season* época *f* de la ser-piente de mar.

si·lo ['sailou] silo *m*, ensiladora *f*.

silt [silt] 1. sedimento *m*, aluvión *m*; 2. obstruirse con sedimentos (*mst* ~ *up*).

sil·ver ['silvə] 1. plata *f*; 2. platear (*a.* ⊕ '~-**plate**); *mirror* azogar; 3. de plata; plateado; ~ *jubilee* vigésimo quinto aniversario *m*; ~ *paper* papel *m* de plata; ~ *wedding* bodas *f/pl.* de plata; **'sil·ver·y** plateado; *voice* argentino.

sim·i·lar ['similə] □ parecido, seme-jante; **sim·i·lar·i·ty** [ˌ'læriti] se-mejanza *f*.

sim·i·le ['simili] símil *m*.

si·mil·i·tude [si'militju:d] simili-tud *f*.

sim·mer ['simə] *v/i.* hervir (*v/t.* cocer) a fuego lento; *fig.* estar a punto de estallar.

sim·per ['simpə] 1. sonrisa *f* afec-tada (*or* boba); 2. sonreír boba-mente.

sim·ple ['simpl] □ sencillo; simple; *style* llano; F bobo; '~-'**heart·ed** □ ingenuo, candoroso; '~-'**mind·ed** □ estúpido, idiota; candoroso; **sim·ple·ton** ['ˌtən] inocentón *m*.

sim·plic·i·ty [sim'plisiti] sencillez *f*; llaneza *f of style*; F simpleza *f*; **sim·pli·fi·ca·tion** [ˌfi'keiʃn] sim-plificación *f*; **sim·pli·fy** ['ˌfai] simplificar.

sim·ply ['simpli] *adv.* sencilla-mente; simplemente.

sim·u·late ['simjuleit] simular; **sim·u·la·tion** simulación *f*.

si·mul·ta·ne·i·ty [siməltə'niəti] si-multaneidad *f*; **si·mul·ta·ne·ous** [ˌl'teinjəs] □ simultáneo.

sin [sin] 1. pecado *m*; 2. pecar.

since [sins] 1. *prp.* desde, a partir de, después de; 2. *adv.* desde en-tonces, después; *long* ~ hace mucho (tiempo); *a short time* ~ hace poco; 3. *cj.* desde que; puesto que, ya que; *it is an hour* ~ *he left* hace una hora que salió.

sin·cere [sin'siə] □ sincero; *Yours* ~*ly* le saluda afectuosamente; **sin·cer·i·ty** [ˌ'seriti] sinceridad *f*.

sine [sain] seno *m*.

si·ne·cure ['sainikjuə] sinecura *f*.

sin·ew ['sinju:] tendón *m*; *fig. mst* ~*s pl.* nervio *m*, fibra *f*; **'sin·ew·y** nervudo, vigoroso.

sin·ful ['sinful] □ pecaminoso; *p.* pecador; **'sin·ful·ness** maldad *f*.

sing [siŋ] [*irr.*] cantar; (*birds*) trinar; (*ears*) zumbar; F ~ *out* vocear; ~ *small* achantarse; ~ *to sleep* arrullar, adormecer cantando; ~ *another song* (*or* tune) bajar el tono, verse obligado a cambiar de opinión.

singe [sindʒ] chamuscar; *hair* que-mar las puntas de.

sing·er ['siŋə] cantor (-a *f*) *m*; (*professional*) cantante *m/f*.

sing·ing ['siŋiŋ] canto *m*; zumbido *m in ears*; ~ *bird* pájaro *m* cantor.

sin·gle ['siŋgl] 1. □ único, solo; simple; *room* individual; *ticket* sen-cillo; (*unmarried*) soltero; ~ *combat* combate *m* singular; ~ *file* fila *f* india; 2. (*mst* ~ *out*) distinguir, singularizar; *escoger*; señalar; 3. *tennis*: ~*s pl.* juego *m* de indi-viduales (*or* de simples); '~-'**breast-ed** sin cruzar; '~-'**cham·ber** *pol.* unicameral; '~-'**en·gin·ed** ✈ mo-nomotor; '~-'**hand·ed** sin ayuda (de nadie); '~-'**heart·ed** □, '~-'**mind·ed** □ resuelto, firme; sincero; '**sin·gle·ness** resolución *f*, firmeza *f of purpose*; '**sin·gle·seat·er** monoplaza *m*; '**sin·gle·stick** *fenc.* (esgrima *f* del) bastón *m*; **sin·glet** ['~it] camiseta *f*; **sin·gle·ton** ['~tən] semi-fallo *m*, carta *f* única de un palo; '**sin·gle·'track** de vía unica.

sin·gly *adv.* individualmente; uno a uno.

sing·song ['siŋsɔŋ] **1.** *(tone)* salmodia *f*, sonsonete *m*; *(songs)* concierto *m* improvisado; **2.** *tone* monótono, cantarín.

sin·gu·lar ['siŋgjulə] □ singular *adj. a. su. m*; **sin·gu·lar·i·ty** [~-'læriti] singularidad *f*.

Sin·ha·lese [siŋhə'li:z] cingalés *adj. a. su. m (-a f)*.

sin·is·ter ['sinistə] □ siniestro.

sink [siŋk] **1.** [*irr.*] *v/i.* menguar, declinar; *(ship)* hundirse; *(sun)* ponerse; ⚕ debilitarse; dejarse caer *into chair*; *my heart sank* se me cayeron las alas del corazón; ~ *in* penetrar, calar; *(words)* tener efecto, hacer mella; *v/t.* sumergir; *ship* hundir; ✗ *shaft* abrir, cavar; *well* perforar; *money* invertir; *teeth* hincar *(into* en); *differences* olvidar, suprimir; **2.** fregadero *m*, pila *f*; ⊕ sumidero *m*; *fig.* sentina *f*; '**sink·er** ✗ plomada *f*; *(fishing)* plomo *m*; '**sink·ing** hundimiento *m*; ~ *fund* fondo *m* de amortización.

sin·ner ['sinə] pecador *(-a f) m*.

Sin·o-... ['sinou] sino...

sin·u·os·i·ty [sinju'ɔsiti] sinuosidad *f*; '**sin·u·ous** □ sinuoso.

si·nus ['sainəs] *anat.* seno *m*; **si·nus·i·tis** [~'saitis] sinusitis *f*.

sip [sip] **1.** sorbo *m*; **2.** sorber.

si·phon ['saifən] **1.** sifón *m*; **2.** sacar con sifón *(a. ~ off)*.

sir [sə:] señor *m (in direct address)*; sir *m (as title)*; *Dear* ♀ muy señor mío.

sire ['saiə] **1.** † *a. zo.* padre *m*; **2.** engendrar, ser el padre de.

si·ren ['saiərin] *all senses:* sirena *f*.

sir·loin ['sə:lɔin] solomillo *m*.

si·roc·co [si'rɔkou] siroco *m*.

sis·sy ['sisi] marica *m*, mariquita *m*.

sis·ter ['sistə] hermana *f (a. eccl.)*; *eccl. (as title)* Sor *f*; ~ *ship* (buque *m*) gemelo *m*; ~ *of charity (or mercy)* hermana *f* de la caridad; **sis·ter·hood** ['~hud] hermandad *f*; cofradía *f* de mujeres; '**sis·ter·in-law** cuñada *f*; '**sis·ter·ly** de *(or* como) hermana.

sit [sit] *v/i.* sentarse *(a. ~ down)*; estar sentado; *(assembly)* reunirse, celebrar junta; *(clothes)* sentar; *(hens)* empollar; posar *as model*; ~ *for portrait* hacerse; *painter* servir de modelo a; ~ *on committee* ser miembro de; *F p.* hacer callar; ser severo con; *objector* reprimir; ~ *up* incorporarse; velar *at night*; *make (a. p.)* ~ *up* sorprender; dar en qué pensar; *v/t.* sentar; *horse* montar; *exam* presentarse para; ~ *out dance* no bailar; *th.* aguantar hasta el fin; *p.* resistir durante más tiempo que; '~-**down strike** huelga *f* de brazos caídos.

site [sait] **1.** sitio *m*; solar *m*, local *m*; **2.** situar.

sit·ter ['sitə] modelo *m* (de pintor); gallina *f* clueca; *sl.* cosa *f* fácil; *sport:* gol *m etc.* que se canta.

sit·ting ['sitiŋ] sesión *f*; nidada *f of eggs*; '~-**room** sala *f* de estar.

sit·u·at·ed ['sitjueitid] situado; sito; **sit·u·a·tion** situación *f*; *(post)* puesto *m*, colocación *f*.

six [siks] seis *(a. su. m)*; *at ~es and sevens* en confusión; **six·teen** ['~'ti:n] dieciséis; '**six·teenth** [~θ] decimosexto; **sixth** [~θ] sexto *(a. su. m)*; **six·ti·eth** ['~tiəθ] sexagésimo; '**six·ty** sesenta.

size¹ [saiz] **1.** tamaño *m*; talla *f*; dimensiones *f/pl.*; extensión *f*; número *m of shoes etc.*; **2.** clasificar según el tamaño; ~ *up* medir *(p.* con la vista); **sized** de ... tamaño.

size² [~] **1.** cola *f*; apresto *m*; **2.** encolar; aprestar.

siz(e)·a·ble ['saizəbl] □ considerable.

siz·zle ['sizl] chisporrotear, churruscar, crepitar (al freírse).

skate [skeit] **1.** patín *m*; *v. roller-*; *ichth.* raya *f*; **2.** patinar; '**skat·er** patinador *(-a f) m*; '**skat·ing-rink** pista *f* de patinaje.

ske·dad·dle [ski'dædl] F poner pies en polvorosa, largarse.

skee·sicks ['ski:ziks] *Am.* F pilluelo *m*.

skein [skein] madeja *f*.

skel·e·ton ['skelitn] **1.** esqueleto *m*;

fig. esquema *m*; ⊕ armazón *f*; **2.** reducido; esquemático; ∼ **key** llave *f* maestra.

skep·tic ['skeptik] *Am. v.* sceptic.

sketch [sket∫] **1.** croquis *m*; bosquejo *m*, boceto *m*; *thea.* pieza *f* corta; **2.** bosquejar, dibujar; **'sketch·y** □ incompleto, superficial.

skew [skju:] oblicuo, sesgado.

skew·er ['skjuə] **1.** broqueta *f*, espetón *m*; **2.** espetar.

ski [ski:] **1.** esquí *m*; **2.** esquiar.

skid [skid] **1.** derrape *m*, patinazo *m*, deslizamiento *m*; ✗ patín *m*; **2.** derrapar, patinar, deslizarse.

skid·doo [ski'du:] *Am. sl.* largarse.

ski·er ['ski:ə] esquiador (-a *f*) *m*.

skiff [skif] esquife *m*.

ski·ing ['ski:iŋ] esquí *m*; **'ski·jump** salto *m* de esquí; **'ski·lift** telesquí *m*, telesilla *f*.

skil(l)·ful ['skilful] □ diestro, hábil; experto; **'skil(l)·ful·ness, skill** [skil] destreza *f*, habilidad *f*; pericia *f*; **skilled** [skild] hábil, experto; *work, man* especializado; cualificado.

skim [skim] *v/t. milk* desnatar; espumar; *(graze)* rozar, rasar; *v/i.:* ∼ **over** pasar rasando; ∼ **through** *fig.* examinar ligeramente, hojear.

skimp [skimp] *v/t.* escatimar; *work* chapucear, frangollar; *v/i.* economizar; **'skimp·y** □ escaso; tacaño.

skin [skin] **1.** piel *f*; cutis *m*; *(animal's)* pellejo *m*; *(hide)* cuero *m*; ♣ corteza *f*; nata *f* on milk; *(wine)* odre *m*; **by** *(or* with*)* the ∼ **of one's teeth** por los pelos; **2.** *v/t.* despellejar *(a. sl.)*; desollar; *fruit* pelar; *tree* descortezar; F ∼ **alive** desollar vivo; *v/i.* ⚓ cicatrizarse *(a.* ∼ **over)**; **'∼·deep** superficial; **'∼·flint** cicatero *m*, tacaño *m*; **'∼·graft·ing** injerto *m* de piel; **'skin·ner** peletero *m*; **'skin·ny** flaco, magro.

skip [skip] **1.** brinco *m*, salto *m*; ✗ jaula *f*; **2.** *v/i.* brincar, saltar (a la comba); *fig.* saltar *from one subject to another*; F escabullirse; *v/t.* *(a.* ∼ **over)** omitir, saltar.

skip·per ['skipə] ⚓ patrón *m*; capitán *m* (*a. sport*).

skip·ping-rope ['skipiŋroup] comba *f*.

skir·mish ['skə:mi∫] **1.** escaramuza *f*; **2.** escaramuzar; **'skir·mish·er** escaramuzador *m*.

skirt [skə:t] **1.** falda *f*; faldón *m of coat*; *(edge)* orilla *f*, borde *m*; **2.** orillar, ladear; **'skirt·ing-board** ⊕ rodapié *m*.

skit [skit] sátira *f*, pasquín *m* (on contra); *thea.* número *m* corto burlesco; **'skit·tish** □ asustadizo (*esp. horse*); caprichoso, coqueta.

skit·tle ['skitl]: ∼**s** *pl.* juego *m* de bolos; *(Am. type in Spain)* juego *m* de las bolas; **'∼·al·ley** bolera *f*.

skiv·vy ['skivi] F *contp.* fregona *f*; esclava *f* del trabajo.

skul·dug·ger·y [skʌl'dʌgəri] *Am.* F trampa *f*, embuste *m*.

skulk [skʌlk] acechar; remolonear; ocultarse (en la sombra *etc.*).

skull [skʌl] cráneo *m*; calavera *f*.

skunk [skʌŋk] *zo.* mofeta *f*; F canalla *m*.

sky [skai] cielo *m*; **'∼·blue** azul celeste; **'∼·high** por las nubes; **'∼·lark 1.** alondra *f*; **2.** F jaranear; **'∼·light** tragaluz *m*; claraboya *f*; **'∼·line** (línea *f* del) horizonte *m*; silueta *f of building etc.*; **'∼·rock·et 1.** cohete *m*; **2.** F subir (como un cohete); **'∼·scrap·er** rascacielos *m*; **sky·ward** (-s) ['∼·wəd(z)] hacia el cielo; **'sky·writ·ing** escritura *f* aérea.

slab [slæb] tabla *f* (*a.* ⊕), plancha *f of wood etc.*; losa *f of stone*; tajada *f* (gruesa) *of meat etc.*

slack [slæk] **1.** flojo (*a.* ✝); *(lax)* descuidado, negligente; *(lazy)* perezoso; *student* desaplicado; ✝ encalmado; *period etc.* de inactividad; ∼ **water**, ∼ **tide** repunte *m* de la marea; **2.** lo flojo; ✝ estación *f (or* temporada *f)* de inactividad; ✗ cisco *m*; ∼**s** *pl.* pantalones *m/pl.* (flojos; *mst* de mujer); **3.** = ∼**en**; = *slake*; F holgazanear; gandulear, racanear; **'slack·en** *v/t.* aflojar (*a.* ∼ **off**); disminuir; *v/i.* aflojarse; *(wind)* amainar; ∼ *up* aflojar el paso; **'slack·er** F gandul *m*, rácano *m*; haragán (-a *f*) *m*; **'slack·ness** flojedad *f*; *(laxity)* descuido *m*; desaplicación *f*, inercia *f in studies*.

slag [slæg] escoria *f*; **'∼·heap** escorial *m*; escombrera *f*.

slain [slein] *p.p. of slay*.

slake [sleik] *all senses:* apagar.

slam [slæm] **1.** golpe *m*; *(door)* portazo *m*; *cards:* bola *f*, capote *m*, slam *m*; **2.** *(door)* cerrar(se) de golpe; colocar *etc.* con violencia; golpear.

slan·der ['slɑ:ndə] 1. calumnia *f*, difamación *f*; 2. calumniar, difamar; decir mal de; '**slan·der·er** calumniador (-a *f*) *m*; '**slan·der·ous** □ calumnioso.

slang [slæŋ] 1. argot *m*, jerga *f*; (*thieves'*) germanía *f*; vulgarismo *m*; 2. poner como un trapo, llenar de insultos; '**slang·y** □ *p.* que emplea (*or th.* lleno de) vulgarismos.

slant [slɑ:nt] 1. inclinación *f*, sesgo *m*; *Am.* F punto *m* de vista, parecer *m*; 2. inclinar(se), sesgar(se); '**slant·ing** □ inclinado, sesgado; '**slant·wise** oblicuamente.

slap [slæp] 1. palmada *f*, manotada *f*; ~ in the face bofetada *f*; *fig.* palmetazo *m*, golpe *m* (rudo); 2. dar una palmada (*or* bofetada) a; pegar; 3. ¡zas!; 4. *adv.* (*full*) de lleno, directamente; (*suddenly*) de golpe; '**~·dash** descuidado, de brocha gorda; '**~·jack** *Am.* torta *f* frita; '**~·stick** payasadas *f*/*pl.*; '**~·up** F de primera.

slash [slæʃ] 1. cuchillada *f*; latigazo *m with whip*; 2. *v/t.* acuchillar, rasgar; azotar *with whip*; F *price* machacar, quemar; *Am.* criticar severamente; *v/i.* tirar tajos (*at* a); '**slash·ing** □ *criticism* severo.

slat [slæt] tablilla *f*, hoja *f*.

slate [sleit] 1. pizarra *f*; *Am.* lista *f* de candidatos; 2. cubrir de pizarra(s); *fig.* censurar, criticar severamente; '**~·'pen·cil** pizarrín *m*; '**slat·er** pizarrero *m*.

slat·tern ['slætə:n] 1. mujer *f* desaseada; 2. (*a.* '**slat·tern·ly**) desaseado.

slaugh·ter ['slɔ:tə] 1. sacrificio *m*, matanza *f*; *fig.* carnicería *f*, mortandad *f*; 2. sacrificar, matar; carnear *S.Am.*; '**slaugh·ter·er** jifero *m*; '**slaugh·ter-house** matadero *m*.

Slav [slɑ:v] eslavo *adj. a. su. m* (a *f*).

slave [sleiv] 1. esclavo (a *f*) *m*; 2. trabajar como un negro, sudar tinta; '**slav·er**[1] ♺ barco *m* negrero; (*p.*) (*a.* '**slave-'driv·er**, '**slave-'trad·er**) negrero *m* (*a. fig.*).

slav·er[2] ['slævə] 1. baba *f*; 2. babear.

slav·er·y ['sleivəri] esclavitud *f*.

slav·ey ['slævi] *sl.* fregona *f*.

Slav·ic ['slævik] eslavo *adj. a. su. m* (*a.* **Slav'on·ic**).

slav·ish ['sleiviʃ] □ servil; '**slav·ish·ness** servilismo *m*.

slaw [slɔ:] *Am.* ensalada *f* de col.

slay [slei] [*irr.*] *lit.* matar; '**slay·er** asesino *m*.

sled [sled], *mst* **sledge**[1] [sledʒ] 1. trineo *m*; 2. *v/i.* ir en trineo; *v/t.* llevar en trineo.

sledge[2] [~] acotillo *m*, macho *m* (*a.* '**~-ham·mer**).

sleek [sli:k] 1. □ liso y brillante; *p. etc.* pulcro, pulido; 2. alisar, pulir; '**sleek·ness** lisura *f etc.*

sleep [sli:p] 1. [*irr.*] *v/i.* dormir; ~ like a log (*or* top) dormir como un lirón; ~ (up)on *s.t.* consultar algo con la almohada; *v/t.* pasar durmiendo (*a.* ~ away); ~ off hangover *etc.* dormir; ~ it off dormir la mona; 2. sueño *m*; go to ~ dormirse (*a. of limb*); put to ~ *p.* dormir, adormecer; *pet* sacrificar; send to ~ dormir; '**sleep·er** durmiente *m*/*f*; ♛ traviesa *f*; (*coach*) coche-cama *m*; cama *f*; be a light (heavy) ~ tener el sueño ligero (profundo); '**sleep·i·ness** somnolencia *f*.

sleep·ing ['sli:piŋ]: ✝ ~ partner socio *m* comanditario; *v. beauty*; '**~-bag** saco *m* de dormir; '**~-car**, '**~·car·riage** ♛ coche-cama *m*; '**~·draught** soporífero *m*; '**~-pill**, '**~-'tab·let** comprimido *m* para dormir, somnífero *m*; '**~·'sick·ness** enfermedad *f* del sueño.

sleep·less ['sli:plis] □ *p.* insomne; desvelado; *night* pasado en vela; '**sleep·less·ness** insomnio *m*.

sleep-walk·er ['sli:pwɔ:kə] somnámbulo (a *f*) *m*.

sleep·y ['sli:pi] *p.* soñoliento; *place* soporífero; *pear* fofo; be ~ tener sueño; '**~·head** F dormilón (-a *f*) *m*.

sleet [sli:t] 1. aguanieve *f*, nevisca *f*; 2. caer aguanieve, neviscar.

sleeve [sli:v] manga *f*; ⊕ manguito *m*, enchufe *m*; *attr.* ... de enchufe; have *s.t.* up one's ~ tener algo en reserva; *laugh up one's* ~ reírse con disimulo; **sleeved** con mangas; '**sleeve·less** sin mangas; '**sleeve-links** *pl.* gemelos *m*/*pl.*

sleigh [slei] *v.* sled.

sleight [slait] (*mst* ~ of hand) escamoteo *m*, prestidigitación *f*.

slen·der ['slendə] □ delgado; *resources etc.* escaso, limitado; '**slen·der·ness** delgadez *f*; escasez *f*.

slept [slept] *pret. a. p.p. of* sleep.

sleuth [slu:θ] (a. '**~-hound**) sabueso m; fig. detective m.

slew[1] [slu:] pret. of slay.

slew[2] [~] torcer(se) (a. ~ round).

slice [slais] **1.** tajada f, lonja f of meat etc.; raja f of sausage; rebanada f, trozo m of bread; (round) rodaja f; (tool) estrelladera f; **2.** cortar, tajar; bread rebanar; (a. ~ off) cercenar.

slick [slik] F **1.** adv. directamente; **2.** adj. p. astuto, mañoso; listo; movement hábil.

slick·er ['slikə] Am. F (p.) embaucador m; Am. (coat) impermeable m.

slid [slid] pret. a. p.p. of slide 1.

slide [slaid] **1.** [irr.] v/i. resbalar; deslizarse (along por); let ~ no ocuparse de; v/t. correr, deslizar; **2.** resbaladero m on ice; ⊕ cursor m; corredera f; (microscope-) portaobjeto m, platina f; (lantern-) diapositiva f; '**slide-rule** regla f de cálculo.

slid·ing ['slaidiŋ] **1.** deslizamiento m; **2.** corredizo; ~ door puerta f de corredera; mot. ~ roof techo m de corredera; ~ scale escala f móvil; ~ seat bancada f corrediza.

slight [slait] **1.** ☐ leve, ligero; insignificante; escaso, tenue; stature delgado, pequeño; not in the ~est ni en lo más mínimo; ~ly un poco; ligeramente; **2.** desaire m, desatención f; **3.** desairar, desatender; menospreciar; '**slight·ing** ☐ menospreciativo; '**slight·ness** insignificancia f; delgadez f.

slim [slim] **1.** ☐ delgado, esbelto; resources, chance escaso; **2.** adelgazar.

slime [slaim] limo m, légamo m; cieno m; baba f of snail; **slim·i·ness** ['slaiminis] lo limoso; viscosidad f.

slim·ness ['slimnis] delgadez f.

slim·y ['slaimi] ☐ limoso, legamoso; baboso; viscoso; p. rastrero; adulón.

sling [sliŋ] **1.** ✗ honda f; ✗ cabestrillo m; ⚓ eslinga f; braga f; **2.** [irr.] lanzar, tirar; (a. ~ away) colgar, suspender; ⚓ eslingar.

slink [sliŋk] [irr.] v/i. andar furtivamente; ~ away escabullirse; irse cabizbajo.

slip [slip] **1.** v/i. deslizarse; (freq. ~ up) resbalar; (bone) dislocarse; F declinar; ~ away, ~ off escabullirse; marcharse desapercibido; ~ back

regresar con sigilo; ~ by pasar inadvertido; ~ through colarse; ~ up resbalar; fig. equivocarse; let ~ chance dejar pasar; secret decir inadvertidamente; v/t. deslizar; bone dislocarse; guard eludir; ~ in remark deslizar, insinuar; ~ into introducir en; ~ off (on) coat etc. quitarse (ponerse) de prisa; it ~ped my mind se me olvidó; F ~ one over on jugarle una mala pasada a; **2.** resbalón m; desliz m (a. fig.); fig. lapso m, equivocación f; ✗ esqueje m; (dress) combinación f; geol. dislocación f; ⚓ (a. ~s pl.) grada f; ~ of paper tira f, papeleta f; F ~ of a girl jovenzuela f; ~ of the pen lapsus m calami; ~ of the tongue lapsus m linguae; give a p. the ~ dar esquinazo a; '**~-knot** lazo m corredizo; '**slip·per** zapatilla f; babucha f; '**slip·per·y** ☐ resbaladizo; skin viscoso; F p. astuto, zorro; **slip·shod** ['~ʃɔd] descuidado; desaseado; '**slip·stream** ✈ viento m de la hélice; '**slip-up** F error m, desliz m; '**slip·way** ⚓ gradas f/pl.

slit [slit] **1.** hendedura f, raja f; resquicio m; **2.** [irr.] hender, rajar, cortar.

slith·er [sliðə] deslizarse, ir rodando.

sliv·er ['slivə] **1.** raja f; **2.** cortar en rajas.

slob·ber ['slɔbə] **1.** baba f; **2.** babear; ~ over entusiasmarse de un modo ridículo por. [endrino m.]

sloe [slou] (fruit) endrina f; (tree)

slog [slɔg] F v/i. afanarse, sudar tinta; v/t. golpear (sin arte).

slo·gan ['slougən] slogan m, lema m; † grito m de combate.

sloop [slu:p] balandra f, corbeta f.

slop [slɔp] **1.:** ~s pl. agua f sucia, lavazas f/pl.; (food) gachas f/pl.; **2.** (a. ~ over) derramar(se), desbordarse.

slope [sloup] **1.** cuesta f, declive m; inclinación f; vertiente f, ladera f of hill; **2.** v/t. inclinar; sesgar; formar en declive; ✗ ~ arms! ¡armas al hombro!; v/i. inclinarse; declinar; sl. ~ off largarse, escabullirse; '**slop·ing** ☐ inclinado; en declive.

slop-pail ['slɔppeil] cubeta f para agua sucia; '**slop·py** ☐ lleno de charcos; mojado; fig. work descuidado; dress desgalichado; F sentimental.

slosh [slɔʃ] F v/i. (a. ~ about) chapotear; v/t. pegar.

slot [slɔt] ✂ muesca f, ranura f; hunt. rastro m.

sloth [slouθ] pereza f; zo. perezoso m; **sloth·ful** ['~ful] □ perezoso.

slot-ma·chine ['slɔtməʃi:n] tragaperras m.

slouch [slautʃ] 1. v/i. estar sentado (or andar etc.) con un aire gacho; caminar arrastrando los pies; agacharse; v/t. hat agachar; 2. postura f desgarbada; ~ hat sombrero m gacho.

slough[1] [slau] fangal m; fig. abismo m.

slough[2] [slʌf] 1. zo. piel f (que muda la serpiente); ✂ escara f; 2. v/i. desprenderse; v/t. mudar, echar de sí (a. ~ off).

slough·y ['slaui] fangoso.

Slo·vak ['slouvæk] 1. eslovaco (a f) m; 2. = **Slo·va·ki·an** eslovaco.

slov·en ['slʌvn] persona f desaseada; **'slov·en·li·ness** desaseo m, dejadez f; **'slov·en·ly** desaseado, desaliñado, dejado; work descuidado.

slow [slou] 1. □ lento; pausado; clock atrasado; (dull) torpe, lerdo; (boring) aburrido; be ~ to tardar en; my watch is (10 minutes) ~ mi reloj atrasa (10 minutos); 2. adv. (a. ~ly) despacio, lentamente; 3. (a. ~ down, ~ up) v/t. retardar; ⊕ reducir la velocidad de, moderar la marcha de; v/i. ir más despacio; moderarse la marcha; '~-coach F torpe m/f; '~-match mecha f tardía; '~-'mo·tion film a cámara lenta; '**slow·ness** lentitud f; torpeza f; '**slow·worm** lución m.

sludge [slʌdʒ] lodo m, fango m; sedimento m fangoso.

slue [slu:] v. slew[2].

slug[1] [slʌg] zo. babosa f.

slug[2] [~] ✂ posta f; typ. lingote m.

slug·gard ['slʌgəd] haragán (-a f) m; '**slug·gish** □ perezoso; tardo; inactivo.

sluice [slu:s] 1. esclusa f; (a. '~-way) canal m; (a. '~-gate) compuerta f; 2. regar, lavar (abriendo la compuerta).

slum [slʌm] barrio m bajo; (house) casucha f, tugurio m; ~s pl. barrios m/pl. bajos.

slum·ber ['slʌmbə] 1. (a. ~s pl.) lit. sueño m (mst tranquilo); fig. in-

actividad f; 2. dormir, dormitar; fig. permanecer inactivo.

slum·brous, slum·ber·ous ['slʌmbrəs, '~bərəs] □ soñoliento; inactivo.

slump [slʌmp] 1. hundirse, bajar repentinamente; dejarse caer pesadamente into chair; 2. ✝ baja f repentina in price; (general) declive m económico, retroceso m; bajón m in morale.

slung [slʌŋ] pret. a. p.p. of sling 2.

slunk [slʌŋk] pret a. p.p. of slink.

slur [slə:] 1. reparo m; borrón m (en la reputación); ♪ ligado m; 2. pasar por encima, ocultar (a. ~ over); syllable comerse; ♪ ligar.

slush [slʌʃ] nieve f a medio derretir; fango m; F sentimentalismo m, cursilería f; '**slush·y** fangoso; F sentimental, cursi.

slut [slʌt] marrana f, mujer f desaseada; '**slut·tish** sucio, desaliñado.

sly [slai] socarrón, taimado; astuto; furtivo; on the ~ a hurtadillas; '~-boots F pajarraco m; '**sly·ness** socarronería f; astucia f.

smack[1] [smæk] 1. sabor(cillo) m, dejo m (of a); 2. saber (of a); ~ of b.s. tener resabios de.

smack[2] [~] 1. (slap) manotada f; golpe m; 2. dar una manotada a, pegar; golpear; lips relamerse; 3. ¡zas!

smack[3] [~] ⚓ queche m.

smack·er ['smækə] sl. beso m sonado; Am. dólar m.

smack·ing ['smækiŋ] F zurra f.

small [smɔ:l] 1. pequeño; chico; menudo; corto, exiguo; insignificante; print minúsculo; voice humilde; p. bajo (de estatura); feel ~ sentirse humillado; v. beer, change, fry, hour, ware, etc.; 2.: ~ of the back parte f más estrecha (de la espalda); F ~s pl. paños m/pl. menores; '~-arms pl. armas f/pl. cortas; '**small-hold-ing** ⚘ parcela f; minifundio m; '**small·ish** más bien pequeño; '**small·ness** pequeñez f; '**small-pox** ✂ viruela f; '**small-talk** cháchara f; vulgaridades f/pl.

smalt [smɔ:lt] esmalte m.

smarm·y ['smɑ:mi] F cobista.

smart [smɑ:t] 1. □ listo, vivo; inteligente; b.s. ladino, astuto; dress etc. elegante; appearance pulcro;

(*tidy*) aseado; *society* de buen tono; *pace* vivo; ~ *aleck* sabelotodo*m*; **2.** escozor *m*; **3.** escocer; picar; ~ *under*, ~ *with* fig. resentirse de; *it makes my tongue* ~ escuece en la lengua; *you shall* ~ *for it* me lo pagarás; '**smart·en** hermosear (*mst* ~ *up*), arreglar; '**smart·ness** elegancia *f*; vivacidad *f* etc.

smash [smæ∫] **1.** romper(se), hacer (se) pedazos; destrozar(se), aplastar(se) (*freq.* ~ *up*); † quebrar; ~ *into* chocar con; **2.** 🚂 etc. choque *m* (violento), accidente *m*; † quiebra *f*; *tennis*: golpe *m* violento; *go to* ~ hacerse pedazos; ~ *hit* sl. exitazo *m*; '~*-and-*'**grab** raid robo *m* relámpago (en joyería etc.); '**smash·er** sl. (*girl*) bombón *m*, guayabo *m*; '**smash·ing** sl. imponente, bárbaro; '**smash-up** colisión *f* violenta.

smat·ter·ing ['smætəriŋ] nociones *f/pl.*

smear [smiə] **1.** manchar(se) (*a.* fig.), embarrar(se), untar(se) (*with* de); **2.** mancha *f* (*a.* fig.), embarradura *f*.

smell [smel] **1.** olor *m* (*of* a); (*bad*) hedor *m*; (*sense of*) olfato *m*; **2.** [*irr.*] oler (*of* a); (*dog*) olfatear; ~ *out* husmear; '~*ing salts* pl. sales *f/pl.* (aromáticas).

smelt[1] [smelt] *pret. a. p.p. of smell* 2.
smelt[2] [~] *ichth.* eperlano *m*.
smelt[3] [~] fundir; '**smelt·er** fundidor *m*; '**smelt·ing-**'**fur·nace** horno *m* de fundición.

smile [smail] **1.** sonrisa *f*; **2.** sonreír (se) (*at* de); fig. ~ *on* favorecer; '**smil·ing** ☐ risueño.

smirch [smə:t∫] *lit.* mancillar; desdorar.

smirk [smə:k] **1.** sonreírse satisfecho; sonreírse afectadamente; **2.** sonrisa *f* satisfecha; sonrisa *f* afectada.

smite [smait] [*irr.*] † golpear (con fuerza); herir; castigar; afligir.

smith [smiθ] herrero *m*.

smith·er·eens ['smiðə'ri:nz] *pl.* F añicos *m/pl.*; *smash to* ~ hacer añicos.

smith·y ['smiði] herrería *f*.

smit·ten ['smitn] **1.** *p.p. of smite*; **2.** fig. ~ *with* afligido por; F *idea* entusiasmado por; *p.* chalado por.

smock [smɔk] **1.** fruncir; **2.** blusa *f* (*a.* '~*-frock*); bata *f*.

smog [smɔg] niebla *f* espesa con humo.

smoke [smouk] **1.** humo *m*; F pitillo *m*, tabaco *m*; F *have a* ~ echar un pitillo; **2.** *v/i.* fumar; (*chimney*) echar humo, humear; *v/t.* fumar; *bacon* etc. ahumar; ~ *out* ahuyentar con humo; '~*-dried* ahumado; '**smoke-less** ☐ sin humo; '**smok·er** fumador (*-a f*) *m*; 🚃 coche *m* fumador; '**smoke-screen** cortina *f* de humo; '**smoke-stack** chimenea *f*.

smok·ing ['smoukiŋ] **1.** el fumar; *no* ~ prohibido fumar; **2.** ... de fumador(es); '~*-com·part·ment* departamento *m* de fumadores; '~*-con·cert* concierto *m* donde se permite fumar; '~*-room* salón *m* de fumar.

smok·y ['smouki] ☐ *fire, chimney* humeante; *room* lleno de humo; *taste, surface* etc. ahumado.

smol·der ['smouldə] = *smoulder*.

smooth [smu:ð] **1.** ☐ liso, terso; suave; llano, igual; *passage, water* tranquilo; *paste* liso, sin grumos; *manner* afable; *style* flúido; *p., b.s.* zalamero, meloso, astuto; *go* ~*ly* ir sobre ruedas; **2.** (*a.* ~ *out*, ~ *down*) alisar; suavizar; allanar; ⊕ desbastar; *p.* ablandar; (*a.* ~ *over*, ~ *away*) suprimir, allanar; ~*ing iron* plancha *f*; '**smooth·ness** lisura *f*; suavidad *f* etc.

smote [smout] *pret. of smite*.

smoth·er ['smʌðə] (*a.* ~ *up*) sofocar, ahogar; *fire* apagar; *yawn* contener; *doubts* etc. suprimir; fig. ~ (*a p.*) *with* llenar de.

smoul·der ['smouldə] arder sin llama; fig. estar latente.

smudge [smʌdʒ] **1.** manchar(se), tiznar(se); **2.** mancha *f*; '**smudg·y** ☐ manchado; borroso.

smug [smʌg] ☐ pagado de sí mismo; presumido, vanidoso; farisaico.

smug·gle ['smʌgl] pasar de contrabando; '**smug·gler** contrabandista *m/f*; '**smug·gling** contrabando *m*.

smut [smʌt] **1.** tizne *m*; tiznón *m*; ♀ tizón *m*; fig. obscenidad *f*; **2.** tiznar(se).

smutch [smʌt∫] v. *smudge*.

smut·ty ['smʌti] ☐ tiznado; ♀ atizonado; fig. obsceno, verde.

snack [snæk] bocadillo *m*, tentempié *m*; '~*-bar* bar *m*; cafetería *f*; cantina *f*.

snaf·fle[1] ['snæfl] bridón *m*.

snaf·fle[2] [✲] *sl*. afanar, guindar.

snag [snæg] nudo *m in wood*; tocón *m of tree*; raigón *m of tooth*; *fig*. tropiezo *m*, pero *m*.

snail [sneil] caracol *m*; *at a ✲'s pace* a paso de tortuga.

snake [sneik] culebra *f*, serpiente *f*; '✲·**weed** bistorta *f*.

snak·y ['sneiki] ☐ serpentino, tortuoso.

snap [snæp] **1.** castañetazo *m of fingers*; chasquido *m of whip*; (*fastener*) corchete *m*, cierre *m*; *Am*. F vigor *m*; *phot*. foto *f*, instantánea *f*; *cold ✲* ola *f* de frío; **2.** repentino, imprevisto; **3.** *v/i*. (*break*) romperse; saltar; (*sound*) chasquear; ✲ *at* querer morder; *fig*. contestar groseramente a; *Am*. F ✲ *into s.t.* emprender algo con vigor; *Am*. F ✲ *out of it* cambiarse repentinamente; ✲ *out of it!* ¡menéate!, ¡ánimo!; *v/t*. romper; hacer saltar; *whip etc*. chasquear; *fingers* castañetear; *phot*. sacar una foto (*or* instantánea) de; ✲ *one's fingers at* tratar con desprecio; ✲ *shut* cerrar de golpe; F ✲ *up* asir; comprar con avidez; **4.** ¡crac!; '✲-**drag·on** cabeza *f* de dragón; '✲-**fas·ten·er** corchete *m* (de presión); '**snap·pish** ☐ arisco; irritable; '**snap·pish·ness** irritabilidad *f*; '**snap·py** *snappish*; F enérgico; F *make it ✲!* ¡pronto!; '**snap·shot 1.** disparo *m* rápido sin apuntar; *phot*. instantánea *f*; **2.** sacar una instantánea de.

snare [snɛə] **1.** trampa *f*, lazo *m*; *fig*. engaño *m*; **2.** coger con trampas; *fig*. hacer caer en el lazo.

snarl [snɑ:l] **1.** gruñir; regañar; **2.** gruñido *m*; regaño *m*.

snatch [snætʃ] **1.** arrebatamiento *m*; ♪ *etc*. trocito *m*; *by ✲es* a ratos; **2.** (✲ *at* tratar de) arrebatar (*from* a); coger (*al vuelo*); ✲ *up* asir.

sneak [sni:k] **1.** *v/i*. ir (✲ *in* entrar) a hurtadillas; ✲ *away*, ✲ *off* escabullirse; *v/t*. F robar a hurtadillas; **2.** soplón (-a *f*) *m*; '**sneak·ers** *pl*. *Am*. F zapatos *m/pl*. ligeros de goma; '**sneak·ing** *manner* ☐ furtivo; *admiration etc*. inexplicable; secreto.

sneer [sniə] **1.** visaje *m* de burla y desprecio; **2.** hacer un visaje de burla y desprecio; ✲ *at* mofarse de,

mirar al desgaire; '**sneer·er** mofador (-a *f*) *m*; '**sneer·ing** ⌐ burlador y despreciativo.

sneeze [sni:z] **1.** estornudar; **2.** estornudo *m*.

snick [snik] tijeretear.

sniff [snif] **1.** *v/i*. oler, ventear; ✲ *at* husmear; F menospreciar; *v/t*. husmear, olfatear; sorber por las narices; **2.** husmeo *m*; venteo *m*; sorbo *m* por las narices; '**sniff·y** F estirado.

snig·ger ['snigə] reírse con disimulo (*at* de).

snip [snip] **1.** tijeretada *f*; recorte *m*; *sl*. ganga *f*; **2.** tijeretear; recortar (*a.* ✲ *off*).

snipe [snaip] **1.** *orn*. agachadiza *f*; **2.** ✕ tirar desde un escondite; '**snip·er** tirador *m* escondido.

snip·pets ['snipits] *pl*. recortes *m/pl*.; *fig*. retazos *m/pl*.

snitch [snitʃ] *sl*. **1.** (*nose*) naipas *f/pl*.; **2.** soplar.

sniv·el ['snivl] lloriquear; gimotear; '**sniv·el·(l)ing** llorón.

snob [snɔb] (e)snob *m/f*; '**snob·ber·y** (e)snobismo *m*; '**snob·bish** ☐ (e)snob.

snoop [snu:p] *sl*. **1.** curiosear, fisgonear, ventear; **2.** fisgón (-a *f*) *m*; '**snoop·er** *sl*. investigador *m* furtivo.

snoot·y ['snu:ti] F fachendón.

snooze [snu:z] F **1.** siestecita *f*, sueñecillo *m*; **2.** dormitar; echar una siestecita.

snore [snɔ:] **1.** ronquido *m* (*a.* '**snor·ing**); **2.** roncar.

snort [snɔ:t] **1.** bufido *m*; **2.** *v/i*. bufar; *v/t*. decir con un bufido.

snot [snɔt] F mocarro *m*; '**snot·ty** F mocoso; *sl*. fachendón; (*angry*) enojado.

snout [snaut] hocico *m*, morro *m*.

snow [snou] **1.** nieve *f*; *sl*. cocaína *f*; **2.** nevar; F *be ✲ed under* estar inundado (*with*, *by* por); *be ✲ed up* estar encerrado (*or* aislado) por la nieve; '✲·**ball 1.** bola *f* de nieve; **2.** *v/t*. lanzar bolas de nieve a; *v/i*. *fig*. aumentar progresivamente; '✲·**bound** aprisionado por la nieve; '✲·**drift** ventisquero *m*; '✲·**drop** campanilla *f* blanca; '✲·**fall** nevada *f*; '✲·**flake** copo *m* de nieve; '✲·**man** figura *f* de nieve;

'~-'plough, *Am.* '~-plow (máquina *f*) quitanieves *m*; '~-shoe raqueta *f* de nieve; '~-storm nevasca *f*; 'snow·y □ nevoso; *fig.* níveo.

snub [snʌb] 1. desairar; 2. desaire *m*; 'snub·ber *mot.* parachoques *m*; 'snub-nosed chato.

snuff [snʌf] 1. rapé *m*, tabaco *m* en polvo; 2. aspirar, sorber por la nariz (*a.* take ~); *fig.* extinguir; '~-box tabaquera *f*; 'snuff·ers *pl.* (*a pair of* ~ unas) despabiladeras *f/pl.*; snuf·fle ['~l] 1. resollar; ganguear; 2. gangueo *m*.

snug [snʌg] □ cómodo; abrigado; *dress* ajustado; ⚓ bien aparejado; 'snug·ger·y cuarto *m* cómodo; snug·gle ['~l] arrimarse (*up to* a); apretarse (para calentarse).

so [sou] así; por tanto, por consiguiente; (*and* ~) conque; ~ *good* tan bueno; ~ *much* tanto; ~ *many* tantos; *I think* ~ creo que sí; *or* ~ o así; más o menos; ~ *am I* yo también; *and* ~ *forth, and* ~ *on* y así sucesivamente; etcétera; *v. far*; ~ *much* ~ tan es así (*that* que); ~ *as to,* ~ *that* (*purpose*) para *inf.*, para que *subj.*; (*result*) de modo que.

soak [souk] remojar(se), empapar(se); F beber mucho; *sl.* desplumar, clavar un precio exorbitante a; *get* ~*ed to the skin* calarse hasta los huesos; *leave to* ~ dejar en remojo; ~ *in* penetrar; ~ *up* absorber, embeber; 2. F borrachín *m*; 'soak·ing remojón *m*.

so-and-so ['souənsou] (*p.*) fulano (a *f*) *m*; F tío *m*; Mr ♀ Don Fulano (de Tal).

soap [soup] 1. jabón *m*; *soft* ~ *sl.* coba *f*; 2. (en)jabonar; '~-box *fig.* caja *f* vacía empleada como tribuna (en la calle); ~ *orator* orador *m* de barricada; '~-dish jabonera *f*; '~-op·er·a *Am. sl.* serial de radiofónico (chabacano); '~-suds *pl.* jabonaduras *f/pl.*; 'soap·y □ jabonoso.

soar [sɔ:] encumbrarse (*a. fig.*); cernerse; volar a gran altura; *fig.* elevarse muchísimo.

sob [sɔb] 1. sollozo *m*; 2. sollozar; 3. F sentimental.

so·ber ['soubə] 1. □ sobrio; serio; (*sensible*) cuerdo; moderado; *colour* apagado; (*not drunk*) no embriaga-

do; 2. calmar(se) (*a.* ~ *down*); F ~ *up* desintoxicar(se), quitar(se) la sopa (a); 'so·ber·ness sobriedad *f*; cordura *f*; so·bri·e·ty [sou'braiəti] moderación *f*; sobriedad *f*.

sob-stuff ['sɔbstʌf] *Am.* sentimentalismo *m*.

so-called ['sou'kɔ:ld] llamado.

soc·cer ['sɔkə] F fútbol *m*.

so·cia·bil·i·ty [souʃə'biliti] sociabilidad *f*; 'so·cia·ble □ sociable.

so·cial ['souʃl] 1. □ social; ~ *democrat* socialdemócrata *m/f*; ~ *insurance* (*or* ~ *security*) seguro *m* social; ~ *services pl.* servicios *m/pl.* sociales; 2. reunión *f* (social), velada *f*; 'so·cial·ism socialismo *m*; 'so·cial·ist socialista *adj. a. su. m/f*; so·cial·ite ['souʃəlait] F persona *f* conocidísima en la buena sociedad; 'so·cial·ize socializar.

so·ci·e·ty [sə'saiəti] sociedad *f*; asociación *f*; (*high* ~) buena sociedad *f*; *friendly* ~ montepío *m*, mutualidad *f*.

so·ci·o·log·i·cal [sousiə'lɔdʒikl] □ sociológico; so·ci·ol·o·gist [~'ɔlədʒist] sociólogo *m*; so·ci·ol·o·gy sociología *f*.

sock[1] [sɔk] calcetín *m*.

sock[2] [~] *sl.* 1. tortazo *m*; *give* (*a p.*) ~*s* pegar; (*defeat*) vencer; 2. pegar.

sock·dol·a·ger [sɔk'dɔlədʒə] *Am. sl.* golpe *m* decisivo.

sock·et ['sɔkit] cuenca *f* of eye; alvéolo *m* of tooth; ⚡, ⊕ enchufe *m*; cañón *m*.

sod [sɔd] césped *m*, terrón *m*.

so·da ['soudə] sosa *f*, soda *f* (*a. drink*); '~-foun·tain sifón *m*; *Am.* fuente *f* de sodas; '~-wa·ter agua *f* de seltz; sifón *m*.

sod·den ['sɔdn] empapado, saturado; *p.* estúpido; embrutecido por el alcohol.

so·di·um ['soudjəm] sodio *m*.

so·ev·er [sou'evə] *in compounds*: ... de cualquier clase *etc.*

so·fa ['soufə] sofá *m*.

sof·fit ['sɔfit] sofito *m*.

soft [sɔft] 1. □ blando; muelle; *sound, air, skin* suave; *water* blando; *metal* dúctil; *colour* delicado; *hat* flexible; *character* débil, afeminado; F *heart* tierno; F *job* fácil; F (*foolish*) estúpido; F *drink* no alcohólico; 2. (*a.* ~*ly*) suavemente, blandamente *etc.*; soft·en ['sɔfn] ablandar(se);

reblandecer; suavizar(se); templar (se); **soft·ness** ['sɔftnis] blandura *f*; suavidad *f*; molicie *f*; ⊕ ductilidad *f*; **'soft·y** mollejón (-a *f*) *m*.

sog·gy ['sɔgi] empapado; esponjoso.

soil¹ [sɔil] tierra *f* (*a. fig.*), suelo *m*.

soil² [⌣] ensuciar(se); manchar(se) (*a. fig.*); '**~-pipe** tubo *m* de desagüe sanitario.

soir·ée ['swɑːrei] sarao *m*, velada *f*.

so·journ ['sɔdʒəːn] **1.** permanencia *f*, estancia *f*; **2.** permanecer, pasar una temporada.

sol·ace ['sɔləs] **1.** consuelo *m*; **2.** consolar. [*m* solar.]

so·lar ['soulə] solar; ~ *plexus* plexo]

sold [sould] *pret. a. p.p. of sell*.

sol·der ['sɔldə] **1.** soldadura *f*; **2.** soldar; **sol·der·ing-i·ron** ['~riŋ-aiən] soldador *m*.

sol·dier ['souldʒə] **1.** soldado *m*; militar *m*; **2.** militar, ser soldado; **'sol·dier·like, 'sol·dier·ly** militar; **'sol·dier·y** soldadesca *f*.

sole¹ [soul] □ único, solo; exclusivo; ~ *agent* agente *m* único; ~ *right* exclusiva *f*.

sole² [⌣] **1.** suela *f*, piso *m of shoe*; *anat.* planta *f*; **2.** solar.

sole³ [⌣] *ichth.* lenguado *m*.

sol·e·cism ['sɔlisizm] solecismo *m*.

sol·emn ['sɔləm] □ solemne; **so·lem·ni·ty** [sə'lemniti] solemnidad *f*; **sol·em·ni·za·tion** ['sɔləmnai-'zeiʃn] solemnización *f*; **'sol·em·nize** solemnizar.

sol·fa [sɔl'fɑː] **1.** solfa *f*; **2.** solfear.

so·lic·it [sə'lisit] solicitar (*a p. for a th. or a th. of a p.* algo a alguien); importunar; intentar seducir; **so·lic·i·ta·tion** solicitación *f*; **so'lic·i·tor** ⚖ *approx.* abogado *m*; procurador *m*; (*oaths, wills etc.*) notario *m*; *Am.* representante *m/f*; ♀ *General* (*British*) subfiscal *m* de la corona; *Am.* procurador *m* general del Estado; **so'lic·it·ous** □ solícito (*about, for* por); ansioso; **so'lic·i·tude** [~tjuːd] solicitud *f*, ansiedad *f*.

sol·id ['sɔlid] **1.** □ sólido (*a. fig.,* ♀); *gold, tyre etc.* macizo; *crowd* denso; *vote* unánime; *a* ~ *hour* una hora entera; ♀ ~ *geometry* geometría *f* del espacio; **2.** sólido *m*; **sol·i·dar·i·ty** [~'dæriti] solidaridad *f*; **so'lid·i·fy** [~fai] solidificar(se); **so'lid·i·ty** solidez *f*.

so·lil·o·quize [sə'liləkwaiz] soliloquiar; **so'lil·o·quy** soliloquio *m*.

sol·i·taire [sɔli'tɛə] solitario *m* (*game, gem*); **sol·i·tar·y** ['~təri] □ solitario; retirado; único; *in* ~ *confinement* incomunicado; **sol·i·tude** ['~tjuːd] soledad *f*.

so·lo ['soulou] *♪, cards:* solo *m*; ✈ ~ *flight* vuelo *m* a solas; **'so·lo·ist** solista *m/f*.

sol·stice ['sɔlstis] solsticio *m*.

sol·u·bil·i·ty [sɔlju'biliti] solubilidad *f*; **sol·u·ble** ['sɔljubl] soluble.

so·lu·tion [sə'luːʃn] *all senses:* solución *f*.

solv·a·ble ['sɔlvəbl] soluble; **solve** [sɔlv] resolver; solucionar; *riddle* adivinar; **sol·ven·cy** ['~vənsi] solvencia *f*; **'sol·vent** solvente *adj.* (♀) *a. su. m* (♧).

som·ber, som·bre ['sɔmbə] □ sombrío.

some [sʌm, *unstressed* səm] **1.** *pron. a. adj.* un poco (de); alguno(s); unos; ciertos; ~ *few* unos pocos; ~ *20 miles* unas 20 millas; *freq. not translated, e. g.* do *you want* ~ *bread?* ¿quiere pan?; *for* ~ *reason (or other)* por alguna que otra razón, por no sé qué razón; F *or Am. this is* ~ *house!* ¡esto es lo que se llama casa!; **2.** *adv.* algo; *Am.* F muy, mucho; '**~·bod·y, '~·one** alguien; F *be* ~ ser un personaje; ~ *else* otra persona; '**~·day** algún día; '**~·how** de algún modo; ~ *or other* de un modo u otro; ~ *or other I never liked him* por alguna que otra razón no me era simpático.

som·er·sault ['sʌməsɔːlt] **1.** salto *m* mortal; (*car*) vuelco *m*; *turn* ~s = **2.** dar saltos mortales; (*car*) volcar.

some...: '**~·thing** ['sʌmθiŋ] algo; alguna cosa; ~ *else* otra cosa; *that is* ~ eso ya es algo; ~ *of a (e.g. painter)* en cierto modo; '**~·time 1.** algún día; alguna vez, en algún tiempo; **2.** antiguo; '**~·times** [~z] algunas veces; a veces; '**~·what** algo, algún tanto; '**~·where** en (*motion* a) alguna parte; ~ *else* en (*motion* a) otra parte.

som·nam·bu·lism [sɔm'næmbjulizm] somnambulismo *m*; **som·'nam·bu·list** somnámbulo (-a *f*) *m*.

som·nif·er·ous [sɔm'nifərəs] □ somnífero.

som·no·lence ['sɔmnələns] somnolencia f; **'som·no·lent** □ soñoliento.

son [sʌn] hijo m.

so·na·ta [sə'nɑːtə] sonata f.

song [sɔŋ] canción f; canto m; cantar m; F for a (mere) ~ medio regalado; F ~ and dance alharaca f; **'~-bird** pájaro m cantor; **'~-book** cancionero m; **'~-hit** canción f de moda; **'song·ster** pájaro m cantor.

son·ic bar·ri·er ['sɔnik 'bæriə] barrera f del sonido.

son-in-law, pl. **sons-in-law** ['sʌn(z)inlɔː] yerno m, hijo m político.

son·net ['sɔnit] soneto m.

son·ny ['sʌni] F hijito m.

so·no·rous [sə'nɔːrəs] □ sonoro, resonante; **so'no·rous·ness** sonoridad f.

soon [suːn] pronto, temprano; ~ after poco después; as (or so) ~ as tan pronto como (a. cj.), luego que; as ~ as possible cuanto antes; **'sooner** más temprano; ~ or later tarde o temprano; ~ than antes que; no ~ ... than apenas; I had (or would) ~ ... preferiría ...; I would just as ~ stay igual me daría quedarme, estaría tan contento de quedarme.

soot [sut] hollín m.

sooth [suːθ]: in ~ en realidad.

soothe [suːð] calmar; aliviar; **'sooth·ing** □ calmante; tranquilizador.

sooth·say·er ['suːθseiə] adivino (a f) m.

soot·y ['suti] □ holliniento.

sop [sɔp] 1. sopa f; fig. dádiva f; compensación f; sl. tonto m; 2. empapar; ~ up absorber.

soph·ism ['sɔfizm] sofisma m.

soph·ist ['sɔfist] sofista m; **so·phis·tic, so·phis·ti·cal** [sə'fistik(l)] □ sofístico; **so'phis·ti·cat·ed** □ sofisticado; **soph·ist·ry** ['sɔfistri] sofistería f.

soph·o·more ['sɔfəmɔː] Am. estudiante m/f de segundo año.

so·po·rif·ic [soupə'rifik] □ soporífero adj. a. su. m.

sop·ping ['sɔpiŋ]: ~ wet hecho una sopa; **'sop·py** sl. tonto; sentimental.

so·pran·o [sə'prɑːnou] soprano f, tiple f.

sor·cer·er ['sɔːsərə] hechicero m, brujo m; **'sor·cer·ess** hechicera f, bruja f; **'sor·cer·y** hechicería f, brujería f.

sor·did ['sɔːdid] □ asqueroso; vil, bajo; **'sor·did·ness** asquerosidad f etc.

sore [sɔː] 1. □ dolorido; doloroso; sensible; inflamado; poet. fuerte, grande; F irritable; F resentido; be ~ doler; 2. llaga f (a. fig.), úlcera f; **'sore·head** Am. F persona f resentida; **'sore·ly** adv. penosamente; con urgencia; muy; **'sore·ness** dolor m; inflamación f.

so·ror·i·ty [sə'rɔriti] Am. univ. hermandad f (de estudiantes).

sor·rel¹ ['sɔrəl] alazán adj. (colour) a. su. m (horse).

sor·rel² [~] ♀ acedura f.

sor·row ['sɔrou] 1. pesar m, dolor m, pena f; 2. apenarse, afligirse (at, for, over de, por); **sor·row·ful** ['~ful] □ pesaroso, afligido.

sor·ry ['sɔri] □ pesaroso, apesadumbrado; apenado; arrepentido (for th. de); condition, plight desastrado, lastimoso; excuse poco convincente; figure ridículo; sight triste; be ~ sentirlo; be ~ for p. compadecer; be ~ for o.s. estar muy alicaído; be ~ that sentir que subj.; be ~ to inf. sentir inf.; (I am) (so) ~! lo siento (mucho); (asking pardon) ¡perdón!

sort [sɔːt] 1. clase f, especie f; a ~ of uno a modo de; in some ~, F ~ of algo; en cierta medida; of all ~s de toda clase; something of the ~, that ~ of thing algo por el estilo; of ~s de poco valor; out of ~s 🎲 indispuesto; de mal humor; it takes all ~s (to make a world) de todo hay en este mundo de Dios; F he's a good ~ es un buen chico; es buena persona; 2. clasificar (a. ~ out); escoger; separar.

sor·tie ['sɔːtiː] salida f.

so-so ['sousou] F regular.

sot [sɔt] borrachín m.

sot·tish ['sɔtiʃ] □ embrutecido (por el alcohol).

sough [sau] 1. susurro m; 2. susurrar.

sought [sɔːt] pret. a. p.p. of seek; **'~-aft·er** solicitado.

soul [soul] alma f (a. fig.); upon my ~! ¡por vida mía!; **'soul·ful** □ sentimental; conmovedor; **'soulless** □ desalmado.

sound[1] [saund] ⌐ sano; firme, sólido; *p.* digno de confianza; *opinion* razonable, bien fundado, ortodoxo; *move* acertado, razonable, eficaz; *sleep* profundo; ✝ solvente.

sound[2] [⌐] 1. sonido *m*; son *m*; ruido *m*; *I don't like the ~ of it* no me gusta la idea; me inquieta la noticia; *~ barrier* barrera *f* del sonido; *~ effects pl.* efectos *m/pl.* sonoros; *~ film* película *f* sonora; *~ track film:* banda *f* sonora; *~ wave* onda *f* sonora; 2. *v/i.* (re)sonar; (*seem*) parecer; *v/t.* sonar; tocar; *alarm* dar la voz de; *praises* entonar; ✖ *~ the charge* tocar el zafarrancho de combate.

sound[3] [⌐] ⚓ estrecho *m*, brazo *m* de mar.

sound[4] [⌐] 1. ✛ sonda *f*; 2. ⚓, ✛ sondar; *chest* auscultar; *intentions*, *p.* sondear (*a. ~ out*).

sound·ing ['saundiŋ] ⚓ sondeo *m*.

sound(·ing)-board ['saund(iŋ)bɔːd] ♪ secreto *m*; caja *f* de resonancia (*a. fig.*).

sound·less ['saundlis] ☐ silencioso; ⊕ insonorizado.

sound·ness ['saundnis] firmeza *f*, solidez *f* etc.

sound-proof ['saundpruːf], **sound-tight** ['~tait] insonorizado.

soup [suːp] (*thin*) caldo *m*, consomé *m*; (*thick*) puré *m*, sopa *f*; *F in the ~* en apuros; *~ tureen* sopera *f*.

sour ['sauə] 1. ☐ agrio (*a. fig.*); acre (*a. fig.*); *milk* cortado; *land* maleado; *go ~* (*milk*) cortarse; 2. agriar(se); (*land*) malear(se); *fig.* amargar (*v/t.*).

source [sɔːs] fuente *f*, nacimiento *m* *of river*; *fig.* fuente *f*; procedencia *f*.

sour·dough ['sauədou] *Am.* explorador en Alaska.

sour·ish ['sauəriʃ] agrete; **sour·ness** agrura *f* (*a. fig.*); acidez *f*.

souse [saus] 1. escabechar; zambullir *into water*; mojar *with water*; *sl. ~d* ajumado; 2. escabeche *m*.

south [sauθ] 1. ⌐ sur *m*, mediodía *m*; 2. *adj.* del sur, meridional; 3. *adv.* al sur, hacia el sur.

South A·mer·i·can ['sauθ ə'merikən] sudamericano.

south...: '~'**east** sudeste *adj.* (*a.* '~'**east·er·ly**, '~'**east·ern**) *a. su. m.*

south·er·ly ['sʌðəli] *direction* hacia

el sur; *wind* del sur; '**south·ern** [~ən] meridional; '**south·ern·er** habitante *m/f* del sur (*Am.* de los estados del sur).

south·ern·most ['sʌðənmoust] (el) más meridional.

south-paw ['sauθpɔː] *Am.* jugador *m* etc. zurdo.

south·ward(s) ['sauθwəd(z)] hacia el sur.

south...: '~'**west** suroeste *adj.* (*a.* '~'**west·er·ly**, '~'**west·ern**) *a. su. m*; '~'**west·er** (*wind*) suroeste *m*; (*hat*) sueste *m.*

sou·ve·nir ['suːvəniə] recuerdo *m.*

sov·er·eign ['sɔvrin] soberano *adj. a. su. m* (*a f*); soberano *m* (*moneda de 1 libra*); '**sov·er·eign·ty** soberanía *f.*

so·vi·et ['souviət] 1. soviet *m*; 2. soviético.

sow[1] [sau] *zo.* cerda *f*; ⊕ galápago *m.*

sow[2] [sou] [*irr.*] sembrar (*a. fig.*); esparcir; plagar *with mines*; '**sow·er** sembrador (-a *f*) *m*; '**sow·ing** siembra *f*; *~ time* sementera *f*; **sown** *p.p. of* **sow**[2].

so·ya ['sɔiə] soja *f*; *~ bean* semilla *f* de soja.

spa [spaː] balneario *m.*

space [speis] 1. espacio *m* (*a. typ.*); *~ helmet* casco *m* sideral; 2. (*a. ~ out*) espaciar (*a. typ.*); '~-**ship** nave *f* espacial, astronave *f.*

spa·cious ['speiʃəs] ☐ espacioso; *room* amplio; *living* holgado; **spacious·ness** amplitud *f*, extensión *f.*

spade [speid] laya *f*, pala *f*; *call a ~ a ~* llamar al pan pan y al vino vino; *cards:* *~s pl.* picos *m/pl.*, pique *m*, (*Spanish*) espadas *f/pl*; '~·**work** trabajo *m* preliminar.

spag·het·ti [spəg'eti] *approx.* fideos *m/pl.*

span[1] [spæn] 1. palmo *m* *of hand*; ojo *m* *of bridge*; ✈ envergadura *f*; *Am.* pareja *f* (de caballos); *fig.* extensión *f*, duración *f*; 2. (*bridge*) extenderse sobre; (*builder*) tender (un puente) sobre; *time* abarcar.

span[2] [⌐] *pret. of* **spin**.

span·gle ['spæŋgl] 1. lentejuela *f*; 2. adornar con lentejuelas; *fig. ~d* estrellado.

Span·iard ['spænjəd] español (-a *f*) *m.*

span·iel ['spænjəl] perro *m* de aguas.

Span·ish ['spæniʃ] español *adj. a. su. m.*

spank [spæŋk] F **1.** zurrar; manotear; ~ *along* ir volando; **2.** manotada *f*; '**spank·er** ⚓ cangreja *f*; '**spank·ing 1.** □ *pace* rápido; F fuerte, bárbaro; **2.** F zurra *f*.

span·ner ['spænə] llave *f* (inglesa).

spar¹ [spɑ:] ⚓ palo *m*, verga *f*.

spar² [~] *boxing*: hacer fintas; amagar (*at* a) (*a. fig.*); *fig.* disputarse (amistosamente); ~*ring partner* sparring *m*.

spar³ [~] *min.* espato *m*.

spare [spɛə] **1.** □ (*lean*) enjuto; (*left over*) sobrante; *room* disponible; para convidados; *time* libre, desocupado; *part* de repuesto, de recambio; ~ *time* ratos *m/pl.* libres, horas *f/pl.* libres, ratos *m/pl.* de ocio; **2.** ⊕ (*pieza f de*) repuesto *m* (*or* recambio *m*); **3.** ahorrar, economizar; pasarse sin; dispensar de, excusar; *life* perdonar; (*and*) *to* ~ de sobra; *have ... to* ~ disponer de; **spare·rib** ['~rib] costilla *f* de cerdo con poca carne.

spar·ing ['spɛəriŋ] □ escaso; parco (*in, of* en), económico; '**spar·ing·ness** parquedad *f*.

spark [spɑ:k] **1.** chispa *f*; *fig.* chispazo *m of wit*; átomo *m of life*; F ~*s sg.* telegrafista *m*; F *bright* ~ tipo *m* muy listo (*or* divertido); **2.** chispear; ~ *off* hacer estallar.

spark(·ing)-plug ['spɑ:k(iŋ)plʌg] bujía *f*.

spar·kle ['spɑ:kl] **1.** centelleo *m*, destello *m*; *fig.* viveza *f*; **2.** centellear, chispear (*a. fig.*); relucir; *fig.* ser muy vivaz; '**spar·kling** centelleante; *eyes, wit* chispeante; *wine* espumoso.

spar·row ['spærou] gorrión *m*; '~-**hawk** gavilán *m*.

sparse [spɑ:s] □ disperso; escaso; *hair* ralo.

spasm ['spæzm] 🗡 espasmo *m*; *fig.* arranque *m*; **spas·mod·ic, spas·mod·i·cal** [~'mɔdik(l)] □ espasmódico.

spat¹ [spæt] *zo.* freza *f*; masa *f* de ostras jóvenes.

spat² [~]: ~*s pl.* botines *m/pl.*

spat³ [~] *pret. a. p.p. of* spit² 2.

spate [speit] avenida *f*; *fig.* torrente *m*; *in* ~ crecido.

spa·tial ['speiʃl] □ espacial.

spat·ter ['spætə] salpicar, rociar (*with* de).

spat·u·la ['spætjulə] espátula *f*.

spav·in ['spævin] esparaván *m*.

spawn [spɔ:n] **1.** freza *f*, huevas *f/pl.*; *fig.* prole *f*; **2.** *v/i.* desovar, frezar; *v/t. contp.* engendrar; '**spawn·ing** freza *f*.

speak [spi:k] [*irr.*] hablar (*to* con, a); *truth* decir; *parl. etc.* hacer uso de la palabra; *teleph.* Brown ~ing! ¡Soy Brown!; *teleph.* *be* ~*ing* estar al habla; *so to* ~ por decirlo así; ~ *for* interceder por; representar; ~ *well for* demostrar el mérito de; ~ *out* hablar claro; osar hablar; ~ *up* hablar alto; ~ *up!* ¡más fuerte!; '~-**eas·y** *Am. sl.* taberna *f* clandestina; '**speak·er** el (la) que habla; orador (-a *f*) *m*; hablante *m/f of language*; *parl.* presidente *m*; *radio*: (*loud-*) altavoz *m*.

speak·ing ['spi:kiŋ] hablante; *likeness* perfecto; *we are not on* ~ *terms* no nos hablamos; '~-**trum·pet** bocina *f*; '~-**tube** tubo *m* acústico.

spear [spiə] **1.** lanza *f*; (*fishing-*) arpón *m*; **2.** alancear, herir con lanza; '~-**head** punta *f* de lanza (*a. fig.*).

spec [spek] 🗡 *sl.* (*on como*) especulación *f*; *sl. on* ~ por si acaso, a ver lo que sale.

spe·cial ['speʃl] **1.** □ especial, particular; **2.** *approx.* guardia *m* auxiliar (= ~ *constable*); número *m* extraordinario (= ~ *edition*); tren *m* especial (= ~ *train*); *Am.* F oferta *f* extraordinaria; *Am.* plato *m* del día; **spe·cial·ist** ['~ʃəlist] especialista *m/f*; **spe·ci·al·i·ty** [speʃi'æliti] especialidad *f*; **spe·cial·ize** ['speʃəlaiz] especializarse (*in, Am. on* en); **spe·cial·ty** ['~ʃlti] 🗡🗡 contrato *m* sellado; especialidad *f*.

spe·cie ['spi:ʃi:] metálico *m*, efectivo *m*; **spe·cies** ['~z] *sg. a. pl.* especie *f*.

spe·cif·ic [spi'sifik] □ específico *adj.* (*all senses*) *a. su. m*; expreso.

spec·i·fi·ca·tion [spesifi'keiʃn] especificación *f*; plan *m* detallado; **spec·i·fy** ['~fai] especificar; designar (*un plan*).

spec·i·men ['spesimin] espécimen *m*, ejemplar *m*.

spe·cious ['spi:ʃəs] □ especioso; '**spe·cious·ness** lo especioso.

speck [spek] **1.** manchita *f*, mota *f*; grano *m* of dust; partícula *f*; *fig.* pizca *f*; **2.** *v.* spec*kle* 2; **speck·le** ['ˌkl] **1.** punto *m*, mota *f*; **2.** motear, salpicar de manchitas.

specs [speks] F gafas *f/pl.*

spec·ta·cle ['spektəkl] espectáculo *m*; (*a pair of* unas) ˌs *pl.* gafas *f/pl.*, anteojos *m/pl*; '**spec·ta·cled** con gafas.

spec·tac·u·lar [spek'tækjulə] □ espectacular; aparatoso.

spec·ta·tor [spek'teitə] espectador (-a *f*) *m*.

spec·tral ['spektrəl] □ espectral (*a. opt.*); **spec·tre** ['ˌtə], **spec·trum** [ˌtrəm] *opt.* espectro *m*.

spec·u·late ['spekjuleit] especular (*on* en; ✝ *in* sobre); **spec·u·la·tion** especulación *f*; **spec·u·la·tive** ['ˌlətiv] □ especulativo; '**spec·u·la·tor** especulador (-a *f*) *m*.

spec·u·lum ['spekjuləm] 🩺 espéculo *m*; *opt.* espejo *m* (metálico).

sped [sped] *pret. a. p.p. of* speed 2.

speech [spiːtʃ] (*faculty*) habla *f*; idioma *m* (*e. g., English* ˌ); (*style, manner*) lenguaje *m*; (*oration*) discurso *m*; *thea.*, 🜨🜨 parlamento *m*; *make a* ˌ pronunciar un discurso; '**ˌ-day** distribución *f* de premios; **speech·i·fy** ['ˌfai] *contp.* disertar prolijamente; '**speech·less** □ mudo; estupefacto.

speed [spiːd] **1.** velocidad *f* (*a.* ⊕, *mot.*); prisa *f*, presteza *f*; *at full* ˌ *a* máxima velocidad, a toda máquina; *good* ˌ! ¡buen viaje!; **2.** *v/i.* apresurarse, darse prisa; *mot.* exceder la velocidad permitida; ˌ *along* ir volando; ˌ *past* pasar como un rayo; *v/t.* *guest* despedir; ˌ *up* ⊕ acelerar; *p.* dar prisa a; *process* activar; '**ˌ-boat** lancha *f* rápida; '**ˌ-cop** F policía *m* de tráfico; '**speed·i·ness** velocidad *f*, rapidez *f*; **speed lim·it** velocidad *f* máxima permitida; límite *m* de velocidad; **speed·om·e·ter** [spi'dɔmitə] velocímetro *m*, cuentakilómetros *m*; '**speed·way** carretera *f* para carreras; *Am.* vía *f* de tráfico rápido; '**speed·well** verónica *f*; '**speed·y** □ veloz, rápido; *answer* pronto.

spe·l(a)e·ol·o·gy [spiːli'ɔlədʒi] espeleología *f*.

spell¹ [spel] tanda *f*, turno *m* of work; rato *m*, temporada *f*; *bad* ˌ mala racha *f*.

spell² [ˌ] **1.** encanto *m*, hechizo *m*; **2.** [*irr.*] *word* escribir; *fig. danger etc.* anunciar, significar; ˌ *out* deletrear; '**ˌ-bind·er** *Am.* orador *m* fascinante; '**ˌ-bound** *fig.* embelesado, hechizado; '**spell·er**: *be a bad* ˌ no saber escribir correctamente las palabras.

spell·ing ['speliŋ] ortografía *f*; '**ˌ-bee** certamen *m* de ortografía; '**ˌ-book** abecedario *m*.

spelt¹ [spelt] *pret. a. p.p. of* spell² 2.

spelt² [ˌ] 🌾 espelta *f*.

spel·ter ['speltə] peltre *m*.

spend [spend] [*irr.*] *v/t. money, effort* gastar; *time* pasar; *anger* (*v/r.*) consumir(se); *v/i.* gastar dinero; '**spend·er** gastador (-a *f*) *m*.

spend·thrift ['spendθrift] derrochador (-a *f*) *m*, pródigo *adj. a. su. m* (a *f*).

spent [spent] **1.** *pret. a. p.p. of* spend; **2.** *adj.* agotado; gastado.

sperm [spəːm] esperma *f*; **sper·ma·ce·ti** [ˌəˈseti] espermaceti *m*; **sper·ma·to·zo·on** [ˌətouˈzouɔn], *pl.* **sper·ma·to·zo·a** ['ˌzouə] espermatozoo *m*.

spew [spjuː] vomitar.

sphere [sfiə] esfera *f* (*a. fig.*); *ast.* esfera *f* celeste; **spher·i·cal** ['sferikl] □ esférico.

sphinc·ter ['sfiŋktə] esfínter *m*.

sphinx [sfiŋks] esfinge *f*.

spice [spais] **1.** especia *f*; *fig.* picante *m*; aliciente *m*; **2.** condimentar; *fig.* dar picante a.

spic·i·ness ['spaisinis] picante *m* (*a. fig.*); *fig.* F sicalipsis *f*.

spick and span ['spikən'spæn] impecablemente limpio; *house etc.* como una tacita de plata; *p.* acicalado, pulcro.

spic·y ['spaisi] □ especiado; picante (*a. fig.*); *fig.* F sicalíptico.

spi·der ['spaidə] araña *f*; ˌ's *web* telaraña *f*; '**spi·der·y** muy delgado; *writing* de patas de araña.

spiel [spiːl] *Am. sl.* arenga *f*.

spiff·y ['spifi] *Am. sl.* guapo.

spig·ot ['spigət] espita *f* of cask; ⊕ espiga *f*.

spike [spaik] **1.** pincho *m*, púa *f*; escarpia *f*, espigón *m*; clavo *m* *on shoes*; 🌾 espiga *f*; **2.** sujetar con pincho *etc.*; *gun* clavar; *fig.* inutilizar; ~d shoe claveteado; **spike·nard** ['~na:d] nardo m; '**spik·y** armado de púas.

spill¹ [spil] 1. [irr.] derramar(se); verter(se); rider desarzonar, hacer caer; Am. sl. ~ the beans tirar de la manta; 2. caída f from horse; vuelco m.

spill² [~] alegrador m, pajuela f.

spill·way ['spilwei] derramadero m.

spilt [spilt] pret. a. p.p. of spill¹ 1.

spin [spin] 1. [irr.] thread hilar; (a. ~ round) girar, hacer girar; top (hacer) bailar; ✶ entrar en barrena; ~ along correr rápidamente; ~ out alargar; 2. vuelta f; ✶ barrena f; F paseo m en coche etc.

spin·ach ['spinidʒ] espinaca f.

spi·nal ['spainl] espinal; ~ column columna f vertebral; ~ cord médula f espinal.

spin·dle ['spindl] (spinning-) huso m; ⊕ eje m; '**spin·dly** leg zanquivano; largo y delgado.

spin·dri·er ['spin'draiə] secador m centrífugo.

spin·drift ['spindrift] ⚓ rocío m.

spine [spain] anat. espinazo m; zo. púa f; ⚘ espina f; lomo m of book; '**spine·less** □ fig. flojo, falto de voluntad.

spin·ner ['spinə] hilandero (a f) m.

spin·ney ['spini] bosquecillo m.

spin·ning...: ~**jen·ny** ['spiniŋ-'dʒeni] máquina f de hilar de husos múltiples; '~**mill** hilandería f; '~**top** peonza f; '~**wheel** torno m de hilar.   [solterona f.\

spin·ster ['spinstə] soltera f; contp.\

spin·y ['spaini] espinoso (a. fig.).

spi·ra·cle ['spaiərəkl] espiráculo m.

spi·rae·a [spai'riə] espirea f.

spi·ral ['spaiərəl] 1. □ (en) espiral; helicoidal; ~ staircase escalera f de caracol; 2. espiral f, hélice f; 3. dar vueltas en espiral.

spire ['spaiə] aguja f; chapitel m.

spir·it ['spirit] 1. espíritu m; ánimo m, brío m; temple m, humor m; espectro m; 🔥 alcohol m; (a. motor ~) gasolina f; ~ lamp lámpara f de alcohol; ~ level nivel m de aire; ~s pl. ánimo m; humor m; ~ of wine espíritu m de vino; keep up one's ~s no desanimarse; in (high) ~s animado; in low ~s abatido; 2.: ~ away, ~ off hacer desaparecer, llevarse misteriosamente.

spir·it·ed ['spiritid] □ animoso, brioso; horse fogoso.

spir·it·less ['spiritlis] □ apocado, sin ánimo.

spir·it·u·al ['spiritjuəl] □ espiritual; '**spir·it·u·al·ism** espiritismo m; **spir·it·u·al·i·ty** [~'æliti] espiritualidad f; **spir·it·u·al·ize** ['~alaiz] espiritualizar.   [t(u)oso.\

spir·it·u·ous ['spiritjuəs] espiri-\

spirt [spə:t] 1. salir a chorros, brotar a borbotones; 2. chorretada f; v. spurt.

spit¹ [spit] 1. espetón m, asador m; lengua f of land; 2. espetar.

spit² [~] 1. saliva f; F be the very ~ of ser la segunda edición (c); 2. [irr.] v/i. escupir (at a, on en); (cat) bufar; ~ with rain chispear; v/t. (mst ~ out) escupir.

spit³ [~] 🔨 azadada f.

spite [spait] 1. rencor m, ojeriza f, despecho m; in ~ of a pesar de, a despecho de; 2. mortificar, causar pena a.

spite·ful ['spaitful] □ rencoroso, malévolo; '**spite·ful·ness** rencor m, malevolencia f.

spit·fire ['spitfaiə] fierabrás m.

spit·tle ['spitl] baba f, saliva f.

spit·toon [spi'tu:n] escupidera f.

spiv [spiv] sl. approx. gandul m; sablista m, chanchullero m.

splash [splæʃ] 1. salpicadura f, rociada f; (noise) chapoteo m; mancha f of colour; F make a ~ impresionar; 2. v/t. salpicar; v/i. chapotear (a. ~ about); F ~ out derrochar dinero; '~**board** guardabarros m, alero m; '**splash·y** □ fangoso.

splay [splei] 1. bisel m; 2. biselar; extender (sin gracia).

splay·foot ['spleifut] pie m aplastado y torcido; ~ed zancajoso.

spleen [spli:n] anat. bazo m; fig. esplín m, spleen m; rencor m.

splen·did ['splendid] □, **splen·dif·er·ous** [~'difərəs] F espléndido; **splen·do(u)r** ['~də] esplendor m, brillantez f.

sple·net·ic [spli'netik] (a. **sple'net·i·cal** [~kl] □) anat. esplénico; fig. malhumorado, irritable.

splice [splais] 1. empalme m; ⊕ (wood) junta f; 2. empalmar; ⊕ juntar; sl. casar.

splint [splint] 1. tablilla f; 2. entablillar.

splin·ter ['splintə] **1.** astilla *f*; ~ *group* grupo *m* disidente, facción *f*; **2.** astillar(se), hacer(se) astillas; '~**bone** peroné *m*; '**splin·ter·less** inastillable.

split [split] **1.** hendedura *f*, raja *f*; *fig.* división *f*, cisma *m*; F *do the* ~s esparrancarse; **2.** partido, hendido; *fig.* dividido; **3.** partir(se); hender (se), rajarse; dividir(se); *sl.* soplar, chivatear (*on* contra); ~ *hairs* ser quisquilloso; ~ *one's sides* desternillarse de risa; ~ *up* separar(se); '**split·ting** *headache* enloquecedor.

splotch [splɔtʃ] borrón *m*, mancha *f*.

splurge [splə:dʒ] F fachenda *f*.

splut·ter ['splʌtə] **1.** farfulla *f* *of speech*; ⊕ chisporroteo *m*; **2.** (*p.*) farfullar; ⊕ chisporrotear.

spoil [spɔil] **1.** (*mst* ~s *pl.*) despojo *m*, botín *m*; *Am. pol.* ~s *system* acaparamiento de los cargos públicos por el partido victorioso; **2.** [irr.] echar (se) a perder; estropear(se); dañar (se); malograr(se); deteriorar(se); *child* mimar; *be* ~*ing for* ansiar; '**spoils·man** ['~zmən] *Am. pol.* miembro del partido victorioso que acepta un cargo público; '**spoil-sport** aguafiestas *m/f*.

spoilt [spɔilt] **1.** *pret. a. p.p. of* *spoil* 2; **2.** *child* consentido, muy mimado.

spoke[1] [spouk] *pret. of speak*.

spoke[2] [~] rayo *m*, radio *m*.

spo·ken ['spoukən] *p.p. of speak*.

spokes·man ['spouksmən] portavoz *m*.

spo·li·a·tion [spouli'eiʃn] despojo *m*; expoliación *f*.

spon·dee ['spɔndi:] espondeo *m* (- -).

spon·du·licks [spɔn'dju:liks] *sl.* parné *m*.

sponge [spʌndʒ] **1.** esponja *f*; (*a.* ~ *cake*) bizcocho *m*; *boxing a. fig.*: *throw up the* ~ darse por vencido; **2.** lavar con esponja; F dar sablazos, vivir de gorra; F ~ *on* vivir a costa de; ~ *up* absorber; '**spong·er** F gorrón *m*, sablista *m/f*.

spon·gi·ness ['spʌndʒinis] esponjosidad *f*; '**spon·gy** esponjoso.

spon·sor ['spɔnsə] **1.** patrocinador *m*; ✝ fiador *m*; **2.** patrocinar; **spon·sor·ship** ['~ʃip] patrocinio *m*.

spon·ta·ne·i·ty [spɔntə'ni:iti] espontaneidad *f*; **spon·ta·ne·ous** [~'teiniəs] □ *all senses*: espontáneo.

spoof [spu:f] *sl.* **1.** *v/t.* engañar; *v/i.* bromear; **2.** engaño *m*; broma *f*.

spook [spu:k] F espectro *m*.

spool [spu:l] **1.** carrete(l) *m*; canilla *f*; **2.** encanillar.

spoon [spu:n] **1.** cuchara *f*; **2.** cucharear (*a.* ~ *out*); *sl.* besuquearse; '~-**drift** ⚓ rocío *m*; '**spoon-fed** *fig.* muy mimado; **spoon·ful** ['~ful] cucharad(it)a *f*; '**spoon·y** F sobón; sentimental; *be* ~ *on* estar tontamente enamorado de.

spo·rad·ic [spə'rædik] □ esporádico.

spore [spɔ:] espora *f*.

sport [spɔ:t] **1.** deporte *m*; juego *m*, diversión *f*; juguete *m*; F (*a. good* ~) buen perdedor *m*; buen chico *m*; *biol.* mutación *f*; ~s *pl.* juegos *m/pl.* (atléticos); **2.** *v/i.* divertirse; juguetear; *v/t.* gastar, lucir; ~ *one's oak* cerrar la puerta (para no recibir visitas); '**sport·ing** □ deportivo; *gun* de caza; *offer* arriesgado; '**spor·tive** □ juguetón; **sports·man** ['~smən] deportista *m*; persona *f* honrada; persona *f* temeraria; '**sports·man·like** deportivo; leal y honrado; '**sports·man·ship** deportividad *f*; '**sports-wear** trajes *m/pl.* de deporte; '**sports·wom·an** deportista *f*.

spot [spɔt] **1.** (*place*) sitio *m*, lugar *m*; (*mark*) punto *m*; (*stain*) mancha *f*; lunar *m*, grano *m* *on face*; F poquito *m*; *radio*: espacio *m* radiofónico (publicitario); *Am.* F *ten* ~ billete *m* de 10 dólares; ~s *pl.* ✝ géneros *m/pl.* vendidos al contado; F *a* ~ *of* un poco de; *on the* ~ en el acto; al punto; *man* sobre el terreno; *sl.* (*put*) *on the* ~ (poner) en un aprieto; **2.** ✝ contante; disponible; **3.** manchar(se); salpicar; F notar, observar; descubrir; encontrar; F ~ *with rain* chispear; '**spot·less** □ nítido; sin manchas, inmaculado; '**spot·less·ness** nitidez *f*; '**spot·light** arco *m*, proyector *m*; *mot.* faro *m* auxiliar orientable; *fig.* luz *f* concentrada; '**spot·ted** manchado; moteado; ~ *fever* tifus *m* exantemático; '**spot·ter** observador *m*; 🚂 *etc.* coleccionista *m* de números de locomotoras *etc.*; *Am.* vigilante *m* secreto; '**spot·ty** manchado (*face* de granos).

spouse [spauz] cónyuge *m/f*.

spout [spaut] **1.** pico *m*; pitón *m*;

caño *m*; chorro *m of water*; ⚓ canalón *m*; *sl.* up the ∼ en prenda; *fig.* arruinado; **2.** *v/t.* arrojar (en chorro); F declamar; *v/i.* chorrear.

sprain [sprein] **1.** torcedura *f*; **2.** torcer(se).

sprang [spræŋ] *pret. of* spring 2.

sprat [spræt] arenque *m* pequeño.

sprawl [sprɔ:l] arrellanarse; tumbarse; (⚓, *town*) extenderse.

spray¹ [sprei] ⚘ ramita *f*.

spray² [∼] **1.** rociada *f*; ⚓ espuma *f*; (*scent-*) atomizador *m*; ✈ riego *m* por aspersión; pulverización *f*; (*machine*) (∼er) pulverizador *m*; **2.** rociar; regar; pulverizar.

spread [spred] **1.** [*irr.*] extender(se); esparcir(se), desparramar(se); propagar(se), difundir(se); (*a.* ∼ out) separar(se), abrir(se); *table* poner; *butter* untar; *wings* desplegar; ∼ o.s. F ponerse a sus anchas; explayarse *in speech*; **2.** *pret. a. p.p. of* 1; **3.** extensión *f*; propagación *f*, difusión *f*; *Am.* ✝ diferencia *f*; envergadura *f of wings*; *sl.* comilona *f*, banquetazo *m*; '∼**·ea·gled** con los miembros extendidos.

spree [spri:] F juerga *f*, parranda *f*; go on the ∼ ir de juerga.

sprig [sprig] ramita *f*; ⊕ puntilla *f*.

spright·li·ness ['spraitlinis] viveza *f*; '**spright·ly** vivo, animado.

spring [spriŋ] **1.** (*season*) primavera *f*; (*water*) fuente *f*, manantial *m*; (*jump*) salto *m*, brinco *m*; ⊕ muelle *m*, resorte *m*; elasticidad *f*; *fig.* móvil *m of action*; hot ∼ fuente *f* termal; **2.** *v/t.* trap hacer saltar; *mine* volar; ⚓ ∼ a leak abrirse una (vía de) agua; ∼ a th. (up)on a p. espetarle algo a alguien, decirle algo a alguien de buenas a primeras; *v/i.* saltar (*over acc.*); brincar; moverse rápidamente; brotar, nacer, proceder (*from* de); ⊕ torcerse, combarse; ∼ at abalanzarse sobre; ∼ up levantarse de un salto; ⚘, *fig.* brotar; (*breeze*) levantarse de pronto; *where have you sprung from?* ¿de dónde diablos ha salido Vd?; **3.** *fig.* primaveral; ⊕ de muelle; '∼**'balance** peso *m* de muelle; '∼**·board** trampolín *m*; '∼**·bolt** pestillo *m* de golpe; '∼**·'clean·ing** limpieza *f* en primavera.

springe [sprindʒ] lazo *m*.

spring gun ['spriŋgʌn] trampa *f* de

alambre y escopeta; '**spring·i·ness** elasticidad *f*; **spring mat·tress** somier *m*; '**spring·tide** ⚓ marea *f* viva; *poet.* = '**spring·time** primavera *f*; '**spring·y** ☐ elástico; *turf* muelle, muy molido.

sprin·kle ['spriŋkl] *v/t.* salpicar, rociar (*with* de); sembrar (*with* de); asperjar *with holy water*; *v/i.* (*rain*) lloviznar; '**sprin·kler** regadera *f*; *eccl.* hisopo *m*; '**sprin·kling** rociada *f*; aspersión *f*; salpicadura *f*; *fig.* a ∼ of unos cuantos.

sprint [sprint] **1.** sprint *m*; **2.** sprintar; '**sprint·er** esprínter *m*.

sprit [sprit] botavara *f*.

sprite [sprait] duende *m*, hada *f*.

sprock·et-wheel ['sprɔkitwi:l] rueda *f* de cadena.

sprout [spraut] **1.** *v/i.* brotar, germinar; crecer rápidamente; *v/t.* echar, hacerse; **2.** vástago *m*, retoño *m*; ∼s *pl.* col *f* de Bruselas.

spruce¹ [spru:s] ☐ apuesto, pulcro.

spruce² [∼] ⚘ pícea *f* (*a.* ∼ fir).

sprung [sprʌŋ] *pret.* (✝) *a. p.p. of* spring 2.

spry [sprai] ágil, activo.

spud [spʌd] ✈ escarda *f*; *sl.* patata *f*.

spume [spju:m] *lit.* espuma *f*.

spun [spʌn] *pret. a. p.p. of* spin 1.

spunk [spʌŋk] coraje *m*, ánimo *m*.

spur [spə:] **1.** espuela *f* (*a. fig.*); *zo.* espolón *m*; *geog.* estribo *m*; *fig.* estímulo *m*, aguijón *m*; on the ∼ of the moment impulsivamente, sin reflexión; win one's ∼s distinguirse; ∼ gear rueda *f* dentada recta; put (*or* set) ∼s to = **2.** espolear; ∼ on estimular, incitar (*to do* a que haga).

spurge [spə:dʒ] euforbio *m*.

spu·ri·ous ['spjuəriəs] ☐ espurio, falso; '**spu·ri·ous·ness** falsedad *f*.

spurn [spə:n] desdeñar, rechazar.

spurt [spə:t] *sport etc.*: **1.** esfuerzo *m* supremo; **2.** hacer un esfuerzo supremo; *v. spirt.*

sput·ter ['spʌtə] *v. splutter.*

spy [spai] **1.** espía *m/f*; **2.** espiar (*on acc.*); columbrar, divisar; ∼ out *land* reconocer; '∼**·glass** catalejo *m*; '∼**·hole** mirilla *f*.

squab·ble ['skwɔbl] **1.** riña *f*, disputa *f*; **2.** reñir, disputar; '**squabbler** pendenciero (a *f*) *m*.

squad [skwɔd] escuadra *f*, pelotón *m*; **squad·ron** ['∼rən] ✕ escuadrón *m*; ✈ escuadrilla *f*; ⚓ escuadra *f*.

squal·id ['skwɔlid] ☐ miserable, sucio; mezquino.

squall[1] [skwɔ:l] **1.** chillido *m*, berrido *m*; **2.** chillar.

squall[2] [~] ♣ ráfaga *f*, racha *f*, chubasco *m*; **'squall·y** chubascoso.

squal·or ['skwɔlə] miseria *f*, suciedad *f*.

squan·der ['skwɔndə] malgastar, despilfarrar; disipar (*on* en).

square [skwɛə] **1.** ☐ cuadrado (*measure, mile,* & *root, etc.*); en ángulo recto (*to, with* con); *fig.* claro y directo; *deal* justo, equitativo; *p.* honrado; *meal* abundante; *be all* ~ estar en paz; (*sport*) ir iguales; *get* ~ (*with*) desquitarse (con); ~ *dance* danza *f* de figuras; ~ *sail* vela *f* de cruz; *Am.* F ~ *shooter* persona *f* honrada; 2 *feet* ~ 2 pies en cuadro; **2.** cuadrado *m* (*a.* &); cuadro *m* (*a.* ✕); ▲, ⊕ escuadra *f*; plaza *f* in *town*; casilla *f* of *chessboard*; **3.** *v/t.* cuadrar (*a.* &); ▲, ⊕ escuadrar; ajustar (*with* con; *a.* ♆); *sl. p.* sobornar; persuadir; ~*d paper* papel *m* cuadriculado; *v/i.* cuadrar, conformarse (*with* con); **'~·ly** *adv.* honradamente; directamente; '~-'**rigged** ... de cruz.

squash [skwɔʃ] **1.** zumo *m* (de limón *etc.*); F apiñamiento *m*, gentío *m*; **2.** aplastar; apretar, apiñar; F *argument* confutar; F *p.* apabullar.

squat [skwɔt] **1.** *p.* rechoncho; *building* desproporcionadamente bajo; **2.** agacharse, sentarse en cuclillas; *sl.* sentarse; establecerse (sin derecho) *on property*; **'squat·ter** intruso *m*, colono *m* usurpador.

squaw [skwɔ:] india *f* norteamericana.

squawk [skwɔ:k] **1.** graznar, chillar; **2.** graznido *m*, chillido *m*.

squeak [skwi:k] **1.** chirriar, rechinar; **2.** chirrido *m*; *have a narrow* ~ escaparse por un pelo; **'squeak·y** ☐ chirriador.

squeal [skwi:l] **1.** chillido *m*; **2.** chillar; *sl.* cantar.

squeam·ish ['skwi:miʃ] ☐ remilgado, escrupuloso, delicado, susceptible; **'squeam·ish·ness** susceptibilidad *f*; repugnancia *f*.

squee·gee ['skwi:'dʒi:] enjugador *m* de goma (*a. phot.*).

squeeze [skwi:z] **1.** *v/t.* apretar, estrujar; oprimir; ~ *out* exprimir; F *p.* excluir; *v/i.* introducirse, deslizarse (*in* en); **2.** estrujón *m*, estrujadura *f*; presión *f*; apretón *m* of *hand*; ♣ restricción *f* of *credit*; F apiñamiento *m*; *tight* ~ aprieto *m*; **'squeez·er** exprimidor *m*.

squelch [skweltʃ] F *v/t.* despachurrar; *v/i.* andar chapoteando.

squib [skwib] buscapiés *m*; *fig.* pasquín *m*.

squid [skwid] calamar *m*.

squif·fy ['skwifi] *sl.* achispado.

squint [skwint] **1.** bizquear; torcer la vista; cerrar casi los ojos; **2.** estrabismo *m*; mirada *f* bizca; F vistazo *m*.

squire ['skwaiə] **1.** *approx.* propietario *m*, hacendado *m*; señor *m*; *Am.* F juez *m* de paz; *hist.* escudero *m*; **2.** *lady* acompañar a.

squir(e)·arch·y ['skwaiərɑ:ki] aristocracia *f* rural.

squirm [skwə:m] F retorcerse.

squir·rel ['skwirəl] ardilla *f*.

squirt [skwə:t] **1.** chorro *m*; jeringazo *m*; F farolero *m*; **2.** *v/t.* jeringar; arrojar a chorros; *v/i.* salir a chorros.

stab [stæb] **1.** puñalada *f*; F tentativa *f*; **2.** apuñalar.

sta·bil·i·ty [stə'biliti] estabilidad *f*.

sta·bi·li·za·tion [steibilai'zeiʃn] estabilización *f*; **sta·bi·lize** ['steibilaiz] estabilizar; **'sta·bi·liz·er** estabilizador *m*.

sta·ble[1] ['steibl] ☐ estable.

sta·ble[2] [~] **1.** cuadra *f*; (*racing-*) caballeriza *f*; **2.** poner (*or* guardar) en una cuadra.

stack [stæk] **1.** ✗ niara *f*, hacina *f*; montón *m* (*a.* F), rimero *m*, pila *f*; ✗ pabellón *m* (de fusiles); canón *m* of *chimney*; **2.** ✗ hacinar; amontonar.

sta·di·um ['steidiəm] estadio *m*.

staff [stɑ:f] **1.** bastón *m*; palo *m*; *eccl. etc.* báculo *m*; *fig.* apoyo *m*; ♪ (*pl. staves* [steivz]) pentagrama *m*; ✗ estado *m* mayor; profesorado *m* of *school*; personal *m* of *office*; (*servants*) servidumbre *f*; **2.** proveer de personal.

stag [stæg] *zo.* ciervo *m*, venado *m*; ♦ especulador *m*; F soltero *m*.

stage [steidʒ] **1.** plataforma *f*, estrado *m*, tablado *m*; *thea.* escena *f*; *fig.* escenario *m*; *fig.* teatro *m*; (*stop*) parada *f*; posta *f*; fase *f*, etapa *f of progress*; *in* ⁓s por etapas; *in* (*or by*) *easy* ⁓s en cortas etapas; *go on the* ⁓ hacerse actor; **2.** *play* representar; *recovery* efectuar, organizar; **'⁓-'box** palco *m* de proscenio; **'⁓-coach** diligencia *f*; ⁓ **di·rec·tion** acotación *f*; **'⁓-door** entrada *f* de artistas; ⁓ **fright** miedo *m* al público; **'⁓-hand** tramoyista *m*; ⁓ **man·ag·er** director *m* de escena; **'stag·er:** *old* ⁓ veterano *m*; **'stag(e)·y** □ teatral.

stag·ger ['stægə] **1.** *v/i.* tambalear, titubear, hacer eses; *v/t.* asombrar, sorprender; *hours*; ⊕ escalonar; **2.** tambaleo *m*; *vet.* ⁓s *pl.* modorra *f*; **'stag·ger·ing** □ *fig.* asombroso.

stag·nan·cy ['stægnənsi] estancamiento *m*; **'stag·nant** □ estancado (*a. fig.*); paralizado; ✝ inactivo; **stag·nate** ['⁓neit] estancarse; paralizarse; **stag'na·tion** estancamiento *m* (*a. fig.*).

stag-par·ty ['stægpɑːti] F tertulia *f* de solteros.

stag·y ['steidʒi] □ teatral.

staid [steid] □ serio, formal; **'staid·ness** seriedad *f*.

stain [stein] **1.** mancha *f* (*a. fig.*); tinte *m*, tintura *f* (*a.* ⊕); **2.** manchar (se) (*a. fig.*); teñir, colorar (*a.* ⊕); ⁓ed glass vidrio *m* de color; **'stain·less** □ inmanchable; *fig.* inmaculado; ⊕ inoxidable.

stair [stɛə] peldaño *m*, escalón *m*; (*flight of*) tramo *m* de) ⁓s *pl.* escalera *f*; **'⁓-car·pet** alfombra *f* de escalera; **'⁓-case** = **'⁓-way** *Am.* escalera *f*; *moving* ⁓ escalera *f* móvil.

stake [steik] **1.** estaca *f*, poste *m*; (*bet*) (a)puesta *f*, parada *f*; *fig.* interés *m*; ⁓s *pl.* premio *m*; *at* ⁓ en juego; en peligro; *Am.* F *pull up* ⁓s mudar de casa; **2.** (*bet*) apostar (*on* a); ✝ aventurar, arriesgar; estacar *with wood* (*a.* ⁓ *off*, ⁓ *out*).

sta·lac·tite ['stæləktait] estalactita *f*.

stale [steil] *food* rancio, añejo, pasado; *bread* duro; *news* viejo; *air* viciado; *joke* mohoso; *p.* cansado.

stale·mate ['steil'meit] **1.** *chess:* tablas *f/pl.* por ahogo; *fig.* paralización *f*; *fig. reach* ⁓ llegar a un punto muerto; **2.** dar tablas por ahogo a.

stalk¹ [stɔːk] ♀ tallo *m*; (*cabbage-*) troncho *m*.

stalk² [⁓] *v/i.* andar con paso majestuoso; *v/t. hunt. etc.* cazar al acecho;

acechar; **'stalk·ing-horse** *fig.* pretexto *m*.

stall [stɔːl] **1.** ✗ pesebre *m*; establo *m*; (*market-*) puesto *m*, caseta *f*; *thea.* butaca *f*; *eccl.* sillería *f*; **2.** *v/t.* ⊕ parar, atascar; ✗ encerrar en establo; *v/i.* ⊕ pararse, atascarse; F buscar evasivas; **'⁓-fed** engordado en establo.

stal·lion ['stæljən] caballo *m* padre.

stal·wart ['stɔːlwət] **1.** (*sturdy*) fornido; *supporter etc.* leal; **2.** *pol.* partidario *m* leal.

sta·men ['steimen] estambre *m*; **stam·i·na** ['stæminə] vigor *m*, resistencia *f*.

stam·mer ['stæmə] **1.** tartamudear, balbucir; **2.** tartamudeo *m*, balbuceo *m*; **'stam·mer·er** tartamudo (*a f*) *m*.

stamp [stæmp] **1.** (*postage-*) sello *m*, estampilla *f S.Am.*; (*fiscal*) timbre *m*; marca *f*, impresión *f*; ⊕ cuño *m*; (*rubber-*) estampilla *f*; patada *f of foot*; (*kind*) temple *m*, calaña *f*; **2.** *v/t. letter* sellar, franquear; estampillar; estampar; imprimir *on memory*; *fig.* marcar, señalar; ⁓ *on* hollar, pisotear; ⁓ *out fire* apagar pateando; *fig.* extirpar; *v/i.* patear, patalear *disapprovingly*; (*horse*) piafar; **'⁓-al·bum** álbum *m* (para sellos); **'⁓-col'lect·ing** filatelia *f*; **'⁓-du·ty** impuesto *m* del timbre.

stam·pede [stæm'piːd] **1.** fuga *f* precipitada, estampida *f S.Am.*; movimiento *m* precipitado y unánime; **2.** (hacer) huir en desorden.

stance [stɑːns] postura *f*.

stanch [stɑːntʃ] **1.** restañar; **2.** *v.* **staunch 1.**

stan·chion ['stɑːnʃn] puntal *m*, montante *m*.

stand [stænd] **1.** [*irr.*] *v/i.* estar de pie; levantarse; (*be situated*) estar (situado); (*remain*) quedarse; (*remain in force*) mantenerse (en vigor); (*last*) (per)durar; (*stop*) pararse; (*measure*) medir; *how do we* ⁓? ¿cómo estamos?; ⁓ *firm* resistir, mantenerse firme; ⁓ *still* estarse quieto; ⁓ *to win* tener probabilidad de ganar; ⁓ *aside* apartarse; ⁓ *back* retroceder; moverse hacia atrás; estar apartado; ⁓ *by* estar alerta; estar cerca; estar a la expectativa; (*abide by*) atenerse a; (*support*) apoyar, sostener, no abandonar;

~ _for_ representar; significar; apoyar, apadrinar; _post, parl._ presentarse como candidato a; F aguantar; ~ _in_ ⚓ acercarse (_to_ a); suplir (_for_ a); ~ _in with_ declararse por; ~ _off_ apartarse (_a._ ⚓); ~ _out_ destacarse (_against sky etc._ contra); _esp. fig._ descollar, sobresalir; no ceder (_for_ hasta obtener); ~ _out against proposal etc._ oponerse a; ~ _out for_ insistir en; ~ _out to sea_ hacerse a la mar; ~ _over_ quedar en suspenso; ~ _to_ ✗ estar sobre las armas; _v. reason;_ ~ _up_ levantarse, ponerse de pie; ~ _up for_ defender; ~ _up to_ resistir resueltamente a; _test_ salir muy bien de; **2.** [_irr._] _v/t._ poner derecho; colocar; (_bear_) aguantar, soportar; _examination_ resistir a; _test_ salir muy bien de; F _drinks_ pagar, invitar a; _I can't_ ~ _him_ no lo puedo ver; _v. chance, ground; sl._ ~ _a p. up_ dar plantón a una p.; **3.** posición _f_, postura _f_; resistencia _f_; (_stall_) puesto _m_; quiosco _m_; _sport:_ tribuna _f_; (_exhibition_) stand _m_; tarima _f_; (_band-_) estrado _m_; ⊕ sostén _m_, pedestal _m_; estante _m_; (_taxi-_) parada _f_, punto _m_; _make a_ ~ resistir (_against_ a).

stand·ard ['stændəd] **1.** patrón _m_, norma _f_, pauta _f_; nivel _m_; modelo _m_; ⚘ árbol _m_ de tronco derecho; (_flag_) estandarte _m_, bandera _f_; gold ~ patrón _m_ oro; ~ _lamp_ lámpara _f_ de pie; ~ _of living_ nivel _m_ de vida; **2.** normal; corriente; standard, estándar; ~ _measure_ medida _f_ tipo; ~ _model_ modelo _m_ standard; ~ _work_ obra _f_ clásica; '**~-bear·er** abanderado _m_; _fig._ jefe _m_; caudillo _m_; **~-gauge** ['~geidʒ] via _f_ normal; **stand·ard·i·za·tion** ['~ai'zeiʃn] normalización _f_, estandar(d)ización _f_; '**stand·ard·ize** normalizar, regularizar, estandar(d)izar.

stand-by ['stændbai] recurso _m_ seguro, persona _f_ confiable, paño _m_ de lágrimas.

stand·ee [stæn'di:] _Am._ espectador _m_ que asiste de pie.

stand-in ['stændin] doble _m/f._

stand·ing ['stændiŋ] **1.** derecho, en (_or_ de) pie; _army, committee_ permanente; _grievance_ constante; _order_ vigente; _start_ parado; _water_ encharcado; ~ _order_ reglamento _m_; **2.** posición _f_; reputación _f_; importancia _f_; (_of_) _long_ ~ de mucho tiempo; '**~-room** sitio _m_ para estar de pie.

stand...: '**~-off** _Am._ reserva _f_; empate _m_; '**~-'off·ish** ☐ reservado; endiosado; poco amable; **~'pat·ter** _Am. pol._ F conservador _m_; '**~-pipe** columna _f_ de alimentación; '**~-point** punto _m_ de vista; '**~-still** parada _f_, paro _m_; alto _m_; inactividad _f_; _be at a_ ~ estar paralizado; _come to a_ ~ pararse, paralizarse.

stank [stæŋk] _pret. of_ stink 2.

stan·nic ['stænik] estánnico.

stan·za ['stænzə] estancia _f_, estrofa _f_.

sta·ple¹ ['steipl] **1.** producto _m_ principal; materia _f_ prima; asunto _m_ principal; fibra _f_ (textil); **2.** principal; corriente.

sta·ple² [~] grapa _f._

star [sta:] **1.** estrella _f_ (_a. fig._); _thea._ estrella _f_, vedette _f_, astro _m_; _typ._ asterisco _m_; _north_ ~ estrella _f_ del norte; _polar_ ~ estrella _f_ polar; ⚥_s and Stripes_ estrellas _f/pl._ y listas; **2.** _v/t._ adornar con estrellas; marcar con asterisco; (_film_) presentar como estrella; _v/i._ ser la estrella; **3.:** ~ _turn_ atracción _f_ especial (_or_ estelar).

star·board ['sta:bəd] **1.** estribor _m_; **2.** _rudder_ volver a estribor.

starch [sta:tʃ] **1.** almidón _m_; _biol._ fécula _f_; **2.** almidonar; '**starch·y** ☐ feculento; _fig._ estirado, entonado.

stare [steə] **1.** mirada _f_ fija; **2.** mirar fijamente (_at acc._); ~ _at_ clavar la vista en; _it's staring you in the face_ salta a la vista; **star·ing** ['~riŋ] ☐ que mira fijamente; _eye_ saltón.

stark [sta:k] (_stiff_) rígido; (_sheer_) completo, puro; severo; (_unadorned_) escueto; ~ _mad_ loco de atar; ~ _naked_ en cueros.

star·ling ['sta:liŋ] estornino _m_ pinto.

star·lit ['sta:lit] iluminado por las estrellas.

star·ring ['sta:riŋ] que presenta como estrella...

star·ry ['sta:ri] estrellado; '**~-'eyed** _fig._ inocentón, ingenuo; lleno de entusiasmo candoroso.

star-span·gled ['sta:spæŋgld]: _Am._ ⚥ _Banner_ bandera _f_ estrellada.

start [sta:t] **1.** comienzo _m_, principio _m_; (_departure_) salida _f_ (_a. of race_); (_advantage_) ventaja _f_; (_surprise_) sobresalto _m_; respingo _m of horse_; _for a_ ~ para empezar; _give a_ ~ (_race_) dar una ventaja; (_surprise_) sobresaltar; **2.** *v/i.* empezar, comenzar, principiar (*to inf. or ger.* a *inf.*); iniciarse; (*depart*) ponerse en camino, salir (*a. in race*); sobresaltarse, sobrecogerse *with surprise* (*at* a); (*motor*) arrancar, ponerse en marcha; ~ *on* emprender; *v/t.* empezar, principiar; iniciar; *motor* arrancar; *vehicle etc.* poner en marcha; *game* levantar; *race* dar la señal de salida a.

start·er ['stɑ:tə] *sport:* stárter *m*, juez *m* de salida; *mot.* (motor *m* de, botón *m* de) arranque *m*.

start·ing ['stɑ:tiŋ]: '~**-han·dle** manivela *f* (de arranque); '~**-point** punto *m* de partida; '~**-post** poste *m* de salida; '~**-switch** botón *m* de arranque.

star·tle ['stɑ:tl] asustar, sobrecoger; **'star·tling** □ alarmante; sorprendente.

star·va·tion [stɑ:'veiʃn] inanición *f*, hambre *f*; *attr.* ... de hambre; **starve** [stɑ:v] *v/i.* morir de hambre; padecer hambre; F tener mucha hambre; *v/t.* hacer morir de hambre; *fig.* privar (*of* de); ~ *out* hacer rendirse por hambre; **starve·ling** ['~liŋ] hambrón *adj. a. su. m* (-a *f*); **'starv·ing** hambriento, famélico.

state [steit] **1.** estado *m* (*a. pol.*), condición *f*; pompa *f*, fausto *m*; *in* ~ con gran pompa; *lie in* ~ estar de cuerpo presente; F *be in a* ~ estar aturrullado; **2.** estatal; del estado; público; *occasion* de gala; *Am.* ♀ *Department* Ministerio *m* de Asuntos Exteriores; *Am.* ♀ *House* edificio *m* del Estado; **3.** declarar, manifestar, afirmar; exponer; *law* formular; *problem* plantear; **'state·less** desnacionalizado; **'state·li·ness** majestad *f*, majestuosidad *f etc.*; **'state·ly** majestuoso, imponente; augusto; *carriage etc.* majestuoso, garboso; ~ *home* casa *f* solariega; **'state·ment** declaración *f*; informe *m*; exposición *f*; relación *f*; ♰ (*a.* ~ *of account*) estado *m* de cuenta(s); **'state·room** camarote *m*.

states·man ['steitsmən] estadista *m*, hombre *m* de estado; **'states·man·like** digno de estadista; **'states·man·ship** habilidad *f* de estadista; arte *m* de gobernar.

State(s') rights ['steit(s)raits] *Am.* derechos *m/pl.* de los Estados.

stat·ic ['stætik] □ *phys.* estático; *fig.* estancado, inactivo; **'stat·ics** *pl. or sg. phys.* estática *f*; *pl. radio:* parásitos *m/pl.*

sta·tion ['steiʃn] **1.** 🚂 *etc.* estación *f*; ⚓ apostadero *m* naval; puesto *m*; situación *f*; condición *f of life*; **2.** colocar, situar; ⚔ apostar, estacionar; **'sta·tion·ar·y** □ estacionario; ~ *engine* máquina *f* fija; **'sta·tion·er** papelero *m*; ~'s papelería *f*; ♀'s' *Hall registro de libros publicados* (*en Londres*) **'sta·tion·er·y** papelería *f*, papel *m* de escribir; **'sta·tion·mas·ter** jefe *m* de estación; **sta·tion wag·on** rubia *f*.

sta·tis·ti·cal [stə'tistikl] □ estadístico; **stat·is·ti·cian** [stætis'tiʃn] estadístico *m*; **sta·tis·tics** [stə'tistiks] *pl.* (*as science, sg.*) estadística *f*.

stat·u·ar·y ['stætjuəri] **1.** estatuario; **2.** (*p.*) estatuario *m*; (*art*) estatuaria *f*; (*collectively*) estatuas *f/pl.*; **stat·ue** ['~tju:] estatua *f*; **stat·u·esque** [~tju'esk] □ estatuario, escultural; **stat·u·ette** [~tju'et] figurina *f*.

stat·ure ['stætʃə] estatura *f*, talla *f*.

sta·tus ['steitəs] estado *m*, condición *f*, rango *m*.

stat·ute ['stætju:t] estatuto *m*; ~ *law* derecho *m* escrito; '~**-book** código *m* de leyes.

stat·u·to·ry ['stætjutəri] □ estatutario; legal.

staunch [stɔ:ntʃ] **1.** □ leal, firme, constante; **2.** *v.* stanch 1.

stave [steiv] **1.** duela *f of barrel*; palo *m*; ♪ pentagrama *m*; **2.** [*irr.*] (*mst* ~ *in*) desfondar; romper; ~ *off* evitar, conjurar, diferir.

staves [steivz] *pl. of staff* 1 pentagrama *m*.

stay [stei] **1.** estancia *f*, permanencia *f*; visita *f*; ⚖ suspensión *f*, prórroga *f*; ⚓ estay *m*; ⊕ sostén *m*; ~*s pl.* corsé *m*; **2.** *v/t.* detener; poner freno a; *hunger* matar, engañar; ⚖ suspender; ⊕ sostener; ~ *one's hand* contenerse; *v/i.* quedar(se), permanecer; hospedarse (*at* en); esperar (*for* hasta); pararse; *they* ~*ed for tea* quedaron a merendar con nosotros; ~ *away* ausentarse; ~ *behind* quedarse; ~ *in* quedarse en casa; ~ *on* quedarse; ~ *out* quedarse fuera; *fig.* no tomar parte (*of* en); *fig.* ~ *put* mantenerse en su lugar; no cejar; ~ *up* velar, no acostarse;

~ing power resistencia *f*; '~-at-home casero *m*, hogareño *m*; 'stay·er (*horse*) caballo *m* apto para carreras de distancia.

stead [sted]: *in his* ~ en su lugar; *stand a p. in good* ~ servirle a uno, serle útil a uno.

stead·fast ['stedfəst] ☐ constante, firme, resuelto; 'stead·fast·ness constancia *f*, resolución *f*.

stead·i·ness ['stedinis] constancia *f*; uniformidad *f etc.*

stead·y ['stedi] 1. ☐ firme, fijo; estable; regular; constante; uniforme; sostenido, ininterrumpido; *p.* juicioso; ✝ en calma; 2. estabilizar; afirmar; *nerves* calmar; 3. *Am.* F novio (a *f*) *m* formal.

steak [steik] biftec *m*; tajada *f*.

steal [sti:l] 1. [*irr.*] *v/t.* hurtar, robar; cautivar; *v/i.*: ~ *away* escabullirse; marcharse sigilosamente; 2. *Am.* robo *m* (*a.* 'steal·ing).

stealth [stelθ] cautela *f*, sigilo *m*; *by* ~ a escondidas; 'stealth·y ☐ sigiloso; furtivo; clandestino.

steam [sti:m] 1. vapor *m*; vaho *m*; *let off* ~ ⊕ descargar vapor; *fig.* desahogarse; 2. ... de vapor; 3. *v/i.* echar vapor; marchar (*or* funcionar) a vapor; navegar *etc.*; (*window*) empañarse; *v/t.* cocer al vapor; *window* empañar; 'steam·en·gine máquina *f* de vapor; 'steam·er ⚓ (buque *m* de) vapor *m*; 'steam-roll·er 1. apisonadora *f*; 2. *fig.* aplastar, arrollar; 'steam·ship = steamer; 'steam·y ☐ lleno de vapor, vaporoso; *window* empañado.

ste·a·rin ['stiərin] estearina *f*.

steed [sti:d] *lit.* corcel *m*.

steel [sti:l] 1. acero *m*; (*sharpener*) chaira *f*, eslabón *m*; 2. de acero; acerado; 3. ⊕ acerar; *fig.* ~ *o.s.* acorazarse; '~-clad revestido de acero; 'steel·y *mst fig.* inflexible; 'steel·yard romana *f*.

steep[1] [sti:p] ☐ empinado, escarpado, abrupto; F exorbitante, excesivo.

steep[2] [~] empapar (*a. fig.*); remojar.

stee·ple ['sti:pl] campanario *m*; aguja *f*; '~-chase carrera *f* de obstáculos; (*horses*) carrera *f* de vallas.

steep·ness ['sti:pnis] lo empinado *etc.*

steer[1] [stiə] 🐂 buey *m*; novillo *m*.

steer[2] [~] dirigir; *car* conducir; *ship*

gobernar; ~ *for* dirigirse a; ~ *clear of* evitar.

steer·age ['stiəridʒ] entrepuente *m*; '~-way empuje *m* del buque (necesario para gobernar).

steer·ing ['stiərin] dirección *f*; ⚓ gobierno *m*; '~-arm *mot.* brazo *m* de dirección; '~-col·umn columna *f* de dirección; '~-wheel volante *m*.

steers·man ['stiəzmən] timonero *m*.

stel·lar ['stelə] estelar.

stem[1] [stem] 1. 🌿 tallo *m*; ⊕ vástago *m*; *gr.* tema *m*; pie *m of glass*; cañón *m of pipe*; 2.: ~ *from* provenir de, resultar de.

stem[2] [~] 1. ⚓ roda *f*, tajamar *m*; *from* ~ *to stern* de proa a popa; 2. *water* represar; *fig.* detener, contener.

stench [stentʃ] hedor *m*. [tener.]

sten·cil ['stensl] 1. ⊕ patrón *m* picado; estarcido *m*; (*typing*) clichém; 2. estarcir.

ste·nog·ra·pher [ste'nɔgrəfə] taquígrafo (a *f*) *m*; ste·nog·ra·phy [ste'nɔgrəfi] taquigrafía *f*.

step[1] [step] 1. paso *m* (*a. fig.*); (*stair*) peldaño *m*, escalón *m*, grada *f*; estribo *m of car*; *fig.* medida *f*, gestión *f*; (*a. flight of*) ~s *pl.* escalera *f*, escalinata *f*; ~s *pl.* (*ladder*) escalera *f* de tijera; *at every* ~ a cada paso; *in* ~ llevando el paso; *fig.* de acuerdo (*with* con); *take* ~s tomar medidas (*to para*); *watch one's* ~ ir con tiento; 2. *v/i.* dar un paso; andar, ir; pisar; ~ *aside* apartarse, hacerse a un lado; ~ *back* retroceder; dar un paso hacia atrás; ~ *down* bajar; *fig.* ceder su puesto; ~ *in* intervenir; ~ *in!* ¡adelante!; ~ *on* pisar; F ~ *on it!* ¡date prisa!; ~ *out* apretar el paso; ~ *this way* haga el favor de pasar por aquí; *v/t.* escalonar; *distance* medir a pasos (*a.* ~ *out*); ~ *up* aumentar, elevar.

step[2] [~]: '~-fa·ther padrastro *m*; '~-son hijastro *m*; *etc.*

steppe [step] estepa *f*.

step·ping-stone ['stepiŋstoun] pasadera *f*; *fig.* escalón *m*.

ster·e·o... ['stiriə]: '~-phon·ic ☐ estereofónico; '~-scope estereoscopio *m*; '~-type 1. clisé *m*, estereotipo *m*; 2. clisar, estereotipar (*a. fig.*).

ster·ile ['sterail] estéril; ste·ril·i·ty [~'riliti] esterilidad *f*; ster·i·lize ['~rilaiz] esterilizar.

ster·ling ['stə:liŋ] **1.** genuino, de ley; *fig.* confiable; *pound ~* libra *f* esterlina; **2.** libras *f/pl.* esterlinas.

stern¹ [stə:n] □ severo, rígido; austero.

stern² [⌐] ⚓ popa *f*. [tero.]

stern·ness ['stə:nnis] severidad *f*, rigidez *f*.

ster·num ['stə:nəm] esternón *m*.

steth·o·scope ['steθəskoup] estetoscopio *m*.

ste·ve·dore ['sti:vidɔ:] estibador *m*.

stew [stju:] **1.** *v/t.* estofar; guisar; *v i. (tea)* pasarse; **2.** estofado *m*; guisado *m*; F apuro *m*.

stew·ard ['stjuəd] mayordomo *m*; administrador *m*; ⚓, ✈ camarero *m*; **'stew·ard·ess** ⚓ camarera *f*; ✈ azafata *f*, aeromoza *f*.

stew...: **'~-pan,** **'~-pot** cazuela *f*, cacerola *f*.

stick¹ [stik] **1.** palo *m*, vara *f*; porra *f*; (*walking-*) bastón *m*; barra *f* of soap etc.; F old *~* tío *m*; *~s pl.* leña *f*; **2.** 𝄞 apoyar con estacas.

stick² [⌐] [*irr.*] **1.** *v/i.* pegarse, adherirse (to a); atascarse *in mud etc.*; estar prendido; pararse, quedar parado; (*stay*) quedarse, permanecer; F *~ around* esperar por ahí; *~ at* persistir en; sentir escrúpulo por; *~ at nothing* no tener escrúpulos, no pararse en barras; *~ fast* quedarse clavado; *~ out* (sobre)salir; F ser evidente; *~ out for* insistir en, no ceder hasta obtener; F *~ to prin·ciple* aferrarse a; *p.* permanecer fiel a; (*follow*) *p.* pegarse a, seguir de cerca; *~ together* quedarse unidos; *~ ub* asomarse por encima; (sobre)salir; (*hair etc.*) estar de punta; F *~ up for* defender; **2.** *v/t.* (*gum etc.*) pegar, encolar (*a. ~ down, ~ together*); (*thrust*) clavar, hincar; (*pierce*) picar; F poner, meter; *~ out* asomar, sacar; *sl. ~ it (out)* aguantar(lo) hasta el final; *sl. ~ up* atracar, encañonar; **'stick·er** F persona *f* perseverante; *Am.* etiqueta *f* engomada; **'stick·i·ness** pegajosidad *f*; viscosidad *f*; **'stick·ing-plas·ter** esparadrapo *m*; **'stick-in-the-mud** tardón *m*; retrógrado *m*.

stick·le·back ['stiklbæk] espinoso *m*; **'stick·ler** rigorista *m/f* (*for* en cuanto a).

stick-up ['stikʌp] *Am. sl.* atraco *m*.

stick·y ['stiki] □ pegajoso; viscoso; F difícil; obstinado; *sl. end* triste.

stiff [stif] **1.** □ tieso, rígido; *collar* duro, almidonado; *door, joint* duro, tieso; *limb* entumecido; aterido *with cold*; *paste* espeso; *breeze* fuerte; *task, climb* difícil; *price* subido; *manner* estirado; F *bored ~* aburrido como una ostra; F *scared ~* muerto de miedo; **2.** *Am. sl.* cadáver *m*; **'stiff·en** atiesar; endurecer(se); (*limb*) entumecerse; *morale etc.* fortalecer(se); **'stiff·ness** entumecimiento *m of limb*; tiesura *f etc.*

sti·fle¹ ['staifl] *vet.* babilla *f*.

sti·fle² [⌐] sofocar(se), ahogar(se); *fig.* suprimir; **'sti·fling** sofocante, bochornoso.

stig·ma ['stigmə] *all senses:* estigma *m*; **'stig·ma·tize** estigmatizar.

stile [stail] escalera *f* para pasar una cerca; △ montante *m*.

sti·let·to [sti'letou] estilete *m*.

still¹ [stil] **1.** *adj.* inmóvil; quieto, tranquilo; silencioso; *wine* no espumoso; **2.** *su. poet.* calma *f*, silencio *m*; *film:* vista *f* fija; **3.** *adv.* todavía, aún; **4.** *cj.* sin embargo, con todo; **5.** calmar, tranquilizar; acallar.

still² [⌐] alambique *m*.

still...: **'~-born** nacido muerto; *~ life* bodegón *m*, naturaleza *f* muerta; **'still·ness** inmovilidad *f*; quietud *f*; **'still·y** *poet.* = *still¹* 1.

stilt [stilt] zanco *m*; **'stilt·ed** hinchado, afectado.

stim·u·lant ['stimjulənt] estimulante *adj. a. su. m*; **stim·u·late** ['~leit] estimular (*to* a); **stim·u·la·tion** estímulo *m*; excitación *f*; **stim·u·la·tive** ['~lətiv] estimulador; **stim·u·lus** ['~ləs] estímulo *m*.

sting [stiŋ] **1.** 🌿, zo. aguijón *m*; picadura *f*; escozor *m*, picazón *m*; *fig.* punzada *f*; **2.** [*irr.*] picar; punzar; escocer; *sl.* clavar; **sting·i·ness** ['stindʒinis] tacañería *f*; **sting·(ing)-net·tle** ['stiŋ(iŋ)netl] ortiga *f*; **stin·gy** ['stindʒi] □ tacaño, cicatero.

stink [stiŋk] **1.** hedor *m*, mal olor *m*; **2.** *v/i.* heder, oler mal (*of* a); *sl.* ser ricacho; *v/t.: ~ out* apestar.

stint [stint] **1.** límite *m*, restricción *f*; destajo *m of work*; tarea *f*; **2.** limitar, restringir; *~ o.s.* estrecharse.

sti·pend ['staipend] estipendio *m*; **sti'pen·di·ar·y** [⌐dʒəri] estipendiario *adj. a. su. m*.

stip·ple ['stipl] puntear, granear.

stip·u·late ['stipjuleit] estipular (*for acc.*); **stip·u·la·tion** estipulación *f.*

stir[1] [stə:] **1.** agitación *f.*; alboroto *m*; conmoción *f*, gran interés *m*; movimiento *m*; meneo *m*; hurgonada *f with poker; cause a ~, make a ~* hacer ruido; **2.** *v/t.* (re)mover; agitar; *fire* hurgar; *liquid* revolver; *emotions* conmover; ~ *up passions* excitar; *rebellion* fomentar; *v/i.* moverse, menearse; *nobody is ~ring* están todavía en cama.

stir[2] [~] *sl.* chirona *f.*

stir·ring ['stə:riŋ] □ emocionante, conmovedor.

stir·rup ['stirəp] estribo *m.*

stitch [stitʃ] **1.** punto *m*, puntada *f*; *⚛* punzada *f*; *be in ~es* desternillarse de risa; **2.** coser (*a. ⚛*), hilvanar.

stoat [stout] armiño *m.*

stock [stɔk] **1.** (*family*) estirpe *f*, raza *f*; *♀* tronco *m of tree*, cepa *f of vine*; *♀* (*grafting*) patrón *m*; *♀* (*flower*) alhelí *m*; (*handle*) mango *m*; *✂* caja *f*; *♰* surtido *m*, existencias *f/pl.*; *♰* capital *m*; *⚒* (*a. live ~*) ganado *m*; (*a. dead ~*) aperos *m/pl.*; *♰ ~s pl.* acciones *f/pl.*, valores *m/pl.*; *⚓ ~s pl.* astillero *m*; *~s pl.* (*punishment*) cepo *m*; *in ~* en almacén, en existencia; *on the ~s ⚓* en vía de construcción; *fig.* en preparación; *take ~ ♰* hacer inventario (*of* de); *v.* asesorarse (*of* de); *v. rolling-~;* **2.** consagrado; acostumbrado; *phrase* hecho; *thea.* de repertorio; **3.** proveer, abastecer; *♰* tener existencias de; *pond etc.* poblar (*with* de); *~ up* almacenar; acumular.

stock·ade [stɔ'keid] estacada *f.*

stock…: '~**breed·er** ganadero *m*; '~**brok·er** bolsista *m*, agente *m* de bolsa; ~ **ex·change** bolsa *f*; '~**hold·er** accionista *m/f.*

stock·i·net ['stɔkinet] tela *f* de punto. [*length*] calceta *f.*

stock·ing ['stɔkiŋ] media *f*; (*knee-*

stock·ist ['stɔkist] distribuidor *m.*

stock…: '~**job·ber** agiotista *m*; '~**job·bing** agiotaje *m*; '~**pile** acumular; '~**still** completamente inmóvil; '~**tak·ing** inventario *m*, balance *m*; ~ *sale* venta *f* por balance; '**stock·y** rechoncho, achaparrado.

stodg·y ['stɔdʒi] □ indigesto, pesado.

sto·ic ['stouik] estoico *adj.* (*a.* '**sto·i·cal** □) *a. su. m*; '**sto·i·cism** estoicismo *m.*

stoke [stouk] cargar, cebar (*a. fig.*), echar carbón a; atizar; '**stok·er** fogonero *m.*

stole[1] [stoul] estola *f.*

stole[2] [~] *pret.*, '**sto·len** *p.p. of steal.*

stol·id ['stɔlid] □ impasible, imperturbable; **sto·lid·i·ty** [~'liditi] impasibilidad *f.*

stom·ach ['stʌmək] **1.** estómago *m*; *fig.* apetito *m*, deseo *m* (*for* de); **2.** *fig.* tragar, aguantar; '**stom·ach·er** peto *m*; **sto·mach·ic** [stə'mækik] □ estomacal *adj. a. su. m.*

stomp [stɔmp] pisar muy fuerte.

stone [stoun] **1.** piedra *f*; hueso *m of fruit;* (*commemorative*) lápida *f*; *♰* cálculo *m*; (*weight*) catorce libras *f/pl.*; **2.** … de piedra; **3.** lapidar, apedrear; *fruit* deshuesar; '~'**blind** completamente ciego; '~**crop** pan *m* de cuco; '~'**dead** más muerto que una piedra; '~'**deaf** sordo como una tapia; '~**ma·son** albañil *m*; cantero *m*; '~**pit**, '~**quar·ry** cantera *f*; '~'**wall·ing** *fig.* táctica *f* de cerrojo; '~**ware** gres *m.*

ston·y ['stouni] *ground* pedregoso; *material* pétreo; *fig. glance* glacial; *heart* empedernido; F ~ *broke* sin un cuarto.

stood [stud] *pret.* a. *p.p. of stand.*

stooge [stu:dʒ] *♩* paniaguado *m*, hombre *m* de paja.

stool [stu:l] taburete *m*, escabel *m*; *♀* planta *f* madre; *♰* evacuación *f*; (*folding*) silla *f* de tijera; *fall between two ~s* terminar siendo ni lo uno ni lo otro; fracasar por no saber a qué carta quedarse; '~**pi·geon** *esp. Am.* soplón *m*, espía *m.*

stoop [stu:p] **1.** *v/i.* encorvarse, inclinarse; (*permanently*) ser cargado de espaldas; *fig.* rebajarse (*to* a); *v/t.* inclinar, bajar; **2.** cargazón *f* de espaldas; inclinación *f*; *Am.* escalinata *f* de entrada.

stop [stɔp] **1.** *v/t.* detener, parar; *abuse, process etc.* poner fin a; *payment* suspender; *supply* cortar, interrumpir; *teeth* empastar; (*forbid*) prohibir, poner fin a; (*a. up*) tapar, cegar; obstruir; ~ *s.o. talking* impedirle a uno hablar; ~ *s.o. going* prohibirle a uno ir; *v/i.* parar(se), detenerse; hacer alto; terminar(se), acabarse; cortarse; (stay) quedarse, hospedarse (at en); ~ ger. dejar de inf.; I ~ped going dejé de ir; it has ~ped raining ha dejado de llover; ~ at nothing no pararse en barras; ~ dead pararse en seco; ~ in no salir; F ~ off interrumpir el viaje (at en); Am. ~ over quedar la noche; 2. parada f; alto m; ⊕ tope m, retén m; ♩ registro m of organ; ♩ llave f; gr. (a. full ~) punto m; come to a ~ venir a parar; put a ~ to poner fin a; '~·**cock** llave f de cierre; '~·**gap** recurso m provisional; (p.) tapa(a)gujeros m; '~·**off**, '~·**o·ver** Am. parada f intermedia; '**stop·page** cesación f; detención f; paro m, suspensión f of work etc.; interrupción f; ⊕ obstrucción f; '**stop·per** 1. tapón m; ⊕ taco m; radio: ~ circuit circuito m anti-resonante; 2. tap(on)ar; '**stop·ping** empaste m of tooth; ~ train tren m ómnibus; '**stop-press news** "al cerrar la edición"; '**stop-watch** cronómetro m.

stor·age ['stɔ:ridʒ] almacenaje m, depósito m; ~ battery acumulador m. **store** [stɔ:] 1. provisión f; (reserve) repuesto m; (~house)§almacén m, depósito m; Am. tienda f; ~s pl. provisiones f/pl., víveres m/pl.; ✕ ~s pl. pertrechos m/pl.; in ~ en almacén, en reserva; be in ~ for a p. esperarle a una p.; set (or put) great ~ by conceder mucha importancia a; 2. almacenar; abastecer; ~ away tener en reserva, guardar, archivar; ~ up amontonar, acumular; '~·**house** almacén m, depósito m; fig. mina f; '~·**keep·er** almacenero m; Am. tendero m; '~·**room** despensa f; ⚓ pañol m. **sto·r(e)y** ['stɔ:ri] piso m. **sto·ried** ['stɔ:rid] de ... pisos. **stork** [stɔ:k] cigüeña f. **storm** [stɔ:m] 1. tormenta f, tempestad f (a. fig.), borrasca f; take by ~ tomar por asalto; ~ cloud nubarrón m; ~ troops pl. tropas f/pl. de asalto; 2. v/t. ✕ asaltar, tomar por asalto; v/i. rabiar, enfurecerse, tronar (at contra); '**storm·y** □ tempestuoso, borrascoso (a. fig.). **sto·ry** ['stɔ:ri] cuento m, histori(et)a f; (joke) chiste m; anécdota f; argumento m, trama f of novel etc.; F mentira f, embuste m; short ~

cuento m; that's (quite) another ~ es harina de otro costal. **sto·ry-tell·er** ['stɔ:ritelə] cuentista m/f; F embustero (a f) m. **stout** [staut] 1. □ robusto, sólido, macizo; p. gordo, corpulento; fig. animoso, valiente; 2. stout m (cerveza fuerte); '~·'**heart·ed** □ valiente; '**stout·ness** gordura f, corpulencia f. **stove** [stouv] 1. estufa f; hornillo m; cocina f de gas etc.; 2. pret. a. p.p. of stave 2; '~·**pipe** tubo m de estufa; Am. F chistera f. **stow** [stou] v/t. meter; esconder; ⚓ arrumar; v/i.: ~ away viajar de polizón; '**stow·age** ⚓ arrumaje m; ⚓ (place) bodega f; '**stow·a·way** polizón m. **strad·dle** ['strædl] esparrancarse encima de; horse montar a horcajadas; ✕ target cubrir, caer a ambos lados de; Am. favorecer a ambos lados en. **strafe** [strɑ:f] bombardear. **strag·gle** ['strægl] rezagarse; extraviarse; vagar; ♧ lozanear; '**strag·gler** rezagado m; ✕ extraviado m; '**strag·gling** □ disperso; desordenado. **straight** [streit] 1. adj. derecho, recto; back erguido; hair lacio; (honest) honrado; answer franco, directo; face serio, impasible; Am. drink sin mezcla; pol. fight sencillo, de dos candidatos; Am. pol. decidido, intransigente; put ~ arreglar; sport: the ~ la recta; 2. adv. derecho; directamente; con franqueza; ~ ahead, ~ on todo seguido; ~ away en seguida; ~ off sin interrupción, de un tirón; F go ~ enmendarse; '**straight·en** v/t. enderezar (a. ~ out); fig. arreglar (a. ~ out); v/i.: ~ up enderezarse; **straight·for·ward** [~'fɔ:wəd] □ honrado, franco; (easy) sencillo. **strain¹** [strein] 1. tensión f, tirantez f; esfuerzo m grande; ⊕ deformación f; ✂ torcedura f of muscle; ✂ agotamiento m nervioso; ♩ ~s pl. aire m, melodía f, compases m/pl.; put a great ~ on someter a gran esfuerzo; 2. v/t. estirar, tender con fuerza, poner tirante; ⊕ machine deformar; ⊕ (filter) colar, filtrar; meaning forzar; ✂ muscle torcer; ✂ eyes forzar, cansar; ~ed *relations* tirante; *v/i.* esforzarse (*after* por conseguir; *at* tirando de).

strain² [~] (*race*) linaje *m*, raza *f*; vena *f of madness*; (*style*) tono *m*, estilo *m*.

strain·er ['streinə] colador *m*.

strait [streit] **1.** *geog.* estrecho *m* (*a.* ~s *pl.*); *fig.* ~s *pl.* estrecheces *f/pl.*, apuro *m*; *in dire* ~s en el mayor apuro; **2.**: ~ *jacket* camisa *f* de fuerza; **'strait·en** estrechar; *in* ~ed *circumstances* apurado, en la necesidad; **strait-laced** ['~leist] gazmoño, remilgado, pudibundo.

strand¹ [strænd] **1.** *poet.* playa *f*, ribera *f*; **2.** ♫ varar(se), encallar; ~ed *fig.* desamparado; inmovilizado.

strand² [~] brizna *f*;' ramal *m of rope*; hebra *f*.

strange [streindʒ] □ extraño, raro, peregrino; desconocido; nuevo, no acostumbrado; *it is* ~ *he has not come* es raro que no haya venido, me extraña que no haya venido; **'strange·ness** extrañeza *f*, rareza *f*; novedad *f*; **'stran·ger** desconocido (a *f*) *m*; forastero (a *f*) *m*; *be no* ~ *to* conocer bien.

stran·gle ['stræŋgl] estrangular; *fig.* ahogar; **'~·hold** *sport*: collar *m* de fuerza; *fig.* dominio *m* completo; *have a* ~ *on* tener asido por la garganta; *fig.* dominar completamente.

stran·gu·late ['stræŋgjuleit] ♣ estrangular; **stran·gu·la·tion** estrangulación *f* (*a.* ♣).

strap [stræp] **1.** correa *f*; tira *f*, banda *f*; **2.** (*tie*) atar con correa; (*beat*) azotar con una correa; **'strap·ping** robusto, fornido.

strat·a·gem ['strætidʒəm] estratagema *f*.

stra·te·gic [strə'ti:dʒik] □ estratégico; **strat·e·gist** ['strætidʒist] estratega *m*; **'strat·e·gy** estrategia *f*.

strat·i·fy ['strætifai] estratificar(se).

stra·to·cruis·er ['streitoukru:zə] avión *m* estratosférico.

strat·o·sphere ['streitousfiə] estratosfera *f*. [estrato *m*; *fig.* capa *f*.]

stra·tum, *pl.* **stra·ta** ['streitə(m)]/

straw [strɔ:] **1.** paja *f*; (*drinking-*) pajita *f*; (*mst* ~ *hat*) sombrero *m* de paja; *it's the last* ~ no faltaba más; **2.** ... de paja; (*colour*) pajizo; ~ *vote Am. pol.* votación *f* de tanteo; **'~·ber·ry** fresón *m*; (*wild*) fresa *f*; ~ *bed* fresal *m*.

stray [strei] **1.** extraviarse; perderse; descarriarse; ~ *from* apartarse de; **2.** (*a.* ~ed) extraviado; errante; aislado; *bullet* perdido; **3.** animal *m* extraviado; *radio:* ~s *pl.* parásitos *m/pl.*

streak [stri:k] **1.** raya *f*, lista *f*; vena *f of madness*; racha *f of luck*; ~ *of lightning* rayo *m* (*a. fig*); **2.** *v/t.* rayar, listar; *v/i.* pasar *etc.* como un rayo; **'streak·y** □ rayado, listado; *bacon* entreverado; *shot* afortunado.

stream [stri:m] **1.** arroyo *m*; corriente *f*; flujo *m*, chorro *m*; *fig.* oleada *f*, torrente *m*; A ~ grupo *m* A; **2.** *v/i.* correr, fluir; ondear, flotar *in wind*; ~ *forth*, ~ *out* brotar, chorrear; (*people etc.*) salir a torrentes; *her eyes were* ~*ing* lloraba a mares; *her face was* ~*ing with tears* su cara estaba bañada de lágrimas; *v/t.* arrojar, derramar; *pupils* clasificar; **'stream·er** flámula *f*; (*paper*) serpentina *f*; ♫ gallardete *m*.

stream·line ['stri:mlain] aerodinamizar; *fig.* coordinar, perfeccionar; ~d perfilado, aerodinámico.

street [stri:t] calle *f*; *attr.* callejero; *Am. on easy* ~ con el bolsillo lastrado; **'~·car** *Am.* tranvía *m*; **'~·walk·er** prostituta *f* de calle.

strength [streŋθ] fuerza *f*; intensidad *f*; resistencia *f*; ⚔ *etc.* número *m*; *on the* ~ *of* fundándose en; **'strength·en** fortalecer(se), reforzar(se), fortificar(se).

stren·u·ous ['strenjuəs] □ vigoroso, enérgico; arduo.

strep·to·my·cin [streptou'maisin] estreptomicina *f*.

stress [stres] **1.** esfuerzo *m*; presión *f*, compulsión *f*; ♣ fatiga *f* (nerviosa); ⊕ tensión *f*, carga *f*; *rhet.* énfasis *m*; *gr.* acento *m*; *lay* ~ (*up*)*on* insistir en; **2.** ⊕ cargar; *rhet.* insistir en, recalcar; *gr.* acentuar.

stretch [stretʃ] **1.** extender(se), estirar(se); alargar(se); dilatar(se), ensanchar(se); *hand etc.* tender(se) (*mst* ~ *out*); *meaning etc.* forzar, violentar; desperezarse *after sleep*; *limb* desentorpecerse; ~ *out on the ground* tenderse en el suelo); **2.** extensión *f*; (*act of stretching*) estirón *m*; ensanche *m*; esfuerzo *m of imagination*; (*distance*) trecho *m*; (*time*) período *m*; *at a* ~ de un tirón;

'**stretch·er** ⊕ ensanchador *m*; ⚒
camilla *f*; ⚓ soga *f*.
strew [stru:] [*irr.*] esparcir; derramar; *ground etc.* sembrar (*with* de);
strewn [stru:n] *p.p. of* strew.
stri·ate ['straiit], **stri·at·ed** [strai-'eitid] estriado.
strick·en ['strikən] afligido (*with* por).
strict [strikt] □ estricto; riguroso; severo; terminante; *~ly speaking* en rigor; '**strict·ness** rigor *m*; severidad *f*; **stric·ture** ['~tʃə] censura *f*; ⚒ constricción *f*.
stride [straid] 1. [*irr.*] *v/t. horse* montar a horcajadas; *v/i.* caminar a paso largo (*a. ~ along*), andar a trancos; 2. zancada *f*, tranco *m*; *get into one's ~* alcanzar el ritmo acostumbrado; *take it in one's ~* sabérselo tomar bien.
stri·dent ['straidnt] □ estridente.
strife [straif] *lit.* disensión *f*, contienda *f*.
strike [straik] 1. huelga *f*; *Am.* F descubrimiento *m* repentino *of oil etc.*; *Am. baseball*: golpe *m*; *be on ~* estar en huelga; *go on ~* ponerse en huelga; 2. [*irr.*] *v/t.* golpear; pegar; herir; *fig.* impresionar; *fig.* dar con; *attitude* tomar, adoptar, asumir; ⚓ *balance* hacer; ⚓ *bargain* cerrar; *blow* asestar; ⚓ *flag* arriar; (*clock*) *hour* dar; *match* frotar, encender; *medal* acuñar; ⚓ *mine* chocar con; *oil* descubrir; ⚒ *root* echar; *work* abandonar; *~ down* derribar; *~ off* borrar; cercenar; quitar de golpe; *~ out* borrar, tachar; *~ up* ♪ iniciar, empezar a tocar; *conversation* entablar; *friendship* trabar; *v/i.* golpear; chocar; ponerse (*or* estar) en huelga; (*clock*) dar (la una *etc.*); (*bell*) sonar; ⚒ echar raíces; ⚓ encallar *on reef*; ⚓ (*flag*) arriar bandera; *~ at* tratar de golpear; *fig.* acometer, amenazar; *~ home* herir en lo vivo; dar en el blanco; *~ into* penetrar en; *~ out on one's own* campear por sus respetos; *~ up* ♪ empezar a tocar; '**~-break·er** esquirol *m*; '**strik·er** huelguista *m/f*; ⊕ percutor *m*.
strik·ing ['straikiŋ] □ impresionante; sorprendente; *colour etc.* llamativo.
string [striŋ] 1. cuerda *f* (*a.* ♪, *a. bow-*); sarta *f of pearls, lies*; (*row*) hilera *f*, fila *f*; ristra *f of onions etc.*; retahíla *f of curses*; ⚒ fibra *f*, nervio *m*; *Am.* F condición *f*; *~s pl.* ♪ instrumentos *m/pl.* de cuerda; *have two ~s to one's bow* tener dos cuerdas en su arco; F *pull ~s* tocar resortes, mover palancas; 2. *violin* encordar; *pearls etc.* ensartar; *Am. sl.* hacer fisga a; *~ out* extender; *sl. ~ up* ahorcar; *~ band*, *~ or·ches·tra* orquesta *f* de cuerdas; **stringed** ♪ ... de cuerda(s).
strin·gen·cy ['strindʒənsi] rigor *m*, severidad *f*; ⚓ tirantez *f*; '**strin·gent** □ riguroso, estricto, severo; ⚓ tirante.
string·y ['striŋi] fibroso.
strip [strip] 1. *v/t.* despojar (*of* de); *p.* desnudar; *clothes* quitar, despojarse de (*a. ~ off*); *gears* estropear; ⊕ desmontar; *v/i.* desnudarse; 2. tira *f*; faja *f*; *comic ~* tira *f* cómica.
stripe [straip] 1. raya *f*, lista *f*; banda *f*; ⚔ galón *m*; 2. rayar, listar.
strip·ling ['stripliŋ] mozuelo *m*.
strive [straiv] [*irr.*] esforzarse (*to* por); luchar (*against* contra); afanarse (*after, for* por conseguir); **striv·en** ['strivn] *p.p. of* strive.
strode [stroud] *pret. of* stride 1.
stroke [strouk] 1. golpe *m* (*a. sport*); jugada *f*; estilo *m of swimming*; brazada *f of swimmer*; remada *f of oar*; (*oarsman*) primer remero *m*; (*caress*) caricia *f*; ⊕ carrera *f*; ⚒ ataque *m* fulminante, apoplejía *f*; campanada *f of bell*; pincelada *f of brush*; rasgo *m*, plumazo *m of pen* (*a. fig.*); *~ of genius* rasgo *m* de ingenio; *~ of lightning* rayo *m*; *~ of luck* racha *f* de suerte; *at a ~* de un golpe; *I haven't done a ~* (*of work*) no he hecho absolutamente nada; 2. acariciar; *chin* pasar la mano sobre.
stroll [stroul] 1. pasearse, deambular, callejear; 2. paseo *m*; *take a ~* dar un paseo; '**stroll·er** paseante *m/f*; *Am.* cochecito *m*; '**stroll·ing** *actor etc.* ambulante.
strong [strɔŋ] □ fuerte; recio, robusto; *accent* marcado; *conviction* profundo; *drink* alcohólico; *emotion* intenso; *language* indecente; fuerte; *situation* dramático; *supporter* acérrimo; *tea* cargado; *terms* enfático; *verb* irregular, fuerte; *they were*

100 ~ eran 100, ascendían a 100; *feel ~ly about* sentir profundamente *acc.*; F *going* ~ sin perder fuerza; lo bien de siempre; '~-**box** caja *f* de caudales); '~-**hold** fortaleza *f*, plaza *f* fuerte; *fig.* baluarte *m*; '~-**point** fuerte *m*; '~-**room** cámara *f* acorazada; '~-'**willed** obstinado.

strop [strɔp] **1.** suavizador *m*; **2.** suavizar.

stro·phe ['stroufi] estrofa *f*.

strove [strouv] *pret. of* strive.

struck[strʌk] *pret. a. p.p. of* strike 2.

struc·tur·al ['strʌktʃərəl] □ estructural; **struc·ture** ['~tʃə] estructura *f*; construcción *f*.

strug·gle ['strʌgl] **1.** luchar (*to, for* por); esforzarse (*to* por); **2.** lucha *f* (*for* por); contienda *f*; esfuerzo *m*.

strum [strʌm] *v/t.* guitar rasguear (sin arte) *v/i.* cencerrear.

strum·pet ['strʌmpit] ramera *f*.

strung [strʌŋ] *pret. a. p.p. of* string 2.

strut [strʌt] **1.** *v/i.* pavonearse, contonearse; *v/t.* ⊕ apuntalar; **2.** (*walk*) contoneo *m*; ⊕ puntal *m*, riostra *f*, tornapunta *f*.

strych·nine ['strikni:n] estricnina *f*.

stub [stʌb] **1.** ✒ tocón *m*; colilla *f of cigarette*; cabo *m of pencil*; talón *m of cheque*; **2.** *land* limpiar (arrancando los troncos); *trunks* desarraigar (*mst* ~ *up*); ~ *out cigarette* apagar; ~ *one's toe* dar un tropezón.

stub·ble ['stʌbl] rastrojo *m*.

stub·bly ['stʌbli] *chin* cerdoso.

stub·born ['stʌbən] □ tenaz, inflexible; *b.s.* terco, testarudo, porfiado; '**stub·born·ness** tenacidad *f*; *b.s.* terquedad *f*, testarudez *f*.

stuc·co ['stʌkou] **1.** estuco *m*; **2.** estucar.

stuck [stʌk] *pret. a. p.p. of* stick 2; *Am.* F ~ *on* chalado por; '~-'**up** empingorotado, finchado, engreído.

stud[1] [stʌd] **1.** tachón *m*; (*boot-*) taco *m*; botón *m* (de camisa); **2.** tachonar; *fig.* sembrar (*with* de).

stud[2] [~] caballeriza *f*; yeguada *f*; '~-**book** registro *m* genealógico de caballos); '~-**horse** caballo *m* padre.

stud·ding ['stʌdiŋ] ⚏ montantes *m/pl.* de tabique.

stu·dent ['stju:dənt] estudiante *m/f*; alumno (a *f*) *m*; investigador (-a *f*) *m;* '**stu·dent·ship** beca *f*.

stud·ied ['stʌdid] □ *insult* premeditado; *pose* afectado.

stu·di·o ['stju:diou] estudio *m* (*a. radio*); taller *m*; ~ *couch* sofá-cama *m*.

stu·di·ous ['stu:djəs] □ estudioso; asiduo, solícito; '**stu·di·ous·ness** aplicación *f*.

stud·y ['stʌdi] **1.** estudio *m* (*a. paint.*, ♪, *room*); (*room*) despacho *m*, gabinete *m*; **2.** estudiar.

stuff [stʌf] **1.** materia *f*, material *m*; (*cloth*) tela *f*, paño *m*; *fig.* cosa *f*; *fig.* F chismes *m/pl.*; ~ *and nonsense!* ¡ni hablar!; **2.** *v/t.* llenar, hinchar, atestar, atiborrar (*with* de); meter sin orden (*into* en); atascar, tapar; *fowl* rellenar; *animal* disecar; ~ *away sl.* zampar; *Am. sl.* ~*ed shirt* tragavirotes *m*; *v/i.* F atracarse, hartarse; '**stuff·ing** borra *f*; *cooking:* relleno *m*; '**stuff·y** □ *room* mal ventilado, sofocante; F relamido; *Am.* F picajoso.

stul·ti·fi·ca·tion [stʌltifi'keiʃn] anulación *f*; situación *f* ridícula; **stul·ti·fy** ['~fai] anular; hacer parecer ridículo; quitar importancia a.

stum·ble ['stʌmbl] **1.** tropezón *m*, traspié *m*; **2.** tropezar (*a. fig.*), dar un traspié; ~ *upon* tropezar con; '**stum·bling-block** *fig.* tropiezo *m*.

stump [stʌmp] **1.** ✒ tocón *m of tree*; muñón *m of leg etc.*; raigón *m of tooth*; cabo *m*; *cricket:* palo *m*; **2.** *v/t.* F confundir, dejar confuso; F *country* recorrer pronunciando discursos; *Am.* F desafiar; *v/i.* cojear; pisar muy fuerte; *sl.* ~ *up* pagar (*for acc.*); '~'**or·a·tor** orador *m* callejero; '**stump·y** □ achaparrado. [*fig.*).]

stun [stʌn] aturdir, atolondrar (*a.*)

stung [stʌŋ] *pret. a. p.p. of* sting 2.

stunk [stʌŋk] *p.p.p. of* stink 2.

stun·ner ['stʌnə] F persona *f* maravillosa; '**stun·ning** □ F bárbaro, imponente.

stunt[1] [stʌnt] F **1.** ✈ vuelo *m* acrobático; (*newspaper etc*) treta *f* publicitaria; maniobra *f* sensacional; **2.** ✈ lucirse haciendo maniobras acrobáticas.

stunt[2] [~] atrofiar, impedir el crecimiento de; '**stunt·ed** enano; raquítico.

stupe [stju:p] fomento *m*, compresa *f*.

stu·pe·fac·tion [stjuːpiˈfækʃn] estupefacción *f.*

stu·pe·fy [ˈstjuːpifai] atolondrar; pasmar, causar estupor (a); dejar estupefacto.

stu·pen·dous [stjuːˈpendəs] □ estupendo.

stu·pid [ˈstjuːpid] □ estúpido; **stupid·i·ty** [stjuːˈpiditi] estupidez *f.*

stu·por [ˈstjuːpə] estupor *m* (*a. fig.*).

stur·di·ness [ˈstəːdinis] robustez *f*, fuerza *f*; **'stur·dy** □ robusto, fuerte; vigoroso; tenaz.

stur·geon [ˈstəːdʒən] esturión *m.*

stut·ter [ˈstʌtə] 1. *v/i.* tartamudear; *v/t.* balbucear; 2. tartamudeo *m.*

sty[1] [stai] 🖈 pocilga *f*, zahurda *f.*

sty(e)[2] [~] 🖈 orzuelo *m.*

style [stail] 1. estilo *m* (*a.* ⚜); moda *f*; elegancia *f*; título *m*; (*of address*) tratamiento *m*; do s.t. in ~ hacer algo lo mejor posible; *live in* ~ darse buena vida; 2. intitular, nombrar; *dress* cortar a la moda.

styl·ish [ˈstailiʃ] □ elegante; a la moda; **'styl·ish·ness** elegancia *f.*

styl·ist [ˈstailist] estilista *m/f*; **stylized** [ˈstailaizd] estilizado.

styp·tic [ˈstiptik] estíptico *adj. a. su. m.*

sua·sion [ˈsweiʒn] persuasión *f.*

suave [swaːv] □ afable, fino; *b.s.* zalamero; **suav·i·ty** [ˈswæviti] afabilidad *f*, finura *f.*

sub [sʌb] F *abbr.* = *submarine*; *subordinate* 2; *subscription*; *substitute* 2.

sub...: *mst* sub...

sub·ac·id [ˈsʌbˈæsid] subácido.

sub·al·tern [ˈsʌbltən] ✗ alférez *m.*

sub·a·tom [ˈsʌbˈætəm] subátomo *m.*

sub·com·mit·tee [ˈsʌbkəmiti] subcomisión *f.*

sub·con·scious [ˈsʌbˈkɔnʃəs] 1. □ subconsciente; 2. subcon(s)ciencia *f.*

sub·con·tract [sʌbˈkɔntrækt] subcontrato *m.*

sub·cu·ta·ne·ous [ˈsʌbkjuːˈteiniəs] □ subcutáneo.

sub·dean [ˈsʌbˈdiːn] subdecano *m.*

sub·di·vide [ˈsʌbdiˈvaid] subdividir(se); **sub·di·vi·sion** [ˈ~viʒn] subdivisión *f.*

sub·due [səbˈdjuː] sojuzgar, avasallar, dominar; suavizar, amansar; **sub'dued** *colour* amortiguado; *emotion* templado; *light* tenue; *p.* deprimido, manso; *voice* bajo.

sub·head(·**ing**) [ˈsʌbhed(iŋ)] subtítulo *m.*

sub·ject [ˈsʌbdʒikt] 1. sujeto; *people* subyugado, esclavizado; ~ to (*liable*) propenso a; ~ to (*exposed*) expuesto a; ~ to the approval of sujeto a la aprobación de; ~ to change without notice sujeto a cambio sin previo aviso; ~ to correction bajo corrección; ~ to a fee sujeto a derechos; 2. *gr.* sujeto *m*; *pol.* súbdito (a *f*) *m*; (-*matter*) tema *m*, materia *f*; materia *f*, asignatura *f in school*; asunto *m* of talk etc.; ♪, *paint.* tema *m*; 🏴 he is a nervous ~ es un caso nervioso; 3. [səbˈdʒekt] someter o test etc.; (*conquer*) dominar, sojuzgar; ~ o.s. to sujetarse a; **sub'jec·tion** sujeción *f*; avasallamiento *m*; **sub·jec·tive** [sʌbˈdʒektiv] □ subjetivo.

sub·join [ˈsʌbˈdʒɔin] adjuntar.

sub·ju·gate [ˈsʌbdʒugeit] subyugar; **sub·ju'ga·tion** subyugación *f.*

sub·junc·tive [səbˈdʒʌŋktiv] (*or* ~ mood) subjuntivo *m.*

sub·lease [ˈsʌbˈliːs], **sub·let** [ˈ~ˈlet] [*irr.* (*let*)] realquilar, subarrendar.

sub·li·mate 1. [ˈsʌblimit] 🜍 sublimado *m*; 2. [ˈ~eit] sublimar (*a.* 🜍); **sub·li'ma·tion** sublimación *f*; **sublime** [səˈblaim] 1. □ (*the lo*) sublime; 2. sublimar; **sub·li·min·al** [sʌbˈliminəl] □ subliminal; **sublim·i·ty** [səˈblimiti] sublimidad *f.*

sub·ma·chine gun [ˈsʌbməˈʃiːnˈgʌn] pistola *f* ametralladora.

sub·ma·rine [ˈsʌbməriːn] submarino *adj. a. su. m.*

sub·merge [səbˈməːdʒ] sumergir (se); **sub'mer·sion** sumersión *f.*

sub·mis·sion [səbˈmiʃn] sumisión *f*; **sub·mis·sive** [ˈ~misiv] □ sumiso.

sub·mit [səbˈmit] *v/t.* someter; *evidence* presentar; *esp. parl.* proponer; *I* ~ that me permito decir que; *v/i.* (*a.* 🜍 ~ o.s.) someterse; *fig.* resignarse (to a).

sub·or·di·nate 1. [səˈbɔːdnit] □ subordinado (*a. gr.*), inferior; 2. [~] subordinado (a *f*) *m*; 3. [~ˈbɔːdineit] subordinar; **sub·or·di·nation** subordinación *f.*

sub·orn [sʌˈbɔːn] sobornar; **subor'na·tion** soborno *m.*

sub·p(o)e·na [səbˈpiːnə] 1. comparendo *m*; 2. mandar comparecer.

sub·scribe [səb'skraib] su(b)scribir (se), abonarse (*to a paper* a un periódico); ✝ su(b)scribir (*for, to acc.*); ~ *to an opinion* su(b)scribir una opinión; **sub'scrib·er** su(b)scriptor (-a *f*) *m*; abonado (a *f*) *m*.

sub·scrip·tion [səb'skripʃn] su(b)scripción *f*; abono *m*; ~ *rate* tarifa *f* de su(b)scripción.

sub·se·quence ['sʌbsikwəns] subsecuencia *f*; **'sub·se·quent** □ subsecuente, posterior (*to* a); ~*ly* con posterioridad, después.

sub·ser·vi·ence [səb'sə:viəns] subordinación *f*; servilismo *m*; **sub'ser·vi·ent** □ subordinado; servil.

sub·side [səb'said] (*water*) bajar; (*house*) hundirse; (*wind*) amainar; (*excitement*) calmarse; ~ *into chair etc.* dejarse caer en; **sub'sid·ence** hundimiento *m*, descenso *m* *of ground*; socavón *m in street*; bajada *f of water etc*; **sub·sid·i·ar·y** [~'sidjəri] **1.** □ subsidiario, auxiliar; ✝ afiliado, filial; **2.** filial *f*, sucursal *f*; **sub·si·dize** ['sʌbsidaiz] subvencionar; **'sub·si·dy** subvención *f*.

sub·sist [səb'sist] subsistir; sustentarse (*on* con); **sub'sist·ence** subsistencia *f*; ~ *allowance* dietas *f/pl*.

sub·soil ['sʌbsɔil] subsuelo *m*.

sub·stance ['sʌbstəns] sustancia *f*; esencia *f*; *man of* ~ hombre *m* acaudalado.

sub·stand·ard [sʌb'stændəd] inferior al nivel normal, deficiente.

sub·stan·tial [səb'stænʃl] □ sustancial, sustancioso; *sum* considerable; *build* sólido; *p.* acomodado.

sub·stan·ti·ate [səb'stænʃieit] establecer, verificar, justificar.

sub·stan·ti·val [sʌbstən'taivl] □ sustantivo; **'sub·stan·tive** □ sustantivo *adj. a. su. m* (*a. gr.*).

sub·sta·tion ['sʌb'steiʃn] ⚡ subestación *f*.

sub·sti·tute ['sʌbstitju:t] **1.** *v/t.* sustituir (*A for B* B por A); *v/i.* F suplir (*for* a); **2.** sustituto (a *f*) *m*; suplente *m/f*; reemplazo *m*; **3.** sucedáneo; de reemplazo; **sub·sti·tu·tion** sustitución *f*; reemplazo *m*.

sub·stra·tum ['sʌb'streitəm] sustrato *m*.

sub·ten·ant ['sʌb'tenənt] subarrendatario (a *f*) *m*.

sub·ter·fuge ['sʌbtəfju:dʒ] subterfugio *m*.

sub·ter·ra·ne·an [sʌbtə'reinjən] subterráneo.

sub·til·ize ['sʌtilaiz] sutilizar.

sub·ti·tle ['sʌbtaitl] subtítulo *m*.

sub·tle ['sʌtl] □ sutil; astuto; *b.s.* insidioso; **'sub·tle·ty** sutileza *f*; astucia *f*.

sub·tract [səb'trækt] ⚡ sustraer, restar; **sub'trac·tion** sustracción *f*, resta *f*.

sub·urb ['sʌbə:b] suburbio *m*, arrabal *m*, barrio *m*; *the* ~*s pl.* los barrios (exteriores); **sub·ur·ban** [sə'bə:bən] suburbano; 🚃 de cercanías.

sub·ven·tion [səb'venʃn] subvención *f*.

sub·ver·sion [sʌb'və:ʃn] subversión *f*; **sub'ver·sive** □ subversivo; **sub·vert** [sʌb'və:t] trastornar, subvertir.

sub·way ['sʌbwei] paso *m* subterráneo; *Am.* metro *m*.

suc·ceed [sək'si:d] tener (buen) éxito, salir bien; ~ *in ger.* lograr *inf.*, conseguir *inf.*; ~ *to crown, post* suceder a; ~ *a p.* suceder a una p.; **suc'ceed·ing** subsiguiente.

suc·cess [sək'ses] (buen) éxito *m*; triunfo *m*; prosperidad *f*; *he was a* (*great*) ~ tuvo (mucho) éxito; *it was a* (*great*) ~ salió (muy) bien; *make a* ~ *of* tener éxito en; **suc'cess·ful** [~ful] □ próspero, afortunado; feliz; *be* ~ tener (buen) éxito; *esp.* ✝ prosperar, medrar; **suc·ces·sion** [~'seʃn] sucesión *f* (*to* a); descendencia *f*; serie *f*; *in* ~ seguidos, uno tras otro; ~ *duty* derechos *m/pl.* de sucesión; **suc·ces·sive** □ sucesivo; **suc'ces·sor** sucesor (-a *f*) *m*.

suc·cinct [sək'siŋkt] □ sucinto.

suc·co(u)r ['sʌkə] **1.** socorro *m*; **2.** socorrer.

suc·cu·lence ['sʌkjuləns] suculencia *f*; **'suc·cu·lent** □ suculento.

suc·cumb [sə'kʌm] sucumbir (*to* a).

such [sʌtʃ] **1.** *adj.* tal, semejante; ~ *a man* tal hombre; *no* ~ *thing* no hay tal cosa; *and* ~ *y tal*; ~ *as* tal como; ~ *as to* de tal manera que, tal que; *as* ~ como tal; ~ *and* ~ tal o cual; ~ *is life* así es la vida; **2.** *adv.:* ~ *a big dog* perro tan grande; **3.** *pron.:* ~ *as* los que; **'such·like 1.** *adj.* tal; **2.** *pron.* tales personas (*or* cosas).

suck [sʌk] **1.** chupar; mamar; ~ *in* sorber; *air* aspirar; ~ *up* absorber;

2. chupada *f*; *give* ~ amamantar; **'suck·er** ⊕ émbolo *m*; ⊕ caño *m* de bomba; ⚡ serpollo *m*, mamón *m*; *Am. sl.* primo *m*, bobo *m*; **'suck·ing**: ~ *pig* lechoncillo *m*; **suck·le** ['~l] *v/t.* amamantar; *fig.* criar; *v/i.* lactar; **'suck·ling** mamón (-a *f*) *m*.

suc·tion ['sʌkʃn] **1.** succión *f*; **2.** ... de succión; aspirante; ~ *pump* bomba *f* aspirante.

sud·den ['sʌdn] □ repentino, súbito; imprevisto; *on a* ~, *(all) of a* ~ de repente; ~*ly* de repente, de pronto; **'sud·den·ness** precipitación *f*, rapidez *f*; lo imprevisto.

su·dor·if·ic [sjuː'dɔrifik] sudorífico *adj. a. su. m.*

suds [sʌdz] *pl.* jabonaduras *f/pl.*

sue [sjuː] *v/t.* procesar; demandar (*a p.* a una p.; *for* por); ~ *for peace* pedir la paz; ~ *out* rogar y obtener; *v/i.* poner pleito.

suede [sweid] suecia *f*.

su·et ['sjuit] sebo *m*; **'su·et·y** seboso.

suf·fer ['sʌfə] sufrir; padecer (⚡ *from* de); aguantar; *(allow)* permitir; ~ *from fig.* adolecer de; **'suf·fer·ance** sufrimiento *m*; *(on por)* tolerancia *f*; ~ *out* rogar y obtener; **'suf·fer·er** víctima *f*; paciente *m/f*; **'suf·fer·ing** dolor *m*.

suf·fice [sə'fais] *v/i.* bastar; *v/t.* satisfacer.

suf·fi·cien·cy [sə'fiʃənsi] cantidad *f* suficiente; suficiencia *f*; **suf'fi·cient** □ suficiente.

suf·fix 1. [sʌ'fiks] añadir (como sufijo); **2.** ['sʌfiks] sufijo *m*.

suf·fo·cate ['sʌfəkeit] sofocar(se), asfixiar(se); **'suf·fo·cat·ing** sofocante; **suf·fo'ca·tion** sofocación *f*, asfixia *f*.

suf·fra·gan ['sʌfrəgən] *(obispo m)* sufragáneo; **'suf·frage** sufragio *m*; aprobación *f*; **suf·fra·gette** [~ə'dʒet] sufragista *f*; **suf·fra·gist** ['~dʒist] sufragista *m/f*.

suf·fuse [sə'fjuːz] bañar *(with* de); difundirse por; **suf'fu·sion** [~ʒn] difusión *f*.

sug·ar ['ʃugə] **1.** azúcar *m a.f*; **2.** azucarar; **'~-ba·sin**, **'~-bowl** azucarero *m*; **'~-cane** caña *f* de azúcar; **'~-loaf** pan *m* de azúcar; **'~-plum** confite *m*; **'~-tongs** *pl.* pinza *f* para azúcar; **'sug·ar·y** azucarado; *fig.* almibarado.

sug·gest [sə'dʒest] sugerir; indicar; **sug'ges·tion** sugestión *f*; sugeren-

cia *f*; indicación *f*; *fig.* sombra *f*, traza *f*.

sug·ges·tive [sə'dʒestiv] □ sugerente; sugestivo; *b.s.* sicalíptico; **sug'ges·tive·ness** *b.s.* sicalipsis *f*.

su·i·cid·al [sjui'saidl] □ suicida; **su·i·cide** ['~said] **1.** suicidio *m*; *(p.)* suicida *m/f*; *commit* ~ = **2.** *Am.* suicidarse.

suit [sjuːt] **1.** traje *m* (*a.* ~ *of clothes*); *(courtship)* galanteo *m*, cortejo *m*; ⚖ pleito *m*, petición *f*; *cards:* palo *m*; *follow* ~ servir del palo; *fig.* hacer lo mismo, seguir la corriente; **2.** *v/t.* adaptar, ajustar, acomodar (*to* a); convenir, satisfacer; *(clothes etc.)* sentar, caer bien a; *be* ~*ed* ir bien juntos; ~ *yourself* como Vd. quiera; *v/i.* convenir; **suit·a·bil·i·ty** conveniencia *f*; idoneidad *f*; **'suit·a·ble** □ conveniente, apropiado; idóneo, adecuado, indicado *(for* para); **'suit·a·ble·ness** *v.* suitability; **'suit·case** maleta *f*; **suite** [swiːt] séquito *m*, comitiva *f*; mobiliario *m*, juego *m of furniture*; *(rooms)* habitaciones *f/pl.* (particulares); ♪ suite *f*; **suit·ing** ['sjuːtiŋ] ⚡ tela *f* para trajes; **'suit·or** pretendiente *m*, galán *m*; ⚖ demandante *m/f*.

sulk [sʌlk] **1.** amohinarse; **2. sulks** *pl.* = **sulk·i·ness** ['~inis] mohina *f*, murria *f*; **'sulk·y** □ mohino, murrio; resentido.

sul·len ['sʌlən] □ hosco, malhumorado, resentido; *sky* plomizo; **'sul·len·ness** hosquedad *f* etc.

sul·ly ['sʌli] *mst fig.* manchar.

sul·phate ['sʌlfeit] sulfato *m*; **sul·phide** ['~faid] sulfuro *m*.

sul·phur ['sʌlfə] **1.** azufre *m*; **2.** azufrar; **sul·phu·re·ous** [sʌl'fjuəriəs] sulfúreo; **sul·phu·ric** [~'fjuərik] sulfúrico; ~ *acid* ácido *m* sulfúrico; **'sul·phu·rize** ⊕ azufrar.

sul·tan ['sʌltən] sultán *m*; **sul·tan·a** [sʌl'tɑːnə] sultana *f*; [səl'tɑːnə] *(fruit)* pasa *f* de Esmirna.

sul·tri·ness ['sʌltrinis] bochorno *m*; **sul·try** ['sʌltri] □ bochornoso; sofocante; *fig.* seductor, provocativo.

sum [sʌm] **1.** suma *f*; total *m*; F problema *m* de aritmética; F ~*s pl.* aritmética *f*; **2.** *(mst* ~ *up)* sumar; *fig.* resumir; F *p.*, *situation* justipreciar; *to* ~ *up* en resumen.

sum·ma·rize ['sʌməraiz] resumir;

'sum·ma·ry 1. ⎓ sumario (a. 🕮); 2. resumen m, sumario m.

sum·mer¹ ['sʌmə] 1. verano m, estío m; fig. of 20 ₋s de 20 abriles; 2. ... de verano; veraniego; estival; v. resort; 3. veranear; '~·house cenador m.

sum·mer² [⌣] ⚠ viga f maestra.

sum·mer·like ['sʌmǝlaik], sum·mer·(l)y ['~ri, '~li] veraniego, estival.

sum·ming-up ['sʌmiŋʌp] recapitulación f. [(a. fig.).\

sum·mit ['sʌmit] cima f, cumbre f/

sum·mon ['sʌmǝn] convocar; llamar; 🕮 citar, emplazar; fig. (mst ~ up) memory evocar; courage cobrar; 'sum·mon·er 🕮 emplazador m;

sum·mons ['~z] 1. 🕮 citación f; llamamiento m, requerimiento m; 2. citar, emplazar.

sump [sʌmp] sumidero m, cárter m.

sump·tu·ar·y ['sʌmptjuǝri] suntuario.

sump·tu·ous ['sʌmptjuǝs] ☐ suntuoso; 'sump·tu·ous·ness suntuosidad f.

sun [sʌn] 1. sol m; 2. ... solar; 3. asolear; ~ o.s. asolearse, tomar el sol (a. '~·bathe); '~·beam ['sʌnbi:m] rayo m de sol; '~·blind store m.

sun·burn ['sʌnbǝːn] solanera f; quemadura f del sol; 'sun·burnt tostado (por el sol), bronceado.

sun·dae ['sʌnd(e)i] helado con frutas, jarabes o nueces.

Sun·day ['sʌndi] domingo m; attr. dominical; ~ best trapos m/pl. de cristianar; dress up in one's ~ best endomingarse; ~ school escuela m en que se da instrucción religiosa (los domingos).

sun·der ['sʌndǝ] poet. romper; separar.

sun·di·al ['sʌndaiǝl] reloj m de sol.

sun·down ['sʌndaun] puesta f del sol; at ~ al anochecer.

sun·dry ['sʌndri] 1. varios, diversos; all and ~ todos y cada uno; 2. sun·dries ['~driz] pl. esp. 🕇 géneros m/pl. diversos.

sun·flow·er ['sʌnflauǝ] girasol m.

sung [sʌŋ] p.p. of sing.

sun·glass·es pl. (a pair of ~ unas) gafas f/pl. de sol.

sunk [sʌŋk] p.p. of sink 1.

sunk·en ['sʌŋkǝn] 1. p.p. of sink 1; 2. adj. sumido, hundido (a. fig.).

sun-lamp ['sʌnlæmp] lámpara f de rayos ultravioletas.

sun·light ['sʌnlait] luz f solar, (luz f del) sol m.

sun·lit ['sʌnlit] iluminado por el sol; 'sun·ny ☐ place (a)soleado; day de sol; fig. alegre, risueño; be ~ hacer sol.

sun...: '~·rise salida f del sol; '~·set puesta f del sol; ocaso m; '~·shade quitasol m; toldo m; '~·shine sol m; hours of ~ horas f/pl. de insolación; mot. ~ roof techo m corredizo; '~·spot mancha f solar; '~·stroke 🞋 insolación f; '~·up salida f del sol.

sup [sʌp] v/i. cenar (off, on acc.); v/t. sorber.

su·per¹ ['sju:pǝ] (abbr.) 1. thea., film: F figurante (a f) m, comparsa m/f; superintendente m; 2. 🕇 F superfino; sl. bárbaro, de rechupete.

su·per...:² [⌣] super...; sobre...; ~·a·'bound sobreabundar (in, with en); ~·a·'bun·dant ☐ sobreabundante; ~·'an·nu·ate ['~rænjueit] jubilar; ~d jubilado; fig. anticuado; ~·an·nu·a·tion jubilación f.

su·perb [sju:'pǝːb] ☐ soberbio; magnífico.

su·per...: '~·car·go sobrecargo m; '~·charged sobrealimentado; '~·charg·er sobrealimentador m; su·per·cil·i·ous [~'siliǝs] ☐ desdeñoso, altanero, arrogante; su·per·cil·i·ous·ness desdén m, arrogancia f; su·per·e·ro·ga·tion ['~rerǝ'geiʃn] supererogación f; su·per·e·rog·a·to·ry ['~re'rɔgǝtǝri] supererogatorio; su·per·fi·cial [~'fiʃl] ☐ superficial; su·per·fi·ci·al·i·ty [~fiʃi'æliti] superficialidad f; su·per·fi·ci·es [~'fiʃi:z] superficie f; 'su·per'fine extrafino, superfino; su·per·flu·i·ty [~'fluiti] superfluidad f; su·per·flu·ous [sju:'pǝ:fluǝs] ☐ superfluo; su·per'heat sobrecalentar; su·per·het ['~'het] radio: superheterodino m.

su·per...: '~·'hu·man ☐ sobrehumano; ~·im'pose sobreponer; ~·in·duce [~'rin'dju:s] sobreañadir; ~·in'tend dirigir; vigilar; supervisar; ~·in'tend·ence superintendencia f; ~·in'tend·ent superintendente m; inspector m; supervisor m.

su·pe·ri·or [sju:'piǝriǝ] 1. ☐ superior; b. s. orgulloso, arrogante; ~ officer oficial m superior; 2. superior

m; *(eccl. a.)* superiora *f*; **su·pe·ri·or·ity** [˴'ɔriti] superioridad *f*.
su·per·la·tive [sju:'pɔ:lətiv] □ superlativo *adj. a. su. m*; **'su·per·man** superhombre *m*; **'su·per·mar·ket** supermercado *m*; **su·per'nat·u·ral** □ *(the lo)* sobrenatural; **su·per·nu·mer·ar·y** [˴'nju:mərəri] supernumerario *adj. a. su. m* (a *f*); *thea.* figurante (a *f*) *m*, comparsa *m/f*; **'su·per·po·si·tion** superposición *f*; **'su·per'scribe** sobrescribir; **su·per'scrip·tion** sobrescrito *m*; **su·per·sede** [˴'si:d] reemplazar; sustituir; **su·per·son·ic** [˴'sɔnik] □ supersónico; **su·per·sti·tion** [˴'sti·ʃn] superstición *f*; **su·per'sti·tious** [˴ʃəs] □ supersticioso; **su·per·struc·ture** ['˴strʌktʃə] superestructura *f*; **su·per·tax** ['˴tæks] impuesto *m* adicional; **su·per·vene** [˴'vi:n] sobrevenir; **su·per·vise** ['˴vaiz] dirigir; vigilar; supervisar; **su·per·vi·sion** [˴'viʒn] superintendencia *f*, vigilancia *f*, supervisión *f*; **su·per·vi·sor** ['˴vaizə] superintendente *m*; inspector *m*; supervisor *m*; **'su·per·vi·so·ry** fiscalizador; de inspector.
su·pine 1. ['sju:pain] *gr.* supino *m*; **2.** [˴'pain] □ supino; *fig.* letárgico, flojo.
sup·per ['sʌpə] cena *f*.
sup·plant [sə'plɑ:nt] suplantar.
sup·ple ['sʌpl] □ flexible; *b.s.* dócil, servil.
sup·ple·ment 1. ['sʌplimənt] suplemento *m*; **2.** ['˴ment] suplir, complementar; **sup·ple'men·tal** □ suplemental; **sup·ple'men·ta·ry** suplementario.
sup·ple·ness ['sʌplnis] flexibilidad *f*.
sup·pli·ant ['sʌpliənt] □ suplicante *adj. a. su. m/f*.
sup·pli·cate ['sʌplikeit] suplicar; **sup·pli'ca·tion** súplica *f*; suplicación *f*.
sup·pli·er [sə'plaiə] suministrador (-a *f*) *m*; ✝ proveedor (-a *f*) *m*.
sup·ply [sə'plai] **1.** suministrar, facilitar; surtir; *city* aprovisionar; *want* suplir; ~ **with** abastecer de, proveer de; **2.** provisión *f*; suministro *m*; ✝ surtido *m*; *mst supplies pl.* provisiones *f/pl.*, víveres *m/pl.*; ✗ pertrechos *m/pl.*; **be in short** ~ andar escaso; ✝ ~ **and demand** oferta y demanda; ~ *teacher* maestro *m* su-

plente; *parl. Committee on ♀ Committee* Comisión *f* del Presupuesto.
sup·port [sə'pɔ:t] **1.** sostén *m*, apoyo *m* (⊕ *a. fig.*); ⚓ soporte *m*, pilar *m*; **in** ~ **of** en apoyo de; **2.** apoyar (⊕ *a. fig.*); sostener, mantener; *campaign* respaldar; ~ *o.s.* mantenerse; *film:* ~*ing programme* películas *f/pl.* secundarias; *thea.* ~*ing role* papel *m* secundario; **sup'port·a·ble** □ soportable; **sup'port·er** partidario (a *f*) *m*; *sport:* seguidor (-a *f*) *m*; ⊕ soporte *m*, sostén *m*; ~*s' club* peña *f* deportiva.
sup·pose [sə'pouz] suponer; presumir; figurarse, imaginarse; F *he is* ~*d to go* debe ir; *let us* ~ pongamos por caso; ~ *or supposing (that)* ...? si...; F ~ *we try y* ¿si probamos?; *he is rich, I* ~ me imagino que es rico; *I* ~ *so* supongo que sí; *(resignedly)* no hay más remedio.
sup·posed [sə'pouzd] □ supuesto; pretendido; **sup'pos·ed·ly** [˴idli] según lo que se supone.
sup·po·si·tion [sʌpə'ziʃn] suposición *f*; **sup·pos·i·ti·tious** [səpɔzi'tiʃəs] □ fingido, espurio; **sup'pos·i·to·ry** [˴təri] supositorio *m*.
sup·press [sə'pres] suprimir; **sup·pres·sion** [sə'preʃn] supresión *f*; **sup'pres·sor** *radio:* supresor *m*.
sup·pu·rate ['sʌpjureit] supurar; **sup·pu'ra·tion** supuración *f*.
su·prem·a·cy [sju'preməsi] supremacía *f*; **su·preme** [sju'pri:m] □ supremo.
sur·charge 1. [sə:'tʃɑ:dʒ] sobrecargar; **2.** ['sɔ:tʃɑ:dʒ] sobrecarga *f*; sobretasa *f*.
surd [sə:d] (número *m*) sordo.
sure [ʃuə] **1.** □ seguro; cierto; *aim etc.* certero; *manner, touch* firme; *to be* ~!, *Am.* ~! ¡claro!; *to be* ~ sin duda; ~ *enough* efectivamente; *Am.* ~ *fire* de éxito seguro; *I am* ~ estoy seguro *(that* de que); *he is* ~ *to return* seguramente volverá; *make* ~ asegurar(se) *(that* de que); *make* ~ *of facts* verificar, cerciorarse de; *p., cooperation etc.* contar con el apoyo de; **2.** *adv. Am.:* *he* ~ *was mean* ése sí que era tacaño; **'sure·ly** seguramente; *I* ~ 'sure·ness seguridad *f etc.*; **'sure·ty** seguridad *f*, fianza *f*; *(p.)* fiador (-a *f*) *m*.
surf [sə:f] oleaje *m*; espuma *f*; rompientes *m/pl.*

sur·face ['sə:fis] **1.** superficie *f*; firme *m of road*; ✕ ∼ *workers* personal *m* del exterior; **2.** *v/t.* ⊕ alisar; recubrir; *v/i.* (*submarine*) emerger.

sur·feit ['sə:fit] **1.** hartura *f*; empacho *m*; exceso *m*; **2.** hartar(se), saciar(se) (*on, with* de).

surf-rid·ing ['sə:fraidiŋ] esquí *m* acuático.

surge [sə:dʒ] **1.** oleada *f*, oleaje *m*; **2.** agitarse, hervir.

sur·geon ['sə:dʒən] cirujano *m*; **sur·ger·y** ['sə:dʒəri] cirugía *f*; (*room*) consultorio *m*; clínica *f*; *Am.* sala *f* de operaciones; ∼ *hours* horas *f/pl.* de consulta; *v. plastic*; **sur·gi·cal** ['sə:dʒikl] □ quirúrgico.

sur·li·ness ['sə:linis] aspereza *f*, malhumor *m*; **'sur·ly** □ áspero, malhumorado, hosco.

sur·mise 1. ['sə:maiz] conjetura *f*; suposición *f*; **2.** [∼'maiz] conjeturar; suponer.

sur·mount [sə:'maunt] superar, vencer; ∼*ed by* (*or with*) coronado de; **sur'mount·a·ble** superable.

sur·name ['sə:neim] **1.** apellido *m*; **2.** apellidar.

sur·pass [sə:'pɑ:s] *fig.* aventajar, exceder, sobrepujar; **sur'pass·ing** □ sobresaliente, incomparable.

sur·plice ['sə:pləs] sobrepelliz *f*.

sur·plus ['sə:pləs] **1.** excedente *m*; sobrante *m*; ✝ superávit *m*; **2.** ... sobrante, de sobra.

sur·prise [sə'praiz] **1.** sorpresa *f*; asombro *m*; ✕ (*a.* ∼ *attack*) rebato *m*; *take by* ✕ sobrecoger; *to my great* ∼ con gran sorpresa mía; **2.** inesperado; **3.** sorprender; ✕ coger por sorpresa; *be* ∼*d at* sorprenderse de; **sur'pris·ing** □ sorprendente.

sur·re·al·ism [sə'riəlizm] surrealismo *m*; **sur're·al·ist** surrealista *m*.

sur·ren·der [sə'rendə] **1.** rendición *f*; abandono *m*; entrega *f of documents*; renuncia *f of rights*; **2.** rendir (se); entregar(se); *rights* renunciar a.

sur·rep·ti·tious [sʌrəp'tiʃəs] □ subrepticio *m*.

sur·ro·gate ['sʌrəgit] sustituto *m*; *eccl.* vicario *m*.

sur·round [sə'raund] cercar, circundar, rodear (*by* de); ✕ copar; sitiar; **sur'round·ing** circundante; **sur'round·ings** *pl.* alrededores *m/pl.*, contornos *m/pl. of place*; *fig.* ambiente *m*.

sur·tax ['sə:tæks] impuesto *m* adicional (sobre ingresos excesivos).

sur·veil·lance [sə:'veiləns] vigilancia *f*.

sur·vey 1. [sə:'vei] reconocer, registrar; inspeccionar, examinar; *surv.* medir; levantar el plano de; **2.** ['sə:vei] reconocimiento *m*; inspección *f*, examen *m*; *surv.* medición *f*; *Economic* ∼ informe *m* económico; **sur·'vey·ing** planimetría *f*; agrimensura *f*; **sur'vey·or** topógrafo *m*; agrimensor *m*.

sur·viv·al [sə'vaivl] supervivencia *f*; **sur·vive** [∼'vaiv] sobrevivir (*acc.* a *acc.*); perdurar; **sur'vi·vor** superviviente *m/f*.

sus·cep·ti·bil·i·ty [səseptə'biliti] susceptibilidad *f*; (*mst* ∼*s pl.*) delicadeza *f*; **sus'cep·ti·ble** □ susceptible; sensible; (*easily moved*) impresionable; *be* ∼ *of* admitir.

sus·pect 1. [səs'pekt] sospechar, recelar; **2.** ['sʌspekt] sospechoso (a *f*) *m*; **3.** [∼] sospechado, sospechoso.

sus·pend [səs'pend] *all senses*: suspender; **sus'pend·ers** *pl.* ligas *f/pl.*; *Am.* tirantes *m/pl.*; **sus'pend·er-belt** pərtaligas *m*.

sus·pense [səs'pens] incertidumbre *f*, duda *f*; ansiedad *f*; *thea. etc.* "suspense" *m*; *in* ∼ en suspenso; **sus·pen·sion** [∼'penʃn] *all senses*: suspensión *f*; ∼ *bridge* puente *m* colgante; **sus'pen·sive** □ suspensivo, interino; **sus·pen·so·ry** [∼'pensəri] suspensorio *adj. a. su. m* (*a.* ∼ *bandage*).

sus·pi·cion [səs'piʃn] sospecha *f*; recelo *m*; suspicacia *f*; *fig.* sombra *f*, traza *f* ligera; **sus·pi·cious** [∼-'piʃəs] □ (*causing suspicion*) sospechoso; (*feeling suspicion*) receloso; suspicaz; **sus'pi·cious·ness** lo sospechoso; suspicacia *f*.

sus·tain [səs'tein] sostener (*a.* ♪), apoyar; sustentar; *loss, injury* sufrir; **sus'tained** ininterrumpido, continuo.

sus·te·nance ['sʌstinəns] sustento *m*, subsistencia *f*.

sut·ler ['sʌtlə] vivandero (a *f*) *m*.

su·ture ['sju:tʃə] **1.** *all senses*: sutura *f*; **2.** ✄ suturar, coser.

su·ze·rain ['su:zərein] soberano (a *f*) *m*; **'su·ze·rain·ty** soberanía *f*.

svelte [svelt] esbelto.

swab [swɔb] **1.** estropajo *m*; ♣ lampazo *m*; ✻ algodón *m*; escob(ill)ón *m*; 2. (*a.* ~ *down*) limpiar.

swad·dle ['swɔdl] 1. empañar; *swaddling clothes pl.* pañales *m/pl.*; 2. pañal *m.*

swag [swæg] *sl.* botín *m*, robo *m.*

swag·ger ['swægə] 1. fanfarronear; pavonearse; 2. F muy elegante; 3. fanfarronada *f*; contoneo *m*; '~-cane bastón *m* ligero de paseo.

swain [swein] zagal *m*; *co.* enamorado *m.*

swal·low¹ ['swɔlou] *orn.* golondrina *f.*

swal·low² [~] 1. trago *m*; 2. tragar (*a. fig.*, *a.* ~ *up*); deglutir; ~ one's words desdecirse; ~ up savings etc. consumir.

swam [swæm] *pret. of swim* 1.

swamp [swɔmp] 1. pantano *m*; marisma *f*; 2. sumergir; inundar; ⚓ hundir; *fig.* abrumar (*with work etc.* de); '**swamp·y** pantanoso.

swan [swɔn] cisne *m.*

swank [swæŋk] *sl.* 1. ostentación *f*; fachenda *f*; (*p.*) currutaco *m*; cursi *m/f*; 2. (*a.* '**swank·y**) ostentoso, fachendoso; muy pera; cursi; 3. fanfarronear; pavonearse; darse charol.

swan·ner·y ['swɔnəri] colonia *f* de cisnes; '**swan-song** canto *m* del cisne.

swap [swɔp] F 1. intercambio *m*, cambalache *m*, canje *m*; 2. intercambiar, cambalachear, canjear.

sward [swɔːd] césped *m.*

swarm¹ [swɔːm] 1. enjambre *m* (*a. fig.*); *fig.* muchedumbre *f*, hormiguero *m*; 2. enjambrar; (*people etc.*) hormiguear, pulular; (*place*) hervir (*with* de).

swarm² [~] trepar (*up* a).

swarth·i·ness ['swɔːðinis] lo atezado; '**swarth·y** □ atezado, moreno.

swash·buck·ler ['swɔʃbʌklə] espadachín *m*, matón *m.*

swas·ti·ka ['swɔstikə] svástica *f.*

swat [swɔt] *fly etc.* aplastar, aporrear.

swath [swɔːθ], *pl.* **swaths** [*a.* ~ðz] ✿ guadañada *f*; ringlera *f* de heno *etc.*

swathe [sweið] fajar, envolver.

sway [swei] 1. vaivén *m*, balanceo *m*; coletazo *m* of train etc. (*a.* '**sway·ing**); *fig.* imperio *m*, dominio *m*;

2. *v/t.* inclinar; hacer oscilar; *fig.* influir en; dominar; *v/i.* oscilar, mecerse; inclinarse, ladearse.

swear [sweə] 1. [*irr.*] *v/i.* jurar (*by* por); decir palabrotas; ~ at maldecir *acc.*, echar pestes de; ~ by tener entera confianza en; ~ to declarar bajo juramento; ~ black and blue echar sapos y culebras; *v/t.* jurar; juramentar; *oath* prestar; ~ in tomar juramento a; 2. F taco *m*, palabrota *f* (*a.* '~-word).

sweat [swet] 1. sudor *m* (*a. fig.* F); *by the* ~ *of one's brow* con el sudor de su frente, a pulso sudando; F *be in a* ~ estar en un apuro, encogérsele a uno el ombligo; 2. *v/i.* sudar; *v/t.* sudar; *workmen* explotar; *metall.* calentar hasta la fusión; ⊕ soldar; '**sweat·er** suéter *m*; '**sweat·ing**, '**sweat·y** sud(or)oso.

Swede [swiːd] sueco (a *f*) *m*; ♀ ♀ nabo *m* sueco.

Swed·ish ['swiːdiʃ] sueco *adj. a.* su. *m.*

sweep [swiːp] 1. [*irr.*] *v/t.* barrer (*a.* ✕); *chimney* deshollinar; ⚓ *mines* rastrear; *fig.* ~ *away* arrebatar, arrastrar; borrar, aniquilar; ~ *out*, ~ *up* barrer; ~ *the board* copar; *v/i.* barrer; (*mst with adv.*, ~ *by etc.*) pasar rápidamente, pasar majestuosamente; rozar; ir volando; descender precipitadamente; 2. barredura *f*, escobada *f*; (*p.*) deshollinador *m*; redada *f by police*; *fig.* extensión *f*; recorrido *m*; *make a clean* ~ *of* cambiar completamente, hacer tabla rasa de; '**sweep·er** barrendero (a *f*) *m*; (*machine*) barredera *f*; '**sweep·ing** □ comprensivo (*or* extenso) pero infundado; (*demasiado*) comprensivo; '**sweep·ings** *pl.* barreduras *f/pl.*; **sweep·stake** ['~steik] swepstake *m* (*lotería en la cual una p. gana todas las apuestas*).

sweet [swiːt] 1. □ dulce; azucarado; suave; *smell* fragante; *land* fértil; (*not stale*) fresco; *face* lindo; *p.* amable, encantador; *th.* admired mono, majo; (*pleasing*) grato; *have a* ~ *tooth* ser goloso; ~ *oil* aceite *m* de oliva; ~ *pea* guisante *m* de olor; ~ *william* minutisa *f*; 2. dulce *m*; caramelo *m*; (*course*) postre *m*; ~s *pl.* dulces *m/pl.*, bombones

mpl., golosinas *f/pl.*; '**~·breads** *pl.*
lechecillas *f/pl.*; '**sweet·en** azucarar; endulzar (*a. fig.*); '**sweet·heart**
novio (a *f*) *m*; '**sweet·ish** algo dulce; '**sweet·meats** *pl.* confites *m/pl.*;
dulces *m/pl.*; '**sweet·ness** dulzura*f*,
suavidad *f etc.*; '**sweet·shop** confitería *f*; '**sweet-smell·ing** fragante.

swell [swel] **1.** [*irr.*] hinchar(se),
inflar(se); crecer (*v/i.*); abultar(se);
aumentar (*v/i. a. v/t.*); *numbers*
engrosar (*v/t.*); ~ *with pride* envanecerse; F *have a ~ed head* subirle
a uno humos a la cabeza; **2.** *Am.* F
muy elegante; *Am. sl.* de órdago,
estupendo; **3.** ♪ crescendo *m*; ⚓
marejada *f*, mar *m* de fondo,
oleaje *m*; F guapo *m*, majo *m*; pez *m*
gordo; '**swell·ing** hinchazón *f*; ⚕
chichón *m*, bulto *m*; protuberancia *f*.

swel·ter ['sweltə] sofocarse de calor,
abrasarse; chorrear de sudor; '**swelter·ing** *heat* sofocante, abrasador.

swept [swept] *pret. a. p.p. of*
sweep **1**; ~ (*back*) *wings* en flecha.

swerve [swəːv] **1.** *v/i.* desviarse
(bruscamente); hurtar el cuerpo;
torcer; *v/t.* desviar; *ball* cortar;
2. desvío *m* (brusco); viraje *m*;
esguince *m*, regate *m*.

swift [swift] **1.** □ rápido, veloz;
repentino; pronto; **2.** *orn.* vencejo *m*
común; '**swift·ness** rapidez *f etc.*

swig [swig] F **1.** tragantada *f*;
2. beber a grandes tragos.

swill [swil] **1.** bazofia *f*; *contp.* aguachirle *f*; (*mst ~ out*) enjuagadura *f*;
2. *v/t.* (*mst ~ out*) enjuagar; beber a
grandes tragos; F emborracharse.

swim [swim] **1.** [*irr.*] *v/i.* nadar;
(*head*) dar vueltas; *go ~ming* ir a
bañarse; *v/t.* (*a. ~ across*) pasar a
nado; **2.**: *go for a ~* ir a nadar;
be in the ~ estar al tanto.

swim·mer ['swimə] nadador (-a *f*)
m.

swim·ming ['swimiŋ] natación *f*;
'**~-'cos·tume** traje *m* de baño;
'**swim·ming·ly** *adv.*: *go ~* ir a las
mil maravillas; '**swim·ming-pool**
piscina *f*.

swin·dle ['swindl] **1.** estafar, timar;
~ *out of* estafar *acc.*, quitar por
estafa; **2.** estafa *f*, timo *m*; '**swin·dler** estafador *m*.

swine [swain] *zo. pl.* puercos *m/pl.*,

cerdos *m/pl.*; F *sg.* canalla *m*;
'**swine·herd** porquero *m*.

swing [swiŋ] **1.** [*irr.*] columpiar(se);
balancear(se); (hacer) oscilar; *arm*
menear; *door* girar; *pol. etc.* bascular; ~ *into action* ponerse en marcha;
sl. ~ *the lead* fingirse enfermo, racanear, hacer el rácano; F *he'll ~*
for it le ahorcarán; **2.** columpio *m*;
(*movement*) vaivén *m*, oscilación *f*;
balance(o) *m*; ♪ swing *m*; ♪ ritmo *m*
agradable; *pol. etc.* movimiento *m*,
viraje *m*; *boxing*: golpe *m* lateral;
in full ~ en plena actividad; F *go*
with a ~ ir sobre ruedas; **3.** ... giratorio; ~ **bridge** puente *m* giratorio;
~ **door** puerta *f* giratoria.

swinge·ing ['swindʒiŋ] □ *fig.* abrumador.

swipe [swaip] **1.** golpear fuertemente; *sl.* apandar, guindar; **2.** golpe *m* fuerte; ~*s pl.* cerveza *f* (floja).

swirl [swəːl] **1.** arremolinarse; remolinar; **2.** remolino *m*; torbellino
m.

swish [swiʃ] *v/t.* (*flog*) zurrar; *cane*
agitar (produciendo un silbido); *v/i.*
silbar; (*dress*) crujir; **2.** silbido *m*;
crujido *m of dress*; **3.** *sl.* guapo,
majo.

Swiss [swis] suizo *adj. a. su. m*
(a *f*).

switch [switʃ] **1.** (*stick*) varilla *f*; cambio *m of policy*; ⚙ agujas *f/pl.*,
desviación *f*; ⚡ interruptor *m*;
llave *f*; **2.** *v/t.* ⚙ desviar; *policy*,
positions cambiar; ~ *on* ⚡ encender,
poner, conectar; ~ *off* ⚡ apagar,
cortar; *v/i.*: ~ *from A to B* (*or ~* [*over*]
to B) dejar A para tomar *etc.* B;
'**~·back** montaña *f* rusa; camino *m*
etc. muy desigual; '**~·board** cuadro
m de distribución; *teleph.* cuadro *m*
de conexión manual; centralita *f*
in office.

swiv·el ['swivl] **1.** eslabón *m* giratorio; **2.** (hacer) girar.

swol·len ['swouln] *p.p. of swell* **1.**

swoon [swuːn] **1.** desmayo *m*;
2. desmayar(se), desvanecerse.

swoop [swuːp] **1.** (*a. ~ down*) precipitarse (*on sobre*); (*bird*) calar;
2. descenso *m* súbito.

swop [swɔp] F *v. swap*.

sword [sɔːd] espada *f*; *put to the ~*
pasar a cuchillo; '**~·fish** pez *m*
espada; '**~·knot** borla *f* de espada.

swords·man ['sɔːdzmən] esgrimidor *m*; espadachín *m*; **'swords-man·ship** esgrima *f*.

sword·stick ['sɔːdstik] bastón *m* de estoque.

swore [swɔː] *pret. of* swear 1.

sworn [swɔːn] *p.p. of* swear 1; *enemy* implacable.

swot [swɔt] *sl.* 1. empollón (-a *f*) *m*; 2. empollar.

swum [swʌm] *p.p. of* swim 1.

swung [swʌŋ] *pret. a. p.p. of* swing 1.

syb·a·rite ['sibərait] sibarita *m/f*.

syc·a·more ['sikəmɔː] sicomoro *m*.

syc·o·phant ['sikəfənt] adulador *m*; **syc·o·phan·tic** [sikə'fæntik] ☐ adulatorio.

syl·lab·ic [si'læbik] ☐ silábico; **syl·la·ble** ['siləbl] sílaba *f*.

syl·la·bus ['siləbəs] programa *m*.

syl·lo·gism ['silədʒizm] silogismo *m*.

sylph [silf] sílfide *f* (*a. fig.*); silfo *m*.

syl·van ['silvən] selvático.

sym·bi·o·sis [simbi'ousis] simbiosis *f*.

sym·bol ['simbəl] símbolo *m*; **sym·bol·ic, sym·bol·i·cal** [ˌ'bɔlik(l)] ☐ simbólico; **sym·bol·ism** ['ˌbəlizm] simbolismo *m*; **'sym·bol·ize** simbolizar.

sym·met·ri·cal [si'metrikl] ☐ simétrico; **sym·me·try** ['simitri] simetría *f*.

sym·pa·thet·ic [simpə'θetik] ☐ compasivo; comprensivo; que simpatiza; simpático; ∼ *strike* huelga *f* por solidaridad; **sym·pa·thize** ['ˌθaiz] compadecerse; ∼ *with* compadecer(se de); **sym·pa·thiz·er** ['ˌθaizə] simpatizante *m/f* (*with* de); partidario (a *f*) *m*; **sym·pa·thy** ['ˌθi] compasión *f*, conmiseración *f*; sentimiento *m*; simpatía *f*.

sym·phon·ic [sim'fɔnik] sinfónico; **sym·pho·ny** ['simfəni] sinfonía *f*.

symp·tom ['simptəm] síntoma *m*; **symp·to·mat·ic** [ˌ'mætik] ☐ sintomático.

syn·a·gogue ['sinəgɔg] sinagoga *f*.

syn·chro·mesh gear ['siŋkroumeʃ-'giə] cambio *m* de velocidad sincronizado.

syn·chro·nism ['siŋkrənizm] sincronismo *m*; **'syn·chro·nize** *v/i.* ser sincrónico; *v/t.* sincronizar; **'syn·chro·nous** ☐ síncrono, sincrónico.

syn·co·pate ['siŋkəpeit] sincopar; **syn·co'pa·tion, syn·co·pe** ['ˌpi] síncopa *f*.

syn·dic ['sindik] síndico *m*; **'syn·di·cal·ism** sindicalismo *m*; **'syn·di·cal·ist** sindicalista *m*; **syn·di·cate** 1. ['ˌkit] sindicato *m*; 2. ['ˌkeit] sindicar.

syn·od ['sinəd] sínodo *m*; **syn·od·al** ['ˌdl] sinodal; **syn·od·ic, syn·od·i·cal** [si'nɔdik(l)] ☐ sinódico.

syn·o·nym ['sinənim] sinónimo *m*; **syn·on·y·mous** [si'nɔniməs] ☐ sinónimo.

syn·op·sis [si'nɔpsis], *pl.* **syn'op·ses** [ˌiːz] sinopsis *f*.

syn·op·tic, syn·op·ti·cal [si'nɔptik(l)] ☐ sinóptico.

syn·tac·tic, syn·tac·ti·cal [sin-'tæktik(l)] ☐ sintáctico; **syn·tax** ['sintæks] sintaxis *f*.

syn·the·sis ['sinθisis], *pl.* **syn·the·ses** ['ˌsiz] síntesis *f*; **syn·the·size** ['ˌsaiz] sintetizar.

syn·thet·ic, syn·thet·i·cal [sin-'θetik(l)] ☐ sintético.

syph·i·lis ['sifilis] sífilis *f*.

syph·i·lit·ic [sifi'litik] sifilítico.

sy·phon ['saifən] *v.* siphon.

Syr·i·an ['siriən] sirio *adj. a. su. m* (a *f*).

sy·rin·ga [si'riŋgə] jeringuilla *f*.

syr·inge ['sirindʒ] 1. jeringa *f*; 2. jeringar.

syr·up ['sirəp] jarabe *m*.

sys·tem ['sistim] sistema *m* (*a.* 🜨); 🜨 constitución *f*; ⊕ mecanismo *m*; ⚡ circuito *m*, instalación *f*; **sys·tem·at·ic** [ˌ'mætik] ☐ sistemático.

T

T [ti:]: F *to a* ⌣ exactamente.
ta [ta:] F ¡gracias!
tab [tæb] oreja *f*, lengüeta *f*; F *keep* ⌣*s on* vigilar, tener a la vista.
tab·ard [ˈtæbəd] tabardo *m*.
tab·by [ˈtæbi] **1.** (*mst* ⌣ *cat*) (*male*) gato *m* atigrado; (*female*) gata *f*; F solterona *f*; F chismosa *f*; **2.** atigrado.
tab·er·nac·le [ˈtæbənækl] tabernáculo *m*.
ta·ble [ˈteibl] **1.** mesa *f*; ⅍ *etc.* tabla *f*; (*statistical*) cuadro *m*; ⚠ tablero *m*; *turn the* ⌣*s on* devolver la pelota a; ⌣ *of contents* tabla *f* (*or* índice *m*) de materias; ⌣ *d'hôte* mesa *f* redonda; **2.** *motion etc.* poner sobre la mesa, presentar; (*index*) catalogar; (*set out*) disponer en una tabla; *Am. bill* dar carpetazo a.
tab·leau [ˈtæblou] cuadro *m* vivo.
ta·ble...: ˈ⌣**·cloth** mantel *m*; ˈ⌣**·land** meseta *f*; ˈ⌣**·lin·en** mantelería *f*; ˈ⌣**·mat** apartador *m*, salvamanteles *m*; ˈ⌣**·nap·kin** servilleta *f*; ˈ⌣**·spoon** cuchara *f* grande, cuchara *f* para servir.
tab·let [ˈtæblit] pastilla *f of soap etc.*; tableta *f*; tabla *f*; bloc *m* (de papel); (*inscribed*) lápida *f*; ⚕ comprimido *m*.
ta·ble...: ˈ⌣**·talk** conversación *f* de sobremesa; ˈ⌣**·ten·nis** tenis *m* de mesa.
tab·loid [ˈtæblɔid] *pharm.* (en forma de) tableta *f*; (*paper*) periódico *m* de formato reducido.
ta·boo [təˈbu:] **1.** tabú, prohibido; **2.** tabú *m*; **3.** declarar tabú, prohibir.
tab·u·lar [ˈtæbjulə] □ tabular; **tab·u·late** [ˈ⌣leit] exponer en forma de tabla, tabular.
tac·it [ˈtæsit] □ tácito; **tac·i·turn** [ˈ⌣tə:n] □ taciturno; **tac·i·tur·ni·ty** taciturnidad *f*.
tack [tæk] **1.** (*nail*) tachuela *f*; *sew.* hilván *m*; ⚓ virada *f*, bordada *f*; ⚓ amura *f of sail*; *fig.* rumbo *m*; línea *f* de conducta; *on the wrong* ⌣

equivocado; **2.** *v/t.* clavar con tachuelas; *sew.* hilvanar; *fig.* añadir (*on, onto* a); *v/i.* ⚓ virar, cambiar de bordada.
tack·le [ˈtækl] **1.** ⚓, ⊕ aparejo *m*; ⚓ jarcia *f*; avíos *m/pl.*, aperos *m/pl.*; *sport:* atajo *m*; blocaje *m*; **2.** agarrar; *sport:* atajar; *problem* abordar; emprender.
tack·y [ˈtæki] pegajoso; *Am.* F desaseado.
tact [tækt] tacto *m*, discreción *f*; **tact·ful** [ˈ⌣ful] □ discreto; diplomático.
tac·ti·cal [ˈtæktikl] □ táctico; **tac·ti·cian** [⌣ˈtiʃn] táctico *m*; **tac·tics** [ˈ⌣iks] *pl.* táctica *f*.
tac·tile [ˈtæktail] táctil.
tact·less [ˈtæktlis] □ indiscreto.
tad·pole [ˈtædpoul] renacuajo *m*.
taf·fe·ta [ˈtæfitə] tafetán *m*.
tag [tæg] **1.** (*label*) etiqueta *f*, marbete *m*; herrete *m*; (*rag*) pingajo *m*; (*end*) rabito *m*; *fig.* dicho *m*; muletilla *f*; **2.** *v/t.* pegar una etiqueta a; F seguir los pasos de; *v/i.* F ⌣ *along* seguir despacio su camino; F ⌣ *on to* unirse a.
tail [teil] **1.** cola *f* (*a. fig.*), rabo *m*; trenza *f of hair*; cabellera *f of comet*; faldón *m*, faldillas *f/pl. of coat*; ⌣*s* cruz *f of coin*; F ⌣*s pl.* frac *m*; *turn* ⌣ volver la espalda; **2.** *v/t.* (*follow*) seguir de cerca, vigilar; (*join*) añadir; *animal* descolar; *v/i.:* ⌣ *away*, ⌣ *off* ir disminuyendo (*into* hasta [ser no más que]); ˈ⌣**·board** escalera *f*; ˈ⌣**·coat** frac *m*; **tailed** con rabo; *long*-⌣ rabilargo; **tail-end** cola *f*; extremo *m*; *fig.* parte *f* que queda; porción *f* restante; ˈ**tail·less** sin rabo; ˈ**tail-light** luz *f* piloto (*or* trasera).
tai·lor [ˈteilə] **1.** sastre *m*; **2.** *suit* confeccionar; *well* ⌣*ed suit* traje *m* que entalla bien; ˈ**tai·lor·ing** sastrería *f*; corte *m*; ˈ**tai·lor-made** hecho por sastre; ⌣ *costume* traje *m* hechura sastre.
tail...: ˈ⌣**-piece** *typ.* florón *m*; *fig.*

apéndice *m*; '~·**plane** (plano *m* de)
cola *f*; '~**-skid** ✈ patín *m* de cola;
'~**-u·nit** conjunto *m* de cola;
'~'**wind** viento *m* de cola.

taint [teint] **1.** infección *f*; mancha *f*;
fig. olor *m* (*of* a); **2.** manchar(se);
corromper(se); viciar(se).

take [teik] **1.** [*irr.*] *v/t.* tomar; coger;
p. llevar; (*by force*) asir; arrebatar;
(*steal*) robar; (*accept*) aceptar; (*tolerate*) aguantar; (*catch*) coger;
comer *at chess*; *city, decision, exercise, food, liberty, note* tomar;
advice seguir; *fence* saltar; *illness*
coger; *journal* abonarse a; *oath*
prestar; *opportunity* aprovechar;
photo, ticket sacar; *step, walk etc.*
dar; *trip* hacer; *for many phrases,
see under the corresponding substantive*; *I ~ it that* supongo que; *it ~s
2 hours* es cosa de 2 horas; tarda
2 horas (*to en*); *it ~s 2 men to lift it*
se necesita 2 hombres para levan-
tarlo; F *we can ~ it* lo aguantamos
todo; *the devil ~ it!* ¡maldición!;
~ *apart* desmontar, descomponer;
~ *away* quitar; llevarse; ✗ restar;
~ *back* recibir devuelto; volver a
quitar (*from* a); (*return*) devolver;
p. recibir otra vez; *words* retractar;
~ *down* bajar; descolgar; ⊕ desmontar; *note* apuntar, poner por
escrito; F *p.* quitar los humos a;
~ *for* tomar por; ~ *from* quitar a;
privar de; ✗ restar de; ~ *in* (*understand*) comprender; (*include*) abarcar; *clothes* achicar; *p.* acoger, recibir; *paper* abonarse a; *sail* desmontar; acortar, disminuir; *work*
aceptar; F engañar; ~ *off clothes*
quitarse; *discount* descontar; F contrahacer, parodiar; ~ *on* (*assume*)
tomar; *duties* tomar sobre sí; F *p.*
desafiar, luchar con; *work* emprender; aceptar; *workmen* contratar; ~ *out* (*extract*) extraer, sacar;
children llevar de paseo; *girl* escoltar, invitar; cortejar; *patent* obtener; *stain* quitar; F ~ *it out of a p.*
(*tire*) cansarle a uno; *b. s.* vengarse
en una p.; ~ *it out on a p.* desahogarse riñendo a una p.; vengarse en
una p.; ~ *over* tomar posesión de;
encargarse de; ~ *to pieces* desmontar; ~ *up* subir; coger; absorber;
carpet quitar; *passengers* tomar;
post tomar posesión de; *residence*
establecer, fijar; *room, time* ocupar,

llenar; *story* empezar a contar;
study dedicarse a; ~ *a p. up
on s.t.* censurar algo a alguien;
(comenzar a) disputar con una p.
sobre algo; *I ~ you up on that* no
puedo aceptar eso; ~ *upon o.s.*
tomar sobre sí; encargarse de; ~ *it
upon o.s. to atreverse a*; **2.** [*irr.*] *v/i.*
pegar; ser eficaz; resultar; ✔ arrai-
gar (*a. fig.*); (*set*) cuajar; (*vaccination*) prender; F (*succeed*) tener éxito; *phot.* he ~*s well* saca buen retrato; ~ *after* parecerse a; salir a; ~ *off*
salir; ✈ despegar; F ~ *on congojarse*; quejarse; *don't ~ on so!* ¡no
te apures!; ~ *over* tomar posesión;
~ *to p.* tomar cariño a; *th.* aficionarse a; ~ *to ger.* aficionarse a *inf.*;
ponerse a *inf.*; F ~ *up with* relacionarse con, estrechar amistad con;
3. toma *f*; *phot.* exposición *f*.

tak·en ['teikn] *p.p. of take*; *be ~
with* estar cautivado por; *be ~ ill*
enfermar; *be ~ up with* estar ocupado en; estar absorto en; F *be ~ in*
tragar el anzuelo; *be ~ in by* dejarse
engañar por; '**take-'off** ✈ despegue *m*; ⊕ toma *f* de fuerza;
F caricatura *f*, parodia *f* (*of, on* de);
'**tak·er** el (la) que acepta *a challenge
etc.*

tak·ing ['teikiŋ] **1.** ☐ F atractivo,
encantador; **2.** toma *f*; '**tak·ings**
pl. ingresos *m/pl.*

talc [tælk], **tal·cum pow·der** ['tæl-
kəm 'paudə] talco *m*.

tale [teil] cuento *m* (*a. b.s.*); fábula *f*;
relación *f*; historia *f*; *tell ~s* (*out of
school*) soplar; chismear; '~·**bear·er**
['~bɛərə] soplón (-a *f*) *m*; chismoso
(a *f*) *m*.

tal·ent ['tælənt] talento *m*; '**tal·ent-
ed** talentoso.

tal·is·man ['tælizmən] talismán *m*.

talk [tɔːk] **1.** conversación *f*; charla *f*;
F palabras *f/pl.*; *there is ~ of ger.*
se habla de *inf.*; ~ *of the town*
comidilla *f* de la ciudad; **2.** hablar
(*to* con); charlar; *sense etc.* decir;
~ *down* ✈ controlar el aterrizaje
de (desde tierra); ~ *into* persuadir a;
convencer; ~ *out of* disuadir de;
~ *over* discutir; hablar de; *past
events* pasar revista a; ~ *over*, ~
round p. convencer; **talk·a·tive**
['~ətiv] ☐ locuaz, hablador; '**talker** hablador (-a *f*) *m*; orador (-a *f*)
m; **talk·ie** ['~i] F película *f* sonora;

'**talk·ing** parlante; *bird* parlero;
talk·ing-to ['ᵔtu:] F rapapolvo *m*.
tall [tɔ:l] alto; grande; *be 6 feet* ᵔ
tener 6 pies de alto; *sl.* ᵔ *order*
cosa *f* muy difícil; *sl.* ᵔ *story, Am.*
ᵔ *tale* cuento *m* exagerado (*or* increíble); '**tall·boy** cómoda *f* alta;
'**tall·ness** altura *f*.
tal·low ['tælou] sebo *m*; '**tal·low·y**
seboso.
tal·ly ['tæli] **1.** (*stick*) tarja *f*; (*account*) cuenta *f*; número *m*;
2. cuadrar, concordar, corresponder
(*with con*).
tal·ly-ho ['tæli'hou] *grito del cazador*
(*de zorras*).
tal·on ['tælən] garra *f*.
ta·lus ['teiləs] **1.** talud *m*; *geol.*
talud *m* detrítico; **2.** *anat.* astrágalo *m*.
tam·a·ble ['teiməbl] domable.
tam·a·rind ['tæmərind] tamarindo
m; **tam·a·risk** ['ᵔisk] tamarisco *m*.
tam·bour ['tæmbuə] **1.** *sew.* tambor
m (para bordar); △ tambor *m*;
2. bordar a tambor; **tam·bou·rine**
[ᵔbə'ri:n] pandereta *f*.
tame [teim] **1.** □ domesticado;
manso; doméstico; amansado; *fig.*
inocuo; F aburrido; **2.** domar,
domesticar; amansar; '**tame·ness**
mansedumbre *f*; '**tam·er** domador
(-a *f*) *m*.
tam-o'-shan·ter [tæmə'ʃæntə] boina *f* escocesa.
tamp [tæmp] apisonar; ✕ atacar.
tam·per ['tæmpə]: ᵔ *with* descomponer, estropear; tocar ajando;
entrometerse en; *document* falsificar; *witness* sobornar.
tam·pon ['tæmpən] tapón *m*.
tan [tæn] **1.** bronceado *m*; (*bark*)
casca *f*; **2.** *leather* curtir, adobar;
(*sun*) tostar(se), broncear(se); F
zurrar; **3.** leonado; *shoes* de color.
tan·dem ['tændəm] **1.** tándem *m*;
2. *adj. a. adv.* ɟ en tándem.
tang¹ [tæŋ] espiga *f of knife*; *fig.*
gustillo *m*, dejo *m*; sabor *m* fuerte
y picante.
tang² [ᵔ] **1.** retintín *m*; **2.** (hacer)
retiñir.
tan·gent ['tændʒənt] tangente *adj.
a. su.* f; *go* (*or fly*) *off at a* ᵔ cambiar
súbitamente de rumbo; **tan·gen-
tial** [ᵔ'dʒenʃl] □ tangencial.
tan·ger·ine [tændʒə'ri:n] mandarina *f*.

tan·gi·bil·i·ty [tændʒi'biliti] tangi-
bilidad *f*; **tan·gi·ble** ['tændʒəbl]
□ tangible; *fig. a.* concreto.
tan·gle ['tæŋgl] **1.** enredo *m* (*a. fig.*),
nudo *m*, maraña *f*; **2.** enredar(se),
enmarañar(se).
tan·go ['tæŋgou] tango *m*.
tank [tæŋk] tanque *m* depósito *m*;
✕ tanque *m*, carro *m* de combate;
ᵔ *car*, ᵔ *truck*, ᵔ *wagon* carro *m*
cuba; 🜂 vagón *m* cisterna; ᵔ *engine*
locomotora *f* ténder; '**tank·age**
cabida *f* de un tanque.
tank·ard ['tæŋkəd] pichel *m*, bock *m*.
tank·er ['tæŋkə] petrolero *m*; tanquero *m S.Am.*
tan·ner¹ ['tænə] curtidor *m*.
tan·ner² [ᵔ] *sl.* (moneda *f* de) seis
peniques *m/pl.*
tan·ner·y ['tænəri] curtiduría *f*.
tan·nic ['tænik] tánico.
tan·nin ['tænin] tanino *m*.
tan·ning ['tæniŋ] curtido *m*; F paliza *f*.
tan·ta·lize ['tæntəlaiz] atormentar,
tentar, dar dentera; '**tan·ta·liz·ing**
□ atormentador.
tan·ta·mount ['tæntəmaunt]: ᵔ *to*
equivalente a.
tan·trum ['tæntrəm] F rabieta *f*.
tap¹ [tæp] **1.** palmadita *f*, golpecito
m; **2.** golpear ligeramente; dar
golpecitos (*v/t. a or* en).
tap² [ᵔ] **1.** (*water*) grifo *m*; (*gas*) llave
f; espita *f of barrel*; ⊕ macho *m* de
terraja; *on* ᵔ servido al grifo; *beer*
sacado del barril; *fig.* a mano, disponible; **2.** *barrel* espitar; *tree* sangrar; *resources* explotar; ɟ *wires*
hacer una derivación en; *teleph.*
wire intervenir, escuchar clandestinamente.
tap-dance ['tæpdɑ:ns] **1.** zapateado
m; **2.** zapatear.
tape [teip] cinta *f* (*a. sport*); cinta *f*
adhesiva; (*ceremonial*) cinta *f* sim-
bólica; cinta *f* magnetofónica *for
recording*; *v.* red ᵔ; '**ᵔ-meas·ure**
cinta *f* métrica; '**ᵔ-re·cord·er**
magnetofón *m*; grabador *m* en cinta; '**ᵔ-re·cord·ing** grabación *f* en
cinta.
ta·per ['teipə] **1.** cerilla *f*; *eccl.* cirio
m; **2.** ahusado; **3.** *v/i.* ahusarse; ᵔ
away, ᵔ *off* ir disminuyendo; *v/t.*
afilar, ahusar; ᵔ*ing* = ᵔ **2.**
tap·es·try ['tæpistri] tapiz *m*; tapicería *f*.

tape-worm ['teipwɔ:m] tenia *f*, solitaria *f*.
ta·pi·o·ca [tæpi'oukə] tapioca *f*.
tap·per ['tæpə] ⚡ manipulador *m*.
tap·pet ['tæpit] ⊕ alza-válvulas *m*.
tap-room ['tæprum] bodegón *m*.
tap-root ['tæpru:t] raíz *f* central.
tap·ster ['tæpstə] mozo *m* de taberna.
tar [tɑ:] **1.** alquitrán *m*; brea *f*; F (*Jack*) ♀ marinero *m*; **2.** alquitranar; embrear; ~ *and feather* emplumar.
ta·ran·tu·la [tə'ræntjulə] tarántula *f*.
tar·di·ness ['tɑ:dinis] tardanza *f*; lentitud *f*; '**tar·dy** □ (*late*) tardío; (*slow*) lento.
tare[1] [tɛə] ⚘ (*mst* ~*s pl.*) arveja *f*; (*Biblical*) cizaña *f*.
tare[2] [~] **1.** ⚘ tara *f*; **2.** destarar.
tar·get ['tɑ:git] blanco *m* (*a. fig.*); ~ *practice* tiro *m* al blanco.
tar·iff ['tærif] tarifa *f*; arancel *m*; *attr.* arancelario.
tar·mac ['tɑ:mæk] alquitranado *m*.
tarn [tɑ:n] lago *m* pequeño de montaña.
tar·nish ['tɑ:niʃ] **1.** deslustrar(se) (*a. fig.*); **2.** deslustre *m*.
tar·pau·lin [tɑ:'pɔ:lin] alquitranado *m*; lienzo *m* alquitranado (*or* encerado).
tar·ry[1] ['tæri] *lit.* tardar; detenerse; quedarse.
tar·ry[2] ['tɑ:ri] alquitranado; embreado.
tart [tɑ:t] **1.** □ ácido, agrio; acre; *fig.* áspero; **2.** tarta *f*, torta *f*; *sl.* puta *f*, fulana *f*.
tar·tan ['tɑ:tən] tartán *m*.
Tar·tar[1] ['tɑ:tə] tártaro *m*; *fig.* arpía *f*, mujer *f* regañona; *catch a* ~ meterse con uno que resulta bastante fuerte.
tar·tar[2] [~] 🔥 tártaro *m*, sarro *m*.
task [tɑ:sk] tarea *f*; faena *f*; *take to* ~ reprender (*for acc.*), llamar a capítulo; **task force** agrupación *f* de fuerzas (para operación especial); '**task·mas·ter** capataz *m*; superintendente *m*; amo *m*.
tas·sel ['tæsl] borla *f*.
taste [teist] **1.** gusto *m*; sabor *m* (*of* a); (*sip*) sorbo *m*; (*sample*) muestra *f*; (*good*) ~ (buen) gusto *m*; *just a* ~ una pizca; *in bad* ~ de mal gusto; *to* ~ al gusto, a discreción; *acquire a* ~ *for* tomar gusto a; *be to one's* ~

gustarle a uno; *have a* ~ *for* gustar de, tener afición a; **2.** *v/t.* gustar; notar (un gusto de); (*try*) probar; *v/i.*: ~ *of* saber a; ~ *good* estar muy rico, estar sabroso, ser sabroso; **taste·ful** ['~ful] □ de buen gusto; elegante.
taste·less ['teistlis] □ insípido, soso; (*in bad taste*) de mal gusto; '**taste·less·ness** insipidez *f*; mal gusto *m*.
tas·ter ['teistə] catador *m*.
tast·y ['teisti] □ F sabroso.
tat[1] [tæt] *v. tit*[1].
tat[2] [~] *sew.* hacer frivolité.
ta-ta ['tæ'tɑ:] F adiós.
tat·tered ['tætəd] andrajoso; en jirones; **tat·ters** ['tætəz] *pl.* andrajos *m/pl.*; jirones *m/pl.*; *in* ~ = tattered.
tat·tle ['tætl] **1.** parlotear; *b.s.* chismear; **2.** charla *f*; *b.s.* chismes *m/pl.*, habilla *f*; '**tat·tler** charlador (-a *f*) *m*; *b.s.* chismoso (a *f*) *m*.
tat·too[1] [tə'tu:] ⚔ (toque *m* de) retreta *f*; espectáculo *m* militar.
tat·too[2] [~] **1.** tatuar; **2.** tatuaje *m*.
tat·ty ['tæti] F desaseado; raído; andrajoso.
taught [tɔ:t] *pret. a. p.p. of* teach.
taunt [tɔ:nt] **1.** mofa *f*; pulla *f*; dicterio *m*; **2.** reprochar con insultos (*for, with acc.*); mofar.
taut [tɔ:t] tieso, tenso, tirante; '**taut·en** *v/t.* te(n)sar; *v/i.* ponerse tieso.
tau·to·log·i·cal [tɔ:tə'lɔdʒikl] □ tautológico; **tau·to·lo·gy** [tɔ:'tɔlədʒi] tautología *f*.
tav·ern ['tævən] taberna *f*; mesón *m*.
taw·dri·ness ['tɔ:drinis] lo charro *etc.*; '**taw·dry** □ charro; barato; deslucido; cursi; de oropel.
taw·ny ['tɔ:ni] leonado.
tax [tæks] **1.** impuesto *m* (*on* sobre), contribución *f*; *fig.* carga *f* (*on* sobre); esfuerzo *m* (*on* para); ~ *evasion* evasión *f* fiscal; **2.** *p.* imponer contribuciones a; *th.* imponer contribución sobre; ⚖ *costs* tasar; *fig. patience* agotar; *resources* someter a esfuerzo excesivo; *p.* acusar (*with* de); censurar (*with acc.*); '**tax·a·ble** imponible; sujeto a impuesto; **tax·a·tion** impuestos *m/pl.*; contribuciones *f/pl.*; sistema *m* tributario; '**tax-col·lec·tor** recaudador *m* de contribuciones; '**tax-'free** exento de contribuciones.

tax·i ['tæksi] **1.** = '~-**cab** taxi *m*; **2.** ir en taxi; ☞ carretear.

tax·i·derm·ist [tæksi'də:mist] taxidermista *m/f*.

tax·i...: '~-**driv·er** taxista *m*; '~-**me·ter** taxímetro *m*; '~-**rank** parada *f* de taxis.

tax·pay·er ['tækspeiə] contribuyente *m/f*.

tea [ti:] té *m*; (*meal*) merienda *f*; high ~ merienda-cena *f*; '~-'**cad·dy** bote *m* para té.

teach [ti:tʃ] [*irr.*] enseñar (*to* a); *fig.* ~ a lesson escarmentar; '**teach·a·ble** educable; '**teach·er** profesor (-a *f*) *m*; maestro (a *f*) *m*; '**teach·er-**'**train·ing** formación *f* pedagógica; '**teach·ing** enseñanza *f*; doctrina *f*; *attr.* docente.

tea...: '~-**co·sy** cubretetera *f*; '~-**cup** taza *f* para té; *storm in a* ~ tormenta *f* en un vaso de agua; '~-**dance** thébaile *m*.

teak [ti:k] (madera *f* de) teca *f*.

team [ti:m] **1.** *sport etc.*: equipo *m*; tiro *m* of horses; yunta *f* of oxen; **2.:** ~ up asociarse; formar un equipo; '~-'**spir·it** compañerismo *m*; camaradería *f*; **team·ster** ['stə] tronquista *m*; *Am.* conductor *m* de camión; '**team-work** cooperación *f*, colaboración *f*; solidaridad *f*.

tea·pot ['ti:pɔt] tetera *f*.

tear[1] [tɛə] [*irr.*] *v/t.* rasgar, desgarrar; romper; *flesh* lacerar; (*snatch*) arrancar; ~ apart despedazar; ~ down building derribar; *hangings, flag, poster etc.* arrancar, quitar (arrancando); ~ off arrancar; ~ up paper etc. romper; plant desarraigar; *v. hair*; *v/i.* rasgarse; *F with adv. or prp.* precipitarse, correr precipitadamente, ir con toda prisa; ~ past pasar como un rayo; **2.** rasgón *m*, desgarrón *m*; *v. wear.*

tear[2] [tiə] lágrima *f*.

tear·ful ['tiəful] □ lloroso, llorón; lacrimoso.

tear-gas ['tiə'gæs] gas *m* lacrimógeno.

tea-room ['ti:rum] salón *m* de té.

tease [ti:z] **1.** *wool* cardar; *fig.* embromar, tomar el pelo a; jorobar; atormentar; **2.** embromador (-a *f*) *m*, guasón (-a *f*) *m*; **tea·sel** ['~l] ⚘ cardencha *f*; ⊕ carda *f*; '**teas·er** F rompecabezas *m*.

tea...: '~-**set** servicio *m* de té; '~-

spoon cucharita *f*; '~-**strain·er** colador *m* de té.

teat [ti:t] pezón *m*; teta *f*; chupador *m* of bottle.

tea-time ['ti:taim] hora *f* del té.

tech·ni·cal ['teknikl] □ técnico; **tech·ni·cal·i·ty** [~'kæliti] tecnicidad *f*; cosa *f* técnica; (*word*) tecnicismo *m*; **tech·ni·cian** [tek'niʃn] técnico *m*.

tech·ni·col·o(u)r ['teknikʌlə] (*attr. en*) tecnicolor *m*.

tech·nique [tek'ni:k] técnica *f*.

tech·no·log·i·cal [teknə'lɔdʒikl] □ tecnológico; **tech·no·lo·gist** [tek-'nɔlədʒist] tecnólogo *m*; **tech·no·lo·gy** tecnología *f*.

tech·y ['tetʃi] *v.* testy.

ted·der ['tedə] heneador *m*.

ted·dy-bear ['tedibɛə] osito *m* de felpa.

te·di·ous ['ti:diəs] □ aburrido, fastidioso; cansado; '**te·di·ous·ness**, **te·di·um** ['ti:diəm] tedio *m*; aburrimiento *m*.

tee [ti:] **1.** tee *m*; **2.:** ~ off golpear desde el tee.

teem [ti:m] hormiguear; abundar (*with* en), hervir (*with* de); ~ with rain diluviar, l!over a cántaros.

teen-ag·er ['ti:neidʒə] joven *m/f* de 13 a 19 años.

teens [ti:nz] *pl.* edad *f* de 13 a 19 años; be in one's ~ tener de 13 a 19 años.

tee·ny ['ti:ni] F chiquito, chiquitín.

tee·ter ['ti:tə] F balancear, oscilar.

teeth [ti:θ] [*pl. of tooth*] dientes *m/pl.*

teethe [ti:ð] endentecer, echar los (primeros) dientes; '**teeth·ing** dentición *f*; ~ ring chupador *m*.

tee·to·tal [ti:'toutl] abstemio; **tee-**'**to·tal·(l)er** abstemio (a *f*) *m*.

tel·e·gram ['teligræm] telegrama *m*.

tel·e·graph ['teligra:f] **1.** telégrafo *m*; *attr.* telegráfico; ~ pole poste *m* telegráfico; **2.** telegrafiar; **tel·e-graph·ic** [~'græfik] □ telegráfico; **te·leg·ra·phist** [ti'legrəfist] telegrafista *m/f*; **te'leg·ra·phy** telegrafía *f*.

tel·e·path·ic [teli'pæθik] □ telepático; **te·le·pa·thy** [ti'lepəθi] telepatía *f*.

tel·e·phone ['telifoun] **1.** teléfono *m*; ~ box, ~ kiosk locutorio *m*, cabina *f* de teléfono; ~ call llamada *f*; ~ directory guía *f* telefónica; ~ ex-

change central *f* telefónica; ~ *operator* telefonista *m/f*; *be on the* ~ estar hablando por teléfono; **2.** llamar al (*or* por) teléfono, telefonear; **tel·e·phon·ic** [ˌ'fɔnik] □ telefónico; **te·leph·o·nist** [ti'lefənist] telefonista *m/f*; **te'leph·o·ny** telefonía *f*.

tel·e·pho·to ['teli'foutou] **1.** telefotografía *f*; **2.** telefotográfico.

tel·e·print·er ['teliprintə] teleimpresor *m*.

tel·e·scope ['teliskoup] **1.** telescopio *m*; catalejo *m*; **2.** telescopar(se); enchufar(se); **tel·e·scop·ic** [ˌ'kɔpik] □ telescópico; de enchufe.

tel·e·type ['telitaip] teletipo *m*; **'te·le'typ·er** teletipista *m/f*.

tel·e·vise ['telivaiz] televisar; **tel·e·vi·sion** ['ˌviʒn] (*attr.* de) televisión *f*; ~ *set* aparato *m* de televisión, televisor *m*.

tell [tel] [*irr.*] *v/t.* decir; *story* contar; conocer (*by* por); distinguir (*from* de); determinar; ~ *a p. to inf.* decirle a uno que *subj.*; *I have been told* (*that*) se me ha dicho (que); *you never can* ~ no se puede saber con certeza; F *you're* ~*ing me!* ¡a quién se lo cuentas!; ~ *off* mandar (*to inf.*); F reñir, regañar; *v/i.* hablar (*about, of* de); hacer mella, surtir efecto (*on* en); ~ *on health etc.* afectar, dejarse ver en; F ~ *on* soplar contra, chivatear contra; **'tell·er** narrador (-a *f*) *m*; *parl.* escrutador *m*; (*bank*) cajero *m*; **'tell·ing** □ eficaz; **tell-tale** ['ˌteil] **1.** revelador; indicador; **2.** soplón (-a *f*) *m*; ♫ axiómetro *m*; ~ *clock* reloj *m* registrador.

te·mer·i·ty [ti'meriti] temeridad *f*.

tem·per ['tempə] **1.** *all senses:* templar; *fig. a.* mitigar, moderar; **2.** humor *m*; disposición *f*; natural *m*; (*anger*) mal genio *m*; (*be in a state de*) *good* ~ buen humor *m*; *keep one's* ~ contenerse; *lose one's* ~ perder la paciencia, enojarse; **tem·per·a·ment** ['ˌrəmənt] temperamento *m*, disposición *f*; excitabilidad *f*; **tem·per·a·men·tal** [ˌ'mentl] □ complexional; caprichoso, excitable; *be* ~ tener genio; **'tem·per·ance** templanza *f*; abstinencia *f* (del alcohol); ~ *hotel* hotel *m* donde no se sirven bebidas alcohólicas; **tem·per·ate** ['ˌrit] □ templado; sobrio, abstemio; ~ *zone* zona *f* templada; **tem·per·a·ture** ['tempritʃə]

temperatura *f*; 🌡 calentura *f*; 🌡 ~ *chart* gráfico *m* de temperatura; **tem·pered** ['tempəd] templado.

tem·pest ['tempist] tempestad *f*; **tem·pes·tu·ous** [ˌ'pestjuəs] □ tempestuoso.

Tem·plar ['templə] *hist.* templario *m*; ♀ estudiante *m* de derecho del *Temple* londinense.

tem·ple¹ ['templ] templo *m*; ♀ Colegio *m* de Abogados (de Londres).

tem·ple² [ˌ] *anat.* sien *f*.

tem·po·ral ['tempərəl] □ temporal; **tem·po·ral·i·ties** [ˌ'rælitiz] *pl.* temporalidades *f/pl.*; **'tem·po·ra·ri·ly** temporalmente; **'tem·po·rar·y** □ temporáneo, provisional; transitorio; *official* interino; *worker* temporero; **'tem·po·rize** contemporizar.

tempt [tempt] tentar, provocar, inducir (*to* a); **temp'ta·tion** tentación *f*; **'tempt·er** tentador *m*; **'tempt·ing** □ tentador; *food* apetitoso; **'tempt·ress** tentadora *f*.

ten [ten] diez (*a. su. m*); decena *f*.

ten·a·ble ['tenəbl] defendible, sostenible.

te·na·cious [ti'neiʃəs] □ tenaz; **te·nac·i·ty** [ti'næsiti] tenacidad *f*.

ten·an·cy ['tenənsi] inquilinato *m*, arriendo *m*.

ten·ant ['tenənt] **1.** arrendatario (a *f*) *m*, inquilino (a *f*) *m*; *fig.* habitante *m/f*; **2.** alquilar; *fig.* ocupar; **'ten·ant·ry** inquilinos *m/pl.*

tench [tenʃ] tenca *f*.

tend¹ [tend] tender (*to, towards* a).

tend² [ˌ] *sick etc.* cuidar; vigilar; *machine* manejar, servir; *cattle* guardar.

tend·en·cy ['tendənsi] tendencia *f*; **ten·den·tious** [ˌ'denʃəs] □ tendencioso.

ten·der¹ ['tendə] □ tierno; *spot* delicado, sensible; 🌡 dolorido.

ten·der² [ˌ] **1.** ⚓ oferta *f*, proposición *f*; *legal* ~ moneda *f* de curso legal; **2.** *v/i.* ⚓ ofertar; *v/t.* ofrecer; *thanks* dar; *resignation* presentar.

ten·der³ [ˌ] ⚓ ténder *m*; ♫ gabarra *f*, embarcación *f* auxiliar.

ten·der·foot ['tendəfut] *Am.* recién llegado *m*; novato *m*; **ten·der·loin** ['ˌlɔin] *Am.* filete *m*; *Am.* F barrio *m* de mala vida; **'ten·der·ness** ternura *f*; sensibilidad *f*.

ten·don ['tendən] tendón *m*.

ten·dril ['tendril] zarcillo *m*; *(vine-)* tijereta *f*.

ten·e·ment ['tenimənt] vivienda *f*; habitación *f*; ⚏ posesión *f* permanente; ~s *pl.* = ~ *house* casa *f* de vecindad.

ten·et ['tiːnet] dogma *m*, credo *m*.

ten·fold ['tenfould] **1.** *adj.* décuplo; **2.** *adv.* diez veces.

ten·nis ['tenis] tenis *m*; '~-**court** pista *f* de tenis, cancha *f* de tenis *S.Am.*; '~-**play·er** tenista *m/f*.

ten·on ['tenən] espiga *f*, almilla *f*; '~-**saw** sierra *f* de espigar.

ten·or ['tenə] tenor *m* (*a.* ♪); curso *m*; tendencia *f*.

tense[1] [tens] *gr.* tiempo *m*.

tense[2] [~] **1.** ☐ tieso, tenso; *situation* crítico, lleno de emoción; **2.** te(n)sar; estirar; '**tense·ness** tirantez *f*; **ten·sile** ['tensail] tensor; de tensión; dúctil; ~ *strength* resistencia *f* a la tensión; **ten·sion** ['~ʃn] tensión *f*; tirantez *f* (*a. fig.*); *fig.* emoción *f*; ansia *f*; ⚡ *high* ~ (*attr.* de) alta tensión *f*.

tent[1] [tent] tienda *f* (de campaña).

tent[2] [~] ⚕ lechino *m*, tapón *m*.

ten·ta·cle ['tentəkl] tentáculo *m*.

ten·ta·tive ['tentətiv] ☐ tentativo; provisional; de ensayo; '~ly provisionalmente, como tanteo.

ten·ter ['tentə] bastidor *m*; '~-**hook** escarpia *f*; *fig.* be on ~s estar en ascuas.

tenth [tenθ] décimo (*a. su. m*).

tent-peg ['tentpeg] estaca *f* de tienda; '**tent-pole** mástil *m* de tienda.

ten·u·i·ty [te'njuiti] tenuidad *f*; raridad *f* *of air*; **ten·u·ous** ['tenjuəs] ☐ tenue; sutil; *air* raro.

ten·ure ['tenjuə] posesión *f*; tenencia *f*, ejercicio *m* *of office*.

tep·id ['tepid] ☐ tibio; **te'pid·i·ty**, '**tep·id·ness** tibieza *f*.

ter·cen·te·nar·y [təːsen'tiːnəri], **ter·cen·ten·ni·al** [~'tenjəl] **1.** de trescientos años; **2.** tricentenario *m*.

term [təːm] **1.** término *m* (*end*, *word*, Å, *phls.*); (*period*) plazo *m*, período *m*; condena *f* *of imprisonment*; mandato *m* *of president*; ⚏, *univ.*, *school*: trimestre *m*; ~s *pl.* condiciones *f/pl.*; ✝ precios *f/pl.*; (*relationship*) relaciones *f/pl.*; *in* ~*s of* en términos de; ✝ *on easy* ~*s* a plazos; *be on good* ~*s with* estar en buenos términos con; *come to* (*or make*) ~*s* llegar a un acuerdo; *fig. come to* ~*s with* conformarse con; **2.** nombrar, llamar; calificar (de).

ter·ma·gant ['təːməgənt] arpía *f*, fiera *f*.

ter·mi·na·ble ['təːminəbl] terminable; '**ter·mi·nal 1.** ☐ terminal (*a.* ⚡); *univ. etc.* trimestral; **2.** ⚡ borne *m*; ⚡ polo *m*; (*port*) terminal *f*; *Am.* 🚂 estación *f* de cabeza; **ter·mi·nate** ['~neit] *v/t. a. v/i.* terminar; **ter·mi'na·tion** terminación *f* (*a. gr.*).

ter·mi·nol·o·gy [təːmi'nɔlədʒi] terminología *f*.

ter·mi·nus ['təːminəs], *pl.* **ter·mi·ni** ['~nai] término *m*; 🚂 estación *f* final (*or de cabeza*).

ter·mite ['təːmait] termita *m*, comején *m*. [común.]

tern [təːn]: *common* ~ charrán *m*

ter·na·ry ['təːnəri] ternario *m*.

ter·race ['terəs] **1.** terraza *f*, terraplén *m*; hilera *f* *of houses*; (*roof*) azotea *f*; **2.** terraplenar.

ter·rain ['terein] terreno *m*.

ter·res·tri·al [ti'restriəl] ☐ terrestre.

ter·ri·ble ['terəbl] ☐ terrible; F malísimo, pésimo.

ter·ri·er ['teriə] terrier *m*.

ter·rif·ic [tə'rifik] ☐ tremendo; F estupendo; imponente; **ter·ri·fy** ['terifai] aterrar, aterrorizar.

ter·ri·to·ri·al [teri'tɔːriəl] **1.** ☐ territorial; ~ *waters pl.* aguas *f/pl.* territoriales (*or jurisdiccionales*); ♀ *Army* reserva *f* (del ejército); **2.** reservista *m*; **ter·ri·to·ry** ['~təri] territorio *m*.

ter·ror ['terə] terror *m*, espanto *m*; '**ter·ror·ism** terrorismo *m*; '**ter·ror·ist** terrorista *m*; '+**er·ror·ize** aterrorizar.

terse [təːs] ☐ breve, conciso, lacónico; '**terse·ness** laconismo *m*.

ter·tian ['təːʃn] ⚕ terciana *f*; **ter·ti·ar·y** ['~ʃəri] terciario *m*.

te·ry·lene ['teriliːn] terylene *m*.

tes·sel·ate ['tesileit] formar con teselas; '~*d* *pavement* mosaico *m*.

test [test] **1.** prueba *f*, ensayo *m*; piedra *f* de toque; examen *m*; *psychological etc.*: test *m*; *acid* ~ *fig.* prueba *f* de fuego; ~ *flight* vuelo *m* de ensayo; *put to the* ~ poner a prueba; **2.** probar, ensayar; examinar; *sight* graduar.

tes·ta·ment ['testəmənt] testamento *m*; **tes·ta·men·ta·ry** [‿'mentəri] testamentario.

tes·ta·tor [tes'teitə] testador *m*.

tes·ta·trix [tes'teitriks] testadora *f*.

test case ['test keis] pleito *m* de ensayo (*para determinar la interpretación de una ley*).

tes·ter[1] ['testə] (*bed*) baldaquín *m*.

test·er[2] [‿] (*p.*) ensayador *m*.

tes·ti·cle ['testikl] testículo *m*.

tes·ti·fy ['testifai] testificar (*that* que); atestiguar (*to acc.*); atestar (*to acc.*) (*a. fig.*).

tes·ti·mo·ni·al [testi'mounjəl] recomendación *f*; certificado *m*; **tes·ti·mo·ny** ['‿məni] testimonio *m*.

test·ing ground ['testiŋ 'graund] zona *f* de pruebas.

test...: ‿ **match** partido *m* internacional; '‿**-pa·per** *school*: papel *m* de examen; ⚗ papel *m* reactivo; '‿**-pi·lot** piloto *m* de pruebas; '‿**-print** *phot.* copia *f* de prueba; '‿**-tube** tubo *m* de ensayo; probeta *f*.

tes·ty ['testi] □, **tetch·y** ['tetʃi] □ enojadizo, picajoso.

te·ta·nus ['tetənəs] tétano *m*.

teth·er ['teðə] 1. atadura *f*, traba *f*; *fig.* be at the end of one's ‿ no poder más, estar para volverse loco; 2. apersogar, atar.

Teu·ton ['tju:tən] teutón *m*; **Teu·ton·ic** [‿'tɔnik] teutónico.

text [tekst] texto *m*; tema *m*; *typ.* ‿ hand letra *f* cursiva grande; '‿**book** libro *m* de texto.

tex·tile ['tekstail] 1. textil; 2. *mst* ‿s *pl.* tejidos *m/pl.*

tex·tu·al ['tekstjuəl] □ textual.

tex·ture ['tekstʃə] textura *f* (*a. fig.*).

than [ðæn, *unstressed* ðən] que; more ‿ I más que yo; more ‿ ten más de diez; not more ‿ ten no más que diez; more money ‿ we have más dinero del que tenemos; more books ‿ we have más libros de los que tenemos; he is more stupid ‿ we thought es más estúpido de lo que creíamos.

thank [θæŋk] 1. dar las gracias a; agradecer (*for acc.*); (no) ‿ you (no) gracias; ‿ you! (*stressed*) ¡a usted!; 2. ‿s *pl.* gracias *f/pl.*; agradecimiento *m*; ‿s to gracias a; **thank·ful** ['‿ful] □ agradecido; I was ‿ to get out me alegré de poder salir; '**thank·less** □ *p.* ingrato; *task* ímprobo, sin recompensa; **thanks-**

giv·ing ['‿sgiviŋ] acción *f* de gracias; *Am.* ♀ (*Day*) Día *m* de acción de gracias.

that [ðæt, *unstressed* ðət] 1. *pron.* (*pl. those*) *m*: ése, aquél (*more remote*); *f*: ésa, aquélla; *neuter*: eso, aquello; (*relative*) que, el cual *etc.*; so ‿'s ‿! se acabó; ‿ is es decir; at ‿ acto seguido, sin más; con todo; like ‿ (*adv.*) de esa manera, de la misma manera; 2. *adj.* (*pl. those*) *m*: ese, aquel (*more remote*); *f*: esa, aquella; 3. *adv.* tan; ‿ far tan lejos; ‿ much tanto; 4. *cj.* que; para que; in ‿ en que, por cuanto; so ‿ (*purpose*) para *inf.*, para que *subj.*; (*result*) de modo que.

thatch [θætʃ] 1. (techo *m* de) paja *f*; 2. poner un techo de paja a; badar.

thaw [θɔ:] 1. deshielo *m*; 2. deshelar (se), derretir(se); *fig.* ablandar(se).

the [ði:; *before vowel* ði, *before consonant* ðə] 1. *article*: el, la; *pl.* los, las; (*stressed*) he's ‿ man for the job es el único hombre para el puesto; it's ‿ thing, my dear es lo último, querida; 2. *adv.* ‿ ... ‿ cuanto más ... (tanto) más.

the·a·tre, *Am.* **the·a·ter** ['θiətə] teatro *m* (*a. fig.*); *lecture* ‿ aula *f*; *operating* ‿ quirófano *m*, sala *f* de operaciones; **the·at·ri·cal** [θi'ætrikl] □ teatral; **the·at·ri·cals** [‿klz] *pl.* funciones *f/pl.* teatrales.

thee [ði:] † *or prov.* te; (*after prp.*) ti; *with* ‿ contigo.

theft [θeft] hurto *m*, robo *m*.

their [ðeə] su(s); **theirs** [‿z] (el) suyo, (la) suya *etc.*

the·ism ['θi:izm] teísmo *m*.

them [ðem, ðəm] *acc.* los, las; *dat.* les; (*after prp.*) ellos, ellas.

theme [θi:m] tema *m*; ‿ song motivo *m* principal.

them·selves [ðʌm'selvz] (*subject*) ellos mismos, ellas mismas; *acc.*, *dat.* se; (*after prp.*) sí (mismos, mismas).

then [ðen] 1. *adv.* entonces; luego; después; by ‿ para entonces; antes de eso; now ‿ ahora bien; there and ‿ en el acto, acto seguido; 2. *cj.* pues; conque; por tanto; 3. *adj.* (de) entonces.

thence [ðens] *lit.* de(sde) allí; por eso.

thence·forth ['ðens'fɔ:θ] *lit.* de allí en adelante; desde entonces.

the·oc·ra·cy [θiˈɔkrəsi] teocracia *f*; **the·o·crat·ic** [θiəˈkrætik] □ teocrático.

the·o·do·lite [θiːˈɔdəlait] teodolito *m*.

the·o·lo·gi·an [θiəˈloudʒiən] teólogo *m*; **the·o·log·i·cal** [ˌˈlɔdʒikl] □ teológico; **the·ol·o·gy** [θiˈɔlədʒi] teología *f*.

the·o·rem [ˈθiərəm] teorema *m*; **the·o·ret·ic, the·o·ret·i·cal** [ˌˈretik(l)] □ teórico; **ˈthe·o·rist** teórico *m*, teorizante *m*; **ˈthe·o·rize** teorizar; **ˈthe·o·ry** teoría *f*; in ~ teóricamente.

the·os·o·phy [θiˈɔsəfi] teosofía *f*.

ther·a·peu·tic [θerəˈpjuːtik] **1.** □ terapéutico; **2.** ~s *pl.* terapéutica *f*; **ther·aˈpeu·tist, ˈther·a·pist** terapeuta *m/f*; **ˈther·a·py** terapia *f*; terapéutica *f*.

there [ðɛə] **1.** *adv.* allí, allá, ahí; F *all* ~ despierto, vivo; F *not all* ~ chiflado, tontiloco; ~ *is*, ~ *are* [ðəˈriz, ðəˈraz] hay; **2.** *int.* ¡vaya!

there...: ˈ~·a·bout(s) por ahí; ~ˈafter después de eso; ˈ~ˈby así, de ese modo; ˈ~ˈfore por (lo) tanto, por consiguiente; ~ˈin en eso; en ese respecto; ~ˈof de eso; de lo mismo; ˈ~ˈupˈon por consiguiente; al momento, en seguida; ~ˈwith con eso, con lo mismo.

ther·mal [ˈθəːməl] □ termal; **ther·mic** [ˈˌmik] □ térmico; **therm·i·on·ic** [ˌˈmiˈɔnik] *radio:* ~ *valve* lámpara *f* termoiónica.

ther·mo·dy·nam·ics [ˈθəːmoudaiˈnæmiks] *sg.* termodinámica *f*.

ther·mo·e·lec·tric cou·ple [ˈθəːmouiˈlektrikˈkʌpl] *par m* termoeléctrico; **ther·mom·e·ter** [θəˈmɔmitə] termómetro *m*; **ther·mo·met·ric, ther·mo·met·ri·cal** [θəːməˈmetrik(l)] □ termométrico; **ther·mo·nu·cle·ar** [ˌˈnjuːkliə] termonuclear; **ther·mo·pile** [ˌˈmoupail] termopila *f*; **Ther·mos** [ˈˌmɔs] (*a.* ~ *flask*, ~ *bottle*) termos *m*; **ther·mo·stat** [ˈˌmoustæt] termóstato *m*.

these [ðiːz] (*pl. of this*) **1.** *pron. m:* éstos; *f:* éstas; **2.** *adj. m:* estos; *f:* estas.

the·sis [ˈθiːsis], *pl.* **the·ses** [ˈθiːsiːz] tesis *f*.

they [ðei] ellos, ellas; ~ *who* los que.

thick [θik] **1.** □ espeso; *smoke etc.* denso; *air (misty)* brumoso; (*foul*) viciado; *liquid* (*cloudy*) turbio; (*stiff*) viscoso; *voice* apagado, indistinto; F *p.* estúpido; F íntimo; *2 inches* ~ 2 pulgadas de espesor; ~ *with place* atestado de; que abunda en; F *be* ~ (*as thieves*) intimar mucho, ser uña y carne; F *be* ~ *with* tener mucha intimidad con; *sl. it's a bit* ~! ¡es demasiado!; F *lay it on* ~ exagerar mucho; **2.:** *in the* ~ *of* en medio de; (*battle*) en lo más reñido de; *through* ~ *and thin* por las buenas y las malas; incondicionalmente; **ˈthick·en** espesar(se); (*plot*) complicarse; **thick·et** [ˈˌit] matorral *m*, espesura *f*; **ˈthick-ˈhead·ed** estúpido, torpe; **ˈthick·ness** espesura *f*; espesor *m*; grueso *m*; densidad *f*; consistencia *f*; **ˈthick·ˈset** rechoncho, grueso; **ˈthick-ˈskinned** *fig.* insensible.

thief [θiːf], *pl.* **thieves** [θiːvz] ladrón (-a *f*) *m*; **thieve** [θiːv] hurtar, robar; **thiev·er·y** [ˈˌvəri], **ˈthiev·ing** robo *m*, latrocinio *m*.

thiev·ish [ˈθiːviʃ] □ ladrón; engatado.

thigh [θai] muslo *m*.

thim·ble [ˈθimbl] dedal *m*; ⚓ guardacabo *m*; **thim·ble·ful** [ˈˌful] dedal *m*; dedada *f*.

thin [θin] **1.** □ delgado; *p.* flaco; *covering* ligero; transparente; *air, scent, sound* tenue; *hair* ralo; *soup etc.* aguado; *crop, crowd* escaso (*a.* ~ *on the ground*); **2.** (*slim*) adelgazar(se); (*weaken*) enflaquecerse; (*a.* ~ *out*) entresacar; aclarar; (*crowd etc.*) reducir(se).

thine [ðain] (el) tuyo, (la) tuya *etc.*

thing [θiŋ] cosa *f*; asunto *m*; ~s *pl.* (*possessions*) efectos *m/pl.*; cosas *f/pl.*; F *the* ~ lo que está de moda; lo importante; F *the* ~ *is* el caso es que; *the best* ~ lo mejor; *the only* ~ lo único; *for one* ~ en primer lugar; *of all the* ~s! ¡qué sorpresa!; (*disgust*) ¡qué asco!; *as* ~s *stand* tal como están las cosas; ~s *are going better* las cosas van mejor; F *have a* ~ *about* estar obsesionado por; F *it's not the* (*done*) ~ eso no se hace; F *know a* ~ *or two* saber cuántas son cinco; *not to know the first* ~ *about* no saber nada en absoluto de.

thing·um(·a)·bob [ˈθiŋəm(i)bɔb] F, **thing·um·my** [ˈˌəmi] F cosa *f*, chisme *m*.

think [θiŋk] [*irr.*] *v/i.* pensar (*about*, *of* en; *of* [*opinion*] de; *to inf.*, *about*, *of ger.*: *all take inf.*); (*believe*) creer; reflexionar; meditar; *I ~ so* creo que sí; *I should ~ so!* ¡ya lo creo!; *v/t.* pensar; acordarse de; *not to know what to ~* no saber a qué carta quedarse; *~ better of it* mudar de parecer; *~ little of* tener en poco; *v. much, nothing; ~ well of* tener buen concepto de; *~ out* resolver; *~ over* meditar *acc.*, pensar *acc.*; *~ up* idear; imaginar; **'think·a·ble** concebible; **'think·er** pensador *m*; **'think·ing 1.** pensante; intelectual, mental; **2.** pensamiento *m*; *way of ~* modo *m* de pensar.

thin·ness ['θinnis] delgadez *f*; tenuidad *f etc.*

third [θəːd] **1.** tercero; *F ~ degree* interrogatorio *m* brutal; *~ party* tercera persona *f*; **2.** tercio *m*; tercera parte *f*; *♪* tercera *f*; **'third·ly** en tercer lugar.

thirst [θəːst] **1.** sed *f*; **2.** tener sed (*after, for* de); **'thirst·y** □ sediento; *land* árido; *F work* sudoroso; *be ~* tener sed.

thir·teen ['θəː'tiːn] trece (*a. su. m*); **'thir'teenth** [~θ] decimotercio, decimotercero; **thir·ti·eth** ['~tiiθ] trigésimo; **'thir·ty** treinta.

this [ðis] (*pl.* these) **1.** *pron.* m: éste; *f*: ésta; *neuter*: esto; **2.** *adj.* m: este; *f*: esta; *~ morning* esta ma-⎫

this·tle ['θisl] cardo *m*.   [ñana.⎰

thith·er ['ðiðə] *lit.* allá.

thole [θoul] escálamo *m*.

thong [θɔŋ] correa *f*.

tho·rax ['θɔːræks] tórax *m*.

thorn [θɔːn] espina *f*; **'thorn·y** espinoso (*a. fig.*).

thor·ough ['θʌrə] □ completo; cabal; concienzudo, minucioso; *~ly freq.* a fondo; **'~bred** (de) pura sangre *m/f*; **'~fare** vía *f* pública; carretera *f*; *no ~* se prohibe el paso!; **'~go·ing** cabal; totalista, de cuerpo entero; **'thor·ough·ness** minuciosidad *f*; lo concienzudo *etc.*

those [ðouz] (*pl. of that* 1, 2) **1.** *pron.* m: ésos, aquéllos (*more remote*); *f*: ésas, aquéllas (*more remote*); *~ who* los que, aquellos que *etc.*; **2.** *adj.* m: esos, aquellos; *f*: esas, aquellas (*v.* 1.).

thou [ðau] † *a. prov.* tú.

though [ðou] **1.** *cj.* aunque; si bien; *as ~* como si *subj.*; **2.** *adv.* sin embargo.

thought [θɔːt] **1.** *pret. a. p.p. of think*; **2.** pensamiento *m*; reflexión *f*; solicitud *f*; *give ~ to* pensar, considerar *acc.*; **'thought·ful** ['θɔːtful] □ (*thinking*) pensativo; (*kind*) atento; considerado; (*far-sighted*) previsor; **'thought·ful·ness** atención *f*; solicitud *f*; previsión *f*.

thought·less ['θɔːtlis] □ irreflexivo; descuidado; inconsiderado; **'thought·less·ness** irreflexión *f*; descuido *m*.

thought-read·ing ['θɔːtriːdiŋ] adivinación *f* de pensamientos.

thou·sand ['θauzənd] **1.** mil; *two ~ people* dos mil personas; **2.** mil *m*; millar *m*; **thou·sandth** ['~zənθ] milésimo (*a. su. m*).

thral(l)·dom ['θrɔːldəm] esclavitud *f*.

thrall [θrɔːl] *poet.* (*p.*) esclavo (a *f*) *m*; (*state*) esclavitud *f*.

thrash [θræʃ] *v/t.* golpear; azotar, zurrar; *~ out* resolver mediante larga discusión; *v/i.: ~ about etc.* sacudirse, dar vueltas; *v. thresh*; **'thrash·ing** paliza *f*; *v. threshing*.

thread [θred] **1.** hilo *m* (*a. fig.*); hebra *f of silkworm*; filete *m*, rosca *f of screw*; *pick* (*or take*) *up the ~* coger el hilo; **2.** *needle* enhebrar; *beads* ensartar; *~ one's way through* abrirse paso por; **'~bare** raído, gastado; **'thread·y** filiforme; fibroso.

threat [θret] amenaza *f*; **'threat·en** amenazar (*to* con); **'threat·en·ing** □ amenazante, amenazador.

three [θriː] tres (*a. su. m*); **'~'col·our** de tres colores; **'~'cor·nered** triangular; *~ hat* tricornio *m*; **'~·di'men·sion·al** tridimensional; **'~fold 1.** *adj.* triple; **2.** *adv.* tres veces; **~·pence** ['θrepəns] tres peniques *m/pl.*; **'~·pen·ny** de 3 peniques; *fig.* despreciable; **~·phase** ['θrifeiz] *⚡* trifásico; **'~·ply** *wood* de 3 capas; *wool* triple; **'~·score** sesenta.

thresh [θreʃ] *↗* trillar; *v. thrash*.

thresh·ing ['θreʃiŋ] *↗* trilla *f*; **'~·floor** era *f*; **'~·ma·chine** trilladora *f*.

thresh·old ['θreʃhould] umbral *m*; *fig. on the ~ of* en los umbrales de, en la antesala de.

threw [θruː] *pret. of throw* 1.

thrice [θrais] † tres veces.

thrift, thrift·i·ness ['θrift(inis)] economía *f*, frugalidad *f*; '**thrift-less** □ malgastador, pródigo; '**thrift·y** □ económico, frugal.

thrill [θril] **1.** emocionar(se), estremecer(se) (*with* de), conmover(se); *be* ～*ed with* estar cautivado por; **2.** emoción *f*; estremecimiento *m*; sensación *f*; '**thrill·er** F novela *f* escalofriante; novela *f* policíaca; '**thrill·ing** □ emocionante; apasionante; cautivador.

thrive [θraiv] [*irr.*] medrar, florecer; **thriv·en** ['θrivn] *p.p. of* thrive; **thriv·ing** ['θraiviŋ] □ floreciente, próspero.

throat [θrout] garganta *f*; cuello *m*; *clear one's* ～ aclarar la voz; '**throat·y** □ gutural, ronco.

throb [θrɔb] **1.** latir, palpitar; (*engine*) vibrar; **2.** (*a.* '**throb·bing**) latido *m*, pulsación *f*; vibración *f*.

throes [θrouz] *pl.* agonía *f*, dolores *m/pl.*; F *be in the* ～ of estar luchando con, sufrir todas las molestias de.

throm·bo·sis [θrɔm'bousis] trombosis *f*.

throne [θroun] trono *m*.

throng [θrɔŋ] **1.** tropel *m*, muchedumbre *f*; **2.** *v/t.* atestar; *v/i.* apiñarse; acudir en tropeles.

throt·tle ['θrɔtl] **1.** ahogar, estrangular (*a.* ⊕.); **2.** gaznate *m*; ⊕ (= '～-**valve**) regulador *m*, válvula *f* reguladora; *mot.* acelerador *m*.

through [θru:] **1.** *prp.* por; a través de; por medio de, mediante, debido a; *Am.* hasta (e incluso); **2.** *adv.* de parte a parte; (desde el principio) hasta el fin; ～ *and* ～ hasta los tuétanos; **3.** *adj.* *train* directo; F, *Am. be* ～ haber terminado; haber acabado (*with* con); '～**out 1.** *prp.* (*time*) durante todo, en todo; (*place*) por todo; **2.** *adv.* (*time*) todo el tiempo, desde el principio hasta el fin; (*place*) en (*or* por) todas partes; en todo.

throve [θrouv] *pret. of* thrive.

throw [θrou] **1.** [*irr.*] echar, lanzar, arrojar, tirar; *bridge* tender; *pot* hacer, dar forma a; *rider* desarzonar; *shadow* proyectar; ⊕ *silk* torcer; *Am.* F *fight* perder con premeditación; ～ *about* esparcir; *money* derrochar; ～ *away* echar; malgastar; *chance* desperdiciar; ～ *back enemy* arrollar; *offer* rechazar; ～ *down ball etc.* echar a tierra; *building* derribar; *challenge* lanzar; ～ *in* añadir; dar de más; *ball* sacar; ～ *off clothes* quitarse; *burden* sacudirse, deshacerse de; *composition* hacer de prisa, improvisar; ～ *out* echar; *p.* poner en la calle; *hint* proferir; *parl. bill* rechazar; ～ *over* abandonar; *friend* despedir; ～ *up defences* levantar rápidamente; *post* renunciar a; *work* abandonar; F devolver, vomitar; *v. sponge*; **2.** tirada *f*, tiro *m*, echada *f*; '～**back** *biol.* reversión *f*; '～**in** *sport*: saque *m*; **thrown** [θroun] *p.p. of* throw.

thru [θru:] *Am.* = through.

thrum[1] [θrʌm] *weaving*: hilo *m* basto.

thrum[2] [～] ♪ *v/t.* guitar rasguear; *v/i.* teclear.

thrush[1] [θrʌʃ] *orn.* zorzal *m*.

thrush[2] [～] 🦠 ubrera *f*; *vet.* higo *m*.

thrust [θrʌst] **1.** estocada *f of sword*; ⚔ avance *m*; ataque *m*; ⊕ *a. fig.* empuje *m*; **2.** *v/t.* empujar (*forward etc.* hacia adelante *etc.*); ～ *aside* rechazar bruscamente; ～ *into* clavar en, hincar en; introducir en; ～ *out* sacar; *hand* tender; ～ *upon* imponer a; *v/i.*: ～ *at* asestar un golpe a; ～ *forward* seguir adelante; ⚔ avanzar; ～ *through* abrirse paso por fuerza.

thud [θʌd] **1.** golpear con ruido sordo; **2.** ruido *m* sordo; (*fall*) baque *m*.

thug [θʌg] asesino *m*; ladrón *m* brutal; hombre *m* rutal, desalmado *m*.

thumb [θʌm] **1.** pulgar *m*; **2.** manosear; (～ *through*) hojear; F ～ *a ride* hacer autostop; '～-**print** F enorme impresión *f* del pulgar; '～-**screw** *hist.* empulgueras *f/pl.*; ⊕ tornillo *m* de orejas; '～-**tack** *Am.* chinche *m*.

thump [θʌmp] **1.** golpazo *m*; porrazo *m*; **2.** *v/t.* golpear; aporrear; *v/i.* caer *etc.* con golpe pesado; (*heart*) latir con golpes pesados; '**thump·ing** F enorme, grandote.

thun·der ['θʌndə] **1.** trueno *m*; *fig.* estruendo *m*; **2.** tronar; *threats etc.* fulminar; '～-**bolt** rayo *m* (*a. fig.*); '～-**clap** tronido *m*; '～-**cloud** nubarrón *m*; '**thun·der·ing** F enorme, imponente; '**thun·der·ous** □ *applause* atronador; '**thun·der·storm** tronada *f*, tempestad *f* de truenos; '**thun·der·struck** *fig.* pasmado, estupefacto; **'thun·der·y** tormen-toso.

Thurs·day ['θəːzdi] jueves *m*.

thus [ðʌs] así; ~ *far* hasta aquí.

thwack [θwæk] *v*. whack.

thwart [θwɔːt] **1.** frustrar, impedir, desbaratar; **2.** ⚓ bancada *f*.

thy [ðai] † tu(s).

thyme [taim] tomillo *m*.

thy·roid ['θairɔid] **1.** tiroideo; **2.** tiroides *m* (*a*. ~ gland).

thy·self [ðai'self] † (*subject*) tú mismo, tú misma; *acc., dat.* te; (*after prp.*) ti (mismo, misma).

tib·i·a ['tibiə] tibia *f*.

tic [tik] 🗲 tic *m*.

tick¹ [~] *zo.* garrapata *f*.

tick² [~] (*mattress-*) funda *f*.

tick³ [~] F: on ~ al fiado.

tick⁴ [~] **1.** tictac *m of clock*; (*mark*) señal *f*, marca *f*; F momento *m*; F on (*or to*) *the* ~ en punto, puntualmente; **2.** *v/i.* hacer tictac; ~ *over mot.* marchar en vacío; *v/t.* poner una señal contra (*a*. ~ off); *sl.* ~ off echar un rapapolvo a.

tick·er-tape ['tikəteip] cinta *f* de cotizaciones.

tick·et ['tikit] **1.** billete *m*; *thea. etc.* entrada *f*, localidad *f*; (*counterfoil*) talón *m*; (*label*) etiqueta *f*, rótulo *m*; *Am.* F multa *f* (*de conductor*); *Am. parl.* candidatura *f*; F *that's the* ~ eso es lo que hacía falta; **2.** rotular, poner etiqueta a; **'~-col·lec·tor** revisor *m*; **'~-win·dow** *esp. Am. thea.* taquilla *f*; 🚪 despacho *m* de billetes.

tick·ing-off ['tikiŋɔf] *sl.* rapapolvo *m*.

tick·le ['tikl] *v/i.* cosquilear, hacer cosquillas a; (*amuse*) divertir; *v/i.*: *my back* ~*s* siento cosquillas en la espalda; **'tick·ler** *radio:* (*or* ~ *coil*) bobina *f* de regeneración; **'tick·ling** cosquillas *f/pl.*; **'tick·lish** □ cosquilloso; *fig.* peliagudo; *be* ~ tener cosquillas, ser cosquilloso.

tid·al ['taidl] □ de marea; ~ *wave* ola *f* de marea.

tide [taid] **1.** marea *f*; *fig.* corriente *f*; marcha *f*; *low* ~ bajamar *f*; *fig.* punto *m* más bajo; *high* ~ pleamar *f*; *fig.* apogeo *m*; *turn of the* ~ cambio *m* de la marea; *fig.* momento *m* del cambio decisivo; **2.**: *fig.* ~ *over* sacar temporalmente de apuro.

ti·di·ness ['taidinis] aseo *m*, buen orden *m*.

ti·dings ['taidiŋz] *pl.* noticias *f/pl.*

ti·dy ['taidi] **1.** □ aseado; ordenado; pulcro; F considerable; **2.** (*a*. ~ *up*) asear; arreglar; poner en orden.

tie [tai] **1.** corbata *f*; lazo *m*; ♪ ligado *m*; △ tirante *m*; *fig.* (*hindrance*) estorbo *m*; (*bond*) vínculo *m*; *sport, voting:* empate *m*; (*match*) partido *m*; **2.** *v/t.* atar; liar; enlazar; ♪ *a. fig.* ligar; *tie* hacer; *fig.* (*a*. ~ *down*) limitar, confinar; (*hinder*) estorbar; ~ *up* atar; envolver; *traffic* obstruir; ⚓ atracar; *v/i. sport etc.*: empatar; ⚓ atracar; **'~-pin** alfiler *m* de corbata.

tier [tiə] fila *f*, grada *f*, grado *m*.

tie-up ['taiʌp] enlace *m*; *esp. Am.* paralización *f by strike*; bloqueo *m of traffic*.

tiff [tif] F riña *f* ligera; pique *m*.

tif·fin ['tifin] (*Indian*) almuerzo *m*.

ti·ger ['taigə] tigre *m/f*; **'ti·ger·ish** □ *fig.* feroz.

tight [tait] □ apretado; estrecho; *clothes* ajustado; (*taut*) tirante; *box* bien cerrado; *curve* cerrado; *situation* difícil; 🌴 *money* escaso; F (*mean*) agarrado; F (*drunk*) borracho; *hold* ~ agarrarse bien; F *sit* ~ estarse quieto; *be in a* ~ *corner* verse en un aprieto; estar en peligro; **'tight·en** (*a*. ~ *up*) apretar(se); atiesar(se); estrechar(se); **'tight-'fist·ed** agarrado; **'tight-'fit·ting** muy ajustado; **'tight·ness** estrechez *f*; tirantez *f*; **'tight-rope walk·er** funámbulo *m*, equilibrista *m/f*; **tights** [~s] *pl.* traje *m* de malla; **'tight·wad** *Am. sl.* cicatero *m*.

ti·gress ['taigris] tigresa *f*.

tile [tail] **1.** (*roof-*) teja *f*; (*floor-*)baldosa *f*; (*coloured*) azulejo *m*; *sl.* sombrero *m*; *sl. on the* ~*s* de juerga; **2.** *roof* tejar; *floor* embaldosar.

till¹ [til] caja *f* registradora, cajón *m*.

till² [~] *prp.* hasta; *cj.* hasta que.

till³ [~] 🗲 cultivar, labrar; **'till·age** cultivo *m*, labranza *f*.

till·er ['tilə] ⚓ caña *f* del timón; 🗲 labrador *m*.

tilt [tilt] **1.** inclinación *f*; ⚔ torneo *m*; (*at*) *full* ~ a toda velocidad; *on the* ~ inclinado; **2.** inclinar(se), ladear(se); ⚔ justar; ~ *at* arremeter contra.

tilth [tilθ] condición *f* (cultivable) de la tierra; *lit.* cultivo *m*.

tim·ber ['timbə] **1.** madera *f* (de construcción); (*beam*) viga *f*; árboles *m*/*pl.* de monte; ⚓ cuaderna *f*; **2.** enmaderar; ⁓*ed* enmaderado; *land* arbolado; '**tim·ber·ing** maderamen *m*; '⁓-**line** límite *m* forestal; '⁓-**yard** almacén *m* de madera.

time [taim] **1.** tiempo *m*; hora *f of day*; (*occasion*) vez *f*; época *f*; plazo *m*; horas *f*/*pl.* de trabajo; ♪ compás *m*; ⁓! ¡la hora!; ⅄ ⁓s por; ⁓ *to go* hora *f* de irse; *what is the* ⁓? ¿qué hora es?; *it is high* ⁓ *that* ya es hora de que; ⁓ *after* ⁓, ⁓ *and again* repetidas veces; *at a* ⁓, *at the same* ⁓ a la vez; *at any* ⁓ a cualquier hora; *at no* ⁓ nunca; *at one* ⁓ en cierta época; *había momentos en que* ...; *at* ⁓s a veces; *behind* ⁓ atrasado; *behind the* ⁓s anticuado; *between* ⁓s en los intervalos; *by that* ⁓ antes de eso; *every* ⁓! sin excepción; *for the* ⁓ *being* por ahora; *from* ⁓ *to* ⁓ de vez en cuando, con el tiempo; *in* (*good*) ⁓ (*early*) a tiempo, con tiempo; (*eventually*) andando el tiempo, con el tiempo; *in no* ⁓ en muy poco tiempo; *on* ⁓ puntual(mente); *beat* (*or keep*) ⁓ llevar el compás; *F do* ⁓ cumplir una condena; *have a bad* ⁓ pasarlo mal; *have a good* ⁓ divertirse (mucho); *darse buena vida*; *have no* ⁓ *for* no poder aguantar; *keep good* ⁓ (*clock*) andar bien; *mark* ⁓ ⚔ llevar el paso; *fig.* hacer tiempo; *take a long* ⁓ *to* tardar mucho en; *take one's* ⁓ no darse prisa; *v. mean*; **2.** *race* cronometrar; medir el tiempo de; *watch* regular; *action* hacer a tiempo oportuno; *the train is* ⁓*d for 5* el tren debe partir (llegar) a las 5; '⁓-**bomb** bomba *f* de relojería; '⁓-**ex·po·sure** *phot.* pose *f*; '⁓-**hon·o(u)red** tradicional, consagrado; '⁓-**keep·er** reloj *m*; cronómetro *m*; (*p.*) cronometrador *m*; '⁓-**lag** intervalo *m*; retraso *m*, retardo *m*; '⁓-**less** eterno; sin limitación de tiempo; '⁓-'**lim·it** limitación *f* de tiempo; plazo *m*; fecha *f* tope; '**time·ly** oportuno; '**time·piece** reloj *m*; '**tim·er** reloj *m* de arena; ⊕ reloj *m* automático; ⊕ distribuidor *m* de encendido *in engine*.

time...: ⁓-**serv·er** ['taimsə:və] con-temporizador *m*; '⁓-'**sig·nal** *radio:* señal *f* horaria; '⁓-**ta·ble** horario *m*; programa *m*.

tim·id ['timid] ☐ tímido; **ti·mid·i·ty** [ti'miditi] timidez *f*.

tim·ing ['taimiŋ] medida *f* del tiempo; realización *f etc.* en momento oportuno *of action*; ⊕ cronometraje *m*; ⁓ *gear* engranaje *m* de distribución.

tim·or·ous ['timərəs] ☐ temeroso, tímido.

tin [tin] **1.** estaño *m*; (*can*) lata *f*; ⊕ hoja *f* de lata, hojalata *f*; *sl.* parné *m*; **2.** de estaño, de hojalata, *F* inferior; ⁓ *soldier* soldado *m* de plomo; **3.** ⊕ estañar; *food* conservar en latas; ⁓*ned meat* carne *f* en lata.

tinc·ture ['tiŋktʃə] **1.** tintura *f* (*a. fig.*); *pharm.* tintura *f*; **2.** tinturar, teñir.

tin·der ['tində] yesca *f* (*a. fig.*); ⁓ *box* yescas *f*/*pl.*

tine [tain] púa *f*.

tin·foil ['tin'fɔil] papel *m* de estaño.

ting [tiŋ] *F v. tinkle*.

tinge [tindʒ] **1.** tinte *m*; dejo *m*, matiz *m* (*a. fig.*); **2.** teñir (*with* de); matizar (*with* de) (*a. fig.*).

tin·gle ['tiŋgl] **1.** sentir comezón; *fig.* estremecerse (*with* de); **2.** (*a.* '**ting·ling**) comezón *f*; estremecimiento *m*.

tink·er ['tiŋkə] **1.** calderero *m* remendón; **2.** *v/t.* remendar chapuceramente (*a.* ⁓ *up*); *v/i.:* ⁓ *with* tratar vanamente de reparar; jugar con; (*spoil*) estropear.

tin·kle ['tiŋkl] **1.** (hacer) retiñir; (hacer) campanillear; **2.** (*a.* '**tink·ling**) retintín *m*; campanilleo *m*.

tin·ny ['tini] ♪ cascado, que suena a lata; *F* desvencijado; '**tin·o·pen·er** abrelatas *m*; '**tin·plate** hojalata *f*.

tin·sel ['tinsl] **1.** oropel *m* (*a. fig.*); **2.** de oropel; **3.** oropelar.

tint [tint] **1.** tinte *m*, matiz *m*; media tinta *f*; **2.** teñir, matizar.

tin·tack ['tintæk] tachuela *f*.

tin·tin·nab·u·la·tion ['tintinæbju-'leiʃn] ⌺ campanilleo *m*.

ti·ny ['taini] menudo, diminuto, chiquitín.

tip [tip] **1.** punta *f*, extremidad *f*; casquillo *m of stick etc.*; embocadura *f of cigarette*; (*dump*) escombrera *f*, depósito *m* de basura; F (*gratuity*) propina *f*; F aviso *m*; soplo *m*; **2.** inclinar(se), ladear(se); *stick etc.* poner casquillo a; F dar propina (*v/t.* a); F *winner* recomendar; F ~ *off*, ~ *the wink* advertir clandestinamente; ~ *over*, ~ *up* volcar(se); '~**-cart** volquete *m*; '~**-off** F advertencia *f* clandestina.

tip-ple ['tipl] **1.** envasar, empinar el codo; **2.** bebida *f* (alcohólica); '**tip-pler** bebedor *m*.

tip-ster ['tipstə] pronosticador *m*.

tip-sy ['tipsi] □ achispado.

tip-toe ['tip'tou]: *on* ~ de puntillas.

tip-top ['tip'tɔp] F de primera, excelente.

tip-up ['tipʌp]: ~ *lorry* basculante *m*; ~ *seat* asiento *m* abatible.

ti-rade [tai'reid] diatriba *f*, invectiva *f*.

tire[1] ['taiə] *v.* tyre.

tire[2] [~] cansar(se) (*of* de); aburrir (se).

tired ['taiəd] □ cansado (*fig. of* de); ~ *out* rendido; '**tired-ness** cansancio *m*.

tire-less ['taiəlis] □ infatigable, incansable.

tire-some ['taiəsəm] □ molesto, fastidioso; aburrido.

ti-ro ['taiərou] novicio *m*, novato *m*.

tis-sue ['tisju:] tejido *m* (*a. anat.*); † (*cloth*) tisú *m*; *fig.* sarta *f of lies etc.*; '~**-pa-per** papel *m* de seda.

tit[1] [tit]: ~ *for tat* donde las dan las toman.

tit[2] [~] = teat.

tit[3] [~] *orn. mst* herrerillo *m*.

Ti-tan ['taitən] titán *m*; **ti-ta-nic** [~'tænik] □ titánico.

tit-bit ['titbit] golosina *f* (*a. fig.*).

tithe [taið] *eccl.* diezmo *m*.

tit-il-late ['titileit] estimular, excitar, titilar; **tit-il-la-tion** estimulación *f*, excitación *f*, titilación *f*.

tit-i-vate ['titiveit] F emperejilar(se), ataviar(se).

ti-tle ['taitl] **1.** título *m*; ⚖ título *m* de propiedad; *sport*: campeonato *m*; ~ *to* derecho *m* a; **2.** (in)titular; ~*d* titulado; '~**-deed** título *m* de propiedad; '~**-hold-er** *sport*: campeón *m*, titular *m*; '~**-page** portada *f*.

ti-trate ['titreit] valorar; **ti'tra-tion** valoración *f*.

tit-ter ['titə] **1.** reírse a disimulo; **2.** risa *f* disimulada.

tit-tle ['titl] *fig.* ápice *m*; '~**-tat-tle 1.** chismes *m/pl.*; **2.** chismear.

tit-u-lar ['titjulə] titular; nominal.

to [tu:; *in the sentence mst* tu, *before consonant* tə] **1.** *not translated before infinitive*: *to do* hacer; *I have letters* ~ *write* tengo cartas que escribir; *the book is still* ~ *be written* el libro está todavía por escribir; *I weep* ~ *think of it* lloro con sólo pensar en ello; **2.** *prp.* a; hacia; para; *I am going* ~ *Madrid* (*Spain*) voy a Madrid (España); *the road* ~ *Madrid* el camino de Madrid; *be kind* ~ *him* sé amable con él; ~ *my way of thinking* según mi modo de pensar; *a quarter* ~ *2* las 2 menos cuarto; *he gave it* ~ *me* me lo dio (a mí); *he gave it* ~ *his friend* se lo dio a su amigo; *secretary* ~ secretario de; *here's* ~ *you!* ¡por Vd.!; *from door* ~ *door* de puerta en puerta.

toad [toud] sapo *m*; '~**-stool** hongo *m* (*freq.* venenoso).

toad-y ['toudi] **1.** pelotillero *m*, adulador *m* servil; **2.** adular servilmente (*to* a); '**toad-y-ing**, '**toad-y-ism** adulación *f* servil.

toast [toust] **1.** pan *m* tostado; tostada *f*; brindis *m* (*to* por); **2.** tostar; *p.* brindar por; '**toast-er** (*electric*) tostadora *f*.

to-bac-co [tə'bækou] tabaco *m*; ~ *pouch* petaca *f*; **to'bac-co-nist** [~kənist] estanquero *m*, tabaquero *m*; ~*'s* (*shop*) estanco *m*, tabaquería *f*.

to-bog-gan [tə'bɔgən] **1.** tobogán *m*; **2.** deslizarse en tobogán.

toc-sin ['tɔksin] campana(da) *f* de alarma.

to-day [tə'dei] hoy; hoy día; ~ *week*, *a week* ~ de hoy en ocho días.

tod-dle ['tɔdl] hacer pinos, andar a tatas; F pasearse, irse (*a.* ~ *off*); '**tod-dler** pequeñito (*a f*) *m* (que aprende a andar).

tod-dy ['tɔdi] ponche *m*.

to-do [tə'du:] F lío *m*, alharaca *f*, alboroto *m*.

toe [tou] **1.** *anat.* dedo *m* del pie; punta *f* del pie; punta *f of sock*; puntera *f of shoe* (*a.* ~ *cap*); **2.** tocar con la punta del pie; ~ *the* (*party*) *line* conformarse; someterse.

toff [tɔf] F currutaco *m*, chuleta *m*.

tof-fee ['tɔfi] caramelo *m*.

to·ga ['tougə] toga *f*.

to·geth·er [tə'geðə] 1. *adj*. juntos; *all* ～ todos juntos; *all* ～*!* (*pulling*) ¡bien, ahora!; 2. *adv*. juntamente, junto; a la vez, a un tiempo; ～ *with* junto con.

tog·gle ['tɔgl] 1. cazonete *m* de aparejo; 2. asegurar con cazonete.

togs [tɔgz] *pl*. F ropa *f*.

toil [tɔil] 1. fatiga *f*; afán *m*; 2. fatigarse; afanarse; ～ *up* subir penosamente.

toi·let ['tɔilit] atavío *m*, tocado *m*; traje *m*; *euph*. wáter *m*, lavabo *m*; '～**-pa·per**, '～**-roll** rollo *m* de papel higiénico; '～**-set** juego *m* de tocador; '～**-soap** jabón *m* de tocador.

toils [tɔilz] *pl*. red *f*, lazo *m*.

to·ken ['toukən] señal *f*; muestra *f*; prenda *f*; prueba *f*; *attr*. simbólico; *in* (*or as a*) ～ *of* en señal de.

told [tould] *pret. a. p.p. of* tell; *all* ～ en total.

tol·er·a·ble ['tɔlərəbl] ☐ tolerable; (*fair*) mediano, regular; '**tol·er·ance** tolerancia *f*; '**tol·er·ant** ☐ tolerante; **tol·er·ate** ['～reit] tolerar; aguantar; **tol·er·a'tion** tolerancia *f*.

toll[1] [toul] peaje *m*; pontazgo *m*; *fig*. mortalidad *f*, número *m* de víctimas; *teleph*. ～ *call* conferencia *f* interurbana; *take* ～ *of* causar bajas en, tener su efecto en; '～**-bar**, '～**-gate** barrera *f* de peaje; '～**-bridge** puente *m* de peaje.

toll[2] [～] *v/i*. doblar (a muerto); *v/t*. tocar (a muerto), tañer, sonar.

tom [tɔm] macho *m* (*esp*. del gato); '～**-cat** gato *m*.

tom·a·hawk ['tɔməhɔːk] tomahawk *m*.

to·ma·to [tə'mɑːtou, *Am*. tə'meitou], *pl*. **to'ma·toes** [～z] tomate *m*.

tomb [tuːm] tumba *f*, sepulcro *m*.

tom·boy ['tɔmbɔi] muchacha *f* traviesa.

tomb·stone ['tuːmstoun] lápida *f* sepulcral.

tome [toum] tomo *m*; *co*. librote *m*.

tom·fool ['tɔm'fuːl] necio *adj. a. su. m*; **tom'fool·er·y** pataratas *f/pl*., payasadas *f/pl*.

tom·my ['tɔmi] F soldado *m* inglés; ～ *gun* pistola *f* ametralladora; F ～ *rot* disparates *m/pl*.

to·mor·row [tə'mɔrou] mañana (*a. su. m*); *the day after* ～ pasado mañana.

tom·tom ['tɔmtɔm] tantán *m*.

ton [tʌn] tonelada *f*; F ～*s pl*. montones *m/pl*.

to·nal·i·ty [tou'næliti] tonalidad *f*.

tone [toun] 1. *all sensès*: tono *m*; *radio*: ～ *control* control *m* de tonalidad; 2. *v/t*. ♪, *paint*. entonar; *phot*. virar; ～ *down* suavizar (el tono de); ～ *up* tonificar, entonar; *fig*. elevar el tono de; *v/i*. armonizar (*in with* con); ～ *down* moderarse.

tongs [tɔŋz] *pl*. (*a pair of* unas) (*sugar-*) tenacillas *f/pl*.; (*coal-*) tenazas *f/pl*.

tongue [tʌŋ] *mst* lengua *f*; ⊕ lengüeta *f* (*a. of scales*); *give* ～ comenzar a ladrar; *hold one's* ～ callar(se); *speak with one's* ～ *in one's cheek* hablar irónicamente; '**tongue-tied** que tiene dificultad al hablar; *fig*. premioso, tímido; '**tongue-twist·er** trabalenguas *m*.

ton·ic ['tɔnik] 1. ☐ tónico; 2. ♪ tónica *f*; ♣ tónico *m* (*a. fig.*).

to·night [tə'nait] esta noche.

ton·nage ['tʌnidʒ] tonelaje *m*.

ton·ner ['tʌnə] de … toneladas.

ton·sil ['tɔnsl] amígdala *f*; **ton·sil·li·tis** [～'laitis] amigdalitis *f*.

ton·sure ['tɔnʃə] 1. tonsura *f*; 2. tonsurar.

ton·y ['touni] *Am. sl*. aristocrático, elegante.

too [tuː] demasiado; (*also*) también; ～ *much* demasiado; (*only*) ～ *well* de sobra.

took [tuk] *pret. of* take.

tool [tuːl] herramienta *f*; utensilio *m*; *fig*. instrumento *m*; (*set of*) ～*s pl*. útiles *m/pl*., utillaje *m*; '～**-bag**, '～**-kit** herramental *m*, bolsa *f* de herramientas; '～**-box** caja *f* de herramientas.

toot [tuːt] 1. sonar (*v/i*. la bocina *etc*.); 2. sonido *m* breve.

tooth [tuːθ] (*pl*. teeth) diente *m*; (*molar*) muela *f*; púa *f of comb*; *false teeth* dentadura *f* postiza; ～ *and nail* encarnizadamente; '～**-ache** dolor *m* (*or* mal *m*) de muelas; '～**-brush** cepillo *m* de dientes; **toothed** [～θt] dentado; con … dientes; '**tooth·ing** △ adaraja *f*; '**tooth·less** ☐ desdentado; '**tooth·paste** pasta *f* dentífrica (*or* de dientes); '**tooth·pick** palillo *m*.

tooth·some ['tuːθsəm] ☐ sabroso.

too·tle ['tuːtl] F *v*. toot.

top¹ [tɔp] **1.** cima *f*, cumbre *f*, ápice *m*; cabeza *f of page, list*; copa *f of tree*; remate *m of roof etc.*; coronilla *f of head*; imperial *f of bus*; (*lid*) tapa *f*; capuchón *m of pen*; *Am. mot.* capota *f*; ⚓ cofa *f*; *sl.* the ∼s *pl.* la flor de la canela; *at* the ∼ *of* a la cabeza de; en la cumbre de; *at* the ∼ *of one's voice* a voz en grito; *from* ∼ *to bottom* de arriba abajo; *de cabo a rabo; from* ∼ *to toe* de pies a cabeza; *on* ∼ ganando; de arriba; *on* ∼ *of* encima de; *fig.* además de; *fig. on* ∼ *of that* por añadidura; **2.** (el) más alto; cimero; *floor* último; *price* tope; *speed* máximo; ∼ *people* la gente bien; **3.** coronar, rematar; *class* estar a la cabeza de; *fig.* superar, aventajar; ✗ descabezar, desmochar; F ∼ *off* rematar; F ∼ *up glass* llenar.

top² [∼] peonza *f*; peón *m*.

to·paz ['toupæz] topacio *m*.

top-boots ['tɔp'buːts] botas *f*/*pl.* de campaña.

top-coat ['tɔpkout] sobretodo *m*.

to·pee ['toupi] casco *m* colonial.

top·er ['toupə] borrachín *m*.

top...: '∼**flight** F sobresaliente; ∼**gal·lant** ['∼'gælənt, ⚓ tə'gælənt] (*or* ∼ *sail*) juanete *m*; ∼ **hat** chistera *f*; '∼-'**heav·y** demasiado pesado por arriba; '∼-'**hole** *sl.* de primera.

top·ic ['tɔpik] asunto *m*, tema *m*; '**top·i·cal** □ (de interés) actual, corriente; ✗ tópico.

top...: '∼**knot** moño *m* (*a. orn.*); F cabeza *f*; '∼**mast** mastelero *m*; '∼**most** (el) más alto; '∼-'**notch** F sobresaliente.

to·pog·ra·pher [tə'pɔgrəfə] topógrafo *m*; **top·o·graph·ic, top·o·graph·i·cal** [tɔpə'græfik(l)] □ topográfico; **to·pog·ra·phy** [tə'pɔgrəfi] topografía *f*.

top·per ['tɔpə] *sl.* chistera *f*; '**top·ping** F estupendo; de primera.

top·ple ['tɔpl] (*mst* ∼ *down*, ∼ *over*) *v/t.* derribar, volcar; *v/i.* volcar(se), venirse abajo.

top·sail ['tɔpsl] gavia *f*.

top-sy-tur·vy ['tɔpsi'təːvi] trastornado; en desorden.

tor [tɔː] colina *f* abrupta y rocosa.

torch [tɔːtʃ] antorcha *f*; *electric* ∼ linterna *f* eléctrica; '∼**bear·er** portahachón *m*; '∼**light** luz *f* de antorcha; ∼ *procession* desfile *m* de portahachones.

tore [tɔː] *pret. of tear¹* 1.

tor·ment 1. ['tɔːmənt] tormento *m*; **2.** [tɔː'ment] atormentar; **tor'men·tor** atormentador (-a *f*) *m*.

torn [tɔːn] *p.p. of tear¹* 1.

tor·na·do [tɔː'neidou], *pl.* **tor'na·does** [∼z] huracán *m*, tornado *m*.

tor·pe·do [tɔː'piːdou], *pl.* **tor'pe·does** [∼z] **1.** *all senses*: torpedo *m*; **2.** torpedear (*a. fig.*); '∼**boat** torpedero *m*; '∼**tube** (tubo *m*) lanzatorpedos *m*.

tor·pid ['tɔːpid] □ aletargado, inactivo; *fig.* torpe, entorpecido; **tor'pid·i·ty, 'tor·pid·ness, tor·por** ['tɔːpə] letargo *m*; *fig.* torpeza *f*, entorpecimiento *m*.

torque [tɔːk] par *m* de torsión.

tor·rent ['tɔrənt] torrente *m* (*a. fig.*); **tor·ren·tial** [tə'renʃl] □ torrencial.

tor·rid ['tɔrid] tórrido; ∼ *zone* zona *f* tórrida.

tor·sion ['tɔːʃn] torsión *f*; '**tor·sion·al** torsional.

tor·so ['tɔːsou] torso *m*.

tort [tɔːt] agravio *m*.

tor·toise ['tɔːtəs] tortuga *f*; '∼**shell** carey *m*.

tor·tu·ous ['tɔːtjuəs] □ tortuoso (*a. fig.*); *p.* torcido.

tor·ture ['tɔːtʃə] **1.** tortura *f*; **2.** torturar; *fig.* torcer, violentar; '**tor·tur·er** verdugo *m*.

To·ry ['tɔːri] tory *adj. a. su. m*/*f*, conservador *adj. a. su. m* (-a *f*).

tosh [tɔʃ] *sl.* música *f* celestial.

toss [tɔs] **1.** meneo *m*, sacudida *f of head*, cogida *f by bull*; caída *f from horse*; echada *f of coin; argue the* ∼ insistir con tesón; *it's a* ∼ *up* puede ser lo uno tanto como lo otro; *win the* ∼ ganar el sorteo; **2.** *v/t.* echar, tirar; lanzar al aire; agitar, menear; sacudir; *head* levantar airosamente; (*bull*) coger; mantear *in blanket; coin* echar a cara o cruz (*a.* ∼ *up*); ∼ *off drink* beber de un trago; *v/i.* agitarse; (∼ *and turn*) revolverse *in bed*; ∼ *up* jugar a cara o cruz (*for acc.*); *sport:* sortear (*for acc.*).

tot¹ [tɔt] F (*drink*) trago *m*, copita *f*; (*child*) nene (a *f*) *m*.

tot² [∼] F: ∼ *up* sumar.

to·tal ['toutl] **1.** □ total; **2.** total *m*; *sum* ∼ (*of people*) colectividad *f*;

3. *v/t.* sumar; *v/i.* ascender a; **to·tal·i·tar·i·an** ['toutæli'tɛəriən] totalitario; **'to·tal·i'tar·i·an·ism** totalitarismo *m*; **to'tal·i·ty** totalidad *f*; **to·tal·i·za·tor** ['ˏtəlaizeitə] totalizador *m*; **to·tal·ize** ['ˏtəlaiz] totalizar.

tote[1] [tout] F llevar, acarrear.

tote[2] [ˏ] F totalizador *m*.

tot·ter ['tɔtə] tambalear(se); estar para desplomarse; **'tot·ter·ing** □, **'tot·ter·y** tambaleante; ruinoso.

touch [tʌtʃ] **1.** *v/t.* tocar; palpar; (*reach*) alcanzar; *food* tomar, probar; *emotions* conmover, enternecer; (*equal*) compararse con, igualar; *sl.* dar un sablazo a (*for* para sacar); ~ *off* hacer estallar (*a. fig.*); ~ *up* retocar (*a. phot.*); *v/i.* estar contiguo; tocarse; pasar rozando; ⚓ ~ *at* tocar en, hacer escala en; ~ *on* aludir brevemente a; **2.** tacto *m*; toque *m*; contacto *m*; ♪ pulsación *f*; *paint.* pincelada *f*; (*master's*) mano *f*; ⚔ ataque *m* leve; *fig.* rasgo *m*; *fig.* poquito *m*; *sport:* touche *f*; *in*(*to*) ~ fuera; *a* ~ *of the sun* una insolación; *be in* ~ (*with*) *th.* estar al tanto (de); *be in* ~ *with p.* estar en comunicación con; *get into* ~ *with* ponerse en contacto con; *keep in* ~ *with p.* mantener relaciones con; *th.* mantenerse al corriente de; **'~·go 1.** difícil; dudoso; **2.**: *it's* ~ está en un vilo (*whether* si); **touched** F chiflado; **'touch·i·ness** susceptibilidad *f*; **'touch·ing 1.** □ conmovedor; **2.** *prp.* tocante a; **'touch-line** línea *f* lateral; **'touch-stone** piedra *f* de toque (*a. fig.*); **'touch-'typ·ing** mecanografía *f* al tacto; **'touch·y** □ quisquilloso, susceptible.

tough [tʌf] **1.** duro; resistente; tenaz; *meat* estropajoso; *task* difícil; *journey* arduo; F *luck* malo; *Am.* F *p.* duro; malvado; criminal; **2.** F *esp. Am.* machote *m*; gorila *m*; pendernciero *m*; criminal *m*; **'tough·en** endurecer; **'tough·ness** dureza *f*; tenacidad *f*; dificultad *f*.

tour [tuə] **1.** viaje *m* (largo); excursión *f*; vuelta *f*; *sport etc.*: jira *f*, gira *f*; *on* ~ en jira; de viaje. **2.** *v/t.* viajar por, recorrer; *v/i.* viajar (de turista); **'tour·er** coche *m* de turismo; **'tour·ing 1.** turismo *m*; **2.** turístico; ~ *car*

coche *m* de turismo; **'tour·ist** turista *m/f*; ~ *agency* agencia *f* de viajes; ~ *class* clase *f* turista, tarifa *f* turística.

tour·na·ment ['tuənəmənt], **tour·ney** ['tuəni] torneo *m*; concurso *m*.

tout [taut] **1.** (*agent*) gancho *m*; (*ticket-*) revendedor *m*; *racing:* pronosticador *m*; **2.** solicitar (*v/i.* .clientes; *for acc.*).

tow[1] [tou] **1.** (*on* a) remolque *m*; *take in* ~ dar remolque a; **2.** remolcar, llevar al remolque.

tow[2] [ˏ] estopa *f*.

tow·age ['touidʒ] (derechos *m/pl.* de) remolque *m*.

to·ward(s) [tə'wɔːd(z)] hacia; (*attitude*) para con; (*time*) cerca de.

tow·el ['tauəl] **1.** toalla *f*; **2.** secar con toalla; **'~-rail** toallero *m*.

tow·er ['tauə] **1.** torre *f* (*church-*) campanario *m*; **2.** elevarse, encumbrarse; ~ *above*, ~ *over* dominar; *fig.* descollar entre; **'tow·er·ing** □ encumbrado; *rage* muy violento.

tow·line ['toulain] sirga *f*; **tow·path** ['toupaːθ] camino *m* de sirga.

town [taun] ciudad *f*; población *f*; pueblo *m*; ~ *clerk* secretario *m* particular del ayuntamiento; ~ *council* ayuntamiento *m*, concejo *m* municipal; ~ *councillor* concejal *m*; ~ *hall* ayuntamiento *m*, casa *f* consistorial; *esp. Am.* ~ *meeting* reunión *f* de los ciudadanos; *new* ~ poblado *m* de absorción; **'~-'plan·ning** urbanismo *m*.

towns·folk ['taunzfouk], **'towns-peo·ple** ciudadanos *m/pl.*

town·ship ['taunʃip] municipio *m*; término *m* municipal.

towns·man ['taunzmən] ciudadano *m*.

tow·rope ['touroup] sirga *f*; cable *m* de remolque.

tox·ic, tox·i·cal ['tɔksik(l)] □ tóxico; **tox·in** ['tɔksin] toxina *f*.

toy [tɔi] **1.** juguete *m*; chuchería *f*; **2.** *attr.* de jugar; muy pequeño; *dog* miniatura; **3.**: ~ *with* jugar con; *food* comer melindrosamente; *idea* acariciar; *affections* divertirse con; **'~-shop** juguetería *f*.

trace[1] [treis] **1.** huella *f*, rastro *m*; vestigio *m*; (*small amount*) pizca *f*; **2.** rastrear; (*find*) encontrar, averiguar el paradero de; *curve etc.*

trazar; *drawing* calcar; ~ *back to* hacer remontar a; ~ *to* rastrear hasta llegar a.

trace² [~] tirante *m*; *kick over the* ~*s* rebelarse.

tra·cer ['treisə] *phys. etc.* trazador; ~ *bullet* bala *f* trazadora; '**trac·er·y** △ tracería *f*.

tra·che·a [trə'kiːə] tráquea *f*.

trac·ing ['treisiŋ] calco *m*; '~**-pa·per** papel *m* transparente.

track [træk] 1. huella *f*; *hunt.*, *sport*: pista *f*; *(path)* senda *f*, camino *m*; 🚗 vía *f*; 🗲 *etc.* trayectoria *f*; *(wheel-)* rodada *f*; ⊕ llanta *f* de oruga; ~ *events pl.* atletismo *m* en pista; *off the* ~ despistado; *be on s.o.'s* ~*s* andar a los alcances de alguien; *keep* ~ *of fig.* estar al tanto de; 2. *(a.* ~ *down)* rastrear; averiguar el origen de; '**track·er** rastreador *m*; ~ *dog* perro *m* rastrero; '**track·less** sin caminos.

tract¹ [trækt] región *f (a. anat.)*; extensión *f*; *digestive* ~ canal *m* digestivo; *respiratory* ~ vías *f/pl.* respiratorias.

tract² [~] tratado *m*; folleto *m*.

trac·ta·ble ['træktəbl] □ tratable, dócil; ⊕ dúctil, maleable.

trac·tion ['trækʃn] tracción *f*; ~ *engine* locomóvil *m*; '**trac·tive** tractivo; '**trac·tor** tractor *m*.

trade [treid] 1. comercio *m*; industria *f*; negocio *m*; *(calling)* oficio *m*; *by* ~ de oficio; *Board of* ♀ Ministerio *m* de Industria y Comercio; 2. *v/i.* comerciar *(in* en, *with* con); F ~ *on* aprovecharse de, explotar; *v/t.* trocar, cambiar *(for* por); ~ *in* dar como parte del pago; '~**-fair** feria *f* de muestras; ~ *mark* marca *f* registrada; ~ *name* razón *f* social; nombre *m* de fábrica; ~ *price* precio *m* al por mayor; '**trad·er** comerciante *m*, traficante *m*; '**trade school** escuela *f* de artes y oficios; '**trades·man** tendero *m*; artesano *m*; ~*'s entrance* puerta *f* de servicio; '**trades·peo·ple** tenderos *m/pl.*

trade(s) un·ion sindicato *m*; gremio *m*; *attr.* sindical, gremial; **trade(s)-un·ion·ism** sistema *m* de sindicatos, sindicalismo *m*; **trade(s)-un·ion·ist** miembro *m* de un sindicato, sindicalista *m/f*.

trade winds ['treid windz] *pl.* vientos *m/pl.* alisios.

trad·ing ['treidiŋ] comercial; mercantil; ~ *post* factoría *f*.

tra·di·tion [trə'diʃn] tradición *f*; **tra·di·tion·al** □ tradicional.

traf·fic ['træfik] 1. *(trade, mot. etc.)* tráfico *m*; *(mot. etc.)* circulación *f*; *(trade)* comercio *m*; *b.s.* trata *f (in* de); *v. jam*; ~ *lights pl.* señales *f/pl.* luminosas, luces *f/pl.* de tráfico; 2. traficar *(in* en); *b.s.* tratar *(in* en); '**traf·fick·er** traficante *m*.

tra·ge·di·an [trə'dʒiːdiən] trágico *m*; **trag·e·dy** ['trædʒidi] tragedia *f*.

trag·ic, **trag·i·cal** ['trædʒik(l)] □ trágico.

trail [treil] 1. rastro *m*, pista *f*; cola *f*; estela *f*; *(path)* sendero *m*; 2. *v/t.* rastrear; seguir la pista de; *(drag)* arrastrar; *arms* bajar; *v/i.* arrastrar(se) *(a.* ✂); *(be last)* rezagarse; ~ *away*, ~ *off* ir desapareciendo; '**trail·er** *mot. etc.* remolque *m*; *film*: tráiler *m*; ✂ planta *f* rastrera.

train [trein] 1. 🚂 tren *m*; *(following)* séquito *m*; recua *f of mules*; cola *f of dress*; reguero *m of powder*; hilo *m of thought*; *by* ~ en tren, por ferrocarril; *in* ~ en preparación; 2. adiestrar(se) *(a.* ✗); preparar; *child etc.* enseñar; *voice etc.* educar; *sport*: entrenar(se); *gun* apuntar *(on* a); *plant* guiar; F 🚂 ir en tren; **train·ee** *approx.* aprendiz *m*. *(esp.* profesional); aspirante *m*; '**train·er** *sport*: entrenador *m (a.* 🗲*)*; *(circus-)* domador *m*.

train·ing ['treiniŋ] educación *f*; preparación *f*; instrucción *f*; orientación *f*; *sport*: entrenamiento *m*; *physical* ~ gimnasia *f*; '~**-col·lege** escuela *f* normal; '~**-ship** buqueescuela *m*.

train-oil ['treinɔil] aceite *m* de ballena.

traipse [treips] *v. trapes.*

trait [trei(t)] rasgo *m*.

trai·tor ['treitə] traidor *m*; *be a* ~ *to* traicionar *acc.*; '**trai·tor·ous** □ traidor; traicionero.

tra·jec·to·ry ['trædʒiktəri] trayectoria *f*.

tram [træm] *(a.* ~*car)* tranvía *m*.

tram·mel ['træml] 1. ~*s pl. fig.* trabas *f/pl.*, impedimento *m*; 2. poner trabas a, impedir.

tramp [træmp] 1. marcha *f* pesada *of feet*; paseo *m* largo, excursión *f* a pie; (p.) vagabundo m; ⚓ (a. ~ steamer) vapor m volandero, mercante m; **2.** v/i. marchar pesadamente; viajar a pie; v/t. pisar con fuerza; recorrer a pie; **tram·ple** ['~l] v/i. patullar; v/t. (a. ~ on, ~ underfoot) pisar, hollar, pisotear.

tram·way ['træmwei] tranvía m.

trance [trɑːns] éxtasis m; arrobamiento m; (spiritualist's) estado m hipnótico, trance m.

tran·quil ['trænkwil] ▢ tranquilo; **tran·quil·(l)i·ty** tranquilidad f; **'tran·quil·(l)ize** tranquilizar; **'tran·quil·(l)iz·er** calmante m.

trans·act [træn'zækt] llevar a cabo; tramitar; despachar; **trans'ac·tion** negocio m, transacción f; tramitación f; ~s pl. memorias f/pl., actas f/pl. of society.

trans·at·lan·tic ['trænzət'læntik] transatlántico.

tran·scend [træn'send] exceder, superar; **tran'scend·ence, tran·'scend·en·cy** [~dəns(i)] superioridad f; phls. tra(n)scendencia f; **tran'scend·ent** ▢ superior; sobresaliente; a. = **tran·scen·den·tal** [~'dentl] ▢ phls. trɔ(n)scendental.

tran·scribe [træns'kraib] transcribir.

tran·script ['trænskript] trasunto m; **tran'scrip·tion** transcripción f.

tran·sept ['trænsept] crucero m.

trans·fer 1. [træns'fɔː] v/t. transferir (a. 🔀); trasladar; transbordar; player traspasar; v/i. trasladarse to post; cambiar (de tren etc.); **2.** ['trænsfə] transferencia f (a. 🔀), traspaso m (a. ✝, sport); transbordo m; traslado m to post; (picture) cromo m, calcomanía f; Am. billete m de transferencia; **trans'fer·a·ble** ▢ transferible; not ~ inalienable; **trans·fer·ee** [~fə'riː] 🔀 cesionario (a f) m; **trans·fer·ence** ['~fərəns] transferencia f; 'trans·fer·or 🔀 cesionista m/f.

trans·fig·u·ra·tion [trænsfigjuɔ·'reiʃn] transfiguración f; **trans·fig·ure** [~'figə] transfigurar.

trans·fix [træns'fiks] traspasar, espetar; ~ed fig. atónito, pasmado (with de).

trans·form [træns'fɔːm] transformar; **trans·for·ma·tion** [~fə'meiʃn]

transformación f; **trans·form·er** [~'fɔːmə] ⚡ transformador m.

trans·fuse [træns'fjuːz] transfundir; blood hacer una transfusión de; fig. impregnar (with de); **trans'fu·sion** [~ʒn] (esp. 🩸) transfusión f.

trans·gress [træns'gres] v/t. violar, transgredir, traspasar; v/i. cometer transgresión; pecar; **trans·gres·sion** [~'greʃn] transgresión f; **trans·gres·sor** [~'gresə] transgresor (-a f) m.

tran·ship [træn'ʃip] transbordar; **tran'ship·ment** transbordo m.

tran·sience, tran·sien·cy ['trænziɔns(i)] lo pasajero; **tran·sient** ['trænziɔnt] **1.** pasajero, transitorio; **2.** Am. transeúnte m.

tran·sis·tor [træn'sistə] 🔀 transistor m.

tran·sit ['trænsit] tránsito m; in ~ de (or en) tránsito.

tran·si·tion [træn'siʒn] transición f, paso m; **tran·si·tion·al** ▢ transicional, de transición.

tran·si·tive ['trɑːnsitiv] ▢ transitivo.

tran·si·to·ry ['trænsitəri] transitorio.

trans·late [træns'leit] traducir (into a); trasladar to post; **trans'la·tion** traducción f; **trans'la·tor** traductor (-a f) m.

trans·lu·cence, trans·lu·cen·cy [trænz'luːsns(i)] translucidez f; **trans'lu·cent** ▢ translúcido.

trans·mi·grate ['trænzmaigreit] transmigrar; **trans·mi'gra·tion** transmigración f.

trans·mis·si·ble [trænz'misəbl] transmisible; **trans'mis·sion** all senses: transmisión f.

trans·mit [trænz'mit] all senses: transmitir; **trans'mit·ter** transmisor m; radio: emisora f; **trans'mit·ting sta·tion** estación f transmisora.

trans·mog·ri·fy [trænz'mɔgrifai] F transformar (como por encanto).

trans·mut·a·ble [trænz'mjuːtəbl] ▢ transmutable; **trans·mu'ta·tion** transmutación f; biol. transformismo m; **trans·mute** [~'mjuːt] transmutar.

tran·som ['trænsəm] travesaño m.

trans·par·en·cy [træns'peərənsi] transparencia f; **trans'par·ent** ▢ transparente (a. fig.).

tran·spi·ra·tion [trænspi'reiʃn] transpiración f; **tran·spire** [~'paiə] transpirar; *fig.* revelarse, divulgarse; F tener lugar, acontecer; *it ⁓s that* se desprende que.

trans·plant [træns'plɑ:nt] trasplantar; **trans·plan'ta·tion** trasplante *m.*

trans·port 1. [træns'pɔ:t] transportar (*a. fig.*); **2.** ['trænspɔ:t] *all senses:* transporte *m; Ministry of ♀ Ministerio m* de Transportes; **trans'port·a·ble** transportable; **trans·por'ta·tion** transportación *f;* transporte(s) *m(pl.);* ⚎⚎ deportación *f.*

trans·pose [træns'pouz] transponer; ♪ transportar; **trans·po·si·tion** [⁓pə'ziʃn] transposición *f (a. ♪).*

trans·ship [træns'ʃip] transbordar.

tran·sub·stan·ti·ate [trænsəb'stænʃieit] transubstanciar; **'tran·sub·stan·ti'a·tion** transubstanciación *f.*

trans·ver·sal [trænz'vɔ:sl] ⊐ (& línea *f*) transversal; **trans·verse** ['⁓vɔ:s] ⊐ transverso, transversal.

trap [træp] **1.** trampa *f;* ⊕ bombillo *m,* sifón *m;* coche *m* ligero de 2 ruedas; *sl.* boca *f; ⁓s pl.* equipaje *m,* cosas *f/pl.;* **2.** entrampar; atrapar; coger (en una trampa); hacer caer en el lazo; **'trap'door** trampa *f; thea.* escotillón *m.*

trapes [treips] F ir (a desgana); andar sin propósito fijo, callejear.

tra·peze [trə'pi:z], **tra'pe·zi·um** [⁓ziəm] trapecio *m;* **trap·e·zoid** ['træpizɔid] trapezoide *m.*

trap·per ['træpə] cazador *m.*

trap·pings ['træpiŋz] *pl.* arreos *m/pl.,* jaeces *m/pl.; fig.* adornos *m/pl.*

trash [træʃ] pacotilla *f,* hojarasca *f,* cachivaches *m/pl.;* **'trash·y** ⊐ baladí, despreciable.

trav·ail ['træveil] † *or lit.* **1.** dolores *m/pl.* del parto; afán *m; be in ⁓ =* **2.** estar de parto; afanarse.

trav·el ['trævl] **1.** *v/i.* viajar (*a.* ✦); ir *at a speed; (wine etc.)* poderse transportar; F ir a gran velocidad; ⊕ *⁓ along etc.* correr por; *v/t.* recorrer; viajar por; **2.** viaje(s) *m(pl.);* el viajar; ⊕ recorrido *m;* **'trav·el(l)ed** que ha viajado mucho; **'trav·el·(l)er** viajero (a *f*) *m;* ✦ viajante *m,* agente *m* viajero *S.Am.; ⁓'s cheque* cheque *m* de viajeros; **'trav·el·(l)ing** *salesman* ambulante; *rug etc.* de viaje; *crane* corredizo.

trav·e·log(ue) ['trævəlɔg] *esp. Am.* película *f* de (*or* conferencia *f* sobre) viajes.

trav·erse ['trævɔ:s] **1.** *mount.* camino *m* oblicuo; ⊕ travesaño *m;* ⚒ través *m;* **2.** atravesar, cruzar; recorrer; ⚒ mover lateralmente.

trav·es·ty ['trævisti] **1.** parodia *f (a. fig.);* **2.** parodiar.

trawl [trɔ:l] **1.** red *f* barredera; **2.** rastrear, pescar a la rastra; **'trawl·er** barco *m* rastreador.

tray [trei] bandeja *f; phot. etc.* cubeta *f.*

treach·er·ous ['tretʃərəs] ⊐ traidor, traicionero; *fig.* engañoso, incierto; *ground* movedizo; **'treach·er·y** traición *f.*

trea·cle ['tri:kl] melado *m,* melaza *f.*

tread [tred] **1.** [*irr.*] *v/i.* andar; poner el pie; *⁓ (up)on* pisar; *v/t.* pisar, pisotear (*a. ⁓ down*); **2.** pisada *f;* paso *m;* huella *f of stair;* huella *f;* (banda *f* de) rodamiento *m of tyre;* suela *f of shoe;* **trea·dle** ['⁓l] **1.** pedal *m;* **2.** pedalear.

trea·son ['tri:zn] traición *f;* **'trea·son·a·ble** ⊐ traidor.

treas·ure ['treʒə] **1.** tesoro *m; ⁓ trove* tesoro *m* hallado; **2.** atesorar (*a. ⁓ up);* apreciar mucho; guardar como un tesoro; **'treas·ur·er** tesorero *m.*

treas·ur·y ['treʒəri] tesoro *m,* tesorería *f; ♀, Am. ♀ Department* Ministerio *m* de Hacienda; ♀ *Bench parl.* Banco *m* Azul; *⁓ bill* vale *m* de la Hacienda; *Am. ⁓ note* bono *m* del Ministerio de Hacienda.

treat [tri:t] **1.** *v/t.* tratar; (*invite*) convidar (*to* a); *v/i.: ⁓ of* tratar de, versar sobre; *⁓ with* negociar con, tratar con; **2.** placer *m,* alegría *f;* (*school-*) excursión *f;* recompensa *f* (especial); convite *m,* extraordinario *m;* F *it's my ⁓* invito yo; **trea·tise** ['⁓iz] tratado *m;* **'treat·ment** tratamiento *m;* **'trea·ty** tratado *m.*

tre·ble ['trebl] **1.** ⊐ triple; ♪ de tiple; *⁓ clef* clave *f* de sol; **2.** ♪ tiple *m/f;* **3.** triplicar(se).

tree [tri:] **1.** árbol *m; v. family;* F *up a ⁓* en un aprieto; **2.** ahuyentar por un árbol; **'tree·less** pelado, sin árboles.

tre·foil ['trefɔil] trébol *m (a. ⚘).*

trek [trek] **1.** emigrar; viajar; F ir

(a desgana); **2.** migración *f*; (*day's*) jornada *f*; F viaje *m* largo y aburrido.

trel·lis ['trelis] **1.** enrejado *m*, espaldar *m*; **2.** proveer de enrejado.

trem·ble ['trembl] **1.** temblar, estremecerse (*at* ante, *with* de); **2.** temblor *m*, estremecimiento *m*.

tre·men·dous [tri'mendəs] □ tremendo, formidable, imponente (*all a.* F).

trem·or ['tremə] temblor *m*; vibración *f*; *without a* ～ sin conmoverse.

trem·u·lous ['tremjuləs] □ trémulo; tímido.

trench [trentʃ] **1.** zanja *f*, foso *m*; ✗ trinchera *f*; ～ *warfare* guerra *f* de trincheras; **2.** zanjar; hacer zanjas *etc.* en; ✗ atrincherar; ✗ excavar, remover; '**trench·ant** □ mordaz, incisivo, agudo; **trench coat** trinchera *f*.

trench·er ['trentʃə] tajadero *m*; '**trench·er·man**: *be a good* ～ tener siempre buen apetito.

trend [trend] **1.** tendencia *f*; dirección *f*; marcha *f*; **2.** tender.

trep·i·da·tion [trepi'deiʃn] turbación *f*, agitación *f*.

tres·pass ['trespəs] **1.** intrusión *f*, entrada *f* sin derecho; violación *f*; *eccl.* pecado *m*; **2.** entrar sin derecho (*on* en); penetrar en finca ajena; ～ *upon* violar; *fig.* abusar de; ～ *against* pecar contra; *no* ～*ing* prohibida la entrada; '**tres·pass·er** intruso (*a f*) *m*; ～*s will be prosecuted* se procederá contra los intrusos.

tress [tres] trenza *f*.

tres·tle ['tresl] caballete *m*; ～ *bridge* puente *m* de caballetes.

tri·ad ['traiəd] tríada *f*.

tri·al ['traiəl] prueba *f*, ensayo *m*; *fig.* aflicción *f*, adversidad *f*; ⚖ proceso *m*, juicio *m*, vista *f* de una causa; F molestia *f*; ～*s sport*, ⊕ *etc.*: pruebas *f/pl.*; *on* ～ a prueba; ⚖ en juicio; ～ *of strength* lucha *f*; ～ *and error* tanteo *m*; *give s.t. a* ～ ensayar, poner a prueba; *bring to* ～, *put on* ～ procesar, encausar; ～ *run*, ～ *trip* viaje *m* de ensayo.

tri·an·gle ['traiæŋgl] triángulo *m* (*a.* ♪); **tri·an·gu·lar** [～'æŋgjulə] □ triangular; **tri·an·gu·late** [～leit] triangular.

trib·al ['traibl] □ trib(u)al; **tribe** [traib] tribu *f* (*a. zo.*); *contp.* tropel *m*; ralea *f*; **tribes·man** ['～zmən] miembro *m* de una tribu.

trib·u·la·tion [tribju'leiʃn] tribulación *f*.

tri·bu·nal [trai'bjuːnl] tribunal *m* (*a. fig.*); **trib·une** ['tribjuːn] tribuna *f*; (*p.*) tribuno *m*.

trib·u·tar·y ['tribjutəri] **1.** □ tributario; **2.** tributario *m*; (*river*) afluente *m*; **trib·ute** ['～bjuːt] tributo *m*; *fig.* homenaje *m*; elogio *m*.

trice [trais]: *in a* ～ en un santiamén.

trick [trik] **1.** engaño *m*; truco *m*; burla *f*; trampa *f*; maña *f*; (*harmless*) travesura *f*; (*illusion*) ilusión *f*; (*conjuring*) juego *m* de manos; peculiaridad *f* *of style etc.*; *cards*: baza *f*; *dirty* ～ faena *f*, mala pasada *f*; ～ *photography* trucaje *m*; ～ *question* pregunta *f* de pega; **2.** engañar, trampear, burlar; ～ *into ger.* lograr con engaños que *subj.*; *be* ～*ed into ger.* dejarse persuadir por engaños a *inf.*; ～ *out* ataviar; ～ *out of* estafar *acc.*; '**trick·er·y** astucia *f*; fraude *m*; malas artes *f/pl.*; **trick·ster** ['～stə] estafador *m*.

trick·le ['trikl] **1.** gotear, escurrir *fig.* salir *etc.* poco a poco; **2.** hilo *m*, chorro *m* delgado.

trick·y ['triki] □ *p.* tramposo; astuto; *situation etc.* delicado, difícil.

tri·col·o(u)r ['trikələ] bandera *f* tricolor.

tri·cy·cle ['traisikl] triciclo *m*.

tri·dent ['traidənt] tridente *m*.

tri·en·ni·al [trai'enjəl] □ trienal.

tri·er ['traiə] persona *f* que se esfuerza mucho.

tri·fle ['traifl] **1.** friolera *f*, bagatela *f*, fruslería *f*; *fig.* pizca *f*; *cooking*: dulce *m* de bizcocho borracho *etc.*; **2.** *v/i.* chancear; jugar (*with* con); *v/t.*: ～ *away* malgastar; '**tri·fler** persona *f* frívola.

tri·fling ['traifliŋ] □ insignificante, fútil.

trig·ger ['trigə] **1.** gatillo *m*; ⊕ disparador *m*; **2.**: ～ *off* hacer estallar (*a. fig.*); *fig.* provocar.

trig·o·no·met·ric, **trig·o·no·met·ri·cal** [trigənə'metrik(l)] □ trigonométrico; **trig·o·nom·e·try** [～'nomitri] trigonometría *f*.

tril·by ['trilbi] F sombrero *m* flexible.

tri·lin·gual ['trai'liŋgwəl] ☐ trilingüe.

trill [tril] 1. trino *m* (*a. ♪*), gorjeo *m*; ♪ quiebro *m*; vibración *f* of *R*; 2. trinar, gorjear; *R* pronunciar con vibración.

tril·lion ['triljən] *British*: trillón *m*; *Am.* billón *m*.

trim [trim] 1. ☐ elegante; aseado; en buen estado; 2. disposición *f*; (buena) condición *f*; recorte *m of hair etc.*; asiento *m of boat*; orientación *f of sails*; 3. arreglar; ajustar; componer; (re)cortar; ☞ podar; *boat* equilibrar; *sails* orientar; *dress* adornar, guarnecer (*with* de); *lamp* despabilar; *wood* alisar; '**trim·ming** guarnición *f*, adorno *m*; orla *f*; ~s *pl.* recortes *m/pl.*; accesorios *m/pl.*; *contp.* arrequives *m/pl.*; '**trim·ness** buen orden *m*; elegancia *f*.

Trin·i·ty ['triniti] Trinidad *f*.

trin·ket ['triŋkit] dije *m*; *contp.* ~s *pl.* baratijas *f/pl.*, chucherías *f/pl.*

tri·o ['tri:ou] trío *m*.

trip [trip] 1. excursión *f*; viaje *m*; tropiezo *m*, zancadilla *f with foot*; ⊕ trinquete *m*, disparo *m*; 2. *v/i.* tropezar (*on, over* en); ir (*or correr etc.*) con paso ligero; *v/t.* (*mst* ~ *up*) echar la zancadilla a; hacer tropezar; *fig.* coger en una falta.

tri·par·tite ['trai'pɑːtait] tripartito.

tripe [traip] tripa *f* (*mst* ~s *pl.*); *cooking*: callos *m/pl.*; *sl.* tonterías *f/pl.*

tri·phase ['trai'feiz] ⚡ trifásico.

trip·li·cate 1. ['triplikit] (*in por*) triplicado; 2. ['~keit] triplicar.

tri·pod ['traipɔd] trípode *m*.

trip·per ['tripə] F excursionista *m/f* (de un día); '**trip·ping** ☐ ligero, ágil.

trip·tych ['triptik] tríptico *m*.

tri·sect [trai'sekt] trisecar.

tris·yl·lab·ic ['traisi'læbik] ☐ trisílabo; **tri·syl·la·ble** ['~'siləbl] trisílabo *m*.

trite [trait] ☐ trillado, trivial, vulgar; '**trite·ness** trivialidad *f*, vulgaridad *f*.

trit·u·rate ['tritjureit] triturar.

tri·umph ['traiəmf] 1. triunfo *m*; 2. triunfar (*over* de); **tri·um·phal** ['~'ʌmfəl] triunfal; ~ *arch* arco *m* triunfal; **tri·um·phant** ☐ triunfante.

triv·i·al ['triviəl] ☐ trivial; frívolo; insignificante; **triv·i·al·i·ty** [~'æliti] trivialidad *f*.

tro·chee ['trouki:] troqueo *m* (-⌣).

trod [trɔd] *pret.*, **trod·den** ['~n] *p.p. of* tread.

trog·lo·dyte ['trɔglədait] troglodita *m*.

Tro·jan ['troudʒn] troyano *adj. a. su. m* (*a f*); *work like a* ~ trabajar como un negro.

trol·l(e)y ['trɔli] carretilla *f*; *Am.* (*a.* '~*-car*) tranvía *m*; (*tea-*) mes(it)a *f* de ruedas; ⚡ trole *m*; ⊕ corredera *f* elevada; '~*-bus* trolebús *m*.

trol·lop ['trɔləp] marrana *f*; ramera *f*.

trom·bone [trɔm'boun] trombón *m*.

troop [tru:p] 1. tropa *f* (*a. ✕*); ✕ escuadrón *m of cavalry*; *thea.* compañía *f*; ~s *pl.* tropas *f/pl.*; 2. reunirse; ~ *away*, ~ *off* marcharse en tropel; '~*-car·ri·er* ⚓ transporte *m*; ✕ camión *m* blindado; '**troop·er** soldado *m* de caballería; = '**troop·ship** transporte *m*.

trope [troup] tropo *m*.

tro·phy ['troufi] trofeo *m*.

trop·ic ['trɔpik] trópico *m*; ~s *pl.* trópicos *m/pl.*; '**trop·ic**, '**trop·i·cal** ☐ tropical.

trot [trɔt] 1. trote *m*; *Am. school sl.* chuleta *f*; F *be always on the* ~ estar siempre ocupado; F *on the* ~ seguidos; 2. trotar; F ~ *out* sacar (para mostrar); *excuses etc.* ensartar.

troth [trouθ] † fe *f*; † *or co.* plight one's ~ desposarse, prometerse.

trot·ter ['trɔtə] (caballo *m*) trotón *m*; *cooking*: pie *m* de cerdo *etc.*

trou·ble ['trʌbl] 1. aflicción *f*, congoja *f*; (*misfortune*) desgracia *f*, apuro *m*; dificultad *f*, disgusto *m*; (*unpleasan·ness*) sinsabor *m*; (*inconvenience*) molestia *f*; *pol.* trastorno *m*; ⚕ mal *m*; ⊕ falta *f*, fallo *m*; *be in* ~ verse en un apuro; *be worth the* ~ valer la pena; *go to great* ~ *to inf.* hacer un gran esfuerzo por *inf.*; *go to the* ~ *of inf.*, *take the* ~ *to inf.* tomarse la molestia de *inf.*; 2. *v/t.* turbar; trastornar; afligir; molestar, fastidiar; incomodar; ~ *a p. for* pedirle a uno; *don't* ~ *yourself* no se moleste; no se preocupe; *v/i.* molestarse; '**trou·bled** *p.* inquieto; apenado; *times* turbulento; *waters*

revuelto, turbio; **trouble·some**
['∼səm] ☐ molesto; dificultoso;
importuno.

trough [trɔf] (*drinking-*) abrevadero
m; (*feeding-*) comedero *m*; (*knead-
ing-*) artesa *f*; canal *m*; seno *m of
wave*; *meteor.* mínimo *m* de presión.

trounce [trauns] zurrar, pegar;
sport etc.: cascar.

troupe [tru:p] compañía *f*.

trou·sers ['trausəz] (*a pair of* un)
pantalón *m*; pantalones *m/pl.*

trous·seau ['tru:sou] ajuar *m*.

trout [traut] trucha *f*.

trow·el ['trauəl] ⚲ desplantador *m*;
△ paleta *f*, llana *f*.

troy (**weight**) [trɔi(weit)] peso *m*
troy.

tru·an·cy ['tru:ənsi] ausencia *f* de
clase sin permiso; **'tru·ant 1.** haragán; **2.** novillero *m*; *play* ∼ hacer
novillos (*or* toros).

truce [tru:s] tregua *f*.

truck[1] [trʌk] (*lorry*) camión *m*;
(*hand-*) carretilla *f*; 🚃 vagón *m*
(de mercancías); vagoneta *f*.

truck[2] [∼] cambio *m*, trueque *m*;
(*mst* ∼ *system*) pago *m* del salario
en especie; *contp.* baratijas *f/pl.*;
have no ∼ *with* no tratar con.

truck·le ['trʌkl] someterse servilmente (*to* a).

truc·u·lence, truc·u·len·cy ['trʌk-
juləns(i)] aspereza *f etc.*; **'truc·u-
lent** ☐ áspero, hosco, arisco; agresivo.

trudge [trʌdʒ] caminar trabajosamente.

true [tru:] (*adv. truly*) verdadero;
account verídico; *p.* leal; *copy* fiel,
exacto; genuino; auténtico; *surface
etc.* uniforme, a nivel; a plomo;
it is ∼ es verdad; ∼ *to life* conforme
con la realidad; *come* ∼ realizarse;
too ∼ *!* tiene Vd. razón; **'∼-'blue** sumamente leal; **'∼-bred** de casta
legítima; **'∼-love** fiel amante *m/f*,
novio (a *f*) *m*.

truf·fle ['trʌfl] trufa *f*.

tru·ism ['tru:izm] truísmo *m*, perogrullada *f*.

tru·ly ['tru:li] verdaderamente; fiel-
mente; efectivamente; *Yours* ∼ su
seguro servidor.

trump [trʌmp] **1.** triunfo *m*; **2.** fallar; ∼ *up* forjar, falsificar; **trump-
er·y** ['∼əri] **1.** hojarasca *f*, oropel *m*;

tontería *f*; **2.** frívolo; (*useless*) inútil;
(*nonsensical*) tonto; (*trashy*) de relumbrón.

trum·pet ['trʌmpit] **1.** trompeta *f*;
∼ *blast* trompetazo *m*; *v. ear-*∼,
speaking-∼; **2.** trompetear; (*elephant*) barritar; *fig.* (*a.* ∼ *forth*)
pregonar (a son de trompeta);
'trum·pet·er trompetero *m*, trompeta *m*.

trun·cate ['trʌŋkeit] truncar; **trun-
'ca·tion** truncamiento *m*.

trun·cheon ['trʌntʃn] (cachi)po-
rra *f*.

trun·dle ['trʌndl] **1.** ruedecilla *f*;
2. (hacer) rodar (*a.* ∼ *along*).

trunk [trʌŋk] ⚲, *anat.* tronco *m*;
(*case*) baúl *m*; (*elephant's*) trompa *f*;
Am. mot. maleta *f*; **'∼-call** conferencia *f* interurbana; **'∼-line** 🚃
línea *f* troncal; *teleph.* línea *f*
principal; **trunks** *pl.* taparrabo *m*.

trun·nion ['trʌnjən] ⊕ muñón *m*.

truss [trʌs] **1.** ⚲ haz *m*, lío *m*; 🔧
braguero *m*; △ entramado *m*;
2. atar, liar; *fowl* espetar; △ apoyar
con entramado.

trust [trʌst] **1.** confianza *f*; crédito
m; obligación *f*, cargo *m*; ⚖ fideicomiso *m*; ♰ trust *m*; ∼ *company*
banco *m* fideicomisario; *breach of* ∼
abuso *m* de confianza; *position of* ∼
puesto *m* de confianza; *in* ∼ en
administración; *on* ∼ a ojos cerrados; ♰ al fiado; **2.** *v/t.* confiar en,
fiarse de; ∼ *a p. with a th.* confiar
algo a alguien; ∼ *a p. to do* confiar
en que uno haga; ∼ *that* esperar
que; ∼ *him to do that!* no me extraña
que lo haya hecho; *I wouldn't* ∼ *him
with your car* no le dejaría usar tu
coche; *v/i.* confiar (*in,* to en).

trus·tee [trʌs'ti:] síndico *m*; depositario *m*; ⚖ fideicomisario *m*; administrador *m*; **trus'tee·ship** cargo
m de fideicomisario *etc.*

trust·ful ['trʌstful] ☐, **'trust·ing** ☐
confiado.

trust·wor·thi·ness ['trʌstwə:ðinis]
confiabilidad *f*; **'trust·wor·thy** *p.*
confiable; *news etc.* fidedigno.

trust·y ['trʌsti] fiel, leal; seguro.

truth [tru:θ, *pl.* ∼ðz] verdad *f*.

truth·ful ['tru:θful] ☐ verídico;
veraz; **'truth·ful·ness** veracidad *f*.

try [trai] **1.** *v/t.* intentar; (*test*) probar, ensayar (*a.* ∼ *out*); ⚖ *p.* pro-

cesar (*for* por); *case* ver; *metall.* refinar; *eyes* cansar, irritar; (*sorely*) afligir; ~ *on clothes* probarse; F ~ *it on* fingirse (enfermo *etc.*); ~ *out* someter a prueba; *v/i.* probar; esforzarse; ~ *to*, F ~ *and inf.* tratar de *inf.*, intentar *inf.*; ~ *for* tratar de obtener; **2.** F tentativa *f*; ensayo *m* (*a. rugby*), prueba *f*; **'try·ing** □ molesto; cansado; penoso; **'try·'on** F trampa *f*; **'try·'out** experimento *m*; prueba *f* (*a. sport*).

tryst [traist, trist] (lugar *m* de una) cita *f*.

Tsar [zɑ:] zar *m*.

T-square ['ti:skwɛə] regla *f* T.

tub [tʌb] **1.** tina *f*; cubo *m*; cuba *f*; F (*bath*) baño *m*; F ⚓ carcamán *f*; **2.** entinar; F tomar un baño; **'tub·by** rechoncho.

tube [tju:b] tubo *m* (*a. television*); *Am. radio*: lámpara *f*; (*a. inner* ~) cámara *f*; 🚇 metro *m*.

tu·ber ['tju:bə] tubérculo *m*; **tu·ber·cle** ['tju:bə:kl] *all senses*: tubérculo *m*; **tu·ber·cu·lo·sis** [tjubə:kju'lou-sis] tuberculosis *f*; **tu'ber·cu·lous** tuberculoso.

tub·ing ['tju:biŋ] tubería *f*; trozo *m* de tubo.

tu·bu·lar ['tju:bjulə] tubular.

tuck [tʌk] **1.** alforza *f*; pliegue *m*; *sl.* dulces *m/pl.*; *sl.* (*a.* ~-*in*) banquetazo *m*; **2.** *v/t.* alforzar; plegar; ~ *away* encubrir, ocultar; *sl. food* zampar; ~ *up sleeves, skirt* arremangar; *bed* guarnecer; *p. in bed* arropar; *v/i.: sl.* ~ *in(to)* comer vorazmente, zampar.

tuck·er [tʌkə] *Am.* F agotar, cansar.

Tues·day ['tju:zdi] martes *m*.

tuft [tʌft] copete *m*; penacho *m*; manojo *m of grass etc.*; **'~-hunt·er** ambicioso *m*; zalamero *m*.

tug [tʌg] **1.** tirón *m*; estirón *m*; ⚓ remolcador *m*; ~ *of war* lucha *f* de la cuerda; *fig.* lucha *f* (decisiva); **2.** tirar de; arrastrar; ⚓ remolcar.

tu·i·tion [tju'iʃn] enseñanza *f*.

tu·lip ['tju:lip] tulipán *m*.

tulle [tju:l] tul *m*.

tum·ble ['tʌmbl] **1.** *v/i.* caer; tropezar (*over on*); desplomarse, hundirse, venirse abajo (*a.* ~ *down*); ~ *out* salir en desorden; F caer en la cuenta (*to* de); *v/t.* derribar; derrocar; desarreglar; ~ *out* echar en des-

orden; **2.** caída *f*; voltereta *f*; *take a* ~ caerse; **'~·down** destartalado, ruinoso; **'tum·bler** (*glass*) vaso *m*; (*p.*) volteador (-a *f*) *m*; *orn.* pichón *m* volteador; seguro *m*, fiador *m of lock.*

tum·brel, tum·bril ['tʌmbrəl, '~-bril] chirrión *m*; ✗ carro *m* de artillería.

tu·mid ['tju:mid] □ túmido.

tum·my ['tʌmi] F estómago *m*.

tu·mo(u)r ['tju:mə] tumor *m*.

tu·mult ['tju:mʌlt] tumulto *m*; **tu·mul·tu·ous** [tju'mʌltjuəs] □ tumultuoso.

tu·mu·lus ['tju:mjuləs] túmulo *m*.

tun [tʌn] tonel *m*; † (*measure*) tonelada *f*.

tu·na ['tju:nə] atún *m*.

tune [tju:n] **1.** aire *m*, tonada *f*; armonía *f*; tono *m*; *in* ~ templado, afinado; *adv.* afinadamente; *fig. be in* ~ *with* concordar con; *out of* ~ destemplado, desafinado; *adv.* desafinadamente; *fig. be out of* ~ *with* desentonar con; *fig. change one's* ~ mudar de tono; F *to the* ~ *of* por la suma de; **2.** ♪ afinar, acordar, templar (*a.* ~ *up*); *radio:* ~ (*in*) sintonizar (*to acc.*); *mot.* ~ *up* poner a punto; **tune·ful** ['~ful] □ melodioso, armonioso; **'tune·less** disonante; **'tun·er** afinador *m*; *radio:* sintonizador *m*.

tung·sten ['tʌŋstən] tungsteno *m*.

tu·nic ['tju:nik] túnica *f*.

tun·ing ['tju:niŋ] ♪ afinación *f*; *radio:* sintonización *f*; **'~-coil** bobina *f* sintonizadora; **'~-fork** diapasón *m*.

tun·nel ['tʌnl] **1.** túnel *m*; ✗ galería *f*; **2.** *v/t.* construir un túnel bajo (*or* a través de); *v/i.* construir un túnel; atravesar por túnel.

tun·ny ['tʌni] atún *m*.

tur·ban ['tə:bən] turbante *m*.

tur·bid ['tə:bid] turbio.

tur·bine ['tə:bin] turbina *f*.

tur·bo·jet ['tə:bou'dʒet] turborreactor (*a. su. m*); **'tur·bo·'prop** turbohélice (*a. su. m*).

tur·bot ['tə:bət] rodaballo *m*.

tur·bu·lence ['tə:bjuləns] turbulencia *f*; **'tur·bu·lent** □ turbulento.

tu·reen [tə'ri:n] sopera *f*.

turf [tə:f] **1.** césped *m*; (*sod*) tepe *m*; (*peat*) turba *f*; *sport:* turf *m*; **2.** encespedar; *sl.* ~ *out* echar.

tur·gid ['tə:dʒid] ☐ turgente; *fig.* hinchado; **tur'gid·i·ty** turgencia *f.*

Turk [tə:k] turco (a *f*) *m*; *fig.* pícaro *m*.

tur·key ['tə:ki] pavo (a *f*) *m*; *Am.* F *talk* ～ no tener pelos en la lengua.

Turk·ish ['tə:kiʃ] turco *adj. a. su. m*; ～ *bath* baño *m* turco; ～ *towel* toalla *f* rusa.

tur·moil ['tə:mɔil] desorden *m*; alboroto *m*, tumulto *m*; disturbio *m*.

turn [tə:n] **1.** *v/t.* volver; ⊕ tornear; *ankle* torcer; *corner* doblar; *handle* girar, dar vueltas a; *key* dar vuelta a; *milk* agriar; *stomach* revolver; F *he's* ～*ed 50* tiene lo menos 50 años; ～ *colour* cambiar de color; ～ *a p. against* predisponerle a uno en contra de; ～ *aside* desviar; ～ *away* apartar; despedir; ～ *back page* doblar; *p.* hacer retroceder; ～ *down page etc.* doblar; *gas etc.* bajar; *offer* rehusar; *p.* no aceptar; ～ *in* doblar hacia adentro; *man* entregar; ～ *into* convertir en, cambiar en; *(translate)* verter a; ～ *off light* apagar; *tap* cerrar; *gas* cortar; *workmen* despedir; ～ *on light* encender; *radio* poner; *tap* abrir; ～ *out light* apagar; *p.* echar, expulsar; *pocket* vaciar; *product* producir, fabricar; *be well* ～*ed out* ir bien vestido; ～ *over* volver; volcar; *pages* pasar; *motor* hacer girar; revolver *in mind*; entregar *(to a)*; ✝ rendir; *v. leaf*; ～ *up* doblar hacia arriba; levantar; *earth* revolver; *gas* abrir (más); *reference* buscar, consultar; *radio* poner más fuerte; *sleeve* arremangar; **2.** *v/i.* volver(se); girar, dar vueltas; *mot.*, 🐎 virar; torcer; *(become)* hacerse *su.*, ponerse, volverse *adj.*; *(milk)* agriarse, cortarse; *(tide)* repuntar; *(weather)* cambiar; ～ *about* dar una vuelta completa; ✗ *about* ～! media vuelta — ¡ar!; ～ *aside*, ～ *away* desviarse, alejarse; volver la espalda; ～ *back* volver (atrás), retroceder; ～ *from* apartarse de; ～ *in* doblarse hacia adentro; F acostarse; ～ *into* convertirse en; ～ *off* desviarse; ～ *on* depender de; *theme* versar sobre; *p.* volverse contra; ～ *out* salir de casa *(or* a la calle)*; resultar; F levantarse *from bed*; ～ *out to be* resultar; ～ *out well* salir bien; ～ *over* revolver(se); *mot.*, 🐎 capotar; volcar; ～ *round*

volverse; girar; ～ *to (for help)* recurrir a, acudir a; *stone etc.* convertirse en; ～ *to* (*adv.*) empezar (a trabajar); ～ *up* doblarse hacia arriba; aparecer; llegar, asistir, presentarse; ～ *upon v.* ～ *on*; **3.** vuelta *f*; giro *m*; revolución *f*; curva *f*, recodo *m in road etc.*; ♣ *etc.* viraje *m*; *mot. etc.* giro *m*; *(change)* cambio *m*; repunte *m*, cambio *m of tide*; *(spell)* turno *m*; oportunidad *f*; propensión *f (for a)*; sesgo *m*, disposición *f of mind*; F susto *m*; F 🟍 vahido *m*, desvanecimiento *m*; *thea.* número *m*; ～ *of phrase* giro *m*; *bad* ～ mala jugada *f*; *good* ～ favor *m*, servicio *m*; *it is my* ～ me toca a mí; *take a* ～ dar una vuelta; *take a* ～ at contribuir con su trabajo a; *take a* ～ *at the wheel* conducir por su turno; *take one's* ～ esperar su turno; *take* ～*s* turnar, alternar; *done to a* ～ en su punto; *at every* ～ a cada paso, a cada momento; *by* ～*s* por turnos; *in* ～ por turno; *in his* ～ a su vez; *out of* ～ fuera de orden; '～**·coat** renegado (a *f*) *m*; '～**-down** doblado hacia abajo; '**turn·er** tornero *m*.

turn·ing ['tə:niŋ] vuelta *f*; ángulo *m*; *the first* ～ la primera bocacalle; '～**-lathe** torno *m* (de tornero); '～**-point** *fig.* punto *m* decisivo, coyuntura *f* crítica.

tur·nip ['tə:nip] nabo *m*.

turn·key ['tə:nki:] llavero *m* (de cárcel); '**turn-out** concurrencia *f*; entrada *f*; ✝ producción *f*; F atuendo *m*; '**turn·o·ver** ✝ (volumen *m* de) transacciones *f/pl.* (*or* operaciones *f/pl.*); movimiento *m* de mercancías; *cooking*: pastel *m* con repulgo; '**turn·pike** barrera *f* de portazgo; *Am.* autopista *f* de peaje *m*; '**turn-stile** torniquete *m*; '**turn-ta·ble** 🎬, *gramaphone*: placa *f* giratoria; '**turn-up** vuelta *f of trousers*; F trifulca *f*; F racha *f* de buena suerte.

tur·pen·tine ['tə:pəntain] trementina *f*.

tur·pi·tude ['tə:pitju:d] *lit.* infamia *f*, vileza *f*.

tur·quoise ['tə:kwɔ:z] turquesa *f*.

tur·ret ['tʌrit] 🜔 torreón *m*; ✗ torre *f*; ♣ torreta *f* (acorazada) 🜔 torreta *f* (de fuego); *Am.* ⊕ cabrestante *m*; ⊕ ～ *lathe* torno *m* revolvedor.

tur·tle ['tɔ:tl] tortuga *f* marina; *turn* ~ ⚓ ·ozobrar; (*car etc.*) volcar.

tur·tle-dove ['tɔ:tldʌv] tórtola *f*.

Tus·can ['tʌskən] toscano *adj. a. su. m* (a *f*).

tusk [tʌsk] colmillo *m*.

tus·sle ['tʌsl] 1. lucha *f*; agarrada *f*, pelea *f*; 2. luchar (*with* con); reñir (*over* a causa de).

tus·sock ['tʌsək] montecillo *m* de hierbas.

tut [tʌt] ¡bah!

tu·te·lage ['tju:tilidʒ] tutela *f*.

tu·tor ['tju:tə] 1. preceptor *m*; ayo *m*; maestro *m* particular; ⚕ tutor *m*; 2. enseñar, instruir; dar enseñanza particular a; **tu·to·ri·al** [tju-'tɔ:riəl] 1. preceptoral; ⚕ tutelar; 2. *univ.* clase *f* particular; **tu·tor·ship** ['tju:təʃip] ⚕ tutela *f*; *univ.* preceptorado *m*.

tux·e·do [tʌk'si:dou] *Am.* smoking *m*.

twad·dle ['twɔdl] disparates *m/pl.*, tonterías *f/pl.*

twang [twæŋ] 1. tañido *m*, punteado *m* of *guitar*; (*mst nasal* ~) gangueo *m*, timbre *m* nasal; 2. *guitar* puntear.

tweak [twi:k] pellizcar retorciendo.

tweed [twi:d] cheviot *m*, mezcla *f* de lana; ~s *pl.* traje *m* de cheviot.

'tween [twi:n] = between.

tweez·ers ['twi:zəz] *pl.* (a pair of ~ unas) bruselas *f/pl.*, pinzas *f/pl.*

twelfth [twelfθ] duodécimo (*a. su. m*); '2-**night** día *m* (*or* noche *f*) de Reyes.

twelve [twelv] doce (*a. su. m*).

twen·ti·eth ['twentiiθ] vigésimo (*a. su. m*).

twen·ty ['twenti] veinte; ~**fold** ['~fould] *adv.* veinte veces (*adj.* mayor).

twerp [twə:p] *sl.* tío *m*; tonto *m*.

twice [twais] dos veces; ~ the sum el doble; ~ as much dos veces tanto.

twid·dle ['twidl] 1. girar; jugar con, revolver ociosamente; 2. vuelta *f* (ligera).

twig¹ [twig] ramita *f*; ~s *pl.* leña *f* menuda.

twig² [~] F caer en la cuenta (*v/t.* de).

twi·light ['twailait] 1. crepúsculo *m* (*a. fig.*); 2. crepuscular; ~ sleep sueño *m* crepuscular.

twill [twil] 1. tela *f* cruzada; 2. cruzar.

twin [twin] gemelo *adj. a. su. m* (a *f*); '~-**'en·gined** ['~endʒind] bimotor; '~-**'jet** birreactor *adj. a. su. m*.

twine [twain] 1. guita *f*, bramante *m*; 2. enroscar(se); (*mst with adv.*) retorcer(se); *fig.* ceñir (*with* de).

twinge [twindʒ] punzada *f*.

twin·ing ['twainiŋ] ♣ sarmentoso.

twin·kle ['twiŋkl] 1. centellear, titilar, parpadear; *fig.* moverse rápidamente; *in the twinkling of an eye* en un abrir y cerrar de ojos; 2. centelleo *m*, parpadeo *m*; *in a* ~ en un instante.

twirl [twə:l] 1. vuelta *f* (rápida), giro *m*; rasgo *m* of *pen*; 2. girar rápidamente; dar vueltas (*v/t.* a).

twist [twist] 1. torcedura *f* (*a.* ⚡); torsión *f*; enroscadura *f*; torzal *m*; rollo *m* of *tobacco*; vuelta *f*, recodo *m in road*; sesgo *m*, peculiaridad *f* of *mind*; F estafa *f*; 2. torcer(se) (*a. fig.*); retorcer(se); enroscar(se); trenzar, entrelazar(se); girar; (*road*) dar vueltas; F estafar; '**twist·er** torcedor *m*; *Am. meteor.* tromba *f*; *baseball:* pelota *f* arrojada con efecto; F estafador *m*, tramposo *m*.

twit [twit]: ~ *a p. with a th.* reprender (para divertirse) algo a alguien.

twitch [twitʃ] 1. *v/i.* crisparse; temblar; *v/t.* tirar ligeramente de; arrancar de un tirón; 2. sacudida *f* repentina; ⚡ tic *m*, contracción *f* nerviosa; *vet.* acial *m*.

twit·ter ['twitə] 1. (*bird*) gorjear; *fig.* agitarse, temblar de inquietud; 2. gorjeo *m*; *fig.* agitación *f*, inquietud *f*; F *be in a* ~ estar muy agitado.

two [tu:] dos (*a. su. m*); *in* ~ en dos; *in* ~s, ~ *by* ~ de dos en dos; *put* ~ *and* ~ *together* atar cabos; '~-**edged** de doble filo (*a. fig.*); '~-**faced** *fig.* doble, falso; '~-**fold** 1. *adj.* doble; 2. *adv.* dos veces; '~-**hand·ed** (*or* para) dos manos; ~**pence** ['tʌpəns] dos peniques *m/pl.*; ~-**pen·ny** ['tʌpni] de dos peniques; *fig.* despreciable; '~-**phase** ⚡ bifásico; '~-**ply** de dos capas; '~-**'seat·er** *mot.* de dos plazas; '~-**'step** paso *m* doble; '~-**'sto·rey** de dos pisos; '~-**'stroke** de dos tiempos; '~-**'tone** *mot.* bicolor; '~-**way** '**switch** ⚡ conmutador *m* de dos direcciones.

ty·coon [tai'ku:n] *Am*. F magnate *m*.
tyke [taik] F perro *m*; chiquillo *m*;
hombre de Yorkshire.
tym·pa·num ['timpənəm] *anat*., △
tímpano *m*.
type [taip] **1.** tipo *m*; *typ*. tipo *m*,
carácter *m*; tipos *m/pl*.; **2.** escribir a
máquina, mecanografiar; '~**script**
(original *m*) mecanografiado; '~
set·ter (*p*.) cajista *m*; (*machine*) máquina *f* de componer; '~**write** [*irr*.
(*write*)] = *type* 2; '~**writ·er** máquina *f* de escribir; ~ *ribbon* cinta *f*
para máquinas de escribir; '~
writ·ing = *typing*.
ty·phoid fiebre *f* tifoidea.
ty·phoon [tai'fu:n] tifón *m*.
ty·phus ['taifəs] tifus *m*.
typ·i·cal ['tipikl] □ típico; **typ·i·fy**
['~fai] simbolizar; representar; ser

ejemplo de; **typ·ing** ['taipiŋ] mecanografía *f*, dactilografía *f*; **typ·ist**
['taipist] mecanógrafo (a *f*) *m*, dactilógrafo (a *f*) *m*.
ty·pog·ra·pher [tai'pɔgrəfə] tipó-
grafo *m*; **ty·po·graph·ic**, **ty·po·
graph·i·cal** [ˌpə'græfik(l)] ⎯ tipográfico; **ty·pog·ra·phy** [ˌ'pɔgrəfi]
tipografía *f*.
ty·ran·nic, **ty·ran·ni·cal** [ti'ræ-
nik(l)] □ tiránico; **tyr·an·nize**
['tirənaiz] tiranizar (*over acc*.); '**tyr·
an·ny** tiranía *f*.
ty·rant ['taiərənt] tirano (a *f*) *m*.
tyre ['taiə] *mot. etc*. neumático *m*,
llanta *f S.Am*.; (*outer cover*) cubierta *f*; (*inner tube*) cámara *f*;
llanta *f*, calce *m of cart*.
ty·ro ['taiərou] *v. tiro*.
Tzar [zɑ:] zar *m*.

U

u·biq·ui·tous [juˈbikwitəs] □ ubicuo; **u'biq·ui·ty** ubicuidad *f*.

ud·der [ˈʌdə] ubre *f*.

ugh [ʌx, uh, ɔːh] ¡puf!

ug·li·fy [ˈʌglifai] F afear.

ug·li·ness [ˈʌglinis] fealdad *f*.

ug·ly [ˈʌgli] □ feo; *wound, situation* peligroso; *vice etc.* feo, asqueroso, repugnante; *sky etc.* amenazador; *rumour etc.* inquietante; F ~ *customer* sayón *m*; persona *f* de mal genio; *be in an* ~ *mood* (*p*.) estar de muy mal humor; (*mob*) amenazar violencia; *turn* ~ (*situation*) ponerse peligroso; F (*p*.) mostrarse violento, ponerse negro.

U·krain·i·an [juːˈkreiniən] ucranio *adj. a. su. m* (a *f*).

u·ku·le·le [juːkəˈleili] guitarra *f* hawaiana.

ul·cer [ˈʌlsə] úlcera *f*; *fig.* llaga *f*; **ul·cer·ate** [ˈ~reit] ulcerar(se); **ul·ce'ra·tion** ulceración *f*; **'ul·cer·ous** ulceroso.

ul·lage [ˈʌlidʒ] ⚓ merma *f* (de un tonel).

ul·na [ˈʌlnə], *pl.* **ul·nae** cúbito *m*.

ul·ster [ˈʌlstə] úlster *m*.

ul·te·ri·or [ʌlˈtiəriə] ulterior; *motive* oculto.

ul·ti·mate [ˈʌltimit] □ último, final; fundamental; sumo; **'ul·ti·mate·ly** últimamente; a la larga.

ul·ti·ma·tum [ʌltiˈmeitəm], *pl. a.* **ul·ti'ma·ta** [ˈ~tə] ultimátum *m*.

ul·ti·mo [ˈʌltimou] ⚓ del mes pasado.

ul·tra [ˈʌltrə] ultra...; '~-**'fash·ion·a·ble** muy de moda; ~-**ma'rine** 1. ultramarino; 2. 🎨, *paint.* azul *m* de ultramar; '~-**'mod·ern** ultramoderno; ~-**mon·tane** [ˈ~mɔntein] ultramontano *adj. a. su. m*; '~-**'short wave** (de) onda *f* extracorta; ~-**'vi·o·let** ultravioleta.

ul·u·late [ˈjuːljuleit] ulular.

um·bel [ˈʌmbl] umbela *f*.

um·ber [ˈʌmbə] tierra *f* de sombra.

um·bil·i·cal [ʌmˈbilikl, ✴ ~ˈlaikl] umbilical; ~ *cord* cordón *m* umbilical.

um·brage [ˈʌmbridʒ] *fig.* resentimiento *m*, pique *m*; *take* ~ ofenderse (*at* por), resentirse (*at* de).

um·brel·la [ʌmˈbrelə] paraguas *m*; ✖ cortina *f* de fuego (antiaéreo); **um'brel·la-stand** paragüero *m*.

um·pire [ˈʌmpaiə] **1.** árbitro *m*; **2.** arbitrar.

ump·teen [ˈʌmtiːn] F muchísimos, tantísimos; **ump'teenth** [ˈ~θ] F enésimo.

un... [ʌn...] in...; des...; no; poco.

un·a·bashed [ˈʌnəˈbæʃt] descarado, desvergonzado.

un·a·bat·ed [ˈʌnəˈbeitid] sin disminución.

un·a·ble [ʌnˈeibl] imposibilitado, incapaz (*to inf.* de *inf.*); *be* ~ *to inf.* no poder *inf.*

un·a·bridged [ˈʌnəˈbridʒd] íntegro.

un·ac·cent·ed [ˈʌnækˈsentid] inacentuado, átono.

un·ac·cept·a·ble [ˈʌnəkˈseptəbl] inaceptable.

un·ac·com·mo·dat·ing [ˈʌnəˈkɔmədeitiŋ] poco acogedor; intransigente.

un·ac·com·pan·ied [ˈʌnəˈkʌmpənid] sin acompañamiento.

un·ac·count·a·ble [ˈʌnəˈkauntəbl] □ inexplicable.

un·ac·cus·tomed [ˈʌnəˈkʌstəmd] insólito; no acostumbrado (*to* a).

un·ac·knowl·edged [ˈʌnəkˈnɔlidʒd] no reconocido.

un·ac·quaint·ed [ˈʌnəˈkweintid]: *be* ~ *with* desconocer, ignorar.

un·a·dorned [ˈʌnəˈdɔːnd] sin adorno, sencillo; escueto.

un·a·dul·ter·at·ed [ˈʌnəˈdʌltəreitid] sin mezcla; puro.

un·ad·vis·a·ble [ˈʌnədˈvaizəbl] · □ poco aconsejable.

un·af·fect·ed [ˈʌnəˈfektid] □ no afectado (*by* por); *fig.* sin afectación, natural.

un·a·fraid [ˈʌnəˈfreid] impertérrito.

un·aid·ed [ˈʌnˈeidid] sin ayuda.

un·al·loyed [ˈʌnəˈlɔid] puro, sin mezcla.

un·al·ter·a·ble [ʌnˈɔːltərəbl] ☐ inalterable.

un·am·big·u·ous [ˈʌnæmˈbigjuəs] ☐ inequívoco.

un·am·bi·tious [ˈʌnæmˈbiʃəs] ☐ poco ambicioso.

un-A·mer·i·can [ˈʌnəˈmerikən] antiamericano. [simpático.\

un·a·mi·a·ble [ʌnˈeimjəbl] ☐ poco\

u·na·nim·i·ty [juːnəˈnimiti] unanimidad f; u·nan·i·mous [juːˈnæniməs] ☐ unánime.

un·an·swer·a·ble [ʌnˈɑːnsərəbl] ☐ incontestable; irrebatible.

un·ap·peal·a·ble [ʌnəˈpiːləbl] ⚟ inapelable.

un·ap·pe·tiz·ing [ˈʌnˈæpitaiziŋ] poco apetitoso.

un·ap·proach·a·ble [ˈʌnəˈproutʃəbl] ☐ inaccesible; p. intratable.

un·ap·pro·pri·at·ed [ˈʌnəˈprouprieitid] no asignado.

un·armed [ˈʌnˈɑːmd] inerme, desarmado.

un·a·shamed [ˈʌnəˈʃeimd; adv. ~midli] ☐ desvergonzado; sin remordimiento.

un·asked [ˈʌnˈɑːskt] no solicitado; sin ser convidado.

un·as·sail·a·ble [ʌnəˈseiləbl] ☐ irrebatible.

un·as·sum·ing [ˈʌnəˈsjuːmiŋ] ☐ modesto, sin pretensiones.

un·at·tached [ˈʌnəˈtætʃt] suelto; p. no prometido; ✂ de reemplazo; ⚟ no embargado.

un·at·tain·a·ble [ˈʌnəˈteinəbl] ☐ inasequible.

un·at·tend·ed [ˈʌnəˈtendid] desatendido; sin guardia.

un·at·trac·tive [ˈʌnəˈtræktiv] ☐ poco atractivo.

un·au·thor·ized [ʌnˈɔːθəraizd] desautorizado.

un·a·vail·a·ble [ˈʌnəˈveiləbl] indisponible; un·a·vail·ing ☐ infructuoso, inútil.

un·a·void·a·ble [ˈʌnəˈvɔidəbl] ☐ inevitable, ineludible.

un·a·ware [ˈʌnəˈwɛə]: be ~ ignorar (of acc., that que); un·a·wares de improviso; inopinadamente; catch a p. ~ coger a una p. desprevenida.

un·backed [ˈʌnˈbækt] fig. sin respaldo; ✝ a descubierto.

un·bal·ance [ˈʌnˈbæləns] desequilibrio m; un·bal·anced desequilibrado.

un·bap·tized [ˈʌnbæpˈtaizd] sin bautizar.

un·bear·a·ble [ʌnˈbɛərəbl] ☐ inaguantable, insufrible.

un·beat·a·ble [ʌnˈbiːtəbl] imbatible; price inmejorable.

un·beat·en [ʌnˈbiːtn] track no trillado; team imbatido; price no mejorado.

un·be·com·ing [ˈʌnbiˈkʌmiŋ] ☐ indecoroso; impropio (for, to de); dress que sienta mal.

un·be·known [ˈʌnbiˈnoun]: ~ to me sin saberlo yo.

un·be·lief [ˈʌnbiˈliːf] descreimiento m; un·be·liev·a·ble ☐ increíble; un·be·liev·er no creyente m/f, descreído (a f) m; un·be·liev·ing ☐ incrédulo.

un·bend [ˈʌnbend] [irr. (bend)] v/t. desencorvar, enderezar (a. ⊕); v/i. fig. relajarse, suavizarse; (p.) hacerse más expansivo; un·bend·ing ☐ inflexible (a. fig.); fig. inconquistable, poco afable.

un·bi·as(s)ed [ˈʌnˈbaiəst] imparcial.

un·bid, un·bid·den [ˈʌnˈbid(n)] sin ser convidado.

un·bind [ˈʌnˈbaind] [irr. (bind)] desatar.

un·bleached [ˈʌnˈbliːtʃt] sin blanquear.

un·blem·ished [ʌnˈblemiʃt] sin tacha.

un·blush·ing [ʌnˈblʌʃiŋ] ☐ desvergonzado.

un·bolt [ˈʌnˈboult] desatrancar.

un·born [ˈʌnˈbɔːn] no nacido aún, nonato.

un·bos·om [ʌnˈbuzm]: ~ o.s. desahogarse, abrir su pecho (to a).

un·bound [ˈʌnˈbaund] book sin encuadernar.

un·bound·ed[ʌnˈbaundid] ilimitado.

un·break·a·ble [ˈʌnbreikəbl] irrompible.

un·bri·dled [ʌnˈbraidld] desenfrenado (a. fig.).

un·bro·ken [ˈʌnˈbroukn] seal intacto; time no interrumpido; horse no domado.

un·buck·le [ˈʌnˈbʌkl] deshebillar.

un·bur·den [ˈʌnˈbɔːdn]: ~ o.s., ~ one's heart desahogarse, aliviarse (of de).

un·bur·ied [ˈʌnˈberid] insepulto.

un·busi·ness-like [ˈʌnˈbiznislaik] poco práctico; informal.

un·but·ton [ʌn'bʌtn] desabotonar.

un·called-for [ʌn'kɔ:ldfɔ:] gratuito, inmerecido; impropio.

un·can·ny [ʌn'kæni] □ misterioso; extraordinario.

un·cared-for ['ʌn'kɛəd'fɔ:] *appearance* de abandono; *p. etc.* abandonado, desamparado.

un·ceas·ing [ʌn'si:siŋ] □ incesante.

un·cer·e·mo·ni·ous ['ʌnseri'mounjəs] □ poco ceremonioso; ~ly sin miramientos.

un·cer·tain [ʌn'sə:tn] □ incierto, dudoso; *be ~ of* no estar seguro de; **un'cer·tain·ty** incertidumbre *f*, duda *f*.

un·chain ['ʌn'tʃein] desencadenar.

un·chal·lenge·a·ble ['ʌn'tʃælindʒəbl] incontestable; **'un'chal·lenged** incontestado.

un·change·a·ble [ʌn'tʃeindʒəbl], **un'chang·ing** □ incambiable, inalterable.

un·char·i·ta·ble [ʌn'tʃæritəbl] □ poco caritativo; despiadado.

un·chaste ['ʌn'tʃeist] □ impúdico, incontinente.

un·checked ['ʌn'tʃekt] **1.** *adj.* desenfrenado; *fact etc.* no comprobado; **2.** *adv.* sin restricción; de una manera desenfrenada.

un·chris·tian ['ʌn'kristjən] indigno de un cristiano.

un·civ·il ['ʌn'sivl] □ incivil; **'un·'civ·i·lized** [~vilaizd] incivilizado, inculto. [mar.]

un·claimed ['ʌn'kleimd] sin reclamar.

un·clas·si·fied ['ʌn'klæsifaid] sin clasificar.

un·cle ['ʌŋkl] tío *m*; *sl.* prestamista *m*, prendero *m*.

un·clean ['ʌn'kli:n] □ sucio; *fig.* impuro.

un·clench ['ʌn'klentʃ] desapretar.

un·clothed ['ʌn'klouðd] desnudo.

un·cloud·ed ['ʌn'klaudid] despejado.

un·coil ['ʌn'kɔil] desenrollar(se).

un·col·lect·ed ['ʌnkə'lektid] sin cobrar.

un·come·ly ['ʌn'kʌmli] desgarbado.

un·com·fort·a·ble [ʌn'kʌmfətəbl] □ incómodo.

un·com·mon [ʌn'kɔmən] **1.** □ poco común, raro; **2.** *adv.* F extraordinariamente.

un·com·mu·ni·ca·tive ['ʌnkə'mju:nikətiv] poco comunicativo.

un·com·plain·ing ['ʌnkəm'pleiniŋ] □ resignado, sumiso.

un·com·pli·men·ta·ry ['ʌn'kɔmpli·'mentəri] poco lisonjero; ofensivo.

un·com·pro·mis·ing ['ʌn'kɔmprə·maiziŋ] □ intransigente.

un·con·cern ['ʌnkən'sə:n] despreocupación *f*; indiferencia *f*; **'un·con·'cerned** [*adv.* ~idli] □ despreocupado; indiferente (*about* a).

un·con·di·tion·al ['ʌnkən'diʃnl] □ incondicional.

un·con·fined ['ʌnkən'faind] ilimitado, libre.

un·con·firmed ['ʌnkən'fə:md] no confirmado.

un·con·gen·ial ['ʌnkən'dʒi:njəl] antipático; incompatible.

un·con·nect·ed ['ʌnkə'nektid] □ inconexo; no relacionado (*with* con).

un·con·quer·a·ble [ʌn'kɔŋkərəbl] □ inconquistable, invencible.

un·con·sci·en·tious ['ʌnkɔnʃi'enʃəs] □ poco concienzudo.

un·con·scion·a·ble [ʌn'kɔnʃənəbl] □ desmedido, desrazonable.

un·con·scious [ʌn'kɔnʃəs] **1.** □ inconsciente (*of* de); no intencional; ⚓ sin sentido, desmayado; **2.** *the ~* lo inconsciente; **un'con·scious·ness** inconsciencia *f*; ⚓ insensibilidad *f*.

un·con·se·crat·ed ['ʌn'kɔnsikreitid] no consagrado.

un·con·sti·tu·tion·al ['ʌnkɔnsti·'tju:ʃnl] □ inconstitucional.

un·con·strained ['ʌnkən'streind] libre, no cohibido.

un·con·test·ed ['ʌnkən'testid] incontestado.

un·con·trol·la·ble [ʌnkən'trouləbl] □ ingobernable.

un·con·ven·tion·al ['ʌnkən'venʃnl] □ poco formalista, desenfadado, poco convencional; original.

un·con·vert·ed ['ʌnkən'və:tid] no convertido (*a.* ✝).

un·con·vinced ['ʌnkən'vinst] no convencido; **'un·con·'vinc·ing** □ poco convincente.

un·cooked ['ʌn'kukd] sin cocer.

un·cork ['ʌn'kɔ:k] descorchar, destapar.

un·cor·rupt·ed ['ʌnkə'rʌptid] incorrupto.

un·count·a·ble ['ʌn'kauntəbl] incontable; **'un'count·ed** sin cuenta.

un·cou·ple ['ʌn'kʌpl] desacoplar.

un·couth [ʌn'ku:θ] ☐ grosero; rústico; tosco.

un·cov·er [ʌn'kʌvə] descubrir.

un·crit·i·cal ['ʌn'kritikl] ☐ falto de sentido crítico; poco juicioso.

un·crowned ['ʌn'kraund] sin corona.

unc·tion ['ʌŋkʃn] unción f (a. fig.); fig. efusión f fingida, fervor m afectado; zalamería f; eccl. extreme ~ extremaunción f; **unc·tu·ous** ['ʌŋktuəs] ☐ untuoso (a. fig.); fig. afectadamente fervoroso; zalamero.

un·cul·ti·vat·ed ['ʌn'kʌltiveitid] inculto (a. fig.).

un·cut ['ʌn'kʌt] sin cortar; diamond en bruto, sin tallar; book intonso.

un·dam·aged ['ʌn'dæmidʒd] ileso, indemne.

un·damped ['ʌn'dæmpt] fig. no disminuido.

un·dat·ed ['ʌn'deitid] sin fecha.

un·daunt·ed [ʌn'dɔːntid] ☐ impávido; intrépido.

un·de·ceive ['ʌndi'si:v] desengañar.

un·de·ci·pher·a·ble ['ʌndi'saifərəbl] indescifrable.

un·de·fend·ed ['ʌndi'fendid] indefenso; tₜₕ ~ suit pleito m perdido por incomparecimiento.

un·de·feat·ed ['ʌndi'fiːtid] invicto.

un·de·filed ['ʌndi'faild] inmaculado.

un·de·fined ['ʌndi'faind] indefinido.

un·de·mon·stra·tive ['ʌndi'mɔnstrətiv] ☐ reservado.

un·de·ni·a·ble ['ʌndi'naiəbl] ☐ innegable.

un·de·nom·i·na·tion·al ['ʌndinɔmi'neiʃnl] ☐ no sectario.

un·de·pend·a·ble ['ʌndi'pendəbl] poco confiable.

un·der ['ʌndə] 1. adv. debajo; abajo; 2. prp. (less precise; a. fig.) bajo, (more precise) debajo de; number inferior a; aged ~ 21 que tiene menos de 21 años; 3. in compounds: ... inferior; ... insuficiente (mente); (clothes) ... interior; '~·'bid [irr. (bid)] ofrecer precio más bajo que; '~·car·riage, F '~·cart ✈ tren m de aterrizaje; '~·clothes, '~·cloth·ing ropa f interior; '~·coat paint. primera capa f; '~·cur·rent corriente f submarina, contracorriente f; fig. nota f callada; '~·cut competitor competir con (rebajando los precios); '~·de'vel·oped subdesarrollado; '~·dog desvalido m; '~·done poco hecho; medio asado;

'~·es·ti·mate subestimar; p. tener en menos de lo que merece; '~·ex·'pose phot. exponer insuficientemente; ~d subexposición; '~·'fed subalimentado; '~·'feed·ing subalimentación f; ~·'foot debajo de los pies; ~·'go [irr. (go)] sufrir, experimentar; ~·'grad·u·ate estudiante m/f (no graduado); '~·ground 1. adj. subterráneo; fig. clandestino; 2. adv. bajo tierra; 3. (= ~ railway) metro m; ⚔ resistencia f; '~·growth maleza f; '~·hand turbio, poco limpio; clandestino; ~ service saque m con la mano debajo del hombro; ~·'lay [irr.] (lay) reforzar; typ. calzar; ~·'lie [irr. (lie)] estar debajo de; servir de base a (a. fig.); ~·line subrayar (a. fig.).

un·der·ling ['ʌndəliŋ] subordinado m, inferior m; secuaz m; **un·der·manned** ['~·'mænd] sin la debida tripulación, sin el debido personal; **un·der·mine** socavar; minar (a. fig.); '**un·der·most** (el) más bajo; **un·der·neath** [~·'ni:θ] 1. pron. debajo de, bajo; 2. adv. debajo; 3. su. superficie f inferior; '**un·der·'nour·ished** desnutrido.

un·der...: '~·pants pl. calzoncillos m/pl.; '~·pass Am. paso m inferior; '~·'pay [irr. (pay)] pagar insuficientemente; ~·'pin apuntalar; ~·'pin·ning apuntalamiento m; ~·'priv·i·leged desvalido; ~·'rate menospreciar; subestimar; ~·'score subrayar; '~·'sec·re·tar·y subsecretario m; '~·'sell [irr. (sell)] p. vender a menor precio que; th. malvender; '~·shirt Am. camiseta f; '~·skirt enaguas f/pl.; '~·side superficie f inferior; revés m; '~·signed infra(e)scrito (a f) m; ~·'sized de dimensión insuficiente; p. sietemesino; ~·'slung mot. debajo del eje; ~·'staffed sin el debido personal; ~·'stand [irr. (stand)] comprender, entender; sobre(e)ntender; give to ~ dar a entender; make o.s. understood hacerse entender; it is understood that se entiende que; an understood thing lo normal; ~·'stand·a·ble ☐ comprensible; '~·'stand·ing 1. entendimiento m; comprensión f; interpretación f; (agreement) acuerdo m; on the ~ that con tal que, bien entendido que; **2.** ☐ inteligente; razonable, compasivo; comprensivo; '~'**state** exponer incompletamente; subestimar; '~'**state·ment** exposición *f* incompleta; subestimación *f*.

un·der...: '~'**stud·y** *thea.* **1.** suplente *m/f*; **2.** aprender un papel para poder suplir a; ~'**take** [*irr.* (*take*)] *task etc.* emprender; *duty etc.* encargase de; ~ **to** *inf.* comprometerse a *inf.*; prometer *inf.*; ~ *that* comprometerse a que, prometer que; ~'**tak·er** director *m* de pompas fúnebres; ~'s funeraria *f*; '~'**tak·ing** empresa *f*; (*pledge*) compromiso *m*, garantía *f*; promesa *f*; '~'**tone** voz *f* baja; trasfondo *m* of *criticism etc.*; **in an ~ en** voz baja; '~'**tow** resaca *f*; '~'**val·ue** valor(iz)ar incompletamente; subestimar; menospreciar; '~'**wa·ter** submarino; '~'**wa·ter·'fish·ing** pesca *f* submarina; '~'**wear** ropa *f* interior; '~'**weight** (*adj.* de) peso *m* insuficiente; '~'**world** infierno *m*; (*criminal*) hampa *f*; '~'**write** [*irr.* (*write*)] † (re)asegurar; '~'**writ·er** (re)asegurador *m*.

un·de·served [ʌndiˈzəːvd] ☐ inmerecido; '**un·de·'serv·ing** indigno.

un·de·sir·a·ble ['ʌndiˈzaiərəbl] ☐ indeseable.

un·de·terred ['ʌndiˈtəːd] sin dejarse intimidar.

un·de·vel·oped ['ʌndiˈveləpt] sin desarrollar; *land* sin explotar; *phot.* sin revelar.   [constante.

un·de·vi·at·ing [ʌnˈdiːvieitiŋ] ☐

un·dies ['ʌndiz] F paños *m/pl.* menores.

un·di·gest·ed ['ʌndiˈdʒestid] indigesto.

un·dig·ni·fied [ʌnˈdignifaid] indecoroso; poco digno.

un·di·min·ished ['ʌndiˈminiʃt] no disminuido.

un·dis'cern·ing ['ʌndiˈsəːniŋ] sin discernimiento.

un·dis·ci·plined [ʌnˈdisiplind] indisciplinado.

un·dis·crim·i·nat·ing ['ʌndisˈkrimineitiŋ] ☐ falto de sentido crítico.

un·dis'guised ['ʌndisˈgaizd] ☐ franco, sin disfraz.

un·dis·mayed ['ʌndisˈmeid] impávido; sin desanimarse.

un·dis·posed-of ['ʌndisˈpouzdɔv] *mst* † no vendido; no invertido.

un·dis·put·ed ['ʌndisˈpjuːtid] ☐ incontestable.

un·dis·tin·guished ['ʌndisˈtiŋgwiʃd] mediocre.

un·dis·turbed ['ʌndisˈtəːbd] sin tocar; *p.* imperturbado.

un·di·vid·ed ['ʌndiˈvaidid] ☐ indiviso; entero.

un·do ['ʌnˈduː] [*irr.* (*do*)] *work* deshacer; *knot* desatar; *clasp* desabrochar; '**un·do·ing** perdición *f*, ruina *f*; **un·done** ['ʌnˈdʌn]: *leave ~* dejar sin hacer; *he is ~* está perdido; *come ~* desatarse.

un·doubt·ed [ʌnˈdautid] ☐ indudable.

un·dreamt [ʌnˈdremt]: ~-*of* no soñado.

un·dress ['ʌnˈdres] **1.** desnudar(se); **2.** traje *m* de casa, des(h)abillé *m*; ✕ traje *m* de cuartel.

un·drink·a·ble [ʌnˈdriŋkəbl] impotable.

un·due ['ʌnˈdjuː] [*adv. unduly*] indebido; excesivo.

un·du·late ['ʌndjuleit] ondular, ondear; '**un·du·lat·ing** ondeante, ondulante; *land* ondulado; **un·du·la·tion** ondulación *f*; '**un·du·la·to·ry** ondulatorio.

un·dy·ing [ʌnˈdaiiŋ] imperecedero, inmarcesible.

un·earned ['ʌnˈəːnd] no ganado.

un·earth ['ʌnˈəːθ] desenterrar; descubrir (*a. fig.*); **un'earth·ly** sobrenatural; espectral; F *hour* inverosímil.

un·eas·i·ness [ʌnˈiːzinis] inquietud *f*, desasosiego *m*; **un'eas·y** ☐ inquieto (*about* por), desasosegado; *feel ~* sentirse mal a gusto.

un·eat·a·ble ['ʌnˈiːtəbl] incomible.

un·e·co·nom·ic, un·e·co·nom·i·cal ['ʌnikəˈnɔmik(l)] ☐ antieconómico.

un·ed·i·fy·ing ['ʌnˈedifaiiŋ] ☐ indecoroso.

un·ed·u·cat·ed ['ʌnˈedjukeitid] ineducado.

un·e·mo·tion·al ['ʌniˈmouʃnl] ☐ que no se deja emocionar; impasible; objetivo.

un·em·ployed ['ʌnimˈplɔid] parado, sin empleo, desocupado; '**un·employ·ment** paro *m* (forzoso), desempleo *m*, desocupación *f*; ~ *benefit* subsidio *m* de paro.

un·end·ing ['ʌnˈendiŋ] ☐ interminable, inacabable.

un·en·dur·a·ble [ˈʌninˈdjuərəbl] □ inaguantable, insufrible.

un·en·gaged [ˈʌninˈgeidʒd] libre.

un·en·light·ened [ˈʌninˈlaitnd] poco instruido; *policy etc.* ignorante, estúpido.

un·en·ter·pris·ing [ˈʌnˈentəpraiziŋ] □ falto de iniciativa.

un·en·vi·a·ble [ˈʌnˈenviəbl] □ poco envidiable.

un·e·qual [ˈʌnˈiːkwəl] □ desigual; ~ *to* sin fuerzas para; ˈun·e·qual(l)·ed inigualado.

un·e·quiv·o·cal [ˈʌniˈkwivəkl] □ inequívoco.

un·err·ing [ˈʌnˈəːriŋ] □ infalible.

un·es·sen·tial [ˈʌniˈsenʃl] □ no esencial.

un·e·ven [ˈʌnˈiːvn] □ desigual; *road* ondulado; ˈun·e·ven·ness desigualdad *f*; lo ondulado.

un·e·vent·ful [ˈʌniˈventful] □ sin incidentes notables.

un·ex·am·pled [ˈʌnigˈzɑːmpld] sin igual.

un·ex·cep·tion·a·ble [ˈʌnikˈsepʃənəbl] □ intachable.

un·ex·pect·ed [ˈʌniksˈpektid] □ inesperado; inopinado.

un·ex·pired [ˈʌniksˈpaiəd] no expirado; *lease, ticket* no caducado; † *bill* no vencido.

un·ex·plained [ˈʌniksˈpleind] inexplicado.

un·ex·plored [ʌniksˈplɔːd] inexplorado.

un·ex·posed [ˈʌniksˈpouzd] *phot.* inexpuesto.

un·ex·pressed [ˈʌniksˈprest] no expresado.

un·ex·pur·gat·ed [ˈʌnˈekspəːgeitid] sin expurgar, íntegro.

un·fad·ing [ʌnˈfeidiŋ] □ *mst fig.* inmarcesible.

un·fail·ing [ʌnˈfeiliŋ] □ *zeal* infalible; *supply* inagotable.

un·fair [ˈʌnˈfɛə] □ *comment* injusto; *practice* sin equidad; *play* sucio; ˈun·fair·ness injusticia *f* etc.

un·faith·ful [ˈʌnˈfeiθful] □ infiel; ˈun·faith·ful·ness infidelidad *f*.

un·fal·ter·ing [ʌnˈfɔːltəriŋ] □ resuelto.

un·fa·mil·iar [ˈʌnfəˈmiljə] desconocido (*to a*); *be* ~ *with* desconocer.

un·fash·ion·a·ble [ˈʌnˈfæʃnəbl] □ fuera de moda.

un·fas·ten [ˈʌnˈfɑːsn] desatar, soltar.

un·fath·om·a·ble [ʌnˈfæðəməbl] □ insondable.

un·fa·vo·(u)r·a·ble [ˈʌnˈfeivərəbl] □ desfavorable.

un·feel·ing [ʌnˈfiːliŋ] □ insensible.

un·feigned [ʌnˈfeind, *adv.* ⁓nidli] □ no fingido.

un·fer·ment·ed [ˈʌnfəːˈmentid] no fermentado.

un·fet·ter [ˈʌnˈfetə] destrabar; **un·ˈfet·tered** *fig.* sin trabas.

un·fin·ished [ˈʌnˈfiniʃt] inacabado, sin acabar; incompleto.

un·fit 1. [ˈʌnˈfit] incapaz (*for de, to de*); no apto (*for para*); *player* lesionado; **2.** [ʌnˈfit] inhabilitar; ˈun·ˈfit·ness incapacidad *f*; un·ˈfit·ted incapacitado (*for para*).

un·flag·ging [ʌnˈflægiŋ] □ incansable.

un·flat·ter·ing [ˈʌnˈflætəriŋ] □ poco lisonjero.

un·fledged [ˈʌnfledʒd] implume.

un·flinch·ing [ʌnˈflintʃiŋ] □ impávido.

un·fly·a·ble weath·er [ˈʌnˈflaiəbl ˈweðə] tiempo *m* que imposibilita la salida de aviones.

un·fold [ˈʌnˈfould] desplegar(se); desdoblar(se); desarrollar(se) (*a. fig.*); revelar; *idea* exponer.

un·fore·see·a·ble [ˈʌnfɔːˈsiːəbl] □ imprevisible; ˈun·fore·ˈseen imprevisto.

un·for·get·ta·ble [ˈʌnfəˈgetəbl] □ inolvidable.

un·for·giv·a·ble [ˈʌnfəˈgivəbl] □ imperdonable; ˈun·for·ˈgiv·ing implacable.

un·for·ti·fied [ˈʌnˈfɔːtifaid] no fortificado; *town* abierto.

un·for·tu·nate [ʌnˈfɔːtʃənit] **1.** □ *p.* desgraciado, desafortunado; malogrado; *event* funesto; *p.'s manner* infeliz; *remark* que trae malas consecuencias; **2.** desgraciado (*a f*) *m*; un·ˈfor·tu·nate·ly por desgracia, desafortunadamente.

un·found·ed [ˈʌnˈfaundid] □ infundado.

un·fre·quent·ed [ˈʌnfriˈkwentid] poco frecuentado.

un·ˈfriend·ly [ˈʌnˈfrendli] poco amistoso, hostil.

un·fruit·ful [ˈʌnˈfruːtful] □ infructuoso.

un·ful·filled [ˈʌnfulˈfild] incumplido.

un·furl [ʌnˈfəːl] desplegar.

un·fur·nished [ˈʌnˈfəːniʃt] desamueblado, sin muebles.

un·gain·li·ness [ʌnˈgeinlinis] torpeza f; **un'gain·ly** torpe, desgarbado.

un·gal·lant [ˈʌnˈgælənt] □ falto de cortesía.

un·gear [ˈʌnˈgiə] ⊕ desembragar.

un·gen·er·ous [ˈʌnˈdʒenərəs] □ poco generoso.

un·gen·tle·man·ly [ʌnˈdʒentlmənli] poco caballeroso.

un·get-at·able [ˈʌngetˈætəbl] inaccesible.

un·glazed [ˈʌnˈgleizd] no vidriado.

un·god·li·ness [ʌnˈgɔdlinis] impiedad f; **un'god·ly** impío, irreligioso; F atroz.

un·gov·ern·a·ble [ʌnˈgʌvənəbl] □ ingobernable.

un·gra·cious [ˈʌnˈgreiʃəs] □ poco afable; descortés, grosero.

un·grate·ful [ʌnˈgreitful] □ desagradecido, ingrato.

un·grudg·ing [ˈʌnˈgrʌdʒiŋ] □ generoso.

un·gual [ˈʌŋgwəl] unguiculado.

un·guard·ed [ˈʌnˈgɑːdid] □ ✕ indefenso; *words* imprudente; *moment* de descuido.

un·guent [ˈʌŋgwənt] ungüento m.

un·gu·late [ˈʌŋgjuleit] (*or* ～ *animal*) ungulado m.

un·ham·pered [ˈʌnˈhæmpəd] no estorbado; libre, sin estorbos.

un·hand [ʌnˈhænd] soltar; **un'hand·y** □ *p.* desmañado; *th.* incómodo.

un·hap·pi·ness [ʌnˈhæpinis] infelicidad f, desdicha f; **un'hap·py** □ *p.* infeliz, desdichado; desgraciado; *event* infausto.

un·harmed [ˈʌnˈhɑːmd] ileso, incólume.

un·har·mo·ni·ous [ˈʌnhɑːˈmounjəs] □ inarmónico.

un·har·ness [ˈʌnˈhɑːnis] desguarnecer.

un·health·y [ʌnˈhelθi] □ *p.* enfermizo; *place* malsano.

un·heard-of [ʌnˈhəːdɔv] inaudito.

un·heed·ed [ʌnˈhiːdid] desatendido.

un·hes·i·tat·ing [ʌnˈheziteitiŋ] □ resuelto; pronto, inmediato; ～*ly* sin vacilar.

un·hinge [ʌnˈhindʒ] desquiciar (*a. fig.*).

un·his·tor·ic, un·his·tor·i·cal [ˈʌnhisˈtɔrik(l)] □ antihistórico.

un·ho·ly [ʌnˈhouli] impío; F atroz.

un·hook [ˈʌnˈhuk] desenganchar; descolgar.

un·hoped-for [ʌnˈhouptfɔː] inesperado; **un'hope·ful** [～ful] □ poco prometedor.

un·horse [ˈʌnˈhɔːs] desarzonar.

un·hurt [ˈʌnˈhəːt] ileso, incólume.

u·ni·corn [ˈjuːnikɔːn] unicornio m.

un·i·den·ti·fied [ˈʌnaiˈdentifaid] sin identificar.

u·ni·fi·ca·tion [juːnifiˈkeiʃn] unificación f.

u·ni·form [ˈjuːnifɔːm] **1.** □ uniforme *adj. a. su. m*; **2.** uniformar; **u·ni'form·i·ty** uniformidad f.

u·ni·fy [ˈjuːnifai] unificar.

u·ni·lat·er·al [ˈjuːniˈlætərəl] □ unilateral.

un·im·ag·i·na·ble [ˈʌniˈmædʒinəbl] □ inimaginable; **'un·im'ag·i·na·tive** [～nətiv] □ poco imaginativo.

un·im·paired [ˈʌnimˈpɛəd] no disminuido, no deteriorado; intacto.

un·im·peach·a·ble [ʌnimˈpiːtʃəbl] □ irrecusable.

un·im·ped·ed [ˈʌnimˈpiːdid] □ sin estorbo.

un·im·por·tant [ˈʌnimˈpɔːtənt] □ insignificante; sin importancia.

un·in·formed [ˈʌninˈfɔːmd] poco instruido, ignorante.

un·in·hab·it·a·ble [ˈʌninˈhæbitəbl] inhabitable; **'un·in'hab·it·ed** inhabitado.

un·in·jured [ˈʌnˈindʒəd] ileso.

un·in·sured [ˈʌninˈʃuəd] no asegurado.

un·in·tel·li·gent [ˈʌninˈtelidʒənt] □ ininteligente; **'un·in'tel·li·gi'bil·i·ty** ininteligibilidad f; **'un·in'tel·li·gi·ble** □ ininteligible.

un·in·tend·ed [ˈʌninˈtendid] □, **un·in·ten·tion·al** [ˈʌninˈtenʃnl] □ involuntario, no intencional; ～*ly* sin querer.

un·in·ter·est·ing [ˈʌnˈintristiŋ] □ falto de interés.

un·in·ter·rupt·ed [ˈʌnintəˈrʌptid] □ ininterrumpido.

un·in·vit·ed [ˈʌninˈvaitid] *guest* no convidado, (*adv.*) sin ser convidado; *comment* gratuito; **'un·in'vit·ing** □ poco atractivo.

un·ion [ˈjuːnjən] unión f (*a.* ⊕); (*marriage*) enlace m; *pol. etc.* sindicato *m*, gremio *m* (obrero); *attr.* gremial; ♀ *Jack* bandera del Reino Unido; ~ *suit Am.* traje *m* interior de una sola pieza; 'un·ion·ism *pol.* (*British*) conservatismo *m*; *v. trade*-; 'un·ion·ist (*British*) conservador (-a *f*) *m*; *v. trade*-; 'un·ion·ize ·agremiar(se).

u·nique [ju:'ni:k] □ único.

u·ni·son ['ju:nizn] ♪ unisonancia *f*; armonía *f* (*a. fig.*); *in* ~ al unísono; u·nis·o·nous [ju:'nisənəs] ♪ unísono.

u·nit ['ju:nit] unidad *f* (*a.* ✂, ♣); ✗ (*measurement*) unidad₁ *f*; ⊕, ✗ grupo *m*; U·ni·tar·i·an [ju:ni'tɛəriən] unitario *adj. a. su. m*; u·ni·tar·y ['_təri] unitario; u·nite [ju:'nait] unir(se), juntar(se); (*marry*) casar, enlazar; ♀d *Kingdom* Reino *m* Unido (*Gran Bretaña e Irlanda del Norte*); ♀d *Nations* Naciones *f/pl.* Unidas; u·ni·ty ['_niti] unidad *f*; unión *f*.

u·ni·ver·sal [ju:ni'və:sl] □ universal; ~ *heir* heredero *m* único; ⊕ ~ *joint* junta *f* cardán, junta *f* universal; ♀ *Postal Union* Unión *f* Postal Universal; ~ *suffrage* sufragio *m* universal; u·ni·ver·sal·i·ty [_'sæliti] universalidad *f*; u·ni·verse ['_və:s] universo *m*; u·ni·'ver·si·ty universidad *f*; *attr.* universitario.

un·just ['ʌn'dʒʌst] □ injusto; un·jus·ti·fi·a·ble [ʌn'dʒʌstifaiəbl] □ injustificable.

un·kempt ['ʌn'kempt] despeinado; *fig.* desaseado, descuidado.

un·kind [ʌn'kaind] □ poco amable, poco compasivo; cruel, despiadado; *remark etc.* malintencionado.

un·known ['ʌn'noun] 1. desconocido; incógnito; *adv.* ~ *to me* sin saberlo yo; 2. desconocido *m*; ♣ *a. fig.* (*a.* ~ *quantity*) incógnita *f*.

un·lace ['ʌn'leis] desenlazar.

un·lade ['ʌn'leid] [*irr.* (*lade*)] descargar.

un·la·dy·like ['ʌn'leidilaik] impropio de una señora.

un·la·ment·ed ['ʌnlə'mentid] no lamentado.

un·latch [ʌn'lætʃ] abrir (levantando el picaporte).

un·law·ful ['ʌn'lɔ:ful] □ ilegítimo, ilegal.

un·learn ['ʌn'lə:n] desaprender;

'un·learn·ed [_id] □ indocto, ignorante.

un·leash ['ʌn'li:ʃ] destraillar; *fig.* desencadenar.

un·leav·ened ['ʌn'levnd] ázimo, sin levadura.

un·less [ən'les, ʌn'les] a menos que, a no ser que.

un·let·tered ['ʌn'letəd] indocto.

un·li·censed ['ʌn'laisənst] sin permiso, sin licencia.

un·like ['ʌn'laik] 1. desemejante; diferente (*a p. de una p.*); ♂ de signo contrario; 2. *prp.* a diferencia de; un·like·li·hood improbabilidad *f*; un·like·ly improbable; inverosímil.

un·lim·it·ed [ʌn'limitid] ilimitado.

un·lined ['ʌn'laind] *coat* sin forro; *face* sin arrugas; *paper* sin rayar.

un·liq·ui·dat·ed ['ʌn'likwideitid] ilíquido.

un·load ['ʌn'loud] descargar; ♣ deshacerse de.

un·lock ['ʌn'lɔk] abrir (con llave); *fig.* resolver.

un·looked-for [ʌn'luktfɔ:] inesperado, inopinado.

un·loose, un·loos·en ['ʌn'lu:s(n)] aflojar, desatar, soltar.

un·lov·a·ble ['ʌn'lʌvəbl] poco apetecible; *p.* antipático; 'un·love·ly desgarbado; 'un·lov·ing □ desamorado; nada cariñoso.

un·luck·y [ʌn'lʌki] □ desgraciado; desdichado; (*ill-starred*) nefasto, de mala suerte; *it's* ~ *to inf.* trae mala suerte *inf.*

un·make ['ʌn'meik] [*irr.* (*make*)] deshacer.

un·man ['ʌn'mæn] acobardar.

un·man·age·a·ble [ʌn'mænidʒəbl] □ inmanejable; *esp. p.* incontrolable.

un·man·ly ['ʌn'mænli] cobarde; afeminado.

un·man·ner·ly [ʌn'mænəli] descortés, mal educado.

un·marked ['ʌn'mɑ:kt] sin marca(r); intacto; (*unnoticed*) inadvertido; *sport*: desmarcado.

un·mar·ket·a·ble ['ʌn'mɑ:kitəbl] invendible.

un·mar·ried ['ʌn'mærid] soltero.

un·mask ['ʌn'mɑ:sk] desenmascarar.

un·matched ['ʌn'mætʃt] incomparable.

un·men·tion·a·ble [ʌn'menʃnəbl]

1. que no debe mencionarse; indecible; 2. *co.* † ~s *pl.* pantalones *m/pl.* (de hombre).

un·mer·ci·ful [ʌn'mɔːsiful] □ despiadado.

un·mer·it·ed ['ʌn'meritid] inmerecido.

un·me·thod·i·cal ['ʌnmi'θɔdikl] poco metódico.

un·mind·ful [ʌn'maindful] □ descuidado; *be* ~ *of* no pensar en.

un·mis·tak·a·ble ['ʌnmis'teikəbl] □ inconfundible; inequívoco.

un·mit·i·gat·ed [ʌn'mitigeitid] no mitigado; *rogue* redomado.

un·mo·lest·ed ['ʌnmou'lestid] indemne.

un·mor·al [ʌn'mɔrəl] amoral.

un·mort·gaged ['ʌn'mɔːgidʒd] libre de hipoteca.

un·mount·ed ['ʌn'mauntid] *rider* desmontado; *stone* sin engastar; *phot.* sin pegar.

un·mourned ['ʌn'mɔːnd] no llorado.

un·moved ['ʌn'muːvd] *mst fig.* impasible, inmoble.

un·mu·si·cal ['ʌn'mjuːzikl] □ inarmónico; *p.* sin instinto musical.

un·named ['ʌn'neimd] sin nombre.

un·nat·u·ral [ʌn'nætʃrl] □ innatural; desnaturalizado; afectado.

un·nav·i·ga·ble ['ʌn'nævigəbl] innavegable.

un·nec·es·sar·y [ʌn'nesisəri] □ innecesario, superfluo.

un·neigh·bo(u)r·ly ['ʌn'neibəli] poco amistoso.

un·nerve ['ʌn'nəːv] acobardar.

un·no·ticed ['ʌn'noutist] inadvertido.

un·num·bered ['ʌn'nʌmbəd] *page etc.* sin numerar; *poet.* innumerable.

un·ob·jec·tion·a·ble ['ʌnəb'dʒekʃnəbl] □ intachable.

un·ob·serv·ant ['ʌnəb'zəːvənt] □ inadvertido; distraído, que no se fija; **'un·ob'served** inadvertido.

un·ob·tain·a·ble ['ʌnəb'teinəbl] inasequible.

un·ob·tru·sive ['ʌnəb'truːsiv] □ discreto; modesto.

un·oc·cu·pied ['ʌn'ɔkjupaid] *house* deshabitado; *territory* sin colonizar; *seat* libre; *post* vacante; *p.* desocupado.

un·of·fi·cial ['ʌnə'fiʃl] □ extraoficial, no oficial.

un·o·pened ['ʌn'oupənd] sin abrir.

un·op·posed ['ʌnə'pouzd] sin oposición.

un·or·gan·ized ['ʌn'ɔːgənaizd] no organizado.

un·or·tho·dox ['ʌn'ɔːθədɔks] poco ortodoxo; *eccl.* heterodoxo.

un·os·ten·ta·tious ['ʌnɔstən'teiʃəs] □ sin ostentación.

un·pack ['ʌn'pæk] desembalar, desempaquetar; *case* deshacer.

un·paid ['ʌn'peid] *bill* a pagar, por pagar; *work* no retribuido.

un·pal·at·a·ble [ʌn'pælətəbl] desabrido (*a. fig.*), intragable (*a. fig.*).

un·par·al·leled [ʌn'pærəleld] incomparable, sin par.

un·par·don·a·ble [ʌn'pɑːdnəbl] □ imperdonable.

un·par·lia·men·ta·ry ['ʌnpɑːli'mentəri] □ antiparlamentario.

un·pat·ent·ed ['ʌn'peitəntid] sin patentar.

un·pa·tri·ot·ic ['ʌnpætri'ɔtik] □ antipatriótico.

un·paved ['ʌn'peivd] sin pavimentar.

un·per·ceived ['ʌnpə'siːvd] inapercibido.

un·per·turbed ['ʌnpə'təːbd] impertérrito.

un·pick ['ʌn'pik] *seam* descoser.

un·pin ['ʌn'pin] desprender.

un·placed ['ʌn'pleist] *sport:* no colocado.

un·pleas·ant [ʌn'pleznt] □ desagradable; *p.* antipático; **un'pleas·ant·ness** lo desagradable; (*quarrel etc.*) desavenencia *f*, disgusto *m*.

un·plumbed ['ʌn'plʌmd] no sondado.

un·po·et·ic, un·po·et·i·cal ['ʌnpou'etik(l)] □ poco poético.

un·po·lished ['ʌn'pɔliʃt] sin pulir; *stone* en bruto; *fig.* grosero, tosco.

un·pol·lut·ed ['ʌnpə'luːtid] impoluto.

un·pop·u·lar ['ʌn'pɔpjulə] impopular; **un·pop·u·lar·i·ty** ['~læriti] impopularidad *f*.

un·prac·ti·cal ['ʌn'præktikl] □ *p.* desmañado; poco práctico; **'un'prac·ticed, 'un'prac·tised** ['~tist] inexperto.

un·prec·e·dent·ed [ʌn'presidəntid] □ inaudito, sin precedente.

un·pre·dict·a·ble ['ʌnpri'diktəbl] ☐ impredictible, incierto; *p.* de (re-) acciones imprevisibles.

un·prej·u·diced ['ʌn'predʒudist] imparcial.

un·pre·med·i·tat·ed ['ʌnpri'medi-teitid] ☐ impremeditado.

un·pre·pared ['ʌnpri'pɛəd, *adv.* ⏴ridli] ☐ no preparado; *p.* desprevenido.

un·pre·pos·sess·ing ['ʌnpri:pə'zes-iŋ] poco atractivo.

un·pre·sent·a·ble ['ʌnpri'zentəbl] mal apersonado.

un·pre·ten·tious ['ʌnpri'tenʃəs] ☐ modesto, sin pretensiones.

un·prin·ci·pled ['ʌn'prinsəpld] nada escrupuloso, sin conciencia.

un·print·a·ble ['ʌn'printəbl] intranscribible.

un·pro·duc·tive ['ʌnprə'dʌktiv] ☐ improductivo.

un·pro·fes·sion·al ['ʌnprə'feʃnl] ☐ *conduct* indigno de su profesión; (*unskilled*) inexperto.

un·prof·it·a·ble ['ʌn'prɔfitəbl] ☐ poco provechoso, nada lucrativo.

un·prom·is·ing ['ʌn'prɔmisiŋ] ☐ poco prometedor.

un·pro·nounce·a·ble ['ʌnprə-'naunsəbl] ☐ impronunciable.

un·pro·pi·tious ['ʌnprə'piʃəs] ☐ impropicio.

un·pro·tect·ed ['ʌnprə'tektid] indefenso.

un·proved ['ʌn'pru:vd] no probado.

un·pro·vid·ed ['ʌnprə'vaidid] desprovisto (*with* de); **un·pro·vid·ed-for** imprevisor; *child* desvalido.

un·pro·voked ['ʌnprə'voukt] sin provocación.

un·pub·lished ['ʌn'pʌbliʃt] inédito.

un·punc·tu·al ['ʌn'pʌŋktjuəl] ☐ impuntual; **un·punc·tu·al·i·ty** ['⏴æliti] impuntualidad *f.*

un·pun·ished ['ʌn'pʌniʃt] impune; *go* ⏴ escapar sin castigo.

un·qual·i·fied [ʌn'kwɔlifaid] *p.* incompetente; *teacher* sin título; *success, assertion* incondicional; F *liar* redomado.

un·quench·a·ble [ʌn'kwentʃəbl] ☐ inextinguible, insaciable (*a. fig.*).

un·ques·tion·a·ble [ʌn'kwestʃənəbl] ☐ incuestionable; **un·ques·tioned** incontestable; **un·ques·tion·ing** ☐ incondicional.

un·qui·et ['ʌn'kwaiət] inquieto.

un·quote ['ʌn'kwout] terminar una cita; "⏴" (*in speech etc.*) fin *m* de la cita; **un·quot·ed** ✝ no cotizado.

un·rav·el [ʌn'rævl] desenmarañar (*a. fig.*).

un·read ['ʌn'red] no leído; **un·read·a·ble** ['ʌn'ri:dəbl] ilegible; *fig.* pesadísimo.

un·read·i·ness ['ʌn'redinis] desprevención *f*; **un·read·y** ☐ desapercibido, desprevenido.

un·re·al ['ʌn'riəl] irreal, ilusorio; **un·re·al·is·tic** ['ʌnriə'listik] ☐ impracticable; fantástico; *p.* poco realista; **un·re·al·i·ty** ['⏴æliti] irrealidad *f*; **un·re·al·iz·a·ble** [⏴laizəbl] irrealizable.

un·rea·son ['ʌn'ri:zn] insensatez *f*; **un·rea·son·a·ble** ☐ irrazonable; *demand* excesivo; **un·rea·son·ing** irracional.

un·re·claimed ['ʌnri'kleimd] *land* no utilizado.

un·rec·og·niz·a·ble ['ʌn'rekəgnaiz-əbl] ☐ irreconocible; **un·rec·og-nized** no reconocido.

un·re·cord·ed ['ʌnri'kɔ:did] no registrado.

un·re·deemed ['ʌnri'di:md] *promise* sin cumplir; *pledge* no desempeñado; *fig.* no mitigado (*by* por).

un·re·dressed ['ʌnri'drest] sin corregir.

un·re·fined ['ʌnri'faind] no refinado; *fig.* inculto.

un·re·flect·ing ['ʌnri'flektiŋ] ☐ irreflexivo.

un·re·formed ['ʌnri'fɔ:md] no reformado.

un·re·gard·ed ['ʌnri'gɑ:did] desatendido.

un·re·gen·er·ate ['ʌnri'dʒenərit] empedernido.

un·reg·is·tered ['ʌn'redʒistəd] no registrado; *letter* no certificado.

un·re·gret·ted ['ʌnri'gretid] no lamentado.

un·re·lat·ed ['ʌnri'leitid] inconexo.

un·re·lent·ing ['ʌnri'lentiŋ] ☐ inexorable, implacable.

un·re·li·a·ble ['ʌnri'laiəbl] *p.* poco confiable; informal; *news* nada fidedigno.

un·re·lieved ['ʌnri'li:vd] ☐ no aliviado.

un·re·mit·ting ['ʌnri'mitiŋ] ☐ infatigable.

un·re·mu·ner·a·tive ['ʌnri'mju:-nərətiv] □ poco lucrativo.

un·re·pealed ['ʌnri'pi:ld] no revocado.

un·re·peat·a·ble ['ʌnri'pi:təbl] que no puede repetirse.

un·re·pent·ant ['ʌnri'pentənt] □ impenitente.

un·re·quit·ed ['ʌnri'kwaitid] □ no correspondido.

un·re·served ['ʌnri'zə:vd, adv. ~vidli] □ no reservado, libre; ~ly sin reserva.

un·re·sist·ing ['ʌnri'zistiŋ] □ sumiso.

un·re·spon·sive ['ʌnris'pɔnsiv] insensible.

un·rest ['ʌn'rest] malestar m, zozobra f; pol. desorden m.

un·re·strained ['ʌnris'treind] □ desenfrenado.

un·re·strict·ed ['ʌnris'triktid] □ sin restricción f.

un·re·vealed ['ʌnri'vi:ld] no revelado.

un·re·ward·ed ['ʌnri'wɔ:did] sin recompensa; un·re'ward·ing sin provecho, infructuoso.

un·rig ['ʌn'rig] desaparejar.

un·right·eous [ʌn'raitʃəs] □ injusto; malvado.

un·ripe ['ʌn'raip] inmaturo, verde.

un·ri·val(l)ed [ʌn'raivəld] sin rival, incomparable.

un·roll ['ʌn'roul] desenrollar.

un·roof ['ʌn'ru:f] destechar.

un·rope ['ʌn'roup] mount. desatar (se).

un·ruf·fled ['ʌn'rʌfld] imperturbable.

un·ruled ['ʌn'ru:ld] paper sin rayar.

un·ru·ly [ʌn'ru:li] revoltoso, ingobernable.

un·sad·dle [ˌʌn'sædl] rider desarzonar; horse desensillar.

un·safe ['ʌn'seif] □ inseguro.

un·said ['ʌn'sed] sin decir.

un·sal(e)·a·ble ['ʌn'seiləbl] invendible.

un·sat·is·fac·to·ry ['ʌnsætis'fæktəri] □ insatisfactorio; un'sat·is·fied insatisfecho; un'sat·is·fy·ing □ insuficiente.

un·sa·vo(u)r·y ['ʌn'seivəri] desabrido; repugnante; p. indeseable.

un·say ['ʌn'sei] [irr. (say)] desdecirse de.

un·scathed ['ʌn'skeiðd] ileso.

un·sci·en·tif·ic ['ʌnsaiən'tifik] □ poco científico.

un·screw ['ʌn'skru:] destornillar.

un·scru·pu·lous [ʌn'skru:pjuləs] □ desaprensivo, poco escrupuloso.

un·seal ['ʌn'si:l] desellar.

un·sea·son·a·ble [ʌn'si:znəbl] □ intempestivo; 'un'sea·soned sin sazonar; sin madurar; wood verde.

un·seat ['ʌn'si:t] rider desarzonar; destituir from post; parl. expulsar.

un·sea·wor·thy ['ʌn'si:wə:ði] innavegable.

un·seem·li·ness [ʌn'si:mlinis] lo indecoroso; un'seem·ly adj. indecoroso.

un·seen ['ʌn'si:n] 1. invisible; inadvertido; 2. (a. ~ translation) traducción f hecha a primera vista.

un·self·ish ['ʌn'selfiʃ] □ desinteresado, altruista.

un·serv·ice·a·ble ['ʌn'sə:visəbl] □ inservible.

un·set·tle ['ʌn'setl] desarreglar; p. inquietar; 'un'set·tled p. inquieto; weather variable; question pendiente; land inhabitado, no colonizado; ✝ market in(e)stable; ✝ account por pagar. [nar.\

un·shack·le ['ʌn'ʃækl] desencade-∫

un·shak·(e)a·ble ['ʌn'ʃeikəbl] □ inquebrantable; un'shak·en impertérrito.

un·shape·ly ['ʌn'ʃeipli] deforme.

un·shav·en ['ʌn'ʃeivn] sin afeitar.

un·sheathe ['ʌn'ʃi:ð] desenvainar.

un·ship ['ʌn'ʃip] desembarcar; rudder desmontar; F deshacerse de.

un·shod ['ʌn'ʃɔd] descalzo; horse desherrado.

un·shrink·a·ble ['ʌn'ʃriŋkəbl] inencogible; 'un'shrink·ing □ impávido.

un·sight·ed ['ʌn'saitid] que tiene impedida la vista; un'sight·ly feo.

un·signed ['ʌn'saind] sin firmar.

un·skil(l)·ful ['ʌn'skilful] □, 'un·skilled inexperto, desmañado; worker no cualificado.

un·skimmed ['ʌn'skimd] sin desnatar.

un·so·cia·ble [ʌn'souʃəbl] □ insociable.

un·sold ['ʌn'sould] sin vender.

un·sol·dier·ly ['ʌn'souldʒəli] indigno de un militar.

un·so·lic·it·ed ['ʌnsə'lisitid] no solicitado.

un·solv·a·ble [ˈʌnˈsɔlvəbl] irresoluble; **'un'solved** no resuelto.

un·so·phis·ti·cat·ed [ˈʌnsəˈfistikeitid] sencillo, cándido.

un·sought [ˈʌnˈsɔːt] no solicitado.

un·sound [ˈʌnˈsaund] □ defectuoso; *opinion* falso, erróneo; *fruit* podrido; of ~ *mind* insano, demente.

un·spar·ing [ˈʌnˈspɛəriŋ] □ generoso, pródigo; *effort* incansable; (*cruel*) despiadado; *be ~ of* no escatimar *acc.*

un·speak·a·ble [ʌnˈspiːkəbl] □ indecible; F horrible

un·spec·i·fied [ˈʌnˈspesifaid] no especificado.

un·spent [ˈʌnˈspent] no gastado.

un·spoiled [ˈʌnˈspɔild] sin menoscabo, intacto.

un·spo·ken [ˈʌnˈspoukn] tácito.

un·sport·ing [ˈʌnˈspɔːtiŋ] □, **un·sports·man·like** [ˈʌnˈspɔːtsmənlaik] antideportivo; nada caballeroso.

un·spot·ted [ˈʌnˈspɔtid] inmaculado.

un·sta·ble [ˈʌnˈsteibl] inestable.

un·stamped [ˈʌnˈstæmpt] ⚭ sin franquear.

un·states·man·like [ˈʌnˈsteitsmənlaik] indigno de un estadista.

un·stead·y [ˈʌnˈstedi] □ inestable, inseguro; inconstante; *p.* irresoluto.

un·stint·ed [ʌnˈstintid] ilimitado, liberal.

un·stop [ˈʌnˈstɔp] destaponar.

un·stressed [ˈʌnˈstrest] inacentuado, átono.

un·string [ˈʌnˈstriŋ] [*irr.* (*string*)] ♪ desencordar; *nerves* trastornar; *pearls* desensartar.

un·stud·ied [ˈʌnˈstʌdid] natural, sin afectación.

un·sub·dued [ˈʌnsəbˈdjuːd] indomado.

un·sub·mis·sive [ˈʌnsəbˈmisiv] □ insumiso.

un·sub·stan·tial [ˈʌnsəbˈstænʃl] □ insustancial.

un·suc·cess·ful [ˈʌnsəkˈsesful] □ *p.* fracasado; *effort etc.* infructuoso, ineficaz; *be ~ malograrse*; *be ~ in ger.* no lograr *inf.*

un·suit·a·ble [ˈʌnˈsjuːtəbl] □ inconveniente, inadecuado; impropio (*for a p.* de una p.); *p.* incompetente; **'un'suit·ed** inapto (*for, to* para); inadecuado.

un·sul·lied [ˈʌnˈsʌlid] inmaculado.

un·sure [ˈʌnˈʃuə] poco seguro.

un·sur·passed [ˈʌnsəˈpɑːsd] insuperado.

un·sus·pect·ed [ˈʌnsəsˈpektid] insospechado; **'un·sus'pect·ing** □ confiado, nada suspicaz.

un·swerv·ing [ˈʌnˈswəːviŋ] □ *resolve* inquebrantable; *course* sin vacilar.

un·sworn [ˈʌnˈswɔːn] no juramentado.

un·sym·pa·thet·ic [ˈʌnsimpəˈθetik] □ incompasivo, indiferente.

un·taint·ed [ˈʌnˈteintid] □ incorrupto; inmaculado.

un·tam(e)·a·ble [ˈʌnˈteiməbl] indomable; **'un'tamed** indomado.

un·tan·gle [ˈʌnˈtæŋgl] desenmarañar.

un·tanned [ˈʌnˈtænd] sin curtir.

un·tar·nished [ˈʌnˈtɑːniʃt] inmaculado.

un·tast·ed [ˈʌnˈteistid] sin probar.

un·taught [ˈʌnˈtɔːt] no enseñado; espontáneo.

un·taxed [ˈʌnˈtækst] libre de impuesto.

un·teach·a·ble [ˈʌnˈtiːtʃəbl] indócil.

un·tem·pered [ˈʌnˈtempəd] ⊕ sin templar.

un·ten·a·ble [ˈʌnˈtenəbl] insostenible.

un·ten·ant·ed [ˈʌnˈtenəntid] desalquilado, desocupado.

un·think·a·ble [ʌnˈθiŋkəbl] inconcebible; **un'think·ing** □ irreflexivo.

un·thread [ˈʌnˈθred] *cloth* deshebrar; *needle* desenhebrar; *pearls* desensartar.

un·thrift·y [ˈʌnˈθrifti] □ gastador.

un·ti·dy [ʌnˈtaidi] □ desaliñado, desaseado; *room* en desorden.

un·tie [ˈʌnˈtai] desatar; soltar.

un·til [ənˈtil, ʌnˈtil] **1.** *prp.* hasta; **2.** *cj.* hasta que.

un·tilled [ˈʌnˈtild] inculto.

un·time·ly [ʌnˈtaimli] intempestivo, prematuro.

un·tir·ing [ʌnˈtaiəriŋ] □ incansable.

un·to [ˈʌntu] † = *to a* etc.

un·told [ˈʌnˈtould] *story* nunca contado; *wealth* incalculable.

un·touch·a·ble [ˈʌnˈtʌtʃəbl] (*India*) intocable *adj. a. su. m/f*; **un'touched** intacto; incólume; *food* sin probar; *phot.* sin retocar; *fig.* insensible (*by* a).

un·to·ward ['ʌntə'wɔ:d] adverso; incómodo.

un·trained ['ʌn'treind] no adiestrado, no entrenado.

un·trans·fer·a·ble ['ʌntræns'fə:rəbl] intransferible.

un·trans·lat·a·ble ['ʌntræns'leitəbl] intraducible.

un·trav·el(l)ed ['ʌn'trævld] *place* inexplorado; *p.* que no ha viajado.

un·tried ['ʌn'traid] no probado; ᵗᵗ *p.* no procesado, *case* no visto.

un·trod, un·trod·den ['ʌn'trɔd(n)] no trillado.

un·trou·bled ['ʌn'trʌbld] tranquilo.

un·true ['ʌn'tru:] □ falso; inexacto; *p.* infiel.

un·trust·wor·thy ['ʌn'trʌstwə:ði] □ indigno de confianza.

un·truth ['ʌn'tru:θ] mentira *f*; **un·'truth·ful** □ mentiroso.

un·tu·tored ['ʌn'tju:təd] no instruido, indocto.

un·twine ['ʌn'twain], **un·twist** ['ʌn'twist] destorcer; desenmarañar.

un·used ['ʌn'ju:zd] inusitado; *stamp etc.* sin usar; no acostumbrado (*to* a);

un·u·su·al [ʌn'ju:ʒuəl] □ insólito, extraordinario; nada usual, poco común.

un·ut·ter·a·ble [ʌn'ʌtərəbl] □ indecible.

un·var·nished ['ʌn'vɑ:niʃt] sin barnizar; *fig.* puro.

un·var·y·ing [ʌn'vɛəriiŋ] □ invariable.

un·veil ['ʌn'veil] quitar el velo a; *statue etc.* descubrir.

un·versed ['ʌn'və:st] poco ducho (*in* en).

un·voiced ['ʌn'vɔist] *opinion* no expresado; *gr.* sordo.

un·vouched-for ['ʌn'vautʃdfɔ:] no garantizado.

un·want·ed ['ʌn'wɔntid] superfluo; *child* no deseado.

un·war·i·ness [ʌn'wɛərinis] imprudencia *f*, falta *f* de precaución.

un·war·like ['ʌnwɔ:laik] pacífico.

un·war·rant·a·ble [ʌn'wɔrəntəbl] □ injustificable; **'un·war·rant·ed** injustificado; desautorizado.

un·war·y ['ʌn'wɛəri] □ imprudente, incauto.

un·wa·ver·ing [ʌn'weivəriŋ] □ inquebrantable, resuelto.

un·wea·ry·ing [ʌn'wiəriiŋ] □ incansable.

un·wel·come [ʌn'welkəm] importuno, molesto.

un·well ['ʌn'wel] indispuesto.

un·whole·some ['ʌn'houlsəm] insalubre; *p. etc.* indeseable.

un·wield·y [ʌn'wi:ldi] pesado; abultado.

un·will·ing ['ʌn'wiliŋ] □ desinclinado; *be* ~ *to* estar poco dispuesto a; ~*ly* de mala gana.

un·wind ['ʌn'waind] [*irr.* (*wind*)] desenvolver.

un·wis·dom ['ʌn'wizdəm] imprudencia *f*; **un·wise** ['ʌn'waiz] □ imprudente, malaconsejado.

un·wit·ting [ʌn'witiŋ] □ inconsciente; ~*ly* sin saber.

un·wont·ed [ʌn'wountid] □ insólito, inusitado. [practicable.\

un·work·a·ble ['ʌn'wə:kəbl] im-∫

un·world·ly ['ʌn'wə:ldli] no mundano, espiritual.

un·wor·thy [ʌn'wə:ði] □ indigno.

un·wound·ed ['ʌn'wu:ndid] ileso.

un·wrap ['ʌn'ræp] desenvolver; *parcel* deshacer.

un·writ·ten ['ʌn'ritn] no escrito; *law* tradicional, tácito.

un·wrought ['ʌn'rɔ:t] no labrado.

un·yield·ing [ʌn'ji:ldiŋ] □ inflexible.

un·yoke ['ʌn'jouk] desuncir.

up [ʌp] **1.** *adv.* arriba; hacia arriba; en el aire, en (lo) alto; (*out of bed*) levantado; (*sun*) salido; (*standing*) de pie, en pie; (*time*) expirado; F *hard* ~ apurado; F *it's all* ~ todo se acabó; *it's all* ~ *with him* no hay remedio para él; F ~ *against it* en apuros; *be* ~ *against p.* tener que habérselas con; F *what's* ~? ¿qué pasa?; *well* ~ *in* fuerte en; ~ *to* hasta; *v. date, mark*; *be* ~ *to* ser capaz de; F *it's not* ~ *to much* no es para mucho; *it is* ~ *to me* me toca a mi; *what are you* ~ *to?* ¿qué haces allí?; **2.** *int.* ¡arriba!; **3.** *prp.* en lo alto de; encima de; ~ *a tree* en un árbol; ~ *the street* calle arriba; **4.** *adj.*: ~ *train* tren *m* ascendente; **5.** *su.*: F *on the* ~ *and* ~ cada vez mejor; *the* ~*s and downs* vicisitudes *f/pl.*, altibajos *m/pl.*; **6.** *vb.*: F *to* ~ *and inf.* ponerse de repente a *inf.*

up-and-com·ing ['ʌpən'kʌmiŋ] F joven y prometedor.

up-and-down ['ʌpən'daun] variable; accidentado.

up·braid [ʌp'breid] reprochar, censurar (*a p. with a th.* algo a alguien).

up·bring·ing ['ʌpbriŋiŋ] educación *f*, crianza *f*.

up·cast ['ʌpkɑːst] ⚒ (*a.* ∼ *shaft*) pozo *m* de ventilación.

up-coun·try ['ʌp'kʌntri] **1.** *adv.* tierra adentro; **2.** *adj.* del interior.

up·cur·rent ['ʌpkʌrənt] 🜛 viento *m* ascendente.

up·end ['ʌp'end] volver de arriba abajo.

up·grade ['ʌpgreid] **1.** cuesta *f*, pendiente *f*; *on the* ∼ *fig.* prosperando; 🜛 mejorando; **2.** ascender.

up·heav·al [ʌp'hiːvl] *geol.* solevantamiento *m*; *fig.* cataclismo *m*, sacudida *f*.

up·hill ['ʌp'hil] **1.** *adv.* cuesta arriba; **2.** *adj. task* arduo.

up·hold [ʌp'hould] [*irr.* (*hold*)] sostener, defender; **up'hold·er** *fig.* defensor (*-a f*) *m*.

up·hol·ster [ʌp'houlstə] (en)tapizar; **up'hol·ster·er** tapicero *m*; **up'hol·ster·y** tapicería *f*; tapizado *m*.

up·keep ['ʌpkiːp] (gastos *m/pl.* de) conservación *f*, entretenimiento *m*.

up·land ['ʌplənd] **1.** (*mst pl.*) tierras *f/pl.* altas; meseta *f*; **2.** de la meseta.

up·lift **1.** [ʌp'lift] *fig.* inspirar, edificar; **2.** ['ʌplift] *fig.* inspiración *f*, edificación *f*.

up·on [ə'pɔn] = *on* en, *s*obre *etc.*

up·per ['ʌpə] **1.** superior; ∼ *class* clase *f* alta; ∼ *deck* (*bus*) piso *m* de arriba; *the* ∼ *hand* la ventaja; **2.** (*mst* ∼*s pl.*) pala *f*; F *on one's* ∼*s* sin un cuarto; ∼**-class** de la clase alta; '∼**-cut** *boxing:* golpe *m* de abajo arriba; '∼**-most** (el) más alto; predominante *in mind.*

up·pish ['ʌpiʃ] □ F, **up·pi·ty** ['ʌpiti] *Am.* F engreído; atrevido.

up·raise [ʌp'reiz] levantar.

up·right **1.** ['ʌp'rait] □ vertical; derecho (*a. adv.*); *fig.* honrado, probo; **2.** ['ʌprait] montante *m*.

up·ris·ing [ʌp'raiziŋ] alzamiento *m*, sublevación *f*.

up·roar ['ʌprɔː] *fig.* alboroto *m*, tumulto *m*; grita *f*; **up'roar·i·ous** □ tumultuoso; clamoroso.

up·root [ʌp'ruːt] desarraigar (*a. fig.*), arrancar.

up·set [ʌp'set] **1.** [*irr.* (*set*)] (*overturn*) volcar, trastornar; (*spill*) derramar; *fig. p. etc.* desconcertar, perturbar, trastornar; *plans* dar al traste con; *stomach* hacer daño a; F ∼ *o.s.* congojarse, apurarse; **2.** vuelco *m*; trastorno *m* (*a.* ⚕); contratiempo *m*; **3.** perturbado, preocupado; 🜛 indispuesto; ∼ *price* precio *m* mínimo *in auction*; **up'set·ting** inquietante; desconcertante.

up·shot ['ʌpʃɔt] resultado *m*; *in the* ∼ al fin y al cabo.

up·side ['ʌpsaid]: ∼ *down* al revés; lo de arriba abajo; *fig.* en confusión; *turn* ∼ *down* trastornar(se).

up·stage ['ʌp'steidʒ] **1.** *adv.* (*be*) en el fondo de la escena; (*go*) hacia el fondo de la escena; **2.** *adj.* F altanero.

up·stairs ['ʌp'steəz] **1.** *adv.* arriba; **2.** *adj.* de arriba; **3.** piso *m* de arriba.

up·start ['ʌpstɑːt] arribista *adj. a. su. m*; advenedizo *adj. a. su. m*.

up·state ['ʌp'steit] *Am.* interior, septentrional (*esp. de Nueva York*).

up·stream ['ʌp'striːm] río arriba.

up·stroke ['ʌpstrouk] plumada *f* (⊕ carrera *f*) ascendente.

up·surge ['ʌpsəːdʒ] acceso *m*, aumento *m* grande.

up·swing ['ʌp'swiŋ] *fig.* mejora *f*, prosperidad *f*.

up·take ['ʌpteik]: F *be quick* (*slow*) *on the* ∼ ser muy listo (torpe).

up·town ['ʌp'taun] hacia (*adj.* de) la parte alta de la ciudad.

up·turn [ʌp'təːn] volver(se) hacia arriba; volcar.

up·ward ['ʌpwəd] **1.** *adj.* ascendente, ascensional; **2.** *adv.* = **up·wards** ['∼z] hacia arriba; ∼ *of* más de.

u·ra·ni·um [juə'reiniəm] uranio *m*.

ur·ban ['əːbən] urbano; **ur·bane** [əː'bein] □ urbano; **ur·ban·i·ty** [əː'bæniti] urbanidad *f*; **ur·ban·i·za·tion** [əːbənai'zeiʃn] urbanización *f*; **'ur·ban·ize** urbanizar.

ur·chin ['əːtʃin] galopín *m*, golf(ill)o *m*.

urge [əːdʒ] **1.** impeler, instar (*to a inf.*, a que *subj.*); incitar (*a p. to a th.*, *a th. on a p.* a una p. a algo); ∼ *on* animar; **2.** impulso *m*; instinto *m*; **ur·gen·cy** ['∼ənsi] urgencia *f*; **'ur·gent** □ urgente.

u·ric ['juərik] úrico.

u·ri·nal ['juərinl] urinario *m*; (*vessel*) orinal *m*; **'u·ri·nar·y** urinario; **u·ri·nate** ['∼neit] orinar; **u·rine** ['∼rin] orina *f*, orines *m/pl*.

urn [ə:n] urna *f*; (*mst tea-*) tetera *f*.

us [ʌs, əs] nos; (*after prp.*) nosotros, nosotras.

us·a·ble ['ju:zəbl] utilizable.

us·age ['ju:zidʒ] uso *m*; tratamiento *m*.

us·ance ['ju:zəns] † plazo *m* a que se paga una letra de cambio; *bill at* ∼ letra *f* de cambio pagadera a plazo.

use 1. [ju:s] uso *m*; utilidad *f*; manejo *m*, empleo *m*; *in* ∼ en uso; *be of* ∼ ayudar; *be of no* ∼ no servir; *it is* (*of*) *no* ∼ *ger.* (*or to inf.*) es inútil *inf.*; *have no* ∼ *for* no necesitar; F tener en poco; *make* ∼ *of* servirse de; *make good* ∼ *of* aprovecharse de; *put to* ∼ servirse de, sacar partido de; **2.** [ju:z] usar; emplear, manejar; utilizar; ∼ *up* consumir, agotar; ∼*d* usado; **used** ['ju:st]: *be* ∼ *to* estar acostumbrado a; *get* ∼ *to* acostumbrarse a; *I* ∼ *to do* solía hacer, hacía; **use·ful** ['ju:sful] ☐ útil; ⊕ ∼ *capacity*, ∼ *efficiency* capacidad *f* útil; ∼ *load* carga *f* útil; **'use·less** ☐ inútil; inservible; *p.* inepto; **'use·less·ness** inutilidad *f*; **us·er** ['ju:zə] usuario (a *f*) *m*.

ush·er ['ʌʃə] **1.** ujier *m*; portero *m*; *thea.* acomodador *m*; **2.** (*mst* ∼ *in*) anunciar; introducir; hacer pasar; *thea.* acomodar.

ush·er·ette [ʌʃər'et] acomodadora *f*.

u·su·al ['ju:ʒuəl] ☐ usual, acostumbrado; corriente; *as* ∼ como de costumbre.

u·su·fruct ['ju:sjufrʌkt] usufructo *m*; **u·su'fruc·tu·ar·y** [∼juəri] usufructuario (a *f*) *m*.

u·su·rer ['ju:ʒərə] usurero *m*; **u·su·ri·ous** [ju:'zjuəriəs] ☐ usurario.

u·surp [ju:'zə:p] usurpar; **u·sur'pa·tion** usurpación *f*; **u'surp·er** usurpador (-a *f*) *m*; **u'surp·ing** ☐ usurpador.

u·su·ry ['ju:ʒuri] usura *f*.

u·ten·sil [ju:'tensl] utensilio *m*.

u·ter·ine ['ju:tərain] uterino; **u·ter·us** ['∼rəs] útero *m*.

u·til·i·tar·i·an [ju:tili'teəriən] **1.** utilitarista *m/f*; **2.** utilitario; **u'til·i·ty 1.** utilidad *f*; *public* ∼ empresa *f* de servicio público; **2.** *attr. clothing etc.* utilitario.

u·ti·li·za·tion [ju:tilai'zeiʃn] utilización *f*; **'u·ti·lize** utilizar.

ut·most ['ʌtmoust] extremo; último; supremo; *do one's* ∼ hacer todo lo posible; *to the* ∼ hasta más no poder.

U·to·pi·an [ju:'toupjən] **1.** utópico; **2.** utopista *m/f*.

u·tri·cle ['ju:trikl] utrículo *m*.

ut·ter ['ʌtə] **1.** ☐ completo, absoluto, total; *fool etc.* de remate; **2.** pronunciar, proferir; *cry* dar; *money* poner en circulación; *to the* ∼ hasta no poder; **'ut·ter·ance** declaración *f*; palabras *f/pl.*; *give* ∼ *to* expresar; **'ut·ter·ly** totalmente, del todo; **ut·ter·most** ['∼moust] más remoto; *v. utmost*.

u·vu·la ['ju:vjulə] úvula *f*; **u·vu·lar** [∼] uvular.

V

va·can·cy ['veikənsi] vacuidad *f*; vacío *m*; vaciedad *f of mind*; cuarto *m* vacante *in boarding-house etc.*; (*office*) vacante *f*; *fill a* ~ proveer una vacante; **va·cant** ['~kənt] □ vacante; vacío; *seat* libre; desocupado; *p.* estólido; *look* vago, distraído.

va·cate [və'keit, *Am.* 'veikeit] *house* desocupar; *post* dejar (vacante); **va·ca·tion 1.** vacación *f*, vacaciones *f/pl.*; **2.** *Am.* tomar vacaciones; **va·ca·tion·ist** *Am.* vacacionista *m/f.*

vac·ci·nate ['væksineit] vacunar; **vac·ci·na·tion** vacunación *f*; **vac·cine** ['~si:n] vacuna *f.*

vac·il·late ['væsileit] vacilar; **vac·il·la·tion** vacilación *f.*

va·cu·i·ty [væ'kjuiti] vacuidad *f* (*mst fig.*); **vac·u·ous** ['~kjuəs] □ *fig.* fatuo, necio; **vac·u·um** ['~əm] vacío *m*; ~ *brake* freno *m* de vacío; ~ *cleaner* aspirador *m*; ~ *flask*, *Am.* ~ *bottle* termos *m*; ~ *tube* tubo *m* al vacío.

va·de-me·cum ['veidi'mi:kəm] vademécum *m.*

vag·a·bond ['vægəbənd] vagabundo *adj. a. su. m* (*a f*); **vag·a·bond·age** ['~bɔndidʒ] vagabundeo *m.*

va·gar·y [və'gɛəri] capricho *m*, extravagancia *f.*

va·gran·cy ['veigrənsi] vagancia *f*; **va·grant 1.** vagabundo; vagante; *fig.* errante; **2.** vagabundo (*a f*) *m.*

vague [veig] □ vago; *p.* indeciso, distraído; **vague·ness** vaguedad *f.*

vain [vein] □ vano; *p.* vanidoso; *in* ~ en vano; ~**·glo·ri·ous** [~'glɔ:riəs] □ vanaglorioso; ~**'glo·ry** vanagloria *f.*

val·ance ['væləns] cenefa *f*, doselera *f.*

vale [veil] *poet. or in names:* valle *m.*

val·e·dic·tion [væli'dikʃn] despedida *f*; **val·e·dic·to·ry** [~təri] (discurso *m*) de despedida.

va·len·cy ['veiⁿnsi] valencia *f.*

val·en·tine ['væləntain] tarjeta *f* del día de San Valentín (*14 febrero*); novio (*a f*) *m* (*escogido en tal día*).

va·le·ri·an [və'liəriən] valeriana *f.*

val·et ['vælit] ayuda *m* de cámara.

val·e·tu·di·nar·i·an ['vælitju:di-'nɛəriən] valetudinario *adj. a. su. m* (*a f*).

val·iant ['væljənt] □ *lit.* esforzado, valiente.

val·id ['vælid] □ válido; valedero; ⚖ vigente; *be* ~ valer; **val·i·date** ['~deit] validar; **va·lid·i·ty** [və'liditi] validez *f*; ⚖ vigencia *f.*

val·ley ['væli] valle *m.*

val·or·i·za·tion [vælərai'zeiʃn] valorización *f*; **'val·or·ize** valorizar.

val·or·ous ['vælərəs] □ *lit.* valeroso.

val·o(u)r ['vælə] *lit.* valor *m*, coraje *m.*

val·u·a·ble ['væljuəbl] **1.** □ valioso; precioso; estimable; **2.** ~*s pl.* objetos *m/pl.* de valor.

val·u·a·tion [vælju'eiʃn] valuación *f*; tasación *f.*

val·ue ['vælju:] **1.** valor *m*; **2.** valorar, tasar (*at en*); estimar, apreciar; tener en mucho; **'val·ue·less** sin valor; **'val·u·er** tasador *m.*

valve [vælv] *anat.*, ⊕ válvula *f*; ⚕, *zo.* valva *f*; *radio:* lámpara *f*, válvula *f*, bulbo *m S.Am.*; ~ *tester* comprobador *m* de lámparas.

va·moose [væ'mu:s] *sl.* largarse, poner pies en polvorosa.

vamp¹ [væmp] **1.** empella *f*; remiendo *m*; **2.** poner empella a; remendar; ♪ improvisar.

vamp² [~] F **1.** vampiresa *f*; **2.** coquetear con.

vam·pire ['væmpaiə] vampiro *m*; *fig.* vampiresa *f.*

van¹ [væn] camioneta *f*; furgoneta *f*; 🚂 furgón *m.*

van² [~] ✕ *a. fig.* vanguardia *f.*

Van·dal ['vændl] **1.** vándalo *m*; **2.** vándalo, vandálico (*a.* **Van·dal·ic** [~'dælik]); **van·dal·ism** ['~dəlizm] vandalismo *m.*

vane [vein] (*weather-*) veleta *f*; paleta *f of propeller*; aspa *f of mill.*

van·guard ['vænɡɑ:d] vanguardia *f.*

va·nil·la [və'nilə] vainilla *f.*

van·ish ['væniʃ] desvanecerse, desaparecer.

van·i·ty ['væniti] vanidad *f*; engreimiento *m*; ~ *case* neceser *m* de belleza, polvera *f* (de bolsillo).

van·quish ['væŋkwiʃ] *lit.* vencer.

van·tage ['vɑːntidʒ] *tennis:* ventaja *f*; '~-point punto *m* panorámico *for views*; lugar *m* estratégico.

vap·id ['væpid] □ insípido.

va·po(u)r·ize ['veipəraiz] vaporizar (se); 'va·po(u)r·iz·er vaporizador *m*.

va·por·ous ['veipərəs] □ vaporoso (*a. fig.*); quimérico.

va·po(u)r ['veipə] 1. vapor *m*; vaho *m*; exhalación *f*; ~ *bath* baño *m* de vapor; 2. *fig.* fanfarronear.

var·i·a·bil·i·ty [vɛəriə'biliti] variabilidad *f*; '**var·i·a·ble** □ variable *adj. a. su. f* (A); '**var·i·ance** desacuerdo *m*; desavenencia *f*; variación *f*; ⅔ discrepancia *f*; *at* ~ en desacuerdo (*with* con); '**var·i·ant** variante *adj. a. su. f*; **var·i·a·tion** variación *f* (*a.* ♪).

var·i·cose ['værikous] varicoso; ~ *veins* varices *f/pl*.

var·ied ['vɛərid] □ variado; **var·i·e·gate** [~rigeit] abigarrar; jaspear; **var·i·e'ga·tion** abigarramiento *m*; **va·ri·e·ty** [və'raiəti] variedad *f* (*a. biol.*); diversidad *f*; *esp.* ♱ surtido *m*; *thea.* ~ *artist* artista *m/f* de variedades; ~ *theatre* teatro *m* de variedades.

va·ri·o·la [və'raiələ] viruela *f*.

var·i·ous ['vɛəriəs] □ vario, diverso.

var·mint ['vɑːmint] F golfo *m*, bribón *m*; *hunt.* bicho *m*.

var·nish ['vɑːniʃ] 1. barniz *m* (*a. fig.*); *fig.* capa *f*, apariencia *f*; *nail* ~ laca *f*, esmalte *m* (para uñas); 2. barnizar; *nails* laquear, esmaltar; *fig.* paliar, dar apariencia respetable a.

var·si·ty ['vɑːsiti] F universidad *f*.

var·y ['vɛəri] variar (*v/i. a. v/t.*); *decision* modificar.

vas·cu·lar ['væskjulə] vascular.

vase [vɑːz] jarrón *m*; florero *m*.

va·se·line ['væsəliːn] vaselina *f*.

vas·sal ['væsl] vasallo *m*; '**vas·sal·age** vasallaje *m*.

vast [vɑːst] □ vasto, inmenso; ~*ly* sumamente, en sumo grado; '**vast·ness** inmensidad *f*, vastedad *f*.

vat [væt] 1. tina *f*, tinaja *f*; 2. poner en tina.

vau·de·ville ['voudəvil] vaudeville *m*.

vault[1] [vɔːlt] 1. ⚠ bóveda *f*; (*wine-*)bodega *f*; (*tomb*) tumba *f*; 2. abovedar.

vault[2] [~] 1. saltar (*v/i. a. v/t.*); 2. salto *m*.

vault·ing ['vɔːltiŋ] abovedado *m*.

vault·ing-horse ['vɔːltiŋhɔːs] potro *m* de madera.

vaunt [vɔːnt] *lit. v/i.* jactarse; *v/t.* jactarse de, hacer alarde de; '**vaunt·ed** cacareado, alardeado; '**vaunt·ing** □ jactancioso.

veal [viːl] carne *f* de ternera.

ve·dette [vi'det] centinela *f* de avanzada.

veer [viə] virar (*a. fig., a.* ~ *round*); (*wind*) cambiar.

veg·e·ta·ble ['vedʒitəbl] 1. vegetal; 2. legumbre *f*; hortaliza *f*; (*in general*) vegetal *m*; ~*s pl. freq.* verduras *f/pl.*; **veg·e·tar·i·an** [~'tɛəriən] vegetariano *adj. a. su. m* (a *f*); '**veg·e·tate** [~teit] vegetar (*a. fig.*); **veg·e'ta·tion** vegetación *f*; '**veg·e·ta·tive** □ vegetativo.

ve·he·mence ['viːiməns] vehemencia *f*; '**ve·he·ment** □ vehemente.

ve·hi·cle ['viːikl] *all senses:* vehículo *m*; **ve·hic·u·lar** [vi'hikjulə] de vehículos; ~ *traffic* circulación *f* rodada.

veil [veil] 1. velo *m* (*a. fig. a. phot.*); 2. velar (*a. fig.*); '**veil·ing** ♱ material *m* para velos; *phot.* velo *m*.

vein [vein] *all senses:* vena *f*; *be in the* ~ estar en vena (*for* para); **veined** venoso; veteado; '**vein·ing** venas *f/pl.*

vel·lum ['veləm] vitela *f*; ~ *paper* papel *m* vitela.

ve·loc·i·ty [vi'lɔsiti] velocidad *f*.

vel·vet ['velvit] 1. terciopelo *m*; *hunt.* piel *f* velluda; *sl.* ganancia *f* limpia; F *on* ~ en situación muy ventajosa; 2. aterciopelado; de terciopelo; **vel·vet·een** [~'tiːn] pana *f*; '**vel·vet·y** aterciopelado.

ve·nal ['viːnl] sobornable, venal; **ve·nal·i·ty** [vi'næliti] venalidad *f*.

vend [vend] *mst* ⅔ vender; vender como buhonero; '**vend·er**, '**vend·or** vendedor (-a *f*) *m*; buhonero *m*; '**vend·i·ble** vendible; '**vend·ing ma·chine** distribuidor *m* automático.

ve·neer [və'niə] 1. chapa *f*, enchapado *m*; *fig.* apariencia *f*, barniz *m*; 2. (en)chapar; *fig.* disfrazar.

ven·er·a·ble ['venərəbl] □ venerable; **ven·er·ate** ['‿reit] venerar; **ven·er'a·tion** veneración *f*.

ve·ne·re·al [vi'niəriəl]: ~ *disease* enfermedad *f* venérea.

Ve·ne·tian [vi'ni:ʃn] veneciano *adj. a. su. m* (a *f*); ~ *blind* persiana *f*.

Ve·ne·zuel·an [veni'zwi:lən] venezolano *adj. a. su. m* (a *f*).

venge·ance ['vendʒəns] venganza *f*; F *with a* ~ con creces, con extremo; **venge·ful** ['‿ful] □ *lit.* vengativo.

ve·ni·al ['vi:niəl] □ venial.

ven·i·son ['venzn] carne *f* de venado.

ven·om ['venəm] veneno *m*; *fig.* virulencia *f*, malignidad *f*; **'ven·om·ous** □ venenoso; *fig.* virulento, maligno.

ve·nous ['vi:nəs] venal, venoso.

vent [vent] 1. respiradero *m*; salida*f*; ⊕ válvula *f* de purga, orificio *m*, lumbrera *f*; *orn.* cloaca *f*; *give* ~ *to* desahogar, dar salida a; 2. ⊕ purgar; *fig.* desahogar, descargar.

ven·ti·late ['ventileit] ventilar (*a. fig.*); **ven·ti'la·tion** ventilación *f* (*a. fig.*); **'ven·ti·la·tor** ventilador *m*.

ven·tral ['ventrəl] □ ventral.

ven·tri·cle ['ventrikl] ventrículo *m*.

ven·tril·o·quism [ven'triləkwizm] ventriloquia *f*; **ven·tril·o·quist** ventrílocuo (a *f*) *m*.

ven·ture ['ventʃə] 1. empresa *f* (arriesgada); riesgo *m*; especulación *f*; *at a* ~ a la ventura; 2. *v/t.* aventurar; *v/i.* aventurarse (*to* a), osar (*to inf.*); ~ (*up*)*on* arriesgarse en; **ven·ture·some** ['‿səm] □ atrevido; emprendedor; azaroso.

ven·ue ['venju:] ᵗᵗ̣ lugar *m* donde se reúne el jurado; F lugar *m* de reunión.

ve·ra·cious [və'reiʃəs] □ veraz; **ve·rac·i·ty** [‿'ræsiti] veracidad *f*.

ver·an·da(h) [və'rændə] veranda *f*.

verb [və:b] verbo *m*; **'ver·bal** □ verbal; **ver·ba·tim** [‿'beitim] palabra por palabra; **ver·bi·age** ['‿biidʒ] palabrería *f*; **ver·bose** [‿'bous] □ verboso; **ver·bos·i·ty** [‿'bositi] verbosidad *f*.

ver·dant ['və:dənt] □ verde; F inocente.

ver·dict ['və:dikt] ᵗᵗ̣ veredicto *m*; fallo *m*, juicio *m*; *fig.* opinión *f*, juicio *m* (*on* sobre); *bring in* (*or return*) *a* ~ dictar un veredicto.

ver·di·gris ['və:digris] verdete *m*, cardenillo *m*.

ver·dure ['və:dʒə] verdura *f*.

verge¹ [və:dʒ] vara *f of office.*

verge² [‿] 1. borde *m*, margen *m*; *fig. on the* ~ *of disaster* a dos dedos de, en el mismo borde de; *madness al borde de*; *discovery, triumph* en la antesala de; *fig. be on the* ~ *of ger.* estar a punto de *inf*; 2.: ~ *on* acercarse a, rayar en.

ver·ger ['və:dʒə] sacristán *m*.

ver·i·fi·a·ble ['verifaiəbl] □ verificable; **ver·i·fi·ca·tion** [‿fi'keiʃn] verificación *f*; **ver·i·fy** ['‿fai] verificar; **ver·i·si·mil·i·tude** [‿si'militju:d] verosimilitud *f*; **'ver·i·ta·ble** □ verdadero; **'ver·i·ty** † *or lit.* verdad *f*.

ver·mi·cel·li [və:mi'seli] fideos *m/pl.*; **ver·mi·cide** ['‿said] vermicida *m*; **ver·mic·u·lar** [‿'mikjulə] vermicular; **ver·mi·form** ['‿fɔ:m] vermiforme; **ver·mi·fuge** ['‿fju:dʒ] vermífugo *m*.

ver·mil·ion [və'miljən] 1. bermellón *m*; 2. de color rojo vivo.

ver·min ['və:min] bichos *m/pl.*; sabandijas *f/pl.*; parásitos *m/pl.* (*a. fig.*); (*fox etc.*) alimañas *f/pl.*; **'ver·min·ous** verminoso; piojoso.

ver·m(o)uth ['və:mu:t] vermut *m*.

ver·nac·u·lar [və'nækjulə] 1. vernáculo; 2. lengua *f* vernácula; F idioma *m* corriente.

ver·nal ['və:nl] vernal.

ver·ni·er ['və:niə] ⚬ vernier *m*.

ver·sa·tile ['və:sətail] □ versátil, flexible, adaptable, hábil para muchas cosas; **ver·sa·til·i·ty** [‿'tiliti] versatilidad *f*, flexibilidad *f*.

verse [və:s] (*stanza*) estrofa *f*; (*poetry*) poesías *f/pl.*; (*line, genre*) verso *m*; versículo *m of Bible*; **versed** versado (*in* en).

ver·si·fi·ca·tion [və:sifi'keiʃn] versificación *f*; **ver·si·fy** ['‿fai] versificar (*v/i. a. v/t.*).

ver·sion ['və:ʃn] versión *f*.

ver·sus ['və:səs] contra.

ver·te·bra ['və:tibrə], *pl.* **ver·te·brae** ['‿bri:] vértebra *f*; **ver·te·bral** ['‿brəl] vertebral; **ver·te·brate** ['‿brit] vertebrado *adj. a. su m*.

ver·tex ['və:teks], *pl. mst* **ver·ti·ces**

['ˌtisiːz] vértice *m*; 'ver·ti·cal □ vertical.

ver·tig·i·nous [vəːˈtidʒinəs] vertiginoso; ver·ti·go [ˈtigou] vértigo *m*.

verve [veəv] energía *f*, entusiasmo *m*, brío *m*.

ver·y [ˈveri] 1. *adv.* muy; (*alone, in reply to question*) mucho; ~ much mucho, muchísimo; *the* ~ *best* el mejor (de todos); ~ *good mst* muy bueno, *but sometimes translated by absolute superlative of adj.*, *e.g.* buenísimo, bonísimo, *and by prefix* re(quete)..., *e.g.* re(quete)bueno; 2. *adj.* mismo; mismísimo; ~ verdadero; *it is* ~ *cold* hace mucho frío; *the* ~ *same* el idéntico; *to the* ~ *bone* hasta el mismo hueso; *it's the* ~ *thing* es exactamente lo que necesitábamos; *the* ~ *idea!* ¡ni hablar!; *the veriest rascal* el mayor bribón.

ves·i·cle [ˈvesikl] vesícula *f*.

ves·pers [ˈvespəz] vísperas *f/pl*.

ves·sel [ˈvesl] vasija *f*, recipiente *m*; *anat.*, ♥ vaso *m*; ♣ buque *m*, barco *m*, bajel *m* (*lit.*).

vest [vest] 1. camiseta *f*; *Am.* chaleco *m*; 2. investir (*with* de); conferir (*in* a), conceder (*in* a); ~*ed rights pl.* derechos *m/pl.* inalienables; ~*ed interests pl.* intereses *m/pl.* creados.

ves·ta [ˈvestə] (*a. wax* ~) cerilla *f*.

ves·tal [ˈvestl] vestal *adj. a. su. f*.

ves·ti·bule [ˈvestibjuːl] vestíbulo *m*; zaguán *m*; *Am.* 🚃 ~ *car* coche *m* de vestíbulo.

ves·tige [ˈvestidʒ] vestigio *m*; ves·tig·i·al vestigial.

vest·ment [ˈvestmənt] vestidura *f*.

vest·pock·et [ˈvestˈpɔkit] *attr.* en miniatura.

ves·try [ˈvestri] sacristía *f*; '~·man miembro *m* de la junta parroquial.

ves·ture [ˈvestʃə] *lit.* vestidura *f*.

vet [vet] F 1. veterinario *m*; 2. repasar, corregir; examinar, investigar; aprobar.

vetch [vetʃ] arveja *f*.

vet·er·an [ˈvetərən] veterano *adj. a. su. m*.

vet·er·i·nar·y [ˈvetnəri] veterinario *adj. a. su. m* (*mst* ~ *surgeon*).

ve·to [ˈviːtou] 1. *pl.* ve·toes [ˈ~z] veto *m*; *put a* (*or one's*) ~ *on* = 2. vedar, vetar.

vex [veks] vejar, fastidiar, enojar; vex·a·tion vejación *f*, enojo *m*;

vex·a·tious □ vejatorio; fastidioso, engorroso; vexed □ enojado, enfadado (*at a th.* de algo, *with a p.* con una p.); ~ *question* cuestión *f* batallona; 'vex·ing □ fastidioso, molesto.

vi·a [ˈvaiə] por (vía de).

vi·a·ble [ˈvaiəbl] viable.

vi·a·duct [ˈvaiədʌkt] viaducto *m*.

vi·al [ˈvaiəl] frasco *m* (pequeño).

vi·ands [ˈvaiəndz] *pl. lit.* manjares *m/pl.* (exquisitos).

vi·at·i·cum [vaiˈætikəm] viático *m*.

vi·brant [ˈvaibrənt] vibrante (*with* de).

vi·brate [vaiˈbreit] vibrar; vi·bra·tion vibración *f*; vi·bra·to·ry [ˈ~brətəri] vibratorio.

vic·ar [ˈvikə] vicario *m*; (*parish priest*) párroco *m*; ~ *general* vicario *m* general; 'vic·ar·age casa *f* del párroco; vi·car·i·ous [vaiˈkɛəriəs] □ .experimentado por otro; (*deputed*) vicario.

vice¹ [vais] vicio *m*.

vice² [ˌ] ⊕ torno *m* (*or* tornillo *m*) de banco.

vice³ 1. [ˈvaisi] *prp.* en lugar de; que sustituye a; 2. [vais] vice...; '~·ad·mi·ral vicealmirante *m*; '~·chair·man vicepresidente *m*; '~·chan·cel·lor vicecanciller *m*; *univ*; rector *m*; '~·con·sul vicecónsul *m*; '~·pres·i·dent vicepresidente *m*; '~·re·gal virreinal; '~·roy [ˈ~rɔi] virrey *m*.

vi·ce ver·sa [ˈvaisiˈvəːsə] viceversa; a la inversa.

vi·cin·i·ty [viˈsiniti] vecindad *f*; proximidad *f* (*to* a); *in the* ~ cerca; *in the* ~ *of 25* alrededor de 25.

vi·cious [ˈviʃəs] □ vicioso; *criticism* virulento, rencoroso; *dog* bravo; *horse* arisco; *phls.* ~ *circle* círculo *m* vicioso.

vi·cis·si·tude [viˈsisitjuːd]: *mst* ~*s pl.* vicisitud *f*.

vic·tim [ˈviktim] víctima *f*; 'vic·tim·ize hacer víctima; escoger y castigar, tomar represalias contra.

vic·tor [ˈviktə] vencedor *m*; Vic·to·ri·an [vikˈtɔːriən] victoriano; vic·to·ri·ous □ victorioso; vic·to·ry [ˈ~təri] victoria *f*.

vict·ual [ˈvitl] 1. abastecer(se), avituallar(se); F comer; 2. ~*s pl.* vitualla(s) *f(pl.)*; víveres *m/pl.*; vict·ual·(l)er [ˈvitlə] abastecedor (-a *f*) *m*;

licensed ~ vendedor *m* de bebidas alcohólicas.

vi·de ['vaidi] vea, véase.

vi·de·li·cet [vi'di:liset] a saber.

vi·de·o ['vidiou] *radio:* ... de video.

vie [vai] rivalizar (con), competir (con); ~ *with s.o.* for s.t. disputar algo a alguien, disputarse algo.

view [vju:] **1.** vista *f*; perspectiva *f*; aspecto *m*; *paint.*, *phot.* panorama *m*; paisaje *m*; (*opinion*) opinión *f*, parecer *m*; *in* ~ visible; *in full* ~ totalmente visible; *in* ~ *of* en vista de; *in my* ~ en mi opinión; *have* (*or keep*) *in* ~ no perder de vista; *be on* ~ estar expuesto; *with a* ~ *to ger.* con miras a *inf.*, con el propósito de *inf.*; **2.** mirar; examinar; contemplar; considerar; **'view·er** espectador (-a *f*) *m*; telespectador (-a *f*) *m*; **'view-find·er** *phot.* visor *m*; **'view·point** mirador *m*, punto *m* panorámico; *fig.* punto *m* de vista.

vig·il ['vidʒil] vigilia *f*, vela *f*; **'vig·i·lance** vigilancia *f*; ~ *committee* comité *m* de vigilancia; **'vig·i·lant** □ vigilante; **vig·i·lan·te** [~'lænti] vigilante *m*.

vi·gnette [vi'njet] *typ.*, *phot.* viñeta *f*.

vig·or·ous ['vigərəs] □ vigoroso; **'vig·o·(u)r** vigor *m*.

vile [vail] □ vil; (*very bad*) horrible, pésimo, asqueroso; **'vile·ness** vileza *f*.

vil·i·fi·ca·tion [vilifi'keiʃn] vilipendio *m*; **vil·i·fy** ['~fai] vilipendiar.

vil·la ['vilə] *hist.* villa *f*; (*seaside etc.*) villa *f*, chalet *m*; (*country house*) quinta *f*.

vil·lage ['vilidʒ] aldea *f*, puebl(ecit)o *m*; lugar *m*; *attr.* aldeano; **'vil·lag·er** aldeano (a *f*) *m*.

vil·lain ['vilən] malvado *m*; *thea. etc.* malo *m*, traidor *m*; *hist.* villano *m*; *co.* tunante *m*; **'vil·lain·ous** □ vil, malvado; F pésimo, malísimo; **'vil·lain·y** maldad *f*, villanía *f*.

vil·lein ['vilin] villano (a *f*) *m*.

vim [vim] F fuerza *f*, energía *f*.

vin·di·cate ['vindikeit] vindicar; justificar; ~ *o.s.* justificarse; **vin·di·ca·tion** vindicación *f*.

vin·dic·tive [vin'diktiv] □ vengativo, vindicativo.

vine [vain] vid *f*; (*climbing*) parra *f*; **'~dress·er** viñador *m*; **vin·e·gar** ['vinigə] **1.** vinagre *m*; **2.** avinagrar (*a. fig.*); **'vin·e·gar·y** vinagroso;

'vine-grow·er viticultor *m*, viñador *m*; **'vine-grow·ing** viticultura *f*; **vine·yard** ['vinjəd] viña *f*, viñedo *m*.

vi·nous ['vainəs] vinoso.

vin·tage ['vintidʒ] **1.** (*season*) vendimia *f*; *the 1949* ~ la cosecha de 1949; **2.**: ~ *wine* vino *m* añejo; vino *m* de marca; F *car etc.* de época, clásico; **'vin·tag·er** vendimiador (-a *f*) *m*; **vint·ner** ['vintnə] vinatero *m*.

vi·o·la ♪ [vi'oulə] viola *f*; ♀ ['vaiələ] viola *f*.

vi·o·late ['vaiəleit] *all senses:* violar; **vi·o'la·tion** violación *f*; **'vi·o·la·tor** violador *m*.

vi·o·lence ['vaiələns] violencia *f*; *do* ~ *to* agredir; *fig.* violentar; *offer* ~ mostrarse violento; **'vi·o·lent** □ violento.

vi·o·let ['vaiəlit] **1.** ♀ violeta *f*; (*colour*) violado *m*; **2.** violado.

vi·o·lin [vaiə'lin] violín *m*; **'vi·o·lin·ist** violinista *m/f*.

vi·o·lon'cel·lo [vaiələn'tʃelou] violoncelo *m*.

vi·per ['vaipə] víbora *f*; **vi·per·ine** ['~rain], **vi·per·ous** ['~rəs] □ *mst fig.* viperino. [ñona.\]

vi·ra·go [vi'reigou] mujer *f* rega-

vir·gin ['və:dʒin] virgen *adj. a. su. f*; **'vir·gin·al** □ virginal; **Vir·gin·ian** [və'dʒinjən] (*or* ~ *tobacco*) tabaco *m* rubio; **vir·gin·i·ty** [və:'dʒiniti] virginidad *f*.

vir·ile ['virail] viril; **vi·ril·i·ty** [vi'riliti] virilidad *f*.

vir·tual ['və:tʃuəl] □ virtual; **vir·tue** ['~tju:] virtud *f*; *in* (*or by*) ~ *of* en virtud de; **vir·tu·os·i·ty** [~tju-'ɔsiti] virtuosismo *m*; **vir·tu·o·so** [~'ouzou] *esp.* ♪ virtuoso *m*; **'vir·tu·ous** □ virtuoso.

vir·u·lence ['viruləns] virulencia *f* (*a. fig.*); **'vir·u·lent** □ virulento (*a. fig.*).

vi·rus ['vaiərəs] virus *m*; ~ *disease* enfermedad *f* por virus.

vi·sa ['vi:zə] **1.** visado *m*; **2.** visar.

vis·age ['vizidʒ] *lit.* semblante *m*.

vis-à-vis ['vi:zə'vi:] respecto de.

vis·cer·a ['visərə] ௶ vísceras *f/pl.*

vis·cid ['visid] □ viscoso.

vis·cose ['viskous] **1.** viscosa *f*; **2.** viscoso; **vis·cos·i·ty** [~'kɔsiti] viscosidad *f*.

vis·count ['vaikaunt] vizconde *m*; **'vis·count·ess** vizcondesa *f*.

vis·cous ['viskəs] □ viscoso.
vi·sé ['vi:zei] v. visa.
vis·i·bil·i·ty [vizi'biliti] visibilidad f;
vis·i·ble ['vizəbl] □ visible.
vi·sion ['viʒn] visión f; 'vi·sion·ar·y
visionario adj. a. su. m (a f).
vis·it ['vizit] 1. v/t. visitar; ~ s.t.
upon a p. castigar una p. con algo;
mandar algo a una p.; v/i. hacer
visitas; Am. F visitarse; 2. visita f;
pay (return) a ~ hacer (pagar) una
visita; vis·it·a·tion eccl. visitación
f; F visita f larga y engorrosa; 'vis-
it·ing ... visitante; ... de visita; ~
card tarjeta f (de visita); 'vis·i·tor
visitante m/f; visita f to house;
turista m/f; forastero (a f) m; ~s'
book libro m de visitas (or de honor).
vi·sor ['vaizə] visera f (a. Am.).
vis·ta ['vistə] perspectiva f, vista f,
panorama m.
vis·u·al ['vizjuəl] □ visual; 'vis·u-
al·ize representarse (en la mente);
imaginarse; situation prever.
vi·tal ['vaitl] □ vital; esencial; p.
enérgico; ~s pl., ~ parts pl. partes
f/pl. vitales; ~ statistics pl. estadística f vital; co. medidas f/pl. vitales; vi·tal·i·ty [~'tæliti] vitalidad f;
vi·tal·ize ['~təlaiz] vitalizar.
vi·ta·min ['vitəmin], vi·ta·mine
['~mi:n] vitamina f; attr. vitamínico; vi·ta·mi·nized ['~minaizd]
reforzado con vitaminas.
vi·ti·ate ['viʃieit] viciar (a. ʀ̵̃ʒ̵̃).
vit·i·cul·ture ['vitikʌltʃə] viticultura f.
vit·re·ous ['vitriəs] □ vítreo.
vit·ri·fac·tion [vitri'fækʃn] vitrifi-
cación f; vit·ri·fy ['~fai] vitrificar
(se).
vit·ri·ol ['vitriəl] vitriolo m; vit·ri-
'ol·ic fig. mordaz, cáustico.
vi·tu·per·ate [vi'tju:pəreit] vituperar, llenar de injurias; vi·tu·per'a-
tion vituperio m, injurias f/pl.; vi-
'tu·per·a·tive [~reitiv] □ vituperioso, injurioso.
Vi·tus ['vaitəs]: St. ~'(s) dance baile
m de San Vito.
vi·va (vo·ce) ['vaivə('vousi)] 1. adj.
oral; 2. adv. de viva voz; 3. examen
m oral.
vi·va·cious [vi'veiʃəs] □ vivaz, animado; alegre; vivaracho; vi·vac·i-
ty [~'væsiti] vivacidad f; alegría f.
viv·id ['vivid] □ impression, memo-

ry etc. vivo; colour, light intenso;
description gráfico; 'viv·id·ness vivacidad f; intensidad f etc.
viv·i·fy ['vivifai] vivificar; vi·vip·a-
rous [~'vipərəs] □ vivíparo; viv-
i·sec·tion [~'sekʃn] vivisección f.
vix·en ['viksn] zorra f, raposa f; fig.
mujer f regañona.
vo·cab·u·lar·y [və'kæbjuləri] vocabulario m.
vo·cal ['voukl] □ vocal (a. ♪); gr.
vocálico; fig. ruidoso, expresivo; ~
cords pl. cuerdas f/pl. vocales; 'vo-
cal·ist cantante m/f; (in cabaret
etc.) vocalista m/f; 'vo·cal·ize ♪
vocalizar; gr. vocalizar(se).
vo·ca·tion [vou'keiʃn] vocación f;
vo'ca·tion·al □ vocacional; ~
guidance guía f vocacional.
voc·a·tive ['vɔkətiv] vocativo m (a. ~
case).
vo·cif·er·ate [vou'sifəreit] vociferar;
vo·cif·er'a·tion vociferación f; vo-
'cif·er·ous □ clamoroso; vocinglero.
vogue [voug] boga f, moda f; in ~ en
boga.
voice [vɔis] 1. voz f (a. gr.); in (good)
~ en voz; with one ~ a una voz, al
unísono; give ~ to expresar; have no
~ in a matter no tener voz en capítulo; 2. expresar; hacerse eco de;
gr. sonorizar(se); voiced gr. sonoro; 'voice·less □ gr. sordo.
void [vɔid] 1. vacío; ʀ̵̃ʒ̵̃ nulo, inválido; ~ of falto de, desprovisto de;
2. vacío m; hueco m; bridge: fallo m;
the ~ la nada; 3. evacuar, vaciar; ʀ̵̃ʒ̵̃
anular.
vol·a·tile ['vɔlətail] volátil (a. fig.);
vol·a·til·i·ty [~'tiliti] volatilidad f;
vol·a·til·ize [vɔ'lætilaiz] volatili-
zar(se).
vol·can·ic [vɔl'kænik] □ volcánico;
vol·ca·no [~'keinou], pl. vol'ca-
noes [~z] volcán m.
vole [voul] campañol m.
vo·li·tion [vou'liʃn] volición f; of
one's own ~ por voluntad propia.
vol·ley ['vɔli] 1. ✗ descarga f; lluvia f
of stones etc.; salva f of applause;
retahíla f of abuse; tennis: voleo m;
2. tennis: ✗ lanzar una descarga; 'vol·ley-ball balón m volea.
volt [voult] voltio m; 'volt·age voltaje m; vol·ta·ic [vɔl'teiik] voltaico; vol·ta·me·ter [vɔl'tæmitə]
voltímetro m.

volte-face ['vɔltfɑːs] viraje *m*, cambio *m* súbito (*or* total) de opinion.
vol·u·bil·i·ty [vɔljuˈbiliti] locuacidad *f*; **vol·u·ble** ['ˌbl] □ locuaz.
vol·ume ['vɔljum] volumen *m*; tomo *m of book*; *fig.* masa *f*; *radio:* ~ *of sound* volumen *m* sonoro; ~ *control* control *m* del volumen sonoro; *speak* ~*s* ser de suma significación; *speak* ~*s for* evidenciar de modo inconfundible; **vo·lu·mi·nous** [vəˈljuːminəs] □ voluminoso.
vol·un·tar·y ['vɔləntəri] 1. □ voluntario; *Am.* ~ *manslaughter* homicidio *m* intencional sin premeditación; 2. solo *m* de órgano; **vol·un·teer** [ˌˈtiə] 1. voluntario *m*; 2. voluntario, de voluntarios; 3. *v/i.* ofrecerse; ✕ alistarse como voluntario; *v/t.* ofrecer; *remark* permitirse hacer.
vo·lup·tu·ar·y [vəˈlʌptjuəri] voluptuoso (a *f*) *m*.
vo·lup·tu·ous [vəˈlʌptjuəs] □ voluptuoso; **vo·lup·tu·ous·ness** voluptuosidad *f*.
vo·lute [vəˈljuːt] voluta *f*; **vo·lut·ed** en la forma de volutas.
vom·it ['vɔmit] 1. vomitar; 2. vómito *m*.
vo·ra·cious [vəˈreiʃəs] □ voraz; **vo·ra·cious·ness, vo·rac·i·ty** [ˌˈræsiti] voracidad *f*.
vor·tex ['vɔːteks], *pl. mst* **vor·ti·ces** ['ˌtisiːz] vórtice *m*.
vo·ta·ry ['voutəri] devoto (a *f*) *m*; partidario (a *f*) *m*.
vote [vout] 1. voto *m*; sufragio *m*; (*a. voting*) votación *f*; *by a majority* ~ por la mayoría de los votos; ~ *of confidence* voto *m* de confianza; *cast a* ~ dar un voto; *put to the* ~, *take a* ~ *on* someter a votación; 2. *v/t.* vo-

tar; ~ *in* elegir; *v/i.* votar (*for* por); F proponer, sugerir (*that* que); ~ *that* resolver (por voto) que; **'vot·er** votante *m/f*; **'vot·ing** votación *f*; ~ *paper* papeleta *f*; ~ *power* potencia *f* electoral.
vo·tive ['voutiv] votivo; ~ *offering* exvoto *m*.
vouch [vautʃ] atestiguar; garantizar, confirmar; ~ *for th.* responder de; *p.* responder por; **'vouch·er** documento *m* justificativo; ✝ comprobante *m*; vale *m*; **vouch'safe** conceder, otorgar; dignarse hacer (*or* dar *etc.*).
vow [vau] 1. voto *m*; promesa *f* solemne; 2. hacer voto (*to* de); jurar; prometer solemnemente.
vow·el ['vauəl] vocal *f*.
voy·age ['vɔidʒ] 1. viaje *m* (por mar); travesía *f*; 2. viajar (por mar); navegar; **voy·ag·er** ['vɔiədʒə] viajero (a *f*) *m*.
vul·can·ite ['vʌlkənait] vulcanita *f*, ebonita *f*; **vul·can·i'za·tion** vulcanización *f*; **'vul·can·ize** vulcanizar.
vul·gar ['vʌlgə] 1. □ vulgar; *b.s.* grosero; (*in bad taste, showy*) cursi; *joke etc.* verde, indecente; ~ *tongue* lengua *f* vulgar; 2.: *the* ~ el vulgo; **'vul·gar·ism** vulgarismo *m*; **vul·gar·i·ty** [ˌˈgæriti] vulgaridad *f*; grosería *f*; indecencia *f*; **'vul·gar·ize** vulgarizar; **Vul·gate** ['vʌlgit] Vulgata *f*.
vul·ner·a·bil·i·ty [vʌlnərəˈbiliti] vulnerabilidad *f*; **'vul·ner·a·ble** □ vulnerable; **'vul·ner·ar·y** vulnerario *adj. a. su. m*.
vul·pine ['vʌlpain] vulpino.
vul·ture ['vʌltʃə] buitre *m*.
vy·ing ['vaiiŋ] *ger. of* vie.

W

wack·y ['wæki] *Am. sl.* chiflado.

wad [wɔd] **1.** taco *m*, tapón *m*; bolita *f* de algodón *etc.*; lío *m* of *papers*;' *Am.* F fajo *m* of *notes*; *sl.* pastel *m*; **2.** rellenar; acolchar; tapar; **'wadding** algodón *m* (en rama); taco *m*, relleno *m*; ☞ algodón *m* absorbente (*or* hidrófilo).

wad·dle ['wɔdl] anadear.

wade [weid] *v/i.* caminar por el agua *etc.*; ~ *ashore* llegar a tierra vadeando; ~ *into* meterse en; F embestir con violencia; ~ *through book* leer a pesar de lo aburrido (*or* difícil *etc.*); *v t.* vadear; **'wad·er** orn. ave *f* zancuda; ~s *pl.* botas *f/pl.* altas.

wa·fer ['weifə] galleta *f*; barquillo *m*; oblea *f* *for sealing*; *eccl.* hostia *f*.

waf·fle ['wɔfl] *approx.* churro *m*, buñuelo *m*; *sl.* palabrería *f*.

waft [wɑːft] **1.** traer, llevar (por el aire); **2.** soplo *m*.

wag¹ [wæg] **1.** menear(se); agitar (se); **2.** meneo *m*.

wag² [~] bromista *m*, zumbón *m*.

wage [weidʒ] **1.** *war* hacer; proseguir; **2.** (*a.* wag·es ['~iz] *pl.*) salario *m*; (*mst day-*) jornal *m*; **wage-earner** ['~ɔːnə] asalariado (a *f*) *m*; obrero *m*.

wa·ger ['weidʒə] *lit.* **1.** apuesta *f*; **2.** apostar (on a, *that* a que).

wag·ger·y ['wægəri] jocosidad *f*; chanzas *f/pl.*; **'wag·gish** ☐ zumbón, divertido.

wag·gle ['wægl] F v. *wag¹*.

wag·(g)on ['wægən] carro *m*; 🚂 vagón *m*, furgón *m*; F be on the (*water*) ~ no beber; **'wag·(g)on·er** carretero *m*; **wag·(g)on·ette** [~'net] break *m*.

wag·tail ['wægteil] *mst* lavandera *f*.

waif [weif] niño (a *f*) *m* abandonado (a); ~s *and strays pl.* niños *m/pl.* desamparados.

wail [weil] **1.** lamento *m*, gemido *m*; (*baby's*) vagido *m*; **2.** lamentarse, gemir; gimotear.

wain [wein] *poet.* carro *m*; *ast.* *Charles's* ♀, *the* ♀ el Carro.

wain·scot ['weinskət] **1.** friso *m*; **2.** poner friso a.

waist [weist] cintura *f*; talle *m*; ⚓ combés *m*; '~·**band** pretina *f*; '~·**coat** chaleco *m*; '~·**deep** hasta la cintura.

wait [weit] **1.** *v/i.* esperar, aguardar (*for acc.*); (*a.* ~ *at table*) servir (*on acc.*); F ~ *about* estar esperando; ~ (*up*)*on p.* presentar sus respetos a; *decision* depender de; *keep s.o.* ~*ing* hacer que uno espere; ~ *and see!* espera y verás; *v/t.* esperar; F *meal* aplazar; **2.** espera *f*; ~s *pl.* murga *f* (de nochebuena); *have a long* ~ tener que esperar mucho tiempo; *be* (*or lie*) *in* ~ acechar (*for acc.*); **'wait·er** camarero *m*; mozo *m*.

wait·ing ['weitiŋ] espera *f*; servicio *m*; *in* ~ de honor; '~·**room** sala *f* de espera.

wait·ress ['weitris] camarera *f*.

waive [weiv] *right* renunciar; *claim* desistir de; **'waiv·er** renuncia *f*.

wake¹ [weik] ⚓ estela *f*; *fig. in the* ~ of siguiendo, como consecuencia de; tras.

wake² [~] **1.** [*irr.*] *v/i.* despertar(se) (*a.* ~ *up*); *v/t.* despertar; *corpse* velar; **2.** *hist.* verbena *f*; vela *f over corpse*; **wake·ful** ['~ful] ☐ despierto; desvelado; **'wak·en** *v/i.* despertar(se); *v/t.* despertar.

walk [wɔːk] **1.** *v/i.* andar; caminar; (*stroll*) pasear(se); (*not ride*) ir a pie; ~ *about* pasearse; ~ *away with* llevarse; *sl.* ~ *into food* atracarse de; *p.* atacar, injuriar; ~ *off with* llevarse; robar; ~ *out* (*strike*) declararse en huelga; retirarse (enfadado) *from conference*; salir repentinamente; F ~ *out on sweetheart* dejar plantado, plantar; dejar; *v/t. child etc.* pasear; *horse* llevar al paso; *distance* recorrer (a pie); (*tire*) cansar con tanto andar; ~ *off* deshacerse de ... andando; **2.** (*stroll*) paseo *m*; (*gait*) andar *m*, paso *m*; (*place*) paseo *m*, alameda *f*; *go for* (*or take*) *a* ~ dar un paseo; ~ *of life* profesión *f*, condición *f*; **'walk·er**

paseante *m/f*, peatón *m*; *be a great* ~ ser gran andarín; **'walk·er-'on** F figurante (a *f*) *m*.

walk·ie-talk·ie ['wɔːki'tɔːki] transmisor-receptor *m* portátil.

walk·ing ['wɔːkiŋ] 1. excursionismo *m* a pie; el pasearse; 2. ambulante; *Am.* F ~ *papers pl.* despedida *f*; ~ *race* carrera *f* pedestre; ~ *tour* excursión *f* a pie; '~-**stick** bastón *m*.

walk...: '~-**out** huelga *f*; salida *f*; '~-**over** *racing*: walkover *m*; *fig.* triunfo *m* fácil; '~-**up** *Am. house* sin ascensor.

wall [wɔːl] 1. (*mst interior*) pared *f*; muro *m*; (*garden-*) tapia *f*; (*city-*) muralla *f*; *go to the* ~ ser desechado por inútil; quedar arrinconado; 2. murar; *city* amurallar;· ~ *up* emparedar; cerrar con muro.

wal·la·by ['wɔləbi] ualabi *m*.

wal·let ['wɔlit] cartera *f*.

wall...: '~-**flow·er** alhelí *m*; *fig. be a* ~ comer pavo; '~-**fruit** fruta *f* de espalera; '~-**map** mapa *m* mural.

wal·lop ['wɔləp] F 1. golpear fuertemente; zurrar; 2. golpazo *m*; zurra *f*; *sl.* cerveza *f*; **'wal·lop·ing** F grandote.

wal·low ['wɔlou] revolcarse; *fig.* nadar (*in* en).

wall...: '~-**pa·per** papel *m* pintado, papel *m* de empapelar; '~-**sock·et** enchufe *m* de pared.

wal·nut ['wɔːlnʌt] nuez *f*; (*tree*, *wood*) nogal *m*.

wal·rus ['wɔːlrəs] morsa *f*.·

waltz [wɔːls] 1. vals *m*; 2. valsar.

wan [wɔn] □ pálido, macilento.

wand [wɔnd] vara *f of office*; (*magic*) varita *f*.

wan·der ['wɔndə] errar, vagar; extraviarse; deambular (*a.* ~ *about*); *fig.* divagar *in mind*; salirse (*from theme etc.* de); **'wan·der·er** vagabundo (a *f*) *m*; nómada *m/f*; **'wan·der·ing** 1. □ errante; errabundo; *fig.* distraído; 2. ♗ delirio *m*; ~*s pl.* viajes *m/pl.*; errabundeo *m*.

wane [wein] 1. (*moon*) menguar; *fig.* disminuir; 2. (*a.* **'wan·ing**) menguante *f*; mengua *f*; *on the* ~ (*moon*) menguante; *fig.* menguando.

wan·gle ['wæŋgl] *sl.* 1. chanchullo *m*, trampa *f*; 2. mamarse, agenciarse; **'wan·gler** chanchullero *m*.

wan·ness ['wɔnnis] palidez *f*.

want [wɔnt] 1. (*lack*) falta *f*, carencia *f*; (*need*) necesidad *f*; (*poverty*) indigencia *f*; *for* ~ *of* por falta de; *be in* ~ estar necesitado; *fill a long-felt* ~ llenar un bien sentido vacío; *Am.* F ~ *ad* anuncio *m* clasificado; 2. *v/i.*: *be* ~*ing* faltar; *be* ~*ing in* estar falto de; ~ *for* necesitar, carecer de; *it* ~*s of* falta; *v/t.* querer, desear; (*need*) necesitar; (*lack*) carecer de; *he* ~*s energy* le falta energía; ~ *a p. to do* querer que una p. haga; F *you* ~ *to be careful* hay que tener ojo; ~*ed* (*in adveris*) necesítase; (*police*) se busca; **'want·ing** defectuoso; deficiente (*in* en), falto (*in* de).

wan·ton ['wɔntən] 1. □ (*playful*) juguetón; (*rank*) lozano; caprichoso; *b.s.* lascivo; *destruction* sin propósito; 2. libertino (a *f*) *m*; 3. retozar; **'wan·ton·ness** lascivia *f etc.*

war [wɔː] 1. guerra *f*; *attr.* ... de guerra, bélico; *at* ~ en guerra; *make* ~ hacer la guerra (*on* a); *cold* ~ guerra *f* fria; *hot* ~ guerra *f* a tiros; ~ *of nerves* guerra *f* de nervios; ~ *criminal* criminal *m* de guerra; ~ *dance* danza *f* guerrera; ~ *horse* corcel *m*; ~ *memorial* monumento *m* a los caídos; ♀ *Office*, *Am.* ♀ *Department* Ministerio *m* de Guerra; 2. *lit.* guerrear.

war·ble [wɔːbl] 1. trinar, gorjear; 2. trino *m*, gorjeo *m*; **'war·bler** mosquitero *m*, curruca *f etc.*

ward [wɔːd] 1. (*p.*) pupilo (a *f*) *m*; (*wardship*) tutela *f*, custodia *f*; (*hospital*) sala *f*, crujía *f*; distrito *m* (electoral) *of city*; guarda *f of key*; *in* ~ bajo tutela; *casual* ~ asilo *m* para pobres; *Am. pol.* F ~ *heeler* muñidor *m*; F *walk the* ~*s* hacer práctica de clínica; 2.: ~ *off* desviar, parar; *fig.* evitar, conjurar; **'ward·en** guardián *m*; *univ. etc.* director *m*; (*in titles*) alcaide *m*; **'ward·er** carcelero *m*, vigilante *m*; **'ward·robe** guardarropa *m*; vestidos *m/pl.*; *thea.* vestuario *m*; ~ *dealer* ropavejero *m*; ~ *trunk* baúl *m* ropero; **'ward·room** ⚓ cuarto *m* de los oficiales; **'ward·ship** tutela *f*.

ware [wɛə] loza *f*; ~*s pl.* mercancías *f/pl.*; *small* ~*s pl.* mercería *f*.

ware·house 1. ['wɛəhaus] almacén *m*,

depósito *m*; **2.** [ˈˌhauz] almacenar; ˌ·**man** [ˈˌhausmən] almacenista *m*.
war…: **ˈˌ·fare** guerra *f*; **ˈˌ·head** punta *f* de combate *of torpedo*; cabeza *f* de guerra *of rocket*.
war·i·ly [ˈwɛərili] cautelosamente; **war·i·ness** [ˈˌinis] cautela *f*, precaución *f*.
war·like [ˈwɔːlaik] guerrero, belicoso; castrense.
war-loan [ˈwɔːloun] empréstito *m* de guerra.
warm [wɔːm] **1.** ⬚ caliente (*a.* F = *near*); *day, greeting* caluroso; *climate* cálido; *heart* afectuoso; *argument* acalorado; *be* ˌ (*p.*) tener calor; (*weather*) hacer calor; (*th.*) estar caliente; **2.** *v/t.* calentar; *heart* alegrar, regocijar; F zurrar; ˌ *up food* recalentar; *v/i.* (*a.* ˌ *up*) calentarse; (*argument*) acalorarse; *sport:* hacer ejercicios (para entrar en calor); ˌ *to* (*heart*) ir cobrando afición a; **ˈwarm·ing** F zurra *f*.
war-mon·ger [ˈwɔːmʌŋgə] incendiario *m* de la guerra.
warmth [wɔːmθ] calor *m*; *fig.* cordialidad *f*; entusiasmo *m*; ardor *m*.
warn [wɔːn] avisar; advertir (*of acc.*); prevenir (*against* contra); amonestar (*to inf.*); ˌ *off* expulsar *from racecourse etc.*; *he was* ˌ*ed off the subject* le advirtieron que no se metiese en el asunto; **ˈwarn·ing** aviso *m*; advertencia *f*; *be a* ˌ servir de escarmiento (*to* a); *attr.* de aviso; de alarma; admonitorio.
warp [wɔːp] **1.** (*weaving*) urdimbre*f*; alabeo *m of wood*; ⚓ espía *f*; *fig.* sesgo *m*; **2.** *v/i.* (*wood*) alabearse, torcerse; ⚓ espiarse; *v/t. wood* alabear, torcer; ⚓ mover con espía; *fig.* pervertir.
warp·ing [ˈwɔːpiŋ] ⚓ torsión *f*.
war·plane [ˈwɔːplein] avión *m* militar.
war·rant [ˈwɔrənt] **1.** garantía *f*; autorización *f*, justificación *f*; ✝ cédula *f*, vale *m*; ⚎ mandato *m*, orden *f* (*of arrest* de prisión); **2.** *esp.* ✝ garantizar; autorizar, justificar; *I* ˌ (*you*) se lo aseguro; **ˈwar-rant·a·ble** justificable; *stag* de edad para cazar; **ˈwar·rant·ed** ✝ garantizado; **war·ran·tee** [ˌˈtiː] persona *f* afianzada; **ˈwar·rant-of-fi·cer** ⚓ contramaestre *m*; ✗ suboficial *m*; **ˈwar·ran·tor** [ˌtɔː] ga-

rante *m/f*; **ˈwar·ran·ty** ✝ garantía *f*; *v. warrant*.
war-ren [ˈwɔrin] conejera *f*.
war·ri·or [ˈwɔriə] guerrero *m*.
war·ship [ˈwɔːʃip] buque *m* de guerra.
wart [wɔːt] verruga *f* (*a.* ⚘); **ˈwart·y** verrugoso.
war·y [ˈwɛəri] ⬚ cauto, cauteloso, prudente.
was [wɔz, wəz] *pret. of be*.
wash [wɔʃ] **1.** *v/t.* lavar (*a.* ˌ *up*, ˌ *out*); *dishes a.* fregar; bañar; ˌ *away* quitar lavando; (*river*) llevarse; ˌ*ed out sl.* rendido; ˌ*ed up sl.* deslomado; *sl.* fracasado; ˌ *one's hands of* desentenderse de; *v/i.* lavarse; lavar la ropa; (*water*) moverse; ˌ *up* lavar (*or* fregar) los platos; **2.** lavado *m*; ropa *f* (para lavar); (*hung to dry*) tendido *m*; ⚓ estela *f*, remolinos *m/pl.*; movimiento *m of water*; ✗ disturbio *m* aerodinámico; (*hair-*) champú *m*; *contp.* aguachirle *f*; **ˈwash·a·ble** lavable; **ˈwash-ba·sin** palangana *f*, lavabo *m*.
wash·er [ˈwɔʃə] ⊕ arandela *f*; (*tap-*) zapatilla *f*; **ˈˌ·wom·an** lavandera *f*.
wash·ing [ˈwɔʃiŋ] **1.** ropa *f* (para lavar); lavado *m*; ˌ*s pl.* lavadura *f*; **2.:** ˌ *machine* lavadora *f*; ˌ *powder* jabón *m* en polvo; **ˈˌ·up** platos *m/pl.* (para lavar); fregado *m*, lavado *m* (de platos).
wash…: **ˈˌ·leath·er** gamuza *f*; **ˈˌ·out** *sl.* fracaso *m*; **ˈˌ·rag** *Am.* paño *m* de cocina; **ˈˌ·stand** lavabo *m*, lavamanos *m*; **ˈˌ·tub** tina *f* (de lavar); **ˈwash·y** aguado, insípido; *fig.* flojo, insulso.
wasp [wɔsp] avispa *f*; ˌ*s' nest* avispero *m* (*a. fig.*); **ˈwasp·ish** ⬚ irascible; punzante.
wast·age [ˈweistidʒ] merma *f*, pérdida *f*; desgaste *m*.
waste [weist] **1.** (*rejected*) desechado; (*useless*) inútil; (*left over*) sobrante; *land* baldío, yermo; *lay* ˌ asolar, devastar; ˌ *paper* papel *m* viejo, papeles *m/pl.* usados; *biol.* ˌ *products pl.* desperdicios *m/pl.*; ˌ *steam* vapor *m* de escape; **2.** despilfarro *m*, derroche *m*; pérdida *f of time*; desgaste *m*; desperdicio(s) *m(pl.)*; desecho *m*, basura *f*; (*land*) yermo *m*; *go* (*or run*) *to* ˌ perderse; **3.** *v/t.* malgastar; desperdiciar; derrochar; *time* perder; *v/i.* (des)gas-

tarse; perderse; ~ *away* consumirse, mermar; **waste·ful** ['~ful] □ pródigo; despilfarrado; antieconómico; **'waste·ful·ness** despilfarro *m etc.*; **'waste-pa·per bas·ket** cesto *m* (para papeles); **'waste-pipe** tubo *m* de desagüe; **'wast·er** artículo *m* imperfecto; **wast·rel** ['weistrəl] derrochador *m*.

watch [wɔtʃ] **1.** reloj *m*; vigilia *f*; vigilancia *f*; ⚔, ⚓ guardia *f*, ⚓ vigía(s) *m*(*pl.*); (*night-*) ronda *f*; *be on the* ~ estar a la mira (*for* de); *keep* ~ estar de guardia; *keep* ~ *over p.* velar; *th.* vigilar por; **2.** *v/i.* velar; ~ *for* esperar; acechar; ~ *out* tener cuidado (*for* con); ~ *over* vigilar; *v/t.* mirar; observar; vigilar; guardar; **'~-chain** cadena *f* de reloj; **'~-dog** perro *m* guardián; **'watch·er** observador *m*; **watch·ful** ['~ful] □ vigilante; **'watch·ful·ness** vigilancia *f*, desvelo *m*.

watch...: **'~-mak·er** relojero *m*; **'~-man** guardián *m*; (*night-*) sereno *m*; **'~-tow·er** atalaya *f*; **'~-word** ⚔ santo *m* y seña; *pol. etc.* lema *m*, consigna *f*.

wa·ter ['wɔːtə] **1.** agua *f*; *high* ~ pleamar *f*; *low* ~ bajamar *f*; *by* ~ por agua; por mar; *of the first* ~ de lo mejor; *drink* (*or take*) *the* ~s tomar las aguas; *get into deep* ~s meterse en honduras; F *get into hot* ~ cargársela (*for, over* en el asunto de); *hold* ~ retener el agua; *fig.* ser lógico; **2.** acuático; de agua, para agua; ~ *supply* abastecimiento *m* de agua; **3.** *v/t.* land, plant regar; *cattle* abrevar; *wine* aguar (*a.* ~ *down*); *v/i.* suavizar, diluir; *v/i.* (*mouth*) hacerse agua; (*eyes*) llorar; **'~-borne** llevado por barco *etc.*; **'~-bot·tle** cantimplora *f*; **'~-car·ri·er** aguador *m*; **'~-cart** cuba *f* de riego; **'~-clos·et** (*mst abbr.* W.C.) wáter *m*, inodoro *m*; **'~-col·o(u)r** acuarela *f*; **'~-cooled** refrigerado por agua; **'~-cool·ing** refrigeración *f* por agua; **'~-course** lecho *m*; arroyo *m*; **'~-cress** berro *m*; **'~-di·vin·er** zahorí *m*; **'~-fall** cascada *f*, salto *m* de agua; **'~-fowl** *pl.* aves *f/pl.* acuáticas; **'~-front** *esp. Am.* terreno *m* ribereño; **'wa·ter·i·ness** acuosidad *f*.

wa·ter·ing ['wɔːtəriŋ] riego *m*; **'~-can** regadera *f*; **'~-place** (*spa*) balneario *m*; ✐ abrevadero *m*.

water...: **'~-jack·et** camisa *f* de agua; **'~-lev·el** nivel *m* del agua; ⚓ línea *f* de agua; **'~-lil·y** nenúfar *m*; **'~-line** línea *f* de flotación; **'~-logged** anegado; empapado; **'~-man** barquero *m*; **'~-mark** filigrana *f*; **'~-mel·on** sandía *f*; **'~-mill** molino *m* de agua; **'~-pipe** caño *m* de agua; **'~-po·lo** polo *m* acuático; **'~-pow·er** fuerza *f* hidráulica; **'~-proof 1.** impermeable *adj. a. su. m*; **2.** impermeabilizar; **'~-shed** línea *f* divisoria de las aguas; cuenca *f*; **'~-side** orilla *f* del agua; **'~-ski·ing** esquí *m* acuático; **'~-spout** tromba *f* marina; **'~-tank** cisterna *f*; **'~-tight** estanco, hermético; *fig.* irrecusable; completamente lógico; **'~-wave 1.** ondulación *f* al agua; **2.** ondular al agua; **'~-way** canal *m*, vía *f* fluvial; **'~-wings** *pl.* nadaderas *f/pl.*; **'~-works** *pl., a. sg.* central *f* depuradora; **'wa·ter·y** acuoso; *eye* lagrimoso; *sky* que amenaza lluvia; *fig.* insípido; pálido.

watt [wɔt] vatio *m*.

wat·tle ['wɔtl] zarzo *m*; *orn.* barba *f*.

wave [weiv] **1.** ola *f*; onda *f* (*a. phys., radio*); (*hair*) ondulación *f*; *fig.* oleada *f* *of strikes etc.*; señal *f*, además *m of hand*; *cold* ~ ola *f* de frío; **2.** *v/t.* agitar; *weapon etc.* blandir; *hair* ondular; ~ *aside* rechazar; ~ *a p. on* hacer señales a una p. para que avance; *v/i.* ondear; agitar el brazo; ~ *to a p.* hacer señales (con la mano) a una p.; **'~-length** longitud *f* de onda; **'~-me·ter** ondímetro *m*.

wa·ver ['weivə] vacilar, titubear.

wave...: **'~-range** *radio*: gama *f* de ondas; **'~-trap** *radio*: trampa *f* de ondas.

wav·y ['weivi] ondulado; ondeado.

wax[1] [wæks] **1.** cera *f*; **2.** encerar.

wax[2] [~] [*irr.*] (*moon*) crecer; (*with adj.*) ponerse.

wax·en ['wæksn] de cera; ceroso; **'wax·work** figura *f* de cera; ~s *pl.* museo *m* de (figuras de) cera; **'wax·y** ⸛ ceroso; *sl.* enojadizo.

way [wei] camino *m* (*to* de); vía *f*; dirección *f*, sentido *m*; distancia *f*, trayecto *m*; viaje *m*; paso *m* (*a.* ~ *through*); costumbre *f*; respecto *m*; estado *m*; progreso *m*; (*means*) manera *f*, modo *m*; medio *m*; estilo *m of life*; ~ *in* entrada *f*; ~ *out* salida *f*; *a good* ~ un buen trecho; *this* ~

por aquí; de este modo; ~s *and means* pl. medios m/pl.; *across the* ~ enfrente; *by the* ~ de paso; a propósito; *by* ~ *of* por vía de; *fig.* a título de; *in a* ~ en cierto modo; *in every* ~ bajo todas los aspectos; *in no* ~ de ningún modo; *in a bad* ~ en mal estado; F *in a big* ~ en grande, en gran escala; *on the* ~ en el camino; *on the* ~ *to* camino de; *out of the* ~ arrinconado, aislado; insólito; *under* ~ en marcha; *be in the* ~ estorbar; *feel* f *one's* ~ andar a tientas; *fig.* proceder con tiento; *get* (*or have*) *one's* ~ salirse con la suya; *get out of the* ~ quitar(se) de en medio; *give* ~ ceder (*to* el paso a); romperse; *mot.* ceder el paso; *go a long* ~ *towards* ger. contribuir mucho a *inf.*; *go one's own* ~ ir a la suya; *go out of one's* ~ desviarse del camino; *fig.* darse la molestia (*to inf. de inf.*); *have a* ~ *with* manejar bien; *have a* ~ *with people* tener don de gentes; *lead the* ~ ir primero; *lose one's* ~ extraviarse, errar el camino; *make one's* ~ abrirse camino (*through* por); dirigirse (*to* a); *make* ~ *for* hacer lugar para; *see one's* ~ *to* ger. *or inf.* ver la forma de *inf.*; *Am.* ~ station estación f de paso; *Am.* ~ *train* tren m ómnibus; '~-**bill** hoja f de ruta; '~-**far·er** viajero (a f) m; caminante m/f; ~'**lay** [*irr.* (*lay*)] asechar; detener; '~-**side 1.** (*by the* al) borde m del camino; **2.** junto al camino.

way·ward ['weiwəd] voluntarioso; caprichoso; '**way·ward·ness** voluntariedad f; lo caprichoso.

we [wi:, wi] nosotros, nosotras.

weak [wi:k] □ débil; flojo; *sound* tenue; ~ *point* flaco m; '**weak·en** debilitar(se); atenuar(se); enflaquecer(se); '**weak·ling** canijo m; cobarde m; '**weak·ly** enclenque, achacoso; '**weak-'mind·ed** imbécil; vacilante; '**weak·ness** debilidad f; flaco m; *have a* ~ *for* ser muy aficionado a.

weal[1] [wi:l] verdugón m.

weal[2] [wi:l] † bienestar m.

wealth [welθ] riqueza f; caudal m; *fig.* abundancia f; '**wealth·y** □ rico, acaudalado.

wean [wi:n] destetar; *fig.* ~ *from*, ~ *of* apartar gradualmente de; '**wean·ing** destete m, ablactación f.

weap·on ['wepən] arma f.

wear [weə] **1.** [*irr.*] v/t. *clothes etc.* llevar; *shoes* calzar; *smile, look* tener; exhibir; ~ *away*, ~ *down*, ~ *out* (des)gastar; consumir; *patience* cansar; agotar; ~ *o.s. out* matarse; v/i. (*well*) durar; ~ *well* conservarse bien; ~ *away* desgastarse; ~ *off* pasar, desaparecer; ~ *on* (*time*) pasar (despacio); ~ *out* gastarse, usarse; **2.** desgaste m, deterioro m, uso m (a. ~ *and tear*); durabilidad f; (*clothes*) ropa f; moda f; *for everyday* ~ para todo trote; *for hard* ~ resistente, duradero; *the worse for* ~ deteriorado.

wea·ri·ness ['wiərinis] cansancio m; aburrimiento m.

wea·ri·some ['wiərisəm] □ fastidioso; aburrido.

wea·ry ['wiəri] **1.** □ (*tired*) cansado (*of* de), fatigado; (*tiring*) fastidioso, aburrido; **2.** v/t. cansar; aburrir; v/i. cansarse (*of* de).

wea·sel ['wi:zl] comadreja f.

weath·er ['weðə] **1.** tiempo m; (*harsh*) intemperie f; *under the* ~ F indispuesto; *sl.* borracho; *make heavy* ~ *of* encontrar difícil; **2.** *attr.* ⚓ de barlovento; intemperie; **3.** v/t. ⚓ (a. ~ *out*) *storm* aguantar (a. *fig.*); *cape* doblar; *fig.* superar; *geol.* desgastar; *wood* curar al aire; v/i. curtirse a la intemperie; *geol.* desgastarse; ~-**beat·en** ['~bi:tn] curtido por la intemperie; '~-**board** tabla f de chilla; '~-**bound** atrasado por el mal tiempo; '~-**bu·reau** servicio m meteorológico; '~-**chart** mapa m meteorológico; '~-**cock** veleta f; '~-**fore·cast** parte m (*or* boletín m) meteorológico; '~-**proof** a prueba de la intemperie; '~-**sta·tion** estación f meteorológica; '~-**strip** burlete m; '~-**vane** veleta f.

weave [wi:v] **1.** [*irr.*] tejer; trenzar; *fig.* urdir, tramar; **2.** tejido m; '**weav·er** tejedor m; '**weav·ing** tejeduría f; *attr.* ... para tejer; de tejido(s).

web [web] tela f; tejido m; (*spider's*) telaraña f; *orn.* membrana f; ⊕ alma f; *printing:* rollo m de papel; **webbed** palmeado; '**web·bing** cincha f; '**web-'foot·ed** palmípedo.

wed [wed] v/t. casarse con; *fig.* casar; v/i. casarse; '**wed·ded** conyugal; *fig.* ~ **to** aferrado a; **'wed·ding 1.** boda *f*, bodas *f*/*pl.*; casamiento *m*; **2.** *attr.*: ~ *breakfast* banquete *m* nupcial; ~ *cake* pastel *m* de boda; ~ *day* día *m* de boda; ~ *dress* traje *m* de novia; ~ *march* marcha *f* nupcial; ~ *ring* anillo *m* de boda.

wedge [wedʒ] **1.** cuña *f*; calce *m*; **2.** calzar, acuñar; ~ *in* introducir apretadamente, encajar.

wed·lock ['wedlɔk] matrimonio *m*.

Wed·nes·day ['wenzdi] miércoles *m*.

wee [wi:] *Scot.* or *F* pequeñito, diminuto.

weed [wi:d] **1.** mala hierba *f*; *F* tabaco *m*; **2.** escardar; desherbar; ~ *out fig.* escardar, extirpar, eliminar; '~**·kill·er** herbicida *m*.

weeds [wi:dz] *pl.* (*mst widow's* ~) ropa *f* de luto.

weed·y ['wi:di] lleno de malas hierbas; *F* flaco, desmirriado.

week [wi:k] semana *f*; *this day* ~, *a* ~ *today* de hoy en ocho días; ~ *in*, ~ *out* semana tras semana; '~**-day** día *m* laborable; '~**end 1.** fin *m* de semana, weekend *m*; **2.** pasar el fin de semana; '**week·ly 1.** semanal; **2.** semanalmente; **3.** (*a.* ~ *paper*) semanario *m*, hebdomadario *m*.

weep [wi:p] [*irr.*] llorar, lamentar (*for acc.*); *tears* derramar; '**weep·ing 1.** lloroso; ~ *willow* sauce *m* llorón; **2.** llanto *m*, lágrimas *f*/*pl.*

wee·vil ['wi:vil] gorgojo *m*.

weft [weft] trama *f*.

weigh [wei] **1.** *v*/*t.* pesar (*a. fig.*, ~ *up*, *words etc.*); ~ *against* considerar en relación con; ~ *anchor* zarpar; ~ *down* sobrecargar; *fig.* agobiar (*with de*); *v*/*i.* pesar; *he* ~*s 80 kilos* pesa 80 kilos; ~ *in with* intervenir afirmando; ~ *on* ser gravoso a; ~ *with* influir en; **2.**: ♣ *under* ~ en marcha; '**weigh·bridge** báscula-puente *f*; '**weigh·ing-ma·chine** báscula *f*.

weight [weit] **1.** peso *m* (*a. fig.*); pesa *f*; ~*s and measures pl.* pesos *m*/*pl.* y medidas; *carry great* ~ influir poderosamente (*with en*); *putting the* ~ lanzamiento *m* de pesos; ~ *lifting* levantamiento *m* de pesos; **2.** (sobre)cargar; sujetar con un peso; ponderar *statistically*; '**weight·i·ness** peso *m*; *fig.* importancia *f*; '**weight·less** ingrávido; '**weight·y** ... pesado; *fig.* importante, de peso.

weir [wiə] presa *f*; pesquera *f*.

weird [wiəd] ☐ fantástico, sobrenatural; horripilante; *F* extraño.

welch [welʃ] *sl.* dejar de pagar una apuesta (*on a*).

wel·come ['welkəm] **1.** ☐ bienvenido; grato; *you are* ~ *to inf.* Vd. es muy dueño de *inf.*; *you are* ~ *to it* está a su disposición; *F you're* ~! no hay de qué; *iro.* ¡buen provecho le haga!; (*you are*) ~! ¡(sea Vd.) bienvenido!; **2.** bienvenida *f*; (buena) acogida *f*; **3.** dar la bienvenida a; acoger; recibir; '**wel·com·ing** ☐ acogedor.

weld [weld] **1.** ⊕ soldar; *fig.* unir, unificar (*into para formar*); **2.** (*or* ~ *ing seam*) soldadura *f*; '**weld·er** soldador *m*; '**weld·ing** ⊕ soldadura *f*; *attr.* ... soldador.

wel·fare ['welfɛə] bienestar *m*; prosperidad *f*; asistencia *f* social; ~ *centre* centro *m* de asistencia social; ~ *state* estado *m* benefactor; ~ *worker* empleado (*a f*) *m* de asistencia social.

well[1] [wel] **1.** pozo *m*; *fig.* fuente *f*, manantial *m*; ⊕ pozo *m* (de petróleo); hueco *m of stairs*; **2.** (*a.* ~ *up*) brotar, manar.

well[2] [~] **1.** *adv.* bien; ~ *done!* ¡bien!; ~ *and good* enhorabuena; *he's* ~ *past 50* tiene mucho más de 50 años; *v. as*; **2.** *pred. adj.* bien (de salud); *it is just as* ~ *that* menos mal que; **3.** *int. etc.* ¡vaya!; bien; pues; ~ *then* pues bien; '~**-ad·vised** bien aconsejado; '~**-at'tend·ed** muy concurrido; '~**-be'haved** bien educado; '~**'be·ing** bienestar *m*; '~**-'bred** bien criado; cortés; '~**-dis'posed** bien dispuesto; benévolo (*to*, *towards con*); '~**-'favo(u)red** bien parecido; '~**-in'formed** (*in general*) instruido; bien enterado (*about matter de*).

Wel·ling·tons ['weliŋtənz] *pl.* botas *f*/*pl.* de goma.

well...: '~**-in'ten·tioned** bienintencionado; '~**-'judged** bien calculado; '~**-'known** familiar, conocido; '~**-'man·nered** cortés, urbano; '~**-'mean·ing** bienintencionado; '~**-nigh** casi; '~**-'off** *F* acomodado; '~**-'read** muy leído; '~**-'spo·ken** bienhablado; '~**-'timed** oportuno; '~**-to-'do** acomodado, pudiente; '~**-'turned** *fig.* elegante; '~**-'wish·er**

amigo (a f) m; '~-'**worn** fig. traído y llevado, trillado.
Welsh[1] [welʃ] **1.** galés, de Gales; **2.** (language) galés m; '~-**man** galés m.
welsh[2] [~] v. welch.
welt [welt] **1.** vira f of shoe; (weal) verdugón m; **2.** poner vira a; F zurrar.
wel·ter ['weltə] **1.** revolcarse; estar empapado (in de); **2.** confusión f; mar m of blood etc.; '~-**weight** wélter m.
wen [wen] lobanillo m.
wench [wentʃ] moza f, mozuela f.
wend [wend]: ~ one's way dirigirse (to a).
went [went] pret. of go 1.
were [wə:, wə] pret. of be.
west [west] **1.** oeste m, occidente m; **2.** adj. del oeste, occidental; **3.** adv. al oeste, hacia el oeste; sl. go ~ romperse; fracasar; (die) reventar.
west·er·ly ['westəli] direction hacia el oeste; wind del oeste.
west·ern ['westən] **1.** occidental; **2.** Am. ♀ película f que se desarrolla en el Oeste de EE. UU.; '**west·ern·er** habitante m/f del oeste; '**west·ern·most** (el) más occidental.
west·ward(s) ['westwəd(z)] hacia el oeste.
wet [wet] **1.** mojado; place húmedo; weather lluvioso; day de lluvia; paint fresco; Am. F antiprohibicionista; v. blanket 1; ~ paint! ¡ojo, se pinta!; ~ steam vapor m húmedo; ~ through mojado hasta los huesos; **2.** humedad f; (rain) lluvia f; **3.** mojar; F bargain cerrar con un brindis; ~ one's whistle remojar el gaznate.
wet·back ['wetbæk] Am. sl. inmigrante m/f ilegal (desde Méjico).
wet·ness ['wetnis] humedad f; (raininess) lo lluvioso.
weth·er ['weðə] carnero m castrado.
wet-nurse ['wetnə:s] nodriza f.
whack [wæk] F **1.** golpear (ruidosamente); pegar; ~ golpe m (ruidoso); sl. tentativa f; sl. parte f, porción f; sl. have a ~ at probar, tratar de hacer; '**whack·ing** F **1.** zurra f; **2.** grandote, imponente.
whale [weil] ballena f; F a ~ of ... un enorme ...; F have a ~ of a time pasarlo en grande; '~-**bone** ballena f; '**whal·er** (p.) ballenero m; (boat)

ballenera f; '**whale-oil** aceite m de ballena.
whal·ing ['weiliŋ] pesca f de ballenas; ~ station estación f ballenera.
whang [wæŋ] F **1.** golpe m resonante; **2.** golpear de modo resonante.
wharf [wɔ:f] (pl. a. **wharves** [wɔ:vz]) muelle m; **wharf·age** ['~idʒ] muellaje m.
what [wɔt] **1.** relative lo que; know ~'s ~ saber cuántas son cinco; ~ money I had el dinero que tenía; cuanto dinero tenía; ~ with one thing and another entre lo uno y lo otro; ... and ~ not y qué sé yo qué más; **2.** interrogative qué; cuál; ~? (surprise etc., asking for repetition) ¿cómo?; what book do you want? ¿qué libro quieres?, ¿cuál de los libros quieres?; ~ about...? ¿qué te parece...?; ~ hay en cuanto a...?; ~ about that book? ¿y el libro aquel?; ~ about me? ¿y yo?; ~ for? ¿para qué?; ¿por qué?; ~ of it?, Am. so ~? y eso ¿qué importa?; ~ if...? ¿y si...?; ~ next? ¿y luego?; ahora ¿qué?; F ~'s his name Fulano; **3.:** ~ luck! ¡qué suerte!; ~ a...! ¡qué...!; '**what(·so)·ev·er** 1. cual(es)quiera que; todo lo que; **2.:** ~ he says diga lo que diga; nothing ~ nada en absoluto; ~ next! ¡es el colmo!
wheat [wi:t] trigo m; attr. triguero; '**wheat·en** de trigo.
whee·dle ['wi:dl] engatusar (into ger. para que subj.); sonsacar (a th. out of a p. algo a alguien).
wheel [wi:l] **1.** rueda f; Am. bicicleta f; (steering-) volante m; ⚓ timón m; ✗ conversión f; **2.** v/t. hacer girar, hacer rodar; bicycle empujar; child pasear; v/i. girar, rodar; (birds) revolotear; ✗ cambiar de frente; ~ round (p.) girar sobre los talones; '~-**bar·row** carretilla f; ~ **base** mot. distancia f entre ejes; battalla f; '~-**chair** silla f de ruedas; '**wheeled** rodado; 4-~ de 4 ruedas; ~ traffic circulación f rodada; '**wheel·spi·der** estrella f de rueda; '**wheel·wright** ruedero m; carretero m.
wheeze [wi:z] **1.** resollar (con ruido); **2.** resuello m (ruidoso), respiración f sibilante; sl. truco m, treta f, idea f; '**wheez·y** □ que resuella (con ruido).

whelk [welk] buccino *m*.

whelp [welp] *lit.* **1.** cachorro *m*; **2.** parir.

when [wen] **1.** ¿cuándo?; **2.** cuando.

whence [wens] *lit.* **1.** ¿de dónde?; **2.** por consiguiente.

when(·**so**)·**ev·er**[wen(sou)'evə]siempre que, cuandoquiera que; ~ *you like* cuando quieras.

where [weə] **1.** ¿(a)dónde?; **2.** donde; **~·a·bouts 1.** ['weərə'bauts] ¿dónde?; **2.** ['~] paradero *m*; **~'as** mientras (que); por cuanto; 🕀 considerando que; **~'at** con lo cual; **~'by** por lo cual, por donde; **'~·fore** por qué; por tanto; **~'in** en donde; **~'of** de que; **~'on** en que; **~·so'ev·er** dondequiera que; **~·up'on** acto seguido, después de lo cual; **wher·'ev·er 1.** dondequiera que; **2.** ¿dónde?; **where·with·al** [weəwi'ðɔːl] F medios *m/pl.*, conquibus *m*.

wher·ry ['weri] chalana *f*.

whet [wet] *tool* afilar, amolar; *fig.* estimular, aguzar.

wheth·er ['weðə] si; ~ ... *or sea* ... sea; ~ *or no* en todo caso.

whet·stone ['wetstoun] muela *f*, piedra *f* de amolar.

whew [hwuː] ¡vaya!

whey [wei] suero *m*.

which [witʃ] **1.** ¿cuál(es)?; ¿qué?; ~ *book do you want?* ¿cuál de los libros quieres?, ¿qué libro quieres?; ~ *way?* ¿por dónde?; **2.** que; el (la, los, las) que; el (la) cual, los (las) cuales; lo cual (*e.g.*, *he came early*, *which was awkward* llegó temprano, lo cual creó dificultades); **~·ev·er** [~'evə] *pron.* cualquiera; el (la) que; **2.** *adj.* cualquier.

whiff [wif] soplo *m* (fugaz); vaharada *f*; fumada *f* of smoke.

whif·fle·tree ['wifltriː] volea *f*.

Whig [wig] † whig *m* (*liberal inglés*).

while [wail] **1.** rato *m*; *a good* ~ un buen rato; *for a* ~ durante un rato; F *worth* ~ que vale la pena; **2.**: ~ *away* entretener, pasar; **3.** (*a.* **whilst** [wailst]) mientras (que).

whim [wim] capricho *m*, antojo *m*; ⊕ malacate *m*.

whim·per ['wimpə] **1.** *v/i.* lloriquear, gimotear; *v/t.* decir lloriqueando; **2.** lloriqueo *m*, gimoteo *m*.

whim·si·cal ['wimzikl] ☐ caprichoso, fantástico; **whim·si·cal·i·ty** [~'kæliti] capricho *m*, fantasía *f*.

whim·s(e)y ['wimzi] fantasía *f* amena, extravagancia *f*; *v.* whim.

whin [win] tojo *m*.

whine [wain] **1.** *v/i.* gimotear, quejarse; (*bullet*) silbar; *v/t.* decir gimoteando; **2.** gimoteo *m etc.*

whin·ny ['wini] **1.** relinchar; **2.** relincho *m*.

whip [wip] **1.** *v/t.* azotar; fustigar (*a. fig.*); *fig. esp. Am.* F derrotar; *cream* batir; ♨ envolver con cuerda *etc.*; ~ *away* arrebatar (*from* a); *parl.* ~ *in* llamar (para que vote); ~ *off* (on) *clothes* quitarse (ponerse) de prisa; ~ *out* sacar de repente; ~ *up* avivar; *v/i.* agitarse; ~ *round* volverse de repente; F hacer una colecta; **2.** látigo *m*; azote *m*; *parl.* llamada *f*; (*p.*) oficial *m* disciplinario de partido; F ~ *round* colecta *f*; '~**·cord** tralla *f*; '~'**hand** ventaja *f*, dominio *m*; *have the* ~ llevar la ventaja.

whip·per... ['wipə]: '~-'**in** *hunt.* montero *m* que cuida los perros de caza; *parl. v.* whip **2**; '~**·snap·per** mequetrefe *m*; rapaz *m*.

whip·pet ['wipit] perro *m* lebrel.

whip·ping ['wipiŋ] flagelación *f*; vapuleo *m*; '~-**boy** cabeza *f* de turco; '~-**top** peonza *f*.

whip·saw ['wipsɔː] sierra *f* cabrilla.

whirl [wəːl] **1.** *v/i.* arremolinarse, girar; (*head*) dar vueltas; *v/t.* hacer girar; agitar; llevar muy rápidamente; **2.** giro *m*, vuelta *f*; remolino *m*; serie *f* vertiginosa of *pleasures*; *in a* ~ (*head*) dando vueltas; **whirl·i·gig** ['~igig] tiovivo *m*; '**whirl·pool**, '**whirl·wind** torbellino *m*, remolino *m*.

whir(r) [wəː] **1.** zumbar, rechinar; **2.** zumbido *m*, rechino *m*.

whisk [wisk] **1.** (*brush*) escobilla *f*; (*fly-*) mosqueador *m*; *cooking*: batidora *f*; **2.** *v/t.* dust quitar; *cooking*: batir; ~ *away* escamotear, arrebatar; llevar rápidamente; *v/i.* zamparse, desaparecer de repente; '**whisk·er** pelo *m* (de la barba); ~*s pl.* patillas *f/pl.*, bigotes *m/pl.* (*a. zo.*).

whis·k(e)y ['wiski] whisky *m*.

whis·per ['wispə] **1.** *v/i.* cuchichear; susurrar (*a. fig.*, *leaves*); *v/t.* decir al oído (*to* a); **2.** cuchicheo *m*; *fig.* susurro *m*; *fig.* rumor *m*.

whist [wist] whist *m*.

whis·tle ['wisl] **1.** silbar (*at* acc.); ~

up llamar con un silbido; 2. ♪ silbato *m*, pito *m*; (*sound*) silbido *m*, silbo *m*; ~ **stop** *Am.* población *f* pequeña.

whit[1] [wit]: *not a* ~ ni pizca.

Whit[2] [~] 1. ... de Pentecostés; 2. Pentecostés *f*.

white [wait] 1. blanco; *face* pálido; F honorable; *turn* ~ (*p.*) palidecer; ~ *coffee* café *m* con leche; ~ *heat* candencia *f*; ~ *horses* (*sea*) palomas *f/pl.*; ~ *lead* albayalde *m*; ~ *lie* mentirilla *f*; ~ *slave trade* trata *f* de blancas; 2. blanco *m* (*a. of eye*); clara *f* del huevo; (*p.*) blanco (a *f*) *m*; '~·**bait** salmonetes *m/pl.*; '~·**col·lar** profesional; de oficina; *work* oficinesco; '~·'**hot** candente; *fig.* violento, ardiente; '**whit·en** blanquear (*v/i. a. v/t.*); (*p.*) palidecer; '**white·ness** blancura *f*; '**whit·en·ing** tiza *f*; jalbegue *m*; **White Pa·per** *pol.* Libro *m* Blanco.

white...: '~·**smith** hojalatero *m*; '~·**wash** 1. jalbegue *m*; F encubrimiento *m* de faltas; 2. enjalbegar, blanquear; F paliar (*p.* las faltas de).

whith·er ['wiðə] *lit.* ¿adónde?

whit·ing[1] ['waitiŋ] blanco *m* de España.

whit·ing[2] [~] *ichth.* pescadilla *f*.

whit·ish ['waitiʃ] blanquecino.

whit·low ['witlou] panadizo *m*.

Whit·sun ['witsn] 1. ... de Pentecostés; 2. Pentecostés *f*; ~·**day** ['wit'sʌndi] domingo *m* de Pentecostés; ~**tide** ['witsntaid] Pentecostés *f*.

whit·tle ['witl] *stick* cortar pedazos a; *fig.* ~ *away*, ~ *down* mermar (*or* reducir) poco a poco.

whiz(z) [wiz] 1. silbar; (*arrow*) rehilar; F ~ *along* pasar como un rayo; 2. silbido *m*, zumbido *m*.

who [hu:] 1. que; quien(es); 2. ¿quién(es)?; ~ *goes there?* ¿quién vive?; *Who's Who* Quién es Quién.

whoa [wou] ¡so!

who·dun·it [hu:'dʌnit] *sl.* novela *f* policíaca.

who·ev·er [hu:'evə] 1. quienquiera que, cualquiera que; 2. F ¿quién?

whole [houl] 1. □ todo; entero; total; ⚕ sano; intacto; *the* ~ *world* el mundo entero; *Am.* F *made out of* ~ *cloth* enteramente imaginario; ~ *milk* leche *f* sin desnatar; 2. todo *m*; conjunto *m*; total *m*; totalidad *f*; *the* ~ *of London* todo Londres; *as a* ~ en su totalidad, en conjunto; *on the* ~ en general; '~·**'heart·ed** □ incondicional; *cien por cien*; '~·**'length** *portrait* de cuerpo entero; '~·**meal** de trigo entero; '~·**sale** 1. (*a.* ~ *trade*) venta *f* al (por) mayor; 2. al (por) mayor; *fig.* en masa; general; '**whole·sal·er** mayorista *m*; **wholesome** ['~səm] □ saludable, sano; apetitoso; '**whole·time** *v.* full-time.

whol·ly ['houlli] enteramente.

whom [hu:m] *acc. of* who.

whoop [hu:p] 1. alarido *m*, grito *m*; 2. gritar (fuertemente); *Am. sl.* ~ *it up* armar una gritería; **whoop·ee** ['wu:pi:] F: *make* ~ divertirse una barbaridad; **whoop·ing-cough** ['hu:piŋkɔf] tos *f* ferina, coqueluche *f*.

whop [wɔp] *sl.* pegar; cascar; '**whop·per** *sl.* enormidad *f*; (*lie*) mentirón *m*; '**whop·ping** *sl.* enorme, grandísimo.

whore [hɔ:] puta *f*.

whorl [wə:l] ⊕ espiral *f*; *zo.* espira *f*; ⚘ verticilo *m*.   [dano *m.*\
whor·tle·ber·ry ['wə:tlberi] arán-\

whose [hu:z] *genitive of* who: 1. cuyo; de quien; 2. ¿de quién?; **who·so·ev·er** [hu:sou'evə] quien(es)quiera que.

why [wai] 1. ¿por qué?; ¿para qué?; 2. vamos; pero; ¡hombre!; 3. *su.* porqué *m*.

wick [wik] mecha *f*.

wick·ed ['wikid] □ malo, malvado; inicuo; *co.* F horroroso; '**wick·ed·ness** maldad *f*.

wick·er ['wikə] (*attr.* de) mimbre *m or f*; '~·**work** 1. rejilla *f*; cestería *f*; 2. de mimbre.

wick·et ['wikit] postigo *m*, portillo *m*; *cricket:* (*stumps*) palos *m/pl.*; (*pitch*) terreno *m*.

wide [waid] 1. □ ancho; extenso; amplio; *difference* considerable; *v. mark;* *be 3 feet* ~ ser ancho de 3 pies, tener 3 pies de ancho; 2. *adv.* lejos; *v. awake;* ~ *open* abierto de par en par; *Am. sl. city* que tiene mano abierta para el juego; *far and* ~ por todas partes; '~·**an·gle** *phot.* de ángulo ancho; **wid·en** ['waidn] ensanchar(se); '**wide·ness** anchura *f*; '**wide·spread** extenso, muy difundido.

wid·ow ['widou] viuda f; **'wid·owed** viudo; be ~ enviudar; **'wid·ow·er** viudo m; **wid·ow·hood** ['~hud] viudez f.

width [widθ] anchura f; extensión f; (cloth) ancho m; 2 feet in ~ ancho de 2 pies.

wield [wi:ld] lit. manejar, empuñar; power ejercer; ~ a pen menear cálamo.

wife [waif] (pl. wives) mujer f, esposa f; **'wife·ly** de esposa.

wig [wig] peluca f; **'wig·ging** F peluca f.

wig·gle ['wigl] menear(se) rápidamente.

wight [wait] co. criatura f.

wig·wam ['wigwæm] tienda f de pieles rojas.

wild [waild] **1.** □ salvaje; ǂ silvestre; feroz; violento; weather tormentoso; child etc. desmandado, desgobernado; (rash, foolish) insensato, temerario; (frantic) frenético; F (angry) negro; muy enfadado; ~ beast fiera f; run ~ vivir desenfrenadamente; ǂ crecer libre; F be ~ about andar loco por; **2.** ~s pl. v. wilderness; **'wild·cat 1.** zo. gato m montés; Am. empresa f arriesgada; Am. pozo m de petróleo de exploración; **2.** fig. quimérico; arriesgado; indisciplinado; Am. ilícito; **wil·der·ness** ['wildənis] desierto m, yermo m; **wild·fire** ['waildfaiə]: spread like ~ propagarse como la pólvora; **'wild-goose chase** empresa f desatinada; **'wild·ness** ferocidad f; violencia f etc.

wiles [wailz] engaños m/pl., ardides m/pl., mañas f/pl.

wil·ful ['wilful] □ p. voluntarioso; act premeditado, intencionado.

wil·i·ness ['wailinis] astucia f.

will [wil] **1.** voluntad f; placer m; ⚖ testamente m; against one's ~ a desgana; at ~ a voluntad; with a ~ resueltamente; v. free-~; **2.** [irr.] v/aux. que forma el futuro etc.: he ~ come vendrá; I ~ do it sí que lo haré; **3.** querer; lograr por fuerza de voluntad; ⚖ legar.

will·ing ['wiliŋ] □ complaciente; gustoso; pred. be ~ to estar dispuesto a; ~ly de buena gana; **'will·ing·ness** buena voluntad f, complacencia f.

will-o'-the-wisp ['wiləðwisp] fuego m fatuo; fig. quimera f.

wil·low ['wilou] sauce m; **'wil·low·y** fig. esbelto, cimbreño.

will-pow·er ['wilpauə] fuerza f de voluntad.

wil·ly-nil·ly ['wili'nili] a la fuerza, quiera o no quiera.

wilt¹ [wilt] † tú harás etc.

wilt² [~] marchitar(se); fig. acobardarse; languidecer.

wil·y ['waili] □ astuto, mañoso.

wim·ple ['wimpl] griñón m.

win [win] **1.** [irr.] v/t. ganar; lograr; sympathy captar; metal arrancar; ⚒ sl. agenciarse; ~ over, ~ round conquistar; v/i. ganar; triunfar; ~ through to alcanzar; **2.** victoria f.

wince [wins] estremecerse, hacer una mueca de dolor.

winch [wintʃ] manubrio m, torno m.

wind¹ [wind, poet. a. waind] **1.** viento m; fig. (breath) aliento m; ✿ flatulencia f; ♪ instrumento m de viento; be in the ~ estar pendiente; get ~ of husmear (a. fig.); sl. get the ~ up encogérsele a uno el ombligo; sl. put the ~ up s.o. meterle a uno el ombligo para dentro; F raise the ~ dar un sablazo; conseguir dinero; throw to the ~s desechar; **2.** hunt. husmear; ✿ dejar sin aliento.

wind² [waind] [irr.] v/t. enrollar, envolver (a. ~ up); handle dar vueltas a; watch dar cuerda a; wool devanar, ovillar; horn sonar; ~ one's arms round rodear de los brazos; ~ up concluir; ✝ liquidar; v/i. serpentear; dar vueltas; ~ round etc. enroscarse; (re)torcerse.

wind... [wind]: **'~·bag** charlatán m; **'~·fall** fruta f caída; fig. golpe m de suerte inesperado; **'~·gauge** anemómetro m; manga f.

wind·ing ['waindiŋ] **1.** (handle) vuelta f; (watch) cuerda f; (road etc.) tortuosidad f; ✦ bobinado m, devanado m; **2.** serpentino; sinuoso; tortuoso; ~ staircase escalera f de caracol; **'~-sheet** mortaja f; **'~-up** conclusión f; ✝ liquidación f.

wind-in·stru·ment ['windinstrumənt] instrumento m de viento.

wind·jam·mer ['winddʒæmə] buque m de vela (grande y veloz).

wind·lass ['windləs] torno m.

wind·mill ['windmil] molino *m* (de viento); (*toy*) molinete *m*.

win·dow ['windou] ventana *f*; (*shop*-) escaparate *m*; ventanilla *f of vehicle*; '**~-dress·er** escaparatista *m/f*; '**~-dress·ing** decoración *f* de escaparates; *fig.* camuflaje *m*.

win·dow...: **~ en·ve·lope** sobre *m* de ventanilla; '**~-frame** marco *m* (de ventana); '**~-pane** cristal *m*; '**~-shade** *Am.* visillo *m*, transparente *m*; '**~-sill** alféizar *m*.

wind...: '**~-pipe** tráquea *f*; '**~-screen**, *Am.* '**~-shield** parabrisas *m*; **~ wiper** limpiaparabrisas *m*; '**~-tun·nel** túnel *m* aerodinámico.

wind·ward ['windwəd] **1.** de barlovento; **2.** (*to a*) barlovento *m*.

wind·y ['windi] ☐ ventoso; *day* de mucho viento; *place* expuesto al viento; *fig. speech* palabrero; **be ~** hacer viento; *sl.* pasar miedo.

wine [wain] vino *m*; '**~-glass** vaso *m* para vino; '**~-grow·er** viñador *m*; '**~-mer·chant** vinatero *m*; '**~-press** lagar *m*; '**~-skin** pellejo *m*, odre *m*.

wing [wiŋ] **1.** ala *f* (*a. pol.*, ✗, ▲); F brazo *m*; *mot.* guardabarros *m*; *sport:* exterior *m*; *thea.* **~s** *pl.* bastidores *m/pl.*; **be on the ~** estar volando; **take ~** irse volando; **2.** *v/t. bird* herir en el ala; *p.* herir en el brazo; **~ one's way** volar; *v/i.* volar; '**~-case**, '**~-sheath** *zo.* élitro *m*; '**~-chair** sillón *m* de orejas; **winged** [~ŋd] alado; '**wing·nut** tuerca *f* mariposa; '**wing·span**, '**wing·spread** envergadura *f* (de alas).

wink [wiŋk] **1.** guiño *m*; pestañeo *m*; F *have* (*or take*) 40 **~s** descabezar el sueño; F *not get a ~ of sleep* no pegar los ojos; F *tip the ~* advertir clandestinamente; **2.** *v/t. eye* guiñar; *v/i.* guiñar el ojo; parpadear, pestañear, (*light*) titilar; **~ at** guiñar el ojo a; *fig.* hacer la vista gorda a.

win·kle ['wiŋkl] **1.** bigarro *m*; **2.** F **~ out** hacer salir; sacar con dificultad.

win·ner ['winə] ganador (-a *f*) *m*, vencedor (-a *f*) *m*.

win·ning ['winiŋ] **1.** ☐ vencedor, victorioso; *shot etc.* decisivo; *ways* encantador, persuasivo; **2.** **~s** *pl.* ganancias *f/pl.*; '**~-post** poste *m* de llegada.

win·now ['winou] aventar; **~ing machine** aventadora *f*.

win·ter ['wintə] **1.** invierno *m*; *attr.* invernal, de invierno; **~ sports** *pl.* deportes *m/pl.* de invierno; **2.** invernar.

win·try ['wintri] invernal; *fig.* frío, glacial.

wipe [waip] **1.** enjugar; limpiar; **~ off** guitar frotando; borrar; **~ out** (*delete*) borrar, cancelar; (*destroy*) destruir, extirpar; aniqui ar; *debt* liquidar; *sl.* **~ the floor with** cascar; **2.** limpión *m*; limpiadura *f*; F golpe *m*.

wire ['waiə] **1.** alambre *m*; F telegrama *m*; *attr.* ... de alambre; *sl.* *pull* **~s** tocar resortes; tener un buen enchufe; **2.** *v/t. house* instalar el alambrado de; *fence* alambrar; F telegrafiar; *v/i.* F poner un telegrama; '**~-cut·ters** *pl.* cizalla *f*; '**~-gauge** calibre *m* para alambres; '**~-haired** de pelo áspero; '**wire·less 1.** radio *f*, radiorreceptor *m* (*a.* **~ set**); radiotelegrafía *f* (*a.* **~ telegraphy**); radiograma *m* (*a.* **~ message**); **2.** *attr.* radiofónico; **~ opera·tor** (radio)telegrafista *m*; **~ station** estación *f* radiotelegráfica, emisora *f*; **3.** transmitir por radio(telegrafía); '**wire·net·ting** red *f* de alambre; '**wire-pull·er** *sl.* enchufista *m*; '**wire-pull·ing** *sl.* empleo *m* de resortes.

wir·ing ['waiəriŋ] instalación *f* de alambres; alambrado *m*; **~** alambres *m/pl.* tensores; **~ diagram** esquema *m* del alambrado; '**wir·y** ☐ delgado pero fuerte; nervudo.

wis·dom ['wizdəm] sabiduría *f*; prudencia *f*; **~ tooth** muela *f* del juicio.

wise¹ [waiz] ☐ (*learned*) sabio; (*sensible etc.*) prudente; juicioso; acertado; *Am. sl.* **~ guy** sabelotodo *m*; *Am.* F **be ~ to** conocer el juego de; *Am.* F **get ~** caer en el chiste; *Am.* F **put a p. ~** ponerle a uno al tanto (*to, on* de).

wise² [~] † guisa *f*, modo *m*.

wise·a·cre ['waizeikə] sabihondo *m*; '**wise·crack** *Am.* **1.** cuchufleta *f*; **2.** cuchufletear.

wish [wiʃ] **1.** desear (*for acc.*; *to inf. inf.*); anhelar (*for acc.*); **~ good morning** dar los buenos días (*a*); I **~** I could *inf.* ¡ojalá pudiera! *inf.*; ~ *a p. well* desearle a uno mucha suerte; **2.** deseo *m* (*for de*; *to inf. de inf.*); anhelo *m*; *best* ~*es* enhorabuena *f*; *with best* ~*es* (*in letter*) saludos *m/pl.*; **wish-ful** ['~ful] □ deseoso (*to inf. de inf.*); ~ *thinking* espejismo *m*, ilusionismo *m*; **'wish(·ing)-bone** espoleta *f*.

wish-wash ['wiʃwɔʃ] F aguachirle *f*; **'wish·y-wash·y** F soso, insípido.

wisp [wisp] manojito *m of grass*; mechón *m of hair*; jirón *m of cloud*.

wist·ful ['wistful] □ pensativo; anhelante; melancólico.

wit [wit] **1.** ingenio *m* (*a. p.*); agudeza *f*; sal *f*; (*p.*) chistoso *m*; ~*s pl.* juicio *m*; inteligencia *f*; *be at one's* ~*'s end* estar para volverse loco; *have* (*or keep*) *one's* ~*s about one* tener ojo; *live by one's* ~*s* campar de golondro; *out of one's* ~*s* fuera de sí; **2.**: *to* ~ a saber.

witch [witʃ] bruja *f*, hechicera *f*; ~ *doctor* hechicero *m*; **'~·craft** brujería *f*; **'~·hunt** lucha *f* contra la subversión; *b.s.* persecución *f* (política).

with [wið] con; en compañía de; (*towards*) para con; de (*e.g., tremble with fear* temblar de miedo); *covered with* cubierto de; *the man with the grey suit* el del traje gris); a (*e. g., with all speed* a toda prisa); según (*e. g., it varies with the season* varía según la estación); sin (*e. g., with no trouble at all* sin dificultad alguna).

with·al [wi'ðɔːl] † además, también.

with·draw [wið'drɔː] [*irr.* (*draw*)] *v/t.* retirar; sacar; retractar; *v/i.* retirarse (*from* de); recogerse; *sport:* abandonar; **with'draw·al** retirada *f* (*a.* ✕, ✝); retiro *m* (*a.* ✝); *sport:* abandono *m*.

withe [wiθ] mimbre *m or f*.

with·er ['wiðə] (*a.* ~ *away*) *v/i.* marchitarse; *v/t.* marchitar; *fig.* aplastar, confundir; **'with·er·ing** □ abrasador; *look* lleno de desprecio.

with·ers ['wiðəz] *pl.* cruz *f*.

with·hold [wið'hould] [*irr.* (*hold*)] retener; negar (*from* a); *payment* suspender; *reason etc.* no revelar (*from* a); **with'in 1.** *adv. lit.* dentro; *from* ~ desde dentro; **2.** *prp.* dentro de; al alcance de (*a.* ~ *reach of*); ~ *call* al alcance de la voz; ~

doors dentro de la casa; ~ *an inch of fig.* a dos dedos de; ~ *a mile of* a poco menos de una milla de; **with-'out 1.** *adv. lit.* (a)fuera; *from* ~ desde fuera; **2.** *prp.* sin; *lit.* fuera de; *v. do*; **3.** *cj.* sin que; **with'stand** [*irr.* (*stand*)] resistir a, aguantar.

with·y ['wiði] mimbre *m or f*.

wit·less ['witlis] □ tonto, insensato.

wit·ness ['witnis] **1.** (*p.*) testigo *m/f*; testimonio *m*; *in* ~ *of* en fe de; *bear* ~ atestiguar (*to acc.*); **2.** presenciar; atestiguar (*to acc.*); *will etc.* firmar como testigo; **'~·stand** barra *f* (*or puesto m*) de los testigos.

wit·ti·cism ['witisizm] agudeza *f*, chiste *m*; **'wit·ti·ness** agudeza *f*, gracia *f*; **'wit·ting·ly** a sabiendas; **'wit·ty** □ ingenioso, chistoso, gracioso.

wives [waivz] *pl. of wife.*

wiz·ard ['wizəd] **1.** hechicero *m*, brujo *m*; F as *m*; **2.** *sl.* (*a.* **wiz** [wiz]) estupendo; mono.

wiz·en·(ed) ['wizn(d)] arrugado, apergaminado.

wo(a) [wou] ¡so!

woad [woud] ♀ hierba *f* pastel.

wob·ble ['wɔbl] bambolear, tambalearse; ⊕ oscilar; *fig.* vacilar.

wo(e) [wou] *lit. or co.* aflicción *f*, dolor *m*; ~ *is me!* ¡ay de mí!; **'~·be·gone** abatido, desconsolado; **wo(e)·ful** □ triste, afligido; lamentable.

woke [wouk] *pret. a. p.p. of wake²*.

wold [would] *approx.* páramo *m*, rasa *f* ondulada.

wolf [wulf] **1.** [*pl.* **wolves**] lobo (a *f*) *m*; *sl.* mujeriego *m*; *cry* ~ gritar ¡el lobo!; **2.** F zampar, engullir; **'wolf·ish** □ lobuno.

wolf·ram ['wulfrəm] wolfram *m*, volframio *m*.

wolves [wulvz] *pl. of wolf 1.*

wom·an ['wumən] (*pl.* **women** ['wimin]) **1.** mujer *f*; F criada *f*; *young* ~ joven *f*; **2.** femenino; de mujer; ~ *doctor* médica *f*; **'wom·an-hat·er** misógino *m*; **wom·an-hood** ['~hud] (*quality*) feminidad *f*; (*age*) edad *f* adulta; (*in general*) mujeres *f/pl.*, sexo *m* femenino; **'wom·an·ish** □ afeminado; mujeril; **'wom·an·kind** mujeres *f/pl.*, sexo *m* femenino; **'wom·an·like** mujeril; **'wom·an·ly** femenino, mujeril.

womb [wu:m] matriz *f*, útero *m*; *fig.* seno *m*.

wom·en ['wimin] *pl. of* woman; ~'s rights *pl.* derechos *m/pl.* de la mujer; ~'s team equipo *m* femenino; **wom·en·folk** ['~fouk] las mujeres.

won [wʌn] *pret. a. p.p. of* win 1.

won·der ['wʌndə] **1.** *(object)* maravilla *f*, prodigio *m*; *(feeling)* admiración *f*; *it is no ~ that* no es mucho que; *work ~s* hacer milagros; **2.** admirarse, maravillarse *(at* de); preguntarse *(if, whether* si); *I ~ if she'll come* ¿si vendrá?; **won·der·ful** ['~ful] □ maravilloso; **'won·der·ment** asombro *m*, admiración *f*; **'won·der-struck** pasmado.

won·drous ['wʌndrəs] □ *lit.* maravilloso.

won·ky ['wɔŋki] *sl.* poco firme; desvencijado.

won't [wount] = will not.

wont [wount] **1.** *pred.* acostumbrado; *be ~ to do* soler hacer; **2.** costumbre *f*; **'wont·ed** acostumbrado.

woo [wu:] *lit.* cortejar, galantear; *fig.* tratar de conquistar.

wood [wud] *(trees)* bosque *m*; *(material)* madera *f*; *(fire-)* leña *f*; *sport:* bola *f*; *♪* instrumento *m* de viento de madera; *~s pl.* bosque *m*; **~·bine**, **~·bind** ['~bain(d)] madreselva *f*; **'~·carv·ing** escultura *f* en madera; **'~·cock** chocha *f* perdiz; **'~·craft** destreza *f* en la montería; **'~·cut** grabado *m* en madera; **'~·cut·ter** leñador *m*; **'wood·ed** arbolado, enselvado; **'wood·en** □ de madera; *fig.* inexpresivo; rígido; **'wood-en·grav·ing** grabado *m* en madera.

wood...: **'~·land 1.** bosque *m*, arbolado *m*; monte *m*; **2.** selvático; **'~·lark** totovía *f*; **'~·louse** cochinilla *f*; **'~·man** leñador *m*; **'~·peck·er:** *green ~* pito *m* real; **'~·pi·geon** paloma *f* torcaz; **'~·pile** montón *m* de leña; **'~·pulp** pulpa *f* de madera; **'~·shav·ings** *pl.* virutas *f/pl.*; **'~·shed** leñera *f*; **'~·wind** *(or ~ instruments) pl.* instrumentos *m/pl.* de viento de madera; **'~·work** carpintería *f*, ebanistería *f*, *△* maderaje *m*; **'~·worm** carcoma *f*; **'wood·y** *tissue* leñoso; *country* arbolado.

woo·er ['wu:ə] pretendiente *m*.

woof [wu:f] trama *f*.

wool [wul] lana *f*; *attr.* de lana, lanar; *dyed in the ~ fig.* acérrimo, intransigente; **'~·gath·er·ing 1.** absorción *f*; *go ~* estar en Babia; **2.** absorto; **wool·(l)en 1.** de lana; lanero; **2.** *~s pl.* géneros *m/pl.* de lana; **'wool·(l)y 1.** lanudo, lanoso; *paint.* borroso; *ideas* vago, confuso; **2.** F woollies *pl.* ropa *f* de lana.

wool...: **'~·sack** saco *m* de lana *(silla del Gran Canciller en la Cámara de los Lores)*; **'~·sta·pler** lanero *m*.

Wop [wɔp] *sl.* italiano *m*.

word [wə:d] **1.** palabra *f*; vocablo *m*; *(news)* noticia *f*; *⚔* santo *m* y seña; *the ♀* el Verbo; *~s pl. fig.* palabras *f/pl.* mayores; *♪* letra *f*; *by ~ of mouth* de palabra; *~ for ~* palabra por palabra; *in other ~s* en otros términos; *my ~!* ¡caramba!; *be as good as one's ~* cumplir lo prometido; *not breathe a ~* no decir palabra; *eat one's ~s* desdecirse; *give one's ~* dar *(or* empeñar*)* su palabra; *have a ~ with* cambiar unas palabras con; *have ~s* reñir; *leave ~* dejar dicho; *send ~* mandar recado; *take a p. at his ~* cogerle a uno la palabra; *take my ~ for it* se lo aseguro; **2.** redactar; expresar; **'~·book** vocabulario *m*; **'word·i·ness** verbosidad *f*; **'word·ing** fraseología *f*, términos *m/pl.*; **'word-'per·fect** *thea.* que sabe perfectamente su papel.

word·y ['wə:di] □ verboso.

wore [wɔ:] *pret. of* wear 1.

work [wə:k] **1.** trabajo *m*; labor *f*; *(lit. etc.)* obra *f*; *~s pl. ⊕* fábrica *f*; *(mechanism)* mecanismo *m*; *(lit. etc.)* obras *f/pl.*; *public ~s pl.* obras *f/pl.* públicas; *~s council* consejo *m* de obreros; *at ~* trabajando; *be in ~* tener un empleo; *be out of ~* estar desempleado; *make short ~ of* concluir con toda rapidez; F comerse rápidamente; *put (or throw) out of ~* privar de trabajo; *set to ~* poner (se) a trabajar; **2.** *v/i.* trabajar *(at* en; *hard* mucho); *⊕* funcionar, marchar; obrar; *(remedy)* surtir efecto, ser eficaz; *~ loose* soltarse; *~ out* resultar; resolverse; *~ out at (cost)* llegar a; *v/t. p.* hacer trabajar; *⊕* manejar; hacer funcionar; *land* cultivar; *mine* explotar; *passage* pagar trabajando; *wonders etc.* hacer, efectuar; *wood* tallar; *sew.*

bordar; F conseguir, agenciarse; ~ in introducir; ~ off deshacerse de ... trabajando; ~ on influir, trabajar; ~ one's way abrirse camino; ~ out calcular; mine etc. agotar; ~ up business desarrollar; feeling excitar (into hasta); theme elaborar; ~ o.s. up exaltarse.

work·a·ble ['wə:kəbl] ⊏ practicable; factible; práctico; 'work·a·day de cada día; fig. prosaico; 'work·box neceser m de costura; 'work·day día m laborable; 'work·er trabajador (-a f) m; obrero (a f) m; operario (a f) m; zo. abeja f obrera; 'work·house asilo m de pobres; 'work·ing 1. funcionamiento m; explotación f; ✗ ~s pl. labores f/pl.; 2. obrero; de trabajo; in ~ order funcionando; ~ capital capital m de explotación; ~ class clase f obrera; ~ day (week-day) día m laborable; (number of hours) jornada f; ~ expenses m. gastos m/pl. de explotación; ~ man obrero m; ~ party comisión f de investigación. **work·man** ['wə:kmən] obrero m; trabajador m; operario m; '~·like bien ejecutado, competente; 'work·man·ship hechura f; confección f; arte m, artificio m.

work...: ~·out ['wə:kaut] Am. sport: entrenamiento m, ejercicio m; '~·room, '~·shop taller m; '~·shy perezoso.

world [wə:ld] mundo m; attr. mundial; fig. a ~ of la mar de; for all the ~ like (or as) (if) exactamente como (si); in the ~ eccl. en el siglo; bring into the ~ echar al mundo; come down in the ~ venir a menos; feel on top of the ~ estar como un reloj; see the ~ ver mundo; think the ~ of tener un altísimo concepto de; ~ champion campeón m mundial; ~ power potencia f mundial; Am. ⦵ Series Serie f Mundial; 'world·li·ness mundanería f.

world·ly ['wə:ldli] mundano; '~-'wis·dom mundología f (F), astucia f; '~-'wise que tiene mucho mundo; astuto.

world-wide ['wə:ld'waid] mundial, universal.

worm [wə:m] 1. gusano m; (earth-) lombriz f; fig. (p.) persona f vil; ⊕ filete m; ⊕ tornillo m sin fin; 2. fig. insinuarse (into en); ~

o.s. through etc. atravesar serpenteando; ~ a secret out of a p. arrancar mañosamente (or sonsacar) un secreto a una p.; '~-drive transmisión f por tornillo sin fin; '~-eat·en wood carcomido; cloth apolillado; '~-gear engranaje m de tornillo sin fin; = '~-wheel rueda f de tornillo sin fin; '~-wood ♣ ajenjo m; fig. amargura f; 'worm·y gusano m; carcomido.

worn [wɔ:n] p.p. of wear 1; '~-'out gastado; inservible; anticuado; be ~ (p.) estar rendido.

wor·ri·ment ['wʌrimənt] F inquietud f; 'wor·ry 1. inquietar(se), preocupar(se) (about, over por); molestar(se); (dog) pillar, morder sacudiendo; atacar; 2. inquietud f, preocupación f; cuidado m; molestia f.

worse [wə:s] 1. peor (a. ⚘); ~ and ~ cada vez peor; ~ than ever peor que nunca; so much the ~ tanto peor; the ~ for wear deteriorado; grow ~, make ~ empeorar; ~ luck! ¡por desgracia!; he is none the ~ for it no se ha hecho daño; no se ha perjudicado; 2. peor m; from bad to ~ de mal en peor; 'wors·en empeorar.

wor·ship ['wə:ʃip] 1. culto m; adoración f; oficio m; Your ⚘ (judge) señor juez; (mayor) señor alcalde; 2. adorar; venerar; wor·ship·ful ['~ful] in titles: excelente; 'wor·ship·(p)er adorador (-a f) m; devoto (a f) m.

worst [wə:st] 1. adj. a. adv. peor; 2. lo peor; at (the) ~ en el peor de los casos; do your ~! ¡haz todo lo que quieras!, ¡haga cuanto daño quiera!; get the ~ of it llevar la peor parte; if the ~ comes to the ~ si pasa lo peor; the ~ of it is (that) lo malo es que; 3. vencer.

wor·sted ['wustid] estambre m.

worth [wə:θ] 1. (worthy of) digno de; (equal to) equivalente a; be ~ valer; merecer; ~ reading que vale la pena de leerse; ~ seeing digno de verse; ~ a million fig. que vale un dineral; 2. valor m; valía f; mérito m; 'wor·thi·ness ['~ðinis] mérito m, merecimiento m; 'worth·less ['~θlis] ☐ sin valor; indigno; inútil; despreciable; 'worth·'while valioso, digno de atención *etc.*; *be* ~ valer la pena; **wor·thy** ['wɔːði] **1.** ⎯ digno (*of* de); meritorio; benemérito; *be* ~ *of* merecer *acc.*, ser digno de; **2.** dignidad *f*, notable *m*; *co.* personaje *m*.

would [wud] [*pret. of will*] *v/aux.* *que forma el condicional etc.*; ~ *that* ...! ¡ojalá (que)...!

would-be ['wudbi] supuesto; llamado; que presume de; aspirante a.

wouldn't ['wudnt] = *would not*.

wound¹ [wuːnd] **1.** herida *f*; **2.** herir; '**wound·ing** ⬚ *tone* hiriente.

wound² [waund] *pret. a. p.p. of* **wind².**

wove *pret.*, **wo·ven** ['wouv(n)] *p.p. of* **weave** 1.

wow [wau] *Am. sl.* exitazo *m*.

wrack¹ [ræk] ⚘ fuco *m*.

wrack² [~] = **rack².**

wraith [reiθ] fantasma *m*.

wran·gle ['ræŋgl] **1.** reñir indecorosamente (*over* a causa de); **2.** riña *f* indecorosa.

wrap [ræp] **1.** *v/t.* envolver (*a.* ~ *up*); *fig. be* ~*ped up in* estar absorto en; F *p.* estar prendado de; *v/i.*: ~ *up* arroparse, arrebujarse; **2.** bata *f*, abrigo *m*; '**wrap·per** envase *m*; (*postal*) faja *f*; '**wrap·ping** envase *m*, envoltura *f*; ~ *paper* papel *m* de envolver (*or* embalar).

wrath [rɔːθ] *lit. or co.* cólera *f*, ira *f*; **wrath·ful** ['~ful] ⬚ colérico, iracundo.

wreak [riːk] *lit. vengeance* tomar (*on* en); *wrath* descargar (*on* en); ~ *havoc* hacer estragos.

wreath [riːθ], *pl.* **wreaths** [~ðz] (*funeral*) corona *f*; guirnalda *f*; espiral *f*, penacho *m* (*of smoke*); **wreathe** [riːð] [*irr.*] *v/t.* enguirnaldar; ceñir; tejer; ~*d in smiles* muy risueño; *v/i.* enroscarse, formar espirales.

wreck [rek] **1.** ⚓ (*act*) naufragio *m*; (*ship*) buque *m* naufragado; *fig.* ruina *f*, destrucción *f*; F *he's a* ~ está hecho polvo; **2.** ⚓ hacer naufragar; 🚂 hacer descarrilar; *fig.* arruinar, acabar con; ⚓ *be* ~*ed* naufragar; '**wreck·age** ⚓ pecios *m/pl.*; restos *m/pl.*; escombros *m/pl. cf house etc.*; (*act*) naufragio *m* (*a. fig.*), ruina *f*; '**wreck·er** ⚓ raquero *m*; demoledor *m*; *Am.* 🚂 descarrilador *m*; '**wreck·ing**: ~ *service mot.* servicio *m* de auxilio.

wren [ren] chochón *m*.

wrench [rentʃ] **1.** arrancar; arrebatar (*from a p.* a una p.); torcer (*a.* 🦴); ~ *open* forzar; ~ *out* sacar violentamente; **2.** arranque *m*; 🦴 torcedura *f*; ⊕ llave *f* inglesa; *fig.* sacudida *f*, choque *m*; dolor *m*, momento *m* angustioso (de separación *etc.*).

wrest [rest] arrancar, arrebatar (*from* a); *fig.* sacar a duras penas.

wres·tle ['resl] **1.** *v/i.* luchar (*a. fig.*); *v/t.* luchar contra; **2.** = '**wres·tling** lucha *f* (libre).

wretch [retʃ] desgraciado (a *f*) *m*; *poor* ~ pobrecito *m*; *co.* (*little* ~) pícaro *m*.

wretch·ed ['retʃid] ⬚ miserable, desgraciado; *th.* pobre, mezquino; *taste etc.* pésimo; '**wretch·ed·ness** miseria *f*; vileza *f etc.*

wrick [rik] **1.** torcer; **2.** torcedura *f*.

wrig·gle ['rigl] menearse; culebrear; ~ *out of* escaparse mañosamente de; *fig.* zafarse de.

wring [riŋ] [*irr.*] *clothes* escurrir, exprimir el agua de; *hands* retorcer; *neck* torcer; *heart* acongojar; *money, truth* sacar (*or* arrancar) por fuerza (*from, out of* a); ~*ing wet* muy mojado; '**wring·er** secadora *f*, escurridor *m*.

wrin·kle¹ ['riŋkl] **1.** arruga *f*; **2.** arrugar(se); *brow* fruncir.

wrin·kle² [~] truco *m*; idea *f*.

wrist [rist] muñeca *f*; ~ *watch* reloj *m* de pulsera; **wrist·let** ['ristlit] pulsera *f*, brazalete *m*.

writ [rit] *mst* ⚖ orden *f*, mandato *m*, auto *m*; *Holy* ♀ Sagrada Escritura *f*; ~ *for an election* autorización *f* para celebrar elecciones; ~ *of attachment* orden *f* de detención; ~ *of execution* auto *m* de ejecución.

write [rait] [*irr.*] *v/t.* escribir; redactar; ~ *down* poner por escrito; ✝ bajar el precio de; ✝ reducir el valor nominal de; ~ *off debt* cancelar; F dar por perdido; ~ *out* copiar; (*in full*) escribir sin abreviar; ~ *up ledger etc.* poner al día; *fig.* escribir una crónica de; describir exageradamente; *thea.* dar bombo a; *v/i.* escribir; ~ *back* contestar; ~ *for* paper colaborar en; ~ *off* escribir con prontitud (*for* pidiendo); F *nothing to* ~ *home about* nada de particular; '~**-off** ✝ carga *f* por depreciación; F pérdida *f* total.

writ·er ['raitə] escritor (-a *f*) *m*, autor (-a *f*) *m*; *the (present)* ~ el que esto escribe; *Scot.* ~ *to the signet* notario *m*; ~'s *cramp* calambre *m* de los escribientes.

write-up ['rait'ʌp] F (*report*) crónica *f*; *b. s.* bombo *m*, valoración *f* excesiva.

writhe [raið] retorcerse, contorcerse, debatirse.

writ·ing ['raitiŋ] (*in general*) el escribir; ʹ(*hand-* etc.) escritura *f*, letra *f*; (*thing written, work*) escrito *m*; profesión *f* de autor; *in* ~ por escrito; *attr.* ... de escribir; '~-**case** recado *m* de escribir; '~-**desk** escritorio *m*; '~-**pad** taco *m* de papel, bloc *m*; '~-**pa·per** papel *m* de escribir.

writ·ten ['ritn] *p.p. of* write; *adj.* escrito.

wrong [rɔŋ] **1.** □ (*mistaken, false*) erróneo, incorrecto, equivocado; (*unfair*) injusto; (*wicked*) malo; inoportuno; impropio; *be* ~ (*p.*) no tener razón; equivocarse; *the* ~ *way* (*round*) al revés; *be the* ~ *side of 60* pasar ya de los 60; *there is something* ~ *with* algo le pasa a; F *what's* ~ *with...?* ¿qué le pasa a...?

what's ~ *in kissing?* ¿por qué no nos podemos besar?; *what's* ~ *in smoking?* por qué es pecado el fumar?; **2.** *adv.* mal; al revés; injustamente; *go* ~ funcionar mal; *fig.* extraviarse; **3.** mal *m*; injusticia *f*, entuerto *m*, agravio *m*; perjuicio *m*; *be in the* ~ no tener razón, equivocarse; *put a p. in the* ~ lograr que una p. parezca equivocada; echar la culpa a una p.; **4.** agraviar, ofender; ser injusto con; '~'**do·er** malhechor (-a *f*) *m*; '~'**do·ing** maldad *f*, perversidad *f*; **wrong·ful** ['~ful] □ injusto; ilegal; '**wrong'head·ed** □ obstinado, perversamente equivocado; '**wrong·ness** injusticia *f*; error *m*.

wrote [rout] *pret. of* write.

wroth [rouθ] † iracundo.

wrought [rɔːt] **1.** † *pret. a. p.p. of* work 2; *lit.* he ~ *great changes* llevó a cabo (*or* efectuó) grandes reformas; **2.** *adj.* ⊕ forjado, labrado; ~ *iron* hierro *m* forjado (*or* batido).

wrung [rʌŋ] *pret. a. p.p. of* wring.

wry [rai] □ torcido, tuerto; *fig.* pervertido; ~ *face* mueca *f*.

X

X [eks] Ⱥ *a. fig.* X.

X-ray ['eks'rei] **1.** F radiografía *f*; ~s *pl.* rayos *m*/*pl.* X; **2.** radiográfico; **3.** radiografiar.

xy·log·ra·pher [zai'lɔgrəfə] xiló-

grafo *m*; **xy·lo·graph·ic, xy·lo·graph·i·cal** [ˌ~lə'græfik(l)] xilográfico; **xy·log·ra·phy** [~'lɔgrəfi] xilografía *f*.

xy·lo·phone ['zailəfoun] xilófono *m*.

Y

yacht [jɔt] **1.** (*mst large*) yate *m*, (*small*) balandro *m*; **2.** pasear en yate; **'yacht·ing** paseo *m* en yate; regatas *f/pl*. de balandros; *attr.* de balandros; de balandristas; **'yachts·man** deportista *m* náutico; balandrista *m*.

ya·hoo [jə'hu:] patán *m*.

yam [jæm] batata *f*, ñame *m*.

yank¹ [jæŋk] F **1.** *mst* ~ out sacar de un tirón; **2.** tirón *m*.

Yank² [˷] *v.* Yankee.

Yan·kee ['jæŋki] F yanqui *adj. a. su. m*; ~ *Doodle canción nacional norte-americana*.

yap [jæp] **1.** dar ladridos agudos; F charlar neciamente; F protestar (neciamente); **2.** ladrido *m* agudo.

yard¹ [jɑ:d] yarda *f* (= *91,44 cm.*); *approx.* vara *f*; ⚓ verga *f*.

yard² [˷] corral *m*; patio *m*.

yard...: '~arm verga *f*; penol *m*; '~stick *fig.* criterio *m*, norma *f*.

yarn [jɑ:n] **1.** hilo *m*, hilaza *f*; F cuento *m* (inverosímil); *spin a* ~ = **2.** F contar cosas inverosímiles.

yar·row ['jærou] milenrama *f*.

yaw [jɔ:] **1.** ⚓ guiñada *f*; ✈ derrape *m*; **2.** ⚓ hacer una guiñada; ✈ derrapar.

yawl [jɔ:l] yola *f*.

yawn [jɔ:n] **1.** bostezar; *fig.* ~ing muy abierto; **2.** bostezo *m*.

ye [ji:, ji] † vosotros, vosotras.

yea [jei] † sí (*a. su. m*); sin duda.

year [jə:, jiə] año *m*; ~ *of grace* año *m* de gracia; '~book anuario *m*; **'year·ling** primal *adj. a. su. m* (-a*f*); **'year·ly** anual(mente *adv.*).

yearn [jə:n] anhelar, añorar, ansiar (*after, for acc.*); suspirar (*for* por); ~ *to* anhelar *inf.*; **'yearn·ing** anhelo *m*, añoranza *f*.

yeast [ji:st] levadura *f*; **'yeast·y** □ espumoso; *fig.* frívolo.

yegg(·man) *Am. sl.* ladrón *m* (de cajas fuertes).

yell [jel] **1.** gritar; chillar; decir a gritos; **2.** grito *m*, alarido *m*; chillido *m*.

yel·low ['jelou] **1.** amarillo; F (*cow-*ardly*) blanco; ~ *fever*, F ♀ *Jack* fiebre *f* amarilla; ~ *press* periódicos *m/pl.* sensacionales; **2.** amarillo *m*; **3.** *v/i.* amarillecer, amarillear; *v/t.* volver amarillo; '~back F novelucha *f*; '~ham·mer escribano *m* cerillo; **'yel·low·ish** amarillento.

yelp [jelp] **1.** gañido *m*; **2.** gañir.

yen [jen] *Am. sl.* deseo *m* vivo.

yeo·man ['joumən] *approx.* labrador *m* rico, pequeño terrateniente *m*; ~ *of the guard* alabardero *m* de la Casa Real; **'yeo·man·ry** *approx.* clase *f* de los labradores ricos; ✕ caballería *f* voluntaria.

yep [jep] *Am.* F sí.

yes [jes] sí (*a. su. m*); ~-man ['~mæn] *sl.* pelotillero *m*.

yes·ter·day ['jestədi] ayer (*a. su. m*); ~ *afternoon* ayer por la tarde; *the day before* ~ anteayer; **'yes·ter'year** *poet.* antaño (*a. su. m*).

yet [jet] **1.** *adv.* todavía, aún; *as* ~ hasta ahora; *not* ~ todavía no; **2.** *cj.* sin embargo; con todo.

yew [ju:] tejo *m*.

yield [ji:ld] **1.** *v/t. crop, result* producir, dar (de sí); *profit* rendir; (*give up*) entregar; *v/i.* ✎ *etc.* producir, rendir; (*surrender*) rendirse, someterse; ceder; consentir (*to* en); **2.** ✎ cosecha *f*; producción *f*; † rendimiento *m*, rédito *m* on *capital*; **'yield·ing** □ flexible (*a. fig.*); *fig.* complaciente, dócil.

yo·del, yo·dle ['joudl] **1.** canto *m* a la tirolesa; **2.** cantar a la tirolesa.

yoke [jouk] **1.** ✎ yunta *f*; *fig.* yugo *m*; ⊕ horquilla *f*; (*shoulder-*) balancín *m*; *sew.* canesú *m*; **2.** ✎ uncir; acoplar; *fig.* unir.

yo·kel ['joukl] F palurdo *m*, patán *m*.

yolk [jouk] yema *f* (de huevo).

yon [jɔn], **yon·der** ['jɔndə] † *or prov.* **1.** aquel; **2.** allá, a lo lejos.

yore [jɔ:] *lit.:* of ~ antaño, en otro tiempo.

you [ju:] **1.** *familiar, with second p. verb:* (*nominative*) *sg.* tú, *pl.* vosotros, vosotras; (*acc. dat.*) *sg.* te, *pl.* os; (*after prp.*) *sg.* ti, *pl.* vosotros, vosotras; *with* ~ (*sg. reflexive*) contigo; **2.** *formal, with third p. verb*: (*nominative*) *sg.* usted, *pl.* ustedes; (*acc. dat.*) *sg.* le, la, *pl.* les; (*after prp.*) *sg.* usted, *pl.* ustedes; *with* ~ (*sg. a. pl. reflexive*) consigo; **3.** *when impersonal, often translated by reflexive*: ~ *can see it from here* se ve desde aquí; *you can't smoke here* no se puede fumar aquí; *also by* uno: *you never know whether...* uno nunca sabe si...

young [jʌŋ] **1.** joven; *brother etc.* menor; ~ *man* joven *m*; **2.** *zo.* cría *f*, hijuelos *m*/*pl.*; *the* ~ *pl.* los jóvenes, la juventud; *with* ~ encinta; **'young·ish** bastante joven; **'young·ster** joven *m/f*, jovencito (*a f*) *m*.

your [jɔː, juə, jə] tu(s); vuestro(s), vuestra(s); su(s); **yours** [jɔːz, juəz] (el) tuyo, (la) tuya *etc.*; (el) vuestro, (la) vuestra *etc.*; (el) suyo, (la) suya *etc.*; (*ending letter*) cordialmente; **your'self,** *pl.* **your·selves** [~'selvz] (*subject*) tú mismo, vosotros mismos; usted(es) mismo(s); *acc., dat.* te, os, se; (*after prp.*) ti, vosotros, sí (mismo[s]); *f forms have* a(s).

youth [juːθ], *pl.* **youths** [juːðz] juventud *f*; (*p.*) joven *m*, mozo *m*; ~ *hostel* albergue *m* para jóvenes; **youth·ful** ['~ful] □ juvenil; joven; **'youth·ful·ness** juventud *f*; vigor *m*, espíritu *m* juvenil.

Yu·go·slav ['juːgouslaːv] yugo(e)slavo *adj. a. su. m* (*a f*).

Yule [juːl], **Yule·tide** ['juːltaid] *lit.* Navidad *f*; ~ *log* leño *m* de Navidad.

Z

zeal [ziːl] celo *m*, entusiasmo *m*; **zeal·ot** ['zelət] fanático *m*; **'zeal·ot·ry** fanatismo *m*; **'zeal·ous** □ celoso (*for* de); entusiasta (*for* de); apasionado (*for* por).

ze·bra ['ziːbrə] cebra *f*.

ze·bu ['ziːbuː] cebú *m*.

ze·nith ['zeniθ] cenit *m*; *fig.* apogeo *m*.

zeph·yr ['zefə] céfiro *m* (*a.* ✝ *cloth*).

ze·ro ['ziərou] **1.** cero *m*; **2.** nulo; ~ *hour* ✗ hora *f* de ataque.

zest [zest] gusto *m*, entusiasmo *m* (*for* por).

zig·zag ['zigzæg] **1.** zigzag *m*; **2.** (en) zigzag; **3.** zigzaguear, hacer eses.

zinc [ziŋk] **1.** cinc *m*; **2.** cubrir con cinc.

Zi·on·ism ['zaiənizm] sionismo *m*; **'Zi·on·ist** sionista *adj. a. su. m.*

zip [zip] **1.** pasar silbando; **2.** silbido *m*, zumbido *m*; F energía *f*; ~ *fastener* = **'zip·per** (cierre *m* de) cremallera *f*, cierre *m* relámpago; **'zip·py** F enérgico; rápido.

zith·er ['ziθə] cítara *f*.

zo·di·ac ['zoudiæk] zodíaco *m*; **zo·di·a·cal** [zou'daiəkl] zodiacal.

zon·al ['zounl] □ zonal; **zone** [zoun] zona *f*.

Zoo [zuː] F jardín *m* (*or* parque *m*) zoológico; casa *f* de fieras.

zo·o·log·i·cal [zouə'lɔdʒikl] □ zoológico; ~ [zu'lɔdʒikl] *gardens pl. v.* Zoo; **zo·ol·o·gist** [zou'ɔlədʒist] zoólogo *m*; **zo'ol·o·gy** zoología *f*.

zoom [zuːm] F **1.** zumbar; ✈ empinarse; **2.** zumbido *m*; ✈ empinadura *f*.

Zu·lu ['zuːluː] zulú *m*.

zy·mot·ic [zai'mɔtik] ☷ cimótico.

Nombres propios*
Proper Names **

A

Aa·chen ['ɑːxən] Aquisgrán.
Ab·er·deen [æbə'diːn] *Ciudad de Escocia.*
A·bra·ham ['eibrəhæm] Abraham, Abrahán.
Ab·ys·sin·i·a [æbi'sinjə] Abisinia *f.*
A·chil·les [ə'kiliːz] Aquiles.
Ad·am ['ædəm] Adán.
Ad·e·laide ['ædəleid] *Ciudad de Australia.*
A·den ['eidn] Adén.
Ad·olf ['ædɔlf], **A·dol·phus** [ə'dɔlfəs] Adolfo.
A·dri·at·ic (**Sea**) [eidri'ætik ('siː)] (Mar *m*) Adriático *m.*
Ae·ge·an Sea [iː'dʒiːən'siː] Mar *m* Egeo.
Ae·ne·as [iː'niːæs] Eneas.
Aes·chy·lus ['iːskiləs] Esquilo.
Ae·sop ['iːsɔp] Esopo.
Af·ghan·i·stan [æf'gænistæn] Afganistán *m.*
Af·ri·ca ['æfrikə] Africa *f.*
Ag·nes ['ægnis] Inés.
Aix-la-Chap·elle ['eiksla:ʃə'pel] Aquisgrán.
A·jax ['eidʒæks] Ayax.
Al·a·bam·a [ælə'bɑːmə, *Am.* ælə'bæmə] *Estado de EE.UU.*
A·lad·din [ə'lædin] Aladino.
Al·am·o ['æləmou] *Misión del Alamo, en la ciudad de San Antonio, Tejas (tomada en 1836 por Méjico).*
A·las·ka [ə'læskə] *Estado de EE.UU. al oeste del Canadá.*
Al·ba·ni·a [æl'beinjə] Albania *f.*
Al·bert ['ælbət] Alberto.
Al·ber·ta [æl'bəːtə] *Provincia del Canadá.*
Al·bi·on ['ælbjən] *poet.* Albión *f.*
Al·der·ney ['ɔːldəni] 1. *Isla británica de las Islas Normandas;* 2. *Raza bovina.*

A·lec *nombre cariñoso de Alexander; smart* ~ sabelotodo *m.*
Al·ex·an·der [ælig'zaːndə] Alejandro; ~ the Great Alejandro Magno.
Al·ex·an·dri·a [ælig'zaːndriə] Alejandría.
Al·fred ['ælfrid] Alfredo.
Al·ge·ri·a [æl'dʒiəriə] Argelia *f.*
Al·giers [æl'dʒiəz] Argel.
Al·ice ['ælis] Alicia.
Alps [ælps] *pl.* Alpes *m/pl.*
Al·sace ['ælsæs] Alsacia *f.*
Al·sace-Lor·raine ['ælsæslɔ'rein] Alsacia-Lorena *f.*
Am·a·zon (*river*) ['æməzn] Amazonas *m.*
A·me·lia [ə'miːljə] Amalia.
A·mer·i·ca [ə'merikə] América *f.*
A·nac·re·on [ə'nækriːən] Anacreonte. [lucía *f.*]
An·da·lu·sia [ændə'luːsjə] Anda-]
An·des ['ændiːz] *pl.* Andes *m/pl.*
An·drew ['ændruː] Andrés.
An·gle·sey ['æŋglsi] *Condado galés.*
An·gou·lême ['ɑːguː'leːm] Angulema.
An·jou ['ɑː'ʒuː] Anjeo *m.*
Ann(e) [æn] Ana; ~ Boleyn Ana Bolena.
An·nap·o·lis [ə'næpəlis] *Capital del Estado norteamericano de Maryland. Sede de la Academia de Marina.*
An·tho·ny ['æntəni] Antonio.
An·til·les [æn'tiliːz] *pl.* Antillas *f/pl.*
An·ti·och ['æntiɔk] Antioquía.
Ant·werp ['æntwəːp] Amberes.
Ap·pa·lach·i·ans [æpə'leitʃiənz] *pl.* Montes *m/pl.* Apalaches.
Ap·pen·ines ['æpenainz] *pl.* Apeninos *m/pl.*
A·pu·le·ius [æp'juːleiəs] Apuleyo.
A·qui·nas [ə'kwainəs] Aquino.
A·ra·bia [ə'reibjə] Arabia *f.*
A·ra·gon ['ærəgən] Aragón *m.*

** This list is the work of the editorial staff of the publishers.

* Esta lista es obra de la redacciòn de la casa editora.

Ar·ca·dy ['ɑ:kədi] Arcadia *f.*

Ar·chi·me·des [ɑ:ki'mi:di:z] Arquímedes.

Ar·dennes [ɑ:'den] Ardenas *f/pl.*

Ar·gen·ti·na [ɑ:dʒən'ti:nə] la Argentina.

Ar·gen·tine ['ɑ:dʒəntain]: the ~ la Argentina.

Ar·gyll·shire [ɑ:'gailʃiə] *Condado escocés.*

Ar·is·tot·le ['æristɔtl] Aristóteles.

Ar·is·to·phan·es [æris'tɔfəni:z] Aristófanes.

Ar·i·zo·na [æri'zounə] *Estado de EE.UU.*

Ar·kan·sas 1. ['ɑ:kənsɔ:] *Estado de EE.UU.;* **2.** [ɑ:'kænsəs] *Río de EE.UU.*

Arles [ɑ:l] Arlés.

Ar·me·ni·a [ɑ:'mi:njə] Armenia *f.*

Ar·thur ['ɑ:θə] Arturo; *King* ~ El Rey Artús (*or* Arturo).

As·cot ['æskət] *Pueblo de Inglaterra con hipódromo de fama.*

A·sia ['eiʃə] Asia *f*; ~ *Minor* Asia *f* Menor.

As·syr·i·a [ə'siriə] Asiria *f.*

A·sun·ción [ɑ:su:n'sjɔn] *Capital del Paraguay.*

Ath·ens ['æθinz] Atenas.

At·kins ['ætkinz]: *Tommy* ~ *El soldado raso inglés.*

At·lan·tic (O·cean) [ət'læntik ('ouʃn)] (Océano *m*) Atlántico *m.*

Auck·land ['ɔ:klənd] *Puerto de Nueva Zelanda.*

Au·gus·tine [ɔ:'gʌstin] Agustín.

Au·gus·tus [ɔ:'gʌstəs] Augusto.

Aus·tra·lia [ɔ:s'treiljə] Australia *f.*

Aus·tri·a ['ɔ:striə] Austria *f.*

Au·vergne [ou'veən] Auvernia *f.*

A·vi·gnon ['ævinjɔ] Aviñón.

A·von ['eivən, 'ævən] *Río de Inglaterra.*

Ayr·shire ['ɛəʃiə] *Condado escocés.*

A·zores [ə'zɔ:z] *pl.* Azores *f/pl.*

B

Bab·y·lon ['bæbilən] Babilonia *f.*

Bac·chus ['bækəs] Baco.

Ba·ha·mas [bə'hɑ:məz] *pl.* Islas *f/pl.* ▸ Bahama, las Bahamas.

Bâle [bɑ:l] Basilea.

Ba·le·ar·ic Isles [bæli'ærik'ailz] *pl.* Islas *f/pl.* Baleares.

Bal·kans ['bɔ:lkənz] Balcanes *m/pl.*

Bal·tic Sea ['bɔ:ltik'si:] Mar *m* Báltico.

Bal·ti·more ['bɔ:ltimɔ:] *Puerto en la costa oriental de EE.UU.*

Bar·thol·o·mew [bɑ:'θɔləmju:] Bartolomé.

Basle [bɑ:l] Basilea.

Basque Coun·try ['bɑ:sk'kʌntri] País *m* Vasco.

Basque Pro·vin·ces ['bɑ:sk'prɔvinsiz] Las Vascongadas.

Ba·var·i·a [bə'veəriə] Baviera *f.*

Ba·yonne [bai'jɔn] Bayona.

Be·a·trice ['biətris] Beatriz.

Bede [bi:d] Beda.

Bed·ford·shire ['bədfədʃiə] *Condado inglés.*

Be·el·ze·bub [bei'elzibʌb] Belcebú.

Bel·fast ['belfɑ:st] *Capital de Irlanda del Norte.*

Bel·gium ['beldʒəm] Bélgica *f.*

Bel·grade [bel'greid] Belgrado.

Ben [ben] *nombre cariñoso de Benjamin.*

Ben·e·dict ['benidikt] Benito; (*pope*) Benedicto.

Ben·gal [beŋ'gɔ:l] Bengala *f.*

Ben·ja·min ['bendʒəmin] Benjamín.

Ben Ne·vis [ben'nevis] *Pico más alto de Gran Bretaña (1343 m).*

Ber·lin [bə:'lin] Berlín.

Ber·mu·da [bə:'mju:də] Islas *f/pl.* Bermudas.

Ber·nard ['bə:nəd] Bernardo.

Berne [bə:n] Berna. [belita.}

Bess, Bessie, Bessy ['bes(i)] Isa-}

Beth·le·hem ['beθli:hem] Belén.

Bet·ty ['beti] Isabelita.

Bill, Bil·ly ['bil(i)] *nombre cariñoso de William.*

Bir·ming·ham ['bə:miŋəm] *Gran ciudad industrial de Inglaterra; Ciudad de Alabama.*

Bis·cay ['biskei]: *Bay of* ~ Golfo *m* de Vizcaya.

Black Sea ['blæk'si:] Mar *m* Negro.

Blue Beard ['blu:biəd] Barba Azul *m.*

Bob(·by) ['bɔb(i)] *nombre cariñoso de Robert.*

Boc·cac·cio [bɔ'kɑ:tʃiou] Bocacio.

Boer War ['bɔ: 'wɔ:] Guerra *f* Boer, Guerra *f* del Transvaal.

Bo·go·tá [bɔgou'tɑ:; bougə~] *Capital de Columbia.*

Bo·he·mi·a [bou'hi:mjə] Bohemia *f.*

Bo·liv·i·a [bə'liviə] Bolivia *f.*

Bom·bay [bɔm'bei] *Puerto de la India.*

Bor·deaux [bɔ:'dou] Burdeos.

Bosch [bɔʃ] El Bosco.

Bos·phor·us ['bɔsfərəs] Bósforo *m*.

Bos·ton ['bɔstən] *Ciudad de EE.UU. con la Universidad de Harvard en el barrio de Cambridge.*

Bour·bon ['buːbən] Borbón.

Bra·si·lia [brə'ziliə] *Capital del Brasil.*

Bra·zil [brə'zil] El Brasil.

Bridg·et ['bridʒit] Brígida.

Brigh·ton ['braitn] *Ciudad en el sur de Inglaterra.*

Bris·tol ['bristl] *Puerto y ciudad industrial en el suroeste de Inglaterra.*

Bri·tain ['britən] Gran Bretaña *f*.

Brit·ish Isles ['britiʃ'ailz] Islas *f/pl.* Británicas.

Brit·ta·ny ['britəni] Bretaña *f*.

Broad·way ['brɔːdwei] *Avenida de Nueva York con centro teatral, bares de noche etc.*

Brook·lyn ['bruklin] *Barrio de Nueva York.*

Bruges [bruːʒ] Brujas.

Brus·sels ['brʌslz] Bruselas.

Brut·us ['bruːtəs] Bruto.

Buck·ing·ham ['bʌkiŋəm], **Bucking·ham·shire** ['~ʃiə] *Condado inglés.*

Bud·dha ['bʌdə] Buda.

Bue·nos Ai·res ['bweinəs 'ai(ə)riz] *Capital de la Argentina.*

Bul·gar·i·a [bʌl'gɛəriə] Bulgaria *f*.

Bur·gun·dy ['bəːgəndi] Borgoña *f*.

Bur·ma ['bəːmə] Birmania *f*.

By·zan·ti·um [bai'zæntiəm] Bizancio.

C

Cae·sar ['siːzə] César.

Cain [kein] Caín; F *raise* ~ armar la gorda.

Cal·cut·ta [kæl'kʌtə] Calcuta.

Cal·i·for·nia [kæli'fɔːnjə] *Estado de EE.UU.*

Cal·vin ['kælvin] Calvino.

Cam·bridge ['keimbridʒ] *Ciudad universitaria inglesa;* v. Boston.

Ca·me·roons [kæmə'ruːnz] *pl.* Camerón *m*.

Can·a·da ['kænədə] El Canadá.

Can·ar·y Isles [kə'nɛəri'ailz] *pl.* Islas *f/pl.* Canarias.

Can·ter·bur·y ['kæntəbəri] Cantórbery.

Cape Horn [keip'hɔːn] Cabo *m* de Hornos.

Cape of Good Hope ['keipəvgud-'houp] Cabo *m* de Buena Esperanza.

Cape Verde Islands ['keip'vəːd-'ailəndz] *pl.* Islas *f/pl.* de Cabo Verde.

Ca·ra·cas [kə'rækəs] *Capital de Venezuela.*

Car·diff ['kaːdif] *Puerto en el sudeste de Gales (Gran Bretaña).*

Car·di·gan·shire ['kaːdiɡənʃiə] *Condado galés.*

Ca·rib·be·an (Sea) [kæri'biːən ('siː)] Mar *m* Caribe.

Car·mar·then·shire [kə'maːðənʃiə] *Condado galés.*

Car·nar·von·shire [kə'naːvənʃiə] *Condado galés.*

Car·pa·thi·ans [kaː'peiθjənz] *pl.* Montes *m/pl.* Cárpatos.

Car·thage ['kaːθidʒ] Cartago.

Cas·pi·an Sea ['kæspiən'siː] Mar *m* Caspio.

Cas·san·dra [kə'sændrə] Casandra.

Cas·si·us ['kæsiəs] Casio.

Cas·tile [kæs'tiːl] Castilla *f*.

Ca·ta·lo·ni·a [kætə'louniə] Cataluña *f*.

Cath·e·rine, Cath·a·rine ['kæθərin] Catalina.

Ca·to ['keitou] Catón.

Ca·tul·lus [kə'tʌləs] Catulo.

Cau·cas·us ['kɔːkəsəs] Cáucaso *m*.

Cec·i·ly ['sisili] Cecilia.

Cey·lon [si'lɔn] Ceilán *m*.

Cham·pagne [ʃæm'pein] Champaña *f*.

Chan·nel Isles ['tʃænəl'ailz] *pl.* Islas *f/pl.* Normandas. [magno.]

Char·le·magne ['ʃaːləmein] Carlo-

Charles [tʃaːlz] Carlos.

Char·lie ['tʃaːli] Carlitos.

Char·lotte ['ʃaːlət] Carlota.

Chesh·ire ['tʃeʃə] *Condado inglés.*

Chi·ca·go [ʃi'kaːgou] *Ciudad norteamericana, situada en el medio oeste de EE.UU.*

Chil·e, Chil·i ['tʃili] Chile *m*.

Chi·na ['tʃainə] China *f*.

Christ [kraist] Cristo.

Chris·to·pher ['kristəfə] Cristóbal.

Ci·ce·ro ['sisərou] Cicerón.

Cin·cin·na·ti [sinsi'næti] *Ciudad de EE.UU., a orillas del río Ohio.*

Cin·der·el·la [sində'relə] La Cenicienta.

Clem·ent ['klemənt] Clemente.

Cleve·land ['kliːvlənd] *Ciudad industrial y de comercio de EE.UU., puerto del Lago Erie.*

Co·logne [kə'loun] Colonia.

Col·o·ra·do [kɔləˈrɑːdou] *Nombre de dos ríos y de un estado de EE.UU.*

Co·lom·bi·a [kəˈlʌmbiə] Colámbia *f.*

Co·lum·bi·a [kəˈlʌmbiə] *Capital del estado norteamericano de Carolina del Sur.*

Co·lum·bus [kəˈlʌmbəs] Colón.

Con·fu·cius [kənˈfjuːʃəs] Confucio.

Con·go [ˈkɔŋgou] El Congo.

Con·nect·i·cut [kəˈnetikət] *Río y estado de EE.UU.*

Con·stance [ˈkɔnstəns] Constanza.

Con·stan·ti·no·ple [kɔnstænti-ˈnoupl] Constantinopla.

Co·pen·ha·gen [koupnˈheign] Copenhague.

Cor·do·va [ˈkɔːdəvə] Córdoba.

Cor·inth [ˈkɔrinθ] Corinto.

Corn·wall [ˈkɔːnwəl] Cornualles *m.*

Cor·si·ca [ˈkɔːsikə] Córcega *f.*

Co·run·na [kəˈrʌnə] La Coruña.

Co·sta Ri·ca [ˈkɔstə ˈriːkə] Costa Rica *f.*

Cov·en·try [ˈkɔvəntri] *Ciudad industrial de Inglaterra.*

Crete [ˈkriːt] Creta *f.*

Croe·sus [ˈkriːsəs] Creso.

Cu·ba [ˈkjuːbə] Cuba *f.*

Cu·pid [ˈkjuːpid] Cupido.

Cyc·lops [ˈsaiklɔps] Cíclope *m.*

Cyp·rus [ˈsaiprəs] Chipre *f.*

Czech·o·slo·va·ki·a [ˈtʃekouslou-ˈvækiə] Checoslovaquia *f.*

D

Dal·ma·tia [dælˈmeiʃə] Dalmacia *f.*

Da·mas·cus [dəˈmæskəs] Damasco.

Dam·o·cles [ˈdæməkliːz] Dámocles *f.*

Dan [daen] *nombre cariñoso de Daniel.*

Da·niel [ˈdænjəl] Daniel.

Da·nube [ˈdænjuːb] Danubio *m.*

Daph·ne [ˈdæfni] Dafne.

Dar·by and Joan [ˈdɑːbiəndˈdʒoun] *el matrimonio ideal de personas ya de edad, que siguen viviendo en el mayor contento.*

Dar·da·nelles [dɑːdəˈnelz] *pl.:* the ∼ los Dardanelos.

Da·ri·us [dəˈraiəs] Darío.

David [ˈdeivid] David.

Dead Sea [ˈdedˈsiː] Mar *m* Muerto.

Del·a·ware [ˈdeləweə] *Río y estado de EE.UU., nombre de una tribu de los indios norteamericanos.*

Del·hi [ˈdeli] *Ciudad de la India.*

Del·phi [ˈdelfai] Delfos.

De·mos·the·nes [diˈmɔsθəniːz] Demóstenes.

Den·mark [ˈdenmɑːk] Dinamarca *f.*

Der·by [ˈdɑːbi] *Ciudad industrial de Inglaterra y capital del condado de Derbyshire.*

Der·by·shire [ˈdɑːbiʃiə] *Condado inglés.*

De·troit [dəˈtrɔit] *Ciudad industrial del Estado de Michigan (EE.UU.).*

Dev·on·shire [ˈdevnʃiə] *Condado inglés.*

Di·a·na [daiˈænə] Diana.

Dick [dik] *nombre cariñoso de Richard.*

Dix·ie [ˈdiksi] **1.** *El Sur de EE.UU.;* **2.** *Título de una canción famosa.*

Do·mi·ni·can Re·pub·lic [dəˈminikənriˈpʌblik] República *f* Dominicana.

Do·mi·tian [dəˈmiʃən] Domiciano.

Don Quix·ote [dɔnˈkwiksət] Don Quijote.

Do·ro·thy [ˈdɔrəθi] Dorotea.

Do·ver [ˈdouvə] *Puerto en el sur de Inglaterra.*

Down·ing Street [ˈdauniŋˈstriːt] *Calle de Londres con la sede del Primer Ministro; fig. el Gobierno de Gran Bretaña.*

Dres·den [ˈdrezdən] Dresde.

Dub·lin [ˈdʌblin] Dublín *(Capital de Irlanda).*

Dun·kirk [dʌnˈkəːk] Dunquerque.

Dü·rer [ˈdjuərə] Durero.

Dur·ham [ˈdʌrəm] *Condado inglés.*

E

East [iːst] Oriente *m;* Far ∼ Extremo Oriente *m;* Middle ∼ Oriente *m* Medio; Near ∼ Próximo Oriente *m.*

East In·dies [ˈiːstˈindiz] *pl.* Indias *f/pl.* Orientales.

Ed(·die) [ˈed(i)] *nombre cariñoso de Edward.*

E·den [ˈiːdn] Edén *m.*

Ed·in·burgh [ˈedinbərə] Edimburgo *(Capital de Escocia).*

Ed·ward [ˈedwəd] Eduardo.

E·gypt [ˈiːdʒipt] Egipto *m.*

Ei·re [ˈɛərə] *Nombre de Irlanda (desde 1937 hasta 1949).*

E·lea·nor [ˈelənə] Leonor.

E·li·za·beth [iˈlizəbəθ] Isabel.

E·ly·si·um [iˈliziəm] Elíseo *m.*

El Sal·va·dor [el sælvədɔː] El Salvador.

E·m(m)a·nu·el [iˈmænjuəl] Manuel.

E·mi·ly [ˈemili] Emilia.

Eng·land [ˈiŋglənd] Inglaterra *f.*

Eng·lish Chan·nel ['iŋgliʃ'tʃaenəl] Canal *m* de la Mancha.

Ep·som ['epsəm] *Pueblo inglés en el condado de Surrey donde se verifica una célebre carrera de caballos.*

E·ras·mus [i'ræzməs] Erasmo.

Er·nest ['ə:nist] Ernesto.

Es·sex ['esiks] *Condado en el sudeste de Inglaterra.*

E·thi·o·pi·a [i:θi'oupiə] Etiopía *f.*

E·ton ['i:tn] *Pueblo inglés con colegio del mismo nombre.*

Eu·clid ['ju:klid] Euclides.

Eu·gene ['ju:dʒi:n] Eugenio.

Eu·phra·tes [ju'freiti:z] Eufrates *m.*

Eur·i·pi·des [ju'ripidi:z] Eurípides.

Eu·rope ['juərəp] Europa *f.*

Eur·y·di·ce [ju'ridisi] Eurídice.

Eve [i:v] Eva.

F

Falk·land Isles ['fɔ:klənd 'ailz] Islas *f/pl.* Malvinas.

Faust [faust] Fausto.

Fer·di·nand ['fə:dinənd] Fernando.

Fin·land ['finlənd] Finlandia *f.*

Flan·ders ['flɑ:ndəz] Flandes *m.*

Flor·ence ['flɔrəns] Florencia *f.*

Flor·i·da ['flɔridə] *Península y estado de EE.UU.*

France [frɑ:ns] Francia *f.*

Fran·ces ['frɑ:nsis] Francisca.

Fran·cis ['frɑ:nsis] Francisco.

Frank [fræŋk] Paco.

Fred(·dy) ['fred(i)] *nombre cariñoso de Frederick.*

Fred·e·rick ['fredrik] Federico.

French West Af·ri·ca ['frentʃ'west-'æfrikə] Africa *f* Occidental Francesa.

Fries·land ['fri:zlənd] Frisia *f.*

G

Ga·len ['geilən] Galeno.

Ga·li·lee ['gælili] Galilea *f.*

Gan·ges ['gændʒi:z] *El río* Ganges *de la India.*

Ga·ronne [gə'rɔn] Garona *m.*

Gas·co·ny ['gæskəni] Gascuña *f.*

Gaul [gɔ:l] Galia *f.*

Ge·ne·va [dʒi'ni:və] Ginebra.

Gen·o·a ['dʒenouə] Génova.

Geof·frey ['dʒefri] Geofredo.

George [dʒɔ:dʒ] Jorge.

Geor·gia ['dʒɔ:dʒiə] *Estado de EE.UU.*

Ger·ma·ny ['dʒə:məni] Alemania *f.*

Ger·trude ['gə:tru:d] Gertrudis.

Geth·se·ma·ne [geθ'seməni] Getsemaní.

Get·tys·burg ['getizbə:g] *Pueblo del Estado de Pensilvania (EE.UU.).*

Gha·na [gɑ:nə] Ghana *f.*

Ghent [gent] Gante.

Gib·ral·tar [dʒib'rɔltə] Gibraltar; *Rock of* ~ Peñón *m* de Gibraltar; *Straits of* ~ *pl.* Estrecho *m* de Gibraltar.

Giles [dʒailz] Gil.

Gi·ronde [dʒi'rɔnd] Gironda *m.*

Gla·mor·gan·shire [glə'mɔ:gənʃiə] *Condado galés.*

Glas·gow ['glɑ:sgou] *Puerto y la ciudad más grande de Escocia.*

Glouces·ter ['glɔstə] *Ciudad en el suroeste de Inglaterra.*

Glouces·ter·shire ['~ʃiə] *Condado inglés.*

God·frey ['gɔdfri] Godofredo.

Gold Coast ['gould'koust] Costa *f* de Oro.

Go·li·ath [gə'laiəθ] Goliat.

Grand Can·yon [grænd'kænjən] *Cañón hondo del río Colorado en el Estado de Arizona (EE.UU.).*

Great Brit·ain ['greit'britən] Gran Bretaña *f.*

Greece [gri:s] Grecia *f.*

Green·land ['gri:nlənd] Groenlandia *f.*

Green·wich ['grinidʒ] *Barrio de Londres.*

Green·wich Vil·lage ['~ 'vilidʒ] *Barrio de los artistas de Nueva York.*

Greg·o·ry ['gregəri] Gregorio.

Gua·te·ma·la [gwæti'mɑ:lə] **1.** Guatemala *f;* **2.** *Capital de este país.*

Guern·sey ['gə:nzi] Guernesey *m.*

Gui·a·na [gi'ɑ:nə] Guayana *f.*

Guin·ea ['gini] Guinea *f.*

Guin·e·vere ['gwiniviə] Ginebra.

Guin·ness ['ginis] *Marca de fábrica de cerveza irlandesa.*

Guy [gai] Guido.

H

Ha·dri·an ['heidriən] Adriano.

Hague [heig] *the* ~ La Haya.

Hai·ti ['heiti] Haití *m.*

Ham·burg ['hæmbə:g] Hamburgo.

Ham·let ['hæmlit] *Personaje dramático del poeta Shakespeare.*

Hamp·shire ['hæmpʃiə] *Condado inglés.*

Han·ni·bal ['hænibəl] Aníbal.

Haps·burg ['hæpsbə:g] Habsburgo.

Har·le·quin ['hɑːlikwin] Arlequín.
Har·ry ['hæri] Enrique.
Har·vard U·ni·ver·si·ty ['hɑːvəd juːniˈvɜːsiti] *Universidad de fama de los EE.UU.*
Has·tings ['heistiŋz] *Ciudad en el sur de Inglaterra.*
Ha·van·a [həˈvænə] La Habana.
Ha·wai·i [hɑːˈwaiiː] *Islas f/pl.* Hawai.
Heb·ri·des ['hebridiːz] *pl.* Hébridas *f/pl.*
Hel·en ['helin] (H)Elena.
Hen·ry ['henri] Enrique.
Her·cu·les ['hɜːkjuliːz] Hércules.
Her·e·ford·shire ['herifədʃiə] *Condado inglés.*
He·rod ['herəd] Herodes.
Hert·ford·shire ['hɑːfədʃiə] *Condado inglés.*
Hi·ma·la·ya [himəˈleiə] (los montes) Himalaya *m.* [*m.*]
Hin·du·stan [hindu'stæn] Indostán
Hip·po·cra·tes [hiˈpɔkrətiːz] Hipócrates.
Hol·land ['hɔlənd] Holanda *f.*
Hol·ly·wood ['hɔliwud] *Ciudad de California y centro de la industria del cine de EE.UU.*
Ho·ly Land ['houliˈlænd] Tierra *f* Santa.
Ho·mer ['houmə] Homero.
Hon·du·ras [hɔnˈdju(ə)rəs] Honduras *m.*
Hor·ace ['hɔris] Horacio.
Hud·son ['hʌdsn] *Río en el este de EE.UU. con la ciudad de Nueva York en su estuario.*
Hugh [hjuː] Hugo.
Hun·dred Years' War ['hʌndridˈjiəzˈwɔː] Guerra *f* de los Cien Años.
Hun·ga·ry ['hʌŋgəri] Hungría *f.*
Hu·ron ['hjuərən]: *Lake* ~ El lago Huron.
Hyde Park ['haidˈpɑːk] *Parque público de Londres.*

I

I·be·ri·a [aiˈbiəriə] Iberia *f.*
Ice·land ['aislənd] Islandia *f.*
I·da·ho ['aidəhou] *Estado de EE.UU.*
Ig·na·ti·us [igˈneiʃəs] Ignacio.
Il·li·nois [iliˈnɔi] *Río y estado de EE.UU.*
In·dia ['indjə] La India.
In·di·an·a [indiˈænə] *Estado de EE.UU.*

In·dian O·cean ['indjənˈouʃn] Océano *m* Indico, Mar *m* de las Indias.
In·dies ['indiz] Indias *f/pl.*
In·do·ne·sia [indouˈniːziə] Indonesia *f.*
I·o·wa ['aiouə, 'aiəwə] *Estado de EE.UU.*
I·rak, I·raq [iˈrɑːk] El Irak.
I·ran [iˈrɑːn] El Irán.
Ire·land ['aiələnd] Irlanda *f.*
I·saac ['aizək] Isaac.
Is·a·bel ['izəbel] Isabel.
I·sol·de [iˈzɔldə] Iseo, Isolda.
Is·rael ['izreil] Israel *m.*
It·a·ly ['itəli] Italia *f.*
I·vo·ry Coast ['aivəriˈkoust] Costa *f* de Marfil.

J

Jack [dʒæk] Juanito; ~ *Frost personificación del hielo;* ~ *Ketch el verdugo; before you can say* ~ *Robinson en un decir Jesús;* ~ *Tar el marinero.*
Ja·cob ['dʒeikəb] Jacob.
Ja·mai·ca [dʒəˈmeikə] Jamaica *f.*
James [dʒeimz] Diego; Jaime; (*Saint*) Santiago; (*British kings*) Jacobo.
Jane [dʒein] Juana.
Ja·pan [dʒəˈpæn] El Japón.
Je·ho·vah [dʒiˈhouvə] Jehová.
Jer·e·my ['dʒerəmi] Jeremías.
Jer·i·cho ['dʒerikou] Jericó.
Jer·ome [dʒəˈroum] Jerónimo.
Jer·sey ['dʒɜːzi] **1.** *Isla británica de las Islas Normandas;* **2.** ~ **City** *Ciudad a orillas del Hudson* (*EE.UU.*).
Je·ru·sa·lem [dʒəˈruːsələm] Jerusalén.
Je·sus ['dʒiːzəs] Jesús; **Je·sus Christ** ['dʒiːzəsˈkraist] Jesucristo.
Jim(·my) ['dʒim(i)] *nombre cariñoso de James; Jim Crow el negro estadounidense; segregado, relativo a la segregación racial.*
Joan [dʒoun] Juana; ~ *of Arc* Juana de Arco.
Job [dʒoub] Job; ~*'s comforter el que, bajo pretexto de animar a una persona triste, le desconsuela todavía más.*
Jock [dʒɔk] *el escocés típico.*
Joe [dʒou] Pepe; *Am. sl.* tío *m*, individuo *m.*
John [dʒɔn] Juan; ~ *Bull personificación de Inglaterra.*

John·ny ['dʒɔni] Juanito.
Jor·dan ['dʒɔːdn] *(river)* Jordán *m;* *(country)* Jordania *f.*
Jo·seph ['dʒouzif] José.
Jo·se·phine ['dʒouzifiːn] Josefina.
Josh·u·a ['dʒɔʃjuə] Josué.
Jove [dʒouv] Júpiter; *by* ~*!* |caramba!
Ju·dae·a [dʒuːˈdiə] Judea *f.*
Ju·dah ['dʒuːdə] Judá *f.*
Ju·das ['dʒuːdəs] Judas.
Ju·go·sla·vi·a [juːgouˈslaːviə] Jugo(e)slavia *f.*
Jul·iet ['dʒuːljet] Julieta.
Ju·lius ['dʒuːljəs] Julio.
Ju·pi·ter ['dʒuːpitə] Júpiter.

K

Kan·sas ['kænzəs] *Río y estado de EE.UU.*
Kash·mir [kæʃˈmiə] Cachemira *f.*
Kate [keit] *nombre cariñoso de Catherine etc.*
Kath·er·ine ['kæθərin]*,* **Kath·leen** ['kæθliːn] Catalina.
Ken·ne·dy Air·port ['kenədi ɛə:pɔːt] *(anteriormente Idlewild) Aeropuerto internacional de Nueva York.*
Kent [kent] *Condado inglés.*
Ken·tuck·y [kenˈtʌki] *Río y estado de EE.UU.*
Ken·ya ['kiːnjə, 'kenjə] *Pico y estado del Africa oriental.*
King Lear [kiŋ 'liə] *Personaje dramático del poeta Shakespeare.*
Kings·ton ['kiŋstən] *Capital de Jamaica.*
Kit(·**ty**) ['kit(i)] *nombre cariñoso de Catherine etc.*
Ko·re·a [kəˈriə] Corea *f.*

L

Lab·ra·dor ['læbrədɔː] *Península en el este del Canadá.*
Lake Dis·trict ['leikˈdistrikt] *País m de los Lagos.*
Lan·ca·shire ['læŋkəʃiə] *Condado inglés.*
Lan·ce·lot ['lɑːnslət] Lanzarote.
La Paz [lɑːˈpæz] *Capital de Bolivia.*
Lap·land ['læplənd] Laponia *f.*
Lat·in A·mer·i·ca ['lætinəˈmerikə] América *f* Latina.
Lat·ium ['leiʃəm] Lacio *m.*
Lau·rence ['lɔrəns] Lorenzo.
Lau·sanne [louˈzæn] Lausana.

La·za·rus ['laezərəs] Lázaro.
Le·an·der [liˈaendə] Leandro.
Leb·a·non ['lebənən] Líbano *m.*
Leeds [liːdz] *Ciudad industrial en el norte de Inglaterra.*
Lee·ward Isles ['liːwədˈailz] *pl.* Islas *f/pl.* de Sotavento.
Leg·horn ['leghɔːn] Liorna.
Leices·ter ['lestə] *Capital del condado inglés de Leicestershire* ['~ʃiə].
Lei·ces·ter·shire ['lestəʃiə] *Condado inglés.*
Len·in·grad ['leniŋgræd] Leningrado.
Le·the ['liːθiː] Lete(o) *m; fig.* olvido *m.*
Ley·den ['leidn] Leide(n), Leida.
Lib·y·a ['libiə] Libia *f.*
Liège [liˈeiʒ] Lieja.
Lille [liːl] Lila.
Li·ma ['liːmə] *Capital del Perú.*
Lin·coln·shire ['liŋkənʃiə] *Condado inglés.*
Lis·bon ['lizbən] Lisboa.
Liv·er·pool ['livəpuːl] *Puerto y ciudad industrial de Inglaterra.*
Li·vy ['livi] Livio.
Loire [lwɑːr] Loira *m.*
Lom·bar·dy ['lɔmbədi] Lombardía *f.*
Lon·don ['lʌndən] Londres.
Lor·raine [lɔˈrein] Lorena *f.*
Los An·ge·les [lɔsˈændʒiliːz, *Am.* 'æŋgilis] *Ciudad de California (EE.UU.).*
Lou·is ['luːi] Luis.
Lou·i·si·an·a [luiːsiˈænə] *Estado de EE.UU.*
Lou·vain [luˈvein] Lovaina.
Low Coun·tries ['loukʌntriz] *pl.* Países *m/pl.* Bajos.
Luc·an ['luːkən] Lucano.
Luc·re·tia [luːˈkriʃə] Lucrecia.
Luc·re·tius [luːˈkriːʃəs] Lucrecio.
Luke [luːk] Lucas.
Lu·ther ['luːθə] Lutero.
Lux·em·bourg ['lʌksəmbəːg] Luxemburgo *m.*
Lyons ['laiənz] Lyón, León de Francia.

M

Mac·beth [mækˈbeθ] *Personaje dramático del poeta Shakespeare.*
Ma·chia·vel·li [mækiəˈveli] Maquiavelo.
Ma·dei·ra [məˈdiərə] Madera *f.*
Mad·i·son ['mædisn] *Capital del Estado de Wisconsin (EE.UU.).*

Ma·dras [mə'dræs] *Puerto de la India.*

Mag·da·len ['mægdəlin] *Magdalena f.*

Ma·gel·lan [mə'gelən] *Magallanes;* ~ *Straits pl.* Estrecho *m* de Magallanes.

Ma·hom·et [mə'hɔmit] *Mahoma (Fundador del Islam).*

Maine [mein] *Estado de EE.UU.*

Mainz [maints] *Maguncia.*

Ma·jor·ca [mə'dʒɔ:kə] *Mallorca f.*

Ma·la·ya [mə'leiə] *Malaya f, Malaca f.*

Mal·ta ['mɔ:ltə] *Malta f.*

Ma·na·gua [ma:'na:gwa] *Capital de Nicaragua.*

Man·ches·ter ['mæntʃistə] *Ciudad industrial en el noroeste de Inglaterra.*

Man·hat·tan [mæn'hætn] *Isla y centro de la ciudad de Nueva York.*

Man·i·to·ba [mæni'toubə] *Provincia del Canadá.*

Mar·ga·ret ['ma:gərit] *Margarita.*

Mar·ie An·toin·ette ['mæriæntwə-'net] *María Antonieta.*

Mark [ma:k] *Marcos.*

Mars [ma:z] *Marte.*

Mar·seill·aise [ma:sə'leiz] *Marsellesa f.*

Mar·seilles [ma:'seilz] *Marsella f.*

Mar·tial ['ma:ʃəl] *Marcial.*

Mar·tin·ique [ma:ti'ni:k] *Martinica f.*

Mar·y ['mɛəri] *María;* ~ *Queen of Scots* María Estuardo.

Mar·y·land ['mɛərilænd] *Estado de EE.UU.*

Mas·sa·chu·setts [mæsə'tʃu:sets] *Estado de EE.UU.*

Ma·t(h)il·da [mə'tildə] *Matilde.*

Mat·thew ['mæθju:] *Mateo.*

Mau·rice ['mɔris] *Mauricio.*

Mau·ri·tius [mə'riʃəs] *Mauricio m, Isla f de Francia.*

Mec·ca ['mekə] *La Meca.*

Med·i·terr·a·ne·an (Sea) [meditə-'reinjən (si:)] *(Mar m) Mediterráneo m.*

Mel·bourne ['melbən] *Melburne (Gran ciudad de Australia del Sur).*

Mer·cu·ry ['mə:kjuri] *Mercurio.*

Mes·si·ah [mi'saiə] *Mesías m.*

Meuse [mə:z] *Mosa m.*

Mex·i·co ['meksikou] *Méjico m; (in Mexico)* México m.

Mi·am·i [mai'æmi] *Ciudad en el Estado de Florida (EE.UU.).*

Mich·ael ['maikl] *Miguel.*

Mich·el·an·gel·o ['maikl'ænʒəlou] *Miguel Angel.*

Mich·i·gan ['miʃigən] *Estado de EE.UU.; Lake* ~ El lago Michigan *(el tercero de los cinco Grandes Lagos de Norteamérica).*

Mid·as ['maidəs] *Midas.*

Mid·dle·sex ['midlseks] *Condado inglés.*

Mid·west [mid'west] *El Medio Oeste de EE.UU.*

Mi·lan [mi'læn] *Milán.*

Min·ne·ap·o·lis [mini'æpəlis] *Ciudad en el Estado de Minnesota (EE.UU.).*

Min·ne·so·ta [mini'soutə] *Estado de EE.UU.*

Mi·nor·ca [mi'nɔ:kə] *Menorca f.*

Mis·sis·sip·pi [misi'sipi] *Misisipí m (Estado y el río más grande de EE.UU.).*

Mis·sou·ri [mi'suəri, Am. mi'zuəri] *Río y estado de EE.UU.*

Mo·ham·med [mou'hæmed] *Mahoma.* [EE.UU.]

Mon·tan·a [mɔn'ta:nə] *Estado de EE.UU.*

Mon·te·vid·e·o [mɔntivi'deiou] *Capital del Uruguay.*

Mont·gom·er·y·shire [~ʃiə] *Condado galés.*

Mont·re·al [mɔntri'ɔ:l] *Ciudad del Canadá.*

Mo·roc·co [mə'rɔkou] *Marruecos m.*

Mos·cow ['mɔskou] *Moscú.*

Mo·selle [mə'zel] *Mosela m.*

Mo·ses ['mouziz] *Moisés.*

N

Na·ples ['neiplz] *Nápoles.*

Nap·ol·eon [nə'pouliən] *Napoleón.*

Nar·bonne [na:'bɔn] *Narbona.*

Na·tal [nə'tæl] *Provincia de la Unión Sudafricana.*

Na·varre [nə'va:] *Navarra f.*

Naz·a·reth ['næzəriθ] *Nazaret.*

Ne·bras·ka [ni'bræskə] *Estado de EE.UU.*

Nep·tune ['neptju:n] *Neptuno.*

Ne·ro ['niərou] *Nerón.*

Neth·er·lands ['neðələndz] *pl.* (Los) Países *m/pl.* Bajos.

Ne·vad·a [ne'va:də] *Estado de EE.UU.*

New Bruns·wick [nju:'brʌnzwik] *Provincia del Canadá.*

New·cas·tle ['nju:ka:sl] *Puerto en el condado de Northumberland (Gran Bretaña).*

New Eng·land [nju:'iŋɡlənd] *Los estados de la Nueva Inglaterra en el nordeste de Norteamérica.*

New·found·land [nju:'faundlənd, 'nju:fəndlænd] *Terranova f.*

New Guin·ea [nju:'ɡini] *Nueva Guinea f.*

New Hamp·shire [nju:'hæmpʃiə] *Estado de EE.UU.*

New Jer·sey [nju:'dʒə:zi] *Estado de EE.UU.*

New Mex·i·co [nju:'meksikou] *Estado de EE.UU.*

New Or·le·ans [nju:'ɔ:liənz] *Nueva Orleans f.*

New South Wales ['nju:'sauθ'weilz] *Nueva Gales f del Sur.*

New York ['nju:'jɔ:k] *Nueva York (Ciudad y estado de EE.UU.).*

New Zea·land [nju:'zi:lənd] *Nueva Zelanda f.*

Ni·ag·a·ra [nai'æɡərə] *Niágara (Cataratas del río San Lorenzo).*

Nic·a·ra·gua [nikə'ræɡwə] *Nicaragua f.*

Nice [ni:s] *Niza.*

Nich·o·las ['nikələs] *Nicolás.*

Nick [nik] *nombre cariñoso de Nicholas; Old ~ el diablo.*

Ni·ge·ri·a [nai'dʒiəriə] *Estado del Africa occidental.*

Nile [nail] *Nilo m.*

No·ah ['nɔ:ə] *Noé.*

Nor·folk ['nɔ:fək] *1. Condado inglés; 2. Puerto en Virginia (EE.UU.).*

Nor·man·dy ['nɔ:məndi] *Normandía f.*

North Af·ri·ca ['nɔ:θ'æfrikə] *Africa f del Norte.*

North Car·o·li·na [nɔ:θkærə'lainə] *Estado de EE.UU.*

North Da·ko·ta [nɔ:θdə'koutə] *Estado de EE.UU.*

North·ern Ire·land ['nɔ:ðən'aiələnd] *Irlanda f del Norte.*

North Sea ['nɔ:θ'si:] *Mar m del Norte.*

North·um·ber·land [nɔ:'θʌmbələnd] *Condado inglés.*

Nor·way ['nɔ:wei] *Noruega f.*

Not·ting·ham·shire ['nɔtiŋəmʃiə] *Condado inglés.*

No·va Sco·tia ['nouvə'skouʃə] *Nueva Escocia f (Provincia del Canadá).*

O

Oc·ta·vian [ɔk'teivjən] *Octavio.*

Oed·ip·us ['i:dipəs] *Edipo.*

O·hi·o [ou'haiou] *Afluente del Misisipi y estado de EE.UU.*

O·kla·ho·ma [ouklə'houmə] *Estado de EE.UU.*

Ol·i·ver ['ɔlivə] *Oliverio.*

O·lym·pus [ə'limpəs] *Olimpo.*

On·tar·i·o [ɔn'teəriou] *Provincia del Canadá; Lake ~ El lago Ontario.*

Or·e·gon ['ɔriɡən] *Estado de EE.UU.*

Ork·ney Is·lands ['ɔ:kni'ailəndz] *pl. (Las) Orcadas f/pl. (Archipiélago situado al norte de Escocia).*

Or·phe·us ['ɔ:fiəs] *Orfeo.*

Ost·end [ɔs'tend] *Ostende.*

Ot·ta·wa ['ɔtəwə] *Capital del Canadá.*

Ov·id ['ɔvid] *Ovidio.*

Ox·ford ['ɔksfəd] *Ciudad universitaria inglesa.*

Ox·ford·shire ['~ʃiə] *Condado inglés.*

P

Pa·cif·ic (O·cean) [pə'sifik('ouʃn)] *(Océano m) Pacífico m.*

Pad·dy ['pædi] *nombre cariñoso de Patrick; el irlandés típico.*

Pa·ki·stan [pæki'stæn] *Pakistán m.*

Pal·es·tine ['pælistain] *Palestina f.*

Pall Mall ['pel'mel] *Nombre de una calle de Londres.*

Pan·a·ma [pænə'mɑ:] *Panamá m.*

Par·a·guay ['pærəɡwai] *El Paraguay.*

Par·is ['pæris] *París.*

Par·nas·sus [pɑ:'næsəs] *Parnaso.*

Pat [pæt] *nombre cariñoso de Patrick.*

Pat·rick ['pætrik] *Patricio.*

Paul [pɔ:l] *Pablo.*

Pearl Har·bour ['pə:l'hɑ:bə] *Puerto cerca de Honolulu, Hawai (Ataque aéreo a la flota estadounidense en 1941).*

Peg·a·sus ['peɡəsəs] *Pegaso.*

Pe·kin(g) [pi:'kin, pi:'kiŋ] *Pekín.*

Penn·syl·va·nia [pensil'veinjə] *Estado de Pensilvania (EE.UU.).*

Per·pi·gnan [pərpi'njɑ̃] *Perpiñán.*

Per·sian Gulf ['pə:ʃən'ɡʌlf] *Golfo m Pérsico.*

Pe·ru [pə'ru:] *El Perú.*

Pe·ter ['pi:tə] *Pedro.*

Pet·rarch ['petrɑ:k] *Petrarca.*

Phil·a·del·phi·a [filə'delfjə] Filadelfia (*Gran ciudad en el este de EE.UU.*).
Phil·ip ['filip] Felipe.
Phil·ip·pines ['filipi:nz] *pl.* Filipinas *f/pl.* (*islas en el Océano Pacífico*).
Phoe·nix ['fi:niks] *Capital del Estado de Arizona (EE.UU.).*
Pic·ar·dy ['pikədi] Picardía *f.*
Pic·ca·dil·ly [pikə'dili] *Avenida principal en la parte occidental de Londres.*
Pied·mont ['pi:dmənt] Piamonte *m.*
Pi·late ['pailət] Pilatos.
Pin·dar ['pində] Píndaro.
Pitts·burgh ['pitsbə:g] *Ciudad del Estado de Pensilvania (EE.UU.).*
Pi·us ['paiəs] Pío.
Pla·to ['pleitou] Platón.
Pli·ny ['plini] Plinio.
Plut·arch ['plu:ta:k] Plutarco.
Plu·to ['plu:tou] Plutón.
Plym·outh ['plimθ] 1. *Puerto en el sur de Inglaterra;* 2. *Ciudad del Estado de Massachusetts (EE.UU.).*
Po·land ['poulənd] Polonia *f.*
Pol·y·ne·sia [pɔli'ni:ziə] Polinesia *f* (*islas en el este del Océano Pacífico*).
Pom·pei·i [pɔm'peii:] Pompeya.
Pom·pey ['pɔmpi] Pompeyo.
Pon·tius Pi·late ['pɔntjəs'pailət] Poncio Pilatos.
Port-au-Prince [pɔrto'prɛ̃:s] *Capital de Haití.*
Port·o Ric·o ['pɔ:tou'ri:kou] Puerto Rico *m.*
Ports·mouth ['pɔ:tsməθ] *Principal puerto militar de Inglaterra en la costa del Canal de la Mancha.*
Por·tu·gal ['pɔ:tjugəl] Portugal *m.*
Po·to·mac [pə'toumæk] *Río que forma el límite de los Estados de Maryland y Virginia occidental (EE.UU.).*
Prague [prɑ:g] Praga.
Pro·vence [prɔ'vã:s] Provenza *f.*
Prus·sia ['prʌʃə] Prusia *f.*
Psy·che ['saiki:] Psique.
Pto·le·my ['tɔləmi] Tolomeo.
Punch [pʌntʃ] Polichinela.
Pyr·e·nees [pirə'ni:z] Pirineo *m,* Pirineos *m/pl.*
Py·tha·go·ras [pai'θægərəs] Pitágoras.

Q

Qui·to ['ki:tou] *Capital del Ecuador.*

R

Ra·chel ['reitʃəl] Raquel.
Ra·leigh ['rɔ:li] *Capital del Estado de Carolina del Norte (EE.UU.).*
Ra·phael ['ræfail] Rafael.
Rat·is·bon ['rætizbɔn] Ratisbona.
Ray·mond ['reimənd] Raimundo, Ramón.
Re·bec·ca [ri'bekə] Rebeca.
Red-Rid·ing Hood ['red'raidiŋhud] Caperucita Roja.
Red Sea ['red'si:] Mar *m* Rojo.
Reg·i·nald ['redʒinld] Reinaldos, Reginaldo.
Rhine [rain] Rin *m.*
Rhine·land ['rainlənd] Renania *f.*
Rhode Is·land [roud'ailənd] *Estado de EE.UU.*
Rhodes [roudz] Rodas *f* (*isla del Mar Mediterráneo*).
Rho·de·si·a [rou'di:ziə] Rodesia *f.*
Rhone [roun] Ródano *m.*
Rich·ard ['ritʃəd] Ricardo.
Rich·mond ['ritʃmənd] 1. *Capital del Estado de Virginia (EE.UU.);* 2. *Barrio de Nueva York; barrio de Londres.*
Rob·ert ['rɔbət], **Rob·in** ['rɔbin] Roberto.
Roch·elle (La) [lærɔʃ'el] La Rochela.
Rock·y Moun·tains ['rɔki'mauntinz] *pl.* Montes *m/pl.* Rocosos (*Sierra principal en el oeste de EE.UU.*).
Rod·er·ick ['rɔdrik] Rodrigo.
Ro·land ['roulənd] Roldán, Rolando.
Rome [roum] Roma.
Rose [rouz] Rosa.
Rou·en ['ru:ã:] Ruán.
Rous·sil·lon ['ru:sijɔ̃] Rosellón *m.*
Ru·ma·ni·a [ru:'meinjə] Rumania *f.*
Rus·sia ['rʌʃə] Rusia *f.*

S

Saar [sɑ:] Sarre *m.*
Sac·ra·men·to [sækrə'mentou] *Capital del Estado de California (EE.UU.).*
Sa·har·a [sə'hɑ:rə] Sahara *m.*
Sal·lust ['sæləst] Salustio.
Sam [sæm] *nombre cariñoso de Samuel;* Uncle ∼ *personificación de Estados Unidos.*
Sam·son ['sæmsn] Sansón.
Sam·u·el ['sæmjuəl] Samuel.

San Fran·cis·co [sænfrən'siskou] *La ciudad de San Francisco (EE.UU.).*

San Jo·sé [sænho'zei] *Capital de Costa Rica.*

San Juan [sæn'hwɑːn] *Capital de Puerto Rico.*

San Sal·va·dor [sæn'sælvədɔ:] *Capital de El Salvador.*

San·ta Claus ['sæntə'klɔːz] *San Nicolás (que el día de Navidad trae regalos para los niños).*

San·ti·ago de Chi·le [sænti'ɑːgou dei'tʃili] *Capital de Chile.*

San·to Do·min·go ['sæntoudə-'miŋgou] *Capital de la República Dominicana.*

Sa·ra·gos·sa [særə'gɔsə] Zaragoza.

Sar·di·nia [sɑ:'dinjə] Cerdeña *f.*

Sas·katch·e·wan [səs'kætʃiwən] *Río y provincia del Canadá.*

Sa·tan ['seitən] Satanás.

Sat·urn [sae'tən] Saturno.

Sau·di A·ra·bia ['sɔːdiə'reibjə] Arabia *f* Saudita.

Saul [sɔ:l] Saúl.

Sa·voy [sə'vɔi] Saboya *f.*

Sax·o·ny ['sæksəni] Sajonia *f.*

Scan·di·na·via [skændi'neivjə] Escandinavia *f.*

Scheldt [ʃelt] Escalda *m.*

Sci·pi·o ['skipiou] Escipión.

Scot·land ['skɔtlənd] Escocia *f*; ~ Yard *oficina central de la policía de Londres; nombre de la brigada criminal inglesa.*

Scrooge [skruːdʒ] *el avariento típico (personaje del Christmas Carol, de Dickens).*

Se·at·tle [si'ætl] *Puerto en la costa del noroeste de EE.UU.*

Seine [sein] Sena *m.*

Seoul [soul] *Capital de la Corea del Sur.*

Ser·bi·a ['sə:biə] Servia *f.*

Se·ville ['səvil] Sevilla.

Shef·field ['ʃefi:ld] *Ciudad industrial en el norte de Inglaterra.*

Si·am [sai'æm] Siam *m.*

Si·be·ri·a [sai'biəriə] Siberia *f.*

Sib·yl ['sibil] Sibila.

Sic·i·ly ['sisili] Sicilia *f.*

Si·er·ra Le·one [si'erəli'oun] Sierra *f* Leona.

Si·mon ['saimən] Simón; F *simple* ~ simple *m*; novato *m.*

Sin(d)·bad ['sinbæd] Simbad.

Sin·ga·pore [siŋgə'pɔ:] Singapur.

Sing Sing ['siŋ'siŋ] *Prisión de la ciudad de Ossining, en el Estado de Nueva York (EE.UU.).*

Smyr·na ['smə:nə] Esmirna.

Snow·don ['snoudn] *Pico en Gales (Gran Bretaña).*

Snow·white ['snouwait] Blancanieves.

Soc·ra·tes ['sɔkrəti:z] Sócrates.

Sol·o·mon ['sɔləmən] Salomón.

So·ma·li·land ['sə'mɑ:lilænd] Somalia *f.*

Som·er·set·shire ['sʌməsitʃiə] *Condado inglés.*

Soph·o·cles ['sɔfəkli:z] Sófocles.

Sou·dan [su:'dæn] Sudán *m* (*Estado de Africa*).

South Af·ri·ca, Un·ion of ['ju:njən-əvsauθ'æfrikə] Unión *f* Sudafricana.

South A·mer·i·ca ['sauθə'merikə] América *f* del Sur.

South·amp·ton [sauθ'æmptən] *Puerto en el sur de Inglaterra.*

South Car·o·li·na ['sauθkærə'lainə] *Estado de EE.UU.*

South Da·ko·ta ['sauθdə'koutə] *Estado de EE.UU.*

So·vi·et Un·ion ['souviet'ju:njən] Unión *f* Soviética.

Spain [spein] España *f.*

Spar·ta [spɑ:tə] Esparta.

Staf·ford·shire ['stæfədʃiə] *Condado inglés.*

Ste·phen ['sti:vn] Esteban.

St. Lou·is [snt'lu:is] *Ciudad industrial y de comercio a las orillas del Misisipí (EE.UU.).*

Stock·holm ['stɔkhɔlm] Estocolmo.

Stras·bourg ['stræzbə:g] Estrasburgo.

Strat·ford ['strætfəd] *Nombre de varias poblaciones de Inglaterra y de EE.UU.;* ~ on Avon *Lugar de nacimiento de Shakespeare.*

Stu·art ['stju:ət] Estuardo.

Su·dan [su:'dæn] Sudán *m.*

Su·ez Ca·nal ['su:izkə'næl] Canal *m* de Suez.

Suf·folk ['sʌfək] *Condado inglés.*

Sur·rey ['sʌri] *Condado en el sur de Inglaterra.*

Su·san ['su:zn] Susana.

Sus·sex ['sʌsiks] *Condado en la costa meridional de Inglaterra.*

Swe·den ['swi:dn] Suecia *f.*

Swit·zer·land ['switsələnd] Suiza *f.*

Syd·ney ['sidni] *Puerto y ciudad industrial de Australia.*
Sy·ra·cuse ['sairəkju:z] Siracusa.
Sy·ri·a ['siriə] Siria *f.*

T

Ta·cit·us ['taesitəs] Tácito.
Taf·fy ['tæfi] (=*David*) *el galés típico.*
Ta·gus ['teigəs] Tajo *m.*
Tam·ma·ny ['tæməni] *Organización del Partido Democrático en Nueva York.*
Tan·gier [tæn'dʒiə] Tánger.
Ted(·dy) ['tedi] *nombre cariñoso de Edward etc.*
Te·gu·ci·gal·pa [təgu:si'gælpə] *Capital de Honduras.*
Ten·nes·see [tene'si:] *Río y estado de EE.UU.*
Ter·ence ['terəns] Terencio.
Ter·ry ['teri] *nombre cariñoso de Terence.*
Tex·as ['teksəs] Tejas (*Estado de EE.UU.*).
Thames [temz] Támesis *m.*
Thebes [θi:bz] Tebas.
The·re·sa [tə'ri:zə] Teresa.
Ther·mo·py·lae [θə:'mɔpili:] Las Termópilas.
The·seus [θi:sju:s] Teseo.
Thes·sa·ly ['θesəli] Tesalia *f.*
Thom·as ['tɔməs] Tomás.
Ti·ber ['taibə] Tíber *m.*
Ti·bet [ti'bet] el Tíbet.
Tim [tim] *nombre cariñoso de Timothy.*
Tim·o·thy ['timəθi] Timoteo.
Ti·ti·an ['tiʃiən] el Ticiano.
To·go·land ['tougoulænd] Togolandia *f.*
Tom(·my) ['tɔm(i)] *nombre cariñoso de Thomas;* ~ *Atkins El soldado raso inglés.*
Ton·y ['touni] *nombre cariñoso de Anthony.*
To·ron·to [tə'rɔntou] *Ciudad del Canadá.*
Tou·lon [tu'lõ] Tolón.
Tou·louse [tu'lu:z] Tolosa (*de Francia*).
Tour·aine [tu'rein] Turena *f.*
Tra·fal·gar [trə'fælgə] *Promontorio cerca de Gibraltar.*
Trans·vaal ['trænsva:l] Transval.
Trent [trent] (*Italy*) Trento.
Tris·tram ['tristrəm] Tristán.
Troy [trɔi] Troya.

Tu·nis ['tju:nis] Túnez.
Turk·ey ['tə:ki] Turquía *f.*
Tus·ca·ny ['tʌskəni] la Toscana.
Tyre [taiə] Tiro.
Ty·rol [ti'rɔl] El Tirol.

U

U·kraine [ju:'krein] Ucrania *f.*
U·nit·ed States (of A·mer·i·ca) [ju:'naitid'steits(əvə'merikə)] *pl.* (Los) Estados *m/pl.* Unidos (de América).
U·ru·guay ['urugwai] El Uruguay.
U·tah ['ju:ta:] *Estado de EE.UU.*

V

Van·cou·ver [væn'ku:və] *Isla y ciudad en la costa occidental del Canadá.*
Vat·i·can ['vætikən] Vaticano *m* (*palacio papal en Roma; fig. el gobierno papal*).
Ve·las·quez [və'læski θ] Velázquez.
Ven·e·zue·la [vene'zweilə] Venezuela *f* (*estado sudamericano*).
Ven·ice ['venis] Venecia.
Ve·nus ['vi:nəs] Venus.
Ver·mont [və:'mɔnt] *Estado de EE.UU.*
Ver·sailles [veə'sai] Versalles.
Ve·su·vi·us [vi'su:viəs] Vesubio.
Vi·en·na [vi'enə] Viena.
Vin·cent ['vinsənt] Vicente.
Vir·gil ['və:dʒil] Virgilio.
Vir·gin·ia [və'dʒinjə] *Estado de EE.UU.*
Vosges [vouʒ] *pl.* Vosgos *m/pl.*
Vul·can ['vʌlkən] Vulcano.

W

Wales [weilz] Gales *f.*
Wall Street ['wɔ:lstri:t] *Calle de Nueva York y centro financiero de EE.UU.*
Wal·ter ['wɔltə] Gualterio.
War·saw ['wɔ:sɔ:] Varsovia.
War·wick·shire ['wɔrikʃiə] *Condado inglés.*
Wash·ing·ton ['wɔʃiŋtən] **1.** *Estado de EE.UU.;* **2.** *Capital federal y sede del gobierno de EE.UU.*
Wa·ter·loo [wɔ:tə'lu:] *Pueblo cerca de Bruselas (Bélgica); 1815 derrota de Napoleón I por los ingleses y los prusianos.*
Wel·ling·ton ['weliŋtən] *Capital y puerto principal de Nueva Zelanda.*

West In·dies ['west'indiz] *pl.* Antillas *f/pl.*

West·min·ster ['westminstə] *Barrio de Londres.*

West·mor·land ['westmələnd] *Condado inglés.*

West Vir·gin·ia ['westvə'dʒinjə] *Estado de EE.UU.*

White·hall ['wait'hɔːl] *Calle de Londres con edificios del gobierno inglés.*

White House ['wait'haus]: the ~ La Casa Blanca (*sede oficial y residencia del presidente de EE.UU.*) en la ciudad de Washington.

Wight: Isle of ~ [wait] *Isla en la costa meridional de Inglaterra.*

Will [wil], **Will·iam** ['wiljəm] Guillermo; ~ the Conqueror Guillermo el Conquistador.

Wim·ble·don ['wimbldən] *Barrio de Londres* (*campeonatos de tenis*).

Wis·con·sin [wis'kɔnsin] *Estado de EE.UU.*

Worces·ter·shire ['wustəʃiə] *Condado inglés.*

Wy·o·ming [wai'oumiŋ] *Estado de EE.UU.*

X

Xen·o·phon ['zenəfən] Jenofonte.

Y

Yale U·ni·ver·si·ty [jeil'juːni'vəː-siti] Universidad de Yale (*en el estado norteamericano de Connecticut*).

Yel·low·stone ['jeloustoun] *Río y parque nacional de EE.UU.*

York [jɔːk] *Ciudad y sede arzobispal en el condado de York o Yorkshire en el norte de Inglaterra.*

York·shire ['jɔːkʃiə] *Condado inglés.*

Yo·sem·i·te [jou'semiti] *Valle y parque nacional de EE.UU.*

Yu·go·sla·vi·a [juːgou'slɑːviə] Yugo(e)slavia *f.*

Z

Zi·on ['zaiən] Sión *m.*

Zu·lu·land ['zuːluːlænd] Zululandia *f.*

Abreviaturas británicas y americanas

British and American abbreviations

Cada artículo contiene el texto completo de la abreviatura británica y, a ser posible, la abreviatura española con su texto completo entre paréntesis. El asterisco (*) significa: véase **Pesos y medidas**.

A

a. *acre**.

A. 1. *adults* (película *f*) apta para mayores; **2.** *argon* argón, argo *m*.

A.A. 1. *Automobile Association equivalent to* Real Automóvil Club *m* de España; **2.** *anti-aircraft* antiaéreo.

A.A.A. 1. *Amateur Athletic Association* Federación *f* de Atletismo (de Aficionados); **2.** *American Automobile Association equivalent to* Real Automóvil Club *m* de España.

A.B. 1. *able-bodied seaman* marinero *m* de primera; **2.** *Am.* = **B.A.**

A.B.C. *American Broadcasting Company* compañía americana de radiodifusión.

A-bomb *atomic bomb* bomba A (bomba *f* atómica).

abp. *archbishop* arz. (arzobispo *m*).

Ac. *actinium* actinio *m*.

A/C *account* (*current*) cta, c.ta (cuenta *f* [corriente]).

A.C. 1. *alternating current* C.A. (corriente *f* alterna); **2.** *aircraftman* soldado raso de las fuerzas aéreas.

acc(t). *account* c.ta, cta (cuenta *f*).

A.D. *Anno Domini* ['ænou'dɔminai] A.C. (año de Cristo), d. de J.C. (después de Jesucristo).

A.D.C. *aide-de-camp* ['eiddə'kɑ̃:ŋ] edecán *m*.

ad lib. *ad libitum* (*Latin = at pleasure*) a voluntad, a discreción.

Adm. *Admiral* almirante *m*.

admin. *administration* admón. (administración *f*).

advt. *advertisement* anuncio *m*.

AEC *Atomic Energy Commission* Comisión *f* de la Energía Atómica.

A.E.F. *American Expeditionary Forces* Fuerzas *f/pl.* Expedicionarias Americanas.

AFL-CIO *American Federation of Labour and Congress of Industrial Organizations* confederación general de los sindicatos de EE.UU.

A.F.N. *American Forces Network* Red *f* de Radiodifusión de las Fuerzas Armadas de EE.UU.

Ag. *argentum* plata *f*.

AGM *Annual General Meeting* junta *f* anual.

A.l. *first class* de primera clase.

A.I.D. *artificial insemination by donor* inseminación *f* artificial por donante.

Al. *alumin(i)um* aluminio *m*.

Ala. *Alabama* estado de EE.UU.

Alas. *Alaska* estado de EE.UU.

Am. 1. *America* América *f*; **2.** *American* americano.

a.m. *ante meridiem* (*Latin = before noon*) de la mañana, antes del mediodía.

A.M. *Am.* = **M.A.**

anon. [ə'nɔn] *anonymous* anónimo.

A.O.B. *any other business* ruegos *m/pl.* y preguntas.

A.P. *Am. Associated Press* agencia de información.

A.P.O. *Army Post Office* Oficina *f* de Correos del Ejército.

Ar. 1. *argon* argón, argo *m*; **2.** *argentum* plata *f*.

A.R.C. *American Red Cross* Cruz *f* Roja Americana.

Ariz. *Arizona* estado de EE.UU.

Ark. *Arkansas* estado de EE.UU.

A.R.P. *Air-Raid Precautions* servicios de defensa civil (*contra bombardeo aéreo*).

arr. *arrives* llega.

art. *article* art., art.º (artículo *m*).

As. *arsenic* arsénico *m.*

A./S. *account sales* cuenta *f* de ventas.

A.S. *Anglo-Saxon* anglosajón *adj. a. su. m.*

assn. *association* asociación *f.*

asst. *assistant* asistente.

atty. *attorney* abogado *m.*

Au. *aurum* oro *m.*

Aug. *August* ag. (agosto *m*).

av. *average* promedio *m.*

avdp. *avoirdupois sistema de pesos británico y estadounidense.*

Av(e). *avenue* Av(da). (avenida *f*).

A.W.O.L. *Am. absent without leave* ausente sin permiso.

B

B. *boron* boro *m.*

b. *born* n. (nacido).

B.A. *Bachelor of Arts* Lic. en Fil. y Let. (Licenciado [a *f*] *m* en Filosofía y Letras).

Ba. *barium* bario *m.*

B.A.O.R. *British Army of the Rhine* Ejército *m* Británico del Rin.

Bart. *Baronet título de la nobleza británica.*

Battn. *battalion* Bón. (batallón *m*).

B.B.B.C. *British Board of Boxing Control* Comité *m* Ejecutivo de Boxeo Británico.

B.B.C. *British Broadcasting Corporation* la BBC (Radio *f* Nacional de Gran Bretaña).

B.C. *before Christ* a. J.C. (antes de Jesucristo).

B.C. *British Columbia* Columbia Británica.

B.Com. *Bachelor of Commerce* Licenciado *m* en Comercio.

B.D. *Bachelor of Divinity* Licenciado *m* en Teología.

Be. *beryllium* berilio *m*, glucinio *m.*

B/E *Bill of Exchange* letra *f* de cambio.

B.E.A. 1. *British European Airways* la BEA (Líneas *f/pl.* Aéreas Británicas en Europa); 2. *British Electricity Authority* Empresa *f* Nacional de Electricidad (Británica).

B.Ed. *Bachelor of Education* Licenciado (a *f*) *m* en Educación.

Beds. *Bedfordshire condado inglés.*

Benelux *Belgium, Netherlands, Luxembourg unión arancelaria de estos países.*

Berks. *Berkshire condado inglés.*

B.F. *bloody fool* idiota *m.*

b/f(wd). *brought forward* suma *f* del anterior.

B.F.N. *British Forces Network* Red *f* de Radiodifusión de las Fuerzas Armadas de Gran Bretaña.

b.h.p. *brake horse power* potencia *f* al freno.

Bi. *bismuth* bismuto *m.*

B.I.F. *British Industries Fair* Feria *f* de Muestras de la Industria Británica.

bk. 1. *bank* Bº (banco *m*); 2. *book* lib.º (libro *m*).

bl. *barrel* brl. (barril *m*).

B/L. *bill of lading* conocimiento *m.*

B.L. *Bachelor of Law* Licenciado *m* en Derecho.

bldg. *building* edificio *m.*

B.Litt. *Bachelor of Letters* Licenciado (a *f*) *m* en Letras.

bls. 1. *bales* balas *f/pl.*; 2. *barrels* brls. (barriles *m/pl.*).

blvd. *boulevard* bulevar *m.*

B.M. 1. *British Museum* Museo *m* Británico; 2. *Bachelor of Medicine* Licenciado (a *f*) *m* en Medicina.

B.M.A. *British Medical Association* Asociación *f* Médica de Gran Bretaña.

B.Mus. *Bachelor of Music* Licenciado (a *f*) *m* en Música.

B.O. *body odour* (*las iniciales son eufemismo*) olor *m* a sudor.

B.O.A.C. *British Overseas Airways Corporation* Líneas *f/pl.* Aéreas Británicas de Ultramar.

bot. 1. *bought* comprado; 2. *bottle* botella *f.*

Bp. *bishop* ob., obpo (obispo *m*).

B.R. *British Railways* Ferrocarriles *m/pl.* Británicos.

B/R. *bills receivable* obligaciones *f/pl.* por cobrar.

Br. *bromine* bromo *m.*

Br(it). 1. *Britain* Gran Bretaña *f*; 2. *British* británico.

Bros. *brothers* Hnos. (hermanos *m/pl.*).

B/S. *bill of sale* 1. hipoteca *f* de bienes (*fianza de un préstamo*); 2. *Am.* escritura *f* de venta.

B.Sc. *Bachelor of Science* Licenciado (a *f*) *m* en Ciencias.

B.Sc. Econ. *Bachelor of Economic Science* Licenciado (a *f*) *m* en Ciencias Económicas.

B.S.G. *British Standard Gauge* ancho *m* normal británico.

bsh. *bushel**.

B.S.I. *British Standards Institution* Instituto *m* de Normas (*pesos, medidas, etc.*) Británico.

B.S.T. *British Summer Time* hora *f* de verano (*en Gran Bretaña*).

Bt. *Baronet título de la nobleza británica.*

bt. *f(wd). brought forward* suma *f* del anterior.

B.T.U. *British Thermal Unit* unidad *f* termal británica.

bu. *bushel**. [*inglés.*]

Bucks. *Buckinghamshire condado*

B.U.P. *British United Press agencia de información.*

bus. *bushel**.

B.V.M. *Blessed Virgin Mary* Nª Srª (Nuestra Señora).

B.W.I. *British West Indies* Antillas *f/pl.* Británicas.

C

c. **1.** *cent(s)** céntimo(s) *m(pl.)* (*moneda americana*); **2.** *circa* h. (hacia); **3.** *cubic* cúbico.

C. *carbon* carbono *m*.

C. *Celsius, centigrade termómetro centígrado.*

C/A. *current account* c/c (cuenta *f* corriente).

Ca. *calcium* calcio *m*.

C.A. *Central America* América *f* Central.

Cal(if). *California estado de EE.UU.*

Cambs. *Cambridgeshire condado inglés.*

Can. **1.** *Canada* el Canadá; **2.** *Canadian* canadiense.

Cantab. *Cantabrigiensis* (*Latin = of Cambridge*) de la Universidad de Cambridge.

Cantuar. *Cantuariensis* (*Latin = of Canterbury*) de Cantórbery.

Capt. *Captain* capn. (capitán *m*).

carr. *carriage* porte *m*.

Cb. *columbium* columbio *m*.

C.B. **1.** (*a.* C/B) *cash book* libro *m* de caja; **2.** *Companion of the Bath título honorífico británico*; **3.** *confined to barracks* (*men*) arresto *m* menor en cuartel; (*officers*) arresto *m* en banderas.

C.B.C. *Canadian Broadcasting Corporation* Radio *f* Nacional del Canadá.

c.c. *cubic centimetre* c.c., c³ (centímetro *m* cúbico).

Cd. *cadmium* cadmio *m*.

C.D. **1.** *Civil Defence* defensa *f* civil (*contra bombardeo aéreo*); **2.** *Corps Diplomatique* Cuerpo *m* Diplomático.

Ce. *cerium* cerio *m*.

C.E. *civil engineer* ingeniero *m* civil.

cert. *certificate* certificado *m*.

cf. *confer* comp. (compárese, cotéjese, confróntese).

c/f(wd). *carried forward* suma y sigue.

ch. **1.** *chain**; **2.** *chapter* c., cap., cap.º (capítulo *m*).

C.H. *Companion of Honour título honorífico británico.*

chq. *cheque* ch. (cheque *m*).

c/i *certificate of insurance* certificado *m* de seguro.

C.I.C. **1.** *Capital Issues Committee* Comisión *f* de Control de Emisión de bonos etc.; **2.** *Am. Counter Intelligence Corps* Cuerpo *m* de Contraespionaje.

C.I.D. *Criminal Investigation Department* Departamento *m* de Investigación Criminal *equivalent to* Brigada *f* Criminal.

c.i.f. *cost, insurance, freight* c.i.f., c.s.f. (costo, seguro, flete).

C. in C. *Commander in Chief* comandante *m* en jefe.

ck(s). *cask* brl. (barril *m*).

Cl. *chlorine* cloro *m*.

cl. *class* clase *f*.

cm. *centimetre* cm. (centímetro *m*).

Co. **1.** *Company* C., Cía etc. (compañía *f*); **2.** *county* condado *m* (*en EE.UU. e Irlanda*).

Co. *cobalt* cobalto *m*.

c/o. *care of* c/d (en casa de); a/c (al cuidado de).

C.O. *Commanding Officer* (comandante *m* en) jefe *m*.

C.O.D. *cash* (*Am. collect*) *on delivery* pagar contra recepción, cóbrese a la entrega.

C. of E. *Church of England* Iglesia *f* Anglicana.

Col. **1.** (*a.* **Colo.**) *Colorado estado de EE.UU.*; **2.** *Colonel* Cnel (coronel *m*); **3.** *column* col. (columna *f*).

Conn. *Connecticut estado de EE.UU.*

Cons. *Conservative* conservador *adj. a. su. m (-a f).*

coop., co-op. *cooperative* cooperativo (*adj.*); cooperativa (*su.*).

cp. *compare* comp. (compárese).

C.P. 1. *Communist Party* P.C. (Partido *m* Comunista); **2.** *carriage paid* P.P. (porte *m* pagado).

c.p. 1. *candle power* potencia lumínica; **2.** *chemically pure* químicamente puro.

Cpl. *Corporal* cabo *m*.

Cr. *credit* haber *m*.

Cr. *chromium* cromo *m*.

Cs. *caesium* cesio *m*.

C.S. *Civil Service* burocracia *f* oficial del Estado.

C.S.M. *Company Sergeant-Major* approx. brigada *m* (*de compañia*).

ct(s). *cent(s)** céntimo(s) *m(pl.)* (*moneda americana*).

Cu. *cuprum* cobre *m*.

cub. *cubic* cúbico.

cu.ft. *cubic foot**.

cu. in. *cubic inch**.   [contado.|

c.w.o. *cash with order* pago *m* al|

cwt. *hundredweight**.

D

d. 1. *penny, pence** penique(s) *m(pl.)* (*moneda inglesa*); **2.** *date* fha. (fecha *f*); **3.** *died* m. (murió).

D.A. 1. *deposit account* approx. cuenta *f* de ahorros); **2.** *Am. District Attorney* fiscal *m* de distrito.

D.A.R. *Daughters of the American Revolution* Hijas *f/pl.* de la Revolución Americana (*organización femenina patriótica*).

D.B. *Day Book* libro *m* diario.

D.C. 1. *direct current* C.C. (corriente *f* continua); **2.** *District of Columbia* Washington, *capital de EE.UU., y sus alrededores*.

D.C.L. *Doctor of Civil Law* Doctor *m* en Derecho Civil.

d-d *damned* condenado.

D.D. *Doctor of Divinity* Doctor *m* en Teología.

DDT *dichloro-diphenyl-trichloro-ethane* DDT (*insecticida*).

Dec. *December* dic.ᵉ (diciembre *m*).

Del. *Delaware* estado *de EE.UU.*

dep. *departs* sale.

Dept. *Debartment* departamento *m*.

D.G. *Dei Gratia* (*Latin = by the grace of God*) por la gracia de Dios.

dis(t). *discount* d.ᵗᵒ (descuento *m*).

dist. *district* distrito *m*, región *f*.

div. *dividend* dividendo *m*.

do. *ditto* íd. (ídem, lo mismo).

doc. *document* documento *m*.

dol. *dollar** dólar *m* (*moneda americana*).

doz. *dozen* dⁿᵃ (docena *f*).

D.P. *displaced person* desplazado (a *f*) *m*.

D.Phil. *Doctor of Philosophy* Doctor *m* en Filosofía.

Dpt. *Department* departamento *m*.

dr. *dra(ch)m**.

Dr 1. *Doctor* Dr (doctor *m*); **2.** *debtor* Dr. (el debe).   [vista.|

d.s., d/s. *days after sight* a ... días|

D.Ts. *delirium tremens* delírium *m* tremens.

D.V. *Deo volente* (*Latin = God willing*) D.m. (Dios mediante).

Dy. *dysprosium* disprosio *m*.

E

E. *East(ern)* E (este [*m*]).

E. & O.E. *errors and omissions excepted* s.e.u.o. (salvo error u omisión).

ea. *each* c/u (cada uno).

Ebor. *Eboracensis* (*Latin = of York*) de York.

E.C. *East Central* parte este del centro de Londres (*distrito postal*).

ECOSOC *Economic and Social Council* m Económico y Social (*de las Naciones Unidas*).

Ed., ed. 1. *edition* ed. (edición *f*); **2.** *editor* director *m*, editor *m*, redactor *m*; **3.** *Edward* Eduardo.

EE, E/E. *errors excepted* salvo error.

e.g. *exempli gratia* (*Latin = for example*) p.ej. (por ejemplo).

E.long. *east longitude* longitud oriental.

Enc(l). *enclosure(s)* adjunto.

Eng(l). 1. *England* Inglaterra *f*; **2.** *English* inglés *adj. a. su. m.*

E.P. *extended play* duración *f* ampliada.

E.P.U. *European Payments Union* Unión *f* Europea de Pagos.

Erb. *erbium* erbio *m*.

Esq. *Esquire* D. (Don) (*Esq., en el sobre después del apellido; Don, en el sobre delante del nombre de pila*).

et al. *et alii* (*Latin = and others*) y otros.

etc., &c. *et cetera* (*Latin = and the rest*) etc. (etcétera).

et seq. *et sequentia* (*Latin = and the following*) y sigs. (y siguientes).

E.T.U. *Electrical Trades Union* Sindicato *m* de Electricistas.

Eu. *europium* europio *m.*

ex div. *ex dividend* sin dividendo.

ex int. *ex interest* sin interés.

F

f. 1. *farthing**; **2.** *fathom**; **3.** *foot, feet** pie(s) *m(pl.)*; **4.** *following* sgte. (siguiente); **5.** *feminine* f. (femenino).

F. *Fahrenheit* termómetro *Fahrenheit.*

F. *fluorine* flúor *m.*

F.A. *Football Association* Federación *f* de Fútbol. [*renheit.*\

Fahr. *Fahrenheit* termómetro *Fah-*

F.A.O. *Food and Agriculture Organization* FAO (Organización *f* de Agricultura y Alimentación).

F.B.I. 1. *Federation of British Industries* Federación *f* de Industrias Británicas; **2.** *Federal Bureau of Investigation* Departamento *m* de Investigación Criminal *equivalent to* Brigada *f* Criminal.

F.C. *Football Club* C.F. (Club *m* de Fútbol).

F.C.C. *Federal Communication Commission* Comisión *f* Federal de Comunicaciones.

Fe. *ferrum* hierro *m.*

Feb. *February* feb.º (febrero *m*).

ff. *following* sigs. (siguientes).

FIFA *Fédération Internationale de Football Association* Federación *f* Internacional de Football Association.

Fla. *Florida* estado de EE.UU.

F/Lt. *Flight Lieutenant* teniente *m* de aviación.

fm. *fathom**.

F.M. *Field Marshal* mariscal *m* de campo, *approx. equivalent to* Capitán *m* General de Ejército.

F.O. *Foreign Office* Ministerio *m* de Asuntos Exteriores.

fo(l). *folio* f.º, fol. (folio *m*).

f.o.b. *free on board* f.a.b. (franco a bordo).

for. *foreign* extranjero.

f.o.r. *free on rail* libre en la estación ferroviaria.

F.P. 1. *freezing point* punto *m* de congelación; **2.** *fire-plug* boca *f* (para agua).

Fr. 1. *France* Francia *f*; **2.** *French* francés *adj. a. su. m*; **3.** *Father* P., Pe. (Padre *m*); **4.** *Friar* Fr. (Fray *m*).

fr. *franc(s)* franco(s) *m(pl.)*.

Fri. *Friday* vier. (viernes *m*).

ft. *foot, feet** pie(s) *m(pl.)*.

FTC *Federal Trade Commission* Comisión *f* Federal de Comercio.

fur. *furlong**.

G

g. 1. *gauge* entrevía *f*, ancho *m*; **2.** *gramme(s)* gr(s). (gramo[s] *m[pl.]*); **3.** *guinea**; **4.** *grain**.

Ga. *Georgia* estado de EE.UU.

Ga. *gallium* galio *m.*

gal. *gallon**.

G.A.T.T. *General Agreement on Tariffs and Trade* Acuerdo *m* General Arancelario y Comercial.

G.B. *Great Britain* Gran Bretaña *f.*

G.C. *George Cross* condecoración *británica.*

G.C.B. *Knight Grand Cross of the Bath* título honorífico británico.

G.C.E. *General Certificate of Education* Diploma *m* General de Educación, *approx.* bachillerato *m.*

Gd. *gadolinium* gadolinio *m.*

Ge. *germanium* germanio *m.*

Gen. *General* Genl (general *m*).

Ger. 1. *Germany* Alemania *f*; **2.** *German* alemán *adj. a. su. m.*

G.H.Q. *General Headquarters* Cuartel *m* General.

gi. *gill**.

G.I. *Am. government issue* propiedad *f* del Estado; *por extensión, el soldado raso americano.*

Gl. *glucinium* glucinio *m.*

gl. *gill**.

Glam. *Glamorgan(shire)* condado *galés.*

Glos. *Gloucestershire* condado *inglés.*

G.M.T. *Greenwich Mean Time* tiempo *m* medio de Greenwich.

gns. *guineas* pl. of *guinea**.

G.O.P. *Am. Grand Old Party* Partido *m* Republicano.

Govt. *Government* gob.no (gobierno *m*).

G.P.O. *General Post Office* Oficina *f* Central de Correos.

gr. 1. *grain**; **2.** *gross* bruto; **3.** *gross* gruesa *f* (= *12 docenas*).

gr. wt. *gross weight* peso *m* bruto.

gs. *guineas* pl. of *guinea**.

G.S. *General Staff* E.M. (Estado *m* Mayor).

Gt. Br. *Great Britain* Gran Bretaña *f.*

guar. *guaranteed* garantizado.

H

h. *hour(s)* hora(s) *f(pl.).*

H. *hydrogen* hidrógeno *m.*

Hants. *Hampshire condado inglés.*

H-bomb *hydrogen bomb* bomba H (bomba *f* de hidrógeno).

h. & c. *hot and cold* (tiene agua) caliente y fría.

He. *helium* helio *m.*

H.E. 1. *high explosive* alto explosivo *m*; **2.** *His Excellency* S.E. (Su Excelencia).

Herts. *Hertfordshire condado inglés.*

Hg. *hydrargyrum (mercury)* mercu-)
hhd. *hogshead* pipa *f.*   [rio *m.*)

H.I. *Hawaiian Islands* Islas *f/pl.* Hawai.

H.M. *His (Her) Majesty* S.M. (Su Majestad).

H.M.S. *His (Her) Majesty's Ship* buque *m* (de guerra) de Su Majestad.

Ho. *holmium* holmio *m.*

H.O. *Home Office* Ministerio *m* del Interior.

Hon. 1. *Honorary* honorario, de honor; **2.** *Honourable título de la nobleza británica.*

H.P., h.p. 1. *horse-power* h.p. (caballos *m/pl.*, caballaje *m*); **2.** *high pressure* de alta presión; **3.** *hire purchase* compra *f* a plazos.

H.Q. *Headquarters* Cuartel *m* General.

H.R. *Am. House of Representatives* Cámara *f* de Diputados.

H.R.H. *His (Her) Royal Highness* S.R.A. (Su Real Alteza).

hrs. *hours* horas *f/pl.*

H.T. *Hawaii Territory* Territorio *m* de Hawai.

H.T., h.t. *high tension* (de) alta)
ht. *height* altura *f.*   [tensión *f.*)

Hunts. *Huntingdonshire condado inglés.*

I

I. *Island, Isle* isla *f.*

I. *iodine* iodo *m*, yodo *m.*

Ia. *Iowa estado de EE.UU.*

I.A.A.F. *International Amateur Athletic Federation* Federación *f* Internacional de Atletismo (de Aficionados).

I.A.T.A. *International Air Transport Association* I.A.T.A. (Asociación *f* Internacional del Transporte Aéreo).

ib(id). *ibidem (Latin = in the same place)* ibíd. (ibídem).

I.B. 1. *Invoice Book* libro *m* de facturas; **2.** *International Brigade* Brigadas *f/pl.* Internacionales.

I.C. *Intelligence Corps approx.* S.I.M. (Servicio *m* de Información Militar).

I.C.A.O. *International Civil Aviation Organization* O.A.C.I. (Organización *f* de Aviación Civil Internacional).

I.C.F.T.U. *International Confederation of Free Trade Unions* Confederación *f* Internacional de Sindicatos Libres.

I.C.I. *Imperial Chemical Industries* Industrias *f/pl.* Químicas Imperiales.

Id(a). *Idaho estado de EE.UU.*

id. *idem (Latin = the same)* íd. (ídem).

i.e. *id est (Latin = that is)* esto es, a saber.

I.H.P., i.h.p. *indicated horse-power* potencia *f* indicada en caballos.

Ill. *Illinois estado de EE.UU.*

I.L.O. *International Labour Organization* Organización *f* Internacional del Trabajo.

I.L.P. *Independent Labour Party* Partido *m* Laborista Independiente.

I.M.F. *International Monetary Fund* F.M.I. (Fondo *m* Monetario Internacional).

Imp. *Imperial** imperial.

in. *inch(es)** pulgada(s) *f(pl.).*

In. *indium* indio *m.*

Inc. *Am. Incorporated* S.A. (Sociedad *f* Anónima).

inc(l). 1. *including* que incluye; **2.** *inclusive* inclusivo.

incog. *incognito* de incógnito.

Ind. *Indiana estado de EE.UU.*

ins. *insurance* seguro *m.*

Inst. *Institute* Instituto *m.*

inst. *instant* cte (corriente, de los corrientes).

Io. *ionium* ionio *m.*

I.o.M. *Isle of Man.*

I.o.W. *Isle of Wight.*

I.O.U. *I owe you* pagaré (*m*).

I.Q. *Intelligence Quotient* cociente *m* intelectual.

Ir. 1. *Ireland* Irlanda *f*; **2.** *Irish* irlandés *adj. a. su. m.*

Ir. *iridium* iridio *m.*

I.R.A. *Irish Republican Army* Ejército *m* Republicano Irlandés.

Is. *Island, Isle* isla *f.*

I.T.A. *Independent Television Authority* Comisión *f* de la Televisión *f* Independiente.

I.T.V. *Independent Television* Televisión *f* Independiente.

I.U.S. *International Union of Students* Asociación *f* Internacional de Estudiantes.

I.W.W. *Am. Industrial Workers of the World* Confederación *f* Mundial de Obreros Industriales.

J

Jan. *January* en.º (enero *m*).

J.P. *Justice of the Peace* juez *m* de paz.

Jr., Jun(r). *junior* hijo.

K

K. *kalium* potasio *m.*

Kan(s). *Kansas estado de EE.UU.*

K.C. 1. *Knight Commander* título honorífico británico; **2.** *King's Counsel* abogado *m* (*de categoría superior*).

K.C.B. *Knight Commander of the Bath* título honorífico británico.

Ken. *Kentucky estado de EE.UU.*

kg. *kilogramme* Kg. (kilogramo *m*).

K.K.K. *Ku Klux Klan* Ku Klux Klan organización terrorista del Sur de EE.UU.

km. *kilometre* Km. (kilómetro *m*).

K.O., k.o. *knock(ed) out* k.o. (fuera de combate).

Kr. *krypton* criptón *m.*

Kt. *Knight* título de la nobleza británica.

kw. *kilowatt* kv. (kilovatio *m*).

Ky. *Kentucky estado de EE.UU.*

L

L. *Liberal* liberal *adj. a. su. m/f.*

l. 1. *left* izquierdo; a la izquierda; **2.** *line* línea *f*; **3.** *link**; **4.** *litre* l. (litro *m*).

£ *pound sterling* libra *f* esterlina.

£A *Australian pound* libra *f* australiana.

La. *Louisiana estado de EE.UU.*

La. *lanthanum* lantano *m.*

Lab. 1. *Labour* laborista *adj. a. su. m f.*; **2.** *Labrador* Tierra *f* del Labrador.

lab. *laboratory* laboratorio *m.*

Lancs. *Lancashire condado inglés.*

lat. *latitude* latitud *f.*

lb. *pound** libra *f.*

L.C. *letter of credit* carta *f* de crédito.

l.c. *typ. lower case* minúscula *f.*

L.C.C. *London County Council* Consejo *m* del Condado de Londres.

L.C.J. *Lord Chief Justice* justicia *m* mayor. [primera.)

L/Cpl. *Lance-Corporal* soldado *m)*

£E *Egyptian pound* libra *f* egipcia.

Leics. *Leicestershire condado inglés.*

Li. *lithium* litio *m.*

L.I. *Long Island* Long Island.

Lieut. *lieutenant* teniente *m.*

Lincs. *Lincolnshire condado inglés.*

ll. *lines* líneas *f/pl.*

Ll.B. *legum baccalaureus* (*Latin = Bachelor of Laws*) Licenciado *m* en Leyes.

Ll.D. *legum doctor* (*Latin = Doctor of Laws*) Doctor *m* en Leyes.

loc. cit. *loco citato* (*Latin = in the place cited*) en el lugar citado.

log. *logarithm* logaritmo *m.*

lon(g). *longitude* longitud *f.*

LP *long-playing* (de) larga duración *f.*

L.P. 1. *Labour Party* Partido *m* Laborista; **2.** (*a.* **l.p.**) *low pressure* de baja presión.

L.s.d. *librae, solidi, denarii* (*Latin = pounds, shillings, pence*);* F dinero *m.*

Lt. *Lieutentant* T(en)te (teniente *m*).

Lt-Col. *Lieutenant-Colonel* teniente coronel *m.*

Ltd. *limited* S. A. (sociedad *f* anónima).

Lt-Gen. *Lieutenant-General* teniente general *m.*

Lu. *lutecium* lutecio *m.*

M

m *minim*.*

m. 1. *male* macho *m*; **2.** *masculine* m (masculino); **3.** *metre* m. (metro *m*); **4.** *mile** milla *f*; **5.** *minute* m (minuto *m*); **6.** *married* se casó con.

M.A. *Master of Arts* Maestro *m* en Artes.

Maj. *Major* comandante *m.*

Maj.-Gen. *Major-General* general *m* de división.

Man., Manit. *Manitoba provincia canadiense.*

Mass. *Massachusetts estado de EE. UU.*

M.B. *Medicinae baccalaureus (Latin = Bachelor of Medicine)* Licenciado *m* en Medicina.

M.B.S. *Mutual Broadcasting System compañía americana de radiodifusión.*

M.C. 1. *Master of Ceremonies* maestro *m* de ceremonias; 2. *Am. Member of Congress* miembro *m* del Congreso; 3. ✠ *Military Cross condecoración británica.*

M.D. 1. *medicinae doctor (Latin = Doctor of Medicine)* Doctor *m* en Medicina; 2. *mentally deficient (su.)* retrasado *m* mental.

Md. *Maryland estado de EE.UU.*

Me. *methyl* metilo *m.*

Me. *Maine estado de EE.UU.*

Messrs *Messieurs* sres. (señores *m/pl.*).

mfs. *manufacturers* fabricante *m.*

mg. *milligramme* mg (miligramo *m*).

Mg. *magnesium* magnesio *m.*

Mgr. *Monsignor* Mons. (Monseñor *m*).

M.I. (5) *Military Intelligence* (5) *servicio secreto y de contraespionaje.*

Mich. *Michigan estado de EE.UU.*

min. *minute* minuto *m.*

Minn. *Minnesota estado de EE.UU.*

misc. *miscellaneous* misceláneo, vario.

Miss. *Mississippi estado de EE.UU.*

mm. *millimetre* mm (milímetro *m*).

Mn. *manganese* manganeso *m.*

Mo. *molybdenum* molibdeno *m.*

Mo. *Missouri estado de EE.UU.*

M.O. 1. *money order* giro *m* postal; 2. *medical officer* médico *m.*

Mon. 1. *Monday* lun. (lunes *m*); 2. *Monmouthshire condado anglogalés.*

Mont. *Montana estado de EE.UU.*

MP, M.P. 1. *Member of Parliament* miembro *m* del Parlamento; 2. *Military Policeman* policía *m* militar, vigilancia *f.*

m.p.g. *miles per gallon* (*) millas por galón (de gasolina).

m.p.h. *miles per hour* (*) millas por hora.

Mr *Mister* Sr (Señor *m*).

Mrs ['misiz] Sra (Señora *f*); † *or Scots = Mistress* ['mistris].

MS *manuscript* MS (manuscrito *m*).

M.S. *motorship* motonave *f.*

MSS *manuscripts* MSS (manuscritos *m/pl.*).

Mt *Mount* montaña *f*, monte *m.*

M.T.B. *motor torpedo-boat* torpedero *m.*

M(dd)x. *Middlesex condado inglés.*

N

n. 1. *neuter* neutro; 2. *noun* sustantivo *m.*

N. *North(ern)* N (norte [*m*]).

N. *nitrogen* nitrógeno *m.*

Na. *natrium (sodium)* sodio *m.*

NAAFI *Navy, Army and Air Force Institutes servicio de cantinas etc. para las fuerzas armadas.*

NATO *North Atlantic Treaty Organization* OTAN (Organización *f* del Tratado del Atlántico del Norte).

Nb. *niobium* niobio *m*, columbio *m.*

N.B. 1. *nota bene (Latin = note well)* N.B. (nótese bien); 2. *New Brunswick* Nuevo Brúnswick.

N.B.C. *National Broadcasting Company compañía americana de radiodifusión.*

N.B.G. *euph. no bloody good* absolutamente inútil.

N.C. *North Carolina estado de EE.UU.*

N.C.B. *National Coal Board* Empresa *f* Nacional de Carbón.

N.C.O. *non-commissioned officer* sargento *m or* cabo *m.*

Nd. *neodymium* neodimio *m.*

n.d. *no date* s.f. (sin fecha).

N.Dak. *North Dakota estado de EE.UU.*

Ne. *neon* neón *m.*

N.E. *North East(ern)* NE (noreste [*m*]).

Nebr. *Nebraska estado de EE.UU.*

nem. con. *nemine contradicente (Latin = with none voting against)* por unanimidad.

Neth. *Netherlands* Los Países Bajos.

Nev. *Nevada estado de EE.UU.*

N.F. *Newfoundland* Terranova *f.*

N.F.U. *National Farmers' Union* Asociación *f* Nacional de Agricultores.

N.H. *New Hampshire estado de EE.UU.*

N.(H.)I. *National (Health) Insurance* Seguro *m* Social Nacional.

N.H.S. *National Health Service* Servicio *m* Nacional de Sanidad.

Ni. *nickel* níquel *m.*

N.J. New Jersey *estado de EE.UU.*

N.Mex. New Mexico *estado de EE.UU.*

No. *number* núm., No. (número *m*).

non seq. *non sequitur* (*Latin = it does not follow*) no sigue.

Northants. Northamptonshire *condado inglés.*

Northumb. Northumberland *condado inglés.*

Notts. Nottinghamshire *condado inglés.*

Nov. November nov.ᵉ (noviembre *m*).

n.p. or d. *no place or date* s.l. ni f. (sin lugar ni fecha).

nr. *near* cerca de.

N.S.P.C.C. National Society for the Prevention of Cruelty to Children Sociedad *f* Nacional Protectora de los Niños.

N.S.W. New South Wales Nueva Gales *f* del Sur.

N.T. New Testament N.T. (Nuevo Testamento *m*).

Nt. *niton* nitón *m*.

nt. wt. *net weight* p.º n.º (peso *m* neto).

N.U.M. 1. National Union of Mineworkers Sindicato *m* Nacional de Mineros; **2.** National Union of Manufacturers Asociación *f* Nacional de Fabricantes.

N.U.R. National Union of Railwaymen Sindicato *m* Nacional de Ferroviarios.

N.W. North West(ern) NO (noroeste [*m*]).

N.Y. New York *estado de EE.UU.*

N.Y.C. New York City Ciudad *f* de Nueva York.

N.Z. New Zealand Nueva Zelanda *f*.

O

O. 1. Ohio *estado de EE.UU.*; **2.** *order* pedido *m*.

O. *oxygen* oxígeno *m*.

O., Ont. Ontario Ontario.

O.A.S. Organization of American States O.E.A. (Organización de los Estados Americanos).

ob. *obiit* (*Latin = died*) m. (murió).

O.B.E. Officer of the British Empire *título honorífico británico.*

O.C. Officer Commanding *oficial que manda un pelotón, una expedición etc.*

Oct. October oct.ᵉ (octubre *m*).

O.E. Old English inglés *m* antiguo.

O.E.D. Oxford English Dictionary *el mayor de los diccionarios de la lengua inglesa.*

O.E.E.C. Organization for European Economic Cooperation O.E.C.E. (Organización *f* Europea de Cooperación Económica).

O.F. Old French a.f. (antiguo francés *m*).

O.H. *on hand* en existencia.

O.H.M.S. On His (Her) Majesty's Service en el servicio de Su Majestad.

O.K. *all correct* (?) bien, en buen orden; V.º B.º (visto bueno) (*y véase esta voz en el diccionario*).

Okla. Oklahoma *estado de EE.UU.*

O.M. Order of Merit *título honorífico británico.*

o.p. *out of print* agotado.

op. cit. *opere citato* (*Latin = in the work cited*) obr. cit. (obra *f* citada).

o.r. *owner's risk* bajo la responsabilidad de los clientes (*or* usuarios).

Ore(g). Oregon *estado de EE.UU.*

Os. *osmium* osmio *m*.

Oxon. *Oxoniensis* (*Latin = of Oxford*) de la Universidad de Oxford.

oz. *ounce*(s)* onza(s) *f*(*pl.*).

P

p. 1. *pole, perch**; **2.** *page* pág. (página *f*).

P. *phosphorus* fósforo *m*.

Pa. Pennsylvania *estado de EE.UU.*

p.a. *per annum* (*Latin = yearly*) por año.

Pan. Panama Panamá *f*.

par(a). *paragraph* párrafo *m*.

P.A.U. Panamerican Union Unión *f* Panamericana.

Pb. *plumbum* plomo *m*.

P.C. 1. *postcard* tarjeta *f* postal; **2.** *police constable* guardia *m*; **3.** *Privy Council(lor)* (miembro *m* del) Consejo *m* de Su Majestad.

p.c. *per cent* P%, %, p. c. (por cien[to]).

pcl. *parcel* paquete *m*.

pcs. *pieces* pzs (piezas *f*/*pl.*).

pd. *paid* pagado.

Pd. *palladium* paladio *m*.

PEN Club Poets, Playwrights, Editors, Essayists and Novelists *asociación internacional de escritores etc.*

Penn(a). *Pennsylvania estado de EE.UU.*

per pro(c). *per procurationem* (*Latin = by proxy*) p.o. (por orden), p.p. (por poder).

Ph.D. *philosophiae doctor* (*Latin = Doctor of Philosophy*) Doctor *m* en Filosofía.

P.I. *Philippine Islands* Islas *f/pl.* Filipinas.

pk. *peck*.*

P/L. *profit and loss* ganancias *f/pl.* y pérdidas *f/pl.*

p.m. *post meridiem* (*Latin = after noon*) de la tarde.

P.M. *Prime Minister* Primer Ministro *m*.

P.M.G. *Postmaster-General* Director *m* General de Correos y Telecomunicación.

P.O. 1. *Post Office* (Oficina *f* de) Correos *m/pl.*; **2.** *postal order* giro *m* postal; **3.** *Pilot Officer* oficial *m* piloto.

P.O.B. *Post Office Box* apartado *m*.

pop. *population* h. (habitantes *m/pl.*).

P.O.S.B. *Post Office Savings Bank* Caja *f* Postal de Ahorros.

P.O.W. *prisoner of war* prisionero *m* de guerra.

p.p. 1. *v. per pro(c).*; **2.** *past participle* participio *m* del pasado.

pp. 1. *pages* págs. (páginas *f/pl.*); **2.** ♪ pianissimo.

Pr. 1. *praseodymium* preseodimio *m*; **2.** *propyl* propilo *m*.

P.R. *proportional representation* representación *f* proporcional.

P.R. *Puerto Rico* Puerto Rico *m*.

P.R.O. *Public Relations Officer* director *m* de relaciones públicas.

Prof. *Professor* Prof. (profesor *m*).

pro tem. *pro tempore* (*Latin = for the time*) interino, en el ínterin.

prox. *proximo* (*Latin = next month*) pr. fr. (próximo futuro).

P.S. *postscript* P.D. (posdata *f*).

pt. 1. *pint *;* **2.** *point* punto *m*.

Pt. *platinum* platino *m*.

P.T. *physical training* educación *f* física.

P.T.A. *Parent-Teacher Association* Asociación *f* de Padres y Profesores.

Pte. *private* soldado *m* raso.

P.T.O. 1. *please turn over* véase al dorso; **2.** *power take-off* toma *f* de fuerza.

Pvt. *Private* soldado *m* raso.

PW. *prisoner of war* prisionero *m* de guerra.

P.W.D. *Public Works Department* O.P. (Obras *f/pl.* Públicas).

Q

Q. *question* pregunta *f*.

q. *query* interrogación *f*, duda *f*.

Q., Que. *Quebec* Quebec.

Q.C. *Queen's Counsel* abogado *m* (*de -categoría superior*).

Q.E.D. *quod erat demonstrandum* (*Latin = that which was to be proved*) lo que había que demostrar.

Q.M. *Quartermaster* furriel *m*, comisario *m*.

qr. *quarter *.*

qt. *quart *.*

q.t. *quiet: sl. on the ~* sigilosamente.

qto. *quarto* in-4º (en cuarto).

qu. *query v. q.*

quot. *quotation* cotización *f*.

q.v. *quod vide* (*Latin = which see*) v. (véase), vid. (vide).

qy. *query v. q.*

R

R. 1. *River* río *m*; **2.** *Réaumur* termómetro Réaumur.

r. *right* derecho, a la derecha.

Ra. *radium* radio *m*.

R.A. 1. *Royal Academician* miembro *m* de la **2.** *Royal Academy* Real Academia *f* de Bellas Artes.

R.A.C. *Royal Automobile Club* equivalent to Real Automóvil Club *m* de España.

R.A.F. *Royal Air Force* Fuerzas *f/pl.* Aéreas Británicas.

Rb. *rubidium* rubidio *m*.

R.C. *Roman Catholic* católico (romano).

Rd. *road* calle *f*.

R.D. *refer to drawer* devuélvase al firmante.

R.E. *Royal Engineers* Cuerpo *m* de Ingenieros.

recd. *received* recibido.

ref. *in reference to* con referencia a respecto de.

regd. *registered* certificado.

reg. tn. *register ton *.*

ret. *retired* retirado.

Rev. *Reverend* R., Rdo (Reverendo).

Rh. *rhodium* rodio *m*.

R.I. *Rhode Island estado de EE.UU.*

R.I.P. *requiescat in pace (Latin = may he rest in peace)* R.I.P., q.e.p.d. (que en paz descanse).

Rly. *railway* f.c. (ferrocarril *m*).

R.N. *Royal Navy* Marina *f* Real.

R.P. *reply paid* C.P. (contestación *f* pagada).

r.p.m. *revolutions per minute* r.p.m. (revoluciones *f/pl.* por minuto).

R.R. *railroad* f.c. (ferrocarril *m*).

R.S.M. *Regimental Sergeant-Major approx.* brigada *m (de regimiento).*

R.S.P.C.A. *Royal Society for the Prevention of Cruelty to Animals* Real Sociedad *f* Protectora de Animales.

R.S.V.P. *répondez s'il vous plait (French = please reply)* S.R.C. (se ruega contestación).

Rt. Hon. *Right Honourable* título honorífico británico.

Ru. *ruthenium* rutenio *m*.

R.U. *Rugby Union* Federación *f* de Rugby.

Ry. *railway* f.c. (ferrocarril *m*).

S

s. 1. *second* segundo *m*; **2.** *shilling* * chelín *m*.

S. *South(ern)* S (sur [*m*]).

S. *sulphur* azufre *m*.

s.a. *sine anno (Latin = without year)* s.a. (sin año).

Sa. *samarium* samario *m*.

S.A. 1. *South Africa* Africa *f* del Sur; **2.** *South America* América *f* del Sur; **3.** *Salvation Army* Ejército *m* de Salvación.

Sask. *Saskatchewan provincia canadiense.*

Sat. *Saturday* sáb. (sábado *m*).

Sc. *scandium* escandio *m*.

S.C. 1. *South Carolina estado de EE.UU.*; **2.** *Security Council* Consejo *m* de Seguridad.

sc(il). *scilicet (Latin = namely)* a saber.

S. Dak. *South Dakota estado de EE.UU.*

Se. *selenium* selenio *m*.

S.E. 1. *South East(ern)* SE (sudeste [*m*]); **2.** *Stock Exchange* Bolsa *f*.

SEATO *South East Asia Treaty Organization* OTASE (Organización *f* del Tratado de la Asia Sudeste).

sec. *second* segundo *m*.

Sec. *Secretary* Srio (secretario *m*).

Sen(r). *senior* padre.

Sept. *September* sept.ᵉ (setiembre *m*).

S(er)gt. *Sergeant* sargento *m*.

sh. *shilling* * chelín *m*.

SHAPE *Supreme Headquarters Allied Powers Europe* Cuartel *m* General Supremo de los Aliados en Europa.

Si. *silicon* silicio *m*.

S.J. *Society of Jesus* C. de J. (Compañía *f* de Jesús.)

Sm. *samarium* samario *m*.

S.M. *Sergeant-Major approx.* brigada *m*.

Sn. *stannum* estaño *m*.

Soc. 1. *Society* sociedad *f*; **2.** *Socialist* socialista *adj. a. su. m/f.*

SOS *save our souls* SOS.

sp.gr. *specific gravity* peso *m* específico.

Sq. *square* plaza *f*.

sq. *square* cuadrado *m*.

sq. ft. *square foot* * pie *m* cuadrado.

Sr. *senior* padre.

Sr. *strontium* estroncio *m*.

SS *Saints* SS (santos *m/pl.*).

S.S. *steamship* vapor *m*.

st. *stone* *.

St. 1. *Saint* S. (San[ta]); **2.** *Street* calle *f*; **3.** *station* estación *f*.

Staffs. *Staffordshire condado inglés.*

St. Ex. *Stock Exchange* Bolsa *f*.

stg. *sterling* moneda *f* esterlina.

sub. *substitute* sustituto *m*, suplente *m/f*.

Sun. *Sunday* dom.º (domingo *m*).

suppl. *supplement* suplemento *m*.

s.v. *sub voce (Latin = under the word specified)* s.v. (sub voce).

S.W. *South West(ern)* SO (suroeste [*m*]).

T

t. *ton* * tonelada *f*.

Ta. *tantalum* tantalio *m*.

T.A. *Territorial Army* Reserva *f* del Ejército.

Tb. *terbium* terbio *m*.

TB *tuberculosis* tuberculosis *f*.

tbs. *tablespoon* cuchara *f* de mesa.

T.C.D. *Trinity College, Dublin* universidad irlandesa.

T.D. 1. *Am. Treasury Department* Ministerio *m* de Hacienda; **2.** *Territorial Decoration* condecoración británica.

Te. *tellurium* telurio *m.*
Tel. *telephone* tel. (teléfono *m*).
Tenn. *Tennessee estado de EE.UU.*
Tex. *Texas estado de EE.UU.*
T.G.W.U. *Transport and General Workers' Union* Sindicato *m* de Obreros de Transportes etc.
Th. *thorium* torio *m.*
Thurs. *Thursday* juev. (jueves *m*).
Ti. *titanium* titanio *m.*
Tl. *thallium* talio *m.*
Tm. *thulium* tulio *m.*
Tn. *thoron* toro *m.*
T.N.T. *trinitrotoluene* trinitrotoluene *m.*
T.O. *Telegraph (Telephone) Office* Oficina *f* de Telégrafos (Teléfonos).
Tr. *terbium* terbio *m.*
T.T. 1. *teetotaller* abstemio *m*; 2. *Tourist Trophy premio de carreras de motociclismo*; 3. *tuberculin tested* a prueba de tuberculinas.
T.U. *Trade(s) Union* sindicato *m.*
T.U.C. *Trade(s) Union Congress* Confederación *f* de Sindicatos.
Tues. *Tuesday* mart. (martes *m*).
TV *television* T.V. (televisión *f*).
T.V.A. *Tennessee Valley Authority* Empresa *f* de Colonización del Tennessee Valley (*EE.UU.*).

U

U. *universal* (película *f*) apta para menores.
U. *uranium* uranio *m.*
U.A.R. *United Arab Republic* R.A.U. (República *f* Arabe Unida).
u.c. *typ. upper case* mayúscula *f.*
U.K. *United Kingdom* Reino *m* Unido (*Inglaterra, Escocia, Gales e Irlanda del Norte*).
ult. *ultimo (Latin = last month)* p. pdo. (próximo pasado).
U.M.W. *Am. United Mine Workers* Sindicato *m* de Mineros.
U.N. *United Nations* N.U., NN.UU. (Naciones *f/pl.* Unidas).
UNA *United Nations Association* Asociación *f* de las Naciones Unidas.
UNESCO *United Nations Educational, Scientific and Cultural Organization* UNESCO (Organización *f* de las Naciones Unidas para la Educación, la Ciencia y la Cultura).
Univ. *university* universidad *f.*

UNO *United Nations Organization* ONU (Organización *f* de las Naciones Unidas). [*mación.*｜
U.P. *United Press agencia de infor-*｜
U.P.U. *Universal Postal Union* U.P.U. (Unión *f* Postal Universal).
U.S.(A.) *United States (of America)* EE.UU. (Estados *m/pl.* Unidos [de América]).
USAF(E) *United States Air Force (Europe)* Fuerzas *f/pl.* Aéreas de Estados Unidos (en Europa).
U.S.N. *US Navy* Marina *f* Estadounidense.
U.S.P. *US Pharmacopoeia* Farmacopea *f* Estadounidense.
U.S.S.R. *Union of Soviet Socialist Republics* U.R.S.S. (Unión *f* de las Repúblicas Socialistas Soviéticas).
Ut. *Utah estado de EE.UU.*

V

v. 1. *verse* verso *m*; estrofa *f*; (*Biblical*) vers.º (versículo *m*); 2. *versus (Latin = against)* contra; 3. *vide (Latin = see)* v. (véase), vid. (vide); 4. *volt* v. (voltio *m*).
V.1 *flying bomb* bomba *f* volante.
V.2 *rocket bomb* bomba *f* cohete.
V., Vd. *vanadium* vanadio *m.*
V. & A. *Victoria and Albert (Museum) museo de Londres.*
Va. *Virginia estado de EE.UU.*
V.C. 1. *Vice-Chancellor* vicecanciller *m*, rector *m* (*de universidad*); 2. *Victoria Cross condecoración británica.*
V.D. *venereal disease* enfermedad *f* venérea.
VE Day *Victory in Europe Day día de la victoria en Europa (8 mayo 1945).*
V.H.F. *very high frequency* M.F. (modulación *f* de frecuencia).
V.I.P. *very important person* personaje *m* importante.
viz. *videlicet (Latin = namely)* v.gr. (verbigracia).
V.J. Day *Victory over Japan Day día de la victoria en la guerra de Lejano Oriente (15 agosto 1945).*
vol(s). *volume(s)* t. (tomo[s] *m* [*pl.*]).
vs. *versus (Latin = against)* contra.
Vt. *Vermont estado de EE.UU.*
v.v. *vice versa (Latin = conversely)* viceversa.

W

w. *watt* w. (vatio *m*).

W. *West(ern)* O (oeste [*m*]).

W. *wolframium (tungsten)* volframio *m*, tungsteno *m*.

War. *Warwickshire condado inglés.*

Wash. *Washington estado de EE.UU.*

W.C. 1. *West Central parte oeste del centro de Londres (distrito postal);* **2.** *water closet* W.C. (wáter *m*, inodoro *m*).

W.D. *War Department* Ministerio *m* de Guerra.

W.E.A. *Workers' Educational Association* Asociación *f* para la Educación Obrera. [*m*).⎫

Weds. *Wednesday* miérc. (miércoles⎭

W.F.T.U. *World Federation of Trade Unions* Federación *f* Mundial de Sindicatos.

W.H.O. *World Health Organization* O.M.S. (Organización *f* Mundial de la Salud).

W.I. *West Indies* Antillas *f|pl.*

Wilts. *Wiltshire condado inglés.*

Wis. *Wisconsin estado de EE.UU.*

W/L, w.l. *wave length* longitud *f* de onda.

W.O. 1. *War Office* Ministerio *m* de Guerra; **2.** *Warrant Officer* ⚓ contramaestre *m*; ✕ suboficial *m*.

Worcs. *Worcestershire condado inglés.*

W.P. *weather permitting* si lo permite el tiempo.

W/T *wireless telegraphy (telephony)* telegrafía *f* (telefonía *f*) sin hilos.

wt. *weight* peso *m*.

W.U.S. *World University Service* Servicio *m* Mundial Univetsitario.

W.Va. *West Virginia estado de EE.UU.*

Wyo. *Wyoming estado de EE.UU.*

X

X, Xe. *xenon* xenón *m*.

x-d. *ex dividend* sin dividendo.

Xmas *Christmas* Navidad *f*.

Y

Y, Yt. *yttrium* itrio *m*.

Yb. *ytterbium* iterbio *m*.

yd. *yard* * yarda *f*.

Y.H.A. *Youth Hostel Association* Asociación *f* de Albergues para la Juventud.

Y.M.C.A. *Young Men's Christian Association* Asociación *f* Cristiana para los Jóvenes.

Yorks. *Yorkshire condado inglés.*

yr. 1. *year* año *m*; **2.** *your* s/ (su).

yrs. 1. *years* años *m|pl.*; **2.** *yours* suyo.

Y.W.C.A. *Young Women's Christian Association* Asociación *f* Cristiana para las Jóvenes.

Z

Zr. *zirconium* circonio *m*, zirconio *m*.

Numerales
Numerals

Números cardinales — Cardinal numbers

0 nought *cero*	40 forty *cuarenta*
1 one *uno, una*	50 fifty *cincuenta*
2 two *dos*	60 sixty *sesenta*
3 three *tres*	70 seventy *setenta*
4 four *cuatro*	80 eighty *ochenta*
5 five *cinco*	90 ninety *noventa*
6 six *seis*	100 a (one) hundred *cien(to)*
7 seven *siete*	101 a hundred and one *ciento uno*
8 eight *ocho*	110 a hundred and ten *ciento diez*
9 nine *nueve*	200 two hundred *doscientos -as*
10 ten *diez*	300 three hundred *trescientos -as*
11 eleven *once*	400 four hundred *cuatrocientos -as*
12 twelve *doce*	500 five hundred *quinientos -as*
13 thirteen *trece*	600 six hundred *seiscientos -as*
14 fourteen *catorce*	700 seven hundred *setecientos -as*
15 fifteen *quince*	800 eight hundred *ochocientos -as*
16 sixteen *dieciséis*	900 nine hundred *novecientos -as*
17 seventeen *diecisiete*	1000 a thousand *mil*
18 eighteen *dieciocho*	1959 nineteen hundred and fifty-nine *mil novecientos cincuenta y nueve*
19 nineteen *diecinueve*	
20 twenty *veinte*	
21 twenty-one *veintiuno*	2000 two thousand *dos mil*
22 twenty-two *veintidós*	1 000 000 a (one) million *un millón (de)*
30 thirty *treinta*	
31 thirty-one *treinta y uno*	2 000 000 two million *dos millones (de)*

Números ordinales — Ordinal numbers

(The ordinal numbers in Spanish agree with the noun in number and gender, *primero -a -os -as* etc.)

1 first *primero*	14 fourteenth *decimocuarto*
2 second *segundo*	15 fifteenth *decimoquinto*
3 third *tercero*	16 sixteenth *decimosexto*
4 fourth *cuarto*	17 seventeenth *decimoséptimo*
5 fifth *quinto*	18 eighteenth *decimoctavo*
6 sixth *sexto*	19 nineteenth *decimonoveno, decimonono*
7 seventh *séptimo*	
8 eighth *octavo*	20 twentieth *vigésimo*
9 ninth *noveno, nono*	21 twenty-first *vigésimo primero, vigésimo primo*
10 tenth *décimo*	
11 eleventh *undécimo*	22 twenty-second *vigésimo segundo*
12 twelfth *duodécimo*	30 thirtieth *trigésimo*
13 thirteenth *decimotercero, decimotercio*	31 thirty-first *trigésimo primero, trigésimo primo*

40 fortieth *cuadragésimo*	500 five hundredth *quingentésimo*
50 fiftieth *quincuagésimo*	600 six hundredth *sexcentésimo*
60 sixtieth *sexagésimo*	700 seven hundredth *septingenté-*
70 seventieth *septuagésimo*	*simo*
80 eightieth *octogésimo*	800 eight hundredth *octingentésimo*
90 ninetieth *nonagésimo*	900 nine hundredth *noningentésimo*
100 hundredth *centésimo*	1000 thousandth *milésimo*
101 hundred and first *centésimo*	2000 two thousandth *dos milésimo*
primero	1 000 000 millionth *millonésimo*
110 hundred and tenth *centésimo*	2 000 000 two millionth *dos milloné-*
décimo	*simo*
200 two hundredth *ducentésimo*	En inglés, los números ordinales
300 three hundredth *trecentésimo*	suelen abreviarse 1st., 2nd., 3rd.,
400 four hundredth *cuadringenté-*	4th., 5th., *etc.*; in Spanish, the ordinal
simo	numbers may be written 1º, 2º, *etc.*

Fractions and other numerals — Números quebrados y otros

$1/2$ one (a) half *medio, media*;	single *simple*
$1^1/_2$ one and a half *uno y medio*;	double *doble, duplo*
$2^1/_2$ two and a half *dos y medio*;	treble, triple, threefold *triple*
$1/2$ hour *media hora*;	fourfold *cuádruplo*
$1^1/_2$ kilometres *kilómetro y medio*	fivefold *quintuplo etc.*
$1/3$ one (a) third *un tercio, la tercera*	once *una vez*
parte;	twice *dos veces*
$2/3$ two thirds *dos tercios, las dos*	three times *tres veces etc.*
terceras partes	seven times as big *siete veces más*
$1/4$ one (a) quarter *un cuarto, la*	*grande*; twice more *dos veces más*
cuarta parte;	firstly *en primer lugar*
$3/4$ threequarters *tres cuartos, las*	secondly *en segundo lugar etc.*
tres cuartas partes;	$7 + 8 = 15$ seven and eight are
$1/4$ hour *un cuarto de hora*;	fifteen *siete y* (or *más*)
$1^1/_4$ hours *hora y cuarto*	*ocho son quince*
$1/5$ one (a) fifth *un quinto*;	$10 - 3 = 7$ three from ten leaves
$3^4/_5$ three and four fifths *tres y*	seven *diez menos tres*
cuatro quintos	*resta siete, de tres a diez*
$1/11$ one (an) eleventh *un onzavo*;	*van siete*
$5/12$ five twelfths *cinco dozavos*;	$2 \times 3 = 6$ two times three are six
$75/100$ seventy-five hundredths *seten-*	*dos por tres son seis*
ta y cinco centésimos	$20 \div 4 = 5$ twenty divided by four
$1/1000$ one (a) thousandth *un milé-*	is five *veinte dividido*
simo	*por cuatro es cinco.*

Nota sobre el verbo inglés

a) Conjugación

Modo indicativo.

1. **El tiempo presente** tiene la misma forma que el infinitivo en todas las personas menos la 3a del singular; en ésta, se añade una -s al infinitivo, p. ej. *he brings*, o se añade -es si el infinitivo termina en sibilante (ch, sh, ss, zz), p. ej. *he passes*. Esta s tiene dos pronunciaciones distintas: tras consonante sorda se pronuncia sorda, p.ej. *he paints* [peints]; tras consonante sonora se pronuncia sonora, p.ej. *he sends* [sendz]; -es se pronuncia también sonora, sea la e parte de la desinencia o letra final del infinitivo, p.ej. *he washes* ['wɔʃiz], *he urges* ['ɔːdʒiz]. Los verbos que terminan en -y la cambian en -ies en la tercera persona, p.ej. *he worries, he tries,* pero son regulares los verbos que en el infinitivo tienen una vocal delante de la -y, p.ej. *he plays.* El verbo *be* es irregular en todas las personas: *I am, you are, he is, we are, you are, they are.* Tres verbos más tienen forma especial para la tercera persona del singular: *do—he does, go—he goes, have—he has.*

   En los demás tiempos, todas las personas son iguales. **El pretérito y el participio del pasado** se forman añadiendo -ed al infinitivo, p.ej. *I passed, passed,* o añadiendo -d a los infinitivos que terminan en -e, p.ej. *I faced, faced.* (Hay muchos verbos irregulares: *v.* abajo). Esta -(e)d se pronuncia generalmente como [t]: *passed* [paːst], *faced* [feist]; pero cuando se añade a un infinitivo que termina en consonante sonora o en sonido consonántico sonoro o en *r*, se pronuncia como [d]: *warmed* [wɔːmd], *moved* [muːvd], *feared* [fiəd]. Si el infinitivo termina en -d o -t, la desinencia -ed se pronuncia [id]. Si el infinitivo termina en -y, ésta se cambia en -ie antes de añadirse la -d: *try—tried* [traid], *pity—pitied* ['pitid]. **Los tiempos compuestos del pasado** se forman con el verbo auxiliar *have* y el participio del pasado, como en español: **perfecto** *I have faced,* **pluscuamperfecto** *I had faced.* Con el verbo auxiliar *will (shall)* y el infinitivo se forma **el futuro**, p.ej. *I shall face,* y con el verbo auxiliar *would (should)* y el infinitivo se forma **el condicional**, p.ej. *I should face.*

   En cada tiempo existe además una forma continua, que se forma con el verbo *be* (= estar) y el participio del presente (*v.* abajo): *I am going, I was writing, I had been staying, I shall be waiting,* etc.

2. **El subjuntivo** ha dejado casi de existir en inglés, salvo en algún caso especial (*if I were you, so be it, it is proposed that a vote be taken,* etc.). En el presente, tiene en todas las personas la misma forma que el infinitivo, *that I go, that he go,* etc.

3. **El participio del presente** y **el gerundio** tienen la misma forma en inglés, añadiéndose al infinitivo la desinencia -ing: *painting, sending.* Pero 1) Los verbos cuyo infinitivo termina en -e muda la pierden al añadir -ing, p.ej. *love—loving, write—writing* (excepciones que conservan la -e: *dye—dyeing, singe—singeing, shoe—shoeing*); 2) El participio del presente de los verbos *die, lie, vie* etc. se escribe *dying, lying, vying* etc.

4. Existe una clase de verbos ligeramente irregulares, que terminan en consonante simple precedida de vocal simple acentuada; en éstos, antes de añadir la desinencia -ing o -ed, se dobla la consonante:

to lob	lobbed	lobbing
to wed	wedded	wedding
to beg	begged	begging
to step	stepped	stepping
to quit	quitted	quitting
to compel	compelled	compelling
to control	controlled	controlling
to bar	barred	barring
to stir	stirred	stirring

Los verbos que terminan en -l, -p, aunque precedida de vocal átona, tienen doblada la consonante en los dos participios en el inglés escrito en Gran Bretaña, aunque no en el de Estados Unidos:

to travel	travelled	travelling
	Am. traveled	*Am.* traveling
to worship	worshipped	worshipping
	Am. worshiped	*Am.* worshiping

Los verbos que terminan en -c la cambian en -ck al añadirse las desinencias -ed, -ing:

to traffic	trafficked	trafficking

5. **La voz pasiva** se forma exactamente como en español, con el verbo *be* y el participio del pasado: *I am obliged, he was fined, they will be moved,* etc.

6. Cuando se dirige uno directamente a otra(s) persona(s) en inglés se emplea únicamente el pronombre *you,* con las formas correspondientes del verbo (2a persona del plural). *You* traduce por tanto el *tú, vosotros, usted y ustedes* del español. La segunda persona del singular en inglés (*thou*) no se emplea más que dialectalmente o en el rezo.

b) Los verbos irregulares ingleses

Se citan las tres partes principales de cada verbo: infinitivo, pretérito, participio del pasado.

abide - abode - abode
arise - arose - arisen
awake - awoke - awoke, awaked
be (am, is, are) - was (were) - been
bear - bore - borne (*llevado*), born (*nacido*)
beat - beat - beaten, beat
become - became - become
beget - begot, † begat - begotten
begin - began - begun
belay - belayed, belaid - belayed, belaid
bend - bent - bent
bereave - bereaved, bereft - bereaved, bereft
beseech - besought - besought
bestrew - bestrewed - bestrewed, bestrewn
bestride - bestrode - bestridden

bet - bet, betted - bet, betted
bid - bade, bid - bidden, bid
bind - bound - bound
bite - bit - bitten
bleed - bled - bled
blow - blew - blown
break - broke - broken
breed - bred - bred
bring - brought - brought
build - built - built
burn - burnt, burned - burnt, burned
burst - burst - burst
buy - bought - bought
can - could
cast - cast - cast
catch - caught - caught
chide - chid - chid, chidden
choose - chose - chosen

cleave - clove, cleft - cloven, cleft
cling - clung - clung
clothe - clothed, *lit.* clad - clothed, *lit.* clad
come - came - come
cost - cost - cost
creep - crept - crept
cut - cut - cut
dare - dared, † durst - dared
deal - dealt - dealt
dig - dug - dug
do - did - done
draw - drew - drawn
dream - dreamt, dreamed - dreamt, dreamed
drink - drank - drunk
drive - drove - driven
dwell - dwelt - dwelt
eat - ate - eaten
fall - fell - fallen
feed - fed - fed
feel - felt - felt
fight- fought - fought
find - found - found
flee - fled - fled
fling - flung - flung
fly - flew - flown
forbear - forbore- forborne
forbid - forbad(e) - forbidden
forget - forgot- forgotten
forgive - forgave - forgiven
forsake - forsook - forsaken
freeze - froze - frozen
geld - gelded, gelt - gelded, gelt
get - got - got, *Am.* gotten
gild - gilded, gilt - gilded, gilt
gird - girded, girt - girded, girt
give - gave - given
go - went - gone
grave - graved - graved, graven
grind - ground - ground
grow - grew - grown
hang - hung, ₮ hanged - hung, ₮ hanged
have - had - had
hear - heard - heard
heave - heaved, ⚓ hove - heaved, ⚓ hove
hew - hewed - hewed, hewn
hide - hid - hidden, hid
hit - hit - hit
hold - held - held
hurt - hurt - hurt
keep - kept - kept
kneel - knelt, kneeled - knelt, kneeled
knit - knitted, knit - knitted, knit
know - knew - known

lade - laded - laded, laden
lay - laid - laid
lead - led - led
lean - leaned, leant - leaned, leant
leap - leaped, leapt - leaped, leapt
learn - learned, learnt - learned, learnt
leave - left - left
lend - lent - lent
let - let - let
lie - lay - lain
light - lighted, lit - lighted, lit
lose - lost - lost
make - made - made
may - might
mean - meant - meant
meet - met - met
mow - mowed - mowed, mown
must - must
falta el presente - **ought**
pay - paid - paid
pen - penned, pent - penned, pent
put - put - put
read [ri:d] - read [red] - read [red]
rend - rent - rent
rid - rid - rid
ride - rode - ridden
ring - rang - rung
rise - rose - risen
rive - rived - riven
run - ran - run
saw - sawed - sawn, sawed
say - said - said
see - saw - seen
seek - sought - sought
sell - sold - sold
send - sent - sent
set - set - set
sew - sewed - sewed, sewn
shake - shook - shaken
shall - should
shave - shaved - shaved, (*mst adj.*) shaven
shear - sheared - shorn
shed - shed - shed
shine - shone - shone
shoe - shod - shod
shoot - shot - shot
show - showed - shown
shred - shredded - shredded, shred
shrink - shrank - shrunk
shut - shut - shut
sing - sang - sung
sink - sank - sunk
sit - sat - sat
slay - slew - slain
sleep - slept - slept

slide - slid - slid
sling - slung - slung
slink - slunk - slunk
slit - slit - slit
smell - smelt, smelled - smelt, smelled
smite - smote - smitten
sow - sowed - sown, sowed
speak - spoke - spoken
speed - sped, ⊕ speeded - sped, ⊕ speeded
spell - spelt, spelled - spelt, spelled
spend - spent - spent
spill - spilt, spilled - spilt, spilled
spin - spun, span - spun
spit - spat - spat
split - split - split
spoil - spoiled, spoilt - spoiled, spoilt
spread - spread - spread
spring - sprang - sprung
stand - stood - stood
stave - staved, stove - staved, stove
steal - stole - stolen
stick - stuck - stuck
sting - stung - stung
stink - stunk, stank - stunk
strew - strewed - (have) strewed, (be) strewn
stride - strode - stridden

strike - struck - struck
string - strung - strung
strive - strove - striven
swear - swore - sworn
sweep - swept - swept
swell - swelled - swollen
swim - swam - swum
swing - swung - swung
take - took - taken
teach - taught - taught
tear - tore - torn
tell - told - told
think - thought - thought
thrive - throve - thriven
throw - threw - thrown
thrust - thrust - thrust
tread - trod - trodden
wake - woke, waked - waked, woke(n)
wear - wore - worn
weave - wove - woven
weep - wept - wept
wet - wetted, wet - wetted, wet
will - would
win - won - won
wind - wound - wound
work - worked, ⊕ wrought - worked, ⊕ wrought
wring - wrung - wrung
write - wrote - written

Weights and Measures

Pesos y Medidas

1. Linear Measures
Medidas de Longitud

1 inch (in.)
= 2,54 cm.
1 foot (ft.)
= 12 inches = 30,48 cm.
1 yard (yd.)
= 3 feet = 91,44 cm.

2. Distance and Surveyors' Measures
Medidas de Distancia y de Agrimensura

1 link (li., l.)
= 7.92 inches = 20,12 cm.
1 rod (rd.), pole o perch (p.)
= 25 links = 5,029 m.
1 chain (ch.)
= 4 rods = 20,12 m.
1 furlong (fur.)
= 10 chains = 201,17 m.
1 (statute) mile (mi.)
= 1,760 yards = 1609,34 m.

3. Nautical Measures
Medidas Náuticas

1 fathom (fm.)
= 6 feet = 1,83 m.
1 cable('s) length
= 100 fathoms = 183 m.
Am. 120 fathoms = 219 m.
1 nautical mile (n. m.)
= 10 cables' length = 1852 m.

4. Square Measures
Medidas Cuadradas

1 square inch (sq. in.)
= 6,45 cm².
1 square foot (sq. ft.)
= 144 square inches
= 929,03 cm².

1 square yard (sq. yd.)
= 9 square feet = 0,836 m².
1 square rod (sq. rd.)
= 30.25 square yards = 25,29 m².
1 rood (ro.)
= 40 square rods = 10,12 áreas.
1 acre (a.)
= 4 roods = 40,47 áreas.
1 square mile (sq. mi.)
= 640 acres = 2,59 km².

5. Cubic Measures
Medidas de Cubicación

1 cubic inch (cu. in.)
= 16,387 cm³.
1 cubic foot (cu. ft.)
= 1728 cubic inches
= 0,028 m³.
1 cubic yard (cu. yd.)
= 27 cubic feet = 0,765 m³.
1 register ton (reg. tn.)
= 100 cubic feet = 2,832 m³.

6. British Measures of Capacity
Medidas de Capacidad (Gran Bretaña)

Dry and Liquid Measures
Medidas para Aridos y Líquidos

1 British o Imperial gill (gi., gl.)
= 0,142 l.
1 British o Imperial pint (pt.)
= 4 gills = 0,568 l.
1 British o Imperial quart (qt.)
= 2 Imp. pints = 1,136 l.
1 British o Imp. gallon (Imp.gal.)
= 4 Imp. quarts = 4,546 l.

Dry Measures
Medidas para Aridos

1 British o Imperial peck (pk.)
= 2 Imp. gallons = 9,087 l.
1 Brit. o Imp. bushel (bu., bsh.)
= 4 Imp. pecks = 36,36 l.

1 Brit. *o* **Imperial quarter (qr.)**
   = 8 Imp. bushels = 290,94 l.

Liquid Measure
Medida para Líquidos

1 Brit. *o* **Imp. barrel (bbl., bl.)**
   = 36 Imp. gallons = 1,636 Hl.

7. Measures of Capacity (U.S.A.)
Medidas de Capacidad (EE.UU.)

Dry Measures
Medidas para Aridos

1 U.S. dry pint
   = 0,550 l.
1 U.S. dry quart
   = 2 dry pints = 1,1 l.
1 U.S. peck
   = 8 dry quarts = 8,81 l.
1 U.S. bushel *(granos)*
   = 4 pecks = 35,24 l.

Liquid Measures
Medidas para Líquidos

1 U.S. liquid gill
   = 0,118 l.
1 U.S. liquid pint
   = 4 gills = 0,473 l.
1 U.S. liquid quart
   = 2 liquid pints = 0,946 l.
1 U.S. gallon
   = 4 liquid quarts = 3,785 l.
1 U.S. barrel
   = 31¹/₂ gallons = 119 l.
1 U.S. barrel petroleum
   = 42 gallons = 158,97 l.

8. Apothecaries' Fluid Measures
Medidas de Boticario

1 minim (min., m.)
   = 0,0006 dl.
1 fluid drachm, *Am.* **dram (dr. fl.)**
   = 60 minims = 0,0355 dl.
1 fluid ounce (oz. fl.)
   = 8 fluid dra(ch)ms = 0,284 dl.

1 pint (pt.)
   = 20 fluid ounces = 0,568 l.
   Am. 16 fluid ounces = 0,473 l.

9. Avoirdupois Weight
Peso Avoirdupois

1 grain (gr.)
   = 0,0648 gr.
1 drachm, *Am.* **dram (dr. av.)**
   = 27.34 grains = 1,77 gr.
1 ounce (oz. av.)
   = 16 dra(ch)ms = 28,35 gr.
1 pound (lb. av.)
   = 16 ounces = 0,453 kg.
1 stone (st.)
   = 14 pounds = 6,35 kg.
1 quarter (qr.)
   = 28 pounds = 12,7 kg.
   Am. 25 pounds = 11,34 kg.
1 hundredweight (cwt.)
   = 112 pounds = 50,8 kg.
   (*a.* long hundredweight:
   cwt. l.)
   Am. 100 pounds = 45,36 kg.
   (*a.* short hundredweight:
   cwt. sh.)
1 ton (tn., t.)
   = 2240 pounds (= 20 cwt. l.) =
   1016 kg. (*a.* long ton: tn. l.)
   Am. = 2000 pounds (= 20 cwt. sh.)
   = 907,18 kg.
   (*a.* short ton: tn. sh.)

10. Troy and Apothecaries' Weight
Peso Troy y de Boticario

1 grain (gr.)
   = 0,0648 gr.
1 scruple (s. ap.)
   = 20 grains = 1,296 gr.
1 pennyweight (dwt.)
   = 24 grains = 1,555 gr.
1 dra(ch)m (dr. t. *o* **dr. ap.)**
   = 3 scruples = 3,888 gr.
1 ounce (oz. ap.)
   = 8 dra(ch)ms = 31,104 gr.
1 pound (lb. t. *o* **lb. ap.)**
   = 12 ounces = 0,373 kg.

LANGENSCHEIDT
STANDARD DICTIONARIES

Second Part

Spanish/English

by

C. C. SMITH

G. A. DAVIES

H. B. HALL

Contents
Materias

○ 1966 Langenscheidt KG, Berlin und München

Preface

We believe that this work will be found to serve—within the obvious limits of its size—a very wide range of purposes.

The dictionary is up-to-date in several senses. First, it has a good selection of the hundreds of neologisms which scientific progress and other agents in modern life are annually creating, many of them not hitherto treated in any Spanish-English dictionary. Second, we have included a greater proportion than is normal of colloquial words, idioms and phrases, even clichés and slang, in the belief that this will better meet the needs of a public more given than ever to travelling abroad, maintaining correspondence overseas, listening to foreign broadcasts, engaging in business with foreign companies, and learning languages for practical rather than for literary or academic ends. Third, large numbers of words are drawn from sport, radio, television, the cinema, and from other spheres which are equally the creation of our own times. Fourth, some attempt has been made to indicate important words used in Spanish America but not in Spain. Fifth, the writing of Spanish words has been governed by the *Nuevas Normas* issued by the Academy in 1952 and revised in 1959.

It is hoped that the introductory note on the sound-system of Spanish, whose writing so nearly perfectly represents the pronunciation, will obviate the need for a phonetic transcription of every headword. This is, however, provided in those rare cases (chiefly words of recent foreign origin) where spelling and pronunciation are not in accord. Within each entry, the reader is offered many defining words to help his choice of an exact translation, and is given help with grammatical constructions.

The appendices contain: a list of important proper names (personal, historical, geographical); a list of abbreviations, with an expansion and where possible a translation of each; a note on the Spanish verb system and a chart of the conjugation of regular and irregular verbs; a table of numerals; and a table of weights and measures.

Although we claim to make certain useful innovations in the dictionary, it leans heavily—as all dictionaries must—upon its predecessors. Among them a special debt must be recognized to the large Spanish-English dictionaries of Williams, Raventós, Amador and Cuyás-Llano, and to the smaller works of Calvert and Brown. The technical dictionaries of Sell and Castilla have also been consulted. Among Spanish dictionaries, we have used the official dictionary of the Academy and the *Diccionario General Ilustrado* of Vox, together with the *Pequeño Larousse Ilustrado* and the Espasa-Calpe *Enciclopedia*. Two other compilations have been extremely helpful: Gerrard and Heras' *Beyond the Dictionary in Spanish*, and Lyon's *Pitfalls of Spanish Vocabulary*.

Apart from this, we are indebted to a number of people, many of them past or present members of the University of Leeds, for expert advice generously given during many months of work. Sr Agustín de Irízar and Dr Manuel Bermejo Marcos have been untiring in their efforts to solve our problems. Much help has also come from Srta María Victoria Alvarez, Srta Paloma de Hita, Professor R. F. Brown, and Mr Peter Saword; also from Professor Keith Whinnom, and Colonel Enrique Navasa of Madrid. To all of them our warmest thanks.

C.C.S.
G.A.D.
H.B.H.

Prólogo

Creemos que la presente obra podrá resolver un buen número de problemas no solucionados hasta ahora por los diccionarios ya existentes.

Nuestro diccionario está al día en varios sentidos. Primero, contiene una buena selección de los centenares de neologismos forjados todos los años por el progreso científico y otros agentes de la vida de nuestra época, muchos de ellos no incluidos hasta la fecha en ningún diccionario español-inglés. Segundo, figura aquí una representación importante—en general, mayor que la que suele figurar en diccionarios de este tipo—de palabras, giros y frases, incluso de clichés y términos de argot, tomados de la lengua hablada actual, con lo cual creemos que podrán satisfacerse mejor las necesidades de un público más aficionado que nunca a viajar por el extranjero, a mantener correspondencia con otros países, a escuchar emisiones extranjeras, a comerciar con empresas de ultramar, y a aprender idiomas con fines más bien prácticos que literarios o eruditos. Tercero, gran número de palabras nos han sido suministradas por los deportes, la radio, la televisión, el cine y otras tantas formas de actividad que son igualmente creación de nuestra época. Cuarto, hemos indicado voces importantes que figuran en el habla hispanoamericana, pero que no aparecen en la de España. Quinto, respecto a la ortografía de las voces españolas, nos hemos atenido a las *Nuevas Normas* publicadas por la Real Academia de la Lengua en 1952 y corregidas en 1959.

Creemos que la nota preliminar sobre el sistema fonético del español, cuya ortografía representa casi perfectamente la pronunciación, nos excusa de poner una pronunciación figurada tras cada voz-guía; pero ponemos ésta en aquellos casos—nada frecuentes, y en su mayor parte extranjerismos de origen reciente—donde la ortografía no concuerda con la pronunciación. Dentro de cada artículo, el lector encontrará muchas definiciones que le ayudarán a elegir la traducción exacta. Además, hemos incluido las construcciones gramaticales.

En los apéndices se encontrará: una lista de nombres propios importantes (personales, históricos, geográficos); una lista de abreviaturas, con su forma completa correspondiente, y donde esto ha sido posible, una traducción; una nota sobre los verbos españoles y un cuadro de los verbos regulares e irregulares; una tabla de números; y un cuadro de pesos y medidas.

Aunque pretendemos haber introducido en este diccionario ciertas innovaciones útiles, nos hemos apoyado mucho en la labor de nuestros antecesores, cosa inevitable en este tipo de trabajo. Entre ellos, debemos destacar una deuda especial a los grandes diccionarios español-inglés de Williams, Raventós, Amador y Cuyás-Llano, y las obras de menor volumen de Calvert y de Brown. Hemos consultado también los diccionarios técnicos de Sell y de Castilla. Entre los diccionarios españoles hemos hecho uso del *Diccionario de la Real Academia de la Lengua* y del *Diccionario General Ilustrado* de Vox, además del *Pequeño Larousse Ilustrado* y de la *Enciclopedia Espasa-Calpe*. Otros dos compendios nos han sido sumamente útiles: *Beyond the Dictionary in Spanish* de Gerrard y Heras, y *Pitfalls of Spanish Vocabulary* de Lyon.

Hemos de poner de manifiesto la deuda que tenemos con varias personas—muchas de ellas miembros antiguos o actuales de la Universidad de Leeds—por los sagaces consejos que tan generosamente nos ofrecieron durante los largos meses de trabajo. Destaquemos a don Agustín de Irízar y al Dr. don Manuel Bermejo Marcos, quienes se han mostrado en todo momento incansables en sus esfuerzos por resolver nuestros problemas. También hemos recibido una ayuda apreciable de las Srtas. María Victoria Alvarez y Paloma de Hita, del Profesor R. F. Brown, de Mr Peter Saword, del Profesor Keith Whinnom, y del Coronel don Enrique Navasa, de Madrid. A todos ellos, nuestro más sincero agradecimiento.

C.C.S.
G.A.D.
H.B.H.

Directions for the use of the dictionary

Advertencias para facilitar la consulta del diccionario

1. Arrangement. A strict alphabetical order has been maintained throughout. The following will therefore be found in alphabetical order: the irregular forms of verbs; the various forms of the pronouns and article, etc.; and compounds.

Proper names and abbreviations are collected in special lists at the end of the dictionary.

2. Vocabulary. In many cases, the rarer words formed with e.g. *-idad, -ción, -ador, -ante, -oso, in-, des-* are excluded, to avoid extending the dictionary beyond all reasonable limits. The reader having some slight acquaintance with the processes of word-formation in the two languages will be able to look up the root word and form derived words from it.

Abstract nouns are often dealt with very briefly when they are adjacent to a root-word which has been fully dealt with. Thus the entry **elegancia** *f* elegance *etc.* means: see the adjective *elegante* and form other abstract nouns accordingly.

3. Separation of different senses. The various senses of each Spanish word are made clear:

a) by symbols and abbreviated categories (see list on pp. 12 and 13);

b) by explanatory additions in italics, which may be a synonym (e.g. *emparejar [aparear]* match), or a complement (e.g. *enloquecedor jaqueca* splitting), or the ob-

1. El orden alfabético queda rigurosamente establecido. Ocupan su lugar alfabético, por tanto: las formas irregulares de los verbos; las diferentes formas de los pronombres y del artículo, etcétera, y las palabras compuestas.

Los nombres propios y las abreviaturas van reunidos en listas especiales que se imprimen como apéndices.

2. Vocabulario. En muchos casos se excluyen las palabras derivadas menos corrientes, que se forman, p.ej., con *-idad, -ción, -ador, -ante, -oso, in-, des-*, a fin de no extender más de lo razonable los límites del diccionario. El lector que tenga algún conocimiento de cómo se forman las palabras derivadas en los dos idiomas podrá buscar la palabra radical y formar sobre ella las derivadas que quiera.

Los sustantivos abstractos están tratados a menudo en forma somera cuando la palabra radical se ha tratado en forma extensa. Por tanto, el artículo **elegancia** *f* elegance *etc.* quiere decir: véase el adjetivo *elegante* para formar luego los sustantivos abstractos correspondientes.

3. Separación de las diversas acepciones. Las diversas acepciones de cada palabra española se indican:

a) mediante signos y categorías abreviadas (véase la lista en las págs. 12 y 13);

b) mediante aclaraciones impresas en bastardilla, las cuales pueden ser un sinónimo (p.ej., *emparejar [aparear]* match), o complemento (p.ej., *enloquecedor jaqueca* split-

ject of a transitive verb (e.g., *echar mirada* cast), or the subject of an intransitive or reflexive verb (e.g., *empalmar [trenes]* connect), or again some other indication which while not exactly synonymous will none the less help the user in his search through the article for the required word.

Sometimes, e.g. with many abstract nouns, these explanations are omitted, but can easily be supplied from the adjacent entry for the corresponding adjective or other root-word.

In the first (English-Spanish) part of the dictionary all these indications are in English, and in this second (Spanish-English) part they are in Spanish. This arrangement is in accordance with the best modern theory. The indications have been kept as simple as possible and users knowing little of the other language should not find them difficult to understand when translating from the foreign language into their own. The abbreviations, largely English but often bilingual, are of course the same in both parts.

It must be emphasized that such indications and explanations are intended only as the most elementary guide to the user, and are in no way complete definitions or exclusive rules about usage. There are many cases in which, given the limited space available, it has not been possible to provide indications of any sort.

4. The different parts of speech are indicated by numbers within each entry; the grammatical indication *adj.*, *adv.*, etc., is omitted in all cases where the category is obvious.

5. The gender of every Spanish noun headword is indicated. In the case of a noun referring to a person which has a form for each gender, both are given; where the final o or e changes to *a* for the feminine, we write *pasajero m, a f* passenger;

ting), u objeto de verbo transitivo (p.ej. *echar mirada* cast) o sujeto de verbo intransitivo o reflexivo (p.ej. *empalmar [trenes]* connect), u otra indicación no precisamente sinónima pero que todavía le podrá ayudar al lector en la elección de la palabra justa.

Estas aclaraciones suelen omitirse en el caso de muchos sustantivos abstractos, etcétera, pero es fácil suplirlas refiriéndose al artículo del adjetivo o palabra radical correspondiente.

En la 1a parte (Inglés-Español) de este diccionario todas estas indicaciones van en inglés, y en esta 2a parte (Español-Inglés) van en español. Esto está de acuerdo con la más autorizada teoría actual. Las indicaciones son las más sencillas posibles para que el lector que no domine muy bien el otro idioma pueda comprenderlas sin demasiada dificultad al traducir una palabra de la lengua extranjera a la suya propia. Las abreviaturas, en inglés en su mayoría pero bilingües muchas, son desde luego idénticas en ambas partes.

Hay que insistir en que estas indicaciones y aclaraciones se le ofrecen al lector como guías sumamente sencillas y elementales, nada más; no pretenden de ningún modo formular definiciones completas ni ofrecer reglas exclusivas para el uso. Y son muchos los casos donde, dentro de los límites del diccionario, no ha sido posible dar indicación alguna.

4. Las diferentes partes de la oración están indicadas dentro de cada artículo mediante números; las indicaciones gramaticales *adj.*, *adv.* etcétera están suprimidas cuando la categoría es obvia.

5. Se indica el género de cada sustantivo español que encabeza artículo. En el caso de los sustantivos de persona que tienen distintas formas para los dos géneros, se ponen las dos formas; cuando la o o la e final se cambia en *a* para formar el

where the *a* has to be added for the feminine, we write *escritor m, -a f* writer. In this second class, some endings carry an accent in the masculine which is not needed in the feminine, and this suppression is not indicated in the dictionary. The endings affected are: *-án, -ín, -ón* and *-és*, so that *danés m, -a f* means *danés m, danesa f.*

femenino, ponemos *pasajero m, a f* passenger; cuando hay que añadir una *a* para la forma femenina, ponemos *escritor m, -a f* writer. En ciertas desinencias de esta segunda clase, el acento que lleva el género masculino se suprime en el femenino, supresión que no está indicada en el diccionario. Estas desinencias son: *-án, -ín, -ón, -és,* de manera que *danés m, -a f* quiere decir: *danés m, danesa f.*

6. Phonetic transcription. This is given only in rare cases in which the pronunciation of a Spanish word does not correspond perfectly to its spelling. For the rest it will be sufficient for the reader to consult pp. 14—16 to know from its written form how any Spanish word is pronounced and stressed.

6. La pronunciación figurada se da únicamente en aquellos casos excepcionales donde la pronunciación de una palabra española (generalmente un extranjerismo) no concuerda con su escritura. Para las demás, bastará con que el lector consulte las págs. 14—16 para saber cómo hay que pronunciar y acentuar cualquier palabra española.

7. Translation. In rare cases, accurate single-word translation is impossible or meaningless. Recognizing this obvious linguistic fact, we have in such cases either provided an explanation in italics, or have introduced the translation with the warning abbreviation *approx.* (= approximately).

7. La traducción. En muy contados casos, la traducción exacta o resulta imposible o carece de sentido práctico. Ante este innegable hecho lingüístico, ponemos en dichos casos o una explicación en bastardilla, o, como advertencia al lector, la abreviatura *approx.* (= aproximadamente).

8. Brackets enclosing part of a word. When certain letters stand within brackets, we indicate

8. El paréntesis que encierra parte de una palabra. Cuando ciertas letras están en paréntesis, indicamos

a) two forms that may be used indifferently, e.g. *sond(e)ar;*

a) dos formas que se pueden usar sin distinción, p.ej., *sond(e)ar;*

b) two forms that may for convenience be run together because the translation of both is the same, e.g. *abarquillar(se)*, since the English word "curl up" covers both the transitive and reflexive senses.

b) dos formas que pueden ponerse juntas porque se traducen las dos por la misma palabra, p.ej. *abarquillar(se)*, puesto que la palabra inglesa "curl up" traduce los dos sentidos transitivo y reflexivo.

9. As appendices, the reader will find: a list of proper names, a list of abbreviations, a table of numerals, a table of the conjugation of Spanish regular and irregular verbs (to which the numbers and letters placed after verb headwords refer, e.g. *abalanzar* [1f], *vender* [2a]), and a table of weights, measures and coinage.

9. Como apéndices, el diccionario tiene: una lista de nombres propios, una lista de abreviaturas, una tabla de numerales, una tabla de la conjugación de los verbos españoles regulares e irregulares (tabla a la cual se refieren los números y letras colocados tras cada verbo que encabeza artículo, p.ej. *abalanzar* [1f], *vender* [2a]), y una tabla de pesos, medidas y moneda.

Key to the symbols and abbreviations

Explicación de los signos y abreviaturas

1. Symbols — Signos

~ ~ is the mark of repetition or tilde (swung dash). Sometimes when several compound words have their first element in common, that element is replaced by the thick tilde: **radio...: ⁓captar, ⁓difusión.** The thin tilde (⁓) used within the entry indicates the repetition of the headword, e.g. **rato...** *un buen ⁓, ⁓s pl. perdidos, pasar el ⁓.*

When the initial letter of the headword changes from a capital to a small letter, or vice versa, the normal tilde mark is replaced by the sign ⚥: **sede...** *Santa ⚥.*

~ ~ es la tilde o raya que indica repetición. Alguna vez cuando varias palabras compuestas tienen el primer elemento en común sustituimos ese elemento por la raya gruesa: **radio...: ⁓captar, ⁓difusión.** La tilde delgada (⁓) empleada dentro del artículo indica la repetición de la palabra que encabeza el artículo, p.ej. **rato...** *un buen ⁓, ⁓s pl. perdidos, pasar el ⁓.*

El signo ⚥ significa la repetición de la palabra que encabeza el artículo con inicial cambiada (mayúscula en minúscula o viceversa): **sede...** *Santa ⚥.*

F	familiar, colloquial, *familiar, coloquial.*	🚂	railway, *ferrocarriles.*
†	archaic, *arcaico.*	✈	aviation, *aviación.*
⚹	rare, little used, *raro, poco usado.*	📬	postal affairs, *correos.*
🕮	scientific, learned, *científico, culto.*	♪	music, *música.*
⚘	botany, *botánica.*	🏛	architecture, *arquitectura.*
⊕	technology, handicrafts, *tecnología, artes mecánicas.*	⚡	electrical engineering, *electrotecnia.*
⚒	mining, *minería.*	⚖	jurisprudence, *jurisprudencia.*
⚔	military, *milicia.*	A	mathematics, *matemáticas.*
⚓	nautical, *náutica.*	✦	farming, *agricultura.*
♀	commerce, *comercio.*	℞	chemistry, *química.*
		✚	medicine, *medicina.*

2. Abbreviations — Abreviaturas

a.	and, also, y, *también*	*m/pl.*	masculine plural, *masculin al plural*
abbr.	abbreviation, *abreviatura*		
acc.	accusative, *acusativo*	*mst*	mostly, *por la mayor part*
adj.	adjective, *adjetivo*	*opt.*	optics, *óptica*
adv.	adverb, *adverbio*	*orn.*	ornithology. *ornitología*
Am.	Americanism, *americanismo*	*o.s., o.s.*	oneself, *uno mismo, sí mismo*
anat.	anatomy, *anatomía*	*p., p.*	person, *persona*
approx.	approximately, *aproximadamente*	*paint.*	painting, *pintura*
		parl.	parliamentary, *parlamentario*
ast.	astronomy, *astronomía*		
attr.	attributive, *atributivo*	*pharm.*	pharmacy, *farmacia*
biol.	biology, *biología*	*phls.*	philosophy, *filosofía*
b.s.	bad sense, *mal sentido, peyorativo*	*phot.*	photography, *fotografía*
		phys.	physics, *física*
cj.	conjunction, *conjunción*	*physiol.*	physiology, *fisiología*
co.	comic(al), *cómico*	*pl.*	plural, *plural*
comp.	comparative, *comparativo*	*poet.*	poetry, poetic, *poesía, poético*
contp.	contemptuous, *despectivo*	*pol.*	politics, *política*
dat.	dative, *dativo*	*p.p.*	past participle, *participio del pasado*
eccl.	ecclesiastical, *eclesiástico*		
e.g.	for example, *por ejemplo*	*pred.*	predicative, *predicativo*
esp.	especially, *especialmente*	*pret.*	preterit(e), *pretérito*
etc.	et cetera, *etcétera*	*pron.*	pronoun, *pronombre*
euph.	euphemism, *eufemismo*	*prov.*	provincialism, *provincialismo*
f	feminine, *femenino*	*prp.*	preposition, *preposición*
fenc.	fencing, *esgrima*	*rhet.*	rhetoric, *retórica*
fig.	figurative, *figurativo, figurado*	*S.Am.*	Spanish Americanism, *hispanoamericanismo*
f/pl.	feminine plural, *feminino al plural*	*sew.*	sewing, *costura*
		sg.	singular, *singular*
freq.	frequently, *frecuentemente*	*sl.*	slang, *argot, germanía*
gen.	generally, *generalmente*	*s.o., s.o.*	someone, *alguien*
geog.	geography, *geografía*	*s.t., s.t.*	something, *algo*
geol.	geology, *geología*	*su.*	substantive, *sustantivo*
ger.	gerund, *gerundio*	*subj.*	subjunctive, *subjuntivo*
gr.	grammar, *gramática*	*sup.*	superlative, *superlativo*
hist.	history, *historia*	*surv.*	surveying, *topografía*
hunt.	hunting, *montería*	*tel.*	telegraphy, *telegrafía*
ichth.	ichthyology, *ictiología*	*teleph.*	telephony, *telefonía*
indic.	indicative, *indicativo*	*th.*	thing, *cosa*
inf.	infinitive, *infinitivo*	*thea.*	theatre, *teatro*
int.	interjection, *interjección*	*typ.*	typography, *tipografía*
iro.	ironical, *irónico*	*univ.*	university, *universidad*
lit.	literary, *literario*	*v.*	vide (see), *véase*
m	masculine, *masculino*	*v/aux.*	auxiliary verb, *verbo auxiliar*
metall.	metallurgy, *metalurgia*	*vet.*	veterinary, *veterinaria*
meteor.	meteorology, *meteorología*	*v/i.*	intransitive verb, *verbo intransitivo*
m/f	masculine and feminine, *masculino y femenino*	*v/r.*	reflexive verb, *verbo reflexivo*
min.	mineralogy, *mineralogía*	*v/t.*	transitive verb, *verbo transitivo*
mot.	motoring, *automovilismo*		
mount.	mountaineering, *alpinismo*	*zo.*	zoology, *zoología*

The pronunciation of Spanish

Accentuation

1. If the word ends in a vowel, or in *n* or *s*, the penultimate syllable is stressed: *espada, biblioteca, hablan, telefonean, edificios.*

2. If the word ends in a consonant other than *n* or *s*, the last syllable is stressed: *dificultad, hablar, laurel, niñez.*

3. If the word is to be stressed in any way contrary to rules **1** and **2**, an acute accent is written over the stressed vowel: *rubí, máquina, crímenes, carácter, continúa, autobús.*

4. **Diphthongs and syllable division.** Of the 5 vowels, *a e o* are considered "strong", *i* and *u* "weak":
   a) A combination of weak + strong forms a diphthong, the stress falling on the stronger element: *reina, baile, cosmonauta, tiene, bueno.*
   b) A combination of weak + weak forms a diphthong, the stress falling on the second element: *viuda, ruido.*
   c) Two strong vowels together remain as two distinct syllables, the stress falling according to rules **1** and **2**: *ma/estro, atra/er.*
   d) Any word having a vowel combination not stressed according to these rules bears an accent: *traído, oído, baúl, río.*

Value of the letters

Since the pronunciation of Spanish is (in contrast with English) adequately represented by orthography, the Spanish headwords have not been provided with a transcription in the I.P.A. alphabet, except in a very few cases of recent loan-words whose spelling and pronunciation are not in accord. The sounds of Spanish are described below, each with its corresponding I.P.A. symbol.

The pronunciation described is that of educated Castilian, and does NOT refer to that of certain Spanish provinces or of Spanish America (although a few outstanding features of the latter's pronunciation are mentioned).

It should be further realized that it is impossible to explain adequately the sounds of one language in terms of another; what is said below is no more than a very approximate guide.

Vowels

Spanish vowels are clearly and sharply pronounced, and single vowels are free from the tendency to diphthongization which is noticeable in English. When they are in an unstressed position they are relaxed only very slightly, again in striking contrast to English. Stressed vowels are more open and short before *rr* (compare *parra* with *para*, *perro* with *pero*).

a   [a]   Not so short as in English *fat*, nor so long as in English *father*: *paz, pata.*

e   [e]   Like *e* in English *they* (but without the following sound of *y*): *grande, pelo.* A shorter sound when followed by a consonant in the same syllable, like *e* in English *get*: *España, renta.*

— 15 —

i	[i]	Like *i* in English *machine*, though somewhat shorter: *pila*, *rubí*.
o	[o]	Not so short as in English *hot*, nor so long as in English *November*: *solo*, *esposa*. A shorter sound when followed by a consonant in the same syllable, like *o* in English *hot*: *costra*, *bomba*.
u	[u]	Like *oo* in English *food*: *puro*, *luna*. Silent after *q* and in *gue*, *gui*, unless marked with a diaeresis (*antigüedad*, *argüir*).
y	[i]	when a vowel (in the conjunction *y* "and" and at the end of a word), is pronounced like *i*.

Diphthongs

ai	[aj]	like *i* in English *right*: *baile*, *vaina*.
ei	[ej]	like *ey* in English *they*: *reina*, *peine*.
oi	[oj]	like *oy* in English *boy*: *boina*, *oigo*.
au	[aw]	like *ou* in English *rout*: *causa*, *áureo*.
eu	[ew]	like the vowel sounds in English *may-you*, without the sound of the *y*: *deuda*, *reuma*.

Semiconsonants

i, y	[j]	like *y* in English *yes*: *yelo*, *tiene*; in some cases in *S.Am.* this *y* is pronounced like the *s* [ʒ] in English *measure*: *mayo*, *yo*.
u	[w]	like *w* in English *water*: *huevo*, *agua*.

Consonants

b, v		These two letters represent the same value in Spanish. There are two distinct pronunciations:
	[b]	1. At the start of the breath-group and after *m*, *n* the sound is plosive like English *b*: *batalla*, *venid*; *tromba*, *invierno*.
	[β]	2. In all other positions the sound is a bilabial fricative, unknown in English, in which the lips do not quite meet: *estaba*, *cueva*, *de Vigo*.
c	[k]	1. *c* before *a*, *o*, *u* or a consonant is like English *k*: *caló*, *cobre*.
	[θ]	2. *c* before *e*, *i* is like English *th* in *thin*: *cédula*, *cinco*. In *S.Am.* this is pronounced like English voiceless *s* in *chase* [s]. N.B. In words like *acción*, both types of *c*-sound are heard [kθ].
ch	[tʃ]	like English *ch* in *church*: *mucho*, *chocho*.
d		Three distinct pronunciations:
	[d]	1. At the start of the breath-group and after *l*, *n*, the sound is plosive like English *d*: *doy*, *aldea*, *conde*.
	[ð]	2. Between vowels and after consonants other than *l*, *n* the sound is relaxed and approaches English voiced *th* [ð] in *this*: *codo*, *guardar*; in parts of Spain it is further relaxed and even disappears, particularly in the *-ado* ending. 3. In final position, this type 2 is further relaxed or altogether omitted: *usted*, *Madrid*.
f	[f]	like English *f*: *fuero*, *flor*.
g		Three distinct pronunciations:
	[x]	1. Before *e*, *i* is the same as the Spanish *j* (below): *coger*, *general*.

	[g]	**2.** At the start of the breath-group and after *n*, the sound is that of English *g* in get: *Granada, rango*.
	[γ]	**3.** In other positions the sound is as in **2** above, but with no more than a close approximation of the vocal organs: *agua, guerra*.

N.B. In the group *gue, gui* the *u* is silent (*guerra, guindar*) unless marked with the diaeresis (*antigüedad, argüir*). In the group *gua* all letters are sounded.

h	[-]	always silent: *honor, buho*.
j	[x]	A strong guttural sound not found in English, but like the *ch* in Scots *loch*, Welsh *bach*, German *Achtung*: *jota, ejercer*. Silent at the end of the word: *reloj*.
k	[k]	like English *k*: *kilogramo, kerosene*.
l	[l]	like English *l*: *león, pala*.
ll	[ʎ]	approximating to English *lli* in *million*: *millón, calle*. In *S.Am.* like the *s* [ʒ] in English *measure*.
m	[m]	like English *m*: *mano, como*.
n	[n]	like English *n*: *nono, pan*; except before *v*, when the group is pronounced like *mb*: *enviar, invadir*.
ñ	[ɲ]	approximating to English *ni* in *onion*: *paño, ñoño*.
p	[p]	like English *p*, but without the slight aspiration which follows it: *Pepe, copa*. Silent in *septiembre, séptimo*.
q	[k]	like English *k*; always in combination with *u*, which is silent: *que, quiosco*.
r	[r]	a single trill stronger than any *r* in English, but like Scots *r*: *caro, querer*. Somewhat relaxed in final position. Pronounced like *rr* at the start of a word and after *l, n, s*: *rata*.
rr	[rr]	strongly trilled: *carro, hierro*.
s	[s]	voiceless *s*, like *s* in English *chase*: *rosa, soso*. But before a voiced consonant (*b, d*, hard *g, l, m, n*) is a
	[z]	voiced *s*, like English *s* in *rose*: *desde, mismo, asno*. Before "impure *s*" in recent loan-words, an extra *e*-sound is inserted in pronunciation: *e-sprint, e-stand*.
t	[t]	like English *t*, but without the slight aspiration which follows it: *patata, tope*.
v	[-]	see *b*.
w	[-]	found in a few recent loan-words only; usually pronounced like an English *v* or like Spanish *b, v*: *wáter*.
x	[gs]	like English *gs* in *big sock*: *máximo, examen*. Before a consonant like English *s* in *chase*: *extraño, mixto*.
z	[θ]	like English *th* in *thin*: *zote, zumbar*. In *S.Am.* like English voiceless *s* in *chase*.

The Spanish Alphabet

a [a], b [be], c [θe], ch [tʃe], d [de], e [e], f ['efe], g [xe], h ['atʃe], i [i], j ['xota], k [ka], l ['ele], ll ['eʎe], m ['eme], n ['ene], ñ ['eɲe], o [o], p [pe], q [ku], r ['ere], rr ['erre], s ['ese], t [te], u [u], v ['uve], x ['ekis], y [i'γrjeγa], z ['θeta] *or* ['θeda].

The letters are of the feminine gender: "Madrid se escribe con una *m* mayúscula."

A

a a) *lugar:* *a la mesa* at the table; *al lado de* at the side of; *a la derecha* on the right; *a retaguardia* in the rear; *subir a un tren* get on a train; *caer al mar* fall into the sea; *distancia:* *a 2 km. (de)* 2 km. away (from); *dirección:* *fue a la estación* he went to the station; *ir a casa* go home; b) *tiempo:* *¿a qué hora?* (at) what time?; *a las 3* at 3 o'clock; *a la noche* at nightfall; *a 15 de mayo* on the fifteenth of May; *a los 30 años* at 30 years of age; *a los pocos días* within a few days; c) *manera etc.:* *a la española* in the Spanish fashion; *a escape* at full speed; *a pie* on foot; *a solicitud* on request; d) *modo, velocidad:* *poco a poco* little by little; *paso a paso* step by step; *a 50 km. por hora* at 50 km. an hour; e) *medio, instrumento:* *bordado a mano* hand-embroidered; *girar a mano* turn by hand; *a sangre y fuego* by fire and sword; *a puñetazos* with (his) fists; *a nado* (by) swimming; *a lápiz* in pencil; f) *precio:* *¿a qué precio?* at what price?; *a 20 pesetas el kilo* at (or for) 20 pesetas a kilo; g) *propósito:* *¿a qué?* why?, for what purpose?; h) *sabor, olor:* *saber a vinagre* taste of vinegar; i) *dativo:* (*le*) *doy el libro a Juan* I give the book to John; j) *objeto personal (no se traduce):* *vio a su padre* he saw his father; k) *construcción con verbo:* *voy a comer* I am going to eat; *decidirse a inf.* decide to *inf.*; l) *se lo compré a él* I bought it from him; m) *al entrar* on entering; n) *equivale a si:* *a no ser él mi padre* if he were not my father; *a saberlo yo* had I known; *a decir verdad* to tell the truth; o) *elíptico:* *a que no lo adivinas* I bet you won't guess.

abacería *f* grocer's (shop), grocery store; **abacero** *m* grocer, provision merchant; *esp.* ⚓ chandler.

ábaco *m* abacus.

abad *m* abbot.

abadejo *m* *ichth.* cod(fish); (*insecto*) Spanish fly.

abadesa *f* abbess; **abadía** *f* abbey; (*oficio*) abbacy.

abajadero *m* slope, incline.

abajeño *S.Am.* 1. lowland; 2. *m*, *a f* lowlander.

abajo (*situación*) down, below, underneath; (*movimiento*) down, downwards; downstairs *en casa*; *¡~ X!* down with X!; *aquí ~* down here; *del rey ~* from the king down; *desde ~* from (down) below; *hacia ~* down(wards); *más ~* lower down; *la parte de ~* the lower part; *~ de prp.* below.

abalanzar [1f] weigh, balance; (*lanzar*) hurl; *~se* spring (*a* at); rush (*a* into); pounce, hurl o.s. (*sobre* on).

abaldonar [1a] degrade, debase; affront.

abalorio *m* glass bead; bead work, beading; *no valer un ~* be not worth a brass farthing.

abanderado *m* standard-bearer; ensign; **abanderar** [1a] ⚓ register; **abanderizar** [1f] organize into bands; *~se* join a band, band together.

abandonado abandoned; *lugar etc.* deserted; godforsaken; *aspecto etc.* forlorn; *edificio* derelict; (*desaliñado*) slovenly, careless; **abandonar** [1a] *v/t.* abandon, leave (behind); forsake; (*salir de*) leave; (*huir*) flee, leave; *fig.* drop, give up; (*no hacer caso*) ignore; *v/i. deportes:* withdraw, scratch; *~se* (*desánimo*) give in, lose heart; (*desaliño*) let o.s. go, get slovenly; *~ a* yield to, give o.s. over to; **abandono** *m* abandonment; dereliction *de edificio, deber;* desertion *de hogar;* (*desaliño*) slovenliness; *fig.* abandon *de vida;* profligacy; indulgence (*a* in); *deportes:* withdrawal, scratching; *por ~* by default.

abanicar(se) [1g] fan (o.s.); **abanico** *m* fan; fan-shaped object; (*ventana*) fanlight; ⚓ derrick;

abaniqueo m fanning; gesticulation con manos.

abaratar [1a] v/t. cheapen, make
cheaper; precio lower; v/i., ~se get
cheap, get cheaper.

abarca f sandal; brogue.

abarcar [1g] embrace, include,
take in, extend to; contain, comprise; tiempo span; S.Am. corner,
monopolize.

abarquillar(se) [1a] curl up, roll
up; (esp. papel) crinkle.

abarraganarse [1a] live together
(as man and wife).

abarrancadero m fig. pitfall, difficult situation; **abarrancar** [1g]
(lluvia) open fissures in; ~se fall
into a pit; fig. get into difficulties.

abarrotar [1a] ⚓ stow, pack tightly; fig. overstock; ~se S.Am. ♰ become a glut on the market; **aba-
rrote** m ⚓ stowing, packing; ~s pl.
S.Am. groceries; tienda de ~s
grocer's (shop); **abarrotero** m
S.Am. grocer.

abastar [1a] supply; **abastecedor** m,
-a f supplier, purveyor, victualler;
abastecer [2d] supply, provide,
provision (de with); **abastecimiento** m supply, provision; (acto)
supplying, provisioning; catering;
abastero m S.Am. cattle-dealer;
abasto m supply; provisioning; dar
~ a supply.

abatanado skilled, skilful; **abatanar** [1a] ⊕ full, mill.

abatí m S.Am. maize, corn Am.

abatido (ruin) abject, despicable;
ánimo downcast, dejected, depressed; prostrate (por dolor etc.
with); ♰ depreciated; **abatimiento** m △ etc. knocking down,
dismantling; fig. dejection, depression, low spirits; gloom;
abatir [3a] casa etc. knock down,
dismantle; tienda take down; árbol
fell; 🗲 shoot down; bandera strike,
lower; fig. humble, humiliate;
(desanimar) discourage, get s.o.
down, depress; prostrate de dolor;
~se (ave) swoop, pounce; fig. be
disheartened, get depressed.

abdicación f abdication; **abdicar**
[1g] abdicate (en in favour of), renounce.

abdomen m abdomen; **abdominal**
abdominal.

abducción f 🖋 abduction.

abecé m ABC; rudiments; **abecedario** m alphabet; (libro) primer,
spelling-book.

abedul m (silver) birch; vara de ~
birch.

abeja f bee; ~ machiega, ~ reina
queen bee; ~ obrera worker; **abejar**
m apiary; **abejarrón** m bumble-
bee; **abejaruco** m bee-eater;
abejón m drone; **abejorro** m
bumble-bee; (escarabajo) cock-
chafer.

abellacado mean, villainous.

aberenjenado violet-coloured.

aberración f aberration (a. ast.,
opt.); **aberrar** [1k] be mistaken.

abertura f (agujero) aperture, opening, gap; (grieta) slit, crack, cleft;
geog. (ensenada) cove; (valle) wide
valley, gap; fig. openness, frankness.

abeto m fir; ~ blanco silver fir; ~ del
Norte, ~ rojo spruce.

abierto 1. p.p. of abrir; **2.** adj.
open, opened; campo, mente, rostro
open; ciudad open, unfortified; p.
frank, forthcoming; S.Am. conceited.

abigarrado variegated, many-
coloured; animal piebald; fig.
motley; (inconexo) disjointed; **abigarramiento** m variegation; motley colouring; **abigarrar** [1a]
variegate; paint etc. in a variety of
colours.

ab intestato 🕀 intestate; fig.
neglected.

abisinio adj. a. su. m, a f Abyssinian.

abismal abysmal; **abismar** [1a]
fig. cast down, humble; (dañar)
spoil, ruin; ~se S.Am. be surprised;
~ en plunge into, sink into; dolor
etc. give o.s. over to; estar abismado
en be lost in; **abismo** m abyss (a.
fig.); estar en el borde del ~ be on
the brink of ruin.

abjurar [1a] abjure, forswear (a. ~
de).

ablactación f weaning.

ablandar [1a] v/t. soften; vientre
loosen; mot. run in; fig. soothe,
mollify; v/i. (viento) moderate;
(frío) become less severe; ~se
soften, get soft; ⊕ melt; (rigor etc.)
relent; moderate; become less
severe; (esp. p.) mellow.

ablativo m ablative (case).

abnegación f self-denial, abnegation; **abnegado** self-denying; **ab-negarse** [1h *a.* 1k] deny o.s., go without.

abobado stupid(-looking); **aboba-miento** *m* stupidity; **abobar** [1a] make stupid; ~se get stupid.

abocado *vino* smooth; **abocar** [1g] *v/t.* seize with the mouth; ✗ bring up; *vino* pour, decant; *v/i.* ♎ enter a river (*or* channel); ~se approach; ~ con meet, have an interview with.

abocinado trumpet-shaped; **aboci-nar** [1a] F fall on one's face.

abochornado flushed, overheated; *fig.* ashamed (de at); **abochornar** [1a] burn up, overheat; *fig.* shame, embarrass; ~se feel overheated; ♀ wilt; ~ de *fig.* feel ashamed at.

abofetear [1a] slap in the face.

abogacía *f* legal profession; **abo-gado** *m* lawyer; ~ de secano quack lawyer; ejercer de ~ practise law; recibirse de ~ be called to the bar; **abogar** [1h] advocate, plead; ~ por hold a brief for (*a. fig.*); *fig.* advo-cate, champion.

abolengo *m* ancestry, lineage; (*herencia*) inheritance.

abolición *f* abolition; **abolicio-nista** *m/f* abolitionist; **abolir** [3a; *defective*] abolish; revoke.

abolsado full of pockets, baggy; **abolsarse** [1a] be baggy, form pockets.

abolladura *f* dent; (*arte*) emboss-ing; **abollar** [1a] dent; bruise; (*arte*) emboss, do repoussé work on; ~se get dented *etc.*; **abollonar** [1a] *metal* emboss.

abombado convex; *S.Am.* (*atur-dido*) stunned; (*borracho*) drunk; **abombar** [1a] make convex; F stun, confuse; ~se *S.Am.* (*pudrirse*) decompose; be stunned; get drunk.

abominable abominable; **abomi-nación** *f* abomination (*a. fig.*), execration; **abominar** [1a] abhor, detest (*a.* ~ de).

abonable payable; **abonado** 1. trustworthy; 2. *m*, a *f* subscriber *a periódico etc.*; ⬟, *thea. etc.* season-ticket holder; **abonador** *m*, -a *f* ✝ guarantor.

abonanzar [1f] clear up (*a. fig.*); ♎ abate, calm down.

abonar [1a] 1. *v/t. p.* vouch for, guarantee; ✝ credit, pay; improve (*a.* ✗); ✗ manure, dress, fertilize;

v. cuenta; 2. *v/i.* clear (up); 3. ~se subscribe (*a periódico etc.* to); be-come a member (*a sociedad* of); ⬟, *thea.* take out a season-ticket; **abonaré** *m* promissory note; **abono** *m* ✝ *etc.* voucher, guarantee; subscription *a periódico;* ⬟, *thea.* season-ticket; improvement *de tie-rras;* ✗ (*sustancia*) manure, dress-ing, fertilizer; ~ (de temporada) sea-son-ticket; ~ químico (chemical) fertilizer; ~ verde leaf-mould.

abordable *p., lugar* approachable; *lugar* easy of access; **abordaje** *m* ♎ boarding; **abordar** [1a] *v/t.* ♎ board; (*atracar*) dock; *p.* accost, *fig.* approach; *problema* tackle; *tarea etc.* undertake, get down to; *tema* broach, begin on; *v/i.* ♎ (*chocar*) run foul; (*aportar*) put in (en at).

aborigen *adj. a. su. m* aboriginal.

aborrascarse [1g] get stormy.

aborrecer [2d] hate, detest; (*abu-rrir*) bore; *nido* abandon; **aborre-cible** hateful, abhorrent; invidious; **aborrecido** (*aburrido*) boring; **aborrecimiento** *m* hatred, hate, abhorrence; (*aburrimiento*) bore-dom.

aborregado: *cielo* ~ mackerel sky.

abortar [1a] abort; ✠ have a mis-carriage; *fig.* miscarry, fail; **abor-tivo** abortive; **aborto** *m* abortion; ✠ miscarriage; ⚖ (*criminal*) abor-tion; *fig.* monster; **abortón** *m* abortion (*animal*).

abota(r)garse [1h] become bloated, swell up.

abotonador *m* button-hook; **abo-tonar** [1a] *v/t.* button (up); *v/i.* ♀ bud.

abovedado *m* △ vaulting; **above-dar** [1a] arch, vault.

abozalar [1a] muzzle.

abra *f* (*ensenada*) bay, cove; (*valle*) dale; *geol.* fissure.

abracadabra *f* hocus-pocus.

abrasado burnt up; *fig.* ashamed; ~ en cólera in a raging temper; **abrasador** burning, scorching; *fig.* withering; **abrasar** [1a] burn (up); ♀ *etc.* parch; (*frío*) scorch, nip; (*viento*) sear; *dinero* squander; *fig.* shame; ~se burn; be parched; *fig.* burn (de amores with love), be on fire; ~ de sed (*de calor*) be dying of thirst (of the heat).

abrasión f graze, abrasion; **abrasivo** m abrasive.

abrazadera f bracket, brace, clasp; typ. bracket.

abrazar [1f] embrace (a. fig.); clasp, take in one's arms, hug; fig. take in, include; doctrina espouse; negocio take charge of; ~se a, con, de embrace; clasp; **abrazo** m embrace, hug; un ~ (afectuoso, cordial etc.) (en carta) best wishes, kind regards; with love from s.o.

ábrego m south-west wind.

abrelatas m tin-opener.

abrevadero m drinking-trough; (lugar) watering-place; **abrevar** [1a] animal water, give a drink to; tierra irrigate; pieles soak; ~se (animal) quench its etc. thirst; fig. ~ en sangre wallow in blood.

abreviación f abbreviation; reduction; **abreviadamente** in an abridged form; **abreviar** [1b] v/t. palabra etc. abbreviate; materia abridge, reduce; período shorten, lessen; suceso hasten; fecha bring forward; v/i. be quick; be short; **abreviatura** f abbreviation.

abrigada f, **abrigadero** m shelter, wind-break; **abrigado** sheltered, protected; enramada etc. cosy.

abrigar [1h] shelter, protect (de viento etc. from, against); (vestido etc.) keep warm, cover; (ayudar) aid, support; esperanzas etc. harbour, cherish, entertain; ~se take shelter (de aguacero etc. from); ⚓ seek shelter (de temporal from); protect o.s.; wrap o.s. up con ropa; **abrigo** m shelter; esp. ⚓ haven; (sobretodo) (over)coat; fig. covering, protection de ropa; (ayuda) aid, support; al ~ de sheltered from; viento in the lee of; peligro safe from; de mucho ~ ropa warm, heavy; ~ antiaéreo air-raid shelter; ~ de pieles fur coat.

abril m April; fig. springtime (de la vida of life); ~es pl. years (of one's youth); de 20 ~es of 20 summers; estar hecho un ~ be dressed to kill; **abrileño** April attr.

abrillantar [1a] ⊕ cut into facets; (pulir) polish, brighten; fig. enhance.

abrir [3a; p.p. abierto] 1. v/t. open (a. fig.); ~ (con llave) unlock; ⚒ cut open; agujero make; zanja dig;

pozo sink; lámina engrave; grifo etc. turn on; camino clear, make; senda beat; bosque clear; cuenta open; lista, procesión head; apetito whet; 2. v/i. ⚘ etc. open, unfold; v. ojo; 3. ~se (puerta etc.) open; (flor etc.) open out; (extenderse) spread (out); ~ a, ~ con unbosom o.s. to, be frank with.

abrochador m button-hook; **abrochar** [1a] button; hook, fasten (up) con corchete; clasp con hebilla etc.

abrogación f abrogation; **abrogar** [1h] abrogate, repeal.

abrojo m caltrop (a. ✕); thistle.

abroncar [1g] F (avergonzar) shame; ridicule; (enfadar) annoy.

abroquelarse [1a] fig.: ~ con, ~ de shield o.s. with.

abrumador crushing, overwhelming; (molesto) wearisome; **abrumar** [1a] crush, oppress; swamp, weigh down (de trabajo with); ~se get foggy.

abrupto steep, abrupt.

abrutado brutish.

absceso m. abscess.

absentismo m absenteeism; absentee landlordism; **absentista** m/f absentee; absentee landlord.

ábside m apse; **absidial** apsidal.

absintio m absinth.

absolución f absolution; ⚖ acquittal; **absoluta** f authoritative assertion, dictum; ✕ discharge; ✕ tomar la ~ leave the service; **absolutamente** absolutely; positively; just; ~ nada nothing at all; **absolutismo** m absolutism; **absoluto** absolute (a. ⚙, pol.); fig. utter, absolute; genio tyrannical; fe implicit; phls. lo ~ the absolute; en ~ nothing at all; ¡en ~! certainly not!; está prohibido en ~ it is absolutely forbidden; no sabe nada en ~ he knows nothing at all; **absolutorio** ⚖ of acquittal.

absolver [2h; p.p. absuelto] absolve; ⚖ acquit, clear (de of); release (de empeño from).

absorbente 1. absorbent; fig. absorbing; (que exige tiempo) demanding; 2. m: ~ higiénico sanitary towel; **absorber** [2a] absorb (a. fig.), suck up; imbibe, take in; ✝ capital use up; fig. engross; ~se become absorbed (en in); **absorción** f absorption (a. fig.); fig. engrossment; **absorto** *fig.* absorbed, engrossed (**en** in); (*admirando*) entranced, amazed; intent (**en** *proyecto* on); ~ **en** *meditación* buried in thought.

abstemio abstemious, temperate; (*por completo*) teetotal.

abstención *f* abstention; nonparticipation; **abstencionista** *m/f* non-participant; **abstenerse** [2l] abstain, refrain (**de** *inf.* from *ger.*); forbear (**de** *inf.* to *inf.*); **abstinencia** *f* abstinence; (*ayuno*) fast; *fig.* forbearance; **abstinente** abstemious.

abstracción *f* abstraction; omission; (*distracción*) absence of mind, engrossment; ~ **hecha de** leaving *s.t.* on one side; **abstracto** abstract; **en** ~ in the abstract; **abstraer** [2p] *v/t.* abstract; *v/i.* (**a.** ~**se**): ~ **de** do without, leave aside; ~**se** be abstracted, be absorbed; **abstraído** absentminded; withdrawn.

abstruso abstruse.

absuelto 1. *p.p.* of *absolver*; 2. *adj.* acquitted; absolved.

absurdo 1. absurd; preposterous; farcical; 2. *m* absurdity; farce.

abubilla *f* hoopoe.

abuchear [1a] F hoot at, howl down, *approx.* boo; **abucheo** *m* F hooting, *approx.* booing.

abuela *f* grandmother; *fig.* old woman; F ¡cuéntaselo a tu ~! tell that to the Marines!; **abuelita** *f* F grandma, granny; **abuelito** *m* F grandpa, grandad; **abuelo** *m* grandfather; *fig.* (*antepasado*) ancestor; (*viejo*) old man; ~s *pl.* grandparents.

abulense *adj. a. su. m/f* (native) of Avila.

abulia *f* lack of will-power; **abúlico** lacking in will-power, weak-willed.

abultado bulky, massive, unwieldy; **abultar** [1a] *v/t.* make large, enlarge; *fig.* exaggerate; *v/i.* be bulky; *fig.* loom large.

abundamiento *m* abundance, plenty; **a** *mayor* ~ furthermore; **abundancia** *f* abundance, plenty; **en** ~ in plenty, in abundance; **abundante** abundant, plentiful; heavy, copious; generous; **abundar** [1a]: ~ **de**, ~ **en** abound in, teem with, be rich in; ~ **en** *la opinión de* wholeheartedly agree with.

abur *v. agur.*

aburilar [1a] engrave.

aburrido wearisome, tiresome, boring; ghastly F; *rutina* humdrum; (*que está* ~) bored; **aburrimiento** *m* boredom, weariness, tedium; **aburrir** [3a] bore, weary; annoy, tire; F *tiempo* spend, while away; *dinero* blue; ~**se** be bored, get bored (**con**, **de**, **por** with).

abusar [1a] go too far, take an unfair advantage; ~ **de** *autoridad*, *hospitalidad* abuse; *dinero* misapply; *confianza* betray; *amistad* presume upon; *amigos* impose upon; **abusión** *f* abuse; superstition; **abusivo** improper, corrupt; **abuso** *m* abuse; misuse, misapplication *etc.*; **abusón** F uppish.

abyecto *condición* abject; (*ruin*) craven, vile.

acá here, around here, over here; hither *lit.*; ~ **y** *a*(*cu*)*llá* here and there; **de** ~ *para allá* to and fro; **de** *ayer* ~ since yesterday; *más* ~ nearer, more this way; *muy* ~ right here; ¡ven ~! come (over) here!

acabado 1. perfect, complete; *fig.* consummate, polished; *salud* ruined, wrecked; ~ **de** *llegar* just after arrival; 2. *m* finish; **acabador** *m* ⊕ finisher; **acabamiento** *m* completion, finishing; (*fin*) end; (*muerte*) death.

acabalar [1a] complete.

acabar [1a] 1. *v/t.* finish, conclude, complete; put the finishing touches to; (*matar*) kill off; 2. *v/i.* finish, come to an end; (*morir*) die; ~ **con** make an end of, put paid to; destroy; *recursos* use up; *letra* end with; ~ **de** *inf.* have just *p.p.*: *acabo de hacerlo* I have just done it; *acababa de hacerlo* I had just done it; ~ **en** *punta etc.* end in; ~ *mal* come to a bad (*or* sticky) end; ~ **por** *inf.*, ~ *ger.* end up by *ger.*, finish up by *ger.*; F *es cosa de nunca* ~ there's no end to it; 3. ~**se** stop, come to an end (*a. fig.*); (*morir*) die; (*estar terminado*) be all over; (*existencias*) run out; (*suministro*) fail; *se me acabó el dinero* I ran out of money; F ¡(*todo*) *se acabó!* it's all up!; F *se acabó para él* he's had it; F *el acabóse* the pay-off, the end.

acabildar [1a] organize into a group, get together.

acabóse v. acabar.
acacia f acacia; ~ falsa locust tree.
acachetear [1a] slap, box.
academia f academy; ~ gastronómica domestic science college; académico 1. academic (a. fig.); 2. m academician, member of an academy.
acaecer [2d] happen, occur, befall; acaecimiento m happening, occurrence.
acalorado heated, hot; (fatigado) tired (out); fig. discusión heated; partidario passionate; acaloramiento m ardour, heat; passion, anger; acalorar [1a] (ejercicio) warm, make hot; (fatigar) tire; fig. pasiones inflame, incite; (animar) encourage, stir up; ~se (tomar calor) get too hot, become overheated; (irritarse) get het up (por about) F, get angry (por about); (discusión) become heated.
acallar [1a] silence (a. fig.), hush, quieten (down); fig. assuage, pacify.
acamar [1a] beat down, lay.
acampanado bell-shaped.
acampar [1a] ✗ (en)camp.
acampo m common pasture.
acanaladura f groove; △ fluting; acanalar [1a] groove; △ flute; papel etc. corrugate.
acanallado disreputable, raffish; low.
acantilado 1. costa (en escalones) shelving; rocky; (escarpado) precipitous, steep; 2. m cliff.
acanto m acanthus.
acantonar [1a] quarter (en on).
acaparador m monopolizer, monopolist; profiteer; acaparamiento m monopolizing (de of), cornering the market (de in); hoarding de víveres; acaparar [1a] monopolize; corner, corner the market in; víveres hoard; hog F.
acápite m S.Am. paragraph; punto ~ full stop, new paragraph.
acaramelado fig. over-sweet, over-polite.
acar(e)ar [1a] ps. bring face to face; peligro etc. face (up to).
acardenalarse [1a] get bruised, go black and blue.
acariciar [1b] caress; animal pat, fondle; esperanza cherish, harbour; proyecto have in mind.
ácaro m zo. mite.

acarrear [1a] transport, cart, haul; (río) bring (down), carry; fig. occasion, bring in its train (or wake); acarreo m haulage, cartage (a. precio); geol. terrenos de ~ drift.
acartonarse [1a] get like cardboard; fig. (p.) become wizened.
acaso 1. adv. perhaps, maybe; por si ~ (just) in case; 2. m chance, accident; al ~ at random.
acatamiento m respect, esteem; acatar [1a] respect, esteem; treat with deference; revere; ley accept, adhere to.
acatarrarse [1a] catch a cold; S.Am. F get boozed.
acato m respect, esteem.
acaudalado wealthy, well-off; acaudalar [1a] accumulate, acquire.
acaudillar [1a] lead, command.
acceder [2a] accede, agree (a to).
accesible accessible; ~ a open to, accessible to; accesión f (acto) assent (a to); (cosa) accessory; (entrada) access, entry; ✗ attack, onset; accésit m second prize, consolation prize; acceso m (acto de entrar) admittance; (camino) access, approach (a. ✗); ✗ attack, fit; fig. fit de generosidad etc.; outburst, fit de cólera; de fácil ~ easy to approach; ~s pl. approaches; accesoria f annex, outbuilding; accesorio 1. accessory; dependent; (secundario) incidental; 2. m accessory, attachment; ~s pl. ⊕ accessories; thea. properties.
accidentado ✗ in a faint; (turbado) upset; vida stormy, troubled, eventful; terreno hilly, rough; superficie uneven; accidental accidental; unintentional; incidental, casual; accidentarse [1a] faint (after an accident); accidente m accident; misadventure, mishap; ✗ faint(ing fit); gr. accidence; roughness, unevenness de terreno; por ~ by accident.
acción f action; ✝ share; ✗ action, engagement; thea. action, plot; ~es pl. ✝ stock(s), shares; thea. ~ aparte by-play; ~ de gracias thanksgiving; ~ liberada stock dividend; ~ preferente preference share; ~ primitiva ordinary share; ⚖ ejercitar una ~ bring an action; accionado m ⊕ action; accionar [1a] v/t. ⊕ work,

drive; *v/i.* gesticulate; **accionista** *m/f* shareholder, stockholder.

acebo *m* holly (tree).

acecinar [1a] salt, cure; ~se get very thin.

acechadura *f* ambush; **acechador** *m*, -a *f* spy, watcher; **acechar** [1a] spy on, lie (*or* be) in wait for; *hunt. etc.* stalk; **acecho** *m* ambush; *al* ~, *en* ~ in wait, on the watch; *cazar al* ~ stalk; **acechón** F spying, prying; F *hacer la acechona* spy, pry.

acedar [1a] make sour; *fig.* sour, embitter; (*molestar*) vex; ~se turn sour; ♀ turn yellow.

acedera *f* sorrel.

acedía *f* sourness (*a. fig.*); (*des-abrimiento*) unpleasantness; asperity *de genio*; ♂ heartburn; **acedo** sour (*a. fig.*), acid; disagreeable.

aceitar [1a] oil, lubricate; **aceite** *m* oil; (*a.* ~ *de oliva*) olive oil; (*perfume*) essence; ~ *alcanforado* camphorated oil; ~ *combustible* fuel oil; ~ *de hígado de bacalao* cod-liver oil; ~ *de linaza*, ~ *secante* linseed oil; ~ *mineral* petroleum; ~ *de ricino* castor oil; **aceitera** *f* oilcan; **aceitero** 1. oil *attr.*; 2. *m* oil merchant; **aceitón** *m* thick dirty oil; **aceitoso** oily, greasy; **aceituna** *f* olive; **aceitunado** olive (-coloured); **aceitunero** *m*, a *f* dealer in olives; **aceituno** 1. *S.Am.* olive(-coloured); 2. *m* olive (tree).

aceleración *f* acceleration, speeding-up; **acelerada** *f* acceleration, speed-up; **aceleradamente** speedily, swiftly; **acelerador** *m* accelerator; **acelerar** [1a] accelerate; *paso* quicken; *fig.* speed up, expedite; ~ *la marcha* go faster, accelerate; ~se hasten, hurry.

acémila *f* beast of burden; mule; **acemilero** *m* muleteer.

acemite *m* bran and flour mixed; (*potaje*) porridge.

acendrado pure, refined (*a. fig.*); **acendrar** [1a] purify; ⊕, *estilo* refine.

acensuar [1d] tax.

acento *m* accent; stress; ~ *agudo* acute accent; **acentuar** [1e] accent, accentuate; stress.

aceña *f* water-mill; **aceñero** *m* miller.

acepción *f* meaning, sense; preference.

acepilladura *f* (wood-)shaving; **acepillar** [1a] brush; ⊕ plane, shave.

aceptable acceptable; palatable; **aceptación** *f* acceptance (*a.* ✝); approval, approbation; **aceptar** [1a] accept; *trabajo* accept, take on, undertake; *hechos* face; ~ *a inf.* agree to *inf.*; **acepto:** ~ *a*, ~ *de* acceptable to, welcome to, welcomed by. [nel).\

acequia *f* irrigation ditch (*or* chan-)

acera *f* pavement, sidewalk *Am.*; row *de casas.*

acerado ⊕ steel *attr.*; (*cortante*) biting, cutting (*a. fig.*); *fig. dicho etc.* caustic; **acerar** [1a] ⊕ turn into steel; put a steel tip *etc.* on; *fig.* make sharp, make biting.

acerbidad *f* acerbity; harshness; **acerbo** sour, sharp (*a. fig.*); *lenguaje etc.* harsh, scathing.

acerca: ~ *de* about, concerning, on.

acercamiento *m* bringing (*or* drawing) near; *pol.* rapprochement; approach; **acercar** [1g] bring near(er); ~se approach (*a acc.*), come near (*a* to); ~ *a* go up to; *fig.* verge on, approach.

acería *f* steelworks.

acerico *m* small cushion; *sew.* pincushion.

acero *m* steel (*a. fig.*); ~ *colado* cast steel; ~ *en lingotes* ingot steel; ~ *al manganeso* manganese steel; F *tener buenos* ~s (*ser valiente*) have a lot of pluck; (*tener hambre*) be ravenous.

acérrimo staunch, out-and-out, fierce.

acerrojar [1a] bolt, lock.

acertado right, correct; (*prudente*) wise, sound; (*hábil*) skilful; *dicho* well-aimed; apt; *idea* bright, well-conceived; *en esto no anduvo muy* ~ it was rather unwise of him; he was far off the mark; **acertar** [1k] *v/t. blanco etc.* hit; *solución* guess right, get right; do *s.t.* right; *v/i.* (*dar en el blanco*) hit the mark; (*tener razón*) be right, guess right; (*tener éxito*) succeed; ~ *a inf.* (*hacer por casualidad*) happen to *inf.*; (*lograr*) succeed in *ger.*, manage to *inf.*; ~ *con* happen (up)on, hit on; find.

acertijo *m* riddle, puzzle.

acervo *m* heap; ~ *común* undivided estate.

acetato *m* acetate; **acético** acetic.

acetileno *m* acetylene.
acetona *f* acetone; **acetoso** acetous, acid.
acetre *m* small bucket; *eccl.* holy water container.
acezar [1f] pant, puff (and blow).
aciago ill-fated, black, of ill omen.
aciano *m* cornflower.
acíbar *m* aloes; *fig.* bitterness, affliction; **acibarar** [1a] make bitter (with aloes); *fig.* embitter; ~ *la vida a* make *s.o.'s* life a burden.
acicalado *arma* bright and clean; *p.* spruce, neat; *b.s.* dressed to kill, dressy F; **acicalar** [1a] polish, clean; *fig.* dress up, bedeck; ~se *fig.* spruce o.s. up, get dressed up.
acicate *m* spur; *fig.* spur, incentive.
acidez *f* acidity; **acidificar** [1g] acidify; **ácido 1.** *fruta etc.* sharp, sour, acid; **2.** *m* acid; ~ *carbólico* carbolic acid; ~ *clorhídrico* hydrochloric acid; ~ *nítrico* nitric acid; ~ *oxálico* oxalic acid; ~ *sulfúrico* sulphuric acid; **acidular** [1a] acidulate; **acídulo** acidulous.
acierto *m* (*tiro*) good shot, hit (*a. fig.*); *fig.* (*acción*) good choice, wise move; (*conjetura*) good guess; (*habilidad*) skill; aptness *de observación*; (*éxito*) success; (*tino*) discretion.
acitrón *m* candied citron.
aclamación *f* acclamation; *por* ~ by acclamation; **aclamar** [1a] acclaim; ~ *a uno por jefe* hail s.o. as leader.
aclaración *f* explanation; rinsing; clearing; brightening (up); **aclarar** [1a] *v/t. asunto* clarify, explain, cast light on; *ropa* rinse; *bosque* clear, thin (out); *salsa* thin; *v. voz*; *v/i.* (*tiempo*) brighten (up), clear (up); **aclaratorio** explanatory; illuminating.
aclimatación *f* acclimatization; **aclimatar** [1a] acclimatize; ~se get acclimatized.
acobardar [1a] cow, intimidate, unnerve; ~se flinch, shrink (back) (*ante* from, at), get frightened.
acobrado copper-coloured.
acocear [1a] kick; *fig.* ill-treat, trample on.
acochinar [1a] F bump off.
acodado elbowed, elbow *attr.*
acodalar [1a] shore up, prop up.
acodar [1a] *vid etc.* layer; ~se lean (*sobre* on).

acodiciarse [1b]: ~ *a* covet.
acodo *m* ⚯ layer.
acogedor *ambiente*, *p.* welcoming, hospitable; *cuarto* snug; **acoger** [2c] *visita etc.* welcome, receive; *fugitivo* harbour, give refuge to; *noticia* admit, accept; ~se take refuge (*a* in); ~ *a* *fig.* pretexto take refuge in; *promesa* avail o.s. of; **acogida** *f* welcome, reception; acceptance; meeting-place *de aguas*; asylum.
acogollar [1a] *v/t.* cover up, protect; *v/i.* sprout.
acogotar [1a] kill (with a blow on the neck); *p.* knock down.
acohombrar [1a] earth up.
acojinar [1a] ⊕ cushion.
acolchar [1a] *sew.* quilt; pad.
acólito *m* acolyte (*a. fig.*), server; *fig.* minion.
acollador *m* ⚓ lanyard.
acollar [1m] ⚯ earth up; ⚓ caulk.
acomedido *S.Am.* obliging.
acometer [2a] attack, set upon, assail; *fig. tarea etc.* undertake, have a go at F; (*sueño etc.*) overcome, overtake; (*dudas*) assail; **acometida** *f* attack, assault; ⚡ connection; **acometimiento** *m* attack; **acometividad** *f* aggressiveness, fight; enterprise, energy *en dificultades*.

acomodable adaptable; **acomodación** *f* accommodation; **acomodadizo** accommodating, obliging; acquiescent; **acomodado** (*conveniente*) suitable; *precio* moderate; *p.* wealthy, well-to-do, well-off F; **acomodador 1.** obliging; **2.** *m* *thea.* usher; **acomodadora** *f* *thea.* usherette; **acomodamiento** *m* convenience; (*arreglo*) transaction, agreement.
acomodar [1a] **1.** *v/t.* (*componer*) arrange; (*encontrar sitio para*) fit in, find room for, accommodate; *acción* suit, adapt (*a* to); *ejemplo* apply (*a* to); *instrumento* adapt (*a uso* for); adjust, put right; *criado etc.* place (*a. fig.*); *thea.* show to a seat; *visitantes* make comfortable; *enemigos* reconcile; **2.** *v/i.* suit, fit; be suitable; **3.** ~se (*conformarse*) comply; adapt o.s.; ~ *a circunstancias* adapt o.s. to; *situación nueva* settle down to; ~ *a inf.* settle down to *inf.*; ~ *con* reconcile o.s. to; (*avenirse*) come to

an agreement with; *dictamen* comply with; ~ de provide o.s. with.

acompañado *sitio* busy, frequented; *p.* assistant; **acompañamiento** *m* accompaniment (*a.* ♪); (*p.*) escort; (*ps.*) retinue; *thea.* extras; *sin* ~ unaccompanied; **acompañanta** *f* chaperon, escort; ♪ accompanist; **acompañante** *m* companion; escort; ♪ accompanist; **acompañar** [1a] accompany (*a.* ♪), go with; *mujer freq.* chaperon; enclose *en carta*; ~ *a la puerta freq.* see out; ~ *a una p.* en join a p. in; *le acompaño en sus sentimientos* I sympathize with you (in your loss); *seguir acompañando a* keep with, stay with; ~*se con* ♪ accompany o.s. on.

acompasado rhythmic, regular, measured; *fig.* (*hablando*) slow (of speech); (*andando*) slow, steady; **acompasar** [1a] ♪ mark the rhythm of; ♪ measure with a compass; ~ *la dicción* speak with a marked rhythm.

acomunarse [1a] join forces.

acondicionado ⊕ conditioned; *bien* ~ (*genio*) nice; (*estado*) well set-up, in good condition; *mal* ~ (*genio*) bad-tempered; (*estado*) badly off, in bad condition; **acondicionador** *m*: ~ *de aire* air-conditioner; **acondicionamiento** *m*: ~ *de aire* air-conditioning; **acondicionar** [1a] arrange, prepare; ⊕ condition.

aconcharse [1a] lean (*a* against); ⚓ run aground.

acónito *m* aconite.

aconsejable advisable, politic; *poco* ~ inadvisable; **aconsejar** [1a] advise, counsel; *virtud etc.* preach; ~*se* seek (*or* take) advice; ~ *con*, ~ *de* consult with; ~ *mejor* think better of it.

aconsonantar [1a] rhyme (*con* with).

acontecer [2d] happen, occur; **acontecimiento** *m* happening, event; new development.

acopiar [1b] gather together, collect; *miel* hive; **acopio** *m* (*acto*) gathering, collecting; store (*a. fig.*), collection.

acoplado *m S.Am.* trailer; **acoplador** *m radio*: coupler; **acoplamiento** *m* ⊕ coupling; joint; ⚡ hook-up, connection; ~ *de manguito* sleeve coupling; ~ *universal*

universal joint; **acoplar** [1a] ⊕ (*unir*) join, couple, fit together; (*encajar*) fit (into place); ⚡ connect, join up; *bueyes* yoke, hitch; *S.Am.* 🐾 couple (up); ~*se zo.* mate, pair; F be reconciled.

acoquinar [1a] scare; ~*se* F get the jitters, get scared.

acorazado 1. armour-plated, iron-clad; F forbidding; **2.** *m* battleship; **acorazar** [1f] armour-plate; ~*se fig.* arm o.s., steel o.s. (*contra* against).

acorchado spongy, cork-like.

acordada *f* 🔒 decree; **acordadamente** by common consent; unanimously; **acordado** agreed; *lo* ~ that which has been agreed upon; **acordar** [1m] **1.** *v/t.* decide, resolve (*que subj.* to *inf.* [*or* that *subj.*]; *inf.* to *inf.*); remind (*algo a alguien* s.o. of s.t.); ♪ tune; *colores* blend; *diversos pareceres* reconcile; **2.** *v/i.* agree; correspond; **3.** ~*se* agree, come to an agreement (*con* with); ~ (*de*) remember; *si mal no me acuerdo* if my memory serves me right; *se acordó hacer* it was agreed to do; **acorde 1.** agreed; in accord; ♪ in harmony, in tune, harmonious; *estar* ~ *con* be in agreement with; **2.** *m* harmony, chord.

acordeón *m* accordion.

acordonado corded, ribbed; **acordonar** [1a] tie up; *corsé* lace up; *lugar* cordon off; *moneda* mill.

acornar [1m], **acornear** [1a] butt; (*penetrando*) gore.

acorralado cornered, at bay; **acorralamiento** *m* corralling; *fig.* intimidation; **acorralar** [1a] *animales* pen, corral, round up; *p.* corner (*a. fig.*); *fig.* intimidate.

acorrer [2a] run (up), hasten (*a* to).

acortar [1a] shorten, cut down; *camino, paso, vela* shorten; *cuento* cut short; *S.Am. fig.* tone down; ~*se fig.* be slow, be timid.

acosar [1a] pursue, hound (*a. fig.*); *fig.* harass, badger, bait; **acoso** *m* pursuit; *fig.* harrying, baiting.

acostar [1m] lay (down); *niño etc.* put to bed; ⚓ bring alongside (*a acc.*); ~*se* lie down; go to bed; *S.Am.* (*mujer*) be confined; *estar acostado* be lying down; be in bed.

acostumbrado usual, customary, habitual; *estar* ~ *a* be accustomed

to, be used to; **acostumbrar** [1a]
v/t. accustom, get *s.o.* used (*a* to);
inure (*a apuros etc.* to); *v/i.*: ~ (*a*)
inf. be in the habit of *ger.*, be accustomed to *inf.*; **~se** accustom o.s.,
get accustomed (*a* to).

acotación *f* (*mojón*) boundary mark;
surv. elevation mark; (*apunte*) marginal note; *thea.* stage direction;
acotar [1a] *terreno* survey, mark
out; *árbol* lop, top; *página* annotate;
oferta accept; F (*escoger*) choose;
F (*atestiguar*) vouch for.

acotillo *m* sledge(-hammer).

acoyundar [1a] yoke.

acre *olor* acrid, pungent; *sabor* tart,
sharp; *genio* disagreeable, sour.

acrecencia *f* increase, growth; 🏛
accretion; **acrecentar** [1k] increase; *p.* promote, advance;
acrecer [2d] increase.

acreditación *f* accrediting; clearance *por policía*; **acreditado** ac-
credited; reputable; reputed (*de* to
be); **acreditar** [1a] *embajador etc.*
accredit (*cerca de* to); 🕇 credit;
(*afamar*) do credit to, add to the
reputation of; (*garantizar*) vouch
for, guarantee; **~se** get a reputation
(*de* tor); justify o.s.

acreedor 1. deserving (*a* of); **2.** *m*,
-a *f* creditor; ~ *hipotecario* mort-
gagee; **acreencia** *f* S.Am. credit
balance.

acribar [1a] sift, riddle; **acribillado** (*balas*) peppered, riddled;
(*agujeros*) honeycombed; **acribillar** [1a] pepper, riddle (*a balas etc.*
with); fill (*a puñaladas* with); *fig.*
pester, harass.

acriminación *f* incrimination;
acriminador incriminating; **acriminar** [1a] incriminate.

acrimonia *f* acridness, pungency;
fig. acrimony; **acrimonioso** acri-
monious.

acriollarse [1a] S.Am. go native.

acrisolar [1a] ⊕ purify, refine; *fig.*
verdad etc. reveal, show, declare;
clarify, bring out.

acristianar [1a] F Christianize; *niño*
baptize.

acritud *f* = *acrimonia*.

acrobacia *f* acrobatics (*a.* ✈); ~
aérea aerobatics; **acróbata** *m/f*
acrobat; **acrobático** acrobatic.

acta *f* minutes, record *de reunión*;
transactions *de sociedad*; certificate

de elección; ~ *notarial* affidavit;
levantar ~ take the minutes; *levantar*
~ *de* minute (*v/t.*); **~s** *pl.* life, acts
de santo; minutes, record *de reunión*.

actitud *f* attitude (*a. fig.*), posture;
outlook; *en* ~ *de inf.* getting ready
to *inf.*; **activar** [1a] activate, energize; *trabajo* expedite, speed up;
fuego brighten up; **actividad** *f* activity; promptness *en obrar*; bustle,
movement *de muchedumbre etc.*; *en*
~ in operation, in action; *volcán* in
eruption; *en plena* ~ in full swing;
activista *m/f* activist, member of a
ginger group; **activo 1.** active (*a.*
gr.); *fig.* active, energetic; prompt;
(*ocupado*) busy; *en* ~ on active
service; **2.** *m* 🕇 assets; ~ *de la quiebra* bankrupt's estate.

acto *m* act, action; ceremony,
function; *thea.* act; ~s *pl. de los*
Apóstoles Acts (of the Apostles);
~ *de fe* act of faith; *en el* ~ forthwith, immediately; on the spot; ~
continuo straight afterwards, there
and then.

actor *m* actor; *fig.* protagonist;
actora: *parte* ~ prosecution;
plaintiff; **actriz** *f* actress; *primera* ~
leading lady.

actuación *f* action; performance
(*a. thea.*), behaviour; S.Am. role;
actual present(-day); *cuestión* topical; **actualidad** *f* present (time);
(*cuestión*) question of the moment,
live issue; *en la* ~ at the present
time, nowadays; *ser* (*or correr*) *de* ~
be current, be alive; *ser de gran* ~
be of immediate interest; be highly
topical; **~es** *pl.* current events;
(*película*) news-reel; **actualmente**
at present, at the moment, nowadays.

actuar [1e] *v/t.* actuate, set in
motion, operate; work; *v/i.* act (*de*
as); perform; ⊕ operate; ~ *sobre*
act on.

actuario *m* 🏛 clerk; 🕇 ~ (*de seguros*) actuary.

acuadrillar(se) [1a] band together.

acuarela *f* water-colour; **acuarelista** *m/f* water-colourist.

acuario *m* aquarium.

acuartelado *heráldica*: quartered;
acuartelar [1a] quarter, billet;
~se withdraw to barracks.

acuático aquatic, water *attr.*;
acuátil aquatic.

acucia f diligence; (*prisa*) haste; (*deseo*) keen desire; **acuciante** pressing; **acuciar** [1b] urge on, hasten, prod (on); (*desear*) desire keenly; **acucioso** diligent, keen; (*deseoso*) eager.

acuclillarse [1a] squat (down).

acuchillado *fig.* experienced, wary; **acuchillar** [1a] stab (to death), knife; *sew.* slash; *madera* hack, gash; ~se fight with knives.

acudir [3a] come up *al ser llamado etc.*; come to the rescue *para socorrer*; come, turn up (*a cita* for, at), present o.s.; (*replicar*) respond, answer; ✗ produce, yield; ~ *a* call on, turn to, have recourse to; *médico* go to see.

acueducto m aqueduct.

ácueo aqueous.

acuerdo m agreement, understanding; (*conformidad*) accord; harmony; (*recuerdo*) remembrance; *parl.* resolution; ~ *verbal* verbal (*or* gentleman's) agreement; *de* ~ in agreement; ¡*de* ~! I agree!, agreed!; *de* ~ *con* in accordance with; *de común* ~ with one accord; *estar de* ~ *con* agree with, be in agreement with; *llegar a un* ~ come to an understanding (*con* with); *ponerse de* ~ come to an agreement, agree; *tomar un* ~ pass a resolution.

acuitar [1a] afflict, grieve; ~se be grieved (*por* by, at).

acular [1a] back (*a* against); F corner.

acullá over there, yonder.

acumulación f accumulation (*a. acto*); pile; hoard; **acumulador** m accumulator, storage battery; **acumular(se)** [1a] accumulate, gather, pile up; **acumulativo** accumulative.

acuñación f minting; **acuñar** [1a] *moneda* coin, mint; *medalla* strike; ⊕ (*meter cuñas*) wedge.

acuoso watery; *fruta* juicy.

acurrucarse [1g] squat; huddle up, curl up.

acusación f accusation; *esp.* 🜨 charge, indictment; *negar la* ~ plead not guilty; **acusado 1.** marked, pronounced; **2.** m, a f accused, defendant; **acusador 1.** accusing, reproachful; **2.** m, -a f accuser; **acusar** [1a] accuse (*de* of); 🜨 accuse, indict (*de, por* of, on a

charge of); *fig.* culpable point to, proclaim the guilt of; (*mostrar*) show, reveal; *cartas* show, declare; *recibo* acknowledge; ~se confess (*de su.* to; *de adj.* to being); **acusativo** m accusative (case); **acusatorio** accusatory; **acuse** m acknowledgement (*de recibo* of receipt); **acusón** F **1.** tell-tale; **2.** m, -a f tell-tale; gossip.

acústica f acoustics; **acústico 1.** acoustic; **2.** m hearing aid.

achacar [1g]: ~ *a* attribute to, impute to, put *s.t.* down to; **achacoso** sickly, infirm; indisposed, ailing.

achaflanar [1a] chamfer, bevel.

achantarse [1a] F hide away; sing small.

achaparrado *árbol* dwarf, shrub-sized; *p.* stocky, thick-set, stumpy.

achaque m 🜨 sickliness, infirmity; ailment; (*asunto*) matter, subject; pretext; defect, fault; F 🜨 period, monthlies; ~s *pl.* mañaneros morning sickness.

achatar [1a] flatten.

achicado child-like.

achicador m scoop, baler; **achicar** [1g] make smaller; *sew.* take in; (*humillar*) humble; intimidate, browbeat; ⚓ bale (out); *S.Am.* F kill; ~se *fig.* eat humble pie, submit to humiliation.

achicoria f chicory.

achicharradero m hot-house, inferno; **achicharrar** [1a] *cocina*: fry crisp; (*demasiado*) overcook, burn; scorch, overheat; F plague; *S.Am.* squeeze; ~se get burnt, get scorched *etc.*

achinado *S.Am.* degraded; coarsened; (*color*) coppery; **achinar** [1a] F scare.

achispado lit-up, jolly; **achisparse** [1a] get tipsy.

achocar [1g] dash (*or* hurl) against a wall; stone *con piedra*; club *con palo*; F hoard.

achocharse [1a] F get doddery, begin to dodder, be in one's second childhood.

achubascarse [1g] (*cielo*) become threatening.

achuchar [1a] F crush, squeeze; (*azuzar*) urge on; **achuchón** m F squeeze; (*empujón*) push, jostle.

achula(pa)do ill-mannered, uncouth; spivvish *sl.*

achurar [1a] *S.Am.* wound; kill.
adagio *m* adage; ♩ adagio.
adalid *m* leader, champion.
adamado effeminate; F *mujer*⎫
adamantino adamantine. [flashy.⎰
adamascado damask; **adamascar**
[1g] damask.
adán *m* F slovenly fellow.
adaptabilidad *f* adaptability; **adaptable** adaptable; *p. freq.* versatile;
adaptación *f* adaptation; **adaptador** *m* adapter; **adaptar** [1a] adapt;
fit, make suitable (*para* for); ⁓se
adapt o.s. (*a* to).
adaraja *f* △ toothing.
adarga *f* (oval) shield.
adarme: *por* ⁓s in driblets.
adecentar [1a] make decent, tidy up.
adecuado adequate; fit, suitable (*a, para* for); **adecuar** [1d] fit, adapt.
adefesio *m* F (*disparate*) absurdity,
piece of nonsense; (*traje*) outlandish dress; (*p.*) queer bird.
adehala *f* (*propina*) gratuity, tip;
bonus *sobre pago*.
adelantado 1. precocious, advanced;
reloj fast; (*atrevido*) forward; ✝
por ⁓ in advance; **2.** *m* ✝ governor,
captain-general; **adelantamiento**
m advancement, furtherance; progress, improvement; **adelantar**
[1a] *v/t.* move forward, move on;
fecha, reloj put forward; *pago*
advance; (*pasar*) overtake, outstrip;
fig. further, advance; *v/i.* make
headway, get on; progress, improve; (*reloj*) be fast, gain; ⁓se go
forward, go ahead; (*reloj*) be fast,
gain; ⁓ *a* get ahead of (*a.* ⁓ *de*);
overtake (*a. mot.*); *fig.* steal a
march on, beat *s.o.* to it; **adelante**
ahead; forward(s), onward(s); ¡⁓!
(*a interlocutor*) go ahead!, go on!,
fire away!; (*a visita*) come in!;
más ⁓ further on; later; (*de aquí o
de hoy*) *en* ⁓ from now on, in the
future; *por el camino* ⁓ from the
opposite direction; **adelanto** *m*
advance (*a.* ✝), progress, advancement.
adelfa *f* rose-bay.
adelgazamiento *m* slimming; **adelgazar** [1f] *v/t.* make thin; (*régimen
etc.*) help *s.o.* to slim; *vara* pare;
fig. purify, refine; *entendimiento*
sharpen; *v/i.* grow thin; (*de propósito*) slim, reduce; *fig.* split hairs;
⁓se grow thin.

ademán *m* gesture, movement;
flourish, motion *de mano*; *paint.
etc.* attitude; ⁓es *pl.* manners; *en* ⁓
de inf. as if to *inf.*; *hacer* ⁓ *de inf.*
make a move to *inf.*; *hacer* ⁓es
gesture, make signs.
además 1. *adv.* besides, moreover,
further(more); **2.** ⁓ *de prp.* besides,
not to mention, aside from *Am.*;
⁓ *de eso* moreover.
adentellar [1a] sink one's teeth
into.
adentrar(se) [1a]: ⁓ *en* penetrate
into, go into, get into, get inside;
adentro 1. = *dentro*; *v. tierra*;
2. ⁓s *m/pl.* innermost being; *para
sus* ⁓ to o.s.
adepto *m* follower, supporter.
aderezar [1f] prepare, get ready;
p. etc. make beautiful, dress up;
fig. embellish, adorn; *comida* season, garnish; *ensalada* dress;
bebidas mix, blend; *tela* gum;
aderezo *m* (*acto*) preparation;
dressing; (*efecto*) adornment; *cocina*: seasoning, dressing; equipment; set *de joyas*; gumming *de
tela*.
adeudado in debt; **adeudar** [1a]
v/t. dinero owe; *impuestos* be liable
for; *cuenta* debit, charge to; *v/i.*
become related (by marriage); ⁓se
run into debt; **adeudo** *m* debt;
customs duty *en aduana*; debit *en
cuenta*.
adherencia *f* adherence; *fig.* connection; **adherente 1.**: ⁓ *a* adhering to, sticking to; **2.** *m* follower,
adherent; **adherir(se)** [3i] adhere,
stick (*a* to); ⁓ *a fig.* espouse,
embrace; adhere to; **adhesión** *f*
adhesion; *fig.* support, adherence;
adhesivo *adj. a. su. m* adhesive.
adición *f* addition, adding-up;
(*cuenta*) bill, check *Am.*; acceptance;
adicional additional, extra; **adicionar** [1a] (*sumar*) add (up); add
(*a* to).
adicto 1.: ⁓ *a* devoted to; given to;
2. *m* supporter.
adiestrar [1a] (*enseñar*) train, teach;
(*guiar*) guide, lead; ⁓se train o.s.
(*a inf.* to *inf.*).
adinerado moneyed, well-off F.
adiós 1. *int.* good-bye!; **2.** *m* good-bye; farewell; ¡**adiosito!** F bye-bye!, cheerio!
adiposo adipose, fat.

aditamento m addition.
adivinación f prophecy, divination; guessing;~ de pensamientos thought-reading; **adivinanza** f riddle, conundrum; **adivinar** [1a] porvenir etc. prophesy, foretell; (descubrir) guess; pensamientos read; enigma solve; **adivino 1.** m, a f fortune-teller; **2.** m zo. praying mantis.
adjetivar [1a] gr. modify; make attributive; fig. apply epithets to; **adjetivo 1.** m adjective; **2.** adjectival.
adjudicación f award; **adjudicar** [1g] award, adjudge; knock down en subasta (a to, en for); ~se algo appropriate.
adjuntar [1a] subjoin, append; enclose en carta; **adjunto 1.** joined on; fig. attached (a to); p. assistant; enclosed en carta; remitir ~ enclose; lo remitimos ~ we enclose it, we send it herewith; **2.** m addition, adjunct; (p.) assistant.
adjutor m, -a f assistant.
adminículo m accessory; ~s pl. emergency kit.
administración f administration; management; running; en ~ in trust; obras en ~ books handled by us, books for which we are agents; **administrador** m, -a f administrator; (jefe) manager; (síndico) steward; (land) agent de finca; ~ de correos postmaster; es buena ~a (en casa) she's a good manager; **administrar** [1a] administer; manage; run; justicia dispense, administer; **administrativo** administrative; managerial.
admirable admirable; **admiración** f admiration; wonder(ment); **admirador** m, -a f admirer; **admirar** [1a] (respetar) admire; look up to; (sorprender) cause surprise (to), astonish; me admira su atrevimiento I am amazed at your boldness; ~se be surprised, be amazed. wonder (de at); **admirativo** admiring, full of admiration.
admisible admissible; excusa etc. legitimate; **admisión** f admission (a to); (recepción) acceptance; ⊕ intake, inlet; **admitir** [3a] admit (a. fig.; a to, en into); accept, recognize; fig. be susceptible of; propina, explicación accept; dilación permit, allow; dudas leave room for.
admonición f warning; **admonitorio** warning attr.
adobado m pickled meat; **adobar** [1a] dress, prepare; carne pickle; piel tan, dress; (guisar) cook, prepare; **adobe** m adobe; **adobo** m preparation, dressing; pickle.
adocenado commonplace, ordinary.
adoctrinar [1a] indoctrinate (en with).
adolecer [2d] fall ill (de with); ~ de suffer from (a. fig.).
adolescencia f adolescence; **adolescente** adj. a. su. m/f adolescent.
adonde 1. where; **2.** ¿adónde? where (to)?
adopción f adoption; **adoptar** [1a] adopt (a. fig.); fig. embrace; actitud adopt, strike, take up; parl. pass, approve; **adoptivo** adoptive; hijo adopted.
adoquín m squared stone, sett; **adoquinado** m paving (of blocks); **adoquinar** [1a] pave (with setts).
adorable adorable; **adoración** f adoration; worship; **adorar** [1a] adore; worship.
adormecedor which sends one to sleep, soporific; a. fig. lulling; **adormecer** [2d] send to sleep; fig. calm, lull; ~se fall asleep, drowse (off); (miembro) get numb, go to sleep; fig. ~ en persist in; **adormecido** drowsy; numb; fig. inactive; **adormecimiento** m drowsiness; numbness; **adormidera** f poppy; **adormilarse** [1a], **adormitarse** [1a] doze.
adornar [1a] adorn, embellish (de with); sew. trim (de with); cuarto decorate; comida garnish; p. grace; le adornan mil virtudes he is blessed with every virtue; **adornista** m/f decorator; **adorno** m adornment; ornament; decoration; sew. trimming; motif en diseño; ~s pl. fig. trappings.
adosar [1a] lean (a against).
adquirir [3i] acquire; obtain; ✝ purchase; earn; hábito acquire, form; **adquirido** acquired; mal ~ ganancias ill-gotten; **adquisición** f acquisition; ✝ purchase; **adquisitivo** acquisitive; ✝ poder purchasing; **adquisividad** f acquisitiveness.

adrede on purpose, intentionally.
adrenalina *f* adrenalin.
adscribir [3a; *p.p. adscrito*]: ~ *a* assign to; *adscrito a(l servicio de)* attached to.
aduana *f* customs; custom-house; (*derechos de*) ~ customs duty; *libre de* ~ customs-free; **aduanero 1.** customs *attr.*; **2.** *m* customs-officer.
aducir [3o] adduce, bring forward; *prueba* furnish.
adueñarse [1a]: ~ *de* take possession of.
aduje *etc. v. aducir.*
adulación *f* flattery, adulation; **adulador** *m*, **-a** *f* flatterer; **adular** [1a] flatter, fawn on, make up to; **adulón** F **1.** cringing, fawning; **2.** *m*, **-a** *f* toady, creep.
adúltera *f* adulteress; **adulteración** *f* adulteration; **adulterar** [1a] *v/t.* adulterate; *v/i.* commit adultery; **adulterino** adulterous; *moneda* falsified, counterfeit; **adulterio** *m* adultery, misconduct; **adúltero 1.** adulterous; *fig.* corrupt; **2.** *m* adulterer.
adulto *adj. a. su. m*, **a** *f* adult, grown-up.
adunar [1a] join, unite.
adustez *f* grimness, austerity; **adusto** *región etc.* scorching; *fig.* austere, grim; *estilo* severe.
aduzco *etc. v. aducir.*
advenedizo 1. foreign, (from) outside; *contp.* upstart, parvenu; **2.** *m*, **a** *f* foreigner, outsider; *contp.* upstart, parvenu; **advenimiento** *m* advent; accession *al trono*; **adventicio** adventitious.
adverbial adverbial; **adverbio** *m* adverb.
adversario *m*, **a** *f* adversary, opponent; **adversidad** *f* adversity; **adverso** *suerte* adverse, untoward; *lado* opposite.
advertencia *f* (*amonestación*) warning; caveat; (*recordatorio*) reminder; foreword *en libro*; **advertido** capable; (*despierto*) wide-awake; **advertir** [3i] *v/t.* notice, observe; (*enseñar*) point out, draw attention to; (*aconsejar*) advise (*que* that); (*amonestar*) warn (of); caution; *v/i.*: ~ *en* notice, observe; (*tener en cuenta*) take notice of.
Adviento *m* Advent.

advocación *f eccl.* name, dedication; *bajo la* ~ *de* in the name of.
adyacente adjacent (*a. Ꭺ*).
aechaduras *f/pl.* chaff; *v. ahechar.*
aeración *f* aeration; **aéreo** aerial, air *attr.*; *ferrocarril etc.* overhead; **aerodinámico** aerodynamic; *mot. etc.* streamlined; *v. túnel*; **aerodinamizar** [1f] streamline; **aeródromo** *m* aerodrome, airfield; **aerofoto** *f* aerial photograph; **aerolito** *m* aerolite; **aeromodelismo** *m* aeromodelling; **aeromoza** *f S.Am.* air hostess, stewardess; **aeronáutica** *f* aeronautics; **aeronáutico** aeronautic(al); **aeronave** *f* airship; **aeropuerto** *m* airport; **aerostática** *f* aerostatics; **aerostático** aerostatic(al); *v. globo*; **aeróstato** *m* aerostat, balloon; **aerotransportado** airborne; **aerovía** *f* airway.
afabilidad *f* affability, geniality, good nature; **afable** affable, genial, good-natured; *trato* easy, smooth.
afamado famed, noted (*por* for); **afamar** [1a] make famous.
afán *m* industry, exertion; anxiety; zeal, desire, urge (*de* for); **afanarse** [1a] exert o.s., strive, labour (*por inf.* to *inf.*); F drudge (*or* toil) away (*en* at); **afanoso** *trabajo* laborious, heavy; *tarea* troublesome, uphill; *p.* solicitous.
afasia *f* aphasia.
afeamiento *m* defacing; disfigurement; condemnation; **afear** [1a] deface, make ugly; *esp. cara* disfigure; *fig.* condemn, decry.
afección *f* affection (*a. ✱*); (*alteración*) change, effect; ~ *cardíaca* heart complaint, heart trouble; ~es *pl. del alma* emotions; **afectación** *f* affectation, pose; pretence, affectation *de ignorancia etc.*; **afectado** affected, unnatural; *estilo* stilted, precious, affected; **afectar** [1a] (*dejarse sentir en*) affect, have an effect on; (*conmover*) affect, move; (*fingir*) affect, pretend; *celo etc.* put on a show of; desire; ~ tie up, encumber; *por lo que afecta a* regarding, as for; **afectísimo** *mst* affectionate; *suyo* ~ yours truly; **afectivo** affective; **afecto 1.** affectionate, fond; ✞ subject to tax; tied; ~ *a* fond of; inclined to; ~ *de* afflicted with; **2.** *m* affection, fond-

ness (a for); emotion, feeling; **afectuosidad** f fondness, affection; **afectuoso** affectionate.

afeitada f, **afeitado** m shave, shaving; **afeitar** [1a] barba shave; cara make up, paint; cola trim; planta prune; ~se (have a) shave; **afeite** m make-up, cosmetic; (aderezo) putting right, fixing.

afelpado plush(y), velvety.

afeminación f effeminacy; **afeminado 1.** effeminate, sissy sl.; **2.** m effeminate person, sissy sl.; (maricón) nancy sl.

aferrado stubborn; fig. ~ a, ~ en opinión etc. wedded to; **aferrar** [1k] v/t. grapple, seize; ⚓ grapple; vela, bandera furl; v/i., ~se grapple (with, together); ⚓ (anclar) anchor, moor; ⚓ (asirse) grapple; fig. ~ a, ~ en stick to.

afestonado festooned.

afianzamiento m guarantee, security; ⚖ bail; fig. backing; **afianzar** [1f] muro support, prop up; (sujetar) fasten; (asir) seize; fig. (apoyar) back, support; p. etc. guarantee, vouch for.

afición f fondness, liking (a for), taste (a música etc. for); (pasatiempo) hobby; (ps.) fans, public; pinta de ~ he paints as a hobby; tomar ~ a take (a liking) to; **aficionado 1.** (no profesional) amateur; ~ a música etc. fond of, with a taste for; deportes etc. keen on; estar ~ a like, be fond of; ser muy ~ a be very keen on; **2.** m, a f (no profesional) amateur; enthusiast; deportes: fan, follower (a of); thea., cine: fan; ~ a la música etc. music- etc. lover, lover of music etc.; tenis para ~s amateur tennis; es un simple ~ he's just an amateur; **aficionar** [1a] make s.o. keen (a algo on); inspire affection in s.o. (a alguien for s.o.); ~se a, ~ de get fond of, take (a fancy) to; deporte etc. become a follower (or fan) of; ~ a inf. become fond of ger.

afiladera f grindstone; **afilado** filo sharp, keen; punto tapering; **afilador** m (p.) knife-grinder; ⊕ strop; **afiladura** f sharpening, whetting; **afilalápices** m pencil-sharpener; **afilar** [1a] sharpen, make sharp, put an edge on; put a point on; navaja strop; ~se get

sharp etc.; (cara) get peaked, grow thin; (dedo) taper.

afiliación f affiliation; **afiliado** affiliated (a to); ⚕ subsidiary; **afiliarse** [1a]: ~ a affiliate (o.s.) to.

afiligranado ⊕ filigreed; fig. delicate, fine.

afilón m strop.

afín 1. (colindante) bordering; related, similar; ideas kindred, akin; **2.** m/f relation by marriage.

afinación f refining; ♩ tuning; **afinado** in tune; **afinador** m ♩ tuning-key; (p.) tuner; **afinar** [1a] v/t. perfect; ⊕ purify, refine; fig. refine, polish; ♩ tune; v/i. sing (or play) in tune.

afinidad f affinity (a. 🜨); fellow-feeling; kinship (con with); por ~ by marriage.

afino m ⊕ refinement.

afirmación f affirmation, assertion; **afirmar** [1a] (reforzar) strengthen, secure; (estabilizar) steady; (declarar) affirm, assert; state, lay (it) down (que that); ~se steady o.s.; **afirmativa** f affirmative; **afirmativo** affirmative; positive.

aflicción f sorrow, affliction, trial; **aflictivo** distressing; pena corporal; **afligido 1.** distressed, heart-broken; stricken (por with); **2.**: los ~s m/pl. the bereaved; **afligir** [3c] afflict; (pena etc.) grieve, trouble, pain; ~se grieve (con, de, por at).

aflojamiento m slackening, loosening (a. 🜨); fig. relief, relaxation; **aflojar** [1a] v/t. cuerda, paso slacken; tornillo etc. loosen (a. 🜨, a. fig.); presión release; fig. relax; v/i. fig. (ablandarse) relent; grow cool (en devoción in); get slack (en estudios in); ~se slacken (off); work loose etc.; fig. (calor, 🜨) abate; (devoción) cool (off); (interés) flag.

afloramiento m outcrop; **aflorar** [1a] crop out, crop up, outcrop.

afluencia f (flujo) inflow, influx; (gente etc.) crowd, jam; attendance en reunión; abundance; eloquence; **afluente 1.** flowing; eloquent; **2.** m geog. tributary, feeder; **afluir** [3g] flow (a. fig.; a into); **aflujo** m 🜨 afflux, congestion.

aforador m gauger; **aforar** [1a] ⊕ gauge; fig. appraise, value.

aforismo m aphorism; **aforístico** aphoristic.

aforo m gauging, fig. appraisal.

aforrar [1a] line, face; ~se put on plenty of underclothes; F feed one's face, tuck it away.

afortunado fortunate, lucky; *tiempo* stormy.

afrancesado *adj. a. su. m,* **a** *f* Francophile; **afrancesarse** [1a] go French; become Gallicized.

afrecho *m* bran; ~ *remojado* mash.

afrenta *f* affront; indignity, outrage; **afrentar** [1a] affront; dishonour; ~se be ashamed (de of); **afrentoso** insulting, outrageous.

africano *adj. a. su. m,* **a** *f* African.

afrodisíaco *adj. a. su. m* aphrodisiac.

afrontar [1a] confront, bring face to face; *enemigo etc.* face (up to).

afuera 1. *adv.* outside; ¡~! out of the way!; **2.** ~s *f/pl.* outskirts; suburbs.

afufar [1a] F beat it, clear off.

agachada *f* F trick, dodge; **agachadiza** *f* snipe; F *hacer la* ~ pretend not to have been seen; **agachar** [1a] F *cabeza* bow; *sombrero* slouch; ~se crouch, double up; (*esconderse*) duck; (*retirarse*) go into hiding, make o.s. scarce, lie low.

agalla *f* ♣ gall(-nut); ~ (*de roble*) oak-apple; *ichth.* gill; F *tener* (*muchas*) ~s have guts.

ágape *m hist.* love-feast; F banquet.

agarrada *f* F scrap, brawl; **agarradero** *m* handle, grip; ⊕ lug; F pull, influence; **agarrado** F stingy, tight(-fisted); **agarrafar** [1a] F grab hold of; **agarrar** [1a] *v/t.* grip, grasp, lay (*or* catch) hold of; grab *con fuerza*; F get, wangle; *v/i.* take hold (de of); *S.Am.* ~ *para* strike out for; ~se grasp one another, grapple; ~ *a* hold on to, seize; grip; *carretera* hold; ~ *de* seize, fasten (up)on; F *se le agarró la fiebre* the fever took hold of him; **agarro** *m* grasp, hold.

agarrotar [1a] *fardo* tie tight; *p.* squeeze tight; *reo* garrotte; (*camisa*) be tight for; ~se ✱ stiffen; ⊕ seize up.

agasajar [1a] treat kindly, make much of; (*con banquete etc.*) regale, entertain lavishly; give *s.o.* a royal welcome; **agasajo** *m* consideration, kindness; (*regalo*) royal welcome, lavish hospitality.

ágata *f* agate.

agave *f* agave, American aloe.

agavilladora *f* ✦ binder; **agavillar** [1a] bind (in sheaves); ~se F gang up, band together.

agazapar [1a] F catch, grab (hold of); ~se F (*esconderse*) hide; (*agacharse*) crouch down, duck.

agencia *f* agency (*a. fig.*); bureau; *S.Am.* pawnshop; ~ *de noticias* news-agency; ~ *de transportes* carriers, removal business; ~ *de turismo*, ~ *de viajes* tourist office, travel agency; **agenciar** [1b] bring about, engineer; procure, obtain; *trato* negotiate; *b.s.* wangle; ~se manage, get along; **agencioso** active, diligent.

agenda *f* notebook; (*diario*) engagement diary. [ment diary.]

agente *m* agent; ~ (*de policía*) policeman; ~ *de cambio* bill broker; ~ *de negocios* broker; ~ *provocador* agent provocateur; ~ *marítimo* shipping agent; ~ *de publicidad* ✝ advertising agent; *thea. etc.* publicity agent; ~ *de transportes* carrier; ~ *de turismo* travel agent; courier; *S.Am.* ~ *viajero* commercial traveller, salesman.

agestado: *bien* ~ well-favoured; *mal* ~ ill-favoured.

agible workable, feasible.

agigantado gigantic; **agigantar** [1a] make *s.t.* (seem) huge.

ágil agile, nimble, quick; **agilidad** *f* agility *etc.*; **agilitar** [1a] enable, make it easy for; ~se limber up.

agio *m* speculation; agio; **agiotaje** *m* speculation; (stock-)jobbery, jobbing; **agiotista** *m* speculator; jobber.

agitación *f* waving; shaking *etc.*; ⚓ roughness; *fig.* ~ (*de ánimo*) agitation; (*movimiento*) bustle, stir, flurry; (*tumulto*) stir, ferment; **agitado** ⚓ rough, choppy; ✈ bumpy; *fig.* agitated, upset, excited; **agitador** *m* (*p.*) agitator, rabble-rouser; ⊕ agitator, shaker.

agitanado gipsy-like.

agitar [1a] *bandera etc.* wave; *brazo* shake, wave; *ala* flap; (*circularmente*) whirl; *líquido* shake up, stir; *fig.* stir up; (*inquietar*) worry, make anxious; ~se shake, wave to and fro; (*bandera etc.*) flutter, flap; ⚓ get rough; *fig.* get excited, get worked up; get worried.

aglomeración f mass, agglomeration; ~ de *tráfico* traffic jam; **aglomerar(se)** [1a] form a mass, agglomerate; (*gente*) crowd together.

aglutinación f agglutination; **aglutinar(se)** [1a] agglutinate.

agnado adj. a. su. m, a f agnate.

agobiador, agobiante *carga* oppressive; *trabajo* overwhelming; *pobreza* grinding; **agobiar** [1b] weigh down, bow down (de with); oppress, burden (a. *fig.*); (*agotar*) exhaust, wear out; ~se con, ~ de be weighed down with (a. *fig.*), bow beneath; **agobio** m burden; oppression; ✠ nervous strain, anxiety.

agolpamiento m rush, crush, throng de gente etc.; bunch de cosas; crop de penas; flood de lágrimas; **agolparse** [1a] crowd together, throng; (*penas*) come on top of one another; (*lágrimas*) come in a flood.

agonía f agony; throes (a. *fig.*); (*ansia*) yearning; **agónico** fig. agonizing; **agonizante 1.** dying; **2.** m/f dying person; *eccl. monk who assists the dying*; **agonizar** [1f] v/t. F harass, pester; v/i. be in the throes of death.

agorar [1n] predict, prophesy; **agorero 1.** p. who prophesies; *ave* of ill omen; **2.** m, a f fortune-teller, soothsayer.

agostar [1a] *plantas* parch, burn up; *tierra* plough (in summer); ~se wither; fig. fade away; **agostizo** ✍ sickly, weak; **agosto** m August; fig. harvest; F *hacer su* ~ feather one's nest; make hay while the sun shines.

agotable exhaustible; **agotado** exhausted, worn out; *libro* out of print; *batería* run down; ✝ *estar* ~ be sold out; **agotamiento** m exhaustion (a. ✠); depletion, draining; ~ *nervioso* strain; **agotar** [1a] exhaust (a. ✠); *cisterna* drain, empty; *filón* work out; *provisión, recursos* drain, deplete, use up; *p.* tire, wear out; *paciencia* exhaust; ~se be(come) exhausted; (*suministro* etc.) be used up, give out, run out; (*filón*) peter out; (*libro*) go out of print.

agraceño tart, sour. [print.]

agraciado graceful; *cara* etc. attractive, nice; blessed (de with); **agraciar** [1b] improve the looks of, make more attractive; *reo* pardon; (*favorecer*) reward (con with).

agradable pleasant, enjoyable, nice; *p.* nice ([*para*] con to), agreeable; **agradar** [1a] please, be pleasing to.

agradecer [2d] *p.* thank; *favor* be grateful (*or* thankful) for; *agradezco tu carta* I am grateful for your letter; *se lo agradezco* I am grateful to you, I am much obliged; *agradecería que* I should be much obliged if; *¡se agradece!* much obliged; **agradecido** grateful (a to; por for); appreciative; *muy* ~ much obliged (*por* for); **agradecimiento** m gratitude.

agrado m affability; (*gusto*) taste, liking; *no es de mi* ~ it is not to my liking.

agrandar [1a] make bigger, enlarge; *dificultad* magnify.

agranujado *piel* pimply.

agrario agrarian; *reforma* etc. freq. land *attr.*

agravación f, **agravamiento** m aggravation, worsening; increase de pena, impuesto; ✠ change for the worse; **agravante 1.** aggravating; **2.** f additional burden; unfortunate circumstance; **agravar** [1a] weigh down, make heavier; *pena, impuesto* increase; *dolor, situación* make worse; *pueblo* oppress; ~se worsen, get worse.

agraviar [1b] wrong, offend; ~se take offence, be offended (de, por at); **agravio** m offence, wrong; a. ⚖ grievance; ~s pl. de hecho assault and battery; **agravioso** offensive, insulting.

agraz m sour grape; (*zumo*) sour grape juice; fig. bitterness, displeasure; en ~ prematurely; **agrazar** [1f] v/t. embitter; (*disgustar*) annoy; v/i. taste sour, have a sharp taste; **agrazón** m F annoyance, bother.

agredir [3a; *defective*] assault, attack, do violence to.

agregado m (*conjunto*) aggregate; (*p.*) attaché; ⊕ concrete block; *S.Am.* tenant; **agregar** [1h] (*añadir*) add (a to); (*juntar*) gather, collect; *p.* appoint, attach (a to); ~se be joined (a, con to, with).

agremiar [1b] form into a union; ~se form a union.

agresión f aggression; **agresivo** aggressive; fig. pushing, assertive, militant; **agresor** *m*, **-a** *f* aggressor, assailant.

agreste rural, country *attr.*; *fig.* rustic, countrified.

agrete sourish.

agriar [1b *or* 1c] (make) sour; *fig.* exasperate; **~se** turn (sour); *fig.* get exasperated, get irritated.

agrícola agricultural, farming *attr.*; **agricultor 1.** agricultural, farming *attr.*; **2.** *m*, **-a** *f* farmer, agriculturalist; **agricultura** *f* agriculture, farming.

agridulce bittersweet.

agrietar [1a] crack (open), make cracks in; **~se** crack (open); get cracked; (*manos*) chap.

agrifolio *m* holly.

agrimensor *m* (land-)surveyor; **agrimensura** *f* (land-)surveying.

agrio 1. sour, acid, tart (*a. fig.*); *fig.* disagreeable; *camino* uneven, rough; *materia* fragile, breakable; *color* harsh, garish; **2.** *m* (sour) juice; **~s** *pl.* citrus fruits.

agronomía *f* agronomy, agriculture; **agrónomo 1.** agricultural, farming *attr.*; *ingeniero* ~ **= 2.** agricultural adviser, farming expert; **agropecuario** farming (and stock-breeding) *attr.*

agrupación *f*, **agrupamiento** *m* association, group; (*acto*) grouping (together), coming together; **agrupar** [1a] group (together); (*apiñar*) bunch (*or* crowd) together; **~se** (*ps.*) crowd (around); (*cosas*) cluster, bunch together; *pol. etc.* rally, come together.

agrura *f* sourness (*a. fig.*).

agua *f* **1.** water; (*lluvia*) rain; ⚓ (*estela*) wake; (*abertura*) leak; ⚠ slope of a roof; ~ *bendita* holy water; ~ *blanda* soft water; ~ *corriente* running water; ~ *de bebida* drinking-water; ~ *de Colonia* eau-de-Cologne; ~ *dulce* fresh water; *de* ~ *dulce pez etc.* freshwater; ~ *de espliego* lavender water; ~ *llovediza*, ~ (*de*) *lluvia* rainwater; ~ (*de*) *manantial* spring water; ~ *potable* drinking-water; ~ *abajo* downstream; ~ *arriba* upstream; *bailarle el* ~ *a* dance attendance on; *echar el* ~ *launch*; *echar el* ~ *a su molino* be on the make; *hacer* ~ leak, take in water; *se me hace la boca* ~ my mouth waters; *que hace* ~ *tela* moiré; *pescar en* ~ *turbia* fish in troubled waters; *retener el* ~ hold water; *volverse* ~ *de cerrajas* (*proyecto etc.*) come to nothing; ¡*hombre al* ~! man overboard!; **2.** **~s** *pl.* waters; ⚓ tide; ☄ urine; sparkle *de joya*; ~ *jurisdiccionales*, ~ *territoriales* territorial waters; ~ *mayores* excrement; ~ *menores* urine; ~ *minerales* mineral waters; ~ *residuales* sewage; *hacer* ~ make water, relieve o.s.; *nadar entre dos* ~ sit on the fence.

aguacero *m* (heavy) shower; **aguacha** *f* stagnant water; **aguachirle** *f* slops, swill; *fig.* dishwater; (*cosa*) trifle, mere nothing; **aguada** *f* ⚓ water supply; ☄ flooding; *paint.* water colour, wash; **aguado** watery, watered (down); *sopa* thin; *fig. fiesta etc.* spoiled, interrupted; **aguador** *m* water-carrier, water-seller; **aguaducho** *m* freshet; **aguafiestas** *m/f* wet blanket, killjoy; **aguafuerte** *f* etching; *grabar al agua fuerte* etch; **aguaje** *m* (*marea*) (spring) tide; current; (*provisión*) water supply; **aguamanil** *m* ewer, water-jug; (*palangana*) wash-stand; **aguamar** *m* jelly-fish; **aguamarina** *f* aquamarine; **aguanieve** *f* sleet; **aguanoso** watery, wet; *terreno* water-logged.

aguantar [1a] *v/t.* *techo* hold up; *aliento* hold; *dolor etc.* endure, withstand; *tempestad* weather; (*tolerar*) bear, stand, put up with; *v/i.* last, hold out; **~se** hold o.s. back, restrain o.s.

aguar [1i] water (down); *fig.* mar, spoil; *v. fiesta.*

aguardada *f* wait(ing); **aguardadero** *m* *hunt.* stand, hide; **aguardar** [1a] *v/t.* wait for, await; *v/i.* wait; *b.s.* lie in wait.

aguardiente *m* brandy; ~ *de caña* rum.

aguarrás *m* (oil of) turpentine.

aguatero *m* *S.Am.* water-seller.

aguatocha *f* pump.

aguaturma *f* Jerusalem artichoke.

aguaza *f* sap.

aguazal *m* puddle.

agudeza *f* acuteness, sharpness (*a. fig.*); (*chiste*) witticism; (*lo ingenioso*) wit(tiness); **agudo** sharp, pointed; ☄, ♪, *gr.* acute; *nota* high

(-pitched); *sonido* piercing; *sabor etc.* pungent; *sentido* keen, acute; *pregunta* searching; *crítica* sharp, trenchant; (*gracioso*) lively, witty; *ingenio* ready, lively.

agüero *m* (*arte*) augury; (*pronóstico*) forecast; (*señal*) omen; **de buen ~** lucky, propitious; **de mal ~** ill-omened, of ill omen. [harden.]

aguerrir [3a; *defective*] inure,]

aguijada *f* goad; **aguijar** [1a] *v/t.* goad (*a. fig.*); *fig.* urge on, incite; *v/i.* hurry along, make haste; **aguijón** *m* goad; *zo.* sting; ♀ prickle, sting; *fig.* spur, incitement; '*dar coces contra el ~* kick against the pricks; **aguijonazo** *m* prick; *zo.*, ♀ sting; **aguijonear** [1a] = *aguijar*.

águila *f* eagle; *fig.* superior mind, genius; (*astuto*) wily bird; **~ pescadora** osprey.

aguileña *f* columbine.

aguileño *nariz* aquiline; *cara* sharp-featured.

aguilera *f* eyrie; **aguilón** *m* large eagle; jib *de grúa*; △ gable(-end); **aguilucho** *m* eaglet.

aguinaldo *m* Christmas (*or* New Year) gift; (*propina*) gratuity.

aguja *f sew.* needle; (*roma*) bodkin; hand *de reloj*; gnomon *de reloj de sol*; pointer *de esfera*; △ spire, steeple; 🚂 (*a. ~s pl.*) points, switch rail; **~s pl. anat.** ribs; **~ capotera**, **~ de zurcir** darning-needle; **~ de gancho** crochet hook; **~ hipodérmica** hypodermic needle; **~ magnética**, **~ de marear** compass (needle); **~ de** (*hacer*) *media* knitting-needle; *buscar una ~ en un pajar* look for a needle in a haystack; **agujazo** *m* jab, prick; **agujereado** full of holes; *vasija* leaky; **agujerear** [1a] make holes in; pierce; **agujero** *m* hole; (*alfiletero*) needle-case; ⊕ **~ de hombre** manhole; **agujetas** *f/pl.* ♀ stitch; **agujón** *m* hatpin.

¡agur! F so long!; *iro. etc.* good-bye.

agusanado maggoty.

agustin(ian)o *adj. a. su. m*, *a f* Augustinian.

aguzar [1f] sharpen (*a. fig.*); *apetito* whet; *v.* oreja, vista.

¡ah! ah!; ha!; **¡~ del barco!** ship ahoy!

ahechar [1a] sift; *trigo* winnow.

aherrojar [1a] fetter, put in irons; *fig.* subjugate, oppress.

aherrumbrarse [1a] get rusty; (*agua*) taste of iron.

ahí there, just there; **de ~ que** with the result that; **por ~** over there, that way; somewhere around; *fig.* more or less; **¡~ va!** there he goes!; (*sorpresa*) goodness me!; **estará por ~** he's knocking around somewhere.

ahijado *m*, **a** *f* godchild; *fig.* protegé(e); **ahijar** [1a] *v/t. p.* adopt; *animal* mother; *fig.* impute (*a* to); *v/i.* have children.

ahilar [1a] *v/t.* line up; *v/i.* go in single file; **~se** ♀ faint with hunger; (*planta*) grow poorly; (*árbol*) grow tall; (*vino etc.*) go sour, go bad.

ahincadamente earnestly, hard; **ahincado** earnest, emphatic, energetic; **ahincar** [1g] press, urge; **~se** make haste, hurry up; **ahinco** *m* earnestness, intentness, energy; **con ~** earnestly, hard.

ahitar [1a] surfeit, cloy; **~se** stuff o.s. (*de* with) F; ♀ have (*or* get) indigestion; **ahito 1.** surfeited, satiated; *fig.* fed up (*de* with); **2.** *m* ♀ indigestion; *fig.* surfeit, satiety.

ahogadero *m* (*collar*) throatband; halter, headstall *de caballo*; *fig.* Black Hole of Calcutta; **ahogado** *cuarto* close, stifling; *fig.* spent up; **ahogar** [1h] drown *en agua*; suffocate, smother *por falta de aire* (*a. fig.*); *fuego* put out, extinguish; *proyecto de ley* kill; *planta* soak; *fig.* afflict, oppress; **morir ahogado** = **~se** drown; (*suicidarse*) drown o.s.; suffocate; **ahogo** *m* ♀ shortness of breath, tightness of the chest; *fig.* affliction, sorrow; ✝ stringency, embarrassment; **perecer por ~** drown; **ahoguío** *m* = *ahogo* ♀.

ahondar [1a] *v/t.* deepen, make deeper; *fig.* penetrate, go into; *v/i.* **~ en** penetrate, go (deep) into; **~se** go (*or* sink) in more deeply.

ahora 1. *adv.* now; (*hace poco*) (just) now; (*dentro de poco*) in a little while; **desde ~** from now on, henceforward; **hasta ~** up till now, as yet, hitherto; **por ~** for the present; **~ mismo** right now, this very minute; **2.** *cj.* now; **~ bien** now then; **~ pues** well then; **~ ... ~** whether ... or.

ahorcajarse [1a] sit astride; **~ en** straddle.

ahorcar [1g] hang; *v. hábito*; ~se be hanged; (*suicidarse*) hang o.s.

ahorita *esp. S.Am.* F right away.

ahormar [1a] adjust (*a* to); *zapatos* break in, stretch; *fig.* make *s.o.* see sense.

ahorquillado forked; **ahorquillar** [1a] (*asegurar*) prop up, stay; *alambre etc.* shape like a fork; ~se fork, become forked.

ahorrar [1a] *mst* save; *disgusto, peligro* avoid; *esclavo* free; *fig.* save (*de* from); ~se spare o.s., save o.s.; *no* ~(*las*) *con nadie* be afraid of nobody; **ahorrativo** thrifty; *b.s.* stingy; **ahorro** *m* economy, saving; ~s *pl.* savings.

ahoyar [1a] make holes in, dibble.

ahuchar [1a] hoard, put by.

ahuecar [1g] *v/t.* hollow (out), make a hollow in; (*mullir*) loosen, soften; *voz* deepen, make solemn; *v/i.* F beat it; ~se F put on airs.

ahumado 1. *tocino etc.* smoked; *cristal etc.* smoky; **2.** *m* smoking, curing; **ahumar** [1a] *v/t. tocino etc.* smoke, cure; (*ahuyentar*) smoke out; *v/i.* (give out) smoke; ~se (*comida*) taste burnt; (*cuarto*) be smoky, get smoked up; F get boozed.

ahusado tapering; **ahusarse** [1a] taper.

ahuyentar [1a] drive away, scare away; *fig.* banish, put out of mind; ~se run away.

airado angry, furious; *vida* immoral, depraved; **airar** [1a] anger, irritate, ~se get angry (*de, por* at).

aire *m* air (*a. fig.: aspecto, elegancia*); (*viento*) wind, draught; ♪ tune, air; ~ *colado* draught; ~ *comprimido* compressed air; ~ *de familia* family resemblance; ~ *líquido* liquid air; ~ *viciado* stale air, fug; *al* ~ *fig.* (up) in the air; *al* ~ *libre adj.* outdoor; *adv.* in the fresh (*or* open) air; outdoors; *de buen* (*mal*) ~ in a good (bad) temper; *cambiar de* ~(*s*) have a change of air; *darse* ~s put on airs; *darse* ~s *de* boast of being; *tener* ~ *de* look like; *tomar el* ~ go for a stroll; *volar por los* ~s fly through the air.

airear [1a] air, ventilate; ~se take the air; ✗ catch a chill.

airosidad *f* grace(fulness), elegance; **airoso** *lugar* airy; *tiempo* blowy; *cuarto* draughty; *fig.* graceful, elegant; airy, jaunty; (*con lucimiento*) successful; *quedar* ~, *salir* ~ come out with flying colours.

aislación *f* insulation; ~ *de sonido* sound-proofing; **aislacionismo** *m* isolationism; **aislado** isolated; cut off; (*retirado*) lonely, out of the way; ⚡, ⊕ insulated; **aislador** ⚡ **1.** insulating; **2.** *m* insulator, non-conductor; **aislamiento** *m* isolation; ⚡ insulation; *material*, **aislante** *m* ⚡ insulator; **aislar** [1a] isolate (*a. fig.*), separate, cut off (*de* from); ⚡ insulate; ~se isolate o.s. (*de* from); live in isolation.

¡ajá! fine!, (jolly) good!

ajamiento *m* (c)rumpling, crushing; *fig.* abuse.   [to fat.)

ajamonarse [1a] F get plump, run)

ajar [1a] (c)rumple, mess up; *esp. vestido* crush; batter; *p.* abuse; dress down; ~se get (c)rumpled *etc.*; ✿ fade.

ajardinar [1a] landscape.

ajedr(ec)ista *m/f* chess player; **ajedrez** *m* chess; (*fichas*) chess set, chessmen; **ajedrezado** chequered.

ajenjo *m* ✿ wormwood; (*bebida*) absinth.

ajeno (*de otro*) somebody else's, not one's own, other people's; (*de fuera*) outside; alien, foreign (*a manera de pensar etc.* to); (*impropio*) unsuitable; inappropriate (*a, de* to, for); different; ~ *a control etc.* outside, beyond; ~ *de preocupaciones etc.* without, free from; *los bienes* ~s, *lo* ~ other people's property; *estar* ~ *de sí* be detached.

ajetreado *vida* tiring, busy; **ajetrearse** [1a] bustle about; (*afanarse*) slave (away); (*fatigarse*) tire o.s. out; **ajetreo** *m* (*trajín*) bustle, much coming and going; (*afanes*) drudgery.

ají *m* chilli, red pepper; **ajiaceite** *m* sauce of garlic and olive oil; **ajilimoje** *m*, **ajilimójili** *m* F pepper and garlic sauce; ~s *pl.* F bits and pieces; buttons and bows; **ajo** *m* (clove of) garlic; F ✝ shady deal; F (*palabra*) swear-word, dirty word; *harto de* ~s badly brought up, brought up in the gutter; F *tieso como un* ~ hoity-toity, high and mighty; F *soltar* ~s *y cebollas* swear black and blue, swear like a trooper.

ajobar [1a] carry on one's back; **ajobo** *m* load; *fig.* burden, trouble.

ajorca *f* bracelet, bangle.

ajornalar [1a] hire by the day.

ajuar *m* household furnishings *de casa*; dowry *de novia*; trousseau.

ajuiciado sensible; **ajuiciar** [1b] bring to one's senses.

ajustado right, fitting; *ropa* close-fitting, tight, clinging; **ajustador** *m* waistcoat; corselet; ⊕ finisher; fitter; **ajustar** [1a] **1.** *v/t.* ⊕ (*encajar etc.*) fit (*a* to, into); (*cerrar, ponerse etc.*) fasten; *mecanismo* adjust, regulate; (*corregir*) put right, set right; (*adaptar, cambiar*) adjust, adapt (*a* to); *agravio* pay off; *boda* arrange; *criado* hire, engage; *cuenta* settle; *página* make up; *precio* fix; **2.** *v/i.* fit; ~ *bien* be a good fit; **3.** ~**se** (*convenir*) fit, go; adapt o.s., get adjusted (*a* to); conform (*a* to); (*ponerse de acuerdo*) come to an agreement (*con* with); **ajustamiento** *m* † settlement; **ajuste** *m* ⊕ *etc.* fitting; adjustment; *sew.* fit, fitting; engagement *de criado*; † settlement; reconciliation; *typ.* making up; ⚖ retaining fee; *mal* ~ maladjustment.

ajusticiar [1b] execute.

al = *a* + *el*; ~ *llegar* on arriving.

ala wing (*a.* ✕, △, *pol. a. fig.*); ✈ wing, main plane; △ (*alero*) eaves; *anat.* auricle; blade *de hélice*; leaf *de mesa*; brim *de sombrero*; ~*s pl. fig.* courage; F *ahuecar el* ~ beat it; F *arrastrar el* ~ (*enamorado*) court; (*alicaído*) be depressed; *caérsele a uno las* ~*s* lose heart; *cortar las* ~*s a fig.* clip *s.o.'s* wings; F *tomar* ~*s* get saucy.

alabador approving, eulogistic; **alabamiento** *m* prɛise; **alabancioso** F boastful; **alabanza** *f* praise; eulogy; ~*s pl.* praises; *cantar las* ~*s de* sing the praises of; **alabar** [1a] praise; ~**se** be pleased, be satisfied; (*jactarse*) boast (*de* of being).

alabarda *f* halberd; **alabardero** *m* halberdier; *thea.* claqueur.

alabastro *m* alabaster (*a. fig.*); **alabastrino** alabaster *attr.*

alabear(se) [1a] warp; **alabeo** *m* warping; *tomar* ~ warp.

alacena *f* recess cupboard.

alacrán *m* scorpion.

alacridad *f* alacrity, readiness.

alada *f* fluttering; **alado** winged; *fig.* swift.

alagartado motley, variegated.

alambicado *fig.* given sparingly (*or* grudgingly); *estilo etc.* subtle, precious; **alambicar** [1g] distil; *fig.* scrutinize; *estilo* make over-subtle; **alambique** *m* still; *por* ~ sparingly; *pasar por* ~ *fig.* go through *s.t.* with a tooth-comb.

alambrada *f* barbed-wire entanglement; **alambrado** *m* (*valla*) wire fence; (*red*) wire mesh; ⚡ wiring; **alambre** *m* wire (*a.* ♪); ~ *cargado* live wire; ~ *forrado* covered wire; ~ *de púas* barbed wire; **alambrar** [1a] wire; **alambrera** *f* wire mesh; wire cover *para carne etc.*; fireguard *para lumbre.*

alameda *f* ♀ poplar grove; (*paseo*) walk; **álamo** *m* poplar; ~ *blanco* white poplar; ~ *de Italia* Lombardy poplar; ~ *negro* black poplar.; ~ *temblón* aspen.

alamparse [1a]: ~ *por* have a craving for.

alano *m* mastiff.

alarde *m* ✕ review; *fig.* display, parade; *hacer* ~ *de* make a show (*or* parade) of; **alardeado** vaunted; **alardear** [1a] boast, brag; **alardeo** *m* boasting, bragging.

alares *m/pl. sl.* trousers, pants.

alargadera *f* ⚗ adapter; ⊕ extension; **alargamiento** *m* elongation, extension *etc.*; **alargar** [1h] lengthen, prolong; extend; (*estirar*) stretch; (*pasar*) reach, hand; *mano* reach out; *cuello* crane; *cuerda* pay out; *paso* hasten; *cuento* spin out; *sueldo* increase; ~**se** (*días etc.*) draw out, lengthen; (*irse*) go away, withdraw; (*discurso etc.*) be long-winded, drag out; *se alargó en la conferencia* his lecture was long drawn-out.

alarido *m* yell, shriek, howl; *dar* ~*s* yell *etc.*

alarma *f* alarm (*a. fig.*); ~ *aérea* air-raid warning; ~ *falsa* false alarm; *de* ~ warning *attr.*, alarm *attr.*; *dar la* ~ raise the alarm; **alarmante** alarming, startling; **alarmar** [1a] ✕ call to arms, alert, sound the alarm among; *fig.* alarm; ~**se** be (*or* become) alarmed; **alarmista** *m/f* alarmist.

alazán *adj. a. su. m* sorrel.

alba f dawn; *eccl.* alb; (*al*) *romper el* ~ (at) dawn.
albacea m executor; f executrix.
albahaca f basil.
albanega f hair-net.
albanés *adj. a. su.* m, **-a** f Albanian.
albañal m sewer, drain; ⚹ dung-heap, compost heap.
albañil m bricklayer; mason, builder;
 albañilería f (*obra*) brickwork; masonry; (*arte*) bricklaying; building.
albarán m "to let" sign (*freq. a white cloth*).
albarda f pack-saddle; **albardilla** f cushion, pad; △ cope, coping; (*tocino*) lard; (*batido*) batter.
albaricoque m apricot; **albaricoquero** m apricot (tree).
albayalde m white lead.
albedrío m (*a. libre* ~) free-will; (*capricho*) whim, fancy; *al* ~ *de uno* at one's own pleasure, to suit o.s.
albéitar m vet(erinary surgeon).
alberca f pond, cistern; *S.Am.* swimming-pool.
albergar [1h] *v/t.* harbour, shelter; lodge, put up; *v/i.,* ~**se** (find) shelter; lodge; **albergue** m shelter, refuge (*a. mount.*); (*alojamiento*) lodging; *zo.* lair; ~ *de carretera* road-house; ~ *para jóvenes* youth hostel; *dar* ~ *a* give *s.o.* lodging, take *s.o.* in.
albero 1. white; **2.** m pipeclay; (*paño*) tea towel; **albillo** white; **albina** f salt lake, salt marsh; **albino** *adj. a. su.* m, **a** f albino; **albis:** F *quedarse in* ~ not have a clue; **albo** *lit.* white.
albogue m rustic flute; (*gaita*) bagpipes; ~**s** *pl.* (*platillos*) cymbals.
albóndiga f *approx.* rissole, meat ball.
albor m whiteness; (*luz*) dawn (light); ~ *de la vida* childhood, youth; ~**es** *pl.* dawn; **alborada** f dawn; ✗ reveille; *poet.,* ♪ aubade; **alborear** [1a] dawn.
albornoz m burnous(e) *de árabe*; bathing-wrap, bath-robe.
alborotadizo turbulent; *p.* restive, jumpy; **alborotado** hasty, rash; **alborotador 1.** riotous; boisterous; **2.** m, **-a** f agitator; rioter; mischief-maker; **alborotar** [1a] *v/t.* disturb, agitate, stir up; *S.Am.* excite curiosity in; *v/i.* make a

racket; ~**se** (*p.*) get excited; (*turba*) riot; (*mar*) get rough; **alboroto** m (*vocerío etc.*) disturbance, racket, uproar; (*motín*) riot; (*pelea*) brawl; (*sobresalto*) scare, alarm.
alborozado merry, gay; **alborozar** [1f] cheer (up), gladden; ~**se** be glad; **alborozo** m merriment, gaiety; jollification.
albricias f/*pl.* reward (for p. bringing good news); ¡~! good news!; jolly good!, congratulations!; *en* ~ *de* as a token of.
álbum m album.
albumen m ⚘ albumen; (*clara*) white of an egg; **albúmina** f ⚘ albumin; **albuminoso** albuminous.
albur m *ichth.* dace; *fig.* risk, chance.
albura f whiteness; white *de huevo*.
alcabala f *hist.* sales tax.
alcachofa f artichoke.
alcahueta f procuress, bawd; (*mensajera*) go-between; F gossip, tale-bearer; **alcahuete** m procurer, pimp; go-between; *thea.* drop-curtain; **alcahuetear** [1a] procure; **alcahuetería** f procuring, pandering.
alcaide m † *castillo:* governor, castellan; *cárcel:* (*jefe*) governor; (*subordinado*) warder, jailer.
alcaldada f arbitrary action; abuse of power; **alcalde** m mayor; F *tener el padre* ~ have influence; **alcaldear** [1a] F lord it, be bossy; **alcaldesa** f mayoress; **alcaldía** f mayoralty; (*casa*) mayor's residence (*or* office).
álcali m alkali; **alcalino** alkaline.
alcance m reach *de mano* (*a. fig.*); ✗ range; *hunt.* pursuit; ✆ special delivery; (*periódico*) stop press; ✝ deficit; *fig.* scope *de programa etc.*; purview *de libro etc.*; range, grasp *de inteligencia*; (*talento*) capacity; significance, import; *al* ~ within reach (de of; *a. fig.*); ✗ within range; *al* ~ *del oído* within hearing, within earshot; *al* ~ *de la voz* within call; *de cortos* ~**s** dim(-witted); *fuera de su* ~ out of one's reach; *fig.* over one's head; *andar* (*or* ir) en los ~**s** *a* spy on *s.o.*; *poner al* ~ *de* make *s.t.* accessible to; **alcancía** f money-box; *S.Am. eccl.* collection box.
alcándara f clothes rack; *orn.* perch.
alcandora f beacon.
alcanfor m camphor; **alcanforar** [1a] camphorate.

alcantarilla f sewer; conduit; (a. boca de ~) drain; S.Am. cistern; **alcantarillado** m sewer system, drains; **alcantarillar** [1a] lay sewers in, provide sewers for.

alcanzadizo easily attainable (or reachable); **alcanzado** hard up, broke; **alcanzar** [1f] v/t. (llegar) reach; (igualarse) catch up with, overtake; época live through, live on into; (coger) grasp, catch (hold of); (con sentidos) perceive; problema etc. grasp, understand; empleo get, obtain; v/i. reach (a, hasta to or acc.); ~ a inf. manage to inf.; ~ para todos be enough, go round.

alcaparra f ⚘ caper.

alcaraván m stone curlew.

alcaravea f carraway.

alcaudón m shrike.

alcayata f meat hook; ⊕ tenterhook.

alcazaba f citadel.

alcázar m fortress, citadel; royal palace; ⚓ quarter-deck.

alcazuz m liquorice.

alce m zo. elk; naipes: cut; ~ de América moose.

alción m orn. kingfisher; (mitológico) halcyon.

alcista ✝ 1. bull(ish); 2. m bull.

alcoba f bedroom.

alcohol m alcohol; ~ desnaturalizado, ~ metilado methylated spirit; lámpara de ~ spirit lamp; **alcohólico** adj. a. su. m, a f alcoholic; **alcoholismo** m alcoholism; **alcoholizado** m, a f alcoholic; **alcoholizar** [1f] alcoholize.

alcor m hill.

alcornoque m cork oak; fig. blockhead.

alcorza f cocina: icing, frosting; fig. delicate little thing; **alcorzar** [1f] cocina: ice.

alcubilla f reservoir.

alcucero F having a sweet tooth; (goloso) greedy.

alcurnia f ancestry, lineage.

alcuza f olive-oil bottle; S.Am. cruet.

alcuzcuz m approx. couscous (paste of flour and honey).

aldaba f (door-)knocker; (barra etc.) bolt, cross-bar; hitching-ring para caballo; tener buenas ~s have pull, have influence; **aldabada** f knock (on the door); fig. fright; **alda-**

billa f latch, catch; **aldabón** m = aldaba; (asa) handle.

aldea f village; **aldeano** 1. village attr.; b.s. uncouth, rustic; 2. m, a f villager; **aldehuela** f hamlet; **aldeorrio** m F rural backwater.

alderredor = alrededor.

aleación f alloy; **alear**[1] [1a] metall. alloy.

alear[2] [1a] orn. flap (its wings); (p.) move one's arms up and down; fig. ✿ convalesce.

alebrarse [1a] lie flat; fig. cower.

aleccionador instructive, enlightening; **aleccionar** [1a] teach, give lessons to; instruct, coach.

alechugar [1h] fold, pleat.

aledaño 1. bordering; 2. m boundary, limit.

alegación f allegation; **alegar** [1h] plead (a. ⚖️); allege; autoridades etc. quote, bring up; dificultades plead; razones put forward, adduce; **alegato** m ⚖️ (escrito) bill; (exposición) pleading.

alegoría f allegory; **alegórico** allegoric(al); **alegorizar** [1f] allegorize.

alegrador 1. cheering; 2. m spill; **alegrar** [1a] gladden, cheer (up); (avivar) brighten up, cheer up, enliven; fuego stir up, brighten up; toro excite; ⚓ cabo slacken; ~se be glad, be happy, rejoice; cheer up (de noticia at); F (achisparse) get merry; ~ de, ~ con, ~ por be glad (because) of, rejoice at; ~ de inf. be happy (or glad) to inf.; **alegre** p., cara etc. happy; ánimo joyful, glad; carácter cheerful, gay, sunny; música etc. gay, merry; noticia cheering, good; color bright, gay; (osado) reckless; F merry, tipsy; ~ (de corazón) light-hearted; **alegría** f happiness; joy(fulness), gladness; gaiety, merriment etc.; **alegrón** m sudden joy; flare-up de fuego.

alejamiento m (acto) removal; (lo remoto) remoteness; distance; **alejar** [1a] move s.t. away (de from), remove; place at a distance; peligro remove; ~se move away (de from); move to a distance; go away; (peligro etc.) recede.

alelar [1a] stupefy; make dull; ~se (viejo) get feeble-minded; fig. gape stupidly.

aleluya 1. f (grito) hallelujah; paint.

Easter print; F (*versos*) doggerel; F (*p. etc.*) bag of bones; **2.** *m* Easter-time.

alemán 1. *adj. a. su. m*, **-a** *f* German; **2.** *m* (*idioma*) German.

alentada *f* deep breath; **alentado** (*animoso*) brave; (*altanero*) haughty; **alentador** encouraging; **alentar** [1k] encourage, inspire (*a inf.* to *inf.*); *resistencia* bolster up; *espíritu* buoy up; ⁓**se** ✗ get well.

alerce *m* larch.

alergia *f* allergy.

alero *m* △ eaves; *mot.* mudguard; wing; **alerón** *m* aileron.

alerta 1.: ¡⁓! watch out!; *estar* (*ojo*) ⁓ be on the alert, stand by; **2.** *m* alert.

aleta *f* small wing; *ichth.* fin; flipper *de foca* (*a. sl.* = *mano*); *mot.* wing; ⊕, ✗ blade.

aletargar [1h] benumb, drug; ⁓**se** become lethargic.

aletazo *m orn.* flap of the wing, wingbeat; *ichth.* movement of the fin; **aletear** [1a] flap its wings, flutter; **aleteo** *m* fluttering, flapping; *fig.* palpitation.

aleudar [1a] leaven.

aleve = *alevoso*; **alevosía** *f* treachery, perfidy; **alevoso 1.** treacherous, perfidious; **2.** *m* traitor.

alfabético alphabetic(al); **alfabetizar** [1f] make literate, teach to read and write; **alfabeto** *m* alphabet.

alfalfa *f* lucerne, alfalfa.

alfanje *m* cutlass; *zo.* swordfish.

alfaque *m* bar, shoal.

alfar *m* (*taller*) pottery; (*arcilla*) clay; **alfarería** *f* pottery; (*tienda*) pottery stall; **alfarero** *m* potter, **alfarjía** *f* door-frame; window-frame; (*larguero*) batten.

alféizar *m* (*puerta*) splay(ing), embrasure; (*ventana*) (window)sill.

alfeñicarse [1g] F get awfully thin; (*remilgarse*) be prim and proper, be finicky; **alfeñique** *m* almond paste; F (*p.*) delicate sort, mollycoddle; (*remilgo*) squeamishness; affectation.

alférez *m* ✗ second lieutenant, subaltern; ⁓ *de fragata approx.* midshipman; ⁓ *de navío* sub-lieutenant.

alfil *m ajedrez*: bishop.

alfiler *m* pin; (*broche*) brooch, clip;

⁓**es** *pl. fig.* pin-money; ⁓ *de corbata* tiepin; ⁓ *de seguridad* safety-pin; F *de 25* ⁓**es** dressed to kill; F *pedir para* ⁓**es** ask for a tip; F *prendido con* ⁓**es** shaky, suspect; **alfilerar** [1a] pin (up); **alfilerazo** *m* pin-prick (*a. fig.*); **alfiletero** *m* needle-case.

alfolí *m* ⚓ granary; salt warehouse.

alfombra *f* carpet (*a. fig.*); (*esp. pequeña*) rug; ⁓ *de baño* bath mat; **alfombrado** *m* carpeting; **alfombrar** [1a] carpet (*a. fig.*); **alfombrero** *m* carpet-maker; **alfombrilla** *f* rug; ✗ German measles.

alforfón *m* buckwheat.

alforjas *f/pl.* saddle-bags; (*comestibles*) provisions; *sacar los pies de las* ⁓ go off on a different tack.

alforza *f* pleat, tuck; *fig.* scar, slash.

alga *f* seaweed, alga ⬚.

algaida *f* (*bosquecito*) thicket; (*matorral*) bush, undergrowth; ⚓ dune.

algalia *f* civet.

algarabía *f* Arabic; *fig.* gibberish; F (*palabras atropelladas*) gabble; (*gritería*) din, hullabaloo.

algarada *f* outcry; *hacer una* ⁓ kick up a fuss.

algarrada *f hist.* catapult; *toros*: bull-baiting.

algarroba *f* carob (bean); **algarrobo** *m* carob tree, locust tree.

algazara *f* (*Moorish*) battle-cry; *fig.* uproar, din.

álgebra *f* algebra; **algebraico** algebraic.

álgido ✗ cold, chilly; F culminating, decisive.

algo 1. *pron.* something; ⁓ *es* ⁓ something is better than nothing; *eso ya es* ⁓ that is something; ¡*por* ⁓ *será!* there must be some reason behind it!; *tomar* ⁓ have a drink; **2.** *adv.* rather, somewhat; *es* ⁓ *grande* it's on the big side, it's rather big.

algodón *m* cotton; ✿ cotton plant; ✗ swab; wadding *para orejas etc.*; ⁓ *hidrófilo* cotton wool; ⁓ *pólvora* gun-cotton; *estar criado entre* ⁓**es** be born with a silver spoon in one's mouth; **algodonar** [1a] stuff (with cotton), wad; **algodonero 1.** cotton *attr.*; **2.** *m* (*p.*) cotton-dealer; ✿ cotton plant; **algodonosa** *f* cotton-grass; **algodonoso** cottony.

alguacil m bailiff, constable.
alguien someone, somebody.
alguno 1. adj. (*algún delante de su. m singular*) some, any; (*tras su.*) (not ...) any; *algún libro que otro* some book or other; an occasional book; *no tengo dinero* ~ I haven't any money; *v. otro, tanto etc.*; **2.** pron. some; one; someone, somebody; ~s pl. some; ~ de ellos one of them; ~ que otro one or two, an occasional one; *¿ha venido* ~ *?* has somebody (*or* anybody) come?; *tengo* ~s I have some, I have a few.
alhaja f jewel, gem; (*mueble*) fine piece; F (*p.*) treasure, gem; *buena* ~ *iro.* fine one, rogue; **alhajar** [1a] *casa* furnish, appoint (in good taste).
alharaca f fuss, ballyhoo, song and dance; *hacer* ~s make a fuss, create; **alharaquiento** demonstrative, emotional.
alhelí m wallflower; stock.
alheña f privet; (*tizón*) mildew.
alhóndiga f corn exchange.
alhucema f lavender.
aliado 1. allied; **2.** m, **a** f ally; **alianza** f alliance (a. *fig.*); (*anillo*) wedding ring; *Biblia*: ♀ Covenant; **aliar** [1c] ally; ~se become allied; form an alliance.
alias adv. a. su. m alias.
alicaído with drooping wings; *fig.* ♣ weak, drooping; (*abatido*) downcast, down in the mouth.
alicantina f trick, ruse.
alicantino adj. a. su. m, **a** f (native) of Alicante.
alicates m/pl. pliers.
aliciente m incentive, inducement; *esp. b.s.* lure; mainspring (*a, de, para acción etc.* for).
alienación f alienation (a. ♣); ♣ mental derangement; **alienado 1.** insane, mentally ill; **2.** m, **a** f mad person, lunatic; **alienar(se)** = *enajenar(se)*; **alienista** m/f psychiatrist, alienist.
aliento m (*un* ~) breath; (*acto*) breathing; *fig.* bravery, strength; *de un* ~ in one breath; *fig.* in one go; *sin* ~ out of breath; *cobrar* ~ take heart; *dar* ~ *a* encourage; *le huele mal el* ~ his breath smells; *tomar* ~ take breath.
aligación f bond, tie; *metall.* alloy.

aligerar [1a] *carga* lighten (a. *fig.*); (*abreviar*) shorten; *fig.* ease, relieve, alleviate; *paso* quicken; ~se de ropa put on lighter clothing.
alijar [1a] *barco* unload; (*aligerar*) lighten; *contrabando* land; *madera* sandpaper; **alijo** m (*acto*) unloading; lightening; contraband; ~ de armas cache of arms.
alimaña f animal; *esp.* vermin.
alimentación f nourishment, feeding; (*comida*) food; ⊕ feed, supply; *fig.* nurture, fostering; ⊕ *dispositivo etc.* de ~ = **alimentador** m ⊕, ⚡ feed(er); **alimentar** [1a] feed, nourish (a. *fig.*); *fig. familia* maintain; (*criar*) bring up, nurture; *pasión etc.* foster, add fuel to; ⊕ feed; ~se feed (de, con on); **alimenticio** *manjar* nourishing; nutritious, nutritive; *valor etc.* food *attr.*; *artículos* ~s foodstuffs; **alimentista** m/f pensioner; **alimento** m food (a. *fig.*); *fig.* incentive; encouragement; ♣ ~s pl. alimony, allowance; **alimentoso** nourishing.
alindado foppish, dandified; **alindar**[1] [1a] make pretty, make nice; *p.* get up F.
alindar[2] [1a] *v/t. surv.* mark out; *v/i.* be adjacent, adjoin.
alineación f alignment (a. ⊕); line-up; *fuera de* ~ out of alignment; **alinear** [1a] align, line (up); ✗ form up; ~se line up; ✗ *etc.* fall in, form up.
aliñar [1a] *cocina*: dress, season; *S.Am. hueso* set; **aliño** m dressing, seasoning; (*acto*) preparation.
aliquebrado F drooping, crestfallen.
alisador m ⊕ (*p.*) polisher; (*instrumento*) smoothing blade; **alisar**[1] [1a] smooth (down); polish; *esp.* ⊕ surface, finish; *pelo* smooth, sleek.
alisar[2] m, **aliseda** f alder grove.
alisios m/pl. (a. *vientos* ~) trade winds.
aliso m alder.
alistamiento m enlistment, recruitment; **alistar** [1a] (put on a) list; enroll *como miembro*; ✗ enlist; ⚓ clear (for action); ~se enroll; ✗ enlist, join up.
aliteración f alliteration; **aliterado** alliterative.

aliviar [1b] lighten (*a. fig.*); *fig.* relieve, give relief to, soothe; (*acelerar*) haste, speed up; *paso* quicken; ~ *de peso etc.* relieve s.o. of; ~**se** get (*or* gain) relief; (*confesarse*) unburden one's heart (*de* of); **alivio** *m* relief (*a. ⚕*), alleviation; mitigation; (*mejora*) betterment; ~ *de luto* half-mourning.

aljaba *f* quiver.

aljama *f* Moorish (*or* Jewish) gathering; △ mosque *de moros*, synagogue *de judíos*; **aljamía** *f* *Castilian written in Arabic characters.*

aljibe *m* (rainwater) cistern; ⚓ water-tender; *mot.* oil-tanker.

aljofaina *f* (wash-)basin, (wash-) bowl.

aljófar *m* pearl (*a. fig.*).

aljofifa *f* floor-cloth; **aljofifar** [1a] wash, mop (up).

alma *f* soul; spirit; *fig.* (*p.*) (living) soul; (*aliento, fuente de inspiración*) heart and soul, life-blood, moving spirit; crux, heart *de asunto*; ⚘ pith; ⊕, ⚡ core; ✕ bore; F ~ *de caballo* twister; F ~ *de Caín* fiend; ~ *de Dios* good soul; *¡~ mía!* my precious!; *con* (*toda*) *el* ~ heart and soul; *con toda mi* ~ with all my heart; *arrancársele a uno el* ~ be deeply shocked (*por at, by*); *caérsele a uno el* ~ *a los pies* be deeply moved; (*desanimarse*) be disheartened; *echarse el* ~ *a las espaldas* not be in the least concerned; *entregar* (*or rendir*) *el* ~ give up the ghost; *írsele a uno el* ~ *tras* be taken up with, fall for; F *me llegó al* ~ it came home to me; *tener el* ~ *en un hilo* have one's heart in one's mouth; *volver a uno el* ~ *al cuerpo* calm down, recover one's peace of mind.

almacén *m* (*depósito*) warehouse, store (*a. fig.*); (*tienda*) shop; (*tienda grande*) department store; (*muebles*) depository; ✕ magazine; *S.Am.* grocer's (shop); ~ *de depósito* bonded warehouse; *en* ~ in store; **almacenaje** *m* storage (charge); ~ *frigorífico* cold-storage; **almacenar** [1a] put in store, store (up); (*esp. tienda*) stock up, lay in stock; *fig.* keep, collect; *b.s.* hoard; **almacenero** *m* storekeeper, warehouseman; *S.Am.* grocer;

almacenista *m* warehouse (*or* shop) owner, warehouseman.

almadía *f* raft.

almadraba *f* tunny-fishing; (*red*) tunny-net(s).

almadreña *f* wooden shoe, clog.

almagrar [1a] raddle, ruddle; *fig.* defame; **almagre** *m* red ochre, ruddle.

almanaque *m* almanac; F *hacer* ~*s* muse.

almazara *f* oil mill.

almeja *f* shell-fish, clam.

almena *f* merlon; ~*s pl.* battlements; **almenado** battlemented, castellated.

almenara *f* beacon; (*araña*) chandelier.

almendra *f* ⚘ almond; (*hueso*) kernel, stone; drop *de araña*; ~ *garapiñada* praline; ~ *tostada* burnt almond; F *de la media* ~ kid-glove, finicky; **almendrada** *f* almond shake; **almendrado 1.** almond-shaped, pear-shaped; **2.** *m* macaroon; **almendral** *m* almond grove; **almendrera** *f*, **almendro** *m* almond (tree); **almendruco** *m* green almond.

almiar *m* haycock; hayrick.

almíbar *m* syrup; **almibarado** syrupy (*a. fig.*); *fig.* sugary, honeyed, over-sweet; **almibarar** [1a] preserve (*or* serve) in syrup; ~ *las palabras* use honeyed words.

almidón *m* starch; **almidonado** starched; F dapper, spruce; **almidonar** [1a] starch.

almilla *f* bodice; ⊕ tenon; (*carne*) breast of pork.

alminar *m* minaret.

almirantazgo *m* admiralty; **almirante** *m* admiral.

almirez *m* (metal) mortar.

almizcle *m* musk; **almizcleño** musky; **almizclero** *m* (*ciervo*) musk-deer; (*roedor*) musk-rat, musquash.

almo *poet.* nourishing; venerable.

almodrote *m* cheese and garlic sauce; F hotchpotch.

almohada *f* cushion *de silla*; pillow *de cama*; (*funda*) pillow-case; ~ *neumática* air-cushion; *consultar algo con la* ~ sleep on s.t.; **almohadilla** *f* small cushion, small pillow; ⊕ pad; ~ (*de entintar*) ink-pad; △ projection, relief;

almohadillado 1. padded, stuffed; *piedra* dressed; **2.** *m* ashlar, dressed stone; **almohadón** *m* sofa cushion; hassock *para pies.*

almohaza *f* curry-comb; **almohazar** [1f] *caballo* curry, groom, brush down; *pieles* dress.

almoneda *f* (*subasta*) auction; (*saldo*) clearance sale; **almoned(e)ar** [1a] (put up for) auction.

almorranas *f/pl.* piles.

almorzar [1f *a.* 1m] *v/t.* have for lunch, lunch on; *v/i.* (have) lunch; (*desayuno*) (have) breakfast; *vengo almorzado* I've had lunch.

almuecín *m*, **almuédano** *m* muezzin.

almuerzo *m* lunch; formal luncheon; (*desayuno*) breakfast; (*de boda*) wedding breakfast; (*juego*) dinner service.

alnado *m*, **a** *f* stepchild.

alocado mad, wild.

alocución *f* allocution.

áloe *m* ✿ aloe; *pharm.* aloes.

alojamiento *m* lodging(s), digs F; ✗ (*acto*) billeting; (*casa*) billet, quarters (*a.* ♉); **alojar** [1a] lodge, put *s.o.* up; accomodate, house; ✗ billet, quarter; ~se lodge; ✗ be billeted, be quartered.

alondra *f* (*a.* ~ *común*) lark.

alongar [1m] = *alargar;* ~se remove, move away.

alpargata *f* rope sandal; rubber and canvas sandal; **alpargatilla** *m/f* crafty sort.

alpende *m* lean-to; tool-shed.

alpestre Alpine; *fig.* mountainous, wild; **alpinismo** *m* mountaineering; **alpinista** *m/f* mountaineer, climber; alpinist; **alpino** Alpine.

alpiste *m* ✿ canary grass; (*semilla*) bird-seed; F brandy; F *quedarse uno* ~ have one's trouble for nothing.

alquería *f* farmhouse.

alquiladizo 1. for rent; for hire; **2.** *m*, **a** *f* hireling; **alquilar** [1a] (*dueño*): *casa* rent (out), let; *coche etc.* hire out; (*inquilino etc.*): *casa, garaje, televisor* rent; *coche etc.* hire; *autocar* hire, charter; ~se (*casa*) be let (*en precio* at, for); (*taxi etc.*) be out for hire, be on hire; (*anuncio*): se *alquila* (*casa*) to let; (*en general*) on hire; **alquiler** *m* (*acto*) letting; hire, hiring; renting;

(*precio*) rent(al); rent *de casa;* ~ *de caballos* livery; *de* ~ for hire, on hire; *control de* ~es rent control; *exento de* ~es rent-free.

alquimia *f* alchemy; **alquímico** alchemic(al); **alquimista** *m* alchemist.

alquitara *f* still; **alquitarar** [1a] distil.

alquitrán *m* tar; ~ *de hulla,* ~ *mineral* coal tar; **alquitranado 1.** tarry; **2.** *m* (*firme*) tarmac; (*lienzo*) tarpaulin; **alquitranar** [1a] tar.

alrededor 1. *adv.* around; **2.** *prp.* ~ *de* around, about; *fig.* about, in the region of; **3.** ~es *m/pl.* outskirts, environs *de ciudad;* (*contornos*) surroundings, neighbourhood; setting *de local.*

alsaciano *adj. a. su. m,* **a** *f* Alsatian.

alta *f* ✚ discharge (from hospital); *dar de* ~ discharge (from hospital); cure; ✗ pass (as) fit; *darse de* ~ join, be admitted.

altanería *f meteor.* upper air; soaring *de ave; hunt.* falconry; *fig.* haughtiness; **altanero** *ave* high-flying, soaring; *fig.* haughty; high-handed.

altar *m* altar; ~ *mayor* high altar.

altavoz *m radio:* loud-speaker; ✦ amplifier.

alterabilidad *f* changeability; **alterable** alterable; **alteración** *f* alteration; (*deterioro*) change for the worse, upset, disturbance; (*emoción*) agitation, strong feeling; (*altercado*) quarrel, dispute; ✚ irregular pulse; **alterado** *fig.* agitated, upset, disturbed; *estómago* upset, disordered; **alterar** [1a] alter, change; ✚ *etc.* change for the worse, upset; *b.s.* falsify; (*perturbar*) disturb, stir up; excite; ~se *fig.* be disturbed, be upset (*por* by); (*leche*) go sour; (*voz*) falter.

altercado *m* argument, altercation; **altercar** [1g] quarrel, argue, bicker.

alternación *f* alternation, rotation; (*entre sí*) interchange; **alternador** *m* ✦ alternator; **alternar** [1a] *v/t.* alternate (*con* with); interchange; vary; *v/i.* alternate; take turns; change about; ⊕ reciprocate; *sl.* pub-crawl; ~ *con amigos* go around with; *sociedad* move in; ~ *de igual*

a igual be on the same footing;
alternativa *f* service by rotation;
(trabajo) shift work; *(elección)*
alternative, choice; *no tener* ~ have
no alternative; ~s *pl. esp.* ups and
downs, fluctuations; **alternativo,**
alterno alternate; alternating (*a.*
♪); (*a elegir*) alternative.
alteza *f* height; *fig.* sublimity;
(título) highness.
altibajos *m/pl.* ups and downs,
unevenness *de terreno*; *fig.* ups and
downs, vicissitudes.
altillo *m* hillock; *S.Am.* attic.
altimático *cabina etc.* pressurized.
altímetro *m* altimeter.
altiplanicie *f* high plateau.
altísimo very high; *el* ♀ The
Almighty.
altisonante high-flown, high-
sounding.
altitud *f* height; *geog.*, *✗* altitude.
altivarse [1a] put on airs; **altivez** *f*
haughtiness, arrogance; **altivo**
haughty, arrogant.
alto¹ 1. *adj. mst* high; *p.*, *edificio,*
árbol tall; *agua* deep; *mar* (*abierto*)
high, deep, open; (*agitado*) rough,
high; *voz* loud; *hora(s)* late, small;
clase, país, piso, río upper; *fig.*
elevated, high, sublime; (*el*) *más* ~
uppermost, highest, top; *de* ~
high (*adv.*); *de lo* ~ from above;
en (*lo*) ~ up, high (up); *en lo* ~ *de*
up, on top of; *por lo* ~ overhead;
tiene 2 metros de ~ it is 2 metres
high; 2. *adv.* lanzar high (up);
gritar loudly; *v. pasar etc.*; 3. *m*
geog. height, hill; ⚠ upper floor,
upper flat.
alto² *m* ✗ *etc.* halt; *esp. fig.* stop,
standstill; *¡~ ahí!* halt!, stop!;
¡~ al fuego! cease fire!; *hacer* ~ halt
(*a.* ✗), stop.
altoparlante *m* loud-speaker.
altozano *m* hill(ock); hilly part *de*
ciudad; *S.Am.* paved terrace.
altramuz *m* lupin(e).
altruísmo *m* altruism; **altruísta**
1. altruistic, unselfish; 2. *m/f*
altruist, unselfish person.
altura *f mst* height; height, tallness,
stature *de p.*; depth *de agua*;
height, altitude *de monte*; *geog.*
latitude; ⚓ high seas; ♪ pitch; *fig.*
loftiness, sublimity; ~s *pl. geog. a.*
fig. heights; *eccl.* heaven; ~ *de*
caída (*agua*) head; ~ *de elevación*

lift; *a la* ~ *de geog.* on the same
latitude as; ⚓ *a la* ~ *de Vigo* off
Vigo; *estar a la* ~ *de tarea etc.* be
up to, measure up to; *estar a la* ~
de las circunstancias be up to the
mark; *de* ~ high; *pesca etc.* deep-
water *attr.*; *en las* ~s on high;
tiene 2 metros de ~ it is 2 metres
high; *✗ tomar* ~ climb.
alubia *f* haricot (bean).
alucinación *f* hallucination, delusion; **alucinar** [1a] hallucinate,
delude; *fig.* fascinate; ~se be
hallucinated, be deluded.
alud *m* avalanche.
aludir [3a]: ~ *a* allude to, mention
(in passing); *el aludido* the aforesaid; *darse por aludido* take the hint.
alumbrado 1. F lit-up, tight; 2. *m*
lighting (system); illumination;
~ *fluorescente* fluorescent lighting;
~ *de gas* gaslight; ~ *público* street
lighting; *red de* ~ electricity grid;
3. *m*, a *f hist.* illuminist; **alumbra-**
miento *m ✗* lighting, illumination;
✗ childbirth; *tener un feliz* ~ be
safely delivered; **alumbrar** [1a]
v/t. light (up), illuminate; *p.* light
the way for; *ciego* give sight to;
agua strike, find; *fig.* enlighten;
v/i. ✗ give birth; *✗* esto *alumbra*
bien this gives a good light; ~se *✗*
light (up); F get tipsy.
alumbre *m* alum.
alúmina *f* alumina; **aluminio** *m*
aluminium, aluminum *Am.*
alumnado *m* student body; **alumno**
m, a *f univ. etc.* student, pupil; *✗*
foster child, ward; *antiguo* ~ old
boy *de colegio*; old student *de*
universidad; old pupil *de profesor.*
alunado lunatic, insane; *tocino*
tainted.
alusión *f* allusion, mention, reference; *hacer* ~ *a* allude to, refer
to; **alusivo** allusive.
aluvial alluvial; **aluvión** *m* alluvion
(*a. ✗*); (*depósito*) alluvium; *geol.*
de ~ alluvial; ~ *de improperios*
shower of insults.
álveo *m* bed (of a stream).
alveolar alveolar; **alvéolo** *m*
alveolus, cell *de panal*; *anat.* socket.
alvino abdominal, bowel *attr.*
alza *f ✗* rise, advance; ✗ rear sight;
✗ al ~ going up, buoyant; *✗ jugar*
al ~ bull, speculate; **alzada** *f*
height *de caballo*; *✗* appeal;

alzado 1. elevated, raised; *precio* fixed, settled; **2.** *m* △ front elevation; *typ.* gathering; **alzamiento** *m* (*acto*) lift(ing), raising; rise, advance *de precio*; (*quiebra*) fraudulent bankruptcy; (*postura*) higher bid; *pol.* (up)rising, revolt; **alzaprima** *f* (*palanca*) lever; (*cuño*) wedge; ♪ bridge; **alzar** [1f] raise, lift (up), hoist; *mantel etc.* put away; (*llevarse*) take away; *cosecha* get in; *hostia* elevate; *pantalón* hitch up; *typ.* take up and arrange; ¡~! up (you get)!; ~**se** rise (up); *pol.* revolt, rise; ✝ go bankrupt (fraudulently); ~ *con* make off with; ~ *a mayores* get stuck up; **alzaválvulas** *m* ⊕ tappet.

allá (over) there; (*tiempo*) way back, long ago; F ¡~ tú! that's your concern!, that's your look-out!; *más* ~ further away (*or* over); farther on; *más* ~ *de* beyond, past; *límites* outside; *el más* ~ *fig.* the beyond; *por* ~ thereabouts; ✕ ¿*quién va* ~? who goes there?; ¡~ *voy*! I'm coming!

allanamiento *m* levelling, flattening; ♣♣ submission (*a* to); ~ *de morada* house-breaking; **allanar** [1a] *v/t.* (*hacer llano*) level (out), flatten; even; (*alisar*) smooth (down); *dificultad* smooth away, iron out; *país* subdue; *esp.* ♣♣ permit entry into; *morada* break into; *v/i.* level out; ~**se** level out, level off; (*caer*) tumble down; ~ *a* accept, conform to.

allegadizo gathered at random; **allegado 1.** near, close; *p.* related (*de* to); **2.** *m*, **a** *f* (*pariente*) relation, relative; (*secuaz*) partisan, follower; **allegar** [1h] gather (together), collect; (*añadir*) add; ~**se** go up (*a* to); (*llegar*) arrive, approach; ~ *a secta* become attached to; *dictamen* agree with.

allende beyond; ~ *de* besides; (*de*) ~ *los mares* (from) overseas.

allí there; ~ *dentro* in there; *de* ~ *a poco* shortly after(wards); *por* ~ (down) that way.

ama *f* mistress *de casa*; (*dueña*) owner, proprietress; foster mother *que cría*; (*de pensión etc.*) landlady; *S.Am.* ~ *de brazos* nursemaid; ~ *de casa* housekeeper, housewife; ~ *de cría*, ~ *de leche* wet-nurse, foster-mother; ~ *de llaves* housekeeper; matron *de colegio*.

amabilidad *f* kindness; amiability; *tener la* ~ *de inf.* be kind enough to *inf.*; **amable** kind; lovable; amiable, nice; *ser* ~ *con* be kind to; *qué* ~ *ha sido Vd. en inf.* how kind of you to *inf.*; **amado** *m*, **a** *f* love(r), sweetheart; **amador 1.** loving; **2.** *m*, **-a** *f* lover.

amadrigar [1h] welcome (with open arms); ~**se** go into its hole, burrow; *fig.* go into retirement; withdraw into one's shell.

amaestrado *animal* trained, performing; *proyecto* well-contrived; **amaestramiento** *m* training *etc.*; **amaestrar** [1a] *animal* train; *caballo* break in; *p.* train, coach.

amagar [1h] *v/t.* threaten, show signs of, portend; *v/i.* threaten, be impending; *esp. fig.* be in the offing; ⚔ show the first signs; ✕, *fenc.* feint; ~ *a inf.* threaten to *inf.*, show signs of *ger.*; **amago** *m* threat; (*indicio*) sign, symptom; ✕, *fenc.* feint.

amainar [1a] *v/t. vela* take in, shorten; *furia* calm; *v/i.*, abate (*a. fig.*); (*viento etc.*) slacken, moderate; *amainó en su furia* his rage subsided; ~**se** abate; slacken; lessen; **amaine** *m* abatement *etc.*

amaitinar [1a] spy on, pry into.

amalgama *f* amalgam; *fig.* concoction, medley; **amalgamación** *f* amalgamation; **amalgamar** [1a] amalgamate (*a. fig.*); *fig.* mix (up); combine; ~**se** amalgamate (*a. fig.*).

amamantar [1a] suckle.

amancebado: *vivir* ~*s* = **amancebarse** [1a] live in sin.

amancillar [1a] stain, spot; *fig.* tarnish.

amanecer 1. [2d] dawn; appear (at dawn); (*p.*) wake up (*en* in), find o.s. at dawn; *fig.* begin to show; **2.** *m* dawn; *al* ~ at dawn; **amanecida** *f* dawn.

amanerado mannered, affected; **amaneramiento** *m* affectation; *lit.* mannerism (of style); **amanerarse** [1a] become affected (*or* mannered).

amanojar [1a] gather *s.t.* by the handful.

amansado tame; **amansador** *m*, **-a** *f* tamer; *S.Am.* horse-breaker;

amansar [1a] *animal* tame; *caballo* break in; *p.* subdue; *pasiones* soothe; **~se** (*pasión etc.*) moderate, abate.

amante 1. loving, fond; **2.** *m/f* lover; *f* mistress; **~s** *pl.* lovers.

amanuense *m* amanuensis; scribe.

amañado (*hábil*) skilful, adroit; (*contrahecho*) fake(d), phon(e)y *sl.*; **amañar** [1a] do skilfully, do cleverly; fake; **~se** be handy, be expert; **~** *a inf.* settle down to *inf.*; **~** *con* get along with; **amaño** *m* skill, expertness; **~s** *pl.* ⊕ tools; (*traza*) intrigue, guile; **tener ~** *para* have an aptitude for.

amapola *f* poppy.

amar [1a] love.

amaraje *m* ✈ landing (on the sea); ditching.

amaranto *m* əmaranth.

amarar [1a] land (on the sea); ditch *para evitar accidente.*

amargar [1h] *v/t.* make bitter; *fig.* embitter, spoil, upset; *v/i.* taste bitter; **~se** get bitter; *fig.* become (*or* grow) embittered; **amargo 1.** bitter (*a. fig.*); *fig.* embittered; **2.** *m* bitterness; **~s** *pl.* bitters; **amargor** *m*, **amargura** *f* bitterness (*a. fig.*); *fig.* grief, affliction.

amaricado *F* effeminate; **es un ~** he's a nancy-boy.

amarillear [1a] show yellow; be yellowish; **amarillecer** [2d] (turn) yellow; **amarillento** yellowish; *tez etc.* sallow; **amarillez** *f* yellow(ness); sallowness; **amarillo** *adj. a. su. m* yellow.

amarra *f* mooring line, painter; **~s** *pl.* moorings; *fig.* support, protection; **echar las ~s** moor; **amarradero** *m* (*poste*) bollard; (*cuerdas*) moorings; (*sitio*) berth; **amarraje** *m* mooring charges; **amarrar** [1a] *v/t. barco* moor; *cuerda* lash, belay; hitch, tie (up); *S.Am.* tie; *cartas* stack; *v/i. F* get down to it.

amartelado in love; love-sick; **andar ~** *de* be in love with; **amartelamiento** *m* infatuation; **amartelar** [1a] *p.* woo, court; *corazón* win; **~se** fall in love.

amartillar [1a] hammer; *pistola* cock.

amasadera *f* kneading trough; **amasador** *m* baker; **amasadora** *f* kneading machine; **amasadura** *f*

(*acto*) kneading; (*masa*) batch; **amasamiento** *m* kneading; ✻ massage; **amasar** [1a] *masa* knead; *harina, yeso* mix; *patatas* mash; *comida* prepare; ✻ massage; F cook up; **amasijo** *m* kneading; mash *etc.*; F (*mezcla*) hotchpotch; (*complot*) plot.

amatista *f* amethyst.

amatorio love *attr.*; amatory, amorous.

amazacotado heavy, clumsy (*a. fig.*); *fig.* shapeless, jumbled; *obra freq.* stodgy.

amazona *f* amazon; (*jinete*) horsewoman; *contp.* horsy type.

ambages *m/pl.* beating about the bush, circumlocutions; **sin ~** in plain language; **ambagioso** roundabout, involved.

ámbar *m* amber; **~ gris** ambergris; **ambarino** amber *attr.*

ambición *f* ambition; **ambicionar** [1a] strive after, seek, be cut for; hanker after; covet; **ambicioso 1.** ambitious; *b.s.* pretentious; **2.** *m,* **a** *f* ambitious person, careerist; **~ de figurar** social climber.

ambidextro ambidextrous.

ambiente 1. ambient; **2.** *m* atmosphere (*a. fig.*); *fig.* climate; (*que rodea*) milieu, environment, surroundings.

ambigú *m* buffet supper, cold supper.

ambigüedad *f* ambiguity; **ambiguo** ambiguous; *género* common; (*incierto*) uncertain; (*evasivo*) noncommittal, equivocal; *cumplido* backhanded.

ámbito *m* ambit, compass; △ confines.

ambos, ambas *adj. a. pron.* both; **~ a dos** both.

ambrosia *f* ambrosia (*a. fig.*); **ambrosíaco** ambrosial.

ambulancia *f* ambulance; ✕ field hospital; **~ de correos** post-office coach; **ambulante** (*que anda*) walking; (*que viaja*) roving, itinerant; *actor* strolling; *vendedor* travelling.

amedrentar [1a] scare; intimidate; **~se** be frightened, get scared.

amelonado F love-sick.

amén 1. *m* amen; F **decir ~ a todo** agree to anything; **2.** *prp.:* **~ de** except (for); (*además de*) besides.

amenaza f threat, menace; **amenazador, amenazante** threatening, menacing; intimidating; **amenazar** [1f] v/t. threaten, menace; ~ de muerte threaten with death; v/i. threaten, loom, impend; ~ con inf. threaten to inf.

amenguar [1i] lessen, diminish; fig. defame, dishonour.

amenidad f pleasantness etc.; **amenizar** [1f] make pleasant, make nice; add charm to; conversación liven up; **ameno** pleasant, agreeable, nice; trato, estilo etc. pleasant; lectura light; escritor delightful.

amento m catkin.

americana f coat, jacket; **americanismo** m americanism; S.Am. pol. Yankee imperialism; **americanizar** [1f] americanize; **americano** adj. a. su. m, a f (norte-) American; (sud-, central-) Latin-American.

amerizar [1f] ⚓ land (on the sea).

ametralladora f machine-gun; **ametrallar** [1a] machine-gun.

amiba f, **amibo** m amoeba.

amiga f friend; (novia) girl-friend, sweetheart; b.s. mistress; fig. lover (de of); **amigable** friendly; fig. harmonious; **amigarse** [1h] get friendly; b.s. live in sin.

amígdala f tonsil; **amigdalitis** f tonsilitis.

amigo 1. friendly; ~ de given to, fond of; ser muy ~s be very good friends; 2. m friend; (novio) boy-friend, sweetheart; b.s. lover; fig. lover (de of); ~ de confianza intimate; F ¡~ mío! my friend!; old boy!; hacerse ~ de make friends with; esp. b.s. get in with; ser ~ de fig. be fond of; **amigote** m F old pal; **amiguita** f girl-friend.

amiláceo starchy.

amilanar [1a] intimidate, cow; ~se be cowed, be scared.

aminorar [1a] lessen; gastos etc. cut down; paso slacken.

amistad f friendship; ~es pl. (ps.) friends, acquaintances; estrechar ~ con get friendly with; F hacer las ~es make it up; romper las ~es fall out; **amistado** friendly (con with); **amistar** [1a] bring together, make friends; ~se become friends; (después de riña) make it up; ~ con make friends with; **amistoso** friendly; (de vecino) neighbourly.

amnesia f loss of memory, amnesia; ~ temporal black-out.

amnistía f amnesty; **amnistiar** [1c] amnesty, grant an amnesty to.

amo m master de casa etc.; head of the family; (dueño) owner, proprietor; boss, overseer en el trabajo; ~ de casa householder.

amodorramiento m sleepiness, drowsiness; **amodorrarse** [1a] get sleepy, get drowsy; (dormirse) go to sleep.

amohinar [1a] vex, annoy; ~se get vexed, get annoyed; (esp. niño) sulk.

amojonar [1a] mark out.

amolador 1. F tedious; 2. m (knife-)grinder; **amolar** [1m] grind, sharpen; F bore; pester; **amoladura** f grinding.

amoldar [1a] mould (a. fig.; a modelo on); adapt (a circunstancias to); ~se fig. adapt o.s., adjust o.s. (a to).

amonarse [1a] F get tight.

amondongado flabby, gross.

amonedar [1a] coin, mint.

amonestación f warning; esp. ⚖ caution; eccl. (marriage) banns; correr las ~es publish the banns; **amonestador** warning attr., cautionary; **amonestar** [1a] (advertir) warn; (recordar) remind; (reprobar) reprove, admonish; eccl. publish the banns of.   [ammonia.\

amoníaco 1. ammoniac(al); 2. m\

amontonamiento m accumulation, piling up; **amontonar** [1a] heap (up), pile (up), accumulate; nieve, nubes bank (up); esp. nieve drift; bienes hoard, store (up); fig. citas etc. pile up; alabanzas etc. heap (sobre on); ~se pile (up), accumulate, collect; (arena, nieve) drift; (nubes) gather, pile up; (gente) crowd (together), huddle together; F get annoyed, go up in smoke.

amor m love (a for; de of); (p.) love; ~es pl. love-affair, romance; ~ cortés courtly love; ~ fracasado disappointment in love; ~ interesado cupboard love; ~ maternal mother love; ¡~ mío! (my) darling!; ~ a la patria love of one's country; ~ propio amour propre, self-respect; al ~ del agua with the current; al ~ de la lumbre by the fireside; *por* ～ for love; *por el* ～ *de* for the love of; *por el* ～ *de Dios* for God's sake; *hacer el* ～ *a* make love to; *picar a uno en el* ～ *propio* wound s.o.'s self respect.

amoral amoral, unmoral.

amoratado purple; blue (*de frío* with cold).

amorcillo *m* flirtation, light-hearted affair.

amordazar [1f] *perro* muzzle (*a. fig.*); *p.* gag (*a. fig.*).

amorfo formless, shapeless, amorphous *esp.* ⛏.

amorío *m* (*a.* ～*s pl.*) love-affair, romance; ～ *secreto* intrigue; **amoroso** *p.* loving, affectionate; *b.s.* (*a. co.*) amorous; *carta, poesía etc.* of love, love *attr.*; *fig.* 𝄞 workable; ⊕ malleable; *tiempo* mild, pleasant.

amorrar [1a] F bow one's head; *fig.* sulk.

amortajar [1a] shroud, lay out.

amortecer [2d] *ruido* muffle, deaden; ♪, *fuego* damp (down); ～**se** 🌡 faint, swoon; **amortecimiento** *m* muffling, deadening; 🌡 fainting.

amortiguación *f* deadening, muffling; absorbing, cushioning; **amortiguador 1.** deadening *etc.*; **2.** *m* damper; ⊕ shock-absorber; 🚗 buffer; *mot. a.* bumper; ～ *de luz* dimmer; **amortiguar** [1i] **1.** *mst* = *amortecer*; *choque* absorb; *golpe* cushion; *luz* dim; *color* tone down, kill.

amortizable ✝ redeemable; **amortización** *f* 🏛 amortization; ✝ redemption; *v. fondo*; **amortizar** [1f] 🏛 amortize; *préstamo* pay off, refund; *empleo* declare redundant; ～ *por desvalorización* write off.

amoscarse [1g], **amostazarse** [1f] F get peeved, get ratty.

amotinado mutinous; **amotinador 1.** mutinous, riotous; **2.** *m* mutineer, rioter; **amotinamiento** *m* mutiny, rising, insurrection; **amotinar** [1a] incite to mutiny (*or* riot); ～**se** mutiny, riot; rise up, rebel; *fig.* be upset, get upset.

amovible (re)movable, detachable; *empleado etc.* temporary.

amparador 1. helping, protecting; **2.** *m*, **-a** *f* protector; **amparar** [1a] (*ayudar*) help; protect, shelter (*de* from); ～**se** seek help; seek pro-tection *etc.*; defend o.s. (*contra* against); ～ *a* have recourse to; ～ *con*, ～ *de* seek the protection of; **amparo** *m* help; protection; refuge, shelter; defence; favour.

amperímetro *m* ammeter; **amperio** *m* ampere.

ampliación *f* enlargement (*a. phot.*); (*ensanche*) extension; **ampliadora** *f* phot. enlarger; **ampliar** [1c] amplify; enlarge (*a. phot.*); (*ensanchar*) extend; *poderes* extend, widen; *declaración* amplify, elaborate; **amplificación** *f* amplification (*a. rhet., phys.*); ⚡ gain; **amplificador** *m* radio: amplifier; **amplificar** [1g] enlarge; amplify (*a. rhet., phys.*); **amplio** *espacio etc.* ample; *vestido* full, roomy; *falda* full; *cuarto* spacious, big; *poderes* ample, wide, generous; (*robusto*) assertive, full-blooded; *dibujo* bold; **amplitud** *f* ampleness, fullness *etc.*; *ast.* amplitude; *esp. fig.* breadth, extent.

ampo *m* dazzling white(ness); *como el* ～ *de la nieve* white as the driven snow.

ampolla *f* 🌡 blister; (*burbuja*) bubble; (*vasija*) flask; 🌡 (*vasija*) ampoule; **ampollarse** [1a] blister; **ampolleta** *f* (*vasija*) vial; (*reloj*) sand-glass, hour-glass; bulb *de termómetro*.

ampón *paquete* bulky; *p.* tubby.

ampulosidad *f* bombast, pomposity; **ampuloso** bombastic, pompous.

amputación *f* amputation; **amputar** [1a] amputate, cut off.

amuchachado boyish.

amueblado furnished; **amueblar** [1a] furnish; appoint.

amujerado effeminate.

amuleto *m* amulet, charm.

amuñecado doll-like.

amura *f* beam *de barco*; tack *de vela*; *cambiar de* ～ go about.

amurallar [1a] wall (in).

amurar [1a] ⚓ tack.

amusgar [1h] *orejas* throw back; *ojos* narrow.

anabaptista *m/f* anabaptist.

anacarado mother-of-pearl *attr.*

anacoreta *m/f* anchorite, anchoret.

anacronismo *m* anachronism; (*objeto*) out-of-date object, bric-à-brac.

ánade *m* duck; ~ *real* mallard;
anadear [1a] waddle; **anadón** *m*
duckling.
anales *m/pl.* annals.
analfabetismo *m* illiteracy; **analfabeto** *adj. a. su. m*, **a** *f* illiterate.
analgesia *f* analgesia.
análisis *mst m* analysis; † ~ *de
mercados* market research; **analista** *m* 🜚 analyst; **analítico**
analytic(al); **analizador** *m* analyst; **analizar** [1f] analyse; *gr.*
parse.
analogía *f* analogy; **análogo**
analogous, similar.
ananá(s) *m* pineapple.
anaquel *m* shelf; **anaquelería** *f*
shelves, shelving.
anaranjado *adj. a. su. m* orange.
anarquía *f* anarchy; **anárquico**
anarchic(al); **anarquismo** *m* anarchism; **anarquista 1.** anarchic(al); *pol.* anarchist(ic); **2.**
m/f anarchist.
anatema *mst m* anathema; **anatematizar** [1f] *eccl.* anathematize;
(*maldecir*) curse; *fig.* reprimand.
anatomía *f* anatomy; **anatómico
1.** anatomical; **2.** *m* = **anatomista**
m/f anatomist; **anatomizar** [1f]
anatomize; *paint. músculos etc.*
bring out, emphasize.
anca *f* haunch; rump, croup *de
caballo;* F buttock; ~*s pl.* rump;
F *no sufre* ~*s* he can't take a joke.
anciana *f* old woman, old lady;
ancianidad *f* old age; **anciano
1.** old, aged; **2.** *m* old man; *eccl.*
elder.
ancla *f* anchor; ⚓ ~ *de la esperanza*
sheet-anchor; *fig.* ~ *de salvación*
sheet-anchor; **echar** (*levar*) ~*s* drop
(weigh) anchor; **ancladero** *m*
anchorage; **anclar** [1a] (drop)
anchor.
ancón *m* cove.
áncora *f* anchor (*a.* ⊕, *fig.*).
ancheta *f* † (*géneros*) small
amount; (*ganancia*) gain, profit.
ancho 1. wide, broad; *esp. fig.*
ample, full; *ropa* loose(-fitting);
falda full; *fig.* liberal, broad
(-minded); ~ *de conciencia* not
over-scrupulous; *de 3 metros,
3 metros de* ~ 3 metres wide,
3 metres in width; F *ponerse a sus*
~*as* spread o.s., be at one's ease;
le viene muy ~ (*chaqueta etc.*) it's

on the big side for him; *fig.* I bet
he's crying his eyes out; *le viene
muy* ~ *el cargo* the job is too much
for him; **2.** *m* width, breadth; 🜚
gauge.
anchoa *f* anchovy.
anchura *f* width, breadth, wideness;
esp. fig. ampleness *etc.* (*v. ancho*);
anchuroso *calle etc.* broad; *lugar*
spacious.
andadas *f/pl. hunt.* tracks; *volver
a las* ~ back-slide, return to one's
old ways; **andaderas** *f/pl.* go-cart; **andadero** *sitio* passable,
easily traversed; **andado** worn,
well-trodden; (*común*) ordinary;
ropa worn, old; **andador 1.** fast-walking; (*carácter*) fond of walking, fond of gadding about; **2.** *m*,
-**a** *f* walker; (*callejero*) gadabout;
3. ~*es pl.* leading-strings; **andadura** *f* (*acto*) walking; (*paso*) gait,
walk; pace *de caballo*.
andaluz *adj. a. su. m*, -**a** *f* Andalusian; **andaluzada** *f* F tall story.
andamiada *f*, **andamiaje** *m*
scaffold(ing), staging; **andamio** *m*
scaffold(ing); (*tablado*) stage, stand;
~ *óseo* skeleton.
andana *f* row, line; *llamarse* ~ go
back on one's word.
andanada *f* ⚓ broadside; (*tribuna*)
covered grandstand; *fig.* scolding,
telling-off F; *soltar la* (or *una*) ~ *a*
haul *s.o.* over the coals.
andante 1. walking; *caballero*
errant; **2.** *m* ♪ andante; **andanza** *f*
fortune, fate.
andar 1. [1q] *v/t. camino* walk;
distancia go, cover; *v/i.* (*a pie*)
walk, go; (*moverse*) move; (*comportarse*) behave; (*reloj, trabajo etc.*)
go; ⊕ go, run, work; (*horas*) pass,
elapse; ~ *adj.* be, feel; *anda muy
alegre* he's very cheerful; *seguir
andando* go on walking, carry on
walking; *ando escribiendo un libro*
I'm in the course of writing a book;
venimos andando we came on foot,
we walked; *¿cómo anda eso?* how
are things going?; *¿cómo andas de
dinero?* how are you off for money?;
¡anda! (*ánimo*) come on!, go on!;
(*sorpresa*) you don't mean to say!,
get along with you!; *¡anda, anda!*
don't be silly!; *¡andando!* that's
all!; ~ *a caballo etc.* ride, go on;
puñetazos go about it with; ~ *a una*

be at one, agree; ~ *bien (reloj)* keep (good) time; ~ *en pleitos* be engaged in, be involved in; ~**se** (= *v/i.*, but freq. indicates personal involvement): ~ *con circunloquios etc.* make use of, use; ~ *en* indulge in; *se me anda la cabeza* my head is spinning; *¡todo se andará!* it will all work out!; *(promesa)* it shall be done!; **2.** *m* gait, pace; *a largo* ~ in time, in due course; *estar a un* ~ be on the same level.

andariego = *andador*; **andarín** *m* walker; *ser gran* ~ be a great walker; **andas** *f/pl. (silla)* litter, sedan chair; portable platform *en procesión; (féretro)* bier; **andén** *m* ⚓ platform; *(acera)* footpath, sidewalk *Am.*; ⚓ quayside.

andino Andean.

andito *m* balcony.

andorga *f* F belly.

andorrear [1a] F gad about, bustle around; **andorrero** *m*, **a** *f* F gadabout.

andrajo *m* rag, tatter; *(p.)* scallywag, good-for-nothing; *(cosa)* trifle; ~**s** *pl.* rags, tatters; **andrajoso** ragged, in tatters.

andrómina *f* F *(cuento)* fib, tale; *(engaño)* trick, fraud.

andurriales *m/pl.* out of the way place, wilds.

aneblar [1k] cover with mist *(or* cloud); *fig.* cast a cloud over, darken; ~**se** cloud over, get misty; get dark.

anécdota *f* anecdote, story; **anecdótico** anecdotal; *contenido* ~ story content, story value.

anegación *f* flooding *etc.*; **anegadizo** *terreno* subject to flooding; **anegar** [1h] *(ahogar)* drown (en in; *a. fig.*); *(inundar)* flood; *fig.* destroy, overwhelm; ~**se** *(p.)* drown *(a. fig.); (campos)* be flooded; *(barco)* sink, founder; ~ *en llanto* dissolve into tears.

anejo 1. attached; dependent; ~ *a* attached to, joined on to; *edificio* ~ = **2.** *m* 🔺 annexe, out-building; *fig.* dependency, supplement *de revista.*

anemómetro *m* anemometer.

anémona *f*, **anemone** *f* anemone; ~ *de mar* sea anemone.

anestesia *f* anaesthesia; **anestesiar** [1b] anaesthetize, give an anaes-

thetic to; **anestésico** *adj. a. su. m* anaesthetic.

anexar [1a] annex; *adjunto* attach, append; **anexión** *f* annexation; **anexo 1.** *documento, edificio* attached; dependent *(a. eccl.); llevar algo* ~ have s.t. attached; **2.** *m* annexe; dependency *(a. eccl.).*

anfibio 1. amphibious; amphibian *(a. ✈)*; **2.** *m* amphibian.

anfiteatro *m* amphitheatre; *thea.* balcony, dress-circle; ~ *anatómico* dissecting room.

anfitrión *m lit. a. co.* host; **anfitriona** *f* hostess.

ánfora *f* amphora; *S.Am.* ballot-box.

anfractuosidad *f (desigualdad)* roughness; *(vuelta)* bend, turning; *anat.* convolution, fold.

angarillas *f/pl.* hand-barrow; *(cestas)* panniers; *(vinagrera)* cruet-stand.

ángel *m* angel; ~ *custodio*, ~ *de la guarda* guardian angel; *tener* ~ have charm; **angelical, angélico** angelic(al); **angelón** *m*: F ~ *de retablo* fat old thing; **angelote** *m (p.)* chubby child; **ángelus** *m* Angelus.

angina *f* angina, quinsy; ~ *de pecho* angina pectoris; *tener* ~**s** have a sore throat.

anglicano *adj. a. su. m*, **a** *f* Anglican; **anglicismo** *m* Anglicism; **anglófilo** *adj. a. su. m*, **a** *f* Anglophile; **anglosajón** *adj. a. su. m*, **-a** *f* Anglo-Saxon.

angostar(se) [1a] narrow; **angosto** narrow; **angostura** *f* narrowness; ⚓ strait, narrows; *geog.* narrow defile.

angra *f* cove, creek.

anguila *f* eel; ~ *de mar* conger eel; ⚓ ~**s** *pl.* slipway.

angular angular; *piedra* corner *attr.*; **ángulo** *m* angle *(a. ✈); (esquina)* corner, turning; ⊕ knee, bend; ~ *agudo (obtuso, recto)* acute (obtuse, right) angle; *phot. de* ~ *ancho* wide-angle; *en* ~ *at* an angle; **anguloso** angular; *camino etc.* full of corners.

angustia *f* anguish, distress; 💊 ~ *vital* anxiety state; **angustiado** distressed, anguished; *(avaro etc.)* grasping, mean; **angustiar** [1b] grieve, distress; ~**se** be distressed (*por* at); break one's heart; **angustioso** anguished, distressed; *voz* anxious; *situación* distressing, heartbreaking.

anhelante 𝕤 (*a. respiración* ~) panting; *fig.* (*ansioso*) eager; (*nostálgico*) wistful, longing; **anhelar** [1a] *v/t.* be eager for; yearn for, pine for; *v/i.* 𝕤 gasp, pant; ~ *inf.* yearn to *inf.*; ~ *por inf.* aspire to *inf.*; ~ *por su.* hanker after *su.*; **anhelo** *m* eagerness; yearning, longing (*de, por* for); appetite (*de, por* for); **anheloso** 𝕤 gasping, panting; *respiración* heavy, difficult; *fig.* eager.

anidar [1a] *v/t.* shelter, take in; *v/i. orn.* make its nest; *fig.* live, make one's home.

anieblar [1a] = **aneblar**.

anilina *f* aniline.

anillado ringed; *forma* ring-shaped; **anillar** [1a] make into a ring; (*sujetar*) (fasten with a) ring; **anillo** *m* ring (*a. ast.*); cigar band; ~ *de boda* wedding ring; *fig. de* ~ honorary; *venir como* ~ *al dedo* be just right; meet the case perfectly.

ánima *f* soul; soul in purgatory; *eccl. las* ~s sunset bell, Angelus.

animación *f* liveliness, life; vivacity *de carácter*; sprightliness *de movimientos*; (*movimiento*) bustle, life, animation; **animado** lively, gay; sprightly, vivacious; in high spirits; *fiesta* gay, merry; (*concurrido*) well attended; busy; *zo.* animate.

animadversión *f* censure, animadversion; (*ojeriza*) ill-will.

animal 1. animal; *p.* stupid; **2.** *m* animal; *fig.* (*estúpido*) blockhead; F beast, brute; **animalada** *f* F stupidity; (*palabra*) silly thing (to say); **animálculo** *m* animalcule; **animalejo** *m* small creature; **animalidad** *f* animality; **animalucho** *m* F ugly brute.

animar [1a] *biol.* give life to, animate; *fig.* (*alegrar*) cheer up; (*estimular*) ginger up; *fuego, vista, cuarto* brighten up; *discusión* enliven, liven up; (*alentar*) encourage (*a inf.* to *inf.*); ~se (*p.*) brighten up, cheer up; (*reunión, discusión*) get livelier, brighten up (*cobrar ánimo*) take heart, feel encouraged; (*atreverse*) dare, make up one's mind (*a inf.* to *inf.*); ¡*anímate*! buck up!;

make up your mind!; **ánimo** *m* soul; spirit (*a. fig.*); (*valor*) courage, nerve; energy; attention, thought; ¡~! *deportes:* go it!, come along!; *cobrar* ~ pluck up courage, take heart; *dar* ~(*s*) *a, infundir* ~ *a* encourage; *dilatar el* ~ gladden the heart; *estar con* ~ *de, tener* ~s *para* be in the mood for, feel like.

animosidad *f* (*valor*) courage, nerve; (*ojeriza*) animosity, ill-will; **animoso** spirited, brave; ready (*para* for).

aniñado *cara etc.* childlike, of a child; *b.s.* childish, puerile; **aniñarse** [1a] act childishly.

aniquilación *f*, **aniquilamiento** *m* annihilation, obliteration; **aniquilar** [1a] annihilate, destroy; ~se be wiped out; *fig.* 𝕤 waste away; (*hacienda*) be frittered away; deteriorate, decline.

anís *m* ♀ anise; (*grana*) aniseed; (*bebida*) approx. anisette; F *llegar a los* ~es turn up late; **anisete** *m* anisette.

aniversario *m* anniversary.

ano *m* anus.

anoche last night; *antes de* ~ the night before last; **anochecedor** *m*, -**a** *f* late bird; **anochecer 1.** [2d] get dark; arrive at nightfall; **2.** *m* nightfall, dusk; *al* ~ at nightfall; **anochecida** *f* nightfall, dusk.

anodino anodyne (*a. su.*); *fig.* harmless, inoffensive; *b.s.* insipid, dull.

ánodo *m* anode.

anomalía *f* anomaly; **anómalo** anomalous.

anonadación *f*, **anonadamiento** *m* annihilation *etc.*; **anonadar** [1a] annihilate, destroy; *fig.* overwhelm; ~se be humiliated; (*desanimarse*) be discouraged.

anónimo 1. anonymous; nameless; ♰ *sociedad* limited; **2.** *m* (*en general*) anonymity; (*p.*) s.o. unknown; (*carta*) anonymous letter.

anormal abnormal; **anormalidad** *f* abnormality.

anotación *f* (*acto*) annotation; note; *S.Am.* score; **anotar** [1a] annotate; (*apuntar*) note (down), jot down; ♰ book; *S.Am.* score.

ánsar *m* goose; **ansarino** *m* gosling.

ansia *f* 𝕤 anxiety, tension; (*angustia*) anguish; (*deseo*) longing, yearning (*de* for); ~s *pl.* 𝕤 nausea;

ansiar [1b] *v/t.* long for, yearn for, covet; ~ *inf.* long to *inf.*, crave to *inf.*; *v/i.*: ~ *por* be head over heels in love with; **ansiedad** *f* anxiety (*a.* 🟊); solicitude; suspense; **ansioso** anxious (*a.* 🟊), worried; solicitous; ~ *de*, ~ *por* eager for, greedy for, avid for.

antagónico antagonistic, opposed; **antagonismo** *m* antagonism; **antagonista** *m/f* antagonist.

antañazo a long time ago; **antaño** last year; *fig.* long ago.

antártico Antarctic.

ante[1] *m* elk; buffalo; (*piel*) buckskin, suède.

ante[2] *juez etc.* before, in the presence of; *enemigo, peligro etc.* in the face of, faced with; *asunto* with regard to.

anteanoche the night before last; **anteayer** the day before yesterday.

antebrazo *m* forearm.

antecámara *f* antechamber, anteroom; lobby.

antecedente 1. previous, preceding; **2.** *m* antecedent (*a.* 🄰, *gr.*, *phls.*); ~s *pl.* record, past history; ~s *pl. penales* criminal record; *sin* ~s with a clean record; *estar en* ~s know all about it; *poner en* ~s put *s.o.* in the picture; **anteceder** [2a] precede, go before; **antecesor 1.** preceding; **2.** *m*, -a *f* predecessor; (*abuelo*) ancestor, forefather.

antedatar [1a] antedate.

antedicho aforesaid, aforementioned.

antediluviano antediluvian.

anteiglesia *f eccl.* porch.

antelación: *con* ~ = **antemano:** *de* ~ in advance, beforehand.

antena *f zo.* antenna, feeler; *radio:* aerial, antenna; ~ *de cuadro* loop aerial; ~ *direccional* directional aerial; ~ *interior* indoor aerial.

antenombre *m* title.

anteojera *f* spectacle case; ~s *pl.* blinkers; **anteojero** *m* spectacle maker; optician; **anteojo** *m* telescope, spyglass (*a.* ~ *de larga vista*); eye-glass; ~s *pl.* spectacles, glasses; *mot. etc.* goggles; blinkers *de caballo*; ~ *binóculo* binoculars, field-glasses; ~s *pl. de concha* horn-rimmed spectacles; ~ *prismático* prism binoculars; ~ *de teatro* opera-glasses.

antepagar [1h] pay beforehand, prepay.

antepasado 1. before last; **2.** *m* forbear, forefather.

antepecho *m* balcony, ledge *de ventana*; parapet, guard-rail *de puente etc.*; 🪖 breastwork, parapet.

antepenúltimo last but two, antepenultimate.

anteponer [2r] place *s.t.* in front; *fig.* prefer; ~se come in front, come in between; ~ *a fig.* overcome.

anteproyecto *m* preliminary sketch (*or* plan); *fig.* blueprint.

antepuerto *m* outer harbour.

antera *f* anther.

anterior (*orden*) preceding, previous; anterior (*a. gr.*); (*delantero*) front, fore; (*tiempo*) previous (*a* to), earlier (*a* than), former; **anterioridad** *f* precedence; priority; *con* ~ previously; *con* ~ *a* prior to.

antes 1. *adv.* before; formerly; (*en otro tiempo*) once, previously; (*con anticipación*) sooner, before now; ~ (*bien*) rather, on the contrary; ~ *que* (*tiempo*) before I did; (*preferencia*) rather (*or* sooner) than I; *cuanto* ~, *lo* ~ *posible* as soon as possible; *mucho* ~ long before; *poco* ~ just before; **2.** *prp.:* ~ *de* before; ~ *de inf.* before *ger.*; ~ *de terminada la función* before the show was over; **3.** *cj.:* ~ (*de*) *que* before.

antesala *f* antechamber; *hacer* ~ wait to be received; *fig.* cool one's heels.

anti... anti...; ~**adherente** nonstick; ~**aéreo** anti-aircraft; *cañón* ~ anti-aircraft gun; ~**biótico** *m* antibiotic; ~**ciclón** *m* anticyclone.

anticipación *f* anticipation, forestalling; 🕇 advance; *con* ~ in advance; *llegar con bastante* ~ arrive in good time; *llegar con 5 minutos de* ~ arrive 5 minutes early; **anticipadamente** in advance; **anticipado** future, prospective; 🕇 advance; **anticipar** [1a] *fecha etc.* advance, bring forward; 🕇 advance; ~ *con placer* look forward to; ~ *las gracias* thank in advance; ~se take place (*or* happen) early; ~ *a acción* anticipate, forestall; *suceso* be ahead of; *p.* steal a march on; ~ *a inf. vb.* ahead of time; **anticipo** *m* foretaste; (*préstamo*) advance;

(*pago*) advance payment; ♂ retainer, retaining fee.

anti...: ~**clerical** anticlerical; ~**conceptivo** *m* contraceptive; ~**congelante** *m* (*a. solución* ~) anti-freeze, de-freezer; ~**corrosivo** anti-corrosive; ~**constitucional** unconstitutional; ~**cristo** *m* Antichrist.

anticuado old-fashioned, out-of-date; *máquina etc.* antiquated; obsolete; **anticuarse** [1d] become old-fashioned; become antiquated; **anticuario** *m* ⏹ antiquarian; ✝ antique-dealer.

anti...: ~**derrapante** non-skid; ~**deslizante** non-slipping; *mot.* non-skid; ~**deslumbrante** anti-dazzle; ~**detonante** *mot.* anti-knock.

antídoto *m* antidote (*a. fig.*; de against, for to).

anti...: -**económico** uneconomic(al); wasteful; ~**estético** inartistic; unsightly, offensive; ~**fascista** *adj. a. su. m/f* anti-fascist; ~**faz** *m* mask; veil; ~**friccional** anti-friction *attr*.

antigualla *f* antique; F relic; (*cuento*) old story; (*p.*) has-been; ~s *pl. contp.* junk; **antiguamente** (*en lo antiguo*) in ancient times, of old; (*antes*) formerly, once; **antiguar** [1i] attain seniority; ~se = **anticuarse**; **antigüedad** *f* antiquity; ✝ seniority; ~es *pl.* antiquities; **antiguo 1.** old; ancient; (*anterior*) former, late, one-time; *alumno etc.* old, former; ✝ *más* ~ senior (*que* to); *socio más* ~ senior partner; *de* ~ from time immemorial; **2.**: *los* ~s *pl.* the ancients.

antihalo *m phot.* antihalo.

antihigiénico insanitary, unhygienic.

antílope *m* antelope.

antimonio *m* antimony.

antioxidante anti-rust.

antipara *f* screen.

antiparras *f/pl.* F glasses, specs.

antipatía *f* dislike (*hacia* for), aversion (*hacia* to, from); antipathy, unfriendliness (*entre* between); **antipático** disagreeable, unpleasant, not nice; *ambiente* uncongenial; *me es muy* ~ I don't like him at all; **antipatizar** [1f] *S.Am.* feel unfriendly; ~ *con* dislike.

antipatriótico unpatriotic.

antípoda 1. antipodal; *fig.* contrary, quite the opposite; **2.** *m* antipode; ~s *f/pl. geog.* antipodes.

antirresbaladizo *mot.* non-skid.

antisemita *m/f* anti-semite; **antisemítico** anti-semitic; **antisemitismo** *m* anti-semitism.

antiséptico *adj. a. su. m* antiseptic.

antitesis *f* antithesis; **antitético** antithetic(al).

antojadizo capricious; given to sudden fancies; faddy; **antojado** eager, desirous; **antojarse** [1a] take a fancy to; ~ *que* imagine that, have the feeling that; *se me antoja visitar la ciudad* I have a mind to visit the city; *no se le antoja ir* he doesn't feel like going; **antojo** *m* caprice, whim, passing fancy; (*juicio*) hasty judgement; craving *de encinta*; ⚹ mole, birthmark; *a su* ~ as one pleases.

antología *f* anthology.

antónimo *m* antonym.

antorcha *f* torch; *fig.* lamp.

antracita *f* anthracite.

ántrax *m* anthrax.

antro *m* cavern.

antropofagía *f* cannibalism; **antropófago 1.** man-eating, anthropophagous ⏹; **2.** *m*, *a f* cannibal; **antropoide** anthropoid; **antropología** *f* anthropology; **antropólogo** *m* anthropologist.

antruejo *m* carnival.

antuviada *f*, **antuvión** *m* (sudden) blow (*or* bump); *de* ~ suddenly, unexpectedly.

anual annual; **anualidad** *f* ✝ annuity; (*suceso*) annual occurrence; **anuario** *m* yearbook.

anubarrado cloudy, overcast.

anublar [1a] *cielo* cloud; (*oscurecer*) darken, dim (*a. fig.*); ♀ dry up, wither; ~se cloud over; darken; *fig.* fade away.

anudar [1a] knot, tie; join, unite (*a. fig.*); *narración* resume, take up again; *voz* strangle; ~se get into knots *etc.*; ♀ *etc.* remain stunted; ~*le a uno la lengua* get tongue-tied.

anulación *f* annulment *etc.*; **anular**[1] [1a] annul, cancel, nullify; *ley* revoke; set aside; *decisión* override, overrule; *p.* remove (from office), discharge; *gol* disallow; ~se be deprived of authority, be removed; (ser postergado) be passed over; be humiliated.

anular² **1.** ring(-shaped); **2.** *m* ring finger.

anunciación *f* announcement; (*día de*) *la* ♀ Lady Day, The Annunciation (*25 March*); **anunciante** *m/f* ✝ advertiser; **anunciar** [1b] announce; proclaim; *brindis* propose; (*pronosticar*) foretell; *b.s.* forebode, foreshadow; ✝ advertise; **anuncio** *m* announcement; proposal; ✝ (*esp. impreso*) advertisement; (*cartel*) placard, poster; *thea. etc.* bill; notice *en tablón*; (*indicio*) sign, omen; ~ *luminoso* illuminated sign; ~s *pl. por palabras* classified advertisements, small ads.

anuo annual.

anverso *m* obverse.

anzuelo *m* (fish-)hook; *fig.* lure, bait; *picar en* (*or tragar*) *el* ~ swallow the bait, be taken in.

añada *f* ✔ year, season; (*terreno*) piece of land.

añadido *m* false hair, switch; **añadidura** *f* addition; ✝ extra measure; *de* ~ extra, into the bargain; *por* ~ besides, in addition, over (and above); **añadir** [3a] add (*a* to); (*aumentar*) increase; *fig.* add, lend (*a* to).

añagaza *f* decoy, lure (*a. fig.*); *fig.* bait, enticement.

añal 1. *suceso* yearly; ✔ *etc.* year-old; **2.** *m* year-old lamb *etc.*

añascar [1g] F get together bit by bit.

añejar [1a] age, make old; *b.s.* make stale; ~se age; (*vino etc.*) improve with age; *b.s.* get stale, go musty; **añejo** old; *vino* mellow, mature; *b.s.* stale.

añicos *m/pl.* bits, pieces, shreds; *splinters de madera*; *hacer* ~ *papel etc.* tear up; *madera etc.* smash to smithereens.

añil *m* indigo (*a.* ⚘); blue *para lavado*.

añinos *m/pl.* lamb's-wool.

año *m* year; ~s *pl.* (*cumpleaños*) birthday; ~ *bisiesto* leap-year; ~ *de Cristo* Anno Domini (A.D.); ~ *de gracia* year of grace; ~ *luz* light-year; *el* ~ *de la nana* the year dot; ~ *de nuestra salud* year of our Lord; ♀ *Nuevo* New Year; *día de* ♀ *Nuevo* New Year's Day; *un* ~ *con otro* in

an average year, on a yearly average; *de pocos* ~s small, young; *entrado en* ~s elderly, advanced in years; *¡mal* ~ *para él!* he's got a hard time coming!; *por los* ~s *de 1600* about (the year) 1600; *¡por muchos* ~s! here's luck!; F *estar de buen* ~ be in good shape, be fat; *v. tener.*

añojal *m* fallow (land).

añojo ✔ yearling calf.

añoranza *f* longing, nostalgia (*de for*), hankering (*de after*); sense of loss (*de pérdida after*); **añorar** [1a] long for, pine for, hanker after; *muerto etc.* grieve for, mourn.

añoso aged, full of years.

añublo *m* mildew, blight.

añudar [1a] = *anudar.*

añusgar [1h] choke; ~se F get cross.

aojar [1a] put the evil eye (*or hoodoo*) on; **aojo** *m* evil eye, hoodoo.

aovado egg-shaped, oval; **aovar** [1a] lay eggs.

apabullar [1a] F squash, flatten (*a. fig.*).

apacentadero *m* pasture (land); **apacentar** [1k] pasture, graze; *fig. rebaño* minister to; *entendimiento* feed; *b.s.* feed, gratify, pander to; ~se ✔ graze; *fig.* feed (*con, de on*).

apacibilidad *f* gentleness *etc.*; **apacible** gentle, mild, meek; *tiempo* mild, calm; *viento* gentle; (*ánimo*) even-tempered, peaceable.

apaciguamiento *m* appeasement *etc.*; **apaciguar** [1i] pacify, appease, mollify; (*aquietar*) calm down; ~se calm down, quieten down.

apadrinar [1a] *empresa etc.* sponsor; *escritor* be a patron to; *eccl. niño* act as godfather to; *novio* be best man for; *fig.* support, approve.

apagado *volcán* extinct; *color* dull, lustreless; *voz* quiet; *sonido* muted, muffled; *p.* listless, spiritless; **apagafuego** *m* fire-extinguisher; **apagar** [1h] *fuego* put out, extinguish; ⚡ *luz* turn off, turn out, switch off; *radio etc.* switch off; *color* tone down; *sonido* muffle; ♪ mute; *sed* quench, slake; *cal* slake; *afecto, dolor* kill, deaden; (*aplacar*) calm, soothe; ~se go out; be extinguished; (*sonido etc.*) die away; (p.) calm down; **apagón** m ✗ black-out; ∦ power-cut.

apalabrar [1a] agree to; p. engage; ~se come to an agreement (con with).

apalancamiento m leverage; **apalancar** [1g] lever (up).

apaleamiento m beating etc.; **apalear** [1a] beat, thrash; alfombra beat; ✗ winnow; ~ oro, ~ plata be rolling in money; **apaleo** m ✗ winnowing.

apanalado honeycombed.

apandar [1a] F swipe, knock off.'

apandillar [1a] form into a gang; ~se band together, gang up.

apantanar [1a] flood, make swampy.

apañado fig. handy, skilful; (apropiado) suitable (para for); F ¡estás ~! you've had it!; **apañar** [1a] (coger) pick up; (asir) take hold of; b.s. steal, swipe; (ataviar) dress up; F (arropar) wrap up; ~se para inf. contrive to inf.; ~las por su cuenta fend for o.s.; **apaño** m F (remiendo) mend, repair; (habilidad) knack, handiness; (lío) mess.

apañuscar [1g] F rumple, crumple; S.Am. jam together; (robar) steal, swipe.

aparador m sideboard, buffet; (vitrina) show-case; (escaparate) shop-window; ⊕ workshop; **aparar** [1a] arrange; adorn; ✗ weed, clean; falda etc. stretch out.

aparato m 🔥 etc. apparatus; (dispositivo) device, piece of equipment; ⊕ machine; radio etc.: set; teleph. instrument; phot., gimnasia etc.: apparatus, equipment; fig. ostentation, show; sign, symptom (a. 🩹); 🩹 (vendaje) bandage; (apósito) application; ~ eléctrico meteor. display of lightning; ~s pl. de mando controls; ~s pl. de relojería clockwork; ~s pl. sanitarios bathroom fixtures; **aparatosidad** f ostentation etc.; **aparatoso** ostentatious, showy; pretentious; caída, función etc. spectacular.

aparcería f partnership; **aparcero** m partner; sharecropper Am.; S.Am. companion.

aparear [1a] make even, level up; animales pair, mate; fig. pair (off), match.

aparecer [2d] appear; turn up,

show up; loom (up) en niebla etc.; **aparecido** m ghost, spectre.

aparejado fit, ready (para for); **aparejador** m foreman, overseer; △ architect's assistant, builder; **aparejar** [1a] prepare, get ready; meteor. threaten; caballo harness; ⚓ fit out, rig out; paint. etc. prime, size; ~se prepare o.s., get ready (para for); **aparejo** m preparation; (caballo) harness; ⚓ rigging; ⊕ lifting gear, (block and) tackle; △ bond; paint. priming, sizing; ~s pl. ⊕ tools, gear, equipment.

aparentar [1a] feign, affect; edad seem to be, look; ~ inf. make as if to inf.; **aparente** apparent, seeming; manifestación outward, visible; convenient, suitable; esp. b.s. plausible; **aparición** f appearance; (espectro) apparition; de próxima ~ libro forthcoming; **apariencia** f appearance, look(s) (exterior) outside; esp. b.s. semblance, (outward) show; probability; ~s pl. thea. décor; salvar las ~s keep up appearances, save one's face.

apartadero m mot. lay-by; 🚂 siding; **apartadijo** m (small) portion; = **apartadizo** m recess, alcove, nook; **apartado** 1. isolated, remote, secluded; camino devious; 2. m (a. ~ de correos) post-office box; (cuarto) spare room; typ. paragraph; section de documento; **apartamento** m esp. S.Am. flat; **apartamiento** m (acto) withdrawal etc.; (efecto) isolation, remoteness; (lugar) secluded spot; **apartar** [1a] separate, take away (de from); isolate; ✂ etc. sort (out); (quitar de en medio) move away; p. (a un lado) take aside, draw aside; turn away, dissuade; side-track (de propósito from); (a. ~ de sí) put aside, put out of one's mind; ⚒ extract; ~se (dos ps.) separate (a. casados); (alejarse) move away; withdraw, retire (de from); (mantenerse aparte) keep away (de from), stand aside; ~ de camino leave, turn from; **aparte** 1. apart, aside (de from); 2. m thea. aside; typ. (new) paragraph, indention.

apasionado passionate; (fogoso) fiery, impassioned, intense; (aficionado) passionately fond (a, por of); **apasionamiento** m passion,

enthusiasm (de, por for); great
fondness (de, por for); (amorío)
infatuation; **apasionante** thrilling,
exciting; **apasionar** [1a] stir
deeply, make a strong appeal to;
enamorado infatuate; afflict, torment; ~se get excited; ~ de, ~ por
be mad about, enthuse over;
(enamorarse) fall in love with.

apatía f apathy; 🐾 listlessness;
apático apathetic; 🐾 listless.

apátrida stateless.

apatuscar [1g] F hurry, botch;
apatusco m F frills, buttons and
bows.

apeadero m 🚂 halt; (alojamiento)
(temporary) lodging, pied à terre;
apear [1a] help s.o. down (de
from); (bajar) take s.t. down;
árbol fell; caballo hobble; rueda
scotch (a. fig.); ⚓ prop up;
surv. measure, survey; problema
solve, work out; dificultad overcome; F make s.o. budge (de
opinión from); (tratamiento) drop;
~se dismount, get down (de
caballo from); 🚂 etc. get off, get
out; (hospedarse) stay, put up (en
at); F back down.

apechugar [1h]: ~ con F put up
with, swallow.

apedazar [1f] cut (or tear) into
pieces; (remendar) mend, patch.

apedrear [1a] v/t. stone, pelt with
stones; v/i. hail; ~se be damaged
by hail; **apedreo** m stoning;
meteor. hail.

apegadamente devotedly; **ape-
gado:** ~ a attached to, fond of;
apegarse [1h] a become attached
to, grow fond of; **apego** m: ~ a
attachment to, fondness for.

apelación f appeal; sin ~ without
appeal, final; interponer ~ give
notice of appeal; **apelante** m/f
appellant; **apelar** [1a] 🏛 appeal
(de against); ~ a fig. appeal to;
have recourse to.

apeldar [1a]: F ~las beat it.

apelmazado compressed, compact;
líquido thick, lumpy; escritura
clumsy; **apelmazar** [1f] compress;
~se cake; get lumpy.

apelotonar [1a] make into a ball;
~se (gente) crowd together.

apellidar [1a] name; (calificar)
call; proclaim (por rey as); ~se be
called, have as a surname; **apellido**

m surname; name; (mote) nickname; ~ de soltera maiden name.

apenar [1a] grieve, trouble; ~se
grieve, sorrow.

apenas scarcely, hardly (a. ~ si);
(only) just; ~ ... cuando no sooner ...
than.

apendectomía f appendectomy;
apéndice m appendix (a. 🐾);
appendage; esp. 🏛 schedule;
apendicitis f appendicitis.

apercibimiento m preparation;
provision; (aviso) warning, notice;
🏛 summons; **apercibir** [3a] prepare; provide; ánimo prepare
(para for); (avisar) warn; 🏛 serve
a summons on, summon; ~se get
(o.s.) ready, prepare (o.s.) (para for);
~ de provide o.s. with.

apercollar [1m] grab by the neck;
(acogotar) fell (with a blow to the
neck).

apergaminado parchment-like; p.
wizened.

aperitivo m appetizer; (bebida)
aperitif.

apero m tools, equipment, gear;
🌱 implements, tackle (a. ~s pl.);
S.Am. riding outfit.

aperreador F tiresome; **aperrear**
[1a] set the dogs on; F (molestar)
bother, plague; (cansar) tire out;
~se F slave (away), overwork.

apersogar [1h] tether.

apersonado: bien ~ presentable;
apersonarse [1a] 🏛 appear;
appear in person; ✝ have a
business interview.

apertura f mst opening; 🏛 reading
(of a will).

apesadumbrado grieved, distressed; **apesadumbrar** [1a],
apesarar [1a] grieve, distress,
sadden; ~se be grieved etc. (con,
de at).

apesgar [1h] weigh down, over-
burden.

apestado de infested with; **apestar**
[1a] v/t. 🐾 infect (with plague);
fig. corrupt, vitiate; (fastidiar)
annoy, bother; v/i. stink; **apestoso**
(que huele) stinking; olor pestilential; F sickening, annoying.

apetecer [2d] v/t. crave (for), long
for, hunger for; v/i.: me apetece la
leche I fancy some milk, I could do
with some milk; me apetece ir
I feel like going; **apetecible**

desirable; tempting; **apetencia** f
hunger; *fig.* hunger, craving,
desire (*de* for); **apetite** m appetizer; *fig.* incentive; **apetito** m
appetite (*a. eccl.*); *esp. fig.* relish;
abrir el ~ whet one's appetite;
apetitoso appetizing; inviting,
tasty; *p.* fond of delicate fare.
apiadar [1a] move to pity; *víctima*
= ~se *de* take pity on.
apicarado *niño* spoilt, naughty;
apicararse [1a] go to the bad.
ápice m apex; *fig.* whit, iota; *estar
en los* ~*s de* be well up in.
apicultor m, -a f bee-keeper;
apicultura f bee-keeping, api-
culture.
apilar(se) [1a] pile up, heap up.
apiñado jammed, packed, congested (*de* with); *barrio* overcrowded; **apiñadura** f, **apiñamiento** m congestion; squeeze,
squash, jam; **apiñar** [1a] squeeze
(together); bunch (*or* herd) together *en grupo*; overcrowd *en
barrio*; ~se (*gente*) crowd together;
(*esp. cosas*) be squashed (*or*
jammed) together.
apio m celery.
apiolar [1a] F (*prender*) nab;
(*matar*) do away with, bump off.
apiparse [1a] F guzzle.
apisonadora f road-roller, steam-
roller; **apisonar** [1a] roll; tamp,
ram *con pisón*.
apitonar [1a] *v/t. huevo* crack,
break through; *v/i.* sprout, begin
to show; ~se F have words, have a
slanging match.
aplacar [1g] appease, placate; calm
down.
aplanamiento m smoothing *etc.*;
aplanar [1a] smooth, level, roll
flat, make even; F knock out, bowl
over; ~se △ collapse; F lose heart.
aplastante overwhelming, crushing;
aplastar [1a] squash, flatten (out);
fig. leave *s.o.* speechless, flatten;
S.Am. tire out.
aplaudir [3a] applaud, cheer;
aplauso m applause; ~s *pl.* applause, cheering, clapping; *fig.*
acclaim.
aplazamiento m postponement *etc.*;
aplazar [1f] postpone, defer, put
off; *sesión* hold over, adjourn; *cita*
set a time *etc.* for; (*convocar*) summon, convene.

aplebeyar [1a] degrade, demean;
~se lower o.s., demean o.s.
aplicabilidad f applicability; **aplicable** applicable; **aplicación** f
application (*a. ⚙*); (*asiduidad*) industry, studiousness; **aplicar** [1g]
mst apply (*a* to); *manos, color etc.*
lay (*sobre* on); *hombres etc.* assign
(*a, para* to); *delito* impute; *bienes*
adjudge; *p.* enter, put in (*a profesión*
for); ~se *algo* claim for o.s.; ~ *a*
apply to, be applicable to; *estudio
etc.* apply o.s. to, give one's mind to.
aplomar [1a] △ plumb; make perpendicular; ~se collapse, fall to the
ground; **aplomo** m *fig.* seriousness,
gravity; (*seguridad*) nonchalance,
aplomb, self-possession; (*atrevimiento*) coolness.
apocado (*de poco ánimo*) spiritless;
spineless; (*tímido*) diffident; (*vil*)
common, mean.
apocalíptico apocalyptic; *estilo* obscure, enigmatic; F frightening.
apocamiento m spinelessness *etc.*;
apocar [1g] make smaller, reduce;
fig. limit; (*despreciar*) belittle, run
down; humiliate; ~se humble o.s.
apócrifo apocryphal.
apodar [1a] nickname, dub; label.
apoderado m agent, representative;
⚖ proxy; **apoderar** [1a] authorize,
empower; ⚖ grant power of attorney to; ~se *de* (*asir*) seize, take hold
of; *fig.* get hold of, take possession
of.
apodo m nickname; label.
apogeo m *ast.* apogee; *fig.* peak,
summit, zenith.
apolilladura f moth-hole; **apolillado** moth-eaten; **apolillarse** [1a]
get moth-eaten.
apologética f apologetics; **apología**
f defence; encomium, eulogy; **apologista** m/f apologist.
apoltronado idling, lazy; **apoltro-
narse** [1a] get lazy; loaf around.
apoplejía f stroke, apoplexy; **apo-
pléctico** apoplectic.
aporcar [1g] earth up.
aporrar [1a] F be unable to say a
word, dry up; ~se F become a bore
(*or* nuisance).
aporreado *vida* poor, wretched;
p. rascally; **aporrear** [1a] beat,
club; beat up; *mesa, teclas etc.*
thump (on), pound (on); *fig.* bother, pester; ~se slave away, be

always at it; **aporreo** *m* beating (-up).

aportación *f* contribution; ~es *pl. de la mujer* dowry; **aportar** [1a] *v/t.* bring; contribute; *(aducir)* bring forward; ꬳ bring as a dowry; *v/i.* reach port; F come out at an unexpected place; **aporte** *m S.Am.* contribution.

aportillar [1a] *muralla* breach; *(romper)* break down, break open; ~se fall, collapse.

aposentar(se) [1a] lodge, put up; **aposento** *m* room; *(hospedaje)* lodging. [session of.}
aposesionarse [1a]: ~ *de* take pos-}
aposición *f* apposition.

apósito *m* ꬳ (external) application; *(cataplasma)* poultice.

aposta(damente) purposely; **apostadero** *m* station, stand; ⚓ naval station; **apostar**[1] [1a] ꭗ post, station.

apostar[2] [1m] *v/t. dinero* lay, wager, stake *(a* on); *v/i.* bet *(a, por* on; *a que* that); *v/i., ~se compete (con* with), be rivals; ~*las a,* ~*las con* compete with *(en punto a* for, in).

apostasía *f* apostasy; **apóstata** *m/f* apostate; **apostatar** [1a] *eccl.* apostatize *(de* from); *fig.* change sides.

apostema *f* abscess.

apostilla *f* note, comment; **apostillar** [1a] annotate.

apóstol *m* apostle; **apostólicamente** F unostentatiously; **apostólico** apostolic.

apostrofar [1a] apostrophize; insult; *(reconvenir)* rebuke; **apóstrofe** *m or f* apostrophe; taunt, insult; rebuke, expostulation; **apóstrofo** *m gr.* apostrophe.

apostura *f* gracefulness; neatness.

apoteósico *éxito etc.* huge, tremendous; **apoteosis** *f* apotheosis *(a. fig.).*

apoyador *m* support, bracket, clamp; **apoyapié** *m* foot-rest; **apoyar** [1a] *v/t. codo etc.* lean, rest *(en, sobre* on); ⚠ *etc.* support, hold up; *fig. (respaldar)* support, back; *(ayudar)* aid, stand by; *b.s.* abet; *(confirmar)* support, bear out; *v/i.,* ~*se en base* rest on; *edificio* abut on; *bastón* lean on; *p.* rely on; *argumento* rest on; *datos* base o.s. on; **apoyo** *m* support *(a. fig.); fig.* backing, help; approval; favour.

apreciable appreciable, considerable; *(tasable)* measurable; *fig.* worthy, estimable; **apreciación** *f* appreciation, appraisal; ⳙ valuation; **apreciar** [1b] value, assess *(en* at; *a. fig.); esp. fig.* estimate; *música etc.* appreciate; *(tener en mucho)* esteem, value *(por* for); ~ *en mucho* set great value on; **aprecio** *m* appreciation, appraisal; esteem; *tener en gran* ~ esteem; **apreciativo** of appraisal *etc.*

aprehender [2a] *criminal* apprehend; *bienes* seize; *fig.* perceive; **aprehensión** *f* capture; seizure; *fig.* perception.

apremiador, apremiante *mandato* urgent; *razón* pressing, compelling; **apremiar** [1b] *(obligar)* compel, force; *(instar)* urge on, press; *(dar prisa a)* hurry; *(oprimir)* oppress; *el tiempo apremia* time presses; **apremio** *m* compulsion *etc.;* ⳙ writ, judgement; summons; *por* ~ *de tiempo* because of pressure of time.

aprender [2a] learn *(a inf.* to *inf.).*

aprendiz *m,* -a *f* apprentice *(de* to); *(principiante)* learner; *poner de* ~ apprentice *(con p.* to); **aprendizaje** *m* apprenticeship; F *pagar su* ~ learn the hard way.

aprensar [1a] *uvas* crush, press; *fig.* oppress, crush; *(angustiar)* distress.

aprensión *f* apprehension, fear, worry; *(infundada)* strange notion; **aprensivo** apprehensive, worried; timid; ꬳ hypochondriac.

apresador *m,* -a *f* captor; **apresamiento** *m* capture *etc.;* **apresar** [1a] *p.* capture, take prisoner; ꬳ seize; *(asir)* seize, grasp.

aprestado ready; ~ *para inf.* calculated to *inf.;* **aprestar** [1a] prepare, make *(or* get) ready; *paint.* prime; *tela* size; ~se prepare, get ready *(para inf.* to *inf.);* ~ *para la lucha* gird o.s. for the fray; **apresto** *m (acto)* preparation; *(equipo)* kit, outfit; *paint.* priming; size; sizing.

apresuración *f* haste(ning); **apresurado** hasty, hurried, quick; **apresuramiento** *m* haste(ning); **apresurar** [1a] hurry (up, along); hustle *sin ceremonia; paso etc.* speed up, accelerate; ~se hasten, make haste *(a, en, por inf.* to *inf.).*

apretadamente hard, tight(ly); **apretadera** f strap, rope; ~s pl. F pressure; **apretado** vestido etc. tight; lugar (pequeño) cramped; (lleno) chock-a-block; dense, thick; escritura close, cramped; lance etc. tight, difficult, dangerous; F stingy, tight(-fisted); ~ de dinero short of money; **apretador** m ⊕ wedge; **apretar** [1k] **1.** v/t. tuerca etc. tighten; lío etc. squeeze; contenido pack in, pack tight; p. hug, squeeze (a to; entre brazos in); mano clasp, grip; (saludo) shake; puño clench; dientes set, grit; botón press; (vestido) be tight for, be small on; (zapato) pinch; fig. disciplina tighten up; afflict; (angustiar) distress (a. ✠); (acosar) harass (a. ✗), pester (por for); ✗ ataque intensify; **2.** v/i. (vestido) be tight; (zapato) pinch; (empeorar) get worse; insist; ~ a correr break into a run; ~ con enemigo close with; ¡aprieta! stuff and nonsense!; **3.** ~se (estrecharse) (get) narrow; (ps.) squeeze up, huddle together; fig. be distressed etc.

apretón m squeeze, pressure; (abrazo) hug; (ahogo) distress; F dash, run; ~ de manos handshake; estar en un ~ be in a quandary; **apretujar** [1a] F squeeze etc. hard; p. hug; sandwich entre dos cosas; **apretujón** m F (hard) squeeze; hug; crush, squash de gente; **apretura** f = apretujón; fig. distress; **aprieto** m crush, jam, squeeze; fig. (apuro) fix, quandary; (aflicción) distress; estar en un ~ be in a hole, be in trouble; poner en un ~ put in a fix.

aprisa quickly, hurriedly.

aprisco m sheep-fold.

aprisionar (encarcelar) imprison; shackle, fetter (a. fig.).

aprobación f approval etc.; **aprobado 1.** approved; worthy, excellent; **2.** m univ. etc. pass (mark); **aprobar** [1m] v/t. approve (de as); endorse; consent to; examen, estudiante, parl. pass; v/i. univ. pass; **aprobatorio** approving, of approval.

aproches m/pl. ✗ approaches.

aprontamiento m quick service, quick dispatch; **aprontar** [1a] get ready quickly; dinero hand over without delay.

apropiación f adaptation etc.; **apropiado** appropriate (a, para to), suitable (a, para for); **apropiar** [1b] adapt, fit (a to); apply (a caso, p. to); (dar) give, bequeath; ~se algo appropriate.

apropincuarse [1d] co. approach.

aprovechable available; useful; **aprovechado** (frugal) thrifty; (ingenioso) resourceful; (aplicado) industrious; tiempo well-spent; **aprovechamiento** m use etc.; (ventaja) profit, advantage; (adelanto) improvement, progress; **aprovechar** [1a] v/t. (explotar) make (good) use of, use; oferta etc. take advantage of; enseñanza etc. profit by; ocasión seize, avail o.s. of; posibilidades make the most of; v/i. be of use; progress, improve (en in); ~ a p. be of use to, profit; ~ poco be of little avail; ¡que aproveche! hoping that those eating will enjoy their meal; ~se de = v/t.

aproximación f approach; (efecto) nearness, closeness; ⅄ etc. approximation; (lotería) consolation prize; **aproximado** approximate; near, rough; **aproximar** [1a] bring near(er), draw up (a to); ~se come near(er), approach; ~ a near, approach; fig. approximate to; **aproximativo** approximate, near.

aptitud f (idoneidad) suitability (para for); (capacidad) aptitude, ability; **apto** suitable, fit (para su. for); ~ a inf., ~ para inf. quick to inf.; ~ para inf. suitable for ger.

apuesta f bet, wager.

apuesto neat, spruce; esp. iro. dapper, natty.

apuntación f note; ♪ notation; **apuntado** pointed, sharp; ⚠ pointed, Gothic; **apuntador** m thea. prompter.

apuntalamiento m underpinning; **apuntalar** [1a] prop (up), shore (up), underpin; ⊕ strut.

apuntamiento m (apunte) note; ✗ aiming; ⚜ judicial report; **apuntar** [1a] **1.** v/t. fusil aim (a at), train (a on); blanco aim at; (señalar) point out; (tomar nota) note (down), take a note of; tantos score; partida enter; herramienta sharpen; (remendar) patch; (zurcir) darn; naipes: stake, put up; thea. prompt; ~ que point out that; **2.** v/i. (bozo etc.)

begin to show; (*día*) dawn; F ~ *y no dar* fail to keep one's word; **3.** ~**se** turn sour; F get tight; **apunte** *m* note; jotting; (*partida*) entry; (*dibujo*) sketch; *thea.* (*p.*) prompt, prompter; (*libro*) prompt-book; *naipes*: stake; *sacar* ~**s** take notes.

apuñalar [1a] stab, knife; *v. mirada*.

apuñar [1a] seize (in one's fist); **apuñ(et)ear** [1a] punch, pummel.

apuradamente F precisely; **apurado** (*pobre*) needy, hard up; (*difícil*) hard, dangerous; exact; **apurar** [1a] *líquido*, *vaso* drain; *surtido* exhaust, finish, use up; (*llevar a cabo*) carry out, finish; ⊕ refine, purify; (*averiguar*) verify, check (on); (*molestar*) annoy; (*apremiar*) hurry, press; ~**se** fret, worry, upset o.s. (*por over*); *S.Am.* hurry; ~ *por inf.* strive to *inf.*; **apuro** *m* (*a.* ~**s** *pl.*) hardship, need, distress; (*aprieto*) difficulty, fix; *estar en el mayor* ~, *verse en* ~**s** be in trouble; be up against it; *pasar* ~**s** suffer hardship; *sacar de* ~ get *s.o.* out of a jam.

aquejar [1a] (*molestar*) worry, harass; (*afligir*) distress; (*fatigar*) weary.

aquel, aquella *adj.* that; *aquellos, aquellas pl.* those.

aquél, aquélla *pron.* that (one); (*el anterior*) the former; *aquéllos, aquéllas pl.* those; (*los anteriores*) the former; **aquél** *m* F charm; (*sex*)-appeal, it F.

aquello *pron.* that.

aquí here; ~ *dentro* in here; ~ *mismo* right here, on this very spot; *de* ~ from here; (*tiempo*) from now; *de* ~ *a 8 días* in a week's time, within a week; *de* ~ *en adelante* from now on; *de* ~ *para allá* to and fro; *de* ~ *que* hence; *hasta* ~ so far, as far as here; (*tiempo*) up till now; *por* ~ this way; *por* ~ (*cerca*) hereabouts, round here.

aquiescencia *f* acquiescence.

aquietar [1a] quieten (down), calm; pacify; *temores* allay.

aquilatar [1a] *metall.* assay; *fig.* weigh up, test, value.

aquilón *m* north wind.

ara *f* altar; (*piedra*) altar stone; *en* ~**s** *de* in honour of.

árabe 1. Arab(ic); ⚠ Moresque; **2.** *m/f* Arab; **3.** *m* (*idioma*) Arabic;

arabesco 1. Arab(ic); **2.** *m* ⚠ arabesque; **arábigo 1.** Arab(ic); **2.** *m* Arabic; F *está en* ~ it's Greek to me; *hablar en* ~ talk double Dutch; **arabista** *m/f* Arabist.

arable arable.

arácnido *m* arachnid.

arada *f* (day's) ploughing; (*terreno*) ploughed land; **arado** *m* plough; (*reja*) (plough)share; **arador** *m* ploughman.

aragonés *adj. a. su. m*, -**a** *f* Aragonese.

arambel *m* tatter, shred.

arana *f* trick, swindle; (*mentira*) lie.

arancel *m* tariff, duty; ~ *protector* protective tariff; **arancelario** tariff *attr.*, customs *attr.*

arándano *m* bilberry, whortleberry; ~ *agrio* cranberry.

arandela *f* ⊕ washer; candle-stand *para vela*.

araña *f zo.* spider; (*a.* ~ *de luces*) chandelier; *fig.* sponger; *b.s.* sponger; **arañar** [1a] scratch; F scrape together; **arañazo** *m* scratch.

arar [1a] plough; till.

arbitrador *m*, -**a** *f* arbiter, arbitrator; **arbitraje** *m* arbitration; ✝ arbitrage (*de cambio* of exchange); **arbitram(i)ento** *m* arbitrament; **arbitrar** [1a] *deportes*: (*tenis*) umpire; (*fútbol, boxeo*) referee; ⚖ *etc.* arbitrate; *phls.* judge, determine freely; ~**se** get along, manage; **arbitrariedad** *f* arbitrariness; (*acto*) outrage, arbitrary act; ⚖ illegal act; **arbitrario** arbitrary; **arbitrio** *m* (*albedrío*) free-will; (*medio*) means, expedient; ⚖ adjudication; ~**s** *pl.* ✝ excise taxes; **arbitrista** *m/f* armchair politician; bright-eyed idealist; **árbitro** *m* arbiter, moderator; *deportes*: umpire, referee.

árbol *m* ♀ tree; ⊕ axle, shaft; ⚓ mast; ~ *frutal* fruit tree; ~ *genealógico* family tree, pedigree; ~ *de levas* camshaft; ~ *motor* drive; **arbolado 1.** *paisaje* wooded; *avenida* lined with trees; ⚓ having a mast; **2.** *m* woodland; **arboladura** *f* ⚓ masts and spars; **arbolar** [1a] *bandera* hoist; ⚓ mast; (*arrimar*) put up (*a against*); ~**se** rear up, get up on its hind legs; **arboleda** *f* grove, plantation; **arboledo** *m* woodland; **ar-**

bóreo zo. arboreal; *forma* tree-like;
arborescente arborescent; **arboricultura** f arboriculture.
arbotante m flying buttress.
arbusto m shrub.
arca f (*caja*) chest, coffer; ♪ hutch;
(*depósito*) tank, reservoir; ‿s pl.
safe, strong-room; ‿ de agua freq.
water-tower; ‿ de la alianza Ark
of the Covenant; ‿ de Noé Noah's
Ark.
arcada f arch(es) de puente; ⚠ series of arches, arcade; ✻ retching.
arcadio adj. a. su. m, a f Arcadian.
arcaduz m pipe, conduit; (*cangilón*)
bucket; *fig.* ways and means.
arcaico archaic; **arcaísmo** m
archaism; **arcaizante** archaic; p.,
estilo given to archaisms.
arcano 1. secret, enigmatic, recondite; **2.** m mystery, (great) secret.
arcángel m archangel.
arcar [1g] = arquear ⚠, ⊕.
arce m maple (tree).
arcediano m archdeacon.
arcén m border, edge; ⚠ curb.
arcilla f clay; ‿ de alfarería, ‿ figulina potter's clay, argil; **arcilloso**
clay(ey); argillaceous ▥.
arcipreste m archpriest.
arco m ⚠, anat. arch; ♪, ✦ arc;
✗ (long)bow; ♪ bow; hoop de
barril etc.; ✦ (luz) spotlight; ‿ de
herradura Moorish arch; ‿ iris rainbow; ‿ ojival pointed arch; ‿ triunfal triumphal arch; ‿ voltaico arc-
lamp.
arcón m bin, bunker.
archidiácono m archdeacon.
archiducado m archduchy; **archiduque** m archduke; **archiduquesa**
f archduchess.   [aire.)
archimillonario m multimillion-)
archipámpano m F co. Lord Muck.
archipiélago m archipelago; F
labyrinth de calles etc.
archivador m (p.) filing-clerk;
(*mueble*) filing-cabinet; **archivar**
[1a] file (away); store away; deposit
in the archives; F hide away; **archivero** m, a f filing-clerk en oficina;
▥ archivist, keeper; registrar;
archivo m archives; registry; ≈
Nacional Record Office; ‿s pl. ✦
etc. files; ▥, hist. muniments,
records.
ardentía f ✻ heartburn; ⚓ phosphorescence.

arder [2a] burn (a. fig.); (resplandecer) glow, blaze; fig. (espada etc.)
flash; ‿ de, ‿ en amor etc. burn with;
‿ en guerra be ablaze with; ‿ sin
llamas smoulder; ‿se burn up,
burn away; ♀ be parched.
ardid m ruse, device, scheme; ‿es pl.
wiles.
ardiente burning (a. fig.); (radiante)
glowing, blazing; color bright, glowing; flor bright red; fiebre, deseo etc.
burning; interés keen, lively; partidario passionate, ardent.
ardilla f squirrel; F andar como una
‿ be always on the go.
ardimiento m burning; fig. courage, dash.
ardite: F no me importa un ‿ I don't
care a hang; F no vale un ‿ it's not
worth a brass farthing.
ardor m heat, warmth; fig. (celo)
ardour, eagerness; heat de disputa
etc.; (valor) courage, dash; ‿ de
estómago heartburn; **ardoroso**
burning, fiery; fig. enthusiastic;
lively, vigorous.
arduo arduous, hard, tough, strenuous.
área f area (a. ⚐); (medida) are;
‿ de castigo penalty area; ‿ de
meta goal area.
arena f sand; grit; (circo) arena; ‿s
pl. ✻ stones, gravel; ‿ movediza
quicksand; ‿s pl. de oro fine gold;
arenal m sandy ground, sands;
(cantero) sandpit; ⚓ quicksand;
arenar [1a] (sprinkle with) sand;
⊕ polish (or rub) with sand.
arenga f harangue (a. F); **arengar**
[1h] harangue.
arenillas f/pl. ✻ gravel.
arenisca f sandstone; grit; **arenisco** sandy; gravelly, gritty; **arenoso** sandy, sand attr.
arenque m herring; ‿ ahumado
kipper.
arete m earring.
argadijo m ⊕ reel, bobbin; F busybody.
argado m prank, trick.
argalia f catheter.
argamandijo m F set (of tools etc.).
argamasa f ⚠ mortar; plaster.
árgana f ⊕ crane.
argelino adj. a. su. m, a f Algerian.
argén m argent; **argentado** silvery;
⊕ silvered; **argentar** [1a] silver
(a. ⊕, fig.); **argénteo** silver(y)

(*a. fig.*); ⊕ silver-plated; **argentería** *f* silver (*or* gold) embroidery (*or* filigree); **argentino**[1] silvery.

argentino[2] *adj. a. su. m*, **a** *f* Argentinian.

argento *m poet.* silver; ~ *vivo* quicksilver.

argolla *f* (large) ring; knocker *de puerta*; *deportes*: croquet.

argonauta *m* Argonaut (*a. zo.*).

argot *m* slang.

argucia *f* sophistry, hair-splitting.

argüir [3g] *v/t.* argue; indicate, point to; impute (*a* to); accuse (*de* of); *v/i.* argue (*contra* against, with); **argumentación** *f* argumentation; (line of) argument; **argumentador** argumentative; **argumentar** [1a] argue; **argumento** *m* argument; line of argument, reasoning; *thea. etc.* plot.

aria *f* aria.

aridecer [2d] *v/t.* make arid; *v/i.*, ~se become arid (*or* dry); **aridez** *f* aridity, dryness (*a. fig.*); **árido 1.** arid, dry (*a. fig.*); **2.** ~s *m/pl.* dry goods (*esp.* ✗).

ariete *m* battering ram.

arillo *m* earring.

ario *adj. a. su. m*, **a** *f* Aryan, Indo-European.

arisco (*displicente*) fractious, cross; (*áspero*) surly; (*huraño*) shy, unsociable; *caballo* vicious.

arista *f* ♀ beard; *mount.* arête; A edge; △ arris; △ ~ *de encuentro* groin.

aristocracia *f* aristocracy (*a. fig.*); **aristócrata** *m/f* aristocrat; **aristocrático** aristocratic.

aristón *m* △ edge, corner.

aritmética *f* arithmetic; **aritmético 1.** arithmetical; **2.** *m* arithmetician.

arlequín *m fig.* buffoon; **arlequinada** *f* (piece of) buffoonery; tomfoolery; **arlequinesco** *fig.* ridiculous, grotesque.

arma *f* arm, weapon; ~s *pl.* arms (*a. heráldica*); ~ *arrojadiza* missile; ~ *atómica* atomic weapon; ~ *blanca* steel (blade); ~s *pl. cortas* small-arms; ~ *de fuego* firearm, gun; ~ *de infantería* infantry arm; ¡~s al hombro! slope arms!, shoulder arms!; *alzarse en* ~s rise up in arms; ¡*descansen* ~s! order arms!; *estar sobre las* ~s stand by; *pasar por las*

~s shoot; *tocar* (*al*) ~ (sound the) call to arms; *tomar las* ~s take up arms.

armada *f* fleet; navy; *la* ♀ *Invencible* the Armada (*1588*).

armadijo *m* trap, snare.

armadillo *m* armadillo.

armado ⊕ reinforced; **armador** *m* shipowner; (*corsario*) privateer; **armadura** *f* ✗ (suit of) armour; ⊕ *etc.* frame(work); ✗ armature; *anat.* skeleton; ♪ key signature; **armamento** *m* ✗ (*acto*) arming; (*conjunto*) armament(s); ⚓ equipment, fitting-out.

armar [1a] *p. etc.* arm (*de, con* with; *a. fig.*); *arma* load; ⊕ *etc.* mount, assemble, put together; △ set (*sobre cimientos* on; *a. fig.*); ⚓ equip, fit out; *hormigón* reinforce; *tienda* pitch, set up; *trampa* set; *fig.* prepare, arrange; *jaleo etc.* stir up, start; *caballero* dub, knight; *pleito* bring; F ~*la* raise the very devil, start a row; ~*se* arm o.s. (*de* with; *a. fig.*); *fig.* get ready; *S.Am.* put money in one's pocket.

armario *m* cupboard; (*ropa*) wardrobe; ~ (*para libros*) book-case.

armatoste *m contp.* hulk; *esp.* ⊕ contraption; *mot.* crock, grid; F fat old thing.

armazón *f* frame(work); body; ✗ chassis; △ *etc.* shell, skeleton; frame, carcass *de mueble*.

armella *f* eye-bolt, screw-eye.

armenio *adj. a. su. m*, **a** f Armenian.

armería *f* museum of arms; ✗ armoury; (*tienda*) gun-shop; **armero** *m* gunsmith, armourer; (*estante*) gun-rack.

armiño *m zo.* stoat; (*piel, heráldica*) ermine.

armisticio *m* armistice.

armón *m* ✗ limber.

armonía *f* harmony (*a. fig.*); *en* ~ in harmony (*con* with); **armónica** *f* harmonica; ~ (*de boca*) mouth-organ, harmonica; **armónico 1.** ♪ harmonic; *sonido* harmonious; **2.** *m* harmonic, overtone; **armonio** *m* harmonium; **armonioso** harmonious (*a. fig.*); *melodía* tuneful; **armonizar** [1f] *v/t.* harmonize, bring into harmony (*a. fig.*); *diferencias* reconcile; *v/i.* harmonize (*con* with); (*colores etc.*) go together; tone (*con* in with).

arnés *m* ✂ armour; ~es *pl.* harness; *fig.* gear, outfit.
árnica *f* arnica.
aro *m* hoop, ring; ~ de émbolo piston-ring; F entrar por el ~ have no option.
aroma *m* aroma, fragrance; bouquet de vino; **aromático** aromatic; **aromatizar** [1f] give fragrance to; *líquido* spice, flavour (with herbs).
arpa *f* harp.
arpado toothed, jagged; *poet.* sweet-singing.
arpar [1a] scratch, claw (at); (*romper*) tear up, tear to pieces.
arpeo *m* grapnel, grappling-iron.
arpía *f* harpy; *fig.* (*regañona*) termagant, shrew; (*flaca*) bag of bones.
arpillera *f* sacking, sackcloth.
arpista *m/f* harpist.
arpón *m* gaff, harpoon; **arpon(e)ar** [1a] harpoon.
arquear [1a] *v/t.* ⚓ arch; ⊕ *lana* beat; ⚓ gauge; *v/i.* F retch; ~se arch; (*superficie*) camber; **arqueo** *m* arching; ⚓ tonnage, burden; ✝ checking (of contents).
arqueología *f* archaeology; **arqueólogo** *m* archaeologist.
arquería *f* arcade; **arquero** *m* archer, bowman; ✝ cashier.
arquetipo *m* archetype.
arquimesa *f* desk, escritoire.
arquitecto *m* architect; ~ de jardines landscape-gardener; **arquitectónico** architectural, architectonic; **arquitectura** *f* architecture.
arrabal *m* suburb; ~es *pl.* outskirts, outlying area; **arrabalero 1.** suburban; F common, ill-bred; **2.** *m*, a *f* suburbanite; F common sort.
arracada *f* earring (with pendant).
arracimado clustered, clustering; **arracimarse** [1a] cluster (or bunch) together.
arraigado (firmly) rooted; *fig.* ingrained; ✝ property-owning; **arraigar** [1h] *v/t.* establish, strengthen (en fe etc. in); *v/i.* ⚘ root, take root (a. fig.), strike root; *v/i.*, ~se (*p.*) become a property-owner, settle en lugar; *fig.* establish a hold; ~ en p. (*costumbre*) grow on; **arraigo** *m* hold (a. fig.); ✝ property, real estate; ⚘ de fácil ~ easily-rooted.

arrancada *f* sudden start; quick acceleration; **arrancadero** *m* starting-point; **arrancado** F on the rocks, broke; (*malo*) terrible; **arrancador** *m* *mot.* starter; **arrancamiento** *m* pulling out *etc.*;
arrancar [1g] **1.** *v/t.* & *etc.* pull up, root out; (*arrebatar*) snatch away (a, de from); *página, botón etc.* tear off; *espada etc.* wrest, wrench (a from); *motor* start; *fig. victoria* snatch, wrest; *apoyo* win, get; *promesa etc.* force out (a of) con fuerza, wangle out (a of) con astucia; *p.* tear away (de vicio from); *suspiro* fetch, utter; **2.** *v/i. mot. etc.* start; pull away (*salir*) start out; F get away (de from); *fig.* ~ de arise from, spring from (a. ⚠).
arranchar [1a] *costa* skirt, sail close to; *velas* brace; *S.Am.* snatch away, snaffle; ~se gather together; (*comer*) mess together.
arranque *m* (*sudden*) start, jerk; ⚠, *anat.* starting-point; *fig.* impulse; (*ira*) fit, outburst; (*ingenio*) sally; ~ (*automático*) (self-)starter. [per.\
arrapiezo *m* rag; F whipper-snap-/
arras *f/pl.* deposit, pledge; *13 coins given by bridegroom to bride.*
arrasar [1a] *v/t.* raze, demolish; (*allanar*) level, flatten; *vasija* fill to the brim; *v/i. meteor.* clear (up); ~se en lágrimas (*ojos*) fill with tears.
arrastradizo dangling, trailing; *fig.* maltreated; **arrastrado 1.** F poor, wretched; (*bribón*) rascally; **2.** *m* rascal; **arrastrar** [1a] *v/t.* drag (along), pull, haul; (*hacer bajar*) drag down (a. fig.); *falda etc.* trail; *palabras* drawl; *afecto* draw (tras to); *público* win over, carry; *v/i.*, ~se (*reptar*) crawl, creep; (*p.*) drag o.s. along; (*colgar*) drag, trail, touch the ground; ⚘ trail; (*horas, obra*) drag; (*humillarse*) grovel, creep; **arrastre** *m* drag(ging) *etc.*; (*transporte*) haulage; *natación:* crawl; ~ de espaldas back-stroke.
arrayán *m* myrtle.
¡arre! gee up!, get up!
arreador *m* foreman; *S.Am.* whip; **arrear** [1a] *v/t.* urge on; (*enjaezar*) harness; *v/i.* F hurry along; F ¡arrea! get a move on!; (*sorpresa*) get along with you!

arrebañaduras *f/pl.* scrapings, remains; **arrebañar** [1a] scrape together; (*comer*) eat up, clear up.

arrebatadizo excitable; hot-tempered, irascible; **arrebatado** *movimiento* sudden, violent; (*impetuoso*) rash, reckless; (*absorto*) rapt; *cara* flushed; **arrebatamiento** *m* snatching *etc.*; *fig.* fury; ecstasy; **arrebatar** [1a] (*quitar*) snatch (away) (*a* from); (*con fuerza*) wrench, wrest (*a* from); (*llevarse*) carry away (*or* off); *parte* rip off; *fig.* captivate; *público* move, stir; ♀ parch; ~se get carried away (*en* by); *cocina:* burn; **arrebatiña** *f* = *rebatiña;* **arrebato** *m* fury; ecstasy, rapture.

arrebol *m* red, glow *de cielo;* (*afeite*) rouge; **arrebolar** [1a] redden; ~se redden, flush; (*maquillarse*) rouge.

arrebozar [1f] = *rebozar.*

arrebujar [1a] jumble up; (*cubrir*) wrap up, cover; ~se wrap (*o.s.*) up (*con* with, in).

arreciar [1b] grow worse, get more severe; ~se ♂ get stronger, pick up.

arrecife *m* causeway; ♧ reef; ~ *de coral* coral reef.

arrechucho *m* F fit, outburst; ✗ (queer) turn.

arredrar [1a] drive back; *fig.* scare, daunt; ~se draw back, move away (*de* from), shrink (*ante* at, before); *fig.* get scared (*sin* ~ nothing daunted.

arregazado *falda etc.* tucked up; *nariz* turned up; **arregazar** [1f] tuck up.

arreglado regulated, (well-)ordered; *fig.* moderate; *vida* of moderation, orderly; **arreglar** [1a] arrange, order, regulate; adjust (*a* to); (*componer*) put in order, put straight; ⊕ fix, repair; *aspecto, pelo, cuarto etc.* tidy up; *disputa* settle, make up; *cita, detalles* arrange, fix up; ~se come to terms (*a, con* with; *a.* ✝); F ~*las* get by; manage (*para inf.* to *inf.*); *todo se arreglará* it will be all right, things will work out; **arreglo** *m* arrangement *etc.;* settlement; (*regla*) rule, order; (*acuerdo*) agreement; ♩ setting; *con* ~ *a* in accordance with; *vivir con* ~ live quietly.

arregostarse [1a]: F ~ *a* take a fancy to; **arregosto** *m* F fancy, taste (*de* for).

arrellenarse [1a] lounge, sprawl; *fig.* be happy in one's work.

arremangado *nariz* turned up, retroussé; **arremangar** [1h] turn up, roll up; *falda etc.* tuck up; ~se roll up one's sleeves *etc.;* *fig.* take a firm stand.

arremeter [2a] *v/t. caballo* spur on; *v/i.* rush forth, attack; *fig.* (*vista*) offend; ~ *a,* ~ *con*(*tra*) attack, rush at; *fenc.* lunge at; **arremetida** *f,* **arremetimiento** *m* attack; lunge *con arma;* (*impetu*) (on)rush; (*empujón*) push.

arremolinarse [1a] (*gente*) crowd around; (*agua*) swirl; (*polvo etc.*) whirl.

arrendable rentable; *casa* to let; **arrendador** *m,* **-a** *f* (*dueño*) lessor; (*inquilino*) tenant.

arrendajo *m* jay.

arrendamiento *m* (*acto*) letting *etc.;* (*precio*) rent(al); (*documento*) contract; *contrato de* ~ lease; *tomar en* ~ rent; **arrendar**[1] [1k] (*dueño*): *casa* let, lease; *máquina etc.* hire out; (*inquilino etc.*): *casa* rent, lease; *máquina etc.* hire.

arrendar[2] [1k] tie, tether.

arrendatario *m,* **a** *f* tenant, lessee; leaseholder; hirer.

arreo *m* adornment; ~*s pl.* harness, trappings; (*equipo*) gear.

arrepentido 1. sorry, regretful (*de* for); (*a. eccl.*) repentant; **2.** *m,* **a** *f* penitent; **arrepentimiento** *m* repentance; regret; **arrepentirse** [3i] repent (*de* of); ~ *de* regret.

arrequives *m/pl.* F best clothes; trimmings, buttons and bows; *fig.* circumstances.

arrestado bold, daring; **arrestar** [1a] arrest, take into custody; ~se *a* rush boldly into; **arresto** *m* arrest; (*reclusión*) imprisonment; ✗ detention; *fig.* boldness, daring.

arriada *f* flood; **arriarse** [1c] flood, become flooded.

arriar [1c] *vela etc.* lower, haul down; *cable* slacken; F let go.

arriate *m* ✍ bed, border; trellis *de madera;* (*camino*) road.

arriba a) *situación:* above; on top; upstairs *en casa;* (*movimiento*) up, upwards; upstairs *en casa;* b) *de la cintura* (*para*) ~ from the waist up;

de 5 libras para ~ from 5 pounds upwards; *de* ~ *abajo* from top to bottom; from beginning to end; *por la calle* ~ up the street; *desde* ~ from (up) above; *hacia* ~ up(wards); *más* ~ higher up; further up; c) ~ *de prp.* above; further up than; d) *attr.: de* ~ upper; *la parte de* ~ the upper part; *los de* ~ those above; those on top; ⊕ *de* ~ overhead; *lo* ~ *escrito* what we have said above; e) *int.* ¡~! up you get!; ¡~ *España!* Spain for ever!

arribada *f* ⚓ arrival; ~ *forzosa* ⚓ emergency call (*or* stop); **arribar** [1a] ⚓ put into port; arrive; (*noticia*) come to hand; F 🦅, ✝ recover; ~ *a inf.* manage to *inf.*; **arribeño** *m*, a *f S.Am.* highlander; inlander; **arribista** *m/f* parvenu, upstart; **arribo** *m* arrival.

arriendo *m* = *arrendamiento*.

arriero *m* muleteer.

arriesgado risky, dangerous, hazardous; *p.* bold, daring; **arriesgar** [1h] *vida etc.* risk, endanger; *conjetura* hazard; *posibilidades* jeopardize; *dinero* stake; ~se take a risk, expose o.s. to danger; ~ *a inf.* risk *ger.*; ~ *en empresa* venture upon.

arrimadero *m* support; **arrimadizo** *fig.* **1.** parasitic, sycophantic; **2.** *m*, a *f* toady, sycophant; **arrimado** *imitación* close; **arrimar** [1a] (*acercar*) move up, bring close (*a* to); *escala etc.* lean (*a* against); *carga* stow; *golpe etc.* give; (*quitar*) move out of the way; (*arrinconar*) put away; *p.* push aside; (*deshacerse de*) get rid of; (*abandonar*) lay aside; ~se come close(r) *etc.*; (*unirse*) join together; ~ *a* come close to (*a. fig.*); lean on; (*afectuoso*) cuddle (*or* snuggle) up to; *fig.* seek the protection of; **arrimo** *m* support (*a. fig.*);(*afición*) attachment;**arrimón** *m* loafer; sponger; F *estar de* ~ hang (*or* loaf) around.

arrinconado *fig.* forgotten, neglected; **arrinconar** [1a] *fig.* lay aside, put away; (*deshacerse de*) get rid of; *p.* push aside; *asunto* shelve; *enemigo* corner; ~se withdraw from the world. [resolute; agile.]

arriscado *geog.* craggy; *fig.* bold,⌉ **arriscar** [1g] risk; ~se take a risk;⌋ (*engreírse*) grow conceited.

arrivista = *arribista*.

arroba *f measure of weight* = *11.502 kg.*; *variable liquid measure*.

arrobamiento *m* ecstasy, rapture; tránce; **arrobar** [1a] entrance; ~se go into ecstasies; (*espiritista*) go into a trance.

arrodillado kneeling, on one's knees; **arrodillarse** [1a] kneel (down), go down on one's knees.

arrogancia *f* arrogance; pride; **arrogante** arrogant; brave.

arrogarse [1h] *algo* arrogate to o.s.

arrojadizo: *v. arma;* **arrojado** *fig.* daring, dashing; **arrojallamas** *m* flamethrower; **arrojar** [1a] throw; (*con fuerza*) fling, hurl; *deportes: pelota* bowl, pitch; *pesa* put; *pesca:* cast; *humo* emit, give out; *flores* put out; 🦅, ✝ yield, produce; *fig.* ~ *de sí* cast from one, fling aside; ~se throw o.s. (*a* into, *por* out of); *fig.* rush, fling o.s., plunge (*a, en* into); **arrojo** *m* daring, dash.

arrollador *fig.* sweeping, overwhelming; devastating; **arrollar** [1a] (*enrollar*) roll (up); *esp.* ⊕, ⚡ coil, wind; (*agua etc.*) sweep away; *enemigo* throw back, rout; *mot.* knock down; *fig. p.* dumbfound, leave speechless.

arromar [1a] blunt, dull.

arropar [1a] wrap (up); tuck up *en cama;* ~se wrap up; tuck o.s. up.

arrope *m* syrup.

arrostrar [1a] *v/t.* face (up to), brave; *v/i.:* ~ *a* show a liking for; ~ *con,* ~ *por* = *v/t.;* ~se throw o.s. into battle.

arroyada *f* gully; (*crecida etc.*) flood; **arroyo** *m* stream, brook, watercourse; gutter *en calle;* F *poner en el* ~ put out of the house.

arroz *m* rice; ~ *con leche* rice pudding; F ~ *y gallo muerto* lots to eat, slap-up meal.

arruga *f* wrinkle, line; crease, fold; **arrugado** wrinkled, lined; creased, crinkly; **arrugar** [1h] *cara* wrinkle, line; *ropa* crease, pucker; (*ajar*) crumple; *papel* crease; *entrecejo* knit, pucker up; ~se get wrinkled *etc.;* ♀ shrivel up.

arruinamiento *m* ruin(ation); **arruinar** [1a] ruin (*a.* ✝, *fig.*), destroy; demolish; *esperanzas* wreck, blight; ~se ⚠ fall into ruins, fall down; ✝ be ruined; *fig.* go to rack rand ruin

arrullar [1a] v/t. niño lull to sleep; F say sweet nothings to; v/i. coo; ~se bill and coo (a. F); **arrullo** m cooing; ♪ lullaby.

arrumaje m ⚓ stowage; **arrumar** [1a] stow.

arrumbar[1] [1a] put aside, put on one side, forget; p. silence en conversación.

arrumbar[2] [1a] ⚓ take one's bearings; ~se ⚓ get seasick.

arrurruz m arrowroot.

arsenal m ⚓ (naval) dockyard, shipyard; ✕ arsenal; fig. storehouse, mine.

arsénico 1. arsenical; **2.** m arsenic.

arte m a. f art; (maña) trick, cunning; (habilidad) knack; (hechura) workmanship; ~ griego Greek art; ~ mecánica mechanical skill; ~ de vivir art of living; no tener ~ ni parte en have nothing to do with; ~s mst f/pl. univ. arts; bellas ~ fine arts; ~ liberales liberal arts; malas ~ trickery, guile; ~ y oficios arts and crafts; **artefacto** m ⊕ appliance, contrivance; esp. arqueología: artefact; F mot. old crock.

artejo m knuckle, joint.

artería f cunning, artfulness.

arteria f artery (a. fig.); ⚡ feeder; **arterial** arterial; **arteriosclerosis** f arteriosclerosis.

artero cunning, artful.

artesa f (kneading-)trough; ✕ ~ oscilante cradle.

artesanía f handicraft, skill; (arte, hechura) craftsmanship; **artesano** m craftsman, artisan.

artesiano: pozo ~ Artesian well.

artesón m kitchen tub; △ panel; mou**l**ding de techo; coffer; **artesonado** m panelling; stuccoed (or plaster) ceiling; coffered ceiling; **artesonar** [1a] mould, stucco; panel.

ártico arctic.

articulación f anat., ⊕ joint; gr. etc. articulation; ~ esférica ball-and-socket joint; ~ universal universal joint; **articulado** anat., ⊕ articulated, jointed; **articular** [1a] articulate; ⊕ join (together, up); 𝓰𝓻 etc. article; **articulista** m/f article writer, contributor (to paper); **artículo** m article (a. gr., 𝓰𝓻, ✝); anat. articulation, joint; entry en libro de consulta; ~s pl. de

consumo consumer goods; ~ de fondo leader, leading article, editorial; eccl. ~ de la muerte point of death; ~s pl. de primera necesidad basic commodities; ~ suelto oddment.

artífice m/f artist, craftsman; maker; fig. architect; **artificial** artificial; b.s. imitation attr.; **artificio** m (arte) art, skill; (hechura) workmanship, craftsmanship; ⊕ contrivance, appliance; fig. artifice; b.s. (piece of) double-dealing; **artificioso** artistic, fine, skilful; fig. cunning, artful; **artilugio** m contp. ⊕ gadget; (treta) gimmick; (que no se nombra) thingummy.

artillería f artillery; cannon (pl.); **artillero** m ✕ artilleryman; ✕, 🏹, ⚓ gunner.

artimaña f trap; fig. cunning.

artista m/f artist; thea. etc. artiste; ~ de cine film actor (f actress); **artístico** artistic.

artrítico arthritic; **artritis** f arthritis.

arveja f vetch.

arzobispado m archbishopric; **arzobispal** archiepiscopal; **arzobispo** m archbishop.

arzón m saddle-tree.

as m ace; one en dado; fig. ace, wizard.

asa[1] f handle; fig. handle, pretext; F ser muy del ~ be well in.

asa[2] f ⚕ juice.

asado 1. roast(ed); bien ~ well done; poco ~ underdone; **2.** m roast (meat); **asador** m spit, broach; (máquina) roasting jack; **asaduras** f/pl. entrails, offal; F tiene ~ he's as lazy as they come.

asaetear [1a] hit (with an arrow); fig. bother, pester.

asalariado 1. paid; wage-earning; **2.** m, a f wage-earner.

asaltar [1a] fortaleza etc. storm, rush; p. fall on, attack; fig. (duda) assail; (pensamiento) cross one's mind; (muerte etc.) overtake; **asalto** m attack, assault; fenc., boxeo: round; por ~ by storm.

asamblea f assembly; ✕ llamar a ~ assemble, muster.

asar [1a] roast; fig. pester, plague (con with); ~se fig. (a. ~ vivo) be boiling hot, be nearly roasted.

asaz † *a. lit.* very, exceedingly; enough.

asbesto *m* asbestos.

ascendencia *f* ancestry, line; **ascendente** ascending; upward; *carrera, plumada, tren* up...; *marea* incoming; **ascender** [2g] *v/t.* promote, raise (*a* to); *v/i.* (*subir*) go up, ascend; (*en rango*) be promoted, move up; ♱ boom; ⚥ ∼ *a* amount to, add up to; **ascendiente 1.** = *ascendente*; **2.** *m/f* ancestor; **3.** *m* ascendancy, influence (*sobre* over).

ascensión *f* ascent; *eccl.* ascension; *fig.* = *ascenso*; *eccl. Día de la ♀* Ascension Day; **ascensional** *ast.* ascendant, rising; *movimiento* upward; **ascensionista** *m/f* balloonist; **ascenso** *m* promotion, rise; grade; **ascensor** *m* lift, elevator *Am.*; ⊕ elevator; **ascensorista** *m/f* lift-attendant.

asceta *m/f* ascetic; **ascético** ascetic; **ascetismo** *m* asceticism.

asco *m* loathing, disgust, revulsion; (*cosa*) abomination, disgusting thing; *coger* ∼ *a* get sick of; *dar* ∼ *a* sicken, disgust; *me da* ∼ *el queso* I loathe cheese; F *estar hecho un* ∼ be filthy; *hacer* ∼s *de* turn up one's nose at.

ascua *f* live coal, ember; *¡*∼*s!* ouch!; F *arrimar el* ∼ *a su sardina* know which side one's bread is buttered; make the most of one's opportunity; F *estar en* ∼s be on tenterhooks; F *sacar el* ∼ *con la mano del gato* get s.o. else to do the dirty work.

aseado clean, neat, tidy, trim; **asear** [1a] adorn, embellish; (*limpiar*) tidy up; ∼*se* tidy (o.s.) up.

asechanza *f* trap, snare (*a. fig.*); **asechar** [1a] waylay, ambush; *fig.* set a trap for.

asediador *m* besieger; **asediar** [1b] besiege; *fig.* pester; (*amor*) chase, set one's cap at; **asedio** *m* siege; ♱ run (*de* on).

asegurado *m*, **a** *f* insured, insurant; **asegurador** *m* fastener; (*p.*) insurer, underwriter; **asegurar** [1a] (*fijar*) secure, fasten; *cimientos etc.* make firm; *fig.* guarantee, assure; affirm (*que* that); ♱ insure (*contra* against); *sitio* make secure (*contra ataque* against); *derechos etc.* safeguard; *se lo aseguro* I assure (*or* promise) you; *le aseguré de mi fide-* lidad I assured him of my loyalty; ∼*se* make o.s. secure (*de peligro* from); ∼ *de hechos* make sure of.

asemejar [1a] *v/t.* make alike; *fig.* liken (*a* to); ∼*se* be alike; ∼ *a* be like, resemble.

asendereado *camino* beaten, well trodden; *vida* wretched, of drudgery; **asenderear** [1a] chase up hill and down dale.

asenso *m* assent; *dar* ∼ *a* give credence to.

asentada *f* sitting; *de una* ∼ at one sitting; **asentaderas** *f/pl.* F behind, bottom; **asentado** *fig.* established, settled; **asentador** *m* ⚒ stonemason; (*suavizador*) strop; **asentar** [1k] **1.** *v/t. p.* seat, sit *s.o.* down; *cosa* place; fix; *tienda* pitch; *cimientos* make firm; *ciudad* found; *tierra* level, tamp down; *golpe* fetch; *cuchillo* sharpen; *fig.* establish, consolidate; (*anotar*) enter, set down; *principio* lay down; ⚖ award; *impresión* fix in the mind; (*conjeturar*) suppose; **2.** *v/i.* be suitable, suit; **3.** ∼*se* seat o.s.; *fig.* establish o.s.; (⚒, *líquido*) settle.

asentir [3i] assent; ∼ *a* consent to; *petición* grant; *arreglo* accept; *verdad* give in to.

asentista *m* contractor; supplier.

aseo *m* tidiness; cleanliness; *cuarto de* ∼, ∼s *pl. euph.* cloakroom, toilet.

aséptico aseptic; free from infection.

asequible obtainable, available; *fin* attainable.

aserradero *m* sawmill; **aserrador** *m* sawyer; **aserradura** *f* saw-cut; ∼*s pl.* sawdust; **aserrar** [1k] saw (up).

aserto *m* assertion.

asesina *f* murderess; **asesinar** [1a] murder; *pol. etc.* assassinate; *fig.* plague (to death); **asesinato** *m* murder; *pol.* assassination; ∼ *legal* judicial murder; **asesino 1.** murderous; **2.** *m* murderer, killer; *pol. etc.* assassin; *fig.* thug, cut-throat.

asesor *m*, **-a** *f* adviser; consultant; **asesorar** [1a] advise; act as a consultant to; ∼*se* seek (*or* take) advice (*con, de* from); consult; ∼ *de situación* take stock of; **asesoría** *f* (task of) advising; (*honorarios*) adviser's fee.

asestar [1a] (*apuntar*) aim (*a* at); *arma* shoot, fire; *golpe* deal, strike; *fig.* try to hurt.

aseveración *f* assertion, contention;
aseveradamente positively; **ase-**
verar [1a] assert, asseverate.

asexual asexual.

asfaltado *m* asphalting; asphalt
(pavement *etc.*); **asfaltar** [1a]
asphalt; **asfalto** *m* asphalt.

asfixia *f* asphyxia ⏚; suffocation,
asphyxiation; **asfixiador, asfi-**
xiante asphyxiating, suffocating;
gas poison *attr.*; **asfixiar** [1b]
asphyxiate; suffocate; ⚒ gas; **~se**
be asphyxiated, suffocate.

asgo *v. asir.*

así 1. *adv.* a) so, in this way, thus;
thereby; F ~ ~ not too bad, middling; ~ *pues* and so, so then; o ~
or so; ~ *que* ~ anyway; F ~ *que así*
it makes no odds; ~ *es que* and so
(it is that); ¡~ *sea!* so be it!; b) *comp.*
etc.: ~ *como* (in the same way) as;
as well as; ~ *A como B* both A and B;
~ *adj. que* so *adj.* that; ~ *de grande*
so big, as big as that; **2.** *adj.*: *un*
hombre ~ such a man, a man like
that; ~ *es la vida* such is life; **3.** *cj.*:
~ *como,* ~ *que as* soon as.

asiático 1. Asian, Asiatic; **2.** *m,* a *f*
Asian.

asidero *m* hold(er), handle; *fig.*
handle, pretext.

asiduo 1. assiduous; frequent, regular, persistent; **2.** *m,* a *f* habitué,
regular.

asiento *m* seat, place; site *de pueblo*
etc.; ⚖ settling; (*fondo*) bottom;
sediment; (*partida*) entry; ⚓ trim;
seat(ing) *de válvula; fig.* stability;
(*cordura*) wisdom, judgement; ~s *pl.*
buttocks; *tome Vd.* ~ take a seat.

asignación *f* assignment *etc.*; ✝
allowance, salary; **asignar** [1a]
assign, apportion; *premio* award;
tarea set; *causas* determine; **asig-**
natura *f univ.* course, subject.

asilado *m,* a *f* inmate.

asilo *m eccl. a. pol.* asylum; *fig.*
shelter, refuge; home *de viejos;*
poor-house, workhouse *de pobres;*
~ *de huérfanos* orphanage; ~ *para*
locos lunatic asylum.

asimilación *f* assimilation; **asimi-**
lar [1a] assimilate; = *asemejar(se).*

asimismo likewise, in like manner.

asir [3a; *present like salir*] *v/t.* seize,
grasp (*con* with, *de* by); *pie etc.*
catch, get caught (*en* in); *v. brazo;*
v/i. ⚘ take root; **~se a,** ~ *de* take

hold of, seize (*a. fig.*); ~ *con* grapple
with.

asirio Assyrian.

asistencia *f* attendance (*a.* ⚛),
presence (*a at*); (*ayuda*) help;
(domestic) help; ⚛ nursing; ~s *pl.*
allowance, maintenance; ~ *médica*
medical attendance; ~ *social* welfare (work); **asistenta** *f* assistant;
(*criada*) charwoman, daily help;
asistente *m* assistant; ⚒ orderly,
batman; ~s *pl.* people present, those
present; **asistir** [3a] *v/t.* help, aid;
rey etc. attend, accompany; ⚛ attend; *v/i.* attend (*a acc.*), be present
(*a* at); *escena freq.* be a witness of.

asma *f* asthma; **asmático** *adj. a. su.*
m, a *f* asthmatic.

asna *f* she-ass; **asnada** *f* silly thing;
asnal asinine (*a. fig.*); F beastly;
asnería *f* silly thing; **asno** *m*
donkey, ass (*a. fig.*); F fathead.

asociación *f* association; society;
✝ partnership; **asociado 1.** asso-
ciate(d); **2.** *m,* a *f* associate, partner; **asociar** [1b] associate (*a, con*
with); *esfuerzos etc.* pool, put together; *categoría etc.* bracket (*con*
with); *socio* take into partnership;
~se associate with; team up, join forces
(*con* with); ✝ become partners,
enter into partnership.

asol(an)ar [1a] 𝄐 dry up, parch.

asolar [1m] destroy, raze (to the
ground), lay waste; **~se** (*líquido*)
settle.

asolear [1a] put (*or* keep) in the sun;
~se sun o.s., bask; (*tostarse*) get
sunburnt.

asomada *f* brief appearance; surprise view; **asomar** [1a] *v/t.* show,
put out, stick out (*a, por* at,
through); (*falda etc.*) let *s.t.* show;
v/i. begin to show, appear; loom
up *en niebla etc.*; **~se** show, stick
out; (*costa etc.*) loom up; ~ *a,* ~ *por*
show o.s. at, lean (*or* hang) out of;
F get merry.

asombradizo easily alarmed; **asom-**
brador = *asombroso;* **asombrar**
[1a] shade, cast a shadow on; *color*
darken; *fig.* (*asustar*) frighten;
(*admirar*) amaze, astonish; **~se** be
amazed (*de* at); be shocked; ~ *de*
inf. be surprised to *inf.*; **asombro**
m fear, fright; surprise, astonishment; F spook; **asombroso** amazing, astonishing.

asomo *m* appearance; sign, indication; hint, trace; *ni por* ～ by no] **asonada** *f* mob, rabble. [means.]

asonancia *f* assonance; *fig.* no tener ～ *con* bear no relation to; **asonantar** [1a] assonate (*con* with); **asonante 1.** assonant; **2.** *f* assonance; **asonar** [1m] assonate.

asordar [1a] deafen.

aspa *f* cross (X); △ cross-piece; sail *de molino*; ⊕ reel, winding-frame; **aspado** F trussed up (*en* in); **aspar** [1a] ⊕ wind, reel; F vex, annoy; ～**se** writhe; F go all out (*por* for).

aspaventero 1. fussy; excitable, emotional; **2.** *m*, *a f* fussy *etc.* person; **aspaviento** *m* fuss.

aspecto *m* aspect; look(s), appearance *de p. etc.*; aspect, side *de problema*; *a(l) primer* ～ at first sight; *bajo ese* ～ from that point of view.

aspereza *f* roughness *etc.* (*v. áspero*).

asperges *m* F sprinkling; *quedarse* ～ come away empty-handed.

asperillo *m* sourness; bitterness.

asperjar [1a] sprinkle (*eccl.* with holy water).

áspero rough *al tacto*; *filo* jagged; *terreno* rough; *país* rugged; tart, sour, bitter *al gusto*; *voz* harsh, rasping; *clima* hard; *trato* surly, gruff; *genio* sour, surly; **asperón** *m* sandstone; ⊕ grindstone.

aspersión *f* sprinkling; ✗ spraying.

áspid *m* asp.

aspillera *f* loophole, embrasure.

aspiración *f* breath; inhalation; *phonet.* aspiration; ♪ short pause; ⊕ air intake; **aspirada** *f* aspirate; **aspirado** aspirate; **aspirador 1.** ⊕ suction *attr.*; **2.** *m* ～ *de polvo* = **aspiradora** *f* vacuum cleaner; **aspirante 1.** ⊕ suction *attr.*; **2.** *m/f* applicant, candidate (*a* for); **aspirar** [1a] *v/t.* breathe in, inhale; *phonet.* aspirate; ⊕ suck in; *v/i.* aspire (*a* to; *a inf.* to *inf.*).

aspirina *f* aspirin.

asquear [1a] *v/t.* loathe; *v/i.* feel loathing, feel disgust; **asqueroso** loathsome, disgusting, nasty; sickening; F lousy, awful; *p.* (*delicado*) squeamish.

asta *f* shaft *de lanza etc.*; (*lanza*) spear, lance; flag-staff *de bandera*; (*mango*) handle; *zo.* horn; *a media* ～ at half-mast.

ástaco *m* crayfish.

astado 1. horned; **2.** *m* bull.

aster *m* aster.

asterisco *m* asterisk.

astigmático astigmatic; **astigmatismo** *m* astigmatism.

astil *m* handle; shaft *de saeta*; beam *de balanza*.

astilla *f* splinter, chip; *hacer(se)* ～**s** = **astillar(se)** [1a] splinter, chip; ～**se** F be (full to) bursting; **astillero** *m* shipyard, dockyard.

astracán 1. F grotesque; **2.** *m* astrakhan.

astrágalo *m* △, ✗ astragal; △ beading; *anat.* talus, astragalus.

astral of the stars, astral.

astreñir [3h *a.* 3i] = **astringir**; **astringente 1.** astringent, binding; **2.** *m* astringent, binding medicine; **astringir** [3c] *anat.* contract; ✗ bind; *fig.* bind, compel.

astro *m* star (*a. cine*), heavenly body; F beauty; **astrología** *f* astrology; **astrológico** astrological; **astrólogo 1.** astrological; **2.** *m* astrologer; **astronauta** *m* astronaut; **astronave** *f* space-ship; **astronomía** *f* astronomy; **astronómico** astronomical (*a. fig.*); **astrónomo** *m* astronomer.

astroso dirty, untidy, shabby; (*desgraciado*) unfortunate; (*vil*) contemptible.

astucia *f* astuteness *etc.*; (*una* ～) trick, piece of trickery.

asturiano *adj. a. su. m*, *a f* Asturian.

astuto astute, shrewd, smart; *b.s.* crafty, cunning.

asueto *m* (*a. día de* ～) day off, holiday; (*tarde*) afternoon off.

asumir [3a] assume, take on; *actitud* strike.

asunción *f* assumption; *eccl.* ♀ Assumption.

asunto *m* matter, thing; (*negocio*) business, affair; (*tema*) subject; ～ *concluido* that's an end of the matter; ～**s** *pl.* exteriores foreign affairs; *Ministerio de* ♀**s** *Exteriores* Foreign Office, State Department *Am.*

asurar [1a] burn; ✝ parch; *fig.* worry.

asustadizo easily frightened; jumpy, panicky F; *caballo* skittish; **asustar** [1a] frighten, scare; startle, alarm;

~se be frightened *etc.* (*con, de, por* of, at).

atabal *m* kettledrum; **atabalear** [1a] (*caballo*) stamp; drum *con dedos*.

atacable attackable; **atacado** F dithery; (*tacaño*) mean, stingy; **atacador 1.** *m*, -a *f* attacker; **2.** *m* ✗ ramrod; **atacadura** *f* fastening, fastener; **atacar** [1g] (*embestir*) attack (*a.* ♠, ✗, *fig.*); corner, press hard *en discusión*; (*atar*) fasten, button, do up; ✗, *cañón* ram, tamp; *costal etc.* stuff, pack.

ataderas *f/pl.* F garters; **atadero** *m* (*cuerda*) rope, cord; (*parte*) place for tying; (*broche etc.*) fastening; (*anillo*) ring; F eso no tiene ~ you can't make head or tail of it; **atadijo** *m* F loose bundle; **atado 1.** *fig.* timid, shy, inhibited; **2.** *m* bundle; (*manojo*) bunch; **atadora** *f* ✔ binder; **atadura** *f* (*acto*) fastening *etc.*; (*cuerda*) string, cord; ⚓ lashing; ✔ tether; *fig.* bond, tie.

atafagar [1h] suffocate, overcome; *fig.* pester the life out of.

ataguía *f* coffer-dam, caisson.

atajar [1a] *v/t.* stop, intercept; head off; *deportes:* tackle; △ partition off; *escrito* cross off; *discusión* cut short; *discurso* interrupt; (*terminar*) call a halt to, put a stop to; *v/i.* take a short cut; *mot.* cut corners; ~se be abashed; (*nervioso*) be all of a dither F; **atajo** *m* short cut (*a. fig.*); *deportes:* tackle; echar por el ~ *fig.* get out of it, get out quick.

atalaya 1. *f* watch-tower; *fig.* height, vantage-point; **2.** *m* lookout, sentinel; **atalayador** *m*, -a *f* look-out; *fig.* snooper, spy; **atalayar** [1a] watch (over), guard; *p.* spy on.

atañer [2f; *defective*]: ~ a concern; en lo que atañe a with regard to; no me atañe it's no concern of mine.

ataque *m* attack (*a, contra* on; ✗ de of; *a. fig.*); ✗ *a.* raid; ~ al corazón, ~ cardíaco heart-attack; ✗ ~ fulminante stroke, seizure.

atar [1a] tie (up), fasten; ✔ tether; *fig.* paralyse, root to the spot; F ~ corto a keep a close watch on; F no ~ ni desatar talk nonsense; get nowhere; ~se *fig.* get stuck (*en dificultades* in); ~ a opinión stick to.

atardecer 1. [2d] get dark, get late; **2.** *m* late afternoon, evening ; al ~ at dusk.

atareado very busy; **atarear** [1a] give a job to, assign a task to; ~se be very busy (*con, en* with); ~ a *inf.* be very busy *ger.*

atarjea *f* sewage pipe, culvert.

atarugar [1h] (*asegurar*) fasten, wedge, peg; *agujero* plug, stop; (*llenar*) stuff, fill (*de* with); F shut *s.o.* up; ~se F swallow the wrong way, choke.

atascadero *m* mire, bog; *fig.* stumbling-block; difficulties; **atascar** [1g] *agujero* plug, stop; *tubo* obstruct (*a. fig.*), clog (up); ~se ⊕ *etc.* clog, get stopped up; get stuck, get bogged down (*en fango* in; *a. fig.*); (*coches*) get into a jam; (*motor*) stall; get stuck *en discurso*; **atasco** *m* obstruction; *mot. etc.* jam.

ataujía *f* ⊕ damascene (work), damask.

ataviar [1c] (*adornar*) deck, array; (*vestir*) dress up, get up (*con, de* in); **atavío** *m* (*a.* ~s *pl.*) dress, finery; get-up, rig-out F.

atavismo *m* atavism.

ataxia *f* ataxy.

atediante boring, tiresome; **atediar** [1b] bore, tire.

ateísmo *m* atheism; **ateísta** atheistic(al).

atelaje *m* team; (*arreos*) harness.

atemorizar [1f] scare, frighten; ~se get scared (*de, por* at).

atemperar [1a] moderate, temper; adjust, accommodate (*a* to).

atención *f* attention; (*cortesía*) a. civility; ¡~! attention!; (*aviso*) look out!; (*en paquete*) with care; ~es *pl.* attentions; duties, responsibilities; en ~ a in view of; llamar la ~ attract *s.o.'s* attention; llamar la ~ sobre draw *s.o.'s* attention to; prestar ~ listen (*a* to); pay attention (*a* to); **atender** [2g] *v/t.* attend to, pay attention to; ✗ look after; *consejo, voz* heed; ⊕ service; *v/i.:* ~ a = *v/t.*; *detalles etc.* take note of; *necesidad etc.* see about, see to; ~ por answer to the name of.

atenerse [2l]: ~ a verdad stand by, hold to; *regla* abide by, go by; *fuerzas etc.* rely on.

atentado 1. prudent, cautious; **2.** *m* illegal act, offence; assault (*contra* on), attempt (*a, contra vida* on);

(*terrorista etc.*) outrage; **atentar** [1a] *v/t. acto* do illegally; *crimen* attempt; *v/i.*: ~ *a*, ~ *contra* make an attempt on.

atento attentive (*a* to), observant (*a* of); mindful (*a pormenor* of); (*cortés*) polite, thoughtful, kind; ~ *a prp.* in view of; ✝ *su* ~*a carta* your esteemed letter; *atentamente le saluda* yours faithfully.

atenuación *f* attenuation; 🏛️ extenuation; **atenuante:** 🏛️ *circunstancias* ~*s* extenuating circumstances; **atenuar** [1e] attenuate; *delito* extenuate; *importancia* minimize; ~*se* weaken.

ateo 1. atheistic(al); **2.** *m, a f* atheist.

aterciopelado velvety, velvet *attr.*

aterido numb, stiff with cold; **aterirse** [3a; *defective*] get stiff with cold.

aterrada *f* ⚓ landfall.

aterrador frightening, terrifying.

aterraje *m* ✈️ landing.

aterrar[1] [1k] *v/t.* demolish, destroy; cover with earth; *v/i.* ⚓ land; ~*se* ⚓ stand inshore; *navegar aterrado* sail inshore.

aterrar[2] [1a] terrify, fill with terror; ~*se* be terrified (*de* at); panic.

aterrizaje *m* ✈️ landing; ~ *forzoso* forced landing; ~ *a vientre* pancake landing; ~ *violento* crash landing; **aterrizar** [1f] ✈️ land.

aterronarse [1a] get lumpy; (*tierra*) cake.

aterrorizar [1f] terrify; *pol. etc.* terrorize. [possess.]

atesorar [1a] hoard (up); *virtudes*)

atestación *f* attestation; **atestado** *m* 🏛️ affidavit, statement.

atestado[1] (*terco*) stubborn.

atestado[3] *p.p.* cram-full (*de* of), packed (*de* with); **atestar**[1] [1k] pack, stuff, cram (*de* with); *cuba* fill up; F stuff (*de comida* with).

atestar[2] [1a] attest, testify to.

atestiguación *f* deposition; attestation; **atestiguar** [1i] testify to, attest; bear witness to.

atezado tanned, swarthy; black; **atezar** [1f] blacken; ~*se* get tanned.

atiborrar [1a] stuff (*de* with); ~*se* stuff (*o.s.*) (*de* with), gorge (*de* on).

ático 1. Attic; **2.** *m* 🏛️ attic.

atiesar [1a] stiffen; (*apretar*) tighten (up); ~*se* get stiff, stiffen (up) *etc.*; ⚒️ *etc.* bind.

atigrado 1. striped; *gato* tabby; **2.** *m* tabby (cat).

atildado neat, spruce, stylish; **atildar** [1a] *typ.* put a tilde over; *fig.* criticize, find fault with; (*asear*) clean (up), put right; ~*se* titivate, spruce *o.s.* up.

atinado (*discreto*) wise; *juicio* keen; *dicho* pertinent; **atinar** [1a] *v/t.* find, hit on; *v/i.* guess (right); be right, do the right thing; ~ *a blanco* hit; ~ *a*, ~ *con*, ~ *en solución etc.* hit on, guess (right); ~ *a inf.* manage to *inf.*

atiparse [1a] F stuff *o.s.*, guzzle.

atiplado treble; **atiplarse** [1a] speak with a high (*or* squeaky) voice.

atisbadero *m* peep-hole; **atisbador** *m*, -a *f* watcher, spy; **atisbar** [1a] spy on, watch; peep at *por agujero etc.*; **atisbo** *m* watching, spying; *fig.* slight sign, inkling, glimmerings.

atizador *m* poker; ⊕ feed(er); ~ *de la guerra* warmonger; **atizar** [1f] (*remover*) poke, stir; stoke *con combustible*; *vela* snuff; *fig.* rouse, stir up; F *puntapié* give; ¡*atiza!* gosh!

atizonar [1a] ⚘ blight, smut.

atlas *m* atlas.

atleta *m/f* athlete; *fig.* giant; **atlético** athletic(al); *deportes* ~*s* = **atletismo** *m* athletics.

atmósfera *f* atmosphere; *fig.* sphere (of influence); feeling *hacia una p.*; *radio: mala* ~ atmospherics; **atmosférico** atmospheric.

atocinado F fat, well-upholstered; **atocinar** [1a] *puerco* cut up; *carne* cure; F do in, cut up; ~*se* F (*irritarse*) get het up; (*enamorarse*) get it bad.

atolón *m* atoll.

atolondrado thoughtless, reckless; **atolondramiento** *m* bewilderment; amazement; thoughtlessness; **atolondrar** [1a] stun, bewilder, amaze.

atolladero *m* mire, muddy spot; F *estar en un* ~ be in a hole; **atollarse** [1a] stick in the mud; *fig.* get into a hole.

atómico atomic; **atomizador** *m* atomizer; (scent-)spray; **átomo** *m* atom (*a. fig.*); *fig.* tiny particle, speck; spark *de vida*.

atonal atonal; **atonalidad** *f* atonality, serial music; **atonía** *f* atony; **atónico** atonic.

atónito thunderstruck (*con, de, por* by); aghast (*con, de, por* at).

átono atonic, unstressed.

atontado dim(-witted), muddleheaded; **atontar** [1a] bewilder, confuse.

atorar [1a] obstruct, stop up; **~se** choke, swallow the wrong way.

atormentador *m*, **-a** *f* tormentor; **atormentar** [1a] torture (*a. fig.*); *fig.* torment; plague; (*aliciente*) tantalize.

atornillar [1a] (*poner*) screw on; (*apretar*) screw up; *dos cosas* screw together.

atortolar [1a] F (*acobardar*) rattle; (*aturdir*) flabbergast.

atortujar [1a] squeeze flat.

atosigar [1h] poison; *fig.* harass, plague; put the pressure on.

atrabancar [1g] rush; **~se** be in a fix.

atrabiliario *fig.* difficult, moody, morose; **atrabilis** *f fig.* difficult temperament, bad temper.

atracadero *m* berth, wharf; **atracador** *m* gangster, hold-up man; **atracar** [1g] *v/t.* ♻ bring alongside, tie up; *p.* hold up, waylay; F stuff; *v/i.* come alongside, tie up; **~ al muelle** berth, dock; **~se** F stuff (*o.s.*) (*de* with), overeat.

atracción *f* attraction; attractiveness, appeal *de p.*; (*diversión*) amusement; **~es** *pl. thea.* entertainment; (*cabaret*) floor show; **~ sexual** sex appeal.

atraco *m* hold-up; **atracón** *m* F blow-out; *darse un* **~** make a pig of o.s. (*de* over).

atractivo 1. attractive; *fuerza f de atracción; fig.* charming, engaging, fetching F; **2.** *m = atracción*.

atraer [2p] attract; draw; *imaginación etc.* appeal to; *atención a.* engage; *dejarse* **~** *por* allow o.s. to be drawn to(wards).

atragantárse [1a] choke (*con* on), swallow the wrong way; F get all mixed up, lose the thread.

atramparse [1a] fall into a trap;

(*tubo*) clog; (*pestillo*) stick, catch; F get stuck, get into a hole.

atrancar [1g] *v/t. puerta* bar; *tubo* clog, stop up; *v/i.* F take big steps; skip a lot *leyendo*; **atranco** *m = atascadero*.

atrapar [1a] F nab, catch; *empleo etc.* get, land (*o.s.*); (*engañar*) take in.

atrás *ir* back(wards); *estar* behind; (*tiempo*) previously; *de* **~** back *attr.*; *desde muy* **~** a long time (ago); *días* **~** days ago; *hacia* **~** back, backwards; **atrasado** slow (*a. reloj*), late, behind (time); overdue; *país* backward; (*pobre*) poor, needy; **~** (*en los pagos*) behind, in arrears; **~** *de noticias* behind the times; **atrasar** [1a] *v/t.* slow up, slow down, retard; *reloj* put back; *v/i.* (*reloj*) lose; *mi reloj atrasa* (*10 minutos*) my watch is (10 minutes) slow; **~se** be behind; be slow, be late; ♻ be in arrears; **atraso** *m* slowness *de reloj*; (*demora*) time-lag, delay; backwardness *de país*; ♻ **~s** *pl.* arrears; **~s** *pl.* backlog *de pedidos etc.*; *salir del* **~** make up leeway.

atravesado (*ojo*) squinting, cross-eyed; *animal* mongrel, cross-bred; *fig.* wicked; **atravesar** [1k] (*cruzar*) go over, go across, cross (over); *madero etc.* lay across (*en la calle* the street); pierce (*con, de bala* with); *periodo etc.* go through; *dinero* bet, stake; *S.Am.* ♻ monopolize, corner; F *le tengo atravesado* I can't stand him; **~se** (*espina*) get stuck; *se me atraviesa X* I can't stand X; **~** *en conversación* butt into; *negocio ajeno* meddle in.

atrayente = *atractivo*.

atrenzo *m S.Am.* trouble, fix.

atreverse [2a] dare (*a inf.* to *inf.*); **~** *a empresa* (dare to) undertake; *competidor* compete with; **~** *con(tra)* be cheeky to; **atrevido** daring, bold; *b.s.* forward, impudent; **atrevimiento** *m* daring, boldness; (spirit of) adventure; *b.s.* impudence.

atribución *f* attribution; functions, powers *de cargo*; **atribuible** attributable; **atribuir** [3g]: **~** *a* attribute to, put *s.t.* down to; *funciones* assign to; **~se** assume, claim for o.s.

atribular(se) [1a] grieve.

atributivo attributive (*a. gr.*); **atributo** *m* attribute.

atrición *f eccl.* attrition.

atril *m eccl.* lectern; ♪ music-stand; ♪ rostrum *de director*; book-rest.

atrincherar [1a] entrench, fortify (with trenches); ～se entrench, dig in.   [*eccl., anat.*).

atrio *m* inner courtyard, atrium (*a.*)

atrocidad *f* atrocity, outrage; F (*dicho*) stupid remark; F ¡qué ～! how dreadful!

atrofia *f* atrophy; **atrofiar(se)** [1b] atrophy.

atronado reckless, thoughtless; **atronador** deafening; *aplausos* thunderous; **atronamiento** *m fig.* stunning; bewilderment; **atronar** [1m] deafen; *res* stun; *fig.* bewilder.

atropelladamente pell-mell, helter-skelter; **atropellado** hasty *en obrar*; brusque, abrupt *en hablar*; **atropellar** [1a] 1. *v/t.* (*pisar*) trample underfoot; (*derribar*) knock down (*a. mot.*); (*empujar*) push past; hustle *por puerta*; *héroe* mob; *trabajo* hurry through; *obligación* disregard; *oposición* ride roughshod over; (*injuriar*) insult, outrage; 2. *v/i.*: ～ *por* push one's way through; *fig.* disregard; 3. ～se act *etc.* hastily; **atropello** *m mot.* accident; *fig.* outrage, excess; disregard (de for).

atroz atrocious, outrageous; F terrific, huge.

atuendo *m* pomp, show; (*vestido*) rig(-out), attire.

atufar [1a] *fig.* anger, vex; ～se (*comida*) go smelly; (*vino*) turn sour; *fig.* get vexed (*con, de at*, with).

atún *m* tunny; F nitwit.

aturar [1a] F close (up) tight.

aturdido thoughtless, reckless; **aturdimiento** *m fig.* bewilderment *etc.*; **aturdir** [3a] stun, daze *con golpe*; (*vino etc.*) fuddle, stupefy; *fig.* (*desconcertar*) bewilder, perplex; (*pasmar*) stun, dumbfound; (*confundir*) confuse, fluster; ～se be stunned; get bewildered *etc.*

aturrullar [1a] F bewilder, perplex muddle.

atusar [1a] trim *con tijeras*; smooth *con mano*; comb *con peine*; ～se dress swankily.

audacia *f* boldness, audacity; **audaz** bold, audacious.

audible audible; **audición** *f* hearing; ♪ (*prueba*) audition; ♪ concert; **audiencia** *f* audience (con with, of); hearing (*a. 🜨*); 🜨 (*tribunal*) high court; **audífono** *m* hearing aid; **audiofrecuencia** *f* audiofrequency; **audión** *m* audion; **auditivo** 1. hearing *attr.*, auditory; 2. *m teleph.* earpiece, receiver; **auditor** *m* (*a.* ～ *de guerra*) judge-advocate; **auditorio** *m* (*ps.*) audience; (*sala*) auditorium.

auge *m* peak, summit, heyday; (*aumento*) increase; ✝ boom; *estar en* ～ thrive, be in its heyday; ✝ boom.

augurar [1a] (*cosa*) augur, portend; (*p.*) predict; **augurio** *m* augury, omen, portent; prediction; ～s *pl. fig.* best wishes.

augusto august; stately.

aula *f* classroom; *univ.* lecture-room.

aulaga *f* furze, gorse.

aullar [1a] howl; **aullido** *m*, **aúllo** *m* howl.

aumentador *m* ∉ booster; **aumentar** [1a] *v/t.* increase, add to, augment; enlarge (*a. phot.*); *opt.* magnify; *precio* increase, put up; ∮, *producción etc.* boost, step up; *v/i.*, ～se (be on the) increase; rise, go up; (*valor*) appreciate; **aumentativo** *gr.* augmentative; **aumento** *m* increase, rise; enlargement (*a. phot.*); *opt.* magnification; ✝ ～ (*en valor*) appreciation; *ir en* ～ (be on the) increase.

aun even; ～ (*siendo esto*) *así* even so; ～ *cuando* although; *ni* ～ not even.

aún still, yet; ～ *no ha venido* he still has not come, he has not come yet.

aunar [1a] join, unite; ～se join up, combine.

aunque although, even though; ～ *más* however much.

¡aúpa! up (you get)!; ¡～ *Madrid!* up Madrid!; F *de* ～ posh, swanky; **aupar** [1a] F help up; *pantalón* hitch up; *fig.* boost, praise up.

aura *f* (*gentle*) breeze; *fig.* popularity, popular favour.

áureo *poet.* golden; **aureola** *f*, **auréola** *f opt. a. eccl.* aureole; *opt. a. fig.* halo.

aurícula *f* auricle; **auricular**

1. auricular, of the ear, aural; 2. *m anat.* little finger; *teleph.* receiver, earpiece; ⁓es *pl.* earphones, headphones.

aurora *f* dawn (*a. fig.*); ⁓ *boreal,* ⁓ *polar* aurora borealis.

auscultar [1a] *⚕* sound.

ausencia *f* absence; **ausentarse** [1a] go away, absent o.s.; stay away; **ausente** 1. absent; missing (de from); away from home; 2. *m/f* absentee; ⚖ missing person.

auspiciar [1b] *S.Am.* support, foster; **auspicio** *m fig.* protection, patronage; *bajo los* ⁓s *de* under the auspices of.

austeridad *f* austerity *etc.*; **austero** austere; *p.* stern, severe; *sabor* harsh.

austral southern.

australiano *adj. a. su. m,* **a** *f* Australian. [Austrian.]

austríaco *adj. a. su. m,* **a** *f* |

austro *m* south wind.

autarquía *f* autarchy, self-sufficiency.

auténtica *f* certificate; authorized copy; **autenticar** [1a] authenticate; **autenticidad** *f* authenticity; **auténtico** authentic, genuine, real.

auto[1] *m* ⚖ edict, judicial decree; writ (*de ejecución* of execution); *thea. approx.* mystery play; ⁓s *pl.* ⚖ documents, proceedings; ⁓ *de fe* auto-da-fé; ⁓ *del nacimiento* nativity play; ⁓ *sacramental* eucharistic play; F *estar en* ⁓s be in the know; F *poner en* ⁓s put *s.o.* in the picture.

auto[2] *m mot.* car.

auto[3] ... self-..., auto...; ⁓**biografía** *f* autobiography; ⁓**biográfico** autobiographic(al); ⁓**biógrafo** *m,* **a** *f* autobiographer; ⁓**bombo** *m* self-advertisement; *hacer* ⁓ shoot a line; ⁓**bote** *m* motorboat; ⁓**bús** *m* (omni)bus; ⁓**car** *m* (motor-)coach.

autocracia *f* autocracy; **autócrata** *m/f* autocrat; **autocrático** autocratic.

autocrítica *f* self-examination, self-criticism.

autóctono autochthonous.

autodeterminación *f* self-determination; **autodidacta** self-educated, self-taught; **autódromo** *m* race-track; **autoexpresión** *f* self-expression; **autógena** *f* welding.

auto...: ⁓**giro** *m* autogiro; ⁓**gobierno** *m* self-government; ⁓**grafía** *f* autography; ⁓**gráfico** autographic; **autógrafo** *adj. a. su. m* autograph.

autómata *m* automaton (*a. fig.*), robot; *fig.* puppet; **automático** automatic; self-acting.

auto...: ⁓**matización** *f* automation; ⁓**motor** *m* Diesel train; ⁓**motriz** self-propelled; ⁓**móvil** 1. self-propelled; 2. *m* car, motorcar, automobile *Am.*; *ir en* ⁓ go by car, motor; ⁓**movilismo** *m* motoring; ⊕ car industry; ⁓**movilista** 1. (*a.* ⁓**movilístico**) motoring; car *attr.*, automobile *attr. Am.*; 2. *m/f* motorist.

autonomía *f* autonomy, home rule; ⚓, ✈ range; *de gran* ⁓ long-range; **autónomo** autonomous, independent.

autopista *f* motorway, motor-road, turnpike *Am.*

autopropulsado self-propelled.

autopsia *f* postmortem, autopsy.

autor *m,* **-a** *f* author, writer; perpetrator *de crimen;* creator, originator *de idea;* **autora** *f* authoress; **autoridad** *f* authority; *fig.* show, pomp; ⁓es *pl.* authorities; **autoritario** authoritarian; peremptory, dogmatic; **autorización** *f* authorization, licence (*para inf.* to *inf.*); **autorizado** authorized; official; **autorizar** [1f] authorize (*a inf.* to *inf.*); license; give (*or* lend) authority to.

autorretrato *m* self-portrait.

autorzuelo *m* scribbler, hack.

autoservicio *m* self-service restaurant.

autostop *m* hitch-hiking; *hacer* ⁓ hitch-hike.

auxiliar 1. auxiliary (*a. gr.*); subsidiary; 2. *m/f* assistant; 3. [1b] help, assist; **auxilio** *m* help, assistance; relief; ⁓ *social* social work; welfare (service); *primeros* ⁓s *pl.* first-aid.

avahar [1a] *v/t.* blow on; *v/i.,* ⁓**se** (give off) steam.

aval *m* endorsement.

avalancha *f* avalanche.

avalar [1a] † endorse (*a. fig.*); *p.* answer for.

avalent(on)ado arrogant, boastful.

avalorar [1a] = *valorar; fig.*

encourage; **avaluar** [1e] = *valorar*.

avance *m* advance (*a.* ✗); ✝ (*anticipo*) advance (payment), credit; balance; ⚡ lead; ⊕ feed; **avanzada** *f* ✗ outpost; (*tropa*) advance party; **avanzado** advanced (*de edad* in years); *fig.* advanced, avant-garde; *hora* late; **avanzar** [1f] *v/t.* advance (*a.* ✝), move on, move forward; *proposición* advance, put forward; *v/i.*, ~se advance (*a.* ✗); move on, push on; (*noche etc.*) advance, draw on; **avanzo** *m* ✝ balance(-sheet); (*presupuesto*) estimate.

avaricia *f* miserliness, avarice; greed(iness); **avaricioso, avariento** miserly, avaricious; **avaro 1.** miserly, mean; greedy; sparing, chary (*de alabanzas* of); *ser* ~ *de palabras* be a man of few words; **2.** *m*, a *f* miser.

avasallar [1a] subdue, enslave; ~se *fig.* submit, yield.

avatar *m* change, transformation.

ave *f* bird; ~ *can(t)ora* song-bird; ~ *de corral* chicken, fowl; *pl. a.* poultry; ~ *de paso* bird of passage (*a. fig.*), migrant; ~ *de rapiña* bird of prey; ~ *zancuda* wader.

avecin(d)arse [1a] take up one's residence, settle.

avechucho *m* F ragamuffin, ne'er-do-well.

avefría *f* lapwing.

avejentar(se) [1a] age (before one's time).

avejigar(se) [1h] blister.

avellana *f* hazel-nut; **avellanado** *color* hazel, nut-brown; *piel etc.* shrivelled, wizened; **avellanar 1.** *m* hazel wood; **2.** [1a] ⊕ countersink; ~se shrivel up; **avellanera** *f*, **avellano** *m* hazel.

avemaría *f* Ave Maria; *al* ~ at dusk; F *en un* ~ in a twinkling; F *saber como el* ~ know inside out.

avena *f* oat(s); *de* ~ oaten; *copos de* ~ rolled oats.

avenado a bit mad.

avenamiento *m* drainage; **avenar** [1a] drain. [✝ deal.｜

avenencia *f* agreement, bargain;｜

avenida *f* avenue; flood, spate *de río*; (*afluencia*) gathering.

avenir [3s] reconcile; ~se come to an agreement, be reconciled (*con*

with); ~ *a inf.* agree to *inf.*; ~ *con* be in agreement with, conform to; *p.* get along with; F *¡allá te las avengas!* that's your look-out!

aventador *m* 𝄪 winnowing fork; fan, blower *para fuego*; **aventadora** *f* winnowing machine.

aventajado outstanding, superior; ~ *de estatura* very tall; **aventajar** [1a] (*exceder*) surpass, outstrip, beat; (*preferir*) put *s.t.* first; ~ *con mucho* outclass; ~ *en un punto* go one better than; ~se *a* surpass; get the advantage of.

aventar [1k] 𝄪 winnow; fan, blow (on); (*viento*) blow away; F throw out; ~se fill, swell (up); F beat it.

aventura *f* (*lance*) adventure; *b.s.* escapade; (*casualidad*) chance, coincidence; (*riesgo*) risk, danger; **aventurado** risky, hazardous; **aventurar** [1a] venture; *vida* risk, hazard; *capital* stake; ~se venture, take a chance; ~ *a inf.* venture to *inf.*, risk *ger.*; **aventurera** *f* adventuress; **aventurero 1.** adventurous; **2.** *m* adventurer; ✗ soldier of fortune; fortune-hunter, social climber *en sociedad*.

avergonzado ashamed (*de, por* at); *expresión* shamefaced; **avergonzar** [1f *a.* 1m] (put to) shame; abash; embarrass; ~se be ashamed (*de, por* of, at, about; *de inf.* to *inf.*).

avería[1] *f* *orn.* aviary; (*bandada*) flock of birds.

avería[2] *f* damage; *mot. etc.* breakdown; fault *de construcción*; **averiado** damaged; *mot. quedar* ~ have a breakdown; **averiar** [1c] damage; ~se get damaged.

averiguable ascertainable; **averiguación** *f* ascertainment *etc.*; **averiguar** [1i] find out, ascertain; look up *en libro*; investigate, inquire into; ~se *con* F tie *s.o.* down; (*entenderse*) get along with.

aversión *f* aversion (*hacia, por algo* to; *a alguien* for); disgust, distaste; *cobrar* ~ *a* take a strong dislike to.

avestruz *m* ostrich.

avetado veined, streaked, grained.

avetoro *m* bittern.

avezado accustomed; **avezar** [1f] accustom; ~se get accustomed (*a* to).

aviación *f* aviation; (*cuerpo*) air-force; **aviador** *m* aviator, airman, flyer.

aviar [1c] v/t. get ready, prepare; equip, provide (de with); F get s.o. ready; S.Am. lend; F estar aviado be in a mess; F dejar aviado leave s.o. in the lurch; v/i. F hurry up; ¡vamos aviando! let's get a move on!

avícola granja chicken attr., poultry attr.; **avicultor** m poultry farmer, poultry keeper; (canarios etc.) bird-fancier; **avicultura** f esp. poultry keeping.

avidez f greed(iness), avidity; **ávido** greedy, avid (de for).

avieso distorted (a. fig.); p. perverse, wicked.

avilés adj. a. su. m, -a f (native) of Avila.

avillanado rustic, boorish.

avinagrado sour, jaundiced; **avinagrar(se)** [1a] (turn) sour.

avío m preparation, provision; S.Am. loan; ¡al ~! get on with it!; hacer su ~ ✝ make one's pile; iro. make a mess of it; ~s pl. kit, tackle, gear; iro. paraphernalia.

avión m (aero)plane, airplane Am.; orn. martin; ~ de caza pursuit plane; ~ de combate fighter; ~ a chorro, ~ a reacción jet plane; en ~ by air; ✇ por ~ (by) airmail; **avioneta** f light aircraft.

avisado prudent, wise; mal ~ rash; **avisador** m, -a f informant; b.s. informer; thea. etc. messenger boy; **avisar** [1a] inform, notify, let s.o. know; (amonestar) warn; ~ con una semana de anticipación give a week's notice; **aviso** m (consejo) advice; (noticia) piece of information, tip; (advertencia) warning; prudence, discretion; con poco tiempo de ~ at short notice; hasta nuevo ~ until further notice; salvo ~ en contrario unless otherwise informed; según (su) ~ as (you) ordered; estar sobre ~ be on the look-out.

avispa f wasp; F wily bird; **avispado** F wide awake, sharp; **avispar** [1a] caballo spur on; F stir up, wake up; ~se fret, be worried; **avispero** m wasps' nest (a. fig.); F mess; **avispón** m hornet.

avistar [1a] descry, sight; ~se have an interview (con with).

avituallar [1a] victual, provision.

avivar [1a] fuego stoke (up); color, luz make brighter; fig. enliven, revive; interés whip up; efecto enhance, heighten; disputa add fuel to; combatientes urge on; v. ojo; ~se revive etc.

avizor 1.: estar ojo ~ be on the alert; 2. m watcher; ~es pl. sl. peepers; **avizorar** [1a] watch, spy on.

avutarda f great bustard.

axioma m axiom; **axiomático** axiomatic.

axiómetro m ⚓ tell-tale.

ay 1. int. ¡~! dolor físico: ouch!; pena: oh!, oh dear!; rhet. alas!; admiración: oh!; ¡~ de mí! poor me!, it's very hard (on me)!; ¡~ del que ...! woe betide the man who ...!; 2. m sigh; groan, cry de dolor.

aya f governess.

ayear [1a] cry with pain; heave sighs.

ayer yesterday.

ayo m tutor.

ayuda 1. f help, aid, assistance; ✒ enema; 2. m page; ~ de cámara valet; **ayudador** m, -a f, **ayudante** m/f helper, assistant; esp. ⊕ mate; ✗ adjutant; ~ de laboratorio laboratory assistant, lab-boy F; **ayudar** [1a] help, aid, assist (a inf. to inf., in ger.); help out; (servir) be of use to, serve; ~ a salir etc. help s.o. out.

ayunar [1a] fast (a on); fig. go without; **ayunas**: en ~ without breakfast; F estar etc. en ~ be (left) in the dark; (no entender) miss the point; **ayuno** 1. fasting; fig. without; F in the dark (de about); 2. m fast(ing); v. ayunas.

ayuntamiento m town (or city) council; (edificio) town (or city) hall; ~ sexual sexual intercourse.

azabache m min. jet.

azacán m, -a f drudge.

azada f hoe; **azadón** m (large) hoe, mattock; **azadonar** [1a] hoe.

azafata f air hostess, stewardess.

azafrán m ⚘ crocus; cocina: saffron.

azahar m orange blossom.

azalea f azalea.

azar m (el ~) chance, fate; (desgracia) misfortune, piece of bad luck; al ~ at random; v. juego; **azararse** [1a] go wrong; (p.) get rattled; **azaroso** risky, hazardous, chancy; (desgraciado) unlucky; vida eventful.

ázimo unleavened.

azogado 1. *fig.* restless, fidgety; *temblar como un* ~ shake like a leaf; **azogar** [1h] *espejo* silver; ~**se** F be restless, get agitated; **azogue** *m* mercury, quicksilver; F *ser un* ~ be always on the go; F *tener* ~ be fidgety.

azoico azoic.

azor *m* goshawk.

azoramiento *m* confusion; excitement; embarrassment; **azorar** [1a] disturb, upset; excite; embarrass; (*animar*) egg on; ~**se** be disturbed *etc.*

azotacalles *m* loafer, lounger; gadabout; **azotado** variegated; **azotaina** *f* F spanking; **azotar** [1a] whip, flog; *niño* thrash, spank; (*mar, lluvia etc.*) lash; *calles* loaf around; **azotazo** *m* lash(ing); spank(ing) *en nalgas*; **azote** *m* whip, lash; (*golpe*) spank; *fig.* scourge; F ~**s** *y galeras* the same old stuff.

azotea *f* flat roof, terrace (roof).

azteca *adj. a. su. m/f* Aztec.

azúcar *m a. f* sugar; ~ *blanco* castor sugar; ~ *cande* rock candy; ~ *moreno,* ~ *terciada* brown sugar; ~ *en terrón* lump sugar; **azucarado** sugary, sweet (*a. fig.*); **azucarar** [1a] sugar; (*bañar*) coat with sugar; F sugar (over); *p.* sweeten; **azucarero 1.** sugar *attr.*; **2.** *m* sugar-bowl, sugar-basin.

azucena *f* (Madonna) lily; ~ *atigrada* tiger lily.

azud *m*, **azuda** *f* water-wheel; (*presa*) dam.

azuela *f* adze.

azufrar [1a] sulphur(ize ⊕); **azufre** *m* sulphur, brimstone.

azul 1. blue; **2.** *m* blue; blueness; ~ *celeste* sky-blue; ~ *de cobalto* cobalt blue; ~ *eléctrico* electric blue; ~ *de mar,* ~ *marino* navy blue; ~ *de Prusia* Prussian blue; ~ *de ultramar* ultramarine; **azulado** blue; bluish; **azular** [1a] dye (*or* colour) blue.

azulejar [1a] tile; **azulejo** *m* glazed tile.

azulina *f* cornflower; **azulino** bluish.

azumbrado F tipsy; **azumbre** *m* *liquid measure* = 2.016 *litres.*

azuzar [1f] *perro* set on; *fig.* irritate; (*estimular*) egg on.

B

baba f spittle, slobber; *biol.* mucus; slime *de caracol*; caérsele *a uno la* ~ (*alegre*) jump for joy; (*bobo*) get soft; *echar* ~ slobber; F say nasty things (*contra* about); **babador** m bib; **babaza** f slime, mucus; *zo.* slug; **babear** [1a] slobber, drivel; F be sloppy, drool (over women).

babel m *or* f babel, bedlam; confusion, mess.

babeo m slobbering, drooling; **babero** m bib.

babieca F 1. simple-minded, stupid; 2. m/f blockhead, dolt.

babilonia f babel, bedlam.

babilonio adj. a. su. m, a f Babylonian.

babilla f *vet.* stifle.

bable m Asturian dialect.

babor m port (side), larboard; *de* ~ port, larboard attr.

babosa f slug; **babosear** [1a] slobber over, drool over (*a.* F *fig.*); **baboseo** m slobbering; F calf love, infatuation; **baboso** slobbering *etc.*; F sloppy (over women); (*adulón*) fawning, snivelling; (*sucio*) dirty; (*bobo*) silly.

babucha f slipper, mule.

baca f top *de autobús*; luggage hold *para equipaje*; (*cubierta*) rain-proof cover.

bacalao m cod(fish); F wet fish, drip; F *cortar el* ~ be the boss; give the keynote *en conversación*.

bacanal 1. bacchanal(ian), bacchantic; 2. f orgy; ~es pl. bacchanalia; **bacante** f bacchanal, bacchante; *fig.* drunken and riotous woman.

bacía f (barber's) bowl; basin, vessel.

bacilar bacillary; **bacilo** m bacillus, germ; ~ *de Koch* T.B. germ.

bacín m large chamber-pot; beggar's bowl; F wretch; **bacineta** f small chamber-pot; beggar's bowl.

bacteria f bacterium, germ; **bacteriano, bactérico** bacterial; **bacteriología** f bacteriology; **bacteriológico** bacteriological; **bacteriólogo** m bacteriologist.

báculo m staff (*a. eccl.*); *fig.* staff, prop, support.

bache m rut, (pot-)hole; ~ *de aire* air-pocket.

bachiller 1. garrulous; 2. m, -a f *pupil who has passed his school-leaving exam.*; † *univ.* bachelor; *fig.* windbag; **bachillerato** m school-leaving examination; **bachillerear** [1a] F prattle (away); **bachillería** f F prattle; (piece of) nonsense.

badajo m (bell) clapper; F chatterbox.

badajocense, badajoceño adj. a. su. m, a f (native) of Badajoz.

badana f (dressed) sheepskin; F *zurrar la* ~ *a* tan s.o.'s hide; *fig.* haul s.o. over the coals.

badil m, **badila** f fire-shovel, *approx.* poker.

badulaque m F nitwit, simpleton; *S.Am.* boor, ill-bred fellow.

bagaje m ✕ baggage; (*acémila*) beast of burden; *fig.* equipment.

bagatela f trinket, knick-knack; *fig.* trifle; ~s pl. trivialities, things of no importance.

¡bah! *desprecio:* bah!, pooh!; *incredulidad:* hum(ph)!, ho!

bahía f bay.

bahorrina F slop, filth; *fig.* riff-raff.

bailable 1. that you can dance to; 2. m ballet; dance number; **bailadero** m dance-hall, dance-floor; **bailador** m, -a f dancer; **bailar** [1a] v/t. dance; *peonza etc.* spin; v/i. dance (*a. fig.*); (*peonza*) spin (round); (*retozar*) jump (about); F ~ *al son que tocan* conform; adapt o.s. to circumstances; F *éste es otro que bien baila* here's another one (of the same kind); **bailarín** m, -a f (professional) dancer; ballet dancer; f *thea.* ballerina; dancing-girl; **baile** m (*acto*) dancing; dancing; (*reunión*) ball, dance; *thea.* ballet; ~ *de candil* village dance, hop; ~ *de etiqueta* dress ball, formal dance; ~ *de máscaras* masked ball; ~ *de San Vito*

St Vitus's dance; ~ de *trajes* fancy (dress) ball; **bailotear** [1a] dance about, hop around.

baivel *m* △ bevel.

baja *f* ✝ drop, fall; ✗ casualty; (*puesto*) vacancy; ✝ *etc.* dar ~, ir de (*or* en) ~ lose value; dar de ~ mark absent; drop *de lista*; darse de ~ drop out, retire; F seguir en ~ go from bad to worse.

bajá *m* pasha.

bajada *f* slope; (*acto*) going down, descent; **bajamar** *f* low tide; **bajar** [1a] 1. *v/t.* *objeto* take down, get down; lower, let down; *brazo*, *ojos*, *precio*, *voz etc.* lower; *p.* help down, lead down; *cabeza* bow, bend; *gas*, *radio etc.* turn down; *escalera* go down, descend; *fig.* humiliate; 2. *v/i.* go down, come down (a to); (✝, *agua*) fall; 🛢 *etc.* get off, get out; ~ de get off, get out of; 3. ~se bend down; *fig.* lower o.s., humble o.s.

bajel *m lit.* vessel, ship.

bajero lower, under-...; **bajeza** *f* meanness *etc.*; lowliness *etc.*; (*acto*) vile deed, mean thing; *v. bajo.*

bajío *m* shoal, sandbank; shallows; *S.Am.* lowland.

bajista *adj. a. su. m* ✝ bear.

bajo 1. *mst* low; *terreno* low(-lying); (*inferior*) lower, under(most); *agua* shallow; (a. ~ de cuerpo) short; *cabeza* bent, lowered; *ojos* downcast; *sonido*, *voz* deep, low; (*débil*) low, faint; *color* dull; *fig.* mean, common; *calidad* low, poor; *condición* low(ly); *tarea* menial; ~ de ley base; por lo ~ secretly; **2.** *m* deep place, depth; 🎵 = *bajío*; 🎵 bass; △ ground-floor (flat); **3.** *adv.* down; *hablar* in a low voice; **4.** *prp.* under(neath); *reinado* in; *punto de vista* from; *palabra*, *pena* on.

bajón *m* decline (a. 🎺) drop; slump *en moral*; 🎵 bassoon.

bajorrelieve *m* bas-relief.

bajura *f* lowness, lack of height; shortness *de p.*

bala *f* ✗ bullet; ✝ bale; ~ de cañón cannon-ball; ~ perdida stray shot; ~ trazadora tracer bullet; F como una ~ like a shot.

balada *f lit.*, 🎵 ballad.

baladí trivial, paltry, footling; *material* trashy.

baladrar [1a] scream, screech; **ba-**ladrero noisy, riotous; **baladro** *m* scream, screech.

baladrón 1. boastful; **2.** *m*, -a *f* braggart; **baladronada** *f* boast; boasting; (*acto*) (piece of) bravado; **baladronear** [1a] boast, brag; (*acto*) show brave.

balalaika *f* balalaika.

balance *m* to-and-fro motion; rocking, swinging; ⚓ roll(ing); *fig.* hesitation; ✝ balance(-sheet); ✝ stock-taking *de existencias*; ~ de comercio balance of trade; ~ de pagos balance of payments; **balancear** [1a] *v/t.* balance; *v/i.*, ~se rock, swing; ⚓ roll; *fig.* hesitate, waver, be in two minds; **balanceo** *m* = *balance*; **balancín** *m* balance beam; ⊕ beam; ⊕ (*eje*) rocker(-arm); swingle-tree *de coche*; yoke *para transportar*; ⚓ outrigger; see-saw *de niños*; balancing-pole *de volatinero.*

balandra *f* sloop; **balandrista** *m* yachtsman; **balandro** *m* yacht; small sloop.

balanza *f* scales, weighing-machine; balance (a. ✝, ♒); *ast.* ♎ Scales; *fig.* judgement; ~ romana steelyard; en la ~ in the balance.

balar [1a] bleat. [ballast.]

balastar [1a] 🛢 ballast; **balasto** *m*]

balaustrada *f* balustrade; banisters *de escalera*; **balaustre** *m* baluster; banister *de escalera.*

balazo *m* shot; 🔫 bullet wound.

balbucear [1a], **balbucir** [3f; *defective*] stammer, stutter; babble; (*niño*) lisp, make the first sounds; **balbuceo** *m* stammer *etc.*

balcón *m* balcony; (*barandilla*) railing; *fig.* vantage-point; **balconero** *m* cat-burglar.

baldaquín *m* canopy, tester.

baldar [1a] cripple; *naipes*: trump; *fig.* put out, inconvenience.

balde[1] *m esp.* ⚓ (canvas) pail, bucket; (zinc) bath.

balde[2]: de ~ free, for nothing; (*sobrante*) over; en ~ in vain, for nothing.

baldear [1a] wash (down), swill; (*achicar*) bale out.

baldío uncultivated; waste; *argumento etc.* empty, baseless; *p.* idle.

baldón *m* affront, insult; (*oprobio*) stain; **baldonar** [1a] insult; stain; disgrace.

baldosa f (floor-)tile; **baldosado** m tiled floor; **baldosar** [1a] tile.
balduque m (official) red tape.
balear[1] [1a] S.Am. shoot (at).
balear[2] adj. a. su. m/f; **baleárico** (native) of the Balearic Isles.
balido m bleat(ing).
balín m small bullet; ~es pl. (buck-) shot.
balística f ballistics.
balita f small bullet; S.Am. marble.
baliza f (lighted) buoy, marker.
balneario 1. thermal, medicinal; spa, health attr.; estación ~a = **2.** m health-resort, spa.
balompié m football.
balón m (foot)ball; ✝ bale; ~ volea volley-ball; **baloncesto** m basket-ball; **balonmano** m handball.
balota f ballot; **balotar** [1a] ballot.
balsa[1] f ⚓ balsa.
balsa[2] f geog. pond; F ser una ~ de aceite be like the tomb, be as quiet as a Sunday-school party.
balsa[3] f ⚓ raft; **balsadera** f, **balsadero** m ferry.
balsámico balsamic, balmy; fig. soothing, healing; **bálsamo** m balsam, balm (a. fig.).
balsear [1a] río cross by ferry; ps. etc. ferry across; **balsero** m ferryman.
baluarte m bulwark (a. fig.).
balumba f (great) bulk; big pile; **balumbo** m bulky thing.
ballena f whale; (lámina) whale-bone; stay de corsé; **ballenera** f whaler; **ballenero 1.** whaling attr.; **2.** (p. a. barco) whaler.
ballesta f cross-bow; 🐞, mot. spring; **ballestero** m cross-bowman.
ballet [bæ'le] m ballet.
bambalear [1a] = bambolear; fig. not be safe (or firm).
bambalinas f/pl. thea. flies.
bambarria m/f F dolt.
bambolear(se) swing, sway; (mueble) wobble; roll, reel al andar; **bamboleo** m sway(ing) etc.
bambolla f F show, ostentation; fuss; **bambollero** F showy, flashy.
bambú m bamboo.   [monplace.}
banal banal; p. superficial, com-}
banana f banana (tree); prov. a. S.Am. banana; **bananal** m banana plantation; **bananero 1.** banana attr.; **2.** m = **banano** m banana (tree).

banasta f large basket, hamper; **banastro** m large round basket.
banca f (asiento) bench; (frutería) fruit-stall; ✝ banking; juegos: bank; hacer saltar la ~ break the bank; **bancada** f stone bench; ⊕ bench; ⚓ thwart; **bancal** m 🌿 patch, plot; (rellano) terrace; **bancario** ✝ bank attr., banking attr.; financial; **bancarrota** f (esp. fraudulent) bankruptcy; fig. failure; hacer ~ go bankrupt; **banco** m (asiento) bench (a. ⊕), form esp. en escuela; ✝ bank; ⚓ bank, shoal; (peces) shoal; min. stratum, layer; ~ de ahorros savings-bank; ~ de arena sandbank; ~ de crédito credit bank; ~ de liquidación clearing house; ~ de sangre blood bank.
banda f (faja) sash, band; (cinta) ribbon; zone, strip; ♪, radio: band; side de mar, barco; billar: cushion; (ps.) band, gang; orn. flock; ~ de rodamiento tread; ~ sonora sound-track; de la ~ de acá (on) this side; F cerrarse a la ~ stand firm; **bandada** f flock (a. fig.), flight.
bandearse [1a] move[?] to and fro; fig. get along, shift for o.s.
bandeja f tray; salver; S.Am. (meat-etc.)dish.
bandera f flag, banner; ✕ colours; ~ de parlamento flag of truce, white flag; ~ de proa jack; a ~s desplegadas in the open; con ~s desplegadas with flying colours (a. fig.); dar a uno la ~ give pride of place to s.o.; **bandería** f faction; **banderilla** f banderilla; F poner una ~ a taunt; give s.o. what for; **banderín** m little flag; pennant; ✕ recruiting post; 🐞 signal; **banderita** f small flag; día de la ~ flagday; **banderola** f (signalling-)flag; ✕ pennant, pennon.
bandidaje m banditry; **bandido** m bandit; outlaw; desperado; F rascal; F co. ¡~! you beast!, you so-and-so!; **banditismo** m banditry.
bando m edict, proclamation; faction, party; ~s pl. marriage banns.
bandolera f bandoleer; **bandolerismo** m brigandage, banditry; **bandolero** m brigand, bandit.
bandullo m F guts, belly.
bandurria f bandurria (a kind of lute).
banjo m banjo.

banquero m banker (a. juegos).
banqueta f stool.
banquetazo m F spread, feast; **banquete** m banquet; (esp. en casa particular) dinner-party; **banquetear** [1a] banquet, feast.
banquillo m bench; footstool; ♣ʰₜ approx. dock.
banquisa f ice-field; (trozo) ice-floe.
bañador 1. m, -a f bather; 2. m ⊕ tub, trough; (traje) bathing-costume; **bañar** [1a] bathe; bath en bañera; dip (a. ⊕); (mar) bathe, wash; fig. bathe (con, de, en in); (luz etc.) bathe, flood, fill, suffuse (de with); estar bañado en agua de rosas walk on air; ~se bath en bañera; bathe en mar etc.; ir a ~ go for a bathe; **bañera** f bath(-tub); **baño** m bath (a. ⊕, ✱); (bañera) bath(-tub); (en general) bathing; paint. coating, wash; cocina: coating; ~s pl. ✱ baths; spa; ~ de asiento hip-bath; ~ de ducha shower-bath; ~ turco Turkish bath; F dar un ~ a teach a lesson to; ir a ~s take the waters.
bao m ⚓ beam.
baque m thud, bump, bang.
baquelita f bakelite.
baqueta f ramrod; ~s pl. ♪ drumsticks; a la ~ severely, harshly; tyrannically; correr ~s run the gauntlet; ser un ~ inured, used to it; ser un ~ know one's way about; **baquetear** [1a] fig. bother; put out; **baqueteo** m imposition, awful bind F.
bar m bar, approx. public house; snack-bar.
barahunda f uproar; racket, din; hubbub.
baraja f pack (of cards); fig. confusion, mix-up; **barajadura** f shuffling, shuffle; **barajar** [1a] v/t. shuffle; fig. mix up, shuffle around; v/i. quarrel; ~se get jumbled up, get mixed up.
baranda f rail(ing); billar: cushion; **barandal** m, **barandilla** f rail(ing), hand-rail; banisters de escalera; balustrade.
baratear [1a] sell cheaply; sell at a loss; **baratero** m cheap; **baratija** f trinket, trifle; ✝ freq. novelty; ~s pl. cheap goods, b.s. junk; **baratillo** m (géneros) second-hand goods; (tienda) second-hand shop, junk shop;

(puesto) bargain counter; (venta) bargain sale; de ~ gimcrack; **barato** 1. cheap; de ~ for nothing; dar de ~ admit (for the sake of argument), grant; echar (or meter) a ~ heckle, barrack; 2. m bargain sale; F cobrar el ~ (be a) bully; **baratura** f cheapness.
baraúnda f = barahunda.
barba 1. f chin; (pelo) beard (a. ✿); whiskers; orn. wattle; ~ cerrada, ~ bien poblada full beard; ~s pl. de chivo goatee; ~ honrada distinguished personage; a ~ regalada abundantly, fully; en las ~s de under the (very) nose of; por ~ apiece, per head; decir algo en sus propias ~s a say s.t. to s.o. to his face; hacer la ~ shave (o.s.); hacer la ~ a shave; fig. (fastidiar) pester; (adular) fawn on; 2. m thea. old man's part; (malo) villain.
barbacoa f S.Am. barbecue.
barbado 1. bearded; 2. m ✿ seedling; plantar de ~ transplant; **barbar** [1a] grow a beard; ✿ strike root.
barbárico barbaric; **barbaridad** f barbarity (a. fig.); fig. atrocity, outrage; F huge amount; ~es pl. fig. nonsense; terrible things, awful things; naughty things; F una ~ (como adv.) terribly, awfully; nos divertimos una ~ we had a tremendous time; ¡qué ~! how awful!; **barbarie** f barbarism, barbarousness; (crueldad) barbarity; **barbarismo** m gr. barbarism; fig. = barbaridad; F lack of polish; **bárbaro** 1. hist. barbarian, barbarous; fig. barbarous, cruel; (arrojado) daring; (inculto) rough, unpolished; F smashing, tremendous; F ¡qué ~! my (goodness)!, cor!; **barbarote** m F brute.
barbear [1a] be as tall (or high) as (a. v/i. ~ con).
barbechar [1a] leave fallow; (arar) plough for sowing; **barbechera** f, **barbecho** m fallow (land); firmar como en un barbecho sign a blank cheque.
barbería f barber's (shop); (oficio) hairdressing; **barbero** m barber, hairdresser.
barbi...:~cano grey-bearded, white-bearded; **~hecho** freshly shaven; **~lampiño** smooth-faced, beard-

less; **~lindo** dapper, spruce; *b.s.* dandified.

barbilla *f* (tip of the) chin.

barbiponiente F beginning to grow a beard; *fig.* raw, novice.

barbo *m* barbel.

barbón *m* man with a beard; *zo.* billy-goat; F greybeard.

barbot(e)ar [1a] mutter, mumble; **barboteo** *m* mutter(ing) *etc.*

barbudo bearded; with a long beard.

barbulla *f* uproar, clamour, hullabaloo; **barbullar** [1a] babble away, talk noisily.

barca *f* (small) boat; **~ de pesca, ~ pesquera** fishing-boat; **barcada** *f* boat-load; (*viaje*) boat trip, crossing; **barcaza** *f* lighter, barge; **~ de desembarco** landing craft.

barcelonés *adj. a. su. m,* **-a** *f* (native) of Barcelona.

barcia *f* chaff.

barco *m* boat; (*grande*) ship, vessel; **~ de guerra** warship; **~ minero** collier; **~ náufrago** shipwreck; **~ de vela** sailing-ship.

barda *f* thatch (on wall); **bardal** *m* thatched wall.

bardana *f* burdock.

bardar [1a] thatch.

bardo *m* bard.

bario *m* barium.

barítono *m* baritone.

barjuleta *f* knapsack; ⊕ tool-bag.

barlovento *m* windward.

barniz *m* varnish; *cerámica*: glaze; ✂ dope; (*afeite*) make-up; *fig.* veneer; smattering *de conocimientos*; **dar de ~** varnish; **barnizado** *m* varnishing; **barnizar** [1f] varnish; polish; glaze.

barométrico barometric(al); **barómetro** *m* barometer.

barón *m* baron; **baronesa** *f* baroness; **baronía** *f* barony.

barquero *m* boatman, waterman; **barquía** *f* skiff, row(ing)-boat.

barquilla *f* ✂ gondola, nacelle, car; ⊕ log.

barquillero *m* wafer seller; **barquillo** *m* *cocina*: *approx.* horn, cone, rolled wafer; (*helado*) cornet.

barquinazo *m* F tumble, hard fall; *mot.* jolt; (*vuelco*) spill, overturning.

barra *f* bar (*a.* ⊕, ⚖, *fig.*); ⊕ rod; ⚖ *a.* dock; stick, bar *de jabón etc.*; *heráldica*: bend; **~ de cortina** curtain-rod; **~ de labios** lipstick; **~s**

pl. paralelas bars; **las ~s de Aragón** the pallets of Aragon; **llevar a la ~** bring *s.o.* to justice; **no pararse en ~s** stick (*or* stop) at nothing.

barraca *f* hut, cabin; *esp.* Valencian thatched house; *S.Am.* storage shed.

barragana *f* concubine.

barranca *f*, **barranco** *m* gully, ravine; *fig.* obstacle.

barrar[1] [1a] daub, smear.

barrar[2] [1a], **barrear** [1a] barricade.

barredera *f* (street-)sweeper; **~ de alfombras** carpet-sweeper; **barredura** *f* sweep(ing); **~s** *pl.* sweepings; (*desperdicios*) refuse; **barreminas** *m* minesweeper.

barrena *f* auger; bit, drill *de berbiquí etc.*; (*esp.* **~ de mano**) gimlet; ✂ spin; ✂ **~ de percusión** jumper; ✂ **entrar en ~** go into a spin; **barrenar** [1a] drill (through); ⊕ scuttle; F upset, make a mess of; ⚖ violate, infringe.

barrendero *m,* **a** *f* sweeper.

barrenillo *m* *zo.* borer; **barreno** *m* large drill, borer; (*agujero*) bore, bore-hole; ✂ blast hole; ⊕ **dar ~ a** scuttle.

barreño *m* washing-up bowl, pan.

barrer [2a] *v/t.* sweep (out, clean *etc.*); (*a. fig.*) sweep away; clear (de of); ✂, ⊕ rake; *v/i.* sweep; F **~ hacia dentro** look after number one.

barrera *f* barrier (*a. fig.*), rail; ✂ *etc.* barricade; **~ (de fuego)** barrage; 🚃 level-crossing gate; *fig.* obstacle; refuge, help; **~ de fuego móvil** creeping barrage; **~ de portazgo** toll-gate, turnpike; **~ racial** colour-bar; **~ del sonido** sound barrier.

barriada *f* quarter, district.

barrica *f* large barrel.

barricada *f* barricade.

barrido *m* = *barredura*; F **vale tanto para un ~ como para un fregado** he can turn his hand to anything.

barriga *f* belly (*a. de vasija*); ⚠ bulge; **barrigón, barrigudo** pot-bellied.

barril *m* barrel; **de ~** *cerveza etc.* draught *attr.*; **barrilero** *m* cooper; **barrilete** *m* keg; ⊕ dog, clamp; chamber *de revólver.*

barrio *m* quarter, district; suburb; F **el otro ~** the other world; **~s** *pl.*

bajos poor quarter, working-class district; *b.s.* slums, slum area.

barrisco: *a* ~ jumbled together; indiscriminately.

barritar [1a] (*elefante*) trumpet.

barrizal *m* muddy place, mire; **barro** *m* mud; *cerámica*: clay; (*búcaro*) earthenware pot; *anat.* pimple (on the face); ~*s pl.* earthenware; crockery; *de* ~ *búcaro etc.* earthen(ware); F *tener* ~ *a mano* be in the money.

barroco 1. baroque; *lit.* mannered, full of conceits; *b.s.* extravagant, in bad taste; **2.** *m* the Baroque (style *etc.*). [*cara* pimply.|

barroso muddy; mud-coloured;|

barrote *m* (heavy) bar.

barruntar [1a] guess, conjecture; **barrunte** *m* sign, indication; **barrunto** *m* guess, conjecture; = *barrunte*.

bartola: *tumbarse a la* ~ be lazy, take it easy.

bártulos *m/pl.* things, belongings, bits and pieces; goods; ⊕ tools; kit; F *liar los* ~ pack up (one's traps); F *preparar los* ~ get ready, get set.

barullo *m* uproar, din.

barzón *m* saunter, stroll; *dar* ~*es* = **barzonear** [1a] stroll around, wander around.

basa *f* △ base (of a column); *fig.* basis, foundation.

basáltico basaltic; **basalto** *m* basalt.

basar [1a] base; *fig.* base, found, ground (*sobre* on); ~*se en* de based on; base o.s. on, rely on.

basca *f* 𝕏 (*mst* ~*s pl.*) queasiness, nausea; F fit of rage, tantrum; *dar* ~*s a* make *s.o.* sick, turn *s.o.'s* stomach; **bascosidad** *f* filth, dirt; **bascoso** 𝕏 queasy; squeamish; *S.Am.* filthy.

báscula *f* scales, weighing-machine; **basculante** *m* tip-up lorry; **báscula-puente** *f* weighbridge; **bascular** [1a] tilt, tip up; (*oscilar*) rock to and fro; *pol. etc.* swing.

base *f* *mst* base; ⊕ mount(ing); bed; *surv.* base(-line); *fig.* basis, foundation; ~ *aérea* air-base; ~ *avanzada* forward base; ~ *naval* naval base; *a* ~ *de* on the basis of; by means .of; **básico** ♪ basic.

basílica *f* *esp. hist.* basilica; *eccl.* large church, privileged church.

basilisco *m* basilisk; F *estar hecho un* ~ be hopping mad.

basquear [1a] feel sick; *hacer* ~ *a* make *s.o.* sick, turn *s.o.'s* stomach.

basquiña *f* skirt.

basta *f* tacking stitch.

bastante 1. *adj.* enough (*para* for; *para inf.* to *inf.*); **2.** *adv.* (*que basta*) enough; (*más o menos*): ~ *bueno* quite good, fairly good, rather good, goodish; **bastantemente** sufficiently, fully; **bastar** [1a] be enough, be sufficient (*para inf.* to *inf.*); suffice, be (quite) enough; *¡basta!* that's enough!; right!, stop!; *¡basta ya!* that's quite enough (of that)!; *basta y sobra* that's more than enough; ~*se a sí mismo* be self-sufficient.

bastardear [1a] *v/t.* debase; adulterate; *v/i. & a. fig.* degenerate; fall away (*de* from); **bastardía** *f* bastardy; *fig.* wicked thing; **bastardilla:** (*letra*) ~ italic(s); *en* ~ in italics; *poner en* (*letra*) ~ italicize; **bastardo** *adj. a. su. m*, *a f* bastard; ⚠ *etc.* hybrid.

bastear [1a] *sew.* baste, tack.

bastidor *m* frame (*a. sew.*, ⊕); frame, case *de ventana etc.*; (*con lienzo*) stretcher; *thea.* wing; *thea. a. fig. entre* ~*es* behind the scenes; (*de*) *entre* ~*es* off-stage; *dirigir entre* ~*es* work the oracle.

bastilla *f* hem; **bastillar** [1a] hem.

bastimentar [1a] supply, provision; **bastimento** *m* supply, provision; ♺ vessel.

basto 1. coarse, rough; (*grosero*) rude, ill-mannered; **2.** *m* pack-saddle; *naipes*: ~*s pl.* clubs.

bastón *m* (walking-)stick; 𝕏 *etc.* baton; *heráldica*: pallet, pale; *fig.* control, command; ~ *de estoque* swordstick; ~ *de mando* baton; sign of authority; ~ *de montaña* walking-stick; *empuñar el* ~ take charge; *meter el* ~ intervene; **bastonazo** *m* blow with a stick; caning; **bastonear** [1a] beat (with a stick), cane; **bastonero** *m* master of ceremonies.

basura *f* rubbish, refuse; (*esp. papeles*) litter; (*polvo*) dust; ✧ dung, manure; **basurero** *m* (*p.*) dustman; scavenger; (*sitio*) rubbish dump; ✧ dung-heap.

bata *f* dressing-gown; housecoat;

négligée; smock *de encinta*; ♎ *etc.* laboratory coat.

batacazo *m* thud, bump.

batahola *f* F hullabaloo, rumpus.

batalla *f* battle; *esp. fig.* fight, contest; *fig.* (inner) struggle, agitation (of mind); *mot.* wheel base; ~ *campal* pitched battle; *librar (trabar)* ~ do (join) battle; **batallador** *m* fighter; *fenc.* fencer; **batallar** [1a] battle, fight (*con* with, against; *por* over); *fig.* vacillate, waver; **batallón 1.** *cuestión etc.* vexed; **2.** *m* battalion.

batán *m* fulling mill; *(máquina)* fulling hammer; **batanar** [1a] full, beat; F = **batanear** [1a] F *(zurrar)* give *s.o.* a hiding; *(sacudir)* give *s.o.* a shaking; **batanero** *m* fuller.

bataola *f* = **batahola**.

batata *f* sweet potato, yam; *S.Am.* bashfulness.

batatazo *m* F stroke of luck, fluke.

batayola *f* ♎ rail.

batea *f* *(bandeja)* tray; *(artesilla)* deep trough; ♎ flat-bottomed boat; 🚋 truck, wagon, flat-car.

batel *m* small boat, skiff; **batelero** *m* boatman.

batería *f* *mst* battery; ⚡ bank *de luces*; *thea.* footlights; ~ *de cocina* kitchen utensils.

batida *f* ✕, *hunt.* drive; ✕ reconnaissance; *fig.* search; **batidero** *m* continuous beating (*or* striking), rough ground; F coming and going; **batido 1.** *seda* shot, chatoyant; *camino* well-trodden, beaten; **2.** *m* *cocina*: batter; ~ *(de leche)* milkshake; **batidor** *m* ⊕, *hunt.* beater; ✕ scout; *(peine)* comb; = **batidora**; **batiente** *m* *(marco)* jamb *de puerta*, frame, case *de ventana*; *(hoja)* leaf *de puerta*; ♪ damper; ♎ open coastline; **batidora** *f* whisk; ⚡ (electric) mixer; **batintín** *m* gong.

batir [3a] **1.** *v/t.* *metall., hunt.*, ✕, *adversario, alas, huevos, marca* beat; *campo, terreno* comb, reconnoitre; *casa* knock down; *costa* beat (on); *crema* whip; *chocolate* mill; *manos* clap; *mantequilla* cream; *moneda* mint; *pelo* comb; *privilegio* do away with; *talones, vuelo* take to; *tiendas* strike; *toldo etc.* take down; *(sol)* beat down on; **2.** *v/i.* ✿ beat (violently); **3.** ~**se** (have a) fight.

batista *f* cambric, batiste.

bato *m* simpleton.

batracio *adj. a. su. m* batrachian.

batucar [1g] shake (up).

batueco *m* F stupid, silly.

batuque *m* *S.Am.* F to-do, rumpus.

baturrillo *m* hotchpotch.

baturro 1. uncouth; **2.** *m*, **a** *f* Aragonese peasant.

batuta *f* ♪ baton; F *llevar la* ~ be the boss, rule the roost.

baúl *m* (♎ cabin) trunk; F corporation; ~ *mundo* large (*or* Saratoga) trunk; ~ *ropero* wardrobe trunk.

bauprés *m* bowsprit.

bausán *m* dummy, straw man; F simpleton.

bautismal baptismal; **bautismo** *m* baptism; F *romper el* ~ *a* break *s.o.'s* nut; **Bautista** *m*: *El* ~, *San Juan* ~ St. John the Baptist; **bautisterio** *m* baptistery; **bautizar** [1f] baptize *(a. fig.)*; *fig.* name, give a name to; F *vino* water; F *p.* drench, soak; **bautizo** *m* baptism; christening.

bauxita *f* bauxite.

baya *f* berry.

bayeta *f* baize; *(trapo)* floor-cloth.

bayo 1. biscuit(-coloured); *caballo* bay *approx.*; **2.** *m* *approx.* bay (horse).

bayoneta *f* bayonet; **bayonetazo** *m* bayonet thrust, bayonet wound.

baza *f* *naipes*: trick; F *hacer* ~ get on; F *meter* ~ butt in, shove one's oar in; *meter* ~ *en* interfere in; F *no dejar meter* ~ *a* not let *a p.* get a word in edgeways.

bazar *m* bazaar.

bazo 1. yellowish-brown; **2.** *m* *anat.* spleen.

bazofia *f* left-overs; (pig)swill, hogwash *Am.* *(a. fig.)*; *fig.* vile thing, filth.

bazucar [1g], **bazuquear** [1a] stir, shake; **bazuqueo** *m* stirring, shaking; ~ *gástrico* rumblings (in the stomach).

be¹: *por* ~ down to the last detail; *tener algo las tres* ~s be really very nice.

be² *m* baa.

beata *f* lay sister; sister of charity; F devout woman; *b.s.* goody-goody; **beatería** *f* cant, sanctimoniousness; **beatificación** *f* beatification; **beatificar** [1g] beatify; **beatitud** *f* beatitude, blessedness; *Su* ♀ His Holiness; **beato 1.** happy, blessed;

pious; *b.s.* hypocritical; sanctimonious, canting; **2.** *m approx.* lay brother; F devout man.
bebé *m* baby.
bebedero 1. drinkable, good to drink; **2.** *m* drinking-trough; spout *de vasija*; **bebedizo 1.** drinkable; **2.** *m* 🛠 potion; † philtre, (love-) potion; **bebedor 1.** hard-drinking, bibulous; **2.** *m*, -a *f* (hard) drinker, toper; **beber 1.** *m* drink(ing); **2.** *v/t.* drink (up); *esp. fig.* drink in, imbibe; ～ *con la lengua* lap up; ～ *de* drink out of; drink (*a. b.s.*); ～ *mucho*, ～ *a pote* drink a lot, be a heavy drinker; **beberrón** = *bebedor*; **bebible** drinkable, good to drink; **bebida** *f* drink (*a. alcohol*); beverage; ～ *alcohólica* liquor, alcoholic drink; *dado a la* ～ hard-drinking, given to drink; **bebido** tipsy, merry; **bebistrajo** *m* F filthy stuff (to drink).
beca *f* scholarship, grant (for study); insignia; **becario** *m*, **a** *f* scholar, scholarship-holder.
becerrillo *m* calf-skin; **becerro** *m* yearling calf; ⊕ calf-skin; *eccl.* record (book).
becuadro *m* ♪ natural (sign).
bedel *m esp. univ. approx.* porter.
beduino 1. *adj. a. su. m*, **a** *f* Bedouin; **2.** *m fig.* barbarian.
befa *f* jeer; **befar** [1a] scoff at, jeer at.
befo 1. thick-lipped; (*zambo*) knock-kneed; **2.** *m* lip.
begonia *f* begonia.
beige [beis] *m* beige.
bejuco *m* liana.
beldad *f* beauty (*a. p.*).
belén *m eccl.* crib, nativity scene; *fig.* confusion, bedlam; (*lance*) risky venture.
beleño *m* henbane.
belfo = *befo*.
belga *adj. a. su. m/f*, **bélgico** Belgian.
belicista militaristic, war-minded; **bélico** warlike; *material etc.* war *attr.*; **belicoso** warlike; militant; **beligerancia** *f* belligerancy; militancy, warlike spirit; **beligerante** *adj. a. su. m/f* belligerent.
belitre *m* rogue, scoundrel.
belvedere *m* belvedere.
bellaco 1. wicked; astute, sly, cunning; **2.** *m*, **a** *f* scoundrel, rogue; miscreant; (*astuto*) knowing one.

belladona *f* deadly nightshade, belladonna (*a.* 🐾).
bellaquear [1a] cheat, be crooked; *S.Am.* (*caballo*) rear; *fig.* be stubborn; **bellaquería** *f* (*acto*) dirty trick; (*dicho*) mean (*or* nasty) thing to say; (*maldad*) wickedness.
belleza *f* beauty, loveliness; (*p.*) beauty, lovely thing; **bello** beautiful, lovely; *lo* ～ *ideal* beau ideal.
bellota *f* ♀ acorn; perfume-box; F *anat.* Adam's apple.
bemol *m* ♪ flat; F *esto tiene muchos* ～*es* this is a tough one.
benceno *m* benzene; **bencina** *f mot.* benz(ol)ine, motor-spirit.
bendecir [*approx.* 3p] bless; consecrate; (*alabar*) praise, extol; ～ *la mesa* say grace; **bendición** *f* blessing, benediction; (*de la mesa*) grace; ～*es pl.* nupciales wedding ceremony; *echar la* ～ give one's blessing (*a. fig.*); F *echar la* ～ *a* say good-bye to; have no more to do with; F *llovía que era una* ～ you should have seen how it rained; **bendito** saintly, blessed; *agua* holy; (*feliz*) happy; F simple (-minded); **bendícite** *m* grace; **benedictino** *adj. a. su. m* Benedictine (*a. licor*); F ser *obra de* ～ be a long job.
beneficencia *f* (*virtud*) doing good; charity; (*obra*) benefaction; (*fundación*) charity, charitable organization; **beneficiado** *m eccl.* incumbent, beneficiary; **beneficial:** *terreno* ～ glebe(land); **beneficiar** [1b] *v/t.* benefit, be of benefit to; 🌱 cultivate; ⚒ *mina* exploit, work; *material* process, smelt; ⚑ sell at a discount; *empleo* bribe one's way into; *v/i.* be of benefit; ～*se* take advantage of; **beneficiario** *m*, **a** *f* beneficiary; **beneficio** *m* benefit, good; (*donativo*) benefaction; *eccl.* living, benefice; ⚑, 🌱 yield, profit; ⚒ processing, smelting; *thea.* benefit (performance); *a* ～ *de* for the benefit of; **beneficioso** beneficial, useful, profitable; **benéfico** good (*a, para* for); *obra etc.* charitable (*para con* towards).
benemérito worthy, meritorious; *un* ～ *de la patria* a national hero; *la* ♀*a* the Civil Guard, the police.
beneplácito *m* approval, consent.
benevolencia *f* benevolence, kind-

(li)ness; **benévolo** benevolent, kind(ly); well-disposed (*con* to, towards).

benignidad *f* kind(li)ness *etc.*; **benigno** kind(ly); gracious, gentle; *clima* kindly, mild; ♂ mild; *tumor* benign.

benito = *benedictino*.

benjamín *m* baby (of the family); favourite child.

beodez *f* drunkenness; **beodo** drunk(en).

berberecho *m* zo. cockle.

berberí, berberisco Berber.

berbiquí *m* (carpenter's) brace; ~ *y barrena* brace and bit.

bereber *adj. a. su. m/f* Berber.

berenjena *f* aubergine, egg-plant; **berenjenal** *m* aubergine bed; *fig.* rare how-d'ye-do, fine pickle; *en buen* ~ *nos hemos metido* we've got ourselves into a fine mess.

bergante *m* scoundrel, rascal.

bergantín *m* brig.

berilo *m* beryl.

bermejo red(dish), russet; *esp. pelo* red(dish), auburn; *gato* ginger; **bermellón** *m* vermilion.

bernardina *f* F tall story.

berrear [1a] low, bellow; F fly off the handle; **berrenchín** *m* F rage, tantrum; **berrido** *m* lowing, bellow(ing); ♪ screech (*a. fig.*); **berrinche** *m* F rage, tantrum.

berro *m* water-cress.

berza *f* cabbage; F *mezclar* ~*s con capachos* be all over the place, jumble things up; **berzal** *m* cabbage patch. [levee.)

besamanos *m* royal audience,)

besar [1a] kiss; *fig.* graze, touch; ♨ *a* ~ chock-a-block; ~ *la mano*, ~ *los pies fig.* pay one's respects (*a* to); ~*se* kiss (each other); *fig.* bump heads together; **beso** *m* kiss; *echar un* ~ *a* blow a kiss to.

bestia 1. *f* beast; ~ *de carga* beast of burden; ~ *negra* bête noire, pet aversion; **2.** *m/f* dunce, ignoramus; (*rudo*) boor; F beast; F ¡~! you idiot!; F ¡*no seas* ~! don't be an idiot!; **bestial** beastly, bestial; *apetito* terrific; F stunning, swell; **bestialidad** *f* bestiality; *fig.* (piece of) stupidity.

besucar [1g] F pet, neck.

besugo *m* sea bream; *fig. de* ~ *ojos* bulging; (*tristes*) like a spaniel's;

besuguera *f* ♨ fishing-boat; *cocina*: fish-pan.

besuquearse [1a] F pet, neck; **besuqueo** *m* F petting, necking.

bético *lit.* Andalusian.

betún *m* ♏ bitumen; (*zapatos*) shoe-polish, blacking; F *darse* ~ swank, show off.

bezo *m* thick lip; ♂ proud flesh; **bezudo** thick-lipped.

bi... bi...

biberón *m* feeding-bottle.

Biblia *f* Bible; *fig. saber la* ~ know everything; **bíblico** biblical.

bibliografía *f* bibliography; **bibliográfico** bibliographic(al); **bibliógrafo** *m* bibliographer; **bibliomanía** *f* bibliomania; **bibliómano** *m* bibliomaniac.

biblioteca *f* library; (*estante*) bookcase; ~ *circulante* lending (*or* circulating) library; ~ *de consulta* reference library; **bibliotecario** *m*, *a f* librarian.

bicarbonato *m*: ~ *sódico*, ~ *de sosa* bicarbonate of soda; cooking-soda.

biceps *m* biceps.

bici *f* F (push)bike; **bicicleta** *f* (bi)cycle; *andar en* ~, *ir en* ~ ride a bicycle, (bi)cycle.

bicoca *f* F trifle.

bicolor two-colour; *mot.* two-tone.

bicha *f euph.* snake; *fig.* bogy; **bicho** *m* small animal, largish insect *etc.*, bug *Am.*; *toros*: fighting bull; (*p.*) odd bird, queer fish; ~*s pl.* vermin; *mal* ~ *fig.* nasty piece of work; *S.Am. de puro* ~ out of spite; F *todo* ~ *viviente* every living soul; every man-jack; *S.Am. tener* ~ have a raging) **bidé** *m* bidet. [thirst.)

bidón *m* drum, can.

biela *f* connecting-rod.

bielda *f approx.* pitchfork; **bieldar** [1a] winnow; **bieldo** *m* winnowing rake.

bien 1. *m* good; (*beneficio*) advantage, profit; (*bienestar*) welfare, wellbeing; property, possession; *mi* ~ (*p.*) my dear(est); ~ *público* common good; *sumo* ~ highest good; *en* ~ *de* for the good of; *hacer* ~ do good; be charitable; **2.** ~*es pl.* wealth, riches; property, possessions; ~ *dotales* dowry; ~ *heredables* hereditament; ~ *inmuebles*, ~ *raíces* real estate, realty; landed property; ~ *mostrencos*

unclaimed (*or* ownerless) property; ~ *muebles* personal property; (goods and) chattels; ~ *relictos* estate, inheritance; ~ *de la tierra* produce; ~ *vinculados* entail; *decir mil* ~ *de* speak highly of; **3.** *adv.* well; (*correctamente*) right; (*de buena gana*) gladly, readily; easily; ~ ... ~ either ... or; ~ (*así*) *como* just as, just like; *de* ~ *en* ~ better and better; *más* ~ rather; *o* ~ *o* else; ~ *que mal* one way or another, by hook or by crook; **4.** (*como int.*) ¡~! all right!, okay!; jolly good!; ¡*muy* ~! (*a orador etc.*) hear hear!; yes indeed!; ¡*hizo muy* ~! and he was quite right too!; **5.** *cj.* ~ *que, si* ~ although; *a* ~ *que* perhaps; *no* ~ no sooner, as soon as.
bienal biennial (*a. planta* ~).
bien...: ~andante happy; prosperous; **~andanza** *f* happiness; prosperity; **~aventurado** happy, fortunate; *eccl.* blessed; F simple, naïve; **~aventuranza** *f* wellbeing, prosperity; *eccl.* (state of) blessedness; *las* ~*s pl.* the Beatitudes; **~estar** *m* wellbeing, welfare; **~hablado** nicely-spoken; **~hadado** lucky; **~hechor 1.** beneficent; **2.** *m* benefactor; **~hechora** *f* benefactress; **~intencionado** well-meaning.
bienio *m* (period of) two years.
bien...: ~oliente fragrant; **~querencia** *f* affection; (*buena voluntad*) goodwill; **~querer 1.** [2u] like, be fond of; **2.** *m* affection; goodwill.
bienquistar [1a] bring together, reconcile; **~se** become reconciled; **bienquisto** well thought-of, well-liked (*con, de, por* by).
bienvenida *f* welcome; greeting; (*llegada*) safe arrival; *dar la* ~ *a* welcome; **bienvenido** welcome; ¡~! welcome! [decently.]
bienvivir [3a] live in comfort; live)
bifásico ⚡ two-phase.
biftec *m* (beef)steak.
bifurcación *f* fork, junction *en camino*; branch; **bifurcado** forked; **bifurcarse** [1g] (*caminos etc.*) fork, branch; bifurcate; diverge.
bigamia *f* bigamy; second marriage *de viudo*; **bígamo 1.** bigamous; twice married; **2.** *m, a f* bigamist.
bigardear [1a] F loaf around; **bigardo** *m* loafer.
bigarro *m* zo. winkle.
bigornia *f* (double-headed) anvil.

bigote *m* (*a.* ~*s pl.*) moustache; whiskers *de gato etc.*; **bigotudo** with a big moustache.
bilateral bilateral (*a.* ✝), two-sided.
bilbaíno *adj. a. su. m,* **a** *f* (native) of Bilbao.
bilbilitano *adj. a. su. m,* **a** *f* (native) of Calatayud.
biliar bile *attr.*; gall *attr.*
bilingüe bilingual.
bilioso bilious (*a. fig.*); *fig.* peevish, difficult; **bilis** *f* bile (*a. fig.*); *descargar la* ~ vent one's spleen; *exaltársele a uno la* ~ get annoyed, get cross.
billar *m* billiards; (*mesa*) billiard-table; ~ *automático*, ~ *romano* pintable.
billete *m* ticket; ✝ (bank-)note, bill *Am.*; (*carta*) note, letter; ~ *de abono* season-ticket; ~ *amoroso* love-letter, billet-doux; ~ *de banco* bank-note, bill *Am.*; ~ *de ida y vuelta* return ticket; ~ *kilométrico approx.* runabout ticket, mileage book; *medio* ~ half-fare; ~ *sencillo* single ticket; **billetera** *f* wallet, billfold *Am.*
billón *m* (*Gran Bretaña*) billion; (*EE.UU.*) trillion.
bimba *f* top hat.
bimotor twin-engined.
binadera *f,* **binador** *m* hoe; **binar** [1a] hoe, dig over.
binario binary; ♪ *compás* two-four.
binocular binocular; **binóculo** *m* binoculars; *thea.* opera-glasses; (*gafas*) pince-nez.
biografía *f* biography, life; **biográfico** biographic(al); **biógrafo** *m,* **a** *f* biographer.
biología *f* biology; **biológico** biologic(al); **biólogo** *m* biologist.
biombo *m* (folding) screen.
bioquímica *f* biochemistry; **bioquímico 1.** biochemical; **2.** *m* biochemist.
bipartido bipartite.
bípedo *adj. a. su. m,* **a** *f* biped; F man.
biplano *m* biplane.
biplaza *m* ✵ two-seater.
birimbao *m* Jew's harp.
birlar [1a] knock down (*or* kill) with one shot; F *p.* swindle out of, do out of; *cosa* pinch; *le birlaron el empleo* he was done out of the job.
birlibirloque: *por arte de* ~ (as if) by magic.

birlonga: *a la* ~ carelessly, sloppily.
birmano *adj. a. su. m*, a *f* Burmese.
birreactor *adj. a. su. m* 🛩 twin-jet.
birreta *f* biretta, cardinal's hat;
  birrete *m eccl.* biretta; *univ. approx.* cap, mortar-board F.
birria *f* F (*feo*) monstrosity, ugly old thing; (*inútil*) bungling piece of work; useless object.
bis 1. *adv.* twice; *thea.* ¡~! encore!;
  2. *m* encore.
bisabuela *f* great-grandmother;
  bisabuelo *m* great-grandfather; ~s *pl.* great-grandparents.
bisagra *f* hinge; F waggle *de caderas.*
bisar [1a] *thea. etc.* repeat.
bisbisar [1a] mutter, mumble;
  bisbiseo *m* mutter(ing), mumbling.
biscuter *m* mini-car.
bisecar [1g] bisect; **bisección** *f* bisection.
bisel *m* bevel(-edge); **biselado** bevel *attr.*; **biselar** [1a] bevel; *superficie* splay.
bisemanal twice-weekly.
bisiesto: *v. año* ~.
bisílabo two-syllabled.
bismuto *m* bismuth.
bisnieto *m* great-grandson; ~s *pl.* great-grandchildren.
bisojo cross-eyed, squinting.
bisonte *m* bison.
bisoñada *f* naïve remark; **bisoño 1.** green, inexperienced; *soldado* raw; **2.** *m*, a *f* greenhorn; 🗡 recruit, rookie.
bisté *m*, **bistec** *m* (beef)steak.
bisturí [1g] *v/t.* scalpel. [paste.\
bisutería *f* imitation jewellery,/
bitácora *f* binnacle.
bituminoso bituminous.
bivio *m S.Am.* road junction.
bizantino 1. Byzantine; *fig.* decadent; *discusión* pointless; *over-subtle*, Jesuitical; **2.** *m*, a *f* Byzantine.
bizarría *f* gallantry; generosity; (*esplendor*) show; **bizarro** gallant; generous; (*gallardo*) dashing, smart.
bizcar [1g] *v/t.* wink; *v/i.* squint; **bizco** cross-eyed, squinting; *mirada* ~a squint; F *quedarse* ~ be dumbfounded.
bizcocho *m* sponge (cake); biscuit; (*loza*) biscuit (ware); ⚓ hardtack, ship's biscuit; ~ *borracho* tipsy cake.

bizma *f* poultice; **bizmar** [1a] poultice.
biznieto *etc. v.* bisnieto.
blanca *f* (*p.*) white woman; ♪ minim; F *estar* (*or quedarse*) *sin* ~ be broke; **blanco 1.** white; *piel* white, light; *tez* fair; *página, verso* blank; F yellow, cowardly; **2.** *m* white(ness); (*p.*) white (man); 🗡 target (*a. fig.*); (*página etc.*) blank (space); interval; ~ *del ojo* white of the eye; ~ *de plomo* white lead; *en* ~ blank; *calentar al* ~ make white-hot; *dar en el* ~ hit the mark (*a. fig.*); *dejar en* ~ leave blank; *firmar en* ~ sign a blank cheque; *pasar la noche en* ~ not sleep a wink; *poner los ojos en* ~ roll one's eyes; *quedarse en* ~ fail to see the point; not understand a word; **blancor** *m* whiteness; **blancote** (sickly) white; F *p.* yellow; **blancura** *f* whiteness.
blandear[1] [1a] = *blandir.*
blandear[2] *v/t. fig.* convince, persuade; *v/i.*, ~se soften, yield, give in.
blandengue *m* F softie.
blandir [3a; *defective*] *v/t.* brandish, wave aloft; *v/i.* ~se wave to and fro.
blando *mst* soft; *pasta etc.* smooth; *carne b.s.* flabby; *fig.* mild, gentle; mellow; *p. b.s.* soft, indulgent; sensual; F cowardly; *clima* mild; *palabras* bland; *ojos* tender; ~ *de boca fig.* talkative, loose-tongued; **blanducho** F on the soft side, softish; *esp. carne* flabby, loose; **blandujo** F on the soft side; **blandura** *f* softness *etc.*; (*halago*) flattery, flattering words; (*requiebro*) sweet nothings.
blanquear [1a] *v/t. tela etc.* bleach, whiten; *pared* whitewash; ⊕ blanch; *v/i.* (*volverse*) turn white, whiten; (*mostrar*) show white; **blanqueador** *m*, -a *f* bleacher; **blanquecer** [2d] = *blanquear*; **blanquecino** whitish; **blanqueo** *m* bleaching *etc.*; **blanquillo** *pan etc.* white; **blanquimiento** *m* bleacher, bleaching solution.
blasfemador 1. blaspheming, blasphemous; **2.** *m*, -a *f* blasphemer; **blasfemar** [1a] blaspheme (*contra* against); *fig.* curse (and swear); ~ *de* curse, revile; **blasfemia** *f eccl.* blasphemy; insult; (*palabrota*) oath, swear-word; **blasfemo** = *blasfemador.*

blasón *m* (*en general*) heraldry; (*escudo*) coat of arms, escutcheon; (*señal*, *pieza*) armorial bearings, charge; *fig.* honour, glory; **blasonar** [1a] *v/t.* (em)blazon; *v/i.* boast (*de* of being), brag.

bledo: F *no se me da un* ~ I don't care two hoots (*de* about).

blenda *f* blende.

blinda *f* = *blindaje*; **blindado** ✕ armoured; ⊕ shielded; **blindaje** *m* ✕, ⚓ armour(-plating); ⊕ shield; **blindar** [1a] ✕ armour; ⊕ shield.

bloc *m* (writing-)pad; calendar pad.

blocao *m* blockhouse; pillbox.

blonda *f* blond (lace); **blondo** blond; light; *esp. pelo* flaxen.

bloque *m* ⚠, ⊕ block; *fig.* group; *pol.* bloc; *en* ~ *en bloc*; ~ *de cilindros* cylinder block; **bloquear** [1a] ✕, ⚓ blockade; *mot.* brake, pull up; ⌖ freeze, block; **bloqueo** *m* blockade; ⌖ freeze, squeeze; ⚓ burlar (*or* forzar) *el* ~ run the blockade.

blufar [1a] bluff; **bluff** *m* [blœf] bluff; *hacer un* ~ *a* bluff.

blusa *f* blouse; jumper *de lana*; overalls *de obrero*.

boa *f* boa.

boato *m* show(iness), ostentation; pomp, pageantry *de ceremonia etc.*

bobada *f* silly thing; *decir* ~*s* talk a lot of nonsense, talk rot; *¡no digas* ~*s!* get along with you!; **bobalías** *m/f* F dolt, ass; **bobalicón** F 1. utterly stupid, quite silly; 2. *m*, -a *f* nitwit, mutt; **bobático** F half-witted, doltish; **bobear** [1a] (*hablar*) talk (a lot of) twaddle; (*obrar*) act like a fool; fool around; **bober(í)a** *f* = *bobada*.

bóbilis: F *de* ~ ~ (*gratis*) for nothing; (*sin trabajo*) for jam, without lifting a finger.

bobina *f* bobbin, spool (*a. phot.*), reel; ⚡ coil; **bobinado** *m* ⚡ winding; **bobinar** [1a] wind (on to a spool *etc.*).

bobo 1. (*corto*) stupid, simple; (*tonto*) silly; (*ingenuo*) naïve, green; ~ *con* crazy about, mad about; 2. *m*, a *f* fool, dolt, mutt; (*ingenuo*) greenhorn; *thea.* clown, funny man.

boca *f* mouth; muzzle *de fusil*; (cutting) edge *de escoplo etc.*; pincer *de crustáceo*; *fig.* mouth, entrance; (*sabor*) taste, flavour; ~ *de agua* fire-plug; ~ *de escorpión fig.* evil tongue; ~ *del estómago* pit of the stomach; ~ *de mina* pit-head; ~ *de riego* hydrant; *a* ~ by word of mouth; *a* ~ *de cañón* at close range; *a* ~ *de jarro beber* immoderately; ✕ at close range; point-blank; ~ *abajo* (*arriba*) face downward (upward); *andar etc. de* ~ *en* ~ (*cuento*) go round, be common talk; F *¡cállate la* ~*!* shut up!, hold your tongue!; *meterse en la* ~ *del lobo* put one's head in the lion's mouth; *no decir esta* ~ *es mía* not open one's mouth; *quedarse con la* ~ *abierta fig.* be dumbfounded; *tapar la* ~ *a* shut *s.o.* up.

bocacalle *f* street entrance; *la primera* ~ the first turning; **bocacha** *f* F big mouth; ✕ blunderbuss; **bocadear** [1a] divide into pieces; **bocadillo** *m* snack; meat (*or* cheese *etc.*) roll, sandwich; **bocado** *m* mouthful; (*un poco de comida*) morsel, bite; (*mordedura*) bite; (*parte del freno*) bit; (*freno*) bridle; **bocal** *m* pitcher; jar; **bocallave** *f* keyhole; **bocamanga** *f* cuff, wristband; **bocamina** *f* pit-head, mine entrance; **bocanada** *f* mouthful *de vino etc.*; puff *de humo*, *viento*; F ~ *de gente* crush; **bocera** *f* smear (on lips), moustache (*fig.*).

boceto *m* sketch, outline.

bocina *f* ♩ trumpet; horn (*a. mot.*, *gramófono*); (*portavoz*) megaphone, speaking-trumpet; ear-trumpet *de sordo*; *mot. tocar la* ~ = **bocinar** [1a] *mot.* hoot, blow the horn, honk; speak through a megaphone; **bocinazo** *m mot.* hoot, honk, toot.

bocio *m* goitre.

bock *m* beer-glass, tankard.

bocón 1. big-mouthed; F boastful; 2. *m*, -a *f* F braggart.

bocoy *m* hogshead, large cask.

bocha *f* bowl; *juego de las* ~*s* bowls.

bochinche *m* uproar, din; *prov.* pub; *S.Am.* general stores.

bochorno *m* sultry weather, sultriness; stifling atmosphere; (*viento*) hot summer breeze; *fig.* 🌡 turn F; flush *de cara*; embarrassment; (*fig.*) dishonour, stigma; **bochornoso** *tiempo* sultry, thundery; *ambiente etc.* stifling; *fig.* embarrassing; *b.s.* shameful, degrading.

boda f wedding (a. ~s pl.), marriage; wedding reception; F ~ de negros rowdy party; ~s pl. de diamante (oro, plata) diamond (golden, silver) wedding.

bodega f wine-cellar; (despensa) pantry; (depósito) store-room, ⚓ warehouse; ⚓ hold de barco; S.Am. grocery store; **bodegón** m cheap restaurant; b.s. low dive; paint. still life.

bodijo m F quiet wedding; b.s. unequal match, misalliance.

bodoque m pellet; lump; F nitwit.

bodorrio m = bodijo.

bofe m lung; ~s pl. lights de animal; F echar los ~s slog, slave; F echar los ~s por go all out for.

bofetada f slap in the face (a. fig.); dar de ~s hit, punch; **bofetón** m (hard) slap.

boga[1] f vogue (por for), popularity; en ~ in fashion, in vogue.

boga[2] ⚓ **1.** f rowing; **2.** m/f rower; **bogada** f stroke (of an oar); **bogador** m, -a f rower; **bogar** [1h] row; (navegar) sail; **bogavante** m ⚓ stroke; zo. lobster.

bogotano adj. a. su. m, a f (native) of Bogotá.

bohardilla f = buhardilla.

bohémico geog., **bohemio** adj. a. su. m, a f fig., **bohemo** adj. a. su. m, a f geog. Bohemian.

boicotear [1a] boycott; **boicoteo** m boycott(ing).

boina f beret.

boj m ♀ box(-wood).

bol m (punch-)bowl; (bolo) ninepin.

bola f ball; ⚓ signal (with disks); naipes: slam; (betún) blacking, shoe-polish; F fib; ~s pl. ⊕ ball-bearings; S.Am. hunt. bolas; (juego de [las]) ~s American skittles; ~ de naftalina mothball; ~ de nieve snowball; F ¡dale ~! come off it!; v. pie; dejar que ruede la ~ let things take their course; **bolada** f throw; S.Am. ✝ lucky break.

bolardo m bollard.

bolchev(iqu)ismo m Bolshevism; **bolchev(iqu)ista** adj. a. su. m/f Bolshevist.

boleada f S.Am. hunt; **boleadoras** f/pl. S.Am. bolas; **bolear** [1a] v/t. F throw; S.Am. hunt; v/i. play for fun; F tell fibs; S.Am. play a dirty trick; ~se (caballo) rear; fig. stum-

ble; S.Am. make a mistake; **bolera** f (sitio) bowling-alley, skittle-alley; **bolero** m bolero. [(juego) skittles.]

boleta f pass, ticket; ✝ authorization, permit; S.Am. ballot (paper); **boletería** f S.Am. 🚋 booking-office; thea. box-office; **boletín** m (informe etc.) bulletin; = boleta; ~ de inscripción registration form; ~ meteorológico weather-forecast; ~ naviero shipping register; ~ de noticias news-bulletin; ~ oficial (del Estado) official gazette; ~ de pedido application form; **boleto** m S.Am. ticket.

bolichada f F lucky break, stroke of luck; de una ~ at one stroke; **boliche** m (bola) jack; (juego) bowls; (pista) bowling green; ⊕ small furnace; S.Am. skittles.

bólido m meteorite.

bolígrafo m ball-point pen.

bolillo m bobbin (for making lace); S.Am. bread roll; ~s pl. toffee-bars.

bolina f ⚓ bowline; F racket, row, uproar; ⚓ de ~ close-hauled.

bolita f pellet; (canica) marble.

boliviano adj. a. su. m, a f Bolivian.

bolo m ninepin; naipes: slam; pharm. large pill; (juego de) ~s pl. ninepins, skittles; echar a rodar los ~s fig. create a disturbance.

bolonio m, a f F dunce, ignoramus.

bolsa f purse para dinero; (saquillo) bag, pouch; handbag de mujer; ⚒, geol. pocket; bag en vestido, tela; S.Am. sack; anat. cavity, sac; ✝ stock exchange, stock market; fig. fortune; ~ de agua caliente hot-water bottle; ~ de aire air-pocket; ~ de granos corn-exchange; ~ de herramientas tool-bag, tool-kit; S.Am. ~ negra black market; ~ de trabajo labour exchange, employment bureau; hacer ~ (vestido) bag; (arrugarse) pucker (up); jugar a la ~ play the market.

bolsillo m pocket (a. fig.); (saquillo) purse, money-bag; de ~ pocket attr., pocket-size; **bolsín** m ✝ bucket-shop, kerb market; **bolsista** m (stock-)broker; S.Am. pickpocket; **bolso** m bag, purse; ~ de mano, ~ de mujer handbag, purse Am.; hacer ~ (vela) belly.

bollería f pastry shop, bakery; **bollero** m baker, muffin-man;

bollo *m cocina*: muffin, bun, roll; dent *en metal*; *sew.* puff; ✵ bump, lump; F to-do, mix-up; **bollón** *m* (ornamental) stud; (*pendiente*) button earring.

bomba *f* pump; glass, globe *de lámpara*; ✺ bomb; ✗ shell; *S.Am.* (*burbuja*) bubble; (*chistera*) top hat; ¡~! attention please!; ~ *de aire* air-pump; ~ *aspirante* suction pump; ~ *atómica* atomic bomb; *mot.* ~ *de gasolina* fuel-pump; (*garaje*) petrol-pump; ~ *de hidrógeno* hydrogen bomb; ~ *impulsora* force-pump; ~ *incendiaria* incendiary bomb; ~ *de incendios* fire-engine; ~ *de mano* grenade; ~ *de relojería*, ~ *de retardo* time-bomb; ~ *revienta-manzanas* blockbuster; *a prueba de ~s* bombproof; *caer como una ~* fall like a bombshell; *dar a la ~* pump; F *estar a tres ~s* be very cross; *estar echando ~s* be boiling hot.

bombardear [1a] ✗, *phys.* bombard (*a. fig.*; de with); ✗ shell; ✺ bomb, raid; **bombardeo** *m* ✗ bombardment (*a. phys.*), shelling; ✺ bombing; ~ *aéreo* (air-)raid; **bombardero 1.** bombing; **2.** *m* bomber.

bombasí *m* fustian. [bomber.]

bombear [1a] ✗ shell; *sew.* pad; *S.Am. agua* pump (out); *fig.* = *dar bombo a*; ~**se** ▲ camber; (*madera etc.*) bulge; **bombeo** *m* camber; crown *de carretera*; bulging, warping.

bombero *m* fireman; (*cuerpo de*) ~*s pl.* fire-brigade.

bombilla *f* ⚡ bulb; chimney *de lámpara*; ~ *de flash*, ~ *fusible* flash-bulb.

bombo 1. F dumbfounded; **2.** *m* ♪ bass drum; ⚓ lighter; F excessive praise; *thea. etc.* write-up, ballyhoo; F *dar ~ a* praise to the skies; *thea.* write up, ballyhoo *Am.*; *S.Am. irse al ~* fail, come to grief.

bombón *m* sweet, candy *Am.*; chocolate; F (*p.*) good sort; (*mujer*) peach; (*cosa*) beauty.

bombona *f* carboy.

bombonera *f* sweet-box; F cosy little place.

bonachón good-natured, kindly; *b.s.* naïve, unsuspecting.

bonaerense *adj. a. su. m/f* (native) of Buenos Aires.

bonancible *meteor.* calm, fair; **bonanza** *f* ⚓ fair weather; *min.* bonanza; ✢ prosperity, bonanza; ✢ *estar en ~* be booming; ⚓ *ir en ~* have fair weather; *fig.* go well,

bonazo = *buenazo*. [prosper.]

bondad *f* goodness; kind(li)ness *etc.*; *tener la* ~ *de inf.* be so kind (*or* good) as to *inf.*; **bondadoso** kind(ly), kind-hearted, good(-natured).

bonete *m eccl.* hat, biretta; *univ. approx.* cap, mortar-board F; F *a tente* ~ doggedly.

bonificación *f* improvement (*a.* ✎); ✢ allowance, discount; **bonificar** [1g] improve (*a.* ✎).

bonísimo *sup. of* bueno.

bonitamente stealthily, craftily; little by little; **bonito[1]** pretty, nice (*a. fig.*).

bonito[2] *m* tunny, bonito.

bono *m* voucher; ✢ bond.

boqueada: *dar la última* ~ breathe one's last; **boquear** [1a] *v/t.* pronounce, say; *v/i.* be at one's last gasp; *fig.* be in its last stages; **boquera** *f* ✎ sluice; ✺ lip sore; ~*s pl.* F hunger; **boquerel** *m* nozzle; **boquerón** *m* wide opening; *ichth.* anchovy; **boquete** *m* gap, opening, hole; **boquiabierto** open-mouthed; *fig.* aghast; *estar* ~ gape; *mirar* ~ gape (at); **boquifresco** F outspoken; cheeky; **boquilla** *f* ♪ mouthpiece; ⊕ nozzle; burner *de gas*; stem *de pipa*; cigarette-holder; **boquirroto** F talkative, garrulous; **boquirrubio** = *boquirroto*; (*candoroso*) simple, naïve; glib, indiscreet.

bórax *m* borax.

borboll(e)ar [1a] bubble, boil up; *fig.* splutter; **borbollón** *m* bubbling, boiling; *a* ~*es* impetuously, with a rush; **borbollonear** [1a] = *borboll(e)ar*.

borbónico Bourbon *attr.*

borbotar [1a] (*fuente*) bubble up, gush forth; bubble, boil *al hervir*; **borbotón** *m* = *borbollón*; *hablar a* ~*es* talk impetuously, splutter; *manar a* ~*es* gush forth.

borceguí *m* high shoe, laced boot, buskin; bootee *de niño*.

borda *f* ⚓ gunwale; ⚓ (*vela*) mainsail; (*choza*) hut; ⚓ *de fuera de* ~ outboard *attr.*; *tirar por la* ~

throw overboard; **bordada** f ♻
tack; *dar* ~s ♻ tack; F keep on going
to and fro.
bordado m embroidery, needlework; **bordadora** f needlewoman;
bordadura f embroidery; **bordar**
[1a] embroider (*a. fig.*).
borde m edge; side *de camino etc.*;
brink *de abismo*; lip *de taza*; brim,
rim *de vaso*; ledge *de ventana*; *sew.*
selvage; ♻ board; ~ *del camino*
roadside, verge; ~ *del mar* seaside,
sea-shore; *al* ~ *de* at the side (*or*
edge) of; **bordear** [1a] *v/t.* skirt,
go along the edge of; *v/i.* ♻ tack;
bordillo m kerb.
bordo m ♻ side; (*bordada*) tack; *a* ~
on board; *al* ~ alongside; *de alto* ~
large, seagoing; *fig.* of importance,
influential.
bordón m pilgrim's staff; *fig.* guide,
helping hand; ♪ bass string; *poet.*
refrain; *fig.* = **bordoncillo** m pet
phrase.
boreal north(ern).
Borgoña m (*a. vino de* ~) burgundy.
borla f tassel; pompon *en sombrero*;
tuft *de hebras*; bob *de pelo*; powder-
puff *para empolvarse*; *univ.* doctor's
insignia.
borne m ⚡ terminal.
borneadizo easily warped; flexible;
bornear [1a] *v/t.* twist, bend; △
put in place, align; *v/i.* ♻ swing at
anchor; ~se warp, bulge; **borneo**
m twisting, bending; swaying *al*⎰
boro m boron.   [*bailar.*⎱
borona f maize, corn *Am.*; millet;
(*pan*) maize bread.
borra f (*lana*) thick wool, flock;
stuffing *de almohada*; (*pelusa*) fluff;
♀ down; sediment, lees; F (*palabras*)
useless talk; F (*cosas*) trash; ~ *de*
algodón cotton waste.
borrachear [1a] (go on the) booze;
borrachera f (*estado*) drunkenness; (*a. juerga de* ~) spree, binge;
fig. great excitement; *tomar una* ~
go on a spree; **borrachez** f
drunkenness; *fig.* mental disturbance; **borrachín** m drunkard, sot,
toper; **borracho 1.** drunk; (*de costumbre*) drunken, hard-drinking,
fond of the bottle; *bizcocho* tipsy;
color violet; *fig.* blind, wild (*de ira*
etc. with); **2.** m, a f drunk(ard), sot.
borrador m rough copy, first draft;
(*libro*) book for rough work; ✝ day-

book; (*goma*) rubber, eraser;
duster *para pizarra*; **borradura** f
erasure; **borrajear** [1a] scribble;
(*distraído*) doodle; **borrar** [1a]
erase, rub out *con borrador*; cross
out *con rayas*; blot, smear *con tinta*;
fig. erase, wipe away, wipe out;
imagen blur, blot out.
borrasca f storm (*a. fig.*); *meteor.*
a. depression, cyclone; (*riesgo*)
hazard; (*contratiempo*) setback;
borrascoso stormy (*a. fig.*); *viento*
squally, gusty; *fig.* = **borrasquero**
riotous, wild.
borrego m, a f (yearling) lamb;
F simpleton; **borreguillo** m fleecy
cloud; ~s *pl.* mackerel sky.
borrica f donkey, she-ass; F ass (of
a woman); **borricada** f piece of
nonsense; **borrico** m donkey, ass
(*a. fig.*); ⊕ saw-horse; **borricón** m
F, **borricote** m F poor devil; **borri-**
quete m ⊕ saw-horse.
borrón m blot, smudge; (*borrador*)
rough draft, sketch (*a. paint.*); *fig.*
blemish; stain, stigma, slur *en repu-*
tación; *lit.* estos ~es these humble
jottings; **borronear** [1a] = **borra-**
jear; **borroso** *líquido* muddy, dirty;
imagen blurred, indistinct; *paint.*
woolly; *superficie* smudgy.
borujo m lump; pack; **borujón** m ⚸
lump, bump; (*lío*) bundle; **boru-**
joso lumpy.
boscaje m small wood, grove; *paint.*
woodland scene; **boscoso** wooded;
bosque m wood(s), woodland;
(*grande*) forest; **bosquecillo** m
copse, spinney.
bosquejar [1a] sketch, outline (*a.*
fig.); ⊕ design; *proyecto* draft;
bosquejo m sketch, outline (*a.fig.*);
draft *de proyecto*.   [yawn.⎱
bostezar [1f] yawn; **bostezo** m⎰
bota f boot; (*odre*) leather wine-
bottle; ~s *pl. de campaña* top-
boots; ~s *pl. de goma* gum-boots;
~s *pl. de montar* riding-boots;
morir con las ~s *puestas* die in harness; F *ponerse las* ~s strike lucky,
make one's pile.
botado cheeky; *S.Am. niño* abandoned; *S.Am.* ✝ dirt-cheap.
botador m ♻ (punting) pole; ⊕
claw-hammer; *S.Am.* spendthrift;
botadura f launching; **botalón** m
boom, outrigger; ~ *de foque* jib-
boom.

botánica f botany; **botánico 1.** botanic(al); **2.** m, a f = **botanista** m/f botanist.

botar [1a] v/t. hurl, fling; *pelota* pitch; *barco* launch; *timón* put over; *S.Am.* throw away; *fortuna* fritter away; v/i. *mot. etc.* bump, bounce; (*caballo*) buck; ~se *S.Am.* throw o.s. (a into); **botaratada** f F wild thing; wild scheme; **botarate** m F wild fellow, madcap; *S.Am.* spendthrift.

botarga f motley, clown's outfit; (*p.*) clown.

botavara f ⚓ boom, sprit.

bote[1] m (*golpe*) thrust, blow; buck de caballo; bounce de pelota etc.; dar ~s bounce; esp. mot. bump, jolt; estar de ~ en ~ be packed, be crowded out.

bote[2] m (*vasija*) can, tin; pot, jar; *naipes*: jackpot; *mot.* F jalop(p)y.

bote[3] m ⚓ boat; ~ de paso ferry-boat; ~ de remos row(ing)-boat; ~ de salvamento, ~ salvavidas lifeboat. [jar.\

botella f bottle; ~ de Leiden Leyden\

botica f chemist's (shop), drug store *Am.*; F de todo como en ~ everything under the sun; **boticario** m chemist, druggist.

botija f earthenware jug; F estar hecho una ~ be as fat as a sow; **botijo** m earthenware jar (with spout and handle); v. tren.

botillería f refreshment stall.

botín[1] m ✕ booty, plunder, spoils.

botín[2] m (*polaina*) spat; = **botina** f bootee; high shoe.

botiquín m medicine chest; (a. ~ de emergencia) first-aid kit.

boto 1. dull, blunt; *fig.* dull, slow (-witted); **2.** m leather wine-bottle.

botón m sew., ♂ button; ~ (de camisa) stud; ~ (de puerta) doorknob; *radio*: knob; tip de florete; ♀ bud; F (*mujer*) peach; ♀ ~ de oro buttercup; kingcup; F ni un ~ not a sausage; **botonar** [1a] *S.Am.* button (up); **botones** m buttons, bellboy, bellhop *Am.*

bóveda f ⚐ vault; dome; cavern; ~ celeste arch of heaven; **bovedilla**: F subirse a las ~s go up in smoke.

bovino bovine.

boxeador m boxer; **boxear** [1a] box; **boxeo** m boxing.

boya f ⚓ buoy; float de red.

boyada f drove of oxen.

boyante buoyant; *fig.* lucky; **boyar** [1a] float. [cattle dog.\

boyero m oxherd, drover; (*perro*)\

bozal 1. (*novato*) raw, green; *potro* wild, untamed; F silly, stupid; *S.Am.* speaking broken Spanish; **2.** m muzzle; *S.Am.* halter.

bozo m (*vello*) down (on upper lip); (*boca*) mouth, lips; halter, headstall de caballo.

bracear [1a] swing one's arms; (*nadar*) swim, esp. crawl; *fig.* wrestle, struggle; **bracero** m (unskilled) labourer, navvy; farm labourer; servir de ~ be an escort; de ~ = **bracete**: de ~ arm in arm.

braco 1. pug-nosed; **2.** m hunt. setter.

bráctea f bract.

braga f ⊕ rope, sling; F nappy, diaper *Am.* de niño; ~s pl. breeches de hombre; knickers, panties de mujer; **bragado** *fig.* energetic; b.s. wicked; **bragadura** f anat. crotch; sew. gusset; **bragazas** m henpecked husband; **braguero** m ♂ truss; **bragueta** f fly, flies; **braguillas** m F brat.

brama f zo. rut.

bramante m twine, fine string.

bramar [1a] roar, bellow (a. fig.); (*viento*) howl, roar; (*mar*) thunder, roar; **bramido** m roar, bellow etc.

branquia f gills.

brasa f (live) coal; estar en ~s fig. be on tenterhooks; estar hecho una ~ be very flushed; **brasero** m brazier; hist. stake.

brasileño adj. a. su. m, a f Brazilian.

bravata f threat; (piece of) bravado; echar ~s = **bravear**; **braveador 1.** blustering, bullying; **2.** m bully; **bravear** [1a] boast, talk big; bluster.

bravera f vent, chimney.

braveza f ferocity; meteor. etc. fury; (*valor*) bravery, courage; **bravío 1.** fierce, ferocious; (*indómito*) untamed, wild; *fig.* uncouth, coarse; **2.** fierceness; **bravo 1.** (*valiente*) brave; b.s. boastful, blustering; fine, excellent; (*guapo*) spruce, fine; sumptuous, magnificent; *animal* fierce; *mar* rough; *paisaje* rugged; *genio* bad-tempered, irri-

table; (*enojado*) very cross; ¡~!
bravo!; 2. *m* thug; **bravucón** *m* F
boaster, braggart; **bravura** *f* ferocity; (*valor*) bravery; = *bravata*.
braza *f* approx. fathom (= *1.67 m.*);
(*cabo*) brace; **brazada** *f* (*remo*,
natación) stroke; (*brazado*) armful; ~ de pecho breast-stroke;
brazado *m* armful; **brazal** *m* arm-
band; ✝ irrigation channel; **brazalete** *m* bracelet, wristlet; **brazo**
m arm (*a.* ⊕, *fig.*); zo. foreleg; ⚮
limb, branch; (*soporte*) bracket; *fig.*
energy, enterprise; (*valor*) courage;
~s *pl. fig.* backers, protectors;
(*obreros*) hands, workers; ~ derecho
fig. right-hand man; ~ de dirección
steering-arm; ~ de lámpara lamp-
bracket; ~ de lámpara de gas gas-
bracket; ~ de mar sound, arm of
the sea; F estar hecho un ~ de mar
be dressed up to the nines; a ~
partido hand to hand; con los ~s
abiertos with open arms (*a. fig.*);
asidos del ~ arm in arm; cruzarse
de ~s fold one's arms; estarse con
los ~s cruzados *fig.* (sit back and)
do nothing; F no dar su ~ a torcer
stand fast, not give in; mover a ~
manhandle; F tener ~ (*voz*) be
husky; **brazuelo** *m* zo. shoulder.
brea *f* tar, pitch; **brear** [1a] F abuse,
ill-treat; (*zumbar*) make fun of;
~ a golpes beat up.
brebaje *m* pharm. potion, mixture;
b.s. brew, nasty stuff (to drink).
brécoles *m/pl.* broccoli.
brecha *f* ⚔ breach; ⚠ gap, opening;
abrir ~ en muro breach; abrir (or
hacer) ~ en *fig.* make an impression
on.
brega *f* (*lucha*) struggle; (*riña*)
quarrel, row; (*chasco*) trick, joke;
F andar a la ~ slog away; dar ~ a
play a trick on; **bregar** [1h] struggle, fight (*con* with, *against*; *a. fig.*);
(*ajetrearse*) slog away.
breña *f*, **breñal** *m* scrub, rough
ground; **breñoso** rough, scrubby.
brete *m* fetters, shackles; *fig.* tight
spot, jam; poner en un ~ get *s.o.* in
a fix.
bretones *m/pl.* Brussels sprouts.
breva *f* ⚮ (early) fig; flat cigar;
F chicken-feed, cinch; ¡no caerá esa
~! no such luck!
breve 1. short; brief (*esp. de duración*); estilo terse; en ~ before long,

shortly; 2. *m* ♪ breve; eccl. (papal)
brief; **brevedad** *f* shortness; brev-
ity; conciseness de estilo; con la
mayor ~ as soon as possible; **breviario** *m* breviary; *fig.* compendium; (*lectura*) bedside companion.
brezal *m* moor(land), heath; **brezo**
m heather.
briba: andar (or vivir) a la ~ loaf
around; **bribón 1.** idle, loafing;
(*bellaco*) rascally; 2. *m*, -a *f* loafer;
rascal, scamp; **bribonada** *f* dirty
trick; **bribonear** [1a] loaf around;
bribonería *f* idle life; (*bellaquería*)
roguery.
brida *f* bridle; ⊕ fishplate; ⊕
(*anillo*) collar; a toda ~ at top speed;
bridón *m* snaffle; ⚔ bridoon.
brigada 1. *f* ⚔ brigade; squad, gang
de obreros etc.; ~ sanitaria sanitation
department; 2. *m* approx. staff
sergeant; **brigadier** *m* brigadier.
brigantino adj. a. su. *m*, a *f*
(native) of Corunna.
brillante 1. brilliant (*a. fig., p.*),
shining, bright; joya, escena glittering; aspecto gay; conversación
scintillating; 2. *m* brilliant; **brillantez** *f* brilliance etc.; **brillar** [1a]
shine (*a. fig., p.*); glitter, gleam,
glisten; beam con sonrisa; glow,
light up (*de emoción* with); ~ por su
ausencia be conspicuous by one's
absence; **brillo** *m* shine etc.; lustre,
sheen esp. de superficie; glow,
radiance; *fig.* splendour, brilliance;
sacar ~ a polish, shine.
brin *m* fine canvas, duck.
brincar [1g] v/t. niño dandle; F
pasaje skip, miss out; v/i. skip,
jump, leap about; F go off the deep
end, blow one's top (*por* at); **brinco**
m jump, leap, skip; en un ~ in a
trice.
brindar [1a] v/t. offer (*a* to; *a
alguien con algo* s.t. to s.o.); toro
etc. dedicate; invite (*a inf.* to inf.);
fig. sombra etc. lend, offer; v/i.
invite; ~ a, ~ por drink (a toast) to,
toast; ~se a inf. offer to inf.;
brindis *m* toast.
brío *m* (freq. ~s pl.) spirit, dash,
nerve; determination, resolution;
(*garbo*) jauntiness; cortar los ~s a
clip s.o.'s wings; **brioso** spirited,
dashing; determined, resolute;
jaunty.
briqueta *f* briquette.

la fiesta de las bromas
= April Fool's Day

brisa f breeze.
británico British; **britano 1.** esp.
hist. British; **2.** m, a f hist. a. poet.
Briton.
brizna f strand, thread, filament;
fragment, piece.
broca f sew. reel, bobbin; ⊕ drill,
bit; tack de zapato; ~ de avellanar
countersinking bit.
brocado 1. brocaded; **2.** m brocade.
brocal m curb de pozo; cigarette-
holder.
brocha f (large paint-)brush; ~ de
afeitar shaving-brush; de ~ gorda
fig. slapdash, crude; **brochada** f,
brochazo m brush-stroke; (pintura) dab (of paint).
broche m clasp (a. de libro), fastener;
(joya etc.) brooch.
brochón m whitewash brush.
broma f (chanza) joke, leg-pull;
prank; ~ (estudiantil) rag; (algazara)
fun, merriment; ~ pesada practical
joke, hoax; b.s. poor sort of joke; en
~ in fun; lo decía en ~ I was only
joking; estar de ~ be in a joking
mood; no estoy para ~s I'm in no
mood for jokes; gastar una ~ play
a joke (a on); **bromear** [1a] joke
(a. ~se); rag; (burlarse) pull s.o.'s
leg; **bromista 1.** fond of joking
etc.; **2.** m/f (salado) joker, wag;
(chancero) leg-puller.   [bromide.]
bromo m bromine; **bromuro** m⟩
bronca f F (riña) row, scrap, wrangle; (reprensión) rap over the
knuckles; (broma) poor sort of joke;
armar una ~ start a row; echar una
~ a rap s.o. over the kuckles.
bronce m bronze; ~ de cañón gun-
metal; ~ dorado ormolu; **bronceado 1.** bronze(-coloured); piel
tanned, sunburnt; **2.** m ⊕ bronze
finish; tan de piel; **broncear(se)**
[1a] ⊕ bronze; piel tan, bronze,
brown.
bronco superficie rough, unpolished;
metal brittle; voz gruff, harsh;
♪ rasping, harsh; trato gruff;
(grosero) uncouth, coarse; **bron-
quedad** f roughness etc.
bronquial bronchial.
bronquina f F scrap, quarrel.
bronquitis f bronchitis.
broquel m shield (a. fig.); **bro-
quelarse** [1a] shield o.s.
broqueta f skewer.
brota f shoot, bud; **brotar** [1a] v/t.

♀ sprout, put out; fig. pour out;
v/i. ♀ sprout, bud; (agua etc.) spring
up, gush forth; (río) rise; ✗ break
out, show; fig. spring up; **brote** m
♀ shoot, bud; ✗ rash, pimples;
✗ outbreak de enfermedad.
broza f ✗ chaff de trigo etc.; (hojas
etc.) dead leaves, dead wood;
(maleza) brushwood; fig. rubbish,
refuse; (escrito) trash.
bruces: de ~ face downwards; caer
de ~ fall flat on one's face.
bruja f witch; F hag, harridan; orn.
owl; **brujería** f sorcery, witchcraft,
magic; **brujo** m sorcerer, magician,
wizard.
brújula f ⚓ compass; fig. guide; ~
giroscópica gyro-compass; F perder
la ~ lose one's touch; **brujulear**
[1a] cartas uncover; F (adivinar)
guess; (gestionar) manage, contrive.
bruma f (esp. sea-)mist, fog;
brumoso misty, foggy.
bruñido m (acto) polish(ing);(efecto)
shine, gloss; **bruñidor** m, -a f
polisher, burnisher; **bruñir** [3h]
polish, burnish; ~se F put on make-
up.
brusco ataque sudden; movimiento
brusque; curva sharp; fig. brusque,
abrupt, off-hand.
bruselas f/pl. (unas a pair of)
tweezers.
brusquedad f suddenness etc.;
hablar con ~ speak sharply.
brutal 1. brutal; (brusco) sudden,
unexpected; F terrific; **2.** m brute;
brutalidad f brutality, bestiality;
(acto) piece of brutality, crime;
stupidity; F terrific; **bruto** 1. brute, brutish; bestial; (malcriado) uncouth,
coarse; material rough, unpolished;
peso gross; stupid; F terrific; en ~
(in the) rough; raw; piedra unpolished; **2.** m brute; F dolt.
bruza f brush para caballo (a. typ.);
scrubbing-brush para fregar.
bu m F bogy (man); hacer el ~ a
scare.   [tumour.⟩
búa f pimple; **buba** f, **bubo** m⟩
bucal oral, of the mouth.
bucanero m buccaneer.
búcaro m (fragrant) clay; (vasija)
vase.
buccino m whelk.
bucear [1a] dive; work as a diver;
fig. delve, search below the surface;
buceo m diving.

buces v. bruces.
bucle m curl, ringlet; *fig.* curve, bend, loop.
bucólica f pastoral poem, bucolic; F meal; **bucólico** pastoral, bucolic.
buchada f = bocanada; **buche** m orn. crop; zo. a. F maw; F belly; (*bocado*) mouthful; *sew.* pucker; *fig.* inside, bosom; *sew.* hacer ~ be baggy, pucker; F *llenar bien el* ~ tuck in; F *sacar el* ~ show off; F *sacar el* ~ a make s.o. talk.
budín m pudding.
budión m butterfly fish.
buen v. bueno; **buenamente** (*fácilmente*) easily, freely; (*de buena gana*) willingly, voluntarily; **buenaventura** f (good) luck; fortune; *decir la* ~ a tell s.o.'s fortune; **buenazo** kind(ly), good-natured.
bueno 1. mst good; p. good, kind, nice; *calentura* high; *constitución* sound, strong; *doctrina* sound; *sociedad* polite; *tiempo* good, fine, fair; *iro.* fine, pretty; F (*sencillo*) gullible, naïve; ~ *para inf.* suitable for ger., good for ger.; ser ~ *para con* be kind to; ~ *de comer* (*sabroso*) good to eat; (*sano*) fit to eat; *el* ~ *de Pedro* good old Peter; de ~as a primeras (*de pronto*) suddenly, out of nowhere; (*en seguida*) straightaway; por las ~as gladly, willingly; por las ~as o por las malas by fair means or foul; por las ~as y las malas through thick and thin; estar ~ be well; F *está* ~a she's pretty hot; F *¡esta buenísima!* she looked a real treat!; F *estar de* ~as be in a good mood; *¡ésa sí que es* ~a! that's a good one!; **2.** (*como int. etc.*): *¡*~*!* all right!, well then!; *duda:* come, come!, come off it!; *sorpresa:* you don't say!; *mandato:* *¡*~ (está)! that's enough!, that'll do!; *¿adónde* ~? where are you off to?; *¡cuánto* (or *tanto*) ~ por aquí! hullo (there)!, it's good to see you!; F *¡*~*as!* hullo!; **3.** cj.: ~ que although, even though.
buey m bullock, steer; ox *para labrar etc.*; F ~ suelto free man, free agent; (*soltero*) bachelor; *trabajar como un* ~ work like a Trojan.
búfalo m buffalo.
bufanda f scarf, muffler.
bufar [1a] snort (a. *fig.*; de with); (*gato*) spit.
bufete m desk; ⚖ lawyer's office.

bufido m snort (a. *fig.*; de of).
bufo 1. farcical, slapstick; *ópera comic*; **2.** m clown; **bufón 1.** funny, comical, clownish; **2.** m, -a f buffoon, clown; *hist.* jester; **bufonada** f (*acto*) buffoonery, clowning; (*dicho*) joke; (*sátira*) comic piece; **bufonearse** [1a] clown, play the fool; (*burlarse*) joke; **bufonesco** ~ bufón 1.
bugui-bugui m boogie-woogie.
bugle m bugle. [(*desván*) garret.|
buhard(ill)a f dormer window;|
buho m (a. ~ real) (eagle) owl; *fig.* unsociable person, hermit.
buhonero m pedlar, hawker.
buitre m vulture.
bujería f trinket, gewgaw.
bujía f candle; (*candelero*) candlestick; ⚡ candle power; *mot.* (sparking-)plug.
bula f (papal) bull; F *no poder con la* ~ have no strength left for anything; F *no me vale la* ~ *de Meco* I'm done for, I haven't a chance in hell.
bulbo m ⚘, ⚕ bulb; *S.Am. radio:* valve; **bulboso** ⚘ bulbous; bulb-shaped.
bulevar m boulevard, avenue.
búlgaro adj. a. su. m, a f Bulgarian.
bulón m bolt; spring pin.
bulto m (*volumen*) bulk(iness), volume, mass(iveness); (*que se distingue mal*) shape, form; ⚕ swelling, lump; (*fardo*) package, bundle, bale; bust; *S.Am.* brief-case; ~s pl. de mano hand luggage; a ~ in the mass, broadly; de (*mucho*) ~ heavy, massive; *fig.* important; de poco ~ small, which does not take up much room; F *buscar el* ~ a steal up behind; F *escurrir el* ~ dodge, get out of it.
bulla f (*ruido*) noise, uproar; (*movimiento*) bustle; fussing about; (*gente*) crowd; *meter* ~ kick up a row; **bullaje** m crush, crowd; **bullanga** f disturbance, riot, unrest; **bullanguero 1.** riotous, rowdy; **2.** m, a f rioter, troublemaker; **bullebulle** m/f busybody, mischief-maker; (*inquieto*) fusspot; **bullicio** m (*ruido*) uproar; rowdiness; din, hum *de calle etc.*; (*movimiento*) bustle; (*alboroto*) uproar, confusion, disturbance; **bullicioso** *multitud, asamblea* noisy; *calle*

bustling, busy, noisy; (*alborotador*) riotous, turbulent; (*inquieto*) restless; **bullir** [3h] *v/t.* move; *v/i.* (*hervir*) boil (*a. fig.*); (*con burbujas*) bubble (up); (*moverse*) move about, get around; bustle around; *fig.* teem, swarm (de, en with); ~se stir, budge.

buñuelo *m approx.* doughnut, fritter; F botched job, mess.

buque *m* ship, boat, vessel; (*casco*) hull; (*cabida*) capacity, tonnage; ~ almirante flagship; ~ de carga freighter; ~-escuela training-ship; ~ de guerra warship; man-of-war †; ~ mercante merchantman; ~ minador minelayer; ~ nodriza mothership; ~ (de) vapor steamer, steamship; ~ de vela, ~ velero sailing-ship.

burbuja *f* bubble; *hacer* ~s = **burbujear** [1a] bubble, form bubbles.

burdégano *m* hinny.

burdel *m* brothel.

burdo coarse.

burgalés *adj. a. su. m*, **-a** *f* (native) of Burgos.

burgués 1. middle-class, bourgeois (*a. contp.*); (*de ciudad*) town *attr.*; **2.** *m*, **-a** *f* bourgeois, member of the middle class; townsman *de ciudad*; **burguesía** *f* middle class, bourgeoisie.

buril *m* burin, graver; **burilar** [1a] engrave.

burla *f* (*palabra*) gibe, taunt; (*chanza*) joke; (*chasco*) trick, hoax, practical joke; (*engaño*) trick, deception; (*esp.* ~*s pl.*) mockery, ridicule, joking, fun; ~ *burlando* unawares; (*con disimulo*) on the quiet; de ~s in fun; *gastar* ~s con make fun of; *hacer* ~ de todo make fun of everything; **burladero** *m* refuge, covert (in bullring); **burlador 1.** *m*, **-a** *f* wag, practical joker, leg-puller F; **2.** *m* seducer.

burlar [1a] *v/t.* (*zumbar*) take in, hoax; (*engañar*) deceive; *enemigo etc.* outwit, outmanoeuvre; *ambición* frustrate; *bloqueo* run; *deseos etc.* disappoint; *cheat s.o.* of; *mujer* seduce; *v/i.*, ~se joke, banter; scoff; *yo no me burlo* I'm in dead earnest; ~ de make fun of, poke fun at, scoff at; **burlería** *f* trick; (*cuento*) tall story, fairy tale; **burlesco** funny, comic; (*satírico*) mock, burlesque.

burlete *m* weather-strip.

burlón 1. joking, bantering; *tono* mocking; *esp. risa* sardonic; **2.** *m*, **-a** *f* wag, joker, leg-puller F; *b.s.* scoffer.

buró *m* bureau, (roll-top) desk.

burocracia *f* public service, civil service; *esp. b.s.* bureaucracy; *contp.* officialdom; *fig.* red tape; **burócrata** *m/f* civil servant, administrative official; *contp.* bureaucrat, pen-pusher; **burocrático** bureaucratic; official.

burra *f* donkey, she-ass; *fig.* stupid woman; (*sufrida*) drudge, slave; **burrada** *f fig.* silly thing, piece of stupidity; *decir* ~s talk nonsense; **burro 1.** *m* donkey, ass; ⊕ sawhorse; *fig.* ass, dolt; ~ de carga *fig.* glutton for work; *b.s.* drudge, slave; F ~ cargado de letras pompous ass.

bursátil stock-market *attr.*

burujo *m etc. v.* borujo.

busca *f* search, hunt (de for); *en* ~ de in search of; *buscada* f = busca; **buscador** *m*, **-a** *f* searcher; **buscapié** *m* hint; **buscapiés** *m* squib, cracker.

buscar [1g] **1.** *v/t.* look for, search for; seek (for, after); hunt for, have a look for; *enemigo* seek out; *cita* look up; *ganancia* be out for; *palabra* grope for; *camorra* ask for; *ir a* ~ (go and) fetch; **2.** *v/i.* look, search; **3.** ~se: *se busca* (*aviso*) wanted; F *buscársela* manage to get along; (*camorra*) look for trouble, ask for it.

buscarruidos *m* troublemaker; **buscavidas** *m/f* snoop, busybody; (*trabajador*) hard worker, hustler *Am.*; *b.s.* social climber, go-getter; **buscón** *m b.s.* petty thief, smalltime crook; **buscona** *f* whore; *v.* buscón.

busilis *m* F (real) difficulty, snag; *dar en el* ~ put one's finger on the spot; *ahí está el* ~ there's the snag.

búsqueda *f* = busca.

busto *m* bust.

butaca *f* armchair, easy-chair; *thea.* stall.

butano *m*: *gas* ~ butane (*or* cylinder) gas.

buz *m* kiss (of respect); F *hacer el* ~ bow and scrape.

buzo *m* diver.

buzón *m* ⚍ letterbox; canal, conduit; *echar al* ~ post.

C

¡ca! F get away with you!, not a bit of it!, oh no!

cabal 1. adj. exact, right; finished, complete, consummate; *esfuerzo etc.* all-out, thorough; *estar en sus* ~es be in one's right mind; 2. adv. exactly; perfectly (right); 3. int. quite right!

cábala f fig. cabal, intrigue; ~s pl. guess, supposition.

cabalgada f troop of riders; ✗ cavalry raid; cabalgadura f mount, horse; *(de carga)* beast of burden; cabalgar [1h] v/t. *yegua* cover; v/i. ride (on horseback); cabalgata f ride; *(desfile)* cavalcade.

cabalista m fig. schemer; cabalístico cab(b)alistic(al); fig. occult, mysterious.

caballa f mackerel.

caballar horse *attr. (a. rostro)*, equine; caballejo m pony; *b.s.* nag; caballerear [1a] put on airs, pretend to be somebody; caballeresco *hist.* of chivalry, chivalric; *sentimientos* fine, noble; *carácter* gentlemanly; *trato* chivalrous; caballerete m F stuck-up young fellow, dude *Am.*; caballería f mount, steed; horse, mule *etc.*; ✗ cavalry; *(orden)* order of knighthood; *hist.* knighthood, chivalry; ~ andante knight-errantry; F andarse en ~s overdo the compliments; caballeriza f stable *(a. fig., deportes)*; stud *de cría*; ~ de alquiler livery stable; caballerizo m groom, stable-man.

caballero 1. riding, mounted (en on); *fig.* persistent, obstinate (en in); 2. m gentleman; mister, sir *en trato directo*; *hist.* knight, noble, nobleman; knight *de Malta etc.*; ~ andante knight-errant; ~ de industria swindler, adventurer; *armar* ~ a knight; *ser cumplido* ~, *ser todo un* ~ be a real gentleman; *es un mal* ~ he's no gentleman; caballerosidad f gentlemanliness; chivalry; nobility; caballeroso gentlemanly; chivalrous; caballerote m F so-called gentleman.

caballete m ✗, △ ridge; *(madero)* trestle; cap *de chimenea*; paint. easel; bridge *de nariz*.

caballista m horseman; caballito m little horse, pony; ~ *(de niños)* hobby-horse; ~ del diablo dragon-fly; ~ de mar sea-horse; ~s pl. merry-go-round.

caballo m horse; *ajedrez*: knight; *naipes*: queen; ⊕ saw-horse; ⊕ ~ *(de fuerza)* horse-power; ~ de *balancín*, ~ *mecedor* rocking-horse; ~ de batalla *fig.* forte, speciality; ~ blanco backer; F ~ de buena boca accomodating fellow; ~ de carga pack-horse; ~ de carrera(s) race-horse; ~ de caza hunter; ~ de guerra war-horse; ~ padre stallion; ~ de tiro cart-horse, draught-horse; *a* ~ on horseback; *a* ~ de astride, on; *a mata* ~ at breakneck speed; ✗ de *a* ~ mounted; *ir (or montar) a* ~ ride (on horseback); caballón m ✗ ridge; caballuno horse-like, horsy.

cabaña f cabin, hut; *(rebaño)* flock; *billar*: balk; ~ de madera log-cabin; cabañero m shepherd.

cabaret [kaβa're] m cabaret; night-club.

cabás m satchel.

cabe m: F ~ de *pala* windfall, lucky break; F dar un ~ a do harm to.

cabecear [1a] v/t. sew. bind; *deportes*: head; v/i. nod; *(negación)* shake one's head; ⊕ pitch; *mot.* lurch; *(carga)* slip; cabeceo m nod; shake of the head; ⊕ pitching; *mot.* lurch(ing); cabecera f head *de cama, mesa, puente etc.*; head-board *de cama*; end *de cuarto etc.*; *(almohada)* pillow, bolster; *geog.* administrative centre, chief town; *typ.* headline; *(adorno)* head-piece; heading *de documento*; de ~ *libro* bedside attr.; *médico* family attr.; *a la* ~ de at *s.o.'s* bedside.

cabecilla 1. m/f F hothead, wrong-headed sort; 2. m ringleader.

cabellera f head of hair; *(peluca)* wig; scalp *de piel roja*; *ast.* tail; cabello m hair *(a. ~s pl.)*; ~ merino thick curly hair; ♀ ~s pl. de Venus maidenhair; en ~ with one's hair down; en ~s bare-headed; pendiente de un ~ hanging by a thread; F asirse de un ~ use any excuse; traído por los ~s irrelevant, quite off the point; símil far-fetched; **cabelludo** hairy; shaggy; ♀ fibrous; v. cuero.

caber [2m] **1.** fit, go (en caja into); ~ en espacio be contained in; cabe(n) X there is room for X; en esta caja no cabe it won't go into this box, this box won't hold it; ¿cabemos todos? is there room for us all?; no cabe por esta puerta it won't get through this door; **2.** fig. be possible; ~ a befall, happen to; (suerte) fall to (one's lot); no cabe más that's the limit; no ~ (en sí) de alegría etc. be bursting with; no ~ en sí be swollen-headed; cabe preguntar si one may ask if; todo cabe en ese chico that lad is capable of anything; no cabe en él hacerlo it is not in him to do it; v. duda, suerte.

cabestrillo m ✂ sling; **cabestro** m halter; (buey) leading ox; F pimp; llevar del ~ fig. lead by the nose.

cabeza f mst head; top, summit de monte; top, head de lista etc.; geog. capital; fig. origin, beginning; (p.) head, chief; F ~ de chorlito nitwit; ~ de dragón snapdragon; ~ de familia head of the household; ~ de guerra warhead; ~ de partido county town; ~ de playa beachhead; ~ de puente bridgehead; ~ de turco scapegoat, whipping-boy; a la ~ de at the head of; de ~ estar on end; caer head first, headlong; por ~ per head; F tocado de la ~ touched, round the bend; F alzar la ~ ✝ get on one's feet again; ✂ be up and about; calentarse la ~ get fagged out; escarmentar en ~ ajena learn by another's mistakes; F ir de ~ be snowed under; írsele a uno la ~ be giddy; meterse de ~ en plunge into; metérsele a uno en la ~ get s.t. into one's head; perder la ~ lose one's head; F romperse la ~ rack one's brains; F sentar la ~ settle down; subírsele a uno a la ~ (vino a. fig.) go to one's head; volver la ~ look round.

cabezada f (golpe) butt con cabeza, blow on the head en cabeza; (movimiento) nod; ♩ pitch(ing); dar ~s

nod; darse de ~s fig. rack one's brains; **cabezazo** m butt; deportes: header; **cabezo** m hillock, small hill; (cumbre) top; ♩ reef; **cabezón 1.** = cabezudo; **2.** m hole for the head; collar-band; llevar de los ~es force s.o. to go; **cabezota 1.** f big head; **2.** m/f F pig-headed sort; **cabezudo** big-headed; fig. pig-headed; vino heady; **cabezuela** f ♀ head.

cabida f space, room; capacity (a. ♩); extent de terreno; tener ~ para have room for, hold.

cabildear [1a] lobby; **cabildero** m lobbyist, intriguer; **cabildo** m eccl. chapter; pol. town council; (junta) chapter etc. meeting.

cabillo m end; ♀ stalk, stem.

cabina f ✈, ♩ etc. cabin; ✈ a. cockpit; ~ de teléfono, ~ telefónica telephone box (or kiosk).

cabio m joist, rafter; lintel de puerta.

cabizbajo fig. crestfallen, dejected.

cable m cable (a. ♩, ✐, medida), rope, hawser; ~ de remolque towline, towrope; **cablegrafiar** [1c] cable; **cablegrama** m cable(gram).

cabo m end (a. fig.); geog. cape; (mango) handle; ♩ cable, rope; ⊕ thread; end, bit que queda; stub, stump de vela, lápiz etc.; (p.) chief, head; ✂ corporal; ~s pl. accessories del vestido; ~s pl. fig. odds and ends; ~ suelto loose end; al (fin y al) ~ in the end; al ~ de at the end of; de ~ a rabo from beginning to end; atar ~s put two and two together; dar ~ a finish off; dar ~ de put an end to; llevar a ~ carry s.t. out; negocio transact; decisión implement; ponerse al ~ de get the point of.

cabotaje m ♩ coasting trade.

cabra f (she-)goat, nanny-goat F.

cabrahigo m wild fig.

cabrerizo 1. goat attr.; **2.** m = cabrero m goatherd.

cabrestante m capstan.

cabria f hoist, derrick.

cabrio m = cabio.

cabrío 1.: macho ~ he-goat, billygoat; **2.** m flock of goats.

cabriola f caper; gambol; prance; dar ~s = **cabriolar** [1a] cut capers; (cordero) gambol; (caballo) prance; frisk about.

cabriolé m cab(riolet).

cabritilla *f* kid(skin); **cabrito** *m zo.* kid; *carne de ~* kid; F *a ~* astride; **cabrón** *m fig.* cuckold, complaisant husband; (*como injuria, a. co.*) bastard; **cabronada** *f* F (*mala pasada*) dirty trick; (*trabajo*) tough job, fag; **cabruno** goat *attr.*

cabuya *S.Am.*: *dar ~* moor, tie up; F *ponerse en la ~* cotton on.

cacahuete *m* peanut, monkey-nut; (*planta*) groundnut.

cacao *m* cocoa; *S.Am.* chocolate.

cacareado vaunted, much boasted of; **cacarear** [1a] *v/t.* boast about, make much of; *v/i.* (*gallina*) cackle; (*gallo*) crow; **cacareo** *m* cackling; crowing (*a. fig.*).

cacatúa *f* cockatoo.

cacería *f* (*partida*) shoot, hunt; (*pasatiempo*) shooting, hunting; (*muertos*) bag.

cacerola *f* (sauce)pan; casserole.

cacique *m S.Am.* chief, headman; *pol.* (local) boss; **caciquismo** *m* (system of) dominance by the local boss.

caco *m* pickpocket; F coward.

cacofonía *f* cacophony.

cacto *m* cactus.

cacha *f* handle; *S.Am.* horn; F *hasta las ~s* up to the hilt.

cachar [1a] *plato* smash, break; *madera* cut with the grain; ✓ plough up.

cacharro *m* earthenware pot, crock; *fig.* piece of junk; F *mot. etc.* jalop(p)y, old crock; *~s pl.* earthenware, (coarse) pottery.

cachaza *f* calm; *b.s.* slowness; (*bebida*) rum; **cachazudo 1.** calm, phlegmatic; slow; **2.** *m* slow sort.

cachear [1a] frisk (for weapons).

cachería *f S.Am.* F small business, sideline.

cachete *m* punch in the face; ✗ swollen cheek; = **cachetero** *m* dagger; **cachetina** *f* fist fight.

cachicán 1. F sly, crafty; **2.** *m* ✓ foreman, gaffer; F sly fellow.

cachigordo F squat, chunky.

cachiporra *f* truncheon *de policía*; cosh, blackjack *de criminal*.

cachivache *m* (*p.*) useless fellow; *~s pl.* pots and pans; *contp.* junk.

cacho 1. bent, crooked; **2.** *m* crumb *de pan*; (*pedazo*) bit, slice; *ichth.* chub; F *estar fuera de ~* be in safe keeping.

cachondeo *m* F farce, poor show; **cachondo** *zo.* in rut, on heat; *sl. mujer* hot, sexy.

cachorr(ill)o *m* pocket pistol; **cachorro** *m,* **a** *f* (*perro*) pup(py); (*león etc.*) cub.

cachupín *m,* **-a** *f* Spanish settler in America.

cada each; (*con número etc.*) every; *~ 2 semanas* every 2 weeks; *~ cual, ~ uno* each one, everyone; *¿~ cuánto?* how often?

cadalso *m* scaffold; ⊕ platform.

cadáver *m* (dead) body, corpse; carcass *de animal*; **cadavérico** *fig.* cadaverous; ghastly, deathly pale.

cadena *f* chain; *~ perpetua* life imprisonment; *phys. en ~* chain *attr.*

cadencia *f* cadence, rhythm; ♪ (*trozo*) cadenza; **cadencioso** rhythmic(al).

cadeneta *f* chain stitch.

cadera *f* hip.

cadetada *f* F thoughtless action, irresponsible act; **cadete** *m* cadet.

caducar [1g] (*viejo*) dodder, be in one's dotage; get out of date *por antiguo*; ⚖, ♰ expire, lapse; **caduco** decrepit, feeble; ⚘ deciduous; *bienes* perishable, fleeting; ⚖ which has lapsed.

caer [2o] *mst* fall (down *etc.*; *a. ~se*); (*viento, sol etc.*) go down; (*cortina*) hang; (*color*) fade; (*conversación*) flag; (*costumbre*) lapse; F *no caigo* I don't get it; F *ya caigo* I get it; *~ a, ~ hacia* look towards, look out on to; *~ bien a* (*vestido*) suit, look well on; *~ de suyo* be obvious, go without saying; *~ de tonto etc.* be very silly *etc.*; *~ en capítulo* come in; *fecha* fall on; *~ en que* realize that; *~ por fecha* fall around; *~ sobre* fall on; (*animal*) pounce on; *dejar ~* drop; *tono* lower; *dejarse ~* let o.s. go (*or* fall); *fig.* be wily; *estar al ~* be on the point of falling.

café *m* coffee; (*casa*) café; (*color de*) *~* coffee-coloured; *~ cantante approx.* night-club; *~ con leche* white coffee; *~ solo* black coffee; **cafeína** *f* caffeine; **cafetal** *m* coffee plantation; **cafetera** *f* coffee-pot; (*eléctrica, filtradora*) percolator; *approx.* kettle *para hervir agua*; **cafetería** *f* cafeteria; milk-bar;

cafetero *m*, **a** *f* café proprietor; **cafetín** *m* little café; **cafeto** *m* coffee plant.

cáfila *f* F flock; string *de disparates*.

cafre 1. Kaffir; *fig.* cruel; (*zafio*) uncouth; **2.** *m f* Kaffir.

cagada *f* shit; *fig.* shocking mistake; **cagado** F yellow, funky; **cagar** [1h] *v/t.* shit; *fig.* make a mess of; *v/i.* (have a) shit; **cagatinta(s)** *m* pen-pusher; **cagón** F = *cagado*.

caída *f* fall (*a. fig.*); (*tropezando*) tumble; (*declive*) drop; *geol.* dip; fold *de cortina*; set, hang *de vestido*; *fig.* decline; collapse, downfall; *thea.* flop; *la ⌇ the* Fall; ⌇*s pl.* ⊕ shoddy; ⌇*s pl.* F witty remarks; ⌇ *de agua* waterfall; ⌇ *de cabeza* header; *a la ⌇ de la tarde* in the evening; *a la ⌇ del sol* at sunset; **caído 1.** fallen; *cabeza etc.* drooping; *cuello* turn-down; *fig.* crestfallen, dejected; ⌇ *de color* pale; **2.** ⌇*s m/pl.*: *los* ⌇ the fallen; ✝ income due; *monumento a los* ⌇ war memorial.

caigo *etc. v.* caer.

caimán *m* alligator, caiman.

caimiento *m* fall; ✿ decline.

cairel *m* wig; (*fleco*) fringe; **cairelar** [1a] fringe.

caja *f* box (*a.* ⊕, ✎); case (*a. typ., de reloj, violín etc.*); chest; *mot.* body; *radio*: cabinet; (*ataúd*) coffin, casket *Am.*; ✕ drum; well *de escalera*; ⊕ housing, casing; ✿ seed-case, capsule; ✝ cash-box; ⌇ (*de caudales*) safe, strong-box; ✝ cash-desk; cashier's office; ⌇ (*de fusil*) (gun)stock; ⌇ (*postal*) *de ahorros* (post-office) savings-bank; ⌇ *de cambio* (*de marchas*), ⌇ *de velocidades* gear-box; ⌇ *de construcciones* approx. building society; ⌇ *de eje* axle box; ⌇ *de empalmes* junction box; ⌇ *de fuego* fire-box; ⌇ *de fusibles* fuse box; ⌇ *de grasas* journal-box; ⌇ *de herramientas* tool-box; ⌇ *de menores* petty cash; ⌇ *de música* musical box; ⌇ *registradora* cash register; ⌇ *de registro* manhole; ⌇ *de resonancia* sounding-board (*a. fig.*); ⌇ *de sebo* grease-box, grease-cup; ⌇ *sorpresa* jack-in-the-box; *despedir con* ⌇*s destempladas* send *s.o.* packing.

cajero *m*, **a** *f* ✝ cashier, (bank) teller; **cajeta** *f* small box; **cajetilla**

f packet, pack *Am.*; **cajista** *m* compositor, type-setter; **cajita** *f* small box; ⌇ *de cerillas* box of matches, match-box; **cajón** *m* big box, case; drawer *de armario etc.*; space *entre estantes*; ✝ till; (*casilla*) stall; ⊕ (*a.* ⌇ *hidráulico*, ⌇ *de suspensión*) caisson; ⌇ *de embalaje* packing case; F ⌇ *de sastre* odds and ends; (*p.*) muddle-headed fellow; *ser de* ⌇ be the usual thing, be a matter of course; **cajonería** *f* set of drawers.

cal *f* lime; ⌇ *apagada* slaked lime; ⌇ *viva* quicklime; F *de* ⌇ *y canto* strong, tough.

cala *f* *geog.* creek, cove, inlet; ⚓ fishing-ground; hold *de barco*; ✁ probe (*a. fig.*); ⌇ *de construcción* slipway.

calabacín *m* ✿ marrow; F dolt; **calabaza** *f* pumpkin, gourd; F dolt; F *dar* ⌇*s a estudiante* fail; *novio* jilt; *recibir* ⌇*s* get jilted; F *salir* ⌇ be a flop; **calabazada** *f* butt (with the head); blow on the head; **calabazazo** *m* F bump on the head.

calabobos *m* drizzle.

calabozo *m* (*cuarto*) cell; (*cárcel*) prison; ✕ F glasshouse; † dungeon.

calabrote *m* ⚓ hawser.

calada *f* soaking *etc.*; F *dar una* ⌇ *a* haul *s.o.* over the coals; **calado** *m* ⊕ fretwork; *sew.* drawn thread work; ⚓ draught.

calafate *m* caulker; **calafatear** [1a] caulk.

calamar *m* squid.

calambre *m* (*a.* ⌇*s pl.*) cramp.

calamidad *f* calamity; F (*'p.*) dead loss; F *es una* ⌇ it's a great pity; F *¡vaya* ⌇! what bad luck!

calamina *f* calamine.

calamitoso *adj.* calamitous.

cálamo *m* *poet.* pen; ♩ reed; *empuñar el* ⌇ take up the pen; *menear* ⌇ wield a pen.

calamocano F merry, tipsy.

calamoco *m* icicle.

calamorra *f* F nut, noddle.

calandrar [1a] calender; **calandria¹** *f* ⊕ calender.

calandria² *f* calandra lark.

calaña *f* model, pattern; *fig.* nature, stamp, kind.

calañés *m* Andalusian hat *with turned-up brim*.

calar[1] **1.** lime *attr.*; **2.** *m* limestone quarry.

calar[2] **[1a] 1.** *v/t.* (*líquido*) soak; pierce *con barrena*; ⊕ *metal* cut openwork in; *madera* cut fretwork in; *bayoneta, mastelero* fix; *puente, red* lower; *sombrero* pull down; *p., situación* size up; *p., intención* see through; *secreto* find out; **2.** *v/i.* (*líquido*) sink in; (*zapato*) leak, let in water; ⚓ draw; (*ave,* 𝇋) swoop (down); (*motor*) stop; **⁓se** get soaked (*hasta los huesos* to the skin), get drenched; (*ave*) swoop (down); *sombrero* pull down; *gafas* stick on, (*ya puestas*) push back.

calavera 1. *f* skull; **2.** *m* gay dog; *b.s.* rake; **calaverada** *f* madcap escapade, foolhardy thing; **calaverear [1a]** F be a gay dog; *b.s.* lead a wild life.

calcañal *m*, **calcañar** *m* heel.

calcar [1g] trace; *fig.* ⁓ *en* base on, model on.

calcáreo lime *attr.*, calcareous ⛰.

calce *m* (*llanta*) tyre; (*cuña*) wedge; (*hierro*) iron tip.

calceta *f* (knee-length) stocking; (*grillete*) fetter, shackle; *hacer* ⁓ knit; **calcetería** *f* hosiery; hosier's (shop); **calcetero** *m*, **a** *f* hosier; **calcetín** *m* sock.

calcificar(se) [1g] calcify; **calcina** *f* concrete; **calcinación** *f* calcination; **calcinar [1a]** calcine; burn, reduce to ashes; F bother; **calcio** *m* calcium.

calco *m* tracing; **calcomanía** *f* transfer.

calculable calculable; **calculador** calculating; (*máquina*) **calculadora** *f* computer, calculating machine; **calcular [1a]** calculate; add up, work out; *fig.* reckon (*que* that); **cálculo** *m* calculation; reckoning; estimate; 𝄽 (gall)stone; ⁓ *de coste* costing; ⁓ *diferencial* differential calculus; ⁓ *mental* mental arithmetic; *según mis* ⁓*s* according to my reckoning; *obrar con mucho* ⁓ act cautiously.

caldas *f/pl.* hot springs.

caldeamiento *m* warming, heating; **caldear [1a]** heat (up), warm (up); *estar caldeado* be very hot; **⁓se** get overheated, get very hot.

caldera *f* boiler (*a.* ⊕); kettle; *S.Am.* coffee-pot; F *las* ⁓*s de Pedro*

Botero hell; **calderero** *m* boiler-maker; ⁓ *remendón* tinker; **caldereta** *f* small boiler; *cocina*: fish stew; lamb stew; *eccl.* = **calderilla** *f eccl.* holy water vessel; ✝ copper(s), small change; **caldero** *m* copper; ⁓ *de colada* ladle; **calderón** *m* large boiler, cauldron; *typ.* paragraph sign; ⚓ hold.

caldo *m* broth; consommé, clear soup; (*aderezo*) dressing, sauce; ⁓*s pl.* liquid derived from fruit *etc.*; ⁓ *concentrado de carne* beef-tea; ⁓ *de cultivo* culture-medium; F *hacer el* ⁓ *gordo* play into *s.o.'s* hands.

cale *m* slap, smack.

calefacción *f* heating; *de* ⁓ heating *attr.*; ⁓ *central* central heating.

cal(e)idoscopio *m* kaleidoscope.

calendario *m* calendar; F *hacer* ⁓*s* muse.

caléndula *f* marigold.

calentador *m* heater; ⁓ (*de inmersión*) immersion heater; ✝ ⁓ *de cama* warming-pan; ⁓ *a gas* gas heater, geyser *de baño*; **calentamiento** *m* heating; **calentar [1k]** *v/t.* *horno etc.* heat (up); *comida, cuarto, piernas, silla etc.* warm (up); *negocio etc.* speed up, get moving; F warm, tan; ⁓ *al blanco* (*al rojo*) make white-hot (red-hot); *v/i.* be hot, be warm; **⁓se** heat (up), (get) warm, get hot; warm o.s. *a la lumbre*; *fig.* (*disputa*) get heated; (*exaltarse*) get excited; *zo.* be on heat; **calentura** *f* 𝄽 temperature, fever; **calenturiento** feverish.

calera *f* limestone quarry; (*horno*) = **calero** *m* lime-kiln.

calesa *f* chaise, buggy.

calesera *f Andalusian jacket.*

calesín *m* gig, fly.

calesitas *f/pl.* *S.Am.* merry-go-round.

caleta *f* cove, inlet.

caletre *m* F gumption.

calibrador *m* gauge; callipers; **calibrar [1a]** gauge; calibrate; **calibre** *m* 𝄽 calibre (*a. fig.*), bore; ⚒ gauge; = *calibrador*; ⁓ *estrangulado* choke-bore.

calicó *m* calico.

calidad *f* quality; ✝ *a.* grade; (social) standing; character; term, stipulation *en contrato*; ⁓*es pl.* (moral) qualities; gifts; *a* ⁓ *de que* provided that; *de* ~ of quality; of importance; *en* ~ *de* in the capacity of.

cálido hot; *color* warm.

calidoscopio *m* kaleidoscope.

calienta-camas *m.* ⚡ electric blanket; **calienta-platos** *m* hotplate; **caliente** hot; warm; *disputa* heated; *batalla* raging; (*fogoso*) fiery; *zo.* on heat; *en* ~ hot; *fig.* at once; *montar en* ~ shrink on.

califa *m* caliph; **califato** *m* caliphate.

calificación *f* qualification; assessment; label; mark *en examen*; **calificado** qualified; well-known, eminent; *prueba, rival* undisputed; *robo* proven, manifest; **calificar** [1g] qualify (*de* as; *a. gr.*); *p.* (*acreditar*) distinguish, give *s.o.* his fame; ennoble; *examen* mark; *escritos* correct; ~ *de* call, label; characterize as, describe as; ~*se* S.Am. register as a voter.

caliginoso *poet.* darkling, misty.

caligrafía *f* penmanship, calligraphy; **caligráfico** calligraphic.

calina *f* haze, mist.

calistenia *f* calisthenics.

cáliz *m eccl.* chalice, communion cup; *poet.* cup, goblet; ♀ calyx.

caliza *f* limestone; **calizo** lime *attr.*; *terreno* limy.

calma *f* calm; calmness; ⚓ calm weather; (*lentitud*) slowness, laziness; lull (*en* in), cessation (*de* of); ~ *chicha* dead calm; *con* ~ calmly; *en* ~ calm; *fig.* in abeyance; ↟ steady; *perder la* ~ get ruffled; **calmante** soothing; sedative (*a. su. m*); **calmar** [1a] *v/t.* calm (down), quieten (down); *dolor* relieve; *nervios* soothe, steady; *v/i.* abate, fall; ~*se* calm down *etc.*; **calmoso** calm; F slow, lazy.

caló *m* gipsy slang; slang; *Madrid equivalent of Cockney.*

calofriarse [1c] feel chilly, get the shivers; **calofríos** *m/pl.* chill(y sensation), shivers.

calor *m* heat (*a.* ⊕, *phys., fig. de batalla, disputa etc.*); (*esp. agradable*) warmth (*a. fig. de acogida etc.*); ~ *rojo* red heat; *¡qué* ~*! isn't it hot!; *entrar en* ~ get warm, begin to feel warm; warm up *con ejercicios*; *hace* (*mucho*) ~ it is (very) hot; *tener* ~ be hot, feel hot; **caloría** *f* calorie;

calórico caloric; **calorífero 1.** heat-producing; **2.** *m* heating system; furnace, stove; **calorífico** calorific; **calorifugar** [1h] *caldera* lag; **calorífugo** heat-resistant, non-conducting; (*incombustible*) fireproof.

calta *f* (*a.* ~ *palustre*) marsh-marigold.

calumnia *f* slander; (*esp. escrito*) libel (*de* on); **calumniador** *m*, **-a** *f* slanderer; libeller; **calumniar** [1b] slander; malign; libel; **calumnioso** slanderous; libellous.

caluroso warm, hot; *fig.* warm, enthusiastic.

calva *f* bald patch; ♀ clearing.

Calvario *m* Calvary; (*estaciones del*) ~ Stations of the Cross; ♀ *fig.* cross; F string of debts.

calvatrueno *m* F bald pate; (*p.*) madcap; **calvero** *m* glade, clearing; **calvicie** *f* baldness; ~ *precoz* premature baldness.

calvinismo *m* Calvinism.

calvo 1. bald; hairless; *terreno* barren, bare; **2.** *m* bald man.

calza *f* wedge, scotch, chock; F stocking; ~*s pl.* hose, breeches; tights; *en* ~*s prietas fig.* in a fix.

calzada *f* highway, roadway; causeway; (*carriage-*)drive *a casa*; **calzado 1.** *p.p.* ~ *de* shod with, wearing; **2.** *m* footwear; **calzador** *m* shoehorn; **calzar** [1f] **1.** *v/t. p. etc.* put shoes on, provide with footwear; *zapatos etc.* put on; *número* wear, take; *bala* take; wedge, scotch, chock *con calce*; **2.** *v/i.*: *calza bien* he wears good shoes; F *calza poco* he's pretty dim; **3.** ~*se* *zapatos etc.* put on; wear; *fig.* get; *p.* keep under one's thumb.

calzo *m* wedge, scotch; ⚓ chock, skid; **calzón** *m* (*a.* ~*es pl.*) breeches; shorts; *S.Am.* trousers; ~*es pl. blancos* (under)pants, drawers; F *ponerse etc. los* ~*es* wear the trousers; **calzonazos** *m* F easy-going (*or* weak-willed) fellow; (*marido*) henpecked husband; **calzoncillos** *m/pl.* (under)pants.

callada: F *a las* ~*s, de* ~ on the quiet; *dar la* ~ *por respuesta* say nothing; **callado** silent, quiet; reserved, secretive; **callandico** F, **callandito** F softly, stealthily; **callar** [1a] **1.** *v/t. secreto* keep; *trozo* *etc.* pass over (in silence), not mention; *cosa vergonzosa* keep quiet about, hush up; **2.** *v/i.*, **~se** keep quiet, be (*or* remain) silent; (*cesar*) stop talking (*or* ♪ playing, ⊕ working *etc.*), become quiet; (*mar, viento*) be hushed; ¡*calla!*, ¡*cállate!* shut up!, hold your tongue!; ¡*calla! fig.* you don't say!; *hacer* ~ make *s.o.* stop talking *etc.*, shut *s.o.* up F.

calle *f* street; road; *deportes:* lane; ~ *de dirección única* one-way street; ~ *mayor* high street, main street; F *dejar en la* ~ put *s.o.* out of a job; F *echar por la* ~ *de en medio* push on regardless; *hacer* ~ clear the way; F *poner en la* ~ kick out, chuck out; F *quedarse en la* ~ not have a penny to one's name;

calleja *f = callejuela;* **callejear** [1a] stroll around; *b.s.* hang about, loaf; **callejero** street *attr.;* (*p.*) fond of walking about town; **callejón** *m* alley(way), lane, passage; ~ *sin salida* cul-de-sac; *fig.* blind alley; impasse; **callejuela** *f* narrow street, side street; alley(way); *fig.* way out (of it).

callista *m/f* chiropodist; **callo** *m* corn *esp. en pie;* callus; ~*s pl. cocina:* tripe; *criar etc.* ~*s* have no feelings, be a callous type; **callosidad** *f* callosity, hardness (on hands *etc.*); **calloso** callous; *manos* horny, hard.

cama *f* bed; ✗ bedding, litter; *zo.* lair; floor *de carro;* ~ *de matrimonio* double-bed; ~ *turca* divan bed; ✗ *caer en* (*la*) ~ fall ill, take to one's bed; ✗ *estar en* ~, *guardar* ~ be confined to bed; *hacer* (*or poner*) *la* ~ *a* work harm for *s.o.* behind his back; *levantarse por los pies de la* ~ get out of bed on the wrong side; **camada** *f zo.* litter, brood; (*capa*) layer; course *de ladrillos;* (*ps.*) gang.

camafeo *m* cameo.

camal *m* halter.

camaleón *m* chameleon.

camamila *f* camomile.

camándula *f* rosary; F *tener muchas* ~*s* be a sly one, be a bit of a rogue; **camandulear** [1a] be a hypocrite, be over-devout; **camandulería** *f* prudery, priggishness; **camandulero** F hypocritical.

cámara *f* room; chamber (*a.* ⊕, ⚓, 🐟, *parl.*); *parl. a.* house; ⚓ (*camarote*) cabin; ⚓ (*sala*) saloon; ✗ *a.*

breech; ✗ granary; *anat.* cavity; *phot.* (*a.* ~ *fotográfica*) camera; *mot.* (*a.* ~ *de aire*) inner tube, tyre; 🐟 ~*s pl.* diarrhoea; ~ *cinematográfica* cinecamera; ♀ *de Comercio* Chamber of Commerce; ~ *de gas* gas-bag; ♀ *de los Comunes* (*Lores*) House of Commons (Lords); ~ *de niebla* cloud chamber; ~ *de televisión,* ~ *televisora* television camera; *a* ~ *lenta* slow-motion; *de* ~ royal.

camarada *m* comrade, companion; mate; **camaradería** *f* comradeship; team-spirit *en deportes etc.*

camarera *f* waitress *en restaurante;* (chamber)maid *en hotel;* ⚓ stewardess; parlour-maid *en casa;* lady's maid *de dama;* **camarero** *m* waiter; ⚓ steward; chamberlain *de rey.*

camarilla *f* clique, coterie; caucus *de partido.*

camarín *m eccl.* niche for an image; *thea.* dressing-room; (*tocador*) boudoir; (*pieza retirada*) side room.

camaró(n) *m* shrimp.

camarote *m* ⚓ cabin, stateroom.

camastro *m* rickety old bed; **camastrón** F sly, not to be trusted.

cambalache *m* swap, exchange; **cambalach(e)ar** [1a] swap, exchange.

cámbaro *m* crab. [change.)

cambiable changeable; exchangeable; **cambiante 1.** fickle, temperamental; **2.** *m* money-changer; ~*s pl.* changing colours, iridescence.

cambiar [1b] **1.** *v/t.* change, exchange (*con, por* for); change, turn (*en* into); ✝ *a.* trade (*por* for); (*de sitio*) shift, move; *saludos etc.* exchange; **2.** *v/i.*, **~se** change (*a...a* ~ *de*); ~ *de sitio* shift, move; ~ *de sombrero etc. con* exchange hats *etc.* with; **cambiazo** *m* ✝ F switch; *dar el* ~ switch the goods; **cambio** *m* change; (*trueque*) exchange; ✝ (*tipo*) rate of exchange; (*vuelta*) change; turn *de marea;* change, shift, switch *de política etc.;* ✝ *libre* ~ free trade; (*palanca de*) ~ *de marchas* gearlever, gear-shift *Am.*; ~ *de tiempo* change in the weather; 🚂 ~ *de vía* points; *a* ~ *de, en* ~ *de* in exchange for; *en* ~ instead, in return; (*por otra parte*) on the other hand; **cambista** *m* money-changer.

camelar [1a] F *mujer* flirt with; cajole, blarney.

camelia f camellia.
camelo m F flirtation; (chasco) joke, hoax, (mentira) cock-and-bull story; (halago) (piece of) blarney; dar ~ a make fun of; me huele a ~ it's fishy.
camello m camel (a. ⚓). [ridge.\
camellón m drinking-trough; ⚔\
camerino m thea. dressing-room.
camero for a big bed.
camilla f ⚕ stretcher; sofa, couch; table with heater underneath.
caminante m/f wayfarer, traveller; walker; **caminar** [1a] v/t. distancia cover, travel, do; v/i. travel, journey; (andar) walk; (rio, fig.) move, go; F ~ derecho behave properly; **caminata** f F hike, ramble; jaunt, outing; **caminero** v. peón.
camino m road; way (de to; a. fig.); esp. fig. course, path; ~ de, on the way to; ~ de entrada approach (road); ~ de herradura bridle-path; ~ real high-road (a. fig.); ~ de Santiago Milky Way; ~ de sirga towpath; ~ trillado well-trodden path; fig. beaten track; ~ vecinal country road, lane; a medio ~ half-way; de ~ attr. travelling; (adv.) in passing; 2 horas de ~ 2 hours' journey; en el ~ on the way, en route; abrir(se) ~ make one's way (por through); fig. find a way; allanar el ~ smooth the way; echar ~ adelante strike out; errar el ~ lose the way; llevar por mal ~ lead astray; partir el ~ con meet s.o. half-way; ponerse en ~ set out, start; traer a buen ~ put s.o. on the right road.
camión m mot. lorry, truck Am.; (carro) heavy wagon, dray; S.Am. bus; ~ blindado troop-carrier; ~ de la basura, dust-cart; **camionaje** m haulage, cartage; **camioneta** f van.
camisa f shirt; ~ (de mujer) chemise; ⊕ jacket (a. de libro), sleeve; ⚕ skin; mantle de luz; folder de legajo; ~ de agua water-jacket; ~ de fuerza strait jacket; en (mangas de) ~ in one's shirt-sleeves; en ~ fig. without a dowry; dejar sin ~ fleece; **camisería** f outfitter's; **camisero** m, a f shirt-maker; outfitter; **camiseta** f vest, undershirt Am.; deportes: singlet; **camisón** m (de noche) nightdress, nightgown.
camomila f camomile.

camorra f F row, set-to, to-do; armar ~ kick up a row; **camorrista** F 1. fond of scraps; 2. m quarrelsome sort; hooligan.
campal batalla pitched.
campamento m camp; encampment; ~ de trabajo labour camp.
campana f bell; eccl. fig. parish (church); ~ de bucear diving-bell; ~ de cristal bell-glass; glass cover; a ~ herida, a toque de ~ to the ring of bells; F oír ~s y no saber dónde get hold of the wrong end of the stick; **campanada** f stroke (of the bell); (sound of) ringing; F commotion; **campanario** m belfry, church tower; **campanear** [1a] ring out; campaneado fig. much talked-of; **campanero** m ⊕ bell-founder; ♪ (bell-)ringer.
campanilla f handbell; ⚡ electric bell; (burbuja) bubble; (adorno) tassel; ⚘ bell-flower; ~ azul harebell; ~ blanca snowdrop; F de muchas ~s big, grand; **campanillazo** m loud ring; **campanillear** [1a] tinkle, ring; **campanilleo** m tinkling, ringing.
campante outstanding; b.s. (a. tan ~) self-satisfied, smug.
campanudo bell-shaped; falda wide; lenguaje high-flown, bombastic; orador pompous.
campaña f geog. (flat) countryside, plain; ✗, pol., fig. campaign; ⚓ cruise, expedition, trip; ✗ season; ✗ de ~ freq. field attr.; ✗ batir la ~ reconnoitre; hacer ~ campaign (en pro de for).
campañol m vole.
campar [1a] ✗ etc. camp; (descollar) stand out, excel; **campear** [1a] (animales) go to graze; (trigo) show green; ✗ reconnoitre; S.Am. scour the countryside.
campechano hearty, good-hearted, open; generous.
campeón m champion; **campeonato** m championship.
campero (out) in the open; open-air attr.; ✗ sleeping in the open.
campesino 1. country attr.; zo. field attr.; contp. rustic; 2. m, a f peasant (a. contp.); countryman (-woman); farmer; **campestre** country attr.; ⚘ wild; **campiña** f flat stretch of farm-land; countryside.

campo *m* ✓ field (*a. fig., phys., heráldica*); (*despoblado*) country (-side); *deportes*: field, ground, pitch; (golf-)course; (*campamento*) camp; (*fondo*) background; ~ de aterrizaje landing ground; ~ de aviación airfield; ~ de batalla battle-field; ~ de concentración concentration camp; ~ de deportes playing-field, recreation ground; ~ de minas minefield; ~ petrolífero oilfield; ~ raso open country; a ~ raso in the open; ~ santo cemetery, churchyard; ~ de tiro range; a ~ traviesa cross-country; dejar el ~ libre leave the field open (*para* for); levantar el ~ strike camp; *fig.* give up; reconocer el ~ reconnoitre; **campo-santo** *m* cemetery, churchyard.
camuesa *f* pippin; **camueso** *m* pippin tree; F dolt.
camuflaje *m* camouflage; **camuflar** [1a] camouflage.
can *m zo.* dog; ✕ trigger; △ corbel.
cana *f* (*a. ~s pl.*) white hair, grey hair; F echar una ~ al aire let one's hair down; F peinar ~s be getting on.
canadiense *adj. a. su. m/f* Canadian.
canal *mst m geog.* ⚓ channel (*a. radio*), strait(s); navigation channel de puerto; (*artificial*) canal, water-way; ✓ (*a. ~ de riego*) irrigation channel; *geog.* narrow valley; *anat.* canal, tract; △ gutter, spout; drain pipe; (*estría*) groove; ⊕ conduit; pipe de agua, gas; (*res*) dress-ed carcass; ~ de navegación ship-canal; abrir en ~ cut down the middle, slit open; **canaladura** *f* = acanaladura; **canalete** *m* paddle; **canalización** *f* canalization; ⊕ piping; ⚡ wiring; mains de gas etc.; *S.Am.* sewerage system; **canalizar** [1f] río canalize; aguas harness; aguas de riego channel; ⊕ pipe; **canalizo** *m* navigable channel; **canalón** *m* △ spout; drain pipe; (*sombrero*) shovel hat.
canalla 1. *f* rabble, riff-raff, mob; **2.** *m* swine, rotter; **canallada** *f* dirty trick; (*dicho*) nasty thing; **canallesco** mean, rotten; *diversión* low.
canana *f* cartridge belt.
canapé *m* sofa, settee.
canario 1. *adj. a. su. m,* **a** *f* (native) of the Canary Isles; **2.** *m orn.* canary; **3.** *int.* well I'm jiggered!

canasta *f* (round) basket; *naipes*: canasta; **canastilla** *f* small basket; layette de niño; **canastillo** *m* wicker tray; **canasto** *m* hamper; basket; ¡~s! heavens above!
cancamurria *f* F blues; **cancamusa** *f* F trick; armar una ~ a throw sand in *s.o.'s* eyes.
cáncano *m* F louse; andar como ~ loco go round in circles.
cancel *m* wind-proof door; (*mueble*) folding screen; **cancela** *f* lattice gate.
cancelación *f* cancellation; **cancelar** [1a] cancel; deuda write off, wipe out; *fig.* dispel, do away with; banish (from one's mind).
cáncer *m* cancer; *ast.* ♋ Cancer; **cancerado** cancerous; *fig.* corrupt; **cancerarse** [1a] (*úlcera*) become cancerous; (*p.*) have cancer; *fig.* become corrupt; **canceroso** cancerous.
canciller *m* chancellor; **cancilleresco** *fig.* formal, ruled by protocol; **cancillería** *f* chancellery.
canción *f* song; *poet.* lyric, song; ~ de cuna lullaby; cradle song; ~ infantil nursery-rhyme; F volvemos a la misma ~ here we go again; **cancionero** *m* ♩ song-book; *poet.* anthology, collection of verse.
cancro *m* ♣ canker; ♣ cancer.
cancha *f* field, ground; *pelota*: court; *S.Am.* caballos: racecourse, race-track; gallos: cockpit; ~ de tenis tennis-court; (*espacio*) open space; *S.Am.* estar en su ~ be in one's element; **canchear** [1a] be out for a good time.
candado *m* padlock; clasp de libro; **candar** [1a] lock up, put away.
cande: v. azúcar.
candeal pan white.
candela *f* candle; *phys.* candle-power; (*candelero*) candlestick; F light para cigarrillo; F arrimar ~ a give *s.o.* a hiding; **candelaria** *f* Candlemas; **candelero** *m* candlestick; (*velón*) oil lamp; F en ~ high up; F poner en ~ give *s.o.* a high post; **candelilla** *f* bougie; ♣ blossom, catkin; *S Am.* glow-worm; **candelizo** *m* F icicle.
candente hierro white-hot, red-hot; glowing, burning; *cuestión* burning.
candidato *m* candidate (*a* for); **candidatura** *f* candidature.

candidez *f* candour *etc.*; (*dicho*) silly remark; **cándido** *poet.* snow-white; *fig.* guileless, innocent; *b.s.* naïve; (*tonto*) stupid.

candil *m* oil lamp; F *arder en un ~* (*vino*) be very strong; *fig.* be pretty strong stuff; **candilejas** *f/pl. thea.* footlights.

candonga *f* F (*lisonja*) blarney; (*engaño*) trick; (*chasco*) hoax, practical joke; teasing; F *dar ~ a* tease, kid; **candongo** F **1.** (*lisonjero*) smooth; (*astuto*) sly; (*holgazán*) lazy; **2.** *m, a f* cajoler, toady; sly sort; lazy blighter; **candonguear** [1a] F *v/t.* tease, kid; *v/i.* shirk, dodge work; **candonguero** = *candongo.*

candor *m poet.* pure whiteness; *fig.* innocence, guilelessness; **candoroso** innocent, guileless; *confesión etc.* frank, candid.

canela *f* cinnamon; F lovely thing; ¡*~*! good gracious!; *~ de la China* cassia; **canelo 1.** cinnamon(-coloured); **2.** *m* cinnamon (tree).

canelón *m* = *canalón*; (*carámbano*) icicle.

canesú *m sew.* yoke; (*vestido*) under-bodice, camisole.

cangilón *m* pitcher; bucket, scoop *de noria etc.*

cangreja *f* ⚓ spanker.

cangrejo *m*: *~* (*de río*) crayfish; *~* (*de mar*) crab; ⚓ gaff.

canguelo *m* F funk.

canguro *m* kangaroo.

caníbal 1. cannibalistic, man-eating; *fig.* savage; **2.** *m* cannibal.

canica *f* marble; (*juego*) marbles.

canicie *f* whiteness of the hair.

canícula *f* dog-days; **canicular 1.**: *calores ~es* midsummer heat; **2.** *~es m/pl.* dog-days.

canijo F weak, sickly.

canilla *f anat.* shin(-bone), arm-bone; ⊕ bobbin, spool; spout, cock *de tonel*; rib *de tela*; *S.Am.* tap; F *irse de ~* be taken short; *fig.* talk nineteen to the dozen.

canino 1. canine, dog *attr.*; *hambre* ravenous; **2.** *m* canine (tooth).

canje *m* exchange, interchange; **canjear** [1a] exchange, interchange.

cano white-haired; (*con algunas canas*) grey(-haired); *fig.* aged, venerable; *poet.* snow-white.

canoa *f* canoe; boat, launch; *~ automóvil* motor-launch.

canódromo *m* dog-track.

canon *m eccl.*, ♪, *paint.* canon; ✝ tax; ♪ rent; *typ. gran ~* canon; *~es pl.* ⚖ canon law; **canonical** canonical; *vida* easy; **canonicato** *m* canonry; F cushy job; **canónico** canonical; **canóniga** *f* F nap before lunch; F *coger una ~* have one over the eight; **canónigo** *m* canon; **canonización** *f* canonization; **canonizar** [1f] canonize; *fig.* applaud, show approval of; **canonjía** *f* canonry; F cushy job.

canoro *ave* (sweet-)singing; *voz etc.* melodious.

canoso grey(-haired); *barba* grizzled.

canotaje *m* boating.

cansado tired, weary (de of); ✍ exhausted; *vista* tired, strained; (*que cansa*) tedious, trying, tiresome; *pluma etc.* well-worn, past its best; **cansancio** *m* tiredness, weariness; *esp.* ✍ fatigue; (*tedio*) boredom; F *estar muerto de ~* be dog-tired; **cansar** [1a] **1.** *v/t.* tire, weary *esp. lit.*; ✍ exhaust; *fig.* bother, bore (*con* with); *apetito* jade; *paciencia* wear out; *tierra* exhaust; *vista* tire, strain, try; **2.** *v/i.* tire; (*p.*) be trying, be tiresome; **3.** *~se* tire, get tired (*con, de* of); tire o.s. out (*en inf. ger.*); **cansera** *f* F bother.

cantábrico Cantabrian.

cantador *m, -a f* folk-singer, singer of popular songs.

cantal *m* boulder; (*cantizal*) stony ground.

cantante 1. singing; *v. voz*; **2.** *m/f* (professional) singer; vocalist; **cantar** [1a] **1.** *v/t.* sing (*fig.* the praises of); chant; F *~ las claras* speak up; (*con descaro*) be cheeky; **2.** *v/i.* sing; *zo.* chirp; ⊕ squeak, grind; F squeal, blab; *~ a dos voces* sing a duet; F *~ de plano* tell all one knows; **3.** *m* song, poem; *~ de gesta* epic; ♀ *de los* ♀*es* Song of Songs, Canticles; F *ése es otro ~* that's another story.

cántara *f* large pitcher; *liquid measure = 16.13 litres.*

cantárida *f*: (*polvo de*) *~* Spanish fly, *pharm.* cantharides.

cantarín 1. fond of singing; *tono* singsong; **2.** *m, -a f* singer.

cántaro m pitcher; (*cabida*) pitcherful; F a ~s in plenty; *llover* cats and dogs.

cante m: ~ flamenco, ~ jondo Andalusian gipsy singing.

cantera f (stone-)quarry, pit; *fig.* talent, genius; **cantería** f (*arte, obra*) masonry, stonework; (*porción*) piece of masonry; **cantero** m (stone-)mason; quarryman; (*extremo*) end; ~ de pan crust.

cántico m *eccl.* canticle; *fig.* song.

cantidad f quantity; amount, number; sum *de dinero*; (*una*) *gran* ~ de a great quantity of, lots of; *phys.* ~ de movimiento momentum; en ~ in quantity.

cantil m (*escalón*) coastal shelf; (*acantilado*) cliff.

cantilena f ballad, song; F *la misma* ~ the same old song.

cantimplora f water-bottle, canteen; decanter *para vino*; ⊕ syphon.

cantina f 🚂 refreshment room, buffet; ✕ *etc.* canteen; snack-bar; (*bodega*) wine-cellar; (*fiambrera*) lunch-box.

cantizal m stony ground.

canto[1] m (*acto, arte*) singing; (*pieza*) song; *eccl.* chant(ing); *poet.* lyric, song; *canto de épica*; ~ del cisne swan-song; ~ llano plainsong; *al* ~ *del gallo* at cockcrow, at daybreak.

canto[2] m (*borde*) edge; rim; (*extremo*) end, point; (*esquina*) corner; back *de cuchillo*; crust *de pan*; (*piedra*) rock, boulder (a. ~ *rodado*); (*guijarro*) pebble; *de* ~ on edge, edgeways; on end; *faltar a uno el* ~ *de un duro* F have a narrow shave; *tener 2 cm. de* ~ be 2 cm. thick.

cantón m corner; *pol., heráldica:* canton; ✕ cantonment; **cantonada:** *dar* ~ *a* give a shake *s.o.* off; **cantonear** [1a] loaf around; **cantonera** f corner-band *de libro*; corner table; corner cupboard; **cantonero** m loafer, good-for-nothing.

cantor 1. (sweet-)singing; **2.** m, -a f singer; *orn.* singing bird, songster.

cantorral m stony ground.

canturía f singing, vocal music; singing exercise; *b.s.* monotonous singing; **canturrear** [1a], **canturriar** [1b] hum, croon.

canuto m = cañuto.

caña f 🌿 reed; (*tallo*) stem, cane; *anat.* shin(-bone); arm-bone; leg *de*

media, bota; ✕ gallery; (*vaso*) (long) glass; *S.Am.* rum; ~ de azúcar, ~ melar sugar-cane; ~ de pescar fishing-rod; ~ del timón tiller.

cañada f *geog.* gully; (*grande*) glen; (*a. real* ~) drover's road.

cañamazo m canvas; burlap; **cañameño** hempen; **cañamero** hemp *attr.*

cañamiel f sugar-cane.

cáñamo m hemp; (*tela*) hempen cloth; **cañamón** m hemp-seed; ~es *pl.* bird-seed.

cañaveral m reed-bed; 🌿 sugar-cane plantation.

cañería f pipe, piece of piping; pipeline; (*desagüe*) drain; ♪ organ pipes; ~s *pl.* pipes, piping; ~ *maestra* water- *etc.* main; **cañero** m plumber, fitter; **cañete** m small pipe; **cañizo** m 🌿 hurdle (for drying fruit *etc.*).

caño m tube, pipe (a. ♪); (*albañal*) drain, sewer; jet, spout *de fuente*; ⚓ channel; ✕ gallery; (*bodega*) wine cellar; **cañón** m ⊕ tube, pipe (a. ♪); ✕ gun, cannon; barrel *de fusil, pluma*; stem *de pipa*; shaft, stack *de chimenea*; *mount.* chimney; *S.Am.* canyon; ~ *antiaéreo* anti-aircraft gun; *de dos* ~es *fusil* double-barrelled; **cañonazo** m gunshot; F bolt from the blue; ~s *pl.* gunfire; *salva de 21* ~s 21-gun salute; **cañonear** [1a] shell; **cañoneo** m shelling, gunfire; **cañonera** f embrasure; **cañonero** m ⚓ gun-boat.

cañoso reedy.

cañutero m pincushion; **cañutillo** m glass tube; *sew.* gold (or silver) twist; **cañuto** m ⊕ tube, container; 🌿 internode; F tell-tale.

coaba f mahogany.

caolín m kaolin.

caos m chaos; **caótico** chaotic.

capa f (*vestido*) cloak; *eccl.* (a. ~ *pluvial*) cope; *toros:* cape; wrapper *de cigarro etc.*; layer *de atmósfera, piel etc.*; *geol.* stratum, bed; *cocina:* coating; *paint.* coat; covering *de nieve*; film, layer *de polvo*; pall *de humo*; *fig.* varnish; *b.s.* cloak, mask; *primera* ~ undercoat, ground; ~ *aguadera* raincoat; F ~ *rota* secret emissary; ~ *social* social level; *de 3* ~s *madera* 3-ply; *so* ~ *de* under the guise of; *abrirse de* ~ pluck up

courage; F *andar de* ~ *caída* be in
a bad way; *echar una* ~ *a* cover up
for; *estar(se)* etc. *a la* ~ ⚓ lie to;
hacer de su ~ *un sayo* do what one
likes with one's own things.
capacidad f capacity (*a. phys.*, ✝);
size *de sala* etc.; *fig.* (cap)ability,
capacity; intelligence; efficiency; ~
para aptitude for; ~ *adquisitiva,* ~
de compra purchasing power; ~ *de
carga* carrying capacity; ~ *útil* effective capacity; **capacitar** [1a]:
~ *para inf.* enable *s.o.* to *inf.*; ~ *para
su.* qualify *s.o.* for *su.*; ~*se para*
qualify for, fit o.s. for.
capacha f frail, basket; **capacho** m
wicker basket; ⚒ hod.
capar [1a] castrate; *fig.* cut down,
curtail.
caparazón m caparison; *zo.* shell;
nose-bag *para pienso.*
caparrón m bud.
caparrosa f vitriol; ~ *azul* copper
sulphate, blue vitriol.
capataz m foreman; *esp.* 🖊 overseer, bailiff.
capaz a) *p.* (cap)able, efficient,
competent (*a.* 🖋; *de inf.* to *inf.*); ~
de capable of; ~ *para* qualified for;
ser ~ *de inf.* be capable of *ger.*, be
up to *ger.*; *¡sería* ~*!* one could well
believe it of him!; ⊕ ~ *de funcionar*
operational; b) *cabida*: large, capacious; ~ *de,* ~ *para* that holds, with
room for, with a capacity of.
capcioso wily, deceitful.
capear [1a] *v/t.* wave the cape at;
F take *s.o.* in; ⚓ *temporal* ride out;
v/i. ⚓ ride out the storm; lie to.
capellán m chaplain; (*en general*)
priest; ~ *castrense* army chaplain;
capellanía f chaplaincy.
capero m hat-stand, hall-stand.
capereza f (pointed) hood; ⊕ cowl,
cowling; cowl *de chimenea.*
capibara f *S.Am.* capybara.
capigorra m F, **capigorrón** m F
loafer, idler.
capilar 1. capillary (*a. anat., phys.*),
hair *attr.*; *tubo* etc. ~ = **2.** m capillary; **capilaridad** f capillarity.
capilla f *eccl.* chapel; ♪ choir;
(*capucho*) hood, cowl; *typ.* proof-
sheet; ~ *ardiente* funeral chapel;
oratory *en casa;* ~ *de la Virgen* Lady
Chapel; ~ *mayor* choir, chancel;
typ. *en* ~*s* in proof; F *estar en* (*la*) ~
fig. be on tenterhooks; **capillo** m

bonnet *de niño;* hood *de halcón;* =
capullo.
capirotazo m flip, flick.
capirote m hood; hennin *de mujer;*
hood *de halcón;* flip, flick *con dedos;*
capirucho m F hood.
capitación f poll-tax, capitation.
capital 1. *mst* capital; *característica*
main, principal; *enemigo, pecado*
mortal; *importancia* supreme, para-
mount; *punto* essential, fundamental; *lo* ~ the main thing; **2.** f *pol.*
capital *de país;* chief town, centre
de región; ~ *de provincia* approx.
county town; **3.** m ✝ capital; ~ *de
explotación* working capital; ~ *social*
share capital; **capitalismo** m cap-
italism; **capitalista 1.** capitalist(ic);
2. m/f capitalist; **capitalización** f
capitalization; **capitalizar** [1f]
capitalize; *interés* compound.
capitán m captain (*a.* ~ *de navío*);
~ *de fragata* commander; ~
general approx. field-marshal; ~
de puerto harbour-master; **capitana** f flagship; **capitanear** [1a]
captain, lead (*a. fig.*), command;
capitanía f captaincy, captainship;
(*grupo*) company; (*derechos*) harbour-dues.
capitel m ⚒ capital.
capitolio m capitol; *fig.* imposing
edifice; F *subir al* ~ get to the top.
capitulación f agreement; ⚔ capi-
tulation; ~*es pl.* (*de boda*) marriage
contract; **capitular**[1] *eccl.* chapter
attr.; **capitular**[2] [1a] *v/t.* agree to;
🖋 charge (*de* with); *v/i.* come to
terms (*con* with); ⚔ capitulate;
capítulo m chapter (*a. eccl.*); item
de presupuesto; heading; (*sala*)
chapter-house; *eccl.* reprimand; ~
de culpas charge; ~*s pl.* matrimonia-
les marriage contract; *llamar* etc. *a*
~ take *s.o.* to task.
capó m *mot.* bonnet, hood *Am.*
capón[1] m rap on the head.
capón[2] m (*p.*) eunuch; (*pollo*) capon;
caponera f 🖋 chicken-coop; *fig.*
open house; *sl.* clink.
capota f *mot.* hood, top *Am.*; bonnet *de mujer.*
capotaje m somersault; ✈ loop;
capotar [1a] ✈, *mot.* turn over;
capote m cloak (with sleeves);
toros: bullfighter's cloak (*a.* ~ *de
brega*); F frown; *naipes:* slam;
meteor. mass of dark clouds; *a* (*or*

para) mi ~ to my way of thinking; *decir para su ~* say to o.'s.; **capotear** [1a] *fig.* get out of, duck, shirk; *(engañar)* bamboozle.

capricho *m* whim, (passing) fancy, caprice *(a. ♪)*; *(deseo)* keen desire, sudden urge *(por* for); *b.s.* craze, fad, pet notion; freak (of the imagination); *(en general)* whimsicality; *por puro ~* just to please oneself; *fue un ~ suyo* it was one of his mad ideas; *tiene sus ~s* he has his moods; **caprichoso, caprichudo** capricious; *niño etc.* wayward; *(inconstante)* temperamental, moody; *idea, obra* fanciful, whimsical; *(con ideas raras)* full of one's own pet notions.

cápsula *f* cap *de botella;* ♀, *anat., pharm.* capsule; ♀ boll *de algodón etc.;* case *de cartucho;* ~ *fulminante* detonating-cap, percussion-cap; **capsular** capsular; *en forma ~* in capsule form.

captar [1a] *confianza etc.* win, get; *voluntad* gain control over; *aguas* dam, harness; *(entender)* catch, get the drift of; *radio:* pick up; **captura** *f* capture, seizure; **capturar** [1a] capture, seize, take.

capucha *f* hood; *eccl.* cowl; top *de pluma;* *gr.* circumflex accent; **capuchina** *f* *eccl.* Capuchin sister; ♀ nasturtium; **capuchino** *m* Capuchin; **capucho** *m* cowl, hood; **capuchón** *m* lady's hooded cloak; *mot.* valve-cap. [*de bellota.*|

capullo *m* *zo.* cocoon; ♀ bud; cup|

capuz *m* hood; *eccl.* cowl; *(capote)* cloak; *(chapuz)* dive.

caqui *m* khaki.

cara *f* face *(a. fig.)*; side *de disco, sólido;* △ façade, front; *(superficie)* surface, face; heads *de moneda; fig.* look, appearance; ~ *de aleluya* cheerful face; ~ *o cruz* heads or tails; ~ *de cuchillo* hatchet face; ~ *de hereje* ugly face; *(triste)* hangdog look; ~ *de juez* grim-looking face; *mala ~ (ademán)* pout, grimace, face F; ~ *de pascua* smiling face; ~ *de viernes* hang-dog look; ~ *de vinagre* sour expression, sourpuss *sl.;* ~ *a ~* face to face; ~ *adelante (atrás)* facing forwards (backwards); *a ~ descubierta* openly; *de ~* opposite, facing; in the face; *dar ~ a* face up to; *dar la ~ por otro* answer for s.o. else; *echar (or jugar) a ~ o*

cruz toss (up) *(acc.* for); *echar algo en ~ a* reproach *s.o.* for *s.t.;* bring up, allude to; *hacer ~ a* face *(a. fig.)*; *enemigo* face up to, stand up to; F *lavar la ~ a* lick *s.o.'s* boots; *poner mala ~* pout, make a face F; *tener ~ de inf.* look as if *condicional;* *tener buena ~ ♂* look well; look nice; *tener mala ~ ♂* look ill; look bad; *tener ~ de roñoso* look mean; *nos veremos las ~s* well we shall see.

carabina *f* ✕ carbine; F chaperon; *hacer etc. de ~* go as chaperon, play gooseberry; F *ser la ~ de Ambrosio* be quite useless; **carabinero** *m* carabineer.

caracol *m* *zo.* snail; *(concha)* snail shell, sea-shell; *(pelo)* curl; *¡~es!* great Scott!; *de ~ escalera* spiral; *en ~* spiral, corkscrew *attr.;* *hacer ~es (p.)* zigzag; *b.s.* reel, stagger; *(caballo)* = **caracolear** [1a] caracole.

carácter *m* character *(a. biol.)*; *typ.* *(una letra)* character; *(cursivo etc.)* hand(writing); *(condición)* position; *de ~ (firme etc.)* of character; *de ~ ... ...-natured; thea. de ~ heroico* cast in a heroic mould; *de medio ~* of an ill-defined nature; *caracteres pl.* (de imprenta) type(-face); **característica** *f* characteristic; **característico** characteristic (de of); **caracterizado** distinguished, of note; **caracterizar** [1f] characterize; distinguish, set apart; *(enaltecer)* confer distinction on; *thea.* play with great effect; *~se thea.* make up, dress for the part.

carajo *m* F prick; *¡~!* hell!

¡caramba! *sorpresa:* well I'm blessed!, good gracious!; *enfado:*\

carámbano *m* icicle. [damn it!|

carambola *f* *billar:* cannon; *fig.* trick, ruse; *por ~* by chance; in a roundabout way.

caramelo *m* sweet, toffee, caramel.

caramillo *m* ♪ recorder, pipe; *poet.* reed; *(montón)* untidy heap; *(chisme)* (piece of) gossip; *armar etc. un ~* start a gossipping campaign; **caramilloso** F fussy.

carantamaula *f* F *(cara)* ugly mug; **carantoña** *f* F *(cara)* ugly mug; *(mujer)* mutton dressed up as lamb; *~s pl.* petting, fondling; *hacer ~s a* make faces at; *(amor)* make sheep's eyes at; coax, wheedle.

carapacho *m* shell; *meterse en su* ~ go into one's shell.
caraqueño *adj. a. su. m*, **a** *f* (native) of Caracas.
carátula *f* mask.
caravana *f* caravan; *fig.* group; *en* ~ in a gang; **caravasar** *m* caravan-serai.
¡caray! F gosh!, well I'm jiggered!
carbohidrato *m* carbohydrate.
carbólico carbolic.
carbón *m min.* coal (*a.* ~ *de piedra*); ⚡ carbon; ~ *bituminoso* soft coal; ~ *de leña*, ~ *vegetal* charcoal (*a. paint.*); ~ *menudo* small coal, slack; (*papel*) ~ carbon (paper); *copia al* ~ carbon copy; **carbonato** *m* carbonate; **carboncillo** *m paint.* charcoal; *mot.* carbon; **carbonear** [1a] make charcoal of; **carbonero 1.** coal *attr.*; charcoal *attr.*; **2.** *m* coal merchant; charcoal-burner; **carbónico** carbonic; **carbonilla** *f* small coal; cinder; *mot.* carbon; **carbonización** *f* 🔥 carbonization; charring; **carbonizar** [1f] 🔥 carbonize; char; *leña* make charcoal of; *quedar carbonizado* ⚡ be electrocuted; (*edificio etc.*) be reduced to ashes; ~**se** 🔥 carbonize; be charred; be reduced to ashes; **carbono** *m* carbon; **carbonoso** carbonaceous.
carbunclo *m min.*, **carbunco** *m* 🗡 carbuncle.
carburador *m* carburettor; **carburante** *m* fuel; **carburar** [1a] carburet; **carburo** *m* carbide.
carcaj *m* quiver; *S.Am.* rifle-case.
carcajada *f* (loud) laugh, guffaw, peal of laughter; *reírse a* ~*s* roar with laughter; *soltar una* (*or la*) ~ burst out laughing.
carcamal *m* F old crock; **carcamán** ⚓ tub.
cárcel *f* prison, jail; ⊕ clamp; *poner en la* ~ send to jail, put in prison; **carcelario** prison *attr.*; **carcelería** *f* imprisonment, detention; **carcelero 1.** prison *attr.*; **2.** *m* warder, jailer.
carcoma *f* woodworm; *fig.* anxiety, perpetual (cause for) worry; (*p.*) spendthrift; **carcomer** [2a] bore into, eat away; *fig.* undermine; *fortuna* eat away; ~**se** get worm-eaten; *fig.* be eaten away; **carcomido** worm-eaten, wormy.
carda *f* (*acto*) carding; (*instrumento*)

card, comb; teasel (*a.* ⚘); *fig.* rap over the knuckles; **cardar** [1a] card, comb; F ~ *la lana a* haul *s.o.* over the coals.
cardenal *m* cardinal; 🗡 bruise; **cardenalato** *m* cardinalate.
cardencha *f* ⚘, ⊕ teasel.
cardenillo *m* verdigris; **cárdeno** purple, violet; lurid; *agua* opalescent.
cardíaco 1. cardiac, heart *attr.*; **2.** *m*, **a** *f* heart case.
cardinal cardinal.
cardo *m* thistle.
cardumen *m* shoal.
carear [1a] *v/t. ps.* bring face to face; *textos* compare, collate; *v/i.*: ~ *a* face towards; ~**se** come face to face, meet; ~ *con* face (up to).
carecer [2d]: ~ *de* lack, be in need of, want (for).
carena *f* ⚓ careening; F ragging; *dar* ~ *a* = **carenar** [1a] careen.
carencia *f* lack (*de* of), need (*de* for); deficiency (*a.* 🗡); **carencial:** *mal* ~ deficiency disease.
careo *m* confrontation; collation.
carero F expensive, dear.
carestía *f* scarcity, shortage; famine; ✝ high price(s); ~ *de la vida* high cost of living; *año de* ~ lean (*or* bad) year.
careta *f* mask; ⚒ *etc* respirator; ~ *antigás* gas-mask, respirator; *quitar la* ~ *a* unmask.
carey *m* tortoiseshell; *zo.* turtle.
carga *f* (*acto*) loading; charge *de cañón*, *caballería*, *horno*, ⚡; (*peso*) load (*a.* ⊕, ⚡); ⚓ cargo; *fig.* load, burden, onus; obligation(s), responsibilities (*propiedad etc.*) encumbrance; (*cuidado*) worry, anxiety; tax (*sobre recursos* on); ⚡ ~ *máxima* peak load; ~ *personal* personal commitments; ⚒ ~ *de pólvora* blast; ⚓ ~ *de profundidad* depth charge; ~ *útil* pay-load; F *a* ~*s* galore, in plenty; ⊕ *con plena* ~ at full load; *de* ~ loading *attr.*; *bestia* pack-, of burden; *echar la* ~ *a* put the blame (*or* onus) on; F *echarse con la* ~ throw up the sponge; F *llevar la* ~ carry the can; *tomar* ~ load; *volver a la* ~ keep at it, return to the attack.
cargadero *m* loading point; ⚠ lintel; **cargado** loaded; *esp. fig.* laden (*de* with); ⚡ charged, live;

~ (con *bala*) live; *dado* loaded; *té etc.* strong; *cielo* overcast; (*bochornoso*) sultry; F *mujer* in the family way; ~ *de años* very old; *v. espalda*; **cargador** *m* loader; ⚓ stevedore; ✂ ramrod; filler *de pluma*; ~ (*de acumulador*) (battery-) charger; **cargamento** *m* cargo, freight; (*acto*) loading; **cargante** F boring, tiresome; *niño* trying; *tarea* irksome.

cargar [1h] **1.** *v/t.* load (*de* with; *a, en* on); (*demasiado*) overload; weigh down on; *cañón* load; ⚔, *enemigo* charge; *horno* stoke; *sl. estudiante* plough; *impuestos* increase (*a* on); *velas* take in; *S.Am.* wear; *fig.* burden, load down (*con, de* with); encumber (*de deudas* with); *imaginación* fill (*de* with); *culpa* lay (*a* on); *responsabilidad* entrust (*a* to), *b.s.* saddle (*a* on); (*imputar*) charge (*de adj.* with being; *con su.* with); F annoy, bore; **2.** *v/i.* load (up), take on a load; ⚓ take on (*a* cargo); *meteor.* turn, veer (*a, hacia* to); (*acento*) fall (*sobre* on); (*ps.*) crowd together; F overeat; drink too much; ~ *con peso* take, carry; *esp. fig.* shoulder; (*llevarse*) take *s.t.* away; ~ *sobre* (△, *responsabilidad*) rest on; (*importunar*) pester; **3.** ~**se** *peso etc.* take on o.s.; *meteor.* become overcast; F get bored, get annoyed; ~ *de* be full of, be loaded with; *fig.* get one's fill of; F ~*la* get into hot water; ¡*algún día me lo cargaré!* I'll get him one day!

cargazón *f* load; ⚓ cargo; ⚓ heaviness; *meteor.* mass of heavy cloud; ~ *de espaldas* stoop; **cargo** *m* load, weight; *fig.* obligation, duty; responsibility; (*custodia*) charge, care; (*empleo*) post; ✝ debit; ⚖ *etc.* charge; *girar* (or *librar*) *a* ~ *de* draw on; *hacer* ~ *de* charge *s.o.* with; *hacerse* ~ *de* take charge of; see about; (*darse cuenta de*) realize; *ser en* ~ *a* be indebted to; *vestir el* ~ look the part.

cariacontecido down in the mouth; aghast *de sobresalto*.

cariado rotten, carious 🦷; **cariarse** [1b] decay, become decayed.

caricatura *f* caricature; *fig.* caricature (of a man); **caricaturista** *m/f* caricaturist; **caricaturizar** [1f] caricature.

caricia *f* caress; pat, stroke *a perro etc.*; *fig.* endearment.

caridad *f* charity, charitableness; *hacer la* ~ *a* give alms to.

caries *f* (dental) decay, caries.

carilla *f* mask; *typ.* page.

carinado *zo.*, ♀ keeled.

cariño *m* affection, love; fondness, liking (*a* for); ~*s* *pl.* endearments, show of affection; *tener* ~ *a* be fond of; *tomar* ~ *a* take (a liking) to; **cariñoso** affectionate, fond, loving.

cariparejo F poker-faced; **carirredondo** F round-faced.

caritativo charitable (*con, para* towards).

cariz *m* look (of the sky); F look; F *esto va tomando mal* ~ this is getting to look bad.

carlinga *f* ✈ cockpit.

carlismo *m* Carlism; **carlista** *adj. a. su. m/f* Carlist.

carlota *f* charlotte.

carmen *m* △ *prov.* villa.

carmenar [1a] *pelo* untangle; *seda etc.* unravel; *lana* card; F pull *s.o.'s* hair; F (*desplumar*) fleece, swindle.

carmesí *adj. a. su. m* crimson; **carmín** *m* carmine; ♀ dog-rose; **carmíneo** carmine, crimson.

carnada *f* bait (*a. fig.*); **carnal** carnal, of the flesh; *pariente* full, blood-; *primo* first; **carnalidad** *f* lust, carnality; **carnaval** *m* carnival; (*época*) Shrovetide.

carne *f* *anat.*, ♀, *eccl.* flesh; meat *de comer*; ~ *adobada* salt meat; ~ *congelada* frozen (or chilled) meat; ~ *de carnero* mutton; ~ *de cerdo* pork; ~ *de cordero* lamb; ~ *de gallina* *fig.* goose-flesh; ~ *de membrillo* quince-jelly; ~ *mollar* lean meat; ~ *picada* mince(d meat); ~ *de ternera* veal; ~ *de vaca* beef; ~ *de venado* venison; *de* ~ *y hueso* of flesh and blood; *de abundantes* (or *muchas*) ~*s* fat; *de pocas* ~*s* thin; *en* ~ *viva* on the raw; *en* ~*s* with nothing on; F *cobrar* (or *criar, echar*) ~*s* put on weight; *perder* ~*s* lose weight; *no ser ni* ~ *ni pescado* be nondescript, be quite undistinguished.

carnear [1a] *S.Am.* slaughter; F take in.

carnero *m* *zo.* sheep; (*macho*) ram; (*carne*) mutton.

carnestolendas *f/pl.* Shrovetide.
carnet [kar'ne] *m* notebook; travel voucher *de turista*; ~ *(de identidad)* identity card; *mot.* ~ *(de conducir)* driving licence.
carnicería *f* butcher's (shop); *fig.* carnage, slaughter; *hacer una* ~ *de* massacre; **carnicero** *m* 1. *zo.* carnivorous; F fond of meat; F *fig.* savage, inhuman; 2. *m* (*p.*) butcher (*a. fig.*); *zo.* carnivore; **cárnico** meat *attr.*
carnívoro 1. carnivorous; 2. *m* carnivore.
carnoso *anat.*, ♀ fleshy; meaty; *p.* = **carnudo** beefy, fat.
caro ✝ dear, expensive; *p.* dear, beloved.
caroca: F *hacer* ~*s* put it on, give o.s. airs.
carótida *f* carotid (artery).
carpa *f* carp; ~ *dorada* goldfish.
carpanta *f* F raging hunger.
carpeta *f* folder, file, portfolio; (*cartera*) brief-case; table-cover *de mesa*; **carpetazo:** *dar* ~ *a* shelve, put on one side.
carpetovetónico terribly Spanish, as Spanish as they come.
carpintería *f* (*arte*) carpentry, joinery; carpenter's shop; **carpintero** *m* carpenter; ~ *(de blanco)* joiner; ~ *de carretas* wheelwright; ~ *de ribera* ship's carpenter.
carraca *f* ⚓ *contp.* tub, hulk; ♪ rattle; **carraco** F 1. feeble, decrepit; 2. *m* old crock.
carrasca *f* kermes oak.
carraspear [1a] be hoarse, have a frog in one's throat; **carraspera** *f* hoarseness.
carrera *f* run (*a.* ♪, ⚓, *béisbol etc.*); (*certamen*) race; (*pista*) track; (*calle*) avenue; (*raya*) parting, run, ladder *en medias*; *ast.* course; (*hilera*) row, line; ▲ beam; ⊕ stroke *de émbolo*, lift *de válvula*; *fig.* course of human life; (*profesión*) career; *univ.* (degree-)course, studies; ~*s pl.* racing, races; *de* ~*(s)* racing ~; race-; ~ *ascendente* upstroke; ~ *corta* dash, short run; ~ *de caballos* horse-race; ~ *descendente* downstroke; ~ *del émbolo* piston-stroke; ~ *de Maratón* Marathon (race); ~ *de obstáculos* obstacle race; ~ *de relevos* relay race; ~ *de resistencia* endurance

race; ~ *de vallas* hurdle-race, hurdles; ~ *caballos*: steeplechase; *a* ~ *(abierta)* at full speed; *correr a* ~ *tendida* career, go full out; *dar* ~ *a* give *s.o.* his education; *dar libre* ~ *a* give free rein to; *no poder hacer* ~ *con* make no headway with; **carrerista** 1. horsy; 2. *m/f* racing man (*or* woman); punter *que apuesta.*
carreta *f* cart; ~ *de mano* = *carretilla*; **carretada** *f* cart-load; *a* ~*s* in loads, galore; **carretaje** *m* cartage, haulage; **carrete** *m* reel (*a. de caña*), spool (*a. phot.*), bobbin; ⚡ coil; ~ *de inducción* induction coil; **carretear** [1a] *v/t.* cart, haul; *carro* drive; *v/i.* ✈ taxi; ~*se* pull hard; **carretel** *m* reel, spool.
carretera *f* (main) road, highway; *por* ~ by road; **carretería** *f* wheelwright's; (*conjunto*) carts; **carretero** *m* carter; (*constructor*) wheelwright, cartwright; *jurar como un* ~ swear like a trooper; **carretilla** *f* truck, trolley; hand-cart, barrow; ✍ wheelbarrow; go-cart *de niño*; F *de* ~ by heart; **carretón** *m* small cart; = *carretilla.*
carricoche *m* caravan, covered wagon; F old crock; **carricuba** *f* water-cart.
carril *m* (*surco*) rut, track; ✍ furrow; (*camino*) cart-track, lane; 🚃 rail.
carrillo *m* cheek, jowl; ⊕ pulley; F *comer a dos* ~*s* eat a lot; *fig.* get the best of both worlds.
carrizal *m* reed-bed; **carrizo** *m* reed.
carro *m* cart, wagon; *S.Am.* car; ✝ (*a.* ~ *de guerra*) chariot; ⚔ car; carriage *de máquina de escribir*; (*carga*) cart-load; ~ *alegórico* float; ~ *blindado* armoured car; ~ *de combate* tank; ~ *cuba* tank truck; ~ *fuerte* heavy trolley, platform carriage; ~ *fúnebre* hearse; ~ *de mudanza* removal van; ~ *de riego* water-cart.
carrocería *f mot.* coachwork, body; **carromato** *m* covered wagon.
carroña *f* carrion; **carroño** foul, putrid.
carroza *f* (state) coach, carriage; float *en desfile*; ⚓ awning; **carruaje** *m* carriage; vehicle.

carta f letter; document; *naipes*: (playing) card; *hist.* charter; ⚓ (*a. ~ de marear*) chart; ~ *adjunta* covering letter; ~ *blanca* carte blanche, free hand; ~ *certificada* registered letter; ~ *de crédito* letter of credit; ~ *de figura* court-card; ~ *geográfica* map; ~ *meteorológica* weather map; ~ *de naturaleza* naturalization papers; ~ *partida* ⚓ charter-party; ~ *de pedido* order; *S.Am.* ~ *postal* postcard; ~ *de privilegio* charter; ~ *de recomendación* letter of introduction; ~ *de solicitud* (letter of) application; ~ *de venta* bill of sale; *a ~ cabal* thoroughly, in every way; *a ~s vistas* with one's cards on the table; *a la ~* à la carte; *echar las ~s* tell one's fortune; *poner las ~s boca arriba* put one's cards on the table; *no saber a qué ~ quedarse* not know what to think; *tomar ~ en* take part in, intervene in; *¡~ canta!* there it is in black and white!

cartabón m set-square *de dibujante*; △ bevel; *surv.* quadrant.

cartapacio m (*cartera*) brief-case; *escuela*: satchel; (*cuaderno*) note-book.

cartearse [1a] correspond (*con* with).

cartel m poster, placard, bill; *escuela*: wall chart; † cartel; F *thea.* tener ~ be all the rage; **cartelera** f hoarding, billboard *Am.*; *thea. fig.* list of plays; *mantenerse en la ~* run, be on; **cartelero** m bill-sticker.

carteo m correspondence.

cárter m housing, case; ~ *del cigüeñal* crank-case.

cartera f wallet, pocketbook; portfolio (*a. pol.*), letter-file; (*bolsa*) brief-case; *sew.* (pocket-) flap; *pol. sin* ~ without portfolio; **carterista** m pickpocket; **cartero** m postman.

cartílago m cartilage ⬜, gristle; **cartilaginoso** cartilaginous ⬜, gristly.

cartilla f primer; ~ (*de ahorros*) deposit book; ~ (*de identidad*) identity card; ~ (*de racionamiento*) ration book; F *leer la ~ a* give *s.o.* a severe ticking-off; F *no saber la ~* not know a blind thing.

cartografía f map-making, carto-graphy; **cartógrafo** m map-maker, cartographer.

cartomancia f fortune-telling (*with cards*).

cartón m cardboard, pasteboard; *paint.* cartoon; board *de libro*; (*caja*) cardboard box, carton; ~ *piedra* papier mâché.

cartuchera f cartridge-belt; **cartucho** m cartridge; roll *de monedas*; paper cone; ~ *sin bala*, ~ *en blanco* blank cartridge; *hastar quemar el último* ~ to the last ditch.

cartulina f fine cardboard.

casa f house; (*hogar*) home; (*piso*) flat, apartment; (*ps.*) household; (*a. ~ de comercio*) firm, business house; (*descendencia*) house, line; square *de tablero*; ~ *de banca* banking-house; ~ *de campo* country house; ~ *de citas*, ~ *pública*, ~ *de putas* brothel; ~ *consistorial* town hall, civic centre; ~ *de corrección* reformatory, remand home; ~ *de correos* post-office; ~ *editorial* publishing house; ~ *embrujada*, ~ *de fantasmas* haunted house; ~ *de empeños* pawnshop; ~ *de fieras* zoo, menagerie; ~ *de guarda* lodge; ~ *de huéspedes* boarding-house; ~ *de locos*, ~ *de orates* asylum; ~ *de maternidad* maternity hospital; ~ *matriz* head office; ~ *de* (*la*) *moneda* mint; ~ *de pisos* block of flats; ~ *real* royal house (*or* family); ~ *religiosa* monastery; convent; ~ *solariega* ancestral home, family seat; ~ *de vecindad* tenements, apartment house *Am.*; *a* ~ home(wards); *ir a* ~ *de Juan* go to John's; *de* ~ home, household *attr.*; *deporte, ropa* indoor; *animal* pet; *en* ~ (at) home; indoors; *en* ~ *de* ⅋ care of; *estar en* ~ *de Juan* be at John's; *por la* ~ about the house; *abandonar la* ~ leave home, move out; *echar la* ~ *por la ventana* go to a lot of expense; *estar de* ~ be in one's every-day clothes; *hacer* ~ get rich; *llevar la* ~ keep house; *poner* ~ set up house; *aquí tiene Vd. su* ~ you're always very welcome; *voy para* ~ I'm off home.

casaca f dress coat; *cambiar de* ~, *volver* ~ be a turncoat.

casación f cassation, annulment.

casada f married woman; **casadero**

marriageable; **casado 1.** married; *mal* ~ unhappily married; *estar* ~ *con* be married to; **2.** *m* married man.

casamata *f* casemate.

casamentero *m*, **a** *f* matchmaker; **casamiento** *m* marriage; wedding (ceremony); *prometer en* ~ betroth.

casar[1] *m* hamlet.

casar[2] [1a] *v/t.* (*sacerdote*) marry, join in marriage; *hija* marry (off), give in marriage (*con* to); *fig.* match; *v/i.*, ~**se** marry (*con acc.*), get married (*con* to); *fig.* match.

casca *f* tan, bark (for tanning).

cascabel *m* (little) bell; *de* ~ *gordo* pretentious; *poner el* ~ *al gato* bell the cat; **cascabelear** [1a] *v/t.* beguile, take *s.o.* in; *v/i.* jingle; *fig.* behave frivolously; **cascabeleo** *m* jingle; **cascabelero** F feather-brained; **cascabillo** *m* (little) bell; ♀ husk, chaff; ♀ acorn cup.

cascada *f* waterfall, cascade.

cascado *p.* broken down, infirm; *cosa* broken (down); *voz* harsh, unmelodious.

cascajo *m* (piece of) grit, (piece of) gravel; *esp.* △ rubble; F junk, rubbish; (*trasto*) old crock; F *estar hecho un* ~ be a wreck; **cascajoso** gritty, gravelly.

cascanueces *m* (*un* a pair of) nutcrackers.

cascar [1g] *v/t.* crack, split; *nueces* crack; *salud* break; F bash, slosh; F *deportes:* beat hollow, wipe the floor with; *v/i.* chatter (away); ~**se** crack, split; (*salud*) crack up; (*voz*) break, crack.

cáscara *f* shell *de huevo, nuez, edificio*; rind, peel *de fruta*; husk *de grano*; *S.Am.* bark; ¡~s! well I'm blowed!; F *ser de la* ~ *amarga* be wild; *pol.* have advanced ideas; **cascarón** *m* (broken) egg-shell; **cascarrabias** *m* F quick-tempered fellow.

casco *m anat.* skull; ✗ *etc.* helmet; crown *de sombrero*; skin *de cebolla*; ⚓ hull; ⚓ (*viejo*) hulk; hoof *de caballo*; piece *de vasija*; (*tonel*) cask, barrel; ⊕ casing; △ city area; ~*s pl.* F nut; ~ *protector* crash helmet; *ligero* (*or alegre*) *de* ~*s* feather-brained, dim; F *romper los* ~*s a* break *s.o.'s* head; F *romperse los* ~*s* rack one's brains.

cascote *m* (piece of) rubble, (piece of) debris; *S.Am.* old fogey.

caseína *f* casein.

casería *f* country house; *S.Am.* ♀ clientèle; **caserío** *m* hamlet, settlement; (*casa*) country house; **casero 1.** domestic, household *attr.*; *pan etc.* home-made; *tela* homespun; *traje* (for use about the) house, indoor; *función* family *attr.*; *p.* home-loving; **2.** *m*, **a** *f* (*dueño*) landlord; (*custodio*) caretaker; (*gerente*) house-agent; (*inquilino*) tenant; (*que queda en casa*) stay-at-home, home-lover; *S.Am.* customer; **caserón** *m* big tumbledown house, barracks (of a place); **caseta** *f* stall, booth *de mercado*; *deportes:* pavilion; bathing-hut *de playa*.

casi nearly, almost; ~ *nada* next to nothing; ~ *nunca* hardly ever; *2 años o* ~ *2* years or thereabouts; ~ ~ very nearly.

casilla *f* △ hut, cabin; 🚃 cab; *thea.* box-office; pigeon-hole *de casillero*; compartment *de caja*; square *de papel, tablero*; *S.Am.* ✆ box-number; F *sacar de sus* ~*s* shake *s.o.* up; (*irritar*) make *s.o.* go off the deep end; F *salir de sus* ~*s* fly off the handle; **casillero** *m* (set of) pigeon-holes.

casimir *m* cashmere.

casinista *m* clubman; **casino** *m* club; casino *para jugar.* [*campo.*\

casita *f* little house; cottage *de*\

caso *m* case (*a.* ✗, *gr.*); (*suceso*) event, occurrence; (*ejemplo*) case, instance; *en* ~ *de* in the event of; (*en*) ~ *que, en el* ~ *de que* in case *verb*, in the event of *ger.*; *en tal* ~ in such a case; *en todo* ~ in any case; *en último* ~ in the last resort; *según el* ~ as the case may be; *el* ~ *es que* the fact is that; *hablar al* ~ speak to the point; F *hacer* (*or venir*) *al* ~ be relevant; be suitable; *hacer* ~ a mind, notice; ¡*no haga Vd.* ~! never mind!, take no notice!; F *hacer* ~ *de* take into account; *p.* take notice of; *sin hacer* ~ *de* regardless of; *hacer* ~ *omiso de* not mention, pass over; *pongamos por* ~ let us suppose that; *servir para el* ~ serve one's purpose; ¡*vamos al* ~! let's get to the point!; *verse en el* ~ *de inf.* find o.s. obliged to *inf.*

casorio *m* F hasty (*or* unwise) marriage.

caspa *f* dandruff, scurf.

¡cáspita! my goodness!; come off it!

casquete *m* ✗ helmet; skull-cap; ~ *polar* polar cap.

casquijo *m* gravel.

casquillo *m* tip, cap; ferrule (*de bastón*; case *de cartucho*); *S.Am.* horseshoe.

casquivano F scatter-brained.

casta *f* caste; *biol.* breed, race; *fig.* quality; *venir de* ~ be natural to one.

castaña *f* chestnut; ~ (*de Indias*) horse-chestnut, conker F; (*moño*) bun; castañar *m* chestnut grove; castañero *m*, a *f* chestnut seller; castañeta *f* snap; ♪ ~s *pl.* castanets; castañetazo *m* click *de castañuelas*; snap; crack; castañetear [1a] *v/t. dedos* snap; *v/i.* ♪ play the castanets; (*dedos*) snap, click; (*dientes*) chatter, rattle; (*huesos*) crack; castaño 1. chestnut (-coloured); 2. *m* chestnut (tree); ~ (*de Indias*) horse-chestnut (tree); F *pasar de* ~ *oscuro* be too much; castañuelas *f/pl.* castanets; castañuelo chestnut.

castellanizar [1f] give a Spanish form to; castellano *adj. a. su. m*, a *f* Castilian.

casticidad *f* purity, correctness; casticismo *m* love of purity and correctness (*in language etc.*); casticista *m/f* purist; castidad *f* chastity, chasteness.

castigador *m* F seducer; castigar [1h] punish (*de, por* for); *deportes*: penalize; *esp. fig.* castigate, chastise; *cuerpo* mortify; *estilo* refine; castigo *m* punishment, penalty (*a. deportes*); *esp. fig.* castigation; refinement.

castillejo *m* ⚓ scaffolding; go-cart *de niño*; castillo *m* castle; ~ *en el aire* castle in Spain; ~ *de naipes* house of cards; ~ *de proa* forecastle.

castizo *biol.* pure-bred, pedigree; *fig.* pure, correct; authentic, genuine; F *es un tipo* ~ he's one of the best; casto chaste, pure.

castor *m* beaver; castóreo *m* *pharm.* castor.

castración *f* castration; castrar [1a] castrate; *animal a.* geld, doctor F; ✿ cut back.

castrense army *attr.*, military.

casual fortuitous, chance *attr.*; (*no esencial*) incidental; *gr.* case *attr.*; casualidad *f* chance, accident; *por* ~ by chance; *da la* ~ *que* as it happens, it happens that; *entrar por* ~ drop in; *se encontraba allí por* ~ he happened to be there; ¡qué ~ *encontrarle a Vd.!* fancy meeting you!

casuc(h)a *f* hovel, slum, shack.

casuista *m/f* casuist; casuística *f* casuistry.

casulla *f* chasuble.

cata *f* testing, sampling; *S.Am.* test bore; F *ir en* ~ *de* go in search of; catacaldos *m* F rolling stone; dilettante *en artes*; (*entrometido*) meddler.

cataclismo *m* cataclysm.

catacumba *f* catacomb.

catador *m* taster, sampler; (*aficionado*) connoisseur; catadura *f* tasting, sampling; F mug.

catalán 1. *adj. a. su. m*, -a *f* Catalan, Catalonian; 2. *m* (*idioma*) Catalan; catalanismo *m* movement for Catalan autonomy.

catalejo *m* (spy)glass, telescope.

catalizador *m* catalyst.

catalogar [1h] catalogue; catálogo *m* catalogue.

cataplasma *f* poultice; F bore.

¡cataplum! bang!, crash!

catapulta *f* catapult.

catar [1a] (*probar*) taste, sample, try; *fig.* examine, have a look at; (*mirar*) look at; (*buscar*) look out for; ¡cata!, ¡cátale! just look at him!; ¡cátate eso! you just think!

catarata *f* waterfall; ✚ cataract.

catarral catarrhal; catarro *m* cold; (*permanente*) catarrh; ~ *crónico del pecho* chest trouble.

catarsis *f* catharsis.

catástrofe *f* catastrophe; catastrófico catastrophic.

catavinos *m* wine-sampler; F boozer.

catecismo *m* catechism.

catecúmeno *m*, a *f* catechumen; *fig.* convert.

cátedra *f univ.* chair, professorship; (*asignatura*) subject; (*aula*) lecture-room, classroom; (*ps.*) class, group; ~ *del Espíritu Santo* pulpit; *explicar una* ~ hold a chair (de of); catedral *f* cathedral; catedrático *m univ.*

professor, lecturer; ~ de instituto grammar school teacher.

categoría f category; class, group; standing, rank en sociedad etc.; de ~ important, of importance; de segunda ~ freq. second-rate; categórico categorical, positive; mentira downright; orden express.

catequizar [1f] catechize, instruct in Christian doctrine; F win s.o. over, talk s.o. round.

caterva f host, throng.

catódico cathode attr.; cátodo m cathode.

catolicismo m (Roman) Catholicism; católico adj. a. su. m, a f (Roman) Catholic; adj. fig. sure, beyond doubt; F no estar muy ~ be none too good; ⚕ be under the weather.

catorce fourteen; (fecha) fourteenth.

catre m cot de niño; ~ (de tijera) camp-bed, folding-bed; catrecillo m camp-stool, folding-seat.

cauce m river-bed; ↗ irrigation channel.

caución f caution, wariness; ⚖ bail; (palabra) pledge, security; admitir a ~ admit to bail; caucionar [1a] ⚖ bail; daño prevent.

cauchero rubber attr.; caucho m rubber; (impermeable) raincoat; ~ esponjoso foam rubber.

caudal m volume, flow de río; fortune, property, wealth de p.; wealth, abundance, stock de cosas; caudaloso río large, carrying much water; fig. wealthy, rich.

caudillaje m leadership; caudillo m leader, chief; pol. el ♀ chief of state.

causa f cause (a. pol.); reason; grounds de queja; ⚖ suit, case; ⚖ prosecution de oficio; a (or por) ~ de on account of, because of, owing to; sin ~ for no good reason; hacer ~ común con make common cause with; instruir ~ take legal proceedings; causal 1. causal; 2. f reason, grounds; causalidad f causality; causar [1a] cause; gastos, trabajo entail; enojo, protesta provoke; causativo causative.

cáustico adj. a. su. m caustic (a. fig.).

cautela f caution, cautiousness, wariness; (astucia) cunning; cautelar [1a] guard against; ~se be on one's guard (de against); cauteloso cautious, careful, wary; (astuto) cunning.

cauterio m cautery; fig. eradication; cauterización f cauterization; cauterizar [1f] cauterize; fig. eradicate; p. reproach.

cautivar [1a] take s.o. prisoner; fig. espíritu enthral; auditorio charm, captivate, win over; corazón steal; cautiverio m, cautividad f captivity; esp. fig. bondage; cautivo adj. a. su. m, a f captive.

cauto cautious, wary, careful.

cava f cultivation; cavar [1a] v/t. dig; pozo sink; v/i. dig; ✠ go deep; fig. delve (en into); medidate deeply (en on).

caverna f cave, cavern; cavernícola m/f cave-dweller; cavernoso cavernous; cave attr.; montaña etc. honeycombed with caves; voz hollow.

caviar m caviar(e).

cavidad f cavity, hollow.

cavilación f deep thought; = cavilosidad; cavilar [1a] ponder (deeply), brood over; be obsessed with; cavilosidad f (unfounded) suspicion; caviloso suspicious.

cayado m ↗ crook; eccl. crosier.

caz m mill-race.

caza 1. f (en general) hunting; shooting con escopeta; (una ~) hunt; chase, pursuit; (animales) game; ~ furtiva poaching; F ~ de grillos wild-goose chase; ~ mayor big game; a ~ de in search of; andar a ~ de go out for; dar ~ give chase; dar ~ a go after, chase; hunt down; fig. search out; ir a la ~, ir de ~ go hunting; go out shooting; F levantar la ~ set the ball rolling; 2. m ✈ fighter; ~-bombardero fighter-bomber; ~ nocturno night-fighter; cazadero m hunting-ground; cazador m hunter, huntsman; ~ (de alforja) trapper; ~ furtivo poacher; cazadora f huntress; hunting jacket; cazar [1f] animales hunt; total de muertos bag; (perseguir) chase, go after, hunt down; F (obtener) get hold of, wangle; p. win over halagando, take in engañando; (sorprender) catch out.

cazcalear [1a] F buzz about, fuss around.

cazo m ladle; ~ (de cola) glue-pot; cazolero = cominero; cazoleta f

bowl *de pipa*; guard *de espada*; ⊕
housing; **cazonete** *m* toggle;
cazuela *f* pan, casserole (*a. plato*);
pan *de arma*; *thea.* gods.
cazurro sullen.
ce: ¡⌐! hey!; F ⌐ *por* be down to the
last detail.
cebada *f* barley; ⌐ *perlada* pearl
barley; **cebadal** *m* barley-field;
cebadera *f* nose-bag; ⊕ hopper;
cebadura *f* ⚭ fattening; ⊕ stok-
ing; ✂ priming; **cebar** [1a] **1.** *v/t.*
✎ feed, fatten (*con* on); *arma*,
lámpara, *máquina* prime; *cohete*
light; *horno* stoke; *fig.* feed (*con*
with); *ira* inflame; *esperanza*
nurse, cherish; **2.** *v/i.* grip, go in,
catch; **3.** ⌐se *en víctima* vent one's
fury on, batten on; (*peste*) rage
among; *estudio* devote o.s. to.
cebellina *f zo.* sable.
cebo *m* ✎ feed; ✂ charge, priming;
⊕ oven load; *pesca*: bait (*a. fig.*).
cebolla *f* onion; bulb *de tulipán etc.*;
⌐ *escalonia* shallot; **cebollana** *f*
chive; **cebollino** *m* young onion,
spring onion; (*simiente*) onion seed;
(*cebollana*) chive.
cebón 1. fat, fattened; **2.** *m* fattened
animal.
cebra *f* zebra.
ceca: *andar de* ⌐ *en Meca* go from
place to place.
cecear [1a] lisp; *pronounce* [s] *as* [θ];
ceceo *m* lisp(ing); *pronunciation
of* [s] *as* [θ]; **ceceoso** lisping, with
a lisp.
cecina *f* dried meat.
cedazo *m* sieve.
ceder [2a] *v/t.* hand over, give up,
yield; *cosa querida* part with; ⚖
grant; *propiedad* make over;
territorio cede; *v/i.* give in, yield
(*a* to); (*disminuir*) decline, go down;
(*viento*, ✎ *etc.*) abate; ⌐ *de pretensión* give up; ⌐ *en honra etc.* redound to.
cedizo high, tainted.
cedro *m* cedar.
cédula *f* document, (slip of) paper,
certificate; ✝ warrant; ⌐ *en blanco*
blank cheque; ⌐ *personal*, ⌐ *de
vecindad* identity card; *dar* ⌐ *a*
license.
céfiro *m* zephyr (*a. tela*).
cegajoso weepy.
cegar [1h *a.* 1k] *v/t.* (make) blind;
(*tapar*) block up, stop up; *v/i.* go

blind; *fig.* = ⌐se become blinded
(*de* by); **ceguedad** *f*, **ceguera** *f*
blindness (*a. fig.*).
ceja *f anat.* eyebrow; △ *etc.* projection; ⊕ rim, flange; *geog.* brow,
crown; *meteor.* cloud-cap; *fruncir
las* ⌐s knit one's brow, frown;
quemarse las ⌐s burn the midnight
oil; *tener a uno entre* ⌐ *y* ⌐ look
with disfavour on s.o.
cejar [1a] (move) back; *fig.* give
way, back down; climb down *en
discusión*; relax, weaken *en esfuerzo*;
no ⌐ keep it up, hold out; *no* ⌐ *en
trabajo etc.* keep at; *sin* ⌐ un-
flinchingly.
cejijunto with bushy eyebrows; *fig.*
scowling, frowning.
celada *f* ambush, trap (*a. fig.*);
celador *m* guard, watchman; ⊕
maintenance man; ⚡ linesman;
mot. parking attendant.
celaje *m* △ skylight; *fig.* sign,
token; ⌐s *pl.* sunset clouds.
celar[1] [1a] *v/t.* keep a watchful eye
on, keep a check on; see that *leyes
etc.* are kept, see that *justicia* is
done; *v/i.:* ⌐ *por* watch over, guard.
celar[2] [1a] (*encubrir*) conceal, hide.
celda *f* cell; **celdilla** *f zo.* cell;
cavity, hollow; △ niche.
celebérrimo *sup. of célebre*; **celebración** *f* celebration *etc.*; **celebrante** *m eccl.* celebrant; **celebrar**
[1a] *v/t. aniversario, suceso feliz*
celebrate; *misa* say; *matrimonio*
perform, celebrate; *reunión* hold;
fiesta keep; (*alabar*) praise;
(*aprobar*) applaud, welcome; *ch'se*
laugh at; *ventajas* preach; ⌐ *inf.*
be glad to *inf.*; *lo celebro* I'm
very glad; *v/i. eccl.* say mass; ⌐se
(*tener lugar*) take place, be held;
célebre famous, noted, celebrated
(*por* for); F funny, witty; F ¡*fue* ⌐!
it was killing!; **celebridad** *f*
celebrity; (*festejo*) celebration(s).
celeridad *f* speed, swiftness; *con* ⌐
quickly, speedily; promptly.
celeste celestial; *ast.* heavenly;
color sky-blue; **celestial** heavenly
(*a. fig.*), celestial; F silly.
celestina *f* bawd, procuress.
celibato *m* celibacy; F bachelor;
célibe 1. single, unmarried; **2.** *m/f*
unmarried person; celibate.
celo *m* zeal, fervour; conscientious-
ness; *b.s.* envy, distrust; *zo.* rut

heat; *época de* ~ mating season; *caer etc.* en ~ be on heat, rut; ~s *pl.* jealousy; *dar* ~s give occasion for jealousy; *tener* ~s be jealous (de of).
celofán *m* cellophane.
celosía *f* lattice, blind, shutter; *fig.* jealousy; **celoso** (*con celo*) zealous (de for), keen (de about, on); (*con celos*) jealous (de of); (*receloso*) suspicious; ⊕ very sensitive.
celta 1. Celtic; **2.** *m/f* Celt; **3.** *m* (*idioma*) Celtic; **celtibérico, celtíbero** *adj. a. su. m,* **a** *f* Celtiberian; **céltico** Celtic.
célula *f* cell; ~ *fotoeléctrica* photoelectric cell; **celular** cellular; **celuloide** *m* celluloid; **celulosa** *f* cellulose.
cementar [1a] ⊕ case-harden.
cementerio *m* cemetery, graveyard.
cemento *m* cement (*a. anat.*); (*hormigón*) concrete.
cena *f* supper, evening meal; (*oficial, de homenaje etc.*) dinner.
cenáculo *m lit.* group, coterie.
cenador *m* arbour; (*casita*) summerhouse.
cenagal *m* quagmire, morass; F sticky business; **cenagoso** muddy, boggy.
cenar [1a] *v/t.* have for supper, sup on, sup off; *v/i.* have one's supper *etc.,* dine; *venir etc. cenado* have had one's supper.
cenceño thin, skinny.
cencerrada *f noisy serenade given to widower who remarries*; **cencerrear** [1a] (*cencerro*) jangle; ♪ play terribly; ⊕ *etc.* rattle, clatter; **cencerreo** *m* jangle *etc.*; **cencerro** *m* cowbell; *a* ~s *tapados* stealthily.
cendal *m* gauze.
cenefa *f* border (*a.* △), trimming, edge.
cenicero *m* ash-tray *para cigarro*; ash-pan *de hogar*; ash-tip *para basuras*; **ceniciento** ashen, ash-coloured.
cenit *m* zenith.
ceniza *f* ash(es); ~s *pl. fig.* ashes, mortal remains; **cenizo** *m* F wet blanket; **cenizoso** ashy; *fig.* ashen.
cenotafio *m* cenotaph.
censo *m* census *de población*; (*impuesto*) tax; ground-rent *de propiedad*; (*hipoteca*) mortgage; ~ *electoral* electoral roll; F *ser un* ~ be

a constant source of trouble; **censor** *m* censor; *fig.* critic; **censual** census *attr. etc.*; **censura** *f pol. etc.* censorship; (*crítica*) censure, stricture; criticism, judgement *de obra*; **censurable** reprehensible, blameworthy; **censurar** [1a] *pol. etc.* censor; (*criticar*) censure, condemn; find fault with; blame.
centaura *f* centaury.
centauro *m* centaur.
centavo *adj. a. su. m* hundredth; *S.Am.* cent.
centella *f* (*chispa*) spark (*a. fig.*); (*rayo*) flash of lightning; **centelleante** sparkling (*a. fig.*); flashing; **centell(e)ar** [1a] sparkle (*a. fig.*); flash; (*metal etc.*) gleam, glint; (*estrella*) twinkle; **centelleo** *m* sparkling, flashing *etc.*
centena *f* hundred; **centenar** *m* hundred; *a* ~es by the hundred, in hundreds; **centenario 1.** *adj. a. su. m* centenary; **2.** *m,* **a** *f* centenarian.
centeno *m* rye.
centésimo *adj. a. su. m* hundredth; **centígrado** centigrade; **centigramo** *m* centigram; **centímetro** *m* centimetre; **céntimo 1.** hundredth; **2.** *m* cent (*hundredth part of a peseta*).
centinela *m/f* sentry, guard, sentinel; *estar etc. de* ~ be on guard; *hacer* ~ *fig.* keep watch, be on the look-out.
centolla *f* (large) crab.
centón *m sew.* patchwork quilt; *lit.* cento.
central 1. central, middle; *esp. fig.* pivotal; **2.** *f* ✝ head office; ~ *de correos* main post-office; ~ *depuradora* waterworks; ~ *eléctrica* power-station; ~ *telefónica* telephone exchange; **centralita** *f teleph.* switchboard; **centralización** *f* centralization; **centralizar** [1f] centralize; **céntrico** central, middle; *lugar* central, convenient; **centrífugo** centrifugal; **centrípeto** centripetal; **centro** *m* centre (*a.* ⚛), middle; *fig.* centre, hub *de actividad etc.*; (*objeto*) goal, purpose; ~ *de gravedad* centre of gravity; ~ *de mesa* centre-piece; ~ *social* community centre; *deportes:* delantero ~ centre forward;

medio ~ centre half; *hallarse en su* ~ be in one's element; **centro-americano** Central American.

centuplicar [1g] centuple; **cén-tuplo 1.** hundredfold, centuple; **2.** *m* centuple.

centuria *f* century.

ceñido *vestido* tight, close-fitting; *fig.* sparing, frugal; ~ *y corto* straight to the point; **ceñir** [3h a. 3l] *espada* gird on; *cinturón etc.* put on; (*llevar*) wear; *frente etc.* bind, encircle (*con, de* with); wreathe (*con, de flores etc.* with); (*atar*) tie; *fig.* (*mar etc.*) girdle, surround; ✗ besiege; *narración* cut down; ~se ✝ tighten one's belt; limit o.s., be brief *en palabras*; ~ a *tema* limit o.s. to, concentrate on; *se ciñó la corona* he became king.

ceño *m* frown, scowl; *meteor.* threatening look; *mirar con* ~ (*v/i.*) frown, scowl; (*v/t.*) frown at, give *s.o.* black looks; **ceñudo** frowning; *mirada etc.* black, grim.

cepa *f* stump *de árbol*; stock *de vid*; (*vid*) vine; △ pier; *fig.* stock; *de buena* ~ *p.* of good stock; *cosa* of good quality.

cepillar [1a] brush; ⊕ plane; *univ. sl.* plough; **cepillo** *m* brush; ⊕ plane; *eccl.* poor-box; ~ *de dientes* tooth-brush; ~ *para las uñas* nail-brush.

cepo *m* ⚭ branch; *hunt.* snare, trap; ✗ *etc.* mantrap; stocks *de reo*; ⊕ reel; *eccl.* poor-box.

cera *f* (bees)wax; ~ (*de lustrar*) (wax) polish; ~s *pl.* honeycomb.

cerámica *f* (*arte*) ceramics; (*objetos*) pottery (*a.* ~s *pl.*); **cerámico** ceramic.

cerbatana *f* pea-shooter; ✗ blow-pipe; ♪ ear-trumpet.

cerca[1] *f* fence; (*tapia*) wall; ~ (*viva*) hedge.

cerca[2] **1.** *adv.* near(by), close; *de* ~ near; ✗ *etc.* at close range; *examinar* closely; *por aquí* ~ somewhere round here, nearby; **2.** *prp.* ~ *de* near, close to; in the neighbour-hood of; *número* about; (*embajador etc.*) to; ~ *de inf.* near *ger.*, on the point of *ger.*; **3.** *m:* *tiene buen* ~ it looks good close up; ~s *pl. paint.* objects in the foreground.

cercado *m* enclosure; garden, orchard; = *cerca*[1].

cercanía *f* nearness; ~s *pl.* out-skirts *de ciudad*; neighbourhood; *de* ~s 🏘 suburban; **cercano** near, close; *pueblo etc.* nearby, next; *muerte* approaching; ~ *a* near to; **cercar** [1g] fence in, enclose; wall *con tapia*, hedge *con seto*; (*rodear*) surround, ring (*de* with); ✗ besiege; (*esp. enemigo, montañas*) hem in.

cercén: *a* ~ entirely; *cortar a* ~ nip in the bud; **cercenar** [1a] cut the edge off; clip, trim; *extremo* slice off; *moneda* clip; *gastos* cut down,

cerceta *f*: ~ (*común*) teal. [(curtail.)

cerciorar [1a] inform, assure; ~se *de* find out about, make sure of, ascertain.

cerco *m* ⚊ *etc.* enclosure; *S.Am.* hedge; hoop *de tonel*; rim *de rueda*; △ frame; ✗ siege; *meteor.* halo; ✗ *poner* ~ *a* lay siege to.

cerda *f* bristle; horsehair; *hunt.* noose, snare; *zo.* sow; **cerdear** [1a] ♪ rasp, grate; ♪ hold back, jib; **cerdo** *m* pig (*a. fig.*); (*carne de*) ~ pork; **cerdoso** *animal* shaggy, hairy; *barbilla etc.* bristly, stubbly.

cereal 1. cereal, grain *attr.*; **2.** *m* cereal; ~es *pl.* grain, cereals.

cerebral cerebral, brain *attr.*; **cerebro** *m* brain (*a. fig.*).

ceremonia *f* ceremony; *eccl. a.* service; *falta de* ~ informality; *de* ~ *adv.* with all due ceremony; *attr.* formal; *por* ~ as a matter of form; *sin* ~ *adv.* informally, with no fuss; *attr.* informal; *hacer* ~s stand on ceremony; **ceremonial** *adj. a. su.m* ceremonial; **ceremonioso** cere-monious; *recepción* formal; *b.s.* stiff, over-polite.

céreo wax(en).

cereza *f* cherry; (*rojo*) ~ cherry (-red); **cerezo** *m* cherry (tree).

cerilla *f* match; (*vela*) wax taper; *anat.* ear-wax; **cerillo** *m* *S.Am.* match.

cernejas *f/pl.* fetlock.

cerner [2g] *v/t.* sift (*a. fig.*); *fig.* scan; *v/i.* ⚭ bud, blossom; *meteor.* drizzle; ~se (*p.*) waddle; *orn.* hover, soar; *fig.* threaten; ~ *sobre* be poised over, hang over.

cernícalo *m* kestrel; F lout, dolt; F *coger un* ~ get boozed.

cernidillo *m* waddle; *meteor.* drizzle; **cernido** *m* sifting; (*harina*) sifted flour.

cero *m* (*nada*) nothing; ≙ (*cifra*) nought; *phys. etc.* zero; *deportes*: nil; *tenis*: love; F ~ *a la izquierda* nonentity, back-number.

ceroso (*de cera*) waxen; (*parecido a cera*) waxy; **cerote** *m* wax; F funk, jitters.

cerquita quite near, close by.

cerradero 1. *caja* that can be locked; *aparato* locking, lock *attr.*; **2.** *m* strike (*of lock*); purse-strings *de bolsa*; clasp; **cerrado** *asunto* obscure; *p.* (*callado*) quiet, secretive; F ~ (*de mollera*) dense; all-too-typical *de carácter*; with a broad accent *en habla*; *acento* broad, thick; *atmósfera* heavy; *barba* full; *cielo* overcast; *curva* sharp, tight; *noche* dark; *aquí huele a* ~ it's stuffy in here.

cerradura *f* (*acto*) closing, shutting; locking *con llave*; (*aparato*) lock; ~ *de combinación* combination lock; **cerraja** *f* lock; **cerrajero** *m* locksmith.

cerrar [1k] **1.** *v/t.* close, shut; lock (up) *con llave*, bolt *con cerrojo*; *grifo etc.* turn off; *agujero* close (up), stop; *puño* clench, close; *carta* seal; *⚡ circuito* make, close; *puerto* close; *trato* strike; *procesión* bring up the rear of; *cuenta, discusión* close; *fábrica etc.* close down, shut down; **2.** *v/i.* close, shut; (*noche*) set in; ~ *con* close with, close in on; *dejar sin* ~ leave open; **3.** ~**se** close *etc.*; ⚡ close up, heal; ✕ close ranks; *meteor.* cloud over; ~ *en inf.* persist in *ger.*; **cerrazón** *f* threatening sky.

cerrero *animal* wild; *p.* uncouth, rough; **cerril** *terreno* rough; = *cerrero*; **cerro** *m* hill, height; *zo.* neck; *irse etc. por los* ~*s de Ubeda* get off the track; F talk a lot of rubbish.

cerrojo *m* bolt; *táctica de* ~ stonewalling; *echar el* ~ bolt the door.

certamen *m* competition, contest.

certero sure, certain; *tirador* good, crack; *golpe* well-aimed; (*sabedor*) well-informed; **certeza** *f* certainty; *tener la* ~ *de que* know for certain that, be quite sure that; **certidumbre** *f* certainty.

certificación *f* certification; ⋈ registration; ⚖ affidavit; **certificado 1.** ⋈ registered; **2.** *m* certificate; ⋈ registered packet *etc.*; ~ *de aptitud* testimonial; ~ *médico* medical certificate; **certificar** [1g] certify; vouch for *s.o.*; ⋈ register.

cerúleo sky-blue.

cerumen *m* ear-wax.

cervato *m* fawn.

cervecería *f* brewery; (*taberna*) public house, bar; **cervecero** *m* brewer; **cerveza** *f* beer.

cervical neck *attr.*, cervical ⌸; **cerviz** *f* (nape of the) neck; *bajar* (*or doblar*) *la* ~ submit, bow down; *ser duro de* ~ be wild, be headstrong.

cesación *f* cessation; suspension, stoppage; **cesante 1.** out of a job; on half-pay; **2.** *m* civil servant *who has been retired*; **cesantía** *f* state of being a *cesante*; (*paga*) retirement pension; **cesar** [1a] *v/t.* stop; *v/i.* stop, cease; (*empleado*) leave, quit; ~ *de inf.* stop *ger.*, leave off *ger.*; ~ *en el trabajo* give up one's work; *sin* ~ ceaselessly; **cese** *m* ✝ stoppage (of payment); ~ *de hostilidades* cease-fire.

cesión *f* ⚖ grant(ing), cession (*a. pol.*); **cesionario** *m*, **a** *f* grantee, assign; **cesionista** *m/f* grantor, assignor.

césped *m* grass, turf; lawn *esp. de casa*; green *para bolos*; (*tepe*) sod, turf.

cesta *f* basket; *pelota*: wicker racquet; **cestada** *f* basketful; **cestería** *f* wickerwork, basket-work; (*tienda*) basket shop; **cestero** *m*, **a** *f* basket-maker; **cesto** *m* (large) basket; hamper *esp. para comida*; ~ (*de la colada*) clothes-basket; ~ (*para papeles*) waste-paper basket; F idiot; F *estar metido en un* ~ be a spoilt child.

cesura *f* caesura.

cetáceo *adj. a. su. m* cetacean.

cetrería *f* falconry; **cetrero** *m* falconer.

cetrino greenish-yellow; *rostro* sallow; *fig.* jaundiced.

cetro *m* sceptre; *fig.* power, dominion; *empuñar el* ~ ascend the throne.

cianotipia *f*, **cianotipo** *m* blueprint.

cianuro *m* cyanide; ~ *de potasio* cyanide of potassium.

ciar [1c] ⚓ go astern; (*bote*) back

water; *fig.* go backwards; (*ceder*) back down, give in.
ciática *f* sciatica.
cicatear [1a] F be stingy; **cicatería** *f* stinginess; **cicatero 1.** stingy, mean; **2.** *m*, **a** *f* mean sort, skinflint.
cicatriz *f* scar (*a. fig.*); **cicatrización** *f* healing; **cicatrizar(se)** [1f] heal (up); heal over, form a scar.
cicerone *m* guide, cicerone.
ciclamino *m* cyclamen.
cíclico cyclic(al); **ciclismo** *m* cycling; (*carreras*) cycle racing; **ciclista** *m/f* cyclist; **ciclo** *m* cycle; *escuela*: term; course, series *de clases*; **ciclón** *m* cyclone; **ciclotrón** *m* cyclotron.
cicuta *f* hemlock.
cidra *f* citron; **cidro** *m* citron (tree); (*género*) citrus.
ciega *f* blind woman; **ciego 1.** blind (*a. fig.*; *de* with); *caño etc.* blocked, stopped up; *a ~as* blindly (*a. fig.*); *fig.* thoughtlessly; *caminar a ~as* grope one's way; **2.** *m* blind man.
cielo *m* sky; *ast.* sky, heavens; *eccl.* heaven; climate; ~ (*raso*) ceiling; roof *de boca*; canopy *de cama*; ¡~s! heavens above!; *a ~ abierto* in the open air (*a. a ~ raso*); ⚒ opencast; *a ~ descubierto* in the open; F *bajado del ~* marvellous; *cosa llovida del ~* godsend; F *juntársele a uno el ~ con la tierra* be in an awful mess; *tomar el ~ con las manos* ask for trouble, be over-optimistic; *venirse el ~ abajo* rain cats and dogs; *ver el ~ abierto* see a way out.
ciempiés *m* centipede.
cien *v.* ciento; ~ *por ~ fig.* a hundred per cent, wholehearted.
ciénaga *f* marsh, bog.
ciencia *f* science; (*saber en general*) knowledge, learning; ~s *pl.* naturales natural sciences; *hombre de ~* scientist; *saber a ~ cierta* know for certain, know for a fact.
cieno *m* mud, silt, ooze.
científico 1. scientific; **2.** *m* scientist.
ciento *adj. a. su. m* (a) hundred, one hundred; *por ~* per cent.
cierne: *en ~(s)* ⚘ in blossom, in flower; *fig. cosa* in its infancy; *p.* budding.
cierre *m* (*acto*) closing *etc.*; shutdown *de fábrica*; (*huelga*) lock-out; (*mecanismo*) snap(-lock); fastener *de*

vestido; clasp *de libro*; catch *de puerta*; shutter *de tienda*; *mot.* choke; ~ *de cremallera* zip fastener; ~ *metálico* (roll) shutter; **cierro** *m* = *cierre*; *S.Am.* envelope.
cierto (*seguro*) sure, certain; *promesa* definite; (*verdadero*) true; (*determinado*) a certain; ~s *pl.* some, certain; *por ~* indeed, certainly; (*a propósito*) by the way; ¡sí, por ~! yes of course!; *es ~ que* it is true that; *no es ~* it is untrue; *estar en lo ~* be right; *saber de ~* know for certain.
cierva *f* hind; **ciervo** *m* deer; (*macho*) stag; ~ *común* red deer.
cierzo *m* north wind.
cifra *f* ⅋ number, numeral; quantity, amount; ✝ sum; (*escritura*) code, cipher; monogram; abbreviation; *en ~* in code; *fig.* mysteriously; (*en breve*) in a shortened form; **cifrado** in code; **cifrar** [1a] write in code; *fig.* summarize; *esperanza etc.* set, concentrate, place (*en* on).
cigarra *f* cicada.
cigarrera *f* cigar-case; **cigarrería** *f* *S.Am.* tobacconist's (shop); **cigarrillo** *m* cigarette; **cigarro** *m* cigar (*a. ~ puro*); cigarette; ~ *habano* Havana (cigar).
cigüeña *f* *orn.* stork; ⊕ crank, handle; **cigüeñal** *m* crankshaft.
ciliar ciliary.
cilindrada *f* cylinder capacity; **cilindrar** [1a] roll; **cilíndrico** cylindric(al); **cilindro** *m* cylinder (*a.* ⊕); *typ. etc.* roller; ~ *de caminos* (road)roller.
cima *f* top *de árbol*; top, summit *de monte*; *fig.* summit, height; *dar ~ a* complete, carry *s.t.* out successfully.
cimarrón *S.Am.* zo., ⚘ wild.
címbalo *m* cymbal.
cimbel *m* decoy (*a. fig.*).
cimbor(r)io *m* (base of a) dome.
cimbr(e)ar [1a] *vara* shake, swish; bend; F thrash; F *le cimbró de un bastonazo* he gave him one with his stick; ~se sway, swing; (*doblarse*) bend; **cimbreño** pliant; *p.* willowy; **cimbreo** *m* sway(ing) *etc.*
cimentar [1k] ⚒ lay the foundations of; *fig.* found; (*afirmar*) cement, strengthen.
cimera *f* crest; **cimero** top, uppermost.
cimiento *m* foundation, ground-

work; *fig.* basis, source; △ ～s *pl.* foundations.
cinabrio *m* cinnabar.
cinc *m* zinc; ✝ counter.
cincel *m* chisel; **cincelar** [1a] carve, chisel; engrave.
cinco five (*a. su.*); (*fecha*) fifth; *las* ～ five o'clock; F *le dije cuántas son* ～ I told him a thing or two; F *saber cuántas son* ～ know what's what, know a thing or two; F *¡vengan esos* ～! shake!
cincuenta fifty.
cincha *f* girth; **cinchar** [1a] *silla* secure; ⊕ band, hoop; **cincho** *m* (*faja*) belt, sash; ⊕ band, hoop.
cine *m* cinema, movies *Am.*; **cineasta** *m/f* film producer; film actor (*f* actress); film-fan; **cinema** *m* cinema; **cinematografía** *f* films; film-making; **cinematografiar** [1c] film; **cinematográfico** cine..., film *attr.*; **cinematógrafo** *m* cinema(tograph); (*máquina*) cine-projector; (*teatro*) cinema. [*ciento*.]
cinerario *urna* cinerary; = *ceni-*]
cinética *f* kinetics; **cinético** kinetic.
cingalés *adj. a. su. m*, **-a** *f* Sinhalese.
cínico 1. cynical; *fig.* brazen, shameless; **2.** *m*, **a** *f* cynic; *fig.* humbug;
cinismo *m* cynicism; *fig.* shamelessness, effrontery; humbug.
cinta *f sew. etc.* ribbon; band, strip; tape *de papel, magnetofón, a. deportes*; *cine*: film; (*rollo*) reel; kerb *de acera*; △ fillet; ～ *adhesiva* adhesive tape; ～ *aisladora* insulating tape; ～ *de freno* brake-lining; ～ *para máquina de escribir* typewriter ribbon; ～ *métrica* tape-measure; **cintero** *m* girdle *de mujer*; (*maroma*) rope; **cinto** *m* ✕ belt; girdle; *armas de* ～ side-arms; **cintura** *f anat.* waist; waistline; (*faja*) girdle; *meter en* ～ keep *s.o.* under; make *s.o.* see reason; *tener poca* ～ have a slim waist; **cinturón** *m* belt; girdle; ～ *de seguridad* safety-belt.
cipayo *m* sepoy.
cipo *m* memorial stone; milestone *de camino*.
ciprés *m* cypress (tree).
circo *m* circus.
circuir [3g] circle, surround; **circuito** *m* circuit (*a.* ∮); *deportes*: lap; circumference; ～ *en bucle* loop-line; ～ *cerrado* closed circuit, loop; *corto* ～ short-circuit; **circulación** *f*

circulation (*a.* ✝, ✍); *mot.* (movement of) traffic; *fig.* propagation; ～ *rodada* wheeled traffic; ✝ *poner en* ～ issue, put into circulation; **circulante** circulating; **circular 1.** *adj. a. su. f* circular; **2.** [1a] *v/t.* circulate; *v/i.* circulate (*a.* ✝, ✍, *fig.*); *mot.* move (freely); (*p.*) walk round, move about (*a.* ～ *por*); *¡circulen!* move along!; *hacer* ～ *ps.* move on, *coches* keep moving; **círculo** *m* circle (*a. fig.*); club; (*aro*) ring, band; (*extensión*) compass, extent; ♀ *Polar Artico* Arctic Circle; ～ *vicioso* vicious circle.
circun... circum...; ～**cidar** [1a] circumcise; *fig.* curtail; moderate; ～**cisión** *f* circumcision; ～**dante** surrounding; ～**dar** [1a] surround; ～**ferencia** *f* circumference; ～**flejo** *m* circumflex; ～**locución** *f*, ～**loquio** *m* roundabout expression, circumlocution; ～**navegación** *f* circumnavigation; ～**navegar** [1h] sail round, circumnavigate; ～**scribir** [3a; *p.p. circunscrito*] circumscribe (*a. fig.*); *fig.* limit; ～**se** *fig.* be limited, be confined (*a* to); ～**scripción** *f* circumscription; *pol. etc.* (sub)division; ～**spección** *f* cautiousness, circumspection; prudence; ～**specto** circumspect, prudent, deliberate; *palabras* guarded; ～**stancia** *f* circumstance; situation; *en las* ～*s* in (*or* under) the circumstances; ～**stanciado** detailed, minute; ～**stancial** circumstantial; *arreglo* makeshift, emergency *attr.*; ～**stante 1.** surrounding; present; **2.** *m/f* onlooker, bystander; ～**vecino** adjacent, surrounding.
cirio *m eccl.* (wax) candle.
cirro *m* cirrus.
ciruela *f* plum; ～ *claudia* greengage; ～ *damascena* damson; ～ *pasa* prune; **ciruelo** *m* plum (tree); F dolt.
cirugía *f* surgery; ～ *estética*, ～ *plástica* plastic surgery; **cirujano** *m* surgeon.
ciscar [1g] F dirty, soil; ～*se* soil *o.s.*; **cisco** *m* slack; F row, shindy; F *armar un* ～, F *meter* ～ start a row; F *estar hecho* ～ be done up.
cisma *m eccl.* schism; *pol. etc.* split; *fig.* disagreement; **cismático** *eccl.* schismatic(al); *fig.* trouble-making; dissident.

cisne *m* swan.

cisterna *f* (water-)tank, cistern.

cistitis *f* cystitis.

cita *f* engagement, appointment, meeting; (*lugar*) rendezvous; (*con novia etc.*) date; *lit.* quotation; reference; *darse* ~ make a date (*con* with); **citación** *f lit.* quotation; ⚖ summons, citation; **citar** [1a] make an appointment (*or* date) with; ⚖ summon; *lit.* quote, cite; *toro* incite; *la cité para las 6* I arranged to meet her at 6.

cítara *f* zither; *hist.* lyre.

cítrico citric.

ciudad *f* city; town; **ciudadanía** *f* citizenship; ~ *de honor* freedom of a city; **ciudadano 1.** civic, city *attr.*; **2.** *m*, **a** *f* city-dweller; *pol.* citizen; ~*s pl. freq.* townsfolk, townspeople; ~ *de honor* freeman of a city; **ciudadela** *f* citadel; **cívico 1.** civic; *fig.* public-spirited, patriotic; domestic; **2.** *m S.Am.* policeman; **civil 1.** civil (*a. fig.*); ⚔ *guerra* civil; *población* civilian; **2.** *m* policeman; **civilidad** *f* civility; **civilización** *f* civilization; **civilizar** [1f] civilize; ~*se* become civilized; **civismo** *m* public spirit; patriotism; community spirit.

cizalla *f* (*una a pair of*) (metal-) shears; wire-cutters; ~*s pl.* clippings.

cizaña *f* ♀ darnel; *Biblia:* tares; *fig.* vice, harmful influence; *sembrar* ~ sow discord; **cizañero** *m*, **a** *f* trouble-maker.

clamar [1a] *v/t.* cry out for; *v/i.* cry out (*contra* against, *por* for); **clamor** *m* (*grito*) cry; (*protesta*) outcry, clamour; (*ruido*) noise, clamour; (*toque*) knell; **clamorear** [1a] *v/t.* cry out for, clamour for; appeal for; *v/i.* (*campana*) toll; **clamoreo** *m* clamour; (*protesta*) outcry; **clamoroso** noisy; loud, shrieking; *éxito* resounding.

clandestinidad *f* secrecy; **clandestino** secret, clandestine; *pol. etc. a.* underground, under-cover.

clara *f* white of an egg; bald spot *en cabeza*; *meteor.* bright interval.

claraboya *f* skylight.

clarear [1a] *v/t.* brighten; *color* make lighter; *v/i.* dawn; *meteor.* clear up; ~*se* (*tela*) be transparent; F give the game away.

clarete *m* claret.

claridad *f* brightness *etc.*; clearness, clarity (*a. fig.*); ~*es pl.* plain speaking, blunt remarks; **clarificación** *f* clarification (*a. fig.*); illumination; **clarificar** [1g] illuminate, light up; clarify (*a. fig.*); *bosque* clear.

clarinada *f* F uncalled-for remark.

clarinete *m* clarinet.

clarividencia *f* far-sightedness; discernment; clairvoyance; **clarividente 1.** far-sighted; discerning; **2.** *m/f* clairvoyant(e).

claro 1. *adj. día, ojos etc.* bright; *agua, lenguaje, prueba, voz* clear; *cristal* clear, transparent; *cuarto, cerveza, color* light; *contorno* clear, distinct, bold; *líquido* thin; (*ralo*) thin, sparse; *fig.* illustrious; ~ *como la luz del día* plain as a pike-staff; *más* ~ *que el sol* as clear as day (light); ¡~! naturally!, of course!; ¡(*pues*) ~! I quite agree with you!; ~ (*que*) ..., ~ *está* naturally..., of course...; ¡~ *que sí!* of course it is!; *a las* ~*as* clearly; openly; *poner* (*or sacar*) *en* ~ explain, clarify; **2.** *adv.* clearly; *hablar* ~ *fig.* speak plainly; **3.** *m* opening, gap; space; △ light, window; *paint* highlight, light tone; clearing *en bosque*.

clase *f mst* class; (*género*) *a.* sort, kind; *univ. a.* lecture; (*sala*) classroom; *univ.* lecture-room; ~ *alta* upper class(es); ~ *baja* lower class (-es); ~ *media* middle class(es); ~ *obrera* working class; ~ *turista* tourist class; ⚔ ~*s pl.* (*de tropa*) non-commissioned officers; *de una misma* ~ of the same kind; *toda* ~ *de* every kind of, all manner of; *de toda* ~ of every kind, of all sorts; *dar* ~ give a lesson; *dar* ~*s* (*enseñar*) teach; (*aprender*) learn; F *fumarse la* ~ cut a class.

clásico 1. classical; *esp. fig.* classic; traditional; typical; *coche etc.* vintage; (*común*) ordinary; **2.** *m* classic; (*erudito*) classicist.

clasificación *f* classification; rating (*a.* ⚓); **clasificador** *m* filing cabinet; **clasificar** [1g] classify; grade, rate; sort (out).

claudia *f* greengage.

claudicar [1g] limp; *fig.* act crookedly; (*ceder*) give way, abandon one's principles.

claustro *m* cloister (*a. fig.*); *univ. approx.* senate.

cláusula f clause.

clausura f (acto) closing (ceremony), closure; eccl. monastic life; eccl. de ~ convento enclosed; **clausurar** [1a] close; suspend, adjourn.

clava f club; **clavado** vestido just right; a las 5 ~as at 5 sharp; estar ~ (reloj) be stopped (en at); quedar ~ fig. be dumbfounded; **clavar** [1a] clavo knock in, drive in; tablas nail (together); (asegurar) fasten, pin, fix; puñal stick, thrust (en into); joya set; cañón spike; vista fix (en on), rivet (en to); F diddle, sting.

clave 1. f ♪ clef; △ keystone; fig. key (de to); ~ de sol treble clef; 2. adj. key attr.

clavel m carnation; **clavellina** f pink.

clavero m ♀ clove (tree); (p.) keeper of the keys.

clavetear [1a] puerta etc. stud; cordón etc. put a tip on; fig. close, clinch, wind up.

clavícula f collar-bone, clavicle.

clavija f pin, peg (a. ♪), dowel; ⚡ plug; F apretar las ~s a put the screws on.

clavillo m pin, rivet; ♀ clove.

clavo m nail; spike; stud; ♀ clove; 💊 (callo) corn; (dolor) sharp pain; fig. anguish; ~ de rosca screw; F dar en el ~ hit the nail on the head; F remachar el ~ make matters worse; F ser de ~ pasado be as plain as a pike-staff; (fácil) be a cinch.

claxon m mot. horn; tocar el ~ sound one's horn, hoot.

clemencia f clemency, mercy; **clemente** ~ merciful, forgiving; lenient.

cleptomanía f kleptomania; **cleptómano** m, a f kleptomaniac.

clerecía f priesthood; (ps.) clergy; **clerical** clerical; **clericalismo** m clericalism; **clericato** m, **clericatura** f priesthood; **clérigo** m (esp. católico) priest; (esp. anglicano) clergyman; **clero** m clergy.

cliché m typ. stencil; lit. cliché; = clisé.

cliente m/f ✝ customer, client (a. ⚖️); 💊 patient; **clientela** f customers, clients, clientèle; 💊 practice, patients.

clima m climate; **climático** climatic.

clincha f clinch.

clínica f clinic, hospital; (esp. privado) nursing home; (que enseña) teaching hospital; (enseñanza) clinical training; ~ de reposo convalescent home; **clínico** clinical.

clip m paper-clip; (joya) clip.

clisar [1a] stereotype; **clisé** m typ. cliché, plate; phot. plate.

clisos m/pl. sl. peepers.

cloaca f sewer (a. fig.).

cloquear [1a] cluck.

cloral m chloral; **clorhídrico** hydrochloric; **cloro** m chlorine; **cloroformizar** [1f] chloroform; **cloroformo** m chloroform; **cloruro** m chloride; ~ de cal chloride of lime.

club m club.

clueca broody (f hen).

coacción f coercion, duress; **coactivo** coercive.

coadjutor m coadjutor; **coadyuvar** [1a] assist, contribute to.

coagulación f coagulation; **coagular(se)** [1a] coagulate.

coalición f coalition.

coartada f alibi; **coartar** [1a] limit, restrict.

coba f F (embuste) neat trick; (halago) soft soap; dar ~ a soap s.o. up, play up to s.o.

cobalto m cobalt.

cobarde 1. cowardly; faint-hearted; 2. m/f coward; **cobardear** [1a] be a coward, show cowardice; **cobardía** f cowardice; faint-heartedness; **cobardón** m real coward.

cobaya f, **cobayo** m guinea-pig.

cobertera f lid, cover; **cobertizo** m shed; outhouse; lean-to; (refugio) shelter; **cobertor** m bed-spread; **cobertura** f cover(ing); bedspread de cama.

cobija f coping tile; S.Am. blanket; S.Am. ~s pl. bedclothes; **cobijar** [1a] cover (up), close; fig. take in, give shelter to; ~se take shelter; **cobijo** m fig. cover, shelter; lodging en casa.

cobista F 1. smarmy; 2. m/f smarmy sort.

cobrable, **cobradero** precio chargeable; suma recoverable; **cobrador** m ✝ collector; conductor de autobús; (perro) retriever; **cobranza** f = cobro; **cobrar** [1a] 1. v/t. (recuperar) recover; precio charge; *suma* collect; *cheque* cash; *sueldo* draw, get; *hunt.* retrieve; *cuerda* pull in; *fig. golpe* get; *cariño* take (*a* to); *crédito, fama, odio* get, acquire; *ánimo* summon up, muster; *fuerzas* gather; *carnes* put on; *S.Am.* press (for payment); † *por* ~ outstanding; receivable; **2.** *v/i.* (*en empleo*) get one's pay; F *¡vas a ~!* you'll cop it!; **3.** ~se 💥 recover; (*volver en sí*) come to; ~ *de pérdida* make up for.

cobre *m* copper; ♪ brass (*a.* ~s *pl.*); *cocina:* copper pans; *batirse el* ~ go all out (*por inf.* to *inf.*); (*disputa*) get really worked up; **cobreño** copper *attr.,* coppery; **cobrizo** coppery.

cobro *m* recovery; collection *etc.;* † *poner en* (*or al*) ~ make *s.t.* payable; (*cuenta*) send out a bill.

coca *f* F nut; (*golpe*) rap on the nut; kink *en cuerda.*

cocaína *f* cocaine.

cocción *f* cooking *etc.;* ⊕ baking, firing.

cóccix *m* coccyx.

cocear [1a] kick (*a.* F).

cocer [2b *a.* 2h] *v/t.* cook; (*hervir*) boil; *pan* bake; ⊕ bake; *barros* fire; *v/i.* cook; boil; (*vino*) ferment; ~se 💥 be in continual pain; F *no se le cuece el pan* he's like a cat on hot bricks; **cocido** *m* stew (*of meat, bacon a. vegetables*).

cociente *m* quotient; ~ *intelectual* intelligence quotient (I.Q.).

cocina *f* kitchen; (*arte,* ~ *francesa etc.*) cooking, cookery, cuisine; (*aparato*) stove, cooker; *de* ~ *utensilio etc.* kitchen *attr.;* *libro etc.* cookery *attr.;* ~ *económica* range, cooker; ~ *de* (*or a*) *gas* gas-stove, gas-cooker; ~ *de petróleo* oil-stove; **cocinar** [1a] *v/t.* cook; *v/i.* do the cooking; F meddle; **cocinero** *m,* **a** *f* cook; **cocinilla** *f* spirit stove; chafing dish *para mesa.*

coco[1] *m* ♀ coconut; = *cocotero.*

coco[2] *m* bogy man; (*mueca*) face; *hacer* ~s *a* make faces at; (*amor*) make eyes at; *parecer un* ~ be an ugly devil.

cocodrilo *m* crocodile.

cócora *m/f* F bore.

cocotero *m* coconut palm.

cóctel *m* (*fiesta*) cocktail party; (*bebida*) cocktail.

cochambre *m* F filthy thing.

coche *m* (motor-)car, automobile *Am.;* † coach, carriage (*a.* 🚗); ~ *de alquiler,* ~ *de punto* taxi; ~ *blindado* armoured car; ~-*cama* sleeper, sleeping-car; ~-*comedor* dining-car; ~s *pl. de choque* dodgems; ~ *fúnebre* hearse; ~-*habitación* caravan; ~-*salón* saloon-car; ~ *de turismo* tourer; *ir en* ~ go by car; drive, motor; *ir en* ~ *de San Fernando* ride Shank's mare; **cochecillo** *m:* ~ *de inválidos* invalid carriage; **cochecito** *m* (*de niño*) pram, perambulator; **cochera** *f* coach-house; ~ *de alquiler* livery stable; **cochero** 1.: *puerta* ~*a* carriage entrance; **2.** *m* coachman.

cochina *f* sow; *fig.* trollop; **cochinada** *f* F, **cochinería** *f* F filth(iness); (*acto*) dirty trick; (*palabra*) beastly thing; *hacer una* ~ play a dirty trick (*a* on); **cochinilla** *f zo.* woodlouse; (*colorante*) cochineal; **cochinillo** *m* sucking pig; **cochino 1.** filthy, dirty (*a. fig.*); (*sin valor*) rotten, measly; **2.** *m* pig (*a. fig.*); **cochiquera** *f,* **cochitril** *m* pigsty (*a.* F).

cochura *f* = *cocción;* (*pan*) batch of dough.

codal *m* ♀ vine shoot; ⚓ strut, prop; frame *de sierra.*

codazo *m* jab, poke (with one's elbow); (*ligero*) nudge; **codear** [1a] elbow, jostle; *abrirse paso codeando* elbow one's way through; ~se *con* hobnob with, rub shoulders with.

códice *m* manuscript, codex.

codicia *f* greed(iness), lust (*de* for); keen desire (*de* for); **codiciable** covetable; **codiciar** [1b] covet.

codicilo *m* codicil.

codicioso greedy, covetous; F hard-working.

codificación *f* codification; **codificar** [1g] codify; **código** *m* 📖, *tel.* code; ~ *de circulación* highway code; ~ *de leyes a.* statute-book; ~ *penal* penal code.

codillo *m zo.* knee; ⊕ elbow (joint); ♀ stump; (*estribo*) stirrup; **codo** *m* elbow; *zo.* knee; ⊕ elbow (joint); *dar de(l)* ~ *a nudge; fig.* despise; F *empinar el* ~ knock them back; *hablar por los* ~s talk too much; F *mentir por los* ~s tell the most frightful lies.

codorniz *f* quail.
coeducación *f* co-education.
coeficiente *adj. a. su. m* coefficient.
coercer [2b] coerce, constrain; **coerción** *f* coercion, constraint; **coercitivo** coercive.
coetáneo *adj. a. su. m*, **a** *f* contemporary.
coexistencia *f* coexistence; **co-existente** coexistent; **coexistir** [3a] coexist (*con* with).
cofa *f* ⚓ top; ~ *mayor* maintop.
cofia *f* (mob-)cap *de criada etc.*; (*red*) hair-net.
cofrade *m* member (of a brotherhood *etc.*); **cofradía** *f* brotherhood, fraternity; (*gremio*) guild.
cofre *m* chest; **cofrecito** *m* casket.
cogedero 1. ready to be picked; 2. *m* handle; **cogedor** *m* dustpan; (*pala*) shovel.
coger [2c] *flores etc* pick, gather, collect; (*recoger*) take (up), gather (up); (*asir*) catch (hold of), take hold of, seize; ~ (*al vuelo*) snatch; *catarro, frío* catch; (*conseguir*) get (hold of); (*apresar*) trap; *dedos* catch (en in); (*toro*) toss, gore; (*alcanzar*) catch up with; (*noche*) overtake; (*sorprender*) catch; (*encontrar*) find; (*entender*) catch, gather, take in; (*contener*) take; *extensión* cover; **cogida** *f* ⚐ picking, harvesting; *toros*: goring; **cogido** 1.: ~*s de la mano* hand in hand; 2. *m* fold, gather.
cognado *adj. a. su. m*, **a** *f* cognate.
cognición *f* cognition.
cogollo *m* heart *de lechuga, col*; head *de col*.
cogotazo *m* blow on the back of the neck, rabbit punch; **cogote** *m* back of the neck, nape.
cogujón *m* point, corner.
cogulla *f* cowl.
cohabitación *f* cohabitation; **cohabitar** [1a] live together, cohabit (*a. b.s.*).
cohechar [1a] bribe; **cohecho** *m* bribe.
coheredero *m*, **a** *f* coheir(ess *f*).
coherencia *f* coherence; *phys.* cohesion; **coherente** coherent; **cohesión** *f* cohesion; **cohesivo** cohesive; **cohesor** *m radio*: coherer.
cohete *m* rocket; ~ *de señales* distress signal, flare.
cohibición *f* restraint; inhibition;

cohibido restrained, restricted; (*carácter*) inhibited, full of inhibitions; self-conscious; **cohibir** [3a] restrain, check; inhibit.
cohombro *m* cucumber.
cohonestar [1a] gloss over, explain away, whitewash.
coime *m* croupier.
coincidencia *f* coincidence; *en* ~ *con* in agreement with; **coincidente** coincident(al); **coincidir** [3a] coincide (*con* with).
coito *m* (sexual) intercourse, coitus ⚕.
cojear [1a] limp, be lame (*de* in); (*mueble*) wobble, rock; F slip up, be at fault (*de* in); *sabemos de qué pie cojea* we know his weaknesses; **cojera** *f* lameness; (*visible*) limp.
cojijoso peevish.
cojín *m* cushion; **cojinete** *m* small cushion, pad; ⊕ ~ (*a bolas*) (ball-)bearing; ⊕ journal-box; 🚋 chair.
cojo 1. lame, limping; crippled; *mueble* wobbly; *fig.* lame, shaky; 2. *m*, **a** *f* lame person; cripple.
cok *m* coke.
col *f* cabbage; ~ (*rizada*) kale; ~ *de Bruselas* Brussels sprouts; ~ *de Saboya* savoy; *entre* ~ *y* ~, *lechuga* variety is the spice of life.
cola[1] *f zo.*, ✈, *ast.* tail (*a. de frac*); (*extremo*) (tail-)end; bottom *de clase*; train *de vestido largo*; (*ps. etc.*) queue, line; ⊕ ~ *de milano* dovetail; *a la* ~ at the back, behind; *de* ~ *posición* rear; *hacer* ~ queue (up), line up; *tener* ~, *traer* ~ have serious consequences.
cola[2] *f* glue; ~ (*de retal*) size; ~ *de pescado* fish glue; (*gelatina*) isinglass.
colaboración *f* collaboration; *lit.* contribution (*a, en* to); **colaborador** *m*, **-a** *f* collaborator; *lit.* contributor; **colaborar** [1a] collaborate; ~ *a lit.* contribute to, write for.
colación *f* collation (*a. eccl.*); (*merienda*) snack; (*boda*) reception, wedding breakfast; *S.Am.* sweet; *sacar a* ~ bring up, drag in; *traer a* ~ adduce as proof; **colacionar** [1a] collate.
colada *f* wash(ing); (*lejía*) bleach; *geog.* defile; **coladera** *f*, **coladero** *m*, **colador** *m* (tea- *etc*) strainer;

colander *para legumbres*; **colado** ⊕ *hierro* cast; *aire* ~ draught; **coladura** *f* straining; F (piece of) nonsense; *(plancha)* blunder; ~*s pl.* dregs.

colapso *m* collapse, breakdown.

colar [1m] *v/t. líquido* strain; *ropa* bleach; pass, squeeze *(por* through); F **palm** *s.t.* off, foist *s.t.* off *(a* on); *moneda* pass; *noticia* make *s.o.* believe; *v/i. (líquido)* filter, percolate; *(aire)* get in *(por* through); = ~**se** slip through; *(p.)* slip in, sneak in; F *(mentir)* fib; *(equivocarse)* make a slip, put one's foot in it.

colcha *f* bedspread, counterpane; **colchón** *m* mattress.

colear [1a] wag its *etc.* tail; F *todavía colea* it's still not settled.

colección *f* collection; **coleccionador** *m* collector; **coleccionar** [1a] collect; **coleccionista** *m/f* collector; **colecta** *f* collection (for charity); *eccl.* collect; **colectar** [1a] collect; **colecticio** ✕ untrained, raw; *tomo* omnibus; **colectividad** *f (conjunto)* sum total, whole; group; ~ *(social)* whole community; *pol.* collective ownership; **colectivismo** *m* collectivism; **colectivo** collective *(a. gr.)*; *acción freq.* joint, group *attr.*; **colector** *m* collector *(a. ⚡)*; *(canal)* sewer.

colega *m* colleague.

colegial 1. school *attr.*, college *attr.*; *eccl.* collegiate; **2.** *m* schoolboy; **colegiala** *f* schoolgirl; **colegiata** *f* collegiate church; **colegio** *m (mst independent)* grammar school, high school; primary school; *univ., eccl.,* ✖ *etc.* college.

colegir [3c *a.* 3l] gather, collect; conclude, gather (de from).

cólera 1. *f* anger; *physiol.* bile; *montar en* ~ get angry; **2.** ✖ *m* cholera; **colérico** angry, irate; irascible.

coleta *f* pigtail; F postscript; *cortarse la* ~ quit; **coletazo** *m* lash, blow with the tail; 🔒 *etc.* sway(ing).

coleto *m* F body; *decir para su* ~ say to o.s.; *echarse algo al* ~ eat (or drink) *s.t.* up.

colgadero *m* hook, hanger, peg; **colgadizo 1.** hanging; **2.** *m* lean-to, penthouse; **colgado** *fig.* uncertain, doubtful; F *dejar* ~ let *s.o.* down,

disappoint; F *quedarse* ~ be disappointed; **colgadura(s)** *f(pl.)* hangings, drapery; **colgajo** *m* rag, tatter; ⚘ bunch; **colgante 1.** hanging; drooping, floppy; *puente* suspension *attr.*; **2.** *m (joya)* drop, pendant; ⚠ festoon.

colgar [1h *a.* 1m] **1.** *v/t.* hang *(a.* 🎼; de from, en on); *ropa etc.* hang up; *pared* decorate with hangings, drape; *univ.* F plough; *culpa* pin *(a* on); *que me cuelguen si lo hago* I'll be hanged if I will; **2.** *v/i.* hang (de on, from); droop, dangle; *teleph.* hang up, ring off; *fig.* ~ *de* hang on.

colibrí *m* humming-bird.

cólico *m* colic.

colicuar [1d] melt, fuse.

coliflor *f* cauliflower.

coligado allied, in league; **coligarse** [1h] join together, make common cause.

colilla *f* fag-end, stub.

colimbo *m* grebe.

colina *f* hill.

colindante adjoining, neighbouring.

colisión *f* collision *(a. fig.)*; *fig.* clash.

colmado 1. full (de of), overflowing (de with); **2.** *m* grocer's (shop); cheap restaurant; **colmar** [1a] fill (up), fill to overflowing; *esperanzas etc.* fulfil, more than satisfy; ~ *de fig.* shower with, overwhelm with; ~ *de favores* lavish favours upon.

colmena *f* (bee)hive; *fig.* hive; **colmenar** *m* apiary; **colmenero** *m* bee-keeper.

colmillo *m anat.* eye-tooth, canine; *zo.* fang; tusk *de elefante*; F *escupir por el* ~ brag, talk big.

colmo *m fig.* height *de locura etc.*; *a(l)* ~ in plenty; *con* ~ *llenar* to overflowing; *para* ~ *de desgracias* to make matters worse; *¡es el* ~*!* it's the limit!, it's the last straw!

colocación *f (acto)* placing *etc.*; position; *(puesto)* job, situation; ✝ investment; **colocar** [1g] put, place (in position); arrange; ✝ invest; *tropas etc.* position, station; *p.* place (in a job), find a situation for; ~**se** be placed *(a. deportes) etc.*; *(p.)* get a job.

colodión *m* collodion.

colodrillo *m* back of the neck.

colofón *m* colophon.

colofonia f rosin, colophony.
colombiano adj. a. su. m, **a** f Colombian.
colon m anat., gr. colon.
colonia f colony; (barrio) suburb; sew. silk ribbon; ~ veraniega holiday camp; **colonial** colonial; productos imported; **colonización** f colonization; settlement; **colonizador** m colonist; settler; pioneer; **colonizar** [1f] colonize; settle; **colono** m pol. colonist, settler; ✱ (tenant) farmer.
coloquial colloquial; **coloquio** m conversation, talk; ⛿ colloquium; lit. dialogue.
color m colour; (matiz) hue; (colorante) dye; fig. colour(ing); ~es pl. ✗ colours; de ~ p. etc. coloured; zapatos brown; en ~es pelicula colour attr.; ~ local local colour; v. rosa; so ~ de under pretext of; v. subido; mudar de ~ change colour, blanch; (sonrojarse) blush; sacar los ~es a make s.o. blush; le salieron los ~es she blushed; **coloración** f colo(u)ration, colouring; zo. etc. markings; **colorado** coloured; (rojo) red; chiste blue, rude; argumento plausible; ponerse ~ blush; **coloradote** red-faced; **colorante** m colouring (matter); **colorar** [1a] colour, dye (de azul blue); stain (a. ⊕); **colorear** [1a] v/t. motivo show in a favourable light; acción etc. gloss over; v/i. redden, show red; **colorete** m rouge; **colorido** m colour(ing); **colorines** m/pl. bright colours; ¡qué ~ tiene! (niño) what rosy cheeks he's got!; **colorir** [3a; defective] v/t. colour; fig. gloss over; v/i. take on a colour; **colorista** m/f colourist. [(a. fig.).\
colosal colossal; **coloso** m colossus/
columbrar [1a] glimpse, spy, sight; fig. guess.
columna f mst column; ⚠ a. pillar (a. fig.); quinta ~ fifth column; ~ vertebral spinal column; **columnata** f colonnade; **columnista** m columnist.
columpiar [1b] swing; ~se swing (to and fro); seesaw; (cuerpo etc.) sway; waddle al andar; **columpio** m swing; (tabla) seesaw.
colusión f collusion.
colza f rape, colza.

collado m hill; (desfiladero) pass.
collar m (adorno) necklace; collar de perro (a. ⊕); (insignia) chain (of office); ~ de fuerza stranglehold.
coma[1] f gr. comma; sin faltar una ~ down to the last detail.
coma[2] m ✱ coma.
comadre f ✱ midwife; F best friend, crony; (chismosa) gossip; **comadrear** [1a] F gossip; **comadreja** f weasel; **comadreo** m F, **comadrería** f F gossip(ing); **comadrero** m, **a** f gossip, busybody; **comadrón** m accoucheur; **comadrona** f midwife.
comandancia f command; (grado) rank of major; **comandante** m commandant, commander; (grado) major; **comandar** [1a] command; lead; **comandita** f sleeping partnership; **comanditario** socio sleeping; **comando** m command; ✗ (grupo) commando; (abrigo) duffel coat; ~ a distancia remote control.
comarca f region, part (of the country); **comarcano** neighbouring, bordering.
comba f bend; esp. bulge, warp, sag; (juego) skipping; (cuerda) skipping-rope; saltar a la ~ skip; **combadura** f bend(ing) etc.; camber de carretera; **combar** [1a] bend, curve; ~se bend, curve; (madera) bulge, warp, sag.
combate m fight, engagement, combat; fig. battle, struggle; ~ singular duel, single combat; fuera de ~ out of action; boxeo: knocked out; poner fuera de ~ boxeo: knock out; **combatiente** m combatant; **combatir** [3a] v/t. ✗ attack; costa beat upon; mente assail, harass; tendencia etc. combat, fight against; v/i., ~se fight, struggle (con, contra against); **combatividad** f fighting spirit, fight; b.s. aggressiveness; **combativo** fighting attr.; aggressive.
combés m ⚓ waist.
combinación f combination; (arreglo) arrangement, set-up; (proyecto) idea, scheme; (prenda) slip; ⛴ connexion; (bebida) cocktail; ~es pl. fig. plans, measures; **combinar** [1a] combine; colores etc. blend, mix; plan work out; ~se combine.

combo bent, warped.
combustible 1. combustible; **2.** *m* fuel, combustible; **combustión** *f* combustion.
comedero 1. eatable; **2.** *m* ↗ trough, manger; (*comedor*) dining-room.
comedia *f* play, drama (*a. fig.*); (*festiva*) comedy; (*fingimiento*) farce, pretence; **hacer la ～** make believe; **ir a la ～** go to the play; **comediante** *m*, **a** *f* (*esp.* comic) actor (actress *f*).
comedido courteous, polite; moderate; **comedimiento** *m* courtesy *etc.*; **comedirse** [3l] be restrained (*en* in), restrain o.s.; be moderate.
comedón *m* blackhead.
comedor 1. = *comilón 1*; **2.** *m* dining-room; (*muebles*) dining-room suite.
comején *m* termite, white ant.
comendador *m* commander (*of an order of knighthood*); **comendatorio** *f* of recommendation.
comensal *m/f* dependant; (*compañero*) companion at table, fellow-diner.
comentador *m* commentator; **comentar** [1a] comment on; expound; **comentario** *m* comment(s), remarks; *esp. lit.* commentary; **～s** *pl.* gossip, tittle-tattle; **comentarista** *m* commentator; **comento** *m* comment; *lit.* commentary; *b.s.* lie, pretence.
comenzar [1f *a.* 1k] begin, start (*diciendo* by saying; *a inf.* to *inf.*; *con* with; *por su.* with *su.*; *por inf.* by *ger.*).
comer [2a] **1.** *v/t.* eat; ⊕ *etc.* eat away, corrode; (*consumir*) use up, eat up; *color* fade; *renta* enjoy; *ajedrez:* take; F ～ *vivo* have it in for; *me come la pierna* my leg is itching; *sin ～lo ni beberlo* without having a hand in it; **2.** *v/i.* eat; have a meal, *esp.* (have) lunch; *dar de ～ a* feed; *ser de buen ～* eat anything; *tener qué ～ fig.* have enough to live on; *pero ¡～ y callar!* but I'd better shut up!; **3. ～se** *comida* eat up (*a. fig.*); *consonante* drop; *sílaba* slur over; *texto* skip; *fig.* ～ *unos a otros* be at loggerheads.
comerciable marketable; *fig.* sociable; **comercial** commercial, business *attr.*, trading *attr.*; *barrio*

freq. shopping *attr.*; **comercializar** [1f] commercialize; **comerciante** *m/f* trader, dealer, merchant; ～ *al por mayor* wholesaler; ～ *al por menor* retailer; **comerciar** [1b] (*ps.*) have dealings; ～ *con mercancías*, ～ *en* deal in, handle; ～ *con p., país* trade with, do business with; **comercio** *m* (*en general*) trade, business, commerce; (*negocio particular*) trade, traffic; (*conjunto de comerciantes*) business interest(s), (big) business; (*sociedad*) business, firm; (*tienda*) shop; *fig.* intercourse; ～ *exterior* foreign trade; ～ *sexual* sexual intercourse.
comestible 1. eatable; ⅋ *etc.* edible; **2.** *m* food(-stuff); **～s** *pl.* food (-stuffs); (*comprados*) groceries; *tienda de ～s* grocer's (shop).
cometa¹ *m ast.* comet.
cometa² *f* kite.
cometer [2a] *crimen etc.* commit; *error* make; *negocio* entrust (*a* to); *gr.* use; **cometido** *m* assignment, commission.
comezón *f* itch (*a. fig.*; *de inf.* to *inf.*; *por* for), itching; tingle, tingling (sensation) *de calor etc.*; *sentir ～* itch *etc.*
comible F eatable, palatable.
cómica *f* (*esp.* comic) actress; comedienne; **comicastro** *m* ham; **comicidad** *f* comicalness, humour; **cómico 1.** comic(al), funny; comedy *attr.*; *autor* dramatic; **2.** *m* (*esp.* comic) actor; comedian.
comida *f* (*alimento*) food; (*acto*) eating; (*a hora determinada*) meal; *esp.* lunch, dinner; (*manutención*) keep, board; **comidilla** *f* F hobby, first love; ～ *de la ciudad* talk of the town; **comido: estar ～** have had lunch *etc.*; F ～ *por servido* it just doesn't pay.
comienzo *m* beginning, start; (*a. ⚙*) onset; birth, inception *de proyecto etc.*
comilón F **1.** fond of eating; *b.s.* greedy; **2.** *m*, **-a** *f* big eater; *b.s.* pig; **comilona** *f* F spread, blow-out.
comillas *f/pl.* quotation marks, inverted commas.
comino: *no vale un ～* it's not worth tuppence.
comisaría *f* police-station; = **comisariato** *m* commissariat;

comisario m commissary (a. ✗);
~ de policía police superintendent;
comisión f commission (a. ✝);
parl. etc. committee; ✝ (junta)
board; (encargo) assignment, commission; ~ permanente standing
committee; ~ planificadora planning
board; **comisionado** m com-
missioner; parl. etc. committee
member; ✝ member of the board;
comisionar [1a] commission;
comisionista m commission agent;
comiso m (acto) confiscation;
(cosas) confiscated goods.

comisquear [1a] F keep on nibbling
away (at).

comistrajo m F awful meal; fig.
hotchpotch.

comisura f join; ~ de los labios
corner of the mouth.

comité m committee.

comitiva f retinue, suite.

como a) comp. su.: like, the same as;
verb: as; algo así ~ something like;
~ si as if; v. así, tal etc.; la manera ~
sucedió the way it happened; b) en
calidad de: as; c) cj. causa: as,
since; condición: if; ~ no venga
mañana if he doesn't come tomorrow, unless he comes tomorrow; ~
sea as the case may be; ~ no sea
para inf. unless it be to inf.; ~ ~
quiera as you like; (porque) because; así ~, tan luego ~ as soon
as; libre ~ estaba free as he was.

cómo a) interrogative: how?; (por
qué) why?, how is it that ...?;
¿~ está Vd.? how are you?; ¿~ es?
what's he like?, what does he look
like?; ¿~ es de grande? how big is
it?; ¿~ así?, ¿~ eso? how can that
be?, how come?; (enfado) what do
you mean?; ¿~ no? why not?; ¿a ~
es el pan? how much is the bread?;
b) int. ¿~? (pidiendo repetición) eh?,
what did you say?; (sorpresa)
what?; (enfado) how dare you!;
¡~! of course!; c) su.: el porqué y
el ~ de the whys and wherefores of.

cómoda f chest of drawers; **comodidad** f comfort, convenience;
(self-)interest, advantage; ~es pl.
de la vida good things of life;
comodín m naipes: joker; fig.
stand-by, useful gadget; **cómodo**
comfortable; cuarto etc. freq. snug,
cosy; convenient, handy; **comodón**
F comfort-loving.

comodoro m commodore.

compacto compact; typ. etc. close.

compadecer [2d] (a. ~se de) pity,
be sorry for; sympathize with; ~se
con agree with; harmonize with.

compadre m godfather; F friend,
pal; **compadrear** [1a] F be pals.

compaginar [1a] arrange; typ.
make up; ~ con reconcile s.t. with,
bring s.t. into line with; ~se agree,
tally (con with).

compañerismo m comradeship;
deportes etc.: team-spirit; **compañero** m, a f companion; partner;
mate; ~ de armas comrade in
arms; ~ de clase schoolmate; ~ de
juego playfellow; ~ de rancho
messmate; ~ de viaje fellow-trav-
eller (a. fig.); **compañía** f company; ~ inversionista investment
trust; ~ de seguros insurance
company; ~ tenedora holding
company; ♀ de Jesús Society of
Jesus.

comparable comparable; **comparación** f comparison; en ~ con in
comparison with, beside; **comparado** comparative; **comparar** [1a]
compare (con with, to); liken (con
to); **comparativo** adj. a. su. m
comparative.

comparecencia f ⚖ appearance
(in court); **comparecer** [2d] ⚖
appear (in court); **comparendo** m
⚖ summons; subpoena.

comparsa 1. m/f extra (a. thea.),
super(numerary); 2. f masquerade;
thea. = **comparsería** f extras.

compartimiento m division, sharing; (departamento) a. ⚓ compartment; **compartir** [3a] divide up,
share (out); opinión share; ~ con
share with.

compás m ⚐ compasses; ⚓ compass; ♩ (tiempo) time, measure;
(ritmo) beat, rhythm; (división) bar;
fig. rule; a ~ in time; llevar el ~
beat (or keep) time; **compasado**
measured, moderate; **compasar**
[1a] = acompasar; fig. arrange,
organize.

compasión f pity, compassion;
¡por ~! for pity's sake!; **compasivo**
compassionate; understanding,
sympathetic.

compatibilidad f compatibility;
compatible compatible, consistent
(con with).

compatriota *m/f* compatriot, fellow-countryman (-woman).

compeler [2a] compel (*a inf.* to *inf.*).

compendiar [1b] abridge, summarize; **compendio** *m* abridgement, summary; (*libro*) compendium, digest; en ~ in brief; **compendioso** compendious, brief.

compenetración *f* *fig.* mutual understanding, natural sympathy; **compenetrarse** [1a] 🜨 *etc.* interpenetrate; *fig.* share each other's feelings; ~ de *algo* enter into (the spirit of); *p.* share the feelings of; absorb, take in.

compensación *f* compensation; 🜨 redress; *esp. fig.* recompense; 🜨 clearing; **cámara de** ~ clearing house; **compensador** compensatory; **compensar** [1a] *pérdida* compensate for, make up (for); *error* redeem; *p.* compensate.

competencia *f* competition (*a.* 🜨); rivalry; 🜨 competence; (*idoneidad*) suitability; (*incumbencia*) domain, field; *a* ~ vying with each other; en ~ de in competition with; *hacer* ~ *con* compete against (or with); *ser de la* ~ *de* be within *s.o.'s* province; **competente** *trabajo,* 🜨 competent; (*apropiado*) suitable, adequate; **competer** [2a]: ~ *a* be incumbent on; **competidor 1.** competing; **2.** *m, -a f* competitor (*a.* 🜨); rival (*a* for); **competir** [3l] compete (*a.* 🜨, *deportes*; *con* with, against; *para* for); *fig.* ~ *con* rival, vie with.

compilación *f* compilation; **compilar** [1a] compile.

compinche *m* F pal, chum.

complacencia *f* pleasure, satisfaction; willingness *en obrar*; **complacer** [2x] please; *cliente* oblige; *tirano* humour; *deseo* gratify; ~**se** en tàke pleasure in *su.,* *ger.*; be pleased to *inf.*; **complacido** complacent; satisfied; **complaciente** genial, cheerful; obliging, helpful *en ayudar.*

complejidad *f* complexity; **complejo** *adj. a. su. m* complex; ~ **de** *inferioridad* inferiority complex.

complementar [1a] complement; complete, make up; **complementario** complementary; **complemento** *m* complement (*a. gr.,* 🝑);

fig. perfection, culmination; ~ (*in*)*directo* (in)direct object.

completar [1a] complete; make up; *pérdida* make good; *fig.* perfect; **completo** complete; 🜨 *etc.* full; *registro* thorough; *pensión* inclusive, all-in; *por* ~ completely, utterly.

complexión *f* *physiol.* constitution; **complexionado: bien** ~ strong, robust; *mal* ~ weak, frail; **complexional** *physiol.* constitutional; (*genio*) temperamental.

complicación *f* complication (*a.* 🜨); complexity, complex structure; **complicado** complex, complicated; *método freq.* elaborate; ~ *con* mixed up with; **complicar** [1g] complicate; ~**se** get complicated; (*embrollarse*) get tangled, get involved; **cómplice** *m/f* accomplice; **complicidad** *f* complicity, implication (en in).

complot [kom'plo] *m* plot, intrigue.

componedor *m* *typ.* composing stick; **componenda** *f* compromise; *b.s.* shady deal; **componente 1.** component; **2.** *m* 🜨, 🜨 component, ingredient *de bebida etc.*; **componer** [2r] compose (*a. typ.,* ♪), constitute, make up; *typ. a.* set up (in type); *lit.* write; *salón* decorate; *p.* dress up; *comida etc.* prepare; *lo roto,* 🜨 repair, mend, overhaul; *diferencias, enemigos* reconcile; *disputa* settle; *mal asunto* patch up; F 🝑 settle; *ánimo* quieten, soothe; ~**se** (*mujer*) dress up; make up; ~(*las*) *con* come to terms with; ~ *de* be composed of, be made up of; F ~*las para inf.* manage to *inf.*, contrive to *inf.*

comportable bearable; **comportamiento** *m* behaviour; 🜨 performance; **comportar** [1a] put up with, bear; ~**se** behave, conduct o.s.; **comporte** *m = comportamiento.*

composición *f* *mst* composition; make-up; (*ajuste*) settlement; (*convenio*) agreement; **compositor** *m* composer; **compostura** *f* composition, make-up; (*reparo*) mending, repair(ing); (*aseo*) neatness; (*mesura*) sedateness; (*ajuste*) arrangement, settlement.

compota *f* compote, preserve; sauce *de manzanas etc.*

compra *f* purchase; ~*s pl.* shopping; ~ *a plazos* hire-purchase; *ir de* ~*s* shop, go shopping; **comprador** *m*, **-a** *f* shopper, customer *en tienda*; purchaser, buyer *de articulo*; **comprar** [1a] buy, purchase (*a* from); *fig.* buy off, bribe; ~ *a plazos* buy on hire-purchase; **compraventa** *f* † contract of sale; (*tienda*) antique shop.

comprender [2a] *v/t.* (*abarcar*) comprise, include; (*entender*) understand; *no comprendido* not including; *todo comprendido* everything included, all in; *v/i.* understand, see; *¿comprendes?* see?; *¡ya comprendo!* I see; **comprensible** understandable, comprehensible (*para* to); **comprensión** *f* understanding; grasp; inclusion; **comprensivo** understanding; intelligent; (*que incluye*) comprehensive.

compresa *f* compress; ~ *higiénica* sanitary towel; **compresibilidad** *f* compressibility; **compresión** *f* compression; *índice de* ~ compression ratio; **compresor** *m* compressor; **comprimido 1.** *aire* compressed; **2.** *m pharm.* (*esp.* sleeping-)tablet; **comprimir** [3a] compress (*a.* ⊕); squeeze, press down; *fig.* restrain, repress; *lágrimas* keep back.

comprobación *f* checking *etc.*; (*prueba*) proof; *en* ~ *de* in (*or* as) proof of; **comprobador** *m*: ~ *de lámparas* valve tester; **comprobante 1.** of proof; **2.** *m* proof; † voucher, guarantee; **comprobar** [1m] check, verify; prove; ⊕ test, overhaul; ~ *que* establish that.

comprometer [2a] (*poner en peligro*) jeopardize, endanger; *reputación* compromise; put *s.o.* in a compromising situation; ~ *a* nail *s.o.* down to, hold *s.o.* to; *asunto* agree to entrust *s.t.* to; ~ *a inf.*, ~ *a que subj.* force *s.o.* to *inf.*; ~*se* get involved (*en* in); † commit o.s.; ~ *a inf.* engage to *inf.*, undertake to *inf.*; *se compromete a todo* he'll say yes to anything; **comprometido** embarrassing; † *etc.* estar ~ be (already) engaged; **compromiso** *m* obligation, pledge, undertaking; (*cita*) engagement; compromising situation; (*aprieto*) tight corner, predicament; † *libre de* ~,

sin ~ without obligation; *por* ~ out of a sense of duty; *poner en un* ~ place *s.o.* in an embarrassing situation; *le puse en el* ~ *de inf.* I placed him in the position of having to *inf.* [hatch *en puerta*.]

compuerta *f* sluice, flood-gate;)

compuesto 1. *p.p. of componer*; *estar* ~ *de* be composed of, be made up of; **2.** *adj.* ⚘, ♃, *gr.* compound; ♀, △ *etc.* composite; *fig.* composed, calm; **3.** *m* compound (*a.* ⚘).

compulsar [1a] ⚖ check; make a copy of; **compulsión** *f* compulsion; **compulsivo** compulsory; compelling, compulsive.

compunción *f* compunction; (*tristeza*) sorrow; **compungido** remorseful, sorry; **compungirse** [3c] feel remorse (*por* at), feel sorry (*por* for).

computar [1a] calculate, reckon; **cómputo** *m* calculation, computation; estimate.

comulgante *m/f* communicant; **comulgar** [1h] *v/t.* administer communion to; *v/i.* take communion.

común 1. common (*a* to; *a. b.s.*); *opinión a.* widespread, generally held; *de* ~ *con* in common with; *en* ~ in common; *attr.* joint; *fuera de lo* ~ out of the ordinary; *por lo* ~ generally; *hacer en* ~ do *s.t.* all together; **2.** *m*: *el* ~ *de las gentes* most people, the common run (of people); **comuna** *f* commune; **comunal** communal.

comunicable communicable; F sociable; **comunicación** *f* communication; (*ponencia*) paper; (*parte*) message; **comunicado** *m* communiqué; **comunicar** [1g] *mst* communicate (*a.* △; *con* with); *noticia* give, convey, deliver (*a* to); (*legar*) bestow (*a* on); *periodismo*: report (*de* from); ~ *que* report that, inform *s.o.* that; *teleph.* estar *comunicando* be engaged; ~*se* (*ps.*) communicate; be in touch; △ (*inter*)communicate; **comunicativo** communicative; *fig.* sociable; *risa etc.* infectious; **comunidad** *f* community; **comunión** *f* communion; **comunismo** *m* communism; **comunista 1.** communist(ic); **2.** *m/f* communist.

con with; (*a pesar de*) in spite of,

despite; (*para* ~) to, towards; ~ *llegar tan tarde* arriving so late; ~ *que* whereupon; (*resumen*) and so, so (then); *v. todo, tal.*

conato *m* attempt, endeavour (*de inf.* to *inf.*); (*empeño*) effort; ᵗⁱᵗ ~ *de* attempted; *poner* ~ *en* put everything into.

concatenación *f* concatenation, linking; **concatenar** [1a] link together, concatenate.

concavidad *f* concavity; (*sitio*) hollow; **cóncavo 1.** concave; hollow; **2.** *m* hollow, cavity.

concebible conceivable, thinkable; **concebir** [3l] conceive.

conceder [2a] (*otorgar*) grant; concede; admit (*que* that); *premio* award.

concejal *m* (town) councillor; **concejo** *m* council; ~ *municipal* town council.

concentración *f* concentration (*a.* 🜋); **concentrar** [1a] concentrate (*a.* 🜋; ⚔ *en lugar* in; *en escena* on); *fig.* restrain, conceal; ~*se* concentrate (*a.* ⚔), be concentrated; centre (*en* on).

concepción *f* conception; (*facultad*) understanding; **concepto** *m* concept (*a. phls.*), notion; opinion; *lit.* conceit; *bajo todos los* ~*s, por todos* ~*s* from every point of view; *en* ~ *de* by way of; *en mi* ~ in my view; *tener buen* ~ *de, tener en buen* ~ think well of; **conceptuar** [1e]: ~ *de*, ~ *por* deem *s.t.* to be, judge *s.t.* to be; ~ *como* regard *s.t.* as; **conceptuoso** witty; *estilo* mannered.

concerniente: ~ *a* concerning, relating to.

concertar [1k] *v/t.* (*arreglar*) arrange; *convenio etc.* conclude; *precio* fix (*en* at); *p.* reconcile (*con* with); harmonize; ♪ tune up; *v/i.* agree (*a. gr.*); harmonize; ~*se* agree; be(come) reconciled.

concertina *f* concertina.

concesión *f* grant, award; ✝, *fig.* concession; **concesionario** *m* concessionaire; licensee; **concesivo** concessive (*a. gr.*).

conciencia *f* (*conocimiento*) knowledge, awareness; *phls.* consciousness; (*moral*) conscience; moral sense; *a* ~ conscientiously; *en* ~ with a clear conscience; **concienzudo** conscientious, thorough.

concierto *m* order, concert; ♪ harmony; (*pieza*) concerto; (*función*) concert; (*convenio*) agreement; *de* ~ in concert.

conciliación *f* conciliation; (*semejanza*) affinity, similarity; favour; **conciliador 1.** conciliatory; **2.** *m* conciliator; **conciliar** [1b] reconcile; *respeto etc.* win; ~ *el sueño* get to sleep; ~*se algo* win, gain; **conciliatorio** conciliatory; propitiatory.

concilio *m* *eccl.* council.

concisión *f* conciseness, terseness; **conciso** concise, terse.

concitar [1a] stir up, incite.

conciudadano *m*, **a** *f* fellow-citizen.

cónclave *m* conclave.

concluir [3g] *v/t.* end; conclude (*de* from; *a uno de s.o.* to be); convince; (*acallar*) silence; *v/i.* end (*gr. etc. con, en, por* in); *¡vamos a* ~ *de una vez!* let's get it over!; ~ *de inf.* finish *ger.*; **conclusión** *f* conclusion; *en* ~ lastly, in conclusion; **concluyente** conclusive.

concomitancia *f* concomitance; **concomitante** concomitant.

concordancia *f* concordance (*a. eccl.*); *gr.*, ♪ concord; **concordante** concordant; **concordar** [1m] *v/t.* reconcile; *gr.* make *s.t.* agree; *v/i.* agree (*a. gr.*); ~ *con* agree with, tally with, fit in with; **concordato** *m* concordat; **concorde** in agreement; *poner* ~*s* bring about agreement between; **concordia** *f* concord, harmony; conformity, agreement; (*sortija*) ring.

concreción *f* concretion; ✹ stone; **concretar** [1a] *fig.* make *s.t.* concrete; reduce to its essentials, boil down; *para* ~ to sum up; to be more specific; ~*se a inf.* confine o.s. to *ger.*; **concreto 1.** concrete; *aceite* thick; *fig. punto etc.* definite, actual, specific; *en* ~ to sum up; exactly, specifically; *nada en* ~ nothing in particular; **2.** *m* concretion; *S.Am.* concrete.

concubina *f* concubine; **concubinato** *m* concubinage.

concupiscencia *f* lust, concupiscence; **concupiscente** lewd, lustful.

concurrencia *f* (*asistencia*) attendance, turn-out; (*multitud*) crowd, gathering; ✝ competition; concurrence de circunstancias etc.; **concurrente** present; concurrent; ✝ competing; **concurrido** lugar crowded; (función) well attended; **concurrir** [3a] (reunirse) gather, meet (a at, en in); fig. come together, conspire (para inf. to inf.); coincide (con with); ✝ etc. compete; (convenir) agree; co-operate (en in); ~ a concurso compete in, take part in; éxito contribute to; ~ con dinero contribute; **concursante** m/f contestant, participant; **concurso** m (reunión) gathering; concurrence de circunstancias; (ayuda) help; competition (a. a puesto), contest; (función) show, exhibition; deportes: match, meeting; tenis: tournament; ~ hípico horse-show; ~ radiofónico quiz (show); por ~ by competition; attr. competitive.

concusión f ⚖ extortion; **concusionario** m extortioner.

concha f zo. shell; (marisco) shellfish; (carey) tortoiseshell; thea. prompt-box; meterse en su ~ retire into one's shell; F tener muchas ~s be wide awake.

conchabarse [1a] F gang up (contra on).

condado m hist. earldom; (tierras, provincia) county; **conde** m earl, count.

condecoración f ✗ etc. decoration; insignia; **condecorar** [1a] decorate (con with).

condena f sentence; term; ~ a perpetuidad life sentence; cumplir su ~ serve one's sentence; **condenable** condemnable; **condenación** f condemnation; = condena; eccl. damnation; F ¡~! damn!; **condenado** 1. F damned, ruddy; 2. m, a f ⚖ criminal, convicted person; eccl. one of the damned; ~ a muerte condemned man; **condenador** condemnatory; **condenar** [1a] condemn (a to); esp. ⚖ convict, find guilty (por ladrón of stealing); ⚖ sentence (a multa to, a presidio to hard labour); eccl. damn; ⚠ close up; ~se ⚖ confess (one's guilt); eccl. be damned.

condensable condensable; **condensación** f condensation; **condensador** m ⊕, ⚡ condenser; **condensar** [1a] condense.

condesa f countess.

condescendencia f willingness (to help); acquiescence (a in); **condescender** [2g] acquiesce, say yes; ~ a consent to, say yes to; ~ en inf. agree to inf.

condestable m hist. constable; ⚓ gunner.

condición f condition; ~ (social) status, position; character, nature; ~es pl. ✝ etc. conditions, terms; circumstances; humilde ~ humble origin; ~es pl. de vida living conditions; a ~ (de) que on condition that; de ~ attr. noble; de ~ ... ...-natured; estar en ~es de inf. be in a condition (or fit state) to inf.; be in a position to inf.; **condicionado**, **condicional** conditional (a. gr.).

condimentar [1a] season; flavour; (con especias) spice; **condimento** m seasoning; flavour(ing); dressing.

condiscípulo m, a f fellow-student.

condolencia f condolence; **condolerse** [2h]: ~ de be sorry for; ~ por sympathize with.

condominio m ⚖ joint ownership; pol. condominium.

condonación f condonation, forgiveness; **condonar** [1a] acto condone; deuda forgive, forget.

conducción f leading etc.; transport(ation); piping de aguas; mot. driving; phys. conduction; ✝ agreement; ~ a (la) derecha right-hand drive; **conducente** conducive (a to); **conducir** [3o] 1. v/t. lead, guide (a to); conduct; negocio conduct, manage; mot. drive; mot., ⚓ steer; carga transport, convey; 2. v/i. mot. etc. drive; ~ a lead to; resultado etc. make for; 3. ~se behave, conduct o.s.; **conducta** f ✝ etc. management, direction; conduct, behaviour de p.; mala ~ misbehaviour, misconduct; **conductibilidad** f conductibility; conductivity; **conductivo** phys. conductive; **conducto** m conduit (a. ✦); tube; esp. anat. duct, canal; fig. agency; (p.) agent, intermediary; por ~ de through; **conductor** 1. leading, guiding; phys. conductive; 2. m phys. conductor; ⚡ lead; 3. m, -a f leader, guide; mot. etc. driver.

condueño m, a f part-owner.

condumio m F food.

conectar [1a] ⚡, ⊕ connect (up); (*poner*) switch on; *boxeo: golpe* land; ~ *a tierra* ⚡ earth; ⚡ *estar conectado* be on; **conectivo** connective.

conejal m, **conejar** m, **conejera** f warren, burrow; F den, dive; **conejillo** m: ~ *de Indias* guinea-pig; **conejo** m rabbit.

conexión f connexion (a. ⚡); relationship; **conexo** connected, related.

confabulación f plot, intrigue; ⚡ ring; **confabularse** [1a] plot, scheme.

confección f (*acto*) making; (*arte*) workmanship; *pharm.* confection, concoction; (*traje*) ready-made suit; **confeccionado** *ropa* ready-made, ready-to-wear; **confeccionar** [1a] make (up).

confederación f confederacy; confederation, league; **confederado** *adj. a. su. m* confederate; **confederarse** [1a] form a confederation, confederate.

conferencia f (*discurso*) lecture; *pol. etc.* meeting, conference; *teleph.* call; ~ *interurbana* long-distance call, trunk-call; ~ *de prensa* press-conference; **conferenciante** m/f lecturer; **conferenciar** [1b] be in conference, confer; **conferencista** m/f S.Am. lecturer; **conferir** [3i] v/t. *dignidad* confer, bestow (*a* on); *premio* award (*a* to); *negocio* discuss; compare (*con* with); v/i. confer.

confesante m penitent; **confesar** [1k] v/t. confess (a. *eccl.*), own up to, admit; v/i., ~se confess (*con* to), make one's confession; **confesión** f confession; **confesional** confessional; **confes(i)onario** m confessional; (*garita a.*) confession box; **confesor** m confessor.

confiabilidad f reliability, trustworthiness; **confiable** reliable, trustworthy; **confiado** (*presumido*) vain, conceited; (*crédulo*) unsuspecting, gullible; ~ *en sí* (*mismo*) self-confident, self-reliant; **confianza** f confidence (*en* in); trust (*en* in), reliance (*en* on); familiarity (*con* with); ~ *en sí* (*mismo*) self-confidence; *b.s.* conceit; *con toda* ~ with complete confidence; *de* ~ p. reliable, trustworthy; *amigo* intimate; *puesto* responsible; *manera*

etc. informal; *en* ~ trustingly; (*en secreto*) in confidence, confidentially; *tener* ~ *con* be on close terms with; **confiar** [1c] v/t.: ~ *a*, ~ *en* entrust *s.t.* to; v/i. (have) trust; ~ *en* trust, trust in (*or* to); rely on, count on; *éxito etc.* be confident about; ~ *en que* trust that; **confidencia** f confidence; *hacer* ~*s a* confide in, reveal secrets to; **confidencial** confidential; **confidente** m, *a* f confidant(e f).

configuración f shape, configuration; ~ *del terreno* lie of the land; **configurar** [1a] form, shape.

confín m limit, boundary; horizon; ~*es* pl. confines (a. fig.); **confinar** [1a] v/t. confine (*a*, *en* in); v/i.: ~ *con* border on; ~*se* shut o.s. up.

confirmación f confirmation (a. *eccl.*); **confirmar** [1a] confirm (a. *eccl.*; *de*, *por* as); endorse, bear out; **confirmatorio** confirmative, confirmatory.

confiscación f confiscation; **confiscar** [1g] confiscate.

confitar [1a] preserve; *frutas* candy; *fig.* sweeten; **confite** m sweet; **confitería** f confectionery; (*tienda*) confectioner's, sweetshop; **confitero** m, *a* f confectioner; **confitura** f preserve; (*mermelada*) jam.

conflagración f conflagration; *fig.* flare-up.

conflicto m conflict (a. fig.); (*apuro*) difficulty, fix; ~ *laboral* labour dispute.

confluencia f confluence (a. ⚡); **confluente** 1. confluent; 2. m confluence; **confluir** [3g] meet, join; *fig.* come together.

conformación f structure, form; conformation; **conformar** [1a] v/t.: ~ *a*, ~ *con* adjust *s.t.* to, bring *s.t.* into line with; v/i. agree (*con* with); ~*se* conform; ~ *con original* conform to; *regla* comply with, abide by; *política etc.* fall into line with, adjust o.s. to; *destino* resign o.s. to; **conforme** 1. *adj.* similar; in agreement, in line (*con* with); (*ps.*) agreed; 2. *prp.*: ~ *a* in conformity with, in accordance with; *carácter etc.* in keeping with; 3. *cj.* as; (*luego que*) as soon as; ~ ... *así* as ... so; 4. *int.* ¡~! agreed!, right!, O.K.!; **conformidad** f similarity, conformity; agreement;

proportion; resignation (*con* to); forbearance; *de ~ con* in accordance with; *en ~* accordingly.

confort *m* comfort; **confortable** comfortable; *noticia etc.* comforting; **confortante** comforting; **confortar** [1a] invigorate, strengthen; *afligido* comfort.

confraternidad *f* confraternity; *fig.* good understanding, intimacy.

confrontación *f* confrontation; **confrontar** [1a] *v/t. ps.* bring face to face, confront (*con* with); *textos* compare; *v/i.* border (*con* on); *~se con* face, confront.

confundir [3a] (*mezclar*) mix, mingle (*con* with); *b.s.* mix up, jumble up; (*equivocar*) confuse (*con* with); mistake (*con* for), mix up; *enemigo* confound; floor *en debate*; *ánimo* perplex, bewilder; (*humillar*) make *s.o.* feel small; **confusamente** in (utter) confusion; *recordar* hazily; **confusión** *f* confusion; **confuso** *mst* confused; *cosas a.* mixed up, in disorder; *recuerdo a.* hazy.

confutación *f* confutation; **confutar** [1a] confute.

congelación *f* congealing; freezing (*a.* ✝); ❄ frost-bite; *~ de salarios* wage-freeze; **congelado** *carne* chilled, frozen; ❄ frost-bitten; **congelar(se)** [1a] (*esp. sangre*) congeal; (*agua a. fig.*) freeze; ❄ get frost-bitten.

congenial kindred; **congeniar** [1b] get on (*con* with).

congénito congenital.

congestión *f* congestion; **congestionar** [1a] produce congestion in, congest.

conglomeración *f* conglomeration; **conglomerado** *adj. a. su. m* conglomerate; **conglomerar(se)** [1a] conglomerate.

congoja *f* anguish, distress; **congojoso** distressing, heartbreaking.

congraciador ingratiating; **congraciarse** [1b] *con* get into *s.o.'s* good graces; *b.s.* ingratiate o.s. with, get in with.

congregación *f* gathering, assembly; *eccl.* congregation; **congregar(se)** [1h] gather, congregate; **congresista** *m/f* delegate, member (of a congress); **congreso** *m* congress.

congrio *m* conger (eel).

congruencia *f* suitability; congruence (*a.* ⅍), congruity; **congruente, congruo** suitable; congruent (*a.* ⅍), congruous.

cónico conical; ⅍ *sección* conic; **conífera** *f* conifer; **conífero** coniferous.

conjetura *f* conjecture, surmise; *por ~* by guesswork; **conjetural** conjectural; **conjeturar** [1a] guess (at) (*de, por* from); *~ que* surmise that, infer that.

conjugación *f* conjugation (*a. biol.*); **conjugar** [1h] conjugate.

conjunción *f* conjunction; **conjuntiva** *f* conjunctiva; **conjuntivitis** *f* conjunctivitis; **conjuntivo** conjunctive; *tejido* connective; **conjunto 1.** united, joint; related *por afinidad*; **2.** *m* whole; (*vestido*, ♪) ensemble; *thea.* chorus; *de ~ attr.* overall; *en ~* altogether, as a whole; *en su ~* in its entirety.

conjura(ción) *f* conspiracy, plot; **conjurado** *m*, a *f* conspirator, plotter; **conjurar** [1a] *v/t.* (*suplicar*) entreat, beseech; swear *s.o.* in *con juramento*; *diablo* exorcize; *peligro* stave off, ward off; *v/i.*, *~se* plot, conspire (together); **conjuro** *m* conjuration, incantation; (*súplica*) entreaty.

conllevar [1a] *penas* help *s.o.* to bear; *p. etc.* put up with.

conmemoración *f* commemoration; **conmemorar** [1a] commemorate; **conmemorativo** commemorative; memorial *attr.*

conmensurable commensurable.

conmigo with me; with myself.

conminar [1a] threaten; **conminatorio** threatening.

conmiseración *f* pity, sympathy; (*acto*) commiseration.

conmoción *f geol.* shock (*a. fig.*); *fig.* commotion, disturbance; *~ cerebral* concussion; **conmovedor** (*enternecedor*) moving, touching; poignant; (*que perturba*) disturbing; (*emocionante*) exciting, stirring; **conmover** [2h] shake, disturb; *fig.* move, touch; shock, disturb.

conmutador *m* ⚡ switch; **conmutar** [1a] exchange (*con, por* for); ⚞ *etc.* commute (*en* into).

connatural innate, inherent.

connivencia *f* connivance; (*complot*) conspiracy.

connotación f connotation; (*parentesco*) distant relationship; **connotar** [1a] connote.

cono m cone (*a.* ⚕).

conocedor m, **-a** f connoisseur, (good) judge (*de* of); expert (*de* in); **conocer** [2d] v/t. know; be familiar with; distinguish, tell (*en*, *por* by); *peligro etc.* recognize; (*llegar a* ⁓) p. meet; *lugar etc.* (get to) know; (*entender*) understand, know about; *¿de qué le conoces?* how do you know him?; *dar a* ⁓ introduce; *darse a* ⁓ make a name for o.s.; v/i. know; ⁓ *de*, ⁓ *en* know a lot about; ⁓*se* know o.s.; (*dos ps.*) (*estado*) know each other; (*acto*) meet, get to know each other; *se conoce que* it is known that, it is established that; **conocible** knowable; **conocido 1.** *p. etc.* well-known; familiar; noted (*por* for); **2.** m, **a** f acquaintance; **conocimiento** m knowledge; understanding; 🕉 consciousness; (*p.*) acquaintance; ⚓ bill of lading; ⁓s *pl.* knowledge (*de* of); information (*de* about); *obrar con* ⁓ *de causa* know what one is up to; *perder* (*recobrar*) ⁓ lose (regain) consciousness; *poner en* ⁓ *a* inform, let *s.o.* know; *tener* ⁓ *de* know about, have knowledge of; *venir en* ⁓ *de* learn of, hear about.

conque 1. (and) so, (so) then; **2.** m F condition (*para* of).   [Cuenca.]
conquense *adj. a. su. m/f* (native) of
conquibus m F wherewithal.

conquista f conquest; **conquistador** m, **-a** f conqueror; *hist.* conquistador; **conquistar** [1a] conquer (*a* from); *fig.* win over, win round.

consabido well-known, well established; above-mentioned.

consagración f consecration; **consagrado** consecrated (*a* to); *expresión* time-honoured; **consagrar** [1a] consecrate (*a* to); deify; *tiempo etc.* devote (*a* to); *palabra* sanction, authorize; ⁓*se a* devote o.s. to.

consanguíneo related by blood, consanguineous; **consanguinidad** f blood-relationship, consanguinity.

consciente conscious (*de* of).

consecución f acquisition; *de difícil* ⁓ difficult to get hold of; **consecuencia** f consequence, outcome;

consistency *de conducta*; *como* ⁓ in consequence; *de* ⁓ of consequence; *en* ⁓ accordingly; *en* ⁓ *de* as a consequence of; *traer a* ⁓ bring *s.t.* up; **consecuente** *phls.* consequent; *conducta etc.* consistent; **consecutivo** consecutive (*a. gr.*); **conseguir** [3d *a.* 3l] obtain, get, secure; ⁓ *inf.* succeed in *ger.*; *conseguí que se fuera* I managed to make him go.

conseja f (fairy-)tale; **consejero** m, **a** f adviser; *pol.* councillor; **consejo** m (*dictamen*) advice, counsel; (*un* ⁓) piece of advice; hint; *pol. etc.* council; ⚖ tribunal, court; ✝ *etc.* board; ⁓ *de administración* board of directors; ⁓ *de guerra* (*sumarísimo*) (drumhead) court-martial; ⁓ *de ministros* cabinet.

consenso m (unanimous) assent, consensus; **consentido** *niño* spoilt; *marido* complaisant; **consentidor** (*débil*) weak(-minded); *madre* indulgent; *marido* complaisant; **consentimiento** m consent; **consentir** [3i] v/t. consent to; permit, allow (*a.* ⚖; *que alguien subj.* s.o. to *inf.*); (*tolerar, admitir posibilidad*) admit; *niño* pamper, spoil; v/i. consent, say yes, agree (*en* to); (*ceder*) give in; (*creer*) believe (*en que* that); ⁓ *con* be indulgent with; = ⁓*se* ⊕ loosen, give; (*rajándose*) split, crack (up).

conserje m porter; caretaker, janitor; **conserjería** f porter's office.

conserva f (*en general*) preserved foods; (*fruta etc.*) preserve(s); (*mermelada*) jam; (*carne etc.*) pickle; ⁓s *pl. alimenticias* canned goods; *en* ⁓ preserved; pickled; canned; **conservación** f preservation *etc.*; △ *freq.* upkeep; **conservador 1.** preservative; *pol.* conservative; *ser* ⁓ *de salud etc.* preserve; **2.** m, **-a** f *pol.* conservative; **3.** m 🏛 curator; **conservar** [1a] p., *salud, frutas,* ⊕ conserve; can, tin *en lata*; *costumbres, hacienda etc.* keep up; *amigos, secreto* keep; (*guardar*) keep; ⁓*se* last (out); ⁓ (*bien*) keep (well); 🎖 take good care of o.s.; ⁓ *con* (or *en*) *salud* keep well; **conservatismo** m conservatism; **conservativo** preservative, conservative; **conservatorio** m ♪ conservatoire; **conservero** *industria* canning *attr.*

considerable considerable, substantial, sizeable; **consideración** f consideration; respect, regard; en ~ a considering, in consideration of; por ~ a out of respect for; sin ~ hablar inconsiderately; sin ~ a irrespective of; ser de ~ be important, be of consequence; **considerado** (amable) considerate, thoughtful; respected; deliberate; **considerar** [1a] consider (que that; como as, to be, or acc.), regard (como as); show consideration for, respect.

consigna f ✗ order; ✗, pol. watchword; ⛟ cloakroom, left-luggage office; **consignación** f consignment; deposit; **consignador** m consignor; **consignar** [1a] (enviar) consign; dispatch, remit (a to); deposit; renta etc. assign (para to); (citar) point out, record; **consignatario** m ✝ consignee; ✝ agent; ⅔ assign(ee).

consigo with him, with her, with you etc.

consiguiente consequent (a upon); por ~ consequently, so, therefore.

consistencia f consistency, consistence etc.; **consistente** consistent; solid, substantial; razón etc. sound, valid; **consistir** [3a]: ~ en consist of (or in); lie in; be due to.

consistorio m eccl. consistory; pol. town council.

consocio m fellow-member; ✝ partner, associate. [sole.]

consola f console-table; ♪, ⌂ con-~]

consolación f consolation; **consolador 1.** consoling, comforting; **2.** m, -a f comforter; **consolar** [1m] console, comfort; ~se find consolation (con in).

consolidación f consolidation; **consolidados** m/pl. consols; **consolidar** [1a] consolidate (a. ✝, fig.); deuda fund; fig. a. strengthen, cement.

consomé m clear soup, consommé.

consonancia f consonance (a. gr.), harmony; fig. harmony, conformity; en ~ con in accordance with; **consonante 1.** adj. a. su. f consonant; **2.** m rhyming word, rhyme; **consonar** [1m] ♪ be in harmony (a. fig.); lit. rhyme.

consorcio m ✝ consortium; association; fig. harmony, good fellowship; **consorte** m/f consort; fig.

partner, companion; ⅔ ~s pl. partners in crime.

conspicuo eminent, prominent.

conspiración f conspiracy; **conspirador** m, -a f conspirator; **conspirar** [1a] conspire, plot (contra against); ~ a inf. conspire to inf.

constancia f constancy; steadiness etc.; proof, evidence; dejar ~ de place s.t. on record; fig. show evidence of; trabajar con ~ work steadily; **constante 1.** constant; steady; amigo etc. faithful, staunch; (duradero) lasting; **2.** f ↯ constant; **constar** [1a]: ~ de be clear from, be evident from; consist of; ~ en be on record in; ~ por be shown by; hacer ~ record; certify; reveal (que that); consta que it is a fact that; me consta que I have evidence that; conste que ⅔ etc. let it be on record that; F remember that, bear in mind that; no consta it is not listed; (libro) not available.

constelación f constellation; climate; **constelado** starry, full of stars; fig. bespangled (de with).

consternación f consternation, dismay; **consternar** [1a] (fill with) dismay.

constipado m ✹ cold; **constiparse** [1a] catch a cold; estar constipado have a cold.

constitución f constitution; **constitucional 1.** constitutional; **2.** m constitutionalist; **constituir** [3g] constitute; colegio etc. set up, establish; principios etc. erect (en into); ~ en oficial etc. make; obligación force s.o. into; ~se en, ~ por set (o.s.) up as; **constitutivo** adj. a. su. m constituent; **constituyente** pol. constituent.

constreñir [3h a. 3l] force (a inf. to inf.); ✹ constipate; **constricción** f constriction; **constrictor 1.** ✹ costive, binding; **2.** m anat. constrictor.

construcción f building, construction (a. gr.); ~ de buques shipbuilding; en (vía de) ~ under construction; **constructor 1.** building, construction attr.; **2.** m builder; ~ de buques shipbuilder; **construir** [3g] construct (a. ↯), build; edificio freq. put up; gr. construe.

consuelda f comfrey.

consuelo m consolation, solace; joy, comfort.

consuetudinario habitual; ⚖ common.

cónsul m consul; **consulado** m (cargo) consulship; (oficina) consulate; **consular** consular.

consulta f consultation; (parecer) opinion; ⚖ (horas de) ～ surgery (hours); de ～ libro etc. reference attr.; **consultación** f consultation; **consultar** [1a] consult; referencia look up; asunto discuss, take up (a, con with); (aconsejar) advise; **consultivo** consultative; **consultor** m consultant; **consultorio** m information bureau; ⚖ surgery, consulting room; problem (or advice) page de periódico.

consumación f consummation; end, extinction; **consumado** consummate, perfect; accomplished (en in); **consumar** [1a] carry out, accomplish; matrimonio consummate.

consumición f consumption etc.; food or drink taken in a café etc.; **consumido** F ⚖ skinny; fidgety, fretful; **consumidor** m ⟰ consumer; (cliente) customer; **consumir** [3a] mst consume; F get on s.o.'s nerves, get s.o. down; wear s.o. out; ～se burn out, be consumed en fuego; ⚖ waste away (a. fig.); fig. pine away, mope (de because of); **consumo** m, **consunción** f consumption.

consuno: de ～ together, with one accord.

contabilidad f accounting, book-keeping; (profesión) accountancy; **contable** m accountant; book-keeper.

contacto m contact; poner(se) en ～ con put (get) into touch with.

contado 1. adj. ～s pl. few; rare; son ～s los que there are few who; ～as veces seldom; **2.** adv.: al ～ cash down, (for) cash; por de ～ naturally; **contador** m counter de café; ⟰ accountant, book-keeper; ⊕ meter; ～ de gas gas-meter; **contaduría** f accountancy; book-keeping; (oficina) accounts department; thea. box-office.

contagiar [1b] infect (con with; a. fig.); ～se become infected; ～ de ⚖ catch; herejía be tainted with; **contagio** m contagion (a. fig.); (enfermedad) infection; **contagioso** contagious, catching (a. fig.); ⟰ infectious.

contaminación f contamination; (baldón) stain; **contaminar** [1a] contaminate (a. fig.); agua pollute; vestido soil; texto corrupt; eccl. profane; (pervertir) defile, stain; ～se be contaminated (con, de by).

contante ready; v. dinero; **contar** [1m] v/t. ⚖ etc. count (por dedos on); (considerar) count (entre among, por as); historia tell; ～ inf. count on ger., expect to inf.; sin ～ not counting, not to mention; except for; cuenta 20 años he's 20; tiene los días contados his days are numbered; v/i. count; ～ con rely on, count on; (poseer, tener) have; no ～ con freq. not bargain for.

contemplación f contemplation; ～es pl. indulgence; sin ～es without any explanation, without more ado; no me vengas con ～es don't come to me with excuses; **contemplar** [1a] gaze at, look at; fig., eccl. contemplate; show consideration for; **contemplativo** contemplative.

contemporáneo adj. a. su. m, a f contemporary; **contemporizador** m time-server; **contemporizar** [1f] temporize.

contención f ⚒ etc. containing, containment; (contienda) contention; rivalry; ⚖ suit; **contencioso** contentious; ⟰ captious; **contender** [2g] contend; compete, be rivals (en in); ～ con fight with, fig. dispute with (sobre over); **contendiente** m contestant.

contener [2l] contain (a. ⚒), hold; multitud keep in check; rebeldes keep down; emoción keep back, bottle up; cólera contain; bostezo, risa smother; ～se fig. hold o.s. in check, contain o.s.; **contenido 1.** fig. restrained; **2.** m contents; content.

contentadizo: bien (mal) ～ easy (hard) to please; **contentamiento** m contentment; **contentar** [1a] satisfy, content; ⟰ endorse; ～se con, ～ de be contented with, be satisfied with; ～ con inf. content o.s. with ger.; **contento 1.** contented; (alegre) pleased; glad, happy; estar ～ de be glad about; (satisfecho) be pleased with; quedar ～ de inf. be content to inf.; no *caber de* ⏑ jump for joy; **2.** *m* joy, contentment; *a* ⏑ to one's satisfaction.

contérmino conterminous.

contero *m* △ beading.

contertuli(an)o *m*, **a** *f* fellow-member (of a *tertulia*).

contestable debatable; **contestación** *f* answer, reply; ₮₮ ⏑ *a la demanda* plea; **contestar** [1a] answer (*a. v/i.* ⏑ *a*); ₮₮ corroborate.

contexto *m lit.* context; (*enredo*) interweaving, web; **contextura** *f* contexture; make-up *de p.*

contienda *f* struggle, contest.

contigo with you; (†, *a. Dios*) with thee.

contigüidad *f* nearness, closeness; adjacency; **contiguo** adjacent (*a* to), adjoining.

continencia *f* continence; **continental** continental; **continente 1.** continent; **2.** *m geog.* continent; (*vasija*) container; *fig.* air, mien; (*porte*) bearing.

contingencia *f* contingency; **contingente 1.** contingent; **2.** *m* contingent (*a.* ✕); contingency; ✝ *etc.* quota.

continuación *f* continuation; *a* ⏑ later (on); below *en texto*; *decir a* ⏑ go on to say; *a* ⏑ *de* after; **continuar** [1e] *v/t.* continue, go on with; *v/i.* continue, go on (*con* with; *ger.* ger.); ⏑ *con salud* keep in good health; ⏑ *en su puesto* stay at one's job, carry on with one's work; *continuará* (*cuento*) to be continued; ⏑(*se*) *con geog.,* △ adjoin, connect with; **continuidad** *f* continuity; continuance; **continuo 1.** continuous; continual; ⊕ *cinta etc.* endless; *p.* persevering; *a la* ⏑*a,* (*de*) ⏑ continuously; **2.** *m* continuum.

contonearse [1a] swagger, strut; **contoneo** *m* swagger, strut.

contorno *m* form, shape; *paint. etc.* outline; ⏑*s pl.* environs; *en* ⏑ around.

contorsión *f* contortion; **contorsionista** *m/f* contortionist.

contra 1. *prp.* against (*a. en* ⏑ *de*); △ opposite, facing; *ir en* ⏑ *de* run counter to, go against; **2.** *adv.* (*en*) ⏑ against; *opinar etc. en* ⏑ disagree; **3.** *m v.* pro; **4.** *f fenc.*

counter; ✝ bind, snag; *llevar la* ⏑ *a* oppose, contradict.

contra...: ⏑**almirante** *m* rear-admiral; ⏑**atacar** [1g] counter-attack; ⏑**ataque** *m* counter-attack; ⏑**bajo** *m* double-bass; ⏑**balancear** [1a] counterbalance; ⏑**balanza** *f* counterbalance; contrast; ⏑**bandista** *m/f* smuggler; ⏑**bando** *m* (*acto*) smuggling; (*géneros*) contraband; ⏑ *de armas* gun-running; *de* ⏑ contraband *attr.*; *pasar de* ⏑ smuggle (in *or* out).

contracción *f* contraction.

contracorriente *f* cross-current; undercurrent.

contractable contractible; **contráctil** *m* contractile; **contractual** contractual.

contra...: ⏑**decir** [3p] contradict; ⏑**dicción** *f* contradiction; *fig.* incompatibility; *espíritu de* ⏑ contrariness; ⏑**dictorio** contradictory.

contraer [2p] *mst* contract; *discurso* condense; *contrato etc.* enter into; *costumbre* acquire.

contra...: ⏑**espionaje** *m* counter-espionage; ⏑**fuerte** *m* △ buttress; *geog.* spur; ⏑**golpe** *m* counter-stroke; ⏑**hacer** [2s] copy, imitate; *moneda* counterfeit; *documento* forge, fake; *p.* impersonate; ⏑**hecho** counterfeit, fake(d); *anat.* hunch-backed; ⏑**hechura** *f* counterfeit; counterfeiting *etc.*; ⏑**jugada** *f* counter-move.

contralto 1. *f* contralto; **2.** *m* counter-tenor.

contra...: ⏑**luz:** *a* ⏑ against the light; ⏑**maestre** *m* ⊕ foreman; ⚓ warrant-officer; ⚓ boatswain; ⏑**mandar** [1a] countermand; ⏑**mandato** *m* countermand; ⏑**marca** *f* countermark; ⏑**marcar** [1g] countermark; ⏑**marcha** *f* ✕ counter-march; *mot. etc.* reverse; ⏑**marchar** [1a] countermarch; ⏑**orden** *f* counter-order; ⏑**pelo:** *a* ⏑ *acariciar etc.* the wrong way; *fig.* against the grain; ⏑**pesar** [1a] (counter-) balance (*con* with); *fig.* offset, compensate for; ⏑**peso** *m* counterbalance, counterweight; ✝ make-weight; ⏑**poner** [2r] compare; (*oponer*) ⏑ *a* set *s.t.* up against; ⏑**posición:** *en* ⏑ *a* in contrast to; ⏑**producente** self-defeating;

boomerang *attr.*; **~punto** *m* counterpoint.

contrariar [1c] go against, be opposed to; (*estorbar*) impede, thwart; (*molestar*) annoy; **contrariedad** *f* opposition; obstacle; (*disgusto*) bother, annoyance; **contrario 1.** contrary (*a* to); (*nocivo*) harmful (*a* to); (*enemigo*) hostile (*a* to); *lado* opposite; *suerte* adverse; *al ~, por lo ~* on the contrary; *al ~ de* unlike; *en ~* to the contrary; *lo ~* the opposite, the reverse; *de lo ~* otherwise; *todo lo ~* quite the reverse; *llevar la ~a a* oppose, contradict; **2.** *m*, **a** *f* (*p.*) enemy, adversary; ♔ *etc.* opponent; **3.** *m* contrary, reverse (*de* of); obstacle.

contra...: ♔rreforma *f* Counterreformation; **~rrestar** [1a] counteract, offset; *pelota* return; **~rresto** *m* counteraction; **~sentido** *m* misinterpretation; contradiction; (*disparate*) piece of nonsense; **~seña** *f* countersign (*a.* ✗); *thea.* ticket.

contrastar [1a] *v/t.* resist; ♔ *metal* assay, hallmark; *medidas* check; *radio*: monitor; *v/i.* contrast (*con* with); *~ a, ~ con(tra)* face up to; **contraste** *m* contrast; ♔ assay; (*marca del*) ~ hallmark; *en ~ con* in contrast to; *por ~* in contrast.

contrata *f* contract; *por ~* by contract; **contratante** *m* ♔ contracting party; ♔ contractor; **contratar** [1a] negotiate for, contract for; *p.* hire, engage; *jugador etc.* sign up.

contratiempo *m*: setback, reverse.

contratista *m/f* contractor; **contrato** *m* contract.

contra...: ~tuerca *f* locknut; **~vención** *f* contravention, infringement; **~veneno** *m* antidote (*de* to); **~venir** [3s]: *~ a* contravene, infringe; **~ventana** *f* shutter.

contribución *f* contribution; (*carga*) tax; *~es pl.* taxes, taxation; *exento de ~es* tax-free; **contribuir** [3g] contribute (*a, para* to, towards; *a inf.* to ger.); pay (in taxes); **contribuyente** *m* contributor; *esp.* taxpayer.

contrición *f* contrition.

contrincante *m* opponent; rival.

contristar [1a] sadden.

contrito contrite.

control *m* control; inspection,

check(ing); ♔ (*cuenta*) audit; *perder ~* get out of control, lose control; **controlar** [1a] control; inspect, check; ♔ audit.

controversia *f* controversy; **controvertible** controversial; **controvertir** [3i] argue (*v/t.* over).

contumacia *f* obstinacy *etc.*; ♔ contempt (of court); **contumaz** obstinate; wayward, perverse; ♔ guilty of contempt, contumacious.

contumelia *f* contumely; **contumelioso** contumelious.

contundente *fig.* convincing, impressive; **contundir** [3a] bruise, contuse.

conturbar [1a] trouble, dismay.

contusión *f* bruising, contusion.

convalecencia *f* convalescence; **convalecer** [2d] get better, convalesce (*de* after); **convaleciente** *adj. a. su. m/f* convalescent.

convección *f* convection.

convencer [2b] convince (*de* of, *de que* that); **convencimiento** *m* (act of) convincing; conviction.

convención *f* convention; **convencional** conventional; **convencionalismo** *m* conventionalism.

convenible suitable; *p.* accomodating; *precio* fair; **conveniencia** *f* suitability *etc.*; (*conformidad*) agreement; conformity; *~s pl.* ♔ property; (*decoro*) decencies; **conveniente** (*apropiado*) suitable, fit(ting); proper, right; (*útil*) useful, profitable; *juzgar ~* see fit (*inf.* to *inf.*); **convenio** *m* agreement; **convenir** [3s] agree (*con* with; *en* about, on; *en inf.* to *inf.*; *en que* that); *~ a* suit, be suited to; be suitable for, befit; *impersonal: ~ inf.* be as well to *inf.*, be important to *inf.*; *conviene beber agua* it's a good thing to drink water; *conviene a saber* namely; **~se** come to an agreement, agree.

conventículo *m* conventicle; **convento** *m* monastery; *~* (*de monjas*) convent, nunnery; **conventual** conventual.

convergencia *f* convergence; *fig.* common direction; concurrence; **converger** [2c], **convergir** [3c] converge (*en* on); *fig.* concur, be in accord (*con* with).

conversación *f* conversation, talk; **conversar** [1a] converse.

conversión f conversion; ⚙ wheel; **converso** m, **a** f convert; **convertible** convertible; **convertidor** m ⊕, ⚡ converter; **convertir** [3i] convert (a. ⊕, ⚡, ✝; en into, eccl. a to); ojos, armas, pensamientos turn; ~se eccl. be(come) converted; ~ en turn into, become.

convexidad f convexity; **convexo** convex.

convicción f conviction; **convicto** convicted, found guilty.

convidada: F dar una ~, pagar la ~ stand a round; **convidado** m, **a** f guest; **convidar** [1a]: ~ a invite s.o. to; bebida esp. treat to, stand; fig. stir to, move to; ~ a uno con offer s.t. to s.o.; ~se volunteer.

convincente convincing.

convite m invitation; party, banquet.

convivencia f living together, life together; **convivir** [3a] live together; share the same life; ~ con fig. exist side by side with.

convocar [1g] summon; call.

convoy m ⚓ convoy; 🚂 train; F procession; **convoyar** [1a] escort.

convulsión f convulsion (a. fig.); **convulsionar** [1a] convulse; **convulsivo** convulsive; **convulso** convulsed (de with).

conyugal married, conjugal; **cónyug(u)e** m/f spouse, partner; ~s pl. married couple, husband and wife.

coñac m brandy.

¡coño! (enojo) damn it all!; (sorpresa) well I'm damned!; (injuria a p.) idiot!

cooperación f co-operation; **cooperador** m, **-a** f co-operator; **cooperar** [1a] co-operate (a in); ~ en take part (together) in; **cooperario** m co-operator; **cooperativa** f co-operative; (mutual) association; **cooperativo** co-operative.

coordenada f ⚗ co-ordinate; **coordinación** f co-ordination; **coordinar** [1a] co-ordinate.

copa f mst glass; poet. goblet; deportes: cup (a. fig. de dolor); crown de sombrero; 🌳 top; naipes: ~s pl. hearts; F llevar una ~ de más have one over the eight; tomar unas ~s have a drink or two.

copar [1a] ✕ surround; naipes: sweep the board (a. fig.).

copear [1a] F have a drink.

copete m anat. tuft (of hair); forelock de caballo; orn., geog. crest; de alto ~ aristocratic; important; tener mucho ~ be stuck-up; **copetín** m S.Am. cocktail; **copetudo** tufted; fig. stuck-up.

copia f copy; abundance; ~ al carbón carbon copy; ~ en limpio fair copy; **copiante** m/f copyist; **copiar** [1b] copy (a. fig.); dictado take down; **copioso** copious, plentiful; **copista** m/f copyist.

copita f (small) glass.

copla f verse; ♩ popular song, folk-song; ~s pl. verse(s), poetry; ~s pl. de ciego doggerel.

copo m ⊕ tuft; ~ de nieve snowflake.

copudo bushy, thick.

coque m coke.

coqueluche f whooping-cough.

coqueta 1. flirtatious, flighty, coquettish; **2.** f flirt, coquette; **coquetear** [1a] flirt (con with); **coqueteo** m, **coquetería** f flirtation; flirtatiousness, coquetry; fig. affectation; **coquetón 1.** (majo) smart; hombre attractive (to women); mujer = coqueta; **2.** m lady-killer.

coquitos: hacer ~ pull faces.

coraje m (ira) anger; (ánimo) (fighting) spirit; **corajina** f F (fit of) temper; **corajudo** quick-tempered.

coral[1] ♩ **1.** choral; **2.** m chorale.

coral[2] m zo. coral; **coralina** f coralline; **coralino** coral attr.

Corán m Koran.

coraza f hist. cuirass; ⚓ armour-plate; zo. shell.

corazón m heart (a. fig.); naipes: ~es pl. hearts; duro de ~ hard-hearted; de ~ adv. willingly; de buen ~ kind-hearted; de todo ~ from the heart; con el ~ en la mano frankly, sincerely; llevar el ~ en la mano wear one's heart on one's sleeve; poner el ~ en set one's heart on; tener el ~ para inf. have the heart to inf.; no tener ~ para not feel up to; estar enfermo del ~ have heart trouble; **corazonada** f rash impulse; presentiment, hunch F.

corbata f (neck)tie; ~ de lazo = **corbatín** m bow-tie.

corbeta f corvette.

corcel m steed, charger.

corcova f hunchback, hump; **corcovado 1.** hunchbacked; **2.** m,

a *f* hunchback; **corcovar** [1a] bend (over); **corcovear** [1a] buck, plunge; **corcovo** *m* buck; *fig.* crookedness.

corchea *f* ♪ quaver.

corcheta *f sew.* eye; **corchete** *m* snap-fastener, clasp; *sew.* hook and eye; *typ.* bracket; ⚎ † constable.

corcho *m* cork; cork mat *para mesa*; *pesca*: float; **corchoso** corky.

cordaje *m* rigging.

cordel *m* cord, line; *a* ～ in a straight line; **cordelero** *m* cord-maker, rope-maker; **cordería** *f* cordage.

corderillo *m*, **corderina** *f* lamb-skin; **cordero** *m*, **a** *f* lamb (*a. fig.*); (*piel de*) ～ lambskin.

cordial 1. cordial; heartfelt; *pharm.* tonic; **2.** *m* cordial; **cordialidad** *f* warmth, cordiality; frankness.

cordillera *f* (mountain-)range.

cordobán *m* cordovan (leather); **cordobana: F** *andar a la* ～ go about with nothing on; **cordobés** *adj. a. su. m*, **-a** *f* Cordovan.

cordón *m* cord (*a. anat.*); (shoe-) lace *de zapato*; ⚡ flex; ⚓ strand *de cabo*; cordon *de policía etc.* (*a.* ✗, ⚎); *de 3* ～*es lana* 3-ply; ～ *sanitario* sanitary cordon; ～ *umbilical* umbilical cord; **cordoncillo** *m sew.* rib; milling, milled edge *de moneda*.

cordura *f* good sense, wisdom.

corear [1a] *fig.* answer in a chorus; say all together; **corifeo** *m* cory-phaeus; *fig.* leader; **corista 1.** *m/f eccl.* chorister; **2.** *f thea.* chorus-girl.

cormorán *m*: ～ (*grande*) cormorant.

cornada *f* goring; **cornadura** *f*, **cornamenta** *f* horns; antlers *de ciervo*.

cornamusa *f* bagpipe; *hunt.* hunt-ing-horn.

córnea *f* cornea.

cornear [1a] gore, butt.

corneja *f* crow; ～ *negra* carrion crow.

córneo horny, corneous ◻.

corneta 1. *f* bugle; ～ (*de llaves*) cornet; ～ (*de monte*) hunting-horn; **2.** *m* ✗ bugler; ♪ cornet-player.

cornezuelo *m* (*hongo*) ergot.

cornisa *f* cornice (*a. mount.*); **cornisamento** *m* entablature.

cornucopia *f* cornucopia; **cornudo 1.** horned; **2.** *m* cuckold.

coro *m* ♪ (*pieza*), *thea.*, *fig.* chorus;

ps., eccl., ♫ choir; *a* ～ in a chorus; *a* ～*s* in turn; *de* ～ by heart, by rote; *hacer* ～ *de* (*or a*) *palabras* echo.

corola *f* corolla; **corolario** *m* corollary.

corona *f* crown; *ast.* corona; *meteor.* halo; *eccl.* tonsure; ～ (*de flores*) chaplet; wreath; **coronación** *f* coronation; = **coronam(i)ento** *m* crowning, conclusion; ♫ crown, coping stone; **coronar** [1a] crown (*con*, *de* with; *por rey acc.*); **coronario** coronary.

coronel *m* colonel; ～ *de aviación* group-captain.

coronilla *f* crown, top of the head; **F** *bailar de* ～ slog away; **F** *estar hasta la* ～ be fed up.

corpa(n)chón *m* F, **corpazo** *m* F carcass.

corpiño *m* bodice.

corporación *f* corporation; asso-ciation; **corporal** corporal, bodily; *higiene etc.* personal; **corporativo** corporate; **corpóreo** corporeal, bodily; **corpulencia** *f* stoutness *etc.*; **corpulento** stout; *esp. p.* well-built, burly; **Corpus** *m* Cor-pus Christi; **corpúsculo** *m* cor-puscle.

corral *m* (farm)yard; ～ *de madera* timber-yard; **F** ～ *de vacas* slum; ～ *de vecindad* tenement; *hacer* ～*es* play truant; **corralillo** *m* playpen.

correa *f* (leather) strap; thong; *esp.* ⊕ belt; (*calidad*) leatheriness; ～ *sin fin* endless belt; ～ *de trans-misión* driving-belt; ～ *transporta-dora* conveyor (belt); *besar la* ～ eat humble pie; **F** *tener* ～ be able to take it; **correaje** *m* belts, straps; ⊕ belting.

corrección *f* correction; (*castigo*) punishment; (*formalidad*) correct-ness; **correccional** *m* reformatory; **correctivo** *adj. a. su. m* corrective; **correcto** correct (*a. fig.*), right; *fig.* polite; *facciones etc.* regular; **corrector** *m typ.* proof-reader.

corredera *f* slide; ⊕ slide-valve; ⚓ log; *de* ～ *puerta etc.* sliding; **corredizo** sliding; *nudo* running, slip *attr.*; *grúa* travelling; **corredor** *m*, **-a** *f* runner; ✝ agent, broker; ～ *automovilista* racing motorist; ～ *de bolsa* (stock-)broker; ～ *de casas* house-agent; ～ *de fincas rurales*

land-agent; F ~ de noticias gossip;
corredurÃa f brokerage.
corregidor m hist. chief magistrate;
corregir [3c a. 3l] correct; put
right; (castigar) punish, reprimand;
fig. temper.
correlaciÃ³n f correlation; **correlacionar** [1a] correlate; **correlativo** adj. a. su. m correlative.
correligionario m, a f co-
religionist.
correntÃ³n F gadabout; (bromista)
jolly, fond of a lark.
correo m 🕭 post, mail (a. ~s pl.);
(p.) courier; 🕭 postman; ✗
dispatch-rider; (tren) ~ mail-train;
(casa de) ~s pl. post-office; ~ aÃ©reo
airmail; ~ diplomÃ¡tico courier;
~ urgente special delivery; a vuelta
de ~ by return (of post); por ~ by
post, through the post; echar al ~,
poner en el ~ post, mail.
correoso leathery, tough.
correr [2a] **1.** v/t. terreno traverse,
travel over; ✗ overrun; caballo
race; toros fight; (acosar) chase,
pursue; cortina draw (back); vela
(un)furl; pestillo shoot; llave turn;
silla pull up, draw up; fig. p.
embarrass, cover with confusion;
aventura have; riesgo run; sl. clase
cut; F ~la have one's fling; (juerga)
go on the spree; **2.** v/i. run (a.
liquido, plazo, fig.); (liquido a.)
flow; (surtidor) play; (viento)
blow; (tiempo) pass, elapse; (moneda) pass; (doctrina etc.) circulate,
be commonly held; (rumor) go
round; a todo ~ at full speed;
a todo turbio ~ however bad things
may be; que corre mes etc. current;
♈ ~ a, ~ por sell at; ~ con be in
charge of; gastos meet; (entender)
understand; **3.** ~se (deslizarse)
slide (por along); (derretirse) melt;
(vela) gutter; fig. get embarrassed;
(excederse) go too far; **correrÃa** f ✗
raid, foray; excursion.
correspondencia f correspondence
(a. 🕭); communication(s), contact
entre lugares etc.; 🕭 connexion;
return de afecto; gratitude; **corresponder** [2a] correspond (con
to), tally (con with); ▲ communicate; 🕭 connect (con with); ~ a
correspond to; afecto, favor return,
reciprocate, repay (con with);
(deber) fall to; (asunto) concern; ~se

correspond (a. 🕭; con with); (en
afecto etc.) agree; have regard
for one another; **correspondiente**
1. a. 🕭 corresponding; respective;
2. m correspondent; **corresponsal**
m (newspaper) correspondent.
corretaje m brokerage; **corretear**
[1a] gad about; (jugando) run
around; **corretero** m, a f
gadabout; **correve(i)dile** m F
gossip.
corrida f run, dash; ~ de toros
bullfight; de ~ fast; **corrido** fig.
sheepish, abashed; (experimentado)
wise, knowing; ~ de vergÃ¼enza
covered with shame; de ~ fluently.
corriente 1. agua etc. running;
estilo flowing, fluid; mes etc.
present; cuenta current; moneda
accepted, normal; common, ordinary, everyday; procedimiento normal, standard; (sabido) well-
known; noticia topical; F ~ y
moliente regular; **2.** m current
month; el 10 del ~ the 10th inst.;
estar al ~ de be informed about;
be well up with; mantenerse al ~ de
keep in touch with; tener al ~ de
keep s.o. informed about; **3.** f
current (a. fig., ⚡; alterna alternating, continua direct), stream; ~ de
aire draught; ~ submarina undercurrent; con ~ alambre live; dejarse
llevar de la ~ fig. follow the crowd.
corrillo m knot of people, huddle;
fig. clique, coterie.
corrimiento m 🦴 discharge; ~ (de
tierras) landslide; fig. embarrassment, sheepishness.
corro m ring, circle (of people);
open space; hacer ~ make room.
corroboraciÃ³n f corroboration etc.;
corroborar [1a] strengthen; fig.
corroborate; **corroborativo** cor-
roborative.
corroer [2za] corrode (a. fig.); geol.
erode.
corromper [2a] v/t. corrupt (a.
fig.); madera rot; comida, placeres
spoil; juez bribe; mujer seduce; F
annoy, put out; v/i. smell bad.
corrosiÃ³n f corrosion; geol. erosion;
corrosivo adj. a. su. m corrosive.
corrupciÃ³n f corruption; corrupt-
ness; ♈, 🏛 a. graft; rotting etc.;
corruptela f corruption; abuse;
bad habit; **corruptible** corruptible; comida etc. perishable; **co-**

rruptivo corruptive; **corrupto** corrupt; **corruptor 1.** corrupting; **2.** *m*, **-a** *f* corrupter.

corsario *m* privateer, corsair.

corsé *m* corset.

corso *adj. a. su. m*, **a** *f* Corsican.

corta *f* felling, clearing.

corta...: ~**bolsas** *m* pickpocket; ~**césped** lawn-mower; ~**circuitos** *m* circuit-breaker.

cortado *leche* sour; *estilo* abrupt; ~ *a pico* precipitous; **cortador 1.** cutting; **2.** *m*, **-a** *f* cutter (*a.* ⊕); **cortadura** *f* cut; (*acto*) cutting (*a. de periódico*); *geog.* pass; **cortalápices** *m* pencil-sharpener; **cortante 1.** cutting; *frío* bitter; *viento* biting; **2.** *m* cleaver, chopper.

corta...: ~**papeles** *m* paper-knife; ~**pisa** *f sew.* trimming; *fig.* (*gracia*) charm, wit; conditions; difficulty; ~**plumas** *m* penknife.

cortar [1a] **1.** *v/t.* cut (*a.* ⚔, *naipes*); (*recortar, suprimir*) cut out; (*amputar*) cut off; *carne* carve; *árbol etc.* cut down; *enemigo, provisión, región* cut off; *conversación* cut into, interrupt; (*acortar*) cut short; *agua, gas,* ⚡ cut off, turn off; ~ *de vestir sew.* cut out; *fig.* backbite; **2.** *v/i.* cut (*a. naipes*); (*frío etc.*) be biting; **3.** ~**se** (*manos*) get chapped; (*leche*) turn (sour); (*p.*) get embarrassed, get tongue-tied.

corte[1] *m* cut; (*acto*) cutting; (*filo*) edge; (*tela*) piece, length; △, ⚔ (cross-)section; ⚡ failure, cut; ⊕ job; ⚒ stint; (*sastrería*) tailoring; cut, style *de traje*; (*marca*) make; ~ *de corriente* power-cut.

corte[2] *f* court (*a. S.Am.* ⚖); (*patio*) court(yard); (*corral*) yard; (*ciudad*) capital (city); *la* ♀ *freq.* Madrid; ~s *pl.* Spanish parliament; ~s *pl.* constituyentes constituent assembly; *hacer la* ~ *a* pay court to.

cortedad *f* shortness *etc.*; *fig.* bashfulness; backwardness *etc.*

cortejar [1a] attend; *mujer, poderoso* court; **cortejo** *m* courting; (*séquito*) entourage; (*agasajo*) treat; (*p.*) beau; (*desfile*) procession; ~ *fúnebre* funeral procession.

cortés polite, courteous; *amor* courtly; **cortesana** *f* courtesan; **cortesanía** *f* politeness, good manners; **cortesano 1.** of the court; = *cortés;* **2.** *m* courtier;

cortesía *f* politeness; courtesy; title; *de* ~ *entrada* complimentary.

corteza *f* bark *de árbol*; peel, skin, rind *de fruta*; crust *de pan*; *fig.* outside; (*grosería*) coarseness.

cortijo *m* farm(house).

cortina *f* curtain; ~ *de humo* smoke-screen.

corto short; brief; slight; (*escaso*) scant(y), deficient; (*defectuoso*) defective; *fig.* (*timido*) bashful, shy; tongue-tied; (*lerdo*) backward, stupid; *quedarse* ~ not know what to say; ~**circuito** *m* short-circuit; *poner(se) en* ~ short-circuit; ~**metraje** *m cine:* short.

coruñés *adj. a. su. m*, **-a** *f* (native) of Corunna.

corvadura *f* curve (*a.* △), bend; curvature; **corvo** curved, arched.

corvejón *m* hock *de caballo*; spur *de gallo*.

corzo *m*, **a** *f* roe(-deer).

cosa *f* thing; (*algo*) something; (*no* ... ~) nothing; ~ *de* about, a matter of; *es* ~ *de 2 horas* it takes about 2 hours; *¡~s pl. de Juan!* one of John's tricks!; that's typical of John!; *¡~s pl. de España! contp.* what can you expect in Spain?; *otra* ~ something else; *poca* ~ nothing much; ~ *rara* strange thing; *¡~ (más) rara!* how strange!; the funny thing is ...!; *a* ~ *hecha* as good as done; *como si tal* ~ as if nothing had happened; *es poca* ~, *no es gran* ~ it isn't up to much; *tal como están las* ~s as things stand; *ni* ~ *que valga* nor anything of the sort; *las* ~s *van mejor* things are going better.

cosaco *adj. a. su. m*, **a** *f* Cossack.

coscoja *f* kermes oak.

coscorrón *m* bump on the head.

cosecha *f* crop, harvest (*a. fig.*); (*acto*) harvesting; (*época*) harvest-time; *de* ~ *propia* ♀ home-grown; *de su propia* ~ *fig.* out of one's own head, of one's own invention; *la* ~ *de 1949* (*vino*) the 1949 vintage; **cosechadora** *f* ⊕ (combine) harvester; **cosechar** [1a] harvest, gather (in); *esp. fig.* reap; **cosechero** *m*, **a** *f* harvester, reaper.

coseno *m* cosine.

coser [2a] sew (up, on); stitch (up; *a.* ⚕); *fig.* join closely (con to); *v.* *puñalada; ser cosa de* ~ *y cantar* be plain sailing, be a cinch; ~se con become attached to; **cosido** m sewing.

cosmético adj. a. su. m cosmetic.

cósmico cosmic; **cosmografía** f cosmography; **cosmógrafo** m cosmographer; **cosmonauta** m cosmonaut; **cosmopolita** adj. a. su. m/f cosmopolitan.

cosquillar [1a] tickle; **cosquillas** f/pl. tickling (sensation); F buscarle a uno las ~ stir s.o. up; hacer ~ a tickle; fig. tickle s.o.'s curiosity; tener ~ be ticklish; tener malas ~ be touchy; **cosquillear** [1a] tickle; **cosquilleo** m tickling (sensation); **cosquilloso** ticklish; fig. touchy.

costa[1] f ✝ cost, price; ~s pl. ⚖ costs; ✝ a ~ at cost; a ~ de at the expense of; a toda ~ at any price.

costa[2] f ♹ coast; coastline, (sea-)shore; **costado** m anat., ♹ side; ✗ flank; de cuatro ~s downright; por los cuatro ~s on both sides of the family; **costal** m sack, bag; F ~ de huesos bag of bones; **costaneras** f/pl. ⚠ rafters; **costanero** steep; ♹ coastal.

costar [1m] cost (a. fig.); fig. cost dear(ly); cuesta caro it costs a lot; cueste lo que cueste cost what it may.

costarricense adj. a. su. m/f, **costarriqueño** adj. a. su. m, a f Costa Rican.

coste m cost, price; **costear**[1] [1a] pay for, defray the cost of; (poder ~) afford.

costear[2] [1a] ♹ (sail along the) coast.

costera f side de paquete; geog. slope; ♹ coast; pesca: fishing season; **costero** coastal; coasting.

costilla f rib; ~s pl. F back; F mi ~ my better half; medir las ~ a tan; **costilludo** strapping.

costo m cost; ~ de la vida cost of living; **costoso** costly, expensive.

costra f crust; ✿ scab; **costroso** crusty, incrusted; ✿ scabby.

costumbre f custom, habit; ~s pl. customs, ways; (moralidad) morals; de ~ usual(ly); como de ~ as usual; tener por ~ inf. be in the habit of ger.

costura f sewing, needlework, dressmaking; (unión) seam; alta ~ fashion-designing; de ~ francesa medias fully-fashioned; sentar las ~s

a fig. tan; **costurera** f dressmaker, seamstress.

cota f: ~ de malla coat of mail.

cotejar [1a] compare, collate; **cotejo** m comparison, collation.

cotí m ticking.

cotidiano daily, everyday.

cotiledón m cotyledon.

cotización f quotation, price en bolsa; quota; dues de asociación; **cotizar** [1f] quote (en at); cuota fix.

coto m ✔ enclosed pasture; preserve de caza; (mojón) boundary post; ~ cerrado fig. closed shop; poner ~ a put a stop to.

cotorra f parrot; (urraca) magpie; **cotorrear** [1a] chatter (away); **cotorreo** m chatter, gabble; **cotorrera** f F chatterbox.

coturno m buskin; de alto ~ lofty, elevated.

coy m ♹ hammock.

coyuntura f anat. joint; fig. juncture, occasion; opportunity.

coz f kick (a. ✗); (culata) butt; F insult; dar coces, dar de coces a kick; v. aguijón; tirar coces lash out (a. fig.).

crac m ✝ crash; ¡~! snap!, crack!

crampón m crampon.

cráneo m skull, cranium ⚕.

crápula f drunkenness; fig. dissipation; **crapuloso** drunken; fig. dissipated.

crasitud f fatness; **craso** p. fat; líquido thick, greasy; fig. gross, crass.

cráter m crater.

creación f creation; **creador** 1. creative; 2. m, -a f creator; originator; **crear** [1a] create, make; idea etc. originate; found, establish.

crecer [2d] mst grow (a. fig.; en in); increase; (luna) wax; (precio, río) rise; (días) get longer; dejar ~ barba grow; ~se assume greater authority (or importance); **creces** f/pl. increase; F con ~ with a vengeance; devolver etc. with interest; **crecida** f spate, flood; **crecido** large; ⚘, p. etc. (full-)grown; río in flood; **creciente** 1. growing, increasing; ast. cuarto ~ crescent (moon); 2. m crescent; 3. f ♹ ~ (del mar) high tide; ast. crescent moon; **crecimiento** m growth, increase; ✝ rise in value.

credenciales f/pl. credentials; **credibilidad** f credibility; **crediticio** ✝ credit attr.; **crédito** m mst credit; authority, standing; (creencia) belief; a ~ on credit; abrir ~ a give credit to; dar ~ a fig. believe (in).

credo m creed; F en menos que se canta un ~ in a jiffy; **credulidad** f credulity, gullibility; **crédulo** credulous, gullible; **creederas:** F tiene buenas ~ he'll swallow anything; **creencia** f belief; **creer** [2e] believe (en in; que that); think (que that); creo que sí (no) I (don't) think so; lo creo I think so; ¡ya lo creo! you bet (your life)!, rather!; ~se believe o.s. (to be); **creíble** believable, credible.

crema f (nata) cream (a. fig.); (natillas) custard, cream; (salsa) sweet sauce; (cosmético) cold cream.

cremación f cremation.

cremallera f ⊕ rack; (cierre de) ~ zip fastener.

crémor m: ~ (tártaro) cream of tartar; **cremoso** creamy.

crencha f parting.

creosota f creosote.

crepitar [1a] (leña etc.) crackle; (tocino) sizzle; crepitate (a. ⚡).

crepuscular twilight; luz ~ = **crepúsculo** m twilight, dusk.

cresa f maggot.

crespo curly; estilo involved; p. cross; **crespón** m crape.

cresta f crest.

creta f chalk; **cretáceo** cretaceous.

cretinez f utter stupidity; **cretino** m cretin (a. fig.).

cretona f cretonne.

cretoso chalky.

creyente m/f believer.

creyón m crayon.

cría f keeping, breeding etc.; (pequeño) young child or animal; (conjunto) litter, young, brood; de ~ attr. breeding; ~ de ganado cattle-breeding, stock-raising; **criada** f maid, servant; ~ por horas charwoman; ~ para todo maid-of-all-work, general; **criadero** m ♣ nursery; zo. breeding-ground; ⚒ vein; **criado 1.**: bien ~ well-bred, well brought up; mal ~ ill-bred; **2.** m servant; **criador** m breeder; **crianza** f raising, rearing;

physiol. lactation; fig. breeding; sin ~ ill-bred; **criar** [1c] ganado etc. keep, breed, raise; (educar) bring up; (cebar) fatten; ~ (a los pechos) breast-feed, nurse; (tierra) produce, grow; fig. foster, nurture; necesidad etc. create; ~se ⚱ etc. grow; **criatura** f creature (a. fig.); (nene) infant, baby.

criba f sieve, screen; **cribar** [1a] sift, sieve, screen.

cric m ⊕ jack.

crimen m crime; **criminal** adj. a. su. m/f criminal; **criminalidad** f criminality.

crin f mane (a. ~es pl.); horsehair.

crío m F kid, child.

criollo adj. a. su. m, a f Creole.

cripta f crypt.

crisálida f chrysalis.

crisis f crisis; ~ nerviosa nervous breakdown; llegar a la ~ come to a head.

crisma f eccl. chrism; sl. nut, bean; sl. romper la ~ a brain.

crisol m crucible; fig. melting-pot.

crispar [1a] make s.t. twitch; ~se twitch.

cristal m glass, crystal (a. phys., poet.); (hoja) pane (of glass); (espejo) mirror; de ~ glass attr.; ~es pl. emplomados leaded lights; ⚓ ~ de patente bull's-eye; ~ de roca rock crystal; ~ tallado cut glass; **cristalería** f (arte) glasswork; (fábrica) glass-works; (objetos) glassware; **cristalino** phys. crystalline; agua limpid; **cristalización** f crystallization; **cristalizar(se)** [1f] crystallize.

cristianar [1a] F baptize; **cristiandad** f Christendom; **cristianismo** m Christianity; **cristianizar** [1f] Christianize; **cristiano 1.** adj. a. su. m, a f Christian; **2.** m F (p.) (living) soul; (idioma) Spanish; **cristo** m crucifix.

criterio m criterion; yardstick; (juicio) judgement; formar un ~ sobre arrive at an assessment of.

crítica f criticism; (reseña) review, notice; b.s. gossip; **criticador 1.** critical; **2.** m, -a f critic; **criticar** [1g] criticize; **crítico 1.** critical; **2.** m critic; **criticón 1.** fault-finding, (over-)critical; **2.** m, -a f faultfinder, critic; **critiquizar** [1f] F be over-critical of, be down on.

croar [1a] croak.

croata *adj. a. su. m/f* Croat(ian).

croché *m* crochet (work); *hacer ~* crochet.

cromado chromium-plated, chrome; **cromo** *m* chromium; *paint.* transfer; F colour reproduction, picture; **cromolitografía** *f* chromolithograph.

crónica *f* chronicle; account; *(periódico)* newspaper; *(artículo)* report; feature story; *~ literaria* literary page; **crónico** chronic; *vicio* ingrained; **cronista** *m/f* chronicler; *(periodista)* reporter, feature-writer; **cronología** *f* chronology; **cronológico** chronological; **cronometrador** *m* time-keeper; **cronometraje** *m* ⊕ timing; **cronometrar** [1a] time; **cronómetro** *m* chronometer; *deportes etc.*: stop-watch.

croqueta *f* croquette, rissole *approx.*

croquis *m* sketch.

crótalo *m* rattlesnake.

cruce *m* crossing; ♄ *etc.* intersection; *~ de caminos* cross-roads; *teleph.* hay un *~ en las líneas* the wires are crossed; **crucero** *m* ⚓ *(barco)* cruiser; ⚓ *(viaje)* cruise; △ transept; *(encrucijada)* cross-roads, crossing *(a.* ⚅); **cruceta** *f* cross-piece; **crucificar** [1g] crucify; *fig.* mortify; **crucifijo** *m* crucifix; **crucifixión** *f* crucifixion; **cruciforme** cruciform; **crucigrama** *m* crossword.

crudeza *f* rawness *etc.*; *con ~ hablar* harshly, roughly; **crudo** *comida, seda, tiempo etc.* raw; *(áspero)* rough; *agua, verdad* hard; *legumbres etc.* green, uncooked; *fruta* unripe; *pan* doughy; *fig. expresión, manera* crude.

cruel cruel; **crueldad** *f* cruelty.

cruento *lit.* gory, bloody.

crujía *f* △ corridor; △ bay *entre muros*; ⚓ ward; *pasar etc. una ~* have a tough time.

crujido *m* rustle *etc.*; **crujir** [3a] *(hojas, papel, seda)* rustle; swish *por el aire*; *(madera)* creak; *(hueso)* crack; *(tierra)* crunch; *(dientes)* gnash, grind.

crup *m* ⚕ croup.

crustáceo *m* crustacean.

cruz *f* cross *(a. fig.)*; tails *de moneda*; crown *de ancla*; *zo.* withers; *~ de*

Malta Maltese cross; ♀ *Roja* Red Cross; *¡~ y raya!* that's quite enough!; *en ~* crosswise; *(brazos)* crossed; *firmar con una ~* make one's mark; *hacer la ~ a* have done with; *hacerse cruces* cross o.s.; *fig.* show one's surprise; *quedar en ~* be in an agonizing situation; **cruzada** *f* crusade; **cruzado** 1 crossed; *chaqueta* double-breasted; *zo.* cross-bred, hybrid; 2. *m hist.* crusader; *~s pl. paint.* shading; **cruzar** [1f] *mst* cross; *palabras* have, exchange; *~se* pass each other.

cuaco *m S.Am.* horse.

cuaderna *f* ⚓ timber; ⚓ frame; **cuaderno** *m* notebook; *(folleto)* folder; *~ de bitácora, ~ de trabajo* log-book.

cuadra *f* ♞ stable; ⚔ ward; *(sala)* hall; ✖ hut; *S.Am.* △ block; **cuadrada** *f* breve; **cuadrado** 1. square *(a.* ♈*); tela* chequered; *p.* square-shouldered; *niño* bonny; *b.s.* stupid; 2. *m* square; *(regla)* ruler; ⊕ die; *sew.* gusset; *typ.* quadrat; **cuadragésimo** fortieth; **cuadrante** *m* ♈, ⚓ quadrant; *radio etc.*: dial; **cuadrar** [1a] *v/t.* square *(a.* ♈*); (agradar)* please; *(convenir)* suit; *v/i.: ~ con* square with, tally with; *~se* ✖ stand to attention; F get very solemn; *(resistir)* refuse to budge; **cuadratura** *f* quadrature; **cuadricular** squared; **cuadrilátero** *adj. a. su. m* quadrilateral; *boxeo*: ring; **cuadrilongo** *adj. a. su. m* oblong.

cuadrilla *f* party, gang; *esp.* ✖ squad; group; *toros*: matador's team; **cuadrillero** *m* chief, leader; ⊕ foreman.

cuadrito *m*: *cortar en ~s pl. cocina*: dice.

cuadro *m* square *(a.* ♈*); (tabla)* table, chart; ♪ *etc.* panel; *paint.* picture *(a. televisión)*, painting; *(marco, bastidor)* frame; pane *de vidrio*; ♞ bed; ✖ *(ps.)* staff, cadre; *thea.* scene; *lit.* (vivid) picture; *~ alpino* rock-garden; *teleph. ~ de conexión manual*, ♪ *~ de distribución* switchboard; *~ vivo* tableau; *a ~s tela* check; *2 metros en ~* 2 metres square; **cuadrúpedo** *adj. a. su. m* quadruped; **cuádruple** quadruple; **cuadruplicar(se)** [1g] quadrupl(icat)e; **cuádruplo** *m* quadruple.

cuajada *f* curd; (*requesón*) cream cheese; **cuajado** *fig.* dumbfounded; F asleep; ~ de full of; **cuajaleche** *m* ♀ bedstraw; **cuajar** [1a] *v/t. leche* curdle; *sangre etc.* coagulate, congeal; F be to *s.o.'s* liking; *v/i.* F (*proyecto*) take shape; (*tener éxito*) come off; ~se curdle *etc.*; set; *fig.* sleep soundly; F ~ de fill with; **cuajarón** *m* clot; **cuajo** *m* rennet; *de* ~ by the roots.

cual 1. *adj.* (such) as, of the kind (that); **2.** *pron. el etc.* ~ which; (*p.*) who; *lo* ~ (a fact) which; *con lo* ~ at which, whereupon; *por lo* ~ (and) so, and because of this; whereby; **3.** *prp.* ~ *su.* like; ~ *verb* (just) as; ~ ... *tal su.*: like ... like; *verb*: just as ... so; *a* ~ *más* vying with each other; *gritar a* ~ *más* see who can shout the loudest; **4.** *cj.*: ~ *si* as if; *v. tal.*

cuál which (one)?; ~(es) ... ~(es) some ... some; *si* ..., *¿*~ *debe ser el hijo?* if ..., what must the son be like?

cualidad *f* quality, characteristic; *phls. etc.* property; **cualitativo** qualitative.

cualquier(a), *pl.* **cualesquier(a) 1.** *adj.* any (... you like); ~ *que* whichever, whatever; **2.** *pron.* anyone; ~ *que* (*cosa*) whichever; (*p.*) whoever; *un* ~ a nobody.

cuan: *tan* ... ~ as ... as.

cuán how.

cuando 1. *cj.* when; (*aunque*) (even) if, although; (*puesto que*) since; ~ *más* at most; ~ *menos* at least; ~ *quiera* whenever; *de* ~ *en* ~ from time to time; **2.** *prp.* at the time of.

cuándo when?; ~ ... ~ sometimes ... sometimes; *¿de* ~ *acá?* how come?

cuantía *f* quantity; importance; *de mayor* ~ first-rate; *de poca* ~ of small account, not much of a ...; **cuantioso** large, substantial; numerous; **cuantitativo** quantitative.

cuanto 1. *adj.* all that, as much as, whatever; ~s *pl.* all that; *unos* ~s a few, some; ~s *más* ... *tantos más* the more ... the more; *creía* ~as *historias escuchaba* he believed all the stories he heard; **2.** *pron.* all that (which), as much as; ~s *pl.* all

those that, as many as; *v. tanto;* ~(s) *más, mejor* the more the merrier; **3.** *adv. a. cj.*: *en* ~ inasmuch as; *tiempo*: as soon as, directly; (*en*) ~ *a* as for, with regard to; ~ *más* at least; ~ *más adv.* the more *adv.*; ~ *más que* all the more because; *por* ~ ... *por tanto* inasmuch as ... therefore; ~ *más* ... *menos* the more ... the less.

cuánto how much?; ~s *pl.* how many?; ~ (*tiempo*) how long?; *¿a* ~s *estamos?* what is the date?; *¡*~ *me alegro!* I'm so glad!

cuarenta forty; **cuarentena** *f* (about) forty; ⚓ quarantine.

cuaresma *f* Lent; **cuaresmal** Lenten.

cuarta *f* ♫ quarter, fourth; ⚓ point; span *de mano*; **cuartazos** *m* F fat old thing; **cuartear** [1a] quarter; (*descuartizar*) cut up; *brújula* box; ~se crack, split.

cuartel *m* ✗ barracks; *heráldica*: quarter; ✗ bed; ~es *pl.* ✗ quarters; ~ *general* headquarters; *no dar* ~ give no quarter; **cuarteto** *m* ♪ quartet; *poet.* quatrain; **cuartilla** *f* (*hoja*) sheet; *anat.* pastern; **cuartillo:** F *andar a tres* ~s be on the rocks.

cuarto 1. fourth; **2.** *m* ♫, *ast.* quarter; △ room; joint *de carne*; ~s *pl.* F dough, brass; ~ *de baño* bathroom; ~ *creciente* (*menguante*) first (last) quarter; ~ *de hora* quarter of an hour; *las 2 y* ~ a quarter past 2; *las 2 menos* ~ a quarter to 2; ~ *oscuro* dark room; ~ *trasero* hindquarters; *cocina*: rump; F *de tres al* ~ worthless; *en* ~ *typ.* quarto; F *por cuatro* ~s for a song; F *sin un* ~ stony broke; F *tener* ~s be rolling in it; F *no tener un* ~ not have a cent.

cuarzo *m* quartz.

cuaternario quaternary; **cuatrillizos** *m/pl.*, ~**as** *f/pl.* quadruplets; **cuatrimotor** four-engined.

cuatro four (*a. su.*); (*fecha*) fourth; *las* ~ four o'clock; F *más de* ~ quite a few; **cuatrocientos** four hundred.

cuba *f* cask, barrel; (*abierta*) vat; F boozer.

cubano *adj. a. su. m,* **a** *f* Cuban.

cubeta *f* keg; (*cubo*) pail; *phot.* tray.

cubicar [1g] ♫ cube; *phys.* determine the volume of; **cúbico** cubic

(-al); *raíz* cube *attr.*; **cubículo** *m* cubicle.

cubierta *f* cover(ing); ⊕ casing; ⚓ deck; (*sobre*) envelope; cover, jacket *de libro*; *mot.* outer cover, tyre; ~ *de cama* coverlet; **cubierto** 1. *p.p. of cubrir*; 2. *m* ⚓ roof; place *en mesa*; (*juego*) knife fork and spoon; (*comida*) meal; ~s *pl.* cutlery; ~ *de 30 pesetas* 30 peseta menu; *precio de* ~ cover charge; *ponerse a* ~ take cover, shelter (de from).

cubil *m* den, lair.

cubilete *m cocina*: copper pan; (*juego*) dice-box.

cubismo *m* cubism; **cubista** *m* cubist.

cúbito *m* ulna.

cubo *m* bucket, pail; tub; ⊕ drum; hub *de rueda*; ⚒ cube; ~ *de basuras* dustbin.

cubrecama *m* coverlet.

cubrir [3a; *p.p. cubierto*] *mst* cover (up, over; *con*, de with); ⚓ roof; *deuda* repay; *fuego* bank up; *vacante* fill; *me cubre* (*agua*) I'm out of my depth; ~**se** (*con sombrero*) put on one's hat.

cuca *f sl.* tart, whore.

cucaña *f* F cinch; **cucañero** *m*, **a** *f* F fly one; (*gorrón*) hanger-on; (*ambicioso*) social climber.

cucaracha *f* cockroach.

cuclillas: *sentarse en* ~ squat, sit on one's heels.

cuclillo *m* cuckoo; F cuckold.

cuco 1. (*bonito*) pretty, cute; *situación* fine; (*taimado*) crafty; 2. *m orn.* cuckoo; F gambler.

cucurucho *m* (paper) cone, cornet; (*sombrero*) horn, hennin.

cuchara *f* spoon; scoop (*a.* ⚒); ⊕ ladle; **cucharada** *f* spoonful; *meter su* ~ butt in *en conversación*; meddle *en asunto*; **cucharear** [1a] spoon out, ladle out; ⚒ pitch; **cucharetear** [1a] F *fig.* meddle; **cucharilla** *f*, **cucharita** *f* small spoon, teaspoon; **cucharón** *m* ladle.

cuchichear [1a] whisper; **cuchicheo** *m* whispering.

cuchilla *f* (large) knife; chopper *de carnicero*; runner *de patín*; blade *de arma*; *geog.* ridge; **cuchillada** *f* (*golpe*) slash; (*herida*) gash; ~s *pl. sew.* slash, slit; *fig.* fight; **cuchille-**

ría *f* cutlery; ✝ cutler's (shop); **cuchillero** *m* cutler; **cuchillo** *m* knife; ⚒ upright; *pasar a* ~ put to the sword.

cuchipanda *f* F feed, beano.

cuchitril *m* den, hole; ⚒ hovel.

cuchufleta *f* F joke, crack.

cuelga *f* ♀ bunch; F birthday present; ~**capas** *m* coat-hanger; (*mueble*) hall-stand.

cuello *m* neck; collar *de camisa*; F *levantar el* ~ get on one's feet again.

cuenca *f* wooden bowl; *anat.* (eye-) socket; *geog.* bowl; basin, catchment area *de río*; ~ *hullera*, ~ *minera* coalfield; **cuenco** *m* saucer, shallow basin; *fig.* hollow.

cuenta *f* ⚒ calculation, count(ing); reckoning; ✝ account, bill; ~ (*de banco*) bank-account; (*registro*) check, tally; (*exposición*, *narración*) account; bead *de rosario*; *boxeo*: count; ~ *corriente* current account; ~ *de diversos* sundries; ~ *de gastos* expense account; ~ *indistinta*, ~ *en participación* joint account; *a* ~ on account; *de* ~ *attr.* important; *de* ~ *y riesgo de* at s.o.'s own risk; *en resumidas* ~s in short, in a nutshell; *por su propia* ~ on one's own account, for o.s.; *abonar en* ~ *a* credit to (*s.o.'s account*); *ajustar* ~s settle up (*con* with); *ajustar* ~s *viejas fig.* pay off old scores; F *le ajusté las* ~s I told him where to get off; F *caer en la* ~ catch on (*de* to), twig; *cargar en* ~ *a* charge to (*s.o.'s account*); *correr por* ~ *de* be s.o.'s business; F *esto corre por mi* ~ this one's on me; *dar* ~ (*de narrar*) give an account of; (*explicar*) account for; F finish off; *dar buena* ~ *de sí* give a good account of o.s.; *darse* ~ (*de*) realize; *sin darse* ~ without noticing; *pedir* ~s *a* bring to account; *perder la* ~ lose count; *tener en* ~ bear in mind, take into account; F *no tener* ~ *inf.* be no point in *ger.*; *¡vamos a* ~s! let's get down to business!

cuentacorrentista *m/f* depositor.

cuentakilómetros *m approx.* milometer; speedometer.

cuentista *m/f* story-teller (*a. b.s.*); *lit.* short story writer; (*chismoso*) gossip.

cuento *m* story, tale (*a. b.s.*); *lit.* (short) story; F trouble; ~ *de hadas* fairy-tale; ~ de viejas old wives' tale; sin ~ countless; dejarse de ~s come to the point; es el ~ de nunca acabar it's an endless business; F ¡es puro ~! it's all my eye!, rubbish!; traer a ~ bring up, b.s. drag in; venir a ~ be apt.

cuerda f rope; (delgado) string (a. ♪), cord (a. anat.); ♩, anat., poet. chord; anat. tendon; spring de reloj; ♪ (tenor etc.) voice; ~ de arco bowstring; ~ floja tight-rope; ~ de plomada plumb-line; ~ salvavidas lifeline; ~ de tripa (♪ cat)gut; ~s pl. vocales vocal cords; F bajo ~ on the side; aflojar (apretar) la ~ fig. ease (tighten) up; dar ~ a reloj wind (up).

cuerdo sensible; sane.

cuerna f drinking-horn; ♪ horn; antler de ciervo; **cuerno** m mst horn; antler de ciervo; ~ de la abundancia horn of plenty; poner en los ~s place in danger; poner los ~s a cuckold; saber a ~ quemado fig. leave a nasty taste; F ¡vaya al ~! go to hell!

cuero m leather; zo. skin, hide; pelt de conejo, zorro; (odre) wine-skin; ~ cabelludo scalp; en ~s stark naked; F estar hecho un ~ be as drunk as a lord.

cuerpo m mst body (a. ♩, ast.); (talle) build, figure; (grueso) bulk; ♏ substance; sew. bodice; (libro) volume; ♠ wing, part; ✕, baile, diplomática: corps; (personal) force, brigade; corporation; carreras: length; ~ de baile corps de ballet; ~ de bomberos fire-brigade; ~ del delito corpus delicti; ~ de sanidad medical corps; ~ a ~ hand to hand; a ~, en ~ without a coat; a ~ de rey like a prince; de (mucho) ~ vino full-bodied; de ~ entero full-length; fig. thoroughgoing; de medio ~ half-length; en ~ y alma fully; dar ~ a thicken; dar con el ~ en tierra fall down; estar de ~ presente be laid out, (rey etc.) lie in state; hacer del ~ relieve o.s.; hurtar el ~ swerve, dodge; tomar ~ grow, get bigger.

cuervo m raven.

cuesco m ♀ stone.

cuesta f slope; hill en carretera; ~ abajo downhill; ~ arriba uphill; a ~s on one's back; echar etc. a ~s take on one's shoulders; hacérsele a uno ~ arriba inf. go against the

grain to inf., find it hard to inf.; ir ~ abajo fig. go downhill.

cuestación f (charity) collection.

cuestión f matter, question, issue; b.s. quarrel, dispute; ♉ problem; ~ batallona vexed question; ~ candente, ~ palpitante burning question; en ~ in question, at issue; **cuestionable** questionable; **cuestionar** [1a] question, argue about; **cuestionario** m questionnaire; question-paper en examen.

cueva f cave; cellar de casa.

cuévano m pannier.

cuidado m (esmero) care; (aprensión) worry, concern; (negocio) concern, affair; ¡~! look out!, mind!; (en paquete) with care; ¡~ con ...! care-ful with ...!; beware of ...!; ¡~ con inf.! be careful to inf., see you inf.; ¡~ conmigo! you watch your step!; al ~ de care of; enfermar de ~ fall seriously ill; estar con ~ be anxious; ♂ estar de ~ be gravely ill; ¡no hay ~!, ¡pierda Vd. ~! don't worry!; poner ~ en inf. take great care in ger.; tener ~ take care; be careful (con of), watch out (con for); tener ~ de mind; v. tener, traer; **cuidadoso** careful; mindful (de of); solicitous (de for); concerned, anxious (de, por resultado etc. about).

cuidar [1a] v/t. take care of, look after (a. ♩); see to; v/i.: ~ de look after; obligación attend to; ~ de que see (to it) that; ~se ♂ look after o.s.; b.s. look after number one; ~ de worry about; ~ de inf. be careful to inf.

cuita f worry, affliction; **cuitado** worried; timid.

cuja f bedstead.

culata f zo. haunch; butt de fusil; breech de cañón; head de cilindro; **culatazo** m kick, recoil.

culebra f snake; ~ de cascabel rattlesnake; **culebrear** [1a] wriggle (along).

culí m coolie.

culibajo F dumpy.

culinario culinary.

culminación f culmination; **culminante** highest, top(most); fig. outstanding; **culminar** [1a] culminate, reach its highest point.

culo m arse; (asentaderas) bottom.

culpa f fault, blame; esp. ♃ guilt; echar la ~ a blame (de for); tener *la* ~ be to blame (*de* for); *Vd. tiene la* ~ it's your fault; **culpabilidad** *f* guilt; **culpable 1.** *p.* to blame, at fault; *esp.* ⚖ guilty; *acto* to be condemned, ⚖ culpable; *confesarse* ~ plead guilty; **2.** *m/f* culprit; *esp.* ⚖ offender, guilty party; **culpado 1.** guilty; **2.** *m*, **a** *f* culprit; ⚖ accused; **culpar** [1a] blame; condemn; ~ *de* accuse *s.o.* of being.

cultivable cultivable; **cultivadora** *f* ⊕ cultivator; **cultivador** *m*, **-a** *f* farmer, cultivator; grower; **cultivar** [1a] cultivate (*a. fig.*); *tierras a.* work, till; *plantas a.* grow; *memoria etc.* develop; **cultivo** *m* cultivation; (*plantas*) crop; *biol.* culture; **culto 1.** cultured, refined; *gr.* learned; **2.** *m* worship; cult (*a* of); *rendir* ~ *a* worship; *fig.* pay homage to; **cultura** *f* culture; education; *de* (*gran*) ~ *attr.* cultured; **cultural** cultural.

cumbre *f* summit, top; *fig.* summit, height.

cumpleaños *m* birthday; **cumplido 1.** full, complete; *p.* courteous; **2.** *m* courtesy; ~*s pl.* compliments; *de* ~ *attr.* formal; *por* ~ as a compliment; out of politeness; *¡sin* ~*s!* make yourself at home!; *venir de* ~ come out of a sense of duty.

cumplimentar [1a] congratulate; (*visitar*) pay one's respects to; ⚖ carry out; **cumplimentero** effusive; **cumplimiento** *m* (*acto*) fulfilment *etc.*; (*cumplido*) compliment; courtesy; *de* ~ *attr.* courtesy *attr.*; *por* ~ as a matter of courtesy; *hacer* ~*s* pay compliments.

cumplir [3a] *v/t. amenaza, deber, promesa* carry out, fulfil; *deseo* realize; *acto* perform; *años* reach; *condena* serve; *hoy cumplo 6 años* I'm 6 (years old) today; *¡que los cumplas muy felices!* many happy returns of the day!; *v/i.* (*plazo etc.*) expire; ✗ finish one's service; *no le cumple a él inf.* it is not his place to *inf.*; ~ *con* = *v/t.*; *p.* do one's duty by; ~ *por* act on behalf of; *por* ~ as a mere formality; ~*se* be fulfilled *etc.*; (*plazo*) expire.

cumulativo cumulative; **cúmulo** *m* heap; *fig.* lot; *meteor.* cumulus.

cuna *f* cradle (*a.* ⚓, *fig.*); (*asilo*) home; *fig.* family; birth.

cundir [3a] spread (*a. fig.*); (*arroz*)

swell; *fig.* multiply; *b.s.* be rampant, be rife.

cuneiforme cuneiform.

cuneta *f* ditch, gutter.

cuña *f* wedge; chock *de rueda*.

cuñada *f* sister-in-law; **cuñado** *m* brother-in-law.

cuñete *m* keg.

cuño *m* (die-)stamp; *fig.* stamp.

cuota *f* quota; share; ~ (*de socio*) membership fee; ~ *de enseñanza* school fees.

cupe *etc. v. caber.*

cupo *m* quota; share.

cupón *m* coupon.

cúpula *f* dome, cupola.

cuquería *f* craftiness.

cura[1] *m*: ~ (*párroco*) parish priest; (*en general*) priest.

cura[2] *f* (*acto*) healing; cure; (*método*) cure, treatment; ~ *de reposo* rest-cure; ~ *de urgencia* emergency treatment, first-aid; *tener* ~ be curable; *F no tiene* ~ it's quite hopeless; **curable** curable; **curación** *f* = *cura*[2]; ~ *primera* first-aid; **curandero** *m* quack; **curar** [1a] *v/t. enfermedad, p., carne* cure (*de* of); *llaga* heal (*a. fig.*); (*tratar*) treat; *piel* tan; *madera* season; *mal etc.* remedy, put right; *v/i.*: ~ *de* look after; *palabras etc.* take notice of; ~*se* recover (*de* from), get better; **curativo** healing; curative.

curda: F *estar* (*con la*) ~ be tight.

cureña *f* gun-carriage; F *a* ~ *rasa* out in the open.

curiosear [1a] *v/t.* (*mirar*) glance at, look over; (*husmear*) nose out; *tiendas etc.* have a look round; *v/i.* poke about, nose around; *b.s.* snoop; **curiosidad** *f* curiosity; *b.s.* inquisitiveness; (*objeto*) curio; (*aseo*) cleanness; **curioso 1.** curious; *b.s.* inquisitive; (*aseado*) neat, clean; (*esmerado*) careful; F queer; ~ *de* eager for; ~ *por inf.* eager to *inf.*; **2.** *m*, **a** *f* bystander, onlooker; *b.s.* busybody; F queer; *los* ~*s de la literatura* those interested in literature.

curro *prov.* smart; *b.s.* showy; **currutaco** F **1.** swell, showy; **2.** *m* toff.

cursado experienced, skilled; **cursante** *m/f S.Am.* student; **cursar** [1a] *v/t. lugar* frequent; *asignatura* take; *solicitud* facilitate, dispatch;

v/i.: *el mes que cursa* the present month.

cursi 1. (*de mal gusto*) in bad taste, vulgar; pretentious, posh, genteel; affected; (*llamativo*) loud, flashy; (*desaseado*) shabby-genteel, dowdy; **2.** *m/f* = cursilón; **cursilería** *f* vulgarity, pretentiousness *etc.*; **cursilón** *m*, **-a** *f* F posh sort, one of the genteel sort; flashy type.

cursivo cursive.

curso *m* course; *univ.* (*ps., año*) year; *moneda de ~ legal* legal tender; *dar ~ a solicitud* deal with; **cursor** *m* ⊕ slide.

curtido 1. *piel* leathery; *tez* tanned, weather-beaten; *estar ~ en* be skilled in; be accustomed to; **2.** *m* tanning; *~s pl.* tanned hides; **curtidor** *m* tanner; **curtiduría** *f* tannery;

curtir [3a] tan (*a. fig.*); (*acostumbrar*) inure, harden.

curva *f* curve; *mot. etc. a.* bend; *~ de nivel* contour line; **curvatura** *f* curvature; **curvo** curved.

cúspide *f geog.* peak; ⅄ apex.

custodia *f* care, safe keeping; ⚖ *etc.* custody; (*p.*) guard; *eccl.* monstrance; *~ preventiva* protective custody; **custodiar** [1b] keep; (*vigilar*) guard, watch over; **custodio** *m* guard(ian), keeper; caretaker *de casa.*

cutáneo cutaneous.

cúter *m* cutter.

cutí *m* ticking.

cutícula *f* cuticle.

cutis *m* skin, complexion.

cuyo whose; *en ~ caso* in which case.

¡cuz, cuz! here boy! (*dog*).

Ch

chabacanería *f* (piece of) vulgarity, bad taste; (*objeto*) shoddy piece of work; (*dicho*) platitude; (*dicho grosero*) coarse thing; **chabacano** vulgar, in bad taste; shoddy; crude, coarse.

chabola *f* shack.

chacal *m* jackal.

chacarero *m S.Am.* farm labourer.

chacolotear [1a] clatter.

chacota *f* fun and games, high jinks; *echar a ~, hacer ~ de* make fun of; **chacotear** [1a] have fun; **chacotero** fond of a laugh.

chacra *f S.Am.* small farm.

chacha *f* F (nurse)maid.

cháchara *f* F small-talk, chatter; **chacharear** [1a] F chatter, jaw; **chacharero** *m*, **a** *f* F chatterbox.

chacho *m* F boy, lad.

chafallar [1a] F botch, make a mess of; **chafallo** *m* F botched job.

chafar [1a] (*aplastar*) flatten; (*arrugar*) crumple; F bring *s.o.* up short.

chafarote *m* cutlass; F sword.

chafarrinón *m* stain, spot; *echar un ~ a* throw dirt at (*a. fig.*).

chaflán *m* bevel, chamfer; **chaflanar** [1a] bevel, chamfer.

chagrén *m* shagreen.

chaira *f* steel *de carnicero*; shoemaker's knife.

chal *m* shawl.

chalado F dotty, round the bend; *estar ~ por* be crazy about.

chalán *m* (*esp.* horse-)dealer.

chalana *f* wherry, scow.

chalanear [1a] *v/t. p.* beat down, haggle with; *negocio* handle cleverly; *v/i.* bargain shrewdly.

chalar [1a] F drive *s.o.* round the bend; *~se* go crazy; *~ por* be crazy about.

chaleco *m* waistcoat, vest *Am.*; *~ salvavidas* life-jacket.

chalet [tʃa'le] *m* (*rural*) villa, cottage; (*suizo*) chalet; house *en ciudad*; *golf*: clubhouse.

chalina *f* cravat.

chalote *m* shallot.

chalupa 1. *f* (open) boat, launch; **2.** *m sl.* madman; **3.** *adj. sl.* crazy.

chamarasca *f* brushwood (fire).

chamarra *f* sheepskin jacket.

chamba *f* F fluke.

chambelán *m* chamberlain.

chambón F awkward, clumsy; (*con suerte*) lucky; **chambonada** *f* F clumsiness; (*chiripa*) fluke.

champiñón *m* mushroom.

chambra *f* housecoat.

chamizo *m* F den, joint.

champaña *m* champagne.
champú *m* shampoo.
champurrar [1a] *bebidas* mix.
chamullar [1a] *sl.* speak, talk.
chamuscar [1g] scorch, singe;
  chamusquina *f* F row, shindy;
  huele a ~ it smells fishy.
chancear(se) [1a] crack jokes; fool
  around (*con* with), play about;
  chancero 1. fond of joking *etc.*;
  2. *m* one for a lark.
chancillería *f* chancery.
chancla *f* old shoe; = **chancleta**
  1. *f* slipper; **2.** *m/f* F good-for-
  nothing; **chanclo** *m* clog; galosh,
  overshoe *de goma.*
chanchi *sl.* **1.** *adv. sentar etc.*
  marvellously; *me fue ~* I had a fine
  time; **2.** *adj.*: *¡estás ~!* I think
  you're wonderful!
chancho *S.Am.* **1.** dirty; **2.** *m* pig.
chanchullero *m* F crook, twister;
  chanchullo *m* F dirty business,
  fiddle, wangle; *andar en ~s* be on
  the fiddle.
chanflón misshapen; (*basto*) coarse,
  crude.
changarro *m* *S.Am.* small shop.
chantaje *m* blackmail; **chantajista**
  m blackmailer, racketeer.
chantre *m* precentor.
chanza *f* (*dicho*) joke; (*hecho*) piece
  of tomfoolery; *~s pl.* banter; tomfoolery; *de ~* in fun.
chao *m* chow.
chapa *f* plate, sheet *de metal*; metal
  top *de botella*; check *de guardarropa etc.*; board, panel *de madera*;
  (*enchapado*) veneer; (*afeite*) rouge;
  flush *en mejillas*; *fig.* good sense;
  chapado: *~ a la antigua* old-
  fashioned.
chapalear [1a] splash (about); (*ola*)
  lap; = **chacolotear.**
chapar [1a] plate, cover *con metal*;
  veneer *con madera*; F *respuesta* come
  out with.
chaparra *f* kermes oak.
chaparrada *f*, **chaparrón** *m*
  downpour, cloudburst.
chapear [1a] = *chapar.*
chapeta *f* flush (on the cheeks).
chapín *m* clog.
chapitel *m* capital; spire *de torre.*
chapotear [1a] *v/t.* sponge (down),
  wet; *v/i.* splash *para salpicar*; paddle *con pies*; dabble *con manos.*
chapucear [1a] botch, bungle;

chapucería *f* botched job, shoddy
  piece of work; **chapucero 1.** *objeto*
  badly made; *trabajo* clumsy, ama-
  teurish; *p.* bungling, slapdash; **2.** *m*
  bungler, bungling amateur.
chapurr(e)ar [1a] *bebidas* mix;
  idioma speak badly.
chapuz *m* ducking; dive; (*obra mala*)
  botched job; (*insignificante*) odd
  job; *dar ~* duck, dive; **chapuzar**
  [1f] *v/t.* duck, dip; *v/i.*, *~se* duck,
  dive.
chaqué *m* morning coat; **chaqueta** *f*
  jacket.
chaquete *m* backgammon.
chaquetón *m* reefer, shooting-
  jacket.
charada *f* charade.
charanga *f* brass band; **charan-
  guero** = *chapucero.*
charca *f* pond, pool; **charco** *m*
  puddle; pool *de tinta etc.*; F *pasar el
  ~* cross the water.
charla *f* talk (*a. radio etc.*), chat;
  b.s. chatter; (*chismes*) gossip; **charlador** talkative, gossipy; **charla-
  duría** *f* small-talk, gossip; **charlar**
  [1a] chat, talk; *b.s.* chatter; **charlatán 1.** talkative; **2.** *m*, **-a** *f* chatterbox, gossip; (*embaidor*) trickster;
  ⚕ quack; **charlatanismo** *m*
  charlatanism; ⚕ quackery.
charnela *f* hinge.
charol *m* varnish; (*cuero*) patent
  leather; F *darse ~* swank; **charolar**
  [1a] varnish, japan.
charrada *f* (piece of) bad breeding,
  coarse thing; F example of bad
  taste; flashy ornament; **charrán** *m*
  rascal; **charranada** *f* dirty trick.
charretera *f* epaulette.
charro 1. *p.* coarse, ill-bred; *cosa*
  flashy, tawdry; *vestido* loud; **2.** *m*,
  a *f fig.* coarse person; flashy
  person.
chascar [1a] *v/t.* *lengua* click; (*ronzar*) crunch; (*engullir*) swallow;
  v/i. crack; **chascarrillo** *m* funny
  story; **chasco** *m* trick, joke; (*decepción*) disappointment; *dar ~ a* pull
  s.o.'s leg; *dar un ~ a* play a trick on;
  llevarse un ~ be disappointed.
chasis *m* chassis.
chasquear¹ [1a] *p.* play a trick on;
  (*zumba*) pull *s.o.'s* leg; (*decepcionar*)
  disappoint; *promesa* break.
chasquear² [1a] *v/t.* *látigo* crack;
  lengua click; *dedos* snap; *v/i.* (*ma-*

dera) crack; **chasquido** *m* crack; click; snap.

chatarra *f* scrap-iron, junk.

chateo *m* (*ir de* go on a) pub-crawl.

chato 1. *p.* snub-nosed; *nariz* snub; *cosa* low, flat; *S.Am.* common; *S.Am.* ¡*a mía*! darling!; **2.** *m* small (wine-)glass.

chatunga *f sl.* smart piece.

¡**chau**! *S.Am.* hullo there!; (*despedida*) so long!

chauvinismo *m* chauvinism; **chauvinista 1.** chauvinistic; **2.** *m/f* chauvinist.

chaval *m* F lad, boy, kid; **chavala** *f* F girl, kid.

chaveta *f* cotter(-pin); F *perder la* ~ go off one's rocker; F *perder la* ~ *por* be crazy about.

¡**che**! *S.Am.* hey!

checo 1. *adj. a. su. m*, **a** *f* Czech; **2.** *m* (*idioma*) Czech; **checoslovaco** *adj. a. su. m.* **a** *f* Czecho-Slovak.

chelín *m* shilling.

cheque *m* cheque; ~ *cruzado* crossed cheque; ~ *de viajeros* traveller's cheque.

chica *f* girl; (*chacha*) maid.

chicle *m* chewing-gum.

chico 1. small, little; **2.** *m* boy; F (*hombre, camarada*) lad, fellow, chap; *los* ~s (*pequeños*) kids, children; ~ *de la calle* street urchin; *es buen* ~ he's a good lad.

chicolear [1a] F say nice things; flirt; **chicoleo** *m* F compliment; flirting; *decir* ~s say nice things; **chicolero** F flirtatious.

chicoria *f* chicory.

chicota *f* F fine girl; **chicote** *m* F fine lad; cigar (stub).

chicha[1] *f S.Am.* maize liquor, corn-juice *Am.*; F *ni* ~ *ni limonada* not one thing or the other; (*sin interés*) dull.

chicha[2] F meat; *tener pocas* ~s be thin; *fig.* be weak.

chicharrero *m* oven, hot-house; F suffocating heat; **chicharro** *m* caranx, horse-mackerel; **chicharrón** *m* fried crackling; *estar hecho un* ~ *cocina*: be burnt to a cinder; (*p.*) be as red as a lobster.

chichear [1a] F hiss.

chicho *m* hair-curler.

chichón *m* ⚕ bump, swelling.

chifla *f* hiss(ing), whistle; **chiflado** F daft, barmy; **chifladura** *f* hiss-

ing, whistling; F daftness; (*acto*) daft thing; crazy idea; **chiflar** [1a] *thea.* hiss; *vino* knock back; ~*se* go barmy; ~ *por, a.* estar *chiflado por* be crazy about.

chileno, chileño *adj. a. su. m*, **a** *f* Chilean.

chilla[1] *f hunt.* call.

chilla[2] *f*: (*tabla de*) ~ weatherboard, clapboard *Am.*

chillar [1a] (*gato etc.*) howl; (*ratón*) squeak; (*ave*) squawk, screech; (*p.*) (let out a) cry, yell; (*tocino*) sizzle; (*puerta*) creak; (*radio*) blare; (*frenos*) screech; (*colores*) jar; **chillido** *m* howl *etc.*; **chillón** *niño* noisy; *sonido, voz* shrill, strident; *color* gaudy, lurid.

chimenea *f* (*exterior*) chimney; ⚓ funnel; ⚒ shaft; (*hogar*) hearth; ~ (*francesa*) fireplace; (*marco de*) ~ chimney-piece.

chimpancé *m* chimpanzee.

china[1] *f* china.

china[2] *f geol.* pebble; **chinarro** *m* large pebble, stone.

china[3] *S.Am.* (*novia*) girl-friend; (*querida*) mistress; (*criada*) maid; (*niñera*) nursemaid.

chinchar [1a] F pester; *S.Am.* do in.

chinche *f* bug; F bore, tiresome person; *morir como* ~s die like flies; = **chincheta** *f* drawing-pin.

chinchilla *f S.Am.* chinchilla.

chinchoso F tiresome.

chinela *f* slipper; (*chanclo*) clog.

chinesco Chinese; **chino**[1] **1.** *adj. a. su. m*, **a** *f* Chinese; **2.** *m* (*idioma*) Chinese; F double Dutch.

chino[2] *m*, **a** *f S.Am.* half-breed.

chino[3] *m geol.* pebble.

chinorri *f sl.* dame, wench.

chipirón *m* squid.

chiquero *m* pigsty; pen *de toro*.

chiquilicuatro *m* F schemer.

chiquillada *f* childish prank; *contp.* childish thing (to do); **chiquillería** *f* F (*una* ~) crowd of youngsters; *la* ~ the kids; **chiquillo** *m*, **a** *f* kid, youngster; **chiquitín** F **1.** tiny; **2.** *m*, -*a f* tiny tot; **chiquito 1.** small, tiny; **2.** *m*, **a** *f* kid, youngster; F *andarse en* ~*as* beat about the bush, hum and ha.

chiribita *f* spark; ~s *pl.* F spots before the eyes; F *echar* ~s blow one's top; *le hacían* ~s *los ojos* his eyes lit up.

chiribitil *m* garret; (*escondrijo*) cubby-hole; F (*cuarto*) hole.

chirigota *f* F joke; (*p.*) laughing-stock.

chirimbolos *m/pl.* F kitchen things.

chirimoya *f* custard-apple.

chiripa *f* billar: lucky break; F fluke, stroke of luck; **chiripero** *m* lucky sort.

chirivía *f* parsnip.

chirle F tasteless, wishy-washy.

chirlo *m* gash; (*cicatriz*) long scar.

chirona *f* sl. jug, quod.

chirriar [1b] (*grillo*) chirp; (*ave*) chirp, squawk; (*rueda*) creak, squeak; (*frenos*) screech; (*tocino*) sizzle; (*p.*) sing (*or* play) out of tune; **chirrido** *m* chirp(ing) etc.

chirrión *m* tumbrel.

¡chis! sh!

chisgarabís *m* F meddler, interfering sort.

chisme *m* (*murmuración*) (piece of) gossip, tale; (*trasto*) thing; ⊕ gadget; ⁓s *pl.* gossip, tittle-tattle; (*trastos*) things, odds and ends; ⊕ tackle, paraphernalia; **chismear** [1a] gossip, tell tales; **chismería** *f*, **chismografía** *f* gossip, scandal; **chismoso 1.** gossipy; **2.** *m, a f* gossip, scandal-monger.

chispa 1. *f* spark (*a.* ⚡); *fig.* sparkle; (*gota*) drop; caen ⁓s it's drizzling; F no dar ⁓ be utterly dull; sl. estar con la ⁓, tener la ⁓ be tight; ser una ⁓, tener (mucha) ⁓ be a lively sort; **2.** *adj.* sl.: estar ⁓ be tight; **chispazo** *m* spark (*a.* fig.); (*cuento*) gossip, scandal; **chispeante** *fig.* sparkling; **chispear** [1a] spark; (*relucir*) sparkle (*a.* fig.); *meteor.* spot with rain; **chispita** *f* F drop (of wine); **chisporrotear** [1a] (*leña*) crackle; (*aceite etc.*) splutter; (*tocino*) sizzle.

chistar [1a]: no ⁓ not open one's mouth; sin ⁓ (ni mistar) without a word.

chiste *m* joke, funny story; (*suceso*) funny thing; ⁓ goma shaggy dog story; caer en el ⁓ get it; no veo el ⁓ I don't see the joke.

chistera *f* F top hat.

chistoso 1. funny, witty; **2.** *m, a f* wit.

chistu *m* (*Basque*) flute.

chita: a la ⁓ callando quietly; F on the quiet, on the sly.

chiticalla *m/f* F clam.

¡chito!, **¡chitón!** sh!

chivatazo *m* sl. tip-off; **chivatear** [1a] F split (*contra* on), squeal; **chivato** *m* zo. kid; F stool-pigeon, informer; *S.Am.* rascal; **chivo** *m* billy-goat.

chocante shocking; (*sorprendente*) startling, striking; **chocar** [1a] *v/t.* shock; startle; ⚡ give a shock to; *vasos* clink; *mano* shake; sl. please; F **¡chócala!** shake (on it)!; *v/i.* ⚔ clash; *mot.* etc. collide; (*vasos*) clink; (*platos*) clatter; ⁓ con(tra) knock into, run into; *mot.* etc. hit, collide with, crash into.

chocarrería *f* coarse joke; **chocarrero** coarse, dirty.

chocolate *m* chocolate; drinking-chocolate; **chocolatera** *f* chocolate pot; F *mot.* crock; ⚓ hulk.

chocha perdiz *f* woodcock.

chochear [1a] dodder, be in one's dotage; (*enamorado*) be soft; **chochera** *f*, **chochez** *f* dotage; (*acto*) silly thing.

chochín *m* wren.

chocho doddering; *enamorado* silly, soft.

chófer *m* driver; (*empleado*) chauffeur.

cholo *adj. a. su. m, a f S.Am.* half-breed.

cholla *f* F nut.

chopa *f* sl. jacket.

chopo *m* ♣ black poplar; ⚔ F gun.

choque *m* shock (*a.* ⚡, ⚔); (*impacto*, jar, jolt; blast *de explosión*; *mot.*, 🚂 crash, smash, collision; (*ruido*) crash, clatter; clink *de vasos*; ⚔ *a.* fig. clash.

choquezuela *f* knee-cap.

chorizo *m* sausage, salami.

chorlito *m* plover; *v.* cabeza.

chorra *f* sl. luck; ¡qué ⁓ tiene! look at that for jam!

chorrear [1a] *v/t.* ⚔ sl. dress down; *v/i.* spirt, gush (forth), spout (out); (*gotear*) drip; F trickle (away etc.); ⁓ de sudor run with; **chorrera** *f* spout; channel; **chorretada** *f* spirt, squirt; **chorro** *m* jet (*a.* ⊕, ⚔), spirt, spout; *fig.* stream; ⚔ a ⁓ jet *attr.*; a ⁓s fig. in plenty; llover a ⁓s pour; salir a ⁓s squirt out, gush forth.

chotacabras *m* nightjar.

chotis *m* schottische.

chova *f* chough.
choza *f* hut, shack.
christmas ['krismas] *m* F Christmas card.
chubasco *m* squall, heavy shower; **chubascoso** squally, stormy; **chubasquero** *m* oilskins.
chuchería *f* knick-knack; (*golosina*) titbit, sweet.
chucho *m* F dog; ¡~! down!
chufa *f* earth-almond, chufa.
chula *f* flashy sort; *S.Am.* girl-friend; **chulada** *f* vulgar thing; mean trick; (*gracioso*) funny thing; **chulear** [1a] F make fun of; *sl.* pinch, swipe; **chulería** *f* funny thing; (*aire*) flamboyant manner; **chulesco** = *chulo*.
chuleta *f* chop, cutlet; *univ. sl.* crib.
chulo 1. pert, saucy; *b.s.* common, flashy; **2.** *m lower-class madrileño*; *b.s.* spiv; (*alcahuete*) pimp.
chumacera *f* ball-bearing.
chumbera *f* prickly pear; **chumbo** *v. higo*.
chunga *f* F (*chiste*) joke; bit of fun; *estar de* ~, *tomar las cosas en* ~ =

chungar(se) [1a] F take things as a joke, joke, have a bit of fun.
chupada *f* suck; pull *de cigarro*; **chupado** F skinny; *falda* tight; ~ *de cara* lantern-jawed; **chupador** *m* teething ring; teat *de biberón*; **chupar** [1a] suck; ♀ absorb, take in; *pipa* puff at; F *p.* milk; *caudal* eat away; F *a. S.Am.* smoke; *S.Am.* (*beber*) drink; *sl.* ¡chúpate eso! put that in your pipe and smoke it!; ~**se** waste away; **chupatintas** *m contp.* pen-pusher; **chupete** *m* dummy; *S.Am.* lollipop; **chupón** *m* ♀ sucker; pull *de cigarro*; (*p.*) swindler.
churre *f* thick grease; (*mugre*) filth.
churro *m* fritter.
churruscar(se) [1g] burn.
chus: *no decir* ~ *ni mus* not say a word.
chuscada *f* funny thing; **chusco** funny, droll.
chusma *f* rabble, riff-raff.
chutar [1a] *deportes*: shoot.
chuzo *m* pike; *llover a* ~*s* rain cats and dogs.

D

dable possible, feasible.

¡daca! hand it over!

dactilar v. huella; **dactilografía** f typing; **dactilógrafo** m, a f typist.

dádiva f gift, present; fig. sop; **dadivosidad** f generosity; **dadivoso** generous, open-handed, bounteous.

dado[1] m die; ~s pl. dice.

dado[2] p.p. of dar; dada su corta edad in view of his youth; ~ a given to; ~ que given that; granted that; **dador** m, -a f giver, donor; bearer de carta.

dafodelo m daffodil.

daga f dagger.

dalia f dahlia.

daltoniano colour-blind; **daltonismo** m colour-blindness.

dama f lady; (noble) lady, gentlewoman; (querida) mistress; juego de damas: king; (juego de) ~s pl. draughts; primera ~ thea. leading lady; pol. first lady; ~ de honor lady-in-waiting; maid of honour en boda.

damajuana f demijohn.

damasco m damask; **damasquinado** ⊕ damask; **damasquinar** [1a] damask.

damisela f † damsel.

damnificar [1g] hurt, injure; los damnificados those affected, those who have suffered loss; the injured parties.

danés 1. adj. Danish; **2.** m, -a f Dane; **3.** m (idioma) Danish.

danza f dance; (arte) dancing; F (negocio) shady business; F (jaleo) row, rumpus; ~ de figuras square dance; ~ guerrera war dance; meterse en la ~ get caught up in a shady business; **danzante** m, a f dancer; F (activo) hustler, person who is always on the go; (casquivano) scatter-brain; **danzar** [1f] dance (a. fig.); F meddle, shove one's oar in; **danzarín** m, -a f dancer; F = danzante F.

dañado bad; **dañar** [1a] hurt, harm, damage; (echar a perder) spoil; ~se get damaged; spoil; 🛠 hurt o.s.; **dañino** harmful, destructive; **daño** m damage; hurt, harm, injury; ♱ loss; S.Am. witchcraft; 🛠 ~s pl. y perjuicios damages; por mi ~ to my cost; hacer ~ a = dañar; estómago upset; hacerse ~ hurt o.s.; **dañoso** harmful, bad, injurious.

dar [1r] **1.** v/t. mst give; (pasar) pass, hand; permiso etc. grant, concede; fig. lend, give; batalla fight; buenos días etc. wish; cartas deal; cosecha produce, yield; ejemplo set; golpe give, strike; fetch; grito give, utter; hora strike; paseo, paso take; tema para discusión propose; ir dando cuerda pay out; ¡dale! boxeo etc.: hit him!; deportes: get on with it!; iro. look at him!; what again?; are you still at it?; (bastante) that's enough!; **2.:** lo mismo da it makes no odds; lo mismo me da it's all the same to me; ¿qué más da? what does it matter?; never mind!; **3.** v/i. con prp. (para muchas frases, v. el correspondiente su. o verbo): ~ a (ventana) look on to, overlook; (casa) face (towards); ~ con p. meet, run into; idea, solución etc. hit (up)on, strike; dio con la cabeza contra un árbol he hit his head against a tree; ~ con algo en el suelo knock s.t. to the ground, drop s.t.; no doy con el nombre I can't think of the name; ~ consigo en land in, end up in; ~ contra hit, strike; ~ de v. espalda etc.; ~ de sí (tela) give, stretch; 🌳 yield (well), produce (a lot); ~ en hábito, trampa fall into; cárcel end up in; chiste see, catch on to; ~ en inf. begin to inf.; persist in ger.; ~ por consider (as); le ha dado por inf. he has taken to ger.; ~ sobre overlook; **4.** ~se (entregarse) give o.s. up; (producirse, existir) occur, be found; no se le da nada he doesn't give a damn; ~ a devote o.s. to; b.s. abandon o.s. to, indulge in; v.

conocer *etc.*; ~*las* de pose as, fancy o.s. as; ~ *por* consider o.s.

dardo *m* dart, shaft.

dares y tomares *m/pl.* F arguments, bickerings; *andar en* ~ *con* argue with.

dársena *f* ⚓ dock.

Darvinismo *m* Darwinism.

data *f* date; ✝ item; **datar** [1a] date (*de* from).

dátil *m* ♀ date; **datilera** *f* date (-palm).

dativo *m* dative (case).

dato *m* fact, piece of information, datum; ~*s pl.* data, facts, information; ~*s pl. personales* personal details, facts about o.s.

de a) *posesión, pertenencia*: of; *tras sup.*: *el mejor del mundo* the best in the world; *los árboles del jardín* the trees in the garden; b) *materia*: *una moneda de plata* a silver coin, a coin of silver; *tras verbo*: *amueblado de nogal* furnished in walnut; *vestido de negro* dressed in black; *contenido*: *un vaso de vino* a glass of wine; *asunto*: *un libro de física* a physics book; *acerca de*: of, about, concerning; c) *partitivo*: *uno de ellos* one of them; ⅗ *de cada* 7,6 6 out of (every) 7; d) *comp.*: *más de 20* more than 20; e) *origen, procedencia*: from; *de A a B* from A to B; *de puerta en puerta* from door to door; f) *que va a*: *el camino de Madrid* the road to Madrid, the Madrid road; g) *tiempo*: *a las 6 de la mañana* at 6 in the morning; *de día* by day; *edad*: *un niño de 8 años* an 8-year old boy, a boy of 8; *cuando*: *de niño* as a child; h) *causal*: *de miedo* for fear; *de puro cansado* out of sheer tiredness; i) *en cuanto a*: *mejor de salud* better in health; j) *aposición*: *la ciudad de Roma* the city of Rome; *frases*: F *el animal de Juan* that beast (of a) John; *el pobre de Juan* poor (old) John; k) *agente de pasivo*: *amado de todos* beloved of all *lit.*, loved by all; l) *condicional*: *de serle a Vd. posible* if you can; *de no ser así* if it were not so.

dé *v. dar.*

deambular [1a] stroll, saunter; wander (about).

deán *m* eccl. dean.

debajo (*a. por* ~) underneath,

below; ~ *de* under(neath), below; beneath.

debate *m* debate, discussion; **debatir**[1] [3a] *v/t.* debate, discuss.

debatir[2] [3a] *v/i.* struggle; flail about.

debe *m* debit (side).

deber 1. [2a] *v/t.* owe; *v/i.*: ~ *inf.* must *inf.*, have to *inf.*; *debería inf.*, *debiera inf.* ought to *inf.*, should *inf.*; *debíamos ir* we were to go, we were to have gone; ~ *de inf.* must *inf.*; *debe de haber ido* he must have gone; *no debe* (*de*) *ser muy difícil* it can't be very difficult; ~*se a* be owing to, be due to, be on account of; ~ *a que* be because, be due to the fact that; *puede* ~ *a que* it may be because; **2.** *m* duty, obligation; ✝ debt; ~*es pl. escuela*: homework; **debidamente** duly, properly, in due form; **debido** due, right, just; *como es* ~ as is only right, as is proper; ~ *a* owing to, due to, through; ~ *a ello* because of this; ~ *a que* because (of the fact that).

débil *mst* weak; feeble; *salud a.* poor; *esfuerzo a.* half-hearted; *luz* dim; *grito etc. a.* faint; **debilidad** *f* weakness *etc.*; *esp.* 🍎 debility; ~ *senil* senility; **debilitación** *f* weakening, enfeeblement, debilitation; **debilitar** [1a] weaken, debilitate (*esp.* 🍎); *resistencia etc.* impair, lower; ~*se* get weak(er).

debutar [1a] make one's début.

década *f* decade.

decadencia *f* decadence, decline; **decadente** decadent, effete; **decaer** [2o] decay, decline; flag; ~ *de ánimo* lose heart.

decaimiento *m* decay; weakness.

decano *m univ. etc.* dean; (*más antiguo*) doyen.

decantar[1] praise, laud.

decantar[2] [1a] *vino etc.* decant.

decapitar [1a] behead, decapitate.

decena *f* (about) ten; **decenal** decennial.

decencia *f* decency *etc.*

decenio *m* decade.

decente decent; seemly, proper; (*limpio*) clean; modest.

decepción *f* disappointment; (*engaño*) deception; **decepcionante** disappointing; **decepcionar** [1a] disappoint.

decidido determined, decided; **decidir** [3a] decide (*inf.* to *inf.*); *cuestión* settle, decide; ~se decide, make up one's mind (*a inf.* to *inf.*).

decidor witty, lively.

décima *f* tenth; *eccl.* tithe; *poet. a* 10-*line stanza;* **decimación** *f* decimation; **decimal 1.** *adj. a. su. m* decimal; **2.** *f:* ~ *periódica pura* recurring decimal; **décimo 1.** tenth; **2.** *m* tenth; (tenth part of a) lottery ticket; **decimoctavo** *etc. v.* Apéndice.

decir 1. [3p] say; tell; *verdad* speak, tell; *misa* say; (*texto*) say, read; (*llamar*) call; ~ *bien* be right; ~ *mal* be wrong; ~ *para* (*or entre*) *sí* say to o.s.; ~ *que sí* say yes; *es* ~ that is (to say); *por mejor* ~ or rather; *por* ~*lo así* so to speak; *no hay más que* ~ there is nothing more to be done about it; *no hay que* ~ *que* it goes without saying that; *no hay para qué* ~ of course; *dar que* ~ *a la gente* make people talk; *me permito* ~ *que* I submit that, I venture to say that; *querer* ~ mean (con *by*); *¡digo, digo!* just listen to this!; now wait a minute!; *como quien dice,* como si dijéramos so to speak, in a manner of speaking; *usted dirá* it's for you to say; (*echando vino etc.*) say when; *ello dirá* the event will show; *el qué dirán* what people (will) say; *¡diga(me)! teleph.* hullo!; *diga lo que diga* whatever he says; F *¡no me diga(s)!* blow me!, I'm blowed!; *no digamos* not exactly, not really; *mejor dicho* rather; *no es para dicho* it's not fit to be told; *lo dicho freq.* what has been said; *dicho y hecho* no sooner said than done; ~se: se *dice* it is said, they say; (*cuento*) the story goes; *se me ha dicho que* I have been told that; **2.** *m* saying; *al* ~ *de* according to.

decisión *f* decision; (*ánimo*) determination; *forzar una* ~ force the issue; **decisivo** decisive; *consideración* overriding; *voto* casting.

declamación *f* declamation; recitation; **declamador** *m* orator; *b.s.* ranter; **declamar** [1a] *v/t.* declaim; recite; *v/i.* hold forth, speak out (*contra* against); *b.s.* rant; **declamatorio** declamatory.

declarable declarable; **declaración** *f* declaration; pronouncement; statement; 🏛 evidence; *naipes:* bid; ~ *de derechos* bill of rights; ~ *de renta* tax-return; *prestar* ~ give evidence; **declarado** professed, declared; **declarar** [1a] declare; pronounce, state; profess; 🏛 (*testigo*) testify, give evidence; (*juez*) find; *naipes:* bid; ~se declare o.s.; 🔥 *etc.* break out; ~ *por* side with, come out on the side of.

declinación *f* decline, falling-off; *ast.,* 🜨 declination; *gr.* declension; **declinar** [1a] *v/t.* decline, refuse; 🏛 reject; *gr.* decline, inflect; *v/i.* decline, fall off; degenerate; (*terreno etc.*) slope (away); *gr.* decline.

declive *m* slope, incline, declivity; ~ *económico* slump; *en* ~ sloping; downhill.

decolorar [1a] discolour; ~se get discoloured.

decoración *f* decoration; ~ *de interiores* interior decoration; *thea.* (*a.* ~*es pl.*) = **decorado** *m thea.* scenery, set; **decorador** *m,* -a *f* decorator; **decorar**[1] [1a] decorate, adorn.

decorar[2] [1a] *lección* learn, memorize.

decorativo decorative, ornamental.

decoro *m* decorum, propriety; proprieties; honour; respect; modesty; **decoroso** decorous, proper, seemly; respectful; decent; modest.

decrecer [2d] decrease; (*aguas etc.*) go down; **decremento** *m* decrease.

decrépito decrepit; **decrepitud** *f* decrepitude.

decretar [1a] decree, ordain; *premio* award, adjudge; **decreto** *m* decree; *parl.* act; ~-*ley m* decree, law.

dechado *m* model, paragon; pattern; *sew.* sampler.

dedada *f* thimbleful; pinch *de rapé etc.*; spot, dab *de mermelada etc.*; **dedal** *m* thimble; *fig.* thimbleful; **dedalera** *f* foxglove.

dedicación *f* dedication (*a* to); *eccl.* consecration; *fig.* devotion (*a* to); *en* (*or con*) *plena* ~ full-time; **dedicar** [1g] dedicate; *eccl. a.* consecrate; *libro* dedicate, *ejemplar* inscribe; *tiempo etc.* devote, give (*a* to), put in (*a* at); ~se *a* devote o.s. to; *trabajo a.* be engaged in;

estudio a. go in for, take up; *¿a qué se dedica Vd.?* what do you do?, what is your line of business?; **dedicatoria** *f* inscription, dedication; **dedicatorio** dedicatory.

dedil *m* finger-stall.

dedillo: F *saber al* ~ have *s.t.* at one's fingertips, have *s.t.* (off) pat.

dedo *m* finger; ~ *(del pie)* toe; F spot, bit; ~ *anular* ring finger; ~ *auricular*, ~ *meñique* little finger; ~ *del corazón*, ~ *cordial* middle finger; ~ *índice* forefinger, index finger; ~ *pulgar* thumb; *(del pie)* big toe; *a dos* ~*s de* within an inch *(or* ace) of; on the verge of; *chuparse los* ~*s* eat with relish; smack one's lips *(a. fig.)*; *no mamarse el* ~ be pretty smart; *meter el* ~ *en la boca a* try to get *s.o.* to talk; *poner el* ~ *en la llaga* put one's finger on the spot; *no tener dos* ~*s de frente* be an oaf.

deducción *f* deduction; **deducible** deducible; inferable; **deducir** [3o] deduce *(de, por* from); infer; **deduct; deductivo** deductive.

defección *f* defection, desertion; **defectible** fallible, imperfect; **defectivo** defective *(a. gr.)*; **defecto** *m* defect, flaw; ⊕, ⚰ fault; *(esp. moral)* shortcoming, failure; lack, absence; ~ *de fonación* speech defect, impediment; **defectuoso** defective, faulty, unsound.

defender [2g] defend *(a.* ⚖; *contra* against, *de* from); protect *(contra, de frío etc.* against, from); *causa* champion, uphold; ~*se* defend o.s.; F manage, get along, keep one's end up; **defendible** defensible; **defensa 1.** *f* defence *(a.* ⚖, *deportes)*; shelter, protection; ⚓ *etc.* fender; ⚔ ~*s pl.* defences, defence works; **2.** *m deportes:* back; **defensiva** *f* defensive; *estar a la* ~ be on the defensive; **defensivo** defensive; **defensor** *m,* -a *f* defender; protector; champion, upholder *de causa;* ⚖ counsel (for the defence; *a. abogado* ~).

deferencia *f* deference; **deferente** deferential; **deferir** [3i] *v/t.* ⚖ refer, delegate *(a* to); *v/i.:* ~ *a* defer to.

deficiencia *f* deficiency, defect; **deficiente** deficient, wanting (en

in); defective; **déficit** *m* ⚰ deficit; *fig.* shortage.

definible definable; **definición** *f* definition; **definido** definite *(a. gr.)*; **definir** [3a] define; **definitiva: en** ~ definit(iv)ely; **definitivo** definitive.

deflación *f* deflation; **deflacionar** [1a] deflate; **deflacionista** deflationary.

deformación *f* deformation; distortion *(a. radio)*; ⊕ strain; **deformar** [1a] deform; distort; ⊕ strain; **deforme** deformed, misshapen; abnormal; **deformidad** *f* deformity, malformation; abnormality; *fig.* moral shortcoming.

defraudar [1a] cheat, defraud; deceive; *esperanzas* cheat, disappoint, dash.

defuera *(a. por* ~) outwardly, on the outside.

defunción *f* decease, demise.

degeneración *f* degeneration; *(moral)* degeneracy; **degenerado** *adj. a. su. m,* a *f* degenerate (type); **degenerar** [1a] degenerate *(en* into).

deglución *f* swallowing; **deglutir** [3a] swallow.

degollación *f* throat-cutting; *(a.* ⚖) beheading, decapitation; **degolladero** *m anat.* neck, throat; *(matadero)* slaughter-house; *(cadalso)* scaffold; **degollar** [1n] cut the throat of; behead, decapitate; *fig.* massacre; *comedia etc.* murder, make nonsense of.

degradación *f* degradation; ✗ demotion, reduction in rank; **degradar** [1a] degrade, debase; ✗ demote, reduce (in rank); ~*se* demean o.s.

degüello *m = degollación;* shaft, slender part *de arma; entrar a* ~ *en* put *the inhabitants of* to the sword.

degustación *f* tasting.

dehesa *f* pasture, meadow; range.

deidad *f* deity; divinity; **deificar** [1g] deify; apotheosize *(a. fig.)*; **deísmo** *m* deism; **deísta 1.** deistic(al); **2.** *m/f* deist.

dejación *f* ⚖ abandonment, relinquishment; **dejadez** *f* neglect, slovenliness *etc.*; **dejado** slovenly; *(flojo)* lazy, slack; *(abatido)* dejected.

dejar [1a] **1.** *v/t. mst* leave; *empresa, trabajo freq.* give up; *pasajero* drop, set down; ✝ *pérdida* show, leave; (*prestar*) lend; (*omitir*) forget, leave out; (*desamparar*) abandon, forsake; (*permitir*) let (*inf. inf.*), allow (*inf.* to *inf.*); ~ *atrás* leave behind, outstrip, outdistance; ~ *así las cosas* leave it at that; leave things as they are; ~ *para después* leave till later, put off; ~ *entrar* let in; ~ *salir* let out; ~ *por* leave *s.t.* as (being); *deja mucho que desear* it leaves much to be desired; *¡deja eso!* drop that!, stop that!; *v. caer etc.; como dejo dicho* as I have said; *dejado de la mano de Dios* beyond redemption; godforsaken; **2.** *v/i.:* ~ *de inf.* (*cesar*) stop *ger.*, leave off *ger.*; give up *ger.*; (*omitir*) fail to *inf.*, neglect to *inf.*; *no deja de extrañarme* I cannot but be surprised; *no poder* ~ *de inf.* not be able to help *ger.*; **3.** ~**se** let o.s. go, get slovenly; ~ *decir que* let slip that; ~ *persuadir* allow o.s. to be persuaded; ~ *de bromas etc.* cut out, stop; *¡déjese de eso!* stop that!, cut it out! F.

dejo *m* (*gustillo*) after-taste, tang; *fig.* touch, smack; (*habla*) (trace of) accent.

delación *f* denunciation, accusation; information.

delantal *m* apron.

delante in front (*a. por* ~); ahead; ~ de in front of; ahead of; **delantera** *f* front (part); *thea.* front row; (*ventaja*) lead, advantage; *coger* (or *tomar*) *la* ~ *a* get ahead of; get a start on; *llevar la* ~ lead; *tomar la* ~ take the lead; **delantero 1.** *fila, parte* front; *pata* fore; foremost *en progreso etc.; línea etc.* forward; **2.** *m* forward.

delatar [1a] denounce; inform against; (*traicionar*) betray (*a. fig.*); **delator** *m*, **-a** *f* accuser; informer; betrayer.

dele *m typ.* dele.

delectación *f* delight.

delegación *f* delegation; *parl.* ~ (*de poderes*) devolution; (*oficina*) local office; ~ *de hacienda* local Treasury office; (*comisaría*) police-station; **delegado** *m*, **a** *f* delegate; ✝ agent; **delegar** [1h] delegate (*a* to).

deleitable enjoyable, delectable (*esp. co., lit.*); **deleitar** [1a] delight; ~**se con**, ~ **de** (take) delight in;

deleite *m* pleasure, delight, joy; **deleitoso** delightful, pleasing, pleasurable.

deletéreo deleterious.

deletrear [1a] spell out; *fig.* decipher, interpret.

deleznable (*que rompe*) fragile, brittle; (*resbaladizo*) slippery; *fig.* frail; ephemeral, insubstantial.

delfín *m* dolphin.

delgadez *f* thinness *etc.*; **delgado** thin; *p. a.* slim, slender, slight; *fig.* delicate, light; (*agudo*) clever.

deliberación *f* deliberation; **deliberar** [1a] *v/t.* debate; ~ *inf.* decide to *inf.*; *v/i.* deliberate (*sobre* on), debate; **deliberativo** deliberative.

delicadeza *f* delicacy *etc*; **delicado** delicate; dainty; *color* soft, delicate; *distinción* nice; *punto* tender, sensitive; sore; *situación* delicate, tricky; (*difícil de contentar*) hard to please, fastidious; (*ingenioso*) subtle; squeamish, over-scrupulous.

delicia *f* delight(fulness); **delicioso** delicious; delightful.

delimitación *f* delimitation; **delimitar** [1a] delimit, define.

delincuencia *f* delinquency, criminality; ~ *de menores* juvenile delinquency; **delincuente 1.** delinquent, criminal; **2.** *m/f* delinquent, criminal, offender; ~ *juvenil* juvenile delinquent; ~ *sin antecedente penal* first offender.

delineación *f* delineation; **delineante** *m* draughtsman; **delinear** [1a] delineate, outline.

delinquir [3e] commit a crime, offend.

deliquio *m* swoon.

delirante delirious; light-headed; **delirar** [1a] be delirious, rave; *fig.* talk nonsense; **delirio** *m* delirium; ravings, wanderings; *fig.* frenzy; (*disparates*) nonsense; *fig. con* ~ madly; F *¡el* ~*!* it was great!; **delirium** *m* **tremens** delirium tremens.

delito *m* crime, offence; *fig.* misdeed.

delta *m* (*geog.*) *a. f* delta.

delusorio delusive; **deludir** [3a] delude.

demacración *f* emaciation; **demacrado** emaciated; **demacrarse** [1a] waste away.

demagogia *f* demagogy; **dema-**

gógico demagogic(al); **demagogo** *m* demagogue.

demanda *f* demand (*a.* ✝), request (*de* for); inquiry; petition; *thea.* call; ⚖ action, lawsuit; *en* ∼ *de* in search of; *entablar* ∼ take legal proceedings, bring an action; ✝ *tener* ∼ be in demand; **demandado** *m*, **a** *f* defendant; respondent *en divorcio*; **demandador** *m*, **-a** *f*, **demandante** *m/f* plaintiff, claimant; **demandar** [1a] demand; claim; ⚖ sue (*a una p.* a *p.*; *de*, *por* for).

demarcación *f* (*línea de* line of) demarcation; **demarcar** [1g] mark out, demarcate.

demás 1. *adj.* other, rest of the; **2.** *pron.*: *lo* ∼ the rest; *los* ∼ the others, the rest (of them); *por lo* ∼ for the rest, otherwise; **3.** *adv.* = *además*; *por* ∼ in vain; moreover; *y* ∼ etcetera; *v. estar de más*; **demasía** *f* (*superávit*) surplus; *fig.* excess, outrage; wicked thing; insolence; *en* ∼ too much, excessively; **demasiado 1.** *adj.* too much; overmuch; ∼*s pl.* too many; **2.** *adv.* too; too much, excessively; ∼ *bueno* too good (*para* for; *para inf.* to *inf.*).

demencia *f* madness, insanity; **demente 1.** mad, insane, demented; **2.** *m/f* lunatic.

demérito *m* demerit; unworthiness.

democracia *f* democracy; **demócrata** *m/f* democrat; **democrático** democratic; **democratizar** [1f] democratize.

demoler [2h] demolish (*a. fig.*), pull down; **demolición** *f* demolition.

demoníaco demoniac(al), demonic; **demonio** *m* demon; devil (*a. fig.*); *¡(qué)* ∼*!* confound it!; oh hell!; *¿qué* ∼*s?* what the hell?; *¿dónde* ∼*s ...?* where the devil ...?; *ir como el* ∼ go hell for leather; *¡que se lo lleve el* ∼*!* to hell with it!; **demontre** *m* F = *demonio*.

demora *f* delay; ⚓ bearing; **demorar** [1a] *v/t.* delay, hold up (*or* back); *v/i.* stay on, linger on, delay.

demostrable demonstrable; **demostración** *f* demonstration; show *de cariño etc.*; gesture; **demostrar** [1m] show, demonstrate; prove;

demostrativo *adj. a. su. m* demonstrative.

demudar [1a] change, alter; ∼*se* change colour, change countenance; *sin* ∼ without a flicker of emotion.

denegación *f* refusal, rejection; **denegar** [1h *a.* 1k] refuse, reject; ⚖ deny, reject, overrule.

dengoso affected, finicky; **dengue** *m* affectation, finickiness; prudery; *hacer* ∼*s* be finicky; *no me vengas con* ∼*s* I don't want to hear your silly complaints; **denguero** = *dengoso*. [insult.]

denigrar [1a] denigrate, revile;]

denodado bold, intrepid.

denominación *f* naming, designation; denomination; **denominador** *m* denominator; ∼ *común* common denominator; **denominar** [1a] name, designate; denominate.

denostar [1m] insult, abuse.

denotar [1a] denote; reveal, indicate, show.

densidad *f* density (*a. phys.*); thickness *etc.*; **denso** *mst* dense; *humo, líquido a.* thick; solid; *libro* heavy, dry.

dentado *rueda* cogged, toothed; *filo* jagged; *sello* perforated; ⚘ dentate; **dentadura** *f* denture, set of teeth; *mala* ∼ bad teeth; ∼ *postiza* false teeth, denture(s); **dental** *adj. a. su. f* dental; **dentar** [1k] *v/t.* furnish with teeth *etc.*; ⊕ *etc.* indent; *filo* make jagged; *sello* perforate; *sin* ∼ *sello* imperforate; *v/i.* teethe; **dentellada** *f* bite, nip; (*señal*) tooth-mark; *a* ∼*s* with one's teeth; **dentellar** [1a] chatter; *el miedo le hizo* ∼ fear made his teeth chatter; **dentellear** [1a] bite, nibble (at); **dentera** *f* the shivers F; F envy, jealousy; *dar* ∼ *a* set *s.o.'s* teeth on edge, give *s.o.* the shivers; *fig.* (*deseo*) make *s.o.'s* mouth water; **dentición** *f* teething; dentition; *estar con la* ∼ be teething; **dentífrico 1.** tooth *attr.*; **2.** *m* dentifrice; **dentista** *m* dentist.

dentro 1. inside; *sentir etc.* inwardly; (*en casa*) indoors; (*a. hacia* ∼, *para* ∼) in, inwards; *de* ∼, *desde* ∼ from inside; *por* ∼ (on the) inside; **2.** *prp.*: ∼ *de estar* in, inside, within; *meter* into, inside.

denudación *f* denudation; **denudar** [1a] denude; lay bare.

denuedo *m* boldness, daring.
denuesto *m* insult.
denuncia *f* denunciation (*a.* ⚖️); ⚖️ accusation; **denunciable** *ofensa* indictable; **denunciación** *f* = *denuncia*; **denunciador** *m*, **-a** *f*, **denunciante** *m/f* accuser; informer; **denunciar** [1b] (*publicar*) proclaim; (*pronosticar*) announce, foretell; (*comunicar*) give notice of; (*mostrar*) reveal; ⚖️ denounce, accuse.
deparar [1a] provide, present (with); offer; ... *que deparó la suerte* which presented itself.
departamental departmental; **departamento** *m* department; compartment *de caja etc.* (*a.* 🚂); ∼ *de máquinas* engine-room.
departir [3a] talk, chat.
depauperar [1a] impoverish; ⚕️ weaken, deplete.
dependencia *f* dependence (*de* on); reliance (*de* on); dependency (*a. pol.*); ✝ branch-office; 🏠 out-building, outhouse; (*negocio*) (piece of) business, affair; (*ps.*) sales staff, employees; ∼*s* *pl.* accessories; **dependienta** *f* sales-girl, shop-assistant, clerk *Am.*; **dependiente 1.** dependent (*de* on); **2.** *m* employee; ✝ salesman, shop-assistant, clerk *Am.*
depilatorio *adj. a. su. m* depilatory.
deplorable deplorable; lamentable, regrettable; **deplorar** [1a] deplore, regret.
deponente *adj.* (*gr.*) *a. su. m* (⚖️) deponent.
deponer [2r] *v/t.* (*bajar*) lay down; (*apartar*) lay aside; (*quitar*) remove, take away, take down; *rey* depose; *ministro* remove from office; *v/i.* ⚖️ give evidence.
deportación *f* deportation; **deportado** *m*, **a** *f* deportee; **deportar** [1a] deport.
deporte *m* sport; game; **deportista 1.** sports *attr.*; sporting; **2.** *m* sportsman; **3.** *f* sportswoman; **deportividad** *f* sportsmanship; **deportivo** *club*, *periódico etc.* sports *attr.*; *actitud etc.* sporting, sportsmanlike.
deposición *f* deposition (*a.* ⚖️); removal; ⚖️ evidence.
depositador *m*, **-a** *f* ✝ depositor; **depositar** [1a] *mst* deposit; store,

put away, lodge; entrust (*en* to); ∼**se** (*líquido*) settle; **depositaría** *f* depository; trust; **depositario 1.** deposit *attr.*; **2.** *m*, **a** *f* depositary, trustee; repository *de secreto etc.*; **depósito** *m* (*almacén*) store (-house), warehouse, depot; ✕ depot, dump; reservoir, tank *de líquido*; ✝, 🔧 deposit; ∼ *de agua* water-tank, cistern; ∼ *de basura* (rubbish-)tip, dump; ∼ *de cadáveres* mortuary; ∼ *de equipajes* cloakroom; ∼ *de gasolina* petrol tank; ∼ *de maderas* timber-yard; ✝ *en* ∼ in bond.
depravación *f* depravity, depravation; **depravado** depraved; **depravar** [1a] deprave.
depreciación *f* depreciation; **depreciar(se)** [1b] depreciate.
depresión *f mst* depression (*a.* ⚕️, ✝, *meteor.*); drop, fall *de mercurio*; dip *de horizonte, camino*; (*hueco*) depression, hollow; **depresivo**, **deprimente** depressing; **deprimido** ⚕️ depressed; **deprimir** [3a] depress (*a.* ⚕️, *fig.*); *nivel* lower, reduce; *fig.* humiliate; (*rebajar*) belittle, disparage.
depuración *f* purification; *pol.* purge; **depurador** *m* purifier; **depurar** [1a] purify, cleanse, purge (*a. pol.*).
derecha *f* right hand; (*lado*) right side; *pol.* right; *a la* ∼ *estar* on the right, *torcer etc.* (to the) right; *a* ∼*s* rightly; **derechamente** straight, directly; *fig.* properly, rightly; **derechazo** *m boxeo*: right; **derechista 1.** right-wing; **2.** *m/f* right-winger.
derecho 1. *adj. lado, mano* right; (*recto*) straight; (*vertical*) upright, erect, straight, standing; *más* ∼ *que una vela* as straight as a die; **2.** *adv.* straight, direct; (*verticalmente*) straight, upright; **3.** *m* right (*a* to, *de inf.* to *inf.*); ⚖️ (*ciencia*) law; (*en abstracto*) justice; right side *de papel*; ∼*s* *pl.* ✝ due(s); (*profesionales*) fee(s); (*impuestos*) tax(es); ∼*s* *pl.* de aduana, ∼*s* *pl.* arancelarios customs duty; ∼*s* *pl.* de autor royalties; ∼ *canónico* canon law; ∼*s* *pl.* civiles civil rights; ∼ *consuetudinario* common law; ∼ *divino* divine right; ∼*s* *pl.* de entrada import duties; ∼ *de gentes*,

~ *internacional* international law; ~ *de paso* right of way; ~ *penal* criminal law; ~ *preferente* preferential duty; ~s *pl. de puerto* harbour-dues; *con* ~ rightly, justly; *con* ~ *a* with a right to; *conforme a* ~ according to law; *por* ~ *propio* in his own right; *según* ~ by right(s); F ¡*no hay* ~! it's not fair!; *reservados todos los* ~s copyright; *tener* ~ *a* have a right to, be entitled to.

derechura *f* straightness; directness; *fig.* rightness; *en* ~ *hablar* plainly; *hacer* right away.

deriva *f* ⚓ drift; leeway *de rumbo*; *a la* ~ adrift, drifting; *ir a la* ~ drift; **derivación** *f* derivation (*a. gr.*); origin, source; ⚡ shunt; *hacer una* ~ *en alambre* tap; **derivado 1.** derivative (*a. gr.*); **2.** *m* derivative (*a. gr.*); 🝔 by-product; **derivar**[1] [1a] *v/t.* derive (*de* from); *v/i.*, ~**se** derive, be derived.

derivar[2] [1a] ⚓ drift.

derivativo *adj. a. su. m* derivative.

dermatología *f* dermatology; **dermatólogo** *m* dermatologist.

derogación *f* repeal, abolition; *hacer* ~ *a* = **derogar** [1h] repeal, abolish.

derramadero *m* spillway; **derramamiento** *m* spilling *etc.*; **derramar** [1a] pour out; spill; (*esparcir*) scatter, spread; *sangre* shed; *lágrimas* weep; *fig. noticia* spread; (*malgastar*) squander, waste; ~**se** spill, overflow, run over; (*sangre*) flow, be shed; (*esparcirse*) scatter; spread; **derrame** *m* spilling *etc.*; (*salida*) overflow, outflow; (*pérdida*) leakage, waste; 🝔 discharge.

derrapar [1a] *mot.* skid; ⚓ yaw; **derrape** *m* skid; yaw.

derredor: *al* ~ (*de*), *en* ~ (*de*) around, about.

derrelicto *m esp.* ⚓ derelict.

derrengado bent, crooked; (*cojo*) lame; **derrengar** [1h] bend, twist; ~ (*a palos*) break *s.o.'s* back, cripple.

derretido melted; *metal* molten; *estar* ~ *por* be crazy about; **derretir** [3l] melt; *nieve a.* thaw; *fortuna* squander; ~**se** melt; run; thaw; ~ *por* be crazy about; F fret and fume.

derribar [1a] *casa* knock down, pull down; *puerta* batter down; *res* throw, fell; *adversario* knock down, lay out F; *hunt.*, 🦌 shoot down, bring down; *gobierno etc.* overthrow; *fig.* humiliate; ~**se** fall down, collapse; (*p.*) throw o.s. to the ground; **derribo** *m* knocking down *etc.*; ~s *pl.* debris, rubble.

derrocadero *m* cliff, precipice; **derrocar** [1g] hurl down *desde lo alto*; *casa* knock down; *gobierno etc.* overthrow; oust, topple (*de* from); *fig.* humble; ~**se** *por* throw o.s. over.

derrochador *adj. a. su. m* spendthrift; **derrochar** [1a] waste, squander; lavish; **derroche** *m* waste, squandering; lavish expenditure, extravagance.

derrota[1] *f* ⚓ course; (*camino*) road, path, way.

derrota[2] *f* defeat, rout; débâcle; **derrotar** [1a] defeat, rout; *ropa* tear; *salud etc.* ruin.

derrotero *m* ⚓ course; *fig.* course, plan of action.

derrotismo *m* defeatism; **derrotista** *m/f* defeatist.

derruir [3g] demolish, tear down.

derrumbadero *m* cliff; *fig.* pitfall, hazard; **derrumbamiento** *m* headlong fall; collapse (*a. fig.*), caving in; **derrumbar** [1a] hurl down, throw down; ~**se** (*p. etc.*) hurl o.s. (*por* over); fall headlong (*por* down); (*edificio a. fig.*) collapse; (*techo*) fall in, cave in.

desabillé *m* deshabille.

desabotonar [1a] *v/t.* unbutton; *v/i.* ❀ blossom; ~**se** come undone.

desabrido *sabor* tasteless, insipid (*a. fig.*); (*áspero*) harsh, rough; *debate* bitter; *p.* surly; *contestación* sharp.

desabrigado *fig.* unprotected, defenceless; **desabrigo** *m* bareness, exposure; *fig.* unprotectedness; destitution.

desabrimiento *m* insipidness *etc.*; (*sentimiento*) depression, uneasiness; *con* ~ *contestar* sharply; **desabrir** [3a] *fig.* embitter.

desabrochar [1a] undo, unfasten; *fig.* penetrate; ~**se** F unbosom o.s. (*con* to).

desacatador disrespectful; **desa-**

catar [1a] be disrespectful to; **desacato** m disrespect; *esp.* ⚖ (act of) contempt.

desacertado mistaken, wrong; (*imprudente*) unwise; *observación etc.* infelicitous; **desacertar** [1k] be wrong; **desacierto** m mistake, miscalculation, miss; (*dicho etc.*) unfortunate remark.

desacomodado unemployed; badly off; **desacomodar** [1a] put out, inconvenience; *criado* discharge; ⁓se lose one's post.

desaconsejado ill-advised.

desacoplar [1a] ⚡ disconnect; ⊕ uncouple.

desacorde discordant.

desacostumbrado unusual, odd; **desacostumbrar** [1a]: ⁓ a uno de break s.o. of the habit of, wean s.o. away from.

desacreditar [1a] discredit, bring into disrepute; (*denigrar*) run down.

desacuerdo m disagreement; error; (*olvido*) forgetfulness; en ⁓ con out of keeping with, at variance with.

desadvertido careless.

desafecto m disaffection; ill-will, dislike.

desafiador 1. defiant; challenging; **2.** m, -a f challenger; **desafiar** [1c] defy; challenge; dare; ⁓ a inf. challenge s.o. to inf., dare s.o. to inf.

desaficionarse [1a]: ⁓ de come to dislike.

desafinado out of tune, off key; **desafinar** [1a] be (or go) out of tune; F speak out of turn.

desafío m challenge (a. fig.); defiance; ✕ duel.

desaforado lawless, disorderly; (*grande*) huge; *grito etc.* mighty; ser un ⁓ be a violent sort; **desaforarse** [1m] act in an outrageous way; get worked up. [lucky.⟩

desafortunado unfortunate, un-⟩ **desafuero** m excess, outrage.

desagradable disagreeable, unpleasant; **desagradar** [1a] displease; dissatisfy; **desagradecido** ungrateful; **desagradecimiento** m ingratitude; **desagrado** m displeasure; dissatisfaction.

desagraviar [1b] *daño* make amends for; *p.* make amends to, indemnify; ⁓se get one's own back; restore

one's honour; **desagravio** m amends, compensation; en ⁓ de as amends for.

desagregación f disintegration; **desagregar(se)** [1h] disintegrate.

desaguadero m drain (a. fig.; de on); **desaguar** [1i] v/t. drain, empty; fig. squander; v/i.: ⁓ en drain into; **desagüe** m drainage, draining; (*caño etc.*) outlet, drain; de ⁓ tubo etc. waste attr., outlet attr.

desaguisado 1. illegal; **2.** m offence, outrage.

desahogado (*descarado*) impudent, brazen; (*despejado*) free; *vida* comfortable; **desahogar** [1h] *dolor etc.* ease; *p.* console; *pasión* vent; ⁓se make things more comfortable; get out of trouble (or debt etc.); (*hablar*) relieve one's feelings, get s.t. off one's chest; (*confesarse*) unbosom o.s.; **desahogo** m (*alivio*) relief; (*medio para aliviarse*) outlet (de for); (*descaro*) impudence; (*libertad*) excessive freedom; comfort, comfortable circumstances; vivir con ⁓ be comfortably off.

desahuciado *caso* hopeless, bad; **desahuciar** [1b] eject, evict; oust; *enfermo* give up hope for; **desahucio** m ejection, eviction.

desairado unattractive, shabby; quedar ⁓ be unsuccessful, come off badly; **desairar** [1a] slight, snub; **desaire** m slight, snub; (*falta de garbo*) lack of charm.

desalentar [1k] make breathless; fig. discourage; ⁓se get discouraged; **desaliento** m discouragement; depression; (*debilidad*) weakness.

desaliñado slovenly, down-at-heel; '(*temporalmente*) untidy, dishevelled; (*descuidado*) slovenly, careless; **desaliño** m slovenliness etc.

desalmado cruel, brutal; **desalmarse** [1a]: ⁓ por long for, crave.

desalojar [1a] v/t. oust, eject, dislodge (a. ✕); v/i. move out.

desalquilado vacant; **desalquilar** [1a] vacate; ⁓se become vacant.

desamar [1a] dislike, detest.

desamarrar [1a] untie; ⚓ cast off.

desamor m coldness, indifference; dislike; **desamorado** cold-hearted.

desamparado helpless, abandoned; **desamparar** [1a] desert, abandon, forsake; **desamparo** m (*acto*) desertion etc.; (*estado*) helplessness.

desamueblado unfurnished; **des-amueblar** [1a] remove the furniture from, clear out.

desandar [1q]: ~ *el camino*, ~ *lo andado* retrace one's steps, go back.

desangramiento: *morir de* ~ bleed to death; **desangrar** [1a] bleed; *lago* drain; *fig.* bleed white; ~se lose a lot of blood; bleed to death.

desanidar [1a] *v/t.* oust, dislodge; *v/i.* (begin to) fly.

desanimado downhearted, low-spirited; lifeless; **desanimar** [1a] discourage, depress; ~se get discouraged; **desánimo** *m* discouragement, despondency; lifelessness.

desanudar [1a] untie; disentangle.

desapacible *mst* unpleasant; *ruido* sharp, jangling; *tono* harsh; *debate* bitter; *sabor* sharp.

desaparecer [2d] *v/t.* hide, remove, take away; *v/i.* disappear; vanish; drop out of sight; *(efectos etc.)* wear off; **desaparecido** missing; **desaparición** *f* disappearance.

desapasionado dispassionate.

desapego *m* coolness, indifference (*a* towards).

desapercibido *(desprevenido)* unprepared; *(inadvertido)* unnoticed.

desaplicación *f* slackness, laziness; **desaplicado** slack, lazy.

desapoderado *(precipitado)* headlong; wild; *gula etc.* excessive; *orgullo* overweening.

desaprensión *f* freedom from worry, nonchalance; unscrupulousness; **desaprensivo** unworried, nonchalant; *b.s.* unscrupulous.

desapretar [1k] loosen.

desaprobación *f* disapproval; **desaprobar** [1m] disapprove of, frown on; *petición* reject.

desapropiar [1b] divest, deprive (*de* of).

desaprovechado unproductive, below expectations; *estudiante etc.* slack; **desaprovechar** [1a] *v/t.* waste, fail to make the best use of; *v/i.* lose ground, slip back.

desarbolar [1a] dismast.

desarmar [1a] *v/t.* ✗ disarm; ⊕ dismantle, take to pieces, take apart, strip (down); *fig. cólera etc.* calm, appease; *v/i.* disarm; **desarme** *m* disarmament.

desarraigar [1h] root out, uproot,

dig up; *fig.* eradicate; **desarraigo** *m fig.* eradication.

desarrebujar [1g] *enredo* disentangle; *(descubrir)* uncover, unwrap; *fig.* explain, elucidate.

desarreglado out of order; *(desaliñado)* slovenly, untidy; *conducta etc.* disorderly; **desarreglar** [1a] disarrange, disturb; upset, mess up; **desarreglo** *m* disorder; confusion, chaos; *vivir en el mayor* ~ live in complete chaos.

desarrimado *m* lone wolf.

desarrollar [1a] *lo arrollado* unroll, unwind, unfold; *ecuación* expand; *tesis* expound; *fig.* develop; evolve; ~se *fig.* develop; unfold; evolve; **desarrollo** *m* development; evolution; growth; run *de juego etc.*

desarroparse [1a] undress, uncover o.s.

desarrugar [1h] smooth (out).

desarticulado disjointed; **desarticular** [1a] separate, take apart; *huesos* put out.

desarzonar [1a] throw, unseat.

desaseado *(sucio)* dirty, slovenly; *(desaliñado)* untidy, unkempt, shabby; **desasear** [1a] dirty, soil; mess up; **desaseo** *m* dirtiness *etc.*

desasimiento *m* loosening *etc.*; *fig.* detachment, disinterest; **desasir** [3a; *present like salir*] loosen, let go; ~se de let go of; *fig. (ceder)* give up; *(deshacerse de)* get rid of; *situación* extricate o.s. from.

desasosegado uneasy; restless; **desasosegar** [1h *a.* 1k] disturb, make uneasy; make restless; **desasosiego** *m* disquiet, uneasiness, anxiety; restlessness.

desastrado dirty, shabby; *(infeliz)* unlucky; **desastre** *m* disaster; **desastroso** disastrous.

desatado *fig.* wild, violent; **desatar** [1a] untie, undo, unfasten, loose(n); *fig.* solve, unravel; ~se come undone *etc.*; *fig. (hablar)* get worked up; *(obrar)* go too far, forget o.s.; *(tempestad)* burst, break; *(calamidad)* fall *(sobre on)*; ~ *de compromiso* get out of; ~ *en injurias etc.* burst into, (begin to) pour out.

desatascar [1g] *carro* pull out of the mud; *cañería* clear; *fig.* get *s.o.* out of a jam.

desatención *f* inattention; *(grosería)* discourtesy; **desatender** [2g] ignore, disregard, pay no attention to; *deber* neglect; (*ofender*) slight; **desatentado** thoughtless, inconsiderate; (*imprudente*) unwise; excessive, extreme; **desatento** inattentive; heedless, careless; (*grosero*) unmannerly.

desatinado foolish; nonsensical, silly; wild; **desatinar** [1a] *v/t.* perplex, bewilder; *v/i.* act foolishly; blunder (along); (*hablar*) talk nonsense; (*como loco*) rave; **desatino** *m* foolishness, folly; (*despropósito*; *esp.* ⁓s *pl.*) nonsense, silly things.

desatornillar [1a] unscrew.

desatrancar [1g] *puerta* unbar; *pozo* clean out; *cañería* clear.

desatufarse [1a] go out for a breather; *fig.* calm down.   [warranted.\

desautorizado unauthorized; un-/

desavenencia *f* disagreement; friction, unpleasantness, rift; **desavenido** in disagreement, incompatible; **desavenir** [3s] cause a rift between, split; ⁓se disagree (*con* with), fall out (*con* with).

desaventajado unfavourable.

desayunar(se) [1a] (have) breakfast (*con* on); *estar desayunado* have had breakfast; ⁓ *de fig.* get the first news of; **desayuno** *m* breakfast.

desazón *f* (*soso*) tastelessness; poorness *de suelo*; *fig.* 🜊 trouble, discomfort; *fig.* annoyance, frustration; **desazonar** [1a] *comida* make tasteless; *fig.* upset, annoy; ⁓se feel off colour.

desbancar [1g] F *juego*: *v/t.* bust; *v/i.* go bust.

desbandada: *a la* ⁓ in disorder; **desbandarse** [1a] 🗡 *etc.* (*irse*) disband; (*huir*) flee in disorder; disperse in confusion.

desbarajustar [1a] throw into confusion; **desbarajuste** *m* confusion, disorder, chaos.

desbaratar [1a] *v/t.* ruin, spoil, mess up F; *proyecto, tentativa* thwart, foil; *teoría* debunk F; *fortuna* squander; 🗡 *etc.* throw into confusion; ⊕ take to pieces; *v/i.* talk nonsense; ⁓se F blow up, go off the deep end.

desbarbar [1a] cut (back), trim (off); F shave (*a.* ⁓se).

desbarrancadero *m S.Am.* precipice.

desbarrar [1a] F talk a lot of rubbish.

desbastar [1a] ⊕ plane (down), smooth (out, down); F knock the corners off; **desbaste** *m* ⊕ planing *etc.*

desbocado *caballo* runaway; *p.* foulmouthed; **desbocar** [1g]: ⁓ *en* (*río*) run into, flow into; (*calle*) open into; ⁓se (*caballo*) bolt; (*p.*) let loose a stream of insults *etc.*, start to swear.

desbordar(se) [1a] overflow, run over; *fig.* lose one's self-control, fly off the handle; ⁓ *de alegría* be bursting with.

desbravador *m* horse-breaker; **desbravar** [1a] *v/t.* break in, tame; *v/i.*, ⁓se get less wild; diminish; (*licor*) lose its strength.

descabalgar [1h] dismount.

descabellado *p.* dishevelled; *proyecto etc.* wild, crazy; **descabellar** [1a] *p. etc.* dishevel, rumple; *toro* kill with a thrust in the neck.

descabezado headless; *fig.* wild, crazy; **descabezar** [1f] behead; *árbol* lop, poll; *planta* top; *fig.* dificultad begin to get over; *trabajo* be over the worst part of; *v. sueño*; ⁓se rack one's brains.

descalabrado: *salir* ⁓ come out the loser (*de* in); **descalabrar** [1a] hit *etc.* in the head; (*en general*) hit, hurt; (*romper*) damage, smash; **descalabro** *m* blow, setback, misfortune; (*daño*) damage; 🗡 defeat.

descalificación *f* disqualification; **descalificar** [1g] disqualify.

descalzar [1f] *zapato etc.* take off; *p.* take off *s.o.'s* shoes *etc.*; ⁓se take off one's shoes *etc.*; (*caballo*) lose a shoe; **descalzo** bare-foot(ed), shoeless *etc.*; *eccl.* discalced; *estar* ⁓ *freq.* have one's shoes off; *ir* ⁓ go bare-footed.

descamarse [1a] scale (off).

descaminado *fig.* misguided, ill-advised; **descaminar** [1a] mislead, put on the wrong road; *fig.* lead astray; *S.Am.* hold up.

descamisado 1. ragged, wretched; 2. *m* poor devil, wretch.

descampado: *al* ⁓ in the open air; *en* ⁓ in open country.

descansadero *m* stopping-place, resting-place; **descansado** rested, refreshed; *vida* free from care; (*que tranquiliza*) restful; **descansar**

[1a] v/t. (ayudar) help, give a hand to; (apoyar) rest, lean (sobre on); ¡descansen armas! order arms!; v/i. (no trabajar) rest, take a rest, have a break (de from); (dormir) rest, sleep; (enfermo) rest, lie down; (yacer) lie; ✝ lie fallow; no ~ freq. not have a moment's rest; ¡que Vd. descanse!, ¡descanse bien! sleep well!; ~ en △, ⊕ rest upon, be supported by; fig. rely on; **descansillo** m △ landing; **descanso** m (reposo) rest; (pausa) rest, break; (alivio) relief; deportes: half-time, interval; thea. interval; △ landing; ⊕ support, rest; bracket; sin ~ trabajar etc. without a break.

descarado shameless, brazen; cheeky, saucy; blatant; **descararse** [1a] behave in an impudent way (con towards); ~ a pedir have the nerve to ask (for).

descarburar [1a] decarbonize.

descarga f unloading; firing, discharge; ~ (cerrada) volley; ⚡ discharge; **descargadero** m wharf; **descargador** m docker; **descargar** [1h] 1. v/t. barco, carro etc. unload; arma fire, shoot, discharge; ⚡ discharge; golpe let fly (en at), strike (en on); fig. p. relieve, release (de obligación from); clear, acquit (de culpa of); free (de deuda of); conciencia ease; ira etc. vent (en on); 2. v/i. ⚡ discharge; (tempestad) burst, break; ~ en (río) flow into; (calle etc.) open into; 3. ~se resign; ⚖ clear o.s. (de of); ~ de get rid of, disburden o.s. of; ~ en uno de algo unload s.t. on to s.o.; **descargo** m unloading de barco etc.; ✝ receipt, voucher; ✝ discharge de deuda; ⚖ (alegato) evidence; ⚖ acquittal (de acusación of); release (de obligación from); **descargue** m unloading.

descarnado lean, scrawny F; cadaverous; **descarnar** [1a] hueso remove the flesh from; fig. wear down, eat away; ~se lose flesh.

descaro m shamelessness; impudence, cheek; blatancy.

descarriar [1c] misdirect, put on the wrong road; ~se stray; fig. go astray.

descarrilamiento m derailment; **descarrilar** [1a] (a. ~se S.Am.) be derailed, go off the rails; fig. wander from the point.

descartar [1a] discard, reject; ~se naipes: discard; ~ de shirk; **descarte** m naipes: discard; fig. excuse.

descascar [1g] peel; shell; ~se smash to pieces; F chatter; **descascarar** [1a] peel; shell; ~se peel (off).

descendedero m ramp; **descendencia** f descent (de from), origin; (hijos) offspring; **descendente** descending, downward; tren down; **descender** [2g] v/t. get down, take down; escalera go down; v/i. descend, come down, go down; (fluir, pasar) run, flow; ~ de descend from, be descended from; fig. derive from; **descendiente** m/f descendant; **descendimiento** m descent (a. eccl.); **descenso** m descent; (disminución) fall, decline, falling-off (de in); (socavón) subsidence; (desnivel) slope, drop.

descentrado off centre; **descentralización** f decentralization; **descentralizar** [1f] decentralize.

descercar [1g] ciudad relieve; **descerco** m relief.

descerrajado F raving mad; (malo) wicked; **descerrajar** [1a] break open; F tiro let off.

descifrable decipherable; **descifrar** [1a] decipher, read; mensaje en cifra decode; fig. puzzle out, make out.

desclasificación f disqualification; **desclasificar** [1g] disqualify.

descocado F cheeky; brazen, forward; **descocarse** [1g] F be cheeky etc.; **descoco** m F cheek; brazenness.

descoger [2c] spread out, unfold.

descolar [1a] tail, dock.

descolgar [1h a. 1m] take down, get down, unhook; ~se let o.s. down (de from; con by); come down; fig. turn up unexpectedly; ~ con fig. come out with.

descoloramiento m discolouration; **descolorar(se)** [1a] discolour; **descolorido** faded, discoloured; fig. colourless.

descollante outstanding; **descollar** [1m] stand out.

descombrar [1a] clear, disencumber.

descomedido excessive; intemperate; (grosero) rude, disrespectful; **descomedimiento** m rudeness *etc.*; **descomedirse** [3l] be rude *etc.*

descompaginar [1a] mess up, disorganize.

descompasado out of all proportion; **descompasarse** [1a] be rude.

descomponer [2r] *orden* disturb, upset, disarrange; *facciones* distort; *fig.* shake up, put out; (*desmontar*) take apart; (*estropear*) tamper with, put out of order; *conjunto* split up; *ps.* create bad feeling between; *calma* ruffle, disturb; (*pudrir*) rot, decompose; ⚗ separate into its elements; ~se (*pudrirse*) rot, decompose; (*irritarse*) lose one's temper; ~ *con* fall out with; **descomposición** *f* disturbance *etc.*; distortion; *opt.* dispersal; (*putrefacción*) decomposition (*a.* ⚗); *fig.* discomposure; **descompostura** *f* disorder, disorganization; (*desaseo*) untidiness; *fig.* discomposure; (*descaro*) brazenness; **descompuesto** out of order; *rostro* twisted; *fig.* (*descarado*) brazen; (*descortés*) rude; (*colérico*) angry.

descomunal huge, enormous.

desconcertado disconcerted, taken aback; puzzled, bewildered; **desconcertador, desconcertante** disconcerting, upsetting, embarrassing; **desconcertar** [1k] ⊕ put out of order, damage; *anat.* dislocate; *proyecto* dislocate, throw out of gear; *orden* disturb; *p.* disconcert, put out; embarrass; (*problema*) baffle; puzzle, bewilder; **desconcierto** *m* disorder, confusion; ⊕ damage; *fig.* (*desavenencia*) disagreement; embarrassment; bewilderment.

desconcharse [1a] peel off, flake off.

desconectar [1a] ⚡, ⊕ disconnect.

desconfiado distrustful, suspicious; **desconfianza** *f* distrust; **desconfiar** [1c]: ~ *de* distrust, mistrust, suspect.

desconformar(se) [1a] disagree, dissent; **desconforme** in disagreement, dissident; **desconformidad** *f* disagreement (*con* with), dissent (*de* from).

desconocer [2d] not know; be ignorant of, be unfamiliar with; (*no reconocer*) not recognize; (*fingiendo*) pretend not to know; ignore, disregard; (*rechazar*) disown, repudiate; **desconocido 1.** unknown (*de, para* to); strange, unfamiliar; (*cambiado*) much changed; (*ingrato*) ungrateful; **2.** *m*, **a** *f* stranger; **desconocimiento** *m* ignorance; repudiation; ingratitude.

desconsideración *f* inconsiderateness; **desconsiderado** inconsiderate.

desconsolado disconsolate; *rostro* woebegone; **desconsolador** distressing; **desconsolar** [1m] grieve, distress; **desconsuelo** *m* grief, distress.

descontable discountable.

descontaminación *f* decontamination; **descontaminar** [1a] decontaminate.

descontar [1m] take away; ✝ discount (*a. fig.*), rebate; (*a. dar por descontado*) take for granted, assume.

descontentadizo hard to please; restless, unsettled; **descontentar** [1a] displease; **descontento 1.** dissatisfied (*de* with); discontented; disgruntled (*de* at); **2.** *m* dissatisfaction, displeasure; *esp. pol.* discontent.

descontinuación *f* discontinuation; **descontinuar** [1e] discontinue.

descorazonar [1a] *fig.* discourage; ~se get discouraged.

descorchador *m* corkscrew; **descorchar** [1a] ✓ *árbol* strip, bark; *botella* uncork, open.

descornar [1m] dehorn, poll.

descorrer [2a] *cortina* draw back.

descortés discourteous, rude; **descortesía** *f* discourtesy, rudeness.

descortezar [1f] *árbol* skin, bark; *pan* cut the crust off; F polish up a bit.

descoser [2a] unpick, unstitch; ~se burst at the seams, come apart; F fart; **descosido 1.** big-mouthed; (*desastrado*) shabby, slovenly; **2.** *m sew.* tear; F *comer como un* ~ eat an awful lot.

descoyuntar [1a] put out of joint, dislocate; *fig.* bother, annoy.

descrédito *m* discredit; disrepute; **descreer** [2e] disbelieve (*a. eccl.*); **descreído 1.** unbelieving; godless; **2.** *m*, **a** *f* unbeliever; **descreimiento** *m* unbelief.

describir [3a; *p.p.* descrito] describe (*a.* 📐); **descripción** *f* description; **descriptible** describable; **descriptivo** descriptive.

descrismar [1a] F bash *s.o.* on the head; **~se** F blow one's top.

descuajar [1a] dissolve; ♀ uproot; *fig.* eradicate; F discourage.

descuajaringarse [1h] F be dogtired; *S.Am.* fall to bits.

descuartizar [1f] carve up.

descubierto *situación* open, exposed; ✗ *freq. a.* under fire; *p.* bareheaded; *cabeza* bare; ✝ *a* ~ unbacked; *a(l)* ~ in the open; ✝ *en* ~ overdrawn; *poner al* ~ lay *s.t.* bare; *quedar al* ~ be exposed; **descubridero** *m* look-out; **descubridor** *m* discoverer; ✗ scout; **descubrimiento** *m* discovery; detection; **descubrir** [3a; *p.p.* descubierto] discover; detect; spot; bring to light, unearth, uncover; *petróleo etc.* strike; (*alcanzar a ver*) see; (*mostrar*) reveal; *estatua etc.* unveil; **~se** take off one's hat; (*saludo*) raise one's hat.

descuento *m* discount, rebate; *a* ~ below par; *al* ~ at a discount.

descuidado careless, slack, negligent; forgetful; (*desaseado*) slovenly, unkempt; (*desprevenido*) off one's guard; **descuidar** [1a] *v/t.* neglect, disregard; *v/i.*, **~se** not worry, not bother (*de* about); ¡*descuide Vd.!* don't worry!; **descuidero** *m* sneak thief; **descuido** *m* carelessness, slackness *etc.*; (*un* ~) oversight, mistake; *al* ~ nonchalantly; *por* ~ by an oversight.

desde *tiempo* since; *tiempo, lugar* from; ~ *hace 3 días* for 3 days; *estos últimos 3 días*; ~ ... *hasta* from ... to; ~ *que* since.

desdeñable contemptible; **desdeñador** = *desdeñoso*; **desdeñar** [1a] scorn, disdain, despise; turn up one's nose at; **~se de** *inf.* not deign to *inf.*; **desdeñoso** scornful, disdainful, contemptuous.

desdibujarse [1a] blur, fade (away).

desdicha *f* unhappiness; wretchedness; (*una* ~) misfortune; **desdichado 1.** unhappy, unlucky; wretched; **2.** *m* poor devil, wretch.

desdinerarse [1a] F cough up.

desdoblar [1a] unfold, spread out; ♗ break down (*en* into).

desdorar [1a] tarnish (*a. fig.*); **desdoro** *m* blot, stigma.

deseable desirable; **desear** [1a] want, desire, wish for; *desearía tiempo* I should like time; ~ *inf.* want to *inf.*, wish to *inf.*

desecación *f* desiccation; **desecar** [1g] dry up (*a. fig.*), desiccate.

desechar [1a] *desechos etc.* throw out; *lo inútil* jettison, scrap; *consejo, miedo etc.* cast aside; *proyecto, oferta* reject; *cargo* throw up; *talento etc.* underrate; blame, censure; *llave* turn; **desecho** *m* residue, waste; chaff *de grano*; *fig.* contempt, low opinion; **~s** *pl.* rubbish, debris, waste.

desembalar [1a] unpack.

desembanastar [1a] unpack; *secreto* blurt out, give away.

desembarazado (*despejado*) free, open; (*sin carga*) light; *fig.* free and easy; **desembarazar** [1f] *camino, sala* clear (*de* of); *fig.* ~ de rid *s.o.* of; **~se de** get rid of, free o.s. of; **desembarazo** *m* freedom; lack of restraint.

desembarcadero *m* quay, landing-stage; **desembarcar** [1g] *v/t. ps.* land, put ashore; *mercancías* unload; *v/i.* land, disembark, go ashore; **desembarco** *m* landing (*a. de escalera*) *etc.*

desembargar [1h] free.

desembarque *m* unloading, landing.

desembaular [1a] unpack, get out; F unburden o.s. of.

desembocadura *f* mouth; outlet, outfall; opening *de calle*; **desembocar** [1g]: ~ *en* (*río*) flow into; (*calle*) open into, meet; *fig.* end in.

desembolsar [1a] pay out; **desembolso** *m* outlay, expenditure; ~ *inicial* deposit.

desembragar [1h] disengage, disconnect; *mot.* declutch; **desembrague** *m* disengagement; *mot.* declutching.

desembriagar(se) [1h] sober up.

desembrollar [1a] F unravel.

desembuchar [1a] disgorge; F spill the beans; ¡*desembucha!* out with it!

desemejante dissimilar; unlike (*a.* ~ *de*); **desemejanza** *f* dissimilarity; **desemejar** [1a] *v/t.* alter, change (for the worse); *v/i.* not look alike.

desempacar [1g] unpack.

desempacho *m* ease, confidence.

desempaquetar [1a] unpack, unwrap.

desempatar [1a] break the tie between; **desempate** *m* (*a. partido de* ~) play-off.

desempeñar [1a] *prenda* redeem; *deudor* free from debt; *p.* get out of a jam; *deber* discharge; perform; *papel* play; **desempeño** *m* discharge *etc. de deber*; *thea.* performance, acting.

desempleado out of work, unemployed; **desempleo** *m* unemployment.

desempolvar [1a] dust.

desencadenar [1a] unchain; *esp. fig.* unleash; ~se *fig.* break loose; (*tempestad, fig.*) burst.

desencajado *cara* contorted; *ojos* wild; **desencajar** [1a] dislocate; ⊕ disconnect; **desencajonar** [1a] take out, unpack.

desencallar [1a] refloat.

desencantar [1a] disenchant, disillusion; **desencanto** *m* disenchantment, disillusion(ment).

desenconar(se) [1a] *fig.* calm down; (*odio*) die down, abate.

desencorvar [1a] unbend, straighten.

desenchufar [1a] disconnect, unplug.

desenfadaderas: F *tener buenas* ~ be unflappable, be good at getting out of jams; **desenfadado** free, uninhibited; unconventional; **desenfadar(se)** [1a] calm down; **desenfado** *m* freedom, lack of inhibition.

desenfocado out of focus.

desenfrenado wild; (*vicioso*) unbridled, licentious; **desenfrenarse** [1a] lose all control; run riot, (go on the) rampage; indulge one's passions; (*tempestad*) burst, rage; **desenfreno** *m* wildness, lack of control; (*vicio*) licentiousness.

desenganchar [1a] unhook, unfasten; ⊕ disengage; *caballo* unhitch.

desengañar [1a] undeceive; disabuse (*de* of); ~se see the light; become disillusioned; *¡desengáñese Vd.!* don't you believe it!; **desengaño** *m* disillusion(ment); (*chasco*) disappointment.

desenlace *m* outcome; *lit.* ending, dénouement; ~ *fatal* tragic ending;

desenlazar [1f] undo, unlace; ~se *lit.* end, turn out.

desenmarañar [1a] unravel, disentangle.

desenmascarar [1a] unmask, expose, show up.

desenojar [1a] appease, calm down.

desenredar [1a] free, disentangle (*a. fig.*); *fig.* resolve, straighten out; ~se *fig.* get clear of trouble; ~ *de* get out of; **desenredo** *m* disentanglement; *lit.* dénouement.

desenrollar(se) [1a] unroll, unwind.

desensillar [1a] unsaddle.

desentenderse [2g]: ~ *de* wash one's hands of; affect ignorance of; *hacerse el desentendido* pretend not to have noticed.

desenterrar [1k] unearth, dig up (*a.* F); *muerto* disinter.

desentonar [1a] be out of tune (*con* with; *a. fig.*); ~se *fig.* speak disrespectfully; **desentono** *m* *fig.* rudeness, rude tone of voice.

desentorpecer [2d] stretch; F polish *s.o.* up a bit.

desentramparse [1a] F get out of the red.

desentrañar [1a] disembowel; *fig.* puzzle out, get to the bottom of.

desentrenado out of practice.

desentumecer [2d] *miembro* stretch; *músculos* loosen up.

desenvainar [1a] *espada* unsheathe; ♀ shell; F bring out, show.

desenvoltura *f* ease, assurance; *b.s.* boldness; brazenness; **desenvolver** [2h; *p.p.* desenvuelto] *paquete* unwrap; *rollo* unwind; *enredo* disentangle; (*desarrollar*) develop; **desenvolvimiento** *m* development; **desenvuelto** *fig.* free and easy, self-assured; *b.s.* bold; *mujer* brazen.

deseo *m* wish, desire (*de* for; *de inf.* to *inf.*); **deseoso** *de inf.* desirous of *ger.*, eager to *inf.*

desequilibrado unbalanced (*a. fig.*); (*desigual*) one-sided, lopsided; **desequilibrar** [1a] unbalance; throw off balance; **desequilibrio** *m* unbalance (*a.* ⚕).

deserción *f* desertion; **desertar** [1a] desert (*a.* ~ *de*); **desertor** *m* deserter.

deservicio *m* disservice.

desescarchador *m* *mot.* defroster.

desesperación *f* despair, desperation; F *ser una ~* be unbearable; **desesperado** desperate; in despair; *condición* hopeless; **desesperanzar** [1f] deprive of hope; **desesperar** [1a] drive to despair; F drive to distraction; *v/i.,* *~se* despair (*de* of), lose hope; get desperate.

desestimar [1a] have a low opinion of; belittle, disparage; (*rechazar*) reject; discount.

desfachatado F brazen, barefaced; cheeky; **desfachatez** *f* F brazenness; face, cheek.

desfalcar [1g] embezzle; **desfalco** *m* embezzlement.

desfallecer [2d] *v/t.* weaken; *v/i.* get weak; faint away; (*voz*) fail; *~ de ánimo* lose heart; **desfallecimiento** *m* weakness; faintness.

desfavorable unfavourable; **desfavorecer** [2d] disfavour.

desfiguración *f* disfiguration *etc.;* **desfigurado** *phot.* blurred; **desfigurar** [1a] *rostro* disfigure; *cuadro etc.* deface; *voz* alter, disguise; *suceso etc.* distort, misrepresent.

desfiladero *m* defile, pass; **desfilar** [1a] parade; (*a. ~ ante*) march past, file past; **desfile** *m* procession; ✠ parade, march past.

desflorar [1a] deflower; *asunto* treat superficially.

desfogar [1h] vent (*a. fig.*); *~se fig.* let o.s. go, blow off steam; **desfogue** *m* vent; *fig.* venting.

desfondar [1a] stave in (*a.* ⚓); ✚ plough deeply.

desgaire *m* (*desaliño*) slovenliness; (*descuido*) nonchalance; *al ~* in a slovenly way; scornfully; *mirar al ~* sneer at.

desgajar [1a] tear off, break off; *~se* come off, break off; *fig.* tear o.s. away (*de* from); (*cielo*) get stormy.

desgalichado F clumsy, sloppy.

desgana *f* lack of appetite; *fig.* disinclination, reluctance; *a ~* reluctantly; **desganado:** *sentirse ~* have no appetite; **desganarse** [1a] lose one's appetite; *fig.* get fed up.

desgañitarse [1a] F bawl, scream o.s. hoarse.

desgarbado clumsy, ungainly; (*desaliñado*) slovenly.

desgarrador *fig.* heartbreaking, heartrending; **desgarrar** [1a] tear, rip up; *fig.* rend, shatter; **desgarro**

m tear; *fig.* effrontery; boastfulness; **desgarrón** *m* big tear.

desgastar [1a] wear away; *geol.* erode, weather; *cuerda etc.* chafe, fray; *metal* corrode; *fig.* spoil, ruin; *~se* wear away *etc.;* ✗ get weak, wear o.s. out; **desgaste** *m* wear; erosion *etc.;* attrition (*a.* ✗); (*pérdida*) waste, wastage.

desglosar [1a] remove, detach.

desgobernado uncontrollable, undisciplined; **desgobernar** [1k] misgovern, misrule; *asunto* mismanage, handle badly; *anat.* dislocate; **desgobierno** *m* misgovernment; mismanagement.

desgoznar [1a] unhinge, take off the hinges; *~se fig.* go off the rails; be thrown out of gear.

desgracia *f* (*mala suerte*) misfortune; (*suceso*) mishap, misfortune; (*pérdida de favor*) disgrace; (*aspereza*) unfriendliness; *por ~* unfortunately; *caer en la ~* fall into disgrace; **desgraciadamente** unfortunately; more's the pity; **desgraciado 1.** unlucky, unfortunate; wretched; (*sin gracia*) graceless; (*desagradable*) unpleasant; **2.** *m,* **a** *f* wretch, unfortunate.

desgranar [1a] *trigo* thresh; *racimo* pick the grapes from; *guisantes* shell; *~se* ⚘ fall, seed; (*cuentas*) come unstrung.

desgreñado dishevelled; **desgreñar** [1a] tousle, ruffle.

desguarnecer [2d] ⊕ strip down; *plaza* abandon, dismantle; *caballo* unharness.

desguazar [1f] ⚓ break up; *madera* dress.

deshabitado uninhabited; **deshabitar** [1a] move out of.

deshabituarse [1e] lose the habit.

deshacer [2s] *lo hecho* undo, unmake; spoil, destroy; (*dividir*) cut up; (*romper*) pull to pieces; ⊕ take apart; *maleta* unpack; *paquete* open; (*desgastar*) wear down; (*liquidar*) melt, dissolve; *agravio* right; *enemigo* rout; *tratado* violate; *miembro* (*a. ~se*) hurt, bump (*contra* on); *~se* fall to pieces, come apart *al caer etc.;* (*liquidarse*) melt; (*afligirse*) grieve; get impatient *esperando;* ✗ get weak; *~ de* get rid of; *carga* throw off; ⚓ dump, unload; part with *de mala gana; ~ en*

lágrimas dissolve into; *cumplidos etc.* overdo, be lavish with; ~ *por inf.* struggle to *inf.*
desharrapado ragged, shabby.
deshebillar [1a] unbuckle.
deshebrar [1a] unthread.
deshecho 1. *p.p. of deshacer*; undone; *salud* broken; F *estoy* ~ I'm worn out; **2.** *adj. lluvia* violent; *suerte* tremendous.
deshelar [1k] thaw, melt (*a.* ~se); 𝕏 de-ice.
desherbar [1k] weed.
desheredar [1a] disinherit.
desherrarse [1f] lose a shoe.
deshidratación *f* dehydration; **deshidratado** dehydrated.
deshielo *m* thaw.
deshilachar [1a] pull threads out of; ~se fray; **deshilar** [1a] unravel.
deshilvanado *fig.* disconnected, disjointed; **deshilvanar** [1a] untack.
deshinchar [1a] *neumático* let down; *cólera* give vent to; ~se 𝕏 go down; F get down off one's high horse.
deshojado leafless; *flor* stripped of its petals; **deshojar** [1a] strip the leaves (*or* petals) off; ~se lose its leaves *etc.*
deshollinador *m* sweep; **deshollinar** [1a] sweep; F take a close look at.
deshonestidad *f* indecency *etc.*; **deshonesto** indecent, lewd, improper; **deshonor** *m* dishonour; insult (*de* to); **deshonorar** [1a] dishonour; be unworthy of; (*afear*) spoil, disfigure; (*despedir*) dismiss; **deshonra** *f* dishonour, disgrace, shame; shameful act; *tener algo a* ~ think s.t. shameful; **deshonrar** [1a] dishonour, disgrace; insult; *mujer* seduce; **deshonroso** dishonourable, ignominious.
deshora: *a* ~ at the wrong time; (*sin avisar*) unexpectedly; *hacer etc. a* ~ *freq.* mistime.
deshuesar [1a] *carne* bone; ⚘ stone.
desiderátum *m* desideratum.
desidia *f* laziness, idleness; **desidioso** lazy, idle.
desierto 1. *casa etc.* deserted; *isla* desert; *paisaje* bleak, desolate; *certamen*: void; **2.** *m* desert; wilderness.
designación *f* designation, appointment; **designar** [1a] designate,

appoint; name; **designio** *m* design, plan.
desigual unequal; *superficie* uneven, rough, bumpy; *filo* ragged; *progreso etc.* erratic; *distribución* uneven, patchy; *contienda* unequal, one-sided; *tiempo* changeable; *fig.* arduous, tough; **desigualdad** *f* inequality; unevenness *etc.*
desilusión *f* disappointment; disillusion(ment); **desilusionar** [1a] disappoint, let down; disillusion; ~se get disillusioned.
desinencia *f gr.* ending.
desinfección *f* disinfection; **desinfectante** *m* disinfectant; **desinfectar** [1a] disinfect.
desinflación *f* disinflation; deflation; **desinflacionar** [1a] ✝ deflate; **desinflar** [1a] deflate.
desintegración *f*: ~ *nuclear* nuclear fission.
desinterés *m* disinterestedness; **desinteresado** disinterested; unselfish.
desintoxicarse [1g] sober up.
desistir [3a] desist; ~ *de* desist from; *derecho etc.* waive.
desjarretar [1a] hamstring; F 𝕏 lay out.
deslavazado faded, colourless.
desleal disloyal; **deslealtad** *f* disloyalty.
desleído *ideas* woolly; **desleír** [3m] dissolve; dilute; *fig.* be long-winded about.
deslenguado foul-mouthed.
desliar [1c] untie, undo; ~se come undone.
desligar [1h] untie, undo; *fig.* detach, separate; (*desenredar*) unravel; absolve, free (*de juramento* from).
deslindar [1a] mark out; *fig.* define.
desliz *m mot.* skid; *esp. fig.* slip, lapse; **deslizadero** *m* slippery spot; **deslizadizo** slippery; **deslizamiento** *m* slide, sliding; skid; glide; ~ *de tierra* landslide; **deslizar** [1f] *v/t.* slide (*por* along), slip (*en* into, *por* through); *observación* slip in; *secreto* let slip; *v/i.*, ~se (*resbalar*) slip (*en up on*); slide (*por* along); *mot.* skid; (*culebra etc.*) glide, slither; (*introducirse*) squeeze in; (*huir*) slip away; (*secreto*) slip out; (*equivocarse*) slip up, blunder; *b.s.* get into bad ways.

deslomar [1a] break the back of; ~se F work one's guts out.

deslucido unadorned; dull, lifeless; undistinguished; *quedar etc.* ~ *fig.* be unsuccessful; **deslucimiento** *m* dullness *etc.*; **deslucir** [3f] tarnish, dull; *fig.* spoil, fail to give life to; ~se *fig.* be unsuccessful.

deslumbrador dazzling (*a. fig.*), glaring; **deslumbramiento** *m* glare, dazzle; *fig.* confusion, bewilderment; **deslumbrante** dazzling; **deslumbrar** [1a] dazzle (*a. fig.*), blind; *fig.* confuse, bewilder.

deslustrado dull, lustreless (*a. fig.*); *vidrio* frosted, ground; **deslustrar** [1a] tarnish (*a. fig.*), dull; **deslustre** *m* dullness; *fig.* stain, stigma.

desmadejar [1a] take it out of, enervate.

desmallarse [1a] (*medias*) ladder.

desmán *m* excess; piece of bad behaviour.

desmandado uncontrollable, out of hand; obstreperous; **desmandarse** [1a] behave badly, be insolent; get out of hand.

desmanotado awkward.

desmantelamiento *m* dilapidation; (*acto*) dismantling; **desmantelar** [1a] dismantle; *casa* abandon, forsake; ~se get dilapidated.

desmaña *f* awkwardness *etc.*; **desmañado** awkward, clumsy; unpractical.

desmarcado *deportes*: unmarked.

desmayado ✻ unconscious; ✻ *fig.* weak, faint; languid; *color* pale; **desmayar** [1a] *v/t.* dismay, distress; *v/i.* lose heart, get depressed; ~se faint; **desmayo** *m* ✻ faint(ing fit); ✻ (*en general*) unconsciousness; *fig.* depression; *con* ~ *hablar* in a small voice, falteringly.

desmedido excessive, disproportionate; *ambición etc.* boundless; **desmedirse** [3l] forget o.s., go too far.

desmedrar [1a] *v/t.* impair; *v/i.* decline, fall off; **desmedro** *m* decline, deterioration.

desmejorar [1a] spoil, impair; ~se decline, deteriorate; ✻ lose one's health; lose one's charms; *queda muy desmejorada* she's lost her looks; she's looking quite ill.

desmelenado dishevelled.

desmembración *f* dismemberment; **desmembrar** [1k] dismember.

desmemoriado forgetful, absentminded; **desmemoriarse** [1b] get absentminded.

desmentida *f* denial; *dar una* ~ *a* give the lie to; **desmentir** [3i] *v/t.* give the lie to; *acusación* deny, refute; *carácter* belie; *rumor* scotch, scout; *teoría* explode; *v/i.*: ~ *de* belie.

desmenuzable crumbly, crumbling, flaky; **desmenuzar** [1f] *pan* crumble; *carne* chop (up), mince; *queso etc.* shred; *fig.* take a close look at.

desmerecer [2d] *v/t.* be unworthy of; *v/i.* deteriorate, lose value; ~ *de* compare unfavourably with; not live up to; *no* ~ *de* be every bit as good as; **desmerecimiento** *m* unworthiness.

desmesurado disproportionate, inordinate; *ambición etc.* boundless; (*descarado*) impudent; **desmesurarse** [1a] forget o.s.

desmigajar [1a], **desmigar** [1h] crumble.

desmilitarización *f* demilitarization; **desmilitarizar** [1f] demilitarize.

desmirriado F ✻ run down, under the weather; weedy *de natural*.

desmochar [1a] top; *árbol* lop, pollard; *texto etc.* cut.

desmontable detachable; **desmontaje** *m* ⊕ dismantling *etc.*; **desmontar** [1a] *v/t.* ⊕ dismantle, take to pieces, strip (down); △ knock down; *escopeta* uncock; *vela* take in; *solar* level, clear; *árboles* fell; (*ayudar a bajar*) help *s.o.* down; *v/i.*, ~se dismount, alight; **desmonte** *m* ⊕ *dismantling etc.*; levelling; ⚒ cutting.

desmoralización *f* demoralization; **desmoralizador** demoralizing; **desmoralizar** [1f] *ejército* demoralize; *costumbres etc.* corrupt.

desmoronadizo crumbling, crumbly; **desmoronado** dilapidated, tumbledown; **desmoronarse** [1a] *geol.* crumble; (*casa*) fall into disrepair, get dilapidated; (*caer*) collapse; *fig.* decline, decay.

desmovilización *f* demobilization; **desmovilizar** [1f] demobilize.

desmultiplicar [1g] ⊕ gear down.

desnacionalizado *p.* stateless.
desnatar [1a] *leche* skim; *fig.* take the cream off; *leche sin ~* whole milk.
desnaturalizado unnatural; **desnaturalizar** [1f] alter fundamentally; pervert, corrupt; *intenciones* misrepresent; *~se* (*p.*) give up one's nationality.
desnivel *m* unevenness; *fig.* inequality, difference, gap; **desnivelar** [1a] make uneven.
desnucar [1g] break the neck of; *res* fell; *~se* break one's neck.
desnudar [1a] strip (*a.* ⚥, *fig.*; *de* of); undress; *brazo etc.* bare; *espada* draw; *~se* undress, get undressed, strip; *~ de hojas etc.* shed; *fig.* cast aside; **desnudez** *f* nakedness, nudity; bareness (*a. fig.*); **desnudismo** *m* nudism; **desnudista** *m/f* nudist; **desnudo 1.** naked, nude; bare; *fig.* (*sin adorno*) bare; (*pobre*) penniless; *verdad etc.* plain; *~ de* devoid of, bereft of; **2.** *m* nude.
desnutrición *f* malnutrition, undernourishment; **desnutrido** undernourished.
desobedecer [2d] disobey; **desobediencia** *f* disobedience; **desobediente** disobedient.
desobstruir [3g] unblock, clear.
desocupación *f* leisure; *b.s.* idleness; (*paro*) unemployment; **desocupado** *cuarto* vacant, unoccupied; *tiempo* spare, leisure *attr.*; *p.* at leisure; *b.s.* idle; (*parado*) unemployed; (*libre*) free, not busy; **desocupar** [1a] *casa etc.* vacate; *cajón* empty.
desodorante *m* deodorant; **desodorizar** [1f] deodorize.
desoír [3q] ignore, disregard.
desojarse [1a] strain one's eyes.
desolación *f* desolation; *fig.* grief; **desolar** [1m] lay waste; *~se* grieve.
desolladero *m* slaughter-house; F talking-shop; **desollado** F brazen, barefaced; **desollador** *m* *fig.* extortioner, robber; **desolladura** *f* ⚕ graze, bruise; **desollar** [1m] skin, flay; F *~ vivo* make *s.o.* pay through the nose; (*criticar*) flay.
desorbitado: *con los ojos ~s* wide-eyed, pop-eyed.
desorden *m mst* disorder; turmoil, confusion; (*objetos*) litter, mess;

fig. loose living; **desordenado** disordered; *conducta etc.* disorderly; *objetos, cuarto* untidy; *niño etc.* wild, unruly; *país* lawless; **desordenar** [1a] throw into confusion, mess up, disarrange.
desorganización *f* disorganization, disruption; **desorganizar** [1f] disorganize, disrupt.
desorientar [1a] make *s.o.* lose his way; *fig.* confuse; *~se* lose one's bearings.
desovar [1a] spawn; (*insecto*) lay eggs; **desove** *m* spawning; egg-laying; **desovillar** [1a] unwind; unravel (*a. fig.*).
despabiladeras *f/pl.* (*unas* a pair of) snuffers; **despabilado** wide awake (*a. fig.*); **despabilar** [1a] *vela* snuff; *lámpara* trim; *fig. p.* wake up, liven up; F (*robar*) swipe; (*matar*) do in; *fortuna* squander; *negocio* do quickly; *~se* wake up (*a. fig.*); *S.Am.* clear out; *¡despabílate!* get a move on!
despacio 1. slowly; gently; gradually; *¡~!* gently!, easy there!; **2.** *m S.Am.* delaying tactic; **despacioso** slow, phlegmatic; **despacito** = *despacio.*
despachaderas: F *tener buenas ~* be practical, be on the ball; **despachante** *m S.Am.* clerk; **despachar** [1a] *v/t.* (*concluir*) dispatch, settle; *negocio* do, transact; (*enviar*) dispatch, send, post; (*dar prisa a*) expedite; (*vender*) deal in; (*despedir*) send packing; F kill, dispatch; *v/i.* get it settled, come to a decision; (*darse prisa*) hurry; **despacho** *m* office *para negocios*; study *en casa*; (*tienda*) shop; (*mensaje*) dispatch; *~ (de aduana)* clearance; *~ de billetes* booking-office; *tener buen ~* be on top of one's job.
despachurrar [1a] F squash, crush, squelch; *comida* mash; *cuento* make a mess of; *p.* flatten, knock sideways.
despampanante F stunning, tremendous; **despampanar** [1a] *v/t.* ⚕ prune; F knock *s.o.* sideways, bowl *s.o.* over; *v/i.* F talk freely; *~se* F get a nasty knock.
desparej(ad)o uneven; odd.
desparpajo *m* ease of manner, self-confidence, charm *en el trato*; *b.s.*

glibness; savoir faire *en obrar*; *b.s.* (*descaro*) nerve, cheek.

desparramado wide, open; **desparramar** [1a] scatter, spread (*por* over); *fortuna* squander; ~se F have a whale of a time.

despatarrada *f* F the splits; **despatarrarse** [1a] F do the splits; sprawl on the floor.

despavorido terrified.

despeado foot-sore; **despearse** [1a] get foot-sore.

despectivo contemptuous, scornful; derogatory; *gr.* pejorative.

despechar [1a] spite; (*irritar*) stir up, enrage; **despecho** *m* spite; despair; *a* ~ *de* in spite of; *orden etc.* in defiance of; *por* ~ out of spite.

despedazar [1f] tear apart, tear to pieces; *fig. honra* ruin; *corazón* break.

despedida *f* farewell, send-off; leave-taking; dismissal; *de* ~ farewell *attr.*, parting *attr.*; **despedir** [3l] *amigo* see off *en estación*, see out *en puerta*; *importuno* send away; *obrero* dismiss, discharge, sack; *olor* emit, give off; (*soltar*) get rid of; ~ *de sí fig.* put out of one's mind; ~se say good-bye, take one's leave; ~ *de* say good-bye to, take leave of; see off *en estación etc.*

despegar [1h] *v/t.* unstick, detach; *sobre* open; *v/i.* ✈ take off; ~se come unstuck; ~ *con* not go well with; **despego** *m* = *desapego*; **despegue** *m* ✈ take-off.

despeinado dishevelled, unkempt; **despeinar** [1a] tousle, ruffle.

despejado clear, open; *cielo* cloudless; *fig. p.* bright, smart; **despejar** [1a] clear (*a. deportes*); *fig.* clear up, clarify; ⚕ find; ~se *meteor.* clear up; *fig.* amuse o.s., relax; be free and easy *en el trato*; **despeje** *m* *deportes*: clearance; **despejo** *m* self-confidence, ease of manner; brightness.

despellejar [1a] skin (*a. sl.*).

despenar [1a] F bump off, do in.

despendedor extravagant.

despensa *f* pantry, larder; ⚓ *etc.* store-room; (*comida*) stock of food; **despensero** *m* butler, steward.

despeñadero *m* cliff; *fig.* risk, danger; **despeñadizo** precipitous; **despeñar** [1a] hurl (*por* over,

down); ~se hurl o.s. down; fall headlong; *fig.* ~ *en* plunge into; **despeño** *m fig.* failure, collapse.

despepitarse [1a] bawl, shriek; ~ *por* be crazy about.

desperdiciar [1b] waste, fritter away; *oportunidad* throw away; **desperdicio** *m* waste, wasting; ~s *pl.* rubbish, refuse; scraps; *biol.* waste products; F *no tener* ~ be just fine.

desperdigar [1h] scatter, separate.

desperezarse [1f] stretch (o.s.).

desperfecto *m* (*daño*) slight damage; (*falta*) flaw, imperfection.

despernado weary, foot-sore.

despertador *m* alarm-clock; (*p.*) knocker-up; *fig.* warning; **despertamiento** *m* awakening; *eccl. etc.* revival; **despertar** [1k] *v/t.* wake (up); *fig. recuerdos* revive, recall; *esperanzas* raise; (*excitar*) arouse, stir up; *v/i.*, ~se wake up, awaken.

despiadado merciless, remorseless.

despicar [1g] satisfy; ~se get satisfaction, get even.

despierto awake; *fig.* alert, watchful; (*listo*) wide awake.

despilfarrado(r) extravagant, wasteful; (*andrajoso*) shabby; **despilfarrar** [1a] waste, squander; **despilfarro** *m* extravagance, waste, wastefulness; (*desaseo*) shabbiness, slovenliness.

despintar [1a] *v/t.* take the paint off; *fig.* spoil, alter, distort; *v/i.*: ~ *de* be unworthy of; ~se fade, lose its colour; *no se me despinta* I always remember it (*or* him *etc.*).

despiojar [1a] delouse; F rescue *s.o.* from the gutter.

despique *m* revenge.

despistado F **1.** (all) at sea, off the beam; absentminded; **2.** *m* absentminded sort; **despistar** [1a] *hunt. a. fig.* throw *s.o.* off the scent; *fig.* mislead; **despiste** *m mot.* swerve; F absence of mind; confusion; (*desliz*) slip; *tener un terrible* ~ be hopelessly unpractical.

desplacer 1. [2x] displease; **2.** *m* displeasure.

desplantador *m* trowel; **desplantar** [1a] pull up, uproot; *fig.* move out of vertical.

desplazado *m*, **a** *f* outsider; misfit; (*refugiado*) displaced person; **des-**

plazamiento *m* ⚓ displacement; **desplazar** [1f] ⚓ displace; *fig.* displace, take the place of; ⁓**se** move, shift; (*p.*) go, travel.

desplegar [1h *a.* 1k] (*en general*) open (out), unfold; *alas etc.* spread; *velas* unfurl; ✕ deploy; *energía etc.* display; *lo oculto* clarify, elucidate; ⁓**se** open (out) *etc.*; **despliegue** *m* *fig.* display; ✕ deployment.

desplomarse [1a] ⚠ lean, bulge; (*caer*) collapse, tumble (down); ✈ make a pancake landing; *fig.* (*p.*) crumple up; (*gobierno*) collapse; **desplome** *m* collapse *etc.*; ✈ pancake landing; *fig.* collapse, downfall.

desplumar [1a] pluck; *fig.* fleece.

despoblación *f* depopulation; ⁓ *del campo* drift from the land; **despoblado** *m* deserted spot, uninhabited place; **despoblar** [1m] depopulate; *fig.* lay waste.

despojar [1a]: ⁓ *de* strip of; *esp. fig.* divest of, denude of; ⚖ dispossess of; ⁓**se de** *ropa* strip off, take off; *hojas etc.* shed; *fig.* divest o.s. of, give up; **despojo** *m* (*acto*) spoliation, despoilment; (*lo robado*) plunder, spoils; ⁓**s** *pl.* leavings, scraps; offal *de animal*; (*restos mortales*) mortal remains; ⚠ rubble; *geol.* debris.

despolvorear [1a] dust.

desportilladura *f* chip; **desportillar(se)** [1a] chip.

desposado recently married; *los* ⁓**s** the bridal couple; **desposar** [1a] marry; ⁓**se** get engaged; (*casarse*) get married.

desposeer [2e] dispossess (*de* of), oust (*de* from); ⁓**se de** give up; **desposeído**: *los* ⁓**s** *m/pl.* *fig.* the have-nots; **desposeimiento** *m* dispossession.

desposorios *m/pl.* engagement.

déspota *m* despot; **despótico** despotic; **despotismo** *m* despotism.

despotricar [1g] F rant, carry on.

despreciable *p.* despicable; (*de baja calidad*) trashy, worthless; miserable; (*muy pequeño*) negligible; **despreciar** [1b] scorn, despise, look down on; (*desairar*) slight, spurn; (*subestimar*) underrate; ⁓**se de** *inf.* think it beneath one to *inf.*; **despreciativo** *tono etc.* contemptuous; *observación* dis-

paraging, derogatory; **desprecio** *m* scorn, contempt.

desprender [2a] unfasten, detach; separate; *gas etc.* give off; ⁓**se** ⊕ *etc.* work loose, fall off, fly off; ⁓ *de* give up; *fig.* follow from, be implied by; *se desprende que* we learn that; **desprendimiento** *m* *fig.* disinterestedness; generosity; ⁓ *de tierras* landslide.

despreocupación *f* unconcern *etc.*; **despreocupado** unconcerned, nonchalant, carefree; unconventional, free and easy; impartial.

desprestigiar [1b] disparage, run down; cheapen; ⁓**se** lose caste, lose prestige; **desprestigio** *m* loss of prestige; unpopularity.

desprevención *f* unreadiness; lack of foresight; **desprevenido** unprepared; *coger* ⁓ catch *s.o.* unawares (*or* off guard).

desproporción *f* disproportion; **desproporcionado** disproportionate.

despropósito *m* (piece of) nonsense, silly thing.

desprovisto *de* devoid of.

después 1. *adv.* afterwards, later; (*en orden*) next; (*desde entonces*) since (then); (*luego*) next, then; *poco* ⁓ soon after; **2.** *prp.*: ⁓ *de* after; since; ⁓ *de inf.* after *ger.*; *el primero* ⁓ *de* the next to; ⁓ *de descubierta América* after the discovery of America; **3.** *cj.*: ⁓ (*de*) *que* after.

despuntado blunt; **despuntar** [1a] *v/t.* blunt; *v/i.* ♀ sprout, begin to show; (*alba*) dawn, appear; (*p.*) sparkle; (*descollar*) stand out.

desquiciar [1b] *puerta* unhinge (*a. fig.*); *fig.* upset, turn upside down; (*turbar*) disturb; F lever *s.o.* out.

desquitarse [1a] get satisfaction; ✝ get one's money back; (*vengarse*) get even (*con* with), get one's own back (*con* on); **desquite** *m* revenge, retaliation; (*partido de*) ⁓ return match.

desrazonable unreasonable.

destacado outstanding; **destacamento** *m* ✕ detachment; **destacar** [1g] emphasize, give due prominence to; *paint.* make *s.t.* stand out; ✕ detach, detail; ⁓**se** stand out (*a. paint. etc.*); ⁓ *contra*, ⁓ *en*,

~ *sobre* stand out against; *cielo etc.* be silhouetted against.

destajar [1a] arrange for, contract for; *baraja* cut; **destajero** *m*, **destajista** *m* pieceworker; **destajo** *m* (*en general*) piecework, contract work; (*tarea*) job, stint; *a* ~ by the job; *fig.* eagerly, keenly; *trabajar a* ~ be on piece-work; *trabajo a* ~ piece-work; F *hablar a* ~ talk nineteen to the dozen.

destapar [1a] *botella* open, uncork; *caja* open, take the lid off; *fig.* reveal; **destaponar** [1a] uncork.

destartalado *casa* tumbledown; (*mal dispuesto*) rambling; *máquina etc.* rickety.

destazar [1f] cut up.

destejer [2a] undo, unravel; *fig.* upset.

destellar [1a] flash; sparkle; glint, gleam; **destello** *m* flash *etc.*

destemplado ♪ out of tune; *voz* harsh, unpleasant; **destemplanza** *f* *meteor.* inclemency, bleakness; ♪ indisposition; *fig.* lack of moderation; **destemplar** [1a] upset, disturb; ♪ untune; ~se ♪ get out of tune; *fig.* get worked up; **destemple** *m* upset (*a.* ♂), disturbance. [out of.\
desteñir [3l] fade, take the colour⌡

desternillarse [1a]: *v. risa.*

desterrado *m*, *a f* exile; **desterrar** [1k] exile; banish (*a. fig.*).

destetar [1a] wean; **destete** *m* weaning.

destierro *m* exile.

destilación *f* distillation; **destilador** *m* ⚗ still; (*p.*) distiller; **destilar** *v/t.* distil; *sangre etc.* ooze, exude; *v/i.* fall (drop by drop); filter through; **destilatorio** *m* still; **destilería** *f* distillery.

destinar [1a] destine (*a, para* for, to); intend, mean (*a, para* for); *fondos etc.* earmark (*a* for); *empleado* appoint, assign (*a* to); ✕ *etc.* post (*a* to); *estar destinado a inf.* be destined to *inf.*; *venir destinado a* (*carta*) be addressed to; **destinatario** *m*, **a** *f* addressee; **destino** *m* (*suerte*) destiny, fate; (*blanco*, ⚓ *etc.*) destination; (*puesto*) job, post; *con* ~ *a* bound for; *salir con* ~ *a* leave for.

destitución *f* dismissal; **destituir** [3g] dismiss, remove (*de* from).

destorcer [2b *a.* 2h] untwist; *vara etc.* straighten; ~se ⚓ get off course.

destornillador *m* screw-driver; **destornillar** [1a] unscrew; ~se *fig.* go out of one's mind.

destrabar [1a] loosen; *preso* unfetter.

destraillar [1a] unleash.

destral *m* hatchet.

destreza *f* skill, handiness, dexterity.

destripaterrones *m* F clodhopper; **destripar** [1a] gut, draw, paunch; disembowel; *fig.* mangle, crush; *cuento* spoil.

destronar [1a] dethrone; *fig.* overthrow.

destroncar [1g] ♀ chop off; *p.* maim; *fig.* ruin; *animal* wear out.

destrozar [1f] smash (*a.* ✕), shatter; mangle; tear to pieces, *esp. fig.* ravage, ruin; **destrozo** *m* destruction; massacre *de ps.*; *esp.* ~s *pl.* ravages, havoc; **destrozón** F hard on one's clothes.

destrucción *f* destruction; **destructible** destructible; **destructivo** destructive; **destructor 1.** destructive; **2.** *m* destroyer (*a.* ⚓); **destruir** [3g] destroy; ruin, wreck; *argumento* demolish; ~se ⚗ cancel out.

desuncir [3b] unyoke.

desunión *f* disconnection, separation; *fig.* disunity; **desunir** [3a] separate, sever; ⊕ disconnect, disengage; *fig.* cause a rift between.

desuñarse [1a] work one's fingers to the bone (*por inf.* to *inf.*).

desusado obsolete, out of date; ~ *de no longer in use by*; **desusar** [1a] stop using; ~se go out of use; **desuso** *m* disuse; *caer en* ~ fall into disuse; *caído en* ~ obsolete.

desvaído gaunt; *color* dull.

desvainar [1a] shell.

desvalido *niño etc.* helpless; *p.* destitute; *pol.* underprivileged.

desvalijar [1a] rob, plunder.

desvalimiento *m* helplessness.

desvalorización *f* devaluation; **desvalorizar** [1f] devalue.

desván *m* loft, attic.

desvanecer [2d] make *s.o.* disappear; *duda etc.* dispel; ~se disappear, vanish; (*atenuarse*) melt away, dissolve; evaporate; *esp. fig.* fade away, fade out (*a. radio*); ♂

faint; **desvanecimiento** m disappearance etc.; 🗲 fainting fit; dizzy spell; fig. vanity; radio: fading.

desvarar [1a] refloat.

desvariar [1c] rave, talk nonsense; 🗲 be delirious; **desvario** m delirium; fig. whim, strange notion; esp. ⹁s pl. ravings, ramblings.

desvelado sleepless, wakeful; vigilant; **desvelar** [1a] keep s.o. awake; ⹁se stay awake, have a sleepless night; ⹁ por su. be much concerned about; ⹁ por inf. do everything possible to inf.; **desvelo** m watchfulness, vigilance; ⹁s pl. care, concern.

desvencijado ramshackle, rickety; **desvencijarse** [1a] fall apart, break down.

desventaja f disadvantage; (estorbo) handicap, liability; **desventajoso** disadvantageous.

desventura f misfortune; **desventurado 1.** unfortunate; miserable, wretched; **2.** m, a f wretch, unfortunate.

desvergonzado 1. shameless; impudent; unblushing; **2.** m, a f shameless person; **desvergonzarse** [1f a. 1m] behave in a shameless way, be impudent (con to); **desvergüenza** f shamelessness; impudence; ¡qué ⹁! what a nerve!; what a shocking thing!; tener la ⹁ de inf. have the nerve to inf.

desviación f deflection, deviation (a. de brújula); mot. diversion; (carretera) bypass; fig. departure (de from); **desviar** [1c] turn aside, deflect, divert (a. fig., mot.; de from); ⚡ switch; golpe parry, ward off; fig. dissuade, side-track (de propósito from); ween away (de mala compañía from); ⹁se deviate (de curso etc. from); turn aside, turn away; mot. etc. swerve; ⚓ sheer off; ⚓ go off course; wander (de tema from); **desvío** m deflection, deviation; mot. etc. swerve; (camino) detour; 🚢 siding; fig. coldness, dislike.

desvirtuar [1e] impair, spoil; detract from; ⹁se spoil.

desvivirse [3a]: ⹁ por su. crave, be crazy about; ⹁ por inf. go out of one's way to inf., be eager to inf.

detallado detailed; conocimiento intimate; **detallar** [1a] itemize, specify; suceso etc. tell in detail; **detalle** m detail; item; F token, (nice) gesture ⹁s pl. a. particulars; al ⹁ retail; en ⹁ in detail; F ¡qué ⹁! how sweet of you!; vender al ⹁ retail; **detallista** m/f retailer.

detective m detective.

detector m ⚡, radio: detector.

detención f stoppage, hold-up; (retraso) delay; ⚖ detention; ⹁ ilegal unlawful detention; **detener** [2l] (parar) stop, hold up, check; (guardar) keep, hold (back), retain; p. (retrasar) keep, delay; (abordar) stop, accost; ⚖ detain; ⹁se stop (a inf. to inf.); delay, linger; pause antes de obrar; **detenidamente** thoroughly; at (great) length; **detenido** cuento detailed; lengthy; examen thorough; fig. timid; (escaso) sparing, niggardly; **detenimiento**: con ⹁ thoroughly.

detergente adj. a. su. m detergent.

deteriorar [1a] spoil, damage, impair; ⹁se deteriorate, spoil; **deterioro** m deterioration; damage; (desgaste) wear (and tear).

determinable determinable; **determinación** f determination; decision; **determinado** (resuelto) determined, purposeful; (cierto) certain, set; un libro ⹁ a given book, some particular book; **determinante** adj. a. su. m determinant; **determinar** [1a] mst determine; fecha, precio a. fix; contribución, daños a. assess; curso a. shape; pleito decide; ⹁ a uno a inf. lead s.o. to inf.; ⹁ inf. = ⹁se a inf. decide to inf., determine to inf.

detestable detestable, odious; damnable; **detestación** f detestation, loathing; **detestar** [1a] detest, hate, loath.

detonación f detonation; **detonador** m detonator; **detonar** [1a] detonate, explode.

detracción f disparagement; **detractor 1.** slanderous; **2.** m, -a f slanderer, detractor.

detrás behind; por ⹁ behind; atacar etc. from behind, from the rear; ⹁ de behind; por ⹁ de fig. behind s.o.'s back.

detrimento m damage, detriment.

detrito m detritus, debris.

deuda f debt; (en general) indebtedness; (pecado) sin; ⹁s pl. (pasivas) liabilities; ~ pública national debt; lleno de ~s heavily in debt; estar en ~ owe (por for); estar en ~ con be indebted to; **deudo** m relative; **deudor 1.** saldo debit attr.; le soy muy ~ I am much indebted to you; **2.** m, -a f debtor.

devanadera f sew. reel, winding-frame; **devanado** m ∮ winding; **devanar** [1a] wind; v. seso.

devanear [1a] rave, talk nonsense; **devaneo** m ravings, nonsense; ✿ delirium; (amorío) affair.

devastación f devastation; **devastar** [1a] devastate, lay waste.

devengar [1h] sueldo draw; interés earn, bear.

devenir 1. [3s] become; **2.** m evolution, process of development.

devoción f devotion (a to); devoutness, piety; fig. liking (a for); estar a la ~ de be completely under s.o.'s thumb; tener gran ~ a be greatly devoted to; tener por ~ inf. be in the habit of ger.; **devocionario** m prayerbook.

devolución f return; ✝ repayment, refund; **devolver** [2h; p.p. devuelto] return, give back, send back; ✝ repay, refund; golpe return; restore (a estado primitivo to); F throw up; ~se S.Am. return.

devorador devouring; **devorar** [1a] devour (a. fig.).

devoto 1. eccl. devout; devoted; obra etc. devotional; **2.** m, a f eccl. devout person; worshipper en iglesia; fig. devotee, votary; los ~s the faithful.

deyección f (a. ~es pl.) ✿ motion; geol. debris, lava.

di etc. v. dar.

día m day; daytime; daylight; ¡buenos ~s! good morning!, good day!; ocho ~s freq. week; quince ~s freq. fortnight; ~ de boda wedding day; ~ feriado, ~ festivo, ~ de fiesta holiday; eccl. feast day; ~ hábil working day; ⚖ court-day; ~-hombre man-day; ~ laborable working day, week-day; ~ libre free day; day off; ~ malo, ~ nulo off day; ♘ de la Raza Columbus Day (12 October); ~ señalado red-letter day; todo el santo ~ the whole day long; al ~ 'up to date; (proporción) a day; a los pocos ~s within a few days; al otro ~ on the following day; el otro ~ the other day; otro ~ some other day; another day; algún ~ some day, sometime; F ¡cualquier ~! not on your life!; de ~ by day, in the daytime; del ~ fashionable, up to date; el ~ de hoy today; v. hoy; el mejor ~ some fine day; el ~ menos pensado when you least expect it; en pleno ~ in broad daylight; en ~s de Dios never; ~ tras ~ day after day, day in day out; un ~ sí y otro no on alternate days, every other day; ✝ poner al ~ write up; ponerse al ~ get up to date, catch up; vivir al ~ live from hand to mouth.

diabetes f diabetes; **diabético** adj. a. su. m, a f diabetic.

diabla: F a la ~ any old how; **diablillo** m F imp, monkey; **diablo** m devil (a. fig.); ¡(qué) ~(s)! the devil!, oh hell!; F como el ~ like the devil; un ruido de todos los ~s a hell of a noise; pobre ~ poor devil; F ahí será el ~ there'll be the devil to pay; F tener el ~ en el cuerpo (niño) be full of mischief; ¡vete al ~! go to hell!; **diablura** f devilry; (de niño) mischief; ~s pl. monkey tricks; **diabólico** diabolic(al), devilish, fiendish.

diaconía f deaconry; **diaconisa** f deaconess; **diácono** m deacon.

diadema f diadem; tiara de mujer.

diáfano diaphanous, transparent; filmy; agua limpid.

diafragma m diaphragm; **diagnosis** f diagnosis; **diagnosticar** [1g] diagnose; **diagnóstico** m diagnosis; diagonal adj. a. su. f diagonal; **diagrama** m diagram.

dialéctica f dialectics; **dialéctico** dialectic(al); **dialecto** m dialect.

dialogar [1h] v/t. write in dialogue form; v/i. talk, converse; **diálogo** m dialogue.

diamante m diamond; naipes: ~s pl. diamonds; **diamantino** diamond-like, adamantine; **diamantista** m diamond-cutter; ✝ diamond merchant.

diametral diametrical; **diámetro** m diameter.

diana f ✖ reveille.

¡diantre! F oh hell!

diapasón m diapason; ~ (normal) tuning-fork.

diapositiva *f* (lantern-)slide; *phot.* transparency.
diario 1. daily; day-to-day; everyday; **2.** *m* (*periódico*) newspaper, daily; (*relación personal*) diary; ✝ daybook; (*gastos*) daily expenses; ~ de a bordo, ~ de navegación logbook; a ~ daily; **diarista** *m/f* diarist.
diarrea *f* diarrhoea.
diarrucho *m S.Am.* F rag.
diatermia *f* diathermy.
diatónico diatonic.
diatriba *f* diatribe, tirade.
dibujante *m* ⊕ draughtsman (*a. paint.*), designer; cartoonist *de periódico*; **dibujar** [1a] draw, sketch; ⊕ design; *fig.* draw, depict; **~se** *contra* be outlined against;
dibujo *m* (*en general*) drawing, sketching; (*un* ~) drawing, sketch; ⊕ design; cartoon *de periódico*; caricature; *fig.* description; *cine:* ~ animado cartoon.
dicción *f* diction; (*palabra*) word; **diccionario** *m* dictionary; ~ geográfico gazetteer.
diciembre *m* December.
dictado *m* dictation; title of honour; ~s *pl.* dictates; *escribir al* ~ take dictation, take down; **dictador** *m* dictator; **dictadura** *f* dictatorship; **dictáfono** *m* dictaphone; **dictamen** *m* opinion, dictum; judgement; *tomar* ~ *de* consult with; **dictaminar** [1a] *v/t. juicio* pass; *v/i.* pass judgement (en on); **dictar** [1a] dictate; inspire; *sentencia* pass, pronounce; *S.Am. clase* give, *conferencia* deliver; **dictatorial, dictatorio** dictatorial; **dicterio** *m* taunt, insult.
dicha *f* happiness; (*suerte*) (good) luck; *por* ~ by chance.
dicharachero *m* F witty person; *b.s.* coarse sort; **dicharacho** *m* dirty thing, coarse remark.
dicho 1. *p.p. of decir*; ~ y hecho no sooner said than done; *lo* ~, ~ I stand by what I said; **2.** *m* (*proverbio*) saying; tag; (*chiste*) bright remark; F insult; F ~ gordo rude thing.
dichoso (*feliz*) happy; (*con suerte*) lucky; (*que trae dicha*) blessed (*a.* F).
didáctico didactic.
dieciséis *etc. v.* Apéndice.
diente *m* tooth (*a.* ⊕, *fig.*); cog *de*

rueda; ~ de ajo clove of garlic; ~ canino canine (tooth); ~ incisivo incisor; ~ de leche milk tooth; ✠ ~ de león dandelion; ~s *pl. postizos* false teeth; *daba* ~ *con* ~ his teeth were chattering; he was trembling like a leaf; F *enseñar los* ~s show fight, turn nasty; F *estar a* ~ be ravenous; *hablar entre* ~s mumble; *hincar el* ~ *en* sink one's teeth into; *fig.* get one's knife into; *tener buen* ~ be a hearty eater.
Diesel: *motor* ~ Diesel engine.
diestra *f* right hand; **diestro 1.** (*derecho*) right; (*hábil*) skilful (*en* in, at); handy, deft *con manos*; (*sagaz*) shrewd; *b.s.* sly; *a* ~ *y siniestro* wildly, all over the place; **2.** *m toros:* matador.
dieta *f* diet (*a. pol.*); ~s *pl.* subsistence allowance; *estar a* ~ (be on a) diet; *poner a* ~ put on a diet; **dietético 1.** dietary; **2.** *m* dietician.
diez ten (*a. su.*); (*fecha*) tenth; *las* ~ ten o'clock; **diezmar** [1a] decimate (*a. fig.*); **diezmo** *m* tithe.
difamación *f* slander, defamation; libel (de on); **difamador 1.** slanderous, libellous, defamatory; **2.** *m*, **-a** *f* defamer; scandal-monger; **difamar** [1a] slander, defame; libel *esp. por escrito*; malign; **difamatorio** = difamador 1.
diferencia *f* difference; *a* ~ *de* unlike; in contrast to; *con corta* ~ more or less; *partir la* ~ split the difference; *fig.* meet s.o. half-way; **diferencial 1.** differential; *impuesto* discriminatory; **2.** *f* ⊕, *mot.* differential; **diferenciar** [1b] *v/t.* differentiate between; *v/i.* differ (de from), be in disagreement (en over); **~se** (*discordar*) differ (de from); (*ser diferente*) be distinguishable; differentiate (*a.* ✠ *etc.*); *fig.* distinguish ó.s.; **diferente** different (de from); unlike (de *acc.*); ~s *pl.* (*varios*) several; **diferir** [3i] *v/t.* defer, put off, hold over; *v/i.* differ, be different (de from).
difícil difficult, hard (de *inf.* to *inf.*); *es* ~ *que* it is unlikely that, it is doubtful if; **difícilmente** with difficulty; ~ *será verdad* this can hardly be true; **dificultad** *f* difficulty; trouble; objection; **dificultar** [1a] make *s.t.* difficult; hinder, obstruct; interfere with; ~ que think

it unlikely that; **dificultoso** awkward, troublesome; F ugly; F (*que estorba*) awkward, full of silly objections.

difteria *f* diphtheria.

difundir [3a] spread, diffuse, disseminate; *alegría etc.* radiate.

difunto dead, defunct; *el ~, la ~a* the deceased; *el ~ rey* the late king; *día de* ♀s All Souls' Day.

difusión *f* spread, diffusion, dissemination; (*prolijidad*) diffuseness; **difusivo** diffusive; **difuso** widespread; *luz* diffused; (*prolijo*) diffuse, discursive.

digerible digestible; **digerir** [3i] digest (*a. fig.*); (*tragar*) swallow; (*aguantar*) stomach; **digestibilidad** *f* digestibility; **digestible** digestible; **digestión** *f* digestion; **digestivo** digestive; **digesto** *m* 👥 digest.

digitación *f* ♪ fingering; **digital 1.** digital; *huella etc.* finger *attr.*; **2.** *f* ⚘ foxglove; **dígito** *m* digit.

dignación *f* condescension; **dignarse** [1a]: *~ inf.* condescend to *inf.*; deign to *inf.*; **dignatario** *m* dignitary; **dignidad** *f* (*gravedad*) dignity; (*cargo*) rank; (*respeto*) self-respect; (*p.*) worthy, dignitary; **dignificar** [1g] dignify; **digno** (*honrado*) worthy; (*grave*) dignified; (*apropiado*) fitting; *~ de* worthy of, deserving; fit for; *~ de mención* worth mentioning; *~ de verse* worth seeing; *ser ~ de a.* deserve.

digresión *f* digression.

dije¹ *etc. v.* decir.

dije² *m* trinket; medallion, locket; amulet; F (*p.*) treasure, gem.

dilación *f* delay; procrastination; *sin ~* without delay, forthwith.

dilapidar [1a] squander.

dilatación *f* dilat(at)ion; *phys.* expansion; *fig.* calm; **dilatado** vast, extensive; numerous; (*prolijo*) long-winded; **dilatar** [1a] stretch, dilate, distend, expand (*a. phys.*); *fama etc.* spread; (*retrasar*) delay, put off; protract; *~se* stretch *etc.*; *fig.* be long-winded; *~ en, ~ sobre* dilate upon, linger over; **dilativo** dilatory; **dilatorias** *f/pl.* delaying tactics.

dilema *m* dilemma.

diletante *m/f* dilettante.

diligencia *f* diligence; † stage-

coach; (*prisa*) speed; F errand, piece of business; *~s pl. previas* inquest; F *hacer una ~* run an errand; *poner ~ en inf.* be careful to *inf.*; **diligenciar** [1b] see about; **diligente** diligent, assiduous; (*pronto*) quick; *poco ~* slack.

dilucidar [1a] elucidate.

dilución *f* dilution; **diluir** [3g] dilute, water down (*a. fig.*).

diluvial *geol.* diluvial; **diluviar** [1b] pour (with rain); **diluvio** *m* deluge, flood (*a. fig.*).

dimanar [1a]: *~ de* arise from.

dimensión *f* dimension; *~es pl.* dimensions, size.

dimes y diretes: F *andar en ~ con* argue with.

diminutivo *adj. a. su. m* diminutive; **diminuto** tiny, minute; dwarf; miniature.

dimisión *f* resignation; **dimitir** [3a] resign (*de* from).

dinamarqués = danés.

dinámica *f* dynamics; *fig.* dynamic; **dinámico** dynamic (*a. fig.*).

dinamita *f* dynamite.

dínamo *f* dynamo. [nastic.\

dinastía *f* dynasty; **dinástico** dy-/

dinerada *f*, **dineral** *m* mint of money; *valer un ~* cost (*or.* be worth) a fortune; **dinerillos** *m/pl.*: *tener ~* have a bit of money; **dinero** *m* money; currency, coinage *de un país*; *hombre de ~* man of means; *~ contante* cash; *~ contante y sonante* hard cash, ready money; *andar mal de ~* be badly off; *dar ~* (*negocio*) make money, pay.

dintel *m* lintel.

diocesano *adj. a. su. m* diocesan; **diócesi(s)** *f* diocese.

Dios *m* God; ♀ god; *~ delante* with God's help; *~ mediante* God willing, D.V.; *¡~ mío!* good gracious!; I ask you!; *a ~ gracias* thank heaven; *a la buena de ~* innocently; *a la de ~* (es Cristo) rashly; *una de ~ es Cristo* a bust-up; *armar la de ~ es Cristo* raise hell; *¡por ~!* for goodness sake!, hang it (all)!; *como ~ manda* as is proper; *¡plegue a ~!* please God!; *~ sabe* God knows; *¡válgame ~!* bless my soul!; *vaya con ~* goodbye; F *iro.* and the best of luck; **diosa** *f* goddess.

diploma *m* diploma; **diplomacia** *f* diplomacy; **diplomado** qualified;

diplomática f diplomatics; (*carrera*) diplomatic corps; **diplomático 1.** diplomatic; tactful; **2.** m diplomat(ist) (*a. fig.*).

dipsomanía f dipsomania; **dipsomaníaco** m, a f dipsomaniac.

diptongo m diphthong.

diputación f deputation, delegation; ~ *provincial* approx. county council (offices); **diputado** m, a f delegate; ~ (*a Cortes*) deputy, member of Parliament; **diputar** [1a] delegate, depute.

dique m (*muro*) dike, sea-wall; (*malecón*) jetty, mole; dam *en río*; dock *de puerto*; ~ *de carena* graving dock; ~ *flotante* floating dock; ~ *seco* dry dock; entrar en ~, hacer ~ dock; poner un ~ a *fig.* check, restrain.

diré etc. v. decir.

dirección f (*línea de movimiento*) direction; way; (*tendencia*) trend, course; (*gobierno*) direction; ✝ etc. management; leading, leadership *de partido* etc.; ♪ conductorship; *mot.* etc. steering; *fig.* guidance; ✝ (*cargo*) directorship; (*junta*) (board of) directors; (*despacho*) manager's office; (*señas*) address; ~ *prohibida* no entry, no thoroughfare; *mot. de ~ columna* etc. steering *attr.*; (*calle de*) ~ *única* one-way (street); ⚡ conmutador de 2 ~es 2-way switch; en la ~ de in the direction of; **direccional** directional; **directivo** *junta* etc. managing, governing; *clase* managerial; administrative; **directo 1.** direct (*a. fig.*), straight; 🚋 through, nonstop; **2.** m *tenis* etc.: forehand; **director 1.** leading, guiding; = directivo; **2.** m director (*a.* ✝, *eccl.*); ✝ manager, executive; editor *de periódico*; ♪ ~ (*de orquesta*) conductor; headmaster *de escuela*; *univ.* master *de colegio*, warden *de residencia*; ~ *de escena* stage manager; producer; ~ *gerente* managing director; **directora** f headmistress (*a.* ~ *de colegio*); *univ.* warden; **directorio** m (*norma*) directive; (*junta*) directorate; ✝ board of directors; (*libro*) directory.

dirigencia f leadership; **dirigente** m leader; **dirigible 1.** *buque* etc. navigable; **2.** m dirigible; **dirigir** [3c] direct (*a, hacia* at, to, towards); *carta, palabra, protesta* address (*a*

to); *libro* dedicate (*a* to); *mirada* turn, direct; ⚓, *mot.* etc. steer; *empresa* run, manage, operate; ♪ conduct; *p.* guide, advise (*en* in); *partido* lead, head; *periódico* edit; *manga* play (*a* on); *actores* produce; *fig. curso* shape; *esfuerzos* concentrate (*a* on), direct (*a* towards); ~se a go to, make one's way to; ⚓ etc. steer, for, make for; *p.* address (o.s. to); apply to *solicitando*; ~ *hacia* head for.

discernidor discerning, discriminating; **discernimiento** m discernment, discrimination; *edad de* ~ years of discretion; **discernir** [3i] discern; distinguish (*de* from); *premio* award.

disciplina f *mst* discipline; doctrine; **disciplinar** [1a] discipline; (*enseñar*) school, train; **disciplinario** disciplinary; ✗ punishment *attr.*; **discipulado** m discipleship; **discípulo** m, a f disciple; pupil.

disco m disk; *deportes:* discus; 🎯 signal; *teleph.* ~ (*de marcar*) dial; ~ (*de gramófono*) (gramophone) record; ~ *microsurco* long-playing record; **discóbolo** m discus-thrower.   [chievous.|

díscolo uncontrollable; *niño* mis-|

disconforme etc. v. desconforme.

discontinuo discontinuous (*a.* ⚡).

discordante discordant; **discordar** [1m] (*ps.*) disagree (*de* with), differ (*de* from); ♪ be out of tune; **discorde** discordant; (*ps.*) in disagreement; ♪ *sonido* discordant; *instrumento* out of tune; **discordia** f discord, disagreement.

discoteca f record library.

discreción f discretion, tact; discrimination; wisdom, shrewdness; secrecy; wit; *a* ~ at one's discretion; ✗ unconditionally; *cocina:* to taste; *comer* etc. ad-lib F; **discrecional** discretionary; optional; *parada* request *attr.*

discrepancia f discrepancy, disagreement; divergence; **discrepante** divergent; dissenting; **discrepar** [1a] differ (*de* from), disagree (*de* with).

discretear [1a] try to be clever, be frightfully witty; **discreto** discreet; tactful; unobtrusive; (*sagaz*) wise, shrewd; (*ingenioso*) witty; *phys.* etc. discrete.

discriminación *f* : ~ *racial* racial discrimination, **discriminar** [1a] *S.Am.* discriminate against.

disculpa *f* excuse, plea; apology; **disculpable** pardonable, excusable; **disculpar** [1a] excuse, pardon; exonerate (*de* from); ~se apologize (*con* to, *de* for).

discurrir [3a] *v t.* invent, think up; *v i.* (*andar*) roam, wander; (*agua*) flow; (*tiempo*) pass; (*meditar*) reason; (*hablar*) discourse (*sobre* about, on); ~ *en* reflect on; **discurso** *m* speech, address; (*en general*, *tratado*) discourse; course *del tiempo*.

discusión *f* discussion; argument; **discutible** debatable, arguable; **discutidor** argumentative; **discutir** [3a] *v/t.* discuss, debate, talk over; argue about; contradict; *v/i.* argue (*sobre* about, over); ¡*no discutas!* don't argue!

disecar [1g] *anat.* dissect (*a. fig.*); stuff *para conservar*; **disección** *f* dissection.

diseminar [1a] scatter; *esp. fig.* disseminate, spread.

disensión *f* dissension.

disentería *f* dysentery.

disentimiento *m* dissent; **disentir** [3i] dissent (*de* from).

diseñador *m* designer; **diseñar** [1a] draw, sketch; ⊕ design; **diseño** *m* drawing, sketch; ⊕ *etc.* design.

disertación *f* dissertation, disquisition; **disertar** [1a]: ~ *acerca de* discuss, expound on.

disfavor *m* disfavour.

disforme badly-proportioned; monstrous; (*feo*) ugly.

disfraz *m* disguise; mask *de cara*; fancy dress *para baile*; **disfrazado** de disguised as, in the guise of; *ir* ~ *de* masquerade as; **disfrazar** [1f] disguise (*de as*; *a. fig.*); *fig.* conceal, cloak; ~se *de* disguise o.s. as.

disfrutar [1a] *v/t.* enjoy; *v/i.* F enjoy o.s.; ¡*cómo disfruto!* this is the life!; ~ *con*, ~ *de* enjoy; **disfrute** *m* enjoyment.

disgregación *f* disintegration; **disgregar(se)** [1h] disintegrate.

disgustar [1a] displease, annoy; ~se be annoyed, get angry (*con*, *de* about); (*enemistarse*) fall out (*con* with); (*aburrirse*) get bored (*de* with); **disgusto** *m* (*desazón*) displeasure, annoyance; (*pesadumbre*) grief, chagrin; (*molestia*) trouble, bother, difficulty; (*disputa*) quarrel, unpleasantness; *a* ~ against one's will.

disidencia *f* dissidence; *eccl.* dissent; **disidente 1.** dissident, dissentient; **2.** *m*/*f* dissident, dissentient; *esp. eccl.* dissenter, nonconformist; **disidir** [3a] dissent.

disílabo 1. disyllabic; **2.** *m* disyllable.

disimulación *f* dissimulation, pretence; **disimulado** furtive, covert, underhand; **disimular** [1a] *v/t.* (*ocultar*, *fingir no sentir*) hide; cloak, disguise; (*perdonar*) excuse; *falta de otro* overlook, condone; *ofensa* pass off; *v/i.* dissemble, pretend; **disimulo** *m* dissimulation; indulgence; *con* ~ craftily.

disipación *f* dissipation (*a. fig.*); **disipado** dissipated, raffish; (*mani-rroto*) extravagant; **disipador** *m* spendthrift; **disipar** [1a] dissipate; *nubes, ilusiones* dispel; *fortuna* fritter away (*en* on); ~se vanish; ♏ evaporate.

dislate *m* silly thing, absurdity.

dislocación *f* dislocation; *geol.* slip; **dislocar** [1g] dislocate.

disminución *f* diminution, decrease *etc.*; *sin* ~ unabated; **disminuir** [3g] *v/t. a. v/i.* diminish, decrease, lessen.

disociación *f* dissociation; **disociar** [1b] dissociate, separate.

disoluble dissoluble, dissolvable; **disolución** *f* dissolution; ♏ solution; (*moral*) dissoluteness; **disoluto** dissolute, dissipated; **disolvente** *adj. a. su. m* dissolvent; **disolver(se)** [2h; *p.p.* disuelto] dissolve (*a. fig.*), melt.

disonancia *f* discord, dissonance; **disonante** discordant, dissonant; **disonar** [1m] ♪ be discordant, sound wrong; *fig.* lack harmony; be out of keeping (*con* with).

dispar unequal, disparate; **disparada** *f S.Am.* sudden flight; *a la* ~ like a shot; **disparado**: *ir* ~ go hell for leather; *salir* ~ be off like a shot; **disparador** *m* ✕ trigger; escapement *de reloj*; *phot.*, ⊕ release; F *poner en el* ~ drive s.o. nuts; **disparar** [1a] *v/t.* ✕ shoot, fire; let off; *piedra etc.* throw, let fly (*contra* at); *v/i.* ✗ fire *etc.*; = *disparatar*; ⁓se ✗ go off; (*caballo*) bolt, run away; (*p. etc.*) rush off, dash away.

disparatado absurd, nonsensical, crazy; **disparatar** [1a] talk nonsense; **disparate** *m* silly thing, foolish remark (*or* idea *etc.*), absurdity; ⁓s *pl.* nonsense, rubbish.

disparidad *f* disparity.

disparo *m* ✗ shot, report; ⊕ trip, release; *fig.* = *disparate*.

dispendio *m* waste; extravagance; **dispendioso** expensive.

dispensa *f eccl. etc.* dispensation; exemption *de examen*; **dispensable** dispensable; **dispensación** *f* dispensation; **dispensador** *m* dispenser; **dispensar** [1a] (*distribuir*) dispense; (*eximir*) exempt, excuse (*de inf.* from *ger.*); *falta* excuse, pardon; ¡*dispense Vd.!* excuse me!; *no puedo* ⁓*me de inf.* I cannot help *ger.*; ⁓ *que subj.* excuse *s.o.* for *ger.*; **dispensario** *m* dispensary.

dispepsia *f* dyspepsia; **dispéptico** dyspeptic.

dispersar [1a] disperse, scatter (*a.* ✗ ⁓se); *manifestación etc.* break up; **dispersión** *f* dispersion (*a. phys.*), dispersal; **disperso** scattered; (*escaso*) sparse.

displicencia *f* indifference; bad temper, peevishness; **displicente** disagreeable, peevish, bad-tempered; fretful.

disponer [2r] *v/t.* (*arreglar*) arrange, dispose, lay out; line up *en fila*; (*preparar*) get ready (*para* for); (*determinar*) decide; ⁓ *que* order that, arrange that, provide that; *v/i.*: ⁓ *de* (*usar*) make use of, avail o.s. of; (*tener listo*) have *s.t.* available, have at one's disposal; ⁓se *a inf.*, ⁓ *para inf.* get ready to *inf.*

disponibilidad *f* availability; **disponible** available; on hand, spare; **disposición** *f* (*arreglo*) arrangement, disposition; lay-out (*a.* △); (*temperamento*) disposition; aptitude (*para* for), turn (of mind); ⁓es *pl.* preparations (*para* for), measures; ⁓ *de ánimo* attitude of mind; *última* ⁓ last will and testament; *a la* ⁓ *de* at the disposal of; *a la* ⁓ *de Vd.*, *a su* ⁓ at your service; *está a su* ⁓ you are welcome to it; *en* ⁓ *de inf.* in a position to *inf.*

dispositivo *m* device, appliance, gadget.

dispuesto 1. *p.p. of disponer*; *bien* ⁓ well-disposed (*hacia* towards); △ well designed; *mal* ⁓ ✗ indisposed; *poco* ⁓ *a inf.* reluctant to *inf.*, loath to *inf.*; *estar* ⁓ *a inf.* be prepared to *inf.*, be disposed to *inf.*; **2.** *adj.* handsome; graceful; (*hábil*) clever.

disputa *f* dispute, argument; *en* ⁓ at issue; *sin* ⁓ beyond dispute; **disputable** debatable, disputable; **disputador 1.** disputatious; **2.** *m* disputant; **disputar** [1a] *v/t.* dispute, challenge; debate; *v/i.* debate (*de, sobre* on; *con* with); argue (*de, sobre* about); ⁓se *algo* fight for.

distancia *f* distance (*a. fig.*); ⁓ *focal* focal distance; *a* ⁓ at a distance; *a gran* ⁓, *a larga* ⁓ *attr.* long-distance; *mantener a* ⁓ keep *s.o.* away, hold *s.o.* off; *mantenerse a* ⁓ keep one's distance, stand aloof; **distanciar** [1b] *objetos* space out; *rival* outdistance; ⁓se (*dos ps.*) be estranged; ⁓ *de rival* get ahead of; **distante** distant; **distar** [1a]: *dista 10 km. de aquí* it is 10 km. (away) from here; *dista mucho* it is a long way away; ¿*dista mucho?* is it far?; *dista de ser adj.* it is a long way from being *adj.*

distender [2g] distend; **distensión** *f* distension.

dístico *m* distich.

distinción *f* distinction (*a. honor*), difference; (*lo distinto*) distinctness; *fig.* elegance; *a* ⁓ *de* unlike; **distingo** *m* reservation; objection; subtle distinction; **distinguible** distinguishable; **distinguido** distinguished; *modales etc.* gentlemanly, ladylike; elegant; **distinguir** [3d] (*divisar*) distinguish, make out; (*separar*) distinguish (*de* from, *entre* between), tell (*de* from); (*caracterizar*) distinguish, mark; single *s.o.* out; *amigo* have a special regard for; honour, bestow an honour upon; ⁓se distinguish o.s.; stand out, be distinguished; **distintivo 1.** distinctive; *señal* distinguishing; **2.** *m* badge; *fig.* distinguishing mark, characteristic; **distinto** different, distinct (*de* from); clear, distinct; ⁓s *pl.* (*varios*) several.

distorsión *f radio:* distortion.

distracción f distraction; amusement; absence of mind; *por ~* through sheer forgetfulness; **distraer** [2p] *v/t.* distract, divert, lead *s.o.* away (*de* from); (*entretener*) amuse; (*moralmente*) lead *s.o.* astray; *v/i.*: *el paseo distrae* walking is a relaxation; *~se* amuse o.s.; **distraído** absentminded; vague, dreamy; *b.s.* inattentive, lackadaisical.

distribución f distribution; (*arreglo*) arrangement; ⊕ timing gears; **distribuido:** △ *bien ~* well designed; **distribuidor** m distributor (*a. mot.*); ✝ dealer, stockist; *~ automático* vending machine; **distribuidora** f ✝ distributor(s); **distribuir** [3g] distribute; hand out; give out, send out; ⅋ deliver; △ design, plan; **distributivo** distributive (*a. gr.*).

distrito m district, administrative area; ⅋ circuit; *~ electoral* constituency *de diputado*, ward *de concejal*.

disturbio m disturbance; *~ aerodinámico* wash.

disuadir [3a] dissuade (*de inf.* from *ger.*), deter, discourage; **disuasión** f disuasion *etc.*; **disuasivo** deterrent, dissuasive.

disyuntivo disjunctive (*a. gr.*).

diurno day *attr.*, diurnal ◷.

diva f prima donna.

divagación f digression; *~es pl.* wanderings, ramblings; **divagador** rambling; **divagar** [1h] ramble *en discurso*; wander *en mente*; (*salir del tema*) digress.

diván m divan.

divergencia f divergence; **divergente** divergent; **divergir** [3c] diverge.

diversidad f diversity, variety; **diversificación** f diversification; **diversificar** [1g] diversify.

diversión f amusement, entertainment; pastime; ⅋ diversion; *~es pl. de salón* indoor games; **diverso** 1. diverse; different (*de* from); *~s pl.* several, various, sundry; 2. *m/pl.* ✝ (*en lista*) miscellaneous.

divertido *libro etc.* entertaining, enjoyable; *fiesta* merry, gay; *chiste, p.* funny, amusing; *S.Am.* tight; **divertimiento** m amusement, entertainment; **divertir** [3i] amuse,

entertain; *~se* have a good time, amuse o.s. (*en hacer* doing); *~ con amor etc.* toy with.

dividendo m dividend; **dividir** [3a] divide (up; *en* into, *por* by); share (out), split (up).

divieso m boil.

divinidad f divinity; godhead; (*dios pagano*) god(dess *f*); *fig.* beauty; **divinizar** [1f] deify; *fig.* exalt; **divino** divine (*a. fig.*).

divisa f emblem, badge; *heráldica:* motto, device; *~s pl.* ✝ foreign exchange; *control de ~s* exchange control.

divisar [1a] make out; (e)spy.

divisible divisible; **división** f division (*a. ✕*); *pol. etc.* split; **divisional** ✕ divisional; **divisor** m: *máximo común ~* highest common factor; **divisoria** f *geog.* divide; **divisorio** dividing; *línea ~a de las aguas* watershed.

divorciado m, **a** f divorcee; **divorciar** [1b] divorce (*a. fig.*); *~se* get divorced, get a divorce (*de* from); **divorcio** m divorce.

divulgación f disclosure *etc.*; **divulgar** [1h] *secreto* divulge, disclose, let out; (*publicar*) spread, circulate; popularize; *~se* (*secreto*) leak out; (*rumor*) get about.

dobladillar [1a] hem; **dobladillo** m hem; turn-up *de pantalón*; **doblado** double; (*cuerpo*) thickset; *terreno* rough; (*taimado*) sly; **dobladura** f fold, crease; **doblaje** m *cine:* dubbing; **doblar** [1a] *v/t.* double (*a. thea., bridge*); (*plegar*) fold (up), crease; *página etc.* turn down; *dobladillo etc.* turn up; (*torcer*) bend; ⚓ *cabo* round; *esquina* turn, round; *cine:* dub; *v/i.* (*torcer*) turn; ♪ toll; *thea.* stand in; *~se* double (*plegarse*) fold (up); bend, buckle; (*ceder*) give in (*a* to), yield.

doble 1. double (*a. ⚓, sentido*); *fondo* false; *mando* dual; *paño extra* thick; *p.* two-faced, deceitful; 2. *m* (*pliegue*) fold, crease; ♪ knell; ♪ tolling; *el ~* twice the quantity; ✝ twice the amount; *pagar el ~ por* pay twice as much for; *ser el ~ de p.* be the double of; *tenis etc.*: *juego de ~s* doubles; *al ~* doubly; 3. *m/f cine etc.*: double, stand-in.

doblegar [1h] (*plegar*) fold; (*torcer*)

bend; *p.* persuade, sway; (*rendir*) force *s.o.* to give in; ~se (*p.*) give in.
doblez 1. *m* fold, crease; **2.** *f* double-dealing, duplicity.
dócar *m* dog cart.
doce twelve (*a. su.*); (*fecha*) twelfth; *las* ~ twelve o'clock; **docena** *f* dozen; ~ *de fraile* baker's dozen; *a* ~s by the dozen.
docente educational; *centro, personal* teaching *attr.*; **dócil** docile; obedient; gentle; **docilidad** *f* docility; gentleness.
docto 1. learned; **2.** *m* scholar; **doctor** *m* doctor; **doctora** *f* ℱ blue-stocking; ℱ woman doctor; **doctorado** *m* doctorate; **doctoral** doctoral; **doctorarse** [1a] take one's doctorate.
doctrina *f* doctrine; teaching; (*saber*) learning; **doctrinal** doctrinal; **doctrinar** [1a] teach; **doctrinario** *adj. a. su. m* doctrinaire.
documentación *f* documentation; papers *de identidad*; **documental** *adj. a. su. m* documentary; **documento** *m* document; record; certificate; ℱ exhibit.
dogal *m* halter; noose *de verdugo*; *estar con el* ~ *al cuello* be in an awful jam.
dogma *m* dogma; **dogmático** dogmatic(al); **dogmatismo** *m* dogmatism; **dogmatizador** *m* dogmatist; **dogmatizar** [1f] dogmatize.
dogo *m* bulldog. ⁻
dólar *m* dollar.
dolencia *f* ailment, complaint; **doler** [2i] ℱ hurt, pain; ache; *fig.* grieve, distress; *me duele el costado* my side hurts, I have a pain in my side; ~se *de* be sorry for, grieve for; (*compadecer*) pity, sympathize with; (*pecados*) repent of; (*quejarse*) complain about; (*a voces*) moan, groan; **doliente 1.** ℱ suffering, ill; sad, sorrowful; **2.** *m/f* sufferer; mourner *en entierro*.
dolomita *f* dolomite.
dolor *m* ℱ pain, ache; pang; (*pesar*) grief, sorrow; regret; ~ *de cabeza* headache; ~ *de muelas* toothache; **dolorido** ℱ sore, tender, aching; *p.* grief-stricken; *tono* plaintive, pained; **doloroso** painful, grievous.
domable tamable; **domador** *m*, **-a** *f* trainer, tamer; ~ *de caballos*

horse-breaker; **domar** [1a] tame, train; *fig.* master, control; **domeñar** [1a] = *domar*.
domesticación *f* domestication; taming; **domesticado** tame; (*de casa*) pet; **domesticar** [1g] tame, domesticate; **domesticidad** *f* (*animal*) (state of being in) captivity; (*p.*) domesticity, homeliness; **doméstico 1.** *animal* tame, pet; *vida* home *attr.*, family *attr.*, domestic; *gastos* housekeeping *attr.*; *quehaceres* household *attr.*; **2.** *m*, **a** *f* domestic.
domiciliar [1b] domicile; house; ~se take up (one's) residence; **domiciliario** house *attr.*, domiciliary; **domicilio** *m* home; ⚏, ℱℱ domicile, dwelling, abode; ✝ ~ *social* head office; *deportes: a* ~ at home; *servicio a* ~ delivery service.
dominación *f* domination; dominance; rule, power; **dominador** controlling; *carácter* domineering; **dominante** dominant (*a.* ♪); *carácter* domineering, masterful; *amor* possessive; **dominar** [1a] dominate, subdue; *p. etc.* overpower; *pasión* control, master; *lengua* know well, have a command of; (*edificio etc.*) dominate, tower over, look down on; ~se control o.s.
domingo *m* Sunday; ♀ *de Ramos* Palm Sunday; ♀ *de Resurrección* Easter Sunday; **dominguero** F, **dominical** Sunday *attr.*; **dominicano** Dominican; **dominico** *m* Dominican.
dominio *m* dominion, power, sway (*sobre* over); *esp. fig.* grip, hold (*de* on); command *de lengua*; (*superioridad*) ascendancy; (*tierras*) domain; *de* ~ *público noticia* generally known; ~ *sobre sí mismo* self-control.
dominó *m* (*ficha, vestido*) domino; (*juego de*) ~ dominoes.
don[1] *courtesy title, used before Christian names; on envelopes Señor Don* = *Esquire; in other cases not translated.*
don[2] *m* gift (*a. fig.*); ~ *de acierto* happy knack; ~ *de lenguas* gift for languages; ~ *de mando* leadership, ✗ generalship; *tener* ~ *de gentes* have a way with people, be a good mixer, have charm; **donación** *f* donation; ℱℱ gift; *escritura de* ~

deed of gift; **donador** *m*, **-a** *f* donor.

donaire *m* charm, wit *de habla*; grace, elegance; *(chiste)* witticism.

donante *m/f* donor; ~ *de sangre* blood donor; **donar** [1a] grant, donate; **donativo** *m* contribution, donation.

doncella *f* virgin; *esp. lit.* maid(en); *(criada)* (lady's) maid; **doncellez** *f* maidenhood; *anat.* maidenhead.

donde where; in which; *en* ~ wherein; *por* ~ whereby; *¿dónde?* where? *(a. a* ~*)*; *¿de dónde vienes?* where do you come from?; *¿por dónde?* *(lugar)* whereabouts?; *(dirección)* which way?; *(motivo)* why?; **dondequiera 1.** *adv.* anywhere; *por* ~ all over the place; **2.** *cj.* wherever.

donoso witty, funny; *iro.* fine.

donostiarra *adj. a. su. m/f* (native) of San Sebastián.

doña *courtesy title, used before Christian names; mst not translated.*

dorado 1. golden; gilded; ⊕ *etc.* gilt; **2.** *m* gilding; **dorador** *m* gilder; **doradura** *f* gilding; **dorar** [1a] gild *(a. fig.)*; *cocina:* brown.

dormidera *f* ♀ poppy; *tener buenas* ~*s* get off to sleep easily; **dormilón 1.** sleepy; **2.** *m*, **-a** *f* sleepyhead; lieabed; **dormir** [3k] *v/t.* send to sleep; *resaca etc.* sleep off; *siesta* have; *v/i.* sleep; *quedarse dormido* drop off, go to sleep; *durmiendo se me pasó la hora* I overslept; ~*se* go to sleep *(a. miembro)*, fall asleep; **dormirela** *f* nap; **dormitar** [1a] doze, snooze; **dormitorio** *m* bedroom; *dormitory de colegio etc.*

dorsal back *attr.*, dorsal ⑫; **dorso** *m* back *(a. fig.)*.

dos two *(a. su.)*; *(fecha)* second; *las* ~ two o'clock; *los* ~ *(ambos)* both of them *etc.*; *tenis: a* ~ deuce; *de* ~ *en* ~ in twos, two by two; *en* ~ *in* two; *en un* ~ *por tres* in a second; *para entre los* ~ between you and me; **doscientos** two hundred.

dosel *m* canopy; **doselera** *f* valance.

dosis *f* dose; *(inyección)* shot.

dotación *f* endowment; *(ps.)* staff; ⚓ complement, crew; **dotado de** ⊕ *etc.* equipped with, fitted with; *(p.)* endowed with; **dotar** [1a] *mujer* give a dowry to; *la dotó de X ptas* he gave her X ptas as a dowry;

fundación endow *(de with; a. fig.)*; *puesto* fix a salary for; ~ *de* ⚓ man with; *(taller etc.)* staff with; ⊕ equip with, fit with; **dote** *mst f* dowry, marriage portion; *fig.* gift, talent, endowment.

doy *v. dar.*

dozavo *adj. a. su. m* twelfth; *en* ~ *typ.* in duodecimo.

dracma *f* drachm, dram.

draga *f* dredge; *(barco)* dredger; **dragado** *m* *(a. obras de* ~*)* dredging; **dragaminas** *m* minesweeper; **dragar** [1h] dredge; *minas* sweep.

dragón *m* dragon; ✕ dragoon; **dragona** *f* ✕ shoulder-knot.

drama *m* drama *(a. fig.)*; **dramática** *f* dramatic art, drama; **dramático 1.** dramatic; **2.** *m* dramatist; **dramatizar** [1f] dramatize; **dramaturgo** *m* dramatist, playwright.

drástico drastic.

drenar [1a] drain.

dríada *f* dryad.

driblar [1a] *deportes:* dribble.

dril *m* duck, drill.

driza *f* halyard.

droga *f* drug *(a. b.s.)*, medicine; substance; *fig.* *(trampa)* trick; *(molestia)* nuisance; **droguería** *f* chemist's (shop).

dromedario *m* dromedary.

druida *m* druid.

dual *gr.* dual; **dualismo** *m* dualism.

ducado *m* duchy, dukedom; † ducat; **ducal** ducal.

dúctil soft, ductile; *fig.* easy to handle; **ductilidad** *f* softness, ductility.

ducha *f* shower(-bath); ❀ douche; **duchar** [1a] ❀ douche; ~*se* have a shower(-bath).

ducho: ~ *en* skilled in, well versed in.

duda *f* doubt; misgiving; suspense; *fuera de toda* ~ past all doubt; *sin* ~ no doubt, doubtless; *no cabe* ~ *(de)* que there can be no doubt that; *poner en* ~ call in question; **dudar** [1a] *v/t.* doubt; *v/i.* doubt *(que, si whether)*; ~ *de* doubt; mistrust; ~ *en inf.* hesitate to *inf.*; **dudoso** doubtful, dubious, uncertain; *punto debatable; resultado* indecisive. **duela** *f* stave. [indecisive.]

duelista *m* duellist; **duelo**[1] *m* ✕ duel; *batirse en* ~ (fight a) duel.

duelo[2] *m* grief, sorrow; bereavement;

mourning *por muerto*; (*ps.*) mourners; ~s *pl.* hardships.

duende *m* imp, goblin; (*fantasma*) ghost; **duendecillo** *m* gremlin, jinx *Am.*

dueña *f* owner; proprietress; mistress *de casa etc.*; (*dama*) lady; † duenna; **dueño** *m* owner; proprietor; master; ~ *de sí mismo* self-possessed; *ser* ~ *de* own, be the owner of; *situación* be the master of; *ser muy* ~ *de inf.* be perfectly free to *inf.*; *ser* ~ *del baile* be the master of the situation.

duermevela *f* F nap, snooze.

dulcamara *f* nightshade.

dulce 1. *mst* sweet; *carácter, clima* mild, gentle; *agua* fresh; *metal* soft; 2. *m* sweet, candy *Am.*; **dulcificar** [1g] sweeten; *fig.* soften, make more gentle; **dulzarrón** F sickly-sweet, cloying; *fig.* sugary, sickening; **dulzura** *f* sweetness; gentleness *etc.*

dumping *m* ♣ dumping; *hacer* ~ dump (goods).

duna *f* dune.

dúo *m* duet.

duodecimal duodecimal; **duodécimo** twelfth.

duplicación *f* duplication; **dupli-**cado *adj. a. su. m* duplicate; *por* ~ in duplicate; **duplicador** *m* duplicator; **duplicar** [1g] duplicate; repeat; ♣ double; **duplicidad** *f* deceitfulness, duplicity.

duque *m* duke; **duquesa** *f* duchess.

durabilidad *f* durability; **durable** durable, lasting; **duración** *f* duration; length of time; *de larga* ~ *disco* long-playing; **duradero** *tela* hard-wearing, serviceable; durable; (*que perdura*) lasting, permanent; **durante** during; ~ *todo el año* all the year round; *habló* ~ *una hora* he spoke for an hour; **durar** [1a] *cierto tiempo* last, go on for; (*permanecer,* ~ *en pie*) stand, survive; (*recuerdo etc.*) survive, endure; (*tela*) wear (well).

durazno *m* peach (tree).

dureza *f* hardness *etc.*

durmiente 1. sleeping; 2. *m/f* sleeper; 3. *m* 👁 sleeper.

duro 1. hard; *pan* stale; (*resistente*) tough; *fig. p. etc.* hard (*con* on), cruel (*con* to), callous; *estilo* harsh; ~ *de oído* hard of hearing; ♪ tone-deaf; F *ser* ~ *de pelar* (or *roer*) be a tough job; 2. *m Spanish coin* = 5 *pesetas*.

dux *m* doge.

E

e and.

¡ea! come on!; here!, hey!

ebanista m cabinet-maker; **ebanistería** f cabinet-making, woodwork.

ébano m ebony.

ebonita f ebonite.

ebrio intoxicated, drunk; blind *de ira.*

ebullición f boiling.

ebúrneo ivory.

ecléctico adj. a. su. m eclectic.

eclesiástico 1. ecclesiastic(al); **2.** m clergyman, priest; ecclesiastic.

eclipsar [1a] eclipse (a. *fig.*); *fig.* outshine, overshadow; **eclipse** m eclipse (a. *fig.*); **eclíptica** f ecliptic.

eclisa f fishplate.

eco m echo; *hacer ~ fig.* correspond; *hacerse ~ de* echo; voice; *tener ~* catch on.

economato m co-operative store; company store *para empleados;* ✕ *approx.* NAAFI shop.

economía f economy; (*un ahorro*) economy, saving; (*virtud*) thrift, thriftiness; *~ dirigida* planned economy; *~ política* economics; **económico** economic(al); (*que ahorra*) economical, thrifty; (*barato*) economical, inexpensive; **economista** m/f economist; **economizar** [1f] economize (en on); save *para la vejez etc.;* b.s. skimp, pinch.

ecuación f equation; **ecuador** m equator; **ecuánime** *carácter* equable, level-headed; *estado* calm, composed; **ecuanimidad** f equanimity, level-headedness; composure; **ecuatorial** equatorial.

ecuatoriano adj. a. su. m, a f Ecuador(i)an.

ecuestre equestrian.

ecuménico oecumenical.

eczema f eczema.

echada f throw, pitch, shy, cast; toss *de moneda;* S.Am. boast; **echadizo** spying; *propaganda* secretly spread; *material* waste; **echado:** *estar ~* lie, be lying (down).

echar [1a] **1.** (*arrojar*) throw; cast, pitch, fling, toss; *desperdicios etc.* throw away; *p.* eject, turn out *de un sitio;* expel *de una sociedad;* dismiss *del trabajo; carta* post; *cimientos* lay; *culpa* lay, put (a on); *freno* put on, apply; *humo etc.* emit, give off; *impuesto* levy, impose; *líquido* pour (out); *llave* turn; *mirada* cast; *partida* play, have; *pelo etc.* begin to grow, sprout; *pestillo* slide; *pitillo* smoke, have; *raíz* strike; *retoño* put forth; *sangre* shed, lose; *suertes* cast, draw; *~ a inf.* begin to *inf.; ~ abajo* demolish; *fig.* overthrow; *~ atrás* push back; *~ de menos* miss; *~la de pose* as, give o.s. the airs of, fancy o.s. as; *~ de sí* throw off; *piel* slough (off); *~ por dirección* take, turn to; *calle* go down; **2. ~se** (*arrojarse*) throw o.s.; (*tenderse*) lie (down), stretch out; *~ a inf.* begin to *inf.; ~las de pose* as, fancy o.s. as; *~ sobre* rush at, fall upon.

echazón f jettison; jetsam.

edad f age; *de ~* elderly; *de corta ~* young; *de mediana ~, de ~ madura* middle-aged; ♀ *Media* Middle Ages; *mayor ~* majority; *mayor de ~* of age, adult, grown-up; *menor ~* minority; *menor de ~* under age, juvenile; *a una ~ avanzada* at an advanced age, late in life; *~ viril* manhood.

edecán m aide-de-camp.

edén m paradise, (garden of) Eden.

edición f *mst* edition; issue, publication; ♀*es* pl. Pérez Pérez Publications; *~ príncipe* first edition; *ser la segunda ~ de* be the very image of.

edicto m edict, proclamation.

edificación f 🏠 construction, building; *fig.* edification, uplift; **edificante** edifying, improving; **edificar** [1g] build; *fig.* edify, improve, uplift; **edificio** m building; *fig.* edifice, structure.

editar [1a] (*publicar*) publish; (*corregir etc.*) edit; **editor 1.** publishing *attr.*; **2.** *m* (*que publica*) publisher; (*que corrige etc.*) editor; **editorial 1.** publishing *attr.*; *política etc.* editorial; **2.** *m* leading article, editorial; **3.** *f* publishing house.

edredón *m* eiderdown.

educable teachable, educable; **educación** *f* education; training; (*crianza*) upbringing; (*modales*) manners, breeding; *mala* ~ *freq.* bad manners; *sin* ~ *freq.* bad-mannered; ¡qué falta de ~! what bad manners!; how coarse!; **educacional** educational; **educacionista** *m/f* education(al)ist; **educado** well-mannered; cultivated; *mal* ~ ill-mannered, unmannerly; **educando** *m*, a *f* pupil; **educar** [1g] educate; train; (*criar*) bring up; **educativo** educative.

efectismo *m* straining after effect; **efectista** sensational; **efectivamente** sure enough; (*realmente*) in fact, really; (*contestación*) precisely; **efectivo 1.** effective; (*real*) actual, real; *hacer* ~ *cheque* cash, clear; **2.** *m* cash; specie; ~s *pl.* ✕ effectives, establishment; *en* ~ in cash; **efecto** *m* effect; impression, impact; ~s *pl.* (*propiedad*) effects; (*capital etc.*) assets; (*enseres*) things; *esp.* ✝ goods, articles, merchandise; ~ calorífico heat-value; ~s *pl.* de consumo consumer goods; ~s *pl.* de escritorio writing materials; ~s *pl.* sonoros sound effects; *al* ~ for the purpose; *en* ~ (*como contestación*) (yes) indeed; (*en realidad*) in fact; in effect; *hacer* ~ make an impression; *poner en* ~ give effect to; *surtir* ~ (*dar resultado*) work, take effect; (*dejarse sentir*) tell (en on); (*idea etc.*) get across.

efectuación *f* accomplishment; **efectuar** [1e] effect, effectuate; *parada etc.* make; (*causar*) bring about; *proyecto, reparación* carry out; *recuperación etc.* stage, make; ~se take place; be carried out.

efervescencia *f* effervescence (*a. fig.*); **efervescente** effervescent (*a. fig.*).

eficacia *f* efficacy; efficiency; **eficaz** effective, efficacious, effectual; (*que funciona bien*) efficient; (*que se deja sentir*) telling; **eficiencia** *f* efficiency; **eficiente** efficient.

efigie *f* effigy.

efímero ephemeral, short-lived.

efluvio *m* effluvium.

efusión *f* effusion (*a. fig.*), outpouring (*a. fig.*); *fig. b.s.* gush; ~ de sangre bloodshed; **efusivo** effusive; *gracias* warmest; *b.s.* gushing.

égida *f* aegis.

egipcio *adj. a. su. m*, **a** *f* Egyptian.

eglefino *m* haddock.

égloga *f* eclogue.

egocéntrico self-centred; **egoísmo** *m* egoism; selfishness; **egoísta 1.** egoistic(al); selfish; **2.** *m/f* egoist; **egotismo** *m* egotism; **egotista 1.** *adj.* egotistic(al); **2.** *m/f* egotist.

egregio eminent, distinguished.

¡**eh**! hey!, heigh!; hi!; hoy!

eje *m* ⊕ axle de ruedas; (*árbol, husillo*) shaft, spindle; ⚡, *phys., geog., pol.* axis; *fig.* (*centro*) hinge, hub; (*esencia*) crux, core; central idea; ~ de balancín rocker (shaft); ~ del cigüeñal crankshaft; ~ flotante floating axle.

ejecución *f* execution (*a.* ♫♫, ♪); fulfilment; enforcement *de ley*; ♪ performance, rendition; *poner en* ~ carry into effect; **ejecutante** *m/f* performer; **ejecutar** [1a] execute (*a.* ♫♫, ♪); perform (*a.* ♪); *órdenes* fulfil; **ejecutivo 1.** executive; (*apremiante*) pressing, insistent; (*sin demora*) prompt; **2.** *m* executive; **ejecutor** *m*: ~ testamentario executor; **ejecutoria** *f* letters patent; (*genealogía*) pedigree.

¡**ejem**! hem!

ejemplar 1. exemplary; **2.** *m* example; copy *de libro*; *zo. etc.* specimen; (*modelo*) model, example; **ejemplaridad** *f* exemplariness; **ejemplificar** [1g] exemplify; be illustrative of; **ejemplo** *m* example, instance; (*lección*) object-lesson; *por* ~ for example, for instance; *sin* ~ unexampled; *dar* ~ set an example.

ejercer [2b] exercise; *influencia* exert, bring to bear; *poder* exercise, wield; *profesión* practise (de as), follow; **ejercicio** *m* exercise (*a.* ✕); practice; tenure *de oficio*; ✝ fiscal year; ~ de castigo escuela: imposition; *hacer* ~s take exercise; **ejercitar** [1a] exercise; *profesión* practise; ✗ *etc.* train, drill; ~se exercise; practise; train; **ejército** *m* army.

ejido *m* common.

el 1. *artículo:* the; **2.** *pron.:* ~ de that of; ~ de *Juan* John's; ~ de *Madrid* the Madrid one, the one from Madrid; *v. que.* [him; it.]

él (*p.*) he; (*cosa*) it; (*tras prp.*)

elaboración *f* elaboration *etc.*; **elaborar** [1a] elaborate; *producto* make, manufacture, prepare; *metal, madera etc.* work; *proyecto* work on, work up.

elasticidad *f* elasticity; give, spring(iness); *fig.* resilience; **elástico 1.** elastic; *superficie etc.* springy; *fig.* resilient; **2.** *m* elastic.

elección *f* choice, selection; *pol. etc.* election; **electivo** elective; **electo** elect; **elector** *m*, -a *f* elector; **electorado** *m* electorate; **electoral** electoral; *potencia etc.* voting *attr.*

electricidad *f* electricity; **electricista** *m* electrician; **eléctrico** electric(al); **electrificar** [1g], **electrizar** [1f] electrify (*a. fig.*); **electrocutar** [1a] electrocute; **electrodinámica** *f* electrodynamics; **electrodo** *m* electrode; **electrólisis** *f* electrolysis; **electromotor** *m* electric motor; **electrón** *m* electron; **electrónica** *f* electronics; **electrónico** electronic; *electron attr.*; **electrotecnia** *f* electrical engineering.

elefante *m*, **a** *f* elephant; **elefantino** elephantine.

elegancia *f* elegance *etc.*; **elegante** elegant; *movimiento etc.* graceful; (*distintivo*) stylish; (*majo*) smart; (*de moda, sociedad*) fashionable; (*de buen gusto*) tasteful; *frase etc.* polished, well-turned.

elegía *f* elegy; **elegíaco** elegiac.

elegibilidad *f* eligibility; **elegible** eligible; **elegido** elect; **elegir** [3c *a.* 3l] choose, select; *pol. etc.* elect.

elemental elementary; elemental; **elemento** *m mst* element (*a. ⚡*); ⚡ cell *de pila*; *fig.* ingredient; factor *de situación*; ~s *pl. fig.* (*medios*) means, resources; (*materia*) material, ingredients.

elenco *m* catalogue, list; *thea.* cast.

elevación *f* elevation; height, altitude; *fig.* exaltation; rise *de*

precios etc.; **elevado** elevated; *edificio etc.* high; *fig. posición etc.* exalted, high, lofty; *estilo* grand; **elevador** *m* hoist; *S.Am.* lift; ~ de granos elevator; **elevar** [1a] raise (*a. ⚡, precios*), lift (up), elevate; exalt *a dignidad*; *producción* step up; ⚡ boost; ~se rise; (*edificio etc.*) soar, tower; *fig.* get conceited.

elidir [3a] elide.

eliminación *f* elimination, removal; *deportes:* ~ progresiva knock-out; **eliminar** [1a] eliminate, remove; *necesidad etc.* obviate; **eliminatoria** *f deportes:* heat.

elipse *f* ellipse; **elipsis** *f* ellipsis; **elíptico** elliptic(al).

elisión *f* elision.

elixir *m* elixir.

elocución *f* elocution.

elocuencia *f* eloquence; **elocuente** eloquent.

elogiar [1b] praise, eulogize; **elogio** *m* praise, eulogy; tribute.

elucidar [1a] elucidate.

eludible avoidable; **eludir** [3a] elude, evade, escape; avoid.

ella (*p.*) she; (*cosa*) it; (*tras prp.*) her; it; **ellas** *pl.* they; (*tras prp.*) them.

ello it; ~ es que the fact is that; ~ dirá the event will show; F ¡a por ~! here goes!

ellos *pl.* they; (*tras prp.*) them.

emanación *f* emanation (*a. phys.*); (*olor*) effluvium; **emanar** [1a]: ~ de emanate from, come from, originate in.

emancipación *f* emancipation; **emancipar** [1a] emancipate.

embadurnar [1a] (be)daub, smear.

embaidor *m* trickster, cheat; **embaimiento** *m* imposture; **embaír** [3a; *defective*] impose upon.

embajada *f* embassy; **embajador** *m* ambassador.

embalador *m*, -a *f* packer; **embalaje** *m* packing; **embalar** [1a] *v/t.* pack, bale, parcel up; *v/i.* F *deportes:* sprint; *mot.* step on it.

embaldosado *m* tiled floor; **embaldosar** [1a] tile.

embalsadero *m* boggy place.

embalsamar [1a] embalm.

embalsar [1a] dam (up); *este mes se han embalsado X metros cúbicos* reservoir stocks have gone up by X

cubic metres this month; **embalse**
m dam; reservoir.

embanderar [1a] bedeck with flags.

embarazada pregnant; **em-barazar** [1f] (*estorbar*) obstruct, hamper, hinder; (*empreñar*) make pregnant, get with child; **em-barazo** *m* (*estorbo*) obstacle, hindrance; (*preñado*) pregnancy; **em-barazoso** awkward, inconvenient; embarrassing.

embarcación *f* craft, boat, vessel; (*embarco*) embarkation; **embarca-dero** *m* pier, landing-stage, jetty; **embarcar** [1g] *ps.* embark, put on board; *cargamento* ship; *fig.* launch (en empresa on); ~se embark, go on board; *fig.* get involved (en in); **embarco** *m* embarkation.

embargar [1h] *propiedad* seize, distrain upon, impound; (*estorbar*) impede; *sentidos* blunt, paralyse; **embargo** *m* ♈ seizure, distraint; ♊ indigestion; sin ~ still, however, none the less.

embarque *m* shipment, loading (of cargo).

embarradura *f* smear.

embarrancarse [1g] run into a ditch, get stuck.

embarrar [1a] smear, bedaub (de with), begrime.

embarullar [1a] make a mess of, muddle.

embate *m* ✂ sudden attack; brunt de ataque; dashing, breaking de olas; ~s *pl.* de la fortuna blows of fortune.

embaucador *m*, **-a** *f* trickster, swindler; humbug; impostor; **em-baucamiento** *m* swindle; humbug; **embaucar** [1g] trick, fool, impose upon, bamboozle F.

embaular [1a] pack (into a trunk); F stuff o.s. with, tuck into.

embazar [1f] *v/t.* (*teñir*) dye brown; (*pasmar*) astound; (*estorbar*) hinder; *v/i.* be dumbfounded; ~se have had enough.

embebecer [2d] entertain; ~se be lost in wonder.

embeber [2a] *v/t.* absorb, soak up; *esp. fig.* imbibe; *vestido* take up, gather in; (*introducir*) insert; contain; *v/i.* shrink; ~se (*absorto*) be absorbed; (*extático*) be en-raptured; ~ de *fig.* imbibe, be soaked in.

embelecar [1g] deceive, cheat; **embeleco** *m* fraud, deceit; F bore.

embelesado spellbound; **embe-lesador** ravishing, entrancing; **embelesar** [1a] enrapture, en-thrall, fascinate; **embeleso** *m* rapture, bliss, delight.

embellecer [2d] embellish, beau-tify; **embellecimiento** *m* embel-lishment.

embestida *f* assault, onslaught; charge de toro etc.; **embestir** [3l] assault, assail; rush upon; (*toro*) charge; F pester (for a loan).

embetunar [1a] *zapatos* black.

emblandecer [2d] soften; *fig.* mollify.

emblanquecer [2d] whiten, bleach.

emblema *m* emblem, device.

embobamiento *m* wonderment; **embobarse** [1a] gape, be amazed (con, de, en at); **embobecer** [2d] make silly.

embocadura *f* mouth de río; tip de cigarrillo; ♩ mouthpiece; bit de freno; thea. proscenium arch; **embocar** [1g] put into the mouth; F comida cram, scoff; ~ algo a uno make s.o. believe s.t., put one over on s.o.

embolado *m* thea. minor role; F trick.

embolia *f* clot; embolism; ~ cerebral clot on the brain.

embolismar [1a] gossip about; **embolismo** *m* confusion, mess; F (*chismes*) gossip; F (*engaño*) hoax.

émbolo *m* piston; plunger.

embolsar [1a] pocket; *pago* col-lect.

emboque *m* F trick, hoax.

emboquillado *cigarrillo* tipped.

emborrachar [1a] intoxicate, get drunk; ~se get drunk (con, de on).

emborrar [1a] (*llenar*) stuff; F = embocar.

emborronar [1a] *papel* scribble over, cover with scribble; *carta*, *renglones* scribble.

emboscada *f* ambush; **embos-carse** [1g] lie in ambush, hide.

embotado dull, blunt (a. fig.); **em-botar** [1a] blunt, dull (a. fig.); *fig.* weaken, enervate.

embotellamiento *m* traffic jam de coches; bottle-neck en calle estrecha (a. fig.); **embotellar** [1a] bottle; *fig.* bottle up.

embozado muffled up; **embozar** [1f] muffle (up); *fig.* cloak, disguise; **~se** muffle o.s. up; **embozo** *m* covering of the face, muffler, mask; (*cama*) turned-down bedclothes; *fig.* cunning, concealment; *sin ~* frankly, openly.

embragar [1h] *engranaje* engage; *piezas* connect, couple; **embrague** *m* clutch; **~ de disco** disc clutch.

embravecer [2d] *v/t.* enrage; *v/i.* ⚓ flourish; **~se** (*mar*) get rough.

embrear [1a] tar, cover with pitch.

embriagador intoxicant, intoxicating; *vino etc.* heady; **embriagar** [1h] make drunk, intoxicate; *fig.* enrapture; **~se** get drunk; **embriaguez** *f* drunkenness, intoxication; *fig.* rapture.

embrión *m* embryo; *en ~* in embryo; **embrionario** embryonic.

embrocación *f* embrocation.

embrocar [1g] *hilos* wind (on a bobbin); *zapatos* tack; (*vaciar*) empty; (*volver boca abajo*) invert, turn upside down.

embrollar [1a] muddle, entangle, dislocate; *esp. ps.* embroil; **~se** get into a muddle; **~ en** get involved in; **embrollo** *m* (*enredo*) tangle, muddle; (*situación difícil*) imbroglio; (*lío*) embroilment, entanglement; **embrollón** *m*, **-a** *f* troublemaker.

embromar [1a] tease, make fun of, rag; (*engañar*) hoodwink, kid F; **~se** *S.Am.* loiter; (*aburrirse*) get bored.

embrujar [1a] *p.* bewitch; *casa* haunt.

embrutecer [2d] brutalize, coarsen.

embuchado *m* pork sausage; F blind; **embuchar** [1a] stuff (with mincemeat); F *comida* bolt.

embudar [1a] fit with a funnel; *fig.* trick; **embudo** *m* funnel; *fig.* trick.

emburujar [1a] jumble (up), pile (up).

embuste *m* (*mentira*) lie, story F; (*engaño*) trick, fraud; imposture, (piece of) chicanery; **~s** *pl.* trinkets; **embustería** *f* imposture, trick; **embustero** 1. deceitful; 2. *m*, *a f* liar, story-teller F; cheat.

embutido *m* *cocina:* sausage; ⊕ inlay, marquetry; **embutir** [3a] stuff, cram; ⊕ inlay; F *comida* cram, scoff; F **~ algo a uno** make s.o. swallow s.t.

emergencia *f* (*acto*) emergence;

(*caso de urgencia*) emergency; **emergente** resultant; **emerger** [2c] emerge; (*submarino*) surface.

emeritense *adj. a. su. m/f* (native) of Mérida.

emético *adj. a. su. m* emetic.

emigración *f* (e)migration; **emigrado** *m*, **a** *f* emigrant; *esp. pol.* emigré; **emigrante** *adj. a. su. m/f* emigrant; **emigrar** [1a] (e)migrate.

eminencia *f* (*colina etc., título, fig.*) eminence; (*lo muy alto*) loftiness; *fig.* prominence; **eminente** (*muy alto*) lofty; *fig.* eminent; prominent, distinguished.

emisario *m* emissary; **emisión** *f* emission; issue; *radio:* (*acto*) broadcasting; (*una ~*) broadcast, programme; **emisor** *m* transmitter; **emisora** *f* radio station; **emitir** [3a] emit, give off (*or* forth, out); *moneda, sellos* issue; *moneda falsa* utter; *empréstito* float, launch; *radio:* broadcast.

emoción *f* emotion; (*entusiasmo etc.*) excitement; (*estremecimiento, escalofrío*) thrill; tension *al esperar etc.*; **emocionado** deeply moved; **emocionante** exciting, thrilling, moving; **emocional** emotional; **emocionar** [1a] (*entusiasmar*) excite, thrill; (*conmover*) move; **~se** get excited; be moved.

emolumentos *m/pl.* emoluments.

emotivo emotive.

empacar [1g] pack (up); **~se** be obstinate; (*cortarse*) get rattled F; *S.Am.* balk, shy.

empachado awkward; **empachar** [1a] upset, cause indigestion to; **~se** get embarrassed; become bashful; **empacho** *m* 🎣 indigestion; *fig.* embarrassment, bashfulness; **empachoso** indigestible; *fig.* embarrassing, shaming, shameful.

empadronamiento *m* census(-taking), registration; **empadronar** [1a] take the census of, register.

empalagar [1h] (*empachar*) pall (*a on; a. fig.*), cloy (*a. fig.*); (*fastidiar*) bore, weary; **empalago** *m* cloying, disgust; *fig.* bore(dom); **empalagoso** sickly, rich, gooey F; *fig.* wearisome, trying.

empalar [1a] impale; **empalizada** *f* stockade.

empalmar [1a] *v/t. cuerda* splice; *fig.* couple, join; *v/i.* (*líneas*) join, meet; (*trenes*) connect (con with); **empalme** *m* splice; ⊕ joint, connection; 👷 junction *de líneas*; connection *de trenes*.

empanada *f* (meat) pie, patty; *fig.* shady business; **empanar** [1a] roll in bread-crumbs, roll in pastry.

empantanar [1a] flood, swamp; *fig.* bog down; ~se *fig.* get bogged down.

empañado *ventana* misty, steamy; **empañar** [1a] *niño* swaddle, wrap up; *ventana etc.* mist; *imagen* blur (*a. fig.*); *honor* tarnish; ~se (*imagen etc.*) dim, blur; (*ventana etc.*) film over, get misty.

empapar [1a] soak, saturate, steep (*a. fig.*); (*lluvia etc.*) drench; ~se en soak up; *fig.* steep o.s. in.

empapelado *m* papering, paper-hanging; **empapelador** *m* paper-hanger; **empapelar** [1a] *pared* paper; *caja* line with paper; *objeto* wrap in paper.

empaque *m* packing; *fig.* appearance, presence; solemnness; *S.Am.* brazenness; **empaquetador** *m*, -a *f* packer; **empaquetadura** *f* packing; ⊕ gasket; filling; **empaquetar** [1a] pack (up), parcel up, package.

emparedado *m* sandwich; **emparedar** [1a] immure, confine.

emparejar [1a] *v/t.* (*aparear*) match; (*allanar*) level; *v/i.* catch up (con with); ~se match.

emparentado related by marriage (con to); **emparentar** [1k] become related by marriage; ~ con familia marry into.

emparrado *m* (trained) vine.

empastar [1a] paste; *libro* bind (in stiff covers); *diente* fill, stop; **empaste** *m* filling.

empatar [1a] *deportes*: draw, tie; *pol. etc.* tie; **empate** *m* draw, tie en juego; dead heat en carrera; *pol. etc.* tie.

empavesado *m* bunting; **empavesar** [1a] deck; *buque* dress.

empecatado incorrigible; (*desgraciado*) ill-fated.

empedernido (*cruel*) heartless; (*sin compasión*) obdurate; *pol. etc.* die-hard; inveterate *en un hábito*; *corazón* stony; **empedernir** [3a; *defective*] harden; ~se harden one's heart.

empedrado 1. *superficie* pitted; *cara* pockmarked; (*manchado*) dappled, flecked; **2.** *m* paving; **empedrar** [1k] pave.

empeine *m* groin; instep *de pie*; ~s *pl.* 🞧 tetter.

empelotarse [1a] F get muddled; (*reñir*) get involved in a row.

empella *f* vamp.

empellón *m* push, shove; *a* ~es roughly; *dar* ~es jostle.

empeñar [1a] pawn, pledge; *fig.* engage, compel; ~se insist (en on), persist (en in); (*obligarse*) bind o.s.; ~ en inf. insist on ger., be set on ger.; ~ por intercede for, mediate on behalf of; **empeño** *m* pledge; obligation; determination, insistence; (*esfuerzo*) endeavour; con ~ insistently; (*con ilusión*) eagerly.

empeoramiento *m* deterioration, worsening; **empeorar** [1a] *v/t.* make worse, worsen; *v/i.*, ~se get worse, worsen, deteriorate.

empequeñecer [2d] dwarf; (*despreciar*) belittle; (*quitar importancia a*) minimize.

emperador *m* emperor; **emperatriz** *f* empress.

emperejilarse [1a] F dress up, titivate, doll (o.s.) up.

empernar [1k] bolt.

empero but, yet, however.

emperrarse [1a] F (*obstinarse*) get stubborn; (*irritarse*) lose one's temper.

empezar [1f *a.* 1k] begin, start (*a inf.* to inf.; *por inf.* by ger.).

empinado *cuesta* steep; (*alto*) high; **empinar** [1a] *v/t. vaso etc.* raise; (*enderezar*) straighten; *v. codo; v/i.* F drink; ~se (*p.*) stand on tiptoe; (*caballo*) rear; (*edificio*) tower; 🞧 soar, zoom.

empingorotado F stuck-up.

empírico empiric(al); **empirismo** *m* empiricism.

emplastar [1a] plaster, poultice; *cara* make up; F *negocio* block; **emplasto** *m* plaster, poultice; *fig.* makeshift arrangement; F weakling.

emplazamiento *m* 🜨 summons; ✗ emplacement; **emplazar** [1f] summon(s).

empleado *m*, a *f* employee; clerk *en oficina etc.*; **emplear** [1a] use; employ; *tiempo* occupy, spend; ~ mal misuse; **empleo** *m* use; (*trabajo en* *general*) employment; (*puesto*) employment, job; *sin ~* unemployed; *pleno ~* full employment.

emplomar [1a] lead, cover (*or* weight *etc.*) with lead.

emplumar [1a] *v/t.* (tar and) feather; *v/i.* = **emplumecer** [2d] fledge, grow feathers.

empobrecer [2d] *v/t.* impoverish; *v/i.*, *~se* become poor; **empobrecimiento** *m* impoverishment.

empolvado powdery; *superficie etc.* dusty; **empolvar** [1a] *cara* powder; *superficie* cover with dust; *~se* (*p.*) powder o.s., powder one's face; (*superficie*) gather dust, get dusty.

empollar [1a] *v/t.* incubate; hatch; *v/i.* (*gallina*) sit, brood (*a. fig.*); (*insectos*) breed; F swot, cram; **empollón** *m*, *-a f* F swot.

emponzoñamiento *m* poisoning; **emponzoñar** [1a] poison (*a. fig.*); *fig.* corrupt.

emporcar [1g *a.* 1m] dirty, foul.

emporio *m* emporium; mart.

empotrar [1a] embed; ⊕ build in.

emprendedor enterprising, go-ahead, pushful; **emprender** [2a] undertake, take on, tackle; (*empezar*) begin on, embark (up)on; F *~la con p.* (*para aclarar*) have it out with, tackle; (*reñir*) fall out with.

empreñar [1a] *p.* make pregnant, get with child; *animal etc.* impregnate; *~se* become pregnant.

empresa *f* enterprise, undertaking (*a.* ✝); venture; ✝ company, concern; *thea.* management; **empresario** *m thea.* manager; showman; impresario *de ópera etc.*; promoter *de boxeo etc.*

empréstito *m* (public) loan; *~ de guerra* war-loan.

empujadora-niveladora *f* bull-dozer.

empujar [1a] push, shove; (*introducir*) push, thrust (en into); (*propulsar*) drive, propel; *botón* press; *fig. p.* sack, give the push to F; (*para obtener algo*) work behind the scenes for, intrigue for; **empuje** *m* push, shove; (*presión*) pressure; *fig.* push, (pushfulness), energy, drive; ⊕ thrust; **empujón** *m* push, shove; dig, poke *con dedo etc.*; *a ~es* roughly; (*a intervalos*) by fits and starts.

empulgueras *f/pl.* thumb-screw.

empuñadura *f* hilt *de espada*; grip *de herramienta*; opening *de cuento*; **empuñar** [1a] grasp, grip, clutch.

emulación *f* emulation; **emulador** **1.** emulous (de of); **2.** *m*, *-a f* rival; **emular** [1a] emulate, rival; **émulo** **1.** emulous; **2.** *m* rival, competitor.

emulsión *f* emulsion.

en (*dentro*) in; (*hacia dentro*) into; (*sobre*) on, upon; (*en un lugar, ciudad etc.*) in, at; (*por un precio*) for, at; (*porcentaje*) by; *está ~ la caja* it's in the box; *meter ~ la caja* put in(to) the box; *está ~ la mesa* it's on the table; *~ Madrid* in Madrid; *pasan un mes ~ Lloret* they're spending a month at Lloret; *en un 20 por ciento* by 20 per cent; *le conocí ~ su andar* I recognized him by his walk; *~ viéndole* (*pasado*) the moment I saw him; (*presente, futuro*) the moment I see him; *~ que* in that; *¿~ qué lo notas?* how can you tell?

enaguas *f/pl.* petticoat, slip.

enaguazar [1f] flood.

enajenación *f* alienation; estrangement; (*distracción*) absentmindedness; *~ mental* derangement; **enajenar** [1a] *propiedad* alienate; *derechos* dispose of; *p.* drive mad; *~se* (*estar absorto*) be lost in wonder; (*amigos*) become estranged; *~ de algo* deprive o.s. of.

enaltecer [2d] exalt, extol.

enamoradizo susceptible (to women); **enamorado:** *estar ~ de* be in love with; **enamoramiento** *m* falling in love; **enamorar** [1a] inspire love in, win the love of; *~se* fall in love (de with); **enamoricarse** [1g] be just a bit in love (de with).

enangostar(se) [1a] narrow.

enano 1. dwarf; stunted; **2.** *m* dwarf; midget; *contp.* runt.

enarbolar [1a] raise, hang out, hoist; *~se* (*caballo*) rear.

enarcar [1g] *barril* hoop; *cejas* arch, raise.

enardecer [2d] *fig.* fire, inflame; *~se* get excited; blaze (de with).

enarenar [1a] sand; *~se* ⚓ run aground.

encabezamiento *m* (*título, titular*) heading, headline; caption *de dibujo etc.*; preamble *de documento*; ✝ billhead; (*oficial*) register; **encabezar** [1f] head, lead; *papel* put a heading to; *dibujo etc.* caption; (*empadronar*) take a census of; *vino* fortify.

encabritarse [1a] rear; prance.

encadenación *f*, **encadenamiento** *m* chaining; *fig.* connexion, concatenation; **encadenar** [1a] (en-) chain; (*trabar*) shackle; *fig.* connect, link.

encajadura *f* (*acto*) insertion, fitting; (*hueco*) socket; (*ranura*) groove; **encajar** [1a] **1.** *v/t.* (*introducir*) insert, fit (*into* en); (*unir*) join, fit together; ⊕ encase, house *en caja*; F *observación* intrude, get in; F *cuento* come out with, tell at the wrong time; F *golpe* land; F (*lanzar*) chuck (*a* at); F (*hacer escuchar*) make s.o. listen to; F ~ *algo a uno* palm (*or* foist) s.t. off on s.o.; **2.** *v/i.* fit (properly); *fig.* be appropriate; ~ *con* fit, match; (*cuadrar*) square with, be in line with; **3.** ~**se** F (*introducirse*) squeeze in; *fig.* intrude (en upon), gate-crash (en *acc.*); **encaje** *m* (*acto*) insertion, fitting; (*hueco*) socket; (*ranura*) groove; (*caja*) housing; *sew.* lace; (*taracea*) inlay, inlaid work, mosaic; ~ *de aplicación* appliqué (work); **encajera** *f* lace-maker.

encajonado *m* coffer-dam; **encajonar** [1a] pack *en caja etc.*; box (up); ⊕ *etc.* box in, (en)case; squeeze in, squeeze through *en sitio estrecho*.

encalabrinar [1a] 🔊 make s.o. dizzy; F get s.o. worked up; F *amante* hook, click with; ~**se** F get an obsession, get the bit between one's teeth.

encaladura *f* whitewash(ing); 🌱 liming; **encalar** [1a] *pared* whitewash; 🌱 lime.

encalmado ⚓ becalmed; 🌱 slack; **encalmarse** [1a] be becalmed.

encalvecer [2d] go bald.

encalladero *m* shoal, sandbank; **encalladura** *f* stranding; **encallar** [1a] run aground, run ashore; *fig.* fail; get stuck, get tied up *en negocio*.

encallecido hardened.

encamarse [1a] take to one's bed; (*animal*) crouch, hide; (*trigo*) be laid.

encaminar [1a] guide, set on the right road (*a* to); *energías* direct (*a* towards); ~**se** *a* set out for, take the road to, make for; *fig.* be directed at, be intended for.

encandecer [2d] make white-hot.

encandilado F high, erect; **encandilar** [1a] dazzle, bewilder; *lumbre* poke; *emoción* kindle; ~**se** (*ojos*) glow, sparkle, glitter.

encanecer(se) [2d] (*pelo*) grey; (*p.*) grow old; (*mohoso*) go mouldy.

encanijado puny; **encanijarse** [1a] grow weak, begin to look ill.

encanillar [1a] (wind on a) spool.

encantado delighted, charmed, pleased; *casa* rambling; *lugar* romantic; (*distraído*) absentminded; (*absorto*) in a trance; *¡~!* how do you do?, pleased to meet you; *yo, ~* it's all right with me; **encantador 1.** enchanting, charming, delightful, lovely; **2.** *m, -a f* magician; *fig.* charmer; **encantamiento** *m* enchantment; **encantar** [1a] bewitch; *fig.* enchant, charm, delight; fascinate; *nos encantó la ciudad* we were charmed with the city; **encanto** *m* charm, spell, enchantment, delight; *el niño es un ~* the child is a real treasure; *la casa es un ~* it's a marvellous house.

encañada *f* ravine; **encañado** *m* conduit; **encañar** [1a] *v/t. agua* pipe; *terreno* drain; *planta* stake; *v/i.* form stalks; **encañonar** [1a] *v/t.* pipe; *sl.* stick up, hold up; *v/i.* grow feathers.

encapotado *cielo* overcast; **encapotarse** [1a] (*p.*) frown; (*cielo*) cloud over.

encapricharse [1a] persist in one's foolishness; ~ *por* take a fancy to, get infatuated with.

encapuchado hooded.

encarado: *bien* ~ having good features, good-looking; *mal* ~ ill-favoured, terribly plain.

encaramar [1a] raise, lift up; (*alabar*) extol; F elevate; ~**se** perch; ~ *a* climb, get to the top of.

encarar [1a] *v/t. arma* point, aim; *problema* face; *v/i.*, ~**se con** face, confront.

encarcelación *f*, **encarcelamiento** *m* imprisonment; **encarcelar** [1a] imprison, jail.

encarecer [2d] *v/t.* 🌱 put up the price of; *p.* recommend; (*alabar*) extol; exaggerate; *dificultad* stress; *v/i.*, ~**se** get dearer; **encarecidamente** insistently; **encarecimiento** *m* 🌱 rise in price; *fig.* exaggeration, overrating; *con* ～ insistently.

encargado 1.: ～ *de* in charge of; **2.** *m* agent, representative; person in charge; *univ.* ～ *de curso* lecturer in charge; ～ *de negocios* chargé d'affaires; **encargar** [1h] (*encomendar*) entrust; charge (*un deber with a duty*), commission; recommend; (*pedir*) order; ～se *de* (*tomar sobre sí*) take charge of, take over; (*cuidar de*) look after, see about; ～ *de inf.* undertake to *inf.*, see about *ger.*; **encargo** *m* (*deber etc.*) charge, commission, assignment, job; (*pedido*) order; (*puesto*) office, post; *por* ～ *de* on the orders of; on behalf of.

encariñarse [1a]: ～ *con* grow fond of.

encarnación *f* incarnation; embodiment; **encarnado** (*color*) red, flesh-coloured; *tez* florid; (*que ha encarnado*) incarnate; **encarnar** [1a] *v/t.* embody, personify; *anzuelo* bait; *v/i.* become incarnate; (*herida*) heal (up); (*arma*) enter the flesh; **encarnecer** [2d] put on flesh; **encarnizado** *ojo* bloodshot; *batalla* bloody, bitter, fierce; **encarnizamiento** *m* bitterness; **encarnizar** [1f] *fig.* (*irritar*) enrage; make cruel; ～se (*irritarse*) get angry; (*luchar*) fight fiercely; ～ *en carne* gorge on; *víctima* treat cruelly.

encarpetar [1a] file away, pigeon-hole.

encarrilar [1a] set on the right road, direct; *fig.* put on the right track, set right; *ir encarrilado fig.* be on the right track; *b.s.* be in a rut.

encartar [1a] *criminal* outlaw; (*empadronar*) enrol, register.

encasar [1a] *hueso* set.

encasillar [1a] pigeon-hole; file, classify.

encasquetar [1a] *sombrero* pull on tight, jam on; *idea* put into *s.o.'s* mind; ～se get an idea firmly fixed.

encastillado △ castellated; *fig.* haughty; **encastillar** [1a] fortify; ～se ✗ take to the hills; *fig.* refuse to yield.

encauchar [1a] rubberize.

encausar [1a] prosecute, put on trial.

encáustico encaustic; **encausto** *m* encaustic.

encauzar [1f] channel; *fig.* channel, guide.

encefálico encephalic.

encenagado mud-stained; *fig.* sunk in vice; **encenagarse** [1h] get muddy; *fig.* wallow in vice.

encendedor *m* lighter; (*p.*) lamp-lighter; **encender** [2g] light, set fire to, ignite; kindle (*a. fig.*); *cerilla* strike; *luz, ⚡* turn on, switch on; *fig.* inflame; ～se catch (fire), ignite; (*arder más*) flare up; *fig.* (*p.*) get excited; (*cara*) blush; **encendido 1.** *adj. luz* on, *alambre* live; (*color*) glowing (de with); *cara* red, inflamed; **2.** *m mot.* ignition, firing; **encendimiento** *m* burning, kindling; *fig.* (*ardor*) eagerness; intensity.

encerado 1. waxy, wax-coloured; **2.** *m* oilcloth; ✚ sticking-plaster; *escuela*: blackboard; **enceradora** *f* polishing machine; **encerar** [1a] wax; *suelo* polish.

encerradero *m* fold, pen; **encerrar** [1k] enclose, shut in, shut up; lock in, lock up *con llave*; (*rodear etc.*) confine, hem in; *fig.* contain, include; (*implicar*) involve, imply.

encespedar [1a] turf.

encía *f* gum.

encíclica *f* encyclical.

enciclopedia *f* encyclopaedia; **enciclopédico** encyclopaedic.

encierro *m* confinement, shutting-up; (*lugar*) enclosure; (*prisión*) prison; *toros*: corralling.

encima (*en el aire*) above, over, overhead; (*en la cumbre*) at the top; on top; (*sobre*) on; (*además*) besides, over and above; ～ *de* on, upon; on top of; *por* ～ over; *fig.* superficially; *por* ～ *de* over; *¿tienes cambio* ～? have you any change on you?

encina *f* holm-oak, ilex; **encinar** *m* wood of holm-oaks.

encinta pregnant; *zo.* with young; *mujer* ～ expectant mother; *dejar* ～ get with child.

encintado *m* kerb(stone).

encizañar [1a] *fig.* sow discord (*v/t.* among).

enclaustrar [1a] cloister; *fig.* hide away.

enclavar [1a] nail; (*traspasar*) pierce; F cheat; ～se interlock; **enclave** *m* enclave; **enclavijar** [1a] peg, pin.

enclenque weak(ly), sickly.
enclocar [1g *a.* 1m], **encloquecer** [2d] go broody.
encobar [1a] brood, sit.
encocorar [1a] F vex; ~se get upset.
encoger [2c] *v/t.* shrink; *p.* intimidate, fill with fear; *v/i.*, ~se shrink, contract; (*p.*) (*acobardarse*) cringe; (*desanimarse*) get disheartened; ~ *de hombros* shrug (one's shoulders); **encogido** shrunken, contracted; *p.* bashful; **encogimiento** *m* shrinkage, contraction; *fig.* bashfulness; ~ *de hombros* shrug.
encojar [1a] cripple, lame; ~se go lame; F pretend to be ill.
encolar [1a] glue; size *antes de pintar*; (*pegar*) stick (down, together).
encolerizar [1f] provoke, anger, incense; ~se get angry, see red.
encomendar [1k] commend, entrust; ~se *a* send greetings to.
encomiar [1b] extol, praise.
encomienda *f* (*encargo*) charge, commission; recommendation; protection; *hist.* land or office held from military order (*in America, from king*).
encomio *m* praise, tribute.
enconar [1a] 🗲 inflame; *p.* irritate, provoke; ~se fester; *fig.* fester, rankle; **encono** *m* rancour, spite, spitefulness, bad blood; **enconoso** resentful, rancorous.
encontradizo: *hacerse el* ~ contrive an apparently chance meeting; **encontrado** opposed, contrary, conflicting; **encontrar** [1m] find; meet; *esp. fig.* encounter; ~se be, be situated (*en* in); (*ps.*) meet; (*coches etc.*) collide; (*opiniones*) clash, conflict; ~ *adj. etc.* be, feel, find o.s.; ~ *con* meet (with), encounter; **encontrón** *m*, **encontronazo** *m* crash, collision.
encopetado (*linajudo*) of noble birth; (*que presume*) high and mighty, haughty; **encopetarse** [1a] give o.s. airs, get conceited.
encorar [1m] cover with leather.
encorchar [1a] cork; *abejas* hive.
encordar [1m] *raqueta, violín* string; (*atar*) lash with ropes; **encordelar** [1a] tie with string.
encornado: *bien* ~ with good horns; **encornadura** *f* horns.
encorralar [1a] corral, pen.
encorvada *f* stoop; F *hacer la* ~

malinger, pretend to be ill; **encorvadura** *f* bend(ing); curving, curvature; **encorvar** [1a] bend, curve; hook; inflect; ~se bend (over, down), stoop; (*romperse*) buckle.
encrespado curly; **encrespador** *m* curling-tongs; **encrespar** [1a] *pelo* curl; *plumas* ruffle; *agua* ripple; ~se curl; ripple; (*mar*) get rough; (*p.*) get angry.
encrestado haughty.
encrucijada *f* cross-roads, intersection.
encuadernación *f* binding; (*taller*) bindery; **encuadernador** *m* bookbinder; **encuadernar** [1a] bind; *sin* ~ unbound.
encuadrar [1a] frame; (*encajar*) fit in, insert.
encubierta *f* fraud; **encubierto** hidden, under-cover; **encubridor** 1. concealing; 2. *m*, -a *f* 🙾 accessory (after the fact), abettor; **encubrimiento** *m* concealment; 🙾 abetment; **encubrir** [3a; *p.p.* encubierto] hide, conceal, cloak; 🙾 *crimen* conceal, abet; *sospechoso* harbour.
encuentro *m* meeting (*a. deportes*), encounter (*a.* ⚔, *deportes*); collision *de coches etc.*; clash *de opiniones*; *salir al* ~ *a*, *ir al* ~ *de* go to meet (*a. fig.*).
encuesta *f* poll; (*investigación*) inquiry, probe F.
encuitarse [1a] grieve.
encumbrado high, lofty, towering; **encumbramiento** *m* (*acto*) raising; (*altura*) height, loftiness; *fig.* exaltation; **encumbrar** [1a] raise (up); *p.* (*elevar*) exalt; (*ensalzar*) extol; ~se (*edificio*) tower; soar (*a. fig.*); (*p.*) be proud.
encurtido *m* pickle; **encurtir** [3a] pickle.
enchapado *m* plating; veneer; **enchapar** [1a] plate *con metal*; veneer *con madera etc.*
encharcada *f* pool, puddle; **encharcado** stagnant; **encharcar** [1g] swamp, cover with puddles; ~se fill (*or* get covered) with water.
enchufable ⚡ plug-in; **enchufar** [1a] connect, fit together; (*como telescopio*) telescope; ⚡ plug in; ✝ merge; **enchufe** *m* ⊕ joint, connexion; (*manguito*) sleeve; (*hueco*) socket; ⚡ plug, point, socket; F

(*p. etc.*) connexion, useful contact; (*sinecura*) cushy job; F *tener un buen* ~ pull wires, have useful contacts; **enchufismo** *m* F wire-pulling, getting things done through contacts; **enchufista** *m* F wire-puller, contact man.

ende: † *por* ~ therefore.

endeble ⚔ feeble, frail; *fig.* flimsy; **endeblez** *f* feebleness; *fig.* flimsiness.

endecasílabo 1. hendecasyllabic; **2.** *m* hendecasyllable.

endecha *f* dirge; **endecharse** [1a] grieve, mourn.

endémico endemic; *fig.* rife.

endemoniado possessed of the devil; *fig.* devilish, fiendish; furious, wild; **endemoniar** [1b] F provoke, stir up.

endentadura *f* serration; **endentar** [1k] ⊕ mesh, engage; **endentecer** [2d] teethe.

enderezado favourable, opportune; **enderezar** [1f] (*poner derecho*) straighten (out), unbend; (*poner vertical*) set up, right (*a.* ⚓); *fig.* direct; dedicate; (*gobernar*) manage; (*arreglar*) put in order; ~se straighten (up), draw o.s. up; ⚔ flatten out; ~ *a inf.* take steps to *inf.*

endeudarse [1a] run into debt.

endiablado devilish, fiendish; *co.* impish, mischievous; *cara* ugly; *S.Am.* complicated.

endibia *f* endive.

endilgar [1h] F send, direct; ~ *algo a uno* (*encajar*) spring s.t. on s.o., unload s.t. on to s.o.

endiosamiento *m* pride, vanity; absorption; **endiosar** [1a] deify; ~se give o.s. airs; (*absorto*) be absorbed.

endocrino endocrine.

endogamia *f* inbreeding; *engendrado por* ~ inbred.

endomingado in one's Sunday best, dressed up; **endomingarse** [1h] dress up (in one's Sunday best).

endosante *m/f* endorser; **endosar** [1a] endorse; **endosatario** *m* endorsee; **endoso** *m* endorsement.

endrina *f* sloe; **endrino** *m* sloe (bush), blackthorn.

endulzar [1f] sweeten (*a. fig.*); soften, mitigate.

endurecer [2d] harden, toughen (*a. fig.*); stiffen; *fig.* inure (*a* to);

~se harden, set; *fig.* become cruel; **endurecido** hard; *fig.* hardy, inured *a fatigas etc.*; (*cruel*) callous, hard-boiled F; **endurecimiento** *m* (*acto*) hardening; (*estado*) hardness; *fig.* callousness.

enebro *m* juniper.

enema *f* enema.

enemiga *f* enmity; **enemigo 1.** enemy, hostile; *fig.* inimical (*de* to); **2.** *m*, **a** *f* enemy; **enemistad** *f* enmity; **enemistar** [1a] set at odds, make enemies of; ~se fall out (*con* with), become enemies.

energía *f* energy; ⊕, ⚡ *etc.* power, energy; *fig.* drive, go F; ~ *atómica* atomic energy; **enérgico** energetic; *tono etc.* emphatic; *p.* energetic, vital, active; *esfuerzo* strenuous; *campaña* high-pressure; *medida etc.* bold, drastic.

energúmeno *m*, **a** *f* person possessed of the devil; *fig.* demon, madman.

enero *m* January.

enervación *f* enervation; **enervador** enervating; **enervar** [1a] enervate.

enésimo nth, umpteenth F.

enfadadizo irritable; **enfadar** [1a] annoy, anger, vex; ~se get angry, be cross (*de* at, *con* with); **enfado** *m* annoyance, irritation; (*afán*) trouble, bother; **enfadoso** annoying, vexatious; (*fatigoso*) irksome.

enfangar [1h] cover with mud; ~se *fig.* F get involved in dirty work; (*depravarse*) wallow in vice.

énfasis *m* emphasis; stress; **enfático** emphatic; positive.

enfermar [1a] *v/t.* make ill; *v/i.* fall ill, be taken ill; **enfermedad** *f* illness, sickness, disease; *fig.* malady; ~ *profesional* occupational disease; ~ *del sueño* sleeping-sickness; *una* ~ *que duró 3 meses* an illness which lasted 3 months; *una* ~ *muy peligrosa* a very dangerous disease; **enfermería** *f* sick-bay *de colegio etc.*; (*hospital*) infirmary; **enfermera** *f* nurse; ~ *jefa* matron; **enfermero** *m* male nurse; ⚔ orderly; **enfermizo** sickly, infirm; unhealthy; *mente* morbid; **enfermo 1.** ill, sick; ~ *de amor* lovesick; *caer* ~, *ponerse* ~ fall (take *Am.*) ill; **2.** *m*, **a** *f* patient, invalid.

enfilada *f* enfilade; **enfilar** [1a] ⚔

enfilade; (*alinear*) line up; (*ensartar*) thread.

enflaquecer [2d] *v/t.* make thin; weaken; *v/i.*, **~se** get thin, lose weight; *fig.* weaken; **enflaqueci-miento** *m* loss of weight; *fig.* weakening.

enflautado F pompous.

enfocar [1g] *phot. etc.* focus; *fig. problema* approach, consider, look at; size up; envisage; **enfoque** *m phot. etc.* focus(ing); (*aumento*) magnification; *fig.* grasp.

enfoscar [1g] fill with mortar; **~se** (*p.*) sulk; plunge (en *negocio* into); (*cielo*) cloud over.

enfrascar [1g] bottle; **~se** get entangled, get involved; bury o.s. (en *libro* in).

enfrenar [1a] *caballo* bridle; ⊕ brake; *fig.* restrain.

enfrentar [1a] *v/t.* put face to face, confront; *v/i.* face; **~se con** face (up to).

enfrente (en el *lado opuesto*) opposite; (*delante*) in front; (en *pugna*) against, in opposition; **~ de** opposite (to); la *casa de* **~** the house opposite.

enfriadera *f* cooling-jar; **enfria-dero** *m* cold-storage; **enfriamiento** *m* cooling; ✖ cold; **enfriar** [1c] cool (*a. fig.*), chill; **~se** cool (down or off); *fig.* grow cold, cool off.

enfundar [1a] sheathe, (put in its) case; (*llenar*) stuff.

enfurecer [2d] enrage, madden; **~se** (*p.*) get furious; (*mar*) get rough.

enfurruñarse [1a] F get angry; (*ponerse mohino*) sulk.

engaitar [1a] F wheedle, humbug, talk round.

engalanar [1a] adorn, (be)deck; **~se** dress up.

enganchar [1a] hook, hitch; (*colgar*) hang up; *caballo* harness; ⊕ couple; *fig.* inveigle, rope in; ✖ persuade to join up; **~se** get hooked up, catch; ✖ enlist; **enganche** *m* (*acto*) hook-ing (up); 📞, ⊕ coupling; ✖ recruit-ing, enlisting; (*dinero*) bounty.

engañabobos *m* (*p.*) trickster; (*trampa*) trick, trap; **engañadizo** gullible; **engañador 1.** deceptive; **2.** *m*, **-a** *f* cheat, impostor, deceiver; **engañar** [1a] deceive, fool F; (*ti-mar*) cheat, trick; mislead con *conse-jos falsos*; beguile con *encantos*;

delude con *promesas vanas*; *hambre* stay; *tiempo* kill, while away; *de-jarse* **~** por be taken in by; **~se** (*equivocarse*) be mistaken; delude o.s. con *esperanzas etc.*; **engañifa** *f* F trick, swindle; **engaño** *m* deceit; (*timo etc.*) fraud, trick; (*apariencia falsa*) sham; (*decepción*) delusion; (*equivocación*) mistake, misunder-standing; **~s** *pl.* wiles; **engañoso** *p. etc.* deceitful; *apariencia etc.* deceptive; *consejo etc.* misleading.

engarabitarse [1a] F climb, shin up; (*aterirse*) get stiff with cold.

engarce *m* linking, connection; set-ting *de joya*; **engarzar** [1f] *cuentas* thread; *joya* mount, set; (*rizar*) curl; *fig.* link, connect.

engastar [1a] set, mount; **engaste** *m* setting, mount(ing).

engatado thievish; **engat(us)ar** [1a] F coax, cajole, inveigle (*para que* into *ger.*).

engendrar [1a] beget, breed (*a. fig.*); generate (*a.* ⚡); *fig.* engender; **engendro** *m biol.* foetus; *fig.* bungled affair, abortion; F *mal* **~** bad lot.

englobar [1a] lump together.

engolfar [1a] ⚓ lose sight of land; **~se** en *fig.* plunge into; launch (out) into.

engolondrinarse [1a] F give o.s. airs; (*enamoricarse*) have a flirtation.

engolosinar [1a] tempt, entice; **~se** con grow fond of; grow accustomed to.

engolletarse [1a] give o.s. airs.

engomar [1a] gum, stick.

engordar [1a] *v/t.* fatten; *v/i.* get fat, fill out; F get rich; **engorde** *m* fattening.

engorrar [1a] *S.Am.* vex, bother; **engorro** *m* bother, nuisance; **en-gorroso** bothersome, vexatious, trying.

engranaje *m* gear(s), gearing, mesh; (*dientes*) gear-teeth; **engranar** [1a] *v/t.* gear; put into gear; **~ con** gear into, engage (with); *v/i.* interlock; ⊕ engage (con in, with), mesh (con with); *estar engranado* be in mesh.

engrandecer [2d] enlarge, magnify (*a. fig.*); (*alabar*) extol; exalt; **en-grandecimiento** *m* enlargement; *fig.* exaltation *etc.*

engrane *m* mesh(ing).

engrasador *m* greaser; **~ de com-**

presión grease-gun; **engrasar** [1a] grease, oil, lubricate; **engrase** *m* greasing, lubrication.

engreído conceited, proud, stuck-up F; **engreimiento** *m* conceit, vanity; **engreír** [3l] make conceited; *S.Am.* spoil; ~se get conceited; ~ con *S.Am.* grow fond of.

engrosar [1m] *v/t.* (*aumentar*) increase, swell; (*ensanchar*) enlarge; (*espesar*) thicken; *v/i.* get fat; ~se swell, expand.

engrudar [1a] paste; **engrudo** *m* paste.

enguijarrado *m* cobbles; **enguijarrar** [1a] cobble.

enguirnaldar [1a] garland; *fig.* wreathe.

engullir [3a *a.* 3h] gulp (down), bolt, gobble.

enhebrar [1a] thread.

enhestar [1k] (*poner derecho*) erect; (*elevar*) raise high, hoist up; **enhiesto** (*derecho*) erect; (*p.*) bolt upright; (*elevado*) lofty.

enhilar [1a] *aguja* thread; (*ordenar*) arrange, order.

enhorabuena *f* congratulations; ¡~! (*aprobación*) well and good; (*felicitación*) congratulations!, best wishes!; *dar la* ~ *a* congratulate; ¡**enhoramala!** good riddance!; ¡*vete* ~! go to the devil!

enhuerar [1a] addle.

enigma *m* enigma; puzzle; **enigmático** enigmatic(al); puzzling.

enjabonar [1a] soap; lather; F (*dar jabón*) soap up; F (*injuriar*) abuse.

enjaezar [1f] harness.

enjalbegar [1h] whitewash; *cara* paint.

enjambrar [1a] *v/t.* hive; *v/i.* swarm; **enjambre** *m* swarm (*a. fig.*).

enjarciar [1b] rig.

enjaular [1a] cage; coop up, pen in; F jail.

enjertar [1a] = *injertar*.

enjoyar [1a] set with precious stones; *fig.* (be)jewel, embellish.

enjuagar [1h] *platos, boca etc.* rinse; *cubo etc.* swill (out); **enjuague** *m* (*acto*) rinse, rinsing; (*licor*) mouthwash; *fig.* intrigue, scheme.

enjugamanos *m S.Am.* towel; **enjugar** [1h] wipe; dry; *deuda* wipe out.

enjuiciamiento *m* judgement; ⚖️

(*civil*) lawsuit, (*criminal*) trial; ~ *civil* civil suit; ~ *criminal* criminal prosecution; **enjuiciar** [1b] examine, judge; ⚖️ (*procesar*) prosecute, try; sentence.

enjundia *f fig.* substance; (*vigor*) drive.

enjuto lean, spare; (*seco*) wizened; *v. pie.*

enlabiar [1b] take in, bamboozle F; **enlabio** *m* humbug, honeyed words.

enlace *m* link, connexion (*a.* 🚂), tie-up; ⚔️ *etc.* liaison; 🔧 linkage; (*casamiento*) union.

enladrillado *m* brick paving; **enladrillar** [1a] pave with bricks.

enlatar [1a] can, tin.

enlazar [1f] *v/t.* connect, link, tie (together), knit (together); *S.Am.* lasso; *v/i.* 🚂 connect; ~se (*unirse*) link (up), be linked; (*engranar*) interlock; (*familias*) become connected by marriage.

enlodar [1a], **enlodazar** [1f] muddy, cover with mud; *fig.* (*manchar*) stain; defame.

enloquecedor maddening; *jaqueca* splitting; **enloquecer** [2d] *v/t.* madden, drive mad; *v/i.* go mad; **enloquecimiento** *m* madness.

enlosar [1a] pave.

enlucido *m* plaster; **enlucidor** *m* plasterer; **enlucir** [3f] plaster; *metal* polish.

enlutado in mourning; **enlutar** [1a] dress in mourning; *fig.* darken; ~se go into mourning.

enmaderado timbered; **enmaderamiento** *m* timbering; **enmaderar** [1a] timber.

enmarañar [1a] (en)tangle; *fig.* complicate, involve; confuse, make a mess of; ~se get tangled etc.

enmascarar [1a] mask; *fig.* mask, disguise; ~se *fig.* masquerade (*de* as).

enmendación *f* emendation *etc.*; **enmendar** [1k] emend, correct; *ley etc.* amend; reform *moralmente etc.*; *pérdida* repair, make good; ~se reform, mend one's ways; **enmienda** *f* emendation; amendment; compensation.

enmohecer [2d] rust; 🌱 make mouldy; ~se rust; 🌱 get mouldy; **enmohecido** rusty; 🌱 mouldy, mildewed.

enmudecer [2d] v/t. silence; v/i., ~se (callar) be silent; remain silent (debiendo hablar); (perder el habla) become dumb.

enmugrecer [2d] (be)grime.

ennegrecer [2d] blacken, dye etc. black.

ennoblecer [2d] ennoble; fig. embellish, adorn, dignify.

enojadizo short-tempered, testy, peevish; **enojar** [1a] anger; annoy, vex; ~se get angry, lose one's temper, get annoyed (con, contra with; de at); **enojo** m anger; annoyance, vexation; **enojoso** irritating, annoying.

enorgullecer [2d] fill with pride; ~se swell with pride; ~ de be proud of, pride o.s. on.

enorme enormous, huge; fig. heinous; **enormidad** f fig. enormity, heinousness de pecado etc.; (maldad) wickedness; (acto) monstrous thing.

enrabiar [1b] enrage.

enraizar [1f] take root.

enramada f arbour, bower.

enrarecer [2d] v/t. rarefy, thin; v/i., ~se (gas etc.) become rarefied, grow thin; (escasear) get scarce.

enredadera f (en general) creeper, climber; (especie) bindweed.

enredador m, -a f (chismoso) gossip, busybody; (embustero) mischiefmaker; **enredar** [1a] (coger con red) net; (enmarañar) (en)tangle; (entretejer) intertwine; (mezclar) mix up, make a mess of; fig. (meter en empeño) embroil, involve, implicate; sow discord between; ~se get (en)tangled; fig. get involved; **enredo** m tangle (a. fig.); fig. (confusión) entanglement, mess; mix-up F, maze de detalles etc.; (lío) embroilment; thea. etc. plot; **enredoso** tangled, tricky.

enrejado m lattice(-work) de ventana; trellis de jardín; (cerca) railing(s); onpenwork; **enrejar** [1a] ventana fix a grating to; (cercar) fence, put railings round.

enrevesado v. revesado.

enriquecer [2d] enrich, make rich; ~se get rich, prosper; **enriquecimiento** m enrichment.

enriscado craggy; **enriscar** [1g] raise; ~se hide among rocks.

enristrar [1a] string; dificultad straighten out.

enrizar(se) (1f) curl.

enrocar [1g] ajedrez: castle.

enrojecer [2d] v/t. redden; metal make red-hot; v/i., ~se blush, redden.

enrolarse [1a] S.Am. enlist, enrol.

enrollar [1a] roll (up), wind (up), coil.

enronquecer [2d] v/t. make hoarse; v/i. grow hoarse, get hoarse; **enronquecido** hoarse.

enroque m ajedrez: castling.

enroscadura f twist; kink; coil; **enroscar(se)** [1g] (torcer) twist, twine; (rizar) curl (up); alambre etc. coil, wind; esp. fig. wreathe.

ensacar [1g] sack, bag.

ensalada f salad; fig. (confusión) mix-up F; (mezcla) medley; mot. traffic jam; **ensaladera** f salad bowl; **ensaladilla** f (Russian etc.) salad.

ensalmador m bone-setter, quack; **ensalmar** [1a] hueso set; cure by quack remedies; **ensalmo** m ✖ quack treatment; (fórmula) charm, incantation; (como) por ~ as if by magic.

ensalzamiento m exaltation; **ensalzar** [1f] exalt; (alabar) extol.

ensamblador m joiner; **ensambladura** f joint; (arte) joinery; ~ dentada joggle; ~ francesa scarf; ~ de inglete mitre joint; **ensamblar** [1a] join; assemble.

ensanchador m ⊕ stretcher; **ensanchar** [1a] enlarge, widen, extend; (estirar) stretch; sew. let out; ~se stretch, expand; **ensanche** m enlargement, widening; extension, expansion; stretch(ing); new development de ciudad etc.; sew. room to let out.

ensangrentado blood-stained, gory, **ensangrentar** [1k] stain with blood; ~se fig. get angry; ~ con, ~ contra treat cruelly, treat vindictively.

ensañamiento m cruelty, barbarity; **ensañar** [1a] enrage; ~se en vent one's anger on; delight in tormenting (or hurting).

ensartar [1a] cuentas etc. string; aguja thread; fig. reel off, trot out.

ensayar [1a] test, try (out); metal assay; thea., ♪ rehearse; ~se practise; ~ a inf. practise ger.; **ensayista** m/f essayist; **ensayo** m test, trial; assay *de metal*; (*entrenamiento*) practice; *lit.* essay; *thea.*, ♪ rehearsal; *rugby*: try; ~ *general* dress rehearsal; *de* ~ tentative; *viaje etc.* trial *attr.*; *vuelo* test *attr.*; *hacer* ~s practise (*en* on).

enselvado wooded.

ensenada *f* inlet, cove, creek.

enseña *f* standard, ensign; **enseñado** trained, informed; *bien* ~ *perro* house-trained; **enseñanza** *f* teaching, instruction, education; schooling; tuition; *primera* ~, ~ *primaria* elementary education; *segunda* ~ secondary education; ~ *superior* higher education; **enseñar** [1a] (*instruir*) teach; train; (*mostrar*) show; (*indicar*) point out; ~**se** *a* accustom o.s. to.

enseñorearse [1a]: ~ *de* take possession of, take over.

enseres *m/pl.* goods and chattels; (*accesorios*) gear, equipment.

ensiladora *f* silo; **ensilar** [1a] store in a silo.

ensillar [1a] saddle (up).

ensimismamiento *m* reverie, brown study; **ensimismarse** [1a] be absorbed, be in a brown study; *S.Am.* be conceited.

ensoberbecerse [2d] become proud; (*mar*) get rough.

ensombrear [1a] overshadow; **ensombrecer** [2d] darken; ~**se** become gloomy.

ensordecedor deafening; **ensordecer** [2d] *v/t. p.* deafen; *ruido* muffle; *v/i.* go deaf; (*fingir*) pretend not to hear.

ensortijar [1a] curl; *nariz* ring.

ensuciamiento *m* soiling; *mst fig.* pollution; **ensuciar** [1b] soil, dirty, mess up, (be)foul; *fig.* defile, pollute; ~**se** soil o.s. *en vestido*, wet one's bed *en cama*.

ensueño *m* dream, reverie; *de* ~ dream-like.

entablado *m* (floor-)boarding; **entabladura** *f* boarding, planking; **entablar** [1a] ⊕ board (up); ⚔ splint; ⚕ bring, institute; *tablero* set up; *conversación etc.* enter into, strike up; ~**se** (*viento*) settle.

entablillar [1a] ⚔ splint.

entallador *m* sculptor; engraver; **entalladura** *f*, **entallamiento** *m* sculpture; carving; engraving; (*corte*) slot, groove; **entallar** [1a]

v/t. (*esculpir*) carve; (*grabar*) engrave; (*hacer cortes en*) notch, slot; *v/i.* (*vestido*) fit; *traje que entalla bien* well tailored suit.

entallecer [2d] shoot, sprout.

entapizado ⚘ overgrown (*de* with); **entapizar** [1f] upholster; *pared* hang with tapestry; *silla etc.* cover with fabric.

entarascar(se) [1g] F dress up, doll up.

entarimado *m* (floor-)boarding; (*mosaico*) inlaid floor; ~ (*de hojas quebradas*) parquet; **entarimar** [1a] board, plank.

entarugado *m* block flooring, block paving.

ente *m* entity, being; F guy, ass.

enteco weak(ly), sickly.

entelerido shivering with cold (*or* fright); *S.Am.* frail.

entendederas *f/pl.* F: *tener malas* ~, *ser corto de* ~ be slow on the uptake; **entendedor** *m*, *-a f* understanding person; *al buen* ~ *pocas palabras* a word to the wise man is enough.

entender [2g] *mst* understand; (*tener intención, querer decir*) intend, mean; (*creer*) believe; *no entiendo palabra* it's Greek to me; *a mi* ~ in my opinion; ~ *de* know about, be good at, be experienced as (*carpintería a carpenter*); *no* ~ *de a.* be no judge of; ~ *en* (*versado*) be familiar with, know all about; (*que trata*) deal with; *dar a* ~ give to understand, imply; purport; *hacer* ~ put across; *hacerse* ~ make o.s. understood, get across; *lograr* ~ manage to understand, get the hang of; ~**se** have one's reasons; (*dos ps.*) understand one another, get along well together; *se entiende que* it is understood that; *eso se entiende* that is understood; ~ *con* know how to manage *en el trato*; (*acuerdo*) come to an agreement with; *eso no se entiende conmigo* that's not my concern; **entendido** (*sabio*) wise, knowing; (*enterado*) (well-) informed; *bien* ~ *que* on the understanding that; *no darse por* ~ pretend not to understand; **entendimiento** *m* understanding; (*inteligencia*) mind; (*juicio*) judgement.

entenebrecer [2d] darken; *asunto* fog; ~**se** get dark.

enterado knowledgeable, (well-) informed; *S.Am.* conceited; *estar~* be informed (*de* about), be in the know; **enterar** [1a] inform; *~se de* learn, find out, hear of, get to know (about).

entereza *f* entirety; *fig.* integrity, strength of mind; fortitude; firmness; (*severidad*) strictness.

entérico enteric; **enteritis** *f* enteritis.

enterizo in one piece, one-piece.

enternecedor moving, pitiable; **enternecer** [2d] soften; *fig.* touch, move (*to pity etc.*); *~se* be touched, be moved; **enternecimiento** *m* compassion, tenderness.

entero 1. entire, whole; complete; *fig.* (*recto*) upright; firm; (*sano*) sound; robust; ⅄ integral, whole; *por ~* wholly, completely; **2.** *m* ⅄ integer.

enterrador *m* grave-digger; **enterramiento** *m* burial, interment; **enterrar** [1k] bury (*a. fig.*), inter.

entibiar [1b] cool (*a. fig.*), take the chill off.

entibo *m* ⚒ prop.

entidad *f* entity; ✝ firm, concern; *pol. etc.* body, organization; *de ~* of moment, of consequence.

entierro *m* burial, interment; (*funeral, procesión*) funeral; F treasure trove.

entintar [1a] ink (in).

entoldado *m* awning; (*tienda grande*) marquee; **entoldar** [1a] put an awning over; (*adornar*) decorate (with hangings); *~se* (*cielo*) cloud over; (*p.*) give o.s. airs.

entomología *f* entomology.

entonación *f* intonation; *fig.* conceit; **entonado** haughty, starchy; ♪ in tune; **entonar** [1a] *v/t.* *canción etc.* intone; (*afinar*) sing in tune; *nota* pitch, give *para empezar*; *phot., paint.,* tone; ♪ tone up; *alabanzas* sound; *v/i.* be in tune; *~se* give o.s. airs.

entonces then, at that time; (*siendo así*) and so; well then; *desde ~* since then; ɛver since; *en aquel ~* at that time.

entono *m* (*acto*) intoning; (*canto afinado*) being in tune; *fig.* haughtiness.

entontecer [2d] *v/t.* make silly; *v/i.,* *~se* get silly.

entornar [1a] half-close; *puerta* leave ajar; (*volcar*) upset.

entorpecer [2d] dull, (be)numb, stupefy; *fig.* obstruct, set back, slow up; **entorpecimiento** *m* numbness, torpor; *fig.* obstruction, delay, slowing-up.

entrada *f* (*en general*) entrance, way in; (*parte de edificio etc.*) porch, doorway, gateway, entrance-hall; (*acto*) entry (*en* into); admission (*en academia etc.* to); (*derecho*) right of entry; beginning *de año etc.*; *thea. etc.* (*localidad*) ticket; (*total*) house; *deportes:* (*total*) gate; *béisbol etc.:* innings; influx *de turistas etc.*; *cocina:* entrée; ⊕ input, intake; ✝ entry *en libro mayor*; (*ingresos*) income, receipts; *~ de favor, ~ de regalo* complimentary ticket, pass; *~ llena* full house; *derechos de ~* import duties; *dar ~ a* admit; give an opening to; *prohibida la ~* keep out, no admittance.

entramado *m* ⚠ truss.

entrambos *lit.* both.

entrampar [1a] trap, (en)snare; F (*enredar*) mess up; ✝ burden with debts; *~se* F get into a mess; ✝ get into debt.

entrante 1. *p.* incoming; *mes etc.* next; *ángulo* re-entrant; **2.** *m* inlet.

entrañable (*querido*) intimate, dearly-loved; (*afectuoso*) affectionate; **entrañar** [1a] (*introducir*) bury deep; (*contener*) contain, harbour; *~se* become very intimate; *~ en* reach the heart of; **entrañas** *f/pl.* entrails, bowels (*a. fig.*), inside(s) F; *fig.* (*lo más oculto*) innermost parts; (*centro, ánimo*) heart; disposition.

entrar [1a] **1.** *v/t.* (*hacer entrar*) bring in, show in; (*influir*) get at, influence; ✗ attack; (*estudio etc.*) attract; *no me entran las matemáticas* I can't get the hang of maths; **2.** *v/i.* go in, come in, enter; (*año etc.*) begin; *~ a inf.* begin to *inf.*; *~ bien* (*convenir*) be fitting; (*venir al caso*) be to the point; *~ en* enter, go into; *esp. fig.* enter into; (*encajar*) fit into; *sociedad* join, be admitted to; *profesión* adopt; *número* be one of, be counted among; (*río*) flow into.

entre between *dos,* among(st) *varios;* (*en medio de*) in the midst of; ᵥ tú y yo (between) the two of us; de ᵥ out of, from among; decir ᵥ sí say to o.s.

entre... inter...; ᵥ**abierto** half-open; ᵥ**acto** m interval; ᵥ**ayudarse** [1a] help one another; ᵥ**cano** greyish; ᵥ**cejo** m space between the eyebrows; fig. frown; fruncir el ᵥ frown; ᵥ**coger** [2c] catch, intercept; fig. press; (hacer callar) silence; ᵥ**cortado** intermittent; ᵥ**cortar** [1a] partially cut; interrupt.

entrecruzar [1f] interlace; ᵥse biol. interbreed.

entre...: ᵥ**cubiertas** f/pl. between-decks; ᵥ**chocarse** [1g] collide; ᵥ**dicho** m prohibition, ban; ♊ injunction; ᵥ**fino** medium-quality.

entrega f (acto) delivery; surrender; instalment, part de novela etc.; ℅ post, delivery; ᵥ contra paga (or reembolso) cash on delivery; ᵥ en fecha futura forward delivery; **entregar** [1h] (dar, poner en manos) deliver; hand (over), hand in; (ceder) surrender; give up, part with; sl. ᵥla kick the bucket; ✝ a ᵥ to be surrender; ᵥse surrender, give in; ᵥ a devote o.s. to, indulge in; b.s. abandon o.s. to; ᵥ de take possession of.

entre...: ᵥ**lazar(se)** [1f] entwine, interlace; ᵥ**listado** striped; ᵥ**medias** (in) between; in the meantime; ᵥ**més** m thea. interlude; ᵥes pl. hors d'oeuvres; ᵥ**meter** [2a] insert; v. entrometer; ᵥ**mezclar** [1a] intermingle; intersperse.

entrenador m deportes: trainer (a. ⚒), coach; **entrenamiento** m training; **entrenar** [1a] train, coach; ᵥse train.

entre...: ᵥ**oir** [3q] half-hear; ᵥ**paño** m (door-)panel; (estante) shelf; ᵥ**pierna(s)** f (pl.) crotch, crutch; ᵥ**puente** m between-decks; steerage; ᵥ**sacar** [1g] pelo, árboles etc. thin out; (escoger) pick out; (examinar) sift; ᵥ**sijo** m mesentery; fig. secret; difficulty, snag; tener muchos ᵥs be complicated; (p.) be very deep; ᵥ**suelo** m mezzanine, entresol; ᵥ**tanto 1.** adv. meanwhile, meantime; **2.** m meantime; ᵥ**tejer** [2a] entwine, interweave; (trabar) mat; palabras etc. put in, insert; ᵥ**tela** f interlining; ᵥs pl. heartstrings; ᵥ**telar** [1a] interline.

entretener [2l] (divertir) entertain; (ocupar) keep (occupied); keep in suspense; engage en conversación; (demorar) hold up, delay; tiempo while away; ⊕ maintain; **entretenida:** dar (con) la ᵥ a hedge with, keep s.o. talking; **entretenido** entertaining, amusing; **entretenimiento** m entertainment, amusement; recreation; (manutención) upkeep; ⊕ maintenance.

entre...: ᵥ**ver** [2v] glimpse; fig. guess, suspect; ᵥ**verado** tocino streaky; ᵥ**verar** [1a] intermingle; mix up; ᵥ**vero** m jumble, mix-up F; ᵥ**vía** f ⛟ gauge.

entrevista f interview, conference; **entrevistar** [1a] interview; ᵥse con interview, have an interview with.

entristecer [2d] sadden, grieve; ᵥse grow sad, grieve.

entrometerse [2a] meddle, interfere (en in, with), intrude; **entrometido 1.** meddlesome, interfering; **2.** m, a f busybody.

entroncar [1g] be related, be connected (con to, with), join; S.Am. ♊ connect (con with).

entronizar [1f] enthrone; fig. exalt.

entronque m relationship, connexion; S.Am. ⛟ junction.

entruchada f F trap, trick; **entruchar** [1a] F decoy, lure.

entuerto m wrong, injustice.

entumecer [2d] (be)numb; ᵥse (miembro) get numb, go to sleep; (río) swell; (mar) surge; **entumecido** stiff, numbed, cramped; **entumecimiento** m stiffness etc.

enturbiar [1b] agua muddy, disturb; fig. obscure, fog, confuse.

entusiasmar [1a] excite, fire, fill with enthusiasm; ᵥse get excited (por about, over); ᵥ por be enthusiastic about, be keen on, rave about; **entusiasmo** m enthusiasm (por for); keenness, zeal, zest; **entusiasta 1.** enthusiastic; keen (de on); zealous (de for); **2.** m/f enthusiast; fan F; **entusiástico** enthusiastic.

enumeración f enumeration; **enumerar** [1a] enumerate.

enunciación f enunciation; declaration; **enunciar** [1b] enunciate; declare.

envainar [1a] sheathe; sl. ¡enváinala! shut your trap!

envalentonamiento *m* boldness, daring; *b.s.* bravado; **envalentonar** [1a] embolden; *b.s.* fill with Dutch courage; ~se take courage; put on a bold front.

envanecer [2d] make vain; ~se grow vain; swell with pride (*con, de at*).

envasar [1a] *v/t.* pack(age), wrap; bottle; can, tin; *v/i. fig.* tipple; **envase** *m* (*acto*) packing *etc.*; (*recipiente en general*) container; (*papel*) wrapping; bottle; (*lata*) can, tin; *sin* ~ loose, unwrapped; ~s *pl.* a *devolver* returnable empties.

envedijarse [1a] get tangled.

envejecer [2d] *v/t.* age, make old; *v/i.*, ~se age, grow old, get old; **envejecido** aged, (looking) old.

envenenador *m*, **-a** *f* poisoner; **envenenamiento** *m* poisoning; **envenenar** [1a] poison (*a. fig.*); *relaciones etc.* embitter.

enverdecer [2d] turn green.

envergadura *f* ⚓ breadth; ✕ ~ (de *alas*) wingspan; (*extensión*) expanse, spread, span; *fig.* scope, compass, reach.

envés *m* back, wrong side *de tela*; flat *de espada*; F *anat.* back.

enviado *m* envoy; **enviar** [1c] send (*por* for).

enviciar [1b] corrupt; *fig.* vitiate; ~se con (*or en*) become addicted to.

envidar [1a] bid.

envidia *f* envy, jealousy; *tener* ~ *a* envy; **envidiable** enviable; **envidiar** [1b] envy, begrudge (*algo a uno* a p. a th.); (*desear*) covet; **envidioso** envious, jealous; (*deseoso*) covetous.

envilecer [2d] debase, degrade; ~se degrade o.s.; grovel; **envilecimiento** *m* degradation.

envío *m* (*acto*) sending, dispatch; ✝ consignment *de mercancías*, remittance *de dinero*; ⚓ shipment; *gastos de* ~ postage and packing.

envión *m* push, shove.

envite *m* stake, side-bet; *fig.* (*ofrecimiento*) offer; (*empujón*) push, shove.

enviudar [1a] become a widow(er), be widowed.

envoltorio *m* bundle; **envoltura** *f* cover(ings), casing, wrapping; ⚓, ✕ *etc.* envelope; ~s *pl.* swaddling clothes; **envolvedor** *m* cover, wrapping; **envolvente** *movimiento* encircling, enveloping; **envolver** [2h; *p.p.* envuelto] (*con papel etc.*) wrap (up), tie up, do up; (*con ropa*) wrap, swathe; (*contener, ceñir*) envelop, enfold; muffle *contra frío, ruido etc.*; ✕ encircle, surround; *fig.* involve, imply; ~se *fig.* become involved; **envolvimiento** *m* envelopment; ✕ encirclement; *fig.* involvement.

enyesado *m* plastering; **enyesar** [1a] plaster.

enzarzar [1f] *fig.* involve, entangle; ~se get involved, get tied up.

épica *f* epic; **épico** epic.

epicúreo *adj. a. su. m* epicurean.

epidemia *f* epidemic; **epidémico** epidemic.

epidermis *f* epidermis.

Epifanía *f* Epiphany.

epígrafe *m* inscription; (*lema*) motto, device; (*título*) title; (*titular*) headline.

epigrama *m* epigram; **epigramático** epigrammatic(al).

epilepsia *f* epilepsy; **epiléptico** *adj. a. su. m*, **a** *f* epileptic.

epilogar [1h] sum up; **epílogo** *m* epilogue.

episcopado *m* (*oficio*) bishopric; (*período*) episcopate; (*obispos*) bishops, episcopate, episcopacy; **episcopal** episcopal.

episodio *m* episode; incident; **episódico** episodic(al).

epístola *f* epistle; **epistolar** epistolary; **epistolario** *m* collected letters.

epitafio *m* epitaph.

epíteto *m* epithet.

epitomar [1a] condense, abridge, epitomize; **epítome** *m* compendium, epitome.

época *f* period, time, epoch; *de* ~ period *attr.*; *coche etc.* vintage; *hacer* ~ be a landmark, be epoch-making.

epopeya *f* epic (*a. fig.*).

equidad *f* equity (*a. ⚖*); fairness, impartiality.

equidistante equidistant.

equilátero equilateral.

equilibrar [1a] (*poner en equilibrio*) balance, poise; (*igualar*) balance, adjust, redress; **equilibrio** *m* balance, equilibrium; *esp. fig.*

poise; ~ *político* balance of power;
equilibrista *m/f* tight-rope walker,
acrobat.

equino equine ♋, horse *attr.*

equinoccio *m* equinox.

equipaje *m* luggage, piece of
luggage; (*equipo*) equipment, kit;
⚓ crew; *hacer el* ~ pack (up);
equipar [1a] equip, furnish, fit
out, fit up (*con* with).

equiparar [1a] consider equal,
equalize, put on a level (with);
compare; ~*se con* rank with.

equipo *m* equipment, outfit, kit;
shift *de obreros*; (*grupo, deportes
etc.*) team; (*acto*) fitting-out.

equitación *f* (*acto*) riding; (*arte*)
horsemanship; *escuela de* ~ riding-
school.

equitativo equitable, reasonable;
trato fair, square.

equivalencia *f* equivalence; **equivalente** *adj. a. su. m* equivalent
(*a* to); **equivaler** [2q]: ~ *a* be
equivalent to; amount to; (*en nivel,
grado*) rank as, rank with.

equivocación *f* mistake, error;
(*descuido*) oversight; (*malentendido*)
misunderstanding; *por* ~ in error,
by mistake; **equivocado** wrong,
mistaken; *cariño etc.* misplaced;
equivocar [1g] mistake (*A con B*
A for B); ~*se* be wrong, make a
mistake; be mistaken (*con* for);
~ *de casa* go to the wrong house;
equívoco 1. equivocal, ambiguous;
2. *m* equivocation, ambiguity;
(*palabra*) ambiguous word, word
having two meanings; (*juego de
palabras*) pun, word-play.

era[1] *etc. v. ser.*

era[2] *f* era, age; ~ *atómica* atomic age.

era[3] *f* ✸ threshing-floor; (*cuadro*)
bed, plot.

erario *m* exchequer, treasury.

erección *f* erection; *fig.* establishment.

eremita *m* hermit; recluse.

ergio *m* erg.

erguido erect; *cuerpo etc.* straight;
erguir [3n] (*levantar*) raise; (*poner
derecho*) straighten; ~*se* straighten
up; *fig.* swell with pride.

erial 1. uncultivated; **2.** *m* common;
(*yermo*) waste land.

erigir [3c] erect, build, raise; *fig.*
establish; ~ *en* set *s.o.* up as; ~*se en*
set up as.

erisipela *f* erysipelas.

erizado bristly; bristling (*de* with);
erizarse [1f] bristle; (*pelo*) stand
on end; **erizo** *m zo.* hedgehog; ♀
bur; F surly fellow; ~ *de mar* sea-
urchin.

ermita *f* hermitage; **ermitaño** *m*
hermit.

erosión *f* erosion; **erosionar(se)**
[1a] erode; **erosivo** erosive.

erótico erotic; *poesía etc.* love *attr.*;
erotismo *m* eroticism; **erotomanía** *f* (pathological) eroticism;
erotómano (pathologically) erotic.

errabundeo *m* wanderings;
errabundo wandering.

erradicar [1g] eradicate.

erradizo wandering, **errado** (*equivocado*) mistaken; (*inexacto*) wide
of the mark; (*imprudente*) unwise;
errante (*no fijo*) wandering,
roving, itinerant; (*perdido*) stray;
fig. errant; **errar** [1l] *v/t. tiro,
vocación* miss; (*no cumplir*) fail (in
one's duty to); *v/i.* wander, rove,
roam (about); = ~*se* err, go
astray; ~ *en vocación* miss; **errata** *f*
misprint, erratum; **errático** erratic.

erre: F ~ *que* ~ obstinately.

erróneo wrong, mistaken, erroneous;
error *m* error, mistake; fault;
fallacy *en teoría etc.*; ~ *de imprenta*
misprint; ~ *judicial* miscarriage of
justice; ~ *de pluma* clerical error.

eructar [1a] belch; **eructación** *f*,
eructo *m* belch, eructation ♋.

erudición *f* erudition, learning,
scholarship; **erudito 1.** erudite,
learned, scholarly; **2.** *m, a f*
scholar.

erupción *f* eruption (*a.* ✸); outbreak; ~ (*cutánea*) rash; *entrar en* ~
erupt; **eruptivo** eruptive.

esa *etc. v. ese.*

esbeltez *f* slenderness *etc.*; **esbelto**
slim, slender, svelte.

esbirro *m* myrmidon, henchman;
(*alguacil*) constable, bailiff.

esbozar [1f] sketch, outline; **esbozo**
m sketch, outline.

escabechar [1a] pickle, souse; F do
in, carve up; F *univ.* plough;
escabeche *m* pickle, souse; (*pescado*) soused fish; *esp.* pickled tunny-
fish.

escabel *m* (foot)stool.

escabiosa *f* scabious.

escabrosidad f roughness, ruggedness etc.; **escabroso** terreno rough, rugged; (desigual) uneven; fig. (áspero) harsh; asunto difficult, thorny; cuento risky, scabrous.

escabullirse [3a] make o.s. scarce, slip away, clear out; ~ por slip through.

escafandra f diving-suit.

escala f (escalera) ladder; (graduación etc.) scale (a. ♪, ♪); range de velocidades etc.; ♫ port of call; (parada) intermediate stop; ~ móvil sliding scale; según ~ to scale; sin ~s non-stop; en gran(de) ~ on a large scale, in a big way; hacer ~ en put in at, call at; **escalada** f scaling, climbing; **escalafón** m establishment, list of officials, scale.

escalamera f rowlock.

escalar [1a] scale, climb; casa burgle, break into.

escaldado F wary, fly; mujer loose. **escaldadura** f scald; **escaldar** [1a] scald; metal make red-hot.

escalera f stairs, staircase en casa; (flight of) steps esp. al descubierto; (escala) ladder; mot. tailboard; ~ de caracol spiral staircase; ~ de incendios fire-escape; ~ mecánica, ~ móvil, ~ rodante escalator, moving staircase; ~ de servicio backstairs; ~ de tijera steps, stepladder.

escalfador m chafing-dish; **escalfar** [1a] huevo poach.

escalinata f (flight of) steps.

escalofriado chilly; **escalofrío** m chill (a. ♯); (estremecimiento) shivering, shiver(s).

escalón m step, stair de escalera; rung de escala; fig. (grado) stage, grade; stepping-stone, ladder hacia un fin etc.; ✗ echelon; **escalonar** [1a] spread out at intervals; step; horas, ⊕ stagger; ✗ echelon.

escalpar [1a] scalp.

escalpelo m scalpel.

escama f zo. scale; fig. (resentimiento) grudge; (recelo) suspicion; **escamado** distrustful, wary; **escamar** [1a] scale; F make wary, make suspicious; ~se F get wary, get suspicious, be once bitten twice shy; **escamón** apprehensive, suspicious.

escamondar [1a] prune (a. fig.).

escamoso pez scaly; sustancia flaky.

escamoteador m conjurer; fig. swindler; **escamot(e)ar** [1a] whisk away, make s.t. vanish; carta palm; F steal, swipe; **escamoteo** m sleight of hand, conjuring; (un ~) conjuring trick.

escampar [1a] v/t. clear out; v/i. clear up, stop raining; fig. give up.

escampavía f revenue cutter.

escanciador m wine-waiter; **escanciar** [1b] vino pour (out), serve; vaso drain.

escandalizar [1f] scandalize, shock; ~se be shocked; be offended; **escándalo** m scandal; (alboroto, protesta etc.) row, uproar; bad example; armar un ~ make a scene; **escandaloso** scandalous, shocking; ofensa etc. flagrant; vida etc. disorderly; niño etc. undisciplined, uncontrollable.

escandallo m ♫ lead.

escandinavo adj. a. su. m, a f Scandinavian.

escandir [3a] scan; **escansión** f scansion.

escantillón m pattern, template, scantling.

escaño m bench, settle.

escapada f (huida) escape; (travesura) escapade; flying visit; ~ en una tabla narrow squeak; **escapar** [1a] escape (a acc., de from); run away; ~ de manos elude; ~se escape; run away; get out; (gas etc.) leak (out); ~ con make off with; se me escapa fig. it eludes me; ~le algo a uno fig. (decir etc.) let s.t. slip; (no ver) escape one's notice.

escaparate m show-case, display cabinet; shop-window de tienda; **escaparatista** m/f window-dresser.

escapatoria f (huida) escape, getaway; fig. loophole, excuse; escape del trabajo etc.

escape m escape, flight, get-away; ⊕ exhaust (a. tubo de ~, gases de ~); leak(age) de gas, líquido; ⊕ escapement; a ~ at full speed; ⊕ de ~ exhaust attr.; **escapismo** m escapism.

escapular scapular; **escapulario** m scapular(y).

escaque m square (of chessboard).

escara f ♯ crust, slough.

escarabajear [1a] v/t. F bother, worry; v/i. wriggle, squirm; (escribir) scrawl, scribble; **escarabajo** m beetle; ⊕ flaw; F runt, dwarf; ~s *pl.* F scrawl.

escáramujo *m* dog-rose, brier; (*fruta*) hip.

escaramuza *f* skirmish, brush; **escaramuzar** [1f] skirmish.

escarapela *f* rosette, cockade; F set-to.

escarbadientes *m* toothpick; **escarbador** *m* scraper; **escarbar** [1a] scratch; *lumbre* poke; *dientes* pick; *fig.* delve into.

escarcha *f* (hoar)frost; **escarchado** *fruta* crystallized; **escarchar** [1a] *v/t. pastel* ice; *v/i.* freeze.

escarcho *m* roach.

escarda *f* weeding-hoe; (*labor*) weeding, hoeing; **escardar** [1a] weed (out) (*a. fig.*); **escardillo** *m* weeding-hoe.

escariador *m* reamer; **escariar** [1b] ream.

escarificación *f* ✄, ✂ scarification; **escarificador** *m* scarifier; **escarificar** [1g] scarify.

escarlata *f* scarlet; scarlet cloth; **escarlatina** *f* scarlet fever.

escarmenar [1a] *lana* comb; *fig.* punish; F do out of *s.t.* bit by bit.

escarmentar [1k] *v/t.* punish severely, teach a lesson (to); *v/i.* learn one's lesson; **escarmiento** *m* punishment; warning, lesson; *para ~ de* as a lesson to; *servir de ~* be a warning (*a* to).

escarnecer [2d] scoff at, ridicule; **escarnio** *m* jibe, jeer; derision.

escarola *f* endive.

escarolar [1a] curl; frill.

escarpa *f* scarp, escarpment, slope; **escarpado** steep, sheer; craggy; **escarpadura** = *escarpa*; **escarpar** [1a] *terreno* (e)scarp; (*raspar*) rasp.

escarpia *f* spike, tenterhook.

escarpín *m* (*zapato*) pump; (*calcetín*) extra sock; ~*es pl.* ankle socks *de muchacha.*

escasear [1a] *v/t.* be sparing with, skimp; *v/i.* be scarce, get scarce, fall short; **escasez** *f* scarcity, shortage; (*tacañería*) stinginess; **escaso** scarce; scant(y); (*miserable*) meagre, skimpy; *cosecha, público* thin, sparse; *posibilidad, recursos* slim, slight; *dinero* tight; *provisión* short; *p.* (*tacaño*) stingy; (*económico*) sparing; ~ *de* short of;

6 *metros* ~*s* barely 6 metres; *por una cabeza* ~*a* by a short head.

escatimar [1a] skimp, give grudgingly, stint, be sparing of; *esfuerzo* spare; **escatimoso** scrimpy, mean.

escena *f mst* scene; (*parte del teatro*) stage; ~ *muda* by-play; *poner en* ~ stage, perform; **escenario** *m* (*parte del teatro*) stage; scene, setting *de acción*; *cine:* continuity; **escénico** scenic; **escenógrafo** *m* scene-painter.

escepticismo *m* scepticism; **escéptico 1.** sceptical; **2.** *m*, a *f* sceptic, doubter.

escindir [3a] split; **escisión** *f* scission; *fig.* split, division; ~ *nuclear* nuclear fission.

esclarecer [2d] *v/t.* (*aclarar*) explain, elucidate; illuminate; *fig.* ennoble; *v/i.* dawn; **esclarecido** illustrious.

esclavina *f* cape, tippet.

esclavitud *f* slavery, bondage; **esclavizar** [1f] enslave; **esclavo** *adj. a. su. m*, a *f* slave.

esclerosis *f* sclerosis.

esclusa *f* lock, sluice; flood-gate.

escoba *f* broom; **escobada** *f* sweep; **escobar** [1a] sweep; **escobazo** *m* quick sweep; *echar a* ~*s* kick out; **escobilla** *f* whisk; brush (*a. ⚡*); **escobillón** *m* ⚓, ⊕ swab; **escobón** *m* long-handled broom; scrubbing-brush *para fregar*; ⚓, ⊕ swab.

escocer [2b a. 2h] *v/t.* annoy; *v/i.* smart, sting; ~*se* chafe.

escocés 1. Scots, Scotch, Scottish; **2.** *m* Scot(sman); (*idioma*) Scots; **escocesa** *f* Scot(swoman).

escofina *f* rasp; **escofinar** [1a] rasp.

escoger [2c] choose, select, pick out; elect *en elección*; **escogido** select, choice; *obras* selected.

escolar 1. scholastic; school *attr.*; **2.** *m* pupil, schoolboy; **escolástica** *f*, **escolasticismo** *m* scholasticism; **escolástico 1.** scholastic; **2.** *m* schoolman.

escolta *f* escort; **escoltar** [1a] escort, guard, protect; ⚓ convoy, escort.

escollo *m* reef, rock; *fig.* pitfall, stumbling-block.

escombrar [1a] clear out, clean out; **escombrera** *f* tip, dump; *metall.* slag-heap; **escombro** *m* *ichth.*

mackerel; ~s *pl.* debris, wreckage, rubble.

escondedero *m* hiding-place; **esconder** [2a] hide, conceal (de from); ~se hide; lurk; **escondid-(ill)as:** *a* ~ by stealth, on the sly; *a* ~ de behind the back of; **escondite** *m* hiding-place, cache; (*juego*) hide-and-seek; **escondrijo** *m* hiding-place, hide-out; *fig.* nook.

escopeta *f* shotgun; ~ de viento air-gun; **escopetazo** *m* (*tiro*) gunshot; (*herida*) gunshot wound; *fig.* bad news, blow; **escopetear** [1a] shoot at (with a shotgun); ~se *a* shower one another with; **escopeteo** *m* shooting; burst; lively exchange *de injurias etc.*; **escopetero** *m* gunsmith.

escoplear [1a] chisel; **escoplo** *m* chisel.

escora *f* ⚓ level line; (*inclinación*) list.

escorbuto *m* scurvy.

escoria *f metall.* slag, dross; scum (*a. fig.*); **escorial** *m* slag-heap, dump.

escorpión *m* scorpion.

escorzar [1f] foreshorten; **escorzo** *m* foreshortening.

escota *f* ⚓ sheet.

escotado décolleté, low(-necked); **escotadura** *f* low neck; *thea.* large trapdoor; **escotar** [1a] *v/t. sew.* cut to fit; *río etc.* draw water from; *v/i.* pay one's share; **escote** *m sew.* (low) neck, décolletage; share *de dinero*; ir *a* ~, pagar *a* ~ pay one's share.

escotilla *f* hatch(way); **escotillón** *m* trapdoor.

escozor *m* smart, sting; *fig.* grief.

escriba *m* scribe; **escribanía** *f* (*escritorio*) writing-desk; writing-case; (*tintero*) inkstand; (*oficio*) clerkship; **escribano** *m* ⚖ clerk; † notary; ~ municipal town clerk; **escribiente** *m* amanuensis; (*empleado*) clerk; **escribir** [3a; *p.p.* escrito] write; (*ortografiar*) spell; ¿cómo se escribe eso? how is that spelled?; el que esto escribe the (present) writer; **escrito 1.** *p.p.* of escribir; **2.** *adj.* written; **3.** *m* writing, document; manuscript; ⚖ brief; ~s *pl.* writings, works; por ~ in writing, in black and white; poner por ~ write down, commit to

writing; **escritor** *m*, **-a** *f* writer; **escritorio** *m* writing-desk, bureau; (*caja*) writing-case; (*oficina*) office; **escritorzuelo** *m* hack, penny-a-liner; **escrituario** Scriptural; **escritura** *f* (*acto*, *arte*) writing; (*símbolos*) writing, script; (*propia de p.*) (hand)writing; ⚖ deed, document; indenture *de aprendiz*; ~ aérea sky-writing; ~ normal longhand; *Sagrada* ♀ Scripture; ~ de traspaso conveyance; **escriturar** [1a] ⚖ execute by deed; *actor etc.* book.

escrófula *f* scrofula; **escrofuloso** scrofulous.

escroto *m* scrotum.

escrupulizar [1f] scruple; (*dudar*) hesitate; **escrúpulo** *m* (*inquietud*) scruple (*a. pharm.*); (*duda*) hesitation; = **escrupulosidad** *f* scrupulousness; **escrupuloso** scrupulous; (*minucioso etc.*) particular, precise.

escrutador 1. searching; **2.** *m parl.* teller; returning officer, scrutineer *en elecciones*; **escrutar** [1a] scrutinize; *votos* count; **escrutinio** *m* scrutiny, count *de votos*; (*votación*) ballot; (*examen*) scrutiny.

escuadra *f* △ square; ~ (de hierro) bracket, angle-iron; ⚔ squad; ⚓ fleet, squadron; ~ de delineante set-square; ~ falsa bevel square; *a* ~ square, at right-angles; fuera de ~ out of true; **escuadrar** [1a] square; **escuadrilla** *f* ✈ squadron, flight; ⚓ flotilla; **escuadrón** *m* ⚔ squadron.

escuálido pale, weak; (*enjuto*) skinny, scraggy.

escucha 1. *f* (*acto*) listening; *eccl.* chaperon; estar *a la* ~ listen in; **2.** *m* ⚔ scout; *radio:* monitor; **escuchar** [1a] *v/t.* listen to; *consejos etc. a.* mind, heed, pay attention to; *v/i.* listen.

escudar [1a] shield (*a. fig.*); ~se shelter, shield o.s.

escudero *m hist.* squire; page.

escudete *m sew.* gusset.

escudilla *f* bowl, basin.

escudo *m* shield (*a. fig.*); ~ de armas coat of arms.

escudriñar [1a] scrutinize, scan, examine; inquire into, investigate.

escuela *f* school; *phls.* school (of thought); ~ de artes y oficios trade school; ~ *automovilista* driving school; ~ *elemental*, ~ *primaria* elementary school, primary school, grade school *Am*.; ~ de *hogar* domestic science college; ~ *nocturna* night-school; ~ *normal* training-college; ~ de *párvulos* infant school, kindergarten.

escueto plain, unadorned; bare, bald.

esculpir [3a] sculpture, carve; *inscripción* cut; **escultor** *m* sculptor; **escultura** *f* sculpture, carving; **escultural** sculptural; *figura* statuesque.

escupidera *f* spittoon; *S.Am.* chamber-pot; **escupidura** *f* spit, spittle; phlegm; **escupir** [3a] spit (*a* at, *en* on); (*echar fuera*) spit out; *fig. llamas etc.* belch, spit, hurl forth; (*echar de sí*) throw off; cast aside.

escurreplatos *m* plate-rack.

escurribanda *f* F loophole, way out; ⚕ looseness; ⚕ running de *úlcera*.

escurridero *m* draining-board; **escurridizo** slippery; **escurrido** *S.Am.* abashed; **escurridor** *m* wringer *para ropa*; plate-rack *para platos*; colander *para legumbres*; **escurrideras** *f/pl.* dregs, lees; **escurrir** [3a] *v/t. ropa* wring (out); *platos*, *líquido* drain; *v/i.* (*líquido etc.*) drip, trickle; (*superficie*) be slippery; ~se drain; slip, slide *en hielo etc.*; F (*p. etc.*) sneak off; (*deslizarse*) glide away; (*palabra*) slip out.

esdrújulo *adj. a. su. m* (*word*) having dactylic stress [— ‿ ‿].

ese[1] *f*: hacer ~s zigzag; (*borracho*) reel, stagger.

ese[2], **esa** *adj.* that; **esos**, **esas** *pl.* those.

ése, **ésa** *pron.* that (one); (*el anterior*) the former; *ésa* your town, the place where you are; **ésos**, **ésas** *pl.* those; (*los anteriores*) the former; *ni por ésas* on no account.

esencia *f* essence; core de *problema etc.*; **esencial** *adj. a. su. m* essential; *lo* ~ the main thing.

esfera *f* sphere; globe; face de *reloj*, dial de *instrumento*; *fig.* sphere, plane; field de *actividad*; ~ de *acción* scope; **esférico** spherical; **esferoide** *m* spheroid.

esfinge *f* sphinx (*a. fig.*).

esfínter *m* sphincter.

esforzado valiant; vigorous, energetic; **esforzar** [1f *a.* 1m] *v/t.* strengthen, invigorate; (*animar*) encourage; ~se strain, exert o.s.; ~ *en inf.*, ~ *por inf.* strive to *inf.*, struggle to *inf.*, endeavour to *inf.*; **esfuerzo** *m* effort, endeavour, exertion; stress; stretch, effort de *imaginación*; (*ánimo*) courage, spirit; *sin* ~ effortlessly; *no escatimar* ~s spare no effort (*para inf.* to *inf.*).

esfumar [1a] *paint.* shade, tone down; ~se fade away; (*p.*) make o.s. scarce.

esgrima *f* (*deporte*) fencing; (*arte*) swordsmanship; **esgrimidor** *m* fencer; (*que maneja bien la espada*) swordsman; **esgrimir** [3a] *v/t.* wield (*a. fig.*); *v/i.* fence.

esguince *m* swerve, avoiding action; ⚕ sprain; *fig.* (*disgusto*) scowl; (*desdén*) scornful look.

eslabón *m* link de *cadena* (*a. fig.*); steel *para sacar fuego*, *afilar*; ⊕, ⚓ shackle; ~ *giratorio* swivel; **eslabonar** [1a] (inter)link; *fig.* link, knit together.

eslavo 1. *adj. a. su. m*, **a** *f* Slav; **2.** *m* (*idioma*) Slavonic.

eslinga *f* ⚓ sling; **eslingar** [1h] sling.

eslora *f* ⚓ length.

eslovaco 1. Slovakian; **2.** *m*, **a** *f* Slovak.

esloveno 1. Slovenian; **2.** *m*, **a** *f* Slovene.

esmaltar [1a] enamel; *uñas* varnish, paint; *fig.* embellish, adorn with different colours; **esmalte** *m* enamel (*a. anat.*); (*obra*) smalt; ~ (*para uñas*) nail-varnish; *fig.* lustre.

esmerado painstaking, careful, neat.

esmeralda *f* emerald.

esmerarse [1a] take pains, take great care (*en* over); (*lucirse*) shine, do well.

esmerejón *m* merlin.

esmeril *m* emery; **esmerilar** [1a] polish with emery.

esmero *m* care(fulness), neatness; refinement, niceness; *poner* ~ *en* take care over.

esmirriado *v.* desmirriado.

esnob 1. *p.* snobbish; (*de buen tono etc.*) posh; **2.** *m/f* snob; **esnobismo** *m* snobbery.

eso *pron.* that; ~ es that's right, that's it; ¡~ a él! that's his look-out!; *v. sí¹; a ~ de las 5* (round) about 5 o'clock; *antes de ~* before then, by that time; *por ~* therefore, and so.

esófago *m* oesophagus, gullet.

esotérico esoteric.

espabilar [1a] snuff; **~se** F: ¡*espabílate!* get a move on!

espacial spatial; *viaje etc.* space *attr.*; **espaciar** [1b] space (out) (*a. typ.*); *noticia* spread; **~se** (*dilatarse*) expatiate, spread o.s.; (*esparcirse*) relax, take one's ease; **espacio** *m* space (*a. typ.*); (*lugar*) space, room; ♪ interval; (*tardanza*) delay, slowness; ~ *exterior* outer space; ~ *muerto* clearance; ~ *vital* living space, Lebensraum; **espacioso** spacious, roomy; capacious; *movimiento* slow, deliberate.

espada 1. *f* sword; *entre la ~ y la pared* between the devil and the deep blue sea; *naipes:* **~s** *pl.* spades; **2.** *m* swordsman; *b.s.* bully, swash-buckler; *toros:* matador.

espadaña *f* bulrush.

espadín *m* dress-sword, ceremonial sword; **espadón** *m* broadsword; ✂ F brass hat.

espalda *f* back, shoulder(s) (*mst* **~s** *pl.*); *a ~s* (*vueltas*) treacherously; *a ~s de uno* behind one's back; *~ con ~* back to back; *de ~s a* with one's back to; *cargado de ~s* round-shouldered; *caer de ~s, dar de ~s* fall on one's back; *echar a las ~s* forget about; *echar sobre las ~s* take on, take charge of; *volver la ~* (*apartarse*) turn away; (*huir*) turn tail; *volver las ~s a p.* cold-shoulder.

espaldar *m* back *de silla*; ✿ espalier, trellis; **espaldarazo** *m* slap on the back; accolade; **espaldera** *f* espa-lier, trellis; **espaldilla** *f* shoulder-blade; **espaldón** *m* mortise.

espantable = *espantoso*; **espantada** *f* (*huida*) stampede; (*miedo*) cold feet; **espantadizo** shy, timid; **espantajo** *m* scarecrow (*a. fig.*); *fig.* sight, fright; (*coco*) bogy; **espantapájaros** *m* scarecrow.

espantar [1a] scare, frighten (away, off); (*horrorizar*) appal; **~se** get scared, get frightened; (*admirarse*) be amazed; **espanto** *m* fright, ter-ror; (*asombro*) consternation; (*ame-*

naza) menace; *S.Am.* ghost; **espantoso** frightful, dread(ful); appal-ling.

español 1. Spanish; **2.** *m*, **-a** *f* Spaniard; **3.** *m* (*idioma*) Spanish; **españolismo** *m* (*amor*) love of Spain, love of things Spanish; (*lo típico*) Spanishness; (*giro*) Spanish turn of phrase; **españolizar** [1f] make Spanish, hispanicize; **~se** adopt Spanish ways.

esparadrapo *m* sticking-plaster.

esparaván *m orn.* sparrow-hawk; *vet.* spavin.

esparcido scattered; *fig.* jolly, cheerful; **esparcimiento** *m* scat-tering, spreading; *fig.* (*descanso*) relaxation, recreation; (*alegría*) joviality; **esparcir** [3b] scatter, spread, sow; **~se** *fig.* relax.

espárrago *m* asparagus.

esparrancado (with legs) wide apart, set wide; **esparrancarse** [1g] F do the splits.

esparto *m* esparto grass.

espasmo *m* spasm; jerk; **espasmó-dico** spasmodic(al); jerky, fitful.

espato *m geol.* spar.

espátula *f* spatula; *paint.* palette knife.

especia *f* spice; **especiado** spicy, spiced.

especial (e)special; *en ~* especially; **especialidad** *f* speciality; line F; **especialista** *m/f* specialist; **espe-cializarse** [1f] specialize (*en* in, *on Am.*).

especie *f biol.* species; (*clase*) sort, kind; (*asunto*) matter; (*noticia*) news, rumour; pretext; *pagar en ~* pay in kind.

especificación *f* specification; **es-pecificar** [1g] specify; itemize; **específico 1.** specific; **2.** *m* (*natu-ral*) specific; (*fabricado*) patent medicine; **espécimen** *m* specimen; **especioso** specious, plausible.

espectacular spectacular; **espectá-culo** *m* spectacle; show, entertain-ment; sight; **espectador** *m*, **-a** *f* spectator; onlooker, looker-on.

espectral *opt.* spectral; ghostly, un-earthly; **espectro** *m opt.* spec-trum; spectre, ghost.

especulación *f* speculation; **espe-culador** *m*, **-a** *f* speculator; **espe-cular** [1a] *v/t.* contemplate, re-flect on; *v/i.* speculate (*en* on; ✝

sobre in); **especulativo** speculative.

espejado glassy, bright; **espejear** [1a] shine, glint; **espejismo** *m* mirage (*a. opt.*), wishful thinking; **espejo** *m* mirror (*a. fig.*), (looking-) glass; *fig.* model; ~ *retrovisor* driving mirror. [holing.\

espeleogía *f* spel(a)eology, pot-\
espelta *f* spelt.

espeluznante hair-raising; lurid.

espera *f* wait; waiting; ⚖ stay, respite; (*paciencia*) restraint; *en* ~ *de* waiting for; **esperanza** *f* hope; prospect; *dar* ~*s de* hold out a prospect of; *tener la* ~ *puesta en* set one's heart on; pin one's faith to; **esperanzador** encouraging, hopeful; **esperanzar** [1f] give hope to, buoy up (with hope); **esperar** [1a] **1.** *v/t.* (*tener esperanza de*) hope for; expect (*de* of); (*estar en espera de*) await, wait for; *niño* expect; *ir a* ~ go to meet; **2.** *v/i.* (*tener esperanza*) hope; (*estar en espera*) wait; (*permanecer*) stay; ~ *que indic.* hope that; ~ *que subj.* expect that; ~ *(a) que subj.* wait until; ~ *inf.* hope to *inf.*; ~ *en Dios* trust in God; ~ *desesperando* hope against hope.

esperma *f* sperm; ~ *de ballena* = **espermaceti** *m* spermaceti; **espermatozoo** *m* spermatozoon.

esperpento *m* F (*p.*) fright, guy; nonsense.

espesar [1a] thicken; *tela* weave tighter; ~*se* thicken, get thicker; coagulate, solidify; **espeso** thick, dense; *pasta etc.* stiff; (*sucio*) dirty; **espesor** *m* thickness, density; *tener 2 metros de* ~ be 2 metres thick; **espesura** *f* thickness; dirtiness; ⚘ thicket.

espetar [1a] *carne* skewer, spit; *p.* run through; (*en general*) impale, transfix; *orden* rap out; *sermón etc.* read; F ~ *algo a uno* spring s.t. on s.o.; ~*se* F get on one's high horse; F (*asegurarse*) steady o.s., settle o.s.

espetón *m* skewer, spit; (*alfiler*) pin; (*golpe*) jab, poke.

espía *m/f* spy.

espiantar [1a] *S.Am.* F hop it, scram.

espiar [1c] spy (*v/t.* on).

espichar [1a] *v/t.* prick; *v/i.* F peg out; **espiche** *m* spike, peg.

espiga *f* ⚘ ear *de trigo*, spike *de flores*; ⊕ spigot; (*clavo*) tenon, peg, pin; ✂ fuse; clapper *de campana*; tang *de cuchillo*; ⚓ masthead; **espigadera** *f*, **espigador** *m*, -a *f* gleaner; **espigado** ⚘ ripe, ready to seed; *p.* tall, grown-up; **espigar** [1h] *v/t.* glean (*a. fig.*); ⊕ tenon; *v/i.* (*trigo*) form ears, come into ear; run to seed; (*p.*) ~*se* shoot up; **espigón** *m zo.* sting; (*púa*) spike; ⚘ ear; point *de herramienta etc.*; ⚓ breakwater; **espigueo** *m* gleaning.

espina *f* ⚘ thorn, spine, prickle; *ichth.* fish-bone; ~ (*dorsal*) spine; *fig.* suspicion, doubt; *dar mala* ~ *a* worry; *estar en* ~*s* be on tenterhooks; *sacarse la* ~ get even.

espinaca(s) *f(pl.)* spinach.

espinal spinal; **espinapez** *m* ⊕ herring-bone; **espinar** [1a] *fig.* hurt *s.o.'s* feelings, sting; **2.** *m* thorn-brake; *fig.* difficulty; **espinazo** *m* spine, backbone.

espineta *f* spinet.

espinilla *f anat.* shin-(bone); ✿ blackhead.

espino *m* hawthorn; **espinoso 1.** ⚘ thorny, prickly; *pez* spiny; *fig.* thorny, knotty; **2.** *m* stickleback.

espionaje *m* spying, espionage.

espira *f* ⚡ spiral; ✦ turn (*a. de espiral*); *zo.* whorl.

espiráculo *m* spiracle; blow-hole.

espiral 1. spiral, helical; corkscrew *attr.*; **2.** *m* hairspring; **3.** *f* spiral; wreath *de humo etc.*; ⊕ whorl.

espirar [1a] *v/t.* exhale, breathe out; *v/i.* breathe; *poet.* blow gently.

espiritado F like a wraith; **espiritismo** *m* spiritualism; **espiritista** *m/f* spiritualist; **espiritoso** *licor* spirituous; *p.* spirited; **espíritu** *m* spirit; mind; soul; ghost; ⚡ *Santo* Holy Ghost; ~ *de vino* spirits of wine; **espiritual** spiritual; unwordly; ghostly; **espiritualidad** *f* spirituality.

espita *f* spigot, tap, cock; F drunkard, soak; **espitar** [1a] tap, broach.

espleen *m v.* spleen.

esplendidez *f* splendour; magnificence *etc.*; **espléndido** splendid; magnificent, grand; (*liberal*) generous, lavish; **esplendor** *m* splendour; brilliance; glory; **esplendoroso** magnificent; brilliant.

esplénico splenetic.

espliego *m* lavender.
esplín *m v.* spleen.
espolada *f* prick with a spur; F ~ *de vino* drink of wine; **espolazo** *m* = *espolada*; **espolear** [1a] spur; *fig.* spur on; **espoleta** *f* ⚔ fuse; *anat.* wish-bone; **espolón** *m zo.*, *geog.* spur; ⚓ ram; ⚓ sea-wall, dike; cutwater *de puente*; △ buttress; (*paseo*) promenade; F chilblain.
espolvorear [1a] dust.
espondeo *m* spondee (— —).
esponja *f* sponge; F sponger; **esponjar** [1a] make spongy; *lana etc.* make fluffy; ~**se** *fig.* swell with conceit; F ✷ glow with health; look prosperous; **esponjosidad** *f* sponginess; **esponjoso** spongy; porous; (*empapado*) soggy.
esponsales *m/pl.* betrothal.
espontanearse [1a] (*falta*) own up; (*cosa íntima*) unbosom o.s.; **espontaneidad** *f* spontaneity; **espontáneo** spontaneous; impromptu.
espora *f* spore.
esporádico sporadic.
esportillo *m* basket, pannier; **esportón** *m* large basket.
esposa *f* wife; ~**s** *pl.* handcuffs, manacles; *poner las* ~**s** *a* = **esposar** [1a] handcuff; **esposo** *m* husband; ~**s** *pl.* husband and wife, couple.
esprínter *m* sprinter.
espuela *f* spur (*a. fig.*); ~ *de caballero* larkspur.
espuerta *f* basket, pannier.
espulgar [1h] delouse, rid of fleas; *fig.* scrutinize.
espuma *f* ⚓ *etc.* foam, spray, surf; froth *en cerveza etc.*; (*desechos*) scum; ~ (*de jabón*) lather; ~ *de caucho*, ~ *de látex* foam rubber; ~ *de mar* meerschaum; *echar* ~ foam; **espumadera** *f* (*paleta*) skimmer; spray nozzle *de atomizador*; **espumajear** [1a] froth at the mouth; **espumajoso** foamy, frothy; **espumar** [1a] *v/t.* skim; *v/i.* foam, froth; **espumarajo** *m* froth (at the mouth); **espumoso** foamy, frothy; *vino* sparkling.
espurio spurious; *p.* bastard.
esputar [1a] spit; **esputo** *m* spit, spittle; ✷ sputum.
esqueje *m* slip, cutting.
esquela *f* note; ~ (*de defunción*) announcement of death.

esqueleto *m* skeleton (*a. fig.*).
esquema *m* diagram, plan, scheme; (*dibujo*) sketch; **esquemático** diagrammatic; schematic.
esquí *m* ski; (*deporte*) skiing; ~ *acuático* water-skiing; surf-riding; **esquiador** *m*, -a *f* skier; **esquiar** [1c] ski.
esquife *m* skiff.
esquila[1] *f* (*campanilla*) handbell; (*cencerro*) cow-bell.
esquila[2] *f* shearing; **esquilador** *m* shearer; **esquilar** [1a] shear, clip; **esquileo** *m* shearing.
esquilimoso F finicky.
esquilmar [1a] *cosecha* harvest; *suelo* exhaust, impoverish (*a. fig.*); **esquilmo** *m* harvest, yield.
esquimal *adj. a. su. m/f* Eskimo.
esquina *f* corner; **esquinado** having corners; *fig.* unsociable, prickly; **esquinazo** F: *dar* ~ *a* dodge, give *a p.* the slip.
esquirla *f* splinter.
esquirol *m* blackleg, scab.
esquisto *m* schist.
esquivar [1a] avoid, shun, elude, side-step; ~ *inf.* avoid *ger.*, be chary of *ger.*; **esquivez** *f* aloofness *etc.*; **esquivo** aloof, shy; evasive *en contestar etc.*; (*desdeñoso*) scornful.
esquizofrenia *f* schizophrenia; **esquizofrénico** schizophrenic.
esta *etc. v.* **este**[2].
estabilidad *f* stability; **estabilización** *f* stabilization; **estabilizador** *m* stabilizer; **estabilizar** [1f] stabilize; steady; *precios* peg; **estable** stable; steady; firm; ✝ regular.
establecer [2d] establish; set up, found; *gente etc.* settle; *afirmación etc.* substantiate; *residencia* take up; ~**se** establish o.s., settle *en casa, ciudad etc.*; ✝ set up in business; **establecimiento** *m mst* establishment (*a. acto*); institution; settlement; ⚖ statute. [*Am.*]
establo *m* cow-shed, tall; barn *esp.*
estaca *f* stake, paling; (tent-)peg *de tienda*; (*porra*) cudgel; ♀ cutting; **estacada** *f* (*cerca*) fencing, fence; ✗ palisade, stockade; F *dejar en la* ~ leave in the lurch; F *quedar en la* ~ succumb; (*fracasar*) fail disastrously; **estacar** [1g] *terreno* stake out (*or* off); *animal* tie to a stake; ~**se** remain rooted to the spot.

estación f 🎏 etc. station (a. fig.), a. depot Am.; season del año; ~ balnearia spa, health resort; ~ carbonera coaling station; ~ depuradora sewage farm; ~ de empalme, ~ de enlace junction; ~ de gasolina petrol station; ~ muerta off season; ~ de servicio service station; ~ veraniega summer resort; estacional seasonal; estacionamiento m mot. parking; estacionar [1a] station; mot. park; ~se remain stationary; (colocarse) station o.s.; mot. park; estacionario stationary.

estada f stay.

estadía f ✝ demurrage; S.Am. stay.

estadio m deportes: stadium; (fase) stage, phase.

estadista m pol. statesman; ⚤ statistician; estadística f statistics; (official) returns; estadístico 1. statistical; 2. m statistician.

estado m state (a. pol.); condition; status; class, rank; list de empleados etc.; (resumen) summary; (informe) report, statement; ~ de ánimo state of mind; ~ benefactor welfare state; en buen ~ in good condition, in good order; ~ civil marital status; ~ de cuenta(s) statement of account; ~ de guerra state of war; hombre de ~ statesman; ~ llano third estate, commoners; ~ mayor staff; ~ de sitio state of siege; ~ tapón buffer state.

estadounidense United States attr.

estafa f swindle, trick; ✝ racket F, ramp F; estafador m swindler, trickster; racketeer F; estafar [1a] swindle, twist F.

estafeta f post; (oficina) (sub) post-office; (p.) courier; ~ diplomática diplomatic bag.

estalactita f stalactite; estalagmita f stalagmite.

estallar [1a] burst, explode, go off; (como volcán) erupt; (látigo) crack; fig. break out, flare up; hacer ~ set off, spark off; estallido m explosion, report; crash, crack; fig. outbreak.

estambre m worsted; ⚲ stamen.

estameña f serge; bunting.

estampa f typ. print, engraving; (imprenta) printing-press; fig. stamp, aspect; fig. (huella) imprint; dar a la ~ print; estampado 1. vestido print(ed); 2. m (cotton)

print; estampar [1a] typ. print, engrave, stamp; esp. fig. imprint.

estampía: de ~ suddenly, unexpectedly.

estampida f S.Am. stampede; = estampido m report; boom, crash, bang.

estampilla f (rubber) stamp; S.Am. (postage) stamp; estampillar [1a] stamp.

estancado stagnant (a. fig.); fig. static; estancamiento m stagnancy, stagnation (a. fig.); fig. deadlock; estancar [1g] aguas stem, check; negocio suspend; negociación bring to a standstill, deadlock; mercancía monopolize (officially), b.s. corner; ~se stagnate.

estancia f (permanencia) stay; (morada) dwelling, abode; (cuarto) living-room; poet. stanza; S.Am. farm, ranch; estanciero m S.Am. farmer, rancher.

estanco 1. water-tight; 2. m state monopoly; (tienda) tobacconist's (shop).

estandar(d)ización f standardization; estandar(d)izar [1f] standardize.

estandarte m standard, banner.

estanque m pond, pool, small lake; reservoir para riego etc.

estanquero m tobacconist.

estante m (mueble) rack, stand; book-case; (una tabla) shelf; estantería f shelves, shelving.

estantigua f apparition; F fright, sight.

estañar [1a] tin; (soldar) solder; estaño m tin.

estaquilla f peg, pin; estaquillar [1a] pin, peg (down).

estar [1p] be; (~ en casa etc.) be in; stand; (asistir) be present (en at); estoy leyendo I am reading; ¿cómo estás? how are you (keeping)?; ¿cómo estamos? how do we stand?; deportes: what's the score?; ¿está Juan? is John in?; ~ a 10 ptas cost 10 ptas, stand at 10 ptas; estamos a 3 de mayo today is the third of May; ¿a cuántos estamos? what date is it?; está bien all right; (basta) that will do; ~ bien a suit; be fitting for; ~ bien con be on good terms with; ~ con ⚔ have; ~ de rango be acting as, be an acting ...; ~ de más be superfluous; (p.) be in the way;

~ en asunto be mixed up in; ~ en que understand that; ~ en sí be in one's right mind; ~ fuera (de casa) be out; (de ciudad) be away, be out of town; ~ mal ♣ be ill; ~ mal con be on bad terms with; have a low opinion of; F no está mal it's not bad; ~ para inf. be about to inf.; ~ para su. be in the mood for; ~ por inf. (dispuesto a) be inclined to inf.; (que queda por) be still to be p.p., remain to be p.p.; está por ver it remains to be seen; ~ por su. be in favour of; ~ por p. side with, support; ~se stay (at home etc.); ¡estáte quieto! keep still!

estarcido m stencil; estarcir [3b] stencil.

estatal state attr.

estática f statics; estático static.

estatificar [1g] nationalize.

estatua f statue; estatuaria f statuary; estatuario statuesque.

estatuir [3g] establish, enact; (arreglar) arrange; (demostrar) prove; estatura f stature, height; estatutario statutory; estatuto m statute; by-law de municipio etc.; (standing) order de comité etc.

estay m ♣ stay.

este¹ 1. parte east(ern); dirección easterly; viento east(erly); 2. m east.

este², esta this; estos, estas pl. these.

éste, ésta this (one); (último) the latter; éstos, éstas pl. these; (últimos) the latter.

estela f ♣ wake, wash; trail de cohete etc.; ⚠ stela; estelar stellar; thea. star attr.

estenografía f shorthand, stenography; estenografiar [1c] take down in shorthand; estenógrafo m, a f stenographer, shorthand writer.

estentóreo stentorian.

estepa f steppe.

estera f mat, matting.

estercoladura f manuring; estercolar [1a] manure, dung; estercolero m dungheap, dunghill.

estereo...: ~fónico stereophonic; ~scopio m stereoscope; ~tipar [1a] stereotype (a. fig.); ~tipo m stereotype.

estéril sterile, barren; esterilidad f sterility; esterilizar [1f] sterilize.

esterilla f mat.

esterlina: libra ~ pound sterling.

esternón m breast-bone, sternum ⏄.

estero m matting; geog. estuary, inlet.

estertor m death-rattle. [inlet.]

estética f aesthetics; estético aesthetic.

estetoscopio m stethoscope.

esteva f plough-handle; estevado bow-legged, bandy-legged.

estiaje m low water.

estiba f ✂ rammer; ♣ stowage; estibador m stevedore, longshoreman; estibar [1a] pack tight; ♣ stow, house.

estiércol m dung, manure.

estigma m stigma; mark; brand; estigmatizar [1f] stigmatize.

estilar [1a] v/t. draw up in due form; v/i., ~se be in fashion, be worn; ~ inf. be customary to inf.

estilete m stiletto.

estilista m/f stylist; estilizado stylized; estilo m style (a. ♀); (pluma) stylus; (modo, manera) manner; natación: stroke; algo por el ~ something of the sort, that sort of thing; y otros por el ~ and such like.

estilográfica f fountain-pen.

estima f esteem; ♣ dead reckoning; estimable estimable, reputable; cantidad considerable; estimación f (acto) estimation; (aprecio, tasa) estimate, estimation; (estima) regard, esteem; estimar [1a] (juzgar, medir) estimate, reckon, gauge; (respetar etc.) esteem, value, respect; think a lot of; (considerar) think, reckon (que that).

estimulante 1. stimulating; 2. m stimulant; estimular [1a] stimulate; encourage; excite; prompt; discusión etc. promote; estímulo m stimulus, stimulation; encouragement; inducement.

estío m summer.

estipendio m stipend.

estipulación f stipulation; proviso, condition; estipular [1a] stipulate.

estirado fig. stiff, starchy; (mojigato) prim; (tacaño) tight-fisted.

estirajar [1a] F = estirar [1a] stretch, pull out; (demasiado) strain; cuello crane; ropa run the iron over; poderes extend unduly; dinero, discurso spin out; ~se stretch; estirón m pull, tug; stretch; dar un ~ fig. shoot up.

estirpe *f* stock, race, lineage.

estival summery, summer *attr.*

esto *pron.* this; con ~ herewith; en ~ at this point; en ~ de in the matter of; ~ es that is to say.

estocada *f* (sword-)thrust, stab, lunge.

estofa *f fig.* quality, class; estofado *m* stew, hot-pot; estofar [1a] *cocina*: stew; *sew.* quilt.

estoicismo *m* stoicism; estoico 1. stoic(al); 2. *m* Stoic.

estola *f* stole.

estolidez *f* stupidity; estólido stupid.

estomacal *adj. a. su. m* stomachic; stomach *attr.* estomagar [1h] give indigestion to; F annoy; estómago *m* stomach; F tener buen ~ (*no ofenderse*) be thick-skinned; *b.s.* have an elastic conscience, be none too scrupulous.

estopa *f* tow; ⚓ oakum; estopilla *f* cheese-cloth.

estoque *m* rapier; ⚘ gladiolus; estoquear [1a] stab.

estorbar [1a] *v/t.* hinder, impede, obstruct; get in the way of; interfere with; *v/i.* be in the way; estorbo *m* hindrance, obstruction, obstacle; drag; curb.

estornino *m* starling.

estornudar [1a] sneeze; estornudo *m* sneeze.

estoy *etc. v.* estar.

estrabismo *m* squint.

estrada *f* road, highway.

estrado *m* dais, stage; ♪ bandstand; † drawing-room; ~s *pl.* law-courts; citar para ~s subpoena.

estrafalario F outlandish, eccentric, screwball *Am.*; *vestido* slovenly, sloppy.

estragar [1h] corrupt, ruin; pervert; spoil; estrago *m* ruin, destruction; ~s *pl.* havoc, ravages; hacer ~s en(tre) play havoc with, wreak havoc among.

estrambótico F odd, eccentric.

estrangul *m* ♪ mouthpiece.

estrangulación *f* strangulation; estrangulador *m* ⊕ throttle; choke; estrangular [1a] strangle; ✚ strangulate; ⊕ throttle; ⊕ choke.

estraperlista *m* black marketeer; estraperlo *m* black market.

estratagema *f* stratagem; estra-

tega *m* strategist; estrategia *f* strategy; generalship; estratégico strategic.

estratificar(se) [1g] stratify; estrato *m* layer, stratum.

estratosfera *f* stratosphere; estratosférico stratospheric; avión ~ stratocruiser.

estraza *f* rag.

estrechar [1a] narrow; *vestido* reduce, take in; (*apretar*) tighten (up); squeeze; *mano* grasp, shake; hug, enfold en *brazos*; *fig.* constrain, compel; ~se narrow; tighten (up); *fig.* get very friendly (con with); stint o.s., economize; estrechez *f* narrowness; tightness; *fig.* closeness, intimacy *de amistad*; austerity, privation; ~ de miras narrow-mindedness; insularity; estrecheces *pl. fig.* straits; estrecho 1. narrow; tight; *cuarto* cramped; *fig. amistad, relación* close, intimate; strict, rigid; austere; (*tacaño*) mean; 2. *m* strait(s), narrows.

estregadera *f* scrubbing-brush; scraper en la *puerta*; estregar [1h a. 1k] rub, scrape; (*con agua etc.*) scrub, scour.

estrella *f* star (*a. fig., thea.*); *zo.* blaze; ✗ pip, star en *uniforme*; ~ fija fixed star; ~ fugaz shooting-star, falling-star; ~ polar pole-star; ~ de rabo comet; nacer con ~ be born under a lucky star; F ver las ~s see stars; estrelladera *f* slice (*tool*); estrelladero *m* pan; estrellado *cielo* starry; *vestido* spangled; *huevo* fried; estrellar [1a] shatter, smash, dash; *huevo* fry; ~se shatter, dash (*contra* against); (*coche etc.*) smash (*contra* into); *esp.* ⚔ crash (*contra* into); ~ con come up against; estrellón *m S.Am.* crash.

estremecer [2d] shake (*a. fig.*); ~se (*edificio etc.*) shake; (*p.*) tremble (ante at, de *miedo* with); shudder (*de horror* with); shiver (de *frío* with); tingle, thrill (*de emoción* with); estremecimiento *m* shaking; trembling; shudder *etc.*

estrenar [1a] use (*or* wear *etc.*) for the first time; *thea.* perform for the first time; *película* give its première, release; ~se make one's début; (*comedia*) open; estreno *m* first appearance *etc.*; début *esp. de p.*; *thea.* first night; *cine*: première, release.

estreñido constipated; estreñi-miento *m* constipation; estreñir [3h *a.* 3l] constipate, bind.

estrépito *m* noise, racket, row, din; estrepitoso noisy, loud, deafening; *p., fiesta etc.* rowdy.

estreptomicina *f* streptomycin.

estría *f* groove; △ flute, fluting; estriado grooved, striate(d); △ fluted; estriar [1c] groove, striate; △ flute.

estribación *f* geog. spur; ~es *pl.* foothills; estribar [1a]: ~ en be supported by; *fig.* rest (up)on, be based (up)on.

estribera *f* stirrup.

estribillo *m* poet. refrain; ♪ chorus; *fig.* pet word, pet phrase.

estribo *m* stirrup; ⊕ bracket, brace; geog. spur; △ buttress, abutment; △ pier; *mot.* running-board, step; *fig.* basis, foundation; *perder los ~s* lose one's head; get hot under the collar *en conversación.*

estribor *m* starboard.

estricnina *f* strychnine.

estricto strict.

estridente strident, raucous; jangling; estridor *m* screech.

estro *m* inspiration.

estrofa *f* verse, stanza.

estropajo *m* scourer *para fregar*; dish-cloth, swab; F dirt, rubbish; estropajoso F *carne* tough; *habla* indistinct; *p.* slovenly.

estropear [1a] *p.* hurt, maim; *mecanismo etc.* damage, tamper with; (*echar a perder*) spoil, ruin; *texto etc.* mangle; ~se get damaged; spoil, go bad; estropicio *m* F (*destrozo*) breakage, smashing; *fig.* rumpus, fuss.

estructura *f* structure; frame; estructural structural; estructurar [1a] construct, organize.

estruendo *m* crash, din, clatter, thunder; *fig.* uproar, confusion; estruendoso noisy; *esp. p.* obstreperous.

estrujadura *f* squeeze, press(ing); estrujar [1a] squeeze, press, crush; F drain, bleed white; estrujón *m* squeeze, press(ing); F crush, jam.

estuario *m* estuary.

estucar [1g] stucco; estuço *m* stucco, plaster.

estuche *m* (*caja*) box, case; (*vaina*)

sheath; ~ *de afeites* vanity case; F *ser un* ~ be quite an expert.

estudiante *m/f* student; estudiantil student *attr.*; estudiantina *f* student band; estudiar [1b] study; estudio *m* mst study (*a. paint.,* ♪; *cuarto particular*); *paint., cine, radio:* studio; (*proyecto preliminar*) plan, design (*de for*); planning (*de for*); (*reconocimiento general*) survey; (*erudición*) learning; (*aplicación*) studiousness; estudioso studious; bookish.

estufa *f* stove; heater; ✠ hot-house; ~ *de gas* gas-fire; ~ *de petróleo* oil-stove; estufilla *f* small brazier; muff *para manos.*

estulticia *f* stupidity; estulto stupid.

estupefacción *f* stupefaction; estupefaciente *adj. a. su. m* narcotic; estupefacto stupefied, thunderstruck, speechless; *dejar* ~ leave speechless, stupefy.

estupendo stupendous; F marvellous, terrific, great; ¡~! wonderful!, that's fine!

estupidez *f* stupidity, foolishness; estúpido stupid, foolish.

estupor *m* stupor (*a. fig.*); *fig.* amazement.

estuprar [1a] rape; estupro *m* rape.

esturión *m* sturgeon.

estuve *etc. v. estar.*

etapa *f* stage, phase; *deportes:* lap, leg; ✗ ration; ✗ (*lugar*) stopping-place.

etcétera et caetera; and so on.

éter *m* ether; etéreo ethereal; eterizar [1f] etherize.

eternidad *f* eternity; eternizar [1f] etern(al)ize; perpetuate; *b.s.* prolong endlessly; eterno eternal.

ética *f* ethics; ético[1] ethical.

ético[2] ✚ consumptive; *fig.* frail.

etimología *f* etymology; ~ *doble* doublet; etimológico etymological.

etíope *adj. a. su. m/f* Ethiopian.

etiqueta *f* (*ceremonial*) etiquette; punctilio, formality; (*rótulo*) label, ticket; *de* ~ *traje* formal; etiquetero ceremonious, punctilious; prim.

etnografía *f* ethnography; etnología *f* ethnology.

eucalipto *m* eucalyptus, gum-tree.

Eucaristía *f* Eucharist.

eufemismo *m* euphemism; **eufemístico** euphemistic(al).

eufonía *f* euphony; **eufónico** euphonic, euphonious.

euforia *f* euphoria, exuberance; **eufórico** euphoric, exuberant.

eugenesia *f*, **eugenismo** *m* eugenics.

eunuco *m* eunuch.

¡eureka! eureka!

europeizar [1f] Europeanize, make a part of Europe; **europeo** *adj. a. su. m*, **a** *f* European.

éuscaro *adj. a. su. m* Basque.

eutanasia *f* euthanasia, mercy killing.

evacuación *f* evacuation; **evacuado** *m*, **a** *f* evacuee; **evacuar** [1d] evacuate; void; *vientre* have a movement of; *fig. encargo* fulfil; *negocio* transact.

evadido *m* fugitive; escaped prisoner; **evadir** [3a] evade; **~se** escape, break out.

evaluación *f* evaluation; **evaluar** [3c] evaluate.

evanescente evanescent.

evangélico evangelic(al); **Evangelio** *m* Gospel; **evangelizador** *m* evangelist; **Evangelista** *m* Evangelist; **evangelizar** [1f] evangelize.

evaporación *f* evaporation; **evaporar(se)** [1a], **evaporizar(se)** [1f] evaporate (*a. fig.*); vapourize.

evasión *f* escape; *fig.* evasion; **~ fiscal** tax evasion; **evasiva** *f* evasion; loophole, excuse; **evasivo** evasive, non-committal; elusive.

evento *m* (unforeseen) event, eventuality, contingency; **eventual** *trabajo etc.* temporary, casual; (*interino*) acting; stopgap; (*sujeto a contingencia*) conditional; fortuitous.

evidencia *f* (*lo evidente*) obviousness; (*prueba etc.*) evidence; **evidenciar** [1b] show, prove, make evident; **evidente** obvious, evident.

evitable avoidable, preventable; **evitar** [1a] *peligro etc.* avoid, escape; *molestia* save; (*precaver*) prevent; *tentación etc.* shun; **~** *inf.* avoid *ger.*, be chary of *ger.*

evocación *f* evocation; invocation; **evocador** evocative; reminiscent; **evocar** [1g] *recuerdo etc.* evoke, call up, conjure up; *espíritus etc.* invoke, call up.

evolución *f* evolution (*a. biol.*); ✕ manoeuvre; change *de política etc.*; **evolucionar** [1a] evolve (*a. biol.*); ✕ manoeuvre; (*política etc.*) change; **evolutivo** evolutionary.

ex... ex-; former, late; **~** *ministro* ex-minister.

exacción *f* exaction, extortion; demand; levy.

exacerbar [1a] exacerbate, aggravate.

exactitud *f* exactness *etc.*; **exacto** exact, accurate, precise; right, correct; punctual; *¡~!* quite right!, just so!

exageración *f* exaggeration; **exagerado** exaggerated; *relato etc. a.* highly-coloured, overdone; *precio etc.* excessive, steep F; *p.* fulsome, demonstrative; theatrical; (*raro*) peculiar, odd; **exagerar** [1a] exaggerate; overdo, overstate; enlarge upon.

exaltación *f* exaltation; over-excitement; **exaltado 1.** exalted; *carácter* hot-headed, excitable; *estado temporal* over-excited, worked up; *pol.* extreme; **2.** *m pol.* extremist, hothead; **exaltar** [1a] exalt; (*celebrar*) extol; elevate *a dignidad*; (*inflamar*) excite, work up, fire; **~se** get excited, get worked up, work o.s. up.

examen *m* examination (*a. univ. etc.*); inspection; interrogation; test; (*indagación*) inquiry (*de* into); **examinador** *m* examiner; **examinando** *m*, **a** *f* examinee; **examinar** [1a] examine; inspect, scan, go over, go through; (*poner a prueba*) test; *sospechoso* interrogate; investigate, inquire into, look into; **~se** sit an examination (*de* in).

exangüe bloodless; *fig.* weak.

exánime lifeless; *fig.* in a faint.

exasperación *f* exasperation; **exasperar** [1a] exasperate, irritate; **~se** lose patience.

excarcelación *f* release; **excarcelar** [1a] release.

excavación *f* excavation; **excavador** *m* excavator (*p.*); **excavadora** *f* excavator (*machine*); **excavar** [1a] excavate; (*ahuecar*) hollow (out).

excedente 1. excessive; (*sobrante*) excess, surplus; **2.** *m* excess, surplus; **exceder** [2a] exceed, surpass; outdo; transcend *en importancia* *etc.*; ~ de exceed; ~se excel o.s.; *b.s.* overreach o.s., overdo it.

excelencia *f* excellence; ♀ Excellency; *por* ~ par excellence; **excelente** excellent.

excelso lofty, sublime.

excéntrica *f* ⊕ eccentric; **excentricidad** *f* eccentricity; **excéntrico 1.** eccentric; erratic; **2.** *m* eccentric.

excepción *f* exception; *a* ~ *de* with the exception of; *hacer una* ~ make an exception; **excepcional** exceptional; **excepto** except (for), excepting; **exceptuar** [1a] except, exclude; ₤₮ *etc.* exempt.

excesivo excessive; over...; *(indebido)* unreasonable, undue; **exceso** *m* excess *(a. fig.)*; extra; surfeit *esp. de comida*; ~ *de peso* excess luggage; *en* ~ *de* in excess of, over and above; *llevar al* ~ carry to excess, overdo.

excisión *f* excision.

excitabilidad *f* excitability; **excitable** excitable; temperamental; highly strung; **excitación** *f* excitation, excitement; ~ *loca* hysteria; **excitador** *m* ⚡ discharger; **excitante 1.** exciting; ⚗ stimulating; **2.** *m* stimulant; **excitar** [1a] excite *(a.* ⚡*)*; *dudas, esperanzas* raise; *emoción* rouse, stir up; ⚡ energize.

exclamación *f* exclamation; **exclamar** [1a] exclaim; cry, shout.

excluir [3g] exclude; shut out; *posibilidad etc.* preclude, rule out; **exclusión** *f* exclusion; *con* ~ *de* to the exclusion of; **exclusiva** *f* sole right; **exclusive** exclusively; **exclusivista** exclusive; *grupo etc.* clannish; **exclusivo** exclusive; sole.

excombatiente *m* exserviceman.

excomulgar [1h] *eccl.* excommunicate; ban; **excomunión** *f eccl.* excommunication; ban.

excoriar [1b] skin, flay; ~se graze o.s., skin o.s.

excrecencia *f* excrescence.

excreción *f* excretion; **excremental** excremental; **excremento** *m* excrement; **excretar** [1a] excrete.

exculpación *f* exoneration, exculpation; ₤₮ acquittal; **exculpar** [1a] exonerate, exculpate; ₤₮ acquit (de of).

excursión *f* excursion; *(mst breve)* outing, trip; ~ *(a pie)* hike ♀, rambling; sightseeing; **excursionista** *m/f* hiker ♀, rambler *por el campo*; tripper *esp. que va a la costa*; *(turista)* sightseer.

excusa *f* excuse; apology.

excusable excusable; **excusado 1.** unnecessary, superfluous; exempt *(de impuesto* from); reserved; ~ *es decir* needless to say; **2.** *m* lavatory; **excusar** [1a] *(disculpar)* excuse; *(evitar)* avoid, prevent; *(prescindir de)* forget about, do without, not bother with; spare; ~se apologize.

execrable execrable; **execración** *f* execration; **execrar** [1a] execrate.

exención *f* exemption; immunity; **exentar** [1a] exempt (de from); **exento** exempt *(de impuesto etc.* from); free *(de cuidados etc.* from); *lugar* clear, open.

exequias *f/pl.* funeral rites, obsequies.

éxeunt exeunt.

exhalación *f* exhalation; *astr.* shooting-star; vapour; **exhalar** [1a] exhale; *vapor etc.* emit, give out; *suspiro* breathe, heave.

exhaustivo exhaustive; **exhausto** exhausted.

exhibición *f* exhibition, show; **exhibicionista** *m/f* exhibitionist; **exhibir** [3a] exhibit, show.

exhortación *f* exhortation; **exhortar** [1a] exhort; **exhorto** *m* ₤₮, *eccl.* charge.

exhumación *f* exhumation; **exhumar** [1a] exhume.

exigencia *f* demand, requirement; exigency; **exigente** exigent, exacting; particular; **exigir** [3c] *rentas etc.* exact *(a* from); *(pedir)* demand, require *(a* of), call for *(a* from); *exige mucho* he's very demanding.

exiguo meagre, scanty, exiguous.

exilado *m*, *a f* exile; **exilar** [1a], **exiliar** [1b] exile; **exilio** *m* exile.

eximio select; *p.* distinguished, eminent.

eximir [3a] exempt, free, excuse *(de* from).

existencia *f* existence; being; ♰ *en* ~ in stock; ~*s pl.* ♰ stock; **existencialismo** *m* existentialism; **existente** in existence, in being, existent; *esp. texto* extant; **existir** [3a] exist; be.

éxito *m* result, outcome; (*buen*) ~ success; *fig.*, *thea.*, ♪ hit; ~ de *librería* best seller; *tener* (*buen*) ~ be successful; *tener* ~ *en* be successful in, make a success of.

éxodo *m* exodus.

exonerar [1a]: ~ *de deber etc.* relieve of, free from.

exorbitancia *f* exorbitance; **exorbitante** exorbitant.

exorcismo *m* exorcism; **exorcista** *m/f* exorcist; **exorcizar** [1f] exorcize.

exornar [1a] adorn, embellish.

exótico exotic.

expansible expandable; **expansión** *f* expansion; *fig.* (*desahogo*) expansiveness; (*solaz*) relaxation; **expansionar** [1a] expand; ~se *fig.* (*confesarse*) open one's heart; (*esparcirse*) relax; **expansivo** expansive (*a. fig.*); *fig.* affable, good-natured.

expatriación *f* expatriation; exile; **expatriado** *m*, a *f* expatriate; exile; **expatriarse** [1b] expatriate o.s., go into exile.

expectación *f* expectation; **expectante** expectant; **expectativa** *f* expectation; hope; prospect; ~ *de vida* expectation of life; *estar a la* ~ *de* look out for.

expectorar [1a] expectorate.

expedición *f* expedition (*a. fig.*); *fig.* speed; **expedicionario** expeditionary; **expedidor** *m* ♣ shipper.

expediente *m* (*medio*) expedient, makeshift, device; ⚖ action, proceedings; (*papeles*) dossier, file.

expedir [3l] *mercancías* send, forward; *negocio* dispatch; *órdenes etc.* issue; **expeditivo** expeditious.

expeler [2a] expel, eject.

expendedor *m*, -a *f* dealer, retailer; tobacconist; *thea.* ticket agent; **expendeduría** *f* tobacconist's (shop); **expender** [2a] (*gastar*) expend; (*vender*) sell retail; be an agent for; *moneda falsa* pass.

expensas *f/pl.* expense(s); ⚖ costs; *a* ~ *de* at the expense of.

experiencia *f* experience; ⫠ experiment; **experimentado** experienced; **experimental** experimental; **experimentar** [1a] *v/t.* experience, undergo, go through; *emoción* feel; ⊕ test; *v/i.* experi-

ment (*con* with, *en* on); **experimento** *m* experiment.

experto 1. expert, skilled, experienced; **2.** *m* expert.

expiación *f* expiation; **expiar** [1c] expiate, atone for.   [1a] expire.⎫
expiración *f* expiration; **expirar**⎬

explanación *f* levelling; *fig.* explanation, elucidation; **explanar** [1a] level; 🚇 grade; *fig.* explain, elucidate; unfold.

explayar [1a] extend, enlarge; ~se spread, open out; *fig.* spread o.s. *en discurso*; (*esparcirse*) relax; ~ *con* confide in, unbosom o.s. to.

explicable explicable, explainable; **explicación** *f* explanation; **explicar** [1g] (*declarar*, *aclarar*, *justificar*) explain; *doctrina etc.* expound; *curso* lecture on; *conferencia* give; ~se explain o.s.; *no me lo explico* I can't understand it; **explicatorio** explanatory.

explícito explicit.

exploración *f* exploration; **explorador** *m* explorer; pioneer; ✕ *etc.* scout; (*niño*) ~ Boy Scout; **exploradora** *f* Girl Guide; **explorar** [1a] explore; open up, pioneer; ✕ *etc.* scout.

explosión *f* explosion (*a. fig.*); *fig.* outburst; *hacer* ~ explode; **explosivo** *adj. a. su. m* explosive.

explotación *f* exploitation; ✕ working etc.; **explotar** [1a] *v/t.* exploit (*a. b.s.*); ✕ work; develop; operate; *recursos* tap; *v/i.* explode.

exponente *m/f* exponent; **2.** *m* 🅐 index, exponent; **exponer** [2r] expose (*a. phot.*); *vida etc.* risk; *cuadro etc.* show, exhibit; *argumento, hechos* set forth, expound, state; *idea* unfold; ⚖ *acusación* bring; *niño* abandon; ~se *a* expose o.s. to, lay o.s. open to.

exportable exportable; **exportación** *f* (*acto*) export(ation); (*mercancías*) export(s); **exportador** *m* exporter; shipper; **exportar** [1a] export.

exposición *f* (*acto*) exposing, exposure (*a. phot.*), exposition; *paint. etc.* exhibition, show; ✝ show, fair; statement of *hechos etc.*; petition *a autoridades*; **exposímetro** *m* exposure meter; **expósito** *m*, a *f* foundling (*a. niño* ~); **expositor** *m*, -a *f* exhibitor; exponent *de teoría*.

expresado above-mentioned; **expresar** [1a] express; voice; phrase, word, put; ~se express o.s.; **expresión** f expression; ~es pl. fig. greetings; **expresivo** expressive; affectionate; **expreso 1.** express, specific, clear; **2.** m 🚂 express (train); (p.) special messenger; por ~ by express delivery.

exprimelimones m lemon-squeezer; **exprimidera** f, **exprimidor** m squeezer; **exprimir** [3a] squeeze out, express.

exprofeso on purpose.

expropiación f expropriation; **expropiar** [1b] expropriate.

expuesto 1. p.p. of exponer; **2.** adj. lugar exposed; (peligroso) dangerous; artículo on show, on view; ~ a exposed to, open to.

expugnar [1a] take by storm.

expulsar [1a] expel, eject, turn out; **expulsión** f expulsion, ejection; **expulsor** m ⊕ ejector.

expurgar [1h] expurgate; **expurgatorio** expurgatory.

exquisito exquisite; delicious; (culto) genteel, refined; b.s. affected.

extasiarse [1c] go into ecstasies, rhapsodize (ante over); **éxtasis** m ecstasy; rapture; trance de espiritista etc.; **extático** ecstatic, rapturous.

extender [2g] extend; stretch, expand; (desenvolver, desplegar) spread (out), open (out), lay out; lo espeso, lo amontonado spread; cheque etc. make out; documento draw up; write out; ~se extend etc.; (ocupar espacio) extend, lie; (ocupar tiempo) extend, last (de from, a to, till); fig. range entre dos puntos etc.; fig. spread o.s. en discurso; ~ a (propagarse, influir) extend to; (alcanzar, subir a) reach, amount to, run into; **extendido** spread out, open; miembro outstretched; fig. prevalent, widespread.

extensible extending, extensible; **extensión** f (acto, propagación) extension; (dimensión) extent, size; (lo espacioso) spaciousness; expanse, stretch de terreno etc.; span, duration de tiempo etc.; range entre dos puntos etc.; ♪ range, compass; fig. (alcance) scope, range, reach; **extensivo** extensive; **extenso** extensive; broad, spacious; imperio far-flung; relato full; (general) widespread; por ~ in full, at (great) length.

extenuación f emaciation; **extenuado** emaciated; **extenuar** [1e] emaciate; weaken.

exterior 1. exterior, external, outer; manifestación etc. outward; comercio etc. foreign; **2.** m exterior, outside; (aspecto) outward appearance; deportes: wing; del ~ noticias, correo etc. foreign, from abroad; **exterioridad** f externals; (aspecto) outward appearance; **exteriorizar** [1f] reveal, express outwardly.

exterminar [1a] exterminate; **exterminio** m extermination.

externo 1. external; outward; **2.** m, a f day pupil.

extinción f extinction; **extinguir** [3d] extinguish; exterminate; **extinto** extinct; **extintor** m (fire-)extinguisher.

extirpación f extirpation, eradication; **extirpar** [1a] extirpate, eradicate, stamp out.

extra 1. extra; **2.** m extra en cuenta; **3.** m/f cine: extra; **4.** F: ~ de besides, in addition to.

extracción f extraction (a. ⚒); drawing en lotería.

extracorto onda ultra-short.

extractar [1a] libro abridge; **extracto** m ♏ extract; lit. abstract.

extradición f extradition; **extradicionar** [1a] extradite.

extraer [2p] extract (a. ♈, ⚒), take out.

extra...: ~fino superfine; ~judicial extrajudicial; ~limitarse [1a] go too far, exceed one's authority; ~muros adv. outside the city.

extranjerismo m foreign word (or expression etc.); **extranjero 1.** foreign; **2.** m, a f (p.) foreigner; **3.** m (un país) foreign country; (en general) foreign lands, foreign parts; en el ~ abroad; ir al ~ go abroad.

extrañamiento m estrangement; **extrañar** [1a] find strange, wonder at; amigo estrange; (desterrar) banish; S.Am. miss; me extraña su conducta I am surprised at your conduct; ~se be amazed, be surprised (de at); (amigos) become estranged; (rehusar) refuse; **extra-**

ñeza f strangeness, oddity; surprise, amazement; estrangement; **extraño** (*raro*) strange, odd; (*extranjero*) foreign; (*que no tiene que ver*) **extraneous**; ~ a unconnected with.

extraoficial unofficial; informal.

extraordinario 1. extraordinary; unusual; *edición*, *número* special; *precio etc.* extra, supplementary; **2.** m treat; (*plato*) extra dish.

extravagancia f extravagance; eccentricity; (*capricho*) vagary; (*tonterías*) nonsense (a. ~s *pl.*); **extravagante** extravagant; eccentric; fancy *attr.*; (*tonto*) nonsensical.

extraviado stray, lost; **extraviar** [1c] *p.* lead astray; mislead, misdirect *en camino etc.*; *cosa* mislay, misplace; ~se go astray (*a. fig.*), get lost, stray, wander; &c miscarry; **extravío** m (*pérdida*) misplacement, loss; wandering; deviation (*from* de); *fig.* misconduct, evil ways.

extremado extreme; intense; **extremar** [1a] carry to extremes; ~se do one's utmost; ~ en *inf.* go to great lengths to *inf.*

extremaunción f extreme unction.

extremeño *adj. a. su.* m, **a** f (native) of Extremadura.

extremidad f extremity; tip; edge; ~es *pl.* extremities *del cuerpo*; **extremista** m/f extremist; **extremo 1.** extreme; (*sumo*) utmost; (*más remoto*) outermost; (*último*) last; **2.** m end; extreme; (*sumo grado*) highest degree; *fig.* great care; *con* ~ in the extreme; with a vengeance; *por* ~ extremely; *deportes*: ~ derecho outside right; *hacer* ~s gush; *pasar de un* ~ a otro go from one end to the other; *fig.* pass from one extreme to the other; **extremoso** effusive, gushing.

extrínseco extrinsic.

extrovertido m, **a** f extrovert.

exuberancia f exuberance; ♀ luxuriance; **exuberante** exuberant; ♀ luxuriant.

exudación f exudation; **exudar** [1a] exude, ooze.

exultación f exultation; **exultar** [1a] exult.

exvoto m votive offering.

eyector m ⊕ ejector.

F

fábrica f ⊕ factory, works, plant, mill; ⚔ fabric; ⚠ masonry; (*edificio*) building, structure; ✝ (*marca*) make; ~ *experimental* pilot plant; ~ *de gas* gas-works; ✝ *en* ~ *precio* ex-factory; **fabricación** f manufacture, making; make; *de* ~ *casera* home-made; *de* ~ *propia* our own make; ~ *en serie* mass production; **fabricante** m manufacturer, maker; **fabricar** [1g] ⊕ manufacture, make; ⚠ build; *fig.* fabricate, invent; (*juntar*) put together; ~ *en serie* mass-produce; **fabril** manufacturing.

fábula f fable; rumour; (*cuento*) tale; story, plot *de comedia etc.*; (*p.*) laughing-stock; **fabuloso** fabulous; mythical.

facción f *pol. etc.* faction; feature *de cara*; ⚔ *estar de* ~ be on duty; **faccioso 1.** factious; rebellious; **2.** m rebel.

faceta f facet (*a. fig.*).

facial facial; *valor* face *attr.*

fácil easy, simple; (*pronto*) ready; *explicación b.s.* glib; facile; *p.* compliant; *mujer* loose; *es* ~ *que* it is likely that; **facilidad** f ease, facility; ~*es* pl. facilities; **facilitar** [1a] (*hacer fácil*) facilitate, help; (*proveer*) provide, supply; *me facilitó el libro* he let me have the book, he supplied me with the book.

facineroso *adj. a. su.* m criminal.

facsímil(e) *adj. a. su.* m facsimile; **facsimilar** [1a] facsimile; autotype.

factible feasible; workable.

facticio artificial, factitious.

factor m factor (*a.* ✝, ⚥); ✝ agent; ⚙ clerk; **factoría** f factory; ✝ agency, trading post.

factótum m factotum, jack-of-all-trades; *b.s.* busybody.

factura f invoice, bill; **facturar** [1a] ✝ invoice; ⚙ register, check *Am.*

facultad f (*potencia*) faculty (*a. univ.*); (*derecho etc.*) power (*de of su.*, *to inf.*); permission; **facultar** [1a] authorize; **facultativo 1.** optional; ✠ medical; **2.** m doctor, practitioner.

facundia f eloquence, fluency; **facundo** eloquent, fluent.

facha f F look; (*p.*) sight, object; ⚓ *ponerse en* ~ bring to, lie to.

fachada f ⚠ façade (*a. fig.*), frontage; *typ.* frontispiece; F outward show.

fachenda f F swank; **fachendear** [1a] F show off, swank; **fachendón** F, **fachendoso** F swanky, snooty, conceited.

faena f (*tarea*) task, job; (*deber*) duty; ⚔ fatigue; F (*trabajo ingrato*) fag, sweat; F (*mala pasada*) dirty trick; *S.Am.* gang of workers; *toros*: play with the cape; ~*s* pl. chores.

faisán m pheasant.

faja f strip, band *de tela etc.*; (*vestido*) sash (*a.* ⚔), belt; (*corsé*) girdle, corset; ⚙ wrapper; *fig.* strip, belt, zone; **fajar** [1a] *v/t.* wrap, swathe; *v/i.* F ~ *con* go for, lay into; **fajín** m ⚔ sash; **fajina** f ⚔ shock, rick; (*leña*) faggots, kindling; ⚔ bugle-call; **fajo** m sheaf *de papeles*; roll, wad *de billetes*.

falacia f deceit.

falange f phalanx; ♀ *Spanish Fascist party.*

falaz p. deceitful; *doctrina etc.* fallacious; *apariencia etc.* deceptive, misleading.

falda f skirt; (*regazo*) lap; *geog.* slope, hillside; *cosido a las* ~*s de* tied to the apron-strings of.

faldellín m short skirt; underskirt; **faldero:** F *es muy* ~ he's a great one for the ladies; **faldillas** f/pl. tail *de traje*, coat-tails; **faldón** m skirt, tail *de traje*; flap; ⚠ gable.

falencia f deceit; mistake.

falena f moth.

falibilidad f fallibility; **falible** fallible.

falsario m, a f forger; (*mentiroso*) liar; **falseador** m, -a f forger;

falsear [1a] *v/t.* falsify, forge, fake; juggle with; *cerradura* pick; *v/i.* buckle, give way; ♪ be out of tune; **falsedad** *f* falsity, falseness *etc.* (*v. falso*); **falsete** *m* ⊕ bung; ♪ falsetto; **falsía** *f* falsity *etc.*; **falsificación** *f* falsification; forgery; fabrication; **falsificador** *m*, -a *f* forger; **falsificar** [1g] falsify; forge, fake, counterfeit; *elección* rig, fiddle; *razones* misrepresent; **falso** *mst* false; counterfeit, fake; *moneda* bad; (*simulado*) bogus, sham; (*insincero*) hollow, insincere; (*traidor*) treacherous; *testimonio* perjured, untrue; *opinión* unsound; en ~ without proper support; *jurar* en ~ perjure o.s.

falta *f* lack, want, need; absence; (*escasez*) shortage; (*defecto en el obrar*) failure, shortcoming; (*equivocación*) fault, mistake; (*desperfecto*) fault; ⊕ trouble; ⚖ default; *deportes*: foul; *tenis*: fault; ~ de freq. non-...: ~ de asistencia non-attendance; *a* ~ de *prp.* failing; = por ~ de for want of, for lack of; sin ~ without fail; *hacer* ~ be necessary; *me hace (mucha)* ~ I need it (badly); *el hombre que hace* ~ the right man.

faltar [1a] (*estar ausente*) be missing, be lacking; be absent; (*necesitarse*) be needed; (*acabarse, fallar, dejar de ayudar a*) fail; default *en pago etc.*; *faltan 5* there are 5 missing, five short; *faltan 3 días para el examen* the exam is 3 days off; *falta poco para terminar* it's almost over; it's almost finished; *le falta dinero* he needs money, he lacks money; ¡*no faltaba más!* it's the limit!, it's the last straw!; ~ *a cita* break, not turn up for; *clase* be absent from, cut, miss; *decencia* offend against; *deber* neglect; *palabra* go back on.

falto short, deficient; (*apocado*) poor, wretched; ~ de short of; *cualidades etc.* wanting in, lacking in, void of.

faltriquera *f* fob, (watch-)pocket.

falúa *f* tender, launch.

falla *f* fault (*a. geol.*), failure; ~ de encendido, ~ de tiro misfire.

fallada *f naipes*: ruff.

fallar [1a] *v/t. naipes*: trump, ruff; ⚖ pronounce sentence on; *v/i.*

(*tiro*) miss; (*escopeta etc.*) misfire, fail to go off; (*cuerda, soporte etc.*) give way, snap; (*frenos, memoria, cosecha etc.*) fail; (*proyecto*) fail, miscarry; ⚖ find, pass judgement; *el amigo me ha fallado* my friend has failed me (*or* let me down).

falleba *f* bolt.

fallecer [2d] pass away, die; **fallecido** late; **fallecimiento** *m* decease, demise.

fallido unsuccessful; ✝ (*a. su. m*) bankrupt; ⊕ (*a. su. m*) dud.

fallo *m* decision, ruling; ⚖ sentence, verdict; findings; ⊕ trouble; *deportes*: mistake, mix-up; *naipes*: void (*a* in).

fama *f* fame; reputation; rumour; glory; *mala* ~ *esp. de p.* notoriety; ✝ *etc.* bad reputation.

famélico starving, famished.

familia *f* family; household; *venir de* ~ run in the family; **familiar 1.** (*conocido; sin ceremonia*) familiar; (*relativo a la familia*) family *attr.*; (*doméstico*) homely; *palabra* colloquial; *estilo etc.* informal; **2.** *m* (*conocido*) close acquaintance; (*pariente*) relation, relative; **familiaridad** *f* familiarity *etc.*; **familiarizar** [1f] familiarize, acquaint; ~*se* become familiar; ~ *con* become conversant with, get to know.

famoso famous; F great.

fanal *m* lantern; (*torre*) lighthouse; (*campana*) bell-glass.

fanático 1. fanatical; bigoted; **2.** *m* fanatic; bigot; fiend F (*de* for); **fanatismo** *m* fanaticism; bigotry.

fandango *m* fandango.

fanega *f* grain measure = 55.5 *litres*; ground area = 1.59 *acres*.

fanfarrear [1a] = *fanfarronear*; **fanfarria** *f* bluster, bragging; ♪ fanfare; **fanfarrón 1.** blustering, boastful; **2.** *m* blusterer, braggart; bully; **fanfarronada** *f* bluster, bluff, swagger; **fanfarronear** [1a] bluster, rant; swagger; **fanfarronería** *f* blustering, bragging.

fangal *m* bog, quagmire; **fango** *m* mud, mire, slush; **fangoso** muddy, slushy.

fantasía *f* fantasy; imagination; fancy; ♪ fantasia; *de* ~ *artículo* fancy; *joya* imitation; **fantasioso** F vain, stuck-up; **fantasma 1.** *m* ghost, phantom; F solemn and vain person; **2.** *f* bogey; **fantasma-goría** *f* phantasmagoria; **fantasmal** phantom *attr.*; **fantástico** fantastic; weird; unreal(istic); fanciful, whimsical.

fantoche *m* puppet; nincompoop.

faquir *m* fakir.

faramalla *f* F claptrap; sham; trash.

farándula *f* † troupe of strolling players; F claptrap, pack of lies; **farandulero 1.** theatre *attr.*; **2.** *m*, a *f* † strolling player; *b.s.* cheat, plausible rogue.

faraute *m* herald; F busybody.

fardel *m* knapsack; F rag-bag; = **fardo** *m* bundle; bale, pack.

farfulla 1. *f* F splutter, jabber; **2.** *m/f* F gabbler, jabberer; **farfullar** [1a] F splutter, jabber, gabble; *trabajo* bungle.

farináceo starchy, farinaceous.

faringe *f* pharynx.

farisaico pharisaical, hypocritical; smug; **fariseo** *m* pharisee, hypocrite.

farmacéutico 1. pharmaceutical; **2.** *m* chemist, pharmacist, druggist; **farmacia** *f* (*ciencia*) pharmacy; (*tienda*) chemist's (shop); **farmacología** *f* pharmacology.

faro *m* beacon; ⚓ (*torre*) lighthouse; ⚓ lantern, light; *mot.* headlamp, headlight; ~ *piloto*, ~ *trasero* tail-light, rear-lamp; **farol** *m* lantern, lamp; street lamp; 🚗 headlight; F swank; **farola** *f* street lamp; **farolear** [1a] F swank; brag; **farolero** *m* lamp-post; (*p.*) lamp-lighter; F swank; **farolillo** *m* fairy light; ♣ Canterbury bell.

fárrago *m* medley, hotchpotch.

farsa *f* farce; *fig.* humbug, masquerade; **farsante** *m* F humbug, fraud, fake.

fas: *por* ~ *o por nefas* by hook or by crook, rightly or wrongly.

fascículo *m* fascic(u)le.

fascinación *f* fascination; **fascinador** fascinating; **fascinar** [1a] fascinate; captivate; bewitch.

fascismo *m* Fascism; **fascista** *adj. a. su. m/f* fascist.

fase *f* (*a. ☽*) phase; stage.

fastidiar [1b] annoy, bother, vex; bore; irk; *¡no me fastidies!* stop bothering me!; *¡no fastidies!* you

don't mean it!, you're kidding!; **fastidio** *m* annoyance, bother, nuisance; boredom; *¡qué* ~*!* what a nuisance!; **fastidioso** annoying, vexing; tedious, tiresome; irksome.

fastos *m/pl.* annals.   [lavish.)

fastuoso magnificent, pompous,)

fatal fatal; fateful; irrevocable; F ghastly; **fatalidad** *f* fate; (*desgracia*) mischance, ill-luck; fatality; **fatalismo** *m* fatalism; **fatalista 1.** fatalistic; **2.** *m/f* fatalist.

fatídico prophetic.

fatiga *f* fatigue (*a.* ⊕); weariness; (*trabajo*) toil; (*apuro*) hardship; **fatigar** [1h] tire, weary; (*molestar*) annoy; **fatigoso** *trabajo etc.* tiring, exhausting; *p.* tired; (*penoso*) laboured; F trying, tiresome.

fatuidad *f* inanity, fatuity; (*presunción*) conceit; **fatuo** inane, fatuous; conceited.

fauces *f/pl. anat.* gullet; *fig.* jaws.

fauna *f* fauna.

fauno *m* faun.

fausto *m* splendour, pomp, luxury.

fautor *m* accomplice; instigator.

favor *m* favour; (*servicio*) favour, good turn, kindness; protection; *a* ~ *de política* in favour of; *medio* with the help of; *p.* on behalf of; *noche etc.* under cover of; *por* ~ please; *hacer el* ~ *de su.* oblige with *su.*; *¿me hace el* ~ *de inf.?* would you be so kind as to *inf.*?, please *inf.*; *haga el* ~ *de esperar* kindly wait; **favorable** favourable; auspicious; (*benévolo*) kind; **favorecer** [2d] favour; help; treat favourably; (*fortuna etc.*) smile on; (*traje, retrato*) flatter; **favoritismo** *m* favouritism; **favorito** *adj. a. su. m*, a *f* favourite (*a. deportes*).

faz *f lit., fig.* face; aspect.

fe *f* faith (*en in*); belief; fidelity; certificate; ~ *de bautismo* birth certificate; ~ *de erratas* errata; *a* ~ *mía* on my honour; *de buena* ~ in good faith; *en* ~ *de* in witness of; *dar* ~ *de* testify to.

fealdad *f* ugliness.

febrero *m* February.

febrífugo *adj. a. su. m* febrifuge.

febril fevered, feverish (*a. fig.*); *fig.* hectic.

fécula *f* starch; **feculento** starchy.

fecundación *f* fertilization; ~ *artificial* artificial insemination;

fecundar [1a] fertilize; **fecundidad** f fertility; *esp. fig.* fruitfulness; **fecundizar** [1f] fertilize; **fecundo** fertile; prolific; *esp. fig.* fruitful.

fecha f date; ~ *tope* closing date; *de larga* ~ long-dated; *hasta la* ~ (up) to date; **fechar** [1a] date.

fechoría f misdeed.

federación f federation; **federal** federal; **federativo** federative.

feérico fairy.

fehaciente reliable; authentic.

felicidad f happiness; good luck; success; ~*es pl.* congratulations; best wishes; **felicitación** f congratulation; **felicitar** [1a] congratulate.

feligrés m, **-a** f parishioner; **feligresía** f parish.

felino feline, catlike.

feliz *mst* happy; (*de buena suerte*) lucky; (*de buen éxito*) successful.

felpa f plush; F (*zurra*) hiding; F (*regaño*) talking-to; **felpar** [1a] cover with plush; *fig.* carpet; **felpudo 1.** plush(y); **2.** m doormat.

femenil feminine, womanly; **femenino 1.** feminine; ♀ female; *equipo* ~ women's team; **2.** m *gr.* feminine.

fementido treacherous, false.

feminidad f femininity; **feminismo** m feminism; **feminista** m/f feminist.

fenecer [2d] v/t. finish, close; v/i. (*morir*) die; perish; (*acabar*) come to an end; **fenecimiento** m death; end, close.

fenicio *adj. a. su.* m Phoenician.

fénix m phoenix; *fig.* marvel.

fenomenal phenomenal; F tremendous, terrific; **fenómeno** m phenomenon; (*cosa anormal*) freak.

feo 1. ugly; unsightly; hideous; *olor etc.* nasty; *juego, tiempo* foul, dirty; **2.** m F insult; *hacer un* ~ *a* insult; **feote, feota** F shockingly ugly.

feraz fertile.

féretro m coffin, bier.

feria f (*mercado etc.*) fair, market; carnival; (*descanso*) holiday; ⚜ (agricultural) show; ~ *de muestras* trade-fair; **feriado:** *día* ~ holiday; **ferial** m market; **feriante** m/f stall-holder; **feriar** [1b] v/t. buy, sell (in a market); v/i. take time off.

ferino savage; *v. tos.*

fermata f ♪ run.

fermentación f fermentation; **fermentar** [1a] ferment; **fermento** m ferment; leaven(ing).

ferocidad f fierceness *etc.*; **feroz** fierce, ferocious, savage, wild.

férreo iron; 🚂 rail...; **ferrería** f ironworks, foundry; **ferretería** f (*material*) ironmongery, hardware; (*tienda*) ironmonger's (shop), hardware shop; **ferretero** m ironmonger; **férrico** ferric; **ferrocarril** m railway, railroad *Am.*; ~ *elevado* overhead railway; **ferrohormigón** m ferro-concrete; **ferroso** ferrous; **ferroviario 1.** railway *attr.*; **2.** m railwayman.

fértil fertile, fruitful; rich (*en* in); **fertilidad** f fertility, fruitfulness; **fertilizante** m fertilizer; **fertilizar** [1f] fertilize; enrich.

férula f ferule, birch; *fig.* domination, rule.

férvido fervid, ardent; **ferviente** fervent; **fervor** m fervour, ardour; **fervoroso** fervent, ardent.

festejar [1a] entertain, fête, feast; (*galantear*) woo, court; *S.Am.* beat; **festejo** m entertainment, feast; courting; **festín** m feast, banquet; **festival** m festival; **festividad** f festivity, merry-making; (*día*) holiday; (*agudeza*) wit; **festivo** (*alegre*) festive, gay; (*chistoso*) humorous, droll; (*agudo*) witty; jovial; *poema* burlesque, humorous; *día* ~ holiday.

festón m *sew.* festoon, scallop; garland *de flores*; **festonear** [1a] *sew.* festoon, scallop; garland.

fetiche m fetish; mumbo jumbo F.

fetidez f rankness *etc.*; **fétido** rank, stinking, fetid.

feto m foetus.

feúcho F horribly ugly.

feudal feudal; **feudalidad** f feudality; **feudalismo** m feudalism; **feudatario** *adj. a. su.* m feudatory; **feudo** m fief; manor; ~ *franco* freehold.

fiable trustworthy.

fiado: *al* ~ on credit, on trust; **fiador** m (*p.*) *esp.* ⚖ surety, guarantor; *esp.* ♱ sponsor; ⊕ catch, trigger; (*cierre etc.*) fastener; ⚒ safety-catch; tumbler *de cerradura*; F bottom; *salir* ~ *por* go bail for, stand security for.

fiambre 1. cold; *noticia* stale; **2.** m

(*carne etc.*) cold meat, cold food; F (*noticia*) (piece of) stale news; F (*chiste*) old joke, chestnut; F (*p.*) corpse, stiff; **fiambrera** *f* lunch-basket, dinner-pail *Am.*

fianza *f* surety (*a. p.*), security; deposit; ~ *de aduana* bond; ~ *carcelera* bail; **fiar** [1c] *v/t.* entrust (*a* to); *p.* guarantee, stand security for, go bail for; ✝ sell on credit; *v/i.* trust (*en* in); *de* ~ reliable; ~**se** *de* trust in, rely (up)on.

fiasco *m* fiasco.

fíat *m* fiat.

fibra *f* fibre; grain *de madera*; *fig.* vigour, sinews; ~**s** *pl. del corazón* heartstrings; **fibrina** *f* fibrin; **fibroso** fibrous.

ficción *f* fiction; invention, fabrication; **ficticio** fictitious, imaginary.

ficha *f* *juegos*: counter, piece, marker; *póker*: chip; ~ (*del dominó*) domino; (*como moneda*) check, tally; (*papeleta etc.*) (index) card, record card; ✝ plug; **fichar** [1a] *v/t.* file; *v/i.* sign on (*por* for); **fichero** *m* card-index; (*mueble*) filing-cabinet.

fidedigno trustworthy, reliable.

fideicomisario 1.: *banco* ~ trust company; **2.** *m* trustee; **fideicomiso** *m* trust.

fidelidad *f* fidelity, loyalty; (*exactitud*) accuracy; *de alta* ~ high-fidelity, hi-fi.

fideos *m/pl.* vermicelli.

fiduciario *adj. a. su. m* fiduciary.

fiebre *f* fever (*a. fig.*); ~ *aftosa* foot-and-mouth disease; ~ *amarilla* yellow fever; ~ *del heno* hay fever.

fiel 1. faithful, loyal; (*exacto*) accurate, true; **2.** *m* pointer, needle *de balanza*.

fieltro *m* felt; (*sombrero*) felt hat.

fiera *f* wild beast; (*p.*) fiend; (*mujer*) dragon, termagant; *casa* (*or* colección*) *de* ~**s** zoo, menagerie; **fiereza** *f* fierceness; cruelty; **fiero** fierce; cruel; (*horroroso*) frightful; (*feo*) ugly.

fiesta *f* (*día*) holiday; *eccl.* feast, day *de santo etc.*; (*alegría, diversión*) festivity, celebration; party *esp. en casa particular*; fête, festival *en pueblo etc.*; *día de* ~ holiday; ~ *de guardar*, ~ *de precepto* holy day; ~ *nacional* national sport (*i.e.*

bullfighting); *por fin de* ~ to round it all off; *aguar la* ~ be a killjoy, spoil the fun; F *estar de* ~ be in a good mood; F *no estar para* ~**s** be in no mood for jokes; *hacer* ~**s** *a* make a great fuss of; F *tengamos la* ~ *en paz* none of that, cut it out.

figura *f* *mst* figure; (*forma exterior, trazado*) shape; image; (*cara*) face; ~ *de nieve* snowman; *hacer* ~ cut a figure; **figurado** figurative; **figurante** *m*, *a* *f* *thea.* super (numerary), walker-on; *fig.* figure-head; **figurar** [1a] *v/t.* figure, shape; represent; *v/i.* figure (*como* as, *entre* among); ~**se** suppose, imagine, figure *Am.*; *¡figúrate!, ¡figúrese!* just imagine!; (*ya*) *me lo figuraba* I thought as much; **figurativo** figurative.

figurín *m* fashion-plate, model; **figurina** *f* figurine, statuette; **figurón** *m* F pompous ass.

fijación *f* (*acto*) fixing; (*psicológica*) fixation; **fijador** *m* *phot.* (*líquido*) fixer; (*cubeta*) fixing-bath; hair-lotion *para pelo*; **fijar** [1a] fix (*a. phot.*); secure, fasten; *sello etc.* stick (on), affix; *cartel* post; *fecha, hora, precio* fix, set; *pelo* set; *residencia* take up; *atención* focus, fix (*en* on); (*decidir*) settle (on), determine; *prohibido* ~ *carteles* stick no bills; ~**se** settle, lodge; *¡fíjese!* just imagine!; ~ *en* (*notar*) notice; (*atender*) pay attention to; (*mirar fijamente*) stare at; seize upon; **fijativo** *adj. a. su. m* fixative; **fijeza** *f* firmness; fixity; *mirar con* ~ stare at; **fijo** fixed; firm, steady, secure; permanent; determined; *de* ~ certainly, without doubt; F *ésa es la* ~*a* that's for sure; F *ésta es la* ~*a* this is it.

fil *m* *derecho* leapfrog.

fila *f* row (*a. thea.*), line, file; rank (*a.* ✗); F dislike; ~ *india* Indian file; *de dos* ~**s** *chaqueta* double-breasted; *en* ~ in a row; ✗ *en* ~**s** on active service; with the colours; ✗ *romper* ~**s** fall out, dismiss.

filamento *m* filament.

filantropía *f* philanthropy; **filantrópico** philanthropic; **filántropo** *m* philanthropist.

filatelia *f* philately, stamp-collecting; **filatelista** *m/f* philatelist, stamp-collector.

filete *m* △, *cocina*: fillet; ⊕ worm; thread *de tornillo*; *sew.* narrow hem.

filfa *f* F fake, fraud, hoax.

filiación *f* filiation; connexion *de ideas*.

filial 1. filial; ✝ subsidiary; **2.** *f* ✝ subsidiary.

filibustero *m* pirate, freebooter.

filigrana *f* filigree; *typ.* watermark; F clever piece of play.

filípica *f* philippic.

filipino 1. Philippine; **2.** *m*, a *f* Philippine, Filipino.

filisteo *m* Philistine; *fig.* big man, giant.

film *m* film; **filmación** *f* filming; **filmar** [1a] film, shot; **fílmico** film *attr.*

filo *m* edge, cutting edge, blade; dividing line; *de dos* ~s doubleedged; *por* ~ exactly.

filo... philo...

filocomunista 1. fellow-travelling, pro-Communist; **2.** *m/f* fellowtraveller, pro-Communist.

filología *f* philology; **filológico** philological; **filólogo** *m* philologist.

filón *m* seam, vein, lode; F goldmine.

filosofal: *piedra* ~ philosopher's stone; **filosofar** [1a] philosophize; **filosofía** *f* philosophy; **filosófico** philosophic(al); **filósofo** *m* philosopher.

filoxera *f* phylloxera.

filtración *f* filtration; *(accidental)* leakage; **filtrar** [1a] *v/t.* filter; strain; *v/i.*, ~se filter through, percolate, seep; **filtro** *m* filter; ✝ philtre.

filván *m* feather-edge.

fin *m* *(término)* end, ending; *(objeto)* purpose, aim; ~ *de semana* weekend; *a* ~ *de inf.* in order to *inf.*; *a* ~ *de que* so that; *a* ~es *de mayo* at *(or* about) the end of May; *al* ~ finally, at the end; *en* ~ *(como exclamación)* well (then), well now; *en* ~, *por* ~ *(finalmente)* finally, at last; *(en suma)* in short; *al* ~ *y al cabo* in the end; *sin* ~ endless(ly); ⊕ endless; *poner* ~ *a* stop, put a stop to.

finado 1. late; **2.** *m*, a *f* deceased.

final 1. final, last, ultimate; eventual; **2.** *m* end; ♪ finale; **3.** *f* *deportes*: final; **finalidad** *f* object, purpose; **finalista** *m/f* finalist; **finalizar** [1f] *v/t.* finish; *v/i.* end.

financiar [1b] finance; **financiero 1.** financial; **2.** *m* financier; **finanzas** *f/pl.* finance.

finar [1a] die.

finca *f* property; (country) estate; country house; *S.Am.* ranch.

finchado F stuck-up.

finés *v.* *finlandés*.

fineza *f* fineness *de material etc.*; *(regalo)* little gift; *naipes*: finesse; *fig.* kindness, courtesy.

fingido false, mock; sham, fake; make-believe; **fingimiento** *m* simulation; pretence; **fingir** [3c] pretend; sham, fake; invent; make believe; ~ *dormir*, ~se *dormido* pretend to be asleep; ~se *su.* pretend to be *su.*

finiquitar [1a] *cuenta* close, balance up; **finiquito** *m* settlement.

finlandés 1. Finnish; **2.** *m*, -a *f* Finn; **3.** *m* *(idioma)* Finnish.

finito finite.

fino fine; *material etc.* delicate, thin; *producto* select, quality *attr.*; *gusto* discriminating; *inteligencia etc.* acute, shrewd; *ironía etc.* subtle; *oído* sharp; *p. etc.* polite, courteous, refined; *b.s.* cunning.

finta *f* feint; *boxeo*: *hacer* ~s spar.

finura *f* fineness *etc.*　　　[✝ firm.)

firma *f* signature; *(acto)* signing;)

firmamento *m* firmament.

firmante *adj. a. su. m/f* signatory; *el abajo* ~ the undersigned; **firmar** [1a] sign.

firme 1. firm; steady, secure; *superficie etc.* hard, firm; *mercado* steady; *precio* set, stable; *p.* staunch, steadfast; ✂ ~s! attention!; ✝ *en* ~ firm; **2.** *m* surface; **firmeza** *f* firmness *etc.*

fiscal 1. fiscal; **2.** *m* prosecutor, counsel for the prosecution, district attorney *Am.*; **fiscalizar** [1f] inspect; oversee; *b.s.* pry into; ⚖ prosecute; **fisco** *m* exchequer.

fisga *f* *fig.* banter; *hacer* ~ *a* make fun of, tease; **fisgar** [1h] *v/t.* *pez* harpoon; *fig.* pry into; *v/i.* pry; *(burlarse)* mock, scoff; **fisgón 1.** F nosy, prying; **2.** *m*, -a *f* Nosey Parker; **fisgonear** [1a] F = *fisgar*; **fisgoneo** *m* F nosiness.

física *f* physics; ~ *nuclear* nuclear physics; **físico 1.** physical; **2.** *m* physicist; ⚕ ✝ physician; *anat.* physique; *(aspecto)* appearance.

físil fissile.
fisiografía f physiography.
fisiología f physiology.
fisión f fission; ~ *nuclear* nuclear fission; **fisionable** fissionable.
fisonomía f physiognomy, features.
fístula f fistule.
fisura f fissure.
fláccido flaccid, flabby.
flaco 1. thin, lean, skinny; *fig.* weak; *memoria* bad, short; **2.** m weakness, weak point, foible; **flacura** f thinness *etc.*
flagelación f flagellation, whipping; **flagelar** [1a] flagellate, whip; *fig.* flay.
flagrante flagrant; *en* ~ red-handed.
flamante brilliant; *fig.* brand-new.
flameante flamboyant (*a.* △); **flamear** [1a] flame; (*bandera*) flutter.
flamenco[1] m *orn.* flamingo.
flamenco[2] **1.** Flemish; Andalusian gipsy *attr.*; F flashy, gaudy; **2.** m, a f Fleming; **3.** m (*idioma*) Flemish.
flámula f streamer.
flan m cream caramel, caramel custard.
flanco m flank; **flanquear** [1a] flank; ⚔ outflank.
flaquear [1a] weaken, flag; slacken; (*viga etc.*) give (way); **flaqueza** f leanness *etc.*; weakness, frailty; *fig.* failing, weakness *de la carne etc.*
flash m newsflash; *phot.* flash(light).
flato m flatulence, wind; *S.Am.* gloominess; **flatulencia** f flatulence; **flatulento** flatulent.
flauta f flute; **flautín** m piccolo.
flebitis f phlebitis.
fleco m fringe *de pelo etc.*; (*adorno*) tassel; ~s *pl.* gossamer.
flecha f arrow; *alas en* ~ swept back wings; **flechar** [1a] wound *etc.* with an arrow, wing; *arco* stretch; F make a hit with; **flechazo** m arrow wound; F love at first sight; **flechero** m archer, bowman.
flema m phlegm (*a. fig.*); **flemático** phlegmatic, matter-of-fact.
flemón m gumboil.
flequillo m fringe.
fletamento m charter(ing); **fletar** [1a] charter; freight; **flete** m freight; (*precio*) freightage.
flexibilidad f flexibility *etc.*; **flexible 1.** flexible; supple, pliable; *sombrero* soft; *p.* compliant, readily

persuaded; **2.** ´m soft hat; ≠ flex; **flexión** f flexion; *gr.* inflection; **flexional** *gr.* inflected; **flexor:** (*músculo*) ~ flexor.
flirtear [1a] flirt; **flirteo** m (*en general*) flirting; (*un* ~) flirtation.
flojear [1a] weaken; slacken; **flojedad** f looseness, slackness *etc.*; **flojel** m nap *de paño*; *orn.* down; **flojera** f F = *flojedad*; **flojo** (*no tirante*) loose, slack; (*no apretado*) loose; (*débil*) weak, feeble; limp; *viento* light; *vino etc.* weak; *precio* low, sagging; *mercado* slack, dull; *p.* lax, lazy, slack; *estudiante* weak.
flor f flower (*a. fig.*), blossom; bloom *en fruta*; grain *de cuero*; ~ *de la vida* prime of life; ~ *y nata fig.* cream; élite, the pick; *a* ~ *de* (on a) level with; *a* ~ *de agua* at water level; awash; *en* ~ in flower; *echar* ~es *a* pay compliments to, flirt with; **flora** f flora; **floración** f flowering; bloom; **floral** floral; **florar** [1a] flower; **florear** [1a] *v/t.* adorn with flowers; *v/i.* ♪ play a flourish; **florecer** [2d] ♀ flower, bloom; *fig.* flourish, thrive; **floreciente** ♀ in flower, blooming; *fig.* flourishing, thriving; **florecimiento** m flowering; *fig.* flourishing; **floreo** m *fenc.*, ♪ flourish; *fig.* witty talk; **florero** m vase; **florescencia** f florescence; **floresta** f wood, grove, glade; beauty spot; *lit.* anthology.
florete m foil.
floricultura f flower-growing.
florido *campo etc.* flowery; *estilo etc.* flowery, florid; *calidad* select; **florilegio** m anthology; **florista** m/f florist; **floristería** f florist's.
florín m florin.
florón m △ finial; *typ.* tail-piece.
flota f (*en general*) shipping; (*escuadra*) fleet; **flotación** f floating, flotation; **flotador** m float; **flotante** floating; *fig.* hanging loose; **flotar** [1a] float; ride; hang loose; stream *al viento*; **flote:** *a* ~ afloat; *poner a* ~, *sacar a* ~ (re)float, raise; *ponerse a* ~ *fig.* get out of a jam; **flotear** [1a]: ~ (*en el aire*) hover; **flotilla** f flotilla.
fluctuación f fluctuation; *fig.* uncertainty; **fluctuante** fluctuating; **fluctuar** [1e] fluctuate; (*p.*) waver, hesitate.

fluidez f fluidity; *fig.* fluency; **flúido** 1. fluid; *fig.* fluent, smooth; 2. *m* fluid; ~ *eléctrico* electric current; **fluir** [3g] flow, run.

flujo *m* flow; flux; stream; ♃ rising tide; ~ *de sangre* haemorrhage; ~ *de vientre* diarrhoea.

fluorescencia f fluorescence; **fluorescente** fluorescent.

fluvial river *attr.*

flux *m naipes*: flush.

fobia f phobia.

foca f seal.

focal focal; **foco** *m* focus (*a. fig.*); source *de calor, luz*; ⚡ floodlight; *fig.* centre; hotbed *de vicios etc.*

fofo soft, spongy; insubstantial.

fogarada f, **fogata** f blaze, bonfire.

fogón *m* stove, kitchen range; 🚂 firebox; ⊕ vent; ♃ galley; **fogonazo** *m* flash; **fogonero** *m* stoker, fireman.

fogosidad f fire, dash, verve; **fogoso** (high-)spirited, mettlesome, ardent; *caballo* fiery, frisky.

foliación f foliation; **foliar** [1b] foliate, number the pages of; **folio** *m* folio.

folklore *m* folklore; **folklórico** folk *attr.*, folklore *attr.*

follaje *m* ♣ foliage, leaves; *fig.* (*adorno*) excessive ornamentation; (*palabras*) verbiage.

folletín *m* newspaper serial; **folletista** *m* pamphleteer; **folleto** *m* pamphlet; folder, brochure, leaflet.

follón 1. (*perezoso*) lazy, slack; (*arrogante*) puffed-up, blustering; 2. *m* ♣ sucker; (*p.*) good-for-nothing, layabout F; F (*jaleo*) rumpus, row, shindy; F *hacer* ~ (*estudiantes*) have a rag, riot.

fomentación f 🩹 fomentation; **fomentar** [1a] encourage, promote, foment (*a.* 🩹), further, foster; *rebelión* stir up; **fomento** *m* encouragement *etc.*; 🩹 fomentation; *Ministerio de* ♀ *ministry responsible for public works, agriculture etc.*

fonda f inn; 🚂 buffet.

fondeadero *m* anchorage; berth; **fondear** [1a] *v/t. fondo* sound; *barco* search; *fig.* examine; *v/i.* drop anchor.

fondero *m S.Am.* innkeeper.

fondillos *m/pl.* seat (of trousers).

fondista *m/f* innkeeper.

fondo *m* (*parte más baja*) bottom (*a.* ♃); (*parte más lejana*) back, far end; (*profundidad*) depth; ♃, *paint., sew.* ground; *paint., fig.* background; (*esencia*) substance, matter; disposition *de p.*; † fund; *fig.* fund, reservoir *de humor etc.*; † ~s *pl.* funds; finance; ~ *de amortización* sinking fund; *doble* ~, ~ *falso* false bottom; *bajos* ~s *pl. sociales* dregs of society; *a* ~ thoroughly; *al* ~ *de escena etc.* at the back of; *deportes*: *de* ~ long-distance, endurance *attr.*; *en el* ~ *fig.* at bottom, at heart; *dar* ~ anchor; *echar a* ~, *irse a* ~ sink.

fonética f phonetics; **fonético** phonetic; **fonetista** *m/f* phonetician.

fonógrafo *m S.Am.* gramophone, phonograph; **fonología** f phonology.

fontanal *m*, **fontanar** *m* spring.

fontanería f plumbing; **fontanero** *m* plumber.

foque *m* jib.

forajido *m* outlaw, bandit, desperado.

forastero 1. alien, strange; 2. *m*, *a* f stranger, outsider, visitor.

forcej(e)ar [1a] struggle, wrestle; flounder (about); **forcejudo** strong, powerful.

fórceps *m* forceps.

forense forensic.

forestal forest *attr.*; *v. repoblación etc.*

forja f forge; foundry; (*acto*) forging; **forjado** wrought; **forjar** [1a] forge, shape; *fig.* concoct.

forma f form, shape; (*modo*) way, means; formula; *typ.* format; ~s *pl.* social forms, conventions; *de esta* ~ in this manner; *de* ~ *que* so that; *de todas* ~s anyway, at any rate; *en debida* ~ duly; *estar en* ~ be in (good) form; *ver la* ~ *de inf.* see one's way to *ger.* or *inf.*; **formación** f formation; education; training *para profesión*; **formal** (*relativo a la forma*) formal; *asunto* serious; official; *permiso etc.* formal, express; *promesa* definite; *manera* earnest; *p.* reliable, dependable; (*de edad*) adult, grown-up; **formalidad** f formality; form; seriousness *etc.*; *pura* ~ matter of form; **formalismo** *m* conventionalism; (*administrativo* *etc.*) red tape; **formalista** *m/f* formalist; **formalizar** [1f] formalize; formulate; regularize, put in order; ⁓**se** take offence; grow serious; **formar** [1a] (*dar forma a*) form, shape; (*reunir, componer*) form, make up; *proyecto* make, lay; *tropas* parade; *alumno* train; ⁓**se** form, shape; develop; ✕ *etc.* form up, line up; **formativo** formative; **formato** *m* format.

fórmico: *ácido* ⁓ formic acid.

formidable formidable, redoubtable; tremendous (*a.* F).

formón *m* chisel.

fórmula *f* formula; (*receta*) formula, prescription; *por pura* ⁓ just for form's sake; **formulación** *f* formulation; **formular** [1a] formulate; *queja* lodge; *pregunta* frame, pose; **formulario 1.** formulary; **2.** *m* formulary; form.

fornicación *f* fornication; **fornicar** [1g] fornicate.

fornido strapping, hefty.

foro *m hist.* forum; ✝ bar; *thea.* backstage.

forraje *m* fodder, forage; (*acto*) foraging; F hotchpotch; **forrajear** [1a] forage.

forrar [1a] *mst* line; *ropa* line, pad; *libro etc.* cover; ⊕ face; ⊕ lag *para retener el calor*; **forro** *m* lining, padding; cover; ⊕ facing, sheathing; F *ni por el* ⁓ not by a long shot.

fortalecer [2d] strengthen; ✕ *etc.* fortify; *moral* stiffen; encourage *en una opinión etc.*; **fortalecimiento** *m* strengthening *etc.*; **fortaleza** *f* ✕ fortress, stronghold; (*fuerza*) strength; fortitude, resolution; **fortificación** *f* fortification; **fortificar** [1g] fortify; *fig.* strengthen; **fortín** *m* pillbox, bunker; fort.

fortuito fortuitous; accidental, chance *attr.*

fortuna *f mst* fortune; luck; *por* ⁓ luckily; ⚓ *correr* ⁓ weather a storm; *probar* ⁓ try one's luck, have a shot F.

forzado forced; **forzar** [1f *a.* 1m] force, compel (*a inf.* to *inf.*); *puerta* break open; *cerradura* pick; *propiedad* enter by force; *mujer* ravish, rape; *sentido, ojos* strain; **forzoso** necessary; inescapable; *aterrizaje* forced; **forzudo** strong, tough.

fosa *f* grave; *anat.* fosse.

fosfato *m* phosphate; **fosforera** *f* match-box; **fosforescencia** *f* phosphorescence; **fosforescente** phosphorescent; **fosfórico** phosphoric; **fósforo** *m* match; 🜔 phosphorus; **fosforoso** phosphorous.

fósil *adj. a. su. m* fossil (*a. fig.*); **fosilizado** fossilized.

foso *m* pit; ditch, trench; ✕ fosse, moat; *thea.* pit; ⁓ *de reconocimiento* inspection pit; *venirse al* ⁓ flop.

fotinga *f S.Am.* F jalopy.

foto *f* F photo; ⁓**copia** *f* photocopy, print; ⁓**cromía** *f* colour photography; ⁓**eléctrico** photo-electric; ⁓**génico** photogenic (*a.* F); ⁓**grabado** *m* photogravure; ⁓**grafía** *f* (*arte*) photography; (*foto*) photograph; ⁓ *instantánea* snapshot; ⁓**grafiar** [1c] photograph; ⁓**gráfico** photographic; **fotógrafo** *m* photographer; **fotómetro** *m* exposure meter, photometer; **fotosíntesis** *f* photosynthesis; **fotostatar** [1a] photostat; **fotóstato** *m* photostat; **fototelegrafía** *f* phototelegraphy; **fototipo** *m* phototype.

fox [fos] *m* foxtrot.

frac *m* dress-coat, tail-coat.

fracasar [1a] fail; fall through; **fracaso** *m* failure.

fracción *f* ✚ *etc.* fraction; division; (*partido*) faction, splinter group; (*acto*) breaking; **fraccionamiento** *m* breaking-up; **fraccionar** [1a] break up, divide; **fraccionario** fractional.

fractura *f* fracture, break; ⁓ *complicada* compound fracture; **fracturar** [1a] fracture, break.

fragancia *f* fragrance, perfume; **fragante** fragrant, sweet-smelling; *crimen* flagrant.

fragata *f* frigate.

frágil fragile; brittle; *fig.* frail; **fragilidad** *f* fragility; brittleness; *fig.* frailty.

fragmentario fragmentary; *b.s.* scrappy; **fragmento** *m* fragment; scrap, piece, bit.

fragor *m* crash, clash; din; uproar.

fragosidad *f* roughness *etc.*; (*camino*) rough road; **fragoso** rough, uneven; *terreno* difficult; *selva* dense.

fragua f forge; **fraguar** [1i] v/t. ⊕ forge; fig. mentira concoct; complot hatch; v/i. ⊕ set.

fraile m friar; monk; F priest; **frailuno** contp. monkish.

frambuesa f raspberry; **frambueso** m raspberry(-cane).

francachela f F spree, jamboree; (comida) spread.

francés 1. French; despedirse a la ~a take French leave; **2.** m (p.) Frenchman; (idioma) French; **francesa** f Frenchwoman.

franciscano adj. a. su. m Franciscan.

francmasón m (free)mason; **francmasonería** f (free)masonry.

franco 1. frank, open, forthright; (pleno) full; (liberal) generous; ✝ free; camino open; ~ a bordo free on board; v. porte; **2.** hist. Frankish; ~-español Franco-Spanish; **3.** m franc; hist. Frank.

francote blunt, bluff.

francotirador m sniper.

franchute m, a f F Frenchy.

franela f flannel.

frangollar [1a] F bungle, botch, rush.

franja f fringe, trimming; band (a. fig.).

franquear [1a] contribuyente exempt; esclavo free, liberate; derecho grant, allow; camino clear; río etc. cross; ✉ frank, stamp; ~se fall in with s.o.'s wishes; open one's heart (a, con to); **franqueo** m franking; postage; **franqueza** f frankness etc.; **franquicia** f exemption; ~ postal privilege of franking letters.

frasco m flask, bottle.

frase f sentence; (locución) phrase; ~ hecha stock phrase, cliché; idiom; proverb; **fraseología** f phraseology.

fraternal brotherly, fraternal; **fraternidad** f brotherhood, fraternity; **fraternización** f fraternization; **fraternizar** [1f] fraternize; **fraterno** brotherly, fraternal.

fratricida 1. fratricidal; **2.** m fratricide (p.); **fratricidio** m fratricide (act).

fraude m fraud; false pretences; dishonesty; **fraudulencia** f fraudulence; **fraudulento** fraudulent; dishonest.

fray m eccl. brother.

frecuencia f frequency (a. ✻); alta ~ high frequency; con ~ frequently; **frecuentador** m, -a f frequenter; **frecuentar** [1a] frequent; haunt; **frecuente** frequent; common; costumbre etc. prevalent, rife.

fregadero m (kitchen) sink; **fregado** m scrub(bing); washing-up de platos; F (enredo) mess; F (jaleo) row; **fregador** m (pila) sink; (trapo) dish-cloth; (estropajo) scrubber, scourer; **fregar** [1h a. 1k] scrub, scour; suelo scrub, mop; platos wash; **fregasuelos** m mop; **fregona** f kitchen-maid; contp. skivvy.

freiduría f fried-fish shop; **freír** [3m; p.p. frito] fry.

fréjol m kidney bean.

frenar [1a] brake; fig. check, restrain.

frenesí m frenzy; **frenético** frantic, frenzied; wild.

freno m ⊕ brake; bit de caballo; fig. check, curb; ~ de mano hand-brake.

frenología f phrenology.

frente 1. f forehead, brow; (cara) face; **2.** m todos sentidos: front; al ~ in front; ✝ carried forward; de ~ mover forward; marchar abreast; chocar head on; ¡de ~ (mar)! by the right quick march!; del ~ brought forward; en ~ opposite, in front; hacer ~ a resist; gastos meet; ⚓ tempestad ride out; **3.** prp.: ~ a opposite (to); in front of; fig. as opposed to.

fresa f ♀ (mst wild) strawberry; bit, drill de dentista; ⊕ milling cutter; **fresadora** f milling machine; **fresal** m strawberry bed; **fresar** [1a] mill.

fresca f fresh air, cool air; F piece of one's mind; tomar la ~ get some fresh air; **frescachón** glowing with health; bouncing; mujer buxom; **fresco 1.** mst fresh; (algo frío) cool; agua cold; huevo new-laid; F fresh, saucy, cheeky; F quedarse tan ~ not bat an eyelid, remain unmoved; **2.** m fresh air, cool air; ♠ etc. fresco; al ~ in the open air, out of doors; tomar el ~ take the air, get some fresh air; **frescor** m freshness; coolness; **frescote** F blooming; buxom; **frescura** f freshness; coolness; F cheek, sauce, nerve.

fresno m ash (tree).

fresón m strawberry.
fresquera f meat-safe.
freza f spawn; (acto, época) spawning; **frezar** [1f] spawn.
friable friable.
frialdad f coldness; coolness, indifference.
fricasé m fricassee.
fricción f rubbing, rub; ⊕ friction (a. fig.); ✗ massage; **friccionar** [1a] rub; ✗ massage.
friega f rubbing; ✗ massage; F bother, fuss; S.Am. thrashing; **friegaplatos** m dish-washer.
frigidez f frigidity; **frígido** frigid.
frigorífico 1. refrigerating; camión ～ refrigerator lorry; 2. m refrigerator; S.Am. cold-storage plant; ⚓ refrigerator ship.
frío 1. cold; bala spent; 2. m cold; coldness; hace (mucho) ～ it is (very) cold; tener ～ be cold, feel cold; **friolento** chilly, shivery; **friolera** f trifle, mere nothing; **friolero** chilly, shivery.
frisar [1a] v/t. tela frizz, rub; v/i. get along; ～ en border on; años be getting on for.
frizo m frieze; wainscot, dado.
fritada f fry; **frito** 1. fried; F tener ～, F traer ～ defeat; worry to death; F el inglés me trae ～ English just gets me down; F ese hombre me trae ～ that chap is forever bothering me; 2. m fry; ～s pl. variados mixed grill.
frivolidad f frivolity etc.; **frívolo** frivolous; pretexto etc. flimsy, trivial; p. shallow; charla idle.
fronda f frond; **frondosidad** f leafiness; luxuriance; **frondoso** leafy; luxuriant.
frontal adj. a. su. m frontal.
frontera f frontier, border; **fronterizo** frontier attr., border attr.; casa opposite.
frontis m façade; **frontispicio** m frontispiece.
frontón m △ pediment; deportes: pelota court.
frotación f, **frotadura** f rub, rubbing; ⊕ friction; **frotar** [1a] rub; cerilla strike; quitar frotando rub off; **frote** m rub, rubbing.
fructífero productive; fig. fruitful; **fructificar** [1g] produce, yield a crop; fig. yield (a profit); **fructuoso** fruitful.

frugal frugal; thrifty; **frugalidad** f frugality; thrift(iness).
fruición f enjoyment, delight.
frunce m, **fruncido** m, **fruncimiento** m pleat, gather(ing), pucker; **fruncir** [3b] pucker, wrinkle, ruffle; sew. pleat, gather, pucker; labios purse; entrecejo knit.
fruslería f trifle.
frustrar [1a] frustrate, thwart, balk; ～se fail, miscarry.
fruta f fruit; fig. result; ～ de sartén fritter; **frutal** 1.: árbol ～ = 2. m fruit tree; **frutar** [1a] fruit; **frutería** f fruiterer's (shop); **frutero** 1.: plato ～ fruit-dish; 2. m fruiterer; **fruticultura** f fruit-growing; **frutilla** f S.Am. strawberry; **fruto** m fruit; fig. fruits, profit, results; dar ～ fruit.
fu: ni ～ ni fa neither one thing nor the other.
fucilazo m sheet lightning.
fuco m. wrack.
fucsia f fuchsia.
fuego m fire; light para cigarrillo; ⚓ beacon; ✗ rash; ✗ ¡～! fire!; ～s pl. artificiales fireworks; ～ fatuo will-o'-the-wisp; abrir ～ open fire; echar ～ por los ojos glare, look daggers; hacer ～ fire (sobre at, on); jugar con ～ play with fire; pegar ～ a set fire to; poner a ～ y sangre lay waste; romper el ～ open up.
fuelle m bellows (a. phot.); mot. folding hood; F tell-tale.
fuente f fountain, spring; (plato) large dish, bowl; fig. source; ～ termal hot spring.
fuer: a ～ de hombre honrado as an honest man.
fuera 1. adv. outside; out; away; deportes: (pelota) estar in touch, out; poner into touch; (equipo) jugar away (from home); ¡～ (de aquí)! off with you!; por ～ on the outside; v. estar; 2. prp.: ～ de out of, outside (of); fig. in addition to, besides, beyond; ～ de eso apart from that; ～ de mentir short of lying; ～ de sí beside o.s.
fuero m jurisdiction; (código) code (of laws); charter de ciudad; privilege de grupo.
fuerte 1. strong; sturdy; vigorous; golpe hard; calor etc. intense; comida, gasto, lluvia heavy; ruido

loud; ~ *en* well up in; **2.** *adv.*
strongly; *golpear* hard; *tocar* loud,
loudly; *poner más* ~ *radio* turn up;
3. *m* ✕ fort, strongpoint; ♪, *fig.*
forte.
fuerza *f* strength; force; power (*a.*
𝄌); intensity; heaviness; effect *de*
argumento etc.; ~*s pl.* ✕ forces;
strength *de p.*; ~ *de gravedad* force
of gravity; ~ *mayor* force majeure;
act of God; ~ *motriz* motive power;
a la ~ by force, willy-nilly; *a* ~ *de*
by dint of; *a viva* ~ *entrada* forced;
por ~ perforce; *por* ~ *mayor* under
coercion; by main force; *hacer* ~
de vela crowd on sail; *tener* ~*s*
para have the strength to *inf.* (for
su.).
fuga *f* flight, escape; leak *de gas etc.*;
♪ fugue; *poner en* ~ put to flight;
apelar a la ~, *darse a la* ~, *ponerse*
en ~ take to flight; **fugarse** [1h]
flee, escape; ~ (*de la ley*) abscond;
~ *con* run away with; **fugaz** (*pasa-*
jero) fleeting, short-lived; (*difícil de*
coger) elusive; **fugitivo** *adj. a. su.*
m, **a** *f* fugitive; = *fugaz*.
fui, fuimos *etc. v. ir, ser.*
fulana *f* F tart, whore; **fulano** *m*, **a**
f (*Mr etc.*) So-and-so.
fulcro *m* fulcrum.
fulero F useless.
fulgente, fúlgido brilliant, bright;
fulgor *m* brilliance, glow; **fulgu-**
rante shining, bright; **fulgurar**
[1a] shine, gleam; flash; **fulguroso**
shining, flashing.
fulminación *f* fulmination; **ful-**
minante *polvo etc.* fulminating;
🜊 fulminant; F *éxito etc.* tremendous; **fulminar** [1a] *v/t.* fulminate; *amenazas etc.* thunder; ~ *con*
la mirada look daggers at; *v/i.*
fulminate, explode; **fulminato** *m*
fulminate.
fullería *f* cardsharping; trick; **fu-**
llero *m* (card)sharper; F cheat,
crook; dodger.
fumada *f* whiff (*or* puff) of smoke;
fumadero *m* smoking-room; ~ *de*
opio opium den; **fumador** *m*, **-a** *f*
smoker; **fumar** [1a] smoke; *prohi-*
bido ~ no smoking; ~*se* F *sueldo*
squander; *clase* cut; **fumarada** *f*
(*humo*) puff of smoke; pipeful *de*
tabaco.
fumigación *f* fumigation; **fumigar**
[1h] fumigate.

funámbulo *m*, **a** *f* tight-rope
walker.
función *f* function; duty; *thea.*
show, entertainment; performance;
~ *taquillera* draw; *entrar en* ~*es* take
up one's duties; **funcional** func-
tional; **funcionamiento** *m* functioning; ⊕ *etc.* working, running;
performance; behaviour; ⊕ *en* ~ in
order, in operation; *en pleno* ~ *socie-*
dad etc. going; **funcionar** [1a]
function; work, run, go (*a.* ⊕); perform (*a.* ⊕); behave; *no funciona*
(*como letrero*) out of order; *hacer* ~
operate; **funcionario** *m* official,
functionary; civil servant.
funda *f* case, sheath; (*bolsa*) hold-
all.
fundación *f* foundation; **fundador**
m, **-a** *f* founder; **fundamental**
fundamental; basic; essential; **fun-**
damentar [1a] lay the foundations
of; base (*en* on); **fundamento** *m*
foundation; basis; (*trabajo prelimi-*
nar) groundwork; (*razón, motivo*)
ground(s); reliability, trustworthiness *de p.*; ~*s pl. fig.* fundamentals;
fundar [1a] found, set up, establish,
institute; endow *con dinero*; *argu-*
mento etc. base (*en* on); *bien fundado*
well grounded.
fundente 1. melting; **2.** *m* 🜋 flux;
🜊 dissolvent; **fundible** fusible;
fundición *f* (*acto*) fusion; ⊕ (*acto*)
melting, smelting; (*fábrica*) foundry, forge; *typ.* fount; **fundidor** *m*
smelter, founder; **fundir** [3a] fuse;
⊕ (*derretir*) melt (down), smelt;
(*formar*) found, cast; ~*se* fuse (*a.* 𝄌),
merge, blend; (*metal*) melt; 𝄌 blow,
burn out.
fúnebre funereal; (*relativo a funeral*)
funeral *attr.*; *fig.* mournful, lugu-
brious; **funeral 1.** funeral *attr.*;
2. *m*, ~*es pl.* funeral; **funeraria** *f*
undertaker's; *director de* ~ funeral
director; **funerario, funéreo** fu-
ner(e)al.
funesto ill-fated, unfortunate; disastrous, fatal (*para* for).
fungoso fungous.
funicular *adj. a. su. m* funicular.
furgón *m* waggon, van; luggage-van
(*a.* ~ *de equipajes*); guard's van (*a.*
~ *de cola*); **furgoneta** *f* van.
furia *f* fury; rage; *a toda* ~ like fury;
hecho una ~ furiously angry; **furi-**
bundo, furioso furious; violent;

frantic; **furor** m rage; passion; frenzy; *hacer* ~ be all the rage (*or* go).

furriel m ✗ *approx.* quartermaster.

furtivo furtive; stealthy; sly, shifty; *edición* pirated.

furúnculo m boil.

fuselaje m fuselage.

fusible 1. fusible; **2.** m fuse; *caja de* ~s fuse box.

fusil m rifle; gun; **fusilamiento** m shooting, execution; **fusilar** [1a] shoot, execute; **fusilazo** m rifleshot; **fusilero** m rifleman, fusilier.

fusión f fusion (*a. fig.*); melting *de metal*; ✝ merger; **fusionar(se)** [1a] fuse; ✝ merge.

fusta f long whip; (*leña*) brushwood.

fustán m fustian.

fuste m wood; shaft *de arma etc.*; (*silla*) saddle-tree; *de* ~ *fig.* of consequence, important.

fustigar [1h] whip, lash (*a. fig.*).

fútbol m football; **futbolista** m footballer.

futesa f trifle, mere nothing.

fútil trifling; **futilidad** f trifling nature, unimportance.

futura f ⚥ reversion; F fiancée; **futurismo** m futurism; **futuro 1.** future; **2.** m future (*a. gr.*); F fiancé; ~s *pl.* ✝ futures; *en el* ~, *en lo* ~ in (the) future.

G

gabacho m, a f F Frenchy, froggy.

gabán m overcoat, top-coat.

gabardina f gaberdine; mackintosh, raincoat.

gabarra f lighter, barge.

gabarro m flaw; vet. pip; fig. error; (estorbo) snag.

gabinete m study, library; (despacho) office; consulting room; (cuarto particular) private (sitting-)room; laboratory; museum; pol. cabinet; de ~ p. armchair attr.; ~ de lectura reading room.

gacela f gazelle.

gaceta f gazette, journal; S.Am. newspaper; **gacetero** m journalist; **gacetilla** f gossip column; news in brief; F gossip; **gacetillero** m gossip columnist; contp. penny-a-liner; **gacetista** m/f gossip.

gacha f thin paste; ~s pl. pap; approx. porridge.

gachí f sl. dame, girl.

gacho drooping, floppy; borde etc. turned down; sombrero slouch; a ~as on all fours.

gachón F nice, charming.

gaditano adj. a. su. m, a f (native) of Cadiz.

gafa f grapple; ~s pl. spectacles, glasses; **gafancia** f F constant bad luck; **gafar** [1a] hook, claw; F bring bad luck to, put a hoodoo on; **gafe**: F ser ~ have constant bad luck.

gaita f (a. ~ gallega) bagpipe; (dulzaina) flageolet; (organillo) hurdy-gurdy; estar de ~ be merry; **gaitero** 1. gaudy, flashy; (alegre) merry; 2. m piper.

gaje m (mst ~s pl.) pay, emoluments, perquisites; ~s pl. del oficio iro. occupational risks.

gajo m (rama) (torn-off) branch; small cluster de uvas; segment de fruta; (punta) prong; geog. spur.

gala f full dress; elegance, gracefulness; fig. cream, flower, chief ornament; ~s pl. finery, trappings; de ~ state, (full-)dress, gala attr.;

hacer ~ de parade, show off; glory in; tener a ~ inf. be proud to inf.

galafate m cunning thief.

galán m handsome fellow; ladies' man; (amante) gallant, beau; thea. ~ joven juvenile lead; primer ~ leading man; **galano** smart, spruce; gaily dressed; fig. elegant; **galante** gallant, attentive (to women); mujer flirtatious; b.s. licentious; **galantear** [1a] court, woo; flirt with; **galanteo** m courting; flirtation; **galantería** f courtesy, compliment; gallantry; **galanura** f prettiness, charm, elegance.

galápago m zo. freshwater tortoise; metall. pig, ingot; (silla) light saddle.

galardón m lit. reward, prize; **galardonar** [1a] reward; obra give an award (or prize) to.

galaxia f galaxy.

galeón m galleon.

galeote m galley-slave.

galera f ⚓, typ. galley; (carro) (covered) wagon; ⚕ hospital ward; **galerada** f galley(-proof).

galería f mst gallery; (pasillo) passage; ~ de tiro shooting-gallery.

galés 1. Welsh; 2. m (p.) Welshman; (idioma) Welsh; **galesa** f Welsh-\ [woman.)

galga f boulder.

galgo m, a f greyhound; F ¡échale un ~! search me!

galicano Gallican; Gallic; **galicismo** m Gallicism; **gálico** m syphilis.

galimatías m gibberish, double Dutch; rigmarole.

galo 1. Gallic; 2. m, a f Gaul.

galocha f clog, patten.

galón m braid; ✂ stripe, chevron; **galonear** [1a] (trim with) braid.

galopada f gallop; **galopante** ⚕ galloping; **galopar** [1a] gallop; **galope** m gallop; a ~, de ~ at a gallop; in great haste; a ~ tendido at full gallop; medio ~ canter.

galopín m ragamuffin, urchin; (bribón) rogue; ⚓ cabin-boy; F smart Alec.

galpón *m S.Am.* (large) shed.
galvánico galvanic; **galvanismo** *m* galvanism; **galvanizar** [1f] galvanize (*a. fig.*); electroplate; **galvanoplástico** galvanoplastic.
gallardear [1a] be graceful; bear o.s. well; **gallardete** *m* pennant, streamer; **gallardía** *f* gracefulness *etc.*; **gallardo** graceful, elegant; (*excelente*) fine; (*apuesto*) upstanding; (*bizarro*) dashing, gallant.
gallear [1a] bluster, throw one's weight about; (*descollar*) excel, stand out.
gallego *adj. a. su. m*, **a** *f* Galician.
gallera *f* cockpit.
galleta *f* biscuit; wafer; F slap; **galletero** *m* biscuit-barrel.
gallina 1. *f* hen, fowl; ~ *ciega* blindman's-buff; ~ *de Guinea* guineafowl; **2.** *m/f* F coward, funk; **gallinero** *m* henhouse, coop; *thea.* gods, gallery; (*voces*) babel; (*p.*) chicken-farmer *que cría*; poulterer *que vende*; **gallipavo** *m* ♪ false note; **gallito** *m* cock o'-the walk; **gallo** *m* cock, rooster; ♪ false note, break in the voice; F boss; ~ *de pelea* fighting-cock; *alzar el* ~ put on airs, brag.
gama[1] *f zo.* doe.
gama[2] *f* (*letra*) gamma; ♪ scale; range, gamut *de colores etc.*; ~ *de frecuencias* frequency-range; ~ *de ondas* wave-range.
gamba *f* prawn; *sl.* 100 pesetas.
gamberrada *f* F piece of hooliganism; **gamberrear** [1a] F go around causing trouble, act like a hooligan; loaf; **gamberrismo** *m* F hooliganism; **gamberro** *m* F lout, hooligan.
gambito *m* gambit.
gamella *f* trough.
gamo *m* buck (of fallow-deer).
gamuza *f zo.* chamois; (*cuero*) chamois leather, wash-leather; (*trapo*) yellow duster.
gana *f* desire; appetite; inclination; *de buena* ~ willingly, readily; *de mala* ~ unwillingly, reluctantly, grudgingly; *dar etc. de mala* ~ (be-) grudge; *me da la* (*real*) ~ *de inf.* I feel like *ger.*, I want to *inf.*; *tener* ~*s de inf.* feel like *ger.*, care to *inf.*, have a mind to *inf.*
ganadería *f* livestock; (strain of) cattle; (*cría*) cattle-raising, stock-breeding; (*granja*) cattle ranch,

stock farm; **ganadero** *m* stock-breeder, rancher *Am.*; cattle-dealer; **ganado** *m* (*en general*) livestock; (*vacas*) cattle; (*rebaño*) herd, flock; ~ *mayor* cattle horses and mules; ~ *menor* sheep and goats; ~ *porcino* pigs; ~ *vacuno* cattle.
ganador 1. winning; **2.** *m*, -**a** *f* winner; **ganancia** *f* gain; ✝ profit; (*aumento*) increase; ~*s pl.* winnings, earnings; ~*s pl. y pérdidas* profit and loss; **ganancial** profit *attr.*; **ganancioso 1.** (*provechoso*) gainful, profitable, lucrative; (*ganador*) winning; **2.** *m*, **a** *f* gainer *en trato*; winner *en juego*.
ganapán *m* (*recadero*) messenger, porter; (*jornalero*) casual labourer; F boor.
ganar [1a] *v/t.* gain; ✝ earn; (*vencer*) win; (*obtener*) get; ✂ conquer, take; (*llegar a*) reach; *tantos* score; *p.* (*atraer*) win over; (*vencer*) beat, outstrip (*en* at, in); *v/i.* thrive, improve.
ganchillo *m* crochet-hook; crochet (work); **gancho** *m* hook; F (*p.*) tout; (*atractivo*) sex appeal, charm; *S.Am.* hairpin; **ganchoso**, **ganchudo** hooked.
gandul F **1.** idle, good-for-nothing, lazy; **2.** *m*, -**a** *f* loafer, good-for-nothing, slacker, spiv; **gandulear** [1a] F loaf, idle, slack; **gandulería** *f* F loafing, laziness.
ganga *f* bargain; gift F.
gangoso nasal, with a twang.
gangrena *f* gangrene; **gangrenarse** [1a] become gangrenous; **gangrenoso** gangrenous.
gángster *m* gunman, gangster.
ganguear [1a] speak with a (nasal) twang; **gangueo** *m* (nasal) twang.
ganoso anxious, keen (*de inf.* to *inf.*).
gansada *f* F (piece of) stupidity; **ganso 1.** *m* gander; **2.** *m*, **a** *f* goose; *fig.* dolt, dope F; (*rústico*) bumpkin.
ganzúa *f* picklock.
gañán *m* farmhand.
gañido *m* yelp, howl; **gañir** [3h] (*perro*) yelp, howl; (*ave*) croak; (*p.*) wheeze.
gañón *m* F, **gañote** *m* F throat, gullet.
garabatear [1a] hook; (*escribir*) scribble; F beat about the bush;

garabato *m* hook, meat-hook; pothook (*a. fig.*); (*letra*) scrawl; F sex appeal.

garaje *m* garage.

garambaina *f* tawdry finery; ～s *pl.* F grimaces; (*letra*) scrawl.

garante *m/f* guarantor; surety; **garantía** *f* guarantee; ♪♪ warranty; (*prenda*) security; (*promesa*) undertaking; **garantir** [3a; *defective*], **garantizar** [1f] guarantee, warrant, vouch for.

garañón *m* stud jackass.

garapiña *f* sugar icing; coagulated liquid; **garapiñar** [1a] ice (with sugar); (*helar*) freeze, clot; *fruta* candy; **garapiñera** *f* freezer.

garatusa: *hacer* ～s *a* coax, wheedle.

garbanzo *m* chick-pea; ～ *negro fig.* black sheep.

garbera *f* ✛ shock.

garbillar [1a] ✛ sift; ✗ riddle, screen; **garbillo** *m* sieve, riddle.

garbo *m* jauntiness; graceful bearing; elegance; glamour, attractiveness; gallantry; generosity; **garboso** (*airoso*) jaunty; sprightly, graceful; elegant, spruce; *mujer* glamorous, attractive; generous.

garceta *f*: ～ *común* little egret.

garduña *f zo.* marten; **garduño** *m*, a *f* sneak-thief.

garete: *al* ～ adrift.

garfa *f* claw; **garfada** *f* clawing.

garfio *m* hook; gaff; ⊕ grapple, grappling-iron, claw; *mount.* climbing-iron.

gargajear [1a] spit phlegm, hawk; **gargajo** *m* phlegm.

garganta *f* throat; gullet; *geog.* gorge, ravine; *instep de pie*; neck *de botella*; ♪ singing voice; **gargantear** [1a] warble, quaver; **gargantilla** *f* necklace.

gárgara *f* gargling; *hacer* ～s gargle; **gargarismo** *m* gargle; **gargarizar** [1f] gargle.

gárgol *m* groove.

gárgola *f* gargoyle. [pipe.\

garguero *m* gullet; (*traquea*) wind-⌋

garita *f* cabin, hut; ✗ sentry-box; (*portería*) porter's lodge; (*atalaya*) look-out; F water-closet; ～ *de señales* signal-box.

garito *m* gambling-den.

garlito *m* fish-trap; *fig.* snare, trap; *caer en el* ～ fall into the trap; *coger en el* ～ catch in the act.

garlopa *f* jack-plane.

garra *f* claw; talon; *fig.* hand; ～s *pl.* grip; *fig.* jaws; *caer en las* ～s *de* fall into the clutches of.

garrafa *f* carafe, decanter; large bottle.

garrafal enormous, terrific; *error etc.* monumental.

garrapata *f zo.* tick; F disabled horse; **garrapatear** [1a] scribble, scrawl; **garrapato** *m* (*mst* ～s *pl.*) scribble, scrawl.

garrido neat, graceful; (*hermoso*) handsome, pretty.

garrocha *f* goad; *toros*: spear; *deportes*: vaulting-pole.

garrón *m* spur, talon; (*pata*) paw.

garrote *m* cudgel, club; ✗ tourniquet; garrotte *para estrangular*; *dar* ～ *a* garrotte; **garrotillo** *m* ✗ croup.

garrucha *f* pulley.

garrulería *f* chatter; **garrulidad** *f* garrulity; **gárrulo** garrulous, chattering; *ave* chirping; *viento* noisy.

garúa *f S.Am.*, ⚓ drizzle.

garulla *f* loose grapes; F (*golfo*) urchin; (*turba*) mob, rabble.

garza *f* (*a.* ～ *real*) heron; ～ *imperial* purple heron.

garzo blue(ish).

gas *m* gas; fumes; (*a.* ～ *del alumbrado*) coal-gas; ～ *asfixiante* poison gas; ～es *pl.* de escape exhaust (fumes); ～ *hilarante* laughing gas; ～ *lacrimógeno* tear-gas; ～ *de los pantanos* marsh gas; ～ *pobre* producer gas.

gasa *f* gauze; (*paño*) crape.

gaseiforme gaseous, gasiform; **gaseosa** *f* aerated water, mineral water; *esp.* (ginger-)pop, fizz F; ～ *de limón* lemonade; **gaseoso** gaseous; aerated, gassy; *bebida* fizzy; **gasista** *m* gas-fitter; **gas-oil** [ga'sojl] *m* diesel oil; **gasolina** *f* petrol, motor-spirit, gasoline *Am.*; **gasolinera** *f* motorboat; **gasómetro** *m* gasometer.

gastable expendable; **gastado** spent; (*usado*) worn-out; *vestido* shabby, threadbare; *fig.* outworn, hackneyed; **gastador 1.** extravagant, wasteful; **2.** *m*, -a *f* spender, spendthrift; **3.** *m* ♪♪ convict; ✗ sapper; **gastar** [1a] *dinero* spend, expend, lay out (*en* on); (*perder*) waste; (*desgastar*) wear away, wear down, wear out; (*agotar*) use up; *ropa etc.* wear, sport; show habitually; possess; *bromas* crack; F ~*las* behave, act; ~*se* wear out; waste; (*agotarse*) run out; **gasto** *m* (*acto*) spending; (*lo gastado*) expenditure, expense; ✝ cost; (*desgaste*) wear; consumption; (*rate of*) flow *de gas etc.*; ✝ ~*s pl.* expenditure, expenses; ~*s pl. de acarreo* haulage; ~*s pl. de explotación* operating costs; ✝ ~*s pl. generales* overheads; ✝ ~*s pl. menores* petty cash; *cubrir* ~*s* cover expenses; *meterse en* ~*s* (*con*) go to (the) expense (of); **gastoso** extravagant.

gástrico gastric; **gastritis** *f* gastritis; **gastronomía** *f* gastronomy; **gastronómico** gastronomic; **gastrónomo** *m*, **a** *f* gastronome(r), gastronomist.

gata *f* (she-)cat; F Madrid woman; *meteor.* hill cloud; *a* ~*s* on all fours; *andar a* ~*s* creep, crawl; **gatada** *f* sly trick; **gatear** [1a] *v/t.* claw, scratch; F pinch, swipe; *v/i.* (*subir*) clamber; (*ir a gatas*) creep, crawl.

gatillo *m* dental forceps; ✂ trigger, hammer; *zo.* nape; F young thief.

gato *m* (tom)cat; ⊕, *mot.* jack; ⊕ grab; ✝ money-bag; F sneak-thief; F native of Madrid; ~ *de algalia* civet cat; ~ *montés* wildcat; ~ *de tornillo* screw-jack; *dar* ~ *por liebre* cheat, put one over *on s.o.*; *aquí hay* ~ *encerrado* there's more in this than meets the eye, I smell a rat; **gatuno** catlike, feline.

gatuperio *m* (*mezcla*) hotchpotch; (*trampa*) snare, fraud.

gaucho *S.Am.* **1.** *m* cowboy, herdsman, gaucho; **2.** gaucho *attr.*; *fig.* (*taimado*) sly; (*grosero*) coarse.

gaudeamus *m* F beano.

gaveta *f* drawer; ✝ till.

gavia *f* ✓ ditch; ⚓ (main) topsail.

gavilán *m orn.* sparrow-hawk.

gavilla *f* ✓ sheaf; (*ps.*) gang, band.

gaviota *f* (sea)gull.

gayo (*alegre*) merry; (*vistoso*) showy.

gayola *f* cage; F jail.

gaza *f* loop; ⚓ bend, bight.

gazafatón *m* F = *gazapatón*; **gazapa** *f* F fib, lie; **gazapatón** *m* F (*plancha*) bloomer; (*disparate*) piece of nonsense; **gazapera** *f* rabbit-warren; F den of thieves; (*riña*)

brawl; **gazapo** *m* young rabbit; (*p.*) sly fellow; (*plancha*) blunder.

gazmoñada *f*, **gazmoñería** *f* hypocrisy, cant; (*recato excesivo*) prudery; (*gravedad afectada*) demureness; **gazmoñ(er)o 1.** hypocritical, canting; strait-laced, prudish; demure; **2.** *m*, **a** *f* hypocrite; prude (*mst f*); prig.

gaznápiro *m*, **a** *f* simpleton, booby.

gaznate *m* (*garganta*) gullet; (*traquea*) windpipe, throttle; F *remojar el* ~ wet one's whistle.

gazpacho *m* cold soup of oil, vinegar, garlic, onion, bread etc.

gazuza *f* F hunger.

géiser *m geog.* geyser.

gelatina *f* gelatin(e), jelly; ~ *explosiva* gelignite; **gelatinizar(se)** (1f) gelatinize; **gelatinoso** gelatinous.

gema *f* gem; ♀ bud.

gemelo 1. twin; *buque* sister *attr.*; **2.** *m*, **a** *f* twin; ~*s pl.* cuff-links; *opt.* field-glasses, binoculars; ~*s pl. de teatro* opera-glasses.

gemido *m* groan; moan; wail; **gemir** [3l] groan; moan; wail; lament; (*viento, animales*) howl, whine.

gen *m* gene.

genciana *f* gentian.

gendarme *m* gendarme; **gendarmería** *f* gendarmerie.

genealogía *f* genealogy; pedigree; **genealógico** genealogical.

generación *f* generation; (*hijos*) progeny; (*descendencia*) succession; **generador 1.** generating; **2.** *m* generator (*a.* ✗, ⊕).

general 1. general; universal; (*corriente*) prevailing, rife; (*vasto*) wide; *en* ~, *por lo* ~ generally, for the most part; **2.** *m* general; ~ *de brigada* brigadier; ~ *de división* major-general; **3.** ~*es f/pl.* personal particulars; **generalato** *m* generalship; **generalidad** *f* generality; majority; vagueness; ♀ *former Catalan government*; **generalísimo** *m* generalissimo; **generalización** *f* generalization; **generalizar** [1f] generalize; make widely known, bring into general use; ~*se* become general.

generar [1a] generate (*a.* ✗); **generativo** generative.

genérico generic; **género** *m* ▥ genus; (*clase*) kind, nature; *lit.*

genre; *gr.* gender; † line; (*paño*) cloth, material; ~ *chico thea.* comic one-act pieces; ~ *humano* human race, mankind; ~s *pl.* † goods, merchandise, wares; ~s *pl.* de *punto* knitwear.

generosidad *f* generosity; nobility; valour; **generoso** generous, liberal (*con*, *para* to, with); noble; magnanimous; valiant; *vino* rich, full-bodied.

genésico genetic; **génesis 1.** *f* genesis; **2.** *m* ♀ Genesis; **genética** *f* genetics; **genético** genetic.

genial inspired, of genius; (*propio del genio de uno*) in character; (*placentero*) pleasant, cheerful; **genialidad** *f* genius; temperament; eccentricity; (*una* ~) stroke of genius; **genio** *m* temper; disposition; character, nature; (*inteligencia superior*) genius; (*deidad*) spirit; *buen* ~ good nature; *mal* ~ (bad) temper; *de mal* ~ bad-tempered, ill-tempered, cross; *corto de* ~ slow-witted; *tener* ~ be temperamental.

genista *f* broom, genista.

genital genital; (*órganos*) ~es *pl.* genitals; **genitivo 1.** reproductive, generative; **2.** *m* genitive (case).

genocidio *m* genocide.

genovés *adj. a. su. m*, **-a** *f* Genoese.

gente *f* people; folk; followers; troops; nation; (*parientes*) relatives, folks F; F ~ *bien* upper-class people, posh people; respectable people; ~ *de bien* honest folk, decent people; ~ *menuda* (*sin importancia*) small fry; (*niños*) children; (*humildes*) humble folk; ¡~ *de paz!* friend!; ~ *de pelo* well-to-do folk; ~ *de medio pelo* people of limited means; ~ *principal* nobility, gentry; **gentecilla** *f* unimportant people; *contp.* riff-raff; **gentil 1.** graceful, elegant; (*amable*) charming; F *iro.* remarkable, pretty; *eccl.* pagan, heathen; **2.** *m/f* gentile, heathen; **gentileza** *f* grace, charm, elegance; (*bizarría*) dash; (*ostentación*) show; politeness, courtesy; **gentilhombre** *m* † gentleman; **gentilicio** national; tribal; family *attr.*; **gentílico** heathen(ish), pagan; **gentío** *m* crowd, throng; mob; **gentualla** *f*, **gentuza** *f* rabble, mob; riff-raff.

genuflexión *f* genuflection.

genuino genuine, real; pure; true.

geodesia *f* geodesy; **geofísica** *f* geophysics; **geografía** *f* geography; **geográfico** geographic(al); **geógrafo** *m* geographer; **geología** *f* geology; **geológico** geologic(al); **geólogo** *m* geologist; **geometría** *f* geometry; ~ *del espacio* solid geometry; **geométrico** geometric (al); **geopolítica** *f* geopolitics.

geranio *m* geranium.

gerencia *f* (*en general*) management; (*cargo*) managership; (*oficina*) manager's office; **gerente** *m* manager; executive.

geriatría *f* geriatrics.

germanesco slang; **germanía** *f* thieves' slang, cant.

germánico Germanic; **germano** German(ic).

germen *m biol.*, ⚕ germ; *fig.* germ, seed, source; **germicida 1.** germicidal; **2.** *m* germicide; **germinación** *f* germination; **germinal** germinal; **germinar** [1a] germinate; sprout.

gerundense *adj. a. su. m/f* (native) of Gerona.

gerundiano bombastic.

gerundio *m* gerund, present participle.

gesta *f* † heroic deed(s).

gestación *f* gestation.

gestear [1a] (*cara*) grimace; (*manos*) gesticulate; **gesticulación** *f* grimace; gesticulation; **gesticular** [1a] grimace; gesticulate.

gestión *f* negotiation; (*dirección*) management, conduct (of affairs); (*diligencia*; *esp.* ~es *pl.*) effort, measure, step; **gestionar** [1a] negotiate; manage; promote; (take steps to) procure.

gesto *m* (expression of one's) face; (*mueca*) grimace; gesture *con manos*; *estar de buen* (*mal*) ~ be in a good (bad) humour; *hacer* ~s make (*or* pull) faces; gesture; *hacer un gesto de asco* look disgusted; *poner mal* ~ make a wry face.

gestor *m* manager; promoter; agent; **gestoría** *f* agency (for dealing with government departments).

giba *f* hump, hunch(back); F nuisance, bother; **gibar** [1a] F annoy, bother; **giboso** hunch-backed, humped.

giganta *f* giantess; ⚙ sunflower; **gigante 1.** giant, gigantic; **2.** *m* giant; **gigantesco** gigantic, giant, mammoth; **gigantón** *m*, **-a** *f* giant (carnival) figure.

gilda *f* F lollipop.

gimnasia *f* gymnastics; physical training; ~ *respiratoria* deep breathing; **gimnasio** *m* gymnasium; **gimnasta** *m/f* gymnast; **gimnástico** gymnastic.

gimotear [1a] F whine; wail; (*lloriquear*) snivel, grizzle; **gimoteo** *m* F whining *etc.*

ginebra *f* gin; *fig.* bedlam, confusion.

ginecología *f* gynaecology; **ginecólogo** *m* gynaecologist.

gira *f* trip, outing; picnic *con comida*; *deportes etc.*: tour.

girado *m*, *a* *f* ✝ drawee; **girador** *m*, **-a** *f* ✝ drawer.

girald(ill)a *f* weathercock.

girar [1a] *v/t.* ⊕ *etc.* turn, twist, rotate; ✝ *letra* draw, issue; *v/i.* rotate, turn (round), go round, revolve; (*esp. rápidamente*) gyrate, whirl, spin; (*de un lado a otro*) swivel, swing; (*sobre gozne*) hinge; (*sobre pivote*) pivot; ✝ do business; ✝ ~ *a cargo de,* ~ *contra* draw on; ✝ ~ *en descubierto* overdraw; ~ *hacia la izquierda* turn (to the) left.

girasol *m* sunflower.

giratorio gyratory; *puerta etc.* revolving; *puente etc.* swivel(ling), swing *attr.*; **giro** *m* turn (*a. fig.*); revolution, rotation, gyration; *fig.* trend, course; *gr.* turn of phrase, expression; (line of) business; ✝ draft; ✝ ~ *en descubierto* overdraft; ~ *postal* approx. money-order, postal order; *tomar otro* ~ change one's mind; **girocompás** *m* gyro-compass; **giroscópico** gyroscopic; **giroscopio** *m* gyroscope.

gitanada *f* gipsy trick; *fig.* fawning, wheedling; **gitanear** [1a] wheedle, cajole; **gitanería** *f* (*gitanos*) band of gipsies; (*dicho*) gipsy saying; (*mimos*) wheedling, cajolery; **gitanesco** gipsy *attr.*; **gitano 1.** gipsy *attr.*; (*taimado*) sly; (*zalamero*) smooth-tongued; (*insinuante*) engaging; **2.** *m*, **a** *f* gipsy.

glaciación *f* glaciation; **glacial** glacial; *viento etc.* icy, freezing; *fig.* cold, stony, indifferent; **glaciar** *m* glacier.

glacis *m* glacis.

gladiador *m* gladiator.

gladio *m*, **gladiolo** *m* gladiolus.

glándula *f* gland; **glandular** glandular.

glasear [1a] *papel etc.* glaze.

glauco light green, sea-green.

gleba *f* clod.

glicerina *f* glycerine.

global global; total, overall; *cantidad* lump *attr.*; *investigación etc.* comprehensive, full; **globo** *m* globe, sphere; ~ (*aerostático*) balloon; ~ *cautivo* captive balloon; ~ *del ojo* eyeball; *en* ~ all in all, as a whole; ✝ in bulk; **globosidad** *f* globosity; **globoso, globular** globular, spherical; **glóbulo** *m* globule; corpuscle *de sangre.*

gloria *f* glory; *una vieja* ~ a has-been; *saber a* ~ taste wonderful, be delicious; *estar en la* ~, *estar en sus* ~*s* be in one's element; **gloriarse** [1c] glory, rejoice (*en* in); boast (*de* of); **glorieta** *f* summer-house, bower *de jardín*; circus, street intersection; **glorificación** *f* glorification; **glorificar** [1g] glorify; ~*se* glory (*de,* *en* in); **glorioso** glorious; *santo* blessed, in glory; *b.s.* proud, boastful; *la Gloriosa eccl.* the Virgin; F *the 1868 revolution.*

glosa *f* gloss; **glosar** [1a] gloss; *fig.* put an unfavourable construction on, criticize; **glosario** *m* glossary.

glosopeda *f* foot-and-mouth disease.

glotis *f* glottis.

glotón 1. gluttonous; **2.** *m*, **-a** *f* glutton, gourmand; **glotonear** [1a] gormandize; **glotonería** *f* gluttony.

glucosa *f* glucose, grape-sugar.

gluglú *m* (*agua*) gurgle; (*pavo*) gobble; *hacer* ~ gurgle; gobble; **gluglutear** [1a] (*pavo*) gobble.

glutinoso glutinous.

gnómico gnomic.

gnomo *m* gnome.

gnóstico *adj. a. su. m,* **a** *f* gnostic.

gobernable governable; ⚓ navigable; **gobernación** *f* governing, government; *Ministerio de la* ⅀ *approx.* Home Office, Ministry of the

Interior; **gobernador 1.** governing; **2.** *m* governor; **gobernalle** *m* rudder, helm; **gobernante 1.** ruling; **2.** *m/f* ruler; **3.** *m* F (self-appointed) boss; **gobernar** [1k] *v. t.* govern, rule; (*manejar*) manage, handle; guide, direct; ⚓ steer, sail; ~ *mal* misgovern; *v/i.* govern; ⚓ handle, steer; **gobierno** *m* government; (*puesto*) governorship; control; management; guidance; ⚓ helm, steering; ~ *de la casa* housekeeping; *para tu* ~ for your guidance.

gobio *m* gudgeon.

goce *m* enjoyment; possession.

godo 1. Gothic; **2.** *m,* **a** *f* Goth; *S.Am. contp.* Spaniard; *S.Am. pol.* conservative, reactionary.

gol *m* goal (*score*). [ogee.

gola *f* throat, gullet; ✂ gorget; ◬

goleta *f* schooner.

golf *m* golf.

golfear [1a] loaf; live a street-urchin's life; **golfería** *f* (*ps.*) street-urchins; (*vida*) loafing, life in the gutter; (*mala pasada*) dirty trick; **golfillo** *m* street-urchin, guttersnipe; **golfo**[1] *m* — *golfillo*; F loafer, tramp.

golfo[2] *m geog.* gulf, bay; open sea.

golilla *f* ruff.

golondrina *f* swallow; ~ *de mar* tern; **golondrino** *m* tramp; ✂ deserter; **golondro** *m* F whim, fancy; *campar de* ~ sponge, live by one's wits.

golosina *f* titbit (*a. fig.*), delicacy, sweet; (*cosa inútil*) bauble; (*antojo*) fancy; (*gusto por dulces*) sweet tooth; (*gula*) greed; **goloso** sweet-toothed; (*glotón*) greedy.

golpe *m* blow, knock (*a. fig.*); (*palmada*) smack; (*latido*) beat; (*choque*) shock, clash; surprise; *deportes*: stroke, hit, shot *con palo, raqueta etc.*; punch, blow *en boxeo*; kick, shot *en fútbol etc.*; (*multitud*) crowd, mass; (*pestillo*) spring lock; (*cartera*) pocket flap; ~ *bien dado* hit; ~ *de agua* heavy fall of rain; ~ *de estado* coup d'état; ~ *de fortuna* stroke of luck; ~ *franco* free-kick; ~ *de gente* crowd; ~ *de gracia* coup de grâce; ~ *de mano* rising; ~ *de mar* heavy sea, surge; ~ *maestro* masterstroke; ~ *de vista* glance; *de* ~ suddenly; *de un* ~ at one

stroke, outright; *abrir de* ~ fling open; *abrirse de* ~ fly open; *cerrar de* ~ slam; F *dar* ~ be a sensation, be a big hit; *dar* ~*s en* thump, pound (at); **golpear** [1a] *v/t.* strike, knock, hit; thump, bang *con ruido*; (*repetidamente*) beat; punch *con puño*; (*zurrar*) thrash; *v/i.* throb; ⊕ knock; **golpecito** *m* tap, rap; **golpeo** *m* knocking *etc.*; ⊕ knock; **golpeteo** *m* knocking; rattling; hammering; drumming.

gollería *f* (*golosina*) titbit; extra, special treat.

gollete *m* throat; (*cuello*) neck (*a. de botella*).

goma *f* gum; (*caucho*) rubber; (*liga*) rubber (*or* elastic) band; *S.Am.* F hangover; ~ *arábiga* gum arabic; ~ *de borrar* rubber, eraser; ~ (*elástica*) India rubber; **gomita** *f* elastic band; **gomoso 1.** gummy, sticky; **2.** *m* F toff, dandy.

góndola *f* gondola.

gong(o) *m* gong.

gorda *f* F: *hist. la* ♀ *the 1868 revolution*; *se armó la* ~ there was a great hullabaloo; *ahora nos va a tocar la* ~ now we're for it.

gordal fat, thick, big.

gordi(n)flón F podgy, fat, chubby.

gordo 1. fat; *p. a.* stout, plump; (*craso*) greasy, oily; (*grande*) big; *premio* first, big; (*basto*) coarse, gross; *agua* hard; *algo* ~ something really big; *hablar* ~ talk big; **2.** *m* fat, suet; F first prize; F *fig. sacarse el* ~ bring home the bacon; **gordura** *f* corpulence, stoutness; (*grasa*) grease, fat.

gorgojo *m* weevil, grub; *fig.* dwarf.

gorgoritear [1a] F trill, warble; **gorgorito** *m* F trill, quaver.

gorgotear [1a] gurgle; **gorgoteo** *m* gurgle.

gorguera *f* ruff; ✂ gorget.

gorigori *m* F dirge, wailing racket.

gorila *m* gorilla; F tough, thug.

gorja *f* gorge, throat; F *estar de* ~ be very cheerful.

gorjear [1a] warble, chirp, twitter; ~*se* (*niño*) gurgle, crow; **gorjeo** *m* warble *etc.*

gorra 1. *f* (peaked) cap; bonnet; ~ *de visera* peaked cap; **2.** *m* (*a.* **gorrero** *m*) cadger, sponger; F *colarse de* ~ gate-crash; F *ir etc. de* ~ scrounge, cadge, sponge.

gorrinería f dirt; fig. dirty trick;
gorrino m, **a** f small pig; hog
(a. fig.).
gorrión m sparrow.
gorrista m/f F sponger.
gorro m cap; bonnet; ~ de baño bath-
ing-cap; ~ de dormir nightcap.
gorrón[1] m pebble; ⊕ pivot, journal.
gorrón[2] m F cadger, sponger; **gorronear** [1a] F scrounge, cadge,
sponge.
gota f drop; bead, blob; 🞋 gout; ~
a ~ drop by drop; caer a ~ drip;
parecerse como dos ~s de agua be
as like as two peas; **goteado** speck-
led; **gotear** [1a] drip; dribble;
trickle (a. fig.); (vela) gutter; ~(se)
leak; **goteo** m drip(ping) etc.;
gotera f leak; drip(ping); (cenefa)
valence; 🞋 ailment; lleno de ~s p.
full of aches and pains.
gótico Gothic; fig. noble.
gotita f droplet.
gotoso gouty.
gozar [1f] v/t. enjoy; possess, have;
v/i. enjoy o.s.; ~ de = v/t.; ~se rejoice; ~ en inf. take pleasure in ger.
gozne m hinge.
gozo m joy, gladness; pleasure, delight, enjoyment; un ~ para la retina
a joy to see, a sight for sore eyes;
F ¡mi ~ en el pozo! I'm sunk!; no
caber de ~ be beside o.s. with joy;
gozoso glad, joyful (con, de about
at).
grabación f recording; ~ en cinta
tape-recording; **grabado** m engraving, print; (esp. en libro) illustration, picture; ~ al agua fuerte
etching; ~ al agua tinta aquatint;
~ en cobre copperplate; ~ en madera
woodcut; **grabador** m engraver;
grabadora f recorder; ~ de cinta
tape-recorder; **grabar** [1a] engrave; record en disco etc.; fig. engrave, imprint; ~ algo en el ánimo
impress s.t. on one's mind.
gracejo m wit, humour; repartee
(en contestar).
gracia 1. f grace (a. eccl.); favour,
pardon; gracefulness, attractiveness; (agudeza) wit, (chiste) joke;
(esencia de chiste) point; F name;
¿cuál es su ~? what's your name?;
¡qué ~! what a nerve!, the very
idea!; de ~ free, for nothing; en ~ a
on account of, for the sake of; sin ~
graceless; caer en ~ a find favour

with, make a hit with F; dar en la ~
de decir harp on; hacer ~ a strike
s.o. as funny; tener ~ be funny;
2. ~s pl. thanks; ¡~! thank you!;
muchas ~ many thanks, thanks very
much; ~ a thanks to; ¡~ a Dios!
thank goodness!; ¡y ~! iro. and be
thankful!; dar las ~ a thank; **graciable** gracious; affable; (fácil de
conceder) easily granted; **grácil**
slender; small; delicate; **gracioso
1.** (elegante) graceful; (afable)
gracious; attractive; (agudo) witty;
(divertido) funny, amusing; (gratuito) free; lo ~ del caso es que the
funny thing about it is that; **2.** m
thea. fool, funny man.
grada f step de escalera; thea. etc.
tier, row (of seats); ⚓ slipway, slips;
✗ harrow; ~ de discos disk harrow;
gradación f gradation; rhet. cli-
max; gr. comparison; **gradar** [1a]
harrow; **gradería** f flight of steps;
thea. etc. rows of seats, tiers.
grado m (peldaño) step; univ., ⚕,
phys. a. fig. degree; (nivel) level;
(rango) grade, rank; escuela: class,
year; ~s pl. eccl. minor orders; ~ de
elaboración stage of production; de
(buen) ~ willingly; de ~ en ~ by
degrees; de ~ o por fuerza willy-
nilly; de mal ~, (a) mal mi etc. ~
unwillingly; en sumo ~ in the extreme, vastly.
graduable adjustable; **graduación**
f gradation; graduation; grading;
✗ rank; alcoholic strength; **graduado** m, **a** f graduate; **gradual**
gradual; **graduar** [1e] (clasificar)
grade; termómetro etc. graduate;
(medir) gauge, measure; ⊕ calibrate; vista test; univ. confer a
degree (✗ rank) on; ~se graduate,
take one's degree (en in); ✗ take a
commission; ~ de receive the degree
of.
gráfica f graph; **gráfico 1.** graphic
(a. fig.); pictorial, illustrated; **2.** m
⚕ graph; chart; diagram; (horario)
time-table; ~ de temperatura temperature chart.
grafito m graphite, blacklead.
grafología f graphology.
grajear [1a] caw; (niño) gurgle;
grajilla f jackdaw; **grajo** m rook.
grama f grass.
gramática f grammar; F ~ parda
native wit; **gramatical** grammati-

cal; **gramático 1.** grammatical; **2.** *m* grammarian.
gramo *m* gram(me).
gramófono *m*, **gramola** *f* gramophone, phonograph *Am.*
gran *v.* grande.
grana[1] *f* ♀ seeding; (*época*) seeding-time; (*semilla*) small seed; dar en ~ go (*or* run) to seed.
grana[2] *f* zo. cochineal; kermes; (*color*) scarlet; (*paño*) scarlet cloth; de ~ scarlet.
granada *f* ♀ pomegranate; ✗ grenade *de mano*, shell *de cañón*; ~ de mano hand-grenade; ~ fallida dud; a prueba de ~ shell-proof; **granadero** *m* grenadier.
granadino *adj. a. su. m*, **a** *f* (native) of Granada.
granado[1] *m* ♀ pomegranate tree.
granado[2] notable, distinguished; select; mature; (*alto*) tall; lo más ~ the pick.
granar [1a] run to seed.
granate *m* garnet.
granazón *f* seeding.
grande 1. big, large; (*a. fig.*) great; (*grandioso*) grand; *número, velocidad* high; (*alto*) tall; en ~ as a whole; on a large scale, in a big way; F estar en ~ be going strong; F pasarlo en ~ have a whale of a time; F vivir en ~ live in style; **2.** *m* ~ (*de España*) grandee; los ~s the great; **grandemente** greatly; extremely; **grandeza** *f* bigness; greatness; (*grandiosidad*) grandeur; (*tamaño*) size; (*nobleza*) nobility; **grandilocuencia** *f* grandiloquence; **grandílocuo** grandiloquent; **grandiosidad** *f* grandeur, magnificence; **grandioso** magnificent, grand; (*esp. b.s.*) grandiose; **grandor** *m* size; **grandote** F whacking big; **grandullón** overgrown, oversize.
graneado granulated; **granear** [1a] *semilla* sow; *cuero* grain; (*puntear*) stipple; **granel: a** ~ (*sin orden*) at random; (*en montón*) in a heap; ✝ in bulk, loose; dar in abundance, lavishly; **granero** *m* granary (*a. fig.*); **granilla** *f* grain (in cloth).
granítico granite *attr.*; **granito** *m* granite; ✗ pimple.
granizada *f* hailstorm; hail (*a. fig.*); = **granizado** *m* iced drink; **granizar** [1f] hail; *fig.* shower; **granizo** *m* hail.

granja *f* farm; farmhouse; (*quinta*) country house; (*vaquería*) dairy; ~ avícola poultry farm.
granjear [1a] gain, earn; win; ~se algo win (for o.s.).
granjería *f* farming; farm earnings; profit; **granjero** *m* farmer.
grano *m* grain (*a. pharm.*); (*semilla*) seed; (*baya*) berry; bean *de café*; (*partícula*) speck; ✗ pimple, spot; ✗ ~s *pl.* grain, cereals; con un ~ de sal with a pinch of salt; ir al ~ come to the point, get down to brass tacks; **granoso** granular.
granuja *m* ragamuffin, urchin; rogue.
granujiento, granujoso pimply.
granulación *f* granulation; **granular** granular; **granular(se)** [1a] granulate; **gránulo** *m* granule.
grapa *f* clip; paper-fastener; staple *de dos puntas*; 🔩 cramp.
grasa *f* fat; (*unto*) grease; (*sebo*) suet; (*aceite*) oil; (*mugre*) filth; ✗ ~s *pl.* slag; ~ de ballena blubber; **grasiento** greasy, oily; filthy; **graso 1.** fatty; greasy; **2.** *m* fattiness; greasiness.
grata *f* ✝ favour; **gratificación** *f* (*premio*) reward; (*propina*) tip, gratuity; bounty; indulgence; **gratificar** [1g] tip; reward; (*dar gusto*) gratify; *deseo* indulge; se gratificará (*anuncios*) a reward is offered; **gratis** free (of charge), for nothing, gratis; **gratitud** *f* gratitude; **grato** pleasing, pleasant; welcome, gratifying; (*agradecido*) grateful; nos es ~ informarle we are pleased to inform you; **gratuito** free; *observación etc.* gratuitous, uncalled-for; *acusación* unfounded; **gratulatorio** congratulatory. [*de camino*.]
grava *f* gravel; crushed stone; metal.
gravamen *m* obligation; burden; (*carga*) encumbrance; *impuestos*: assessment; **gravar** [1a] encumber, burden; *impuestos*: assess; **gravativo** burdensome.
grave (*de peso*) heavy; *fig.* grave, serious; important, momentous; *enfermedad* grave; *herida, pérdida* grievous, severe; *p.* sedate, dignified; ♪ low, deep; gr. palabra paroxitone; *acento* grave; estar ~ be critically ill; **gravedad** *f* gravity (*a. phys.*) *etc.*; herido de ~ severely injured (*or* wounded).

grávido pregnant (*a. fig.*).

gravitación *f* gravitation; **gravitacional** gravitational; **gravitar** [1a] *phys. etc.* gravitate; ~ *sobre* (*descansar*) rest on; (*pesar*) weigh down on; *fig.* be a burden to; **gravitatorio** gravitational; **gravoso** onerous; oppressive; burdensome; † costly; (*molesto*) tiresome; *ser* ~ *a* weigh on.

graznar [1a] squawk; (*grajo*) caw, croak; (*ganso*) cackle; (*pato*) quack; **graznido** *m* squawk *etc.*

greda *f geol.* clay; (*de batán*) fuller's earth; **gredoso** clayey.

gregario gregarious; herd *attr.*; (*servil*) slavish.

gremial 1. guild *attr.*; trade(s) union *attr.*; **2.** *m* guild-member; trade-unionist; **gremio** *m* guild, corporation; association; (*obrero*) trade(s) union.

greña *f* (*mst pl.*) shock (*or* mat, mop) of hair; *fig.* entanglement, tangle; *andar a la* ~ squabble; **greñudo** dishevelled.

gres *m geol.* potter's clay; (*loza*) earthenware, stoneware.

gresca *f* (*jaleo*) uproar, hubbub; (*riña*) row, brawl.

grey *f eccl.* flock, congregation.

grial *m* Grail.

griego 1. Greek; **2.** *m,* **a** *f* Greek; F cheat; **3.** *m* (*idioma*) Greek; *fig.* gibberish, double Dutch.

grieta *f* fissure, crack; crevice; chink; chap *en piel*; **grietarse** [1a] = agrietarse.

grifo *m* tap, cock, faucet *Am.*; (*servido*) *al* ~ on tap, (on) draught.

grilla *f* female cricket; F *ésa es* ~ (*y no canta*) that's a cock-and-bull story.

grillete *m* fetter, shackle.

grillo *m zo.* cricket; ♀ shoot, sprout; ~*s pl.* fetters, irons; *fig.* shackles.

grima *f* annoyance; horror; *me da* ~ it gets on my nerves; (*escalofrío*) it gives me the shivers.

grímpola *f* pennant.

gringo *m,* **a** *f contp.* foreigner (*mst English or N. American*); F *hablar en* ~ talk double Dutch.

gripe *f* influenza, 'flu.

gris 1. grey; *día* dull, gloomy; **2.** *m* grey; F *hace* ~ there's a nasty cold wind; **grisáceo** greyish.

grisú *m* ⚒ fire-damp.

grita *f* uproar, outcry; *dar* ~ *a* hoot, boo; **gritar** [1a] shout, yell, cry out; (*desaprobar*) hoot; (*bramar*) bellow; **gritería** *f,* **griterío** *m* shouting, uproar; **grito** *m* shout, yell; cry; hoot; bellow; scream; call; *a* ~ *herido, a* ~ *pelado, a voz en* ~ at the top of one's voice; F *poner el* ~ *en el cielo* kick up a great fuss; **gritón** screaming, shouting.

groenlandés 1. Greenland *attr.*; **2.** *m,* **-a** *f* Greenlander.

grosella *f* (red) currant; ~ *espinosa* gooseberry; **grosellero** *m* currant (bush).

grosería *f* coarseness *etc.*; (*dicho*) rude thing; **grosero** (*basto*) coarse, rough; discourteous, rude; indelicate, gross; vulgar; (*zafio*) loutish; **grosor** *m* thickness; **grosura** *f* fat; (*régimen*) meat diet.

grotesco grotesque, bizarre, absurd.

grúa *f* ⊕ crane; derrick; ~ *puente* overhead crane.

gruesa *f* gross.

grueso 1. thick; (*corpulento*) fat; *p.* stout, thick-set; (*abultado*) large, bulky; (*basto*) coarse; (*poco agudo*) dull; *artillería, mar* heavy; **2.** *m* (*grosor*) thickness; (*bulto*) bulk; (*parte principal*) major portion; ✗ main body; *el* ~ *del pelotón carreras*: the ruck; *en* ~ in bulk.

grulla *f orn.* (*a.* ~ *común*) crane.

grumete *m* cabin-boy.

grumo *m* clot *de sangre*; dollop; cluster *de uvas*; ~ *de leche* curd; **grumoso** clotted, lumpy.

gruñido *m* grunt; growl; snarl; **gruñir** [3h] (*esp. cerdo*) grunt; (*perro, oso*) growl, snarl; *fig.* grumble; (*puerta etc.*) creak; **gruñón** F grumpy.

grupa *f* crupper, horse's hindquarters; **grupera** *f* pillion.

grupo *m* group (*a. pol.*); cluster; bunch F; clump *de árboles*; ⊕ unit, set; ~ *electrógeno* generating set, power-plant; ~ *de presión* pressure-group.

gruta *f* cavern, grotto.

guaca *f S.Am.* Indian tomb; buried treasure; **guacamayo** *m* macaw.

guaco *m S.Am. zo.* curassow (*kind of turkey*).

guachapear [1a] *v/t.* paddle in,

splash; *fig.* botch, bungle; *v/i.* rattle, clatter.

guacho *S.Am.* motherless, orphaned; *zapato etc.* odd.

guadal *m S.Am.* bog; dune.

guadamecí *m* embossed leather.

guadaña *f* scythe; **guadañadora** *f* mowing-machine; **guadañar** [1a] scythe, mow; **guadañero** *m* mower.

guagua *f* trifle; *S.Am.* bus; (*rorro*) baby; de ~ free, for nothing.

gualdo yellow, golden.

gualdrapa *f* trappings; F tatter.

guano *m* guano.

guantada *f*, **guantazo** *m* slap; **guante** *m* glove; ~s *pl. fig.* tip, commission; ~ *con puño* gauntlet glove; ~s *pl. de cabritilla* kid gloves; *como un* ~ *ajustarse* like a glove; *convenir* down to the ground; *arrojar* (*recoger*) el ~ throw down (take up) the gauntlet; F *echar el* ~ *a* lay hands on, seize; *echar un* ~ make a collection (*a beneficio de* for); **guantelete** *m* gauntlet; **guantero** *m*, **a** *f* glover.

guapear [1a] F swagger; cut a dash; bluster; **guapetón** F very good-looking; (*bizarro*) dashing; (*ostentoso*) flashy; **guapeza** *f* prettiness; dash *etc.*; **guapo 1.** *mujer* pretty; *hombre* handsome; good-looking; (*aseado*) smart; (*ostentoso*) flashy; (*valiente*) dashing, bold; **2.** *m* F lover, gallant; (*matón*) bully; (*fanfarrón*) braggart; (*elegante*) swell.

guarda 1. *m* guard; keeper, custodian; ~ *de coto* gamekeeper; **2.** *f* guard(ing); (safe) keeping, custody; observance *de ley*; flyleaf, endpaper *de libro*; ward *de cerradura*; guard *de espada* (*a.* ⊕).

guarda...: ~**barro(s)** *m* mudguard; ~**bosque** *m* ranger, forester; gamekeeper; ~**brisa** *m mot.* windscreen; ~**cabo** *m* ⚓ thimble; ~**cenizas** *m* ash-pan; ~**costas** *m* revenue cutter.

guardador watchful; (*tacaño*) stingy.

guarda...: ~**espaldas** *m* henchman, bodyguard; ~**fango** *m* mudguard; ~**frenos** *m* brake(s)man; ~**fuego** *m* fire-guard; fender; ~**lmacén** *m/f* storekeeper; ~**lodos** *m* mudguard; ~**mano** *m* guard (*of sword*); ~**meta** *m* goalkeeper; ~**muebles** *m* furniture repository; ~**pelo** *m* locket; ~**polvo** *m* dust-cover, dust-sheet; (*vestido*) dust-coat; overall(s).

guardar [1a] (*retener*) keep; (*proteger*) guard (de against, from); preserve, save (de from); (*poner aparte*) put away, lay by; (*vigilar*) watch; *ganado* tend; *fiesta*, *mandamiento* observe; ¡*guarda!* look out!; ~**se** de avoid; look out for; ~ de *inf.* keep from *ger.*, avoid *ger.*, guard against *ger.*; F ~ *la a* keep a rod in pickle for, have it in for.

guardarropa 1. *m* cloakroom, checkroom *Am.*; (*mueble*) wardrobe; **2.** *m/f* cloakroom attendant; **guardarropía** *f thea.* wardrobe; (*accesorios*) properties, props F; de ~ make-believe, fake.

guardavía *m* 🚂 linesman.

guardia 1. *f* (✗ *servicio*, *regimiento*, *esgrima*) guard; police; custody, care; defence, protection; ⚓ watch; ♀ Civil Civil Guard; ~s *pl.* montadas horse guards; ~ *municipal* town police; ~ *real* household troops; *en* ~ on guard; *estar de* ~ be on guard, be on duty; keep watch; *montar la* ~ mount guard; *relevar la* ~ change guard; **2.** *m* ✗ guard(sman); policeman; ~s *pl. de asalto* shock troops; ~ *civil* civil guard; ~ *marina* midshipman.

guardián *m*, **-a** *f* keeper, custodian; warden; (*vigilante*) watchman.

guardilla *f* attic, garret.

guardoso careful; *b.s.* niggardly.

guarecer [2d] shelter, protect, take in; preserve; ~**se** shelter, take refuge (de from).

guarida *f zo.* lair, den; (*refugio*) shelter, cover; hide-out, haunt *de p.*

guarismo *m* figure, numeral.

guarnecer [2d] (*adornar*) garnish, embellish (de with); equip, provide (de with); ✗ man, garrison; *sew.* trim; *frenos* line; *pared* plaster; *joya* set; **guarnecido** *m* plaster; **guarnición** *f* equipment, provision; fitting; ✗ garrison; ⊕ packing; *sew.* trimming, binding; lining *de frenos*; setting *de joya*; guard *de espada*; ~**es** *pl.* harness de caballo; fittings, fixtures; ~**es** *pl. del alumbrado* light-fittings; **guarnicionar** [1a] garrison; **guarnicionero** *m* harness-maker.

guarra f sow; **guarro 1.** m pig; **2.** filthy.

guasa f F (*sosería*) dullness; (*burla*) joke; badinage, kidding; de ~ jokingly.

guasearse [1a] F joke, kid, rag; **guaso** *S.Am.* coarse, uncouth; **guasón** m, -a f F joker, tease; (*lerdo*) dolt.

guatemalteco adj. a. su. m, a f Guatemalan.

guateque m F do, party, celebration.

guau 1. bow-wow!; **2.** m bark.

guayaba f guava (jelly).

guayacán m lignum vitae.

gubernamental 1. governmental; loyalist; **2.** m/f loyalist; **gubernativo** governmental.

gubia f gouge.

guedeja f long hair, lock; mane de *león*.

guerra f war; warfare; conflict, struggle, fight; ~ *atómica* atomic warfare; ~ *fría* cold war; ~ de guerrillas guerrilla warfare; ~ *mundial* world war; ~ de nervios war of nerves; ~ *relámpago* blitzkrieg; ~ a tiros shooting war, hot war; de ~ military, war *attr.*; Ministerio de ♀ War Office, War Department *Am.*; en ~ con at war with; dar ~ a (*molestar*) be a nuisance to, annoy; (*bromear*) hacer la ~ make war (a on); **guerrear** [1a] wage war, fight; *fig.* resist, put up a fight; **guerrero 1.** fighting; war *attr.*; warlike, martial; **2.** m warrior, soldier, fighting-man; **guerrilla** f guerrilla band, band of partisans; **guerrillero** m guerrilla, partisan, irregular.

guía 1. m/f (*p.*) guide; leader; adviser; **2.** m ✗ marker; **3.** f (⊕, *fig.*, *libro*) guide; (*acto*) guidance; guide-book, handbook; guide-post; handle-bars de *bicicleta*; (*caballo*) leader; ~s pl. reins; *cine*: ~ *sonora* sound track; ~ *telefónica*, ~ de teléfonos telephone directory; ~ del viajero guide-book; ~ *vocacional* vocational guidance; **guiar** [1c] guide; lead; manage; *planta* train; ⚓ etc. steer; *mot.* drive; ✗ pilot; ~se por go by, be guided (*or* ruled) by.

guija f pebble; cobble de calle; **guijarral** m stony place; shingle de

playa; **guijarro** m pebble; boulder; **guijarroso** *playa* pebbly, shingly; *terreno* boulder-strewn; **guijo** m (*grava*) gravel; granite chips *para carretera*; shingle de *playa*.

guillame m rabbet plane.

guillotina f guillotine (a. ⊕); **guillotinar** [1a] guillotine.

guinda f morello cherry.

guindaleza f hawser.

guindar [1a] hang on high; F pinch, swipe, snaffle.

guindilla m F cop, policeman.

guindola f lifebuoy.

guiñada f wink; blink; ⚓ yaw.

guiñapo m rag, tatter; (*p.*) slovenly person.

guiñar [1a] wink; blink; ⚓ yaw; **guiño** m wink; hacer ~s a wink at, make eyes at.

guión m (*p. etc.*) leader; *typ.* hyphen, dash; (*escrito*) explanatory text, hand-out F; *cine*: script, scenario; *eccl.* processional cross (*or* banner); royal standard; ~ de *codornices* corncrake; **guionista** m/f script writer.

guirigay m gibberish, jargon; (*ruido*) hubbub.

guirnalda f garland, chaplet; wreath *esp.* de *entierro*.

guisa: a ~ de as, like, in the manner of; de tal ~ in such a way.

guisado m stew; **guisante** m pea; ~ de olor sweet pea; **guisar** [1a] (*cocinar*) cook; (*hervir*) stew; *fig.* prepare, arrange; **guiso** m cooked dish; seasoning; **guisote** m F contp. stew, concoction; grub.

guita f twine; *sl.* dough, lolly.

guitarra f guitar; **guitarrista** m/f guitarist.

gula f gluttony; **gulusmear** [1a] (*comer*) nibble titbits; (*oler*) sniff the cooking.

gurrumino F **1.** uxorious; **2.** m henpecked husband.

gusanillo m: F andarle a uno el ~ be peckish; F matar el ~ take a nip first thing in the morning; **gusano** m worm; maggot, grub; caterpillar de mariposa etc.; *fig.* meek creature; ~ de luz glow-worm; ~ de seda silkworm; **gusanoso** worm-eaten, maggoty.

gustación f tasting, trying; **gustar** [1a] v/t. taste, try, sample; v/i. please, be pleasing; la comedia no *gustó* the play was not much liked, the play was a flop; *me gustan los plátanos* I like bananas; *¿te gustaría ir a Madrid?* would you like to go to Madrid?; *¿te gustó la comedia?* did you enjoy the play?; *si Vd. gusta* if you don't mind; *¿Vd. gusta?* would you care for some?; *como Vd. guste* as you wish; ~ *de inf.* be fond of *ger.*, have a taste for *ger.*, enjoy *ger.*; **gustazo** *m* great (*or* fiendish) pleasure; **gustillo** *m* suggestion, touch, tang.

gusto *m* taste; (*sabor*) flavour; (*placer*) pleasure; (*afición*) liking (*por* for); (*capricho*) fancy, whim; *¡tanto* ~*!* how do you do?; *a* ~ at will; (*a sus anchas*) at ease, in comfort; *encontrarse a* ~ be happy, like it (here *etc.*); *al* ~ to taste; *a* ~ *de* to the liking of; *con mucho* ~ gladly, with pleasure; *de buen (mal)* ~ in good (bad) taste; *dar* ~ *a* please; *ser del* ~ *de* be to the liking of; *tener* ~ *en inf.* be glad to *inf.*; *tengo mucho* ~ *en conocerle* I'm very glad to meet you; *tomar* ~ *a* take a liking to; **gustoso** (*sabroso*) tasty, savoury; (*agradable*) pleasant; *lo haré* ~ I'll do it with pleasure.

gutapercha *f* gutta-percha.

gutural guttural, throaty.

H

ha *v.* haber.

¡ha! ah!

haba *f* (broad) bean; *en todas partes cuecen ⁓s* it's the same the whole world over; *son ⁓s contadas* it's a certainty, it's a cert F.

habano *m* Havana (cigar).

hábeas corpus *m* habeas corpus.

haber 1. [2k] *v/t.* catch, lay hands on; † have; *bien haya* blessed be; *que Dios haya* God rest his *etc.* soul; *habidos y por haber* present and future; *v/aux.* have; ⁓ *de inf.* have to *inf*; must *inf.*; be (due) to *inf.*; *¿qué he de hacer?* what am I to do?, what must I do?; *ha de ser tonto* he must be a fool; *ha de cantar esta noche* he is to sing tonight; *verbo impersonal*: hay: (*sg.*) there is, (*pl.*) there are; *hay sol* it is sunny; *¿cuánto hay de aquí a Madrid?* how far is it to Madrid?; *¡no hay de qué!* you're welcome!, don't mention it!; *¿qué hay?* what's the matter?; *¿hay plátanos?* (*en tienda*) have you any bananas?; *años ha* years ago; *habrá ocho días* about a week ago; ⁓ *que inf.* be necessary to *inf.*; *hay que comer para vivir* one must eat to live; *no hay que decírselo* there's no need to tell him; he mustn't be told; ⁓*se: tener que habérselas con* have to deal with, be up against; 2. *m* property, goods (*mst ⁓es pl.*); income; ✝ assets, credit (side).

habichuela *f* kidney bean.

hábil clever, skilful; proficient, expert, good (*en* at); capable; *b.s.* cunning; fit (*para* for); ♂♀ competent; habilidad *f* cleverness, skill *etc.*; habilidoso clever; habilitación *f* qualification; financing; equipment; habilitado *m* paymaster; habilitar [1a] enable, capacitate; entitle, qualify; empower; equip, fit out; ✝ *p.* finance.

habitable (in)habitable; habitación *f* (*cuarto*) room; (*morada*) dwelling, habitation; residence; (*alojamiento*) lodging(s); *biol.* habitat; ⁓ *doble*

double room; ⁓ *individual* single room; ⁓ *lacustre* lake-dwelling; habitante *m* inhabitant; occupant *de casa*; habitar [1a] *v/t.* inhabit, live in, dwell in; *casa* occupy; *v/i.* live, dwell; habitat *m* habitat.

hábito *m todos sentidos*: habit; F *ahorcar* (*or colgar*) *los ⁓s* leave the priesthood; *tomar el ⁓* enter religion; take holy orders.

habituado *m*, a *f* habitué; habitual habitual, customary; *mst b.s.* inveterate; *criminal* hardened; regular; habituar [1e] habituate, accustom (*a* to); ⁓*se a* become accustomed to, get used to.

habla *f* (*facultad*) speech; (*idioma*) language; (*regional*) dialect, speech; talk, speech *de clase, profesión etc.*; *al* ⁓ in communication, in conversation; *teleph.* speaking, on the line; ⚓ within hail; *de* ⁓ *española* Spanish-speaking; *dejar sin* ⁓ dumbfound; *negar* (*or quitar*) *el* ⁓ *a* not be on speaking terms with; *perder el* ⁓ be speechless; hablado: *bien* ⁓ well-spoken; *mal* ⁓ coarse, rude; (*indecente*) foul-mouthed; hablador 1. talkative; 2. *m*, -a *f* talker, chatterbox; (*y chismoso*) gossip; habladuría *f* rumour; malicious remark; (*chismes*) idle chatter, (piece of) gossip; hablanchín F, hablantín F talkative, chatty; hablante 1. speaking; 2. *m/f* speaker.

hablar [1a] speak, talk (*con* to); *habla bien el español, pero habla tonterías* he speaks Spanish well, but he talks nonsense; *que hable él* let him have his say; *¡ni ⁓!* no fear!, not likely!, the very idea!; ⁓ *alto* speak up; ⁓ *claro* speak out; ⁓*lo todo* talk too much; ⁓ *por* (*sólo*) ⁓ talk for the sake of talking; *estar hablando* (*retrato*) be a speaking likeness; ⁓*se: se habla español* Spanish (is) spoken here; *se habla de inf.* there is talk of *ger.*; *no nos hablamos* we are not on speaking terms.

hablilla f rumour; idle gossip, tittle-tattle.

hacedero practicable, feasible; **hacedor** m, -a f maker; ♀ Maker.

hacendado 1. landed, property-owning; **2.** m, a f landowner, man etc. of property; S.Am. rancher; **hacendero** industrious, thrifty; **hacendista** m economist, financial expert; **hacendoso** diligent, hard-working; bustling, busy.

hacer [2s] **1.** v/t. a) make; create; ⊕ manufacture; ⚠ build, construct; compose, fashion, form; b) do; perform; practise; put into practice, execute; cause; compel, oblige; effect; (proveer) provide (con, de with); accustom (a to); suppose a. p. to be; c) ♉ amount to, make; apuesta lay; ✝ balance strike; cama make; comedia perform, do; comida prepare, cook, get; corbata tie; dinero earn, make; discurso make, deliver; guerra wage; humo give off, produce; maleta pack; objeción raise; papel play, act, take; pregunta put, pose; prodigios work; sombra cast; visita pay; d) ~ adj. turn adj., render adj., send (esp. p. F) adj.; e) ~ inf. have (or make) a p. inf.; have (or get) s.t. p.p.; hágale entrar show him in, have him come in; me hago cortar el pelo I have (or get) my hair cut; ~ que subj. see to it that; f) ~ bien do good; ~ bien (mal) en inf. be right (wrong) to inf.; ~ bueno acusación make good; F la ha hecho buena he's made a hash of it; te hacíamos en Madrid we thought (or supposed) you were in Madrid; nos hizo con dinero he provided us with money; ¿qué (le) hemos de ~? what's to be done (about it)?; tener que ~ have s.t. to do; **2.** v/i. be important, matter, signify; (convenir) be suitable, be fitting; ~ a todo (p.) be good for anything; la llave hace a las dos puertas the key fits (or does for) both doors; ~ que hacemos pretend to be busy; ¿hace? will it do?, is it a go? F; no le hace never mind, it doesn't matter; ~ como que, ~ como si act as if; ~ de act as; ~ para inf., ~ por inf. make to inf.; try to inf.; dar que ~ give trouble; make work; **3.** verbo impersonal: a) meteor.

be; v. calor, tiempo etc.; b) hace 2 horas que llegó he arrived 2 hours ago, it is 2 hours since he arrived; está aquí desde hace 2 horas he has been here for 2 hours; v. tiempo; **4.** ~se (transformarse) become, grow, get (or come) to be, turn (into); (crecer) grow; (fingirse) pretend to be; cortesías exchange; ~ soldado become a soldier, turn soldier; ~ viejo grow old, get old; ~ a become accustomed to; ~ atrás fall back: ~ con, ~ de appropriate, get hold of; se me hace imposible creerlo I find it impossible to believe it; ¡eso no se hace! that isn't done, that's not on! F.

hacia toward(s); (cerca de) about, near; ~ abajo down(wards); ~ adelante forward(s); ~ arriba up(wards); ~ atrás back(wards); ~ las 3 at about 3 o'clock.

hacienda f (landed) property; (finca) (country) estate; fortune; S.Am. ranch; (ganado) livestock; ~s pl. household chores; ~ pública public finance; (Ministerio de) ♀ Exchequer, Treasury.

hacina f esp. ⚹ stack, rick; (montón) pile, heap; **hacinamiento** m stacking etc.; **hacinar** [1a] stack; pile (up), heap (up); accumulate.

hacha¹ 1. f axe, chopper; (ligera) hatchet; ✕ (a. ~ de armas) battle-axe; **2.**: ♀ ser un ~ be a wizard, be brilliant.

hacha² f torch; large candle.

hachazo m axe-blow, axe-stroke, hack.

hache f letter H; llámele Vd. ~ call it what you will, it's all the same.

hachear [1a] v/t. hew; v/i. wield an axe; **hachero** m woodcutter, lumberjack; ✕ sapper.

hacho m beacon; **hachón** m (large) torch.

hada f fairy; ~ madrina fairy godmother; de ~s fairy attr.; **hadado**: bien ~ lucky; mal ~ ill-fated; **hado** m fate, destiny.

haga, hago v. hacer.

¡hala! hi (there)!, hoy!; ⚓ etc. heave!

halagar [1h] show affection to, make up to F; (acariciar) caress; cajole, blandish para persuadir; (adular) flatter; (agradar) gratify; **halago** m caress; cajolery; blan-

dishment(s); flattery; gratification;
delight; **halagüeño** flattering;
pleasing, attractive, alluring; *perspectiva* hopeful.
halar [1a] ✢ *v/t.* haul (at, on), pull;
v/i. pull ahead.
halcón *m* falcon; ~ común peregrine;
halconería *f* falconry, hawking;
halconero *m* falconer.
halibut *m* halibut.
halo *m* halo.
hall [xol] *m* hall; *thea.* foyer.
hallar [1a] *mst* find; discover;
locate; come across *sin buscar*;
(*averiguar*) find out; ~se find o.s.;
be; *se halla en Burgos* he is in
Burgos; *se hallaba muy enfermo* he
was very ill; ~ con obstáculo encounter; ~ en todo have a hand in
everything; **hallazgo** *m* (*acto*)
finding; discovery; (*cosa hallada*)
find; (*recompensa*) reward (to
finder); *100 ptas de* ~ 100 ptas
reward.
hamaca *f* hammock; **hamaquear**
[1a] *S.Am.* rock.
hambre *f* hunger (*a. fig.*; de for);
famine; starvation; *fig.* longing (de
for); ~ *canina* ravenous hunger;
entretener el ~ stave off hunger;
matar el ~ satisfy one's hunger;
(*hacer*) *morir de* ~ starve (to death);
padecer ~ starve; *pasar* ~ go
hungry; *tener* ~ be hungry; *esp. fig.*
hunger (de after, for); **hambrear**
[1a] *v/t.* starve; *v/i.* starve, go
hungry; **hambriento** hungry, famished, starving; *fig.* starved (de of),
longing (de for).
hamburguesa *f* hamburger.
hamo *m* fish-hook.
hampa *f* rogue's life, vagrancy;
underworld, low life; (*a. gente del*~)
riff-raff; **hampón** *m* tough, rowdy,
thug.
hámster *m* hamster.
han *v. haber.*
handicap *m* handicap; **handicapar**
[1a] *deportes:* handicap.
hangar *m* hangar.
haragán 1. idle, good-for-nothing;
2. *m*, **-a** *f* idler, loafer, good-for-
nothing; **haraganear** [1a] idle;
lounge, lie (about), hang about;
haraganería *f* idleness *etc.*
harapiento, haraposo in rags,
ragged, tattered; **harapo** *m* rag,
tatter; *hecho un* ~ in rags.

harén *m* harem.
harina *f* flour, meal; (*polvo*)
powder; ~ *de avena* oatmeal; ~ *de
huesos* bone-meal; ~ *lacteada*
malted milk; ~ *de maíz* cornflour,
corn-meal; *es* ~ *de otro costal* that's
(quite) another story, that's a horse
of a different colour; **harinero
1.** flour *attr.*; **2.** *m* (*p.*) flour
merchant; flour bin; **harinoso**
floury, mealy.
harnero *m* sieve.
harpillera *f* sacking, sackcloth.
hartar [1a] satiate, stuff, surfeit,
glut (con with); *fig.* (*aburrir*) weary,
bore; (*agobiar*) overwhelm (de
with); ~ *de palos a* shower blows
on; ~se gorge (con on), eat one's
fill (con of); *fig.* weary (de of); get
fed up (de with) F; **hartazgo** *m*
glut, repletion, surfeit; bellyful F;
darse un ~ *de* eat one's fill of; *fig.*
overdo; **harto 1.** *adj.* full (de of),
glutted (de with); *fig.* tired (de of),
fed up (de with); **2.** *adv.* quite,
very; enough; **hartura** *f* surfeit,
glut; abundance; *fig.* full satisfaction (of a desire); *con* ~ in
abundance.
has *v. haber.*
hasta 1. *prp. espacio:* as far as, up
to, down to; *tiempo:* till, until; as
late as, up to; pending; *cantidad:*
as much as, as many as; *v. ahora,
vista etc.*; **2.** *adv.* even; quite;
3. *cj.* even, also; ~ *que* until.
hastial[1] *m* △ gable-end.
hastial[2] *m* hulking lout.
hastiar [1c] (*cansar*) weary; (*repugnar*) disgust; (*disgustar*) annoy;
(*aburrir*) bore; **hastío** *m* weariness;
disgust; annoyance; boredom.
hatajo *m* F lot; **hato** *m* ⚕ herd;
flock *de ovejas*; group *de ps.*; *b.s.*
gang; *S.Am.* cattle ranch; *fig.* lot;
(*víveres*) provisions; (*ropa*) clothes;
personal effects; F *liar el* ~ pack
up; F *menear el* ~ *a* beat up;
revolver el ~ stir up trouble.
hay *v. haber.*
haya *f* beech (tree); **hayuco** *m*
beechnut, beechmast.
haz[1] *m* ⚕ sheaf *de mieses etc.*, truss
de paja; bundle *de leña etc.*; *haces* pl. *hist.* fasces; ~ *de luz* beam
of light.
haz[2] *f mst fig. or lit.* face; (*superficie*)
surface; right side *de tela*; ~ *de la*

tierra face of the earth; **de dos haces** *fig.* two-faced.

haz[3] *v.* hacer.

hazaña *f* feat, exploit, (heroic) deed; achievement; **hazañería** *f* fuss; **hazañoso** heroic, valiant, dauntless.

hazmerreír *m* butt, laughing-stock, joke (*p.*).

he[1] *v.* haber.

he[2]: *mst lit.* ~ **aquí** here is, here are; **lo (and behold)!**; **¡heme (or héteme) aquí!** here I am!; **¡helos allí!** there they are!

hebdomadario *adj. a. su. m* weekly.

hebilla *f* buckle, clasp.

hebra *f* (length of) thread; strand; fibre; grain *de madera*; ⚒ vein; *fig.* thread (of the conversation); **~s** *pl. poet.* hair; **pegar la ~** start a conversation.

hebraico Hebraic; **hebreo 1.** *adj. a. su. m,* **a** *f* Hebrew; **2.** (*idioma*) Hebrew.

hebroso fibrous; **carne** stringy.

hecatombe *f* hecatomb.

hectárea *f* hectare.

héctico 🞗 consumptive.

hectolitro *m* hectolitre.

hechicera *f* sorceress, witch; enchantress; **hechicería** *f* sorcery, witchcraft; spell, enchantment (*a. fig.*); *fig.* charm, fascination; **hechicero 1.** magic; bewitching, enchanting (*a. fig.*); *fig.* charming; **2.** *m* wizard, sorcerer; witch doctor *de salvajes*; **hechizar** [1f] bewitch (*a. fig.*), cast a spell on; *b.s.* bedevil; *fig.* charm, enchant, delight; **hechizo 1.** artificial, false; (*amovible*) detachable; ⊕ manufactured; **2.** *m* magic; charm, spell (*a. fig.*); *fig.* glamour; **~s** *pl.* (woman's) charms.

hecho 1. *p.p. of* hacer; **¡~!** done!, it's a deal!; **a lo ~, pecho** what's done can't be undone; **bien ~** well-made; *p.* well proportioned; **¡bien ~!** well done!, quite right!; **estar ~ un ...** be like a ...; **estar ~ a** be accustomed to, be hardened to; **2.** *adj.* complete, mature; (*acabado*) finished; *sew.* ready-made, ready-to-wear; **frase** stock; **~ y derecho** complete, proper, fully-fledged; **3.** *m* deed, act, action; fact; (*elemento*) factor; (*asunto*) matter;

(*suceso*) event; **los ~s de los Apóstoles** the Acts of the Apostles; **el ~ es que** the fact is that; **a ~** continuously; all together; indiscriminately; **de ~** in fact, as a matter of fact; **volvamos al ~** let's get back to the matter in hand.

hechura *f* make, making; creation; creature (*a. fig.*); form, shape; build *de p.*; cut *de traje*; (*artesanía*) workmanship; **de ~ sastre** tailormade; **somos ~ de Dios** we are God's handiwork.

heder [2g] stink, reek (*a* of); *fig.* annoy, be intolerable; **hediondez** *f* stench; stinking thing; **hediondo** stinking, foul-smelling; filthy (*a. fig.*); intolerable.

hedonismo *m* hedonism.

hedor *m* stench, stink, reek.

hegemonía *f* hegemony.

helada *f* frost; freeze(-up); **~ blanca** hoarfrost; **heladera** *f* refrigerator; **helado 1.** frozen (*a. fig.*); freezing, icy; (*preso*) ice-bound; *fig.* chilly, disdainful; **2.** *m* ice(-cream); iced drink; **helar** [1k] freeze; ice; chill (*a. fig.*); (*pasmar*) astonish; (*desalentar*) dishearten; **~se** freeze; be frozen; (*avión, riel etc.*) ice (up); (*coagularse*) set.

helecho *m* fern, bracken.

helénico Hellenic, Greek; **heleno** *m,* **a** *f* Hellene, Greek.

hélice *f* spiral; 🜨, ✈, *anat.* helix; ⚓ screw, propeller; ✈ propeller, airscrew; **helicoidal** spiral, helicoid(al).

helicóptero *m* helicopter.

helio *m* helium; **heliograbado** *m* heliogravure; **heliógrafo** *m* heliograph; **heliotropo** *m* heliotrope.

hembra *f zo.,* ⚀, ⊕ female; *zo.* she-...; *orn.* hen; *sew.* eye; ⊕ nut; **F** woman; **un pez ~** a female fish; **una real ~** a fine figure of a woman; **hembrilla** *f* ⊕ nut.

hemiciclo *m* semicircle; semicircular theatre; *parl.* floor; **hemisferio** *m* hemisphere; **hemistiquio** *m* hemistich.

hemofilia *f* haemophilia; **hemorragia** *f* haemorrhage; **hemorroides** *f/pl.* haemorrhoids.

henal *m* hayloft; **henar** *m* meadow, hayfield.

henchir [3h] fill (up), stuff, cram; **~se** (*p.*) stuff o.s.

hendedura f cleft, split; (incisión) slit; (grieta) crack; mst geol. rift, fissure; **hender** [2g] cleave (a. fig.); split; crack; slit con cuchillo; fig. make a way through; **hendidura** f = hendedura.

henil m hayloft; **heno** m hay.

hepático hepatic.

heptágono m heptagon.

heráldica f heraldry; **heráldico** heraldic; **heraldo** m herald (a. fig.).

herbáceo herbaceous; **herbaje** m herbage, grass, pasture; **herbaj(e)ar** v/t. put to pasture, graze; v/i. graze, browse; **herbario** 1. herbal; 2. m herbarium; (p.) herbalist; **herbazal** m grassland; **herbívoro** herbivorous; **herbolario** 1. crazy; 2. m herbalist; **herborizar** [1f] gather herbs; (como estudio) botanize; **herboso** grassy.

hercúleo Herculean.

heredable (in)heritable; **heredad** f (country) estate, farm; domain; landed property; **heredar** [1a] inherit (de from), be heir to; p. name as one's heir; **heredera** f heiress; **heredero** m heir (de to), inheritor (de of); owner of an estate; ~ forzoso heir apparent, heir at law; ~ único universal heir; **hereditario** hereditary.

hereje m/f heretic; **herejía** f heresy (a. fig.).

herencia f inheritance; estate; legacy; esp. fig. heritage; biol. heredity.

herético heretic(al).

herida f wound, injury; (ofensa) insult, outrage; fig. affliction; **herido** 1. injured; ✗ wounded; 2. m injured (✗ wounded) man; los ~s pl. the wounded; **herir** [3i] hurt, injure; esp. ✗ wound (a. fig.); (golpear) strike, hit; (sol) beat down on; ♪ pluck, strike; fig. touch, move; fig. offend.

hermafrodita adj. a. su. m hermaphrodite.

hermana f sister (a. eccl.); (cosa) twin; **hermanar** [1a] match; (unir) join; harmonize; **hermanastro** m stepbrother; **hermandad** f brotherhood (a. fig.), sisterhood; fig. close relationship; **hermano** 1. m brother (a. fig., eccl.); (cosa) twin; ~s pl. brother(s) and sister(s); ~

carnal blood brother; ~ de leche foster brother; ~ político brother-in-law; 2. adj. similar, matching; sister attr. (fig.).

hermético hermetic, air-tight; water-tight; fig. impenetrable.

hermosear [1a] beautify, make beautiful; adorn; **hermoso** beautiful; esp. hombre handsome; lovely; fine, splendid; **hermosura** f beauty; loveliness; (p.) belle, beauty.

hernia f rupture, hernia.

héroe m hero; **heroicidad** f (act of) heroism; **heroico** heroic; **heroicocómico** mock-heroic; **heroína**[1] f heroine.

heroína[2] f pharm. heroin.

heroísmo m heroism.

herpes m/pl. or f/pl. ✗ shingles, herpes.

herrador m farrier; **herradura** f horseshoe; curva en ~ mot. hairpin bend; **herraje** m ironwork, metal fittings; **herramental** m tool-bag, tool-kit; **herramienta** f tool, implement; appliance; set of tools; F (bull's) horns; F (dientes) teeth; ~ de filo edge-tool; ~ mecánica power-tool; **herrar** [1k] caballo shoe; ganado brand; ⊕ bind (or trim) with iron; **herrería** f smithy, blacksmith's (shop), forge; (fábrica) ironworks; (oficio) blacksmith's trade; fig. uproar.

herrerillo m tit.

herrero m (black)smith.

herrete m tag, metal tip; S.Am. branding-iron.

herrumbre f rust; fig. taste of iron; a prueba de ~ rust-proof, rust-resistant; **herrumbroso** rusty.

hervidero m boiling, bubbling, seething (a. fig.); (fuente) bubbling spring; fig. swarm, throng; **hervidor** m approx. kettle; boiling-pan; cooker; **hervir** [3i] boil, seethe (a. fig.); (mar) surge; ~ de, ~ en swarm with, teem with; **hervor** m boiling, seething; fig. fire (of youth), restlessness; alzar el ~ come to the boil.

heterodino adj. a. su. m heterodyne.

heterodoxo unorthodox, heterodox.

heterogéneo heterogeneous.

hético = héctico.

hexágono m hexagon.

hez f: mst pl. heces sediment, lees;

dregs (*a. fig.*); excrement; *fig.* scum.

hiato *m gr.*, ✗ hiatus.

hibernación *f* hibernation; **hibernal** wintry, winter *attr.*; **hibernar** [1a] hibernate.

híbrido hybrid.

hice *v.* hacer.

hidalga *f* noblewoman; **hidalgo 1.** noble, illustrious; (*propio de* ∼) gentlemanly; generous; **2.** *m* nobleman; **hidalguía** *f* nobility)

hidra *f* hydra. [(*esp.* of conduct).]

hidratar(se) [1a] hydrate; **hidrato** *m* hydrate.

hidráulica *f* hydraulics; **hidráulico** hydraulic, water *attr.*; *fuerza* ∼*a* water-power.

hidro(avión) *m* seaplane; flying boat; **hidrocarburo** *m* hydrocarbon; **hidrodinámica** *f* hydrodynamics; **hidroeléctrico** hydroelectric; **hidrófilo** absorbent, F bibulous; **hidrofobia** *f* hydrophobia; rabies; **hidrófobo** hydrophobic; **hidrófugo** damp-proof, water-repellent; **hidrógeno** *m* hydrogen; **hidrom(i)el** *m* mead; **hidropesía** *f* dropsy; **hidrópico** dropsical; **hidroplano** *m* seaplane; **hidrostática** *f* hydrostatics; **hidrostático** hydrostatic; **hidróxido** *m* hydroxide.

hiedra *f* ivy.

hiel *f* bile, gall (*a. fig.*); *fig.* bitterness, sorrow; ∼es *pl.* troubles; *echar la* ∼ overwork.

hielo *m* ice; frost; freezing; *fig.* coldness, indifference; ∼ *a la deriva*, ∼ *movedizo* drift-ice; *romper el* ∼ *fig.* break the ice.

hiena *f* hyena.

hierba *f* grass; *esp.* ✗ herb; small plant; ∼s *pl.* pasture; ∼ *cana* groundsel; ∼*mora* nightshade; ∼ *rastrera* cotton-grass; *mala* ∼ weed; *fig.* bad influence; ∼**buena** *f* mint.

hierro *m* iron; head *de lanza etc.*; (*de marcar*) brand; ∼s *pl.* irons; ∼ *acanalado*, ∼ *ondulado* corrugated iron; ∼ *colado*, ∼ *fundido* cast-iron; ∼ *forjado* wrought iron, ∼ *en lingotes* pig-iron; ∼ *viejo* scrap-iron; *a* ∼ *candente*, *batir de repente* strike while the iron's hot; *machacar en* ∼ *frío* beat one's head against a wall, flog a dead horse.

higa *f* scorn, contempt.

hígado *m* liver; ∼s *pl.* F guts, pluck; F *echar los* ∼s wear o.s. out.

higiene *f* hygiene; **higiénico** hygienic; sanitary; healthy.

higo *m* ✿ (green) fig; *vet.* thrush; ∼ *chumbo*, ∼ *de tuna* prickly pear; *de* ∼s *a brevas* once in a blue moon; *no se me da un* ∼ I don't care a rap (*de* about).

higrómetro *m* hygrometer.

higuera *f* fig-tree.

hija *f* daughter, child (*a. fig.*); **hijastro** *m* stepson; **hijito** *m* F sonny; **hijo** *m* son, child (*a. fig.*); F (*vocativo*) son(ny), my boy; ∼s *pl.* children, son(s) and daughter(s); (*prole*) offspring, descendants; ∼ *de leche* foster child; ∼ *político* son-in-law; *Juan Lanas* ∼ Juan Lanas Junior; **hijuela** *f* little girl; ⊕ accessory; ✂ portion, inheritance; **hijuelo** *m* little boy; ✿ shoot; *zo.* young.

hila *f* row, line; ∼s *pl.* ✗ lint.

hilacha *f*, **hilacho** *m* ravelled thread; fraying; ∼ *de vidrio* spun glass.

hilada *f* row, line; △ course.

hilado *m* (*acto*) spinning; (*hilo*) yarn, thread; **hilandería** *f* (*arte*) spinning; (*fábrica*) (spinning-)mill; **hilandero** *m*, a *f* spinner; **hilar** [1a] spin; *fig.* reason, infer; ∼ *delgado* draw it fine.

hilarante hilarious; *gas* laughing; **hilaridad** *f* hilarity, mirth.

hilaza *f* yarn, (coarse) thread; *descubrir la* ∼ show o.s. in one's true colours.

hilera *f* row, rank (*a.* ✗); line, string; *sew.* fine thread; ✗ drill.

hilo *m* thread (*a. fig.*); yarn; (*tejido*) linen; (*alambre*) (thin) wire; trickle *de líquido*; string *de perlas etc.*; *fig.* train *del pensamiento*; course *de la vida*; *a* ∼ uninterruptedly; *al* ∼ *sew.* on the straight; *colgado de un* ∼ hanging by a thread; *coger el* ∼ pick (or take) up the thread; *irse tras el* ∼ *de la gente* follow the crowd; *perder el* ∼ *de* lose the thread of.

hilván *m sew.* tacking, basting; **hilvanar** [1a] *sew.* tack, baste; *fig.* throw together, knock up.

himen *m* hymen, maidenhead; **himeneo** *m* Hymen.

himnario *m* hymnal, hymnbook; **himno** *m* hymn; ∼ *nacional* national anthem.

hincapié: *hacer* ~ make a stand; *hacer* ~ *en* dwell on, insist on, emphasize.

hincar [1g] thrust (in); *clavo etc.* drive (in), sink; *pie* set (firmly); *v. diente, rodilla.*

hincha F **1.** *f* grudge, bad blood, ill-will; (*p., cosa*) pet aversion; **2.** *m/f deportes:* supporter, fan, rooter *Am.;* **hinchado** *lenguaje etc.* high-flown, pompous, stilted; *p.* vain, puffed-up; **hinchar** [1a] swell; distend; inflate, pump up, blow up *con aire; fig.* exaggerate; ~se swell (up), get distended; *fig.* be(come) puffed up (*or* vain); **hinchazón** *f* swelling; bump, lump; *fig.* vanity, conceit *de p.;* pomposity *de lenguaje.*

hindú *adj. a. su. m,* **-a** *f* Hindu.

hiniesta *f* ♀ broom.

hinojo[1] *m* ♀ fennel. [knee.]

hinojo[2] *m* knee; *de* ~s on bended

hipar [1a] **1.** hiccup, hiccough; (*perro*) pant; *fig.* be worn out; long, yearn (*por* for *su.,* to *inf.*); **2.** [xi'par] whimper.

hipérbola *f* ♈ hyperbola; **hipérbole** *f* rhet. hyperbole; **hiperbólico** hyperbolic(al); exaggerated; **hipercrítico** hypercritical, carping, censorious; **hipertrofia** *f* hypertrophy.

hípico equine ♊, horse *attr.*

hipnosis *f* hypnosis; **hipnótico** hypnotic; **hipnotismo** *m* hypnotism; **hipnotista** *m/f* hypnotist; **hipnotizar** [1f] hypnotize, mesmerize.

hipo *m* hiccup(s), hiccough(s); (*deseo*) longing; (*odio*) grudge, enmity; *tener* ~ *contra* have it in for; *tener* ~ *por* long for.

hipocampo *m* sea-horse.

hipocondría *f* hypochondria; **hipocondríaco 1.** hypochondriacal; **2.** *m,* **a** *f* hypochondriac.

hipocresía *f* hypocrisy; **hipócrita 1.** hypocritical; **2.** *m/f* hypocrite.

hipodérmico hypodermic.

hipódromo *m* racecourse; hippodrome.

hipopótamo *m* hippopotamus.

hipoteca *f* mortgage; **hipotecar** [1g] mortgage; **hipotecario** mortgage *attr.*

hipotenusa *f* hypotenuse.

hipótesis *f* hypothesis, supposition; **hipotético** hypothetical.

hiriente offensive; wounding, cutting.

hirsuto hairy, hirsute, bristly; *fig. p.* brusque, rough.

hirviendo boiling; **hirviente** boiling, seething.

hisopear [1a] *eccl.* sprinkle (with holy water); **hisopo** *m eccl.* sprinkler; ♀ hyssop.

hispalense *adj. a. su. m/f* Sevillian.

hispánico Hispanic; **hispanidad** *f* Spanishness; *pol.* (solidarity of the) Spanish world; **hispanismo** *m gr.* Hispanicism; ♐ Hispanism; **hispanista** *m/f* Hispanist; **hispano** Spanish, Hispanic; **hispanoamericano** *adj. a. su. m,* **a** *f* Spanish-American, Latin-American; **hispanófilo** *adj. a. su. m,* **a** *f* Hispanophile.

histérico hysteric(al); *paroxismo* ~ hysterics; **histerismo** *m* hysteria.

histología *f* histology.

historia *f* history; (*narración, cuento*) story; (*esp. inventada*) tale; ~ *pl.* (*chismes*) gossip; ~ *natural* history; ♀ *Sacra,* ♀ *Sagrada* biblical history; Scripture *en la escuela;* ~ *universal* world history; *dejarse de* ~s come to the point; *mujer que tiene* ~ woman with a past; **historiador** *m,* **-a** *f* historian; **historial 1.** historical; **2.** *m* (*historia, antecendentes*) record; (*ficha*) dossier; ⚔ (*case-*)history; **historiar** [1b] tell the (hi)story of; chronicle; (*representar*) depict; **histórico** historical; (*notable*) historic; **historieta** *f* (short) story, tale, anecdote; **historiógrafo** *m* historiographer.

histrión *m* actor, player; buffoon; *b.s.* play-actor; **histriónico** histrionic; **histrionismo** *m* histrionics; (*arte*) acting; (*ps.*) actors.

hita *f* ⊕ sprig, brad; (*mojón*) = **hito** *m* boundary-post, milestone; ⚔ target; *fig.* aim, goal; ~ *kilométrico* kilometre-stone; *a* ~ fixedly; *dar en el* ~ hit the nail on the head; *mirar de* ~ *en* ~ stare at, look *s.o.* up and down.

hocicar [1g] (*puerco*) root; (*con cariño*) nuzzle; (*p.*) fall on one's face; *fig.* run into trouble; **hocico** *m* snout, muzzle *de animal;* F snout, mug *sl. de p.;* *dar de* ~s fall on one's face; *dar de* ~s *contra* bump into; *estar de* ~ be in a bad temper;

meter el ~ meddle; *poner* ~ pull a face.

hockey ['oki] *m* hockey; ~ *sobre patines,* ~ *sobre hielo* ice-hockey.

hogaño *mst* † this year; these days.

hogar *m* hearth, fireplace; ⊕ furnace; 🔥 fire-box; *fig.* home, house; family life; **hogareño** home *attr.*, family *attr.*; fireside *attr.*; *p.* home-loving, stay-at-home.

hogaza *f* large loaf.

hoguera *f* bonfire; *(llamas)* blaze.

hoja *f* ⚘ leaf *(a. de libro, puerta);* ⚘ petal; sheet *de metal, papel;* blade *de espada etc.;* pane *de vidrio;* (*documento*) form; ~ *de afeitar* razor-blade; ~ *de estaño* tinfoil; ~ *de guarda* flyleaf; ~ *de lata* tin(plate); ~ *plegadiza* (table-)flap; ~ *de ruta* way-bill; ~ *de servicios* record of service; ~ *de tocino* flitch, side of bacon; ~ *volante* leaflet, handbill; *doblar la* ~ *fig.* change the subject; *volver la* ~ *fig.* turn over a new leaf; change the subject.

hojalata *f* tin(plate); **hojalatero** *m* tinsmith.

hojaldre *m* puff-pastry.

hojarasca *f* dead (*or* fallen) leaves; *fig.* trifles, trash, rubbish; *(palabras)* empty verbiage.

hojear [1a] turn the pages of, skim (*or* glance) through; **hojoso** leafy; **hojuela** *f* little leaf; *(escama)* flake; *metall.* foil; *cocina:* pancake.

¡hola! *saludo:* hullo!; *extrañeza, represión:* hullo!, hey!, hoy!

holandés 1. Dutch; **2.** *m* Dutchman; **3.** *m* (*idioma*) Dutch; **holandesa** *f* Dutch woman; *a la* ~ *libro* quarter-bound.

holgado (*ocioso*) leisured, idle, unoccupied; *vestido etc.* loose, roomy, baggy; comfortable, cosy; *(casi rico)* comfortably off, well-to-do; **holganza** *f* (*ocio*) ease, leisure; *(descanso*) rest; *(placer)* enjoyment; **holgar** [1h *a.* 1m] *(descansar)* rest, take one's ease; *(estar ocioso)* be idle, be out of work; *(cosa)* be unused; be unnecessary; *(alegrarse)* be pleased (*con, de* with; *about*); *huelga decir* needless to say; ~*se* be glad (*con, de* about, at, of; *de que* that); enjoy o.s.

holgazán 1. idle, lazy; **2.** *m,* **-a** *f* idler, slacker, loafer; bum *Am.* F; ne'erdowell; **holgazanear** [1a]

laze, loaf, slack; **holgazanería** *f* laziness *etc.*

holgorio *m* = *jolgorio.*

holgura *f* enjoyment, merry-making; ease, comfort; looseness, roominess *de vestido;* ⊕ play.

holocausto *m* holocaust, burnt offering; *fig.* sacrifice.

hollar [1m] tread (on); trample underfoot *(a. fig.);* *fig.* humiliate.

hollejo *m* ⚘ skin, peel.

hollín *m* soot; **holliniento** sooty.

hombrachón *m* hulking fellow; **hombrada** *f* manly act; piece of bravado; **hombradía** *f* manliness; courage.

hombre 1. *m* man; *(género humano)* man, mankind; F husband; ~ *de armas* man-at-arms; ~ *de bien* honest man, man of honour; ~ *de la calle* man in the street; ~ *de estado* statesman; ~ *hecho* grown man; ~ *de letras* man of letters; ~ *medio* average man; ~ *de mundo* man of the world; *v. muy;* ~ *de negocios* businessman; *pobre* ~ poor devil; slow-witted fellow; ~ *de pro(vecho)* honest man; man of worth; **2.** *int.* ¡~! *sorpresa:* good heavens!; *confirmación:* you bet!; *condoliéndose:* dear dear; yes I know; *¡pero* ~! *protesta:* but my dear fellow!; heavens man!

hombrear¹ [1a] play the man; *(a.* ~*se)* con try to keep up with.

hombrear² [1a] shoulder; put one's shoulder to.

hombrecillo *m* little man; ⚘ hop.

hombrera *f* shoulder-strap; ✕ epaulette.

hombre-rana *m* frogman.

hombría *f* manliness; ~ *de bien* honesty, uprightness.

hombro *m* shoulder; ~ *a* ~ shoulder to shoulder; ✕ *sobre el* ~ *¡armas!* slope arms!; *arrimar el* ~ put one's shoulder to the wheel, lend a hand; *echar al* ~ shoulder, take upon o.s.; *encogerse de* ~*s* shrug (one's shoulders); *mirar por encima del* ~ look down on, despise.

hombruno mannish, masculine.

homenaje *m* homage *(a. fig.);* allegiance; *fig.* tribute, testimonial; *(don)* gift; *en* ~ *a* in honour of; *rendir* ~ *a* do (*or* pay, render) homage to, swear allegiance to.

homeópata *m* homeopath(ist); **ho-**

meopatía *f* homeopathy; **homeopático** homeopathic.
homicida 1. murderous, homicidal; **2.** *m* murderer; **3.** *f* murderess; **homicidio** *m* murder, homicide; manslaughter.
homilía *f* homily.
homogeneidad *f* homogeneity; **homogéneo** homogeneous; **homología** *f* homology; **homólogo** homologous; **homónimo** *m* homonym; (*p.*) namesake; **homosexual** *adj. a. su. m/f* homosexual.
honda *f* sling, catapult.
hondear [1a] ⚓ sound; (*descargar*) unload.
hondo 1. deep; low; *fig.* profound; *sentimiento* deep, heartfelt; **2.** *m* depth(s); bottom; **hondón** *m* bottom *de vaso, valle*; eye *de aguja*; *geog.* = **hondonada** *f* (*depresión*) hollow; (*tierra baja*) lowland; (*barranco*) gully, ravine; **hondura** *f* depth; profundity; *meterse en ~s* get out of one's depth, get into deep waters.
honestidad *f* decency, decorum *etc.*; **honesto** decent, decorous; modest; chaste; fair, just; honourable; honest.
hongo *m* (*en general*) fungus; (*comestible*) mushroom; (*venenoso*) toadstool; (*sombrero*) bowler (hat), derby *Am.*
honor *m* honour; virtue *esp. de mujer*; (*reputación*) good name; *~es pl.* honours, honorary status; *~ profesional* professional etiquette; *de ~ dama etc.* in waiting, of honour; *en ~ de* in honour of; *hacer ~ a firma* honour; *hacer los ~es de la casa* do the honours; *hacer los debidos ~es a comida* do justice to; *tener el ~ de inf.* have the honour to *inf.*, be proud to *inf.*
honorable honourable, worthy; **honorario 1.** honorary; honorific; **2.** *m* honorarium; *mst ~s pl.* fees, charges.
honra *f* self-esteem; dignity; (*reputación*) good name; honour; chastity; *~s pl.* (*fúnebres*) last honours, obsequies; *¡a mucha ~!* delighted!; *tener a mucha ~ inf.* be proud to *inf,*; *tener algo a mucha ~* be proud of *s.t.*; **honradez** *f* honesty, honourableness, integrity; **honrado** honest, honourable; upright; **hon-**

rar [1a] honour (*a.* ✝); respect, esteem, revere; do honour to; *~se* be honoured (*con* by, with; *de inf.* to *inf.*); **honrilla**: *por la negra ~* for the sake of appearances, out of a sense of shame; **honroso** honourable; respectable, reputable.
hopa *f* cassock.
hora *f* hour; time (of day); *altas ~s pl.* small hours; *~ de comer* mealtime; *time to eat*; *~ de irse* time to go; *~s pl. extraordinarias* overtime; *~-hombre* man-hour; *~s pl. de oficina* business hours; *~s pl. punta* peak hours; *~ de recreo* playtime; *última ~ (periódico)* stoppress; *a última ~* at the last moment; *a buena ~* opportunely; *a la ~* punctually; *en buen(a) ~* fortunately; safely; *en mala ~* unluckily; *fuera de ~s* out of hours; *por ~s* by the hour; *dar ~* fix a time; *dar la ~* strike (the hour); *ya es ~ de que* it is high time that; *¡ya era ~!* about time too! *¿qué ~ es?* what is the time?, what time is it?; *poner en ~ reloj* set; *trabajar por ~s* work part-time; *no ver la ~ de* be hardly able to wait for.
horadar [1a] drill, bore (through); perforate, pierce.
horario 1. hourly; hour *attr.*; time *attr.*; **2.** *m* hour-hand *de reloj*; 🚂 *etc.* time-table, schedule *Am.*
horca *f* gallows, gibbet; ⚒ (pitch-)fork; (*cebollas*) string; **horcadura** *f* fork (of a tree); **horcajadas**: *a ~* astride; **horcajadura** *f anat.* crotch; **horcajo** *m* ⚒ yoke; *geog.* fork (of a river).
horchata *f* orgeat; **horchatería** *f* resfreshment stall; *approx.* ice-cream parlour.
horda *f* horde; (*pandilla*) gang.
horizontal horizontal; flat, level; **horizonte** *m* horizon (*a. fig.*); (*línea del ~*) skyline.
horma *f* ⊕ form, mould; (*a. ~ del calzado*) last, boot-tree; (*muro*) dry stone wall; *hallar la ~ de su zapato* meet one's match.
hormiga *f* ant.
hormigón *m* concrete; *~ armado* reinforced concrete; *~ pretensado* prestressed concrete.
hormiguear [1a] 🐜 itch; (*abundar*) swarm, teem; **hormigueo** *m* 🐜 itch(ing), tingling, creeps F; *fig.* un-

easiness; swarming; **hormiguero**
m anthill (a. fig.); fig. swarm (of
people).

hormón m, **hormona** f hormone.

hornacina f (vaulted) niche.

hornada f batch (of bread), baking;
fig. crop, batch; **hornero** m, a f
baker; **hornillo** m ⊕ small furnace;
stove de cocina; bowl de pipa; ✄
mine; ~ eléctrico hot-plate; ~ de gas
gas-ring; **horno** m ⊕ furnace;
cerámica: kiln; cocina: oven; alto ~
blast-furnace; ~ de cal lime-kiln; ~
crematorio crematorium; ~ de fundición smelting-furnace; ~ de ladrillos brick-kiln.

horóscopo m horoscope.

horqueta f todos sentidos: fork; **horquilla** f ⚹ pitchfork; hairpin para
pelo; fork de bicicleta; ⊕ yoke.

horrendo horrible, dire, frightful.

hórreo m prov. (esp. raised) granary.

horrible horrible, ghastly, dreadful
(a. F); F unspeakable, nasty; **horripilante** hair-raising, horrifying,
weird, creepy F; **horripilar** [1a]
make s.o.'s hair stand on end, give
s.o. the creeps F; **horror** m (sentimiento) horror, dread; abhorrence;
(calidad) horror; repulsiveness;
enormity; (acto) atrocity; ¡qué ~!
how horrible!; F goodness!, well
did you ever!; tener ~ a have a
horror of; tener en ~ abhor, detest;
horrorizar [1f] horrify; terrify;
~se be horrified; **horroroso** horrifying; horrible, frightful, grim (a.
F); F ghastly, dreadful.

horrura f filth, dirt, rubbish.

hortaliza f vegetable; **hortelano** m,
a f (market) gardener.

hortensia f hydrangea.

hortera f wooden bowl; F Madrid:
shop-assistant, grocer's boy.

hortícola horticultural; **horticultor** m, a f horticulturist, gardener;
(m) nurseryman; **horticultura** f
horticulture; gardening.

hosco dark, gloomy; p. surly, sullen,
grim.

hospedaje m (cost of) lodging;
hospedar [1a] put up, lodge,
receive as a guest; ~se put up,
lodge, stop, stay (en at); **hospedera**
f hostess; innkeeper's wife; **hospedero** m host; innkeeper; **hospicio**
m poor-house; hospice; (niños) orphanage; **hospital** m hospital, in-

firmary; esp. eccl. hospice; ~ de
aislamiento, ~ de contagiosos isolation hospital; ✄ ~ de sangre field
dressing-station; **hospitalario**
hospitable; **hospitalidad** f hospitality; **hospitalizar** [1f] send to
hospital.

hosquedad f gloom; sullenness etc.

hostelero m innkeeper; **hostería** f
inn.

hostia f eccl. host; wafer.

hostigar [1h] lash, whip; fig.
harass, plague.

hostil hostile; **hostilidad** f hos-
tility; hostile act; romper las ~es
start hostilities; **hostilizar** [1f] ✄
harass, attack; (enemistar) antag-
onize.

hotel m hotel; (casa) detached house,
mansion, villa; **hotelero 1.** hotel
attr.; **2.** m, a f hotel-keeper.

hoy today; ~ (en) día nowadays; ~
por ~ at the present; (de) ~ en
8 días this day week, a week today;
de ~ a mañana any time now, when
you least expect it; de ~ en adelante
from now on, henceforward; por ~
for the present.

hoya f pit, hole; (tumba) grave; geog.
vale; S.Am. river basin; ⚹ seed-
bed; **hoyada** f depression, hollow;
hoyo m hole (a. golf), cavity; (tumba) grave; ⚹ pock mark; **hoyuelo** m
dimple.

hoz f ⚹ sickle; geog. defile, ravine,
gorge.

hozar [1f] (puerco) root.

hube v. haber.

hucha f bin; (arca) chest; money-
box para dinero; fig. savings;
buena ~ fig. nest-egg.

hueco 1. hollow; (vacío) empty;
blank; (mullido) soft; tierra etc.
spongy; fig. p. conceited; estilo
pompous; voz resounding, boom-
ing; **2.** m hole, hollow, cavity; (intervalo) gap, opening; (vacío) void,
empty space; (puesto) vacancy; ⚠
recess, window; well de escalera; ~-
grabado m photogravure.

huelga f (laboral) strike; (descanso)
rest; (ocio) leisure, b.s. idleness;
⊕ play; ~ de brazos caídos sit-down
strike; ~ de hambre hunger strike;
~ patronal lock-out; ~ por solidaridad sympathetic strike; en ~ on
strike; declararse (or ponerse) en ~
(go on) strike, walk out; **huelgo** m

breath; space; ⊕ play; **huelguista** *m/f* striker.

huella *f* (*impresión de pie*) footprint; (*acto*) tread(ing); (foot)step; (*pista*) track; (*señal*) trace, mark, imprint, sign; tread *de escalón, neumático*; ~ *dactilar*, ~ *digital* finger-print; **huello:** *camino de buen* (*mal*) ~ good (bad) road for walking.

huérfano 1. orphan(ed); *fig.* unprotected, uncared-for; ~ *de madre* motherless; **2.** *m*, **a** *f* orphan.

huero *huevo* addled; *fig.* empty; sterile; dud F.

huerta *f* (large) market garden; ~ (*de árboles frutales*) orchard; *esp.* *Valencia a. Murcia* irrigated region; **huerto** *m* (kitchen) garden, market garden; orchard *de árboles frutales*.

huesa *f* grave.

hueso *m anat.* bone; ♀ stone; core; *fig.* hard work; ~ *de la alegría* funny-bone; ~ *de la suerte* wishbone; ~ *duro de roer* a hard nut to crack; *F la sin* ~ the tongue; *no dejar* ~ *sano* a pull to pieces, walk all over; *estar en los* ~*s* be nothing but skin and bone; **huesoso** bony, bone *attr.*

huésped *m* (*invitado*) guest; boarder, lodger *que paga*; (*que invita*) host; (*amo de la casa*) landlord; **huéspeda** *f* guest *etc.*; hostess; landlady.

huesudo bony; *p.* raw-boned.

hueva *f ichth.* (hard) roe; ~*s pl.* spawn; **huevera** *f* egg-cup; **huevo** *m* egg; ~ *al plato*, ~ *estrellado* fried egg; ~ *en cáscara*, ~ *pasado por agua* boiled egg; ~ *duro* hard-boiled egg; ~ *escalfado* poached egg; ~*s pl.* *revueltos* scrambled eggs.

hugonote *m*, **a** *f* Huguenot.

huida *f* flight, escape; shy(ing) *de caballo*; **huidizo** shy; elusive; (*pasajero*) fleeting; **huir** [3g] *v/t.* run away from, escape (from), flee; (*apartarse*) avoid, shun; *v/i.* run away, flee (de from) (*a.* ~*se*); (*tiempo*) fly.

hule *m* oilcloth, oilskin; (*caucho*) rubber; (*toros:* goring; *F habrá* ~ there's going to be trouble.

hulla *f* (soft) coal; **hullera** *f* colliery; **hullero** coal *attr.*

humanar [1a] humanize; ~*se* become more human; *eccl.* become man; ~ *a inf. S.Am.* condescend to *inf.*; **humanidad** *f* humanity (*a.*

fig.), mankind; F corpulence; ~*es* *pl.* humanities; **humanismo** *m* humanism; **humanista** *m/f* humanist; **humanitario** humanitarian; **humanización** *f* humanization; **humanizar** [1f] humanize; ~*se* become (more) human; **humano 1.** human; (*compasivo*) humane; *ciencias* ~*as* humane learning; **2.** *m* human (being).

humareda *f* cloud of smoke; **humazo** *m* dense (cloud of) smoke; F *dar* ~ *a* smoke out; **humeante** smoking, smoky, fuming; **humear** [1a] *v/t. S.Am.* fumigate; *v/i.* smoke; fume; steam; reek; *fig.* be not yet dead; (*altivecerse*) give o.s. airs.

humectar [1a]🕮 = *humedecer*; **humedad** *f* humidity, damp(ness), moisture, wet(ness); *a prueba de* ~ damp-proof; **humedecer** [2d] damp, moisten, wet; ~*se* get damp *etc.*; **húmedo** damp, humid, moist, wet.

humera *f* F drunkenness.

humero *m* chimney, flue.

húmero *m* humerus.

humildad *f* (*virtud*) humility; (*condición*) humbleness, lowliness; (*acto*) submission; **humilde** humble; *carácter* humble, meek; *condición* low(ly), low-born; *voz* small; **humillación** *f* humiliation, mortification; **humillante** humiliating, humbling; degrading; **humillar** [1a] humiliate, humble; *cabeza* bow, bend; ~*se* humble o.s.; *b.s.* grovel.

humo *m* smoke; fumes; ~*s pl.* (*casas*) homes; *fig.* airs, conceit; *a* ~ *de pajas* thoughtlessly; F *bajar los* ~*s a* take *s.o.* down a peg; *echar* ~, *hacer* ~ smoke; *hacerse* ~, *irse todo en* ~ go up in smoke, vanish without trace; *tener muchos* ~*s* have a swelled head; F *vender* ~*s* brag, talk big.

humor *m* humour (*a. anat.*); temper, mood; (*genio*) disposition; *buen* ~ good humour, high spirits; *estar de buen* (*mal*) ~ be in a good (bad) mood (*or* temper); *seguir el* ~ *a* humour; **humorada** *f* joke, witticism; **humorado:** *bien* ~ good-humoured; *mal* ~ bad-tempered; **humorismo** *m* humour, humorousness; **humorista** *m/f* humorist; **humorístico** humorous, funny, comic.

humoso smoky.

humus *m* humus.

hundido sunken; *ojos* hollow; **hundimiento** *m* sinking *etc.*; **hundir** [3a] sink; submerge, engulf; plunge (en into); *fig.* destroy, ruin; *p.* confound *con razones*; ~**se** ⚓ *etc.* sink; plunge; △ *etc.* collapse, cave in, tumble (down); (*tierra*) subside; *fig.* be destroyed, be ruined; disappear.

húngaro 1. *adj. a. su. m,* **a** *f* Hungarian; **2.** *m* (*idioma*) Hungarian.

huracán *m* hurricane.

huraño shy, diffident; unsociable; *animal* wild, shy.

hurgar [1h] poke; stir (up) (*a. fig.*); *lumbre* poke, rake; *fig.* incite, excite; ~**se** pick one's nose; **hurgón** *m* poker, fire-rake; **hurgonazo** *m* poke; jab; **hurgonear** [1a] *lumbre* poke; thrust at; jab.

hurón *m zo.* ferret; (*p.*) (*entrometido*) busybody, snooper; (*huraño*) shy unsociable person; **huronear** [1a]

fig. ferret out, pry into; **huronera** *f* *fig.* den, lair.

hurtadillas: *a* ~ stealthily, on the sly.

hurtar [1a] steal, thieve; ✝ give short measure; (*mar*) encroach on, erode; *lit.* plagiarize; ~**se** keep out of the way, make off; **hurto** *m* (*acto*) theft, robbery; (*cosa*) thing stolen; ~ *doméstico* burglary, housebreaking; *a* ~ on the sly, by stealth.

húsar *m* hussar.

husillo *m* ⊕ (*eje*) spindle, shaft; (*tornillo*) clamp-screw; (*desagüe*) drain.

husma: *andar a la* ~ go prying around (*de* after); **husmear** [1a] *v/t.* scent, get wind of (*a. fig.*); F smell out, nose out, pry into; *v/i.* (*carne*) smell high; **husmeo** *m* scenting; sniff; F prying; **husmo** *m* high smell, gaminess; *estar al* ~ watch one's chance.

huso *m* spindle (*a.* ⊕); bobbin; drum *de torno*.

¡huy! ow!, ouch!; (*sorpresa*) whew!

huyo *etc. v.* huir.

I

iba etc. v. ir.

ibérico Iberian; **ibero, íbero** adj. a. su. m, **a** f Iberian; **iberoamericano** Latin-American.

iceberg m iceberg.

icono m icon; **iconoclasta 1.** iconoclastic; **2.** m/f iconoclast.

ictericia f jaundice.

ictiología f ichthyology.

ida f going; departure; *fig.* rash act; hastiness; (*rastro*) trail; (*viaje de*) ~ outward journey; ~s *pl. y venidas* comings and goings; ~ *y vuelta* round trip.

idea f idea; notion; opinion; (*ingenio*) inventiveness, talent; ~ *fija* obsession, bee in one's bonnet F; ~ *luminosa* bright idea; F *ni* ~ I haven't a clue; *hacerse etc. una* ~ de get an idea of; *no tengo la menor* ~ I haven't the faintest idea; **ideación** f conception, thinking-out; **ideal 1.** ideal; notional, imaginary; **2.** m ideal; **idealismo** m idealism; **idealista 1.** idealistic; **2.** m/f idealist; **idealizar** [1f] idealize; **idear** [1a] think up; plan, design; invent; **ideario** m body of ideas; ideology.

ídem ditto, idem.

idéntico identical, (very) same; **identidad** f identity; sameness; **identificación** f identification; ~ *errónea* mistaken identify; **identificar** [1g] identify; recognize; pick out; ~*se* identify o.s., be identical (*con* with). [ideological.]

ideología f ideology; **ideológico** |

idílico idyllic; **idilio** m idyll.

idioma m language; speech, idiom *de grupo*; **idiomático** idiomatic.

idiosincrasia f idiosyncrasy.

idiota 1. idiotic, stupid; *p.* simple; **2.** m/f idiot; **idiotez** f idiocy; **idiotismo** m *gr.* idiom(atic expression).

idólatra 1. idolatrous; **2.** m idolater; **3.** f idolatress; **idolatrar** [1a] *ídolo* worship, adore; *fig.* idolize; **idolatría** f idolatry; **ídolo** m idol (a. *fig.*).

idoneidad f suitability; aptitude, ability; **idóneo** suitable; apt, fit, fitting.

iglesia f church; *cumplir con la* ~ fulfil one's religious obligations.

iglú m igloo.

ígneo igneous; **ignición** f ignition.

ignominia f ignominy, shame(fulness), disgrace; **ignominioso** ignominious, shameful, disgraceful.

ignorancia f ignorance; **ignorante 1.** ignorant, uninformed; **2.** m/f ignoramus; **ignorar** [1a] not know, be ignorant (*or* unaware) of, be unacquainted with; *no* ~ be well aware of, know very well.

igual 1. equal (*a* to); (the) same; indifferent; (*parecido*) alike, similar; uniform, constant; (*liso*) smooth, level, even; *clima* equable; *temperamento* even; ~ *que* like, the same as; (*me*) *es* ~ it's all the same (to me); *ir* ~*es* be level, be even; **2.** m/f equal; match (*de* for); *al* ~, *por* ~ equally; *sin* ~ matchless; *no tener* ~ be unrivalled, have no equal; **igualación** f equalization *etc.*; **igualar** [1a] v/t. equalize; (*comparar*) match; *a* equate; (*allanar*) level (up, down), smooth (off), even (out; *a. fig.*); adjust; ✝ agree upon; v/i., ~*se*: ~ *a*, ~ *con* equal, be the equal of; **igualdad** f equality; sameness; evenness, smoothness; ~ *de ánimo* equanimity; **igualmente** equally; likewise; F the same to you.

ijada f flank; loin; ✗ pain in the side, stitch; **ijar** m flank.

ilación f inference; connexion; sequence; **ilativo** inferential.

ilegal illegal, unlawful; **ilegalidad** f illegality.

ilegible illegible, unreadable.

ilegítimo illegitimate; *acto* unlawful; *cosa* false, spurious.

ilerdense adj. a. su. m/f (native) of Lérida.

ileso unharmed, unhurt; untouched.

iletrado uncultured, illiterate.

iliberal illiberal.

ilícito illicit.

ilimitado unlimited, limitless.

ilógico illogical.

iluminación f illumination, lighting; *fig.* enlightenment; **iluminado 1.** illuminated; **2.** *m* visionary; **iluminar** [1a] illuminate; light (up); *fig.* enlighten.

ilusión f illusion; delusion; (*esperanza*) (unfounded) hope, (day-) dream; (*entusiasmo*) excitement, eagerness; (*sentimiento de placer*) thrill; ¡qué ~! how thrilling!; *forjarse* ~es, *hacerse* ~es build up high hopes, indulge in wishful thinking; *este proyecto me hace mucha* ~ I am getting very excited about this scheme; *el viaje me hacía tanta* ~ I was looking forward so much to the trip; **ilusionado** hopeful; excited, eager; *el viaje me trae muy* ~ I am looking forward tremendously to the trip; **ilusionarse** [1a] indulge in wishful thinking; **ilusionismo** *m* wishful thinking; **iluso 1.** (easily) deluded, deceived; **2.** *m*, *a* f visionary, dreamer; **ilusorio** illusory, deceptive; unreal; empty.

ilustración f illustration; picture; *fig.* enlightenment, learning; **ilustrado** illustrated; *fig.* enlightened; **ilustrador 1.** illustrative; *fig.* enlightening; **2.** *m*, -a f illustrator; **ilustrar** [1a] illustrate; *fig.* enlighten, instruct; (*aclarar*) explain; (*hacer ilustre*) make *s.o.* famous; **ilustre** illustrious, famous; **ilustrísimo** most illustrious; *Vuestra* ♀a Your Grace.

imagen f *mst* image; (mental) picture; (*semejanza*) likeness; ~es *pl. rhet.* imagery; *a su* ~ in his own image; *ser la viva* ~ *de* be the living image of; **imaginación** f imagination; (*fantasía*) fancy; **imaginar** [1a] imagine, visualize; (*inventar*) think up; ~se suppose (*que* that); imagine, picture (to o.s.), fancy; *me imagino freq.* I can imagine; ¡imagínate! just fancy!; **imaginario** imaginary, fanciful; **imaginativa** f imaginativeness, imagination; common sense; **imaginativo** imaginative; **imaginería** f statuary; *rhet.* imagery.

imán *m* magnet; **iman(t)ación** f magnetization; **iman(t)ar** [1a] magnetize.

imbatible unbeatable; **imbatido** unbeaten.

imbécil 1. *p.* imbecile, feeble-minded; *cosa* silly; **2.** *m/f* imbecile, idiot; **imbecilidad** f imbecility *etc.*

imberbe beardless.

imborrable ineffaceable.

imbuir [3g] imbue, infuse (*de, en* with).

imitación f imitation; *a* ~ *de* after, in imitation of; *de* ~ imitation *attr.*; **imitador 1.** imitative; **2.** *m*, -a f imitator; follower; **imitar** [1a] imitate; mimic, *b.s.* ape; *cosa b.s.* counterfeit.

impaciencia f impatience; **impacientar** [1a] exasperate, make *s.o.* lose patience; ~se get impatient, fret (*por* at); **impaciente** impatient (*con, de, por* at); fretful.

impacto *m* impact; ⚔ hit; ~ *directo* direct hit.

impar odd (*a.* ♈).

imparcial impartial; **imparcialidad** f impartiality.

impasible impassive, unmoved.

impávido dauntless, unflinching, intrepid.

impecable impeccable, faultless.

impedido disabled, crippled; ~ *para* unfit for; **impedimento** *m* impediment (*a.* ♊), obstacle, hindrance (*a* to); disability; **impedir** [3l] stop, prevent (*inf. or que subj.* [from] *ger.*); deter; (*frustrar*) thwart; (*estorbar*) hamper; **impeditivo** preventive.

impeler [2a] propel, drive; *fig.* impel, drive (*a inf.* to *inf.*).

impenetrable impenetrable (*a. fig.*); impervious; *fig.* unfathomable.

impenitencia f impenitence; **impenitente** impenitent, unrepentant.

impensado unexpected, unforeseen; (*fortuito*) random.

imperante ruling (*a.* ♱), prevailing; **imperar** [1a] rule, reign, *fig.* be in force, prevail; **imperativo 1.** commanding; **2.** *m* imperative (mood).

imperceptible imperceptible.

imperdible *m* safety-pin.

imperdonable unpardonable, unforgivable.

imperecedero undying, imperishable; eternal.

imperfección f imperfection, flaw, fault; **imperfecto** imperfect (*a. gr.*); faulty; (*sin acabar*) unfinished.

imperial 1. imperial; **2.** *f* top, upper deck; **imperialismo** *m* imperialism; **imperialista 1.** imperialistic; **2.** *m/f* imperialist.

impericia *f* unskilfulness; *a prueba de* ~ foolproof.

imperio *m* empire; (*autoridad*) rule, sway; *fig.* pride; **imperioso** imperious, lordly; (*urgente*) peremptory; (*necesario*) imperative.

imperito inexpert, unskilled; (*torpe*) clumsy.

impermeabilizar [1f] waterproof; **impermeable 1.** waterproof; impervious, impermeable; **2.** *m* raincoat, mackintosh.

impersonal impersonal.

impertérrito unafraid, unshaken.

impertinencia *f* irrelevance; impertinence *etc.*; **impertinente 1.** irrelevant; uncalled-for; (*insolente*) impertinent; (*susceptible*) touchy; (*nimio*) fussy; **2.** ~s *m/pl.* lorgnette.

imperturbable imperturbable, unruffled; **imperturbado** unperturbed.

ímpetu *m* impetus, impulse; momentum; (*movimiento*) (on)rush; (*prisa*) haste; violence; **impetuosidad** *f* impetuosity; impetus; **impetuoso** *p.* impetuous; headstrong; *acto* hasty; violent; *torrente* rushing.

impiedad *f* impiety *etc.*; **impío** impious, ungodly; wicked; heartless. [*competencia* cut-throat.)

implacable implacable, relentless;)

implantar [1a] implant, introduce.

implicación *f* contradiction (in terms).

implicar [1g] involve; *p. mst b.s.* implicate; *inferencia* imply; **implícito** implicit, implied.

implorar [1a] implore, beg.

impolítico imprudent; tactless; (*descortés*) impolite.

imponderable imponderable; (*indecible*) unutterable.

imponente 1. imposing, impressive; stately, grand; F terrific, tremendous; **2.** *m/f* ✝ depositor, lender; **imponer** [2r] *mst* impose (*a* on; *a. typ., eccl.*); *obediencia etc.* exact (*a* from); enforce (*a* upon); *tarea* set; *carga etc.* lay, thrust (*a* upon); instruct (*en* in); impute falsely (*a* to); (*impresionar*) impress; ✝ invest, deposit; ~se get one's way, assert o.s.; prevail (*a* over); (*costumbre*) grow up; ~ de acquaint o.s. with; **imponible** taxable.

impopular unpopular; **impopularidad** *f* unpopularity.

importación *f* import(s); (*acto*) importation; *de* ~ imported; **importador** *m*, **-a** *f* importer; **importancia** *f* importance; significance; weight; magnitude; *sin* ~ unimportant, minor; *dar mucha* ~ *a* make much of; *no dar* ~ *a* make light of; *darse* ~ give o.s. airs; **importante** important; significant; weighty; (*grande*) considerable, sizeable; *lo* (*más*) ~ the main thing; **importar**[1] [1a] *v/t.* amount to, be worth; (*llevar consigo*) involve, imply; *v/i.* matter (*a* to), be of consequence; ~ *a* concern; *¡no importa!* it doesn't matter!, never mind!; *no importa* (*el*) *precio* cost no object; *¿te importa prestármelo?* do you mind lending it to me?; *¿qué importa?* what does it matter?, what of it?; **importar**[2] [1a] ✝ import (*a, en* into); **importe** *m* amount, value, cost.

importunar [1a] importune, pester, molest; **importunidad** *f* importunity, pestering; (*incomodidad*) annoyance; **importuno** importunate; inopportune; (*molesto*) troublesome, annoying.

imposibilidad *f* impossibility; inability; **imposibilitado** unable (*para inf.* to *inf.*); ⚕ disabled; (*pobre*) without means; **imposibilitar** [1a] make *s.t.* impossible, preclude; *p.* render unfit (*para* for), incapacitate; *me imposibilitó el salir* it prevented me going out; **imposible 1.** impossible; **2.** *m* the impossible; *hacer los* ~s *para inf.* do everything possible to *inf.*

imposición *f* imposition *etc.*; (*impuesto*) tax; *typ.* make-up; ✝ deposit; ~ *de manos* laying-on of hands.

impostor *m*, **-a** *f* impostor, fraud; **impostura** *f* imposture, fraud, sham; (*imputación*) aspersion, slur.

impotable undrinkable.

impotencia *f* impotence (*a.* ⚕) *etc.*; **impotente** impotent (*a.* ⚕), powerless, helpless.

impracticabilidad *f* impractica-bility; **impracticable** impracti-cable, unworkable; *camino* im-passable.

imprecación *f* imprecation, curse; **imprecar** [1g] imprecate, curse.

imprecisión *f* lack of precision, vagueness.

impredictible unpredictable.

impregnar [1a] impregnate, satu-rate; *fig.* pervade.

impremeditado unpremeditated.

imprenta *f* (*arte*) printing; (*oficina*) press, printing-house; (*letra*) print; (*lo impreso*) printed matter.

imprescindible essential, indispen-sable.

impresión *f typ.* printing; (*letra, phot.*) print; (*tirada*) edition, im-pression; (*marca*) imprint; *fig.* impression; ~ *dactilar*, ~ *digital* finger-print; **impresionable** im-pressionable, sensitive, susceptible; **impresionante** impressive, strik-ing; moving; **impresionar** [1a] impress, strike; move; *disco etc.* record; **impresionista 1.** im-pressionist(ic); **2.** *m/f* impressionist; **impreso 1.** printed; **2.** *m* printed paper (*or* book); ~s *pl.* printed matter; **impresor** *m* printer.

imprevisible unforeseeable; **im-previsión** *f* lack of foresight; thoughtlessness; **imprevisor** thoughtless; happy-go-lucky F; **imprevisto 1.** unforeseen, unex-pected; **2.** ~s *m/pl.* incidentals, unforeseen expenses.

imprimar [1a] *paint.* prime.

imprimir [3a; *p.p. impreso*] *typ.* print; (*estampar*) stamp; *fig.* stamp, imprint (*en* on).

improbabilidad *f* improbability, unlikelihood; **improbable** im-probable, unlikely. [thankless.\

ímprobo dishonest; *tarea* arduous,/

improcedencia *f* wrongness; in-admissibility; **improcedente** not right; ⚖ unfounded, inadmissible.

improductivo unproductive.

impronunciable unpronounceable.

improperio *m* insult, taunt.

impropicio inauspicious.

impropiedad *f* infelicity (of lan-guage); **impropio** improper (*a.* A); (*no apto*) inappropriate, unsuitable (*de, para* to, for); (*ajeno*) foreign (*de* to); *estilo* infelicitous.

impróvido improvident.

improvisación *f* improvisation; *b.s.* makeshift; *esp.* ♪ extemporiza-tion, impromptu; **improvisado** improvised; *b.s.* makeshift; ♪ *etc.* extempore, impromptu; **impro-visar** [1a] improvise; extemporize (*a.* ♪); **improviso** unexpected, unforeseen; *al* ~, *de* ~ unexpect-edly; *hablar etc.* extempore; ♪ impromptu; **improvisto** = *im-proviso.*

imprudencia *f* imprudence *etc.*; **imprudente** unwise, imprudent; rash, reckless; *palabras* indiscreet.

impudencia *f* impudence *etc.*; **impudente** impudent, brazen, shameless; **impudicia** *f* immodesty *etc.*; **impúdico** immodest, lewd, lecherous.

impuesto 1. *p.p.* of *imponer*; **2.** *m* tax, duty, levy (*sobre* on); ~s *pl.* taxation; *sujeto a* ~ taxable; ~ *sobre la renta* income-tax.

impugnar [1a] oppose, contest; *teoría etc.* refute.

impulsar [1a] = *impeler*; **im-pulsión** *f* impulsion; ⊕ drive, propulsion; *fig.* impulse; ~ *por reacción* jet propulsion; **impulsivo** *fig.* impulsive; **impulso** *m* impulse (*a. fig.*), drive, thrust; impetus; *fig.* urge; *a* ~s *del miedo* driven by fear.

impune unpunished; **impune-mente** with impunity; **impunidad** *f* impunity.

impuntual unpunctual; **impun-tualidad** *f* unpunctuality.

impureza *f* impurity; **impurificar** [1g] adulterate; *fig.* defile; **impuro** impure.

imputación *f* imputation; **im-putar** [1a] impute, attribute (*a* to).

inabordable unapproachable.

inacabable endless, interminable; **inacabado** unfinished.

inaccesible inaccessible.

inacción *f* inaction; drift.

inacentuado unaccented.

inaceptable unacceptable.

inactividad *f* inactivity *etc.*; **in-activo** inactive; (*perezoso*) idle, sluggish; ♰ dull.

inadaptación *f* maladjustment; **inadaptado** *m*, **a** *f* (*p.*) misfit.

inadecuado inadequate; unsuit-able, inappropriate.

inadmisible inadmissible.

inadvertencia f inadvertence; (*error*) oversight, slip; **inadvertido** p. unobservant, inattentive; *error* inadvertent; *cosa* unnoticed; *pasar*~ escape notice.

inagotable inexhaustible.

inaguantable intolerable.

inajenable, inalienable inalienable; not transferable.

inalámbrico wireless.

inalterable unalterable, unchanging; *color* fast; **inalterado** unchanged.

inamovible irremovable, fixed.

inanición f inanition, starvation; **inanidad** f inanity.

inanimado inanimate; **inánime** spiritless, lifeless.

inapeable incomprehensible; p. stubborn.

inapelable ⚖ unappealable; *fig.* inevitable.

inapercibido unperceived.

inapetencia f lack of appetite.

inaplicable inapplicable.

inapreciable invaluable, inestimable.

inapto unsuited (*para* for, to).

inarmónico unharmonious, unmusical.

inarrugable crease-resisting.

inarticulado inarticulate.

inasequible unattainable, out of reach; unobtainable.

inastillable non-splinter.

inatacable unassailable.

inaudible inaudible; **inaudito** unheard-of, unprecedented; *fig.* outrageous.

inauguración f inauguration *etc.*; **inaugural** inaugural, opening; *viaje* maiden; **inaugurar** [1a] inaugurate; *exposición etc.* open; *estatua* unveil.

inca m/f Inca; **incaico** Inca.

incalculable incalculable; *riqueza* untold.

incalificable indescribable, unspeakable.

incandescencia f incandescence, white heat, glow; **incandescente** incandescent, white-hot.

incansable tireless, unflagging.

incapacidad f incapacity; incompetence; inability (*para inf.* to *inf.*), unfitness (*para* for); **incapacitado** incapacitated; un-

fitted (*para* for); **incapacitar** [1a] incapacitate, render unfit (*para* for); disqualify (*para* for); **incapaz** incapable (*de* of); unfit; unable (*de inf.* to *inf.*); (*necio*) stupid; ⚖ incompetent.

incasable unmarriageable; (*que no quiere casarse*) opposed to marriage.

incautarse [1a]: ~ *de* ⚖ seize, attach.

incauto unwary, incautious.

incendiar [1b] set on fire, set alight; ~se catch fire; **incendiario 1.** incendiary; *palabras* inflammatory; **2.** m, a f incendiary; **incendio** m fire.

incensar [1k] *eccl.* (in)cense; *fig.* flatter; **incensario** m censer.

incentivo m incentive.

incertidumbre f uncertainty.

incesante incessant.

incesto m incest; **incestuoso** incestuous.

incidencia f incidence (*a.* ⚛); incident; **incidental** incidental; **incidente 1.** incidental; **2.** m incident.

incidir [3a] *v/t. esp.* ⚕ incise; *v/i.*: ~ *en error* fall into; impinge upon.

incienso m incense (*a. fig.*).

incierto uncertain; (*falso*) untrue; inconstant.

incineración f incineration; ~ *de cadáveres* cremation; **incinerador** m incinerator; **incinerar** [1a] incinerate; *cadáver* cremate.

incipiente incipient.

incisión f incision; **incisivo 1.** sharp, cutting; *fig.* incisive; **2.** m incisor.

inciso m *gr.* clause; comma.

incitante provoking, inviting; **incitar** [1a] incite, prompt, spur on (*a* to).

incivil uncivil, rude; **incivilidad** f incivility; **incivilizado** uncivilized.

inclasificable unclassifiable, nondescript.

inclemencia f harshness; *a la* ~ exposed to wind and weather; **inclemente** harsh, severe.

inclinación f inclination (*a. fig.*); (*declive*) slope, incline; (*oblicuidad*) slant, tilt; *de cuerpo*; nod *de cabeza*; (*reverencia*) bow; *fig.* leaning; **inclinado** sloping, leaning, slanting; *plano* inclined; **inclinar** [1a] *v/t.* incline (*a. fig.*;

a inf. to *inf.*); slope, slant, tilt; *cabeza* (*bajar*) bend, nod *asintiendo,* bow *haciendo reverencia;* p. induce, persuade (*a inf.* to *inf.*); *v/i.*: ~ *a p.* resemble; ~se lean; slope; bend; *fig.* be inclined, tend (*a* to); ~ *a p.* resemble.

ínclito illustrious, renowned.

incluir [3g] include; contain, incorporate; (*comprender*) comprise; (*insertar*) enclose; *todo incluido* all found, inclusive terms; **inclusión** *f* inclusion; **inclusive 1.** *adv.* (*a.* **inclusivamente**) inclusive(ly); **2.** *prp.* including; **inclusivo** inclusive; **incluso 1.** *adj.* enclosed; **2.** *prp.* including; (*hasta*) even.

incoar [1a] initiate; **incoativo** *gr.* inchoative, inceptive. [bad.\

incobrable irrecoverable; *deuda*\

incógnita *f* unknown quantity; **incógnito 1.** unknown; **2.** *m* incognito; *de* ~ *adv.* incognito.

incoherencia *f* incoherence; **incoherente** incoherent, disconnected.

incoloro colourless (*a. fig.*).

incólume safe, unharmed.

incombustible incombustible, fireproof.

incomible uneatable, inedible.

incomodar [1a] inconvenience, trouble, put out; ~se get annoyed; **incomodidad** *f* inconvenience; discomfort; annoyance; **incómodo 1.** inconvenient; uncomfortable; (*molesto*) tiresome, annoying; **2.** *m* = incomodidad.

incomparable incomparable.

incomparecimiento: *pleito perdido por* ~ undefended suit.

incompatible incompatible.

incompetencia *f* incompetence; **incompetente** incompetent, unqualified.

incompleto incomplete, unfinished.

incomprensible incomprehensible.

incomunicación *f* isolation; ⚖ solitary confinement; **incomunicado** cut off; ⚖ in solitary confinement, incommunicado; **incomunicar** [1g] isolate, cut off; ⚖ put *s.o.* into solitary confinement.

inconcebible inconceivable, unthinkable.

inconciliable irreconcilable.

inconcluso incomplete, unfinished: **inconcluyente** inconclusive.

incondicional unconditional; *fe* implicit; *apoyo* whole-hearted; *aserto* unqualified; *amigo, partidario etc.* staunch, stalwart.

inconexo unconnected; *fig.* incongruous; (*incoherente*) disjointed, disconnected.

inconfeso unconfessed.

inconfundible unmistakable.

incongruencia *f* incongruity; **incongruente, incongruo** incongruous.

inconmensurable immeasurable, vast; (*desproporcionado*) incommensurate.

inconmovible unshakable.

inconquistable unconquerable; *fig.* unyielding.

inconsciencia *f* unconsciousness; unawareness; thoughtlessness, recklessness; **inconsciente** unconscious, unaware (*de* of); oblivious (*de* of, to); unwitting; (*irreflexivo*) thoughtless, reckless; *lo* ~ the unconscious.

inconsecuencia *f* inconsequence, inconsistency; **inconsecuente** inconsequent(ial), inconsistent.

inconsiderado thoughtless, inconsiderate; (*precipitado*) hasty.

inconsistencia *f* inconsistency *etc.*; **inconsistente** inconsistent; uneven; (*poco firme*) unstable; *argumento etc.* weak; *tela etc.* thin, flimsy; *terreno* loose.

inconsolable inconsolable.

inconstancia *f* inconstancy *etc.*; **inconstante** inconstant, changeable; (*poco firme*) unsteady; *p.* fickle.

inconstitucional unconstitutional.

incontable countless.

incontestable unanswerable; undeniable; **incontestado** unchallenged, unquestioned.

incontinencia *f* incontinence (*a.* ⚕); **incontinente 1.** incontinent (*a.* ⚕); **2.** *adv.* = **incontinenti** instantly, forthwith.

incontrastable *dificultad* insuperable; *argumento* unanswerable; *p.* unshakable.

incontrovertible incontrovertible.

inconveniencia *f* unsuitability; inconvenience; (*dicho*) tactless remark; silly thing; **inconveniente 1.** unsuitable; inconvenient; impolite; **2.** *m* obstacle, difficulty;

(*desventaja*) drawback; objection; *poner un* ~ raise an objection; *no tengo* ~ (*en ello*) I have no objection, I don't mind.

incordiar [1b] F bother, annoy.

incorporación *f* incorporation; association; **incorporado** ⊕ built-in; **incorporar** [1a] incorporate (*a, con, en* in[to], with), embody (*a, con, en* in); mix (*con* with); make *p.* sit up; ~**se** sit up; ~ *a buque etc.* join; **incorpóreo** incorporeal, bodiless.

incorrección *f* incorrectness *etc.*; **incorrecto** wrong, incorrect; *conducta* discourteous, improper; *facciones* irregular; **incorregible** incorrigible.

incorruptible incorruptible; **incorrupto** *cuerpo* uncorrupted; *fig.* pure, chaste.

incredibilidad *f* incredibility; **incredulidad** *f* incredulity, unbelief; **incrédulo** 1. incredulous, sceptical; 2. *m, a f* unbeliever, sceptic; **increíble** incredible, unbelievable.

incremento *m* increase, addition; *tomar* ~ grow, increase.

increpar [1a] rebuke, reprimand.

incriminar [1a] accuse; incriminate; *falta* magnify.

incruento bloodless.

incrustación *f* incrustation; (*taracea*) inlay; **incrustar** [1a] incrust; inlay.

incubación *f* incubation (*a.* 🕯️); **incubadora** *f* incubator; **incubar** [1a] incubate; hatch (*a. fig.*).

íncubo *m* incubus.

incuestionable unquestionable.

inculcar [1g] instil, inculcate (*en* in).

inculpable blameless; **inculpación** *f* accusation; **inculpar** [1a] accuse (*de* of); blame (*de* for).

inculto uncultivated (*a. fig.*); *fig.* uncultured, uncouth; **incultura** *f* *fig.* lack of culture.

incumbencia *f* obligation; *no es de mi* ~ it is not my in province, it has nothing to do with me; **incumbir** [3a]: ~ *a* be incumbent upon (*inf.* to *inf.*); *le incumbe inf.* it is his business (*or* job) to *inf.*

incumplido unfulfilled; **incumplimiento** *m* non-fulfilment; default.

incunables *m/pl.* incunabula.

incurable incurable; *fig.* irremediable.

incuria *f* negligence.

incurrir [3a]: ~ *en error* fall into; *deuda, ira etc.* incur; **incursión** *f* incursion, raid.

indagación *f* investigation, inquiry; **indagar** [1h] investigate, inquire into; (*descubrir*) ascertain.

indebido undue; *b.s.* improper.

indecencia *f* indecency *etc.*; **indecente** indecent, improper; obscene; F wretched, miserable.

indecible indescribable; *b.s.* unspeakable.

indecisión *f* indecision, hesitation; **indeciso** undecided; hesitant; vague; *resultado* indecisive.

indecoroso unseemly, indecorous.

indefectible unfailing, infallible.

indefendible indefensible; **indefenso** defenceless.

indefinible indefinable; **indefinido** indefinite; vague; (*sin definir*) undefined.

indeleble indelible.

indemne undamaged; *p.* unhurt; **indemnización** *f* (*acto*) indemnification; (*pago*) indemnity; ~*es pl.* reparations; **indemnizar** [1f] indemnify, compensate (*de* for).

independencia *f* independence; self-sufficiency; **independiente** 1. independent (*de* of); *cosa a.* self-contained; *p. a.* self-sufficient; 2. *m/f* independent; **independizarse** [1f] become independent.

indescifrable undecipherable.

indescriptible indescribable.

indeseable undesirable.

indeshilachable non-fraying.

indesmallable ladder-proof.

indestructible indestructible.

indeterminado indeterminate; inconclusive; *p.* irresolute.

indiano 1. (Spanish-)American; 2. *m Spaniard returning rich from America, approx.* nabob.

indicación *f* indication, sign; (*sugerencia*) hint; (*dato*) piece of information; reading *de termómetro etc.*; ~*es pl.* instructions, directions; *por* ~ *de* at the suggestion of; **indicado** right, suitable (*para* for); obvious; (*probable*) likely; *él es el más* ~ *para hacerlo* he is the best man to do it; **indicador** *m* indicator (*a.* ⊕,

⌒m); gauge *de gasolina etc.*; (*aguja*) pointer; ∼ *de velocidades* speedometer; **indicar** [1g] indicate; suggest; (*señalar*) point out, point to; ⊕ register, record; (*termómetro etc.*) read; **indicativo** *adj. a. su. m* indicative; **índice** *m mst* index; (*aguja*) pointer, needle; hand *de reloj*; catalogue *de biblioteca*; ∼ *de compresión* compression ratio; ∼ *expurgatorio* Index; **indiciario** *prueba* circumstantial; **indicio** *m* indication, sign; (*prueba*) piece of evidence, clue (de to); (*huella*) trace; ⚖ ∼*s pl.* vehementes circumstantial evidence.

indiferencia *f* indifference *etc.*; **indiferente** indifferent (*a* to); apathetic, unconcerned (*a* about); me es ∼ it makes no difference to me.

indígena 1. indigenous (de to), native; **2.** *m/f* native.

indigencia *f* indigence, poverty; **indigente 1.** indigent, destitute; **2.** *m/f* pauper.

indigestarse [1a] (*p.*) have indigestion; (*comida*) be indigestible; *fig.* be insufferable; **indigestible** indigestible; **indigestión** *f* indigestion; **indigesto** undigested; (*incomible*) indigestible; *fig.* muddled.

indignación *f* indignation; **indignado** indignant (con, contra *p.* with; de, por at, about); **indignante** outrageous, infuriating; **indignar** [1a] anger, make *s.o.* indignant; ∼se get indignant; **indignidad** *f* unworthiness; (*una* ∼) unworthy act; (*afrenta*) indignity; **indigno** unworthy (de of); (*vil*) low.

indio *adj. a. su. m*, a *f* Indian.

indirecta *f* hint; insinuation; ∼ *del padre Cobos* broad hint; *soltar una* ∼ drop a hint; **indirecto** indirect; roundabout; oblique.

indisciplina *f* indiscipline, lack of discipline; **indisciplinado** undisciplined; lax.

indiscreción *f* indiscretion; **indiscreto** indiscreet, tactless.

indisculpable inexcusable.

indiscutible indisputable, unquestionable.

indisoluble indissoluble.

indispensable indispensable, essential.

indisponer [2r] *proyecto* spoil, upset; ⚙ upset, make unfit; ∼ con set *s.o.* against; ∼se ⚙ fall ill; ∼ con *p.* fall out with; **indisponible** unavailable; **indisposición** *f* indisposition; **indispuesto** indisposed.

indisputable indisputable.

indistinción *f* indistinctness; indiscrimination; identity; **indistinguible** indistinguishable; **indistintamente** indiscriminately, without distinction; **indistinto** indistinct; vague; *luz etc.* faint, dim; *elección etc.* indiscriminate.

individual 1. individual; peculiar; *habitación* single; **2.** ∼es *m/pl. tenis:* singles; **individualidad** *f* individuality; **individualista 1.** individualistic; **2.** *m/f* individualist; **individualizar** [1f], **individuar** [1e] individualize; **individuo** *adj. a. su. m*, a *f* individual (*a.* F); member *de sociedad*; **indivisible** indivisible; **indiviso** undivided.

indócil unmanageable, disobedient.

indocto unlearned, ignorant.

indoeuropeo *adj. a. su. m* Indo-European.

índole *f* nature; character, disposition *de p.*; class, kind *de cosa*.

indolencia *f* indolence *etc.*; **indolente** indolent, lazy; apathetic; = **indoloro** painless.

indomable indomitable; *animal* untamable; unmanageable; **indomado** untamed; **indómito** indomitable; *animal* untamed; *b.s.* unruly.

indostanés *adj. a. su. m*, -a *f* Hindustani; **indostánico 1.** Hindustani; **2.** *m* (*a.* **indostaní** *m*) Hindustani.

indubitable indubitable.

inducción *f* inducement, persuasion; *phls.*, ⚡ induction; **inducido** *m* ⚡ armature; **inducir** [3o] induce (*a.* ⚡), persuade (*a inf.* to *inf.*); *phls.* infer; ∼ *en error* lead *s.o.* into; **inductivo** inductive.

indudable undoubted; **indudablemente** undoubtedly, doubtless.

indulgencia *f* indulgence (*a. eccl.*); **indulgente** indulgent.

indultar [1a] ⚖ pardon, reprieve; exempt; **indulto** *m* ⚖ pardon, reprieve; exemption.

indumentaria *f*, **indumento** *m* clothing, dress.

industria f industry; (*destreza*) ingenuity, skill; (*oficio*) trade; ~ *pesada* heavy industry; *de* ~ on purpose; **industrial 1.** industrial; **2.** m industrialist, manufacturer; **industrialismo** m industrialism; **industrializar** [1f] industrialize; **industriarse** [1b] manage, find a way, get things fixed; **industrioso** industrious; (*hábil*) skilful, resourceful.

inédito unpublished.

ineducado uneducated; *b.s.* ill-bred.

inefable ineffable, indescribable.

ineficacia f inefficacy *etc.*; **ineficaz** ineffective, ineffectual; **inefficient**; **ineficiencia** f inefficiency; **ineficiente** inefficient.

inelástico inelastic.

inelegancia f inelegance; **inelegante** inelegant.

inelegible inelegible.

ineluctable, ineludible inescapable.

inenarrable inexpressible.

inencogible unshrinkable, non-shrink.

inepcia f stupidity; = **ineptitud** f ineptitude, incompetence; **inepto** inept, incompetent; stupid.

inequívoco unequivocal, unmistakable.

inercia f inertia *etc.*

inerme unarmed, unprotected.

inerte inert (*a. phys.*); inactive; *fig.* passive; sluggish.

inescrutable inscrutable.

inesperado unexpected, unforeseen.

inestabilidad f instability; **inestable** unstable, unsteady.

inestimable inestimable, invaluable.

inevitable inevitable, unavoidable.

inexacto inaccurate; *hecho* incorrect, untrue.

inexcusable inexcusable; essential.

inexhausto *parte etc.* unused; unspent; (*inagotable*) inexhaustible.

inexistencia f non-existence; **inexistente** non-existent; defunct.

inexorable inexorable.

inexperiencia f inexperience *etc.*; **inexperto** inexperienced, raw; inexpert, unskilled.

inexplicable inexplicable; **inexplicado** unexplained.

inexplorado unexplored.

inexpresable inexpressible; **inexpresivo** inexpressive; wooden, dull.

inexpugnable impregnable; *fig.* firm, unshakable.

inextinguible inextinguishable, unquenchable.

inextricable inextricable.

infalibilidad f infallibility; **infalible** infallible.

infamar [1a] dishonour, discredit; (*defamar*) slander; **infamatorio** defamatory; **infame 1.** infamous, odious; vile; **2.** m/f villain; **infamia** f infamy.

infancia f infancy (*a. fig.*), childhood; (*ps.*) children; **infanta** f infant; *hist.* princess; **infante** m infant; *hist.* prince; ✗ infantryman; **infantería** f infantry; ~ *de marina* marines; **infanticida** m/f infanticide (*p.*); **infanticidio** m infanticide (*act*); **infantil** (*de niños*) infant, children's; (*inocente*) childlike; *b.s.* infantile, childish.

infatigable tireless.

infausto unlucky, unfortunate.

infección f infection (*a. fig.*); **infeccioso** infectious; **infectar** [1a] = *inficionar*; **infecto** foul; *fig.* corrupt, tainted.

infecundo infertile, sterile.

infelicidad f unhappiness; misfortune; **infeliz 1.** unhappy, wretched; unfortunate; **2.** m poor devil; good-natured simpleton.

inferencia f inference.

inferior 1. lower (*a* than); *calidad, rango* inferior (*a* to); ~ *a número* under, below, less than; **2.** m subordinate, inferior; *contp.* underling; **inferioridad** f inferiority; lower position.

inferir [3i] infer, deduce (*de, por* from); (*conducir a*) lead to, bring on; *herida* inflict.

infernáculo m hopscotch.

infernal infernal (*a.* F), hellish; F *un ruido* ~ a hell of a noise.

infértil infertile.

infestación f infestation; **infestar** [1a] overrun, infest; ✗ infect.

inficionar [1a] infect, contaminate (*a. fig.*); *fig.* corrupt.

infidelidad f unfaithfulness *etc.*; **infidencia** f disloyalty, faithlessness; (*acto*) disloyal act; **infiel 1.** unfaithful, disloyal (*a, con, para*

to); *relato* inaccurate; **2.** *m/f*
unbeliever, infidel.
infiernillo *m* spirit lamp; **infierno**
m hell; *fig.* inferno, hell; *en el
quinto* ~ at the back of beyond.
infiltración *f* infiltration; **in-
filtrar** [1a] infiltrate; *fig.* inculcate;
~se filter (en in, through); percolate; *esp. fig.* infiltrate.
ínfimo lowest.
infinidad *f* infinity; *fig.* enormous
number; **infinitesimal** infinitesimal (*a.* Ⱥ); **infinitivo** *m* infinitive
(mood); **infinito 1.** infinite; *fig.*
boundless, limitless; enormous;
2. *m* infinite; Ⱥ infinity; **3.** *adv.*
infinitely, immensely.
inflación *f* inflation (*a.* ✝); swelling; *fig.* conceit; **inflacionista**
inflationary.
inflamable inflammable; **inflamación** *f* ignition, combustion; *fig.*,
𝕤 inflammation; **inflamar** [1a]
set on fire; *fig.* inflame (*a.* 𝕤),
excite; ~se catch fire, flame up;
fig. become inflamed (*a.* 𝕤; de, en
with), get excited.
inflar [1a] inflate (*a. fig.*), blow up;
~se swell.
inflexible inflexible, unyielding;
inflexión *f* inflexion.
infligir [3c] inflict (*a* on).
influencia *f* influence (*sobre* on);
influenciar [1b] influence; **influir**
[3g] have influence, carry weight
(*con* with); ~ *en,* ~ *sobre* influence,
affect; have a hand in; **influjo** *m*
influence (*sobre* on); **influyente**
influential.
información *f* (*una* a piece of)
information; 𝕏 intelligence; (*noticias*) news; 𝕥𝕥 judicial inquiry;
investigation; (*informe*) report;
testimonial *sobre p.*; 𝕥𝕥 *abrir una* ~
institute proceedings; **informador**
m, **-a** *f* informant; **informal**
irregular, incorrect; unconventional; *p.* unreliable, off-hand,
unbusiness-like; **informalidad** *f*
irregularity; unreliability *etc.*; **informar** [1a] *v/t.* inform (de of,
sobre about); (*dar forma a*) shape;
v/i. report (*acerca de* on); 𝕥𝕥 plead;
𝕥𝕥 inform (*contra* against); ~se
inquire (*de* into), find out (*de*
about), acquaint o.s. (*de* with);
informativo informative; news
attr.; *junta etc.* consultative.

informe[1] shapeless.
informe[2] *m* report, statement;
(piece of) information; 𝕥𝕥 plea; ~s
pl. information; data; references;
pedir ~s make inquiries (*a* of;
sobre about); *tomar* ~s gather information.
infortunado unfortunate, unlucky;
infortunio *m* misfortune; mishap.
infracción *f* infringement; breach
de contrato.
infra(e)scrito 1. undersigned; un-
dermentioned; **2.** *m,* **a** *f* undersigned.
infraestructura *f* substructure;
fig. underlying structure.
fraganti: *in* ~ red-handed.
infranqueable impassable; *fig.*
insurmountable.
infrarrojo infra-red.
infrecuente infrequent.
infringir [3c] infringe, contravene.
infructuoso fruitless.
ínfulas *f/pl. fig.* conceit; *darse* ~
put on airs; *tener (muchas)* ~ *de*
fancy o.s. as.
infundado unfounded, groundless.
infundio *m* F fairy-tale, fib.
infundir [3a] infuse (*a, en* into); *fig.*
instil (*a, en* into); ~ *miedo a* fill *s.o.*
with fear; **infusión** *f* infusion.
ingeniar [1b] devise, contrive,
think up; ~se manage, contrive
(*a, para inf.* to *inf.*); make shift
(*con* with); **ingeniería** *f* engineering; **ingeniero** *m* engineer (*a.* ⚓
𝕏); *v. agrónomo;* ~ *de caminos,
canales y puertos* civil engineer;
~ *forestal,* ~ *de montes* forestry
expert; ~ *de minas* mining engineer; ~ *naval* shipbuilder, naval
architect; **ingenio** *m* ingenuity,
inventiveness; talent; wit; (*p.*)
clever person; ⊕ apparatus;
~ *nuclear* nuclear device; *S.Am.*
~ (*de azúcar*) sugar-mill; **ingeniosidad** *f* ingenuity *etc.*; (*una* ~)
clever idea; **ingenioso** ingenious,
clever; resourceful; witty.
ingénito innate.
ingente huge, enormous.
ingenuidad *f* ingenuousness *etc.*;
ingenuo ingenuous, naïve; candid.
ingerir [3i] swallow.
ingle *f* groin.
inglés 1. English, British; **2.** *m* (*p.*)
Englishman, Briton; (*idioma*) Eng-
lish; F creditor; *los* ~es the English,

the British; **inglesa** f English-woman; *montar a la* ～ ride side-saddle; **inglesismo** m Anglicism.
ingobernable uncontrollable.
ingratitud f ingratitude; **ingrato** ungrateful; *tarea* thankless; dis-agreeable; *(desabrido)* harsh.
ingrávido weightless; light.
ingrediente m ingredient.
ingresar [1a] v/t. *dinero* deposit, put in; v/i. enter; ✝ come in; ～ en *sociedad* join, become a member of; **ingreso** m entry (*en* into); ad-mission (*en sociedad* to); ～s pl. income *de p.*; ✝ receipts, takings; ✝ revenue *del gobierno.*
íngrimo *S.Am.* all alone.
inhábil clumsy, unskilful; in-competent; *(inadecuado)* unfit; **in-habilidad** f clumsiness *etc.*; **in-habilitación** f disqualification; disablement; v. *nota*; **inhabilitar** [1a] disqualify (*para* from), render *s.o.* unfit (*para* for).
inhabitable uninhabitable; **in-habitado** uninhabited.
inhalador m ✎ inhaler; **inhalante** m inhalant; **inhalar** [1a] inhale.
inherente inherent (*a* in).
inhibición f inhibition; **inhibir** [3a] inhibit; ～se keep out (*de* of), stay away (*de* from).
inhospitalario inhospitable; *fig.* uninviting, bleak; **inhospitalidad** f inhospitality; **inhóspito** in-hospitable.
inhumación f burial.
inhumanidad f inhumanity; **in-humano** inhuman; *S.Am.* filthy.
inhumar [1a] bury, inter.
iniciación f initiation; beginning; **iniciado** *adj. a. su. m*, **a** f initiate; **iniciador** m pioneer; **inicial** *adj. a. su.* f initial; **iniciar** [1b] initiate (*en* into); *(comenzar)* begin; originate, pioneer, set on foot; **iniciativa** f initiative; resource, enterprise; lead(ership); ～ *privada* private enterprise; *tomar la* ～ take the initiative (*de* in).
inicuo wicked, iniquitous.
inigualado unequalled.
inimaginable unimaginable.
inimitable unimitable.
ininteligente unintelligent; **in-inteligible** unintelligible.
ininterrumpido uninterrupted; sustained, steady.

iniquidad f iniquity, wickedness; injustice.
injerencia f interference, meddling;
injerir [3i] insert, introduce; ✐ graft; *(tragar)* swallow; ～se inter-fere, meddle (*en* in); **injertar** [1a] ✖, ✐ graft (*en* on, in); **injerto** m graft; *(acto)* grafting.
injuria f insult, offence; outrage, injustice; *(daño)* injury, harm; ～s pl. freq. abuse; **injuriar** [1b] insult; revile; outrage, wrong; *(dañar)* injure, harm; **injurioso** insulting; outrageous; harmful.
injusticia f injustice *etc.*; **in-justificable** unjustifiable; **injusto** unjust, unfair; wrong(ful).
inmaculado immaculate.
inmanejable unmanageable.
inmanente immanent.
inmarcesible, inmarchitable im-perishable, undying.
inmaterial immaterial.
inmaturo unripe; *fig.* immature.
inmediaciones f/pl. neighbour-hood, environs; **inmediatamente** immediately, at once; **inmediato** immediate; *(contiguo)* adjoining, next; ～ *a* next to, close to.
inmejorable unsurpassable; per-fect; *precio* unbeatable.
inmemorable, inmemorial im-memorial.
inmensidad f immensity *etc.*; **inmenso** immense, huge, vast; **inmensurable** immeasurable.
inmerecido undeserved.
inmersión f immersion.
inmigración f immigration; **in-migrado** m, **a** f, **inmigrante** *adj. a. su. m/f* immigrant; **in-migrar** [1b] immigrate.
inminente imminent. [in).|
inmiscuirse [*inf. only*] meddle (*en*|
inmoble immovable; motionless; *fig.* unmoved.
inmoderado immoderate; ex-cessive.
inmodestia f immodesty; **in-modesto** immodest.
inmolar [1a] immolate.
inmoral immoral; **inmoralidad** f immorality.
inmortal *adj. a. su. m/f* immortal; **inmortalidad** f immortality; **in-mortalizar** [1f] immortalize.
inmovible, inmóvil immovable, immobile; *(temporalmente)* mo-

tionless, still; *fig.* steadfast; **inmovilidad** *f* immobility *etc.*; **inmovilizar** [1f] immobilize; bring to a standstill; **✝** *capital* lock up; **inmueble** *m* property; ~s *pl.* (*a.* **bienes** ~s) real estate.

inmundicia *f* filth, dirt; (*basura*) rubbish; **inmundo** filthy, dirty, foul.

inmune exempt (*de* from); **⚕** immune (*contra* to); **inmunidad** *f* exemption; immunity; **inmunizar** [1f] immunize.

inmutable immutable, changeless; **inmutarse** [1a] change countenance, lose one's self-possession; *se inmutó* his face fell.

innato innate, inborn.

innatural unnatural.

innavegable unnavigable; *barco* unseaworthy.

innecesario unnecessary.

innegable undeniable.

innoble ignoble, base.

innocuo innocuous, harmless.

innovación *f* innovation; novelty; **innovador** *m*, **-a** *f* innovator; **innovar** [1a] introduce.

innumerable innumerable, countless.

inobediente disobedient.

inobservado unobserved; **inobservancia** *f* neglect.

inocencia *f* innocence; **inocentada** *f* naïve remark *etc.*; (*plancha*) blunder; (*broma*) practical joke; **inocente** innocent (*de* of); (*tonto*) simple; **inocentón** *m*, **-a** *f* F simpleton.

inoculación *f* inoculation; **inocular** [1a] inoculate; *fig.* corrupt, contaminate.

inocuo innocuous, harmless.

inodoro 1. odourless; 2. *m* lavatory.

inofensivo inoffensive, harmless.

inoficioso *S.Am.* useless.

inolvidable unforgettable.

inoperante inoperative.

inopinadamente unexpectedly; **inopinado** unexpected.

inoportuno inopportune, untimely; inconvenient; inexpedient.

inorgánico inorganic.

inoxidable rustless, stainless.

inquebrantable unbreakable; *fig.* unshakable.

inquietador, inquietante disturbing, disquieting; **inquietar** [1a] disturb, upset, worry; (*acosar*) stir up; ~se worry, fret (*de, por* about); **inquieto** restless, unsettled; anxious, worried, uneasy (*por* about); **inquietud** *f* restlessness; anxiety, worry, disquiet.

inquilinato *m* tenancy; (*pago*) rent; (*impuesto de*) ~ rates; **inquilino** *m*, **a** *f* tenant; lessee.

inquina *f* dislike, ill-will; *tener* ~ *a* have one's knife into.

inquirir [3i] inquire into, investigate; **inquisición** *f* inquiry; ♀ Inquisition; **inquisidor** *m* inquisitor.

insaciable insatiable.

insalubre unhealthy, insalubrious; insanitary.

insanable incurable; **insania** *f* insanity; **insano** insane, mad.

insatisfactorio unsatisfactory; **insatisfecho** unsatisfied.

inscribir [3a; *p.p. inscrito*] inscribe (*a. fig.*, **✝**, **Ạ**); (*apuntar*) list; enrol, enter *en padrón etc.*; register, record; ~se enrol, register; **inscripción** *f* inscription; lettering; (*acto*) enrolment *etc.*

insecticida *adj. a. su. m* insecticide; **insectívoro** insectivorous; **insecto** *m* insect.

inseguridad *f* insecurity; **inseguro** unsafe, insecure; (*movedizo*) unsteady; (*dudoso*) uncertain.

inseminación *f* insemination.

insensatez *f* folly; **insensato** senseless, foolish; **insensibilidad** *f* insensitivity; **⚕** unconsciousness; **insensible** insensitive (*a* to); **⚕** unconscious; *miembro* numb; *fig.* unfeeling, callous.

inseparable inseparable.

inserción *f* insertion; **insertar** [1a] insert.

inservible useless, unusable.

insidia *f* snare; **insidioso** insidious.

insigne illustrious, distinguished; remarkable; **insignia** *f* badge, device; (*honorífica*) decoration; (*bandera*) flag; ~s *pl.* insignia.

insignificancia *f* insignificance; (*cosa*) trifle; **insignificante** insignificant; petty, trivial.

insinuación *f* insinuation; **insinuante** insinuating, ingratiating;

insinuar [1e] insinuate, imply, hint at; *observación* slip in; ~se en worm one's way into, creep into; ~ con ingratiate o.s. with.

insipidez f insipidness *etc.*; **insípido** insipid, tasteless; *fig.* dull, flat.

insistencia f insistence; **insistente** insistent; persistent; **insistir** [3a] insist (*en, sobre* on; *en inf.* on *ger.*; *en que* that); ~ en a. stress, emphasize; *idea etc.* press.

insobornable incorruptible.

insociable unsociable.

insolación f exposure (to the sun); ⚕ sunstroke; *horas de* ~ hours of sunshine; **insolar** [1a] expose to the sun; ~se ⚕ get sunstroke.

insolencia f insolence; **insolentarse** [1a] be(come) insolent; **insolente** insolent; (*orgulloso*) haughty; contemptuous; (*no avergonzado*) unblushing; *sonido* grating.

insólito unusual, unwonted.

insoluble insoluble.

insolvencia f insolvency, bankruptcy; **insolvente** insolvent, bankrupt.

insomne sleepless; **insomnio** m sleeplessness, insomnia.

insondable bottomless; *fig.* unfathomable, inscrutable.

insonorizado sound-proof; **insonoro** noiseless, soundless.

insoportable unbearable.

insospechado unsuspected.

insostenible untenable.

inspección f inspection; check; survey; supervision; **inspeccionar** [1a] inspect; (*comprobar*) check; (*velar*) supervise; survey; **inspector** m inspector; superintendent, supervisor.

inspiración f inspiration; **inspirar** [1a] breathe in; *fig.* inspire; ~se en be inspired by, find inspiration in.

instable = *inestable.*

instalación f (*acto, cosas*) installation; (*cosas*) fittings, equipment; ⊕ plant; **instalar** [1a] install, set up; *agua etc.* lay on; ~se settle, establish o.s.

instancia f request; (*escrito*) petition, application; (*hoja*) application form; *a* ~ *de* at the request of; *con* ~ *pedir* insistently.

instantánea f *phot.* snap(shot); **instantáneo** instantaneous.

instante m instant, moment; (*a*) *cada* ~ every moment, all the time; *al* ~ instantly; *en un* ~ in a flash; **instantemente** insistently, urgently; **instar** [1a] urge, press *a*) *inf., a que, para que* to *inf.*).

instaurar [1a] establish; restore.

instigación f instigation; *a* ~ *de* at the instigation of; **instigador** m, -a f instigator; **instigar** [1h] instigate; *p.* induce (*a inf.* to *inf.*),

instilar [1a] instil(l). [abet.]

instintivo instinctive; **instinto** m instinct; impulse, urge.

institución f institution, establishment; **instituir** [3g] institute, establish, set up; **instituto** m institute, institution; *eccl.* rule; ~ (*de segunda enseñanza*) *approx.* grammar school, high school *Am.*; **institutriz** f governess.

instrucción f instruction; (*enseñanza*) education, teaching; ✗ drill; (*conocimientos*) knowledge, learning; 🏛 proceedings; ~es *pl.* instructions, orders, directions; ~ pública (state) education; **instructivo** instructive; *película etc.* educational; **instructor** m instructor, teacher; **instructora** f instructress; **instruido** (well-)educated; **instruir** [3g] instruct (*de, en, sobre* in, about); educate; ✗ drill; 🏛 draw up; ~se learn (*de, en, sobre* about).

instrumental 1. instrumental; **2.** m instruments; **instrumentar** [1a] score; **instrumentista** m/f instrumentalist; **instrumento** m instrument (*a. fig.*); (*herramienta, p.*) tool; (*apero*) implement; 🏛 deed, legal document.

insubordinación f insubordination; unruliness; **insubordinado** insubordinate; unruly, rebellious; **insubordinar** [1a] rouse to rebellion; ~se rebel, be(come) insubordinate.

insuficiencia f insufficiency *etc.*; **insuficiente** insufficient, inadequate; *p.* incompetent.

insufrible unbearable.

insular insular.

insulina f insulin.

insulso tasteless, insipid; *fig.* dull, flat.

insultante insulting; **insultar** [1a] insult; **insulto** m insult.

insumiso rebellious.
insuperable insuperable; *calidad* unsurpassable; **insuperado** unsurpassed.
insurgente *adj. a. su. m/f* insurgent.
insurrección *f* revolt, insurrection; **insurreccionar** [1a] rouse to rebellion; **~se** rise in revolt; **insurrecto** *adj. a. su. m,* **a** *f* rebel.
insustituible irreplaceable.
intacto untouched; (*entero*) intact, whole; (*sin daño*) undamaged.
intachable irreproachable.
intangible intangible, impalpable.
integración *f* integration; **integral** *adj. a. su. f* ℟ integral; **integrante** integral; **integrar** [1a] integrate (*a.* ℟); (*componer*) make up, form; ✝ repay; **integridad** *f* wholeness, completeness; *fig.* integrity; **íntegro** whole, complete; integral; *fig.* upright.
intelectiva *f* intellect, understanding; **intelecto** *m* intellect; brain(s); **intelectual** *adj. a. su. m/f* intellectual; **intelectualidad** *f* intellectuality; (*ps.*) intelligentsia.
inteligencia *f* intelligence; mind, wits; (*comprensión*) understanding; (*trato secreto*) collusion; **inteligente** intelligent, clever; (*instruido*) skilled, trained (en in); **inteligible** intelligible.
intemperancia *f* intemperance; **intemperie** *f* inclemency (of the weather); *a la ~* in the open; **intempestivo** untimely, ill-timed.
intención *f* intention; *segunda ~* underhandedness; *con ~* deliberately; *con la ~ de inf.* intending to *inf.*; *con segunda ~* meaningfully; *b.s.* nastily; *de ~* on purpose; *llamar la ~* catch the eye; *tener la ~ de inf.* intend to *inf.*, mean to *inf.*; **intencionado:** *bien ~* well-meaning; *mal ~* ill-disposed; **intencional** intentional.
intendencia *f* administration, management; ✗ (*Cuerpo de*) ♀ approx. Service Corps; **intendente** *m* manager.
intensar(se) [1a] intensify; **intensidad** *f* intensity *etc.*; ⊕, ⚡ *etc.* strength; **intensificación** *f* intensification; **intensificar** [1g] inten-

sify; **intensivo** intensive; **intenso** *mst* intense; *impresión* vivid; *emoción* strong, powerful.
intentar [1a] attempt, try (*inf.* to *inf.*); (*tener intención*) intend, mean (*inf.* to *inf.*; con by); **intento** *m* intention; (*cosa intentada*) attempt; *de ~* on purpose; **intentona** *f* wild attempt; *pol.* putsch.
inter... inter...; **~acción** *f* interaction, interplay; **~calar** [1a] intercalate, insert; **~cambiable** interchangeable; **~cambiar** [1b] exchange; interchange; **~cambio** *m* exchange; interchange; **~ceder** [2a] · intercede, plead (con with, por for); **~ceptación** *f* interception; stoppage, hold-up; **~ceptar** [1a] intercept, cut off; (*detener*) hold up; **~cesión** *f* intercession; **~conectar** [1a] interconnect; **~confesional** interdenominational; **~continental** intercontinental; **~decir** [3p] forbid; **~dependiente** interdependent; **~dicción** *f* prohibition; **~dicto** *m* interdict.
interés *m* interest (*a.* ✝); (*egoísmo*) self-interest; **~es** *pl.* interests, affairs; *~ compuesto* compound interest; **~es** *pl. creados* vested interests; *~ predominante* controlling interest; *~ simple* simple interest; *en ~ de* in the interest of; *por (el) ~* for money; *dar (or poner) a ~* put out at interest; *poner ~ en* take an interest in; *sentir ~ por* be interested in; **interesado 1.** interested (en in); *b.s.* selfish; mercenary; having an ulterior motive; (*parcial*) biassed; **2.** *m,* **a** *f* person concerned, interested party; (*el que firma*) applicant; **interesante** interesting; **interesar** [1a] *v/t.* (*atraer*) interest (en in), be of interest to; appeal to; (*afectar*) concern, affect (*a.* ✗), involve; *v/i.* be of interest; be important; **~se** be interested, take an interest (en, por in).
inter...: **~estelar** interstellar; **~ferencia** *f* interference; *radio:* jamming; **~ferir** [3i] interfere with; *radio:* jam; **~foliar** [1b] interleave.
ínterin 1. *m* interim; *en el ~* in the interim, in the meantime; **2.** *adv.* meanwhile; **3.** *cj.* while; until;

interino 1. provisional, temporary; *p.* acting; **2.** *m*, **a** *f* stand-in; ♫, *eccl.* locum (tenens).

interior 1. interior, inner, inside; *fig.* inward, inner; *pol.* domestic, internal; *geog.* inland; **2.** *m* interior, inside; *fig.* mind, soul; ~es *pl.* insides; *deportes:* ~ *derecho* inside right; *para mi* ~ to myself; *Ministerio del* ♀ Home Office; Department of the Interior *Am.*; **interiormente** inwardly.

inter...: ~**jección** *f* interjection; ~**lineal** interlinear; ~**locutor** *m*, **-a** *f* speaker; *mi* ~ the person I was talking to; ~**ludio** *m* interlude; ~**mediario 1.** *m*, **a** *f* intermediary; mediator; **2.** *m* ✝ middleman; ~**medio 1.** intermediate, half-way; intervening; **2.** *m* interval (*a. thea.*); recess; *por* ~ *de* through, by means of; ~**mezzo** *m* intermezzo.

interminable unending, endless, interminable.

inter...: ~**mitente** intermittent (*a.* ♫); ~**nacional 1.** international; **2.** ♀ *f pol.* International; ~**nacionalismo** *m* internationalism; ~**nacionalizar** [1f] internationalize.

internado 1. *m*, **a** *f (p.)* internee; **2.** *m* boarding-school; *(estado)* boarding; *(ps.)* boarders; **internamiento** *m* internment; **internar** [1a] *v/t. pol.* intern; *v/i.*, ~**se** *en país* penetrate into; *estudio* go deeply into; **interno 1.** internal; inside; **2.** *m*, **a** *f* boarder.

inter...: ~**pelar** [1a] implore; *parl.* ask *s.o.* for explanations; *(dirigirse a)* address, speak to; ~**planetario** interplanetary; ~**polación** *f* interpolation; ~**polar** [1a] interpolate; interrupt momentarily; ~**poner** [2r] interpose, insert, place between; ~**se** intervene; ~**pretación** *f* interpretation *etc.*; ~**pretar** [1a] *mst* interpret; *(traducir a.)* translate; ♪ render, perform; *thea. papel* play, take; ~ *mal sentido* misinterpret; **intérprete** *m/f* interpreter; translator; ♪, *thea. etc.* exponent, performer.

inter...: ~**regno** *m* interregnum; ~**rogación** *f* interrogation; *(pregunta)* question; *v. punto*; ~**rogar** [1h] question, interrogate; ⚖ examine; ~**rogativo** *gr. adj. a. su. m* interrogative; ~**rogatorio** *m* questioning; *(hoja)* questionnaire; ~**rumpir** [3a] interrupt; cut short, cut off; ∲ switch off; *tráfico etc.* hold up; ~**rupción** *f* interruption; stoppage; ~**ruptor** *m* ∲ switch; ~**secarse** [1g] intersect; ~**sección** *f* intersection; ~**sticio** *m* interstice; interval, gap; *(grieta)* crack; ⊕ clearance; ~**urbano** *teleph.* trunk *attr.*; ~**valo** *m tiempo:* interval (*a.* ♪), break; *espacio:* gap; *a* ~*s* at intervals; intermittently, off and on; ~**vención** *f* intervention; participation; supervision; ✝ audit(ing); ♫ operation; ~**venir** [3s] *v/t.* supervise; ✝ audit; ♫ operate on; *teleph.* tap; *v/i.* intervene (*en* in); *(tomar parte)* take part (*en* in); be involved (*en* in); ~**ventor** *m* inspector, superintendent; ✝ auditor; ~**viú** *f* interview; ~**viuvar** [1a] interview, have an interview with.

intestado intestate.

intestinal intestinal; **intestino 1.** internal; **2.** *m* intestine, gut; ~ *ciego* caecum; ~ *delgado* small intestine; ~ *grueso* large intestine.

intimación *f* notification *etc.*; **intimar** [1a] notify, announce, intimate; order, require; *v/i.*, ~**se** become intimate (*con* with).

intimidación *f* intimidation.

intimidad *f* intimacy, familiarity; privacy; *en la* ~ in private life.

intimidar [1a] intimidate, overawe; bully; ~**se** be intimidated, get apprehensive.

íntimo intimate; *(interior)* innermost; private.

intitular [1a] entitle, call.

intocable *adj. a. su. m/f* untouchable.

intolerable intolerable, unbearable; **intolerancia** *f* intolerance *etc.*; **intolerante** intolerant (*con*, *para* of); bigoted, narrow-minded (*en* about).

intonso *libro* uncut.

intoxicar [1g] poison.

intraducible untranslatable.

intragable unpalatable (*a. fig.*).

intramuros within the city.

intranquilizar [1f] worry; **intranquilo** restless; uneasy, worried.

intranscribible unprintable.

intransferible untransferable.

intransigente intransigent; uncompromising; *esp. pol.* die-hard.

intransitable impassable; **intransitivo** intransitive.

intratable intractable; *p.* unsociable, difficult; *cosa* awkward.

intravenoso intravenous.

intrépido intrepid, undaunted; *b.s.* rash.

intriga *f* intrigue, plot (*a. lit.*), scheme; **intrigante** *m/f* intriguer, schemer; **intrigar** [1h] *v/t.* intrigue, puzzle; interest; *v/i.* intrigue, plot.

intrincado dense, impenetrable; *fig.* intricate; **intrincar** [1g] complicate.

intríngulis *m* F ulterior motive; (*dificultad*) (hidden) snag; (*misterio*) puzzle.

intrínseco intrinsic.

introducción *f* introduction; insertion; **introducir** [3o] introduce; *objeto* put in, insert; *p. a.* bring in, show in; (*ocasionar*) bring on; ~**se** get in, slip in; (*entrometerse*) meddle.

intro...: ~**misión** *f* insertion; *b.s.* interference; ~**spección** *f* introspection; ~**spectivo** introspective; ~**vertido** *adj. a. su. m, a f* introvert.

intrusión *f* intrusion; ⚖ trespass; **intruso 1.** intrusive; **2.** *m, a f* intruder, interloper; gate-crasher *en reunión etc.*; ⚖ trespasser.

intuición *f* intuition; **intuir** [3g] know by intuition; **intuitivo** intuitive.

inundación *f* flood; **inundar** [1a] flood, inundate, swamp (*de, en* with; *a. fig.*).

inusitado unusual, unwonted; (*anticuado*) obsolete.

inútil useless; *es* ~ *inf.* it is no use *ger.*, it's no good *ger.* F; **inutilidad** *f* uselessness; **inutilizar** [1f] make *s.t.* useless; disable; put out of action; (*estropear*) spoil; ⚭ cancel.

invadir [3a] invade (*a. fig.*), overrun; *fig.* encroach upon.

invalidar [1a] invalidate, nullify; **invalidez** *f* nullity *etc.*; **inválido 1.** ⚖ invalid, null (and void); *p.* disabled; **2.** *m,* ✚ *a f* invalid; **3.** *m* ✗ pensioner, disabled soldier *etc.*

invariable invariable.

invasión *f* invasion (*a.* ✗, *fig.*); encroachment (*de* on); *fig.* inroad (*de* into); **invasor 1.** invading; **2.** *m, -a f* invader.

invectiva *f* (*una* a piece of) invective; (*discurso*) tirade; **invectivar** [1a] inveigh against.

invencible invincible; *obstáculo* insuperable.

invención *f* invention; discovery; *poet.* fiction.

invendible unsalable.

inventar [1a] invent; devise; create; (*fingir*) make up; **inventariar** [1a] inventory, make an inventory of; **inventario** *m* inventory; ✚ *a.* stocktaking; **inventiva** *f* ingenuity *etc.*; **inventivo** inventive; ingenious, resourceful; **invento** *m* invention; **inventor** *m, -a f* inventor.

invernáculo *m,* **invernadero** *m* greenhouse, conservatory *de casa*; **invernal** wintry, winter *attr.*; **invernar** [1k] winter; *zo.* hibernate; **invernizo** wintry, winter *attr.*

inverosímil unlikely, improbable, implausible; **inverosimilitud** *f* unlikelihood *etc.*

inversión *f* inversion; reversal; ✚ investment; **inversionista** *m/f* investor; **inverso** inverse; reverse, contrary; *a la* ~*a* the other way round; *fig.* vice-versa.

invertebrado *adj. a. su. m* invertebrate.

invertir [3i] invert, turn upside down; reverse (*a.* ⊕); ✚ invest; *tiempo* spend, put in.

investidura *f* investiture.

investigación *f* investigation, inquiry; 🎓 research (*de* into); **investigador** *m, -a f* investigator; 🎓 research worker; **investigar** [1h] investigate, look into; 🎓 do research into.

investir [3l]: ~ *con,* ~ *de* invest *s.o.* with, confer upon *s.o.*

inveterado *p.* inveterate; *hábito* deep-seated.

invicto unconquered.

invierno *m* winter; *S.Am.* rainy season.

inviolable inviolable; **inviolado** inviolate.

invisibilidad *f* invisibility; **invisible** invisible.

invitación *f* invitation; **invitado** *m, a f* guest; **invitar** [1a] invite (*a inf.* to *inf.*); call on (*a inf.* to *inf.*); attract, entice.

invocar [1g] invoke, call on.

involuntario involuntary; *ofensa etc.* unintentional.
invulnerable invulnerable.
inyección *f* injection; **inyectado:** ~ (en sangre) walk; (en coche) drive; (a caballo etc.) ride; ᵓ be, get along, do; be at stake *en apuesta* (a. *fig.*); *va mucho de uno a otro* there is a great difference between them; *de 5 a 3 van 2 3* from 5 leaves 2; *con éste van 50* that makes 50; *eso no va para ti* that wasn't meant for you; *¿cuánto va?* what do you bet?; *van 5 duros a que no lo dices* I bet you 5 duros you don't say it; **2.** *modismos:* ¡voy! (I'm) coming!; *a eso voy* I'm coming to that; ¡vamos! let's go!, come on!; *fig.* well, after all; ¡vaya! sorpresa: well!, there!, I say!; *aviso:* now now!; ¡vaya ...! what a ...!; ¡vaya, vaya! well I declare!; ¡qué va! F nonsense!, not a bit of it!; ¿quién va? who goes there?; **3.** *dativo:* ¿cómo te va (el libro)? how are you getting on (with the book)?; ¿qué te va en ello? what does it matter to you?; *vestido:* te va muy bien it suits you; **4.** *con prp.:* ~ a *inf.* (*futuro próximo*) be going to *inf.*, be about to *inf.*; *voy a hacerlo en seguida* I am going to do it at once; *fui a verle* I went to see (F and saw) him; ~ de guía act (or go) as guide; *v. para;* ~ por (go to, go and F) fetch, go for; *carrera* go in for; *va por médico* he's going to be a doctor; ¡vaya por X! here's toX!; ~ tras *fig.* chase after; **5.** *v/aux.* mst be; ~ *ger.* be *ger.;* *van corriendo* they are running; *iba oscureciendo* it was getting dark; (ya) *voy comprendiendo* I'm beginning to understand; ~ *p.p.* be *p.p.;* *iba cansado* he was tired; *va vendido todo el género* all the goods are (already) sold; **6.** ~se go (away), leave, depart; (morir) die; (líquido) leak, ooze out; (desbordar) run over; (gastarse) wear out; (envejecer) grow old; (resbalar) slip, lose one's balance; (pared etc.) give way; ¡vete! be off with you!, go away!; ¡vámonos! let's go!

ira *f* anger, rage; *lit.* wrath; fury *de los elementos;* **iracundia** *f* irascibility; ire; **iracundo** irascible; irate.
irakí, iraquí *adj. a. su. m/f* Iraqi.
irascible irascible.
iridescencia *f* iridescence; **iridescente** iridescent; **iris** *m* rainbow; *opt.* iris; **irisado** iridescent.
irlandés 1. Irish; **2.** *m* (*p.*) Irishman; (idioma) Irish; *los* ~es the Irish; **irlandesa** *f* Irishwoman.
ironía *f* irony; **irónico** ironic(al).
irracional 1. irrational (*a.* Ⱥ); unreasoning; **2.** *m* brute.
irradiar [1b] (ir)radiate.
irrazonable unreasonable.
irreal unreal; **irrealidad** *f* unreality; **irrealizable** unrealizable, unattainable.
irrebatible irrefutable, unassailable.
irreconciliable irreconcilable; inconsistent, incompatible.
irreconocible unrecognizable.
irrecuperable irrecoverable.
irrecusable unimpeachable.
irredimible irredeemable.
irreducible irreducible.
irreemplazable irreplaceable.
irreflexivo thoughtless, unthinking; *p.* impetuous.
irrefutable irrefutable.
irregular irregular (*a. b.s.*); abnormal; **irregularidad** *f* irregularity.
irreligioso irreligious, ungodly.
irremediable irremediable.
irreparable irreparable.
irreprochable irreproachable.
irresistible irresistible.
irresoluble unsolvable; **irresoluto** irresolute, hesitant; (*sin resolver*) unresolved.
irrespetuoso disrespectful.
irresponsable irresponsible.
irreverente irreverent, disrespectful.
irrevocable irrevocable.
irrigar [1h] irrigate (*a.* ᵓ).
irrisión *f* derision, ridicule; (objeto) laughing-stock; **irrisorio** derisory, ridiculous.
irritable irritable; **irritación** *f* irritation; **irritador, irritante 1.** irritating; **2.** *m* irritant; **irritar** [1a] irritate (*a.* ᵓ), anger, exasperate; *deseos* stir up; ~se get angry (de at), be exasperated (de with).

irrompible unbreakable.
irrumpir [3a]: ~ *en* burst into, rush into; *país* invade; **irrupción** *f* irruption; invasion.
isabelino *España*: Isabelline; *Inglaterra*: Elizabethan.
isla *f* island; ⚓ block.
Islam *m* Islam; **islámico** Islamic.
islandés 1. Icelandic; **2.** *m*, -a *f* Icelander; **3.** *m* (*idioma*) Icelandic.
isleño 1. island *attr.*; **2.** *m*, a *f* islander; **isleta** *f* islet; **islote** *m* small (rocky) island.
iso... iso...; **isobara** *f* isobar; **isósceles** isosceles; **isoterma** *f* isotherm; **isótopo** *m* isotope.

israelí *adj. a. su. m/f* Israeli; **israelita** *adj. a. su. m/f* Israelite.
istmo *m* isthmus; neck.
italiano 1. *adj. a. su. m*, **a** *f* Italian; **2.** *m* (*idioma*) Italian.
ítem 1. *m* item; **2.** *adv.* item; also, moreover.
itinerario *m* itinerary, route.
izar [1f] ⚓ hoist; *bandera* run up.
izquierda *f* left hand; (*lado*) left side; *pol.* left; *a la* ~ *estar* on the left; *torcer etc.* (to the) left; **izquierdista 1.** left-wing; **2.** *m/f* left-winger, leftist; **izquierdo** left(-hand); (*zurdo*) left-handed; (*torcido*) crooked, twisted.

J

¡**ja!** ha!

jabalí m wild boar; **jabalina** f ✕, deportes: javelin.

jábega f seine, sweep-net; (barco) fishing smack.

jabón m soap; (un ~) piece of soap; ~ de olor, ~ de tocador toilet-soap; ~ en polvo soap-powder, washing powder; dar ~ a soap; F soft-soap; F dar un ~ a tell s.o. off; **jabonado** m soaping; (ropa) wash; **jabona-duras** f/pl. lather, (soap-)suds; **jabonar** [1a] soap; ropa wash; barba lather; F tell s.o. off; **jabon-cillo** m toilet-soap; ~ de sastre French chalk; **jabonera** f soap-dish; **jabonoso** soapy.

jaca f pony.

jácara f lit. comic ballad (of low life); ♪ a merry dance; estar de ~ be very merry; tener mucha ~ have a fund of stories; **jacarandoso** lively.

jacaré m S.Am. alligator.

jacarero m jolly fellow, wag.

jácena f △ girder.

jacinto m ⚘, min. hyacinth.

jaco m nag, hack.

jacobino adj. a. su. m, a f Jacobin.

jactancia f boasting; (cualidad) boastfulness; **jactancioso** boastful; **jactarse** [1a] boast (de about, of; de inf. of ger.).

jade m min. jade.

jadeante panting, gasping; **jadear** [1a] pant, puff (and blow), gasp (for breath); **jadeo** m pant(ing) etc.

jaez m (piece of) harness; fig. kind, sort; jaeces pl. trappings.

jaguar m jaguar.

jalar [1a] F pull, haul; ♣ heave; ~se S.Am. F get drunk; (irse) clear out.

jalbegar [1h] whitewash; F paint; **jalbegue** m whitewash(ing); F paint.

jalde, jaldo bright yellow.

jalea f jelly.

jalear [1a] perros urge on; bailadores encourage (by shouting and clap-ping); **jaleo** m F (jarana) spree, binge; (ruido) row, racket; (lío) row, fuss; armar un ~ kick up a

row; estar de ~ make merry.

jalón m surv. stake, pole; fig. stage; **jalonar** [1a] stake out, mark out; fig. mark.

jamás never; (not) ever; v. nunca, siempre.

jamba f jamb.

jamelgo m F sorry nag, jade.

jamón m ham; ~ en dulce boiled ham; F y un ~ con chorreras and jam on it; **jamona** f F buxom (middle-aged) woman.

jangada f stupid remark; F dirty trick; ♣ raft.

japonés 1. adj. a. su. m, -a f Japa-nese; **2.** m (idioma) Japanese.

jaque m ajedrez: check; F bully; ~ mate check-mate; ¡~ de aquí! get out of here!; dar ~ a check; dar ~ mate (a) (check-)mate; tener en ~ fig. hold a threat over; **jaquear** [1a] check; fig. harass.

jaqueca f headache; dar ~ a bore.

jaquetón m F bully.

jarabe m syrup; sweet drink; ~ de pico mere words, lip-service; F dar ~ a butter s.o. up.

jarana f F spree, binge; (pendencia) rumpus; andar de ~ = **jaranear** [1a] F roister, carouse; lark about; **jaranero** roistering, merry.

jarcia f ♣ rigging (freq. ~s pl.); (fishing-)tackle; fig. heap.

jardín m (flower) garden; ~ de la infancia kindergarten, nursery school; ~ zoológico zoo; **jardinería** f gardening; **jardinero** m, a f gardener.

jarope m syrup; F nasty drink.

jarra f pitcher, jar; de ~s, en ~s (with) arms akimbo.

jarrete m back of the knee; hock de animal.

jarro m jug, pitcher; F echar un ~ de agua a pour cold water on; **jarrón** m vase; △ urn.

jaspe m jasper; **jaspear** [1a] marble, speckle.

jato m, a f calf.

jauja f promised land, earthly para-dise; ¡esto es ~! this is the life!;

¿estamos aquí o en ~? where do you think you are?

jaula f cage (*a.* ✖); crate *de embalaje*; *mot.* lock-up garage; cell *para loco*.

jauría f pack (of hounds).

jayán m hulking great brute.

jazmín m jazmine.

jazz [dʒaz] m jazz.

jeep [dʒip] m jeep.

jefa f (woman) head; manageress; **jefatura** f leadership; (*oficina*) headquarters; ~ *de policía* police headquarters; **jefe** m chief, head, boss F; leader; (*gerente*) manager; ✖ field-officer; ~ *de cocina* chef; ~ *de estación* station-master; ~ *de estado mayor* chief of staff; ~ *de redacción* editor-in-chief; ~ *de taller* foreman; ~ *de tren* guard, conductor *Am.*; *en* ~ in chief.

jején m *S.Am.* gnat.

jengibre m ginger.

jeque m sheik(h).

jerarca m important person; F big shot; **jerarquía** f hierarchy; *fig.* (high) rank; *de* ~ high-ranking; **jerárquico** hierarchic(al).

jerez m sherry; **jerezano** *adj. a. su. m,* a f (native) of Jerez.

jerga f jargon; slang *de ladrones etc.*; (*incomprensible*) gibberish.

jergón m palliasse; F ill-fitting garment; (*p.*) lumpish fellow; **jerigonza** f = *jerga*; F silly thing.

jeringa f syringe; ~ *de engrase* grease-gun; **jeringar** [1h] syringe; inject; squirt; F plague; *~se* F get bored, get annoyed; **jeringazo** m injection; squirt; syringing.

jeringuilla f mock-orange.

jeroglífico 1. hieroglyphic; 2. m hieroglyph(ic); *fig.* puzzle.

jersé m, **jersey** m jersey, sweater, pullover; jumper *de mujer*; cardigan *con mangas*.

jesuita *adj. a. su. m* Jesuit; **jesuítico** Jesuitic(al).

jeta f *zo.* snout; F face, mug; F *fig.* nerve; F *poner* ~ pout.

jíbaro *adj. a. su. m,* a f *S.Am.* peasant, rustic.

jibia f cuttlefish.

jícara f small cup; *S.Am.* gourd.

jifero 1. F filthy; 2. m slaughterer, butcher; (*cuchillo*) knife.

jilguero m goldfinch.

jindama f *sl.* funk.

jinete m horseman, rider; ✖ cavalryman; **jinetear** [1a] *v/t. S.Am.* break in; *v/i.* ride around.

jingoísmo m jingoism; **jingoísta** 1. jingoistic; 2. m/f jingo.

jipijapa m straw hat.

jira f strip *de tela*; excursion, outing; (*merienda*) picnic; (*viaje*) tour; *en* ~ *deportes etc.*: on tour; *ir de* ~ picnic; go on an outing.

jirafa f giraffe.

jirón m rag, shred; *fig.* bit.

jiu-jitsu m ju-jitsu.

jockey ['xoki] m jockey.

jocoserio serio-comic; **jocosidad** f humour; (*chiste*) joke; **jocoso** jocular, comic, humorous.

jofaina f wash-basin.

jolgorio m F fun, merriment; (*un* ~) binge, beano; lark.

jónico △ Ionic.

¡jopo! get out!, be off!

jornada f (day's) journey, stage; (*horas*) working day; ✖ expedition; *fig.* lifetime; *thea.* † act; ✖ *a largas* ~*s* by forced marches; *al fin de la* ~ in the end; **jornal** m (day's) wage; (*trabajo*) day's work; *a* ~ by the day; **jornalero** m (day-)labourer.

joroba f hump, hunched back; *fig.* nuisance; **jorobado** 1. hunchbacked; 2. m, a f hunchback; **jorobar** [1a] F annoy, pester, give *s.o.* the hump.

jota[1] f letter *J*; *fig.* jot, iota; F *no entiendo ni* ~ I don't understand a word of it; *no saber* ~ have no idea.

jota[2] f Spanish dance.

joven 1. young; youthful *en aspecto etc.*; 2. m young man, youth; *los* ~*es* youth; young people; 3. f young woman, girl; **jovencito** m, a f, **jovenzuelo** m, a f youngster.

jovial jolly, jovial, cheerful; **jovialidad** f joviality *etc.*

joya f jewel; *fig.* (*p.*) gem; ~*s pl.* trousseau *de novia*; **joyería** f jewellery; (*tienda*) jeweller's (shop); **joyero** m jeweller; (*caja*) jewel-case.

jubilación f retirement; (*renta*) pension; **jubilado** retired; **jubilar** [1a] *v/t. p.* pension off, retire; *cosa* discard, get rid of; *v/i.* rejoice; *~se* retire; **jubileo** m jubilee; F comings and goings; **júbilo** m jubilation, joy, rejoicing; **jubiloso** jubilant.

jubón *m* jerkin, close-fitting jacket; bodice *de mujer*.

judaísmo *m* Judaism; **judería** *f* ghetto; **judía** *f* Jewess; ♀ kidney bean; ~ *blanca* haricot (bean); ~ *de España* scarlet runner; **judiada** *f* F cruel thing; ♱ extortion.

judicatura *f* judicature; (*empleo*) judgeship; **judicial** judicial.

judío 1. Jewish; *fig.* usurious; **2.** *m* Jew (*a. fig.*).

juego¹ etc. v. jugar.

juego² *m* (*acto*) play(ing); (*diversión*) game (*a. fig.*), sport; gambling *con apuestas*; *naipes*: hand; (*conjunto de cosas*) set; suite *de muebles*; kit, outfit *de herramientas*; pack *de naipes*; ⊕ movement, play; play *de agua, luz etc.*; ~s *pl.* atléticos (athletic) sports; ~ *de azar* game of chance; ~ *de bolas* ball-bearing; ~ *de bolos* ninepins; ~ *de café* coffee-set; ~ *de campanas* peal of bells; ~ *de damas* draughts; ~ *limpio* (*sucio*) fair (foul) play; ~s *pl.* malabares juggling; ~ *de manos* (conjuring-)trick; ~ *de mesa* dinner-service; ~ *de naipes* card game; ♀s *pl.* Olímpicos Olympic Games; ~ *de palabras* pun, play on words; ~ *de prendas* forfeits; ~ *de salón* parlour game; *a* ~ *con* matching; *en* ~ ⊕ in gear; *fig.* at stake; *fuera de* ~ (*p.*) offside; (*pelota*) out; *por* ~ in fun, for fun; *conocer el* ~ *a* know what *s.o.* is up to; *entrar en* ~ take a hand; have a say; *hacer* ~ (*con*) match, go (with); *poner en* ~ set in motion; co-ordinate.

juerga *f* F (*ir de* go on a) binge, spree; **juerguista** *m* F reveller.

jueves *m* Thursday; ♀ *Santo* Maundy Thursday; *no es cosa del otro* ~ it's nothing to write home about.

juez *m* judge (*a. fig.*); ~ *árbitro* arbitrator, referee; ~ *de línea* linesman; ~ (*municipal*) magistrate; ~ *de paz approx.* Justice of the Peace.

jugada *f* play; (*una* ~) move; (*golpe*) stroke, shot; (*echada*) throw; (*mala*) ~ bad turn, dirty trick; **jugador** *m*, -a *f* player; *b.s.* gambler; ~ *de manos* conjurer; **jugar** [1h *a.* 1o] *v/t.* mst play; (*arriesgar*) gamble, stake; *arma* handle; *v/i.* play (*a* at, *con* with); *b.s.* gamble; ~ *con fig.* trifle with; (*hacer juego*) go with, match; ~ *limpio* play the game; *de* ~ toy

attr.; ~se: ~ *el todo por el todo* stake one's all; **jugarreta** *f* F bad move; (*mala pasada*) dirty trick.

juglar *m* † minstrel; juggler, tumbler.

jugo *m* juice; gravy *de carne*; ♀ sap (*a. fig.*); *fig.* essence; substance; **jugoso** juicy; *fig.* pithy, substantial.

juguete *m* toy; *esp. fig.* plaything; **juguetear** [1a] play, romp; **juguetería** *f* toyshop; **juguetón** playful.

juicio *m* judgement; (*seso*) sense; opinion; (*sana razón*) sanity, reason; ⚖ verdict (*a. fig.*); ⚖ (*proceso*) trial; ~ *final* Last Judgement; *a mi* ~ in my opinion; *asentar el* ~ come to one's senses; *estar en su* (*cabal*) ~ be in one's right mind; *pedir en* ~ sue; *perder el* ~ go out of one's mind; **juicioso** judicious; wise, sensible.

julio *m* July.

jumento *m*, **a** *f* donkey (*a. fig.*).

juncia *f* sedge.

junco¹ *m* ♀ rush, reed.

junco² *m* ⚓ junk.

jungla *f* jungle.

junio *m* June.

junquera *f* rush, bulrush; **junquillo** *m* jonquil; (*junco*) reed.

junta *f* (*reunión*) meeting, assembly; session; (*ps.*) board (*a.* ♱), council, committee; (*juntura*) junction; ⊕ joint; ⊕ washer, gasket; ~ *directiva* board of management; ~ *universal* universal joint; *celebrar* ~ sit; **juntamente** together (*con* with); at the same time; **juntar** [1a] join, put together; (*acopiar*) collect, gather (together); *esp. ps.* get together; *dinero* raise; ~se join; (*ps.*) meet, gather (together); associate (*con* with); **junto 1.** *adj.* joined, together; ~s *pl.* together; **2.** *adv.* together; ~ *a* next to, near; ~ *con* together with; (*de*) *por* ~ all together; ♱ wholesale; *todo* ~ all at once.

juntura *f* junction, join(ing); joint (*a. anat.*); ⊕ seam; ⊕ coupling.

jura *f* oath; **jurado** *m* jury; (*p.*) juryman, juror; **juramentar** [1a] swear *s.o.* in; ~se take an oath; **juramento** *m* oath; *b.s.* oath, swear-word; *bajo* ~ on oath; *prestar* ~ take an (*or* the) oath (*sobre* on); *tomar* ~ *a* swear *s.o.* in; **jurar** [1a]

swear (*inf.* to *inf.*; *a. b.s.*); *v. falso*;
⁓*selas a* have it in for; **jurídico**
juridical, legal; **jurisdicción** *f*
jurisdiction; district; **jurisdiccio-**
nal *v. agua*; **jurisprudencia** *f*
jurisprudence, law; **jurista** *m/f*
jurist, lawyer.
justa *f* joust, tournament; *fig.* contest.
justamente justly, fairly; (*exacta-*
mente) just, precisely.
justar [1a] joust, tilt.
justicia *f* justice; fairness; right,
rightness; (*ps.*) police; **en** ⁓ **by**
rights; *hacer* ⁓ *a* do justice to;
justiciable actionable; **justiciero**
(strictly) just; **justificable** justi-
fiable; **justificación** *f* justification;

justificar [1g] justify (*a. typ.*);
(*probar*) substantiate; *sospechoso*
clear (*de* of), vindicate; **justipreciar**
[1b] evaluate; **justiprecio** *m*
evaluation, appraisal; **justo 1.** *adj.*
just, right, fair; (*virtuoso*) righteous;
(*legítimo*) rightful; *cantidad etc.*
exact; (*ajustado*) tight; **2.** *adv.* just;
right; (*ajustadamente*) tightly; *¡*⁓*!*
that's it!; *vivir muy* ⁓ be hard up.
juvenil young; youthful; *obra* early;
juventud *f* youth, early life; (*ps.*)
young people.
juzgado *m* court, tribunal; **juzgar**
[1h] judge (*a. fig.*); ⁂ pass sentence
upon; *fig.* consider, deem; ⁓ **de** pass
judgement upon; *a* ⁓ *por* judging by
(*or* from).

K

kermes(s)e [ker'mes] *f* charitable
fair, bazaar.
kerosén *m*, **kerosene** *m* paraffin.
kilo *m* kilo; ⁓**ciclo** *m* kilocycle; ⁓-
gramo *m* kilogramme; ⁓**metraje** *m*
approx. mileage; **kilómetro** *m* kilo-

metre; **kilovatio** *m* kilowatt; ⁓**s-**
hora *m/pl.* kilowatt-hours.
kiosco *m v. quiosco.*
knock-out [kaw] *m* knock-out
(blow).

L

la 1. *articulo*: the; **2.** *pron.* (*p.*) her; (*cosa*) it; (*Vd.*) you; **3.** *pron. relativo*: ~ de that of; ~ de Juan John's; ~ de Pérez Mrs Pérez; *v.* que.

laberíntico labyrinthine; *casa* rambling; **laberinto** *m* labyrinth, maze (*a. fig.*); *fig.* tangle.

labia *f* F glibness, fluency; *tener mucha* ~ have the gift of the gab; **labial** *adj. a. su. f* labial; **labio** *m* lip (*a. fig.*, 💀); (*reborde*) edge, rim; *fig.* tongue; ~ *leporino* harelip; *no morderse los* ~s be outspoken.

labor *f* labour, work; (*una* ~) piece of work; job; *esp.* 🌾 farm work, ploughing; *sew.* (*una* a piece of) embroidery, sewing; ~ (*de aguja*) needlework; ~es *esp.* ⚒ workings; **laborable** workable; *v.* día; **laboral** labour *attr.*; **laboratorio** *m* laboratory; **laborear** [1a] work (*a.* ⚒); 🌾 till; **laborioso** *p.* hard-working, painstaking; *trabajo* hard, laborious; **labradío** arable; **labrado 1.** worked; ⊕ wrought; *tela* patterned, emboidered; **2.** *m* cultivated field; **labrador** *m* (*dueño*) farmer; (*empleado*) farm-labourer; ploughman *que ara*; (*campesino*) peasant; **labradora** *f* peasant (woman); **labrantío** arable; **labranza** *f* farming; (*hacienda*) farm; **labrar** [1a] work, fashion; 🌾 farm, till; *madera etc.* carve; (*toscamente*) hew; *fig.* bring about; **labriego** *m*, a *f* farmhand; peasant.

laburno *m* laburnum.

laca *f* shellac (*a. goma* ~); (*barniz*) lacquer; (*color*) lake; ~ *negra* japan; ~ (*para uñas*) nail-varnish.

lacayo *m* footman.

lacear [1a] beribbon; (*atar*) tie with bows; (*coger*) snare. [age.]

lacerar [1a] lacerate, tear; *fig.* dam-

lacería *f* want, poverty; distress.

lacio 🌿 witheред; (*flojo*) limp, languid; *pelo* lank.

lacónico laconic, terse; **laconismo** *m* terseness.

lacra *f* 💀 mark; *fig.* defect, blemish; **lacrar**[1] [1a] 💀 strike; *fig.* damage.

lacrar[2] [1a] seal (with wax); **lacre** *m* sealing-wax.

lacrimógeno *v. gas*; **lacrimoso** tearful, lachrymose.

lactancia *f* lactation, nursing; **lactar** [1a] *v/t.* nurse; *v/i.* feed on milk; **lácteo** milky; **láctico** lactic; **lactosa** *f* lactose.

lacustre lake *attr.*

ladear [1a] *v/t.* tilt, tip; *colina etc.* skirt; ⚑ bank; *v/i.* lean, tilt; (*desviarse*) turn off; ~se lean, incline (*a. fig.*; *a* to, towards); *fig.* be even (*con* with); F ~ *con* break with; **ladera** *f* slope, hillside; **ladero** side *attr.*

ladino shrewd, smart, wily.

lado *m* side (*a. fig.*); ⚒ flank; ~ *débil* weak spot; ~ *a* ~ side by side; *al* ~ near, at hand; *al* ~ *de* by the side of, beside; (*casa*) next door to; *al otro* ~ *de* over, on the other side of; *de* ~ *adv.* sideways, edgeways; *de al* ~ *casa* next (door); *de un* ~ *a otro* to and fro; *por el* ~ *de* in the (general) direction of; *por todos* ~s on all sides; all round; *dejar a un* ~ pass over; *echar a un* ~ cast aside; finish; *hacer* ~ make room (*a* for); *hacerse a un* ~ stand aside, move over; *fig.* withdraw; *mirar de* (*medio*) ~ look askance at; steal a look at; *ponerse al* ~ *de* side with; *tener buenos* ~s have good connexions.

ladrar [1a] bark; **ladrido** *m* bark(ing); *fig.* scandal(-mongering).

ladrillado *m* brick floor; **ladrillo** *m* brick; (*azulejo*) tile; block *de chocolate*; ~ *refractario* fire-brick.

ladrón 1. thieving; **2.** *m*, -a *f* thief; **ladronera** *f* den of thieves; (*acto*) robbery.

lagar *m* (wine- *etc.*) press.

lagarta *f* lizard; F bitch; **lagartija** *f* small lizard; **lagarto** *m* lizard; F sly rogue; ~ *de Indias* alligator.

lago *m* lake.

lagotería *f* F wheedling.

lágrima *f* tear; *fig.* drop; ~s *pl. de cocodrilo* crocodile tears; *deshacerse en* ~s burst (*or* dissolve) into tears; *llorar a* ~ *viva* sob one's heart out; **lagrimoso** tearful; *ojos* watery; (*triste*) sad.

laguna *f* pool; *esp.* ⚓ lagoon; *fig.* gap, lacuna ⊞.

laicado *m* laity; **laical** lay; **laico** 1. lay; 2. *m* layman.

lama *f* mud, slime, ooze.

lameculos *m* F bootlicker, toady.

lamentable regrettable (*que* that), lamentable; pitiful; (*quejoso*) plaintive; **lamentación** *f* lamentation; **lamentar** [1a] be sorry, regret (*que* that); *pérdida* lament; *muerto* mourn; ~se wail, moan (*de, por* over); complain (*de, por* at); **lamento** *m* lament; moan, wail; **lamentoso** = *lamentable*.

lamer [2a] lick; (*agua etc.*) lap; **lametada** *f* lick; lap; **lamido** (*flaco*) thin; pale; (*limpio*) scrubbed; (*relamido*) dandified.

lámina *f* sheet *de vidrio, metal etc.*; *metall., phot., typ.* plate; ⊞ lamina; ~*s pl. de cobre etc.* sheet copper *etc.*; **laminado** *metal* sheet *attr.*; ⊞ laminate(d); **laminador** *m* rolling-mill; **laminar** [1a] *metal* roll; ⊞ laminate.

lamiscar [1g] F lick greedily.

lámpara *f* lamp, light; (*bombilla*) bulb; *radio:* valve, tube *Am.*; ~ *de arco* arc-lamp; ~ *de pie* standard lamp; ~ *de soldar* blow-lamp; F *atizar la* ~ fill up the glasses; **lamparilla** *f* small lamp; (*vela*) nightlight; ⚘ aspen; **lamparón** *m* ⚕ scrofula.

lampazo *m* ⚘ burdock; ⚓ swab.

lampiño hairless; *p.* clean-shaven.

lamprea *f* lamprey.

lana *f* wool; fleece; (*tela*) woollen cloth; **lanar** wool *attr.*; *ganado* ~ sheep.

lance *m* (*acto*) throw, cast *de red*; (*jugada*) stroke, move; (*cantidad pescada*) catch; (*suceso*) occurrence, incident, event; (*trance*) critical moment; (*riña*) row; ~ *de honor* duel; *de* ~ second-hand; (*barato*) cheap.

lancero *m* lancer; ~*s pl.* (*baile*) lancers; **lanceta** *f* lancet; ⚕ *abrir con* ~ lance; **lancinante** piercing.

lancha *f* launch; (*bote*) (small) boat; lighter *para carga*; ~ *automóvil*, ~ *motora* motor-launch; ~ *de desembarco* landing craft; ~ *rápida*

speedboat, motor-launch; ~ *salvavidas*, ~ *de socorro* lifeboat; **lanchón** *m* lighter, barge.

lanería *f* woollen goods; (*tienda*) wool shop; **lanero** wool *attr.*, woollen.

langosta *f* lobster; (*insecto*) locust (*a. fig.*); **langostín** *m*, **langostino** *m* prawn.

languidecer [2d] languish, pine (away); **languidez** *f* languor, lassitude; **lánguido** languid; (*débil*) weak; (*sin energía*) drooping, listless.

lanilla *f* nap; (*tela*) thin flannel; **lanoso, lanudo** woolly, fleecy.

lanza *f* spear, lance; pole *de coche*; nozzle *de manga*; ~ *en ristre* ready for action; *medir* ~*s* cross swords; **lanzadera** *f* shuttle; **lanzallamas** *m* flamethrower; **lanzamiento** *m* throw(ing) *etc.*; launch(ing) *de barco*; ⚑ drop (by parachute), jump; ~ *de pesos* putting the weight; **lanzaminas** *m* minelayer; **lanzar** [1f] throw, fling, cast, pitch; hurl *con violencia*; drop *en paracaídas*; ⚘ vomit; *barco*, ⚓ launch; *hojas etc.* put forth; ⚖ dispossess; *grito* give; *desafío* throw down; ~se throw o.s. (*a, en* into); rush (*sobre* at, on), dash; ⚑ jump; *fig.* launch out (*a* into); ~ *sobre* fly at, fall upon; **lanzatorpedos** *m* torpedo-tube.

laña *f* clamp, rivet; **lañar** [1a] clamp (together); *loza* rivet.

lapa *f* limpet.

lapicero *m* propelling pencil; pencil-holder.

lápida *f* memorial tablet, stone; ~ *mortuoria* headstone; ~ *sepulcral* gravestone; **lapidar** [1a] stone (to death); **lapidario** *adj. a. su. m* lapidary.

lápiz *m* pencil; *min.* blacklead, graphite; ~ *labial* lipstick; *a* ~ in pencil.

lapón *m*, **-a** *f* Laplander.

lapso *m* lapse; **lapsus** *m*: ~ *calami* slip of the pen; ~ *linguae* slip of the tongue.

laquear [1a] lacquer; *uñas* varnish.

lares *m/pl. fig.* home.

lard(e)ar [1a] lard, baste; **lardo** *m* lard.

largamente *contar* at length, fully; *vivir* comfortably; generously;

(*largo rato*) long, for a long time; **largar** [1h] let loose, let go; *cable* let out; *velas, bandera* unfurl; F give; **~se** F beat it, hop it; **largo 1.** long; *fig.* generous; abundant; F *p.* sharp; ⚓ loose, slack; ¡~ (*de aquí*)! clear off!; **~s años** long years, many years; *tardar ~a media hora* take a good half hour; *le costó 100 ptas ~as* it cost him all of 100 ptas; *tendido cuan ~ es etc.* full-length; *a la ~a* in the long run; *a lo ~ de* along, alongside; (*tiempo*) throughout; *de ~* in a long dress; *pasar de ~* pass by (without stopping); *ponerse de ~* put on grown-up clothes; *tirar de ~* spend lavishly; **2.** *m* length; *tener 4 metros de ~* be 4 metres long; **largor** *m* length; **larguero** *m* △ jamb; *deportes:* cross-bar; bolster *de cama;* **largueza** *f fig.* generosity; **larguirucho** lanky; **largura** *f* length.
laringe *f* larynx; **laringitis** *f* laryngitis.
larva *f* larva 🜨, grub.
las *v.* **los.**
lascivia *f* lasciviousness; lust; **lascivo** lascivious, lewd; (*juguetón*) playful.
lasitud *f* lassitude, weariness; **laso** weary; (*flojo*) limp, languid.
lástima *f* pity; (*cosa*) pitiful object; (*quejido*) complaint; ¡qué ~! what a pity (or shame)!; *dar etc. ~* be pitiful, cause pity; *es una ~* it's a shame; *es ~ que* it is a pity that; *estar hecho una ~* be a sorry sight; **lastimar** [1a] hurt, injure; offend; (*compadecer*) pity, sympathize with; **~se** hurt o.s. (*con, contra* on); *~ de* complain about; (*compadecer*) feel sorry for; **lastimero** injurious; = **lastimoso** piteous, pitiful.
lastre *m* ballast; *fig.* steadiness, good sense.
lata *f* tinplate; (*envase*) tin, can; (*tabla*) lath; F nuisance, bind; *en ~* tinned, canned; F *dar la ~* be a nuisance, annoy.
latente latent.
lateral lateral, side *attr.*
latido *m* yelp, bark; beat(ing) *etc.*
latifundio *m* large estate.
latigazo *m* (*golpe*) lash (*a. fig.*); (*chasquido*) crack (of a whip); *fig.* harsh reproof; F strong nightcap; **látigo** *m* whip.

latín *m* Latin; **~es** *pl.* Latin tags; **latinajo** *m* F dog-Latin; **~s** *pl.* Latin tags; **latinismo** *m* Latinism; **latino** *adj. a. su. m,* **a** *f* Latin; **latinoamericano** *adj. a. su. m,* **a** *f* Latin-American.
latir [3a] (*perro*) yelp, bark; (*corazón etc.*) beat, throb.
latitud *f* latitude (*a. fig.*); (*anchura*) breadth; (*extensión*) area, extent; **lato** broad, wide.
latón *m* brass.
latoso F boring, annoying, tiresome.
latrocinio *m* robbery, theft.
laucha *f S.Am.* mouse.
laúd *m* ♩ lute.
laudable laudable, praiseworthy; **laudatorio** laudatory.
laurear [1a] crown with laurel; *fig.* reward, decorate; **laurel** *m* laurel; *fig.* laurels; reward.
lava *f* lava.
lavable washable; **lavabo** *m* wash-basin; (*mesa*) wash-stand; (*cuarto*) lavatory; **lavacaras** *m/f* F toady; **lavadero** *m* laundry, wash-house; washing-place *de río;* **lavado** *m* wash(ing); laundry; *~ de cabeza* shampoo; *~ a seco* dry cleaning; **lavadora** *f* washing machine; *~ de platos* dish-washer; **lavadura** *f* washing; (*agua*) dirty water; **lavamanos** *m* wash-basin.
lavanda *f* lavender.
lavandera *f* laundress, washer-woman; *orn.* wagtail; **lavandería** *f S.Am.* laundry; **lavar** [1a] wash; *fig.* wipe out; **~se** (have a) wash; *~ las manos* wash one's hands (*a. fig.*); **lavativa** *f* enema; F annoyance, bother; **lavazas** *f/pl.* dish-water, slops; **lavoteo** *m* F cat-lick, quick wash.
laxante *adj. a. su. m* laxative; **laxar** [1a] ease, slacken; *vientre* loosen; **laxativo** laxative; **laxitud** *f* laxity, slackness; **laxo** slack; *moral* lax.
laya *f* spade; *fig.* kind, sort.
lazada *f* bow, knot; **lazar** [1f] lasso, rope; **lazo** *m* bow, knot, loop; lasso, lariat *para caballos etc.;* snare *para caza menor; fig.* link, bond; (*trampa*) trap; hairpin bend *en carretera;* *~ corredizo* slip-knot, noose; *caer en el ~* fall into the trap; *tender un ~ a* set a trap for.

le *acc.* him; (*Vd.*) you; *dat.* (to) him, (to) her, (to) it; (*a Vd.*) (to) you.
leal loyal, faithful; true; **lealtad** *f* loyalty.
lebrato *m* leveret.
lebrel *m* greyhound.
lección *f* lesson (*a. eccl., fig.*); *univ.* lecture; reading *de MS etc.*; *fig.* warning, example; ~ *práctica* object lesson; **lectivo** school *attr.*; **lector** *m*, **-a** *f* reader; *univ.* conversation assistant; lecturer; **lectura** *f* reading; *de mucha* ~ widely-read.
lecha *f* milt. (soft) roe; **lechada** *f* paste; (*cal*) whitewash; pulp *para papel*; **lechal 1.** sucking; **2.** *m* milky juice; **leche** *f* milk; ~ *desnatada* skimmed milk; ~ *de magnesia* milk of magnesia; ~ *en polvo* powdered milk; **lechecillas** *f/pl.* sweetbreads; **lechera** *f* dairymaid; (*vasija*) milk can; **lechería** *f* dairy, creamery; **lechero 1.** milk *attr.*, dairy *attr.*; **2.** *m* dairyman; (*repartidor*) milkman; **lechigada** *f* litter, brood; *fig.* gang.
lecho *m* mst bed; (*fondo*) bottom; *geol.* layer; ~ *de roca* bed-rock.
lechón *m*, **-a** *f* (sucking) pig; **lechoncillo** *m* sucking pig; **lechoso** milky.
lechuga *f* lettuce; *sew.* frill, flounce; **lechuguino** *m* young lettuce; F toff, masher.
lechuza *f* owl; ~ *común* barn-owl.
leer [2e] read; interpret; † lecture (*en*, *sobre* on); ~ *entre líneas* read between the lines.
lega *f* lay-sister.
legación *f* legation; **legado** *m* legate; ⚖ legacy, bequest.
legajo *m* file, bundle (of documents).
legal legal, lawful; *p.* trustworthy, truthful; **legalidad** *f* legality *etc.*; **legalizar** [1f] legalize; *documento* authenticate.
légamo *m* slime, mud; (*arcilla*) clay; **legamoso** slimy; clayey.
legañoso bleary.
legar [1h] ⚖ bequeath (*a. fig.*), leave; **legatario** *m*, **a** *f* legatee.
legendario legendary.
legibilidad *f* legibility; **legible** legible, readable.
legión *f* legion (*a. fig.*); ⚥ *extranjera* Foreign Legion; **legionario** *adj. a. su. m* legionary.
legislación *f* legislation; **legislador** *m*, **-a** *f* legislator; **legislar** [1a] legislate; **legislativo** legis-|lative.
legista *m* jurist. [lative.]
legitimar [1a] legitimize; legalize; ~*se* prove one's identity; **legitimidad** *f* legitimacy *etc.*; **legitimista** *adj. a. su. m/f* loyalist; **legítimo** legitimate, rightful; just; real, genuine.
lego 1. lay; *fig.* ignorant, uninformed; **2.** *m* layman; *eccl.* lay-brother; *los* ~*s* the laity.
legua *f* league; *a la* ~ far away.
legumbre *f* vegetable; **leguminoso** leguminous.
leíble legible; **leído** *p.* well-read.
lejanía *f* distance, remoteness; **lejano** distant, remote, far(-off).
lejía *f* bleach *para blanquear*; lye; F dressing-down.
lejos 1. far (off, away); ~ *de* far from (*a. fig.*; *de inf.* from *ger.*); *de* ~, *desde* ~ from afar, from a distance; *está muy* ~ it is a long way away (*or* off); *ir* ~ go far; **2.** *m* distant view; (*vislumbre*) glimpse; *paint.* background; *tener buen* ~ look well at a distance.
lelo silly, stupid.
lema *m* (*mote*) motto, device; theme; *pol. etc.* slogan.
lencería *f* draper's (shop); (*géneros*) linen, drapery; lingerie *para mujer*.
lengua *f* tongue (*a. fig.*); (*idioma*) language; ♪ clapper; *mala* ~ gossip, evil tongue; ~ *de tierra* spit (of land); ~ *madre* parent language; ~ *materna* mother tongue; *de* ~ *en* ~ from mouth to mouth; *andar en* ~*s* be the talk of the town; *buscar la* ~ *a* pick a quarrel with; *írsele a uno la* ~ talk too much; *morderse la* ~ hold one's tongue; *tirar de la* ~ *a* make *s.o.* talk; *trabársele a uno la* ~ stammer; **lenguado** *m ichth.* sole; **lenguaje** *m* (*en general*) language, (faculty of) speech; (*modo de hablar*) idiom, parlance, (mode of) speech; *lit. etc.* style, diction; **lenguaraz** *b.s.* foul-mouthed; **lenguaz** garrulous; **lengüeta** *f* tab; ♪, ⊕ tongue (*a. de zapato*); pointer *de balanza*; *anat.* epiglottis; barb *de saeta etc.*; **lengüetada** *f* lick.

lenidad f lenience, lenity; **lenitivo** adj. a. su. m lenitive.

lente mst m lens; eye-glass de miope; ~s pl. glasses; ~ de aumento magnifying glass; ~ de contacto contact lens.

lenteja f lentil.

lentejuela f spangle, sequin.

lentitud f slowness; **lento** slow.

leña f firewood, sticks; F beating; echar ~ al fuego add fuel to the flames; hartar de ~ thrash; llevar ~ al monte carry coals to Newcastle; **leñador** m woodcutter; **leño** m log; (madera) timber, wood; fig. blockhead; **leñoso** woody.

león m lion (a. ast. a. fig.); S Am. puma; ~ marino sea-lion; **leona** f lioness; **leonado** tawny; **leonera** f lion's cage, lion's den; F gambling-den; F (trastera) lumber-room.

leonés adj. a. su. m, -a f Leonese.

leopardo m leopard.

lepra f leprosy; **leproso 1.** leprous; **2.** m, a f leper.

lerdo dull, slow; clumsy al moverse.

les acc. them; (Vds.) you; dat. (to) them; (a Vds.) (to) you.

lesa majestad f lese-majesty.

lesión f wound; injury (a. fig.); **lesionado** jugador unfit; hurt; **lesionar** [1a] injure, hurt; ~se get hurt.

letal soporific; ⚕ deadly, lethal.

letanía f litany; fig. long list, rigmarole.

letárgico lethargic; **letargo** m lethargy (a. fig.).

letón adj. a. su. m, -a f Latvian.

letra f mst letter; (modo de escribir) (hand)writing; ♩ words, lyric; ♱ a. bill, draft; ~s pl. letters, learning; ~s pl. univ. Arts; bellas ~s pl. literature; primeras ~s pl. elementary education, approx. three Rs; ♱ ~ abierta letter of credit, open credit; ♱ ~ de cambio bill of (exchange), draft; ~ cursiva script; ~ gótica black-letter; ~s pl. humanas humanities; ~s pl. de molde print; ~ muerta dead letter; ~s pl. sagradas scripture; ♱ ~ a la vista sight draft; ♱ a ~ vista on sight; a(l pie de) la ~ v. pie; F poner unas (or cuatro) ~s a drop a line to.

letrado 1. learned; b.s. pedantic; **2.** m lawyer.

letrero m sign, notice; (cartel)

placard; (marbete) label; (palabras) words; ~ luminoso illuminated sign.

letrina f lavatory; fig. filthy place.

leucemia f leukemia. [rise.]

leudar [1a] leaven; ~se (pan etc.)]

leva f ⚓ weighing anchor; ✕ levy; ⊕ cam; mar de ~ swell.

levadizo v. puente.

levadura f yeast, leaven.

levantamiento m raising etc.; (sublevación) (up)rising, revolt; ~ de pesos weight-lifting; **levantar** [1a] raise, lift (up); △ erect, build; (recoger) pick up; (poner derecho) straighten; cerco, prohibición, tropa, voz raise; casa (re)move; caza flush; mesa clear; plano draw (up); sesión adjourn; testimonio bear; tienda strike; fig. (excitar) rouse, stir up; (animar) hearten, uplift; ~se rise; get up de cama; (ponerse de pie) stand up; (ponerse derecho) straighten up; (sublevarse) rise, rebel; (sobresalir) stand out; ~ con make off with.

levante m east; east wind; v. Nombres Propios; **levantino** adj. a. su. m, a f Levantine.

levantisco restless, turbulent.

levar [1a]: ~ anclas weigh anchor; ~se set sail.

leve light; fig. slight, trivial; **levedad** f lightness; fig. levity.

levita[1] f frock-coat.

levita[2] m Levite.

léxico 1. lexical; **2.** m lexicon, dictionary; vocabulary; **lexicografía** f lexicography; **lexicógrafo** m lexicographer.

ley f law; parl. act, measure; (regla) rule; fig. loyalty, devotion; (calidad) (legal standard of) fineness; ~ de Lynch mob-law; ~ marcial martial law; a ~ de on the word of; de buena ~ sterling, reliable; de mala ~ base, disreputable; dar la ~ set the tone; tener ~ a be devoted to.

leyenda f legend (a. typ.); inscription.

lezna f awl.

liar [1c] tie (up), bind; paquete do up, wrap up; cigarrillo roll; fig. embroil; F ~las beat it; (morir) kick the bucket; ~se fig. get involved (con with); F ~ a inf. start to inf.

libación f libation; ~es pl. potations.

libanés *adj. a. su. m*, **-a** *f* Lebanese.
libar [1a] suck, sip; (*probar*) taste.
libelo *m* lampoon, libel (*contra* on); ⚖️ petition.
libélula *f* dragonfly.
liberación *f* liberation, release; **liberado** ✝ paid up; **liberal** 1. liberal; generous; 2. *m/f* liberal; **liberalidad** *f* liberality; **liberalismo** *m* liberalism.
libertad *f* liberty, freedom; (*excesiva*) licence; familiarity *en el trato*; ~ *de comercio* free trade; ~ *de cultos* freedom of worship; ~ *de palabra* freedom of speech; *en* ~ at liberty, free; *poner en* ~ set free; **libertador** *m*, **-a** *f* liberator; **libertar** [1a] set free, release, liberate (*de* from); (*eximir*) exempt; (*preservar*) save (*de* from); **libertinaje** *m* profligacy, licentiousness; **libertino** 1. profligate, rakish; (*incrédulo*) free-thinking; 2. *m* libertine, rake; freethinker.
libidinoso lustful, libidinous.
libio *adj. a. su. m*, **a** *f* Libyan.
libra *f* pound; ~ *esterlina* pound sterling.
libraco *m* worthless book.
librado *m*, **a** *f* ✝ drawee; **librador** *m*, **-a** *f* ✝ drawer; **libramiento** *m* delivery, rescue; = **libranza** *f* ✝ draft, bill of exchange; *S.Am.* ~ *postal* money-order; **librar** [1a] save, free, deliver (*de* from); ⚖️ exempt (*de* from); (*confianza*) place; *sentencia* pass; *batalla* join; (*expedir*) issue; ✝ draw; *~se* de get out of, escape; (*deshacerse de*) get rid of; F *de buena nos hemos librado* that was a close shave; **libre** *mst* free (*de* from); (*atrevido*) free, outspoken; *b.s.* loose; *aire* open.
librea *f* livery.
librepensador *m*, **-a** *f* free-thinker; **librepensamiento** *m* free-thinking.
librería *f* (*tienda*) bookshop; ✝ bookselling, book-trade; (*biblioteca*) library; (*armario*) book-case; ~ *de viejo* second-hand bookshop; **librero** *m* bookseller; **libresco** bookish; **libreta** *f* notebook; ✝ account-book; ~ *de banco* pass-book, bank-book; **libreto** *m* libretto; **libro** *m* book; ~ *de actas* minute-book; ~ *de apuntes* notebook; ~ *de caja* cash-book; ~ *de cocina* cookery book; ~

de cuentas account-book; ~ *diario* journal; ~ *de lectura* reader; ~ *mayor* ledger; ~ *parroquial* parish register; ~ *de pedidos* order-book; ~ *de texto* textbook; ~ *de vuelo(s)* log-book; *ahorcar los* ~*s* give up studying; *hacer* ~ *nuevo* turn over a new leaf; **librote** *m* F tome.
licencia *f* *mst* licence; permission; ⚔️ *etc.* leave; *univ.* degree; ⚔️ ~ *absoluta* discharge; ~ *de armas* gun-licence; ~ *de caza* game-licence; *de* ~ on leave; **licenciado** *m*, **a** *f* licentiate, *approx.* bachelor; *S.Am.* lawyer; **licenciar** [1b] license, give a permit to; ⚔️ discharge; *~se univ.* graduate; **licenciatura** *f* degree; (*acto*) graduation; (*estudios*) degree course; **licencioso** licentious.
liceo *m* lyceum.
licitar [1a] bid for; *S.Am.* sell by auction; **lícito** lawful, legal; just; permissible.
licor *m* liquor, spirits; (*dulce*) liqueur; (*en general*) liquid; *~es pl.* espiritosos hard liquor; **licuar** [1d] liquefy; *metal* liquate; **licuefacción** *f* liquefaction.   [fair fight.│
lid *f* fight, contest; *en buena* ~ in a│
líder *m* leader; **liderato** *m* leadership; *deportes:* lead.
lidia *f* *toros:* bullfight(ing); *de* ~ *toro* fighting; **lidiador** *m*, **-a** *f* fighter; *toros:* bullfighter; **lidiar** [1b] *v/t.* fight; *v/i.* fight (*con, contra* against, *por* for); *fig.* contend, struggle (*con* with).
liebre *f* hare; *fig.* coward; *levantar la* ~ blow the gaff.
liendre *f* nit.
lienzo *m* (*un a piece of*) linen; (*pañuelo*) handkerchief; *paint.* canvas; 🏛️ wall.
liga *f* suspender, garter; (*faja*) band; *pol., deportes:* league; *metall.* alloy; (*mezcla*) mixture; ⚘ mistletoe; *orn.* bird-lime; **ligado** *m* ♩ slur, tie; *typ.* ligature; **ligatura** *f* tie, bond; ♪, ♫ ligature; **ligamento** *m* ligament; **ligar** [1h] tie, bind (*a. fig.*); *metall.* alloy; (*unir*) join; ♫ ligature; *~se* band together; **ligazón** *f* bond, union.
ligeramente lightly; *conocer etc.* slightly; **ligereza** *f* lightness *etc.*; (*dicho etc.*) indiscretion; **ligero** light; rapid, swift, agile; *té* weak; (*superficial*) slight; *carácter etc.*

fickle; (*poco serio*) flippant; v. casco; ~ *de ropa* scantily clad; *a la* ~*a* perfunctorily, quickly; without fuss; *de* ~ rashly, thoughtlessly; *juzgar a la* ~*a* jump to conclusions.

lignito *m* lignite.

ligustro *m* privet.

lija *f* ichth. dogfish; ⊕ (*a. papel de* ~) sandpaper; **lijar** [1a] sandpaper.

lila 1. *f* ♀ lilac; **2.** *m* F boob, ninny; **lilailas** *f/pl.* F cunning, tricks.

lima[1] *f* ♀ lime; *jugo de* ~ lime-juice.

lima[2] *f* ⊕ file; *fig.* polish, finish; ~ *para las uñas* nail-file; **limadura** *f* filing; ~*s pl.* filings; **limar** [1a] file; *fig.* polish; (*suavizar*) smooth (over); (*cercenar*) cut down.

limazo *m* sliminess.

limbo *m* limbo; F *estar en el* ~ be bewildered, be distracted.

limeño *adj. a. su. m*, **a** *f* (native) of Lima.

limero *m* ♀ lime (tree).

limitación *f* limitation; **limitado** limited (*a.* †); *p.* slow-witted; **limitar** [1a] *v/t.* limit (*a inf.* to *ger.*); restrict; cut down; *v/i.*: ~ *con* border on, be bounded by; **límite** *m* limit; *geog.* boundary, border; (*fin*) end; **limítrofe** bordering.

limo *m* slime, mud.

limón *m* lemon; **limonada** *f* lemon-ade; ~ (*natural*) lemon-squash; **limonado** lemon(-coloured); **limonero** *m* ♀ lemon (tree).

limosna *f* alms, charity; **limosnero 1.** charitable; **2.** *m* almoner; *S.Am.* beggar.

limoso slimy, muddy.

limpia 1. *f* cleaning; **2.** *m* F bootblack; ~**barros** *m* scraper; ~**botas** *m* bootblack; ~**chimeneas** *m* chimney-sweep; ~**dientes** *m* toothpick; **limpiadura** *f* cleaning; ~*s pl.* scourings, dirt; **limpiaparabrisas** *m* windscreen-wiper; **limpiar** [1b] clean; cleanse (*a. fig.*); wipe *con trapo*; *zapatos* polish, shine; F clean out *en el juego*; *sl.* swipe; ~ *en seco* dry-clean; **límpido** limpid; **limpieza** *f* (*acto*) cleaning etc.; (*calidad*) cleanness, (*a. hábito*) cleanliness; (*moral*) purity; (*destreza*) skill; fair play *en juego*; integrity, honesty; ~ *de sangre* purity of blood; ~ *en seco* dry-cleaning; *hacer la* ~ clean; **limpio** clean (*a. fig.*); pure; (*orde-*

nado) neat, tidy; *juego* fair (*a. adv.*); ✝ clear, net; ~ *de* free from; *en* ~ *copia* fair; *poner en* ~ make a fair copy of; F *estar* ~ not know a thing; F *quedar(se)* ~ be cleaned out (of money); *sacar en* ~ understand, deduce; *no he podido sacar nada en* ~ *de ello* I couldn't make anything of it; **limpión** *m* wipe, (quick) clean; (*p.*) cleaner.

limusina *f* limousine.

linaje *m* lineage, parentage, family; *fig.* class, sort; ~*s pl.* (local) nobility; ~ *humano* mankind; **linajudo** highborn, blue-blooded F.

linaza *f* linseed.

lince *m* lynx; *fig.* sharp-eyed (*or* shrewd) person.

linchar [1a] lynch.

lindante adjoining, bordering; **lindar** [1a] adjoin (*con acc.*), border (*con* on); **linde** *m a. f* boundary; **lindero 1.** adjoining; **2.** *m* edge, border.

lindeza *f* prettiness etc.; (*dicho*) witticism; ~*s pl. iro.* insults; **lindo 1.** pretty, lovely, fine (*a. iro.*); F *de lo* ~ jolly well, good and proper; **2.** *m* fop.

línea *f* line; figure *de p.*; (*contorno*) lines; (*linaje*) line; (*vía*) route; (*clase*) kind; ✗ ~*s pl.* lines; ~ *aérea* overhead cable; 🛪 airline; ~ *de base* surv. base-line; ~ *delantera* forward line; ~ *derivada* teleph. extension; ~ *de flotación* waterline; ~ *de* (*flotación con*) *carga* load-line; ~ *lateral deportes:* touch-line, side-line; ~ *de montaje* assembly line; ~ *de saque* base-line; ✗ *de* ~ regular; *en* ~ in a row, in (a) line; *en su* ~ of its kind; *en toda la* ~ all along the line; *leer entre* ~*s* read between the lines; F *poner unas* ~*s a* drop a line to; **lineal** linear; *dibujo* line attr.; **linear** [1a] line, draw lines on; (*bosquejar*) sketch, outline.

linfa *f* lymph; **linfático** lymphatic.

lingote *m* ingot; *typ.* slug.

lingüística *f* linguistics; **lingüístico** linguistic.

linimento *m* liniment.

lino *m* ♀ flax; (*tejido*) linen.

linóleo *m* linoleum.

linotipia *f* linotype.

linterna *f* lantern (*a.* 🔺), lamp; ⚡ spotlight; ~ *eléctrica* torch, flashlight; ~ *mágica* magic lantern.

lío *m* bundle, parcel, package; ⚓ truss; F (*confusión*) mess, mix-up; F (*apuro*) jam; F (*jaleo*) row, rumpus; F (*amorío*) affair; F *armar un ~* cause trouble; make a fuss, kick up a row; F *hacerse un ~*, F *meterse en un ~* get into a jam.

liquen *m* lichen.

liquidación *f* liquefaction; † liquidation (*a. fig.*), winding-up; † settlement *de cuenta*; (*venta*) (clearance) sale; **liquidador** *m*, **-a** *f* liquidator; **liquidar** [1a] liquefy; †, *pol.*, *fig.* liquidate; † *negocio* wind up; † *cuenta* settle; † *deuda* clear, settle; † *existencias* sell off; **líquido 1.** liquid (*a. gr.*); † net; **2.** *m* liquid, fluid; † net profit; *~ imponible* net taxable income.

lira *f* lyre (*a. fig.*); **lírica** *f* lyrical poetry; **lírico** lyric(al); *thea.* musical.

lirio *m* iris; lily; *~ de los valles* lily of the valley.

lirismo *m* lyricism; *b.s.* effusiveness; sentimentality.

lirón *m* dormouse; *dormir como un ~* sleep like a log (*or* top).

lirondo: *v.* mondo.

lisiado 1. injured; (*tullido*) lame, crippled; **2.** *m*, **a** *f* cripple; **3.** *m*: *~ de guerra* wounded ex-serviceman; **lisiar** [1b] injure (permanently); cripple, maim.

liso smooth, even; *pelo* straight; *fig.* plain; *~ y llano* simple; *400 metros ~s* 400 metres flat.

lisonja *f* flattery; **lisonjear** [1a] flatter; (*agradar*) please, delight; **lisonjero 1.** flattering; pleasing; **2.** *m*, **a** *f* flatterer.

lista *f* list; catalogue; ✗roll(-call); (*tira*) strip; slip *de papel*; stripe *de color*; *~ de correos* poste restante; *~ electoral* electoral roll; *~ (de platos)* menu; *~ de precios* price list; *~ (de tandas etc.)* roster, rota; *pasar ~* call the roll; **listado** striped.

listo ready (*para* for); (*avisado*) clever, smart, sharp; *v.* pasarse.

listón *m* ribbon; ⚖ lath.

lisura *f* smoothness *etc.*; *fig.* naivety.

litera *f* litter; ⚓, 🚃 berth.

literal literal; **literario** literary; **literata** *f* literary lady; *contp.* bluestocking; **literato** *m* man of letters; **literatura** *f* literature.

litigación *f* litigation; **litigante** *adj.*

a. su. m/f litigant; **litigar** [1h] go to law; *fig.* dispute, argue; **litigio** *m* lawsuit, litigation; *fig.* dispute; **litigioso** litigious.

litisexpensas *f/pl.* 🏛 costs.

litografía *f* lithography; (*estampa*) lithograph; **litografiar** [1b] lithograph.

litoral *adj. a. su. m* seaboard, litoral.

litro *m* litre.

lituano *adj. a. su. m*, **a** *f* Lithuanian.

liturgia *f* liturgy; **litúrgico** liturgical.

liviandad *f* fickleness *etc.*; **liviano 1.** *fig.* fickle; frivolous; (*lascivo*) wanton; **2.** *~s m/pl.* lights.

lívido livid, (black and) blue.

living ['liβin] *m* living-room.

liza *f hist.* lists.

lo 1. the, that which is *etc.*; *~ bueno* the good, the good thing, goodness; *~ ... que* how; *no sabe ~ grande que es* he doesn't know how big it is; *~ mío* what is mine; *~ ocurrido* what has happened; *no ~ hay* there isn't any; *a veces no se traduce: ~ sé* I know; *v.* que; **2.** *pron.* (*p.*) him; (*cosa*) it.

loa *f* praise; † *thea.* prologue; short play; **loable** praiseworthy, commendable; **loar** [1a] praise.

lobanillo *m* wen.

lobato *m*, **lobezno** *m* wolf-cub; **lobo** *m* wolf; *~ de mar* sea-dog, old salt; *~ marino* seal; *gritar ¡el ~!* cry wolf; F *pillar un ~* get drunk.

lóbrego murky, gloomy; **lobreguez** *f* murk, gloom(iness).

lóbulo *m* lobe.

local 1. local; **2.** *m* premises, rooms; (*sitio*) site, scene, place; **localidad** *f* locality; *thea.* seat, ticket; **localizar** [1f] locate, place; (*limitar*) localize.

loción *f* lotion; (*acto*) wash; *~ capilar*, *~ para el cabello* hair-restorer.

loco 1. mad; (*disparatado*) wild; ⊕ loose; *más ~ que una cabra* mad as a hatter; *~ de atar* raving mad; *~ por* mad about (*or* on); *volver ~* drive *s.o.* mad; *volverse ~* go mad; *es para volverse ~* it's maddening; *estar para volverse ~* be at one's wit's end; **2.** *m*, **a** *f* madman *etc.*, lunatic.

locomoción *f* locomotion; **locomotora** *f* locomotive, (railway) engine; *~ de maniobras* shunting

engine; **locomóvil** *m* traction engine.
locro *m S.Am.* stew.
locuacidad *f* loquacity *etc.*; **locuaz** loquacious, talkative, voluble; **locución** *f* expression, (turn of) phrase.
locuelo *m*, **a** *f* madcap; **locura** *f* madness, lunacy; (*acto*) crazy thing; ~s *pl.* folly.
locutor *m*, **-a** *f* radio: announcer, commentator; **locutorio** *m eccl.* parlour; telephone box.
locha *f* loach.
lodazal *m* muddy place, quagmire; **lodo** *m* mud, mire; **lodoso** muddy.
logaritmo *m* logarithm.
lógica *f* logic; **lógico 1.** logical; es ~ (*que*) it is natural (that), it stands to reason (that); **2.** *m* logician; **logística** *f* logistics; **logístico** logistic.
lograr [1a] get, obtain; attain, achieve; ~ *inf.* succeed in *ger.*, manage to *inf.*; ~ *que una p. haga* get s.o. to do; **logrero** *m* moneylender, usurer; *S.Am.* sponger; **logro** *m* achievement *etc.*; ✝ profit; *b.s.* usury; *a* ~ at (a high rate of) interest.
logroñés *adj. a. su. m*, **-a** *f* (native) of Logrono.
loma *f* hillock, low ridge.
lombriz *f* (earth)worm; ~ *solitaria* tape-worm.
lomo *m anat.* back; (*carne*) loin; ⚁ balk, ridge; shoulder *de colina*; spine *de libro*; ~s *pl.* ribs.
lona *f* canvas, sail-cloth.
lonche *m S.Am.* lunch.
londinense 1. London *attr.*; **2.** *m/f* Londoner.
longaniza *f* long pork sausage.
longevidad *f* longevity; **longevo** aged.
longitud *f* length; *geog.* longitude; ~ *de onda* wave-length; **longitudinal** longitudinal; **longitudinalmente** lengthwise.
lonja[1] *f* slice; rasher *de tocino etc.*
lonja[2] *f* ✝ exchange, market; (*tienda*) grocer's (shop).
lontananza *f paint.* background; *en* ~ far away.
loor *m* praise.
loquear [1a] play the fool; *fig.* make merry.
loro *m* parrot.

los, las 1. *artículo:* the; **2.** *pron.* them; **3.** *pron. relativo:* ~ *de* those of; ~ *de luan* John's; ~ *de casa* those at home; *v. que.*
losa *f* stone slab, flag-stone; ~ (*sepulcral*) tombstone; (*trampa*) trap.
losange *m* diamond (shape); ⟡, *heráldica:* lozenge.
lote *m* portion, share; ✝ lot; **lotería** *f* lottery; *caerle a uno la* ~ win a prize in the lottery; F strike lucky; **lotero** *m*, **a** *f* lottery-ticket seller.
loto *m* lotus.
loza *f* crockery; ~ *fina* china(ware).
lozanear [1a] ⚘ flourish; (*p.*) be full of life; **lozanía** *f* luxuriance; vigour, liveliness; (*orgullo*) pride; **lozano** ⚘ lush, luxuriant, rank; *p., animal* vigorous, lusty; (*orgulloso*) proud.
lubricidad *f fig.* lubricity; **lúbrico** slippery; *fig.* lewd.
lubri(fi)cación *f* lubrication; **lubri(fi)cador 1.** lubricating; **2.** *m* lubricator; **lubri(fi)cante** *adj. a. su. m* lubricant; **lubri(fi)car** [1g] lubri- \
lucera *f* skylight.   [cate, oil. ⌡
lucerna *f* chandelier.
lucero *m* bright star, *esp.* Venus; ~ *del alba* morning star.
lucidez *f* lucidity; **lúcido** lucid, clear.
lucido splendid, brilliant; elegant; gallant; *quedar(se)* ~ *iro.* make a mess of things.
luciente bright, shining.
luciérnaga *f* glow-worm.
lucimiento *m* brilliance; show; dash; (*éxito*) success.
lucio[1] *m ichth.* pike.
lucio[2] bright, shining.
lución *m* slowworm.
lucir [3f] *v/t.* show off, display, sport; *v/i.* shine (*a. fig.*); (*joyas etc.*) glitter, sparkle; cut a dash *con vestido etc.*; ~*se* dress up; *fig.* shine; *iro.* make a fool of o.s.
lucrativo lucrative, profitable; **lucro** *m* profit.
luctuoso mournful, sad.
lucubración *f* lucubration.
lucha *f* fight, struggle (*por* for); conflict; *fig.* dispute; *deportes:* ~ (*libre*) wrestling; ~ *de clases* class-struggle; **luchador** *m*, **-a** *f* fighter; wrestler; **luchar** [1a] fight, struggle (*por* for; *por inf.* to *inf.*); *deportes:* wrestle (*con* with; *a. fig.*).

ludibrio *m* derision, mockery.
luego immediately; (*después*) then, next; (*dentro de poco*) presently, later (on); ~ *que* as soon as; *¿y* ~? what next?; *desde* ~ of course, naturally; *hasta* ~ see you later.
lugar *m* place, spot; position; (*espacio*) room; (*pueblo*) village; *fig.* reason (*para* for), cause; opportunity; ~ *común* platitude, commonplace; *en* ~ *de* instead of; *en primer* ~ in the first place, firstly; *for one thing*; *en su* ~ in his place; *fuera de* ~ out of place; *dar* ~ *a* give rise to; *dejar* ~ *a* permit of; *hacer* ~ *para* make way (*or* room) for; *ponerse en su* ~ *fig.* stand on one's dignity; *tener* ~ take place; **lugareño 1.** village *attr.*; **2.** *m*, **a** *f* villager; **lugar-teniente** *m* deputy.
lugre *m* lugger.
lúgubre mournful, dismal.
lujo *m* luxury; *fig.* profusion, abundance; *de* ~ *de luxe*, luxury *attr.*; **lujoso** luxurious; ostentatious; profuse, lavish; **lujuria** *f* lust, lechery; **lujuriar** [1b] lust; **lujurioso** lustful, lewd.
lumbago *m* lumbago.
lumbre *f* fire; (*luz, para cigarrillo*, 🜂) light; brilliance, splendour; 🜂 skylight; **lumbrera** *f* luminary (*a. fig.*); 🜂 skylight; ⊕ vent; **luminarias** *f/pl.* illuminations; **luminoso** luminous, bright; *idea* brilliant.
luna *f* moon; (*cristal*) plate-glass;

(*espejo*) mirror; (*lente*) lens; ~ *llena* full moon; *media* ~ half-moon; ~ *de miel* honeymoon; ~ *nueva* new moon; *a la* ~ *de Valencia* disappointed, in the lurch; **lunar 1.** lunar; **2.** *m* spot, mole; (*defecto*) flaw, blemish; ~ *postizo* beauty spot; **lunático** lunatic.
lunes *m* Monday.
luneta *f* lens; *thea.* stall.
lunfardo *m* *S.Am.* thieves' slang.
lupa *f* magnifying glass.
lupanar *m* brothel.
lúpulo *m* ♀ hop.
lusitano *adj. a. su. m*, **a** *f* Portuguese.
lustrar [1a] shine, polish; **lustre** *m* polish, shine, gloss; *esp. fig.* lustre; ~ *para metales* metal polish; *dar* ~ *a* polish; **lustroso** glossy, bright.
luterano *adj. a. su. m*, **a** *f* Lutheran.
luto *m* mourning; *medio* ~ half-mourning; ~ *riguroso* deep mourning; *estar de* ~ be in mourning (*por* for).
luz *f* light (*a.* 🜂, *fig.*); *luces pl. fig.* enlightenment; intelligence; ~ *de costado*, ~ *de situación* side-light; *luces pl. de estacionamiento* parking lights; *luces pl. de tráfico* traffic lights; *a la* ~ *de* in the light of; *a todas luces* anyway; everywhere; *entre dos luces* at twilight; F mellow; *dar a* ~ give birth (*v/t.* to); *fig.* publish; *mot. poner a media* ~ dim; *sacar a* ~ bring to light; *salir a* ~ come to light; (*libro*) appear.

Ll

llaga *f* ulcer, sore (*a. fig.*); (*herida*) wound; affliction; **llagar** [1h] wound, injure.
llama[1] *f* flame, blaze; *fig.* passion.
llama[2] *f zo.* llama.
llamada *f* call (*a.* ⚔, *teleph.*); ring (*or* knock) at the door; (*ademán*) signal, gesture; *typ.* reference (mark); **llamado** so-called; **llamamiento** *m* call; **llamar** [1a] *v/t.* call (*a. fig. a. teleph.*); (*convocar*) call, summon; (*invocar*) call upon (*a inf.* to inf.); beckon *con ademán*; (*atraer*) draw, attract; *v/i.* call;

knock, ring *a puerta*; ~*se* be called; *¿cómo te llamas?* what is your name?; *¡eso sí que se llama hablar!* now you're talking!, that's more like it!
llamarada *f* flare-up, sudden blaze; flush *de cara*; *fig.* outburst, flash.
llamativo gaudy, flashy, showy.
llamear [1a] blaze, flare.
llana *f* 🜂 trowel; = **llanada** *f* plain, level ground; **llanero** *m*, **a** *f* plain-dweller; **llaneza** *f* plainness, simplicity; modesty; (*familiarity*) informality; **llano 1.** level, smooth,

even; (*sin adorno*) plain, simple; (*claro*) clear, plain; (*sin dificultad*) straightforward; *gr.* paroxytone; *a la ~a* simply; *de ~* openly, clearly; **2.** *m* plain, level ground.

llanta *f* rim (of wheel); (*neumático*) tyre; *~ de oruga* track.

llantén *m* plantain.

llanto *m* weeping, crying; *fig.* lamentation.

llanura *f* flatness *etc.*; (*terreno*) plain.

llave *f* key (*a. fig.*); (gas- *etc.*) tap; ⚡ switch; ⊕ spanner; ⊕ key; ♩ stop; ✕, *lucha*: lock; *~ de cierre* stopcock; *mot. ~ de contacto* ignition key; *~ inglesa* (monkey-)wrench; *~ maestra* skeleton key, master-key; *debajo de ~* under lock and key; *echar la ~* (*a*) lock up; **llavero** *m* keyring; (*p.*) turnkey; **llavín** *m* latch-key.

llegada *f* arrival, coming; **llegar** [1h] *v/t.* bring up, draw up; *v/i.* arrive (*a* at), come; (*alcanzar*) reach; (*suceder*) happen; (*bastar*) be enough; *~ a* reach; (*importar*) amount to; (*igualar*) be equal to; *~ a inf.* reach the point of *ger.*; (*lograr*) manage to *inf.*; *~ a saber* find out; *~ a ser* become; *hacer ~ el dinero* make both ends meet; *~se* approach, come near.

llenar [1a] fill, stuff (*de* with); *espacio, tiempo* occupy, take up; *hoja* fill in (*or* up, out *Am.*); (*cumplir*) fulfil; (*satisfacer*) satisfy; (*colmar*) overwhelm (*de* with); *~ de insultos* heap insults upon; *~se* fill up; F stuff o.s.; *fig.* get cross; *~ de polvo* get covered in dust; **lleno 1.** full (*de* of), filled (*de* with); *de ~* fully, entirely; **2.** *m* fill, plenty; *fig.* per-

fection; *thea.* full house; *ast.* full moon.

llevadero bearable; **llevar** [1a] carry (*a.* ⚚); *p., cosa* take (*a* to); *p.* lead (*a* to); *casa, cuentas* keep; *armas, frutos, nombre* bear; *ropa* wear; *tiempo* spend; *precio* charge; *dirección* follow, keep to; *vida* lead; *premio* carry off; (*cercenar*) take off; (*aguantar*) bear, stand; (*dirigir*) manage; *~ p.p.* have (already) *p.p.*; *llevo escritas 3 cartas* I have written 3 letters; *~ mucho tiempo ger.* have been *ger.* a long time; *¿cuánto tiempo llevas aquí?* how long have you been here?; *te llevo 3 años* I am 3 years older than you; *~ adelante* push ahead with; *~ consigo, ~ encima* carry, have with one; F *~la hecha* have got it all worked out; *~las de perder* be in a bad way; *~ lo mejor* (*peor*) get the best (worst) of it; *~ puesto* wear, have on; *no ~las todas consigo* have the wind up; *~se algo* take away, carry off; *~ bien con* get on with.

llorar [1a] *v/t.* weep for, cry over; lament; *muerte* mourn; *v/i.* cry, weep; **lloriquear** [1a] snivel, whimper; **lloriqueo** *m* whimper, whimpering; **llorón 1.** snivelling, whining; **2.** *m*, *-a* *f* cry-baby; **lloroso** tearful; sad.

llovedizo *techo* leaky; *v. agua*; **llover** [2h] rain (*a. fig.*); *como llovido* unexpectedly; *llueva o no* rain or shine; *como quien oye ~* quite unmoved; *v. cielo*; **llovizna** *f* drizzle; **lloviznar** [1a] drizzle; **lluvia** *f* rain; (*cantidad*) rainfall; (*agua*) rainwater; *fig.* shower; mass; hail *de balas*; **lluvioso** rainy, wet.

M

macabro macabre.

macadán *m* macadam; **macadamizar** [1f] macadamize.

macana *f S.Am.* club; F (*disparate*) silly thing; F (*cuento*) fib, tale; F *¡qué ~!* what a bind!; **macanear** [1a] *S.Am.* F fib, lay it on; **macanudo** F smashing, super; (*disparatado*) silly.

macarrón[1] *m* ⚓ bulwark.

macarrón[2] *m*: ~ (*de almendra*) macaroon; ~es *pl.* macaroni; **macarrónico** macaronic; *latín* ~ dog-Latin.

macear [1a] hammer, pound.

macerar(se) [1a] macerate.

macero *m* mace-bearer.

maceta *f* ✿ flower-pot.

macicez *f* massiveness.

macilento wan, haggard; (*flaco*) }
macillo *m* ♪ hammer. [emaciated.}

macis *f* mace (*spice*).

macizo 1. massive; (*bien construido*) stout; *neumático, oro etc.* solid (*a. fig.*); **2.** *m geog.* mass(if); ✗ bed.

macro... macro...

mácula *f* stain, blemish; ~ *solar* sun-spot.

machaca *m/f* (*p.*) pest, bore; **machacar** [1g] *v/t.* pound, crush, mash; F *precio* slash; *v/i.* go on, keep on; nag; ~ *en harp on*; *¡no machaques!* don't go on so!, stop harping on it!; **machacón 1.** tiresome; **2.** *m, -a f* pest, bore.

machado *m* hatchet.

machamartillo: F *a* ~ tightly; *creer etc.* implicitly; *cumplir* to the letter.

machaqueo *m* pounding *etc.*; *fig.* nagging.

machete *m* machete.

machihembrar [1a] ⊕ dovetail.

macho 1. *biol.,* ⊕ male; *fig.* strong, tough; **2.** *m* male; mule; *v. cabrío;* ✗ pin; ⊕ pin, peg; (*martillo*) sledge(-hammer); *sew.* hook; F dolt; **machón** *m* buttress; **machote** *m sl.* he-man, tough guy.

machucar [1g] bruise.

machucho elderly; wise beyond one's years, prudent; sedate.

madeja *f* skein, hank *de lana*; mass *de pelo*; F ~ *de nervios* bundle of nerves.

madera *f* wood; (*trozo*) piece of wood; ~ (*de construcción*) timber; ~ *contrachapeada* plywood; ~ *de deriva* driftwood; *de* ~ wood(en); **maderaje** *m,* **maderamen** *m* woodwork, timbering; **madero** *m* beam; F blockhead.

madrastra *f* stepmother; **madre** *f* mother (*a. attr., eccl., fig.*); *anat.* womb; bed *de río;* (*residuo*) sediment, dregs; *fig.* cradle *de civilización etc.; juegos: la* ~ home; ~ *adoptiva* foster mother; *sin* ~ motherless; *salirse de* ~ overflow; ~selva *f* honeysuckle.

madrigal *m* madrigal.

madriguera *f* den (*a. fig.*); burrow *en tierra.*

madrileño *adj. a. su. m,* **a** *f* (native) of Madrid.

madrina *f* godmother; *fig.* patron, patroness; ~ *de boda approx.* bridesmaid.

madroño *m* strawberry-tree.

madrugada *f* early morning; (*alba*) daybreak; *de* ~ early; *las 3 de la* ~ three o'clock in the morning; **madrugador 1.** that gets up early; **2.** *m,* **-a** early riser, early bird; **madrugar** [1h] get up early; *fig.* get ahead; *deportes:* jump the gun.

madurar [1a] *v/t.* ripen; *fig.* mature; *p.* toughen (up), season; *proyecto etc.* think out; *v/i.* ripen; *fig.* mature; **madurez** *f* ripeness; *fig.* maturity; **maduro** ripe; *fig.* mature; *de edad ya* ~a middle-aged.

maestra *f* teacher (*a. fig.*); ~ (*de escuela*) schoolteacher; **maestranza** *f* ⚓ dockyard; arsenal, armoury; **maestre** *m hist.* (grand-) master; **maestría** *f* mastery; masterliness; *con* ~ in a masterly fashion; **maestro 1.** masterly; main, principal; *llave, obra etc.* master *attr.;* **2.** *m* master (*a. fig.*); ~ (*de escuela*) schoolteacher;

♪ maestro; ~ de ceremonias master of ceremonies; ~ de obras (dueño) (master-)builder; foreman.

magenta f magenta.

magia f magic; **mágico 1.** magic, magical; **2.** m magician. [mind.]

magín m F fancy, imagination;

magisterio m (arte) teaching; teaching profession; (ps.) teachers; **magistrado** m magistrate; **magistral** magisterial; fig. masterly; authoritative; **magistratura** f magistracy.

magnanimidad f magnanimity etc.; **magnánimo** magnanimous, generous; **magnate** m magnate, tycoon esp. Am. F; hist. baron.

magnesia f magnesia; **magnesio** m ⚛ magnesium; phot. flashlight.

magnético magnetic; **magnetismo** m magnetism; **magnetizar** [1f] magnetize; **magneto** f magneto; **magnetofón** m tape-recorder; **magnetofónico** tape attr., recording attr.

magnificencia f magnificence, splendour; **magnificar** [1g] opt. magnify; **magnífico** splendid, wonderful, superb, magnificent; ¡~! splendid!; **magnitud** f magnitude (a. ast.); **magno** lit. great.

magnolia f magnolia.

mago m magician; v. rey.

magra f lean part; (lonja) slice, rasher; ¡~s! rubbish!, not on your life!; **magro** (flaco) skinny; carne lean; (escaso) meagre.

magulladura f bruise; **magullar** [1a] 💥 bruise; batter, bash, mangle.

mahometano adj. a. su. m, a f Mahommedan.

maitines m/pl. matins.

maíz m maize, corn Am.; **maizal** m maize-field.

majada f sheep-fold; (estiércol) dung; **majadería** f silliness; (dicho etc.) silly thing; ~s pl. nonsense; **majadero 1.** silly; **2.** m idiot.

majar [1a] pound, grind, mash; 💥 bruise; fig. bother.

majestad f majesty; stateliness; Su ♀ His (or Her) Majesty; (Vuestra) ♀ Your Majesty; **majestuoso** majestic, stately, imposing.

majo 1. lovely, nice, cute; (elegante) smart, natty; **2.** m toff, masher; flashy sort; (valentón) bully, lout.

majuelo m newly-planted vine.

mal 1. adj. = malo; **2.** adv. badly; (difícilmente) hardly; (equivocadamente) wrong(ly); compuestos: ~ educado ill-mannered, unmannerly; v. parecido etc.; pero digo ~ but I am wrong (to say ...); no, that's not right; ~ que quiere willy-nilly; (bien o mal) any old how; de ~ en peor from bad to worse; ¡menos ~! that's a relief!; menos ~ que it is just as well that; **3.** m evil, wrong; (calamidad) evil; (daño) harm, hurt, damage; (desgracia) misfortune; 💥 disease; illness; ~ caduco epilepsy; ~ de ojo evil eye; caer en el ~ fall into evil ways; echar a ~ scorn; hacer ~ (a) harm, hurt; ¡~ haya ...! a curse on (quien him who); llevar (or tomar) a ~ resent, be offended at; parar en ~ come to a bad end.

mala f mail-bag.

malabarista m/f juggler.

malacate m ⊕ winch, whim.

malaconsejado ill-advised.

malagueño adj. a. su. m, a f (native) of Málaga.

malandante unfortunate.

malandrín m, -a f scoundrel.

malaquita f malachite.

malaria f malaria.

malavenido in disagreement.

malaventura f misfortune; **malaventurado** unfortunate.

malayo 1. Malay(an); **2.** m, a f Malay; **3.** m (idioma) Malay.

malbaratar [1a] ♣ sell off cheap; fig. squander.

malcasado unfaithful.

malcontento 1. discontented; **2.** m, a f malcontent.

malcriado ill-bred, coarse.

maldad f evil, wickedness; (acto) wicked thing.

maldecir [approx. 3p] v/t. curse; (difamar) = v/i.: ~ de run down, disparage; **maldiciente 1.** that speaks ill of everything, forever criticizing; slanderous; (malhablado) foul-mouthed; **2.** m grumbler, malcontent; slanderer; **maldición** f curse; ¡~! curse it!, damn!; **maldita** f F tongue; soltar la ~ talk too freely; (encolerizarse) blow up; **maldito** damned (a. eccl.); (malo) wicked; ~ lo que me importa I don't care a damn; no saber ~a la

cosa de know damn-all about; ¡~ *sea!* damn it!
maleable malleable (*a. fig.*).
maleante 1. wicked; **2.** *m/f* rough type; vagrant; **malear** [1a] damage, spoil; *tierra* sour; *fig.* corrupt; ~se spoil *etc.*, be ruined.
malecón *m* pier, jetty; breakwater, mole.
maledicencia *f* slander, scandal.
maleficio *m* curse, spell; **maléfico** evil, harmful.
malejo F pretty bad. [ing.\
malentendido *m* misunderstand-\
malestar *m* 🞧 discomfort; *fig.* uneasiness, malaise; *pol.* unrest, discontent.
maleta 1. *f* (suit)case; *mot.* boot; *hacer la(s)* ~(s) pack; **2.** *m* F bungler; *thea.* ham; **maletín** *m* small case; *esp.* gladstone bag.
malevolencia *f* malevolence, spite, ill-will; **malévolo** malevolent, spiteful.
maleza *f* (*malas hierbas*) weeds; (*arbustos*) scrub; undergrowth *en bosque*; (*soto*) thicket.
malformación *f* malformation.
malgastador spendthrift, thriftless; **malgastar** [1a] *hacienda* squander; *tiempo* waste; *salud* ruin.
malhablado foul-mouthed.
malhadado ill-starred, ill-fated.
malhecho *m* misdeed; **malhechor** *m*, **-a** *f* evil-doer, malefactor.
malhumorado cross, bad-tempered, peevish.
malicia *f* (*maldad*) wickedness; (*astucia*) slyness; mischief *de niño etc.*; (*mala intención*) malice, maliciousness; **malicioso** wicked; sly; mischievous; malicious.
malignidad *f* malignancy *etc.*; **maligno** malignant (*a.* 🞧), malicious; *influjo etc.* evil, pernicious.
malintencionado unkind, ill-disposed.
malísimo dreadful, appalling.
malmandado F disobedient; obstinate.
malo 1. *mst* bad; *niño* naughty, mischievous; (*equivocado*) wrong; 🞧 ill; ~ *de inf.* hard to *inf.*; *lo* ~ *es que* the trouble is that; *andar a* ~*as con* be on bad terms with; *estar de* ~*as* be out of luck; *ponerse a* ~*as con* fall foul of; *venir de* ~*as* have evil intentions; **2.** *m thea.* villain.

malogrado abortive, ill-fated; *p.* late lamented; **malograr** [1a] spoil; *oportunidad* waste; ~se fail, miscarry, come to grief; (*morir*) come to an untimely end; **malogro** *m* failure; (*muerte*) untimely end; waste *de tiempo etc.*
maloliente stinking, smelly.
malparado: *salir* ~ come off badly (*de* in); **malparar** [1a] damage, harm; ill-treat.
malparir [3a] have a miscarriage; **malparto** *m* miscarriage.
malpensado evil-minded; ¡*no seas* ~! don't be nasty!
malquerencia *f* dislike; **malquistar** [1a] cause a rift between; ~se become estranged; **malquisto** disliked; *dos ps.* estranged.
malsano unhealthy; *mente* morbid; 🞧 sickly.
malsonante nasty, rude.
malsufrido impatient.
malta *f* malt.
maltés *adj. a. su. m*, **-a** *f* Maltese.
maltratamiento *m* maltreatment *etc.*; **maltratar** [1a] ill-treat, maltreat; knock about; abuse *de palabra*; **maltrato** *m* maltreatment *etc.*; **maltrecho** battered, damaged.
malucho F 🞧 poorly.
malva *f* 🌿 mallow; ~ *loca*, ~ *rósea* hollyhock; (*de*) *color de* ~ mauve; *ser como una* ~ be very meek and mild.
malvado 1. wicked, villainous; **2.** *m* villain.
malvarrosa *f* hollyhock; **malvavisco** *m* 🌿 marshmallow.
malvender [2a] sell off cheap.
malversación *f* embezzlement; graft; **malversador** *m* embezzler; **malversar** [1a] embezzle, misappropriate.
malla *f* mesh; network; ✕ (chain-)mail.
mallo *m* mallet.
mallorquín *adj. a. su. m*, **-a** *f* Majorcan.
mamá *f*, **mamaíta** *f* F mummy, mum, mamma.
mamar [1a] suck; *fig.* absorb, acquire in infancy; (*a.* ~se) F *destino* wangle, land; *recursos* milk; *fondos* pocket; *susto* have; *dar de* ~ *a* feed; ~se F get tight; ~ *a uno* get the best of s.o.

mamarracho *m* (*p.*) sight, object; (*obra*) unholy mess, botch; *paint.* daub.

mameluco *m* F chump.

mamífero 1. mammalian; **2.** *m* mammal.

mamola: *dar la ~ a* chuck *s.o.* under the chin.

mamón *m* ♀ sucker.

mamotreto *m* notebook; F whacking big book.

mampara *f* screen; **mamparo** *m* ⚓ bulkhead.

mamporro *m* bump *al caer;* punch, clout.

mampostería *f* △ rubble-work; **mampuesto** *m* (rough) stone; parapet; *de ~* spare, emergency *attr.*

mamut *m* mammoth.

maná *m* manna.

manada *f* ✶ flock, herd; pack *de lobos;* F crowd, mob; **manadero** *m* shepherd, herdsman.

manantial 1. flowing, running; **2.** *m* spring; *fig.* source; **manar** [1a] *v/t.* run with, flow with; *v/i.* flow, pour out; well up; *fig.* abound.

manceba *f* whore; (*concubina*) mistress; **mancebía** *f* brothel; **mancebo** *m* youth.

mancilla *f* stain, blemish; **mancillar** [1a] stain, sully.

manco one-handed, one-armed; (*en general*) crippled, maimed; *fig.* defective.

mancomún: *de ~* (con)jointly; **mancomunar** [1a] *recursos* pool; *intereses* combine; *~se* merge, combine; *~ en* associate in; **mancomunidad** *f* pool; association; *pol.* commonwealth.

mancha *f zo. etc.* spot, mark; spot, fleck *en diseño;* (*suciedad*) spot, stain; smear; blot, smudge *de tinta; fig.* stain *en reputación;* (*defecto*) blemish; (*terreno*) patch; *~ solar* sunspot; **manchado** spotty, smudgy *etc.; esp. animal* dappled, spotted; *esp. ave* pied; **manchar** [1a] spot, mark; (*ensuciar*) soil, stain; smudge; *fig.* stain, soil; *reputación de otro* smear.

manchego *adj. a. su. m*, **a** *f* (native) of La Mancha.

manda *f* bequest; **mandadero** *m*, **a** *f* messenger; (*m*) errand-boy; **mandado** *m* order; commission,

errand; *ir a los ~s* run errands; **mandamiento** *m* order; *eccl.* commandment; ⚖ writ, warrant; **mandar** [1a] **1.** *v/t.* order (*inf.* to *inf.*); (*gobernar*) rule (over); (*acaudillar*) lead, command; (*enviar*) send; (*legar*) bequeath; *~ (para acá y para allá*) order about; *~ hacer algo* get (*or* have) s.t. done; *~ hacer un traje* have a suit made, order a suit; *~ salir* order *s.o.* out; **2.** *v/i.* be in command (*or* control); *b.s.* boss (people about); *~ por* send for; *aquí mando yo* I am the master here, I'm the boss; **3.** *~se* △ communicate (*con* with); ♂ get around (by o.s.); **mandarín** *m* mandarin; *contp.* jack-in-office; **mandarina** *f* tangerine; **mandatorio** *adj. a. su. m* mandatory; **mandato** *m* order; *pol. etc.* mandate; term *de presidente;* ⚖ writ, warrant (*de prisión* of arrest).

mandíbula *f* jaw (*a.* ⊕), mandible ⚙.

mandil *m* (leather) apron; **mandilón** *m* apron; F coward.

mando *m* command, rule, control; leadership; ⊕ drive; ⊕ *~s pl.* controls; ⊕ *de ~* control *attr.; alto ~* high command; *~ a distancia* remote control; ✗ *al ~ de* (*jefe*) in command of; (*subordinado*) under the command of; *tener el ~* be in control.

mandolina *f* mandolin(e).

mandón bossy, domineering.

mandrágora *f* mandrake.

mandria 1. worthless; **2.** *m/f* useless sort.

mandril[1] *m zo.* mandrill.

mandril[2] *m* ⊕ mandrel.

manear [1a] hobble.

manecilla *f* ⊕ pointer, hand; (*broche*) clasp.

manejable manageable; *herramienta etc.* handy; **manejar** [1a] manage, handle (*a. fig.*); *máquina a.* work, run, operate; *S.Am. coche* drive; *~se* ♂ get around; *¿cómo te manejas para hacer eso?* how do you set about doing that?; **manejo** *m* management, handling *etc.; b.s.* intrigue; stratagem; *llevar todo el ~ de* be in sole charge of.

manera *f* way, manner; *~s pl.* manners *de p.; a la ~ de* in (*or* after) the manner of; *de esta ~* (in) this way, like this; *de otra* ~ otherwise; *de ninguna* ~ by no means; *¡de ninguna* ~! certainly not!; *de* ~ *que* so that; *¿de* ~ *que ...?* so ...?; *de todas* ~s at any rate; *en gran* ~ in (a) great measure; *sobre* ~ exceedingly; *no hay* ~ *de inf.* there's no way of *ger.*; *no había* ~ *de disuadirle* there was no dissuading him.

manga *f* sleeve; ~ *(de riego)* hose, hose-pipe; ⚓ wind-sock; ⚓ beam; ~ *(de agua)* cloudburst, ⚓ waterspout; *bridge*: game; ~ *de viento* whirlwind; F *de* ~ *in* league; *de* ~ *ancha* indulgent; *b.s.* not overscrupulous; *en* ~s *de camisa* in one's shirt-sleeves; *sin* ~s sleeveless; F *andar etc.* ~ *por hombro* be in a mess; *sl. pegar las* ~s kick the bucket.

manganeso *m* manganese.

mangante F **1.** brazen; **2.** *m* scrounger; **mangar** [1h] *sl.* swipe.

mango[1] *m* ⚘ mango.

mango[2] *m* handle; **mangonear** [1a]: F ~ *en* meddle in; *estudio etc.* dabble in; **mangoneón** *m* F busybody.

mangosta *f* mongoose.

manguera *f* hose-pipe; ⚓ waterspout.

manguito *m* muff; ⊕ sleeve; ~ *incandescente* gas-mantle.

manía *f* mania; *fig.* mania, rage, craze (de for); *(capricho)* whim; *(rareza)* fad, peculiarity; ~ *persecutoria* persecution mania; *dar en la* ~ *de inf.* take to *ger.*; *tener* ~ *a* dislike, have it in for; *tiene la* ~ *de inf.* he's got the habit of *ger.*; **maníaco 1.** maniac(al); **2.** *m, a f* maniac.

maniatar [1a] tie *s.o.'s* hands.

maniático 1. maniacal; *fig.* mad, crazy; *(testarudo)* stubborn; *(raro)* eccentric, odd; **2.** *m, a f* maniac; *fig.* eccentric, odd type; **manicomio** *m* (lunatic) asylum, mental hospital.

manicura *f* manicure; **manicuro** *m, a f (p.)* manicurist.

manida *f* lair, den.

manido high, gamy.

manifestación *f* manifestation; show; declaration; *pol.* demonstration; **manifestante** *m/f* demonstrator; **manifestar** [1k] show; *(por palabra)* declare, express, state; ~se show, be manifest; *pol.* demonstrate; ~ *en* be evident in; **manifiesto 1.** clear, evident; *verdad* manifest; *error etc.* glaring; obvious; *poner* ~ make clear; *quedar* ~ be plain; **2.** *m* ⚓ manifest; *pol.* manifesto.

manija *f (mango)* handle; *(abrazadera)* clamp, collar; ⚓ coupling.

manilargo *fig.* open-handed.

manilla *f* bracelet; *(grillete)* manacle; *hand de reloj*; **manillar** *m* handle-bar.

maniobra *f* handling; manoeuvre *(a. fig.)*; *fig.* move; *b.s.* stratagem, intrigue; ~s *pl.* ✗ manoeuvres; ⚓ shunting; **maniobrable** manoeuvrable; **maniobrar** [1a] manoeuvre *(a. fig.)*; ⚓ shunt.

maniota *f* hobble.

manipulación *f* manipulation; **manipulador 1.** *m*, -a *f* manipulator; **2.** *m* ✂, *tel.* key, tapper; **manipular** [1a] manipulate; *fig.* handle, manage.

maniquí 1. *m* (tailor's) dummy, manikin; *fig.* puppet; **2.** *f* mannequin.

manirroto lavish, extravagant.

manivela *f* crank; ~ *(de arranque)* starting-handle. [morsel.]

manjar *m* dish; ~ *exquisito* tasty]

mano *f* hand; *zo.* foot; coat *de pintura*; *naipes*: ser ~ lead; *yo soy* ~ it's my lead; ~ *de almirez* pestle; ~s *pl.* muertas mortmain; ~ *de obra* labour; man-power; ~ *de papel* quire; *¡*~s *quietas!* hands off!; *última* ~ finishing touch; *a* ~ by hand; *escribir* in longhand; *a (la)* ~ at hand, on hand, handy; *a* ~ *airada* violently; *a* ~ *salva* without risk; *a* ~s *de dirigir* care of; *¡arriba las* ~s! hands up!; *bajo* ~ in secret, behind the scenes; *con las* ~s *en la masa* red-handed, in the act; *de la* ~ llevar by the hand; *de primera* ~ at first hand; *de segunda* ~ secondhand; *de* ~s *a boca* suddenly, unexpectedly; *de* ~s *de* at the hands of; *recibir* from; *entre* ~s in hand, on hand; *¡fuera las* ~s! hands off!; *asidos de la* ~ hand-in-hand; *cargar la* ~ insist, press hard; *darse las* ~s join hands; *(estrechar)* shake hands; *dejar de la* ~ abandon; *no dejar de la* ~ *libro* not be able to put down; *echar una* ~ lend a hand; *naipes etc.*:

play a game (de of); echar ~ a lay hands on; echar ~ de make use of, resort to; estrechar la ~ a shake s.o.'s hand; ganar por la ~ a steal a march on; hacerse la ~ get one's hand in; hecho a ~ hand-made; tener ~ con have a way with, have influence on; tener buena ~ para be a good hand at; untar la ~ a grease s.o.'s palm; venir a las ~s come to blows; vivir de la ~ a la boca live from hand to mouth.

manojo m handful, bunch; tuft de hierba etc.

manómetro m gauge; ~ de aceite oil-gauge.

manopla f (face-)flannel;† gauntlet.

manoseado fig. hackneyed; **manosear** [1a] handle, finger; (ajar) rumple; b.s. paw, fiddle with, muck about with.

manotada f, **manotazo** m slap, smack; **manotear** [1a] v/t. slap, smack; v/i. gesticulate, use one's hands; **manoteo** m gesticulation.

mansalva: a ~ without risk; a ~ de safe from.

mansedumbre f mildness etc.; **manso** mild, gentle; animal tame.

manta f blanket; ~ (de viaje) rug; F hiding; F liarse la ~ a la cabeza go the whole hog; press on regardless; F tirar de la ~ let the cat out of the bag; **mantear** [1a] toss in a blanket.

manteca f fat; esp. ~ (de cerdo) lard; ~ (de vaca) butter; **mantecado** m approx. ice-cream; **mantecoso** buttery; lardy.

mantel m tablecloth; **mantelería** f table-linen; **mantelillo** m table-runner.

mantener [2l] keep en equilibrio etc.; ⚠ etc. hold up, support; (alimentar) sustain; ⊕ maintain, service; opinión maintain; costumbre, relaciones etc. keep up; ~se sustain o.s., subsist (de on); fig. stand firm; ~ (en vigor) stand; ~ en un puesto keep a job; **mantenimiento** m sustenance; maintenance etc.

mantequera f churn; butter-dish de mesa; **mantequería** f dairy, creamery; **mantequilla** f butter.

mantilla f mantilla; ~s pl. baby clothes; estar en ~s (p.) be very innocent; (proyecto) be in its infancy.

mantillo m humus, mould.

manto m cloak (a. fig.); eccl., ⚕ robe, gown; zo. mantle; ~ (de chimenea) mantel; **mantón** m shawl.

manuable handy; **manual 1.** manual, hand attr.; (manuable) handy; **2.** m manual, handbook; **manubrio** m handle, crank; winch.

manufactura f manufacture; (edificio) factory; **manufacturar** [1a] manufacture; **manufacturero 1.** manufacturing; **2.** m manufacturer.

manuscrito 1. hand-written, manuscript; **2.** m manuscript.

manutención f maintenance (a. ⊕).

manzana f apple; ⚕ block; ~ de la discordia apple of discord, bone of contention; ~ silvestre crab, crab-apple; **manzanilla** f ♣ camomile; (infusión) camomile tea; (vino) manzanilla (a very dry sherry); **manzano** m apple (tree).

maña f (en general) skill, ingenuity; b.s. guile, craft; (una ~) trick, knack; b.s. evil habit; darse ~ para inf. contrive to inf.

mañana 1. f morning; de ~, por la ~ in the morning; muy de ~ early in the morning; **2.** m: el ~ the morrow, the future; **3.** adv. tomorrow; ~ por la ~ tomorrow morning; ¡hasta ~! see you tomorrow!; pasado ~ the day after tomorrow.

mañoso skilful, clever; b.s. wily, sharp.

mapa m map.

mapache m rac(c)oon.

maque m lacquer; **maquear** [1a] lacquer.

maqueta f model.

maquillador m thea. make-up man; **maquillaje** m make-up; **maquillar(se)** [1a] make up.

máquina f machine (a. fig.); 🚂 engine, locomotive; ~ (fotográfica) camera; F bicycle; mot. F car; ⚠ palace, building; fig. scheme (of things), machinery; (proyecto) scheme; ~ de afeitar (safety) razor; ⚡ electric razor; ~ de coser sewing-machine; ~ de escribir typewriter; ~ herramienta machine-tool; ~ infernal infernal machine; ~ de vapor steam-engine; a toda ~ at full speed; acabar (or coser etc.) a ~ machine; escribir a ~ type; hecho a ~

machine-made; *typ.* typed; **maquinación** *f* machination, plot; **maquinador** *m*, **-a** *f* schemer; **maquinal** mechanical (*a. fig.*); **maquinar** [1a] plot; **maquinaria** *f* machinery; plant; **maquinista** *m* ⊕ operator, machinist; ⚓ *etc.* engineer; 🚂 engine-driver, engineer *Am.*

mar *m a. f* sea; ~ de fondo (ground-)swell; F la ~ *adv.* a lot; F la ~ de lots of, no end of; F la ~ de tonto no end of a fool; al ~ caer *etc.* overboard; a ~es copiously; *llorar* a ~es cry one's eyes out; de alta ~ seagoing; en alta ~ on the high seas; por ~ by sea; hacerse a la ~ put to sea.

maraña *f* ❦ thicket; (*enredo*) tangle; *fig.* puzzle, jungle; (*embuste*) trick; **marañero 1.** scheming; **2.** *m* schemer.

marasmo *m* ❦ wasting, consumption; *fig.* paralysis, stagnation.

maravilla *f* marvel, wonder; ❦ marigold; a ~, a las mil ~s wonderfully, extremely well; **maravillar** [1a] surprise, amaze; ~se be amazed (de at); wonder, marvel (de at); **maravilloso** marvellous, wonderful. [edge, border.]

marbete *m* label; tag, docket; *sew.*❘ **marca** *f* mark(ing); stamp; (*fabricación*) make, brand; ⚓ landmark; ♪ beat; *naipes*: bid; *deportes*: record; *hist.* march(es); ~ de fábrica, ~ registrada (registered) trade mark; de ~ outstanding; de ~ mayor most outstanding; **marcación** *f* ⚓ bearing; **marcado** marked, pronounced; *acento* strong, broad; **marcador** *m* marker (*a. billar*); *deportes*: (*p.*) scorer; (*tanteador*) scoreboard; **marcar** [1g] **1.** *v/t.* (*poner señal a*) mark; stamp, brand; *terreno etc.* mark out; (*señalar*) point out; (*reloj etc.*) show; (*termómetro etc.*) read, say; (*aplicar*) designate; ♪ *compás* keep, beat; *paso* mark; *deportes*: score; *teleph.* dial; **2.** *v/i. deportes*: score; *teleph.* dial; **3.** ~se ⚓ take one's bearings.

marcial martial; *porte* military.

marco *m paint.*, △ *etc.* frame; *fig.* setting; ✝ mark; standard *de pesos etc.*; ~ de chimenea chimney-piece; *poner* ~ a *paint.* frame.

marcha *f* ✕, ♪ *a. fig.* march; ⊕ running, functioning; ⊕ (~ atrás *etc.*) gear; *fig.* progress; (*tendencia*) trend, course; (*velocidad*) speed; ⊕ primera ~ low gear; ~ atrás reverse (gear); dar ~ atrás a, poner en ~ atrás coche *etc.* reverse; ~ forzada forced march; ~ nupcial wedding march; a toda ~ (at) full blast; en ~ in motion, going; ⚓ *etc.* under way; ¡en ~! ✕ forward march!; let's go!; *fig.* here goes!; (*a otro*) get going!; sobre la ~ immediately; cerrar la ~ bring up the rear; poner en ~ start; *fig.* set going, set in motion; ponerse en ~ start.

marchar [1a] (*caminar*) go; ✕ march; ⊕ go, run, work; *fig.* go, come along; ~se go (away), leave.

marchitar(se) [1a] wilt, wither, shrivel (up); **marchito** withered; faded (*a. fig.*).

marea *f* tide; (*viento*) sea-breeze; ~ alta high tide, high water; ~ menguante ebb tide; ~ muerta neap tide; ~ viva spring tide; **mareado** ❦ sick; ⚓ seasick; *fig.* giddy, light-headed; F tipsy; **mareaje** *m* navigation; **marear** [1a] sail, navigate; *fig.* make *s.o.* cross; ~se feel sick, feel giddy; ⚓ feel (or be) seasick; **marejada** *f* swell, surge; *fig.* undercurrent; **mareo** *m* sick feeling, travel-sickness; giddiness; ⚓ seasickness; **mareta** *f* surge (*a. fig.*).

marfil *m* ivory.

marga *f* marl.

margarina *f* margarine.

margarita *f* ❦ daisy; *zo.* pearl.

margen **1.** *mst m* border, edge; *typ.*, ✝ *etc.* margin; ~ de error margin of error; ~ de seguridad margin of safety; al ~ in the margin; dar ~ para give occasion for; F dejar al ~ leave out in the cold; **2.** *f* bank de río *etc.*; **marginal** marginal.

marica 1. *f orn.* magpie; **2.** *m* F milksop, sissy; **maricón** *m* F queer, pansy.

maridaje *m fig.* marriage; **marido** *m* husband.

mariguana *f* marijuana.

marimacho *m* F masculine sort of woman.

marina *f* (*arte*) seamanship; (*buques*) shipping; ~ (de guerra) navy; *paint.*

sea-piece; ~ *mercante* merchant navy; **marinería** *f* seamanship; (*ps.*) crew; **marinero 1.** seaworthy; **2.** *m* seaman, sailor; ~ *de primera* able seaman; **marino 1.** sea *attr.*; marine ⨂; **2.** *m* seaman, sailor.

marioneta *f* marionette; *régimen* ~ puppet régime.

mariposa *f* butterfly; ~ (*nocturna*) moth; (*luz*) nightlight; **mariposear** [1a] flutter about; *fig.* act capriciously; (*amor*) flirt.

mariquita 1. *f* lady-bird; **2.** *m* F milksop, sissy.

marisabidilla *f* F blue-stocking.

mariscal *m*: ~ *de campo* field-marshal; † major-general.

mariscos *m/pl.* shell-fish.

marisma *f* marsh, swamp.

marital marital.

marítimo maritime; marine, ꞵea *attr.*; *ciudad etc.* seaside *attr.*; *agente etc.* shipping *attr.*

marjal *m* moor; (*húmedo*) marsh, fen.

marmita *f* pot; *geol.* ~ *de gigante* pot-hole.

mármol *m* marble; **marmóreo** marble (*a. fig.*).

maroma *f* rope.

marqués *m* marquis; **marquesa** *f* marchioness.

marquesina *f* awning; canopy; △ porch; △ cantilever roof.

marquetería *f* marquetry.

marramizar [1f] caterwaul.

marrana *f* sow; F slut; **marrano 1.** dirty; **2.** *m* pig; F dirty pig; *hist.* Jew.

marrar [1a] miss; *fig.* go astray.

marras: F *de* ~ (that) you all know about; old, long-standing.

marrón 1. chestnut; maroon; **2.** *m* chestnut.

marroquí 1. *adj. a. su. m/f* Moroccan; **2.** *m* (*cuero*) Moroccan (leather); **marrueco** *adj. a. su. m*, **a** *f* Moroccan.

marrullería *f* smoothness, glibness; plausible excuses *etc.*; **marrullero 1.** smooth, glib, plausible; **2.** *m* smooth *etc.* sort.

marsopa *f* porpoise; **marsupial** *adj. a. su. m* marsupial.

marta *f* marten; (*piel*) sable.

martes *m* Tuesday; ~ *de carnaval* Shrove Tuesday.

martillar [1a] hammer; **marti-**

llear [1a] ⊕ knock; **martillo** *m* hammer; gavel *de presidente*; (*subastas*) auction-room; ~ *picador* pneumatic drill.

martín *m* **pescador** kingfisher.

martinete *m* △ pile-driver; ⊕ drop-hammer; ♪ hammer.

mártir *m/f* martyr; **martirio** *m* martyrdom; *fig.* torture; **martirizar** [1f] martyr(ize); *fig.* torment, torture.

marxismo *m* Marxism.

marzo *m* March.

más 1. *comp.* more; *sup.* most; (*y*) plus, and; (*más tiempo*) longer; (*más rápidamente*) faster; *un libro de lo* ~ *interesante* a most interesting book; ~ *quiero inf.* I would rather *inf.*; ~ *bien* rather; ~ *de*, ~ *de lo que*, ~ *que* more than; (*poco*) ~ *o menos* more or less; *a* ~ in addition (*de to*), besides (*de acc.*); *a lo* ~ at (the) most; *como el que* ~ as well as anyone, as well as the next man; *cuando* ~ at (the) most, at the outside; *de* ~ (*adicional*) extra; (*superfluo*) too much, too many; *v. estar*; *el que* ~ *y el que menos* every single one; *hasta no* ~ to the limit; *los* ~ most (people); *nada* ~ nothing else; that's all; *ni* ~ *ni menos* just; *no* ~ no more; *haber llegado etc.* just; *no ...* ~ no longer, not any more; *no* ~ *que* only; just; *por* ~ *que* however much (*or* hard) *etc.*; *por* ~ *que yo quisiera* much as I should like; *¿qué* ~? what else?; what next?; *sin* ~ (*ni* ~) without more ado; thereupon, at that; *es* ~ furthermore; *hace no* ~ *de* no longer ago than, only ... ago; **2.** *m* Ⓐ plus (sign); *tiene sus* ~ *y sus menos* it has its good and bad points.

mas *lit.* but.

masa[1] *f* (*pasta*) dough.

masa[2] *f* mass (*a. phys., fig.*); *fig.* bulk, volume; *las* ~*s pl.* the masses; ~ *coral* choir; *en* ~ *en masse*; altogether.

masacrar [1a] massacre.

masaje *m* massage; *dar* ~ *a* massage; **masajista 1.** *m* masseur; **2.** *f* masseuse.

mascar [1g] chew; F mumble.

máscara *f* mask (*a. fig.*); ~ *antigás* gas-mask; ~*s pl.* = **mascarada** *f* masque(rade); **mascarilla** *f* mask;

(*vaciado*) death mask; **mascarón** *m*: ~ de *proa* figure-head.

mascota *f* mascot.

masculinidad *f* masculinity, manliness; **masculino 1.** *biol.* male; *gr.* masculine; *fig.* masculine, manly; **2.** *m gr.* masculine.

mascullar [1a] F mumble, mutter.

masilla *f* putty.

masón *m* (free)mason; **masonería** *f* (free)masonry; **masónico** masonic.

masoquismo *m* masochism.

mastelero *m* topmast.

masticación *f* mastication; **masticar** [1g] masticate, chew; **masticatorio** masticatory, chewing.

mástil *m* pole, post; ⚓ mast; ⚠ upright; ♪ neck; ~ de *tienda* tent-pole.

mastín *m* mastiff; ~ *danés* Great Dane.

mastodóntico *fig.* elephantine.

mastoides *adj. a. su. f* mastoid.

mastuerzo *m* cress; F dolt.

mata *f* ♀ shrub; (*pie de planta*) clump, root; (*hoja*) blade, sprig; mop *de pelo*; ~*s pl.* ♀ scrub.

matachín *m* F bully.

matadero *m* slaughter-house; F drudgery; **matador 1.** killing; **2.** *m*, **-a** *f* killer; *toros*: matador; **matadura** *f vet.* sore, gall; **matafuego** *m* fire-extinguisher; **mátalas callando** *m* F sly sort; **matanza** *f* slaughter, *esp.* ✗ pig-killing; *fig.* massacre; **matar** [1a] kill (*a. fig.*); *fuego* put out; *hambre* stay; *polvo* lay; *color* tone down; *así me maten* for the life of me; ~*se* kill o.s.; get killed *en accidente*; *fig.* wear o.s. out; ~ *por inf.* struggle to *inf.*; **matarife** *m* butcher; ~ de *caballos* knacker; **matasanos** *m* quack.

matasellar [1a] cancel, postmark; **matasello(s)** *m* postmark.

matasiete *m* bully, braggart.

mate[1] dull, matt.

mate[2] *m* (check-)mate; *dar* ~ *a* (check-)mate.

mate[3] *m S.Am.* ♀ maté.

matemáticas *f/pl.* mathematics; **matemático 1.** mathematical; **2.** *m* mathematician.

materia *f* matter (*a. phys.*, ✱); (*componentes*) material, stuff; (*asunto*) subject(-matter); *escuela*:

subject; ~ *colorante* dye-stuff; ~ *prima* raw material; *en* ~ *de* in the matter of, as regards; **material 1.** material; **2.** *m* material; ⊕ equipment, plant; *typ.* copy; ~ *móvil*, ~ *rodante* rolling-stock; **materialismo** *m* materialism; **materialista 1.** materialistic; **2.** *m/f* materialist; **materializar** (-se) [1f] materialize; **materialmente** *freq.* literally.

maternal motherly; maternal; **maternidad** *f* motherhood, maternity; (*a. casa de* ~) maternity hospital; **materno** maternal; *lengua etc.* mother *attr.*; *abuelo* ~ grandfather on the mother's side.

matinal morning *attr.*

matiz *m* shade (*a. fig.*); hue, tint; **matizar** [1f] (*casar*) blend, match; (*colorar*) tinge, tint (*de* with); *matizado de fig.* adorned with.

matón *m* bully, rough, lout.

matorral *m* thicket; brushwood, scrub.

matraca *f* rattle; F terrible bore, nuisance; *dar* ~ *a* give *s.o.* a hell of a time; (*mofarse*) jeer at; **matraquear** [1a] rattle; *fig.* jeer at.

matraz *m* ⚗ flask.

matrero 1. cunning; *S.Am.* suspicious; **2.** *m S.Am.* bandit.

matriarca *f* matriarch; **matricida** *m/f* matricide (*p.*); **matricidio** *m* matricide (*act*).

matrícula *f* list, register (*a.* ⚓), roll; *univ. etc.* (*acto*) matriculation, registration; (*permiso*) licence; *mot.* registration number; **matriculación** *f* registration *etc.*; **matricular(se)** [1a] register, enrol.

matrimonial matrimonial; *vida* married; **matrimonio** *m* (*en general*) marriage, matrimony; (*acto*) marriage; (*ps.*) (married) couple; ~ *civil* civil marriage; ~ *de conveniencia* marriage of convenience; *de* ~ *cama etc.* double; *contraer* ~ (*con*) marry.

matritense *adj. a. su. m/f* (native) of Madrid.

matriz *f anat.* womb; stub *de talonario*; ⊕ mould, die; ⊕ (*tuerca*) nut; *typ.*, ⚒ matrix.

matrona *f* matron.

matutino morning *attr.*

maula 1. *f* piece of junk; white

elephant; *b.s.* dirty trick; **2.** m/f cheat, tricky sort; (*pesado*) bore; **maulero** m, a f cheat.

maullar [1a] mew, miaow; **maullido** m mew, miaow.

mausoleo m mausoleum.

maxilar 1. maxillary; **2.** m jaw, jaw-bone.

máxima f maxim; **máxime** especially; **máximo 1.** maximum; top; *grado etc.* highest; *esfuerzo etc.* greatest (possible); **2.** m = **máximum** m maximum.

maya f ♀ daisy; (*p.*) May Queen.

mayal m ⚹ flail.

mayo m May; (*árbol*) maypole.

mayonesa f mayonnaise.

mayor 1. *adj. altar, calle, misa* high; *parte etc.* main, major (*a. ♩*); *p.* grown-up, of age; (*de edad avanzada*) elderly; **2.** *adj. comp.* bigger, larger, greater (que than); *edad*: older (*que* than), elder; senior (*que* to); *v. edad*; **3.** *adj. sup.* biggest; eldest *etc.*; **4.:** *al por* ~ wholesale; **5.** m chief, head; ⚔ major; ~*es pl.* ancestors; *fig.* elders.

mayoral m ⊕ foreman, overseer; ⚹ head shepherd; † coachman.

mayorazgo m primogeniture; (*finca*) entailed estate; (*p.*) eldest son.

mayordomo m steward, butler.

mayoría f majority; larger part; *la* ~ *de* most; *en su* ~ in the main; **mayorista** m wholesaler; **mayormente** chiefly, mainly.

mayúscula f capital letter; **mayúsculo** *letra* capital; F pretty big, tremendous.

maza f mace; *deportes*: bat; ♩ drumstick; ~ *de gimnasia* Indian club.

mazacote m 🜨 concrete; ⚗ soda; F dry doughy food; F (*p.*) bore.

mazapán m marzipan.

mazmorra f dungeon. [(*p.*) bore.)

mazo m mallet; (*manojo*) bunch;)

mazorca f ♀ spike, clump; ear, cob *de maíz*; *sew.* spindle.

me (*acc.*) me; (*dat.*) (to) me; (*reflexivo*) (to) myself.

meadero m F bog, jakes; **meados** m/pl. F piss.

meandro m meander.

mear [1a] F *v/t.* piss on; *v/i.* piss.

mecánica f mechanics; (*aparato*) mechanism, works; **mecánico**

1. mechanical; machine *attr.*; *oficio* manual; **2.** m mechanic; engineer; machinist; **mecanismo** m mechanism; works; action, movement *de pieza*; *esp. fig.* machinery, structure; **mecanizar** [1f] mechanize; **mecanografía** f typing; ~ *al tacto* touch-typing; **mecanografiado** *adj. a. su.* m typescript; **mecanografiar** [1c] type; **mecanógrafo** m, a f typist.

mecedora f rocking-chair.

mecenas m patron; **mecenazgo** m patronage.

mecer(se) [2b] *cuna etc.* rock; *rama etc.* sway; (*columpiar*) swing; (*agitar*) shake, stir up.

mecha f wick; ⚔ *etc.* fuse; = *mechón*; ~ *tardía* time-fuse; **mechar** [1a] lard; **mechera** f F shoplifter; **mechero** m burner *de lámpara*; (*cada fuego*) jet; (cigarette-) lighter; ~ *encendedor* pilot light; ~ *de gas* gas-burner, gas-jet; **mechón** m lock (of hair).

medalla f medal; = **medallón** m medallion; locket *con pelo etc.*; *typ.* inset. [sandbank.)

médano m, **medaño** m sand-dune;)

media f stocking; ⚹ mean; *hacer* ~ knit; **mediación** f mediation; (*medio*) instrumentality; **mediado** half-full; *a* ~s *de* in the middle of; **mediador** m, -a f mediator; **medial** medial; **medianería** f party wall; **medianero 1.** *pared etc.* dividing; **2.** m mediator; (*mensajero*) go-between; **medianía** f (*punto medio*) half-way (point); (*promedio*) average; (*calidad*) mediocrity; ✝ modest means (*or* circumstances); **mediano** *punto* middle; ♀ *etc.* median; *calidad* middling, medium, average; *b.s.* mediocre, indifferent; **medianoche** f midnight; **mediante** *prp.* by means of, through; **mediar** [1b] be in the middle; *fig.* mediate, intervene; *mediaba el mes de julio* it was half-way through July; *entre A y B median 50 km.* it is 50 km. from A to B.

médica f woman doctor; **medicamento** m medicine, drug; **medicastro** m quack; **medicina** f medicine; **medicinal** medicinal; **medicinar** [1a] treat, prescribe for.

medición *f* measuring, measurement; *surv.* survey(ing).

médico 1. medical; **2.** *m* doctor; medical practitioner; ~ *de cabecera* family doctor; ~ *dentista* dental surgeon; ~ *residente* house-physician.

medida *f* △ measure(ment); (*acto*) measuring; (*regla, vasija*) measure; fitting, size *de zapato etc.*; *fig.* measure, step; *fig.* moderation; *a* ~ *de* in proportion to, according to; *a* ~ *que* as; *hecho a* ~ made to measure; *tomar* ~*s fig.* take steps (*para inf.* to *inf.*); **medidor** *m S.Am.* meter.

medieval medi(a)eval.

medio 1. *adj. punto* mid(way), middle; △ mean; (*corriente*) average; (*mitad de*) half (a); ~ *pan* half a loaf; *a* ~ *tarde* in the middle of the afternoon; *las 2 y* ~*a* half-past 2; *a* ~*as hacer etc.* by halves; *dueño etc.* half; *dormido a* ~*as* half asleep; *ir a* ~*as* go halves (con with); **2.** *adv.* half; ~ *dormido* half asleep; *a* ~ *hacer* half done; **3.** *m* (*punto*) middle; (*mitad*) half; (*ambiente*) milieu, environment; *medium de comunicación etc.*; (*método*) means, way; (*medida*) measure; *deportes:* half-back; ~ *centro* centre half; ~*s pl.* ⊕ means; ~ *ambiente* environment; ~ *de cultivo* culture-medium; *justo* ~ happy medium, golden mean; *de en* ~ middle; *de por* ~, *en* ~ in between; *en* ~ *de* in the middle (*or* midst) of; *por* ~ *de* by means of, through; *v. quitar*; *no regatear* ~ *para inf.* spare no effort to *inf.*

mediocre middling, average; *b.s.* mediocre; **mediocridad** *f* mediocrity; ⊕ modest circumstances.

mediodía *m* midday, noon; *geog.* south.

medir [3l] measure (*a, por metros etc.* in; *a. fig.*); gauge; *surv.* survey; ~ (*con la vista*) size *s.o.* up; *poet.* scan; *mide 1,80 m.* (*p.*) he's 1.80 m. tall; ~*se* act with moderation.

meditabundo pensive, thoughtful; **meditación** *f* meditation *etc.*; **meditar** [1a] *v/t.* ponder, meditate (on); *proyecto* think out, plan; *v/i.* ponder, meditate; muse.

mediterráneo Mediterranean.

médium *m* medium (*p.*).

medra *f* increase; improvement; ⊕ prosperity; **medrar** [1a] (*crecer*) grow; (*mejorar*) improve; ⊕ *etc.* thrive, prosper, do well; *¡medrados estamos!* now we're in a mess!, a fine thing you've done!

medroso fearful, timid; (*horroroso*) dreadful.

médula *f*, **medula** *f anat.* marrow; ⊕ pith; *fig.* essence; ~ *espinal* spinal cord.

medusa *f* jelly-fish.

megaciclo *m* megacycle.

megáfono *m* megaphone.

megalomanía *f* megalomania.

megatón *m* megaton.

mejicano *adj. a. su. m*, **a** *f* Mexican.

mejido *huevo* beaten.

mejilla *f* cheek.

mejillón *m* mussel.

mejor 1. *adj. comp.* better; *sup.* best; *postor* highest; *lo* ~ the best thing (*or* part *etc.*); *a lo* ~ probably, maybe, with any luck; (*inesperadamente*) suddenly; **2.** *adv. comp.* better; *sup.* best; ~ *quisiera inf.* I would rather *inf.*; ~ *que* rather than; ~ *que* ~ all the better; **mejora** *f* improvement; ~*s pl.* △ alterations; repairs; **mejoramiento** *m* improvement.

mejorana *f* marjoram.

mejorar [1a] *v/t.* improve; enhance; *postura* raise; *v/i.*, ~*se* improve (*a. meteor.*); ⚕ recover, get better; ⊕ *etc.* prosper; **mejoría** *f* improvement, recovery.

mejunje *m* F brew, mixture stuff.

melado *m* treacle, syrup.

melancolía *f* gloom(iness), melancholy; ⚕ melancholia; **melancólico** gloomy, sad, melancholy; (*pensativo*) dreamy, wistful.

melaza *f* (*a.* ~*s pl.*) molasses; treacle.

melena *f* long hair, loose hair; *esp.* pony-tail; *zo.* mane; *estar en* ~ have one's hair down; **melenudo** long-haired; with flowing hair; *b.s.* bushy.

melifluo *fig.* mellifluous, sweet.

melindre *m fig.* daintiness; affectation; ~*s pl.* dainty ways; *b.s.* affectation; squeamishness; (*moral*) prudery; *gastar* ~*s* = **melindrear** [1a] F be affected, be finicky; **melindroso** affected; squeamish; finicky; (*moralmente*) prudish.

melocotón *m* peach; **melocotonero** *m* peach (tree).

melodía f melody, tune; (*calidad*) melodiousness; **melodioso** melodious, tuneful.

melodrama m melodrama; **melodramático** melodramatic.

melón m melon; F nut; (*p.*) idiot; **melonada** f F silly thing.

meloso honeyed, sweet; *fig.* gentle, sweet.

mella f notch, nick, dent; (*hueco*) gap; hacer ~ (*reprensión etc.*) sink in, strike home; (*causar efecto*) tell (en on); (*dañar*) do damage (en to); **mellado** *filo* jagged, ragged; gap-toothed; **mellar** [1a] notch, nick, dent; *fig.* damage.

mellizo adj. a. su. m, a f twin.

membrana f membrane; *orn. a.* web.

membrete m note, memo; (*inscripción*) letter-head, heading.

membrillo m ♀ quince; (*carne de*) ~ quince-jelly.

membrudo burly, brawny.

memez f silly thing; **memo** silly, stupid.

memorable memorable; **memorándum** m memorandum; (*librito*) notebook; **memoria** f memory; (*relación*) report, statement; (*nota*) memorandum; (*solicitud*) petition; (*ponencia*) paper; ~s pl. memoirs *de p.*; transactions *de sociedad*; (*saludo*) regards; ~ anual annual report; digno de ~ memorable; flaco de ~ forgetful; de ~ *aprender* by heart; hablar from memory; en ~ de in memory of; hacer ~ de bring up, recall; **memorial** m petition; ⚖ brief; **memorialista** m amanuensis.

mena f ore.

menaje m family, household; (*muebles*) furnishings.

mención f mention; **mencionar** [1a] mention, refer to, name; sin ~ let alone.

mendacidad f mendacity; **mendaz** mendacious, lying.

mendicante adj. a. su. m/f mendicant; **mendicidad** f begging; (*condición*) beggarliness; **mendigar** [1h] beg; **mendigo** m, a f beggar.

mendrugo m (hard) crust.

menear [1a] move; *cabeza etc.* shake, toss; *cola* wag; *caderas* swing, waggle; *cálamo* wield; *negocio* handle; F *peor es meneallo* leave

well alone; ~se F bestir o.s., get a move on; ¡~! get going!; **meneo** m shaking *etc.*; F hiding.

menester 1.: ser ~ be necessary; **2.** ~es pl. duties, jobs; F gear, tackle; F hacer sus ~ euph. do one's business; **menesteroso** needy.

menestral m workman, artisan.

mengano m, a f (Mr *etc.*) So-and-so.

mengua f decrease, dwindling; decline; poverty; en ~ de to the discredit of; **menguado** (*cobarde*) cowardly, spineless; (*tonto*) silly; (*tacaño*) mean; **menguante 1.** dwindling *etc.*; **2.** f ⚓ ebb tide; waning *de luna*; *fig.* decline; **menguar** [1i] decrease, dwindle; (*marea etc.*) go down; (*luna*) wane; *fig.* decline, decay.

mengue m F devil.

meningitis f meningitis.

menor 1. adj. órdenes, ♪ *etc.* minor; **2.** adj. comp. smaller, lesser; *edad*: younger (que than), junior (que to); v. edad; **3.** adj. sup. smallest, least; youngest *etc.*; **4.:** al por ~ retail; por ~ in detail; **5.** m/f minor, young person; apto para ~s cine: U(niversal).

menos 1. prp. except; ⅋ less, minus; 5 ~ 3 son 2 3 from 5 leaves 2; las 2 ~ cuarto a quarter to 2; **2.** adv. comp. less; sup. least; ~ de, ~ de lo que, ~ que less than; lo de ~ the least of it; 5 de ~ 5 short; una libra de ~ a pound less; al ~, (a) lo ~, por lo ~ at least; **3.** cj.: a ~ que unless; **4.** adj. signo minus; **5.** m minus (sign).

menos...: ~cabar [1a] lessen, reduce; (*dañar*) damage, impair; (*deslucir*) discredit; ~cabo m lessening; damage, loss; en ~ de to the detriment of; ~preciar [1b] (*desdeñar*) scorn, despise; (*insultar*) slight; (*subestimar*) underrate; ~preciativo scornful; slighting; ~precio m scorn, contempt.

mensaje m message; **mensajero** m, a f messenger.

menstruación f, **menstruo** m menstruation.

mensual monthly; 100 ptas ~es 100 ptas a month; **mensualidad** f monthly payment (*or* salary *etc.*); **mensualmente** monthly.

ménsula f bracket, corbel.

mensurable measurable; **mensuración** f mensuration.

menta f ♀ mint.

mental mental; *trabajo etc.* intellectual; **mentalidad** f mentality; **mentar** [1k] mention, name; **mente** f mind.

mentecato 1. silly, stupid; **2.** *m,* **a** f idiot.

mentidero m F talking-shop; **mentir** [3i] lie, tell a lie (*or* lies); **mentira** f lie; (*en general*) lying, deceitfulness; *lit. etc.* fiction, invention; ¡*parece* ~! you don't say so!; well (I never)!; *parece* ~ *que* it seems impossible that; *aunque parece* ~ however unlikely it seems; **mentirijillas:** *de* ~ as a joke; *jugar* for fun; **mentirilla** f fib, white lie; **mentiroso 1.** lying, deceitful; **2.** *m,* **a** f liar; **mentís** m denial; *dar el* ~ *a* deny, give the lie to.

mentol m menthol.

mentón m chin.

mentor m mentor.

menú m menu.

menudear [1a] *v/t.* repeat frequently; tell in detail; *v/i.* be frequent, happen frequently; go into detail *contando*; F rain, come thick and fast; **menudencia** f trifle; ~s *pl.* trifles; little things, odds and ends; (*despojos*) offal; **menudeo:** ↑ *al* ~ retail; **menudillos** m/pl. giblets; **menudo 1.** small, tiny; slight, trifling; meticulous; *a* ~ often; *por* ~ in detail; **2.** *m* small change; ~s *pl.* offal.

meñique m little finger.

meollo m *anat.* marrow; *fig.* (*esencia*) gist; (*sustancia*) solid stuff, meat; (*seso*) brains.

mequetrefe m whippersnapper; (*entrometido*) busybody.

meramente merely, solely.

mercachifle m hawker, huckster; **mercadear** [1a] trade; **mercader** m merchant; **mercadería** f commodity; ~s *pl.* merchandise; **mercado** m market; ~ *negro* black market; **mercancía 1.** f commodity; ~s *pl.* goods, merchandise; **2.** ~s m 🚂 goods train; **mercante** ⚓ **1.** merchant *attr.*; **2.** *m* merchant ship; **mercantil** mercantile, commercial, trading *attr.*; *b.s.* mercenary; **mercar** [1g] buy.

merced f: *mst* † favour; benefit;

reward; *vuestra* ~ your honour, your worship; *a* ~ voluntarily; ~ *a* thanks to; *estar a la* ~ *de* be at the mercy of.

mercenario 1. mercenary; **2.** *m* ✗ mercenary; *fig.* hack, hireling.

mercería f haberdashery; (*tienda*) haberdasher's (shop).

mercerizar [1f] mercerize.

mercero m haberdasher.

mercurial mercurial; **mercurio** m mercury.

merecedor deserving (*de* of); **merecer** [2d] *v/t.* deserve; be worth(y of); *alabanza etc.* earn (*a.* ~**se**); (*necesitar*) need; *v/i.* be worthy; ~ *mucho* be very deserving; **merecido 1.:** *bien* ~ *lo tiene* it serves him right; **2.** *m* deserts; *llevar su* ~ get one's deserts; **merecimiento** m deserts; merit, worthiness.

merendar [1k] *v/t.* have *s.t.* for tea; (*acechar*) peep at; (*a.* ~**se**) F wangle; *fortuna* squander; *v/i.* have tea; picnic *en el campo.*

merengue m meringue.

meridiana f couch; chaise-longue; **meridiano** *adj. a. su. m* meridian; *a la* ~*a* at noon; **meridional 1.** southern; **2.** *m/f* southerner.

merienda f tea; (*bocadillo*) snack; packed meal *para viaje*; picnic *en el campo*; F *juntar* ~s join forces.

mérito m merit; worth, value; *hacer* ~ *de* mention; *hacer* ~s strive to be deserving; **meritorio** meritorious, worthy.

merluza f hake; *sl. estar* (*con la*) ~ be sozzled.

merma f decrease; wastage, loss; **mermar** [1a] *v/t.* reduce, deplete; *ración etc.* cut down on; *v/i.* decrease, dwindle; (*líquido*) go down; *fig.* waste away.

mermelada f jam.

mero 1. *adj.* mere; pure, simple; *S.Am.* selfsame, very; **2.** *adv. S.Am.* soon, in a moment.

merodeador m marauder; **merodear** [1a] maraud.

mes m month.

mesa f table; desk *de trabajo*; counter *de oficina*; ▲ landing; *geog.* tableland, plateau; (*junta*) presiding committee, board; ~ *de noche* bedside table; ~ *de operaciones* operating table; ~ *redonda* table d'hôte; *hist. a. pol.* round table;

alzar (or levantar) la ~ clear away; *poner la* ~ lay the table.
mesana *f* mizzen.
mesarse [1a]: ~ *el pelo* tear one's hair.
mescolanza *f* = *mezcolanza.*
meseta *f* tableland, plateau; △ landing; **mesilla** *f* occasional table; ~ *de chimenea* mantelpiece.
mesmerismo *m* mesmerism.
mesón[1] *m phys.* meson.
mesón[2] *m* † inn; **mesonero** *m*, a *f* innkeeper.
mestizar [1f] cross-breed; **mestizo** *adj. a. su. m*, a *f* half-caste, half-breed; *zo.* cross-bred, mongrel.
mesura *f* gravity *etc.*; **mesurado** grave; moderate, restrained; sensible; calm; **mesurarse** [1a] restrain o.s.
meta 1. *f* goal (*a. fig.*); winning-post *en carrera*; **2.** *m* goalkeeper.
metabólico metabolic; **metabolismo** *m* metabolism.
metafísica *f* metaphysics.
metáfora *f* metaphor; **metafórico** metaphoric(al).
metal *m* metal; ♩ brass; timbre *de voz*; *fig.* quality; *el vil* ~ filthy lucre; **metálico 1.** metallic; metal *attr.*; **2.** *m* specie, coin; *en* ~ in cash; **metalífero** metalliferous; **metalistería** *f* metalwork; **metalurgia** *f* metallurgy; **metalúrgico** metallurgic(al).
metamorfosear [1a] metamorphose, transform; **metamorfosis** *f* metamorphosis, transformation.
metano *m* methane.
metedúría *f* smuggling.
meteórico meteoric; **meteorito** *m* meteor; **meteoro** *m fig.* meteor; **meteorología** *f* meteorology; **meteorológico** meteorological, weather *attr.*; **meteorologista** *m/f* meteorologist.
meter [2a] put, insert, introduce (*en* in, into); (*apretando*) squeeze in; smuggle (in) *de contrabando*; *fig.* make, cause; *v. miedo etc.*; ~ *a una p. en* let a p. in for; *¿quién le mete en esto?* who told you to interfere?; ~*se fig.* meddle, interfere (*mucho a* lot); (*hacerse*) *monja* become; *soldado* turn; ~ *a su.* become; (*con ambición*) set o.s. up as; ~ *a inf.* take it upon o.s. to *inf.*; ~ *con* meddle with; *p.* pick a quarrel with; ~ *en*

go into, get into; *fig.* interfere in; *dificultades* get into; *negocio* get involved in; *¡no te metas en lo que no te importa!* mind your own business!; *no* ~ *donde no le llaman* mind one's own business; ~ *en sí mismo* go into one's shell.
meticuloso meticulous, scrupulous.
metido 1. : ~ *en sí* introspective *estar muy* ~ *con* be well in with; *estar muy* ~ *en* be deeply involved in; **2.** *m* shove, punch.
metilo *m* methyl.
metimiento *m* insertion; *fig.* influence.
metódico methodic(al); **método** *m* method; **metodología** *f* methodology.
metraje *m*: (*cinta de*) *largo* ~ full-length film.
metralla *f* shrapnel.
métrica *f* metrics; **métrico** metric, metrical; **metro**[1] *m* 🔔, *poet.* metre; (*de cinta*) tape-measure; (*plegable*) rule; (*recto*) ruler.
metro[2] *m* 🚇 underground, tube, subway *Am.*
metrónomo *m* metronome.
metrópoli *f* metropolis; *pol.* mother country; **metropolitano 1.** *adj. a. su. m eccl.* metropolitan; **2.** *m* 🚇 underground railway.
mexicano *adj. a. su. m*, a *f S.Am.* Mexican.
mezcla *f* mixture; *esp. fig.* blend; medley; △ mortar; *sin* ~ *bebida* neat; **mezclador** *m* mixer; **mezclar** [1a] mix (up); blend; (*unir*) merge; *cartas* shuffle; ~*se* mix, mingle (*con* with); *b.s.* get mixed (en up in); (*entrometerse*) meddle (*en* in); **mezcolanza** *f* hotchpotch, jumble.
mezquindad *f* meanness *etc.*; **mezquino** (*pobre*) poor, wretched; (*avaro*) mean; (*pequeño*) wretchedly small; (*insignificante*) petty, paltry.
mezquita *f* mosque.
mi, mis *pl.* my.
mí me.
miaja *f* crumb, bit.
miasma *m* miasma.
miau *m* mew, miaow.
mica *f min.* mica.
mico *m*, a *f* monkey; F *dar* (*or hacer*) ~ miss a date (*a* with).
micro... micro...
microbio *m* microbe.

microcosmo *m* microcosm.
microfilm *m* microfilm.
micrófono *m* microphone; *teleph.*
mouthpiece.
microfundio *m* small-holding.
micrómetro *m* micrometer.
microscópico microscopic; **microscopio** *m* microscope.
micho *m*, **a** *f* F puss(y).
miedo *m* fear (*a* of); *por ~ de que*
for fear that; *dar* (*or meter*) *~ a*
frighten; *tener ~* be afraid (*a* of);
miedoso scared, fearful; *carácter* \
miel *f* honey. [timid.]
miembro *m* anat. limb; *anat.*, *gr.*,
p. etc. member.
mientes: *parar ~ en* reflect on.
mientras while, as long as; *~* (*que*)
whereas; *~ más ... más* the more ...
the more; *~ tanto* meanwhile.
miércoles *m* Wednesday; *~ de ceniza* Ash Wednesday.
mierda *f* F shit.
mies *f* corn, wheat, grain; *~es pl.*
cornfields.
miga *f* bit; crumb *de pan*; *fig.* substance; F *hacer buenas ~s* get on
well, hit it off (*con* with); **migaja** *f*
bit; crumb *de pan* (*a. fig.*); *~s pl.*
leavings; **migar** [1h] crumble.
migración *f* migration.
migraña *f* migraine.
migratorio migratory.
mijo *m* millet.
mil a thousand; *dos ~* two thousand;
~es pl. thousands.
milagro *m* miracle; *fig. a.* wonder;
por ~ by a miracle; *vivir de ~* have
a hard time of it; **milagroso** miraculous.
milano *m* orn. kite.
mildeu *m* mildew.
milenario 1. millennial; **2.** *m* =
milenio *m* millennium.
milenrama *f* yarrow.
milésimo *adj. a. su. m* thousandth.
milicia *f* (*ps.*) militia; soldiery;
(*profesión*) soldiering; (*período*)
military service (*a.* **mili** *f* F);
(*ciencia*) art of war; **miliciano** *m*
militiaman.
miligramo *m* milligram(me); **mililitro** *m* millilitre; **milímetro** *m*
millimetre.
militante militant; **militar 1.** military; (*guerrero*) warlike; *arte* of war;
2. *m* soldier; serviceman; **3.** [1a]
serve (in the army), soldier; *fig.*

militate (*contra* against); **militarismo** *m* militarism; **militarizar**
[1f] militarize.
milla *f* mile; *~ marina* nautical mile.
millar *m* thousand; *a ~es* in thousands, by the thousand; **millarada**
f (about a) thousand; **millón** *m*
million; *3 ~es de hombres* 3 million
men; **millonario** *m*, **a** *f* millionaire; **millonésimo** *adj. a. su. m*
millionth.
mimar [1a] (*acariciar*) pet, fondle;
fig. pamper, spoil; *poderoso* humour.
mimbre *mst m ♀* osier; (*materia*)
wicker; *de ~(s)* wicker(work) *attr.*;
mimbrear(se) [1a] sway; **mimbrera** *f* osier.
mimeógrafo *m* mimeograph.
mimetismo *m* mimicry; **mímica** *f*
gesticulation; sign language; (*remedo*)
mimicry; (*una ~*) mime; **mímico**
mimic; imitative; **mimo 1.** *m* thea.
etc. mime; *hacer ~ de* mime; **2.** *m*
pampering, indulgence; *hacer ~s a*
make a fuss of; **mimoso** spoilt.
mina *f* mine (*a.* ⚒, ⚓, *fig.*); lead,
refill *de lápiz*; *fig.* storehouse; *~ de*
carbón coal-mine; **minador** *m*
⚒ sapper; ⚒ mining engineer;
(*buque*) *~* minelayer; **minar** [1a]
mine (*a.* ⚒, ⚓); (*cavar lentamente*)
undermine, wear away; *fig.* undermine, sap.
mineral 1. mineral; **2.** *m* ⚒ mineral;
⚒ ore; *~ de hierro* iron ore; **mineralizar** [1f] mineralize; **mineralogía** *f* mineralogy; **mineralogista**
m/f mineralogist; **minería** *f* mining; **minero 1.** mining; **2.** *m* miner.
miniatura 1. *f* miniature; *en ~* in
miniature; **2.** *adj.* miniature; *perro*
etc. toy.
mínimo 1. smallest, least; minimum; minimal; tiny; *sin la más ~a*
dificultad without the slightest difficulty; *ni en lo más ~* not in the
slightest; **2.** *m* minimum; *meteor. ~*
de presión trough; **mínimum** *m*
minimum.
minino *m*, **a** *f* F puss(y).
minio *m* red lead.
ministerial ministerial; **ministerio** *m* ministry; **ministro** *m*
minister; *primer ~* prime minister.
minorar [1a] reduce, lessen; **minoría** *f*, **minoridad** *f* minority.
minucia *f* minuteness; *~s pl.* details,

minutiae; **minuciosidad** f thoroughness etc.; **minucioso** thorough, meticulous; minute.

minué m minuet.

minúscula f small letter; **minúsculo** small (a. typ.), tiny.

minuta f (borrador) first draft; (apunte) minute, memorandum; list; (comida) menu; **minutar** [1a] draft; minute; **minutero** m minute-hand; **minutisa** f sweet william; **minuto** m minute.

mío, mía 1. pron. mine; **2.** adj. (tras su.) of mine.

miope short-sighted; **miopía** f short-sightedness, miopia ⨂.

mira f ⚔ (a. ~s pl.) sights; fig. object, aim; de amplias ~s broad in outlook; de ~s estrechas narrow, narrow-minded; insular, parochial; con ~s a inf. with a view to ger.; estar a la ~ be on the look-out (de for); tener ~s sobre have designs on; **mirada** f look; glance; gaze; expression de cara; ~ fija stare; apuñalar con la ~ look daggers at; echar una ~ a glance at; (vigilar) keep an eye on; **miradero** m cynosure (of all eyes); (asunto) chief concern; (lugar) look-out, vantage-point; **mirado** circumspect; bien ~ well thought-of; **mirador** m △ bay-window, balcony; (lugar) vantage-point; **miramiento** m considerateness; caution; ~s pl. fuss; sin ~s unceremoniously; tratar sin ~s freq. ride rough-shod over.

mirar [1a] **1.** v/t. look at; watch; fig. look on, consider (como as); (reflexionar sobre) think carefully about; (tener cuidado con) watch, be careful about; ~ fijamente stare at; ~ bien like; ~ mal dislike; **2.** v/i. look; ¡mira! look! (protesta) look here!; (aviso) look out!; ~ a fig. aim at, have in mind; (provecho) look to; △ etc. face, open on to; ~ alrededor look around; ~ por ventana look out of; fig. look after; ~ de través squint; **3.** ~se look at o.s.; (recíproco) look at each other; ~ en ello watch one's step.

mirasol m sunflower.

miríada f myriad.

miriápodo m millipede.

mirilla f peep-hole, spy-hole; phot. viewer.

mirlo m blackbird; ~ blanco extraordinary thing; impossible dream.

mirón 1. inquisitive; **2.** m, -a f onlooker; b.s. Nosey Parker; estar de ~ look on.

mirra f myrrh.

mirto m myrtle.

misa f mass; ~ del gallo Midnight Mass; ~ mayor High Mass; ~ rezada Low Mass; **misal** m missal.

misantropía f misanthropy; **misantrópico** misanthropic(al); **misántropo** m misanthrope.

miscelánea f miscellany; **misceláneo** miscellaneous.

miserable 1. (desdichado) wretched; (tacaño) mean; sueldo etc. miserable, pitifully small; conducta contemptible; lugar squalid, sordid; **2.** m/f wretch; (vil) cad; **miseria** f misery, wretchedness; poverty; meanness; F (una ~) pittance; vivir en la ~ live in poverty; **misericordia** f pity; (perdón) forgiveness; mercy; **misericordioso** compassionate; merciful; **mísero** wretched.

misión f mission; **misionero** adj. a. su. m, a f missionary; **misiva** f missive.

mismísimo selfsame, very same; **mismo** same (que as); enfático: en ese ~ momento at that very moment; el ~ obispo the same bishop; el obispo ~ the bishop himself; yo ~ I myself; yo ~ lo vi I saw it myself; es la ~a bondad he is kindness itself; lo ~ the same thing; él hizo lo ~ he did the same, he did likewise; por lo ~ for the same reason; lo ~ que prp. just like; eso ~ digo yo that's just what I say; v. ahora etc.

misoginia f misogyny; **misógino** m misogynist.

misterio m mystery; secrecy; thea. mystery play; **misterioso** mysterious; mystifying, puzzling; **mística** f, **misticismo** m mysticism; **místico 1.** mystic(al); **2.** m, a f mystic; **mistificación** f hoax; hocus-pocus; **mistificar** [1g] hoax; mystify.

mitad f half; (medio) middle; mi cara ~ my better half; ~ y ~ half and half; a ~ de camino etc. half-way there; a ~ de precio half-price; en la ~ de in the middle of; por la ~ partir in halves, down the middle.

mítico mythical.
mitigación *f* mitigation *etc.*; **mitigar** [1h] *efecto* mitigate; *dolor* relieve; *cólera* appease, mollify; *severidad* temper.
mitin *m esp. pol.* meeting.
mito *m* myth; **mitología** *f* mythology; **mitológico** mythological.
mitón *m* mitten.
mitra *f* mitre.
mixomatosis *f* myxomatosis.
mixto 1. mixed; **2.** *m* match; 🚂 passenger and goods train; **mixtura** *f* mixture; **mixturar** [1a] mix.
mnemotécnica *f* mnemonics.
moaré *m* moiré.
mobiliario *m* suite; **moblaje** *m* (suite of) furniture.
mocear [1a] play around; **mocedad** *f* youth; *pasar las* ⁓*es* sow one's wild oats; **mocetón** *m* strapping youth; **mocetona** *f* big girl.
moción *f* motion (*a. parl.*), movement.
mocito 1. very young; **2.** *m*, a *f* youngster.
moco *m* mucus; *metall.* slag; *llorar a* ⁓ *tendido* cry like a baby; **mocoso 1.** snivelling; F ill-bred; **2.** *m* F brat.
mochila *f* rucksack, knapsack; ✖ pack.
mocho 1. *zo.* hornless, polled; ♀ pollard(ed); *torre* flat-topped; (*sin punta*) blunt; F shorn; **2.** *m* butt.
mochuelo *m*: ⁓ (*común*) little owl.
moda *f* fashion; style; *a la* ⁓, *de* ⁓ in fashion, fashionable; *fuera de* ⁓, *pasado de* ⁓ out of fashion, outdated; *muy de* ⁓ very much in the fashion. [manners.)
modal 1. modal; **2.** ⁓*es m/pl.*)
modelado *m* modelling; **modelar** [1a] model (*sobre* on); (*dar forma a*) fashion, shape; **modelo 1.** *adj.* model; **2.** *m* model (*a. fig.*); pattern; **3.** *f* model, mannequin.
moderación *f* moderation; **moderado** moderate (*a. pol.*); **moderar** [1a] moderate; *velocidad etc.* reduce; (*refrenar*) restrain; ⁓*se* (*p.*) control o.s., restrain o.s.
modernidad *f* modernity; **modernismo** *m* modernism; **modernizar** [1f] modernize; **moderno** modern; present-day; up-to-date.

modestia *f* modesty; **modesto** modest.
módico reasonable, moderate.
modificación *f* modification; **modificar** [1g] modify.
modismo *m* idiom.
modista *f* dressmaker; ⁓ (*de sombreros*) milliner; **modisto** *m* fashion-designer.
modo *m* way, manner, mode (*a. ⅃*); method; form *de gobierno etc.*; *gr.* mood; *fig.* moderation; ⁓*s pl.* manners; ⁓ *de empleo* (*en envase*) instructions for use; *a mi* ⁓ *de ver* to my way of thinking; *a su* ⁓ in his own way; *al* ⁓ *inglés* in the English style; *uno a* ⁓ *de* a sort (*or* kind) of; *de ese* ⁓ at that rate; *de este* ⁓ (in) this way, like this; *de otro* ⁓ otherwise; *de un* ⁓ *u otro* somehow or other; *de ningún* ⁓ by no means; *¡de ningún* ⁓*!* certainly not!; *de* ⁓ *que* so that; *¿de* ⁓ *que* ...? so ...?; *de todos* ⁓*s* at any rate; *en cierto* ⁓ in some degree; in a way; *ver el* ⁓ *de inf.* see one's way to *ger. or inf.*
modorra *f* drowsiness, heaviness; *vet.* staggers; **modorro** drowsy; *fig.* dull, stupid.
modoso quiet, nicely behaved.
modulación *f* modulation; *radio*: ⁓ *de frecuencia* frequency modulation; **modular** [1a] modulate.
mofa *f* mockery, derision; (*una* ⁓) taunt, gibe; *hacer* ⁓ *de* = *mofarse de*; **mofador** mocking *etc.*; **mofar** [1a] jeer, sneer; ⁓*se de* make fun of; mock, scoff at, sneer at.
mofeta *f* ✖ fire-damp; *zo.* skunk.
mofletudo fat-cheeked, chubby.
mogol *adj. a. su. m*, -a *f* Mongol, Mongolian; *el gran* ♀ the Great Mogul.
mogollón *m* F sponger, hanger-on; *comer de* ⁓ scrounge a meal.
mohín *m* face, grimace; **mohina** *f* (*disgusto*) annoyance; (*murria*) sulkiness, sulks; (*resentimiento*) grudge; *fácil a las* ⁓*s* easily depressed; **mohino** (*triste*) gloomy, depressed; (*murrio*) sulky; (*malhumorado*) peevish.
moho *m* rust; ♀ mould, mildew; **mohoso** rusty; ♀ mouldy, musty; *chiste* stale.
moisés *m* carry-cot.

mojada *f* wetting, soaking; stab;
mojado wet; soaked; damp,
moist; **mojar** [1a] *v/t.* wet; *(ligera-mente)* moisten; *(completamente)*
drench, soak; *pluma* dip (en into);
(apuñalar) stab; *v/i.*: ~ en F get
mixed up in; **~se** get drenched
etc.

mojicón *m* sponge cake; *(bollo)*
bun; F punch.

mojiganga *f* † masquerade, mum-mery; F pretentious thing.

mojigatería *f* hypocrisy; prudery
etc.; **mojigato 1.** hypocritical;
(beato) sanctimonious; *(puritano)*
prudish; **2.** *m, a f* hypocrite;
prude.

mojón *m* landmark, boundary
stone; *(de camino)* milestone.

mola *f* ❀ mole.

molar *m* molar.

molde *m* mould; cast *de yeso etc.*;
sew. etc. pattern; *esp. fig.* model;
venir de ~ come just right; **moldear**
[1a] mould; *(vaciar etc.)* cast;
moldura *f* △ moulding.

mole *f* mass; bulk; △ pile.

molécula *f* molecule; **molecular**
molecular.

moledor *fig.* **1.** boring; **2.** *m* bore;
moler [2h] grind, mill; pound;
fig. *(fastidiar)* annoy; *(cansar)*
weary; ~ a palos beat *s.o.* up; F
estoy molido I'm done up.

molestar [1a] *(fastidiar)* annoy,
bother; *(incomodar)* bother, put
out; *(perturbar)* upset; *(doler)* hurt,
bother; ¿le molesta el ruido? do you
mind the noise?; ¿le molesta a Vd.
que fume? will it bother you if
I smoke?; **~se** bother *(con about,
en inf. to inf.)*; put o.s. out; *(perder
la calma)* be annoyed, get cross;
molestia *f* annoyance; bother,
nuisance; ❀ *etc.* discomfort; tomarse
la ~ de inf. take the trouble to inf.;
molesto annoying, trying; *p. etc.*
tiresome; *olor etc.* nasty; *trabajo*
irksome; *(sentirse)* bothered; *(in-quieto)* ill at ease; *(incómodo)* un-comfortable.

molicie *f* softness *(a. fig.)*; *fig.*
luxurious living; effeminacy.

molienda *f* grinding, milling; F
weariness; *(una ~)*· nuisance;
molinero *m* miller; **molinete** *m*
(toy) windmill; **molinillo** *m* mill,
grinder *para café etc.*; mincer *para*

carne; **molino** *m* mill; grinder;
~ de viento windmill.

molusco *m* mollusc.

mollar soft, mushy; *carne* lean;
tierra easily worked; **molleja** *f*
gizzard; **mollejón** *m*, **-a** *f* F (big)
softy; **mollera** *f anat.* crown of
the head; *freq.* noddle; F brains;
duro de ~ dense; *(porfiado)* pig-headed; F tener buena ~ have
brains.

momentáneo momentary; **mo-mento** *m* moment; *phys.* momen-tum; al ~ at once; de ~ adv. at (or
for) the moment; de poco ~ un-important; de un ~ a otro at any
moment.

momería *f* mummery, clowning.

momia *f* mummy; **momificar(se)**
[1g] mummify.

momio 1. lean; de ~ free; **2.** *m*
bargain.

momo *m* funny face.

mona *f zo.* monkey; F *(p.)* ape;
(borracho) drunk; *(borrachera)*
drunk, hangover; F coger *(or pillar)*
una ~ get boozed; F dormir la ~
sleep it off; F hecho una ~ quite put
out; F pintar la ~ act important.

monacal monastic; **monacillo** *m*
= monaguillo.

monada *f (bobada)* silly thing;
(estupidez) silliness; *(objeto)* lovely
thing, beauty; *(p.)* pretty girl; *(lo
bonito)* loveliness *etc.*; ~s *pl.*
flattery.

monag(uill)o *m* acolyte, server.

monarca *m* monarch; **monarquía**
f monarchy; **monárquico 1.** mo-narchic(al); *pol.* royalist, mon-archist; **2.** *m* royalist, monarchist;
monarquismo *m* monarchism.

monasterio *m* monastery; **mo-nástico** monastic.

monda *f* ✀ pruning, lopping; *(piel)*
peel(ings), skin; *sl.* es la ~ it's the
limit; *(p.)* co. he's a terror; **monda-dientes** *m* toothpick; **mondaduras**
f/pl. peel(ings), skin; **mondar** [1a]
(limpiar) cleanse; *fruta* peel; *árbol*
prune, lop; *dientes* pick; F *p.* cut
s.o.'s hair; *fig.* fleece; **mondo**
clean; pure; el asunto ~ es esto the
plain fact of the matter is; ~ y
lirondo plain, pure and simple.

mondongo *m* guts.

moneda *f* currency, coinage; *(una ~)*
coin; ~ dura hard currency; ~

suelta change; F *pagar en la misma*~ pay *s.o.* back; **monedero** *m*: ~ *falso* counterfeiter.

monería *f* (*mueca*) funny face; (*mímica*) mimicry; (*broma*) playful trick; pretty ways *de niño*; (*bagatela*) trifle.

monetario monetary, financial.

monigote *m* rag doll; *paint.* daub; (*p.*) colourless individual.

monises *m/pl.* F dough, brass.

monja *f* nun; **monje** *m* monk; **monjil** nun's, monk's, monkish.

mono[1] *m zo.* monkey; (*p.*) clown; *paint.* daub; *estar de* ~*s* be at daggers drawn.

mono[2] *m* overalls, boiler-suit; rompers *de niño*.

mono[3] F pretty, nice.

mono... mono...; ~**cromo** *adj. a. su. m* monochrome; **monóculo** *m* monocle.

mono...: ~**gamia** *f* monogamy; ~**grafía** *f* monograph; ~**grama** *m* monogram; ~**lito** *m* monolith; **monólogo** *m* monologue.

mono...: ~**manía** *f* monomania; ~**motor** ✕ single-engined; ~**plano** *m* monoplane; ~**plaza** *m* ✕ single-seater; ~**polio** *m* monopoly; ~**polista** *m/f* monopolist; ~**polizar** [1f] monopolize; ~**silábico** = **sílabo 1.** monosyllabic; **2.** *m* monosyllable; ~**teísmo** *m* monotheism; ~**tonía** *f* monotony; sameness, dreariness; **monótono** monotonous; *rutina etc.* humdrum, dreary.

monserga *f* gibberish; drivel.

monstruo *m* monster (*a. fig.*); *biol.* freak; **monstruosidad** *f* monstrosity; freak; **monstruoso** monstrous, monster *attr.*; *biol.* freakish; *fig.* monstrous, hideous.

monta *f* ✕ total; *de poca* ~ of small account; *cosa de poca* ~ mere trifle.

montacargas *m* (service) lift, hoist.

montado mounted; ⊕ built-in; *artillería* horse *attr.*; **montador** *m* (*p.*) fitter; **montadura** *f* mounting; (*engaste*) setting; **montaje** *m* ⊕ assembly; △ erection; **montante** *m* ⊕ upright, stanchion; △ transom; ✕ broadsword; ✝ total, amount.

montaña *f* mountain; ~ *rusa* switchback, scenic railway; **mon-**

tañero *m*, **-a** *f* mountaineer; **montañés 1.** mountain *attr.*; **2.** *m*, **-a** *f* highlander; *native of Santander region*; **montañismo** *m* mountaineering; **montañoso** mountainous; mountain *attr.*

montaplatos *m* dumb-waiter.

montar [1a] **1.** *v/t.* *caballo etc.* (*subir*) mount, (*ir*) ride; ⊕ assemble, put together, mount; △ erect; *joya* set; *escopeta* cock; *negocio* start, set up; ✗ amount to (*a. fig.*); **2.** *v/i.* mount (*a, en acc.*), get up (*a, en* on); ✗ ~ *a* amount to; ~ *a caballo* ride; ~ *en cólera* get angry; *tanto monta* it makes no odds.

montaraz 1. *zo.* mountain *attr.*; *fig.* wild; **2.** *m* keeper.

monte *m* mountain, hill; (*bosque*) woodland; (*despoblado*) wilds, wild country; ~ *alto* forest; ~ *bajo* scrub; ~ *de piedad* pawnbroker's; **montecillo** *m* hump, hummock; **montepío** *m* charitable organization, friendly society.

montera *f* cloth cap.

montería *f* hunting; **montero** *m* huntsman, hunter.

montés *gato etc.* wild.

montículo *m* hillock, mound.

montón *m* heap, pile; drift *de nieve*; F stack; F *un* ~ *de gente* masses of people; F *un* ~ *de cosas* heaps of things; ~*es pl.* F tons, loads; *a* ~ together; *a* ~*es* in plenty, galore; *del* ~ perfectly ordinary.

montuoso hilly.

montura *f* (*caballo*) mount; (*silla*) saddle; (*arreos*) harness; ⊕ mounting; *sin* ~ bare-back.

monumental monumental; **monumento** *m* monument (*a. fig.*); (*mausoleo*) memorial; ~*s pl. freq.* sights *de interés turístico.*

monzón *m or f* monsoon.

moña: *sl. estar con la* ~ be sozzled.

moño *m* bun, chignon; *orn.* crest; F *ponerse* ~*s* put it on.

moquero *m* handkerchief.

moqueta *f* moquette.

moquete *m* punch (on the nose).

moquillo *m vet.* distemper; *orn.* pip.

mora[1] *f* mulberry; blackberry *de zarza.*

mora[2]: *ponerse en* ~ default.

morada *f* dwelling, home; (*estancia*) stay; *última* ~ (last) resting-place.

morado purple, dark violet.
morador m, -a f inhabitant.
moral[1] m ♣ mulberry (tree).
moral[2] **1.** moral; **2.** f (ciencia) ethics; (moralidad) morals; morale de ejército etc.; **moraleja** f moral; **moralidad** f morality, morals, ethics; (moraleja) moral; **moralista** m/f, **moralizador** m, -a f moralist; **moralizar** [1f] moralize.
morar [1a] live, dwell; (permanecer) stay.
moratoria f moratorium.
mórbido ⚘ morbid; **morbosidad** f morbidity, morbidness; **morboso** diseased, morbid.
morcilla f black pudding; thea. gag, unscripted bit.
mordacidad f pungency etc.; **mordaz** fig. biting, scathing, pungent; **mordaza** f gag; ⊕ clamp, jaw; **mordedura** f bite; **morder** [2h] bite; ⊕ wear down; ⊕ eat away; fig. gossip about, run down; **mordiscar** [1g] nibble; p. nip; (caballo etc.) champ; **mordisco** m nibble; nip; (bocado) bite.
morena[1] f geol. moraine.
morena[2] f dark girl, brunette; **moreno** (dark) brown; p. dark; (con exceso) swarthy; (de pelo ⌣) dark-haired.
morera f mulberry (tree).
morfina f morphia, morphine; **morfinómano** m drug-addict.
morfología f morphology.
moribundo 1. dying; esp. fig. moribund; **2.** m dying man.
morigerado well-behaved, law-abiding.
morillo m fire-dog.
morir [3k; p.p. muerto] v/t.: fue muerto he was killed; v/i. die (a. fig.); (fuego etc.) die down; 🚂 etc. (línea) end; (calle) come out (en in); ¡muera X! down with X!; ⌣ ahogado drown; ⌣ de frío freeze to death; ⌣ de hambre starve (to death; a. fig.); ⌣se die; (miembro) go to sleep; ⌣ por be dying for; ⌣ por inf. be dying to inf.
morisco 1. Moorish; **2.** m, a f Moorish convert to Christianity; **moro 1.** Moorish; **2.** m, a f Moor; hay ⌣s en la costa you'd better watch out.
morisqueta f dirty trick.
morosidad f slowness; **moroso**

1. slow, dilatory; ✝ slow to pay up; **2.** m ✝ defaulter.
morra f top of one's head; andar a la ⌣ come to blows; **morrada** f butt de carnero; bang on the head.
morral m haversack; hunt. pouch; nose-bag de caballo; F lout.
morriña f F blues; (nostalgia) homesickness.
morro m zo. snout; 🐦 nose; geog. headland; anat. thick lip; andar de ⌣ be at odds; **morrocotudo** F (pistonudo) smashing, super; (fuerte) strong; negocio sticky; important.
morrongo m F cat.
morsa f walrus.
mortaja f shroud; **mortal** adj. a. su. m/f mortal; herida etc. fatal; **mortalidad** mortality; toll, loss of life en accidente; (estadística) death-rate; **mortandad** f death-roll; ⚔ etc. slaughter, carnage; **mortecino** dying, failing; luz dim, fading; color dull; hacer la ⌣a play dead.
mortero m mortar (a. ⚔).
mortífero deadly, lethal; **mortificación** f mortification; humiliation; **mortificar** [1g] mortify; humiliate; (despechar) spite; (doler) hurt, kill; **mortuorio**: esp. casa ⌣a house of the deceased.
morueco m zo. ram.
mosaico[1] eccl. Mosaic.
mosaico[2] m mosaic.
mosca f fly; F ✝ dough; F (p.) nuisance, bore; ⌣s pl. sparks; ⌣ de la carne meat fly; ⌣ doméstica house-fly; ⌣ muerta sly sort; ⌣s pl. volantes spots before the eyes; F aflojar (or soltar) la ⌣ fork out; estar con ⌣ be fed up to the teeth; F papar ⌣s gape, gawk; **moscarda** f blowfly, bluebottle; **moscardón** m = moscarda; (avispón) hornet; F nuisance, pest.
moscatel adj. a. su. m muscatel; F (p.) pest, nuisance.
moscón m F nuisance.
mosqueado spotted; brindled; **mosqueador** m fly-whisk; **mosquearse** [1a] fig. take offence.
mosquete m musket; **mosquetero** m musketeer: thea. † groundling.
mosquita f **muerta** hypocrite; **mosquitero** m mosquito net; **mosquito** m mosquito; gnat.

mostacho *m* moustache.

mostachón *m* macaroon.

mostaza *f* mustard.

mosto *m* must, unfermented grape juice.

mostrador *m* counter; bar *de taberna*; ⊕ dial; **mostrar** [1m] show.

mostrenco ownerless, unclaimed; *título etc.* in abeyance; F *p.* homeless, *animal* stray; *obra* crude; *p.* (*zafio*) dense.

mota *f* burl *de paño*; (*hilacho*) thread; (*punto*) speck; *fig.* fault.

mote *m* nickname; (*lema*) motto.

motear [1a] speckle; dapple.

motejar [1a] nickname; ~ de brand *s.o.* as.

motín *m* revolt, rising; riot.

motivación *f* motivation; **motivar** [1a] cause, give rise to, motivate; justify; **motivo 1.** motive; **2.** *m* motive, reason (*de* for); ♪, *paint.* motif; *con* ~ *de* on the occasion of; (*debido a*) owing to; *con este* ~ for this reason, because of this.

moto *f* F motorbike; ~**carro** *m* three-wheeler; ~**cicleta** *f* motorcycle; ~**ciclista** *m/f* motor-cyclist; ~ de escolta outrider; ~**nave** *f* motor vessel.

motor 1. ⊕ motive; *anat.* motor; **2.** *m* motor, engine; ~ de arranque starter; ~ de combustión interna, ~ de explosión internal combustion engine; ~ a chorro jet engine; ~ de fuera de borda outboard motor; **motora** *f*, **motorbote** *m* motorboat; **motorismo** *m* motor-cycling; *mot.* motoring; **motorista** *m/f* motor-cyclist; *mot.* motorist; **motorizar** [1f] motorize; **motriz** *v.* *fuerza.*

movedizo loose, unsteady; *arenas* shifting; *fig. p. etc.* fickle; *situación etc.* troubled, unsettled; **mover** [2h] move; shift; ~ *cabeza* shake *negando*, nod *asintiendo*; *cola* wag; *fig.* (*promover*) stir up; move (*a compasión* to); ~ *a inf.* prompt *s.o.* to *inf.*, lead *s.o.* to *inf.*; ~**se** move, stir; **movible** movable; mobile; *fig.* changeable; **móvil 1.** = *movible*; **2.** *m* motive (*de* for); **movilidad** *f* mobility; **movilización** *f* mobilization; **movilizar** [1f] mobilize; **movimiento** *m* movement; *phys. etc.* motion;

shake, nod *de cabeza*; ♪ tempo; (*animación*) activity, bustle *en calle etc.*; *thea. etc.* action; *mot. etc.* traffic; (*conmoción*) stir; ~ máximo peak traffic.

moza *f* girl; *contp.* wench; (*criada*) servant; *buena* ~, *real* ~ goodlooking girl; ~ de taberna barmaid; **mozalbete** *m* lad.

mozárabe 1. Mozarabic; **2.** *m/f* Mozarab; **3.** *m* (*idioma*) Mozarabic.

mozo 1. young; (*soltero*) single; **2.** *m* lad; (*criado*) servant; waiter *en café*; 🚂 porter; *buen* ~ handsome fellow; (*fuerte*) well-built fellow; ~ de caballos groom; ~ de cámara cabin-boy; **mozuela** *f* girl; *contp.* wench; **mozuelo** *m* lad.

mucílago *m* mucilage; **mucosa** *f* mucous membrane; **mucosidad** *f* mucus; **mucoso** mucous.

muchacha *f* girl; (*criada*) maid; **muchachada** *f* boyish prank; **muchacho** *m* boy, lad.

muchedumbre *f* crowd; mass, throng, host; *contp.* mob, herd.

mucho 1. *adj.* a lot of; much, great; ~s *pl.* many, lots of; many a; (*como pron.*) ~s *pl.* creen que a lot of people think that; *somos* ~s there are a lot of us; **2.** *adv.* a lot, a great deal, much; *estimar etc.* highly, greatly; *trabajar* hard; *v. sentir*; (~ *tiempo*) long, a long time; (*muchas veces*) often; *¿estás cansado?* — *¡~!* are you tired? — very!; *con* ~ by far, far and away; *ni con* ~ not nearly, nothing like; *ni* ~ *menos* far from it; *v. por*; *no es* ~ *que* it is no wonder that; *no es para* ~ it isn't up to much.

muda *f* change of clothing; *zo.* moult; (*época*) moulting season; *está de* ~ (*muchacho*) his voice is breaking; **mudable** changeable; shifting; *carácter etc.* fickle; **mudanza** *f* (*cambio*) change; removal, move *de domicilio*; ~s *pl. fig.* fickleness; (*humor*) moodiness; **mudar** [1a] *v/t.* change; *piel* slough (off), shed; *v/i.*, ~**se** change (*de ropa, parecer etc. acc.*); (*trasladarse*) move; (*voz*) break; *zo.* moult.

mudez *f* dumbness; **mudo** dumb (*a. fig., de* with); mute (*a. gr.*); speechless; *gr.*, *película* silent; *thea. papel* walking-on.

mueblaje *m* = *moblaje*; **mueble**
1. movable; **2.** *m* piece of furniture;
~s *pl.* furniture; fittings *de tienda*
etc.

mueca *f* face, grimace.

muela *f* millstone *de molino*; grindstone *para afilar*; *anat.* molar, *freq.*
tooth; ~ *del juicio* wisdom tooth.

muellaje *m* wharfage; **muelle¹** *m*
⚓ wharf, quay; 🛳 unloading
bay.

muelle² **1.** soft; *vida* luxurious;
2. *m* ⊕ spring.

muérdago *m* mistletoe.

muerte *f* death; *(asesinato)* murder;
a ~ guerra to the knife; *luchar* to the
death; *de ~* implacably; F *de mala ~*
lousy; **muerto 1.** dead; lifeless;
color dull; F *más ~ que mi abuela*
as dead as a doornail; *más ~ que
una piedra* stone-dead; *dar por ~*
give *s.o.* up for dead; F *no tener
donde caerse ~* be on the rocks; **2.** *m,*
a f dead man *etc.*; *(cadáver)*
corpse; *los ~s pl.* the dead; *tocar a ~*
(campana) toll; **3.** *m naipes*:
dummy.

muesca *f* notch, groove, slot.

muestra *f* ✝ *etc.* sample; sign,
signboard *de tienda etc.*; *(indicio)*
sign, token; model; face *de reloj*;
dar ~s de show signs of; **muestra-
rio** *m* collection of samples; *sew.*
pattern-book.

mugido *m* moo; bellow; **mugir** [3c]
(vaca) moo; *(toro)* bellow.

mugre *f* dirt; grease, grime;
mugriento dirty; greasy, grimy.

mugrón *m* layer *de vid*; sucker.

muguete *m* lily of the valley.

mujer *f* woman; *(esposa)* wife; ~ *de
faena* charwoman; **mujeriego
1.** fond of the women; *a ~as* side-
saddle; **2.** *m* F wolf; **mujeril**
womanly.

mújol *m* (grey) mullet.

mula *f* mule.

muladar *m* dunghill, midden.

mulato *adj. a. su. m,* **a** *f* mulatto.

mulero *m* muleteer.

muleta *f* crutch; *fig.* prop; **muletilla** *f fig.* tag, pet phrase.

mulo *m* mule.

multa *f* fine; penalty; **multar** [1a]
fine (*en 20 ptas* 20 ptas); *deportes*:
penalize.

multi...: ~**color** multicoloured;
~**copista** *m* duplicator; ~**forme**
manifold, multifarious; ~**látero**
multilateral; ~**millonario** *m,* a *f*
multimillionaire; **múltiple** manifold, multifarious; ⅍ multiple;
cuestión many-sided; ~s *pl.* freq.
many.

multiplicación *f* multiplication;
multiplicar(se) [1g] ⅍ multiply;
increase; ⊕ gear up; **multiplici-
dad** *f* multiplicity; **múltiplo** *adj.*
a. su. m multiple; **multitud** *f*
multitude; crowd *de gente etc.*; *la ~
contp.* the masses; F ~ *de* lots of,
heaps of.

mullir [3a] pound, knead; soften;
cama shake up; ✗ *tierra* hoe, loosen;
plantas hoe round.

mundanal, mundano worldly; of
the world; *(de la buena sociedad)*
society *attr.*; fashionable; social;
mundanería *f* worldliness; **mundial** world-wide; *guerra, record etc.*
world *attr.*; **mundo** *m* world (*a.
fig., eccl.*); *(ps.)* people; *(esfera)*
globe; *todo el ~* everybody; *echar
al ~* bring into the world; *tener
(mucho) ~* be sophisticated, be
experienced; *ver (mucho) ~* see life,
knock about F; **mundología** *f* F
worldly-wisdom; **mundonuevo** *m*
peep-show.

munición *f* (*a. ~es pl.*) stores,
supplies; ✗ ammunition, munitions; *de ~* service *attr.*

municipal 1. municipal, town *attr.*;
2. *m* policeman; **municipio** *m*
municipality; township; *(ayuntamiento)* town council.

munificencia *f* munificence; **munífico** munificent.

muñeca *f anat.* wrist; doll; dummy
de modista; **muñeco** *m* figure, guy;
dummy *de sastre*; *(muñeca)* doll;
fig. puppet; F *(niño)* little angel;
(afeminado) sissy; ~ *de nieve*
snowman; **muñequera** *f* wrist
watch.

muñón *m anat.* stump; ⊕ trun-
nion; journal, gudgeon.

mural mural; *mapa etc.* wall *attr.*;
muralla *f* (city) wall, rampart;
murar [1a] wall.

murciélago *m zo.* bat.

murmullo *m* murmur; ripple *etc.*;
murmuración *f* gossip, slander;
murmurador *m,* -a *f* gossip;
grumbler; **murmurar** [1a] murmur; mutter *entre dientes*; whisper

al oído; (multitud etc.) hum; (aguas) ripple; (hojas etc.) rustle; fig. (quejarse) grumble, mutter; (chismear) gossip (de about); ~ de esp. criticize.

muro m wall.

murria f F sulks, blues; tener ~ be down in the dumps; **murrio** sulky; sullen.

mus m a card game.

musa f Muse.

musaraña f zo. shrew; (animalejo) bug, creepy-crawly; mirar a las ~s moon (about).

muscular muscular; **musculatura** f muscles; **músculo** m muscle; **musculoso** muscular.

muselina f muslin.

museo m museum; ~ de arte etc. art gallery.

musgaño m shrew.

musgo m moss; **musgoso** mossy.

música f music; (ps.) band; ~ celestial bunk, drivel; ~ de fondo background music; **musical** = **músico** 1. musical; 2. m, a f musician, player.

musitar [1a] mumble, whisper.

muslo m thigh.

mustio p. depressed, gloomy; ♀ withered.

musulmán adj. a. su. m, -a f Moslem.

mutabilidad f changeability; **mutación** f change, mutation (a. biol., gr.); thea. change of scene.

mutilación f mutilation; **mutilado** m, a f cripple, disabled person; **mutilar** [1a] mutilate (a. fig.); (lisiar) cripple, maim; texto mutilate; cuento garble.

mutis m thea. exit; hacer ~ thea. exit; fig. not say a word; **mutismo** m dumbness; fig. silence.

mutualidad f mutuality; (ayuda) reciprocal aid; ♥ friendly society; **mutuo** mutual (a. ♥), reciprocal; joint.

muy very; greatly, highly; es ~ de él that's just like him; es ~ de lamentar it is much to be regretted; el ~ tonto etc. the big fool etc.; es ~ hombre he's a real man; es ~ mujer she's very feminine.

N

naba f ⚓ rape.
nabab m nabob.
nabo m turnip; ~ *sueco* swede.
nácar m mother-of-pearl; **naca-rado, nacarino** mother-of-pearl *attr.*; pearly.
nacer [2d] be born (*a. fig.*); ⚓ come up, sprout; (*río*) rise; *fig.* spring, arise (de from); **nacido:** ~ *a*, ~ *para* born to (be); *bien* ~ of noble birth; *mal* ~ low-born; **naciente** nascent; recent; *sol* rising; **nacimiento** m birth (*a. fig.*); (*principio*) origin, start, beginning; source *de río*; (*manantial*) spring; (*belén*) nativity (scene); de ~ *ciego etc.* from birth.
nación f nation; de ~ by birth; **nacional** *adj. a. su. m/f* national; *producto freq.* home *attr.*; **nacio-nalidad** f nationality; **naciona-lismo** m nationalism; **nacio-nalista** *adj. a. su. m/f* nationalist; **nacionalizar** [1f] nationalize; naturalize.
nada 1. f nothingness; *la* ~ the void; 2. *pron.* nothing; *¡*~, ~*!* not a bit of it!; *¡*~ *de eso!* nothing of the kind!, far from it!; ~ *más* nothing else; (*solamente*) only; *¡de* ~*!* not at all!, don't mention it!; *por* ~ *llorar etc.* for no reason at all; *por* ~ *del mundo* not for love nor money; *por menos de* ~ for two pins; *¡pues* ~*!* not to worry!; *no ha sido* ~ it's nothing; 3. *adv.:* ~ *fácil* not at all easy, far from easy.
nadaderas f/pl. waterwings; **na-dador** m, **-a** f swimmer; **nadar** [1a] swim; (*corcho etc.*) float; ~ *en fig.* be rolling in, wallow in.
nadería f trifle.
nadie nobody, no-one; *no ... ~* not ... anybody; *un* (*don*) ~ a nobody.
nadir m nadir.
nado: *pasar a* ~ swim (across).
nafta f naphtha; **naftaleno** m, **naftalina** f naphthalene.
naipe m (playing-)card; ~*s pl.* cards.
nalgas f/pl. buttocks.
nana f F granny; ♪ lullaby; *v. año.*

napolitano *adj. a. su. m*, **a** f Neapolitan.
naranja f orange; F *media* ~ better half; **naranjada** f orangeade, orange squash; **naranjado** orange; **naranjal** m orange-grove; **na-ranjo** m orange (tree).
narciso m narcissus; daffodil; *fig.* dandy.
narcosis f narcosis; **narcótico** 1. narcotic; 2. m narcotic; sleeping-pill; drug, dope; **narcotismo** m narcotism; **narcotizar** [1f] drug, dope, narcotize ⚕.
nardo m (spike)nard.
narigada f S.Am. snuff; **narigón, narigudo** big-nosed; **nariz** 1. f nose (*a. fig.*); (*cada orificio*) nostril; bouquet *de vino*; 2. **narices** pl. zo. nostrils; F nose; *¡*~*!* rubbish!; *cerrar la puerta en las* ~ de shut the door in *s.o.*'s face; *dar de* ~ land on one's nose; *hinchársele a uno las* ~ get annoyed.
narración f narration; account, narrative; **narrador** m, **-a** f narrator; **narrar** [1a] tell, narrate; **narrativa** f narrative; **narrativo** narrative.
narval m narwhal.
nasa f ⚓ fish-trap; (*cesta*) basket; bin *para pan etc.*
nasal *adj. a. su.* f nasal; **nasalidad** f nasality; **nasalizar** [1f] nasalize.
nata f cream (*a. fig.*); skin *en natillas etc.*; *v. flor.*
natación f swimming; ~ *de costado* side-stroke.
natal natal; *suelo etc.* native; **natali-cio** *adj. a. su. m* birthday; **natali-dad** f birth-rate.
natillas f/pl. custard.
natividad f nativity; **nativo** native (*a.* ⚒); home *attr.*; natural, innate; **nato** born.
natural 1. *mst* natural (*a.* ♪); native; 2. m/f native (de of), inhabitant; 3. m nature, dispositition; *buen* ~ good nature; *al* ~ *descripción* true to life; (*sin arte*) rough; *bebida etc.* just as it comes; *vivir* according to

nature; *del* ~ from nature, from life; **naturaleza** *f* nature; ~ *muerta* still life; *v. carta*; **naturalidad** *f* naturalness; *con la mayor* ~ as if nothing had happened; *hablar* in an ordinary tone; **naturalismo** *m* naturalism; **naturalista 1.** naturalistic; **2.** *m/f* naturalist; **naturalización** *f* naturalization; **naturalizar** [1f] naturalize.

naufragar [1h] be (ship)wrecked, sink; *fig.* fail; **naufragio** *m* (ship-)wreck; *fig.* ruin; **náufrago 1.** shipwrecked; **2.** *m* shipwrecked sailor *etc.*, castaway.

náusea(s) *f(pl.)* nausea, sick feeling; *fig.* disgust; *dar* ~*s a* sicken; **nauseabundo** nauseating, sickening.

náutica *f* navigation, seamanship; **náutico** nautical.

navaja *f* (clasp-)knife, jack-knife; (*cortaplumas*) penknife; ~ (*de afeitar*) razor; **navajada** *f*, **navajazo** *m* slash.

naval naval.

navarro *adj. a. su. m*, **a** *f* Navarrese.

nave *f* ship; △ nave; ~ *espacial* space-ship; **navegable** navigable; **navegación** *f* navigation; (*viaje*) voyage; (*buques*) shipping; **navegador** *m*, **navegante** *m* navigator; **navegar** [1h] (*ir*) sail; (*dirigir*) navigate.

Navidad *f* Christmas(-time); *por* ~*es* at Christmas(-time).

naviero 1. shipping *attr.*; **2.** *m* shipowner; **navío** *m* ship; ~ *de línea* ship of the line.

nazareno *adj. a. su. m*, **a** *f* Nazarene.

nazi *adj. a. su. m/f* Nazi; **nazismo** *m* Nazism.

neblina *f* mist; **nebulosa** *f* nebula; **nebulosidad** *f* mistiness *etc.*; **nebuloso** *ast.* nebular, nebulous; *cielo* cloudy; *atmósfera* misty; (*tétrico*) gloomy; *idea etc.* nebulous, vague; obscure.

necedad *f* silliness; (*acto, dicho*) silly thing.

necesario necessary; **neceser** *m* hold-all; dressing-case *de tocador*; ~ *de belleza* vanity case; ~ *de costura* workbox; **necesidad** *f* necessity; need (*de* for, of); (*hambre*) hunger; *euph.* business; *de* ~, *por* ~ of necessity; *de primera* ~ absolutely

essential; *en caso de* ~ in case of need; **necesitado** needy, necessitous; *los* ~*s* the needy; **necesitar** [1a] *v/t.* want, need; *acción etc.* necessitate; ~ *inf.* must *inf.*, need to *inf.*; *v/i.*: ~ *de* need; ~*se*: *necesítase* (*anuncios*) wanted.

necio silly, stupid.

necrófago *m* ghoul; **necrología** *f* obituary (notice); **necromancia** *f* necromancy.

néctar *m* nectar.

nefando unspeakable; **nefario** nefarious.

nefasto unlucky, inauspicious.

negación *f* negation; denial; *gr.* negative; **negar** [1h *a.* 1k] *verdad etc.* deny; *permiso etc.* refuse (*a acc.*), withhold (*a* from); *responsabilidad* disclaim; (*vedar*) deny; ~ *que* deny that; ~*se a inf.* refuse to *inf.*; **negativa** *f* negative (*a. phot.*); denial, refusal; **negativo 1.** negative; *⅄* minus; **2.** *m phot.* negative.

negligencia *f* negligence *etc.*; **negligente** negligent; neglectful (*de* of), slack, careless.

negociable negotiable; **negociación** *f* negotiation; clearance *de cheque*; **negociador** *m*, **-a** *f* negotiator; **negociante** *m* businessman; merchant, dealer; **negociar** [1b] *v/t.* negotiate; *v/i.* negotiate; ~ *en* deal in, trade in; **negocio** *m* (*asunto*) affair, (piece of) business; † (*un* ~) deal, transaction; † (*en general*) trade, business; (*puesto*) job; ~*s pl.* business; *buen* ~ (good) bargain; *de* ~*s adj.* business *attr.*; *adv.* on business.

negra *f* negress; **negrero** *m* slave-trader; slave-driver (*a. fig.*); **negrita** *f typ.* bold face; *en* ~*s* in bold type; **negrito** *m* (*muñeca*) golliwog; **negro 1.** black (*a. fig.*); dark; (*sombrío*) gloomy; *p.* negro; F (*enfadado*) peeved; F broke; *suerte* awful, atrocious; ~ *como boca de lobo* pitch dark; F *pasar las* ~*as* have a rough time; **2.** *m* negro; ~ *de humo* lamp-black; *trabajar como un* ~ work like a nigger; **negroide** negroid; **negrura** *f* blackness; **negruzco** blackish.

nene *m*, **a** *f* F baby.

nenúfar *m* water-lily.

neo *m* neon.

neófito *m*, **a** *f* neophyte.

neolatino *lengua* Romance.
neologismo *m* neologism.
neón *m* neon.
neoyorquino *m*, **a** *f* New Yorker.
neozelandés *m*, **-a** *f* New Zealander.
nepotismo *m* nepotism.
nervadura *f* △ rib; **nervio** *m* nerve (*a. fig.*); ♀ rib; *fig.* sinews; vigour; stamina, toughness; crux, key *de cuestión*; *sin* ∼ weak, spineless; *crispar los* ∼*s a* get on *s.o.'s* nerves; *poner los* ∼*s en punta a* jar on, grate on; *tener* ∼ possess character; *tener los* ∼*s en punta* be all keyed up; **nerviosidad** *f*, **nerviosismo** *m* nervousness; (*temporal*) nerves F; **nervioso** *centro*, *célula* nerve *attr.*; *crisis*, *sistema* nervous; *p.* (*con miedo*) nervous, nervy F; highly strung; excitable; (*fuerte*) vigorous; *estilo* energetic; *poner* ∼ *a alguien* get on *s.o.'s* nerves; *ponerse* ∼ get excited, get worked up; **nervudo** wiry, sinewy.
nesga *f sew.* flare, gore; **nesgar** [1h] flare, gore.
neto pure, clean; neat, clear; ✝ net.
neumático 1. pneumatic; **2.** *m* tyre.
neuralgia *f* neuralgia; **neurastenia** *f* nervous exhaustion; neurasthenia 𝕼; excitability; **neurasténico** highly strung, excitable; neurasthenic 𝕼; **neuritis** *f* neuritis; **neurología** *f* neurology; **neurólogo** *m* neurologist; **neurona** *f* nerve-cell; **neurosis** *f* neurosis; ∼ *de guerra* shell-shock; **neurótico** *adj. a. su. m*, **a** *f* neurotic.
neutral *adj. a. su. m/f* neutral; **neutralidad** *f* neutrality; **neutralizar** [1f] neutralize; *fig. a.* counteract; **neutro** *mst* neutral; *género* neuter; *verbo* intransitive.
neutrón *m* neutron.
nevada *f* snow-storm; (*cantidad*) snowfall; **nevado** snow-covered; *fig.* snowy; **nevar** [1k] *v/t.* whiten; *v/i.* snow; **nevasca** *f* snow-storm; **nevera** *f* refrigerator, ice-box (*a. fig.*); **nevisca** *f* light snowfall, flurry of snow; (*aguanieve*) sleet; **neviscar** [1g] snow lightly; sleet; **nevoso** snowy; *temporal* snow *attr.*
nexo *m* link, connexion.
ni nor, neither; ∼ ... ∼ neither ... nor; ¡∼ *una palabra!* not a single word!; ∼ *que* even though; ∼ ... *siquiera* not even.

niara *f* ⚹ stack.
nicotina *f* nicotine.
nicho *m* niche, recess.
nidada *f* (*huevos*) sitting, clutch; (*pollos*) brood; **nidal** *m* nest *de gallina*; (*huevo*) nest-egg; F hangout; **nido** *m* nest (*a. fig.*).
niebla *f* fog; mist; *hay* ∼ it is foggy.
nieta *f* granddaughter; **nieto** *m* grandson; *fig.* descendant; ∼*s pl.* grandchildren.
nieve *f* snow.
nigromancía *f* necromancy, black magic.
nihilismo *m* nihilism; **nihilista** *m/f* nihilist.
nilón *m* nylon.
nimbo *m* halo; *meteor.* nimbus.
nimiedad *f* insignificant detail; *con* ∼ with a lot of details; **nimio** *detalle etc.* tiny, insignificant; *p.* small-minded; (*delicado*) fussy; *lit.* excessive (*en* in).
ninfa *f* nymph.
ningún, **ninguno 1.** *adj.* no; **2.** *pron.* none; (*p.*) nobody, no-one; ∼ *de ellos* none of them; ∼ *de los dos* neither (of them).
niña *f* (little) girl; *anat.* pupil; ∼*s pl. de los ojos de fig.* apple of *s.o.'s* eye; **niñada** *f* childish thing; **niñear** [1a] act childishly; **niñera** *f* nursemaid, nanny F; **niñería** *f* childish thing; *fig.* silly thing; **niñez** *f* childhood; **niño 1.** young; *b.s.* childish; **2.** *m* (little) boy; (*en general*) child; (*no nacido aún, recién nacido*) baby; ∼*s pl.* children; ∼ *expósito* foundling; *desde* ∼ from childhood; ¡*no seas* ∼! don't be so childish!
níquel *m* nickel; chromium-plating; **niquelar** [1a] nickel(-plate); chromium-plate.
níspero *m*, **níspola** *f* medlar.
nitidez *f* spotlessness *etc.*; **nítido** bright, clean, spotless; *phot.* sharp.
nitrato *m* nitrate; **nítrico** nitric; **nitro** *m* nitre; **nitrogenado** nitrogenous; **nitrógeno** *m* nitrogen; **nitroso** nitrous.
nivel *m* level; ∼ *de aire*, ∼ *de burbuja* spirit level; ∼ *de vida* standard of living; *a* ∼ level (*a.* 🚂); true; *al* ∼ *de* (on a) level with; *ocasión* equal to, up to; **nivelación** *f* levelling; **nivelado** level; ⊕ *a.* flush; **niveladora** *f* ⊕ bulldozer; **nivelar** [1a] level; 🚂 *etc.* grade; *fig.* level up, even up.

níveo *fig.* snowy.

no *mst* not; (*usado solo*) no; ¿~? = ¿~ es verdad?; *compuestos:* ~ agresión non-agression; ~ sea que lest; ~ ... sino only; not ... but; ¡que ~! I tell you it isn't!; no I won't!

nobiliario noble; **noble** *adj. a. su. m* noble; **nobleza** *f* nobility, aristocracy.

noción *f* notion, idea; ~es *pl.* elements; smattering; **nocional** notional.

nocivo harmful, injurious.

nocturno night *attr.*; *zo. etc.* nocturnal; **noche** *f* night; night-time; (*más bien tarde*) evening; (*oscuridad*) darkness; ¡buenas ~s! good evening!; (*al despedirse o acostarse*) good night!; esta ~ tonight; de (*la*) ~ función *etc.* late-night *attr.*; ~ toledana sleepless night; de ~, por la ~ at night, by night; de la ~ a la mañana overnight; hacerse de ~ get dark; quedarse a buenas ~s be left in the dark; **Nochebuena** *f* Christmas Eve.

nodo *m* node.

nodriza *f* wet-nurse.

nodular nodular; **nódulo** *m* nodule.

nogal *m*, **noguera** *f* walnut (tree).

nómada 1. nomadic; **2.** *m/f* nomad.

nombradía *f* fame, renown; **nombrado** *fig.* renowned; **nombramiento** *m* naming, designation; nomination; appointment; ⚔ commission; **nombrar** [1a] name; designate; (*proponer*) nominate; (*elegir etc.*) appoint; ⚔ commission; mention; **nombre** *m* name (*a. fig.*); *gr.* noun; ~ (*de pila*) Christian name; *mal* ~ nickname; *por mal* ~ nicknamed; ~ propio proper name (*or* noun); de ~ by name; en ~ de in the name of, on behalf of; sin ~ nameless; poner ~ a call; **nomenclatura** *f* nomenclature.

nomeolvides *f* forget-me-not.

nómina *f* list; ✝ pay-roll; **nominación** *f* nomination; **nominal** nominal; titular; *valor* face *attr.*; *gr.* noun *attr.*; **nominativo** *m* nominative (case).

non odd; andar de ~es have nothing to do; estar de ~ be odd (man out); *fig.* be useless.

nonada *f* trifle, mere nothing.

nonagenario *adj. a. su. m*, **a** *f*

nonagenarian; **nonagésimo** ninetieth.

nonato unborn.

nono ninth.

noqueada *f* knock-out (blow); **noquear** [1a] knock out.

nordeste = noreste.

nórdico Nordic.

noreste 1. *parte* north-east(ern); *dirección* north-easterly; *viento* north-east(erly); **2.** *m* north-east.

noria *f* water-wheel, chain-pump.

norma *f* standard, rule, norm; method; ⊕, ⚠ square; *phys. etc.* ~ de comprobación control; **normal** normal (*a.* ⚕); natural; regular; ancho *etc.* standard; **normalizar** [1f] normalize, standardize; ~se return to normal, settle down.

normando *adj. a. su. m*, **a** *f* Norman.

noroeste 1. *parte* north-west(ern); *dirección* north-westerly; *viento* north-west(erly); **2.** *m* north-west.

norte 1. *parte* north(ern); *dirección* northerly; *viento* north(erly); **2.** *m* north; *fig.* guide; lodestar; north wind; **norteamericano** *adj. a. su. m*, **a** *f* American; **norteño 1.** northern; **2.** *m*, **a** *f* northerner.

noruego 1. *adj. a. su. m*, **a** *f* Norwegian; **2.** *m* (*idioma*) Norwegian.

nos (*acc.*) us; (*dat.*) (to) us; (*reflexivo*) (to) ourselves; (*recíproco*) (to) each other; **nosotros, nosotras** *pl.* we; (*tras prp.*) us.

nostalgia *f* nostalgia, homesickness; **nostálgico** nostalgic, homesick.

nota *f* note (*a.* ♪); *escuela:* report; mark, class *en examen*; ~ de adorno grace note; ~ de inhabilitación endorsement; **notabilidad** *f* notability; (*p.*) notable; **notable 1.** notable, noteworthy (por for, on account of); remarkable; **2.** *m* worthy, notable; **notación** *f* notation; **notar** [1a] note, notice; (*apuntar*) note down; *escrito* annotate; *fig.* criticize; hacer ~ indicate, point out.

notarial notarial; **notario** *m* notary (public).

noticia *f* piece of news; (news) item *en periódico*; (*noción*) knowledge, idea (de of); ~s *pl.* news; **noticiar** [1b] notify; **noticiario** *m radio:* news(-bulletin); *cine:* news-reel; **noticioso** *fuente* well-informed; **notificación** *f* notification; **notifi-**

car [1g] notify; **notorio** well-known; *b.s.* notorious; obvious; blatant, flagrant.

novato 1. raw, green; **2.** *m* beginner, tiro.

novecientos nine hundred.

novedad *f* (*calidad*) newness, novelty, strangeness; (*cambio*) change, new development; (*cosa nueva*) novelty; (*noticia*) news; ~es *pl.* novelties; (*modas*) latest fashions; *sin* ~ as usual; 🏵 the same as before; *llegar* safely, without incident; ⚔ all quiet; **novel 1.** new, inexperienced; **2.** *m* beginner; **novela** *f* novel; ~ *por entregas* serial; ~ *policíaca* detective story, whodunit *sl.*; **novelero** *p.* highly imaginative, romantic; **novelesco** *género* fictional; *suceso* romantic, fantastic; **novelista** *m/f* novelist; **novelón** *m* three-decker novel; **novelucha** *f* F yellowback, shocker.

noveno ninth; **noventa** ninety; **noventón** *adj. a. su. m*, **-a** *f* F nonagenarian.

novia *f* girl-friend, sweetheart; (*prometida*) fiancée; (*casada*) bride; **noviazgo** *m* engagement.

noviciado *m eccl.* novitiate; apprenticeship; **novicio** *m*, **a** *f* novice (*a. eccl.*); beginner; apprentice.

noviembre *m* November.

novilunio *m* new moon.

novilla *f* heifer; **novillada** *f* bull-fight with young bulls; **novillero** *m toros*: novice bullfighter; F truant; **novillo** *m* young bull; steer, bullock; F *hacer* ~s play truant.

novio *m* boyfriend, sweetheart; (*prometido*) fiancé; (*casado*) bridegroom; *los* ~s (*casados*) the bridal couple.

novísimo newest, latest.

nubarrón *m* storm cloud; **nube** *f* cloud (*a. fig.*); 🏵 film; *por las* ~s sky-high; *poner en* (or *por*) *las* ~s praise to the skies.

núbil nubile, marriageable.

nublado 1. cloudy; **2.** *m* storm cloud; *fig.* threat; (*copia*) swarm, abundance; **nubloso** cloudy; *fig.* gloomy.

nuca *f* nape.

nuclear nuclear; **núcleo** *m* nucleus; ⚡ core (*a. fig.*); 🌿 kernel; ~ *rural* village settlement.

nudillo *m* knuckle; **nudo** *m* knot (*a.* ⚓, 🪢, *fig.*); node; centre *de comunicaciones*; (*enredo*) tangle; lump *en garganta*; *fig.* bond, tie; *thea.* plot; **nudoso** *madera* etc. knotty; *tronco* gnarled; *palo* knobbly.

nuera *f* daughter-in-law.

nuestro 1. *adj.* our; (*tras su.*) of ours; **2.** *pron.* ours; *los* ~s (*ps.*) our men, our side.

nueva *f* piece of news; ~s *pl.* news; *me cogió de* ~s it was news to me; **nuevamente** again; recently.

nueve nine (*a. su.*); (*fecha*) ninth; *las* ~ nine o'clock.

nuevo new; (*original*) novel; (*adicional*) further; *más* ~ (*p.*) junior; *de* ~ (all over) again; *¿qué hay de* ~? what's the news?

nuez *f* nut; (*de nogal*) walnut; ~ *de la garganta* Adam's apple; ~ *moscada* nutmeg.

nulidad *f* ⚖ nullity; incompetence *de empleado*; (*p.*) nonentity; **nulo** ⚖ (null and) void; invalid; *p.* etc. useless; *partido* drawn.

numen *m* talent, inventiveness; *de propio* ~ out of one's own head.

numeración *f* numeration; **numeral** numeral; **numerar** [1a] number; **numerario** *m* hard cash; **numérico** numerical; **número** *m* number (*a. de revista* etc.); *thea.* turn, number; item, number *en programa*; ~ *atrasado* back-number; ~ *extraordinario* special edition; *de* ~ *miembro* full; *sin* ~ numberless; **numeroso** numerous.

numismática *f* numismatics; **numismático 1.** numismatic; **2.** *m* numismatist.

nunca never; ever; ~ (*ja*)*más* never again, nevermore; *casi* ~ hardly ever.

nuncio *m eccl.* nuncio.

nupcial wedding *attr.*; **nupcias** *f/pl.* wedding; *casarse en segundas* ~ get married (for) a second time.

nutria *f* otter.

nutrición *f* nutrition, nourishment; **nutrido** *fig.* large, considerable; abundant; ⚔ *fuego* heavy; **nutrimento** *m* nutriment, nourishment; **nutrir** [3a] feed, nourish; (*fortalecer*) strengthen; *fig.* support, foment; **nutritivo** nourishing, nutritious; *valor* nutritional.

nylón *m* nylon.

Ñ

ñame *m* yam.
ñapa *f S.Am.* tip.
ñaque *m* junk.
ñiquiñaque *m* F trash, rubbish.

ñoño 1. whining; spineless; 2. *m*, a *f* drip.
ñudoso = *nudoso*.

O

o or; ~ ... ~ either ... or.
oasis *m* oasis.
obcecación *f* blind obstinacy; obcecar [1g] blind.
obedecer [2d] obey; ~ a (*ceder*) yield to; ~ a(*l hecho de que*) be due to, arise from; obediencia *f* obedience; obediente obedient.
obelisco *m* obelisk.
obenques *m/pl.* ⚓ shrouds.
obertura *f* overture.
obesidad *f* obesity; obeso obese.
óbice *m* obstacle.
obispado *m* bishopric; obispo *m* bishop.
óbito *m* decease.
objeción *f* objection; objetante *m/f* objector; objetar [1a] object; *objeciones* raise; *argumento* put forward; objetividad *f* objectivity; objetivo *adj. a. su. m* objective; objeto *m* object (*a. gr.*); (*fin a.*) end, purpose; (*asunto*) subject-matter.
oblación *f*, oblata *f* oblation; oblato *eccl.* oblate.
oblea *f* wafer.
oblicuidad *f* obliquity; oblicuo oblique; *mirada* sidelong.
obligación *f* obligation; duty (*a, con, para* to); liability, responsibility; ✝ bond; ~ de banco bank-bill; ~s *pl.* ✝ bonds, securities; obligar [1h] force, compel, oblige (*a inf.* to *inf.*); ~se bind o.s. (*a* to); obligatorio obligatory, binding (*a* on), compulsory (*a* for).
oblongo oblong.
oboe *m* oboe.
óbolo *m* mite (*contribution*).
obra *f* work; piece of work; handiwork; ~s *pl. lit. etc.* works; ⚠ repairs, alterations; ~ de about, a matter of; ~s *pl.* de caridad good works; ~ de consulta reference book; ~ de hierro ironwork; ~ maestra masterpiece; ~s *pl. públicas* public works; ~ de romanos herculean task, tremendous undertaking; ¡manos a la ~! let's get on with it!; ⚠ estar en ~s be closed for repairs; poner por ~ carry out, implement; put into practice; obrar [1a] *v/t.* build, make; *madera etc.* work; (*medicina*) work on, have an effect on; *v/i.* act, behave, proceed; *su carta obra en mi poder* your letter is to hand; obrero 1. *clase etc.* working; labour *attr.*; *movimiento* working-class; 2. *m*, a *f* worker (*a. pol.*); 3. *m* workman; man, hand.
obscenidad *f* obscenity; obsceno obscene.
obscu... *v.* oscu...
obsequiar [1b] *amigo etc.* lavish attentions on; ~ (con) present *s.o.* with, give; ~ a alguien con un banquete hold a dinner for s.o.; obsequio *m* attention, courtesy; (*regalo*) present, gift; presentation *en jubilación etc.*; en ~ de in honour of; obsequioso attentive, obliging, helpful; *b.s.* obsequious.
observación *f* observation; (*dicho a.*) remark, comment; observance *de ley*; observador 1. observant; 2. *m*, -a *f* observer; observancia *f* observance; observar [1a] (*ver*) observe; watch; notice, spot F; *ley* observe, keep; *regla* adhere to; observatorio *m* observatory.
obsesión *f* obsession; obsesionante haunting; obsesionar [1a] obsess.

obstaculizar [1f] hold up, hinder; **obstáculo** *m* obstacle; hindrance; handicap.

obstante: no ~ **1.** *adv.* however, nevertheless; **2.** *prp.* in spite of; **obstar** [1a]: ~ *a* hinder, prevent.

obstetricia *f* obstetrics; **obstétrico** *m* obstetrician.

obstinación *f* obstinacy *etc.*; **obstinado** obstinate, stubborn; **obstinarse** [1a]: ~ en *inf.* persist in *ger.*

obstrucción *f* obstruction (*a. parl.*); **obstruccionista** *m/f* obstructionist; **obstructivo** obstructive; **obstruir** [3g] obstruct, block; hinder, interfere with.

obtención *f* obtaining; **obtener** [2l] get, obtain, secure.

obturador *m phot.* shutter; ⊕, *mot.* choke; **obturar** [1a] plug, stop up, seal off; *diente* fill.

obtuso blunt; ⅄, *fig.* obtuse.

obús *m* howitzer; (*granada*) shell.

obviar [1c] *v/t.* obviate, remove; *v/i.* stand in the way; **obvio** obvious. }

oca *f* goose.

ocasión *f* occasion, time; opportunity, chance (*de inf.* to *inf.*); de ~ second-hand; **ocasional** accidental; **ocasionar** [1a] cause, produce, occasion.

ocaso *m ast.* sunset; setting *de astro*; *geog.* west; *fig.* decline.

occidental western; **occidente** *m* west.

oceánico oceanic; **océano** *m* ocean.

ocio *m* leisure; *b.s.* idleness; *ratos de* ~ spare time; **ociosidad** *f* idleness; **ocioso** *p. etc.* idle, lazy; *obra* useless.

ocre *m* ochre.

octagonal octagonal; **octágono** *m* octagon; **octanaje**: *de alto* ~ high octane *attr.*; **octano** *m* octane; **octava** *f* octave; **octavilla** *f* pamphlet; **octavo** *adj. a. su. m* eighth; *typ.* en ~ octavo; **octogenario** *adj. a. su. m, a f* octogenarian; **octogésimo** eightieth; **octosílabo 1.** octosyllabic; **2.** *m* octosyllable; **octubre** *m* October.

ocular 1. ocular; *v. testigo*; **2.** *m* eyepiece; **oculista** *m/f* oculist.

ocultar [1a] hide (*a, de* from); screen, mask; **ocultismo** *m* occultism; **oculto** hidden, concealed; *fig.* secret; *ciencia* occult; *pensamiento* inner; *motivo* ulterior.

ocupación *f* occupation (*a.* ⅄); **ocupante** *m/f* occupant; **ocupar** [1a] *mst* occupy (*a.* ⅄); *puesto a.* fill, hold; *espacio, tiempo a.* take up; (*llenar*) fill (up); *atmósfera* pervade; *p.* keep *s.o.* busy; give employment to; (*molestar*) bother; ~**se** *de* take care of, look after; pay attention to; ~ en be occupied in (*or* with), busy *o.s.* with; engage in; *estar ocupado* (*habitación, silla*) be taken, be occupied; (*p.*) be busy (en with), be engaged (en in); *teleph.* be engaged.

ocurrencia *f* occurrence; incident; (*chiste*) witty remark; (bright) idea; **ocurrente** witty; **ocurrir** [3a] happen, occur; ~**se**: se *le ocurrió inf.* it occurred to him to *inf.*; he took it into his head to *inf.*

ochenta eighty; **ochentón** *adj. a. su. m, -a f* F octogenarian; **ocho** eight (*a. su.*); (*fecha*) eighth; *las* ~ eight o'clock; **ochocientos** eight hundred.

oda *f* ode.

odiar [1b] hate; **odio** *m* hatred; ill-will; ~ *de sangre* feud; *tener* ~ *a* hate; **odioso** odious, hateful; nasty.

odontología *f* odontology 𝔘, dentistry.

odorífero sweet-smelling, odoriferous.

odre *m* wineskin; F old soak.

oeste 1. *parte* west(ern); *dirección* westerly; *viento* west(erly); **2.** *m* west.

ofender [2a] offend; wrong; *reputación etc.* injure; *vista etc.* hurt; (*injuriar*) insult; ~**se** take offence (*de, por* at); take exception (*por* to); **ofensa** *f* offence; insult; **ofensiva** *f* offensive; *tomar la* ~ take the offensive; **ofensivo** offensive (*a.* ⅄); disgusting; (*grosero*) rude; **ofensor** *m*, **-a** *f* offender.

oferta *f* offer (*a.* ✝); proposal, proposition; ✝ tender, bid; ~ *y demanda* supply and demand; ✝ *en* ~ on offer; **ofertorio** *m* offertory.

office ['ofis] *m* pantry.

offset [of'set] *m typ.* offset.

oficial 1. official; **2.** *m* official, officer (*a.* ⅄); (*obrero*) skilled worker; journeyman; clerk *en oficina*; ~ *del día* orderly officer; ~ *de enlace* liaison officer; ~ *mayor* chief clerk; ~ *médico* medical officer; ♣ *primer* ~ mate; **oficiala** *f* (*obrera*) skilled woman worker; clerk *en oficina*; **oficialidad** *f* officers; **oficiar** [1b] officiate (*de as*); **oficina** *f* office; ⚒ orderly room; *pharm.* laboratory; ⊕ workshop; ~ *de informacion(es)* information bureau; **oficinal** officinal; **oficinesco** office *attr.*; clerical; white-collar; **oficinista** *m/f* office worker, clerk; white-collar worker; **oficio** *m* (*profesión*) occupation; ⊕ craft, trade; (*papel*) function; (*cargo*) office; *eccl.* ~ (*divino*) (divine) service; *buenos* ~*s pl.* good offices; *Santo* ♀ Inquisition, Holy Office; *de* ~ by trade, by profession; *miembro* ex officio; (*adv.*) officially; **oficioso** diligent; helpful; *b.s.* officious; (*no oficial*) informal, unofficial.

ofrecer [2d] *mst* offer; present; *bienvenida* extend; *gracias* give, offer; *respetos* pay; ~*se* offer o.s.; volunteer; ~ *a inf.* offer to *inf.*; **ofrecimiento** *m* offer(ing); **ofrenda** *f eccl.* offering; **ofrendar** [1a] give, contribute.

oftalmía *f* ophthalmia; **oftálmico** ophthalmic; **oftalmólogo** *m* ophthalmologist.

ofuscar [1g] dazzle; *fig.* mystify, confuse; *fama* dim.

ogro *m* ogre.

¡oh! o!, oh!

ohmio *m* ohm.

oída *f* hearing; *de* ~*s* by hearsay; **oído** *m* hearing; *anat.*, ♪ ear; ♪ *de* ~ by ear; *aguzar los* ~*s* prick up one's ears; *dar* ~*s* listen (*a* to); *decir al* ~ a whisper to; *prestar* ~ *a* give ear to; *ser todo* ~*s* be all ears; **oidor** *m* † judge; **oigo** *v. oír*; **oír** [3q] hear; (*atender*) listen (to); *misa* attend, go to; ~ *decir que* hear that; ~ *hablar de* hear about, hear of; *¡oye!, ¡oiga!* listen!; (*llamando*) hi!, hey!; (*sorpresa*) I say!; (*rechazando*) the very idea!; *¡oiga! teleph.* hullo!

ojal *m* buttonhole.

¡ojalá! 1. *int.* if only it would! *etc.*; no such luck!; 2. *cj.* ~ (*que*) ... if only ...!; *¡* ~ *pudiera!* I wish I could!

ojazo: *echar los* ~*s a* ogle, make eyes at; **ojeada** *f* glance; *echar una* ~ *a* glance at; **ojear** [1a] eye, stare at; *hunt.* beat; **ojeras** *f/pl.* rings under the eyes; **ojeriza** *f* spite, ill-will; *tener* ~ *a* have a grudge against;

ojeroso seedy; **ojete** *m sew.* eyelet; **ojinegro** black-eyed.

ojiva *f* ogive; **ojival** ogival.

ojo *m* eye (*a. fig.*); span *de puente*; ~ (*de la cerradura*) keyhole; *¡* ~*!* look out!; (*mucho*) ~ *con* be very careful about, beware of; *a los* ~*s de* in the eyes of; *a* ~ *s cerrados* on trust; *a* ~*s vistas* publicly; *con buenos* ~*s* favourably; *en un abrir y cerrar de* ~*s* in the twinkling of an eye; *avivar el* ~ be on the qui vive; F *costar un* ~ *de la cara* cost a small fortune; *echar el* ~ *a* have one's eye on; *guiñar el* ~ wink (*a at*); turn a blind eye (*a* on); *hacer del* ~ wink; *no pegar los* ~*s* not get a wink of sleep; *tener* ~ go very carefully, keep one's wits about one; **ojuelos** *m/pl.* (bright) eyes.

ola *f* wave; ~ *de calor* heat-wave; ~ *de frío* cold wave; ~ *de marea* tidal wave; *batir las* ~*s* ply the seas.

¡olé! bravo!

oleada *f* ♨ big wave; (*movimiento*) surge, swell; *fig.* wave *de huelgas etc.*

oleaginoso oily, oleaginous ⚕.

oleaje *m* surge, swell, surf.

óleo *m paint.*, *eccl.* oil; (*cuadro*) oil-painting; *al* ~ *pintura* oil *attr.*, *pintar* in oils; **oleoducto** *m* pipeline; **oleografía** *f* oleograph.

oler [2i] smell (*a* of, like); **olfatear** [1a] sniff, smell, scent (out; *a. fig.*); *fig.* nose out; **olfativo** olfactory; **olfato** *m* (sense of) smell; scent; **olfatorio** olfactory.

oligarquía *f* oligarchy.

olimpíada *f* Olympiad; **olímpico** Olympian; *v. juego*.

oliscar [1g] *v/t.* smell, sniff; *fig.* look into; *v/i.* smell (bad).

oliva *f* olive; **olivar** *m* olive-grove; **olivo** *m* olive (tree).

olmo *m* elm (tree).

olor *m* smell; odour; scent; *mal* ~ stink, bad smell; **oloroso** sweet-scented, fragrant.

olvidadizo forgetful, absentminded; **olvidado** forgetful; ~ *de* forgetful of, oblivious of (*or* to); **olvidar** [1a] forget; leave behind; omit; ~*se* (*propasarse*) forget o.s.; ~ *de* = *v/t.*; ~*se de inf.* forget to *inf.*; neglect to *inf.*; *se me olvidó* I forgot; **olvido** *m* (*estado*) forgetfulness; oblivion; omission, slip.

olla f pot, pan; (*guisado*) stew; pool de río; *mount.* chimney; ~ *podrida* stew; *fig.* hotchpotch; ~ de *presión* pressure-cooker.

ombligo m navel; F encogérsele a uno el ~ have cold feet.

ominoso ominous; (*terrible*) awful, dreadful.

omisión f omission; failure (de *inf.* to *inf.*); (*dejadez*) neglect; **omitir** [3a] leave out, miss out, omit.

omni...: ~potencia f omnipotence; **~potente** omnipotent; **~presencia** f omnipresence; **~presente** omnipresent; **~sciencia** f omniscience; **~sciente, ~scio** omniscient; **omnívoro** omnivorous.

omóplato m shoulder-blade.

once eleven (*a. su.*); (*fecha*) eleventh; *las* ~ eleven o'clock; **onceno** eleventh.

onda f wave (*a. phys., radio*); ~ corta short wave; de ~ corta short-wave *attr.*; ~ larga long wave; ~ luminosa light wave; *radio:* ~ portadora carrier; ~ sonora sound wave; **ondeante** *superficie* undulating; **ondear** waving; **ondear** [1a] *v/t.* pelo wave; *sew.* pink; *v/i.* (*agua*) ripple; (*movimiento*) undulate; (*bandera etc.*) flutter, wave; (*pelo*) stream *al viento*, flow; **~se** wave; swing; **ondímetro** m wavemeter; **ondulación** f undulation; wave (*a. pelo*), ripple; ~ *permanente* permanent wave; **ondulado** wavy; *camino* uneven; *terreno* rolling, undulating; *hierro, papel* corrugated; **ondulante** = **ondeante**; **ondular** [1a] = **ondear**; **ondulatorio** undulatory.

oneroso onerous, burdensome.

ónice m onyx.

onomástico 1. name *attr.*, of names; **2.** m (*a. fiesta ~a*) saint's day; *approx.* birthday.

onomatopeya f onomatopoeia.

onubense *adj. a. su. m/f* (native) of Huelva.

onza f ounce (*a. zo.*).

opacidad f opacity; **opaco** opaque.

opalescente opalescent; **ópalo** m opal. [optional.)

opción f option (a on); **opcional)**

ópera f opera.

operación f operation; **operador** m, -a f *cine etc.*: operator; **♂** surgeon; **operar** [1a] *v/t.* **♂** operate

on (de for); *v/i.* operate; **~se ♂** have an operation (de for); **operario** m, a f operative; hand; ~ de *máquina* machinist; **operativo** operative.

opereta f operetta, light opera.

opiata f, **opiato** *adj. a. su. m* opiate.

opinar [1a] think; ~ *que* be of the opinion that, judge that; **opinión** f opinion; ~ *pública* public opinion.

opio m opium.

oponer [2r] *dique etc.* set up (a against); *objeción etc.* raise (a to); *resistencia* offer; *dos pareceres* contrast; ~ a *adversario* pit against; ~ A a B play off A against B; **~se a** oppose, be opposed to; defy; resist; *cátedra etc.* put in for.

oportunidad f opportunity (de *inf.* of *ger.*, to *inf.*), chance; (lo *oportuno*) opportuneness, expediency; **oportunismo** m opportunism; **oportunista** m/f opportunist; **oportuno** timely, opportune; expedient; apposite.

oposición f opposition; (*a. ~es pl.*) examination, competition (a for); **opositor** m, -a f competitor, candidate (a for).

opresión f oppression; oppressiveness; **opresivo** oppressive; **opresor** m, -a f oppressor; **oprimir** [3a] oppress; squeeze, press *con presión*; (*vestido*) be too tight for.

oprobio m shame, opprobrium; **oprobioso** shameful, opprobrious.

optar [1a] choose, decide (*entre* between; *por inf.* to *inf.*).

óptica f optics; **óptico 1.** optic(al); **2.** m optician.

optimismo m optimism; **optimista 1.** optimistic, hopeful; **2.** m/f optimist.

óptimo very good; optimum.

opuesto ♂, *lado* opposite; *opinión etc.* contrary, opposing.

opugnar [1a] attack.

opulencia f opulence, affluence; *vivir en la* ~ live in luxury; **opulento** opulent, rich; luxurious.

opúsculo m booklet, short work, tract.

oquedad f hollow; *fig.* hollowness.

ora: ~ ... ~ now ... now.

oración f oration, speech; *eccl.* prayer; *gr.* sentence; **oráculo** m oracle; **orador** m, -a f orator;

speaker; **oral** oral; **orar** [1a] speak, make a speech; *eccl.* pray (*a* to, *por* for).

orate *m/f* lunatic (*a.* F).

oratoria *f* oratory; **oratorio 1.** oratorical; **2.** *m* ♪ oratorio; *eccl.* oratory.

orbe *m* orb; (*mundo*) world; **órbita** *f* orbit (*a. fig.*); *entrar en* ~ go into orbit; **orbital** orbital.

orca *f* grampus.

órdago: F de ~ jolly good, swell *Am.*

ordalías *f/pl. hist.* (trial by) ordeal.

orden[1] *m* order; ~ *del día* agenda; ~ *público* law and order; *del* ~ de of the order of; *en* ~, *por* (*su*) ~ in order; *fuera de* ~ out of order (*a. parl.*); out of turn; *llamar al* ~ call to order; *poner en* ~ put into order; tidy up.

orden[2] *f mst* order; ✝✝ *a.* writ, warrant; ✗ ~ *del día* order of the day; ✝ *a la* ~ to order; *hasta nueva* ~ till further orders; *por* ~ de on the orders of, by order of; *estar a las* ~*es* de be at *s.o.'s* service.

ordenación *f* order; arrangement; *eccl.* ordination; **ordenada** *f* ordinate; **ordenado** orderly, tidy; methodical; **ordenancista** *m* disciplinarian, martinet; **ordenanza 1.** *f* ordinance; decree; **2.** *m* ✗ orderly, batman; **ordenar** [1a] (*arreglar*) arrange, order; marshal; (*poner en orden*) put into order; (*mandar*) order (*inf.* to *inf.*); *eccl.* ordain; ~*se* take (holy) orders.

ordeñadora *f* ⊕ milking-machine; **ordeñar** [1a] milk; **ordeño** *m* milking.

ordinal *adj. a. su. m* ordinal.

ordinariez *f* commonness, coarseness; **ordinario** ordinary; usual; (*sin distinción*) ordinary, mediocre; (*vulgar*) common, coarse; *de* ~ usually.

orear [1a] air; ~*se* take a breather.

orégano *m* marjoram.

oreja *f* ear; (*lengüeta*) tab; (*asa*) lug, handle; *aguzar las* ~*s* prick up one's ears; **orejera** *f* ear-flap; **orejeta** *f* ⊕ lug; **orejudo** big-eared, with big ears.

orfanato *m* orphanage.

orfebre *m* goldsmith, silversmith; **orfebrería** *f* gold *etc.* work.

orfeón *m* glee club, choral society.

orgánico organic; **organillero** *m* organ-grinder; **organillo** *m* barrel-organ, hurdy-gurdy; **organismo** *m biol. etc.* organism; *pol.* organization; **organista** *m/f* organist; **organización** *f* organization; **organizador** *m*, -a *f* organizer; **organizar** [1f] organize; **órgano** *m* organ; (*medio*) means, medium.

orgía *f* orgy.

orgullo *m* pride; (*arrogancia*) haughtiness; **orgulloso** proud; haughty.

orientación *f* orientation; positioning; prospect *hacia sur etc.*; training; ⚓ trim; ~ *sur* southerly aspect, facing south; **oriental 1.** oriental; eastern; **2.** *m/f* oriental; **orientar** [1a] orientate; position; (*dirigir*) guide; train *para profesión*; ⚓ trim; *está orientado hacia el oeste* it faces (*or* looks, points) west; ~*se fig.* take one's bearings; **oriente** *m* east; ♀ Orient (*v. Apéndice*).

orificio *m* orifice; vent.

origen *m* origin; source; *dar* ~ *a* give rise to; **original 1.** original; novel; (*singular*) odd, eccentric; **2.** *m* original (*a. p.*); (*p.*) character; *typ.* copy; **originalidad** *f* originality; eccentricity; **originar(se)** [1a] originate; start, cause; **originario:** ~ de native to.

orilla *f* edge (*a. sew.*); bank *de río*; side *de lago*; shore *de mar*; rim *de taza*; *sew.* border, hem; ~ *del mar* sea-shore; *a* ~*s de* on the banks of; **orillar** [1a] *sew.* edge, trim (*de* with); *lago etc.* skirt; *asunto* touch briefly on; **orillo** *m* selvage, list.

orín *m* rust; *tomarse de* ~ get rusty.

orina *f* urine; **orinal** *m* chamber-pot; **orinar** [1a] urinate; **orines** *m/pl.* urine.

oriundo: ~ de native to; *ser* ~ de come from, be a native of.

orla *f* border, edging, fringe; **orlar** [1a] border, edge (*de* with).

ornamental ornamental; **ornamentar** [1a] adorn; **ornamento** *m* ornament; adornment; ~*s pl. eccl.* ornaments; *fig.* moral qualities; **ornar** [1a] adorn, decorate; **ornato** *m* adornment, decoration.

ornitología *f* ornithology; **ornitológico** ornithological; **ornitólogo** *m* ornithologist.

oro *m* gold; *naipes:* ~*s pl.* diamonds;

~ en barras bullion; ~ batido gold leaf; ~ laminado rolled gold; ~ molido ormulu; F como un ~ spick and span; de ~ gold(en).

oropel m tinsel (a. fig.); de ~ tawdry; flashy; gastar mucho ~ put on a bold front.

oropéndola f (golden) oriole.

orquesta f orchestra; orquestal orchestral; orquestar [1a] orchestrate.

orquídea f orchid, orchis.

ortiga f (stinging-)nettle.

orto...: ~doxia f orthodoxy; ~doxo orthodox; sound; ~grafía f spelling, orthography ⏄; ~gráfico orthographic(al); ~pedia f orthopaedics; ~pédico orthopaedic; ~pedista m/f orthopaedist.

oruga f zo. caterpillar; ⚘ rocket.

orujo m skins and stones of grapes etc. after pressing.

orza f ⚓ luff(ing); orzar [1f] luff.

orzuelo m 💉 stye.

os (acc.) you; (dat.) (to) you; (reflexivo) (to) yourselves; (recíproco) (to) each other.

osadía f daring; osado daring, bold.

osamenta f bones; skeleton.

osar [1a] dare (inf. to inf.).

osario m ossuary, charnel-house.

oscilación f oscillation, swing etc; oscilador m oscillator; oscilar [1a] oscillate, swing, sway; (luz) blink; fig. waver; oscilatorio oscillatory.

ósculo m lit. kiss.

oscurantismo m obscurantism; oscurecer [2d] v/t. obscure, darken; fig. confuse, fog; fama tarnish; v/i. get dark, grow dark; oscuridad f darkness; gloom, gloominess; esp. fig. obscurity; oscuro dark; gloomy; esp. fig. obscure; (borroso) indistinct; a ~as in the dark (a. fig.).

óseo bony, osseous ⏄; osificación f ossification; osificar(se) [1g] ossify.

oso m bear; ~ blanco polar bear; ~ gris grizzly bear; F hacer el ~ play the fool.

ostentación f ostentation; pomp, display; hacer ~ de show off, parade; ostentar [1a] show; b.s. show off, flaunt, display; ostentativo, ostentoso ostentatious.

osteología f osteology.

ostra f oyster; fig. (p.) fixture.

ostracismo m ostracism.

ostral m oyster-bed.

otario S.Am. silly.

otear [1a] spy on, watch from above; fig. examine, look into.

otero m hill, knoll.

otomana f ottoman; otomano adj. a. su. m, a f Ottoman.

otoñada f autumn-time; otoñal autumnal, autumn attr.; otoño m autumn, fall Am.

otorgamiento m consent; (acto) granting; 🏛 execution; otorgar [1h] grant, give (a to); confer (a on); 🏛 execute.

otramente otherwise; in a different way; otro 1. adj. other; another; thea. ¡~a! encore!; ~ que other than; no ~ que no less a person etc. than; F ¡ésa es ~a! here we go again!; los tiempos son ~s times have changed; ser muy ~ be quite changed; 2. pron. another one; el ~ the other (one); los ~s the others, the rest; algún ~ somebody else; ~ me dijo que somebody else told me that; como dijo el ~ as someone said; v. alguno, tanto, uno etc.

ovación f ovation; ovacionar [1a] applaud, cheer.

oval(ado) oval; óvalo m oval.

ovario m biol. ovary.

oveja f sheep, ewe; cargar con la ~ muerta be left holding the baby; ovejuno sheep attr. [Oviedo.]
ovetense adj. a. su. m/f (native) of
oviforme egg-shaped, oviform ⏄.

ovillar [1a] wind; ~se curl up into a ball; ovillo m ball of wool etc.; fig. tangle; hacerse un ~ curl up; cower con miedo; get tied up in knots hablando.

ovíparo oviparous; ovoide adj. a. su. m ovoid.

oxálico oxalic.

oxear [1a] shoo.

oxiacetilénico oxyacetylene attr.

oxidado rusty; 🜍 oxidized; oxidar [1a] 🜍 oxidize; rust; ~se go rusty, get rusty (a. fig.); óxido m oxide; oxigenar [1a] oxygenate; oxígeno m oxygen.

¡oxte! shoo! it; hop it!; sin decir ~ ni moxte without a word.

oye, oyendo etc. v. oír; oyente m/f listener, hearer.

ozono m ozone.

P

pabellón *m* (*edificio*) pavilion; summerhouse, hut *en jardín etc.*; block *de hospital etc.*; (*tienda*) bell-tent; (*colgadura*) canopy, hangings; (*bandera*) flag; ✕ stack; ♪ bell; *anat.* outer ear; ~ *de caza* shooting-box.

pábilo *m*, **pabilo** *m* wick; (*quemado*) snuff.

pábulo *m fig.* encouragement, fuel; food *para pensamiento*; *dar* ~ *a* encourage, add fuel to.

paca *f* bale.

pacato peaceable; timid.

pacer [2d] *v/t. hierba* eat; *ganado* graze; *v/i.* graze.

paciencia *f* patience; forbearance; ¡~ *y barajar!* keep trying!, don't give up!; *perder la* ~ lose one's temper; **paciente** *adj. a. su. m/f* patient; **pacienzudo** patient; long-suffering.

pacificación *f* pacification; peace (of mind), calm; **pacificador** *m*, -**a** *f* peacemaker; **pacificar** [1g] pacify; ~*se* calm down; **pacífico** pacific, peaceable; peace-loving; **pacifismo** *m* pacifism; **pacifista** *adj. a. su. m/f* pacifist.

pacotilla *f fig.* trash; *de* ~ shoddy, catchpenny; F *hacer su* ~ make a modest profit, be doing nicely; F *hacer la* ~ *a* suck up to.

pactar [1a] stipulate, agree to, contract for; covenant; **pacto** *m* pact, covenant, agreement.

pachón 1. *S.Am.* woolly; shaggy; **2.** *m* F dull fellow; (*perro*) pointer.

pachorra *f* F slowness, laziness; **pachorrudo** F slow, sluggish.

pachucho ♀ over-ripe; F droopy, off colour, poorly.

padecer [2d] suffer (*de* from); endure; *error etc.* labour under, be a victim of; **padecimiento** *m* suffering.

padrastro *m* stepfather; *fig.* obstacle; *anat.* hangnail; **padrazo** *m* F indulgent father; **padre** *m* father (*a. eccl.*); *zo.* sire; (*tras nombre*)

senior, the elder; ~*s pl.* parents, father and mother; ancestors; ~ *espiritual* confessor; ~ *de familia* father of a family, man with family responsibilities; ♀ *Nuestro* Lord's Prayer; ♀ *Santo* Holy Father, Pope; F *de* ~ *y muy señor mío* terrific, a ... and a half; **padrino** *m eccl.* godfather; best man *en boda*; second *en duelo*; sponsor, patron *de empresa*.

padrón *m* (*nómina*) poll, census; register *de miembros etc.*; ⊕ *etc.* pattern; △ commemorative column; *fig.* stain; F indulgent father.

paella *f Valencian rice dish with meat, shell-fish etc.*

¡**paf!** bang!; plop!

paga *f* payment; (*sueldo*) pay, wages; fee; F *mala* ~ bad payer; **pagadero** payable, due; **pagado:** ~ *de sí mismo* self-satisfied, smug; **pagador** *m*, -**a** *f* payer; ✕ (*oficial*) ~ paymaster.

paganismo *m* paganism; **pagano** *adj. a. su. m, a f* pagan, heathen.

pagar [1h] pay; repay; pay off; *compra* pay for; *favor, visita* return; *fig.* atone for; ¡*me las pagarás!* I'll pay you out for this!; *a* ~ ✂ postage due; *a* ~, *por* ~ *cuenta* unpaid; ~*se de* be pleased with, take a liking to; ~ *de sí mismo* be conceited, be smug; **pagaré** *m* promissory note, IOU.

página *f* page; **paginación** *f* pagination; **paginar** [1a] paginate.

pago¹ 1. *m* payment; repayment; *fig.* return, reward; ~ *anticipado* advance payment; ~ *al contado* cash (payment); ~ *a cuenta* payment on account; ~ *en especie* payment in kind; ~ *a plazos* deferred payment; ~ *contra recepción* cash on delivery; *en* ~ *de* in payment for; **2.** F paid, quits.

pago² *m* district; estate.

pagoda *f* pagoda.

pagote *m* F scapegoat.

paila *f* large pan.

país *m* country; land, region; *del ~ vino etc.* local; **paisaje** *m* landscape; countryside; scene(ry); **paisajista** *m/f* landscape-painter; **paisanaje** *m* civil population; **paisano 1.** of the same country; **2.** *m, a f* fellow-countryman; ✗ civilian; *S.Am.* peasant; *de ~ soldado* in mufti, in civvies F; *policía* in plain clothes.

paja *f* straw; *fig.* trash; *lit.* padding; *de ~* straw *attr.*; F *hombre de ~* stooge; **pajar** *m* straw-loft; rick.

pájara *f zo.* (hen-)bird; *(cometa)* paper kite; F sharp one; *~ pinta* forfeits; **pajarear** [1a] *fig.* loaf, loiter; *S.Am. (caballo)* shy; **pajarera** *f* aviary; **pajarero 1.** F *p.* merry, bright; *vestido* gaudy; **2.** *m* bird-fancier; *(cazador)* bird-catcher; **pajarilla** *f* paper kite; F *alegrárselas a uno las ~s* laugh o.s. silly; **pajarita** *f* paper kite, paper bird; **pajarito** *m* fledgling; **pájaro** *m* bird; F chap; *(astuto)* clever fellow; F *~ de cuenta* bigwig; *~ carpintero* woodpecker; *~ mosca* humming-bird; **pajarota** *f* F hoax; **pajarraco** *m* F slyboots.

paje *m* page; ⚓ cabin-boy.

pajera *f* straw-loft; **pajita** *f* (drinking-)straw; **pajizo** straw *attr.*; straw-coloured; **pajuela** *f* spill.

pala *f* shovel, spade; scoop; blade *de remo, hélice etc.*; *deportes:* bat, racquet; upper(s) *de zapato;* F wiliness.

palabra *f* word; *(facultad)* (power of) speech; F *¡~!* honestly!, no kidding!; *~ de casamiento* engagement (to marry); *~ de honor* word of honour; *~s pl. mayores* (strong) words; *a media ~* at the least hint; ✗ *bajo ~* on parole; *de ~* by word of mouth; *en una ~* in a word; *por ~* word for word, verbatim; *coger a uno la ~* take a p. at his word; *pedir la ~* ask to be allowed to speak; *tener la ~* have (or hold) the floor; **palabrería** *f* F wordiness; verbiage; palaver; **palabrero 1.** windy, wordy; **2.** *m, a f* windbag; **palabrota** *f* rude word, swear-word.

palaciano, palaciego 1. palace *attr.*, court *attr.*; **2.** *m* courtier; **palacio** *m* palace; *~ de justicia* court-house; *~ municipal* city hall.

palada *f* shovelful; stroke *de remo.*

paladar *m* palate (*a. fig.*), roof of the mouth; *fig.* taste; **paladear** [1a] taste (with pleasure), relish.

paladín *m hist.* paladin; champion.

paladino open, public, clear.

palafrén *m* palfrey.

palanca *f* lever; crowbar; *~ de freno* brake lever; *~ de mando* control column; F *mover ~s* pull strings.

palangana *f* wash-basin; **palanganero** *m* wash-stand.

palanqueta *f* small lever; jemmy *de ladrón.*

palatino *anat.* palatal; *pol.* palatine, palace *attr.*

palco *m* box; *~ de proscenio* stage-box.

palenque *m (defensa)* palisade; *(público)* arena, ring.

paleografía *f* pal(a)eography.

paleontología *f* pal(a)eontology.

palestino *adj. a. su. m, a f* Palestinian.

palestra *f* arena; *fig.* lists; *salir a ~ fig.* take the floor (*or* field).

paleta *f* small shovel, scoop; *(badil)* fire-shovel; ⚒ trowel; *paint.* palette; blade, vane, bucket *de rueda etc.*; **paletilla** *f* shoulder-blade.

paleto *m zo.* fallow-deer; F yokel, country bumpkin.

paliar [1b] palliate, alleviate; *fig.* conceal, gloss over; **paliativo 1.** palliative; *fig.* concealing; **2.** *m* palliative.

palidecer [2d] (turn) pale; **palidez** *f* paleness, pallor *etc.*; **pálido** pale, pallid; wan; sickly.

palillo *m* toothpick; ♪ drumstick; *~s pl.* castanets.

palinodia *f: cantar la ~* recant.

palio *m* cloak; canopy; *eccl.* pall, pallium.

palique *m* F chat; small-talk, chit-chat; *estar de ~* have a chat.

paliza *f* beating, thrashing; drubbing (*a. fig.*).

palizada *f* fenced enclosure; *(defensa)* stockade.

palma *f* ♀, *anat. a. fig.* palm; *llevarse la ~* carry off the palm, triumph; **palmada** *f* slap, pat *en el hombro etc.*; clapping, applause; *dar ~s* clap, applaud; **palmadita** *f* pat, tap.

palmar[1] *m* ♀ palm-grove.

palmar², **palmario** obvious, self-evident; patent.
palmatoria f candlestick; cane *para castigar*.
palmeado webbed.
palmear [1a] clap.
palmera f palm(-tree).
palmeta f cane; (*acto*) caning; *ganar la ~ fig.* get in first; **palmetazo** m caning; *fig.* slap in the face.
palmípedo webfooted.
palmo m span; *avanzar ~ a ~* go forward inch by inch; *conocer a ~s (or ~ a ~)* know every inch of; *crecer a ~s* shoot up.
palmotear [1a] clap; **palmoteo** m applause.
palo m stick; pole; (*material*) wood; handle *de escoba etc.*; (golf- *etc.*) club; ⚓ mast; ⚓ spar; (*golpe*) blow with a stick; *naipes*: suit; *~ dulce* liquorice root; *~ mayor* mainmast; *~ santo* lignum vitae; *dar ~s de ciego* lash out wildly; *dar de ~s* beat; *servir del ~* follow suit.
paloma f dove, pigeon; *fig.* meek and mild person; *~s pl.* ⚓ white horses; *~ mensajera* carrier-pigeon; *~ torcaz* woodpigeon; **palomar** m dovecot(e); **palomino** m young pigeon; **palomitas** f/pl. popcorn; **palomo** m (cock-)pigeon.
palote m: F *no dar ~* not do a stroke.
palote m ♪ drumstick; downstroke *de pluma*, pothook; **palotear** [1a] F wrangle; **paloteo** m F wrangle.
palpable palpable; **palpar** [1a] touch, feel; (*a tientas*) grope along, feel one's way; *sl.* frisk.
palpitación f palpitation *etc.*; **palpitante** palpitating, throbbing; *cuestión* burning; **palpitar** [1a] palpitate, throb; *flutter de emoción*; (*estremecerse*) quiver.
palúdico marshy; ✚ marsh *attr.*, malarial; **paludismo** m malaria.
palurdo 1. rustic; coarse; **2.** m rustic, yokel; *b.s.* lout.
palustre marshy.
pamema f F trifle; *~s pl.* (*cuentas*) humbug, nonsense; (*halagos*) wheedling; *¡déjate de ~s!* stop all that nonsense!
pampas f/pl. *S.Am.* pampas, prairie.
pámpana: F *zurrar la ~ a* tan.
pámpano m vine tendril; vine leaf.

pamplina f ⚘ chickweed; F silly remark, nonsense.
pan¹ m (*en general*) bread; loaf; ⚘ wheat; ⊕ gold leaf, silver leaf; cake *de jabón*; *~ de azúcar* sugar-loaf; F *~ comido* chicken-feed; *~ de cuco* stonecrop; *de ~ llevar tierra* arable; *con su ~ se lo coma* that's his lookout, let him get on with it; *ganarse el ~* earn a living; *llamar al ~ ~ y al vino vino* call a spade a spade; F *venderse como ~ bendito* go like hot cakes.
pan² ... pan ...
pana¹ f velveteen, corduroy.
pana² f *mot.* breakdown.
panacea f panacea, cure-all.
panadería f bakery, bakehouse; baker's (shop); **panadero** m, **a** f baker.
panadizo m ✚ whitlow; F sickly sort.
panal m honeycomb.
panameño adj. a. su. m, **a** f Panamanian.
panamericano Pan-American.
pancarta f placard.
páncreas m pancreas.
pandear(se) [1a] bulge, warp, sag.
pandemonio m pandemonium.
pandeo m bulge, bulging.
pandereta f tambourine; **pandero** m tambourine; F idiot.
pandilla f set; *b.s.* gang, clique; ✚ ring; **pandillero** m *S.Am.* gangster.
pandorga f kite; F fat woman.
panecillo m roll.
panegírico m panegyric.
panel m panel; plywood.
panfleto m lampoon; pamphlet.
paniaguado m protégé; henchman.
pánico adj. a. su. m panic.
panizo m millet; maize.
panorama m panorama; vista; *paint., phot.* view; **panoramicar** [1g] *cine:* pan; **panorámico** panoramic; *punto ~* viewpoint, vantage-point.
pantalón m, *~es pl.* trousers, pants *Am.*; (*de mujer, exterior*) slacks; (*interior*) knickers; *~es pl. cortos* shorts.
pantalla f screen (*a. cine*); (lamp-)shade; *llevar a la ~* film.
pantanal m marshland; **pantano** m marsh, bog, swamp; (*artificial*) reservoir; *fig.* obstacle; **pantanoso** marshy, swampy.

panteísmo *m* pantheism; **panteísta** pantheistic; **panteón** *m* pantheon.
pantera *f* panther.
pantomima *f* pantomime, dumb show.
pantoque *m* bilge; *agua de* ~ bilge-water.
pantorrilla *f* calf (of the leg); **pantorrilludo** fat in the leg.
pantufla *f*, **pantuflo** *m* slipper.
panza *f* paunch, belly; **panzada** *f* F bellyful; *darse una* ~ have a blow-out; **panzón** F, **panzudo** F paunchy, pot-bellied.
pañal *m* nappy, diaper *Am. de niño*; tail *de camisa*; ~es *pl.* swaddling clothes; *fig.* early stages, infancy.
pañero *m* draper, clothier.
pañete *m* light cloth; ~s *pl.* shorts, trunks.
pañito *m*: ~ *de adorno* doily.
paño *m* cloth; stuff; (*medida*) breadth of cloth; duster, rag *para limpiar*; mist, cloudiness *en espejo etc.*; *sew.* panel; ~ *de cocina* dish-cloth; ~ *higiénico* sanitary towel; ~ *de lágrimas* stand-by; ~ *de manos* towel; ~ *mortuorio* pall; ~s *pl. calientes fig.* half-measures; ~s *pl. menores* F underclothes, undies; *al* ~ *thea.* off-stage; *conocer el* ~ know one's business.
pañol *m* ⚓ store-room; ~ (*del agua*) water-store; ~ (*del carbón*) bunker.
pañoleta *f* fichu; **pañolón** *m* shawl; **pañuelo** *m* handkerchief; (head)scarf.
papa¹ *m* pope.
papa² *f esp. S.Am.* potato; ~s *pl.* pap, mushy food.
papá *m* F dad(dy), papa.
papada *f* double chin (*a.* **papadilla** *f*); dewlap *de animal*.
papado *m* papacy.
papagayo *m* parrot; (*p.*) chatter-box.
papaíto *m* F = *papá*.
papal¹ papal.
papal² *m S.Am.* potato field.
papalina *f* cap with ear-flaps; bonnet; F binge.
papamoscas *m orn.* flycatcher; F (*a.* **papanatas** *m* F) simpleton, sucker.
papar [1a] swallow, gulp; F eat; F *fig.* pass over hurriedly.
paparrucha *f* F hoax; worthless book *etc.*

papel *m* paper; piece of paper; *thea.* part, role (*a. fig.*); ~es *pl.* (identification) papers; ~ *de calcar* tracing-paper; ~ *carbón* carbon paper; ~ *cuadriculado* squared paper; ~ *de embalar*, ~ *de envolver* brown paper, wrapping paper; ~ *de empapelar* wallpaper; ~ *del Estado* government bonds; ~ *de estaño* tinfoil; ~ *de estraza* strong wrapping paper; ~ *de filtro* filter-paper; ~ *de fumar* cigarette-paper; ~ *higiénico* toilet-paper, toilet-roll; ~ *de lija* sandpaper; ~ *marquilla* demy; ~ *mojado fig.* scrap of paper; triviality; ~ *moneda* paper money; ~ *ondulado* corrugated paper; ~ *de paja de arroz* rice paper; ~ *pintado* wallpaper; ~ *de plata* silver paper; ~ *secante* blotting-paper, blotter; ~ *de seda* tissue-paper; ~ *sellado* stamped paper; ~ *transparente* tracing-paper; ~ *viejo*, ~es *pl. usados* waste paper; *desempeñar un* ~, *hacer un* ~ play a part (*a. fig.*); *hacer* ~ cut a figure.
papelear [1a] rummage through papers; F make a splash; **papeleo** *m* red tape; **papelería** *f* stationery; (*tienda*) stationer's (shop); (*lío*) sheaf of papers; **papelero** *m*; stationer; paper manufacturer; **papeleta** *f* slip, card; *pol.* voting paper; *escuela*: report; (*empeño*) pawn-ticket; **papelillo** *m* cigarette; **papelón** *m* waste paper; (*cartón*) pasteboard; F impostor; **papelote** *m*, **papelucho** *m* worthless bit of paper.
papera *f* mumps; goitre.
papilla *f* pap; *fig.* guile, deceit.
papiro *m* papyrus.
papirotazo *m*, **papirote** *m* flick.
papismo *m* papistry, popery; **papista 1.** popish; **2.** *m/f* papist.
papo *m* dewlap; crop *de ave*; **papujado** F swollen, puffed up.
paquebote *m* packet(-boat).
paquete *m* parcel (*a.* ✂); packet, pack(age); ⚓ packet(-boat); F toff; ~s *pl. postales* parcel post; ✗ F *meter un* ~ a put on a charge, punish.
par 1. ♪ even; equal; **2.** *m* pair, couple; (*noble*) peer; ~ *de torsión* torque; ~es *o nones* odds or evens; *a* ~es in pairs; *al* ~ equally; together; *de* ~ *en* ~ wide open; *sin* ~

unparalleled; peerless; *no tener ~* have no parallel; **3.** *f* par; *a la ~* equally; at the same time; **✝** at par; *a la ~ que* at the same time as; *golf*: *5 bajo ~ 5* under par; *estar sobre la ~* be at a premium.

para a) *destino, uso, fin*: for, intended for; *un hotel ~ turistas* a hotel (intended) for tourists, a tourist hotel; *una taza ~ el té* a teacup; *lo traje ~ ti* I brought it for you; *nació ~ poeta* he was born to be a poet; *salir ~ Madrid* leave for Madrid; *decir ~ sí* say to o.s.; b) *tiempo*: *~ mañana* for tomorrow; by tomorrow; *quede ~ mañana* let it wait till tomorrow; *va ~ 9 años* (*p.*) he's nearly 9; (*suceso pasado*) it's nearly 9 years ago, it's getting on for 9 years; c) *relación*: (*a. ~ con*) to, towards; *era amable ~* (*con*) *todos* he was kind to everyone; *no hay hombre grande ~ su ayuda de cámara* no man is a hero to (*or* in the eyes of) his valet; d) *contraste*: *~ niño, lo hace muy bien* he does it very well for a child; e) *~ inf.* (*fin*): (in order) to *inf.*; *ahorrar ~ comprar algo* save (in order) to buy s.t.; f) *~ inf.* (*resultado*): *lo encontró ~ volver a perderlo* he found it only to lose it again; e) *~ inf.* (*con bastante, demasiado*): *tengo bastante ~ vivir* I have enough to live on; *es demasiado bueno ~ hacer eso* he is too good to do a thing like that; h) *~ que* in order that, so that; i) *¿~ qué?* why?, for what purpose?; *¿~ qué sirve?* what's it for?; what's the use of ...?

parabién *m* congratulations; *dar el ~ a* congratulate.

parábola *f lit.* parable; *Å* parabola; **parabólico** parabolic.

para...: **~brisas** *m* windscreen, windshield *Am.*; **~caídas** *m* parachute; *lanzar en ~* parachute; *lanzarse en ~* parachute, bale out *en emergencia*; **~caidista** *m* parachutist; *✗* paratrooper; **~choques** *m mot.* bumper, fender *Am.*; *⊕* shock-absorber; *ॐ* buffer.

parada *f* stop; (*acto*) stopping; (*lugar*) stop, stopping-place; (*taxi~*) stand; shut-down, standstill *de industria*; relay *de caballos*; dam *para agua*; stake, bet *en juego*; *✗* parade; *fenc.* parry; *~ discrecional*

request stop; *~ en seco* sudden stop; *formar en ~* parade.

paradero *m* whereabouts; stopping-place; *S.Am.* *ॐ* halt.

paradigma *m* paradigm.

paradisíaco heavenly.

parado slow, inactive; motionless; *salida* standing; *p.* unemployed; *S.Am.* standing up; *S.Am.* proud.

paradoja *f* paradox; **paradójico** paradoxical.

parador *m* ✝ inn; (*moderno*) tourist hotel; (*p.*) heavy gambler.

parafina *f* paraffin wax.

parafrasear [1a] paraphrase; **paráfrasis** *f* paraphrase.

paraguas *m* umbrella.

paraguay(an)o *adj. a. su. m,* **a** *f* Paraguayan.

paragüero *m* umbrella-stand.

paraíso *m* paradise; *thea.* gods, gallery.   [dition.]

paraje *m* place, spot; state, con-]

paralela *f* parallel line; *~s pl.* parallel bars; **paralelismo** *m* parallelism; **paralelo** *adj. a. su. m* parallel (*a. geog.*); *∮ en ~* in parallel; **paralelogramo** *m* parallelogram.

parálisis *f* paralysis; **paralítico** *adj. a. su. m,* **a** *f* paralytic; **paralizar** [1f] paralyse (*a. fig.*); **~se** become paralysed (*a. fig.*); *fig.* come to a standstill; stagnate.

paramento *m* ornament; hangings; trappings *de caballo*; face *de piedra*; *~s pl. eccl.* vestments.

páramo *m* bleak plateau, moor (-land).

parangón *m* comparison; **parangonable** comparable; **parangonar** [1a] compare.

paranoia *f* paranoia.

paraninfo *m univ.* central hall.

parapetarse [1a] protect o.s., take shelter; **parapeto** *m* parapet, breastwork.

parar [1a] **1.** *v/t.* stop; *progreso* check; *atención* fix (en on); *dinero* stake; *fenc.* parry; *golpe, amenaza* ward off; **2.** *v/i.* stop; stay, put up (*en hotel* at); (*terminar*) end up; *~ en* result in; *ॐ* run to; *sin ~* without stopping, without a pause; *ir a ~ a* finish up at, end up at; **3.** *~se* stop; *mot. etc.* stop, pull up, draw up; (*trabajo etc.*) stop, come to a standstill; *S.Am.* stand up; *~ en* pay attention to.

pararrayos *m* lightning-conductor.

parasitario, parasítico parasitic, parasitical; **parásito 1.** parasitic (*de* on); **2.** parasite (*a. fig.*); *radio*: ⁓*s pl.* atmospherics, statics.

parasol *m* parasol.

paratifoidea *f* paratyphoid.

parcela *f* plot, small-holding; **parcelar** [1a] parcel out.

parcial partial, part ...; *p. etc.* partial, prejudiced, partisan; **parcialidad** *f* partiality, prejudice.

parco sparing (*en alabanzas etc.* of); frugal (*en comer* in); temperate.

parchar [1a] *S.Am.* mend, patch; **parche** *m* ✽ sticking-plaster; *mot.* patch; ♪ drum(head).

pardal *m* sparrow; F sly fellow.

¡pardiez! by Jove!

pardillo *m* brown cloth; (*p.*) yokel, rustic; *orn.* (*a.* ⁓ *común*) linnet; *gente del* ⁓ country folk.

pardo 1. brown; dun; *esp. S.Am.* dark grey; *cielo* cloudy, overcast; **2.** *m S.Am.* mulatto; **pardusco** greyish.

parear [1a] match; pair (*a. biol.*); ⁓*se* pair off.

parecer [2d] **1.** seem, look; (*presentarse*) appear, turn up; (*dejarse ver*) show; ⁓ *inf.* seem to *inf.*; *a lo que parece, según parece* apparently, evidently; ⁓ *bien* look well, look all right *por el aspecto*; seem right *por lo justo etc.*; *parece que va a llover* it looks as though (*or* it seems that) it's going to rain; *me parece que sí* I think so; *¿qué te parece?* what do you think (of it)?; *si te parece* if you wish; just as you like; **2.** ⁓*se* look alike; ⁓ *a* resemble, look like; *padre etc.* take after; **3.** *m* opinion, view; looks *de cara*; *a mi* ⁓ in my opinion; *al* ⁓ apparently, evidently; *mudar de* ⁓ change one's opinion.

parecido 1. similar; ⁓ *a* like; *bien* ⁓ good-looking; personable; *mal* ⁓ plain; **2.** *m* resemblance, similarity (*a* to).

pared *f* wall; ⁓ *medianera* party wall; ⁓ *por medio* next door; **paredaño** adjoining, next-door; **paredón** *m* thick wall.

pareja *f* pair, couple; (dancing-) partner; pair of Civil Guards; *correr* ⁓*s* be on a par, keep pace, go together (*con* with); **parejero** *m*

S.Am. race-horse; **parejo** equal; *juntura etc.* even, smooth, flush; *por* ⁓ on a par; *ir* ⁓*s* go neck and neck.

parentela *f* relationship; (*ps.*) relations; **parentesco** *m* relationship, kinship.

paréntesis *m* parenthesis; (*signo*) bracket; *entre* ⁓ *fig. adj.* parenthetic(al); *adv.* by the way, incidentally.

paria *m/f* pariah.

parián *m S.Am.* market.

paridad *f* parity; comparison.

pariente *m, a f* relation, relative; F *la* ⁓*a* the wife, the missus.

parietal parietal.

parihuela *f* stretcher.

parir [3a] *v/t.* give birth to, bear; *v/i.* give birth, be delivered; (*vaca*) calve (*y hay palabras parecidas para otros animales*).

parisién *adj.*, **parisiense** *adj. a. su. m/f* Parisian.

parla *f* chatter, gossip; **parlador** talkative; *ojos etc.* expressive; **parlamentar** [1a] talk, converse; (*enemigos*) parley; **parlamentario 1.** parliamentary; **2.** *m* parliamentarian; member of parliament; **parlamento** *m parl.* parliament; parley *entre enemigos*; *thea.*, 🖙 speech.

parlanchín *m*, **-a** *f* F chatterbox; **parlante** talking; **parlar** [1a] chatter, talk (too much); **parlatorio** *m* chat, talk; **parlero** *p.* garrulous; (*chismoso*) gossiping; *pájaro* talking, song *attr.*; *ojo* expressive; **parleta** *f* F small-talk, idle talk; **parlotear** [1a] prattle, run on; **parloteo** *m* prattle.

parné *m sl.* tin, dough.

paro[1] *m orn.* tit.

paro[2] *m* stoppage, standstill; ⁓ (*forzoso*) unemployment.

parodia *f* parody, travesty (*a. fig.*), take-off F; **parodiar** [1b] parody, travesty, take off F; **parodista** *m/f* parodist.

parola *f* F chit-chat, idle talk; (*soltura*) fluency.

paroxismo *m* paroxysm; ⁓ *de risa* convulsions of laughter.

parpadear [1a] blink, wink; (*luz*) flicker, twinkle; **parpadeo** *m* blink(ing); flicker *etc.*; **párpado** *m* eyelid.

parque m park (a. ✗, mot.); S.Am. ✗ ammunition; ～ de bomberos fire-station; ～ zoológico zoo.

parquedad f sparingness etc.

parquet [par'ke] m parquet.

parra f vine (trained, climbing); hoja de ～ fig. fig-leaf.

párrafo m paragraph; F ～ aparte to change the subject; F echar un ～ have a chat.

parral m vine arbour.

parranda F: andar (or ir) de ～ go on a spree.

parricida m/f parricide (p.); **parricidio** m parricide (act).

parrilla f grating, gridiron; cocina: grill; (restaurante) grill-room.

párroco m parish priest; **parroquia** f parish; parish church; ✝ clientèle, custom(ers); **parroquial** parochial, parish attr.; **parroquiano** m, a f ✝ patron, client, customer.

parsimonia f parsimony; moderation; (lentitud) slowness; con ～ freq. slowly, deliberately, unhurriedly; **parsimonioso** parsimonious; sparing de palabras etc.; (lento) slow, deliberate, unhurried.

parte¹ m teleph. etc. message; ✗ dispatch, communiqué; (informe) report; ～ meteorológico weather-forecast; dar ～ a inform.

parte² f part (a. ♪, thea.); share en repartimiento; ⚖ party; side; ～s pl. fig. parts, talents; ～s pl. (pudendas etc.) private parts; ～ actora prosecution; plaintiff; ～s pl. contratantes contracting parties; ～ del león lion's share; la mayor ～ the majority, most; ～ de la oración part of speech; tercera ～ (p.) third party; ～s pl. vitales vitals, vital parts; de algún tiempo a esta ～ for some time past; de ～ a ～ through and through; de una ～ a otra back and forth; de ～ de on behalf of, from; en ～ in part; en buena ～ in good part; en gran ～ to a great extent; en (or a) alguna ～ somewhere; en (or a) otra ～ somewhere else; en ninguna ～ nowhere; en todas ～s everywhere; por ～s systematically; one thing at a time, bit by bit; por la mayor ～ for the most part; por mi ～ as for me, for my (own) part; por otra ～ on the other hand; por todas ～s everywhere, on all sides; por una ～ on the one hand; echar a mala ～ look upon with disapproval; palabra use incorrectly; ir a la ～ go shares; llevar la peor ～ get the worst of it; ponerse de ～ de side with; tener ～ en share in; tomar ～ en take part in.

partear [1a] mujer deliver.

partenueces m nutcrackers.

partera f midwife.

partición f partition, division; sharing-out.

participación f participation; share en repartimiento; deportes: entry; fig. notification; ～ en los beneficios profit-sharing; **participante** m/f participant; deportes: entrant, entry; **participar** [1a] v/t. inform, notify (of); v/i. participate; deportes: enter (en for); ～ de share in, partake of; ～ en participate in, (have a) share in; **partícipe** m/f participant; **participio** m participle; ～ de pasado past participle; ～ de presente present participle.

partícula f particle.

particular 1. particular; (e)special; private; ～ a peculiar to; **2.** m (p.) private individual; (asunto) particular, point; nada de ～ nothing special; en ～ (en especial) in particular; in private; **particularidad** f particularity, peculiarity; friendship, intimacy; **particularizar** [1f] particularize, specify; ～se be distinguished, stand out.

partida f (salida) departure; certificate de bautismo etc.; entry en registro; ✝ entry, item en lista; ✝ consignment de mercancías; naipes etc.: game; party de personas; mala ～, ～ serrana dirty trick; ✝ ～ doble double-entry; ✝ ～ simple single-entry.

partidario 1. partisan; **2.** m, a f partisan; supporter (de of); follower (de of); **partidismo** m partisan spirit; party politics (b.s.); **partidista** adj. a. su. m/f partisan.

partido 1. divided, split; **2.** m pol. party; deportes etc.: game, match; (ps.) side; geog. district, administrative area; fig. advantage, profit; (apoyo) support; (acuerdo) agreement; de ～ soltero eligible; sacar ～ de profit by (or from), put to use; tomar ～ take sides, take a stand; **partija** f partition, division.

partir [3a] v/t. (rajar etc.) split,
break; nueces etc. crack; (repartir)
divide up, share (out); ✝ divide;
v/i. set off, set out, depart, start (de
from); a ~ de beginning from;
since; a ~ de hoy from today.
partisano m partisan.
partitivo partitive.
partitura f score.
parto m (child)birth, delivery;
labour; fig. product; ~ del ingenio
brain-child; estar de ~ be in labour.
parva f ⚹ unthreshed corn; heap,
pile.
párvulo 1. very small, tiny; fig.
simple, innocent; 2. m, a f child,
infant.
pasa f raisin; ~ de Corinto currant;
~ de Esmirna sultana.
pasable passable.
pasada f (acto) passage, passing;
enough to live on; sew. tacking
stitch; F mala ~ dirty trick; de ~
in passing; **pasadera** f stepping-
stone; ⚓ gangway; **pasadero**
passable, tolerable; **pasadizo** m
passage, corridor; gangway; **pasado**
1. past; semana etc. last; (anticuado)
out-of-date; comida stale, bad;
comida guisada overdone; 2. m past
(a. gr.); ~s pl. ancestors; **pasador**
m bolt, fastener de ventana etc.;
pin para pelo, corbata etc.; cocina:
colander; (p.) smuggler; ~es pl.
cuff-links.
pasaje m (acto, lugar, ♪, lit.) passage;
⚓ (travesía) crossing, voyage; ⚓
(precio) passage-money, fare; arcade
de tiendas; **pasajero** 1. calle etc.
busy; fig. transient, passing,
fleeting; 2. m, a f passenger.
pasamano m rail.
pasante m assistant (teacher etc.).
pasapasa m sleight of hand.
pasaporte m passport.
pasar [1a] 1. v/t. pass; río etc. cross,
go over; (aventajar) surpass, excel;
apuros suffer, endure; armadura
etc. pierce; contrabando smuggle in;
detalle overlook; enfermedad give;
factura send; falta overlook; fruta
dry; lista call; mano pass, run (por
over); mercancías take across, move,
transfer; moneda etc. pass off;
noticia etc. pass on, give; propiedad
transfer; tiempo spend; vehículo
pass, overtake; ~lo bien enjoy o.s.,
have a good time; ~lo mal have a

bad time (of it); ~ por alto detalle
etc. leave out, overlook; p. ignore;
2. v/i. pass; go; (tiempo) pass,
elapse, wear on; (suceso) happen;
(efectos) pass off, wear off; (desaparecer) pass away; (cosa vieja) last
(out); get by, manage con dificultad;
naipes: paso I pass, no bid; ¡pase
Vd.! come in!; after you!; ¿qué
pasa? what's going on?, what's up?;
¿qué le pasa a X? what's the matter
with X?; hacer ~ p. show in; ~ a
inf. go on to inf.; ~ a ser become;
~ adelante proceed; ~ de exceed;
~ de los 60 años be more than 60;
de ahí no paso that is as far as I (can)
go; there I stick; ~ de inf. go
beyond ger.; ~ por ciudad pass
through; casa call at; ~ por encima
(de) pass over; ~ por sabio have a
reputation for learning; hacerse ~
por pass o.s. off as, pose as; ~ sin do
without; 3. ~se (comida) go bad;
~ al enemigo go over to the enemy;
~ de listo be too clever (by half);
~ sin do without, get by without.
pasarela f foot-bridge; ⚓ etc.
gangway, gangplank.   [hobby.)
pasatiempo m pastime, pursuit,)
Pascua f, **pascua** f: ~ de los hebreos
Passover; ~ florida, ~ de Resurrección Easter; ~ de Navidad
Christmas; ~s pl. Christmas holiday, Christmas time (strictly,
Christmas Day to Twelfth Night;
¡Felices ~s! Merry Christmas!; de
~s a Ramos once in a blue moon;
estar como unas ~s be as happy as
a sandboy; **pascual** paschal.
pase m pass.
paseante m/f stroller, walker; F ~ en
corte loafer; **pasear** [1a] v/t. niño
etc. walk, take for a walk; parade
(por las calles through the streets),
show off; v/i., ~se stroll, walk, go
for a walk; ~ en bicicleta go for a
cycle ride, go cycling; ~ a caballo
ride; ~ en coche go for a drive, go
for a run; **paseo** m stroll, walk;
outing; (calle) parade, avenue; ~
(marítimo) promenade, esplanade;
~ en bicicleta, ~ a caballo ride; ~ en
coche drive, run; dar un ~ go for a
walk, take a walk (or stroll); sl.
llevar a ~ take s.o. for a ride;
llevar de ~ niño take out, take for a
walk; F mandar a ~ send s.o.
packing.

pasillo m passage, corridor; ⚓ etc. gangway; thea. short piece, sketch.
pasión f passion; b.s. bias, prejudice; **pasional** p. etc. passionate; crimen passionel; **pasionaria** f passion-flower.
pasito adv. gently, softly.
pasividad f passiveness, passivity; **pasivo 1.** passive; clases ~as pensioners; **2.** m ✝ liabilities; debit side de cuenta.
pasmar [1a] amaze, astound, astonish; stun, dumbfound; ~se be amazed (de at) etc.; **pasmarota(da)** f F exaggerated show of surprise; **pasmo** m amazement, astonishment; awe; fig. wonder, marvel; ✠ lockjaw; **pasmoso** amazing etc., breath-taking; awesome; wonderful, marvellous.
paso¹ fruta dried.
paso² 1. m step, pace; (sonido) footfall, footstep; (huella) footprint; (modo de andar) walk, gait; (velocidad) pace, rate; step, stair de escalera; geog. pass; △ etc. passage, way (through); ⊕, ⚡ pitch; sew. stitch; thea. short piece, sketch; fig. (acto) passing; (cambio) passage, transition; progress, advance; incident, event; (a. mal ~) difficulty, jam F; prohibido el ~ no entry, no thoroughfare; ~ de andadura amble; ~ (en) falso slip, false move; ~ inferior underpass; ~ a nivel level crossing; ~ subterráneo subway; ~ a ~ step by step; a buen ~ quickly, hurriedly; a cada ~ at every step, at every turn; a ese ~ at that rate; a dos ~s near (de to); ✗ a ~ ligero at the double; al ~ in passing; al ~ que while, whereas; de ~ in passing; by the way, incidentally; abrir ~ make (a) way (para for); abrirse ~ force one's way (por through); aflojar el ~ slacken one's pace, slow down; apretar el ~ step (it) out, hurry along; ceder el ~ make way; mot. give way; ceder el ~ a fig. give place to; estar de ~ be passing through; llevar el ~ keep in step, ✗ mark time; llevar al ~ caballo walk; salir al ~ a waylay; confront; salir del ~ get out of a difficulty (or jam F); seguir los ~s a tail, shadow; visitar de ~ drop in (or by, over); volver sobre sus ~s retrace one's

steps; **2.** adv. ¡~! not so fast!, easy there!; hablar muy ~ talk very softly.
paspartú m passe-partout.
pasquín m skit (contra on), lampoon.
pasta f paste; dough para pan (a. sl.); pastry para hojaldre; pulp de madera; (cartón) cardboard; (encuadernación) full leather; filling de diente; ~s pl. pastry, pastries; (fideos) noodles, spaghetti; ~ de dientes toothpaste; de buena ~ kindly; media ~ half-binding.
pastar [1a] graze.
pastel m (dulce) cake; pie de carne etc.; paint. pastel; F plot, undercover agreement; ~es pl. pastry, confectionery; **pastelear** [1a] F stall, spin it out to gain time; **pastelería** f (arte) confectionery, pastry; (conjunto) pastries; (tienda) confectioner's, cake shop; **pastelero** m, a f pastry-cook; confectioner; **pastelillo** m small cake; pat de mantequilla.
pasteurizar [1f] pasteurize.
pastilla f tablet, pastille; cake de jabón etc.; bar de chocolate.
pastinaca f parsnip.
pasto m grazing; (campo) pasture; (comida) feed, grazing; fig. nourishment; fuel para fuego etc.; a ~ abundantly; a todo ~ freely, in great quantity; vino de ~ ordinary wine; **pastor** m shepherd; herdsman, goatherd etc.; eccl. clergyman, protestant minister; **pastora** f shepherdess; **pastoral** adj. a. su. f pastoral; **pastorear** [1a] pasture; eccl. guide, lead; **pastorela** f pastoral, pastourelle; **pastoril** pastoral.
pastoso doughy; pasty; voz rich, mellow.
pastura f pasture; (comida) feed, fodder.
pata f zo. foot, paw, leg; leg de mesa etc.; orn. (female) duck; ~ de cabra crowbar; ~ de gallo crow's feet; F bloomer; F piece of nonsense; ~ hendida cloven hoof; ~s arriba on one's back, upside down; a cuatro ~s on all fours; a la ~ la llana plainly, simply; enseñar la ~, sacar la ~ give o.s. away; F estirar la ~ peg out; F meter la ~ put one's foot in it; butt in; ser ~(s) be even, tie; F tener mala ~ be unlucky.

patada f stamp; (*puntapié*) kick; (*paso*) (foot)step; a ~s on all sides; **patalear** [1a] stamp; kick out, kick about; **pataleo** m stamping; kicking.

patán m F rustic, yokel; *b.s.* lout.

patarata f (piece of) nonsense, absurdity; gush, affectation; ~s *pl.* tomfoolery.

patata f potato; ~s *pl. fritas* chips; ~s *pl. inglesas* crisps; **patatal** m, **patatar** m potato patch.

patatús m F dizzy turn.

pateadura f, **pateamiento** m stamping; kicking; *thea.* noisy protest, the bird F; **patear** [1a] F *v/t.* kick, boot; trample on; *v/i.* stamp (one's foot); *thea.* give the bird to a play; *fig.* bustle about.

patentado patent; proprietary; **patentar** [1a] patent; **patente** 1. patent (*a.* ✝), obvious, (self-)evident; 2. f patent (*a.* ~ de invención); warrant; de ~ patent; *S.Am.* first-class; ~ de privilegio letters patent; ~ de sanidad bill of health; **patentizar** [1f] make evident, reveal.

pateo m F stamping; *thea.* the bird.

paternal fatherly, paternal; **paternidad** f fatherhood; paternity de niño *etc.*; ~ literaria authorship; **paterno** paternal; abuelo ~ grandfather on the father's side.

patético pathetic, moving, poignant; **patetismo** m pathos, poignancy.

patiabierto F bowlegged.

patibulario horrifying, harrowing.

patíbulo m gallows, gibbet.

patidifuso F nonplussed, shattered.

patiestevado bandy-legged.

patillas f/pl. whiskers, sideburns.

patín m skate; runner de trineo; 🛷 skid; 🛷 ~ de cola tail-skid; ~ de ruedas roller skate; **patinadero** m skating-rink; **patinador** m, -a f skater; **patinaje** m skating; **patinar** [1a] skate; (*resbalar*) skid, slip; **patinazo** m skid; **patinet(te)** f scooter.

patio m court, (court)yard, patio; *thea.* pit; ~ de recreo playground.

patita: F poner de ~s en la calle chuck out.

patito m duckling.

patizambo knock-kneed.

pato m duck; ~ (macho) drake; F estar hecho un ~ be slow, be awkward; F pagar el ~ foot the bill, carry the can.

patochada f F blunder.

patología f pathology; **patológico** pathological; **patólogo** m pathologist.

patoso F 1. boring; (*sabihondo*) smart; 2. m bore.

patraña f story, fib; fake, hoax, swindle.

patria f mother country, native land; ~ chica home town *etc.*; *fig.* home.

patriarca m patriarch; **patriarcal** patriarchal.

patricio adj. a. su. m, a f patrician.

patrimonial hereditary; **patrimonio** m inheritance; *fig.* heritage.

patrio native, home attr.; potestad *etc.* paternal; **patriota** m/f patriot; **patriotería** f jingoism, chauvinism; **patriotero** adj. a. su. m, a f jingo, chauvinist; **patriótico** patriotic; **patriotismo** m patriotism.

patrocinador m, -a f sponsor, patron; **patrocinar** [1a] sponsor; back; patronize; **patrocinio** m sponsorship; backing; patronage; **patrón** m landlord de pensión; (jefe) master, boss; ⚓ skipper; *eccl.* patron (saint); = patrono; *sew.* pattern; ⚙ stock; standard para medidas *etc.*; ~ oro gold standard; ~ picado stencil; **patrona** f landlady de pensión; employer, owner; *eccl.* patron (saint); (*patrocinadora*) patron, patroness; **patronal** employer's; *eccl.* of a patron saint; **patronato** m (acto) patronage; ✝ employers' association; board of trustees de obra benéfica *etc.*; board de turismo *etc.*; **patrono** m employer, owner; *eccl.* patron (saint); (*patrocinador*) patron; sponsor; protector.

patrulla f patrol; **patrullar** [1a] patrol (por acc.); police.

patulea f F rabble, mob.

patullar [1a] trample, stamp about; F bustle about; F (*conversar*) chat.

paulatinamente gradually, bit by bit.

paulina f F telling-off, dressing-down; F (carta) poison-pen letter.

pauperismo m pauperism; **paupérrimo** very poor, terribly poor.

pausa f pause; break, respite; ♪ rest;

con ~ slowly; **pausado** slow, deliberate; **pausar** [1a] v/t. slow down; interrupt; v/i. go slow; pause.

pauta f ruler para rayar; standard, norm; model, example; outline, plan, key; **pautar** [1a] papel rule; fig. give directions for.

pava f turkey hen; F plain woman; S.Am. pot, kettle; S.Am. fig. banter; F pelar la ~ do one's courting at a window grille.

pavesa f spark, cinder; estar hecho una ~ be a shadow of one's former self; F ser una ~ be very meek and mild.

pavimentar [1a] pave; **pavimento** m pavement, paving; flooring de casa etc.

pavisoso F, **pavitonto** F nice but a bit simple.

pavo m turkey; sl. 5 pesetas; ~ real peacock; F comer ~ be a wallflower; sl. ponerse hecho un ~, tener mucho ~ blush like a lobster; F ¡no seas ~! don't be an idiot!

pavón m peacock; metall. bluing, bronzing; **pavonar** [1a] metall. blue, bronze; **pavonearse** [1a] swagger, strut, swank F.

pavor m terror, dread; **pavoroso** terrifying, frightful.

payasada f clowning, clownish stunt; ~s pl. tomfoolery; thea. etc. slapstick; **payaso** m clown.

payuelas f/pl. chicken-pox.

paz f peace; peacefulness; rest; en ~ at peace; at rest; dejar en ~ leave alone, leave in peace; descansar en ~ rest in peace; estar en ~ be even (con with), be quits; hacer las paces make peace; make it up; mantener la ~ keep the peace.

pazguato simple, stupid.

pe: de ~ a pa from beginning to end.

peaje m toll; barrera de ~ toll-bar, toll-gate; puente de ~ toll-bridge.

peana f stand, pedestal, base.

peatón m pedestrian, walker; ℧ country postman.

pebete m joss-stick; ✂ fuse; F thing that stinks; S.Am. F kid.

peca f freckle.

pecado m sin; **pecador 1.** sinning, sinful; **2.** m, -a f sinner; **pecaminoso** sinful; **pecar** [1g] sin; go astray; ~ de confiado be too trusting; ~ por exceso de err on the side of.

pececillos m/pl. fry.

pecera f fish-bowl.

pecios m/pl. flotsam, wreckage.

pécora f: F buena ~, mala ~ nasty piece of work, cunning bitch; (puta) whore.

pecoso freckled.

pectoral 1. pectoral; **2.** m eccl. pectoral (cross).

pecuario cattle attr.

peculado m peculation.

peculiar peculiar; typical, characteristic; **peculiaridad** f peculiarity.

peculio m small savings; modest sum.

pecunia f F brass, cash; **pecuniario** pecuniary, money attr.

pechar [1a] pay (as a tax).

pechera f shirt-front; bosom de vestido; (armadura) chest-protector; F bosom; ~ (postiza) dicky.

pechero m commoner, plebeian.

pecho[1] m anat. chest; breast (a. fig.); (esp. de mujer) breast, bosom, bust; ~s pl. breasts, bust; fig. courage, spirit; geog. slope, gradient; ¡~ al agua! courage!; a ~ descubierto unprotected; openly, frankly (a. a ~ abierto); abrir su ~, descubrir su ~ unbosom o.s.; dar el ~ feed, nurse; tomar a ~(s) take to heart; S.Am. tomarse a ~s take seriously, make an issue of.

pecho[2] m tax, tribute.

pechuga f breast de pollo etc.; F breast, bosom de mujer; F geog. slope, hill.

pedagogía f pedagogy; **pedagógico** pedagogic(al); **pedagogo** m pedagogue (a. b.s.); teacher.

pedal m pedal; ~ de acelerador accelerator (pedal); ~ de embrague clutch (pedal); ~ de freno footbrake, brake (pedal); **pedalear** [1a] pedal.

pedante 1. pedantic; **2.** m pedant; **pedantería** f pedantry; **pedantesco** pedantic.

pedazo m piece, bit; scrap; ~ del alma etc. darling, apple of one's eye; F ¡~ de animal!, ¡~ de bruto! you idiot!; you beast!; a ~s in pieces; hacer ~s break to (or in) pieces, pull to pieces; shatter, smash; hacerse ~s fall to pieces, come apart, break up; hecho ~s fig. worn out.

pedernal m flint; flintiness.
pedestal m pedestal, stand, base.
pedestre viaje on foot; pedestrian (a. fig.).
pediatra m/f paediatrician; **pediatría** f paediatrics.
pedicuro m chiropodist.
pedido m request; ✝ order; ~ de repetición repeat order; a ~ on request.
pedigüeño insistent, importunate; niño demanding.
pedimento m petition; ⚖ claim, bill.
pedir [3l] 1. v/t. ask for; request, require; demand; need; beg; paz sue for; comida etc.; ✝ order; me pidió dinero he asked me for money; no me pidas que lo haga don't ask me to do it; ~ prestado borrow (a from); 2. v/i. ask; ~ (por Dios) beg; a ~ de boca just right, just as one would wish.
pedrada f (golpe) hit with a stone; (echada) throw of a stone; fig. snide remark, dig; matar a ~s stone to death; **pedrea** f stone-throwing; meteor. hailstorm; small prizes en lotería; **pedregal** m stony place; **pedregoso** stony, rocky; **pedrera** f stone-quarry; **pedrería** f precious stones, jewels; **pedrisco** m shower of stones; heap of loose stones; meteor. hailstorm; **pedrusco** m rough stone, lump of stone; meteor. hailstorm, hailstones.
pega f (acto) sticking etc.; pitch, varnish de vasija; F (chasco) trick, practical joke; F (zurra) beating-up; F (dificultad) snag; F de ~ fake, sham; pregunta de ~ catch (or trick) question; poner ~s raise objections, make difficulties; **pegadizo** sticky; ♪ infectious; ♪ catchy; p. parasitic; (postizo) sham, imitation; **pegado** m patch, sticking-plaster; **pegajoso** sticky, adhesive; ♪ infectious, catching; ♪ catchy; F (suave) soft, gentle; vicio etc. tempting; p. tiresome; (sobón) sloppy, oily, cloying.
pegar [1h] 1. v/t. stick, glue, gum; unite, join; botón etc. sew on; cartel etc. post, stick; p. strike, slap, smack; enfermedad give; sl. estar pegado not have a clue; estar pegado a fig. be fond of; stick to, be inseparable from; 2. v/i. stick etc.;

(fuego) catch; (colores) match, go together; ⚘ take root; (remedio etc.) take; F eso no pega ni con cola that's miles off the point; F ~ con p. run into; 3. ~se stick etc.; ♣ be catching; cocina: catch; fig. intrude; ~ a p. stick to, attach o.s. to; sl. ~la a marido deceive, cuckold; se la pega su mujer his wife's deceiving him.
pegote m sticking-plaster; F sticky mess; (p.) hanger-on, sponger; **pegotear** [1a] F sponge, cadge.
peina f ornamental comb, back comb; **peinada** f combing; darse una ~ comb one's hair, have a brush up; **peinado** 1. p. overdressed; estilo overdone, overnice; 2. m coiffure, hair-do; hair-style; **peinador** m hairdresser; (vestido) peignoir, dressing-gown; **peinadora** f hairdresser; **peinadura** f combing; ~s pl. combings; **peinar** [1a] pelo comb; do; style; pelo, pieles, caballo style; ~se comb one's hair; **peine** m comb; F buen ~ sly one; a sobre ~ lightly; **peineta** f = peina.
peje m fish; F sly fellow.
pejiguera f F bother, nuisance.
pela f sl. one peseta.
pelado cabeza etc. shorn, hairless; paisaje etc. bare, treeless, bleak; manzana etc. peeled; S.Am. broke, penniless; S.Am. (desvergonzado) shameless; **peladura** f peeling etc.; ~s pl. peelings.
pelafustán m, -a f F good-for-nothing, layabout; **pelagallos** m F tramp, vagrant; **pelagatos** m F wretch, poor devil.
pelaje m coat, fur; fig. appearance, quality.
pelambre m hair; (falta) bare patch; **pelambrera** f thick hair, thick fur.
pelar [1a] cut the hair off, shear; pollo pluck; fruta peel, skin; F fleece, clean out en el juego; F rob; S.Am. (azotar) beat; S.Am. (desacreditar) blacken, slander; ~se (p.) lose one's hair; (capa) peel off; F ~las por crave.
peldaño m step, stair; rung de escala.
pelea f fight, tussle; quarrel; struggle; scuffle, scrimmage; ~ de gallos cock-fight; de ~ gallo fighting; **peleador** combative, quarrelsome; **pelear** [1a] fight; scuffle; struggle;

fig. vie; ~se fight; scuffle; come to blows; (*desavenirse*) fall out (*con* with).

pelechar [1a] moult, shed one's hair; get new hair; F take a turn for the better.

pelele *m* rompers *de niño*; (*figura*) stuffed guy, dummy; F village idiot.

peleona *f* F row, set-to.

pelete *m* F poor fish, nobody; en ~ without a stitch on; **peletero** *m* furrier; skinner.

peliagudo furry; long-haired; F *p.* crafty, clever; F *cosa* ticklish.

pelicano grey-haired.

pelícano *m* pelican.

pelicorto short-haired.

película *f* film; ~ en *colores* colour film; ~ muda silent film; ~ sonora sound film, talkie.

peligrar [1a] be in danger; **peligro** *m* danger; risk; con ~ de *vida etc.* at the risk of; en ~ in danger; at stake; *fuera de* ~ out of danger; *correr* ~ be in danger; run a risk; *poner en* ~ endanger; **peligroso** dangerous; risky; *herida, situación etc.* ugly, nasty.

pelillo *m* slight annoyance; F *echar* ~s *a la mar* make it up, bury the hatchet; *pararse en* ~s be easily upset, make a fuss about nothing at all.

pelinegro black-haired; **pelirrojo** red-haired, red-headed; **pelirrubio** fair-haired.

pelma(zo) *m* F bore; (*que tarda*) lump, sluggard.

pelo *m* hair; coat, fur *de animal*; down *de ave, fruta*; nap, pile *de tela, alfombra*; ~ (*de la barba*) whisker; F *a(l)* ~ just right; ~ *arriba, contra* ~ the wrong way; con ~s y *señales* with chapter and verse; *hombre de* ~ *en pecho* brave man; real man; en ~ bare-back; F naked; F *a medios* ~s tight, half-seas-over; *de medio* ~ trifling; (*postizo*) sham, fake; *cortar un* ~ *en el aire* be pretty smart; *cortarse el* ~ have one's hair cut; F *echar* ~s *a la mar* make it up, bury the hatchet; *escaparse por un* ~ have a narrow escape; *poner los* ~s *de punta* make one's hair stand on end; *tener el* ~ *de la dehesa* betray one's humble origins; *no tener* ~s *en la lengua* be outspoken, not mince words; (*hablar mucho*) talk nineteen to the dozen; *no tener* ~ de

tonto be no fool; F *tomar el* ~ *a* pull one's leg; *venir al* ~ *a* suit down to the ground.

pelón hairless, bald; F stupid; F (*sin dinero*) broke; **pelona** *f* baldness; F death; **peloso** hairy.

pelota *f* ball; (*juego vasco*) pelota; *S.Am.* ferry-boat; ~ *base* baseball; en ~ naked; **pelotari** *m* pelota-player; **pelotear** [1a] *v/t. cuenta* audit; *v/i. tenis etc.*: knock up; *fútbol*: kick a ball about; F bicker, fall out; **peloteo** *m tenis*: knock-up *antes de comenzar*; rally *en el juego*; **pelotera** *f* F, **pelotero** *m* F row, quarrel, argument.

pelotilla: F *hacer la* ~ *a* suck up to, toady to; **pelotillero** *m* F toady, yes-man, stooge.

pelotón *m* ✕ squad, party; small mat, tuft *de pelo*; crowd *de gente*; ~ *de ejecución* firing squad.

peltre *m* pewter, spelter.

peluca *f* wig; F wigging, dressing-down.

peluco *m sl.* watch.

peludo 1. hairy, shaggy; *esp. animal* furry; *barba etc.* bushy; 2. *m* thick mat.

peluquería *f* hairdresser's (shop), barber's (shop); **peluquero** *m* hair-dresser, barber.

pelusa *f* ♀ down; fluff *de tela*; F envy.

pelvis *f* pelvis.

pella *f* ball, pellet; roll, round mass; ♀ head; raw lard *de cerdo*; F sum of money; F *hacer* ~ play truant.

pelleja *f* skin, hide; **pellejería** *f* skins, hides; (*fábrica*) tannery; ~s *pl. S.Am.* upsets, troubles; **pellejo** *m* skin, hide, pelt *de animal*; ♀ peel; (*odre*) wineskin; F drunk, toper; *sl.* (*mujer*) whore; *no quisiera estar en su* ~ I wouldn't like to be in his shoes; F *salvar el* ~ save one's bacon.

pellizcar [1g] pinch, nip; *comida etc.* take a small bit of; **pellizco** *m* pinch, nip; small bit.

pena *f* (*aflicción*) sorrow, distress, grief; ✝ pain(s); (*trabajo*) trouble; hardship; ⚖ punishment, penalty; ✝ forfeit, penalty; ~s *pl. S.Am.* ghosts; ~ *capital* capital punishment; ~ *de muerte* death penalty; *alma en* ~ soul in torment; *a duras* ~s with great difficulty; ¡qué ~! what a shame!; *so* ~ *de* under pain of; *da ~ verle así* it grieves me to see him like that; *es una ~* it's a shame, it's a pity; *merecer la ~, valer la ~* be worthwhile (*ir, de ir* to go, going), be worth the trouble; *no vale la ~ inf. (a.)* there is no point in *ger.*; *que vale la ~ de leerse* (*visitarse*) worth reading (visiting); *morir de ~* die of a broken heart; **penable** punishable.

penacho *m orn.* tuft, crest; plume *de casco*; plume, wreath *de humo*; *fig.* pride, arrogance; panache.

penado 1. grieved; laborious, difficult; **2.** *m* convict.

penal 1. penal; **2.** *m* prison; **penalidad** *f* trouble, hardship; ♯♯ penalty; **penalista** *m* penologist, expert in criminal law; **penálty** *m* penalty.

penar [1a] *v/t.* penalize, punish; *v/i.* suffer; (*alma*) be in torment; *~ por* pine for, long for; *~se* grieve, mourn.

penca *f* ♀ fleshy leaf; *hacerse de ~s* have to be coaxed into doing s.t.

pendencia *f* quarrel, fight, brawl; *armar ~* brawl; **pendenciero 1.** quarrelsome, cantankerous; given to fighting; **2.** *m* brawler; tough F.

pender [2a] hang; dangle; droop; depend; ♯♯ *etc.* be pending; **pendiente 1.** hanging; *asunto etc.* pending, unsettled; *fig.* dependent (de on); *estar ~ de los labios de* hang on *s.o.*'s lips; **2.** *m* earring; **3.** *f geog.* slope, incline; pitch *de techo*.

pendil *m* (woman's) mantle; F *tomar el ~, tomar ~es* pack up, clear out; sneak away.

péndola *f* pendulum *de reloj*; *fig.* pen, quill; **pendolista** *m* penman, calligrapher.

pendón *m* banner, standard; pennon; F tall shabby person; *sl.* whore.

péndulo *m* pendulum.

pene *m* penis.

peneque F pickled.

penetración *f* penetration (*a. fig.*); *fig.* insight, acuteness; **penetrador** penetrating, keen; **penetrante** penetrating; penetrative; *frío* biting; *mirada* searching; keen, acute; *vista, viento* sharp; *sonido* piercing; **penetrar** [1a] *v/t.* penetrate, pierce; permeate; *misterio etc.* fathom, grasp;

intención see through; *v/i.* penetrate (*en, entre, por acc.*); sink in, soak in; *~se de* become imbued with.

penicilina *f* penicillin.

península *f* peninsula; **peninsular** peninsular.

penique *m* penny.

penitencia *f* penitence; (*acto*) penance; *hacer ~ fig.* take pot-luck; **penitenciado** *m S.Am.* convict; **penitencial** penitential; **penitenciar** [1b] impose a penance on; **penitenciaría** *f* prison, penitentiary *esp. Am.* (*a. eccl.*); **penitenciario** *m eccl.* confessor; ♯♯ prison, penitentiary *esp. Am.*; **penitente** *adj. a. su. m/f* penitent.

penol *m* yard-arm.

penoso arduous, laborious; painful, distressing.

pensado: *mal ~* evil-minded, nasty-minded; *de ~* on purpose; **pensador** *m* thinker; **pensamiento** *m* (*facultad, una idea*) thought; (*ideas de p.*) thinking; ♀ pansy; *ni por ~* not on any account; **pensante** thinking; **pensar** [1k] **1.** *v/t. pensamiento etc.* think; *problema* think over, give thought to; *número* think of; *~ inf.* intend to *inf.*, propose to *inf.*, plan to *inf.*; *~ de* think of, have an opinion of; *dar que ~ a* give food for thought to, give pause to; *¡ni ~lo!* not a bit of it!; **2.** *v/i.* think; *~ en* think of, think about, reflect on; *sin ~* unexpectedly; **pensativo** thoughtful, pensive.

penseque *m* F oversight, mistake.

pensión *f* (*renta etc.*) pension; (*casa*) boarding-house, guest-house, lodging-house; lodgings *para estudiantes etc.*; (*que se paga*) board and lodging; *fig.* burden; *~ completa* full board (and lodging); *~ vitalicia* annuity; **pensionado 1.** *m*, a *f* (*p.*) pensioner; **2.** *m* boarding-school; **pensionar** [1a] pension; **pensionista** *m/f* pensioner; (*huésped*) paying guest, lodger; (*alumno*) boarder.

pentagonal pentagonal; **pentágono** *m* pentagon.

pentagrama *m* ♪ stave, staff.

Pentecostés *f* (*hebrea*) Pentecost; (*cristiana*) Whit(sun), Whitsuntide.

penúltimo last but one, next to last, penultimate.

penumbra *f* penumbra, half-light.

penuria f shortage, dearth.

peña f rock; cliff, crag; (*ps.*) group, circle; *b.s.* coterie, clique; ~ *deportiva* supporters' club; **peñascal** m rocky place; **peñasco** m rock; crag; pinnacle of rock; **peñascoso** rocky, craggy; **peñón** m (mass of) rock, crag; el ♀ The Rock (of Gibraltar).

peños m/pl. sl. teeth.

peón m (*peatón*) pedestrian; ✗ infantryman, foot-soldier; ⚓ etc. labourer, builder's mate; *S.Am.* farmhand, peon; (*peonza*) top; *ajedrez*: pawn; ⊕ spindle, axle; ~ *caminero* navvy, road-mender; **peonada** f day's stint.

peonía f peony.

peonza f spinning-top, whipping-top; F busy little person; sl. ir a ~ go on Shanks' pony.

peor adj. a. adv. comp. worse; sup. worst; *cada vez* ~, ~ *que* ~ worse and worse; *de mal en* ~ from bad to worse; *v. tanto*; **peoría** f worsening, deterioration.

pepinillos m/pl. (en vinagre) gherkins; **pepino** m cucumber.

pepita f pip; *metall.* nugget; F *no tener* ~ *en la lengua* be outspoken, not mince words; (*hablar mucho*) talk nineteen to the dozen.

pepitoria f fig. hotchpotch, medley.

péptico peptic.

pequeñez f smallness, small size; shortness de p.; infancy de niño; *contp.* smallmindedness; *pequeñeces* pl. trifles; **pequeño** little, small; *estatura* short; fig. modest, humble; *los* ~s the children.

pera[1] adj. sl.: *muy* ~ posh, classy.

pera[2] f ♀, vet. pip; (*barba*) goatee; ♀ switch; bulb de claxon etc.; F *partir* ~s con be on easy terms with; F *poner a uno las* ~s a cuarto put the screws on; tell a few home truths to; **peral** m pear (tree).

perca f ichth. perch.

percance m mishap, mischance; hitch en proyecto etc.; ✝ perquisite.

percatarse [1a]: ~ de take notice of; guard against.

percebe m barnacle; F idiot.

percepción f perception; appreciation, notion; ✝ collection, receipt; **perceptible** perceptible, noticeable, detectable; **percibir** [3a] *sueldo etc.* receive, get; *impuestos* collect; *impresión etc.* perceive,

see, notice, detect; *peligro etc.* scent, sense.

percusión f percussion; **percusor** m, **percutor** m striker, hammer; **percutir** [3a] strike, tap.

percha f rack, coat-stand; coat-hanger; **perchero** m hall-stand.

perdedor m loser; *buen* ~ good loser, good sport.

perder [2g] lose; *tiempo* waste; *tren etc.* miss; *univ. curso* fail; ✝ etc. forfeit; (*echar a* ~) ruin, spoil; ~ *por 2 a 3* lose (by) 2—3; *echar a* ~ *comida etc.* spoil, ruin; *oportunidad* waste, lose; *echarse a* ~ spoil, be ruined; ~se (*en camino etc.*) lose o.s., get lost, stray; (*material, comida*) be spoiled; (*líquido, provisión*) go (*or* run) to waste; ~ (*de vista*) pass out of sight; ~ *por* be mad about.

perdición f perdition (a. eccl.), undoing, ruin.

pérdida f loss; waste de tiempo; ✝ etc. forfeiture; wastage de líquido etc.; fig. ruination; ✝ con ~ at a loss, at a sacrifice; **perdidizo**: *hacer* ~ hide; lose on purpose; *hacerse el* ~ make o.s. scarce; **perdido 1.** *bala* stray; *momentos* idle, spare; F dirty; F *bebedor etc.* inveterate, hardened; ~ *por* mad about; *dar por* ~ give up for lost; **2.** m rake.

perdigar [1h] *carne* half-cook, brown; **perdigón** m orn. young partridge; ✗ pellet; ~ *zorrero* buckshot; ~es pl. (small-)shot, pellets.

perdiz f partridge.

perdón m forgiveness, pardon (a. ✝): ¡~! sorry!; con ~ if I may, by your leave; *hablando con* ~ if I may say so; *pedir* ~ a ask s.o.'s forgiveness; **perdonable** pardonable, excusable; **perdonador** forgiving; **perdonar** [1a] pardon (a. ✝), forgive, excuse (*algo a alguien* a p. a th.); *vida* spare; (*exceptuar*) exempt; ¡*perdone*! pardon me!, I'm so sorry!; *no* ~ *ocasión* miss no opportunity; *no* ~ *medio de inf.* use all possible means to *inf.*; **perdonavidas** m F bully, tough.

perdulario 1. careless, sloppy; (*moralmente*) vicious; **2.** m rake.

perdurable (ever)lasting; abiding; **perdurar** [1a] last, endure, survive; stand.

perecedero perishable; *vida etc.* transitory; p. mortal; **perecer** [2d] perish; suffer; ~ *ahogado* drown;

~se *por* pine for, crave, be dying for; *mujer* be mad about; ~ *por inf.* crave to *inf.*, be dying to *inf.*; ~ *de risa* die of laughing.

peregrinación *f* long tour, travels; *eccl.* pilgrimage; **peregrinar** [1a] travel extensively (abroad); *eccl.* go on a pilgrimage; **peregrino 1.** *p.* wandering; *ave* migratory; *fig.* strange; *belleza etc.* rare, exotic; **2.** *m*, **a** *f* pilgrim.

perejil *m* parsley; ~es *pl.* F buttons and bows, trimmings; F titles, handles.

perendengue *m* trinket, cheap ornament.

perenne everlasting, undying, perennial (*a.* ♀); *de hoja* ~ evergreen.

perentorio peremptory, authoritative; urgent.

pereza *f* idleness, laziness, sloth (*a. eccl.*); **perezoso 1.** idle, lazy, slothful; slack; *movimiento* sluggish, slow; **2.** *m zo.* sloth.

perfección *f* perfection; completion; *a la* ~ to perfection; **perfeccionamiento** *m* perfection; improvement; **perfeccionar** [1a] perfect; improve; *proceso etc.* complete; **perfectamente** perfectly; ¡~! precisely!, just so!; **perfectibilidad** *f* perfectibility; **perfectible** perfectible; **perfecto 1.** perfect; *proceso etc.* complete; **2.** *m gr.* perfect (tense).

perfidia *f* perfidy, treachery; **pérfido** perfidious, treacherous, disloyal.

perfil *m* profile; *phot. etc.* side view; △, *geol.* (cross-)section; outline *de edificio etc.*; ~es *pl.* finishing touches; **perfilado** *cara* elongated, long; *nariz* well-formed; *avión etc.* streamlined; **perfilar** [1a] outline; *avión etc.* streamline; ~se show one's profile, give a side view; (*edificio etc.*) show in outline; F dress up.

perforadora *f* pneumatic drill; **perforar** [1a] perforate; pierce; puncture *accidentalmente*; *agujero* drill, bore; *pozo* sink; *tarjeta etc.* punch.

performance [per'formans] *m deportes:* performance.

perfumar [1a] scent, perfume; **perfume** *m* scent, perfume; **perfumería** *f* perfume shop; perfumery; **perfumista** *m/f* perfumer.

pergamino *m* parchment.

pergeñar [1a] (*disponer*) arrange, fix up; (*bosquejar*) do roughly, do in rough; **pergeño** *m* rough draft.

pericia *f* skill, skilfulness; expertness, expertise; proficiency; **pericial** *testigo* expert.

perico *m orn.* parakeet; F chamberpot; F *es* ~ *entre ellas* he's a ladies' man. [*ciudad.*\

periferia *f* periphery; outskirts *de*|

perifollo *m* ♀ chervil; ~s *pl.* buttons and bows, frippery.

perífrasis *f* periphrasis; **perifrástico** periphrastic.

perilla *f* pear-shaped ornament; (*barba*) goatee; ~ (*de la oreja*) lobe of the ear; F *venir de* ~(s) come just right, be to the point.

perillán *m* F rogue, crafty sort.

perímetro *m* perimeter.

perinola *f* teetotum.

periódico 1. periodic(al); ♪ recurrent; **2.** *m* (*diario, dominical*) newspaper; (*revista etc.*) periodical; **periodicucho** *m* F rag; **periodismo** *m* journalism; **periodista** *m/f* journalist; *m a.* pressman, newspaperman; **periodístico** journalistic, newspaper *attr.*

período *m* period.

peripecia *f lit.* vicissitude; ~s *pl.* unforeseen changes, ups and downs.

peripuesto F dressy, overdressed.

periquete: F *en un* ~ in a tick.

periquito *m* parakeet.

periscopio *m* periscope.

peristilo *m* peristyle.

peritaje *m* expert work; (*pago*) expert's fee; **perito 1.** skilled, skilful; experienced; qualified; expert, proficient (*en* at, in); **2.** *m* expert; technician; ~ *electricista etc.* qualified electrician *etc.*

peritonitis *f* peritonitis.

perjudicar [1g] damage, harm, impair; *posibilidades etc.* prejudice; **perjudicial** harmful, injurious *a salud etc.*; prejudicial, detrimental (*a, para intereses etc.* to); **perjuicio** *m* (*daño*) damage, harm; ✝ financial loss; (*injusticia*) wrong; prejudice; *en* ~ *de* to the detriment of; *sin* ~ *de* without prejudice to.

perjurar [1a] commit perjury; ~se perjure o.s.; **perjurio** *m* perjury; **perjuro 1.** perjured; **2.** *m* perjurer.

perla f pearl (a. fig.; de of, among); fig. gem; F me está (or viene) de ~s it suits me a treat.

perlático paralytic, palsied; **perlesía** f paralysis, palsy.

permanecer [2d] stay, remain; **permanencia** f (estado) permanence; (período) stay; **permanente 1.** permanent; constant; comisión, ejército standing; **2.** f F perm; hacerse una ~ have one's hair permed.

permanganato m permanganate.

permeable permeable, pervious (a to).

permisible allowable, permissible; **permisivo** permissive; **permiso** m permission; ✗ etc. leave; (documento) permit, licence; ~ de conducir driving licence; ~ de convalecencia sick-leave; ~ de entrada entry permit; ~ de salida exit permit; con ~ if I may; (levantándose de mesa etc.) excuse me; con ~ de Vd. if you don't mind, by your leave; estar de ~ be on leave; **permitir** [3a] allow, permit; permit of; enable; no se permite fumar aquí you can't smoke here, no smoking here; si lo permite el tiempo weather permitting.

permuta f barter, exchange; **permutación** f esp. ⚕ permutation; interchange; ✝ barter, exchange; **permutar** [1a] esp. ⚕ permute; ✝ barter, exchange.

pernear [1a] kick one's legs; F hustle, get cracking; **pernera** f trouser-leg; **perneta: en ~s** bare-legged.

pernicioso pernicious, evil.

pernil m upper leg, haunch de animal; trouser-leg.

pernio m hinge.

perno m bolt.

pernoctar [1a] spend the night.

pero 1. cj. but; yet; **2.** m objection; snag; defect; ¡no hay ~ que valga! there are no buts about it!; poner ~(s) a find fault with, raise objections to.

perogrullada f platitude, truism.

perol m (bowl-shaped) pan.

peroné m fibula, splint(er)-bone.

peroración f peroration; conclusion of a speech; **perorar** [1a] perorate, make a speech; summarize; F orate; **perorata** f long-winded speech.

peróxido m peroxide.

perpendicular 1. perpendicular; at right-angles; **2.** f perpendicular.

perpetración f perpetration; **perpetrador** m, **-a** f perpetrator; **perpetrar** [1a] perpetrate.

perpetuación f perpetuation; **perpetuar** [1e] perpetuate; **perpetuidad** f perpetuity; **perpetuo** perpetual; everlasting; ceaseless; exilio etc. (for) life.

perplejidad f perplexity; bewilderment; dilemma; hesitation; **perplejo** perplexed; dejar ~ perplex, puzzle.

perra f bitch; F ~ chica 5-céntimo coin; F ~ gorda 10-céntimo coin; F ~s pl. small change; sl. cogerse una ~ de get an obsession about (or with), get a thing about; **perrada** f pack of dogs; F dirty trick; **perrera** f kennel; fig. badly-paid job; drudgery; F tantrum; **perrería** f pack of dogs; (ps.) gang of thieves; (palabra) harsh word; F dirty trick; **perrillo** m puppy; (raza pequeña) miniature dog; ✗ trigger; **perrito** m, **a** f puppy.

perro 1. m dog; ~ de aguas spaniel; ~ cobrador retriever; ~ danés Great Dane; ~ dogo bulldog; ~ esquimal husky; ~ faldero lap-dog; ~ guardián watch-dog; ~ del hortelano dog in the manger; ~ de lanas poodle; ~ lebrel whippet; ~ lobo alsatian; ~ marino dogfish; ~ de muestra pointer; setter; ~ pastor sheep-dog; ~ de presa bulldog; ~ raposero foxhound; ~ rastrero tracker dog; ~ de Terranova Newfoundland dog; ~ viejo fig. old hand, wily bird; tiempo de ~s dirty weather; a otro ~ con ese hueso tell that to the Marines; dar a uno ~ keep s.o. waiting; darse a ~s get wild; **2.** wretched, cruel, wicked.

perruna f dog-biscuit; **perruno** ⚥ canine, dog attr.; devoción etc. dog-like.

persa adj. a. su. m/f Persian.

persecución f persecution; (caza) pursuit, chase; **persecutorio**: v. manía; **perseguidor** m, **-a** f persecutor; pursuer; **perseguir** [3d a. 3l] persecute; (dar caza a) pursue, chase; (acosar) harass, beset; pick on; objetivo aim at, pursue.

perseverancia f perseverance; constancy; **perseverante** persevering;

perseverar [1a] persevere; persist (en in).

persiana f (Venetian) blind; slatted shutter.

persignarse [1a] cross o.s.

persistencia f persistence; **persistente** persistent; **persistir** [3a] persist (en in; en inf. in ger.); persevere; continue.

persona f person; ~s pl. freq. people; buena ~ good sort, decent fellow; tercera ~ third party; en ~ in person, in the flesh; en la ~ de in the person of; por ~ per person; **personaje** m personage; thea. etc. character; F ser un ~ be somebody; **personal 1.** personal; **2.** m personnel, staff; (total) establishment; esp. ✠ force; ♣ complement; **personalidad** f personality; **personalismo** m selfishness, egoism; taking things in a personal way; **personalizar** [1f] personalize; embody; virtud personify; ~se become personal; **personarse** [1a] appear in person; **personificación** f personification; embodiment; **personificar** [1g] personify; embody; pick out for individual mention en discurso etc.

perspectiva f (en in) perspective: outlook, prospect para el futuro; appearance; (vista) view, scene.

perspicacia f perspicacity, discernment, perception; **perspicaz** perspicacious, discerning, perceptive; **perspicuo** clear, intelligible.

persuadir [3a] persuade; dejarse ~ be prevailed upon (a inf. to inf.); ~se be persuaded, become convinced; **persuasión** f persuasion; **persuasiva** f persuasion, persuasiveness; **persuasivo** persuasive.

pertenecer [2d] belong (a to); fig. ~ a concern, appertain to; **perteneciente:** ~ a appertaining to; **pertenencia** f ⚖ ownership; (cosa) property, possession; appurtenance, accessory.

pértica f = 2.571 m.; approx. rod.

pértiga f pole.

pertinacia f pertinacity, obstinacy; ✠ persistence; **pertinaz** pertinacious, obstinate; ✠ persistent.

pertinencia f relevance, pertinence; **pertinente** relevant, pertinent, appropriate.

pertrechar [1a] ✠ supply with ammunition and stores etc.; equip; fig.

arrange, prepare; **pertrechos** m/pl. ✠ supplies and stores etc.; ✠ munitions; implements, equipment.

perturbación f (mental) perturbation; pol., meteor., ✠ disturbance; ✠ upset; ~ del orden público breach of the peace; **perturbador 1.** perturbing, disturbing; **2.** m disturber; pol. disorderly element; **perturbar** [1a] (mentalmente) perturb; calma ruffle; orden, ✠ disturb; ✠ etc. upset.

peruano adj. a. su. m, a f Peruvian.

perversidad f perversity, depravity; (acto) wrongdoing; **perversión** f perversion (a. ✠), depravation; **perverso** perverse, depraved; consejo etc. evil; **pervertido** m, a f pervert; **pervertimiento** m perversion, corruption; **pervertir** [3i] pervert, corrupt; texto etc. distort; ~se become perverted.

pervinca f periwinkle.

pesa f weight; deportes: shot; dumbbell para ejercicios.

pesadez f heaviness, weight; slowness etc.

pesadilla f nightmare; (p. etc.) pet aversion.

pesado heavy, weighty; movimiento slow, sluggish; ponderous; sueño deep; libro etc. boring, tedious; stodgy; p. boring, tiresome; **pesadumbre** f sorrow, grief.

pésame: dar el ~ express one's condolences, send one's sympathy (por for, on).

pesantez f weight; gravity.

pesar [1a] **1.** v/t. weigh (a. fig.); v/i. weigh; be heavy; (tiempo) drag; (opinión etc.) count for a lot; mal que le pese whether he likes it or not; me pesa mucho 1 am very sorry about it, it grieves me greatly; pese a in spite of; pese a quien pese regardless of the consequences; **2.** m regret, sorrow; a ~ de in spite of, despite; a mi ~ to my regret; **pesaroso** regretful, sorrowful, sorry.

pesca f fishing; (cantidad pescada) catch; ~ submarina underwater-fishing; ~ de altura deep-sea fishing; F andar a la ~ de fish for; **pescada** f hake; **pescadería** f fish-market; (tienda) fish-shop; **pescadero** m, -a f fishmonger; **pescadilla** f whiting; **pescado** m fish;

pescador *m* fisherman; ~ *de caña* angler.

pescante *m mot.* driver's seat; ⊕ jib; ⚓ davit.

pescar [1g] *v/t.* (*coger*) catch; (*tratar de coger*) fish for; (*sacar del fondo*) dredge up (*a. fig.*); F *puesto* manage to get, land; F *p.* catch unawares, catch (in a lie *etc.*); F *no saber qué se pesca* not have a clue; *v/i.* fish.

pescozudo thick-necked; **pescuezo** *m* neck; scruff of the neck; *fig.* haughtiness.

pesebre *m* manger, crib; stall.

peseta *f* peseta; F *cambiar la* ~ be sick.

pesimismo *m* pessimism; **pesimista 1.** pessimistic; **2.** *m/f* pessimist.

pésimo vile, abominable, wretched.

peso *m* weight; (*que se sostiene*) burden, load; *esp. phys.* gravity; (*balanza*) balance, scales; *S.Am.* peso; *fig.* weight(iness); ~ *atómico* atomic weight; ~ *bruto* gross weight; ~ *específico* specific gravity; ~ *fuerte* heavy-weight; ~ *gallo* bantam-weight; ~ *ligero* light-weight; ~ *medio* middle-weight; ~ *medio fuerte* cruiser-weight; ~ *mosca* fly-weight; ~ *de muelle* spring-balance; ~ *muerto* dead weight; ~ *neto* net(t) weight; ~ *pesado* heavy-weight; ~ *pluma* feather-weight; *de* ~ *fig.* weighty; *en* ~ *echar etc.* bodily; *coger* in the air; *eso cae de su* ~ it goes without saying.

pespunt(e)ar [1a] back-stitch; **pespunte** *m* back-stitch(ing).

pesquera *f* weir *en río*; = **pesquería** *f* fishery, fishing-grounds; **pesquero** fishing *attr.*

pesquisa *f* inquiry, investigation; search; **pesquisar** [1a] inquire into, investigate; **pesquisidor** *m* investigator; (*juez*) examining magistrate.

pestaña *f* eyelash; ⊕ flange; rim *de llanta*; F *no pegar* ~ not get a wink of sleep; **pestañear** [1a] blink, wink; *sin* ~ without batting an eye; **pestañeo** *m* blink(ing), wink(ing).

peste *f* 🐀 plague, epidemic; (*olor*) stink, stench; *fig.* evil, menace; ~ *aviar* fowl pest; ~ *bubónica* bubonic plague; *echar* ~s swear (*contra* at); **pestífero** pestiferous; *olor* foul, noxious; **pestilencia** *f* pestilence,

plague; **pestilencial** pestilential; **pestilente** pestilent.

pestillo *m* bolt, latch, catch.

petaca *f* cigarette-case; tobacco pouch.

pétalo *m* petal.

petardear [1a] *v/t. fig.* cheat, swindle; *v/i. mot.* backfire; **petardista** *m/f* cheat, swindler; blackleg *en huelga*; **petardo** *m* 🗡 petard; (*fuegos artificiales*) cracker; *fig.* swindle, fraud.

petate *m* roll of bedding; F luggage; F (*p.*) trickster; (*despreciable*) poor fish; F *liar el* ~ pack up (and clear out); (*morir*) peg out.

peteretes *m/pl.* sweets.

petición *f* request; petition *a autoridad etc.*; ⚖ suit, plea; *a* ~ by request; *a* ~ *de* at the request of; *cometer* ~ *de principio* beg the question; **peticionario** *m*, **a** *f* petitioner.

petimetre *m* fop, beau.

petirrojo *m* robin.

peto *m* 🗡 breastplate; bodice *de mujer*.

pétreo stony; **petrificación** *f* petrification; **petrificar(se)** [1g] petrify (*a. fig.*).

petróleo *m min.* oil, petroleum; (*como combustible*) oil; paraffin; ~ *crudo* crude oil; **petrolero 1.** oil *attr.*; petrol *attr.*; **2.** *m* (*p.*) oil man; ⚓ (*a. buque* ~) tanker; **petrología** *f* petrology.

petulancia *f* pertness, insolence; **petulante** pert, insolent.

peyorativo pejorative; depreciatory.

pez[1] *m* fish; ~ *espada* swordfish; ~ *sierra* sawfish; F ~ *gordo* big pot, big shot; F *estar* ~ (*en ello*) not have a clue; *estar como el* ~ *en el agua* feel completely at home.

pez[2] *f* pitch, tar.

pezón *m* teat, nipple; ♀ stalk.

pezuña *f* hoof.

piada *f* cheeping; F catch-phrase.

piadoso pious, devout; (*benigno*) merciful, kind (*para con* to).

piafar [1a] paw the ground, stamp.

pianista *m/f* pianist; **piano** *m* piano; ~ *de cola* grand piano; ~ *de media cola* baby grand; ~ *vertical* upright piano.

piar [1c] cheep; F ~ *por* cry for.

piara *f* herd; drove.

pibe *m S.Am.* kid, child.

pica f pike; *poner una ~ en Flandes* bring off something difficult.

picada f sting; bite; peck; **picadero** m riding-school; **picadillo** m minced meat; **picado 1.** *material* perforated; *tabaco* cut; *mar* choppy; **2.** m 🜊 dive; **picador** m horse-trainer; *toros:* picador; 🜊 face-worker; **picadura** f sting, bite; prick(ing); cut tobacco.

picajón, picajoso F touchy.

picante 1. *sabor* hot, peppery; *fig.* piquant, racy, spicy; *observación* sharp, pungent; **2.** m *fig.* piquancy, spiciness; pungency.

picapedrero m stone-cutter, quarryman.

picapleitos m F litigious person.

picaporte m door-handle; latch; *(llave)* latch-key.

picar [1g] **1.** v/t. prick, pierce, puncture; *billete* punch, clip; *papel* perforate; *superficie* pit, pock; *caballo* prick, spur on; *toro* stick; *(insecto)* sting, bite; *(culebra, pez)* bite; *(ave)* peck; *comida* nibble, pick at; *lengua* burn; *carne* mince, chop up; *paint.* stipple; *sew.* pink; *fig.* annoy, bother; pique; **2.** v/i. 🜊 smart; itch; *(sol)* burn, scorch; 🜊 dive; *(por autoencendido)* pink; *~ muy alto* be over-ambitious; *~ en* be something of a; *estudio etc.* dabble in; **3.** *~se (ropa)* get moth-eaten; *(vino)* turn sour; *(fruta)* go off; *(mar)* get choppy; *(p.)* take offence, bridle *(por al)*; *~ de boast of being.

picardear [1a] play about, play up, be mischievous; *~se* go to the bad; **picardía** f *b.s.* crookedness; *(una ~)* dirty trick; naughtiness *de niño*; *(palabra)* rude thing, naughty word; **picaresco** roguish; *lit.* picaresque; **pícaro 1.** *b.s.* crooked, sly, crafty; *mst co.* rascally; *niño* naughty; *S.Am.* funny; **2.** m *lit.* picaro; *b.s.* rascal, rogue; *(niño)* rascal, scamp; **picaruelo** roguish.

picatoste m fried bread.

picaza f magpie.

picazo m jab, poke; **picazón** f 🜊 smarting, itch(ing); sting; F annoyance.

pícea f spruce.

pick-up [pi'ku(p)] m pick-up.

pico m *orn.* beak, bill; *(ave)* woodpecker; spout *de vasija etc.*; *geog.*

peak, summit; *(punta)* sharp point, corner; *(herramienta)* pick(axe); F talkativeness; *20 y ~* 20-odd; *a las 4 y ~* just after 4; F *callar el ~* keep one's trap shut; *irse del ~* talk too much; *ser un ~ de oro*, *tener mucho (or buen) ~* have the gift of the gab.

picor m smarting, itch(ing).

picoso pockmarked.

picota f pillory; *geog.* peak; 🜊 point.

picotada f, **picotazo** m peck; **picotear** [1a] v/t. peck; v/i. F chatter; talk hot air, gas; *~se* F squabble; **picotero F 1.** chattering, talkative; **2.** m, **a** f chatterer, gas-bag.

pictórico pictorial; *dotes etc.* artistic.

pichel m tankard. [tistic.]

pichón m young pigeon; *S.Am.* young bird; F kid; *~ de barro* clay pigeon; **pichona** f F darling.

pie m foot (a. 🜊, *poet.*); foot, base *de columna etc.*; stand, support; trunk *de árbol*; stem *de vaso*, *planta*; sediment *de líquido*; foot *de cama*, *página*; *thea.* cue; catchword; *fig.* foothold *al trepar*; *(estado)* footing; *~ de atleta* athlete's foot; *~ de imprenta* imprint; *~ marino* sealegs; *a ~* on foot; *a cuatro ~s* on all fours; *a ~ enjuto* dry-shod; *fig.* without risk; *a ~ juntillo*, *a ~ juntillas* firmly, absolutely; *al ~* close, handy; ✝ *al ~ de fábrica* cost-price, ex works; *al ~ de la letra* entender, citar literally; *copiar* word for word, exactly; *de ~* standing; up; *de a ~ soldado* foot attr.; *de ~s a cabeza* from head to foot; *en ~* standing; up; *en ~ de guerra* on a war footing; *en un mismo ~ de igualdad* on an equal footing (con with); *dar ~ a* give cause for; *no dar ~ con bola* be continually wide of the mark; *estar de (or en) ~* stand, be standing; *ir a ~* walk, go on foot; *írsele a uno los ~s* slip, stumble; *irse por ~s* make off; *morir al ~ del cañón* die in harness; *nacer de ~(s)* be born with a silver spoon in one's mouth; *poner el ~* tread; *ponerse de (or en) ~* rise, stand up, get up; *volver ~(s) atrás* retrace one's steps.

piedad f piety, devoutness; *(lástima)* pity; *(filial)* piety; *¡por ~!* for pity's sake!; *tener ~ de* take pity on.

piedra *f* stone; rock; *meteor.* hail, hailstone; flint *de mechero*; ~ de *afilar* hone; ~ de *amolar* grind-stone; ~ *angular* corner-stone (*a. fig.*); ~ *arenisca* sandstone; ~ *caliza* limestone; ~ de *escándalo* source of scandal; bone of contention; ~ *fundamental* foundation-stone; ~ de *molino* millstone; ~ *pómez* pumice(-stone); ~ *preciosa* precious stone; *primera* ~ foundation-stone; ~ de *toque* touchstone; *a tiro de* ~ within a stone's throw; *no dejar* ~ *sobre* ~ raze to the ground.

piel *f* skin; (*de animal*) skin, hide, pelt; (*con pelo*) fur; ♀ peel, rind, skin; ~ de *ante* buckskin. buff; ~ de *cerdo* pigskin; ~ de *foca* sealskin; ~ de *Rusia* Russia leather; ~ *roja* *m/f* redskin; ~ de *ternera* calf, calf-leather.

piélago *m lit.* ocean, deep.

pienso[1] *m* ✐ feed, fodder; ~s *pl.* feeding-stuffs.

pienso[2]: ¡ni por ~! the very idea!

pierna *f* leg; downstroke *con pluma*; *en* ~s bare-legged; *dormir a* ~ *suelta* (*or tendida*) sleep soundly.

pieza *f mst* piece; (*cuarto*) room; *hunt.* game, catch, example; *esp.* ⊕ part; *buena* ~, *linda* ~ crafty fellow; ~ de *convicción* convincing argument; ~ *fundida* cast(ing); ~ de *recambio*, ~ de *repuesto* spare part; ~ de *respeto* guest room; *de una* ~ in one piece.

pífano *m* fife.

pifia *f* F blunder, bloomer.

pigmento *m* pigment.

pigmeo *adj. a. su. m* pigmy.

pijama *m* pyjamas.

pijotero F *co.* **1.** wretched, beastly; **2.** *m* beast, rogue.

pila *f* (*montón*) pile, heap, stack; (*fregadero*) sink; (*abrevadero*) trough; *eccl.* font; ⚠ pier of bridge *etc.*; ⚡ battery; ~ *atómica* atomic pile; *sacar de* ~ *a* act as godparent to.

pilar *m* ⚠ pillar, pier; (*mojón*) milestone; basin, bowl *de fuente*.

píldora *f* pill; *dorar la* ~ sugar (*or* gild) the pill.

pileta *f* basin, bowl; sink.

pilón *m* (*abrevadero*) drinking-trough; basin *de fuente*; (*mortero*) mortar; (*azúcar*) loaf sugar; ⚡ pylon.

pilongo thin, lean.

pilot(e)ar [1a] steer; *coche* drive; *avión* pilot; **pilote** *m* ⚠ pile; **piloto 1.** *m* pilot; ~ de *puerto* harbour pilot; ~ de *prueba* test-pilot; **2.** *luz* rear, tail *attr.*

piltrafa *f* skinny meat; ~s *pl.* offal, scraps.

pillada *f* dirty trick; **pillaje** *m* plunder, pillage; **pillar** [1a] plunder, pillage; (*perro*) worry; F catch, seize.

pillastre *m* F scoundrel, rogue; **pillería** *f* dirty trick; (*ps.*) gang of scoundrels; **pillín** *m* F *co.* scamp, rascal; **pillo** F **1.** black-guardly; rotten; *niño* mischievous; (*astuto*) sly, crafty; **2.** *m* rascal, rogue; rotter; *cad*; (*niño*) = **pilluelo** *m* F scamp, rascal; (*golfo*) urchin.

pimentero *m* pepper-pot; ♀ pepper plant; **pimentón** *m* cayenne pepper, red pepper; paprika; **pimienta** *f* pepper, pimento; **pimiento** *m* pepper, pimento; ♀ pepper plant.

pimpollo *m* sucker, shoot *de planta*; (*árbol*) sapling; rosebud; F bonny }

pinabete *m* fir (tree). [child.}

pináculo *m* pinnacle.

pinar *m* pinewood, pine-grove.

pinaza *f* pinnace.

pincel *m* paint-brush; *fig.* painter; **pincelada** *f* (brush-)stroke; *última* ~ *fig.* finishing touch.

pinchar [1a] pierce, prick, puncture (*a. mot.*); *fig.* F prod; *tener un neumático pinchado* have a puncture; *no* ~ *ni cortar* cut no ice; **pinchazo** *m* prick, puncture (*a. mot.*); F prod.

pincho *m* prickle, spike.

pindonga *f* F gadabout.

pingajo *m* F tag; rag, shred.

pinganitos: F *estar en* ~ be high up, be well in.

pingo *m* F rag, shred; (*p.*) raga-muffin; *S.Am.* horse; ~s *pl.* clothes.

pingüe fat, greasy; *fig. ganancia* rich, fat; *negocio* lucrative.

pingüino *m* penguin.

pinitos *m/pl.*: *hacer* ~ toddle, take one's first steps; **pino**[1]: *en* ~ upright, standing; *v. pinitos*.

pino[2] *m* pine (tree); ~ *albar* Scotch pine; ~ *negro* Swiss mountain pine; ~ rodeno cluster pine; ~ de tea pitch-pine; **pinocha** *f* pine-needle; **pinsapo** *m* Spanish fir.

pinta 1. *f* spot, mark; (*punto*) dot, spot; *fig.* look(s), appearance, face; F (*lluvia*) drop of rain; F (*trago*) drop to drink; *naipes*: ¿a qué ~? what's trumps?; 2. *m* F co. es un ~ he's a fly one, he's a wily bird.

pintado spotted, mottled; *fig.* identical; F como el más ~ with the best; F me sienta que ni ~, viene que ni ~ it suits me a treat.

pintar [1a] *v/t.* paint (de rojo red; a. *fig.*); *esp. fig.* depict, picture; describe; F ~la put it on; F no pinta nada he cuts no ice, he doesn't count; *v/i.* paint; ♀ begin to ripen; F show, turn out; ~ como querer indulge in wishful thinking; ~se put on make-up; ¡ojo, se pinta! wet paint!; **pintarraj(e)ar** [1a] *f* daub; **pintarrajo** *m* F daub.

pintiparado identical (a to); just the thing, just right (*para* for); **pintiparar** [1a] F compare.

pintor *m*, -a *f* painter; ~ de brocha gorda house-painter; *b.s.* dauber; **pintoresco** picturesque; **pintura** *f* painting; (*color*) paint; *fig.* description; ~ a la aguada water-colour; ~ al óleo oil-painting.

pinturero F 1. conceited, swanky; 2. *m*, a *f* show-off, swank.

pinza *f* (clothes-)peg; *zo.* claw; **pinzas** *f/pl.* (unas a pair of) ⊕ pincers; (*pequeñas*) tweezers; forceps.

pinzón *m* (a. ~ vulgar) chaffinch; ~ real bullfinch.

piña *f* ♀ pine-cone; (*comestible*) pineapple; (*ps.*) clique, cluster; **piñón** *m* ♀ pine kernel; *orn.*, ⊕ pinion; **piñonate** *m* candied pine kernel; **piñonear** [1a] click; **piñoneo** *m* click.

pío[1] *caballo* piebald.

pío[2] pious, devout; (*benigno*) merciful, kind.

pío[3] *m orn.* cheep; F itch, intense longing; no decir ni ~ not breathe a word.

piojería *f* verminous place; F wretchedness; **piojo** *m* louse; F ~ resucitado jumped-up fellow; parvenu; **piojoso** verminous, lousy; *fig.* mean.

pipa *f* pipe; ♩ reed; cask de vino; ♀ pip.

pipiar [1c] chirp.

pipirigallo *m* sainfoin.

pipiripao *m* F slap-up do, spread.

pipote *m* keg, small cask.

pique *m* pique, resentment; *naipes*: spades; a ~ de in danger of; on the point of; echar a ~ sink; *fig.* wreck, ruin; irse a ~ sink, founder; tener un ~ con have a grudge against.

piqueta *f* pick(axe).

piquete *m* prick, jab; small hole en ropa; ✕ picket.

pira *f* pyre.

piragua *f* canoe; shell; **piragüista** *m* canoeist; oarsman.

piramidal pyramidal; **pirámide** *f* pyramid.

pirarse [1a] F beat it (a. ~las); *clase* cut.

pirata *m* pirate; *fig.* hard-hearted villain; **piratear** [1a] buccaneer; *fig.* rob; **piratería** *f* piracy; **pirático** piratical.

pirenaico Pyrenean.

pirita *f* pyrites.

piro... pyro...

piropear [1a] F say flirtatious things to; **piropo** *m* flirtatious remark, amorous compliment; *min.* garnet, carbuncle; echar ~s a = piropear.

pirotecnia *f* pyrotechnics; **pirotécnico** firework *attr.*, pyrotechnic(al).

pirrarse [1a] F: ~ por rave about, be crazy about.

pirueta *f* pirouette; **piruetear** [1a] pirouette.

pisa *f* tread(ing) *etc.*; **pisada** *f* (*ruido*) footstep, footfall, tread; (*huella*) footprint; **pisapapeles** *m* paper-weight; **pisar** [1a] 1. *v/t.* (*por descuido*) step on; (*apretando*) tread down; (*destruyendo*) trample (on, underfoot), flatten; (*estar una cosa sobre otra*) lie on, cover; ♩ cuerda pluck, tecla strike; *fig.* walk all over, abuse; 2. *v/i.* tread, step; **pisaverde** *m* F toff, swell.

piscina *f* swimming-pool; fishpond.

piscolabis *m* F snack, bite.

piso *m* (*acto*) tread(ing); sole de zapato; (*suelo*) flooring; (*habitaciones*) flat, apartment *Am.*; (*segundo etc.*) floor, storey; ~ alto top floor; ~ bajo ground-floor; ~ principal first floor; casa de dos ~s two-storey house; **pisón** *m* ram, rammer; **pisotear** [1a] tread down); trample (on, underfoot); stamp on; **pisotón** *m* stamp on the foot.

pista *f* track, trail (*a. fig.*); *atletismo etc.*: race-track; ~ de aterrizaje runway; ~ de baile dance-floor; ~ de ceniza dirt-track; ~ de patinaje skating-rink; ~ de tenis tennis-court; *estar sobre la* ~ be on the scent; *seguir la* ~ *a* trail, be on the track of.

pistilo *m* pistil.

pisto *m* vegetable hash; ✱ broth; *a* ~s little by little; sparingly; *darse* ~ give o.s. airs.

pistola *f* pistol; ~ ametralladora tommy gun, sub-machine gun; ~ engrasadora grease-gun; **pistolera** *f* holster; **pistolero** *m* gunman, gangster; **pistoletazo** *m* pistol-shot; **pistolete** *m* pocket pistol.

pistón *m* ⊕ piston; ♪ key, piston; F *de* ~ = **pistonudo** F terrific, smashing.

pitada *f* whistle; hiss(ing) *de desaprobación*; F *dar una* ~ come out with an inappropriate remark.

pitanza *f* dole; F grub.

pitar [1a] blow a whistle; *mot.* sound the horn; *S.Am.* smoke; **pitido** *m* whistle, whistling.

pitillera *f* cigarette-case; **pitillo** *m* cigarette; *echar un* ~ have a smoke.

pito *m* ♪ whistle; *mot.* horn; cigarette; *S.Am.* pipe; *no se me da un* ~ I don't care tuppence (*de* about, for); *no tocar* ~ *en* have nothing to do with; *no vale un* ~ it's not worth tuppence.

pitón[1] *m zo.* python.

pitón[2] *m* horn *de toro etc.*; spout, nozzle *de porrón*; ♧ sprig, young shoot.

pitorrearse [1a]: F ~ *de* scoff at.

pitorro *m* spout, nozzle.

pituitario pituitary; *glándula* ~*a* pituitary.

pivote *m* pivot.

píxide *f* pyx.

pizarra *f min.* slate; *escuela*: blackboard; **pizarrín** *m* slate-pencil; **pizarrón** *m S.Am.* blackboard; *deportes*: scoreboard; **pizarroso** slaty; full of slate.

pizca *f cocina*: pinch; crumb *de pan etc.*; *fig.* trace, speck; *ni* ~ not a bit, not a scrap.

pizcar [1g] F pinch, nip; **pizco** *m* F pinch, nip.

pizpereta *f* F, **pizpireta** *f* F smart little piece.

placa *f* plate (*a. phot.*); plaque *con inscripción etc.*; (*condecoración*) badge; ~ esmerilada focussing screen; ~ giratoria turn-table; ~ de matrícula number-plate.

pláceme *m* congratulations; *dar el* ~ *a* congratulate; **placentero** pleasant, agreeable; **placer**[1] **1.** *v/t.* [2x] please; **2.** *m* pleasure; enjoyment; delight; *a* ~ at one's pleasure.

placer[2] *m min.* placer; ♧ sandbank.

placero *m*, **a** *f* stall-holder, market trader; *fig.* loafer, gossip.

placidez *f* placidity; **plácido** placid.

plaga *f* ✱ etc. plague; ✗ (*zo.*) pest, (♧) blight; *fig.* scourge, calamity; blight; hardship; abundance, glut; **plagar** [1h] infest, plague (*de* with); sow (*de minas* with); *plagado de* full of, infested with; ~*se* become infested with.

plagiar [1b] plagiarize; *S.Am.* kidnap; **plagiario** *m*, **a** *f* plagiarist; **plagio** *m* plagiarism; *S.Am.* kidnapping.

plan *m* (*disposición, intento*) plan, scheme; △, *surv.* plan; (*nivel*) level; (*altitud*) height; F set-up, arrangement; F (*actitud*) attitude; ~ de estudios curriculum; ~ quinquenal five-year plan; F *en* ~ *de as*, on a basis of; *en* ~ *de viaje* making preparations for a trip; *en* ~ *de turismo* as a tourist; *en* ~ *económico* on the cheap; *en ese* ~ in that way; *como sigas en ese* ~ if you go on like that; *estar en* ~ *de divertirse* be out for a good time; *estar en un* ~ *imposible* be on an impossible basis; *sl. tener un* ~ *con casada* be having an affair with.

plana *f typ.* page; *escuela*: copy-writing; ✗, ♧ mayor staff; *a* ~ *y renglón* line for line; *fig.* just right; *enmendar la* ~ *a* find fault with; improve upon.

plancha *f* plate, sheet *de metal*; slab *de madera etc.*; iron *para planchar*; (*acto*) ironing; ♧ gangway; F bloomer; ⊕ ~ *de garnitura* bolster; *hacer la* ~ float; F *hacer (or tirarse) una* ~ make a bloomer, drop a brick; **planchado** *m* ironing;

planchar [1a] iron; *traje* press;
planchear [1a] plate; **plancheta** *f*
surv. plane-table; F *echárselas de* ~
show off.

planeador *m* glider; **planear** [1a]
v/t. plan; *v/i.* glide; soar; **planeo** *m*
glide, gliding.

planeta *m* planet; **planetario**
1. planetary; 2. *m* planetarium.

planicie *f* level ground, flat surface.

planificación *f* planning; **planifi-
cador** planning *attr.*; **planificar**
[1g] plan, organize.

planilla *f* S.Am. pay-roll; (*billete*)
ticket (*a. pol.*).

plano 1. flat, level; smooth; plane
(*esp.* ⚊); *de* ~ clearly, plainly; *confesar* openly; *caer de* ~ fall flat;
rechazar de ~ turn down (flat); 2. *m*
⚊ plane; plan *de edificio etc.*; map,
street-plan *de ciudad*; flat *de espada*;
~ *de cola* tailplane; ~ *focal* focal
plane; ~ *inclinado* inclined plane;
primer ~ foreground; *levantar el* ~
de survey, make a map of.

planta *f* ⚘, ⊕ plant; plantation;
anat. sole, foot; △ (*piso*) floor,
storey; △ (ground-)plan; (*proyecto*)
plan, scheme; establishment *de
personal*; ~ *baja* ground-floor, first
floor *Am.*; ~ *piloto* pilot plant; *de* ~
from the foundations; *echar* ~*s*
swagger, brag; F *tener buena* ~ have
a good presence, be well-built;
plantación *f* plantation; (*acto*)
planting; **plantador** *m* (*p.*) planter;
(*instrumento*) dibber.

plantar [1a] *planta, golpe* plant;
poste etc. fix, set up; *fig.* set up;
F (*a. dejar plantado*) *novio* jilt, walk
out on; (*dejar en apuro*) leave high
and dry; (*en cita*) stand *s.o.* up; F
~ *en la calle* pitch into the street;
obrero sack; ~*se* plant o.s.; (*caballo*)
refuse, balk; F (*llegar*) get (en to),
be (en at).

plantear [1a] establish, set up, get
under way; *problema* pose; *dificultad, cuestión* raise.

plantel *m* ⚘ nursery; (*gente*) body,
group, establishment; (*educacional*)
training establishment.

plantilla *f* inner sole *de zapato*;
sole *de media*; ⊕ template, pattern;
establishment *de personal*; *ser de* ~
be on the establishment.

plantío *m* plot, bed; (*acto*) planting.

plantista *m* boaster, braggart.

plantón *m* ⚘ seedling, cutting; ✂
guard, sentry; F *dar* ~ *a* stand *s.o.*
up; F *estar de* ~ be stuck, have to
wait around.

plañidero mournful, plaintive;
plañir [3h] mourn, grieve over.

plasma *m* plasma.

plasmar [1a] mould, shape; create.

plasta *f* soft mass; flattened mass;
F badly-made thing, bungled job.

plasticidad *f* plasticity; *fig.*
expressiveness, descriptiveness;
plasticina *f* plasticine; **plástico**
1. plastic; *fig.* expressive, descriptive; 2. *m* plastic.

plata *f* silver; *S.Am.* money; *como
una* ~ like a new pin; F *en* ~ briefly;
frankly.

plataforma *f* platform (*a. fig.*);
stage; ⛟ turn-table.

plátano *m* plane (tree); (*fruta*)
banana.

platea *f thea.* pit.

plateado 1. silver *attr.*; silvery; ⊕
silver-plated; 2. *m* silver-plating;
platear [1a] silver; silver-plate;
platería *f* (*arte*) craft of the silversmith; (*tienda*) silversmith's; jeweller's; **platero** *m* silversmith;
jeweller.

plática *f* talk, chat; *eccl.* sermon;
platicar [1g] talk, chat, converse.

platija *f* plaice.

platillo *m* saucer; ♪ ~*s pl.* cymbals;
~ *de balanza* scale; ~ *volante* flying
saucer; *pasar el* ~ pass the hat
round.

platina *f* (microscope-)slide.

platino *m* platinum; *mot.* ~*s pl.*
contact points.

plato *m* plate, dish; (*primero etc.*)
course; (*español, favorito etc.*) dish;
(*porción*) plateful; F *nada entre dos
~s* much ado about nothing; *fregar
(or lavar) los ~s* wash up; F *ser ~ de
segunda mesa* feel neglected, be
left out in the cold; be second-best.

plausible acceptable, admissible;
(*loable*) praiseworthy, commendable.

playa *f* (sea-)shore; beach; seaside
(resort) *para veranear etc.*; *Santander tiene magníficas ~s* Santander
has wonderful beaches; *pasar el
día en la* ~ spend the day on the
beach; *este año vamos a una* ~ this
year we're going to the seaside;
playeras *f/pl.* sandals, sand-shoes;
tennis-shoes; **playero** beach *attr.*

plaza *f* square *en ciudad*; *(mercado)* market place; ⚔ (*a.* ~ *fuerte*) fortified town, stronghold; ♰ town, city, place; ♰ money market; *(sitio)* room, space; place, seat *en vehículo*; *(puesto)* post, job; *(vacante)* vacancy; ~ *de armas* parade ground; ~ *mayor* main square; ~ *de toros* bullring; *mot. etc. de dos* ~s two-seater; ♰ *en esa* ~ there, in your town; *sentar* ~ enlist (de as).

plazo *m* time, period; term; time-limit; expiry date; *esp.* ♰ date; *(pago)* instalment; *dentro de un* ~ *de 2 meses* within a period of 2 months; *a* ~s on credit, on easy terms; by instalments; on hire-purchase; *a corto* ~ short-dated; *a largo* ~ long-dated; *compra a* ~s hire-purchase; *comprar a* ~s buy on hire-purchase.

plazoleta *f*, **plazuela** *f* small square.

pleamar *f* high tide.

plebe *f* common people, the masses; *contp.* plebs; **plebeyo 1.** plebeian; **2.** *m*, a *f* plebeian, commoner.

plebiscito *m* plebiscite.

plegable pliable, pliant; *silla etc.* folding, collapsible; **plegadera** *f* paper-knife; **plegadizo** = *plegable*; **plegado** *m*, **plegadura** *f* fold; pleat; *(acto)* folding; pleating; **plegar** [1h *a.* 1k] fold, bend, crease; *sew.* pleat; ~se fold (up), bend, crease; *fig.* bow, submit.

plegaria *f* prayer.

pleitear [1a] plead, conduct a lawsuit; go to law *(con, contra* with; *sobre* over); **pleitista 1.** litigious; **2.** *m/f* litigious person; **pleito** *m* lawsuit, case; *fig.* dispute, controversy; ~s *pl.* litigation; *andar a* ~s be engaged in lawsuits; *estar a* ~ *con* be at odds with; *poner* ~ *sue (a acc.)*, bring an action (*a* against).

plenario plenary, full.

plenilunio *m* full moon.

plenipotenciario *adj. a. su. m* plenipotentiary.

plenitud *f* plenitude, fullness; abundance; **pleno 1.** *mst fig.* full, complete; *sesión* plenary, full; *en* ~ *día* in broad daylight; *en* ~ *verano* at the height of summer; *en* ~*a vista* in full view; **2.** *m* plenum.

pleonasmo *m* pleonasm.

plétora *f* plethora; abundance,

flood; **pletórico** plethoric; ~ *de* full of, brimming with.

pleuresía *f* pleurisy.

plexo *m*: ~ *solar* solar plexus.

pliego *m (hoja)* sheet; folder; *(carta)* sealed letter; ~ *cerrado* sealed orders; ~ *de condiciones* details, specifications *para oferta etc.*; tender; ~ *suelto* broadsheet; **pliegue** *m* fold *(a. geol.)*; *sew. etc.* pleat, crease, tuck.

plinto *m* plinth.

plisado *m* pleating; **plisar** [1a] pleat.

plomada *f* △ plumb, plummet; ⚓ sinker *de red*; ⚓ (sounding-) lead *para sondar*; **plomar** [1a] seal with lead; **plomería** *f* △ lead roofing; ⊕ plumbing; **plomero** *m* plumber; **plomizo** leaden *(a. fig.)*; lead-coloured; **plomo** *m* 🜍 lead; *(peso)* lead (weight); sinker *de red*; △ plumb-line; ⚔ bullet; ✦ fuse; *a* ~ plumb, true, vertical(ly); *fig.* just right; *andar con pies de* ~ proceed very gingerly; *caer a* ~ fall flat.

plugo, pluguiere *etc. v. placer*[1].

pluma *f orn.* feather; *(de escribir)* pen *(a. fig.)*; *(adorno)* plume; *fig.* penmanship; ~ *estilográfica* fountain-pen; *dejar correr la* ~ let one's pen run on; *escribir al correr de la* ~, *escribir a vuela* ~ write quickly, write freely; *hacer a* ~ *y a pelo* waste nothing; **plumada** *f* stroke of a pen; **plumado** feathered; *pollo* fledged; **plumafuente** *f* *S.Am.* fountain-pen; **plumaje** *m* plumage, feathers; plume, crest *de casco*; **plumazo** *m* feather mattress, feather pillow; *(plumada)* stroke of a pen *(a. fig.)*.

plúmbeo leaden; heavy as lead.

plumero *m* (feather) duster; plume *de casco*; **plumón** *m* down; *(colchón)* feather-bed; **plumoso** downy.

plural *adj. a. su. m* plural; **pluralidad** *f* plurality; majority *de votos etc.*

plus *m* extra pay, bonus.

pluscuamperfecto *m* pluperfect.

plusmarca *f* record.

plusvalía *f* enhanced value, appreciation.

plutocracia *f* plutocracy; **plutócrata** *m/f* plutocrat.

plutonio *m* plutonium.
pluvial rain *attr.*; **pluviómetro** *m* rain-gauge, pluviometer; **pluvioso** rainy.
población *f* population; (*ciudad etc.*) city, town, village; **poblacho** *m* down-at-heel town, decayed village; **poblachón** *m* F dump; **poblado** *m* town, village; inhabited place; built-up area; **poblador** *m*, -a *f* settler, founder.
poblar [1m] *tierra* settle, colonize, people; stock (*de peces* with); plant (*de árboles* with); *poblado de* peopled with, populated with (*or* by); *fig.* full of; **~se** ⚥ come into leaf.
pobo *m* white poplar.
pobre 1. poor (*de in*); *¡~ de mí!* poor (old) me!; **2.** *m/f* poor person; pauper; beggar *que mendiga*; *los ~s pl.* the poor; *un ~* a poor man; *fig.* poor wretch; **pobrete 1.** poor, wretched; **2.** *m*, *a f* poor thing; well-meaning but ineffective person; **pobretería** *f* poverty; (*ps.*) poor people; **pobretón 1.** very poor; **2.** *m* poor man; **pobreza** *f* poverty; want, penury; slender resources.
pocilga *f* piggery, (pig)sty (*a. fig.*).
pócima *f*, **poción** *f* *pharm.* dose, draught; *vet.* drench; *fig.* brew, concoction.
poco 1. *adj.* little, slight, scanty; *~ dinero* little money; *queda ~ vino* there isn't much wine left; *su inteligencia es ~a* his intelligence is slight; *la ganancia es ~a* the profit is small; *~s pl.* few; *~s libros* few books, not many books; *~s son los que ...* there are few who ...; *unos ~s* some few, a few; **2.** *m*: *un ~* a little; *un ~ de dinero* a little money, some money; *un ~ (como adv.)*: *le conozco un ~* I know him slightly, I know him a little; *un ~ mejor* a little better; **3.** *adv.* little, not much; only slightly; *sabe ~* he knows little; *cuesta ~* it doesn't cost much; *a veces se traduce por el prefijo* un-: *~ amable* unkind, *~ amistoso* unfriendly; *a ~* shortly (after); *a ~ de haber salido* shortly after he had gone out; *~ a ~* little by little, gradually; *¡~ a ~!* gently!, easy there!; *dentro de ~* shortly, soon; *en ~ estuvo que se cayese* he almost fell, he very nearly fell; *~ más o*

menos more or less; *por ~* almost, nearly; *hace ~* a short time since; *tener en ~* think little of, have no use for; *vida* hold cheap.
pocho discoloured; *fruta* over-ripe; *S.Am.* chubby, squat.
pochola *f* F nice girl; *¡~!* darling!
poda *f* pruning (season); **podadera** *f* pruning shears, secateurs; pruning knife, bill-hook; **podar** [1a] prune; lop.
podenco *m* hound, hunting-dog.
poder 1. [2t] be able, can; *puede venir* he is able to come, he can come; *no puede venir* he is unable to come, he cannot come, he can't come; (*absoluto*) *los que pueden* those who can, those that are able (to); *puede que subj.* it may be that, it is possible that, perhaps; *puede ser* (it) may be (so); *puede ser que it* may be that; *¿se puede?* may I?; *no ~ con p. etc.* not be able to stand; *carga etc.* not be able to manage; *no ~ más* be exhausted; have had enough; *a más no ~* to the utmost; as hard as possible; *hasta más no ~* to the utmost; *comer etc.* to one's heart's content; *b.s.* excessively; *no ~ menos de inf.* not be able to help *ger.*, have no alternative but to *inf.*; *no puedo menos de creer* I can't help thinking; *~ mucho* have power, have influence; **2.** *m* power; authority; 🕮 power of attorney, proxy; ⊕ power, capacity, strength; ⊕ value; *~ adquisitivo* purchasing power; *~ legislativo* legislative power; (*plenos*) *~es pl.* full power, authority; *a ~ de* by dint of; *en ~ de* in the possession of, in the hands of; *por ~(es)* by proxy.
poderío *m* power; authority, jurisdiction; (*bienes*) wealth, substance.
poderoso powerful; *remedio etc.* potent, efficacious; (*rico*) rich, wealthy.
podómetro *m* pedometer.
podre *f* pus; **podredumbre** *f* rot, rottenness, decay, corruption; 🕮 pus; *fig.* gnawing doubt, uneasiness; **podrido** rotten, bad, putrid; **podrir** = *pudrir*.
poema *m* (*esp.* long) poem; **poesía** *f* poetry; (*una ~*) (*esp.* short *or* lyrical) poem; **poeta** *m* poet; **poetastro** *m* poetaster; **poética** *f* poetics; **poético** poetic(al); **poetisa** *f* poetess;

poetizar [1f] v/t. poeticize; idealize; v/i. write poetry.

pogrom(o) m pogrom.

póker m poker.

polaco 1. Polish; **2.** m, a f Pole; **3.** m (idioma) Polish.

polaina f gaiter, legging.

polar polar; **polaridad** f polarity; **polarización** f polarization; **polarizar** [1f] polarize.

polca f polka.

polea f pulley; tackle-block.

polémica f polemics; controversy; **polémico** polemical.

polen m pollen.

poli m F bobby.

policía 1. m policeman; ~ femenino policewoman; **2.** f police (force); fig. administration, order, (good) government; (cortesía) politeness; ~ militar military police; ~ secreta secret police; **policíaco**: v. novela.

polifacético many-sided, versatile.

polifónico polyphonic.

poligamia f polygamy; **polígamo 1.** polygamous; **2.** m, a f polygamist.

poligloto m, a f polyglot.

poligonal polygonal; **polígono** m polygon.

polígrafo m writer on a wide variety of subjects.

polilla f (clothes-)moth; bookworm.

polio(mielitis) f polio(myelitis).

pólipo m polyp(us).

polisílabo 1. polysyllabic; **2.** m polysyllable.

polisón m bustle.

politeísmo m polytheism.

politene m, **politeno** m polythene.

política f politics; (e.g. ~ de Carlos V, ~ exterior) policy; (cortesía) politeness, good manners; **político 1.** political; polite, courteous; padre etc. ~ father- etc. in-law; familia ~a relatives by marriage, in-laws F; **politicón** ceremonious, obsequious; **politiquear** [1a] F talk politics; **politiqueo** m b.s. party politics; political gossip; **politiquero** m b.s. politician.

póliza f certificate, voucher; (giro) draft, order; (timbre) tax stamp; ~ dotal endowment policy; ~ de seguro(s) insurance policy.

polizón m ♣, ✈ stowaway; vagrant, tramp; viajar de ~ stow away.

polizonte m F copper, cop esp. Am.

polo m geog., ⚡ pole; ⚡ (borne) terminal; (juego) polo; ~ acuático water-polo.

poltrón idle, lazy; **poltrona** f reclining chair, easy-chair.

polvareda f dust cloud; F levantar una ~ cause a rumpus; **polvera** f powder-compact, vanity case; **polvo** m dust; powder; pinch de rapé etc.; ~s pl. face-powder; ~(s) de arroz rice-powder; ~s pl. de blanqueo bleaching-powder; ~(s) de hornear, ~(s) de levadura baking-powder; lleno de ~ dusty, covered with dust; en ~ powdered; F hacer ~ cosa ruin; p. shatter; flatten, crush en discusión; F estoy hecho ~ I'm worn out; hacer morder el ~ make s.o. bite the dust; matar el ~ lay the dust; ponerse ~s powder one's face; quitar el ~ (a) dust; F sacudir el ~ a thrash; beat up.

pólvora f gunpowder; fig. life, liveliness; (mal genio) bad temper; descubrir la ~ set the Thames on fire; F gastar la ~ en salvas fuss around uselessly; propagarse como la ~ spread like wildfire; **polvorear** [1a] powder, dust, sprinkle; **polvoriento** dusty; powdery; **polvorilla** m/f F live wire; **polvorín** m powder-magazine; **polvoroso** dusty; F poner pies en ~ beat it.

polla f orn. pullet; naipes: pool, stake; F chick, girl; **pollada** f hatch, brood; **pollastro** m F sly fellow.

pollera f hen-coop; **pollero** m chicken-farmer; (que vende) poulterer.

pollino m, a f donkey; F ass.

pollita f pullet; **pollito** m chick; F está Vd. hecho un ~ you're looking quite a youngster; **pollo** m chicken; chick de ave no domesticada; F young man, youth; **polluelo** m chick.

pomada f pomade.

pomar m apple-orchard.

pomelo m grapefruit.

pómez: v. piedra.

pomo m (frasco) scent-bottle; pommel de espada; ⚘ fruit having pips.

pompa f pomp; show, display, pageantry; procession; ♣ pump; ~ de jabón soap-bubble; director de ~s fúnebres undertaker; **pomposidad** f pomposity; **pomposo** pompous;

majestic, magnificent; *estilo* pompous, high-flown.
pómulo *m* cheekbone.
ponche *m* punch.
poncho *m* S.Am. poncho, blanket, cape.
ponderación *f* *fig.* deliberation, consideration; exaggeration; high praise; **ponderar** [1a] *fig.* weigh up; ponder (over); exaggerate; (*alabar*) praise highly; *estadística*: weight.
ponedero *m* nest(ing-box); **ponedora** laying; *buena ~* good layer.
ponencia *f* (learned) paper; report.
poner [2r] **1.** put; place; set; arrange; *cuidado* take, exercise (en in); *dinero (inversión)* put, invest; (*juego*) bet, stake; *escaparate* dress; *huevo* lay; *impuesto* impose; *luz, radio etc.* switch on, turn on, put on; *mesa* lay, set; *miedo* cause; *objeción* raise; *obra dramática* perform, put on; *película* show; *problema* set; *ropa* put on; *telegrama* send; *tiempo* take; *tienda* set up; *~ adj.* make, turn; *~ que* suppose that; *~ a alguien a inf.* set s.o. to *inf.*; *~ a alguien de* treat s.o. as; set s.o. up as; *~ aparte* set aside; F *eso pone mucho* that's asking a lot; *teleph.* póngame con el Sr X put me through to Mr X; **2.** *~se* put o.s.; place o.s.; (*sol*) set; *~ adj.* turn; get, become; *~ a inf.* begin to *inf.*, set about *ger.*, proceed to *inf.*; *~ bien con* get in with, get on the good side of; *~ (a) mal con* get the wrong side of.
poney *m* pony.
ponga, pongo *etc. v.* poner.
poniente *m* west; west wind.
pontazgo *m* toll.
pontificado *m* pontificate, papacy; **pontifical** pontifical, papal; **pontificar** [1g] pontificate; **pontífice** *m* pope, pontiff; Sumo ♀ His Holiness the Pope; **pontificio** pontifical, papal.
pontón *m* pontoon; bridge of planks; pontoon bridge; ⚓ hulk.
ponzoña *f* poison; **ponzoñoso** poisonous; *fig.* noxious, harmful.
popa *f* stern, poop; *a ~* abaft, astern; *de ~ a proa* fore and aft; from stem to stern; *v. viento.*
popar [1a] scorn, jeer at.
popelín *m*, **popelina** *f* poplin.
populachería *f* cheap popularity,

playing to the gallery; **populachero** common, vulgar, cheap; **populacho** *m* mob, plebs; lower orders;
popular popular; *palabra* colloquial; **popularidad** *f* popularity; **popularismo** *m* colloquialism; **popularizar** [1f] popularize; *~se* become popular; **populoso** populous.
poquedad *f* scantiness, paucity; fewness; timidity *de carácter*; (*cosa*) trifle; **poquísimo** very little; *~s pl.* very few; **poquito**: *un ~* a little bit (*su. de of*).
por 1. *prp.* **a)** *agente tras verbo pasivo*: by; *instrumento*: comunicar *~ señas* talk by (means of) signs; *~ ferrocarril* by rail; *lo hizo ~ sí mismo* he did it by himself; **b)** *lugar*: *~ la ciudad (pasar)* through the town; (*pasearse*) round the town; *~ Medina* by way of Medina, via Medina (*a.* 🌍); *~ el túnel* through the tunnel; *~ la calle* along the street; *~ todo el país* over the whole country; *errar ~ los campos* wander in the fields; **c)** *tiempo*: *~ la noche* in the night, during the night; *~ Navidades* at (or about) Christmas time; *~ estas fechas* about this time; **d)** *motivo etc.*: *~ temor* out of fear, from fear; *cerrado ~ muerte del dueño* closed owing to (or on account of, because of) owner's death; *~ mí* for me, for my sake; for myself, for my part; *~ la patria* for (the sake of) the country; *~ adj.* as being, as, because it is *etc.*; *lo dejó ~ imposible* he gave it up as impossible; **e)** *en nombre de*: hablo *~ todos* I speak for (or in the name of, on behalf of) everybody; *intercedió ~ mí* he interceded for me (or on my behalf); **f)** *objetivo*: *mi admiración ~ ti* my admiration for you; **g)** *en busca de*: vendrá *~ nosotros* he will come for us; **h)** *quedar etc.*: quedan *cartas ~ escribir* there are still some letters to be written; **i)** *cambio*: *lo compró ~ 150 pesetas* he bought it for 150 pesetas; *te doy éste ~ aquél* I'll give you this one in exchange for (or in place of) that one; **j)** *manera*: *~ docenas* in dozens, by the dozen; *~ escrito* in writing; *~ persona* per person; *120 kms. ~ hora* 120 kms. an hour; *recibir ~ esposa* take as one's wife; **k)** ✕ times; *3 ~ 5*

3 times 5; **2.** *cj. etc.*: ~ *inf.* (*para*) in order to *inf.*; (*causa*) because; ~ *haber venido tarde* through having come late, because he came late; ~ *que subj.* in order that; ~ *difícil que sea* however hard it is; ~ *mucho* (*or más*) *que se esforzara* however hard (*or much*) he struggled; *¿~ qué?* why?; *yo sé ~ qué* I know why.

porcachón F, **porcallón** F filthy, dirty.

porcelana *f* porcelain; (*loza corriente*) china.   [rate.)

porcentaje *m* percentage; *esp.* ⊕)

porcino porcine; *ganado* ~ pigs.

porción *f* portion; part, share; *una* ~ *de cosas etc.* a number of things *etc.*

pordiosear [1a] beg; **pordiosero** *m*, **a** *f* beggar.

porfía *f* persistence, obstinacy, stubbornness; *a* ~ in competition; **porfiado** persistent, obstinate, stubborn; **porfiar** [1c] persist (*en* in), insist; argue obstinately; ~ *por inf.* struggle obstinately to *inf.*

pórfido *m* porphyry.

pormenor *m* detail, particular; **pormenorizar** [1f] detail, set out in detail.

pornografía *f* pornography; **pornográfico** pornographic.

poro *m* pore; **porosidad** *f* porosity, porousness; **poroso** porous.

porque because; ~ *subj.* in order that.

porqué *m* reason (*de* for), why; F quantity, amount; F (*dinero*) wherewithall.

porquería *f* F (*en general*) dirt, filth; nastiness; (*acto*) indecency, indecent act; (*mala pasada*) dirty trick; *la obra es una* ~ the thing's a lot of old rubbish, it's a wretched piece of work; *vender por una* ~ sell for next to nothing; **porqueriza** *f* pigsty; **porquerizo** *m*, **porquero** *m* pigman.

porra *f* stick, cudgel; truncheon *de policía*; (*herramienta*) large hammer; F bore, nuisance; *¡~s!* dash (it)!; (*a otra p.*) get away!, rubbish!; F *mandar a la* ~ chuck out, send packing; F *¡vete a la* ~! go to hell!; **porrada** *f* thwack, thump; F stupidity; F (*montón*) pile, heap; **porrazo** *m* thwack, thump; bump *de caída*; **porrear** [1a] grind away, go on and on.

porreta *f* green leaf *de cebolla etc.*; F *en* ~ stark naked; **porretada** *f* pile, heap; **porrillo:** F *a* ~ in abundance, by the ton; **porro** F dull, stupid; **porrón 1.** slow, stupid; sluggish; **2.** *m* glass wine-jar with long spout.

porta(a)viones *m* aircraft carrier.

portada *f* △ front, façade; (*puerta*) porch, doorway; cover *de revista*; *typ.* frontispiece, title-page; **portado:** *bien* ~ well-dressed; well-behaved; **portador** *m*, **-a** *f* carrier, bearer; ✝ bearer, payee; ~ *de gérmenes* germ-carrier.

porta...: ~**equipajes** *m mot.* boot, trunk *Am.*; ~**estandarte** *m* standard-bearer; ~**fusil** *m* sling; ~**hachón** *m* torch-bearer.

portal *m* vestibule, hall; (*puerta*) porch, doorway; street door *que da a calle*; gate(way) *de ciudad*.

portalámpara *m* socket, lampholder.

portaligas *m* suspender-belt.

portalón *m* △ gate(way); ⚓ gangway.

porta...: ~**manteo** *m* travelling-bag; ~**monedas** *m* pocketbook; purse; ~**objeto** *m opt.* slide; stage; ~**papeles** *m* brief-case; ~**placas** *m* plateholder; ~**plumas** *m* penholder.

portarse [1a] behave; conduct o.s.; *se portó muy bien conmigo* he treated me very well.

portátil portable.

portavoz *m* megaphone; (*p.*) spokesman; *contp.* mouthpiece.

portazgo *m* toll.

portazo *m* bang, slam; *dar un* ~ slam the door.

porte *m* ✝ carriage; porterage; ✇ postage; *fig.* behaviour, conduct, demeanour, bearing; disposition, character; *franco de* ~ ✝ carriage free; ✇ post-free; ~ *pagado* ✝ carriage paid; ✇ post-paid; **portear**[1] [1a] ✝ carry, convey.

portear[2] [1a] slam, bang.

portento *m* marvel, prodigy; **portentoso** marvellous, extraordinary.

porteño *adj. a. su. m*, **a** *f* (native) of Buenos Aires.

porteo *m* carrying, portage.

portería *f* porter's lodge; *deportes*: goal; **portero** *m* porter, janitor, door-keeper; *deportes*: goalkeeper.

portezuela *f* door; *sew.* pocket-flap.

pórtico *m* portico, porch; arcade *de plaza etc.*

portilla *f* porthole; **portillo** *m* gap, opening, breach; (*puerta*) wicket; *geog.* narrow pass.

portón *m* large door, main door.

portorriqueño *adj. a. su. m*, **a** *f* (native) of Porto Rico.

portuario port *attr.*, harbour *attr.*; *trabajador* ~ docker.

portugués 1. *adj. a. su. m*, **a** *f* Portuguese; **2.** *m* (*idioma*) Portuguese.

porvenir *m* future; *en el* ~, *en lo* ~ in the future.

pos: *en* ~ *de* after, in pursuit of; *ir en* ~ *de* chase, pursue.

posada *f* (*mesón*) inn; lodging-house; (*casa*) house, dwelling; (*alojamiento*) lodging.

posaderas *f/pl.* buttocks.

posadero *m*, **a** *f* innkeeper.

posar [1a] *v/t. carga* lay down; *v/i.*, **~se** (*ave*) alight, settle, perch, rest; (*modelo*) sit, pose; (*polvo, líquido*) settle; lodge *en posada.*

posdata *f* postscript.

pose *f* pose; *phot.* time-exposure.

poseedor *m*, **-a** *f* owner, possessor; holder *de marca, oficio*; **poseer** [2e] have; own, possess; *tema, lengua* know perfectly, have a complete mastery of; *ventaja* (*cosa*) have, hold; (*p.*) enjoy; **poseído** possessed; *fig.* crazed; **posesión** *f* possession; tenure *de oficio*; complete mastery *de tema, lengua*; *tomar* ~ take over; *tomar* ~ *de* = **posesionarse** [1a]: ~ *de* take possession of, take over; *oficio* take up; **posesivo** *adj. a. su. m* possessive; **poseso 1.** possessed; **2.** *m*, **a** *f* person possessed.

posfechar [1a] postdate.

posibilidad *f* possibility; chance; **posibilitar** [1a] make possible, facilitate; **posible 1.** possible; feasible; *en lo* ~ as far as possible; *v. pronto; a serme* ~ if I possibly can; *hacer lo* ~ do all in one's power, do as much as possible (*para, por inf.* to *inf.*); **2.** ~**s** *m/pl.* means, assets.

posición *f* position; situation; (*rango*) standing.

positiva *f* *phot.* positive, print; **positivismo** *m* positivism; **positivo 1.** positive (*a., phot.*); **2.** positive, plus; *idea etc.* constructive;

2. *m gr.* positive; *phot.* positive, print.

posma *m* F bore.

poso *m* sediment, deposit, dregs.

posponer [2r] subordinate.

posta 1. *f* relay *de caballos*; (*casa*) post-house; (*etapa, distancia*) stage; stake *en juego*; *hunt.* slug; F *a* ~ on purpose; *por la* ~ post-haste; **2.** *m* courier.

postal 1. postal; **2.** *f* (*a. tarjeta* ~) postcard; ~ *ilustrada* picture-post-card.

poste *m* post, pole; stake *de cerca etc.*; (*a.* ~ *telegráfico*) telegraph pole; ~ *indicador* signpost; ~ *de llegada* winning-post; ~ *de salida* starting-post; F *dar* ~ *a* keep *s.o.* waiting; *oler el* ~ scent danger, smell a rat.

postema *m* ♣ abscess, tumour; *fig.* bore, dull sort.

postergar [1h] delay, postpone; *p.* pass over.

posteridad *f* posterity; **posterior** *lugar*: rear, back; posterior; *tiempo*: later, subsequent; *ser* ~ *a* be later than; **posterioridad:** *con* ~ subsequently; *con* ~ *a* subsequent to, later than.

pos(t)guerra *f* post-war period; *de* (*la*) ~ post-war; *en la* ~ in the post-war period, after the war.

postigo *m* wicket, postern, small door; shutter *de ventana.*

postillón *m* postilion.

postín *m* F side, swank; (*boato*) show, luxury; *de* ~ posh, swanky; luxurious; *darse* ~ swank; **postinero** F posh, swanky.

postizas *f/pl.* castanets; **postizo 1.** *dentadura etc.* false, artificial; *cuello* detachable; *b.s.* sham, phon(e)y *esp. Am.*; dummy; **2.** *m* false hair.

postmeridiano postmeridian; afternoon *attr.* [bidder.)

postor *m* bidder; *mejor* ~ highest↲

postración *f* prostration; ~ *nerviosa* nervous exhaustion; **postrado** prostrate (*a. fig.*); **postrar** [1a] prostrate; *esp.* ♣ weaken, exhaust; (*derribar*) overthrow; **~se** (*acto*) prostrate o.s.; (*estado*) be prostrate.

postre 1. *m* (*a.* ~**s** *pl.*) dessert, sweet; **2.:** *a la* ~ at last, in the end.

postremo, postrero last; rear, hindermost; **postrimerías** *f/pl.*

dying moments; closing stages; *eccl.* four last things.

postulación *f* postulation; **postulado** *m* postulate, assumption, working hypothesis; **postulante** *m/f* petitioner; candidate; **postular** [1a] postulate; (*pedir*) seek, claim, demand.

póstumo posthumous.

postura *f* posture, pose, stance *del cuerpo*; *fig.* position, attitude; *pol. etc.* agreement; bet, stake *en el juego*; bid *en subasta*; *orn.* (*cantidad*) eggs; (*acto*) egg-laying.

potable drinkable; *v. agua.*

potaje *m cocina:* mixed vegetables, stew; dried vegetables; *fig.* medley, mixture.

potasa *f* potash.

potasio *m* potassium.

pote *m* pot, jar; (*tiesto*) flower-pot; (*guiso*) stew; *a* ~ in abundance.

potencia *f* power (*a.* ⚡, *pol.*); potency; ⊕ (horse-)power, capacity; *pol. las* ~s the Powers; ~ *electoral* voting power; ~ *mundial* world power; ⊕ ~ *real* effective power; **potencial 1.** potential; **2.** *m* potential; capacity; *gr.* conditional; **potencialidad** *f* potentiality.

potentado *m* potentate; *fig.* baron, tycoon.

potente powerful; potent; F big, strong.

potestad *f* power; authority, jurisdiction; (*p.*) potentate; ~ *marital* husband's authority.

potingue *m* F concoction, brew.

potosí *m: costar un* ~ cost the earth; *valer un* ~ be worth a fortune.

potra *f zo.* filly; 🩹 rupture, hernia; F *tener* ~ be lucky; **potro** *m zo.* colt; rack *de tormento*; ~ *de madera* vaulting-horse.

poyo *m* stone bench.

pozanco *m* pool, puddle.

pozo *m* well; ⚒ shaft; pool *de río*; *S.Am.* pool, puddle; ~ *artesiano* Artesian well; ~ *negro* cesspool; ~ *de petróleo* oil-well; ~ *de ventilación* upcast, ventilation shaft; *ser un* ~ *de ciencia* be immensely learned.

práctica *f* practice; method; *en la* ~ in practice; *la* ~ *hace maestro* practice makes perfect; *hacer* ~s *de piano etc.* practise; **practicable** practicable; workable, feasible; *thea. puerta* that opens; **practican-**

te 1. practising; **2.** *m/f* practitioner; 🩺 male nurse, medical assistant, orderly; **practicar** [1g] practise; exercise; (*poner por obra*) perform, carry out; *deporte* go in for; *agujero* cut, make; ~**se:** ~ *en la enseñanza* do school practice; **práctico 1.** practical; handy; *proyecto* workable; *p.* practical, down-to-earth; **2.** *m* practitioner; ⚓ pilot.

prader(í)a *f* meadow(land); prairie *en el Canadá etc.*; **prado** *m* meadow, field, pasture.

pragmático pragmatic.

preámbulo *m* preamble; *b.s.* beating about the bush.

prebenda *f eccl.* prebend; F sinecure, soft job; **prebendado** *m* prebendary.

preboste *m* provost.

precalentar [1k] pre-heat.

precario precarious, uncertain.

precaución *f* precaution; (*cualidad*) foresight, forethought; wariness; *tomar* ~es take precautions.

precaver [2a] guard against, forestall; ~**se** be on one's guard (*de* against), be forewarned, beware (*de* of); **precavido** cautious.

precedencia *f* priority, precedence; superiority; **precedente 1.** preceding, foregoing, former; **2.** *m* precedent; *sin* ~ unprecedented; **preceder** [2a] precede, go before; have priority over; *que precede freq.* preceding, foregoing.

preceptista *m/f* theorist; **precepto** *m* precept; order, injunction; rule; **preceptor** *m* teacher; tutor; **preceptorado** *m* tutorship; **preceptoral** tutorial.

preces *f/pl.* prayers, supplications.

preciar [1b] estimate, appraise; ~**se** boast; ~ *de algo* pride o.s. on, boast of; ~ *de* (*ser*) boast of being; ~ *de inf.* boast of *ger.*

precintar [1a] (pre)seal, prepackage; **precinto** *m* seal.

precio *m* (*que se paga*) price; cost; (*valor*) value, worth; ✝ *a.* charge, figure, rate; *fig.* worth *de p. etc.*; *control de* ~s price control; *lista de* ~s price list; ~ *de compra* purchase price; ~ *al contado* cash price; ~ *irrisorio* bargain price; ~ *tope* ceiling price; ~ *de venta* sale price; *al* ~ *de fig.* at the cost of; *poner a* ~ offer a reward for; *no tener* ~ *fig.*

be priceless; **preciosidad** *f* preciousness; (*cosa*) beautiful thing; **preciosismo** *m* preciosity; **precioso** precious; valuable; *fig.* lovely, beautiful; charming, pretty.

precipicio *m* precipice; cliff.

precipitación *f* *meteor.* precipitation, rainfall; (*prisa*) haste; rashness; **precipitado 1.** *prisa* breakneck, headlong; *acción, modo* hasty; (*imprudente*) rash; **2.** *m* 🜍 precipitate.

precipitar [1a] hurl, cast down *desde lo alto*; (*acelerar*) hasten, speed up; precipitate (*a.* 🜍); ~se rush, dash, dart; ~ *sobre* rush at; swoop on; pounce on.

precisamente precisely; ~ *por eso* for that very reason; *vengo* ~ *de allí* it so happens I come from there; **precisar** [1a] *v/t.* (*necesitar*) need, require; fix, determine exactly; *detalles* state precisely; *v/i.* be necessary; **precisión** *f* precision, preciseness, accuracy; need, necessity; ⊕ *de* ~ precision *attr.*; **preciso** necessary, essential; (*exacto*) precise, exact, accurate; *estilo* concise; *es* ~ *que vayas* you must go, it is essential that you should go; *tener las cualidades* ~*as* have the requisite qualities; *tener el tiempo* ~ have just enough time (*para inf.* to *inf.*).

precitado above-mentioned.

preclaro illustrious, famous.

precocidad *f* precociousness *etc.*

preconcebido preconceived; *idea* ~*a* = **preconcepción** *f* preconception.

preconizar [1f] foresee; *se preconiza que* it is foreseen that, it is thought that.

precoz precocious, forward; *calvicie etc.* premature; 💈 *etc.* early.

precursor *m*, **-a** *f* forerunner, precursor.

predecesor *m*, **-a** *f* predecessor.

predecir [3p] foretell, predict.

predestinación *f* predestination; **predestinar** [1a] predestine.

predeterminar [1a] predetermine.

prédica *f* *eccl.* sermon; harangue; **predicación** *f* preaching; sermon; **predicado** *m* predicate; **predicador** *m* preacher; **predicar** [1g] preach (*a. fig.*).

predicción *f* prediction, forecast.

predilección *f* predilection; **predilecto** favourite.

predio *m* property, estate; ~ *rústico* country estate; ~ *urbano* town property.

predisponer [2r] predispose; prejudice (*contra* against); **predisposición** *f* predisposition, inclination; *b.s.* bias, prejudice.

predominante predominant; prevailing, prevalent; ✝ interés controlling; uppermost *en la mente*; **predominar** [1a] predominate, prevail (*v/t.* over); **predominio** *m* predominance; prevalence; superiority (*sobre* over).

preeminencia *f* pre-eminence; superiority; **preeminente** pre-eminent; superior.

preempción *f* pre-emption.

preenfriar [1c] pre-cool.

pre-estreno *m* preview, pressview.

preexistencia *f* pre-existence; **preexistente** pre-existent; **preexistir** [3a] pre-exist, exist before.

prefabricado prefabricated; **prefabricar** [1g] prefabricate.

prefacio *m* preface, foreword.

prefecto *m* prefect.

preferencia *f* preference; priority; *de* ~ *plaza* reserved; **preferente** preferential; preferable; ✝ *acción* preference *attr.*; **preferentemente** preferably; **preferible** preferable; **preferir** [3i] prefer (*A a B* A to B; *hacer* to do, doing).

prefigurar [1a] foreshadow.

prefijar [1a] fix beforehand, prearrange; *gr.* prefix; **prefijo** *m* prefix.

pregón *m* proclamation, announcement; ✝ street cry; **pregonar** [1a] proclaim, announce; *secreto* disclose; *méritos etc.* praise publicly; *mercancías* cry, hawk; **pregonero** *m* town crier.

preguerra *f* pre-war period; *de* (*la*) ~ pre-war; *en la* ~ in the pre-war period, before the war.

pregunta *f* question; F *andar* (*or estar*) *a la cuarta* ~ be broke; *hacer una* ~ ask a question; **preguntar** [1a] *v/t.* ask (*algo a alguien* a p. a th., *a th.* of a p.); *v/i.* ask, inquire; ~ *por p. etc.* ask for; *salud de p. etc.* ask after; ~*se* wonder (*si* if, whether); **preguntón** inquisitive.

prehistórico prehistoric.

preignición f preignition.
prejuicio m prejudice; bias; (acto) prejudgement; tener ~ be biassed; **prejuzgar** [1h] prejudge.
prelado m prelate.
preliminar 1. preliminary; preparatory; **2.** m preliminary.
preludiar [1b] prelude (a. ♪); introduce; **preludio** m prelude (a. ♪).
premarital premarital.
prematuro premature; untimely.
premeditación f premeditation; con ~ with premeditation, deliberately; **premeditado** premeditated; deliberate, wilful; insulto studied; **premeditar** [1a] premeditate.
premiado 1. adj. prize attr.; **2.** m, a f prize-winner; **premiar** [1b] reward, recompense; give an award (or prize) to en certamen; **premio** m reward, recompense; prize en certamen; ✝ premium; ~ gordo first prize, big prize; a ~ at a premium.
premioso vestido tight; (molesto) troublesome, burdensome; orden strict; p. tongue-tied, slow of speech.
premisa f premise.
premonición f premonition; **premonitorio** premonitory.
premura f pressure; (prisa) haste, urgency.
prenatal prenatal, antenatal.
prenda f (empeño) pledge, security; (alhaja) jewel; ~ (de vestir) garment, article of clothing; fig. token, sign, favour; (p.) loved one, darling; ~s pl. qualities, talents, gifts; (juego) forfeits; en ~ de as a pledge of; (dejar) en ~ (leave) in pawn; **prendar** [1a] pledge, pawn; fig. captivate, win over; ~se de take a fancy to; p. fall in love with.
prendedero m, **prendedor** m brooch, clasp, pin.
prender [2a; p.p. a. preso] v/t. seize, grasp; p. capture, catch; ⚖ arrest; pin, attach con alfiler etc.; v/i. ⚘ take root; (fuego) catch; (vacunación etc.) take; ~se (mujer) dress up.
prendería f second-hand shop; pawnbroker's; **prendero** m second-hand dealer; pawnbroker.
prendimiento m capture, seizure.
prensa f press; ⊕ gland, stuffing box; de ~ press attr.; ~ de copiar printing-frame; ~ rotativa rotary press; dar a la ~ publish; entrar en ~ go to press; estar en ~ be in press; tener mala ~ have a bad press; **prensado** m sheen, shine; **prensaestopas** m ⊕ (packing) gland; **prensar** [1a] press; **prensil** prehensile.
preñada pregnant; **preñado 1.** muro bulging, sagging; ~ de full of; **2.** m = **preñez** f pregnancy.
preocupación f worry, concern, preoccupation; prejudice; **preocupado** worried, concerned, preoccupied; **preocupar** [1a] (inquietar) worry, preoccupy, exercise; (predisponer) prejudice; ~se worry, care (de, por about); ¡no se preocupe! don't bother!, don't trouble yourself!; don't worry about it!
preparación f preparation; (instrucción) training; ~ militar etc. military etc. preparedness; **preparador** m deportes: trainer; **preparar** [1a] prepare; ⊕ prepare, process; (aprestar) get ready; (instruir) train; ~se prepare (o.s.); get ready; **preparativo 1.** preparatory; preliminary; **2.** ~s m/pl. preparations; preliminaries; **preparatorio** preparatory.
preponderancia f preponderance; superiority; **preponderante** preponderant; superior; **preponderar** [1a] preponderate; prevail.
preposición f preposition; **preposicional** prepositional.
prepucio m foreskin, prepuce.
prerrogativa f prerogative, privilege.
presa f (acto) capture, seizure; (cosa apresada) prize (esp. ⚓), spoils, booty; (animal que se caza) prey, quarry; (animal cazado) capture, catch; weir, dam, barrage de río; (conducto) ditch, conduit; ~s pl. fangs; hacer ~ seize; ser ~ de be a prey to.
presagiar [1b] betoken, forebode, presage; **presagio** m omen, portent.
presbicia f long-sightedness; **présbita, présbite** long-sighted.
presbiterio m presbitery, chancel; **presbítero** m priest.
presciencia f foreknowledge, prescience; **presciente** prescient.
prescindible dispensable, expendable; **prescindir** [3a]: ~ de do without; dispense with; disregard.

prescribir [3a; *p.p.* prescrito] prescribe; **prescripción** f prescription; **prescrito** prescribed.

presea f jewel.

presencia f presence; ~ de ánimo presence of mind; **presencial** v. testigo; **presenciar** [1b] be present at, witness, watch.

presentable presentable; **presentación** f presentation; introduction; **presentar** [1a] mst present; p. a otra introduce; p. propose, nominate (a puesto for); (mostrar) display, show; thea. perform; demanda put in, present; dimisión tender; película show; proyecto etc. put forward; pruebas submit, present; ¡presenten armas! present arms!; ~se present o.s.; (acudir) turn up; report (en at); run como candidato; ~ a puesto put in for; ~ para examen sit, enter for.

presente 1. present; ¡~! present!; los ~s those present; la ~ this letter; con perdón de los ~s, mejorando lo ~ present company excepted; al ~ at present; hacer ~ state, declare; tener ~ remember, bear in mind; **2.** m present; gr. present (tense).

presentimiento m premonition, presentiment; foreboding; **presentir** [3i] have a presentiment of; ~ que have a presentiment that.

preservación f preservation, protection; **preservar** [1a] preserve, protect (contra from, against).

presidencia f pol. etc. presidency; chairmanship; **presidencial** presidential; **presidente** m, a f pol. etc. president; chairman de comité, reunión; parl. speaker.

presidiario m convict; **presidio** m (cárcel) prison; (condena) hard labour; ✕ (ps.) garrison; (lugar) fortress.

presidir [3a] preside (acc. at, over); take the chair (acc. at).

presilla f fastener, clip; press-stud.

presión f pressure (a. ⊕, meteor.); press, squeeze con mano etc.; ⊕ de ~ pressure attr.; ~ atmosférica atmospheric (or air-)pressure; ~ sanguínea blood-pressure; **presionar** [1a] press.

preso 1. p.p. of prender; **2.** m, a f prisoner, convict.

prestación f lending, loan; **prestado:** dar ~ lend, loan; pedir ~,

tomar ~ borrow; **prestador** m, -a f lender; **prestamista** m moneylender; pawnbroker; **préstamo** m (acto) lending, borrowing; (dinero) loan; **prestar** [1a] v/t. lend, loan; atención pay; ayuda give; juramento take, swear; v/i. give, stretch; ~se (p.) lend o.s., (cosa) lend itself (a to).

presteza f quickness, speed, agility.

prestidigitación f prestidigitation, sleight of hand; **prestidigitador** m conjurer, juggler.

prestigio m prestige; face; (fascinación) spell; (engaño) trick; **prestigioso** famous, of some standing; (fascinador) captivating; (engañoso) illusory.

presto 1. adj. (vivo) quick, prompt; agile, nimble; (dispuesto) ready; **2.** adv. quickly; at once, right away.

presumible presumable, to be presumed; **presumido** conceited; **presumir** [3a] v/t. presume; guess, surmise; v/i. be conceited, presume; give o.s. airs; ~ de fancy o.s. as su., boast of being adj.; ~ de listo think o.s. very clever; según cabe ~ presumably; **presunción** f presumption; conceit; **presunto** supposed, presumed; heredero presumptive; **presuntuoso** conceited, vain; presumptuous; pretentious.

presuponer [2r] presuppose; **presuposición** f presupposition; **presupuestar** [1a] budget for; **presupuestario** budget attr., budgetary; **presupuesto** m ✝ budget; estimate para un proyecto etc.

presura f speed; promptness; (porfía) persistence; **presuroso** quick, speedy; prompt; hasty (a. b.s.).

pretencioso pretentious.

pretender [2a] claim; mujer court; puesto seek, try for; honores etc. aspire to; objeto aim at, try to achieve; ~ que indic. claim that, allege that; ~ que subj. expect that, suggest that, intend that; ~ inf. (intentar) seek to inf., attempt to inf., try to inf.; ~ decir mean (con by); ~ poder inf. claim to be able to inf., purport to inf.; ~ ser su. profess to be, claim to be; **pretendido** supposed, pretended; alleged; **pretendiente 1.** m suitor de mujer; **2.** m, a f claimant; applicant (a puesto for); pretender (a trono to).

pretensado prestressed.

pretensión f (cualidad) claim; aim, object; (pretencioso) pretension; pretence para engañar; tener ~es de have pretensions to.

pretérito 1. past; **2.** m preterit(e), past historic.

preternatural preternatural.

pretextar [1a] plead, use as an excuse; **pretexto** m pretext; pretence; plea, excuse; so ~ de under pretext of.　　　[rail, railing.)

pretil m parapet de puente; hand-)

pretina f girdle, belt.

prevalecer [2d] prevail (sobre over, against); ✿ take root.

prevalerse [2q]: ~ de avail o.s. of.

prevención f (cualidad) forethought, foresight; (prejuicio) prejudice; (estado) preparedness; (acto) prevention etc.; safety measure, precaution; (aviso) warning; (comisaría) police-station; a ~, de ~ spare, emergency attr.; **prevenido** prepared, ready; fig. cautious, forewarned; **prevenir** [3s] prepare, make ready; (impedir) prevent; (prever) foresee, anticipate; provide for; (advertir) (fore)warn (contra against); (predisponer) prejudice (contra against); ~se make ready, get ready; ~ contra prepare for; take precautions against; **preventivo** preventive (a. ✿); precautionary.

prever [2v] foresee, forecast; envisage, visualize.

previo 1. adj. previous, prior; examen preliminary; **2.** prp. after, following.

previsible foreseeable; **previsión** f foresight; far-sightedness; thoughtfulness; (pronóstico) forecast; ~ social social security; **previsor** far-sighted; thoughtful.

prez f honour, glory.

prieto blackish, dark; p. mean; S.Am. dark, brunette.

prima f ✝ bonus, bounty; premium de seguros; subsidy de exportación etc.

primacía f primacy; **primada** f F hoax, trick; piece of stupidity; **primado** m primate; **primal** adj. a. su. m, -a f yearling; **primar** [1a]: ~ sobre take precedence over; **primario** primary; **primato** m primate.

primavera f spring(time); ✿ primrose; **primaveral** spring attr.; springlike.

primera f (a. ~ clase) first class; ~ de cambio first of exchange; F de ~ first-rate, first-class; F estar de ~ ~ feel fine; viajar en ~ travel first; **primeramente** first(ly), in the first place; chiefly; **primerizo** m, a f novice, beginner; **primero 1.** first; primary; foremost; años etc. early; (anterior) former; necesidad basic, prime; urgent; materia raw; a ~s de at the beginning of; ser el ~ en inf. be the first to inf.; **2.** adv. first; (preferentemente) rather, sooner.

primicias f/pl. first-fruits.

primitivo primitive; original; obra etc. early; color prime.

primo 1. ⚹ prime; materia raw; **2.** m, a f cousin; ~ carnal, ~ hermano first cousin; **3.** m F fool, sucker esp. Am.

primogénito first-born; **primogenitura** f primogeniture; birth-right.

primor m beauty, elegance, exquisiteness; (habilidad) skill; es un ~ it's a charming thing, it's a lovely piece of work.

primordial original; hecho etc. basic.

primoroso exquisite, fine, elegant; (hábil) skilful, neat.

princesa f princess; **principado** m principality.

principal 1. principal; chief, main; foremost; piso first; (noble) illustrious; **2.** m principal (a. ✝, ⚹); head, chief.

príncipe m prince; ~ consorte prince consort; v. edición; ~ heredero crown prince; **principesco** princely.

principiante 1. learner, who is beginning; **2.** m, a f beginner, learner, novice; **principiar** [1b] start, begin (a inf. to inf. or ger.; con with); **principio** m beginning, start; origin, source; phls., ciencias etc.: principle; ⌐ etc. element, constituent; cocina: entrée; ~s pl. essentials, rudiments de tema; a ~s del mes at the beginning of the month; a ~s del siglo pasado early last century; al ~ at first; in the beginning; desde el ~ from the first; **en ~** in principle; **en un ~** at first; **por ~** on principle.

principote *m* F swank, swell; parvenu.

pringar [1h] *v/t. cocina*: dip in fat; *asado* baste; *(ensuciar)* stain with fat; *S.Am.* splash; F *(herir)* wound; F *(calumniar)* blacken, run down; *v/i. sl. (perder)* come a cropper, take a beating; ✗ *sl.* sweat one's guts out; F **~** en dabble in, have a hand in; **~se** F make money on the side, clean up a packet; **pringón 1.** F greasy; **2.** *m* grease stain; **pringoso** greasy; **pringue** *m* grease, fat, dripping; grease stain.

prior *m* prior; **priora** *f*, **prioresa** *f* prioress; **priorato** *m* priory.

prioridad *f* priority; seniority.

prisa *f* hurry, haste; speed; urgency; *a ~, de ~* quickly, hurriedly; *a toda ~* as quickly as possible; *correr ~* be urgent; *¿corre ~ este trabajo?* is this work urgent?; *¿te corre ~?* are you in a hurry?; *darse ~* hurry; *¡date ~!* hurry up!, come along!; *despachar de ~ trabajo* hurry along, rush; *estar de ~,* *tener ~* be in a hurry.

prisión *f (acto)* capture, arrest; *(cárcel)* prison; *(período)* imprisonment; **~es** *pl.* shackles; **prisionero** *m* prisoner; *hacer ~* take prisoner.

prisma *m* prism; **prismático 1.** prismatic; **2.** **~s** *m/pl.* prism binoculars.

prístino pristine, original.

privación *f (acto)* deprivation; *(falta)* privation, want; **privado 1.** private; personal; **2.** *m* favourite; *en ~* in private; **privanza** *f* favour; **privar** [1a] *v/t.* deprive (de of), dispossess (de of); starve (de of); *(destituir)* demote, remove (de from); *(vedar)* forbid; *v/i.* be in favour *en corte*; F be in vogue, be the thing; **~se de** deprive o.s. of, give up, forgo; **privativo** exclusive; particular; *~ de* peculiar to, restricted to.

privilegio *m* privilege *(de inf. of ger.)*; ⚖ sole right; *lit.* copyright; *~ de invención* patent.

pro *m* a. *f* profit, advantage; *hombre de ~* worthy man; *los ~s y los contras* the pros and cons; *buena ~ le haga* and much good may it do him; *en ~ de* pro, for.

proa *f* bow(s), prow; *de ~* bow *attr.*, fore.

probabilidad *f* probability, likelihood; chance, prospect; *según toda ~* in all probability; *no tener ~ de ganar* be unlikely to win, have small chance of winning; **probable** probable, likely.

probanza *f* proof, evidence; inquiry.

probar [1m] **1.** *v/t.* prove; establish; *(ensayar)* try, try out, test; *vestido* try on; *comida etc.* taste, sample, try; *no pruebo nunca el vino* I never touch wine; **2.** *v/i.*: *~ a inf.* try to *inf.*; *no me prueba bien el vino* wine doesn't agree with me; *¿probaremos?* shall we try?

probatorio probative, evidential; *documentos ~s de* documents in proof of.

probeta *f* 🧪 test-tube; graduated cylinder; ⊕ test specimen.

probidad *f* integrity, rectitude.

problema *m* problem; puzzle; **problemático** problematic, doubtful.

probo upright, honest.

probóscide *f* proboscis.

procacidad *f* insolence *etc.*; **procaz** insolent, impudent; shameless.

procedencia *f* source, origin; ⚓ port of origin; ⚖ propriety; **procedente** fitting, reasonable; ⚖ proper, lawful; *~ de* coming from, originating in; **proceder 1.** [2a] proceed *(a elección* to; *a inf.* to *inf.*; ⚖ *contra* against); *(portarse)* behave, act; *(convenir)* be proper; *si el caso procede* if the case warrants it; *~ de* proceed from, flow from, spring from; originate in; **2.** *m* course, procedure; behaviour; **procedimiento** *m* procedure; proceeding; process; ⚖ proceedings.

proceloso stormy, tempestuous.

prócer *m* important person, chief, leader.

procesado *m*, **a** *f* accused; **procesal** procedural; ⚖ *costas etc.* legal; **procesar** [1a] ⚖ try, put on trial; prosecute; sue.

procesión *f* procession; F *la ~ va por dentro* still waters run deep.

proceso *m* process *(a. anat.,* 🧪*);* ⚖ trial; prosecution; proceedings, lawsuit.

proclama *f* proclamation; **~s** *pl.* banns; **proclamación** *f* proclamation; acclamation; **proclamar** [1a] proclaim; acclaim.

procreación f procreation; **procreador** procreative; **procrear** [1a] procreate; breed.

procuración f ⚖ letter (or power, warrant) of attorney; proxy; **procurador** m ⚖ attorney, approx. solicitor; pol. (a. ~ a Cortes) member of parliament; deputy, representative; **procurar** [1a] get; seek; cause, produce; ~ inf. try to inf., strive to inf., endeavour to inf.

prodigalidad f extravagance; plenty, abundance; **prodigar** [1h] b.s. waste, squander; alabanzas etc. lavish.

prodigio m prodigy; wonder, marvel; niño ~ child prodigy; **prodigioso** prodigious; marvellous.

pródigo 1. b.s. extravagant, wasteful; prodigal (de of), lavish (de with); hijo ~ prodigal son; **2.** m, a f spendthrift, prodigal.

producción f production; yield; produce; ~ en serie mass production; **producir** [3o] mst produce; cause, generate; ~ en serie mass produce; me produce la impresión de que it gives me the impression that; ~se take place, come about, arise; come into being; se produjo un cambio a change came about; se produjo una explosión there was an explosion.

productividad f productivity; **productivo** productive; ✝ ~ de interés interest-bearing; **producto** m product (a. ♈, ♐, ⊕); production; ✝ proceeds, yield; ~s pl. products, produce (esp. ♪); ~ alimenticio food-stuff; **productor 1.** productive; producing; **2.** m, -a f producer; **produje, produzco** etc. v. producir.

proemio m preface, introduction.

proeza f exploit, heroic deed.

profanación f desecration; **profanar** [1a] desecrate, profane; **profano 1.** profane; indecent, immodest; **2.** m layman.

profecía f prophecy.

proferir [3i] utter; indirecta throw out; injuria hurl, let fly (contra at); suspiro fetch.

profesar [1a] v/t. profess; show, declare; profesión practise; v/i.

eccl. take vows; **profesión** f profession, calling; declaration de fe etc.; de ~ professional; hacer ~ de pride o.s. on; **profesional** adj. a. su. m/f professional; **profesionalismo** m professionalism; **profesor** m, -a f teacher en general; (school)master, (school)mistress de instituto; univ. (que tiene cátedra) professor; (subordinado) lecturer; ~ adjunto, ~ auxiliar approx. assistant lecturer; ~ agregado visiting lecturer; **profesorado** m teaching profession; (ps.) teaching staff; (puesto) professorship.

profeta m prophet; **profético** prophetic(al); **profetizar** [1f] prophesy. [lactic.∫

profiláctico adj. a. su. m prophy-∫

prófugo m fugitive; ⚔ deserter.

profundidad f depth; esp. fig. profundity; ♈ height; tener una ~ de 3 metros be 3 metres deep; poca ~ shallowness; **profundizar** [1f] hoyo deepen, make deeper; (a. v/i. ~ en) estudio extend, make a careful study of; misterio fathom; **profundo** deep; mst fig. profound; conocedor etc. very knowledgeable; tener 3 metros de ~ be 3 metres deep.

profusión f profusion; extravagance; **profuso** profuse.

progenie f progeny; offspring de p.; fig. brood; **progenitor** m ancestor; **progenitura** f offspring.

programa m programme; plan; schedule; ~ de estudios curriculum, syllabus.

progresar [1a] progress, advance; **progresión** f progression (a. ♈); **progresista** adj. a. su. m/f pol., **progresivo** progressive; **progreso** m progress, advance; ~s pl. progress; hacer ~s make progress.

prohibición f prohibition (de of), ban (de on); embargo (de on); **prohibir** [3a] prohibit, forbid (algo a alguien a p. a th.); ban; stop; ~ inf. forbid s.o. to inf.; v. dirección etc.; se prohibe fumar, prohibido fumar no smoking; queda terminantemente prohibido inf. it is strictly forbidden to inf.; **prohibitivo** prohibitive.

prohijar [1a] adopt.

prohombre m leader, top man, man of authority.

prójima f F woman who is no better than she ought to be; **prójimo** m neighbour, fellow-man, fellow-being. [brood, spawn.)

prole f offspring, progeny; b.s.)

proletariado m proletariat(e); **proletario** adj. a. su. m, a f proletarian.

proliferación f proliferation; **proliferar** [1a] proliferate; **prolífico** prolific (en of).

prolijidad f prolixity etc.; **prolijo** prolix, tedious, long-winded.

prologar [1h] preface; libro prologado por X book with a preface by X (or introduced by X); **prólogo** m prologue; preface, introduction de libro etc.

prolongación f prolongation; extension; **prolongar** [1h] prolong; extend; Ᾱ línea produce.

promediar [1b] v/t. divide into two halves; v/i. (interponerse) mediate; antes de ~ el mes before the month is half-way through; **promedio** m average; middle de una distancia.

promesa f promise; **prometedor** promising; perspectiva hopeful, rosy; **prometer** [2a] v/t. promise; pledge; v/i. have (or show) promise; es un chico que promete he's a promising lad; ~se algo expect, promise o.s.; (novios) get engaged; estar prometido be engaged; **prometida** f fiancée; **prometido** m promise; (p.) fiancé.

prominencia f protuberance; esp. fig. prominence; **prominente** prominent; protuberant.

promiscuidad f mixture, jumble, confusion de objetos; promiscuity de vida; **promiscuo** objetos all mixed up, in disorder; ambiguous; vida promiscuous.

promisión v. tierra.

promoción f (ascenso) promotion; (fomento) promotion, advancement, furtherance; Ӿ la ~ de 1960 the 1960 class.

promontorio m promontory, headland.

promotor m, **promovedor** m promoter; pioneer; instigator; **promover** [2h] (ascender) promote; (fomentar) promote, forward, further; proyecto etc. pioneer, set on foot; rebelión stir up, instigate.

promulgación f promulgation; **promulgar** [1h] promulgate; fig. proclaim, announce publicly.

pronombre m pronoun; **pronominal** pronominal.

pronosticación f prediction, prognostication; **pronosticar** [1g] forecast, predict, foretell, prognosticate; **pronóstico** m forecast, prediction; Ӿ prognosis; (señal) omen, prognostic; ~ del tiempo weather-forecast; Ӿ de ~ leve slight, not serious; de ~ reservado of uncertain gravity (or extent).

prontitud f promptness, speed; quickness, keenness de ingenio; **pronto 1.** adj. prompt, quick, speedy; contestación prompt, swift, ♱ early; curación speedy; (listo) ready (para inf. to inf.); **2.** adv. quickly, promptly; soon; at once; early; un poco ~ a bit early, on the early side; lo más ~ posible as soon as possible; tan ~ como as soon as; de ~ suddenly; ¡hasta ~! see you soon!; por de ~, por lo ~ meanwhile, for the present; **3.** m sudden movement, jerk; F strong impulse (or urge).

prontuario m handbook, compendium.

prónuba f bridesmaid.

pronunciación f pronunciation; **pronunciamiento** m Ӿ revolt, insurrection; **pronunciar** [1b] pronounce; utter; discurso make, deliver; ⚖ sentencia pass, pronounce; ~se declare (o.s.) (en favor de in favour of); Ӿ revolt, rebel.

propagación f biol. etc. propagation; fig. spreading, dissemination; **propaganda** f propaganda; ♱ advertising; **propagandista** m/f propagandist; **propagar** [1h] biol. etc. propagate; fig. ideas etc. spread, disseminate.

propalar [1a] divulge, disclose.

propasarse [1a] go to extremes, go too far; forget o.s.

propender [2a] incline, tend (a to); **propensión** f inclination (a for), propensity (a to), tendency (a to, towards); bent (a for); proneness (a to); **propenso:** ~ a inclined to; prone to, subject to; ~ a inf. apt to inf.

propiamente properly; la arquitectura ~ dicha architecture proper.

propiciación f propitiation; **propiciar** [1b] propitiate; **propiciatorio** propitiatory; **propicio** propitious, auspicious; p. kind, helpful.

propiedad f (bienes, finca) property; (atributo) property (a. ⌐m), attribute; (dominio) ownership; (lo propio) appositeness; paint. etc. likeness, resemblance; ~ literaria copyright, rights; en ~ properly; es ~ copyright; **propietaria** f proprietress; **propietario 1.** proprietary; **2.** m proprietor; owner; (terrateniente) landowner, landlord.

propina f tip, gratuity; F de ~ into the bargain; **propinar** [1a] bebida treat to; golpe deal; paliza give; ~se algo treat o.s. to.

propincuidad f propinquity; **propincuo** near.

propio (conveniente) proper, suitable, fitting (para for); (que pertenece a uno) own, one's own; characteristic (de of), peculiar (de to), special; (mismo) same; natural, genuine; el ~ obispo the bishop himself; sus ~as palabras his very words; lo hizo con su ~a mano he did it with his own hand; la casa es la suya ~a the house is his very own; la ciudad tiene un carácter ~ the city has a character of its own; F haré lo ~ que tú I'll do the same as you.

proponente m proposer; **proponer** [2r] propose; teoría etc. propound, put forward; ~se inf. propose to inf., plan to inf.

proporción f proportion; ratio; rate; en ~ con in proportion to; no guardar ~ be out of proportion (con to, with); **proporcionado** proportionate; bien ~ well-proportioned, shapely; **proporcional** proportional; **proporcionar** [1a] provide, supply, give; adjust, adapt.

proposición f proposition; proposal.

propósito m purpose, aim, intention; buenos ~s pl. good resolutions; a ~ (adj.) appropriate, fitting (para for); observación apt, apposite; a ~ (adv.) by the way, incidentally; a ~ de about; de ~ on purpose, purposely, deliberately; fuera de ~ off the point, out of place, irrele-

vant(ly); sin ~ fijo purposeless(ly).

propuesta f proposition, proposal.

propulsión f propulsion; ~ a cohete, ~ cohética rocket propulsion; ~ a chorro, ~ por reacción jet propulsion; **propulsor** m propellent.

prorrata f share, quota; a ~ pro rata, proportionately; **prorratear** [1a] apportion, share out; average; **prorrateo** m apportionment, sharing.

prórroga f prorogation; ✝ extension; ⚖️ stay, respite; deportes: extra time; **prorrogación** f prorogation; **prorrogar** [1h] (suspender) prorogue, adjourn; (suprimir) abolish; (aplazar) postpone; plazo extend; ⚖️ stay, respite.

prorrumpir [3a] burst forth, break forth; ~ en gritos, lágrimas burst into.

prosa f prose; F idle chatter; **prosador** m, **-a** f prose-writer; F chatterbox, great talker; **prosaico** prosaic, prose attr.; fig. prosaic, prosy, ordinary; **prosaísmo** m fig. ordinariness.

prosapia f ancestry, lineage.

proscribir [3a; p.p. proscrito] (prohibir) prohibit, ban; partido etc. proscribe; (desterrar) banish; criminal outlaw; **proscripción** f ban (de on), prohibition (de of); proscription; banishment; **proscrito 1.** p.p. of proscribir; **2.** adj. banned; banished; outlawed; **3.** m exile; outlaw.

prosecución f prosecution, continuation; pursuit; **proseguir** [3d a. 3l] v/t. continue, proceed with, carry on; demanda push; estudio, investigación pursue; v/i. continue, go on.

proselitismo m proselytism; **prosélito** m, **a** f proselyte.

prosista m/f prose-writer.

prosodia f gr. rules for pronunciation and accentuation; poet. prosody.

prosopopeya f F pomposity, solemnity.

prospección f exploration; ⚒️ prospecting (de for); **prospecto** m prospectus; **prospector** m prospector.

prosperar [1a] prosper, thrive, flourish; **prosperidad** f prosperity; success, good fortune; (*período*) good times; **próspero** prosperous, thriving, flourishing; successful; *fortuna etc.* favourable.

prosternarse [1a] prostrate o.s.

prostíbulo *m* brothel.

prostitución *f* prostitution; **prostituir** [3g] prostitute (*a. fig.*); **prostituta** *f* prostitute.

protagonista *m/f* protagonist; main character, (*m*) hero, (*f*) heroine.

protección *f* protection; **proteccionista** *adj. a. su. m/f* protectionist; *impuesto* protective; **protector 1.** protective; *tono* patronizing; **2.** *m*, **-a** *f* protector; guardian; **protectorado** *m* protectorate; **proteger** [2c] protect (*de*, *contra* from, against); shield, shelter; defend; (*alentar*) support, encourage; **protegido** *m*, **a** *f* protegé(e).

proteína *f* protein.

protervo wicked, perverse.

protesta *f* protest; protestation *de amistad etc.*; **protestación** *f* protestation; ~ *de fe* profession of faith; **protestante** *adj. a. su. m/f* Protestant; **protestantismo** *m* Protestantism; **protestar** [1a] protest (*a.* †, ⚖); *contra* a. object; *de que* that); remonstrate; *fe* profess; ~ *de inocencia etc.* protest; **protesto** *m* †, ⚖ protest.

protocolo *m* protocol; etiquette *de sociedad.*

protón *m* proton.

protoplasma *m* protoplasm.

prototipo *m* prototype.

protuberancia *f* protuberance; **protuberante** protuberant.

provecto: *de edad* ~*a* elderly, advanced in years.

provecho *m* advantage, benefit, profit (*a.* †); *negocio de* ~ profitable business; *persona de* ~ useful person, decent sort; ¡*buen* ~! *hoping that those eating will enjoy their meal;* ¡*buen* ~ *le haga!* and much good may it do him!; *sacar* ~ *de* benefit by (*or* from), profit by (*or* from); **provechoso** advantageous, beneficial, profitable (*a.* †).

proveedor *m*, **-a** *f* supplier, purveyor; caterer; ~ *casero* roundsman; **proveer** [2a; *p.p.* *provisto*, *a. proveído*) provide, supply (de

with); *negocio* transact; ⚖ decree; *vacante* fill; ~ *a* cater for.

provenir [3s]: ~ *de* come from, arise from, stem from.

provenzal *adj. a. su. m* Provençal.

proverbial proverbial; **proverbio** *m* proverb.

providencia *f* forethought, foresight, providence; (*Divina*) ♀ Providence; **providencial** providential; **providente**, **próvido** provident.

provincia *f* province; *de* ~(*s*) *freq.* provincial, country *attr.*; **provincial** *adj. a. su. m*, **-a** *f* (*eccl.*) provincial; **provincialismo** *m* provincialism; **provinciano 1.** provincial, country *attr.*; **2.** *m*, **a** *f* provincial, country-dweller.

provisión *f* provision; supply, store; ~*es* *pl.* provisions *etc.*; **provisional** provisional, temporary.

provocación *f* provocation; (*insulto*) affront; **provocador** provocative; **provocar** [1g] *v/t.* provoke; incite, tempt, move; (*fomentar*) promote, forward; *cambio*, *reacción* ect. provoke, bring about, induce; ~ *a cólera* rouse to fury; ~ *a lástima* move to pity; *el mar provoca a bañarse* the sea invites (*or* tempts) one to bathe; *v/i.* F be sick; **provocativo** provocative, provoking.

próximamente approximately; (*pronto*) shortly; **proximidad** *f* proximity, nearness; **próximo** near, next, neighbouring; *pariente* close; *el mes* ~ next month; *el mes* ~ *pasado* last month; *en fecha* ~*a* at an early date; *estar* ~ *a inf.* be on the point of *ger.*

proyección *f* projection; **proyectar** [1a] *película etc.* project, show; *sombra* cast; *casa*, *máquina etc.* plan, design; *viaje etc.* plan; ~ *inf.* plan to *inf.*; *estar proyectado para inf.* be designed to *inf.*; **proyectil** *m* projectile, missile; *esp.* ✕ shell; ~ *dirigido* guided missile; **proyectista** *m/f* designer, planner; **proyecto** *m* project, scheme, plan; (*presupuesto*) detailed estimate; ~ *de ley* bill; ¿*qué* ~*s tienes para las vacaciones?* what are your plans for the holiday?; **proyector** *m cine*: projector; ✄, ✕ searchlight.

prudencia f prudence, wisdom; sound judgement; **prudente** prudent, wise, sensible; judicious.

prueba f proof (a. ⅄, typ.); (indicio) proof, sign, token; ⚖ proof, evidence (a. fig.); (ensayo) test, trial, try-out; phot. proof, print; esp. ⚗ experiment; taste, sample de comida etc.; fitting de vestido; deportes: event; ~s pl. typ. proofs, proof-sheets; ~s pl. ⊕, deportes etc.: trials; ~ documental documentary evidence; ~ eliminatoria heat; ~ de fuego fig. acid test; ~ indiciaria circumstantial evidence; phot. ~ positiva positive print; de ~ freq. test attr., testing; phot. copia de ~ test-print; a ~ on trial, on approval; a ~ de proof against; a ~ de agua waterproof; a ~ de bala bulletproof; a toda ~ foolproof; en ~ de in proof of; poner a ~, someter a ~ (put to the) test, try out.

prurito m ⚕ itch; fig. itch, urge (de inf. to inf.).

prusiano adj. a. su. m, a f Prussian.

psicoanálisis m psychoanalysis; **psicoanalista** m/f psychoanalyst; **psicología** f psychology; **psicológico** psychological; **psicólogo** m psychologist; **psicosis** f psychosis; **psique** f psyche; **psiquiatra** m psychiatrist; **psiquiatría** f psychiatry; **psíquico** psychic(al).

ptomaína f ptomaine.

púa f zo., ⚘ prickle, spike, spine; quill de erizo; ⚘ graft para injertar; tooth de peine; prong de horquilla etc.; barb de anzuelo etc.

pubertad f puberty.

publicación f publication; **publicar** [1g] publish; (dar publicidad a) publicize; secreto disclose, divulge; **publicidad** f publicity; ✝ advertising; **publicista** m/f publicist; **público 1.** public; state attr.; hacer ~ publish, disclose; **2.** m public; thea. etc. audience; deportes etc.: spectators; crowd; un ~ numeroso a large attendance; en ~ publicly, in public.

puchera f F pot; stew; **pucherazo** m F rigging of an election, fiddling with votes; **puchero** m pot; (guisado) stew; F daily bread; F (gesto) pout, face; F hacer ~s pout,

screw up one's face; F volcar el ~ rig an election, fiddle the voting.

puches m/pl. porridge, gruel.

pucho m fag-end; S.Am. tiny amount, trifle.

pude etc. v. poder.

pudendo: partes ~as private parts.

pudibundo modest, shy; chaste; **pudicicia** f modesty; chastity; **púdico** modest, shy; chaste.

pudiendo v. poder.

pudiente well-to-do; powerful.

pudor m modesty, shyness; virtue, chastity; (vergüenza) shame; atentado al ~ indecent offence; **pudoroso** modest, shy; chaste.

pudrición f, **pudrimiento** m rot, rottenness; putrescence; pudrición seca dry-rot; **pudrir** [3a] rot; ~se rot, decay, putrefy; fig. rot, languish en cárcel; die (de aburrimiento etc. of).

pueblada f S.Am. revolt; **pueblero 1.** S.Am. village attr.; **2.** m S.Am. villager; **pueblo** m (nación) people, nation; (plebe) lower orders, common people; (poblado) town, village.

puedo etc. v. poder.

puente m bridge (a. ♪); ⚓ deck; ⚓ ~ (de mando) bridge; ~ aéreo air-lift; ~ colgante suspension bridge; ~ giratorio swing bridge; ~ levadizo drawbridge; ~ de pontones pontoon bridge.

puerca f sow; F slut; **puerco 1.** m pig, hog Am.; F pig; ~ espín porcupine; **2.** dirty, filthy.

puericia f boyhood; **pueril** childish; contp. puerile, childish; **puerilidad** f puerility, childishness.

puerro m leek.

puerta f door; doorway; gate de jardín, ciudad etc.; gateway (a. fig.); ~ accesoria side door; ~ excusada, ~ falsa private door, side door; ~ giratoria swing door, revolving door; ~ principal front door; ~ de servicio tradesman's entrance; ~ trasera back door; ~ ventana french window; ~ vidriera glass door; a ~ cerrada behind closed doors; a las ~s de la muerte at death's door; de ~ en ~ from door to door; tomar la ~ leave, get out.

puerto m ⚓ port, harbour; (ciudad) port; esp. fig. haven; geog. pass;

~ de escala port of call; ~ franco free port; entrar a ~ put in.

puertorriqueño v. portorriqueño.

pues (ya que) since, for, because; (continuativo) then; well; well then; (afirmación) yes, certainly; ~ ... (vacilando) well ...; ahora ~ now, now then; ~ bien well then, very well; ~ sí well yes, yes certainly.

puesta f stake, bet en el juego; orn. egg-laying; ~ del sol sunset; ~ en marcha starting.

puesto 1. p.p. of poner; ir bien ~ be well dressed; con el sombrero ~ with his hat on; **2.** m place, position, situation; (empleo) post, position; ✗ post; booth, stall de mercado; (quiosco) stand; pitch de vendedor ambulante; ~ de escucha listening-post; ~ de policía police-post, police-station; ~ de socorro first-aid post; **3.:** ~ que since, as.

¡puf! ugh!

púgil m boxer; **pugilato** m boxing.

pugna f fig. battle, struggle; estar en ~ con conflict with; **pugnacidad** f pugnacity; **pugnar** [1a] struggle, fight, strive (por inf. to inf.); **pugnaz** pugnacious.

puja f bid; F sacar de la ~ a get ahead of; get s.o. out of a jam.

pujante strong, vigorous; p. strapping; **pujanza** f strength, vigour; **pujar** [1a] v/t. precio raise, push up; v/i. bid up en subasta; naipes: bid; (pugnar) struggle, strain; (no lograr hablar) be at a loss for words, be tongue-tied; falter hablando; (casi lorar) be on the verge of tears.

pujo m fig. strong impulse, strong desire; F try, shot.

pulcritud f neatness etc.; **pulcro** neat, tidy, smart; exquisite, delicate.

pulga f flea; de malas ~s peppery; tener malas ~s be bad-tempered, be short-tempered.

pulgada f inch.

pulgar m thumb; **pulgarada** f pinch, de rapé etc.; flip, flick con el pulgar; (medida) inch.

pulido (pulcro) neat, tidy; trabajo etc. polished; **pulidor** m, -a f polisher; **pulimentar** [1a] polish; (alisar) smooth; **pulimento** m polish; **pulir** [3a] polish; fig. polish up, touch up; F (robar)

pinch; F (vender) flog; ~se fig. acquire polish; dress up.

pulmón m lung; **pulmonar** pulmonary, lung attr.; **pulmonía** f pneumonia.

pulpa f pulp; soft part de carne, fruta; ~ de madera wood-pulp; **pulpejo** m fleshy part, soft part.

pulpería f S.Am. general store.

púlpito m pulpit.

pulpo m octopus.

pulposo pulpy; fleshy.

pulquérrimo sup. of pulcro.

pulsación f pulsation; throb(bing), beat(ing); ♪ touch; tap en máquina de escribir; **pulsador** m push-button; **pulsar** [1a] v/t. ♪ instrumento play; tecla etc. touch, strike, play; botón press, push; ✗ feel the pulse of; fig. sound out, explore; v/i. pulsate, throb, beat.

pulsera f wristlet, bracelet.

pulso m anat. pulse; (muñeca) wrist; fig. steady hand, firmness of touch; (cuidado) care, caution; a ~ by sheer strength; by sheer hard work; fig. the hard way; a ~ sudando by the sweat of one's brow; hecho a ~ dibujo freehand; tomar el ~ a feel the pulse of; tomar a ~ lift clean off the ground; S.Am. F drink in one go.

pulular [1a] swarm, abound.

pulverización f pulverization; spray(ing) de líquido; **pulveriza-dor** m spray(er); **pulverizar** [1f] pulverize; powder; líquido spray; **pulverulento** powdered, powdery.

pulla f taunt, cutting remark; dig; rude word, indecent remark.

¡pum! bang!; pop!

punción f ✗ puncture.

punching ['puntʃin] m punch-ball.

pundonor m point of honour; honour; face (fig.); **pundonoroso** honorable; punctilious, scrupulous.

pungir [3c] prick; sting.

punible punishable; **punición** f punishment; **punitivo** punitive.

punta f point (a. geog.); end, tip; end, butt de cigarro; ⊕ nail; toe de zapato etc.; sour-ness de vino; (pizca) touch, trace, tinge; ~ del pie toe; ~ de lanza spearhead (a. fig.); de ~ on end, endways; estar de ~ be at odds (con with); *hacer* ~ be first, go first; *poner(se) de* ~ (*pelo*) stand on end; *ponerse de* ~ *con* fall out with; *sacar* ~ *a* sharpen, point; *tener* ~ *de loco* have a streak of madness.

puntada *f* stitch (*a. S.Am.* ⚕).

puntal *m* △ prop, shore; stanchion; ⊕ strut; *fig.* prop, support; *S.Am.* snack.

puntapié *m* kick.

punteado *m* ♪ twang(ing), plucking; **puntear** [1a] ♪ pluck, twang; *sew.* stitch; *dibujo etc.* dot, mark with dots; stipple; fleck.

puntera *f* toe (cap); F kick.

puntería *f* aim(ing); (*destreza*) marksmanship; *enmendar la* ~ correct one's aim; *hacer la* ~ de aim, sight; *tener mala* ~ be a bad shot.

puntiagudo sharp(-pointed).

puntilla *f* ⊕ tack, brad; *sew.* narrow lace edging; point *de pluma*; de ~s on tiptoe.

puntillo *m* punctilio; **puntilloso** punctilious.

punto *m* point (*a. fig.*; *sitio, momento, detalle, rasgo, estado, etc.*); (*sitio*) spot, place; dot *señalado en papel etc.*; *gr.* full stop; pip *de carta*; dot, speckle, fleck *de tela*; *sew.* stitch; (*malla*) mesh; *fig.* point of honour; *dos* ~*s gr.* colon; ~ *y coma* semicolon; *¡~ en boca!* mum's the word!; ~ *por* ~ point by point; ~ *de admiración* exclamation mark; ~ *de apoyo* fulcrum; ~ *capital* crucial point, crux; ~*s pl. cardinales* cardinal points; ~ de *congelación* freezing point; ~*s pl.* de *consulta* terms of reference; ~ de *contacto* point of contact; ~ de *ebullición* boiling point; ~ de *fuga* vanishing-point; *de fusión* melting-point; ~ *de honor* point of honour; ~ de *inflamación* flash-point; ~ de *interrogación* question mark; ~ *de media* plain knitting; ~ *muerto* ⊕ dead centre (*a.* ~ *neutral*); *fig.* stalemate, deadlock; ~ *neutro mot.* neutral; ~ de *partida* starting-point; ~*s pl. suspensivos three dots indicating hesitation etc.* (...); ~ de *vista* point of view; *a* ~ ready; *a* ~ *fijo* for sure; *al* ~ at once, instantly; de *todo* ~ completely; en ~ (*hora*) on the dot, sharp; en ~ *a* with regard to; *cocina*: *en su* ~ done to a turn; *hasta cierto* ~ up to a point; *hasta el* ~ de *inf.* to the extent of *ger.*; *hasta tal* ~ *que* to such an extent that; *por* ~*s* one thing at a time; *boxeo*: on points; *bajar de* ~ decline; *estar a* ~ *de inf.* be on the point of *ger.*; *hacer* ~ knit; *poner a* ~ *motor* tune up; *poner en su* ~ bring to perfection; *subir de* ~ grow; *b.s.* get worse.

puntuación *f* *gr.* punctuation; marking *de exámenes*; mark, class *en examen*; *deportes*: score; **puntual** prompt; *cálculo etc.* exact; *p. etc.* reliable, conscientious; **puntualidad** *f* punctuality *etc.*; **puntualizar** [1f] fix in the mind; *suceso* give an exact account of; (*acabar*) finish off; **puntuar** [1e] *v/t. gr.* punctuate; *examen* mark; *v/i. deportes*: score; eso *no puntúa* that doesn't count.

puntura *f* puncture, prick.

punzada *f* puncture, prick; ⚕ stitch *de costado*; ⚕ shooting pain, spasm, twinge; *fig.* pang; **punzante** *dolor* shooting, stabbing; *observación* biting, caustic; **punzar** [1f] *v/t.* puncture, pierce, prick; punch; *v/i.* (*dolor*) shoot, stab, sting; **punzón** *m* punch; graver, burin.

puñada *f* punch, clout.

puñado *m* handful (*a. fig.*).

puñal *m* dagger; **puñalada** *f* stab; *fig.* grievous blow; F *coser a* ~*s* cut up, carve up.

puñetazo *m* punch; *dar un* ~ *a* punch; *dar de* ~*s* punch, pommel.

puño *m anat.* fist; (*contenido*) fistful, handful; (*mango*) handle, haft, hilt; cuff *de camisa*; de *propio* ~ in one's own handwriting; de ~ *y letra* de X in X's own handwriting; *como un* ~ tangible, absolutely real; *por sus* ~*s* by oneself, on one's own; *meter en un* ~ intimidate, cow; domineer.

pupa *f* ⚕ pimple, blister.

pupila *f anat.* pupil; (*p.*) ward; **pupilo** *m* ward; boarder.

pupitre *m* desk.

puré *m* purée, soup; ~ de *patatas* mashed potatoes.

pureza *f* purity.

purga *f* purge (*a. pol.*), purgative; ⊕ *válvula de* ~ vent; **purgación** *f* purging; **purgar** [1h] purge (*a. pol.*); purify, refine; ⊕ vent, drain; *fig. pecado etc.* purge, expiate; ~**se** ⚕ take a purge; *fig.* purge o.s.;

purgativo purgative; **purgatorio** *m* purgatory.

purificación *f* purification; **purificar** [1g] purify; cleanse; ⊕ refine.

Purísima: *la* ~ the Virgin.

purista *m/f* purist.

puritanismo *m* puritanism; **puritano 1.** puritanical; puritan; **2.** *m*, **a** *f* puritan.

puro 1. pure; (*sin mezcla*) pure, unadulterated, unalloyed; *verdad* plain, simple, unvarnished; *cielo* clear; *de* ~ *aburrimiento* out of sheer boredom; *de* ~ *bobo* out of sheer stupidity; **2.** *m* cigar.

púrpura *f* purple; **purpurar** [1a] purple; dye purple; **purpúreo, purpurino** purple.

purulento purulent.

pus *m* pus, matter.

puse *etc. v. poner.*

pusilánime faint-hearted, pusillanimous; **pusilanimidad** *f* faint-heartedness, pusillanimity.

pústula *f* pustule, sore, pimple.

puta *f* whore, prostitute.

putativo supposed, putative.

putrefacción *f* rot(tenness), putrefaction, decay; ~ *fungoide* dry-rot; **putrefacto** rotten, putrid; **putrescente** rotting, putrescent; **pútrido** putrid, rotten.

Q

que 1. *pron. relativo*: (*p.*) (*sujeto*) who, (*acc.*) whom; (*cosa*) which; (*p., cosa*) that; *en muchos casos se puede suprimir*; *el hombre ~ vi* the man (whom) I saw; *el ~* (*p.*) he who, whoever; who, the one who; (*cosa*) which, the one which; *la ~* she who *etc.*; *los ~, las ~* those who *etc.*; *lo ~* what, that which; (*esp. tras coma*) which, something which, a fact which; *lo ~ quiero* what I want; *todo lo ~ vi* all (that) I saw; *lo ~ es eso* as for that; *no tengo nada ~ hacer* I have nothing to do; **2.** *cj.* a) *that*; *en muchos casos se puede suprimir*: *yo sé ~ es verdad* I know (that) it is true; *dice ~ sí* he says yes; *¡~ sí, hombre!* I tell you it is!; *v. sí*[1]; b) (*pues*) for, because; *a menudo no se traduce*: *¡cuidado!, ~ viene un coche* look out! there's a car coming; c) *con subjuntivo*: *quiero ~ lo hagas* I want you to do it; *¡~ lo pases bien!* have a good time!; *¡~ entre!* let him come in!, send him in!; d) *comparaciones*: than; *más ~ yo* more than I; e) *el ~ subj.* the fact that, that; f) *~ ... ~* whether ... or; *yo ~ tú* if I were you; F *¡a ~ no!* I bet it isn't!, I bet you can't!; no, I tell you!

qué 1. *pron. interrogativo*: *¿~?* what?; *¿~ hiciste entonces?* what did you do then?; **2.** *¡~ perro más feo!* what an ugly dog!; *¡~ bonito!* how pretty!; *¡~ asco!* how disgusting!; *¿de ~ tamaño es?* how big is it?, what size is it?; *¿~ edad tiene?* how old is he?; *¡~ de ...!* how many ...!; **3.** *¿a ~?* why?; *¿a mí ~?* what's that got to do with me?; *¿de ~ le conoce?* how do you know him?; F *¿y ~?* so what?; what then?; *sin ~ ni para ~* without rhyme or reason.

quebrada *f* gorge, ravine; gap.

quebradero *m*: F *~ de cabeza* headache, worry; **quebradizo** fragile, delicate, brittle; *hojaldre* short; *salud, virtud* frail; **quebrado 1.** *terreno* rough, broken; *✝* rup-

tured; *✝* bankrupt; **2.** *m* ♭ fraction; **quebradura** *f* fissure, slit; *✝* rupture; **quebraja** *f* fissure, slit; **quebrantadura** *f*, **quebrantamiento** *m* breaking, breakage *etc.*; *✝* exhaustion, fatigue; **quebrantahuesos** *m* bearded vulture; **quebrantar** [1a] break (*a. fig.*); crack; shatter; *caja* break open; *cárcel* break out of; *color* tone down; *S.Am. potro* break in; *resistencia, salud* break, shatter; *p.* annoy; **quebranto** *m* (*acto*) breaking *etc.*; *✝* weakness, poor health; *fig.* (*pérdida*) severe loss; (*pena*) great sorrow.

quebrar [1k] *v/t.* break, smash; *color* tone down; *v/i.* break; *✝* go bankrupt, fail; (*disminuir*) slacken, weaken; *~ con* break with; *~se* break, get broken; *✝* be ruptured.

queche *m* smack, ketch.

queda *f* curfew.

quedar [1a] **1.** (*permanecer en un lugar etc.*) stay, remain; (*sobrar*) be left (over), remain; *~ adj., p.p.* be, remain, stay; keep; *quedé 3 días* I stayed 3 days; *quedan 3* there are 3 left; *me quedan 3* I have 3 left; *no quedan más que ruinas* there are only ruins left, there is nothing but ruins; *la cosa quedó así* there the matter rested; *~ inmóvil* keep still; *~ sentado* remain seated, stay sitting down; *quedó aterrado* he was terrified; *~ a deber* still owe; *~ bien* do o.s. justice, acquit o.s. well; *~ en inf.* agree to *inf.*; *~ en que* agree that; *¿en qué quedamos?* well, what do we say?; *~ por inf.* remain to be *p.p.*, be still to be *p.p.*; *el trabajo queda por hacer* the work is still to be done; *~ por encima de* come off better than, have the laugh of; *~ sin hacer* be left undone; **2.** *~se* stay, remain; stay on, stay behind, linger (on); put up (*en hotel* at); *~ ciego* go blind; *~ con* (*retener*) keep, hold on to, retain; *~ en casa* stay in(doors); *no se quedó en menos* he was not to be outdone; *se me quedan chicos los zapatos* I have outgrown my shoes; ~ *sin gasolina etc.* run out of.

quedo 1. *adj.* quiet, still; **2.** *adv.* softly.

quehacer *m* job, task, duty; ~*es pl. domésticos* household jobs, chores; housekeeping.

queja *f* (*dolor*) moan, groan; whine; (*resentimiento*) complaint, grumble, grouse; ⚖ *etc.* protest, complaint; *tener* ~ *de* have a complaint to make about; **quejarse** [1a] (*dolor*) moan, groan; whine; complain (*de* about, *of*), grumble (*de* about, *at*); protest (*de* about, *at*); **quejido** *m* moan, groan; **quejoso** complaining, querulous; **quejumbroso** whining, plaintive; cantankerous.

quema *f* fire, burning; **quemador** *m* burner; ~ *de gas* gas-burner; **quemadura** *f* burn; scald *de líquido etc.*; (*insolación*) sunburn; blowout *de fusible*; **quemar** [1a] **1.** *v/t.* burn; (*pegar fuego a*) kindle, set on fire; (*líquido*) scald; *boca* burn; *plantas* (*sol*) burn, scorch; (*helada*) burn, frost; *fusible* blow, burn out; F *precio* slash, cut; F *p.* annoy, upset; *v. tierra*; **2.** *v/i. fig.* be burning hot; **3.** ~*se* burn; scorch; feel burning hot; F (*buscando*) be warm; *¡qué te quemas!* you're getting warm!

quemarropa: *a* ~ point-blank.

quemazón *f* burn, burning; *fig.* intense heat; F (*comezón*) itch; F (*palabra*) cutting remark; F (*resentimiento*) pique, annoyance; *S.Am.* F ✝ bargain sale, cut-price sale.

quepo *etc. v. caber.*

querella *f* dispute, controversy; ⚖ *etc.* complaint, charge; **querellante** *m/f* ⚖ plaintiff, complainant; **querellarse** [1a] complain; ⚖ file a complaint, bring an action.

querencia *f zo.* (*guarida*) lair, haunt; *zo.* homing instinct; *fig.* den, haunt, favourite spot; *buscar la* ~ home.

querer 1. [2u] (*amar*) love; (*tener afición a*) like; (*desear*) want, wish; *quiero hacerlo* I want to do it; *quiero que lo hagas* I want you to do it; *te quiero mucho* I love you very much; *en la oficina le quieren mucho* he is well liked in the office; *quisiera saber* I should like to know; *como Vd. quiera* as you please, just as you wish; *como quiera* anyhow, anyway; *como quiera que* whereas;

since, inasmuch as; *quiera o no quiera* willy-nilly; *v. decir*; *quiere llover* it is trying to rain; *sin* ~ inadvertently, unintentionally, by mistake; *lo hizo sin* ~ he didn't mean to do it; **2.** *m* love, affection.

querida *f b.s.* mistress; *¡sí, ~!* yes dear, yes darling; **querido 1.** dear, beloved, darling; **2.** *m b.s.* lover; *¡sí, ~!* yes dear, yes darling; *el* ~ *de las musas* the darling of the muses.

quesera *f* (*p.*) dairymaid; cheesemaker; (*plato*) cheese-dish; **quesería** *f* dairy *en granja*; cheese factory; **quesero** *m* dairyman; cheesemaker; **queso** *m* cheese; ~ *crema* cream cheese; ~ *helado* ice-cream brick; F *me lo dio con* ~ he put one ¡ *¡quiá!* surely not!   [over on me.

quicio *m* hinge; *fig. fuera de* ~ out of joint; *sacar de* ~ exasperate.

quid [kið] *m* gist, core, nub.

quídam ['kiðan] *m* F (*fulano*) somebody or other; *contp.* nobody.

quiebra *f* (*grieta*) crack, fissure; (*pérdida*) loss, damage; ✝ bankruptcy *de p.*, failure *de sociedad*, slump, crash *de economía entera.*

quiebro *m* ♪ trill; *toros:* dodge, avoiding action; F *dar el* ~ *a p.* dodge.

quien (*sujeto*) who, (*acc.*) whom; (*en comienzo de frase*) he *etc.* who, whoever; *el hombre a* ~ *lo di* the man to whom I gave it, the man I gave it to; ~ ... ~ some ... others; *hay* ~ *dice* there are some who say.

quién (*sujeto*) who, (*acc.*) whom; *¿a* ~ *lo diste?* to whom did you give it?, who did you give it to?; *¿de* ~ *es este libro?* whose is this book?

quienquiera whoever.

quieto (*inmóvil*) still; (*silencioso*) quiet; calm, peaceful; *¡estáte* ~*!* keep still!; **quietud** *f* stillness *etc.*

quijotada *f* quixotic act; **quijote** *m* quixotic person, hopelessly unrealistic person; **quijotería** *f*, **quijotismo** *m* quixotism, hopeless lack of realism; **quijotesco** quixotic, hopelessly unrealistic.

quilatar [1a] = *aquilatar*; **quilate** *m* carat.

quilo[1] *m physiol.* chyle; F *sudar el* ~ slave, work like a nigger.

quilo[2] *m* kilogramme.

quilombo *m S.Am.* cottage, hut; *b.s.* brothel.

quilla f ♆, orn., ⚓ keel; *colocar la ~ de* lay down; *dar de ~* keel over.

quimera f fantastic idea, fancy, chimera; *fig.* quarrel, dispute; **quimérico** fantastic, fanciful, chimerical; **quimerista** m/f quarrelsome sort, rowdy, brawler.

química f chemistry; **químico 1.** chemical; **2.** m chemist.

quina f Peruvian bark, quinine.

quincalla f hardware, ironmongery; **quincallería** f hardware shop, ironmonger's (shop); **quincallero** m ironmonger.

quince fifteen (*a. su.*); (*fecha*) fifteenth; *~ días freq.* fortnight; F *dar ~ y raya a* wipe the floor with; **quincena** f fortnight; **quincenal** fortnightly; **quinceno** fifteenth.

quincuagésimo fiftieth; **quingentésimo** five hundredth.

quinielas f/pl. football pool(s).

quinientos five hundred.

quinina f quinine.

quinqué m oil lamp; F *tener mucho ~* be wide awake, know what's going on.

quinquenal quinquennial; *plan ~* five year plan; **quinquenio** m quinquennium, five year period.

quinta f (*casa*) villa, country house; ♪ fifth; ✕ draft; ♣ coughing fit; *la ~ de 1960* the 1960 call-up, the 1960 draft *Am.*

quintaesencia f quintessence.

quintal m *Castilla:* = *46 kg.*; ~ *métrico* = *100 kg.*

quintar [1a] ✕ conscript, draft *Am.*

quintería f farmhouse; **quintero** m farmer; farm-labourer.

quinteto m quintet.

quintilla f 5-line stanza.

quinto 1. fifth; **2.** m ♣ fifth; ✕ conscript, recruit, draftee *Am.*

quintuplicar [1g] quintuple; **quíntuplo** quintuple, fivefold.

quiosco m kiosk *de calle*; summerhouse, pavilion *de jardín*; ~ (*de música*) bandstand; ~ (*de periódicos*) news-stand; ~ *de necesidad* public lavatory.

quiquiriquí m cock-a-doodle-doo.

quirófano m operating theatre.

quiromancia f palmistry, chiromancy.

quiropedia f chiropody, pedicure.

quirúrgico surgical.

quise *etc. v.* querer.

quisicosa f F puzzle(r).

quisquilla f trifle, triviality; (*a. ~s pl.*) quibbling, hair-splitting; *dejarse de ~s* stop fussing, stop quibbling; *pararse en ~s* bicker, quibble; **quisquilloso** touchy, cantankerous; fastidious, pernickety, choosy; captious, hair-splitting.

quiste m cyst.

quisto: *bien ~* well-liked; well received; *mal ~* disliked; unwelcome.

quita...: *~manchas* m (*p.*) drycleaner; (*material*) cleaning material; *~motas* m/f F bootlicker, toady; *~nieves* m: (*máquina*) ~ snow-plough; *~pelillos* m/f F bootlicker, toady; *~pesares* m F consolation, comfort; *~piedras* m cowcatcher.

quitapón: *de ~* detachable.

quitar [1a] **1.** take away, remove (*a* from); *ropa* take off; *pieza* take out, take off, remove; *golpe* avert; *fenc.* parry; *mesa* clear; (*robar*) steal; *abuso, dificultad etc.* do away with, remove; ♣ subtract, take away; *le quitaron el reloj* someone stole his watch; *no quita nada de su valor* it does not detract from its value at all; *me quitaron ese privilegio* they deprived me of that privilege; ~ *que subj.* prevent *ger.*; ~ *frotando etc.* rub *etc.* off; F *¡quita (allá)!* get away with you!; *de quita y pon* detachable; ~ *de en medio* remove, get rid of; ~ *de encima* shake off, get rid of; **2.** *~se ropa* take off; (*mancha*) come out; (*p.*) withdraw (*de* from); ~ *de algo, ~ algo de encima* get rid of s.t., dispose of s.t.; ~ *de en medio* get out of the way; *¡quítate de ahí!* come out of that!, come away from that!

quitasol m sunshade, parasol.

quite m hindrance; *fenc.* parry; (*regate*) dodge, dodging; *estar al ~* be forewarned.

quizá(s) perhaps, maybe; I dare say.

R

rábano *m* radish; ~ *picante* horse-radish; F *tomar el* ~ *por las hojas* bark up the wrong tree, get hold of the wrong end of the stick.
rabear [1a] wag its tail.
rabí *m* rabbi.
rabia *f* ⚕ rabies; *fig.* rage, fury; *me da* ~ it maddens me; *tener* ~ *a* have a grudge against; **rabiar** [1b] *fig.* rage, rave; (*dolor*) be in great pain; *pica que rabia* it stings like the devil; F *esto está que rabia* (*bebida*) it's got a kick to it; ~ *por* be dying for; ~ *por inf.* be dying to *inf.*
rabieta *f* F paddy, tantrum.
rabillo *m* ⚘ stalk; (*con el*) ~ *del ojo* (out of the) corner of one's eye.
rabino *m* rabbi.
rabión *m* rapids.
rabioso ⚕ mad, rabid; *fig.* furious; *partidario* rabid; *dolor* raging, violent; *sabor* hot.
rabo *m* tail; = *rabillo*.
rabona *hacer* ~ play truant.
racanear [1a] F slack, swing the lead; **rácano** *m* F slacker; *hacer el* ~ = *racanear*.
racial racial, race *attr.*
racimo *m* cluster, bunch.
raciocinar [1a] reason; **raciocinio** *m* reason; (*acto*) reasoning; argument.
ración *f* ration; portion, helping *de plato*; *eccl.* prebend; **racional** rational (*a.* Ⱥ); reasonable; **racionalismo** *m* rationalism; **racionalista** *m/f* rationalist; **racionamiento** *m* rationing; **racionar** [1a] ration; **racionero** *m eccl.* prebendary.
racismo *m* racialism.
racha *f meteor.* squall, gust; (*suerte*) stroke of luck; string, series *de sucesos*; *a* ~*s* fits and starts.
rada *f* ⚓ roads(tead).
radar *m* radar.
radiación *f* radiation; *radio:* broadcasting; **radiactividad** *f* radioactivity; **radiactivo** radioactive; **radiado** radio *attr.*, broadcast *attr.*; **radiador** *m* radiator; **radial**

radial; *S.Am.* radio *attr.*; **radiante** radiant (*a. fig.*); **radiar** [1b] *radio:* broadcast; *phys.* radiate.
radical 1. radical; **2.** *m pol.* radical; Ⱥ, *gr.* root; **radicalismo** *m* radicalism; **radicar** [1g] ⚘ *a. fig.* take root; be, be located *en lugar;* (*dificultad etc.*) lie (en in).
radio[1] *m* Ⱥ, *anat.* radius; spoke *de rueda;* ⚛ radium; ⚓, ⚡ ~ *de acción* range; *en un* ~ *de* within a radius of.
radio[2] *f* radio; broadcasting; (*aparato*) radio (set); wireless telegram; **~captar** [1a] monitor; **~difusión** *f* broadcasting; **~escucha** *m/f* listener; **~experimentador** *m* radio fan, ham; **~fonía** *f* radio(phony); **~fónico** radio *attr.*; **~fonógrafo** *m* *S.Am.* radiogram; **~goniómetro** *m* direction-finder; **~grafiar** [1c] ⚕ X-ray; ⚡ radio; **~gráfico** X-ray *attr.*; **~grama** *m* wireless message; **~gramola** *f* radiogram; **~logía** *f* radiology; **~rreceptor** *m* radio set (*or* receiver); ~ *de contrastación* monitor; **~scopia** *f* radioscopy; **~telefonía** *f* radio(telephony); **~telefonía** *f* radio(telephony), wireless; **~telegrafista** *m* wireless operator; **~telescopio** *m* radio-telescope; **~terapia** *f* radiotherapy; **radioyente** *m/f* listener.
raedera *f* scraper; **raedura** *f* scraping; ⚕ abrasion; ~*s pl.* filings, scrapings; **raer** [2z] scrape; (*quitar*) scrape off; (*alisar*) smooth; chafe; ⚕ abrade; **~se** chafe; (*tela*) fray.
ráfaga *f* squall, gust *de viento;* burst *de balas;* flurry *de nieve;* flash *de luz.*
raído *tela* frayed, threadbare; *aspecto* shabby; *fig.* shameless.
raigón *m* ⚘ large root; root, stump;
rail *m* rail. [*de diente.*]
raíz *f* root; *fig.* foundation; origin; ~ *cuadrada* square root; ~ *cúbica* cube root; *a* ~ *de* soon after; as a result of; *de* ~ root and branch; *cortar de* ~ nip in the bud; *echar raíces* take root.

rajá *m* raja(h).

raja *f* crack, split, slit; gash; (*astilla*) sliver, splinter; slice *de melón etc.*; F *sacar* ~ look after number one; ✝ *get a rake-off*; **rajadura** *f* = *raja*; **rajar** [1a] *v/t.* split, crack, slit; *melón etc.* slice; *v/i.* F shoot a line; (*hablar*) chatter; ~se split *etc.*; *sl.* back down, give up.

rajatabla: F *a* ~ down to the last detail, to the letter; at all costs, regardless; *S.Am.* on the dot.

ralea *f* breed, kind, sort.

ralo *pelo* sparse; *tela* loosely-woven; *phys.* rare.

rallador *m* grater; **rallar** [1a] grate; F grate on, annoy; **rallo** *m cocina*: grater; ⊕ large file, rasp.

rallye ['rali] *m mot.* rally; ~**-paper** *m* paper-chase.

rama *f* branch (*a. fig.*); en ~ *algodón* raw; *libro* unbound; *andarse por las* ~s beat about the bush; get bogged down in details; **ramaje** *m* branches; **ramal** *m* strand *de cuerda*; (*ronzal*) halter; *fig.* offshoot; 🚂 branch-line; **ramalazo** *m* (*golpe*) lash; (*señal*) weal, bruise; (*dolor*) stab of pain; (*pesar*) grief, blow.

ramera *f* whore.

ramificación *f* ramification; **ramificarse** [1g] ramify, branch (out).

ramillete *m* bouquet, posy; corsage *en vestido*; cluster; *fig.* collection.

ramita *f* twig, sprig; spray *de flores*.

ramo *m* branch, bough; bunch, bouquet *de flores*; 🎨 touch; *fig.* branch; department *de tienda etc.*; ✝ line; **ramojo** *m* brushwood.

rampa *f* ramp; ~ *de lanzamiento* launching-ramp.

ramplón *zapato* heavy, rough; *fig.* vulgar, common; **ramplonería** *f* vulgarity, coarseness.

rana *f* frog; ~ *toro* bullfrog.

rancidez *f*, **ranciedad** *f* rancidness *etc.*; **rancio** rancid, rank, stale, musty; *fig. abolengo* ancient; *costumbre* time-honoured; *vino* old.

ranchear [1a] *S.Am. v/t.* sack; *v/i.* build a camp, make a settlement; **ranchería** *f* settlement; **ranchero** *m* (mess) cook; *S.Am.* rancher; **rancho** *m* 🍴, ⚓ mess; camp, settlement; *S.Am.* hut; (*finca*) ranch; ⚔ F *asentar el* ~ prepare a meal; *fig.* get things organized, settle in; *hacer* ~ make room; ⚔ *hacer el* ~

have a meal; *hacer* ~ *aparte* set up on one's own.

rango *m* rank; status; class.

ranúnculo *m* buttercup.

ranura *f* groove, slot.

rapacidad *f* rapacity, greed.

rapapolvo *m* F ticking-off; *echar un* ~ a tick off.

rapar [1a] shave, crop; F pinch.

rapaz[1] rapacious, greedy; thieving; *zo.* predatory.

rapaz[2] *m* lad, youngster; *contp.* kid; **rapaza** *f* lass, youngster.

rape *m* quick hair-cut (*or* shave); *fig.* ticking-off; *al* ~ cut close.

rapé *m* snuff.

rapidez *f* speed(iness), rapidity *etc.*; **rápido 1.** rapid, speedy, quick, swift; **2.** *m* express (train); ~s *pl.* rapids.

rapiña *f* robbery (with violence); *de* ~ predatory; *v. ave*; **rapiñar** [1a] F steal, make off with.

raposa *f* vixen, fox (*a. fig.*); **raposo** *m* (dog-)fox.

rapsodia *f* rhapsody.

raptar [1a] abduct, kidnap; **rapto** *m* abduction, kidnapping; *fig.* sudden impulse; *fig.* ecstasy; **raptor** *m* kidnapper.

raquero *m* beachcomber.   [shoe.]

raqueta *f* racquet; ~ *de nieve* snow-

raquítico 🩺 rickety; *fig.* stunted; (*débil*) weak, feeble; **raquitis** *f*, **raquitismo** *m* rickets.

rareza *f* rarity, rareness, scarcity; *fig.* oddity, eccentricity; **raridad** *f* rarity; **rarificar** [1g] rarefy; **raro** rare, scarce, uncommon; *fig.* strange, odd; notable; *es* ~ *que* it is odd that; *¡qué hombre más* ~*!* what an odd man!; *¡cosa más* ~*a!* very strange!

ras *m* level(ness); ~ *con* ~ level; flush; *a* ~ *de* on a level with; flush with; *a* ~ *de tierra* (almost) at ground level; **rasar** [1a] skim, graze; ~se (*cielo*) clear.

rascacielos *m* skyscraper; **rascadera** *f* scraper; **rascador** *m* rasp, scraper; hairpin *para pelo*; **rascar** [1g] scrape (*a.* ♪ *co.*); scratch; rasp; ~se *S.Am.* get drunk; **rascatripas** *m/f* F third-rate violinist; **rascón** sharp, sour.

rasete *m* satinet(te).

rasgado *ojos* large; *boca* wide; **rasgadura** *f* tear, rip; **rasgar** [1h]

tear, rip, slash; *un papel* tear up;
rasgo *m* stroke, flourish *de pluma*;
fig. feature, characteristic; (*acto*)
feat, deed; noble gesture; ~s *pl.*
features *de cara*; ~ *de ingenio* flash
of wit; stroke of genius; *a grandes*
~s in outline; **rasgón** *m* tear, rent;
rasguear [1a] *♪* strum; **rasguñar**
[1a] scratch, scrape; *paint.* outline;
rasguño *m* scratch; *paint.* outline.
raso 1. level, flat, clear; *paisaje*
bare; open; *asiento* backless; *cielo*
cloudless; *soldado etc.* ordinary;
v. soldado; 2. *m sew.* satin; *al* ~ in
the open air; in open country.
raspa *f ichth.* fish-bone; *♀* beard *de
espiga,* stalk *de uvas;* **raspador** *m*
scraper, rasp(er); **raspadura** *f*
scrape *etc.;* erasure; ~s *pl.* filings,
scrapings; **raspante** *vino* sharp;
raspar [1a] *v/t.* scrape, rasp, file
con raspador; piel etc. graze; scale;
palabra erase; F pinch; *S.Am.* F
tick off; *v/i.* (*vino*) be sharp; **raspear** [1a] (*pluma*) scratch.
rastra *f* (*señal*) track, trail; (*carro*)
sledge; *✔* harrow; *⚓* drag, trawl;
dredge; string *de cebollas etc.;* a ~(s)
by dragging; *fig.* unwillingly; *llevar
a* ~ drag; *pescar a la* ~ trawl; **rastreador** *m* tracker; ~ (*barco*) ~
trawler; **rastrear** [1a] *v/t.* (*seguir*)
track, trail; (*encontrar*) track down,
trace; (*llevar*) drag; *⚓* dredge,
drag; *minas* sweep; *v/i.* ✔ rake,
harrow; *⚓* trawl; *✈ etc.* skim the
ground, fly low; **rastrero** *fig.* despicable; **rastrillar** [1a] rake; *lino
etc.* dress; **rastrillo** *m* rake; *✕*
portcullis; ~ *delantero* cowcatcher
Am.; **rastro** *m ✔* rake, harrow;
track, trail *de animal, de cosa arras-
trada; fig.* trace, sign; path *de huracán; sin dejar* ~ without leaving a
trace behind; **rastrojera** *f* stubble-
field; **rastrojo** *m* stubble.
rasurador *m* (electric) razor; **rasu-
rar** [1a] *cara* shave; ~ scrape.
rata 1. *f* rat; 2. *m* F sneak-thief.
rataplán *m* drum-beat, rub-a-dub.
ratear [1a] share out; (*robar*) pilfer,
lift; filch; **ratería** *f* petty larceny,
pilfering; **ratero** 1. light-fingered;
2. *m* pickpocket, small-time thief.
ratificación *f* ratification; **ratificar**
[1g] ratify.
rato *m* (short) time, while, spell; *un*~
(*como adv.*) awhile; *un buen* ~ a good

while; *largo* ~ a long while; ~s *pl.*
perdidos spare time, leisure; *al poco*
~ shortly after; *a* ~s from time to
time; F *pasar el* ~ while away the
time; *pasar un buen* ~ have a good
time; *pasar un mal* ~ have a bad
time of it.
ratón *m,* -a *f* mouse; ~ *de biblioteca*
bookworm; **ratonar** [1a] gnaw,
nibble; **ratonera** *f* mouse-trap;
(*agujero*) mouse-hole.
raudal *m* torrent; *fig.* plenty, abundance; *entrar etc. a* ~es flood in *etc.;*
raudo swift, rushing.
raya *f* stripe, streak *en tela etc.;*
scratch, mark *en piedra etc.;* dash
con pluma (*a. tel.*); line *que subraya
etc.; deportes:* line, mark; parting
de pelo; crease *de pantalón;* boundary, limit; *ichth.* ray, skate; *a* ~
(with)in bounds; *a* ~s *tela* striped;
hacerse la ~ part one's hair; *mantener a* ~ keep off, keep at bay, keep
in check; *pasar de* (*la*) ~ *fig.* go too
far, overstep the mark; *poner a* ~
check, hold back.
rayado 1. striped *etc.;* 2. *m* stripes;
ruling *de papel;* *⊕* rifling.
rayano adjacent; borderline; ~ *en*
bordering on.
rayar [1a] *v/t.* stripe, line, streak;
piedra etc. scratch, score; *papel* rule,
draw lines across; *fusil* rifle; (*tachar*)
cross out; (*subrayar*) underline;
v/i.: ~ *con* border on, be next to;
fig. be equal to, match; ~ *en* border
on (*a. fig.*); *al* ~ *el alba* at first light.
rayo[1] *etc. v. raer.*
rayo[2] *m* (*luz*) ray, beam, shaft;
(*relámpago*) flash of lightning;
thunderbolt *que daña;* spoke *de
rueda;* ~s *pl.* catódicos cathode rays;
~s *pl.* cósmicos cosmic rays; ~s *pl.*
gama gamma-rays; ~ *del* sol sun-
beam; ~s *pl.* X X-rays; *caer como
un* ~ fall like a bombshell; come
down out of nowhere; *entrar* (*salir*)
como un ~ dash in (out); *pasar como
un* ~ flash past.
rayón *m* rayon.
raza[1] *f* race (*a. biol.*); breed, stock,
strain; ~ *humana* human race, man-
kind; *de* ~ *caballo* thoroughbred;
perro etc. pedigree.
raza[2] *f* crack, slit; ray of light.
razón *f* reason; right, justice; *A*
ratio; *S.Am.* message; ~ *de más* all
the more reason; ~ *de ser* raison

d'être; ✝ ~ *social* trade name; *a ~ de* at the rate of; *con ~ o sin ella* rightly or wrongly; *en ~ de* with regard to; *dar ~ de* give an account of, report on; *dar ~ de sí* give an account of o.s.; *meter en ~*, *poner en ~* make *s.o.* see sense; *meterse en ~* listen to reason, see sense; *perder la ~* go mad; *puesto en ~* reasonable; *tener ~* be right; *no tener ~* be wrong; **razonable** reasonable; rational; *aviso, posibilidad etc.* fair; **razonado** reasoned; **razonamiento** *m* reasoning; argument; **razonar** [1a] *v/t.* reason; argue; *problema* reason out; *v/i.* reason; *(dis-)* re[1] ... re .. [*currir*] talk.}

re[2] ... *prefijo de intensificación:* very ...; *rebueno* very good.

reabrir(se) [3a; *p.p. reabierto*] reopen.

reacción *f* reaction (*ante* to); response (*a* to); *~ en cadena* chain reaction; ✖ *a ~* jet(-propelled); **reaccionar** [1a] react (*a, ante* to; *contra* against; *sobre* on); respond (*a* to); **reaccionario** *adj. a. su. m*, **a** *f* reactionary.

reacio obstinate, stubborn.

reacondicionar [1a] recondition.

reactivo *m* reagent; **reactor** *m phys.* reactor; ✖ jet engine; **~generador** *m* breeder reactor.

reafirmar [1a] reaffirm; reassert.

reajustar [1a] readjust; **reajuste** *m* readjustment.

real[1] real; genuine.

real[2] **1.** (*del rey*) royal; *aspecto etc.* kingly; *fig.* royal, splendid, generous; *moza etc.* fine; **2.** *m* fairground; ✝ *coin of 25 cents.*

realce *m* ⊕ raised work, embossing; *paint.* high light; *fig.* lustre, splendour; *fig.* enhancement.

realeza *f* royalty.

realidad *f* reality; truth, sincerity; *en ~* in fact, actually; **realismo** *m* realism; **realista 1.** realistic; **2.** *m/f* realist; **realizable** realizable (*a.* ✝); *objetivo etc.* attainable; **realización** *f* realization (*a.* ✝); fulfilment, achievement; ✝ (*venta*) sale, selling-up; **realizar** [1f] realize (*a.* ✝); *objetivo* fulfil, achieve; *promesa etc.* carry out; ✝ (*vender*) sell out, sell up; *~se* (*sueño etc.*) come true, materialize; **realmente** really, actually; *comer etc.* royally.

realquilar [1a] sublet, sublease; re-let.

realzar [1f] ⊕ emboss, raise; *fig.* enhance, heighten, add to; *paint.* highlight.

reanimar [1a] revive (*a. fig.*); *fig.* encourage; *~se* revive, rally.

reanudación *f* renewal, resumption; **reanudar** [1a] renew; *viaje etc.* resume.

reaparecer [2d] reappear; **reaparición** *f* reappearance; recurrence, return.

reapertura *f* reopening.

reaprovisionar [1a] replenish, restock.

rearmar(se) [1a] re-arm; **rearme** *m* re-armament.

reasegurar [1a] reinsure; **reaseguro** *m* reinsurance.

reasumir [1a] resume, reassume.

reata *f* string of horses *etc.*; (*cuerda*) rope; *de ~* in single file; *fig.* submissively.

rebaja *f* lowering, reduction (*a.* ✝); **rebajamiento** *m = rebaja*; *~ de sí mismo* self-abasement; **rebajar** [1a] reduce (*a.* ✝), lower, cut down; *paint.* tone down; *fig. p.* humble, deflate; *valor* detract from; (*desacreditar*) decry, disparage; *~se* humble o.s.; *~ a inf.* descend to *inf.*, stoop to *inf.*

rebajo *m* ⊕ rabbet; recess.

rebalsa *f* pool, puddle; **rebalsar** [1a] dam (up); *~se* form a pool; become dammed up.

rebanada *f* slice; **rebanar** [1a] slice.

rebaño *m* flock (*a. fig.*), herd.

rebasar [1a] exceed, go beyond, overrun (*a. ~ de*).

rebatible easily refuted; *asiento* tip-up.

rebatiña: F *andar a la ~* scramble, fight (*de* for).

rebatir [3a] *ataque* repel, ward off; *cantidad* reduce; *descuento* deduct; *argumento* rebut, refute.

rebato *m* alarm; ✖ call to arms; ✖ surprise attack; *llamar a ~* sound the alarm.

rebeca *f* cardigan.

rebeco *m* chamois, ibex.

rebelarse [1a] rebel, revolt; resist; **rebelde 1.** rebellious, mutinous; *niño etc.* unruly; stubborn; *ser ~ a fig.* be in revolt against, resist;

2. m/f rebel; ⚖⚖ defaulter; **rebeldía** f rebelliousness, defiance, disobedience; ⚖⚖ default; ⚖⚖ contempt of court; en ~ by default; caer en ~ default; be in contempt; **rebelión** f revolt, rebellion; **rebelón** restive.

reblandecer [2d] soften.

rebolludo thick-set, chunky F.

reborde m ⊕ flange, rim; ledge.

rebosadero m overflow; **rebosante** overflowing (a. fig.; de with), brimful (a. fig.; de of); **rebosar** [1a] run over, overflow (a. fig.; de, en with); ~ en dinero have pots of money; ~ de salud be bursting with health.

rebotar [1a] v/t. clavo etc. clinch; ataque repel; F annoy, upset; v/i. bounce; rebound; (bala) ricochet; ~ de soslayo glance off; **rebote** m bounce; rebound; de ~ on the rebound.

rebozar [1f] muffle up; cocina: roll in flour (or batter etc.); ~se muffle up; **rebozo** m muffler; S.Am. shawl; fig. disguise; de ~ secretly; sin ~ openly, frankly; (adj.) aboveboard.

rebufar [1a] recoil; **rebufo** m recoil.

rebullicio m hubbub, uproar; **rebullir** [3a] stir; show signs of life.

rebusca f search; ✍ gleaning; fig. leavings, remains; **rebuscado** recherché; studied, elaborate; **rebuscar** [1g] search carefully for, hunt out; ✍ glean.

rebuznar [1a] bray; **rebuzno** m bray(ing).

recabar [1a] manage to get.

recadero m messenger; errand-boy; **recado** m message; errand; (regalo) gift; (compras) daily shopping; (seguridad) safety, precaution; v. recaudo; ~ de escribir writing-case; dejar ~ leave a message; enviar a un ~ send on an errand; mander ~ send word.

recaer [2o] fall back, relapse (en into); ✝ suffer a relapse; ~ en heredero pass to; ~ sobre devolve upon; **recaída** f ✝ relapse (a. fig.; en into).

recalar [1a] saturate.

recalcar [1g] (apretar) squeeze, press; cram, stuff (de with); fig. stress; make great play with.

recalcitrante recalcitrant; **recalcitrar** [1a] retreat, back down; resist, be stubborn.

recalentar [1k] overheat; comida etc. warm up.

recalmón m lull.

recamado m embroidery; **recamar** [1a] embroider.

recámara f dressing-room; S.Am. bedroom; ✂ breech (a. ⊕), chamber; F tener mucha ~ be on the careful side.

recambio m ⊕ spare; refill; ✝ re-exchange; de ~ spare.

recapacitar [1a] think over.

recapitulación f recapitulation, summing-up; **recapitular** [1a] recapitulate, sum up.

recargado overloaded; fig. over-elaborate; **recargar** [1h] reload; (demasiado) overload; recharge; (demasiado) overcharge; fig. increase; **recargo** m new burden; extra load; ✝ extra charge, surcharge; increase de impuestos etc.

recatado cautious, circumspect; mujer shy, demure; **recatar** [1a] hide; ~se be cautious; refrain from taking a stand; **recato** m caution; shyness, demureness; modesty.

recaudación f collection; recovery; (oficina) tax office; **recaudador** m: ~ de contribuciones tax-collector; **recaudar** [1a] impuestos collect; deudas recover; fig. watch over, guard; **recaudo** m collection; fig. care, protection; a buen ~ in safe keeping.

recelar [1a] suspect, fear, distrust (a. ~ de, ~se); ~ que suspect that; ~se inf. be afraid of ger.; **recelo** m suspicion, fear; mistrust, misgiving; **receloso** suspicious, distrustful, apprehensive.

recensión f recension.

recepción f reception (a. radio); receipt; admission a academia etc.; (cuarto) drawing-room; reception (desk) en hotel; **receptáculo** m receptacle (a. ♀); holder; **receptivo** receptive; **receptor** m receiver.

receso m S.Am. parl. recess.

receta f cocina: recipe; ✝ prescription; **recetar** [1a] ✝ prescribe.

recial m rapids.

recibidero receivable; **recibidor** m, **-a** f receiver, recipient; receptionist en hotel; **recibimiento** m (cuarto) hall; (grande) reception-room; (acto) reception; **recibir**

[3a] receive; (acoger) welcome, receive, greet; (salir al encuentro de) (go and) meet; título take, receive; ir a ~ (go to) meet; reciben mucho en casa they entertain a good deal; reciben los jueves they receive visitors on Thursdays; ~se de qualify as; **recibo** m = **recibimiento**, **recepción**; ✝ receipt; (cuenta) bill; acusar ~ acknowledge receipt (de of); estar de ~ be at home (to callers); ser de ~ be acceptable.

recién adv. newly; just; lately; ~ **casado** newly wed; ~ **llegado** 1. newly arrived; 2. m, a f newcomer en lugar; late-comer en reunión etc.; ~ **nacido** new-born; ~ **puesto** huevo new-laid; **reciente** recent; pan etc. new, fresh.

recinto m enclosure, compound; precincts; area; place.

recio 1. adj. (fuerte) strong, robust; (grueso) thick, bulky; (duro) hard; (áspero) harsh, rough; voz loud; tiempo severe; 2. adv. hablar loudly.

recipiente m (p.) recipient (a. phys., 🜊); (vaso) vessel, container.

recíproca f 🜊 reciprocal; **reciprocar** [1g] reciprocate; **reciprocidad** f reciprocity; usar de ~ reciprocate; **recíproco** reciprocal.

recitación f recitation; **recitado** m recitation; ♪ recitative; **recital** m recital; **recitar** [1a] recite; **recitativo** adj. a. su. m recitative.

reclamación f claim, demand; objection; protest, complaint; **reclamar** [1a] v/t. claim, lay claim to; press for, demand; socorro etc. beg; ⚖ reclaim; v/i. protest (contra against).

reclamo m orn. (ave) decoy; (grito) call; typ. catchword; fig. lure, inducement; (anuncio) advertisement; slogan; blurb de libro.

reclinar(se) [1a] recline, lean back.

recluir [3g] shut away; ⚖ intern, imprison; **reclusión** f seclusion; ⚖ imprisonment; ~ **perpetua** life imprisonment; **recluso** 1. ⚖ imprisoned; 2. m, a f ⚖ prisoner, inmate; recluse.

recluta 1. m recruit; 2. f = **reclutamiento** m recruitment; **reclutar** [1a] recruit; S.Am. ganado round up.

recobrar [1a] recover, get back;

retrieve; fugitivo recapture; tiempo make up (for); ~se ✗ recover; (volver en sí) come to; fig. collect o.s.; **recobro** m recovery etc.

recocer [2b a. 2h] cook again; (demasiado) overcook; metall. anneal; ~se suffer inwardly.

recodo m turn, bend de camino etc.; loop; ⊕ offset.

recogedor m (p.) picker, harvester; gleaner; (herramienta) rake; scraper; **recoger** [2c] (levantar) pick up; deportes: pelota freq. field, stop; (juntar) collect, gather together; cosecha get in, harvest; frutos pick; noticia pick up, come across; (acoger) take in; (ir por) get, fetch; p. come for; (encoger) contract, draw in; (acortar) shorten; alas fold; ~se withdraw; (acostarse) go to bed, retire; (ir a casa) go home; (refugiarse) take shelter; **recogida** f withdrawal, retirement; 🌾 harvest; 🖂 post, collection; **recogimiento** m (acto) gathering; 🌾 harvesting; eccl. withdrawal, retreat; (estado) seclusion; eccl. quiet time, retreat.

recolección f 🌾 harvest, picking; collection de rentas; gathering de información etc.; (resumen) compilation; eccl. retreat; **recolectar** [1a] 🌾 = recoger.

recomendable recommendable; (aconsejable) advisable; **recomendación** f recommendation; (escrito) reference, testimonial; **recomendar** [1k] recommend; ~ inf. urge to inf.; ~ que request that, ask that.

recomenzar [1f a. 1k] begin again.

recompensa f recompense; reward; compensation (de pérdida for); en ~ in return (de for); **recompensar** [1a] recompense (acc. for); compensate (acc. for); trabajo etc. reward.

recomponer [2r] ⊕ mend, repair; typ. reset.

reconcentrar [1a] concentrate, bring together; sentimiento hide; ~se become absorbed in thought; collect one's wits.

reconciliación f reconciliation **reconciliar** [1b] reconcile.

reconcomio m F suspicion.

recóndito recondite.

reconfortar [1a] comfort; cheer,

encourage; ~se con fortify o.s. with.

reconocer [2d] recognize; know; *culpa, verdad etc. a.* admit, acknowledge; *hechos a.* face; inspect, examine (*a. ⚓*); *terreno* survey; ⚔ reconnoitre; spy out; *reconozco que no es normal* I realize it's not usual; *hay que ~ que* one must admit that; *ya se reconoce que* it is already acknowledged that; **reconocible** recognizable; **reconocido** grateful; **reconocimiento** *m* recognition; admission, acknowledgement; inspection, examination (*a. ⚓*); survey; ⚔ reconnaissance; ⚖ recognizance; (*agradecimiento*) gratitude.

reconquista *f* reconquest; **reconquistar** [1a] reconquer.

reconsiderar [1a] reconsider.

reconstituir [3g] reconstitute, reform; reconstruct; **reconstituyente** *m* tonic, restorative.

reconstrucción *f* reconstruction *etc.*; **reconstruir** [3g] reconstruct; rebuild; *gobierno* reshuffle.

recontar [1m] recount, retell.

reconvención *f* expostulation, remonstrance; ⚖ (counter-)charge; **reconvenir** [3s] reprimand; accuse; ⚖ counter-charge; (*a. ~ a*) expostulate with, remonstrate with.

reconvertir [3i] reconvert.

recopilación *f* summary; compilation; ⚖ code; **recopilar** [1a] compile, collect; *leyes* codify.

record ['rekor] *adj. a. su. m* record.

recordable memorable; **recordación** *f* remembrance; *de feliz ~* of happy memory; **recordar** [1m] *v/t.* remember, recall, recollect; remind (*algo a alguien* a p. of a th.); (*hacer pensar en*) call up, bring to mind; *v/i.*, ~se awaken; **recordativo** reminiscent; *carta ~a* follow-up letter, reminder; **recordatorio** *m* reminder.

recorrer [2a] *país etc.* cross, travel, tour; go through; *plaza etc.* cross; *terreno* (*buscando*) range, scour; *distancia* travel (*a. ⊕*), cover; (*repasar, registrar*) look over, go over, survey; ⊕ repair, overhaul; ~ *de pie* travel on foot, walk; **recorrido** *m* run, journey; (*ruta*) path, route; ✈ flight; distance travelled, run; round *de proveedor*

casero etc.; stroke *de émbolo*; ~ *de aterrizaje* landing run.

recortadito F very particular; **recortar** [1a] *lo sobrante* cut away, cut back, trim; *figura, periódico* cut out; *pelo* trim; *paint.* outline; ~se be outlined, stand out; **recorte** *m* cutting; trim; ~*s pl.* trimmings, clippings; *álbum de ~s* scrap-book.

recostado reclining, recumbent; lying down; **recostar** [1m] lean; ~se lie back, lie down.

recoveco *m* turn, bend *de calle etc.*; ~*s pl.* ins and outs; innermost recesses; *fig.* subterfuges.

recreación *f* recreation; *escuela*: break, playtime; **recrear** [1a] recreate; amuse, entertain; ~se amuse o.s., take recreation.

recrecer [2d] *v/t.* increase; *v/i.* increase; (*ocurrir*) happen again; ~se recover one's good spirits.

recreo *m* recreation, relaxation; amusement; *escuela*: break.

recriminación *f* recrimination; **recriminar** [1a] recriminate; ~se exchange recriminations.

recrudecer [2d] recrudesce, break out again.

recta *f* straight line; *carreras*: the straight; ~ *de llegada* home straight; **rectangular** = **rectángulo 1.** rectangular, oblong; *triángulo etc.* right-angled; **2.** *m* rectangle, oblong.

rectificación *f* rectification; **rectificador** *m* rectifier; **rectificar** [1g] *mst* rectify (*a. fig.*); *trazado etc.* straighten; *cálculo* set right; *cilindro* rebore.

rectilíneo rectilinear.

rectitud *f* straightness; *fig.* rectitude, uprightness; **recto 1.** straight; *ángulo* right; *gr.* literal, proper; *fig.* upright, honest; *juicio* sound; **2.** *m* rectum.

rector 1. governing, managing; **2.** *m* rector; *univ. approx.* vice-chancellor; **3.** *m*, **-a** *f* principal, head *de comunidad.*

recua *f* mule-train; F string, drove.

recubrir [3a; *p.p.* recubierto] recover; cover; ⊕ coat, surface.

recuento *m* recount; inventory; *hacer el ~ de* make a survey of.

recuerdo *m* memory, recollection; (*objeto*) souvenir, momento; ~*s pl.* (*saludo*) regards.

recuero m muleteer.

reculada f recoil; fig. retreat; **recular** [1a] recoil; fig. retreat, fall back; F back down; **reculones: F andar a ~** go backwards.

recuperable recoverable, retrievable; **recuperación** f recovery; **recuperar** [1a] recover, retrieve, recuperate; reclaim; **~se** 🗶 recover, recuperate.

recurrente recurrent; **recurrir** [3a]: **~ a algo** have recourse to, resort to, fall back on; **p.** turn to; **recurso** m recourse, resort; expedient; refuge; ⚖️ appeal; **~s** pl. resources; means.

recusar [1a] ⚖️ reject; challenge.

rechazamiento m rejection etc.; **rechazar** [1f] ataque repel, beat off; oferta reject, refuse, turn down; tentación resist; ⚖️, proyecto de ley reject; **rechazo** m rebound de pelota; recoil de cañón; fig. repulse; **de ~** on the rebound; fig. as a result.

rechifla f (silbo) whistle; hiss; esp. thea. catcall; (silbos) whistling etc.; fig. derision; **rechiflar** [1a] whistle (v/t. at), hiss, catcall.

rechinamiento m creak(ing) etc.; **rechinar** [1a] (madera etc.) creak; (ludir dos cosas) grate, grind; (maquinaria) clank; (motor) whirr, hum; (sonido agudo) squeak; fig. do s.t. with an ill grace; hacer ~ dientes gnash, grind; **rechino** m creak(ing) etc.

rechoncho F thick-set, stocky; squat; plump, tubby.

rechupete: F de ~ comida scrumptious; jolly good.

red f net (a. fig.); (mallas) mesh(es) (a. fig.); 🚂 etc. network, system; agua, ⚡ mains; fig. trap, snare; **~ de alambre** wire-netting; **~ barredera** trawl; **caer en la ~** fig. fall into the trap.

redacción f (acto) writing, redaction; editing; wording; (oficina) newspaper office; (ps.) editorial staff; **redactar** [1a] write; draft, word; periódico edit; **redactor** m, **-a** f (jefe) editor; (subordinado) sub-editor.

redada f (acto) cast; (cantidad) catch, haul (a. fig.); sweep por policía.

redaños m/pl. F pluck, guts.

redarguir [3g] turn an argument against its proposer; ⚖️ impugn.

redecilla f small net; hair-net para\
rededor: al ~ v. alrededor. [pelo.∫

redención f redemption (a. ✝); **redentor 1.** redeeming; redemptive; **2.** m, **-a** f redeemer; ♀ Redeemer.

redicho F affected, refined.

redil m sheep-fold, pen.

redimible redeemable; **redimir** [3a] redeem; cautivo ransom.

rédito m interest, yield, return; **redituar** [1e] yield, produce.

redoblado stocky, thick-set; paso double-quick; **redoblante** m drum; **redoblar** [1a] v/t. redouble; (replegar) bend back, bend over; clavo clinch; v/i. ♪ play a roll on the drum; **redoble** m ♪ drumroll; roll, rumble de trueno.

redoma f flask, phial.

redomado sly, artful; (completo) out-and-out, utter.

redonda: a la ~ round (about); de la ~ in the neighbourhood, of the area; **redondear** [1a] round off; round; **~se** get to be well off; get clear of debts; **redondel** m bullring, arena; **redondez** f roundness; en toda la ~ de la tierra in the whole wide world; **redondilla** f quatrain; **redondo** round (a. fig.); fig. (sin rodeos) square, straightforward; en ~ around; 2 metros en ~ 2 metres round; caer ~ fall senseless.

red(r)opelo m F row; **al ~** the wrong way; against the grain; traer al ~ ride rough-shod over.

redro F (detrás) behind; (atrás) backwards.

redrojo m (p.) puny child, runt.

reducción f reduction, cut; (copia) miniature version; 🗶 setting; **reducible** reducible; **reducido** reduced; limited; número etc. freq. small; precio low; espacio limited, confined, narrow; **reducir** [3f] reduce (a. fig.; a, hasta to); diminish, lessen, cut; fortaleza reduce; país subdue; 🗶 hueso set; **~se** lessen etc.; fig. economize.

reducto m ⚔ redoubt.

reduje m etc. v. reducir.

redundante redundánt, superfluous; **redundar** [1a]: **~ en** redound to.

reedificar [1g] rebuild.
reeditar [1a] republish, reprint; re-edit.
reeducación f re-education.
reelegible re-eligible; **reelegir** [3c a. 3l] re-elect.
reembolsable repayable; ✝ no ~ irredeemable; **reembolsar** [1a] p. reimburse, repay; dinero pay back, refund; ~se reimburse o.s.; dinero recover; **reembolso** m reimbursement; repayment, refund; envío etc. contra ~ cash on delivery.
reemplazar [1f] replace (con with, by), change (con for); **reemplazo** m (acto, p.) replacement; ✗ reserve; ✗ de ~ reserve.
reenviar [1c] forward; (devolver) send back.
reestreno m thea. revival.
reexpedir [3l] carta forward.
refacción f refreshment; S.Am. repair(s); F extra, bonus.
refectorio m refectory.
referencia f reference (a. ✝, recomendación sobre p.); account, report; **referente**: ~ a relating to; **referéndum** m referendum; **referir** [3i] recount, report; cuento tell; ~ que say that; ~ a (dirigir) refer to; ~se a refer to; apply to; por lo que se refiere a as regards, as for.
refilón: mirar de ~ take a quick look at.
refinación f refining; **refinado** refined; **refinadura** f refining; **refinamiento** m fig. refinement; nicety; neatness; **refinar** [1a] refine; estilo etc. polish; **refinería** f refinery; **refino** refined, extra fine.
reflector m reflector; ✗ etc. searchlight; mot. ~ posterior rear reflector; **reflejar** [1a] reflect; mirror; reveal; ~se be reflected; **reflejo 1.** luz reflected; acto reflex; verbo reflexive; **2.** m reflection; gleam, glint; physiol. reflex (action); **reflexión** f reflection, thought; **reflexionar** [1a] v/t. reflect on, think about; v/i. reflect (en, sobre on), muse; think, pause antes de obrar; **reflexivo** thoughtful, reflective; gr. reflexive.
refluir [3g] flow back; **reflujo** m ebb (tide); fig. retreat.
refocilación f (huge) enjoyment, (great) pleasure; (alegría) cheer-

fulness; **refocilar** [1a] give (great) pleasure to; (alegrar) cheer up; ~se con enjoy (hugely), have a fine time with; **refocilo** m = refocilación.
reforma f reform; reformation; (mejora) improvement; ♀ Reformation; ~s pl. ⚠ alterations, repairs; ~ agraria land reform; **reformación** f reform(ation); **reformado** reformed; **reformador** m -a f reformer; **reformar** [1a] reform; (mejorar) improve; revise, reorganize; abusos put right, correct; ⊕ mend, repair; ⚠ alter, repair; ~se reform; (contenerse) restrain o.s.; **reformatorio** m reformatory; **reformista** m/f reformer.
reforzador m ⚡ booster; phot. intensifier; **reforzar** [1f a. 1m] reinforce (a. ✗), strengthen; boost (a. ⚡); fig. buttress, bolster up; (animar) encourage.
refracción f refraction; **refractar** [1a] refract; **refractario** fireproof; fig. refractory, recalcitrant; ser ~ a resist.
refrán m proverb, saying; como dice el ~ as the saying goes.
refregar [1h a. 1k] rub; F dress down, tick off; **refregón** m rub(bing).
refrenar [1a] caballo rein back, rein in; fig. curb, restrain.
refrendar [1a] endorse, countersign; authenticate.
refrescar [1g] v/t. refresh; cool; acción renew; memoria refresh, jog; v/i., ~se (tiempo) cool down, get cooler; (salir) take the air; (beber) take a drink; **refresco** m soft drink; ~s pl. refreshments.
refriega f scuffle, affray.
refrigeración f refrigeration; cooling de motor; ~ por agua water-cooling; **refrigerador** m refrigerator; **refrigerante** refrigerating, cooling; ♒ refrigerant (a. su. m); **refrigerar** [1a] refrigerate; cool; refresh; **refrigerio** m refreshment; cooling drink; fig. relief.
refuerzo m strengthening; brace; ~s pl. reinforcements.
refugiado m, a f refugee; **refugiarse** [1b] take refuge; shelter; go into hiding; se refugió en

Francia he fled to France; **refugio**
m refuge, shelter (*a. fig.*); *eccl.*
sanctuary; *fig.* haven; ~ *antiaéreo*
air-raid shelter; ✗ ~ *subterráneo*
dug-out.

refulgente brilliant, refulgent.

refundición *f* revision, recasting;
(*obra*) adaptation; **refundir** [3a] ⊕
recast; *fig.* revise; *texto* remodel,
adapt, rewrite.

refunfuñar [1a] grunt, growl;
(*murmurar*) grumble; **refunfuño** *m*
grunt, growl; grumble.

refutación *f* refutation; **refutar**
[1a] refute.

regadera *f* watering-can; (*reguera*)
irrigation ditch; sprinkler *para
calle etc.*; **regadío 1.** irrigable;
tierra ~*a*, *tierra de* ~ = **2.** irrigated
land; **regadura** *f* watering, irrigation; sprinkling.

regala *f* gunwale.

regalado dainty, delicate; *vida etc.*
of luxury, comfortable, pleasant;
regalar [1a] *regalo* give; (*dar gratis*) make a present of, give away;
(*acariciar*) caress, fondle; (*halagar*)
make a fuss of; (*convidar*) treat (*con*
to), regale (*con* on, with); *dar medio
regalado* sell for a song; *no lo quisiera ni* ~ I wouldn't want it at any
price; ~*se* regale o.s. (*con* on, with);
indulge o.s.

regalía *f fig.* perquisite, privilege;
bonus; ~*s pl.* royal prerogatives.

regaliz *m*, **regaliza** *f* liquorice.

regalo *m* gift, present; (*comida*)
treat, delicacy; *fig.* pleasure;
comfort, luxury; *de* ~ *entrada*
complimentary; **regalón** F *p.*
pampered, spoiled; *vida* soft,
comfortable.

regañadientes: *a* ~ reluctantly.

regañar [1a] *v/t.* F scold; nag (at);
v/i. (*perro*) snarl, growl; (*p.*) grouse;
(*dos ps.*) quarrel; **regaño** *m* snarl,
growl; (*gesto*) scowl; *fig.* grouse; F
scolding; **regañón** *p.* grumbling,
irritable; *mujer* ~*a* shrew, virago.

regar [1h *a.* 1k] *planta* water; *tierra*
water, irrigate; *calle* hose; *geog.*
(*río*) water; spray *con insecticida
etc.*; (*esparcir*) sprinkle, scatter.

regata¹ *f* ↯ irrigation ditch.

regata² *f* ↯ (*carrera*) race; (*conjunto de carreras*) regatta.

regate *m* swerve, dodge (*a.* F);
regatear¹ [1a] *v/t.* haggle over;

bargain away; (*por menor*) sell
retail; *v/i.* haggle, bargain; F
bicker; F (*hurtar el cuerpo*) swerve,
duck, dodge.

regatear² [1a] ↯ race.

regateo *m* haggling *etc.*; **regatón**¹
1. haggling; F niggling, argumentative; **2.** *m* retailer.

regatón² *m* ferrule *de bastón*.

regazo *m* lap (*a. fig.*).

regencia *f* regency.

regeneración *f* regeneration;
regenerar [1a] regenerate; ⊕
reclaim.

regentar [1a] manage, direct;
preside over; *cátedra* occupy, hold;
b.s. domineer, boss F; **regente
1.** *príncipe* regent; *director etc.*
managing; *fig.* ruling; **2.** *m/f* (*real*)
regent; manager *de fábrica, finca*;
typ. foreman.

regicida *m/f* regicide (*p.*); **regicidio** *m* regicide (*act*).

régimen *m pol.* régime; ✚ diet;
(*reglas*) rules, regulations; system,
regimen; *gr.* government; ~ *alimenticio* diet; ~ *lácteo* milk diet;
regimiento *m* administration *etc.*;
✗ regiment.

regio royal, regal; *apariencia* regal,
kingly; *fig.* royal.

región *f* region; part, area; *anat.*
tract, region; **regional** regional;
local; **regionalismo** *m* region-
alism.

regir [3c *a.* 3l] *v/t. país etc.* rule,
govern (*a. gr.*); *sociedad etc.*
manage, control; (*conducir*) guide,
steer; *v/i.* (*ley, precio*) be in force;
(*condición*) prevail; ↯ obey the
helm; *el mes que rige* the present
month; ~*se por* be ruled by, go by.

registrador *m* recorder, registrar;
inspector; register; **registrar** [1a]
hecho register, record; *partida etc.*
enter; file *en archivo*; *voz etc.*
record; (*examinar*) survey, inspect,
look through; *equipaje* examine; *p.*,
sitio search; **registro** *m* (*acto*)
registration; (*libro, archivo*) register, record; (*archivos*) registry,
record office; (*partida*) entry;
recording *en disco etc.*; ♪ (*extensión, altura*) register; ♪ stop *de
órgano*; ♪ pedal *de piano*; regulator
de reloj; bookmark(er) *para libro*;
damper *de estufa*; (*abertura*) manhole; *typ.* register; survey, inspec-

tion; examination; search; ~ *domiciliario* search of a house; ~ *parroquial* parish register.

regla *f* rule (*a.* ♉, *deportes, eccl.*); regulation; (*base*) law, principle; ruler *para trazar líneas*; order, discipline; ~**s** *pl.* ♪ period; ~ *de cálculo* slide-rule; ~ T T-square; ~ *de tres* rule of three; *en* ~ in order; *por* ~ *general* as a rule; on the average; *hacerse una* ~ *de inf.* make it a rule to *inf.*; *salir de* ~ *go too far*; *ser de* ~ be the rule; **reglaje** *m* ⊕ overhaul; adjustment.

reglamentación *f* regulation; **reglamentar** [1a] regulate, provide regulations for; **reglamentario** regulation *attr.*, set; statutory; **reglamento** *m* regulation, rule; (*código*) rules and regulations; standing order *de asamblea*; by-law *de sociedad, municipio*; ~ *del tráfico* rule of the road.

reglar [1a] *línea* rule; *fig.* regulate; ~**se** *por* conform to, be guided by.

regleta *f* *typ.* space; **regletear** [1a] *typ.* space out.

regocijado merry; exultant; *carácter* jolly, cheerful; **regocijar** [1a] gladden, cheer (up); ~**se** rejoice (*de, por* at); make merry; exult (*por* at, in); **regocijo** *m* joy, rejoicing; elation; gaiety, merriment; ~**s** *pl.* festivities.

regodearse [1a] F crack jokes; ~ *con,* ~ *en* delight in; **regodeo** *m* F delight; amusement.

regoldar [1m] belch.

regordete F chubby, dumpy.

regosto *m* craving (*de* for).

regresar [1a] go back, come back, return; **regresión** *f* regression; retreat; **regresivo** re(tro)gressive; **regreso** *m* return.

regüeldo *m* belch(ing).

reguera *f* irrigation ditch; ⚓ moorings; **reguero** *m* ⚮ irrigation ditch; trickle *de sangre etc.*; (*señal*) streak, track; ~ *de pólvora* train of gunpowder.

regulable adjustable; **regulación** *f* regulation; adjustment; control; **regulador** *m* ⊕ regulator, throttle; governor; control; *radio:* (control) knob; *radio:* ~ *de volumen* volume control; **regular 1.** regular (*a.* ♉, *eccl.*); (*mediano*) fair, middling; medium; F *salud, progreso etc.* fair,

so-so; (*conveniente*) suitable; normal, usual; *por lo* ~ as a rule; **2.** *m eccl.* regular; **3.** [1a] regulate; *esp.* ⊕ adjust; *precios etc.* control; *reloj* put right; *despertador etc.* negocios etc. put in order; **regularidad** *f* regularity; **regularizar** [1f] regularize; standardize.

regurgitar [1a] regurgitate.

rehabilitación *f* rehabilitation; **rehabilitar** [1a] rehabilitate; reinstate *en oficio*; *casa* restore, renovate; ⊕ overhaul.

rehacer [2s] redo, do again; *objeto* remake; (*reparar*) mend, repair; ~**se** ♪ recover; ⚔ rally; **rehecho** *p.* thick-set.

rehén *m* hostage.

rehilar [1a] quiver, reel; (*flecha*) whizz; **rehilete** *m* dart; (*volante*) shuttlecock; *fig.* dig, cutting remark.

rehuir [3g] (*apartar*) remove; (*evitar*) avoid, decline.

rehusar [1a] refuse (*inf.* to *inf.*), decline, turn down.

reidero F laughable; **reidor** laughing, merry.

reimpresión *f* reprint; **reimprimir** [3a] reprint.

reina *f* queen (*a. ajedrez, abeja*); ~ *madre* queen mother; **reinado** *m* reign; **reinante** reigning; prevailing; **reinar** [1a] reign; rule; (*condiciones*) prevail.

reincidir [3a] relapse (*en* into); backslide.

reincorporarse [1a]: ~ *a* rejoin.

reino *m* kingdom.

reinstalar [1a] reinstall; *p.* reinstate.

reintegración *f* ✝ refund, reimbursement; restitution *etc.*; **reintegrar** [1a] ✝ refund, pay back; restore; ~**se** *a* return to; ~ *de* recover, recoup; **reintegro** *m* restoration, restitution.

reinvertir [3i] reinvest; plough back.

reír(se) [3m] laugh (*de* at, over); F (*vestido*) tear; ~ *con alguien* laugh at s.o.'s jokes; ~ *de* (*burlarse*) laugh at, make fun of; *cosa de* ~ joke.

reja *f* grating, grid(iron); grille; bar(s) *de ventana*; ~ (*del arado*) plough-share; **rejado** *m* grille, grating; **rejilla** *f* grating; lattice; screen; wickerwork *de silla etc.*; 🧳 luggage-rack; *radio*: grid, grille; small stove; **rejo** *m* spike, sharp point; *zo.* sting; *fig.* vigour; **rejón** *m* pointed iron bar; *toros*: lance.

rejuvenecer [2d] *v/t.* rejuvenate; *v/i.*, **~se** be rejuvenated.

relación *f* (*conexión*) relation(ship) (con to, with); (*narración*) account, statement, report; tale, recital *de dificultades etc.*; (*informe oficial*) record, return; list; ⚖ ratio; proportion; **~es** *pl.* relation(ship); (*amorosas*) courting, courtship; *llevan 2 años de* **~s** they've been courting 2 years; *buenas* **~s** *pl.* good relations; **~es** *pl.* comerciales business connexions, trade relations; ✝ **~es** *pl.* personales personnel management; **~es** *pl.* públicas public relations; *no guardar* **~** *con* be out of proportion to, bear no relation to; *mantener* **~es** *con* keep in touch with; **relacionado** related; **~** *con* that has to do with; bound up with; **relacionar** [1a] relate (con to); connect (*con* with); **~se** be related; **~** *con* relate to; *p.* get to know.

relai(s) [re'le] *m* ⚡ relay.

relajación *f* relaxation *etc.*; laxity *de moralidad*; ✚ hernia; **relajado** *vida* dissolute; **relajar** [1a] relax, slacken, loosen; *moralidad* weaken; (*distraer*) relax, amuse; **~se** relax; ✚ be ruptured; (*moralidad*) become lax.

relamerse [2a] lick one's lips; *labios* smack, lick; *fig.* gloat (de over); (*afeitarse*) paint one's face; **relamido** prim and proper; affected, too-too F; (*pulcro*) overdressed.

relámpago 1. *m* lightning, flash (*a. fig.*); *pasar como un* **~** go by like lightning; **2.** *attr.* lightning; **relampagueante** lightning; flashing; **relampaguear** [1a] lighten; flash (*a. fig.*); **relampagueo** *m* lightning; flashing.

relanzar [1f] repel, repulse.

relatar [1a] relate, report; *anécdota* tell.

relatividad *f* relativity; **relativo 1.** relative (*a. gr.*; *a* to); comparative; **~** *a* regarding, relating to; **2.** *m gr.* relative.

relato *m* story, tale; (*informe*) report; **relator** *m* narrator, teller; ⚖ court reporter.

releer [2e] re-read.

relegación *f* relegation; exile; **relegar** [1h] relegate; (*desterrar*) exile; **~** *al olvido* banish from memory.

relevación *f* relief (*a.* ⚔); replacement *etc.*; **relevante** outstanding; **relevar** [1a] *v/t.* ⊕ emboss, carve in relief; relieve (*de cargo etc.* of; *a.* ⚔); absolve, exonerate (*de culpa* from); *empleado* replace; *v/i.* stand out; **relevo** *m* relief (*a.* ⚔); (*deportes*: **~s** *pl.* relay (race).

relicario *m* shrine; (*caja*) reliquary.

relieve *m* relief; *fig.* prominence; **~s** *pl.* left-overs; *bajo* **~** bas-relief; *de* **~** *fig.* of importance; *en* **~** in relief, raised; *estampar en* **~** emboss; *poner de* **~** set off (*contra* against); *fig.* emphasize, point out.

religión *f* religion; religious sense, piety; *entrar en* **~** take vows; **religiosa** *f* nun; **religioso 1.** religious (*a. fig.*); **2.** *m* monk.

relimpio F spick and span.

relinchar [1a] neigh, whinny; **relincho** *m* neigh(ing), whinny.

reliquia *f* relic; **~s** *pl.* ⚔ after-effects; *fig.* relics, traces *del pasado etc.*; remains; **~** *de familia* heirloom.

reloj *m* (*grande*) clock; (*portátil*) watch; ⊕ clock, meter; **~** *de arena* sand-glass, hour-glass; **~** *automático* timer; **~** *de bolsillo* pocket watch; **~** *de caja* grandfather clock; **~** *despertador* alarm-clock; **~** *de estacionamiento* parking meter; **~** *de pulsera* wrist watch; **~** *de sol* sun-dial; *como un* **~** like clockwork; *contra el* **~** against the clock; F *estar como un* **~** feel on top of the world; **relojería** *f* (*arte*) watch-making; (*tienda*) watch-maker's shop; (*aparato de*) **~** clockwork; *v. bomba*; **relojero** *m* watch-maker.

reluciente shining, brilliant; glittering, gleaming; sparkling; **relucir** [3f] shine (*a. fig.*); glitter, gleam; sparkle; *sacar a* **~** bring out, show off.

relumbrar [1a] shine; sparkle; glare; **relumbrón** *m* flash; glare; *de* **~** flashy; *vestirse de* **~** dress flashily.

rellano *m* ◭ landing.

rellenado *m* replenishment *etc.*; **rellenar** [1a] refill, replenish; (*henchir*) stuff, cram; pad; *pollo* stuff; ~se F stuff o.s.; **relleno 1.** full, packed; *cocina*: stuffed; **2.** *m* filling, stuffing; padding (*a. fig.*), wadding; *cocina*: stuffing.

remachar [1a] ⊕ *clavo* clinch; *metales* rivet; *fig.* drive home; **remache** *m* rivet; (*acto*) riveting *etc.*

remada *f* stroke; **remador** *m* oarsman.

remanente 1. *phys.* remanent; ⚓ *etc.* surplus.

remansarse [1a] form a pool; eddy; become stagnant; **remanso** *m* pool; eddy; backwater.

remar [1a] row; *fig.* toil.

rematado hopeless, out-and-out; *loco* raving; *tonto* utter; **rematante** *m* highest bidder; **rematar** [1a] *v/t. p., trabajo* finish off; ⚔ *etc.* top, crown; *subasta*: knock down (*a* to, en for); *v/i.* end (⚔ en in); *deportes*: shoot, score; ~se be ruined; **remate** *m* (*fin*) end; (*toque*) finishing touch; ⚔ *etc.* top, crest; (*postura*) highest bid; (*adjudicación*) sale; *bridge*: bidding, auction; de ~ utterly, completely; *tonto etc.* utter; *por ~* finally; *poner ~ a* cap, top.

remedar [1a] imitate, copy; (*para burlarse*) ape, mimic.

remediable that can be remedied; **remediar** [1b] *perjuicio etc.* remedy; *daño etc.* repair; save, help *en peligro*; (*evitar*) prevent (*que* from *ger.*); **remedio** *m* remedy; help; ⚕ recourse; *sin ~* inevitable, having nothing to stop it; F *ni para un ~* not for love nor money; *no hay ~ para él* it's all up with him; *no hay más ~* there's no help for it; *no hay más ~ que inf.* the only thing is to *inf.*; *no tener ~* be unavoidable; (*p. etc.*) be past redemption; *no tengo más ~ que inf.* I have no alternative but to *inf.*

remedo *m* imitation; *b.s.* poor imitation, travesty.

remendar [1k] mend, repair, patch; *fig.* correct; **remendón** *m* cobbler.

remero *m* oarsman.

remesa *f* remittance; shipment, consignment; **remesar** [1a] *dinero* remit, send; *mercancías* send, ship, consign.

remiendo *m* (*acto*) mending *etc.*; (*tela etc.*) mend, patch; spot *en piel*; *fig.* correction; *a ~s* piecemeal.

remilgado (*gazmoño*) prudish,

prim; (*afectado*) affected, overnice; (*delicado*) finicky, fussy; squeamish; **remilgarse** [1h] be fussy *etc.*; **remilgo** *m* prudery; affectation; (*mueca*) simper, smirk.

reminiscencia *f* reminiscence; ♪ *a. fig.* echo.

remirado over-cautious, excessively scrupulous; pernickety; **remirar** [1a] look at again; ~se take great pains (en over).

remisión *f* (*envío*) sending; forgiveness *de pecado etc.*; **remiso** slack, remiss; *movimiento* sluggish; **remisor** *m S.Am.* ⚓ sender; **remitente 1.** ⚓ remittent; **2.** *m/f* sender; **remitir** [3a] *v/t.* send, remit; *pena etc.* forgive, pardon; *lector* refer (*a* to); *sesión* adjourn; *v/i.* slacken, let up; *remite* (*en sobre*) sender; ~se *a* refer to.

remo *m* oar; (*deporte*) rowing; *fig. anat.* arm, leg; *fig.* toil; *a ~ y vela fig.* speedily; *andar al ~* be hard at it; *pasar a(l) ~* row across.

remoción *f* removal.

remojar [1a] soak, steep; dip; F celebrate with a drink; **remojo** *m* soaking *etc.*; *dejar etc. en ~* soak, steep; **remojón** *m* soaking *etc.*

remolacha *f* beet(root); ~ *azucarera* sugar-beet; *azúcar de ~* beet-sugar; *raíz de ~* beetroot.

remolcador *m* ⚓ tug; **remolcar** [1g] (take in) tow; tug; *avión remolcado* sailplane.

remoler [2h] grind up small.

remolin(e)ar(se) [1a] (*agua*) swirl, eddy; whirl, spin *en aire*; (*gente etc.*) swirl, mill around, crowd together; **remolino** *m* (*agua*) swirl, eddy; whirlpool; (*aire*) whirl, whirlwind; (*polvo*) whirl, cloud; (*pelo*) tuft; (*gente*) throng, crush.

remolón 1. slack, lazy; **2.** *m*, **-a** *f* shirker, slacker; *hacerse el ~* = **remolonear** [1a] F shirk, slack; skulk; (*no moverse*) refuse to budge.

remolque *m* towing; (*cable*) tow-rope; (*cosa remolcada*) tow, ship *etc.* on tow; *mot.* trailer; caravan *para turismo*; *a ~* on tow; *dar ~ a* take in tow; *llevar al ~* tow.

remonta *f* ✂ remount; cavalry horses; mending, repair; **remontar** [1a] ✂ remount; *zapatos etc.* mend, repair; *río* go up; *fig.* raise; ~se rise, tower; ⚔ soar (*a. fig.*); *fig.* get excited; ~ *a* go (*or* date) back to.

remoquete *m* punch; *fig.* cutting remark; F (*nombre*) nickname; F (*amoroso*) flirting, spooning; F *dar ~ a* bother.

rémora *f fig.* hindrance.

remorder [2h] *fig. p.* cause remorse to; *conciencia* nag, prick; *mente* prey upon; ~**se** show remorse; **remordimiento** *m* remorse, regret; pang of conscience.

remoto remote (*a. fig.*).

remover [2h] *p., cosa* remove, move; (*agitar*) stir, shake up; *tierra* turn over, dig up; *sentimientos* disturb, upset; **removimiento** *m* removal.

remozarse [1f] look much younger.

rempujar [1a] F push, shove, jostle; **rempujón** *m* F push, shove.

remuneración *f* remuneration; **remunerador** remunerative; rewarding; **remunerar** [1a] remunerate; reward.

renacer [2d] be reborn; ♀ appear again; ✚ recover; *fig.* revive; *hacer ~* revive; **renacimiento** *m* rebirth; revival; ♀ Renaissance.

renacuajo *m* tadpole; F shrimp, runt.

renal kidney *attr.*, renal ⚕.

rencilla *f* (*disputa*) quarrel; (*odio de sangre*) feud; (*rencor*) bad blood, ill-will; *me tiene ~* he's got it in for me; **rencilloso** quarrelsome.

rencor *m* ill-feeling, spite(fulness), rancour; *guardar ~* have a grudge, bear malice (*a* against); **rencoroso** spiteful; vicious, malicious.

rendición *f* surrender; ✝ yield, profits; **rendido** obsequious, submissive; *admirador* humble; ~ (*de cansancio*) worn-out.

rendija *f* crack, crevice, chink; aperture; *fig.* rift, split.

rendimiento *m* ⊕ (*producto*) output; ⊕ efficiency, performance; ✝ yield; *fig.* obsequiousness; (*cansancio*) exhaustion; **rendir** [3l] **1.** *v/t.* (*conquistar*) *país* conquer, subdue; defeat; *fortaleza* take; (*entregar*) surrender; (*sujetar*) overcome; (*devolver*) return, give back; ✝ *producto* produce; *ganancia etc.* yield; *interés, fruto* bear; *gracias* give, render; *homenaje* pay, do; ✗ *guardia* hand over; (*cansar*) tire, wear out; F throw up; *le rindió el*

sueño sleep overcame him; **2.** *v/i.*: *~ bien* yield well; *este negocio no rinde* this business does not pay; **3.** ~**se** ✗ surrender; yield, give up; (*cansarse*) wear o.s. out; *~ a evidencia* bow to.

renegado 1. renegade; F gruff, bad-tempered; **2.** *m, a f* renegade, turncoat; F nasty piece of work; **renegar** [1h *a.* 1k] *v/t.* deny vigorously; detest; *v/i.* turn renegade, *eccl.* apostatize; blaspheme; *~ de* forsake, disown; detest.

renglón *m* line; *leer entre ~es* read between the lines; F *poner unos ~es a* drop a line to.

renguear [1a] *S.Am.* limp.

reniego *m* curse, oath.

reno *m* reindeer.

renombrado renowned; **renombre** *m* renown, fame; (*apellido*) surname.

renovable renewable; **renovación** *f* renewal; renovation; *paint.* redecoration; *etc.*; **renovar** [1m] renew; renovate; *cuarto* redecorate; *aviso etc.* repeat; *moda* reintroduce; *país, organización* transform, reorganize.

renquear [1a] limp.

renta *f* (*ingresos*) income; interest, return; (*acciones*) stock; *~ nacional* national income; *~s pl. públicas* revenue; *~ vitalicia* annuity; **rentar** [1a] yield, produce; **rentero** *m* tenant farmer; **rentista** *m/f* (*accionista*) stockholder; rentier, person of independent means; financial expert; **rentístico** financial.

renuencia *f* reluctance.

renuevo *m* ♀ shoot, sprout; (*acto*) renewal.

renuncia *f* renunciation, surrender; resignation *etc.*; **renunciar** [1b] *v/t.* (*a. v/i. ~ a*) *derecho etc.* renounce (en in favour of), surrender; relinquish; *demanda* drop, waive; *proyecto, hábito* give up; *puesto* resign; *trono* abdicate; *v/i. naipes*: revoke; **renuncio** *m* revoke; F lie, fib; F *coger en un ~* catch out, show up.

reñidero *m*: ~ (*de gallos*) cockpit.

reñido *p.* on bad terms, at odds (con with); *batalla* bitter; *en lo más ~ de* in the thick of; **reñir** [3h *a.* 3l] *v/t.* scold, tell off; *v/i.* (*disputar*) quarrel; (*pelear*) fight, come to blows; (*enemistarse*) fall out (*con with*).

reo *m/f* culprit, offender, criminal; ⚥ defendant, accused.

reojo: *mirar de* ～ look askance (at); F look scornfully at.

reorganización *f* reorganization; **reorganizar** [1f] reorganize.

reorientar [1a] reorientate, read-just.

reóstato *m* rheostat.

repanchigarse, repantigarse [1h] loll (about), lounge, sprawl.

reparación *f* ⊕ repair(ing), mend-ing; *fig.* reparation, redress; ～es *pl.* repairs.

reparador 1. faultfinding; *alimento* fortifying; **2.** *m*, -a *f* ⊕ repairer; (*criticón*) faultfinder, critical ob-server.

reparar [1a] *v/t.* ⊕ repair, mend; (*satisfacer*) make good, make amends for; *fortunas* retrieve; *fuerzas* restore; *error* correct; *golpe* parry; = *v/i.*: = ～ en notice; pay at-tention to; ～se check o.s., restrain o.s.

reparo *m* ⊕ *etc.* repairs; ⚕ restora-tion; 🖋 restorative; criticism; doubt, objection; protection; *fenc.* parry; *poner* ～*s a* raise objections to; find fault with; **reparón** F **1.** critical, faultfinding; **2.** *m*, -a *f* faultfinder.

repartición *f* distribution; division; sharing-out; **repartidor** *m* distri-butor; **repartimiento** *m* distribu-tion; **repartir** [3a] distribute, divide, share (out); parcel out; *tareas etc.* allot; *territorio* partition; *octavillas, vasos etc.* give out, hand round; 🖊 deliver; *naipes:* deal; *castigos* mete out; *thea. papeles* cast; **reparto** *m* = *repartición*; 🖊 delivery; *thea.* cast.

repasar [1a] *lugar* pass by again; *calle* go along again; *fig.* re-examine, review; *texto, lección* read (or go) over; *ropa* mend; *mecanismo etc.* check, overhaul; **repasata** *f* F ticking-off; **repaso** *m* review, revision *etc.*; *sew.* mending; ⊕ check-up, overhaul; F ticking-off; ～ *general* general overhaul; *curso de* ～ refresher course; *ropa de* ～ mending.

repatriado 1. repatriated; **2.** *m*, a *f* repatriate; **repatriar** [1b] repa-

triate; send home; ～se return home.

repecho *m* sharp gradient, steep slope; *a* ～ uphill.

repelente repulsive; repellent; **re-peler** [2a] repel, repulse; *idea etc.* reject.

repensar [1k] reconsider, rethink.

repente *m* start, sudden movement; *fig.* sudden impulse; ～ (*de ira*) fit of anger; *de* ～ suddenly, all at once; **repentino** sudden; swift; *vuelta* sharp; **repentizar** [1f] ♪ sight-read, improvise; **repentón** *m* F violent start.

repercusión *f* repercussion (*a. fig.*), reverberation; **repercutir(se)** [3a] (*cuerpo*) rebound; (*sonido*) reverber-ate, re-echo; *fig.* ～ *en* have reper-cussions on.   [index, repertory.\]

repertorio *m thea. etc.* repertoire;/

repetición *f* repetition; recurrence; *thea.* encore; **repetir** [3l] *v/t.* re-peat; do *etc.* again; *sonido* echo; *lo grabado* play back; *lección etc.* recite, rehearse; *v/i.* repeat; ～se (*p.*) repeat o.s.; (*pintor etc.*) copy o.s.; (*suceso*) recur.

repicar [1g] *campana* ring, peal; *carne* chop up small; ～se boast.

repintar [1a] repaint; ～se use too much make-up.

repipi F (*redicho*) posh, lah-di-dah; arty; (*resabido*) know-all; *niña* ～ little madam.

repique *m* peal(ing), chime; F tiff, squabble; **repiquete** *m* merry (*or* lively) peal; ⚔ clash; **repiquetear** [1a] *campana* ring merrily; ～se F squabble, wrangle; **repiqueteo** *m* merry pealing; rapping, tapping; clatter *de máquina*.

repisa *f* ledge, shelf; bracket; ～ *de chimenea* mantelpiece; ～ *de ventana* windowsill.

replantar [1a] replant.

replegable folding; ⚙ retractable; **replegar** [1h *a.* 1k] fold over; re-fold; ⚙ retract; ～se ⚔ fall back (*sobre* on).

repleto replete, cram-full; obese.

réplica *f* answer, argument; retort, rejoinder; *b.s.* back-chat F; **repli-car** [1g] retort, rejoin; *b.s.* argue, answer back; **replicón** F argumen-tative, saucy; **repliegue** *m* fold, crease; convolu-tion; ⚔ retirement.

repoblación f repopulation; re-stocking; ~ *forestal* (re)afforesta-tion; **repoblar** [1m] *pais* repopu-late; *estanque* restock; ⚕ (re)affo-rest.

repollo m cabbage; **repolludo** round-headed; *fig.* tubby.

reponer [2r] replace, put back; restore; *thea.* revive; (*contestar*) reply; ~se ⚕ etc. recover, pick up; ~ de recover from, get over.

reportaje m report, article; **repor-tar** [1a] fetch, carry; *fig.* restrain; ~se control o.s.; **reporte** m report, news item; **repórter** m, **reportero** m reporter.

reposado quiet, restful; solemn; **reposar** [1a] rest, repose; sleep; (*yacer*) lie; ~se (*líquido*) settle.

reposición f replacement; *thea.* revival; ⚕ etc. recovery.

repositorio m repository.

reposo m rest (a. ⚕), repose.

repostería f (*tienda*) confectioner's (shop); pantry *en casa*; (*arte*) pas-try-making, confectionery; **repos-tero** m, a f pastry-cook, confec-tioner.

reprender [2a] reprimand, take to task (*algo a alguien* s.o. for s.t.); **reprensible** reprehensible; **re-prensión** f reprimand, rebuke.

represa f (*acto*) recapture; (*parada*) check, stoppage; dam, weir *en río*; ~ *de molino* mill-pond.

represalia f reprisal; *tomar ~s* take reprisals, retaliate.

represar [1a] (*tomar*) recapture; (*parar*) halt, check; *agua* dam (a. *fig.*); stem (a. *fig.*).

representación f representation; *thea.* production; performance; acting; *de ~ hombre* of importance; *hacer ~es* a make representations to; **representante** m/f representative (a. ♦); *thea.* performer; **represen-tar** [1a] *mst* represent; stand for; act for; (*informar*) state, declare; (*ser la imagen de*) show, express; *edad* look; *thea.* perform, play; act; ~se *algo* imagine, picture (to o.s.); envisage; **representativo** repre-sentative.

represión f repression; suppression; **represivo** repressive.

reprimenda f reprimand.

reprimir [3a] repress, curb; *levan-tamiento* suppress.

reprobar [1m] condemn, reprove; *univ. etc.* fail; **réprobo** *adj. a. su. m*, a f reprobate; *eccl.* damned.

reprochar [1a] reproach (*algo a alguien* s.o. with *or* for a th.); cen-sure, condemn; **reproche** m re-proach, reproof (a for); reflection (a on).

reproducción f reproduction; **re-producir(se)** [3o] reproduce.

reptil m reptile.

república f republic; **republica-nismo** m republicanism; **republi-cano** *adj. a. su. m*, a f republican.

repudiación f repudiation; **repu-diar** [1b] repudiate; *herencia etc.* renounce; disavow, disown; **repu-dio** m repudiation *etc.*

repudrirse [3a] F eat one's heart out, pine away.

repuesto m store, stock, supply; (*sustituto*) replacement; ⊕ refill; ⊕ (*pieza*) spare (part), extra *Am.*; ⊕ *de ~* spare, extra *Am.*

repugnancia f aversion (*hacia, por* from, to), loathing (*hacia, por* for); disgust; (*desgana*) reluctance; op-position; **repugnante** disgusting, revolting; **repugnar** [1a] disgust, revolt; (*estar en pugna con*) conflict with; contradict; do reluctantly; *me repugna hacerlo* I hate doing it.

repulgado affected; **repulgar** [1h] hem; **repulgo** m hem; *cocina:* fancy edging; F ~ *de empanada* trifle.

repulir [3a] repolish; refurbish; ~se dress up to the nines; spruce o.s. up.

repulsa f rejection, refusal; rebuff; ✄ check; **repulsar** [1a] reject, refuse; ✄ repulse, check; **re-pulsión** f = *repulsa*; (*antipatía*) repulsion (a. *phys.*); **repulsivo** repulsive.

repuntar [1a] (*marea*) turn; ~se (*vino*) turn; F fall out (*con* with); **repunte** m turn of the tide).

reputación f reputation, name; standing; **reputar** [1a] repute, esteem; *bien reputado* highly reputed.

requebrar [1k] say nice things to, try to flirt with; *fig.* flatter; ~ *de amores* a court.

requemado *piel* tanned; parched; overdone; **requemar** [1a] ⚕ etc. parch, scorch; *comida* overdo, burn; *lengua* burn, sting; *sangre etc.* inflame; ~se *(piel)* get tanned; ⚘ get parched, dry up; *fig.* smoulder *(de* with).

requerir [3i] *(necesitar)* require *(a* of), need; *(llamar)* summon; *(enviar por)* send for; intimate, notify; investigate; ~ *de amores a* court.

requesón *m* curd; cream cheese.

requiebro *m* flirtatious remark.

réquiem *m* requiem.

requilorios *m/pl.* F time-wasting formalities; *(adornos)* frills, buttons and bows; *(accesorios)* bits and pieces.

requisar [1a] requisition; **requisición** *f* ✗ requisition; **requisito** *m* requisite; requirement; ~ *previo* prerequisite; *llenar los* ~*s* fulfil the requirements.

res *f* beast, animal; *(esp. como número)* head of cattle; *S.Am.* steak.

resabiado knowing, that has learned his lesson; *(taimado)* crafty; **resabiarse** [1b] acquire a bad habit; get fed up; **resabido** would-be expert, pretentious; **resabio** *m* nasty taste; *fig.* bad habit; *tener* ~*s de* smack of.

resaca *f* ⚓ undertow, undercurrent; F hangover.

resalado witty, lively, vivacious.

resaltar [1a] jut (out); *fig.* stand out; *hacer* ~ throw into relief, set off *(contra* against); **resalte** *m*, **resalto** *m* projection.

resarcimiento *m* indemnification, repayment; **resarcir** [3b] indemnify *(de* for), repay; ~se *de* make up for, retrieve.

resbaladero *m* slippery place, slide; **resbaladizo** slippery; **resbalar** [1a] slip (up); slide; skid; *fig.* slip up; **resbalón** *m* slip *(a. fig.)*; slide; skid; **resbaloso** *S.Am.* slippery.

rescatar [1a] *p.* ransom; *cosa empeñada etc.* redeem; *(salvar)* rescue; *terrenos* reclaim; *tiempo* make up for; **rescate** *m* ransom; redemption; rescue; ~ *de terrenos* land reclamation.

rescindir [3a] rescind.

rescoldo *m* embers; *fig.* scruple, lingering doubt.

rescontrar [1m] ✝ offset, balance.

resecar [1g] dry thoroughly; *(dañar)* parch, scorch; **reseco** very dry; parched.

reseda *f* mignonette.

resentido resentful, sullen; *es un* ~ he's got a chip on his shoulder; *estar* ~ *de* feel the effect of; **resentimiento** *m* resentment; **resentirse** [3i]: ~ *de,* ~ *por* resent; be offended at; *defecto* suffer from; *consecuencias* feel the effects of.

reseña *f* *lit.,* ✗ review; *paint.* sketch; **reseñar** [1a] review; sketch.

reserva *f* reserve *(a.* ♟, ✗); *(acto etc.)* reservation; discretion, reticence; privacy; ~ *de Indios* Indian reservation; ~ *mental* mental reservation; *absoluta* ~, *con la mayor* ~ in the strictest confidence; *a* ~ *de* with the intention of; *de* ~ in reserve; *sin* ~ unreservedly; **reservación** *f* reservation; **reservado** 1. *p.* reserved, reticent; discreet; *lugar* private; *asiento* reserved; 2. *m* ♟ reserved compartment; ~ *de señoras* ladies only compartment; **reservar** [1a] reserve; set aside, keep; *(encubrir)* conceal; ~se save o.s. *(para* for); *(desconfiar)* beware *(de* of); **reservista** *m* reservist.

resfriado *m* cold; chill; **resfriar** [1c] *v/t.* cool *(a. fig.)*, chill; *v/i.* turn cold; ~se ⚕ catch cold; *fig.* cool off.

resguardar [1a] protect, shield *(de* from); ~se shelter; safeguard o.s.; **resguardo** *m* protection; safeguard; shelter; guard; *(documento)* certificate; *(papeleta)* slip, check.

residencia *f* residence; *univ.* hall of residence, hostel; **residencial** residential; **residente** *adj. a. su. m/f* resident; **residir** [3a] reside; live; *fig.* lie; *fig.* ~ *en* consist in, reside in; rest with; **residual** residual, residuary; **residuo** *m* residue; ⅍ remainder; ⅍, ♎ residuum; ~*s pl.* refuse, remains.

resignación *f* resignation; **resignado** resigned; **resignar** [1a] resign; renounce; *mando etc.* hand over *(en* to); ~se resign o.s. *(a* to).

resina *f* resin; **resinoso** resinous.

resistencia *f* resistance *(a.* ✗, *phys.,* ⚡); strength; endurance, stamina, staying power; opposition; *(acto)* stand; ✗ ~ *al avance* drag; ～ *pasiva* passive resistance; **resistente** resistant; tough; *tela etc.* hard-wearing; ♀ hardy; **resistir** [3a] *v/t.* stand, bear; *tentación* resist; *v/i.* resist; (*durar*) last; *esp.* ✗ hold out; fight back; ～ *a* resist, withstand; make a stand against; stand up to; (*soportar*) stand, bear; ～se resist, struggle; ～ *a inf.* refuse to *inf.*, find it hard to *inf.*; **resistor** *m* resistor.

resma *f* ream.

resobado hackneyed, trite.

resol *m* glare of the sun; **resolana** *f*, **resolano** *m* sun-trap.

resolución *f* resolution (*a. parl.*); (*acto*) solving; decision; *fig.* resolution, resolve; boldness; en ～ in short, to sum up; *tomar una* ～ take a decision; **resoluto** = **resuelto**; **resolver** [2h; *p.p. resuelto*] *problema* solve, do; think out, puzzle out; *cuestión* settle; *cuerpo, materia* resolve (en into); *conjunto* analyse, divide (up); ⚗ *etc.* dissolve (away); *acción* decide on; ～se resolve itself, work out; ～ *a inf.* resolve to *inf.*

resollar [1m] puff (and blow); snort; wheeze; F *no* ～ give no sign of life.

resonancia *f* resonance; echo; *tener* ～ *fig.* cause a stir, have repercussions; **resonante** resonant; resounding, ringing, echoing; **resonar** [1m] resound, ring, echo (de with).

resoplar [1a] puff, blow, snort; **resoplido** *m* puff, snort.

resopón *m* nightcap.

resorte *m* ⊕ spring; elasticity, springiness; *fig.* means, expedient; ～ *espiral* coil spring; F *tocar* ～s pull wires.

respaldar [1a] endorse; *fig.* support, back; ～se lean back; sprawl; **respaldo** *m* back *de silla, hoja*; endorsement *en papel*; *fig.* support, backing.

respectar [1a] concern; **respectivo** respective; **respecto** *m* respect, relation; (*con*) ～ *a*, (*con*) ～ *de* with regard to; in relation to; *a ese* ～ on that score; *al* ～ in the matter; *bajo ese* ～ in that respect; **respetabilidad** *f* respectability; **respetable** respectable; worthy; **respetar** [1a] respect; **respeto** *m* respect, regard,

consideration; *de* ～ spare, extra; *por* ～ *a* out of consideration for; ～s *pl.* respects; *campar por sus* ～s strike out on one's own; *b.s.* be self-centred; be bone idle; *estar de* ～ be all dressed up.

réspice *m* F curt reply; (*reprensión*) ticking-off.

respingado *nariz* snub; **respingar** [1h] shy, start; *fig.* kick; **respingo** *m* shy, start; *fig.* gesture of disgust; **respingón** *nariz* snub; *caballo* difficult; *S.Am.* surly.

respiración *f* breathing; **respiradero** *m* ⊕ vent, air-valve; *fig.* respite, breathing-space; **respirar** [1a] breathe; *gas etc.* breathe in; breathe again *después de mal momento*; (*descansar*) get one's breath; *sin* ～ without a break; **respiratorio** respiratory; breathing *attr.*; **respiro** *m* breathing; (*descanso*) breathing-space; lull, respite; (*prórroga*) grace; reprieve.

resplandecer [2d] shine (*a. fig.*); glitter, glow, blaze; **resplandeciente** shining *etc.*; **resplandor** *m* brilliance, radiance; glitter, glow, blaze.

responder [2a] *v/t.* answer; *injuria etc.* answer with; *v/i.* answer, reply; *esp. fig.* respond; (*ser respondón*) answer back; ～ *de*, ～ *por* answer for, be responsible for; **respondón** F cheeky, saucy, pert.

responsabilidad *f* responsibility *etc.*; *de* ～ *limitada* limited liability *attr.*; *bajo mi* ～ on my responsibility; **responsable** responsible (de for); liable (de for); *la p.* ～ the person in charge.

responsorio *m eccl.* response.

respuesta *f* answer, reply; response.

resquebra(ja)dura *f* crack, split; **resquebrajar(se)** [1a] crack, split; **resquebrar** [1k] begin to crack.

resquemar [1a] *lengua* burn, sting; ♀ parch; *comida* burn; **resquemo(r)** *m* burn, sting; burnt taste *de comida*; *fig.* sorrow; resentment.

resquicio *m* chink, crack; *fig.* chance, opening.

resta *f* ⚗ subtraction; (*residuo*) remainder.

restablecer [2d] re-establish; restore; revive; ～se recover.

restallar [1a] crack; (*crujir*) crackle.

restante 1. remaining; *los* ~s the rest; **2.** *m* rest, remainder.

restañar [1a] stanch.

restar [1a] *v/i.* ⒜ subtract, take away; deduct; *pelota* return; *autoridad, valor etc.* reduce; *v/i.* remain, be left.

restauración *f* restoration; **restaurán** *m*, **restaurante** [resto'ran] *m* restaurant; café; **restaurar** [1a] restore; repair; recover.

restitución *f* return, restitution; **restituir** [3g] restore, return.

resto *m* rest; remainder (*a.* ⒜); *deportes:* (*p.*) receiver; (*acto*) return; ~s *pl.* remains; *cocina:* left-overs; ⚓ *etc.* wreckage; ~s *pl. mortales* mortal remains; *echar el* ~ stake all one's money; F go the whole hog; do one's utmost (*por inf.* to *inf.*).

restorán *m S.Am.* restaurant.

restregar [1h *a.* 1k] scrub, rub (hard).

restricción *f* restriction; limitation; restraint; ~ *mental* mental reservation; **restrictivo** restrictive; **restringir** [3c] restrict.

resucitar [1a] *v/t.* resuscitate; *fig.* resurrect, revive; *v/i.* resuscitate; return to life; revive.

resuelto 1. *p.p. of resolver;* **2.** resolute, determined; steadfast; prompt; *estar* ~ *a inf.* be determined to *inf.*

resuello *m* (*respiración*) breathing; (*un* ~) breath; (*ruidoso, penoso*) puff; snort; wheeze; *corto de* ~ short-winded.

resulta: *de* ~s *de* as a result of; **resultado** *m* result, outcome; issue; sequel; effect; *dar* ~ produce results; **resultar** [1a] be, prove (to be), turn out (to be); ~ *de* result from, stem from; be evident from; ~ (*ser*) *verdadero* prove (to be) true; *esto resulta difícil* this is awkward; *resulta que* it emerges that, it appears that; *resulta de todo esto que* it follows from all this that; *ahora resulta que no puedo* now it turns out that I can't; *con todo lo que después resultó* with all that ensued; *no me resultó muy bien aquello* it didn't work out very well for me; F *esto no me resulta* I can't get along with this.

resumen *m* summary, résumé; *en* ~ to sum up, in short; **resumir** [3a] sum up, summarize; ~*se* be included.

resurgimiento *m* resurgence; revival; **resurgir** [3c] revive, reappear; be resurrected; **resurrección** *f* resurrection.

retablo *m* reredos, altar-piece.

retaguardia *f* rearguard; *a* ~ in the rear.

retahíla *f* row, line, string; *fig.* volley, string.

retajar [1a] cut round.

retal *m* remnant, oddment.

retama *f* broom.

retar [1a] challenge; F tick off.

retardar [1a] slow down, slow up, retard; *reloj* put back; **retardo** *m* slowing-up; delay; time-lag; **retardriz** *acción* delaying.

retazo *m* remnant; *fig.* bit, fragment; ~s *pl.* odds and ends; snippets; *labor de* ~s patchwork.

rete... very ...; **retebién** very well, jolly well.

retemblar [1k] shudder, shake (*de* at, with).

retén *m* reserve (*a.* ✗), store; ⊕ stop, catch, lock.

retención *f* retention (*a.* 🗡); ✝ deduction; **retener** [2l] retain, keep (back), hold (back); (*deducir*) withhold, deduct; ⚖ detain; **retenida** *f* guy (rope); **retentivo** retentive (*a.* 🗡).

reticencia *f* irony, sarcasm; (*una* ~) half-truth; **reticente** ironical, sarcastic; misleading, full of half-truths.

retícula *f phot.* screen; *opt.* reticule; **retículo** *m* reticle; network.

retina *f* retina.

retintín *m* tinkle, tinkling; jingle; ring(ing); F nastily sarcastic tone; **retiñir** [3h] tinkle; jingle; ring.

retirada *f* ✗ withdrawal (*a.* ✝), retreat (*a. toque*); recall *de embajador*; (*sitio*) retreat, place of refuge; *batirse en* ~ retreat; **retirado** *oficial* retired; *lugar* secluded, remote; **retirar** [1a] withdraw (*a.* ✗, ✝; *de* from); take away, remove (*a* from); ⊕ *pieza* take out, take off; *tapa* take off; *mano, cubierta* draw back; *embajador* recall; ~*se* ✗ retreat, withdraw; *retire a su cuarto* (*apartarse de la gente*) retire, go into seclusion; shrink back (*ante peligro etc.* at, from); (*jubilarse*) retire; *de-*

portes: drop out, retire; scratch *antes de salida*; **retiro** *m* ✕, ⭻ withdrawal; (*sueldo*) pension, retirement pay; (*jubilación*) retirement; *eccl.* retreat; (*recogimiento*) seclusion; (*lugar*) retreat; *vivir en el* ~ live in retirement (*or* seclusion).

reto *m* challenge; (*amenaza*) threat; *S.Am.* insult.

retocar [1g] retouch, touch up (*a. phot.*).

retoñar [1a] ⚇ sprout; *fig.* reappear, recur; **retoño** *m* ⚇ shoot.

retoque *m* retouching, touching-up; (*última mano*) finishing touch; ⚘ touch.

retorcer [2b *a.* 2h] twist; *manos* wring; *argumento* turn; *sentido* twist; ~se twist, twine; writhe, squirm *de dolor*.

retórica *f* rhetoric; ~s *pl.* quibbles; **retórico 1.** rhetorical; **2.** *m* rhetorician.

retornar [1a] *v/t.* return, give back; turn back; *v/i.* return; **retorno** *m* return; (*pago*) reward, payment; (*cambio*) barter.

retorsión *f* twisting; writhing.

retorta *f* ⚗ retort.

retortero: F *andar al* ~ bustle around, fuss about; F *traer a* ~ lead *s.o.* a dance, push *s.o.* around.

retortijón *m*: ~ *de tripas* gripe.

retozar [1f] frolic, frisk, gambol, romp; **retozo** *m* frolic *etc.*; ~ *de la risa* giggle, titter; **retozón** frisky, playful.

retractar [1a] retract, withdraw; ~se recant, retract.

retraer [2p] bring back, bring again; *fig.* dissuade, discourage; ~se retire, retreat; take refuge; retract; ~ *de* withdraw from, give up; shun; **retraído** retiring, shy; unsociable; *b.s.* backward; **retraimiento** *m* (*acto*) withdrawal *etc.*; (*lugar*) retreat, refuge; (*lo retirado*) seclusion.

retransmisión *f* *radio*: repeat (broadcast); **retransmitir** [3a] repeat; relay.

retrasar [1a] *v/t.* delay, defer, put off; *evolución etc.* retard, slow down; *reloj* put back; *v/i.* (*reloj*) be slow; = ~se (*p.*, ⛴ *etc.*) be late, be behind time; lag behind *en estudios etc.*; **retraso** *m* delay; time-lag; slowness, lateness; *con* ~ late;

behindhand; *con 20 minutos de* ~ 20 minutes late; *tener* ~ be late.

retratar [1a] portray (*a. fig.*); *fig.* describe; **retratista** *m/f* portrait painter; **retrato** *m* portrait; *fig.* description; *fig.* (*imagen fiel*) likeness; *ser el vivo* ~ *de* be the very image of.

retrechería *f* F dodge; **retrechero** F clever, crafty; (*atractivo*) lovely, nice.

retreparse [1a] lean back, lounge.

retreta *f* ✕ (*toque de*) ~ tattoo; retreat.

retrete *m* lavatory.

retribución *f* (*recompensa*) reward, payment; (*pago*) pay; compensation (*a.* ⊕); **retribuido** *puesto* salaried; *trabajo* paid; **retribuir** [3g] reward, repay; pay.

retro... retro...; **~activo** retroactive; retrospective; **~carga:** *de* ~ breech-loading; *arma de* ~ breech-loader; **~ceder** [2a] draw back, stand back; go back, turn back *en viaje etc.*; back down, flinch (*ante peligro* from); (*agua etc.*) fall; ✕ retreat, fall back; (*arma*) recoil; *hacer* ~ force back; **~ceso** *m* backward movement, falling back; ✕ withdrawal; ✕ recoil *de arma*; ⭻ recession, slump; ⚘ renewed attack; **retrógrado** retrograde; *esp. pol.* reactionary; **retrogresión** *f* retrogression.

retronar [1m] rumble.

retro...: ~spección *f* retrospect, retrospection; **~spectivo** retrospective; *cine*: *escena* ~*a* flashback; **~visor** *m*: (*espejo*) ~ driving mirror.

retruécano *m* play on words.

retumbante booming, resounding; *fig.* bombastic; **retumbar** [1a] boom, rumble, reverberate; **retumbo** *m* boom *etc.*

reuma *m* rheumatism; **reumático** rheumatic; **reumatismo** *m* rheumatism.

reunión *f* meeting, gathering; reunion; *pol.* meeting, rally; (*fiesta*) party; **reunir** [3a] *cosas separadas* join (together), (re)unite; *cosas dispersas* gather (together), assemble, get together; *colección* make; *datos etc.* collect; *fondos* raise; *cualidades* combine; ~se (*juntarse*) meet, get together, gather; (*unirse*) unite;

(*concurrir*) conspire; ~ *con* (re)join; meet up with.

revalidar [1a] confirm, ratify.

revalor(iz)ación *f* revaluation; **revalorar** [1a], **revalorizar** [1f] revalue; reassess.

revancha *f* revenge; *deportes*: return match; *tomar su* ~ get one's own back.

revelación *f* revelation; disclosure; **revelado** *m* *phot.* developing; **revelador 1.** revealing, tell-tale; **2.** *m* *phot.* developer; **revelar** [1a] *mst* reveal; disclose, betray, give away; *phot.* develop.

revendedor *m*, **-a** *f* retailer; *b.s.* speculator; *deportes*: ticket-tout; **revender** [2a] resell, retail; *b.s.* speculate in; *entradas* tout.

revenirse [3s] (*encogerse*) shrink; (*vino*) turn sour; (*secarse*) dry out; (*ceder*) give way.

reventa *f* resale.

reventadero *m* rough ground; F tough job, grind; **reventar** [1k] **1.** *v/t.* burst; crush, smash; *fig.* ruin; F (*cansar*) bore to tears; F (*molestar*) rile; F (*hacer trabajar*) overwork, work to death; **2.** *v/i.* burst; explode, pop; (*brotar*) burst forth; (*olas*) break; *fig.* explode (*de ira etc.* with); F die; ~ *de risa* split one's sides; ~ *por inf.* be bursting to *inf.*; **3.** ~**se** burst *etc.*; **reventón** *m* burst; explosion; *mot.* blow-out; *fig.* steep hill, tough climb; (*apuro*) jam; *darse un* ~ sweat, slog (*para inf.* to *inf.*).

rever [2v] review, revive; 🏛 *fallo* review; *pleito* retry.

reverberar [1a] (*ruido*) reverberate; (*luz*) play (*en* on), be reflected (*en* from); **reverbero** *m* reverberation; (*espejo*) reflector; (*farol*) street lamp.

reverdecer [2d] grow green again; *fig.* acquire new vigour.

reverencia *f* reverence; (*saludo*) bow *de hombre*, curtsy *de mujer*; ♀ Your *etc.* Reverence; **reverencial** reverential; **reverenciar** [1b] revere, venerate; **reverendo** respected, reverend; *eccl.* reverend; F solemn; **reverente** reverent.

reversible *mst* reversible; 🏛 reversionary; **reversión** *f* reversion; **reverso** *m* back, other side; reverse *de moneda*; *el* ~ *de la medalla fig.*

the other side of the picture; (*p.*) the exact opposite; **reverter** [2g] revert.

revés *m* (*cara*) back, other side, underside; (*golpe*) slap; *tenis*: backhand; *fig.* reverse, setback; *al* ~ *tela etc.* inside out, upside down; (*adv.*) on the contrary; *al* ~ *de lo que esperaba* contrary to what I expected; *todo le salió al* ~ it all turned out wrong for him; *volver al* ~ turn inside out, turn upside down; **revesado** complicated; *fig.* unmanageable.

revestimiento *m* facing, coating; lining; ✕ revetment; **revestir** [3l] *ropa* put on, wear; *superficie* clothe (*de* in); *esp.* ⊕ face, coat; line; sheathe; *fig. suelo etc.* carpet (*de* with); *cuento* adorn (*de* with); *p.* invest (*con, de* with); *importancia* have; ~**se** be carried away; (*engreírse*) be haughty; ~ *con,* ~ *de autoridad etc.* be invested with.

reviejo very old.

revisar [1a] revise; re-examine; review (*a.* 🏛); check; *esp.* ⊕ overhaul; **revisión** *f* revision; review (*a.* 🏛); check; *esp.* ⊕ overhaul; **revisor** *m*, **-a** *f* reviser; 🚆 ticket-collector, inspector, conductor *Am.*

revista *f* review (*a.* ⚓, ✕), inspection; revision; *thea.* revue; *lit.* review, magazine; 🏛 retrial; *pasar* ~ *a* = **revistar** [1a] ⚓, ✕ inspect, review; **revistero** *m* reviewer, critic; contributor.

revivificar [1g] revitalize; **revivir** [3a] revive, be revived; live again.

revocación *f* revocation, repeal; reversal; **revocar** [1g] *orden etc.* revoke, repeal; *decisión* reverse; dissuade (*de* from); *casa* plaster; whitewash; **revoco** *m* = *revocación*; ⚠ = *revoque*.

revolcar [1g *a.* 1m] *p. etc.* knock down, knock over, send flying; F *adversario* floor; ~**se** roll, flounder about; (*esp. animal*) wallow (*a. fig.*, *en* in); (*empeñarse*) dig one's heels in.

revolear [1a] fly around; **revolotear** [1a] flutter, flit; wheel; hover.

revoltijo *m*, **revoltillo** *m* jumble, mess, litter; *fig.* mess.

revoltoso 1. rebellious, unruly; *niño* naughty; **2.** *m* rebel; *pol.* trouble-maker, agitator.

revolución f mst revolution (a. ⊕); turn; **revolucionar** [1a] revolutionize; **revolucionario** adj. a. su. m, a f revolutionary.

revólver m revolver.

revolver [2h; p.p. revuelto] (agitar, sacudir) shake; líquido stir (up); tierra turn up, turn over; objeto turn round, turn over (or upside down); papeles etc. look through, rummage among; lo ordenado mix up, upset, disarrange; estómago turn; asunto turn over en mente; ánimos upset, sow discord among; p. get into trouble (con with); (envolver) wrap up; ~se turn (right) round, turn over etc.; toss and turn en cama; ast. revolve; (tiempo) change, turn stormy.

revoque m (acto) plastering; whitewashing; (materia) plaster; whitewash.

revuelco m fall, tumble.

revuelo m disturbance; rumpus; de ~ incidentally, in passing.

revuelta f (motín) revolt; disturbance; turn, bend de camino; change de parecer etc.; (disputa) quarrel, row; **revuelto 1.** p.p. of revolver; agua troubled; v. huevo; **2.** adj. in disorder, higgledy-piggledy; (travieso) naughty; asunto complicated.

rey m king (a. naipes, ajedrez); día (or noche) de ♀es Twelfth Night; los ♀es Magos the Magi, the Three Wise Men (equivalent to Santa Claus as bringers of presents).

reyerta f quarrel; fight, brawl.

rezagado m late-comer; loiterer; ✗ straggler; **rezagar** [1h] outdistance, leave behind; (aplazar) postpone; ~se fall (or get left) behind; lag (behind); straggle.

rezar [1f] v/t. say; v/i. pray, say one's prayers; (texto) read, say, run; F grumble; F ~ con have to do with; **rezo** m (acto) praying; (una oración) prayer; (oraciones) prayers; devotions; office, daily service.

rezongar [1h] grumble, mutter; growl; **rezongo** m grumble; growl; **rezongón** grumbling, cantankerous.

rezumar [1a] v/t. ooze, exude; v/i. ooze (out), seep, leak out (a. fig.).

ría[1] etc. v. reír.

ría[2] f estuary; approx. sea-loch, fiord.

riachuelo m brook, stream.

riada f flood.

ribera f shore, beach; bank de río; **ribereño** riverside attr.; esp. ∰ riparian.

ribete m sew. etc. edging, border; fig. addition; fig. trimmings, embellishments de cuento; ~s pl. fig. streak, touch; tener sus ~s de have some pretentions to, have some appearance of being etc.

ricacho m, **ricachón** m F nouveau riche.

rico 1. rich, wealthy; (fértil, suntuoso) rich (en in); comida tasty, delicious; dulces etc. rich; fruto luscious; F cute; F lovely; F sí, rica yes darling; **2.** m, a f rich person, wealthy man etc.; nuevo ~ nouveau riche.

rictus m (involuntary) twisting of the lips; sneer; grin.

ridiculez f absurdity; **ridiculizar** [1f] ridicule, deride; guy; **ridículo** ridiculous, absurd, ludicrous; (delicado) touchy; poner en ~ ridicule, make a fool of; ponerse en ~ make a fool (or exhibition) of o.s.

riego m watering; irrigation; fig. sprinkling; ~ por aspersión spray.

riel m 🚃 rail; metall. ingot.

rielar [1a] poet. shimmer; twinkle.

rienda f rein; a ~ suelta at top speed; fig. without the least restraint; dar ~ suelta a give free rein to; give s.o. his head; deseos indulge; soltar las ~s take off the brakes; kick over the traces.

riente laughing, merry; paisaje smiling, bright.

riesgo m risk; danger; correr ~ de inf. run the risk of ger.

rifa f raffle; (riña) quarrel, fight; **rifar** [1a] v/t. raffle; v/i. quarrel, fight.

rifle m rifle; ~ de repetición repeater; **riflero** m rifleman.

rigidez f rigidity etc.; ~ cadavérica rigor mortis; **rígido** rigid; stiff; fig. strict, stern (con, para towards), unbending; b.s. wooden; hidebound; **rigor** m rigour, severity (a. meteor. etc.); harshness, strictness; stringency; en ~ strictly speaking; ser de ~ be de rigueur, be the order of the day; **rigorismo** m strictness; austerity; **rigorista** m/f strict observer, stickler; **rigurosi-**

dad *f* rigour, severity; **riguroso** rigorous; *crítico, pena, tiempo etc.* severe, harsh; strict; stringent.

rija *f* quarrel, fight; **rijo** *m* lust(fulness); **rijoso** quarrelsome; (*sensual*) lustful.

rima *f* rhyme; ~s *pl.* poems, poetry; *octava* ~ ottava rima; *tercia* ~ terza rima; **rimador** *m*, -a *f* rhymester; **rimar** [1a] rhyme (*con* with).

rimbombancia *f* resonance, echo; *fig.* bombast; showiness, flashiness; **rimbombante** resounding, echoing; *fig.* bombastic; (*vistoso*) showy, flashy.

rimero *m* stack, heap.

rincón *m* (inside) corner; *fig.* corner, nook, retreat; patch *de terreno etc.*; **rinconada** *f* corner.

ringl(er)a *f* row, line; swath *de hierba segada.*

ringorrango *m* F flourish *de pluma;* *fig.* trimmings, frills.

rinoceronte *m* rhinoceros.

riña *f* quarrel; (*con golpes*) fight, scuffle, fracas; ~ *de gallos* cockfight.

riñón *m* anat. kidney; *fig.* heart, core; F *tener el* ~ *bien cubierto* be well-heeled.

río *m* river; ~ *abajo* downstream; ~ *arriba* upstream; ~ *de oro fig.* goldmine; *a* ~ *revuelto* in disorder.

rió *etc. v. reír.*

riolada *f* F flood, stream.

rioplatense *adj. a. su. m/f* (native) of the River Plate region.

riostra *f* brace, strut.

ripio *m* residue, refuse; (*cascote*) debris, rubble; *fig. poet.* word used to fill up the line; (*palabrería*) verbiage, padding; *no perder* ~ not miss a trick.

riqueza *f* wealth, riches; (*fertilidad, sabor, de estilo*) richness; *vivir en la* ~ live in luxury.

risa *f* (*una* ~) laugh; (*en general*) laughter, laughing; *hubo* ~s there was laughter; *el libro es una verdadera* ~ the book's a laugh from start to finish; *cosa de* ~ joke, laughing matter; *¡qué* ~*!* what a joke!, how funny!; *desternillarse de* ~ split one's sides; *morirse de* ~ die of laughing; *tomar a* ~ laugh *s.t.* off.

risco *m* cliff, bluff, crag; **riscoso** craggy.

risible ludicrous, laughable.

risotada *f* guffaw, horse-laugh.

ristra *f* string.

ristre: (*lanza*) *en* ~ at the ready, all set.

risueño smiling; *disposición* cheerful, sunny; *paisaje* smiling; *perspectiva* bright.

rítmico rhythmic(al); **ritmo** *m* rhythm.

rito *m* rite; ceremony; **ritual** *adj. a. su. m* ritual.

rival 1. rival, competing; **2.** *m/f* rival, competitor; **rivalidad** *f* rivalry; enmity; **rivalizar** [1f] compete, vie; ~ *con* rival.

rizado *pelo* curly; *superficie* crinkly; crisp; **rizador** *m* curling-iron, hair-curler; **rizar** [1f] *pelo* curl; crisp; *superficie* crinkle; *agua* ripple, ruffle; ~se curl *etc.*; **rizo 1.** curly; **2.** *m* curl, ringlet; ripple *de agua;* ~s *pl.* ⚓ reefs; ✈ *hacer* (*or rizar*) *el* ~ loop the loop; **rizoso** curly.

roano roan.

robar [1a] *poseedor* rob (*algo a alguien s.o. of s.t.*); *posesión* steal (*a* from); (*secuestrar*) abduct, kidnap; *caja* break into, rifle; *casa* break into, burgle; *cartas* draw, take.

roblar [1a] rivet, clinch.

roble *m* oak (tree); **robledal** *m*, **robledo** *m* oak wood.

roblón *m* rivet.

robo *m* robbery; theft, thieving; ~ *en la vía pública* highway robbery; ~ *relámpago* smash-and-grab raid.

robot *m* robot.

robustecer [2d] strengthen; ~se grow stronger; **robustez** *f* robustness *etc.*; **robusto** robust; strong, sturdy; tough; hardy.

roca *f* rock.

roce *m* rub(bing); *esp.* ⊕ friction; graze *en piel;* *fig.* close contact, familiarity; *tener* ~ *con* be in close contact with.

rociada *f* dash, splash; shower, sprinkling; (*aspersión*) spray; *fig.* shower *de piedras,* hail *de balas;* F *echar una* ~ *a* dress down; **rociador** *m* spray, sprinkler; **rociar** [1c] *v/t.* sprinkle, spray (de with); spatter *de lodo etc.;* *fig.* scatter, shower; *v/i.*: *rocía esta mañana* there is a dew this morning.

rocín *m* hack, nag; F lout; **rocinante** *m* poor old horse.

rocío *m* dew; (*llovizna*) drizzle; *fig.* sprinkling.

rococó *adj. a. su. m* rococo.

rocoso rocky.

roda *f* ⚓ stem.

rodaballo *m* turbot; ~ (*menor*) brill.

rodada *f* rut, (wheel-)track; *S.Am.* fall.

rodado *circulación* wheeled, on wheels; *piedra* rounded; *v. canto*; *caballo* dappled; *estilo* rounded, fluent; **rodaja** *f* (*rueda*) small wheel, castor; disc, round; slice *de pan etc.*; **rodaje** *m* ⊕ (set of) wheels; *cine:* shooting, filming; *mot.* en ~ running-in; **rodante** rolling; **rodapié** *m* skirting-board; **rodar** [1m] *v/t.* *vehículo* wheel; *cosa redonda* roll; *mot.* run in; *película* shoot, film; *v/i.* roll (por along, down *etc.*); go, run, travel *sobre ruedas*; rotate, revolve *en eje*; *fig.* wander about, roam; abound; ~ *por alguien* be at s.o.'s beck and call; *echarlo todo a* ~ spoil everything.

rodear [1a] *v/t.* surround (de by, with); ring, encircle, shut in; *S.Am.* *ganado* round up; *v/i.* go round; (*camino*) make a detour; *fig.* beat about the bush; **~se** turn, toss, twist; **rodeo** *m* detour *de camino*; roundabout way, long way round; *fig.* dodge; pretext; circumlocution; 🐎 cattle-pen; *S.Am.* 🐎 round-up, rodeo; *sin* ~s outright; *andarse con* ~s, *ir por* ~s beat about the bush; *dejarse de* ~s come to the point.

rodera *f* rut, cart-track.

rodete *m* coil, bun *de pelo*; pad *para peso*; ward *de cerradura*; ⊕ articulator.

rodilla *f* knee; (*trapo*) floor-cloth; *de* ~s kneeling; *caer de* ~s fall on one's knees; *estar* (*or hincarse, ponerse*) *de* ~s kneel (down); *hincar la* ~ kneel down; *fig.* bow, humble o.s. (*ante* to); **rodillazo** *m* push with the knee; *dar un* ~ *a* knee.

rodillo *m* roller; *cocina:* rolling pin; ink-roller *para entintar*; ~ *pintor* paint-roller; ~ *de vapor* steam-roller.

rodrigón *m* 🐎 stake, prop.

roedor 1. gnawing (*a. fig.*); **2.** *m* rodent; **roer** [2z] gnaw; nibble;

hueso pick; *metal* corrode, eat into; (*pesar, duda*) gnaw.

rogación *f* petition; *eccl.* rogation; ~s *pl. eccl.* rogations; **rogar** [1h *a.* 1m] *v/t. p.* beg; plead with; *cosa* beg for, ask for, plead for; ~ *que* beg *inf.*; ask that; *v/i.* beg, plead (*por* for); (*orar*) pray; *hacerse* (*de*) ~ have to be coaxed; *no se hizo de* ~ he didn't have to be asked twice.

rojear [1a] redden, turn red; **rojete** *m* rouge; **rojez** *f* redness; **rojillo** *pol.* pink; **rojizo** reddish; ruddy; **rojo 1.** red (*a. pol.*); ruddy; **2.** *m* red (*a. pol.*); ~ *cereza* cherry-red; ~ *de labios* lipstick; *calentar al* ~ make red-hot.

rol *m* list, catalogue, roll; ⚓ muster.

rollizo *p.* plump; stocky, sturdy; *niño* chubby; *mujer* plump, buxom; *objeto* cylindrical.

rollo *m* roll; *cocina:* rolling pin; F awful bore.

romadizo *m* head-cold.

romana *f* steelyard.

romance 1. *lengua* romance; **2.** *m* romance (language); Spanish (language); *lit.* ballad; **romancero** *m* collection of ballads; **románico** *lengua* romance; △ Romanesque, *en Inglaterra* Norman; **romano** *adj. a. su. m*, **a** *f* Roman (*a. typ.*); *v. obra*; **romanticismo** *m* romanticism; **romántico** *adj. a. su. m* romantic.

romaza *f* dock, sorrel.

rombo *m* rhomb(us).

romería *f* *eccl.* pilgrimage; gathering at a shrine; *fig.* trip, excursion; F festivities, fair, open-air dance *etc.*; **romero**[1] *m*, **a** *f* pilgrim.

romero[2] *m* ♣ rosemary.

romo blunt; *p.* snub-nosed.

rompecabezas *m* (*problema*) puzzle, teaser; (*acertijo*) riddle; (*dibujo*) jig-saw puzzle; **rompedero** fragile, breakable; **rompedora-cargadora** *f* ⚒ power-loader; **rompehielos** *m* ice-breaker; **rompeolas** *m* breakwater; **romper** [2a; *p.p.* roto] **1.** *v/t. plato etc.* break, smash, shatter; *cuerda etc.* break, snap; *presa, cerca etc.* break through, breach; *papel, tela* tear (up), rip (up); *ropa* tear; wear out; *tierra* break up; *aguas* cleave; *niebla, nubes* break through; *ayuno* break; *hostilidades* open up, start; *relaciones* break off; **2.** v/i. (día, olas) break; ♀ burst (open); (guerra etc.) break out; (ps.) fall out (con with); ~ a inf. suddenly start to inf.; F de rompe y rasga determined; **rompiente** m (ola) breaker; (escollo) reef; ~s pl. breakers, surf; **rompimiento** m (acto) breaking etc.; (abertura) opening, breach, crack; fig. out break de guerra; break (con p. with); breaking-off de relaciones.

ron m rum.

ronca f F nasty threat; (reprimenda) ticking-off; echar ~s bully.

roncar [1g] snore; (mar etc.) roar; F threaten, bully.

roncear [1a] kill time; work etc. unwillingly; F cajole; **roncería** f time-wasting; unwillingness; F cajolery; **roncero** (tardo) slow; F grumpy; (que halaga) smooth, smarmy.

ronco p. hoarse; throaty, husky; sonido harsh, raucous.

roncha f bruise, weal; swelling de picadura.

ronda f night patrol, (night) watch; beat de policía; (ps.) watch, patrol; (con canto) serenaders; round de bebidas etc.; **rondar** [1a] v/t. patrol, go the rounds of; fig. haunt, hang about; F pester; ~ la calle a una joven hang about the street where a girl lives; luz (mariposa) fly round; v/i. (policía) be on patrol, go the rounds; prowl (round), hang about; roam the streets at night; ♪ go serenading.

rondón: entrar de ~ rush in.

ronquear [1a] talk hoarsely; **ronquedad** f, **ronquera** f hoarseness etc.; **ronquido** m snoring; (un ~) snore; fig. roar.

ronronear [1a] purr; **ronroneo** m purr(ing).

ronzal m halter.

ronzar [1f] crunch, munch.

roña f vet. scab de oveja, mange de perro; ♀ rust; (mugre) filth, grime; = **roñería** f meanness; **roñoso** scabby, mangy; filthy; F mean, stingy.

ropa f clothing, clothes, dress; ~ blanca linen; ~ blanca (de mujer) lingerie; ~ de cama bedclothes, bedding; ~ hecha ready-made clothes; ~ interior underwear, underclothes; ~ lavada, ~ por lavar,

~ sucia laundry, washing; a quema ~ point-blank; tentarse la ~ think long and hard; **ropaje** m (ropa) clothing, (vestido) gown, robe; (paños) drapery; fig. garb; **ropavejero** m old-clothes dealer; **ropería** f clothing trade; (tienda) clothier's; **ropero** m clothier; (mueble) wardrobe.

roque m rook, castle (chess).

roquedal m rocky place.

rorro m F baby, kid.

rosa f rose; red spot, birthmark en cuerpo; caminito de ~s primrose path; ~ de los vientos, ~ náutica compass; color (de) ~ rose, pink; verlo todo color de ~ see everything through rose-coloured spectacles; **rosado** pink, rosy; **rosal** m rose-tree, rose-bush; ~ silvestre dog-rose; ~ trepador rambler rose; **rosaleda** f rose-garden, rose-bed.

rosario m rosary, beads, chaplet; rezar el ~ tell one's beads.

rosbif m roast beef.

rosca f coil, spiral; ⊕ screw, thread de tornillo; cocina: ring-shaped roll etc.; ⚓ en ~ light; F hacer la ~ a suck up to; pasarse de ~ have a crossed thread; F bite off more than one can chew; F tirarse una ~ plough.

róseo roseate, rosy.

roseta f ♀ small rose; rose de regadera; red patch en mejilla; (adorno) rosette; ~s pl. popcorn; **rosetón** m △ rosette; △ rose (window).

rosicler m red of dawn, rosy tint.

rostro m anat. countenance, face; ⚓ beak; hist., zo. etc. rostrum; dar en ~ a alguien con algo throw s.t. in s.o.'s face; hacer ~ a face (up to).

rotación f rotation; revolution; turnover de mano de obra; ~ de cultivos rotation of crops; **rotativo** rotary; revolving; **rotatorio** rotary, rotatory.

roto 1. p.p. of romper; **2.** broken; torn; (andrajoso) ragged; fig. debauched.

rotunda f rotunda.

rotor m rotor.

rotoso S.Am. ragged.

rótula f knee-cap; ⊕ ball-and-socket joint.

rotulación f (acto) labelling; lettering; (profesión) sign-painting; **rotular** [1a] label, ticket; letter; mark, inscribe; (titular) head, entitle;

rotulata *f* label, ticket, tag; **rotulista** *m* sign-painter; **rótulo** *m* label, ticket, tag; inscription, lettering; (shop-)sign *de tienda*; title, heading; *(cartel)* poster.

rotundamente roundly, flatly; **rotundo** *negativa etc.* round, flat; *lenguaje etc.* sonorous.

rotura *f (acto)* breaking *etc.*; *(abertura)* opening, breach, break; tear, hole *en tela etc.*; **roturar** [1a] ♒ break up.

roya *f* ♣ rust, blight.

rozadura *f* rub(bing); chafing; *esp.* ♣ abrasion, graze, sore spot; **rozagante** striking; *b.s.* showy; *fig.* proud; **rozamiento** *m* friction (*a.* ⊕), rubbing; **rozar** [1f] *v/t. a. v/i. tierra* clear; *hierba* crop, graze; nibble; *(ludir)* rub (against, on), chafe, scrape; ♣ *piel* chafe, graze; *(tocar ligeramente)* shave, graze; *superficie* skim; ~**se** *fig.* hobnob, rub shoulders (*con* with).

roznar [1a] *v/t.* crunch, gnaw; *v/i.* bray.

ruano roan.

rubéola *f* German measles.

rubí *m* ruby; jewel *de reloj.*

rubia *f (p.)* blonde; *mot.* shooting-brake; ♣ madder; *sl.* one peseta; ~ *de bote* peroxide blonde; ~ *platino* platinum blonde; **rubicundo** reddish; ruddy; rubicund; **rubio** fair, fair-haired, blond(e); *tabaco* Virginian.

rublo *m* rouble.

rubor *m* bright red; blush, flush *en cara*; *fig.* bashfulness; **ruborizarse** [1f] blush (*de* at, with), flush, redden; **ruboroso** blushing, red; *fig.* bashful.

rúbrica *f* rubric (*a. eccl.*), heading; *(señal)* red mark; flourish *tras firma*; *ser de* ~ be in line with custom; **rubricar** [1g] sign with a flourish; *(y sellar)* sign and seal.

rucio 1. *caballo* (silver-)grey; *p.* grey-haired; **2.** *m* grey.

ruda *f* rue.

rudeza *f* coarseness *etc.*

rudimental, rudimentario rudimentary; **rudimento** *m* rudiment; ~**s** *pl.* rudiments.

rudo *(tosco)* coarse, rough, crude; *(áspero)* rough; *golpe* hard; *(penoso)* hard, tough; *(grosero)* rude, ill-mannered; *(bobo)* simple.

rueca *f* distaff.

rueda *f* wheel; roller, castor *de mueble etc.*; ring, circle *de ps. etc.*; *(suplicio)* rack; *(rebanada)* round; ~ *de cadena* sprocket-wheel; ~ *dentada* gear-wheel; cog(-wheel); ~ *libre* free wheel; ~ *de molino* mill-stone; ~ *de paletas* paddle-wheel; ~ *de recambio* spare wheel; ~ *de trinquete* ratchet-wheel; *en* ~ in a ring; F *hacer la* ~ *a* suck up to; F *ir sobre* ~**s** go with a swing; **ruedecilla** *f* roller, castor; **ruedero** *m* wheelwright; **ruedo** *m (giro)* turn, rotation; edge, circumference; *(estera)* mat; *toros:* bull-ring, arena.

ruego *m* request; entreaty.

rufián *m* pimp, pander; *(brutal)* lout, hooligan.

rufo red-haired, sandy; *(rizado)* curly; *(fuerte)* tough.

rugby *m* rugby.

rugido *m* roar *etc.*; **rugir** [3c] *(león)* roar; *(toro etc.)* bellow; *(tempestad)* roar, howl; *(tripas)* rumble.

rugoso wrinkled, creased.

ruibarbo *m* rhubarb.

ruido *m* noise; sound; *(muy ruidoso)* din, row; noisiness; *fig.* repercussions; *(protestas)* outcry, stir; *mucho* ~ *y pocas nueces* much ado about nothing; *hacer* ~ *fig.*, *meter* ~ make a stir, be a sensation; F *quitarse de* ~**s** keep out of trouble; **ruidoso** noisy, loud; *suceso* sensational; *oposición* vocal, noisy.

ruin *(vil)* mean, despicable; *(pequeño)* small; *(mezquino)* petty; *(avaro)* mean; *trato* shabby, heartless; *animal* vicious.

ruina *f mst* ruin; downfall, collapse, wreck; ~**s** *pl.* ruins; *estar hecho una* ~ be a wreck.

ruindad *f* meanness *etc.*

ruinoso ruinous, tumbledown, ramshackle; *empresa* disastrous; *(sin valor)* worthless.

ruiseñor *m* nightingale.

ruleta *f* roulette.

rumano 1. *adj. a. su. m*, **a** *f* Rumanian; **2.** *m (idioma)* Rumanian.

rumbo *m esp.* ♣ course, direction, bearing; F show(iness), pomp; ~ *nuevo fig.* departure; *con* ~ *a* bound for, headed for; in the direction of; *hacer* ~ *a* set a course for, head for;

F de mucho ~ = **rumbón** F, **rumboso** F very fine, big, splendid; (*generoso*) free with one's money etc.
rumia(ción) *f* rumination; **rumiante** *adj. a. su. m* ruminant; **rumiar** [1b] *v/t.* chew; F chew over, brood on (*or* over); *v/i.* chew the cud; F ruminate, brood.
rumor *m* murmur, mutter, buzz *de voces*; (*voz*) rumour; **rumorear** [1a]: se *rumorea que* it is rumoured that; **rumoroso** noisy, loud; *arroyo etc.* murmuring.
runa *f* rune; **rúnico** runic.
runrún *m* F purr(ing) *de gato*; (*ruido*) murmuring, buzz; (*voz*) buzz.

ruptura *f fig.* rupture; breaking *de contrato*; breaking-off *de relaciones*.
rural rural; country *attr*.
ruso 1. *adj. a. su. m*, **a** *f* Russian; **2.** *m* (*idioma*) Russian.
rusticidad *f* rusticity *etc.*; **rústico 1.** rustic, country *attr.*; *b.s.* coarse, uncouth; en ~a paper-backed; **2.** *m* rustic, yokel.
ruta *f* route; (*señal de carretera*) main road, through road.
rutilante *poet.* shining.
rutina *f* routine; round; *por* ~ as a matter of course; **rutinario** routine; everyday; humdrum; *p.* unimaginative; **rutinero 1.** = *rutinario*; **2.** *m* man who just sticks to routine.

S

sábado *m* Saturday; (*judío*) Sabbath.
sábana *f* sheet; *eccl.* altar-cloth; *sl.* 1000 pesetas.
sabana *f* savanna(h).
sabandija *f* bug, creepy-crawly F; ~s *pl.* vermin.
sabañón *m* chilblain.
sabelotodo *m* F know-all.
saber [2n] **1.** *v/t.* know; (*estar enterado de*) know about, be aware of; *en pretérito freq.* learn, get to know, find out; ~ *inf.* know how to *inf.*, can *inf.*; *hacer* ~ inform; ~ *de* know about, know of; *p. ausente* hear from; *a* ~ namely; *sin* ~lo yo without my knowledge; *vete a* ~ your guess is as good as mine; ¡*qué sé yo!* how do I know?, how should I know?; ¡*qué sé yo qué más!* and what not; *el Sr no sé cuántos* Mr what's his name; *un no sé qué* a certain something; *un no sé qué de elegante* a certain elegance; *demasiado sé que* I know only too well that; *que yo sepa* as far as I know; F ¿*sabe(n)?* you know (what I mean)?; ¿*quién sabe?* who can tell?; *sepa Vd.* I would have you know; **2.** *v/i.*: ~ *a* taste of, taste like; *esp. fig.* smack of; **3.** *m* knowledge, learning; *según mi leal* ~ *y entender* to the best of my knowledge.
sabidillo *m*, **a** *f* know-all; **sabido** well-informed, knowledgeable; *de* ~ for sure; **sabiduría** *f* wisdom; knowledge, learning; **sabiendas**: *a* ~ knowingly; *a* ~ *de que* knowing full well that; **sabihondo** *adj. a.* *su. m*, **a** *f* know-all, smart aleck; **sabio 1.** wise, learned; knowing; *animal* trained; **2.** *m*, **a** *f* learned man *etc.*; wise person; ⚕ scholar, savant; *hist.* sage.
sablazo F: *dar un* ~ raise the wind, make a touch (*de* for); *vivir de* ~s live by sponging.
sable *m* sabre, cutlass.
sablista *m* F sponger, cadger.
sabor *m* taste, flavour; savour(iness); *con* ~ *a miel* honey-flavoured;

saborear [1a] flavour; (*percibir el sabor de*) savour, relish, taste; ~se smack one's lips; **saborete** *m* F slight flavour.
sabotaje *m* sabotage; **saboteador** *m* saboteur; **sabotear** [1a] sabotage.
sabroso tasty, delicious; F salty.
sabueso *m* bloodhound (*a. fig.*).
saburra *f* coat, fur.
saca[1] *f* big sack.
saca[2] *f* (*acto*) taking out; ✝ export, exporting; *estar de* ~ be on sale; F be of an age to marry.
saca...: ~**bocados** *m* ⊕ punch; ~**botas** *m* boot-jack; ~**corchos** *m* corkscrew; ~**cuartos** *m* F, ~**dineros** *m* F cheap trinket; (*maña*) cheat; ~**manchas** *m/f* dry-cleaner; ~**muelas** *m* F dentist; ~**puntas** *m* pencil-sharpener.
sacar [1g] (*extraer*) take out, get out, pull out, draw out; extract (*a.* ⚕); withdraw; (*quitar*) remove; (*exceptuar*) exclude, remove; (*obtener*) get; *arma* draw; *billete, entrada* buy, book; *copia* make; *cuentas* make up; *dinero* draw (out) *de banco*; *foto* take; *lengua, mano etc.* put out, stick out; *mancha* get out, get off; *notas* make; *pelota* (*fútbol*) throw in, (*tenis*) serve; *premio* win; *producto nuevo* bring out; *provecho* derive (*de* from); *publicación* bring out; *puesto* get; *secreto* draw out; *título* (*univ.*) get, take; *verdad* get at; *saca buen retrato* he takes well; F ¿*qué sacas con eso?* what are you driving at?; ¿*de dónde has sacado esa idea?* where did you get that idea?; ~ *de sí* drive *s.o.* crazy.
sacarina *f* saccharin.
sacerdocio *m* priesthood; ministry; **sacerdotal** priestly; **sacerdote** *m* priest; **sacerdotisa** *f* priestess.
saciar [1b] satiate, surfeit (*de* on, with); *hambre, deseos etc.* appease; **saciedad** *f* satiation, surfeit.
saco[1] *m* bag, sack; ✗ kit-bag; *sl.* 1000 pesetas; *S.Am.* jacket; ~ *de*

dormir sleeping-bag; ~ *de viaje* travelling bag.

saco[2] *m* ✕ sack; *entrar a* ~ sack, loot.

sacramental sacramental; *fig.* time-honoured; **sacramento** *m* sacrament; **sacrificar** [1g] sacrifice; slaughter *en matadero*; *perro etc.* put to sleep; **sacrificio** *m* sacrifice; slaughter(ing); **sacrilegio** *m* sacrilege; **sacrílego** sacrilegious; **sacristán** *m* verger, sacrist(an); sexton; **sacristía** *f* vestry, sacristry; **sacro** sacred, holy; **sacrosanto** most holy; sacrosanct.

sacudida *f* shake; jerk; jolt, bump *esp. de vehículo*; shock *de terremoto etc.*; blast *de explosión*; jerk, toss *de cabeza*; *pol. etc.* upheaval; **sacudidura** *f*, **sacudimiento** *m* shaking *etc.*; **sacudir** [3a] (*agitar*) shake; *brazo, pasajeros etc.* jerk, jar, jolt; *cabeza etc.* jerk, toss; (*hacer oscilar*) rock; beat *para quitar polvo*; (*mover de arriba abajo, alas etc.*) flap; (*arrojar*) toss; (*quitar de encima*) shake off; (*debatirse*) thrash about.

sádico sadistic; **sadismo** *m* sadism.

saeta *f* ✕ arrow, dart; hand *de reloj*; ♪ sacred song esp. *during Holy Week*.

saetín *m* mill-race; ⊕ tack.

saga *f* saga.

sagacidad *f* shrewdness *etc.*; **sagaz** shrewd, clever, sagacious.

sagrado 1. sacred, holy; **2.** *m* sanctuary; *acogerse a* ~ seek sanctuary; **sagrario** *m* sanctuary, shrine.

sagú *m* sago.

sahumar [1a] perfume, smoke, fumigate.

saín[1] *f* fat, grease; fish-oil *para alumbrar*; **sainete** *m* = *saín*; sauce, seasoning; *fig.* (*bocado*) titbit; (*sabor*) spice, relish; *thea.* one-act comedy.

sajar [1a] ✗ cut, lance.

sajón *adj. a. su. m*, **-a** *f* Saxon.

sal[1] *f* salt; *fig.* (*donaire*) charm; (*viveza*) liveliness; (*agudeza*) wit, wittiness; ~ *amoníaca* sal ammoniac; ~*es* pl. (*aromáticas*) smelling salts; ~ *de fruta* fruit salts; ~ *gema* rock salt; ~ *de la Higuera* Epsom salts; ~ *de la tierra* salt of the earth; ~ *volátil* sal volatile.

sal[2] *v. salir*.

sala *f* (*a.* ~ *de estar*) drawing-room, sitting-room, lounge; (*pública*) hall; *thea.* house, auditorium; ✗ ward; ⅔ court; ~ *de lo civil* civil court; ~ *de conferencias* lecture-room; ~ *de espectáculos* concert-room, hall; ~ *de espera* waiting-room; ~ *de justicia* law-court; ~ *de lectura* reading room; ~ *de máquinas* engine-room; ~ *de muestras* showroom; ~ *de operaciones* operating theatre; ~ *de recibo* parlour; ~ *de subastas* sale-room; *en* ~ *deporte* indoor.

salacidad *f* salaciousness.

saladar *m* salt-marsh; **salado** salt(y); *fig.* (*encantador*) charming, cute; (*vivo*) lively; *lenguaje etc.* racy; (*agudo*) witty; *S.Am.* ✝ expensive; (*desgraciado*) unlucky.

salamandra *f* salamander.

salamanquesa *f* lizard.

salami *m* salame.

salar [1a] salt, cure; (*sazonar*) add salt to.

salario *m* wage(s).

salaz salacious, prurient.

salceda *f*, **salcedo** *m* willow plantation.

salcochar [1a] boil (in salt water).

salchicha *f* (pork) sausage; **salchichería** *f* pork butcher's; **salchichón** *m* (salami) sausage.

saldar [1a] *cuenta* settle; *cuentas* balance; *existencias* sell off; *libros* remainder; **saldo** *m* (*acto*) settlement; (*cantidad*) balance; (*venta*) (clearance) sale; (*géneros*) remnant(s); ~ *acreedor* credit balance; ~ *deudor* debit balance.

saledizo *m* projection.

salero *m* salt-cellar; (*almacén*) salt store; F wit; charm; (*gancho*) sex appeal; **saleroso** F = *salado*.

salida *f* (*puerta etc.*) way out, exit; ⊕ *etc.* outlet, vent; *geog.* outlet (*al mar* to the sea); (*acto*) going out *etc.*; emergence; 🚂, 🚢 departure; rising *de sol*; *deportes*: start; leak *de gas, líquido*; ✕ sally, sortie; ⊕ output; ✝ (*inversión*) outlay; (*venta*) sale; (*mercado*) outlet, opening; (*resultado*) issue, outcome, result; △ projection; (*escapatoria*) loophole, way out; F crack, joke; ~ *de emergencia* emergency exit;

~ *fácil* ready market; ~ *lanzada* flying start, running start; ~ *de tono* remark out of place; *dar* ~ *a cólera etc.* vent; ✝ place, find an outlet for; ✝ *tener* ~ sell well; F *tener buenas* ~*s* be full of wisecracks.

salido projecting, bulging; *hembra* on heat; **salidizo** *m* projection; **saliente 1.** △ *etc.* projecting; *rasgo* prominent; *sol* rising; *miembro etc.* retiring, outgoing; **2.** *m* projection.

salina *f* salt-mine; ~*s* *pl.* salt-works; **salinidad** *f* salinity, salt(i)ness; **salino** saline, salty.

salir [3r] (*pasar fuera*) come out, go out; appear; emerge (*de* from), issue; arise; (*sol*) rise; *thea.* (*a.* ~ *a escena*) come on, go on; (*partir*) leave, depart (*a.* 🚂, ✈); *para* for); ⚓ sail; ⚘ come up (*a. puesto*); (*escapar*) get out (*de* of), escape (*de* from); (*mancha*) come off; (*sobresalir*) project, jut out, stick out *etc.*; *deportes:* start; *ajedrez:* have first move; *naipes:* lead; (*lotería*) win a prize (*a.* ~ *premiado*); (*resultar*) prove, turn out (to be); *le salió un diente* he cut a tooth; ~ *corriendo etc.* run *etc.* out; ~ *ganando deportes:* win; *fig.* be the gainer; ✝ be in pocket; ~ *perdiendo deportes:* lose; *fig.* be the loser; ✝ be out of pocket; ~ *elegido* be elected; ~ *bien* (*p.*) succeed, make good; pass *an examen*; (*suceso*) go off well; ~ *mal* (*p.*) fail, do badly; (*proyecto etc.*) miscarry; ~ *a calle* open into; *padre* take after; ✝ come to, work out at; ~ *caro* come expensive; ~ *con carta* lead; *novio* go out with; *observación* come out with; *pretensión* succeed in; ~ *de enfermedad* get over; ~ *por fig.* stand security for; ~*se* (*líquido, vasija*) leak; (*desbordarse*) overflow; boil over; ~ *de tema* wander from.

salitre *m* saltpetre.

saliva *f* spit, spittle, saliva; (*no*) *gastar* ~ (not) waste one's breath (*en* on); *tragar* ~ swallow one's feelings; **salivar** [1a] salivate.

salmantino *adj. a. su. m*, **a** *f* Salamancan.

salmo *m* psalm; **salmodia** *f* psalmody; F singsong, drone, monotonous singing; **salmodiar** [1b] drone, sing monotonously.

salmón *m* salmon; **salmonete** *m* (red) mullet.

salmuera *f* pickle, brine.

salobre salt(y).

saloma *f* ♪ (sea-)shanty.

salón *m* lounge, drawing-room; (*público*) hall; *paint.* salon; *esp.* ⚓ saloon; common room *de colegio*; ~ *de baile* ballroom, dance-hall; ~ *de belleza* beauty parlour; ~ *de demostraciones* showroom; ~ *de pintura* art exhibition; ~ *de sesiones* assembly hall; *juego de* ~ parlour game.

salpicadura *f* splash(ing) *etc.*; **salpicar** [1g] splash, spatter (*de* with); sprinkle (*de* with); *fig.* bespatter; pepper; *tela etc.* dot, fleck; *discurso* interlard (*de* with); **salpicón** *m* (*carne*) salmagundi; = *salpicadura.*

salpimentar [1a] season; *fig.* sweeten.

salpresar [1a] salt.

salpullido *m* 🎗 rash; swelling *de picadura.*

salsa *f* sauce; gravy *para carne asada*; dressing *para ensalada*; *fig.* appetizer; ~ *de tomate* tomato sauce; **salsera** *f* sauce-boat; gravy-boat.

saltabanco *m* quack, mountebank; (*malabarista*) juggler; **saltadura** *f* chip; **saltamontes** *m* grasshopper.

saltar [1a] **1.** *v/t.* leap (over), jump (over); vault; skip *en lectura*; **2.** *v/i.* leap, jump, spring (*a* on, *por* over); vault; dive, plunge (*a agua* into); hop, skip *a la comba etc.*; (*rebotar*) bounce, fly up; (*tapón*) pop out; (*botón*) come off; ⊕ (*pieza*) fly off; (*líquido*) spurt up, shoot up; (*vaso*) break, crack, burst; explode; *biol.* ~ *atrás* revert; ~ *sobre* pounce on; *hacer* ~ (*volar*) blow up; *trampa* spring; *caballo* (make) jump; **saltarín** *m*, **-a** *f* dancer; F restless sort.

salteador *m:* ~ *de caminos* highwayman, robber; **salteamiento** *m* hold-up; **saltear** [1a] hold up; *fig.* overcome suddenly.

salterio *m* psalter; ♪ psaltery.

saltimbanqui *m* = *saltabanco.*

salto *m* leap, jump, spring, bound; vault; hop, skip; dive, plunge; pounce *sobre presa*; (*sima*) chasm; passage skipped, part missed *en* *lectura*; ~ *de agua* waterfall; ⊕ chute; ~ *de altura* high-jump; ~ *de cabeza* header; ~ *de cama* négligée; ~ *a ciegas* leap in the dark; ~ *con garrocha*, ~ *con pértiga* pole-vault; ~ *de longitud* long-jump; ~ *mortal* somersault; ~ *de palanca* high-dive; *triple* ~ hop step and jump; ~ *de trampolín* (springboard) dive; *a* ~*s* by leaps and bounds; (*a empujones*) by fits and starts; *de un* ~ in one bound; *bajar etc. de un* ~ jump down *etc.*; *en un* ~ *fig.* in a jiffy; **saltón 1.** *ojos* bulging; *dientes* protruding; **2.** *m* grasshopper.

salubre healthy, salubrious; **salubridad** *f* healthiness; *S.Am.* (public) health; **salud** *f* ✛ health; *fig.* welfare, wellbeing; *eccl.* salvation; *¡(a su)* ~*!* good health!; *beber a la* ~ *de* drink (to) the health of; *estar bien* (*mal*) *de* ~ be in good (bad) health; **saludable** healthy; *fig.* salutary; **saludar** [1a] greet; say hullo to ☥; hail; *esp.* ✕ salute; *fig.* hail, welcome; **saludo** *m* greeting; *esp.* ✕ salute; ~*s* (*en carta*) best wishes; *un* ~ *afectuoso* kind regards; **salutación** *f* greeting.

salva *f* ✕ salute, salvo; (*bienvenida*) greeting; volley, salvo *de aplausos*.

salvabarros *m* mudguard.

salvación *f* *eccl. etc.* salvation; rescue, delivery (*de* from).

salvado *m* bran.

salvador *m*, -a *f* rescuer, deliverer; ♀ Saviour.

salvadoreño *adj. a. su. m*, **a** *f* Salvadoran.

salvaguardar [1a] safeguard; **salvaguardia** *f* safe conduct; *fig.* safeguard.

salvajada *f* barbarity, savage deed *etc.*; **salvaje 1.** *mst* wild; (*feroz*) savage; **2.** *m/f* savage; **salvajería** *f* savagery; (*acto*) barbarity; **salvajino** wild; savage; *carne* gamy; **salvajismo** *m* savagery.

salvamanteles *m* table-mat.

salvamento *m* rescue; salvage; *fig.* salvation; (*lugar*) place of safety; *de* ~ life-saving; *v. bote etc.*; **salvar** [1a] save (*a. eccl.*), rescue (*de* from); *barco etc.* salvage; *arroyo etc.* jump over, clear; *rápidos* shoot; *distancia* cover; *obstáculo* negotiate, clear; *dificultad* get

round; resolve; ~*se* save o.s., escape (*de* from); *eccl.* save one's soul; *salvando prp.* excepting; *sálvese el que pueda* every man for himself; **salvavidas** *m*: (*cinturón*) ~ lifebelt; *v. bote etc.*; **salvedad** *f* reservation, proviso.

salvia *f* ♀ sage.

salvilla *f* salver.

salvo 1. *adj.* safe; saved; **2.** *adv.*, *prp.* except (for), save, barring; *a* ~ safely; out of danger; *a* ~ *de* safe from; *en* ~ out of danger; ~ *que* except that; unless; *dejar a* ~ make an exception of; *poner a* ~ put in a safe place; *ponerse a* ~ escape, reach safety; **salvoconducto** *m* safe conduct; **salvohonor** *m* F backside.

samaritano *adj. a. su. m*, **a** *f* Samaritan; *buen* ~ good Samaritan.

sambenito *m* *fig.* dishonour, disgrace; F *quedó con su* ~ *toda la vida* he was disgraced for life.

san saint (*mst escrito* St.); F *¡voto a* ~*es!* in heaven's name!

sanable curable; **sanalotodo** *m* *fig.* panacea, cure-all; **sanar** [1a] *v/t.* cure (*de* of), heal; *v/i.* (*p.*) recover; (*herida*) heal; **sanativo** healing; **sanatorio** *m* sanatorium; nursing home.

sanción *f* sanction; **sancionar** [1a] sanction.

sancochar [1a] parboil.

sandalia *f* sandal.

sándalo *m* sandal(wood).

sandez *f* foolishness; *sandeces pl.* nonsense.

sandía *f* water-melon.

sandio foolish, silly.

sandunga *f* F charm; wit; **sandunguero** F charming; witty.

saneamiento *m* ⚖ surety; indemnification; drainage; sanitation *de casa*; **sanear** [1a] ⚖ guarantee; indemnify; *terreno* drain.

sangradera *f* ✛ lancet; **sangradura** *f* ✛ bleeding, blood-letting; outlet, draining; **sangrar** [1a] *v/t.* ✛ bleed; *fig.* ↗ *etc.* drain; *árbol, horno* tap; *typ.* indent; *v/i.* bleed; F *estar sangrando* be still fresh; be perfectly clear; **sangre** *f* blood; ~ *azul* blue blood; ~ *fría* sangfroid, coolness; *a* ~ *fría* in cold blood; *a* ~ *y fuego* by fire and sword; without mercy; *mala* ~ bad blood;

pura ~ m/f thoroughbred; de pura ~ thoroughbred; ~ vital life-blood; echar ~ bleed; se me heló la ~ my blood ran cold; sangría f bleeding; tapping etc.; (bebida) approx. fruit-cup; **sangriento** bloody; gory; arma etc. bloodstained; p. bloodthirsty; injuria deadly; **sanguijuela** f leech (a. fig.); **sanguinario** bloodthirsty, bloody; **sanguíneo** vaso etc. blood attr.; fig. blood-red; **sanguinolento** bloody, bloodstained; fig. blood-red.

sanidad f sanitation; (lo sano) health(iness); ~ pública public health; inspector de ~ sanitary inspector; **sanitario** sanitary; instalación ~a sanitation; **sano** p. healthy, fit; comida etc. wholesome; fruta, doctrina etc. sound; F whole, undamaged; ~ y salvo safe and sound; cortar por lo ~ take desperate measures; cut one's losses.

sánscrito adj. a. su. m Sanskrit.

santa f saint.

santabárbara f (powder-)magazine.

santiamén: F en un ~ in a trice.

santidad f holiness, sanctity; saintliness; su ♀ His Holiness; **santificar** [1g] sanctify; hallow, consecrate.

santiguar [1i] make the sign of the cross over; F slap; ~se cross o.s.

santo 1. holy; esp. p. saintly; mártir blessed (a. F); 2. m saint; saint's day; ~ y seña password; fig. watchword; F ¿a ~ de qué? what on earth for?; desnudar a un ~ para vestir a otro rob Peter to pay Paul; F no es ~ de mi devoción I'm not very keen on him; F quedar para vestir ~s be on the shelf; **santuario** m sanctuary; **santurrón** 1. sanctimonious; hypocritical; 2. m, -a f sanctimonious person; hypocrite.

saña f anger, fury (a. fig.); cruelty; **sañoso, sañudo** furious.

sapo m toad; F echar ~s y culebras swear black and blue.

saque m tenis etc.: service, serve; (línea) base-line; (p.) server; fútbol: throw-in; ~ inicial kick-off; ~ de esquina corner-kick; ~ de portería goal-kick.

saqueador m looter; **saquear** [1a] loot, sack, plunder; fig. rifle, ransack; **saqueo** m looting etc.

sarampión m measles.

sarao m soirée, evening party.

sarcasmo m sarcasm; **sarcástico** sarcastic.

sarcófago m sarcophagus.

sardina f sardine; ~ arenque pilchard; **sardinero** sardine attr.

sardo adj. a. su. m, a f Sardinian.

sargentear [1a] v/t. ✗ command; F boss about; v/i. F be bossy; **sargento** m sergeant; **sargentona** f F big blowzy woman.

sargo m bream.

sarmentoso twining; **sarmiento** m vine shoot.

sarna f itch, scabies; vet. mange; **sarnoso** that has the itch; itchy; vet. mangy.

sarraceno adj. a. su. m, a f Saracen.

sarracina f free fight.

sarro m incrustation; fur de vasija, lengua; tartar de dientes; **sarroso** incrusted; furry; covered with tartar.

sarta f, **sartal** m string (a. fig.); line, series.

sartén mst f frying-pan.

sastre m tailor; ~ de teatro costumier; hecho por ~ tailor-made; **sastrería** f tailoring; (tienda) tailor's.

satánico satanic, devilish.

satélite 1. satellite; 2. m satellite (a. pol.); (p.) minion, henchman.

satén m sateen; **satinado** glossy.

sátira f satire; **satírico** satiric(al); **satirizar** [1f] satirize.

sátiro m satyr (a. fig.).

satisfacción f satisfaction; ~ de sí mismo self-satisfaction, smugness; a ~ to one's satisfaction; **satisfacer** [2s] mst satisfy; deuda pay; necesidad, petición meet; (dar placer a) gratify, please; ~se satisfy o.s., be satisfied; (vengarse) take revenge; **satisfactorio** satisfactory; **satisfecho** satisfied; pleased ~ (de sí mismo) self-satisfied, smug.

saturar [1a] saturate; permeate.

saturnino saturnine.

sauce m willow; ~ llorón weeping willow; **saucedal** m willow plantation.

saúco m ♀ elder.

saurio m saurian.

savia f sap.

saxofón m saxophone.

saya *f* skirt; dress; **sayo** *m* smock, tunic; long loose gown.

sayón *m* executioner; F ugly customer.

sazo *m sl.* hankie.

sazón *f* ripeness, maturity; (*ocasión*) season, time; *a la* ~ then, at that time; *en* ~ **♀** ripe; *actuar* opportunely; **sazonado ♀** *etc.* mellow; *plato* tasty; *frase* witty; **sazonar** [1a] *v/t.* season, flavour; *fig.* bring to maturity; *v/i.* ripen.

se 1. *pron. reflexivo:* a) *sg.* himself, herself, itself; (*con Vd.*) yourself; *pl.* themselves; (*con Vds.*) yourselves; b) *recíproco:* each other, one another; c) *con inf.:* oneself, *e.g.* hay que protegerse one must protect oneself; d) *impersonal: freq.* se traduce por la voz pasiva, *por* one, *por* people: se dice que it is said that, people say that; no se sabe por qué it is not known why; se habla español Spanish (is) spoken here; **2.** *pron. personal que corresponde a* le, les: se lo di I gave it to him; se lo buscaré I'll look for it for you.

sé *v.* saber, ser.

sebo *m* grease, fat; tallow *para velas*; suet *para cocina*; **seboso** greasy, fatty; tallowy; suety. ⁰

seca *f* drought; (*época*) dry season; (*arena*) sandbank; **secador** *m:* ~ *para el pelo* hair-dryer; **secadora** *f* wringer; **secano** *m* (*a. tierras de* ~) dry land, unirrigated land; region having little rain; **♏** sandbank; *fig.* very dry thing; **secante 1.** drying; *S.Am.* annoying; *papel* ~ = **2.** *m* blotting-paper; **secar** [1g] dry (up); *superficie* wipe dry; *frente* wipe, mop; blot *con papel secante*; *líquido derramado* mop up; *fig.* annoy, vex; bore; ~**se** (*río etc.*) dry up, run dry; (*p.*) dry o.s.; **♀** dry up, wilt; (*animal*) get thin.

sección *f* section; **♎** (*corte*) cross-section; *fig.* section (*a.* **♐**), division, department *de organización;* ~ *vertical* vertical section; **seccional** sectional; **seccionar** [1a] divide up.

secesión *f* secession.

seco *mst* dry; *legumbres etc.* dried; *planta* dried-up; (*flaco*) lean; (*áspero*) sharp, harsh; *golpe etc.* sharp; (*riguroso*) strict; *respuesta* curt; *estilo* plain, bare; *a* ~*as* simply, just; *en* ~ high and dry (*a. fig.*); *río* dry; *fig.* abruptly; *parar(se) en* ~ stop dead.

secoya *f* sequoia.

secreción *f* secretion; **secretar** [1a] secrete.

secretaría *f* secretariat(e); (*oficio*) secretaryship; (*oficina*) secretary's office; **secretario** *m*, **a** *f* secretary; **secretear** [1a] F talk confidentially; **secreto 1.** secret; (*no visible*) hidden; **2.** *m* secret; (*lo* ~) secrecy; (*escondrijo*) secret drawer, hiding-place; ~ *de correspondencia* sanctity of the mails; ~ *de estado* state secret; ~ *a voces* open secret; *en* ~ in secret; in private; **♏** in camera; *estar en el* ~ be in the secret; *hacer* ~ *de* be secretive about.

secta *f* sect; denomination; **sectario 1.** sectarian; denominational; **2.** *m*, **a** *f* follower, devotee; sectarian.

sector *m mst* sector; section *de opinión.*

secuaz *m* follower; *b.s.* underling.

secuestrador *m*, **-a** *f* kidnapper; **secuestrar** [1a] kidnap; *bienes* seize; **secuestro** *m* kidnapping; **♏** seizure.

secular secular; (*viejo*) age-old, ancient; **secularización** *f* secularization; **secularizar** [1f] secularize.

secundar [1a] second, help; **secundario** *mst* secondary; minor, side...; by...; **secundinas** *f/pl.* afterbirth.

sed *f* thirst (*de* for; *a. fig.*); *apagar la* ~ quench one's thirst; *tener* ~ be thirsty; *fig. tener* ~ *de* thirst for.

seda *f* silk; (*cerda*) bristle; *de* ~ silk(en); *como una* ~ (*adj.*) smooth (as silk); (*adv.*) smoothly; **sedal** *m* fishing-line.

sedante 1. sedative; *fig.* soothing; **2.** *m* = **sedativo** *adj. a. su. m* sedative.

sede *f eccl.* see; seat *de gobierno;* headquarters *de sociedad etc.;* ~ *social* head office; *Santa* **♀** Holy See.

sedentario sedentary.

sedeño silken; silky; **sedería** *f* silks, silk goods; (*comercio*) silk trade; (*tienda*) silk-shop; **sedero** silk *attr.*

sedic(i)ente self-styled, so-called.
sedición f sedition; **sedicioso** 1. seditious; 2. m, a f rebel.
sediento thirsty (a. ✗); fig. eager (de for).
sedimentar [1a] deposit (sediment); ⁓se settle; **sedimentario** sedimentary; **sedimento** m sediment.
sedoso silky.
seducción f (acto) seduction etc.; (aliciente) lure, charm; **seducir** [3o] seduce; entice, lure, lead astray; (cautivar) charm, beguile; (sobornar) bribe; fig. charming, captivating; **seductor** 1. = seductivo; 2. m seducer.
sefardí 1. Sephardic; 2. m/f Sephardi; ⁓es pl. Sephardim.
segador m harvester, reaper; **segadora** f reaper; mower, mowing-machine; ⁓-atadora f binder; ⁓-trilladora f combine (harvester); ⁓ de césped lawn-mower; **segar** [1h a. 1k] trigo etc. reap, cut; heno, hierba mow; fig. cut off; mow down.
seglar 1. secular, lay; 2. m layman.
segmento m segment; ⁓ de émbolo piston-ring.
segregación f segregation; **segregar** [1h] segregate; physiol. secrete.
seguida: de ⁓ uninterruptedly, straight off; en ⁓ at once, right away; **seguido** continued, successive; camino etc. straight; ⁓s pl. in a row, in succession; 3 días ⁓s 3 days running; todo ⁓ adv. straight ahead; **seguimiento** m chase, pursuit; continuation; **seguir** [3d a. 3l] 1. v/t. follow; (cazar) chase, pursue; (acosar) hound; pasos dog; consejo follow, take; curso pursue; continue; 2. v/i. follow; come after, come next; go on, continue; (caminar etc.) proceed; como sigue as follows; ¿cómo sigue? how is he?; ¡siga! go on!; siga a la derecha keep to the right; ⁓ ger. keep (on) ger., go on ger.; ⁓ leyendo etc. read on etc.; ⁓ en su sitio still be in the same place; ⁓ hacer ⁓ forward; ⁓ adelante go on, carry (straight) on; mot. drive on (hasta as far as); ⁓ bueno (tiempo) hold, stay fine; ⁓ con go on with; ⁓ en error

continue in; 3. ⁓se follow, ensue; (sucederse) follow one another; síguese que it follows that.
según 1. prp. according to; in accordance with; ⁓ lo que dice from what he says; ⁓ este modelo on this model; 2. adv. depending on circumstances; ⁓ (y como), ⁓ (y conforme) it (all) depends; 3. cj. as; ⁓ esté el tiempo depending on the weather.
segunda f ♪ second; ⁓ (intención) second (or veiled) meaning; hidden purpose; **segundante** m boxeo: second; **segundero** m second-hand; **segundo** 1. second; 2. m second; ⚓ mate; sin ⁓ unrivalled; **segundón** m second (or younger) son.
seguridad f safety, safeness; security; reliability; (certeza) certainty; ⚖ security, surety; ⁓ colectiva collective security; ⁓ contra incendios fire precautions; de ⁓ cinturón etc. safety attr.; para mayor ⁓ to be on the safe side, tener la ⁓ de que be sure that; **seguro** 1. (sin peligro) safe, sure; secure; (confiable) reliable, dependable; (cierto) certain, sure; (firme) stable, steady; ¿está Vd. ⁓? are you sure?; estar ⁓ de que be sure that; 2. m safety; certainty; confidence; ✝ insurance; (lugar) safe place; tumbler de cerradura; ✂ safety-catch; ⊕ pawl, catch; ⁓ de incendios fire-insurance; ⁓ social social insurance (or security); ⁓ de vida life-insurance; (póliza de) ⁓ sobre la vida life-insurance (policy); a buen ⁓, de ⁓ surely, truly; sobre ⁓ without risk; saber a buen ⁓ know for certain.
seis six (a. su.); (fecha) sixth; las ⁓ six o'clock; **seiscientos** six hundred.
seísmo m earthquake.
selección f selection (a. biol.); ♪ ⁓es pl. selections; **seleccionador** m selector; **seleccionar** [1a] pick, choose; **selectivo** selective (a. radio); **selecto** calidad select, choice; obras etc. selected; club select, exclusive.
seltz [selθ, sel]: agua (de) ⁓ soda-water, seltzer (water).
selva f forest, wood(s); (esp. tropical) jungle; **selvático** ♀ wild; escena etc. sylvan; fig. rustic; **selvoso** wooded.

selladura *f* seal(ing); **sellar** [1a] seal; stamp *con timbre etc.*; **sello** *m* seal; signet; & stamp; ✝ brand, seal; *fig.* (*huella*) impression, mark; hallmark *de calidad*; ✍ capsule, pill; ~ *fiscal* revenue stamp.

semáforo *m* semaphore; 🚦 signal; *mot.* traffic signal.

semana *f* week; ~ *inglesa* five-and-a-half day week; ♀ *Santa* Holy Week; *entre* ~ during the week; **semanal, semanario** *adj. a. su. m* weekly.

semántica *f* semantics.

semblante *m* *lit.* visage; *fig.* appearance, look; *componer el* ~ recover one's composure; *mudar de* ~ change colour; **semblanza** *f* biographical sketch.

sembradera *f*, **sembradora** *f* drill; **sembrado** *m* sown field; **sembrador** *m*, **-a** *f* sower; **sembradura** *f* sowing; **sembrar** [1k] sow; *fig.* sprinkle, scatter, strew (de with); *discordia* sow; *noticia* spread.

semejante 1. similar (*a.* ⅊); ~*s pl.* alike, similar; ~ *a* like; *no hice cosa* ~ I never did such a thing; 2. *m* fellow-man, fellow-creature; *no tiene* ~ it has no equal; **semejanza** *f* similarity, resemblance; *a* ~ *de* like, as; **semejar(se)** [1a] be alike, be similar, resemble each other.

semen *m* semen; **semental** 1. *caballo* stud, breeding; 2. *m* sire; **sementera** *f* (*acto*) sowing; (*campo*) sown land; (*época*) seed-time, sowing time.

semestral half-yearly; **semestre** *m* period of six months.

semi... semi...; half...; ~**breve** *f* semibreve; ~**círculo** *m* semicircle; ~**corchea** *f* semiquaver; ~**final** *f* semi-final.

semilla *f* seed; **semillero** *m* seedbed; nursery; *fig.* hotbed; **seminal** seminal.

seminario *m* seminary; *univ.* seminar; ♀ seed-bed; nursery; **seminarista** *m* seminarist.

semioficial semi-official.

semita 1. Semitic; 2. *m/f* Semite; **semítico** Semitic.

semitono *m* semitone.

semivocal *f* semivowel.

sémola *f* semolina.

sempiterna *f* evergreen; **sempiterno** everlasting.

senado *m* senate; **senador** *m* senator; **senatorial, senatorio** senatorial.

sencillez *f* simplicity *etc.*; **sencillo** 1. simple, straightforward, easy; *billete,* ♀ single; *p. etc.* unsophisticated, natural; *b.s.* simple; *vestido, estilo etc.* simple, plain; 2. *m* S.Am. loose change.

senda *f*, **sendero** *m* (foot)path, track, lane (*a. mot.*).

sendos one ... each; *les dio* ~ *golpes* he struck each of them; *llevaban* ~ *fusiles* they each carried a rifle.

senectud *f* old age; **senil** senile; **senilidad** *f* senility.

seno¹ *m* (*pecho*) breast; (*pechos*) bosom, bust; (*útero*) womb; (*frontal*) sinus; *fig.* bosom; lap; (*hueco*) hollow; *geog.* small bay; ⚓ trough *de ola*; *esconder algo en el* ~ hide s.t. in one's bosom; *en el* ~ *de la familia* in the bosom of the family.

seno² *m* ⅊ sine.

sensación *f* sensation (*a. fig.*); sense, feeling; feel; thrill; *hacer* ~ cause a sensation; **sensacional** sensational; **sensacionalismo** *m* sensationalism.

sensatez *f* good sense, sensibleness; **sensato** sensible.

sensibilidad *f* sensitivity (*a* to); **sensibilizado** *phot.* sensitive; sensitized; **sensible** (*que siente*) sensible; *aparato etc.* sensitive; (*que se conmueve*) sensitive, responsive (*a* to); (*apreciable*) perceptible, noticeable; (*lamentable*) regrettable; *pérdida* considerable; ✍ tender, sore; *phot.* sensitive; ~ *de mejora* capable of improvement; ~ *del honor que se me hace* fully aware of the honour being done me; **sensiblería** *f* sentimentality, mush; squeamishness; **sensiblero** sentimental, mushy; squeamish; **sensitiva** *f* mimosa; **sensitivo** *órgano etc.* sense *attr.*; sensitive; *ser* sentient; **sensorio** sensory; **sensual** sensual, sensuous; **sensualidad** *f* sensuality; **sensualismo** *m* sensualism; **sensualista** *m/f* sensualist.

sentada *f* sitting; *de una* ~ at one sitting; **sentadero** *m* seat; **sentado** sitting, seated; (*establecido*) settled; permanent; *carácter* sedate; sensible; *dar por* ~ take for granted, assume; *dejar* ~ leave a clear impression of; *dejar* ~ *que* lay (it) down that; *estar (or quedar)* ~ sit, be sitting (down), be seated; **sentar** [1k] **1.** *v/t. p.* seat, sit; *(asentar)* set up, establish; ✝ put down (*en la cuenta de* to); **2.** *v/t. a. v/i. (vestido)* fit *por tamaño*, suit *por estilo*; ~ *bien fig.* go down well; ~ *bien a (comida)* agree with; ~ *mal fig.* go down badly, produce a bad impression; ~ *mal a (comida)* disagree with; **3.** ~**se** sit (down); settle (o.s.).

sentencia *f* 🜨 sentence; *(máxima)* dictum, saying; **sentenciar** [1b] *v/t.* 🜨 sentence (*a* to); *v/i.* pronounce, give one's opinion; **sentencioso** sententious; dogmatic; *dicho* pithy; oracular.

sentidamente regretfully; **sentido 1.** *(hondo)* heartfelt, keen; *(que se ofende)* sensitive; *(convincente)* moving, feeling; **2.** *m (facultad)* sense; *(significado)* sense, meaning; *(juicio)* sense, good sense; *(aprecio)* feeling (*de música* for); way, direction; ~ *común* common sense; *doble* ~ double meaning; *en cierto* ~ in a sense; *sin* ~ meaningless; 🜨 senseless, unconscious; *cobrar* ~ begin to mean s.t.; F *costar un* ~ cost the earth; *perder el* ~ lose consciousness; *tener* ~ make sense.

sentimental sentimental; *mirada* soulful; *aventura, vida etc.* love *attr.*; **sentimentalismo** *m* sentimentality; **sentimiento** *m* feeling; sentiment; *(pesar)* grief, regret; consciousness; *v. acompañar.*

sentina *f* ⚓ bilge; *fig.* sink, sewer.

sentir 1. [3i] *v/t.* feel; sense, perceive; *(oír)* hear; *(tener pesar)* regret, be sorry for; *lo siento (mucho)* I am (very *or* so) sorry; *siento tener que hacerlo* I am sorry to have to do it; *dejarse* ~ let itself be felt; *v/i.* judge, think; *sin* ~ inadvertently; *dar que* ~ give cause for regret; ~**se** feel, *e.g.* ~ *enfermo* feel ill, ~ *obligado a* feel obliged to; *(quejarse)* complain, be offended, be resentful; *(quebrarse)* crack; ~ *de* 🜨 have a pain in; *palabra etc.* take offence at; **2.** *m* feeling; opinion; *a mi* ~ in my opinion.

seña *f* sign, token; mark *en cara etc.*; ✗ password; ~*s pl.* address; ~*s pl.*

personales personal description; *por más* ~*s* to clinch the matter; *dar* ~*s de* show signs of; *hablar por* ~*s* talk by signs; *hacer* ~*s a*, *llamar con* ~*s* make signs to, beckon (to).

señal *f* sign, mark; *(indicio)* sign, token, indication; mark(ing) *de identidad*; brand *de animal*; sign, signal *con mano*; *radio, mot.*, 🚂 *etc.* signal; *(mojón)* landmark; bookmark *en libro*; 🜨 scar, mark; *(huella)* trace; ✝ deposit; *(prenda)* pledge, token; ~ *de carretera* road sign; ~ *horaria* time-signal; ~*es pl. luminosas*, ~*es pl. de tráfico* traffic signals; ~ *para marcar* dialling tone; ~ *de ocupado* engaged signal; ~ *de peligro* danger-signal; ✝ *en* ~ as a deposit; *en* ~ *de* as a token of; *sin la menor* ~ *de* without a trace of;

señaladamente especially; **señalado** notable, distinguished; **señalar** [1a] point out, point to, indicate *con dedo*; *(mostrar)* show; *(comunicar)* signal; mark, stamp; *animal* brand; denote; *fecha etc.* fix, set; *p. etc.* appoint, name; 🜨 leave a scar (on); ~**se** *fig.* make one's mark; **señalizar** [1f] signpost.

señor *m* gentleman, man; *(dueño)* master, owner; *(noble, feudal, dueño fig.)* lord; *delante de apellido*: Mister *(escrito* Mr); *en trato directo*: sir; *(a noble)* my lord; *¡sí* ~*!* yes indeed!; *pues sí* ~ well that's how it is; *El* ♀ The Lord; *muy* ~ *mío* Dear Sir; *hacer el* ~ lord it; ~*es pl.* gentlemen; ✝ Messrs; *los* ~*es Smith* the Smiths.

señora *f* lady; *(dueña)* mistress, owner; *(noble)* lady; *(esposa)* wife; *delante de apellido*: Mrs ['misiz]; *en trato directo*: madam; *(a noble)* my lady; *la* ~ *de Smith* Mrs Smith; *Nuestra* ♀ Our Lady *para católicos*, the Virgin (Mary) *para protestantes*.

señorear [1a] rule; lord it over; *pasiones* master; ~**se** control o.s.; ~ *de* seize.

señoría *f* rule, sway; *tratamiento*: *su etc.* ♀ (Your, His) Lordship, (Your, Her) Ladyship; my lord, my lady; **señori(a)l** *fig.* lordly, commanding; **señorío** *m* *hist.* manor; domain; *fig.* dominion, sway, rule (*sobre* over); (*dignidad*) lordliness.

señorita *f* young lady; *delante de apellido*: Miss; *en trato directo freq. no se traduce*; **señorito** *m* young gentleman; (young) master; (*de mucho mundo*) man about town; *contp.* play-boy; **señorón** *m* F big shot.

señuelo *m* decoy; *fig.* bait, lure.

sépalo *m* sepal.

separable separable; ⊕ detachable; **separación** *f* separation (*a.* 🔬); dismissal (*de puesto* from); ⊕ removal; *eccl.* disestablishment; ~ *del matrimonio* legal separation; **separado** separate; *esp.* ⊕ detached; *por* ~ separately; ᭒ under separate cover; *vive* ~ *de su mujer* he is separated from his wife, he doesn't live with his wife; **separador** *m* separator; **separar** [1a] separate (*de* from); sever; divide; (*clasificar*) sort; *mueble etc.* move away (*de* from); ⊕ *pieza* remove, detach; (*despedir*) dismiss; ~**se** separate (*de* from); part company (*de* with); (*piezas*) come apart; retire, withdraw; (*estado etc.*) secede; **separata** *f* offprint; **separatismo** *m* separatism; **separatista** *m/f* separatist.

sepia *f zo.* cuttlefish; *paint.* sepia.

sepsis *f* sepsis.

septentrión *m* north; **septentrional** north(ern).

séptico septic.

se(p)tiembre *m* September.

séptimo *adj. a. su. m* seventh; **septuagenario** *adj. a. su. m*, a *f* septuagenarian; **septuagésimo** seventieth.

sepulcral sepulchral (*a. fig.*); *fig.* gloomy, dismal; **sepulcro** *m* tomb, grave; (*Biblia*) sepulchre; **sepultar** [1a] bury; *fig.* entomb; *fig.* (*esconder*) bury, hide away; **sepultura** *f* (*acto*) burial; (*tumba*) grave; *dar* ~ *a* bury; **sepulturero** *m* gravedigger, sexton.

sequedad *f* dryness *etc.*; **sequía** *f* drought; (*temporada*) dry season.

séquito *m* retinue, entourage; party.

ser 1. [2w] be; a) *identidad*: *soy yo* it's me, it is I *lit.*; *teleph.* ¡*soy Pérez!* Pérez speaking, this is Pérez; b) *origen*: *yo soy de Madrid* I am from Madrid; c) *materia*: *la moneda es de oro* it is a gold coin;

d) *hora*: *es la una* it is one o'clock; *son las 2* it is 2 o'clock; *serán las 9* it will be about 9; *serían las 9* it would be (*or* have been) about 9; e) *posesión*: *el coche es de mi padre* the car belongs to my father; f) *destino*: ¿*qué ha sido de él?* what has become of him?; F ¿*qué es de tu vida?* what's the news?; g) *pasivo*: *ha sido asesinado* he has been murdered; h) *frases*: ~ *para poco* be of next to no use; *de no* ~ *así* were it not so; *a no* ~ *por* but for; were it not *for*; *a no* ~ *que* unless; ¡*cómo ha de* ~! what else do you expect?; *es de esperar que* it is to be hoped that; *es de creer que* it may be assumed that; *es que* the fact is that; *soy con Vd.* I'll be with you in a moment; *siendo así que* so that; *o sea* that is to say, or rather; *sea ... sea* whether ... or whether; *sea lo que sea* (*or fuere*) be that as it may; *no sea que* lest; *érase que se era* once upon a time (there was); *era de ver* you ought to have seen it, it was worth seeing; *presidente que fue* ex-president; former(ly) president; **2.** *m* being; (*vida*) life; essence; ~ *humano* human being.

sera *f* pannier, basket.

seráfico seraphic, angelic; F poor; **serafín** *m* seraph.

serenar [1a] calm; quieten, pacify; *líquido* clarify; ~**se** grow calm; *meteor.* clear up; (*p.*) calm down; (*líquido*) clear.

serenata *f* serenade.

serenidad *f* serenity *etc.*; **sereno**[1] serene, calm; *tiempo* settled, fine; *cielo* cloudless; *temperamento* even; F (*no borracho*) sober.

sereno[2] *m* (night-)watchman; (*rocío*) dew; *al* ~ in the open (air).

serial *m* serial; **serie** *f* series (*a.* 🅰, 🔬, *biol.*); sequence; set; 🔧 *arrollado en* ~ series-wound; *v. fabricar*; *fuera de* ~ out of order, not in the proper order; (*extraordinario*) special.

seriedad *f* seriousness *etc.*; **serio** *mst* serious; grave; solemn; sober, staid; (*confiable*) reliable, trustworthy; (*justo*) fair, fair-minded; (*genuino*) true, real; *en* ~ seriously; *poco* ~ *freq.* frivolous; (*no confiable*) unreliable; *etc.*

sermón *m* sermon (*a. iro.*); **sermonear** [1a] F *v/t.* lecture; *v/i.* sermonize; **sermoneo** *m* F lecture.

serón *m* pannier, large basket.

serpa *f* ♀ runner.

serpentear [1a] *zo.* wriggle, snake; (*camino*) wind; (*río*) wind, meander; **serpenteo** *m* wriggling *etc.*; **serpentín** *m* coil; **serpentina** *f min.* serpentine; (*papel*) streamer; **serpentino** snaky, sinuous; winding; **serpiente** *f* snake; (*mitológica*, *fig.*) serpent; ~ *de cascabel* rattlesnake; ~ *de mar* sea-serpent.

serpollo *m* sucker, shoot.

serraduras *f/pl.* sawdust.

serrallo *m* harem, seraglio.

serranía *f* mountainous area, hill country; **serrano 1.** highland *attr.*, mountain *attr.*; *fig.* rough, rustic; *jugada* dirty; **2.** *m* highlander.

serrar [1k] saw; **serrín** *m* sawdust; **serruchar** [1a] *S.Am.* saw; **serrucho** *m* handsaw.

servible serviceable; **servicial** helpful, obliging; dutiful; **servicio** *m* service (*a.* ✗, *eccl.*, *hotel*, *tenis*); service, set *de vajilla*; *hotel*: service (charge); *S.Am.* lavatory; ~*s pl.* sanitation *de casa*; ~ *activo* active service; ~ *de café* coffee-set; ~ *doméstico* (domestic) service; domestic help; (*ps.*) servants; ~ *militar* military service; ~ *social* social service, welfare work; *al* ~ *de* in the service of; ✗ *etc. de* ~ on duty; ✗ *en condiciones de* ~ operational; *franco de* ~ off duty; *hacer un flaco* ~ *a* play a dirty trick on; ✗ *prestar* ~ serve, see service.

servidor *m*, -a *f* servant; *un* ~ my humble self; ~ *de Vd.* at your service; *su seguro* ~ yours faithfully; **servidumbre** *f* servitude; *fig.* self-control; (*obligación*) compulsion; (*ps.*) servants, staff; ~ *de la gleba* serfdom; ~ *de paso* right of way; **servil** servile; (*rastrero*) grovelling, abject; *imitación* slavish; *oficio* menial; **servilismo** *m* servility *etc.*

servilleta *f* serviette, napkin.

servio 1. Serbian; **2.** *m*, a *f* Serb; **3.** *m* (*idioma*) Serbo-Croat.

servir [3l] *v/t. mst* serve; *ps. a la mesa* wait on; *cargo* carry out, fulfil; *cañón* man; *máquina* tend; (*hacer un servicio a*) do a favour to, oblige; *ser servido de inf.* de pleased to *inf.*;

2. *v/i.* serve (*a.* ✗, *tenis*; *de as*, for); (*ser servible*) be useful, be of use; serve, wait *a la mesa*; (*ser criado*) be in service; ✗ *está sirviendo* he is doing his military service; ~ *en lugar de* do duty for; *para* ~ *a Vd.* at your service; ~ *para* be good for, be used for; *no sirve para nada* (*p.*) he's no earthly use; *¿para qué sirve?* what is the good of it?; (*eso*) *no sirve* that's no good, that won't do; **3.** ~*se* help o.s. *a la mesa*; ~ *inf.* be good enough to *inf.*; deign to *inf.*; *sírvase inf.* please *inf.*; ~ *de* make use of; put to use.

sésamo *m* ♀, *fig.* sesame; *¡*~ *ábrete!* open sesame!

sesear [1a] pronounce c (*before e, i*) *and* z [θ] *as* [s].

sesenta sixty; **sesentón** *adj. a. su. m*, -a *f* F sexagenarian.

seseo *m* pronunciation of c (*before e, i*) *and* z [θ] *as* [s].

sesera *f* brain-pan; F brain(-box).

sesgado slanting, oblique; *gorra etc.* awry; **sesgar** [1h] slant, slope; (*cortar*) cut on the slant; *sew.* cut (on the) bias; ⊕ bevel; (*torcer*) twist to one side; **sesgo** *m* slant, slope; *esp. sew.* bias; (*torcimiento*) warp, twist; *fig.* (mental) twist, turn; *fig.* compromise; *al* ~ slanting; awry; *cortar etc.* on the bias.

sesión *f* session, sitting; meeting; *cine:* ~ *continua* continuous showing; ~ *de espiritismo* séance; *levantar la* ~ adjourn.

seso *m* brain; *fig.* sense, brains; ~*s pl.* brains (*a. cocina*); *devanarse los* ~*s* rack one's brains; *v. tapa;* *perder el* ~ go mad.

sestear [1a] take a siesta (*or* nap).

sesudo sensible, wise; (*inteligente*) brainy.

set *m tenis:* set.

seta *f* mushroom.

setecientos seven hundred; **setenta** seventy; **setentón** *adj. a. su. m*, -a *f* F septuagenarian.

setiembre *m* September.

seto *m* fence; ~ (*vivo*) hedge.

seudo... pseudo...; **seudónimo 1.** pseudonymous; **2.** *m* pseudonym.

severidad *f* severity *etc.*; **severo** *mst* severe; stringent, exacting; hard, harsh; stern; *ser* ~ *con* (*or para*) be hard on.

sevillano *adj. a. su. m*, a *f* Sevillian.

sexagenario *adj. a. su. m,* **a** *f* sexagenarian; **sexagésimo** sixtieth.

sexo *m* sex; *el bello* ~ the fair sex; *el* ~ *débil* the gentle sex.

sextante *m* sextant.

sexto *adj. a. su. m* sixth.

sexual sexual; sex *attr.*; **sexualidad** *f* sexuality.

shock *m* [ʃok] shock.

sí[1] **1.** *adv.* yes; indeed; *enfático etc.*: *él* ~ *fue* he did go, he certainly went; *él no lo sabe pero yo* ~ he doesn't know (it) but I do; *ellos* ~ *vendrán* they are sure to come, they at least will come; F *porque* ~ because that's the way it is; because I say so; *lo hizo porque* ~ *b.s.* he did it out of pure cussedness; *por* ~ *o por no* in any case; *¡eso* ~ *que no!* not on any account!; not a bit of it!; *un día* ~ *y otro no* on alternate days, every other day; **2.** *m* yes; consent; *dar el* ~ say yes.

sí[2] *pron. sg.* himself, herself, itself; *(con Vd.)* yourself; *pl.* themselves; *(con Vds.)* yourselves; *recíproco*: each other; ~ *mismo* himself *etc.*; *(con inf.)* oneself; *de* ~ in itself; spontaneously; *de por* ~ separately, individually; per se; in itself *etc.*; *fuera de* ~ beside o.s.; *por* ~ *(solo)* by oneself *etc.*; *v. dar etc.*

si *cj.* if; whether; ~ *no* if not; otherwise; *¡~ ...?* what if ...?; suppose ...?; *¡~ fuera verdad!* if only it were true!; *¡¿~ vendrá?* I wonder if he'll come?; *¡~ está en América, imbécil!* but he's in America, silly!

siamés *adj. a. su. m,* **-a** *f* Siamese.

siberiano *adj. a. su m,* **a** *f* Siberian.

sibilante *adj. a. su. f* sibilant.

sibilino sibylline.

sicalipsis *f* eroticism, suggestiveness; **sicalíptico** erotic, suggestive.

siciliano *adj. a. su. m,* **a** *f* Sicilian.

sicomoro *m* sycamore.

sidecar ['sajkar] *m* sidecar.

sideral *adj. a.* **sidéreo** sidereal; astral; *casco etc.* space *attr.*

siderurgia *f* iron and steel industry; **siderúrgico** iron and steel *attr.*; *la* ~*a* iron and steel works.

sidra *f* cider.   [harvest.]

siega *f*| reaping, mowing; *(época)*

siembra *f (acto)* sowing; *(campo)* sown field; *(época)* sowing time; *patata de* ~ seed potato.

siempre always; all the time; ever; *como* ~ as usual; *de* ~ usual, inevitable; *lo de* ~ the same old thing; *(de una vez) para* ~ once and for all, for good; *para* ~ for ever; *para (or por)* ~ *jamás* for ever and ever; ~ *que indic.* whenever, as often as; *subj.* provided that.

sien *f anat.* temple.

sierpe *f* snake, serpent.

sierra *f* ⊕ saw; *geog.* mountain range; ~ *de arco (para metales)* hacksaw; ~ *cabrilla* whip-saw; ~ *de calados* fretsaw; ~ *circular* circular saw; ~ *de espigar* tenon-saw; ~ *de vaivén* jig-saw.

siervo *m,* **a** *f* slave; ~ *(de la gleba)* serf.

siesta *f* siesta, (afternoon) nap; *(calor)* hottest part of the day; *dormir (or echar) la* ~ take a nap *(esp.* after lunch).

siete seven *(a. su.)*; *(fecha)* seventh; *las* ~ seven o'clock; F *hablar más que* ~ talk nineteen to the dozen.

sífilis *f* syphilis; **sifilítico** syphilitic.

sifón *m* siphon; ⊕ trap; *con* ~ *bebida* and soda.

sigilo *m* secrecy, discretion; **sigiloso** discreet, secret; reserved.

sigla *f* symbol, abbreviation.

siglo *m* century; *(mucho tiempo)* age; *(época)* age, time(s); *eccl.* world; ♀ *de las Luces* Age of Enlightenment; ♀ *de Oro* Golden Age; *eccl. en el* ~ in the world; *por los* ~s *de los* ~s world without end.

signarse [1a] cross o.s.; **signatura** *f typ.*, ♪ signature; (catalogue-) number *de biblioteca.*

significación *f* significance; **significado 1.** *S.Am.* well-known; important; **2.** *m* meaning *de palabra*; intention; *(importancia)* significance; **significante** significant; **significar** [1g] *v/t. (hacer saber)* make known, signify; *(querer decir)* mean *(para* to), signify; *v/i.* be important; **significativo** significant; *mirada etc.* meaning, expressive.

signo *m mst* sign; & *a.* symbol; mark *en lugar de firma*; ~ *de admiración* exclamation mark; ~ *de interrogación* question mark.

sigo *etc. v. seguir.*

siguiente next, following.

sílaba *f* syllable; **silábico** syllabic.

silba f hiss(ing), catcall; **silbar** [1a] v/t. melodía whistle; silbato blow; comedia etc. hiss (en Inglaterra: boo); v/i. ♪ etc. whistle; (bala etc.) whine; (flecha etc.) whizz, swish; thea. etc. hiss (en Inglaterra: boo, catcall); **silbato** m whistle; **silbido** m, **silbo** m whistle; whistling; hiss, hissing; whine etc.; silbido de oídos ringing in the ears.

silenciador m silencer; **silenciar** [1b] hecho keep silent about; p. silence; **silencio** m silence; quiet; hush; ♪ rest; ¡~! quiet!; en ~ in silence (a. fig.); guardar ~ keep quiet; entregar al ~ forget about; pasar en ~ omit all reference to; **silencioso 1.** silent, quiet; soundless; esp. ⊕ noiseless; **2.** m ⊕ muffler, silencer.

silfide f sylph (a. fig.); **silfo** m sylph.

silicato m silicate; **sílice** f silica.

silo m ✔ silo; fig. cave(rn).

silogismo m syllogism.

silueta f silhouette; outline de edificio; skyline de ciudad; (talle de p.) figure.

silvestre esp. ♀ wild; uncultivated; fig. rustic; **silvicultura** f forestry.

silla f (en general) seat; (mueble) chair; ~ (de montar) saddle; ~ eléctrica electric chair; ~ de manos sedan chair; ~ plegadiza, ~ de tijera camp-stool, folding-chair; ~ de ruedas wheel-chair.

sillar m block (of stone), ashlar.

sillería f (set of) chairs; seating; eccl. stall, choir stalls; △ masonry; **silleta** f small chair; (orinal) bedpan; **sillico** m chamber-pot; commode; **sillín** m saddle; **sillón** m armchair, easy-chair; ~ (de montar) side-saddle; ~ de orejas wing-chair; ~ de ruedas Bath-chair.

sima f abyss, pit; chasm.

simbiosis f symbiosis.

simbólico symbolic(al); token attr.; **simbolismo** m symbolism; **simbolizar** [1f] symbolize; be a token of; typify, represent; **símbolo** m symbol; eccl. creed.

simetría f symmetry; fig. harmony; **simétrico** symmetrical; fig. harmonious.

simiente f seed.

simiesco apish, simian.

símil 1. similar; **2.** m simile; comparison; **similar** similar; **similitud** f similarity, resemblance.

similor m pinchbeck; de ~ fig. fake, sham.

simonía f simony.

simpatía f (afecto) liking (hacia, por for), friendliness (hacia, por towards); congeniality de ambiente; (correspondencia) sympathy; fellow-feeling; (lo atractivo) charm; (no) tener ~ a (dis)like; **simpático** p. nice, likeable; pleasant; ambiente congenial, agreeable; ⨆, phys. etc. sympathetic; **simpatizante** m/f sympathizer (de with); **simpatizar** [1f] get on well together; ~ con p. get on well with; carácter etc. harmonize with, be congenial to.

simple 1. mst simple; (no doble) single; (incauto) gullible, simple; (corriente) ordinary; por ~ descuido through sheer carelessness; **2.** m simpleton; ♀ ~s pl. simples; **simpleza** f silliness; (acto etc.) silly thing; (pequeñez) mere trifle; decir ~s talk nonsense; **simplificar** [1g] simplify; **simplón** F **1.** gullible, simple; **2.** m, -a f simple soul, gullible sort.

simulación f simulation; make-believe; b.s. pretence; **simulacro** m image, idol; (fantasma) vision; (apariencia) semblance, pretence; ~ de combate sham fight; **simular** [1a] simulate; feign, sham.

simultáneo simultaneous.

sin without; with no; ...less; un...; apart from, not counting; ~ gasolina out of petrol; ~ sombrero without a hat, hatless; ~ inf. without ger.; ~ hablar without speaking; ~ almidonar unstarched; ~ lavar unwashed; cuenta ~ pagar bill to be paid, unpaid bill; ~ que subj. without ... ger.; entró ~ que yo le viese he came in without my seeing him.

sinagoga f synagogue.

sinapismo m ✗ mustard plaster; F nuisance, bore.

sincerarse [1a]: ~ a, ~ con open one's heart to; **sinceridad** f sincerity; **sincero** sincere; genuine, heartfelt.

síncopa f ♪ syncopation; gr. syncope; **sincopar** [1a] syncopate; fig. abridge; **síncope** m ✗ fainting fit.

sincrónico synchronous; synchronized; **sincronismo** m synchronism; coincidence *de fechas etc.*; **sincronizar** [1f] synchronize.

sindical trade(s) union *attr.*; **sindical**; **sindicalismo** *m* trade(s)-unionism; syndicalism; **sindicalista** *m/f* trade(s)-unionist; syndicalist; **sindicar** [1g] *obreros* form into a trade union; syndicate; *propiedad* put in trust; **sindicato** *m* syndicate; (*laboral*) trade(s) union; **síndico** *m* trustee; ♠, † approx. (official) receiver.

sinecura *f* sinecure.

sinfín *m* = *sinnúmero*.

sinfonía *f* symphony; **sinfónico** symphonic.

singladura *f* ♣ (day's) run.

singular 1. *mst* singular (*a. gr.*); (*destacado*) outstanding; *combate* single; (*raro*) peculiar, odd; 2. *m gr.* singular; **singularidad** *f* singularity; peculiarity *etc.*; **singularizar** [1f] single out; ~se stand out, distinguish o.s.; be conspicuous.

siniestro 1. left; *fig.* sinister; (*funesto*) disastrous; 2. *m* accident, catastrophe, disaster.

sinnúmero: *un ~ de* a great many, a great amount of.

sino[1] *m* fate, destiny.

sino[2] ... (*chino*) sino...

sino[3] but; except; ~ *que* but.

sínodo *m* synod.

sinónimo 1. synonymous; 2. *m* synonym.

sinopsis *f* synopsis.

sinrazón *f* wrong, injustice.

sinsabor *m* trouble, unpleasantness; (*pesar*) sorrow.

sintáctico syntactic(al); **sintaxis** *f* syntax.

síntesis *f* synthesis; **sintético** synthetic(al); **sintetizar** [1f] synthesize.

síntoma *m* symptom; sign; **sintomático** symptomatic.

sintonía *f radio*: tuning; ♪ signature tune; **sintonización** *f* tuning; **sintonizar** [1f] *radio*: tune; *programa* tune in to; ⚡ syntonize.

sinuosidad *f* sinuosity; **sinuoso** winding, sinuous; wavy.

sinusitis *f* sinusitis.

sinvergüenza *m* F rotter, cad, scoundrel.

siquiera 1. *adv.* at least; *dame un beso ~* give me a kiss at least; *ni ~* not even, not so much as; *ni me*

besó *~* he didn't even kiss me; *tan ~* even; 2. *cj.* even if, even though.

sirena *f* (*p.*) mermaid; (*clásica*) siren; ♪ siren, hooter; *~ de la playa* bathing beauty; *~ de niebla* foghorn.

sirga *f* towrope; **sirgar** [1h] tow.

sirio *adj. a. su. m,* **a** *f* Syrian.

sirte *f* shoal, sandbank.

sirvienta *f* servant, maid; **sirviente** *m* servant; waiter.

sisa *f* petty theft; *sew.* dart; **sisar** [1a] pilfer; *sew.* put darts in, take in.

sisear [1a] hiss; **siseo** *m* hiss.

sísmico seismic; **sismógrafo** *m* seismograph.

sisón 1. thieving, light-fingered; 2. *m*, **-a** *f* petty thief.

sistema *m mst* system; method; framework; **sistemático** systematic; **sistematizar** [1f] systematize; organize.

sitiador *m* besieger; **sitiar** [1b] besiege; *fig.* surround, hem in; **sitio** *m* (*lugar determinado*) place, spot; site, location; (*espacio*) room; ⚔ siege; *en estado de ~* in a state of siege; *under martial law*; *¿hay ~?* is there (any) room?; *hay ~ de sobra* there's plenty of room; *levantar el ~* raise the siege; *poner ~ a* lay siege to; *quedarse en el ~* die on the spot; **sito** situated, located (*en* in); **situación** *f* situation; position; location, locality; (*social*) position, standing; *S. Am. precios de ~* bargain prices; **situado** situated, placed; **situar** [1e] place, put, set; *esp. edificio* site, locate; ⚔ *etc.* post, station; † lay aside; place.

slogan [ez'logan] *m* slogan.

smoking [ez'mokin] *m* dinnerjacket.

snob [ez'nob] *etc. v.* esnob *etc.*

so[1] *prp.* under.

¡so![2] whoa!

soba *f* kneading *de masa*; slap, dab *con mano*; F hiding; F *dar ~ a* tan.

sobaco *m* armpit; armhole *de vestido*.

sobado rumpled, messed up; *libro* well-thumbed, dog-eared; *S. Am.* F terrific; **sobajar** [1a] crush, rumple, mess up; *fig.* humiliate.

sobaquera *f* armhole.

sobar [1a] *masa etc.* knead; squeeze; F (*zurrar*) tan; F (*manosear*) paw, finger, feel; (*novios, a. ~se*) pet, cuddle.

soberanía f sovereignty; **soberano** adj. a. su. m, **a** f sovereign.

soberbia f pride etc.; **soberbio** (orgulloso) proud, haughty; arrogant; magnificent, grand; (colérico) angry.

sobón F (que manosea) too free with his etc. hands; fig. too familiar by half, fresh; (enamorado) mushy, spoony; (taimado) work-shy.

sobornable bribable, venal; **sobornar** [1a] bribe; buy off; **soborno** m bribe; (en general) bribery, graft.

sobra f excess, surplus; ~s pl. leavings, left-overs; scraps; de ~ (adj.) (to) spare, surplus, extra; (adv.) more than enough; (saber) only too well; F estar de ~ (p.) be one (etc.) too many; be left out; b.s. be in the way; **sobradamente** too; (only) too well; **sobradillo** m penthouse; **sobrado 1.** excessive, more than enough; p. wealthy; estar ~ de be well provided for; **2.** m attic, garret.

sobrancero unemployed.

sobrante 1. spare, extra, surplus; **2.** m surplus (a. ✝); ✝ balance in hand; margin; **sobrar** [1a] v/t. exceed, surpass; v/i. be left over, be to spare; remain; be more than enough; nos sobra tiempo we have heaps (or lots, plenty) of time; me parece que aquí sobro it seems I'm not needed here.

sobre[1] m envelope; letter-cover; (señas) address.

sobre[2] on, upon; on top of; (encima de) over, above; (acerca de) about; 1 ~ 4 1 in 4; ~ las 5 about 5 o'clock; ~ inf. on top of (being), in addition to (being).

sobre[3]... super...; over...; ~abundante superabundant; ~abundar [1a] superabound (en in, with); ~alimentado ⊕ supercharged; ~alimentador m ⊕ supercharger; ~alimentar [1a] ⊕ supercharge; p. overfeed; ~calentar [1k] overheat; ~cama m bedspread; ~carga f extra load; (soga) rope; ✝, & surcharge; ~cargar [1h] carro overload; ⨍ etc. overcharge; p. etc. weigh down; ✝, & surcharge; ~cargo m ⚓ supercargo; ~cejo m, ~ceño m frown.

sobrecoger [2c] startle, (take by) surprise; ~se be startled, start (a at,

de with); (achicarse) be overawed, be abashed.

sobre...: ~cubierta f outer cover; jacket de libro; ~dicho above (-mentioned); ~dorar [1a] gild; fig. gloss over.

sobre(e)ntender [2g] understand; deduce, infer; ~se be implied etc.

sobre...: ~(e)xcitado overexcited; ~(e)xcitar [1a] overexcite; ~(e)x-poner [2r] phot. overexpose; ~faz f surface, outside; ~giro m overdraft; ~haz f = ~faz; (cubierta) cover; ~humano superhuman; ~llevar [1a] (help to) carry; fig. carga de otro ease; molestias bear, endure; faltas de otro be tolerant towards; ~manera exceedingly; ~marcha f mot. overdrive; ~mesa f (tapete) table cover; (postre) dessert; (tiempo) sitting on after a meal; de ~ charla etc. after-dinner; reloj etc. table attr.; ~nadar [1a] float; ~natural supernatural; unearthly, weird; ciencia occult; ~nombre m nickname; by-name; title.

sobrentender etc. v. sobre(e)ntender etc.

sobre...: ~paga f rise, bonus; ~parto m ⚕ confinement; morir de ~ die in childbirth; ~pasar [1a] surpass; límite exceed; marca beat; ✗ pista overshoot; ~pelliz f surplice; ~peso m overweight; ~población f overcrowding.

sobreponer [2r] put on top, put one thing on another, superimpose; ~se fig. pull o.s. together; win through en adversidad; make the best of a bad job; ~ a dificultad overcome; susto get over; rival etc. triumph over.

sobre...: ~precio m surcharge; ~producción f overproduction; ~puesto 1. added, superimposed; 2. m addition; ~pujar [1a] outdo; outbid.

sobrero extra, spare.

sobre...: ~saliente 1. outstanding, brilliant; univ. first class; 2. m/f substitute; thea. understudy; 3. m univ. first class, distinction; ~salir [3r] △ etc. project, jut out; stick out (or up), protrude; fig. stand out, excel (en at).

sobresaltar [1a] fall upon, rush at; (asustar etc.) startle; shock; ~se start, be startled (*con*, *de* at); **sobresalto** *m* fright, scare; shock; *de* ~ suddenly.

sobre...: ~**sanar** [1a] ⚕ heal superficially; *defecto* hide, gloss over; ~**scrito** *m* superscription; address *en carta*; ~**seer** [2e] desist; default *en obligación*; ~**seimiento** *m* giving up; default; ⚖ stay of proceedings; ~**sello** *m* double seal; ~**stante** *m* overseer; foreman; ~**stimar** [1a] overvalue; overestimate; ~**sueldo** *m* extra pay, bonus; ~**tasa** *f* surcharge; ~**todo** *m* overcoat; ~**venir** [3s] supervene, ensue; happen (unexpectedly); ~**viviente** 1. surviving; 2. *m/f* survivor; ~**vivir** [3a] survive; ~ *a* survive; outlive, outlast; ~**volar** [1m] fly over.

sobriedad *f* sobriety *etc.*

sobrina *f* niece; **sobrino** *m* nephew.

sobrio sober, moderate; temperate; *fig.* sober, restrained.

socaire *m* lee; *al* ~ to leeward; F *ponerse al* ~ shirk.

socaliñar [1a] get by a swindle; **socaliñero** 1. swindling; 2. *m* swindler.

socapa *f* F subterfuge; *a* ~ surreptitiously.

socarrón sly, crafty, artful; (*guasón*) mocking, with sly humour; malicious; **socarronería** *f* slyness; sly humour *etc.*

socava(ción) *f* undermining; **socavar** [1a] undermine, dig under; *fig.* sap, undermine; **socavón** *m* ⚒ mine gallery, tunnel; hole *en calle*; ⚠ sudden collapse.

sociable *p.* sociable; *animal etc.* social, gregarious; **social** social; ✝ company *attr.*; **socialismo** *m* socialism; **socialista** *adj. a. su. m/f* socialist; **socializar** [1f] socialize, nationalize.

sociedad *f* society; association; ✝ company, firm; ✝ *etc.* partnership *de dos ps.*; *alta* ~, *buena* ~ (high) society; ~ *anónima* limited liability company, corporation; *Pérez y García* ♀ *Anónima* Pérez y García Limited (Incorporated *Am.*); ~ *de control* holding company; ♀ *de las Naciones* League of Nations; ~ *secreta* secret society; ~ *de socorro mutuo* friendly (*or* provident) society.

socio *m*, **a** *f* member *de club etc.*;

fellow *de sociedad científica etc.*; ✝ partner; ✝ associate; F fellow; ~ *comanditario*, ~ *pasivo* sleeping partner; ~ *de honor*, ~ *honorario* honorary member; ~ *de número* full member; **sociología** *f* sociology; **sociológico** sociological; **sociólogo** *m* sociologist.

socorrer [2a] help; *necesidades, ciudad* relieve; **socorrido** *p. etc.* helpful, co-operative; *cosa útil* handy; (*bien provisto*) well-stocked; (*trillado*) hackneyed; **socorro** *m* help, aid; relief (*a.* ✗); ¡~! help!; ~*s pl.* *mutuos* mutual aid; *trabajos de* ~ relief work.

soda *f* ⚗ soda; (*bebida*) soda(-water).

sodio *m* sodium.

soez dirty, obscene; crude.

sofá *m* sofa, settee; ~**cama** *f* studio couch.

sofisma *m* sophism; **sofista** 1. sophistic(al); 2. *m* sophist; **sofistería** *f* (piece of) sophistry; **sofisticado** *p. etc.* sophisticated; **sofístico** sophistic, sophistical; false, fallacious.

sofocación *f* suffocation; *fig.* vexation; annoying rebuff; **sofocante** stifling, suffocating; **sofocar** [1g] choke, stifle, suffocate; *incendio* smother, put out; *fig.* make *s.o.* blush; (*irritar*) make *s.o.* angry; F bother; ~**se** choke *etc.*; (*corriendo etc.*) get out of breath; *fig.* flush, get embarrassed; (*encolerizarse*) get worked up, get hot under the collar; **sofoco** *m* embarrassment; F *pasar un* ~ have an embarrassing time; **sofocón** *m* F stunning blow.

sofrenada *f* sudden check; F ticking-off; **sofrenar** [1a] rein back suddenly; *fig.* restrain; F tick off.

soga *f* rope; halter; *con la* ~ *al cuello* up to one's neck in it; F *dar* ~ *a* make fun of; *echar la* ~ *tras el caldero* throw in one's hand, chuck it all up; F *hacer* ~ lag behind.

soja *f* soya; *semilla de* ~ soya bean.

sojuzgar [1h] subjugate, subdue.

sol *m* sun; sunshine, sunlight; F *como un* ~ bright as a new pin; *de* ~ *día* sunny; *de* ~ *a* ~ from sunrise to sunset; *no dejar a* ~ *ni a sombra* drive *s.o.* from pillar to post, give *s.o.* no respite; *hacer* ~ be sunny; *tomar el* ~ sun o.s., bask.

solado *m* tiling, tiled floor.

solamente only; solely.

solana f sunny spot; (*cuarto*) sun lounge; **solanera** f ☼ sunburn; (*lugar*) sunny spot.

solano m east wind.

solapa f lapel; flap *de sobre*; *fig.* excuse; **solapadamente** in an underhand way, by crooked means; **solapado** sly, sneaky; **solapar** [1a] *fig.* v/t. overlap; (*ocultar*) cover up, keep dark; v/i. overlap; ~se get hidden underneath; **solapo** m sew. lapel; overlap; ~ de F chuck under the chin; F a ~ by underhand methods.

solar[1] m △ lot, site, piece of ground; (*casa*) ancestral home, family seat.

solar[2] solar, sun *attr.*

solar[3] [1m] *calzado* sole; *suelo* floor, tile.

solariego *casa* ancestral; *familia* ancient and noble; *hist.* manorial; *hist.* tierras ~as demesne.

solaz m relaxation, recreation; (*consuelo*) solace; **solazar** [1f] give relaxation to, amuse; (*consolar*) solace, comfort; ~se enjoy o.s., amuse o.s., relax.

solazo m F scorching sun(shine).

soldada f pay, wages.

soldadesca f (brutal and licentious) soldiery; **soldadesco** soldierly; *a la ~a* like a soldier; **soldado** m soldier; ~ de infantería infantryman; ~ de marina marine; ~ primera lance-corporal; ~ raso private.

soldador m soldering-iron; (*p.*) welder; **soldadura** f (*metal*) solder; (*acto*) soldering, welding; (*juntura*) soldered joint, welded seam; ~ autógena welding; **soldar** [1a] ⊕ solder, weld; *fig.* join; *disputa* patch up; correct; ~se (*huesos*) knit.

soleado sunny; **solear** [1a] (put in the) sun.

solecismo m solecism.

soledad f solitude; loneliness; (*lugar*) lonely place.

solemne solemn; dignified; grave, weighty; F *error* terrible; **solemnidad** f solemnity *etc.*; (*acto*) solemn ceremony; formalities; F *pobre de ~* miserably poor; F *rico de ~* stinking with money; **solemnizar** [1f] solemnize; celebrate.

soler [2h; *defective*]: ~ *inf.* be in the habit of *ger.*; *suele venir a las 5* he generally (*or* usually) comes at 5; *solía hacerlo* I used to do it; *como se suele* as is customary.

soleta: F *tomar* ~ beat it.

solevantar [1a] raise up, heave up; *fig.* rouse, stir up.

solfa f ♪ solfa; musical notation; *fig.* music; F tanning; F *poner en ~* make a mockery of; **solfear** [1a] ♪ solfa; F tan; **solfeo** m ♪ solfa; F tanning.

solicitador m, **-a** f, **solicitante** m/f applicant; petitioner; **solicitar** [1a] request, solicit (*algo* a th.; *algo a alguien* a th. of a p.); *puesto etc.* apply for, put in for; *votos* canvass; *atención, phys.* attract; *ser solicitado fig.* be sought after, be in demand; **solícito** diligent, careful; solicitous (*por* about, for); **solicitud** f care, concern; (*acto, petición*) request; application (*de puesto* for); *a ~* on request, on demand; ♱ *dinero* on call.

solidaridad f solidarity; **solidario** jointly liable; *esp.* ⚖ joint and several; *compromiso etc.* mutually binding; ~ de integral with; **solidez** f solidity *etc.*; **solidificar(se)** [1g] solidify; harden; **sólido 1.** solid (*a.* ☀, *fig.*); stable, firm; (*robusto*) strong, stout; hard; *aspecto* solid, massive; (*duradero*) solid, lasting; *argumento* sound; *color* fast; **2.** m solid.

soliloquiar [1b] soliloquize, talk to o.s.; **soliloquio** m soliloquy, monologue.

solista m/f soloist.

solitaria f tape-worm; **solitario 1.** solitary; desolate, lonely, bleak; **2.** m, **a** f (*p.*) recluse, hermit; **3.** m solitaire.

soliviantar [1a] rouse, stir up; win over *con promesas etc.*; **soliviar** [1b] lift up; ~se half rise, get up on one elbow *etc.*

solo 1. (*único*) only, sole; (*sin compañía*) alone, by o.s.; single; (*solitario*) lonely; ♪ solo; *sentirse muy* ~ feel very lonely (*or* isolated); *ni un* ~ *punto* not one single point; *a solas* by o.s., alone; **2.** m ♪, *naipes*: solo.

sólo only, solely; merely; just; *tan* ~ only.

solom(ill)o m sirloin.

solsticio m solstice.

soltar [1m] (*desatar*) untie, unfasten; (*aflojar*) loose(n), slacken; (*desenmarañar*) free; (*dejar caer*) drop, let go of; *mano etc.* release; (*poner en libertad*) release, let go, (set) free;

animal etc. let out, let (*or* set, turn) loose; *amarras* cast off; *carcajada* let out; *dificultad* solve; F *dinero* cough up; ⊕ *embrague* disengage, *freno* release; *exclamación* let out; *golpe* let fly; *injurias* utter, let fly (a string of); *presa* let go of; ~se (*pieza*) (*aflojarse*) work loose; (*desprenderse*) come off, come undone; (*escapar*) get free; (*perfeccionarse*) become expert; *b.s.* let o.s. go; ~ *a inf.* begin to *inf.*

soltera *f* spinster, unmarried woman; **soltero 1.** single, unmarried; **2.** *m* bachelor, unmarried man; **solterón** *m* old (*or* confirmed) bachelor; **solterona** *f* spinster, maiden lady; *contp.* old maid.

soltura *f* (*acto*) release *etc.*; ⊕ looseness *de pieza*; agility, freedom of movement; *fig.* (*desvergüenza*) shamelessness, liberty *de lengua*; (*inmoralidad*) licentiousness; ease, fluency *en hablar*; *hablar idioma con* ~ speak fluently; *ℊ* ~ *de vientre* looseness of the bowels.

soluble soluble; **solución** *f mst* solution; answer (*de problema* to); resolving *de duda*; *thea.* dénouement; ~ *de continuidad* interruption, break in continuity; **solucionar** [1a] (re)solve.

solvencia *f* ✝ solvency; settlement *de cuenta*; *de* ~ discerning; *de toda* ~ *moral* of excellent character, completely trustworthy; **solventar** [1a] ✝ settle, pay; *dificultad* resolve; **solvente** *adj.* (✝) *a. su. m* (⚗) solvent; (*juicioso*) discerning.

sollamar [1a] scorch, singe.

sollo *m* sturgeon.

sollozar [1f] sob; **sollozo** *m* sob.

somanta *f* F tanning.

sombra *f* (*que proyecta un objeto*) shadow; (*para resguardarse del sol*) *luz y* ~) shade; (*oscuridad*) darkness, shadow(s); (*fantasma*) ghost, shade; *fig.* shadow *de duda etc.*; protection, favour; (*atracción*) charm, wit; *paint.* (*tierra de*) ~ umber; *a la* ~ in the shade; F in clink; *ni por* ~ by no means; *dar* ~ *a* shade; *hacer* ~ *a fig.* put *s.t.* in the shade; F *tener buena* ~ be lucky, bring good luck; be likeable; *tener mala* ~ bring bad luck; be not much liked; *no tener* ~ *de* not be a bit like; **sombraje** *m*, **sombrajo** *m* shelter from the sun;

hacer ~*s* get in the light; **sombreado** *m* shading; **sombrear** [1a] shade; *fig.* overshadow.

sombrerera *f* milliner; (*caja*) hat-box; **sombrerería** *f* millinery, hats; (*tienda*) hat shop; **sombrerero** *m* hatter; **sombrerete** *m* little hat; ⊕ bonnet; cowl *de chimenea*; cap *de seta*, *cubo*; **sombrero** *m* hat; headgear; ~ *de candil*, ~ *de tres picos* three-cornered hat, cocked hat; ~ *de copa* top hat; ~ *flexible* soft hat, trilby; ~ *gacho* slouch hat; ~ *hongo* bowler (hat); ~ *de paja* straw hat.

sombrilla *f* parasol, sunshade.

sombrío shady; *fig.* sombre, dismal; *p.* gloomy, morose.

somero superficial, shallow.

someter [2a] *informe etc.* submit, present; (*conquistar*) conquer; ~ *a prueba etc.* subject to, put to; ~se yield, submit.

somier *m* spring mattress.

somnambulismo *m* sleep-walking; **somnámbulo** *m*, *a f* sleep-walker; **somnífero** sleep-inducing; **somnolencia** *f* sleepiness, drowsiness; **somnolento** = *soñoliento*.

somorgujar [1a] duck, submerge; ~se dive, plunge; **somormujo** *m* grebe.

son *m* (pleasant) sound; *fig.* news, rumour; *¿a qué* ~?, *¿a* ~ *de qué?* why?; *a* ~ *de* to the sound of; *en* ~ *de* like, as, in the manner of; *en* ~ *de broma* as a joke; *por este* ~ in this way; *sin* ~ for no reason at all; **sonado** talked-of, famous; sensational.

sonaja *f* little bell; **sonajear** [1a] jingle; **sonajero** *m* rattle.

sonar [1m] **1.** *v/t.* sound; *campana* ring; ♪ play; *sirena*, *narices* blow; **2.** *v/i.* sound; (*campana*) ring; ♪ play; (*reloj*) strike; *gr.* be pronounced; F (*tripas*) rumble; F *fig.* sound familiar, ring a bell; *no me suena* it doesn't ring a bell with me; *su nombre suena mucho* he is much talked about; *no quiero que suene mi nombre* I don't want my name mentioned; F *así como suena* just as I'm telling you; ~ *a* sound like; ~ *a hueco* sound hollow; **3.** ~se (*a.* ~ *las narices*) blow one's nose; *se suena que* it is rumoured that.

sonata *f* sonata.

sonda f (*acto, medida*) sounding; (*instrumento*) ⚓ lead; ⊕ bore; ⚒ probe; ～ *acústica* echo-sounder; **sondaje** m ⚓ sounding; ⊕ boring; *fig.* de ～ exploratory; *organismo de* ～ public opinion poll; **sond(e)ar** [1a] ⚓ sound, take soundings of; ⚒ probe, sound; ⊕ drill, bore into; *fig. terreno* explore; *p., intenciones* sound out; *misterio* plumb; **sondeo** m sounding *etc.*; *fig.* (*encuesta*) poll, inquiry; *pol. etc.* feeler, overture.

soneto m sonnet.

sonido m sound (*a. gr., phys.*); noise.

sonorizar(se) [1f] *gr.* voice; **sonoro** sonorous; loud, resounding; *voz a.* rich; *gr.* voiced; *banda, efectos etc.* sound *attr.*

sonreír(se) [3m] smile (*de* at); **sonriente** smiling; **sonrisa** f smile.

sonrojarse [1a] blush, flush (*de* at); **sonrojo** m blush(ing); *fig.* naughty word, dubious remark.

sonrosado rosy, pink.

sonsacar [1g] remove *s.t.* surreptitiously (*or* craftily); *p.* entice away; *fig. p.* pump, draw out; *secreto* worm out (*a* of).

sonsonete m (*golpecitos*) tapping; din, jangling, rumbling; *fig.* singsong, chant; (*frase con rima*) jingle; (*desprecio*) mocking undertone.

soñación: F *ni por* ～ not on your life; **soñador 1.** dreamy; **2.** m, -a f dreamer; **soñar** [1m] dream (*con* about, of; *con inf.* of *ger.*); ～ *despierto* day-dream; F *ni* ～*lo* not on your life; F *me va que ni soñado* it suits me a treat; **soñera** f drowsiness; **soñolencia** f = somnolencia; **soñoliento** sleepy, drowsy, somnolent; (*que adormece*) soporific.

sopa f soup; sop *en leche*; F *hecho una* ～ soaked to the skin; F *comer la* ～ *boba* scrounge a meal; F *quitar la* ～ *a*, F *quitarse la* ～ sober up.

sopapear [1a] F shake violently; bash, punch; **sopapo** m F punch.

sopesar [1a] lift, try the weight of.

sopetón m punch; *de* ～ unexpectedly; *entrar de* ～ pop in, drop in.

soplado F affected, over-nice; (*engreído*) stuck-up; *sl.* tight, lit up.

soplamocos m F punch on the nose.

soplar [1a] **1.** *v/t.* (*apartar*) blow away; blow up, inflate; *fig.* inspire; (*apuntar*) prompt, help *s.o.* along with; (*robar*) pinch; F (*zampar*) hog, guzzle; *sl.* split on; **2.** *v/i.* blow (*a. viento*); puff; *sl.* split (*contra* on), blab; **soplete** m blowlamp, torch; ～ *oxiacetilénico* oxyacetylene burner; **soplido** m = **soplo** m blow(ing), puff *de boca*; puff, gust *de viento*; *esp.* ⊕ blast; *fig.* instant; F (*aviso*) tip; F (*delación*) tales; = **soplón** m, -a f F (*niño*) tell-tale; informer *de policía*.

soponcio m F dizzy spell.

sopor m ⚒ drowsiness; *fig.* lethargy; **soporífero 1.** soporific; **2.** m nightcap; ⚒ sleeping-draught.

soportable bearable.

soportal m porch; ～es *pl.* arcade *con tiendas*; colonnade.

soportar [1a] (*apoyar*) carry, hold up; (*aguantar*) endure, bear, stand; **soporte** m support; mount(ing); base, stand; holder, bracket.

soprano f soprano.

sor f *eccl.* sister.

sorber [2a] sip; (*chupar*) suck (in); ～ (*por las narices*) sniff; *medicamento* inhale; absorb, soak up; (*tragar*) swallow (up); **sorbete** m sherbet; (*bebida*) iced fruit drink; **sorbetón** m F gulp, mouthful; **sorbo** m sip; gulp, swallow; sniff.

sordera f deafness.

sordidez f nastiness *etc.*; **sórdido** nasty, dirty; *fig.* mean.

sordina f ♪ mute, muffler; damper *de piano*; *a la* ～ on the quiet.

sordo 1. *p.* deaf (*a. fig.*; *a* to); (*silencioso*) quiet, noiseless; *sonido* muffled, dull; *gr.* voiceless; ～ *como una tapia* deaf as a post; *a la* ～*a*, *a* ～*as* noiselessly; **2.** m, *a* f deaf person; *hacerse el* ～ pretend not to hear; *turn a deaf ear* (*a* to); **sordomudo 1.** deaf and dumb; **2.** m, *a* f deaf-mute.

sorna f slyness; *con* ～ slyly, sarcastically. [ness.]

soroche m S.Am. mountain sick-)

sorprendente surprising; amazing; startling; **sorprender** [2a] (*maravillar*) surprise; amaze; (*sobresaltar*) startle; (*coger desprevenido*) (take by) surprise, catch; *conversación* overhear; *secreto* discover; ～se be surprised (*de* at); **sorpresa** f surprise; ¡qué ~!, ¡vaya ~! what a surprise!; coger de ~ take by surprise; ╳ coger por ~ surprise.

sortear [1a] v/t. (rifar) raffle; deportes etc.: toss up for; (evitar) dodge; v/i. toss up; draw lots; (esquivarse) dodge.

sortija f ring; curl, ringlet de pelo; ~ de sello signet-ring.

sortilegio m spell, charm; (brujería) sorcery; (adivinación) fortune-telling.

sosa f soda.

sosegado quiet, calm, peaceful; gentle; restful; **sosegar** [1h a. 1k] v/t. calm (down); quieten; ánimo reassure; dudas allay; v/i. rest; ~se calm down.

sosería f tastelessness etc.

sosiego m quiet(ness), calm, peace, peacefulness.

soslayar [1a] put s.t. sideways, place s.t. obliquely; dificultad get round; pregunta dodge; **soslayo**: al ~, de ~ obliquely, at a slant, sideways; mirada sidelong; mirar de ~ look at s.o. out of the corner of one's eye; fig. look askance at.

soso tasteless, insipid; (sin azúcar) unsweetened; fig. dull, colourless; flat.

sospecha f suspicion; **sospechar** [1a] v/t. suspect; v/i.: ~ de suspect, have one's suspicions about; **sospechoso 1.** suspicious; (no confiable) suspect; **2.** m, a f suspect.

sostén m △ etc. support, prop; stay; stand; bra(ssière) de mujer; fig. support, prop; mainstay, pillar; **sostener** [2l] △, ⊕ support, hold up; lo inestable prop up; peso bear; carga carry; fig. sustain (a. ♪); (entretener) maintain; (tolerar) bear; p. etc. sustain con comida; maintain con dinero; opinión uphold; proposición maintain; presión keep up, sustain; resistencia bolster up; ~ que hold that; ~ support o.s. etc.; (perdurar) last (out); ~ (en pie) stand up; **sostenido** adj. a. su. m ♪ sharp; **sostenimiento** m support; maintenance etc.

sota f jack, knave.

sotabanco m attic, garret.

sotana f cassock; F hiding.

sótano m basement; (almacén) cellar.

sotavento m lee(ward).

sotechado m shed.

soterrar [1k] bury; fig. hide away.

soto m thicket; copse; grove.

soviet m soviet; **soviético** soviet attr.

spleen [es'plin] m boredom, depression.

sprint [es'print] m sprint; **sprintar** [esprin'tar] [1a] sprint.

stand [es'tand] m stand.

stándard [es'tandar] adj. a. su. m standard.

store [es'tor] m sun-blind.

su, sus (un poseedor) his, hers, its, one's; (de Vd.) your; (varios poseedores) their; (de Vds.) your.

suave (blando) soft); (liso) smooth; (dulce, agradable) sweet; aire soft, mild; carácter gentle; docile; modales, movimiento, tacto, viento gentle; música, olor sweet; pasta smooth; ruido soft; sabor smooth, mild; **suavidad** f softness etc.; **suavizador** m razor-strop; **suavizar** [1f] soften; (alisar) smooth (out, down); navaja strop; fig. dureza ease, soften; temper; relax; color tone down; p. mollify, soften; carácter mellow.

sub... mst sub...; under...

subalimentado undernourished, underfed.

subalterno 1. subordinate; auxiliary; minor, inferior; **2.** m subordinate.

subarrendar [1k] sublet, sublease; **subarrendatario** m, a f subtenant.

subasta f auction sale, (sale by) auction; poner en (or sacar a) pública ~ sell by auction; **subastador** m auctioneer; **subastar** [1a] auction (off).

subcampeón m runner-up.

subcomisión f subcommittee.

subconsciencia f subconscious.

subconsciente subconscious.

subcontrato m subcontract.

subcutáneo subcutaneous.

subdesarrollado underdeveloped.

súbdito adj. a. su. m, a f pol. subject.

subdividir(se) [3a] subdivide; **subdivisión** f subdivision.

subestación f substation.

subestimación f underestimation; understatement; **subestimar** [1a] *capacidad, contrario* underestimate, underrate; *propiedad* undervalue; *proposición* understate.

subida f (*acto*) climb(ing) *etc.*; (*cuesta*) slope, hill; (*aumento*) rise, increase; promotion; **subido** *color* bright; *olor* strong; *precio* high, stiff; *calidad* superior; ~ *de color cara* florid, rosy; flushed *de vergüenza*; *cuento* dirty, rude.

subinquilino m, **a** f subtenant.

subir [3a] **1.** v/t. (*levantar*) raise, lift up; (*llevar*) take up; get up; *escalera* climb, go up; *montaña* climb; *p.* promote; *precio, sueldo* raise, put up; ♪ *artículo* put up the price of; ♪ raise the pitch of; **2.** v/i. go up, come up; move up; climb; (*aumentarse*) rise, increase; (*precio, río, temperatura*) rise; (*fiebre*) get worse; (*ser ascendido*) rise, move up; ~ *a* (*precio*) come to; ~ *a*, ~ *en vehículo* get into, get on; *caballo* mount; *árbol* climb; **3.** ~**se** rise, go up; ~ *a*, ~ *en* get into *etc.*

súbito sudden; *de* ~ suddenly.

subjetivo subjective.

subjuntivo m subjunctive (mood).

sublevación f (up)rising; **sublevar** [1a] stir up a revolt among; ~**se** rise, revolt.

sublimación f sublimation; **sublimado** m sublimate; **sublimar** [1a] exalt; *deseos etc.*, ♠ sublimate; **sublime** sublime; high, lofty; noble, grand; *lo* ~ the sublime; **subliminal** subliminal.

submarino 1. underwater; **2.** m submarine.

suboficial m non-commissioned officer.

subordinado *adj. a. su.* m, **a** f subordinate; **subordinar** [1a] subordinate.

subproducto m by-product.

subrayar [1a] underline (*a. fig.*); *lo subrayado es mío* my italics.

subrepticio surreptitious.

subsanar [1a] *falta* overlook; *error* put right; *pérdida* make up; *daño* repair.

subscr... v. **suscr...**

subsecretario m under-secretary.

subsidiario subsidiary.

subsidio m subsidy, grant; aid; (*de seguro social*) benefit; ~ *familiar* family allowance; ~ *de natalidad* maternity benefit; ~ *de paro*

unemployment pay, dole; ~ *de vejez* old age pension.

subsiguiente subsequent.

subsistir [3a] (*vivir*) subsist, live; (*existir aún*) endure, last (out); (*ley etc.*) be still in force; (*edificio*) be still in being.

subst... v. **sust...** [still stand.]

subsuelo m subsoil.

subteniente m second lieutenant.

subterfugio m subterfuge; way out, dodge.

subterráneo 1. underground, subterranean; **2.** m cavern; cellar; *S.Am.* underground.

subtítulo m subtitle, subhead(ing); caption.

suburbano suburban; **suburbio** m suburb; *b.s.* shanty-town.

subvención f subsidy, grant; **subvencionar** [1a] subsidize, aid; **subvenir** [3s]: ~ *a gastos* meet, defray; *necesidades* provide for.

subversión f subversion; (*acto*) overthrow; **subversivo** subversive; **subverter** [3i] subvert; *orden* disturb; undermine.

subyacente underlying.

subyugar [1h] subdue, subjugate; overpower; *ánimos etc.* (come to) dominate.

succión f suction; **succionar** [1a] suck; apply suction to.

suceder [2a] (*ocurrir*) happen; (*seguir*) succeed, follow; (*heredar*) inherit; ~ *a p.* succeed; *puesto, trono* succeed to; *bienes* inherit; ~**se** follow one another; **sucesión** f sucession (*a* to), sequence; (*hijos*) issue, offspring; **sucesivamente** successively; *y así* ~ and so on; **sucesivo** successive; consecutive; *en lo* ~ in the future; (*desde entonces*) thereafter; **suceso** m event, happening; incident; (*resultado*) outcome; **sucesor** m, **-a** f successor; (*heredero*) heir.

suciedad f dirt(iness) *etc.*; (*palabra*) dirty word, obscene remark.

sucinto succinct, concise.

sucio dirty, filthy; grimy, grubby; soiled; *fig.* dirty, obscene; *juego* foul; *color* blurred.

suculencia f succulence; **suculento** succulent; luscious, juicy; *plato* tasty.

sucumbir [3a] succumb (*a* to).

sucursal f branch(-office); subsidiary.

sud *m* south; **sudamericano** *adj. a. su. m, a f* South American.

sudar [1a] sweat (*a.* F); **sudario** *m* shroud.

sudeste 1. *parte* south-east(ern); *dirección* south-easterly; *viento* south-east(erly); **2.** *m* south-east; **sudoeste** *v.* suroeste.

sudor *m* sweat (*a. fig.*); *con el ~ de su frente* by the sweat of one's brow; **sudoriento, sudo(ro)so** sweaty, sweating.

suecia *f* suede.

sueco 1. Swedish; **2.** *m, a f* Swede; F *hacerse el ~* act dumb; **3.** *m* (*idioma*) Swedish.

suegra *f* mother-in-law; **suegro** *m* father-in-law.

suela *f* sole; (*poner*) *media ~* half-sole; F *de siete ~s* downright; *no llegarle a uno a la ~ del zapato* not be able to hold a candle to s.o.

sueldo *m* salary, pay; *a ~* on a salary.

suelo *m* (*tierra*) ground, soil, land; (*superficie de la tierra*) ground; (*piso*) floor; (*material de piso*) flooring; *bottom de vasija*; *~ natal* native land; *caer al ~* fall to the ground; *echarse por los ~s* grovel; F *estar por los ~s* be dirt-cheap.

suelto 1. (*no atado*) loose, free; (*libre*) free, at large; (*sin trabas*) unhampered; (*separado*) detached, unattached; (*no en serie*) odd, separate; *ejemplar, número* single; *fig.* (*ligero*) light, quick; (*hábil*) expert; (*libre, atrevido*) free, daring; *estilo* easy, fluent; *verso* blank; *~ de lengua* (*parlanchín*) talkative; (*respondón*) cheeky; (*soplón*) blabbing; (*obsceno*) foul-mouthed; *~ de vientre* loose; **2.** *m* ✝ loose change; item, short article *en periódico*; *typ.* paragraph.

sueño *m* sleep; (*fantasía*) dream (*a. fig.*); *en(tre) ~s* in a dream; *conciliar el ~* (*p.*) get to sleep; (*droga*) make *s.o.* sleep; *descabezar el ~*, *echar un ~* have a nap; *tener ~* be sleepy; *tener el ~ ligero* be a light sleeper.

suero *m* ✳ serum; whey *de leche*.

suerte *f* (good) luck; fortune, chance; (*hado*) fate, destiny, lot; condition, state; (*género*) kind; *toros*: stage; (*de capa*) play with the cape; *~s pl.* juggling; *buena ~* (good) luck; *mala ~* bad luck, hard luck; *de mala ~* unlucky; *de ~ que* so that; (*en principio de frase*) (and) so; *por ~* luckily; by chance; *caber en ~ a* fall to; *no me cupo tal ~* no such luck; *echar ~s* draw lots; *la ~ está echada* the die is cast; *estar de ~* be in luck; *probar ~* try one's luck, have a go; *quiso la ~ que* as luck would have it; *tener (buena) ~* be lucky; *¡que tengas (mucha) ~!* I wish you luck!; *trae mala ~ inf.* it's unlucky to *inf.*; *unirse a la ~ de* throw in one's lot with.

sueste *m* sou'wester.

suéter *m* jumper, sweater.

suficiencia *f* adequacy, fitness; (*aire de*) ~ self-importance; smugness, self-satisfaction; *darse aires de ~* get on one's high horse; *una ~ de* enough; **suficiente** enough, sufficient; (*apto*) adequate, fit; *b.s.* smug, self-satisfied, superior.

sufijo *m* suffix.

sufragar [1h] *v/t.* aid, support; ✝ defray (the costs of); *v/i. S.Am.* vote; **sufragio** *m* (*derecho de votar*) suffrage, franchise; (*voto*) vote; ballot; (*ayuda*) aid; *~ universal* universal suffrage.

sufrido 1. patient, long-suffering; *color, tela etc.* hard-wearing; *marido* complaisant; **2.** *m* F complaisant husband; **sufrimiento** *m* patience; tolerance; (*padecimiento*) suffering, misery; **sufrir** [3a] *v/t.* (*padecer*) suffer; *pérdida* suffer, sustain; (*experimentar*) undergo, experience; (*soportar*) bear, put up with; (*permitir*) suffer, permit; *v/i.* suffer.

sugerencia *f* suggestion; **sugerente** full of suggestions; **sugerir** [3i] suggest; hint; *pensamiento etc.* prompt; **sugestión** *f* suggestion; hint; prompting; stimulus; (*psychological*) auto-suggestion, self-hypnotism; **sugestionar** [1a] hypnotize; *fig.* influence, dominate the will of; **sugestivo** attractive; (*que hace pensar*) stimulating, thought-provoking.

suicida 1. suicidal; **2.** *m/f* suicide (*p.*); **suicidarse** [1a] commit suicide; **suicidio** *m* suicide (*act*).

suizo¹ *adj. a. su. m, a f* Swiss.

suizo² *m* sugared bun.

sujeción f subjection; (*acto de fijar*) fastening etc.; **sujetador** m fastener; clip *de pluma*; ~ *de libros* bookend; **sujetapapeles** m paperclip; **sujetar** [1a] (*fijar etc.*) fasten, hold in place; (*agarrar*) lay hold of, seize; (*dominar*) subdue; keep down, keep under; ~**se** *a* subject o.s. to, submit to; **sujeto 1.:** ~ *a* subject to, liable to; **2.** m gr. subject; F fellow, character; F mal ~ bad lot.

sulfato m sulphate.

sulfurar [1a] ⚗ sulphurate; *fig.* annoy, rile; ~**se** blow up, see red; **sulfúreo** sulphur(e)ous; **sulfúrico** sulphuric; **sulfuro** m sulphide.

sultán m sultan; **sultana** f sultana.

suma f (*agregado*) sum, total; (*dinero*) sum; (*acto*) adding-up; (*resumen*) summary; substance, essence; ~ *y sigue* carried forward; ~ *global* lump sum; *en* ~ in short; **sumadora** f adding-machine; **sumamente** extremely, highly; **sumar** [1a] add up, total; (*compendiar*) summarize; sum up; ~**se** *a* join, become attached to; **sumario** adj. a. su. m summary (a. ⚗).

sumergir [3c] submerge; sink; dip, plunge, immerse; *fig.* plunge (en into); ~**se** submerge; sink etc.; **sumersión** f submersion, submergence; immersion; *fig.* absorption (en in).

sumidero m drain; overflow; sink; *esp.* ⊕ sump.

suminstrador m, -a f supplier; **suministrar** [1a] supply; **suministro** m supply; ~**s** pl. supplies; ~ *de combustible* fuel supply.

sumir [3a] sink; plunge, immerse; *fig.* plunge (en into); ~**se** sink.

sumisión f submission; (*cualidad*) submissiveness; **sumiso** submissive, obedient; unresisting; (*sin quejar*) uncomplaining.

sumo great, extreme; *sacerdote* high; *pontífice* supreme; *con* ~*a dificultad* with the greatest difficulty; *a lo* ~ at (the) most.

suntuario sumptuary; **suntuoso** *mst* sumptuous; lavish, rich.

supeditar [1a] oppress, crush; (*avasallar*) subdue; *fig.* subordinate (*a* to).

super... super...; over...

superable surmountable; *obra* that can be done.

superabundante superabundant.

superar [1a] surpass *en cantidad*; excel *en calidad*; *dificultad* overcome, surmount; *expectativa* exceed; *límites* transcend; *marca* break, beat.

superávit m surplus.

supercarburante m high-test fuel.

superconsumo m over-consumption.

superchería f fraud, trick(ery); **superchero** fraudulent; bogus.

super...: ~**directa** f mot. overdrive; ~**empleo** m over-employment; ~**entender** [2g] supervise; ~**estructura** f superstructure; ~**ferolítico** F finicky.

superficial *medida* surface attr.; *fig. mst* superficial (a. 🗲); facile; perfunctory; *p. etc.* shallow; **superficie** f surface; area; outside; face; ~ *inferior* underside; *mot.* ~ *de rodadura* tread.

superfino superfine.

superfluo superfluous.

super...: ~**heterodino** m superhet (-erodyne); ~**hombre** m superman; ~**intendencia** f supervision; ~**intendente** m superintendent, supervisor; overseer.

superior 1. upper, higher; *fig.* superior, better; high, higher; first-rate; *clase social etc.* upper; *p.* chief, head ...; *master* ...; ~ *a cifra* more than, larger than; *calidad* better than; *nivel etc.* above, higher than; **2.** m superior; *mis* ~*es* my superiors *en categoría*; *fig.* my betters; **superiora** f mother superior; **superioridad** f superiority. [lative.\
superlativo adj. a. su. m super-\
super...: ~**mercado** m supermarket; ~**numerario** adj. a. su. m, a f supernumerary; ~**poblado** *barrio etc.* overcrowded, congested; *región* over-populated; ~**poner** [2r] superimpose; ~**producción** f overproduction; ~**sónico** supersonic.

superstición f superstition; **supersticioso** superstitious.

supervisar [1a] supervise.

supervivencia f survival; **superviviente** m/f survivor.

suplantar [1a] supplant.

suplefaltas m/f F scapegoat.

suplemental supplemental; **suplementario** *mst* supplementary; *precio etc.* extra; *empleo* ~, *negocio* ~ side-line; *tren* ~ relief train, extra train; **suplemento** *m* supplement; 🚲 excess fare.

suplente 1. substitute, deputy, reserve; *maestro* supply *attr.*; **2.** *m/f* substitute, deputy; *thea. etc.* understudy; *deportes*: reserve.

supletorio supplementary.

súplica *f* supplication; ⚖ petition; ~s *pl.* pleading(s); **suplicante 1.** *tono etc.* imploring; **2.** *m/f* ⚖ *etc.* petitioner; applicant; **suplicar** [1g] *p.* plead with, implore; beg; *ayuda etc.* plead for, beg (for); ⚖ appeal, petition (de against).

suplicio *m* (*castigo*) punishment; (*tormento*) torture; (*dolor*) torment; *fig.* ordeal, anguish.

suplir [3a] *necesidad, omisión* supply; *falta* make good, make up for; supplement; *p. etc.* (*mst* ~ a) replace, take the place of; substitute for.

suponer [2r] *v/t.* suppose, assume; entail, imply *como consecuencia*; *supongo que sí* I suppose so; *Vd. puede* ~ *lo que pasó* you can guess what happened; *v/i.* be important; **suposición** *f* supposition, surmise; *fig.* authority; distinction; (*mentira*) imposture.

supremacía *f* supremacy; **supremo** supreme.

supresión *f* suppression *etc.*; **supresor** *m* *radio*: suppressor; **suprimir** [3a] *rebelión, crítica etc.* suppress; *costumbre, derecho* abolish; *dificultad, desechos* remove, eliminate; *restricciones* lift; *pasaje* delete, cut out.

supuesto 1. *p.p.* of **suponer**; **2.** *adj.* supposed, ostensible; (*sedicente*) self-styled; *nombre* assumed; ~ *que* since, granted that; **3.** *m* assumption, hypothesis; *por* ~ of course; *dar por* ~ take *s.t.* for granted.

supurar [1a] discharge, run, suppurate ⚕.

sur 1. *parte* south(ern); *dirección* southerly; *viento* south(erly); **2.** *m* south.

surcar [1g] *tierra etc.* furrow, plough (through *etc.*); (*hacer rayas*) score, groove; *agua* cleave; **surco** *m* 🎵 *etc.* furrow; (*raya*) groove, line; groove *de disco*; (*arruga*)

wrinkle; *track en agua*; F *echarse en el* ~ lie down on the job.

surgir [3c] arise, emerge, appear; (*líquido*) spout, spurt (up); spring up; loom up; (*dificultad etc.*) arise, crop up; (*p.*) appear unexpectedly; ⚓ anchor.

suroeste 1. *parte* south-west(ern); *dirección* south-westerly; *viento* south-west(erly); **2.** *m* south-west.

surrealismo *m* surrealism; **surrealista** *m/f* surrealist.

surtido 1. mixed, assorted; **2.** *m* (*gama*) range, selection, assortment; (*provisión*) stock, supply; *de* ~ stock; **surtidor** *m* fountain; (*chorro*) jet; ~ *de gasolina* petrol pump; **surtir** [3a] *v/t.* supply, stock; *esp. fig.* provide; *efecto* have, produce; *bien surtido* well stocked (de with); *v/i.* spout, spurt; ⚓ anchor; ~se de provide o.s. with.

susceptible susceptible; sensitive, touchy; impressionable; ~ *de mejora etc.* capable of, open to; *daño* liable to.

suscitar [1a] *rebelión etc.* stir up; provoke; *cuestión, duda etc.* raise.

suscribir [3a; *p.p. suscrito*] subscribe (*a* to); *opinión* subscribe to; (*firmar*) sign; ~se subscribe (*a* to, for); **suscripción** *f* subscription; **suscriptor** *m*, -a *f* subscriber.

susodicho above(-mentioned).

suspender [2a] hang (up), suspend; *fig. mst* suspend; *candidato* fail; (*admirar*) astonish; **suspensión** *f* hanging (up), suspension (*a. mot.*); *fig. mst* suspension; ⚖ stay; ~ *de armas*, ~ *de hostilidades* cease-fire; **suspensivo:** *v. punto;* **suspenso 1.** suspended, hanging; *candidato* failed; *fig.* amazed; bewildered; **2.** *m univ. etc.* fail(ure); *en* ~ *negocio* in suspense, pending; ⚖ in abeyance; *quedar en* ~ stand over.

suspicacia *f* suspicion, mistrust; **suspicaz** suspicious, distrustful.

suspirado longed-for; **suspirar** [1a] sigh (*por* for); **suspiro** *m* sigh; *exhalar el último* ~ breathe one's last.

sustancia *f* substance; essence; *en* ~ in substance; **sustancial** substantial; important, vital; **sustancioso** substantial; *comida* nourishing; **sustantivo 1.** substantive; *gr.* substantival; **2.** *m* noun, substantive.

sustentación *f* lift; = **sustentamiento** *m* maintenance; sustenance; **sustentar** [1a] sustain; maintain; support; (*alimentar*)feed, nourish; *tesis* defend; ~se sustain o.s.; subsist (*con* on); **sustento** *m* sustenance, food; maintenance; *fig.* (*vida que se gana*) livelihood; (*esencia vital*) life-blood.

sustitución *f* substitution; replacement; **sustituir** [3g] *v/t.* substitute (*A por B* B for A), replace (*A por B* A by B, A with B); *v/i.* substitute; deputize; ~ *a* replace; deputize for; **sustituto** *m*, **a** *f* substitute; deputy; replacement.

susto *m* fright, scare; ¡*ay qué* ~! what a fright you gave me!; *darse un* ~ have a fright.

sustracción *f* Å subtraction; deduction; **sustraer** [2p] Å subtract; deduct; (*robar*) steal; ~se *a* withdraw from, contract out of; avoid.

sustrato *m* substratum.

susurrar [1a] whisper; *fig.* (*arroyo*) murmur; (*hojas*) rustle; (*viento*) whisper; *susurran que, se susurra que* it is whispered that; ~se *fig.* be whispered about; **susurro** *m fig.* whisper; murmur; rustle.

sutil *tela etc.* thin, fine; tenuous; (*perspicaz*) keen, observant; *distinción etc.* subtle; **sutileza** *f* thinness *etc.*; subtlety; finesse; **sutilizar** [1f] *v/t.* thin down, fine down; *fig.* polish, perfect; refine (up)on; *b.s.* split hairs about; *v/i.* quibble.

sutura *f* suture; **suturar** [1a] suture.

suyo, suya 1. *pron. a. adj.* (*tras verbo* ser) (*un poseedor*) his, hers, its, one's; (*de Vd.*) your; (*varios poseedores*) theirs; (*de Vds.*) yours; **2.** *adj.* (*tras su.*) of his *etc.*; *de* ~ naturally; intrinsically; *per se*; on its own; *eso es muy* ~ that's just like him; *salirse con la* ~*a* have one's way; carry one's point *en debate*.

svástica *f* swastika.

T

¡**ta!** careful!; easy there!

taba *f* anklebone; (*juego*) knuckle-bones; F *menear las* ~*s* bustle about; F *tomar la* ~ start speaking; show who is boss.

tabacal *m* tobacco field; **Tabacalera** *f Spanish state tobacco monopoly;* **tabacalero 1.** tobacco *attr.*; **2.** *m* tobacconist; **tabaco** *m* tobacco; (*puro*) cigar; (*cigarrillos*) cigarettes; ⚕ tobacco-plant; ~ *en polvo* snuff; ~ *rubio* Virginian tobacco; **tabacoso** *dedos* tobacco-stained.

tabalada *f* F punch; knock, bump *de caída;* **tabalear** [1a] *v/t.* shake, rock; *v/i.* drum · (with one's fingers).

tábano *m* horsefly.

tabaquera *f* (*caja*) snuff-box; bowl *de pipa; S.Am.* pouch; **tabaquería** *f* tobacconist's (shop); **tabaquero** *m* tobacconist.

taberna *f* pub(lic house), bar.

tabernáculo *m* tabernacle.

tabernario *fig.* rude, dirty; **tabernero** *m* publican, landlord; (*empleado*) barman.

tabicar [1g] wall up, partition off; *fig.* cover up; **tabique** *m* partition (wall), thin wall.

tabla *f* (*madera*) plank, board; (*piedra*) slab; *paint.* panel; *anat.* flat (*or* wide) part; ✦ bed, patch; *sew.* broad pleat; ✝ meat stall; *etc.* table; (*lista*) table, list; chart; index *de libro;* ~*s pl. thea.* boards, stage; *fig.* theatre; ~*s pl. ajedrez etc.*: draw; ~ *de dibujo* drawing-board; ~ *de materias* table of contents; ~ *de multiplicar* multiplication table; ~ *de planchar* ironing-board; ~ *de salvación* last resort; thing that saves one's life; *escapar en una* ~ have a narrow escape; *hacer* ~ *rasa de* make a clean sweep of; *quedar* ~*s fig.* be deadlocked; **tablado** *m* plank floor, platform, stand; *thea. etc.* stage; (*cadalso*) scaffold; **tablaje** *m*, **tablazón** *f* planks, planking,

boards; **tablear** [1a] cut into boards; ✦ divide into beds; *sew.* pleat; **tablero** *m* boards, planks; *ajedrez etc.*: board; (*encerado*) blackboard; counter *de tienda;* ✦ switchboard; ~ (*de instrumentos*) instrument panel, *mot.* dashboard; ✦ beds, plots; (*juego*) gambling-den; ~ *de ajedrez* chessboard; ~ *de dibujo* drawing-board; **tableta** *f* small board; (*taco*) tablet; bar *de chocolate;* **tabletear** [1a] rattle; **tablilla** *f* small board; ✂ splint; **tablón** *m* plank, beam; ~ *de anuncios* notice-board.

tabú *m* taboo.

tabuco *m* slum, wretched little place.

tabular [1a] tabulate.

taburete *m* stool.

tacañería *f* meanness; **tacaño** mean, stingy, close-fisted.

tácito tacit; *observación etc.* unspoken; *ley* unwritten; **taciturno** taciturn; (*triste*) moody, sulky, glum.

taco *m* plug, bung, stopper; (*empaquetadura*) wad(ding); *billar:* cue; ⚒ rammer; (*juguete*) popgun; *S.Am.* heel; ~ (*de papel*) writing-pad; F (*bocadillo*) snack; F swig, mouthful *de vino;* F (*palabra*) swear-word, rude word; F *soltar un* ~ swear.

tacón *m* heel; **taconear** [1a] click one's heels *al saludar etc.;* stamp with one's heels.

táctica *f* tactics; *fig.* move; way (of doing things); gambit; **táctico 1.** tactical; **2.** *m* tactician.

táctil tactile; **tacto** *m* (*sentido*) (sense of) touch; touch *de mecanógrafa etc.;* (*acto*) touch(ing), feel; *fig.* tact; *ser áspero etc. al* ~ feel rough *etc.*

tacha[1] *f* ⊕ large tack, stud.

tacha[2] *f* flaw, blemish, defect; *sin* ~ flawless; *poner* ~ *a* find fault with; **tachar** [1a] cross out; *fig.* fault, criticize, attack; ~ *de* accuse of being.

tachines *m/pl. sl.* feet.

tachón[1] *m* ⊕ stud, boss; *sew.* trimming; **tachonar** [1a] ⊕ stud (*a. fig.*).

tachón[2] *m* stroke, crossing-out.

tachoso defective, faulty.

tachuela *f* (tin)tack.

tafetán *m* taffeta, ~es *pl. fig.* flags; F buttons and bows; ~ adhesivo, ~ inglés sticking-plaster.

tafilete *m* morocco leather.

tahona *f* bakery, bakehouse.

tahur *m* gambler; *b.s.* card-sharper, cheat.

taifa *f* F gang of thieves; *hist.* band, faction.

taimado sly, crafty.

taja *f* cut; division; **tajada** *f* slice, cut *de carne etc.*; *S.Am.* cut, slash; F (*ronquera*) hoarseness; F (*borrachera*) drunk; F ⊤ rake-off; F *sacar* ~ look after number one; get something out of it; ⊤ *get a rake-off*; **tajadera** *f* chopper; ⊕ cold chisel; **tajadero** *m* chopping-block; **tajado** *peña* sheer; **tajamar** *m* stem, cutwater; *S.Am.* dyke, dam; **tajante** cutting, sharp; *fig.* incisive, sharp; **tajar** [1a] *carne etc.* slice, cut; chop; hew; **tajo** *m* (*corte*) cut; slash *con espada*; (*filo*) cutting edge; *geog.* sheer cliff; (*tajadero*) chopping-block; *block de verdugo*; (*tarea*) job; *tirar* ~s slash (*a* at).

tal 1. *adj.* such (a); (*con su. abstracto*) such; ~es *pl.* such; el ~ Pérez this Pérez, that fellow Pérez; un ~ Pérez a man called Pérez, one Pérez; **2.** *pron.* (*p.*) such a one, someone; (*cosa*) such a thing, something; F *en la calle de* ~ in such-and-such a street; el ~ this man *etc.* (we're talking about); such a person; ~ *como* such as; *como* ~ as such; ~ *cual libro* an odd book, one or two books; ~ *o cual* such-and-such; ~ *para cual* two of a kind; *sí* ~ yes indeed; *y* ~ and such; ~ *hay que* there are those who; *no hay* ~ nothing of the sort; *no hay* ~ *como inf.* there's nothing like *ger.*; **3.** *adv.* so, in such a way; ~ *como* just as; ~ *cual* (*adv.*) just as it is; *era* ~ *cual deseaba* it was just what he wanted; (*como adj.*) middling, so-so; *¿qué* ~? how goes it?, how's things?; *¿qué* ~ *el libro?* what do you think of the book?;

¿qué ~ *te gustó?* how did you like it?; **4.** *cj.:* *con* ~ *que* provided (that).

talabartería *f* saddlery; **talabartero** *m* saddler.

taladradora *f* drill; ~ *de fuerza* power-drill; **taladrar** [1a] bore, drill, punch, pierce; *que taladra los oídos* ear-splitting; **taladro** *m* drill; gimlet; bore(r); (*agujero*) drill-hole.

tálamo *m* marriage-bed.

talante *m* (*semblante*) look; (*ánimo*) frame of mind; (*deseo*) will, pleasure; (*modo de hacer*) method, way; *de buen* (*mal*) ~ *estar in a* good (bad) mood; *hacer* with a good (bad) grace.

talar [1a] *árbol* fell, cut down; ⚠ *etc.* pull down; *fig.* devastate.

talco *m* talcum powder; *min.* talc.

talcualillo F so-so, middling (*a.* ⚓).

talega *f* bag, sack; nappy *de niño*; **talego** *m* long sack, poke; F (*p.*) rag-bag; F *tener* ~ have money tucked away.

talento *m* talent (*a. hist.*); gift; (*inteligencia*) brains, ability; ~s *pl.* talents; accomplishments; **talentoso** talented, gifted.

talismán *m* talisman.

talmente in such a way, so.

talón *m anat.* heel; stub, counterfoil *de cheque etc.*; 🚆 receipt for luggage; **talonar** [1a] heel; **talonario** *m* (*a. libro* ~) book of tickets; receipt-book; cheque-book; **talonear** [1a] hurry along.

talud *m* slope, bank; *geol.* talus.

talla *f* (*escultura*) carving; (*grabado*) engraving; height, stature *de p.*; size *de traje etc.*; rod, scale *para medir*; ⚖ reward; *obra de* ~ carving; *poner a* ~ offer a reward for; *tener poca* ~ be on the short side; **tallado 1.** carved *etc.*; *bien* ~ shapely, well-formed; **2.** *m* carving *etc.*; **tallar** [1a] *v/t.* carve; shape, work; (*grabar*) engrave; *diamante* cut; *p.* measure; *fig.* value, appraise; *v/i. S.Am.* chat.

tallarín *m* noodle.

talle *m* (*cintura*) waist; (*cuerpo*) figure *esp. de mujer*; build, physique *esp. de hombre*; *fig.* outline; look, appearance.

taller *m* ⊕ workshop, shop; (*grande*) mill, factory; workroom *de sastre*;

studio *de pintor*; ~es *pl.* gráficos printing works; ~ *de máquinas* machine-shop; ~ *de montaje* assembly shop; ~ *de reparaciones* repair shop.

tallo *m* ♀ stem, stalk; blade *de hierba*; (*renuevo*) shoot.

talluda: F *es una* ~ *ya* she's no chicken; **talludo** ♀ tall; *p.* lanky.

tamañito: *dejar* ~ crush, make *s.o.* feel small; **tamaño 1.** (*grande*) so big, such a big; huge; (*pequeño*) so small *etc.*; ~ *como* as big as; **2.** *m* size; capacity, volume; *de* ~ extra(*ordinario*) outsize; *de* ~ *natural* full-size, life-size; ¿*de qué* ~ *es?* how big is it?

tamarindo *m* tamarind; **tamarisco** *m*, **tamariz** *m* tamarisk.

tambalear(se) [1a] (*p.*) stagger, reel, totter; (*cosa*) wobble; (*vehículo*) lurch, sway; *ir tambaleándose* lurch along *etc.*

también also, as well, too; beside(s); *¡*~*!* that as well?, not that too!; *yo* ~ so am I, me too.

tambo *m S.Am.* inn.

tambor *m* ♪, ⊕ drum; *sew.*, ⚠ tambour; *anat.* ear-drum; (*p.*) drummer; *a* ~ *batiente* with flying colours; **tambora** *f* bass drum; **tamboril** *m* small drum; **tamborilada** *f* F, **tamborilazo** *m* F bump on one's bottom; (*espaldarazo*) slap on the shoulder; **tamborilear** [1a] drum *con dedos*; (*lluvia*) patter; **tamborileo** *m* drumming; patter; **tamborilero** *m* drummer. [sieve.)

tamiz *m* sieve; **tamizar** [1f] sift,)

tamo *m* fluff; (*polvo*) dust (*a.* ✗).

tampoco neither, not ... either; nor; *ni éste ni aquél* ~ neither this one nor that one; *yo* ~ *lo sé, yo no lo sé* ~ I don't know either; *ni yo* ~ nor I.

tampón *m* plug (*a.* ✗); ~ (*de entintar*) ink-pad.

tan so; ~ *bueno* so good; *coche* ~ *grande* such a big car; ~ ... *como* as ... as; ~ *es así que* so much so that.

tanda *f* shift, gang, relay *de ps.*; shift, turn, spell *en el trabajo*; turn *de riego etc.*; (*tarea*) job; (*capa*) layer, coat; (*partida*) game; (*lote*) batch; *S.Am. thea.* show; *S.Am.* bad habit.

tándem *m* tandem; ✗ *en* ~ tandem.

tanganillas: *en* ~ unsteadily; **tanganillo** *m* prop, wedge.

tangencial tangential; **tangente** *f* tangent.

tangible tangible.

tango *m* tango.

tanque *m* tank (*a.* ✗); **tanquero** *m S.Am.* ⚓ tanker.

tantán *m* tomtom; **tantarantán** *m* drum-beat, rub-a-dub; F punch.

tanteador *m* scoreboard; (*p.*) scorer; **tantear** [1a] *v/t.* (*examinar*) weigh up; (*ensayar*) feel, test; (*comparar*) measure, weigh; *intenciones, p.*, sound out; *deportes*: keep the score of; *v/i. deportes*: score, keep (the) score; (*ir a tientas*) grope; **tanteo** *m* weighing-up; calculation; trial, test(ing); trial and error; *deportes*: score; *al* ~ by guesswork.

tanto 1. *adj.* so much; ~s *pl.* so many; ~ *como* as much as; ~s *como* as many as; *20 y* ~s 20-odd; *a* ~s *de mayo* on such-and-such a day in May; *a las* ~as in the small hours; **2.** *adv.* so much; as much; *trabajar etc.* so hard; *permanecer etc.* so long; *él come* ~ *como yo* he eats as much as I do; ~ *A como B* both A and B; ~ *más* the more, all the more ... as; ~ *más cuanto que* all the more (...) because; ~ *mejor* all the better; ~ *peor* so much the worse; *no es para* ~ there's no need to make such a fuss; it's not as bad as all that; ~ *que* so much so that; *en(tre)* ~ meanwhile; F *¡ni* ~ *así!* not in the least little bit; *por* (*lo*) ~ so, therefore; **3.** *cj.*: *con* ~ *que* provided (that); **4.** *m* ✝ *etc.* so much, a certain amount; (*ficha*) counter, chip; *deportes*: point, goal; ~ *por ciento* percentage, rate; ✝ *al* ~ at the same price; *algún* ~, *un* ~ rather; *otro* ~ as much again, the same thing again; *estar al* ~ *de* be in touch with, know about; *poner al* ~ *de* give *s.o.* the news about, put *s.o.* in the picture about.

tañer [2f] ♪ play; *campana* ring; **tañido** *m* sound *de instrumento*; ringing *de campana*; twang *de guitarra*; tinkle *al caer etc.*

tapa *f* lid; (*tapón*) top, cap; cover *de libro*; (*plato*) approx. dish of hors d'oeuvres, snack (taken with a drink); ~ *de los sesos* brain-box, brain-pan, skull; *levantarse la ~ de los sesos* blow one's brains out.

tapa(a)gujeros *m* F jerry-builder; *fig.* stopgap.

tapaboca *f*, **tapabocas** *m* slap; (*bufanda*) muffler.

tapacubos *m* hub-cap.

tapadera *f* lid, cover, cap; **tapadero** *m* stopper; **tapadillo**: *de ~* secretly; **tapado** *m S.Am.* (woman's) coat.

tapar [1a] *vasija* put the lid on; *botella* put the cap on, stopper; *cara* cover up; muffle up; (*cegar etc.*) stop (up), block (up); *visión* obstruct, hide; *fig.* conceal; *defecto* cover up; *fugitivo* hide; *delincuente* cover up for; *~se* wrap (o.s.) up.

taparrabo *m* loincloth *de indio etc.*; (bathing-)trunks.

taperujarse [1a] F cover up one's face.

tapete *m* rug; (table-)runner; *~ verde* card-table; *estar sobre el ~* be under discussion.

tapia *f* (garden-)wall; mud wall; **tapiar** [1b] wall in; *fig.* stop up.

tapicería *f* (*colgada*) tapestry, tapestries, hangings; upholstery *de mueble*; (*arte*) tapestry-making; upholstery.

tapioca *f* tapioca.

tapiz *m* tapestry; carpet; **tapizar** [1f] *pared* hang with tapestries; *mueble* upholster; *suelo* carpet (*a. fig.*, con, de with).

tapón *m* stopper, cap *de botella*; (*corcho*) cork; ⊕ plug, bung; wad; 🗡 tampon; **taponar** [1a] stopper, cork; *conducto* plug, stop up; 🗡 tampon; **taponazo** *m* pop.

tapujarse [1a] F muffle o.s. up; **tapujo** *m* muffler; F subterfuge; F *sin ~s* straight, no messing.

taquigrafía *f* shorthand, stenography; **taquígrafo** *m*, **a** *f* shorthand writer, stenographer.

taquilla *f* 🚆 booking-office; *thea.* box-office; (*carpeta*) file; **taquillero 1.** *éxito etc.* box-office attr.; **2.** *m*, **a** *f* clerk.

taquimeca(nógrafa) *f* shorthand typist.

taquímetro *m* speedometer; *surv.* tachymeter.

tara *f* 🏴 tare; (*palito*) tally-stick.

tarabilla 1. *f* F chatter; **2.** *m/f* F (*hablador*) chatterbox; (*casquivano*)

useless sort, dreamer; *soltar la ~* talk nineteen to the dozen.

taracea *f* inlay, marquetry; **taracear** [1a] inlay.

tarado defective, damaged.

tarambana *adj. a. su. m/f* F harum-scarum; crackpot.

tarántula *f* tarantula.

tarar [1a] tare.

tararear [1a] hum.

tarasca *f hist.* (processional) dragon; F old bag; **tarascada** *f* bite; F tart reply, rude answer; **tarascar** [1g] bite, snap at.

tardanza *f* slowness; (*retraso*) delay; **tardar** [1a] take a long time, be long; delay; (*sin partir etc.*) linger (on); (*llegar tarde*) come late, be late; *~ en inf.* be slow to *inf.*, be long in *ger.*; be late in *ger.*; *~ mucho en inf.* take a long time to *inf.*; *~ dos horas en inf.* take two hours to *inf.*; *¿cuánto tardaremos en llegar?* how long shall we take to get there?; *a más ~* at the latest.

tarde 1. *adv.* late; (*demasiado*) too late; *de ~ en ~* from time to time; *~ o temprano* sooner or later; *más ~* later (on); *se hace ~* it is getting late; **2.** *f* (*de 12 a 5 o 6*) afternoon; (*5 o 6 al anochecer*) evening; *¡buenas ~s!* good afternoon, good evening; *de la ~ a la mañana* overnight; *fig.* in no time at all; **tardecer** [2d] get dark; **tardecita** *f* dusk.

tardío (*lento*) slow; (*que llega o madura tarde*) late; (*atrasado*) belated, overdue; **tardo** slow, sluggish; **tardón** F slow; (*lerdo*) dim.

tarea *f* job, task; duty, duties; (*cuidado*) worry; *~ de ocasión* chore; *~ suelta* odd job.

tarifa *f* tariff; rate, charge; price list *en café etc.*; (*pasaje*) fare; *~ turística* tourist class; **tarifar** [1a] price.

tarima *f* platform; (*soporte*) stand; (*asiento*) stool, bench; (*cama*) bunk.

tarja *f* tally; F swipe, slash; **tarjar** [1a] keep a tally of.

tarjeta *f* card; *~ de identidad* identity card; *~ postal* postcard; *~ de visita* visiting card.

tarraconense *adj. a. su. m/f* (native) of Tarragona.

tarro *m* pot, jar.

tarta *f* tart, cake.

tártago: F *darse un ~* slog, sweat.

tartajear [1a] stammer; **tartajoso** stammering, tongue-tied; **tartalear** [1a] F stagger, reel; (*hablando*) get stuck for words; **tartamudear** [1a] stutter, stammer; **tartamudeo** *m* stutter(ing); **tartamudez** *f* stutter, speech defect; **tartamudo** 1. stuttering; 2. *m*, **a** *f* stutterer.

tártaro *m* ⚗ tartar; (*p.*) Tartar.

tarugo *m* wooden peg; (*tapón*) plug, stopper; △ wooden paving-block.

tarumba: F volver ~ daze, fog.

tasa *f* (fixed, official) price; rate; *fig.* estimate; (*acto*) valuation *etc.*; (*medida, norma*) measure, standard; sin ~ boundless, unstinted; **tasable** ratable; **tasación** *f* valuation; fixing *de precios*; *fig.* appraisal; **tasadamente** in moderation, sparingly; **tasador** *m* valuer; **tasar** [1a] *artículo* fix a price for, price (en at); *trabajo etc.* assess, rate (en at); *fig.* appraise; regulate; put a limit on, restrict.

tasca *f* F bar, pub; eating-house; *b.s.* low dive.

tata *f* F maid; (*niñera*) nanny.

tatarabuelo *m* great-great-grandfather.

tatas: F andar a ~ (*niño*) toddle; (*a gatas*) get down on all fours.

¡tate! *admiración:* goodness!, well well!; (*ya caigo*) oh I see; *cuidado:* look out!

tatuaje *m* tattoo; (*acto*) tattooing; **tatuar** [1d] tattoo.

taumaturgo *m* miracle-worker.

taurino bullfighting *attr.*; *zo.* bull *attr.*; **tauromaquia** *f* (art of) bullfighting; **tauromáquico** bullfighting *attr.*

tautología *f* tautology.

taxativo limiting, restricting.

taxi *m* taxi(-cab).

taxidermista *m/f* taxidermist.

taxímetro *m* taximeter, clock F; **taxista** *m* taxi-driver.

taz: *S.Am.* ~ con ~ side by side; equal, even.

taza *f* cup; basin *de fuente*.

tazarse [1f] fray.

tazón *m* large cup, bowl; *prov.* wash-basin.

te (*acc.*) you; (*dat.*) (to) you; (*reflexivo*) (to) yourself; (†, *a Dios*) thee, (to) thee, (to) thyself.

té *m* tea.

tea *f* torch.

teatral of the theatre, theatrical; *fig.* dramatic; *esp. b.s.* histrionic, stagey; **teatralidad** *f* drama, sense of theatre; showmanship; **teatro** *m* theatre (*a.* ✗); scene *de acontecimiento*; (*profesión*) the theatre, the stage; (*obras*) dramatic works; ~ de la ópera opera-house.

tebeo *m* children's comic.

teca *f* teak.

tecla *f* key; F dar en la ~ get the hang of a thing; fall into a habit; **teclado** *m* keyboard; manual *de órgano*; **teclear** [1a] *v/t.* F *asunto* approach from various angles; *v/i.* strum, thrum; F drum *con dedos*; **tecleo** *m* fingering *etc.*; touch, fingerwork.

técnica *f* technique; **tecnicidad** *f* technicality; **tecnicismo** *m* technicality, technical term; **técnico** 1. technical; 2. *m* technician; expert, specialist; **tecnicolor** *m* technicolour; **tecnología** *f* technology; **tecnológico** technological; **tecnólogo** *m* technologist.

tecomate *m* S.Am. gourd.

techado *m* roof; bajo ~ indoors, under cover; **techar** [1a] roof (in, over); **techo** *m*, **techumbre** *f* roof; ceiling *de habitación* (*a.* ✗).

tedio *m* boredom; tedium.

teja *f* tile; a toca ~ on the nail, in hard cash; de ~s abajo in the natural way of things; de ~s arriba with God's help; up aloft; supernatural; as far as the supernatural is concerned; **tejadillo** *m* top, cover; **tejado** *m* (tiled) roof; *fig.* housetop; **tejar** [1a] tile.

tejedor *m*, **-a** *f* weaver; **tejedura** *f* weaving; (*textura*) weave, texture; **tejeduría** *f* weaving; (*fábrica*) textile mill; **tejer** [2a] weave (*a. fig.*); *S.Am.* knit; *fig.* scheme; ~ y destejer blow hot and cold; **tejido** *m* fabric, material; tissue (*a. anat.*); web; (*textura*) weave, texture; ~s *pl.* textiles.

tejo *m* ♀ yew; (*aro*) quoit.

tejoleta *f* bit of tile, sherd; brickbat.

tejón *m* badger.

tela *f* cloth, fabric, material; web *de araña etc.*; (*nata*) skin, film; skin *de fruta*; *sl.* dough; *fig.* subject, matter; ~ de araña spider's web; ~s *pl. del corazón* heartstrings; ~ cru-

zada twill; ~ **metálica** wire fencing; ~ **de punto** stockinet; *hay* ~ *que cortar* (*or para rato*) it's an awkward business, it's a long job; *poner en* ~ *de juicio* (call in) question; test, look closely at.
telar *m* loom; *thea.* gridiron.
telaraña *f* spider's web, cobweb.
tele...: ~**comando** *m*, ~**control** *m* remote control; ~**fonear** [1a] telephone; ~**fonema** *m* telephone message; ~**fónico** telephonic; telephone *attr.*; ~**fonista** *m/f* (telephone) operator, telephonist; **teléfono** *m* telephone; *llamar al* (*or por*) ~ telephone, ring (up).
tele...: ~**fotografía** *f* telephoto; ~**grafía** *f* telegraphy; ~**grafiar** [1c] telegraph; ~**gráfico** telegraphic; telegraph *attr.*; ~**grafista** *m/f* telegraphist; **telégrafo** *m* telegraph; ~**s** *m* F telegram-boy; **telegrama** *m* telegram; **teleimpresor** *m* teleprinter; **telémetro** *m* range-finder.
tele...: ~**patía** *f* telepathy; ~**pático** telepathic; ~**scopar(se)** [1a] telescope; ~**scópico** telescopic; ~**scopio** *m* telescope; ~**spectador** *m*, **-a** *f* (tele)viewer; ~**squí** *m* ski-lift; ~**tipo** *m* teletype; ~**visar** [1a] televise; ~**visión** *f* television; *aparato de* ~ = ~**visor** *m* television set.
telón *m* curtain; *pol.* ~ *de acero* iron curtain; ~ *de boca* front curtain; drop (curtain); ~ *de fondo*, ~ *de foro* backcloth, backdrop; ~ *de seguridad* safety curtain.
tema[1] *m* theme (*a.* ♪); subject (*a. paint.*), topic; motif; *gr.* stem.
tema[2] *f* fixed idea, mania; *tener* ~ be stubborn; *tener* ~ *a* have a grudge against.
temblar [1k] tremble (*ante* at, *de* at, with); shake, quiver, shiver; (*tambalearse*) totter, sway; ~ *de frío* shiver with cold; ~ *por su vida* fear for one's life; **temblequear** [1a] F be all of a quiver; **temblón** **1.** trembling; *álamo* ~ = **2.** *m* aspen; **temblor** *m* tremble, trembling *etc.*; tremor; shiver(ing) *esp. de frío*; ~ *de tierra* earthquake; **tembloroso** trembling.
temer [2a] *v/t.* be afraid of, fear; dread; *v/i.* be afraid; ~ *por* fear for; ~ *inf.*; fear to *inf.*; ~ *que* fear that; be afraid that; *no temas* don't be afraid.

temerario *p.*, *acto* rash, reckless; *juicio* hasty; unfounded; **temeridad** *f* rashness *etc.*, temerity.
temeroso timid; = **temible** dreadful, frightful; *adversario etc.* redoubtable; **temor** *m* fear, dread; (*recelo*) misgiving; *sin* ~ *a* fearless of.
témpano *m*: ~ (*de hielo*) ice-floe; (*grande*) iceberg.
temperamento *m* temperament, nature; *fig.* compromise; **temperancia** *f* temperance; **temperante** *S.Am.* **1.** teetotal; **2.** *m/f* teetotaller; **temperar** [1a] *v/t.* temper, moderate; *pasión etc.* calm; *v/i. S.Am.* go on holiday; **temperatura** *f* temperature; **temperie** *f* (state of the) weather.
tempe~**tad** *f* storm (*a. fig.*); ~ *en un vaso de agua* storm in a teacup; **tempestuoso** stormy (*a. fig.*), rough.
templado moderate, restrained; *agua* tepid; *clima* mild, temperate; ♪ in tune; **templanza** *f* temperance; mildness; **templar** [1a] temper, moderate; (*suavizar*) soften; *temperatura* cool; *solución* dilute; *metal* temper; *colores* blend; ♪ tune (up); ~**se** (*p.*) control o.s.; (*tiempo*) moderate; **temple** *m* temper(ing) *de metal*; ♪ tuning; *meteor.* (state of the) weather; temperature; *fig.* disposition; spirit, mettle; *pintar al* ~, *pintura al* ~ distemper.
templete *m* bandstand.
templo *m* temple; (*cristiano*) church, chapel.
temporada *f* time, period; spell (*a. meteor.*); (*social, deportiva etc.*) season; *en plena* ~ at the height of the season; **temporal 1.** *eccl. etc.* temporal; (*provisional*) temporary; **2.** *m* storm; **temporáneo** temporary; **témporas** *f/pl.* ember-days; **temporero** temporary; **temporizar** [1f] temporize; **tempranal** ♀ *etc.*, **tempranero**, **temprano** early.
tenacidad *f* toughness *etc.*
tenacillas *f/pl.* tongs *para azúcar etc.*; curling-tongs *para pelo*; ✂ *etc.* tweezers, forceps; (*despabiladeras*) snuffers.
tenaz tough, resistant; (*pegajoso*) that sticks fast; *creencia, resistencia* stubborn; *p.* tenacious, persevering.

tenazas *f/pl.* ⊕ (*unas* a pair of) pliers, pincers; tongs *para carbón*.
tenca *f* tench.
tendajo *m* small shop.
tendal *m* awning.
tendalera *f* F mess, litter.
tendejón *m* small shop.
tendencia *f* tendency, trend; inclination; tenor *de observación etc.*; ✝ trend, run *de mercado*; *con ~ a* tending to(wards).
tendencioso tendentious.
ténder *m* ⛟ tender.
tender [2g] 1. *v/t.* stretch; spread (out), lay out; *paint.*, △ put on; *arco* draw; *cable*, *vía* lay; *ferrocarril*, *puente* build; *mano* stretch out; *ropa* hang out; *trampa* set (a for); 2. *v/i.*: *~ a su.* tend to, tend towards, incline to; *~ a inf.* tend to *inf.*; 3. *~se* lie down, stretch (o.s.) out; (*caballo*) run at a full gallop; *naipes*: lay down; F let things go to pot.
tendero *m*, *a f* shopkeeper; *esp.* grocer.
tendido 1. lying (down), flat; 2. *m* laying *de cable etc.*; (*ropa*) washing; (*yeso*) coat of plaster; *toros*: front row.
tendón *m* tendon, sinew.
tendré *etc. v.* tener.
tenducho *m* poky little shop.
tenebroso dark; gloomy, dismal; *asunto* sinister, dark; *negocio* shady; *estilo* obscure.
tenedor *m* fork; (*p.*) holder, bearer; *~ de acciones* stockholder; *~ de libros* book-keeper; *~ de obligaciones* bondholder; **teneduría** *f*: *~ de libros* book-keeping.
tenencia *f* tenure *de oficio etc.*; possession *de propiedad*.
tener [2l] have; have got; (*tener en la mano, asir etc.*) hold; (*retener*) keep; (*contener*) hold, contain; *¿qué tienes?* what's the matter with you?; *~ 9 años* be 9 (years old); *¿cuántos años tienes?* how old are you?; *~ 3 metros de ancho* be 3 metres wide; *eso me tiene sin cuidado* I'm not bothered (about that); *~ puesto el sombrero* have (got) one's hat on; F *no ~las todas consigo* have the wind up; *¡ten!, ¡tenga!* here you are!; (*al lanzar*) catch!; *~ a bien inf.* think it proper to *inf.*; *~ a menos inf.* think it beneath o.s. to *inf.*;

~ en más think all the more of; *~ en menos* think the less of; *~ en mucho* value, esteem; *v. poco*; *~ para sí que* think that; *~ por* consider as; *le tengo por listo* I think him pretty clever; *~ que inf.* have to *inf.*, must *inf.*; *~ trabajo que hacer* have work to do; *~se* hold (fast); stand firm; catch o.s. *al caer*; (*detenerse*) stop; *¡tente! ¡tente!* hold it!, wait a moment!; *~ a stick to*; *~ con* stand up to; *~ en pie* stand up; *~ por* think o.s.
tenería *f* tannery.
tengo *etc. v.* tener.
tenia *f* tape-worm.
teniente *m* lieutenant; *~ coronel* lieutenant-colonel; *~ general* lieutenant-general.
tenis *m* tennis; *~ de mesa* table-tennis; **tenista** *m/f* tennis-player.
tenor¹ *m* ♪ tenor.
tenor² *m* state; (*sentido*) tenor, purport; *a este ~* like this; *a ~ de* on the lines of.
tenorio *m* lady-killer.
tensar [1a] tauten; tense; **tensión** *f* tension; stress, strain; rigidity; *alta ~* high tension; *de alta ~* high-tension; ⚡ *~ excesiva*, *~ nerviosa* (over)strain; *~ superficial* surface tension; **tenso** tense, taut; **tensor** *m* ⊕ guy; *anat.* tensor.
tentación *f* temptation.
tentáculo *m* tentacle, feeler.
tentador 1. tempting; 2. *m* tempter; **tentadora** *f* temptress; **tentar** [1k] (*palpar*) touch, feel; ⚡ probe; *camino* feel; (*intentar*) try, attempt; (*emprender*) undertake; (*seducir*) tempt; lure, entice; **tentativa** *f* try, attempt; effort; *~ de asesinato* attempted murder; **tentativo** tentative.
tentempié *m* F snack, bite.
tenue (*delgado*) thin, slender; *hilo* fine; *esp. fig.* tenuous, slight; *aire, olor* thin; *línea, ruido* faint; *asunto* trifling; **tenuidad** *f* thinness *etc.*
teñir [3h a. 3l] *mst* dye (*de negro* black); colour; stain, tinge.
teocracia *f* theocracy.
teodolito *m* theodolite.
teología *f* theology; **teólogo** *m* theologian.
teorema *m* theorem; **teoría** *f* theory; *~ atómica* atomic theory; *~ cuántica*, *~ de los cuanta* quantum

theory; **teórico 1.** theoretic(al); **2.** *m* = **teorizante** *m* theorist; **teorizar** [1f] theorize.

tepe *m* turf, sod.

tequila *f S.Am.* brandy.

terapeuta *m/f* therap(eut)ist; **terapéutica** *f* therapeutics; = **terapia** *f* therapy; ~ *laboral* occupational therapy.

tercera *f ♪* third; **tercería** *f* mediation; *b s.* procuring; **tercero 1.** *adj. a. su. m ♣* third; **2.** *m,* a *f* go-between; (*árbitro*) mediator; ⅓ third person (*or* party); *b.s.* procurer, pimp; **terceto** *m ♪* trio; *poet.* tercet; ~*s pl.* terza rima; **terciado** *azúcar* brown; **terciar** [1b] *v/t.* slope, slant; *A* divide into three; *v/i.* fill in, stand in; ~ *en* take part in, join in; (*como árbitro*) mediate in; **tercio** *m* third; ⚔ *hist.* regiment.

terciopelo *m* velvet.

terco obstinate, stubborn.

terebrante *dolor* piercing.

tergiversación *f* distortion *etc.*; **tergiversar** [1a] *v/t.* distort, misrepresent; *v/i.* prevaricate; be undecided, blow hot and cold.

terliz *m* tick(ing).

termal thermal; **termas** *f/pl.* hot springs, hot baths; **térmico** thermic.

terminación *f* ending (*a. gr.*), conclusion; **terminacho** *m,* **terminajo** *m* F (*grosero*) rude word, coarse expression; (*feo,bárbaro*) ugly word; (*mal usado*) malapropism, howler; **terminal** *adj. a. su. m* (*♪*), *f* (*puerto*) terminal; **terminante** final, definitive; (*claro*) conclusive; *negativa* flat; *prohibición* strict; **terminar** [1a] end, finish; ~ *de inf.* stop *ger.*; finish *ger.*; ~ *en* end in (*a. fig.*); ~ *por inf.* end (up) by *ger.*; ~*se* come to an end, draw to a close, stop; ~ *hacia* lead to; **término** *m* end, finish; (*mojón*) boundary, limit; ⛫ *etc.* terminus; (*plazo*) period, time; outlying part *de ciudad*; (*palabra, phls.,* ♣) term; (*arbitrio*) compromise solution; *primer* ~ foreground; *segundo* ~ middle distance; *último* ~ background; *en último* ~ *fig.* in the last analysis; ~ *medio* compromise, middle way; (*promedio*) average; *de* ~ *medio* average; *por* ~ *medio* on the average;

~ *municipal* township; *en* ~*s de* in terms of; *en otros* ~*s* in other words; *poner* ~ *a* put an end to; **terminología** *f* terminology.

termita *m* termite.

termodinámica *f* thermodynamics; **termómetro** *m* thermometer; **termonuclear** thermonuclear; **termopila** *f* thermopile; **termos** *m* vacuum (*or* thermos) flask; **termóstato** *m* thermostat.

terne 1. big, tough; *b.s.* bullying; **2.** *m* bully.

ternera *f* (heifer-)calf; (*carne*) veal; **ternero** *m* (bull-)calf.

terneza *f* tenderness; ~*s pl.* sweet nothings, nice things.

ternilla *f* gristle; **ternilloso** gristly.

terno *m* set of three, trio; (*traje*) three-piece suit; F swear-word.

ternura *f* tenderness; (*palabra*) endearment.

terquedad *f* obstinacy.

terrado = *terraza.*

terraja *f* ⊕ die-stock.

terranova *m* Newfoundland (dog).

terraplén *m* ⛏ *etc.* embankment; ✗ terrace; mound; ⚔ rampart, earthwork; **terraplenar** [1a] terrace; *hoyo* fill in; (*levantar*) bank up.

terrateniente *m/f* landowner.

terraza *f* terrace; (*tejado*) flat roof; balcony *de piso*; ✗ flower-bed, border.

terrazgo *m* field, plot; (*pago*) rent.

terremoto *m* earthquake.

terrenal = **terreno 1.** earthly, worldly; **2.** *m geol. etc.* (*superficie*) terrain; (*naturaleza del suelo*) soil, land; (*extensión*) piece of ground, grounds; ✗ plot, patch, field; *deportes:* pitch, ground; *fig.* field, sphere; ~ *de pasto* run, pasture; *sobre el* ~ *fig.* on the spot; *ceder* ~ give ground; *ganar* ~ gain ground; *preparar el* ~ *fig.* pave the way (*a* for).

térreo earthen; (*parecido a tierra*) earthy; **terrero 1.** earthly; earthen; *fig.* humble; **2.** *m* pile, heap; **terrestre** terrestrial, land *attr.*; *vía etc.* overland.

terrible terrible, dreadful; **terrífico** terrifying.

territorial territorial; **territorio** *m* territory.

terrón *m* clod; lump (*a. azúcar*); ✗ patch.

terror *m* terror, dread; **terrorífico** terrifying; **terrorismo** *m* terrorism; **terrorista** *m* terrorist.

terroso earthy; (*sucio*) dirty.

terruño *m* clod, lump; (*espacio*) piece of ground; *fig.* native soil.

terso (*liso*) smooth; (*y brillante*) glossy; (*brillante*) shining, bright; *estilo* smooth, flowing; **tersura** *f* smoothness *etc.*

tertulia *f* (*reunión*) social gathering, get-together F; (*grupo*) party, group, circle; set *de café etc.*; *estar de* ~, *hacer* ~ get together (and talk); **tertuliano** *m*, **a** *f* member of a social gathering *etc.*

terylene *m* terylene.

tesar [1k] tense; ⚓ tauten.

tesis *f* thesis.

teso tense, taut.

tesón *m* insistence; tenacity, firmness *en resistir*.

tesorería *f* treasury; (*oficio*) treasurership; **tesorero** *m*, **a** *f* treasurer; **tesoro** *m* treasure; hoard; (*edificio, ministerio*) treasury; (*diccionario*) thesaurus; ♀ *público* Exchequer, Treasury.

test *m* test.

testa *f* head; (*frente, cara*) front; F brains; ~ *coronada* crowned head.

testador *m* testator; **testadora** *f* testatrix.

testaferro *m* man of straw; figurehead; † dummy.

testamentario 1. testamentary; 2. *m* executor; 3. **a** *f* executrix; **testamento** *m* will, testament; *Antiguo* (*Nuevo*) ♀ Old (New) Testament; **testar** [1a] make a will.

testarada *f* butt with the head; F pig-headedness; **testarudez** *f* stubbornness; **testarudo** stubborn, pig-headed F; **testera** *f* front, face; forehead *de animal*.

testículo *m* testicle.

testificar [1g] give evidence, testify; *fig.* attest; **testigo** *m/f* witness; ~ *de cargo* witness for the prosecution; ~ *de descargo* witness for the defence; ~ *ocular*, ~ *presencial*, ~ *de vista* eye-witness; **testimoniar** [1b] testify to, bear witness to; **testimonio** *m* testimony, evidence; *dar* ~ give evidence; *dar* ~ *de* testify to, give evidence of.

teta *f* breast; (*pezón*) teat.

tétano *m* tetanus.

tetera *f* teapot; tea-urn.

tetilla *f* nipple; teat *de biberón*.

tétrico gloomy; sullen; *luz* dim,⎫
teutónico Teutonic.   [dismal.⎭

textil 1. textile; 2. ~*es* *m*/*pl.* textiles.

texto *m* text; *fuera de* ~ full-page; **textual** textual.

textura *f* texture (*a. fig.*).

tez *f* complexion, skin.

ti you; (†, *a Dios*) thee.

tía *f* aunt; F (*grosera*) coarse woman; (*vieja*) old bag; (*puta*) whore; (*chica*) dame, bird; ~ *abuela* great-aunt; F *¡no hay tu* ~*!* nothing doing!; F *¡cuéntaselo a tu* ~*!* tell that to the Marines!

tiberio *m* F set-to.

tibia *f* tibia.

tibieza *f* lukewarmness *etc.*; **tibio** lukewarm, tepid, cool (*a. fig.*).

tiburón *m* shark.

tic *m* tic.

tictac *m* tick(-tock); *hacer* ~ (*reloj*) tick; (*corazón*) go pit-a-pat.

tiempo *m* time; *meteor.* weather; *gr.* tense; ♪ (*parte*) movement; ♪ (*compás*) time, tempo; *deportes:* half; *los buenos* ~*s* the good old days; *en mis buenos* ~*s* in my prime; ~ *libre* spare time, leisure; *deportes: primer* ~ first half; *a* ~ in (good) time, early; *a un* ~, *al mismo* ~ at the same time; *a su debido* ~ in due course; *al poco* ~ very soon; *con* ~ in (good) time, early; *con el* ~ eventually, in time; *de 4* ~*s motor* 4-stroke; *en* ~ *de Maricastaña, en* ~ *del rey que rabió* long ago, in the year dot; *fuera de* ~ at the wrong time; *más* ~ *quedar etc.* longer; *¿cuánto* ~ *más?* how much longer?; *mucho* ~ a long time; *de mucho* ~ of long standing; *en otro* ~ formerly; *andando el* ~ in due course, in time; *darse buen* ~ have a good time; *hacer* ~ while away the time; *hace buen* ~ it is fine, the weather is good; *hace mucho* ~ a long time ago; *desde hace mucho* ~ for a long time; *hace mucho* ~ *que no le veo* it's a long time since I saw him; *matar el* ~ kill time; *perder el* ~ waste time.

tienda *f* shop, store *esp. Am.*; ~ (*de campaña*) tent; (*toldo*) awning; *poner* ~ set up shop.

tienta *f* 🝐 probe; *fig.* cleverness; *a* ~*s* gropingly; *andar a* ~*s* grope, feel one's way (*a. fig.*); **tiento** *m* (*tacto*) touch, feel(ing); stick *de ciego*; zo. feeler; *fig.* (*seguridad*) steady hand; (*cuidado*) wariness; ♪ flourish; F (*golpe*) punch; (*trago*) swig; *S.Am.* snack; *a* ~ by touch; *fig.* uncertainly; *con* ~ cautiously; *ir con* ~ watch one's step, go carefully; F *dar un* ~ *a* take a swig from.

tierno *mst* tender; (*blando*) soft; *pan* new.

tierra *f ast.* earth; *geog.* world, earth; (*no mar*) land; (*finca. terreno*) land; (*materia del suelo*) ground, earth, soil; (*patria*) native land, one's (own) country; region; ♀ earth; *de batán* fuller's earth; ~ *firme* mainland; dry land; ~ *de nadie* no man's land; ~ *de pan llevar* corn land; ~ *prometida*, ~ *de promisión* promised land; ~ *quemada* scorched earth; ~ *adentro* inland; *up-country*; *por* ~ by land, overland; *caer a* ~ fall down; *dar en* ~ *con, echar por* ~ knock down; *fig.* upset; *echar a* ~ raze to the ground; *echar* ~ *a fig.* hush up; *poner en* ~ ground; ⚡ land; ⚓ *tomar* ~ land.

tieso 1. *adj.* stiff, rigid (*a. fig.*); (*tirante*) taut; *fig.* brave; grave; (*terco*) stubborn; (*engreído*) stuck-up; *tenérselas* ~*as con* stand up to; **2.** *adv.* strongly, hard.

tiesto *m* flower-pot; (*fragmento*) piece of pottery, sherd.

tifoidea: *fiebre* ~ typhoid.

tifón *m* typhoon; (*tromba*) waterspout.

tifus *m* typhus; *thea. sl.* free seats, complimentaries; ~ *exantemático* spotted fever; *thea. sl. entrar de* ~ get in free.

tigre *m* tiger; *S.Am.* jaguar; **tigresa** *f* tigress.

tijera *f* (*p.*) gossip; *tener una* ~ have a sharp tongue; **tijeras** *f/pl.* (*unas* a pair of) scissors; (*grandes, de jardín*) shears, clippers; *de* ~(*s*) folding; **tijeretada** *f*, **tijeretazo** *m* snip, cut; **tijereta** *f* ♀ vine tendril; *zo.* earwig; **tijeretear** [1a] snip, cut, snick.

tildar [1a] *letra* put a tilde over; (*tachar*) cross out; *fig.* brand, stigmatize (*de* as); **tilde** *mst f typ.* tilde (~); *fig.* jot.

tilín *m* tinkle, ting-a-ling; F *hacer* ~ be well liked; F *tener* ~ be nice, have a way with people.

tilo *m* lime (tree).

timador *m* swindler, confidence trickster; **timar** [1a] steal; *p.* swindle; ~*se* F make eyes at each other; ~ *con* make eyes at.

timbal *m* ♪ (kettle)drum; *cocina:* meat pie.

timbrar [1a] stamp; ✆ postmark; **timbre** *m* ✆ stamp; (*impuesto del* ~) tax stamp, stamp-duty; (*campanilla*) bell; *timbre de voz etc.*

timidez *f* timidity *etc.*; **tímido** timid, shy, nervous; bashful, coy.

timo *m* F swindle, confidence trick; (*broma*) gag; *dar un* ~ *a* cheat; (*burlar*) play a joke on.

timón *m* ⚓, ✈ rudder; *esp. fig.* helm; ⚒ beam; ~ *de dirección* rudder; ~ *de profundidad* elevator; **timonel** *m*, **timonero** *m* steersman, helmsman; cox(swain) *de trainera etc.*

timorato god-fearing.

tímpano *m* 🏛, *anat.* tympanum; ♪ (kettle)drum.

tina *f* vat, tub; (*baño*) bath-tub; large jar; ~ *de lavar* washtub; **tinaja** *f* vat; (large earthen) jar.

tinctura *f* tincture (*a. fig.*).

tinerfeño *adj. a. su. m*, **a** *f* (native) of Tenerife.

tinglado *m* platform; (*cobertizo*) shed; *fig.* trick; *conocer el* ~ see through it.

tinieblas *f/pl.* darkness (*a. fig.*), dark, shadows.

tino *m* (*habilidad*) skill, knack; feel, (sure) touch; (*juicio*) good judgement; *a* ~ gropingly; *a buen* ~ by guesswork; *sin* ~ immoderately; (*sin propósito*) foolishly, aimlessly; *coger el* ~ get the hang of it; *perder el* ~ get all mixed up; *sacar de* ~ *a* bewilder.

tinta *f* ink; dye *para teñir*; (*matiz*) tint, shade, hue; ~ *de copiar* copying-ink; ~ *china* Indian ink; ~ *de imprenta* printer's ink; ~ *de marcar* marking-ink; ~ *simpática* invisible ink; *media* ~ half-tone, tint; F *medias* ~*s pl.* half-baked ideas; *de buena* ~ on good authority; F *sudar* ~ slog; **tinte** *m* (*acto*) dyeing; (*materia*) dye(-stuff); (*color*) tint, hue, tinge; ⊕ stain; (*tintorería*) dry-cleaner's; *fig.* disguise; **tinterillo** *m* F pen-pusher; **tintero** *m* inkpot; F *dejar en el* ~, F *quedar* *(sele a uno)* en el ~ forget clean about.

tintín *m* clink, chink *de vasos etc.*; jingle *de cadena etc.*; tinkle, ting-a-ling *de timbre*; **tintinear** [1a] clink *etc.*

tinto dyed; *vino* red; **tintorería** *f* dry-cleaner's *que limpia*; dyer's *que tiñe*; *(arte)* dyeing; *(fábrica)* dyeworks; **tintura** *f* dye; rouge *de cara*; ⊕ stain; *pharm.* tincture; *fig.* smattering.

tiña *f* 🐛 ringworm; F meanness; **tiñoso** scabby, mangy; F mean.

tío *m* uncle; F *(viejo)* old fellow; F *(sujeto)* fellow, chap; ~s *pl.* uncle and aunt; ~ *abuelo* great-uncle; *el ~ Lucas* old Lucas; F *¡qué ~!* the old so-and-so!, what a fellow (he is)!; **tiovivo** *m* roundabout, merry-go-round.

típico typical; *fig.* picturesque; quaint, cute, of interest to (*or* popular with) tourists; *p. fig.* original; **tipismo** *m* quaintness *etc.*

tiple 1. *m* treble, boy soprano; **2.** *f* soprano.

tipo *m* *mst* type; *(clase a.)* sort, kind; *(físico)* shape, figure, build; F fellow, chap; ~s *pl. typ.* type; ~ *bancario* bank-rate; ~ *de cambio* rate of exchange; ~ *de interés* rate of interest; ~ *(de) oro* gold standard; *tiene buen* ~ (*m*) he is well-built; *(f)* she has a good figure; **tipografía** *f* printing; typography; **tipográfico** printing *attr.*; typographical.

típula *f* daddy-long-legs, cranefly.

tiquete *m* S.Am. ticket.

tiquismiquis F **1.** *m* fussy sort; **2.** *m/pl.* silly scruples; *(cortesías)* bowing and scraping; *(molestias)* pinpricks.

tira *f* (long *or* narrow) strip; slip *de papel*; ~ *cómica* comic strip.

tirada *f* *(acto)* throw; distance, stretch; *typ.* printing, edition; ~ *aparte* offprint; *de una* ~ at one stroke, at a stretch; **tirado** ✝ dirt cheap; ⚓ rakish; *letra* cursive; **tirador** *m* handle, knob *de puerta etc.*; bell-rope; ✂ cord; 🏹 (*p.*) shot, marksman; ~ *apostado*, ~ *certero* sniper.

tiralevitas *m* F climber, creep.

tiralíneas *m* drawing-pen; 📐 compasses.

tiranía *f* tyranny; **tiránico** tyrannical; *amor* possessive; *encanto* irresistible; **tiranizar** [1f] *v/t.* tyrannize; *v/i.* be a tyrant, domineer; **tirano 1.** tyrannical; domineering; **2.** *m*, *a f* tyrant.

tirante 1. taut, tight; *relaciones etc.* tense, strained; ✝ tight; **2.** *m* ⚠ tie, brace; ⊕ strut; trace *de guarnición*; shoulder-strap *de vestido*; ~s *pl.* braces, suspenders *Am.*; **tirantez** *f* tautness *etc.*; *fig.* tension; ✝ stringency.

tirar [1a] **1.** *v/t.* throw; cast, toss, sling; *desperdicios* throw away; *(disipar)* waste; *alambre* draw out; *(arrastrar)* haul; *línea* draw; 🏹 shoot, fire; *typ.* print, run off; *beso* blow; ~le de fancy o.s' as, as, pose as; **2.** *v/i.* *(chimenea)* draw; 🏹 fire (*a* at, on), shoot (*a* at); *(atraer)* appeal; (have a) pull; *(durar)* last; ~ *a su.* tend towards; ~ *a color* approach, have a touch of; ~ *a inf.* aim to *inf.*; ~ *a la derecha* turn to the right, keep right; ~ *a viejo* be elderly; ~ *de (arrastrar)* pull, haul; *cuerda etc.* pull on, tug; *(imán)* attract; *espada* draw; *v. largo*; ~ *por calle* turn down, go off along; *a todo* ~ at the most; F *ir tirando* get along, manage; **3.** ~se throw o.s., jump *(por ventana* out of; *risco* over); *(abalanzarse)* rush (*a* at), spring (*a* at, on); *(echarse)* lie down.

tirillas *m* F nobody; *(pequeño)* runt; *(como int.)* little man, buster.

tiritaña *f* F trifle.

tiritar [1a] shiver (*de* with); **tiritón** *m* shiver.

tiro *m* throw; 🏹 shot (*a. deportes, p.*); *(alcance)* range; 🏹 *(sitio)* rifle-range; shooting-gallery *de feria*; team *de caballos*; trace *de guarnición*; *(cuerda)* rope; *sew.* length; flight *de escalera*; *(broma)* practical joke; ~ *con arco* archery; ~ *al blanco* target practice; ~ *de fusil* gunshot; *a* ~ within range; *a* ~ *de fusil* within gunshot; *a* ~ *de piedra* within a stone's throw; *ni a* ~s not for love nor money; *de* ~ *caballo* draught; *de* ~s *largos* all dressed up; *errar el* ~ miss; *hacer* ~ *a* aim at, have designs on; *matar a* ~s shoot; F *salir el* ~ *por la culata* backfire.

tiroideo thyroid; **tiroides** *m* (*a. glándula* ~) thyroid (gland).

tirón *m* pull, tug; jerk; hitch; (*estirón*) stretch; *de un* ~ in one go, straight off; *mover etc. a* ~*es* tug, jerk.

tirotear [1a] blaze away at; ~**se** exchange shots repeatedly; **tiroteo** *m* firing, shooting.

tirria *f* dislike; *tener* ~ *a* have a grudge against.

tísico *adj. a. su. m,* **a** *f* consumptive; **tisis** *f* consumption.

tisú *m* tissue.

titán *m* titan; **titánico** titanic.

títere *m* marionette, puppet; (*teatro de*) ~*s pl.* puppets, puppet-show; **titiritero** *m,* **a** *f* puppeteer; acrobat; (*malabarista*) juggler.

titubeante halting, stammering; **titubear** [1a] (*tambalear*) reel, stagger, totter; (*vacilar*) hesitate; stammer, falter *al hablar;* **titubeo** *m* hesitation *etc.*

titular 1. titular, official; **2.** *m typ.* headline; **3.** *m/f* holder; **4.** [1a] (en)title, call; **titulillo** *m* running title, page heading; F *andar en* ~*s* watch out for every little thing; **título** *m mst* title; headline *de periódico*; (*certificado*) diploma, qualification; *univ.* degree; ✝ bond; ~ (*de nobleza*) title; ~ *de propiedad* title-deed; *a* ~ *de* by way of; as a, in the capacity of; *¿a* ~ *de qué?* by what right? [*escribir.*]

tiza *f* whitening; chalk *para* |

tizna *f* black, grime; *paint.* crayon; **tiznar** [1a] blacken; smudge; (*manchar*) spot, stain; *fig.* stain, tarnish; brand; **tizne** *mst m* (*hollín*) soot; (*suciedad*) smut, grime; **tiznón** *m* smut, spot of soot, smudge; **tizón** *m* half-burned piece of wood; ♉ smut; *fig.* stain; **tizonear** [1a] poke.

tizos *m/pl. sl.* fingers.

toalla *f* towel; ~ *de rodillo* roller towel; **toallero** *m* towel-rail.

tobera *f* nozzle.

tobillera *f* ankle sock; F teenager; **tobillo** *m* ankle.

tobogán *m* toboggan.

toca *f* head-dress.

tocadiscos *m* record-player; juke-box *de café.*

tocado head-dress; (*pelo*) coiffure, hair-do.

tocador[1] *m,* **-a** *f* ♪ player.

tocador[2] *m* (*mueble*) dressing-table; (*cuarto*) boudoir, dressing-room; (*estuche*) toilet-case; *de* ~ *freq.* toilet *attr.*

tocante: ~ *a* with regard to.

tocar[1] [1g] **1.** *v/t.* (*palpar, estar en contacto con*) touch; (*palpar*) feel; (*manosear*) touch, handle; (*chocar*) collide with, hit; ⚓ go aground on; ♪ play; *trompeta* blow; *tambor* beat; *disco* play; *timbre* ring; *tema* touch on; **2.** *v/i.:* ~ *a puerta* knock at; *pariente* be related to; (*caber en suerte*) fall to one's lot (*or* share); *le tocó el premio* he got the prize; (*importar a*) concern, affect; *le toca de cerca* it closely concerns him; (*deber*) *le toca a Vd.* decidir it is for you (*or* up to you) to decide; (*turno*) *me toca a mí* it's my turn (*inf.* to *inf.*), it's my go; *¿a quién le toca* (*jugar*)? whose turn is it?; **3.** *v/i.:* ~ *en* ⚓ touch at, call at; (*estar junto*) be next to; *b.s.* impinge upon; interfere with; **4.** ~**se:** F ~*selas* beat it.

tocar[2] [1g] *pelo* do; arrange, set; ~**se** cover one's head.

tocayo *m,* **a** *f* namesake.

tocino *m* bacon; salt pork.

tocón *m* ♉, *anat.* stump.

todavía still, yet; ~ *no* not yet; ~ *en 1900* as late as 1900.

todo 1. all; whole, entire; every; *velocidad etc.* full; ~ *el dinero* all the money, the whole of the money; *por* ~*a Europa* all over Europe, throughout Europe; ~*s los días* every day; ~ *el que* everyone who; *lo comió* ~ he ate it all; *lo sabe* ~ he knows everything; (*nada menos que*) ~ *un hombre* every inch (*or* bit) a man; ~ *cuanto* all that which; ~*s cuantos* all those who; **2.** *adv.:* *ante* ~ first of all; primarily; *a pesar de* ~, *así y* ~ even so, in spite of everything; all the same; *con* ~ still; however; *del* ~ wholly, completely; *no del* ~ not quite; *después de* ~ after all; *sobre* ~ above all, especially, most of all; F *y* ~ and so on, and what not; **3.** *m* all, everything; (*el* ~) whole; F *ser el* ~ run the show; be the mainstay; ~*s pl.* everybody; every one of them; ~*s y cada uno* all and sundry.

todopoderoso almighty.

toga f hist. toga; univ. etc. gown; ⚖ gown, robe.

tojo m gorse, furze.

toldilla f ⚓ round-house; **toldo** m sunshade, awning; (pabellón) marquee; cloth, tarpaulin de carro; S.Am. hut; fig. pride.

tole m hubbub, uproar; (protesta) outcry; levantar el ~ kick up a fuss; F tomar el ~ get out quick.

toledano adj. a. su. m, **a** f Toledan; noche sleepless.

tolerable tolerable; **tolerancia** f tolerance (a. ⊕), toleration; **tolerante** tolerant; broad-minded; **tolerar** [1a] tolerate; endure, put up with.

tolondro 1. scatter-brained; **2.** m bump, lump.

toma f taking; ✕ capture; 💊 dose; (entrada) inlet, intake; (salida) outlet; ⚡ (a. ~ de corriente) (enlace) lead; (enchufe) plug, point; ~ de declaración taking of evidence; ~ de hábito taking of vows; ~ de posesión taking-over; (presidente etc.) inauguration; ~ de tierra ⚡ groundwire; ⚓ landing; **tomacorriente** m, **tomada** f S.Am. ⚡ plug; **tomado** F tight; ~ (de orín) rusty; **tomadura** f = toma.

tomar [1a] **1.** v/t. mst take; ánimo, fuerzas get, gain; aspecto take on; bebida, comida, lecciones have; costumbre get into, acquire; frío get, catch; ~ por take s.o. for; ~ sobre sí take upon o.s.; ~la con pick a quarrel with; **2.** v/i.: ~ por la derecha turn to the right; ~ por una calle turn down a street; toma y daca give and take; ¡toma! fancy that!; well there you are!; of course!; **3.** ~se: ~ (de orín) go rusty.

tomate m tomato.

tomavistas m phot. (cine)camera.

tomillo m thyme; ~ salsero savo(u)ry.

tomo m volume; (lo grueso) bulk; fig. importance; de ~ y lomo bulky; F big, important.

ton: sin ~ ni son without rhyme or reason.

tonada f tune, song; **tonadilla** f little tune; merry tune; thea. interlude; **tonalidad** f ♪ tonality; ♪ key; shade de color; radio: control de ~ tone control.

tonel m barrel, cask; **tonelada** f ton; **tonelaje** m tonnage; **tonelero** m

cooper; **tonelete** m cask, keg; (falda) short skirt; kilt de hombre.

tongo m F deportes: fixing, nobbling; aquí hay ~ it's been fixed.

tónica f ♪ tonic; (nota) ~ keynote.

tónico 1. 💊, ♪, acento tonic; sílaba accented; **2.** m 💊 tonic (a. fig.); **tonificar** [1g] tone up, fortify; **tonillo** m singsong, monotonous note; **tono** m mst tone; ♪ (calidad etc.) tone; ♪ (altura) pitch; ♪ (de fa etc.) key; ♪ (pieza) slide; (matiz) shade; teleph. ~ de marcar dialling tone; ~ mayor (menor) major (minor) key; ♪ a ~ in key; a ~ con in tune with; de buen ~ fashionable; elegant; genteel; de mal ~ vulgar; bajar el ~ lower one's voice; dar el ~ fig. set the tone; darse ~ put on airs; subir(se) de ~ put it on; live in style.

tonsura f eccl. tonsure; **tonsurar** [1a] eccl. tonsure; ✂ shear.

tontada f rubbish, nonsense; **tontaina** m/f F dimwit; **tontear** [1a] talk nonsense; fool; **tontería** f (lo tonto) silliness; (acto) silly thing; (palabra) a. ~s pl.) nonsense; rubbish; ¡déjate de ~s! come off it!; **tonto 1.** silly, foolish; **2.** m, **a** f fool, idiot; (payaso) funny man, clown; a ~as y a locas all over the place, haphazardly; hacer el ~ play the fool; F hacerse el ~ act dumb; **tontuna** f = tontería.

topacio m topaz.

topar [1a] v/t. (chocar) bump (against, into), knock (against, into); (encontrar, a. v/i. ~ con) run into, bump into; v/i. zo. butt (each other); (juego) take a bet; (tropezar) stumble; (dificultad) lie; (salir bien) succeed, manage it; **tope** m (cabo) butt, end; ⚓ masthead; 🚂 buffer; mot. bumper; ⊕ stop, check; (choque) collision; bump, knock; fig. snag; (riña) quarrel; (reyerta) scuffle; v. fecha etc.; al ~ end to end; hasta el ~ to the brim; estar hasta los ~s ⚓ be loaded to the gunwales; fig. be fed up; ahí está el ~ that's the snag.

topera f molehill.

topetada f, **topetazo** m butt, bump; **topetar** [1a] butt, bump; fig. bump into; **topetón** m bump.

tópico 1. local; **2.** m commonplace, cliché, catch-phrase; S.Am. topic.

topo *m* mole; F great lump.
topografía *f* ⨂ topography; *surv.* surveying; **topográfico** topograph-ic(al); **topógrafo** *m* ⨂ topogra-pher; *surv.* surveyor; **toponimia** *f* study of place-names; *la ~ de Aragón* the place-names of Aragon; **topónimo** *m* place-name.
toque *m* (*acto*) touch (*a. paint.*); (*ensayo*) test, trial; peal(ing) *de campana*; ring *de timbre*; beat *de tambor*; hoot *de sirena*; ✕ (bugle-) call; *S.Am.* turn; *~ de diana* reveille; *~ de difuntos* knell; *~ de queda* curfew; *dar un ~ a* test; *p.* sound out.
toquilla *f* headscarf; shawl.
torada *f* herd of bulls.
tórax *m* thorax.
torbellino *m* (*viento*) whirlwind; (*agua*) whirlpool; *fig.* whirl.
torcedor *m* ⊕ spindle; **torcedura** *f* twist(ing); ✚ sprain, strain; (*vino*) weak wine; **torcer** [2b *a.* 2h] **1.** *v/t.* twist; (*encorvar*) bend, curve; (*alabear*) warp; *manos, cuello* wring; *cara* screw up; *músculo* strain; *tobillo* sprain, twist; *esquina* turn; *fig. sentido* twist; *justicia* pervert; **2.** *v/i.* turn (*a* to); (*pelota*) swerve, spin; **3.** *~se* twist; bend; (*ala-bearse*) warp; (*cambiar de lugar*) slew (round); (*extraviarse*) go astray; (*vino etc.*) turn sour; **torcida** *f* wick; **torcido 1.** twisted; bent; *camino etc.* full of turns, twisty; *fig.* crooked; *S.Am.* un-lucky; **2.** *m* curl *de pelo*; twist *de seda etc.*; **torcimiento** *m* twisting *etc.*
tordo 1. dappled; **2.** *m* thrush.
torear [1a] *v/t. toro* fight, play; *fig.* deceive; (*burlarse*) tease, draw on; *v/i.* fight (bulls); (*como profesión*) be a bullfighter; **toreo** *m* (art of) bullfighting; **torería** *f* (class of) bullfighters; F prank; **torero** *m* bullfighter; **torete** *m* young bull; F bouncing child; **toril** *m* bull-pen.
tormenta *f* storm; *fig.* misfortune; (*confusión*) turmoil, upheaval; **tor-mento** *m* torment; anguish, agony; torture (*a. fig.*); **tormentoso** stormy, wild.
torna *f* return; *volver las ~s* turn the tables (*a* on); *se han vuelto las ~s* now the boot's on the other foot; **tornada** *f* return; **tornadizo**

1. changeable; renegade; **2.** *m,* **a** *f* turncoat, renegade.
tornado *m* tornado.
tornar [1a] *v/t.* give back; (*volver*) turn, make; *v/i.* go back, return; *~ a escribir* write again; *~se* turn, become; **tornasol** *m* ♀ sunflower; ⚗ litmus; sheen *de tela*; **tornaso-lado** iridescent, sheeny; *seda* shot; **tornavía** *f* turn-table; **tornavoz** *f* sounding-board; *eccl.* canopy; *hacer ~* cup one's hands to one's mouth.
tornear [1a] turn (on a lathe).
torneo *m* tournament, competition; *hist.* tourney, joust.
tornero *m* turner, lathe operator.
tornillo *m* (*rosca*) screw; (*torno*) small lathe; ✕ F desertion; *~ de banco* vice, clamp; *~ sin fin* worm (-gear); *apretar los ~s a* put the screws on; *le falta un ~* he has a screw loose.
torniquete *m* turnstile; ✚ tourni-quet.
torniscón *m* F slap (*or* smack) in the face; (*con dedos*) pinch.
torno *m* ⊕ lathe; ⊕, ⚓ winch, drum; (*freno*) brake; bend *de río*; (*vuelta*) turn; *~ de alfarero* potter's wheel; *~ de asador* spit; *~ de banco* vice, clamp; *~ de hilar* spinning-wheel; *~ revolvedor* turret lathe; *~ de tornero* turning-lathe; *en ~* around, round about; *en ~ suyo* about him; *en ~ a* around, about; *labrar a ~* turn on the lathe.
toro *m* bull; *~s pl.* bullfight; (*arte*) bullfighting; *~ de lidia* fighting bull; *echar (or soltar) el ~ a* pull no punches with; *irse a la cabeza del ~* take the bull by the horns; *ver los ~s desde la barrera* sit on the fence.
toronja *f* grapefruit; **toronjil** *m* ♀ balm.
torpe *movimiento* ungainly, heavy; *mente* slow; (*desmañado*) clumsy, awkward; (*tosco*) crude, indecent, lewd; dishonourable.
torpedear [1a] torpedo (*a. fig.*); **torpedero** *m* torpedo-boat; **tor-pedo** *m* torpedo (*a. ichth.*).
torpeza *f* slowness *etc.*
torrar [1a] toast.
torre *f* ⌂ tower; ✕, ⚓, ✈ turret; *radio:* mast; *ajedrez:* rook; *~ de conducción eléctrica* pylon; *~ del homenaje* keep; ⚓ *~ de mando*

conning-tower; ~ de *perforación* oil derrick; ~ de *refrigeración* cooling tower; ⚓ ~ de *vigía* crow's-nest.

torrencial torrential; **torrente** *m* mountain stream, torrent; *fig.* torrent, rush, flood *de palabras etc.*; (*ímpetu*) (on)rush; **torrentera** *f* gully.

torreón *m* △ turret; fortified tower.

torrero *m* lighthouse-keeper.

torreta *f* ⚓, ✈ turret; conning-tower *de submarino*.

torrezno *m* rasher, piece of bacon.

tórrido torrid.

torsión *f* ⊕ torsion; twist; *esp.* ✈ warping; **torsional** torsional.

torso *m* torso; *paint.* head and shoulders; *escultura*: bust.

torta *f cocina*: cake, tart; *fig.* cake; *typ.* fount; F slap; F *costar la* ~ *un pan* come out dearer than expected; F *ser* ~*s y pan pintado* be child's play; **tortazo** *m* F slap.

tortícolis *m* crick in the neck, stiff neck.

tortilla *f* omelet(te); F *hacer* ~ *a p.* beat up; *cosa* smash; *asunto* make a mess of; F *se volvió la* ~ it came out all wrong; *his etc.* luck turned.

tortita *f* pancake.

tórtola *f* turtle-dove; **tórtolo** *m* turtle-dove; F love-bird.

tortuga *f* tortoise; ~ (*marina*) turtle.

tortuoso winding, tortuous; *fig.* devious.

tortura *f* torture (*a. fig.*); **torturar** [1a] torture.

torvo *aspecto* grim; *mirada* fierce.

tos *f* cough(ing); ~ *ferina* whooping-cough.

tosco course, rough, crude; *p. etc.* uncouth.

toser [2a] cough; F *a mí nadie me tose* I'll not stand for that; no-one's going to push me around.

tósigo *m* poison.

tosquedad *f* coarseness *etc* (*v. tosco*).

tostada *f* (piece of) toast; F *dar* (*or pegar*) *una* ~ *a* have *s.o.* on;

tostado 1. *pan* toasted; *color* dark brown; ~ (*por el sol*) sunburnt, tanned; **2.** *m* tan; **tostador** *m* toaster; roaster; **tostadora** *f* ✦ toaster; **tostar** [1m] *pan* toast;

café roast; *fig.* (*calentar*) toast; *p.* tan; ~*se* (*al sol*) tan, get brown; **tostón** *m* toasted chick-pea; roast sucking pig; (*pan*) buttered toast; F (*p.*) bore; F (*obra*) dreadful piece of work.

total 1. *adj.* total; whole; *esp.* ✝ gross; *ruina etc.* utter; **2.** *adv.* all in all; and so; anyway, when all is said and done; ~ *que* the upshot of it was that; to cut a long story short; **3.** *m* total; whole; sum; *en* ~ in all; **totalidad** *f* whole; totality; *en su* ~ as a whole; **totalitario** totalitarian; **totalitarismo** *m* totalitarianism; **totalizador** *m* totalizator; **totalizar** [1f] add up.

tóxico 1. toxic, poisonous; **2.** *m* poison; **toxicómano 1.** addicted to drugs; **2.** *m, a f* drug addict; **toxina** *f* toxin.

tozudo obstinate.

traba *f* link, bond *que une*; lock *que cierra, sujeta*; ✦ hobble; *fig.* hindrance, obstacle; ~*s pl. fig.* trammels; *echar* (*or poner*) ~*s a* shackle; **trabacuenta** *f* mistake; *andar con* ~*s* be engaged in endless controversies; **trabado** *fig.* strong, tough.

trabajado worn out; *estilo etc.* strained; **trabajador 1.** hard-working, industrious; **2.** *m* worker; labourer; **trabajar** [1a] *v/t. madera etc.* work; work on; *p.* work, drive; *p.* (*con maña*) get to work on; *caballo* train; *mente* trouble; *v/i.* work (*de as; en at*); (*torcerse*) warp; ~ *mucho* work hard; ~ *con fig.* (get to) work on; ~ *por inf.* strive to *inf.*; *hacer* ~ *dinero* make work; *agua, recursos* harness; **trabajo** *m* (*en general, a. phys.*) work; (*un* ~) piece of work; (*tarea, colocación*) job; (*fermentación*) working(s); (*los obreros*) labour, the workers; *fig.* trouble, difficulty; ~*s pl. fig.* hardships; *en el propio campo* fieldwork; ~ *a destajo* piecework; ~*s pl.* forzados hard labour; *me cuesta* ~ *inf.* I find it hard to *inf.*; *estar sin* ~ be out of a job; *tomarse el* ~ *de inf.* take the trouble to *inf.*; **trabajoso** hard, laborious; deficient; ✳ sickly.

trabalenguas *m* tongue-twister; **trabar** [1a] join, link; (*aherrojar*) shackle, fetter (*a. fig.*); (*sujetar*) lock, fasten; (*asir*) seize; *caballo* hobble; *sierra* set; *amistad* strike up; *batalla* join; *conversación* start; ~se (*cuerdas*) get tangled; ⊕ lock, jam; **trabazón** *f* link; consistency; *fig.* bond, connexion.

trabucar [1g] turn upside down; *fig.* confuse; *palabras etc.* mix up; ~se get all mixed up; **trabuco** *m hist.* catapult; blunderbuss; (*juguete*) popgun.

tracción *f* traction; haulage; ~ *a las 4 ruedas* 4-wheel drive.

tracería *f* tracery.

tractor *m* tractor; ~ *de oruga* caterpillar tractor.

tradición *f* tradition; **tradicional** traditional; *costumbre freq.* time-honoured; *ley* unwritten; *canción etc.* folk *attr.*

traducción *f* translation; rendering; **traducir** [3f] translate; render; express; **traductor** *m*, -a *f* translator.

traer [2p] bring, get, fetch; (*atraer*) attract, draw; *ropa* wear; (*llevar consigo*) have, carry; (*causar*) bring (about); (*acarrear*) involve, bring in its train; *autoridades* adduce; *me trae sin cuidado* it doesn't bother me; *me trae loco* it's driving me mad; *le trae muy preocupado* he's very worried about it; ~se: ~ *bien* (*mal*) be well (badly) dressed; (*comportarse*) behave properly (badly); ~*las* be up to something; *problema que se las trae* difficult problem.

tráfago *m* ✝ traffic, trade; (*faena*) drudgery, routine job; **traficante** *m* trader; **traficar** [1g] trade, deal (en in); buy and sell; F come and go; **tráfico** *m mot. etc.* traffic; ✝ trade, business, traffic.

tragaderas *f/pl.* throat; F *tener buenas* ~ be gullible; be very easy-going; **tragadero** *m* throat, gullet; **trágala** *m/f* F, **tragaldabas** *m/f* F greedy sort; **tragaleguas** *m/f* F quick walker; great one for walking; **tragaluz** *m* skylight; **tragantada** *f* F swig, mouthful; **tragaperras** *m* (penny-in-the-) slot-machine; **tragar** [1h] **1.** *mst* swallow; (*y terminar*) drink up, swallow down; (*engullir*) gulp (down); (*con dificultad*) get down; **2.** *fig.* (*a.* ~se) *barco etc.* swallow up, engulf; *material* use up, take; *cosa*

desagradable, increíble swallow; *p.* stick, stand; *tenerse tragado algo* have got used to the idea (of s.t. happening); **3.** *v/i. sl.* sleep around.

tragedia *f* tragedy; **trágico 1.** tragic(al); **2.** *m* tragedian.

trago *m* drink, draught; swallow, gulp; F *mal* ~ bad time; nasty blow; *a* ~s little by little; *de un* ~ at one go; *echar un* ~ have a swig; F *pasar un* ~ *amargo* have a rough time of it; **tragón** F greedy.

traición *f* treachery; treason (*a.* 🔏); (*una* ~) betrayal, act of treason; *alta* ~ high treason; **traicionar** [1a] betray, be a traitor to; **traicionero** treacherous.

traída *f*: ~ *de aguas* water supply; **traído** worn, threadbare; ~ *y llevado* knocked about; *fig.* well-worn.

traidor 1. *p.* treacherous; *acto* treasonable; **2.** *m* traitor; betrayer; *thea.* villain; **traidora** *f* traitress.

traílla *f* lead, leash; (*látigo*) lash; (*perros*) team of dogs; ⚒ harrow.

trainera *f* (small) boat, fishing-boat.

traje[1] *etc. v. traer.*

traje[2] *m* (*en general*) dress; costume (*a. de mujer*); suit *de hombre*; *fig.* garb, guise; ~ *de baño* bathing-costume; ~ *de calle* lounge suit; *en* ~ *de calle policía* in plain clothes; ~ *de campaña* battledress; ~ *de ceremonia*, ~ *de etiqueta* full-dress; dress-suit, evening dress; ~ *de cuartel* undress; ~ *hecho* ready-made suit; ~ *de luces* bullfighter's costume; ~ *de malla* tights; ~ *de montar* riding-habit; ~ *de novia* wedding dress; ~ *de paisano* civilian clothes (*v. a. paisano*); **trajear** [1a] clothe, dress; *co.* get up, rig out; ~se dress up *etc.*

trajín *m* haulage, transport; F coming and going; (*bullicio*) bustle; **trajinante** *m* carrier, haulage contractor; **trajinar** [1a] *v/t.* carry, convey; *v/i.* be on the go; hustle, bustle.

tralla *f* whipcord; (*látigo*) lash.

trama *f* weft, woof; *fig.* plot, scheme; *thea. etc.* plot; **tramar** [1a] weave; *fig.* plot, contrive; *complot* hatch; *¿qué estarán tramando?* I wonder what they're up to?

tramitación *f* transaction; steps, procedure; **tramitar** [1a] transact, negotiate; **trámite** *m* (*paso*) movement, transit; (*en negocio*) step, move; ~s *pl.* procedure; ~s *pl. de costumbre* usual channels; ~s *pl. oficiales* official channels.

tramo *m* flight *de escalera*; length, section *de camino etc.*; stretch; span *de puente*; (*terreno*) plot.

tramoya *f* piece of stage machinery; F *armar una* ~ kick up a fuss; **tramoyista** *m* scene-shifter; *fig.* swindler; humbug.

trampa *f* hunt. trap, snare; trapdoor *en suelo*; 🚗 fender *Am.*; *fig.* snare, catch, pitfall; (*ardid*) trick, ruse; (*criminal*) fraud; fiddle F, wangle F; ✝ bad debt; ~ *explosiva* booby-trap; *armar* ~ *a* set a trap for; *caer en la* ~ fall for it; *hacer* ~s cheat; (*con manos*) juggle; *hay* ~ there's a catch somewhere; **trampantojo** *m* F sleight of hand, trick; **trampear** [1a] *v/t.* cheat, swindle; *v/i.* get money by false pretences; *ir trampeando* get by; **trampería** *f* monkey business; **trampista** *m* = *tramposo* 2.

trampolín *m* springboard (*a. fig.*).

tramposo 1. tricky, crooked; 2. *m* twister, crook.

tranca *f* beam, pole; (cross-)bar *de puerta*; *S.Am.* F binge; *a* ~ *y barrancas* through fire and water; **trancada** *f* stride; **trancar** [1g] *v/t.* bar; *v/i.* F stride along; **trancazo** *m* swipe, bang; 🦠 F 'flu.

trance *m* moment, juncture; (*mal paso, apuro*) critical juncture; ~ *mortal* dying moments; *a todo* ~ at all costs; *en* ~ *de* in the act of; *muerte* at the point of.

tranco *m* big step, stride; *a* ~s pell-mell; *en dos* ~s in a couple of ticks.

tranquilidad *f* stillness *etc.*; *con toda* ~ with one's mind at ease; **tranquilizador** *noticia* reassuring; *música etc.* soothing; **tranquilizante** *m* 💊 tranquillizer; **tranquilizar** [1f] still, calm; *ánimo* reassure, relieve; *¡tranquilícese!* calm yourself!; don't worry!; **tranquilo** still, calm, tranquil; (*sin ruido*) quiet; *mar* calm; *ánimo* calm, untroubled.

tranquilla *f* latch; trap, red herring *en conversación*.

trans... trans...; *v. a. tras...*; ~**acción** *f* compromise, settlement; ✝ transaction; (*volumen de*) ~es *pl.* turnover; ~**atlántico** 1. trans-atlantic; 2. *m* liner; ~**bordador** *m* ferry; (*puente*) transporter bridge; ~**bordar** [1a] 🚗 *etc.* transfer; ⚓ tranship; ferry *en río*; *v/i.* 🚗 change; **bordo** *m* transfer; change; ⚓ transhipment; 🚗 *hacer* ~ change (en at); ~**cribir** [3a; *p.p. transcrito*] transcribe; ~**cripción** *f* transcription; ~**currir** [3a] go by, elapse; ~**curso** *m*: *en el* ~ *de* in the course of; ~**eúnte** 1. transitory, transient; 2. *m/f* passer-by; (*que vive fuera*) non-resident; ~**ferencia** *f* transfer (*a.* ⚗️); transference; ~**ferible** transferable; ~**ferir** [3i] transfer; ~**figurar** [1a] transfigure; ~**formable** *mot.* convertible; ~**formación** *f* transformation, change; ~**formador** *m* ⚡ transformer; ~**formar** [1a] transform; change; ~**formismo** *m* biol. transmutation; ~**formista** *m* thea. quick-change actor.

tránsfuga *m* ✗ deserter; *pol.* turncoat.

trans...: ~**fundir** [3a] transfuse; (*comunicar*) tell, spread; ~**fusión** *f* transfusion; ~ *de sangre* blood transfusion; ~**gredir** [3a] transgress; ~**gresor** *m*, -a *f* transgressor.

transición *f* transition; **transicional** transitional.

transido: ~ *de dolor* racked with pain; ~ *de hambre* overcome with hunger.

transigente accommodating, compromising; **transigir** [3c] compromise (*con* with); be tolerant (*con* towards).

transistorio *m* ⚡ transistor.

transitable passable; **transitar** [1a] travel, go from place to place; **transitivo** transitive; **tránsito** *m* (*acto*) transit, passage; (*parada*) stop(ping-place); traffic; transfer *a puesto*; *calle de mucho* ~ busy street; *horas de máximo* ~ rush hours; *de* ~, *en* ~ in transit; *hacer* ~ make a stop; *el* ~ *de este camino es difícil* this road is hard going; **transitorio** transitory.

trans...: ~**lúcido** translucent; ~**marino** overseas; ~**migrar** [1a] (trans)migrate; ~**misión** *f* transmission (a. ⊕, ⚡); radio a. broadcast; ~ en circuito hook-up; ✕ (cuerpo de) ~es pl. signals; ~**misor 1.**: estación ~a transmitting station; **2.** m transmitter; ~**mitir** [3a] mst transmit (a. radio); posesión pass on, hand down; ~**mutación** f transmutation; ~**mutar** [1a] transmute; ~**parencia** f transparency; ~**parentarse** [1a] (vidrio etc.) be transparent; (objeto visto) show through; (intención) be clear; ~**parente 1.** transparent (a. fig.); limpid; filmy; aire etc. clear; **2.** m curtain, blind; ~**piración** f anat. perspiration; ⚕ transpiration; ~**pirar** [1a] anat. perspire; ⚕ transpire; (rezumarse) seep through; fig. transpire, become known; ~**pirenaico** (situado) on the other side of the Pyrenees; tráfico through the Pyrenees.

transponer [2r] move, change the places of, transpose; esquina disappear round; ~**se** hide behind s.t.; (sol) set; (dormirse) get sleepy.

transportable transportable; **transportación** f transportation; **transportador** m ⚔ protractor; **transportar** [1a] transport; haul, carry; ⚓ a. ship; diseño etc. transfer; ♪ transpose; ~**se** fig. get carried away; **transporte** m transport (a. buque); (a. ~s pl.) transportation; fig. transport, ecstasy; ~s pl. (negocio) haulage business; (mudanzas) removals; Ministerio de ♀s Ministry of Transport.

transposición f transposition (a. ♪); move, change of places.

transubstanciación f transubstantiation.

transvasar [1a] decant.

transversal, transverso transverse; oblique; calle etc. cross.

tranvía m tram(car); (sistema) tramway.

trapacear [1a] be on the fiddle; **trapacería** f racket, fiddle; **trapacero** swindling; **trapacista** m racketeer; cheat, swindler.

trápala 1. f uproar, shindy; clatter de caballo; F swindle; **2.** m F talkativeness; **3.** m/f chatterbox; (embustero) cheat, swindler; **trapalear** [1a] F chatter, jabber; (mentir) fib; (trapacear) be on the fiddle; **trapalón** F lying; swindling.

trapatiesta f F roughhouse, shindy.

trapaza f = trapacería.

trapecio m trapeze; ⚔ trapezium.

trapería f rags, old clothes; (tienda) junk shop; **trapero** m ragman.

trapichear [1a] F plot.

trapillo: F estar de ~ be dressed up to the nines; **trapío**: tener buen ~ have real class; have a fine presence.

trapisonda f F (jaleo) row, shindy; (enredo) monkey business, dirty work; (mentira) fib; **trapisondear** [1a] F scheme, plot; **trapisondista** m F schemer, intriguer.

trapito m rag; ~s pl. de cristianar Sunday best; **trapo** m rag; duster; ⚓ canvas, sails; F ~s pl. clothes, dresses; v. trapito; a todo ~ in full sail; F poner como un ~ haul s.o. over the coals; (difamar) tear s.o. to pieces; soltar el ~ burst out laughing; (llorar) burst into tears.

traque m crack, bang; (pólvora) fuse.   [zo.).|

tráquea f windpipe, trachea ⚕ (a.|

tranque(te)ar [1a] v/t. (agitar) shake; rattle con ruido; F muck about with; v/i. crackle, bang como cohete; (máquina, vehículo etc.) rattle; jolt, joggle; **traque(te)o** m crack(le); rattle etc.; **traquido** m crack, bang.

tras 1. prp. lugar: behind, after; tiempo: after; **2.** cj.: ~ de inf. besides ger., in addition to ger.; **3.** m F bottom; **4.** int. ¡~, ~! bang, bang!

tras... trans.; v. a. trans...; ~**alcoba** f dressing-room; ~**cendencia** f importance; result; implications; esp. phls. transcendence; de ~ important, significant; ~ **cendental** far-reaching; momentous, of great significance; esp. phls. transcendent(al); ~**cender** [2g] (oler) smell strongly (a of); (divulgarse) become known, leak out; (extenderse) spread, have a wide effect; ~ a fig. suggest, evoke; ~**cocina** f scullery; ~**colar** [1m] strain; fig. get s.t. across; ~**conejarse** [1a] get lost; ~**corral** m back yard; F bottom.

trasegar [1h a. 1k] v/t. decant; pour into another bottle; botellas rack; fig. upset, turn upside down; puestos reshuffle; v/i. F booze.

trasera f back, rear; **trasero 1.** back, rear, hind; **2.** m hind quarters, rump de animal; bottom de p.; F ~s pl. ancestors.

trasfondo m background; (honduras) uttermost depths; undertone de crítica etc.

trasgo m goblin; imp (a. niño); bogy.

trashumación f migration, move to new pastures; **trashumante** tribu, p. nomadic; ganado migrating, on the move to new pastures; **trashumar** [1a] make the move to new pastures.

trasijado skinny.

traslación f transfer, move, removal (a to); copy(ing); **trasladar** [1a] transfer, move (a to); función postpone; documento copy; (traducir) translate; ~se move; ~ a puesto etc. transfer to, move to; otro sitio move to, go on to, proceed to; **traslado** m transfer, move, copy.

tras...: ~lapar(se) [1a] overlap; **~lapo** m overlap; **~laticio** sentido figurative; **~lucirse** [3f] (cuerpo) be translucent; (hecho) be plain to see; (noticia) leak out; **~luz** m diffused light; reflected light; al ~ against the light; **~nochada** f last night; (vela) sleepless night; (vigilia) watch; ✕ night attack; **~nochado** comida, cuento stale; p. hollow-eyed, run down; **~nochador** m (p.) night-bird; **~nochar** [1a] v/t. problema sleep on; v/i. (sin dormir) have a sleepless night; (pernoctar) spend the night; (estar fuera) stay out all night, have a night on the tiles F; **~oír** [3q] mishear; **~ojado** haggard, hollow-eyed; **~país** m hinterland, interior; **~palar** [1a] shovel; **~papelar** [1a] mislay.

traspasar [1a] (trasladar) move; (cruzar) cross (over); negocio make over, transfer; jugador transfer; esp. ⚙ convey; cuerpo pierce, run through, transfix; ley violate; (dolor) rack, torture; ~se go too far; **traspaso** m move; transfer; esp. ⚙ conveyance; (dolor) anguish, pain.

traspatio m S.Am. back yard.

traspié m stumble, slip; (zancadilla) trip; dar un ~ stumble.

traspintarse [1a] F turn out all wrong.

trasplantar [1a] transplant; ~se fig. emigrate, uproot o.s.

tras...: ~pontín m F bottom; **~portín** m pillion seat; F bottom; **~puesta** f transposition, changing over; removal; geog. fold, rise; (escondite) hiding-place; (patio) back yard; (huida) escape; **~punte** m thea. call-boy; **~quiladura** f shearing; **~quilar** [1a] oveja shear, clip; pelo de p. make a mess of; fig. cut down.

trastada f dirty trick; (broma) practical joke; **trastazo** m whack, thump; **traste** m ♪ fret; S.Am. F backside; F dar al ~ con chuck away; fig. mess up, spoil; **trastear** [1a] v/t. ♪ play (well); toro play; F p. manage, get round; v/i. move things around; S.Am. move house; fig. make bright conversation; **trastera** f lumber-room; **trastería** f lumber, junk; (tienda) junk shop; F = trastada.

trastienda f back room (of a shop); F tener mucha ~ be pretty smart.

trasto m (mueble) piece of furniture; (utensilio) crock; (cosa inútil) piece of junk; thea. furniture and properties; F (p. inútil) dead loss, washout; (p. molesta) nuisance; (p. rara) queer type; ~s pl. tools, tackle; ~s pl. de matar weapons; ~s pl. de pescar fishing-tackle; ~s pl. viejos junk; F coger (or liar) los ~s pack up and go.

trastornar [1a] (volcar) turn upside down; overturn, upset; orden de objetos mix up; fig. (inquietar) trouble; sentidos daze, make dizzy; nervios shatter; orden político etc. disturb; **trastorno** m (acto) overturning etc.; fig. pol. etc. upheaval; disorder, trouble; ⚙ upset, disorder; ~ mental mental disorder, breakdown.

trastrocar [1g a. 1m] reverse, invert, change round; **trastrueco** m, **trastrueque** m reversal etc.

trasunto m copy; fig. (a. ~ fiel) faithful copy, exact image.

trasvolar [1m] fly over.

trata f slave-trade; ~ de blancas white slave trade.

tratable tractable, manageable; p. sociable, easy to get on with.

tratado m lit. treatise, tract; pol. treaty; † etc. agreement.

tratamiento *m* treatment (*a.* 🔧, ⊕); ⊕ processing; treatment, handling *de p.*, *problema*; title, style (of address); *apear el ~* drop *s.o.'s* title; *dar ~ a* give *s.o.* his full title.

tratante *m* dealer, trader (en in).

tratar [1a] 1. *v/t. mst* treat (*a.* ⊕; 🔧 con, por with; *de loco etc.* as); ⊕ *a.* process; (*manejar*) handle, deal with; *~ de p.* (*con título, de tú*) address as; 2. *v/i.*: *~ con* have dealings with; *~* (*acerca*) *de*, *~ sobre* deal with, treat of; *tema* discuss, be about; *~ de inf.* try to *inf.*; *~ en* deal in, trade in; 3. *~se* bien live well, do o.s. well; *se trata de inf.* it is a question of *ger.*; *se trata de su.* it is about *su.*; *¿de qué se trata?* what's it about?; what's wrong?

trato *m* treatment; (*entre ps.*) intercourse, dealings; relationship; manner; title, style (of address); † deal, bargain; *~ colectivo* collective bargaining; *~ comercial* business deal; *~ doble* double-dealing; *~ sexual* sexual intercourse; *de fácil ~* easy to get on with; *cerrar un ~* strike a bargain, do a deal; *hacer un buen ~* drive a good bargain; *¡~ hecho!* it's a deal!; *tener buen ~* be easy to get on with.

través *m* bend, turn; (*torcimiento*) bias; △ cross-beam; 🔧 traverse; *fig.* upset; *a(l) ~ de* through; across; over; *de ~* sideways; crooked; **travesaño** *m* △, ⊕ transome, cross-bar (*a. deportes*); bolster *de cama*;

travesear [1a] play up, be mischievous; *fig.* talk wittily; **travesero** 1. sideways; cross *attr.*; 2. *m* bolster; **travesía** *f* (*calle*) cross-street; main road *dentro de pueblo*; ⚓ crossing, voyage; *S.Am.* plain;

travesura *f* prank, lark, (piece of) mischief; clever trick; (*ingenio*) wit, sparkle; **traviesa** *f* 🚂 sleeper; △ cross-beam; ⚓ crossing, voyage; **travieso** = travesero 1.; *fig. muchacho* naughty, mischievous; (*inquieto*) restless; (*sagaz*) clever.

trayecto *m* (*espacio*) distance, way; (*viaje*) journey *de p.*, run *de vehículo*; flight *de bala etc.*; **trayectoria** *f* trajectory, path.

traza *f* △ *etc.* plan, design; (*medio*) device, scheme; (*aspecto*) looks; *por las ~s* by all the signs; F *darse ~* get along, manage; *discurrir ~s para*

contrive schemes for; *llevar buena ~* look all right; *tener ~s de inf.* look like *ger.*; **trazado** 1.: *bien ~* good-looking; *mal ~* unattractive; 2. *m* (*dibujo*) outline, sketch; (*plano*) plan, lay-out; (*línea*) route; **trazador** 1. *phys.*, 🔧 tracer *attr.*; 2. *m* (*p.*) planner, designer; *phys. etc.* tracer; **trazar** [1f] sketch, outline; design, plan, lay out; *límites* mark out; *línea* draw, trace; *curso etc.* plot; *medios* contrive, devise; **trazo** *m* sketch, outline, line, stroke.

trebejo *m* old-fashioned thing; *ajedrez*: chessman; *~s pl. de cocina* kitchen utensils.

trébol *m* clover, trefoil (*a.* ♣); *naipes*: *~es pl.* clubs.

trece thirteen; (*fecha*) thirteenth; F *estarse etc. en sus ~* stand firm, stick to one's guns.

trecho *m* stretch, way; (*tiempo*) while; *un buen ~* a good way; *a ~s* intermittently; *de ~ en ~* at intervals; *muy de ~ en ~* only once in a while.

tregua *f* 🔧 truce; *fig.* respite, lull, let-up; *no dar ~* give no respite.

treinta thirty; (*fecha*) thirtieth; **treintena** *f* (about) thirty.

trematodo *m* fluke.

tremebundo terrible; **tremendo** (*horrendo*) dreadful, frightful; (*digno de respeto*) imposing; (*muy grande*) tremendous; F terrific, tremendous.

trementina *f* turpentine.

tremolar [1a] *v/t.* hoist; (*agitar*) wave; *fig.* make a show of; *v/i.* flutter, wave; **tremolina** *f* rustle; F bustle, great doings; (*jaleo*) row; **trémulo** quivering, tremulous; *luz* flickering; *voz* timid, small.

tren *m* 🚂 train; 🔧 convoy; ⊕ set *de engranajes etc.*; outfit, equipment *de viaje*; (*ps.*) retinue; (*boato*) pomp; *~ ascendente* up train; *~ de aterrizaje* undercarriage; *~ botijo*, *~ de recreo* excursion train; *~ correo* mail-train; slow train; *~ descendente* down train; *~ expreso* express train; *~ de laminación* rolling mill; *~ de mercancías* goods train; *~ ómnibus* stopping train, local train; *en ~* by train.

trena *f sl.* clink.

trencilla *f*, **trencillo** *m* braid; **trenza** *f* plait, pigtail, pony-tail;

braid; twist *de hebras*; plait *de esparto etc.*; en ~ with one's hair down; **trenzado** *m* plaits; **trenzar** [1f] *pelo* plait, braid; *hebras etc.* twist, intertwine, weave.

trepa 1. *f* climb(ing); *(voltereta)* somersault; *hunt.* hide; ⊕ drilling, boring; *sew.* trimming; grain *en madera*; F slyness; F *(castigo)* hiding; **2.** *m* F social climber; **trepado** *m* ⅋ perforation; **trepador 1.** climbing, rambling; **2.** *m* (*a.* **trepadora** *f*) climber, rambler; **trepar** [1a] *v/t.* climb; ⊕ drill, bore; *sew.* trim; *v/i.* (*a.* ~ *a*) climb (up); clamber up; scale; ⚘ climb (*por* up).

trepe: F echar un ~ *a* tick off.

trepidar [1a] shake, vibrate.

tres three (*a. su.*); *(fecha)* third; *las* ~ three o'clock; **trescientos** three hundred.

tresnal *m* shock, stack.

treta *f fenc.* feint; *fig.* trick, stratagem; wheeze F; gimmick *publicitaria etc.*; *S.Am.* bad habit.

triangular triangular, three-cornered; **triángulo** *m* triangle (*a.* ♪).

tribal tribal; **tribu** *f* tribe (*a. zo.*); **tribual** tribal.

tribulación *f* tribulation.

tribuna *f* rostrum *de orador*; *hist.* tribune; platform *en mitin*; gallery (*a. eccl.*); *deportes:* (grand)stand; ~ *del acusado* dock; ~ *del jurado* jury-box; ~ *de la prensa* press-box; **tribunal** *m* ⚖ court; (*ps.*) court, bench; tribunal *de investigación etc.*; *univ.* board of examiners; *fig.* tribunal; forum *de opinión etc.*; ~ *marítimo* prize court; ~ *de menores* juvenile court; ♀ *Supremo* High Court, Supreme Court *Am.*; en *pleno* ~ in open court.

tributar [1a] *todos sentidos:* pay; **tributario** *adj. a. su. m* tributary; **tributo** *m* tribute (*a. fig.*); (*impuesto*) tax.

tricentenario *m* tercentenary.

triciclo *m* tricycle.

tricolor *m* tricolour.

tricornio *m* three-cornered hat.

tridente *m* trident.

tridimensional three-dimensional.

trienal triennial; **trienio** *m* period of three years.

trifásico ⚡ three-phase, triphase.

trifulca *f* F row, roughhouse.

trigal *m* wheat-field.

trigésimo thirtieth.

trigo *m* wheat; *sl.* dough; ~ *candeal* bread wheat; ~ *sarraceno* buckwheat; *de* ~ *entero* wholemeal; meterse en ~s *ajenos* meddle in s.o. else's affairs (*or* subject *etc.*).

trigonometría *f* trigonometry.

trigueño *pelo* corn-coloured; *tez* olive; *p.* olive-skinned.

triguero 1. wheat *attr.*; **2.** *m* corn-sieve.

trilingüe trilingual.

trilla *f* threshing; **trillado** *camino* beaten, well-trodden; *fig.* trite, hack(neyed); **trillador** *m* thresher; **trilladora** *f* threshing-machine; **trilladura** *f* threshing; **trillar** [1a] thresh; *fig.* frequent.

trillizos *m/pl.* triplets.

trillo *m* threshing-machine.

trillón *m* trillion (*Gran Bretaña*).

trimestral *revista etc.* quarterly; *univ.* terminal, termly; **trimestre** *m* quarter, period of three months; *univ.* term; ⸙ quarterly payment (*or* rent *etc.*).

trinado *m* ♪ trill; *orn.* warble; **trinar** [1a] trill; *orn.* sing, warble; F fume, blow one's top; F *está que trina* he's hopping mad.

trinca *f* group (*or* set) of three; threesome; F gang.

trincar¹ [1g] break up; tear up.

trincar² [1g] (*atar*) tie up; ⚓ lash.

trincar³ [1g] F have a drink.

trinchar [1a] carve, slice; F do in; **trinchera** *f* ⚔ *etc.* trench; entrenchment; ▓ cutting; (*abrigo*) trench coat.

trineo *m* sled(ge), sleigh; ~ *balancín* bobsleigh.

Trinidad *f* Trinity.

trinitaria *f* ⚘ heartsease; pansy *de jardín*.

trino *m* = *trinado*.

trinquete *m* ⚓ (*palo de*) ~ foremast; (*vela*) foresail; ⊕ pawl, trip; ratchet.

trinquis *m* F drink, swig.

trío *m* trio.

tripa *f* intestine, gut; (*panza*) belly; ~s *pl. anat.* insides, guts; *cocina:* tripe; *hacer de* ~s *corazón* pluck up courage; put on a bold front; F *tener malas* ~s be cruel.

tripartito tripartite.

triple 1. triple; threefold; **2.** *m* triple; *es el* ~ *de lo que era* it is three times (*or* treble) what is was; **triplicado** (*por* in) triplicate; **triplicar(se)** [1g] treble, triple; do three times.

trípode *mst m* tripod.

tripón *m* F pot-bellied.

tríptico *m* triptych; (*hoja*) form in three parts.

tripulación *f* crew; **tripulante** *m* crew member, man; **tripular** [1a] man.

trique *m* crack, swish; *a cada* ~ at every turn.

triquiñuela *f* F trick, funny business; *tío* ~s artful old cuss.

tris *m* (*ruido*) crack, tinkle; F trice; *en un* ~ within an inch; *estuvo en un* ~ *que lo hiciera* he very nearly did it.

trisca *f* crushing noise; (*retozo*) romp; (*jaleo*) rumpus, row; **triscar** [1g] *v/t.* (*mezclar*) mix, mingle; (*enredar*) mix up; *sierra* set; *v/i.* stamp one's feet; (*retozar*) romp, frisk about.

trisílabo 1. trisyllabic; **2.** *m* trisyllable.

trismo *m* lockjaw.

triste *mst* sad; *aspecto* sad-looking, gloomy; *carácter* melancholy; (*afligido*) sorrowful; (*sombrío*) gloomy, dismal; *paisaje etc.* desolate, dreary; (*despreciable*) wretched, miserable; *es* ~ *no poder ir* it's a pity we can't go.

tritón *m* zo. newt.

triturar [1a] triturate; grind (up), pound, pulverize.

triunfador 1. triumphant; **2.** *m* victor, winner; **triunfal** triumphal; **triunfante** triumphant; (*jubiloso*) jubilant, exultant; **triunfar** [1a] triumph (*de* over); exult (*de, sobre* over); *naipes*: trump; **triunfo** *m* triumph (*a. fig.*); *fig.* success; *naipes*: trump; *sin* ~ no trumps; *palo de(l)* ~ trump(s suit).

trivial trivial; (*trillado*) trite; (*grosero*) vulgar; **trivialidad** *f* triviality; triteness; *decir* ~es talk in platitudes.

triza *f* shred, bit; ~s *pl. fig.* ribbons; *hacer* ~s shred, tear up; smash to bits.

trocar [1g *a.* 1m] ✝ *etc.* exchange, barter; change (*con, por* for); *posiciones etc.* change over; *palabras* exchange; (*equivocar*) mix up, twist; ~**se** change.

trocha *f* by-path, narrow path; *S.Am.* 🚂 gauge.

trochemoche: *a* ~ helter-skelter, pell-mell; all over the place.

trofeo *m* trophy; *fig.* victory, success.

troglodita *m* caveman, troglodyte; *fig.* brute; (*comilón*) glutton.

troj(e) *f* barn, granary.

trola *f* F fib.

trole *m* trolley; **trolebús** *m* trolleybus.

trolero *m* F fibber.

tromba *f* whirlwind; column *de polvo etc.*; ~ (*marina*) waterspout.

trombón *m* trombone.

trombosis *f* thrombosis.

trompa *f* ♪ horn; (*trompo*) humming-top; trunk *de elefante*; proboscis *de insecto etc.*; *sl.* hooter, conk; *anat.* tube, duct; *sl. cogerse una* ~ get boozed; **trompada** *f* F, **trompazo** *m* F bump, bang; (*golpe*) punch.

trompeta 1. *f* trumpet; **2.** *m* = trompetero; **trompetazo** *m* trumpet blast; blast, blare; **trompetear** [1a] (play the) trumpet; **trompetero** *m* ♪ trumpet-player; ⚔ trumpeter; **trompetilla** *f*: ~ (*acústica*) ear-trumpet.

trompicar [1g] *v/t.* trip up; F fiddle the promotion of; *v/i.* stumble; **trompicón** *m* stumble, trip.

trompis *m* F punch, swipe.

trompo *m* top; F clumsy dancer; **trompón** *m* *S.Am.* bump, bang; F clumsy individual.

tronada *f* thunderstorm; **tronado** F broke; **tronar** [1m] thunder; (*cañón etc.*) thunder, rumble; F fail, be ruined; F ~ *con* fall out with; ~ *contra* denounce, fulminate against; storm at; F *por lo que pueda* ~ just in case.

troncal: *línea* ~ trunk-line; **tronco** *m* ⚘ (*de árbol*), *anat.* trunk; stem, stalk *de flor*; (*leño*) log; team *de caballos*; 🚂 trunk-line; (*familia*) stock; F *estar hecho un* ~ be sleeping like a log.

tronchar [1a] chop off, lop off; (*romper*) smash.

tronera 1. *f* ⚔ loophole, embrasure; 🔺 narrow window; *billar:* pocket; **2.** *m/f* crazy sort.

tronido *m* thunderclap; ~s *pl.* thunder.

trono *m* throne.
tronzar [1f] smash, shatter; *sew.* pleat.
tropa *f* (*gente*) troop, flock, body; ✕ (*soldados*) troop; (*no oficiales*) men, rank and file; *S.Am.* herd; ~s *pl.* troops; **tropel** *m* (*movimiento*) rush, bustle; (*prisa*) rush, hurry; (*confusión*) jumble, mess; (*muchedumbre*) throng; de ~, en ~ in utter chaos; in a mad rush; **tropelía** *f* = *tropel*; *fig.* outrage; **tropero** *m* *S.Am.* cowboy.
tropezar [1f *a.* 1k] trip, stumble (con, en on, over); (*reñir*) fall out (con with); *fig.* ~ con, ~ en dificultad run into, run up against; (*encontrar*) stumble upon; *p.* run into; **tropezón** *m* stumble, trip; *a* ~es by fits and starts; *hablar etc.* falteringly; *dar un* ~ stumble.
tropical tropic(al); **trópico** *m* tropic; ~s *pl.* tropics.
tropiezo *m* stumble, trip; *fig.* snag, obstacle; (*falta*) slip; (*riña*) squabble.
tropo *m* trope, figure of speech.
troquel *m* ⊕ die.
troqueo *m* trochee (-‿).
trotamundos *m* globe-trotter; **trotar** [1a] trot; F be on the go, hustle; **trote** *m* trot; ~ cochinero, ~ de perro jog-trot; *al* ~ at a trot; *fig.* right away; *para todo* ~ for everyday wear; F *andar en malos* ~s have a rough time; F *tomar el* ~ dash off.
trovador *m* troubadour.
troyano *adj. a. su. m,* **a** *f* Trojan.
trozo *m* bit, piece; ♪, *lit. etc.* passage; *a* ~s piecemeal, in bits.
trucaje *m* trick photography; **truco** *m* F trick, wheeze, dodge; ~ de naipes card trick; ~ de propaganda gimmick.
trucha *f* trout; ⊕ derrick, crane.
trueco *m* = *trueque.*
trueno *m* thunder; (*un* ~) clap of thunder; bang, report; F crazy sort; F ~ gordo big row.
trueque *m* exchange; barter; *a* ~ de in exchange for.
trufa *f* truffle; F fib, story; **trufar** [1a] *v/t.* stuff with truffles; *v/i.* F fib.
truhán *m* rogue, crook; (*gracioso*) clown, funny man; **truhanesco** crooked; funny.
truismo *m* truism.

truncar [1g] truncate; cut short, curtail; *escrito etc.* slash.
trust *m* trust, cartel.
tú you; (†, *a Dios*) thou; *tratar etc.* de ~ = *tutear.*
tu, tus *pl.* your; (†, *a Dios*) thy.
tubérculo *m* ♀ tuber; *anat., zo.,* ♣ tubercle; **tuberculosis** *f* tuberculosis; **tuberculoso** tuberculous, tubercular.
tubería *f* tubing; piping, pipes; **tubo** *m* tube (*a. anat., televisión*); pipe; ~ acústico speaking-tube; ~ de aspiración breathing-tube; ~ capilar capillary; ~ de chimenea chimney-pot; ~ de desagüe waste-pipe; drain-pipe; ~ digestivo alimentary canal; ~ de ensayo test-tube; ~ de escape exhaust (pipe); ~ de humo flue; ~ de lámpara lamp-glass; ~ de paso bypass; ~ de rayos catódicos cathode ray tube; **tubular** tubular.
tudesco *adj. a. su. m,* **a** *f* German.
tuerca *f* nut; ~ mariposa wing-nut.
tuerto 1. (*torcido*) twisted, crooked; (*de ojo*) one-eyed, blind in one eye; F *a* ~as one-eyed, back to front; *a* ~as o a derechas rightly or wrongly; by hook or by crook; (*sin pensar*) hastily; 2. *m,* **a** *f* one-eyed person; 3. *m* wrong.
tuétano *m* *anat.* marrow; ♀ pith; *hasta los* ~s through and through; *enamorado hasta los* ~s head over heels in love.
tufarada *f* bad smell; **tufo** *m* vapour, gas; (*olor*) bad smell, stink; F ♣ bad breath; F ~s *pl.* swank.
tugurio *m* ♪ shepherd's hut; (*cuarto*) poky little room; (*casucha*) slum, hovel.
tul *m* tulle, net.
tulipán *m* tulip.
tullido 1. crippled; paralytic; 2. *m,* **a** *f* cripple; **tullir** [3h] cripple, maim; paralyse; *fig.* abuse.
tumba[1] *f* grave, tomb.
tumba[2] *f* (*voltereta*) somersault; **tumbacuartillos** *m* F old soak; **tumbar** [1a] *v/t.* knock down, knock over; F (*vino*) lay *s.o.* out; *v/i.* fall down; ♣ capsize; *estar tumbado* lie, be lying down; ~se lie down; stretch out, sprawl; **tumbo** *m* fall, tumble; (*vaivén*) shake, lurch; *fig.* critical moment; *dar un* ~ tumble; (*a. dar* ~s) lurch;

tumbón F bone-idle; **tumbona** *f* easy-chair.

tumefacción *f* swelling; **túmido** swollen; **tumor** *m* tumour, growth.

túmulo *m* tumulus, barrow; *geog.* mound.

tumulto *m* turmoil, tumult; *pol. etc.* riot; **tumultuario, tumultuoso** tumultuous; riotous.

tuna *f* ♩ *student music group.*

tunante 1. crooked; **2.** *m* rogue, crook; *esp. co.* scamp, villain.

tunda *f* shearing; F hiding; **tundir** [3a] *paño* shear; *hierba* mow, cut; F tan.

túnel *m* tunnel; ~ *aerodinámico* wind-tunnel.

tungsteno *m* tungsten.

túnica *f hist., anat. etc.* tunic; *(vestido largo)* robe, gown.

tuno = *tunante.*

tuntún: F *al (buen)* ~ thoughtlessly, trusting to luck.

tupé *m* toupee; F nerve, cheek.

tupido thick, dense (*a.* F); *paño* close-woven; **tupir** [3a] pack tight, press down; ~se F stuff o.s.

turba[1] *f geol.* peat, turf.

turba[2] *f* crowd; swarm; *(chusma)* mob.

turbación *f* confusion; disturbance; *(de p.)* embarrassment; distress; trepidation; **turbador** disturbing.

turbamulta *f* mob, rabble.

turbante *m* turban.

turbar [1a] *orden etc.* disturb, upset; *agua* stir up; *fig.* darken; *p., ánimo* disturb, upset, worry; *(desconcertar)* embarrass; ~se get embarrassed, feel awkward; get all mixed up, get confused; *(inquietarse)* begin to worry, get upset.

turbina *f* turbine.

turbio *agua* muddy, turbid; *líquido* thick, cloudy; *aguas fig.* dark, troubled; *época, vida* unsettled; *negocio* shady; *medio* dubious; *estilo* confused, obscure.

turbión *m* heavy shower, squall; *fig.* shower; swarm; hail *de balas*.

turbo-hélice *adj. a. su. m* turbo-

prop; **turborreactor** *adj. a. su. m* turbo-jet.

turbulencia *f* turbulence *etc.*; **turbulento** turbulent; *niño* noisy, unruly; *espíritu etc.* restless; *época* troubled; *ejército etc.* mutinous, disorderly.

turca *f* F booze-up, binge; *coger una* ~ get boozed.

turco 1. Turkish; **2.** *m*, **a** *f* Turk; **3.** *m (idioma)* Turkish.

turgente, túrgido swollen, turgid.

turismo *m* tourism; tourist trade; touring; sightseeing; *(coche de)* ~ tourer; **turista** *m/f* tourist; sightseer; visitor, holiday-maker; **turístico** tourist *attr.*

turnar [1a] take turns; **turno** *m (vez)* turn; *(tanda)* spell, shift; turn, go *en juegos*; *por* ~ in rotation, in turn; *por* ~s by turns; *esperar su* ~ take one's turn; *es su* ~, *le toca el* ~ it's his turn; *estar de* ~ be on duty.

turolense *adj. a. su. m/f* (native) of Teruel.

turón *m* polecat.

turquesa *f min.* turquoise; ⊕ mould.

turquí deep blue.

turrón *m sweet made of almond, honey etc. in a hard block, approx.* nougat; F cushy government job.

turulato F dazed, stunned.

¡tus! good dog!; F *sin decir* ~ *ni mus* without a word.

tusar [1a] *S.Am.* cut, shear.

tute *m a card game, approx.* bezique.

tutear [1a] *address · as tú*; be on familiar terms with.

tutela *f* ⚖ guardianship; *fig.* protection, tutelage; *bajo* ~ in ward.

tuteo *m addressing a p. as tú.*

tutiplén: F *comer a* ~ eat hugely.

tutor *m* guardian, tutor; **tutora** *f* guardian; **tutoría** *f* guardianship, tutelage.

tuve *etc. v.* tener.

tuyo, tuya 1. *pron.* yours; (†, *a Dios*) thine; **2.** *adj. (tras su.)* of yours.

U

u or.

ubicación *f* location, position, situation; **ubicar** [1g] *v/t. S.Am.* place, put; *v/i.,* ~**se** be, lie, stand, be located; **ubicuidad** *f* ubiquity; **ubicuo** ubiquitous.

ubre *f* udder; *(cada pezón)* teat; **ubrera** *f* ⚕ thrush.

ucranio *adj. a. su. m,* **a** *f* Ukrainian.

¡uf! *cansancio:* phew!; *repugnancia:* ugh!

ufanarse [1a] boast; ~ **de** pride o.s. on, boast of; **ufanía** *f* pride; *b.s.* vanity, conceit; **ufano** proud; exultant; *(alegre)* cheerful; satisfied (**de** with); easy, smooth *en obrar*; *b.s.* vain, conceited.

ujier *m* usher, attendant.

úlcera *f* ulcer; *(esp. externo)* sore; **ulceración** *f* ulceration; **ulcerar** [1a] ulcerate; make a sore on; ~**se** ulcerate, fester; **ulceroso** ulcerous; full of sores.

ulterior *lugar:* farther, further; *tiempo:* later, subsequent.

ultimación *f* conclusion; **últimamente** lastly, finally; *(recientemente)* lately, of late; **ultimar** [1a] end, finish; *trato etc.* conclude; **ultimátum** *m pol.* ultimatum; **último** (*en* ~ *lugar*) last; latter **de dos**; *(más reciente)* latest; *(más remoto)* furthest; *(extremo)* utmost; *piso* top; *calidad* finest, superior; *este* ~ the latter; *a* ~**s de mes** in the latter part of; *en estos* ~**s años** in the last few years; *por* ~ last(ly), finally; F *estar en las* ~**as** be down and out, be on one's last legs; *llegar el* ~ be last; *ser el* ~ *en inf.* be the last to *inf.*; F *ser la* ~**a** be all the rage.

ultra... ultra...

ultrajador, ultrajante outrageous; insulting, offensive; **ultrajar** [1a] outrage; insult, revile; **ultraje** *m* outrage; insult; **ultrajoso** outrageous.

ultramar: **de** ~, **en** ~ overseas; **ultramarino 1.** overseas; **2.** ~**s** *m/pl.* groceries; *(tienda de)* ~ grocer's (shop).

ultramoderno ultramodern.

ultramontano *adj. a. su. m* ultramontane.

ultranza: *a* ~ to the death; *fig.* regardless, at all costs.

ultratumba: **de** ~ *vida* beyond the grave; *voz* from beyond the grave.

ultravioleta ultra-violet.

ulular [1a] howl, shriek; *(buho)* hoot; **ululato** *m* howl, shriek; hoot.

umbela *f* umbel.

umbilical umbilical.

umbral *m* threshold (*a.* ~**es** *pl. fig.*).

umbrío, umbroso shady; shadowy.

un, una 1. *artículo:* a, *(delante de vocal y h muda)* an; **2.** *adj. numeral:* one; *¡a la una, a las dos, a las tres!* *(subasta)* going, going, gone!; *(carreras)* ready, steady, go!

unánime unanimous; **unanimidad** *f* unanimity; *por* ~ unanimously.

unción *f* *eccl. a. fig.* unction; ⚕ ointment.

uncir [3b] yoke.

undécimo eleventh.

undulación *f etc. v. ondulación etc.*

ungir [3c] anoint (*a. eccl.*), apply ointment to; **ungüento** *m* ointment, salve.

unguiculado ungual; **ungulado** *adj. a. su. m* hoofed (animal), ungulate ⛝.

uni... uni...; one-...

únicamente only; solely.

unicameral single-chamber.

único only; sole, single, solitary; *(singular, extraordinario)* unique; *distribuidor etc.* sole, exclusive; *hijo* ~ only child; *su* ~ *cuidado* his one care; *este ejemplar es* ~ this specimen is unique.

unicolor one-colour; *esp.* ⚘ self.

unicornio *m* unicorn.

unidad *f* unity; oneness; ⚔, ♌, ⊕ *etc.* unit; **unido** united; *(liso)* smooth; *mantener(se)* ~(s) keep together; remain united; **unificación** *f* unification; **unificar** [1g] unite, unify.

uniformar [1a] make uniform; *p.* put into uniform; **uniforme 1.** *mst* uniform; *velocidad etc. a.* steady, unvarying, regular; *superficie a.* level, even, true; **2.** *m* uniform; **uniformidad** *f* uniformity *etc.*

Unigénito: el ~ the only Begotten Son.

unilateral one-sided, unilateral.

unión *f* union (*a.* ✝); (*unidad*) unity; (*casamiento*) union, marriage; ⊕ union, joint; (*punto de*) ~ junction.

unir [3a] *cosas* join; *mst fig.* unite; *sociedades, intereses* merge; *familias, novios* unite (by marriage); ~se join (together) unite; *esp.* ✝ merge; ~ *a* join.

unísono unisonous; *voces etc.* in harmony; *al* ~ in unison, with one voice.

unitario 1. unitary; *eccl.* Unitarian; **2.** *m*, *a* *f* Unitarian.

universal universal; world-wide; **universalidad** *f* universality; generality; **universidad** *f* university; **universitario 1.** university *attr.*; academic; **2.** *m* university teacher, university man; **universo** *m* universe.

uno 1. *adj.* one; identical, one and the same; *Dios es* ~ God is one; *la verdad es una* truth is one and indivisible; ~*s* *pl.* some, a few; *unos 20 km* some 20 km, about 20 km; **2.** *pron.* one; ~ *que vino a verme* someone who came to see me; ~ *no sabe* one does not know; ~ *necesita amigos* a man needs friends; ~ *a* ~ one by one; ~(s) *a otro(s)* one another, each other; ~ *que otro* an occasional, the odd; ~ *y otro* both; *cada* ~ each one, everyone; *en* ~ at one; *una de dos* either one (thing) or the other; *a una* all together; *la una* one o'clock; **3.** *m* one.

untadura *f* (*acto*) smearing *etc.*; ⚕ ointment; ⊕ grease; (*mancha*) smear, dab; **untar** [1a] smear, dab (de with); (*engrasar*) grease, oil; *pan, mantequilla* spread; *fig.* bribe, grease the palm of; **unto** *m* grease; fat *de animal*; **untuoso** greasy, sticky; *mst fig.* unctuous; **untura** *f* = untadura.

uña *f* *anat.* nail; (*garra*) claw; hoof *de caballo*; sting *de alacrán*; ⚓ fluke, bill; ⊕ pallet; ⊕ claw; ♀ ~ *de caballo* coltsfoot; *a* ~ *de caballo* at full gallop; *largo de* ~*s* light-fingered; *comerse las* ~*s* bite one's nails; F *ser* ~ *y carne* be thick (as thieves), be hand in glove; **uña(ra)da** *f* nail-mark; (*arañazo*) scratch; **uñero** *m* ingrowing nail; ⚕ whitlow.

¡upa! up, up!

uranio *m* uranium.

urbanidad *f* refinement, urbanity; **urbanismo** *m* town-planning; **urbanización** *f* urbanization; development; **urbanizado** built-up; **urbanizar** [1f] *terreno* urbanize, develop, build on; *p.* civilize; **urbano** urban, city *attr.*; *fig.* polite, refined, urbane; **urbe** *f* large city, metropolis; *La ⚲ esp.* Madrid.

urdimbre *f* warp; **urdir** [3a] warp; *fig.* contrive, plot, conspire to bring about.

urente burning, stinging.

urgencia *f* urgency; pressure; haste; emergency; pressing need; *de* ~ *medida, salida* emergency *attr.*; *botiquín etc.* first-aid *attr.*; *en caso de* ~ in case of necessity; *pedir con* ~ press for; **urgente** (*que corre prisa*) urgent; (*apremiante*) pressing; *demanda etc.* imperative, insistent; *pedido* rush *attr.*; *carta* express; **urgir** [3c] be urgent, press; ~ *inf.* it is absolutely necessary to *inf.*

úrico uric; **urinario 1.** urinary; **2.** *m* urinal.

urna *f* urn; glass case; ~ *electoral* ballot-box; ~*s* *pl.* electorales *fig.* polling-station; *acudir a las* ~*s* vote, go to the polls.

urraca *f* magpie.

urticaria *f* nettle-rash, hives.

uruguayo *adj. a. su. m*, *a* *f* Uruguayan.

usado used; (*gastado*) worn; *p.* skilled, experienced.

usagre *m* ⚕ impetigo; *vet.* mange.

usanza *f* custom; *a* ~ *de* according to the custom of.

usar [1a] *v/t.*, *a. v/i.* ~ *de* use, make use of; *sin* ~ unused; *sello etc.* mint; ~ *inf.* be accustomed to *inf.*; ~se be used, be in use; (*estilarse*) be in fashion; (*gastarse*) wear out.

usina *f* *S.Am.* factory.

uso *m* (*empleo*) use; (*usufructo*) use, enjoyment; (*deterioro*) wear (and tear); (*costumbre*) usage, custom; (*moda*) fashion, style; *al* ~ in keeping with custom; *al* ~ *de hacer etc.* for the use of; *vestir etc.* in the style of; *en* ~ in use; *hacer* ~ *de* make use of; *hacer ~ de la palabra* speak.

usted, ustedes *pl.* you.

usual usual, customary; **usuario** *m*, **a** *f* user; **usufructo** *m* usufruct, use; ~ *(vitalicio)* life-interest (de in); **usufructuario** *m*, **a** *f* usufructuary.

usura *f* usury, interest; *(ganancia excesiva)* profiteering; **usurario** usurious; **usurear** [1a] lend money at high rates of interest; *fig.* profiteer; **usurero** *m* usurer; *fig.* profiteer.

usurpación *f* usurpation; *fig.* encroachment (de upon), inroad (de into); **usurpador** *m* usurper; **usurpar** [1a] usurp (*a. fig.*); *fig.* encroach upon, make inroads into.

utensilio *m* tool, implement; utensil *esp. de cocina.*

uterino uterine; *hermanos* born of the same mother; **útero** *m* womb, uterus.

útil 1. useful; helpful, handy; usable, serviceable; **2.** *m* usefulness; *~es pl.* (set of) tools, implements, equipment; **utilidad** *f* use(fulness), utility; *(provecho)* profit, benefit, good; **utilitario** utilitarian; *ropa etc.* utility *attr.*; **utilizable** usable; fit for use, ready to use; ⊕ *desechos* reclaimable; **utilización** *f* use, utilization; ⊕ reclamation; **utilizar** [1f] use, make use of, utilize; ⊕ *desechos* reclaim; *recursos naturales, potencia* harness; **utillaje** *m* = *útiles.*

utopía *f* Utopia; **utópico, utopista** *m/f* Utopian.

uva *f* grape; ~ *espina* gooseberry; ~ *pasa* raisin; ~ *de Corinto* currant; *estar hecho una ~* be drunk as a lord.

úvula *f* uvula; **uvular** uvular.

V

va *etc. v. ir.*

vaca *f* cow; *(carne)* beef; *(cuero)* cowhide; ~ *lechera* milker; ~ *marina* sea-cow; ~ *de San Antón* lady-bird; F *pasar las* ~*s gordas* have a whale of a time.

vacación *f* holiday(s), vacation *(a.* ~*es pl.);* *(puesto)* vacancy; ~*es pl. retribuidas* holidays with pay; *de* ~*es* on holiday; *marcharse de* ~*es* go off on holiday; **vacacionista** *m/f* holiday-maker, vacationist *Am.*

vacada *f* herd of cows.

vacante 1. vacant, unoccupied; **2.** *f* vacancy; **vacar** [1g] be vacant, remain unfilled; ~ *a,* ~ *en* engage in, attend to.

vaciadero *m* sink, drain; **vaciado 1.** ⊕ hollow-ground; **2.** *m* cast, moulding; plaster cast *de yeso;* **vaciador** *m* scoop; *(p.)* cutler.

vaciar [1c] *v/t. vasija, bolsillo etc.* empty; *vaso etc.* drain; *contenido* empty out; *líquido* pour away, run off; cast, mould *en molde;* *(ahuecar)* hollow out; *(afilar)* grind, sharpen; *v/i. (río)* flow, empty (en into); ~*se* F tell all one knows, spill the beans.

vaciedad *f = vacuidad; fig.* piece of nonsense; ~*es pl.* nonsense.

vacilación *f* hesitancy, hesitation, vacillation; **vacilante** *luz* flickering; *movimiento* unsteady; *habla* halting; *fig.* hesitant, vacillating; **vacilar** [1a] *(luz)* flicker; *(mueble etc.)* be unsteady, shake; *(habla)* falter; *fig.* hesitate, waver, vacillate; hang back *al avanzar; (memoria)* fail; ~ *en su.* hesitate about; *inf.* hesitate to *inf.*

vacío 1. empty; *puesto etc.* vacant, unoccupied; *papel* blank; *charla* idle; *(inútil)* vain, useless; *(presuntuoso)* vain, proud; **2.** *m phys.* vacuum; *(el espacio, la nada)* void; *(lo vacío)* emptiness; *(un espacio)* empty space, gap; *(hueco)* hollow; *(ijada)* side, ribs; *(puesto)* vacancy; *caer en el* ~ fall flat; *hacer el* ~ *a* send *s.o.* to Coventry; *llenar un bien sentido* ~ fill a long-felt want; ⊕ *mar-*

char en ~ idle, tick over; *(fuera de control)* race.

vacuidad *f* emptiness; vacancy; *mst fig.* vacuity.

vacuna *f* vaccine; **vacunación** *f* vaccination; **vacunar** [1a] vaccinate; **vacuno** bovine; *ganado* ~⎱
vade *m* satchel.   [cattle.⎰

vadeable fordable; *fig.* not insuperable; **vadear** [1a] *v/t. río* ford; *agua* wade through; *fig. dificultad* get around, overcome; *p.* sound out; *v/i.* wade.

vademécum *m* vademecum; *(bolsa)* satchel.

vado *m* ford; *fig.* way out, expedient; *no hallar* ~ see no way out; *tentar el* ~ look into matters, study the ground.

vagabundear [1a] wander, roam; *(holgazanear)* loaf, idle; **vagabundo 1.** vagabond; wandering, vagrant; **2.** *m,* **a** *f* wanderer, rover; *b.s.* tramp, bum *Am.*; vagabond, vagrant; **vagancia** *f* vagrancy; idleness; **vagante** vagrant; **vagar 1.** [1h] wander, rove, roam; prowl *esp. de noche; (cazcalear)* saunter; *b.s.* loiter; *(vivir ocioso)* be idle, be at leisure; *b.s.* loaf; **2.** *m* leisure; *andar de* ~ be at leisure.

vagido *m* wail, cry.

vago 1. vague, indeterminate; *perfil etc.* ill-defined, indistinct; *ideas* vague, woolly; *control etc.* loose, lax; *(holgazán)* lazy; *(errante)* roving, wandering; *en* ~ in vain; *(sin firmeza)* unsteadily; *golpe etc.* in the air; **2.** *m (holgazán)* lazy sort; *(no confiable)* unreliable sort; *(confuso)* woollyminded sort.

vagón *m pasajeros:* carriage, coach; *mercancías:* truck, waggon; ~ *cisterna* tank waggon; ~ *tolva* hopper; **vagoneta** *f* ✕ *etc.* truck; *S.Am.* •delivery van.

vaguear [1a] *= vagar;* **vaguedad** *f* vagueness; indistinctness; *(dicho)* vague remark.

vaharada *f* puff; whiff, reek; **vah(e)ar** [1a] steam, send out vapour,

give out fumes; (*oler*) whiff, reek;
vahido *m* queer turn, dizzy spell;
vaho *m* vapour, steam, fumes; (*olor*)
reek, whiff; (*aliento*) breath.

vaina *f* sheath, scabbard; (⊕,*estuche*)
case; ♀ pod, husk, shell; **vainica** *f*
sew. hemstitch; **vainilla** *f* vanilla.

vaivén *m* oscillation, rocking; swing,
sway; movement to and fro; (*ir y
venir*) coming and going, constant
movement; *fig.* unsteadiness; *pol.
etc.* swing, seesaw; ~es *pl.* ups and
downs.

vajilla *f* (*en general*) crockery; (*una
~*) set of dishes, service; ~ de oro
gold plate; ~ de porcelana china-
ware.

valdré etc. v. *valer.*

vale *m* promissory note, IOU; (*cédula*) voucher, warrant; **valedero**
valid, binding; ~ para 3 meses valid
for 3 months; ser ~ (*afirmación etc.*)
hold good; **valedor** *m*, **-a** *f* protector.

valencia *f* 🜍 valency.

valenciano *adj. a. su. m*, **a** *f*
Valencian.

valentía *f* courage, bravery; (*acto*)
brave deed; *b.s.* boastfulness;
valentón 1. boastful; arrogant;
2. *m* braggart; **valentonada** *f* brag,
bragging, boast(ing).

valer [2q] **1.** *v/t.* (*tener el valor de*) be
worth, be valued at; cost; (*sumar*)
amount to; be equal to, be equivalent to; *castigo etc.* earn; (*ayudar,
servir*) avail, be of help to, protect;
¿*cuánto vale?* how much is it?;
¡*válgame Dios!* goodness!, bless my
soul!; no ~ *nada* be worthless;
v. pena; **2.** *v/i.* (*ser valioso*) be
valuable; (*ser valedero*) be valid;
(*p. etc.*) have one's merits; count
en juegos etc.; es un hombre que vale
he is a man of some quality; ¿*vale?*
is that all right?, will that do?; eso
no vale that won't do, that's no
good; (*juegos etc.*) that doesn't
·count; *más vale así* it's just as well,
it's better this way; *más vale que no
vaya* I had better go; *más vale tarde
que nunca* better late than never; ~
para be useful for; ~ por be worth
be as good as; hacer ~ *derechos* assert; **3.** ~se: no poder ~ be helpless;
~ de make use of, avail o.s.; *derecho*
exercise; ~ por sí mismo help o.s.;
4. *m* value, worth.

valeriana *f* valerian.

valeroso brave; effective, powerful.

valetudinario *adj. a. su. m*, **a** *f*
valetudinarian.

valía *f* value, worth; influence.

validar [1a] ratify, validate; **validez**
f validity; **válido** valid; (*sano*)
strong, fit; **valido** *m pol.* favourite.

valiente brave, gallant; (*excelente*)
fine, first-rate; *iro.* fine.

valija *f* case; 🜍 (*saco*) mail-bag;
(*correo*) mail, post; ~ diplomática
diplomatic bag.

valimiento *m* influence (*cerca de
with*); favour, protection.

valioso valuable; useful, worthwhile; (*rico*) wealthy; (*poderoso*)
powerful.

valor *m* value (a. ♪, ♪); worth;
price; value, denomination de
moneda etc.; importance; (*sentido*)
meaning; (*ánimo*) courage; (*atrevimiento*) nerve, audacity; ♱ ~es *pl.*
securities, bonds, stock; ~ alimenticio food-value; ~es *pl.* en cartera
investments; ~es *pl. habidos* hold-
ings; ~ nominal face value, nominal
value; ~ sentimental sentimental
value; *objetos de ~* valuables; sin ~
worthless.

valoración *f* ♱ valuation; *fig.* assessment; 🜍 titration; **valorar** [1a]
value; price; *esp. fig.* assess, rate,
appraise; 🜍 titrate; **valorizar**
[1f] valorize; = valorar.

vals *m* waltz; **valsar** [1a] waltz.

valuar [1e] etc. = valorar etc.

valva *f* ♀, zo. valve.

válvula *f* valve; ~ de admisión inlet
valve; ~ de escape exhaust valve;
~ de purga vent; ~ de seguridad
safety-valve.

valla *f* fence; (*defensa*) barricade,
stockade; ~ (*de construcción*) hoarding; *fig.* obstacle; *deportes:* hurdle;
v. carrera; **valladar** *m*, **vallado** *m*
= valla; **vallar** [1a] fence in, enclose.

valle *m* valley; ~ de lágrimas vale of
tears.

vallisoletano *adj. a. su. m*, **a** *f*
(native) of Valladolid.

vamos v. ir.

vampiresa *f* vamp; **vampiro** *m*
vampire; *fig.* vampire, bloodsucker.

vanagloria *f* vainglory; **vanaglo-
riarse** [1b]: ~ de boast of; **vanaglorioso** vainglorious, boastful.

vandálico Vandal(ic); **vandalismo** *m* vandalism; **vándalo** *m*, **a** *f* Vandal; *fig.* vandal.

vanguardia *f* van(guard) (*a. fig.*).

vanidad *f* vanity; uselessness *etc.*; **vanidoso** vain, conceited, smug; **vano** useless, vain, idle; (*ilusorio*) vain; (*frívolo*) inane, idle, frivolous; **en ~** in vain.

vapor *m* steam (*a.* ⊕), vapour; (*natural*) vapour, mist; (*con olor*) fumes; 🐟 faintness, giddiness; ⚓ steamer, steamship; 🐟 **~es** *pl.* vapours, hysteria; **~ de agua** water-vapour; **~ correo** mailboat; **~ de ruedas** paddle-steamer; **~ volandero** tramp (steamer); **al ~** by steam; **de ~** steam *attr.*; **cocer al ~** steam; **echar ~** steam; **vaporizador** *m* vaporizer; spray *de perfume etc.*; **vaporizar** [1f] vapourize; *perfume etc.* spray; **vaporoso** steamy, misty, vaporous; *fig.* light, airy.

vapulear [1a] thrash, flog; beat up; **vapuleo** *m* thrashing *etc.*

vaquería *f* dairy; (*vacada*) herd of cows; **vaquer(iz)o** *m* herdsman, cowman, cowboy *Am.*; **vaqueta** *f* cowhide; **vaquill(on)a** *f S.Am.* heifer.

vara *f* stick, rod (*a.* ⊕), bar; wand *de mando*; shaft *de coche*; (*medida*) *approx.* yard (*2.8 feet*); **~ alta** authority, power; **varada** *f* launching; (*encalladura*) stranding; **varadero** *m* shipyard; **varal** *m* long pole, long stick; F lamp-post; **varapalo** *m* long pole; (*golpe*) blow with a stick; F trouble; setback, disappointment.

varar [1a] *v/t.* (*botar*) launch; beach *en playa etc.*; *v/i.*, **~se** run aground, be stranded; *fig.* get bogged down.

varazo *m* blow with a stick; **varear** [1a] *p.* beat, strike; beat *como castigo*; *fruta* knock down; *toro* stir up; *paño* sell by the yard.

varec *m* seaweed.

variabilidad *f* variability; **variable 1.** variable (*a.* 🜂), changeable, up-and-down; **2.** *f* 🜂 variable; **variación** *f* variation (*a.* ♩); **variado** varied; mixed; *superficie etc.* variegated, chequered; **variante** *adj. a. su. f* variant; **variar** [1c] *v/t.* vary, change; alter, modify; *v/i.*

vary; change; range (de from; *a* to); **~ de opinión** change.

várices *f/pl.* varicose veins.

varicela *f* chicken-pox.

variedad *f* variety (*a. biol.*); **teatro de ~es** variety theatre.

varilla *f* (thin) stick; ⊕ rod, bar, link; spoke *de rueda*; rib *de paraguas etc.*; curtain-rod; stay *de corsé*; **~** (*de virtudes, mágica*) wand; F *anat.* jaw-bone; **~ de zahorí** divining-rod; **varillaje** *m* rods, linkage; ribs, ribbing.

vario various, varied; *colorido* variegated, motley; *actividades* multifarious; (*inconstante*) changeable; **~s** *pl.* several, some, a number of.

varioloso pockmarked.

varita *f*: **~ mágica** wand.

varón *m* (*hombre*) man; (*macho*) male; (*de edad viril*) adult male; (*respetable*) worthy man, great man; **hijo ~** male child, boy; **santo ~** nice old chap; **varonil** manly, virile; *biol.* male, masculine.

vasallaje *m hist.* vassalage; *fig.* subjection; **vasallo** *m* vassal.

vasco(ngado) 1. *adj. a. su. m*, **a** *f* Basque; **2.** *m* (*idioma*; *a.* **vascuence** *m*) Basque.

vascular vascular.

vase = **se va**; *v. ir.*

vaselina *f* vaseline; petroleum jelly.

vasija *f* vessel; container.

vaso *m* glass, tumbler; (*en general*) vessel; *hist.* vase; (*cantidad*) glassful; *anat.*, ⚘ vessel, duct; hoof *de caballo*; **~ capilar** capillary; **~ de noche** chamber-pot; **~ sanguíneo** blood-vessel.

vástago *m* ⊕ rod, stem; ⚘ shoot, bud; *fig.* scion, offspring; **~ de émbolo** piston-rod.

vastedad *f* vastness; **vasto** vast, immense.

vate *m* poet, bard; **vaticinar** [1a] prophesy, predict; **vaticinio** *m* prophecy, prediction.

vatio *m* watt.

vaya *v. ir.*

vecinal *camino* local; **vecindad** *f* neighbourhood, vicinity; (*ps.*) neighbourhood, neighbours; **vecindario** *m* neighbourhood; community; (*cifra etc.*) population, inhabitants; **vecino 1.** neighbouring, adjoining; *casa etc.* next; (*cercano*) near, close; *fig.* close, similar (*a* to);

2. *m*, **a** *f* (*de al lado*) neighbour; (*habitante*) resident, inhabitant, citizen.

veda *f* (*acto*) prohibition; (*tiempo*) close season; **vedado** *m* preserve; *cazar etc.* en ~ poach; **vedar** [1a] forbid, prohibit; (*impedir*) stop, prevent; *proyecto etc.* veto.

vedette [be'ðet] *f* star.

vedija *f* tuft of wool (*or* hair); (*greña*) mat, matted hair.

vega *f* fertile plain; water-meadow(s); *S.Am.* tobacco-plantation.

vegetación *f* vegetation; (*desarrollo*) growth; **vegetal 1.** plant *attr.*, vegetable; **2.** *m* plant, vegetable; **vegetar** [1a] grow; *esp. fig.* vegetate; **vegetariano** *adj. a. su. m*, **a** *f* vegetarian; **vegetativo** vegetative.

veguero 1. country *attr.*, lowland *attr.*; **2.** *m* farmer; *S.Am.* tobacco planter; (*puro*) cigar.

vehemencia *f* vehemence *etc.*; **vehemente** vehement, passionate; *partidario etc.* fervent, red-hot; *deseo* eager, fervent.

vehículo *m* vehicle (*a. fig.*).

veinte twenty; (*fecha*) twentieth; **veintena** *f* a score, (about) twenty; **veintiuna** *f* pontoon (*game*).

vejación *f* vexation; **vejamen** *m* vexation; (*reprensión*) sharp rebuke; (*pulla*) taunt.

vejancón *m* F, **vejarrón** *m* F old boy, geezer.

vejar [1a] vex, annoy; **vejatorio** vexatious, annoying.

vejestorio *m*, **vejete** *m* old boy, little old man.

vejez *f* old age; *fig.* old story.

vejiga *f anat.* bladder (*a. de pelota*); (*ampolla*) blister; ~ *natatoria* air-bladder.

vela¹ *f* ♣ sail; (*toldo*) awning; ~ *de cruz* square sail; ~ *mayor* mainsail; F *entre dos* ~*s* half-seas-over; *darse* (*or hacerse*) *a la* ~ (set) sail, get under way.

vela² *f* wakefulness, being awake; (*trabajo*) night work; (*romería*) pilgrimage; (*velación*) vigil; candle; *pasar la noche en* ~ have a sleepless night; **velada** *f* evening party, soirée; party, social *para divertirse*; = *vela*; ~ *musical* musical evening; **velador** *m* candlestick; (*p.*) watchman, caretaker.

velamen *m* sails.

velar¹ [1a] veil (*a. fig.*); *phot.* fog. veil; *fig.* shroud; ~**se** *phot.* fog.

velar² [1a] *v/t.* keep watch over, watch; *enfermo* sit up with; *v/i.* (*no dormir*) stay awake; stay up, sit up at night; *eccl. etc.* keep vigil; (*trabajar*) work late; ~ *por* watch over, look after; ~ *por que* see to it that.

veleidad *f* fickleness; (*capricho*) whim; (*intento*) half-hearted attempt (*de* at); **veleidoso** fickle, inconstant; capricious, flighty.

velero 1. swift; **2.** *m* ♣ sailing-ship; ➤ glider.

veleta *f* weather-vane, weathercock; float *de pescar*; F person who chops and changes.

velo *m* veil; *fig.* veil, shroud, film; pretext; *phot.* fog, veil(ing); ~ *del paladar* soft palate; *tomar el* ~ take the veil.

velocidad *f* speed, pace, rate; velocity; (*ligereza*) swiftness; ⊕, *mot.* speed; (*engranaje*) gear; *de alta* ~ high-speed; ~ *económica* cruising speed; *límite de* ~*s*, ~ *máxima permitida* speed limit; *primera* ~ low gear, bottom gear; *segunda* ~ second gear; *a toda* ~ at full speed; **velocímetro** *m* speedometer; **velódromo** *m* cycle track.

velón *m* oil lamp.

veloz fast, speedy; (*ligero*) swift, quick.

vello *m* down, hair; ♀ bloom; **vellocino** *m* fleece; ~ *de oro* Golden Fleece; **vellosidad** *f* hairiness *etc.*; **vellón** *m* (*lana*) fleece; (*piel*) sheepskin; *metall.* copper alloy; **velloso** hairy; downy; fluffy; **velludo** shaggy.

vena *f anat.* vein; (*filón*) vein, seam; grain *de piedra, madera*; streak *de locura etc.*; *poet.* inspiration; *estar de* ~ be in (good) form; *estar en* ~ be in the vein, be in the mood (*para* for).

venablo *m* dart, javelin; F *echar* ~*s* blow one's top.

venado *m* deer, stag; (*carne*) venison.

venal¹ *anat.* venous.

venal² that can be bought; for sale; *p.* venal, mercenary; *no* ~*es libros* not to be sold; **venalidad** *f* venality.

venatorio hunting *attr.*

vencedor 1. *equipo etc.* winning;

general, país conquering, victorious; **2.** *m*, **-a** *f* winner; victor, conqueror.
vencejo *m* orn. swift; (*lazo*) band, string.
vencer [2b] *v/t. enemigo* defeat, beat, conquer; *deportes*: beat; *rival* surpass, outdo; *pasión etc.* master; *dificultad* get over, surmount; *v/i.* win; ✝ (*plazo*) expire; (*obligaciones*) mature, fall due; **~se** control o.s.; **vencida**: *a la tercera va la ~ (para animar)* third time lucky; (*aviso*) you won't get away with it next time; *ir de ~* be all in, be on one's last legs; **vencido** *equipo etc.* losing; ✝ mature; due, payable; *darse por ~* give in, give up; **vencimiento** *m* ✝ expiration; maturity.
venda *f* bandage; **vendaje** *m* dressing, bandaging; *~ provisional* first-aid bandage; **vendar** [1a] *herida* bandage, dress; *ojos etc.* cover; (*atar*) bind; *fig.* blind.
vendaval *m* gale, strong wind.
vendedor *m* seller, vendor; salesman *de tienda etc.*; *~ ambulante* pedlar, hawker; **vendedora** *f* seller; salesgirl, saleswoman *en tienda etc.*; **vender** [2a] sell; market; *fig.* sell, betray, give away; **~se** sell (*bien etc.*); be sold; *~ a, ~ por* sell at, sell for; fetch; *se vende* (*anuncios*) for sale; **vendible** saleable, marketable.
vendimia *f* grape-harvest; vintage *esp. de 1960 etc.*; *fig.* big profit, killing; **vendimiador** *m*, **-a** *f* vintager; **vendimiar** [1b] pick, gather; *fig.* profit by, take a profit from.
vendré *etc. v. venir.*
veneciano *adj. a. su. m,* **a** *f* Venetian.
veneno *m* poison, venom; **venenoso** poisonous, venomous.
venera *f* zo. scallop; (*cáscara*) scallop-shell.
venerable venerable; **veneración** *f* veneration, worship; **venerar** [1a] venerate, revere, worship.
venéreo venereal.
venero *m* spring; *min.* lode; *fig.* source, origin.
venezolano *adj. a. su. m,* **a** *f* Venezuelan.
vengador 1. avenging; **2.** *m*, **-a** *f* avenger; **venganza** *f* vengeance, revenge; retaliation; **vengar** [1h] avenge; **~se** take revenge (*de* for,

en on); retaliate (*en* on, against);
vengativo vindictive; *medida etc.* retaliatory.
vengo *etc. v. venir.*
venia *f* pardon, forgiveness; (*permiso*) leave, consent; (*saludo*) nod; **venial** venial.
venida *f* (*llegada*) arrival, coming; (*regreso*) return; *fig.* impetuosity, rashness; **venidero** coming, forthcoming, future; *los ~s* future generations, posterity.
venir [3s] come (*a* to; *de* from); *el mes que viene* next month; *eso vengo diciendo* that's what I've been saying all along; *vengo cansado* I'm tired; *¿a qué viene ...?* what's the point of ...?; *¡venga!* come along!; *¡venga un beso!* let's have a kiss!; *¡venga el libro ese!* let's have a look at that book!; *venga lo que viniere* come what may; (*estar a*) *ver ~* sit on the fence, wait and see; *~ a su.* agree to, consent to; *~ a inf.* come to *inf.*; (*terminar*) end by *ger.*, end up *ger.*; (*suceder*) happen to *inf.*; (*acertar*) manage to *inf.*; *~ a ser* (*sumar*) amount to, work out at; (*resultar*) turn out to be; *~ a menos* come down in the world; *~ bien* ✝ *etc.* do well, grow well; (*objeto*) come in handy; *~ bien a* (*vestido*) fit, suit; *te viene muy estrecho* it's too tight for you; *~ en inf.* resolve to *inf.*, agree to *inf.*; *~ por* come for; **~se** ferment; *~ abajo, ~ a tierra* collapse, tumble down.
venoso *sangre* venous; *hoja etc.* veined.
venta *f* sale; selling, marketing; (*mesón*) inn; *~ al contado* cash sale; *~ de liquidación* clearance sale; *~ a plazos* hire-purchase; *~ por balance* stocktaking sale; *~ pública* (public) auction; *precio de ~* selling-price; *de ~* on sale, on the market; *en ~* for sale; *poner a la ~* put on sale, market.
ventada *f* gust of wind.
ventaja *f* advantage; asset; start *en carrera*; *tenis*: vantage; odds *en juego*; (*sobresueldo*) bonus; (*ganancia*) gain, profit; *llevar la ~ a* be ahead of, have the upper hand over; **ventajoso** advantageous; ✝ profitable.
ventana *f* window; *~ de guillotina* sash-window; *~ de la nariz* nostril;

~ *salediza* bay-window; **ventanaje** *m* windows; **ventanal** *m* large window; sash-window; **ventanear** [1a] F be always at the window; **ventanilla** *f* small window; window *de coche etc.*; *anat.* nostril; **ventanillo** *m* small window; peep-hole *en puerta.*

ventarrón *m* gale, high wind.

ventear [1a] *v/t.* (*perro etc.*) sniff, scent; *ropa* air, put out to dry; *fig.* smell out; *v/i.* snoop, come sniffing around; *impersonal:* blow; **~se** (*henderse*) split; (*arruinarse*) spoil (out in the air); **venteo** *m* sniff(ing); *fig.* snooping.

ventero *m*, **a** *f* innkeeper.

ventilación *f* ventilation (*a. fig.*); *fig.* airing, discussion; **ventilado** draughty, breezy; **ventilador** *m* ventilator, (electric) fan; **ventilar** [1a] ventilate (*a. fig.*); *fig.* air, discuss.

ventisca *f* blizzard, snow-storm; **ventiscar** [1g] blow a blizzard; **ventisquero** *m* blizzard; glacier; (*montón*) snowdrift.

ventolera *f* gust of wind; (*molinete*) (toy) windmill; F smugness, conceit; whim, wild idea.

ventosa *f* 🐝 cupping-glass; *zo.* sucker; (*abertura*) vent, air-hole; **ventosear** [1a] break wind; **ventosidad** *f* wind, flatulence; **ventoso** windy.

ventral ventral.

ventregada *f* brood, litter.

ventrículo *m* ventricle.

ventrílocuo *m*, **a** *f* ventriloquist; **ventriloquia** *f* ventriloquism.

ventura *f* luck, (good) fortune; (*dicha*) happiness; *a la* (*buena*) ~ at random; hit or miss; *por* ~ by chance; (*quizá*) perhaps; (*afortunadamente*) luckily; **venturoso** lucky, fortunate, happy.

ver [2v] **1.** *mst* see; (*mirar*) look at; (*examinar*) look into; ⚖ hear, try; *le vi llegar* I saw him arrive; *lo vi hacer* I saw it done; *lo veo* I see; *según voy viendo* as I am now beginning to see; *véase* see, vide; *¡a ~!* let's see, let's have a look; *a mi modo de* ~ in my opinion; ~ *y creer* seeing is believing; *dejarse* ~ (*p.*) show one's face, show up; (*efecto*) become apparent; *dejarse* ~ *en* tell on; *no dejarse* ~

keep away; *echar de* ~ notice; *estar por* ~ remain to be seen; *hacer* ~ *que* make *s.o.* see that; make the point that *en discusión*; *no poder* ~ not be able to stand; *ser de* ~ be worth seeing; *no tener nada que* ~ *con* have nothing to do with; *vamos a* ~ let me see; **2.** **~se** be seen; (*reflexivo*) see o.s.; (*recíproco*) see each other; (*encontrarse*) (*una p.*) find o.s., be; (*dos ps.*) meet; *ya se ve* naturally; *ya se ve que* it is obvious that; ~ *con* see, have a talk with; **3.** *m* sight, vision; (*aspecto*) looks, appearance; opinion; *a mi* ~ in my opinion; *tener buen* ~ look all right.

vera *f* edge, verge; *a la* ~ *de* near, beside.

veracidad *f* truthfulness, veracity.

veranda *f* veranda(h).

veraneante *m/f* holiday-maker, vacationist *Am.*; **veranear** [1a] spend the summer (holiday), holiday; **veraneo** *m* summer holiday; *lugar de* ~, *punto de* ~ summer resort; **veraniego** summer *attr.*; summery; *fig.* slight, trivial; **veranillo** *m*: ~ *de San Martín* Indian summer; **verano** *m* summer.

veras *f/pl.* truth, reality; (*seriedad*) earnestness; serious matters, hard facts; *de* ~ really; (*en serio*) in earnest; *¿de* ~*?* really?, indeed?; *va de* ~ it's the real thing.

veraz truthful, veracious.

verbal verbal; oral.

verbena *f* fair; (*velada*) evening party; *eccl.* night festival; *hist.* wake; ♀ verbena.

verbigracia for example.

verbo *m* *gr.* verb; *el* ♀ the Word; **verborrea** *f* F, **verbosidad** *f* wordiness, verbosity; **verboso** wordy, verbose.

verdad *f* truth; *la* ~ *lisa y llana* the plain truth; *la pura* ~ *es* the fact of the matter is; *a la* ~ really, in truth; *de* ~ real, proper; *en* ~ really, truly; *es* ~ it is true (*que that*); *¿no es* ~*?, ¿*~*?* isn't it?, don't you? etc.*; isn't that so?; *decir cuatro verdades a* tell *s.o.* a few home truths, give *s.o.* a piece of one's mind; **verdaderamente** really, truly, indeed; **verdadero** *historia etc.* true, truthful; *p.* truthful; (*real, cierto*) true, real, veritable.

verde 1. green; *fruta* green, unripe; *madera* unseasoned; (*fresco*) fresh; (*lozano*) young, vigorous, lusty; *cuento etc.* dirty, low, smutty; ¡*están* ~*s!* sour grapes!; F *poner* ~ abuse; run down; dress down; **2.** *m* green; ✿ greenery, foliage; *darse un* ~ take a bit of time off; **verdear** [1a], **verdecer** [2d] (*estar*) look green; (*hacerse*) turn green, grow green; **verdegay** *m adj. a. su.* *m* light green; **verdemar** *m* sea-green; **verdete** *m* verdigris; **verdín** *m* ✿ scum *en estanque*, moss *en árbol*; (*verdete*) verdigris; **verdinegro** dark green; **verdor** *m* greenness; *esp.* ✿ verdure; *fig.* youthful vigour; **verdoso** greenish.

verdugo *m* executioner, hangman; *fig.* (*p.*) tormentor; (*cosa*) torment; ✿ shoot, sucker; (*azote*) lash; = **verdugón** *m* weal, welt.

verdulera *f* *fig.* vulgar woman; **verdulería** *f* greengrocery; (*tienda*) greengrocer's (shop); **verdulero** *m*, a *f* greengrocer.

verdura *f* greenness; *esp.* ✿ greenery, verdure; ~*s* *pl.* greens(tuff), vegetables.

vereda *f* path, lane; *S.Am.* pavement.

veredicto *m* verdict.

verga *f* ♩ yard(-arm), spar; *anat.* penis; **vergajo** *m* pizzle.

vergonzante shame-faced; **vergonzoso** (*tímido*) bashful, shy; (*pudoroso*) modest; (*que causa vergüenza*) shameful, disgraceful; *anat. partes* private; **vergüenza** *f* shame; bashfulness, shyness; modesty; honour; (*oprobio*) shame; ¡*qué* ~*!* shame (on you)!, what a disgrace!; *me da* ~ *inf.* it upsets me to have to *inf.*, I find it embarrassing to *inf.*; *tener* ~ be ashamed (*de inf.* to *inf.*).

vericueto *m* rough track.

verídico true, truthful; **verificable** verifiable; **verificación** *f* checking, check-up, verification; proving; realization *de suceso etc.*; **verificar** [1g] (*comprobar*) check (up on), verify; *hechos* establish, substantiate; *testamento* prove; *contador etc.* inspect; (*efectuar*) carry out; ~*se* (*tener lugar*) take place; (*ser verdad*) prove true, come true.

verismo *m* realism, truthfulness.

verja *f* (*reja*) grating, grill; (*puerta*) (iron) gate; (*valla*) railing(s).

vermicida *m* vermicide; **vermicular** vermicular; **vermiforme** vermiform; **vermífugo** *m* vermifuge.

verminoso verminous.

vermut *m* [ber'mu] vermouth.

vernáculo vernacular; *lengua* ~*a* vernacular.

vernal spring *attr.*, vernal.

vernier *m* vernier.

verónica *f* ✿ veronica, speedwell; *a pass in bullfighting*.

verosímil likely, probable; *relato* credible; **verosimilitud** *f* likeliness, probability; *lit. etc.* verisimilitude; credibility.

verraco *m* boar; **verraquear** [1a] F grunt; (*niño*) howl with rage; **verraquera** *f* violent crying.

verruga *f* wart (*a.* ✿); *fig.* defect; (*p.*) bore, nuisance; **verrugoso** warty.

versado: ~ *en* versed in, conversant with.

versal *adj. a. su. f typ.* capital; **versalitas** *f*/*pl. typ.* small capitals.

versar [1a] turn, go round; ~ *sobre* *fig. materia* deal with, discuss; *tema* turn on.

versátil *miembro etc.* mobile, easily turned; (*inconstante*) changeable; (*talentoso*) versatile; **versatilidad** *f* changeableness *etc.*

versículo *m* verse; **versificación** *f* versification; **versificar** [1g] *v/t.* versify; *v/i.* write verses.

versión *f* version; draft; translation.

verso *m* (*en general*) verse; (*un* ~) line; ~ *suelto* blank verse.

vértebra *f* vertebra; **vertebrado** *adj. a. su. m* vertebrate; **vertebral** vertebral.

vertedero *m* rubbish dump, tip; = **vertedor** *m* (*canal*) overflow, drain; **spillway** *de río*; ♩ scoop (*a. de tendero*), bailer; **verter** [2g] *v/t. líquido, sal etc.* pour (out); (*por accidente*) spill; *luz, lágrimas* shed; *desechos* dump, tip; *vasija* empty, tip up; (*traducir*) translate (*a into*); *v/i.* flow, run.

vertical vertical (*a.* ♈), upright; **vértice** *m* apex, vertex; *anat.* crown of the head.

verticilo *m* whorl.

vertiente *mst f* slope.
vertiginoso giddy, dizzy, vertiginous; **vértigo** *m* giddiness, dizziness, vertigo.
vesícula *f* vesicle; (*ampolla*) blister; ~ biliar gall bladder.
vespertino evening *attr.*
vestal *adj. a. su. f* vestal.
vestíbulo *m* vestibule; hall, lobby; *thea.* foyer.
vestido *m* (*en general*) dress, clothing; dress, frock *de mujer*; (*conjunto*) costume, suit; **vestidor** *m* dressing-room; **vestidura** *f* clothing; ~s *pl. eccl.* vestments.
vestigial vestigial; **vestigio** *m* vestige, trace, sign; relic; ~s *pl.* (*restos*) remains.
vestimenta *f* raiment, clothing.
vestir [3l] 1. *v/t. p. etc.* dress, clothe (*de in*); (*cubrir*) dress, cover, drape (*de in, with*); (*adornar*) dress up; embellish, trim; *vestido* (*ponerse*) put on, (*llevar*) wear; (*sastre*) make clothes for; *vestido de* dressed in, clad in; (*como disfraz etc.*) dressed as; 2. *v/i.* dress (*bien well!*); ~ de dress in, wear; 3. ~se (*p.*) dress, get dressed; (*cubrirse*) get covered (*de with*); *importancia* assume.
vestuario *m* (*vestidos*) clothes, wardrobe; *thea.* (*trajes*) wardrobe; (*cuarto*) dressing-room; ✕ uniform; *deportes:* changing-room, pavilion; (*guardarropa*) cloakroom.
veta *f* seam, vein; grain *en madera etc.*; *fig.* talents, inclinations.
vetar [1a] veto.
veteado 1. veined; *madera etc.* grained; 2. *m* graining.
veterano *adj. a. su. m* veteran.
veterinaria *f* veterinary science; **veterinario** *m* vet(erinary one); **veto** *m* veto; *poner* ~ *a* veto. [geon).]
vetustez *f* great age, antiquity; **vetusto** very old, ancient; hoary.
vez *f* 1. time, occasion; (*caso*) instance; (*turno*) turn; *a la* ~ at a time, at the same time; *a su* ~ in his turn; *alguna* ~ sometimes; *¿le ves alguna* ~? do you ever see him?; (*alg*)*una* (*que otra*) ~ occasionally; *cada* ~ every time; *cada* ~ *más* increasingly, more and more; *le veo cada* ~ *más delgado* he seems to get thinner and thinner; *de una* ~ in one go, at

once, outright; *de una* ~ (*para siempre*) once and for all, for good; *de* ~ *en cuando* now and again, from time to time; *en* ~ *de* instead of; *otra* ~ again; *rara* ~ seldom; *tal* ~ perhaps; *una* ~ (*que*) once; 2. **veces** *pl.* times *etc.*; *dos* ~ twice; *dos* ~ *tanto* twice as much; *a* ~ at times; *algunas* ~ sometimes; *¿cuántas* ~? how many times?, how often?; *las más* ~ in most cases, most times; *muchas* ~ often; *pocas* ~ seldom; *repetidas* ~ repeatedly, time after time; *hacer las* ~ *de* act as, take the place of.
veza *f* vetch.
vía 1. *f* road; route, way; 🚂 (*rieles*) track, line; (*ancho*) gauge; (*número de andén*) platform; *anat.* passage, tract; *fig.* way, means; (*oficial etc.*) channel; ✆ ~ *aérea* airmail; ~ *de agua* leak; ~ *ancha* broad gauge; ~ *doble* double track; *de* ~ *estrecha* narrow-gauge; ~ *férrea* railway; ~ *fluvial* waterway; ♀ *Láctea* Milky Way; ~ *muerta* siding; ~ *normal* standard gauge; ~ *pública* thoroughfare; *en* ~ *de* in process of; *por* ~ *de vía*, by way of; *por* ~ *bucal* orally; *por* ~ *marítima* by sea; *por* ~ *terrestre* overland; 2. *prp.* vía.
viable viable; *proyecto* feasible.
viaducto *m* viaduct.
viajante 1. travelling; 2. *m/f* traveller; 3. *m* ✝ commercial traveller, salesman; **viajar** [1a] travel (*a. ✝*); go; ~ *en coche etc.* ride; ~ *por* travel (through); tour *de vacaciones;* **viaje** *m* journey; ⚓ voyage; (*breve, de excursión*) trip; (*jira, de vacaciones*) tour; (*en general*) travel (*mst* ~s *pl.*); ~ *en coche etc. a.* ride; ~ *de ensayo* trial run, trial trip; ~ *de ida y vuelta* return journey; ~ *de novios* honeymoon; ~ *de recreo* pleasure trip; *¡buen* ~! have a good trip!, bon voyage!; *estar de* ~ be away (on one's travels); be on tour; **viajero** *m*, *a f* traveller; 🚂 *etc.* passenger.
vianda *f* (*a.* ~s *pl.*) food.
viandante *m/f* traveller.
viático *m* travel allowance; food for a journey; *eccl.* viaticum.
víbora *f* viper (*a. fig.*).
vibración *f* vibration; throb(bing); *phonet.* roll, trill; **vibrante** vibrat-

ing; *phonet.* rolled, trilled; *fig.*
vibrant (de with); **vibrar** [1a] *v/t.*
vibrate; *phonet.* roll, trill; *v/i.*
vibrate; throb, pulsate; **vibratorio**
vibratory.

vicario *m eccl.* curate; (*suplente*)
deputy; ~ *general* vicar general.

vice... vice...; **~almirante** *m* vice-
admiral; **~canciller** *m* vice-chancellor; **~cónsul** *m* vice-consul;
~gerente *m* assistant manager;
~presidencia *f* vice-presidency;
vice-chairmanship; **~presidente** *m*
pol. etc. vice-president; vice-
chairman *de comité.*

viceversa vice versa.

viciado *aire* foul, thick, stale; *texto*
corrupt; **viciar** [1b] *aire* make
foul; *comida etc.* taint, spoil; *texto*
corrupt, falsify; *costumbres* corrupt,
pervert; *contrato*, ⚖ nullify;
(*quitar valor a*) vitiate, spoil; **~se**
fig. get depraved; **vicio** *m mst*
vice; defect; *gr. etc.* mistake; *de ~,*
por ~ (*de mimo*) from being spoiled;
(*por costumbre*) out of sheer habit;
vicioso 1. *mst* vicious (*a. phls.*);
gusto etc. depraved; ⊕ defective,
faulty; *niño* spoiled; ♀ rank,
luxuriant; **2.** *m,* **a** *f* addict, fiend.

vicisitudes *f/pl.* vicissitudes.

víctima *f* victim; (*p. o animal*
sacrificado) sacrifice; prey *de ave*
etc.; ser ~ *de fig.* be a prey to.

victoria *f* victory; **victorioso**
vid *f* vine.   [victorious.]

vida *f mst* life; (*duración*) life(time);
(*modo de vivir*) way of life, living;
(*modo de sustentarse*) livelihood;
de ~ airada loose-living; ~ *de perros*
dog's life; *¡~ mía!* my love!; *¡por ~*
mía! upon my soul!; *de por ~* for
life; *de toda la ~* lifelong; *en la ~,*
en mi ~ never in my life; *en ~ in his*
etc. lifetime; *darse buena ~* live in
style, do o.s. proud; *dar mala ~ a*
ill-treat; *estar con ~* be alive; *ga-*
narse la ~ earn a living; *hacer ~ b.s.*
live together.

vidente *m/f* seer; clairvoyant.

vidriado 1. glazed; **2.** *m* glaze,
glazing; (*loza*) glazed earthenware;
vidriar [1b] glaze, glass; **vidriera**
f eccl. stained-glass window; *S.Am.*
shop-window; (*puerta*) ~ glass
door; **vidriería** *f* glass-works;
(*vasos*) glassware; **vidriero** *m*
glazier; **vidrio** *m* glass; ~ *cilindrado*

plate-glass; ~ *de color* stained
glass; ~ *deslustrado* frosted glass,
ground glass; ~ *tallado* cut glass;
F *pagar los ~s rotos* carry the can;
vidrioso glassy; *mirada* glazed,
glassy; (*resbaladizo*) like glass;
(*quebradizo*) brittle; delicate; *p.*
touchy, sensitive.

vieja *f* old woman; **viejo 1.** old;
(*anticuado*) old(-fashioned); *no-*
ticia stale; **2.** *m* old man; ~ *verde*
gay old dog; *b.s.* old goat, dirty
old man.

vienés *adj. a. su. m,* **-a** *f* Viennese.

viento *m* wind (*a. ♪, fig.*, F); air;
hunt. scent; (*cuerda*) guy (rope);
fig. vanity; **~s** *pl. alisios* trade
winds; ⚓ ~ *ascendente* up-current;
~ *contrario* headwind; ~ *de la hélice*
slipstream; ~ *en popa* following
wind; *ir ~ en popa fig.* get along
splendidly; F *beber etc. los ~s por*
be crazy about; *hacer ~* be windy.

vientre *m* belly (*a. fig.*); (*útero*)
womb; (*intestino*) bowels; ✻ ~ *flojo*
looseness of the bowels.

viernes *m* Friday; ♀ *Santo* Good
Friday.

viga *f* △ beam, rafter; girder *de*
metal; (*madero*) balk, timber.

vigencia *f* operation, validity; *en ~*
= **vigente** in force, valid.

vigésimo twentieth.

vigía 1. *f* watchtower; ⚓ reef; **2.** *m*
look-out, watch.

vigilancia *f* vigilance, watchfulness;
vigilante 1. vigilant, watchful;
2. *m* watchman, caretaker; warder
de cárcel; shopwalker *en tienda;*
~ *de noche* night-watchman; **vi-**
gilar [1a] watch (over), keep an
eye on (*a. ~ por*); *trabajo etc.*
supervise, superintend; *máquina*
tend; *frontera* guard, police;
vigilia *f eccl. etc.* vigil; (*día de*)
~ fast-day; (*desvelo*) watchfulness;
(*víspera*) eve; (*trabajo*) study, night
work, lucubrations; *comer de ~*
abstain from meat; *pasar la noche*
de ~ spend a night without sleep.

vigor *m mst* vigour; validity;
(*resistencia*) stamina, hardiness;
(*ímpetu*) drive; *en ~* in force,
operative; *entrar en ~* come into
force; *poner en ~* put into effect,
enforce; **vigorizar** [1f] invigorate;
(*animar*) encourage; **vigoroso** *mst*
vigorous; strong, forceful; *esfuerzo*

a. strenuous; *proyecto etc. a.* bold;
niño etc. a. sturdy.
viguería *f* beams, rafters; (*metal*)
steel frame; **vigueta** *f* joist, small
beam. [Vigo.)
vigués *adj. a. su. m,* **-a** *f* (native) of)
vil villainous, blackguardly; low,
base; *hecho* vile, foul; *tratamiento*
shabby; **vileza** *f* vileness *etc.*; (*acto*)
base deed.
vilipendiar [1b] vilify; (*despreciar*)
despise, scorn; **vilipendio** *m*
vilification; contempt, scorn; **vili-
pendioso** contemptible.
vilo: en ~ in the air; *fig.* all in the
air, undecided.
villa *f* (*romana, quinta, de veraneo*)
villa; (*población*) small town;
(*municipio*) borough; *La* ♀ *esp.*
Madrid; **villalata** *f* shack, tin hut;
villanaje *m* peasantry, villagers.
villancico *m* carol.
villanesco peasant *attr.*; *fig.* rustic;
villanía *f* baseness, villainy; (*acto
etc.*) foul thing; (*nacimiento*) humble
birth; **villano 1.** rustic; *fig.* coarse;
2. *m,* **a** *f hist.* villein; low-born
person; peasant (*a. fig.*).
villorrio *m* one-horse town, dump.
vinagre *m* vinegar; **vinagrera** *f*
vinegar-bottle; *S.Am.* heartburn;
~s *pl.* cruet-stand; **vinagroso**
vinegary; *fig.* bad-tempered.
vinatería *f* wine shop; wine trade;
vinatero 1. wine *attr.*; **2.** *m* wine-
merchant, vintner.
vinaza *f* nasty wine; **vinazo** *m*
strong wine.
vinculación *f* linking *etc.*; ♏ entail;
vincular [1a] (*ligar*) link, bind;
esperanzas base, found (*en* on);
perpetuate; ♏ entail; **vínculo** *m*
link, bond, tie; ♏ entail.
vindicación *f* vindication; **vindicar**
[1g] vindicate; **vindicativo** vindictive.
vine *etc. v.* venir.
vínico wine *attr.*; **vinícola** wine
(-growing) *attr.*; **vinicultor** *m*
wine-grower; **vinicultura** *f* wine-
growing, production of wine;
vinillo *m* weak wine; **vino** *m*
wine; **~** *añejo* mellow wine; **~** *blanco*
white wine; **~** *espumoso* sparkling
wine; **~** *generoso* strong wine,
full-bodied wine; **~** *de Jerez*
sherry; **~** *de mesa,* **~** *de pasto* table
wine; **~** *de Oporto* port (wine); **~** *de*

postre dessert wine; **~** *seco* dry
wine; **~** *tinto* red wine; *dormir el* **~**
sleep off a hangover; **vinoso** like
wine, vinous; *p.* too fond of wine.
viña *f* vineyard; **viñador** *m* vine-
grower; wine-grower; **viñedo** *m*)
viñeta *f* vignette. [vineyard.)
viola *f* ♪, ♀ viola; **violáceo** violet.
violación *f mst* violation; **~** (*de la
ley*) offence, infringement; outrage
(*de on*); rape; **violador** *m,* **-a** *f*
violator *etc.*; **violar** [1a] *mst*
violate; *ley a.* break, offend against;
(*ultrajar*) outrage; *lugar sagrado a.*
desecrate; *mujer* rape.
violencia *f* violence (*a. fig.*); *fig.*
fury; embarrassment; embarrassing
situation; ♏ assault, violence;
hacer **~** *a* = **violentar** [1a] *casa*
break into; ♏ assault; *fig.* do
violence to, outrage; *sentido* distort,
force; **~se** force o.s.; **violento** *mst*
violent; *fig. a.* wild; *postura*
awkward, unnatural; *situación etc.*
awkward, embarrassing; *sentido*
distorted; *mostrarse* **~** turn violent,
offer violence; *sentirse* **~** feel
awkward, feel embarrassed.
violeta *f* violet.
violín *m* violin; (*p.*) = **violinista**
m/f violinist; **violón** *m* double-
bass; F *tocar el* **~** have a silly sort
of job; **violencelista** *m/f* cellist;
violoncelo *m* cello.
vira *f* dart; welt *de zapato.*
virada *f* tack(ing); **viraje** *m* ♏
tack, turn; bend *de camino*;
swerve, turn *de coche*; *pol.* swing
de votos, volte-face *de política*;
phot. toning; **~** *en horquilla* hairpin
bend; **virar** [1a] *v/t.* put about;
phot. tone; *v/i.,* **~se** ♏ go about,
tack; veer (round) (*a. fig.*); *mot.,*
♏ turn, swerve; *pol.* (*votos*)
swing; (*política*) veer round,
change round.
virgen *adj. a. su. f* virgin; **virginal**
maidenly, virginal; **virginidad** *f*
virginity; **virgo** *m* virginity; *ast.* ♀
Virgo.
viril virile; *esp. carácter* manly; *v.
edad*; **virilidad** *f* virility; manliness; (*edad*) manhood.
virola *f* collar; ⊕ ferrule.
virolento pockmarked.
virote *m* arrow; F (*joven*) man
about town; (*p. grave*) solemn
sort.

virreinal viceregal; **virreinato** *m* viceroyalty; **virrey** *m* viceroy.

virtual virtual; *fuerza* potential; *imagen etc.* apparent.

virtud *f* virtue; efficacy; *en ~ de* in (*or* by) virtue of, by reason of; **virtuosismo** *m* virtuosity; **virtuoso 1.** virtuous; **2.** *m* virtuoso.

viruela *f* smallpox, variola; *~s pl.* pock-marks.

virulencia *f* virulence; **virulento** virulent.

virus *m* virus; *enfermedad por ~* virus disease.

viruta *f* ⊕ shaving.

vis *f* **cómica:** *tener ~* be witty, sparkle.

visado *m* visa; *~ de permanencia* residence permit; *~ de tránsito* transit visa.

visaje *m* face, grimace; *hacer ~s* grimace, smirk.

visar *m pasaporte* visa; *documento* endorse, pass.

vísceras *f/pl.* viscera.

viscosidad *f* ⋓ viscosity; stickiness *etc.*; **viscoso** ⋓ viscous, sticky, slimy; *líquido a.* thick.

visera *f* ✕ visor; peak *de gorra*; eye-shade *contra el sol.*

visibilidad *f* visibility; **visible** visible; (*manifiesto*) evident, in evidence; *¿está ~ el duque?* is the duke free?, will the duke see a visitor?

visión *f* sight, vision (*a. eccl.*); (*imaginación vana*) fantasy; *fig.* (*p.*) sight, scarecrow; *~ de conjunto* (complete) picture; F *ver ~es* be seeing things; **visionario** *adj. a. su. m,* **a** *f* visionary.

visita *f* visit; call; (*p.*) visitor, caller; *hacer (pagar) una ~* pay (return) a visit; **visitación** *f eccl.* visitation; **visitador** *m,* **-a** *f* frequent visitor; (*oficial*) inspector; **visitante 1.** visiting; **2.** *m/f* visitor; **visitar** [1a] visit; call on, (go and) see; (*en viaje oficial*) inspect; **visiteo** *m* frequent visiting; **visitero 1.** forever visiting; **2.** *m,* **a** *f* constant visitor.

vislumbrar [1a] glimpse, catch a glimpse of; *fig.* get some idea of, conjecture; **vislumbre** *f* glimpse; (*reflejo*) gleam, glimmer; *fig.* (*esp. ~s pl.*) inkling, general idea.

viso *m* sheen, gloss *de tela*; gleam, glint *de metal*; *~s pl. fig.* appearance; *a dos ~s* having a double purpose; *de ~* of some importance; *hacer ~s* shimmer.

visón *m* (*a. piel de ~*) mink.

visor *m phot.* view-finder; ✸ bomb-sight.

visorio visual.

víspera *f* eve, day before; *~s pl.* vespers, evensong; *la ~ de, en ~s de* on the eve of; *en ~s de inf.* on the point of *ger.*

vista *f* (*facultad, sentido*) sight, vision, eyesight; (*que se dirige a un punto*) eyes, glance, gaze; (*cosa vista*) sight; (*panorama*) view, scene, vista; (*apariencia*) appearance, looks; (*perspectiva*) outlook, prospect; intention; ✝ sight; ⚖ trial *de p.*, hearing *de pleito*; *~s pl.* view, outlook; *corto de ~* short-sighted; *doble ~* second sight; *cine: ~ fija* still; *~ de pájaro* bird's-eye view; ✝ *a la ~* at sight, on sight; *a la ~ de* (with)in sight of; *a ~ de* in sight of; (*ante*) in the presence of; *a primera ~* at first sight, on the face of it; *a simple ~* with the naked eye; *con ~s al mar* overlooking the sea; *con ~s al norte* with northerly aspect; *de ~* (*conocer etc.*) by sight; *en plena ~* in full view; *¡hasta la ~!* cheerio!, so long!; *aguzar la ~* look more closely; *clavar la ~ en* stare at; clap eyes on; *hacer la ~ gorda a* turn a blind eye to, wink at; *medir con la ~* size up; *perder de ~* lose sight of; *no perder de ~* keep in view; *salta a la ~* it hits you in the eye; *torcer la ~* squint.

vistazo *m* look, glance, glimpse; *de un ~* at a glance; *dar un ~* have a look (*a* at); *fig.* pop in; *echar un ~ a* take a look at, glance at.

vistillas *f/pl.* viewpoint, high place.

visto 1. *p.p. of* ver; *~ bueno* passed, approved, O.K.; *bien ~* approved of, thought right; *mal ~* thought wrong; *~ que* seeing that; *por lo ~* evidently; by the look of things; *~ todo esto* in view of all this; *no ~, nunca ~* unheard-of; *está ~ que* it is clear that; **2.:** *~ bueno m* approval, authorization.

vistoso showy, attractive, gay; *b.s.* loud, gaudy.

visual 1. visual; **2.** f line of sight.
vital vital; *espacio* living; **vitalicio
1.** life *attr.*; **2.** *m* life-annuity;
vitalidad f vitality; **vitalizar** [1f]
vitalize; **vitamina** f vitamin;
vitamínico vitamin *attr.*
vitela f vellum.
vitícola vine-growing, vine *attr.*;
viticultor *m* vine-grower; **viticultura** f vine-growing, viticulture.
vitola f *S.Am.* looks, appearance.
¡vítor! hurrah!; **vitorear** [1a] cheer,
acclaim.
vítreo glassy, vitreous ⊕; **vitrifi-
car(se)** [1g] vitrify; **vitrina** f glass
case, show-case; display cabinet
(*a.* ～ *de exposición*); *S.Am.* shop-
window.
vitriolo *m* vitriol.   [uals.)
vitualla(s) f(pl.) provisions, vict-)
vituperar [1a] condemn, inveigh
against, vituperate; **vituperioso**
vituperative; **vituperio** *m* condemnation, vituperation; insult,
affront.
viuda f widow; **viudedad** f widow's
pension; **viudez** f widowhood;
viudo 1. widowed; **2.** *m* widower.
¡viva! *v. vivir.*
vivacidad f vivacity, liveliness *etc.*
vivaque *m* bivouac; **vivaquear** [1a]
bivouac.
vivar *m* (*conejos*) warren; (*peces*)
fish-pond.
vivaracho *p. etc.* jaunty, frisky,
lively; *ojos* lively, intelligent.
vivaz (*de larga vida*) long-lived;
♣ perennial; (*que dura*) enduring,
lasting; active, vigorous; (*lleno de
vida*) lively; (*agudo*) sharp, quick-
witted.
víveres *m/pl.* provisions, supplies,
stores.
vivero *m* fish-pond; ♣ nursery.
viveza f liveliness *etc.* (*v. vivo*).
vividero habitable; **vividor** *m* F
sharp one; wide boy.
vivienda f housing, accommodation;
(*morada*) dwelling; *escasez de* ～s
housing shortage; *problema de la* ～
housing problem.
viviente living; *los* ～s the living.
vivificador, vivificante life-giv-
ing; reviving; **vivificar** [1g] revitalize, enliven, bring to life.
vivíparo viviparous.
vivir 1. [1a] live (*de* by, off, on; *en*
at, in); **¡viva!** hurrah!; **¡viva X!** long

live X!, hurrah for X!; *¿quién vive?*
who goes there?; *dar el quién vive a*
challenge; ～ *para ver* live and learn;
tener con qué ～ have enough to live
on; **2.** *m* life; living; (*modo de* ～)
way of life; *de mal* ～ loose-living;
⚖ criminal, outside the law.
vivisección f vivisection.
vivo 1. (*no muerto*) alive, living; live;
lengua modern, living; (*lleno de
vida*) lively, bright; *dolor* sharp,
acute; *emoción* keen, deep, intense;
inteligencia sharp; *imaginación* lively; *ingenio* ready; *paso* quick, smart;
escena, recuerdo, colorido etc. vivid;
color rich, bright; *carne* raw; *los* ～s
the living; *al* ～ to the life; *herir en lo*
～ cut to the quick; strike home;
2. *m sew.* edging, border.
vizcaíno *adj. a. su. m,* **a** f Biscayan.
vizconde *m* viscount; **vizcondesa** f
viscountess.
vocablo *m* word; *jugar del* ～ (make
a) pun; **vocabulario** *m* vocabulary.
vocación f calling, vocation; **vocacional** vocational.
vocal 1. vocal; **2.** *m* voting member;
3. f vowel; **vocálico** vocalic, vowel
attr.; **vocalizar** [1f] *v/t.* vocalize;
voice; *v/i.* ♪ hum; ～se vocalize;
vocativo *m* vocative (case).
voceador 1. vociferous, loud-
mouthed; **2.** *m* town crier; **vocear**
[1a] *v/t.* (*publicar*) shout, announce
loudly; acclaim loudly; (*llamar*)
shout to; F make a fuss about *s.t.* in
public; *v/i.* shout, bawl; **vocejón** *m*
rough voice; **vocería** f, **vocerío** *m*
shouting, uproar, hullabaloo F;
vocero *m* spokesman; **vociferar**
[1a] vociferate, scream; **vocinglería** f shouting, shrieking, uproar;
vocinglero vociferous, loud-
mouthed; (*parlanchín*) chattering;
fig. blatant.
voladero flying, that can fly; **vola-
dizo** △ projecting; **volador 1.**
flying; *fig.* swift; **2.** *m* rocket;
ichth. flying fish; **voladura** f blow-
ing-up, demolition *etc.*; **volandas:**
en ～, *a las* ～ in the air, through
the air; *fig.* on wings.
volandera f ⊕ washer; grindstone
de molino; F fib; **volandero**
fledged, ready to fly; *p.* restless;
volante 1. flying; *fig.* unsettled]
2. *m mot.* steering-wheel; ⊕ fly-
wheel; balance *de reloj*; (*juego*)

badminton; shuttlecock *con que se juega; sew.* ruffle, frill, flounce; *(papel)* note; **volantón** *m* fledgeling.

volar [1m] *v/t.* explode; *edificio etc.* blow up, demolish; *mina* explode, spring; blast *en cantera; v/i.* fly *(a. fig.)*; flutter; hurtle; *(irse volando)* fly away, disappear; *(ir rápidamente)* fly, run fast, go fast; *(noticia)* spread quickly; *(tiempo)* fly.

volatería *f (aves)* birds, fowls; *(caza)* falconry; fowling *con señuelo.*

volátil ♈ volatile *(a. fig.)*; *(mudable)* changeable; **volatilidad** *f* volatility; **volatilizar(se)** [1f] volatilize, vapourize.

volatín *m,* **volatinero** *m,* **a** *f* tightrope walker, acrobat.   [canic.\

volcán *m* volcano; **volcánico** vol-\

volcar [1g *a.* 1m] *v/t.* overturn, tip over; upset, knock over *por accidente; coche etc.* overturn, turn over; ♧ capsize; *contenido* empty out, dump; *fig. (turbar)* make *s.o.* dizzy; *(hacer cambiar)* make *s.o.* change his mind; tease, irritate; *v/i., ~se* overturn *etc.;* F ~ *por inf.* do one's utmost *to inf.*

volear [1a] volley; **voleo** *m* volley; F *de un ~* at one blow.

volframio *m* wolfram.

volición *f* volition.

volquete *m* tip-cart.

voltaico voltaic; **voltaje** *m* voltage.

volteador *m,* **-a** *f* acrobat; **voltear** [1a] *v/t. (girar)* swing, whirl; *(poner al revés)* turn round; *(volcar)* upset, overturn; transform; *S.Am.* turn; *v/i.* roll over, somersault; **voltereta** *f* somersault, roll; tumble; ~ *sobre las manos* hand-spring.

voltímetro *m* voltmeter; **voltio** *m* volt.

volubilidad *f fig.* fickleness; instability; **voluble** *(que gira)* revolving; ♧ winding; *fig.* fickle, changeable; unstable.

volumen *m mst* volume; *(bulto)* bulk(iness); *radio:* ~ *sonoro* volume (of sound); **voluminoso** voluminous; bulky, big.

voluntad *f mst* will; *(energía)* willpower; *(cariño)* affection, fondness; *buena* ~ goodwill; *mala* ~ illwill, malice; *su santa* ~ his own sweet will; *última* ~ last wish; 🕊 last will and testament; *a* ~ *obrar*

etc. at will; *(cantidad)* ad-lib F; *por* ~ *propia* of one's own free-will; *ganarse la* ~ *de* win over; **voluntariedad** *f* waywardness, wilfulness; **voluntario 1.** voluntary; ✗ volunteer *attr.;* **2.** *m* volunteer; **voluntarioso** wayward, headstrong, wilful.

voluptuosidad *f* voluptuousness; **voluptuoso 1.** voluptuous; *b.s.* sensual; **2.** *m,* **a** *f* voluptuary.

voluta *f* △ scroll, volute; spiral, column *de humo etc.*

volver [2h; *p.p.* vuelto] **1.** *v/t.* turn; turn round; *página etc.* turn (over); *(invertir)* turn upside down; *ojos etc.* turn, cast; *arma etc.* turn *(a* on), direct, aim *(a* at); *puerta* close, pull to; *(devolver)* send back; *favor, visita* return, repay; *(reponer)* put back, replace *(a* in); *(restablecer)* restore *(a* to); ~ *adj.* turn, make, render; *v. loco;* **2.** *v/i.* return, come back, go back, get back; *(torcer)* turn, bend; ~ *a hábito, tema etc.* revert to, return to; ~ *a hacer* do again; ~ *atrás* turn back; ~ *en sí* come to, regain consciousness; ~ *por* stand up for; ~ *sobre sí* recover one's calm; **3.** ~*se* turn (round); *(regresar)* = *v/i.;* *(vino)* turn (sour); *(opinión)* change one's mind; ~ *adj.* turn, become, go, get; ~ *atrás fig.* look back; *(cejar)* back out; ~ *contra* turn on; *v. loco.*

vomitado F sickly, seedy; **vomitar** [1a] vomit, bring up, throw up; *fig. llamas etc.* belch forth, spew; *ganancias* disgorge; *injurias* hurl; **vomitivo** *m* emetic; **vómito** *m* vomit; *(acto)* being sick, vomiting; **vomitona** *f* F bad sick turn.

voracidad *f* voracity, voraciousness.

vorágine *f* whirlpool, maelstrom.

voraz voracious, greedy, ravenous.

vórtice *m* whirlpool, vortex.

vos † ye; *S.Am.* you; **vosear** [1a] *S.Am.* address as *vos (i.e., treat familiarly).*

vosotros, vosotras *pl.* you.

votación *f* vote, voting; *esp. parl.* division; ~ *por manos levantadas* show of hands; *someter a* ~ put to the vote, take a vote on; **votante 1.** voting; **2.** *m/f* voter; **votar** [1a] *v/t. ley* pass; *candidato* vote for; *v/i.* vote *(por* for); vow *a Dios etc.;* *(renegar)* curse, ~ swear; **votivo** votive; **voto** *m pol. etc.* vote; *(p.)*

voter; vow *a Dios etc.*; *(reniego)* curse, swear-word; ~s *pl. fig.* (good) wishes; ~ *de calidad* casting vote; ~ *de confianza* vote of confidence; *echar* ~s curse, swear; *hacer* ~ *de inf.* swear to *inf.*, (make a) vow to *inf.*; *hacer* ~s *para que* earnestly hope that.

voy *etc. v.* ir.

voz *f* voice *(a. gr.)*; *(vocablo)* word; *(voto)* vote, support; *(grito)* shout; noise *de trueno etc.*; rumour, report; *voces pl. (gritos)* shouting; ~ *común* hearsay, rumour; *a una* ~ with one voice; *a media* ~ in a low voice; *v. grito*; *de viva* ~ viva voce; by word of mouth; *en* ~ in (good) voice; *en* ~ *alta* aloud, out loud; *en* ~ *baja* in an undertone; *aclarar la* ~ clear one's throat; *corre la* ~ *de que* there's a rumour going round that; *dar voces* shout, call out; *dar la* ~ *de alarma* sound; *dar cuatro voces* make a great fuss; F *llevar la* ~ *cantante* be the boss; *estar pidiendo a voces* be crying out to *inf.*; *tener* ~ *y voto* have a say; *no tener* ~ *en capítulo* have no say *in a thing.*

vozarrón *m* F loud harsh voice.

vuelco *m* upset, spill, overturning; *dar un* ~ overturn; *(corazón)* jump.

vuelo *m* 🗶 flight; fullness *de vestido*; *(adorno)* lace, frill; 🏛 projecting part; *de mucho* ~ *falda* full; ~ *a ciegas* blind flying; ~ *de ensayo* test flight; ~ *sin motor*, ~ *a vela* gliding; ~ *en picado* dive; *al* ~ on the wing, in flight; *fig.* at once; *alzar el* ~ take flight; F dash off; *tocar a* ~ peal; *tomar* ~ grow, develop.

vuelta *f* turn, revolution; *deportes*: lap, circuit *en carrera*; round *de torneo*; *(jira)* tour; *(paseo)* stroll; *(recodo)* turn, bend, curve; *(regreso)* return; *(devolución)* return, giving back; *(dinero)* change; *(revés)* back,

other side; *(repetición)* repeat; *sew.* cuff; F hiding; ⚓ ~ *de cabo* hitch; ~ *de campana* somersault; ~ *del mundo* journey round the world; *a la* ~ *(de regreso)* on one's return; *(página)* on the next page, overleaf; *a la* ~ *de esquina* round; *años etc.* after, at the end of; *v. correo*; *dar* ~ *a llave* turn; *coche etc.* reverse, turn round; *dar la* ~ *a* go round; *dar una* ~ take a stroll; *dar una* ~ *de campana* turn completely over; *dar media* ~ face about; 🗶 about turn; *dar* ~s turn, go round, revolve; *(camino)* twist and turn; *(cabeza)* (be in a) whirl; *dar* ~s *a manivela etc.* wind, turn; *botón* turn; twirl *en dedos*; *no hay que darle* ~s it's no use going on (with it); *estar de* ~ be back, be home; F be in the know; F be mighty clever; *poner de* ~ *y media* heap insults upon; *no tiene* ~ *de hoja* there's no denying it.

vuelto 1. *p.p. of* volver; **2.** *m* S.Am. change.

vuestro 1. *adj.* your; *(tras su.)* of yours; **2.** *pron.* yours.

vulcanita *f* vulcanite; **vulcanizar** [1f] vulcanize.

vulgar *lengua* vulgar; *opinión etc.* common, general; *término* ordinary, accepted; *(corriente)* ordinary, everyday; banal; trivial, trite; **vulgaridad** *f* commonness *etc.*; *(cosa vulgar)* triviality; ~es *pl. freq.* small-talk; platitudes; **vulgarismo** *m* popular form; *b.s.* slang (word), vulgarism; **vulgarizar** [1f] popularize, vulgarize; *texto etc.* translate into the vernacular; **Vulgata** *f* Vulgate; **vulgo** *m* common people, lower orders, common herd.

vulnerable vulnerable; **vulnerar** [1a] damage.

vulpeja *f* fox; *(hembra)* vixen; **vulpino** vulpine.

W, X

wáter ['bater] *m* lavatory, toilet, water-closet.   [weight.⎱
wélter ['belter] *m boxeo*: welter-⎰
whisk(e)y ['wiski] *m* whisk(e)y.
wolfram ['bolfram] *m* wolfram.

xilófono [s-] *m* xylophone.
xilografía [s-] *f* xylography, wood-engraving.
xilógrafo [s-] *m* xylographer, wood-engraver.

Y

y and; *las 2 y media* half-past two.
ya (*en momento pasado*) already, before now; (*ahora*) now; (*más adelante*) in due course, sometime; (*en seguida*) at once; ¡~! now I remember, of course!; ~, ~ yes, yes; ~ ..., ~ ... (*ora*) now ..., now ...; (*si*) whether ..., or ...; ~ en 1950 as long ago as 1950, as early as 1950; ~ no no longer, not any more; ~ que as, since; now (that).
yacaré *m* crocodile.
yacente *estatua* recumbent; **yacer** [2y] †, *lit.* lie; *aquí yace* here lies; **yacija** *f* bed; (*tumba*) grave, tomb; *ser de mala* ~ sleep badly; (*inquieto*) be restless; (*carácter*) be a bad lot; **yacimiento** *m* bed, deposit.
yámbico iambic; **yambo** *m* iambus.
yanqui *adj. a. su. m/f* Yankee.
yate *m* yacht.
yedra *f* ivy.
yegua *f* mare; **yeguada** *f* stud.
yelmo *m* helmet.
yema *f* yolk *de huevo*; ♀ (leaf-)bud, eye; (*lo mejor*) best part; *fig.* snag; ~ *del dedo* fingertip; ~ *mejida* egg-flip; *dar en la* ~ put one's finger on the spot.
yendo *v. ir.*
yerba *f v.* hierba.

yermar [1a] lay waste; **yermo 1.** waste, uninhabited; **2.** *m* waste (land), wilderness.
yerno *m* son-in-law.
yerro *m* error, mistake.
yerto stiff, rigid.
yesca *f* tinder (*a. fig.*); fuel *de pasión etc.*; ~s *pl.* tinder box.
yesería *f* plastering, plasterwork; **yesero** *m* plasterer; **yeso** *m* *geol.* gypsum; △ *etc.* plaster; (*vaciado*) plaster cast; ~ *mate* plaster of Paris.
yip *m S.Am.* jeep.
yo I; *el* ~ the self, the ego.
yódico iodic; **yodo** *m* iodine; **yoduro** *m* iodide.
yola *f* gig, yawl; *deportes:* sailing-boat, shell.
yugo *m* yoke (*a. fig.*).
yugo(e)slavo *adj. a. su. m*, **a** *f* Jugoslav.
yugular jugular.
yungas *f/pl. S.Am.* valleys.
yungla *f* jungle.
yunque *m* anvil; *fig.* tireless worker, devil for work.
yunta *f* yoke, team *de bueyes*; (*pareja*) couple, pair.
yute *m* jute.
yuxtaponer [2r] juxtapose; **yuxtaposición** *f* juxtaposition.

Z

zabordar [1a] run aground.
zabullir *etc. v.* zambullir *etc.*
zafado *S.Am.* (*vivo*) wide awake; (*descarado*) brazen.
zafar [1a] loosen, untie; ~se keep out of the way, hide o.s. away; ~ *de p. etc.* shake off, dodge, ditch F; *compromiso* wriggle out of.
zafarrancho *m* ⚓ clearing for action; F row, set-to; ~ *de combate* (call to) action stations.
zafio coarse, loutish.
zafiro *m* sapphire.

zafo: *salirse* ~ come out (*de* of) unharmed.
zaga *f* rear; *a la* ~, *en* ~ behind, in the rear; *no ir en* ~ *a* be every bit as good as; *no ir en* ~ *a nadie* be second to none.
zagal *m* lad, youth; 🗡 shepherd boy; **zagala** *f* lass, girl; 🗡 shepherdess.
zagalón *m* big lad; **zagalona** *f* big girl.
zagual *m* puddle.
zaguán *m* vestibule, hall(way).

zaguero rear, back; bottom *en liga*; *p.* slow.

zahareño wild, unsociable.

zaherir [3i] attack, criticize (sarcastically); reproach, upbraid; ~ *con* throw *s.t.* in *s.o.'s* face..

zahorí *m* seer, clairvoyant; (*que busca agua*) water-diviner.

zahurda *f* pigsty.

zaino *animal* chestnut; *p.* treacherous, false.

zalamería *f* flattery, cajolery *etc.*; **zalamero 1.** flattering, cajoling; unctuous, suave, oily; **2.** *m*, *a f* flatterer; suave sort, oily person.

zalea *f* sheepskin.

zalema *f* salaam, bowing and scraping.

zamarra *f* sheepskin (jacket); **zamarrear** [1a] shake, worry; *fig.* shake up, knock about; **zamarro** *m* sheepskin; F yokel; ~s *pl. S.Am.* riding-breeches.

zambo 1. knock-kneed; **2.** *m*, *a f* half-breed (*mixed Indian and Negro*).

zambomba *f* sort of rustic drum; F ¡~! phew!; **zambombo** *m* coarse fellow, yokel.

zambra *f* F uproar, row.

zambucar [1g] F jumble up, mix up.

zambullida *f* dive, plunge; duck, ducking; **zambullir** [3h] duck, plunge; ~se dive, plunge; duck; *fig.* hide, cover o.s. up.

zampabollos *m/f* F (*comilón*) greedy pig, glutton; (*grosero*) coarse sort; **zampar** [1a] whip smartly, shoot (en into); F (*comer*) wolf, demolish, put away; ~se whip, vanish (en into); **zampatortas** *m/f* F = zampabollos; **zampón** F greedy.

zampoña *f* shepherd's pipes.

zampuzar [1f] duck *en agua*; *fig.* = zampar.

zanahoria *f* carrot.

zanca *f* shank; ~s *pl.* F long shanks; **zancada** *f* stride; F *en dos* ~s in a couple of ticks; **zancadilla** *f* trip *con pie*; (*aparato*) booby-trap; (*engaño*) trick; *echar la* ~ *a* a trip (up); **zancajear** [1a] rush around; **zancarrón** *m* F leg-bone; big bone; (*p.*) old bag of bones; **zanco** *m* stilt; *en* ~s *fig.* well up, in a good position; **zancudo** long-legged; *orn.* wading; *ave* ~a wader.

zangamanga *f* F funny business, piece of dirty work; **zanganada** *f* F sauce, saucy remark.

zanganear [1a] F loaf, (be a) spiv; **zángano** *m* drone; F drone, idler, slacker.

zangarrear [1a] strum on a guitar.

zangarri(an)a *f* F 🞰 small upset; headache; *fig.* blues.

zangolotear [1a] F *v/t.* keep playing with, fidget with; *v/i.* (be on the) fidget; ~se (*ventana*) rattle.

zangón *m* big lazy lad.

zanguanga: F *hacer la* ~ swing the lead; **zanguango** F spivvish. .

zanja *f* ditch, trench, drainage channel; *abrir las* ~s lay the foundations; **zanjar** [1a] trench, ditch; *dificultad* get round.

zanquilargo F leggy; **zanquivano** spindly.

zapa¹ *f* (*lija*) shagreen, sharkskin.

zapa² *f* 🞵 (*pala*) spade; (*trinchera*) trench, sap; **zapador** *m* sapper, pioneer.

zapallo *m S.Am.* gourd, pumpkin.

zapapico *m* pick(axe); **zapar** [1a] sap, undermine.

zaparrazo *m* F claw, scratch.

zapata *f* shoe *de freno etc.*; **zapatazo** *m* bump, bang; **zapateado** *m* tap-dance; **zapatear** [1a] *v/t.* kick, prod with one's foot; tap with one's foot; F give *s.o.* a rough time; *v/i.* tap-dance; **zapatería** *f* shoe-shop; (*arte*) shoemaking; **zapatero** *m* shoemaker; ~ *remendón*, ~ *de viejo* cobbler; **zapatilla** *f* slipper *para casa*; pump *para bailar*; ⊕ washer; **zapato** *m* shoe; *como tres en un* ~ like sardines; *saber dónde aprieta el* ~ know which side one's bread is buttered; know where *s.o.'s* weakness lies. [scare away.\

¡**zape!** shoo!; **zapear** [1a] shoo,\

zaque *m* wineskin; F boozer; F *estar hecho un* ~ be sozzled.

zaquizamí *m* poky little place, hole.

zar *m* tsar, czar.

zarabanda *f* sarabande; *fig.* row.

zaragata *f* F row, set-to; **zaragatero** *m* F rowdy, hooligan.

zaragozano *adj. a. su. m*, *a f* (native) of Saragossa.

zaranda *f* sieve; **zarandajas** *f/pl.* F trifles, odds and ends; **zarandear** [1a] siit, sieve; shake up; ~se be on the go, never be still; **zarandillo** *m*

F active person, lively sort; F *traer como un* ~ keep *s.o.* on the go; **zarandón** *m sl.* booze-up.

zarapito *m* curlew.

zarcillo *m* ♀ tendril; (*joya*) earring.

zarco light blue.

zarigüeya *f* opossum.

zarpa *f* claw, paw; F *echar la* ~ grab hold (*a* of); **zarpada** *f* clawing, blow with the paw; **zarpar** [1a] weigh anchor, set sail; **zarpazo** *m* = *zarpada*; *fig.* thud, bump.

zarrapastrón F, **zarrapastroso** ragged, slovenly, shabby.

zarza *f* bramble, blackberry; **zarzal** *m* (clump of) brambles; **zarzamora** *f* blackberry.

zarzo *m* (*tejido*) wattle; hurdle *de cerca etc.*

zarzuela *f* operetta, light opera, musical comedy.

¡zas! bang!, slap!

zascandil *m* F busybody.

zigzag *m* zigzag; *en* ~ *relámpago* forked; **zigzaguear** [1a] zigzag.

zinc *m* zinc.

zipizape *m* F set-to, rumpus.

zócalo *m* socle.

zoclo *m* clog, wooden shoe; galosh, overshoe *de goma.*

zodiacal zodiacal; **zodíaco** *m* zodiac.

zona *f* zone; belt, area; ~ *edificada* built-up area; ~ *de pruebas* testing ground; ~ *tórrida* torrid zone; **zonal** zonal.

zoo... zoo...; **zoología** *f* zoology; **zoológico** zoological; **zoólogo** *m* zoologist.

zopenco F **1.** stupid, silly; **2.** *m* clot, nitwit.

zoquete *m* (*madera*) block, piece; (*pan*) bit of bread; F (*tonto*) chump, duffer; (*grosero*) oaf, lout.

zorra *f* (*en general*) fox; (*hembra*) vixen; F whore; **zorrera** *f* foxhole; F worry, anxiety; **zorrería** *f* foxiness, craftiness; **zorrero** foxy, crafty; **zorro 1.** *m* (dog-)fox; F old fox, crafty sort; F *hacerse el* ~ act dumb; **2.** foxy, crafty, slippery.

zorzal *m* thrush; F sly fellow; *S.Am.* F mutt.

zozobra *f* ⚓ sinking, capsizing; *fig.* worry, anxiety; unrest; **zozobrar** [1a] ⚓ sink, capsize, overturn; *fig.* (*peligrar*) be in danger; (*afligirse*) worry, fret.

zueco *m* clog, wooden shoe.

zulú *m* Zulu.

zumba *f fig.* banter, chaff, teasing; *hacer* ~ *a* rag, tease; **zumbador** *m* ♀ buzzer; **zumbar** [1a] *v/t.* F rag, chaff; *univ. sl.* plough; *golpe* let *s.o.* have; *S.Am.* throw, chuck; *v/i.* (*abeja*) buzz, hum, drone; (*oídos*) sing, ring; (*máquina*) whirr, drone, hum; (*zumbador*) buzz; ~*se de* rag, chaff; **zumbido** *m* buzz(ing) *etc.*; F punch, biff; **zumbón 1.** *p.* waggish, funny; *tono etc.* bantering; **2.** *m,* **-a** *f* wag, funny man *etc.*; banterer, tease.

zumo *m* juice; (*como bebida*) juice, squash; *fig.* solid profit, real benefit; ~ *de limón* lemon-squash; **zumoso** juicy.

zuncho *m* band, hoop, ring.

zupia *f* muddy wine; *fig.* trash.

zurcido *m* darn, mend; **zurcidura** *f* (*acto*) darning, mending; = *zurcido*; **zurcir** [3b] darn, mend, sew up; *fig.* put together; *mentira* concoct, think up.

zurdo left-handed.

zurra *f* dressing, tanning; F (*paliza*) tanning, spanking; (*trabajo*) grind, drudgery; (*riña*) set-to; **zurrador** *m* tanner.

zurrapa *f* dregs; F trash, muck; **zurraposo** thick, muddy.

zurrar [1a] dress, tan; F tan, wallop, spank; ~*se* dirty o.s.

zurriaga *f* whip; **zurriagar** [1h] whip; **zurriagazo** *m* lash; *fig.* bad knock, stroke of bad luck; **zurriago** *m* whip.

zurriar [1b] hum, buzz.

zurribanda *f* F = *zurra* F.

zurriburri *m* F mess, mix-up.

zurrón *m* pouch, bag.

zutano *m,* **a** *f* (Mr *etc.*) So-and-so.

Spanish abbreviations
Abreviaturas españolas

Cada artículo contiene la forma desarrollada de la abreviatura, y, en cuanto ha sido posible, la abreviatura inglesa correspondiente, desarrollándose también ésta entre paréntesis. El asterisco (*) significa: véase la lista de Pesos y Medidas.

A

a *área**.

A: bomba A *bomba atómica* A-bomb (atomic bomb).

A *naipes: as* A (ace).

(a) *alias* alias.

a *arroba* (*v. Diccionario*).

ab.¹ *april* April.

a.c. *año corriente* current year, present year.

A.C. *año de Cristo* A.D. (Anno Domini).

a/c *al cuidado* c/o (care of).

acr. *acreedor* creditor.

A. de C. *año de Cristo* A.D. (Anno Domini).

adj. *adjunto* Enc. (enclosure, enclosed).

admón. *administración* admin. (administration).

a.f. *antiguo francés* O.F. (Old French).

a/f. *a favor* in favour.

afmo. *afectísimo: suyo ~* yours truly.

ag. *agosto* Aug. (August).

a. J.C. *antes de Jesucristo* B.C. (before Christ).

Al.º *Alonso personal name.*

amp. *amperios* amp. (ampères).

Ant.º *Antonio personal name.*

ap. *thea. aparte* aside.

apdo. *apartado (de correos)* P.O.B. (Post Office Box).

art., art.º *artículo* art. (article).

arz. *arzobispo* abp. (archbishop).

atmo. *atentísimo: suyo ~* yours truly.

atta. *atenta.*

atte. *atentamente.*

a/v. *a vista* at sight.

Av., Av.da *Avenida* Av., Ave. (Avenue).

B

B. *eccl. beato* blessed.

B. *Barcelona Spanish city.*

B.A. *Buenos Aires capital of Argentina.*

b.l.m. *besa las manos courtesy formula.*

b.l.p. *besa los pies courtesy formula.*

Bº *banco* bk. (bank).

Bón. *batallón* Battn, Bn. (battalion).

B.p. *bendición papal* papal blessing.

C

c. *capítulo* ch. (chapter).

C. *compañía* Co. (company).

c³ *centímetro cúbico** c.c. (cubic centimetre).

c.ª *compañía* Co. (company).

C.A.E. *cóbrese al entregar* C.O.D. (cash on delivery).

cap. *capítulo* ch. (chapter).

Cap.n *Capitán* Capt. (Captain).

cap.º *capítulo* ch. (chapter).

c.c. *centímetro cúbico** c.c. (cubic centimetre).

C.C. *corriente continua* D.C. (direct current).

c/c *cuenta corriente* C/A (current account).

C.D. *Club Deportivo* S.C. (Sports Club).

c/d *con descuento* with discount.

C. de J. *Compañía de Jesús* S.J. (Society of Jesus).

CECA *Comunidad Europea del Carbón y Acero* ECSC (European Coal and Steel Community).

c.f. *caballo de fuerza* H.P. (horsepower).

C.F. *Club de Fútbol* F.C. (Football Club).

cg. *centigramo** centigramme.

ch. *cheque* chq. (cheque).
Cía *compañía* Co. (company).
c.i.f. *costo, seguro y flete* c.i.f. (cost, insurance, freight).
cl. *centilitro** centilitre.
cm. *centímetro** cm. (centimetre).
cm² *centímetro** *cuadrado* sq. cm. (square centimetre).
cm³ *centímetro cúbico** c.c. (cubic centimetre).
Cnel *Coronel* Col. (Colonel).
col., col.ª *columna* col. (column).
comp. *compárese* cf. (confer).
comp.ª *compañía* Co. (company).
CONDESA *Consorcio de Diarios Españoles, Sociedad Anónima* news-agency.
corrte. *corriente, de los corrientes* inst. (instant).
C.P. *contestación pagada* R.P. (reply paid).
cs. *céntimos; centavos* cents.
c.s.f. *costo, seguro, flete* c.i.f. (cost, insurance, freight).
C.S.I.C. *Consejo Superior de Investigaciones Científicas* Spanish state research organization.
cta, *cuenta* A/C. (account).
cte *corriente, de los corrientes* inst. (instant).
cts. *céntimos; centavos* cents.
c/u *cada uno* ea. (each).

D

D. *debe* debit side.
D. *Don* Esq. (Esquire) (*Sr D., en el sobre delante del nombre de pila*; Esq., *en el sobre después del apellido*).
D *naipes: dama* Q (Queen).
Da. *Doña* title of courtesy to ladies: no equivalent.
D.A. *duración ampliada* E.P. (extended play).
d. de J.C. *después de Jesucristo* A.D. (Anno Domini).
D.F. *Méjico: Distrito Federal* Federal District.
dg. *decigramo** decigramme.
Dg. *decagramo** decagramme.
D.G. de B.B. *Dirección General de Banca y Bolsa* institute for control of investment etc.
D.G.T. *Dirección General del Turismo* state tourist organization.
dho. *dicho* aforesaid.
dic.ᵉ *diciembre* Dec. (December).
dl. *decilitro** decilitre.
Dl. *decalitro** decalitre.

dm. *decímetro** decimetre.
Dm. *decámetro** decametre.
D.m. *Dios mediante* D.V. (Deo volente).
D.n *Don* (*v. D.*).
d.na *docena* doz. (dozen).
do. *descuento* dis., dist (discount).
doc. *docena* doz. (dozen).
D.N.S. *Delegación Nacional de Sindicatos* Spanish state trade union organization.
dom.º *domingo* Sun. (Sunday).
d/p. *días plazo* days' time.
Dr *Doctor* Dr (doctor).
Dr. ✝ *el debe* Dr (debtor).
d.to *descuento* dis., dist (discount).
dup.do *duplicado* duplicate.
d/v. *días vista* d.s., d/s. (days after sight).

E

E *este* E. (East[ern]).
ed. *edición* ed. (edition).
EE.UU. *Estados Unidos* U.S., U.S.A. (United States [of America]).
E.M. *Estado Mayor* staff.
Encia. *Eminencia* Eminence.
ENESA *Empresa Nacional de Electricidad, Sociedad Anónima* Spanish state electricity authority.
en.º *enero* Jan. (January).
ENSIDESA *Empresa Nacional Siderúrgica de Avilés, Sociedad Anónima* state iron and steel company, Avilés.
E.P.D. *en paz descanse* R.I.P. (requiescat in pace).
esq. *esquina* corner.
etc. *etcétera* etc. (et caetera, etcetera).
Exc. *Excelencia* Excellency.
Exmo. *Excelentísimo* courtesy title.

F

f. *femenino* f., fem. (feminine).
fa *factura* bill, account.
f.a.b. *franco a bordo* f.o.b. (free on board).
f.c. *ferrocarril* Rly. (railway).
feb.º *febrero* Feb. (February).
Fern.do *Fernando* personal name.
fha. *fecha* d. (date).
F.M.I. *Fondo Monetario Internacional* I.M.F. (International Monetary Fund).
F.N.M.T. *Finca Nacional de Moneda y Timbre* branch of treasury issuing bank-notes and stamps.

f.º, fol. *folio* fo., fol. (folio).
fr. *francés* Fr. (French).
Fr. *Fray* Fr. (Friar).
Fran.ᶜᵒ *Francisco personal name.*

G

g. *gramo(s)* gr(s). (gramme[s]).
G/ *giro* draft, money-order.
gde. *guarde:* que Dios guarde whom God protect.
Genl *General* Gen. (General).
G.º *Gonzalo personal name.*
gob.ⁿᵒ *gobierno* Govt. (Government).
Gral, gral. *General* Gen. (General).
grs. *gramos* grs. (grammes).

H

h. *habitantes* pop. (population).
h. *hacia* c. (circa).
H. *haber* Cr. (credit).
H: bomba H *bomba de hidrógeno* H-bomb (hydrogen bomb).
hect. *hectárea** hectare.
Hg. *hectogramo** hectogramme.
Hl. *hectolitro** hectolitre.
Hm. *hectómetro** hectometre.
Hnos. *Hermanos* Bros. (Brothers).
H.P. *(inglés = horse-power) caballos, caballaje* H.P. (horse-power).

I

ib., ibid. *ibídem* ibid. (ibidem).
I.C.R.N. *Instituto de Crédito para la Reconstrucción Nacional* state credit bank for industry etc.
igl.ᵃ *iglesia* church.
Il. *Ilustre courtesy title.*
Ilmo. *Ilustrísimo courtesy title.*
Imp. *Imprenta* printers, printing works.
I.N.C. *Instituto Nacional de Colonización* land development corporation.
I.N.I. *Instituto Nacional de Industria* state industrial council.

J

J.C. *Jesucristo* Jesus Christ.
J.E.N. *Junta de Energía Nuclear* Atomic Energy Authority.
juev. *jueves* Thurs. (Thursday).

K

k/c. *kilociclos* k/c. (kilocycles).
Kg. *kilogramo** kg. (kilogramme).
Kl. *kilolitro** kilolitre.
Km. *kilómetro** km. (kilometre).

Km./h. *kilómetros por hora* kilometres per hour.
kv. *kilovatio* kw. (kilowatt).

L

l. ₨ *ley* law.
l. *libro* bk. (book).
l. *litro** l. (litre).
lbs. *libras* lbs. (pounds).
lib. *libra* lb. (pound).
lib., lib.º *libro* bk. (book).
Lic. en Fil. y Let. *Licenciado en Filosofía y Letras* B.A. (Bachelor ot Arts).

M

m. *minuto* m. (minute).
m. *metro** m. (metre).
m. *masculino* m., masc. (masculine).
m. *murió* d. (died).
m² *metro cuadrado** sq. m. (square metre).
m³ *metro cúbico** cu. m. (cubic metre).
M. *Madrid capital of Spain.*
Ma. *María personal name.*
mart. *martes* Tues. (Tuesday).
M.C. *Mercado Común* C.M. (Common Market).
Md. *Madrid capital of Spain.*
M.F. *modulación de frecuencia* F.M. (frequency modulation)
mg *miligramo** mg. (milligramme).
miérc. *miércoles* Weds. (Wednesday).
mm *milímetro** mm. (millimetre).
Mons. *Monseñor* Mgr. (Monsignor).
MS *manuscrito* MS (manuscript).
MSS *manuscritos* MSS (manuscripts).

N

n. *nacido* b. (born).
N *norte* N. (North[ern]).
Na. Sra. *Nuestra Señora* Our Lady, The Virgin.
N.B. *nótese bien* N.B. (nota bene).
NE *noreste* N.E. (North East[ern]).
NN.UU. *Naciones Unidas* U.N. (United Nations).
N.º *número* No. (number).
NO *noroeste* N.W. (North West [-ern]).
NODO *Noticiario y Documentales Cinematográficos* Spanish news-reel etc.
nov.ᵉ *noviembre* Nov. (November).
nra. *nuestra* our.
nro. *nuestro* our.

N.S. *Nuestro Señor* Our Lord.

N.T. *Nuevo Testamento* N.T. (New Testament).

N.U. *Naciones Unidas* U.N. (United Nations).

Núm. *número* No. (number).

O

O *oeste* W. (West[ern]).

O.A.A. *Organización de Agricultura y Alimentación* F.A.O. (Food and Agriculture Organization).

O.A.C.I. *Organización de Aviación Civil Internacional* I.C.A.O. (International Civil Aviation Organization).

ob., obpo. *obispo* Bp. (bishop).

obr. cit. *obra citada* op. cit. (opere citato).

oct.ᵉ *octubre* Oct. (October).

O.E.A. *Organización de los Estados Americanos* O.A.S. (Organization of American States).

O.E.C.E. *Organización Europea de Cooperación Económica* O.E.E.C. (Organization for European Economic Cooperation).

O.M.S. *Organización Mundial de la Salud* W.H.O. (World Health Organization).

ONU *Organización de las Naciones Unidas* UNO (United Nations Organization).

O.P. *Orden de Predicadores* O.S.D. (Order of St. Dominic).

O.P. *Obras Públicas* P.W.D. (Public Works Department).

O.S.B. *Orden de San Benito* O.S.B. (Order of St. Benedict).

OTAN *Organización del Tratado del Atlántico del Norte* NATO (North Atlantic Treaty Organization).

OTASE *Organización del Tratado del Sudeste Asiático* (*or del Asia Sudeste*) SEATO (South East Asia Treaty Organization).

P

p. *punto, puntada* st. (stitch).

P. *papa* pope.

P. *padre* Fr. (Father).

P % *por cien*(to) %, p.c. (per cent).

pág. *página* p. (page).

págs. *páginas* pp. (pages).

p.c. *por cien*(to) %, p.c. (per cent).

P.C. *Partido Comunista* C.P. (Communist Party).

P.D. *posdata* P.S. (postscript).

pdo. *pasado* ult. (ultimo).

Pe. *Padre* Fr. (Father).

p. ej. *por ejemplo* e.g. (exempli gratia, for example).

pmo. *próximo* prox. (proximo).

P.º *Pedro* personal name.

P.º *Paseo* Avenue.

p.º n.º *peso neto* nt. wt. (net weight).

p.o. *por orden* per pro(c)., p.p. (per procurationem, by proxy).

p.p. *por poder* per pro(c)., p.p. (per procurationem, by proxy).

P.P. *porte pagado* C.P. (carriage paid).

p.pdo. *el mes próximo pasado* ult. (ultimo).

pr. fr. *próximo futuro* prox. (proximo).

Prof. *Profesor* Prof. (Professor).

prov. *provincia* province.

P.S. *postscriptum* (posdata) P.S. (postscript).

ptas *pesetas* pesetas.

PYRESA *Prensa y Radio Españolas, Sociedad Anónima* news-agency.

pzs *piezas* pcs. (pieces).

Q

Q.B.S.M. *que besa sus manos* courtesy formula.

Q.B.S.P. *que besa sus pies* courtesy formula.

q.D.g. *que Dios guarde* whom God protect (*used after mention of king*).

q.e.g.e. *que en gloria esté* R.I.P. (requiescat in pace).

q.e.p.d. *que en paz descanse* R.I.P. (requiescat in pace).

q.e.s.m. *que estrecha su mano* courtesy formula.

quil. *quilates* carats.

q.s.g.h. *que santa gloria haya* R.I.P. (requiescat in pace).

qts. *quilates* carats.

R

R *naipes*: *rey* K (King).

R. *Real* Royal.

R. *Reverendo* Rev. (Reverend).

R.A.C.E. *Real Automóvil Club de España* equivalent to British A.A. and R.A.C.

R.A.U. *República Arabe Unida* U.A.R. (United Arab Republic).

Rdo *Reverendo* Rev. (Reverend).

RENFE *Red Nacional de Ferrocarriles Españoles* Spanish railway company.

R.I.P. *requiescat in pace* R.I.P. (requiescat in pace).

R.M. *Reverenda Madre* Reverend Mother.

R.N.E. *Radio Nacional de España Spanish national radio.*

R.O. *real orden* royal decree.

R.P. *Reverendo Padre* Reverend ather.

S

s/ *su* yr. (your).

S. *San(to), Santa* St. (Saint).

S *sur* S. (South[ern]).

s.a. *sin año* s.a. (sine anno).

S.A. *Su Alteza* H.H. (His [or Her] Highness).

S.A. ✝ *Sociedad Anónima* Ltd. (Limited); Inc. *Am.* (Incorporated).

sáb. *sábado* Sat. (Saturday).

SE *sudeste* S.E. (South East[ern]).

sept.ᵉ *septiembre* Sept. (September).

S.E.U. *Sindicato Español Universitario students' union.*

s.e.u.o. *salvo error u omisión* E. & O.E. (errors and omissions excepted).

s.f. *sin fecha* n.d. (no date).

sgte. *siguiente* f. (following).

sigs. *(y) siguientes* et seq. (et sequentia), ff. (following).

S.I.M. *Servicio de Información Militar* M.I. (Military Intelligence).

s.l. ni f. *sin lugar ni fecha* n.p. or d. (no place or date).

s/n. *sin número* not numbered.

S.M. *Su Majestad* H.M. (His [or Her] Majesty).

SO *suroeste* S.W. (South West[ern]).

Sr *Señor* Mr (Mister).

Sra *Señora* Mrs (Mistress).

S.R.C. *se ruega contestación* R.S.V.P. (répondez s'il vous plaît).

Sres *Señores* Messrs (Messieurs).

Srio. *Secretario* Sec. (Secretary).

S.R.M. *Su Real Majestad* H.M. (His [or Her] Majesty)

S.S. *Su Santidad* His Holiness.

SS *Santos* SS (Saints).

s.s.s. *su seguro servidor* yours truly.

s.v. *sub voce* s.v. (sub voce).

T

t. *tomo(s)* vol(s). (volume[s]).

Tel. *teléfono* Tel. (Telephone).

Tente. *Teniente* Lieut. (Lieutenant).

Tlf. *teléfono* Tel. (Telephone).

T.R.B. *toneladas registradas brutas* G.R.T. (gross register tonnage).

Tte *Teniente* Lieut. (Lieutenant).

T.V. *televisión* T.V. (television).

U

Ud. *Usted* you.

Uds. *ustedes* you.

U.E.P. *Unión Europea de Pagos* E.P.U. (European Payments Union).

U.P.U. *Unión Postal Universal* U.P.U. (Universal Postal Union).

U.R.S.S. *Unión de las Repúblicas Socialistas Soviéticas* U.S.S.R. (Union of Soviet Socialist Republics).

V

v. *voltio* v. (volt).

v. *véase* see.

V *naipes: valet* J (Jack).

V. *Usted* you.

Vd. *Usted* you.

Vda de *viuda de* widow of.

Vds. *Ustedes* you.

verso *versículo* v. (verse).

v.g., v. gr. *verbigracia* viz. (videlicet).

vid. *vide* see.

vier. *viernes* Fri. (Friday).

V.M. *Vuestra Majestad* Your Majesty.

V.º B.º *visto bueno* O.K. (all correct?).

vra. *vuestra* yr. (your).

vro. *vuestro* yr. (your).

W

w. *watio* w. (watt).

X

Xpo. *Cristo* Christ.

Proper Names

Nombres propios

A

Abisinia f Abyssinia.
Abrahán Abraham.
Adán Adam.
Adén Aden.
Adolfo Adolf, Adolphus.
Adriano Hadrian.
Adriático m Adriatic.
Afganistán m Afghanistan.
Africa f Africa; ~ del Norte North Africa; ~ Occidental Francesa French West Africa.
Agustín Augustine.
Aladino Aladdin.
Albania f Albania.
Alberto Albert.
Albión f Albion.
Alejandría Alexandria.
Alejandro Alexander; ~ Magno Alexander the Great.
Alemania f Germany.
Alfredo Alfred.
Alicia Alice.
Alpes m/pl. Alps.
Alsacia f Alsace.
Alsacia-Lorena f Alsace-Lorraine.
Alto Volta, El Upper Volta.
Amalia Amelia.
Amazonas m Amazon.
Amberes Antwerp.
América f America; ~ del Sur South America; ~ Latina Latin America.
Ana Ann(e).
Anacreonte Anacreon.
Andalucía f Andalusia.
Andes m/pl. Andes.
Andrés Andrew.
Angulema Angoulême.
Aníbal Hannibal.
Anjeo m Anjou.
Antillas f/pl. West Indies, Antilles.
Antioquía Antioch.
Antonio Anthony.
Apeninos m/pl. Appenines.
Apuleyo Apuleius.
Aquiles Achilles.
Aquino Aquinas.

Aquisgrán Aachen, Aix-la-Chapelle.   [Arabia.]
Arabia f Arabia; ~ Saudita Saudi]
Aragón m Aragon.
Arcadia f Arcady.
Ardenas m/pl. Ardennes.
Argel Algiers.
Argelia f Algeria.
Argentina, La The Argentine.
Aristófanes Aristophanes.
Aristóteles Aristotle.
Arlequín Harlequin.
Arlés Arles.
Armenia f Armenia.
Arquimedes Archimedes.
Arturo Arthur.
Artús: el Rey ~ King Arthur.
Asia f Asia; ~ Menor Asia Minor.
Asiria f Assyria.
Asunción Capital of Paraguay.
Atenas Athens.
Atila Attila.
Atlántico m Atlantic.
Augusto Augustus.
Australia f Australia.
Austria f Austria.
Auvernia f Auvergne.
Aviñón Avignon.
Ayax Ajax.
Azores m/pl. Azores.

B

Babia: estar en ~ go wool-gathering, have one's mind somewhere else.
Babilonia f Babylon.
Baco Bacchus.
Bahamas f/pl. Bahamas.
Balcanes m/pl. Balkans.
Báltico m Baltic.
Barba Azul Bluebeard.
Barcelona Barcelona.
Bartolomé Bartholomew.
Basilea Bâle, Basle.
Baviera f Bavaria.
Bayona Bayonne.
Beatriz Beatrice.
Beda Bede.

Belcebú Beelzebub.

Belén Bethlehem; estar en ~ day-dream, go wool-gathering.

Bélgica f Belgium.

Belgrado Belgrade.

Benedicto Benedict.

Bengala f Bengal.

Benito Benedict.

Benjamín Benjamin.

Berlín Berlin.

Berna Berne.

Bernardo Bernard.

Birmania f Burma.

Bizancio Byzantium.

Blancanieves Snow-white.

Bocacio Boccaccio.

Bogotá Capital of Columbia.

Bolivia f Bolivia.

Bonn Bonn.

Borbón Bourbon.

Borgoña f Burgundy.

Bosco, El Bosch.

Bósforo m Bosphorus.

Brasil, El Brazil.

Bretaña f Brittany.

Brígida Bridget.   [bright.]

Briján: saber más que ~ be very]

Brujas Bruges.

Bruselas Brussels.

Bruto Brutus.

Buda Buddha.

Buenos Aires Capital of Argentina.

Bulgaria f Bulgaria.

Burdeos Bordeaux.

Burundi m Burundi.

C

Cabo m de Buena Esperanza Cape of Good Hope.

Cabo m de Hornos Cape Horn.

Cachemira f Kashmir.

Cádiz Cadiz.

Caín Cain; F pasar las de ~ have a terrible time.

Calcuta Calcutta.

Calvino Calvin.

Camboya f Cambodia.

Camerón m Cameroons.

Canadá, El Canada.

Canal m de la Mancha English Channel.

Cantórbery Canterbury.

Caperucita Roja Red Riding-Hood.

Caracas Capital of Venezuela.

Carlitos Charlie.

Carlomagno Charlemagne.

Carlos Charles.

Carlota Charlotte.

Cárpatos m/pl. Carpathians.

Cartago Carthage.

Casa Blanca, La The White House.

Casandra Cassandra.

Casio Cassius.

Castilla f Castile.

Catalina Catherine, Catharine; Katherine; Kathleen.

Cataluña f Catalonia.

Catón Cato.

Catulo Catullus.

Cáucaso m Caucasus.

Cecilia Cecily.

Ceilán m Ceylon.

Cenicienta, La Cinderella.

Cerdeña f Sardinia.

César Caesar.

Cicerón Cicero.

Cíclope m Cyclops.

Clemente Clement.

Colón Columbus.

Colonia Cologne.

Concha, Conchita pet names for María de la Concepción.

Confucio Confucius.

Congo, El The Congo.

Constantinopla Constantinople.

Constanza Constance.

Copenhague Copenhagen.

Córcega f Corsica.

Córdoba Cordova.

Corea f Korea.

Corinto Corinth.

Cornualles m Cornwall.

Coruña, La Corunna.

Costa f de Marfil Ivory Coast.

Costa Rica f Costa Rica.

Creta f Crete.

Creso Croesus.

Cristo Christ.

Cristóbal Christopher.

Cuba f Cuba.

Cupido Cupid.

Ch

Chad m Chad.

Champaña f Champagne.

Checoslovaquia f Czechoslovakia.

Chile m Chile, Chili.

China f China.

Chipre f Cyprus.

D

Dafne Daphne.

Dahomey o Dahomé Dahomey.

Dalmacia f Dalmatia.

Damasco Damascus.

Dámocles Damocles.

Daniel Daniel.
Danubio *m* Danube.
Dardanelos *m/pl.* Dardanelles.
Darío Darius.
David David.
Delfos Delphi.
Demóstenes Demosthenes.
Diana Diana.
Diego James.
Dinamarca *f* Denmark.
Domiciano Domitian.
Don Quijote Don Quixote.
Dorotea Dorothy.
Dresde Dresden.
Dublín Dublin.
Dunquerque Dunkirk.
Durero Dürer.   [Beauty.\
Durmiente: *la Bella* ~ Sleeping/

E

Ecuador *m* Ecuador.
Edén *m* Eden.
Edimburgo Edinburgh.
Edipo Oedipus.
Eduardo Edward.
Egeo, Mar *m* Aegean Sea.
Egipto *m* Egypt.
Eire *m* Eire.
Elena Helen.
Elíseo *m* Elysium.
Emilia Emily.
Eneas Aeneas.
Enrique Henry, Harry.
Erasmo Erasmus.
Ernesto Ernest.
Escalda *m* Scheldt.
Escandinavia *f* Scandinavia.
Escipión Scipio.
Escocia *f* Scotland.
Esmirna Smyrna.
Esopo Aesop.
España *f* Spain.
Esparta Sparta.
Esquilo Aeschylus.
Estados *m/pl.* Unidos United States.
Esteban Stephen.
Estocolmo Stockholm.
Estonia *f* Estonia.
Estrasburgo Strasbourg.
Estuardo Stuart.
Etiopía *f* Ethiopia.
Euclides Euclid.
Eufrates *m* Euphrates.
Eugenio Eugene.
Eurídice Eurydice.
Eurípedes Euripedes.
Europa *f* Europe.
Eva Eve.

F

Fausto Faust.
Federico Frederick.
Felipe Philip.
Fernando Ferdinand.
Filadelfia Philadelphia.
Filipinas *f/pl.* Philippines.
Finlandia *f* Finland.
Flandes *m* Flanders.
Florencia Florence.   [Main.\
Francfort-del-Meno Frankfurt on/
Francia *f* France.
Francisca Frances.
Francisco Francis.
Frisia *f* Friesland.

G

Gabón *m* Gaboon.
Galeno Galen.
Gales *m* Wales.
Galia *f* Gaul.
Galilea *f* Galilee.
Gante Ghent.
Garona *m* Garonne.
Gascuña *f* Gascony.
Génova Genoa.
Geofredo Geoffrey.
Gertrudis Gertrude.
Getsemaní Gethsemane.
Ghana *f* Ghana.
Gibraltar *m* Gibraltar; *Estrecho de* ~ Straits of Gibraltar; *Peñón de* ~ Rock of Gibraltar.
Gil Giles.
Ginebra Geneva; (*p.*) Guinevere.
Gironda *m* Gironde.
Godofredo Godfrey.
Golfo *m:* Pérsico Persian Gulf.
Golfo *m* de Vizcaya Bay of Biscay.
Goliat Goliath.
Gran Bretaña *f* Great Britain.
Granada Granada.
Grecia *f* Greece.
Gregorio Gregory.
Groenlandia *f* Greenland.
Gualterio Walter.
Guatemala *f* Guatemala.
Guayana *f* Guiana.
Guernesey *m* Guernsey.
Guido Guy.
Guillermo William; ~ *el Conquistador* William the Conqueror.
Guinea *f* Guinea.

H

Habana, La Havana.
Habsburgo Hapsburg.
Haití *m* Haiti.

Hamburgo Hamburg.
Haya, La The Hague.
Hébridas f/pl. Hebrides.
Helena Helen.
Hércules Hercules.
Herodes Herod.
Himalaya m The Himalaya(s).
Hipócrates Hippocrates.
Hispanoamérica f Spanish America.
Holanda f Holland.
Homero Homer.
Honduras f Honduras.
Horacio Horace.
Hugo Hugh, Hugo.
Hungría f Hungary.

I

Iberia f Iberia.
Ibiza f Ibiza.
Ignacio Ignatius.
India, La India.   [East Indies.\
Indias f/pl. Indies; ~ *Orientales)*
Indonesia f Indonesia.
Indostán m Hindustan.
Inés Agnes.
Inglaterra f England.
Irak m Irak, Iraq.
Irán, El Iran.
Irlanda f Ireland; ~ *del Norte* Northern Ireland.
Isaac Isaac.
Isabel Isabel, Elizabeth.
Isabelita Bess(ie), Bessy, Betty.
Iseo Isolde.
Isla f **de Francia** Mauritius.
Islandia f Iceland.
Islas f/pl.: ~ *Bahama* Bahamas; ~ *Baleares* Balearic Isles; ~ *Bermudas* Bermuda; ~ *Británicas* British Isles; ~ *de Cabo Verde* Cape Verde Islands; ~ *Canarias* Canary Isles; ~ *Hawai* Hawaii; ~*Normandas* Channel Isles; ~ *de Sotavento* Leeward Isles.
Isolda Isolde.
Israel m Israel.
Italia f Italy.

J

Jacob Jacob.
Jacobo (*reyes de Escocia e Inglaterra*) James.
Jaime James.
Jamaica f Jamaica.
Japón, El Japan.
Jehová Jehovah.
Jenofonte Xenophon.

Jeremías Jeremy.
Jericó Jericho.
Jerónimo Jerome.
Jerusalén Jerusalem.
Jesús Jesus; ¡~! good heavens!; (*estornudo*) bless you!; en un decir ~ in a trice; *Jesucristo* Jesus Christ.
Job Job.
Jordán m Jordan (*river*).
Jordania f Jordan (*country*).
Jorge George.
José Joseph.
Josefina Josephine.
Josué Joshua.
Juan John; un buen ~, ~ Lanas simple soul.
Juana Jane; Joan; ~ de Arco Joan of Arc.
Juanito Jack; Johnny.
Judá f Judah.
Judas Judas.
Judea f Judaea.
Julieta Juliet.
Julio Julius.
Júpiter Jupiter; Jove.

K

Kenia f Kenya.
Kuwait m, **Estado de** ~ Kuwait, State of ~.

L

Lacio m Latium.
Lanzarote Lancelot.
Laos m Laos.
La Paz *Capital of Bolivia.*
Laponia f Lapland.
Lausana Lausanne.
Lázaro Lazarus.
Leandro Leander.
Leida, Leide(n) Leyden.
Leningrado Leningrad.
León de Francia Lyons.
Leonor Eleanor.   [smart.\
Lepe: saber más que ~ be pretty)
Lete(o) m Lethe.
Letonia f Latvia.
Levante m Levant; *South-east part (or coasts) of Spain.*
Líbano m Lebanon.
Liberia f Liberia.
Libia f Libya.
Lieja Liège.
Lila Lille.
Lima *Capital of Peru.*
Liorna Leghorn.
Lisboa Lisbon.
Lituania f Lithuania.

Livio Livy.
Loira *m* Loire.
Lola, Lolita *pet names for María de los Dolores.*
Lombardía *f* Lombardy.
Londres London.
Lorena *f* Lorraine.
Lorenzo Laurence.
Lovaina Louvain.
Lucano Lucan.
Lucas Luke.
Lucerna Lucerne.
Lucrecia Lucretia.
Lucrecio Lucretius.
Luis Louis.
Lutero Luther.
Luxemburgo *m* Luxembourg.
Lyón Lyons.

M

Madera *f* Madeira.
Madrid Madrid.
Magallanes *m* Magellan; *Estrecho de* ～ Magellan Straits.
Magdalena *f* Magdalen.
Maguncia Mainz.
Mahoma Mahomet.
Malaca *f*, Malaya *f* Malaya.
Málaga Malaga.
Malasia *f* Malaysia.
Malawi *m* Malawi.
Malí *m*, República *f* del ～ Mali.
Mallorca *f* Majorca.
Malvinas *f/pl.* Falkland Isles.
Managua *Capital of Nicaragua.*
Manolo *pet name for Manuel.*
Manuel Emmanuel.
Mar *m*: ～ *Adriático* Adriatic Sea; ～ *Báltico* Baltic Sea; ～ *Caribe* Caribbean (Sea); ～ *Caspio* Caspian Sea; ～ *de las Indias* Indian Ocean; ～ *Mediterráneo* Mediterranean Sea; ～ *Muerto* Dead Sea; ～ *Negro* Black Sea; ～ *del Norte* North Sea; ～ *Rojo* Red Sea.
Marcial Martial.
Marcos Mark.
Margarita Margaret.
María Mary; ～ *Antonieta* Marie Antoinette.
Maricastaña: *en tiempo de* ～ long ago, in the year dot.
Marruecos *m* Morocco.
Marsella Marseilles.
Marsellesa *f* Marseillaise.
Marte Mars.
Martinica *f* Martinique.
Mateo Matthew.

Matilde Mat(h)ilda.
Mauricio Mauritius; (*p.*) Maurice.
Mauritania *f* Mauretania.
Meca, La Mecca.
Mediterráneo *m* Mediterranean.
Méjico *m* Mexico.
Menorca *f* Minorca.
Mercurio Mercury.
Mesías Messiah.
México *m S.Am.* Mexico.
Midas Midas.
Miguel Michael; ～ *Angel* Michaelangelo.
Milán Milan.
Misisipí *m* Mississippi.
Moisés Moses.
Montevideo *Capital of Uruguay.*
Moscú Moscow.
Mosela *m* Moselle.
Montes *m/pl.*: ～ *Apalaches* Appalachian Mountains; ～ *Cárpatos* Carpathian Mountains; ～ *Rocosos* Rocky Mountains.
Munich Munich.
Murcia Murcia.

N

Napoleón Napoleon.
Nápoles Naples.
Narbona Narbonne.
Navarra *f* Navarre.
Nazaret Nazareth.
Nepal *m*, Reino de ～ Nepal, Kingdom of ～.
Neptuno Neptune.
Nerón Nero.
Niágara Niagara.
Nicolás Nicholas.
Niger *m* Niger.
Nigeria *f* Nigeria.
Nilo *m* Nile.
Niza Nice.
Noé Noah.
Normandía *f* Normandy.
Noruega *f* Norway.
Nueva Escocia *f* Nova Scotia.
Nueva Gales *f* del Sur New South Wales.
Nueva Guinea *f* New Guinea.
Nueva York New York.
Nueva Zelanda *f* New Zealand.

O

Océano *m*: ～ *Atlántico* Atlantic Ocean; ～ *Indico* Indian Ocean; ～ *Pacífico* Pacific Ocean.
Octavio Octavian.

Olimpo Olympus.
Oliverio Oliver.
Orcadas *f/pl.* Orkney Islands.
Orfeo Orpheus.
Oriente *m* East; *Extremo* ~ Far East; ~ *Medio* Middle East; *Próximo* ~ Near East.
Ostende Ostend.
Ovidio Ovid.

P

Pablo Paul.
Pacífico *m* Pacific
Paca *pet name for Francisca.*
Paco *pet name for Francisco* Frank.
País *m* **de los Lagos** Lake District.
País *m* **Vasco** Basque Country.
Países *m/pl.* **Bajos** Low Countries; Netherlands.
Pakistán *m* Pakistan.
Palestina *f* Palestine.
Panamá *m* Panama.
Paquita *pet name for Francisca.*
Paquito *pet name for Francisco* Frank.
Paraguay, El Paraguay.
París Paris.
Parnaso Parnassus.
Patillas F the devil, Old Nick; *ser un* ~ be a poor fish, be a nobody.
Patricio Patrick.
Pedro Peter.
Pegaso Pegasus.
Pekín Pekin(g).
Pensilvania *f* Pennsylvania.
Pepa *pet name for Josefa.*
Pepe *pet name for José* Joe.
Pepita *pet name for Josefa.*
Perico *pet name for Pedro* Pete; ~ *el de los Palotes* somebody, so-and-so, any Tom Dick or Harry.
Pero Grullo: *frase de* ~ = *perogrullada.*
Perpiñán Perpignan.
Perú, El Peru.
Petrarca Petrarch.
Piamonte *m* Piedmont.
Picardía *f* Picardy.
Pilatos Pilate.
Píndaro Pindar.
Pío Pius.
Pirineo(s) *m(pl.)* Pyrenees.
Pitágoras Pythagoras.
Platón Plato.
Plinio Pliny.
Plutarco Plutarch.
Plutón Pluto.
Polichinela Punch.

Polinesia *f* Polynesia.
Polonia *f* Poland.
Pompeya Pompeii.
Pompeyo Pompey.
Poncio Pilatos Pontius Pilate.
Portugal *m* Portugal.
Praga Prague.
Provenza *f* Provence.
Prusia *f* Prussia.
Psique Psyche.
Puerto Rico *m* Porto Rico.
Pulgarcito Tom Thumb.

Q

Quito *Capital of Ecuador.*

R

Rafael Raphael.
Raimundo, Ramón Raymond.
Raquel Rachel.
Ratisbona Ratisbon.
Rebeca Rebecca.
Reginaldo, Reinaldos Reginald.
Renania *f* Rhineland.
República *f* **Arabe Unida (R.A.U.) (Egipto** *m***)** United Arab Republic (U.A.R.) (Egypt).
República *f* **Centroafricana** Central African Republic.
República *f* **Dominicana** *f* Dominican Republic.
República *f* **Malgache** Republic of Madagascar.
República *f* **Popular de Mongolia** Peoples's Republic of Mongolia.
República *f* **Socialista Soviética de Bielorusia** Byelorussian Soviet Socialist Republic.
República *f* **Socialista Soviética de Ucraina** Ukrainian Soviet Socialist Republic.
Ricardo Richard.
Rin *m* Rhine.
Roberto Robert.
Rochela, La La Rochelle.
Ródano *m* Rhône.
Rodas *f* Rhodes.
Rodesia *f* Rhodesia.
Rodrigo Roderick.
Roldán, Rolando Roland.
Roma Rome.
Rosa Rose.
Rosellón *m* Roussillon.
Ruán Rouen.
Ruanda *f* Ruanda.
Rumania *f* Rumania.
Rusia *f* Russia.

S

Saboya f Savoy.
Sahara m Sahara.
Sajonia f Saxony.
Salomón Solomon.
Salustio Sallust.
Salvador, El (El) Salvador.
Samuel Samuel.
San José Capital of Costa Rica.
Sansón Samson.
Santander Santander.   [Chile.\
Santiago Saint James; Capital of)
Sarre m Saar.
Satanás Satan.
Saturno Saturn.
Saúl Saul.
Segovia Segovia.
Sena m Seine.
Senegal, El Senegal.
Servia f Serbia.
Sevilla Seville.
Siam m Siam.
Siberia f Siberia.
Sibila Sibyl.
Sicilia f Sicily.
Sierra Leona f Sierra Leone.
Simbad Sin(d)bad.
Singapur Singapore.
Sión m Zion.
Siracusa Syracuse.
Siria f Syria.
Sócrates Socrates.
Sófocles Sophocles.
Somalia f Somaliland.
Sudán m S(o)udan.
Suez, Canal m de Suez Canal.
Suecia f Sweden.
Suiza f Switzerland.

T

Tácito Tacitus.
Tailandia f Thailand.
Tajo m Tagus.
Támesis m Thames.
Tanganica f Tanganyika.
Tánger Tangier.
Tebas Thebes.
Tejas m Texas.
Terencio Terence.
Teresa Theresa.
Termópilas, Las Thermopylae.
Terranova f Newfoundland.
Tesalia f Thessaly.
Tíber m Tiber.
Tibet, El Tibet.
Ticiano Titian.
Tierra f Santa Holy Land.
Timoteo Timothy.

Tiro Tyre.
Tirol, El The Tyrol.
Togolandia f Togoland.
Toledo Toledo.
Tolomeo Ptolemy.
Tolón Toulon.
Tolosa (de Francia) Toulouse.
Tomás Thomas.
Toscana, La Tuscany.
Trento Trent.
Trinidad f y Tobago m Trinidad
and Tobago.
Tristán Tristram.
Troya Troy; ¡arda ~! press on
regardless!; ¡aquí fue ~! now there's
nothing but ruins; that's where the
trouble began; that was a battle\
Túnez Tunis.   [royal.)
Turena f Touraine.
Turquía f Turkey.

U

Ucrania f Ukraine.
Unión f de India Union of India.
Unión f de Repúblicas Socialistas
  Soviéticas (U.R.S.S). Union
  of Soviet Socialist Republics
  (U.S.S.R.).   [South Africa.\
Unión f Sudafricana Union of)
Uruguay m, República f Oriental
  del ~ Uruguay.
Utopia f Utopia.

V

Valencia Valencia.
Varsovia Warsaw.   [ces.\
Vascongadas, Las Basque Provin-)
Vaticano m Vatican.
Velázquez Velasquez.
Venecia Venice.
Venezuela f Venezuela.
Venus Venus.
Versalles Versailles.
Vesubio m Vesuvius.
Vicente Vincent.
Viena Vienna.
Villadiego: F tomar las de ~ beat it.
Virgilio Virgil.
Vizcaya f Biscay.
Vosgos m/pl. Vosges.
Vulcano Vulcan.

Y

Yugo(e)slavia f Jugoslavia.

Z

Zambia f Zambia.
Zaragoza Saragossa.
Zululandia f Zululand.

Numerals — Numerales

Cardinal numbers — Números cardinales

0	cero *nought*	50	cincuenta *fifty*
1	uno, una *one*	60	sesenta *sixty*
2	dos *two*	70	setenta *seventy*
3	tres *three*	80	ochenta *eighty*
4	cuatro *four*	90	noventa *ninety*
5	cinco *five*	100	cien(to) *a (one) hundred*
6	seis *six*	101	ciento uno *a hundred and one*
7	siete *seven*	110	ciento diez *a hundred and ten*
8	ocho *eight*	200	doscientos, -as *two hundred*
9	nueve *nine*	300	trescientos, -as *three hundred*
10	diez *ten*	400	cuatrocientos, -as *four hundred*
11	once *eleven*		
12	doce *twelve*	500	quinientos, -as *five hundred*
13	trece *thirteen*	600	seiscientos, -as *six hundred*
14	catorce *fourteen*	700	setecientos, -as *seven hundred*
15	quince *fifteen*	800	ochocientos, -as *eight hundred*
16	dieciséis *sixteen*	900	novecientos, -as *nine hundred*
17	diecisiete *seventeen*	1000	mil *a thousand*
18	dieciocho *eighteen*	1959	mil novecientos cincuenta y nueve *nineteen hundred and fifty-nine*
19	diecinueve *nineteen*		
20	veinte *twenty*		
21	veintiuno *twenty-one*	2000	dos mil *two thousand*
22	veintidós *twenty-two*	1000000	un millón (de) *a (one) million*
30	treinta *thirty*		
31	treinta y uno *thirty-one*	2000000	dos millones (de) *two million*
40	cuarenta *forty*		

Ordinal numbers — Números ordinales

(The ordinal numbers in Spanish agree with the noun in number and gender, *primero -a -os -as* etc.)

1	primero *first*	15	decimoquinto *fifteenth*
2	segundo *second*	16	decimosexto *sixteenth*
3	tercero *third*	17	decimoséptimo *seventeenth*
4	cuarto *fourth*	18	decimoctavo *eighteenth*
5	quinto *fifth*	19	decimonoveno, decimonono *nineteenth*
6	sexto *sixth*		
7	séptimo *seventh*	20	vigésimo *twentieth*
8	octavo *eighth*	21	vigésimo prim(er)o *twenty-first*
9	noveno, nono *ninth*	22	vigésimo segundo *twenty-second*
10	décimo *tenth*	30	trigésimo *thirtieth*
11	undécimo *eleventh*	31	trigésimo prim(er)o *thirty-first*
12	duodécimo *twelfth*	40	cuadragésimo *fortieth*
13	decimotercero, decimotercio *thirteenth*	50	quincuagésimo *fiftieth*
		60	sexagésimo *sixtieth*
14	decimocuarto *fourteenth*	70	septuagésimo *seventieth*

80 octogésimo *eightieth*	500 quingentésimo *five hundredth*
90 nonagésimo *ninetieth*	600 sexcentésimo *six hundredth*
100 centésimo *hundredth*	700 septingentésimo *seven hundredth*
101 centésimo primero *hundred and first*	800 octingentésimo *eight hundredth*
110 centésimo décimo *hundred and tenth*	900 noningentésimo *nine hundredth*
200 ducentésimo *two hundredth*	1000 milésimo *thousandth*
300 trecentésimo *three hundredth*	2000 dos milésimo *two thousandth*
400 cuadringentésimo *four hundredth*	1000000 millonésimo *millionth*
	2000000 dos millonésimo *two millionth*

En inglés, los números ordinales suelen abreviarse 1st., 2nd., 3rd., 4th., 5th. *etc.*; in Spanish, the ordinal numbers may be written 1°, 2° *etc.*

Fractions and other numerals — Números quebrados y otros

$1/2$ medio, media *one (a) half*; $1^1/_2$ uno y medio *one and a half*; $2^1/_2$ dos y medio *two and a half*; $1/2$ hora *half an hour*; $1^1/_2$ kilómetros *a kilometer and a half*

$1/3$ un tercio, la tercera parte *one (a) third*; $2/3$ dos tercios, las dos terceras partes *two thirds*

$1/4$ un cuarto, la cuarta parte *one (a) quarter*; $3/4$ tres cuartos, las tres cuartas partes *three-quarters*; $1/4$ hora *a quarter of an hour*; $1^1/_4$ horas *an hour and a quarter*

$1/5$ un quinto *one (a) fifth*; $3^4/_5$ tres y cuatro quintos *three and four fifths*

$1/11$ un onzavo *one (an) eleventh*; $5/12$ cinco dozavos *five twelfths*; $75/100$ setenta y cinco centésimos *seventy-five hundreths*

$1/1000$ un milésimo *one (a) thousandth*

simple *single*
    doble, duplo *double*
    triple *treble, triple, threefold*
    cuádruplo *fourfold*
    quíntuplo *fivefold etc.*

una vez *once*
    dos veces *twice*
    tres veces *three times etc.*
    siete veces más grande *seven times as big*; doce veces más *twelve times more*

en primer lugar *firstly*
    en segundo lugar *secondly etc.*

$7 + 8 = 15$ siete y (*or* más) ocho son quince *seven and eight are fifteen*

$10 - 3 = 7$ diez menos tres resta siete, de tres a diez van siete *three from ten leaves seven*

$2 \times 3 = 6$ dos por tres son seis *two times three are six*

$20 \div 4 = 5$ veinte dividido por cuatro es cinco *twenty divided by four is five*.

Note on the Spanish verb

The simple tenses and parts of the three conjugations and of irregular verbs are set out in the following pages, but certain general points may be summarized here:

1. **Compound tenses** etc. are formed with the auxiliary *haber* and the past participle:

perfect:	he mandado (*subj.*: haya mandado)
pluperfect:	había mandado (*subj.*: hubiera mandado, hubiese mandado)
future perfect:	habré mandado
perfect infinitive:	haber mandado
perfect gerund:	habiendo mandado

2. The **imperfect** is regular for all verbs except *ser* (*era* etc.) and *ir* (*iba* etc.).

3. The **conditional** is formed like the future on the infinitive: *mandar/ía*. If the future is irregular, so will be the conditional: *salir — saldré, saldría; decir — diré, diría*.

4. The **imperfect subjunctives** I and II are formed from the 3rd person plural of the preterite, using as a stem what remains after removing the final *-ron* syllable, and adding *-ra* or *-se*:

   mandar: manda/ron — mandara, mandase

   querer: quisie/ron — quisiera, quisiese

   traer: traje/ron — trajera, trajese

   conducir: conduje/ron — condujera, condujese.

5. **Imperative.** The "true" imperative is limited to the familiar forms or true second persons (*tú, vosotros*) used affirmatively: *habla, mándamelo, hacedlo*. The imperative affirmative with *Vd., Vds.* is formed with the subjunctive: *mándemelo Vd., háganlo Vds*. The imperative negative for all persons is formed with the subjunctive: *no lo hagas* (*tú*), *no vayan Vds*.

6. **Continuous tenses** are formed with *estar* and the gerund: *estoy trabajando, estábamos discutiendo*. Other auxiliary verbs may be used according to sense: *vamos avanzando, según voy viendo, vengo diciendo eso*.

7. The **passive** is formed with tenses of *ser* and the past participle: *es recibido, será vencido, fue construido*. In passive uses the past participle agrees in number and gender with the subject: *las casas fueron derribadas*.

First Conjugation

[1a] mandar
Infinitive: mandar   **Gerund:** mandando   **Past Participle:** mandado

Indicative

Present	Imperfect	Preterite
mando	mandaba	mandé
mandas	mandabas	mandaste
manda	mandaba	mandó
mandamos	mandábamos	mandamos
mandáis	mandabais	mandasteis
mandan	mandaban	mandaron

Future	Conditional
mandaré	mandaría
mandarás	mandarías
mandará	mandaría
mandaremos	mandaríamos
mandaréis	mandaríais
mandarán	mandarían

Subjunctive

Present	Imperfect I	Imperfect II
mande	mandara	mandase
mandes	mandaras	mandases
mande	mandara	mandase
mandemos	mandáramos	mandásemos
mandéis	mandarais	mandaseis
manden	mandaran	mandasen

Imperative

Affirmative	Negative
manda (tú)	no mandes (tú)
mande Vd.	no mande Vd.
mandad (vosotros)	no mandéis (vosotros)
manden Vds.	no manden Vds.

	Infinitive	Present Indicative	Present Subjunctive	Preterite
[1b]	**cambiar.** The *i* of the stem is not stressed and the verb is regular	cambio cambias cambia cambiamos cambiáis cambian	cambie cambies cambie cambiemos cambiéis cambien	cambié cambiaste cambió cambiamos cambiasteis cambiaron
[1c]	**variar.** In forms stressed on the stem, the *i* is accented	varío varías varía variamos variáis varían	varíe varíes varíe variemos variéis varíen	varié variaste varió variamos variasteis variaron

Infinitive	Present Indicative	Present Subjunctive	Preterite
[1d] evacuar. The *u* of the stem is not stressed and the verb is regular	evacuo evacuas evacua evacuamos evacuáis evacuan	evacue evacues evacue evacuemos evacuéis evacuen	evacué evacuaste evacuó evacuamos evacuasteis evacuaron
[1e] acentuar. In forms stressed on the stem, the *u* is accented	acentúo acentúas acentúa acentuamos acentuáis acentúan	acentúe acentúes acentúe acentuemos acentuéis acentúen	acentué acentuaste acentuó acentuamos acentuasteis acentuaron
[1f] cruzar. The stem consonant *z* is written *c* before *e*	cruzo cruzas cruza cruzamos cruzáis cruzan	cruce cruces cruce crucemos crucéis crucen	crucé cruzaste cruzó cruzamos cruzasteis cruzaron
[1g] tocar. The stem consonant *c* is written *qu* before *e*	toco tocas toca tocamos tocáis tocan	toque toques toque toquemos toquéis toquen	toqué tocaste tocó tocamos tocasteis tocaron
[1h] pagar. The stem consonant *g* is written *gu* (*u* silent) before *e*	pago pagas paga pagamos pagáis pagan	pague pagues pague paguemos paguéis paguen	pagué pagaste pagó pagamos pagasteis pagaron
[1i] fraguar. The *u* of the stem is written *ü* (so that it should be pronounced) before *e*	fraguo fraguas fragua fraguamos fraguáis fraguan	fragüe fragües fragüe fragüemos fragüéis fragüen	fragüé fraguaste fraguó fraguamos fraguasteis fraguaron
[1k] pensar. The stem vowel *e* becomes *ie* when stressed	pienso piensas piensa pensamos pensáis piensan	piense pienses piense pensemos penséis piensen	pensé pensaste pensó pensamos pensasteis pensaron
[1l] errar. As [1k], but the diphthong is written *ye* at the start of the word	yerro yerras yerra erramos erráis yerran	yerre yerres yerre erremos erréis yerren	erré erraste erró erramos errasteis erraron

Infinitive	Present Indicative	Present Subjunctive	Preterite
[1m] contar. The stem vowel *o* becomes *ue* when stressed	cuento cuentas cuenta contamos contáis cuentan	cuente cuentes cuente contemos contéis cuenten	conté contaste contó contamos contasteis contaron
[1n] agorar. The stem vowel *o* becomes *üe* when stressed	agüero agüeras agüera agoramos agoráis agüeran	agüere agüeres agüere agoremos agoréis agüeren	agoré agoraste agoró agoramos agorasteis agoraron
[1o] jugar. The stem vowel *u* becomes *ue* when stressed; the stem consonant *g* is written *gu* (*u* silent) before *e*; *conjugar*, *enjugar* are regular	juego juegas juega jugamos jugáis juegan	juegue juegues juegue juguemos juguéis jueguen	jugué jugaste jugó jugamos jugasteis jugaron
[1p] estar. Irregular. Imperative: *está (tú)*	estoy estás está estamos estáis están	esté estés esté estemos estéis estén	estuve estuviste estuvo estuvimos estuvisteis estuvieron
[1q] andar. Irregular.	ando andas anda andamos andáis andan	ande andes ande andemos andéis anden	anduve anduviste anduvo anduvimos anduvisteis anduvieron
[1r] dar. Irregular.	doy das da damos dais dan	dé des dé demos deis den	di diste dio dimos disteis dieron

Second conjugation

[2a] **vender**
Infinitive: vender   **Gerund:** vendiendo   **Past Participle:** vendido

Indicative

Present	*Imperfect*	*Preterite*
vendo	vendía	vendí
vendes	vendías	vendiste
vende	vendía	vendió
vendemos	vendíamos	vendimos
vendéis	vendíais	vendisteis
venden	vendían	vendieron

Future	*Conditional*
venderé	vendería
venderás	venderías
venderá	vendería
venderemos	venderíamos
venderéis	venderíais
venderán	venderían

Subjunctive

Present	*Imperfect I*	*Imperfect II*
venda	vendiera	vendiese
vendas	vendieras	vendieses
venda	vendiera	vendiese
vendamos	vendiéramos	vendiésemos
vendáis	vendierais	vendieseis
vendan	vendieran	vendiesen

Imperative

Affirmative	*Negative*
vende (tú)	no vendas (tú)
venda Vd.	no venda Vd.
vended (vosotros)	no vendáis (vosotros)
vendan Vds.	no vendan Vds.

Infinitive	Present Indicative	Present Subjunctive	Preterite
[2b] **vencer.** The stem consonant *c* is written *z* before *a* and *o*	venzo vences vence vencemos vencéis vencen	venza venzas venza venzamos venzáis venzan	vencí venciste venció vencimos vencisteis vencieron
[2c] **coger.** The stem consonant *g* is written *j* before *a* and *o*	cojo coges coge cogemos cogéis cogen	coja cojas coja cojamos cojáis cojan	cogí cogiste cogió cogimos cogisteis cogieron

Infinitive	Present Indicative	Present Subjunctive	Preterite
[2d] merecer. The stem consonant *c* becomes *zc* before *a* and *o*	merezco mereces merece merecemos merecéis merecen	merezca merezcas merezca merezcamos merezcáis merezcan	merecí mereciste mereció merecimos merecisteis merecieron
[2e] creer. Untressed *i* between vowels is written *y*. Past participle: *creído* Gerund: *creyendo*	creo crees cree creemos creéis creen	crea creas crea creamos creáis crean	creí creíste creyó creímos creísteis creyeron
[2f] tañer. Unstressed *i* after *ñ* and *ll* is omitted. Gerund: *tañendo*	taño tañes tañe tañemos tañéis tañen	taña tañas taña tañamos tañáis tañan	tañí tañiste tañó tañimos tañisteis tañeron
[2g] perder. The stem vowel *e* becomes *ie* when stressed	pierdo pierdes pierde perdemos perdéis pierden	pierda pierdas pierda perdamos perdáis pierdan	perdí perdiste perdió perdimos perdisteis perdieron
[2h] mover. The stem vowel *o* becomes *ue* when stressed. Verbs in *-olver* form their past participle in *-uelto*	muevo mueves mueve movemos movéis mueven	mueva muevas mueva movamos mováis muevan	moví moviste movió movimos movisteis movieron
[2i] oler. As [2h], but the diphthong is written *hue* at the start of the word	huelo hueles huele olemos oléis huelen	huela huelas huela olamos oláis huelan	olí oliste olió olimos olisteis olieron
[2k] haber. Irregular throughout. Future: *habré*	he has ha hemos habéis han	haya hayas haya hayamos hayáis hayan	hube hubiste hubo hubimos hubisteis hubieron
[2l] tener. Irregular throughout. Future: *tendré* Imperative: *ten (tú)*	tengo tienes tiene tenemos tenéis tienen	tenga tengas tenga tengamos tengáis tengan	tuve tuviste tuvo tuvimos tuvisteis tuvieron

Infinitive	Present Indicative	Present Subjunctive	Preterite
[2m] caber. Irregular throughout. Future: *cabré*	quepo cabes cabe cabemos cabéis caben	quepa quepas quepa quepamos quepáis quepan	cupe cupiste cupo cupimos cupisteis cupieron
[2n] saber. Irregular throughout. Future: *sabré*	sé sabes sabe sabemos sabéis saben	sepa sepas sepa sepamos sepáis sepan	supe supiste supo supimos supisteis supieron
[2o] caer. Irregular. Unstressed *i* between vowels is written *y*, as [2e]. Past participle: *caído* Gerund: *cayendo*	caigo caes cae caemos caéis caen	caiga caigas caiga caigamos caigáis caigan	caí caiste cayó caimos caisteis cayeron
[2p] traer. Irregular throughout. Past participle: *traído* Gerund: *trayendo*	traigo traes trae traemos traéis traen	traiga traigas traiga traigamos traigáis traigan	traje trajiste trajo trajimos trajisteis trajeron
[2q] valer. Irregular. Future: *valdré*	valgo vales vale valemos valéis valen	valga valgas valga valgamos valgáis valgan	valí valiste valió valimos valisteis valieron
[2r] poner. Irregular throughout. Future: *pondré* Past participle: *puesto* Imperative: *pon (tú)*	pongo pones pone ponemos ponéis ponen	ponga pongas ponga pongamos pongáis pongan	puse pusiste puso pusimos pusisteis pusieron
[2s] hacer. Irregular throughout. Future: *haré* Past participle: *hecho* Imperative: *haz (tú)*	hago haces hace hacemos hacéis hacen	haga hagas haga hagamos hagáis hagan	hice hiciste hizo hicimos hicisteis hicieron
[2t] poder. Irregular throughout. In present tenses like [2h]. Future: *podré* Gerund: *pudiendo*	puedo puedes puede podemos podéis pueden	pueda puedas pueda podamos podáis puedan	pude pudiste pudo pudimos pudisteis pudieron

Infinitive	Present Indicative	Present Subjunctive	Preterite
[2u] querer. Irregular. In present tenses like [2g]. Future: *querré*	quiero quieres quiere queremos queréis quieren	quiera quieras quiera queramos queráis quieran	quise quisiste quiso quisimos quisisteis quisieron
[2w] ser. Irregular throughout. Past participle: *sido* Gerund: *siendo* Future: *seré* Imperfect: *era, eras etc.* Imperative: *sé (tú), sed (vosotros)*	soy eres es somos sois son	sea seas sea seamos seáis sean	fui fuiste fue fuimos fuisteis fueron

[2x] placer. Used only in 3rd person sg. Irregular forms: Present subj. *plega, plegue* or *plazca*; Preterite *plugo* or *plació*; Imperfect subj. I *pluguiera* or *placiera*, Imperfect subj. II *pluguiese* or *placiese*.

[2y] yacer. (Mostly †). Irregular forms: Present indic. *yazco, yazgo* or *yago*; Present subj. *yazca, yazga, yaga* etc. Imperative *yace (tú)* or *yaz (tú).*

[2z] raer. Alternative forms in present tenses: Present indic. *raigo* or *rayo* etc.; Present subj. *raiga* or *raya* etc.

[2za] roer. Alternative forms in present tenses: Present indic. *roigo* or *royo*; Present subj. *roiga* or *roya.*

Third conjugation

[3a] **recibir**
Infinitive: recibir   **Gerund:** recibiendo   **Past Participle:** recibido

Indicative

Present	Imperfect	Preterite
recibo	recibía	recibí
recibes	recibías	recibiste
recibe	recibía	recibió
recibimos	recibíamos	recibimos
recibís	recibíais	recibisteis
reciben	recibían	recibieron

Future	Conditional
recibiré	recibiría
recibirás	recibirías
recibirá	recibiría
recibiremos	recibiríamos
recibiréis	recibiríais
recibirán	recibirían

Subjunctive

Present	Imperfect I	Imperfect II
reciba	recibiera	recibiese
recibas	recibieras	recibieses
reciba	recibiera	recibiese
recibamos	recibiéramos	recibiésemos
recibáis	recibierais	recibieseis
reciban	recibieran	recibiesen

Imperative

Affirmative	Negative
recibe (tú)	no recibas (tú)
reciba Vd.	no reciba Vd.
recibid (vosotros)	no recibáis (vosotros)
reciban Vds.	no reciban Vds.

Infinitive	Present Indicative	Present Subjunctive	Preterite
[3b] **esparcir.** The stem consonant *c* is written *z* before *a* and *o*	esparzo	esparza	esparcí
	esparces	esparzas	esparciste
	esparce	esparza	esparció
	esparcimos	esparzamos	esparcimos
	esparcís	esparzáis	esparcisteis
	esparcen	esparzan	esparcieron
[3c] **dirigir.** The stem consonant *g* is written *j* before *a* and *o*	dirijo	dirija	dirigí
	diriges	dirijas	dirigiste
	dirige	dirija	dirigió
	dirigimos	dirijamos	dirigimos
	dirigís	dirijáis	dirigisteis
	dirigen	dirijan	dirigieron

Infinitive	Present Indicative	Present Subjunctive	Preterite
[3d] distinguir. The *u* after the stem consonant *g* is omitted before *a* and *o*	distingo distingues distingue distinguimos distinguís distinguen	distinga distingas distinga distingamos distingáis distingan	distinguí distinguiste distinguió distinguimos distinguisteis distinguieron
[3e] delinquir. The stem consonant *qu* is written *c* before *a* and *o*	delinco delinques delinque delinquimos delinquís delinquen	delinca delincas delinca delincamos delincáis delincan	delinquí delinquiste delinquió delinquimos delinquisteis delinquieron
[3f] lucir. The stem consonant *c* becomes *zc* before *a* and *o*	luzco luces luce lucimos lucís lucen	luzca luzcas luzca luzcamos luzcáis luzcan	lucí luciste lució lucimos lucisteis lucieron
[3g] concluir. The *i* of *-ió* and *-ie-* changes to *y*; a *y* is inserted before endings not beginning with *i*. Gerund: *concluyendo*	concluyo concluyes concluye concluimos concluís concluyen	concluya concluyas concluya concluyamos concluyáis concluyan	concluí concluiste concluyó concluimos concluisteis concluyeron
[3h] gruñir. Unstressed *i* after *ñ*, *ll* and *ch* is omitted. Gerund: *gruñendo*	gruño gruñes gruñe gruñimos gruñís gruñen	gruña gruñas gruña gruñamos gruñáis gruñan	gruñí gruñiste gruñó gruñimos gruñisteis gruñeron
[3i] sentir. The stem vowel *e* becomes *ie* when stressed; unstressed *e* becomes *i* in 3rd persons of Preterite, 1st and 2nd persons pl. of Present Subjunctive. In *adquirir* etc. the stem vowel *i* becomes *ie* when stressed Gerund: *sintiendo*	siento sientes siente sentimos sentís sienten	sienta sientas sienta sintamos sintáis sientan	sentí sentiste sintió sentimos sentisteis sintieron
[3k] dormir. The stem vowel *o* becomes *ue* when stressed; unstressed *o* becomes *u* in 3rd persons of Preterite, 1st and 2nd persons pl. of Present Subjunctive. Gerund: *durmiendo*	duermo duermes duerme dormimos dormís duermen	duerma duermas duerma durmamos durmáis duerman	dormí dormiste durmió dormimos dormisteis durmieron

Infinitive	Present Indicative	Present Subjunctive	Preterite
[3l] medir. The stem vowel *e* becomes *i* when stressed, and also when unstressed in 3rd persons of Preterite, 1st and 2nd persons pl. of Present Subjunctive. Gerund: *midiendo*	mido mides mide medimos medís miden	mida midas mida midamos midáis midan	medí mediste midió medimos medisteis midieron
[3m] reír. Irregular. Past participle: *reído* Gerund: *riendo*	río ríes ríe reímos reís ríen	ría rías ría riamos riáis rían	reí reíste rió reímos reísteis rieron
[3n] erguir. Irregular. Gerund: *irguiendo* Imperative: *irgue* (tú) or *yergue* (tú)	irgo irgues irgue erguimos erguís irguen *or* yergo yergues yergue erguimos erguís yerguen	irga irgas irga irgamos irgáis irgan *or* yerga yergas yerga yergamos yergáis yergan	erguí erguiste irguió erguimos erguisteis irguieron
[3o] conducir. The stem consonant *c* becomes *zc* before *a* and *o*, as [3f]. Irregular preterite in *-uje*	conduzco conduces conduce conducimos conducís conducen	conduzca conduzcas conduzca conduzcamos conduzcáis conduzcan	conduje condujiste condujo condujimos condujisteis condujeron
[3p] decir. Irregular throughout. Future: *diré* Past participle: *dicho* Gerund: *diciendo* Imperative: *di* (tú)	digo dices dice decimos decís dicen	diga digas diga digamos digáis digan	dije dijiste dijo dijimos dijisteis dijeron
[3q] oír. Irregular. Unstressed *i* between vowels becomes *y*. Past participle: *oído* Gerund: *oyendo*	oigo oyes oye oímos oís oyen	oiga oigas oiga oigamos oigáis oigan	oí oiste oyó oímos oísteis oyeron

Infinitive	Present Indicative	Present Subjunctive	Preterite
[3r] salir. Irregular. Future: *saldré* Imperative: *sal (tú)*	salgo sales sale salimos salís salen	salga salgas salga salgamos salgáis salgan	salí saliste salió salimos salisteis salieron
[3s] venir. Irregular throughout. Future: *vendré* Gerund: *viniendo* Imperative: *ven (tú)*	vengo vienes viene venimos venís vienen	venga vengas venga vengamos vengáis vengan	vine viniste vino vinimos vinisteis vinieron
[3t] ir. Irregular throughout. Imperfect: *iba, ibas* etc. Gerund: *yendo* Imperative: *ve (tú), id (vosotros)*	voy vas va vamos vais van	vaya vayas vaya vayamos vayáis vayan	fui fuiste fue fuimos fuisteis fueron

Weights and Measures
Pesos y medidas

Metric system — Sistema métrico

(The various ancient measures still in use are listed and defined in the main part of the dictionary)

Multiples and fractions formed with the following prefixes are not listed separately:

> *deca-* 10 times; *hecto-* 100 times; *kilo-* 1000 times;
> *deci-* one tenth; *centi-* one hundredth; *milli-* one thousandth

1. Linear measures
Medidas de longitud

1 **centimetre** = 10 millimetres
   = 0.3937 inches

1 **metre** = 100 centimetres
   = 39.37 inches *or* 1.094 yards

1 **kilometre** = 1000 metres
   = 0.6214 mile (almost exactly five-eighths of a mile)

2. Square measures
Medidas cuadradas

1 **square centimetre**
   = 0.155 square inch

1 **square metre**
   = 10.764 square feet

1 **square kilometre**
   = 247.1 acres *or* 0.3861 square mile

1 **are** = 100 square metres
   = 119.6 square yards

1 **hectare** = 100 áreas
   = 2.471 acres

3. Cubic measures
Medidas de cubicación

1 **cubic centimetre**
   = 0.061 cubic inch

1 **cubic metre**
   = 35.31 cubic feet *or* 1.308 cubic yards

4. Measure of capacity
Medida de capacidad

1 **litre** = 1000 cubic centimetres
   = 1.76 pints *or* 0.22 gallon

5. Weights — Pesos

1 **gramme**
   = 0.0352 ounce

1 **kilogramme**
   = 2.2045 pounds

1 **quintal métrico**
   = 100 kilogrammes = 220.45 pounds

1 **tonelada**
   = 1000 kilogrammes = 0.9842 ton

Monetary system

| 100 céntimos | = 1 peseta |

Spaniards often reckon by the
| *real* | = 25 céntimos |
| *duro* | = 5 pesetas |